A
SANSKRIT-ENGLISH DICTIONARY

A SANSKRIT-ENGLISH DICTIONARY

WITH REFERENCES TO THE BEST EDITIONS

OF SANSKRIT AUTHORS

AND

ETYMOLOGIES AND COMPARISONS OF COGNATE WORDS

CHIEFLY IN

GREEK, LATIN, GOTHIC, AND ANGLO-SAXON.

COMPILED BY

THEODORE BENFEY

GYAN

Published by

Gyan Publishing House
5, Ansari Road
Daryaganj, New Delhi-110002
Phone: 011-47034999, 9811692060
E-mail: books@gyanbooks.com

Distribution Network
gyanbooks.com
India, USA, Canada, UK, Australia, France

ISBN: 978-93-6280-252-1 (PB)

First Published, 1866

2nd Impression 2023

Printed at: Gyan Press, Delhi.

A SANSKRIT-ENGLISH DICTIONARY

Compiler: THEODORE BENFEY

A

SANSKRIT-ENGLISH DICTIONARY

WITH REFERENCES TO THE BEST EDITIONS

OF SANSKRIT AUTHORS

AND

ETYMOLOGIES AND COMPARISONS OF COGNATE WORDS

CHIEFLY IN

GREEK, LATIN, GOTHIC, AND ANGLO-SAXON.

COMPILED BY

THEODORE BENFEY

PROFESSOR IN THE UNIVERSITY OF GÖTTINGEN, CORRESPONDING MEMBER OF THE IMPERIAL INSTITUTE OF FRANCE, ETC.

1866.

TO

FRANCIS BOPP,

WHO FIFTY YEARS AGO LAID THE FOUNDATION OF THE SCIENCE OF LANGUAGE IN HIS WORK

'THE SYSTEM OF CONJUGATION IN SANSKRIT COMPARED WITH THE GREEK, LATIN, PERSIAN, AND GERMAN,'

BY HIS GRATEFUL DISCIPLE,

THEODORE BENFEY.

PREFACE.

For some years past there has been no Sanskrit Dictionary available for the English student. The second edition of that by Wilson, published in 1831, has been long exhausted, as also Yates' Abridgment, published in Calcutta in 1846. Dr. Goldstücker's excellent work has not yet reached the end of the first vowel, and the St. Petersburg Dictionary, by Messrs. Böhtlingk and Roth, besides being in German, has only just completed the letter *ph*.

The present work aims at supplying this long-felt want. It does not exceed the limits of one volume, but at the same time it is hoped that it contains all that the student is likely to require. It especially includes all the words occurring in the different Chrestomathies and Selections generally in use (as Lassen's Anthology, my own Chrestomathy, Bopp's Nala, Johnson's Mahâbhârata Selections, &c.), and in the texts usually read by students, as the Hitopadeça, Pañchatantra, Manu's Laws, Çakuntalâ, Vikramorvaçî, Uttararâmacharita, Mâlatîmâdhava, and Meghadûta; but it is also believed to contain most of the words likely to occur in the general classical literature. It does not profess to contain the technical terms of the grammarians or philosophers, nor are purely Vaidik words included, except such as occur in the extracts given in the above-mentioned Chrestomathies.

References have been added to the greater part of the meanings. and sometimes explanations of passages also; but these latter are rarely introduced, for fear of swelling the volume beyond its proper size. For the same reason, compound words are generally printed in roman type, and arranged alphabetically under their last part. Thus the student must look for *a-mañgala, an-amça,* and *megha-dûta* respectively under *mañgala, amça,* and *dûta.* The difficulty arising from this source will soon disappear with practice. If a word, as for instance *chandraçekhara,* is not found under *ch,* its first component part *chandra* will be found; and the student has only to turn to the letter *ç* to find the remaining part *çekhara,* and under it in its place the very word he is in search of.

For the same reason, feminines ending in *â, î, û, ikâ,* are inserted under the corresponding masculines (where there are such) in *a, i, ṛi, n, nt, añch, as, u, aka*; while participles, participles used as substantives, and absolutives are inserted under the verbs to which they belong.

The etymology of every word is given, where ascertainable; but here also, to save space, abbreviations have been used. The several parts of a compound word are separated by hyphens, except in the case of the grammatical element, which is always preceded by +: thus, in p. 2, *a-karuṇa+tva* denotes that this word is compounded of *a* and *karuṇa,* with the affix *tva*; and similarly, in p. 397, *dâçarathi* is analysed as *daçaratha+i.*

As Sanskrit is also of the greatest use in the study of Comparative Grammar, I have added at the end of the principal articles the kindred words in the Greek, Latin, and German (particularly the Gothic and Anglo-Saxon) languages.

I have availed myself of the valuable labours of my predecessors, especially the works, already mentioned, of Wilson, Goldstücker, Böhtlingk, and Roth (as far as published), besides the Çabdakalpadruma of Râja Râdhâkânta Deva, and the various glossaries which have been published for special books; but for the latter half some of these aids have failed me, and I have been chiefly left to my own resources. I must therefore crave the reader's indulgence for the deficiencies and shortcomings which he may discover.

I cannot close this Preface without expressing my sincere thanks to Mr. E. B. Cowell and Professor Max Müller, for the assistance which they have rendered to me while carrying this work through the press.

GÖTTINGEN: *Jan.* 1, 1866.

CONTRACTIONS AND SIGNS.

adhy. = adhyâya.

Amar. = Amaruçataka, ed. Calcutt.

Ânandal. = Ânandalaharî, in Häberlin's Sanskrit Anthology.

Arj. = Arjunasamâgama, an episode of the MBh., ed. Bopp.

A.S. = Anglo-Saxon.

Âtm. = Âtmanepada.

Aufr. Ujjvalad. = Ujjvaladatta, ed. Aufrecht.

Bhag. = Bhagavadgîtâ, ed. Schlegel.

Bhâg. P. = Bhâgavata-Purâṇa, ed. Burnouf.

Bhartṛ. = Bhartṛihari, ed. Bohlen.

Bhâshâp. = Bhâshâparichchheda, in Bibliotheca Indica and in my Sanskrit Chrestomathy.

Bhaṭṭ. = Bhaṭṭikâvya, ed. Calc.

Bhavishyap. = Bhavishya-Purâṇa.

Böhtl. Chr. = Böhtlingk, Sanskrit Chrestomathy.

Böhtl. Ind. Spr.=Böhtlingk, Indische Sprüche (Indian Sentences).

Br. = Brockhaus.

Brâhmaṇ. and Brâhmaṇav. = Brâhmaṇavilâpa, an episode of the MBh., ed. Bopp.

Brahmav. P. = Brahmavaivarta-Purâṇa, ed. Stenzler.

Çâk. = Çâkuntala, ed. Böhtlingk.

Çântiç. = Çântiçataka, in Häberlin's Sanskrit Anthology.

Çârṅg. Paddh. = Çârṅgadhara-Paddhati (MSS. used by Böhtl.).

Çatr. = Çatruñjayamâhâtmya, ed. A. Weber.

Caus. = Causal.

Châṇ. = Châṇakya, published in Häberlin's Anthology, and by Weber in Berl. Monatsb. Hist. Phil. Cl., i.e. in 'Monthly Reports of the Berlin Academy of Sciences, Class of History and Philology,' 1864.

Ch. = Chezy.

Chât. = Châtaka, in Zeitschrift für die Kunde des Morgenlands, i.e. 'Journal for the Knowledge of the Orient,' vol. iv.

Chaur. and Chaurap. = Chaurapañchâçikâ, in Bohlen's ed. of Bhartṛihari.

Chr. = my Sanskrit Chrestomathy.

Çiç. = Çiçupâlavadha, 2. ed. Calc.; the ninth book in my Chr.

ÇKD. = Çabdakalpadruma.

Comp. = Compound.

Çṛiṅgârat. = Çṛiṅgâratilaka, ed. Gildemeister, in his edition of the Meghadûta.

Çrut. and Çrutab. = Çrutabodha, ed. Brockhaus.

Çukas. = Çukasaptati (MSS. of St. Petersburg).

Çvet. Up. = Çvetâçvataropanishad, in Bibliotheca Indica.

d. = distich.

Daçak. = Daçakumâracharita, ed. Wilson, partly in my Chr.

Daçar. = Daça-Rûpa, ed. Fitz-Edward Hall.

denomin. = denominative.

desid. = desiderative.

Dev. = Devîmâhâtmya, ed. Poley.

Draup. = Draupadîpramâtha, an episode of the MBh., ed. Bopp.

frequent. = frequentative.

Ghaṭ. = Ghaṭakarpara, ed. Calc.

Gît. = Gîtagovinda, ed. Lassen.

Goth. = Gothic.

Gött. Gel. Anz. = Göttinger Gelehrte Anzeigen, i.e. 'Scientific Reports published in Göttingen.'

Govardh. Âryas. = Govardhana Âryasaptati, ed. Soma Nath Mookerjea.

Grammar. = Grammarians.

Häb. and Häberl. Chr. or Anth. = Kâvya Sangraha, 'A Sanskrit Anthology,' by John Häberlin.

Hariv. = Harivaṁça, ed. Calc.

Hiḍ. = Hiḍimbavadha, an episode of the MBh., ed. Bopp.

Hit. = Hitopadeça, ed. of Lassen, and when followed by M.M., that of Max Müller. When followed by two Arabian numerals, the first denotes the page, the second the line; when followed by a Roman and Arabian numeral, the first denotes the book, the second the distich.

Icel. = Icelandic.

Indr. = Indralokâgamana, an episode of the MBh., ed. Bopp.

Johns. Sel. = Johnson's Selections from the Mahâbhârata.

Kâm. and Kâmand. Nîtis. = Kâmandakîya Nîtisâra, in Bibliotheca Indica.

Kathâs. = Kathâsaritsâgara, ed. Brockhaus.

Kâvya Prak. = Kâvya Prakaça, 2. ed. Calcutta, 1865.

Kir. and Kirât. = Kirâtârjunîya, 2. ed. Calc., 1846, and the fifth book in my Chr.

Kull. = Kullûka Schol. ed. Man.

Kumâras. = Kumârasambhava, ed. Stenzler.

Kusumâñj. = Kusumâñjali, ed. Cowell.

Lalit. = Lalitavistara, in Bibliotheca Indica.

Lass. = Lassen, Anthologia Sanskritica.

Lass. Pent. = Lassen, Commentatio de Pentapotamia Indica.

Lat. = Latin.

Mahâv. = Mahâvîracharita, ed. Trithen.

Mâlat. = Mâlatîmâdhava, ed. Calc.

Mâlav. = Mâlavikâgnimitra, ed. Tullberg.

Man. = Mânavadharmaçâstra, ed. Haughton and Lois. (i.e. Loiseleur Deslongchamps). Where there is a numeral in brackets, it denotes the verse of Jones' translation.

Mârk. P. = Mârkaṇḍeya-Purâṇa, in Bibliotheca Indica.

Matsyop. = Matsyopâkhyâna, an episode of the MBh., ed. Bopp.

MBh. = Mahâbhârata, ed. Calc.

Megh. = Meghadûta, ed. Gildemeister.

Mit. = Mitâksharâ, ed. Calc., 1829.

Mṛichchh. = Mṛichchhakaṭikâ, ed. Stenzler.

Mudrâr. = Mudrârâkshasa, ed. Calc.

Naish. = Naishadhacharita, ed. Calc.

Nal. = Nala, an episode of the MBh. ed. Bopp.; a numeral in brackets denotes Böhtlingk's ed. in his Chrestomathy.

Nalod. = Nalodaya, ed. Benary.

N.H.G. = New High German.

N.N.L. = New Netherlandis or Dutch.

Nyây. S. = Nyâya-Sûtrâṇi of Gotama, ed. Calc.

O.H.G. = Old High German.

O.N. = Old Norse.

Padmap. = Padma-Purâṇa, ed. Wollheim.

Pâṇ. = Pâṇini, ed. Böhtlingk.

Pañch. = Pañchatantra, ed. Kosegarten; the numerals are used on the same system as in Hit. When there is added 'ed. orn.,' it denotes the fragment of the recensio ornatior, published by Kosegarten.

Par. = Parasmaipada.

Part. = particle.

Pr. = prologue.

Prab. = Prabodhachandrodaya, ed. Brockhaus.

Prâkṛ. = Prâkṛit.

Ragh. = Raghuvaṁça, ed. Stenzler.

Râgh. = Râghavânanda, Sch. ad Man.

Râjat. = Râjataraṅgiṇî, ed. Troyer, the fifth book in my Chrestomathy.

Râm. = Râmâyaṇa, the two first books after the ed. of Schlegel; when that of Gorresio is meant, there is added Gorr.; the remaining books after Gorresio's.

Ratnâv. = Ratnâvalî, 2. ed. Calc.

Rigv. = Rigveda.

Ṛit. = Ṛitusaṁhâra, ed. Bohlen, the first chapter also in Lass., the sixth in my Chrestomathy.

Sâh. D. = Sâhitya Darpaṇa, in Bibliotheca Indica.

Sâṅkhya Aph. = Sâṅkhya Sûtras, in Hall's ed. of Saṅkhya Pravachana Bhâshya in Bibl. Ind.

Sâv. = Sâvitryupâkhyâna, an episode of the MBh., ed. Bopp.

Siddh. K. = Siddhântakaumudî, ed. Calc., 4to.

Siddh. Mukt. = Siddhânta Muktâvalî, ed. Roër in Bibl. Ind.

Skandap. Kâçîkh.= Kâçikhaṇḍa, a part of the Skanda-Purâṇa (MSS.).

Somadev. Nal. = Somadeva's Nala, published by Brockhaus.

Ssk. and Sskr. = Sanskrit.

Suçr. = Suçruta, ed. Calc.; the first numeral denotes the vol., the second the page, the third the line.

Sund. = Sundopasundopâkhyâna, an episode of the MBh., ed. Bopp.

Swed. = Swedish.

Upak. = Upakoça, an episode of the Kathâs., ed. Brockhaus.

Utt. Râmach. = Uttara Râmacharita, 2. ed. Calc., 1862.

Varâh. Bṛih. = Varâhamihira's Bṛihajjâtaka.

Varâh. Bṛih. S. = Varâhamihira's Bṛihatsaṁhitâ.

Vârt.=Vârtika.

Vedântas. = Vedântasâra, in my Chrestomathy.

Vikr. = Vikramorvaçî, ed. Bollensen.

Vop. = Vopadeva, ed. Böhtlingk.

Web. Ind. St. = Weber, Indische Studien, i.e. 'Essays concerning India.'

Yâjñ. = Yâjñavalkya, ed. Stenzler.

Yogas. = Yogasûtrâṇi, ed. Allahabad, 1852–53.

† denotes verbs or meanings for which there are no authoritative references.

S when before, denotes that the word occurs only as latter part of a compound; when after, as former.

° denotes abbreviations, which may be easily supplied from the context.

- denotes, in the etymological analysis, elements which are to be found in the dictionary; in comp. that the word which is the subject of the article must be supplied, as e.g. 1, A, 8, after *An-* must be added *aṁça*; 51, B, 10 bel., before *-paṇa* must be added *ardha*.

+ denotes grammatical elements of a word.

* denotes fictitious forms.

SANSKṚIT DICTIONARY.

अ *A.*

अऽ *a-*, a negative prefix, corresponding to the ἀ-privative in Greek; see *an-*.

अंश् *AṂÇ*, see *aṃs*.

अंश *aṃça*, rarely *aṃsa*, m. **1.** A part, a share. **2.** Booty. **3.** Inheritance, Man. 9, 47. **4.** See *aṃsa*. —**Comp.** *An-*, adj. excluded from a share of the heritage, Man. 9, 201. *Eka-*, m. 1. a single part, Man. 9, 150. 2. a part. *Chaturtha-*, 1. m. a fourth. 2. adj. entitled to a quarter, Man. 8, 210. *Tṛitîya-*, adj. entitled to a third part, Man. 8, 210. *Tri-*, (m.) sing. three shares, Man. 9, 151. *Dvi-*, (m.) sing. two shares, Man. 9, 153.

अंशु *aṃçu* (cf. *ço*), m. A ray of light, a sunbeam.—**Comp.** *Gharma-*, m. the sun. *Tigma-*, m. the sun. *Tîkshṇa-*, I. adj. having hot beams. II. m. 1. the sun. 2. fire. *Daçana-*, m. the brightness of the teeth. *Divya-*, m. the sun. *Dîpta-*, m. the sun. *Prâleya-*, m. the moon. *Sahasra-*, m. the sun. *Sudhâ-*, m. 1. the moon. 2. camphor. *Haṃsa-*, adj. white. *Hima-*, m. 1. the moon. 2. camphor.—Cf. ἀκτίν.

अंशुक *aṃçu+ka*, n. **1.** A leaf. **2.** Fine cloth; cloth; leaf and cloth, Ṛit. 6, 19.—**Comp.** *Chîna-*, n. silk. *Tanu-*, n. a thin cloth. *Patâkâ-*, n. a flag. *Sita-*, adj., f. *kâ*, dressed in a white cloth. *Stana-*, n. a cloth covering the bosom.

अंशुमन्त् *aṃçu + mant*. I. adj., f. *matî*. Radiant. II. m. The sun.

अंस् *AṂS*, also अंश् *AṂÇ*, i. 10, Par. To divide.—With वि *vi*. **1.** To break asunder. **2.** To deceive, Pańch. 202, 25.

अंस *aṃsa*, also अंश *aṃça*, probably from *am* (originally, To be strong), m. and n. The shoulder.—Cf. Goth. amsa; ἄσιλλα; Lat. humerus and ansa.

अंसल *aṃsa+la*, adj., f. *lâ*. Strong.

अंह् *AṂH*, i. 1, Âtm. To go. Caus. To send. † i. 10, Par. To shine, or to speak.

अंहस् *aṃhas* (*h* instead of *gh*, cf. *agha*; from a lost vb. *angh*=ἄγχω), n. **1.** Pain. **2.** Sin.—Cf. ἄχνυμαι, ἄχος, ἀκαχεῖν, ἄγος, and ἐγγύ corresponding to Ved. *aṃhu*; Goth. aggvus; Lat. angustus, angere, anxius, etc.

अंह्रि *aṃhri* (*h* instead of *gh*, cf. *anghri*), m. The foot.

† अक् *AK*, i. 1, Par. To wind or move tortuously.

अकरुणत्व *a-karuṇa+tva* (cf. *karuṇâ*), n. Cruelty.

अकर्णक *a-karṇa+ka*, adj., f. *ṇikâ*. Having no ears. Râm. 5, 17, 24.

अकल्कता *a-kalka+tâ*, f. Honesty.

अकामता *a-kâma+tâ*, f. Exemption from love, Man. 2, 2.

अकिंचित्कर *akiṁchitkara*, i. e. *a-kim-chid-kara*, adj. Innocent, Pańch. 187, 24.

अकुतोभय *akutobhaya*, i.e. *a-kutas-bhaya*, adj., f. *yâ*. Free from any danger.

अकुलता *a-kula+tâ*, f. Low state, Man. 3, 63.

अकुह *akuha*, adj. s. One who does not deceive, an honest man, Râm. 2, 109, 27.—Cf. *a-kuhaka*.

अकृत *a-kṛita*. I. adj., f. *tâ*. 1. Not done. 2. Undone, Man. 8, 117. 3. Not cultivated, Man. 10, 114. 4. Wavering, MBh. 14, 34. II. f. *tâ*. A daughter who is not by a formal declaration, but only mentally, appointed to supply an heir for her father, MBh. 9, 136.—Comp. *Kṛita-*, adj. 1. wrought and unwrought. 2. prepared and not prepared.

अकृतबुद्धित्व *akṛita-buddhi+tva*, n. Rudeness of mind, Bhag. 18, 16.

अक्तु *aktu*, m. Night, Chr. 289, 2 = Rigv. 1, 50, 2.

अक्ष् *AKSH* (probably an old desiderat. of 1. *aç*), i. 1. and ii. 5, *akshṇu*, Par. To pervade, to fill, to accumulate.—With निस् *nis*, To disperse.—With सम् *sam*, To pervade.

1. अक्ष *aksha*, probably from a lost vb. *aksh*, corresponding to *ὀσσ* in *ὄσσομαι*. I. n. 1. The eye; particularly as latter part of comp. adj., f. *kshî*. 2. An organ of sense, Pańch. ii, d. 164. II. m. 1. A die, Man. 4, 74. 2. The name of a plant, Terminalia Bellerica, of which the nuts are used as dice, and the seed for making rosaries.—Comp. *Kamala-patra-*, adj., f. *kshî*, adj. having eyes like lotus-leaves. *Kûṭa-*, m. a false die. *Jâlu-*, m. a lattice window. *Tâmra-*, adj. red-eyed. *Târaka-*, 1. adj. having stars for eyes. 2. m. a proper name. *Tryaksha*, i.e. *tri-*, I. adj. having three eyes. II. m. a name of Rudra-Çiva, and of a demon. *Daçâksha*, i.e. *daçan-*, m. the name of a spell or charm. *Padma-*, adj. lotus-eyed. *Puṇḍarîka-*, m. a name of Vishṇu. *Pushkara-*, adj. lotus-eyed. *Manda-*, n. modesty. *Lohita-*, adj. red-eyed. *Sahasra-*, I. adj. thousand-eyed. II. m. a name of Indra. *Su-*, adj. 1. handsome-eyed. 2. acute.—Cf. *ὄσσομαι*, *ὄκκος*; Lat. oculus; and see *akshi*.

2. अक्ष *aksha*, probably akin to *aj*, m. 1. The axle of a wheel. 2. A wheel. 3. A car.—Comp. *Eka-*, adj. having one axle.—Cf. *ἄξων*; O.H.G. ahsa; A.S. eax; Lat. axis.

अक्षन् *akshan*, see *akshi*.—Comp. *Tryakshan*, i.e. *tri-*, and *hari-*, adj. epithets of Rudra.

अक्षयत्व *a-kshaya+tva*, n. Imperishableness.

अक्षर *a-kshara*. I. adj., f. *râ*. Imperishable. II. n. 1. A word. 2. A syllable. 3. The holy syllable *om*. 4. A letter. 5. A vowel.—Comp. *An-*, adj. one who utters what ought not to be said. *Eka-*, adj. monosyllabic, Man. 2, 83. *Ghuṇa-*, n. a figure bored by a woodworm, and by accident resembling a letter, Râjat. 4, 167 (Pańch. 42, 12, read *ghuṇâkshara*). *Chatur-*, n. four syllables. *Tryakshara*, i.e. *tri-*, adj. triliteral, Man. 11, 265. *Shaḍakshara*, i.e. *shash-*, adj. containing six syllables, Pańch. i. d. 184.

अक्षवती *akshavatî*, i.e. *aksha + vant + î*, f. Gaming with dice.

अक्षि *akshi* (cf. 1. *aksha*), n., in some cases *akshan* is substituted. The eye. —**Comp.** *Agra-*, n. the first look. —Cf. ὄσσι in ὄσσει, ὄκταλλος, ὀφθαλμός; Goth. augo; A.S. aegh, eag.

अक्षिगत *akshi-gata* (vb. *gam*) adj., f. *tâ*. 1. Present, Çiç. 5, 81. 2. Hated.

अक्षौहिणी *akshauhiṇî*, i. e. *aksha -ûh + in + î*, f. A complete army.

† **अग्** *AG*, i, 1, Par. To wind, or move tortuously.

अग *a-ga*, m. 1. A mountain. 2. A tree.

अगतीक *agatîka*, i.e. *a-gati + ka* (*i* is lengthened on account of the metre), adj. Impervious, MBh. 12, 3078.

अगम्यागमनीय *agamyâgamanîya*, i.e. *a-gamya-âgamana + îya* (cf. *gam*), adj. Caused by illicit intercourse, Man. 11, 169.

अगस्ति *agasti*, and **अगस्त्य** *agastya*, m. The name of a Ṛishi, or saint, the son of Mitra and Varuṇa.

अगात्मजा *agâtmajâ*, i. e. *aga -âtmajâ*, f. A name of Pârvatî, the daughter of the Himâlaya, Kir. 5, 13.

अगार *agâra* (probably akin to *agni*, and originally a hearth), n. A house, Man. 9, 265.—**Comp.** *Agnyagâra*, i.e. *agni-*, n. the place where the sacred fire is kept.

अगुरु *a-guru*. I. adj. Short. II. n. Aloe wood (Aquilaria Agallochum *Roxb.*)—**Comp.** *Kâla-*, n. a black sort of Agallochum.

अग्नि *agni* (probably from *ańj* in its original signification, To shine), m. 1. Fire. 2. The sacrificial fire. 3. The deity of fire. 4. The digestive power. —**Comp.** *An-*, adj. without fire, Man. 6, 25. *Âhita-* (vb. *dhâ*), adj. one who keeps up a consecrated fire, Man. 3, 282. *An-âhita-*, adj. one who neglects to keep up a consecrated fire, Man. 11, 14. *Kaṭa-*, m. a fire of dry grass, Man. 8, 377. *Kopa-*, and *krodha-*, m. the fire of wrath. *Jńâna-*, m. the flame of knowledge, Man. 11, 246. *Tṛiṇa-*, m. a fire of dry grass, Man. 8, 168. *Dakshiṇa-*, m. one kind of sacred fire, that which is taken from the domestic fire and is placed to the south. *Dâva-*, m. the fire of a forest conflagration. *Pańchâgni*, i.e. *pańchan-*, adj. one who keeps the five fires constantly burning, Man. 3, 185. *Râjâgni*, i.e. *râjan-*, m. the fire of a king (in wrath), Man. 7, 9. *Visha-*, m. the fire of poison. *Çoka-*, m. the fire of grief. *Huta-* (vb. *hu*), and *homa-*, m. the sacrificial fire.—Cf. Lat. ignis.

ऽअग्निक *-agni + ka*. A substitute for *-agni* at the end of many comp. adj.: e.g. *sa-*, adj., with Agni.

अग्निचित् *agni-chi + t*, adj. One who has arranged a sacrificial fire.

अग्निद *agni-da*, m. An incendiary, Man. 9, 278.

अग्निभु *agni-bhu* (vb. *bhû*), n. Water, Man. 9, 321.

अग्निमन्त् *agni + mant*, adj., f. *matî*. 1. One who maintains a sacrificial fire, Man. 3, 122. 2. Having a good digestion.

अग्निष्टुत् *agnishṭut*, i.e. *agni-stu* + *t*, m. The name of a sacrifice, Man. 11, 74.

अग्निष्टोम *agnishṭoma*, i. e. *agni-stoma*, m. The name of a series of offerings to Agni, forming the first part of the Jyotishṭoma sacrifice, Man. 2, 143.

अग्निष्वात्त *agnishvâtta*, also **अग्नि-स्वात्त** *agni-svâtta* (vb. *svâd*), m. A class of Pitṛis or Manes, viz. those of the Devas and Brâhmaṇas, Man. 3, 195, 199.

अग्निसात् *agni-sât* (*sât* is the original abl. of *sa*), adv. Completely reduced to fire; with *kṛi*, To burn, Daçak. in Chr. 187, 14.

अग्निहोत्रिन् *agnihotrin*, i. e. *agni-hotra* + *in*, m. One who keeps the holy fire, Man. 11, 41.

अग्नीषोम *agnishoma*, i.e. *agni-soma*, m. du. Agni and Soma.

अग्न्याधेय *agnyâdheya*, i. e. *agni-âdheya* (vb. *dhâ*), n. Preparing the holy fire, Man. 2, 143.

अग्न्याहित *agnyâhita*, i.e. *agni-âhita* (vb. *dhâ*), m. One who has arranged a sacred fire, Râm. 6, 93, 30.

अग्र *agra*. I. adj. First, Megh. 4. II. n. **1.** Point, Man. 2, 167. **2.** Summit, top. **3.** Forepart, front. **4.** Beginning, Man. 2, 161. **5.** The first, or best. III. acc. sing. *agram*, adv. Before, *dishṭyâsi me Râghava chakshusho 'graṁ prâptaḥ*, 'fortunately, O descendant of Raghu, are you come before my eyes.' Râm. 6, 36, 72. IV. loc. sing. *agre*. **1.** Before. **2.** First; with abl. Sooner, Man. 3, 114. **3.** Forward, Pańch. 245, 13.—Comp. As former part of a comp. 1. the forepart, the tip: e.g. *agra-nakha*, the tip of the nail. 2. in front: e.g. *agra-yâyin*, adj. going in front, Çâk. d. 185. 3. best: e.g. *agra-vâjin*, m. an excellent horse. As latter part: e.g. *Eka-*, adj. 1. one whose mind is fixed on one object, Bhag. 6, 12. 2. intent. *An-eka-*, adj. inattentive. *Kuça-*, n. the point of a blade of kuça grass. *Daṁshṭrâ-*, n. the point of a tooth. *Dakshiṇâ-*, adj. that of which the points are directed southward. *Druma-*, m. the top of a tree, Râm. 5, 60, 16. *Nakha-*, n. the tip of the nails, Man. 2, 137. *Naga-*, n. the summit of a mountain. *Nâsikâ-*, n. the tip of the nose. *Maṇḍala-*, m. a sword.

अग्रग *agra-ga*, adj. **1.** Going in presence of somebody, Râjat. 5, 196. **2.** Going in front, a leader.—Comp. *Senâ-*, m. the leader of an army.

अग्रगण्य *agra-gaṇya* (vb. *gaṇ*), adj. One who must be considered as the first, Daçak. in Chr. 184, 8.

अग्रज *agra-ja*. I. adj., f. *jâ*. First-born. II. m. **1.** An elder brother, Man. 3, 171. **2.** A Brâhmaṇa, Man. 2, 20.—Comp. *Gada-*, m. the elder brother of Gada, a name of Kṛishṇa.

अग्रणी *agraṇî*, i.e. *agra-nî*, m. A leader.

अग्रतस् *agra* + *tas*. I. adv. **1.** Before. **2.** In front. **3.** Forward. II. preposition with the gen. **1.** Before, Man. 8, 244. **2.** In presence of.—Comp. *Bhairava-*, adv. in the presence of Bhairava.

अग्रसर *agrasara*, i.e. *agra-sṛi* + *a*, adj., f. *rî*. First.—Comp. *Pra-*, adj. First, Çâk. d. 112.

अग्रसरता *agrasara* + *tâ*, f. Going in front, Ragh. 5. 71.

अग्रहार *agra-hâra*, m. A grant of land or villages conferred upon Brâhmaṇas.

अग्राह्यक *a-grâhya* + *ka* (vb. *grah*), adj. Incomprehensible, MBh. 12, 3024.

अग्राह्यनामकता *agrâhyanâmakatâ*, i.e. *a-grâhya-nâman + ka + tâ* (vb. *grah*), f. Condition of having a name not fit to be assumed, Lass. 75, 1.

अग्रेदिधिषू *agredidhishû*, i.e. *agra + i-didhishû*, f. A younger sister married before her elder, Man. 3, 160.

अग्रेसर *agresara*, i.e. *agra + i-sṛi + a*, adj., f. *rî*. Going in front, first.

अग्र्य *agrya*, i.e. *agra + ya*, adj., f. *yâ*. **1.** First. **2.** Best, Man. 12, 30. —Comp. *Dvija-*, m. a Brâhmaṇa, Man. 3, 35.

†**अघ्** *AGH*, i, 10, *aghaya*, Par. To sin.

अघ *agha* (from a vb. *angh*, see *aṁhas*), n. **1.** Sin, Man. 3, 118. **2.** Impurity, Man. 5, 63.—Comp. *An-*, adj., f. *ghâ*, 1. sinless, Man. 12, 1. 2. pure. 3. unblamable, Çâk. d. 43.

अघशंसिन् *aghaçaṁsin*, i. e. *agha-çaṁsa + in*, adj. Wicked, Daçak. 2, 19.

अघायु *aghâyu*, i.e. Ved. *aghâya + u*, adj. Mischievous.

अङ्क् *AṄK*, i, 10 (rather a denominat. derived from *aṅka*), Par. and i. 1, Âtm. **1.** To mark, Pańch. 46, 8. **2.** To adorn, Râjat. 5, 230. **3.** To brand, Man. 9, 240. **4.** To stigmatise, Bhartṛ. 2, 44. **5.** † To go.

अङ्क *aṅka*, i.e. *ańch + a*, m. **1.** A hook. **2.** A mark. **3.** A cipher. **4.** An act in a drama. **5.** The flank. **6.** The lap. **7.** The arm, Vikr. d. 147. **8.** Proximity, Bhartṛ. 2, 23.—Comp. *Kṛita-*, adj. branded, Man. 8, 281. *Jambâla-*, adj. full of swamps. *Makara-*, m. the god of love. *Mṛiga-*, m. the moon. *Valgâ-*, adj. holding a bridle, Râjat. 5, 342. *Svanâmâṅka*, i. e. *Sva-nâman-*, adj. called after his name, 243. Cf. ἄγκη, ἀγκών, ἀγκύλος, ὄγκος; Lat. uncus; O.H.G. ango, anga, angul; A.S. angel, etc.

अङ्कभाज् *aṅka-bhâj* (vb. *bhaj*), adj. Approaching, Kir. 5, 52.

अङ्कुर *aṅkura* (from *ańch*, cf. *aṅka*), m. **1.** A shoot, or sprout, Pańch. i. d. 251. **2.** Intumescence.—Comp. *Abhilâsha-*, m. the germ of desire, Râjat. 5, 376. *Kula-*, m. offspring, a young child, Çâk. d. 178. *Daṁshṭrâ-*, m. the point of a tooth, Bhartṛ. 2, 4. *Rada-*, m. the point of a tooth. *Visha-*, m. a spear, a dart. *Vîja-*, m. a seedling, Pańch. i. d. 254. *Smara-*, m. 1. a lover, a lecher. 2. a finger nail.

अङ्कुरित *aṅkurita*, i.e. *aṅkura + ita*, adj. Furnished with shoots, Vikr. d. 12.

अङ्कुश *aṅkuça*, i.e. *aṅku* (in the Ved. *aṅkûya* from *ańch*, cf. *aṅka*) + *ça*, m. and n. **1.** A hook. **2.** A goad for driving elephants with.—Comp. *Ati-*, adj. unmanageable. *An-*, adj. unruly. *Niraṅkuça*, i.e. *nis-*, adj. 1. unchecked. 2. unruly. 3. independent, free.

अङ्कोठ *aṅkoṭha*, and **अङ्कोल** *aṅkola*, m. A plant, Alangium hexapetalum.

अङ्ख् *AṄKH*, i, 10. **1.** To take hold. **2.** To stop.—With the prepos. **परि** *pari*, To surround.

अङ्ग् *AṄG*, i. 1, Par. and † i. 10, Par. **1.** To go, Nalod. 1, 23. **2.** † i. 10, To mark.—With the prepos. **पलि** *pali* for **परि** *pari*, Caus. To stir up. Pass. To go round.—With **विपलि** *vi-pali*, Caus. Âtm. To cover one's self.

1. **अङ्ग** *aṅga*, n. **1.** A limb, Man. 3, 178. **2.** The penis, Man. 8, 374. **3.** A part, Man. 11, 11. **4.** A supplementary part. **5.** A division of Hindu learning, comprehending such sciences

as are considered dependent upon the Vedas; cf. *angavidyâ.* **6.** An expedient. **7.** The body.—**Comp.** In comp. adj. the fem. ends generally in *gî*, sometimes also in *gû.* *An-*, m. Kâma, the god of love. *An-a-vadya-* (vb. *vad*), adj., f. *gî*, of faultless form. *Ashṭânga*, i.e. *ashṭan-*, adj. consisting of eight parts. *Uttama-*, n. the head, Man, 1, 93. *Eka-*, I. n. one part only. II. m. pl. body-guards. *Kâla-*, adj. having a dark-blue blade, MBh. 4, 231. *Kushṭha-*, adj. leprous. *Kṛiça-*, adj., f. *gî*, meagre. *Khaṭvâ-*, n. one of Çiva's weapons (a club with a skull at the top), also carried by devotees. *Chatur-*, I. adj. consisting of four parts; with *bala*, a complete army, consisting of chariots, elephants, horse, and foot. II. n. 1. a complete army. 2. chess. *Chitra-*, m. a proper name. *Tanu-*, f. *gî*, a delicate woman. *Tanû-ja-*, n. a wing. *Niranga*, i.e. *nis-*, adj. deprived of expedients. *Panchânga*, i.e. *panchan-*, adj. consisting of five parts. *Mahâ-*, m. a camel. *Rakta-*, I. m. 1. a bug. 2. planet Mars. II. n. 1. coral. 2. saffron. *Ratha-*, I. n. 1. any part of a carriage. 2. a wheel. II. m. the ruddy goose, Anas casarca. *Vakra-*, m. 1. the ruddy goose. 2. a goose. *Vara-*, I. m. an elephant. II. n. 1. an elegant body. 2. the head. 3. pudendum, male or female. *Vi-chitra-*, I. adj. 1. handsome. 2. having the body of various colours. II. m. 1. a tiger. 2. a peacock. *Hîna-* (vb. 2. *hâ*), I. adj. maimed, Man. 4, 141. II. f. *gî*, an ant. *Hema-*, I. adj. golden, Râm. 3, 55, 32. II. m. 1. a lion. 2. Brahman. 3. Garuḍa, a fabulous bird.

2. **अङ्ग** *anga* (an old instr. sing. of the last, signifying 'by my body'), particle: **1.** Of asseveration, Indeed, to be sure. **2.** Of solicitation, invocation, Râm. 2, 97, 16. **3.** Of interrogation, Daçak. in Chr. 192, 7. **4.** Again, further, Böhtl. Ind. Spr. 1106.

3. **अङ्ग** *anga*, m. **1.** The name of a country, Bengal proper, and its inhabitants. **2.** The name of a king.

अङ्गक *anga + ka.* **1.** = 1. *anga*, e.g. Body, Çiç. 4, 66. **2.** A substitute for 1. *anga* at the end of comp. adj., f. *gikâ*, e.g. *âlingita-* (vb. *ling*), One whose body is embraced, Râjat. 5, 410.

अङ्गज *anga-ja*, adj. Produced from the body, bodily.

अङ्गण *angaṇa*, for *angana* (q. cf.), n. A court, a yard. Dev. 5, 50.—**Comp.** *Ranga-*, n. the area of an amphitheatre. *Harmya-*, n. the court of a palace.

अङ्गतस् *anga + tas*, adv. From the body, Man. 4, 167.

अङ्गत्व *anga + tva*, n. Corporality.

अङ्गद *anga-da* (vb. 3. *dâ*). I. n. A bracelet. II. m. A proper name.—**Comp.** *Chitra-*, 1. adj. adorned with splendid or variegated bracelets. 2. m. a proper name. 3. f. *dâ*, a proper name.

अङ्गन *ang + ana*, n. **1.** A passage. **2.** A court.—**Comp.** *Raṇa-*, n. a field of battle.

अङ्गना *anganâ* (cf. *anga*), f. **1.** A beautiful woman. **2.** A woman in general. **3.** The female of any animal. —**Comp.** *Kula-*, f. a chaste woman. *Vara-*, f. a lovely woman.

अङ्गरुह *anga-ruh + a*, n. Hair.

अङ्गविद्या *anga-vidyâ*, f. **1.** Such learning as is comprehended under the title *anga*, viz. pronunciation, grammar, prosody, explanation of obscure terms, description of religious rites, and astronomy, Daçak. in Chr. 180, 6. **2.** Palmistry, Man. 6, 40.

अङ्गहीनत्व *anga-hîna + tva* (vb. 2. *hâ*), n. Defect of some limb, Man. 11, 50.

अङ्गार *angâra* (vb. *anj*, cf. *agni*), m. and n. Charcoal, Man. 8, 250.—Comp. *Kula-*, m. or n., an enemy to his own family, Pańch. 211, 14. *Mṛita-*, m. a proper name.

अङ्गारक *angâra + ka*, m. 1. The planet Mars. 2. The name of a king. —Comp. *Sa-*, adj. attended by the planet Mars.

अङ्गिन् *angin*, i.e. *anga + in*, adj., f. *nî*. 1. Having limbs. 2. Having expedients. 3. Chief.—Comp. *Chatur-*, (i.e. *chaturanga + in*), adj., f. *iṇî*, consisting of four parts (Bhâg. P. 1, 10, 32, *inî*).

अङ्गिरस् *angiras*, m. The name of a Ṛishi, or saint.—Comp. *Tṛiṇa-soma-*, m. one of the seven priests attending a sacrifice.

अङ्गीकरण *angîkaraṇa*, i.e. 2. *angu-kṛi + ana*, n. Agreement, consent, Vedântas. in Chr. 213, 19.

अङ्गीकार *angîkâra*, i.e. 2. *anga-kṛi + a*, m. Agreement, Vedântas. in Chr. 213, 22.

अङ्गुरीयक *anguriyaka* = *anguliyaka* (q. cf.).

अङ्गुल *angula* (from a lost base, *angu*) m. 1. A finger's breadth as a linear measure. 2. A substitute for *anguli* at the end of many comp. words: e.g. *daçângula*, i.e. *daçan-*, adj. Ten fingers long, Man. 8, 271.—Comp. *Pańchângula*, i. e. *pańchan-*, m. The castor-oil plant.

ऽअङ्गुलक *-angula + ka*, a substitute for *angula* at the end of comp. words: *shoḍaçângulaka*, i.e. *shoḍaçan-*, adj. Of sixteen fingers' breadth.

अङ्गुलि and अङ्गुली *anguli, î*, f. A finger.—Comp. *Latâ-*, f. a branch serving instead of a finger, Çiç. 9, 4.

अङ्गुलित्र *anguli-tra* (vb. *trâ*), n. A piece of leather or thin iron, worn by archers to prevent the fingers being injured by the bowstring.

अङ्गुलित्रवन्त् *angulitra + vant*, adj. Protected by the *angulitra*.

अङ्गुलीय *angulîya*, i.e. *anguli + îya*, n. A finger-ring.—Cf. Lat. annulus.

अङ्गुलीयक *angulîya + ka*, n. A finger-ring.

अङ्गुष्ठ *angushṭha*, i.e. *angu-stha* (cf. *angula*), m. 1. The thumb. 2. The great toe. 3. A thumb's breadth as a measure.

† अङ्घ् *AṄGH*, i, 1. Âtm. 1. To go. 2. To begin moving. 3. To begin. 4. To hasten. 5. To blame. 6. To despise.

अङ्घ्रि *anghri* (akin to *janghâ* from *janghan*, the frequent. of *han*; the initial consonant is lost, as e.g. in *inaksh* for *ninasksh* and others, and *n* is changed to *r*, as in *pivar + î* fem. of *pîvan*), m. 1. A foot. 2. The root of a tree.—Comp. *Çîrṇa-* (vb. *çṛî*), m. Yama.

अचल *a-chala*. I. adj., f. *lâ*. 1. Immovable. 2. Steady, Pańch. 202, 19. II. m. A mountain.—Comp. *Kula-*, m. a principal mountain. *Tuhina-*, m. Himâlaya. *Mahâ-*, m. a great mountain.

अच्छ *achchha* (akin to 1. *aksha*), adj., f. *chhâ*. Transparent, clear, Megh. 52.—Comp. *Su-*, adj. 1. transparent, 2. pure. 3. white. 4. healthy.

अज् *AJ*, i, 1, Par., in the Vedas also Âtm. 1. To go. 2. To drive; to direct, Chr. 297, 16 = Rigv. 1, 112, 16.

—With the prepos. उद् *ud*, To drive out, Chr. 297, 12 = Rigv. 1, 112, 12. —Cf. ἄγω, πράσσω (πραγ-jω); Lat. ago, igitur (for agitur); ON. aka.

1. अज *a-ja*, adj., f. *jâ*. Unborn.

2. अज *aja*. 1. m. A he-goat. 2. f. *jâ*. A she-goat.—Comp. *Vana-*, m. a wild goat.—Cf. αἴξ, of which the base is ἀγ + ι.

अजगर *ajagara*, i.e. *aja-gṛî* + *a*, m. A large serpent, Boa constrictor.

अजननि *a-jan* + *ani*, f. Privation of birth, used as imprecation, Pańch. i. d. 355.

अजर्य *a-jarya* (vb. *jṛî*), n. Friendship, Ragh. 18, 6.

अजस्र *a-jas* + *ra*, adj., f. *râ*. Continual. acc. *ram*, adv. Continually, always, Man. 1, 57.

अजात *a-jâta* (vb. *jan*), adj., f. *tâ*. 1. Unborn. 2. As former part of comp. adj., Not having, e.g. *ajâta-vyańjana*, adj. beardless. *ajâta-çatru*. 1. Having no enemies. 2. One with whom nobody can contend; epithet and name of Yudhishṭhira and others.

अजाविक *ajâvika*, i.e. *aja-avi* + *ka*, n. sing. Goats and sheep, Man. 8, 235.

अजिन *ajina* (perhaps derived from 2 *aja*), n. The hide of any animal, particularly of the black antelope, used as a covering, Man. 2, 64, as purse, Daçak. 191, 16. — Comp. *Kṛishṇa-*, n. the hide of the black antelope.

अजिर *aj* + *ira*, n. A court, Pańch. 138, 1.—Comp. *Raṇa-*, n. a field of battle.

अजिह्मग *a-jihma-ga*. I. adj. Advancing in a straight path, Man. 6, 31. II. m. An arrow.

अजीगर्त *ajîgarta*, m. The name of a Ṛishi or saint, Man. 10, 105.

अजीर्णिन् *ajîrṇin*, i.e. *a-jîrṇa* + *in* (vb. *jṛî*), adj. Suffering from indigestion.

अज्जुका *ajjukâ*, f. 1. A courtesan (Mṛichchh. 27, 2, Prâkṛ.; in the Ssk. translation *ajjû*). 2. (in Prâkṛ. *ajjû*, and in the Ssk. translation *ajjukâ*, Çâk. p. 105, 3.) A mother.

अज्ञता *a-jńa* + *tâ*, f. Ignorance.

अज्मन् *aj* + *man*, n. Battle, Chr. 297, 17 = Rigv. 1, 112, 17.—Cf. Lat. agmen; -αγμα in κάταγμα, etc.

अज्र *aj* + *ra*, m. A field.—Cf. ἀγρός; Lat. ager; Goth. akrs; A.S. acer.

अञ्च् *AŃCH* (cf. *ańka*), i. 1, Par. Âtm. 1. To go. 2. To ask. 3. To speak indistinctly. 4. To bend, to curve, Nal. 12, 45. 5. To honour, Ragh. 9, 24. 6. i. 10 (rather Caus.). To make clear, to manifest, Gît. 10, 11.—With the prep. उद् *ud*, To rise, Râjat. 5, 362.

अञ्चन *ańch* + *ana*, n. Bending, curving.

अञ्चल *ańch* + *ala*, m. The end or border of a cloth.

अञ्ज् *AŃJ*, ii. 7, *anaj*, *ańj*, Par. (Ved. also Âtm.). To cause to shine by smearing with greasy substances. 1. To anoint, to smear, Man. 5, 25. 2. To adorn, Chr. 294, 1 = Rigv. 1, 92, 1. 3. To make clear. 4. To be beautiful. 5. † To go. Caus. To anoint, Man. 4, 44. † i. 10. To shine.—With the prepos. अभि *abhi*. 1. To anoint, Man. 4, 44. 2. To pollute, Çâk. d. 108.—With वि *vi*. 1. Âtm. To dress one's self, Chr. 290, 4 = Rigv. 1, 64, 4. 2. To make clear, MBh. 2, 2122. *vyakta*, manifest, clear, Râm. 3, 73, 12. acc. sing. *tam*, adv. to be sure, Daçak. in Chr. 199, 11.—**Comp.** *A-vyakta*, adj. 1. invisible, Man. 1, 6. 2. imperceptible, Râm. 1, 70, 9. acc. sing. *tam*, adv. indistinctly, Brâhmaṇav. 3, 21. n. the primary Being, Ragh. 13, 60. Caus. 1. To make discernible, Man. 1, 6. 2. To betray, Man. 10, 58. 3. To show, Râjat. 5, 107. *Vyañjita*, discerned, Man. 9, 36.—With अभिवि *abhi-vi*, 1. To discern clearly, Vedântas. in Chr. 208, 23. 2. To reveal. *Abhivyakta* + *m*, adv. evidently, Nal. 17, 8.—With सम् *sam*, To adorn, Chr. 290, 1=Rigv. 1, 64, 1.—Cf. Lat. unguere; O.H.G. anko, butter; and ἀγ in ἀγλαός, ἀγάλλω.

अञ्जन *añj* + *ana*. I. n. **1.** Anointing, Man. 4, 152. **2.** A collyrium or application to the eyelashes to darken and improve them, Man. 2, 178. **II.** m. **1.** The elephant of the west or south-west quarter. **2.** The name of a mountain. **3.** A particular plant, Pañch. 10, 7. **III.** f. *nâ*. The name of a female monkey, the mother of Hanumant.—**Comp.** *Nirañjana*, i.e. *nis-*, adj., f. *nâ*, artless. *Rasa-*, n. a particular sort of collyrium, Çiç. 9, 21.

अञ्जलि *añjali*, m. **1.** The cavity formed by putting the hands together and hollowing the palms, Man. 4, 63. **2.** This cavity as measure: two handfuls. **3.** Putting the hands together and raising them to the forehead, as humble salutation of inferiors to their superiors.—**Comp.** *Ud-*, adj. with uplifted hands, Daçak. in Chr. 180, 1. *Karṇa-*, m. the auditory passage. *Kṛita-*, adj. with humble salutation, Man. 4, 154. *Jala-*, m. 1. two handfuls of water in honour of a deceased relation. 2. farewell, resignation: *jalâñjalim̃ dattvâ duḥkâya cha sukhâya cha*, 'having completely renounced sorrow and joy,' Râjat. 4, 284. *Brahmâñjali*, i.e. *brahman-*, m. 1. joining both hands together whilst reading the Vedas, Man. 2, 71. 2. paying obeisance to the spiritual preceptor at the beginning or end of a lecture.

अञ्जसा *añjasâ* (instr. sing. of the Ved. *añj* + *as*, n. Smoothness, slip), adv. **1.** Straightforward, directly, Man. 2, 244. **2.** Instantly, Vikr. d. 48. **3.** Truly, Man. 8, 101.

अञ्जि *añj* + *i*, m. **1.** An ornament, Chr. 290, 4=Rigv. 1, 64, 4. **2.** The penis: cf. Lat. inguen.

अट् *AṬ*, i. 1, Par. (in epic poetry also Âtm., MBh. 3, 1586), To roam, with the loc. and acc. MBh. 1, 1031; Daçak. in Chr. 179, 6.—With the preposition परि *pari*, To wander about, Pañch. 55, 1. *Paryaṭita*, n. Wandering about, Pañch. 70, 12.

अटन *aṭ* + *ana*, n. Rambling, Man. 9, 12.—**Comp.** *Bhikshâ-*, n. wandering about for begging alms, Pañch. 116, 17.

अटनि and **अटनी** *aṭanî*, f. The notched extremity of a bow.

अटवी *aṭavî* (vb. *aṭ.*), f. A wood.

† **अट्ट्** *AṬṬ*, i. 1, Âtm. **1.** To transgress. **2.** To kill. i. 10, Par. To slight.

अट्ट *aṭṭa*, m. **1.** A room on the top of a house, a sollar. **2.** A tower, Râm. 5, 56, 142. **3.** As former part of some comp. words, High, lofty, loud. (cf. the next.)

अट्टपतिभागाख्य *aṭṭapatibhâgâkhya*, i.e. *aṭṭa-pati-bhâga-âkhya*, adj. Called the part of the great king, name of a government office, Râjat. 5, 166.

अट्टहास *aṭṭa-hâsa*, m. A horse-laugh.—**Comp.** *Sa-aṭṭahâsa+m*, adv. with a horse-laugh.

अट्टाल *aṭṭâla* (derived from *aṭṭa*), m. A room on the top of a house.

अट्टालक *aṭṭâla+ka*, m. A tower.

अट्या *aṭ+yâ*, f. Wandering about. —**Comp.** *Vṛithâ-*, f. strolling about, Man. 7, 47.

† **अठ्** *AṬH*, i. 1, Par. Âtm. To go.

† **अड्** *AḌ*, i. 1, Par. To strive or endeavour.

† **अड्ड्** *AḌḌ*, i. 1, Par. **1.** To attack. **2.** To connect. **3.** To meditate.

† **अण्** *AṆ*, i. 1, Par. To sound. i. 4, Âtm. To breathe (cf. *an*).

अणिमन् *aṇiman*, i.e. *aṇu+iman*, m. Subtility; the superhuman power of making one's self infinitely small.

अणु *aṇu*. I. adj., f. *ṇu* and *ṇvî*. **1.** Small, minute; *aṇv api*, the least, Man. 3, 51. **2.** Subtile, Hariv. 1241. Comparat. *aṇîyaṅs*, very soft, Daçak. in Chr. 198, 22. II. m. An atom, Bhâshâp. 35.—**Comp.** *Parama-*, m. an atom.

अणुत्व *aṇu+tva*, n. **1.** Smallness. **2.** Condition of being an atom, Bhâshâp. 84.

अणुमात्रिक *aṇumâtrika*, i.e. *aṇu-mâtra+ika*, adj. Composed of atoms, Man. 1, 56.

† **अण्ठ्** *AṆṬH*, i. 1, Âtm. To go.

अण्ड *aṇḍa*, n. **1.** An egg. **2.** A testicle.—**Comp.** *Brahmâṇḍa*, i.e. *brahman-*, n. the world. *Mesha-*, m. Indra; see *pûtyaṇḍa*.

अण्डक *aṇḍa+ka*, n. **1.** A bird's egg. **2.** An egg in general, Çiç. 9, 9.

अण्डज *aṇḍa-ja*. I. adj. Oviparous, Man. 1, 44. II. m. **1.** A bird. **2.** A fish.—**Comp.** *Kâla-*, m. the Indian cuckoo.

अत् *AT*, i. 1, Par. **1.** To go. **2.** To move continually.

अतदर्ह *a-tad-arha*, adj. Not deserving that, Râm. 2, 13, 1.

अतन्द्रित *atandrita*, i.e. *a-tandrâ+ita*, adj., f. *tâ*. Unwearied, not remiss, Man. 2, 186.

अतपस्क *a-tapas+ka*, adj. Impious.

अतस् *a+tas* (cf. *idam*), adv. **1.** abl. of *idam*, From this, Man. 2, 213. **2.** From this place. **3.** From this time, then, now, Man. 5, 26. **4.** From this reason, therefore.

अति *ati*. I. adv. Over, exceedingly, in a high degree, much. Comparat. *ati+tarâm*, very much, Vedântas. in Chr. 217, 10. II. prepos. with the acc. Over, beyond, more than. III. Combined and compounded with verbs and their derivatives. IV. Former part of compound nouns and adverbs, implying: **1.** Exceedingly, much, very: e.g. *ati-guru*, adj. very heavy; *ati-kâya*, adj. having a very large body, gigantic. **2.** Too much: e.g. *ati-praṇaya*, m. exorbitant love, Daçak. in Chr. 182, 10; *atyaçnant*, i.e. *ati-* (vb. 2. *aç*), adj. eating too much. **3.** Surpassing the object denoted by the following part of the comp. These comps. are generally: *a*) adj. e.g. *atîndriya*, i.e. *ati-*, surpassing the senses, transcendental. *b*) adv., e.g. *ati-mâtra+m*. exceedingly, extraordinarily.—Cf. ἔτι; Lat. at in atavus, and et.

अतिक्रम *ati-kram+a*, m. **1.** Transgression (of time), Pañch. 55, 5. **2.** Violation, Man. 11, 120. **3.** Offence. **4.** Irreverence, Man. 3, 63.

—Comp. *Duratikrama*, i.e. *dus-*, adj. 1. hard to be overcome, unconquerable, Man. 11, 238. 2. difficult of accomplishment.

अतिक्रमण *atikramaṇa*, i. e. *ati-kram+ana*, n. 1. Overstepping (of a boundary), Yâjń. 2, 155. 2. Transgression (of time), Pańch. i. d. 170.

अतिक्रमिन् *ati-kram+in*, adj., f. *iṇî*. One who violates.

ऽअतिग *-ati-ga*, adj. 1. Surpassing, (*sarva-loka-*,) Râm. 2, 19, 33. 2. Piercing, (*deha-*,) Ragh. 12, 48.—Cf. *vayotiga*.

अतिथि *atithi* (vb. *at*), m. 1. A guest. 2. The name of a king.—Comp. *Deça-*, m. a foreigner.

अतिथिग्व *atithigva*, m. A name of Divodâsa, Chr. 297, 14=Rigv. i. 112, 14.

अतिथित्व *atithi+tva*, n. Hospitality.

अतिथिधर्मिन् *atithidharmin*, i.e. *atithi-dharma+in*, adj. Having the character of a guest, as guest, Man. 3, 112.

अतिदर्शिन् *atidarçin*, i.e. *ati-dṛiç+in*, adj., f. *nî*. Seeing very far.

अतिदेश *atideça*, i.e. *ati-diç+a*, m. Extension, as e.g. of the signification of a word by analogy, Bhâshâp. 79.

अतिनिर्वसुत्व *atinirvasutva*, i.e. *ati-nis-vasu+tva*, n. Excessive poverty, Râjat. 6, 79.

अतिपत्ति *ati-pat+ti*, f. 1. Lapse (of time). 2. Unsuitableness, Yâjń. 2, 169 (*deça-kâla-atipattau*, 'should time or place not permit').

अतिपात *atipâta*, i.e. *ati-pat+a*, m. 1. Neglect, Câk. 7, 10. 2. Hurting.

अतिपातिन् *atipâtin*, i.e. *ati-pat+in*, adj. 1. Outrunning. 2. Acute (as a disease).

अतिभाव *atibhâva*, i.e. *ati-bhû+a*, m. Overcoming.

अतिमानिता *atimânitâ*, i. e. *ati-mânin+tâ*, f. Excessive self-conceit, Bhag. 16, 3.

अतिमुक्त *ati-mukta* (vb. *much*), m. A large creeper, Gaertnera racemosa.

अतिमुक्तक *atimukta+ka*, m. The name of several plants, as Dalbergia ougeinensis, Gaertnera racemosa, etc.

अतियश *atiyaça*, see *yaças*.

अतिरिक्तता *ati-rikta+tâ* (vb. *rich*), f. Excess, MBh. 2, 2270.

अतिरेक *atireka*, i.e. *ati-rich+a*, m. Excess, high degree.

अतिलुब्धता *ati-lubdha+tâ* (vb. *lubh*), f. Excessive greediness, Böhtl. Ind. Spr. 109.

अतिलोभता *ati-lobha+tâ*, f. Excessive greediness.

अतिवर्तन *ativartana*, i.e. *ati-vṛit+ana*, n. Remission (of a fine), Man. 8, 290.

अतिवर्तिन् *ativartin*, i.e. *ati-vṛit+in*, adj., f. *nî*. 1. Crossing, passing over. 2. Not caring, Daçak. in Chr. 194, 8. 3. Offending, Râm. 4, 16, 37.

अतिवाद *ativâda*, i.e. *ati-vad+a*, m. A reproachful speech, Man. 6, 47.

अतिवाह्य *ati-vâhya* (vb. *vah*), n. Passing (as time), Böhtl. Chr. 217, 38.

अतिवृत्ति *ati-vṛit+ti*, f. Trespass, Daçak. in Chr. 181, 3.

अतिशय *atiçaya*, i.e. *ati-çî+a*, m. 1. Excellence. 2. Excess, Çiç. 9, 77. 3. Plenty, Vikr. d. 157. 4. As former part of comp. words: 1. In a high degree, great, Pańch. 239, 14. 2. Violent.—Comp. *Niratiçaya*, i.e. *nis-*, adj. not to be surpassed, greatest, Pańch. i. d. 36. *Sa-*, adj. most excellent, Man. 9, 114.

अतिशयिन् *atiçayin*, i.e. *atiçaya+in*, adj., f. *nî*. Most excellent, Vikr. d. 159.

अतिशायिन् *atiçâyin*, i.e. *ati-çî+in*, adj. Surpassing, Daçak. in Chr. 182, 1.

अतिसमीपता *ati-samîpa + tâ*, f. Too close proximity, Çiç. 9, 81.

अतिसर्ग *atisarga*, i.e. *ati-sṛij+a*, m. Granting (of a wish), Râm. 4, 52, 21.

अतिसार and **अतीसार** *atisâra*, i.e. *ati-sṛi+a*, m. Diarrhœa.

अतीन्द्रिय *atîndriya*, i.e. *ati-indriya*. I. adj. Surpassing the senses, transcendental, Bhâshâp. 57. II. n. Mind, Man. 1, 7.

अतीव *atîva*, i.e. *ati-iva*, adv. 1. Much, very. 2. Indeed, Çâk. d. 137, v.r.

अतृप्तिता *a-tṛipti + tâ*. f. Insatiableness, Çiç. 9, 64.

अतोर्थम् *atortham*, i.e. *atas-artha+m*, adv. To that end, Râm. 3, 8, 15.

अत्ता *attâ*, f. A mother, Mṛichchh. 27, 2. (Prâkṛ.)

अत्तृ *attṛi*, i.e. *ad+tṛi*, m. One who eats, Man. 5, 30; (a king) who swallows up the possessions of his people, Man. 8, 309.

अत्य *at+ya*, m. A horse, Chr. 290, 6 = Rigv. 1, 64, 6.

अत्यन्त *atyanta*, i.e. *ati-anta*, adj., f. *tâ*. 1. Excessive, very large. 2. Endless, perpetual, Man. 5, 46; eternal. acc. sing. *tam*, adv. 1. very much. 2. for ever, Man. 9, 202.

अत्यय *atyaya*, i.e. *ati-i+a*, m. 1. Passing away, lapse (of time), Man. 8, 145. 2. Death. 3. Danger, Man. 5, 27. 4. Transgression, crime, fault, Man. 8, 243; *dâpyo 'shṭaguṇam atyayam*, 'he shall be fined eight times the amount of the defraudation,' Man. 8, 400.—Comp. *An-*, adj. imperishable. *Kâla-*, m. lapse of time, Man. 8, 145. *Jala-*, m. the end of the rainy season, i.e. autumn. *Tapa-*, m. 1. the end of the hot season, i.e. the rainy season. 2. the end of the heat, i.e. sunset, Çâk. d. 60. *Duratyaya*, i.e. *dus-*, adj., f. *yâ*, 1. hard to be crossed (as a river), MBh. 4, 1970. 2. hard to be attained, 13, 4880. 3. unfathomable, Râm. 3, 71, 15. *Niratyaya*, i.e. *nis-*, adj., f. *yâ*, 1. free from danger. 2. infallible. *Mahâ-*, 1. m. great pain, Chr. 11, 15. 2. adj. very pernicious, Chr. 22, 22. *Su-mahâ-*, adj. very dangerous, Chr. 37, 3.

अत्यर्थम् *atyartham*, i.e. *ati-artha+m*, adv. Exceedingly.

अत्र *a+tra* (cf. *idam*), adv. 1. = the loc. of *idam*, In this, Çâk. d. 59. 2. Here, therein, Man. 3, 235.

अत्रत्य *atra+tya*, adj. Of this place, Daçak. in Chr. 186, 18.

अत्रि *atri*, m. The name of a Ṛishi, or saint, Man. 1, 35.

अत्रिन् *atrin* (for *attrin*, vb. *ad*), adj. A demon, Chr. 292, 10 = Rigv. 1, 85, 10.

अथ *a+tha* (probably for *athâ*, Ved. cf. *idam*), adv. 1. Then, Nal. 17, 35. 2. Now, at the beginning of works and parts of works. 3. But, Nal. 22, 13. 4. In conditional sentences: If, *atha tân nânu gachchhâmi gamishyâmi yamakshayam*, 'if I do not follow them, I shall go to the house of death,' Râm. 2, 60, 3.—With following *u*, (*atho*): 1.

afterwards, then, Chr. 56, 11. 2. and, Man. 2, 430. 3. even, Chr. 3, 1; and 23, 28.—With following *api*: nevertheless, Râm. 2, 29, 7.—With following *vâ*: 1. or also, or, Man. 2, 219. Pañch. i, d. 399, *vâtha* instead of *vâtha vâ* (cf. Pañch. iii, d. 36. *atho vâ*, Man. 3, 202). 2. or even, Bhartṛ. 2, 10. 3. but no, Çâk. 60, 18. 4. it is particularly used to introduce sentences: for, Pañch. 26, 14.—With following *kim*: yes, well (in dialogue, cf. *τί μήν*).—Cf. Lat. at.

अथर्वन् *atharvan* (borrowed from the Zend. *âthra-van*, derived from *âtar*, 'fire'), m. **1.** A priest. **2.** The name of a Ṛishi, or saint. **3.** The Atharvaveda.

अथर्वाङ्गिरस *atharvâṅgirasa*, i.e. *atharvan-aṅgiras + a*. **1.** adj., f. *sî*. Revealed to Atharvan and Angiras, Man. 11, 33. **2.** sing. and pl. The hymns of the Atharvaveda.

अथर्वी *atharvî*, f. (probably from *a-tharvan*), The wife of a priest (?), Chr. 296, 10 = Rigv. 1, 112, 10.

अथो *atho*, see *atha*.

अद् *AD*, ii, 2, Par. (in epic poetry also Âtm. Nal. 12, 35). To eat, Man. 2, 53; to devour, 4, 28. *Svadita*, i.e. *su-adita*, n. Well eaten, a term used after presenting food ('much good may it do you!'), Man. 3, 251; 254. *Adya*, Eatable, Pañch. iv. d. 79 (perhaps it ought to be changed to *âdya*, the regular form).—Cf. *ἔδω*; Lat. edere; Goth. itan; A.S. etan.

ऽअद् *-ad*, latter part of comp. words. One who eats, cf. *kravyâd*.

अदन *ad + ana*, n. Eating, Man. 11, 64.—Comp. *Phala-*, m. a parrot.

अदम्भित्व *adambhitva*, i.e. *a-dambhin + tva*, n. Sincerity.

अदस् *adas*, pronoun, nom. sing. m. and f. *asau*, nom. and acc. sing. n. *adas*; the bases of the remaining cases are *amu*, *amû*, and *amî*. That, you, Man. 10, 128. It is preceded by the relative pronoun, He-who, Man. 1, 7.

अदायिक *adâyika*, i.e. *a-dâya + ika*, adj. For which there are no heirs.

अदिति *a-diti*, f. The name of a female deity, Chr. 298, 25 = Rigv. 1, 112, 25; the mother of the gods, Râm. 3, 20, 15.

अदृश्यता *a-dṛiçya + tâ* (vb. *dṛiç*), f. Invisibility, Bhartṛ. 1, 95.

अदेशकाल *a-deça-kâla*, s. A wrong place and wrong time, Bhag. 17, 22.

अद्भुत *adbhuta*. I. adj., f. *tâ*. Surprising, wonderful; superl. *adbhuta + tama*, most surprising. II. n. A strange phenomenon, Man. 4, 118; a prodigy—Comp. *Atyadbhuta*, i.e. *ati-*, adj. very surprising. *Mahâ-* adj. very surprising.

अद्य *adya*, Ved. also *adyâ*, i. e. *a -div + â* (cf. *idam*), adv. **1.** To-day. **2.** Now.—Cf. Lat. ho-die, *ἤδη*.

अद्यतन *adya + tana*, adj., f. *nî*. **1.** Of to-day, Pañch. 5, 6.—**2.** Of this time, a contemporary, Râjat. 5, 100. 'The Hrishîkeça (i.e. an idol of Vishṇu) of Suyya, reposing in meditation on the bank, may be adored by any contemporary who comes near the temple of Sundarî.'

अद्यतनीय *adyataniya*, i.e. *adya-tana + iya*, adj., f. *yâ*. Of to-day, Pañch. 169, 13.

अद्यूति *adyûti*, i.e. *a-div + ti*, adj. Eager, Chr. 298, 24 = Rigv. 1, 112, 24.

अद्रि *adri*, m. **1.** A stone, Chr. 293, 3 = Rigv. 1, 88, 3. **2.** A mountain. **3.** A cloud, Chr. 291, 5 = Rigv. 1, 85,

5. 4. A proper name.—**Comp.** *Asta-*, m. the mountain called *Asta* (q. cf.). *Kula-*, m. a principal mountain. *Tushâra-*, *tuhina-*, and *prâleya-*, m. Himâlaya.

अद्रिसारमय *adri-sâra + maya*, adj. f. *yi*. Made of iron.

अद्वयत्व *a-dvaya + tva*, n. Absence of duality. *tva + tas*, adv. In consequence of there being no duality, Vedântas. in Chr. 218, 23 (i.e. because he knows that there is no duality, that all is one).

अद्वारतस् *a-dvâra + tas*, adv. By any other aperture than the door, MBh. 13, 4750.

अद्वेषरागिन् *advesharâgin*, i.e. *a-dvesha-râga + in*, adj. Exempt from hatred and affection, Man. 2, 1.

अद्वेष्टृत्व *a-dveshṭṛi + tva*, n. Inoffensiveness, Vedântas. in Chr. 219, 6.

अध *a + dha* (cf. *adhas*), a particle. There, then, Lass. Anth. 98, 14 = Rigv. 5, 9, 5.

अधम *adhama* (an old superlative, akin to *adhas*), adj., f. *mâ*. Extremely low, Man. 6, 65. In Karmadhâraya compounds it is generally the latter part: e.g. *Dvija-*, m. the meanest of twice-born men, Man. 3, 140; *Nara-*, m. the lowest of mortals, Man. 10, 26; *Pâpa-*, m. the lowest of the wicked; *Pârthiva-*, m. the meanest of kings; *Purusha-*, m. the vilest of men; *Çaçaka-*, m. the vilest of hares. —Cf. Lat. infimus.

अधमर्ण *adhamarṇa*, i. e. *adhama-ṛiṇa*, m. A debtor, Man. 8, 47.

अधमर्णिक *adhamarṇika*, i.e. *adhamarṇa + ika*, m. A debtor, Man. 8, 48.

अधर *adhara* (an old comparative, akin to *adhas*). I. adj., f. *râ*. Lower, inferior. II. m. 1. The lower lip Çâk. 102, 10. 2. The lip in general, Çiç. 9, 46.—**Comp.** *Khaṇḍita-*, adj., f. *râ*, with bitten lips, Pañch. 46, 1.—Cf. Lat. inferus; Goth. undar; A.S. under; probably ἔνεροι.

अधरोष्ठ *adharoshṭha*, and **अधरौष्ठ** *adharaushṭha*, i.e. *adhara-oshṭha*, m. 1. The lower lip, Suçr. 1, 114, 19. 2. The lower and the upper lips, the lips, Pañch. 45, 11. — **Comp.** *Anguli-sam-vṛita-*, adj. the lips of which are covered with the finger, Çâk.d. 73. *Vimba-phala-*, adj., f. *shṭhi*, having lips like the Bimba fruit, Râm. 5, 28, 17.

अधस् *a + dhas* (cf. *idam*). I. adv. 1. Underneath. 2. Low, Man. 11, 224. 3. Down, Pañch. i. d. 214; to hell, Man. 7, 53. II. prepos. Under, with the gen., Man. 2, 59, and abl. Pañch. 115, 25. III. doubled: *adhodhas*, i.e. *adhas-adhas*, adv. 1. Lower and lower, Man. 7, 53. 2. One below the other.—Cf. ἔνθεν, and see *adhara*.

अधस्तात् *adhas-tât* (the latter part is the original abl. of *tad*). I. adv. 1. Underneath, below. 2. Down, downward, Man. 4, 54; to hell, 194. II. prepos. Under, with the gen. III. latter part of comp. adv. Under, Pañch. 141, 20.

अधि *a + dhi* (cf. *idam*). I. adv. Above, on high, Chr. 291, 2 = Rigv. 1, 85, 2. II. prepos. Over, on, with the abl., Chr. 287, 7 = Rigv. 1, 48, 7. III. Combined and compounded with verbs and their derivatives. IV. Former part of compounded nouns and adverbs, implying: 1. Over, cf. *adhijya*. 2. Chief, cf. *adhirâja*. 3. Before, cf. *adhyaksha*. 4. Relative to, cf. *adhiyajña*. 5. On, cf. *adhijânu*.—Cf. Lat. ad.

अधिक *adhi + ka*, adj. 1. Exceeding, Man. 3, 49; greater, Râm. 4, 9, 95;

stronger, Pańch. ii. d. 29; more than, with the abl., Man. 9, 154; higher than, with the abl., Bhag. 6, 46; dearer, Râm. 2, 45, 32, Gorr. 2. Surpassing, Man. 11, 185; chief, Hit. pr. d. 48; highest, Bhartṛ. 2, 17. 3. Having an addition, *adhikam̃ mâsam*, 'a month and more,' Râm. 3, 15, 27. 4. Too much, Râm. 6, 16, 78.—acc. sing. *kam*, adv. 1. Much, exceedingly. 2. More; with the abl., Râjat. 5, 419. Comparat. *adhika + tara*, Better than, Çâk. 100, 17.—Comp. 1. exceeding, e.g. *Eka-*, adj. exceeding one, i.e. two, Man. 9, 117. *Sarva-dâna-*, adj. better than any gift, Yajń. 1, 334. *Prâṇa-*, adj. dearer than life. *Varsha-çata-*, adj. longer than a century. 2. exceeded by, particularly after numerals, e.g. *Varshe . . . râjanyabandhor dvâvim̃çe, vaiçyasya dvyadhike tatah*, 'in the twenty-second year for a soldier, for a merchant two years later than that,' Man. 2, 65. *Navatim̃ navâdhikâm*, ninety-nine, Ragh. 3, 69. *Vayodhika*, i.e. *vayas -adhika*, adj. advanced in age, Man. 4, 141. 3. doubled: *Adhikâdhika*, adj. outbidding each other, Râjat. 5, 264.

अधिकरण *adhikaraṇa*, i. e. *adhi -kṛi + ana*, n. 1. Substance, substratum, or site. 2. Court of justice, Daçak. in Chr. 180, 20.—Comp. *Dharma-*, n. 1. administration of justice, Pańch. 97, 1. 2. A court of justice, Pańch. 96, 25. *Râma-*, adj. relating to Râma, Râm. 2, 15, 29. *Samâna-*, I. n. generic property. II. adj. contained in the same subject or category.

अधिकार and **अधीकार** *adhîkâra*, i.e. *adhi-kṛi + a*, m. 1. Superintendence, Vikr. d. 42. 2. Administration. 3. Office, Pańch. 63, 23. 4. Office of a king. 5. Right, title, Man. 2, 16. 6. Topic, main point.—Comp. *Tâmbûla-*, m. the bearer of betel, an officer, Pańch. 63, 22. *Dharma-*, m. administration of justice. *Pṛitanâ-*, adj. relating to battles, MBh. 1, 7166. *Samâna-*, m. 1. equal duty. 2. generic character. *Hṛita-*, adj. 1. deprived of office. 2. deprived of one's right.

अधिकारित्व *adhikâritva*, i.e. *adhikârin + tva*, n. The office of a superintendent, Râjat. 5, 470.

अधिकारिन् *adhikârin*, i. e. *adhi -kâra + in*, adj. 1. One who holds an office, Pańch. i. d. 180. 2. A superintendent, Hit. 61, 7. 3. One who is entitled to, or fit for, something, Vedântas. in Chr. 202, 9. — Comp. *Dharma-*, m. a judge, Pańch. 101, 2.

अधिक्षेप *adhikshepa*, i.e. *adhi-kship + a*, m. 1. Detraction, Râjat. 5, 234. 2. Censure, Daçak. in Chr. 188, 3. 3. Sneer, 184, 16.

अधिगम *adhi-gam + a*, m. 1. Coming to, attaining, Megh. 50. 2. Accession to, Râjat. 5, 45. 3. Gaining, profit, Man. 8, 157. 4. Reading, Man. 2, 2. 5. Perception, Çiç. 9, 19.—Comp. *Dus-*, adj. 1. hard to be attained, Mâlav. 10, 8. 2. difficult to be learned, Kir. 5, 18.

अधिगमन *adhi-gam + ana*, n. 1. Obtaining, Râm. 4, 45, 19. 2. Reading, Man. 11, 65.—Comp. *Dâra-*, n. marriage, Man. 1, 112.

अधिगुण *adhi-guṇa*, adj. Of superior qualities, Megh. 6.

अधिगोप्तृ *adhigoptṛi*, i.e. *adhi-gup + tṛi*, in *dhana-*, m. A name of Kuvera, MBh. 5, 7521.

अधिजनन *adhi-jan + ana*, n. Birth, Man. 2, 169.

अधिजानु *adhi-jânu*, adv. On the knee, Çiç. 9, 54.

अधिज्य *adhi-jya* (cf. *jyâ*), adj. Strung (as a bow), Çâk. d. 6.

अधिज्यता *adhijya*+*tâ*, f. Condition of being strung, Ragh. 11, 14.

अधित्यका *adhi*+*tya*+*kâ*, f. Land on the upper part of a mountain, Hit. 101, 18.

अधिप *adhi-pa* (vb. 2. *pâ*), m. **1.** A lord, Chr. 3, 3. **2.** A king. **3.** A superintendent, Râjat. 5, 238. **4.** A commander.—Comp. *Amara-*, m. a name of Indra, Râm. 2, 74, 19. *Sa-amara-*, adj. with the lord of the gods, Râm. 3, 53, 28. *Jana-*, m. a king. *Jala-*, m. a name of Varuṇa. *Târâ-*, m. the moon, Râm. 3, 58, 4. *Daṇḍa-*, m. lord chief justice, Kathâs. 25, 130. *Daṇḍa-dhara-*, m. a king, Râjat. 4, 655. *Deva-*, m. Indra. *Dvâra-*, m. a porter, a chamberlain, Râjat. 5, 213. *Dharâ-*, m. a king. *Nagara-*, m. chief of the police in a town, Kathâs. 5, 49.

अधिपति *adhi-pati*, m. **1.** A lord, an owner, Man. 8, 37. **2.** A king.—Comp. *Gaṇa-*, m. Çiva, Çiç. 9, 27. *Tri-*, m. epithet of Kṛishṇa-Vishṇu (lord over the three primary qualities), Bhâg. P. 3, 16, 24. *Daçâdhipati*, i.e. *daçan-*, m. a commander of ten men, MBh. 12, 3712. *Dhana-*, m. a name of Kuvera, Kir. 5, 16. *Nagara-*, m. chief of the police in a town, Kathâs. 10, 70.

अधिमन्थ and **अधीमन्थ** *adhî-mantha*, i e. *adhi-manth*+*a*, m. Acute pain in the eyes.

अधिमांसक *adhi-mâṁsa*+*ka*, m. Inflammation of the tonsils.

अधियज्ञ *adhi-yajña*. I. m. The supreme sacrifice, Bhag. 8, 4. II. acc. sing. *ñam*, adv. Concerning sacrifice, Man. 6, 83.

अधियोध *adhi-yodha*, m. A champion (?), Râm. 6, 23, 28.

अधिरथ *adhi-ratha*, m. **1.** A charioteer. **2.** A proper name.

अधिराज *adhirâja*, i.e. *adhi-râjan*, m. A supreme king.

अधिराज्य *adhi-râjya*, n. Supreme sway, Mahâv. 65, 9.

अधिरोपण *adhiropaṇa*, i. e. *adhi-ruh*, Caus. +*ana*, n. Lifting up. *Sâ sehe . . . adhiropaṇam*, She endured being lifted on . . ., Böhtl. Chr. 240, 313.

अधिरोहण *adhirohaṇa*, i. e. *adhi-ruh*+*ana*, n. Mounting, Râm. 5, 85, 29.

अधिवास *adhivâsa*, m., i.e. **1.** *adhi-vas*+*a*. A house, an abode, Dev. 4, 10. **2.** *adhi-vâs*+*a*. Perfuming the person, Bhartṛ. 1, 12.

अधिवासन *adhi-vâs*+*ana*, n. Perfuming the person.

अधिवेश्म *adhiveçma*, i. e. *adhi-veçman*, adv. At home, Çiç. 9, 78.

अधिष्ठातृ *adhishṭhâtṛi*, i. e. *adhi-sthâ*+*tṛi*, m. f. *tri*, n. **1.** Ruling, a ruler. **2.** Protecting.

अधिष्ठान *adhishṭhâna*, i. e. *adhi-sthâ*+*ana*, n. **1.** A resting-place. **2.** A seat, Man. 12, 4. **3.** An abode. **4.** A place, Pañch. 10, 3. **5.** A town, a capital, Râjat. 5, 266. **6.** Dignity, Nal. 26, 28. **7.** Power, Râm. 4, 14, 30.—Comp. *Tri-*, adj. having three bases, Man. 12, 4. *Dharma-*, n. a court of justice, Pañch. 237, 20. *Nis-*, adj. being without a solid base, Râm. 5, 82, 12. *Sa-*, adj. having a solid base, ib. *Su-*, adj., having a solid base, Chr. 25, 52.

अधीकार *adhikâra*; see *adhikâra*.

अधीतिन् *adhîtin,* i.e. *adhi-ita + in* (vb. *i*), adj. Conversant with, Daçak. 140, 3.

अधीन *adhîna,* i.e. *adhas + îna,* adj. Subject, dependent, Ragh. I. 72. It is generally the latter part of compound words: e.g. *adhi-,* adj. Wholly dependent, Man. 8, 65. *tvad-,* adj. Subject to thee, Râm. 2, 72, 52. *para-,* adj. Depending on another, Râm. 3, 37, 6. *sva-,* adj. 1. Independent. 2. Dependent on ourselves, belonging to us, faithful, Pañch. i. d. 196.

अधीरता *a-dhîra + tâ* (cf. *dhîra*), f. 1. Unsteadiness. 2. Pusillanimity.

अधीश *adhi-îça,* m. A lord, Çiç. 9, 38. A chief, Râjat. 5, 300.—**Comp.** *Tri-,* m. epithet of Krishṇa-Vishṇu (the lord over the three primary qualities), Bhâg. P. 3, 2, 21. *Dina-,* m. the sun, Pañch. i. d. 231.

अधुना *adhunâ,* adv. Now.

अधोवेक्षिन् *adhovekshin,* i.e. *adhas -ava-iksh + in,* adj., f. *iṇî,* With downcast eyes, Pañch. i. 214.

अध्यक्ष *adhyaksha,* i.e. *adhi-aksha.* I. adj. Perceptible, Bhâshâp. 48. II. n. Perception, ib. 56; 149. III. m. A superintendent, Daçak. in Chr. 186, 3. —**Comp.** *An-,* adj imperceptible, Bhâshâp. 48. *Açva-,* m. a superintendent of the horses, Pañch. 156, 18. *Koça-,* m. a treasurer, Pañch. 156, 18. *Gaja-,* m. a superintendent of the elephants, Pañch. 156, 18. *Dvâra-,* m. a porter, a chamberlain, Râm. 1, 20, 5. *Sûda-,* m. a superintendent of the kitchen.

अध्यग्नि *adhyagni,* i.e. *adhi-agni,* adv. Before the nuptial fire, Man. 9, 194.

अध्ययन *adhyayana,* i.e. *adhi-i + ana,* n. Reading, study, especially of the sacred books, Man. 1, 88.—**Comp.** *An-,* n. neglecting to read the sacred books, Böhtl. Ind. Spr. 1260.

अध्यर्ध *adhyardha,* i.e. *adhi-ardha,* adj. One and a half, Man. 9, 117.

अध्यवसाय *adhyavasâya,* i.e. *adhi -ava-so + a,* m. Perseverance, Pañch. 60, 6. Constancy, ib. iii. d. 261.

अध्यात्म *adhyâtma,* i.e. *adhi-âtman,* n. The supreme soul, Bhag. 8, 3.

अध्यात्मिक *adhyâtmika,* Man. 6, 83, read *âdhy°,* q. cf.

अध्यापक *adhyâpaka,* i.e. *adhi-i,* Caus. *+ aka,* m. A teacher, Man. 3, 156.

अध्यापकता *adhyâpaka + tâ,* f. Condition of a teacher, Râjat. 5, 469.

अध्यापन *adhyâpana,* i.e. *adhi-i,* Caus. *+ ana,* n. 1. Instructing. 2. Teaching the sacred books, Man. 8, 340.

अध्याय *adhyâya,* i.e. *adhi-i + a,* m. 1. Reading, recitation. 2. The time when the sacred books ought to be read, Man. 4, 102. 3. A section of a book, e.g. the subdivisions of the Râm., MBh. **Comp.** *An-,* m. the time when the sacred books ought not to be read, Man. 2, 106. *Sva-,* m. 1. perusal or study of the Vedas, Man. 2, 105. 2. the Veda. 3. inaudible reading or muttering of prayers. *Niḥsva-,* i.e. *nis -sva-,* adj. not muttering prayers, Hariv. 11187.

अध्यारोप *adhyâropa,* i.e. *adhi-â -ruh,* Caus. *+ a,* m. Erroneous predication, Vedântas. in Chr. 204, 7; 9; 210, 10; 211, 23.

अध्यावाहनिक *adhyâvâhanika,* i.e. *adhi-â-vah + ana + ika,* n. What was given to a wife on the bridal procession, Man. 9, 194.

अध्यास *adhyâsa*, i.e. *adhi-2.as + a*, m. Putting on; *pâdâdhyâse*, 'for putting the foot on a person,' Yâjń. 2, 217.

अध्यासिन् *adhyâsin*, i.e. *adhi-âs + in*, adj., f. *nî*. Sitting on, Pańch. iii. d. 270.

अध्रिगु *adhrigu*, i.e. probably *a-dhṛi + i-gam + u*, ved. adj. Of unrestrained course, Chr. 290, 3 = Rigv. i. 64, 3.

अध्वग *adhvaga*, i.e. *adhvan-ga*. I. adj. f. *gâ*, Being on the road, travelling, Râjat. 5, 9. II. m. A traveller, Man. 11, 1.

अध्वन् *adhvan*, m. A road, Man. 4, 60.—Comp. *Gata-* (vb. *gam*), adj. versed, skilled, MBh. 12, 11876.

अध्वनीन *adhvan + îna* and अध्वन्य *adhvan + ya*, m. A traveller, Yâjń. 1, 111.

अध्वर *adhvara*, i.e. perhaps *a-dhvṛi + a* or *adhvan + a* (with *r* for *n*, cf. *añghri*), m. A sacrifice, Chr. 288, 11 = Rigv. i. 48, 11.

अध्वरग *adhvara-ga*, adj. Belonging to a sacrifice, Draup. 6, 21.

अध्वर्यु *adhvaryu* (i.e. *adhvarya*, a ved. denominat., derived from *adhvara + u*), m. A special priest versed in the Yajurveda, Man. 3, 145.

अन्ऽ *an-*, before consonants अऽ *a-*, an inseparable prefix, implying I. negation, e.g. *a-brâhmaṇa*, m. One who is not a Brâhmaṇa, Man. 7, 85. *a-jńâna*, n. Ignorance, Man. 11, 145. *an-anta*, adj. Endless, Man. 4, 149. In this use it produces very often the opposite signification, e.g. *a-gada*, m. Health, Man. 11, 237. *a-krûra*, adj. Soft, Man. 2, 34. *a-sakṛit*, adv. Often, Man. 3, 233. II. deterioration. 1. Wrong, e.g. *a-kâla*, m. Unseasonable time, Man. 3, 105. 2. Bad, *a-kshetra*, n. A bad field, Man. 10, 71.—Cf. Lat. in-, Goth. and A.S. un-, ἀν- and ἀ-.

अन् *AN*, ii. 1, Par. † i, 4, Âtm. 1. To breathe. 2. To blow (as wind). 3. To live.—Cf. ἄνεμος; Lat. animus, ânus (cf. Sskr. *apâna*); Goth. uz-ana; see *prâṇa*.

अन *ana*, cf. *idam*.

अनडुद्द *anaḍudda*, i.e. *anaḍuh da*, m. The giver of a bull, Man. 4, 231.

अनडुह् *anaḍuh*, i.e. *anas-vah*, m. (nom. sing. *anaḍvân*, voc. *van*; the acc. sing., N.V.A. du. and N.V. pl. have as base *vâh*, the rest *uh*, the final of which becomes *ṭ* in the loc. pl. and *ḍ* before *bh*). A bull, or ox, Man. 11, 136.

अनतिप्रकाशकत्व *an-ati-prakâçaka + tva*, adj. Having the nature of a somewhat insufficient illustrator, Vedântas. in Chr. 205, 5.

अननुभावकता *ananubhâvakatâ*, i.e. *an-anu-bhû + aka + tâ*, f. Unintelligibility, Bhâshâp. 83.

अनन्तकर *anantakara*, i.e. *an-anta -kṛi + a*, adj. Making endless or infinite, Râm. 5, 20, 26.

अनन्तर *an-antara*, I. adj., f. *râ*. 1. Having nothing intermediate, Man. 2, 19. 2. Immediately bordering, next, Nal. 22, 16. 3. Immediately following, Bhâshâp. 123. 4. Of an immediately following caste, Man. 10, 14. 5. Allowing no delay, necessary, Chr. 10, 6. II. *ram*, acc. 1. adv. Next in space, Râm. 2, 87, 5. Next in time, immediately afterwards, then, Râm. 1, 3, 7. Especially compounded with preceding *tad-*, after that, Pańch. 70, 17. 2. prep. with abl. and gen. Immediately after, Bhag. 12, 12; Râm. 5, 73, 28. After, Pańch. 108, 13. — Comp. *Sam-anantara + m*, adv. immediately after, Chr. 14, 20.

अनन्तरज *anantara-ja* (vb. *jan*), m. A son, born by a wife belonging to a caste next to that of her husband, except the fourth, Man. 10, 41.

अनपकर्मन् *an-apa-karman*, n. Subtraction (of what has been given), Man. 8, 4.

अनपक्रिया *an-apa-kriyâ*, f. Non-payment, Man. 8, 214.

अनपसर *an-apasara*, m. One who has no claims (properly: no outlets), Man. 8, 198.

अनपाकर्मन् *anapâkarman* = *anapakarman*.

अनपायिन् *anapâyin*, i.e. *an-apa-i* + *in*, adj., f. *nî*. 1. Not going away, Kathâs. 12, 33. 2. Lasting, Râjat. 5, 32. 3. Immovable. 4. Imperishable.

अनभिस्नेह *anabhisneha*, i. e. *an-abhi-snih* + *a*, adj. Without attachment, Bhag. 2, 57.

अनय, I. *a-naya*, m. 1. Bad conduct, Pañch. 259, 16. 2. Sin, Râm. 5, 24, 28. 3. Wrong, Râm. 6, 40, 5 (*na sa veda nayânayau.* Such a man knows neither right nor wrong). 4. Lewdness, Böhtl. Ind. Spr. 1260. II. *an-aya*, m. 1. Distress, Man. 10, 95. 2. Ill-luck, Chr. 8, 33.

अनर्घत्व *an-arghya* + *tva*, n. Invaluableness, Hit. Pr. d. 4.

अनर्थ *an-artha*. I. m. 1. Disadvantage, Man. 8, 24; *Bhavaty anarthâya*, It becomes prejudicial, Man. 4, 193. 2. Misfortune, Çâk. 81, 8. II. adj., f. *thâ*. 1. Useless, Pañch. 248, 6. 2. Prejudicial, Râm. 6, 21, 5. 3. Poor, Daçak. in Chr. 181, 1. 4. Unhappy, Râm. 3, 75, 40.

अनर्थक *anartha* + *ka*, adj. 1. Useless, Pañch. 183, 2. 2. Vain, Brâhmaṇav. 1, 14. 3. Unmeaning, nonsensical.

अनर्थत्व *an-artha* + *tva*, n. Pañch. i. d. 158, read *anarthitva*; see *arthitva*.

अनर्ह्यता *an-arhya* + *tâ* (vb. *arh*), f. Disproportionateness, Vedântas. in Chr. 215, 12.

अनल *an* + *ala*, m. 1. Fire, Man. 3, 261. 2. The deity of fire, Man. 5, 1. 3. The digestive power. 4. The proper name of a monkey, Râm. 6, 13, 8.—Comp. *Kâla-*, m. the fire of all-destroying Time, Râm. 3, 69, 10. *Dâva-*, m. the fire of a forest conflagration, Pañch. 142, 6. *Baḍavâ-*, m. submarine fire, Böhtl. Ind. Spr. 419.

अनलद *anala da*, adj. Quenching fire, Kirât. 5, 25.

अनवगाहिन् *an-ava-gâh* + *in*, adj. f. *nî*. Not entering, Bhâshâp. 135.

अनवद्यता *an-a-vadya* + *tâ* (cf. *avadya*), f. Blamelessness, Mâlav. 20, 10.

अनवेक्षक *anavekshaka*, i.e. *an-ava-îksh* + *aka*, adj. One who does not take care, Râm. 4, 17, 12.

अनस् *anas*, n. A cart, Man. 8, 209. —Cf. Lat. onus.

अनसूयितृ *anasûyitṛi*, i.e. *an-asûya* + *tṛi*, m. Free from a spirit of detraction, MBh. 1, 5611.

अनसूयु *anasûyu*, i.e. *an-asûya* + *u*, adj. Free from a spirit of detraction.

अनस्थन् *an-asthan* (cf. *asthi*), adj. Boneless, Man. 11, 140.

अनागत *an-â-gata*, (vb. *gam*), adj., f. *tâ*. 1. Not arrived, Râjat. 5, 171. 2. Future, Böhtl. Ind. Spr. 89. *anâgatañ kṛi*, To make dispositions for the future, ib. 88. 3. Not mentioned, Râm. 3, 56, 18.

अनागतवन्त् *anâgata + vant*, adj., f. *vatî.* Full of schemes concerning the future, Pańch. v. d. 59.

अनात्मज्ञ *anâtmajńa*, i.e. *an-âtman -jńa* (vb. *jńâ*), adj. Foolish, Çâk. 78, 15.

अनामिका *anâmikâ*, i.e. *a-nâman + ka*, f. The ring-finger, Yâjń. 3, 278.

अनावृष्टि *anâvṛishṭi*, i.e. *an-â-vṛish + ti*, f. Drought, Lass. 62, 18.

अनाश्रव *anâçrava*, i.e. *an-â-çru + a*, adj., f. *vâ.* Not obeying, Daçak. in Chr. 191, 8.

अनाहिताग्निता *anâhitâgni + tâ* (cf. *agni*), f. Neglecting to keep up the consecrated fire, Man. 11, 65.

अनिमेषता *a-nimesha + tâ* (cf. *nimesha*), f. Not winking, Çiç. 9, 11.

अनिल *an + ila*, m. **1.** Wind. **2.** The deity of wind, Man. 5, 96. **3.** Wind as one of the humors of the body. **4.** A proper name.

अनिवर्तित्व *anivartitva*, i.e. *a-nivartin + tva*, n. Not running away, courageous resistance, Man. 7, 88.

अनिवेदक *anivedaka*, i.e. *a-ni-vid*, Caus. + *aka*, adj. Not reporting, MBh. 13, 2385.

अनीक *an + îka*, m. n. **1.** The face (ved.), front (ved.). **2.** An army, Râjat. 5, 452.—**Comp.** *Agra-*, the van of an army, Man. 7, 193. *Yathâ-anîka + m*, adv. as far as the host extended, MBh. 3, 15715.

अनीरसन *anîrasana*, i. e. *a-nis -rasanâ*, adj. Girded, Kir. 5, 11.

अनु *anu.* I. adv. Afterwards, then, Râm. 2, 84, 4. **II.** prep. **1.** with acc. **a.** Along, Râm. 2, 83, 6. **b.** After, Pańch. 165, 5. **c.** According to, like, Vikr. d. 110. **2.** with abl. In consequence of, Râm. 6, 10, 23. **III.** combined and compounded with verbs and their derivatives. **IV.** former part of compounded nouns and adverbs, implying: After, according to, along, again, secondary, every.—Cf. *ἀνά*, Goth. ana, N.H.G. an.

अनुकम्पक *anu-kamp + aka*, adj. Having tender affection, Man. 6, 8.

अनुकम्पन *anu-kamp + ana*, n. Compassion, Râm. 2, 45, 31.

अनुकम्पा *anu-kamp + â*, f. Compassion, Bhartṛ. 2, 60.—**Comp.** *Sa-anu -kampa*, I. adj. kind. II. *pam*, adv. kindly, Daçak. in Chr. 181, 13.

अनुकम्पिन् *anu-kamp + in*, adj. Having tender affection, Râm. 6, 70, 38.

अनुकल्प *anu-kalpa*, m. A substituted rule, Man. 11, 30.

अनुकाङ्क्षिन् *anu-kâṅksh + in*, adj. Striving for, eager.

अनुकार *anukâra*, i.e. *anu-kṛi + a*, m. **1.** Imitation. **2.** Resemblance.

अनुकारिन् *anukârin*, i.e. *anu-kṛi* or *anukâra + in*, adj. **1.** Acting conformably. **2.** Imitating, Çâk. d. 49. Like, Çâk. 104, 8.—**Comp.** *Hita-*, adj. kind.

अनुकार्य *anu-kârya*, n. What must be done later, Râm. 6, 40, 5.

अनुकीर्तन *anukîrtana*, i.e. *anu-kṛît + ana*, n. Proclaiming, Kathâs. 4, 121.

अनुकूल *anu-kûla*, adj. **1.** Suitable, Râm. 1, 17, 26. **2.** Agreeable, Râm. 5, 31, 45. **3.** Favourable, Pańch. 120, 16.

अनुकूलता *anukûla + tâ*, f. **1.** Favour, Pańch. 263, 13. **2.** Proneness, Bhâshâp. 156.

अनुकूलत्व *anukûla-tva*, n. Favour, Ragh. 1, 42.

अनुकृति *anu-kṛi+ti*, f. Imitation, Megh. 70.

अनुक्रम *anu-kram+a*, m. **1.** Regular order, Yâjń. 1, 19. **2.** Table (of contents), MBh. 1, 2294.—Comp. *Devatâ-*, m. table of the deities, Bhâg. P. 2, 6, 25.

अनुक्रमणिका *anukramaṇikâ*, i.e. *anu-kram+ana+î+ka*, f. Table of contents, MBh. 1, 103.

अनुक्रोश *anukroça*, i.e. *anu-kruç+a*, m. Compassion, Chr. 21, 11.—Comp. *Nis-*, I. m. unmercifulness, Râm. 4, 19, 21. II. adj. merciless. *Sa-*, 1. adj. f. *çâ*, compassionate. 2. *çam*, adv. compassionately, Daçak. in Chr. 179, 16.

अनुक्षणम् *anu-kshaṇa+m*, adv. Every moment, perpetually, Hit. 59, 17.

अनुक्षपम् *anu-kshapa+m* (cf. *kshapâ*), adv. Every night, Kirât. 5, 17.

ऽअनुग *-anu-ga* (vb. *gam*), I. adj., f. *gâ*. **1.** Following, Pańch. i. d. 63. **2.** Corresponding, Man. 8, 239. II. m. A follower, a servant, Râm. 1, 12, 26.—Comp. *Pada-*, m. a follower. *Çrotra-pada-*, adj. agreeable to the ear, Râm. 2, 100, 25, Gorr. *Vaça-*, adj. 1. obedient, submissive. 2. subject, Man. 2, 214. *Sa-*, adj. with one's attendants, Râm. 3, 55, 24. *Sa-bala-*, adj. with (his) army and followers, Chr. 54, 16.

अनुगति *anugati*, i.e. *anu-gam+ti*, f. **1.** Following, Râm. 5, 81, 23. **2.** Assent.

ऽअनुगतिक *-anugati+ka*, adj. Following, Pańch. i. d. 389.

अनुगम *anu-gam+a*, m. **1.** Following, pursuing. **2.** Penetrating.

अनुगमन *anu-gam+ana*, n. Following, Râm. 1, 28, 32.

अनुगामिन् *anugâmin*, i.e. *anu-gam+in-*. I. adj., f. *nî*. Following, pursuing, Râm. 5, 5, 31. II. m. A servant, Chr. 62, 47.

अनुगुण *anu-guṇa*, adj. f. *ṇâ*. Corresponding, conformable, Mṛichchh. 43, 16. Suitable, Daçak. in Chr. 195, 21.

अनुग्रह *anu-grah+a*, m. **1.** Promoting, Râm. 6, 11, 22. **2.** Favour, Pańch. 34, 2. **3.** Help, Böhtl. Ind. Spr. 1643.

अनुग्रहण *anugrahaṇa*, i. e. *anu-grah+ana*, n. **1.** Showing favour, Râm. 2, 1, 19. **2.** Favour.

अनुग्राहक *anugrâhaka*, i. e. *anu-grah+aka*, m. A supporter, Râjat. 5, 259.

अनुचर *anu-char-a*, I. adj. f. *râ*. Following, Ragh. 2, 4. II. m. **1.** A servant, an attendant, Pańch. 68, 11. **2.** A supporter, Râjat. 5, 288. III. f. *râ* (ved. also *rî*), A female servant, Râm. 6, 38, 14.—Comp. *Lakshmaṇa-*, adj. accompanied by Lakshmaṇa, Râm. 1, 24, 3.

अनुचिन्तन *anu-chint+ana*, n. **1.** Thinking, Vedântas. in Chr. 216, 22. **2.** Regretful remembrance.

अनुज *anu-ja* (vb. *jan*), I. adj., f. *jâ*. Younger, Man. 9, 57. II. m. A younger brother. III. f. *jâ*. A younger sister, Râm. 3, 4, 52.

अनुजीविन् *anu-jîv+in*, m. A dependent, a servant, Pańch. i. d. 79.

अनुज्ञा *anu-jńâ*, f. **1.** Permission. **2.** Dismission.—Comp. *Prâpta-* (vb. *âp*), adj. having received the permission to withdraw.

अनुताप *anutâpa*, i.e. *anu-tap+a*, m. Repentance, Man. 11, 227.—Comp. *Puçcha-* (cf. *paçchât*), m. repentance.

अनुतापन *anutâpana,* i.e. *anu-tap + ana,* adj. Afflicting, Râm. 4, 2, 13.

अनुत्सेकिन् *anutsekin,* i.e. *an-utseka + in,* f. *nî.* Humble, Çâk. d. 93.

अनुदर्शन *anudarçana,* i. e. *anu -driç + ana,* n. Consideration, Bhag. 13, 8.

अनुदर्शिन् *anudarçin,* i. e. *anu -driç + in,* adj. Considering, Pañch. iii. d. 169.

अनुदिनम् *anu-dina + m,* adv. Every day, Kirât. 5, 37.

अनुदिवसम् *anu-divasa + m.* adv. Every day, Çâk. 47, 2 (Ch.).

अनुदेहम् *anu-deha + m,* adv. From behind, Çiç. 9, 73.

अनुधावन *anu-dhâv + ana,* n. Cleansing.

अनुध्यान *anudhyâna,* i.e. *anu dhyai + ana,* n. Meditation, Çâk. 57, 13 v.r.

अनुनय *anunaya,* i.e. *anu-nî + a,* m. 1. Reconcilement, Hit. ii. d. 117. 2. Courtesy, Vikr. d. 20.—Comp. *Sa-,* I. adj. kind. II. *yam,* adv. tenderly, Daçak. in Chr. 190, 4.

अनुनयम् *anu-naya + m,* adv. According to propriety, Râm. 4, 26, 10.

अनुनाद *anunâda,* i.e. *anu-nad + a* m. Consequent sound ; echo.—Comp. *Sa-veṇu-viṇâ-paṇava-anunâda + m,* adv. re-echoing with flutes, lutes, and tabors.

अनुनादिन् *anunâdin,* i.e. *anu-nad + in,* adj., f. *nî.* Echoing, Râm. 6, 69, 40.

अनुपदम् *anu-pada + m,* adv. 1. Immediately after, Pañch. 198, 11. 2. In a moment, Çâk. 5, 11. 3. At every step, Çiç. 9, 78.

अनुपदिन् *anu-pad + in,* m. A searcher, Çiç. 9, 70.

अनुपरोधतस् *an-uparodha + tas,* adv. Without inconvenience, Man. 4, 32.

अनुपसंहारिन् *anupasaṁhârin,* i.e. *an-upa-sam-hṛi + in,* adj., f. *iṇî.* Non-exclusive (a subdivision of one of the forms of fallacious middle term), Bhâshâp 71 ; 73.

अनुपातिन् *anupâtin,* i.e. *anu-pat + in,* adj. f. *nî.* Following.

अनुपालन *anupâlana,* i.e. *anu-pâ,* Caus. + *ana,* n. Observance, Râm. 5, 24, 20.—Comp. *Dus-,* adj. hard to be preserved, MBh. 13, 1929.

अनुपालिन् *anupâlin,* i.e. *anu-pâ,* Caus. + *in,* adj. Cherishing, Man. 9, 204.

अनुपूर्व *anu-pûrva,* adj. f. *vâ.* 1. Following whoever or whatever precedes. 2. Regular.

अनुपूर्वशस् *anupûrva + ças,* adv. In regular order, Man. 1, 2 ; with gen. Man. 8, 142.

अनुप्रवेश *anu-praveça,* m. 1. Entering after. 2. Entering (in general).

अनुप्रश्न *anu-praçna,* m. A question, MBh. 12, 4924.

अनुबन्ध *anu-bandh + a,* m. 1. Beginning, Daçak. in Chr. 195, 5. 2. A motive, Man. 8, 126. 3. An indispensable element, Vedântas. in Chr. 202, 8. 4. Uninterrupted succession, Râm. 5, 3, 43. 5. Consequence. 6. Posterity, Râm. 2. 7, 28.

ऽनुबन्धन *-anu-bandh + ana,* n. Uninterrupted connection, Vikr. 55, 10.

ऽनुबन्धिन् *-anubandhin,* i. e. *anubandha + in,* adj., f. *nî.* 1. Connected with, Bhag. 15, 2 ; Daçak, in Chr. 193, 6. 2. Lasting.

अनुबल *anu-bala,* n. The rear of an army, Râm. 1, 1, 46.

अनुबुभूषु *anububhûshu,* i. e. *anu-bubhûsha,* desider. of *bhû* + *u,* adj. Desiring to enjoy, Daçak. in Chr. 201, 14.

अनुभर्तृ *anubhartṛi,* i.e. *anu-bhṛi* + *tṛi,* m., f. *trî,* n. One who imitates, Chr, 294, 6 = Rigv. i. 88, 6.

अनुभव *anubhava,* i.e. *anu-bhû* + *a,* m. **1.** Apprehension, Vedântas. in Chr. 210, 14. **2.** Understanding, Râm. 4, 42, 9 (Hanuman knows well how to finish the work).

अनुभाव *anubhâva,* i.e. *anu-bhû* + *a,* m. **1.** Dignity, authority, Daçak. 196, 14. **2.** Power, Çâk. 31, 2. **3.** A sign, Kathâs. 4, 117; Ragh. 2, 75.—Comp. *Mahâ-,* adj. pre-eminent, just, virtuous.

अनुभाविन् *anubhâvin,* i. e. *anu-bhû* + *in.* I. adj. Seeing, Çâk. 89, 3 (Prâkṛ.). II. m. A witness, Man. 8, 89.

अनुभूति *anu-bhû* + *ti,* f. Apprehension, perception, Bhâshâp. 50.

अनुमति *anumati,* i.e. *anu-man* + *ti,* f. **1.** Assent, Daçak. in Chr. 186, 3. **2.** The goddess of the fifteenth day of the moon's age, Man. 3, 86.

अनुमन्तृ *anu-man* + *tṛi,* m. One who assents, Man. 5, 51.

अनुमरण *anumaraṇa,* i.e. *anu-mṛi* + *ana,* n. Following in death, Hit. iii. d. 28.

अनुमा *anu-mâ,* f. Conclusion, Bhâshâp. 65.

अनुमान *anumâna,* i.e. *anu-mâ* + *ana,* n. **1.** Inferring, Bhâshâp. 139; 140. **2.** Argument, Man. 8, 144; Râm. 6, 23, 2. **3.** Analogy, Vikr. 63, 13.

अनुमानन *anumânana,* i. e. *anu-man,* Caus. + *ana,* n. Inducing to confess, Chr. 53, 2.

अनुमार्दव *anu-mârdava,* n. Compassion, Râm. 5, 37, 31.

अनुमिति *anumiti,* i.e. *anu-mâ* + *ti,* f. Conclusion, Bhâshâp. 51; 65.

अनुयातृ *anu-yâ* + *tṛi,* m. A companion, Râm. 2, 91, 59.

अनुयात्र *anu-yâ-tra,* n. and fem. *trâ.* **1.** Retinue. **2.** Attendance, Râm. 4, 36, 10.—Comp. *Datta-,* adj. accompanied.

अनुयात्रिक *anuyâtrika,* i.e. *anuyâtra* + *ika,* m. A follower, Çâk. 30, 9.

अनुयान *anuyâna,* i.e. *anu-yâ* + *ana,* n. Following, Râm. 2, 105, 10.

अनुयायिता *anuyâyitâ,* i.e. *anu-yâyin* + *tâ,* f. Following, Râm. 2, 90, 20.

अनुयायिन् *anuyâyin,* i.e. *anu-yâ* + *in,* adj. f. *ni,* Following, a follower, Chr. 35, 10.

अनुयुगम् *anu-yuga* + *m,* adv. In proportion to the (four) ages, Man. 1, 84.

अनुयोग *anuyoga,* i.e. *anu-yuj-a,* m. **1.** Question, Çâk. 15, 17. **2.** Inquiry, Daçak. in Chr. 193, 2; 195, 20.

अनुरञ्जक *anu-rañj* + *aka,* adj. Gratifying, Râm. 2, 1, 20, Gorr.

अनुरञ्जन *anu-rañj* + *ana,* n. Loving.

अनुरथ्या *anu-rathyâ,* f. A by-way running along the main street, Râm. 2, 6, 17.

अनुराग *anurâga,* i.e. *anu-rañj* + *a* m. **1.** Redness, Çiç. 9, 1. **2.** Love, Daçak. in Chr. 183, 18. **3.** Good will, Man. 7, 154.—Comp. *Kṛita-,* adj. f. *gâ,* loving, Râm. 2, 12, 98. *Sa-,* adj. impassioned.

अनुरागवन्त् *anurâga+vant*, adj., f. *vatî*. **1.** Enamoured, Hit. 28, 9. **2.** Enamoured or red, Çiç. 9, 10.

अनुरागिता *anurâgitâ*, i.e. *anurâgin +tâ*. f. Attachment.

अनुरागिन् *anurâgin*, i.e. *anurâga +in*, adj. **1.** Attached, Sâh. D. 76, 21. **2.** Causing affection.

अनुरूप *anu-rûpa*, adj., f. *pâ*. Suitable, Sâv. 2, 10; instr. *peṇa*, In proportion, Man. 8, 206. *pam*, adv. According to, Daçak. in Chr. 197, 13.—**Comp.** *Sva-*, adj. Innate, natural.

अनुरूपतस् *anurûpa+tas*, adv. In proportion, M. 7, 125.

अनुरोध *anurodha*, i.e. *anu-rudh + a*, m. **1.** Compliance, Hit. 106, 17. **2.** Obligation, Man. 2, 105.

अनुरोधन *anurodhana*, i. e. *anu -rudh+ana*, n. Compliance, Hit. ii. d. 99.

अनुरोधिता *anurodhitâ*, i.e. *anurodhin+tâ*, f. Compliance.

अनुरोधिन् *anurodhin*, i.e. *anurodha+in*, adj., f. *nî*. **1.** Compliant, Râm. 2, 75, 36. **2.** Acting in conformity with, Râm. 3, 2, 28.

अनुलेप *anulepa*, i.e. *anu-lip+a*, m. Unguent.

अनुलेपन *anulepana*, i.e. *anu-lip+ana*, n. Ointment, Çiç. 9, 24.

अनुलोमन *anulomana*, i.e. *anulomaya+ana*, I, adj. **1.** Putting in due order. **2.** (In medicine) Correcting the vitiated air of the body, or obviating excretory obstructions.

अनुलोमय *ANULOMAYA* (a denominat. derived from *anu-loma*), Par. **1.** To go or touch with the grain. **2.** (In medicine) To direct into the proper channel.

अनुवंश *anu-vaṁça*, m. A genealogical table, MBh. 1, 3762.

अनुवंश्य *anuvaṁçya*, i.e. *anuvaṁça +ya*, adj., f. *yâ*, Referring to genealogical lists, MBh. 3, 8330.

अनुवचन *anu-vach+ana*, n. **1.** Studying, Vedântas. in Chr. 203, 1. **2.** A section.

अनुवर्तन *anuvartana*, i.e. *anu-vṛit +ana*, n. Attending, Hit. 75, 17.

अनुवर्तित्व *anuvartitva*, i.e. *anuvartin +tva*, n. Accommodating one's self to, Pañch. i. d. 79.

अनुवर्तिन् *anuvartin*, i.e. *anu-vṛit+in*, adj., f. *nî*. **1.** Following, Daçak. in Chr. 196, 10. **2.** Obedient, Pañch. i. d. 331.—**Comp.** *Chitta-*, adj. compliant, Lass. 29, 16. *Vṛitta-*, adj. conforming to rule.

अनुवश *anu-vaça*. **I.** m. Obedience, Râm. 2, 8, 29. **II.** adj. Obedient, Râm. 2, 89, 7.

अनुवाक *anuvâka*, i.e. *anu-vach+a*, m. A section.

अनुवाद *anuvâda*, i.e. *anu-vad+a*, m. Report, Lass. 67, 2.—**Comp.** *Vâda-*, m. 1. attack and rejoinder. 2. plaint and reply.

अनुवादिन् *anuvâdin*, i.e. *anuvâda +in*, adj., f. *nî*. **1.** Assenting, Râm. 4, 62, 65. **2.** Harmonizing with, Râm. 5, 14, 10. **3.** Like, Pañch. 248, 11.

अनुविधायिन् *anuvidhâyin*, i. e. *anu-vi-dhâ+in*, adj., f. *nî*. **1.** Compliant, Vikr. 36, 1. **2.** Obedient, Hit. ii. d. 134.

अनुवृत्त *anu-vṛitta* (vb. *vṛit*), adj., f. *tâ*. Oval, Râm. 6, 23, 12.

अनुवृत्ति *anu-vṛit + ti*, f. **1.** Acting in conformity with. **2.** Compliance, Çiç. 9, 58. **3.** Attachment, Vedântas. in Chr. 219, 1.—**Comp.** *Sneha-*, f. affectionate intercourse.

अनुवेध *anuvedha*, i.e. *anu-vyadh + a*, m. Boring.

अनुवेलम् *anu-vela + m* (cf. *velâ*), adv. Continually, Ragh. 3, 5.

अनुवेश *anuveça*, i.e. *anu-viç + a*, m. Entering, MBh. 1, 7772.

अनुव्याहरण *anuvyâharaṇa*, i.e. *anu-vi-â-hṛi + ana*, n. Repetition, Râm. 1, 2, 43.

अनुव्रज्या *anu-vraj + yâ*, f. Attendance on a person departing, Man. 2, 241.

अनुव्रत *anu-vrata*, adj., f. *tâ*. **1.** Devout, Râm. 1, 6, 16. **2.** Faithful, Râjat. 5, 251. **3.** Attached to (with acc.), Nal. 2, 26.

अनुशय *anuçaya*, i.e. *anu-çi + a*, m. **1.** Repentance, Man. 8, 228. **2.** Rescission (as of sale), Man. 8, 5.

अनुशासन *anu-çâs + ana*, n. **1.** Instruction, Man. 2, 159. **2.** Precept, Man. 8, 139. **3.** Explanation, Man. 6, 50.

अनुशासितृ *anu-çâs + itṛi*, m. A teacher, Bhag. 8, 9.

अनुशासिन् *anu-çâs + in*, adj., f. *nî*, Punishing, Vikr. 62, 14.

अनुशिक्षिन् *anuçikshin*, i.e. *anu -çiksha*, desider. of *çak + in*, adj. Practising.

अनुषङ्ग *anushaṅga*, i.e. *anu-sañj + a*, m. Desire.

अनुषङ्गिन् *anushaṅgin*, i.e. *anu-shaṅga + in*, adj. Attached, prevailing, Man. 7, 52.

अनुष्ठातृ *anushṭhâtṛi*, i.e. *anu-sthâ + tṛi*, m. One who performs, Pańch. 253, 12.

अनुष्ठान *anushṭhâna*, i.e. *anu-sthâ + ana*, n. **1.** Performing, Pańch, 79, 22. **2.** Practice, Man. 7, 100. **3.** Study, Râjat, 5, 374.

अनुष्ठापन *anushṭhâpana*, i.e. *anu -sthâ*, Caus. *+ ana*, n. Causing to perform, Daçak. in Chr. 180, 2; 21.

अनुष्ठायिन् *anushṭhâyin*, i.e. *anu -sthâ + in*, adj., f. *nî*, Performing, Daçak. in Chr. 181, 12.

अनुष्णशीत *an-ushṇa-çîta*, adj. Neither hot nor cold, Bhâshâp. 103.

अनुसंधान *anusaṁdhâna*, i.e. *anu -sam-dhâ + ana*, n. Inquiry, Hit. 90, 18; Vedântas. in Chr. 207, 2.

अनुसर *anusara*, i.e. *anu-sṛi + a*, m. A companion, Lass. 20, 6.

अनुसरण *anusaraṇa*, i.e. *anu-sṛi + ana*, n. **1.** Following, Hit. 98, 21. Persecution, Megh. 82. **2.** Searching, Hit, 68, 13. **3.** Conformity, Hit. 9, 8.

अनुसार *anusâra*, i.e. *anu-sṛi + a*, m. **1.** Following. **2.** Conformity. **3.** Rule, Man. 8, 152.

अनुसारिन् *anusârin*, i.e. *anu-sṛi + in*, adj., f. *iṇî*. **1.** Following, Pańch. 98, 23. **2.** Scrutinising, Man. 7, 102. **3.** Observant, Man. 7, 31.—**Comp.** *Kâla-*, m, benzoin, Suçr. 2, 32, 1.

अनुसेविन् *anu-sev + in*, adj., f. *nî*, Addicted to (cruel actions), Râm. 2, 49, 5.

अनुस्मरण *anusmaraṇa*, i.e. *anu -smṛi + ana*, n. Recollection, Râm. 6, 82, 34.

अनुस्यूतत्व *anu-syûta + tva* (vb. *siv*), n. Condition of being sewn on or closely attached (as with a thread), Vedântas. in Chr. 208, 4.

अनूचान *anûchâna* (properly ptcple.

of the pf. Âtm. of *anu-vach*), m. One versed in the Vedas, Man. 2, 154.—Comp. *An-*, m. One who is not versed in the Vedas, Man. 2, 242.

अनूदक *anûdaka*, i.e. *an-udaka* (the *u* is lengthened on account of the metre), n. Want of water, drought, Râm. 1, 20, 16.

अनूदर *anûdara*, i.e. *an-udara* (*u* is lengthened on account of the metre), adj. Without belly, MBh. 14, 1305.

अनूप *anûpa*, i.e. *anu-ap + a*, I. adj., f. *pâ*, Watery, Man. 7, 192. II. m. A shore, Râm. 5, 15, 55.

अनूला *anûlâ*, f. The name of a river.

अनृच् *an-ṛich* and **अनृच** *an-ṛich + a*, m. One not conversant in the Rigveda, Man. 3, 131; 2, 158.

अनृणता *an-ṛiṇa + tâ*, f. **अनृणत्व** *an-ṛiṇa + tva*, n., and **अनृण्यता** *an-ṛiṇyatâ* (Pańch. 255, 11), i.e. *an-ṛiṇa + ya + tâ*, f. Freedom from debt.

अनृतमय *an-ṛita + maya*, adj., f. *yî*, False, Çâk. 68, 13.

अनृतिन् *anṛitin*, i.e. *an-ṛita + in*, adj. Lying, a liar, Man. 4, 214.

अनृशंसत्व *a-nṛiçam̃sa + tva*, n. Mildness, Râm. 2, 46, 8.

अनेकधा *an-eka + dhâ*, adv. In many ways, Bhâshâp. 99.

अनेकशस् *an-eka + ças*, adv. Repeatedly, Chr. 33, 2.

अनेकैकत्वबुद्धि *an-eka-eka + tva-buddhi*, f. Comprehension of manifold unities, Bhâshâp. 108.

अनेहस् *anehas*, i.e. *an-ih + as* (anom.). I. adj. Without a rival. II. m. (nom. sing., *hâ*) Time, Râjat. 5, 405.

अनैकान्त *anaikânta*, i.e. *an-eka-anta + a*, adj. Going astray (one of the five forms of fallacious middle term), Bhâshâp. 70.

अनोकह *an-oka-ha* (vb. 2. *hâ*), m. A tree.

अनोंकृत *anom̃kṛita*, i.e. *an-om-kṛita*, adj. Not accompanied by the mystical syllable *om*, Man. 2, 74.

† **अन्त्** *ANT*, i. 1, Par. To bind.

अन्त *anta*, m. 1. End, Nal. 22, 4. 2. Boundary, Râm. 3, 15, 16. 3. Limit, Râm. 3, 1, 23. 4. Border, Râm. 4, 6, 16. 5. Proximity, Man. 4, 116. 6. Death, Râm, 5, 87, 29.—Comp. *An-*, I. adj. endless, Man. 3, 275. II. m. 1. a name of Vishṇu. 2. Çesha, the chief of the Nâgas, or serpents. *Apara-*, m. 1. the western extremity. 2. pl. the name of a people. 3. completion. 4. death. *Udaka-*, m. the bank of a river, Çâk. 54, 21. *Etad-*, adj., f. *tâ*, ending in this, Man. 1, 50. *Kalpa-*, m. the end of a Kalpa-period, the destruction, the end of the world, Dev. 1, 49; Hit. i, d. 43. *Kṛita-*, I. adj., f. *tâ*, deciding, Bhâg. P. 9, 6, 13. II. m. 1. fate, Râm. 1, 41, 1. 2. a name of the God of Death, Hit. 9, 6. 3. a proved doctrine, Bhag. 18, 13. *Keça-*, *m.* 1. the end of the hair, Râm. 6, 8, 2. 2. a tuft of hair, Pańch. 245, 12. 3. hair, Râm. 5, 35, 21. 4. the ceremony of cutting the hair, Man. 2, 65. *Gata-*, adj. whose end is near, Râm. 2, 12, 31. *Gharma-*, m. the end of the hot season, Megh. 104. *Jana-*, m. an uninhabited country, Suçr. 1, 204, 5. *Tad-*, adj. finding its end thereby, Hit. i. d. 85. *Diç-*, I. m. the end of the world, Kir. 5, 1. II. adj. dwelling at the end of the world, MBh. 10, 260. *Dishṭa-*, m. (vb. *diç*) death, Râm. 2, 111, 3 Gorr. *Dṛishṭa-*, m. (n. Râm. 2, 109, 37 Gorr.) 1. a prototype,

Hariv. 5298. 2. an example, Hit. ii, d. 97. 3. comparison, Chr. 9, 45. *Yajña-*, m. a supplementary sacrifice. *Yuga-*, m. 1. the end of an age. 2. a destruction of the universe. *Svîkâra-*, adj. 1. agreed to. 2. consequent upon a promise.—Cf. Goth. andi, A.S. ende; Lat. uls instead of ultis; see *antara, antima*.

अन्तःपुर *antaḥpura*, i.e. *antar-pura*, n. 1. The palace of a king, Râm. 2, 14, 28. 2. The female apartments, the gyneceum, Man. 7, 221. 3. The wives of a king. Sing. Nal. 17, 31, and plur. Çâk. 30, 12.

अन्तःस्थ *antaḥstha*, i.e. *antar-stha* (vb. *sthâ*), adj., f. *thâ*, Being in the interior, Kathâs. 16, 104.

अन्तक *anta+ka*. I. adj., f. *kâ*, Causing death, Râm. 3, 46, 9. II. m. A name of the god of Death, Böhtl. Ind. Spr. 1520.—Comp. *An-*, adj. endless. *Kâla-*, m. the god of Death, Râm. 6, 67, 2. *Jagadantaka*, i.e. *jagat-*, m. the destroyer of the world, Bhâg. P. 4, 5, 6. *Visha-*, m. Çiva.

अन्तकर *anta-kara*, adj., f. *rî*, Causing death, Râm. 5, 94, 11.

अन्तकृत् *anta-kṛi+t*. I. adj. Causing the end. II. m. Death.

अन्तग *anta-ga* (vb. *gam*), adj., f. *gâ*. 1. Going to the end. 2. Thoroughly conversant in, Man. 3, 145.

अन्ततस् *anta+tas*, adv. 1. With the end or extremity, Man. 2, 62. 2. At the end, lastly, Man. 3, 86.

अन्तर् *antar*. I. adv. Within, Böhtl. Ind. Spr. 119; Vikr. d. 8. II. prep. Within, with gen. Bhag. 13, 15. III. Combined and compounded with some verbs and their derivatives. IV. Former and latter part of compound nouns implying the interior; e.g. *antaḥ-karaṇa*, the internal sense (cf. *karaṇa*); *ambhontar*, i.e. *ambhas-antar* in the water, Yâjñ. 1, 149. *dantântar*, between the teeth, Man. 5, 141.—Cf. Lat. inter.

अन्तर *antara*. I. adj., f. *râ*, Other, Râm. 5, 56, 57. II. n. 1. The interior, Pañch. ii. d. 42; the main substance, Pañch. 167, 6. 2. Interval, Man. 2, 17. *etasminn antare*, In the meanwhile, Râm. 1, 24, 24. *ekântara*, adj. With one class between, Man. 10,13. *dvi-eka-*, adj. With one or two classes between, Man. 10, 7. *kâla-*, n. Lapse of time, Böhtl. Ind. Spr. 1264.—Loc. *antare*, Between, Râjat. 5, 152. 3. A hole, Râm. 3, 35, 84. 4. Distance, Râm. 2, 49, 1. 5. Difference, Râm. 3, 53, 56. 6. Opportunity, Râm. 1, 46, 23. 7. A weak side, Râm. 6, 18, 46. 8. A surety, Pañch. 213, 24; see *antareṇa*. 9. When latter part of compound words it may be translated very often by adjectives, e.g. 'other,' *diç-* and *deça-*, n. A foreign country, Râjat, 6, 16; Man. 5, 78. *sthâna-*, n. Another place, Hit. 25, 9. 'Special,' *kâraṇa-*, A special reason, Nal. 13, 59; Râm. 4, 9, 28. 'Suitable,' e.g. *kâla-*, A suitable time, Pañch. iii. d. 236. 'Relative to,' *mad-*, Relative to myself, Râm. 2, 90, 16 (cf. 92, 21 Gorr.)—Comp. *Divasa-*, adj. one day old, MBh. 11, 98. *Sa-*, adj. with interstices. *Stana-*, n. the heart.—Cf. Lat. interus, interior, alter, and ulterior, ultra (see *anta* and *antima*); Goth. anthar, A.S. other.

अन्तरतस् *antara+tas*, adv. 1. From the interior, Çiç. 9, 19. 2. Within (in his heart), Râm. 3, 62, 1.

अन्तरा *antarâ* (old instr. sing. of *antara* cf. *antareṇa*). I. adv. 1. Amidst, Chr. 14, 17. 2. Between, Râm. 5, 34, 5. 3. In the interval, i.e. between morning and evening, Man. 2, 56. 4. For some time, Râm. 3, 8, 13. 5. Therein, Man. 10, 174. 6. On the way, Daçak. in Chr. 187, 17. 7. Near, Râm. 2, 57, 13. II. prep. 1. Between, with loc., Râm. 2, 40, 44, and acc., Ram. 2, 92, 12. 2. Without.—Cf. *antareṇa*, ἄτερ.

अन्तरात्मन्य *antar-âtman* + *ya*, adj. Internal, Man. 12, 13.

अन्तराय *antarâya*, i.e. *antar-i* + *a*, m. Obstacle, Çiç. 9, 87.

अन्तराल *antarâla*, i.e. *antar-âli*, n. Interval, Daçak. in Chr. 197, 17; Çiç. 9, 2. loc. *le*, While, Pañch. 55, 17.—Comp. *Sa-*, adj., separated, distinct from.

अन्तरिक्ष *antariksha* and **अन्तरीक्ष** *antarîksha*, i.e. *antar-îksh* + *a*, n. The sky, Chr. 41, 21; 30, 8.

अन्तरीक्षग *antarîksha-ga* (vb. *gam*). I. adj. Moving in the air, Râm. 5, 27, 11. II. m. A bird.

अन्तरीय *antarîya*, i.e. *antara* + *îya*, n. A lower garment, Daçak. in Chr. 198, 22.

अन्तरेण *antareṇa* (instr. of *antara*), prep. with acc. 1. Between, Çiç. 3, 3. 2. During, Mâlav. 67, 21. 3. Except, Râm. 3, 25, 1. 4. Without, Râm. 3, 71, 13. 5. Regarding, Çâk. 59, 14.

अन्तर्दशाह *antardaçâha*, i.e. *antar-daçan-ahan*, n. An interval of ten days, Man. 5, 79.

अन्तर्धान *antardhâna*, i.e. *antar-dhâ* + *ana*, n. 1. Disappearance; with *i* or *gam*, to disappear, Râm. 6, 19, 39. 2. Invisibility, Râm. 6, 19, 48.

अन्तर्भाव *antarbhâva*, i.e. *antar-bhû* + *a*, m. Inclusion, being included, Vedântas. in Chr. 207, 1.

अन्तर्यामिन् *antaryâmin*, i.e. *antar-yam* + *in*, m. The soul, Vedântas. in Chr. 204, 19.

अन्तर्वंशिक *antarvaṁçika*, i.e. *antar-vaṁça* + *ika*, m. A superintendent of a gyneceum, Pañch. 156, 17.

अन्तर्वन्त् *antar* + *vant*, adj., f. *vatnî* (ved. *vatî*). A pregnant woman, Râjat. 5, 245.

अन्तवन्त् *anta* + *vant*, adj., f. *vatî*. Having an end, perishable, Bhag. 2, 18.

अन्तिक *anti* + *ka* (from the ved. anti = ἀντί, cf. ἄντα, ἄντην, Lat. ante, Goth. and, e.g. in and-hafjan, to answer; N.H.G. ant-, ent-, e.g. in ant-worten, ent-gegnen), n. Vicinity, Râjat. 5, 57. —abl. *kât*. Near, with acc. Râm. 3, 9, 11. From, with gen. Man. 9, 174.—loc. *ke*. Close to, Nal. 1, 25. In presence of, Man. 2, 202.—Comp. *Keça-*, i.e. *keçânta* + *ika*, reaching to the hair, Man. 2, 46. *Grahaṇa-*, i.e. *grahaṇânta* + *ika*, lasting till the comprehension, Man. 3, 1. *janântikam*, i.e. *jana-antika* + *m*, adv. whispering, speaking aside, Çâk. 13, 12.

अन्तिम *antima* (ved. *antama*), adj., f. *mâ*. Last, Hit. Pr. d. 12.—Cf. Lat. ultimus and intimus; see *anta* and *antara*.

अन्तेवासिन् *antevâsin*, i.e. *anta* + *i-vas* + *in*, m. A pupil, Man. 4, 33.

अन्त्य *antya*, i.e. *anta* + *ya*. I. adj., f. *yâ*. 1. Last, Man. 11, 213. With *daçâ*, State of extremity, Pañch. 70, 5. 2. Lowest, Pañch. iv. d. 76. Of a very low class, Man. 12, 59. II. m. 1. A Chândâla, Man. 2, 238. 2. One of a barbarous nation, Man. 3, 9.

अन्त्यज *antya-ja* (vb. *jan*). I. adj., f. *jâ*, Born in the lowest class, Man. 8, 385. II. m. A man of the lowest tribe, Pañch. i. d. 452. III. f. *jâ*, A woman of the lowest class, Man. 11, 58.

अन्त्यजातिता *antya-jâti* + *tâ*, f. The lowest of human conditions, Man. 12, 9.

अन्त्यावसायिन् *antyâvasâyin*, i.e. *antya-ava-so + in*, m. A man of a degraded tribe; the son of a Nishâdî woman by a Châṇḍâla, Man. 10, 39.

अन्त्र *antra* (for *antara*, cf. ἔντερον, Lat. interiora), n. An intestine (mostly used in the plur.), Râm. 5, 25, 46.—Comp. *Kshudra-*, n. the entrails which are nearer to the heart. *Sthûla-*, n. those which are near the anus, Yâjń. 3, 94; 95.

† **अन्द्** *AND*, i. 1, Par. To bind.

अन्दोलन *andolana*, i.e. *andolaya + ana*, n. Swinging, Râjat. 5, 356.

† **अन्दोलय** *ANDOLAYA* (a denomin. derived from **andola*, based on **andul*, an anomalous frequent. of *dul* for * *dandul*, cf. *aṅghri*). To swing.

अन्ध् *ANDH*, i, 10, Par. (rather denomin. of *andha*) **1.** † To be blind. **2.** To make blind, to obstruct the sight, Çiç. 9, 21.

अन्ध *andha*, adj., f. *dhâ*. **1.** Blind, Pańch. 291, 11. **2.** Obstructing the sight, Man. 8, 94.—Comp. *divâ-*, m. An owl, Pańch. 158, 22.

अन्धक *andha + ka*. **I.** adj., f. *dhikâ*, Blind. **II.** m. A proper name.

अन्धकार *andha + kâra*, m. and n. Darkness, Man. 4, 51.

अन्धकारमय *andhakâra + maya*, adj., f. *yî*. Dark, Kathâs. 4, 51.

अन्धता *andha + tâ*, f. and **अन्धत्व** *andha + tva*, n. Blindness.

अन्धस् *andhas*, n. The sacrificial food (ved.), Chr. 291, 6 = Rigv. i. 85, 6.

अन्ध्र *andhra*, m. **1.** The name of a people. **2.** A man of a low caste, son of a Vaideha by a Kârâvara woman, Man. 10, 36.

अन्न *anna*, i.e. *ad + na*, n. **1.** Food, Man. 3, 182. **2.** Corn, Man. 3, 76. **3.** Boiled rice, Man. 3, 82.—Comp. *Kṛita-*, n. dressed food, Man. 9, 213. *Deva-*, n. food offered to gods, Man. 5, 7. *Dadhi-*, n. rice with curdled milk, Yâjń. 1, 288. *Paryâya-*, n. food prepared for another. *Mishṭa-*, n. a mixture of sugar and acids, etc., eaten with bread or rice. *Râjânna*, i.e. *râjan-*, n. a sort of rice.—Cf. Lat. annona.

अन्नद *anna-da* (vb. *dâ*), adj., f. *dâ*. Giving food, Man. 4, 229.

अन्नमय *anna + maya*, adj., f. *yî*. Consisting of food in a metaphysical sense, i.e. of the essence of the elementary creation, Vedântas. in Chr. 209, 12.

अन्नाद *annâda*, i.e. *anna-ad + a*, adj., f. *dî*. Eating food, Man. 8, 317 (one who eats food given to him by a killer of a Brâhmaṇa).

अन्नाद्य *annâdya*, i.e. *anna-âdya*. **1.** (the latter part being the ptcple. of the fut. pass. of *ad*), n. Proper food, Man. 3, 82. **2.** (the latter part being the adj. *âdya*), Dressed rice, etc., Man. 3, 244.

अन्य *anya*, adj., f. *yâ*, n. *yad*. **1.** Other, Man. 8, 17. **2.** Different, Hit. i. d. 121. **3.** with abl. Other than, Râjat. 5, 178. (*nânyaḥ Çaṅkaravarmaṇaḥ*, no other than Çaṅkaravarman). **4.** One, Pańch. 80, 16. **5.** plur. The others, i. e. the rest, Böhtl. Chr. 219, 161. **6.** acc. sing., n. *yad*. Besides, else, Pańch. 55, 9.—Comparat. *anyatara*, f. *râ*., n. *rad*, Either of two, Man. 2, 111.—Superl. *anyatama*, f. *mâ*, Any one of more than two, Man. 11, 25.—Comp. *an-*, adj., f. *yâ*, fixed on one object, Bhag. 9, 32.—Cf. Lat. alius, ἄνευ, ἄνις, ἄλλος, Goth. alja-, alis, alja, probably also alls, A.S. eall.

अन्यतस् *anya + tas*, adv. **1.** From another, Man. 4, 33. **2.** On the contrary, Pańch. i. d. 109. 3. To another place, Man. 2, 200.

अन्यता *anya + tâ*, f. Difference, Çiç. 4, 55.—Comp. *An-*, f. identity.

अन्यत्र *anya + tra*, adv. 1. Elsewhere. 2. On another occasion, Man. 5, 41. 3. To another subject, Man. 2, 168. 4. With abl., except, without, Bhag. 3, 9.—Cf. Goth. aljathrô, Lat. aliter ἀλλότριος.

अन्यथा *anya + thâ*, adv. 1. In another manner, differently. *anyathâ kṛi*, To change, Böhtl. Ind. Spr. 717. 2. Otherwise, else, Man. 8, 144. 3. Untruly, Râm. 4, 21, 15. 4. Wrongly, illegally, Man. 9. 234. 5. In an opposite way, Pańch. 206, 14; with *kṛi*, To deny.—Cf. Lat. aliuta.

अन्यदा *anya + dâ*, adv. 1. At another time. 2. Once, Pańch. 234, 8.

अन्यदीय *anyadîya*, i.e. *anya + d + îya*, adj. f. *yâ*. 1. Belonging to another. 2. Being in others, Daçak. 187, 23.

अन्यमातृज *anya-mâtṛi-ja* (vb. *jan*), m. A half-brother, born by another mother, Yâjń. 2, 139.

अन्यस्त्रीग *anya-strî-ga* (vb. *gam*), m. An adulterer, Man. 8, 386.

अन्यादृश *anyâdṛiça*, i.e. *anya-dṛiç + a*, adj., f. *çî*, Looking different, Lass. 72, 8.

अन्यूनाधिक *anyûnâdhika*, i.e. *a-nyûna-adhika*, adj., f. *kâ*. Neither too little nor too much, Ram. 6, 16, 78.

अन्येद्युस् *anyedyus*, i.e. *anya + i-div + as*, adv. 1. On the following day, Daçak. in Chr. 197, 9. 2. Once, Pańch. 68, 25.

अन्योदर्य *anyodarya*, i.e. *anya-udara + ya*, m. A half-brother, having the same father but another mother, Yâjń. 2, 139.

अन्योन्य *anyonya*, i.e. *anya + a-anya*, adj. 1. Each other, Man. 7, 89. 2. Mutual, Man. 9, 101.

अन्वक् *anvak*, i.e. *anu-añch*, acc. sing. n. I. adv. Behind, Çiç. 9, 76. II. prep. with acc. After, Ragh. 2, 16.

अन्वय *anvaya*, i.e. *anu-i + a*, m. 1. Following. 2. Connection. 3. The affirmative connection between the major and middle terms, Bhâshâp. 141. 4. Male descendants, Yâjń. 2, 117. 5. Lineage, Ragh. 1, 9. Race, Râjat. 5, 151. Family, Râjat. 5, 41. 6. Succession, inheritance in *anvayâgata*, Inherited, Pańch. 16, 11.—Comp. *Dus-*, adj. 1. hard to be pursued, Râm. 2, 92, 13 Gorr. 2. hard to be performed, MBh. 13, 5854. 3. not easy to be conceived, Bhâg. P. 7, 6, 30. *Nis-*, adj. 1. in absence (cf. *anvayavant*), Man. 8, 332. 2. without descendants, Râjat. 2, 81. 3. not related, Man. 8, 198. *Sa-*, adj. 1. related, Man. 8, 331. 2. in connection with family. 3. with all the family, Pańch. 45, 6. 4. in order or regular succession.

अन्वयवन्त् *anvaya + vant*, adj., f. *vatî*, In presence, Man. 8, 332.

अन्वयिन् *anvayin*, i.e. *anvaya + in*, adj., f. *nî*. 1. Connected with, Bhâshâp. 73. 2. Belonging to a race, Râjat, 5, 246.

अन्वर्थ *anvartha*, i.e. *anu-artha*. I. adj., f. *thâ*, Clear. II. adv. *tham*, Literally.

अन्ववाय *anvavâya*, i.e. *anu-ava-i + a*, m. Race, Sund. 1, 2.

अन्ववेक्षा *anvavekshâ*, i.e. *anu-ava-îksh + â*, f. Regard.

अन्वष्टका *anvashṭakâ*, i.e. *anu-ashṭakâ*, f. The ninth day of the latter half of the months Pausha, Mâgha, and Phâlguna (and, according to another authority, also of the Âgrahâyaṇa), Man. 4, 159.

अन्वहम् *anvaham*, i.e. *anu-aha + m*, adv. Every day, Man. 2, 167.

अन्वाधेय *anvâdheya*, i.e. *anu-â-dheya* (vb. *dhâ*), n. A woman's property, consisting in what she has received after her marriage from her husband's or her father's families, Man. 9, 195.

अन्वाधेयक *anvâdheya + ka*, n. = *anvâdheya*.

अन्वाहार्य *anvâhârya*, i.e. *anu-â-hârya* (vb. *hṛi*), n. The monthly Çrâddha or funeral repast in honour of the manes, held on the day of new moon, Man. 3, 123.

अन्वाहार्यक *anvâhârya + ka*, n. = *anvâhârya*, in *piṇḍa-* (properly, the oblation offered after the funeral cakes), Man. 3, 122.

अन्वेष *anvesha*, i.e. *anu-* 2. *ish + a*, m. Searching, Çâk. d. 22.

अन्वेषक *anveshaka*, i.e. *anu-* 2. *ish + aka*, adj., f. *ikâ*, One who searches, Râm. 4, 61, 12. Who explores, Râjat. 5, 54.

अन्वेषण *anveshaṇa*, i.e. *anu-* 2. *ish + ana*, n. and f. *ṇâ*, Searching, Daçak. in Chr. 179, 5.

अन्वेषिन् *anveshin*, i.e. *anu-* 2. *ish + in*, adj., f. *iṇî*, Searching, Râjat. 5, 463.—Comp. *Hita-*, adj. seeking another's welfare.

अन्वेष्टृ *anveshṭṛi*, i.e. *anu-* 2. *ish + tṛi*, m. A searcher, Nal. 16, 30.

अप् *ap*, f., in the classical literature plur.: N.V. *âpas*, I. *adbhis*, D.A. *adbhyas*. Water, Man. 1, 8. *adbhir dâ*, To give and confirm the gift by pouring water, Man. 9, 168.—Cf. Lat. aqua, amnis, Goth. ahva, A.S. ewe.

1. **अप** *apa*. I. adv. (ved.) Away. II. prep. with abl. Away from, without (very seldom). III. combined and compounded with verbs and their derivatives. IV. former part of compounded nouns and adverbs, implying: Loss, negation, privation, wrong, bad, unnatural.—Cf. ἀπό, Lat. ab, Goth. and A.S. af.

2. **ऽअप** *-ap + a*, a substitute for *ap*, when latter part of a comp. word, e.g. *çushka-*, adj. Of which the water is dried up, Râm. 2, 72, 20.

अपकर्तृ *apakartṛi*, i.e. *apa-kṛi + tṛi*, m. An injurer, Hit. iii. d. 47.

अपकर्ष *apakarsha*, i.e. *apa-kṛish + a*, m. 1. Deterioration. 2. Sinking, Man. 10, 42.

अपकर्षक *apakarshaka*, i.e. *apa-kṛish + aka*, adj. Deteriorating.

अपकर्षण *apakarshaṇa*, i.e. *apa-kṛish-ana*. I. adj., f. *ṇî*, Removing, Râm. 1, 29, 18. II. n. Removal, Yâjń. 1, 191.

अपकार *apakâra*, i.e. *apa-kṛi + a*, m. 1. Injury. 2. Malice, Daçak. in Chr. 191, 22.

अपकारता *apakâra + tâ*, f. An injurious action, Nal. 21, 13.

अपकारिन् *apakârin*, i.e. *apa-kṛi + in*, adj., f. *iṇî*, Mischievous, Man. 11, 31; Böhtl. Ind. Spr. 687.

अपकृत्य *apa-kṛitya*, n. Injury, Pańch. 255, 11.

अपक्रमण *apakramaṇa*, i.e. *apa-kram + ana*, n. Going away, Râm. 2, 34, 40.

अपक्रिया *apa-kriyâ*, f. 1. A wrong (unseasonable) act, Böhtl. Ind. Spr. 890. 2. Wrong manner, Çiç. 9, 68.—Cf. *anapakriyâ*.

अपक्रोश *apakroça*, i.e. *apa-kruç + a*,

m. Reviling, Daçak. in Chr. 192, 21 (ib. 20, read *pârthivaṁ mitho*).

अपक्कता *a-pakva* + *tâ*, f. Immaturity.

अपगम *apa-gam* + *a*, m. **1.** Going away, Megh. 71. **2.** Separation, Böhtl. Ind. Spr. 643. **3.** Passing away (of time), Kathâs. 21, 147.

अपगर्जित *apa-garjita* (vb. *garj*), adj. Without thundering, Kathâs. 19, 94.

अपचमान *a-pachamâna* (vb. *pach*, ptcple. pres. Âtm.), adj. One who by his mode of life is prevented from dressing his food, as a student, a mendicant, and a heretic, Man. 4, 32 (Kull.).

अपचय *apachaya*, i.e. *apa-chi* + *a*, m. Decrease, Hit. iii. d. 131.

ऽअपचायिन् *-apachâyin*, i.e. *apa -chi* + *in*, adj. **1.** Decreasing in, MBh. 3, 11157. **2.** Honouring, MBh. 13, 6705.

अपचार *apachâra*, i.e. *apa-char* + *a*, m. **1.** Death, Daçak. in Chr. 200, 20. **2.** Trespass, fault, Çâk. 110, 23.

अपचारिन् *apachârin*, i.e. *apa -char* + *in*, adj., f. *iṇî*. **1.** Deviating from, Hariv. 1014 (corr. °*châriṇaḥ*). **2.** Adulterous, Man. 8, 317.

अपचिति *apa-chi* + *ti*, f. **1.** Honour, Râm. 2, 74, 26. **2.** Expiation.

अपच्छाय *apachchhâya*, i.e. *apa -chhâya* (cf. *chhâyâ*), adj. Shadowless, Pañch. ii. d. 108 (?).

अपजिहीर्षु *apajihîrshu*, i.e. *apa -jihîrsha*, desid. of *hṛi* + *u*, adj. Desirous of taking away, Râjat. 5, 426.

अपटी *apaṭî*, f. A screen of cloth; see *kshepa*.

अपण्डितता *a-paṇḍita* + *tâ*, f. Foolishness, Bhartṛ. 2, 88.

अपत्य *apa* + *tya*, n. Offspring, Man. 5, 161.—Comp. *An-*, adj., f. *yâ*, childless, without offspring, Man. 9, 190. *Vipanna-* (vb. *pad*), adj. f. *yâ*, having lost a child by abortment, Râjat. 5, 246. *Sa-*, adj. having progeny.

ऽअपत्यता *-apatya* + *tâ*, f. State of having offspring, Man. 3, 16. *an-*, Having no offspring, childlessness, Çâk. 90, 20.

अपत्रपा *apa-trap* + *â*, f. Bashfulness, Daçak. in Chr. 184, 22.—Comp. *Nis-*, adj., f. *pâ*, impudent, Râm. 4, 30, 17.

अपदेश *apadeça*, i.e. *apa-diç* + *a*, m. **1.** Stating, Vedântas. in Chr. 204, 14. **2.** Denunciation, Daçak. in Chr. 193, 13. **3.** Pretext, Man. 4, 198. *apadeçais*, Artfully, Man. 8, 182.—Comp. *Sa-apadeça* + *m*, adv. under a pretext, Daçak. in Chr. 190, 16.

ऽअपदेशिन् *-apadeça* + *in* in *râjaputra-*, adj. Disguised as (Râjputs) Kathâs. 24, 121.

अपदोषता *apa-dosha* + *tâ*, f. Faultlessness, Çiç. 9, 12.

अपध्यान *apadhyâna*, i.e. *apa-dhyai* + *ana*, n. **1.** Disregard, MBh. 1, 8457. **2.** Hurting, Hariv. 9058 (?).

अपध्वंसज *apa-dhvaṁs* + *a-ja* (vb. *jan*), m. The offspring of a father inferior in caste to the mother, Man. 10, 41.

अपनयन *apanayana*, i.e. *apa-nî* + *ana*, n. Removing, Râm. 3, 64, 11; 1, 46, 11.

अपनुत्ति *apanutti*, i.e. *apa-nud* + *ti*, f. **1.** Removing. **2.** Expiation, Man. 11, 209.

ऽअपनुद *apa-nud* + *a*, adj., f. *dâ*. Removing, Râm. 2, 1, 28.

अपनुनुत्सु *apanunutsu*, i.e. *apa -nunutsa*, desider. of *nud* + *u*, adj. Desirous of removing, Man. 11, 101.

अपनोद *apanoda,* i.e. *apa-nud + a,* m. 1. Removal. 2. Expiation, Man. 11, 75.

अपनोदन *apanodana,* i.e. *apa-nud + ana.* I. adj., f. *nî,* Removing, Man. 11, 215. II. n. Expiation, Man. 11, 252.

अपपात्र *apa-pâtra,* adj. Deprived of vessels, Man. 10, 51.

अपपादत्र i.e. *apa-pâda-tra* (vb. *trâ*), adj. Without shoes, Râjat. 5, 194.

अपभ्रंश *apa-bhraṁç + a,* m. Incorrect language, Râjat. 5, 205.

अपमर्द *apamarda,* i.e. *apa-mṛid + a,* m. Dirt, Râm. 3, 2, 3.—Cf. Lat. merda.

अपमर्श *apamarça,* i.e. *apa-mṛiç + a,* m. Touch, Çâk. d. 116, v. r.

अपमान *apamâna,* i.e. *apa-man + a,* m., n. 1. Disrespect, Râm. 1, 12, 14. 2. Token of disrespect, Daçak. in Chr. 181, 1.

अपमानिन् *apamânin,* i.e. *apa-man + in,* adj., f. *nî,* Disregarding, despising.

अपमार्ग *apamârga,* i.e. I. *apa-mṛij + a,* m. Cleansing, Çiç. 9, 36. II. *apa-mârga,* m. A sideway, Pańch. 169, 15.

अपयान *apayâna,* i.e. *apa-yâ + ana,* n. 1. Going away, Çiç. 9, 84. 2. Retreat, flight, Râm. 3, 40, 29.

अपर I. *apa + ra,* adj., f. *râ.* 1. Posterior, Man. 3, 278; with *sandhyâ,* Evening-twilight, Man. 4, 93. 2. Following, Râm. 2, 65, 1. 3. Western, Çiç. 9, 1. 4. Other, Pańch. 55, 13.—acc. *ram,* adv. Moreover, Pańch. 71, 1. II. *a-para,* adj. 1. Inferior, Bhag. 7, 5. 2. Relative, Bhâshâp. 7; 9. 3. Modern, Man. 9, 99.—Comp. *Pûrva-.* I. adj. 1. being before and behind. 2. prior and subsequent. II. n. sing. 1. east and west. 2. connexion, Man. 8, 56 (Proof, and thing to be proved, Ragh.).—Cf. Goth. afar, after, N.H.G. aber.

अपरता *apara + tâ,* f. 1. Relativeness. 2. Condition of being less extensive, Bhâshâp. 8. 3. Shortness of distance and time.

अपरत्र *apara + tra,* adv. In another place, Râm. 3, 15, 26; 27.

अपरत्व *apara + tva,* n. Shortness of distance and time, Bhâshâp. 120.

अपरत्वक *aparatva + ka,* n. = *aparatâ,* Bhâshâp. 3; 85, Shortness of distance and time.

अपरथा *apara-thâ,* adv. Otherwise, Çiç. 9, 67.

अपरस्परसंभूत *aparasparasaṁbhûta,* i.e. *a-paraspara-sam-bhûta* (vb. *bhû*), adj. Not sprung up in a successive order, Bhag. 16, 8.

अपराध *apa-râdh + a,* m. 1. Transgression, Ragh. 1, 6. 2. Offence, Pańch. 40, 23. 3. Crime, Râm. 2, 58, 22. 4. Injury, Râm. 6, 33, 21. 5. *aparâdha + tas,* adv. By the fault, Man. 8, 408.—Comp. *Nis-,* adj. innocent, Pańch. 198, 4. *Sa-,* adj. guilty.

अपराधकृत् *aparâdha-kṛit,* adj. One who has committed a crime, sinful, Çiç. 9, 58.

अपराधिन् *apa-râdh + in,* adj., f. *nî,* Offending, Râm. 5, 91, 8. An offender, Yâjń. 2, 266.

अपरान्तक *aparântaka,* i.e. *apara-anta + ka.* I. m. The name of a people. II. n. A song conducive to final liberation, Yâjń. 3, 113.

अपरावर्तिन् *aparâvartin,* i.e. *a-parâ-vṛit + in,* adj. Not turning the back, not flying.

अपराह्ण *aparâhṇa,* i.e. *apara-ahna,* m., n. 1. The afternoon, Man. 3, 255. 2. Evening, Chr. 34, 16.

अपरिहारवन्त् *a-parihâra+vant*, adj., f. *vatî*, Unavoidable.

अपरेद्युस् *aparedyus*, i.e. *apara+i-div+as*, adv. The following day, Râm. 1, 9, 52; Nal. 13, 35.

अपलताभवन *apa-latâ-bhavana*, adj., f. *nâ*, Without arbours, Kir. 5, 10.

अपवर्ग *apavarga*, i.e. *apa-vṛij+a*, m. Completion; the delivery of the soul from the body; final beatitude, Daçak. in Chr. 181, 10.

अपवर्गद *apavarga-da* (vb. *dâ*), adj., f. *dâ*, Giving final beatitude, Râjat. 5, 44.

अपवर्तन *apavartana*, i.e. *apa-vṛit+ana*, n. 1. Removing. 2. Depriving one of, Man. 9, 79.

अपवाद *apavâda*, i.e. *apa-vad+a*, m. 1. Refutation of an erroneous imputation, Vedântas. in Chr. 211, 24. 2. Insulting, Man. 4, 239. 3. Blame, Pańch. 37, 4.

अपवादिन् *apavâdin*, i.e. *apa-vad+in*, adj., f. *nî*, Blaming, Çâk. 23, 12.

अपवारितक *apa-vârita+ka* (vb. *vṛi*), adj., instr. *kena*, Apart, Mṛichchh. 23, 22.

अपवाहन *apavâhana*, i.e. *apa-vah+ana* (vb. *vah*), n. Removal, Daçak. in Chr. 181, 1.

अपवेध *apavedha*, i.e. *apa-vyadh+a*, m. Boring improperly, Man. 9, 286.

अपशङ्कम् *apa-çańka+m* (see *çańkâ*), adv. Fearless, Çiç. 4, 47.

अपस् *apas*, Ved. (akin to *âp*) I. n. Work, Chr. 292, 9 = Rigv. i. 85, 9. II. adj. Active, diligent, Chr. 294, 3 = Rigv. i. 92, 3.— Comp. *Su-*, adj. making beautiful works, Chr. 292, 9 = Rigv. 1, 85, 9. —Cf. Lat. opus, Ved. *apasya* = Lat. operari, ποιέω for ποσίεω.

अपसद *apa-sad-a*, m. 1. A degraded one, Man. 10, 10. 2. A contemptible individual; in this signification, it is generally the latter part of a comp., e.g. *gaja-*, m. A contemptible elephant, Pańch. 80, 21; *vânara-*, m. A contemptible monkey, Râm. 6, 33, 14.

अपसरण *apasaraṇa*, i.e. *apa-sṛi+ana*, n. Retreating, Pańch. 152, 21.

अपसर्प *apasarpa*, i.e. *apa-sṛip+a*, m. A spy, Daçak. in Chr. 186, 13.

अपसर्पण *apasarpaṇa*, i.e. *apa-sṛip+ana*, n. Retreating, Râm. 6, 92, 9.

अपसव्यवन्त् *apa-savya+vant*, adj. With the sacrificial cord over the right shoulder (cf. *savya*), Yâjń. 1, 250.

अपसार *apasâra*, i.e. *apa-sṛi+a*, m. An outlet, Pańch. 171, 16.

अपस्कर *apaskara*, i.e. *apa-kṛi+a*, m. Excrements, Lass. 4, 16.

अपस्नान *apasnâna*, i.e. *apa-snâ+ana*, n. Water which had been used for bathing, Man. 4, 132.

अपस्मार *apasmâra*, i.e. *apa-smṛi+a*, m. 1. Epilepsy. 2. Madness, Bhartṛ. 1, 88.

अपस्मारिन् *apasmârin* i. e. *apasmâra+in*, adj., f. *iṇî*, Subject to epilepsy, Man. 3, 7.

ऽअपह *-apa-ha* (vb. *han*), adj., f. *hâ*, 1. Removing, Râm. 3, 79, 44; Kir. 5, 22. 2. Destroying, Râjat. 5, 179. 3. Curing, Suçr. 2, 408, 5.—Comp. *visha-*, adj. antidotal.

अपहरण *apaharaṇa*, i.e. *apa-hṛi+ana*, n. 1. Taking away, Daçak. in Chr. 180, 21. 2. Stealing, Man. 9, 293.

अपहर्तृ *apahartṛi*, i.e. *apa-hṛi+tṛi*, m., f. *trî*, n. 1. One who takes away, a thief, Man. 9, 275. **2.** One who withholds another's property, Man. 8, 190. **3.** Removing, expiating, Man. 11, 161.

अपहार *apahâra*, i.e. *apa-hṛi* + *a*, m. **1.** Taking away. **2.** Concealment, Çâk. 13, 22.

अपहारक *apahâraka*, i.e. *apa-hṛi* + *aka*. I. adj., f. *ikâ*, Taking away, stealing, Man. 9, 256. II. m. A thief, Man. 4, 255.

अपहारिन् *aphârin*, i.e. *apa-hṛi* + *in*. I. adj., f. *iṇî*, Taking away; ravishing, Man. 2, 88. II. m. A thief, Pańch. 33, 4.

अपह्नव *apahnava*, i.e. *apa-hnu* + *a*, m. **1.** Denying, Man. 8, 52. **2.** Concealment, Kathâs. 10, 92.

अपाकरिष्णु *apâkarishṇu*, i.e. *apa-â-kṛi* + *ishṇu*, adj. Surpassing, Bhartṛ. 1, 5.

अपाङ्ग *apâṅga*, i.e. *apa-aṅga*, m. The outer corner of the eye, Daçak. in Chr. 190, 15.—In comp. adj. the fem. terminates in *gî* and *gâ*, Râm. 5, 38, 7; 2, 30, 34.—Comp. *Çukla-*, m. a peacock.

अपात्रकृत्या *a-pâtra-kṛityâ*, f. An action by which a person becomes unworthy of receiving a present, Man. 11, 125.

अपात्रीकरण *apâtrîkaraṇa*, i.e. *a-pâtra-kṛi* + *ana*, n. Causing a person to become unworthy of receiving a present, Man. 11, 69.

अपान *apâna*, i.e. *apa-an* + *a*, m. **1.** One of the five vital airs, that which goes downwards, Vedântas. in Chr. 207, 10. **2.** The anus (cf. *an*).

अपाय *apâya*, i.e. *apa-i* + *a*, m. **1.** Going away. **2.** Disappearance. **3.** Diminution, Man. 1, 70. **4.** End, Râjat. 5, 98. **5.** Trespass, injury. **6.** Loss. **7.** Danger. **8.** Calamity.—Comp. *Eka-*, adj. diminished by one, Man. 1, 70. *Nis-*, adj. 1. imperishable, MBh. 12, 8003. 2. infallible, MBh. 3, 2178. *Sa-*, adj. dangerous, Pańch. 192, 7.

अपार्थक *apârthaka*, i.e. *apa-artha* + *ka*, adj. f. *thikâ*, Useless, Man. 8, 78.

अपाश्रय *apâçraya*, i.e. *apa-â-çri* + *a*, m. **1.** Refuge, support, Man. 9, 335. **2.** An awning spread over a court, Râm. 5, 11, 19. **3.** The head, Daçak. in Chr. 198, 20 (Sch. Wils. p. 90).

अपि *api* (properly, Thereto, on, by, cf. ἐπί, Lat. ob) I. part. **1.** Moreover, also, Man. 8, 274; 1, 119. **2.** Even, Man. 2, 150. **3.** Still, Çâk. d. 29. **4.** Though, Çâk. d. 68. **5.** With preceding *yadi*, Although, Man. 9, 145. **6.** With *tathâ*, Even thus, nevertheless, Çâk. 99, 8, **7.** With *tad*, Nevertheless, Bhartṛ. 1, 28. **8.** Only, Pańch. Pr. d. 9. **9.** All together, after numerals and words used in a similar signification, Man. 1, 107 (All four), Man. 2, 14 (after *ubhau*, both); Man. 3, 193 (all together); Böhtl. Ind. Spr. 1047 (after *etâni*, all these); Pańch. 108, 14 (after *aparam*, Every other subject). **10.** A part. of interrogation, Râm. 5, 33, 34. **11.** A part. of desire, O that! Man. 3, 274. **12.** With following *nâma* (base *nâman*), Perhaps, Mṛichchh. 174, 3. O that! Vikr. **13.** Following the interrogat. pron. *kim* or its derivatives: **a.** It makes them indefinite, *ko 'pi* (i.e. *kas api*), Somebody, Bhartṛ. 3, 99 (cf. Lat. quispiam for quis-pi-jam). **b.** Signifies: Even, Kathâs. 4, 55. **c.** Violently, Megh. 110. **14.** Preceding *kiṁ chid* becomes more indefinite, Man. 3, 14. II. conjuuct. **1.** And also, Man. 1, 115. **2.** And, Man. 4, 55. **3.** *api–api*, 'as well as,' Hit. i. d. 159; from the one part — from the other part, Pańch. 113, 8; 9; *api–cha*, Man. 5, 23. **4.** But, Man. 8, 267. **5.** But also, Pańch.

155, 25. **III.** Combined and compounded with verbs and their derivatives. **IV.** Former part of comp. nouns implying 'near to,' 'joined to.'

अपिधान *apidhâna*, i.e. *api-dhâ + ana*, n. A cover.—Comp. *Çilâ-*, adj., f. *nâ*, covered by stones, Râm. 3, 76, 35.

अपूप *apûpa*, m. A cake, Man. 5, 7.

अपूर्वता *a-pûrva + tâ*, f. and **अपूर्वत्व** *a-pûrva + tva*, n. Condition of having no antecedent, i.e. acquiring an understanding of the *only real being* from no other authority than the Vedic texts, Vedântas. in Chr. 216, 10 cf. 3.

अपेक्षा *apekshâ*, i.e. *apa-iksh + a* f. **1.** Consideration, Pańch. 40, 16. **2.** Regard. **3.** Care, Daçak. in Chr. 187, 6. **4.** Expectation, Vedântas. in Chr. 214, 9. **5.** Reference, relation, ib. 208, 5.—Comp. *An-apeksha*, adj., f. *kshâ*. 1. Regardless. 2. Without desire, Bhag. 12, 16. *Nis-*, I. f. indifference, Râm. 2, 116, 5 Gorr. II. adj. 1. Regardless, Daçak. in Chr. 185, 19. 2. Without desire, indifferent, Man. 6, 41. III. *ksham*, adv. 1. Without having any regard, Daçak. in Chr. 192, 22. 2. Accidentally, Pańch. 264, 7.

अपेक्षितत्व *apekshitatva*, i.e. *apa-iksh-ita + tva*, (vb. *iksh*), n. Consideration, Vedântas. in Chr. 216, 1.

अपेक्षिन् *apekshin*, i.e. *apa-îksh + in*, adj., f. *iṇî*. **1.** Regarding. **2.** Expecting, Râjat. 5, 296.—Comp. *An-*, disregarding, Râm. 4, 28, 5. *Dîrgha-*, i.e. *dîrghâpekshâ + in*, adj. patient, enduring, MBh. 7, 5467. *Nis-*, adj. indifferent, ib. 13, 6169.

अपोगण्ड *apogaṇḍa*, adj. Not under sixteen years of age, Man. 8, 148 (v. r.).

अपोह *apoha*, i.e. *apa-ûh + a*, m. Disconnecting reasoning, MBh. 13, 6725.

अपोहन *apohana*, i.e. *apa-vah + ana*, n. Removal, Bhag. 15, 15 (of recollection and knowledge.)

अप्चर *ap-chara*, adj., f. *râ*, Living in water, Man. 7, 72.

अप्नस्वन्त् *apnas + vant* (*apnas*, ved.), adj. Efficacious, Chr. 298, 24 = Rigv. i. 112, 24.

अप्यय *apyaya*, i.e. *api-i + a*, m. Absorption.—Comp. *Loka-îça-prabhava-*, adj. owing both origin and end to the guardians of the world, Man. 5, 97.

अप्रजस् *aprajas*, i.e. probably *a-pra-jan + as*, adj. Childless, Râm. 1, 14, 29.

अप्रतिरथ *a-prati-ratha* (cf. the next), m. A leader in combat, Çâk. d. 95; 192.

अप्रतिवीर्य *a-prati-virya* (*a-prati* is a ved. word, Irresistible), adj. Of irresistible strength, Râm. 4, 35, 4.

अप्राज्ञता *a-prâjña-tâ*, f. Ignorance, Man. 4, 167.

अप्सरस् *apsaras*, i.e. *ap-sṛi + as*, f. The name of female divinities; in the classical poetry the courtesans of paradise.—Comp. *Pańchâpsaras*, i.e. *pańchan-*, n. the name of a pond.

अबाधक *a-bâdha + ka* (see *bâdhâ*) adj., f. *kâ*, Unobstructed, Kathâs. 26, 80.

अब्ज *abja*, i.e. *ap-ja* (vb. *jan*), I. adj., f. *jâ*, Born or produced in or by water, Man. 5, 112. **II.** n. A lotus, —Comp. *Nîla-*, n. a blue lotus.

अब्द *abda*, i.e. *ap-da* (vb. *dâ*) m. **1.** A cloud. **2.** A year, Râjat. 5, 291.—Comp. *Kṛichchhra-*, m. a year of penance, Man. 11, 162. *Tri-*, n. Three years, Man. 8, 30.

अब्धि *abdhi*, i.e. *ap-dhâ* (cf. *nidhi*),

m. The ocean, Kathâs. 12, 113.—**Comp.** *Kshîra-*, m. the sea of milk, Kathâs. 22, 186.

अभि *abhi* (Towards, to). **I.** adv. On, Chr. 295, 10=Rigv. i. 92, 10. **II.** prep. with acc. To, Ved. Chr. 287, 7=Rigv. i. 48, 7; over, Chr. 292, 5=Rigv. i. 86, 5. **III.** Combined and compounded with verbs and their derivatives. **IV.** Former part of compounded nouns and adverbs implying Towards, in presence of, very, cf. e.g. *abhitâmra*; Quite, cf. *abhinava.*—Cf. Goth. bî. The original form of this indeclinable was probably *ambhi*=Gr. ἀμφί; Lat. amb in amb-ire; O.H.G. umbi.

अभिक *abhi-ka* (vb. *kam*) adj., f. *kâ*, Libidinous, Ragh. 19, 4.

अभिकाङ्क्षा *abhi-kâṅksh+â*, f. Desire, Râm. 3, 48, 15 (*svargam abhikaṅkshâ*, Desire of getting into heaven, with accus. like its verbal base).

अभिकाङ्क्षिन् *abhi-kâṅksh+in*, adj., f. *iṇî*, Desiring, Chr. 7, 18.

अभिकाम *abhikâma*, i.e. *abhi-kam +a*. **I.** m. Love. **II.** adj., f. *mâ*, Loving, Râm. 1, 77, 29.—**Comp.** *Sa-*, adj. loving, Nal. 24, 13.

अभिकाल *abhikâla*, m. The name of a town, Râm. 2, 68, 17.

अभिक्रम *abhi-kram+a*, m. An undertaking, Bhag. 2, 40.

अभिख्या *abhi-khyâ*, f. Beauty, Megh. 78.—**Comp.** *Adhika-ud-rechita-abhikhya*, adj. exceedingly beautiful, Râjat. 5, 365. *Hamsa-*, n. silver. *Himâmçu-*, i.e. *hima-amçu-*, n. silver.

अभिगम *abhi-gam+a*, m. **1.** Approaching. **2.** A visit, Megh. 50. **3.** Sexual intercourse, Yâjń. 2, 291.

अभिगमन *abhi-gam+ana*, n. **1.** Approaching. **2.** Mounting, Kathâs. 20, 154. **3.** Sexual intercourse, Pańch. Pr. d. 8.

अभिगामिन् *abhigâmin*, i.e. *abhi-gam+in* adj., f. *nî*, Approaching (for sexual intercourse), Man. 3, 45.

अभिघात *abhighâta*, i.e. *abhi-han*, Caus. +*a*, m. **1.** Striking, Bhâshâp. 117; Kir. 5, 42. **2.** Hurting, affliction, Man. 12, 77.—**Comp.** *Vapra-*, m. butting at a bank or mound.

अभिघातिन् *abhighâtin*, i.e. *abhi-han*, Caus. +*in*, adj., f. *nî*, **1.** Striking. **2.** Hostile, Hit. iv. d. 92.

अभिचार *abhichâra*, i.e. *abhi-char +a*, m. Incantation, making charms for mischievous purposes, Man. 11, 197.

अभिजन *abhi-jan+a*, m. **1.** Race, Râm. 3, 48, 18. **2.** Family, Râm. 5, 87, 15.

अभिजनन *abhi-jan+ana*, n. Production, Häberl. 524, 9.

अभिजनवन्त् *abhijana+vant*, adj., f. *vatî*, Noble, Çâk. d. 94.

अभिजित् *abhi-ji+t*, **I.** m. The name of a sacrifice, Man. 11, 74. **II.** n. The name of the eighth Indian hour (*muhûrta*, comprising 48 minutes) of the day, (i.e. 24 minutes before and 24 minutes after midday), Râm. 6, 112, 70.

अभिज्ञ *abhi-jńa* (vb. *jńâ*), adj., f. *jńâ*, Knowing, conversant with, Râjat. 5, 383.—**Comp.** *An-*, adj. ignorant, Daçak. in Chr. 182, 18.

अभिज्ञता *abhijńa+tâ*, f. Knowledge, Ragh. 7, 61.

अभिज्ञान *abhijńâna*, i.e. *abhi-jńâ +ana*, n. **1.** Remembrance, Râm. 5, 68, 1. **2.** Recognition, Daçak. in Chr. 192, 12. **3.** A token of remembrance, Râm. 2, 100, 6. **4.** A sign by which one proves himself to be a trustee, Daçak. in Chr. 196, 15.

अभितस् *abhi*+*tas*, adv. and prep. with acc. **1.** On both sides, Bhartṛ. 1, 80; Râm. 2, 45, 4. **2.** From every side, round about, Râm. 2, 94, 20. **3.** Near, Kir. 5, 14; also with gen. Râm. 1, 33, 22. **4.** Completely, Kir. 5, 11. **5.** Towards, in presence of.

अभिताप *abhi-tâpa*, m. **1.** Extreme heat, Çiç. 9, 1. **2.** Great pain, Sâv. 5, 69.

अभिताम्र *abhi-tâmra*, adj., f. *râ*, Very red, Kathâs, 14, 30.

अभितिग्मरश्मि *abhi-tigma-raçmi*, adv. Towards the sun, Çiç. 9, 11.

अभिदर्शन *abhidarçana*, i. e. *abhi-dṛç*+*ana*, n. Sight, Man. 9, 274.

अभिदूति *abhidûti*, i.e. *abhi-dûtî* (cf. *dûta*), adv. To a female messenger, Çiç. 9, 56.

अभिद्रोह *abhidroha*, i.e. *abhi-druh*+*a*, m. **1.** Injury, Râm. 1, 26, 20. **2.** Contumely, Man. 8, 271.—Comp. *An-*, m. tenderness, Kathâs. 13, 34.

अभिधा *abhi-dhâ*, f. **1.** A name, Râjat. 5, 379. **2.** The primary sense of a word. —Comp. *Çûravarmâbhidha*, i.e. *çûra-varman-*, adj. called Çûravarman, Râjat. 5, 22.

अभिधान *abhidhâna*, i.e. *abhi-dhâ*+*ana*, n. **1.** A name, Kathâs. 7, 112. **2.** A word.—Comp. *Suyyâ-*, adj., f. *nâ*, called Suyyâ, Rajât. 5, 74.

अभिधायिन् *abhidhâyin*, i.e. *abhi-dhâ*+*in*, adj., f. *nî*, **1.** Speaking, Râm. 5, 14, 41. **2.** Teaching.

अभिधावक *abhi-dhâv*+*aka*, adj. Running towards, hastening, Yâjú. 2, 234.

अभिध्यान *abhidhyâna*, i.e. *abhi-dhyai*+*ana*, n. Desire, covetousness, Man. 12, 5.

अभिनन्द *abhi-nand*+*a*, m., or f. *dâ*, Wish, desire.

अभिनन्दिन् *abhi-nand*+*in*, adj., f. *nî*. **1.** Praising, Râm. 5, 59, 11. **2.** Delighting, Râm. 3, 79, 12.

अभिनम्र *abhi-namra*, adj., f. *râ*, Bent, Ragh. 13, 32.

अभिनय *abhinaya*, i.e. *abhi-nî*+*a*, m. Dramatic performance, Vikr. d. 36.

अभिनव *abhi-nava*, adj., f. *vâ*, Quite new, Râjat. 5, 1. **2.** Fresh, Bhartṛ. 2, 14.

अभिनासिकाविवरम् *abhi-nâsikâ-vivara*+*m*, adv. To the nostril, Çiç. 9, 52.

अभिनिवेश *abhiniveça*, i.e. *abhi-ni-viç*+*a*, m. **1.** Inclination, Vikr. 35, 13. **2.** Adhering, Man. 12, 5. **3.** Tenacity. **4.** Determined resolution. *samupajâtâbhiniveçam*, i.e. *sam-upa-jâta-abhiniveça*+*m*, adv. After having taken a determined resolution, Prab. 67, 14.

अभिनिवेशवन्त् *abhiniveça*+*vant*, adj., f. *vatî*, Adhering, Yâjú. 3, 155.

अभिनिवेशिन् *abhiniveçin*, i.e. *abhiniveça*+*in*, adj., f. *nî*. **1.** Adhering. **2.** Persevering, Daçak. in Chr. 190, 22.

अभिपीतत्व *abhi-pîta*+*tva* (vb. 1. *pâ*), n. Condition of being saturated, MBh. 12, 12844.

अभिपुष्प *abhi-pushpa*, adj. Covered with flowers, Râm. 6, 93, 18.

अभिप्राय *abhiprâya*, i.e. *abhi-pra-i*+*a*, m. **1.** Intention, Pañch. i. d. 366; wish, Râm. 3, 28, 31. **2.** Opinion, Pañch. 150, 25. **3.** Consideration, Vedântas. in Chr. 204, 13 sqq. *Samashṭi-abhiprâyeṇa*, when taken collectively.—Comp. *Sa-*, adj. resolute, Pañch. 122, 13.

अभिप्रेप्सु *abhiprepsu*, i.e. *abhi-pra-ipsa*, desider. of *âp* + *u*, adj. Ardently desiring, Man. 8, 344.

अभिभर्तृ *abhi-bhartṛi*, adv. In the presence of the husband, Çiç. 9, 77; on the husband, ib. 35.

अभिभव *abhibhava*, i.e. *abhi-bhû* + *a*, m. 1. The being overpowered, Çâk. d. 40. 2. Defeat.—Comp. *Nis-*, adj., not surpassable, Bhartṛ. 2, 54.

अभिभवन *abhibhavana*, i.e. *abhi-bhû* + *ana*, n. The being overpowered, Man. 6, 62.

अभिभाविन् *abhibhâvin*, i.e. *abhi-bhû* + *in*, adj. Overpowering, Ragh. 1, 14.

अभिभाषण *abhibhâshaṇa*, i.e. *abhi-bhâsh* + *ana*, n. Allocution.

अभिभाषिन् *abhi-bhâsh* + *in*, adj., f. *iṇî*, Addressing, Râm. 3, 49, 5.

अभिभूति *abhi-bhû* + *ti*, f. Defeat.

ऽअभिमनस् *-abhi-manas*, adj. Wishing for, Râm. 5, 38, 24.

अभिमन्तृ *abhi-man* + *tṛi*, m. One who refers existing objects to one's own self, Man. 1, 14.

अभिमन्त्रण *abhimantraṇa*, i.e. *abhi-mantr* + *ana*, n. Consecration, Yâjń, 1, 237.

अभिमर्द *abhimarda*, i.e. *abhi-mṛid* + *a*, m. Oppression, invasion, Draup. 6, 8.

अभिमर्दन *abhimardana*, i.e. *abhi-mṛid* + *ana*. I. adj., f. *nî*, Oppressing. II. n. Oppression, Râm. 6, 95, 8; invasion, 6, 100, 7.

अभिमर्दिन् *abhimardin*, i.e. *abhi-mṛid* + *in*, adj., f. *nî*, Oppressing.

अभिमर्श *abhimarça*, i.e. *abhi-mṛiç* + *a*, m. Touching improperly, Çâk. d. 116. Sometimes it is written incorrectly with *sh* instead of *ç*, Man. 8, 352.

अभिमर्शक *abhimarçaka*, i.e. *abhi-mṛiç* + *aka*, adj. Touching improperly.—With *sh* instead of *ç* (see the last), Râm. 1, 7, 14.

अभिमर्शन *abhimarçana*, i.e. *abhi-mṛiç-ana*, n. Touching improperly, Yâjń, 2, 284. Also incorrectly (see the last) with *shaṇa* instead of *çana*, Râm. 6, 66, 26.

अभिमर्शिन् *abhimarçin*, i.e. *abhi mṛiç-in*, adj., f. *nî*, Courting, Daçak. in Chr. 195, 4.

अभिमर्ष, -मर्षक, -मर्षण See **अभिमर्श, -मर्शक, -मर्शन.**

अभिमातिन् *abhimâtin*, i.e. *abhi-man* + *ti* + *in*, m. An enemy, Chr. 291, 3 = Rigv. i. 85, 3.

अभिमान *abhimâna*, i.e. *abhi-man* + *a*, m. 1. Referring existing objects to one's own self, egotism, Vedântas. in Chr. 207, 2. 2. Self-conceit, pride, Bhartṛ. 3, 4. 3. Love, Daçak. in Chr. 182, 23.—Comp. *Nis-*, adj. exempt from pride, Bhâg. P. 5, 15, 6. *Sa-*, adj. proud, Râjat. 5, 233.

अभिमानवन्त् *abhimâna* + *vant*, adj., f. *vatî*, Proud.

ऽअभिमानित्व *abhimânitva*, i.e. *abhimânin* + *tva*, n. State of one who refers existing objects to his own self, egotism, Vedântas. in Chr. 209, 11.

अभिमानिन् *abhimânin*, i.e. *abhi-mâna* + *in*, adj., f. *nî*, 1. Proud, Râm. 3, 37, 16. 2. Fancying, Daçak. in Chr. 187, 12 (*narendrâbhimânin*, having the fancy of being a physician).

अभिमुख *abhi-mukha*, adj., f. *khâ* or *khî*. 1. Facing, fronting, Râm. 1, 71, 18: with acc. Directed towards,

Râm. 2, 1, 34; towards, Bhag. 11, 28; opposite, Râm. 5, 71, 9. **2.** Near, Vikr. d. 28. **3.** Ready for, Ragh, 5, 29. **4.** Favourable, Râm. 2, 109, 23. Acc. *kham*, adv. Opposite to, Man. 2, 193; towards, Pańch. 40, 17; to, Râm. 1, 45, 48; near, Megh. 69. Loc. *khe*, adv. Opposite, Râm. 6, 19, 25. — Comp. *Kânana-*, adv. to the wood, Pańch. 63, 3. *Dakshiṇâ-*, adj. turned to the south, Man. 4, 50.

अभियाचना *abhi-yâch + anâ*, f. A request, at the end of the comp. adj. *satya-abhiyâchana*, Fulfilling the requests (which are directed to him), Râm. 2, 55, 6.

अभियातृ *abhi-yâ + tṛi*, m. An aggressor, Râm. 2, 1, 21.

अभियान *abhiyâna*, i.e. *abhi-yâ + ana*, n. **1.** Approaching. **2.** Aggression, Chr. 53, 5.

अभियायिन् *abhiyâyin*, i.e. *abhi-yâ + in*, adj., f. *nî*. **1.** Approaching, Râm. 6, 16, 56. **2.** Assaulting, Ragh. 12, 24.

अभियोक्तृ *abhiyoktṛi*, i.e. *abhi-yuj + tṛi*, m. **1.** An enemy. **2.** A plaintiff, Man. 8, 52.

अभियोग *abhiyoga*, i.e. *abhi-yuj + a*, m. **1.** Exertion, Râm. 5, 51, 16. **2.** Attack. **3.** A charge, Yâjń. 2, 9.

अभियोगिन् *abhiyogin*, i.e. *abhi-yuj + in*, adj. Accusing, a plaintiff, Yâjń, 2, 11.

अभिरचितृ *abhi-raksh + itṛi*, m. A protector, Man. 7, 35.

अभिरति *abhirati*, i.e. *abhi-ram + ti*, f. Delight, Hit. i. d. 129.

अभिराम *abhirâma*, i.e. *abhi-ram + a*, adj., f. *mâ*, Charming, delighting, Râm. 3, 49, 23.

अभिरुचि *abhi-ruch + i*, f. Delight, desire, Bhartṛ. 2, 53.

अभिरुचिर *abhi-ruchira*, adj., f. *râ*, Very beautiful.

अभिरूप *abhi-rûpa*, adj., f. *pâ*. **1.** Suitable. **2.** Beautiful, Man. 9, 88. **3.** Learned, Man. 3, 144.—Comp. *An-*, adj. ugly, Daçak. in Chr. 184, 8.

अभिलक्ष्यम् *abhi-lakshya + m*, adv. Towards the mark, Ram. 2, 63, 22.

अभिलङ्घन *abhi-laṅgh + ana*, n. Jumping over, Râm. 5, 53, 9.

अभिलाष *abhilâsha*, i.e. *abhi-lash + a*, m. Desire, Daçak. in Chr. 182, 8. —Comp. *Nis-*, adj. indifferent, Çâk. d. 104. *Sa-*, adj., f. *shâ*, eager, Dev. 1, 39. *Sâbhilâsha + m*, adv. passionately, Çâk. 33, 13.

अभिलाषक *abilâshaka*, i.e. *abhi-lash + aka*, adj. Desiring.

अभिलाषिन् *abhilâshin*, i.e. *abhi-lash + in*, adj., f. *iṇî*, Desirous, Çâk. d. 21.

अभिलाषुक *abhilâshuka*, i. e. *abhi-lash + uka*, adj., f. *kâ*, Desiring (with acc.), Kir. 11, 18.

अभिवदन *abhi-vad + ana*, n. Address, allocution.

अभिवन्दन *abhi-vand + ana*, n. Respectful salutation. — Comp. *Kṛita-pâda-*, adj., f. *nâ*, literally, having performed a respectful salutation of the feet, i.e. having made a respectful salutation, Kathâs. 22, 131.

अभिवर्तिन् *abhivartin*, i.e. *abhi-vṛit + in*, adj., f. *nî*, Approaching, Râm. 6, 88, 35.

अभिवर्षण *abhivarshaṇa*, i.e. *abhi-vṛish + ana*, n. Raining upon.

अभिवर्षिन् *abhivarshin*, i.e. *abhi-vṛish-in*, adj., f. *iṇī*, Throwing upon, Râm. 1, 28, 22.

अभिवाद *abhivâda*, i.e. *abhi-vad+a*, m. Salutation, Man. 2, 122.

अभिवादक *abhivâdaka*, i.e. *abhi-vad+aka*, adj., f. *dikâ*, Greeting, Nal. 21, 24 (*bhavantaṁ abhivâdakaḥ*, in order to salute you).

अभिवादन *abhivâdana*, i.e. *abhi-vad+ana*, n. Respectful salutation, Man. 2, 124.

अभिवाह्य *abhivâhya*, i.e. *abhi-vah+ya*, n. Offering, Man. 1, 94.

अभिवृद्धि *abhivṛiddhi*, i.e. *abhi-vṛidh+ti*, f. Growth, exaltation, Man. 7, 109.

अभिव्यक्ति *abhivyakti*, i.e. *abhi-vi-añj+ti*, f. Manifestation.

अभिव्यञ्जक *abhivyañjaka*, i.e. *abhi-vi-añj+aka*, adj. Manifesting.

अभिशंसन *abi-çaṁs+ana*, n. Slandering, Man. 8, 268.

अभिशंसिन् *abhi-çaṁs+in*, adj., f. *nî*, Slandering, Yâjñ. 3, 285.

अभिशङ्का *abhi-çaṅk+â*, f. 1. Suspecting, Râm. 6, 66, 26. 2. Fear.

अभिशस्तक *abhi-çasta + ka* (vb. *çaṁs*), adj. 1. Accused, Yâjñ. 1, 223. 2. Inflicted, imprecated.

अभिशस्ति *abhiçasti*, i.e. *abhi-çaṁs+ti*, f. Defamation, calumny.

अभिशान्त्व *abhi-çântv+a*, m. Conciliating manner, Râm. 5, 56, 44 (written with *s* instead of *ç*).

अभिशाप *abhiçâpa*, i.e. *abhi-çap+a*, m. 1. A curse, Râm. 3, 8, 12. 2. A heavy charge. 3. Calumny.

अभिषङ्ग *abhishaṅga*, i.e. *abhi-sañj+a*, m. 1. Attachment. 2. An oath, Chr. 53, 23. 3. A curse. 4. Defeat, Ragh. 2, 30.

अभिषेक *abhisheka*, i.e. *abhi-sich+a*, m. 1. Sprinkling with water, inauguration of a king, Pañch. iii. d. 267. 2. The water used for an inauguration. 3. Ablution, Çâk. 50, 16.

अभिषेचन *abhishechana*, i.e. *abhi-sich+ana*, n. Inauguration of a king, Râm. 3, 53, 5.

अभिष्टव *abhishṭava*, i.e. *abhi-stu+a*, m. Praise.

अभिष्यन्द *abhishyanda*, i.e. *abhi-syand+a*, m. Great increase, Ragh. 15, 29.

अभिष्वङ्ग *abhishvaṅga*, i.e. *abhi-svañj+a*, m. Attachment.—**Comp.** *An-*, adj. without attachment, Bhag. 13, 9.

अभिसंश्रय *abhisaṁçraya*, i.e. *abhi-sam-çri+a*, m. Refuge, Râm. 4, 54, 16.

अभिसंदेह *abhisaṁdeha*, i.e. *abhi-sam-dih+a*, m. The organ of generation, Chr. 58, 8.

अभिसंधक *abhisaṁdhaka*, i.e. *abhi-sam-dha+ka* (vb. *dhâ*), m. A calumniator, Man. 4, 195.

अभिसंधा *abhi-saṁ-dhâ*, f. Promise.—**Comp.** *Satyâbhisaṁdha*, i.e. *satya-*, adj. one who keeps his promises true, Râm. 1, 6, 5.

अभिसंधान *abhi-saṁ-dhâ+ana*, n. 1. Promise. 2. Deceiving, Ragh. 17, 76.—**Comp.** *Satya-*, adj., f. *nâ*, keeping one's promises true, Râm. 5, 31, 21.

अभिसंधि *abhisaṁdhi*, i.e. *abhi-sam-dhâ* (cf. *nidhi*), m. Intention, Pañch. 200, 11.

अभिसंधित *abhisaṁdhita*, see *dhâ* with *abhi-sam*.

अभिसंबन्ध *abhisaṁbandha*, i.e. *abhi-sam-bandh + a*, m. Union, Man. 5, 63.

अभिसर *abhisara*, i.e. *abhi-sṛi + a*, m. Companion, Daçak. in Chr. 187, 1; 201, 6.

अभिसरण *abhisaraṇa*, i.e. *abhi-sṛi + ana*, n. An amorous visit, Daçak. in Chr. 182, 12.

अभिसर्ग *abhisarga*, i.e. *abhi-sṛij + a*, m. Creation.

अभिसान्त्व *abhisântva*, see *abhiçântva*.

अभिसार *abhisâra*, i.e. *abhi-sṛi + a*, m. 1. A lover's appointment, a rendezvous. 2. An attack, Râm. 6, 9, 19. 3. plur. The name of a people.—Comp. *Loha-*, m. lustration of arms.

अभिसारिका *abhisârikâ*, i.e. *abhi-sṛi-aka*, f. A woman who goes to a rendezvous.

अभिसेवन *abhi-sev + ana*, n. Indulgence, habitual practice.

अभिहरण *abhiharaṇa*, i.e. *abhi-hṛi + ana*, n. Conveying, Ragh. 11, 43.

अभिहार *abhihâra*, i.e. *abhi-hṛi + a*, m. 1. Seizing. 2. Robbing. 3. Attack. 4. Arming.—Comp. *Loha-*, m. lustration of arms,

अभीक्ष्णम् *abhîkshṇam*, i.e. probably *abhi-ikshaṇa + m* (cf. *kshaṇa*), adv. 1. Every moment, continually. 2. Repeatedly.—Comp. *An-*, adv. seldom, Râm. 2, 71, 8.

अभीक्ष्णशस् *abhîkshṇa + ças*, adv. Continually, Râm. 2, 46, 6.

अभीतवत् *a-bhîta + vat*, adv. Like a fearless one, Ram. 6, 28, 6.

अभीप्सु *abhîpsu*, i.e. *abhi-îpsa*, desider. of *âp + u*, adj. Desiring, Nal. 5, 2.

अभीमान *abhîmâna = abhimâna*.—Comp. *Nis-*, adj., f. *nâ*, 1. devoid of egotism, MBh. 7, 2019. 2. devoid of pride, MBh. 4, 14668.

अभीशाप *abhîçâpa = abhiçâpa*, Yâjń. 2, 110.

अभीषु *abhîçu*, i.e. *abhi-iç + u*, m. A bridle, Çâk. 5, 15.

अभोग्घन् *abhogghan*, i.e. *a-bhuj-han*, adj. Slaying those who do not feed (the gods), i.e. who do not sacrifice, impious, Chr. 290, 3 = Rigv. 1, 64, 3.

अभ्यङ्ग *abhyaṅga*, i.e. *abi-añj + a*, m. Unction, Man. 2, 178.

अभ्यञ्जन *abhyañjana*, i.e. *abhi-añj + ana*, n. Anointing, Man. 10, 91.

अभ्यधिक *abhyadhika*, i.e. *abhi-adhika*, adj. Exceeding, preeminent, Râm. 5, 82, 13. Superior, Daçak. in Chr. 201, 2. Acc. *kam*, adv. Exceedingly, Râm. 5, 73, 59.

अभ्यनुज्ञा *abhyanujńâ*, i.e. *abhi-anu-jńâ*, f. Permission.—Comp. *An-*, f. want of permission, Daçak. in Chr. 188, 7 (without the permission of the father). *Krita-*, adj., f. *jńâ*, having received the permission to withdraw, dismissed, Râm. 5, 76, 24.

अभ्यनुज्ञान *abhyanujńâna*, i.e. *abhi-anu-jńâ + ana*, n. Assent, Râm. 1, 3, 14.

अभ्यन्तर *abhyantara*, i.e. *abhi-antara*. I. adj., f. *râ*, 1. Interior, Kathâs. 4, 51. Being within, Râm. 6, 112, 43 (in the town). Belonging to, Man. 3, 154. 2. Conversant in, Râm. 6, 5, 19. 3. Intimate, Pańch. i. d. 290 (perhaps to be read *âbhy°*). 4. Secret, Daçak. in Chr. 180, 9. II. n. 1. The interior, the space within, Bhag. 5, 27. 2. An interval, Pańch. 5, 6.

अभ्यन्तरीकरण *abhyantarîkaraṇa*, i.e. *abhyantara-kṛi + ana*, n. Initiation, Daçak. in Chr. 180, 9.

अभ्यर्चन *abhyarchana*, i.e. *abhi-arch* + *ana*, n. Worship, Man. 2, 176.

अभ्यर्ण *abhyarṇa*, i.e. *abhi-arṇa* (vb. *ard*). I. adj., f. *ṇâ*, Near. II. n. Proximity, Râjat. 5, 145.

अभ्यर्थना *abhyarthanâ*, i.e. *abhi-arth* + *ana*, f. Request, Sâv. 4, 27.

अभ्यर्थिन् *abhyarthin*, i.e. *abhi-arth* + *in*, adj., f. *nî*, Requesting.

अभ्यर्हणीयता *abhyarhaṇîyatâ*, i.e. *abhi-arhaṇîya* + *tâ* (vb. *arh*), f. Great venerableness, Man. 9, 23.

अभ्यवहार *abhyavahâra*, i.e. *abhi* -*ava-hṛi* + *a*, m. Eating, Man. 6, 59.

अभ्यवहार्य *abhyavahârya*, i.e. *abhyavahâra* + *ya*, adj. Fit to be taken as food, eatable.

अभ्यसन *abhyasana*, i.e. *abhi*- 2. *as* + *ana*, n. Study, Bhag. 17, 15.—Comp. *An*-, n. laziness, Râm. 5, 19, 22.

अभ्यसूयक *abhyasûyaka*, i.e. *abhi* -*asûya* + *aka*, adj. Detracting, a detractor, Bhag. 16, 18.

अभ्यसूया *abhyasûyâ*, i.e. *abhi* -*asûya* + *a*, f. 1. Detraction, envy. 2. Wrath, Megh. 40.—Comp. *Sa*-, adj. envious, malicious.

अभ्यागम *abhyâgama*, i.e. *abhi-â* -*gam* + *a*, m. A visit, Ragh. 16, 8.

अभ्यागमन *abhyâgamana*, i.e. *abhi* -*â-gam* + *ana*, n. Arrival.

अभ्याघात *abhyâghâta*, i.e. *abhi-â* -*han*, Caus. + *a*, m. Assault (by robbers), Man. 9, 272.

अभ्याश *abhyâça*, i.e. *abhi*- 1. *aç* + *a*, often written *abhyâsa* (q. cf.) but incorrectly. I. adj., f. *çâ*, Near, Kumâras. 6, 2. II. n. Proximity, Râm. 4, 59, 12.

अभ्यास *abhyâsa*, i.e. *abhi*- 2. *as* + *a* (cf. *abhyâça*), m. 1. Repetition, Man. 12, 74. Repetition of words, Vedântas. in Chr. 216, 8; 9. 2. Repeated practice, Râjat. 5, 164; 439. Use, Yâjñ. 3, 68. 3. Reading, Man. 4, 148. Study, Pañch. 220, 4.

अभ्युक्षण *abhyukshaṇa*, i.e. *abhi* -*uksh* + *ana*, n. Sprinkling, Ragh. 16, 57.

अभ्युत्थान *abhyutthâna*, i.e. *abhi* -*ud-sthâ* + *ana*, n. 1. Rising, Râm. 6, 72, 65. 2. Rising from one's seat as mark of respect, Pañch. ii. d. 65. 3. Origin, Bhag, 4, 7. 4. Elevation, dignity, Ragh. 4, 3.

अभ्युत्पतन *abhyutpatana*, i.e. *abhi* -*ud-pat* + *ana*, n. Assault.

अभ्युदय *abhyudaya*, i.e. *abhi-ud-i* + *a*, m. 1. Prosperity, Bhartṛ. 2, 53. Wealth, Daçak. in Chr. 192, 19. 2. A festival, Man. 9, 84.

अभ्युदयिन् *abhyudayin*, i.e. *abhi* -*ud-i* + *in*, adj., f. *nî*, Arising, impending, Râjat. 5, 36.

अभ्युद्गम *abhyudgama*, i.e. *abhi-ud* -*gam* + *a*, m. Rising from one's seat as mark of respect, Kathâs. 24, 122.

अभ्युपगम *abhyupagama*, i. e. *abhi* -*upa-gam* + *a*, m. 1. Arrival. 2. Assenting, agreement, Man. 9, 53. 3. Admitting to be true, Mâlav. 15, 19.

अभ्युपपत्ति *abhyupapatti*, i.e. *abhi* -*upa-pad* + *ti*, f. 1. Defence, Man. 8, 112. 2. Protection, Daçak. in Chr. 179, 19. 3. Assent.

अभ्युपाय *abhyupâya*, i.e. *abhi-upa-i* + *a*, m. An expedient, Daçak. in Chr. 190, 3; 191, 12.

अभ्र् *ABHR*, i. 1, Par. To roam (probably for *babhr*, a mutilated redupl. of *bhram* cf. *andolaya*).

अभ्र *abhra* (akin to *ambhas*), n. **1.** A cloud, especially a rain-cloud, Man. 4, 104. **2.** Atmosphere, Pańch. i. d. 209. Heaven, Çiç. 9, 3.—Cf. *ambhas*, ὄμβρος, Lat. imber, and probably umbra.

अभ्रंलिह *abhraṁliha*, i.e. *abhra* + *m-lih* + *a*. I. adj., f. *hâ*, Touching the clouds, very lofty, Megh. 65. II. m. Wind.

अभ्रावकाशक *abhrâvakâçaka*, i.e. *abhra-avakâça* + *ka*, adj. Uncovered (see the next), Râm. 1, 63, 24.

अभ्रावकाशिक *abhrâvakâçika*, i.e. *abhra-avakâça* + *ika*, adj. Having the clouds for shelter, uncovered, Man. 6, 23 (read आभ्रा° *âbhrâ*°).

अभ्रावकाशिन् *abhrâvakâçin*, i.e. *abhra-avakâça* + *in*, Uncovered (see the last), Râm. 3, 10, 4.

अभ्रि *abhri*, f. A sharp pointed stick, Man. 11, 133.

अभ्रित *abhrita*, i.e. *abhra* + *ita*, adj., f. *tâ*, Clouded, Ragh. 3, 12.

अम् *AM*, i. 1, Par., with prep. also Âtm. **1.** To go. **2.** To sound.—I. 10, Par. To be ill (ved.). The original notion was 'to be hard, strong, powerful.'—Cf. *aṁsa*, *âma*, and many ved. significations and derivatives; Lat. emo, properly 'to take,' demo; περιημεκτέω.

अमन्त्रक *a-mantra* + *ka*, adj., f. *rikâ*, Not accompanied by a *mantra* or vedic verse, Man. 2, 66.

अमम *a-mama* (the latter part is the gen. sing. of the pronoun of the first person, in the sense of a possessive pronoun), adj., f. *mâ*, Devoid of selfish affection, Man. 6, 26.

अमर *amara*, i.e. *a-mṛi* + *a*. I. adj., f. *râ* and *ri*, Immortal, Man. 2, 148; Râm. 1, 34, 16. II. m. **1.** A god, Man. 7, 72. **2.** The name of a Marut and of a mountain.—**Comp.** *Dharâ-*, m. a Brâhmaṇa, Mârk. P. 26, 36. *Sa-*, adj. with the gods, Râm. 3, 53, 28.

अमरत्व *amara* + *tva*, n. Immortality, Arj. 3, 47.

अमरलोकता *amara-loka* + *tâ*, f. The happiness of the world of gods, Man. 2, 5.

अमरावती *amarâvatî*, i.e. *amara* + *vant* + *î*. The capital of Indra, Râm. 3, 53, 37.

अमर्त्यत्व *a-martya* + *tva*, n. Immortality.

अमर्षिन् *amarshin*, i.e. *a-mṛish* + *in*, adj., f. *iṇî*, Unable to endure, impatient, Draup. 7, 1.

अमलय *AMALAYA*, a denom. derived from *a-mala*, Par. To make white, Kir. 5, 44.

अमात्य *amâ* + *tya* (the basis signifies in the Vedas 'in the house'). I. adj. Being in the house. II. m. (A companion of the king) A minister, Râjat. 5, 3.—**Comp.** *Mahâ-*, m. a minister. *Sa-*, adj. with the ministers, Chr. 18, 33. *Sa-janâmâtya*, i.e. *-jana -amâtya*, adj. together with people and ministers, Chr. 53, 25.

अमानन *amânana*, i.e. *a-man* + *ana*, n. Disrespect.

अमानित्व *amânitva*, i.e. *a-mânin* + *tva*, n. Humility, Vedântas. in Chr. 219, 6.

अमावाशी *amâvâśî*, and अमावास्या *amâvâsyâ*, i.e. *amâ* (cf. *amâtya*) *-vâsa* + *ya*, f. The day of the conjunction of the sun and moon, the day of the new moon, Man. 4, 113.

अमित्रता *a-mitra + tâ*, f. Enmity, Pańch. ii. d. 106.

अमित्राय *AMITRÂYA*, a denom. derived from *a-mitra* by *ya*, Âtm. To behave like an enemy, Bhartṛ. 3, 74.

अमीव *am + îva*, n. Pain, Râm. 3, 59, 23.

अमुक *amu + ka* (cf. *adas*), adj., f. *kâ*, Instead of a proper name, Mr. so and so, Yâjń. 2, 86 sqq.

अमुतस् *amu + tas* (cf. *adas*), adv. **1.** = abl. of *adas*, From that, from him, Daçak. in Chr. 179, 8. **2.** From thence, from the other world.

अमुत्र *amu + tra* (cf. *adas*), adv. **1.** There, Daçak. in Chr. 198, 14. **2.** In the other world, Vedântas. in Chr. 203, 6.

अमृत *a-mṛita*. **I.** adj., f. *tâ*, Immortal, Bhag. 14, 27. **II.** m. **1.** A god. **2.** The soul. **III.** n. **1.** The beverage of the gods, nectar. **2.** A medicine preventing old age, prolonging life, and awakening the dead, Lass. 33, 20. **3.** A medicament; nectar and medicament, Çiç. 9, 36. **4.** The residue of sacrificial food, Man. 3, 285. **5.** Unsolicited alms, Man. 4, 4. — **Comp.** *Gava-*, n. *amṛita*, consisting of rays, MBh. 3, 17351.—Cf. *ἄμβροτος*, *ἀμβροσία*.

अमृतत्व *amṛita + tva*, n. Immortality, Man. 6, 60.

अमृतमय *amṛita + maya*, adj., f. *yî*, Like nectar, Pańch. 206, 7.

अमृतलतिका *amṛitalatikâ*, i.e. *amṛita-latâ + ka*, f. A small creeper as beautiful as nectar (denoting a beautiful woman), Çrut. (Br.) 35.

अमृतस्रुत् *amṛita-sru + t*, adj. Shedding nectar, Çiç. 5, 68.

अमृताय *AMṚITÂYA*, denom. derived from *amṛita* by *ya*, Âtm. To be like nectar, Ragh. 2, 61.

† **अम्ब्** *AMB*, i. 1, Par. To go; Âtm. To sound.

अम्बर *ambara* (akin to *ambhas*, cf. *stambh* and *stamba*). **I.** n. **1.** Sky, Râm. 3, 55, 9. **2.** Cloth, Râm, 3, 55, 5. Sky and garment, Çiç. 9, 7. **II.** m. plur. The name of a people.—**Comp.** *Nis-*, adj., f. *râ*, naked, MBh. 12, 7775. *Mada-*, m. an elephant in rut.

अम्बष्ठ *ambashṭha*, m. **1.** The name of a people, MBh. 2, 1189. **2.** The offspring of a Brâhmaṇa father and a Vaiçyâ mother, Man. 10, 8.

अम्बा *ambâ* (voc. sing. *amba*; in the Veda also *ambe*). **1.** f. A mother, Böhtl. Ind. Spr. 855. **2.** A proper name, Chr. 4, 10.—Cf. O.H.G. amma and ama.

अम्बालिका *ambâlikâ*, and **अम्बिका** *ambikâ* (akin to *ambâ*), f. Proper names, Chr. 4, 10.

अम्बु *ambu* (akin to *ambhas*, cf. *ambara*), n. Water, Pańch. iii. d. 33. —**Comp.** *Gharma-*, n. sweat, Suçr. 2, 343, 10. *Tila-*, n. water with sesame, Bhâg. P. 7, 8, 44. *Nis-*, adj. abstaining from water, Bhâg. P. 7, 3, 19.

अम्बुज *ambu-ja* (vb. *jan*). **I.** adj., f. *jâ*, Born in water, Râm. 4, 25, 24. **II.** n. A lotus, Râm. 5, 13, 24.

अम्बुजस्थ *ambuja-stha* (vb. *sthâ*), adj., f. *thâ*, Sitting on a lotus, Ṛit. 6, 14.

अम्बुद *ambu-da* (vb. *dâ*), m. A cloud, Ṛit. 6, 6.

अम्बुधर *ambu-dhara*, m. A cloud, Râm. 5, 16, 29.

अम्बुधि *ambudhi*, i.e. *ambu-dhâ* (cf. *nidhi*), m. The ocean, Râjat. 5, 8.—

Comp. *Kshâra-*, m. the salt ocean, Bhartṛ. 2, 6 (Häb.). *Kshîra-*, m. the sea of milk, Kathâs. 17, 8.

अम्बुमुच् *ambu-much*, m. A cloud, Kir. 5, 12.

अम्बुरुह *ambu-ruh+a*, n. A lotus, Kir. 5, 10.—Comp. *Hema-*, n. a golden lotus, Ṛit. 6, 7.

† अम्भ् *AMBH*, i. 1, Âtm. To sound.

अम्भस् *ambhas*, n. Water, Bhartṛ. 2, 91; Çiç. 9, 31.—Comp. *Ud-*, adj. abounding in water, Ragh. 4, 31. *Gharma-*, n. sweat, Çâk. d. 29. *Lavaṇa-*, n. the sea of salt water, Matsop. 40.

अम्भोज *ambhoja*, i.e. *ambhas-ja* (vb. *jan*), n. A lotus flower, Böhtl. Ind. Spr. 1447.—Comp. *Hema-*, n. a golden lotus flower, Megh. 63.

अम्भोजिनी *ambhojinî*, i.e. *ambhoja+in+î*, f. An assemblage of lotus flowers, Bhartṛ. 2, 15.

अम्भोद *ambhoda*, i.e. *ambhas-da* (vb. *dâ*), m. A cloud, Râm. 5, 40, 7.

अम्भोधर *ambhodara*, i.e. *ambhas-dhara*, m. A cloud, Daçak in Chr. 199, 7.

अम्भोधि *ambhodi*, i.e. *ambhas-dhâ* (cf. *nidhi*), m. The ocean, Kathâs. 19, 105.

अम्भोरुह् *ambhoruh*, and अम्भोरुह *ambhoruha*, i.e. *ambhas-ruh* and *ruh+a*, n. A lotus.

अम्मय *ammaya*, i.e. *ap+maya*, adj., f. *yî*, Consisting of water, watery.

अम्ल *amla*, m. Sourness, Râm. 5, 14, 45; Man. 5, 114 (acids). Perhaps from vb. *am*.—Cf. Lat. ăm+ârus.

अय् AY, see *i*.

अय *aya*, i.e. *i+a*, m. 1. Going. 2. Good luck, Ragh. 4, 26.

अयन *ayana*, i.e. *i+ana*, n. 1. A place of motion, Man. 1, 10. 2. A road. 3. A line, Bhag. 1, 11. 4. The half year, i.e. the sun's road north and south of the equator, Man. 4, 26.—Comp. *Uttarâ-*, Man. 6, 10; and *udagayana*, i.e. *udańch-*, Man. 1, 67, n. the half of the year in which the sun is to the north of the equator. *Dakshiṇâ-*, I. n. the half of the year when the sun moves to the south of the equator, Man. 1, 67. II. adj. lying on the course of the sun to the south of the equator, Bhâg. P. 5, 23, 5. *Gîta-*, n. a procession accompanied by hymns, Bhâg. P. 4, 4, 5. *Guṇa-*, adj. walking the path of virtue, Bhâg. P. 4, 21, 43. *Vârttâ-*, m. a spy.

अयवन्त् *aya+vant*, adj., f. *vatî*, Happy, Kir. 5, 20.

अयस् *ayas* (probably *a-yam+as*), n. Iron. — Comp. *Kṛishṇa-*, n. iron, MBh. 13, 6225 — Cf. Lat. aes; Goth. eis+arn; A.S. isern.

अयस्कान्त *ayas-kânta* (vb. *kam*), m. A loadstone, Ragh. 17, 63.

अयस्मय *ayas+maya*, adj., f. *yî*, Of iron, Arj. 10, 31.

अया *ayâ*, Ved. (old instr. sing. of *idam*) Thus, Chr. 293, 4=Rigv. i. 87, 4; but in this passage rather for *ayâs*.

अयास् *ayâs*, i.e. *a-yas*, adj. Indefatigable (?), Chr. 290, 11=Rigv. i. 64, 11.

अयि *ayi*, 1. A vocative particle, Daçak. in Chr. 182, 16. 2. An interrogative particle, Pańch. 38, 6.

अयुज् *a-yuj*, adj. Odd, Man. 3, 277.

अयुतशस् *a-yuta+ças*, adv. Ten thousand-fold, Indr. 2, 8.

अये *aye*, interj. Oh! Ah! **1.** Of surprise, Vikr. 11, 3. **2.** Of calling, Bhartṛ. 3, 87.

अयोगव *ayogava*, m. An *âyogavî* woman (? cf. *âyogava*), Man. 10, 32.

अयोनिज *a-yoni-ja* (vb. *jan*), adj. Not born in the natural way, Ragh. 11,47.

अयोनिजत्व *ayonija + tva*, n. A supernatural birth, Râjat. 5, 73.

अयोमय *ayomaya*, i.e. *ayas + maya*, adj., f. *yî*, Iron, Man. 11, 103 (read *talpe*, instead of *tapte*).

अर *ara*, i.e. *ṛi + a*, m. The spoke of a wheel, Çâk. d. 166.

अरघट्ट *ara-ghaṭṭ + a*, m. A wheel or a machine for raising water from a well, Pańch. 209, 24.

अरणि and **-णी** *araṇî*, f. Wood used for kindling a fire by attrition, Pańch. i. d. 247; Râm. 2, 104, 24.

अरण्य *araṇya*, n. A forest.—Comp. *Dharma-*, n. 1. a grove where ascetics live, Çâk. 14, 1. 2. The name of a forest, MBh. 13, 7655. *Maha-*, a large forest, Râm. 3, 52, 46.

अरण्यक *araṇya + ka*, n. A forest, Yâjń. 3, 192.

अरण्यानी *araṇyânî*, i.e. *araṇya + î*, f. A large forest, Hit. 17, 4.

अरति *arati* (vb. *ṛi* ?), m. **1.** A disposer, Lass. 101, 4 = Rigv. 7, 16, 1. **2.** *a-rati*, f. Pain, Kir. 5, 31.—Cf. ὑπηρέτης.

अरत्नि *aratni* (vb. *ṛi*; the aff. contains the verb *tan*), m. **1.** The elbow, Draup. 9, 5. **2.** A cubit of the middle length from the elbow to the tip of the little finger, Râm. 4, 40, 43.—Cf. Goth. arms; Lat. armus, arma; ὠλένη; Lat. ulna; O.H.G. elina.

अरत्निक *aratni + ka*, m. The elbow, Yâjń. 3, 86.

अरविन्द *aravinda*, n. A lotus, Ragh. 1, 43.

अराजक *arâjaka*, i.e. *a-râjan + ka*, adj. Without a king, Man. 7, 3.

अराजन्यप्रसूतितस् *a-râjanya-prasûti + tas*, adv. From one who is not born in the military caste, Man. 4, 84.

अराल *arâla*, adj., f. *lâ*, Crooked, Râm. 5, 28, 13.

अरि *ari*, m. **1.** probably *a-râ* (+ *i* ?) An enemy, Pańch. i. d. 267. **2.** *ṛi + i*, A wheel, Pańch. i. d. 324.—**Comp.** *Dânava-*, m. an enemy of the Dânavas.

अरिक्थीय *arikthîya*, i.e. *a-riktha + îya*, adj., f. *yâ*, Incapable of inheriting, Man. 9, 147.

अरित्र *aritra*, i.e. *ṛi + tra*, n. A rudder.—Cf. O.H.G. ruodar; ἐρέτης = Ved. *aritṛi*.

अरिंदम *ariṁdama*, i.e. *ari + m -dam + a*, adj. Victorious, Chr. 21, 14; 31, 13.

अरिष्ट *a-rishṭa* (vb. *rish*). **I.** adj., f. *ṭâ*, Unhurt, Chr. 298, 25 = Rigv. i. 112, 25; Draup. 7, 20. **II.** m. **1.** The soap berry plant, Sapindus saponaria, Yâjń. 1, 186. **2.** The nimb tree, Melia azadaracta, Râm. 2, 94, 9. **3.** A woman's apartment, the lying-in chamber, Ragh. 3, 15; the female apartments, the gyneceum, Râm. 2, 42, 22.

अरिष्टक *arishṭa + ka*, m. The soap berry plant, Sapindus saponaria, Man. 5, 120 (its pounded fruits).

अरिष्टनेमिन् *arishṭanemin* (= *a -rishṭa-nemi*), m. A proper name, Râm. 5, 2, 10.

अरुण *aruṇa* (akin to *arus*, cf. *arusha*).

I. adj., f. *ṇâ* and *ṇî*, Tawny, dark red, Chr. 293, 2=Rigv. i. 88, 2; Râm. 3, 5, 7. II. m. **1.** The dawn, Man. 10, 33. **2.** The sun, Çâk. d. 31 (*pariṇata-*, The setting sun). **3.** A proper name, Dev. 11, 49.

अरुणता *aruṇa+tâ*, f. Tawny (the colour), Çiç. 9, 14.

अरुणप्सु *aruṇa-psu* (the latter part perhaps *bhâs+u*), adj. Tawny, Chr. 288,1=Rigv. i. 49, 1.

अरुणित *aruṇita*, i.e. *aruṇa + ita*, adj., f. *tâ*, Made red, Ṛit. 6, 5; Çiç. 6, 15.

अरुंतुद *arum̃tuda*, i.e. *aru+m-tud +a* (cf. *arus*), adj. **1.** Wounding, Prab. 31, 16. **2.** Causing pain, Prab. 93, 2.

अरुन्धती *a-rundhati* (vb. *rudh*), f. **1.** The wife of Vaçishṭha, Râm. 1, 10, 37. **2.** An asterism, Böhtl. Ind. Spr. 1165.

अरुष *arusha*, i.e. *arus+a*. I. adj., f. *shî*, Tawny, Chr. 294, 1=Rigv. i. 92, 1. II. m. A dark red cloud, Chr. 291, 5=Rigv. i. 85, 5.

अरुस् *arus*, n. A wound.

अरे *are*, interj. of calling to inferiors, sirrah! Prab. 24, 8.

अरेपस् *arepas*, i.e. *a-rip(=lip)+as*, adj. Spotless, pure from sin, Chr. 290, 2=Rigv. i. 64, 2.

अरोगिता *arogitâ*, i.e. *a-rogin+tâ*, f. Health, Hit. Pr. d. 18.

अरोग्यता *arogyatâ*, i.e. *a-roga+ya+tâ*, f. Health, Râm. 2, 70, 7.

† **अर्क्** *ARK*, i. 10, Par. (rather a denom. derived from *arka*). **1.** To praise. **2.** To heat.

अर्क *arka*, i.e. *arch+a*, m. **1.** A ray of light, Chr. 291, 2=Rigv. i. 85, 2. **2.** The sun, Chr. 36, 22. **3.** Swallow wort, Asclepias gigantea, Çâk. d. 41.—Comp. *Jala-*, the reflexion of the sun in water, Bhâg. P. 3, 27, 1. *Bâla-*, m. the rising sun. *Sa-*, adj. with the sun, sunny. *Su-*, adj. flashing beautifully, Chr. 293, 1=Rigv. i, 50, 1.

अर्गल *argala*, m., f. *lâ*, and n. A wooden bolt, or pin for fastening a door, Kathâs. 4, 56; Pañch. 105, 5.—Comp. *An-*, adj. unrestrained, Ragh. 3, 39. *Nis-*, 1. adj. unrestrained, MBh. 3, 16601. 2. acc. *lam*, adv. without constraint, Râjat. 3, 194.

अर्गलित *argalita*, i.e. *argala+ita*, adj. Shut by a pin.

अर्घ् *argh*, i. 1, Par. To be worth, Pañch. i. d. 88.—Cf. *arh*, ἄρχω, ὄρχαμος, ἄρχομαι, ἄργμα.

अर्घ *argh+a* (vb. *argh* or *arh*), m. and n. **1.** Price, cost, Man. 8, 398. **2.** A mode of worship, or reverence, consisting in an oblation of rice, etc., with water or, of water only, Sâv. 3, 6.—Comp. *An-*, I. m. n. wrong price, Yâjñ. 2, 250. II. adj. priceless, inestimable, Kathâs. 24, 148. *Mahâ-*, adj. of great value, Kathâs. 21, 86.

अर्घतस् *argha+tas*, adv. Under the real value, Bhartṛ. 2, 12 (this is the true reading).

अर्घ्य *arghya*, i.e. *argha+ya*. I. adj., f. *yâ*. **1.** Deserving worship, Yâjñ. 1, 357. **2.** Deserving to be entertained, ib. 1, 110. II. n. A respectful oblation to gods or venerable men, consisting of rice, durva grass, flowers, etc., with water, or of water only, Yâjñ. 1, 289.—Comp. *An-*, adj. invaluable, Kathâs. 3, 42.

अर्च् *ARCH*, i. 1 and 10, Par. and Âtm. **1.** To beam, Chr. 291, 2=Rigv. i. 85, 2; to shine, Chr. 294, 3=Rigv. i.

92, 3. **2.** To worship, to honour, Man. 3, 93. To offer respectfully, Man. 4, 235. *an-archita,* Given without due honour, Man. 4, 213.—With the prep. अभि *abhi,* To worship, Man. 8, 391. *abhyarchita,* with gen. Râjatr 5, 101.—With समभि *sam-abhi,* To worship, Yâjń, 1, 179.—With प्रति *prati,* Causal. To return a respectful salutation, with acc. Râm. 2, 71, 31.—With सम् *sam,* To honour, Râm. 2, 3, 48.

अर्चक *arch + aka,* adj. Worshipping, Man. 11, 224.

अर्चन *arch + ana,* n. Worship, Daçak. in Chr. 181, 19.

अर्चा *arch + â,* f. Worship, Chr. 56, 11.

अर्चि *arch + i,* m. Flame, Chr. 288, 13=Rigv. i. 48, 13; Ragh. 12, 11.—Comp. *Sa-,* adj. flaming, Râm. 4, 10, 20.

अर्चितृ *arch-itṛi,* m. A worshipper, Râm. 5, 32, 7.

अर्चिष्मन्त् *archishmant,* i.e. *archis + mant,* adj., f. *matî,* Beaming, flaming, Vikr. d. 43.

अर्चिस् *arch + is,* f. and n. **1.** A ray of light, Chr. 294, 5=Rigv. i. 92, 5. **2.** Flame, Râm. 5, 75, 6; 6, 36, 117.—Comp. *Aruṇa-,* m. the sun, Daçak. in Chr. 184, 5. *Ud-,* adj. radiant, Ragh, 7, 21. *Çânta-* (vb. *çam*), adj. extinguished. *Saptârchis,* i.e. *saptan-,* m. 1. fire. 2. the planet Saturn.

अर्छ् *archh,* see *ṛi.*

1. अर्ज् *ARJ,* i. 1, and 10, Par. To earn, to acquire, MBh. 11, 193; Indr. 3, 7 (Âtm). *sva-arjita* and *svayam-arjita,* adj. Acquired by one's own efforts, Râm. 1, 43, 11; Man. 9, 209.—With the prep. उप *upa,* To acquire, Man. 9, 208.

2. अर्ज् *ARJ,* i. 10, Par. To work, to prepare.—With the prepositions समुप *sam-upa,* To prepare, Chr. 14, 21 (read *tat tu*).

अर्जन *arj + ana,* n. Earning, acquisition, Böhtl. Indr. Spr. 219.

अर्जुन *arj-una* (from a lost vb. akin to *râj*). I. adj., f. *nî,* White, Chr. 288, 3=Rigv. i. 49, 3. **II.** m. **1.** A tree, Terminalia Arjuna, Râm. 3, 19, 13. **2.** The name of the third son of Pâṇḍu, Indr. 1, 10. **III.** f. *nî,* The dawn, Râm, 2, 114, 14.—Cf. ἀργεννός, ἄργυρος; Lat. argentum; the base of these forms is *arj + vant:* cf. also, ἀργός, ἄργιλος, ἀργής, Ἀργυννίς; see *rańj, rajata.*

अर्णव *arṇava* (from *arṇa,* ved. by aff. *va* for *vant*), m. The ocean, Râm. 4, 9, 38.—Comp. *Mahâ-,* m. the ocean. *Lavaṇa-,* m. the sea of salt water, Râm. 1, 1, 70. *Sa-parvata-vana-,* adj., f. *vâ* (viz. *pṛithivî,* earth), with its mountains, forests, and seas, Râm. 1, 16, 32.

अर्त्ति *artti,* i.e. *ard + ti,* f. Pain, Kathâs. 13, 152.

अर्थ् *ARTH,* i. 10 (rather a denom. derived from *artha*) Âtm. To ask, to request; with two acc. Daçak. in Chr. 199, 15. *tvâm tam imam artham arthayate,* He asks this from thee, Pass. Kathâs. 22, 52. *tair evârthyamânas,* Being requested by them.—With the prep. अभि *abhi,* To ask, to request, Prab. 109, 18, with two acc; Par., with acc. and loc. Kathâs. 26, 148. *tvâm bhartṛitve 'bhy arthayishyati,* She will ask thee to become her husband. *abhyarthita,* Asked, Man. 2, 189. n. Desire, Yâjń. 2, 88.—With कद् *kad.* **1.** To treat ill, Böhtl. Indr. Spr. 591. **2.** To reproach, Daçak. in Chr. 200, 15. **3.** To torment, Kathâs. 18, 243.—With

प्र *pra*, To request, Pańch. 255, 22; *prârthayâna* instead of *prârthayamâna*, Râm. 2, 25, 31; with inf. *kim idaṁ prârthitaṁ kartum*, What is this which you intend to do? Nal. 19, 15; Par. Râm. 3, 40, 6; Pańch. 96, 5. *tatprârthita*, i.e. *tad-*, adj. Requested by him, Daçak. in Chr. 197, 8.—Pass. *prârthya*, To be desired, ib. 184, 17.—With अभिप्र *abhi-pra*, To wish, Râm. 2, 11, 3.—With संप्र *sam-pra*, To request, MBh. 5, 18.—With प्रति *prati*, To challenge, Bhaṭṭ. 6, 25. —With सम् *sam* (rather a denom. derived from *samartha*), **1.** To prepare, Râm. 4, 26, 25 (Par.); Chr. 55, 7. **2.** To consider, Râm. 6, 101, 17. **3.** To expect, Vikr. 20, 9. **4.** To interpret, Çâk. d. 67. **5.** To judge, Pańch. 185, 2. **6.** To approve, Pańch. 71, 25 (Par.). **7.** To determine, Râm. 2, 20, 26 Gorr.

अर्थ *artha*, i.e. *ṛi* + *tha*, m. **1.** Desire; *vivâha-*, a marriage suit. **2.** Aim; *siddha-*, one who has obtained his aim, Chr. 62, 60. **3.** Advantage, Bhartṛ. 2, 40. **4.** Business, Man. 2, 67. **5.** Wealth, Pańch. i. d. 197; worldly prosperity, Man. 12, 38 (one of the three aims of men; the two others are *kâma*, pleasure, and *dharma*, virtue); money, Daçak. in Chr. 180, 19. **6.** Cause, Man. 2, 213. **7.** Thing, Man. 8, 170. **8.** Meaning, Man. 3, 186; true sense, Man. 1, 3; thought, word, Çâk. d. 164. **9.** In law: A suit, an action. **10.** The acc. *artham* is used as an adverb, but almost always at the end of a compound word, implying, 'for,' 'on account of,' e.g. *yajńa-siddhi-artham*, For the performance of sacrifices, Man. 1, 23. The dat. *arthâya*, and loc. *arthe*, may be also used at the end of a compound word, or may govern the genitive. Abl. *arthât*, 'to wit,' 'namely,' Sch. Çâk. d. 41.—Comp. *Iti-artha* + *m*, adv. to this end, Brâhmaṇav, 3, 4. *Indriya-*, m. an object of sense, Man. 4, 16. *Etad-artha* + *m*, therefore, Pańch. i. d. 330; in order, Râm. 2, 52, 24. *Kim-*, adj. with what aim, Chr. 57, 24. *Kim-artha* + *m*. adv. why, to what end, Nal. 22, 7. *Kṛita-*, adj. having attained one's end, satisfied, Râm. 4, 34, 22. *Gṛiha-*, m. the business of the house, Man. 2, 67. *Tad-artha* + *m*, adv. therefore, Râm. 1, 73, 4. *Nirartha*, i.e. *nis-*, I. m. nonsense. II. adj. 1. purposeless. 2. poor. 3. unmeaning. *Niçchitârtha*, i.e. *nis-chita-*, (vb. *chi*), adj. completely resolved, Râm. 4, 42, 9. *Para-*, m. 1. great importance. 2. the interests of another. 3. sexual intercourse. *Parama-*, m. 1. the most sublime truth. 2. the whole truth. 3. reality. 4. earnest, Çâk. d. 51. *Purusha-*, m. 1. the object or aim of man. 2. human exertion. *Bhûta-*, m. an element of life. *Mahâ-*, I. m. a principal object. II. adj. 1. significant. 2. dignified. *Yajńa-*, adj. serving for a sacrifice, Bhag. 3, 9. *Yathâ-*, adj. 1. according to the sense. 2. proper, right. *tham*, adv. suitably, properly. *A-yathâ-*, adj. not true, Çâk. d. 54. *Yad-artha* + *m*, adv. for what reason, Chr. 3, 3. *Yâvadartha*, i.e. *yâvant-*, I. adj. as much as may be useful, Man. 2, 182. II. adv. *tham*, as much as may be useful, ib. 2, 51. *Sva-*, I. adj. 1. having one's own object. 2. having a literal meaning. 3. pleonastic. II. m. 1. property. 2. own object. 3. own interest, Bhartṛ. 2, 59.

अर्थकर *artha-kara*, adj., f. *rî*, Useful, Hit. Pr. d. 18.

अर्थकृत् *artha-kṛi* + *t*, adj. Useful, Indr. 5, 56.

अर्थघ्न *artha-ghna*, adj., f. *nî*, Prodigal, Man. 9, 80.

अर्थजात *artha-jâta* (vb. *jan*), n. **1.** Money's worth, Daçak. in Chr. 192, 16. **2.** Financial affairs, Çâk. 90, 13 (Prâkṛ).

अर्थतस् *artha-tas,* adv. Truly, Vedântas. in Chr. 202, 5.

अर्थद *artha-da* (vb. *dâ*), adj. **1.** Useful, Kathâs. 17, 122. **2.** Liberal, Man. 2, 109.

अर्थना *arth + anâ,* f. A request, Naish. 5, 112.

अर्थवत् *artha + vat,* adv. According to the object, Man. 5, 134.

अर्थवन्त् *artha + vant,* adj., f. *vatî.* **1.** Wealthy, Hit. i. d. 175. **2.** Significant, full of meaning, Râm. 1, 14, 35. **3.** True, Pańch. i. d. 152.—Comp. *Mahâ-,* adj. very dignified.

अर्थिता *arthitâ,* i.e. *arthin + tâ,* f. **1.** Desire, Man. 9, 203. **2.** Begging, Hit. i. d. 130.

अर्थित्व *arthitva,* i.e. *arthin + tva,* n. **1.** Condition of one who implores, Megh. 6. **2.** Request, Mâlav. 40, 4.—Comp. *An-,* n. Absence of desire, disdain, Böhtl. Ind. Spr. 87 (Pańch. i. d. 158).

अर्थिन् *arthin,* i.e. *artha + in,* adj., f. *nî.* **1.** Full of desire, Râm. 1, 48, 18; with instr. *bhâryayâ chârthî,* Longing after a wife, Râm. 3, 24, 4. *vadhena mamârthî,* Desiring my death, Böhtl. Chr. 114, 27. **2.** A beggar, Bhartṛ. 2, 36; Daçak. in Chr. 186, 20. **3.** A plaintiff, Man. 8, 62.—Comp. *Chhâyâ-,* adj. desiring shadow. *Dhana-,* adj. greedy for money, Man. 5, 34. *Putra-,* adj. wishing for a son, Man. 3, 48. *Bala-,* adj. desiring power, Man. 2, 37. *Bhâryâ-,* adj. desiring a wife, Chr. 6, 5. *Yuddha-,* adj. seeking war. *Çaraṇa-,* adj. depending on others for protection, unfortunate. *Hita-,* adj. seeking another's welfare, Râm. 3, 48, 15.

अर्थिसात् *arthisât,* i.e. *arthin + sât,* adv. (Given) to mendicants, Râjat. 5, 18.

ऽअर्थीय *-arthîya,* i.e. *-artha + îya,* adj., f. *yâ.* **1.** Fit for, susceptible of, e.g. *yâtanâ-,* susceptible of torment, Man. 12, 16. **2.** Referring to, e.g. *dharma-,* referring to duty, MBh. 1, 600.

अर्थेप्सुता *arthepsutâ,* i.e. *artha-îpsa, îpsa,* desid. of *âp + u + tâ,* f. Desire of wealth, Brâhmaṇav. 1, 18.

अर्थ्य *arthya,* i.e. *artha + ya,* adj., f. *yâ.* **1.** Proper, Râm. 6, 92, 77. **2.** Wealthy.—Comp. *Hema-,* adj. abounding in gold, Pańch. i. d. 377.

अर्द् *ARD,* i. 1, Par. **1.** † To go. **2.** To beg, Ragh. 5, 17. i. 1 and 10, Par. and Âtm. **1.** To kill, Râm. 1, 16, 30. **2.** To hurt; to wound, Pańch. 221, 13. **3.** To afflict; to vex, Râm. 3, 14, 11; 53, 27.—With the prep. **अति** *ati.* To press violently, Bhaṭṭ. 15, 115.—With **अभि** *abhi.* To press; to afflict, Râm. 2, 21, 55; cf. *abhyarṇṇa.*—With **प्रति** *prati.* To press in return, Râm. 6, 92, 52.—With **वि** *vi.* To press. *a-vyarṇṇa.* Not pressed, Bhaṭṭ. 9, 19.—With **सम्** *sam.* To wound, MBh. 3, 761.—Cf. perhaps ἀρδ in ἄρδις.

ऽअर्दन *-ard + ana,* adj. Killing, Râm. 1, 54, 17. *kaiṭabha-* and *jana-,* m. Names of Vishṇu, Bhâg. P. 3, 24, 18; Bhartṛ. 3, 84.

अर्ध *ardha,* i.e. *ṛidh + a.* **I.** adj., f. *dhâ.* Half, halved, Lass. 22, 2.—Often former part of comp. words: *-paṇa,* Half a paṇa, Man. 8, 404. *-ukta,* Half spoken, Pańch. 77, 2. *-dagdha,* Half burnt, Pańch. 98, 1.—When before cardinal numerals it denotes: **1.** A half more, e.g. *-trayodaçan,* thirteen and a half, Yâjń. 2, 265. **2.** A half of the following number more, e.g. *-çata,* hundred and fifty, Man. 8, 331. **3.** Division of the following number,

-*pañchâçat*, twenty-five, Man. 3, 268.—When an ordinal follows a half is added, e.g. -*tṛitîya*, three and a half, Râm. 2, 92, 10.—When it follows a cardinal numeral, this numeral is divided, e.g. *daçârdha*, i.e. *daçan*-, Five, Man. 1, 24. II. n. A half, Man. 8, 296. III. m. A part, e.g. *jaghana*-, the rear of an army, MBh. 5, 5162. *paçcha*-, The hind-part, Çâk. d. 7. *pûrva*-, The former part, Bhartṛ. 2, 5.—Comp. *Chandra*-, m. The half-moon, Râm. 1, 28, 25.

अर्धचन्द्र *ardha-chandra*, m. 1. A half-moon, Râm. 3, 49, 35.—Cf. *ardha-bhâskara*. 2. An arrow with a head like a half-moon, Râm. 3, 34, 30; cf. 6, 36, 77. 3. The hand bent into a semicircle or the shape of a claw, as for the purpose of seizing or clutching any thing. *ardhachandraṁ dâ*. To seize one by the neck, Pañch. 63, 24.

अर्धभाज् *ardhabhâj*, i.e. *ardha-bhaj*, adj. Getting a half of, Man. 8, 39.

अर्धभास्कर *ardha-bhâskara*, m. Noon, Râm. 3, 55, 33 (*ardhachandra*-, loc. At noon on the day of the half-moon, i.e. on the eighth day of the month).

अर्धरात्रार्धदिवस *ardharâtrârdha-divasa*, i. e. *ardha-râtra-ardha-divasa*, m. The equinox, Râm. 3, 55, 35.

अर्धिक *ardhika*, i.e. *ardha+ika*, adj., f. *kî*, Amounting to the half, Yâjń. 2, 296.—Comp. *Tad*-, adj. half that (time), Man. 3, 1.

अर्धिन् *ardhin*, i.e. *ardha+in*, adj., f. *nî*, Entitled to a half, Man. 8, 210.

अर्धोरुक *ardhoruka*, i.e. *ardha-ûru+ka*, n. A petticoat, Daçak. in Chr. 186, 9.

अर्पण *arpaṇa*, i.e. *ṛi*, Caus. +*ana*, n. 1. Offering, Râm. 4, 28, 22. 2. Returning, Hit. 72, 19. 3. Putting on, Ragh. 2, 35.—Comp. *Deva*-, adj. receiving sacrifices (?), MBh. 13, 4202.

† **अर्ब्** *ARB*, i. 1, Par. 1. To go. 2. To kill.

अर्बुद *arbuda*. I. m., n. 1. The shape of the fœtus in the second month after the conception, Yâjń. 3, 75. 2. A hundred millions, Râm. 5, 29, 3. II. m. The name of a mountain, Râm. 6, 2, 27.

अर्भ *arbha*, adj. Small.—Cf. *arbhaka*; ὀρφός; Lat. orbus; Goth. arbja; A.S. orf.

अर्भक *arbha+ka*, m. 1. A child, Ragh. 3, 21. 2. The young of any animal, Çâk. d. 14, v. r.

अर्य *arya*, m., f. *yâ* and *yî*, A man or woman of the third caste, Daçak. in Chr. 186, 17.

अर्यमन् *aryaman*, m. 1. The name of a deity, Râm. 2, 25, 8. 2. The chief of the Pitṛis, or Manes, Bhag. 10, 29.

† **अर्व्** *ARV*, i. 1, Par. To kill, or hurt.

अर्वन् *arvan* and **अर्वन्त्** *arvant*, m. *vatî*, f. A horse, Lass. 102, 3=Rigv. 7, 102, 2.—Cf. perhaps Lat. armentum.

अर्वाक्कालिकता *arvâkkâlikatâ*, i.e. *arvâñch-kâla+ika+tâ*, f. Modern date, Man. 12, 96.

अर्वाञ्च् *arvâñch*, i.e. *arva-añch* (the former part is still questionable), adj., f. *vâchî*; n. *arvâk*, adv. 1. Towards, Chr. 295, 16=Rigv. i. 92, 16. 2. Before, till, with abl., Man. 5, 59. Within, Yâjń. 2, 173. *arvâk saṁvatsarât*, Until one year has elapsed, Man. 8, 30. 3. Near, Çâk. d. 40 v. r.

अर्शस् *arças*, probably *ṛish* + *as* (with *ç* instead of *sh*), n. Hæmorrhoids.

अर्शस *arças* + *a*, adj., f. *sâ*. Subject to hæmorrhoids, Man. 3, 7.

अर्ह् *ARH* (*h* for *gh*, cf. *argh*), i, 1, Par. (in epic poetry also Âtm., Hiḍ. 1, 36). **1.** To deserve, with the acc., Man. 2, 208 (*mânam*, honour); Man. 8, 323 (*vadham*, death); 8, 194 (*daṇḍam*, a fine); 8, 267 (*çatam . . . daṇḍam*, a fine of hundred *paṇas*); 8, 139 (*pañchakaṁ çatam*, with ellipsis of *daṇḍa*, he must pay five in the hundred). **2.** To be entitled to, with the inf., Man. 8, 147. **3.** To be obliged to, with the acc., Çâk. d. 66; with the inf., Man. 8, 155; Naish. 5, 112 (*kartum arhati*, must be done). **4.** To undergo, Man. 8, 145; Râm. 6, 103, 20. **5.** To be worthy, to be equal to, with the acc., Man. 3, 131. **6.** To be able, with the inf., Bhag. 2, 17. **7.** i. 1, and i. 10, Par. To worship or to honour. **8.** The second persons of i. 1, joined with an inf. represent a respectful form of the imperative, *vaktum arhasi*, Say (literally, Be pleased to say, cf. the Lat. dignor, with the inf.), Man. 1, 3.—With the prep. **अभि** *abhi*, *abhyarhita*. Fit, suitable.

अर्ह *arh* + *a*, adj., f. *hâ*. **1.** Deserving, with the acc., Râm. 1, 53, 12; subject to, Man. 8, 240.—With the inf., Bhag. 1, 37 (*nârhâ vayaṁ hantum*, we ought not to be killed). **2.** Entitled to, with the acc., Man. 9, 144; with the inf., Râm. 4, 36, 17. **3.** Worth; *mahâ-*, of great value, Daçak. in Chr. 198, 16. **4.** Fit, suitable, Pañch. 152, 8.—**Comp.** *An-*, adj. 1. not deserving, Draup. 9, 7. 2. unworthy, Brâhmaṇav. 2, 16. *Pûjâ-*, adj. worthy of reverence, Man. 9, 26. *Priya-*, adj. deserving love, amiable, Kir. 5, 51. *Mâna-*, adj. entitled to respect, Man. 2, 137. *Râjârha*, i.e. *râjan-*, adj. royal, suitable to, or fit for a king, Râm. 3, 49, 42. *Satkâra-*, adj. deserving hospitality, Nal. 9, 10. *Sukha-*, adj. deserving pleasure, Râm. 3, 52, 41.

अर्हण *arhaṇa*, i.e. *arh* + *ana*. **I.** n. A token of respect, Man. 3, 54. **II.** f. *ṇâ*, Worship, adoration, Pañch. 236, 24.

अर्हत्व *arha* + *tva*, n. Worthiness, Kathâs. 2, 74.

अर्हन्त् *arhant* (ptcple. of the pres. of *arh*), f. *hati*, Venerable, Çâk. d. 112. —Superlat. *arhattama*, Most venerable, Man. 3, 128.

† **अल्** *AL*, i. 1, Par. **1.** To adorn. **2.** To be able. **3.** To prevent.

अलक *alaka*. **I.** m. and n. A curl, Ṛit. 6, 6. **II.** f. *kâ*, The capital of Kuvera, Megh. 7.—**Comp.** *Latâ-*, m. an elephant.

अलकनन्दा *alakanandâ*, f. The name of a river, and surname of the Ganges.

अलक्त *alakta* (cf. *laktaka*), m. Lac, the red animal dye so called.

अलक्तक *alakta* + *ka*, m. Lac (see the last).

अलक्ष्यजन्मता *alakshyajanmatâ*, i.e. *a-lakshya-janman* + *tâ*. f. Insignificant birth, Kumâras. 5, 72.

अलंकरण *alaṁkaraṇa*, i.e. *alam-kṛi* + *ana*, n. Ornament, Bhartṛ. 2, 88.

अलंकार *alaṁkâra*, i.e. *alam-kṛi* + *a*, m. **1.** Trimming, Râm. 2, 40, 13. **2.** Ornament, trinkets, Daçak. in Chr. 183, 13.

अलंकारक *alaṁkâra* + *ka*, m. Ornament, Man. 7, 220.

अलंकृति *alam̃kṛiti*, i.e. *alam-kṛi + ti*, f. Ornament, Amar. 13.

अलज्जाकर *a-lajjâ-kara*, adj. Not disgracing, Pańch. v. d. 10.

अलम् *alam* (i.e. *ṛi + a + m*, cf. Ved. *aram*, *ἄρα*, *ἀρι-*, *ἐρι-*, *ἄρω*), adv. 1. Fit, able, with loc., Râm. 3, 47, 6; with inf., Râm. 2, 39, 28. 2. Adequate, Megh. 54; with inf., Kir. 5, 17; Daçak. in Chr. 194, 3. 3. Enough, with dat. Man. 11, 76; with inf., Çiç. 9, 87. 4. No more, implying prohibition, no, not; with instr., Daçak. 187, 14 (*çuchâlam*, cease to lament); with inf., Mṛichchh. 45, 6 (*alam̃ suptajanam̃ prabodhayitum*, do not awake the sleeping man); with absolutive, Râm. 2, 28, 5 (*alam̃ vanam̃ gatvâ*, do not go to the forest). 5. Abundant, powerfully, Râm. 5, 3, 21; Râjat. 5, 377. 6. See *kṛi*.

अलर्क *alarka*, m. 1. A fabulous animal, MBh. 12, 87. 2. The proper name of a prince, Râm. 2, 12, 40.

अलस *a-las + a*, adj., f. *sâ*. 1. Weary. 2. Slack, Ṛit. 6, 12. 3. Sleepy, Râjat. 5, 408. 4. Lazy, Pańch. iii. d. 25.—Comp. *Sa-*, adj. languid, Ṛit. 6, 30.

अलात *alâta*, n. A firebrand, Râm. 3, 24, 18.

अलाबु *alâbu*, f. A long gourd, a gourd-bottle, Man. 6, 54.

अलाबुमय *alâbu + maya*, adj., f. *yî*, Made of a gourd, Yâjń. 3, 60.

अलि *ali*, m. A bee.

अलिञ्जर *alińjara*, m. An earthen water jar, Matsyop. 10.

अलिन् *alin*, see the next.

अलिनी *alinî*, f. A swarm of bees (?), Bhartṛ. 1, 5: perhaps ought to be read *alinâm* or *alino*, from अलिन् *alin*, m. A large black bee.

अलिन्द *alinda*, m. 1. A terrace, Çâk. 62, 14. 2. The name of a people, MBh. 6, 371.

अलीक *alîka*. I. adj., f. *kâ*, False, Amar. 23. II. n. 1. Any thing displeasing, Râm. 2, 52, 25. 2. Falsehood, Pańch. 259, 4. 3. Smallness, Pańch. i. d. 205 (smallness and falsehood).

अलेपक *a-lepa + ka*, adj., f. *pakâ* and *pikâ*, Spotless, Vedântas. in Chr. 217, 6.

अलोक्य *alokya*, i.e. *a-loka + ya*, adj., f. *yâ*. 1. Extraordinary. 2. Obstructing the progress to heaven, Man. 2, 161.

अलोमक *a-loma + ka*, adj., f. *mikâ* (ved. also *makâ*). Having no hair, Man. 3, 8.

अलोलुत्व *alolutva* (probably for *a-lolupa + tva*), n. Absence of covetousness, Bhag. 16, 2.

अल्प *alpa*, adj. f. *pâ*. 1. Little, small, Râm. 5, 35, 31; Man. 3, 55; *alpena*, For a small price, Daçak in Chr. 180, 18. 2. Insignificant, Ragh. 2, 47. 3. Of no great value, Daçak. in Chr. 198, 6 (cf. *naya*). 4. Short, Pańch. Pr. d. 10. 5. Feeble, Kathâs. 24, 136. Comparative, *alpîyam̃s*, Man. 8, 36, and *alpatara*.—Comp. *An-*, adj., 1. great, Daçak in Chr. 182, 8. 2. numerous, 187, 5. 3. much, Kathâs. 18, 285. *Alpa-alpa*, adj. very little, Man. 7, 129. *Su-*, adj. 1. very small, Bhartṛ. 2, 23; *svalpena*, for a very short time, Man. 2, 134. 2. very few.

अल्पक *alpa-ka*, adj., f. *pikâ*, Small, Man. 3, 219.

अल्पता *alpa + tâ*, f. and अल्पत्व *alpa + tva*, n. Minuteness, Böhtl. Ind. Spr. 1143.

अल्पदुःखता *alpa-duḥkha + tâ*, f. Having little pain, Arj. 10, 8.

अल्पशस् *alpa-ças*, adv. In a small degree, Man. 12, 20.

अल्पित *alpita*, i.e. *alpa + ita*, adj., f. *tâ*, Diminished, Naish. 1, 15.

अव् *AV*, i. 1, Par. **1.** To please, to satisfy, Ragh. 11, 75. **2.** To be pleased, ved. **3.** To desire, Ragh. 1, 65. **4.** To take care, ved. **5.** To protect, Chr. 291, 13 = Rigv. i. 64, 13; Çâk. d. 1. **6.** † To move. **7.** † To excite affection, or be lovely. **8.** † To know, or apprehend. **9.** † To own (v.r. to be able). **10.** † To obey. **11.** † To act. **12.** † To shine. **13.** † To obtain. **14.** † To embrace. **15.** † To kill or hurt. **16.** † To take (v.r. to burn). **17.** † To be (v.r. to divide). **18.** † To grow. Ptcple. of the pf. pass. *ûta*.—With the prep. प्र *pra*, To help. Chr. 288, 2 = Rigv. i. 49, 2; Chr. 296, 5 = Rigv. i, 112, 5.—With सम् *sam*, To satisfy, Chr. 297, 18 = Rigv. i. 112, 18.—Cf ἄω; Lat. avere and uti (an old denominat.).

अव *ava*, a prefix. Away, off, down. I. Combined and compounded with verbs and their derivatives. II. Former part of compounded nouns. — Cf. *αὐ-* in *αὐερύω, αὖ, αὖτε*; Lat. autem, aut.—This prefix is based on a pronoun *ava*, which is preserved in the Zend language, and in the former part of the compounded pronoun *αὐ-τός*.

अवकर *avakara*, i.e. *ava-kṛi + a*, m. Sweepings, Bhartṛ. suppl. 21.

अवकर्त *avakarta*, i.e. *ava-kṛit + a*, m. A chip, Nal. 10, 22.

अवकर्तन *ava-kṛit + ana*, n. Cutting off, Nal. 10, 16.

अवकाश *ava-kâç + a*, m. **1.** Space, room, Man. 3, 207. **2.** Interval. **3.** Opportunity, Râm. 5, 9, 28; Pańch. iii. d. 263 (264), cf. *vishaya*.—**Comp.** *Nis-*, adj. having no room for moving freely, Bhâg. P. 5, 26, 28. *Sulabha-*, adj. f. *çâ*, getting easily the opportunity (of appearing), Çâk. d. 191.

ऽवकाशद *-avakâça-da* (vb. *dâ*), m. One who gives shelter, Man. 9, 271; 278.

अवकीर्णिन् *avakirṇin*, i.e. *ava-kîrṇa + in* (vb. *kṛî*) adj., f. *nî*, A violator of a vow to be chaste, Man. 2, 187; 3, 155.

अवक्रय *avakraya*, i.e. *ava-krî + a* m. Letting out, Yâjń. 2, 238.

अवक्षेपण *avakshepaṇa*, i.e. *ava-kship + ana*, n. Throwing down. Bhâshâp. 5.

अवगति *avagati*, i.e. *ava-gam + ti*, f. Knowledge.

अवगम *ava-gam + a*, m. Knowledge, Bhag. 9, 2.—**Comp.** *Dus-*, adj. hard to be comprehended, Bhâg. P. 5, 13, 29. *Svatva-*, n. ascertainment of ownership.

अवगाह *ava-gâh + a*, m. Bathing, Ragh. 5, 47.

अवगाहन *ava-gâh + ana*, n. Immersion, Pańch. 31, 2.

अवगुण्ठन *ava-gunṭh + ana*, n. A veil.

अवगुण्ठनवन्त् *avaguṇṭhana + vant*, adj., f. *vati*, Veiled, Çâk. d. 110.

अवगूहन *avagûhana*, i.e. *ava-guh*, Caus. + *ana*, n. Embracing, Prab. 57, 11 (v.r.).

अवग्रह *ava-grah + a*, m. **1.** Obstacle. **2.** Drought, Ragh. 11, 29. **3.** Contempt, Râm. 5, 44, 18. **4.** Nature, original temperament, Mâlav. 70, d. 89

(affection).—**Comp.** *Dus-*, adj. 1. hard to be stopped, Kâm. Nîtis. 8, 66. 2. disagreeable, Bhâg. P. 4, 19, 35. *Nis-*, adj. 1. without any obstacle, MBh. 4, 436. 2. irresistible, Râjat. 5, 52.

अवघट्टन *ava-ghaṭṭ+ana*, n. Rubbing off, Suçr. 1, 362, 6.

अवघर्षण *avagharshaṇa*, i. e. *ava-ghṛish+ana*, n. Rubbing off, Yâjń. 3, 60.

अवघात *avaghâta*, i.e. *ava-han*, Caus. *+a*, m. A violent blow.

अवचय *avachaya*, i.e. *ava-chi+a*, m. Gathering, Daçak. in Chr. 181, 20.

अवचूर्णन *ava-chûrṇ+ana*, n. Sprinkling powders on sores.

अवच्छद *avachchhada*, i. e. *ava-chhad+a*, m. A cover, Râm. 3, 56, 48.

अवच्छेद *avachchheda*, i. e. *ava-chhid+a*, m. Distinction.

अवजय *avajaya*, i.e. *ava-ji+a*, m. Conquering, Ragh. 6, 62.

अवज्ञा *ava-jńâ*, f. Disrespect, Râm. 3, 33, 17; Contempt, Râm. 3, 49, 52; Daçak. in Chr. 189, 7.—**Comp.** *Sa-avajńa*, adj. disdainful; *sâvajńam*, adv. with contempt, Râm. 3, 29, 2.

अवज्ञान *avajńâna*, i.e. *ava-jńâ+ana*, n. Contempt, Hit. 103, 4.

अवट *avaṭa*, m. A pit, Râm. 3, 8, 19.

अवत *avata*, m. A well, Chr. 292, 10=Rigv. i. 85, 10.

अवतंस *ava-taṁs+a*, m. and n. 1. A crest. 2. An ear-ring, Daçak. in Chr. 199, 3. 3. Ornament, Daçak. in Chr. 179, 14.—**Comp.** *Puṇḍarîka-*, adj., f. *sâ*, adorned with white lotus flowers, Râm. 5, 12, 18.

अवतंसक *avataṁsa+ka*, m. and n. An ear-ring, Vikr. d. 141.—**Comp.** *koshṭha-âgâra-*, adj., f. *kâ*, adorned, i.e. furnished with treasuries, Râm. 5, 10, 1.

अवतमस *ava-tamas+a*, n. Slight darkness, Çiç. 11, 57.

अवतरण *avataraṇa*, i.e. *ava-tṛî+ana*, n. 1. Descending, Çâk. 111, 3. 2. Descent especially of a deity from heaven, MBh. 12, 12965.

अवतर्पण *avatarpaṇa*, i. e. *ava-tṛip+ana*, n. A soothing remedy.

अवतस् *ava+tas*, adv. Below, in the lower regions, Kir. 5, 27.

अवतान *avatâna*, i.e. *ava-tan+a*, m. A cover, Râm. 5, 16, 28.

अवतार *avatâra*, i.e. *ava-tṛî+a*, m. 1. Descent. 2. Entering into, Daçak. in Chr. 185, 6. 2. Descent of a deity from heaven, Ragh. 10, 85.

अवतारण *avatâraṇa*, i.e. *ava-tṛî* Caus. *+ana*, n. Causing to descend, Râm. 4, 56, 29.

अवदान *avadâna*, i.e. *ava-dai+ana*, n. A heroic deed, Daçak. in Chr. 187, 24.—**Comp.** *Vîrya-*, n. effecting any thing by prowess.

अवदारण *avadâraṇa*, i.e. *ava-dṛî+ana*, n. Bursting, Ram. 2, 77, 16.

अवद्य *a-vad+ya*, n. Blame, Kathâs. 24, 235.—**Comp.** *An-*, adj., f. *yâ*, blameless, Bhartṛ. 2, 18. *Nis-*, I. adj. blameless, Râm. 6, 99, 51. II. f. blamelessness (?), Indr. 5, 11 (v. r.).

अवधान *avadhâna*, i.e. *ava-dhâ+ana*, n. 1. Attention, Vikr. d. 2. 2. Staring at, Çiç. 9, 11.—**Comp.** *Sa-*, adj. careful, attentive, Yâjń. 3, 112.

अवधारण *avadhâraṇa*, i. e. *ava*

dhṛi + *ana*, n. **1.** Restriction, Prab. 75, 10. **2.** Ascertaining, Vedântas. in Chr. 216, 3.

अवधि *avadhi*, i. e. *ava-dhâ* (cf. *nidhi*), m. **1.** Limit. **2.** End.—**Comp.** *Pratyâgamâvadhi*, i. e. *pratyâgama-*, adv. till (my) return, Kathâs. 4, 100. *Sa-*, adj. with the end, Kathâs. 9, 52.

अवधीर् *AVADHÎR*, i. 10 (rather a denom. of a lost noun, *avadhîra*, from the vb. *dhṛi*, cf. *dhîra*), **Par.** To disdain, to contemn, Çiç. 9, 59.

अवधीरण *avadhîraṇa*, i. e. *avadhîr* + *ana*, n. and f. *ṇâ*. Refusal, Ragh. 8, 47.

अवधीरिन् *avadhîr* + *in*, adj., f. *iṇî*, Surpassing, Daçak. in Chr. 184, 5.

अवधूनन *avadhûnana*, i.e. *ava-dhû*, Caus. + *ana*, n. Shaking, Man. 3, 230.

अवध्यता *a-vadhya* + *tâ*, f., and

अवध्यत्व *a-vadhya* + *tva*, n. Inviolability, Râm. 5, 44, 10; 6, 36, 30.

अवनति *avanati*, i.e. *ava-nam* + *ti*, f. Setting (of the sun), Çiç, 9, 8.

अवनम्र *ava-nam* + *ra*, adj., f. *râ*, Bent, Ṛit. 6, 15.

अवनि and **-नी** *avani*, *avanî*, f. The earth, Bhartṛ. 2, 10; Çiç. 9, 20.

अवनेजन *avanejana*, i. e. *ava-nij* + *ana*, n. Washing, Man. 2, 209.

अवन्ति *avanti*, m. pl. The name of a people, MBh. 6, 350.

अवन्तिन् *avantin*, m. A surname of Avantivarman, Râjat. 5, 17.

अवन्ती *avantî*, f. The name of a city, the modern Oujein, Megh. 31 v. r.

अवपात *avapâta*, i.e. *ava-pat* + *a*, m. **1.** Falling down. **2.** Descent. **3.** A pit for catching game in, Ragh. 16, 78. **4.** (From the causal of *pat*) Striking, wounding, Yâjñ. 2, 277.

अवपातन *avapâtana*, i.e. *ava-pat*, Caus. + *ana*, n. Cutting down, Man. 11, 64.

अवपीडन *ava-pîḍ* + *ana*, n. Hurting, Man. 8, 287.

अवबोध *avabodha*, i.e. *ava-budh* + *a*, m. **1.** Being awake, Bhag. 6, 17. **2.** Full knowledge, Vedântas. in Chr. 219, 8.—**Comp.** *Dus-*, adj. hard to be understood, Bhâg. P. 6, 9, 33.

अवबोधन *avabodhana*, i. e. *ava-budh*, Caus. + *ana*, n. Instruction, Pañch. 5, 13.

अवभास *ava-bhâs* + *a*, m. Appearance.—**Comp.** *An-*, m. non-appearance, Vedântas. in Chr. 217, 11; 12.

अवभासक *ava-bhâs* + *aka*, m. An illuminator, Vedântas. in Chr. 219, 11; cf. 215, 23.

अवभासकत्व *avabhâsaka* + *tva*, n. Illuminating, Vedântas. in Chr. 204, 19.

अवभासना *ava-bhâs* + *anâ*, f. Illuminating, shining, Vedântas. in Chr. 215, 11.

अवभृथ *ava-bhṛi* + *tha*, m. The name of certain ceremonies at the close of a sacrifice, e.g. bathing, Man. 11, 82.

अवम *ava* + *ma*, adj., f., *mâ*, Low.—**Comp.** *An-*, adj. high, illustrious, Draup. 5, 11.

अवमन्तृ *ava-man* + *tṛi*, m. A scorner, Man. 2, 163.

अवमर्द *avamarda*, i.e. *ava-mṛid* + *a*, m. Devastation, Râm. 5, 43, 7.

अवमर्दन *avamardana*, i. e. *ava-mṛid* + *ana*. **I.** adj. Destroying, Râm. 3, 35, 114. **II.** n. Destruction.

अवमर्दिन् *avamardin*, i.e. *ava-mṛid* + *in*, adj., f. *nî*, Destroying, Kathâs. 23, 58.

अवमान *avamâna*, m., and **अवमानन** *avamânana*, n., i.e. *ava-man* + *a* or *ana*, Disrespect, Man. 2, 162.

अवमानिन् *avamânin*, i. e. *ava-man* + *in*, adj., f. *nî*. **1.** One who despises, Râm. 5, 81, 6. **2.** One who undervalues, Çâk, 91, 16.

अवयव *avayava*, i.e. *ava-yu* + *a*, m. **1.** A limb, Daçak. in Chr. 190, 16. **2.** A part, Man. 1, 16.

अवयवशस् *avayava* + *ças*, adv. Limb by limb, Bhâg. P. 3, 30, 28.

अवयविन् *avayavin*, i.e. *avayava* + *in*, adj., f. *nî*, Consisting of parts, Bhâshâp. 155.

अवर *ava* + *ra*. **I.** adj., f. *râ*. **1.** Posterior, Man. 3, 23. **2.** Inferior, Râm. 2, 106, 22. **3.** Low, Râjat. 5, 203. **II.** m. A Çûdra, or one of the fourth caste, Man. 2, 238.—Comp. *Avara-avara*, adj. lowest, Râm. 5, 53, 24.—Preceded by a numeral it implies 'at least,' e.g. *tri-*, three at least, Man. 8, 60; at least three times, Man. 11, 80; also, after *kârshâpaṇa-*, a kârshâpaṇa at least, Man. 8, 274.

अवरज *avara-ja* (vb. *jan*). **I.** adj., f. *jâ*, Younger, Râm. 3, 75, 10. **II.** m. **1.** A younger brother, Râjat. 5, 26. **2.** A Çûdra, or one of the fourth caste, Man. 2, 223.

अवरोध *avarodha*, i.e. *ava-rudh* + *a*, m. **1.** Hindrance. **2.** Blocking up. **3.** The seraglio of a palace, Râjat. 5, 357.

अवरोधक *avarodhaka*, i. e. *ava-rudh* + *aka*, adj. Being about to block up, Râm, 1, 71, 6.

अवरोधन *avarodhana*, i. e. *ava-rudh* + *ana*, n. Blocking up, Râm. 1, 3, 33.

अवरोह *avaroha*, i.e. *ava-ruh* + *a*, m. A pendant branch, one that strikes fresh roots into the earth, as those of the Indian fig-tree, Râm. 2, 52, 96.—Comp. *Dus-*, adj. whither it is difficult to descend, Râjat. 6, 49.

अवरोहण *avarohaṇa*, i.e. *ava-ruh* + *ana*, n. Descending, Kathâs. 20, 179.

अवलक्ष *ava-laksha*, adj. White.

अवलम्ब *ava-lamb* + *a*, m. **1.** Depending, hanging on or from. **2.** A prop.—Comp. *Jâla-*, adj. supported, i.e. borne by a net, Megh. 71. *Nis-*, adj. 1. unsupported. 2. not granting any support. *Sa-*, adj. supported, Ragh. 19, 50. *Sevâ-*, adj. depending on the service of . . ., Bhartṛ. 1, 66. *Hasta-*, adj. supported by the hand of . . ., Vikr. 11, 1.

अवलम्बन *ava-lamb* + *ana*, n. **1.** Supporting one's self, Vedântas. in Chr. 217, 24. **2.** A prop or support, Çâk. d. 100.—Comp. *An-*, n. not supporting one's self, Vedântas. in Chr. 217, 23. *Kara-*, n. taking hold with the hand, Çiç. 9, 82; Hit. 41, 16.

अवलम्बिन् *ava-lamb* + *in*, adj., f. *nî*. **1.** Hanging down. **2.** Hanging, Mṛichchh. 46, 7. **3.** Supporting one's self, Çak. 62, 15.—Comp. *Rajju-*, adj. hanging by a string.

अवलिप्तता *ava-lipta* + *tâ*, f., and **अवलिप्तत्व** *ava-lipta* + *tva*, n. Pride, Bhartṛ. 2, 44.

अवलुञ्चन *ava-luñch* + *ana*, n. Pulling out, Râm. 6, 98, 25.

अवलुण्ठन *ava-luṇṭh* + *ana*, n. Robbing, Kathâs. 22, 71.

अवलुम्पन *avalumpana,* i.e. *ava-lup* + *ana,* n. Leaping away, Lass. 48, 4.

अवलेप *avalepa,* i.e. *ava-lip* + *a,* m. 1. Anointing. 2. Pride, Vikr. 5, 8.—Comp. *An-,* adj. without anointing and without pride, Çiç. 9, 51. *Sa-,* adj. Proud, Daçak. in Chr. 185, 19.

अवलेपन *avalepana,* i.e. *ava-lip* + *ana,* n. Haughtiness, Râm. 1, 44, 9.

अवलोक *ava-lok* + *a,* m. 1. Sight, Çiç. 9, 71. 2. Observation, Vikr. 38, 5.

अवलोकक *ava-lok* + *aka,* m. A spy, Râm. 6, 101, 13.

अवलोकन *ava-loh* + *ana,* n. 1. Sight. 2. Observation. 3. A glance, Ragh. 10, 14.

अवलोकयितृ *avalokayitṛi,* i.e. *ava -lok,* Caus. + *tṛi,* m. An observer, Vedântas. in Chr. 206, 1.

अवशेष *avaçesha,* i.e. *ava-çish* + *a,* m. Residue.—Comp. *Ardha-,* adj. of which a half is left, Râm. 5, 14, 49. *Alpa-,* adj. of which few are left, Râm. 3, 32, 2. *Nis-,* adj. without a residue, whole, Râm. 3, 16, 28. *Sa-,* adj. 1. leaving a residue. 2. imperfect. 3. remaining, *sâvaçesha-bandhana,* adj. still bound, Pańch. 109, 17. 4. till, *mṛid-bhâṇḍa-,* adj. exclusive of the earthen pots, Daçak. in Chr. 188, 14.

अवश्यम् *avaçyam,* i.e. *a-vaça* + *ya* + *m,* adv. 1. Certainly. 2. Inevitably, Man. 12, 68; necessarily. When compounded with a participle of fut. pass. the final *m* is dropped, e.g. *avaçya-karaṇîya,* to be done necessarily, Brâhmaṇav. 3, 16.

अवश्याय *avaçyâya,* i. e. *ava-çyai* + *a,* m. 1. Hoar-frost, Râm. 3, 22, 21. 2. Dew, MBh. 12, 5334.

अवष्टम्भ *avashṭambha,* i.e. *ava-stambh* + *a,* m. 1. Relying on, Pańch. 20, 20. 2. Self-confidence, Pańch, 246, 19. 3. Gold.—Comp. *Sa-,* adj. full of self-confidence, Pańch. i. d. 215; acc. *Sâvashṭambham,* adv. courageously, Kathâs. 25, 97.

अवष्टम्भन *avashṭambhana,* i.e. *ava -stambh* + *ana,* n. Supporting one's self on, being supported by, Pańch. 233, 16.

अवष्टम्भमय *avashṭambha* + *maya,* adj., f. *yî,* Golden, Ragh. 3, 53.

अवस् *av* + *as,* n. Protection, Chr. 288, 14 = Rigv. i. 48, 14.

अवसक्थिका *ava-sakthi* + *kâ,* f. A cloth drawn round the knees and loins of a person sitting on his hams, Man. 4, 112.

अवसर *avasara,* i.e. *ava-sṛi* + *a,* m. 1. Opportunity, Çiç. 9, 41; Râjat. 5, 36. 2. The right time, Kir. 5, 16; with inf., Çâk. 12, 11. 3. Turn, Pańch. 55, 4 (*çaçakasyâvasaraḥ samâyâtaḥ,* The turn of the hare came). 4. Use, Kathâs. 6, 62.—Comp. *An-,* I. m. wrong time, Mṛichchh. 102, 8. II. adj. unseasonable, Hit. 53, 11. *Sarvâvasara* + *m,* i. e. *sarva-,* adv. on every occasion, Lass. 2, 2.

अवसाद *avasâda,* i.e. *ava-sad-a,* m. 1. Sitting down. 2. Exhaustion, 3. Lassitude, want of energy.—Comp. *Nis-,* adj. cheerful, Gît. 11, 1.

अवसादक *avasâdaka,* i.e. *ava-sad,* Caus. + *aka,* adj. Bringing down, impairing, Râm. 4, 26, 19.

अवसान *avasâna,* i.e. *ava-so* + *ana,* n. 1. Termination, end, Çiç. 9, 19; Daçak. in Chr. 201, 4. 2. Death, Pańch. ii. d. 123.

अवसानिक *avasânika,* i.e. *avasâna* + *ika,* adj., f. *ikâ,* Concluding, Râm. 2, 56, 25 (perhaps the masc. must be read *-sânaka*).

अवसेक *avaseka*, i.e. *ava-sich + a*, m. Sprinkling, Mṛichchh. 47, 1.

अवसेचन *avasechana*, i.e. *ava-sich + ana*, n. Water used for washing, Man. 4, 151.

अवस्कन्द *ava-skand + a*, m. Assault, Pańch. iii. d. 37.

अवस्कन्दिन् *ava-skand + in*, adj., f. *nî*, Assailing, Mahâv. 72, 7.

अवस्कर *avaskara*, i.e. *ava-kṛi + a*, m. **1.** Ordure, Râjat. 5, 406. **2.** The privy, Râjat. 5, 412.

अवस्त्रता *a-vastra + tâ*, f. Nakedness, Nal. 10, 16.

अवस्था *ava-sthâ*, f. **1.** State, Pańch. 44, 1. **2.** Condition, Râm. 3, 44, 13.—Comp. *Tad-*, adj., f. *thâ*, being in this state. *Antya-*, adj. being in the lowest condition, Pańch. iv. d. 76. *Kṛita-*, adj. brought into court, Man. 8, 60.

अवस्थान *avasthâna*, i.e. *ava-sthâ + ana*, n. **1.** Standing-place, Râm. 5, 15, 8. **2.** Position, Pańch. 9, 14. **3.** State, Pańch. 107, 8. **4.** Abiding, Pańch. 19, 5; duration, Râjat. 5, 278. **5.** Perseverance, Vedântas. in Chr. 217, 3.—Comp. *An-*, I. n. unsteadiness, mobility. II. adj. unsteady. III. m. wind.

अवस्थापन *avasthâpana*, i. e. *ava-sthâ*, Caus. *+ ana*, n. Setting out for sale, Daçak. in Chr. 180, 15.

अवस्थिति *avasthiti*, i.e. *ava-sthâ + ti*, f. Abode, Kathâs. 9, 67.—Comp. *An-*, f. unsteadiness.

अवहार *avahâra*, i.e. *ava-hṛi + a*, m. Suspension of fighting, Chr. 37, 31.

अवहास *avahâsa*, i.e. *ava-has + a*, m. Jest, Bhag. 11, 42.

अवहेल *avahela*, i.e. *ava-heḍ + a*, n. and f. *lâ*, Contempt.—Comp. *Sa-*, adj. despising.

अवाञ्च् *avâńch*, i.e. *ava-ańch*, adj., f. *vâchî*, Downward, headlong, Man. 3, 249; acc. ntr. *avâk*, adv. Downwards, Vedântas. in Chr. 207, 10; headlong, Man. 8, 75.—Cf. *οὐκ*.

अवान्तर *avântara*, i.e. *ava-antara*, adj. Included, Vedântas. in Chr. 203, 3.

अवाप्ति *avâpti*, i. e. *ava-âp + ti*, f. Acquisition, Vedântas. in Chr. 204, 3.

अवि *avi*, m. A sheep; f. an ewe, Man. 3, 6.—Cf. Lat. ovis, οἶς; O.H.G. awi; A.S. eav; Goth. avistr.

अविवेकता *a-viveka + tâ*, f. Want of discrimination or judgment.

अविषयीकरण *avishayikaraṇa*, i.e. *a-vishaya-kṛi + ana*, n. The non-acquiring of an understanding, Vedântas. in Chr. 216, 9; 10.

अवेक्षण *avekshaṇa*, i.e. *ava-îksh + ana*, n. Attention, care, Ragh. 14, 85.—Comp. *An-*, n. want of attention, Böhtl. Ind. Spr. 1260.

अवेक्षा *avekshâ*, i.e. *ava-îksh + â*, f. Careful attention, Man. 7, 101.—Comp. *An-*, f. Want of attention, Man. 7, 111 (instr. rashly). *Su-*, adj. well taken care of, Râm. 5, 75, 1.

अवेक्षिन् *avekshin*, i. e. *ava-îksh + in*, adj., f. *iṇî*, Looking, Pańch. i. d. 214.

अव्यथि *a-vyath + i*, adj. Fearless, Chr. 296, 6 = Rigv. 1, 112, 6.

अव्रतिक *avratika*, i.e. *a-vrata + ika*, adj. One who neglects his religious duties, Indr. 2, 5.

1. **अश्** *AÇ*, ii. 5, *açnu*. Âtm. **1.** To pervade, to occupy, Yâjń. 1, 260. **2.** To attain, Vedântas. in Chr. 203, 2; ved. ii. 2, Par. Chr. 294, 8 = Rigv. i. 92,

8. 3. † To heap or crowd.—With the prep. उप *upa*, To attain, Man. 6, 82.— With वि *vi*, To pervade, Ragh. 4, 15.— With सम्‌ *sam*, To attain, Man. 2, 233.

2. अश्‌ *AÇ*, ii. 9, *açnâ*, *nî*, Par. (in epic poetry also Âtm. MBh. 3, 14686) **1.** To eat, Man. 1, 95. *an-açnâna*, Not eating, Chr. 57, 23. **2.** To enjoy, Bhag. 9, 20. Caus. To cause to eat, Man. 3, 83. *an-âçita*, Not satiated, Râm. 5, 17, 34. —With the prep. अति *ati*, To eat before another, MBh. 3, 14686.—With उप *upa*. **1.** To eat up, to consume, Dev. 5, 61. **2.** To enjoy, Râm. 1, 62, 6. *upâçnîyât*, instead of °*çnîy*°, on account of the metre, MBh. 12, 3266.—With समुप *sam-upa*, To enjoy, MBh. 3, 12631. —With परि *pari*, To eat, MBh. 3, 13354.—With प्र *pra*. **1.** To begin eating, Râm. 3, 63, 28. **2.** To take in the mouth only, Man. 2, 62. **3.** To eat, Man. 5, 103. **4.** To drink, Chr. 47, 39 (Âtm.). **5.** To enjoy one's self, MBh. 3, 8083 (Âtm.). Caus. To cause to eat or devour, Kathâs. 9, 10; Man. 3, 260. *prâçita*, n. An oblation to the Pitṛis, or Manes, Man. 3, 73; 74.—With सम्‌ *sam*, To eat, Pańch. iv. d. 84.

अशंकुसुक *açam̃kusuka*, Firm, Man. 6, 43; see *sam̃kasuka*.

अशन 2. *aç* + *ana*, n. **1.** Eating, Pańch. 236, 22. **2.** Food, Man. 3, 59.— Comp. *Ati-*, n. excess of eating, Man. 2, 56. *Adhi-*, n. Eating too often. *An-*, I. adj. consisting in abstinence, Bhâg. P. 2, 6, 20. II. n. 1. hunger, Daçak. in Chr. 181, 9. 2. fasting, Râjat. 5, 428 (plur.). *Nis-*, adj. abstaining from food, Hariv. 2539. *Mûla-phala-*, n. feeding on roots and fruits, Man. 6, 75. *Piçita-*, n. eating flesh, Çâk. d. 75. *Sa-*, adj. consisting of nourishment, Bhâg. P. 2, 6, 30. *Havis-*, m. fire. *Huta-* (vb. *hu*), m. 1. fire. 2. the deity of fire. 3. Çiva.

अशनि 1. *aç* + *ani*, f. (seldom m. Râm. 3, 4, 45) and अशनी 1. *aç* + *anî*, f. (Chr. 40, 12) Indra's thunderbolt, Ragh. 3, 56.

अशिरस्क *a-çiras* + *ka*, adj. Headless, Draup. 8, 30.

अशिशिरता *a-çiçira* + *tâ*, f. Heat, Megh. 82.

अशीत *açîta*, i.e. *açîti* + *a*, ord. num. Eightieth. *eka-*, Eighty-first, MBh. i; adhy. 81. *tri-*, Eighty-third, adhy. 83. *dvi-*, Eighty-second, adhy. 82.

अशीति *açîti* (cf. *ashṭan*), card. num., f. Eighty, with genitive of the numbered objects, Man. 11, 220; in the same case, Râm. 2, 32, 19.—Comp. *Eka-*, eighty-one. *Pańchâçîti*, i.e. *pańchan-*, eighty-five.

अशीतिक *açîti* + *ka*, adj. Measuring eighty, Râm. 5, 6, 21.

अशीतितम *açîti* + *tama*, ord. num. f. *mî*. Eightieth. *eka-*, Eighty-first. *tri-*, Eighty-third. *nava(n)-*, Eighty-ninth. *pańcha(n)-*, Eighty-fifth.

अशेषतस्‌ *a-çesha* + *tas*, adv. Entirely, Man. 1, 59.

अशेषय *AÇESHAYA* (a denom. derived from. *a-çesha*). To complete, Kumâras. 7, 29.

अशोक *a-çoka*. I. adj. Free from sorrow, Nal. 12, 107. II. m. A shrub, Jonesia Asoka, Ṛit. 6, 16. III. n. An asoka-flower, Ṛit. 6, 6.—Comp. *Nîla-*, m. an asoka with blue flowers, Râm. 3, 17, 10.

अश्मन्‌ *aç* + *man* (see vb. *ço*), m. A stone.—Comp. *A-sita-*, m. an emerald, Kir. 5, 48. *Mahâ-*, m. a ruby, Kir. 5,

8. *Sûrya-*, m. the sun-stone. *Harita-*, n. 1. blue vitriol. 2. a turquoise; an emerald.—Cf. the next and ἄκμων; also ved. *açna*, stone, and Goth. auhns.

अश्मन्तक *aç+mant+aka* (see the last), n. A stove, Daçak. in Chr. 192, 19.

अश्ममय *açmamaya*, i.e. *açman+maya*, adj., f. *yî*, Made of stone, Man. 5, 111.

अश्मसारमय *açmasâramaya*, i.e. *açman-sâra+maya*, adj., f. *yî*, Made of iron, Râm. 4, 22, 15.

अश्मान्तक *açmântaka*, The name of a plant, Man. 2, 43 (probably=*açmantuka*, m. A species of Oxalis).

अश्र *aç+ra* (see vb. *ço*). I. A substitute for *açri*, when latter part of comp. adj., implying An angle, e.g. *chatur-*, adj. Quadrangular, regular, Kumâras. 1, 32 (written with *s* instead of *ç*). II. n. A tear, Kathâs. 13, 126; Man. 3, 229 (with *s* instead of *ç*).—Comp. *Sa-*, adj. weeping, Megh. 100.—Cf. the next, and ἄκρος, ἄκρα, Lat. acer.

अश्रि *aç+ri* (see vb. *ço*), f. 1. Edge, Kumâras. 2, 20. 2. A corner, an angle, Râm. 1, 13, 28.—Cf. ὄκρις.

अश्रु *aç+ru* (see vb. *ço*), n. A tear, Râm. 2, 48, 2.—Comp. *Ud-*, adj. shedding tears, Ragh. 12, 14.

अश्रुतवत् *a-çru+ta+vat*, adv. As if not heard, Râjat. 5, 53.

अश्लीक *açlîka*, i.e. *a-çrî+ka* (*l* for *r*), adj. Bringing misfortune, Man. 4, 206.

अश्व *aç+va* (see vb. *ço*). I. m. A horse, Man. 7, 96. II. f. *vâ*, A mare, Râjat. 5, 415.—Comp. *An-*, m. one who is not a horse, Pañch. iv. d. 49. *Indriya-*, m., plur. the horse-like organs of sense, Kir. 5, 50. *Gava-*, n. bulls and horses, MBh. 1, 3654. *Vija-*, m. a stallion, Râjat. 5, 280. *Vṛihadaçva*, i.e. *vṛihant-*, m. a proper name. *Sa-*, adj. with horses. *Saptâçva*, i.e. *saptan-*, m. the sun. *Hata-* (vb. *han*), adj. having the horses killed.—Cf. Lat. equus; ἴκκος, ἵππος; Goth. aihvs.

अश्वक्रन्द *açva-krand+a*, m. The name of a bird, MBh. 1, 1488.

अश्वतर *açva+tara*. I. m. 1. A mule, Râm. 2, 91, 53. 2. One of the chiefs of the Nâgas or serpent race, MBh. 1, 1555. II. f. *tarî*. 1. A female mule. 2. Probably the name of a kind of serpent, which, according to a popular opinion, used to die when pregnant with or bringing forth young, Râm. 3, 49, 49.

अश्वत्थ *açvattha*, m. The holy fig-tree, Ficus religiosa, Bhag. 15, 1.

अश्वत्थामन् *açvatthâman*, i.e. *açva-sthâ+man*, m. A proper name, Bhag. 1, 8.

अश्वमेधिक *açvamedhika*, i. e. *açva-medha+ika*, adj. Referring to the sacrifice of a horse, MBh. 1, 354.

अश्वयुज् *açva-yuj*, adj. On which horses are put, Râm. 5, 27, 14.

अश्ववार *açvavâra*, i.e. *açva-vṛi+a*, m. A horseman, Râm. 5, 73, 11.

अश्वस्तनिक *açvastanika*, i.e. *a-çvas+tana+ika*, adj. Not having for to-morrow, Man. 4, 7.

अश्वावन्त् *açvâvant*, i.e. *açva+vant*, adj., f. *vatî*, Abounding in horses, Chr. 287, 2=Rigv. i. 48, 2.

अश्विन् *açvin*, i.e. *açva+in*, m., du. Two deities, Râm. 1, 24, 8.—Cf. the Dioscuri.

अश्व्य *açvya*, i.e. *açva+ya*, m. A patronymic: a son of Açva, Chr. 296, 10=Rigv. i. 112, 10.

† अष् *ASH*, i. 1, Par. Âtm. 1. To

go. **2.** To take. **3.** To shine (v.r. *as*, cf. 3. *as*).

अष्टक *ashṭaka*, i.e. *ashṭan+ka*. **I.** adj. Eight-fold, Man. 7, 48. **II.** f. *kâ*. **1.** The eighth day after the full moon, Man. 4, 113; especially those on which the Pitṛis or Manes are worshipped. **2.** Worship of the Pitṛis, Râm. 2, 108, 14. **III.** n. An octad, a collection of eight things.—Comp. *Tri-*, n. a kind of vessel, Suçr. 1, 171, 19. *Ashṭâshṭaka*, i.e. *ashṭan-*, n. sixty-four (arts), Râm. 3, 53, 41.

अष्टतय *ashṭataya*, i.e. *ashṭan+taya*, n. A complex of eight, Lass. 89, 1.

अष्टधा *ashṭadhâ*, i.e. *ashṭan+dhâ*, adv. Eight-fold, Bhag. 7, 4.

अष्टन् *ashṭan*, i.e. *aç+tan* (cf. *açîti*; the vb. is doubtful), card. num., adj. Eight, Hiḍ. 2, 9.—Comp. *Tri-*, Twenty-four, Man. 9, 94.—Cf. ὀκτώ = *ashṭau*; Lat. octo; Goth. ahtau; A.S. ĕhta.

अष्टम *ashṭama*, i.e. *ashṭan+ma*. **I.** ord. num., f. *mî*, Eighth, Man. 2, 36. **II.** m. An eighth, Man. 10, 120. **III.** f. *mî*, The eigth day of a lunar half month, Râjat. 5, 327; 412.—Cf. Lat. octavus; ὄγδοος.

अष्टमक *ashṭama+ka*, adj. Eighth, Yâjñ. 2, 244.

अष्टा *ashṭâ*, a substitute of *ashṭan* in the former part of many comp. words, especially before numerals, e.g. *ashṭâ -daçan*, Eighteen.

अष्टादश *ashṭâ-daça*, ord. num., f. *çî*, Eighteenth, Chr. 51.

अष्टादशन् *ashṭâ-daçan*, card. num. adj. Eighteen, Man. 8, 3.—Cf. Lat. octodecim.

अष्टापद *ashṭâ-pada*. **I.** n. A board for draughts, dice, etc., Hariv. 6752. **II.** m. and n. Gold, Kumâras, 7, 10.

अष्टापाद्य *ashṭâpâdya*, i. e. *ashṭâ -pâda+ya*, adj. Eight-fold, Man. 8, 337.

अष्ट्रा *ashṭrâ*, i.e. *aç+tra* (vb. *ço*, cf. Lat. incitare), f. A goad.

अष्ठीला *ashṭhîlâ* (probably from *asthi*), f. **1.** A kernel, MBh. 3, 10629. **2.** A ball, MBh. 1, 4494.

1. **अस्** *AS*, ii. 2, Par. (Âtm. when combined with *vi-ati* and as auxiliary vb.; e.g. *sṛishṭâḥ smahe*, MBh. 13, 13). **1.** To exist, Bhag. 2, 12. **2.** To be, Man. 1, 5; with an adv., MBh. 3, 4041; with participles, Man. 8, 94. *asti*, So it is, Çâk. 14, 16. *asti*, Once, Pañch. 132, 22. With *na*, Not, it implies very often 'to be lost,' e.g. MBh. 3, 10284. **3.** With a gen. To belong. *kasyâsi*, Whose are you, Nal. 12, 118. *santi me*, I have, Man. 8, 87. *tavâsmi*, I am thy captive, Man. 7, 91. **4.** With a dat. To suffice, Man. 11, 85. **5.** With a loc. or with *prati*, To be affected against, Çâk. 17, 13; 14. *Sant*, participle of the present (cf. Lat. præ-sens), 1. Being, Hit. i. d. 75. 2. Being in the true sense of the word, Right, Bhâshâp. 138. 3. Virtuous, Chr. 8, 22. 4. Steady, Daçak. in Chr. 189, 10. 5. Venerable, Râjat. 5, 79. 6. Excellent, Kir. 5, 9. fem. *Satî*, A virtuous wife, Lass. 41, 11. Comp. *mahâ-satî*, a very virtuous wife, Pañch. 38, 12. n. *Sat*, Entity, Man. 1, 11. superl. *sat+tama*, adj., f. *mâ*, Most excellent. In comp. words of the Kharmadhâr. class it forms the latter part, e.g. *dvija-sattama*, 1. A Brâhmaṇa, Man. 1, 33. 2. A most excellent Brâhmaṇa, Chr. 15, 30. *brâhmaṇa-*, m. Chr. 22, 15; *bharata-*, 25, 55; *bhârata-*, 40, 17; *bhṛigu-*, 45, 11; *mṛiga-*, Ram. 3, 49, 25; *ratha-*, Chr. 63, 64; *râjasattama*, i.e. *râjan-*, 53, 5.—Comp. *A-sant*, adj. wicked, Pañch. i. d. 182; heretic, Man. 11, 65. f. *A-satî*, an unchaste woman, Pañch. 185, 15. *A-sat*, n. non-entity, Man. 1,

11.—With the prepositions व्यति *vi-ati*, Âtm. To outweigh, Bhaṭṭ. 2, 35.—With आविस् *âvis*, To be visible, to appear, Daçak. in Chr. 186, 17 (corr. *âvir âsît*).—With उप *upa*, To be near, Chr. 12, 2.—With प्रादुस् *prâdus*, **1.** To be conspicuous, Man. 1, 6. **2.** To appear, Chr. 13, 6. **3.** To spring up, Chr. 31, 10.—Cf. *εἰμί*, e.g. *ἐστί = asti*; Lat. sum, est; Goth. im, ist; A.S. ëom, is.

2. अस् *AS*, i, 4, Par. **1.** To throw, Râm. 2, 67, 18. **2.** To leave, Kathâs. 6, 141. Aor. *âstham*, Ragh. 12, 23. Part. of the perf. pass. *asta* (*asita*, Râm. 4, 13, 54).—With the prep. अति *ati*, To surpass, Râm. 2, 23, 37.—With व्यति *vi-ati*, To cross, Man. 2, 72.—With अप *apa*. **1.** To drive away, Amar. 2. **2.** To put off, Nalod. 3, 8. **3.** To lay aside, Râm. 2, 32, 30. **4.** To leave, Pańch. Pr. d. 10. Absolutive *apâsya*, Except, Hit. iii. d. 139.—With अभि *abhi*, also Âtm. Man. 4, 149; sometimes i. 1, Par. Man. 11, 106. **1.** To discharge (an arrow), MBh. 1, 5497. **2.** To do repeatedly; to repeat, Man. 2, 79. **3.** To practise, Daçak. in Chr. 187, 1. **4.** To study, Pańch. 244, 1.—With उद् *ud*. **1.** To cast upward, MBh. 3, 430. **2.** To lift up, Çâk. 34, 1; to raise, Çiç. 9, 74.—With पर्युद् *pari-ud*, To heap round about, MBh. 2, 1805.—With व्युद् *vi-ud*, To cast off, Bhag. 18, 51.—With नि *ni*, also i. 1 Par. Man. 6, 46. **1.** To cast down, Râm. 3, 58, 2; to put down, Chr. 27, 12. **2.** To resign, Râm. 2, 46, 20. **3.** To put on, Râm. 2, 28, 27; Daçak. in Chr. 189, 6. **4.** To support, Çâk. d. 161. **5.** To put in, Bhartṛ. 2, 77; to settle, Yâjń. 2, 185; to appoint, MBh. 12, 4336. **6.** To intrust, Râm. 3, 51, 18.—**Comp.** partic. *Chitra-nyasta*, adj. painted, MBh. 9, 43. *Su-nyasta*, gracefully reposing, Râm. 5, 14, 23. Caus., to cause to put down, Chr. 43, 31.—With उपनि *upa-ni*. **1.** To put near, Râm. 4, 4, 17. **2.** To intrust, MBh. 3, 11551. **3.** To prove, Hit. 120, 5. **4.** To hint, Çâk. 65, 15. Comp. partic. *An-upa-nyasta*, unproved, Yâjń. 2, 19.—With समुपनि *sam-upa-ni*, To prove, Hit. 103, 3.—With परिनि *pari-ni*, To stretch, Kathâs. 6, 121.—With प्रतिनि *prati-ni*, To put down for every one, Râm. 2, 40, 16.—With विनि *vini*, **1.** To put off and down, Pańch. 230, 18. **2.** To put down, Nal. 24, 45. **3.** To divide, Râm. 1, 13, 28. **4.** To direct, Râm. 2, 60, 7. **5.** To put in, Pańch. 236, 9.—Comp. partic. *Su-vi-nyasta*, well arranged, Râm. 5, 13, 37.—With संनि *sam-ni*, **1.** To put down, MBh. 3, 16708. **2.** To abandon, Man. 6, 95; to abandon all worldly concerns, i.e. to become an anchorite, Man. 6, 94. **3.** To put together, Râm. 3, 35, 63. **4.** To put on, MBh. 3, 740. **5.** To intrust, Râm. 4, 28, 5.—With निस् *nis*, **1.** To throw out, to expel, Çiç. 9, 62; Ṛit. 6, 23; Râm. 3, 75, 24. **2.** To drive back, Râm. 3, 42, 42; to send back, Çiç, 9, 33. **3.** To destroy, Hit. i, d. 63.—With परा *parâ*, To leave, Kir. 5, 27.—With परि *pari*, **1.** To spread, Kir. 5, 34. **2.** To put around, MBh. 2, 1898. **3.** To turn round, Kumâras. 3, 68. **4.** To surround, Kumâras. 1, 45; to enchase, Daçak. in Chr. 198, 23. **5.** To turn over, Man. 11, 183. **6.** To turn away, Bhartṛ. 3, 29.—Caus. to cause to drop, Ragh. 13, 28.—With विपरि *vi-pari*, To invert, Mṛichchh. 115, 4.—With प्र *pra*, To

throw, Man. 11, 73.—With वि *vi*, **1.** To separate, Man. 7, 159; Vedântas. in Chr. 205, 3; to divide, MBh. 1, 4263; pf. *vivyâsa*, MBh. 1, 2212, instead of *vyâsa*, as if the combined *vyas* was a simple vb. *vyasta*, different, Prab. 97, 19; MBh. 3, 17052.—With सम् *sam*, To unite, Man. 7, 57; Vedântas. 205, 3. *samasta*. 1. United, Man. 3, 85. 2. All, Râjat. 5, 62. 3. Whole, Pañch. 69, 15.—**Comp.** *Yâvatsamasta*, i.e. *yâvant-*, large as it is, Pañch. 31, 17.

† 3. अस् *AS*, i. 1, Par. Âtm. **1.** To go. **2.** To take. **3.** To shine (v.r. *ash.*)

असन् *asan*, see *asṛij*.

असन 2. *as* + *ana*. I. n. Discharging (as arrows), Chr. 297, 21 = Rigv. i. 112, 21. II. m. The name of a tree, Terminalia alata tomentosa, Râm. 2, 94, 8.—**Comp.** *Ishu-*, n. a bow, Ragh. 11, 37. *Çara-*, n. a bow.

असमञ्ज *asamañja* and असमञ्जस् *asamañjas*, m. A proper name, Râm. 1, 39, 16; 1, 40, 16 Gorr.

असमवायित्व *asamavâyitva*, i.e. *a -samavâyin* + *tva*, n. Condition of not being in an intimate relation, Bhâshâp. 96.

असमावृत्तिक *asamâvṛittika*, i.e. *a -sam-âvṛitta* + *ika* (? see *vṛit*), m. A student before he has completed his studies, Man. 11, 157.

असि *asi*, m. A sword, Râm. 3, 50, 2.—Cf. Lat. ensis, ἄορ, cf. *akshan* = *akshi*, and πῖαρ = *pîvan*.

असु *asu*, i.e. 1. *as* + *u*, m. plur. **1.** The five vital breaths, or airs of the body (cf. Vedântas. in Chr. 207, 9). **2.** Life, Daçak. in Chr. 189, 6.—**Comp.** *Gata-* (vb. *yam*), adj. lifeless, Böhtl. Ind. Spr. 266. *A-gata-*, adj. living, ib.

असुर *asura*, i.e. 1. *as* + *ura*, I. adj. Eternal, Chr. 290, 2 = Rigv. i. 64, 2. II. m. An Asura, or demon, Kir. 5, 30. III. f. *rî*, A female Asura, or demon, MBh. 3, 12203.—**Comp.** *Deva-*, I. m. pl. the gods and the demons, Râm. 1, 45, 27. II. adj. 1. referring to the gods and the demons, Râm. 1, 34, 8 Gorr. 2. n. elliptically (supply *yuddha*), the war between the gods and the demons, Râm. 3, 53, 8.

असू *a-sû*, adj. Sterile, Chr. 296, 3 = Rigv. i. 112, 3.

असूय *ASÛYA* (an old denom. based on 2. *as*), Par. Âtm. **1.** To detract, scorn, MBh. 4, 99. **2.** To reprove, Râjat. 5, 196. **3.** To be angry, Mâlav. 51, 18.—**Comp.** *An-asûyant*, free from a spirit of detraction, Bhag. 3, 31. Caus. *asûyaya*, To chastise, Nal. 14, 17. —With the prep. अभि *abhi*, To blame, Sâv. 5, 90. *Asûyâm*, instead of *asûyeyam*, MBh. 1, 4377.

असूयक *asûyaka*, i.e. *asûya* + *aka*, adj., f. *yikâ*, A scorner, Man. 2, 114.—**Comp.** *An-* (i.e. *anasûya* + *ka*, see *asûyâ*), adj. free from a spirit of detraction, Nal. 12, 46.

असूया *asûyâ*, i.e. *asûya* + *a*, f. **1.** Detraction, Man. 7, 48. **2.** Ill-will, Râm. 4, 14, 20.—**Comp.** *An-asûya*, I. adj. free from a spirit of detraction, Man. 4, 158. II. f. *yâ*, a proper name, Çâk. 9, 7. *Sa-*, adv. angrily, Vikr. 30, 14.

असृज् *asṛij*, i.e. *asar-*, for 1. *as* + *an*, which is the base of several cases, *-j* (vb. *jan*), n. Blood, Pañch. 21, 12.—With *asan*, cf. Lat. san + ies; with *asar*, Lat. assir, ἔαρ; with **asan-j*, Lat. sanguis.

अस्त 1. *as* + *ta*, I. n. Home. II. m. **1.** Sun-set, Pañch. iii. d. 187; Çiç. 9, 5. The acc. sing. *astam*, combined like a prefix, with *i*, *gam*, *yâ*, implies, To set, Daçak. 184, 1. **2.** The western mountain, behind which the sun is supposed to set, Râm. 4, 37, 4. IV. n. Death, Kathâs. 13, 74; Râjat. 5, 126.—Comp. *Sûrya-*, n. sunset.

अस्तमन *astamana* (a syncope of *astam-ayana*), n. Sun-set, Pańch. ii. d. 7.

अस्तमय *astamaya*, i.e. *astam-i + a*, m. Sun-set, Kir. 5, 35.

अस्तृ 2. *as + tṛi*, m. A shooter, Chr. 290, 10=Rigv. i. 64, 10.

अस्त्र 2. *as + tra*, n. 1. A missile weapon, Çâk. 94, 10; an arrow, Vikr. d. 18. 2. A bow, Arj. 8, 2.—Comp. *Ishu-*, n. the art of discharging arrows, Chr. 22, 16; 51, 2. *Kusuma-*, m. the god of Love, Ragh. 7, 58. *Kṛita-*, adj. conversant with the use of missile weapons, MBh. 3, 228. *Daṇḍa-*, n. the name of a fabulous weapon, Râm. 1, 56, 9. *Mahâ-*, n. a great missile weapon, Chr. 44, 4.

अस्थन् *asthan*, see *asthi*.

अस्थि *asthi*; several cases have *asthan* as their base, n. 1. A bone, Bhartṛ. 2, 9. 2. A kernel, seed, Man. 4, 78.—Cf. ὀστέον; Lat. os, gen. ossis, for ostis.

अस्थिक *asthi + ka*, 1. n. A small bone, Bhartṛ. 2, 23. 2. A substitute for *asthi*, when latter part of comp. adj., e.g. *an-*, Boneless, Yâjń. 3, 275. *dṛiḍha -gulpha-çirâ-*, adj. Having strong ancles, nerves, and bones, Râm. 5, 32, 11.

अस्थिदन्तमय *asthi-danta + maya*, adj., f. *yî*, Made of bones and ivory, Man. 5, 121.

अस्थिमन्त् *asthi + mant*, adj., f. *matî*, Having bones, Man. 11, 140.

अस्थिमय *asthi-maya*, adj., f. *yî*, Full of bones, Râjat. 5, 272.

अस्मद् *asmad*, First person. pronoun, I; nom. sing. *aham*, plur. *vayam*; the bases of the other cases are, *ma*, *âva*, *na*, *asma*.—Cf. ἐγώ, ἐμοῦ, μοῦ, νῶϊ, ἄμμες; Lat. ego, me, nos; Goth. ik, mis, veis, unsis; A.S. ic, më, vit, unc.

अस्मदीय *asmad + îya*, adj., f. *yâ*, Our, Daçak. in Chr. 195, 1.

अस्मयु *asmayu*, i.e. **asmaya* (a denominat. of *asmad* by *ya*) + *u*, adj. Favourable to us, Lass. p. 100, 8=Rigv. vii. 15, 8.

अस्यवामीय *asya vâm + îya*, n. The Vedic hymn beginning with the words *asya vâm* (Rigv. i. 164), Man. 11, 250.

अस्र *asra*, see *açra*.

1. **अह्** *AH* (*h* for *gh*; cf. Lat. adag + ium, ajo for agjo, nego; Goth. aikan), forms only 2. sing. and du., and 3. sing. du., and plur. of the redupl. pf. 1. To say, speak, Man. 9, 47. 2. To specify, Man. 8, 122. 3. To call, MBh. 3, 16065. 4. To pronounce, Man. 9, 44. —With the prep. **प्र** *pra*, 1. To pronounce, Man. 9, 45. 2. To say, Vedântas. in Chr. 204, 8.—With **प्रति** *prati*, To answer, Hit. 10, 2.—Cf. **ह्**=*âha*.

† 2. **अह्** *AH*, ii. 5, *ahnu*, Par. To pervade, or occupy (v.r. *aḍ*).

1. **अह** *aha*, a particle; Certainly, Chr. 287, 4=Rigv. i. 48, 4.

2. **ऽअह** *-aha*, a substitute for *ahan*, when part of compound words. Day, e.g. *agha-*, n. A day of impurity, Man. 5, 84. *anirdaçâha*, i.e. *a-nis-daçan-*, adj. f. *hâ*, Not out of the ten days (of impurity which follow birth or death), Man. 8, 242. *ekâdaçâha*, i.e. *ekâdaçan -aha*, adj. Lasting eleven days, MBh. 13, 4938. *ekâha*, i.e. *eka-aha*, m. One day, Man. 5, 59. *katipayâha*, i.e. *ka-*

tipaya-, Some day, Chr. 52, 19 (sing); Pańch. 9, 6 (plur). *kshapâha*, i.e. *kshapâ-*, A day and night, Man. 1, 68. *tri-*, I. n. Three days, Man. 4, 110. II. adj. Lasting three days, Râm. 1, 13, 43. . *daçâha*, i.e *daçan-*, n. An interval of ten days, Man. 5, 59. *pańchâha*, i.e. *pańchan-*, n. A period of five days, Kathâs. 41, 26. *puṇya-*, n. A holy day, Chr. 25, 20. *saptâha*, i.e. *saptan-*, n. Seven days, a week.

अहंकार *ahaṁkâra*, i.e *aham-kâra*, m. **1.** Conceiving objects with the notion that they refer to one's own self, egotism, Vedântas. in Chr. 207, 3. **2.** Pride, Râm. 4, 6, 22. **3.** Self-conceit, Daçak. in Chr. 192, 4; arrogance, Râjat. 5, 234.—**Comp.** *Nis-*, adj. free from selfishness, MBh. 15, 882.

अहंकृत *ahaṁkṛita*, i.e. *aham-kṛita*, adj. **1.** Selfish, Bhag. 18, 17. **2.** Proud, Yâjń. 3, 151. **3.** Arrogant, Brâhmaṇav. 2, 11.—**Comp.** *An-*, adj. not arrogant, Man. 9, 335. *Nis-*, adj. 1. Impersonal, Bhâg. P. 6, 16, 8. 2. Not selfish, Bhâg. P. 3, 32, 6.

अहंकृति *ahaṁkṛiti*, i.e. *aham-kṛi + ti*, f. **1.** Selfishness, Bhartṛ. 3, 95. **2.** Pride, Râjat. 5, 481.

अहन् *ahan*; several cases have as their base *ahas*, which is used also as former part of compound words, n. A day, Çiç. 9, 23. Ved. *ahâ* for *ahâni*, Chr. 289, 7 = Rigv. i. 50, 7.

अहम् *aham* (see *asmad*). Former part of many compound words, implying the first person, e.g. *ahaṁkâra*, see above; *aham-pûrva*, see *pûrva*.

अहर्पति *aharpati*, i.e. *ahan-pati*, m. The sun, Ragh. 10, 55.

अहल्या *ahalyâ*, f. The wife of Gautama, Daçak. in Chr. 182, 10.

अहह *ahaha*, interj. **1.** of surprise, Bhartṛ. 2, 28; **2.** of pain, Bhartṛ. 2, 29; **3.** of pleasure, Vikr. 65, 11; **4.** of calling, Hit. 12, 3.

अहार्यत्व *a-hârya + tva* (vb. *hṛi*), n. Condition of not being easily taken away, Hit. Pr. d. 4.

अहि *ahi*, i.e. probably **aṁh + i* (cf. *aṁhas*), A snake, Kir. 5, 47.—**Comp.** *Andha-*, m. a kind of snake. —Cf. ἔχις; Lat. anguis; probably also ὄφις.

अहिर्ब्रध्न *ahirbradhna*, i.e. *ahi + s -bradhna*, m. The name of a Rudra or deity, MBh. 5, 3899.

अहीन *ahîna*, m. The name of a sacrifice, Man. 11, 197.

अहो *aho*, interj. **1.** of calling, Pańch. 45, 12; **2.** of grief, Pańch. 21, 3; **3.** of regret, Çâk. d. 35; **4.** of contempt, Pańch. Pr. d. 8; **5.** of surprise, Pańch. 76, 24; **6.** of praise, Hit. 17, 5.

अहोरात्र *ahorâtra*, i.e. *ahan-râtra*, m. and n. A day of twenty-four hours or thirty *muhûrtas*, Man. 1, 64.

ऽअह्न *-ahna*, i.e. *ahan + a*, A substitute for *ahan* in the latter part of some compound words, e.g. *parâhna* and *parâhṇa*, i.e. *para-*, m. The afternoon. *pûrva-*, and *pra-*, m. The forenoon, Man. 2, 256. *madhya-*, m. Noon, Lass. 73, 18. *sâya-*, m. Evening.

अह्नाय *ahnâya*, (properly dat. sing. of the preceding), adv. Soon, Ragh. 5, 71.

आ *Â*.

1. **आ** *â*, interj. of reminiscence. Ah! Prab. 46. 4.

2. **आ** *â*. I. prep. **1.** With abl., implying: **a.** Limit inceptive: From,

Chr. 295, 17=Rigv. i, 92, 17; Daçak. in Chr. 196, 17. b. Limit conclusive: Until, with abl., Bhartṛ. 2, 97. 2. With loc., On, Chr. 291, 4=Rigv. i. 85, 4; In, Chr. 297, 17=Rigv. 1, 112, 17. II. Combined and compounded with verbs and their derivatives. III. Former part of compounded nouns and adverbs: signifying 1. From, e.g. *â-kumâra +m*, adv. From (my) youth, MBh. 3, 1403. 2. Up to, till, e.g. *â-gopâla*, adj. Reaching up to the herdsmen, MBh, 2, 531. *â-maraṇa+m*, adv. Till death, Pańch. i. d. 44. Compounded adverbs of this kind, when they are former part of a compound word, drop the final *m*, e.g. *â-yojana-su-gandhi*, adj. Spreading fragrance as far as a yojana, MBh. 1, 6965. 3. A little, as former part of adj. or participles, e.g. *â-pita*, adj. Yellowish, Râm. 2, 76, 4.

आकत्थन *â-katth+ana*, adj. Boasting, Râm. 6, 3, 28.

आकम्प *â-kamp+a*, m. Shaking, Râm. 3, 62, 31.—Comp. *An-*, adj. unshakeable, Vikr. d. 160.

आकर *âkara*, i.e. *â-kṛi+a*, m. 1. A multitude, Râm. 5, 17, 18. 2. A mine, Man. 7, 62.—Comp. *Kusuma-*, m. spring (literally, Having plenty of flowers), Bhag. 10, 35. *Padma-*, m. a pond abounding in lotus flowers. *Ratna-*, m. 1. the ocean. 2. a proper name.

आकरिन् *âkarin*, i.e. *âkara+in*, adj., f. *iṇî*, Born in mines, Kir. 5, 7.

आकर्णन *âkarṇana*, i.e. *âkarṇaya +ana*, n. Hearing, Kathâs. 16, 67.

आकर्णय *ÂKARṆAYA*, a denominative derived from *â-karṇa*, Par. To hear, Pańch. 19, 10.—With the prepos.

सम् *sam*, To perceive, Pańch. 19, 14.

आकर्ष *âkarsha*, i.e. *â-kṛish+a*, m. 1. Attraction, Prab. 61, 16. 2. Playing with dice, MBh. 2, 2116. 3. A proper name, MBh. 2, 1270.

आकर्षण *âkarshaṇa*, i.e. *â-kṛish+ana*, n. Attracting, drawing near, drawing on, MBh. 1, 7109.—Comp. *Khalîna-*, pulling of a bridle, Pańch. 258, 22.

आकल्प *âkalpa*, i.e. *â-kḷip+a*, m. Ornament, Daçak. in Chr. 195, 5.

आकस्मिक *âkasmika*, i.e. *a-kasmât*, abl. of *kim +ika*, adj., f. *kî*, Sudden, Râjat. 5, 54.

आकाङ्क्षा *â-kâṅksh+â*, f. 1. Wish, Amar. 41. 2. A necessary supply, Bhâshâp. 83.

ऽआकाङ्क्षिन् *-â-kâṅksh+in*, adj., f. *iṇî*, Desiring, Râm. 1, 20, 5.—Comp. *nirâkâṅkshin*, i.e. *nis-*, adj. devoid of desire, MBh. 14, 537.

आकार *âkâra*, i.e. *â-kṛi+a*, m. 1. Form, Çâk. 103, 18. 2. Countenance, Daçak. in Chr. 196, 24.—Comp. *Guńjâ-phala-sama-âkâra*, adj. like the fruit of the guńjâ, Böhtl. Ind. Spr. 119. *Dvidhâ-*, adj., of two kinds, Pańch. iii. d. 35. *Nis-*, adj. 1. deprived of one's natural form, Râm. 2, 124, 24 Gorr. 2. disguised, MBh. 1, 5787. 3. unassuming, ib. 5, 1395. *Vṛithâ-*, m. a vain, or useless appearance, Pańch. i. d. 62.

आकारण *âkâraṇa*, i.e. *â-kṛi*, Caus. *+ana*, n. Calling up, Pańch. 227, 23.

आकारवन्त् *âkâra+vant*, adj., f. *vatî*. 1. Embodied, Kathâs. 17, 50. 2. Well-shaped, Nal. 5, 5.

आकालिक *âkâlika*, adj., f. *kâ*, i.e. I. *a-kâla+ika*, Unseasonable, Kumâras. 3, 34. II. *â-kâla+ika*, What must be deferred till the same time next day, Man. 4, 103.

आकाश *â-kâç+a*, m. 1. The fifth element, æther, Man. 1, 75. 2. Sky,

Pańch. 47, 14. **3.** The open air, Man. 3, 90; Nal. 14, 10. **4.** The loc. sing. *çe* denotes in dramatic language that which is spoken off the stage, Mṛichchh. 32, 18.—**Comp.** *Nis-*, adj. filled, Râm. 5, 64, 24.

आकाशग *âkâça-ga* (vb. *gam*). I. adj., f. *gâ*, Moving in or through the sky, Râm. 2, 33, 8; 1, 38, 7. II. m. A bird, Chr. 41, 21.

आकिंचन्य *âkiñchanya*, i. e. *a-kim-chana + ya*, n. Poverty.

आकुञ्चन *â-kuńch + ana*, n. Bending together, Bhâshâp. 5.

आकुल *âkula*, i. e. probably *â-kṛî + a*, adj., f. *lâ*. **1.** Crowded. **2.** Fully occupied. **3.** Confounded. **4.** Distressed. **5.** Perplexed.—**Comp.** *An-*, adj., composed. *Pari-*, adj. 1. full of. 2. confused. 3. agitated. *Sam-*, adj. 1. agitated, bewildered, confused. 2. crowded, thronged.

आकुलता *âkula + tâ*, f. Disturbance, MBh. 3, 401.

आकुलत्व *âkula + tva*, n. **1.** Crowd, MBh. 3, 13711. **2.** Disturbance, Bhartṛ. 1, 17. **3.** Commotion, Çiç. 9, 42.

आकुलय *ÂKULAYA* (a denomin. derived from *âkula*), Par. To disturb, Pańch. 129, 18. *âkulita*, Distressed, Râm. 2, 98, 11.

आकूत *â-kû + ta* (vb. *kû*, has no correspondent signification, but cf. κο, in ἔκομεν, κών, κοέω, κοῷ, κοάσαι, ἐκοάϑη, and ἀκούω), n. Intention, Amar. 4.—**Comp.** *Sa-*, adj. 1. intentional, Lass. 83, 2. 2. significant. 3. wanton. Acc. *tam*, adv. intentionally, Kathâs. 6, 141.

आकूति *â-kû + ti* (see the last), f. Intention, MBh. 3, 15530.

आकृति *â-kṛi + ti*, f. Form, Çâk. d. 19; figure, Hiḍ. 2, 2; appearance, Brâhmaṇav. 1, 28.—**Comp.** *Nis-*, I. adj. 1. shapeless, Hariv. 12090. 2. ugly, Mârk. P. 8, 83. 3. one who disregards his religious duties, Man. 3, 154. 4. annihilating, Bhâg. P. 1, 6, 4. II. m. a proper name. *Vâmana-*, adj. dwarf-shaped.

आकृतिमन्त् *âkṛiti + mant*, adj., f. *matî*, Embodied, Kathâs. 10, 88.

आकृष्टि *âkṛishṭi*, i. e. *â-kṛish + ti*, f. **1.** Drawing, Amar. 1. **2.** Attraction, Hit. i. d. 90.

आक्रन्द *â-krand + a*, m. **1.** Calling loud, Man. 8, 292. **2.** Cry of lamentation, Kathâs. 10, 94. **3.** A king, whose kingdom lies next but one, Man. 7, 207; cf. Kâm. Nîtis. viii. 17; 43; 46; sqq.—**Comp.** *An-*, adj., f. *dâ*, not crying, MBh. 1, 6568. *Durâkrandam*, i.e. *dus-âkranda + m*, adv. miserably, Pańch. iv. d. 31 (thus to be read).

आक्रन्दन *â-krand + ana*, n. Crying, lamenting, Pańch. 145, 25.

आक्रन्दिन् *â-krand + in*, adj., f. *nî*, Calling lamentably.

आक्रम *â-kram + a*, m. Beginning, Kathâs. 25, 64.—**Comp.** *Dus-*, adj. 1. difficult to be attained, MBh. 7, 8861. 2. difficult to be attacked, Râm. 1, 23, 16.

आक्रमण *âkramaṇa*, i.e. *â-kram + ana*, n. **1.** Ascending, Râm. 2, 31, 5. **2.** Increase. **3.** Entering.

आक्रान्ति *âkrânti*, i.e. *â-kram + ti*, f. Ascending, Kathâs. 22, 7.

आक्रीड *â-krîḍ + a*. I. m. and n. A royal garden, Râm. 5, 9, 10; MBh. 3, 10823. II. m. Sport.—**Comp.** *Deva-*, m. a play-ground of the gods, Hariv. 6980.

आक्रोश *âkroça*, i. e. *â-kruç + a*,

m. **1.** Abuse, Yâjń 2, 302 **2.** A curse. —**Comp.** *Durâkroçam*, i.e. *dus-âkroça* + *m*, adv. with terrible curses, Râm. 4, 9, 19.

आक्रोष्टृ *âkroshṭṛi*, i.e. *â-kruç* + *tṛi*, m. An abuser, MBh. 1, 3557.

आक्षेप *âkshepa*, i.e. *â-kship* + *a*, m. **1.** Convulsion, Kumâras. 7, 95. **2.** Putting on, Kumâr. 7, 17. **3.** Throwing away. **4.** Reproach, Bhartṛ. 2, 59; blame, Bhartṛ. 3, 29.—**Comp.** *Çara-*, m. a flight of arrows. *Sa-âkshepa* + *m*, adv. revilingly, Pańch. 24, 12.

आखण्डल *â-khaṇḍ* + *ala*, m. A name of Indra, Çâk. d. 187.

आखु *âkhu*, i.e. *â-khan* + *u*, m. A rat, a mouse.—**Comp.** *Vana-*, m. A hare.

आखेट *âkheṭa*, m. Hunting, Kathâs. 15, 120.

आखेटक *âkheṭa* + *ka*, m. **1.** A hunter, Pańch. i. d. 432. **2.** Hunting, Kathâs. 9, 74.

आख्या *â-khyâ*, f. A name, Çâk. 105, 7.—**Comp.** *Udaya-âkhya*, adj. called Udaya, Böhtl. Chr. 228, 166. *Kim-*, adj. how called, Çâk. 104, 13. *Daçâbda-*, i.e. *daçan-abda-*, adj. declared to be of ten years, Man. 2, 134 (i.e. a citizen may be considered as equal to another citizen who is ten years older or younger than himself).

आख्याति *â-khyâ* + *ti*, f. **1.** A tale, a report. **2.** Appellation, Kathâs. 18, 5.

आख्यान *âkhyâna*, i.e. *â-khyâ* + *ana*, n. **1.** A tale. **2.** A legend, Nal. 6, 9.

आख्यानक *âkhyâna* + *ka*, n. A little tale, Pańch. 72, 16.

आख्यापन *âkhyâpana*, i.e. *â-khyâ*, Caus. + *ana*, n. Invitation to give a report.

आख्यायिका *âkhyâyikâ*, i.e. *â-khyâ* + *aka*, f. A tale, MBh. 2, 453, with short final on account of the metre.

आख्यायिन् *âkhyâyin*, i.e. *â-khyâ* + *in*, adj., f. *nî*, Reporting, Çâk. d. 22.

आगति *âgati*, i.e. *â-gam* + *ti*, f. **1.** Arrival, Çiç. 9, 43. **2.** Concern, Daçak. in Chr. 193, 9 (that you have something to do with the theft).—**Comp.** *Gata-*, f. literally, coming and going, i.e. origin and disappearance, Râm. 2, 110, 1.

आगत्व *â-ga* + *tva* (vb. *gam*), n. Concern, Dacak. in Chr. 193, 4 (*tadâgatvena châham apadeçyah*, And you will denounce that I have to do with that; *châ°* must be read instead of *nâ°*).

आगन्तु *âgantu*, i.e. *â-gam* + *tu*, adj. **1.** One who arrives, Hit. 18, 2. **2.** Incidental, adventitious.

आगन्तुक *âgantu* + *ka*. **I.** adj. **1.** Arriving. **2.** Incidental. **II.** m. **1.** A stranger, Hit. 70, 12. **2.** An estray (Jur.), Yâjń. 2, 163. **3.** A vagabond, Daçak. in Chr. 181, 4.

आगम *â-gam* + *a*, m. **1.** Arrival, Râm. 2, 25, 19. **2.** Occurrence, Yâjń. 2, 92. **3.** Stream, Man. 8, 252. **4.** Afflux of wealth, Bhartṛ. 2, 39. **5.** Report, Yâjń. 2, 212. **6.** Knowledge, Râm. 6, 4, 30. **7.** Art, Mâlav. 15, d. 16. **8.** Sacred science, Kir. 5, 22. **9.** A work on sacred science, Kir. 5, 18. **10.** A precept, MBh. 3, 1163. **11.** A legal title, Man. 8, 202. —**Comp.** *An-*, m. not returning, MBh. 3, 8868. *Artha-*, m. revenue, Hit. Pr. d. 18. *Jalada-*, m. the approach of the rainy season, Nal. 21, 4. *Dina-*, m. daybreak, Hariv. 4287. *Dus-*, m. illegal afflux of wealth, MBh. 5, 1513. *Dhana-*, m. afflux of wealth, Man. 8, 347. *Dharma-*, m. a code of law, Mârk. P. 23, 36. *Pushpa-*, m. spring, Ṛit. 6, 34. *Hima-*, m. winter.

आगमन *â-gam+ana*, n. **1.** Coming, arrival, Nal. 3, 21. **2.** Origin, Râm. 4, 2, 29. **3.** Sexual intercourse, Râjat. 5, 399.—**Comp.** *An-*, m. non-returning, Pańch. 89, 8.

आगमनतस् *âgamana+tas*, adv. In consequence of the arrival, Indr. 5, 23 (thus to be read).

आगमवन्त् *âgama+vant*, adj., f. *vatî*, Having sexual intercourse, MBh. 1, 3025.

आगमापायिन् *âgamâpâyin*, i.e. *âgama-apâya+in*, adj. Coming and going, Bhag. 2, 14.

आगस् *âgas*, n. Crime, Man, 9, 241; fault, Çiç. 9, 60; sin, Ragh. 2, 32.—**Comp.** *An-*, adj. faultless, Brâhmaṇav. 2, 14. *Kṛita-*, adj. guilty, Amar. 43. *A-kṛita-*, adj. innocent, Râm. 1, 7, 13. *Nis-*, adj. innocent, Râjat. 5, 172.

आगस्त्य *âgastya*, i.e. *agasti+ya* or *agastya+a*, adj. Referring to Agasti, or Agastya, MBh. 1, 442.

आगामिन् *âgâmin*, i.e. *â-gam+in*, adj., f. *nî*. **1.** Arriving. **2.** Future, next, Pańch. 169, 8.

आगार *âgâra* (perhaps *agâra+a*), n. A house, Daçak. in Chr. 187, 1.—**Comp.** *Agni-*, m. a building for keeping the sacred fire, Man. 4, 58. *Antar-*, m. a private chamber, Yâjń. 2, 31. *Âyudha-*, n. an arsenal, Man. 9, 280. *Kûṭa-*, n. an apartment on the top of a house, Râm. 5, 12, 45. *Koça-*, or *kosha-*, m. and n. a treasury, Râm. 6, 111, 52. *Koshṭha-*, m. and n. a treasury, Man. 9, 280. *Kautuka-*, m., n. a nuptial apartment, Kumâras. 7, 94. *Garbha-*, the sanctuary of a temple, Kathâs. 7, 71. *Deva-*, and *devatâ-*, m. a temple, Râm. 2, 71, 36; Man. 9, 280. *Prekshâ-*, a temporary structure consisting of stalls for spectators. *Bandha-a-*, a jail, Daçak. in Chr. 197, 17. *Bhâṇḍa-*, I. m. a store-room. II. n. a treasury, Râjat. 5, 10. *Muktâ-*, n. the pearl oyster.

आगुरव *âgurava*, i.e. *agurû+a*, adj., f. *vî*, Produced by agallochum, Çiç. 4, 52.

आग्नीध्र *âgnîdhra*, i.e. *agni-indh+ra+a*, m. A priest (who kindles the sacrificial fire?).

आग्नेय *âgneya*, i.e. *agni+eya*. **I.** adj., f. *yî*, Belonging or relating to fire or the deity of fire, Man. 9, 310. **II.** m. pl. The name of a people.

आग्रयण *âgrayaṇa* (from *agra*). **I.** n. Offering of new grain, MBh. 3, 14188, and in the vedic literature; in the classic books it is spelled *âgrâyaṇa*, e.g. Râm. 3, 22, 6; Yâjń. 1, 25; Man. 6, 10, Lois. **II.** m. A name of Agni.

आग्रह *â-grah+a*, m. **1.** Favour, Kumâras. 5, 7. **2.** Pertinacity, Çukasapt. 6; 8; Kathâs. 25, 9.—**Comp.** *Dus-*, m. blameable pertinacity, Bhâg. P. 3, 5, 43.

आग्रहिका *â-grah+ikâ*, f. (of *aka*) Help, Daçak. in Chr. 188, 19.

आग्रायण *âgrâyaṇa*, see *âgrayaṇa*.

आघात *âghâta*, i.e. *â-han*, Caus. + *a*, m. **1.** Beating, Râjat. 5, 417. **2.** A stroke, Bhartṛ. 2, 83. **3.** A cast, Râjat. 5, 463. **4.** A gust, Râjat. 5, 330. **5.** Killing, Bhartṛ. 2, 60 (read *prâṇâ°*). **6.** A slaughter-house, Mṛichchh. 161, 11. **7.** An execution-place, Hit. iv. d. 64.—**Comp.** *Taṭa-*, m. butting at a bank or mound, Kumâras. 2, 50. *Paksha-*, m. Hemiplegy. *Çara-*, m. shooting with a bow.

आघृणि *âghṛiṇi*, i.e. *â-ghṛi+ni*, adj. Radiant, Lass. 99, 5 (read *pûshann-âghṛiṇe*)=Rigv. iii, 62, 7.

आघोषणा *âghoshaṇâ*, i.e. *â-ghush* + *ana*, f. A proclamation, Pańch. 261, 9.

आघ्राणतस् *âghrâṇatas*, i.e. *â-ghrâ* + *ana* + *tas*, adv. By smelling, Kathâs. 13, 64.

आङ्ग *âṅga*, i.e. 3. *aṅga* + *a* adj., f. *gî*, An inhabitant of Anga, MBh. 1, 3772.

आङ्गारक *âṅgâraka*, i.e. *aṅgâra* + *ka*, n. A multitude of firebrands, Pańch. iii. d. 166.

आङ्गिरस *âṅgirasa*, i.e. *aṅgiras* + *a*, patronym., f. *sî*, A descendant of Angiras.

आचमन *â-cham* + *ana*, n. Rinsing the mouth, Yâjń. 1, 242.

आचरण *âcharaṇa*, i.e. *â-char* + *ana*, n. **1.** Arrival, Chr. 287, 3 = Rigv. i. 48, 3. **2.** Conduct, MBh. 15, 312.

आचाम *âchâma*, i.e. *â-cham* + *a*, m. The water or scum of boiled rice.

आचार *âchâra*, i.e. *â-char* + *a*, m. **1.** Rule of conduct, Man. 2, 69. **2.** Good custom, good conduct, Sâv. 6, 16. **3.** Conduct, Râm. 6, 10, 24. **4.** Sacred usage, Ragh. 2, 10. **5.** Use, Çâk. d. 100. **6.** Rule, MBh. 3, 166.—Comp. *Dakshiṇa-*, adj. conducting one's self honestly, MBh. 4, 167. *Duḥkha-*, adj., f. *râ*, one who is difficult to deal with, MBh. 4, 274. *Dus-*, I. m. bad conduct, ib. 12, 4539. II. adj., f. *râ*, following bad customs, Man. 4, 157. *Kâma-*, adj. following one's own will, Daçak. in Chr. 200, 8. *Sadâchâra* i.e. *sant-* (ptcple. pres. of 1. *as*), m. 1. approved usage, Man. 2, 18. 2. virtuous conduct.

आचारतस् *âchâra* + *tas*, adv. From immemorial custom, Man. 1, 110.

आचारवन्त् *âchâra* + *vant*, adj., f. *vatî*, Virtuous, Râm. 5, 21, 9.—Comp. *Sadâchâra* + *vant*, i.e. *sant-* (see *âchâra*), adj. one who observes the approved usages, Man. 4, 158.

आचार्य *âchârya*, i.e. *âchâra* + *ya*, m. A spiritual guide or teacher; he who invests the student with the sacrificial thread and instructs him in the Vedas, etc., Man. 2, 40.—Comp. *Kula-*, m. a family priest, Bhâg. P. 9, 1, 9. *Nâṭya-*, m. a dancing master, Mṛichchh. 49, 2.

आचार्यक *âchârya* + *ka*, n. in *nâṭya-*, Teaching the scenic art, i.e. dancing and acting, Pańch. iii. d. 268.

आचार्यता *âchârya* + *tâ*, f., and

आचार्यत्व *âchârya* + *tva*, n. The condition of a teacher, Chr. 28, 32; Çiç. 9, 87.

आचार्यवन्त् *âchârya* + *vant*, adj. Having a teacher, Vedântas. in Chr. 216, 12.

आच्छाद *âchchhâda*, i.e. *â-chhad* + *a*, m. Cloth, Man. 7, 126.

आच्छादकत्व *âchchhâdaka* + *tva*, i.e. *â-chhad* + *aka* + *tva*, n. Covering, Vedântas. in Chr. 204, 22.

आच्छादन *âchchhâdana*, i. e. *â-chhad* + *ana*, n. **1.** Covering, Pańch, 22, 17. **2.** Cloth, Man. 3, 59.

आच्छादिन् *âchchhâdin*, i. e. *â-chhad* + *in*, adj., f. *nî*, Covering, Çâk. d. 18.

आज *âja*, i.e. 2. *aja* + *a*, adj. **1.** Coming from goats. **2.** Made of goat's flesh, Râm. 2, 91, 66.

आजनन *â-jan* + *ana*, n., and

आजाति *âjâti*, i.e. *â-jan* + *ti*, f., New birth, transmigration, MBh. 1, 4561; Man. 4, 166.

आजानेय *âjâneya*, i.e. *â-jan+i+eya*, I. adj, f. *yî*, Of good race, MBh. 2, 1733. II. m. A horse of good breed, draup. 7, 10.

आजि *âji*, i.e. *aj+i*, f. and m. 1. Battle, Arj. 10, 74. 2. Level ground, field of battle, Chr. 36, 12.

आजिहीर्षु *âjihîrshu*, i.e. *â-jihîrsha*, desider. of *hṛi* + *u*, adj. Desiring to fetch, with acc., MBh. 3, 11078.

आजीव *â-jîv+a*, m. 1. Livelihood, MBh. 14, 956. 2. Profession, Daçak. in Chr. 180, 8.—Comp. *Raṅga-*, m. 1. a painter. 2. an actor. *Strî-*, m. one who subsists by (the harlotry of) a wife, Man. 11, 63.

आजीवन *â-jîv+ana*, n. Livelihood, Böhtl. Ind. Spr. 1264.

आजीव्य *âjîvya*, i.e. *âjîva+ya*, I. adj. Granting livelihood, MBh. 14, 1330. II. n. Provisions, MBh. 3, 8452.—Comp. *Su-*, adj. yielding an easy subsistence, Man. 7, 69.

ऽआज्ञत्व *-âjñatva* in *a-khaṇḍita-*, i.e. *a-khaṇḍita-âjña*, from *âjñâ*, +*tva*, n. The whole authority, Râjat. 6, 229.

आज्ञा *â-jñâ*, f. 1. An order, Râjat. 5, 3. 2. Authority, Bhartṛ. 2, 40.—Comp. *An-*, f. want of assent, Man. 9, 199.

आज्ञाकर *âjñâ-kara*, m., f. *rî*, A servant, Çâk. 110, 14.

आज्ञाकरत्व *âjñâkara+tva*, n. The office of a servant, Vikr. d. 60.

आज्य *âjya*, i.e. *â-añj+ya*, n. Butter in a liquid state, which is poured on a sacrificial fire.—Comp. *Vara-*, n. choicest liquid butter.

आज्यप *âjya-pa* (vb. 1.*pâ*), m. The Pitṛis or Manes of the Vaiçyas, Man. 3, 197.

आज्यभुज् *âjya-bhuj*, m. A name of Agni, Râm. 3, 20, 38.

आञ्छ् *ÂÑCHH*, i. 1, Par. To stretch.

आञ्जन *âñjana*, i.e. *â-añj+ana*, n. and f. *nî*, Ointment.

आटविक *âṭavika*, i.e. *aṭavi+ika*, m. 1. One who lives in forests, MBh. 3, 15255. 2. A forest keeper.

आटोप *âṭopa*, m. 1. Inflation. 2. Pride, Pañch. i. d. 229; 46, 4.—Comp. *Sa-*, adj. 1. swollen, big, Pañch. 93, 8. 2. Proud. Acc. *pam*, adv. arrogantly, proudly, Hit. 58, 15.

आडम्बर *âḍambara*, m. A drum, Râm. 5, 13, 51 (where erroneously is read *âḍampara*).

आढक *âḍhaka* (a transformation of *ardha+ka*), m.n. A measure of grain, equal to 7 lb. 11 oz. avoirdupois, Hit. Pr. d. 19.

आढ्य *âḍhya*, i.e. probably a transformation of *ṛidh+a+ya*. adj., f. *yâ*. 1. Wealthy, Chr. 61, 38. 2. Abounding in.—Comp. *Ratna-*, adj. abounding in jewels.

आढ्यता *âḍhya+tâ*, f. Wealth, Râjat. 5, 272.

आत् *ât* (the regular abl. sing. n. of the pronoun *idam*) adv. Then, Chr. 293, 5=Rigv. i. 87, 5.

आतङ्क *âtaṅka*, i.e. *â-tañch+a*, m. 1. Sickness, Yâjñ. 3, 245. 2. Affliction, Vikr. 41, 20. 3. Agitation, fear.—Comp. *Nashṭa-âtaṅka+m*, adv. fearless, Çâk. d. 14 n. *Nis-*, adj. 1. without ailment, Dev. 12, 30. 2. not causing ailment, MBh. 2, 285.

आततायिन् *âtatâyin*, i.e. *â-tata* (vb. *tan*) +*vin* (*y* instead of *v* as in *kiyant* for *kim+vant*), I. adj. Assailing, Chr. 3, 1. II. m. A felon, a murderer, a thief, Man. 8, 350.

आतप *â-tap+a*, m. **1.** Sunshine, Pañch. ii. d. 136. **2.** Heat of the sun, Çâk. 31, 8.—Comp. *An-*, adj. shadowy, Bhartṛ. 2, 86. *Bâla-*, m. the rays of the rising sun, Man. 4, 69. *Sûrya-*, m. sunshine, Pañch. 121, 13; heat of the sun, Ṛit. 1, 10.

आतपत्र *âtapa-tra* (vb. *trâ*), n. A parasol, Kir. 5, 39.—Comp. *Uchchhilîndhra-*, i.e. *ud-çilîndhra-*, adj., f. *râ*, having raised mushrooms instead of parasols, Megh. 11.

आतपवन्त् *âtapa+vant*, adj., f. *vatî*, Irradiated by the sun.

आतिथेय *âtitheya*, i.e. *atithi+eya*, I. adj., f. *yî*. **1.** Proper for a guest, Çâk. 7, 11. **2.** Hospitable, Ragh. 12, 25. II. n. Hospitality, Man. 3, 18.

आतिथ्य *âtithya*, i.e. *atithi+ya*, n. Hospitable salutation, Chr. 13, 8.

आतिरैक्य *âtiraikya*, i.e. *atireka+ya*, n. Having some redundant member, Man. 11, 50.

आतुर *âtura*, adj., f. *râ*. **1.** Diseased, Râm. 3, 55, 36. **2.** Wounded, Râm. 3, 50, 19, **3.** Agitated by a morbid desire; *pradharshayitum âturaḥ*, Desirous to violate her, Nal. 11, 36.—Comp. *An-*, adj. 1. free from illness, Man. 2, 187. 2. indefatigable, Ragh. 1, 21.

आत्तगन्ध *âtta-gandha*, i.e. *â-datta-* (vb. *dâ*), adj. Strangled, Çâk. 93, 2.

ऽआत्म *-âtma*, A substitute for *âtman* when latter part of compound words, e.g. *pratyaya-*, adj. Trustworthy, Râm. 2, 109, 19.

ऽआत्मक *-âtmaka*, i.e. *âtman+ka*, adj., f. *mikâ*, A substitute for *âtman*, when latter part of a comp. adj., e.g. *ashṭâdaçâtmaka*, i. e. *ashṭâ-daçan-âtmaka*, adj. Eighteenfold, Râm. 1, 13, 30. *ubhaya-*, adj. Having the nature of both, Man. 2, 92. *karuṇa-*, adj. Compassionate, Râm. 1, 10, 6. *kâla-*, adj. Governed by fate, MBh. 13, 52 sqq. *dâha-*, adj. Easily flashing up, Çâk. d. 40. *vishaya-*, adj. Sensual, Man. 2, 29. *sadasad-*, i.e. *sant-a-sant-* (cf. vb. 1. *as*), adj. Having the nature of entity and non-entity, Man. 1, 11.

आत्मकाम *âtmakâma*, i.e. *âtman-kam+a*, adj., f. *mâ*, Selfish, Râm. 2, 70, 10.

आत्मकीय *âtmakîya*, i.e. *âtman+ka+îya*, adj. Own, MBh. 1, 4712.

आत्मज *âtmaja*, i.e. *âtman-ja* (vb. *jan*), I. m. A son, Man. 7, 14. II. f. *jâ*, A daughter, Râm. 1, 1, 69.—Comp. *Dharma-*, m. epithet of Yudhishṭhira, Lass. 15, 11. *Nanda-*, I. m. a name of Kṛishṇa, Gît. 8, 11. II. f. *jâ*, a name of Durgâ, MBh. 4, 179. *Varuṇa-*, f. *jâ*, spirituous liquor.

आत्मज्ञ *âtmajña*, i.e. *âtman-jña* (vb. *jñâ*), adj., f. *ñâ*, Knowing the Supreme Being, Vedântas. in Chr. 219, 5.—Comp. *An-*, adj. foolish, Çak. 78, 15.

आत्मन् *âtman*, i.e. probably **avâ* (=*vâ*) +*tman* (cf. ἀϋτμήν, ἀϋτμή, ἀτμή, ἀτμός), m. **1.** Breath. **2.** The soul. Bhâshâp. 97. **3.** One's own self, Man. 4, 254. **4.** Self, own; used, but only in the sing., as reflective pronoun of all the three persons, e.g. *darçayâtmânam*, Show thyself, Nal. 11, 8. *gopâyanti kulastriyaḥ* । *âtmânam âtmanâ*, Virtuous wives protect themselves by means of themselves, Nal. 18, 8. **5.** The instr. sing. compounded with following ordinal numbers denotes one's self as making up the number, e.g. *âtmanâ-saptama*, Himself as the seventh, i.e. he with six. **6.** The body. **7.** Intellect, understanding. **8.** The soul of the universe, Vedântas. in Chr. 202, 4. **9.** The initial *â* when preceded by *e* or *o* is sometimes in vedic and epic writings irregularly dropped, e.g. Draup. 5, 9.—**Comp.** I. When latter part it denotes often, 1. nature, mind, e.g. *Kṛita-*, adj. whose mind is improved, Pańch. ii. d. 15. *A-kṛita-*, adj. whose mind is not improved, Man. 6, 73. *Jita-*, adj. one who has subdued his mind, who restrains himself, Pańch. 131, 19. *A-jita-*, adj. one who has not subdued his mind, Man. 7, 34. *Prîta-*, adj. with an affectionate mind, Man. 1, 60. *Çânta-* (vb. *çam*), adj. with a tranquil mind, Man. 1, 52. 2. natural disposition, e.g. *karmâtman*, i.e. *karman-*, adj. having a natural disposition for action, Man. 2, 53. *Kâma-*, adj. voluptuous, Man. 7, 27. *Chala-*, adj. unsteady, Râm. 4, 55, 7. *Dharma-*, adj. just, Râm. 1, 1, 29. *Pâpa-*, adj. wicked, Pańch. 37, 19. *Mahâ-*, adj. magnanimous, Pańch. ii. d. 153. *Sûtra-*, m. having the nature of a thread, Vedântas. in Chr. 208, 3. 3. *Antar-*, m. the soul, Râjat. 5, 194. *Kevala-*, m. being the absolute unity, Kumâras. 2, 4. *Chatur-*, adj. having four faces, Râjat. 5, 25. *Chhâyâ-*, m. an image, Megh. 41. *Jagat-*, m. the soul of the world, Râm. 6, 82, 153. *Jîva-*, m. the individual soul, Bhâg. P. 6, 16, 2. *Datta-*, (vb. *dâ*), adj. one who has given himself (as a son to another), Yâjń. 2, 131. *Dvâdaçâtman-*, i.e. *dvâdaçan-*, adj. appearing in twelve forms, MBh. 3, 156. *Parama-*, m. the universal soul. *Bhâvita-* (vb. *bhû*), adj. 1. intent upon. 2. having obtained (the union with) the universal soul, Pańch. iii. d. 63. *Bhûta-*, m. 1. the elementary or vital principle. 2. the body. 3. Brahman. 4. Çiva. 5. war. *Manda-*, adj. dull, foolish. *Viçva-*, m. the soul of the universe, a name of Vishṇu. — Cf. O. H. G. atum, A.S. aedhm, and see above.

आत्मनीन *âtman + îna*, adj. 1. Appropriate. 2. Suitable (as diet).

आत्मंभू *âtmabhû*, i.e. *âtman-bhû*, adj. Self-existing, epithet of Brahman, Çâk. d. 186; of Vishṇu, Çiva and Kâma.

आत्मभूत *âtmabhûta*, i. e. *âtman-bhûta* (vb. *bhû*), adj. Attached to one's person.

आत्मंभरि *âtmaṁbhari*, i. e. *âtman-bhṛi + i*, adj. Selfishly voracious, Pańch. ed. orn. i. d. 215.

आत्मंभरित्व *âtmaṁbhari + tva*, n. Selfishness, Kathâs. 26, 228.

आत्मवत्ता *âtmavattâ*, i.e. *âtmavant + tâ*, f. Self-control, Man. 11, 86.

आत्मवन्त् *âtmavant*, i.e. *âtman + vant*, adj., f. *vatî*. 1. One who has subdued his senses; endowed with self-control, Râm. 3, 51, 44. 2. Sensible, Man. 5, 43.—**Comp.** *An-*, adj. one who has no self-control, Nal. 20, 31.

आत्मसात् *âtmasât*, i.e. *âtman-sât* (cf. *agnisât*), adv. 1. In one's mind, Man. 6, 25. 2. On one's self, Yâjń. 3, 54. 3. Under one's self, MBh. 3, 493.

आत्मीभाव *âtmîbhâva*, i. e. *âtman-bhû + a*, m. Becoming the universal soul, Bhartṛ. 3, 64.

आत्मीय *âtmîya*, i.e. *âtman + îya*, I. adj., f. *yâ*, Own, poss. pron. of the refl. of all the three persons, Hit. 52, 16; Pańch. 63, 23. II. m. A friend, Bhartṛ. 2, 47.—**Comp.** *An-*, adj. not belonging to one's self, Pańch. 132, 18.

आत्यन्तिक *âtyantika*, i.e. *atyanta + ika*, adj., f. *kî*, Continual, Man. 2, 242.

आत्ययिक *âtyayika*, i.e. *atyaya + ika*, adj. What must be done instantly, Man. 7, 165.

आत्रेय *âtreya*, i.e. *atri + eya*. I. patronym., f. *yî*, A descendant of Atri, MBh. 3, 971. II. f. *yî*, A woman who has bathed after temporary uncleanness, Man. 11, 87.

आथर्वण *âtharvaṇa*, i.e. *atharvan* + *a*, adj., f. *ṇî*, Belonging to the Atharvaveda, Daçak. in Chr. 201, 11.

ऽआद *-âda*, i.e. I. *ad* + *a*, adj., f. *dî*, Eating, e.g. *purushâda*, i.e. *purusha-*, Eating men. *pṛishṭha-mâṁsa-*, m. A backbiter, a slanderer. *mânusha -mâṁsa-*, Eating men's flesh, Hiḍ. 2, 2. II. *â-da* (vb. *dâ*), adj. Taking.

ऽआदक *-âdaka*, i.e. *ad* + *aka*, adj. Eating, e.g. *purusha-*, Eating men, Hiḍ. 2, 30.

आदर *âdara*, i.e. *â-dṛi* + *a*, m. 1. Regard, Kumâras. 6, 13. 2. Concern, Pañch. iii. d. 262. 3. Care, Daçak. in Chr. 180, 10. 4. Love, Pañch. iv. d. 7 (*âdarât*, passionately). 5. Interest, Daçak. in Chr. 190, 8. 6. Respect, Kir. 5, 16.—**Comp**, *Ati-*, m. excessive regard, Pañch. i. d. 463. *An-*, m. carelessness, Pañch. 202, 5, Bhartṛ. 2, 28 (*rât*, easily). *Sa-*, adj., f. *râ*. 1. impassioned, Ṛit. 6, 14. 2. respectful, Kathâs. 2, 67. Acc. sing. *ram*, adv. considerately, Pañch. 33, 16; respectfully, Pañch, 71, 6.

आदर्श *âdarça*, i.e. *â-dṛiç* + *a*, and

आदर्शक *âdarça* + *ka*, m. A mirror, Bhag. 3, 38.

आदातृ *â dâ* + *tṛi*, m. A receiver, Man. 4, 193.—**Comp**. *An-*, m. a non-receiver, Man. 6, 8.

आदान *âdâna*, i.e. *â-dâ* + *ana*, n. 1. Seizing, Vedântas. in Chr. 209, 20. Seizure, Kumâras. 5, 11; Man. 7, 204. 2. Taking, receiving, Man. 11, 15. Receipt, Râjat. 5, 265.—**Comp**. *Adhyayana-*, n. learning the Veda, Man. 11, 62. *Nis-*, adj. not taking, MBh. 3, 8501. *Rasa-*, n. drying up. *Su-*, *n.* taking with justice, Man. 8, 172.

आदानवन्त् *âdâna* + *vant*, adj., f. *vatî*, Taking away, MBh. 3, 8501.

आदायिन् *âdâyin*, i.e. *â-dâ* + *in*, adj., f. *nî*. 1. Taking, MBh. 12, 5969 (*a -sam-mata-*, taking without assent, a thief). 2. Robbing, Man. 7, 123. 3. Bringing, Râjat. 5, 272.

आदि *âdi*, i.e. *âdya*, with *i* for *ya*, 1. m. Beginning, Man. 1, 8; 4, 25. 2. indecl. First, MBh. 2, 2008.—**Comp**. When latter part of a comp. adj. 1. having first, beginning with, e.g. Man. 3, 205, *Daiva-âdi-anta*, beginning and ending with an offering to the gods. 2. other, et-cetera, e.g. Man. 1, 58, *Marîchi-âdîn munîn*, Marîchi and the other Munis (properly, as before 'The Munis beginning with Marîchi'); Man. 3, 104, *Anna-âdi-dâyin*, giving food, etc. 3. the like, Man. 9, 260, *Evam-âdîn . . . kaṇṭakân*, these and the like thorny weeds. 4. more, e.g. Man. 8, 407, *Garbhiṇî dvimâsâdiḥ*, a woman who is pregnant two months or more. These adj. when without subst. are neuters: e.g. Nal. 13, 43, *evam-âdîni . . . vilapya*, lamenting thus and similarly; Hit. 12, 16, *ato 'haṁ bravîmi kaṅkaṇasya tu lobhenety-âdi*, therefore I say, *kaṅkaṇasya* et -cetera, i.e. the verse beginning with *kaṅkaṇasya tu lobhena*. Man. 8, 31, the masc. is used.

ऽआदिक *-âdi* + *ka*, adj., f. *kâ*, a substitute for *âdi* as latter part of a compound adj., e.g. Man. 2, 143, *agnishṭoma-âdikân makhân*, the agnishṭoma and the other sacrifices.

आदितस् *âdi* + *tas*, adv. 1. From the beginning, Chr. 11, 22. 2. First, Man. 1, 34.—**Comp**. *Râma-darçana -âditas*, after having seen Râma, Râm. 1, 51, 7.

आदित्य *âditya*, i.e. *aditi* + *ya*, m. 1. The name of a class of deities, sons of Aditi, Man. 3, 284. 2. The sun, Vedântas. in Chr. 205, 24. 3. A deity in general, MBh. 18, 215.—**Comp**. *Ati-*, adj. surpassing the sun, Megh. 44. *Su-gandha-*, m. a proper name, Râjat. 5, 268.

आदित्सु *âditsu*, i.e. *â-ditsa*, desid. of *dâ* + *u*, adj. Desirous to take, Hit. ii. d. 106.

ऽआदिन् *-âdin*, i.e. *ad* + *in*, adj., f. *nî*, Eating, e.g. *ekânna-*, i.e. *eka-anna-*, adj. Eating the food of one person only, Man. 2, 188.

आदिम *âdi* + *ma*, adj., f. *mâ*, First, Bhâshâp. 20; 115.

आदिमन्त् *âdi* + *mant*, adj., f. *matî*, Having a beginning, Yâjń. 3, 183.—Comp. *An-*, adj. without any beginning, Bhag. 13, 12.

आदिश् *â-diç*, f. Advise.

आदिष्टिन् *âdishṭin*, i.e. *â-dishṭa* + *in* (vb. *diç*), m. A student, Man. 5, 88.

आदीपक *â-dîp* + *aka*, m. An incendiary, MBh. 12, 3215.

आदेश *âdeça*, i.e. *â-diç* + *a*, m. **1.** Report, tidings, Yâjń. 2, 304. **2.** Instruction, Vedântas. in Chr. 216, 15. **3.** Order, Râm. 3, 53, 29. **4.** Prediction, Man. 9, 250.

आदेशक *âdeçaka*, i.e. *â-diç* + *aka*, adj. Announcing.—Comp. *Çiva-*, m. a fortuneteller, Mâlav. 69, 13.

आदेशतस् *âdeça* + *tas*, adv. According to a command, Pańch. ii. d. 199 (with the gen.).

आदेशन *âdeçana*, i.e. *â-diç* + *ana*, n. Performance, Man. 2, 173.

आदेशिन् *âdeçin*, i.e. *â-diç* + *in*, adj., f. *nî*, Commanding, Ragh. 4, 68 (*kapola-pâṭala-*, Commanding paleness to the cheeks of . . ., i.e. frightening).

आद्य *âdya*, i.e. *ât* + *ya* for *iya* (cf. *turya* = *turiya*, *vasyaṁs* = *vasiyaṁs*, etc.), adj., f. *yâ*. **1.** First, Man. 7, 92. **2.** Preeminent, MBh. 1, 8130.—Comp. *Âdya-âdya*, each preceding, Man. 1, 20. Like *Âdi* (q. cf.), other, et-cetera, e.g. *anna-*, adj. food, etc., Pańch. i. d. 188.

आद्यन्तवन्त् *âdyantavant*, i. e. *âdi-anta* + *vant*, adj., f. *vatî*, Having beginning and end, Bhag. 5, 22.

आद्रिसार *âdrisâra*, i.e. *adri-sâra* (see *sâra*) + *a*, adj. Of iron, Râm. 6, 18, 31.

आधमन *âdhamana*, i.e. *â-dhmâ* + *ana*, n. A pledge, Man. 8, 165.—Comp. *Yoga-*, n. a fraudulent pledge.

आधान *âdhâna*, i.e. *â-dhâ* + *ana*, n. **1.** Adding, Man. 2, 176. **2.** Preparing the holy fire, MBh. 3, 8194. **3.** Lighting the nuptial fire, Man. 5, 186. **4.** Conception, Megh. 3. **5.** Pledging, Yâjń. 2, 238. **6.** Using, Ragh. 1, 24.—Comp. *Garbha-*, n. a ceremony performed previous to conception. *Purîsha-*, n. the strait-gut.

आधायक *âdhâyaka*, i.e. *â-dhâ* + *aka*, adj. Bestowing.

आधार *âdhâra*, i.e. *â-dhṛi* + *a*, m. **1.** A prop, support, Râm. 5, 3, 77; Vedântas. in Chr. 202, 4. **2.** A canal, Yâjń. 3, 144. **3.** A basin round the foot of a tree, Çâk. d. 14. **4.** A dike, Ragh. 5, 6. —Comp. *Jala-*, or *toya-*, m. a reservoir of water, Yâjń. 3, 144; Çâk. d. 14.

आधि *âdhi*, m., i.e. **I.** *â-dhâ* (cf. *nidhi*), A pledge, Man. 8, 143. **II.** *â-dhyai*, Mental agony, Daçak. in Chr. 184, 7.

आधिक्य *âdhikya*, i.e. *adhika* + *ya*, n. **1.** Excess, Vedântas. in Chr. 206, 19. **2.** Preeminence, Râm. 5, 90, 24. **3.** Superiority, Man. 7, 169.

आधिदैविक *âdhidaivika*, i. e. *adhi-deva* + *ika*, adj. Treating of the deities, Man. 6, 83.

आधिपत्य *âdhipatya* i.e. *adhipati* + *ya*, n. Sovereign dominion, Man. 12, 100.

आधिवेदनिक *âdhivedanika*, i. e. *adhi-vedana* + *ika*, n. Property given to a first wife upon marrying a second.

आधोरण *âdhoraṇa*, i.e. *â-dhor* + *ana*, m. The driver of an elephant, Daçak. in Chr. 188, 17.

आध्यात्मिक *âdhyâtmika*, i. e. *adhi-âtman* + *ika*, adj., f. *kâ* and *kî*, Referring to or treating of the universal soul; sacred, Man. 2, 117.

आध्वनिक *âdhvanika*, i.e. *adhvan* + *ika*, adj. Travelling, MBh. 1, 3031.

आनक *ânaka*. m. A drum, Bhag. 1, 13.—Comp. *Çata-*, m. a cemetery.

आनडुह *ânaḍuha*, i.e. *anaḍuh* + *a*, adj. Coming from a bull (as its flesh or hide).

आनति *ânati*, i.e. *â-nam* + *ti*, f. 1. Bowing, Amar. 22. Salutation, Kathâs. 23, 17. 2. Homage, Râjat. 5, 215.

आनन *ânana*, i.e. *an* + *ana*, n. 1. The mouth, the face, Ṛit. 6, 30. 2. A point, Râm. 6, 79, 69.—Comp. *Chatur-*, adj. having four faces, Bhâg. P. 5, 1, 30. *Daçânana*, i.e. *daçan-*, adj. epithet of Râvaṇa, Râm. 3, 39, 8. *Nâga-*, m. a peacock, Pañch. i. d. 175 (perhaps to be changed to *nâgâçana*, i.e. *nâga-açana*). *Pañchânana*, i.e. *pañchan-*. 1. Çiva. 2. used at the end of names of scholars, Chr. 234, 6. 3. f. *nî*, perhaps a name of Durgâ. *Mahâ-*, adj. having a great mouth, Hiḍ. 3, 2. *Su-hasa-*, adj. having a cheerfully smiling face.

आनन्तर्य *ânantarya*, i.e. *an-antara* + *ya*, n. Absence of an interval, Man. 10, 28. Instr. *yeṇa*, Instantly, Râm. 4, 23, 6.

आनन्त्य *ânantya*, i.e. *ananta* + *ya*, n. Eternity, Man. 3, 266.

आनन्द *â-nand* + *a*, m. 1. Joy, Râm. 1, 1, 17. 2. Sensual pleasure, Vedântas. in Chr. 209, 20. 3. Happiness, bliss, ib. 202, 3; 5.—Comp. *Nis-*, adj., f. *dâ*, joyless, Râm. 2, 47, 10. *Parama-*, m. 1. the highest bliss. 2. the universal soul.

आनन्दक *â-nand* + *aka*, adj. Delighting, Hit. i. d. 204 v. r.

आनन्दन *â-nand* + *ana*, n. Delight, Hit. i. d. 204.

आनन्दमय *ânanda* + *maya*, adj., f. *yî*, Full of joy or happiness, Kathâs. 23, 85; Vedântas. in Chr. 204, 22.

आनन्दयितृ *ânanday'tṛi*, i.e. *â-nand*, Caus. + *tṛi*, m., f. *trî*, n. Giving pleasure, Ragh. 14, 26.

आनन्दिन् *ânandin*, i.e. *ânanda* + *in*, adj., f. *nî*, Joyful, Râm. 6, 11, 45.

आनयन *ânayana*, i.e. *â-nî* + *ana*, n. 1. Bringing near, Râm. 1, 12, 27. 2. Escorting, Çâk. 48, 21.

आनर्त *ânarta*, m., pl. The name of a people and their country (also sing.), Râm. 4, 43, 13.

आनाथ्य *ânâthya*, i.e. *a-nâtha* + *ya*, n. Want of protection, Kathâs. 3, 8.

आनाय *ânâya*, i.e. *â-nî* + *a*, m. A net.

आनायिन् *ânâyin*, i.e. *ânâya* + *in*, m. A fisher, Ragh. 16, 55.

आनाह *ânâha*, i.e. *â-nah* + *a*, m. 1. Obstruction. 2. Length.

आनीति *â-nî* + *ti*, f. Bringing near, Râm. 1, 8, 29.

आनुकूल्य *ânukûlya*, i.e. *anukûla* + *ya*, n. 1. Suitability, Yâjñ. 1, 74. 2. Compliance with (gen.), Râjat. 5, 132. 3. Favour, Kathâs. 19, 1.

आनुपूर्व *ânupûrva*, i.e. *anupûrva* + *a*,

I. n. Regular succession, order, Man. 2, 41. II. f. *rvî*, see the next.

आनुपूर्व्य *ânupûrvya*, i.e. *anupûrva* + *ya*, n. and fem. *vî*, Regular succession, order, Man. 9, 149; Râm. 3, 70, 20.

आनुलोम्य *ânulomya*, i.e. *anu-loma* + *ya*, n. Direct or natural order, Man. 10, 5.

आनुवेश्य *ânuveçya*, i.e. *anu-veça* + *ya*, m. A neighbour who lives next but one, Man. 8, 392.

आनुषक् *ânushak*, i.e. *anu-sañj*, adv. Continually, Lass. 98, 7 = Rigv. v. 9, 1.

आनुषङ्गिक *ânushañgika*, i.e. *anushañga* + *ika*, adj. Connected, adherent, accustomed to live (there), Pañch. 10, 5.

आनूप *ânûpa*, i.e. *anûpa* + *a*. I. adj. Watery, marshy. II. m. Any animal frequenting marshy places.

आनृण्य *ânṛiṇya*, i.e. *an-ṛiṇa* + *ya*, n. Freedom from debt; acc. with *gam*, to pay, Man. 4, 257.

आनृण्यता *ânṛiṇya* + *tâ*, f. Freedom from debt, Râm. 2, 24, 32.

आनृशंस्य *ânṛiçaṁsya*, i.e. *a-nṛiçaṁsa* + *ya*, n. Mildness, Man. 8, 411.

आन्तर *ântara*, i.e. *antara* + *a*, m. A subject, MBh. 12, 3346; 3913.

आन्तरिक्ष *ântariksha* and आन्तरीक्ष *ântarîksha*, i.e. *antarîksha* + *a*, adj. Proceeding from the air or sky; airy, MBh. 2, 1636; Râm. 2, 25, 20.

आन्दोलन *ândolana* = *andolana*, n. A swinging motion, Chaurap. 12.

आन्ध्य *ândhya*, i.e. *andha* + *ya*, n. Blindness, Vedantâs. in Chr. 218, 16.

आन्वाहिक *ânvâhika*, i.e. *anvaham* + *ika*, adj., f. *kî*, Daily, Man. 3, 67.

आप् *ÂP*, i. 1 and 10; ii. 5, *âpnu*, Par. (in ved. and epic writings also Âtm., MBh. 14, 597. Originally also *ăp*; cf. the ved. desiderative *ap* + *sa*; Lat. ăpiscor, ops, opto, cœpi, copia; πρέπειν, i.e. originally προ-ἔπειν). **1.** To attain, Ragh. 8, 24. **2.** To incur, Man. 8, 188. **3.** To obtain, Man. 1, 63. *âpta* (cf. Lat. aptus). **1.** Fit, Ragh. 3, 12. **2.** Trusted, Man. 7, 80; just, 8, 63. **3.** Near, Man. 5, 101; a friend, ib. 8, 64. **4.** Large, Man. 7, 79. **Comp.** *An-âpta*, unapt, Man. 8, 294.—Desid. *îpsa*, To desire to obtain, MBh. 1, 1090. *îpsita*. **1.** Desired, Nal. 3, 2. **2.** Loved, Nal. 1, 4. **3.** Ordained, Man. 2, 48. n. A wish, Kathâs. 22, 170. **Comp.** *Yathâ-îpsita*, adj. as desired, Sund. 4, 5; acc. *tam*, adv. 1. According to one's wish. 2. Willingly. 3. Independently.—With the prep. अभि *abhi*, desid. To desire, Man. 136; with infin., Chr. 11, 14.—With अव *ava*. **1.** To attain, Kathâs. 1, 27. **2.** To meet, Kathâs. 3, 46. **3.** To obtain, Vikr. d. 105. *an-avâpta*, adj. Not obtained, Man. 9, 209.—With प्रत्यव *prati-ava*, To recover, Çiç, 5, 40.—With समव *sam-ava*. **1.** To meet, Râm, 4, 44, 71. **2.** To incur, Chr. 23, 20. **3.** To obtain, Râm. 3, 55, 40.—With परि *pari*, To cease, MBh. 15, 1073. *paryâpta*. **1.** Adequate, Bhag. 1, 10. **2.** Sufficient, Man. 11, 7. **3.** Enough (no more), Chr. 42, 13. **4.** Full, Kumâras. 7, 26. **5.** Many, Daçak. in Chr. 185, 10. **6.** Large, Man, 3, 40. **Comp.** *A-paryâpta*, adj. inadequate; with infin., Râm. 3, 51, 7. *Ati-*, adj. excessive, Ragh. 15, 18. *Su-*, adj. well finished, Man. 7, 76. *A-paryâptavant*, adj. unable, Ragh. 16, 28.—Desid. **1.** To demand, Man. 8, 161. **2.** To desire, MBh. 1, 5515; Âtm., MBh. 2, 563. **3.** To take care, MBh. 3, 17327. **4.** To defend, MBh. 4, 480.—With प्र *pra*. **1.** To reach, Râm. 3, 22, 37. To attain, Râjat. 5, 57. **2.** To meet, Pańch. i. d. 328. **3.** To incur, Man. 8, 355. **4.** To obtain, Man. 3, 277. **5.** To get in, Man. 11, 263. **6.** To find, Yâjń. 3, 142; Râjat. 5, 406. *prâpta.* **1.** Proper, right, Daçak. in Chr. 188, 4. **2.** Having obtained, Man. 7, 2. *astam̃ prâpta*, Dead, Kathâs. 13, 74. **3.** Having arrived, Nal. 23, 18.—Comp. *A-prâpta*, adj. 1. not finished, pending, Yâjń. 2, 243. 2. not of age, Man. 9, 88. 3. not obtained, Bhâshâp. 114. *Krama-*, adj. obtained by succession, Nal. 12, 49. Comp. ptcple. of the fut. pass., *Dushprâpya*, i.e. *dus-prâpya*, adj. difficult to be attained, Râm. 4, 17, 44.—Caus. *prâpaya.* **1.** To bring, Râm. 4, 62, 19. **2.** To cause to obtain, MBh. 2, 171. **3.** To appoint, Râjat. 5, 424. **4.** To give, Daçak. in Chr. 197, 15.—With अनुप्र *anu-pra.* **1.** To recover, Râm. 1, 1, 80. **2.** To find, Chr. 70, 54. **3.** To incur, Chr. 54, 11. **4.** To imitate, Ragh. 4, 22. **5.** To arrive, Râm. 3, 75, 2. *anuprâpta*, Having attained, MBh. 1, 5874; come, Râm. 3, 27, 9.—With समनुप्र *sam-anu-pra.* **1.** To attain, Râm. 2, 52, 76. **2.** To obtain, MBh. 2, 1616. *samanuprâpta*, Having attained, Râm. 3, 30, 1.—With उपप्र *upa-pra*, To come near, Râm. 3, 75, 17 (the ptcple. of the pf. pass. in active signification).—With संप्र *sam-pra.* **1.** To attain, Râm. 6, 109, 1. **2.** To obtain, Man. 12, 74. *sam̃prâpta*, Having arrived, Man. 3, 99. *a-sam̃prâpya*, Without touching, Chr. 40, 17.—With अनुसंप्र *anu-sam-pra*, To attain, Râm. 3, 68, 7. *anusam̃prâpta*, Having arrived, Râm. 2, 65, 11.—With अभिसंप्र *abhi-sam-pra.* **1.** To attain, Râm. 2, 55, 21. **2.** To obtain, Râm. 4, 3, 27. *abhisam̃prâpta*, Having arrived, MBh. 3, 11366.—With उपसंप्र *upa-sam-pra*, To attain, MBh. 3, 2337. *upasam̃prâpta.* **1.** Having incurred, MBh. 1, 5188. **2.** Come, MBh. 3, 14378.—With वि *vi.* **1.** To pervade, MBh. 12, 124. **2.** To occupy, Bhag. 10, 16. **3.** To fill, Chr. 33, 5. *vyâpta*, That which has inherent properties, e. g. smoke, as invariably accompanied by fire, Bhâshâp. 67. *vyâpya*, n. That which is invariably accompanied by something else, as smoke by fire; the sign or middle term in an inference. Absol. *a-vyâpya*, Not having pervaded, Bhâshâp. 26.—With सम् *sam*, To obtain, Râm. 3, 2, 28. *samâpta*, Finished, Râm. 3, 49, 27. Caus. To finish, Man. 8, 420. Desid. To desire, Râm. 3, 5, 22.—With परिसम् *pari-sam*, To bring to a full conclusion, Bhag. 4, 33. *parisamâpta*, Sufficient, Çâk. d. 105.—Cf. O.H.G. uobjan, and see above.

आप *âpa*, m. One of the eight deities, called Vasus, MBh. 3, 14208.

आपगा *âpagâ*, i.e. *ap + a-ga* (vb. *gam*), f. **1.** A river, Râjat. 5, 140. **2.** The name of a river, MBh. 3, 6038.—Comp. *Sura-*, f. the Ganges, Kir. 5, 40.

आपगेय *âpageya*, i.e. *âpagâ + eya*, patronym. m. The son of a river, a surname of Kṛishṇa, MBh. 2, 1340, and Bhîshma, Chr. 15, 3.

आपण *â-paṇ + a*, m. A market, Daçak. in Chr. 192, 10.—Comp. *Antar-*, m., the interior part of a market, Râm. 1, 5, 8 Gorr.

आपतन *â-pat + ana*, n. **1.** Happening. **2.** Appearing.

आपत्ति *âpatti*, i.e. *â-pad + ti*, f. **1.** Undergoing, obtaining. **2.** Misfortune, Lass. 30, 9.—Comp. *Artha-*, f. presumption (the fifth *pramâṇa* of the Pûrva and Uttara mîmânsâ), Bhâshâp. 142.

आपथी *âpathî* (probably *â-patha*

+*i*). An impediment on a road (?), Chr. 290, 11 = Rigv. i. 64, 11.

आपद् *â-pad*, f. **1.** Calamity, Daçak. in Chr. 194, 14. **2.** Necessity, Man. 9, 82.—**Comp.** *An-*, f. absence of misfortune, Man. 4, 2. *Nis-*, I. f. absence of misfortune, MBh. 12, 9671. II. adj. free from calamity, Ragh. 1, 64.

आपात *âpâta*, i.e. *â-pat* + *a*, m. **1.** Attack, Arj. 7, 10. **2.** Running on, Man. 11, 9; running in, Yâjń. 3, 154. **3.** Throwing down, Megh. 49.

आपाततस् *âpâta* + *tas*, adv. Instantly, Vedântas. in Chr. 202, 10.

आपातिन् *âpâtin*, i.e. *â-pat-in*, adj. f. *nî*, Happening, Kathâs. 18, 49.

आपान *âpâna*, i.e. *â-pâ* + *ana*, n. **1.** A banquet, MBh. 1, 620. **2.** A place for drinking, Râm. 1, 3, 28.

आपीड *â-pîḍ* + *a*, m. **1.** Squeezing. **2.** A chaplet tied on the crown of the head, Daçak. in Chr. 188, 22.—**Comp.** *Gala-*, m. strangling. *Bhuja-*, m. clasping or enfolding in the arms.

आपीडित *âpîḍita*, i.e. *âpîḍa* + *ita*, adj. Adorned with chaplets, Nal. 12, 102.

आपूरण *âpûraṇa*, i.e. *â-pûr* + *ana*, n. Filling, Pańch. 96, 20.

आपोमय *âpomaya*, i.e. *âpas* (plur. of *ap*) + *maya*, adj. Consisting of water, MBh. 1, 6859.

आपोशान *âpoçâna*, i.e. *apo 'çâna* + *a*, n. The name of a prayer beginning with the words *apo 'çâna*, Yâjń. 1, 106.

आप्ति *âp* + *ti*, f. Acquisition, Pańch. ii. d. 49.—**Comp.** *An-*, f. non-effecting of a purpose, Man. 9, 290.

आप्यायन *â-pyây* + *ana*. **I.** adj. **1.** Causing corpulency. **2.** Causing wellbeing. **II.** n. **1.** Satisfying, Man. 3, 211. **2.** Advancement, Man. 3, 213.

आप्लवन *âplavana*, i.e. *â-plu* + *ana*, n. Bathing, MBh. 1, 1814; v.r. Man. 5, 115.

आबन्ध *â-bandh* + *a*, m. A tie or bond.

आबन्धन *â-bandh* + *ana*, n. Girding round, Râm. 2, 23, 31.

आबाध *â-bâdh* + *a*, m. Injury, Man. 4, 51.—**Comp.** *An-*, adj. unobstructed, Râm. 3, 44, 30. *Dus-*, adj. irresistible, MBh. 13, 724. *Nis-*, adj. 1. unmolested, Hiḍ. 4, 12. 2. not injuring, Hariv. 11811.

आब्दिक *âbdika*, i.e. *abda* + *ika*, adj. Yearly, Man. 7, 3. — **Comp.** *Shash-triṁçat-*, adj. lasting thirty-six years, Man. 3, 1.

आभरण *âbharaṇa*, i.e. *â-bhṛi* + *ana*, n. Ornaments, as jewels, etc., Râm. 3, 55, 6.—**Comp.** *Tapta-*, n. an ornament made of refined gold, Râm. 3, 58, 19.

आभा *â-bhâ*, f. **1.** Splendour, light, Pańch. iv. d. 58. **2.** When latter part of a compound adj., often Like; e.g. Râm. 3, 55, 28, *giri-çṛiṅga-âbha*, Like the peak of a mountain.—**Comp.** *Vajra-*, I. adj. like a diamond. II. m. a precious opal.

आभाष *â-bhâsh* + *a*, m., and **आभाषण** *âbhâshaṇa*, i.e. *â-bhâsh* + *ana*, n. Addressing, speaking to, Râm. 3, 26, 12; Râjat. 5, 462.

आभास् *â-bhâs*, f. Light, MBh. 3, 10980.

आभास *â-bhâs* + *a*, m. **1.** Splendour, Râm. 6, 77, 17. **2.** Light, Vedântas. in Chr. 219, 11. **3.** Appearance, Kathâs. 12, 16. **4.** Semblance, Bhâshâp. 70.—Comp. *Rasa-*, m. the semblance of sentiment, as e.g., a sentiment attributed to an irrational animal. *Hetu-*, m. fallacious reason or middle term.

आभिजात्य *âbhijâtya*, i.e. *abhi-jâta* (vb. *jan*) + *ya*, n. Nobility, Râm. 2, 35, 15.

आभिमुख्य *âbhimukhya*, i.e. *abhimukha* + *ya*, n. Front, direction towards, Pańch. i. d. 370 (with *yâ*, to attack).

आभिषेचनिक *âbhishechanika*, i. e. *abhishechana* + *ika*, adj., f. *kî*, Referring or serving to the inauguration of a king, Râm. 6, 112, 69.

आभीर *âbhîra*, m. **1.** The name of a people, MBh. 2, 1192. **2.** The offspring of a Brâhmaṇa by an Ambashṭha woman, Man. 10, 15.

आभील *â-bhî* + *la*, adj. Terrible, MBh. 3, 388.

आभू *â-bhû*, adj. Helping, Chr. 290, 1; 6 = Rigv. i. 64, 1; 6.

आभोग *âbhoga*, i.e. *â-bhuj* + *a*, m. **1.** Crookedness, MBh. 3, 9957; vault, Râm. 2, 65, 3; roundness, Megh. 89. **2.** Fullness, plenty, Çâk. 8, 1. **3.** The expanded hood of the Cobra capella, MBh. 16, 118.—Comp. *Stana-*, m. a man with a breast like a woman's.

आभ्यन्तर *âbhyantara*, i.e. *abhyantara* + *a*, adj. Interior, MBh. 2, 202.—Comp. *Gaṇa-*, m. the member of a corporation, MBh. 3, 154.

आभ्यासिक *âbhyâsika* (with *s* for *ç*), i.e. *abhyâça* + *ika*, adj. Standing near together, MBh. 1, 7577.

ऽआभ्युदयिक *-âbhyudayika*, i. e. *abhyudaya* + *ika*, adj. Causing prosperity, increase, Man. 12, 88.—Comp. *An-*, Not causing prosperity, Mṛichchh. 111, 5.

आम् *âm*, A particle of reminiscence: Ah! Vikr. 38, 17.

आम *âma*, i.e. *am* + *a*, adj., f. *mâ*. **1.** Raw, undressed, Man. 4, 223. **2.** Unbaked (as a pot), Pańch. iii. d. 13.—Cf. ὠμός.

आमन्त्रण *âmantraṇa*, i.e. *â-mantr* + *ana*, n. **1.** Calling, addressing. **2.** Invitation, Pańch. 34, 17.

आमय *âmaya*, i.e. *am*, Caus. + *a* (anomal.), m. Sickness, Râjat. 5, 209.—Comp. *An-*, I. adj. 1. healthy, Draup. 4, 10. 2. being in a good condition, Râm. 2, 72, 52. 3. unharmed, Râm. 1, 44, 58. II. n. health, Çâk. 64, 23; well-being, Râm. 2, 89, 6. *Nis-*, I. adj. 1. healthy, Indr. 3, 8. 2. full, Hariv. 3639. 3. pure, Râm. 1, 62, 18. II. n. health, Râm. 1, 41, 21. *Sa-*, adj. sick.

आमयावित्व *âmayâvitva*, i.e. *âmayâvin* + *tva*, n. Dyspepsia, Man. 11, 51.

आमयाविन् *âmayâvin*, i.e. *âmaya* + *vin*, adj., f. *nî*, Subject to dyspepsia, Man. 3, 7.

आमरणान्त *âmaraṇânta*, i. e. *â-maraṇa-anta*, adj. Lasting till death, Hit. i. d. 180.

आमरणान्तिक *âmaraṇântika*, i.e. *âmaraṇânta* + *ika*, adj. Lasting till death, Man. 9, 101.

आमर्द *âmarda*, i.e. *â-mṛid* + *a*, m. Pulling (as of hair), Çâk. d. 173.

आमर्दिन् *âmardin*, i.e. *â-mṛid* + *in*, adj., f. *nî*, Destroying, Râm. 4, 14, 16.

आमर्ष *âmarsha* = *a-marsha* in *nis-âmarsha*, = *nis-amarsha*, Devoid of energy, Râm. 2, 10, 14 Gorr.

आमलक *âmalaka*, m., f. *kî*, and *n.* Emblic myrobalan.

आमिष *âmisha*, m. and n. Flesh, Pañch. i. d. 449.—Comp. *Khaḍga-*, n. the flesh of a rhinoceros, Man. 3, 272. *Nis-*, adj. 1. fleshless, Bhartṛ. 2, 9. 2. free of covetousness, Man. 6, 49.

आमिषता *âmisha + tâ*, f. and आमिषत्व *âmisha + tva*, n. Being an object of covetousness, Ragh. 12, 11; Daçak. 194, 6 Wils.

आमुख *â-mukha*, n. Prelude.

आमुष्मिक *âmushmika*, i.e. *amushmin*, loc. sing. of *adas*, + *ika*, adj., f. *kî*, Belonging to the next life, Daçak. in Chr. 179, 19.

आमोक्षण *âmokshaṇa*, i.e. *â-moksh* + *ana* (v. r.), n. Binding on, Râm. 2, 23, 39, Schl.

आमोचन *âmochana*, i.e. *â-much* + *ana*, n. Binding on, Râm. 2, 20, 43 Gorr.

आमोद *âmoda*, i.e. *â-mud* + *a*, m. **1.** Pleasure, Kir. 5, 26. **2.** A fragrancy, strong smell, Ṛit. 6, 34.—Comp. *Sa-*, adj. fragrant.

ऽआमोदिन् *-âmodin*, i.e. *â-mud* + *in*, adj. Smelling, Râjat. 5, 357.

आम्नाय *âmnâya*, i.e. *â-mnâ* + *a*, m. **1.** Holy tradition, Man. 7, 80. **2.** A Veda, Daçak. 140, 3.—Comp. *Dus-*, adj. hard to be transmitted, MBh. 14, 1441.

आम्भस *âmbhasa*, i.e. *ambhas* + *a*, adj. Full of water, Matsyop. 43.

आम्र *âmra*, m. The mango tree, Mangifera indica, Nal. 12, 4.—Comp. *Râjâmra*, i.e. *râjan-*, m. a superior sort of mango.

आम्रात *âmrâta* (derived from the last), and आम्रातक *âmrâta + ka*, m. The hog-plum, Spondias mangifera, Râm. 3, 17, 7.

आय *âya*, i.e. *â-i* + *a*, m. **1.** Gain, Böhtl. Ind. Spr. 219. **2.** Revenue, Man. 8, 419.

आयतन *âyatana*, i.e. *â-yat* + *ana* n. **1.** A place, Chāṇ. 32. **2.** A seat, Man. 6, 77; Pañch. 32, 23. **3.** An outhouse, Yâjñ. 2, 154. **4.** An altar, Pañch. 199, 12.—Comp. *Deva-* and *devatâ-*, n. a temple, Man. 4, 46; 8, 248.

आयति *âyati*, i.e. *â-yam* + *ti*, and, on account of the metre, *tî*, Râm. 3, 44, 11, f. **1.** Dignity, Kathâs. 24, 119; Râjat. 5, 189. **2.** Future time, Man. 4, 70.

आयत्तता *â-yatta* + *tâ* (vb. *yat*) f., Dependence, Dev. 1, 29.

आयस *âyasa*, i.e. *ayas* + *a*, **I.** adj., f. *sî*, Of iron, Man. 8, 315; **II.** n. Iron, Yâjñ. 1, 305.

आयाग *âyâga*, i.e. *â-yaj* + *a*, m. A sacrificial gift, Râm. 1, 33, 13.

आयान *âyâna*, i.e. *â-yâ* + *ana*, n. Coming near, MBh. 3, 11029 (p. 570).

आयाम *âyâma*, i.e. *â-yam* + *a*, m. **1.** Stopping, Vedântas. in Chr. 217, 14. **2.** Oppression, Râjat. 5, 165 (perhaps is to be read *âyâsa*, q. cf.). **3.** Length, Râm. 1, 40, 18.

आयामवन्त् *âyâma* + *vant*, adj., f. *vatî*, and आयामिन् *âyâmin*, i.e. *âyâma* + *in*, adj., f. *nî*, Long, Vikr. d. 4; Daçak. in Chr. 200, 11.

आयास *âyâsa*, i.e. *â-yas* + *a*, m. **1.** Effort, Böhtl. Ind. Spr. 997. **2.** Fatigue, Râm. 3, 55, 17. **3.** Trouble, Çâk. d. 37. **4.** Oppression, Râjat. 5, 174 (Chr. 261, 191, read *âyâso*). **5.** Weariness, Râm. 6, 7, 1.—Comp. *An-*, adj. easy, Çâk. 22, 17.

आयासक *âyâsaka,* i.e. *â-yas* Caus. + *aka,* adj., f. *ikâ,* Causing fatigue, Bhartṛ. 3, 64.

आयासिन् *âyâsin,* i.e. *âyâsa + in,* adj., f. *ni,* Endeavouring, Çâk. d. 34.

आयुःशेषता *âyuḥçeshatâ,* i.e. *âyus -çesha + tâ,* f. Condition of having saved only the life, Pańch. 127, 3 (I came off scarcely alive).

आयुध *â-yudh + a,* n., A weapon, Man. 7, 93.—Comp. *Indra-* n. the rainbow, Man. 4, 59. *Sa-indra-,* adj. with a rainbow. *Ud-,* adj. with raised weapons, Chr. 4, 17. *Kusuma-,* m. the god of love, Ṛit. 6, 33. *Chakra-,* m. a name of Vishṇu, Râm. 6, 102, 12. *Tridaça-,* n. the rainbow, Ragh. 9, 54. *Nis-,* adj., f. *dhâ,* disarmed, Man. 7, 92. *Sa-,* adj. armed, Pańch. 44, 23. *Hala-,* m. Baladeva.

आयुधिक *âyudhika,* i. e. *âyudha + ika,* and **आयुधिन्** *âyudhin,* i.e. *âyudha + in,* m. A warrior, MBh. 16, 212; Râm. 2, 53, 30.

आयुधीय *âyudhîya,* i. e. *âyudha + îya,* adj. Military, Man. 7, 222.

आयुर्वेदमय *âyurvedamaya,* i. e. *ayus-veda + maya,* adj. Containing the Ayurveda (see *veda*), Râm. 1, 45, 32.

ऽआयुष *-âyusha,* i.e. *âyus + a,* A substitute for *âyus* when latter part of compound words: e. g. *chira-,* adj. Long living, Pańch. 245, 35; *purusha-,* n. The duration of a man's life.

आयुष्काम *âyushkâma,* i.e. *âyus -kam + a,* adj. Desirous of long life, Man. 9, 41.

आयुष्मन्त् *âyushmant,* i.e. *âyus + mant,* adj., f. *matî,* Long-lived, Man. 2, 152. Used in dramas as an honorific address.

आयुष्य *âyushya,* i.e. *âyus + ya,* I. adj., f. *yâ,* Procuring long life, Man. 1, 106. II. n. Long life, Man. 2, 52.—Comp. *An-,* adj. prejudicial to long life, Man. 2, 57.

आयुस् *âyus,* n. Life, Man. 1, 84.—Comp. *Alpa-,* adj. short-lived, Man. 4, 157. *Kshîṇa-* (vb. *kshi*), adj. lifeless, Sâv. 2, 23. *Gata-,* adj. 1. lifeless, Pańch. 101, 23. 2. whose life is forfeited, Râm. 6, 1, 10. *Dîrgha-,* adj. 1. long-lived, Râm. 1, 6, 18. 2. wished to be long-lived, Râm. 3, 1, 11. *Pari-mita-* (vb. *mâ*), adj. short-lived, Râm. 3, 55, 20. *Çata-,* m. a man a hundred years old, Lass. 32, 18; an old man. Cf. *αἰές, αἰεί, αἰών,* Lat. aevum, Goth. aivs.

आयोग *âyoga,* i. e. *â-yuj + a,* m. Presenting with flowers, perfumes, Râm. 5, 17, 15 (*bhramara-,* A present of flowers made to the bees).

आयोगव *âyogava,* m., f. *vî,* Offspring of a Çûdra by a Vaiçya woman, Man. 10, 12; 16.

आयोधन *âyodhana,* i.e. *â-yudh + ana,* n. 1. Battle, Ragh. 5, 71. 2. A field of battle, Draup. 8, 30.

आरक्ष *â-raksh + a,* m. Guard, protection, Man. 3, 204; Râm. 5, 75, 2.

आरक्षक *â-raksh + aka,* and **आरक्षिक** *ârakshika,* i.e. *â-raksha + ika* (?), m. A policeman, Pańch. 129, 5; Daçak. in Chr. 195, 11.

आरट्ट *âraṭṭa* (a dialectical change of *â-râshṭra*), m. pl. The name of a people and country, MBh. 8, 2056.

आरट्टज *âraṭṭa-ja* (vb. *jan*), adj. Born in Âraṭṭa, Râm. 5, 12, 36.

आरण *âraṇa,* An abyss, Chr. 296, 6 = Rigv. i. 112, 6.

आरण्य *âraṇya*, i.e. *araṇya* + *a*, adj., f. *yâ*. **1.** Living in forests, MBh. 1, 3637. **2.** Growing in forests, MBh. 1, 6658; wild, Man. 10, 89.

आरण्यक *âraṇya* + *ka*, **I.** adj. Referring to forests, MBh. 15, 532; produced in forests, Râm. 2, 36, 6. **II.** m. An anchorite, Çâk. d. 46. **III.** n. The name of a book, Man. 4, 123.

आरब्धि *ârabdhi*, i.e. *â-rabh* + *ti*, f. An enterprise, Râjat. 5, 190.

आरम्भ *ârambha*, i.e. *â-rabh* + *a*, m. **1.** A beginning, Megh. 37. **2.** Exertion, effort, Daçak. in Chr. 198, 22. **3.** An enterprise, Râm. 4, 30, 14.—**Comp.** *Chitra-*, adj. painted, Vikr. d. 4. *Chitrârpita-*, i.e. *chitra-arpita-* (vb. *ṛi*), adj. painted, Ragh. 2, 31. *Nis-*, adj. devoid of exertion, inactive, MBh. 5, 1027.

आरम्भण *ârambhaṇa*, i.e. *â-rabh* + *ana*, n. Commencement (support, according to the Sch. of the Chhând.-up. 385), Vedântas. in Chr. 216, 18.

आरम्भता *ârambha* + *tâ*, f. Commencement, Kathâs. 16, 79.

आरम्भिन् *ârambhin*, i.e. *ârambha* + *in*, adj. One who begins many things.

आरव *ârava*, i.e. *â-ru* + *a*, m. Sound, Râm. 4, 50, 23.

आरा *ârâ*, f. An awl.—Cf. O.H.G. âla; A.S. âl, ael.

आरात् (abl. sing. of ved. *âra*) adv. **1.** From afar, MBh. 1, 6447. **2.** Instantly.

आराधन *â-râdh* + *ana*. **I.** adj. Who or what conciliates, wins. **II.** n. **1.** Acquirement, Bhartṛ 3, 5. **2.** Accomplishment (representation), Çâk. 12, 1. **3.** Gratification. **4.** Adoration, Kathâs. 17, 26.

आराधयितृ *ârâdhayitṛi*, i.e. *â-râdh*, Caus. + *tṛi*, m. An adorer, Çâk. 39, 13.

आराधयिष्णु *ârâdhayishṇu*, i.e. *â-râdh*, Caus. + *ishṇu*, adj. Gratifying, adoring, Râm. 3, 17, 30.

आराम *ârâma*, i.e. *â-ram* + *a*, m. **1.** Pleasure, Bhag. 3, 16. **2.** A garden, Daçak. in Chr. 197, 17.—**Comp.** *Antar-*, adj. one who finds his pleasure in his soul, Bhag. 5, 24.

आराव *ârâva*, i.e. *â-ru* + *a*, m. **1.** Sound, Nal. 13, 16. **2.** Scream, MBh. 1, 6846.

आरिराधयिषु *ârirâdhayishu*, i.e. *â-rirâdhayisha* (desider. of the Caus. of *râdh*) + *u*, adj. Desirous of conciliating or winning, MBh. 1, 4784.

आरुणि *âruṇi*, i.e. *aruṇa* + *i*, patronym. m. A descendant of Aruṇa, surname of Uddalaka, MBh. 1, 684, and of Vainateya, MBh. 1, 2548.

आरुणी *âruṇî*, i.e. *aruṇa* + *a* + *î*, f. Tawny, viz. an antelope, Chr. 290, 7 = Rigv. i. 64, 7.

आरुरुक्षु *âurukshu*, i.e. *â-ruruksha* (desider. of *ruh*) + *u*, adj. Desiring to ascend, MBh. 3, 11108; to acquire, Bhag. 6, 3.

ऽआरुह *-â-ruh* + *a*. Latter part of comp. words: e.g. *gaja-*, m. The rider of an elephant, Râm. 5, 12, 31 (in *para-*, adj. Having excellent riders, etc). *dus-*, adj. Hard to be ascended, Râm. 2, 117, 13 Gorr.

आरोग्य *ârogya*, i.e. *a-roga* + *ya*, n. Health, Râm. 1, 15, 13.—**Comp.** *An-*, adj. prejudicial to health, Man. 2, 57. *Saha-*, adj. convalescent, well.

आरोढृ *âroḍhṛi*, i.e. *â-ruh* + *tṛi*, m. One who mounts, Yâjń. 2, 303.

आरोप *âropa*, i.e. *â-ruh*, Caus. + *a*,

m. Attributing to, predication, Çâk. d. 35 Sch.

आरोपक *âropaka*, i.e. *â-ruh*, Caus. + *aka*, m. A planter, Man. 3, 163.

आरोपण *âropaṇa*, i.e. *â-ruh*, Caus. + *ana* n. 1. Causing to ascend, Kathâs. 17, 84 (viz. to heaven, i.e to die); Râm. 5, 15, 46. 2. Putting on, Ragh. 7, 25. 3. Stringing (a bow), Râm. 1, 66, 27.—Comp. *Vṛiksha-*, n. planting trees.

आरोह *âroha*, i.e. *â-ruh* + *a*, m. 1. A rider, Hariv. 13464. 2. Mounting, Kathâs. 25, 142; Râjat. 5, 310. 3. A heap, Râm. 1, 5, 14. 4. The buttocks, Râm. 3, 52, 27.—Comp. *Açva-*, m. a horseman, Kathâs. 10, 124. *Gaja-*, and *hasty-âroha*, i.e. *hastin-*, m. a rider on an elephant, Râm. 3, 57, 23; Draup. 8, 22. *Dus-*, adj., f. *hâ*, hard to be ascended, Râm. 2, 105, 6. *Vara-*, I. m. 1. a rider on an elephant or horse. 2. an elephant-driver. II. f. *hâ*, 1. an elegant woman. 2. the hip or flank. *Sa-*, adj., f. *hâ*, rising, Râm. 5, 73, 6. *Syandana-*, m. a warrior who fights in a car.

आरोहक *ârohaka*, i.e. *a-ruh* + *aka*, m. A rider, Pañch. 129, 18.

आरोहण *ârohaṇa*, i.e. *â-ruh* + *ana*, 1. Ascending, MBh. 1, 372. 2. A stage, MBh. 14, 282. 3. A ladder, Râm. 5, 14, 14.—Comp. *Durga-*, adj. of difficult ascent, Râm. 3, 76, 28. *Pavitra-*, n. the name of a festival, Pañch. 34, 18. *Sukha-*, adj. of easy ascent, MBh. 2, 1281.

आरोहणिक *ârohaṇika*, i.e. *ârohaṇa* + *ika*, adj. Referring to the ascension (viz. to heaven), MBh. 1, 553.

आरोहिन् *ârohin*, i.e. *â-ruh* + *in*, adj. f. *iṇî*, Ascending, Pañch. iii. d. 264.

आर्जव *ârjava*, i.e. *ṛiju* + *a*, n. Candour, Man. 11, 222; Bhartṛ 2, 19.—Comp. *An-*, n. dishonesty, Man. 9, 17.

आर्जुनेय *ârjuneya*, i.e. *arjuna* + *eya*, patronym. m. A descendant of Arjuna (?), Chr. 298, 23 = Rigv. i. 112, 23.

आर्तव *ârtava*, i.e. *ṛitu* + *a*. I. adj., f. *vâ*, Seasonable, Râm. 2, 30, 16. II. n. 1. The menstrual discharge, Man. 4, 40; Râjat. 5, 391. 2. The approved time for cohabitation, Man. 3, 48, cf. 46.—Comp. *An-*, adj. unseasonable.

आर्त्त *ârtta*, written **आर्त** *arta*, (an anomalous ptcple. of the pf. pass. of *â-ard*) adj., f. *tâ*. 1. Injured, Man. 4, 236; hurt, Yâjñ. 3, 248. 2. Distressed, Man. 6, 16. 3. Afflicted, Daçak. in Chr. 179, 19.—Comp. *Bhaya-*, adj., distressed with fear.

आर्त्तता *ârtta* + *tâ* (written **आर्तता**) f. Painfulness.

आर्त्ति (आर्ति) *ârtti*, i.e. *â-ard* + *ti* (cf. *ârtta*), f. Pain, Daçak. in Chr. 197, 17.—Comp. *Kṛitrima-*, adj. feigning sorrow, Daçak. in Chr. 192, 8.

आर्द्र *ârdra*, adj., f. *râ*. 1. Wet, Megh. 87. 2. Fresh, Amar. 2. 3. Mild, Pañch. 8, 19.—Comp. *Sa-*, adj. Wet. Cf. probably ἄρδω (although beginning with F, Fαρδ, Fραδ), ῥαίνω, ῥαθάμιγξ.

आर्द्रय *ÂRDRAYA*, a denomin. derived from the last, Par. To moisten, Bhartṛ. Suppl. 7.

आर्धिक *ârdhika*, (i.e. probably *ardha* + *ika*), m. A labourer in tillage, Man. 4, 253.

आर्य *ârya*. I. m., f. *yâ*, 1. Originally the name of the immigrated Indian people in opposition to the old inhabitants. In later times, the name of the three upper castes in opposition to the fourth, Yâjñ. 2, 294; or to barbarians, MBh. 14, 2137. II. fem. *yâ*, The name of a metre, Râjat. 5. 35. III. adj., f. *yâ*. 1. Respectable, venerable, Man. 8, 75 ; Daçak. in Chr. 186, 17. 2. Apposite, Râm 2, 115, 6.—Comp. *An-*, adj. and subst. 1. A barbarian, Man. 9, 260. 2. Unworthy, Râm. 3, 51, 25. 3. Inhabited by barbarians, Çâk. Ch. 139, 7.

आर्यक *ârya+ka*, m. 1. A grandfather, Râm. 5, 61, 15. 2. A proper name, Mṛichchh. 35, 22 ; MBh. 1, 1552.

आर्यता *ârya+tâ*, f. and **आर्यत्व** *ârya+tva*, n. Venerableness, Man. 7, 211 ; Râjat. 1, 110.— Comp. *An-*, f. Want of virtuous dignity, Man. 10, 58. Dishonourableness, Hit. iv. d. 23.

आर्ष *ârsha*, i.e. *ṛishi+a*, I. adj. f. *shî*. 1. Referring to the Ṛishis. 2. Ordained by or practised by the Ṛishis, Man. 3, 21; 12, 106. II. m. A form of marriage, Man. 3, 53. III. n. Holy lineage.

आर्षभ *ârshabha* i.e. *ṛishabha+a*, adj. Proceeding from a bull, Man. 9, 50 (n. its strength).

आलक्षण्य *âlakshaṇya*. i.e. *a-lakshaṇa+ya*, n. Inclination to sin, Man. 9, 19 (Kull.).

आलङ्घन *â-laṅgh+ana*, n. Covering, Daçak. in Chr. 182, 11.

आलम्ब *â-lamb+a*, I. adj. Hanging down, Râm. 3, 22, 17. II. m. Support, Râjat. 5, 310 (in Chr. p. 271, corr. -बद्दे-). —Comp. *An-*, adj. unsupported, Râm. 2, 48, 22. *Dus-*, adj., f. *bâ*, difficult to get a footing in, Râm. 5, 73, 6. *Nis-*, adj. having no support, Râm. 1, 44, 2. *Matta-* (vb. *mad*), m. a fence round the walls of a palace. *Sa-*, adj. supported, Kathâs. 12, 175.

आलम्बन *a-lamb+ana*, n., 1. Supporting, Megh. 4. 2. Support, Pañch. i. d. 34.—Comp. *Nis-*, adj. having no support, Râm. 5, 3, 64.

आलम्बिन् *â-lamb+in*, adj., f. *nî*. 1. Hanging down, Ṛit. 6, 24. 2. Dependent, MBh. 3, 9924. 3. Depending on, Hit. pr. d. 19.

आलम्भ *âlambha*, i.e. *â-labh+a*, m. 1. Touching, Man. 2, 79. 2. Cutting, Man. 11, 144. 3. Killing, Megh. 46.—Comp. *Dus-*, adj., f. *bhâ*, difficult to be seized, MBh. 13, 4707.

आलम्भिन् *âlambhin*, i.e. *â-labh+in*, adj., f. *nî*, Touching, Râjat. 5, 88.

आलय *âlaya*, i.e. *â-lî+a*, m. and n. (Râm. 5, 23, 31), 1. A house. 2. A seat. —Comp. *Kṛita-*, adj. 1. having settled. 2. Inhabiting, Râm. 3, 1, 18. *Tridaça-*, m. 1. the heaven. 2. a deity. *Deva-*, m. a temple. *Padma-*, adj., f. *yâ*, dwelling in a lotus flower. *Mânasa-*, m. a wild swan, or goose. *Hima-*, m. the Himâlaya range of mountains.

आलवाल *âlavâla*, n. A basin for water round the root of a tree, Vikr. d. 41.

आलस्य *âlasya*, i. e. *alasa+ya*, n. Idleness, Bhartṛ. 2, 74.

आलान *âlâna*, n., 1. A post to which an elephant is tied, Mâlav. 62, d. 76. 2. The rope that ties him, Ragh. 4, 69.

आलानिक *âlânika*, i.e. *âlâna+ika*, adj. Serving for a post, etc. (see the preceding), Ragh, 14, 38.

आलाप *âlâpa*, i.e. *â-lap+a*, m. 1. Speaking. 2. Conversation, Pañch. 46, 12.—Comp. *Kathâ-*, m. conversation, Hit. 26, 22.

आलापवन्त् *âlâpa+vant*, adj., f. *vatî*, Addressing, Amar. 42.

आलापिन् *âlâpin*, i.e. *â-lap+in*, adj., f. *nî*, Speaking.

आलि *âli*, i.e. *â-lî*, I. m. A bee, Pañch. i. d. 203. II. Also *âlî*, f. 1. A woman's female friend, Kumâras. 5, 83. 2. A line, Amar. 89; Pañch. 203, 6.—Comp. *Sûtra-âlî*, f. a necklace.

आलिङ्ग *â-liṅg+a*, m. Embracing, Daçak. in Chr. 201, 14.

आलिङ्गन *â-liṅg+ana*, n. An embrace, Megh. 71.

आलु *âlu*, n. A vessel, Hit. iii. d. 52.

आलुञ्चन *â-luñch+ana*, n. Darting on, Mṛichchh. 50, 15.

आलेप *âlepa*, i.e. *â-lip+a*, m., and

आलेपन *âlepana*, i.e. *â-lip+ana*, n. 1. Smearing, anointing. 2. Ointment.

आलोक *âloka*, i.e. *â-lok+a*, m. 1. Sight, Megh. 38; Çâk. d. 9 (first look). 2. Light, Râm. 4, 50, 52. 3. Appearance, Daçak. in Chr. 186, 15. 4. Flattery, panegyric, Ragh. 2, 9.—Comp. *Dus-*, adj. difficult to be perceived, Gît. 2, 20. *Nis-*, adj., f. *kâ*, 1. without moving the eyes, Râm. 2, 111, 14. 2. invisible, MBh. 1, 1475. *Sukha-*, adj., f. *kâ*, charming, Vikr. d. 109. *Sûrya-*, m. sunshine.

आलोकन *â-lok+ana*, n. Looking, Vikr. d. 150.

आलोकनीयता *â-lokanîya+tâ* (vb. *lok*), f. Visibility, Kumâras. 2, 24.

ऽआलोकिन् *-âlokin*, i.e. *âloka+in*. Bhartṛ. 1, 69, at the end of the comp. word *vikasita-kumuda-indîvara-âloka+in*, adj., f. *nî*, Looking like a lotus whose flowers are expanded; literally, having the appearance of a lotus, etc.

आलोचक *â-loch+aka*, adj. Causing sight.

आलोचन *â-loch+ana*, n. and f. *nâ*, Consideration.

आलोडन *âloḍana*, i.e. *â-luḍ+ana*, n. Mixing.

आवन्त्य *âvantya*, i.e. *avanti+ya*, m. 1. An inhabitant of Avanti, MBh. 3, 15253. 2. The son of a Vrâtya or outcast Brâhmaṇa, Man. 10, 21.

आवपन *â-vap+ana*, n. 1. Sowing seed. 2. Any vessel.

आवरण *âvaraṇa*, i.e. *â-vṛi+ana*, n. 1. Covering, Vedântas. in Chr. 205, 23. 2. A cover, Çâk. d. 77. 3. Protection, Râm. 6, 99, 33. 4. A shield, Çiç. 5, 66. 5. Obstruction, Man. 3, 163. 6. A lock, Ragh. 16, 7.—Comp. *Gâtra-*, n. a shield, MBh. 7, 79. *Deha-*, n. an armour, MBh. 7, 4423.

आवर्त *âvarta*, i.e. *â-vṛit+a*, m. 1. Turning, a turn. 2. A whirlpool, Böhtl. Ind. Spr. 392. 3. A curl, Nal. 19, 14.—Comp. *Ârya-*, m. the holy land, extending from the eastern to the western sea, and bounded on the north and south by the Himâlaya and Vindhya mountains, Man. 2, 22. *Dakshiṇâ-*, adj. 1. turned to the right, Bhâg. P. 5, 23, 5. 2. turned to the south, MBh. 6, 5671. *Nandi-*, m. a certain diagram, MBh. 7, 2930. *Brahmâvarta*, i.e. *brahman-*, m. the country between the rivers Sarasvatî and Dṛishadvatî, Man. 2, 17. *Râjâvarta*, i.e. *râjan-*, m. an inferior kind of diamond. *Shoḍaçâvarta*, i.e. *shoḍaçan-*, m. a conch shell. *Su-dus-*, adj. very difficult to be dissuaded, MBh. 12, 579. *Sûrya-*, m. 1. a plant, Cleome viscosa. 2. a sun-flower. *Hṛid-*, m. a lock of hair on a horse's neck or breast.

आवर्तिन् *âvartin*, i.e. *â-vṛit+in*, adj., f. *nî*, Returning, Hit. i. d. 201.

आवलि and **ली** *âvali*, f. A row, Hit. i. d. 90.

आवश्यक *âvaçyaka*, i.e. *avaçya+m*

+*ka*, I. adj. Necessary, inevitable, Bhâshâp. 21. II. n. Necessity, that which must be done, Bhâg. P. 5, 8, 1.

आवश्यकता *âvaçyaka*+*tâ*, f. Inevitability, Hit. 116, 10.

आवसति *â-vas*+*ati* (for original -°*ti*, fem. of the pres. partic.), f. Night, Arj. 1, 13.

आवसथ *â-vas*+*atha*, m. **1.** A resting-place, Man. 3, 107. **2.** A house. **3.** The mansion of the holy fire, Man. 4, 151. —Comp. *Deva-*, m. a temple, Râjat. 4, 325.

आवसथ्य *âvasathya*, i.e. *âvasatha*+*ya*, m. The holy fire, MBh. 3, 14181.

ऽआवह -*â-vah*+*a*, adj., f. *hâ*. **1.** Bringing, Râm. 1, 23, 13. **2.** Causing, Ragh. 14, 5.—Comp. *Dus-*, adj., f. *hâ*, difficult to be lead, MBh. 12, 12459. *Mala-*, adj. 1. soiling. 2. defiling.

आवाप *âvâpa*, i.e. *â-vap*+*a*, m. **1.** An arm-guard, Râm. 6, 92, 15. **2.** Watching the enemies, Çiç. 2, 88.—Comp. *Çara-*, m. a bow, MBh. 1, 7073.

आवास *âvâsa*, i.e. *â-vas*+*a*, m. A house.—Comp. *Bhoga-*, m. the harem.

आवाहन *âvâhana*, i.e. *â-vah*+*ana*, n. Invitation.

आविक *âvika*, i.e. *avi*+*ka*, I. adj. **1.** Coming from a sheep, e.g. *kshîra*, 'the milk of an ewe,' Man. 5, 8. **2.** Woollen, Man. 2, 41. II. n. A woollen cloth, Man. 5, 120.—Comp. *Pañchâvika*, i.e. *pañchan-*, n. the five productions from a sheep.

आविकसौत्रिक *âvika-sautrika*, i.e. *âvika-sûtra*+*ika* (v.r. -*sûtrika*, perhaps better), adj. Consisting of woollen threads, Man. 2, 44.

आविल *âvila*, adj., f. *lâ*. **1.** Turbid, Nal. 13, 7 (6). **2.** Without splendour, Râm. 5, 18, 3. **3.** Stained, Chr. 40, 11; Foul, Çântiç. 3, 2.—Comp. *An-*, adj. 1. pure, Râm. 3, 76, 11. 2. healthy, Man. 7, 69. *Pari-*, adj. very turbid, Ragh. 7, 37.

आविलय *ÂVILAYA*, a denomin. derived from *âvila*, Par. To sully, Çâk. d. 117.

आविस् *âvis*, adv. and prepos., combined or compounded with *as*, *kṛi*, *bhû*, and their derivatives, Manifest.

आवीतिन् *âvîtin*, i.e. *â-vîta*+*in* (vb. *vye*), adj. in *prâchîna-âvîtin*, m. A Brâhmaṇa wearing his cord over his right shoulder, Man. 2, 63.

आवृत् *â-vṛit*, f. **1.** Order, arrangement, Man. 3, 214 (see Lois.). **2.** Manner, Man. 3, 248. **3.** A ceremony, Man. 2, 66.

आवृत्ति *â-vṛit*+*ti*, f. Returning, Kathâs. 14, 64.

आवेग *âvega*, i.e. *â-vij*+*a*, m. Trouble, hurry.—Comp. *Ati-*, m. excessive trouble, Prab. 92, 8.

आवेदक *âvedaka*, i.e. *â-vid*+*aka*, adj. One who makes known.

ऽआवेदिन् -*âvedin*, i.e. *â-vid*+*in*, adj., f. *nî*, Announcing.

आवेश *âveça*, i.e. *â-viç*+*a*, m. Entering.

आवेशन *âveçana*, i.e. *â-viç*+*ana* n. **1.** A workshop, Man. 9, 265. **2.** Possession by demons.

आवेष्ट *â-veshṭ*+*a*, m. Wrapping round, Yâjñ. 2, 217.

ऽआश -*âça*, i.e. **2.** *aç*+*a*, m. Eating, e.g. *prâtar-*, m. Breakfast, Lass. 76, 19; *havya-* (vb. *hu*) and *huta-* (vb. *hu*), m. Agni, or fire.

आशंसा *â-çaṁs*+*â*, f. Wish, Ragh. 12, 44.—Comp. *Sa-*, adj. full of desire, Kir. 5, 23. -*çam*, adv. uttering a benediction, Vikr. 11, 4.

आशंसिन् *â-çaṁs+in*, adj., f. *nî*, Announcing, Râm. 6, 90, 32.

आशङ्का *â-çaṅk+â*, f. 1. Fear, Bhartṛ. 3, 4. 2. Suspicion, Kathâs. 14, 56.—Comp. *Gata-* and *Nashṭa-*, adj., f. *kâ*, fearless. *Sa-*, adj. disheartened, Pañch. 47, 15.

ऽआशङ्किन् *-â-çaṅk+in*, adj., f. *nî*, Apprehending, Râm. 2, 71, 32.

आशय *âçaya*, i.e. *â-çî+a*, m. 1. A seat, Kathâs. 20, 128. 2. A den, MBh. 3, 1387. 3. An asylum, Pañch, 141, 1. 4. The stomach, Daçak. 189, 11 (Wils.). 5. The heart, Daçak. in Chr. 188, 1; Mind, Bhag. 10, 20. 6. Intention, Kathâs. 12, 73.—Comp. *Ama-*, m. the part of the belly about the navel. *Krûra-*, adj., f. *yâ*, containing cruel animals and wicked intentions, Bhartṛ. 1, 80. *Garbha-*, m. the womb, MBh. 14, 501. *Toya-*, m. a pond, a river. *Dus-*, I. m. a bad abode, Bhâg. P. 3, 24, 36. II. adj. having wicked intentions, Kathâs. 20, 3. *Dushṭa-* (vb. *dush*), adj. having wicked intentions, Pañch. 51, 25. *Pakva-*, m. the abdomen, MBh. 3, 13973. *Mahâ-*, I. adj. 1. magnanimous; 2. liberal. II. m. a gentleman. *Mûtra-*, m. the lower belly. *Vi-rata-* (vb. *ram*), adj. resigning worldly intentions, Pañch. ii. d. 189. *Sukha-*, adj. hoping for pleasure, Pañch. ii. d. 160.

आशा *âçâ*, f. I. i. e. 1. *aç+a*, A quarter, a region, Râm. 3, 22, 8. II. i.e. *â-çaṁs*, 1. Desire, Hit. d. 105. 2. Hope, Daçak. 191, 5.—Comp. *Dus-*, f. want of hope, Râjat. 3, 213. *Dhana-*, f. desire of wealth, Hit. i. d. 105. *Nis-*, adj., f. *çâ*, hopeless, Râm. 4, 19, 4. *Bhagna-* (vb. *bhañj*), adj. disappointed. *Hata-* (vb. *han*), adj. hopeless, desperate, Mâlav. 36, 20.

आशावन्त् *âçâ+vant*, adj., f. *vatî*, Full of hope, Hit. i. d. 72.

ऽआशित्व *-âçitva*, i.e. *âçin+tva*, n. Eating, e.g. *an-âçitva*, Hunger, MBh. 3, 13477.

ऽआशिन् *-âçin*, i.e. 2. *aç+in*, adj., f. *nî*, Eating, Man. 2, 118.—Comp. *Nirâmisha-*, i.e. *Nis-*, adj. not feeding on meat, Hit. 19, 1. *Pavana-*, m. a snake. *Pûrva-*, adj., eating before (others), MBh. 5, 1291.

आशिस् *âçis*, i.e. *â-çâs*, f. Benediction, Râm. 2, 32, 11.—Comp. *Jaya-*, f. cheering, congratulation, Râm. 3, 35, 105.

आशीविष *âçî-visha* (*âçî*, according to the grammarians, a serpent's fang), m. A snake, MBh. 3, 544.

आशु *âçu*, i.e. probably *aç* (see *ço*) + *u*, adv. Quickly. Cf. ὠκύς, Lat. ocius, accipiter=ved. *âçupatvan*, aquila.

आशुग *âçu-ga* (vb. *gam*), I. adj., f. *gâ*, Moving quickly, Man. 4, 68. II. m. An arrow.

आशुत्व *âçu+tva*, n. Quickness, Arj. 6, 18.

आशौच *âçaucha*, i. e. *a-çuchi+a*, n. Impurity, Man. 5, 59. — Comp. *Sûtyâçaucha*, i.e. *Sûti-*, n. impurity from child-birth.

आश्चर्य *âçcharya*, i. e. *â-char+ya* I. adj., f. *yâ*, Astonishing, wonderful, Daçak. in Chr. 179, 11. II. n. A surprising phenomenon, Râm. 5, 49, 27. —Comp. *Sa-*, adj. wonderful, Bhartṛ. 2, 59. *-yam*, adv. with surprise.

आश्चर्यमय *âçcharya+maya*, adj., f. *yî*, Wonderful, Kathâs. 26, 64.

आश्च्योतन *âçchyotana*, i.e. *â-çchyut* +*ana*, Sprinkling.

आश्रम *â-çram+a*, m. and n. 1. An hermitage. 2. A religious order of which there are four (or only three, Man. 2, 230) kinds referable to the different periods of a Brâhmaṇa's life, Man. 3, 2.—Comp. *Kâma-*, m. and n. the hermitage of the god of love. *Gṛiha-*, m. the second order, that of the householder, Man. 6, 1. *Jyeshṭha-*, adj. being in the most eminent order, Man. 3, 78.

आश्रमिन् *âçramin*, i.e. *âçrama* + *in*, adj. Belonging to one of the religious orders, Man. 6, 91.—Comp. *Gṛiha-*, m. a Brâhmaṇa fulfilling the duties of a householder, Mârk. P. 29, 30.

आश्रय *âçraya*, i.e. *â-çri* + *a*, m. **1.** A seat, Pańch. 51, 20; Ragh. 11, 26 (a quiver). **2.** An abode. **3.** A retreat, Man. 7, 27. **4.** An asylum, Pańch. 211, 4. **5.** Protection, Pańch. i. d. 43. **6.** Recourse, Man. 2, 11; refuge, Ragh. 12, 35. **7.** Dependence, Yâjń. 2, 48. **8.** Support, Pańch. 155, 8; help, Pańch. 95, 14. **9.** Base, Vedântas. in Chr. 212, 3; the subject (in Logic), Bhâshâp. 74. **10.** Reference, Yâjń. 3, 143; Daçak. in Chr. 185, 17.—Comp. *Garta-*, adj. living in holes, Man. 7, 72. *Nis-*, adj., f. *yâ*, having no support, MBh. 8, 1905. *Para-*, m. 1. dependence from another, Hariv. 5154. 2. the refuge of the enemies, Bhâg. P. 1, 4, 12. *Vana-*, I. adj. who or what is in a forest. II. m. a raven. *Vâṇa-*, m. a bow.

ऽआश्रयण *-âçrayaṇa*, i.e. *â-çri* + *ana*, adj., f. *ṇî*. **1.** Taking refuge. **2.** Referring to, Vikr. d. 51.

आश्रयाशवत् *açrayâçavat*, i.e. *â-çraya-âça* + *vat*, adv. Like fire, Hit. ii. d. 165.

आश्रयिन् *âçrayin*, i.e. *âçraya* + *in*, adj., f. *ṇî*. **1.** Seated, Ragh. 6, 4. **2.** Lodging, Çâk. 78, 19.

आश्रव *âçrava*, i.e. *â-çru* + *a*, adj., f. *vâ*, Obedient.—Comp. *An-*, adj., f. *vâ*, not obeying.

आश्रितत्व *â-çrita* + *tva* (vb. *çri*), n. Dependence, Bhâshâp. 23.

आश्लेष *âçlesha*, i.e. *â-çlish* + *a*, m. An embrace, Megh. 105.

आश्वयुज *açvayuja*, i.e. *açva-yuj* + *a*, m. The month Âçvina (September-October), Man. 6, 15.

आश्वास *âçvâsa*, i.e. *â-çvas* + *a*, m. **1.** Recreation. **2.** Rest, repose, Râjat. 5, 315. **3.** Appeasing, Kathâs. 9, 64.

आश्वासन *âçvâsana*, i.e. *â-çvas* + *ana*, n. Recreation, Pańch. 70, 21.

आश्विन *âçvina*, i.e. *açvin* + *a*, adj. Directed to the Açvins, Chr. 296.

आषाढ *âshâḍha*, i.e. *a-sâḍha*, old ptcple. of the pf. pass. of *sah*, + *a*, m. **1.** The name of a month (June-July), Râjat. 5, 126. **2.** A staff carried by an ascetic in that month. **3.** A proper name, MBh. 1, 2699.

1. **आस्** *âs*, an interj. **1.** Of anger: Ah! Pańch. 36, 21. **2.** Of fear, Prab. 31, 10. **3.** Of recollection, Prab. 72, 11. **4.** Of joy, Prab. 29, 9.

2. **आस्** *ÂS*, ii. 2, Âtm. (in epic poetry sometimes Par., MBh. 14, 2871). **1.** To sit, Râm. 1, 50, 10; with the acc., Vikr. 27, 16. **2.** To abide, MBh. 3, 12723. **3.** To stay, Râm. 3, 9, 32. **4.** To perform, Nal. 7, 3 (Böhtl.). **5.** To spend time in doing something, to do something a long time; the action being expressed, a. By a participle, Pańch. 36, 20 (*svâkâram nigûhann âste*, He conceals the state of his mind). b. By an absolutive, Man. 7, 195; Râm. 4, 57, 23 (*prâyam* [hardly acc. of *prâya*] *âsmahe*, we are starving). **6.** To exist, Râjat. 5, 99; to be, Pańch. 89, 10; Râjat. 5, 3 (corr. *âsâtâm*). With an adv. *tûshṇîm*, silent, Pańch. 21, 10; *evam*, thus, Râm. 5, 57, 15. With an

instrumental, Pańch. i. d. 106, 'with fearless mind.' With a dative, Hit. i. d. 207, *âstâm tushṭaye*, it may be gratifying. **7.** To cease, Pańch. 106, 19; *âstâm*, 'enough,' Hit. 122, 19. Ptcple. of the pres. *âsîna*, Man. 1, 1. Of the pf. pass. *âsita*, passed, Râm. 1, 3, 4 (what came to pass with Râma, etc.); n. Seat, Râm. 2, 58, 10. **Comp.** *Dus-*, n. Unsuitable manner of sitting, MBh. 3, 14669.—With the prepos. अधि *adhi*, **1.** To sit down, Râm. 5, 57, 6. **2.** To sit down on, with acc., Râm. 2, 81, 11. **3.** To take for his seat, Râm. 2, 99, 11; to occupy, Râm. 6, 2, 34. **4.** To inhabit, Râm. 3, 54, 5. **5.** To enter, MBh. 3, 13330. **6.** To live as wife of, MBh. 1, 7265. Part. of the pf. pass. *adhyâsita*, Being the subject, Lass. 92, 2.—With समधि *sam-adhi*, **1.** To occupy, Ragh. 13, 52. **2.** To inhabit, Râm. 6, 4, 52.—With अनु *anu*, **1.** To sit down after, Ragh. 2, 24. **2.** To attend, Çâk. 33, 3. **3.** To perform, Râm. 2, 50, 34.—With उद् *ud*, To be indifferent, Çiç. 2, 42. Ptcple. of the pres. *udâsîna*, One who is indifferent, neither friend nor enemy, Man. 7, 155.—With उप *upa*, **1.** To sit near, Man. 4, 154. **2.** To attend, Bhag. 12, 2. **3.** To honour, MBh. 3, 12611. **4.** To partake, Man. 3, 104; MBh. 17, 2871. **5.** To attain, Yâjń. 3, 192. **6.** To sit, Man. 2, 103. **7.** To occupy, Man. 5, 93. **8.** To perform, Râm. 4, 24, 11; Daçak. in Chr. 184, 3. **9.** To undergo, MBh. 3, 15634. **10.** To stay, Râm. 1, 36, 1. **11.** To spend time, doing something (cf. the simplex), the action being expressed, **a.** By a participle, Bhag. 12, 6; **b.** By an absolutive, Râm. 1, 44, 1. **12.** To expect, MBh. 3, 1215.—With पर्युप *pari-upa*, **1.** To surround, MB. 2, 280; Nal. 1, 11. **2.** To sit on, Man. 2, 75. **3.** To dwell round (with the acc.), MBh. 3, 10412. **4.** To partake, Arj. 8, 21. **5.** To attend respectfully, Man. 7, 37.—With समुप *sam-upa*, **1.** To sit, Râm. 2, 105, 1. **2.** To perform, Râm. 4, 10, 24. **3.** To honour, Mṛichchh. 37, 4.—With सम् *sam*, **1.** To sit together, MBh. 2, 304. **2.** To sit together with (with the acc.), MBh. 1, 2104; with the instr., Sâv. 6, 27. **3.** To sit, Man. 2, 101. **4.** To be a match, MBh. 3, 372.—With प्रतिसम् *prati-sam*, To be able to resist (with the acc.), MBh. 3, 17314.—Cf. ἧμαι, ἧσται = *âste*; concerning the spir. asper cf. ἡμεδ- in ἡμεδ-απός = *asmad*.

आसङ्ग *âsaṅga*, i.e. *â-sańj + a*, m. **1.** Being attached, Çâk. d. 132. **2.** Attachment, Pańch. v. d. 93.—**Comp.** *Uttara-*, m. an upper and outer garment, Pańch. 236, 8.

आसत्ति *âsatti*, i.e. *â-sad + ti*, f. Juxtaposition (of words), Bhâshâp. 81; 82. Connection, Bhâshâp. 63.

आसन *âs + ana*, m. and n. **1.** Sitting, Man. 6, 22; Daçak. in Chr. 180, 22 (*vigṛihya-*, Sitting separately, not together). **2.** Sitting in some peculiar posture for pious purposes, Vedântas. in Chr. 217, 14; 16. **3.** Sitting encamped, Man. 7, 160. **4.** Dwelling, Man. 2, 215. **5.** A seat, Man. 3, 208; Bhag. 6, 11.—**Comp.** *Ardha-*, n. half a seat, Çâk. 97, 10. *Kamala-* and *Jalaja-*, m. a name of Brahman. *Dharma-*, n. the seat of a judge, Man. 8, 23. *Nṛipa-*, n. a throne. *Padma-*, I. n. 1. a seat consisting of a lotus-flower. 2. a kind of posture when absorbed in meditation. II. adj. dwelling in a lotus-flower. *Bhadra-*, n. 1. a throne. 2. a peculiar posture, in which abstract meditation is performed by a devotee. *Vîra-*, n. 1. a field of battle. 2. a bivouac. 3. a kneeling posture, Man. 11, 110. *Çakra-*, n. a throne, Pañch. iii. d. 270. *Saha-*, n. sitting on the same seat. *Siṁha-*, n. a throne.

आसव *âsava*, i.e. *â-su+a*, m. A distilled spirit, MBh. 16, 30.—Comp. *Madhu-*, m. a spirit distilled from the blossoms of the Bassia latifolia. *Surâ-*, n. an inebriating liquor, Man. 11, 95. *Smara-*, m. saliva.

आसादन *âsâdana*, i. e. *â-sad+ana*, n. Attacking, MBh. 2, 808.

आसार *âsâra*, i.e. *â-sṛi+a*, m. 1. A hard shower, Pañch. 94, 3. 2. A king whose dominions are separated by other intervening states, Kâmand. Nîtis. 8, 17. — Comp. *Dhârâ-*, m. a hard shower, Vikr. d. 70. *Pushpa-*, m. a shower of flowers, Megh. 44. *Sa-*, adj., f. *râ*, rainy.

आसिधार *âsidhâra*, i.e. *asi-dhârâ +a*, adj. As difficult as standing on the edge of a sword (cf. *vrata*), Ragh. 13, 67.

आसिसादयिषु *âsisâdayishu*, i. e. *â-sisâdayisha*, desid. of *sad*, *+u*, adj. Desirous of attacking, Râm. 6, 76, 6.

आसुर *âsura*, i.e. *asura+a*, adj., f. *rî*. 1. Belonging to the Asuras or demons, Arj. 10, 30. 2. Demon-like, Bhag. 9, 12 ; wicked, Daçak. in Chr. 182, 13 : that form of marriage is so called in which the bridegroom gives to the bride, her father, and paternal kinsmen, as much as he can afford, Man. 3, 31.

आसेध *âsedha*, i.e. *â-sidh+a*, m. Arrest.—Comp. *Sthâna-*, m. confinement to a place.

आसेवा *â-sev+â*, f. Intercourse.—Comp. *Dus-*, adj., f. *vâ*, hard to have intercourse with, Râm. 3, 23, 15.

ऽस्रासेविन् *-â-sev+in*, adj., f. *nî*, Addicted, Râjat. 5, 207.

आस्कन्द *â-skand+a*, m. Mounting, Kathâs. 26, 36.

आस्कन्दिन् *â-skand+in*, I. adj., f. *nî*, Jumping on, Ragh. 17, 52. II. m. A donor, Kathâs. 24, 87.

आस्तर *âstara*, i.e. *â-stṛi+a*, m. A layer, Kathâs. 22, 196.

आस्तरण *âstaraṇa*, i.e. *â-stṛi+ana*, n. 1. A layer, MBh. 3, 15142. 2. Lying, Pañch. i. d. 190. 3. A cover, Râm. 3, 49, 15.

आस्तरणवन्त् *âstaraṇa+vant*, adj., f. *vatî*, Covered with blankets, or carpets, Râm. 4, 44, 99 ; MBh. 1, 7943.

आस्तरणिक *âstaraṇika*, i. e. *âstaraṇa+ika*, adj. Spread sacrificial grass, Râm. 6, 96, 15 (Sch.).

आस्तिक *âstika*, i.e. *asti*, third ps. of the pres. of 1. *as*, *+ika*, m. A believer, religious, pious, Râm. 2, 109, 37.

आस्तिक्य *âstikya*, i. e. *âstika + ya*, n. Devoutness, Bhag. 18, 72.

आस्था *â-sthâ*, f. 1. Stay, Bhartṛ. 1, 93. 2. Trust, Bhartṛ. 2, 96. 3. Regard, Bhartṛ. 3, 59.—Comp. *An-*, f. disregard, Kumâras. 6, 63 ; no matter, 6, 12. *Jâta-*, adj., f. *thâ*, full of hope, Daçak. in Chr. 200, 6.

आस्थान *âsthâna*, i.e. *â-sthâ+ana*, n. and f. *nî*, An assembly, Râjat. 5, 35.

आस्पद *âspada*, i.e. perhaps *ât-pada*, n. 1. A place, Râjat. 5, 44. 2. A palace, Râjat. 5, 235. 3. A position, Man. 7, 184. — Cf. perhaps Lat. oppidum.

ऽस्रास्पदता *-âspada + tâ*, f. Condition of being the place of, Kathâs. 7, 81 (confidence).

आस्फालन *âsphâlana*, i.e. *â-sphal* Caus. + *ana*, n. Flapping, striking against, Pańch. iii. d. 237, Kumâras. 3, 22.

आस्फोट *âsphoṭa*, i. e. *â-sphuṭ+a*, m. **1.** Clapping with the hands, MBh. 2, 900. **2.** Clapping, clap in general, MBh. 3, 11141.

आस्फोटन *âsphoṭana*, i.e. *â-sphuṭ* + *ana*, n. Clapping of the hands, Râm. 5, 10, 13.

आस्य *âsya* (vb. *an*, cf. *ânana*), n. **1.** The mouth, Man. 1, 94. **2.** The face, Çringârat. 1. **3.** An organ of speech, as the lips, the teeth, etc., Pańch. v. d. 44.—**Comp.** *Uraga-*, n. A kind of spade, Daçak. in Chr. 198, 9. *Daçâsya*, i.e. *daçan-*, adj. epithet of Râvaṇa. *Dîrgha-*, adj. having a long face. *Pańcha(n)-*, I. adj. 1. having five faces. 2. having five edges, MBh. 7, 1710. II. m. A lion. *Pâṇi-*, adj. one whose hand is his mouth, Man. 4, 117. *Manda-*, n. modesty. *Markaṭa-*, n. copper. *Sthûla-*, m. a snake.—Cf. os, ôra, probably ἠϊών.

आस्या *âs-yâ*, f. Sitting.

आस्वाद *â-svâd+a*, m. Taste, Kumâras. 3, 31; Yâjń. 3, 229; Pańch. 263, 22; i. d. 429.

आस्वादक *â-svâd + aka*, adj. Enjoying.

आस्वादन *â-svâd+ana*, n. Tasting, enjoying, Pańch. 35, 6; Vedântas. in Chr. 218, 2.

आहंकार्य *âhaṁkârya*, i. e. *ahaṁkâra+ya*, adj. Subject to selfishness, Vedântas. in Chr. 209, 21.

ऽआहर *-âhara*, i.e. *â-hṛi+a*, adj. Bringing, Ragh. 1, 49.—**Comp.** *Dus-*, adj. difficult to be accomplished, MBh. 2, 664.

आहरण *âharaṇa*, i.e. *â-hṛi+ana*, n. **1.** Fetching, Çâk. 7, 9. **2.** Accomplishment, MBh. 14, 2072.

आहर्तृ *âhartṛi*, i. e. *â-hṛi+tṛi*, m. **1.** An acquirer, Râm. 5, 95, 34; with acc., Vikr. d. 139 (causing). **2.** One who accomplishes, Nal. 12, 45.

आहव *âhava*, i.e. *â-hve+a*, m. War, battle.—**Comp.** *Mahâ-*, m. a great battle or fight.

आहार *âhâra*, i. e. *â-hṛi+a*, m. Food, Pańch. 55, 19.—**Comp.** *An-*, I. m. non-eating, Hit. 24, 12. II. adj. one who abstains from eating, Râm. 3, 75, 30. *Ekâhâra*, i.e. *eka-âhâra*, adj. eating only once a day, MBh. 13, 5159. *Nis-*, adj. without food, Râm. 1, 48, 31. *Paksha-*, adj. taking food only twice a month, MBh. 3, 15409. *Phala-*, adj., f. *rî*, in order to fetch fruits, Sâv. 4, 23. *Çâka-*, adj. living upon potherbs, Bhartṛ. 2, 79. *Su-*, adj. easily to be procured, Râm. 2, 31, 26. *Svechchhâ-*, i.e. *sva-ichchhâ-*, adj. omnivorous.

आहिण्डिक *âhiṇḍika*, m. The son of a Nishâda by a Vaidehî woman, Man. 10, 37.

आहितुण्डिक *âhituṇḍika*, i.e. *ahi -tuṇḍa+ika*, n. A snake catcher, a juggler, Pańch. iii. d. 67.

आहुति *â-hu+ti*, f. An oblation to the deities, Man. 2, 106.

आहो *âho*, part. Or, Çâk. d. 125.

आह्निक *âhnika*, i.e. *ahan+ika*, I. adj. Daily, MBh. 3, 10772. II. n. A religious ceremony which must be performed every day, Râm. 1, 25, 2.—**Comp.** *Gava-*, n. the daily food of a cow, MBh. 13, 6175.

आह्लाद *â-hlâd+a*, m. Joy, Pańch. v. d. 46.

आह्लादन *â-hlâd+ana*, n. Delighting, delight, Daçak. in Chr. 182, 23.

ऽआह्व *-âhva*, see *âhvâ*.

आह्वय *âhvaya*, i. e. *â-hve+a*, m. **1.** Betting, Man. 8, 7. **2.** As latter part of a comp. adj., Called, e. g. *râmâyaṇa-* called Râmâyaṇa, Râm. 1, 4, 1. *gajâhvaya, gajasâhvaya, nâgasâhvaya* and *vâraṇasâhvaya*, i. e. *-sa-âhvaya*, Called by the name of an elephant, i.e. Hâstinapura from *hastin*, an elephant, and *pura*, a town, MBh. 3, 270 and 9, and 1, 1786. *gaṇḍa-sâhvayâ*, f. The name of a river, probably=Gaṇḍakî, MBh. 3, 14230. *chakra-sâhvaya*, m. The ruddy goose, Anas casarca Gm., Râm. 4, 51, 38; cf. *sâhvaya*.—**Comp.** *Hima-*, m. camphor.

ऽआह्वयन *-âhvayana*, i.e. *â-hve+ana*, n. Latter part of comp. adj., *ratha-anga-*, called after a part of a cart, i.e. *chakra-vâka*, The name of a bird, from *chakra*, a wheel, Râm. 2, 95, 11.

आह्वा *âhvâ*, i. e. *â-hve + â*, f. A name.—**Comp.** *Chakra-*, m. the ruddy goose, Anas casarca Gm., Kathâs. 14, 62. *Sûrya-*, n. 1. copper. 2. gigantic swallow-wort.

आह्वान *âhvâna*, i.e. *â-hve+ana*, n. **1.** Calling, summons, Pañch. iii. d. 44. **2.** An invocation, Man. 9, 126. **3.** A challenge, Râm. 4, 13, 40.

इ *I.*

इ *I*, **A.** ii. 2, Par. (in epic poetry also Âtm. MBh. 5, 192). **1.** To go, Chr. 296, 8=Rigv. i. 112, 8, *etave* ved. inf. **2.** To go to (with the acc.), Râm. 2, 67, 1; with *punar*, to return, MBh. 2, 58. **3.** To undergo, with abstracts, e. g. *çudratâm*, Man. 4, 245, the condition of a Çûdra, i.e. to become a Çûdra; *çosham*, Chât. 9, dryness, i. e. to become dry; *prîtim*, Nal. 16, 23, joy, i.e. to rejoice; *vaçam*, Hit. 1, 32, power, i.e. to become subject. **4.** To go away, Râm. 3, 1, 28. **5.** To return, Râm. 1. 42, 9. **6.** To attain, Vedântas. in Chr. 205, 2. **B.** अय् *AY*, according to the grammarians, i. 1, Par. and Âtm. To go. **C.** ई *Î*, i. 4, Âtm. (properly the pass. voice of *I*), To go, Chr. 287, 5= Rigv. i. 48, 5. ii. 2, Par., **1.** To go. **2.** To pervade. **3.** To conceive. **4.** To desire. **5.** To throw. **6.** To eat. Comp. ptcple. of the pf. pass. *durita*, i.e. *dus-*, n. Sin, Hariv. 11059.—With the prep. अति *ati*, A. *I*, **1.** To pass over, Râm. 1, 21, 19; 3, 74, 7. **2.** To surpass, Man. 8, 151, also in the pass. voice or *Î*, i. 4, Âtm., MBh. 2, 1473. **3.** To conquer, Hit. i. d. 18. **4.** To pass into, to enter, Man. 4, 73. **5.** To avoid, Man. 12, 90. **6.** To trespass, Râm. 2, 112, 18. The partic. of the pf. pass. *atîta*, **1.** Passed, Man. 7, 178. **2.** Dead, Man. 5, 71. **3.** Having passed over, Megh. 30. **4.** Conquered, Vedântas. in Chr. 202, 5. **5.** Having let pass away, Râm. 4, 28, 17. **6.** Sluggish, Râm. 4, 31, 8.—With अभ्यति *abhi-ati*, **1.** To pass over, Râm. 2, 70, 27. **2.** To pass away, MBh. 3, 12547. *abhyatîta*, Dead, Man. 4, 252.—With व्यति *vi-ati*, **1.** To pass over, Râm. 2, 113, 4. **2.** To conquer, MBh. 1, 6257. **3.** To swerve (with the abl.), Râm. 4, 17, 32. **4.** To disregard, Naish. 5, 113. **5.** To pass away, Râm. 2, 50, 37. *vyatîta*. 1. Passed, Chr. 16, 20. 2. Dead, MBh. 1, 4592.—With समति *sam-ati*, **1.** To pass. Râm. 2, 71, 17; MBh. 3, 10435. **2.** To surpass, Kir. 5, 20. **3.** To avoid, Bhag. 14, 26. **4.** To pass away, Râm. 2, 27,

19.—With अधि *adhi*, Âtm. (in epic poetry also Par.), To study, Man. 2, 107; MBh. 3, 13689 (Par.); to learn. MBh. 3, 10713 (Par.). Ptcple. of the pres. compounded with *an-*, *anadhiyâna*, Unlearned, Man. 2, 157. *adhîta*, in pass. and act. sense, Learned, having learned, Sâv. 6, 11; Hit. Pr. d. 23. *dus-*, adj. Learned wrongly, Châṇ. 98.—Caus. *adhy-âpaya*, To teach (with two acc.), Man. 2, 140.—With प्राधि *pra-adhi* in *prâdhîta*, Well-read, Man. 7, 85.—With प्रत्यधि *prati-adhi*, To study one by one, MBh. 3, 4182.—With समधि *sam-adhi*, To peruse, MBh. 6, 93.—With अनु *anu*, 1. To follow, Râm. 6, 10, 4. 2. To visit, Nal. 2, 9. 3. To obey, MBh. 3, 1143. *anvita*, 1. Following, Râm. 3, 40, 31. 2. Possessed of, having, Pańch. iii. d. 238; Râm. 1, 7,16; 3, 20, 3. 3. Followed, rendered, Çâk. d. 141.—Comp. *Kula-*, adj. descended from a high family, Pańch. i. d. 466.—With समनु *sam-anu* in *samanvita*, Possessed of, having, Râm. 1, 4, 26; 4, 8, 52.—With अन्तर् *antar* in *antarita*, 1. Plunged, Pańch. 117, 5. 2. Hidden, Çâk. 9, 18. 3. Obstructed, Pańch. i. d. 140. B. *AY*, with *antar*, to get between, Mṛichchh. 35, 11 (cf. Lat. interire).—A. *I*, with अप *apa*, To go away, Chr. 289, 2=Rigv. i. 50, 2; Man. 8, 292. *apeta*, 1. Come off, Pańch. 91, 6. 2. Having swerved from, Ram. 2, 109, 32. 3. When being the former part of a comp. adj., Without, e.g. *apeta-bhî*, Fearless, Man, 7, 197. Comp. *An-apeta*, not having swerved from, Râm. 5, 48, 7.—With व्यप *vi-apa*, 1. To come asunder, to separate, MBh. 12, 868. 2. To leave, Man. 11, 97. *vyapeta*, 1. Having swerved from, Yâjń. 2, 5. 2. When being the former part of a comp. adj., Without, e.g. *vyapeta-bhî*, Fearless, Bhag. 11, 49.—With अभि *abhi*, 1. To come near, to approach, Sâv. 6, 4; also with *sakâçam*, *samîpam*, Pańch. 46, 4; 200, 2. 2. To enter, Man. 8, 75. 3. To attain, Pańch. 2, 6. 4. To undergo, Pańch. i. d. 132; Râm. 3, 49, 26, *grahaṇam*, to be caught.—With समभि *sam-abhi*, 1. To approach, Râm. 2, 97, 18. 2. To follow, Çiç. 1, 72.—With अव *ava*, 1. To understand, MBh. 3, 235. 2. To know, Ragh. 2, 56. 3. To consider, Çâk. d. 108. 4. To believe, Vikr. 8, 18.—With समव *sam-ava* in *samaveta*, 1. Having met, Man. 2, 139. 2. United, Râm. 4, 28, 12; intimately united, Bhâshâp. 17.—With अस्तम् *astam*, A. *I*, 1. To set, Man. 4, 75. 2. To die, Râm. 2, 102, 9.—B. *AY*, To set, Prab. 112, 6.—With आ *â*, A. *I*, 1. To approach, Man. 2, 120. 2. To come, Nal. 7, 4. 3. To undergo, Râm. 2, 62, 20; Daçak. in Chr. 189, 4, *mûlaharatvam*, To become utterly ruined.—With अभ्या *abhi-â*, 1. To approach, Nal. 18, 14 (13). 2. To undergo, Râm. 1, 35, 14 (To go to rest).—With समभ्या *sam-abhi-â*, To approach, Pańch. 40, 21.—With उपा *upa-â*, 1. To approach, Dev. 13, 3. 2. To cling to, Bhartṛ. 3, 64. 3. To undergo, MBh. 1, 1258 (to become tranquil).—With अभ्युपा *abhi-upa-â*, To approach, Râm. 6, 9, 99.—With अनुपर्या *anu-pari-â*, To walk round about, MBh. 14, 468.—With प्रत्या *prati-â*, To return, MBh. 3, 2744.—With समा *sam-â*, 1. To go together, Pańch. 45, 15. 2. To meet, MBh. 12, 868; Râm. 3, 43, 42. 3. To unite, Râm. 1, 77, 29. 4. To assemble,

Man. 2, 152. **5.** To enter, Hit. iii. d. 173. —With उद् *ud*, A. *I*, **1.** To proceed, Ragh. 7, 23; Prab. 107, 18. **2.** To rise, Râm. 4, 38, 12; Ragh. 17, 77; Man. 4, 37. **3.** To rise against (with acc.), MBh. 3, 1921. *udita*, **1.** Risen, Man. 2, 15. **2.** Sprung up, Kir. 5, 5. **3.** Commenced, Râjat. 5, 117. B. *AY*, To rise, Râm. 3, 12, 4; Mṛichchh. 25, 24; Âtm., Prab. 91, 10. C. *Î*, To rise, Bhaṭṭ. 18, 20; 8, 35. *udîta*, Naish. 6, 52.—With अभ्युद् *abhi-ud*, A. *I*, **1.** To rise, Râm. 1, 19, 8. **2.** To appear, Man. 4, 104. **3.** To spring up, Prab. 116, 19. **4.** To rise over (with acc.), Man. 2, 219. **5.** To rise against, MBh. 3, 210 (*iyât* either for *iyât* or from *î* Par.). *abhyudita*, Surprised by the rising sun, Man. 2, 221. B. *AY*, To rise over, MBh. 4, 488 (fut. ii.).—With प्रोद् *pra-ud*, A. *I*, To rise, Bhartṛ. 1, 66.—With प्रत्युद् *prati-ud*, To rise and go to meet, MBh. 13, 147.—With समुद् *sam-ud*, **1.** To rise together, Râm. 2, 1, 26. **2.** To rise, Râm. 2, 83, 9. *samudita*, **1.** Lofty, Kir. 5, 1. **2.** Endowed, Arj. 10, 10.—With उप *upa*, **1.** To approach, Pańch. ii. d. 18; with *samîpam*, Çâk. d. 139; to approach carnally, Man. 11, 172. **2.** To undergo, Ṛit. 6, 7; *vistaratâm*, To spread; Râm. 2, 21, 7, *bâlyam*, To become childish. **3.** To reach, to devolve upon, Hit. Pr. d. 30. *upeta*, **1.** Approached, MBh. 3, 3003. **2.** Living under, Râm. 3, 76, 13. **3.** Undergone, Daçak. in Chr. 183, 12. **4.** Accompanied, Chr. 56, 16. **5.** Possessed of, having, Râm. 3, 55, 6. Ptcple. of the fut. pass. *upeya*, To be expedited, Man. 7, 215. n. Aim, Mâlav. 10, 3.—Comp. *An-upeya*, not to be approached carnally, Man. 11, 172.—B. *AY*, To approach, MBh. 14, 781.—With अभ्युप *abhi-upa*, A. *I*, **1.** To approach, Bhartṛ. 3, 83. **2.** To attain, Pańch. 40, 13. **3.** To undergo, Râm. 5, 90, 41, *sakhitvam naḥ*, he may become our friend. **4.** To assent, Daçak. in Chr. 189, 22.—With समोप *sam-â-upa* in *samopeta*, Possessed of, having, Pańch. i. d. 463. —With समुप *sam-upa*, **1.** To assemble, MBh. 1, 6937. **2.** To meet, Pańch. 35, 2. **3.** To approach, Râm. 1, 73, 1. **4.** To reach, to devolve upon, Râm. 4, 21, 29. **5.** To undergo, Çiç. 9, 68; *vishatâm*, to become poison. *samupeta*, **1.** Approached, MBh. 2, 1219. **2.** Endowed, Nal. 12, 46.—With निस् *nis*, To go out (with abl.), Râm. 2, 42, 1.—With परा *parâ*, **1.** To run away, Pańch. v. d. 74. **2.** To approach, MBh. 1, 7204. **3.** To attain, MBh. 3, 255. *pareta*, Dead, Yâjń. 2, 29.—Cf. Lat. perire.—With पला *palâ* (for *parâ*), B. *AY*, Âtm. (in epic poetry also Par., MBh. 2, 613), To run away, to show one's heels.—With प्रपला *pra-palâ*, To run away. *palâyita*, Run away, Râjat. 5, 260. —With विपला *vi-palâ*, To fly away in different directions, Râm. 2, 78, 13; *vi-a-palâyata* as if *palây* was a simplex. —With परि *pari*, A. *I*, **1.** To walk around, Râm. 4, 61, 47; Draup. 7, 8 (as a sign of honour). **2.** To turn over in one's mind, MBh. 3, 12508; Râm. 5, 81, 4. *parîta*, Surrounded, Râm. 1, 49, 16. **2.** Filled, Râm. 2, 76, 23. **3.** Seized, Nal. 14, 5; 15, 18 (17). **4.** Surrounding, MBh. 12, 2167. **5.** Expired, Râm. 3, 57, 18.—With अनुपरि *anu-pari*, To roam about, Râm. 6, 3, 29.—With अभिपरि *abhi-pari*; *abhiparîta*, **1.** Seized, MBh. 3, 997. **2.** Filled, Râm. 4, 1, 2.—With विपरि *vi-pari*; *viparîta*, **1.** Inverted, Mṛichchh. 22, 6. **2.** Contrary, Man. 7, 34; Râm. 5, 81, 15. 3. Perverse, MBh. 3, 110. 4. Unfavourable, MBh. 16, 1. n. A kind of love-making, Râjat. 5, 372.—With प्र *pra*, 1. To proceed, to spring up, MBh. 3, 13116. 2. To come to, MBh. 3, 13385. 3. To die, Man. 2, 111. *preta*, Dead, Man. 2, 247. Absol. *pretya*, In the other world, Man. 2, 9.—With अभिप्र *abhi-pra*, 1. To approach, Râm. 2, 3, 31. 2. To consider, Râm. 2, 49, 16. *abhipreta*, 1. Intended, Pańch. 191, 11. 2. Desired, Râm. 2, 21, 35. 3. Beloved, Çâk. 87, 16.—With विप्र *vi-pra*, To withdraw, MBh. 1, 6392.—With प्रति *prati*, 1. To go to, MBh. 3, 12359. 2. To return, Ragh. 5, 35. 3. To learn exactly, to be convinced of (with acc.), Prab. 25, 4. 4. To believe, Râm. 5, 31, 62. *pratîta*, 1. Agreed, Man. 3, 3. 2. True, Daçak. in Chr. 192, 1. 3. Known, Ragh. 13, 35. 4. Convinced, Hit. 12, 2. 5. Resolved, MBh. 14, 241. 6. Cheerful, Râm. 5, 95, 44. Caus. *praty-âyaya*, To convince, Çâk. d. 127. — With संप्रति *sam-prati*, To believe, Râm. 5, 31, 61.—With वि *vi*, 1. To traverse, Chr. 289, 7=Rigv. i. 50, 7. 2. To leave, MBh. 3, 8557. *vîta*, when the former part of a comp. adj., Devoid of, Man. 6, 32.—With अपवि *apa-vi*, B. *AY*, To deny, Man. 8, 51; 60; 332.—With सम् *sam*, A. *I.*, 1. To assemble, Râm. 1, 44, 21. 2. To meet with, Râm. 6, 18, 5. 3. To become united, Nal. 14, 23. Pass., To be united, to be treated in the same manner with (instr.), Böthl. Ind. Spr. 280. 4. To arrive, Pańch. 53, 23. 5. To go, Pańch. 226, 12. 6. To attain, Pańch. i. d. 221. 7. To begin, MBh. 4, 348. *samita*, 1. Assembled, MBh. 3, 10651. 2. United with, MB. 14, 2630.—Cf. εἶμι (=*emi*), ἴενται=*iyante*, οἴω, οἴομαι οἶμαι=*ava-i*; Lat. ire; Goth. ï in ïddja, etc.

इक्षु *ikshu* (akin to *ish*), m. Sugar cane, Man. 9, 39.—Comp. *Kâshṭha-*, m. a kind of sugar cane, Suçr. 1, 186, 15.

इक्ष्वाकु *ikshvâku*, m. 1. The name of the first king of Ayodhya, Râm. 1, 70, 20. 2. A descendant of that king, Râm. 1, 70, 11.

† इख् *IKH* and इङ्ख् *IṄKH*, i. 1, Par. To go.

इङ्ग् *IṄG* (probably a denomin. derived from *iṅga*), i. 1, Par. (in epic poetry also Âtm., Bhag. 14, 23), To move, MBh. 3, 8756. *iṅgita*, n. Gesture, Man. 7, 67.

इङ्ग *iṅga*, i.e. *iṅj* (cf. Bṛih. Ar. Up. 6, 4, 23, akin to *ej* and *vij*)+*a*, adj., f. *gâ*, Moveable, MBh. 3, 8756.—Comp. *Nis-*, adj. immoveable, MBh. 12, 1558.

इङ्गुद *iṅguda*, I. m. and *dî* f. The name of a plant, Terminalia catappa. II. n. Its nut.

इच्छा *ichchhâ*, i.e. *ichchh*, base of the pres. of 2. *ish*, +*a*, f. Wish, desire, Vedântas. in Chr. 203, 19; Bhag. 5, 28. Will, Daçak. in Chr. 191, 10. *ichchhayâ âtmanaḥ*, Voluntarily, Man. 11, 73.—Comp. *An-*, f. absence of intention; °*chhhayâ*, involuntarily, Man. 11, 124.—Comp. *Mahâ-ichchha*, adj. 1. high-minded. 2. liberal. *Yathechchham*, i.e. *yathâ-ichchha*+*m*, adv. according to one's wish, Daçak. in Chr. 189, 21. *Sva-*, f. wilfulness, following one's own inclination, Pańch. 87, 11.

इच्छु *ichchh*+*u* (see the last), adj. Wishing, Çiç. 9, 82.

इज्या *ijyâ*, i.e. *yaj*+*yâ*, f. Sacrifice, Man. 1, 89.—Comp. *Bhûta-ijya*, adj.

one who makes oblations to the Bhûtas, Bhag. 9, 25.

इट् *IṬ*, i. 1, Par. To go.

इडा *iḍâ* (akin to *iḍ*), f. 1. Refreshment, ved. Chr. 288, 16=Rigv. i. 48, 16 (written *iḷa*). 2. Oblations to the deities, MBh. 2, 1304. 3. Speech, Hariv. 14036. 4. Earth, MBh. 3, 14750. 5. The wife of Budha, MBh. 1, 3141.

इतर *i-tara* (from the pronominal base *i*, see *idam*), adj., f. *râ*, n. *rad* (ved. *ram*, cf. Lat. iterum), 1. Other, Man. 1, 70; *itara-itarair atha vâ itaraiḥ*, By these or those, MBh. 2, 2503. 2. Contrary, e.g. *vijayâya itarâya vâ*, To victory or defeat, MBh. 1, 4092. —Comp. *Itara-itara*, adj., used generally only in the oblique cases of the sing., 1. mutual, with each another, Pańch. ii. d. 136. 2. several, Man. 3, 35.—When the latter part of a comp. word it signifies, I. negation of the former part, e.g. *Dvija-*, m. one who is not a Brâhmaṇa, Ragh. 9, 76. *Nara-*, m. 1. a superhuman being, Bhâg. P. 4, 6, 9. 2. an animal, 3, 13, 49. II. the contrary, e.g. *Dakshiṇa-*, adj. left, Kumâras. 4, 19. *Parusha-*, adj. mild, Ragh. 5, 68. *Sabhya-*, adj. vulgar, Bhartṛ. 3, 57. *Savya-*, adj. right, Ragh. 12, 90. *Sahaja-*, adj. not innate, accidental. *Sita-*, adj. black.

इतरतस् *itara + tas*, adv., Repeated; *itarataç chetarataḥ*, Hither and thither, Râm. 2, 105, 13.

इतरथा *itara + thâ*, adv. Else, Çiç. 9, 13.

इतरेतरतस् *itaretaratas*, i.e. *itara -itara + tas*, adv. One from the other, MBh. 1, 7403.

इतस् *i + tas* (from the pronominal base *i*, see *idam*), I. = the abl. of *idam*, Daçak. in Chr. 182, 2 (from this person, i.e. from myself); Hiḍ. 1, 5, than this, i.e. than I. II. adv. 1. From hence, from this place, Râm. 3, 54, 28; from this time, MBh. 3, 204; therefore, Râm. 5, 81, 45. 2. Hither, Râm. 5, 13, 9; Ragh. 2, 34, against myself. 3. *itas -itas*, Here—there, Çâk. 29, 20; *itaç chetaç cha*, Here and there, Pańch. 20, 25.

इति *iti* (probably a case of an original *i + tya*, see *idam*), adv. 1. Thus, Man. 2, 237. 2. It is used in quoting words or thoughts of one's self or some other: Man. 2, 129, *tâṁ brûyâd bhavatîti*, He may address her thus (i.e. by the word), *bhavati*; Chr. 4, 15, *avocam . . . bhîshmaḥ çântanavaḥ kanyâ haratîti*, I spoke thus: ' Bhîshma the son of Çântanu robs the girls,' i.e. I rob, etc.; Nal. 16, 9, *tarkayâm âsa bhaimîti*, he thought thus: ' she is the daughter of Bhîma '; Nal. 20, 14, *na hi jânâmi bhaved evaṁ na veti*, I do not know (thus): may it be so or not, i.e. I do not know if it be thus or not. Generally words expressing ' to say,' or ' to think,' are wanting, e.g. Pańch. 68, 25, *akuto pi bhayam iti*, ' There is no danger from any quarter ' thus (thinking); Nal. 14, 14, *na tvâṁ vidyur janâ iti*, ' People will not know thee ' thus (thinking). Sometimes is added *kṛitvâ* or *ha*, e.g. MBh. 1, 1522, *sakheti kṛitvâ*, Thinking you are my friend, Man. 9, 45. 3. It often follows a question without expressing a distinct meaning, e.g. Hit. 53, 18. 4. It is used to denote the conclusion of a book or chapter, Râm. 1, end. 5. With preceding *kim*, Why, Daçak. in Chr. 197, 22.

इतिकर्तव्यता *iti-kartavya + tâ*, **इतिकार्यता** *iti-kârya + tâ*, and **इतिकृत्यता** *iti-kṛitya + tâ* (vb. *kṛi*), f. Business, Sâv. 3, 7; MBh. 3, 10031; 1, 7929.

इतिहास *itihâsa*, i.e. *iti-ha-âsa* (the

last part is the third sing. of the pf. of 1. *as*) m. Traditional account, a legend, Man. 3, 232.

इत्थम् *ittham*, i.e. *id* + *tham*, adv. Thus, Daçak. in Chr. 197, 10.

इत्था *itthâ*, i.e. *id* + *thâ*, adv. Thus, Chr. 295, 17 = Rigv, 1, 92, 17.—Cf. Lat. ita.

इद् *i* + *d* (properly the acc. n. of the pronominal base *i* = Lat. id, Goth. ita, O.H.G. iz), a ved. part. laying a stress upon the preceding word, Chr. 290, 8 = Rigv. i. 64, 8.

इदम् *i* + *d-am*, pron. sbst. and adj. The bases of the declension are *a* m. and n., *â* f., *i* n. *î* f., *i-ma* m. and n. *i-mâ* f., *a-na* m. and n. *a-nâ* f., and *e-na* m. and n. *e-nâ* f. This, Man. 2, 163; Nal. 7, 17 (16). Combined with other pronouns it may be translated Here, e.g. with the first psn., Chr. 24, 44, *ayam̃ gachchhâmi*, Here I go; with *tad*, Râm. 5, 13, 31; with *yad*, Hiḍ. 3, 19; with *kim*, Hit. 18, 11.—Cf. Lat. is, ea, id; Goth. is, ita.

इदानीम् *idânîm*, i.e. *i* + *dâ* + *na* + *î* + *m* (*idâ* ved., and, properly then, cf. *ἰδέ*), adv. **1.** Now, Ṛit. 6, 29. **2.** Presently, Çâk. 94, 2.—Cf. Lat. idoneus.

इध्म *idhma*, i.e. *indh* + *ma*, m. Fuel, Râm. 3, 21, 5.

† **इन्द्** *IND*, i. 1, Par. To have supreme power.

इन्दीवर *indîvara*, n. and m. The blue lotus, Nymphæa cærulea, Indr. 1, 8; Daçak. in Chr. 199, 4.

इन्दु *indu*, m. The moon, Râm. 3, 50, 12.—Comp. *A-bâla-*, m. the full moon, Ragh. 6, 53. *Vadana-*, m. a moon-like face, Çiç. 9, 30.

इन्द्र *indra*, m. **1.** The name of a deity, originally the supreme god of the Hindus, Râm. 1, 1, 83. **2.** First, a king, especially as latter part of comp. words, e.g. *khaga-*, m. The king of the birds, Pañch. i. d. 356; *gaja-*, m. A huge elephant, Nal. 12, 54 (40); *jana-*, m. A king (of the people), Râm. 2, 100, 14. *tṛiṇa-*, m. The palmyra tree, MBh. 13, 6861. *deva-*, m. Indra, Arj. 4, 5. *naga-*, m. The Himâlaya, Ragh. 2, 28. *nara-*, m. **1.** A king, Man. 9, 253. **2.** A physician, Daçak. in Chr. 187, 12. *mahâ-*, m. **1.** Indra. **2.** A range of mountains, the northern part of the Ghats. *mṛiga-*, m. A lion. *yaksha-*, m. Kuvera, the god of wealth. *râkshasa-*, m. Râvaṇa, the king of the Râkshasas, or demons, Râm. 3, 55, 35. *râjendra*, i.e. *râjan-*, m. An emperor, a powerful king, Chr. 41, 5. *sura-*, m. Indra, Bhartṛ. 2, 11. *sa-*, adj. With Indra, Râm. 3, 51, 6.

इन्द्रकोषक *indra-kosha* + *ka*, m. A projection of the roof of a house forming a kind of balcony, Râm. 5, 9, 17.

इन्द्राणी *indrâṇî*, i.e. *indra* + *î*, f. The wife of Indra, MBh. 1, 7351.

इन्द्रिय *indriya*, i.e. *indra* + *iya*, n. **1.** Power, Chr. 291, 2 = Rigv. i. 85, 2. **2.** Semen virile, Man. 4, 220. **3.** An organ of sense, Man. 1, 15.—Comp. *Antar-*, n, the internal sense, i.e. the faculty of thinking, Vedântas. in Chr. 217, 19. *Karmendriya*, i.e. *karman-*, n. an organ of action, e.g. the hand, foot, etc., Man. 2, 91. *Jita-*, adj. one who has subdued his senses, Râm. 3, 49, 53. *Nis-*, adj., f. *yâ*, 1. having lost the use of a limb, Man. 9, 201. 2. powerless, Man. 9. 18 (? see Sch.). *Buddhi-* (or *jñâna-*), n. an organ of perception and intellect, as the mind, eye, ear, etc., Man. 2, 91. *Sa-*, adj. with the organs of sense, Man. 1, 55.

इन्ध् *INDH*, ii. 7, Âtm., pf. *îdhe*, **1.** To kindle; pass. *idhya*, MBh. 3, 10821;

ptcple. pf. *iddha,* Man. 8, 215. **2.** To shine.—With the prep. सम् *sam,* To kindle, MBh. 3, 10658. Cf. ἰθαρός, αἴθω, αἰθήρ; Lat. aestus; O.H.G. eit.

इन्धन *indh + ana,* n. Fuel, Man. 7, 118. — **Comp.** *Agni-,* n. kindling a sacrificial fire, Man. 2, 108. *Ap-,* adj. having water for fuel, Ragh. 13, 14.

इन्धनवन्त् *indhana + vant,* adj., f. *vatî,* Possessed of fuel, Râm. 5, 75, 6.

इन्व् *INV,* i. 1, Par. (properly *i,* ii. 5 *i + nu,* which form is in the Vedas the base of the pres.), **1.** To pervade. **2.** To please. **3.** To satisfy. In the Veda especially: to further.—Cf. ἀνύω for αἰνύω, cf. γάννυμαι under *ju.*

इभ *ibha,* m. An elephant, Râjat. 5, 315. — **Comp.** *Gandha-,* m. a kind of elephant, Râjat. 1, 300. *Jala-gandha-,* m. a kind of elephant, or a *gandhebha* (see the preceding) living in water, Râjat. 5, 107. *Digibha,* i.e. *diç-,* m. an elephant of a quarter or point of the compass, one of eight attached to the north, north-east, etc., supporting the globe, Bhâg. P. 5, 14, 39.

इभ्य *ibhya-,* i.e. *ibha + ya,* adj., f. *yâ,* Wealthy, Daçak. in Chr. 186, 19. —Cf. probably ἴφιος, ἴφθιμος.

इयत्ता *iyattâ,* i. e. *iyant + tâ,* f. Quantity, Ragh. 6, 77.

इयन्त् *iyant,* i.e. *i + vant,* cf. ved. *î-vant,* with *y* for *v,* adj., f. *yatî.* **1.** So much, Kathâs. 4, 95. **2.** So large, Kathâs. 12, 8.

इरा *irâ,* f. **1.** Water. **2.** The name of an Apsaras, MBh. 2, 393.

इरिण *iriṇa,* i.e. *irâ + in + a,* n. Barren soil, Man. 3, 142.

इल् *IL,* i. 6, Par. **1.** To sleep. **2.** To go, Hariv. 620. † **3.** To throw; in this signification also i. 10, Par.

ऽइव *-iva,* i.e. curtailed *i + vat* (see *idam*), indecl. **1.** Like, Man. 2, 79. **2.** In some way, Daçak. in Chr. 195, 14. **3.** Almost, Nal. 17, 12. **4.** Scarcely, Chr. 36, 15. **5.** With *na,* Not very, Nal. 25, 19. **6.** With *kim,* Indeed, Çâk. 97, 15.

1. इष् *ISH,* i. 4, Par. **1.** To throw, ved. **2.** To go.—With the prep. अनु *anu,* To search, Daçak. in Chr. 192 10, (cf. 2. *ish*).—With प्र *pra,* Caus. **1.** To throw, Râm. 3, 35, 46. **2.** To direct, Çâk. d. 35. **3.** To send, Râm. 3, 64, 7. **4.** To make known, Râm. 1, 71, 17; *preshita,* Banished, Râm. 2, 68, 8; m. A messenger, Çâk. 29, 12. — With अनुप्र *anu-pra,* Caus. To send after, Râm. 4, 37, 10.—With संप्र *sam-pra,* To throw, Chr. 30, 7. Caus. **1.** To send, MBh. 2, 1179. **2.** To send away, Râm. 4, 56, 17.—Cf. ἵημι.

2. इष् *ISH,* i. 6, Par. (base of the pres. impf. imprt. and potent. *ichchha,* but cf. *anu-*), **1.** To wish, Sâv. 5, 100; Yâjń. 1, 130. **2.** To cherish, Man. 2, 159. **3.** To chose, Man. 8, 384. **4.** To approve, Man. 8, 366. Pass., To be fixed or determined, Bhâshâp. 12; Yâjń. 3, 18; Man. 8, 322. Comp. part. of the pres. *an-ichchhant,* **1.** Not desiring, Râm. 5, 24, 8. **2.** Unwilling, Pańch. 55, 4. Ptcple. of the pf. pass., *ishṭa,* Desired, good, Nal. 1, 1. m. A lover, Çâk. d. 78.—**Comp.** *An-ishṭa,* 1. disagreeable, Râm. 3, 14, 23. 2. disapproved, Man. 9, 319. 3. wicked, Hit. i. d. 5. n. evil occurrence, Kathâs. 18, 86. *Yathâ-ishṭa + m,* adv. 1. according to one's wish, Bhartṛ. 2, 81. 2. carelessly, Man. 2, 198.—Ptcple. of the fut. pass. *eshṭavya* (anomal.), Desirable, MBh. 3, 8075; n. wish, MBh. 14, 1600. —With

the prep. अनु *anu*, **1.** To search, Man. 6, 84; with *isha* as base of the present, etc., MBh. 3, 15753. **2.** To try, Man. 8, 190. **3.** To ask, Man. 4, 33. Comp. ptcple. of the fut. pass., *dus-*, Difficult to be searched through, Râm. 4, 86, 6.—Caus. **1.** To search, Pańch. 214, 19. **2.** To expect, Pańch. 182, 24.—With पर्यनु *pari-anu*, To search, MBh. 1, 1668.—With समनु *sam-anu*, To search through, Râm. 3, 66, 1.—With अभि *abhi*, *abhishṭa*, **1.** Desired, Vedântas. in Chr. 202, 4. **2.** Agreeable, Pańch. 77, 24.—With आ *â*, *eshṭavya* (anomal.), Desirable, MBh. 3, 8075; n. Wish, MBh. 14, 1600.—With पर्या *pari-â*, *paryeshṭavya* (see the last), To be searched, MBh. 9, 229.—With प्रति *prati*, **1.** To receive, Sâv. 3, 12. **2.** To obey, Râm. 1, 34, 30.—With संप्रति *sam-prati*, To assent, Râm. 1, 52, 13. Cf. ἰότης, perhaps ἵμερος.

3. इष् *ISH*, ii. 9, *ishṇâ*, Par. **1.** † To repeat an act. **2.** ved. To further, Chr. 297, 16=Rigv. i. 112, 16.

4. इष् *ish*, f. A desirable object, comfort, Chr. 288, 15=Rigv. i. 48, 15.

इषीका 1.*ish*+*îkâ*, f. Reed, MBh. 1, 4332.—Comp. *Çara-*, f. an arrow, Râm. 2, 104, 43, Gorr.

इषु 1.*ish*+*u*, m. and f. An arrow.—Comp. *Kusuma-*, m. the god of love. *Pańcheshu*, i.e. *pańchan-*, m. the god of love. *Pushpa-*, m. the god of love Cf. ἰός.

इषुधि *ishudhi*, i. e. *ishu-dhâ* (see *nidhi*), m. and f. A quiver.—Comp. *Mahâ-*, a great quiver.

इष्टका *ishṭaka*, f. A brick, Râjat. 5, 463.

इष्टतस् *ishṭa*+*tas* (vb. 2. *ish*), adv. According to one's wish, Râm. 1, 34, 35.

इष्टाकृत *ishṭâkṛita*, i. e. *ishṭa-â* (?) *-kṛita*, n. The name of a sacrifice, MBh. 3, 10513.

इष्टापूर्त *ishṭâpûrta*, i.e. *ishṭa-â-pûrta* (vb. *yaj* and *prî*), n. Sacrifices and pious works, Râm. 1, 23, 8.

इष्टि *ishṭi*, f. I. 2.*ish*+*ti*, Wish. II. *yaj*+*ti*, **1.** Sacrificing, Chr. 296, 1=Rigv. i. 112, 1. **2.** Sacrifice, Man. 4, 10.—Comp. *Jâta-* (vb. *jan*), f. a sacrifice on the birth of a child, Vedântas. in Chr. 202, 16.

इष्टिका *ishṭikâ*=*ishṭakâ*, MBh. 14, 2633.

इष्मिन् 1.*ish*+*min*, adj. Hastening, Chr. 293, 6=Rigv. i. 87, 6.

इष्वास *ishvâsa*, i.e. *ishu*-2.*as*+*a*, m. **1.** An archer, Râm. 1, 1, 12. **2.** A bow, Râm. 3, 49, 43.—Comp. *Mahâ-*, m. an archer.

इह *iha*, i.e. *i*+*dha*, which appears still in the Vedas, cf. *idam*, adv. **1.** In this case, Chr. 55. **2.** Here, Man. 9, 8; in this world, Man. 3, 181. **3.** Hither, Chr. 13, 13.

इहत्य *iha*+*tya*, adj. Of this place, Kathâs. 13, 10.

इळा *iḷâ*, see *iḍâ*.

ई *Î*.

ई *Î*, see *i*.

ईक्ष् *ÎKSH* (like *aksh* in 1.*aksha*, a desider. of a lost vb., see *aksha*), i. 1, Âtm. (in epic poetry also Par., MBh. 15, 826). **1.** To look, Kathâs. 25, 148.

To behold, Çiç. 9, 61. To perceive, Bhag. 6, 29. **2.** To mind, Kumâras. 5, 82; *îkshita*, n. A look, Çâk. d. 44.—With the prep. अधि *adhi*, To suspect, Hit. iv. d. 101 (*satye py apâyam adhîkshate*, Suspects injury even in truth).—With अप *apa*, **1.** To see, Râm. 5, 42, 6. **2.** To mind, Pańch. v. d. 61. To pay regard to, Kathâs. 17, 12. **3.** To intend, Vedântas. in Chr. 215, 13. **4.** To require, Bhâshâp. 63. **5.** To expect, Bhartṛ. 3, 66. *an-apekshita*, adj. **1.** Not minded, Man. 8, 309; unregarded, Daçak. in Chr. 193, 3. **2.** Regardless, Prab. 34, 15.—With व्यप *vi-apa*, **1.** To look back, Râm. 2, 86, 22. **2.** To mind, Ragh. 19, 6.—With अव *ava*, **1.** To look at, MBh. 1, 5923; Râm. 3, 50, 11 (*avekshya-avekshya*, ever pursuing with his eyes). **2.** To perceive, Râm. 2, 45, 5. **3.** To consider, Man. 7, 10. **4.** To mind, MBh. 2, 2158; to regard, Râm. 6, 7, 48. *dus-avekshita*, n. An unsuitable look, MBh. 3, 14669. *su-avekshita*, adj. Well pondered, Râm. 4, 31, 5.—With अन्वव *anu-ava*, **1.** To look at, Râm. 1, 64, 9. **2.** To look round, Râm. 5, 16, 38. **3.** To perceive, Râm. 1, 3, 5. **4.** To reflect, Man. 6, 65.—With अभ्यव *abhi-ava*, To look at, MBh. 2, 2686.—With न्यव *ni-ava*, To ponder, MBh. 12, 4975.—With निरव *nis-ava*, To perceive, Mṛichchh. 86, 1.—With पर्यव *pari-ava*, To regard (?), MBh. 14, 636.—With प्रत्यव *prati-ava*, **1.** To look at, Râm. 2, 39, 1. **2.** To inspect one after the other, Çâk. 80, 21. **3.** To mind, Râm. 2, 32, 34.—With समव *sam-ava*, **1.** To look at, Ṛit. 6, 17; to behold, MBh. 4, 218. **2.** To consider, Râm. 2, 78, 4. **3.** To reflect, Râm. 1, 50, 10. **4.** To pay regard to, Râm. 4, 19, 2.—With उद् *ud*, **1.** To look up to, Râm. 5, 30, 12. **2.** To look at, Man. 4, 77. **3.** To see, Râm. 2, 22, 7. **4.** To wait, Man. 9, 90; to expect, Râm. 6, 109, 5.—With अभ्युद् *abhi-ud*, To look at, Râm. 6, 11, 2.—With प्रत्युद् *prati-ud*, To look at, Râm. 2, 9, 19.—With समुद् *sam-ud*, **1.** To look, Râm. 3, 73, 3. **2.** To perceive, Râm. 5, 2, 1. **3.** To look up to one, Chr. 3, 7.—With उप *upa*, **1.** To look at, Nal. 22, 5. **2.** To pay regard to, Chr. 55, 5. **3.** To examine, Râm. 4, 29, 29. **4.** To descry, Râm. 5, 29, 4. **5.** To overlook, Pańch. 66. 11; Râm. 2, 23, 16; to disregard, Râjat. 5, 47; to neglect, Râm. 4, 17, 5. **6.** To let escape, Man. 8, 344.—With अभ्युप *abhi-upa*, To forsake, MBh. 16, 160.—With समुप *sam-upa*, To neglect, MBh. 2, 1960.—With निस् *nis*, **1.** To behold, MBh. 2, 2463. **2.** To look at, Man. 4, 38. **3.** To look about, Pańch. iv. d. 63, 64 (pass. on account of the metre). **4.** To perceive, Kathâs. 2, 19. **5.** To consider, Râm. 5, 84, 5.—With संनिस् *sam-nis*, To perceive, Râm. 2, 21, 55.—With परि *pari*, **1.** To look round, Râm. 5, 17, 2. **2.** To examine, Man. 9, 14. **3.** To perceive, Râjat. 5, 109. *a-parîkshita*, adj. Inconsiderate, Lass. 15, 5; foolish, Lass. 14, 20.—See *ku-*; *su-*, adj. Well considered, Pańch. v. d. 16. *dushparîkshya*, i. e. *dus-parîkshya*, adj. Difficult to be examined, MBh. 3, 12481. Comp. absol. *a-parîkshya*, Without due consideration, Pańch. v. d. 16. Caus. *parîkshaya*, To cause to be examined, Man. 7, 194.—With प्र *pra*, **1.** To look at, Râm. 2, 97, 13. **2.** To suffer patiently, MBh. 3, 526. **3.** To perceive, Pańch. 23, 11. *prekshita*, n. A look, Daçak.

in Chr. 190, 15. *prekshaṇîya*, Worthy to be looked at, Indr. 5, 13.—Comp. *Dushprekshaṇîya* and *dushprekshya*, i.e. *dus-*, adj. difficult to be looked at, MBh. 1, 2112; Râm. 3, 30, 35.—With अनुप्र *anu-pra*, To see, Draup. 5, 23.—With अभिप्र *abhi-pra*, **1.** To look at, Draup. 8, 39. **2.** To perceive, MBh. 3, 888.—With उत्प्र *ud-pra*, **1.** To look up to, Râm. 5, 85, 5 (*utprekshyâmas*, ii. 2, Par.). **2.** To perceive, Amar. 38.—With उपप्र *upa-pra*, To overlook, MBh. 1, 3022.—With विप्र *vi-pra*, To look in different directions, Râm. 3, 52, 3.—With संप्र *sam-pra*, **1.** To behold, Bhag. 6, 13. **2.** To perceive, Chr. 22, 21. **3.** To consider, Man. 7, 127.—With अभिसंप्र *abhi-sam-pra*, To behold, MBh. 1, 3011.—With प्रति *prati*, **1.** To wait, Daçak. in Chr. 181, 15; To expect, MBh. 3, 1726. **2.** To endure, Man. 9, 77. Comp. ptcple. of the pres. *a-pratîkshamâṇa*, adj. Not expecting, Daçak. in Chr. 201, 1.—With संप्रति *sam-prati*, To wait, MBh. 1, 2903; Râm. 3, 52, 37; literally: do not dwell here waiting, i.e. do not stay here a moment; to expect, Râm. 1, 73, 13.—With वि *vi*, **1.** To look, Man. 2, 192; pass. to appear, Vikr. d. 132. **2.** To consider, Man. 7, 140. Ptcple. of the pf. pass. *vîkshita*, n. A look, Ṛit. 6, 11, v.r.—With अनुवि *anu-vi*, **1.** To look at, MBh. 4, 1235. **2.** To examine, Râm. 5, 19, 34.—With अभिवि *abhi-vi*, **1.** To look at, Man. 7, 6. **2.** To perceive, Râm. 3, 53, 62. **3.** To consider, MBh. 15, 379 (read *-vîkshate*).—With उद्वि *ud-vi*, **1.** To look up, Amar. 24. **2.** To look to, Çâk. d. 161. **3.** To consider, Pañch. i. d. 265.—With समुद्वि *sam-ud-vi*, **1.** To look at, Râm. 3, 4, 34. **2.** To perceive, MBh. 3, 12425.—With उपवि *upa-vi*, To look at, Râm. 2, 58, 32.—With प्रतिवि *prati-vi*, To perceive, Râm. 1, 15, 26. *dushprativîkshaṇîya* and *dushprativîkshya*, i.e. *dus-*, adj. Difficult to be looked at, MBh. 6, 137; Râm. 2, 23, 3.—With संवि *sam-vi*, To perceive, Râm. 5, 46, 10.—With सम् *sam*, **1.** To look to, Man. 6, 68. **2.** To behold, Râm. 3, 52, 11; to perceive, Hiḍ. 4, 26. **3.** To mind, Râm. 2, 61, 12. **4.** To consider, Man. 7, 26. Comp. ptcple. of the pf. pass. *a-samîkshita*, adj. Unperceived, Râm. 5, 81, 8; of the fut. pass. *dus-samîkshya*, adj. Difficult to be looked at, MBh. 7, 1928.—With अभिसम् *abhi-sam*, To perceive, Râm. 2, 100, 39.—With प्रसम् *pra-sam*, **1.** To see, Man. 7, 214. **2.** To perceive, Râm. 3, 52, 52. **3.** To consider, Man. 5, 49.

ईक्षण *îkshaṇa*, i.e. *îksh* + *ana*, n. **1.** Sight, Kathâs. 18, 300. **2.** Care, Man. 7, 141; superintendence, Man. 9, 11. **3.** The eye, Hiḍ. 3, 20.—Comp. *A-sita-*, adj., f. *ṇâ*, black-eyed, Râm. 3, 52, 40. *Madirâ-*, f. *ṇâ*, a fascinating woman, Çâk. d. 67.

ईक्षणिक *îkshaṇika*, i.e. *îkshaṇa* + *ika*, m., f. *kâ*, A fortune-teller, Man. 9, 258.

ईक्षितृ *îkshitṛi*, i.e. *îksh* + *tṛi*, m. An inspector, Man. 8, 91.

† ईख् *ÎKH*, i. 1, Par. To go.

ईङ्ख् *ÎṄKH*, i. 1, Par. To vacillate.—With प्र *pra*, To tremble, Bhartṛ. 1, 66.

† ईज् *ÎJ* and ईञ्ज् *ÎÑJ*, i. 1, Âtm. **1.** To go. **2.** To blame.

ईड् *ÎḌ* (a change of *ishṭ*, a denominative based on 2. *ish*), ii. 2, Âtm. and † i. 10, Par. **1.** To implore, Chr. 296, 1 =Rigv. i. 112, 1. **2.** To praise, Râm. 3, 9, 8.

ईति *i+ti*, f. Calamity, MBh. 3, 11258.—Comp. *Nis-*, adj. free from calamities, Ragh. 1, 63.

ईदृक्ता *îdṛiktâ*, i.e. *îdṛiç + tâ*, f. Quality, Ragh. 13, 5.

ईदृक्ष *îdṛiksha*, i.e. *id-dṛiç+sa* (see *idam*), adj. Such, Kathâs. 25, 176.

ईदृश् *îdṛiç*, i.e. *id-dṛiç* (see the last), adj. Such, Kathâs. 25, 176.

ईदृश *îdṛiça*, i.e. *id-dṛiç+a* (see *îdriksha*), adj., f. *çî*, Such, Pañch. 206, 6.

ईदृशक *îdṛiça+ka*, adj. Such, MBh. 2, 1644.

ईप्सा *îpsâ*, i.e. *îpsa*, desider. of *âp*, +*a*, f. Desire, MBh. 14, 1025.—Comp. *Yathâ-*, fem., instr. sing., according to one's desire, MBh. 3, 116.

ईप्सु *îpsu*, i.e. *îpsa*, desider. of *âp*, +*u*, adj. Desiring, Man. 2, 61.—Comp. *Dharma-*, adj. anxious to perform one's duty, Man. 10, 127.

ईम् *îm* (an old acc. of *î*, f. of *i*, see *idam*), a ved. part. which lays a stress upon the preceding word, Chr. 292, 11 =Rigv. i. 85, 11 (cf. *ιν* in *οὑτοσιν*, also ved. *î*=*ι* in *οὑτοσ-ί*, etc.).

ईर् *ÎR* (akin to *ṛi*), ii. 2, Âtm. († i. 1 and 10, Par.) **1.** To go. **2.** To shake, to throw.—Caus. **1.** To move, MBh. 13, 1839. **2.** To throw, MBh. 3, 709. **3.** To excite, Râm. 5, 11, 8. **4.** To utter (a sound), MBh. 1, 4565; to pronounce, MBh. 14, 941.—With the prep. उद् *ud*, ptcple. of the pf. pass. *udîrṇa*, **1.** Excited, MBh. 3, 973. **2.** Lofty, MBh. 1, 5138. Caus. **1.** To lift up, Râm. 2, 57, 3. **2.** To throw, Râm. 1, 55, 22. **3.** To excite, Râm. 2, 93, 14. **4.** To cause, Daçak. in Chr. 182, 23. **5.** To utter Man. 2, 161. **6.** To speak, Lass. 73, 8. **7.** To show, Kumâras. 2, 6. **8.** *udîrit a* Quick, Prab. 14, 14.—With अभ्युद् *abhi-ud*, Caus. To utter, MBh. 1, 2170. —With समुद् *sam-ud*, *samudîrṇa*, Excited, Râm. 4, 43, 69. Caus. **1.** To raise, Chr. 29, 29. **2.** To throw, Râm. 1, 56, 15. **3.** To excite, MBh. 3, 5073. **4.** To utter, Kathâs. 24, 41.—With प्र *pra*, Caus. **1.** To move, Ragh, 15, 23. **2.** To turn, Çâk. d. 35, v. r. **3.** To push on, Râjat. 5, 329; 330. **4.** To send, Râm. 3, 50, 23. **5.** To excite, Megh. 71. **6.** To ask, Daçak. in Chr. 182, 1. —With संप्र *sam-pra*, Caus. To push forward, Pañch. 222, 2.—With सम् *sam*, Caus. **1.** To move, Râm. 5, 16, 45. **2.** To lift up, MBh. 3, 12185. **3.** To utter, Râm. 4, 6, 21.—With अभिसम् *abhi-sam*, Caus. To move, MBh. 10, 579.

ईरिण *îriṇa* (cf. *iriṇa*), n. A desert, MBh. 13, 7257.

† ईर्क्ष्य् *ÎRKSHY*, i. 1, Par. To envy (cf. *îrshy*).

ईर्षा *îrshâ*, i.e. *îrshy+a*, f. Envy, jealousy, Râm. 4, 24, 37.

ईर्षित *îrshita*, ptcple. of the pf. pass., and ईर्षितव्य *îrshitavya*, ptcple. of the fut. pass. of *îrshy*, Hit. i. d. 107 v. r.; Prab. 49, 11.

ईर्षु *îrshu*, i.e. *îrshy+u*, adj. Envious, Hit. i. d. 22.

ईर्ष्य् *ÎRSHY* (probably *îrshya*, and originally an anomal. frequentat. of *rish*), i. 1, Par. **1.** To envy, Hit. i. d. 107, v.r. **2.** To be jealous, Prab. 49, 11.

ईर्ष्या *irshy*+*â*, f. **1.** Envy, Man. 7, 48. **2.** Jealousy, Bhartṛ. 1, 2.—**Comp.** *Sa-irshya*+*m*, adv. full of jealousy, Pańch. 27, 10.

ईर्ष्यालु *irshyâ* + *lu*, adj. Jealous, Râjat. 5, 316.

ईश् *ÎÇ*, ii. 2, Âtm. **1.** To possess, to be master (with gen.), MBh. 3, 955. **2.** To be able (with loc.), MBh. 13, 26; cf. *içâna*.—With **परि** *pari*, To be able (with infin.), Skandap. Kâçîkh. 19, 51. —Cf. Goth. aigan, A.S. agan.

ईश *iç*+*a*, m., f. *çâ*, **1.** A proprietor, Pańch. i. d. 16. **2.** A master, MBh. 1, 1532. **3.** A ruler, Man. 9, 245. **4.** A name of Çiva, MBh. 13, 588.—**Comp.** *An-*, m., f., not being master, Man. 9, 104. *Amara-*, m. a name of Çiva, Râm. 6, 35, 3. *Avani-*, m. a king, Chaurap. 22. *Kshiti-*, m. a king, Ragh. 2, 67. *Gaurî-*, m. a name of Çiva, MBh. 14, 210. *Chaṇḍî-*, m. a name of Çiva, Bhâg. P. 4, 5, 17. *Jagadîça*, i.e. *jagat-*, m. a name of Vishṇu, Gît. 1, 5. *Jana-*, m. a king, Hariv. 8403. *Jala-*, m. 1. the ocean, Bhâg P. 8, 7, 26. 2. a name of Varuṇa, Bhâg. P. 3, 18, 1. *Jîvita-*, m. a name of Yama, Ragh. 11, 20. *Tiryagîça*, i.e. *tiryańch-*, m. a name of Kṛishṇa, MBh. 7, 6471. *Deva-*, m. the lord of the gods, Râm. 1, 63, 3. *Nadî-*, m. the ocean, Pańch. ii. d. 27. *Bhûta-*, m. Çiva. *Rohiṇî-*, m. the moon. *Viṁçati-*, m. a lord of twenty towns, Man. 7, 115. *Vijaya-*, m. a name of Çiva, Râjat. 5, 46. *Vitta-*, m. a name of Kuvera, Man. 7, 4. *Svarga -loka-*, m. 1. Indra. 2. the body.

ईशा *iç*+*â* (also **ईषा** *ishâ*), f. The pole of a car, Râm. 6, 69, 46.—**Comp.** *Ratha-*, f. the pole of a car, Chr. 34, 14.

ईशान *iç*+*âna* (properly the ptcple. of the pres.), **I.** adj. Ruling, Chr. 293, 4=Rigv. i. 87, 4. **II.** m. A name of Çiva, MBh. 3, 8169. **III.** f. *ni*, A surname of Durgâ, Dev. 8, 21.—**Comp.** *Gaṇa-içâna*, Gaṇeça, MBh. 1, 75.

ईशानकृत् *içana-kṛi* + *t*, adj. Behaving as master, Chr. 290, 5=Rigv. i. 64, 5.

ईशितृ *içitṛi*, i.e. *iç*+*tṛi*, m. A ruler, Prab. 108, 15.

ईशित्व *içitva*, i. e. *için*+*tva*, n. Supremacy, MBh. 14, 1053.

ईशिन् *iç*+*in*, adj. m. A governor, Man. 7, 116.

ईश्वर *içvara*, i.e. *iç*+*van*+*a* (with *r* for *n*), **I.** m., f. *ri*, **1.** A ruler, Man. 1, 99; f. *ri*, Râm. 3, 61, 29. **2.** An owner, **II.** m. **1.** A lord. **2.** A husband, Nal. 4, 2. **3.** A king, Man. 4, 153. **4.** A wealthy man, Pańch. 110, 23; ii. d. 70. **5.** The supreme deity, Man. 7, 14. **6.** A name of Çiva, Kathâs. 10, 33. **III.** f. *râ* and *ri*, A surname of Durgâ, Kir. 5, 33.—**Comp.** *An-*, adj. repugnant to the nature of the supreme deity, Man. 6, 72. *Amara-*, m. a name of Vishṇu, Râm. 1, 77, 29; of Indra, Ragh. 19, 15. *Alakâ-*, m. a name of Kuvera, Ragh. 19, 15. *Avanti-*, m. the name of a sanctuary, Râjat. 5, 45. *Âtmeçvara*, i.e. *âtman-*, m. one who has subdued his senses, Kumâras. 3, 40. *Kavi-*, m. the chief of the wise men, Bhartṛ. 2, 21. *Kâvyadevî-*, m. a sanctuary of Çiva, erected by the princess Kâvyadevî, Râjat. 5, 41. *Kshiti-*, m. a king, Ragh. 3, 3. *Gaṇa-*, m. the chief of a troop, Râm. 4, 28, 22. *Chakra-*, m. a name of Vishṇu, Râjat. 4, 276. *Chaṇḍâ-*, m. a name of Çiva, Megh. 34. *Jagadîçvara*, i.e. *jagat-*, m. a name of Çiva, Râm. 3, 53, 60. *Jana-*, m. a king, Râm. 1, 43, 17. *Jala-*, m. a name of Varuṇa. MBh. 1, 8175. *Tuṅga-*, m. a sanctuary of Çiva, Râjat 2, 14. *Tri-diva-*, m.

a name of Indra, Râm. 1, 48, 17. *Tri-pura-*, the name of a locality, Râjat. 6, 135; of a sanctuary, Râjat. 5, 46. *Dina-* and *divasa-*, m. the sun, Bhartṛ. 2, 27; 86. *Deva-*, m. the lord of gods, Râm. 1, 25, 13. *Deha-*, m. the soul, Mârk. P. 26, 18. *Dvija-*, m. the moon, Hariv. 2476. *Dhana-*, m. a name of Kuvera, Draup. 2, 3. *Nandîçvara*, i.e. *nandi-* or *nandin-*, m. 1. a name of Çiva, MBh. 12, 10431. 2. a proper name, Bhâg. P. 4, 2, 20. *Prâṇa-*, m. a husband. *Niçâ-prâṇa-*, m. the moon. *Bhûta-*, m. Çiva. *Mahâ-*, m. Çiva. *Yoga-*, m. 1. a teacher of sacred science, Pañch. 24, 23. 2. a magician. 3. a deity, the object of devout contemplation. 4. Krishṇa. *Çûra-*, m. a sanctuary built by Çûra, Râjat. 5, 38. *Sâmbâ-*, m. a sanctuary built by Sâmbavatî, ib. 295. *Sura-*, I. m. Çiva. II. f. *rî*, a name of Durgâ, Râjat. 5, 37; 40, 41.

ईश्वरता *îçvara + tâ*, f. and **ईश्वरत्व** *îçvara + tva*, n. Supremacy, Prab. 108, 15; MBh. 2, 1695.

ईष् *ÎSH* (akin to 1. *ish*), i. 1, Âtm. **1.** To go, to hasten, to fly. † **2.** To kill. † **3.** To see (or to give). † i. 1, Par. To glean.

ईषत् *îshat* (probably ntr. of the ptcple. of the present of *îksh*, with *sh* for *ksh*), adv. **1.** A little, Daçak. in Chr. 198, 18. **2.** When the former part of a comp., especially when followed by a word denoting the partic. of the fut. pass.: Easily, e.g. *îshat-kârya* (vb. *kṛi*), Easy to be made, Râm. 4, 54, 12 (*vidâraṇe*, easy to be cleft). *îshat-kara* (vb. *kṛi*), Easy to be performed, Prab. 36, 6.

ईषा *îshâ*, see *îçâ*.

ईह् *ÎH*, i. 1, Âtm. (sometimes Par.) **1.** To aim at, Man. 4, 15. **2.** To desire, Bhartṛ. 2, 6. **3.** To desire to perform, Man. 3, 205. Comp. ptcple. of the pres. *an-îhamâna*, Not desiring, Yâjñ. 2, 116. Ptcple. of the pf. pass., *îhita*, Desired, Prab. 104, 5. n. **1.** Exertion, Man. 9, 208. **2.** Desire, MBh. 1, 1370. —Comp. *Âyati-*, adj. referring to future time, Râm. 3, 44, 11.—With the prep. **सम्** *sam*, To desire, Pañch, iii.d. 87; i. d. 105 (Par.). *samîhita*, n. Desire, Hit. 44, 7.

ईहा *îh + â*, f. **1.** Exertion, Râm. 3, 43, 38. **2.** Desire, MBh. 3, 95.—Comp. *An-îha* and *nis-*, adj. devoid of energy, MBh, 3, 1240; 14, 1302. *Nis-îhâ*, f. indifference, Bhâg. P. 4, 22, 24.

ईहातस् *îhâ-tas*, adv. By exertion, Man. 9, 205.

उ *U.*

उ, I. interj. of anger, of command, Kumâras. 1, 26. **II.** a part. (cf. *ud*), **1.** Also. **2.** Now, Chr. 289, 1 = Rigv. i. 50, 1. Lengthened *û*, Chr. 296, 1 = Rigv. i. 112, 1.—Cf. *atho* under *atha*, *kim*, and the ved. combination *sa u*, with οὐ in οὖ-τος.

† **उ** *U*, i. 1, Âtm. To sound.

उक्ति *ukti*, i.e. *vach + ti*, f. **1.** Speaking, Man. 8, 104. **2.** Speech, Pañch. 44, 20. — Comp. *Dus-*, f. offending speech, Bhâg. P. 3, 18, 6. *Vakrokti*, i.e. *vakra-*, f. 1. equivoque, pun. 2. sarcasm. 3. hint. *Hita-*, f. 1. good advice. 2. tenderness, compassion.

उक्थ *uktha*, i.e. *vach + tha*, n. Praise, Chr. 292, 4 = Rigv. i. 86, 4.

उक्थ्य *ukthya*, i.e. *uktha + ya*, I. adj. Praiseworthy, Chr. 288, 12 = Rigv. i. 48, 12. **II.** n. The name of the second day of the horse-sacrifice, Râm. 1, 13, 44.

उक्ष् *UKSH*, i. 1, Par. (ved. also

Âtm.), **1.** To sprinkle, Chr. 293, 2=Rigv. i. 87, 2; Chr. 36, 15. **2.** To wet, MBh. 13, 1791.—With the prep. अभि *abhi,* To sprinkle on, Çâk. 41, 4.—With प्र *pra,* **1.** To hallow (by sprinkling) for a sacrifice, Man. 5, 27. **2.** To sacrifice, Râm. 1, 13, 29; 31, Gorr.—With संप्र *sam-pra,* To sprinkle on, Yâjń. 1, 24.—With सम् *sam,* **1.** To wet, Râm. 3, 75, 8. **2.** To endow, Râm. 2, 91, 33.

उक्षणज *ukshaṇaja,* i.e. *uksh+ana-ja* (vb. *jan*), adj. Sprung up by consecration, Ragh. 5, 27.

उक्षन् *uksh+an,* m. An ox or bull, Kir. 5, 42. **2.** A ved. epithet of the Maruts who, by bringing rain (i.e. by sprinkling), impregnate the earth like bulls, Chr. 290, 2=Rigv. i. 64, 2.—Cf. Goth. auhsa, base auhsan; A.S. oxa; the ved. fem. is *vaçâ,* probably=Lat. vacca.

उक्षित *ukshita,* ptcple. of the pf. pass. of *uksh,* and ved. also of *vaksh,* q. cf.

† **उख्** *UKH,* and **उङ्ख्** *UṄKH,* i. 1 Par. To go, to move.

उग्र *ugra,* probably *vaj+ra,* **I.** adj. f. *râ,* **1.** Very strong (ved.). **2.** Terrible, Râm. 4, 22, 35; Bhag. 11, 31. **3.** Cruel, Man. 4, 212. **4.** Rigorous, Man. 6, 75. Compar. *ugratara,* as rigorous as possible, Man. 6, 24. **II.** m. and f. *râ,* The offspring of a Kshatriya father and a Çûdrâ mother, Man. 10, 9; 19. **III.** m. A proper name, MBh. 1, 2738. —Comp. *Ati-,* adj. excessively cruel, Pańch. iii. d. 76.

उच् *UCH,* i. 4, Par. To like, to be accustomed to. Ptcple. of the pf. pass. *uchita,* **1.** Used, Râm. 4, 8, 57. **2.** Accustomed to (with the gen.), Nal. 23, 22. **3.** Suitable, proper, Pańch. 176, 1; Râjat. 5, 184; Râm. 1, 44, 56.—Comp. *A-tathâ-,* adj. not thus used to, Nal. 15, 18. *An-,* adj. 1. inappropriate, Pańch. 61, 3. **2.** unused to, Râm. 2, 58, 5. *Yathâ-,* adj. used, Hit. 42, 3. *A-yathâ-uchita,* adj. inappropriate, Pańch. i. d. 193 (former part of a comp. word, in the sense of the adv. °*ta+m*).—With the prep. सम् *sam,* in the ptcple. of the pf. pass. *samuchita,* Used to, Daçak. in Chr. 181, 16.

उचितत्व *uchita+tva* (see the last), n. Convenience, MBh. 1, 7465.

उच्च *uchcha,* i.e. *ud-ańch+a,* **I.** adj. f. *châ,* **1.** High, Kir. 5, 5. **2.** Deep, Chaurap. 44. **3.** Loud, Bhartṛ 3, 85. **II.** *uchchais* (instr. pl.), adv. **1.** High, Kumâras. 6, 72. **2.** Loud, Nal. 11, 2. **3.** Much, excessively, Amar. 94. **4.** Powerfully, Pańch. iv. d. 22. **III.** m. Culmination, Râm. 1, 19, 2.—Comp. *An-,* adj. low, Râjat. 5, 478.

उच्चकैस् *uchchakais,* i.e. *uchcha+ka,* instr. pl., adv. Very loud, Pańch. ii. d. 166.

उच्चता *uchcha+tâ,* f. Superiority, MBh. 3, 10635.

उच्चय *uchchaya,* i.e. *ud-chi+a,* m. **1.** Gathering, Daçak. in Chr. 181, 20. **2.** Collection, Çâk. d. 42. **3.** Plenty, Râm. 5, 13, 61.—Comp. *Çilâ-,* m. a mountain, Kir. 5, 10. *Salila-,* adj. having plenty of water, MBh. 3, 8334. *Sthûla-,* m. 1. a hollow at the root of an elephant's tusk. 2. the middle pace of an elephant. 3. pimples on the face. 4. a hill at the foot of a mountain.

उच्चाटन *uchchâṭana,* i.e. *ud-chaṭ+ana,* n. **1.** Ruin, Prab. 61, 16. **2.** The name of one of the arrows of Kâma, Lass. 7, 3.

उच्चार *uchchâra,* i.e. *ud-char+a,* m. Voiding excrements, Man. 4, 50.

उच्चारण *uchchâraṇa*, i.e. *ud-char* Caus., + *ana*, n. Pronunciation, Çiç. 4, 18; recitation, MBh. 3, 14037.

उच्चारित्र *uchchâritra*, i.e. *ud-châritra* in *mâtra-*, n. Immoral conduct, Râjat. 6, 166.

उच्चावच *uchchâvacha*, i.e. *uchcha -ava-añch* + *a*, adj. High and low, various, Man. 12, 14.

उच्चैस्तर *uchchais* + *tara* (see *uchcha*), adj. Very tall, Pañch. 161, 14. °*tarâm*, adj. Higher, Kumâras. 7, 68.

उच्चैस्तरत्व *uchchaistara* + *tva*, n. Being excessively high, Pañch. 33, 6.

उच्छ् *UCHCHH*, see 2. *vas*.

उच्छित्ति *uchchhitti*, i.e. *ud-chhid* + *ti*, f. Extermination, Kathâs. 15, 82.

उच्छिलीन्ध्र *uchchhilîndhra*, i.e. *ud -çilîndhra*, I. n. A mushroom, Megh. 11. II. adj. Covered with mushrooms, ib. v. r. (read *uchchhil*°).

उच्छिष्टता *uchchhishṭatâ*, i.e. *ud -çishṭa* + *tâ* (vb. *çish*), f. Impurity, Pañch. 89, 3.

उच्छीर्षक *uchchhîrshaka*, i.e. *ud -çîrshan* + *ka*, I. adj. Having the head erect. II. n. A pillow, Man. 3, 89.

उच्छुष्क *uchchhushka*, i.e. *ud-çushka*, adj., f. *kâ*, Dried up, Mṛichchh. 2, 12.

उच्छृङ्खल *uchchhṛiṅkhala*, i.e. *ud -çṛiṅkhala*, adj., f. *lâ*, 1. Unrestrained, Hit. iii. d. 97. 2. Wicked, Kathâs. 18, 123.

उच्छेत्तृ *uchchhettṛi*, i.e. *ud-chhid* + *tṛi*, m. A destroyer, Râm. 3, 36, 11.

उच्छेद *uchchheda*, i.e. *ud-chhid* + *a*, m. 1. Chopping off, Kathâs. 18, 29. 2. Destruction, Pañch. ii. d. 196.—Comp. *Dus-*, adj. difficult to be destroyed, Prab. 76, 9.

उच्छेदन *uchchhedana*, i.e. *ud-chhid* + *ana*, n. Extermination, Pañch. 53, 25.

उच्छेदिन् *uchchhedin*, i.e. *ud-chhid* + *in*, adj., f. *nî*, Destroying, Hit. Pr. 9.

उच्छेष *uchchhesha*, i.e. *ud-çish* + *a* m. Residue, MBh. 13, 1621.

उच्छेषण *uchchheshaṇa*, i.e. *ud-çish* + *ana*, n. Residue, Man. 3, 246.

उच्छोषण *uchchhoshaṇa*, i.e. *ud -çush* + *ana*, I. adj. Drying up. II. n. Drying up, Râm. 5, 72, 2.

उच्छ्रय *uchchhraya*, i.e. *ud-çri* + *a*, m. Elevation, Râm. 1, 13, 24.—Comp. *Mahâ-*, adj. lofty, Râm. 3, 74, 14. *Su -kṛita-*, adj. very lofty, MBh. 1, 6963.

उच्छ्राय *uchchhrâya*, i.e. *ud-çri* + *a*, m. 1. Rising, Kir. 5, 31; Kathâs. 25, 45. 2. Elevation, Râjat. 5, 261.—Comp. *Çṛiṅga-*, m. a lofty top, Megh. 59.

ऽउच्छ्रायवन्त् *-uchchhrâya* + *vant*, in *mahâ-*, adj. Very tall, Pañch. 104, 6. *patâkâ-*, adj. Having tall flags, MBh. 1, 4995.

उच्छ्रिति *uchchhriti*, i.e. *ud-çri* + *ti*, f. Exaltation, an exalted birth, Man. 5, 40.

उच्छ्वास *uchchhvâsa*, i.e. *ud-çvas* + *a* m. 1. Breathing, Râm. 1, 65, 7. 2. Growing a little more conspicuous (of a colour), Çâk. d. 142. 3. Breath, Vikr. d. 105. 4. Sighing, Megh. 100. 5. A division of a book, Daçak. in Chr. 179, 4.—Comp. *Nis-*, adj., f. *sâ*, without breathing, Râm. 5, 25, 48.

उच्छ्वासिन् *uchchhvâsin*, i.e. *ud -çvas* + *in*, adj., f. *nî*, 1. Sighing, Megh. 100. 2. Rising, Vikr. d. 7. 3. Growing conspicuous (as colour), Kumâras. 7, 82.

उच्छ् *UCHH*, see 2. *vas*.

उज्जयिनी *ujjayinî*, i.e. *ud-ji* + *in* + *î*, f. The city Oujein, Daçak. in Chr. 192, 12.

उज्ज्वल *ujjvala*, i.e. *ud-jval* + *a*, adj., f. *lâ*, **1.** Splendid, Daçak. in Chr. 195, 24. **2.** Clear, Bhartṛ. 2, 16. **3.** Beautiful, Çiç. 9, 47.

उज्ज्वलन *ujjvalana*, i.e. *ud-jval* + *ana*, n. Fire (?), Râm. 2, 40, 14.

उज्जृम्भ *ujjṛimbha*, i. e. *ud-jṛimbh* + *a*, adj. **1.** Yawning. **2.** Open. **3.** Expanded, blown.

उज्झ् *UJJH* (a dialect. form of *ud -hâ*), i. 6, Par. **1.** To abandon, Râjat. 5, 349. **2.** To let fall, Kir. 5, 6. **3.** To throw, Râjat. 5, 108. *ujjhita*, **1.** Devoid of, Râjat. 5, 4. **2.** Risked, Râjat. 5, 131.—With the prep. **प्र** *pra*, **1.** To abandon, Pañch. v. d. 22. **2.** To avoid, Hit. i. d. 17 n.—With **सम्** *sam*, To abandon, Pañch. i. d. 343. *samujjhita*, Free from, Prab. 11. 9.

उञ्छ् *UŃCHH*, i. 1 and 6, Par. To collect the gleanings of the harvest, Man. 3, 100 —With the prep. **प्र** *pra*, To wipe out, Mṛichchh. 140, 23.

उञ्छ *uńchh* + *a*, m. Gleaning grains, Man. 10, 112.—**Comp.** *Çila-*, m. gleaning ears and grains, Man. 7, 33.

उटज *uṭaja*, i.e. perhaps *vaṭa-ja* (vb. *jan*), m. and n. A hut made of leaves, the residence of anchorites, Râm. 1, 48, 22.—**Comp.** *Saha-*, m. A hut made of leaves, the residence of anchorites.

† **उठ्** *UṬH* or **ऊठ्** *ÛṬH*, i. 1, Par. To strike.

उडु *uḍu*, f. and n. A star, Mâlav. 64, d. 82.

उडुप *uḍupa*, i. e. **I.** *uḍu* (perhaps akin to *udan*, and a dialectical form of *udra* in *samudra*) *-pa* (vb. 2. *pâ*), m. and n. A raft, Mṛichchh. 123, 20. **II.** *uḍu-pa* (vb. 2. *pâ*), m. The moon.

उडुम्बर *uḍumbara*, see *udumbara*.

उड्डयन *uḍḍayana*, i.e. *ud-ḍî* + *ana*, n. Flying up, Pañch. 115, 5.

उत *uta*, part. **1.** And, Chr. 34, 7. **2.** Also, Chr. 3, 8. **3.** *uta—uta*, As well as, MBh. 3, 10684. **4.** *uta—vâ—uta—uta*, As well as, as also, and, MBh. 5, 916; 917. **5.** *uta vâ*, Or, Brâhmaṇav. 3, 5. **6.** part. of interrogation, What, how. In a disjunctive interrogation: Or, Bhartṛ. 3, 77; also with following *vâ*, Pañch. 68, 14; also with following *âho* (*utâho*), Nal. 12, 120; also with following *âho svid*, Nal. 19, 27-29; also with following *svid* only, Pañch. 41, 1; seldom with preceding *kim* (*kim uta*), Mṛchchh. 172, 3. **7.** preceded by *kim* (*kim uta*), Much less, Râm. 4, 35, 8. **8.** preceded by *prati* (*praty uta*), Even, Pañch. iii. d. 27.

उतथ्य *utathya*, m. The name of a Muni, Man. 3, 16.

उत्क *utka*, i.e. *ud-ka* (vb. *kam*), adj., f. *kâ*, Desirous, Megh. 11.—**Comp.** *Sa-*, adj. desirous, Kathâs. 26, 271.

उत्कट *utkaṭa*, i. e. *ud-kaṭa* (*kaṭa* is probably a change of *kashṭa*), adj., f. *ṭâ*. **1.** Excessive, Râm. 5, 13, 37. **2.** Abounding in, Râm. 2, 55, 30. **3.** Drunk, MBh. 2, 2160. **4.** Furious, Râm. 6, 73, 7.—**Comp.** *Ati-*, adj. exceedingly great, Hit. i. d. 78. *Mada-*, I. adj. I. arrogant. 2. furious. II. m. an elephant in rut.

उत्कण्ठ् *UTKAṆṬH* (properly a denomin. derived from *utkaṇṭhâ*), Par. **1.** To long for, Râm. 2, 53, 2. **2.** To sorrow, Çâk. 60, 5.—Caus. *utkaṇṭhaya*, To make desirous, Bhartṛ. 1, 42.

उत्कण्ठ *utkaṇṭha*, i.e. *ud-kaṇṭha*, I. adj. Having the neck erect. II. f. *ṭhâ*, 1. Longing for, Daçak. in Chr. 190, 18. 2. Regret, sorrow, Çâk. d. 81.—Comp. *Sa-*, adj., f. *ṭhâ*, 1. ardently longing, Râjat. 5, 93. 2. regretting, grieving. *-ṭham*, adv. sorrowfully, Kir. 5, 51.

उत्कम्प *utkampa*, i.e. *ud-kamp + a*, I. adj. Trembling. II. m. Trembling, Megh. 68. — Comp. *Gati-*, m. haste, Megh. 68. *Sa-*, adj., f. *pâ*, Trembling, Vikr. 28, 10.

उत्कम्पिन् *utkampin*, i.e. *ud-kamp + in*, adj., f. *nî*, Causing to tremble, Râm. 1, 74, 10.

उत्कर *utkara*, i.e. *ud-kṛî + a*, m. A heap, plenty, Râm. 6, 79, 38.—Comp. *Mûshika-*, m. a mole-hill, Mṛichchh. 47, 6. *Prakîrṇa-kusuma-*, adj., f. *râ*, strewed with plenty of flowers, Râm. 1, 77, 7.

उत्कर्ष *utkarsha*, i.e. *ud-kṛish + a*, I. adj. Boasting. II. m. 1. Excess, Daçak. in Chr. 192, 21. 2. Distinction, Çâk. d. 38. 3. Exaltation, Man. 10, 42; an exalted rank, Man. 4, 244.

उत्कर्षण *utkarshaṇa*, i.e. *ud-kṛish + ana*, n. Putting off (his clothes), MBh. 2, 1665 (cf. 1667).

उत्कलिका *utkalikâ*, i.e. *utka + la + ika*, f. Longing for, Kathâs. 22, 105.

उत्कषण *utkashaṇa*, i.e. *ud-kash + ana*, n. Tearing up, Megh. 16.

ऽउत्किर *-utkira*, i.e. *ud-kṛî + a*, adj., f. *râ*, Heaping up, Kumâras. 5, 26.

उत्कुट *utkuṭa*, adj. 1. Stretched out. 2. Erect. 3. (Sitting) with the legs under one's body, Fausböll, Dhammap. 306.

उत्कूज *utkûja*, i.e. *ud-kûj + a*, m. Cry, Râm. 5, 17, 8.

उत्कूर्दन *utkûrdana*, i.e. *ud-hurd + ana*, n. Leaping, jumping aloft, Pañch. 124, 17.

उत्कोच *utkocha*, i.e. *ud-kuch + a*, m. Bribe, Râjat. 5, 363.

उत्कोचक *utkochaka*, i.e. *ud-kuch + aka*, I. adj., One who receives bribes, Man. 9, 258. II. (n.) The name of a holy place, MBh. 1, 6914.

उत्क्रमण *utkramaṇa*, i.e. *ud-kram + ana*, n. Departure, Man. 6, 63.

उत्क्रोश *utkroça*, i.e. *ud-kruç + a*, m. An osprey.

उत्क्षेप *utkshepa*, i.e. *ud-kship + a*, m. 1. Tossing up, Megh. 48. 2. Stretching out, Çâk. d. 126.

उत्क्षेपक *utkshepaka*, i.e. *ud-kship + aka*, m. A purloiner, Yâjñ. 2, 274.

उत्क्षेपण *utkshepaṇa*, i.e. *ud-kship + ana*, n. 1. Tossing up, Bhâshâp. 5. 2. Lifting up, Çâk. d. 29.

उत्तंस *uttaṁsa*, i.e. *ud-taṁs + a*, m. 1. An ear-ring, Râjat. 5, 138. 2. A crest.

उत्तंसित *uttaṁsita*, i.e. *uttaṁsa + ita*, adj. Adorned with, Bhartṛ. 3, 1.

उत्तम *uttama*, i.e. *ud + tama*, I. adj., f. *mâ*. 1. Supreme, Chr. 289, 10=Rigv. i. 50, 10. 2. Chief, principal, Pañch. 16, 20; best, Man. 4, 229; greatest, Râm. 5, 33, 35; better, Pañch. 241, 24. 3. Last, MBh. 1, 4674 (cf. ὕστατος). II. acc. sing. n. *mam*, adv. 1. Most, Râm. 2, 30, 2. 2. Very loudly, Chr. 25, 60. —Comp. *An-*, adj. (literally, having no superior), 1. insurmountable, Daçak. in Chr. 182, 24; most lofty, Râm. 3, 52, 22. 2. most rigorous, Râm. 1, 62, 6.

3. most excellent, Râm. 3, 53, 18. *Dvija-*, m. a Brâhmaṇa, Man. 2, 49. *Purusha-*, m. 1. an excellent man, an excellent servant. 2. a name of Vishṇu. 3. a proper name. *Maṇḍala-*, n. a principal kingdom, Râjat. 5, 262. *Mṛiga-*, m. a most excellent antelope, Râm. 3, 49, 54. *Raghu-*, m. chief of the race of Raghu, Râm. 3, 50, 6. *Ratha-*, m. an excellent cart, Bhag. 1, 24. *Çara-*, m. a very good arrow, Râm. 3, 50, 16. *Sevaka-*, m. an excellent servant, Böhtl. Ind. Spr. 1435.

उत्तमर्ण *uttamarṇa*, i. e. *uttama* + *ṛiṇa*, m. A creditor, Man. 8, 47.

उत्तमर्णिक *uttamarṇika*, i. e. *uttamarṇa*+*ika*, m. A creditor, Man. 8, 48.

उत्तर *uttara*, i.e. *ud*+*tara*, I. adj., f. *râ*. **1.** Superior, Ragh. 1, 60; more powerful, Chr. 289, 10=Rigv. i. 50, 10. **2.** Northern, Pańch. 241, 7. *uttareṇa* (instr. sing.), adv. and prep. (with the gen. abl. and acc.), To the north, Megh. 73. **3.** Left (not right), MBh. 1, 7212. **4.** Posterior, Man. 2, 136; subsequent, Hit. i. d. 143; becoming, fit, Daçak. in Chr. 180, 6. **5.** Future, Râm. 2, 88, 22. **6.** Answering, Râm. 3, 18, 48; Chr. 59, 24. **II.** m. The name of a mountain, Kathâs. 25, 23. **III.** f. *râ*, **1.** The north, Kathâs. 18, 57. **2.** A proper name, MBh. 1, 169. **IV.** n. **1.** Superiority, MBh. 1, 4986; power, Râm. 5, 70, 18. **2.** Answer, Râm. 3, 70, 7; defence, Lass. 90, 4.—**Comp.** *Adhara-*, I. adj. 1. lower and higher, Yâjń. 1, 96. 2. confused, Man. 8, 53. II. n. a state of confusion, topsy-turvy, Man. 7, 21; useless discussion, Çâk. 69, 17. *uttarottara*, i.e. *uttara-*, I. adj. 1. always the subsequent, Yâjń. 2, 136. 2. always increasing, Pańch. 84, 25. II. *-ram*, adv. higher and higher, MBh. 14, 1016; more and more, Hit. 20, 20. III. n. useless discussion, Hit. 21, 3. *Asrottaram*, i. e. *asra-uttara* + *m*, adv. with tears in the eyes, Kumâras. 5, 61. *Klinna-paksha-*, adj. of which the upper parts of the wings are wet, Daçak. 1, 16. *Guṇa-*, m. superior virtue, Râm. 5, 2, 4; n. MBh. 3, 13922. *Dakshiṇa-*, turned to the south and to the north, Mârk. P. 16, 34. *Dadhi-*, n. cream of curdled milk, Suçr. 1, 159, 11. *Duḥkha-*, adj., f. *râ*, accompanied by pain, Çâk. 61, 18. *Dharma-*, adj. attached to virtue, Ragh. 13, 7. *Nis-*, adj., f. *râ*, unable to answer, Pańch. 112, 18. *Prâguttareṇa*, i.e. *prâńch-*, adv. north-eastwards. *Vishṭara-*, adj. covered with Kuça grass, MBh. 3, 1881. *Saptottara*, i.e. *saptan-*, adj., f. *râ*, having a surplus of seven (with *çata*, hundred and seven), Yâjń. 3, 102.—Cf. ὕστερος.

उत्तरण *uttaraṇa*, i.e. *ud-tṛî* + *ana*, n. Crossing, passing over, Pańch. 33, 15.

उत्तरतस् *uttara*+*tas*, adv. To the north, Râm. 4, 55, 20.

उत्तरा *uttarâ* (an old instr. sing. of *uttara*), adv. To the north, e.g. in *-mukha*, adj. Looking to the north, MBh. 2, 1084.

उत्तरीय *uttarîya*, i.e. *uttara* + *îya*, and **उत्तरीयक** *uttarîya*+*ka*, n. An upper and outer garment, Pańch. 236, 9.

उत्तरेद्युस् *uttaredyus*, i.e. *uttara* + *i-div* + *as*, adv. The following day, Daçak. in Chr. 183, 5.

उत्तान *uttâna*, i.e. *ud-tan* + *a*, adj., f. *nâ*, Lying supinely, Daçak. in Chr. 198, 20 (referring to the hand lying with the palm turned upwards).

उत्तार *uttâra*, i.e. *ud-tṛî*+*a*, m. Crossing, passing over, Prab. 83, 10.

उत्तारण *uttâraṇa*, i.e. *ud-tṛî-ana*,

I. adj. Causing to cross, MBh. 14, 194. II. n. Deliverance, Râm. 4, 52, 18.

उत्ताल *uttâla*, i.e. *ud-tâla*, adj., f. *lâ*, Formidable, Kathâs. 25, 36.

उत्तितीर्षु *uttitîrshu*, i.e. *ud-titîrsha*, desider. of *tṛî*, + *u*, adj. Desirous to step out, MBh. 11, 160.

उत्तुङ्ग *uttuṅga*, i.e. *ud-tuṅga*, adj., f. *gâ*. 1. Prominent, Bhartṛ. 1, 72. 2. High, Pańch. iii. d. 260.

उत्तेजन *uttejana*, i.e. *ud-tij* + *ana*, n. Instigation.

उत्थ *uttha*, i.e. *ud-stha* (vb. *sthâ*), adj. 1. Rising, Chaurap. 18. 2. Springing up, Pańch. 257, 4; proceeding, Pańch. i. d. 400; Bhâshâp. 119; Râjat. 5, 167.

उत्थान *utthâna*, i.e. *ud-sthâ* + *ana*, I. n. 1. Rising, Bhartṛ. 3, 10; of the moon, Ragh, 6, 31. 2. Resurrection, MBh. 3, 10811. 3. Exertion, Man. 9, 215. II. m. A causer, MBh. 13, 1242. —Comp. *An-*, n. want of exertion, Râjat. 5, 252. *Su-*, adj. clever.

उत्थानवन्त् *utthâna* + *vant*, adj., f. *vatî*, Strenuous, MBh. 2, 1941.

उत्थापन *utthâpana*, i.e. *ud-sthâ*, Caus., + *ana*, n. 1. Raising, MBh. 1, 1885. 2. Leading away, Lass. 24, 9.

उत्थायिन् *utthâyin*, i.e. *ud-sthâ* + *in*, adj., f. *nî*, Rising, MBh. 1, 3628. 2. Appearing, MBh. 1, 2332.

उत्थितता *utthitatâ*, i.e. *ud-sthita* + *tâ* (vb. *sthâ*), f. Veneration, MBh. 3, 14687.

उत्पतन *utpatana*, i.e. *ud-pat* + *ana*, n. Jumping, Pańch. 118, 13.

उत्पतिष्णु *utpatishṇu*, i.e. *ud-pat* + *ishṇu*, adj. 1. Rising, Ragh. 4, 47. 2. Being about to jump, Pańch. iii. d. 40.

उत्पत्ति *utpatti*, i.e. *ud-pad* + *ti*, f. 1. Springing up, Çriṅgârat. 20. 2. Birth, Man. 3, 16; second birth, 2, 68. 3. Produce, Râjat. 5, 69.—Comp. *An-*, f. absence of production, Daçak. in Chr. 182, 4.

उत्पत्तिमन्त् *utpatti* + *mant*, adj. Produced, born.

उत्पथ *utpatha*, i.e. *ud-patha*, m. Wrong way, Chr. 22, 25.

उत्पल *utpala*, i.e. probably *ud-paṭ* + *a* (with *l* for *ṭ*), I. n. A blue lotus, Nymphæa cærulea, Bhartṛ. 2, 56. II. m. A proper name, Râjat. 5, 127.—Comp. *Nîla-*, m. a blue lotus, Nymphæa cyanea Roxb., Râm. 4, 44, 91.

उत्पलिन् *utpalin*, i.e. *utpala* + *in*, I. adj., f. *nî*, Abounding with lotus-flowers, Râm. 3, 78, 26. II. f. *nî*, An assemblage of lotus-flowers, MBh. 3, 8564.

उत्पवन *utpavana*, i.e. *ud-pû* + *ana*, n. Purifying, Man. 5, 115 (Lois.).

उत्पाटन *utpâṭana*, i.e. *ud-paṭ* + *ana*, n. 1. Eradication, Râm. 6, 83, 34. 2. Destruction, Râjat. 5, 292.

उत्पाटिन् *utpâṭin*, i.e. *ud-paṭ* + *in*, adj., f. *nî*, Pulling out, Pańch. i. d. 26.

उत्पात *utpâta*, i.e. *ud-pat* + *a*, m. 1. A jump, Râm. 5, 53, 25. 2. A portent, MBh. 1, 8287; an omen, Man. 6, 50.—Comp. *Mahâ-*, adj. terrible, Pańch, 114. 14.

उत्पाद *utpâda*, i.e. *ud-pad* + *a*, m. Producing, causing, Yâjń. 2, 225 (shedding).

उत्पादक *utpâdaka*, i.e. *ud-pad* + *aka*, I. adj. A producer, a causer, Man. 4, 168 (a shedder). II. m. A father, Man. 2, 146.

उत्पादन *utpâdana*, i.e. *ud-pad* +

ana, I. adj., f. *nî,* Producing, MBh. 1, 7834. II. n. Producing, Man. 9, 27.

उत्पादिन् *utpâdin,* i.e. I. *utpâda* + *in,* adj., f. *nî,* Produced, Hit. i. d. 202. II. *ud-pad* + *in,* adj., f. *nî,* Producing, causing, Yâjń. 2, 224.

उत्पीड *utpîḍa,* i.e. *ud-pîḍ* + *a,* m. 1. Drawing out, MBh. 3, 825 (of an arrow). 2. Forcing, Megh. 88 (tears). 3. Pressing, Prab. 71, 10. 4. Foam, Râm. 5, 4, 5.—Comp. *Sa-,* adj. covered with foam, Râm. 4, 15, 23.

उत्पीडन *utpîḍana,* i. e. *ud-pîḍ* + *ana,* n. Pressing, Ṛit. 1, 20.

उत्प्रास *utprâsa,* i.e. *ud-pra-*2. *as* + *a,* m. Excess.—Comp. *Sa-,* I. adj. violent. II. m. a horse-laugh. III. m. and n. irony.

उत्प्लवन *utplavana,* i.e. *ud-plu* + *ana,* n. Taking off (?) Man. 5, 115, v.r.

उत्फाल *utphâla,* i.e. *ud-phal* + *a,* m. Jumping up, Kathâs. 26, 20.

उत्फुल्ल *utphulla,* see *phal.*

उत्स *utsa* (akin to *und*), m. A fountain, ved. a cloud, Chr. 290, 6 = Rigv. i. 64, 6.

उत्सङ्ग *utsańga,* i.e. *ud-sańj* + *a,* m. 1. The lap, Râm. 6, 71, 11; figuratively, Daçak. 199, 7; Râjat. 5, 6. 2. The slope of a mountain, Ragh. 6, 3. 3. A roof, Pańch. 128, 8.

उत्सङ्गिन् *utsańgin,* i.e. *utsańga* + *in,* adj., f. *nî,* Deep, Râm. 6, 23, 13.

उत्सधि *utsadhi,* i. e. *utsa-dhâ* (cf. *nidhi*), m. A reservoir of water, a cloud (ved.), Chr. 293, 4 = Rigv. i. 88, 4.

उत्सर्ग *utsarga,* i.e. *ud-sṛij* + *a,* m. 1. Emission, Megh. 19. 2. Evacuation, Pańch. 34, 22; Man. 12, 21. 3. Abandoning, Nal. 10, 12; relinquishing, Man. 11, 193 (194); dismission, Chr. 9, 37. 4. Donation, Sâv. 1, 8. 5. The name of a ceremony, when suspending the reading of the Veda, Man. 4, 119. 6. Setting at liberty. 7. A general rule, Kumâras. 2, 27.—Comp. *Vṛisha-,* m. setting a bull at liberty on occasion of a sacrifice or obsequial oblation, Pańch. 9, 3.

उत्सर्जन *utsarjana,* i. e. *ud-sṛij* + *ana,* n. 1. Rejection, Chr. 9, 38. 2. The name of the ceremony, *utsarga* (q. cf.), Man. 4, 96.

उत्सर्पिन् *utsarpin,* i.e. *ud-sṛip* + *in,* adj., f. *iṇî,* Soaring upwards, Çâk. 101, 5.

उत्सव *utsava,* i.e. *ud-su* + *a,* m. A festival, Daçak. in Chr. 180, 5; figuratively, Amar. 23.—Comp. *Baddha-* (vb. *bandh*), adj., f. *vâ,* celebrating a festival, Kathâs. 25, 269.

उत्सादन *utsâdana,* i.e. *ud-sad* + *ana,* n. 1. Destruction, Râm. 1, 74, 21. 2. Cleaning with perfumes, Man. 2, 209.

उत्सारण *utsâraṇa,* i.e. *ud-sṛi* + *ana,* n. Removal, Râm. 6, 33, 13.

उत्साह *utsâha,* i.e. *ud-sah* + *a,* m. 1. Effort, Draup. 8, 56. 2. Energy, Pańch. i. d. 44. 3. Ardour, Râm. 3, 33, 4. 4. Perseverance, Pańch. 79, 1; will, Çâk. 23, 12. — Comp. *Krita-,* adj., f. *hâ,* having made an effort, Sâv. 4, 21. *Dus-,* adj. difficult to be resisted, MBh. 9, 1130. *Nis-,* I. m. want of energy, Hariv. 14493. II. adj., f. *hâ,* 1. devoid of energy, Pańch. 123, 23. 2. desponding, Râm. 1, 21, 6. *Mahâ-,* I. adj. possessing great energy, persevering. II. m. 1. exertion. 2. a king possessing all the powers of monarchy. *Yathâ-utsâha* + *m,* adv. according to one's power or ability, Man. 5, 86. *Sa-,* I.

adj. 1. energetic. 2. persevering. II. *-ham*, adv. carefully, Pańch. i. d. 15.

उत्साहवन्त् *utsâha+vant*, adj., f. *vatí*, Energetic.

उत्साहिन् *utsâhin*, i.e. *utsâha+in*, adj., f. *ní*, Full of ardour, Pańch. ii. d. 89.

उत्सुक *utsuka*, i.e. *ud-su-ka* (vb. *kam*), adj., f. *kâ*. 1. Longing for. 2. Languid. 3. Uneasy, Râm. 1, 17, 28. 4. Proud, Râm. 4, 9, 37.—Comp. *Nis-*, adj. careless, Arj. 10, 14. *Pari-*, adj. 1. longing for. 2. languid. 3. sad. *Sa-*, adj. languid, Ṛit. 1, 6.

उत्सुकता *utsuka+tâ* f. 1. Longing for, love, Çiç. 9, 2. 2. Care, zeal, Pańch. 40, 14.—Comp. *An-*, f. modesty, Vikr. 12, 6.

उत्सेक *utseka*, i.e. *ud-sich+a*, m. Pride, Râm. 4, 9, 88; 5, 3, 10.—Comp. *An-*, m. meekness, Bhartṛ. 2, 54.

उत्सेध *utsedha*, i.e. *ud-sidh+a*, m. Height, Râm. 6, 83, 23; figuratively, 6, 82, 44.—Comp. *Navotsedha*, i.e. *navan-*, adj., f. *dhâ*, having an elevation of nine (viz. fathoms), MBh. 3, 10207.

उत्स्वप्नाय *UTSVAPNÂYA*, a denomin. derived from *ud-svapna*, Âtm. To speak sleeping, Mâlav. 55, 22.

उद् *ud* (properly acc. sing. n. of *u*, probably an obsolete pronominal base, akin to *va* in *ava*, *eva*, etc.), a prefix, *Up, out*. I. Combined and compounded with verbs and their derivatives, q. cf. II. Former part of comp. nouns, e.g. *ud-ayudha*, adj. With raised weapon (literally, having a weapon upward), Chr. 4, 17. *utpakshman*, i.e. *ud-*, adj. The eye-lids of which are elevated, Çâk. d. 90. *ud-dâma*, adj. Unfettered (literally, having the fetter out), Râm. 2, 23, 21.—Cf. ὕστερος, ὕσταρος for ὑδ+τερο, ταρο, Goth. and A.S. ut; O.H.G. ûz.

उद *uda*, a substitute for *udaka* in comp. words, e.g. *uda-kumbha*, m. A water-pot, Man. 2, 182. *kshâra-*, m. The salt ocean, Bhâg. P. 5, 1, 34. *kshîra-*, m. The sea of milk, Râm. 4, 37, 28. *gandha-*, Fragrant water, Bhâg. P. 9, 11, 26. *ghṛita-*, m. The sea of clarified butter, Râm. 4, 40, 49. *lohita-*, adj., f. *dâ*, With blood-red water, Râm. 4, 44, 65. *çânti-*, n. Lustral water.

उदक *udaka*, i. e. *udan+ka*, n. 1. Water, Man. 2, 99. 2. The ceremony of pouring water at obsequies, Man. 5, 88. 3. Religious ablution, MBh. 1, 790.—Comp. *Kâma-*, n. an optional oblation of water, Yâjń. 3, 4. *Kâla-*, the name of a sea, Râm. 4, 40, 36. *Kuça-*, n. water (boiled) with kuça-grass, Man. 11, 212. *Kṛita-*, adj. 1. one who has performed the ceremony of pouring water at obsequies, Râm. 1, 25, 3. 2. one who has performed his religious ablution, MBh. 3, 8141. *Tila-*, n. water with sesame, Man. 3, 223. *Maṇḍa-*, n. 1. variegated colour. 2. painting figures. *Samâna-*, m. a kinsman connected by oblations of water only to the manes of common ancestors, i.e. when the *sapiṇḍas* are excluded, a relation from the seventh to the fourteenth degree.

उदक्या *udakyâ*, i.e. *udaka+ya*, f. A woman in her courses, Man. 4, 57.

उदग्र *ud-agra*, adj., f. *râ*. 1. Pointing upwards, lofty, Râm. 5, 54, 19; figuratively, Ragh. 2, 53. 2. Uppermost, Vikr. d. 156. 3. Excited, Râm. 6, 14, 15.

उदञ्च् *ud-ańch*, adj., f. *udîchî*. 1. Upper, upwards. 2. Northern, Megh. 58. *udak* (acc. sing. n.), adv. To the north, Man. 3, 217.

उदञ्चन *ud-anch+ana*, m. A pail, Daçak. 152, 4.

उदधि *udadhi*, i.e. *uda-dhâ* (cf. *nidhi*), m. The ocean, Daçak. in Chr. 188, 21.—Comp. *Kshâra-*, m. the salt ocean, Bhâg. P. 5, 20, 2. *Kshîra-*, m. the sea of milk, MBh. 12, 12778. *Mahâ-*, m. the great ocean.

उदन् *udan*, i.e. *und+an*, n. Water, Chr. 291, 5=Rigv. i. 85, 5.—Cf. ὕδωρ, with ρ for *n*; cf. also Lat. udor; Goth. vato, base vatan, represents the organic form of the vb. *und*, viz. *vad*; O.H.G. wazar has *r* instead of *n*, like the Greek.

उदन्त *ud-anta*, m. Tidings, Kathâs. 10, 55.

उदन्वन्त् *udan+vant*, m. The ocean, Ragh. 4, 32.

उदय *udaya*, i.e. *ud-i+a*, m. 1. Rising, Râm. 4, 34, 32 (of the ocean); Ragh. 12, 36 (of the moon); Man. 10, 33 (appearance of dawn); figuratively, Ragh. 9, 9; Râjat. 5, 311. 2. The eastern mountain behind which the sun is supposed to rise, Râm. 4, 58, 5. 3. Beginning, Bhâg. P. 1, 7, 12. 4. Appearance, Çâk. d. 67. 5. Prosperity, Râjat. 5, 336. 6. Consequence, Man. 4, 70. 7. Gain, Râm. 3, 2, 22; revenue, Man. 7, 55. 8. A gate (?), Râm. 2, 48, 29.—Comp. *Karuṇa-*, adj. causing compassion, MBh. 1, 436. *Chandra-*, m. the rise of the moon, Suçr. 2, 485, 21. *Dus-*, adj. appearing with difficulty, Bhâg. P. 3, 15, 50. *Mahâ-*, I. m. 1. prosperity. 2. final beatitude. 3. sovereignty. 4. a lord. 5. the country of Kanoj. 6. a proper name, Râjat. 5, 28. II. n. Kanoj. *Yathâ-udaya+m*, adv. in proportion to one's income, Yâjń. 2, 43. *Sa-*, adj. 1. with profit. 2. with interest.

उदयन *udayana*, i.e. *ud-i+ana*, I. n. Rising (of the sun), Chr. 287, 7=Rigv. i. 48, 7; Râm. 4, 40, 43. II. m. A proper name, Kathâs. 9, 599.

उदयवन्त् *udaya + vant*, adj., f. *vatî*, Risen, Çiç. 9, 43.

उदर *udara*, i.e. *ud-ṛi+a*, n. 1. The belly. 2. The interior part, Bhartṛ. 2, 26.—Comp. *Kṛiça-*, adj., f. *rî*, slender, Vikr. d. 154. *Jala-*, n. dropsy, MBh. 3, 14664. *Dagdha-* (vb. *dah*), n. a hungry stomach, Hit. i. d. 62. *Nis-nata-* (vb. *nam*), adj., f. *rî*, having a protuberant belly, Râm. 6, 74, 8. *Brahmâṇḍabhâṇḍa-*, i.e. *brahman-aṇḍa-bhâṇḍa-*, n. the interior of the vessel-like egg of Brahman, Bhartṛ. 2, 93. *Mahâ-*, adj., f, *rî*, having a large belly, Râm. 3, 23, 15. *Lamba-*, m. 1. a glutton. 2. Gaṇeça. *Sa-*, m. a brother, Râjat. 5, 42. *Saha-*, m. a brother of whole blood.

उदरंभरि *udarambhari*, i.e. *udara+m-bhṛi+i*, adj. Voracious, Mâlav. 14, 4.

उदरिन् *udarin*, i.e. *udara+in*, adj., f. *iṇî*, Paunch-bellied, Kathâs. 20, 109.—Comp. *Udaka-*, adj. hydropic.

उदर्क *udarka*, i.e. *ud-rich-a* (anomal.), m. 1. Future time, Nal. 21, 26. 2. Consequence, Râm. 6, 93, 14.—Comp. *Çubha-*, adj., f. *kâ*, causing happiness, Kathâs. 9, 58. *Sa-*, adj. with towers (?), MBh. 2, 1299. *Sukha-*, adj. causing happiness, Man. 9, 25.—*A-sukha-*, adj. causing pain, Man. 4, 176.

उदात्त *udâtta*, see *dâ* with the prep. *ud-â*.

उदान *udâna*, i.e. *ud-an+a*, m. One of the five vital airs, that which has its place in the throat and passes upward and outward, Vedântas. in Chr. 207, 11.

उदार *udâra*, i.e. *ud-ṛi + a*, adj., f. *râ* and *rî*, **1.** Distinguished, Nal. 1, 8. **2.** Excellent, Râm. 1, 35, 8. **3.** Great, MBh. 3, 13158. **4.** Gentle, Râm. 1, 33, 3. **5.** Munificent, Daçak. in Chr. 183, 4.

उदारक *udâra + ka*, adj. A poor munificent person, Daçak. in Chr. 186, 21; used as surname of one who has ruined himself by munificence, 187, 16.

उदारता *udâra + tâ*, f. Generosity, Kathâs. 21, 103.—**Comp.** *Ati-*, f. Excessive munificence, Daçak. in Chr. 186, 20.

उदासीनता *ud-âsîna + tâ* (vb *âs*), f. Indifference, carelessness, Pañch. 86, 12.

उदाहरण *udâharaṇa*, i.e. *ud-â-hṛi + ana*, n. **1.** Speaking, Kumâras. 6, 65. **2.** Declaration, Vikr. d. 32. **3.** An example.

उदीच्य *udîchya*, i. e. *udañch + ya*, **I.** adj. Northern. **II.** m. The country to the north and west of the river Çarâvatî, MBh. 3, 14774. pl. Its inhabitants, Râm. 2, 82, 7.

उदीप *udîpa*, i. e. *ud-ap + a*, m. Inundation, Râjat. 5, 269.

उदीरण *udîraṇa*, i.e. *ud-îr + ana*, n. **1.** Throwing, MBh. 3, 16525. **2.** Pronunciation, Kumâras. 2, 12.

उदुम्बर *udumbara*, also उडुम्बर *uḍumbara*, m. The glomerous fig tree, Ficus glomerata, Nal. 12, 4.

उदूखल *udûkhala*, cf. *ulûkhala*, n. A mortar, Râm. 6, 96, 13.

उद्गति *udgati*, i. e. *ud-gam + ti*, f. Springing up (of flowers), Kathâs. 17, 113.

उद्गम *ud-gam + a*, m. **1.** Springing up, Ragh. 4, 9. **2.** A shoot, Kir. 5, 38. **3.** Appearance, Bhartṛ. 2, 62. **4.** Departing, Kathâs. 4, 128.

उद्गमन *ud-gam + ana*, n. Springing up, appearance.

उद्गमनीय *ud-gamanîya* (vb. *gam*), n. A pair of bleached clothes, Daçak. in Chr. 181, 18.

उद्गातृ *udgâtṛi*, i.e. *ud-gai + tṛi*, m. A reciter of the Sâma Veda, Man. 8, 209.

उद्गार *udgâra*, i.e. *ud-gṛî + a*, m. **1.** Spitting, Râm. 4, 15, 23; figuratively, Ragh. 4, 57 (exhalation); Bhartṛ. 2, 29 (throwing out). **2.** Saliva, MBh. 3, 15549. **3.** Roar, MBh. 3, 11140.

उद्गारिन् *udgârin*, i.e. *ud-gṛi + in*, adj., f. *iṇî*, Spitting, Râm. 3, 33, 37; figuratively, Ragh. 13, 47 (uttering); Megh. 26 (exhaling).

उद्गिरण *udgiraṇa*, i.e. *ud-gṛî + ana*, n. Vomiting, Vedântas. in Chr. 207, 15.

उद्गीथ *udgîtha*, i.e. *ud-gai + tha*, n. A portion of the Sâma Veda, Dev. 4, 9.

उद्घट्टन *ud-ghaṭṭ + ana*, n. **1.** Rubbing, exciting. **2.** Inflammation, Megh. 62.

उद्घर्षण *udgharshaṇa*, i.e. *ud-ghṛish + ana*, n. Thrashing, Mṛichchh. 34, 3.

उद्घाटक *udghâṭaka*, i.e. *ud-ghaṭ + aka*, m. A key, Mṛichchh. 48, 5.

उद्घाटन *udghâṭana*, i.e. *ud-ghaṭ + ana*, n. A key, Hit. i. d. 146.

उद्घात *udghâta*, i.e. *ud-han*, Caus., *+ a*, m. **1.** A toss, Çâk. d. 192; pain, Kathâs. 17, 3. **2.** Height, Râm. 5, 4, 12. **3.** A beginning, Ragh. 4, 20.—**Comp.** *An-*, adj. unhurt, Râm. 2, 72.

उद्घातिन् *udghâtin*, i.e. *udghâta* + *in*, adj., f. *nî*, Rugged, Çâk. 5, 12.

उद्दान *uddâna*, i.e. *ud-do* + *ana*, n. Binding, MBh. 12, 4902.

उद्दीपन *ud-dîp* + *ana*, n. Inflaming, Ṛit. 6, 27.

उद्देश *uddeça*, i.e. *ud-diç* + *a*, m. 1. Pointing to, Kathâs. 10, 110. 2. Reference, Kathâs. 20, 210; Pańch. 119, 3 (on account of). 3. A sketch, Indr. 4, 16. 4. Exposition, Râm. 4, 17, 12. 5. A region, Râm. 5, 51, 5; a quarter, Daçak. in Chr. 179, 8; a part, Hiḍ. 1, 16; a seat, Râm. 6, 33, 47.—Comp. *Yathâ-uddeça* + *m*, adv. according to the command, Râm. 2, 99, 1. *Raṇa-*, m. a field of battle, Râm. 5, 56, 126. *Vana-*, m. the part of a forest.

उद्देशतस् *uddeça* + *tas*, adv. Shortly, Bhag. 10, 24.

उद्द्योत *uddyota*, i.e. *ud-dyut* + *a*, I. adj. Resplendent, Râm. 1, 15, 19. II. m. Splendour, Lass. 2, 11.

उद्धर *uddhara*, i.e. *ud-hṛi* + *a*, adj. Pulling out, MBh. 3, 11188.

उद्धरण *uddharaṇa*, i.e. *ud-hṛi* + *ana*, n. 1. Plucking out. 2. Eradication, Lass. 31, 16. 3. Deliverance, Râjat. 5, 114; Hit. i. d. 27.

उद्धर्तृ *uddhartṛi*, i.e. *ud-hṛi* + *tṛi*, m. A deliverer, Kathâs. 5, 40.—Comp. *Chaura-*, m. the officer charged with the pursuit of thieves, Yâjń. 2, 271.

उद्धर्ष *uddharsha*, i.e. *ud-dhṛish* + *a*, m. Daring, undergoing, Râm. 4, 9, 47.

उद्धर्षण *uddharshaṇa*, i.e. I. *ud-hṛish* + *ana*, adj. Comforting, Râm. 2, 2, 1. II. *ud-dhṛish* + *ana*, n. Encouragement, MBh. 15, 476.

उद्धार *uddhâra*, i.e. *ud-hṛi* + *a*, m. 1. Deliverance from. 2. Taking out, separating what ought to be avoided, Man. 10, 85 (*uddhṛitoddhâra*, adj. What ought to be avoided being avoided). 3. A selected part, Man. 7, 97. 4. Debt, Daçak. 111, 12, Wils.—Comp. *Vaira-*, m. revenge. *Çalya-*, m. 1. extraction of foreign substances from the body. 2. cleansing and purifying a new house. *Çâpa-*, m. deliverance from a curse.

उद्धारण *uddhâraṇa*, i.e. *ud-dhṛi* Caus., + *ana*, n. Payment, Pańch. 138, 14.

उद्धुर *ud-dhur* + *a*, adj. Brisk, Kathâs. 22, 193.

उद्धूलय *UDDHÛLAYA*, a denom. derived from *ud-dhûli*, Par. To strew over, Kathâs. 18, 240.

उद्धृति *uddhṛiti*, i.e. *ud-hṛi* + *ti*, 1. Pulling out (as an arrow). 2. Preservation, Râjat. 5, 477.

उद्बन्ध *ud-bandh* + *a*, m., and **उद्बन्धन** *ud-bandh* + *ana*, n. Hanging, Kathâs. 13, 100.

उद्भव *udbhava*, i.e. *ud-bhû* + *a*, m. 1. Birth. 2. Origin, Man. 11, 244. 3. When latter part of a comp. adj., Produced, Man. 6, 13; sprung from, Râjat. 5, 244.—Comp. *Kshata-*, blood. *Jala-*, I. adj. produced by water. II. m. the name of a country, MBh. 2, 1078. *Tanu-*, m. a son. *Padma-*, 1. adj. sbst. born in a lotus-flower, a name of Brahman. 2. m. a proper name. *Saṁmûrchhana-*, m. a fish, or aquatic animal. *Soma-*, f. *vâ*, the Narmadâ river.

उद्भावन *udbhâvana*, i.e. *ud-bhû* Caus., + *ana*, n. Neglect, MBh. 1, 5070.

उद्भावयितृ *udbhâvayitṛi*, i.e. *ud-bhû* Caus., + *tṛi*, One who raises or exalts, Daçak. 180, 3.

उद्भासिन् *ud-bhâs+in*, adj., f. *nî*, Resplendent, Râjat. 5, 482.

उद्भासुर *ud-bhâs+ura*, adj. Shining, Amar. 76.

उद्भिज्ज *udbhijja*, i.e. *udbhid-ja* (vb. *jan*), adj., f. *jâ*, Sprouting, Vedântas. in Chr. 209, 5.

उद्भिद् *ud-bhid*, and **उद्भिद** *ud-bhid+a*, adj. Sprouting, MBh. 1, 3587.

उद्भूति *ud-bhû+ti*, f. Growth, prosperity, Vikr. d. 162.

उद्भेद *udbheda*, i.e. *ud-bhid+a*, m. **1.** Opening, Çâk. d. 80. **2.** Appearance, Bhartṛ. 1, 49. **3.** A spring or fountain, Râm. 2, 94, 13. **4.** Treason, Kathâs. 3, 42.—Comp. *Gaṅgâ-*, m. (the source of the Ganges) a holy place, MBh. 3, 8043.

उद्भ्रान्तक *ud-bhrânta + ka* (vb. *bhram*), f. Soaring up, Çâk. 92, 19.

उद्यम *ud-yam+a*, m. and n. **1.** Raising, Pańch. ii. d. 138. **2.** Effort, Pańch. 185, 2. **3.** Energy, Böhtl. Ind. Spr. 470.—Comp. *Kṛita-*, adj., f. *mâ*, having made an effort, Kumâras. 5, 3. *Daṇḍa-*, m. and n. (?) severe punishment, Pańch. i. d. 421. *Nis-*, adj., f. *mâ*, lazy, Râm. 4, 9, 49. *Mahâ-*, I. m. great effort. II. adj. making a strenuous effort, Râjat. 5, 136 (with infin.); 188 (with dat.).

उद्यमिन् *ud-yam+in*, adj., f. *nî*, Exerting one's self, Bhartṛ. 3, 45.

उद्यान *udyâna*, i.e. *ud-yâ+ana*, m. and n. A grove, a garden, Pańch. ii. d. 178.—Comp. *Puṇya-*, adj., f. *nâ*, having pure gardens, Râm. 2, 71, 19.

उद्यानक *udyâna+ka*, n. A grove, Râm. 3, 61, 18.

उद्योग *udyoga*, i.e. *ud-yuj+a*, m. and n. Exertion, Râm. 3, 31, 34.—Comp. *An-*, m. and n. want of exertion, Böhtl. Ind. Spr. 1400. *Nis-*, adj., f. *gâ*, 1. Lazy, Sund. 4, 3. 2. disheartened, Râm. 6, 21, 16. *Sa-*, adj. 1. active, persevering. 2. violent (as a disease), Râjat. 5, 123.

उद्योगिन् *udyogin*, i.e. *ud-yuj+in*, or *udyoga+in*, adj. Exerting one's self, Pańch. i. d. 220.

उद्रेक *udreka*, i.e. *ud-rich+a*, m. **1.** Excess, MBh. 3, 13169. **2.** Excellence, MBh. 14, 1012.—Comp. *Sattva-*, m. superabundance of wisdom, MBh. 3, 15818.

उद्वर्तन *udvartana*, i.e. *ud-vṛit+ana*, n. **1.** Jumping, Megh. 41. **2.** What has served for rubbing the body with, Man. 4, 132.

ऽउद्वस *-udvasa*, Râjat. 5, 378, Uninhabited (?).

उद्वह *ud-vah+a*, I. adj., f. *hâ*, Supporting, continuing, Râm. 1, 13, 56. II. m. A son, an offspring, Indr. 5, 28.—Comp. *Dus-*, adj. difficult to be borne, MBh. 5, 3147. *Raghu-*, m. Râma. *Rata-*, m. the Indian cuckoo.

उद्वहन *ud-vah+ana*, n. **1.** Lifting up, Ragh. 13, 8. **2.** Bearing, Pańch, 68, 23; having, Râjat. 5, 384. **3.** Riding, Man. 8, 370.

उद्वाष्पत्व *ud-vâshpa+tva*, n. Shedding tears, Vikr. d. 29.

उद्वास्य *udvâsya* (based on *ud-*1.*vas*), adj. Referring to the slaughter of sacrifices, Râm. 1, 13, 4.

उद्वाह *udvâha*, i.e. *ud-vah+a*, m. Marriage, Kathâs. 17, 68.—Comp. *Kṛita-*, adj., f. *hâ*, married.

उद्वाहिक *udvâhika*, i.e. *udvâha+ika*, adj. Relating to nuptials, Man. 9, 65.

उद्वीचण *udvikshaṇa*, i.e. *ud-vi-iksh* + *ana*, n. Looking at, sight, Ragh. 3, 1.

उद्वेग *udvega*, i.e. *ud-vij*+*a*, m. **1.** Going upwards, MBh. 1, 1214 (fluctuation). **2.** Violent motion, Daçak. 189, 6. **3.** Uneasiness, distress, Râm. 6, 99, 28.—**Comp.** *An-*, m. absence of uneasiness, Râm. 3, 14, 20. *Nis-*, adj. fearless, MBh. 3, 7537. *Sa-*, I. adj. fearful, Pańch. 29, 15. II. *-gam*, adv. eagerly, Pańch. 157, 4.

उद्वेगिन् *udvegin*, i.e. *udvega*+*in*, adj., m. A coward, Pańch. iii. d. 241.

उद्वेजन *udvejana*, i.e. *ud-vij*+*ana*, n. Terror, Man. 9, 248 ; aversion, 8, 352.

† **उध्रस्** *UDHRAS* (a combination of *ud-dhras*, q. cf.), ii. 9; i. 10, Par. To glean. i. 10, Par. To throw upward.

उन्द् *UND* (cf. *udan*, and Lat. unda), ii. 7, Par. To wet, or moisten.—With the prep. **वि** *vi*, To moisten, Chr. 291, 5=Rigv. i. 85, 5.

उन्दरु *undaru*, **उन्दुर** *undura*, and **उन्दुरु** *unduru*, m. A rat.

उन्नतत्व *unnatatva*, i.e. *ud-nata*+*tva* (vb. *nam*), n. Majesty, Ragh. 5, 37.

उन्नति *unnati*, i.e. *ud-nam*+*ti*, f. **1.** Rising, Pańch. i. d. 166. **2.** Increase, Pańch. iii. d. 58. **3.** Loftiness, Bhartṛ. 2, 20.

उन्नतिमन्त् *unnati*+*mant*, adj., f. *matî*, **1.** Prominent, Çiç. 9, 72. **2.** Lofty, Kathâs. 24, 20.—**Comp.** *Naya-sâhasa-unnati*+*mant*, endowed (i. e. performed) with wisdom, power, and majesty, Pańch. iii. d. 264.

उन्नमन *unnamana*, i.e. *ud-nam*+*ana*, n. Erecting.

उन्नम्रता *unnamratâ*, i.e. *ud-nam*+*ra*+*tâ*, f. Lifting up, Râjat. 5, 223.

उन्नयन *unnayana*, i.e. *ud-nî*+*ana*, n. **1.** Raising, lifting up. **2.** Inference.—**Comp.** *Sîmanta-*, n. (arranging of the hair) a purificatory and sacrificial ceremony observed by women in the sixth or eighth month of their first pregnancy.

उन्नाद *unnâda*, i.e. *ud-nad*+*a*, m. Sound, MBh. 3, 11563.

उन्मत्तक *unmattaka*, i.e. *ud-matta*+*ka* (vb. *mad*) n. A madman, Yâjú. 2, 140.

उन्मथन *unmathana*, i.e. *ud-math*+*ana*, n. **1.** Shaking, Suçr. 1, 25, 17. **2.** Throwing down by shots, Râm. 6, 91, 13.

उन्मद *unmada*, i.e. *ud-mad*+*a*. **I.** m. Ecstasy, insanity. **II.** adj., f. *dâ*. **1.** Drunk, Prab. 3, 12. **2.** Thoughtless, Pańch. 176, 1. **3.** Furious, Dev. 4, 22—**Comp.** *Mahâ-*, m. 1. intoxication, literally and figuratively. **2.** A sort of fish.

उन्मनस् *unmanas*, i. e. *ud-manas*, adj. **1.** Desirous. **2.** Agitated, Ragh. 11, 22.

उन्मनस्क *unmanas*+*ka*, adj. Agitated, Mṛichchh. 76, 4.

उन्मनाय *UNMANÂYA*, a denomin. derived from *unmanas* by *ya*, Âtm. To be beside one's self, Daçak. in Chr. 181, 14 (*ud-amanâyata*).

उन्माथ *unmâtha*, i.e. *ud-math*+*a*, m. Shaking, Prab. 8, 5.

उन्माथिन् *unmâthin*, i.e. *unmâtha*+*in*, adj., f. *nî*, Shaking, Prab. 41, 2.

उन्माद *unmâda*, i.e. *ud-mad*+*a*, m. Madness, Râm. 5, 31, 40.—**Comp.** *Kṛita-*, adj., f. *dâ* (MBh. 14, 2009), feigning madness, Kathâs. 18, 242. *Sa-*, adj. mad.

उन्मादन *unmâdana*, i. e. *ud-mad*, Caus., + *ana*, m. Causing madness, the name of one of the five arrows of Kâma, Lass. 7, 3.

उन्मार्ग *unmârga*, i.e. *ud-mârga*, m. **1.** A wrong road. **2.** Improper conduct.

उन्मार्जन *unmârjana*, i. e. *ud-mṛij*, Caus., + *ana*, n. Eclipsing, Prab. 81, 10.

ऽउन्मिश्र *-unmiçra*, i.e. *ud-miçra*, adj., f. *râ*, Mixed, Râm. 3, 34, 34.

उन्मीलन *unmîlana*, i. e. *ud-mîl* + *ana*, n. **1.** Opening of the eye, MBh. 1, 84. **2.** Springing up, appearance.

उन्मुखता *unmukhatâ*, i.e. *ud-mukha* + *tâ*, f. Having the face uplifted, Kathâs. 25, 248.

उन्मूलन *unmûlana*, i. e. *ud-mûl* + *ana*, n. Eradication, Ragh. 2, 34; figuratively, Prab. 67, 16.

उन्मेष *unmesha*, i.e. *ud-mish* + *a*, m. **1.** Opening of the eye-lids, Râm. 6, 102, 25. **2.** Flashing (of lightning), Megh. 79. **3.** Opening (of buds), Kumâras. 2, 33. **4.** Appearance, Prab. 118, 4.

उन्मेषण *unmeshaṇa*, i.e. *ud-mish* + *ana*, n. Awaking, appearance.

उप *upa*, ind. Under, on, near. **I.** adv. Near, further (ved.). **II.** prep. Near to (with the acc.), MBh. 1, 4099. **III.** Combined and compounded with verbs and their derivatives (q. cf.). **IV.** Former part of comp. nouns and adv. implying Inferiority, Nearness, e. g. *upa-vana* (lit., an inferior, a small, forest), n. A grove. *upa-kîchaka*, m. A partisan of the Kîchakas (a people). *upa-graha*, m. A minor planet or any secondary heavenly body, as a comet, etc. *upa-kanyâ-pura* + *m*. adv. Near the gynœceum.—Cf. Goth. uf, e.g. in ufdaupjan (to submerge), ufsneithan (to cut up), and ufhaban (to lift); Lat. sub is compounded with *sa*, corresponding to a Sskr. *sa-upa*; likewise ὑπό.

उपकण्ठ *upa-kaṇṭha*, **I.** adj., f. *ṭhâ*, Near, Bhartṛ. 3, 24. **II.** m. n. Proximity, Pañch. 74, 21; 222, 1.

उपकरण *upakaraṇa*, i. e. *upa-kṛi* + *ana*, n. Benefitting, Pañch. 86, 3. **2.** Implements, Yâjñ. 2, 276. **3.** Complement, Man. 2, 105 (of the Veda, viz. the Vedângas).—Comp. *Karmopakaraṇa*, i.e. *karman-*, adj. assisting by labour, Man. 10, 120. *Çastra-*, n. military apparatus.

उपकर्तृ *upakartṛi*, i.e. *upa-kṛi* + *tṛi*, m. An assistant, MBh. 3, 1049.

उपकान्तम् *upa-kânta* + *m* (vb. *kam*), adv. The lover being near at hand, Kir. 5, 19.

उपकार *upakâra*, i. e. *upa-kṛi* + *a*, m. **1.** Benefitting, Man. 8, 265 (in order to benefit them). **2.** Favour, MBh. 3, 15024. **3.** Assistance, Vikr. 11, 11. —Comp. *Sa-*, adj., f. *râ*. 1. beneficial, Man. 8, 143 (which may be used for one's profit). 2. equipped, stocked. 3. assisted, befriended.

उपकारक *upakâraka*, i.e. *upa-kṛi* + *aka*, adj., f. *rikâ*. **1.** Benefitting, Hit. 97, 21. **2.** Helping, Bhâshâp. 102. —Comp. *Sa-*, i.e. *sa-upakâra* + *ka*, one who has been benefitted, Pañch. 239, 4.

उपकारिन् *upakârin*, i. e. *upa-kṛi* + *in*, adj., f. *iṇî*. **1.** Benefitting; a benefactor. **2.** Supporting.—Comp. *Para-*, adj. supporting others.

उपकार्या *upakâryâ* (properly ptcple. of the fut. pass. of *kṛi*), f. A king's house, Râm. 1, 73, 37.

उपकूलम् *upa-kûla+m*, adv. Near the bank (of a river), Ragh. 15, 28.

उपकृति *upa-kṛi+ti*, f. A benefit, a service, Bhartṛ. 2, 54.

उपकृतिमन्त् *upakṛiti+mant*, adj., f. *matî*, Benefitting, Çiç. 9, 33.

उपक्रम *upa-kram+a*, m. **1.** A beginning, Vedântas. in Chr. 216, 3, cf. 5. **2.** Deliberate commencement, a design, Pańch. 263, 2. **3.** First designed work, Râjat. 5, 98. **4.** Proceeding, Râm. 5, 65, 8. **5.** An expedient, Man. 7, 107. **6.** Practice of medicine, Suçr. 1, 5, 11. **7.** Use (medical), Kathâs. 17, 37.—Comp. *Nis-*, adj. without commencement, Bhâg. P. 6, 9, 44.

उपक्रिया *upakriyâ*, i.e. *upa-kṛi+yâ*, f. Service, Râjat. 5, 177.

उपक्रीडा *upa-krîḍ+â*, f. A playground, Râm. 3, 78, 27.

उपक्रोश *upakroça*, i. e. *upa-kruç+a*, m. Blame, Râm. 3, 62, 26.

उपक्रोशन *upakroçana*, i.e. *upa-kruç+ana*, n. Censure, Daçak. in Chr. 180, 24.

उपक्षेप *upakshepa*, i. e. *upa-kship+a*, m. **1.** Dropping, Daçak. in Chr. 193, 14. **2.** Mentioning.

ऽउपग *-upa-ga* (vb. *gam*), adj., f. *gâ*. **1.** Joining, MBh. 13, 992. **2.** Getting, Man. 1, 46.

उपगति *upagati*, i.e. *upa-gam+ti*, f. Approach, Çiç. 9, 75.

उपगम *upa-gam+a*, m. Approach, Ragh. 6, 69.—Comp. *Viçvâsa-*, m. getting confidence, Çâk. d. 14.

उपगमन *upa-gam+ana*, n. **1.** Attainment, MBh. 1, 4140. **2.** Undergoing, Râm. 4, 53, 20.

उपगामिन् *upagâmin*, i. e. *upa-gam+in*, adj., f. *nî*. **1.** Approaching, Kathâs. 18, 102. **2.** Undergoing, 22, 2.

उपगिरि *upa-giri*, m. A country, bordering on mountains, MBh. 2, 1012.

उपग्रहण *upagrahaṇa*, i.e. *upa-grah+ana*, n. Holy study, Râm. 1, 4, 4.

उपग्राह *upagrâha*, i.e. *upa-grah+a*, m. A present, MBh. 2, 1898.

उपघात *upaghâta*, i. e. *upa-han*, Caus., *+a*, m. Damage, Yâjń. 2, 256.

उपघातक *upaghâtaka*, i. e. *upa-han*, Caus., *+aka*, adj. Injuring, Râm. 1, 2979.

उपघोषण *upaghoshaṇa*, i.e. *upa-ghush+ana*, n. Proclaiming, Daçak. in Chr. 180, 13.

उपघ्न *upaghna*, i.e. *upa-han+a*, m. Support.

उपचक्र *upa-chakra*, m. The name of a bird akin to the *chakra* or *chakravâka*, MBh. 3, 11613.

उपचय *upachaya*, i.e. *upa-chi+a*, m. Increase, Çiç. 9, 29.

ऽउपचायित्व *-upachâyitva*, i.e. *upachâyin+tva*, n. Veneration, MBh. 14, 2198.

ऽउपचायिन् *-upachâyin*, i. e. *upa-chi+in*, adj. **1.** Increasing, MBh. 13, 6275. **2.** Honouring, MBh. 4, 595.

उपचार *upachâra*, i.e. *upa-char+a*, m. **1.** Homage, Çâk. d. 66. **2.** Service, Vikr. 56, 9. **3.** Courting, Man. 8, 357. **4.** Means of doing homage, garlands, etc., Ragh. 7, 4. **5.** Practice, Man. 1, 111; performance, Man. 9, 259. **6.** Ceremony, Kumâras. 7, 86. **7.** Physicking, Suçr. 1, 117, 7; medical use, Vikr. 19, 17. **8.** Behaviour, Râm. 5, 32, 8.—Comp. *Dus-*, adj., f. *râ*, difficult to be treated, Pańch. 203, 5. *Sopa-*

chāram, i. e. *sa-upachāra + m,* adv. respectfully, Rām. 5, 90, 5.

उपचारिन् *upachārin,* i. e. *upa -char + in,* adj., f. *iṇī,* Serving, Rām. 1, 6, 16.

उपचिति *upa-chi + ti,* f. Collection, store.

उपच्छन्दन *upachchhandana,* i. e. *upa-chhand + ana,* n. Persuading, Daçak. in Chr. 196, 13.

उपजल्पिन् *upa-jalp + in,* adj., f. *nī,* Advising, giving advice, MBh. 1, 5396.

उपजाप *upajāpa,* i.e. *upa-jap + a,* m. Sowing disunion, Pańch. i. 337.

उपजापक *upajāpaka,* i.e. *upa-jap + aka,* adj. Inciting, encouraging, Man. 9, 275.

उपजिगमिषु *upajigamishu,* i.e. *upa -jigamisha,* desider. of *gam,* + *u,* adj. Desiring to approach, Megh. 43.

उपजिह्वा *upa-jihvā,* f. The uvula, or soft palate, Yājń. 3, 97.

उपजीवक *upa-jīv + aka,* adj. 1. Maintaining one's self by, Rām. 1, 6, 11. 2. Dependent, Kathās. 17, 46.

उपजीवन *upa-jīv + ana,* n. Maintenance, Man. 9, 207.

उपजीविन् *upa-jīv + in,* adj., f. *nī,* 1. Maintaining one's self by, Man. 9, 257. 2. Practising, MBh. 3, 12851. 3. Dependent, Rām. 6, 5, 4.—Comp. *Ātmopajīvin,* i.e. *ātman-,* adj. one who subsists by labour, Man. 7, 138; 8, 362 (by the intrigues of his wife, Kull.). *Gandha-,* adj. trading with perfumes, Rām. 2, 83, 14. *Tāmra-,* m. a coppersmith, Rām. 2, 90, 27 Gorr.

उपजोषम् *upa-josha + m,* adv. Silently, Çāk. 66, 16 v.r.—Comp. *Yathā-,* adv. Satisfactorily, Rām. 2, 89, 23.

उपतटम् *upa-taṭa + m,* adv. On a slope, Megh. 58.

उपताप *upatāpa,* i.e. *upa-tap + a,* m. 1. Heat. 2. Pain, Çāk. 38, 7 v.r. 3. Disease, MBh. 3, 13333.

उपतापिन् *upatāpin,* adj., f. *nī,* i.e. I. *upa-tap + in,* Causing pain, MBh. 1, 3630. II. *upatāpa + in,* Affected with illness, Man. 11, 1.

उपत्यका *upa + tya + kā,* f. The land lying along the foot of a mountain, Draup. 5, 5.

उपदा *upa-dā,* f. A present, Ragh. 4, 70.

उपदिग्धता *upa-digdha + tā* (vb. *dih*), f. Being covered, Kām. Nītis. 7, 24.

उपदिश् *upa-diç,* f. An intermediate quarter or point of the compass, e.g. north-east, etc., Rām. 1, 76, 23.

उपदेश *upadeça,* i.e, *upa-diç + a,* m. 1. Instruction, Bhartṛ. 2, 12. 2. Advice, Rām. 4, 40, 4. 3. A pretext, Man. 9, 268.—Comp. *Dharma-,* m. instruction concerning duty, Man. 8, 272. *Yathopadeçam,* i.e. *yathā-upadeça + m,* adv. according to the rule, MBh. 3, 8710. *Hita-,* m. friendly or good advice.

उपदेशता *upadeça + tā,* f. Condition of being the rule, Kumāras. 5, 36 (*te çīlam—upadeçatām gatam,* Thy virtue has become the rule).

उपदेशना *upadeçanā,* i.e. *upa-diç,* Caus., + *ana,* f. A sermon (concerning duty), Pańch. 165, 17.

उपदेशिन् *upadeçin,* i.e. *upa-diç + in,* adj., f. *nī,* Teaching, a teacher, Hit. i. d. 9.

उपदेष्टृ *upadeshṭṛi,* i.e. *upa-diç + tṛi,* m. A teacher, Pańch. 156, 17.

उपदोह *upadoha*, i.e. *upa-duh + a*, m. A milk-pail, MBh. 3, 12527.

उपद्रव *upadrava*, i.e. *upa-dru + a*, m. 1. Distress, Râm. 2, 108, 14; Pańch. i. d. 368. 2. Mischief, Böhtl. Ind. Spr. 11.—Comp. *Nis-*, adj., f. *vâ*. 1. unharmed, Böhtl. Ind. Spr. 1607; Râm. 5, 73, 56 (in an astrological sense). 2. free from danger, Pańch, 264, 25.

उपद्रष्टृ *upadrashṭṛi*, i.e. *upa-dṛiç + tṛi*, m. A spectator, Bhag. 13, 22.

उपधर्म *upa-dharma*, m. A subordinate duty, Man. 2, 237.

उपधा *upa-dhâ*, f. 1. A false pretence, Man. 8, 193. 2. Deceit, Hit. iii. d. 16.

उपधान *upadhâna*, i.e. *upa-dhâ + ana*, n., and f. *nî*, A pillow, Râm. 2, 42, 15; MBh. 1, 7165.—Comp. *Gaṇḍa-upadhâna*, n. a pillow, Suçr. 2, 41, 9.

उपधायिन् *upadhâyin*, i.e. *upa-dhâ + in*, adj., f. *nî*, Putting under, Kumâras. 5, 12.

उपधारण *upadhâraṇa*, i.e. *upa-dhṛi*, Caus., + *ana*, n. Consideration, MBh. 1, 5561.

उपधि *upadhi*, i.e. *upa-dhâ* (cf. *nidhi*), m. Fraud, Man. 8, 165.—Comp. *Nis-*, adj. guileless, Lass. 88, 5. *Sa-*, adj. guileful, Kir. 1, 45.

उपधिक *upadhi + ka*, m. An extorter of money by threats, Man. 9, 258.

उपनय *upanaya*, i.e. *upa-nî + a*, m. 1. Supplying, MBh. 3, 70. 2. Applying, Râm. 5, 37, 30.

उपनयन *upanayana*, i.e. *upa-nî + ana*, n. 1. Bringing, Vikr. 76. 2. The initiation of the three first classes, Man. 2, 108.

उपनायन *upanâyana*, i.e. *upa-nî + ana*, n. The initiation of the three first classes, Man. 2, 36.

उपनिक्षेप *upanikshepa*, i.e. *upa-ni-kship + a*, m. A deposit, Yâjń. 2, 25.

उपनिधि *upanidhi*, i.e. *upa-ni-dhâ* (cf. *nidhi*), m. A deposit, Man. 8, 145.

उपनिपातिन् *upanipâtin*, i. e. *upa-ni-pat + in*, adj., f. *nî*, Meeting, Çâk. 81, 8.

उपनिषद् *upanishad*, i.e. *upa-ni-sad*, f. A portion of the religious writings of the Hindus, Vedântas. in Chr. 202, 7.

उपनेतृ *upanetṛi*, i. e. *upa-nî + tṛi*, m., f. *trî*, n. One who brings near, Kumâras. 1, 61.

उपन्यास *upanyâsa*, i.e. *upa-ni-2. as + a*, m. 1. Giving, Râjat, 5, 461. 2. Declaration, Çâk. 36, 15 (Prâkṛ.). 3. Law, Man. 9, 31. 4. Pretext, Amar. 23.

उपपति *upa-pati*, m. An adulterer, Man. 3, 155.

उपपत्ति *upapatti*, i.e. *upa-pad + ti*, f. 1. Taking place, happening, Bhag. 13, 9; appearance, MBh. 14, 496; success, Vedântas. in Chr. 216, 4, cf. 17. 2. Suitableness, Râjat. 5, 374; 378.—Comp. *An-*, I. f. 1. not taking place, Bhâshâp. 81. 2. failure, Vedântas. in Chr. 205, 11. II. adj. not suitable, Râjat. 5, 378.

उपपातक *upa-pâtaka*, n. A lesser crime, Yâjń, 2, 210.

उपपातकिन् *upapâtakin*, i.e. *upa-pâtaka + in*, adj., f. *nî*, One who has committed a lesser crime, Man. 11, 107.

उपपादन *upapâdana*, i.e. *upa-pad*, Caus., + *ana*, n. Causing to spring up, MBh. 14, 506.

उपपार्श्व *upa-pârçva*, m. and n. The

shoulder (? perhaps the haunch), Nal. 19, 17.

उपपीडन *upa-pîḍ + ana*, n. Tormenting, Man. 6, 62.

उपपौरिक *upa-paurika* (the latter part is derived from *pura*, by the aff. *ika*), adj. Belonging to a suburb (?), Daçak. in Chr. 189, 6.

उपप्रदान *upapradâna*, i.e. *upa-pra-dâ + ana*, n. Bribe, Râm. 5, 81, 37.

उपप्रलोभन *upapralobhana*, i.e. *upa-pra-lubh*, Caus., + *ana*, n. Alluring, Daçak. in Chr. 185, 22; 198, 4.

उपप्रेक्षण *upaprekshaṇa*, i.e. *upa-pra-îksh + ana*, n. Overlooking, MBh. 1, 7757.

उपप्लव *upaplava*, i. e. *upa-plu + a*, m. **1.** Assault, MBh. 1, 3534. **2.** A portent, or natural phenomenon so considered, Ragh. 5, 6. **3.** An eclipse, Râm. 2, 65, 2 Gorr. **4.** Misfortune, Kumâras. 2, 32.—Comp. *Nis-*, adj. unharmed, Çâk. d. 31, v. r. *Vana-*, m. the conflagration of a forest, Megh. 17. *Sa-*, m. the sun or moon in eclipse. *Salila-*, m. inundation, Râjat. 5, 70.

उपप्लविन् *upaplavin*, i.e. *upaplava + in*, adj., f. *nî*, Assailed, Ragh. 13, 7.

उपबन्ध *upa-bandh + a*, m. A kind of sitting (or of love-making ?), Chaurap. 48.

उपभाषा *upa-bhâshâ*, f. A subordinate dialect, Lass. 67, 7.

उपभोग *upabhoga*, i.e. *upa-bhuj + a*, m. **1.** Eating, Kathâs. 8, 23. **2.** Enjoyment, Man. 2, 94. **3.** Use, Man. 8, 285.

उपभोगिन् *upabhogin*, i. e. *upa-bhuj + in*, adj., f. *nî*, Enjoying, MBh. 3, 13067.

उपमर्द *upamarda*, i.e. *upa-mṛid + a*, m. Destruction, Kathâs. 12, 143.

उपमर्दक *upamardaka*, i.e. *upa-mṛid + aka*, adj. Destroying, Kathâs. 7, 12.

उपमा *upa-mâ*, f. **1.** Comparison, Bhâshâp. 79. **2.** Likeness, MBh. 1, 6401; Bhag. 6, 19; *âtmânam upamâm kṛitvâ*, comparing thyself (viz. with others), Râm. 5, 23, 5.—Comp. *An-upama*, adj., f. *mâ*, incomparable, Ram. 4, 62, 17. *Alabdhopama*, i.e. *a-labdha-* (vb. *labh*), adj., f. *mâ*, incomparable, MBh. 3, 16517. *Nis-*, adj. not having his like, Bhartṛ. 2, 9.—As latter part of a comp. adj. it denotes very often, Like; e. g. *amaropama*, i. e. *amara-*, adj., f. *mâ*, God-like, Nal. 5, 46. *amṛita-*, adj., f. *mâ*, Amṛita-like, Nal. 12, 58.

उपमान *upamâna*, i. e. *upa-mâ + ana*, n. **1.** Comparison (the third *pramâṇa*), Bhâshâp. 139. **2.** Likeness, Kumâras. 4, 5. **3.** An image, Vikr. d. 22.

उपमिति *upamiti*, i.e. *upa-mâ + ti*, f. Comparison.

उपयन्तृ *upayantṛi*, i. e. *upa-yam + tṛi*, m. A husband, Ragh. 7, 1.

उपयम *upa-yam + a*, m. Marriage.

उपयाचन *upa-yâch + ana*, n. Solicitation.—Comp. *Satya-*, adj. fulfilling, or granting what is requested, Râm. 2, 68, 16.

उपयान *upayâna*, i.e. *upa-yâ + ana*, n. Approach, Râm. 3, 9, 22.

उपयायिन् *upayâyin*, i.e. *upa-yâ + in*, adj., f. *nî*. Approaching, Râm. 2, 97, 3.

उपयोग *upayoga*, i.e. *upa-yuj + a*, m. Employment, use, Kumâras. 1, 7.

उपयोगिन् *upayogin*, adj., f. *nî*, i.e. **1.** *upa-yuj + in*, Using, Daçak. 198, 16,

Wils. **2.** *upayoga + in*, Serviceable, Kathâs. 12, 42.

उपरति *uparati*, i.e. *upa-ram + ti*, f. **1.** Ceasing, Dev. 11, 8. **2.** Resigning, indifference, Vedântas. in Chr. 203, 13, cf. 16.

उपरम *upa-ram + a*, m. **1.** End, Râm. 4, 19, 13. **2.** Death, MBh. 1, 4897.

उपरमण *uparamaṇa*, i.e. *upa-ram + ana*, n. Ceasing, resigning, Vedântas. in Chr. 203, 16.

उपराग *uparâga*, i.e. *upa-rañj + a*, m. **1.** Painting, Çâk. d. 80, v.r. **2.** An eclipse, MBh. 3, 13476. **3.** Calamity, Ragh. 16, 7.—Comp. *nirvishayoparâga*, i.e. *nis-vishaya-*, adj., f. *gâ*, unharmed by objects of the senses, Prab. 48, 13.

उपरि *upari*, indecl. Over, above, on. **I.** adv. Above, MBh. 1, 571 ; upwards, Pañch. ii. d. 74 ; moreover, MBh. 1, 294. **II.** prep. **1.** Over, with the loc., Râm. 6, 85, 3 ; with the acc., 6, 3, 26 ; with the gen. MBh. 1, 507. **2.** On, with the gen., Yâjń. 2, 253 (adding to). **3.** Concerning, with the gen., Pańch. 94, 12 ; on account of, 214, 6. **III.** Former part of comp. nouns and former and latter part of comp. adv., e.g. *upari-purusha*, adj. Mounted by a man Daçak. in Chr. 188, 16. *karparopari*, i.e. *karpara-*, adv. Over earthen pots, Pańch. 218, 12. *taruvaropari*, i.e. *taru-vara-*, adv. On an excellent tree, Râm. 3, 35, 92. *kathitavelopari*, i. e. *kathita-velâ-*, adv. After the appointed time, Lass. 44, 15. — Doubled *uparyupari*, i.e. *upari-upari*. **1.** adv. Always higher, Hit. ii. d. 2 (those who look always above themselves, i.e. to their superiors) ; one above another, Vedântas. in Chr. 209, 2. **2.** prep. Over, with acc., MBh. 1, 4648 ; with gen., Nal. 1, 2.—Cf. *upa* and ved. *upara*, of which it is probably the loc. sing. slightly changed ; Goth. ufar- ; concerning Lat. super and Gr. ὑπέρ (properly ὑπερι in aeol. ὑπέρρ, ep. ὑπειρ.) cf. *upa*.

उपरिष्टात् *uparishṭât*, i.e. ved. *upara + bhis* (instr. pl.) + *tât*. **I.** adv. **1.** Above, Râm. 4, 28, 26. **2.** Afterwards, Yâjń. 1, 106. **II.** prep. **1.** Over, on, with the gen., MBh. 3, 13654. **2.** Concerning, Daçak. in Chr. 197, 19.

उपरोध *uparodha*, i.e. *upa-rudh + a*, m. **1.** Obstacle, MBh. 3, 13670. **2.** Disturbance, Vikr. 44, 12 ; Çâk. 8, 9. **3.** Injury, Man. 11, 10.

उपरोधन *uparodhana*, i.e. *upa + rudh + ana*, n. Obstacle, Râm. 5, 81, 17.

उपरोधिन् *uparodhin*, adj., f. *nî*, i.e. **I.** *upa-rudh + in*, Disturbing, Ragh. 18, 17. **II.** *uparodha + in*, Interrupted, Çâk. d. 81, v. r.

उपल *upala*, m. **1.** A stone, Man. 11, 167. **2.** A rock, Kir. 5, 15.—Comp. *Tapana-*, m. A fabulous gem = *sûrya-kânta*, Râjat. 3, 296. *Rasa-*, n. A pearl.

उपलचण *upalakshaṇa*, i. e. *upa-laksh + ana*, n. **1.** Seeing after, Çâk. 46, 6. **2.** A mark, Vikr. 69, 10. **3.** Including.

उपलब्धि *upalabdhi*, i.e. *upa-labh + ti*, f. **1.** Acquisition, Vikr. 65, 11. **2.** Perception, MBh. 14, 683. **3.** Knowledge, Vedântas. in Chr. 206, 5.—Comp. *An-*, f. Non-perception (the sixth *pramâṇa* of the Pûrva and Uttara mimâm̃sâ).

उपलम्भ *upalambha*, i.e. *upa-labh + a*, m. **1.** Acquisition, Râm. 5, 34, 23. **2.** Observation, Çâk. 13, 23. **3.** Perception, Chr. 59, 22 (*tad-upalambha-sam̃yukta*, according with what he had heard) ; feeling, Ragh. 14, 2.

उपलम्भक *upalambhaka*, i. e. *upa*

-*labh*, Caus., + *aka*, adj. Causing perception, Bhâshâp. 99.

उपलिप्सु *upalipsu*, i.e. *upa-lipsa*, desid. of *labh*, + *u*, adj. Desirous to learn, Daçak. in Chr. 179, 11.

उपलेपन *upalepana*, i.e. *upa-lip* + *ana*, n. Smearing, especially with cowdung, Pañch. 116, 21.

उपवन *upa-vana*, n. A grove, Râm. 3, 52, 38.

उपवर्णन *upa-varṇ* + *ana*, n. Description, Hit. 35, 19.

उपवास *upavâsa*, i.e. *upa-vas* + *a*, m. and n. Fasting, Man. 2, 188.—Comp. *Sa-*, adj. keeping a fast.

उपवासक *upavâsa* + *ka*, n. Fasting, MBh, 3, 13649.

उपवासिन् *upavâsin*, i.e. *upa-vas* + *in*, adj., f. *nî*, Fasting, Râjat. 5, 401. —Comp. *Mâsa-*, f. ironically, a lascivious woman, Lass. 41, 12.

उपवाहिन् *upavâhin*, i.c. *upa-vah* + *in*, adj., f. *nî*, Flowing to, MBh. 1, 2367.

उपवीणय *UPAVÎṆAYA*, a denom. derived from *upa-vîṇâ*, Par. To entertain somebody (acc.) by playing on the *vîṇâ* or Indian lyre, Ragh. 8, 33.

उपवीतिन् *upavîtin*, i.e. *upa-vîta* (vb. *vye*) + *in*, adj. Wearing the sacrificial cord on the left shoulder, Man. 2, 63.—Comp. *Yajña-*, i.e. *yajñopavîta* + *in*, adj., invested with the sacred thread.

उपवृत्ति *upa-vṛit* + *ti*, f. Collecting, holding, Prab. 40, 3.

उपवेद *upa-veda*, m. A subordinate Veda, a class of writings, MBh. 2, 450.

उपवेश *upaveça*, i.e. *upa-viç* + *a*, m. 1. Encampment, Râm. 5, 92, contents. 2. Undergoing, Râm. 5, 32, 25.

उपवेशन *upaveçana*, i.e. *upa-viç* + *ana*, n. Undergoing, Pañch. 50, 15.

उपवेशिन् *upaveçin*, i.e. *upa-viç* + *in*, adj., f. *nî*, Undergoing, Râjat. 5, 467.

उपशम *upa-çam* + *a*, m. 1. Ceasing, MBh. 1, 758. 2. Calmness, Bhartṛ. 2, 80.

उपशमन *upa-çam* + *ana*, n. Appeasing, Pañch. 118, 22.

उपशल्य *upa-çalya*, m. A space near a village, Ragh. 15, 60.

उपशान्ति *upaçanti*, i.e. *upa-çam* + *ti*, f. Ceasing, Hit. ii. d. 155.

उपशायिन् *upaçâyin*, i.e. *upa-çî* + *in*, adj., f. *nî*. 1. Sleeping, Râm. 5, 14, 21. 2. Going to rest, MBh. 1, 3628.

उपशोभन *upaçobhana*, i.e. *upa-çubh*, Caus., + *ana*, n. Trimming, Râm. 6, 112, 21.

उपशोषण *upaçoshaṇa*, i.e. *upa-çush*, Caus., + *ana*, adj. Drying up, Prab. 29, 6.

उपश्रुति *upa-çru* + *ti*, f. A voice heard in the night, considered as a deity, MBh. 5, 426 sqq.

उपश्लेष *upaçlesha*, i.e. *upa-çlish* + *a*, m. An embrace, Prab. 15, 7.

उपसंहार *upasaṁhâra*, i.e. *upa-sam-hṛi* + *a*, m. 1. Drawing back, Arj. 5, 6. 2. Comprehension, compendium, Vedântas. in Chr. 216, 3; 5.

उपसंक्षेप *upasaṁkshepa*, i.e. *upa-sam-kship* + *a*, m. Summary, Râm. 1, 3, contents.

उपसंग्रह *upasaṁgraha*, i.e. *upa-sam-grah* + *a*, m. 1. Touching (one's feet), Pańch. 206, 21 (as a token of respect. 2. Collecting, Râm. 1, 3, 24.

उपसंग्रहण *upasaṁgrahaṇa*, i.e. *upa-sam-grah* + *ana*, n. Respectful salutation (by touching one's feet, see the last), Man. 2, 72.

उपसदन *upa-sad* + *ana*, n. 1. Approaching for receiving instruction, MBh. 3, 17169. 2. Presence, Râm. 1, 50, 14 (*yajńa-*, i.e. at the sacrifice).

उपसंध्यम् *upasaṁdhyam*, adv. (from *upa-saṁdhyâ*), Near the twilight, Çiç, 9, 5.

उपसंन्यास *upasaṁnyâsa*, i.e. *upa-sam-ni-* 2. *as* + *a*, m. Abandoning, resigning, MBh. 3, 125.

उपसर्ग *upasarga*, i.e. *upa-sṛij* + *a*, m. 1. A portent, supposed to announce future evil, Dev. 12, 7. 2. A preposition. —Comp. *Sa-*, adj., f. *gâ*, portentous, Râm. 3, 44, 11; possessed by an evil spirit, Râm. 5, 18, 13.

उपसर्जन *upasarjana*, i.e. *upa-sṛij* + *ana*, n. 1. Obscuration, Man. 4, 105. 2. A representative, Man. 9, 121.

उपसर्पण *upasarpaṇa*, i.e. *upa-sṛip* + *ana*, n. Approach, Vikr. 64, 8.

उपसर्पिन् *upasarpin*, i.e. *upa-sṛip* + *in*, adj., f. *iṇî*, Approaching, MBh. 1, 1200.—Comp. *Dus-*, adj. approaching carelessly, Man. 7, 9.

उपसेवक *upa-sev* + *aka*, adj. Courting as a gallant, Yâjń. 3, 136.

उपसेवन *upa-sev* + *ana*, n. 1. Veneration, MBh. 3, 14677. 2. Service, devotion to, Man. 4, 134; MBh. 3, 28.

उपसेवा *upa-sev* + *â*, f. 1. Attendance, Man. 3, 64. 2. Devotion to, pursuing, MBh. 2, 2577. 3. Indulgence, Man. 12, 32.

ऽउपसेविन् *-upa-sev* + *in*, adj., f. *nî*. 1. Respecting, Man. 2, 121. 2. Serving, 11, 43. 3. Practising, Pańch. iii. d. 208 (*ye hitaṁ vâkyam utsṛijya viparîtopasevinaḥ*, they who neglecting good advice, follow the contrary).

उपस्कर *upaskara*, i.e. *upa-kṛi* + *a*, m. (and n. Chr. 36, 18). 1. Implements, MBh. 2, 2063; household implements, Man. 12, 66. 2. A broom (? vb. *kṛi*), Man. 3, 68.—Comp. *Su-*, adj. well furnished with the necessary implements, Chr. 25, 52. *Susaṁskṛita-*, i. e. *su-sam-kṛi* + *ta-*, f. *râ*, one who takes great care of the household furniture, Man. 5, 150.

उपस्तम्भ *upa-stambh* + *a*, m. A support, Hit. 29, 19.

उपस्तुत *upa* + *stuta* (vb. *stu*), m. A proper name, Chr. 295, 15 = Rigv. i. 112, 15.

उपस्थ *upa-stha* (vb. *sthâ*), m. and n. 1. The lap (ved.). 2. The male or female organs of generation, Vedântas. in Chr. 207, 8.—Comp. *Ratha-*, m. and n. the charioteer's seat for driving.—Cf. πόσθη.

उपस्थान *upasthâna*, i. e. *upa-sthâ* + *ana*, n. 1. Waiting on, Râm. 4, 44, 111; Vikr. 5, 5. 2. Being at one's command, Yâjń. 3, 160. 3. Assembly, MBh. 2, 1757.—Comp. *An-*, n. want of compliance, Râm. 6, 72, 49.

उपस्नेह *upasneha*, i.e. *upa-snih* + *a*, m. Humectation, Râm. 5, 75, 11.

उपस्पर्शन *upasparçana*, i. e. *upa-spriç* + *ana*, n. Bathing, MBh. 3, 8053.

उपस्वेद *upasveda*, i.e. *upa-svid* + *a*, m. Moisture; in the comp. word *sa-*, adj. Moistened, MBh. 1, 1033.

उपहर्तृ *upahartṛi*, i.e. *upa-hṛi* + *tṛi*, m. One who serves (meat), Man. 5, 51.

उपहस्तिका *upahastikâ*, i.e. *upa-hasta* + *ka*, f. A box, Daçak. 135.

उपहार *upahâra*, i.e. *upa-hṛi* + *a*, m. **1.** A complimentary present to a superior, Vedântas. in Chr. 204, 6. **2.** Exultation (which comprehends laughter, dance, song, bowing, recital of prayer, etc.), Daçak. in Chr. 181, 20 (?).

उपहास *upahâsa*, i.e. *upa-has* + *a*, m. Sneering, Ragh. 12, 37.—**Comp.** *Sopahâsam*, i.e *sa-upahâsa* + *m*, adv. Sneeringly, Pańch. 227, 4.

उपहास्यता *upa-hâsya* + *tâ* (vb. *has*), f. Derision, Ragh. 1, 3.

उपह्वर *upahvara*, i.e. *upa-hvṛi* + *a* **I.** m. **1.** A slope, Chr. 293, 2 = Rigv. i. 87, 2. **II.** loc. sing. *re*, **1.** Near, Arj. 1, 5. **2.** Privately, Daçak. in Chr. 189, 1; 192, 7; 193, 1.

उपांशु *upâṁçu*, i.e. *upa-aṁçu*, **I.** m. A low muttered prayer, Man. 2, 8. **II.** adv. Secretly, MBh. 3, 17309.

उपाकर्मन् *upâkarman*, i.e. *upa-â-kṛi* + *man*, n. The beginning of holy study, Man. 4, 119.

उपाख्यान *upâkhyâna*, i.e. *upa-â-khyâ* + *ana*, n. An episode, MBh. 1, 101.

उपाख्यानक *upâkhyâna* + *ka*, n. A tale, Pańch. 222, 23.

उपाङ्ग *upa-aṅga*, n. A supplement, Nal. 12, 17.

उपाञ्जन *upâńjana*, i.e. *upa-ańj* + *ana*, n. Smearing with cow-dung, Man. 5, 105.

उपादान *upâdâna*, i.e. *upa-â-dâ* + *ana*, n. **1.** Seizure, Man. 8, 417. **2.** Learning, Hit. 4, 13, v. r. **3.** Material cause, Bhâshâp. 149.

उपाधि *upâdhi*, i.e. *upa-â-dhâ* (cf. *nidhi*), m. **1.** Deception, Râm. 2, 111, 29. **2.** Modifying circumstance, Bhâshâp. 46. **3.** A condition supplied to limit a too general middle term, Bhâshâp. 137.—**Comp.** *An-*, m. natural disposition, Prab. 101, 11 (this country is beautiful naturally and not through any accidental circumstance).

ऽउपाधिता *-upâdhi* + *tâ*, f. in the comp. words *utkṛishṭa-*, Vedântas. in Chr. 204, 17; *nikṛishṭa-*, 205, 3; *aspashṭa-*, 205, 5. The affix *tâ* does not belong to *upâdhi* alone, but to its combination with the preceding part, e.g. *utkṛishṭopâdhi*, etc., and these compounds are of the Bahuvrîhi class. *utkṛishṭopâdhi* (vb. *kṛish* with the prep. *ud*) as Bhvr. and adj. would denote 'Having an excellent disguise;' with the aff. *tâ*, Condition of having an excellent disguise. *ni*° (vb. *kṛish* with the prep. *ni*), Condition of having a vile disguise; *aspashṭa-* (*a-sp*°), Condition of having an indistinct disguise.

उपाध्याय *upâdhyâya*, i. e. *upa-adhi-i* + *a*, m. A spiritual preceptor who gives instruction in a part only of the Veda, Man. 2, 141; a spiritual preceptor in general, Çâk. 61, 11; Râm. 1, 11, 13 (19 Gorr.).—**Comp.** *Paṭṭa-*, m. a dispatcher of documents (master of the rolls?), Râjat. 5, 396. *Mahâ-*, m. a reverend master, Chr. 175, l. 17. *Mahâ-mahâ-*, m. a very reverend master. Chr. 235, 6.

उपाध्यायानी *upâdhyâyânî*, i. e. *upâdhyâya* + *î*, f. The wife of a teacher, MBh. 1, 750.

उपानह् *upânah*, i. e. *upa-nah*, f.

(nom. sing. *upânat*, inst. du. *upânadbhyâm*, loc. pl. *upânatsu*). A shoe, Man. 2, 178.

उपान्त *upânta*, i. e. *upa-anta*, n. Proximity, Râjat. 5, 450.

उपान्तिक *upântika*, i. e. *upânta+ika*, n. Vicinity, Pańch. 167, 15.

उपाय *upâya*, i.e. *upa-i+a*, m. **1.** Approach, Bhartṛ. 3, 10. **2.** Means of success, Man. 7, 177. **3.** An expedient in general, Man. 9, 110. **4.** Craft, Böhtl. Ind. Spr. 498.

उपायन *upâyana*, i.e. *upa-i+ana*, n. A present, Râm. 2, 70, 23.

उपार्जन *upârjana*, i. e. *upa-arj+ana*, n. Acquisition, Böhtl. Ind. Spr. 215.

उपालम्भ *upâlambha*, i. e. *upa-â-labh+a*, m. Blame, Chr. 10, 2.—Comp. *Sa-*, adj. censuring, Râm. 6, 99, 27.

उपालम्भन *upâlambhana*, i.e. *upa-â-labh+ana*, n. Blame, Çâk. 59, 14.

उपावर्तन *upâvartana*, i. e. *upa-â-vṛit+ana*, n. Return.

उपाश्रय *upa-âçraya*, m. A retreat, refuge, MBh. 15, 152; 3, 17262.

उपासक *upâsaka*, i.e. *upa-âs+aka*, m. **1.** A servant, Kathâs. 19, 78. **2.** A worshipper, Mṛichchh. 113, 11.

उपासङ्ग *upâsańga*, i.e. *upa-â-sańj+a*, m. A quiver, MBh. 2, 1916.

उपासन *upâsana*, i.e. *upa-âs+ana*. I. n. **1.** Attendance, Man. 3, 107. **2.** Practice, Mṛichchh. 2, 11. **3.** Religious contemplation, Vedântas. in Chr. 202, 12, cf. 18, 3. **4.** The sacred fire, Yâjń. 3, 45. II. f. *nâ*, Service, Chât. 10.

उपासितृ *upâsitṛi*, i.e. *upa-âs+tṛi*, m. A worshipper, Râm. 5, 32, 6.

उपास्ति *upâsti*, i.e. *upa-âs + ti*, f. Service, Lass. 56, 20.

उपेक्षक *upekshaka*, i.e. *upa-îksh+aka*, adj. Indifferent, Man. 6, 43.

उपेक्षण *upekshaṇa*, i.e. *upa-îksh+ana*, n. Indulgence, tolerance, Hit. ii. d. 119.

उपेक्षा *upekshâ*, i.e. *upa-îksh+a*, f. **1.** Indifference, MBh. 14, 1049. **2.** Neglect, Râm. 4, 12, 35. **3.** Want of attention, Bhâshâp. 159.

उपेतृ *upetṛi*, i.e. *upa-i+tṛi*, m. One who must use expedients, Man. 7, 215.

उपेन्द्र *upendra*, i.e. *upa-indra*, m. A name of Vishṇu, Râm. 1, 1, 6; Vedântas. in Chr. 209, 19.

उपोद्घात *upodghâta*, i. e. *upa-ud-han*, Caus., *+a*, m. An introduction, Kathâs. 3, 65.

उप्ति *upti*, i.e. *vap+ti*, f. Sowing, Man. 9, 330.

उब्ज् *UBJ*, i. 6, Par. (originally a denom. derived from *ubja*, i.e. *ubh*= ὑφ in ὑφός, and *ja* from *jan*). To incurvate, to restrain.—With the prep. **निस्** *nis*, To let loose, to set free, Chr. 292, 9=Rigv. i. 85, 9.

उभ् *UBH*, and **उम्भ्** *UMBH*, i. 6, Par. To fill (ved.), ii. 9, Par. To compress (properly 'to incurvate'= ὑφ, see the last, an old form of **kubh*, *kumbh*).

उभ *ubha* (for original *ambha*= ἄμφω, Lat. ambo, Goth. bai), numeral, m. f. n. dual. Both, Man. 2, 14.

उभय *ubha+ya*, numeral, m. f. n. without dual. Both, Man. 2, 55.

उभयतस् *ubhaya+tas*, adv. **1.** On

both sides, Man. 8, 315. 2. In the one and the other case, Man. 1, 47.

उभयत्र *ubhaya + tra*, adv. In both instances, Man. 3, 125.

उभयथा *ubhaya + thâ*, adv. In both cases, Prab. 77, 3; Vikr. 43, 17 (on both reasons).

उमा *umâ*, f. Pârvatî, or Durgâ, the wife of Çiva, Râm. 1, 36, 15.

उम्भ् *UMBH*, see *ubh*.

उरग *uraga*, i.e. *uras-ga* (vb. *gam*). I. m. A snake, Kir. 3, 33. II. f. *gî*, A female snake, Prab. 77, 7. III. f. *gâ*, The name of a city.—**Comp.** *Kṛishṇa-*, m. a black kind of snake, Draup. 5, 8. *Mahâ-*, m. a sort of demi-god of the serpent genus, inhabiting Pâtâla. *Hṛita-*, adj. robbed of (its) snakes.

उरण *uraṇa*, i.e. *vṛi + ana* (cf. *ûrṇa*), m. A lamb, MBh. 12, 6535.

उरभ्र *urabhra*, i.e. *vṛi + a* (akin to *ûrṇâ*)-*bhṛi + a*, m. A ram.

उरश्छद *uraçchhada*, i.e. *uras -chhad + a*, m. Mail.—**Comp.** *Kâñchana-*, adj. having a mail of gold, Râm. 3, 67, 16.

उरस् *uras*, probably for *varas*, i.e. *vṛi + as*, and akin to *uru*, n. The breast, Daçak. in Chr. 184, 8.

ऽउरस्क *-uras-ka*, a substitute for *uras*, when latter part of comp. adj., e.g. *mahâ-* and *vipula-*, adj. Having a broad chest, Râm. 3, 36, 6.

उरसिज *uras + i-ja* (vb. *jan*), m. The female breast, Râm. 1, 9, 38.

उरीऽ *urî-*, see *kṛi*.

उरु *uru*, i.e. *vṛi + u*, adj., I. f. *urvî*, Large, MBh. 1, 1222. Comparat. *varîyaṁs*, superl. *varishṭha*, MBh. 14, 879. II. f. *Urvî*, the earth, Râm. 4, 44, 130. —Cf. εὐρύς, Ῥεία.

उरोज *uroja*, i.e. *uras-ja* (see *urasija*), m. The female breast, Çiç. 9, 44; 86.

† उर्द् *URD*, or ऊर्द् *ÛRD*, i. 1, Âtm. 1. To measure. 2. To play.

† उर्व् *URV*, i. 1, Par. To kill or hurt.

उर्वशी *urvaçî*, f. The name of an Apsaras, Vikr. d. 110, etc.

उर्विया *urviyâ*, adv. (probably for *ûrvyâ*, instr. sing. fem. of *uru*), Far and wide, Chr. 294, 9=Rigv. i. 92, 9.

उर्वीभृत् *urvî-bhṛi + t* (see *uru*), m. A mountain, Amar. 93.

उलण्ड् *ULAṆḌ*, see *laṇḍ*.

उलूक *ulûka*, m. 1. An owl, Bhartṛ. 2, 89. 2. A name of Indra, Chr. 46, 26. 3. The name of a country, its people (plur.), and its king, MBh. 1, 335, etc. **Comp.** *Kumbha-*, m. A kind of owl, MBh. 13, 5499.—Cf. Lat. ulula, A.S. and O.H.G. ûla.

उलूखल *ulûkhala* (cf. *udûkhala*), n. A mortar, Pañch. 249, 8.

ऽउलूखलिक *-ulûkhalika*, i.e. *ulûkhala + ika*, adj. A substitute for the last, when latter part of comp. adj., e.g. *danta-*, adj. One who uses his teeth as a mortar or pestle, Man. 6, 17.

ऽउलूखलिन् *-ulûkhalin*, i.e. *ulûkhala + in*, in *danta-*, adj. Using his teeth as a mortar or pestle, Râm. 1, 52, 26 Gorr.

उल्का *ulkâ*, i.e. probably *jval + ka*, f. 1. A firebrand, Râm. 3, 75, 51. 2. Fire falling from heaven, a meteor, Man. 1, 38.—**Comp.** *Tṛiṇa-*, f. a burning bunch of grass, Hit. i. d. 81. *Mahâ-*,

f. a great fireball, Man. 4, 103.—Cf. Lat. Vulcanus.

उल्मुक *ulmuka*, i.e. perhaps *jval+man+ka*, cf. *ulkâ*, I. n. A firebrand, Pańch. 38, 20. II. m. A proper name, MBh. 2, 1275.

उल्लङ्घन *ullańghana*, i.e. *ud-lańgh+ana*, n. Transgress, Kathâs. 22, 57.

उल्लाप *ullâpa*, i.e. *ud-lap+a*, m. Violent cry, Bhartṛ. 3, 6 (perhaps, with the former part *khala-*, a comp. of the Bahuvr. class, denoting a tyrant, cf. Galanos' translation).

उल्लापिक *ullâpika*, i.e. *ullâpa+ika* (?), adj. Betraying (?), Chr. 57, 22.

उल्लापिन् *ullâpin*, i.e. *ud-lap+in*, adj., f. *nî*, Calling out, Amar. 36.

उल्लास *ullâsa*, i.e. *ud-las+a*, m. 1. Skipping, Amar. 48. 2. Joy, Sâh. D. 83, 8.—Comp. *Chidullâsa*, i.e. *chit-*, adj. rejoicing the mind, Bhâg. P. 9, 11, 33.

उल्लासन *ullâsana*, i.e. *ud-las+ana*, n. Delighting, making happy, Râjat. 5, 243 (*hastâgraveshṭanollâsanaspṛiçaḥ khaḍgasya*, Of the sword which seemed to rejoice at being grasped by his hand).

उल्लुञ्चन *ulluńchana*, i.e *ud-luńch+ana*, n. Pulling, Yâjń. 2, 217.

उल्लेख *ullekha*, i.e. *ud-likh+a*, m. Description, Kathâs. 25, 225.

उल्लेखन *ullekhana*, i.e. *ud-likh+ana*, n. Scraping, Man. 5, 124.

उल्व *ulva*, n. 1. Amnium, the caul, Ait. Br. 1, 3. 2. The womb, Bhag. 3, 38.—Cf. Lat. vulva.

उल्वण *ulvaṇa* (probably akin to *uru*, of which the original form has been *urvan*, cf. εὐρυν-ω for εὐρυνjω), adj., f. *ṇâ*. 1. Abundant, MBh. 3, 340. 2. Evident, Râjat. 5, 148 (incarnate).—Comp. *Ati-*, adj. very violent, Râm. 3, 30, 29.

उशनस् *uçanas*, m., nom. sing. *uçanâ*, The name of a Ṛishi or saint, Râm. 6, 31, 14; identified with Çukra, regent of the planet Venus, MBh. 1, 3204.

उशीनर *uçînara*, m. The name of a country, its people (pl.), and its king, MBh. 1, 227.

उशीर *uçîra*, m. and n. The root of a fragrant grass, Andropogon muricatum, Râm. 2, 55, 14.

उष् *USH*, i. 1, Par. 1. To burn; to burn up, Man. 4, 189. 2. To chastise, Man. 9, 273.—Cf. αὔω, εὔω, εὔσανα, εὔστρα; Lat. uro prurire; O.H.G. usilvar, yellow, probably Lat. aurum.—Cf. 2. *vas*.

उषती *ushatî* (ptcple. of an aor. of *ush* ?), f. Inauspicious, MBh. 1, 3558.

उषर्बुध् *usharbudh*, i.e. *ushas-budh*, adj. Early awake, Chr. 295, 18=Rigv. i. 92, 18.

उषस् *ushas*, i.e. 2. *vas+as*, f. The dawn, morning, Kir. 5, 40; ved. nom. pl. *ushâsas*, Chr. 294. 2=Rigv. i. 92, 2. The deity of the dawn, Chr. 287, sqq. —Cf. aeol. αὔως (=the original nom. sing. *vasâs*), ἠώς; Lat. aurora.

उष्ट्र *ushṭra*, I. m. A camel, Man. 3, 162. II. f. *ushṭrî*, A she-camel, Pańch. 87, 6.—Comp. *Khara-*, n. an ass and a camel, Yâjń. 2, 160.

उष्ट्रिका *ushṭrikâ*, i.e. *ushṭrî+ka*, f. A she-camel, Pańch. 228, 16.

उष्ण *ushṇa*, i.e. *ush+na*, I. adj., f. *ṇâ*, Hot, Vedântas. in Chr. 203, 17. II. m. and n. The hot season, Man. 11, 113.—Comp. *Ati-*, adj. exceedingly hot, Man. 3, 236. *An-*, adj. not hot, Man. 2, 61; chilly, Çiç. 9, 3.

उष्णग *ushṇa-ga* (vb. *gam*), m. The hot season, Râm. 5, 31, 16.

उष्णता *ushṇa+tâ*, f., and **उष्णत्व** *ushṇa+tva*, n. Heat, MBh. 3, 15101.

उष्णालु *ushṇâlu*, i. e. *ushṇa+âlu*, adj. Hot, Vikr. d. 41.

उष्णिमन् *ushniman*, i. e. *ushṇa+iman*, m. Heat, Çiç. 9, 65.

उष्णीष *ushṇîsha*, m. and n. A diadem, a turban, Chr. 25, 56; Râjat. 5, 206.

उष्णीषिन् *ushṇîshin*, i.e. *ushṇîsha+in*, m. A name of Çiva, MBh. 13, 1158.—Comp. *Kańchukoshṇîshin*, i. e. *kańchuka-ushṇîsha+in*, the affix belonging to both parts of the compound, wearing jackets and turbans, Râm. 6, 99, 23.

उष्मन् *ush+man*, m. **1.** Heat, MBh. 9, 13969. **2.** Ardour, Pańch. ii. d. 67; Çiç. 9, 85. **3.** Hot moisture, Man. 1, 45. — Comp. *Dhana-*, m. ardent longing for wealth, Man. 9, 231. *Nidhâna-*, m. ardour, courage, caused by the possession of a treasure, Pańch. 118, 15. *Nis-*, adj. cold, MBh. 14, 476.

उसर् *usar*, i.e. 2. *vas+ar* (*r* for *n*, and originally for *vasant*, identic with *ushas* for *vasant*), f. Dawn, morning; acc. pl. *usras*, Lass. 100, 15=Rigv. vii. 15, 8. — Cf. *ἦρι*=loc. *vasri*, *ἄριστον*, breakfast, *αὔριον*.

उस्र *usra*, i. e. 2. *vas+ra*, **I.** m. A ray of light, Kir. 5, 31. **II.** f. *râ*, A cow, Chr. 293, 1=Rigv. i. 87, 1; Chr. 294, 4=Rigv. i. 92, 4.

उस्रिया *usriyâ*, i.e. *usra+iya*, f. A cow, Chr. 297, 12=Rigv. i. 112, 12.

† **उह्** *UH*, i. 1, Par. To hurt or to kill.

ऊ *Û*.

ऊ *Û*, see *u*.

† **ऊठ्** *ÛṬH*, see *uṭh*.

ऊढि *ûḍhi*, i.e. *vah+ti*, f. Bringing, Râjat. 5, 173.

ऊति *ûti*, f. i.e. **I.** *av+ti*, **1.** Assistance, Chr. 288, 14=Rigv. i. 48, 14; help, Lass. 98, 16=Rigv. v. 9, 6; *ûtî*, ved. instr. sing. Chr. 291, 13=Rigv. i. 64, 13. **2.** Quickness, Bhâg. P. 8, 5, 44. **II.** *ve+ti*, Web, tissue, Bhâg. P. 2, 10, 1; 4.

ऊधन् *ûdhan*, and, with *r* for *n*, **ऊधर्** *ûdhar*, and **ऊधस्** *ûdhas*, based on original **vad-dhant* (cf. *udan*, vb. *dhâ*, and *payodhas*), n. An udder. —Cf. *οὖθαρ*, uber; O.H.G. ûtar; A.S. uder.

ऊधस्य *ûdhas+ya*, n. Milk.

ऊधस्वन्त् *ûdhas+vant*, adj., f. *vatî*, Having exuberant udders.

ऊन् *ÛN*, i. 10, Par. (properly a denom. of the following), To detract.

ऊन *ûna* (probably for *van+na* from *van*=Goth. van, vans; cf. O.H.G. wênag, few, perhaps *εὖνις*, etc.), adj., f. *nâ*. **1.** Lessened, Yâjń. 2, 295. **2.** Inferior, Man. 9, 123. **3.** Wanting, usually as former or latter part of a comp., e.g. *alpa-*, adj. Wanting a little, Man. 8, 217. *kiṁchid-*, adj. A little less, Sâv. 4, 26. *tri-bhâga-*, adj. Reduced by a third, Râjat. 5, 170. *daçona*, i.e. *daçan-*, adj. Wanting ten, Râm. 1, 46, 12. If one only is wanting, *eka* may be added, e.g. *ekonachatvâriṁça*, i.e. *eka-ûna-*, ord. The thirty-ninth, MBh. 1, adhy. 39, but usually it is dropped, e.g. *ûna*

-vimça, ord. The nineteenth, MBh. 3, adhy. 19. As former part, e.g. *ûna-dvi-vârshika* (i.e. *-dvi-varsha+ika*), adj. A child under two years, Man. 5, 68; *ûna-shoḍaçavarsha* (i.e. *-shash-daçan-varsha*), adj. Under sixteen years, Râm. 1, 22, 2.—Cf. probably Lat. un-, or unde-, e.g. in unde-viginti = *ûna-vimçati*.

† ऊय् *ÛY*, i. 1, Âtm. (properly *ve*, i. 4, Âtm.). To sew, to weave.

ऊरी *ûrî*, see *kṛi*.

ऊरु *ûru*, perhaps akin to *uru*, m. The thigh, Râm. 3, 52, 32. When the latter part of a comp. adj., the fem. ends in *ru*, or *rû*, e.g. *vâmoru*, i.e. *vâma-*, f. *rû*, Having beautiful thighs, MBh. 1, 1903; but *ru* (against the grammatical rule), MBh. 1, 2988. *karabhopamoru*, i.e. *karabha-upama-ûru*, f. *rû*, and *karabhoru*, i.e. *karabha-* f. *rû*, Having thighs like the proboscis of an elephant, Ragh. 6, 83; Çâk. d. 69. *rambha-*, f. *rû*, Having bambu-like thighs, Mâlav. d. 45. *vara-*, f. *ru*, Having beautiful thighs, Râm. 3, 52, 53.—Comp. *An-*, I. adj. thighless. II. m. Aruṇa, the charioteer of the sun, Skândap., Kâçîkh. 2, 13.

ऊरुज *ûru-ja*, adj. Born from the thigh, MBh. 1, 6820.

ऊर्ज् *ÛRJ*, i. 10, Par. (properly a denomin. derived from the next). 1. To nourish, to strengthen. 2.† To live. *ûrjita*, 1. Swollen, Râjat. 5, 214. 2. Strong, Hariv. 9920. 3. Distinguished, Ragh. 9, 38. 4. Violent, Râm. 2, 85, 2.—Cf. ὀργάω, ὀργάς, perhaps Lat. urgere.

ऊर्ज् *ûrj*, f. Strength, food, Chr. 295, 17 = Rigv. i. 92, 17; Bhâg. P. 4, 24, 38.

ऊर्ज *ûrj+a*, m. Strength, Man. 2, 55.

ऊर्जस्कर *ûrjaskara*, i.e. *ûrj+as-kṛi+a*, adj. Causing strength, MBh. 3, 14181.

ऊर्जस्वल *ûrjas+vala*, adj., and

ऊर्जस्विन् *ûrjas+vin*, adj., f. *nî*, Strong, Ragh. 2, 50.

ऊर्जावन्त् *ûrj+â+vant*, adj., f. *vatî*, Abundant with food, MBh. 13, 1842.

ऊर्ण *ûrṇa*, i.e. *vṛi+na*, n., and f. *ṇâ*, Wool, MBh. 2, 1847.—Comp. *Karṇorṇa*, i.e. *karṇa-*, adj. having wool near the ears, Bhâg. P. 4, 6, 21. *Patrorṇa*, i.e. *patra-*, n. 1. Wove silk. 2. A garment of wove silk.—Cf. Goth. vulla; A.S. vull; Lat. vellus, οὖλος.

ऊर्णमय *ûrṇa+maya*, adj., f. *yî*, Woollen.

ऊर्णु *ÛRṆU*, ii. 2, Par., Âtm. (properly vb. *vṛi*, ii. 5). To cover; Âtm. To hide one's self, Bhâg. P. 2, 9, 27.—With the prep. अप *apa*, To discover, Chr. 294, 4 = Rigv. i. 92, 4.—With वि *vi*, To discover, Chr. 295, 11 = Rigv. i. 92, 11.

ऊर्द् *ÛRD*, see *urd*.

ऊर्ध्व *ûrdhva*, i.e. *ṛidh+va*, adj., f. *vâ*. 1. Erect, Hiḍ. 3, 2. 2. Raised (as dust), Man. 11, 110. 3. Upper, MBh. 1, 1034. 4. The name of a kind of flying, Pañch. ii. d. 57. *vam*, adv. 1. Upwards, Râm. 4, 8, 5. 2. Above, Man. 1, 92. 3. After, Râm. 3, 53, 4; after death, Man. 9, 104.—Cf. ὀρθός; Lat. arduus.

ऊर्ध्वग *ûrdhva-ga* (vb. *gam*), adj., f. *gâ*. 1. Going upwards, MBh. 3, 850. 2. Being in the air.

ऊर्ध्वपुण्ड्रक *ûrdhva-puṇḍra+ka*, m. A perpendicular line on the forehead made with sandal, etc.; a sectarial mark, Lass. 70, 11.

ऊर्मि *ûrmi*, probably *hvṛi*+*mi*, m. and f. A wave, Bhartṛ. 2, 4.—**Comp.** *Kshîra-*, a wave of the sea of milk, Ragh. 4, 27.

ऊर्मिन् *ûrmin*, i.e. *ûrmi*+*in*, adj., f. *ṇî*, Wavy (ved.).—**Comp.** *Mahâ-*, adj. having great waves, MBh. 3, 793.

ऊर्मिमन्त् *ûrmi*+*mant*, adj., f. *matî*, adj. Surgy, Râm. 4, 9, 38.

ऊर्व *ûrva*, m. The name of a saint from whose thighs (*ûru*) proceeded the submarine fire, Hariv. 2527 sqq.

† ऊष् *ÛSH*, ii. 1, Par. To be diseased.

ऊष *ûsha*, I. m. Saline earth, Man. 5, 120. II. f. *shî*, Salt ground, Bhâg. P. 1, 15, 21.

ऊषण *ûshaṇa*, i.e. *ûsh*(=*ush*)+*ana*, n. Pepper.

ऊषर *ûsha*+*ra*, adj., f. *râ*, Impregnated with saline particles, MBh. 13, 3341. 2. Salt ground, barren land, Man. 2, 112.

ऊष्मन् *ûshman* (=*ushman*). 1. Heat, MBh. 14, 468. 2. A name comprising the sibilants and *h*, Bhâg. P. 3, 12, 47.

ऊष्मप *ûshmapa*, i.e. *ûshman-pa* (vb. 1.*pâ*). I. adj. Drinking the steam of food only, MBh. 13, 646. II. m. pl. The name of a class of Pitṛis or Manes, MBh. 2, 341.

1. ऊह् *ÛH*, i. 1, Âtm., with prepositions also Par. To apprehend, MBh. 1, 5228.—Caus. To observe, MBh. 2, 1240.—With the prep. अपि *api*, To understand, Hit. iii. d. 33.—With अभि *abhi*, To infer, Kathâs. 7, 11.

2. ऊह् *ÛH* (derived from *vah*, and appearing only after prep.), i. 1, Par. and Âtm. *ûhyamânâ*, Râjat. 5, 33, is to be corrected to *uhy°*, pass. of *vah*, Being carried.—With the prep. अप *apa*. 1. To remove, Man. 8, 414; 11, 102 (Âtm.); *apohita*, Prab. 116, 7.—2. To press, to follow immediately, Ragh. 19, 5. 3. To avoid, Man. 10, 86 (Âtm.).—With the prep. व्यप *vi-apa*. 1. To remove, Man. 2, 102. 2. To expiate, Man. 11, 81. 3. To keep off, Râm. 6, 75, 57 (Âtm.).—With उद् *ud*. To raise, Bhâg. P. 4, 8, 15.—With उप *upa*, To bring near, Râm. 2, 52, 6.—Pass. To begin, MBh. 2, 2051. *upoḍha*, Produced, Çâk. d. 169.—With समुप *sam-upa* in *samupoḍha*, 1. Near, Man. 6, 41. 2. Commenced, Râm. 2, 75, 29.—With प्रति *prati*, *pratyûḍha*. 1. Denied, Râm. 5, 31, 14. 2. Exceeded, Bhâg. P. 4, 22, 38. 3. Interrupted, Man. 5, 84.—With वि *vi*, To arrange an army, Man. 7, 191. *vyûḍha*, Large, Râm. 6, 36, 45.—With निर्वि *nis-vi*, *nirvyûḍha*. 1. Brought out, MBh. 1, 6257. 2. Achieved, Kathâs. 17, 159.—With प्रतिवि *prati-vi*, To arrange an army against, MBh. 3, 16370, *pratyavyûhat*, instead of *prativy-auhat*; *prativyûḍha*, Large, Râm. 6, 35, 18.

ऊह *ûh*+*a*, m. Connected reasoning, MBh. 13, 6725.—**Comp.** *An-ûha*, adj. without (long) reflection, quick, Bhâg. P. 3, 5, 48; 18, 12. *Durûha*, i.e. *dus-*, adj. difficult to be inferred, Man. 11, 238. v.r.

ऋ ṚI.

ऋ ṚI, i. 1, *ṛichchha* (in epic poetry also *archchha* = ἔρχομαι), ii. 3; 5; 9 Par. **1.** To go. **2.** To go to. **3.** To undergo. With abstracts (cf. *i*): Man. 1, 53, *glânim ṛichchhati*, To become inert; MBh. 3, 2166, *mṛityum*, To die; *archh*, Nal. 7, 4; MBh. 3, 84; Nalod. 2, 10, *yuddharaṅgatâm âra*, To become the field of battle. **4.** To rise, *ṛi-ṇu*. **5.** To meet, Man. 8, 351; to attain, Nalod. 1, 32; to fall on, Man. 8, 18, *ṛichchha*. **6.** To gain, to acquire. **7.** To move, to raise, ved. ii. 3, *iyarmi*. **8.** To open, ii. 5. **9.** To attack, MBh, 4, 1059, *ṛichchha*. **10.** To hurt; *ṛita*, and *ṛite*, see separately.—Caus. *arpaya*, **1.** To cast; *arpita*, thrown, Ragh, 8, 87; turned, Bhag. 8, 7. **2.** To fasten, Çâk. d. 133. **3.** To pierce. **4.** To put, Ragh. 9, 74. **5.** To deliver, Yâjń. 2, 65; Daçak. in Chr. 183, 24; 201, 11. **6.** To restore, Man. 8, 191.—*arpita*. **1.** Cut in, Çâk. d. 74. **2.** Written, Ragh. 17, 79.—Comp. *Chitra-*, adj. painted, Çâk. d. 143.—With the prepos. अभि *abhi*, To attack, MBh. 3, 11726, *ṛichchha*, 11875 *archchha*.—With आ *â*. **1.** To meet, MBh. 3, 17226. **2.** To adapt (ved.).—With प्र *pra*, To rise, Chr. 288, 3=Rigv. i. 49, 3.—With प्रति *prati*, Caus. **1.** To fasten, Ragh. 6, 28. **2.** To deliver, Ragh. 15, 41. **3.** To restore, Daçak. in Chr. 195, 15; 189, 15; 192, 16. —With वि *vi*, To open, Chr. 288, 15= Rigv. i. 48, 15.—With सम् *sam*, Caus. **1.** To cast, MBh. 1, 6978. **2.** To deliver, Pańch. 36, 13. **3.** To restore, Hit. 72, 20.—*samarpita*. **1.** Fastened, Kumâras. 5, 63. **2.** Put together, Daçak. in Chr. 200, 2. **3.** Resting, Râm. 1, 77, 25. **4.** Painted, Ragh. 3, 15.—Cf. ἔρχομαι, ὄρνυμι, ἄρνυμαι, ἄρος, μισθαρνέω, ἰάλλω, ὄλλυμι (Lat. abolere), ἄρω, ἀρτίζω; Lat. orior, adorior, adolesco, adultus; Goth. alds; A.S. ald; O.H.G. arnên.

ऋक्वन् *ṛikvan*, i. e. *ṛich* + *van*. **I.** adj. Praising. **II.** m. A praiser, Chr. 293, 5=Rigv. i. 87, 5.

† ऋक्ष् ṚIKSH (?), ii. 5, Par. To kill or hurt.

ऋक्ष *ṛiksha*, **I.** m. A bear, Râm. 3, 52, 45. **II.** f. *kshî*, A she-bear, Râm. 1, 16, 21. **III.** m. and n. **1.** A star, Râm. 5, 73, 57; MBh. 13, 625. **2.** Bears and stars, Çiç. 9, 31. **IV.** m. and f. *kshâ*, Proper names, MBh. 1, 3722; 3790.—Cf. ἄρκτος; Lat. ursus.

ऋक्षवन्त् *ṛiksha* + *vant*, m. The name of a mountain, Râm. 6, 3, 10.

ऋच् ṚICH, i. 1, Par. **1.** To shine, ved. **2.** i. 1, and † i. 6, Par. To praise, ved. **3.** To honour, Man. 3, 93; anomal. absol. *archya*, Man. 1, 4.—Caus. *archaya*, To honour, Man. 2, 181. *archita*, Respectfully bestowed, Man. 4, 235.—With the prep. अभि *abhi*, To honour, Man. 8, 391.—With समभि *sam-abhi*, To honour, Yâjń. i. 226; to adore, 2, 112. —With प्रति *prati*, **1.** To salute in turn, Râm. 2, 71, 31. **2.** To salute one by one, MBh. 1, 7211.—With सम् *sam*, To adore, Râm. 2, 3, 48; to honour, MBh. 3, 11090 (properly 10190).

ऋच् *ṛich*, f. **1.** A verse or text of the Vedas, Man. 11, 142. **2.** The Ṛigveda, Man. 1, 23.—Comp. *An-*, adj. unlearned in holy texts, Man 3, 131. *Try-ṛich*, i.e. *tri-*, f. pl. three holy verses, Man. 2, 77.

ऽऋच *-ṛich* + *a*. A substitute for *ṛich* when being the latter part of a comp., e. g. *an-*, adj. Unlearned in holy texts, Man. 2, 158. *tryṛicha*, i.e. *tri-*, n. A strophe consisting of three verses, Man. 11, 254.

ऋचीक *ṛichîka*, m. **1.** The name of a saint, Râm. 1, 35, 7. **2.** The name of a country, Daçak. 193, 11.

ऋछ् *ṚICHH* (properly the base of the pres. etc. of *ṛi*, q. cf.), i. 6, Par.; ep. also Âtm. (MBh. 4, 1056), **1.** To go. **2.** To attack, MBh. 3, 16375, *ânarchha*, pf. **3.** † To fail in faculties. **4.** † To become stiff.

ऋज् *ṚIJ* (for primitive *raj*), i. 1, Âtm. **1.** † To go. **2.** † To stand or to be firm. **3.** † To gain. **4.** † To be strong. **5.** To live.—Ved. i. 4, Par., and Âtm. **1.** To stretch. **2.** To desire, to strive for.—Cf. *raj* under *ṛiju*, *ὀρέγω*, *ὀρέγνυμι*, *ὀριγνάομαι*, Lat. regere, rectus; Goth. rakjan; A.S. reccan; Goth. raihts, etc.

ऋजीष *ṛijîsha* (vb. *ṛiñj*), n. The name of a hell, Man. 4, 90.

ऋजीषिन् *ṛijîshin* (vb. *ṛij*), adj. Quick, Chr. 291, 12=Rigv. i. 64, 12.

ऋजु *ṛij-u*, adj. **1.** Straight, Man. 2, 47. **2.** Right, Râm. 4, 34, 31.—Comparat. *ṛijîyaṁs*, and ved. also *rajîyaṁs*; superl. *ṛijishṭha*, and ved. also *rajishṭha*.—**Comp.** *An-*, adj. crooked, Man. 4, 177.—Cf. *ὄργυια*, f. of *ὀργυ*, properly the measure of a tall upright man, i.e. six feet in general.

ऋजुता *ṛiju+tâ*, f. **1.** Straightness, Kumâras. 4, 23. **2.** Plainness, Amar. 67.

† **ऋञ्ज्** *ṚIÑJ*, i. 1, Âtm. To fry.

† **ऋण्** *ṚIṆ*, ii. 8, Par., Âtm. (properly the base of the pres. etc. of *ṛi*, ii. 5), To go.

ऋण *ṛiṇa*, n. Obligation, Man 6, 35; a debt, Man. 9, 218.—**Comp.** *An-*, adj. free from obligation or debt, Man. 9, 106.

ऋणयावन् *ṛiṇa-yâ+van*, m. A pursuer of debts, Chr. 293, 4=Rigv. i. 87, 4.

ऋणवन्त् *ṛiṇa+vant*, adj., f. *vatî*, Indebted, Hit. Pr. d. 20, v. r.

ऋणिन् *ṛiṇin*, i.e. *ṛiṇa+in*, adj., f. *nî*. **1.** Obligated, MBh. 1, 8341. **2.** m. A debtor, Yâjń. 2, 86.

ऋत् *ṚIT*, the base of the pres., impf., imptve., and potent., and optionally of all the other forms, is **ऋतीय** *ṛitîya*, Âtm. (properly a denomin. derived from *ṛiti*). **1.** † To blame. **2.** To pity, Mâlav. 55, 23. **3.** † To rival. **4.** To domineer. **5.** † To go.

ऋत *ṛi+ta*, I. adj., f. *tâ*, True, Man. 8, 82. **II.** n. **1.** Truth, Râm. 5, 31, 19. **2.** Gleaning, Man. 4, 5—**Comp.** *An-*, I. adj. untrue, Râm. 3, 53, 18; unjust, Man. 4, 170. II. n. 1. untruth, Râm. 3, 53, 16; a lie, Chr. 48, 12. 2. agriculture, Man. 4, 5. *Apânṛita*, i.e. *apa-an-ṛita*, adj. true, Râm. 2, 34, 38. *Satya-an-*, I. adj. true and false at the same time, Pańch. 98, 17. II. n. commerce, traffic.—Cf. Lat. ratus, irritus; *ἄρτιος*, *ἀνάρτιος*, *ἀνάρσιος*, *ἀλιτέω*, *ἀλιταίνω*, *ἀλιτεύω*, *ἀλιτήμων*.

ऋतंभर *ṛitaṁbhara*, i. e. *ṛita+m-bhṛi+a*, I. m. A name of Brahman, Bhâg. P. 6, 13, 17. **II.** f. *râ*, Understanding, Prab. 68, 3.

ऋतवन्त् *ṛita+vant*, adj., f. *vatî*, Possessing truth, Bhâg. P. 1, 15, 19.

ऋतस्तुभ् *ṛita-stubh*, adj. Praising truth, Chr. 297, 20=Rigv. i. 112, 20.

ऋति *ṛi+ti*, f. **1.** Way, Lass. 2, 8. **2.** Attack (ved.).

ऋतीषह् *ṛitîshah*, i.e. *ṛiti-sah*, adj.

Braving an attack, Chr. 291, 15= Rigv. i. 64, 15.

ऋतु *ṛi+tu*, m. **1.** Order (ved.). **2.** Right time, Chr. 288, 3=Rigv. i. 49, 3. **3.** A season (of the year), Man. 3, 217. **4.** The menstrual discharge, MBh. 14, 2739. **5.** The season approved for sexual intercourse, Man. 3, 46, sqq.—Comp. *An-*, m. wrong season, Man. 4, 104; for sexual intercourse, 5, 153. The aff. *tu* is a form of *tvan* and *ṛi* of *ar*; the older form would be * *artvan* =Lat. ordo, base ordon.—Cf. ἀρτύνω for ἀρτυν-jω, ἀρτύς, ἀρτύω.

ऋतुमती *ṛitumatî*, i.e. *ṛitu+mant +î*, f. **1.** A woman in her courses, Suçr. 1, 317, 4. **2.** A marriageable girl, Man. 9, 89. **3.** A woman in the period approved for sexual intercourse, MBh. 1, 750.

ऋते *ṛite* (loc. sing. ntr. of the ptcple. pf. pass. of *ṛi*, To go; properly, In deficiency), prep. with abl. and acc. **1.** Wanting, Yâjñ. 2, 117. **2.** Except, MBh. 3, 16144; 3090. **3.** Without, Daçak. in Chr. 182, 4; 191, 1.

ऋत्विज् *ṛitvij*, i.e. *ṛitu-yaj*, m. A priest, who receives a stipend for preparing the holy fire and conducting sacrifices, Man. 2, 143.

ऋद्धि *ṛiddhi*, i.e. *ṛidh+ti*, f. **1.** Plenty, Indr. 5, 26. **2.** Wealth, Kumâras. 2, 58. **3.** Prosperity, Râm. 2, 105, 33. **4.** Perfection, Bhâg. P. 9, 21, 12. **5.** The deity of wealth, MBh. 13, 6750.

ऋद्धिमन्त् *ṛiddhi+mant*, adj., f. *matî*. **1.** Wealthy, Râm. 5, 9, 63. **2.** Prosperous, MBh. 3, 244. **3.** Resplendent, Daçak. in Chr. 187, 3; beautiful, MBh. 3, 11077 (p. 572).

ऋध् *ṚIDH*, i. 4, Par., ii. 5, Par. and ved. also i. 6 and ii. 7. **1.** To prosper, Man. 9, 322 (ii. 5); MBh. 2, 1693 (i. 4); pass. To prosper, MBh. 3, 8488. **2.** To augment (ved.). **3.** † To please; *ṛiddha*, Prosperous, Ragh. 2, 50. —With **सम्** *sam*, To prosper, Man. 9, 315 (ii. 5), MBh. 2, 1960 (i. 4); *samṛiddha*. **1.** Completed, Râm. 1, 44, 60. **2.** Abundant, Râm. 2, 104, 26. **3.** Abounding in (with instr. or abl.), Daçak. in Chr. 184, 14; Man. 3, 6. **4.** Wealthy, Daçak. in Chr. 185, 15.—Cf. ἄλθω; also ἀλδαίνω, etc., and ὀρόδαμνος; but *ṛidh* being compounded, viz. *ṛi -dhâ*, and the Vedas having a vb. *ṛid*, which may be considered also as derived from *ṛi*, the base ἀλδ or ὀροδ may be another derivation from *ṛi*; cf. also Lat. ordior.

† **ऋफ्** *ṚIPH*, and **ऋम्फ्** *ṚIMPH*, i. 6, Par. To injure, to kill.—Cf. *riph*.

ऋभु *ṛibhu*, i.e. *rabh+u*, m. The name of certain deities, MBh. 3, 15459.

ऋम्फ् *ṚIMPH*, see *ṛiph*.

ऋष् *ṚISH*, i. 6, Par., ved. also i. 1, Par. **1.** † To go. **2.** To flow, to rain, to drip (ved. i. 1). **3.** To pierce (ved. i. 6).—Cf. Lat. rigare, rivus; Goth. rign; A.S. regen.

ऋषभ *ṛishabha*, i.e. *ṛish+an-bha* (vb. *bhâ*), m. **1.** A bull, Bhâg. P. 1, 14, 19. **2.** Chief, Bhâg. P. 2, 4, 22; especially as latter part of compound words, 'best, excellent,' e.g. *pârthivarshabha*, i.e. *pârthiva-*, m. An excellent king, Chr. 55, 4. *purusha-*, m. An excellent man, Râm. 3, 49, 11. *bharata-*, m. A noble descendant of Bharata, Chr. 24, 48. *siṁha-*, m. A fierce lion.

ऋषि *ṛish+i* (for original *ṛishan*, cf. *akshi* for *akshan*, *asthi* for *asthan*, etc., =ἄρσην, ἄῤῥην), m. **1.** A bard or author of sacred hymns, Chr. 287, 1. 3; Man. 11, 243. **2.** An old saint, MBh. 12,

12724; Hariv. 417, seq. **3.** A pious person, especially an anchorite, Man. 4, 94.—**Comp.** *Devarshi*, i.e. *deva-ṛishi*, m. a sage of the class of demi-gods, as Nârada, VP. 284; Râm. 1, 1, 83. *Brahmarshi*, i.e. *brahman-* and *viprarshi*, i.e. *vipra-*, m. a sage of the class of Brâhmaṇas, as Vaçishṭha, VP. 284; Chr. 22, 20; 14, 17. *Râjarshi*, i.e. *râjan-*, m. a prince who has adopted a life of devotion, as Viçvâmitra, VP. 284; Chr. 11, 16; Pańch. 76, 9. *Saptarshi*, see separately.

ऋषित्व *ṛishi-tva*, n. State of a *ṛishi*, MBh. 13, 2896.

ऋष्टि *ṛishṭi*, i.e. *ṛish* + *ti*, f. **1.** A spear, Chr. 290, 4 = Rigv. i. 64, 4. **2.** A sword, Arj. 10, 20.

ऋष्टिमन्त् *ṛishṭi* + *mant*, adj., f. *matî*, Bearing spears, Chr. 293, 1 = Rigv. i. 88, 1.

ऋष्य *ṛishya*, m. The painted or white-footed antelope, Bhâg. P. 3, 31, 36; in *ṛishyarûpin*, i.e. *-rûpa* + *in*, adj. Having the shape of an antelope. In the Veda it is written *ṛiçya*; cf. O.H.G. elah, ἄλκη.

ऋष्यक *ṛishya* + *ka*, adj. Of the colour of the painted antelope, Râm. 5, 12, 35.

ऋष्यमूक *ṛishya-mûka*, m. The name of a mountain, Râm. 1, 3, 22.

ऋष्व *ṛishva*, adj. Lofty, Chr. 290, 2 = Rigv. i. 64, 2.

ॠ *Ṛî*.

† **ॠ** *Ṛî*, ii. 5, To go (cf. *ṛi* and *ir*).

ए *E*.

एक *e-ka* (*e*, old loc. sing. of the pronom. base *a*, cf. *idam* and *etat*; *ka* cf. *kim*), num., m., f. *kâ*, and n. I. sing. **1.** One (cf. *enad*), Man. 2, 43; *ekasmât*, At once, Râjat. 5, 407. **2.** Alone, Man. 1, 3; Only, Hit. i. d. 81; *puṇyaika-karman*, i.e. *puṇya-eka-karman*, adj. Practising only virtue. **3.** Same, Man. 8, 204; Pańch. iv. d. 10. **4.** Preeminent, chief, Megh. 31. **5.** When immediately repeated, 'one by one,' Râm. 2, 91, 51. **6.** A, an, Pańch. 242, 6, *purusham ekam*, 'a man.' **7.** Somebody, Kathâs. 18, 330. **II.** plur. Some, Man. 9, 61. **III.** Former and latter part of compounds, e.g. *Eka-chara*, adj. living alone, Man. 5, 17. *An-*, adj. many, Man. 5, 159; several, Yâjń. 2, 120; manifold, Yâjń. 3, 144. *Karapâdaikahînaka*, i.e. *kara-pâda-eka-hîna* + *ka*, adj. one who has had a hand and foot cut off, Yâjń. 2, 274. *Tad-eka*, one of these, Hit. 25, 10.—Cf. Lat. acquus.

एकक *eka* + *ka*, adj. **1.** Solitary, Pańch. iii. d. 51. **2.** Same, Man. 9, 38.

एकचित्तता *eka-chitta* + *tâ*, f. **1.** Fixing one's mind only on one object, Pańch. 244, 23. **2.** Unanimity.

एकज *eka-ja* (vb. *jan*), adj. Solitary, Hiḍ. 1, 39.

एकत *eka* + *ta*, m. The name of a deity, MBh. 12, 12772.

एकतम *eka* + *tama*, adj., f. *mâ*, n. *mad*, **1.** One of many, Pańch. 169, 15. **2.** One of two, Pańch. 92, 5. **3.** A, an, Râm. 5, 14, 2.

एकतर *eka* + *tara*, adj., f. *râ*, n. *ram*, One of two, Râm. 6, 6, 12.

एकतस् *eka* + *tas*, adv. **1.** = abl. of *eka*, Râjat. 5, 90. **2.** On one side, Kir. 5, 2; *ekatas-ekatas*, on one side, on the other, Böhtl. Ind. Spr. 523.

एकता *eka* + *tâ*, f. 1. Unity, Prab. 18, 9. 2. Harmony, Râm. 4, 33, 26. 3. Conjunction, MBh. 3, 14272.

एकतीर्थिन् *ekatîrthin*, i.e. *eka-tîrtha* + *in*, adj. Dwelling in the same religious retreat, Yâjñ. 2, 137.

एकत्र *eka* + *tra*, adv. 1. = loc. of *eka*, Man. 5, 136. 2. At the same place, MBh. 3, 1446. 3. Together, Pañch. 25, 10.

एकत्व *eka* + *tva*, n. Unity, MBh. 14, 952.

एकदा *eka* + *dâ*, adv. 1. Once, Râjat. 5, 249. 2. Sometimes, Pañch. iii. d. 60.

एकधा *eka* + *dhâ*, adv. Once, MBh. 14, 1166.

एकपत्निता *ekapatnitâ*, i.e. *eka-patnî* + *tâ*, f. Having one wife in common, MBh. 1, 7274.

एकपत्नीत्व *eka-patnî* + *tva*, n. Faithfulness to a husband, Râm. 5, 49, 21.

एकपदी *eka-pad* + *î*, f. A path, Râm. 4, 31, 13.

एकमय *eka* + *maya*, adj., f. *yî*, Only consisting of, in *chârana-* (of mimes), Kathâs. 23, 85.

एकरात्रिक *ekarâtrika*, i.e. *eka-râtra* + *ika*, adj. Sufficing for one night (or day), Man. 4, 223.

एकरूपता *eka-rûpa* + *tâ*, f. Equality, Pañch. ii. d. 7.

एकल *eka* + *la*, adj., f. *lâ*, Solitary, alone, Bhâg. P. 5, 7, 10.

एकवर्णिक *ekavarṇika*, i.e. *eka-varṇa* + *ika*, adj. Incumbent on one caste only, MBh. 3, 11298.

एकवस्त्रता *eka-vastra* + *tâ*, f. Having one garment only, Nal. 10, 16.

एकशस् *eka* + *ças*, adv. One by one, Râm. 4, 8, 12.

एकश्रुतधरत्व *ekaçrutadharatva*, i.e. *eka-çru* + *ta-dhṛi* + *a* + *tva*, n. Retaining what one has heard once, Kathâs. 2, 40.

एकस्थ *eka-stha* (vb. *sthâ*), adj. United, Râm. 3, 30, 26.

एकस्थता *ekastha* + *tâ*, f. Union, MBh. 1, 5328.

एकांशता *ekâm̃çatâ*, i.e. *eka-am̃ça* + *tâ*, f. Being a part, Ragh. 3, 66.

एकाकिन् *ekâkin*, i.e. probably *eka -eka* + *in* (anom.), adj., f. *nî*, Solitary, alone, Man. 4, 258.

एकाग्रतस् *ekâgratas*, i.e. *eka-agra* + *tas*, adv. Attentively, Lass. 21, 2.

एकात्म्य *ekâtmya*, i.e. *eka-âtman* + *ya*, adj. 1. Alone, Bhâg. P. 4, 21, 29. 2. Homogeneous, Bhâg. P. 4, 13, 8.

एकादश *ekâdaça*, i.e. *ekâdaçan* + *a*. I. ord. numb., f. *çî*. 1. The eleventh, Man. 3, 47. 2. Lasting eleven (months), MBh. 13, 4247. II. f. *çî*, The eleventh day of the half month, MBh. 13, 4234.—Comp. *Vṛishabhaikadaça*, i. e. *vṛishabha-*, adj., f. *çâ*, having a bull as the eleventh, i.e. ten (cows) with a bull, Man. 11, 116 (117).

एकादशक *ekâdaçaka*, i.e. *ekâdaçan* + *ka*, adj. Consisting of eleven, MBh. 13, 4914.

एकादशन् *ekâdaçan*, i.e. *eka-daçan*, card. numb. pl. Eleven, Man. 2, 89.

एकादशम *ekadâçama*, i.e. *ekâdaçan* + *ma*, ord. numb. Eleventh, Bhâg. P. 8, 13, 25.

एकादशिन् *ekâdaçin*, i.e. *ekâdaçan* + *in*, I. adj. Consisting of eleven, MBh.

13, 10668. II. f. *nî*, Eleven (hymns), Yâjń. 3, 309.

एकान्त *ekânta*, i.e. *eka-anta*, I. adj., f. *tâ*, Alone, Râm. 4, 28, 1; only, Bhartṛ. 2, 7; Pańch. 154, 20 (the only one, i.e. indispensable). II. m. and n. 1. A solitary place, Pańch. iii. d. 6. 2. An extreme, Râm. 4, 21, 36. 3. One only, MBh. 12, 13618. III. The acc. *tam*, instr. *tena*, and loc. *te*, are used as adv. 1. Exclusively, Bhag. 6, 16; Pańch. 247, 8. 2. Privately, Daçak. in Chr. 197, 10. 3. Necessarily, MBh. 3, 1240. IV. As former part of comp. words, 1. Perfect, Râm. 6, 93, 24. 2. Altogether, Sund. 1, 15. 3. Necessary, Ragh. 2, 57. V. As latter part, Only, Pańch, 2, 21. *an-*, adj., f. *tâ*, Relative, Bhartṛ. 2, 37.

एकान्ततस् *ekânta* + *tas*, adv. Thoroughly, Bhartṛ. 3, 14.

एकान्तर *ekântara*, i.e. *eka-antara*, adj., f. *râ*, Separated by one caste, Man. 10, 9 (the father belonging, e.g. to the Kshatriyas, the mother to the Çûdras, the Vaiçyas being between them). *dvjekântara*, i.e. *dvi-eka-*, adj. Being separated by one or two castes.

एकान्तत्व *ekânta* + *tva*, n. Exclusive adoration, Bhâg. P. 7, 9, 35.

एकान्तित्व *ekântitva*, i.e. *ekântin* + *tva*, n. Identity, Bhâg. P. 9, 2, 11.

एकान्तिन् *ekântin*, i.e. *ekânta* + *in*, adj., f. *nî*, Adoring one being only, Bhâg. P. 6, 9, 38.

एकायन *ekâyana*, i.e. *eka-ayana*, I. adj. 1. Passable by one only, MBh. 3, 11136. 2. Adoring one only, MBh. 12, 7872. II. n. 1. A solitary place, MBh. 3, 11695. 2. Adoration of one only, MBh. 14, 532.

एकार्थ *ekârtha*, i.e. *eka-artha*, m. The same intention, Nal. 3, 7.

एकार्थता *ekârtha* + *tâ*, f. Having the same intention, MBh. 1, 3413.

एकीभाव *ekîbhâva*, i.e. *eka-bhû* + *a*, m. Union, Vedântas. in Chr. 217, 10.

एकैक *ekaika*, i.e. *eka-eka*, I. adj., f. *kâ*. 1. Every one, Draup. 8, 17. 2. One successively, Kathâs. 18, 265. II. *kam*, adv. One by one, Râm. 1, 13, 27. III. comparat. *ekaikatara*, adj. Always one of many, Bhâg. P. 2, 10, 41.

एकैकशस् *ekaika* + *ças*, adv. 1. One by one, Nal. 1, 25. 2. One after another, Râm. 4, 45, 16.

एकैकश्य *ekaikaçya*, i.e. *ekaikaças* + *ya*, n. Singleness, MBh. 3, 14903 (fighting one by one).

एकोदक *ekodaka*, i.e. *eka-udaka*, m. A kinsman who is connected by oblations of water only to the manes of common ancestors, Man. 5, 71.

एज् *EJ*, i. 1, Par. 1. To stir, MBh. 1, 800. Ptcple. of the pres. Living, Bhâg. P. 7, 3, 22. 2. To tremble, to quake, cf. *ejatka*. 3. † i. 1, Âtm. To shine.—Caus. To move, to turn, Bhâg. P. 5, 2, 14.—Cf. ἐπ-είγω, αἴγειρος, αἰγίς; Lat. aeger.

एजत्क *ejatka*, i.e. *ejant* + *ka* (vb. *ej*), adj. Trembling, Bhâg. P. 9, 6, 42.

† **एठ्** *EṬH*, i. 1, Âtm. To annoy, to resist.

एडक *eḍaka*, m. A ram, MBh. 3, 10935.

एडूक *eḍûka*, m. A building enclosing bones (a Buddhistic *stûpa*), MBh. 3, 10374.

एण *eṇa*, m., f. *ṇî*, A kind of antelope, Man. 3, 269.

एतद् *e-tad* (cf. *eka* and *enad*),

demonst. pron. This here, Nal. 20, 17; this, Man. 3, 147; with the first person, Hiḍ. 4, 15; with the second, Nal. 11, 9; with *tad*, Kathâs. 3, 48; with *idam*, Pańch. Pr. 3; with *kim*, Çâk. 101, 19; with *yad*, Man. 1, 71.

एतदात्म्य *etadâtmya*, i.e. *etad-âtman* + *ya*, adj. Having the nature of this, Vedântas. in Chr. 216, 6.

एतर्हि *etarhi*, i.e. *etad* + *rhi*, adv. Now, Bhâg. P. 1, 17, 43.

एतादृश् *etâdṛiç*, i.e. *etad-dṛiç*, adj. Such, Bhâg. P. 9, 11, 17.

एतादृश *etâdṛiça*, i.e. *etad-dṛiç* + *a*, adj., f. *çî*, Such, MBh. 3, 579.

एतावत्त्व *etâvattva*, i.e. *etâvant* + *tva*, n. **1.** Greatness, Bhâg. P. 2, 5, 10. **2.** Sufficiency, Bhâg. P. 4, 30, 28 (*etâvattvam—bhâvyam*, it must be sufficient).

एतावन्त् *etâvant*, i.e. *etad* + *vant*, I. adj., f. *vatî*. **1.** So much, Man. 9, 45. **2.** Such a one, Brâhmaṇ. 1, 8; such, Daçak. in Chr. 188, 4; *etâvati*, In this distance, Çâk. 8, 10. **3.** With *kim*, Of this kind, Kathâs. 20, 58. II. *vat* (acc. sing. n.), adv. **1.** So far, Râm. 4, 40, 68. **2.** Thus, Hit. 27, 19.

एध् *EDH* (a form of *ardh*, the original form of *ṛidh*), i. 1, Âtm. (in epic poetry also Par., MBh. 3, 15031). **1.** To prosper, MBh. 2, 510. **2.** To increase, Râm. 2, 52, 34; to grow up, Çâk. d. 51.—Caus. *edhaya*. **1.** To cause to prosper, Bhâg. P. 7, 1, 11. **2.** To glorify, Kumâras. 6, 90.—With the prep. **अधि** *adhi*, To increase, Bhâg. P. 5, 11, 17.—With **सम्** *sam*, To increase, Bhâg. P. 3, 21, 25. *samedhita*, **1.** Strengthened, MBh. 3, 10443. **2.** United, Râm. 2, 64, 35. Caus. To cause to prosper, MBh. 13, 7510.

एध *edha*, i.e. *indh* (or rather *idh*) + *a*, m. Wood for fuel, Man. 4, 247.

एधस् *edhas*, I. n. *indh* + *as* (see the last), Wood for fuel, Man. 11, 70. II. *edh* + *as*, Prospering; in *sukham-edhas*, adj. Well prospering, MBh. 13, 5191.

एनद् *enad*, i.e. *e-na* (cf. *etad* and *eva*; *na* is an old pron. base), pron. which forms only the acc. sing., du. pl., instr. sing., and gen. loc. du., which are substituted for the corresponding cases of *idam* and *etat*, This, when used substantively, He, She, It, and without any stress, Man. 2, 50.—Cf. Goth. ainaha, ains; A.S. ân; Lat. oinos, unus; οἴνη.

एनस् *enas*, n. **1.** Sin, Man. 5, 34. **2.** Fault, Daçak. in Chr. 194, 17.—Comp. *An-*, I. adj. guiltless, Man. 8, 19. II. m. a proper name, Hariv. 669.

एनस्विन् *enas* + *vin*, adj., f. *nî*, m. A sinner, Man. 11, 189.

एरक *eraka*, I. m. A proper name, MBh. 1, 2154. II. f. *kâ*, The name of a grass, MBh. 1, 620; bent-grass, Bhâg. P. 1, 3, 18.

एरण्ड *eraṇḍa*, m. The castor oil plant, Ricinus communis, Pańch. i. d. 108.

एर्वारु *ervâru*, m. and f. A kind of cucumber, Cucumis utilissimus, Roxb., Yâjń. 3, 142.

एला *elâ*, f. Small cardamoms, Ragh. 6, 64.

एव *e-va* (cf. *enad*, *va* is an old pronominal base), a particle (properly an old instr. sing.). **1.** Only, Man. 1, 91; 2, 87; 190; Çâk. 69, 15. **2.** Still, Man. 2, 168. **3.** Just, Man. 5, 61; Pańch. 223, 9. **4.** Also, Man. 1, 48. **5.** Very (especially after *tad*), Man. 3, 23.—Cf. οἶος, οἰαδόν.

एवम् *e-va + m* (see the preceding), a particle (originally acc. sing. n.), Thus, Pañch. 24, 4. Very often former part of comp. words, e.g. *evaṁrûpa*, adj., f. *pâ*, Having such a form, Râm. 3, 52, 36. *evaṁvidha* (cf. *vidhâ*), adj. Of such a kind, Çâk. d. 104. *evaṁgata* (vb. *gam*), adj. Being in this state, Râm. 2, 39, 31; loc. sing. *te*, Under these circumstances, Chr. 23, 33. *evaṁ-guṇa*, I. m. Such a quality, Râm. 1, 1, 20. II. adj. Having such qualities, Nal. 6, 12. *evam-âdi*, adj. Beginning thus, i.e. This and the like, Man. 9, 260. *evam-bhû + ta*, adj. Being thus, such a one, Hit. 7, 13.

एष् *ESH* (cf. 1, 2. *ish*), i. 1, Âtm. (after *anu* and *pari* in epic poetry also Par.). **1.** To go. **2.** To strive to attain, Bhâg. P. 3, 13, 44. **3.** To search, Bhâg. P. 9, 4, 52.—With the prep **अनु** *anu*, To search, MBh. 1, 5253; to investigate, Râm. 1, 3, 2.—With **परि** *pari*, To search, MBh. 13, 4033 (Par.).

एषण *eshaṇa*, i.e. *ish + ana*, I. n. **1.** Wish, desire, Bhâg. P. 7, 9, 39. **2.** Searching MBh. 1, 8399. II. f. *ṇâ*, Desire, Râjat. 5, 281.

एषिन् *eshin*, i.e. *ish + in*, adj., f. *iṇî*, Wishing, MBh. 3, 12513.—**Comp.** *Dhana-*, adj. one who asks payment of a debt, Man. 8, 60. *Sarva-bhûta-hita-*, adj. wishing the well-being of all creatures, Chr. 26, 64.

ऐ *AI.*

ऐकध्यम् *aikadhyam*, i.e. *ekadhâ + ya + m*, adv. At once.

ऐकपत्य *aikapatya*, i.e. *eka-pati + ya*, n. Supreme power, Bhâg. P. 7, 3, 37.

ऐकमत्य *aikamatya*, i.e. *eka-mati + ya*, I. n. Unanimity, Hit. 19, 22. II. adj. Unanimous, Râm. 5, 77, 15.

ऐकशफ *aikaçapha*, i.e. *eka + çapha + a*, adj. Belonging to a quadruped with a hoof not cloven, Man. 5, 8.

ऐकागारिक *aikâgârika*, i. e. *eka -âgâra + ika*, m., f. *kî*, A thief, Daçak. in Chr. 197, 18.

ऐकाग्र्य *aikâgrya*, i.e. *eka-agra + ya*, n. Attention fixed on one subject, Vedântas. in Chr. 202, 20.

ऐकाङ्ग *aikâṅga*, i.e. *eka-aṅga + a*, m. One of the bodyguards, Râjat. 5, 249.

ऐकात्म्य *aikâtmya*, i.e. *eka-âtman + ya*, n. Unity with the universal soul.

ऐकाधिकरण्य *aikâdhikaraṇya*, i.e. *eka-adhikaraṇa + ya*, n. Residing in the same subjects, Bhâshâp. 68.

ऐकान्तिक *aikântika*, i.e. *ekânta + ika*, adj. **1.** Perfect, Bhag. 14, 27. **2.** Exclusive, Bhâg. P. 3, 20, 2.—**Comp.** *An-*, adj. 1. indeterminate, Pañch. 58, 22. 2. going astray, (a fallacious middle term,) Bhâshâp. 71.

ऐक्य *aikya*, i.e. *eka + ya*, n. Unity, Vedântas. in Chr. 203, 23.

ऐक्षव *aikshava*, i.e. *ikshu + a*, I. adj., f. *vî*, Made of sugar. II. n. Sugar.

ऐक्ष्वाक *aikshvâka*, i.e. *ikshvâku + a*, patron., f. *kî*, Descended from Ikshvâku, Râm. 2, 36, 1; MBh. 1, 3719.

ऐङ्गुद *aiṅguda*, i.e. *iṅguda + a*, adj. Produced from the inguda plant, Râm. 2, 103, 29.

ऐण *aiṇa*, i.e. *eṇa + a*, adj. Belonging to the black antelope (as flesh), Yâjñ. 1, 258.

ऐणेय *aiṇeya*, i.e. *eṇa + eya*, I. adj.

Belonging to a she-antelope, Râm. 2, 56, 18. II. m.=*eṇa*, Draup. 4, 15.

ऐतिहासिक *aitihâsika*, i.e. *itihâsa*+*ika*, adj. Occurring in old legends, Prab. 91, 7.

ऐतिह्य *aitihya*, i. e. *iti-ha*+*ya*, n. Oral tradition, Râm. 5, 87, 23.

ऐन्दव *aindava*, i.e. *indu*+*a*, adj., f. *vî*, Referring to the moon, lunar, Man. 11, 125.

ऐन्द्र *aindra*, i.e. *indra*+*a*, adj., f. *rî*. 1. Belonging to Indra, Arj. 4, 82. 2. Like that which belongs to Indra, Man. 5, 93. 3. Indra-like, Man. 8, 344. 4. Devoted to Indra, MBh. 3, 1494.

ऐन्द्रजालिक *aindrajâlika*, i.e. *indra-jâla*+*ika*, I. adj., f. *kî*, Referring to witchcraft, Prab. 101, 4. II. m. A wizard, Prab. 55, 1.

ऐन्द्रद्युम्न *aindradyumna*, i.e. *indra-dyumna*+*a*, 1. adj. Relating to Indradyumna (a proper name), MBh. 1, 325. 2. The name of a locality, MBh. 3, 10624.

ऐन्द्रशिर *aindra-çira*, m. A kind of elephant, Râm. 2, 70, 22.

ऐन्द्राग्न्य *aindrâgnya*, i.e. *indra-agni*+*ya*, adj. Sacred to Indra and Agni, MBh. 12, 2307.

ऐन्द्रि *aindri*, i.e. *indra*+*i*, patron. Offspring of Indra, MBh. 1, 2751.

ऐन्द्रिय *aindriya*, i.e. *indriya*+*a*, adj. Referring to the senses, Bhâg. P. 3, 10, 15; sensual, 3, 25, 26.

ऐन्द्रियक *aindriya*+*ka*, adj. Perceptible by the senses, Bhâg. P. 7, 2, 48.

ऐन्द्रियेधी *aindriyedhî*, i.e. *aindriya*+*i-dhî*, adj. Attached to sensuality, Bhâg. P. 5, 18, 22.

ऐन्धन *aindhana*, i. e. *indhana*+*a*, adj. Consisting of fuel, epithet of the sun, MBh. 3, 149.

ऐरावण *airâvaṇa*, i.e. *irâvan*+*a* (the base is curtailed *irâvant*, ved., and cf. *irâvati*), m. Indra's elephant, MBh. 1, 1151.

ऐरावत *airavata*, i.e. *irâvant*+*a* (see the last), I. m. 1. Indra's elephant, considered as the elephant of the east quarter, MBh. 1, 2627. 2. A kind of elephant, Râm. 2, 70, 22. 3. A patronymic name of a Nâga, MBh. 1, 829. 4. The name of the northern path of the moon, MBh. 3, 11836. II. m. and n. A particular shape of the rainbow, Ragh, 1, 36. III. m., f. *tî*, and n. Lightning, MBh. 13, 7391. IV. m. The orange-tree; n. its fruit, Suçr. 1, 211, 11. V. f. *tî*, The name of a river, MBh. 8, 2055.

ऐल *aila*, i.e. *iḷâ* (=*iḍâ*) +*a*. A metronymic name of Purûravas, MBh. 1, 3149.

ऐश *aiça*, i.e. *îça*+*a*, adj. Belonging to Çiva, Bhâg. P. 9, 10, 6.

ऐशानी *aiçânî*, fem. of *aiçâna*, i.e. *îçâna*+*a*, The north-east quarter, Vikr. 6, 4.

ऐश्वर *aiçvara*, i.e. *îçvara*+*a*, adj., f. *rî*. 1. Befitting a lord, majestic, MBh. 1, 3315; 14, 411; powerful, Râm. 3, 10, 21. 2. Belonging to Çiva, Ragh. 11, 76.

ऐश्वर्य *aiçvarya*, i.e. *îçvara*+*ya*, n. 1. Control, Man. 6, 95. 2. Dominion, Râm. 5, 22, 31. 3. Supreme dominion, Man. 4, 235. 4. Superhuman power, Bhâg. P. 3, 25, 37.—**Comp.** *Dhana*-, n. the dominion over wealth, Man. 7, 42.

ऐश्वर्यवन्त् *aiçvarya*+*vant*, adj., f. *vatî*, Endowed with superhuman power, MBh. 15, 389.

ऐषीक *aishîka,* i.e. *ishîkâ + a,* adj. Made of reeds, Râm. 1, 29, 7.

ऐष्टिकपौर्तिक *aishṭikapaurtika,* i.e. *ishṭi + ika-pûrti + ika,* adj. Referring to sacrifices and pious works (cf. *ishṭâpûrta*), Man. 4, 227.

ऐहलौकिक *aihalaukika,* i.e. *iha-loka + ika,* adj. Belonging to this world, MBh. 3, 12616.

ऐहिक *aihika,* i.e. I. *iha + ika,* adj. Terrestrial, temporal, Daçak. in Chr. 179, 19. II. *îhâ + ika,* n. Business; in *tryahaihika,* i.e. *tri-aha-aihika,* adj. m. A shopkeeper who gathers as much corn only as may suffice for three days, Man, 4, 7.

ओ *O.*

ओक *oka,* i.e. *uch + a,* m. A house; in *an-oka-çâyin,* adj. Not sleeping in a house, MBh. 1, 3631.

ओकस् *okas,* i.e. *uch + as,* n. A dwelling-place, Bhâg. P. 3, 3, 15; a house, MBh. 2, 805.—**Comp.** *Ambara-,* m. a god, Kumâras. 5, 79. *Araṇya-,* m. an anchorite, Çâk. d. 81. *Kânana-,* m. a monkey, Râm. 5, 65, 7. *Jala-,* I. adj. living in water, MBh. 13, 2650. II. f. a leech, Suçr. 1, 28, 10. *Tri-diva-* and *diva-,* m. a god, Man. 1, 95; 11, 242. *Mânasa-,* m. the wild swan or goose. *Vana-,* I. adj. living in woods, Chr. 25, 61. II. m. 1. an anchorite, Chr. 11, 18. 2. a wild beast, Râm. 3, 49, 39. 3. a monkey, 6, 26, 5. *Vâri-,* m. a leech, Man. 7, 129. *Vâsa-,* n. the private apartments; a sleeping-room. *Vila-,* m. any animal living in holes, Man, 10, 49. *Svarga-,* m. a deity.

† **ओख्** *OKH,* i. 1, Par. **1.** To be dry (cf. *ush, sh* is often changed to *kh*). **2.** To be able.

ओघ *ogha,* i.e. probably *vah + a,* m. **1.** A stream, Man. 9, 54. **2.** A multitude, MBh. 1, 4448. **3.** Density, Çiç. 9, 27.—**Comp.** *Çara-,* m. a multitude of arrows, Chr. 34, 15. *Sarva-,* m. 1. assembling a complete army. 2. great speed.

ओघवन्त् *ogha + vant,* I. adj., f. *vatî,* Rapid, MBh. 3, 10538. II. m. A proper name, MBh. 13, 121. III. f. *vatî,* A proper name, ib.

ओंकार *oṁkâra,* i.e. *om-kṛi + a,* m. **1.** The holy syllable *om,* Man. 2, 75. **2.** Thanksgiving, Râjat. 5, 134. **3.** Grumbling, Pañch. 158, 7.

† **ओज्** *OJ,* i. 1, and i. 10, Par. **1.** To be strong. **2.** To live.

ओजस् *ojas,* i.e. *vaj + as,* I. n. **1.** Strength, Matsyop. 2. **2.** Light, splendour, Man. 12, 18. **II.** *ojasâ* (instr.), adv. Powerfully, Chr. 291, 4 = Rigv. i. 85, 4; courageously, Râm. 3, 53, 22.—**Comp.** *Amitaujas,* i.e. *a-mita-* (vb. *mâ*), adj. all-mighty, Man. 1, 4. *Mahaujas,* i.e *mahâ-,* adj. eminent in power, Man. 1, 61.—Cf. Lat. augus in augus + tus, and *αὐγή, -αὐγες* in *ἀνταυγής, ές.*

ओजस्विन् *ojas + vin,* adj., f. *nî,* Strong, MBh. 14, 100.

ओड्र *oḍra,* m. pl. The name of a people and their country, now Orissa, Man. 10, 44.

† **ओण्** *OṆ,* i. 1, Par. To take away (probably a form of *arṇ* for *arṇu,* i.e. *ṛi* ii. 5, cf. *ἄρνυμαι*).

ओदती *odatî* (fem. of a ptcple. of *ud = und*), f. The dawn, Chr. 287, 6 = Rigv. i. 48, 6.

ओदन *odana,* i.e. *ud* (= *und*) + *ana,* m. and n. **1.** A pap, see comp. **2.** Boiled rice, Man. 8, 329.—**Comp.** *Kshi-*

raudana, i.e. *kshîra-*, m. rice boiled with milk, MBh. 13, 947. *Guḍodana* (sic instead of °*ḍau*°), i.e. *guḍa-*, boiled rice with sugar, MBh. 13, 6162. *Tila-*, n. a dish of rice, milk, and sesamum, Râm. 2, 69, 10 (*tilodana* instead of °*lau*°). *Dadhi-*, m. a mess prepared of curds, Yâjń. 1, 303. *Mâṅsa-bhûtodana* (instead of °*tau*°), i.e. *-bhûta-*, a dish of rice and meat (?), Râm. 2, 52, 83. *Çâli-*, boiled rice, Bhartṛ. 2, 79.

ओम् *om*, ind. A mystic word prefacing all prayers, Pańch. 33, 11; used at the commencement and end of holy recitations, Man. 2, 74; 73; and writings, Man.; used to commence respectful salutations, and on other occasions, e.g. Man. 2, 75; and the subject of many mystical speculations, Man. 2, 79; 84.

ओम्यावन्त् *omyâvant*, i.e. *av* + *man* + *ya* + *vant*, adj., f. *vatí*, Agreeable, Chr. 296, 7=Rigv. i. 112, 7; kind, Chr. 297, 20=Rigv. i. 112, 20.

ओलण्ड् *OLAṆḌ*, see *laṇḍ*.

ओषधि and **धी** *oshadhi*, i.e. *ush* + *a-dhâ* (cf. *nidhi*), f. **1.** A plant, Man. 1, 46. **2.** A medicinal herb, Chaurap. 47. —Comp. *Mahaushadhi*, i.e. *mahâ-*, f. a kind of sensitive plant, Mimosa pudica.

ओषधिज *oshadhi-ja* (vb. *jan*), adj. Produced from plants, Kir. 5, 14 (i.e. a phosphorescent light).

ओष्ठ *oshṭha*, i.e. probably *ava-stha* (vb. *sthâ*), m. **1.** The lip, Man. 8, 282. **2.** The upper lip, Bhâg. P. 4, 8, 46. In comp. words a preceding *a* may be dropped, and the fem. of a comp. adj. may end in *ṭhâ* or *ṭhî*, e.g. *ruchira-dantaushṭhî*, Having beautiful teeth and lips, Râm. 3, 52, 16. *bimboshṭha*, adj. Having bimba-like lips, Kathâs. 4, 8. *sańdashṭaushṭha*, i.e. *sam-dashṭa-oshṭha* (vb. *daṅç*), adj. Biting the lips, MBh. 3, 427. *sphuradoshṭha*, i.e. *sphurant-oshṭha*, adj., f. *ṭhî*, With trembling lips, Indr. 5, 51.

औ *AU*.

औक्थ्य *aukthya*, i.e. *uktha* + *ya*, n. A complex of hymns (?), MBh. 3, 10686.

औग्र्य *augrya*, i. e. *ugra* + *ya*, n. Formidableness.

औत्कण्ठ्य *autkaṇṭhya*, i.e. *utkaṇṭhâ* + *ya*, n. Desire, Bhâg. P. 1, 6, 17.

औत्कण्ठ्यवन्त् *autkaṇṭhya* + *vant*, adj., f. *vatî*, Desirous, Bhâg. P. 2, 6, 33.

औत्तमि *auttami*, i.e. *uttama* + *i*, patron. m. The name of a Manu, Man. 1, 62.

औत्तर *auttara* (? if correct it would be *uttara* + *a*), adj. Inhabiting the north, MBh. 3, 10546 (probably it must be corrected *yatrott*°).

औत्तानपाद *auttânapâda*, and **-पादि** *-pâdi*, i.e *uttâna-pâda* (a proper name) + *a* or *i*, patron. m. Dhruva or the polar star, MBh. 13, 195; Bhâg. P. 4, 8, 82.

औत्पत्तिक *autpattika*, i.e. *utpatti* + *ika*, adj. Innate, Bhâg. P. 3, 15, 45.

औत्पातिक *autpâtika*, i.e. *utpâta* + *ika*, adj., f. *kî*, Prodigious, Râm. 5, 52, 1.

औत्सुक्य *autsukya*, i.e. *utsuka* + *ya*, I. n. **1.** Perturbation, Râm. 3, 1, 4. **2.** Desire, MBh. 3, 114. **II.** instr. *yena*, adverbially, Quickly, Pańch. 35, 9; 95, 25.—Comp. *Manda-*, adj. having no great desire, Çâk. 18, 22. *Sa-*, adj., f. *yâ*, full of desire, Pańch. 185, 20.

औदक *audaka*, i.e. *udaka* + *a*, adj. **1.** Referring to water, Man. 3, 215. **2.** Aquatic, Man. 1, 44; 6, 13.

औदञ्चन *audañchana*, i. e. *udañchana* + *a*, adj. Contained in a tub, Bhâg. P. 8, 24, 19.

औदरिक *audarika*, i.e. *udara* + *ika*, adj., f. *kî*, Gluttonous, Vikr. 39, 14.

औदर्य *audarya*, i.e. *udara* + *ya*, adj. Being in the womb, Bhâg. P. 3, 24, 4.

औदार्य *audârya*, i.e. *udâra* + *ya*, n. **1.** Excellence, Nal. 16, 17. **2.** Dignity, Râm. 3, 18, 25. **3.** Generosity, Daçak. in Chr. 187, 24.

औदासीन्य *audâsînya*, i.e. *ud-âsîna* + *ya* (vb. *âs*), and **औदास्य** *audâsya*, i. e. *ud-âs* + *a* + *ya*, n. Indifference, apathy, Daçak. in Chr. 183, 17; Vedântas. in Chr. 219, 2.

औदुम्बर *audumbara*, i.e. *udumbara* + *a*, I. adj., f. *rî*, Made of Udumbara wood, Man. 2, 45. II. m. pl. The name of a people, MBh. 2, 1869. III. f. *rî*, A branch of the Udumbara tree, Râm. 1, 4, 21.

औद्धारिक *auddhârika*, i.e. *uddhâra* + *ika*, adj. Deducted, Man. 9, 150.

औद्वाहिक *audvâhika*, i.e. *udvâha* + *ika*, adj. Received on account of marriage, Man. 9, 206.

औपधर्म्य *aupadharmya*, i. e. *upa-dharma* + *ya*, n. A false doctrine, heresy, Bhâg. P. 2, 7, 37.

औपनायनिक *aupanâyanika*, i. e. *upa-nâyana* + *ika*, adj. Relating to the initiation, Man. 2, 68.

औपनिषद *aupanishada*, i.e. *upanishad* + *a*, adj., f. *dî*, Contained in an Upanishad, Man. 6, 29.

औपपत्तिक *aupapattika*, i.e. *upapatti* + *ika*, adj. Suitable, MBh. 13, 2742.

औपम्य *aupamya*, i.e. *upamâ* + *ya*, n. Resemblance. Only at the end of comp. words, *an-*, adj. Incomparable, Râm. 6, 87, 10; *âtmaupamya*, i.e. *âtman-*, n. Taking one's self as measure, Hit. i. d. 10 (*âtmaupamyena*, as they wish for themselves); *svapna-*, n. Resemblance to a dream, Bhâg. P. 9, 19, 28; *vâtya-*, adj. Resemblance to a storm, Bhâg. P. 5, 14, 9.

औपयिक *aupayika*, i.e. *upâya* + *ika*, the *â* of the base shortened (*aupâyika* with *â*, MBh. 5, 7019, and Chr. 18, 37, see n.), adj., f. *kî*, Suitable, Râm. 2, 54, 38.

औपल *aupala*, i.e. *upala* + *a*, adj., f. *lî*, Made of stone, Man. 4, 194.

औपवास्य *aupavâsya*, i.e. *upavâsa* + *ya*, n. Fasting, Râm. 2, 87, 18.

औपवाह्य *aupavâhya*, i.e. *upa-vah* + *a* + *ya*, adj. Serving for riding on, Râm. 2, 39, 10.

औपस्थ्य *aupasthya*, i.e. *upastha* + *ya*, n. Sexual intercourse, Bhâg. P. 7, 6, 13.

औपहारिक *aupahârika*, i.e. *upahâra* + *ika*, n. Oblation, MBh. 13, 6039.

औपाधिक *aupâdhika*, i.e. *upâdhi* + *ika*, adj. Reflectional, conditional (as the crystal's red colour from a china rose near it).

औपासन *aupâsana*, i.e. *upâsana* + *a*, m. The sacred fire, Yâjñ. 3, 17.

औरभ्र *aurabhra*, i.e. *urabhra* + *a*, adj. Belonging to a ram, MBh. 3, 268.

औरभ्रिक *aurabhrika*, i.e. *urabhra* + *ika*, m. A shepherd, Man. 3, 166.

औरश *auraça*, i.e. *uraçâ* + *a*, m. An inhabitant of Uraçâ, Râjat. 5, 216.

औरस *aurasa*, i.e. *uras* + *a*, I. adj., f. *sî*, Dwelling in one's breast, innate, Man. 3, 1314. II. m. A legitimate son, Man. 9, 166; Yâjń. 2, 128.

और्ण *aurṇa*, i.e. *ûrṇa* + *a*, adj., f. *ṇî*, Woollen, MBh. 2, 1823.

और्ध्वदेह *aurdhvadeha*, i.e. *ûrdhva-deha* + *a*, n. Obsequies of a deceased person, Râm. 2, 83, 24.

और्ध्वदेहिक *aurdhvadehika*, i. e. *ûrdhva-deha* + *ika*, I. adj. 1. Serving for the acquisition of merit, Man. 11, 10. 2. Belonging to the obsequies of a deceased person, Pańch. 9, 3. II. n. Obsequies, Râm. 4, 24, 24.

और्व *aurva*, i.e. *ûrva* + *a*, I. m. The patronymic name of a Ṛishi or saint, MBh. 1, 2610. II. adj., f. *vî*. 1. Produced by Ûrva, MBh. 1, 1242. 2. adj. or m. (supple *agni*), Submarine fire, Râjat. 3, 170.

औशनस *auçanasa*, i.e. *uçanas* + *a*, I. adj., f. *sî*. 1. Belonging to Uçanas. 2. Descended from Uçanas, Bhâg. P. 7, 5, 48; 9, 18, 20. II. n. 1. A law-book ascribed to Uçanas, Pańch. 253, 12. 2. The name of a holy place, MBh. 3, 7005.

औशिज *auçija*, i.e. *uçij* (i.e. probably *vaç* + *i-j*, vb. *jan*), + *a*, adj. Covetous (?), Chr. 297, 11 = Rigv. i. 112, 11.

औशीनर *auçînara*, i.e. *uçînara* + *a*, I. m. The king of the Uçînaras, MBh. 1, 3669. II. f. *rî*, A proper name, Vikr. 30, 18.

औशीर *auçîra*, i.e. *uçîra* + *a*, n. 1. The handle of a fan, MBh. 12, 2299. 2. A bed, Daçak. in Chr. 200, 8. 3. An ointment made of Uçîra, Çâk. d. 57, v.r.

औषध *aushadha*, i.e. *oshadhi* + *a*, m. and n. A medicine, Man. 8, 324.—Comp. *Mahâ-*, I. n. 1. garlic. 2. long pepper. II. n. and f. *dhî*, dry ginger.

औषधि and **औषधी** *aushadhî* = *oshadhi*, Kir. 5, 24; MBh. 13, 454.

औष्ट्र *aushṭra*, i. e. *ushṭra* + *a*, adj. Produced from a camel, Man. 5, 8.

औष्ण्य *aushṇya*, i.e. *ushṇa* + *ya*, n. Heat, Yâjń. 3, 77.

औष्म्य *aushmya*, i.e. *ushman* + *ya*, n. Heat, Ragh. 17, 33.

क *K.*

क *ka*, I. see *kim*. II. m. (properly nom. sing. of *kim*), A name of the highest deities, viz. Prajâpati, Bhâg. P. 6, 6, 2; Brahman, MBh. 1, 32; Vishṇu, 13, 7027. III. n. Water, Yâjń. 2, 108.

† **कंस्** *KAṄS* (or **कश्** *KAÇ*, or **कस्** *KAS*), ii. 2, Âtm. 1. To go. 2. To command (v.r. to destroy).

कंस *kaṅsa*, I. m. A proper name, MBh. 1, 357. II. f. *sâ*, A proper name, Hariv. 2029. III. m. n. Bell metal.

कंसवती *kaṅsavatî*, i. e. *kaṅsa* + *vant* + *î*, f. A proper name, Bhâg. P. 9, 24, 24.

† **कक्** *KAK*, i. 1, Âtm. 1. To be proud. 2. To be unsteady. 3. To be thirsty.

ककुत्स्थ *kakutstha*, i.e. *kakud-stha* (vb. *sthâ*), m. A proper name, Râm. 1, 70, 38.

ककुद् *kakud* (a reduplicated form of a lost base, *kud*, probably akin to κῦδος, etc., cf. *kakudmant*), f. **1.** A summit, Bhâg. P. 5, 25, 7. **2.** The hump of the Indian bull, Bhâg. P. 9, 6, 15. — **Comp.** *Tri-*, m. a name of Kṛishṇa, or Vishṇu, MBh. 12, 1508.

ककुद *kakud+a*, m. and n. **1.** Chief, Râm. 6, 37, 12. **2.** The hump of the Indian bull, MBh. 13, 835. **3.** An ensign or symbol of royalty, Ragh. 3, 70. —**Comp.** *Tri-*, adj. having three horns, MBh. 12, 13252.

ककुद्मन्त् *kakud+mant*, I. adj., f. *mati*, Having a hump, Ragh. 4, 29. **II.** m. **1.** A mountain, Ragh. 13, 47. **2.** A bull having a hump, Kumâras. 1, 27.— Cf. Lat. cacumen.

ककुद्मिन् *kakud+min*, I. adj., f. *nî*, Having a hump, MBh. 13, 4935. **II.** m. **1.** A bull having a hump, Bhâg. P. 3, 3, 4. **2.** A proper name, Hariv. 644.

ककुद्रुम *kakudruma*, i. e. *kakud -druma*, n. A proper name, Pańch. i. d. 290.

ककुद्वन्त् *kakud+vant*, m. A bull having a hump, Râm. 5, 7, 11.

ककुन्दर *kakundara*, and **कुकुन्दर** *kukundara*, n. The cavities of the loins, Yâjń. 3, 96.

ककुभ् *kakubh* (a reduplicated form of a lost base, *kubh*; cf. κῦφός, Lat. cubare, and *kumbh*), f. **1.** A summit (ved.). **2.** A quarter or point of the compass, Kathâs. 21, 13. **3.** A proper name, Bhâg. P. 6, 6, 4.

ककुभ *kakubh+a*, m. **1.** A tree, Terminalia Arjuna, Râm. 1, 26, 15. **2.** A certain musical mode, Vikr. 61, 1. **3.** The name of a mountain, Bhâg. P. 5, 19, 16.

† **कक्क्** *KAKK*, see *kakh*.

कक्कोल *kakkola*, m. (?) A plant bearing a berry, the inner part of which is an aromatic substance, Râm. 3, 39, 22.

† **कक्ख्** *KAKKH*, see *kakh*.

कक्ष *kaksha*, I. m. **1.** A spreading creeper, MBh. 3, 12548; weed, Man. 7, 110. **2.** A dry wood, Râm. 5, 5, 24. **3.** A forest, MBh. 15, 1082. **4.** The side or flank, Râm. 6, 36, 108 (of an army). **5.** pl. The name of a people, MBh. 6, 356. **II.** m. and f. *kshâ*. **1.** The armpit, Râm. 4, 10, 19; Mṛichchh. 34, 11. **2.** The end of the lower garment tucked into the waistband, MBh. 2, 902; Pańch. 32, 25 (used for keeping money). **III.** f. *kshâ*. **1.** A girdle, MBh. 4, 1749. **2.** A wall, Râm. 2, 32, 32. **3.** An enclosure, a part of an edifice, Man. 7, 224. —**Comp.** *Hiraṇya-*, adj., f. *kshâ*, wearing a golden girdle, MBh. 4, 2108. *Hema-*, adj. having a golden wall, Râm. 3, 54, 15.

कक्षघ्न *kakshaghna*, i.e. *kaksha-han +a*, adj. Destroying a dry wood, MBh. 1, 5756.

कक्षीवन्त् *kakshîvant*, m. The name of a Ṛishi, Chr. 297, 11=Rigv. i. 112, 11.

कक्ष्य *kakshya*, i.e. *kaksha+ya*, I. f. *yâ*, **1.** A girdle, MBh. 2, 900. **2.** An upper garment, Kathâs. 18, 5. **3.** An enclosed court, MBh. 2, 827; Râm. 2, 57, 22. **II.** n. **1.** The cup of a balance, Mit. 145, 20. **2.** A certain part of a chariot, Râm. 6, 106, 23.—**Comp.** *Suvarṇa-*, adj. having a golden girth, Râm. 2, 92, 32. *Saptakakshya*, i.e. *saptan-*, having seven courts, Râm. 4, 33, 24.

† **कख्** *KAKH*, or **कक्ख्** *KAKKH*,

or कक्क् *KAKK*, or खक्ख् *KHAKKH*, i. 1. Par. To laugh.—Cf. Lat. cachinnus; καχάζω, καγχάζω, καγχαλάω; O.H.G. hôh (sneer).

† कग् *KAG*, i. 1, Par. To perform an action.

† कङ्क् *KAṄK*, i. 1, Âtm. To go.

कङ्क *kaṅka*, I. m. **1.** A heron, Râm. 6, 90, 25. **2.** The name of a king, MBh. 1, 227. **3.** pl. The name of a people, MBh. 2, 1850. **II.** f. *kâ*, A proper name, Hariv. 2029.

कङ्कट *kaṅkaṭa* (for *kaṅkatra*, from the base *kañch*, cf. *kañchuka*), m. Mail, Râm. 5, 80, 32.

कङ्कण *kaṅkaṇa* (a reduplicated form of *kaṇ*, and aff. *a*), m. and n. **1.** An ornament, MBh. 3, 15757. **2.** A bracelet, Bhartṛ. 2, 63. **3.** The name of a certain weapon, Râm. 1, 29, 13; 56, 12 (Gorr. has *kiṅkiṇî*, q. cf.).

कङ्कणिन् *kaṅkaṇin*, i.e. *kaṅkaṇa* + *in*, adj., f. *nî*, Wearing a bracelet, Kathâs. 22, 91.

कङ्कत *kaṅkata* (perhaps for **kaṅkarta*, i.e. an old redupl. form of *kṛit* and aff. *a*) m., f. *tî*, and n. A comb, Râm. 2, 91, 70.

कङ्काल *kaṅkâla*, m. A skeleton, Sund. 2, 24.

कच् *KACH*, i. 1, Âtm. **1.** To bind. **2.** † To shine. † i. 1, Par. To sound.—Cf. *kañch* and *kâñch*.

कच *kach* + *a*, m. **1.** The hair, MBh. 1, 4982. **2.** A proper name, MBh. 1, 3193.—Comp. *Utkacha*, i.e. *ud-*, adj. 1. blown, Bhâg. P. 3, 23, 38. 2. opened, MBh. 1, 6079 (?) *Vi-*, adj., f. *châ*. 1. bald, MBh. 1, 6078. 2. blown, Kir. 5, 13; Indr. 5, 8.

कचाकचि *kachâkachi*, i.e. *kacha-kacha* + *i*, adv. Seizing one another by the hair, MBh. 8, 2377.

कच्चिद् *kachchid*, see *kad*.

कच्छ *kachchha* (a form of *kaksha*, q. cf.), m. and n. A shore or bank, land contiguous to water, Pañch. 8, 17.—Comp. *Mahâ-*, m. 1. the ocean. 2. Varuṇa. 3. a mountain.

कच्छप *kachchha-pa* (vb. *pâ*), m. **1.** A tortoise, Pañch. 51, 13. **2.** A proper name: **a.** of a Nâga, MBh. 1, 4828; b. of a country, Kathâs. 18, 253.

कच्छू *kachchhû*, f. Scab, Suçr. 1, 269, 12.

† कज् *KAJ* (?), i. 1, Par. To be glad.

कज्जल *kajjala*, i.e. *kad-jala*, n. **1.** A collyrium prepared from lamp-black. **2.** Shame, Bhâg. P. 6, 2, 27.

† कञ्च् *KAÑCH*, i. 1, Âtm. **1.** To bind. **2.** To shine.—Cf. *kach*, and *kâñch*.

कञ्चुक *kañch* + *uka*, m. **1.** A jacket, Râm. 6, 99, 23; Kathâs. 18, 16. **2.** Dress, MBh. 12, 816. **3.** Mail, Bhâg. P. 8, 7, 15. **4.** The skin of a snake, Pañch. i. d. 73 (and mail).—Comp. *Utkañchuka*, i. e. *ud-*, adj. naked, Bhartṛ. 1, 49. *Mukta-*, m. a snake that has cast his slough. *Su-bhâshita-rasa-âsvâda-jâta-româñcha-kañchuka*, adj. covered with a mail-like horripilation (a token of pleasure), produced by tasting the flavour of beautiful words, MBh. 12, 816.

कञ्चुकित *kañchukita*, i.e. *kañchuka* + *ita*, adj., f. *tâ*, Armed with a coat of mail, Bhartṛ. 3, 66.

कञ्चुकिन् *kañchukin*, i.e. *kañchuka*

+ *in*, m. An attendant on the women's apartments, Pańch. 156, 20.

कञ्चुलिका *kańchulikâ*, i.e. *kańch* + *ula*+*ka*, f. A bodice, Amar. 28.

कंज *kañja*, i.e. *ka*+*m-ja* (vb. *jan*), n. A lotus, Râm. 4, 41, 59; Bhâg. P. 3, 14, 14.

कञ्जिका *kańjikâ*, f. A plant, Siphonanthus indica, Pańch. 184, 18.

† **कट्** *KAṬ*, i. 1, Par. **1.** To go. **2.** To rain. **3.** To encompass.—Cf. *prakaṭaya*.

कट *kaṭa* (for **karta*, i.e. *kṛit*+*a*), m. **1.** A twist of straw, a mat, Man. 2, 204. **2.** The hip, MBh. 13, 2796. **3.** The temples of an elephant, Ragh. 4, 57. **4.** A certain cast in a game of hazard, Mṛichchh. 33, 10. **5.** The name of a Râkshasa, Râm. 5, 12, 13.—**Comp.** *Baddha-*, adj., f. *ṭâ*, made of plaited grass, Râm. 2, 56, 17. *Çruti-*, m. 1. penance. 2. a snake. *Sa-*, adj. bad, vile. *Sam-*, I. adj. (properly 'having the hips thronged together'). 1. crowded. 2. impervious. 3. narrow, contracted. II. n. 1. a defile. 2. difficulty, trouble. III. m. a proper name. *Mahâ-sam-*, adj. full of great difficulties, Bhartṛ. 2, 98.

कटक *kaṭaka*, m. and n. **1.** A bracelet, Kathâs. 9, 73. **2.** The hill of a mountain. **3.** An army.

कटकटा *kaṭakaṭâ*, Imitation of the sound of fisticuffs, MBh. 3, 11516.

कटकटापय *KAṬAKAṬÂPAYA*, a denomin. derived from the last, To gnash, Râm. 2, 35, 1.

कटङ्कट *kaṭaṅkaṭa*, m. A surname of Çiva, MBh. 12, 10372.

कटपूतन *kaṭapûtana*, m. A demon, called Kaṭapûtana, Man. 12, 71.

कटाक्ष *kaṭâksha*, i.e. *kaṭa-aksha*, m. A side-look, MBh. 1, 3009; an amorous look, Daçak. in Chr. 190, 12.

कटाह *kaṭâha*, I. m. and n. A frying vessel, MBh. 14, 1927. **II.** m. The name of a *dvîpa* of the grand divisions of the terrestrial world, Kathâs. 18, 74.

कटि and **कटी** *kaṭi̇̂* (cf. *kaṭa*), f. **1.** The hip, MBh. 1, 6293. **2.** The buttocks, Man. 8, 281.

कटिका *kaṭi*+*kâ*, f. The hip, MBh. 13, 5390.

कटु *kaṭu* (for *kartu*, i.e. *kṛit*+*u*), adj., f. *ṭu* or *ṭvi*, Sharp, pungent; of taste, Pańch. 61, 11; of smell, MBh. 14, 1408; of the wind, Râm. 3, 22, 11; of words, Pańch. i. d. 191.

कटुक *kaṭu*+*ka*, I. adj., f. *kâ*, Sharp, pungent; of taste, Kathâs. 11, 23; of smell, Râm. 3, 16, 17; of words, MBh. 13, 6645. **II.** n. Pungency.—**Comp.** *Sa-*, adj. Harsh, MBh. 2, 1551.

कटुता *kaṭu*+*tâ*, f. Wickedness, Hariv. 1022.

कटोदक *kaṭa-udaka*, n. Obsequies of a deceased person, Bhâg. P. 7, 2, 17.

† **कठ्** *KAṬH* (a form of *kashṭ* in *kashṭa*), i. 1, Par. To live in distress.

कठ *kaṭha*, m. The name of a sage, MBh. 1, 962.

कठिन *kaṭhina*, perhaps for *kashṭa* +*ina* (cf. *kaṭh*), I. adj., f. *nâ*. **1.** Hard, solid, Pańch. 190, 16; Bhartṛ. 2, 77. **2.** Cruel, Kathâs. 19, 89. **II.** f. *nî*, Chalk, Pańch. Pr. 7. **III.** n. A pat, MBh. 3, 8484.

कठिनता *kaṭhina*+*tâ*, f., and **कठिनत्व** *kaṭhina*+*tva*, n. Hardness, Bhâg. P. 3, 26, 36.

कठोर *kaṭhora*, i.e. probably *kashṭa* + *var* (for *van*) + *a* (cf. *kaṭhina*), adj. **1.** Hard, solid, Bhâg. P. 3, 19, 15. **2.** Full grown, Mṛichchh. 115, 13. **3.** Sharp, Bhâg. P. 5, 13, 3. **4.** Violent, Pańch. 93, 1. **5.** Loud, Pańch. 248, 17. **6.** Hard-hearted, Pańch. iv. d. 62.

† कड् *KAḌ*, i. 1 and 6, Par. To be glad. i. 6, Par. To eat. i. 10, Par. To remove the husk of grain.

† कड्ड् *KAḌḌ*, i. 1, Par. To be rough (a dialectical form of *kashṭ*; cf. *kaṭh*).

† कण् *KAṆ*, i. 1, Par. **1.** To sound. **2.** To cry as in distress. **3.** To go. i. 10, Par. To wink, to cover the eye with the lids.

कण *kaṇa*, I. m. **1.** Grain, Hit. 9, 14; broken rice, Man. 11, 92; also the fine red powder which adheres to the rice berry beneath the husk. **2.** A drop, Bhartṛ. 3, 15; spray, Çâk. d. 55. **3.** A spark, Pańch. 93, 3. **4.** A little bit, Prab. 29, 13. **II.** f. *ṇâ*, Long pepper, Suçr. 2, 418, 16.—**Comp.** *Tushâra-*, *tuhina-*, m. a flake of snow, Kathâs. 19, 50; Amar. 54.

कणप *kaṇapa*, m. A kind of spear, MBh. 1, 8257; with *n* instead of *ṇ*, MBh. 3, 810.

कणभ *kaṇabha*, m. A kind of fly (an autumn fly ?), Suçr. 2, 258, 1.

कणशस् *kaṇa* + *ças*, adv. In small pieces, Kumâras. 4, 27.

कणाद *kaṇâda*, m. The name of a sage, the founder of the Vaiçeshika or atomic school of philosophy.

कणान्नता *kaṇânnatâ*, i.e. *kaṇa* -*anna* + *tâ*, f. Eating broken rice, Man. 11, 167.

कणिक *kaṇika*, i.e. *kaṇa* + *ika*, I. m. **1.** Seed, Bhâg. P. 7, 9, 33. **2.** A proper name, MBh. 1, 5544. **II.** f. *kâ*, A drop, Megh. 96.

† कण्ट् *KAṆṬ*, i. 1, Par. To go.

कण्टक *kaṇṭaka* (the base *kaṇṭ* is a dialect. form of *kṛint* (originally *karnt*), the base of the present, etc. of *kṛit*), m. **1.** A thorn, Böhtl. Ind. Spr. 483. **2.** A sharp bone, Man. 8, 95. **3.** An enemy, Pańch. 176, 8; a wicked person, Man. 9, 252; 253. **4.** Stinging pain, Suçr. 1, 93, 4. **5.** Obstacle, Hit. iii. d. 76.—**Comp.** *A-*, adj., f. *ikâ*, free from thorns, i.e. obstacles, Râm. 2, 46, 29; from danger, 2, 81, 6; from harm, 3, 53, 15. *Amara-*, n. the name of the eastern table-land of the Vindhya mountain, Râm. 2, 73, 3 Gorr. *Nishkaṇṭaka*, i.e. *nis-*, adj. = *akaṇṭaka*, MBh. 4, 266. *Bhûrja-*, m. the son of an outcast Brâhmaṇa, Man. 10, 21. *Sa-*, adj. thorny.

कण्टकित *kaṇṭakita*, i.e. *kaṇṭaka* + *ita*, adj., f. *tâ*. **1.** Thorny, Draup. 1, 14. **2.** With bristling hair (a sign of pleasure or love, according to the Hindus), Râjat. 5, 2; Çâk. d. 63.

कण्टकिन् *kaṇṭakin*, i.e. *kaṇṭaka* + *in*, adj., f. *nî*. Thorny, MBh. 1, 2851.

† कण्ठ् *KAṆṬH*, i. 1, Par., Âtm., i. 10, Par. **1.** To grieve. **2.** To desire, to long for.—Cf. *utkaṇṭh*.

कण्ठ *kaṇṭha* (probably a dial. form of **kandhra*, for *kandhara*), m. **1.** The neck, Râm. 2, 66, 32 Gorr. **2.** The throat, Mṛichchh. 128, 20; Man. 11, 205. **3.** Voice, MBh. 3, 829. **4.** Proximity, Pańch. 247, 14. **5.** The proper name of a Ṛishi, Râm. 4, 18, 11 —When latter part of a comp. adj., f *ṭhî* and *ṭhâ*, e.g. *açru-* adj. With tears in the throat, i.e. the voice interrupted by tears, Râm. 2, 74, 28; f. *ṭhî*, Daçak in Chr. 191, 3. *nishka-*, I. adj., f. *ṭhî*, Wearing a golden ornament on the neck, MBh. 3, 14694. II. m. A golden ornament of the neck, 13, 4928. *nîla-*, I. adj. With a blue throat, MBh. 10, 454. II. m. 1. A peacock, Megh. 77. 2. A name of Çiva, Râm. 5, 89, 41. III. f. *ṭhî*, A peahen, 5, 11, 23. *mukta-kanṭha+m* (vb. *much*), adv. Aloud, as shouting or crying. *çiti-*, m. 1. A peacock. 2. A gallinule. 3. Çiva. *çrî-*, m. 1. Çiva. 2. A proper name. *sanna-* (vb. *sad*), adj. Choked, scarcely able to articulate. *sûtra-*, m. 1. A Brâhmaṇa. 2. A wagtail. 3. A dove.

कण्ठीरव *kanṭhîrava*, i.e. *kanṭhî-* (f. of *kanṭha* with the same signification) *ru+a*, m. A lion, Pańch. iii. d. 28.

कण्ठ्य *kanṭhya*, i.e. *kanṭha+ya*, adj. 1. Being at the throat. 2. Salutary to the throat. 3. Guttural.

† **कण्ड्** *KAṆḌ*, i. 1, Âtm. To be glad. i. 1 and i. 10, Par. To remove the husk of grain. i. 10, Par. To preserve.—Cf. *kad*.

कण्डन *kaṇḍ+ana*, I. n. The chaff, Suçr. 1, 38, 4. II. f. *nî*, A mortar, Man. 3, 68.

कण्डु, I. *kaṇḍu*, and, usually, **कण्डू** *kaṇḍû*, f. The itch, Bhâg. P. 2, 7, 13. II. *kaṇḍu*, m. The name of a Ṛishi, Râm. 2, 21, 31.

कण्डूति *kaṇḍûti*, i. e. *kaṇḍûya+ti*, f. Wantonness, Râjat. 5, 281.

कण्डूय *KAṆḌÛYA*, a denominative derived from *kaṇḍu*, Par. (Âtm. MBh. 13, 5023). 1. To scratch, MBh. 1, 5932. 2. To rub, Çâk. d. 144. 3. To stroke, Man. 4, 82. *khara-kaṇḍûyita*, n. (proverbially) Scratching with a thorn for 'doing an absurd action,' MBh. 3, 1329.

कण्डूयन *kaṇḍûyana*, i.e. *kaṇḍûya+ana*, n. 1. Itching, Bhâg. P. 8, 7, 10. 2. Scratching, 3, 31, 26. 3. Stroking, Vikr. d. 151.

कण्डूयनक *kaṇḍûyana+ka*, adj. Titillating, Böhtl. Ind. Spr. 1106.

कण्डूयितृ *kaṇḍûyitṛi*, i.e. *kaṇḍûya+tṛi*, m., f. *tṛî*, n. Who or what rubs, Ragh. 13, 43.

कण्व *kaṇva*, m. The name of a Ṛishi, MBh. 1, 2874. Superl. *kaṇva+tama*, The first of the Kaṇva tribe, Chr. 287, 4=Rigv. i. 48, 4.

कतक *kataka*, m. The nut plant, Strychnos potatorum, which clears water, Man. 6, 67.

कतम *ka+tama*, superl. of *kim*, pron. n. °*mad*. Who, what, which of many, MBh. 1, 4312; of two, 13, 3044 —With *na* and *api*, Not the least, Bhâg. P. 7, 15, 59.

कतर *ka+tara*, compar. of *kim*, pron. n. °*rad*, Who, what, which of two, MBh. 1, 3645; of many, Vikr. 5, 14.—Cf. Lat. uter for cuter (ubi: alicubi), utrum; κότερον, ὁ-πότερος; Goth. hvathar; A.S. hvädher.

कति *kati*, i.e. *ka*, base of *kim+ti*, pron. 1. How many, Râm. 5, 73, 2. 2. Some, Pańch. 171, 2; usually with following *chid*, Pańch. 87, 22; with *api*, Amar. 25. 3. A proper name, Hariv. 1461.—Cf. Lat. quot.

कतिधा *kati+dhâ*, adv. In how many ways, Bhâg. P. 3, 6, 11.

कतिपय *katipaya* (from *kati*), adj., f. *yâ* and *yî*, Some, Pańch. 9, 6.

कत्थ् *KATTH*, i. 1, Âtm. 1. To boast, Chr. 24, 39. 2. To praise, Râm. 3, 55, 8. 3. To blame, Bhâg. P. 8, 7,

33.—With the prep. वि *vi*, 1. To boast, Râm. 6, 36, 42. 2. To disparage, MBh. 4, 1299. Caus. To humble, Draup. 9, 10.

कत्थन *katth + ana*, I. adj. Boasting, a boaster, Râm. 1, 6, 10. II. n. Boasting, Râm. 3, 35, 23.

† **कत्र्** *KATR*, see *kartr*.

कथ् *KATH*, i. 10, Par., in epic poetry also Âtm. (probably a denomin. of *katham*). 1. To tell, MBh. 1, 2206; Âtm. ib. 3, 13180; to tell of, with the acc., Çâk. 7, 18. 2. To announce, MBh. 14, 144. 3. To declare, Man. 7, 157. 4. To command, Pańch. 57, 22; Vikr. d. 7. 5. To converse, Râm. 2, 57, 1; Brâhmaṇ. 1, 11.—Pass. To be called, Hit. Pr. d. 32.—Anomalous ptcple. of the pres. Âtm. *kathayâna*, MBh. 2, 1906. *kathita*, n. Talk, Çâk. 33, 3.—With the prep. प्र *pra*, To announce, Râm. 5, 1, 93.—With सम् *sam*, 1. To tell, Bhâg. P. 8, 5, 13. 2. To explain, MBh. 3, 14000.

कथक *kath + aka*, adj. Telling, Çântiç. 2, 27. m. A narrator, MBh. 1, 7778.

कथन *kath + ana*, n. Relating, Bhartṛ. 2, 54.

कथम् *ka + tha + m* (cf. *him*), adv. 1. In what manner, Nal. 3, 10. 2. How, Çâk. 14, 13; Man. 5, 2. 3. What, Çâk. 94, 1 (*katham̃ mâm evoddiçati*, What! dares he defy me?). 4. Whence, Çâk. 98, 23.—With following *api*, 1. By some means, by accident, Pańch. 127, 25; 261, 13. 2. A little, Çâk. d. 73. 3. Slowly, with difficulty, Pańch. 236, 7. 4. *katham̃katham api*, Not without great pain, Daçak. in Chr. 187, 11.—With following *nu*, 1. How now? Nal. 17, 20 (19). 2. How much more? Çâk. d. 81; with *na*, How much less? Râm. 1, 33, 9.—With following *chana*, 1. In any manner, Man. 5, 143; with *na*, In no manner, never, Man. 4, 11. 2. Not without difficulty, Râm. 1, 67, 4. 3. *katham̃katham chana*, A little, Vikr. 29, 15.—With following *chid*, 1. A little, Çâk. 65, 1. 2. Scarcely, Râm. 3, 24, 20. 3. With difficulty, Pańch. 9, 5; MBh. 13, 2797. *katham̃ chid api*, Even a little, Man. 3, 190; Scarcely, Râm. 6, 99, 50. *katham̃ chid—na*, In no way, Râm. 5, 75, 7. *na katham̃ chid api*, Never, Chr. 19, 4. *na katham̃ chid—na*, By all means, Arj. 10, 17.—Comp. *Yathâ-katha + m*, adv. with following *chid*, by all means, Man. 11, 220 (221).

कथा *kath + â*, f. 1. A tale, Ram. 1, 2, 38. 2. A speech, discourse, Man. 3, 231; Çâk. d. 76. 3. Mention, Nal. 21, 33. 4. With preceding *kâ* (fem. of *kim*), and a following loc., or *prati* with acc., No question, out of the question, Ragh. 10, 29 (you are out of the question); in a prodosis, Çâk. d. 52, *kâ kathâ vâṇasam̃dhâne*, There is no need to fix the arrow to the bow; in an apodosis, Kathâs. 4, 123, how much less?—Comp. *Dharma-*, f. a conversation concerning law or duty, Pańch. 117, 13. *Purâ-*, f. a tale of past ages. *Sam-*, f. conversation.

कथानक *kath + âna + ka*, n. A little tale, Lass. 15, 13.

कथामय *kathâ + maya*, adj., f. *yî*, Consisting of tales, Kathâs. 8, 1.

कथावशेषता *kathâvaçeshatâ*, i. e. *kathâ-avaçesha + tâ*, f. Condition of one of whom nothing but the mention is left, i.e. death, Prab. 83, 1.

कद् *ka + d* (the old nom. acc. sing. n. of *kim*; cf. Lat. quod; O.H.G. huaz; A.S. hvät). 1. With following *chid*, **कच्चिद्** *kach chid*, particle of interrogation, Perhaps, Nal. 4, 24. **2.** As former part of compound nouns, Bad, e.g. *kad-anna*, n. Bad food, Bhâg. P. 5, 9, 9. *kad-apatya*, adj. Having a bad offspring, 4, 13, 43. *kad-indriya*, n. pl. The paltry organs of sense, 8, 3, 28. **3.** Combined with vb. *dâ*, To blame, 7, 5, 28; with *arth*, q.v.

कद् *KAD*, or † **कन्द्** *KAND*, or † **क्रन्द्** *KRAND*, or † **क्लन्द्** *KLAND*, i. 1, Âtm. **1.** † To be confused. **2.** † To confound. **3.** To kill; *chakâda*, Râm. 6, 65, 23.

कदन *kad+ana*, n. Killing, Râm. 6, 65, 23.

कदम्ब *kadamba*, **I.** m. A tree, Nauclea cadamba (its flower, when full-blown, is covered with projecting anthers), Râm. 5, 74, 4; Kir. 5, 9. **II.** n. Plenty, Çâk. 87, 15 (Prâkṛ.).

कदम्बक *kadamba+ka*, n. Plenty, Çâk. d. 39.

कदर्थ् *KADARTH*, see *arth*.

कदर्थ *kadartha*, see *kadarthî* under *kṛi*.

कदर्थन *kadarthana*. i.e. *kad-arth+ana*, n. and f. *nâ*, Tormenting, Daçak. 169, 7.

कदर्य *kad-arya*, adj., f. *yâ*, Avaricious, Man. 4, 210.

कदल *kadala*, **I.** m. and f. *lî*, The plaintain tree, Musa sapientum, Megh. 75. **II.** f. *lî*, A kind of deer, MBh. 2, 1743.

कदलिका *kadalikâ*, i.e. *kadalî+ka*, f. The plaintain tree, Prab. 65, 13.

कदा *ka+dâ* (see *kim*), adv. At what time, Nal. 22, 7. With following *chana*, **1.** Once, some time; preceded by *na*, Never, Man. 2, 58. **2.** Perhaps, Pañch. 22, 10. With following *chid*, Once, Brâhmaṇ. 1, 2; preceded by *na*, Never, Man. 4, 74. **3.** Followed by *api*, and preceded by *na*, Never, Hit. 58, 12.—Cf. Lat. quando, quandoque = *kâda chid*.

कद्रू *kadrû*, f. The wife of Kaçyapa, and mother of the serpent race, MBh. 1, 1074.

कन् *KAN*, i, 1, Par. (perhaps proceeded from *kam*, q. cf., by *kam+nâ*, ii. 9, cf. *raṇ*). **1.** To love, to be satisfied, etc. (ved.). **2.** † To shine. **3.** † To go.

कनक *kan+aka*, n. Gold, Ṛit. 6, 28; 30.

कनकमय *kanaka+maya*, adj., f. *yî*, Golden, Pañch. 235, 13.

कनप *kanapa*, see *kaṇapa*.

कनिष्ठ *kanishṭha*, superl. of *alpa* and *yuvan*, f. *shṭhâ*. **1.** Smallest, very small, Râm. 3, 51, 7. **2.** Youngest, Man. 9, 113. **3.** with and without *anguli*, f. The little finger, Yâjñ. 1, 19.

कनिष्ठिका *kanishṭhikâ*, i.e. *kaṇishṭha+ka*, f. The little finger, MBh. 13, 5059.

कनीयंस् *kanîyaṁs*, **I.** comparative of *alpa* and *yuvan*, f. *yasî*, Very small, Pañch. 16, 7. **II.** m. A younger brother, Râm. 1, 26, 5.

कनीयस *kanîyasa*, i. e. *kanîyaṁs+a*, adj. **1.** Smaller, MBh. 13, 2560. **2.** Younger, MBh. 1, 3518.

कन्था *kanthâ*, f. A patched cloth, Bhartṛ. 3, 16. — Cf. perhaps Lat. cento (?).

† **कन्द्** *KAND*, i. 1, Par. **1.** To call. **2.** To cry or shed tears.—Cf. *kad*.

कन्द् *kanda*, m. A bulbous root, Pańch. ii. d. 161.—**Comp.** *Mahâ-*, m. 1. garlic. 2. a sort of yam. 3. a plant, Hingtsha repens. *Rakta-*, m. 1. coral. 2. a sort of onion.

कन्दट *kandaṭa*, n. The white esculent water lily.

कन्दद *kanda-da* (vb. *dâ*), adj. One who makes roots (?), MBh. 12, 10403.

कन्दर *kandara* (probably *ka* + *m*, old nom. and acc. n. of *kim*, *-dṛi* + *a*), m., f. *rî*, and n. A cave, Pańch. 93, 8.

कन्दरवन्त् *kandara* + *vant*, adj., f. *vatî*, Abundant in caves, Râm. 3, 21, 13.

कन्दर्प *kandarpa* (probably *kam*, see *kandara*, *-dṛip* + *a*), m. **1.** A name of the god of love, Râm. 1, 25, 10. **2.** Love, MBh. 1, 7920.

कन्दल *kandala* (perhaps *kam*, see the last, and *dala*), n. **1.** The flower of the *kandalî* (q. cf.), Bhartṛ. 1, 43. **2.** A new shoot. — **Comp.** *Rakta-*, *ratna-*, and *hema-*, m. coral.

कन्दली *kandalî*, see the last, f. The plaintain tree, Musa sapientum, Vikr. d. 78.

कन्दलिन् *kandalin*, i.e. *kandala* + *in*, adj., f. *nî*, Abundant in new shoots, Bhartṛ. 1, 42.

कन्दु *kandu*, m. f. An iron pan, Mâlav. 24, 21 (Prâkṛ.).

कन्दुक *kanduka*, I. m. A ball for playing with, Bhartṛ. 2, 83. II. n. A pillow, Bhartṛ. 3, 42.

कन्धर *kandhara* [i.e. *kam* (see *kandara*), according to the grammarians, Head, *-dhṛi* + *a*], m., and f. *râ*, The neck, Yâjń. 2, 220. — **Comp.** *Utkandhara*, i.e. *ud-*, adj., f. *râ* (cf. Kathâs. 20, 8), with raised neck, Pańch. 249, 5. *Daçakandhara*, i.e. *daçan-*, adj. having ten necks, epithet of Râvaṇa, MBh. 3, 16516.

कन्यका *kanyakâ*, i.e. *kanyâ* + *ka*, f. A girl, Pańch. 44, 18.

कन्यकुब्ज *kanyakubja*, i. e. *kanyâ* *-kubja* (with shortened *â*), f. The name of a town, Râm. 1, 34, 37.

कन्यस *kanyasa*, i.e. *kanyaṁs* (for *kanîyaṁs*) + *a*, adj., f. *sî*, Younger, Râm. 5, 33, 10.

कन्या *kanyâ* (akin to *kanîyaṁs*), f. **1.** A girl, Nal. 1, 8. **2.** A virgin, Man. 8, 367. **3.** A daughter, Man. 9, 71.—**Comp.** *Kâçi-*, f. a daughter of the king of the Kâçis, Chr. 20, 18. *Jahnu-*, f. a name of the Gangâ, Bhartṛ. 3, 79. *Sama-*, f. a girl fit to be married.

कन्यात्व *kanyâ* + *tva*, n. Virginity, MBh. 1, 2406.

कन्यामय *kanyâ* + *maya*, adj., f. *yî*, Consisting of a girl, Ragh. 16, 86.

कप् *KAP*, see *krap*.

कप *kapa*, m. The name of a kind of demons, MBh. 13, 7329 sqq.

कपट *kapaṭa*, m. and n. Fraud, Pańch. 217, 15.

कपर्द *kaparda*, m. **1.** A small shell used as a coin, a cowrie. **2.** The braided hair of Çiva.

कपर्दक *kaparda* + *ka*, m. and

कपर्दिका *kapardikâ*, f. A small shell used as a coin, Hit. 115, 2.

कपर्दिन् *kapardin*, i. e. *kaparda* + *in*, m. A name of Çiva, MBh. 3, 1624.

कपाट *kapâṭa*, m., f. *ṭî*, and n. **1.** A half of a folding-door, Râm. 5, 15, 10. **2.** A door, Mṛichchh. 16, 17.

ऽकपाटक *-kapâṭa+ka,* a substitute for the last when latter part of a comp. adj. *sphâṭika-uru-,* adj. Having large folding-doors of crystal, MBh. 2, 1673. f. *ṭikâ,* Bhâg. P. 3, 15, 29.

कपाल *kapâla* (probably for **kar-pâla;* cf. *karpara*), I. m., f. *lî,* An earthen water-pot, especially of the religious mendicants, Man. 6, 44; Bhartṛ. 3, 24; of beggars in general, Daçak. in Chr. 194, 1. II. m. and n. 1. Either half of a water-jar, Bhâshâp. 10. 2. The skull, MBh. 14, 273. III. m. 1. A potsherd. 2. Either half of an egg, Kathâs. 2, 15. 3. The glene, Suçr. 1, 265, 8. 4. A kind of leprosy, Suçr. 1, 268, 1.

कपालिक *kapâlika,* I. = *kâpâlika* II. (q. cf.), Pańch. i. d. 239 (with shortened *a* on account of the metre?). II. f. *kâ,* i.e. *kapâla+ka,* f. A potsherd, Man. 4, 78.

कपालिन् *kapâlin,* i.e. *kapâla+in,* I. adj., f. *nî,* Wearing skulls (as a necklace), Kumâras. 5, 78; covered with skulls, Bhâg. P. 4, 4, 16. II. m. and f. A follower of a certain sect, Prab. 56, 13. III. m. A name of Çiva, MBh. 2, 1641; of one of the Rudras, 1, 2567. IV. f. *nî,* A name of Durgâ.

कपि *kapi,* i.e. *kamp+i,* m. 1. A monkey, Man. 11, 154. A name of Vishṇu, MBh. 13, 7045.

कपिञ्जल *kapiñjala,* m. 1. A bird, the francoline partridge, Bhâg. P. 6, 9, 5. 2. A proper name, Pańch. 163, 20.

कपित्थ *kapittha* (probably *kapi-stha,* vb. *sthâ*), I. m. A tree, Feronia elephantum, Corr., MBh. 1, 2830. II. n. Its fruit, Suçr. 1, 148, 16.

कपित्थक *kapittha+ka,* m. A tree, Feronia elephantum, Corr., Râm. 5, 16, 2.

कपित्व *kapi+tva,* n. Condition of a monkey, Râm. 5, 2, 15.

कपिल *kapi+la,* I. adj., f. *lâ,* Reddish, Man. 3, 8 (with reddish hair), Râm. 6, 3, 2. II. m. The name of a sage, MBh. 3, 1896; of a mountain, Bhâg. P. 5, 16, 27. III. f. *lâ.* 1. A reddish or brown cow, MBh. 3, 8067. 2. A proper name, MBh. 1, 2520. 3. The name of a river, MBh. 3, 14233.

कपिश *kapi+ça,* adj. Reddish, Çâk. d. 75; brown, Vikr. d. 26; Megh. 21.

कपीन्द्र *kapîndra,* i.e. *kapi-indra,* m. A name of Vishṇu, MBh. 13, 7002.

कपीवन्त् *kapîvant,* i.e. *kapi+vant,* I. m. The name of a sage, Hariv. 426. II. f. *vatî,* The name of a river, Râm. 2, 71, 15.

कपोत *ka-pota* (see *kim*), I. m. A dove or pigeon, Pańch. iii. d. 139. II. f. *tî,* A she-pigeon, Pańch. iii. d. 179.

कपोतक *kapota+ka,* m., f. *tikâ,* A little pigeon, Pańch. ii. 9; iii. 144.

कपोल *kapola,* m. A cheek, Pańch. d. 225.—Comp. *Su-,* adj., f. *lâ,* having beautiful cheeks, Bhâg. P. 4, 25, 22.

कपोलकाष *kapolakâsha,* i.e. *kapola -kash+a,* m. That which rubs the cheeks (viz. of the elephants), as a branch, etc., Kir. 5, 26.

कफ *kapha,* m. Phlegm, one of the three humours of the body, Suçr. 1, 4, 8.

कफल *kapha+la,* adj. Phlegmatic, causing or exciting phlegm, Suçr. 1, 224, 7.

† **कब्** *KAB,* or **कव्** *KAV,* i. 1, Âtm. 1. To colour. 2. To praise.

कबन्ध *kabandha,* and **कवन्ध** *ka-*

vandha, m. and n. **1.** A headless trunk, especially one retaining the power of action, Böhtl. Ind. Sp. 166. **2.** A belly, MBh. 3, 806. **3.** A cloud, or vapour, MBh. 3, 13087. **4.** The name of a demon, Râm. 3, 75, 24, sqq. — Cf. Κάανθος.

कम् *ka+m* (old acc. s. n. of *kim*), a particle, Indeed, Chr. 293, 2=Rigv. i. 88, 2. —Cf. κέν.

कम् *KAM*, i. 10, Âtm. (in epic poetry also Par., Hiḍ. 4, 4; Râm. 3, 51, 28), in the pres., impf., imptive., and potent., and optionally in all the other forms, *kâmaya*. **1.** To love, MBh. 1, 2400; Râm. 1, 34, 16. **2.** To desire, Sâv. 5, 52; to wish, with infin., MBh. 1, 6582; to intend, with infin., MBh. 3, 2249.—Anom. ptcple. of the pres. *kâmayâna*, e.g. MBh. 13, 1891; *kâmamana* (probably to be corrected to *kâmayâna*), Râm. 5, 24, 37; 38.—Pf. pass. *kânta*. **1.** Loved, Hiḍ. 4, 35. **2.** Amiable, graceful. —**Comp.** *Chandra-*, m. the moon-stone. *Ramâ-*, m. Vishṇu. *Ravi-*, m. the sun-stone. *Râdhâ-*, m. Vishṇu. *Sûrya-*, m. 1. the sunstone, Çâk. d. 40; a gem. 2. Hibiscus phœniceus.—Compar. *kânta* + *tara*, Most beautiful, Râm. 3, 17, 6. *kâmita*, n. Wish, MBh. 1, 2187. — Ptcple. of the fut. pass. *kamanîya*. **1.** To be loved, Kumâras. 1, 37. **2.** Beautiful, Bhartṛ. 1, 45. *kâmya*, see separately.—Caus. To cause to desire, Râm. 3, 38, 20 (Par.); Ṛit. 6, 30 (Âtm.).— With the prep. **अति** *ati*, in *ati-kânta*, adj. Excessively loved, Bhartṛ. 2, 30. —With **अभि** *abhi*, To desire, MBh. 1, 3347.—With **नि** *ni*, To desire, Bhâg. P. 5, 18, 21. — Cf. Lat carus = *kam-ra*, Beautiful, charming (Grammarians), amo (cf. *katara*), amœnus, etc.; κῆδος (aff. δος = *tvas*) κεδνός, etc.; probably O.H.G. gaman, A.S. gamene.

कमठ *kamaṭha*, m. **1.** A tortoise, Pañch. ii. d. 199. **2.** A proper name, MBh. 2, 117.

कमण्डलु *kamaṇḍalu*, m. (and n). A water-pot used by ascetics and religious students, Man. 2, 64; Râm. 3, 52, 9.

कमन *kam+ana*, adj. Desirable, Bhâg. P. 1, 9, 33.

कमल *kam+ala*, I. n. **1.** A lotus, Nelumbium, Megh. 32. **2.** Water, Kir. 5, 25. **II.** f. *lâ*. **1.** A name of Lakshmî, Bhâg. P. i. p. xcv. **2.** A proper name, Râjat. 4, 424.—**Comp.** *Kara-kamala*, n. a lotus-like hand, Ṛit. 3, 23. *Vikasita-vadana-kamala*, adj., f. *lâ*, opening her lotus-like mouth, Pañch, 129, 10. *Vikasita-nayana-vadana-kamala*, opening his lotus-like eyes and mouth, 192, 11. *Sa-*, adj. abounding in lotus-flowers, Kir. 5, 25.

कमलाहास् *KAMALÂHÂS*, a denomin. derived from *kamala-â-hâsa*, Par. To smile like a lotus, Lass. 67, 15.

कमलिनी *kamalinî*, i.e. *kamala* + *in* + *î*, f. A group of lotus flowers, Megh. 90.

कम्प् *KAMP*, i. 1, Âtm. (in epic poetry also Par., MBh. 4, 1290). **1.** To move to and fro, Râm. 1, 14, 18. **2.** To tremble, Râm. 3, 53, 61. Comp. ptcple. of the pf. pass. *â-kampita*, n. Trembling a little, Ragh. 2, 13. Caus. To cause to tremble, Râm. 1, 74, 13; 3, 33, 38 (Âtm.). Comp. ptcple. of the pf. pass. *a-kampita*, Without being stirred, by themselves, MBh. 4, 1290. Comp. ptcple. of the fut. pass. *a-kampya*, immoveable, Râm. 3, 53, 43. —With the prep. **अनु** *anu*, To pity, with loc. and acc., MBh. 14, 29; Râm. 3, 37, 15. Ptcple. of the pf. pass. *anu-*

kampita, n. Compassion, Bhâg. P. 1, 9, 22. Caus. To pity, Kumâras. 4, 39. —With समनु *sam-anu*, To pity, Ragh. 9, 14.—With अभि *abhi*, To tremble, MBh. 3, 15721 (? v.r.).—With आ *â*, Caus. To cause to tremble, MBh. 1, 1165. *âkampita*, Excited, Ṛit. 6, 32.— With उद् *ud*, To tremble, Kathâs. 15, 2.—With प्र *pra*, To tremble, Râm. 1, 65, 13. Caus. To cause to tremble, Râm. 3, 25, 26. Comp. ptcple of the fut. pass. *dushprakampya*, i. e. *dus-*. **1.** Difficult to be made to tremble, Hariv. 12824. **2.** Difficult to be made to reel, MBh. 5, 718.—With संप्र *sam-pra*, Caus. To cause to tremble, Râm. 5, 6, 16.—With प्रति *prati*, Caus. **1.** To cause to tremble, MBh. 4, 298.—With वि *vi*. **1.** To tremble, Bhag. 2, 31.—**2.** To retreat (with abl., from), MBh. 4, 109. **3.** To change, Râm. 2, 60, 17. *vikampita*, Trembling, Ṛit. 1, 3. Caus. To cause to tremble, Ragh. 11, 19.— With सम् *sam*, To tremble, MBh. 4, 574. Caus. To cause to tremble, MBh. 1, 1167.—Cf. perhaps κάμπτω καμπύλος.

कम्प *kamp* + *a*, m. Trembling, Bhartṛ. 1, 50.—**Comp.** *Nishkampa*, i.e. *nis-*, adj., f. *pâ*, unmoved, unmovable. *Kshiti-*, *bhû-* and *bhûmi-*, m. an earthquake, MBh. 7, 7867; Râm. 1, 41, 15.

कम्पन *kamp* + *ana*, **I.** adj., f. *nâ*. **1.** Causing to tremble, MBh. 13, 662. **II.** m. **1.** A certain weapon, Râm. 6, 7, 24. **2.** A proper name, MBh. 2, 117. **3.** The name of a country, Râjat. 5, 446. **III.** f. *nâ*, The name of a river, MBh. 3, 8094. **IV.** n. Trembling, MBh. 3, 13539.—**Comp.** *Sa-*, adj., f. *nâ*, accompanied by earthquakes, Chr. 36, 23. *Sva-*, m. wind. *Hṛidaya-*, adj. agitating the heart, causing it to throb (with indignation), Draup. 4, 22.

† कम्ब् *KAMB*, see *karb*.

कम्बल *kambala*, **I.** m. and n. **1.** A woollen blanket, MBh. 3, 181. **2.** A woollen garment, Râjat. 5, 460. **II.** m. The name of a Nâga, MBh. 1, 1555.— Comp. *Pâṇḍu-*, m. 1. a white woollen blanket. 2. a kind of stone.

कम्बु *kambu*, m. and n. **1.** A shell, Bhâg. P. 4, 7, 20. **2.** A bracelet (made of shells, MBh. 2, 2067), MBh. 4, 54.

कम्बोज *kamboja*, m. pl. The name of a country and its inhabitants.

कर *kara*, i.e. **A.** *kṛi* + *a*, **I.** latter part of comp. adj. and subst., f. *rî*, Making, causing, producing; e.g. *vaira-*, Causing enmity, Man. 9, 227. *a-yaças-*, Causing disgrace, Hiḍ. 3, 18. *deha-*, m. A father, MBh. 5, 3657. **II.** m. **1.** The hand, Man. 5, 136. **2.** An elephant's trunk, Nal. 13, 12. **B.** *kṛî* + *a*, m. **1.** A ray of light, Râm. 6, 11, 44. **2.** Hail. **3.** Royal revenue, Man. 7, 128; toll, Man. 7, 127.—**Comp.** *Agra-*, m. 1. the tip of the extended hand. 2. the extremity of the hand and of a ray, Çiç. 9, 34. *A-tushâra-kara*, m. the sun, Çiç. 9, 7. *Kula-kara*, m. ancestor, MBh. 1, 6562. *Chitra-*, m. a painter, Kathâs. 5, 30. *Dina-*, *divasa-*, and *divâ-*, m. the sun, Bhartṛ. 2, 65. *Dushkara*, i.e. *dus-*, adj., f. *rî*, difficult, Man. 7. 55; *dushkaraṁ yadi*, scarcely, Râm. 2, 73, 7. *Padma-*, I. m. a lotus-like hand, Bhâg. P. 7, 9, 26. II. adj., f. *râ*, holding a lotus, Prab. 86, 3. III. f. *râ*, a name of Çrî, Bhâg. P. 4, 20, 27. *Bhoga-*, adj., f. *rî*, procuring food, Bhartṛ. 2, 17. *Çûlodyatakara*, i.e. *çûla-udyata-* (vb. *yam*), adj. with a spear in his uplifted hand. *Sa-*,adj. I. bearing toll. 2. with rays. *Su-*, I. adj., f. *rî*. 1. easy, Man. 7, 55. 2. doing well.

II. f. *râ*, a tractable cow. III. n. charity, benevolence. *A-su-*, adj. to be shunned, Bhartṛ. 2, 61.

करक *karaka*, m., i.e. A. *kṛi* + *aka*, The waterpot of the student or ascetic, Man. 4, 66. B. *kṛî* + *aka*, Hail, Megh. 55.

करकासार् *KARAKÂSÂR*, a denominative derived from *karaka-âsâra*, Par. To rain like a shower of hail, Lass. 67, 16.

करङ्क *karaṅka*, m. The skull, Mâlat. 79, 18.

करज *kara-ja* (vb. *jan*), m. A finger nail, Man. 4, 70.

करञ्ज *karañja*, m. The name of a plant, Pongamia glabra, Vent., MBh. 3, 14488 sqq.

करञ्जक *karañja* + *ka*, m. = the last, Râm. 3, 79, 37.

करट *karaṭa*, m. 1. An elephant's temples, MBh. 3, 16039; Bhartṛ. 3, 73. *karaṭâ-mukha*, with lengthened *a*, MBh. 3, 441, etc., perhaps on account of the metre. 2. A crow, Bhâg. P. 5, 14, 29. 3. pl. The name of a people, MBh. 6, 370.—**Comp.** *Pra-bhinna-*, m. an elephant in rut, or from whose temples the juice is exuding, Sund. 2, 20.

करटक *karaṭa* + *ka*, m. 1. A crow, Mṛichchh. 104, 13 (Prâkṛ.). 2. A proper name, Pańch. 9, 19.

करण *karaṇa*, i.e. *kṛi* + *ana*, I. adj., f. *ṇî*, Making, causing, e. g. *vaidhavya-*, Causing widowhood, Râm. 6, 95, 27. *saṁjiva-*, Causing health, Râm. 6, 26, 5. II. n. 1. Making, MBh. 3, 15297; performing, Pańch. 40, 15. 2. Action, Râm. 1, 11, 17. 3. Instrument, Bhâshâp. 57. 4. An organ of sense, Ragh. 8, 38. 5. The body, Kumâras. 4, 5. 6. A document, Man. 8, 51. 7. Musical time, Kumâras. 6, 40. III. m. The son of a Vrâtya Kshatriya, Man. 10, 22.—**Comp.** *A-*, n. non-doing, Vedântas. in Chr. 202, 15. *Anta-*, adj. causing destruction, Man. 9, 221. *Antaḥkaraṇa*, i.e. *antar-*, n. the internal sense, Vedântas. in Chr. 206, 24; the heart, Çâk. d. 21. *A-hita-*, n. a wicked action, Bhartṛ. 1, 87. *Trivṛit-*, n. triplication, Vedântas. in Chr. 208, 20. *Prahâra-*, n. beating, Pańch. 245, 12. *Virûpa-*, n. disfiguring, Râm. 1, 3, 19. *Çesha-*, n. doing what is still to be done, Râm. 4, 17, 56.

करण्ड *karaṇḍa*, m. and n. (Böhtl. Ind. Spr. 392), A basket or covered box of wicker work, Bhartṛ. 2, 82.

करण्डक *karaṇḍa* + *ka*, m. A box, Çâk. 89, 15 (Prâkṛ.).—**Comp.** *Pushpa-*, n. the name of a garden, Mṛichchh. 148, 19. *Bhramara-*, m. (?) a dark lantern, Daçak. in Chr. 186, 11. *Rakshâ-*, n. an amulet, Çâk. 105, 15 (Prâkṛ.).

करतोया *karatoyâ*, i.e. *kara-toya*, f. The name of a river, MBh. 2, 374.

करतोयिनी *karatoyinî*, i.e. *kara-toya* + *in* + *î*, f. The name of a river, MBh. 13, 4887.

करद *kara-da* (vb. *dâ*), adj. 1. Paying taxes, MBh. 1, 7170. 2. Tributary, 3, 15288.

करंधम *karaṁdhama*, i.e. *kara* + *m-dhmâ* + *a*, m. A proper name, MBh. 14, 78.

करपाल *kara-pâla*, करबाल *karabâla*, and करवाल *karavâla* (with *b*, *v* for *p*), m. A sword, MBh. 1, 1432.

करप्रद *kara-pra-da* (vb. *dâ*), adj. Tributary, MBh. 3, 14774.

करबाल *karabâla*, see *karapâla*.

करभ *kara-bha* (vb. *bhâ*), m. 1.

The metacarpus, the hand from the wrist to the root of the fingers, MBh. 3, 16138. **2.** An elephant's trunk, Ragh. 6, 83. **3.** A young elephant, Bhâg. P. 8, 2, 22. **4.** A young camel, Pañch. 229, 5. **5.** A camel, MBh. 2, 1200.

करभक *karabha + ka*, m. A proper name, Çâk. 29, 15.

करमर्द *karamarda*, i.e. *kara-mṛid + a*, **I.** m. A small acanthaceous tree, Carissa carandas, Lin., MBh. 1, 11571. **II.** n. Its fruit, Suçr. 1, 210, 18.

करम्ब *karamba*, m. = *karambha*, q. cf.

करम्बित *karambita*, i.e. *karamba + ita*, adj. Mingled, Gît. i. 27.

करम्भ *karambha*, **I.** m. **1.** A cake of flour or meal mixed with curds, Man. 12, 76. **2.** Mixture, Bhâg. P. 3, 26, 45 (a mixed smell). **3.** A proper name, Râm. 4, 39, 35. **II.** f. *bhâ*, A proper name, MBh. 1, 3775.—Cf. perhaps κάραβος, ἔδεσμα ὠπτημένον ἐπ' ἀνθράκων.

करम्भक *karambha + ka*, m. A cake, Râjat. 5, 16.

कररुह *kara-ruh + a*, m. A finger nail, Megh. 94.

करवीर *kara-vîra*, m. **1.** A fragrant plant, Oleander or Nerium odorum, Râm. 3, 17, 10. **2.** The name of a magical weapon, Râm. 1, 30, 7. **3.** The name of a Nâga, MBh. 1, 1557. **4.** The name of a mountain, Bhâg. P. 5, 16, 28. **5.** The name of a city, MBh. 13, 1730.

करस्थालिन् *karasthâlin*, i.e. *kara-sthâla + in*, m. A name of Çiva, MBh. 13, 1243.

करायिका *karâyikâ*, f. A small kind of crane, Pañch. 157, 3.

कराल *karâla*, adj., f. *lâ*, **1.** Gaping, Mṛichchh. 47, 2. **2.** Formidable, Hiḍ. 2, 5; MBh. 2, 296. **II.** m. **1.** A certain beast, Suçr. 1, 200, 8. **2.** The name of a locality, Râjat. 1, 97. **III.** f. *lâ*, A name of Durgâ, Mâlat. 75, 6.—**Comp.** *A-*, adj. Mild, Bhâg. P. 3, 13, 28. *Daṁshṭrâ-*, adj. Gaping with projecting teeth, Hiḍ. 2, 3. *Vi-*, adj. Formidable.

करालता *karâla + tâ*, f. Formidableness, Pañch. 217, 23, °*tâṁ gataḥ*, It became formidable.

करिन् *karin*, i.e. *kara + in*, **I.** m. An elephant, Kir. 5, 7. **II.** f. *iṇî*, A female elephant, Bhartṛ. 3, 82.—**Comp.** *Dikkarin*, i.e. *diç-*, m. an elephant of a quarter or point of the compass, one of the eight supporting the globe, Bhâg. P. 8, 10, 24. *Vana-*, m. a wild elephant. *Sura-*, m. an elephant of the gods, Kir. 5, 26.

करीर *karîra*, **I.** m. and n. The shoot of a bamboo, Suçr. 1, 28, 6. **II.** m. A leafless plant, Capparis aphylla, Roxb., Bhartṛ. 2, 89.

करीष *karîsha*, i.e. *kṛî + îsha*, m. and n. **1.** Dry dung, Râm. 2, 100, 7; 3, 3, 2. **2.** Dry cow-dung, Man. 8, 250.

करुण *karuṇa*, **I.** adj., f. *ṇâ*, **1.** Doleful, Vikr. 4, 1; Râm. 2, 63, 32. **2.** Lamentable, Râm. 3, 51, 25. **II.** *ṇam* (acc. sing. n.), adverbially, Miserably, Râm. 1, 2, 14; Çiç. 9, 67. **III.** m. Moving compassion, one of the *rasas*, or sentiments of a poetical production, Râm. 1, 4, 7. **IV.** f. *ṇâ*, Compassion, Bhâg. P. 1, 2, 3. —**Comp.** *A-karuṇa*, adj., f. *ṇâ*, cruel, Çiç. 9, 67; Bhâg. P. 9, 14, 37. *Nishkaruṇa*, i.e. *nis-*, adj. cruel, Pañch. iv. d. 16. *Sa-*, adj. compassionate, Bhâg. P. 1, 13, 12.

करुणवेदिता *karuṇaveditâ*, i.e. *karuṇa-vedin + tâ*, f. Benignity of heart, Man. 7, 211.

करुणाय *KARUṆÂYA*, a denom. derived from *karuṇa* by *ya*, Âtm., but in epic poetry also Par. To be in distress, MBh. 3, 336 (Par.).

करुणावन्त् *karuṇâ + vant*, adj., f. *vati*, Distressed, Râm. 5, 33, 14.

करूष *karûsha*, m. pl. The name of a people, MBh. 2, 124; Râm. 1, 26, 20. —Comp. *Nishkarûsha*, i.e. *nis-* (*kṛî* + *ûsha*), adj. free from dirt, Râm. 1, 27, 20 Gorr.

करूषक *karûsha + ka*, I. m. A proper name. II. n. A certain fruit, MBh. 3, 10039.

करेणु *kareṇu* (base *kara*), I. m. f. A male or female elephant, MBh. 13, 4899; 1, 4477. II. m. The name of a plant, Suçr. 2, 171, 16.

करेणुक *kareṇu + ka*, I. n. The fruit of the plant *kareṇu*. II. f. *kâ*, A female elephant, Pańch. 43, 5.

करोट *karoṭa*, I. m. A basin; probably also cymbals in *ṭakkarâghâtasaṭâm̃kârakaroṭikâḥ* Râjat, 5, 417. II. m., and f. *ṭâ* and *ṭi*, The skull, Râjat. 6, 157.

कर्क *karka*, m. A white horse, MBh. 13, 4921.

कर्कट *karkaṭa*, a form of **karkarta*, i.e. an old reduplicated form of *kṛit* + *a*, I. m. 1. A crab, Pańch. iv. d. 10. 2. The sign of the zodiac, Cancer, Râm. 1, 19, 2. 3. The name of a plant, Suçr. 2, 253, 12. II. f. *ṭî*, A female crab, MBh. 4, 272. III. m., f. *ṭî*, The curved end of the beam of a balance, Pańch. ii. d. 74.—Cf. Lat. cancer; καρκίνος.

कर्कटक *karkaṭa + ka*, I. m. 1. A crab, Pańch. 1, 237. 2. The name of a plant, Suçr. 2, 527, 4. 3. The name of a Nâga, Râm. 5, 78, 9. II. f. *kî*, A female crab, Draup. 5, 9. III. n. A poisonous bulbous plant, Suçr. 2, 252, 7.

कर्कटिका *karkaṭikâ*, i.e. *karkaṭa* + *ka*, f. The name of a plant, probably a sort of cucumber, Pańch. 248, 2.

कर्कन्धु *karkandhu*, I. m., and f. *dhû*, The jujube, Zizyphus jujuba. II. n. Its fruit, Yâjń. 1, 240; also the fem. *dhû*, Bhâg. P. 3, 31, 32. III. m. A proper name, Chr. 296, 6 = Rigv. i. 112, 6.

कर्कर *karkara*, I. adj., f. *râ*, Hard, Mâlat. 79, 18. II. m. The name of a Nâga, MBh. 1, 1561. III. f. *rî*, A small water-jar, Bhartṛ. 1, 47.—Cf. perhaps Lat. calculus, calx; κρόκη, κροκάλη, κάχληξ.

कर्कश *karkaça*, adj., f. *çâ*. 1. Hard, Böhtl. Ind. Spr. 740. 2. Firm, Bhartṛ. 2, 56. 3. Cruel, Râm. 3, 36, 23.

कर्कशत्व *karkaça + tva*, n. 1. Hardness, Kumâras. 1, 36. 2. Harshness, MBh. 13, 542.

कर्कोटक *karkoṭaka*, I. m. 1. The name of a Nâga or snake, Nal. 14, 4. 2. A plant, Momordica mixta, Suçr. 1, 137, 15. II. n. Its fruit, 2, 343, 1.

† **कर्ज्** *KARJ*, i. 1, Par. To pain or make uneasy.

† **कर्ण्** *KARṆ*, i. 10, Par. To pierce or bore.—Cf. *âkarṇaya*.

कर्ण *karṇa*, m. 1. The ear, Man. 8, 125; with *dâ*, To listen, Çâk. 8, 21. 2. A rudder, Râm. 6, 23, 30. 3. A proper name, MBh. 1, 2427.—Comp. When the latter part of a comp. adj. the f. ends in *ṇâ* and *ṇî*. *Açva-*, m. a timber tree, Vatica robusta, Râm. 1, 26, 15. *Utkarṇa*, i.e. *ud-*, adj. with the ears erect, Ragh. (Calc. ed.) 15, 11. *Kumbha-*, m. 1. a name of Çiva, MBh. 12, 10350. 2. the name of a Râkshasa, Râm. 1, 3,

34. *Go-*, m. 1. a kind of deer, Antelope picta, Râm. 2, 103, 41. 2. a kind of arrow, MBh. 8, 4668. 3. a span from the tip of the thumb to that of the little finger, MBh. 2, 2324. 4. the name of a holy place, Râm. 1, 42, 13. 5. a name of Çiva, Kathâs. 22, 218. *Chatushkarṇa,* i.e. *chatur-*, adj. heard only by four ears, Pańch, i. d. 112. *Tri-*, adj., f. *ṇî,* having three ears, Râm. 5, 18, 24. *Dadhi-*, m. a proper name, Pańch. 165, 9. *Lamba-*, m. 1. a goat. 2. an elephant. 3. a Râkshasa. *Vi-*, adj. earless. *Çańku-*, I. adj., f. *ṇâ,* having ears like a javelin, MBh. 1, 6662; *ṇî,* Râm. 5, 18, 24. II. m. 1. an ass. 2. a proper name, Pańch. 87, 12. *Shaṭkarṇa,* i.e. *shash-*, adj. heard by six ears, Lass. 3, 10. *Stabdha-* (vb. *stambh*), adj. having the ears erect. *Hastikarṇa,* i.e. *hastin-*, m. 1. the castor oil tree. 2. the Butea frondosa. 3. a demigod. 4. the name of a district, Râjat. 5, 32.

कर्णकुब्ज *karṇa-kubja,* n. The name of a city, Lass. 8, 9.

कर्णग्राहवन्त् *karṇagrâhavant,* i.e. *karṇa-grah + a + vant,* adj., f. *vatî,* Having a helmsman, Râm. 2, 52, 5.

कर्णधार *karṇadhâra,* i.e. *karṇa-dhṛi + a,* m. A helmsman, Râm. 2, 52, 75.—**Comp.** *A-*, adj., f. *râ,* without a pilot, Hit. iii. d. 2.

कर्णवन्त् *karṇa + vant,* adj. f. *vatî,* Having ears, Râm. 2, 45, 15.

कर्णश्रव *karṇaçrava,* i.e. *karṇa-çru + a,* adj. Heard by the ear, Man. 4, 102.

कर्णाकर्णि *karṇâkarṇi,* i.e. *karṇa-karṇa + i,* adv. From ear to ear, Râm. 6, 21, 39. .

कर्णाट *karṇâṭa,* I. m. pl. The name of a country and its inhabitants, MBh. 3, 16352. II. f. *ṭî,* A proper name, Râjat. 4, 152.

कर्णाटक *karṇâṭa + ka = karṇâṭa,* m. Bhâg. P. 5, 6, 8.

कर्णिका *karṇikâ,* i.e. *karṇa + ka* or *ika,* f. 1. An ornament of the ear, Daçak. in Chr. 199, 1. 2. The pericarp of the lotus, Râm. 3, 22, 25. 3. The name of an Apsaras, MBh. 1, 428.—**Comp.** *Padma-karṇika* (perhaps to be corrected to °*ṇikâ*), the pericarp of a lotus, i.e. a manner of arraying an army, MBh. 7, 2674.

कर्णिकार *karṇikâra,* I. m. The name of a plant, Pterospermum acerifolium, Râm. 3, 21, 15. II. n. Its flower, Ṛit. 6, 6.

कर्णिन् *karṇin,* i.e. *karṇa + in,* adj. 1. Mischievously barbed, Man. 7, 90. 2. In *-ardhakuṇḍalakarṇin,* MBh. 13, 886, where the aff. *in* belongs to *-ardha-kuṇḍala-karṇa,* not to *karṇa* alone: Wearing in his ear half an ear-ring.

कर्णीरथ *karṇîratha* (cf. *ratha*), m. A litter, Râjat. 5, 218.

कर्णीसुत *karṇîsuta* (cf. *su*), m. A proper name, Daçak. in Chr. 185, 16.

कर्णोपकर्णिका *karṇopakarṇikâ,* i.e. *karṇa-upa-karṇa + ka,* f. Gossip, Pańch. 36, 19.

† **कर्त्** *KART,* see *kartṛ*.

कर्तन *kartana,* i. e. *kṛit + ana,* n. Cutting, Yâjń. 2, 229.

कर्तव्यता *kartavya + tâ* (vb. *kṛi*), f. Business, Man. 7, 61.

कर्तुकाम *kartukâma,* i. e. *kartum-kâma* (vb. *kṛi*), adj. Desiring to do, Râm. 3, 49, 51.

कर्तुमनस् *kartumanas,* i.e. *kartum*

-*manas* (vb. *kṛi*), adj. Intending to do, Pańch. 12, 19.

कर्तृ *kartṛi*, i.e. *kṛi*+*tṛi*, m., f. *trî*, and n. 1. An agent, a maker, Râm. 4, 24, 5; Man. 4, 172; 3, 160; 5, 105 (n.); Kathâs. 25, 153 (f.). 2. A founder, MBh. 13, 1662. 3. Creator, Râm. 3, 69, 7. 4. An author, Pańch. ii. d. 34.—Comp. *Âdi-*, m. the first creator, Râm. 6, 102, 18. *Dina-*, m. the sun, Hariv. 9367. *Mishṭa-*, m. a confectioner. *Râjya-*, m. an officer of the government, Râm. 2, 67, 1. *Çarîra-*, m. a father, Chr. 15, 28. *Su-varṇa-*, m. a goldsmith. *Hema-*, m. a kind of bird (?), Man. 12, 61.

ऽकर्तृक -*kartṛi*+*ka*, a substitute for *kartṛi*, when the latter part of a comp. adj., e.g. *sa-*, adj., f. *kâ*, Accompanied by an agent, Bhâshâp. 46.

कर्तृत्व *kartṛi*+*tva*, n. Being agent, MBh. 3, 1232.

कर्त्तरि and री *karttarî* (for *karttrî*, i.e. *kṛit*+*tṛi*+*î*), f. Scissors, Suçr. 2, 13, 16.

† कर्त्र् *KARTR*, or कर्त् *KART*, or कत्र् *KATR*, i. 10, Par. To loosen (akin to *kṛit*, a denominative).

कर्त्त्रिका *karttrikâ*, i.e. 1. *kṛit*+*tṛi*+*î*+*ka*, f. A hunter's knife, Hit. 43, 19 v. r.—With *karttṛi*, cf. Lat. culter.

† कर्द् *KARD*, i. 1, Par. To grumble, as the bowels.

कर्दम *kardama*, I. m. 1. Mud, Yâjń. 1, 197; Râm. 3, 78, 31 (*rudhira-kardama*, Gore, Pańch. iii. d. 107). 2. Dregs, MBh. 14, 2683. 3. A certain plant, Suçr. 2, 100, 20. 4. The name of a Nâga, MBh. 1, 1561; of a Prajâpati, 12, 2211. II. adj. Soiled, Suçr. 2, 309, 5.—Comp. *Kshâra-*, m. the name of a hell, Bhâg. P. 5, 26, 7. *Yaksha-*, m. a sort of perfumed paste.

कर्पट *karpaṭa* (this and some of the following words seem to be derived from a base *karp*=Lat. carpo), m. and n. Rags, Pańch. 236, 25.

कर्पण *karpaṇa* (see the last), A spear, Daçak. 56, 17.

कर्पर *karpara* (see *karpaṭa*), n. 1. A pot, Pańch. 218, 11. 2. A potsherd, Pańch. 217, 22.—Comp. *Ghaṭa-*, m. a broken jar, Ghaṭak. 22.

कर्पास *karpâsa* (see *karpaṭa*), m. and n. Cotton, Suçr. 2, 481, 13.

कर्पूर् *KARPÛR*, a denominative derived from the next, Par. To smell like camphor, Lass. 67, 15.

कर्पूर *karpûra*, m. and n. Camphor, Pańch. 47, 7.

† कर्ब् *KARB*, and कम्ब् *KAMB*, i. 1, Par. To go.

कर्बु *karbu*, adj. Of a spotted or variegated colour, Yâjń. 3, 166.

कर्बुर *karbu*+*ra*, or कर्वुर *karvura* (with *b* for *v*), adj., f. *râ*. 1. Of a variegated colour, Suçr. 1, 40, 12. 2. Grey, Kumâras. 4, 27.—Cf. probably Κέρβερος.

ऽकर्मक -*karmaka*, i.e. *karman*+*ka*, A substitute for *karman* when the latter part of a comp. adj., e. g. *ad-bhuta-*, adj. One who has done surprising works, MBh. 3, 8102.

कर्मकर *karmakara*, i. e. *karman*-*kṛi*+*a*, adj., f. *rî*, A hired labourer, a servant, Pańch. 10, 4; Kathâs. 13, 94. —Comp. *Gṛiha-*, m. a domestic servant, Pańch. 30, 2.

कर्मकार *karmakâra*, i.e. *karman*-*kṛi*+*a*, adj. A hired labourer, Pańch. 116, 20.

कर्मकृत् *karmakṛit*, i. e. *karman -kṛi + t*, m. A workman, Râjat. 5, 90. —Comp. *Krûra-*, i.e. *krûrakarman-*, adj. doing cruel works, Man. 12, 58. *Sva-*, m. an independent workman.

कर्मज *karmaja*, i.e. *karman-ja* (vb. *jan*), adj. Proceeding from actions, Man. 12, 3.

कर्मठ *karmaṭha* (base *karman*, probably a dialect. form of *karmastha*), adj. Eager, Râjat. 5, 24.

कर्मतस् *karmatas*, i.e. *karman + tas*, adv. **1.** Out of one's works (or with, etc. ?), Man. 12, 98. **2.** Concerning one's business, Daçak. in Chr. 186, 8.

कर्मन् *karman*, i.e. *kṛi + maṇ*, n. **1.** Action, Bhâshâp. 5; Sâv. 2, 28. **2.** Work, Çâk. 22, 17. **3.** Business, Bhag. 18, 42 sqq.; Pańch. 7, 9. **4.** Religious action as sacrifice, etc., Chr. 296, 2 = Rigv. i. 112, 2. **5.** The actions of a former life as the cause of men's subsequent births and fate, Pańch. v. d. 77; cf. *karmatas*, and Pańch. 134, 9.—**Comp.** *Adbhuta-*, adj. one who performs surprising deeds, Râm. 1, 21, 18. *An-ârya-*, adj. one who acts like one who is not an Ârya (like a Çûdra), Man. 10, 73. *Antya-*, n. funeral rites, Man. 11, 197. *Indra-*, m. a name of Vishṇu, Râm. 6, 102, 16. *Kâla-*, m. (?) death, Râm. 6, 72, 11. See *Ku-*; *Kṛita-*, adj. one who has done his duty, Râm. 1, 66, 1. *Keça-*, n. dressing of the hair, MBh. 4, 78. *Krûra-*, I. n. 1. a cruel deed, Suçr. 1, 106, 1. 2. a hard work, Çâk. d. 37 v. r. II. adj. 1. practising cruel deeds, Pańch. i. d. 74 2. f. *aṇî*, cruel, Râm. 2, 75, 6. *Gṛiha-*, n. domestic business, Pańch. 121, 14. *Grâmya-*, n. sensual pleasure, Bhâg. P. 5, 14, 31. *Chitra-*, n. a picture, Kathâs. 6, 50. *Chûḍâ-*, n. the ceremony of tonsure, Man. 2, 35. *Chaura-*, n. roguery, Pańch. 96, 22. *Jâta-*, n. the ceremony on the birth of a child, Man. 2, 27. *Jâla-*, n. fishery, MBh. 13, 2653. *Toya-*, n. a religious ceremony performed with water, MBh. 1, 589. *Tri-*, adj. one who performs the three duties of a Brâhmaṇa, MBh. 13, 6455. *Dâra-*, n. marriage, Man. 4, 5. *Durga-*, n. defences, Râm. 5, 49, 14. *Dushkarman*, i.e. *dus-*, I. n. a bad action, MBh. 5, 415. II. adj. wicked, MBh. 5, 4478. *Dushkṛita-*, i.e. *dus-kṛita-*, m. a sinner, Man. 4, 248. *Nâma(n)-*, n. the ceremony of giving a name to a child, Râm. 1, 19, 14. *Nau-*, n. labour in boats, Man, 10, 34. *Puṇya-*, adj. having done meritorious actions, Indr. 1, 22. *Putra-*, n. a ceremony or sacrifice on the birth of a son, Chr. 55, 4. *Mûla-*, n. a machination with (poisonous) roots, Man. 9, 290 *Yathâ-*, acc. adv. according to the work (allotted to them), Man. 1, 41. *Viçva-*, m. 1. the sun. 2. a son of Brahman, the artist of the gods. 3. a saint. *Shaṭk°*, i.e. *shash-*, m. a Brâhmaṇa who performs the six acts proper for him. *Sa-*, adj. 1. performing any act. 2. following the same business. *Sajja-*, n. preparation. *Su-*, I. adj. 1. one who performs beautiful works, Râjat. 5, 115. 2. virtuous. II. m. the artist of the gods. *Hîna-*, adj. neglecting religious acts.

कर्मनाशा *karmanâçâ*, i.e. *karman -naç + a*, f. The name of a river, the water of which destroys religious merit, Bhâshâp. 161.

कर्ममय *karmamaya*, i.e. *karman + maya*, adj., f. *yî*. **1.** Produced by action, MBh. 3, 129. **2.** Having the nature of action, MBh. 14, 1456. **3.** Active, Bhâg. P. 7, 9, 21.

कर्मरङ्ग *karmaranga*, m. A plant, Averrhoa carambola, Lin., Râm. 3, 17, 8.

कर्मवन्त् *karmavant*, i.e. *karman* + *vant*, adj., f. *vatî*, Working, MBh. 3, 1263.

कर्मान्त *karmânta*, i.e. *karman-anta*, m. **1.** Business, Râm. 5, 12, 39; Man. 8, 419 (public affairs). **2.** Cultivated land, Man. 7, 62.

कर्मान्तर *karmântara*, i.e. *karman-antara*, n. A pause in the performance of sacred actions, Râm. 1, 13, 21.

कर्मान्तिक *karmântika*, i.e. *karmânta* + *ika*, m. A workman, Râm. 1, 12, 7.

कर्मार *karmâra* (base *karman*), m. A blacksmith, Man. 4, 215.

कर्मिन् *karmin*, i.e. *karman* + *in*, adj., f. *iṇî*. **1.** Attached to worldly action, Bhag. 6, 46. **2.** When latter part of a compound word, the aff. *in* generally belongs to the whole compound, not to *karman* alone, e.g. *an-ârya-karmin* is *anâryakarman* + *in*, adj. Doing the work of an Anârya, Man. 10, 73. *pâpa-karmin* is *pâpakarman* + *in*, m. A sinner, MBh. 18, 51. *puṇya-vâgbuddhikarmin*, is *puṇya-vâch-buddhi-karman* + *in*, adj. Pure in word, mind, and action, MBh. 17, 96.

† **कर्व्** *KARV*, i. 1, Par. To be proud.—Cf. *garv*.

कर्वट *karvaṭa*, I. m. and n. A market town, Yâjń. 2, 167. II. m. pl. The name of a country or people, MBh. 2, 1098.

कर्शन *karçana*, i.e. *kṛiç* + *ana*, I. adj. Causing to grow lean, Suçr. 1, 189, 1. II. m. Fire, MBh. 13, 6307.

कर्ष *karsha*, i.e. *kṛish* + *a*, I. m. Dragging, Yâjń. 2, 217. II. m. and n. A certain weight, equal to 16 mâshas, about 280 troy grains, Suçr. 2, 175, 15.

कर्षक *karshaka*,, i.e. *kṛish* + *aka*, m. A cultivator, one who lives by tillage, Yâjń. 2, 265.

कर्षण *karshaṇa*, i.e. *kṛish* + *ana*, n. **1.** Bringing, Çâk. 69, 15, v.r. **2.** Tormenting, Man. 7, 112. **3.** Bending (a bow), Ragh. 11, 46. **4.** Tillage, Man. 4, 5. **5.** Cultivated land, MBh. 3, 10082. **6.** At the end of a compound adj. Overpowering, e.g. *çatru-*, Overpowering his enemies, Râm. 4, 38, 51.

कर्षिन् *karshin*, i.e. *kṛish* + *in*, I. adj., f. *iṇî*. **1.** Dragging, Mṛichchh. 96, 6. **2.** Attracting, Ragh. 19, 11. II. m. A cultivator, Kathâs. 18, 41.

कर्षू *karshû*, i.e. *kṛish* + *u*, f. A furrow, an incision, Suçr. 2, 33, 17.

कर्हि *ka* + *rhi* (see *kim*), adv. At what time; with following *chid*, At any time, Nal. 24, 22; with a negation, Never, e.g. *na karhi chid*, Man. 2, 4. With following *api*, Sometimes, Bhâg. P. 5, 17, 24.

† 1. **कल्** *KAL*, i. 1, Âtm. **1.** To sound. **2.** To count.

2. **कल्** *KAL* (akin to *kṛî*), i. 10, in three forms, *kalaya*, *kalâpaya*, and *kâlaya*, Par. (*kâlaya* Âtm. Râm. 4, 18, 28): *kalaya*, **1.** To impel, Kathâs. 18, 90; *kâlaya*, to drive, MBh. 4, 1007, Bhâg. P. 3, 30, 1. *kalita*, Incited by, Çiç. 9, 59; greedy of, Râm. 5, 83, 10. Comp. *Dhairya-*, adj. steady, calm.— **2.** *kâlaya*, To drive onwards, MBh. 1, 6690; to pursue, Râm. 4, 18, 28. **3.** *kâlaya*, To provoke, Râm. 3, 41, 26. **4.** etc. *kalaya*, To bear, Gît. 1, 16. **5.** To perform, Bhartṛ. 3, 20. **6.** To put in, to fasten, Gît. 12, 26. **7.** To utter, Gît. 11, 9. **8.** To endow, Çiç. 9, 59. **9.** To reckon, Bhartṛ. 2, 37. **10.** To perceive, Çiç. 9, 83. **11.** To consider, Çiç. 9, 58. **12.** † To go: cf. *ud*.—With the prep. **आ** *â*: *kalaya*, **1.** To shake,

MBh.1. 2858. **2.** To catch, Çiç. 9, 72. **3.** To fasten, Kathâs. 20, 52; Çiç. 9, 45. **4.** To surrender, Bhâg. P. 5, 20, 2. **5.** To regard, Prab. 5, 5. **6.** To perceive, Hit. 38, 10.—With **प्रत्या** *prati-â, kalaya,* To enumerate one by one, Daçak. in Chr. 185, 10.—With **उद्** *ud,* I. *kalaya,* To loosen, to deliver, Bhâg. P. 7, 8, 26; *utkalita,* **1.** Opened, Pañch. 184, 18 (where *kâl°* must be changed to *kal°*). **2.** Joyful, Bhâg. P. 7, 8, 34. II. *kalâpaya,* To beg for dismission, Pañch. 244, 25.—With **परि** *pari,* I. *kâlaya,* To pursue, MBh. 15, 1060. II. *kalaya,* To reckon, Çiç. 8, 9. To perceive, Naish. 2, 54.—With **प्र** *pra, kâlaya,* **1.** To drive onwards, MBh. 1, 7178. **2.** To pursue, 3, 10778.—With **सम्** *sam, kâlaya,* **1.** To drive, Hariv. 1191. **2.** To put to flight, MBh. 4, 1981. —Cf. Lat. celer, cello, procella; κέλλω, ὀκέλλω, κέλης, κέλομαι, κελεύω, κολετράω; O.H.G. halôn, holôn, holên.

कल *kala,* I. adj., f. *lâ,* **1.** Dumb (ved.). **2.** Low, Brâhmaṇ. 3, 21; soft, Çâk. d. 85; Ṛit. 6, 29. *kalam,* adv. Softly, Râm. 1, 19, 10. **3.** Indistinct, confused, Megh. 31. **4.** Uttering a low sound, Vikr. d. 119. II. m. A kind of Pitṛis or Manes, MBh. 2, 463. III. Often in compound words after *açru* and *vâshpa,* adj. Indistinct on account of tears, Râm. 2, 106, 33; 2, 34, 53. *vâshpa-kala + m,* adv. MBh. 3, 10839. *vâshpa-kalâ,* f. A torrent of tears, Bhâg. P. 3, 22, 55.—Comp. *Mada-,* 1. adj. speaking like a drunken person. 2. m. an elephant in rut; see *kalâ.*

कलकल *kala-kala,* m. **1.** A confused noise, Râm. 3, 34, 34. **2.** A name of Çiva, MBh. 12, 10378.

कलङ्क *kalaṅka* (probably an anomalous compound, *kala-aṅka*), m. **1.** A spot, Râm. 6, 86, 42. **2.** The rust of iron, Ragh. 13, 15. **3.** Defamation, Pañch. 4, 6, 3.—Comp. *Hariṇa-,* m. the moon.—Cf. *kâla*; κελαινός, κηλίς, κηλάς; Lat. cāligo.

कलङ्कय *KALAṄKAYA,* a denom. derived from the last, Par. To disgrace, Daçak. 124, 1. *kalaṅkita,* **1** Painted, Bhartṛ. 1, 9. **2.** Disgraced, Kathâs. 12, 24.

कलत्र *kalatra,* n. A wife, Bhartṛ. 2, 58.—Comp. *Sa-,* adj. with his wife, Pañch. 46, 14.

कलत्रवन्त् *kalatra + vant,* adj. **1.** Having a wife, Mṛichchh. 67, 3. **2.** With his wives, Râjat. 5, 427.

कलत्रिन् *kalatrin,* i.e. *kalatra + in,* adj. Having a wife. *vasumatyâ nṛipâḥ kalatriṇaḥ,* Kings are wedded to the earth, i.e. the earth is the wife of kings, Ragh. 8, 82.

कलधौत *kala-dhauta,* I. n. **1.** Gold, Gît. 8, 4. **2.** Silver, Çiç. 4, 41. II. adj. Golden, Râm. 3, 60, 12.

कलन *kalana* (cf. *kalaṅka*), I. n. A spot, Bhâg. P. 3, 31, 2. II. f. *nâ,* Subjection, Ânandal. 29. III. As latter part of a comp., Bhartṛ. 3, 72, causing, perhaps to be corrected to *karaṇa.*

कलभ *kalabha* (cf. *karabha*), m. **1.** A young elephant, Pañch. 159, 16. **2.** A young camel, Pañch. 229, 3.

कलम *kalama,* m. A kind of rice, Râm. 5, 74, 11.—Cf. κάλαμος; Lat. calamus; O.H.G. halm; A.S. haelme.

कलविङ्क *kalaviṅka,* m. A sparrow, Man. 5, 12.

कलश *kalaça,* or **कलस** *kalasa,* I. m. (and f. *çî,* and n.), A water-pot, a cup, Pañch. 252, 10; i. d. 225; designation of the ocean when churned, MBh. 1, 1149. **II.** f. *çi*, **1.** A plant, Hemionitis cordifolia, Roxb., Suçr. 1, 139, 15. **2.** The name of a holy place, MBh. 3, 650.

कलह *kalaha*, m. and n. Quarrel, MBh. 2, 1780.—Comp. *Vâkkhalaha*, i.e. *vâch-*, m. a contest about words, Prab. 55, 12. *Çushka-*, m. a quarrel about trifles, Pańch. 171, 25. *Sa-*, adj. quarreling, Kir. 5, 13.

कलहंस *kala-ham̃sa*, m., f. *sî*, A kind of duck or goose, Râm. 2, 82, 9; Kir. 5, 13; Ragh. 8, 58.

कलहाय *KALAHÂYA*, a denom. derived from *kalaha* by *ya*, To quarrel, Pańch. 207, 22 (Par.).

कला *kalâ*, i. e. *kṛi* + *a*, f. **1.** A small part, Man. 8, 36. **2.** A part, Man. 2, 86. **3.** The sixteenth part of the moon's disc, Hit. pr. d. 1. **4.** Interest on capital, Çiç. 9, 32 (at the same time, a sixteenth part of the moon's disc). **5.** A division of time, Man. 1, 64. **6.** One of the seven elements of the human body, as blood, etc., Suçr. 1, 326, 13. **7.** One of the sixty-four mechanical or elegant arts, Râm. 1, 9, 8; Daçak. in Chr. 180, 7; 9.—Comp. *Nishkala*, i.e. *nis-*, adj., f. *lâ*, 1. undivided, MBh. 13, 1044. 2. maimed, infirm, MBh. 3, 13851. *Sa-kala*, adj. f. *lâ*, 1. whole, Vikr. d. 95. 2. all, Pańch. 53, 21; 55, 12.

कलाप *kalâ-pa* (vb. 2. *pâ*), m. **1.** A bundle, MBh. 3, 10772. **2.** A string, Kumâras. 1, 43 (of pearls). **3.** A band (of belts, laces, etc., worn by women round the waist), Ṛit. 3, 20; Bhartṛ. 1, 56. **4.** Totality, Bhâg. P. 9, 4, 21; perfection, Pańch. v. d. 23. **5.** A quiver, MBh. 3, 11454. **6.** A peacock's tail, Pańch. ii. d. 85.

कलापक *kalâpa* + *ka*, m. **1.** A string, MBh. 3, 10055. **2.** A band, Çiç. 9, 45.

कलापवन्त् *kalâpa* + *vant*, adj., f. *vatî*, MBh. 1, 1957 in *tatâyudha-*, i.e. *tata-âyudha-* (vb. *tan*), the aff. *vant* belongs to the whole comp., Wearing a strung bow and a quiver.

कलापशस् *kalâpa* + *ças*, adv. (Made) into bundles, MBh. 13, 4509.

कलापिन् *kalâpin*, i.e. *kalâpa* + *in*, **I.** adj. **1.** Wearing a quiver, MBh. 4, 141 (the aff. *in* belongs to the whole comp.). **2.** With its tail spread out, MBh. 3, 11585 (a peacock). **II.** m. **1.** A peacock, Pańch. ii. d. 85. **2.** A proper name.

कलाभृत् *kalâ-bhṛi* + *t*, m. An artist, Man. 2, 134.

कलाय *kalâya*, m. **1.** Peas, MBh. 13, 5469. **2.** An unknown plant, Çiç. 13, 21.

कलावन्त् *kalâ* + *vant*, **I.** m. The moon, Kumâras. 5, 71. **II.** f. *vatî*, A proper name, Kathâs. 9, 38.

कलि *kali*, i.e. *kṛi* + *i*, m. **1.** A die (ved.). **2.** The game at dice personified, Nal. 6, 14. **3.** The fourth age of the world, Man. 9, 302. **4.** Quarrel, MBh. 3, 12282; Hit. iii. d. 47. **5.** A very wicked king, MBh. 12, 361; 363. **6.** The name of an inferior deity, MBh. 1, 2552. **7.** A proper name, Chr. 297, 15 = Rigv. i. 112, 15.

कलिका *kalikâ*, i.e. *kalâ* + *ka*, f. **1.** The sixteenth part of the moon's disc, Bhartṛ. 3, 1. **2.** A bud, Ṛit. 6, 17.

कलिङ्ग *kalińga*, m. pl. The name of a people and their country, Râm. 2, 71, 16.

कलिन्द *kalinda*, **I.** m. The name of a mountain, on which the Yamunâ rises, Gît. 3, 2; Râm. 2, 71, 6. **II.** f. *kalindî*, Râm. 2, 55, 4; 12; 13; it must be corrected to *kâl°*.

कलिल *kalila* (vb. *kṛî*) I. adj., f. *lâ*, Filled, MBh. 1, 3717. **II.** n. Confusion, Bhag. 2, 52.

कलुष *kalusha* (cf. *kalaṅka* and *kalmasha*), I. adj., f. *shâ*. **1.** Turbid, Vikr. d. 8. **2.** Impure, Man. 10, 57. **3.** Choked, Çâk. d. 81. **4.** Unable, Ragh. 5, 64. **II.** n. **1.** Dirt, Ṛit. 3, 22. **2.** Impurity, Râm. 2, 97, 27.

कलुषाय *KALUSHÂYA*, a denom. derived from the last by *ya*, Âtm. To become turbid.

कलेवर *kalevara*, n. The body, Bhag. 8, 5.—**Comp.** *Dushka°*, i.e. *dus-*, n. the vile body, Bhâg. P. 5, 19, 13.

कल्क *kalka*, m. (and n.) **1.** Sediment, Yâjñ. 1, 276. **2.** Paste, Daçak. in Chr. 199, 13. **3.** Foulness, MBh. 1, 268.—**Comp.** *Tila-*, m. a paste of ground sesame, Mârk. P. 35, 10.

ऽकल्कक *-kalka+ka*, a substitute for the last, when the latter part of comp. adj., *a-* adj. Candid, MBh. 3, 4053.

कल्कन *kalkana* (akin to *kalka*), n. Fraud, Bhâg. P. 1, 14, 4.

कल्कि *kalki* (MBh. 3, 13111), and

कल्किन् *kalkin* (MBh. 3, 13101), m. A name of Vishṇu in his tenth or future avatâra.

कल्प *kalpa*, i.e. *kḷip+a*, I. adj., f. *pâ*. **1.** Able, Bhâg. P. 1, 6, 7; with infin., 4, 13, 42. **2.** Being a match for, able to protect (with gen.), Bhâg. P. 8, 23, 22. **II.** m. **1.** A sacred precept, Man. 5, 74. **2.** A rule, Man. 3, 147. **3.** Performance, MBh. 13, 4728; usage, Daçak in Chr. 189, 17; an act, Çâk. 99, 15. **4.** Manner, Man. 1, 112. **5.** The rules concerning rites, one of the six Vedângas, Man. 2, 140. **6.** A designation of Vishṇu as containing all the sacred precepts, MBh. 13, 953; of Çiva, 12, 10368. **7.** A day of Brahman, a period of 1000 yugas, the duration of the world, Bhâg. P. 3, 11, 23. **8.** Toxicology, Suçr. 1, 8, 5. **III. Comp.** when the latter part of a comp. adj., f. *pâ*, almost like, Râm. 1, 5, 21; 3, 52, 46. *A-*, adj. unable, with loc., Bhâg. P. 7, 12, 23; with infin., 4, 3, 21. *Purâ-*, m. 1. a former creation, Man. 9, 227. 2. a tale of past ages. *Pûrva-*, m. time of old, MBh. 9, 2732. *Prathama-*, m. a principal rule, Man. 11, 30. *Prasanna-* (vb. *sad*), adj. almost quiet, Daçak. in Chr. 200, 6. *Yathâ-kalpa+m*, adv. according to rule, Râm. 1, 11, 14.

कल्पक *kalpa+ka*, m. Rite, MBh. 14, 1571.

कल्पन *kalpana*, i.e. *kḷip+ana*, I. n. **1.** Determination, Prab. 111, 8. **2.** Caparisoning or decorating an elephant, Daçak. 53, 13. **3.** Ornament, MBh. 13, 2784. **II.** f. *nâ*. **1.** A rule, Man. 9, 116. **2.** Performance, Mṛichchh. 47, 17. **3.** Making, Bhâg. P. 2, 5, 42; 4, 18, 32. **4.** Imagination. — **Comp.** *A-satkalpanâ*, i.e. *a-sant-* (vb. *as*), f. deceit, Çâk. 66, 3.

कल्पलतिका *kalpalatikâ*, i.e. *kalpa-latâ+ka*, f. A creeper yielding all wishes, Bhartṛ. 1, 89.

कल्मष *kalmasha* (cf. *kalusha*), m. and n. **1.** Dirt, sediment, Bhâg. P. 8, 7, 43. **2.** A spot, Râm. 2, 36, 27; Daçak. in Chr. 186, 9. **3.** Guilt, Man. 12, 104; sin, 12, 22.—**Comp.** *A-*, adj. sinless, Lass. 52, 7. *Nishkalmasha*, i.e. *nis-*, adj., f. *shâ*, spotless, sinless, Pañch. iii. d. 212. *Vi-*, adj., f. *shâ*, sinless, Râm. 2, 29, 16. *Vi-gata-*, adj. 1. Unsoiled. 2. Pure. *Vîta-*, i.e. *vi-ita*, adj. free from sin or soil.

कल्माष *kalmâsha* (cf. the last), I. adj., f. *shî*, Of a mixed or variegated colour, spotted, MBh. 2, 1043; Râm. 1, 52, 20. **II.** m. The name of a Nâga, MBh. 1, 1552. **III.** f. *shî*, **1.** A cow of variegated colour, Râm. 5, 13, 16. **2.** The name of a river, MBh. 2, 2575.

कल्माषपाद *kalmâsha-pâda*, m. A proper name, Râm. 1, 70, 39.

कल्य *kalya* (i.e. *kṛi* + *ya*, cf. *kalyâṇa*, of which the lingual *ṇ* proves that the original form was *karyâṇa*, cf. also *καιρός*), **I.** adj., f. *yâ*. **1.** Healthy, MBh. 2, 1974. **2.** Ready, MBh. 1, 865. **II.** n. Dawn, MBh. 1, 6304. **III.** *kalya* + *m*, adv. At break of day, MBh. 1, 6304. *kalyam-kalyam*, Every morning, Râm. 4, 44, 112.—Comp. *Ati-kalyam*, adv. too early in the morning, Man. 4, 140.

कल्यपाल *kalyapâla*, see *kalpa-pâla*.

कल्यवर्त *kalyavarta*, m. **1.** *kalya* -*vṛit* + *a*, Breakfast. **2.** A trifle, Mṛichchh. 34, 10.

कल्याण *kalyâṇa* (cf. *kalya*), **I.** adj., f. (*ṇâ*, and) *ṇî*. **1.** Prosperous, Nal. 12, 92. **2.** Blessed, Man. 8, 91; Nal. 8, 10. **II.** n. **1.** Prosperity, welfare, Man. 3, 60. **2.** A virtuous action, Râm. 2, 54, 29. **3.** An entertainment, Man. 8, 392.

कल्याणक *kalyâṇa* + *ka*, adj., f. *ṇikâ*. **1.** Prosperous, Râm. 6, 23, 7. **2.** Useful, excellent, Suçr. 2, 285, 3.

कल्याणिन् *kalyâṇin*, i.e. *kalyâṇa* + *in*, adj. f. *nî*, Blessed, Kathâs. 26, 49.

† **कल्ल्** *KALL*, i. 1, Âtm. **1.** To sound indistinctly. **2.** To be mute.

कल्लोल *kallola*, i.e. *kad-lola*, m. A billow, Bhartṛ. 3, 37.

कल्लोलिनी *kallolinî*, i.e. *kallola* + *in* + *î*, f. A river, Prab. 73, 1.

कल्हण *kalhaṇa*, m. The name of the author of the Râjataraṅgiṇî.

† **कव्** *KAV*, see *kab*.

कवऽ *kava-*, i.e. *ka-va* (cf. *kim* and *kva*). Former part of comp. words, denoting inferiority, cf. *kavoshṇa*.

कवक *kavaka*, n. A mushroom, Man. 5, 3.

कवच *kavacha*, m. and n. Mail, Râm. 3, 50, 3.—Comp. *Nârî-*, adj. having wives as a coat of mail, protected by wives, Bhâg. P. 9, 9, 40. *Nivâta-*, (wearing an impenetrable coat of mail), m. a class of demons, Arj. 5, 10. *Sa-*, adj. clad in armour, mailed.

कवचिन् *kavachin*, i.e. *kavacha* + *in*, **I.** adj. Mailed, Râm. 3, 56, 30. **II.** m. A proper name, MBh. 1, 2733.

कवन्ध *kavandha*, see *kabandha*.

कवर *kavara*, m., f. *rî*, and n. A braid of hair, Amar. 59.

कवरीभृत् *kavarî-bhṛi* + *t*, in *nava -chandrikâ-kusuma-tamaḥ-kav*°, adj. Wearing darkness (i. e. black) like a braid of hair, adorned with the young moon as with fresh flowers, Çiç. 9, 28.

कवल *kavala* (cf. *kavi*, iii.), m. **1.** A mouthful, Bhartṛ. 2, 22; a morsel, Râm. 2, 41, 9. **2.** Water for rinsing the mouth, Suçr. 1, 39, 3.

कवलित *kavalita*, i.e. *kavala* + *ita*, adj. Devoured, Pañch. 213, 6.

कवाट *kavâṭa*, *ṭî*=*kapâṭa*, *ṭî*, q. cf., Râm. 2, 71, 34 (and at the end of a comp. adj. *kavâṭaka*, Kathâs. 19, 24).

कवि *kavi*, i.e. *kû* + *i*, **I.** adj. Wise (ved.). **II.** m. **1.** A wise man, Man. 7, 49. **2.** A poet, Râjat. 5, 203. **3.** A proper name, MBh. 13, 4123. **III.** f. The bit of a bridle, Râm. 1, 53, 18 (cf. *kavala*).—Comp. *Su-*, m. an excellent poet, Râjat. 5, 204.—Cf. κοας in εὐρυ-κόας Λαο-κόων, i.e. ΛαϜο-κόϜων, and *kû*.

कविता *kavi + tâ*, f. Poetry, Râm. Pr. 1.—Comp. *Su-*, f. excellent poetical talent, Bhartr̥. 2, 18.

कवित्व *kavi + tva*, n. Poetic art, Lass. 5, 18; pl. Daçak. 196, 5.

कवोष्ण *kavoshṇa*, i.e. *kava-ushṇa*, adj. Slightly warm, Ragh. 1, 67.

कव्य *kavya*, i.e. *kavi + ya*, n. An oblation to deceased ancestors (the wise men of old), Man. 1, 95.

† **कश्** *KAÇ*, i. 1, Par. To sound. —Cf. *kaṁs*, *kas*, *chhash* and *çaç*.

कश *kaça*, m., and f. *â*, A whip, MBh. 3, 13268; 13272; also **कषा** *kasha*, Râm. 3, 30, 23.

कशिपु *kaçipu*, m. and n. A cushion, Bhâg. P. 2, 2, 4.—Comp. *Hiraṇya-*, m. a Daitya, or demon, slain by Vishṇu.

कशेरु *kaçeru*; also **कसेरु** *kaseru*, m. and f. (*rû*) and n. A kind of grass, Suçr. 1, 377, 18; 2, 223, 11.

कशेरुक *kaçeru + ka*; also **कसेरुक** *kaseruka*, m., and f. (*kâ*) and n. A kind of grass, Suçr. 1, 156, 21.

कशोजू *kaçojû*, i. e. *kaças-jû*, adj. Hastening to the water (passing a river?), Chr. 297, 14=Rigv. i. 112, 14.

कश्मल *kaçmala*, I. m. and n. **1.** Fainting, Chr. 31, 15; 35, 4. **2.** Pusillanimity, MBh. 1, 2060. **3.** Weakness, Bhâg. P. 3, 14, 15. II. adj., f. *lâ*, Dirty, Lass. 75, 11.

कश्मीर *kaçmîra*, m. The name of a country, Cashmere, Râjat. 1, 27.

कश्यप *kaçyapa*, m. The name of a Muni, or sage, Man. 9, 129.—Comp. *Bhû-*, m. a name of Vasudeva.

कष् *KASH* (probably a dialectical form of *harsh*, vb. *kr̥ish*). **1.** i. 1, Par., Âtm. To scratch, to itch, Bhâg. P. 2, 7, 13 (*kashâṇa*, anomalous, or ii. 2). **2.** i. 1, Par. To injure, to destroy, Prab. 90, 3.—Cf. *chhash*, *vrûs*, and *çaç*.

कष *kash + a*, m. The touch-stone, Mr̥ichchh. 48, 12.

कषण *kashaṇa*, i.e. *kash + ana*, n. Rubbing, Kir. 5, 47.

कषा *kashâ*, see *kaça*.

कषाय *kashâya* (probably vb. *kr̥ish*), I. adj., f. *yâ*. **1.** Being of an astringent taste, MBh. 14, 1411. **2.** Fragrant, Megh. 32. **3.** Red, subst. m. and n., red colour, Yâjñ. 1, 272; MBh. 14, 1263; of a colour composed of red and yellow, Mr̥ichchh. 113, 3. II. m. and n. **1.** An astringent juice, Man. 11, 153. **2.** A decoction, Suçr. 2, 175, 9. **3.** Ointment, MBh. 13, 5970. **4.** Dirt, Bhâg. P. 2, 6, 45; impurity, 4, 22, 20. **5.** Stupor, Vedântas. in Chr. 218, 1.—Comp. *a-nishkashâya*, i.e. *a-nis-*, adj. full of impure passions, MBh. 12, 568.

कषायित *kashâyita*, i.e. *kashâya + ita*, adj. Coloured, Prab. 102, 9.

कष्ट *kashṭa*, i.e. *kash + ta*, I. adj. **1.** Bad, Râm. 3, 51, 23; comparat. worse, Man. 7, 53. **2.** Miserable, Bhartr̥. 2, 22. **3.** Heavy, Yâjñ. 3, 29. **4.** Severe, Man. 12, 78. **5.** Dangerous, Man. 7, 186; 210. **6.** Pernicious, Man. 7, 50. II. n. **1.** A blameable action, Râm. 1, 2, 32. **2.** Misfortune, Hit. 72, 15. **3.** Misery, Pañch. 123, 22. Acc. *kashṭam*, adv. Woe! Râm. 3, 79, 46.—Comp. *Adhi-*, n. excessive misery, Bhâg. P. 5, 7, 12.

कस् *KAS* (or **कश्** *KAÇ*), i. 1, Par. To go, Nal. 2, 2.—With the prep. **निस्** *nis*, Caus. To turn out, Pañch. 127, 16 (with *ç* instead of *s*); 224, 5.—Comp. ptcple. of the pf. pass. *danta-nishkâçita*, Hit. 91, 16, showing his teeth (perhaps from *kâç*, q. cf.).—With प्र *pra*, Caus. To cause to open, Ghaṭ. 19.—With वि *vi*, **1.** To burst, Suçr. 1, 247, 12. **2.** To open as a flower, Mâlat. 15, 3. **3.** To rejoice, Bhartṛ. 2, 71. Caus. To cause to blow, Bhartṛ. 2, 65 (*ç* for *s*).—With अनुवि *anu-vi*, To blossom, Bhâg. P. 3, 15, 17.—With प्रवि *pra-vi*, To blow, Çiç. 11, 63.—Cf. *kam̃s*.

कसेरु *kaseru*, and कसेरुक *kaseru-ka*, see *kaçeru* and *kaçeruka*.

कस्तूरिका *kastûrikâ*, and कस्तूरी *kastûrî*, f. Musk, Pañch. 47, 8; Çṛiñgârat. 7.

कस्मात् *kasmât* (abl. sing. n. of *kim*), adv. Why, on what account, Râm. 1, 9, 26.—Comp. *A*-, adv. 1. without a cause, Hit. i. d. 102. 2. instantly, Hit. 18, 2. 3. Suddenly, Sâv. 6, 53.

कह्लार *kahlâra*, n. The white esculent water-lily, Ṛit. 3, 15.

काऽ *kâ-* (see *kim*), former part of comp. words, Bad.—Cf. e.g. *kâpatha*, *kâpurusha*, *kôshṇa*.

† कांश् *KÂM̃S*=*kâç*, i. 1, Âtm.

कांस्य *kâm̃sya*, i.e. *kam̃sa*+*ya*, **I.** adj. Made of brass, Man. 4, 65. **II.** n. **1.** Brass, Man. 5, 114. **2.** A drinking vessel, MBh. 2, 1751.

काक *kâka* (onomatop.), I. m. A crow, Man. 7, 21. II. f. *kî*. **1.** A female crow, Pañch. 52, 23. **2.** A proper name, MBh. 3, 14396.—Comp. *Bhû*-, m. a small kind of heron.

काकतालीय *kâkatâlîya*, i.e. *kâka-tâla*+*îya*, adj. literally, Resembling the crow and the palmyra tree, an unknown fable, and denoting, **1.** Inconsiderate, Râm. 3, 45, 17. °*yam*, adv. By accident, MBh. 12, 6596.

काकतालीयवत् *kâkatâlîya* + *vat*, adv. By accident, Hit. Pr. 34.

काकरुक *kâkaruka* (perhaps *kâka-ru*+*ka*), and काकरूक *kâkarûka*, adj., f. *kâ*, Timid, Pañch. 9, 15.

काकलि and काकली *kâkali*[2] (cf. *kala*), f. **1.** A soft sound, Ṛit. 1, 8; Bhartṛ. 1, 35. **2.** *kâkalî*, A dog-whistle, used for trying whether one be asleep or awake, Daçak. in Chr. 186, 10.

काकाण्डक *kâkâṇḍaka*, i.e. *kâka-aṇḍa*+*ka*, The name of an unknown plant, MBh. 3. 12880.

काकिणी *kâkiṇî*, and काकिनी *kâkinî* (perhaps *kâka* + *in*+*î*), f. A small coin, a quarter of a Paṇa, Pañch. ii. d. 70.

काकु *kâku*, f. Change of voice in fear, grief, etc.; Vikr. d. 42, *asmâkam . . . pratidinam iyam . . . sevâkâku-pariṇatir abhût*, My lot is to be obliged by my office to use every day another voice.

काकुत्स्थ *kâkutstha*, i.e. *kakutstha*+*a*, patron. A descendant of Kakutstha, Râm. 1, 23, 3.

काकोल *kâkola* (cf. *kâka*), I. m. A raven, Man .5, 14. II. n. A division of the infernal regions, or hell, Yâjñ. 3, 223.

काकोलूकीय *kâkolûkîya*, i.e. *kâka-ulûka*+*îya*, n. The war of the crows and owls, Pañch. 148, 1.

काक्षीवत *kâkshîvata*, i. e. *kakshîvant*+*a*, patron., f. *tî*, A descendant of Kakshîvant, MBh. 1, 4695.

काचीवन्त् *kâkshîvant=kakshîvant*, MBh. 1, 224.

काङ्क्ष् *KÂṄKSH* (an old desider. of *kam*, **kaṅkaṁs*, by intermediate *kaṅkas*), i. 1, Par. (in epic poetry also Âtm., MBh. 13, 769). **1.** To wish, Bhag. 12, 17. **2.** To desire, Râm. 4, 17, 18. **3.** To wait for, MBh. 3, 414. **4.** To attend to (with the dat.), Râm. 2, 25, 43. *kâṅkshita*, n. Desire, Râm. 5, 29, 9.—With the prep. **अनु** *anu*, To desire, MBh. 2, 2135 (Âtm.). — With **अभि** *abhi*, To desire, Râm. 2, 49, 15. Caus. To desire, MBh. 3, 12457.—With **आ** *â*, **1.** To desire, MBh. 1, 4286. **2.** To strive for, Yâjń. 1, 153. **3.** To seek (with the gen.), Man. 2, 162. **4.** To turn towards, Man. 3, 258. **5.** To want, Man. 10, 121. **6.** To expect, Râm. 2, 5, 19.—With **प्रत्या** *prati-â*, To expect, MBh. 12, 4870 (Âtm.); to wait for, 4, 734 (Âtm.). — With **समा** *sam-â*, To desire, MBh. 4, 1664. — With **प्र** *pra*, To desire, Suçr. 1, 52, 6.—With **प्रति** *prati*, To long for, Râm. 2, 112, 12 (Âtm.).—With **वि** *vi*, To intend, Hariv. 13136.—Cf. perhaps Goth. huhru; A.S. hungor.

काङ्क्षा *kâṅksh+â*, f. Desire, Nal. 16, 1.

काङ्क्षिता *kâṅkshitâ*, i.e. *kâṅkshin+tâ*, f. Desire, Râm. 2, 34, 28.

काङ्क्षिन् *kâṅksh+in*, adj., f. *iṇî*. **1.** Desiring (with acc.), Râm. 2, 110, 20. **2.** Expecting, Râm. 5, 33, 27.

काच *kâcha*, m. **1.** Glass, Pańch. i. d. 87. **2.** A disease of the eyes, Suçr. 2, 305, 4 sqq.

† **काञ्च्** *KAŃCH*, i. 1, Âtm. **1.** To shine. **2.** To bind.—Cf. *kach*, *kańch*.

काञ्चन *kâńchana*, I. n. **1.** Gold, Man. 2, 239. **2.** Wealth, Bhartṛ. 2, 33. II. adj., f. *nî*, Golden, Man. 5, 112; Râm. 3, 52, 21. III. m. A proper name, Bhâg. P. 9, 15, 3.

काञ्चनमय *kâńchana+maya*, adj., f. *yî*, Golden, Pańch. 236, 5.

काञ्चनवर्मन् *kâńchana-varman*, m. A substitute for the proper name Hiranyavarman, Chr. 53, 21.

काञ्चनीय *kâńchanîya*, i.e. *kâńchana+îya*, adj., f. *yâ*, Golden, MBh. 13, 5039.

काञ्चि *kâńchi*, m. pl. **1.** The name of a people, MBh. 1, 6684. **2.** see *kâńchî*.

काञ्ची *kâńchî*, f. A woman's zone or girdle, usually adorned by small bells, Râm. 5, 10, 12.—Comp. *Sva-kara-avalambana-vi-mukta-galat-kala-kâńchi*, adv. so that her girdle fell down with a sound when loosened by his taking hold of it with his hand, Çiç. 9, 82.

काञ्जिक *kâńjika*, n. Sour gruel, Suçr. 1, 34, 4.

काठिन्य *kâṭhinya*, i.e. *kaṭhina+ya*, n. **1.** Hardness, Çâk. d. 58. **2.** Firmness, Râjat. 5, 440.

काण *kâṇa* (probably a syncope of *eka-akshan+a* by intermediate *kâkshṇa*; cf. Lat. coeles, i.e. *coelo+vit, see *çashpa*), adj., f. *ṇâ*. **1.** One-eyed, monoculous, Man. 3, 155. **2.** Perforated, Pańch. ii. d. 74. **3.** Blind, Vedântas. in Chr. 210, 20; Hit. Pr. d. 11; Bhartṛ. 3, 5 (used of a worn-out coin).

काणेलीमातृ *kâṇelî-mâtṛi*, m. An abusive word; according to glosses: A son of an unmarried woman, Mṛichchh. 14, 5.

काण्ड *kâṇḍa*, m. and n. **1.** The part of a plant from one joint to another (ved.). **2.** A slip, Man. 1, 46. **3.** A stalk, Râm. 2, 91, 15. **4.** A switch, Râm. 2, 89, 19 (97, 24 Gorr.). **5.** An arrow, Hit. 85, 5. **6.** The section of a book, Bhâg. P. 4, 24, 9; Râm. (title of the first, of the second book, etc.); e.g. *âraṇyaka-*, The section comprising the sojourn in the forest (title of the third book). **7.** A bone, Suçr. 2, 31, 5. **8.** A multitude, Mâlav. d. 43; Râm. 1, 30, 15 (corr. *kâṇḍa* for *kaṇḍa*).—Comp. *A-*, adj., f. *ḍâ*. 1. unjust, Râjat. 4, 655. 2. sudden, Hit. iv. d. 82; loc. *ḍe*, suddenly, Çâk. d. 45. *Jaṅghâ-*, a stalk-like leg, Daçak. in Chr. 198, 19. *Danta-*, a stem-like tusk, 188, 18.

कातर *kâtara*, i.e. *katara* + *a* (properly, irresolute), adj., f. *râ*, Timid, Râm. 4, 9, 103; disheartened, Çâk. 56, 13.—Comp. *A-*, adj. resolute, courageous, Râm. 3, 19, 27. *Sa-*, adj. cowardly, Nal. 13, 18.

कातरता *kâtara* + *tâ*, f., and

कातरत्व *kâtara* + *tva*, n. Fear, Çâk. d. 59; Pañch. 216, 11.

कातर्य *kâtarya*, i.e. *kâtara* + *ya*, n. Fear, Râm. 4, 9, 100; apprehension (care), Ragh. 17, 47.

कात्यायन *kâtyâyana*, i.e. *kati*, or *kâtya* + *âyana*, I. patron., f. *nî*, A descendant of *Kati* or *Kâtya*, used as proper name, Râm. 2, 67, 2. II. f. *nî*, A name of Durgâ, Dev. 8, 28.

कादम्ब *kâdamba*, I. m. A kind of goose, Râm. 3, 78, 27. II. i.e. *kadamba* + *a*, n. The flower of the Nauclea cadamba, Roxb., Ragh. 13, 27.—Cf. perhaps, Lat. columba; κόλυμβος; O.H.G. tûba; A.S. dûua.

कादम्बरी *kâdambarî* (for *kâdamba-vârî*), f. **1.** The rain-water which collects in the hollow of the tree Nauclea cadamba when the flowers are in perfection, and which is supposed to be impregnated with their honey, Hariv. 5417. **2.** A spirituous liquor, Çâk. 76, 6 (Prâkṛ.). **3.** A proper name, Sâh. D. 79, 18.

काद्रवेय *kâdraveya*, i.e. *kadrû* + *eya*, metron. m. A serpent, MBh. 1, 2549.

कानक *kânaka*, i.e. *kanaka* + *a*, adj. Golden, Suçr. 1, 99, 5.

कानन *kânana*, n. **1.** A forest, Hiḍ. 1, 42. **2.** A grove, Râm. 3, 68, 12.—Comp. *Krîḍâ-*, n. a grove, Bhartṛ. 3, 15. *Maṇi-*, n. 1. a wood abounding in jewels. 2. the throat.

कानीन *kânîna*, i.e. *kanîna* (ved. young) + *a* (cf. *kanyâ*), adj., f. *nî*. **1.** A son, a daughter, of an unmarried woman, Man. 9, 172. **2.** Serviceable for the pupil of the eye, Suçr. 2, 353, 13.

कान्तक *kânta* + *ka* (see *kam*), m. A proper name, Daçak. in Chr. 195, 13.

कान्तत्व *kânta* + *tva* (vb. *kam*), n. Charm, grace, MBh. 3, 14437.

कान्ताय *KÂNTÂYA*, a denominative derived from *kânta* (vb. *kam*) by *ya*, Âtm. To play the lover, Bhartṛ. 1, 50.

कान्तार *kântâra*, m. and n. **1.** A large forest, Râm. 2, 28, 6. **2.** Wilderness, Râm. 4, 44, 27. **3.** A difficult road, Daçak. in Chr. 188, 10.

कान्तारक *kântâra* + *ka*, m. pl. The name of a people, MBh. 2, 1117.

कान्ति *kânti*, i.e. *kam* + *ti*, f. Beauty, Indr. 5, 7.—Comp. *Sûrya-*, f. 1. sunshine. 2. the flower of the sesamum.

कान्तिमत्ता *kântimattâ*, i.e. *kântimant* + *tâ*, f. Beauty, Kumâras. 4, 5.

कान्तिमन्त् *kânti* + *mant*, adj., f. *matî*, Beautiful, Râm. 4, 44, 103.

कांदिश् *kâm̃diç*, i.e. *kâm* (acc. sing. f. of *kim*) -*diç* (based on an acc. *kâm̃ diçam*, literally 'to what quarter'), adj. Fugitive, MBh. 12, 6320.

कांदिशीक *kâm̃diç* + *îka*, adj. Fugitive, Çukas. 62.

कान्यकुब्ज *kânyakubja*, i.e. *kanyakubja* + *a*, n. The name of a city, the modern Canouj, Pańch. 244, 22.

कापथ *kâ-patha*, m. A bad road, Râm. 2, 108, 7.

कापाल *kâpâla*, i.e. *kapâla* + *a*, adj. Made of skulls, Râm. 1, 56, 12.

कापालिक *kâpâlika*, i.e. *kapâla* + *ika*, I. m. A follower of a certain Çaiva sect, Bhartṛ. 1, 64. II. adj. Practised by a Kâpalika, Prab. 57, 12.—Cf. *kapâlika* I.

कापालिन् *kâpâlin*, m. 1.=*kapâlin* III. MBh. 13, 1217 (perhaps with lengthened *a* on account of the metre). 2. A proper name, Hariv. 9196.

कापिल *kâpila*, i.e. *kapila* + *a*, adj. Referring or peculiar to Kapila, Râm. 1, 41, 3; MBh. 12, 12218.

कापिलेय *kâpileya*, i.e. *kapila* + *eya*, m. A descendant of Kapila, MBh. 12, 7886.

कापिशायन *kâpiçâyana*, n. A spirituous liquor, Çiç. 10, 4.

कापुरुष *kâ-purusha*, I. m. 1. A contemptible man, Pańch. i. d. 31. 2. A coward, Râm. 6, 89, 5. II. adj. Cowardly, Râm. 6, 88, 13.

कापेय *kâpeya*, i.e. *kapi* + *eya*, adj., f. *yî*, Peculiar to monkeys, Râm. 6, 111, 19.

कापोत *kâpota*, i.e. *kapota* + *a*, I. adj., f. *tî*, peculiar to pigeons, MBh. 3, 15408. II. f. *tî*, The name of a plant, Suçr. 2, 173, 12.

काम *kâma*, i.e. *kam* + *a*, I. m. 1. Wish, Râm. 2, 90, 23. 2. Desire, Indr. 5, 61. 3. Love, Man. 2, 94; 214. 4. Intention, Man. 9, 248. 5. A desired object, Man. 9, 304. 6. The god of love, Indr. 5, 49. II. acc. *kâmam*, adv. 1. At one's pleasure, Man. 2, 189. 2. Willingly, MBh. 3, 298; Ragh. 12, 75. 3. With following *na*, Rather than, Hit. i. d. 125; Man. 9, 89. 4. Indeed, Çak. 26, 16. 5. Only, Râm. 5, 94; 21. III. When the latter part of a comp. adj., f. *mâ*. 1. Desiring, Man. 2, 37. 2. Loving, Râm. 3, 55, 29. 3. An infin. ending in *tum* drops its final before it; cf. *kartukâma*.—Comp. *A*-, adj., f. *mâ*, exempt from desire, Man. 2, 4. 2. unwilling, without one's consent, Man. 8, 364. *Artha*-, I. m. du. wealth and pleasure, Daçak. in Chr. 181, 24. II. adj. desiring wealth, Nal. 17, 47. *Nishkâma*, i.e. *nis*-, adj. disinterested, Man. 12, 89. *Pum̃s*-, adj., f. *mâ*, wishing for a lover or husband, Hiḍ. 3, 15. *Priya*-, adj. benevolent, Brâhmaṇ. 2, 23. *Bandhu*-, adj. one who loves his kinsmen, Brâhmaṇ. 1, 23. *Yathâ-kâma* + *m*, adv. at pleasure. *Vîta*-, i.e. *vi-ita*-, adj. free from desire. *Sa*-, I. adj. 1. one who has attained his desire, Râm. 3, 52, 52. 2. being in love, Ṛit. 6, 2. II. -*mam*, adv. 1. with pleasure, Pańch. 44, 9. 2. indeed, Daçak. in Chr. 195, 4 (for aught I care). *Svapna*-, adj. wishing to sleep. *Hita*-, adj. wishing well to, friendly to, Pańch. i. d. 360.

कामकार *kâma-kâra*, m. Free will, Râm. 3, 66, 6.

कामकारतस् *kâmakâra + tas*, adv. Voluntarily, Man. 11, 41.

कामग *kâma-ga* (vb. *gam*), I. adj., f. *gâ*, 1. Coming by one's own free will, Nal. 18, 23. 2. Going as one lists, Râm. 3, 48, 5. II. f. *gâ*, A lascivious woman, Yâjń. 3, 6.

कामगम *kâma-gam + a*, adj., f. *mâ*, Going as one lists, Râm. 5, 13, 5.—Comp. *Sarva-*, yielding every desired object, MBh. 13, 357.

कामचर *kâma-char + a*, adj. One who comes by his own free will, MBh. 4, 222.

कामचरत्व *kâmachara + tva*, n. Roving at will, Kathâs. 18, 208.

कामचार *kâmachâra*, i. e. *kâma -char + a*, I. adj. Going as one lists, MBh. 13, 4175. II. m. Free will, intention, Yâjń. 2, 162.

कामचारतस् *kâmachâra + tas*, adv. Through sensual indulgence, Man. 2, 220.

कामज *kâma-ja* (vb. *jan*), adj. Produced from love of pleasure, Man. 7, 46; 9, 107.

कामठ *kâmaṭha*, i. e. *kamaṭha + a*, adj. Belonging or proper to the tortoise, Râm. 1, 45, 30.

कामतस् *kâma + tas*, adv. 1. By inclination, Man. 3, 12. 2. At one's pleasure, 5, 90. 3. Intentionally, 4, 207.—Comp. *A-*, adv. 1. unwillingly, Man. 2, 181. 2. unintentionally, 9, 242.

कामत्व *kâma-tva*, n. Love of pleasure, Lass. 40, 5.

कामदुघ *kâmadugha*, i. e. *kâma -duh + a*, adj., f. *ghâ*, Yielding every wish, MBh. 13, 3165.

कामदुह् *kâma-duh*, adj., nom. sing. *-dhuk*, Yielding every wish, MBh. 13, 2700.

कामदुह *kâma-duh + a*, adj., f. *hâ*, Yielding every wish, MBh. 3, 12725.

कामन्दकि *kâmandaki*, patron. (*kamandaka + i*). A proper name, Pańch. 122, 1.

काममय *kâma + maya*, adj., f. *yî*, Meeting all wishes, Râm. 4, 33, 6.

कामया *kâma + yâ*, adv. (either the ved. instr. sing. of *kâma*, or that of a lost noun *kâmâ*), For my sake, MBh. 2, 728.

कामरसिक *kâmarasika*, i. e. *kâma -rasa + ika*, adj. Libidinous, Bhartṛ. 3, 51.

कामरूपधर *kâmarûpadhara*, i. e. *kâma-rûpa-dhṛi + a*, adj., f. *râ*, Changing one's shape as one lists, Râm. 1, 9, 27.

कामरूपिन् *kâmarûpin*, i. e. *kâma rûpa + in*, adj., f. *iṇî*, Changing one's shape as one lists, MBh. 3, 367.

कामल *kâmala*, I. (m. and) f. *lâ*, A disease of the bile, Suçr. 1, 193, 15. II. f. *lî*, A proper name, Hariv. 1453.

कामलिन् *kâmalin*, i. e. *kâmala + in*, adj., f. *nî*, Jaundiced, Suçr. 2, 469, 3.

कामवन्त् *kâma + vant*, adj., f. *vatî*, Loving, MBh. 1, 3869.

कामसू *kâma- û*, adj. Granting desires, Ragh. 5, 33.

कामात्मता *kâmâtmatâ*, i.e. *kâmâtman + tâ*, f. Sensuality, Man. 2, 2.

कामात्मन् *kâmâtman*, i. e. *kâma -âtman*, adj. Voluptuous, Man. 7, 27.

कामिक *kâmika*, i.e. *kâma + ika*, I.

adj., f. *kî*. **1.** Wished, wish, MBh. 13, 6025. **2.** Wishing, 1969. **3.** In *sarva-kâmika* the aff. *ika* belongs to the comp. *sarva-kâma*, Attaining all one's desires, MBh. 3, 13860.

कामिता *kâmitâ*, i.e. *kâmin* + *tâ*, f. Love, Hit. i. d. 104.

कामिन् *kâmin*, i. e. *kama* + *in*, **I.** adj., f. *nî*. **1.** Desiring, MBh. 13, 7060. **2.** Having sexual intercourse, MBh. 1, 4185. **II.** m. A lover, MBh. 4, 978. **III.** f. *nî*, A beloved one, Man. 8, 112.—**Comp.** *A-*, m. one who is not in love, Pañch. i. d. 180. *Kâma-*, adj. fostering wishes, Bhag. 2, 70. *Sarva-*, i. e. *sarvakâma* + *in*, adj. abounding in all pleasures, Sund. 1, 31 (v.r.).

कामुक *kâmuka*, i.e. *kam* + *uka*, **I.** adj., f. *kâ* and *kî*, Desirous, Râm. 2, 74, 7. **II.** m. A lover, Râm. 5, 16, 42.—**Comp.** *Vañchitâneka-*, i.e. *vañchita-an-eka-*, adj., f. *kâ*, one who has deceived many lovers, Kathâs. 12, 190.

कामुकत्व *kâmuka* + *tva*, n. Lasciviousness, Megh. 25.

काम्पिल्य *kâmpilya*, i.e. *kâmpila* (the name of a country) + *ya*, **I.** adj., f. *yâ*, Belonging to Kâmpila, Kathâs. 25, 53; with *pura* or *purî*, or without a subst., ntr. Its capital, MBh. 1, 5512; Râm. 1, 34, 46; Chr. 52, 14. **II.** m. A proper name, Bhâg. P. 9, 21, 32.

काम्बोज *kâmboja*, i.e. *kamboja* + *a*, **I.** adj. Originating from Kamboja, Râm. 5, 12, 36. **II.** m. The king of Kamboja, MBh. 1, 6995. **III.** m. pl. The name of the people and of the country of Kamboja, MBh. 1, 2668.

काम्य *kâmya*, i.e. **I.** the ptcple. of the fut. pass. of *kam*. **1.** Amiable, Ragh. 6, 30. **2.** Agreeable, Râm. 5, 43, 13. **3.** Precious, Râm. 2, 25, 9. **II.** *kâma* + *ya*, adj. Connected with a wish, interested, Man. 12, 89. **III.** f. *yâ*, The name of an Apsaras, MBh. 1, 4820. **IV.** f. *yâ*, Desire, Man. 5, 27.—**Comp.** *Itaretarakâmyâ*, i.e. *itara-itara-*, f.; instr. sing. according to their several fancies, Man. 3, 35. *Tvaddhitakâmyâ*, i.e. *tvad-hita-*, f. desire of benefitting thee, Chr. 15, 2. *Badha-kâmyâ*, f. intention to hurt, Man. 4, 165. *Sarva-kâmya*, adj. deserving to be wished for by every one, Sund. 4, 7. *Hita-*, f. *yâ*, concern for another's welfare.

काम्यक *kâmya* + *ka*, n. The name of a forest, MBh. 3, 218.

काम्यता *kâmya* + *tâ*, f. Beauty, MBh. 13, 1032.

काय *kâya*, **I.** (base *ka*, a name of the god Prajâpati). **1.** m. A nuptial form called Prâjâpatya, Man. 3, 38. **2.** n. The root of the little finger, Man. 2, 59. **II.** i.e. *chi* + *a*, m. The body, Bhag. 5, 11.—**Comp.** *Ati-*, I. adj. gigantic, Râm. 5, 56, 124. II. m. the name of a Râkshasa, Râm. 6, 51, 3 sqq. *Pûrva-*, m. the fore-part of the body, Çâk. d. 7. *Yaçaḥ-kâya*, m. a body consisting of glory, i.e. glory, Bhartṛ. 2, 21. *Svarṇa-*, m. Garuḍa.

कायस्थ *kâya-stha* (vb. *sthâ*), m. A mixed tribe or caste, the writer caste; a writer, Râjat. 5, 174; 264; 438.

कायिक *kâyika*, i.e. *kâya* + *ika*, adj., f. *kâ* (Man. 8, 153) and *kî*. **1.** Corporeal, bodily, Man. 12, 8; Suçr. 1, 12, 2. **2.** (viz. *vṛiddhi*, Immoderate profits) from a pledge to be used by way of interest, Man. 8, 153.

1. **कार** *kâra*, i.e. *kṛi* + *a*, **I.** adj., f. *rî*. Latter part of a comp. adj. Making, a maker of, e.g. *andha-kâra*, *mâlâ-kâra*, *ratha-kâra*. *danta-*, m. An artist in ivory, Râm. 2, 83, 14. *dyûta-* (vb. *div.*) m. A gamester, Pañch. i.

d. 431. *parva(n)-*, adj. Working at festivals. *bhasma(n)-*, m. A washerman. *su-varṇa-*, *svarṇa-*, and *hema-*, m. A goldsmith. II. m. Latter part of comp. substantives, Making, action. Cf. e. g. *kâma-kâra*, *purusha-kâra*; especially used after letters to form their name, e.g. *a-kâra*, the letter *a*; *u-kâra*, the letter *u*; *ma-kâra*, the letter *ma(m)*, Man. 2, 76.

2. कार *kâra*, i.e. *kara* + *a*, adj. Produced by hail, Suçr. 1, 170, 1.

कारक *kâraka*, i.e. *kṛi*+*aka*, I. adj., f. *rikâ*, Making. Latter part of nominal comps., e.g. *kshema-*, adj. Causing security, Pańch. v. d. 89. *gṛiha-*, m. A carpenter, Yâjń. 3, 146. *priya-*, adj. Causing love, Man. 7, 204; *guru-vachana-*, adj. Performing the order of one's teacher; *mańgala-*, adj. Giving joy, MBh. 2, 1925; *çilpa-*, adj. Versed in an art, Mâlav. 65, 15. II. m. An agent; doing, Yâjń. 2, 233; causing, 3, 150; an author, MBh. 13, 247. *siṁha-*, m. A maker of lions, Pańch. v. d. 31. III. f. *rikâ*, A metrical explanation, a memorial verse, MBh. 2, 453.

कारण *kâraṇa*, i.e. *kṛi*, Caus., + *ana*. I. m. 1. Motive, Pańch. iii. d. 99. 2. Cause, Suçr. 1, 310, 4; Kathâs. 3, 31 (with the loc.). 3. Primary cause, Man. 5, 152; Bhartṛ. 2, 82. 4. An element, Yâjń. 3, 148. 5. Basis, Man. 11, 84. 6. Argument, Nal. 16, 27; proof, Man. 8, 200. 7. An instrument, a means, Râm. 1, 65, 10 (cf. Gorr. 1, 67, 4, who reads *upâyaiḥ*). 8. An organ of sense, Ragh. 16, 22. 9. Abl. *kâraṇât*, and loc. *ṇe*, On account of, Râm. 5, 56, 136; 5, 28, 9. Instr. *ṇena*, By some reason, Châṇ. 23. *yena kâraṇena*, Because, Pańch. 175, 10. *kiṁ punaḥ kâraṇam*, From what motive, MBh. 1, 3600. II. f. *ṇâ*, Torture, Daçak. in Chr. 195, 16. — Comp. *A-*, adj. 1. unreasonable, Pańch. 246, 6. 2. *A-kâraṇam* and *a-kâraṇena*, without cause, Vikr. d. 54; Yâjń. 2, 234. *Anna-kâraṇam*, on account of (supplying) food, Man. 5, 94. *Kârya-*, n. aim and motive, Pańch. i. d. 462. *Nishkâraṇa*, i.e. *nis-*, adj. 1. not proceeding from any cause, Bhâg. P. 8, 3, 15. 2. disinterested, Pańch. ed. orn. 41, 19. 3. Acc. *ṇam*, and abl. *ṇât*, adv. without a special motive, MBh. 12, 4993; Râm. 6, 10, 23. *Yatkâraṇam*, and *ṇât*, i.e. *yad-*, adv. because, Pańch. 30, 21; 135, 16.

कारणतस् *kâraṇa*+*tas*, adv. By some reason, Ragh. 10, 19. *kârya-*, adv. From the relation of cause and effect, Hit. i. d. 33.

कारणता *kâraṇa*+*tâ*, f., and कारणत्व *kâraṇa* + *tva*, n. Causality, Kumâras. 2, 6; Bhâshâp. 14. Being the cause, Bhâg. P. 3, 26, 26.

कारणिक *kâraṇika*, i.e. *karaṇa* + *ika*, m. A judge, Pańch. 237, 20.

कारण्डव *kâraṇḍava*, m. A sort of duck, Râm. 2, 27, 18.

कारंधम *kâraṁdhama*, i.e. *karaṁdhama*+*a*, patron. I. m. MBh. 14, 63. II. n. The name of a holy place, MBh. 1, 7843.

कारयितृ *kârayitṛi*, i.e. *kṛi*, Caus., + *tṛi*, m. Giving the power of acting, MBh. 3, 7000; Man. 12, 12.

कारा *kârâ*, f. A gaol, Daçak. in Chr. 198, 9.

कारावर *kârâvara*, m. The name of a mixed caste, viz. of the offspring of a Nishâda by a Vaidehî woman, Man. 10, 36.

कारिन् *kârin*, i.e. *kṛi*+*in*, adj., f. *iṇî*, An agent, Râm. 2, 78, 8; MBh. 13, 4304; acting, Man. 7, 26.—It is generally the latter part of a comp. adj., e.g. *a-kârya-*, adj. **1.** One who does a wrong action, Man. 11, 239. **2.** One who does not what ought to be done, i.e. who neglects his duty, Man, 5, 107. *a-klishṭa-*, adj. Indefatigable, Râm. 3, 31, 1. *âpta-*, adj. Acting properly, Man. 9, 12 (in a trustworthy manner). *keça-*, m. f. *iṇî*, A hair-dresser, MBh. 4, 412. *kshipra-*, adj. Clever, Râm. 3, 36, 10. *gṛiha-*, m. A kind of wasp. Man. 12, 66. *tatkarmakârin*, i.e. *tad-karman-*, adj. Doing the same, Man. 9, 261. *dṛiḍha-*, adj. Persevering in good actions, Man. 4, 246. *vighna-*, adj. **1.** Obstructing. **2.** Fearful.

कारीष *kârîsha*, i.e. *karîsha* + *a*, I. adj. Sprung up from dung, Suçr. 1, 224, 11. II. n. A great quantity of dung, Hariv. 4355.

कारु *kâru*, i.e. *kṛi* + *u*, adj. and s., f. *rû*, Working, an artisan, Man. 8, 360.

कारुक *kâru* + *ka*, m., and f. *kâ*, An artisan, Man. 4, 219.

कारुणिक *kâruṇika*, i.e. *karuṇa* + *ika*, adj. Compassionate, MBh. 4, 1500.

कारुणिकता *kâruṇika* + *tâ*, f. Compassion, Bhâg. P. 5, 13, 24.

कारुण्य *kâruṇya*, i.e. *karuṇa* + *ya*, n. Compassion, Pañch. ii. d. 25.

कारुष *kârusha*, m. The offspring of a Vrâtya, or an outcast of the Vaiçya tribe, Man. 10, 23.

कारूष *kârûsha*, m. **1.** The name of a country, MBh. 2, 1864. **2.** pl. Its people, Bhâg. P. 9, 2, 16. **3.** Its king, Hariv. 4954.

कारूषक *kârûsha-ka*, adj. Belonging to the Kârûshas, MBh. 1, 2700.

कार्कश्य *kârkaçya*, i.e. *karkaça* + *ya*, n. **1.** Hardness, Pañch. i. d. 205. **2.** Harshness, Amar. 24. **3.** Rough labour, MBh. 13, 5551.

कार्तयुगऽ *kârtayuga-*, i. e. *kṛita-yuga* + *a*, adj. Belonging to the age called Kṛita, MBh. 1, 3600.

कार्तवीर्य *kârtavîrya*, i.e. *kṛita-vîrya* + *a*, patron. m. A name of the Arjuna killed by Paraçurâma, MBh. 3, 141.

कार्तस्वर *kârtasvara*, i.e. *kṛita-svara* + *a*, n. Gold, MBh. 13, 4196.

कार्तान्तिक *kârtântika*, i. e. *kṛita-anta* + *ika*, m. An astrologer, Daçak. in Chr. 180, 13; 197, 12.

कार्त्तिक *kârttika*, i.e. *kṛittikâ* + *a*, I. m. The name of a month (October-November), MBh. 2, 918. II. f. *kî*, The day of this month on which the moon is full, MBh. 3, 4073.

कार्त्तिकेय *kârttikeya*, i.e. *kṛittikâ* + *eya*, m. The god of war, Râm. 1, 37, 20.

कार्त्स्न *kârtsna*, i. e. *kṛitsna* + *a*, n. Totality, Suçr. 1, 94, 11.

कार्त्स्न्य *kârtsnya*, i. e. *kṛitsna* + *ya*, n. Totality; instr. *yena*, Comprehensively, Man. 3, 183.

कार्दम *kârdama*, i.e. *kardama* + *a*, adj. **1.** Muddy, Râm. 5, 27, 16. **2.** Belonging to the Prajâpati Kardama, Bhâg. P. 3, 24, 6.

कार्पटिक *kârpaṭika*, i.e. *karpaṭa* + *ika*, m. A pilgrim, Skandap. Kâçîkh. 12, 14; 30, 66.

कार्पण्य *kârpaṇya*, i.e. *kṛipaṇa* + *ya*, n. **1.** Misery, Bhag. 2, 7; Râm. 5, 19, 17. **2.** Compassion, Bhâg. P. 5, 8, 10.

कार्पास *kârpâsa*, i. e. *karpâsa* + *a*, I. adj., f. *sî*, Made of cotton, Man. 2,

44. II. m. and n. 1. Cotton, Man. 8, 326. 2. Cotton cloth, Suçr. 1, 25, 3.

कार्पासिक *kârpâsika*, i.e. *karpâsa* + *ika*, adj. Made of cotton, Râm. 5, 49, 5.

कार्मिक *kârmika*, i.e. *karman* + *ika*, n. A figured web, Yâjń. 2, 180.

कार्मुक *kârmuka*, i.e. *krimuka* (the name of a tree, ved.) + *a*, n. A bow, Man. 11, 138.—**Comp.** *Bhîma-*, adj., f. *kâ*, having formidable bows, MBh. 4, 1241.

कार्मुकाय *KÂRMUKÂYA*, a denomin. derived from the last by *ya*, Âtm. To become a bow, Çringârat. 13.

कार्मुकिन् *ârmukin*, i.e. *kârmuka* + *in*, adj. Wearing a bow, Râm. 3, 55, 12.

कार्य *kârya*, I. ptcple. of the fut. pass. of 1. *kṛi*, cf. *kṛi*. 1. What ought to be made, to be done, etc., Man. 3, 248; superl. *kâryatama*, That which must be done first, Râm. 5, 77, 16. 2. With an instr. To be used; use, Pańch. i. d. 81 (*triṇena kâryam̃ bhavatiçvarâṇâm*, kings use a blade of grass); with *na*, No use, Râm. 1, 30, 5 (we do not care for possessing the earth); 2, 21, 60 (I am indifferent to life and joy). II. n. 1. Intention, Râm. 1, 18, 15. 2. Duty, Man. 3, 80. 3. Service, Man. 10, 47. 4. Business, Man. 9, 299; affairs, 7, 59. 5. A law-suit, 8, 43. 6. Effect, Vedântas. in Chr. 207, 22.—**Comp.** *A-*, I. adj. not to be done. II. n. a wrong action. *Agni-*, n. the management of the sacrificial fire, Man. 2, 69. *Udaka-*, n. 1. ablution, MBh. 1, 791. 2. obsequies, Râm. 3, 73, 38. *Eka-*, I. n. the same work, MBh. 2, 791. II. adj. having the same intention, Pańch. 182, 5. *Kṛita-*, adj. 1. having accomplished a business, Yâjń. 2, 189. 2. satisfied, Râm. 6, 97, 21; 2, 99, 11. 3. not wanting (with instr.), MBh. 13, 3862. *Gṛiha-*, n. the affairs of the house, Man. 5, 150. *Charmakârya*, i.e. *charman-*, n. leather work, Man. 10, 49. *Deva-*, n. an oblation to the deities, Man. 3, 203. *Dharma-*, n. a sacred duty, Man. 9, 76. *Pitṛi-*, n. an oblation to the Pitris or Manes, Man. 3, 203. *Putra-*, n. a ceremony or sacrifice on the birth of a son, Chr. 50, 16. *Mitra-*, n. duty, service, of a friend, Râm. 6, 107, 12. *Samûha-*, n. the affairs of a community, Yâjń. 2, 189.

कार्यत्व *kârya* + *tva*, n. Condition of being an effect, Bhâg. P. 3, 26, 26.

कार्यवत्ता *kâryavattâ*, i.e. *kâryavant* + *tâ*, f. Business, Râm. 5, 46, 17.

कार्यवन्त् *kârya* + *vant*, adj., f. *vatî*, Occupied, Man. 9, 74.

कार्यार्थ *kâryârtha*, i.e. *kârya-artha*, m. An important matter, Man. 7, 167. Acc. °*tham*, adv. 1. For a special end, Man. 7, 164. 2. On account of judicial proof, 8, 110. 3. For the purpose of work, 10, 55.

कार्यार्थिन् *kâryârthin*, i.e. *kârya* -*arthin*, adj. Demanding justice, Mṛichchh. 138, 9.

कार्यिक *kâryika*, i. e. *kârya* + *ika*, adj. Demanding justice, Man. 7, 124.

कार्यिन् *kâryin*, i.e. *kârya* + *in*, adj. Demanding justice, Man. 8, 2.

कार्श्य *kârçya*, i.e. *kṛiça* + *ya*, n. 1. Meagerness, Megh. 30. 2. Smallness, Ragh. 5, 21.

कार्षक *kârshaka*, i.e. *kṛishi* + *aka*, m. A husbandman, Râjat. 5, 169.

कार्षापण *kârshâpaṇa*, i.e. *karsha* -*âpaṇa* + *a*, m. and n. A coin, Man. 8, 136.

कार्षिक *kârshika,* i.e. *karsha* + *ika,* adj. Being of the weight of a karsha, Man. 8, 136.

कार्ष्ण *kârshṇa,* i.e. *kṛishṇa* + *a,* adj. f. *ṇî.* **1.** Made of the hide of the black antelope, Man. 2, 41. **2.** Composed by Kṛishṇa, MBh. 1, 261.

कार्ष्णायस *kârshṇâyasa,* i.e. *kṛishṇâyas,* or °*yasa* + *a,* I. adj., f. *sî,* Of iron, Man. 11, 133. **II.** n. Iron, Man. 10, 52.

कार्ष्णि *kârshṇi,* i.e. *kṛishṇa* + *i,* patron., m. Offspring of Kṛishṇa, MBh. 1, 4812.

कार्ष्ण्य *kârshṇya,* i.e. *kṛishṇa* + *ya,* n. **1.** Blackness, MBh. 1, 4236. **2.** Darkness, Râjat. 5, 94 (in a comp. adj. *vyakta-,* vb. *añj* with *vi,* Dark).

† **काल्** *KÂL,* i. 10 (rather a denom. derived from the next), Par. To count time.

1. **काल** *kâla,* m. **1.** Due season, Man. 2, 80; instr. *kâlena,* In due season, Man. 9, 246. **2.** Time, Man, 1, 24; 7, 183; instr. *kâlena,* and abl. *kâlât,* In the long run, Pańch. 32, 24; Man. 8, 251; gen. *dîrghasya kâlasya,* After a long time, Nal. 18, 1; *kasya chit kâlasya,* After some time, Çâk. 110, 15. **3.** Meal-time; there are two meal-times a day, therefore, *shashṭha kâla,* The sixth meal-time = the evening of the third day, MBh. 13, 5175; Râm. 3, 31, 47. **4.** A period, Râjat. 5, 73. **5.** Death, Bhâg. P. 9, 9, 2. **6.** Time personified, fate, MBh. 13, 56; Râm. 6, 70, 35; endowed with the attributes of Yama, the regent of the dead, Râm. 1, 21, 13; 3, 35, 43, etc.—**Comp.** *A-,* m. unseasonableness, Sund. 2, 31; loc. *le,* unseasonably, Man. 3, 105. *Âdi-,* m. beginning of time, Râm. 3, 20, 6. *Ṛitu-,* m. 1. seasonable time, MBh. 3, 14763. 2. time approved for sexual intercourse, Man. 3, 45. *Eka-kâla* + *m,* adv. once, Man. 6, 55. *Kârya-,* m. time of action, Böhtl. Ind. Spr. 1809. *Kṛita-,* I. m. appointed time, Yâjń. 2, 184. II. adj. having waited a certain time, MBh. 2, 1875. *Chaturtha-kâla* + *m,* adv. at the fourth meal-time, i.e. on the evening of every second day, Man. 11, 109. *Tad-kâla* + *m,* adv. instantly, Pańch. 192, 6. *Tâvatkâla* + *m,* i.e. *tâvant-,* adv. such a long time, MBh. 3, 16889. *Tri-,* n. 1. past, future, and present time, Bhâg. P. 5, 23, 8. 2. morning, noon, and evening, MBh. 13, 6607. *Dushkâla,* i.e. *dus-,* m. the formidable, all-destroying, time, Râm. 2, 33, 21; a name of Çiva, MBh. 12, 10418. *Nitya-kâla* + *m,* adv. continually, Man. 2, 58. *Parva(n)-,* m. the periodic change of the moon. *Prâpta-kâla* + *m* (vb. *âp* with *pra*), adv. in due season, Pańch. 16, 6. *A-prâpta-kâla* + *m,* adv. Out of due season, Böhtl. Ind. Spr. 173. *Yathâ-kâla* + *m,* adv. At the proper time, Man. 2, 39. *Sa-kâla* + *m,* adv. Betimes, early in the morning. *Sûrya-,* m. day.

2. **काल** *kâla* (cf. *kalańka*), **I.** adj., f. *lî,* Dark blue, black, Râm. 6, 67, 2; MBh. 16, 57. **II.** m. **1.** A black and poisonous snake, Coluber naga, Lass. 16, 13. **2.** The black in the eye, Suçr. 2, 336, 20. **3.** A name of Rudra, Bhâg. P. 3, 12, 12. **4.** A proper name, Hariv. 189. **5.** The name of a mountain, Râm. 4, 44, 21. **III.** f. *lâ.* **1.** The name of several plants, Suçr. 1, 131, 19, etc. **2.** A proper name, MBh. 1, 2520. **3.** The name of a female demon, Hariv. 11552. **IV.** f. *lî.* **1.** A name of Durgâ, MBh. 4, 195. **2.** A surname of Satyâvatî, Chr. 6, 1.—**Comp.** *Bhadra-kâlî,* f. 1. a name of Durgâ. 2. a fragrant grass, Cyperus. *Mahâ-,* I. m. a name of Çiva. II. f. *lî,* Durgâ.—Cf. κελαινός, etc., under *kalańka.*

कालक *kâla + ka*, I. m. **1.** The black in the eye, Suçr. 2, 304, 2. **2.** A sort of grain, Suçr. 1, 73, 5. **3.** The name of a Râkshasa, or demon, Râm. 3, 29, 30; of an Asura, Hariv. 2286. II. f. *kâ*, The name of a female demon, MBh. 3, 12203.—Comp. *Tila-*, m. a mole, a dark spot on the body, Suçr. 1, 31, 18.

कालकञ्ज *kâlakañja*, m. The name of a Dânava tribe, MBh. 3, 12198.

कालकूट *kâla-kûṭa*, I. m. and n. A kind of poison, MBh. 3, 540. II. m. The name of a people, MBh. 1, 4637.

कालज्ञ *kâla-jña* (vb. *jñâ*), adj. Knowing the proper season, Man. 7, 217.

कालञ्जर *kâlañjara*, m. The name of a range of mountains, MBh. 3, 8198.

कालतस् *kâla + tas*, adv. In the long run, Kathâs. 6, 101.

कालता *kâla + tâ*, f. Seasonableness, Ghaṭ. 19.

कालपाशिक *kâlapâçika*, i.e. *kâla -pâça + ika*, m. A hangman, Mudrâr. 21, 1.

कालमाल *kâlamâla*, i.e. *kâla-mâlâ*, m. A vegetable, Ocimum sanctum, Suçr. 1, 138, 16.

कालयाप *kâlayâpa*, i. e. *kâla-yâ*, Caus., + *a*, m. Procrastination, Hit. iii. d. 90.

कालवन्त् *kâla + vant*, adj., f. *vatî*, Long, Râm. 6, 22, 17.

कालानुसारिवा *kâlânusârivâ*, i. e. *kâla-anusârin + vâ* (fem. of *va*, i.e. mutilated *vant*), f. Benzoin, Suçr. 2, 94, 21.

कालानुसार्य *kâlânusârya*, i.e. *kâla -anusâra + ya*, n. m. and f. *yâ*, Benzoin, Suçr. 2, 275, 16.

कालाप *kâlâpa*, i.e. **1.** *kalâpa + a*, m. Hair, Çântiç. 1, 27. **2.** *kalâpin + a*, m. A proper name, MBh. 2, 113.

कालापक *kâlâpa + ka*, n. The name of a grammar, Kathâs. 7, 13.]

कालायस *kâlâyasa*, i.e. *kâla-ayas + a*, n. Iron, Râm. 5, 37, 38.

कालायसमय *kâlâyasa + maya*, adj., f. *yî*, Of iron, Râm. 5, 49, 32.

1. **कालिक** *kâlika*, i.e. 1. *kâla + ika*, adj. **1.** f. *kâ*, Referring to time, Bhâshâp. 120. **2.** Seasonable, MBh. 3, 868. **3.** f. *kî*, Long, Râm. 2, 41, 12.—Comp. *A-kâlika + m*, adv. without delay, MBh. 4, 908. *Ashṭama-*, adj. one who eats only on the evening of every fourth day, Man. 6, 19 (cf. 1. *kâla*, **3.**). *Eka-kâlika + m*, adv. eating once a day, Man. 11, 123. *Chaturtha-*, adj. one who eats only on the evening of every second day, Man. 6, 19 (cf. 1. *kâla*, **3.**). *Nishkâlika*, i.e. *nis-kâla + ika*, adj. one whose lifetime is elapsed (or °*kam*, adv., without delay), MBh. 8, 3628. *Mâsa-* adj., monthly, MBh. 2, 2080.

2. **कालिका** *kâlikâ*, i.e. 2. *kâla + ka*, f. **1.** A multitude of clouds, Ragh. 11, 15. **2.** The liver, Mit. 1, 31. **3.** A blood-vessel in the ear, Suçr. 1, 55, 1. **4.** The name of several plants, Suçr. 2, 499, 2. **5.** A name of Durgâ, MBh. 2, 457. **6.** The name of a river, MBh. 3, 8134.

कालिङ्ग *kâliṅga*, i.e. *kaliṅga + a*, I. m. **1.** A prince of the Kaliṅgas, Ragh. 4, 40. **2.** pl. = Kaliṅga, a people, MBh. 8, 2066. II. f. *gî*, A princess of the Kaliṅgas, MBh. 1, 3775.

कालिङ्गक *kâliṅga + ka*, m. A prince of the Kaliṅgas, MBh. 2, 1270.

कालिञ्जर *kâliñjara*, m. The name

of a mountain, Kathâs. 22, 161 (cf. *kâlañjara*).

कालिदास *kâlidâsa*, i. e. *kâlî-dâsa* (with *i* shortened), m. A proper name, Çâk. 3, 12.

कालिन्द *kâlinda*, i. e. *kalinda* + *a*, **I.** n. A water melon, Suçr. 1, 156, 21. **II.** f. *dî*. **1.** A proper name, Râm. 1, 70, 33. **2.** The Yamunâ, Pañch. 25, 3. —**Comp.** *Yama-kâlindî*, f. The wife of the sun.

कालिमन् *kâliman*, i. e. 2.*kâla* + *iman*, m. Blackness, Çiç. 4, 57.

कालिय *kâliya*, i.e. 2.*kâla* + *iya*, m. The name of a Nâga, MBh. 1, 1551.

ऽकालीन -*kâlîna*, i.e. 1.*kâla* + *îna*, latter part of compound words derived from nouns ending in *kâla*, adj. Referring to the time of, e.g. *utpattikâlîna*, i. e. *utpatti-kâla* + *îna*, adj. At the time of production, Bhâshâp. 77. *samâna*-, adj. Occurring or produced at the same period.

कालीय *kâlîya*, i.e. 2.*kâla* + *îya*, n. A dark kind of sandal, Suçr. 2, 120, 15.

कालीयक *kâlîya* + *ka*, **I.** n. A dark kind of sandal, Râm. 6, 96, 3. **II.** m. The name of a Nâga, MBh. 1, 1555.

कालुष्य *kâlushya*, i.e. *kalusha* + *ya*, n. **1.** Foulness, Kathâs. 19, 95. **2.** Unfairness, Râjat. 5, 63.

कालेय *kâleya*, i.e. 2.*kâla* + *eya*, **I.** n. A dark kind of sandal, Kumâras. 7, 9. **II.** m. The name of a tribe of Daityas, MBh. 3, 8719; 8769.

कालेयक *kâleya* + *ka*, **I.** n. A yellow fragrant wood, Suçr. 1, 146, 3. **II.** m. **1.** One of the interior parts of the body not yet identified, Suçr. 1, 208, 3. **2.** A kind of jaundice, Suçr. 2, 469, 4.

काल्य *kâlya*, i. e. *kalya* + *a*, n. Dawn, Râm. 2, 34, 34.

कावेरी *kâverî*, f. The name of a river, MBh. 2, 372.

काव्य *kâvya*, i.e. *kavi* + *ya*, **I.** adj., f. *yâ*, Coming from old sages, MBh. 2, 2097. **II.** m. **1.** A class of Pitṛis or Manes, Man. 3, 199. **2.** patron. Surname of Uçanas, MBh. 1, 3188. **III.** m. A bard, MBh. 2, 453. **IV.** n. A poem, Râm. 1, 2, 38.—**Comp.** *Mahâ*-, n. a classical poem, Chr. 170.

काश् *KÂÇ*, i. 1, Âtm. (in epic poetry also Par.), † i. 4, Âtm. **1.** To be visible, Râm. 3, 29, 8. **2.** To shine, MBh. 1, 7008. *kâçita*, Resplendent, Râm. 6, 26, 48.—With the prepos. उद् *ud*, To shine, Bhâg. P. 1, 11, 2.—With संनि *sam-ni*, Caus. To reveal, MBh. 14, 1283.—With निस् *nis*, cf. *kas*.—With प्र *pra*, **1.** To be visible, MBh. 3, 9990. **2.** To appear, Râm. 6, 20, 10. **3.** To shine, MBh. 3, 13750. Caus. **1.** To show, Çâk. 12, 11; Râm. 4, 42, 14. **2.** To illumine, MBh. 4, 232. **3.** To make known, Lass. 3, 9.—With अभिप्र *abhi-pra*, To shine, Râm. 5, 73, 6.—With संप्र *sam-pra*, **1.** To appear, MBh. 3, 13982. **2.** To shine, Râm. 5, 5, 23. Caus. To discover, MBh. 1, 87.—With वि *vi*, To appear, Râm. 5, 40, 10. Caus. To illumine, MBh. 1, 7856. — With सम् *sam*, To appear, Râm. 2, 65, 14.

काश *kâç* + *a*, m. and n. A species of grass, Saccharum spontaneum, Râm. 2, 28, 22. When the latter part of a comp. adj., f. *çâ*, e.g. *kusumita-nava*-, adj., f. *çâ*, Covered with fresh blossoming Kâça, Ṛit. 3, 28.—Cf. *kâsa*.

काशमय *kâça + maya*, adj., f. *yî*, Made of Kâça-grass, Bhâg. P. 3, 22, 31.

काशि *kâçi*, I. m. 1. A proper name, Hariv. 1734. 2. The king of Kâçi, Chr. 19, 6. 3. pl. The name of a people, MBh. 13, 1949. II. f. *çi* and *çî*. 1. The name of Benares, Râm. 1, 12, 22. 2. *çî*, A proper name, Hariv. 9204.

ऽकाशिन् *-kâç + in*, adj., f. *nî*, latter part of comp. adj. Shining like, e.g. *matta-*, Like one delighted, charming, Râm. 5, 18, 37. 2. Shining on account of, e.g. *jaya-* and *jita-*, On account of victory, victorious, proud on account of triumphs, Bhâg. P. 4, 10, 15; Chr. 16, 12.—Cf. *kâsin*.

काशिष्णु *kâç + ishṇu*, adj. Resplendent, Bhâg. P. 4, 30, 6.

काशेय *kâçeya*, i.e. *kâçi + eya*, I. m. A son of Kâçi, Hariv. 1734. II. f. *yî*, A daughter of Kâçi, MBh. 1, 3785.

काश्मरी *kâçmarî*, i.e. *kâç + man + î*, f. A plant, Gmelina arborea, Râm. 2, 94, 9.

काश्मर्य *kâçmarya*, i.e. *kâç + man + ya*, m. A plant, Gmelina arborea, MBh. 13, 2773.

काश्मीर *kâçmîra*, i.e. *kaçmîra + a*, I. adj., f. *rî*. 1. Trained in Cashmere, MBh. 4, 254 (a horse). 2. An inhabitant of Cashmere, MBh. 3, 5032. II. m. 1. A king of Cashmere, Mudrâr. 18, 17. 2. Cashmere, Râm. 4, 43, 32. III. n. Saffron, Bhartṛ. 1, 48.

काश्मीरक *kâçmîra + ka*, adj. Belonging to Cashmere, MBh. 2, 1025 (the inhabitants); 2, 1271 (the king).

काश्मीरिक *kâçmîrika*, i.e. *kâçmîra + ika*, adj. Referring to Cashmere, Chr. 245, l. 2.

काश्य *kâçya*, i.e. *kâçi + ya*, adj., and f. *yâ*. 1. Belonging to the Kâçis; a king of the Kâçis, MBh. 1, 4128. 2. f. A daughter of the king of the Kâçis, MBh. 1, 3829.

काश्यप *kâçyapa*, i.e. *kaçyapa + a*, f. *pî*. I. adj. Belonging to Kaçyapa, MBh. 13, 7237. II. patron. m. A descendant of Kaçyapa, Râm. 1, 9, 28.

काश्यपेय *kâçyapeya*, i.e. *kaçyapa + eya*, patron. m. A name of the Âdityas, MBh. 13, 7094; of the sun, 1, 1247.

काषाय *kâshâya*, i.e. *kashâya + a*, adj., f. *yî*. 1. Red, Sâv. 3, 18. 2. s. A red cloth, Râm. 3, 52, 9.

काष्ठ *kâshṭha*, I. n. A piece of wood, Man. 8, 372. II. m. A proper name, MBh. 2, 415. *kâshṭhâ*, q.v.—**Comp.** *Daṇḍa-*, n. a wooden staff, Çâk. 21, 1. *Danta-*, n. a small piece of wood for cleaning the teeth, MBh. 13, 4998.

काष्ठकूट *kâshṭhakûṭa*, m. A kind of bird, probably = *kâshṭha-kuṭṭa*, Pañch. 80, 12.

काष्ठभारिक *kâshṭhabhârika*, i.e. *kâshṭha-bhâra + ika*, m. One who carries wood, Kathâs. 6, 42.

काष्ठमय *kâshṭha + maya*, adj., f. *yî*. Made of wood, Man. 2, 157.

काष्ठलोष्टमय *kâshṭha-loshṭa-maya*, adj., f. *yî*, Made of wood or clay, Man. 8, 289.

काष्ठा *kâshṭhâ*, f. 1. Aim, MBh. 3, 10424; limit, boundary, Kumâras. 5, 28. 2. Place, Bhâg. P. 3, 18, 12. 3. A quarter or point of the compass, Bhâg. P. 4, 24, 1. 4. A lunar station, Bhâg. P. 1, 12, 31. 5. A measure of time, MBh. 1, 1292. 6. A proper name, Bhâg. P. 6, 6, 25.

काष्ठिक *kâshṭhika*, i.e. *kâshṭha* + *ika*, I. m. One who carries wood, Kathâs. 6, 43. II. f. *kâ*, A small piece of wood, Pańch. 194, 12.

कास् *KÂS*, i. 1, Âtm. To cough, Suçr. 1, 38, 10.—Cf. O.H.G. huosta; A.S. hvosta.

कास *kâs* + *a*, m. Cough, Bhâg. P. 3, 30, 17; with *ç* instead of *s*, Çântiç. 2, 27.

कासमर्द *kâsamarda*, i.e. *kâsa-mṛid* + *a*, and कासमर्दक *kâsamarda* + *ka*, m. A plant, Cassia sophora, Suçr. 1, 138, 17.

कासवन्त् *kâsa* + *vant*, adj., f. *vatî*, Subject to cough, Suçr. 2, 506, 4.

कासार *kâsâra*, m. A pond, Bhartṛ. 1, 39.

कासिन् *kâsin*, i.e. *kâsa* + *in*, adj., f. *nî*, Subject to cough, Suçr. 1, 116, 9; with *ç* instead of *s*, Pańch. v. d. 41.

कासीस *kâsîsa*, n. Green vitriol, Suçr. 1, 132, 17.

काहल *kâhala*, m. A large drum, Pańch. 20, 8. f. A musical instrument, probably a large drum, Râjat. 5, 464.

काहलि *kâhali*, i.e. *kâhala* + *i*, m. A name of Çiva, MBh. 13, 1179.

कि *KI*, ii. 3, Par. To know, ved., cf. *chi*; the original form was *ski*, Lat. scio.

किंवदन्ती *kiṁvadantî*, i.e. *kim-vadantî* (participle pres. f. of *vad*), f. Report, Hit. 39, 7.

किंशुक *kiṁçuka*, i.e. *kim-çuka*, I. m. A tree bearing beautiful red blossoms, Butea frondosa, Man. 8, 246. II. n. Its blossom, Suçr. 1, 224, 1.

किंकर *kiṁkara*, i.e. *kim-kṛi* + *a*, I. m. and f. *rî*, A servant, Râm. 1, 18, 13; MBh. 4, 634. II. m. 1. A tribe of demons, Râm. 1, 3, 30. 2. The name of a people, Râm. 4, 44, 13.

किंकरत्व *kiṁkara* + *tva*, n. The condition of a slave, Pańch. iv. d. 8.

किंकर्तव्यता *kiṁkartavyatâ*, i.e. *kim-kartavya* + *tâ*, and किंकार्यता *kiṁkâryatâ*, i.e. *kim-kârya* + *tâ* (vb. *kṛi*), f. Condition of one who does not know what to do, Daçak. in Chr. 199, 9; Kathâs. 10, 101.

किङ्किणी *kiṅkiṇî* (onomatop.) f., and किङ्किणीक *kiṅkiṇî* + *ka*, m. and n. A small bell, Râm. 3, 28, 32.

किङ्किणीकिन् *kiṅkiṇîkin*, i.e. *kiṅkiṇika* + *in*, adj., f. *nî*, Adorned with small bells, Indr. 5, 12.

किञ्जल्क *kiñjalka*, m. A filament, especially of the lotus, Bhâg. P. 3, 15, 43; 2, 2, 9; MBh. 3, 12880.

किञ्जल्किन् *kiñjalkin*, i.e. *kiñjalka* + *in*, adj., f. *nî*, Consisting of filaments, Dev. 5, 51.

† किट् *KIṬ*, i. 1, Par. 1. To go. 2. To fear. 3. To alarm.

किटकिटाय *KIṬAKIṬÂYA* (onomatop.), Âtm. To gnash, Suçr. 2, 195, 3.—Cf. *katakatâpaya*.

किट्ट *kiṭṭa*, n. Excretion, dirt, Suçr. 1, 328, 14; with *lauham*, Rust of iron, Suçr. 2, 469, 10.

किण *kiṇa*, m. A scar or callosity, Çâk. d. 13.

किणवन्त् *kiṇa* + *vant*, adj., f. *vatî*, Callous, MBh. 4, 633.

किण्व *kiṇva*, n. Ferment, a material used to produce fermentation in the manufacture of spirits from sugar, etc., Man. 8, 326.

कित् *KIT* (akin to *ki*), ii. 3, Par. To perceive, to know (ved.). Frequent. *chekit*, To see, Bhâg. P. 6, 16, 48. Desider. *chikitsa*. **1.** To cure, Bhartṛ. 1, 83; to administer remedies, Pańch. 183, 22 (read *chikitsyamâno*). *chikitsita*, n. Physic, Man. 10, 47. *chikitsya*, Curable, MBh. 12, 418. Comp. *A*-, adj. incurable, Yâjń. 2, 140. — **2.** † To chastise. **3.** † To remove. **4.** † To destroy. **5.** † To coerce.—Caus. of the desider. *chikitsaya*, To cure, Mâlav. 47, 11.—Caus. or i. 10, Par. *ketaya*. **1.** To invite, MBh. 13, 1596; Man. 3, 190. **2.** † To dwell. **3.** † To desire.—With the prepos. वि *vi*, desider. To doubt, MBh. 5, 2701. *vichikitsita*, Uncertain, Bhâg. P. 2, 4, 10.—Cf. *saṁket*.

कितव *kitava* (akin to *kit*), m. **1.** A gamester, Man. 3, 151. **2.** A cheat, Bhâg. P. 8, 20, 3; a rogue, Megh. 110. **3.** pl. The name of a people, MBh. 2, 1832.—Comp. *Dhûrta*-, m. a professed gambler, Yâjń. 2, 199.

किंनर *kiṁnara*, i.e. *kim-nara*, m. and f. *rî*, A class of demigods attached to the service of Kuvera, Man. 1, 39. **2.** A proper name, Râjat. 1, 197.

किम् *kim*, except for the nom. and acc. sing. ntr., the base of the msc. and n. and most derivatives is *ka*, of the fem. *kâ*, **I.** interrog. pron., sbst., and adj. Who, what, which, Man. 8, 414; 9, 170; 8, 161.—With gen. Who, what in proportion to, Kumâras. 3, 10: *ke mama dhanvino nye*, What may the other archers be able to do against me?—With instr. Away with, e.g. *kiṁ vilambena*, Do not tarry, Râm. 3, 35, 35. *kiṁ bahunâ*, In short, Pańch. 5, 3. *kim anena*, No question, Çâk. 91, 7.—With instr. and gen. *kiṁ te jńâtair mahâdhanurdharaiḥ*, What have you to do with knowing the great archers? Draup. 7, 4.—Instead of the instr. may be used also the absolutive, *kiṁ te sûryam nipâtya*, What matters it to you to bring down the sun? MBh. 13, 4628.—Joined with the demonstr. pron. *idam*, e.g. *ko yam*, Who there? Hit. 18, 11.—Doubled, e.g. *kiṁkiṁ na karoti*, What, what does he not? Pańch. i. d. 338.—It joins two questions in one sentence, e.g. *kâ vâm kaṁ varam ichchhati*, Who of you chooses the one and who the other boon? Râm. 1, 39, 12. **II.** Indefin. pron. **1.** Some, Bhag. 2, 21; generally followed by, **a.**, *cha*, Bhâg. P. 3, 3, 11; preceded by the relat. pron. *yad*, Whoever, whatever, Man. 12, 95. **b.** *cha na*, Anybody, Nal. 17, 44 (40); anything, Man. 8, 76; some, Bhâg. P. 5, 23, 4; doubled, *kâṁçchana- kâṁçchana*, Several, Râm. 2, 96, 34; preceded by the relat. pron. *yad*, Whatever, Nal. 4, 2. **c.** *chid*, Anybody, Man. 8, 212; any, 8, 232; whoever, Sâh. D. 7, 12; somebody, Nal. 14, 2. *kaṁ chit kâlam*, Some time, Râm. 3, 21, 31. *kaç chid—kaç chid*, Some one—another, Râm. 1, 4, 18; preceded by the relat. pron. *yad*, *α*. Whatever, Man. 2, 7. *β*. Some trifle, Man. 9, 115. **d.** *api*, see *api*. **2.** Any, Yajń. 3, 133. **3.** Joined with *na*, Nobody, Bhartṛ. 3, 99.—With *cha na* or *na—cha na*, Nothing, nobody, Nal. 15, 16; Man. 4, 134. *mâ kiṁ cha na*, Not at all, Bhâg. P. 1, 13, 39. *na hi kiṁ cha na*, Never, MBh. 1, 6132.—With *na—chid*, Nobody, nothing, Nal. 3, 24; not any, Man. 1, 81.—With *na—api*, Nobody, Bhartṛ. 3, 99; not the least, Pańch. 157, 6. **III.** *kim* (acc. sing. ntr.) adv. **1.** Why, Nal. 11, 3. **2.** A particle of interrog., e.g. *sâmyam ichchhasi kim*, Are you really desirous of readmission to equality? Man. 11, 195.—With following *u*, *kim u*, How much more? Man. 7, 55.—With following *cha*, Further, Kathâs. 2, 1; Pañch. 226, 11; Hit. 4, 18; go on, Çâk. 89, 17.—With following *tu*, But, MBh. 1, 1916.—With following *nu*, **1.** It lays a stress on the interrogation, Draup. 5, 13. **2.** How much less? Bhag. 1, 35.—With following *punar*, How much less? Ram. 1, 22, 21.— A following *vâ* increases the doubt, Çâk. 105, 7; Pañch. 44, 21.—In disjunctive questions we find, *kim—kiṁ vâ*, Çṛiṅgârat. 7. *kim—kiṁ vâ—kiṁ vâ*, Pañch. 34, 15 (*tat kim ... çastreṇa mârayâmi, kiṁ vâ visham pra yachchhâmi, kiṁ vâ paçudharmeṇa vyâpâdayâmi*, Shall I kill him with a knife, or shall I give him poison, or shall I kill him like a beast?). *kim—kim—vâ—atha*, Mṛichchh. 171, 14. *kim—uta*, Mṛichchh. 147, 22. *kim—uta vâ*, Pañch. 68, 14. *kim—uta—uta*, Bhartṛ. 3, 77. *kim—uta—atha vâ*, Kathâs. 17, 112. *kim—uta—âho svid*, Çâk. 106. *kim—atha vâ—uta*, Râm. 5, 51, 7. *kim* is sometimes the former part of a compound word, e.g. *kiṁrûpa*, adj. How shaped? Pañch. 258, 13. *kiṁchid* is also the latter part of compound words, e.g. *kiṁchijjña*, adj. Knowing a little, Bhartṛ. 2, 8. *a-kiṁchid*, Nothing at all, MBh. 13, 2334. **IV.** *kena*, instr. How so? Râm. 6, 12, 4.—Cf. *kasmât* separately. —Cf. κο, πο, e.g. κῇ, πῇ, πόθι, etc.; Lat. quis, qui, etc.; Goth. hvas; A.S. hva.

किमिच्छक *kimichchhaka*, i. e. *kim-ichchhâ+ka*, adj. Desirable, MBh. 13, 2111.

किमीय *kim+îya*, adj. To whom belonging, Daçak. 195, 10.

कियन्त् *kiyant*, i.e. *kim+vant* (*y* for original *v*), adj., f. *yatî*, acc. sing. n. *yat*, also adv. **1.** How great, MBh. 14, 766. **2.** How long, Râm. 2, 92, 8. **3.** How much, Kathâs. 2, 17. **4.** Of what value, Kathâs. 3, 49; Bhâg. P. 1, 13, 22. **5.** How little, Pañch. i. d. 46. **6.** Some, Pañch. 246, 13. **7.** A little, Pañch. 229, 20; with following *api*, However small, Pañch. 221, 21.

किर *kira*, i.e. *kṛî+a*, m. A hog. —Comp. *Mṛitkirâ*, i.e. *mṛid-*, f. *râ*, an earth worm.

किरण *kiraṇa*, i.e. *kṛî+ana*, m. A ray of light, Pañch. 223, 3; Daçak. in Chr. 199, 1.—Comp. *Tushâra-*, m. the moon, Çiç. 9, 27.

किरात *kirâta*, m., f. *tî*, The name of a people, MBh, 2, 584; Ragh. 16, 57.

किरातार्जुनीय *kirâtârjunîya*, i. e. *kirâta-arjuna+îya*, n. The title of a poem describing the combat of Arjuna with Çiva in the shape of a Kirâta, Chr. 170.

किरीट *kirîṭa*, m. and n. A diadem, Arj. 5, 13.

किरीटिन् *kirîṭin*, i. e. *kirîṭa+in*, adj., f. *nî*, Adorned by a diadem (a name of Arjuna), Bhag. 11, 17.

† **किल्** *KIL*, i. 6, Par. **1.** To be white. **2.** To play. i. 10, Par. *kelaya*, To throw (v.r.).

किल *kila*, adv. Indeed, Chr. 14, 18; Pañch. 167, 1.

किलकिल *kilakila*, (cf. **2.**) m. **1.** A name of Çiva, MBh. 12, 10365. **2.** *lâ*, onomatop. A cry expressing joy, Râm. 6, 26, 47.

किलाट *kilâṭa*, m. and f. *ṭî*, A kind of coagulated milk, Suçr. 1, 179, 17.

किल्बिष *kilvisha*, n. **1.** Fault, Man. 8, 235. **2.** Crime, 8, 296. **3.** Sin, Bhag. 3, 13. **4.** Injury, MBh. 1, 882.—Comp. *Chaura-*, n. an offence equal to larceny, Man. 8, 198. *Râma-*, n. an offence against Râma, Râm. 3, 46, 19.

किल्विषिन् *kilvishin*, i.e. *kilvisha* + *in*, adj., f. *iṇî*. **1.** Guilty, Man. 8, 18. **2.** A sinner, 8, 141.

किशलय *kiçalaya*, see *kisalaya*.

किशोर *kiçora*, m. and f. *rî*. **1.** A colt, Râm. 2, 40, 39; 5, 26, 21. **2.** A youth, Bhâg. P. 4, 12, 20; 24, 11. **3.** m. The name of a Dânava, Hariv. 2439.

† **किष्क्** *KISHK*, i. 10, Âtm. To kill, to injure.

किष्किन्ध *kishkindha*, m. The name of a mountain, Râm. 4, 8, 37; MBh. 2, 1122.

किष्किन्ध्या *kishkindhyâ*, f., = *kishkindha*, Râm. 6, 82, 88.

किष्कु *kishku*, m. and f. **1.** The fore-arm, Râm. 5, 32, 11. **2.** A span, as measure, MBh. 3, 10454.

किसलय *kisalaya*, also *kiçalaya*, n. A young shoot, Râm. 4, 50, 28; Megh. 11 (with *ç*).—Comp. *Karu-*, n. a finger, Daçak. in Chr. 191, 17 (with *ç*).

किसलयित *kisalayita*, i.e. *kisalaya* + *ita*, adj. Having young shoots, Bhartṛ. 1, 6.

कीकट *kîkaṭa*, m. **1.** pl. The name of a people, Bhâg. P. 1, 3, 24. **2.** A proper name, Bhâg. P. 5, 4, 10.

कीकस *kîkasa*, n. A bone, Lass. 95, 13.

कीचक *kîchaka*, m. **1.** A kind of bamboo, Arundo karka, Roxb., Râm. 4, 44, 76. **2.** A hollow bamboo, Ragh. 2, 12. **3.** pl. The name of a people, MBh. 1, 6085.

† **कीट्** *KIṬ*, i. 10, Par. To tinge (or bind).

कीट *kîṭa*, m. (and f. *ṭî* and n.) A worm, Man. 1, 40. An insect, Man. 2, 201.—Comp. *Keça-*, m. a louse, Man. 4, 207. *Pakshikîṭa*, i.e. *pakshin-*, m. an insect-like bird, a paltry bird, Pañch. 75, 19. *Yama-*, m. an earthworm. *Çûra-*, m. an inferior warrior, Mahâvîrach. 109, 10.

कीटज *kîṭa-ja* (vb. *jan*), n. Silk, Man. 11, 168.

कीदृश् *kîdṛiç*, i.e. *kim-dṛiç*, adj. Who or what like, of what kind? Pañch. 63, 10.—Cf. Lat. qualis, and the next.

कीदृश *kîdṛiça*, i.e. *kim-dṛiç* + *a*, adj., f. *çî*, Who or what like, of what kind? Pañch. 130, 10.—Cf. πηλίκος.

कीनाश *kînâça*, I. m. **1.** The chief servant in husbandry, Man. 9, 150. **2.** A poor labourer, or in general a poor man, MBh. 13, 3743. **II.** adj., f. *çâ*, Covetous, Daçak. in Chr. 193, 11.

कीर *kîra*, m. **1.** A parrot, Lass. 19, 14.—Comp. *Vâkkîra*, i.e. *vâch-*, m. a wife's brother.

कीर्तन *kîrtana*, i.e. *kṛît* + *ana*, n., and f. *nâ*, Mention, report, Pañch. 163, 21; Dev. 12, 21.

कीर्तन्य *kîrtanya*, a contraction of *kîrtanîya*, ptcple. of the fut. pass. of *kṛît*, adj. Memorable, Bhâg. P. 3, 15, 18.

कीर्ति *kîrti*, i.e. *kṛî* + *ti*, f. **1.** Renown, Man. 2, 9. Personified, MBh. 1, 2578.—Comp. *Divâ-*, m. a man of a low or impure caste, a Chaṇḍâla, Man. 5, 85. *Dushkîrti*, i.e. *dus*, adj. infamous, Bhâg. P. 8, 19, 43.

कीर्तिमन्त् *kîrti* + *mant*, I. adj., f. *matî*, Renowned, Râm. 1, 2, 45. **II.** m. A proper name, MBh. 13, 4356.

कीर्तिमय *kîrti* + *maya*, adj., f. *yî*, Made (wreathed) of glory, Bhâg. P. 4, 15, 15.

† **कील्** *kîl*, i. 10, Par. To bind.

कील *kîla*, m. **1.** A stake, MBh. 3, 650. **2.** A pin, Pañch. 44, 14. **3.** A wedge, Pañch. i. d. 26. **4.** A pillar Râjat. 5, 107.—**Comp.** *Indra-*, m. the name of a mountain, Râm. 2, 80, 18. *Guda-*, m. hemorrhoids, Suçr. 1, 198, 13. *Rata-* (vb. *ram*), m. a dog.

कीलक *kîla+ka*, m. A wedge, Pañch. 10, 7.

कीलाल *kîlâla*, i.e. *kim-lal+a*, m. **1.** A sweet drink (ved.). **2.** Blood, Prab. 54, 3.

कीलालज *kîlâla-ja* (vb. *jan.*), n. Flesh, MBh. 3, 15341.

कीलालप *kîlâla-pa* (vb. 1.*pâ*), adj. Drinking blood, MBh. 3, 13241.

कीलित *kîlita*, i.e. *kîla+ita*, adj., f. *tâ*, Bolted, Gît. 12, 13.

कीश *kîça*, m. A monkey, Pañch. 94, 15.

1. **कुऽ** *ku-*, a contraction of *ka+va*, from *kim*. Former part of compound words, implying, **I.** Inferiority, wickedness, e.g. *ku-karman*, **1.** n. A wicked action, Pañch. v. d. 64. **2.** adj. Doing wicked actions, Bhâg. P. 1, 16, 22. *ku-kṛitya*, n. A shameful action, Pañch. 237, 21. *ku-go*, m. An infirm bull, Râm. 6, 112, 6. *ku-jananî*, f. A bad mother, Râm. 6, 82, 118. *ku-janman*, adj. Having a bad origin, Bhâg. P. 4, 4, 22. *ku-tanaya*, m. A son who has not turned out well, Pañch. i. d. 85. *ku-tapasvin*, m. A bad ascetic, Pañch. 126, 1. *ku-tarka*, m. A false doctrine, Râjat. 5, 378. *ku-dṛishṭa*, adj. Imperfectly seen, Pañch. v. d. 1. *ku-dṛishṭi*, f. A false system, Man. 12, 95. *ku-dhî*, adj. sbst. A fool, Pañch. i. d. 38. *ku-nadikâ*, f. An insignificant rivulet, Pañch, i. d. 31. *ku-patha*, m. **1.** An erroneous way, Bhâg. P. 6, 7, 14. **2.** A proper name, Hariv. 203. *ku-parîkshaka*, m. A bad estimator, Bhartṛ. 2, 12. *ku-parîkshita*, adj. Imperfectly examined, Pañch. v. d. 1. *ku-putra*, m. A contemptible son, Man. 9, 161. *ku-purusha*, m. **1.** A contemptible man, MBh. 13, 108. **2.** A coward, 5, 5493. *ku-plava*, m. A frail boat, Man. 9, 161. *ku-buddhi*, adj. **1.** Foolish, Bhâg. P. 5, 5, 17. **2.** Mischievous, Pañch. i. d. 444. *ku-bhṛitya*, m. A bad servant, Pañch. 83, 13. *ku-mati*, **A.** f. **1.** Perversity, Daçak. in Chr. 181, 7. **2.** Error, Bhâg. P. 1, 9, 36. **B.** adj. Foolish, Bhâg. P. 1, 15, 17. *ku-mantra*, m. An evil advice, Bhâg. P. 3, 3, 13. *ku-mantrin*, m. A bad counsellor, Râjat. 5, 455. *ku-mârga*, m. An erroneous way, Pañch. 122, 24. *ku-mitra*, n. A false friend, Pañch. iii. d. 61. *ku-medhas*, adj. Mischievous, Bhâg. P. 3, 20, 33. *ku-râjan*, m. A contemptible king, Pañch. v. d. 64. *ku-rûpa*, adj. Ugly, Pañch. v. d. 17. *ku-varsha*, m. A heavy shower, Râm. 6, 89, 15. *ku-vâkya*, n. Injurious speech, Pañch. v. d. 64. *ku-vivâha*, m. A culpable marriage, Man. 3, 63. *ku-sachiva*, m. A bad counsellor, Râjat. 5, 439. *ku-sṛiti*, adj. Walking in error; a sinner, Bhâg. P. 8, 23, 7. **II.** Surprise: How, cf. e.g. *kumâra*; how much? cf. e.g. *kumuda*.

2. **कु** *KU*, see *kû*.

3. **कु** *ku*, f. The earth, Bhâg. P. 6, 1, 42.

† **कुंश्** *KUṀÇ*, or **कुंस्** *KUṀS*, i. 1 and 10, Par. To shine or speak.

† **कुक्** *KUK*, i. 1, Âtm. To take.

कुकुन्दर *kukundara*, see *kakundara*.

कुकुर *kukura*, **1.** see *kurkura*. **2.** m. The name of a prince, MBh. 13,

7679.' 3. pl. The name of a people, Râm. 4, 41, 14.

कुक्कुट *kukkuṭa*, onomatop. (cf. Lat. cucurire), I. m. A cock, Man. 3, 239 (a dog, Châṇ. 98, in Monatsber. der Berliner Ak. Hist. Phil. 1864, p. 413, read *kukkura*). II. f. *ṭî*, The silk cotton tree, Bombax heptaphyllon, Suçr. 2, 387, 1.—Comp. *Grâma-*, m. a town-cock, Man. 5, 12. *Jala-*, m. a kind of water-bird, Râm. 4, 13, 8. *Vana-*, m. wild fowl.

कुक्कुटक *kukkuṭa* + *ka*, m. A man of a mixed caste, one sprung from a Çûdra by a Nishâdî woman, Man. 10, 18.

कुक्कुटाण्डक *kukkuṭâṇḍaka*, i.e. *kukkuṭa-aṇḍa* + *ka*, A kind of rice, Suçr. 1, 196, 2.

कुक्कुभ *kukkubha*, i.e. *kukku* (onomatop.) *-bha* (vb. *bhâ*), m. A wild cock, Phasianus gallus, MBh. 13, 2835.

कुक्कुर *kukkura*. 1. see *kurkura*. 2. m. The name of a muni, or sage, MBh. 2, 113. 3. m. pl. The name of a people, MBh. 2, 1872.

कुक्षि *kukshi* (vb. *kuch*), m. 1. The belly, Râm. 1, 70, 34. 2. Cavity, Pańch. i. d. 281. 3. A cavern, Ragh. 2, 38. 4. A bay, MBh. 3, 793. 5. A proper name, Râm. 1, 70, 21.

कुङ्कुम *kuṅkuma*, n. Saffron, Crocus sativus, Bhartṛ. 1, 9.

कुच् *KUCH*, see *kuńch*.

कुच *kucha*, i.e. *kuch* + *a*, m. The female breast, Râm. 2, 29, 22.

† कुज् *KUJ*, i. 1, Par. 1. To steal or rob. 2. To be crooked (cf. *kuńch*).

कुज *kuja*, i.e. 3. *ku-ja* (vb. *jan*), m. The planet Mars, Bhâg. P. 2, 7, 34.

I. कुञ्च् *KUŃCH*, i. 1, and कुच् *KUCH*, i. 6, Par. 1. To straiten, to make narrow, Ṛit. 4, 16. 2. To bend, Râm. 5, 55, 27; Pańch. 50, 10. 3. To crisp, MBh. 1, 2170. II. † कुच् *kuch*, i. 1, Par. 1. To sound high. 2. To go. 3. To polish. 4. To be crooked. 5. To draw furrows. 6. To resist. — With the prepos. आ *â*, *âkuńchita*, 1. Compressed, Râm. 3, 31, 21. 2. Contracted, Bhartṛ. 1, 3. 3. Crisped, MBh. 13, 882. —With वि *vi*, *vikuńchita*, 1. Frowning, MBh. 1, 4112. 2. Crisped, Ṛit. 3, 19. Caus. *kuńchaya*, To turn backwards (?), Râm. 5, 5, 18.—With सम् *sam*, *kuch*. 1. To contract one's self, Pańch. 3, 40. 2. To close, Daçak. in Chr. 184, 8. *saṁkuchita*, 1. Contracted, Bhartṛ. 3, 74. 2. Shut, Râm. 4, 30, 20. Comp. *A-saṁkuchita*, adj. not wrinkled, Suçr. 1, 66, 6.—Caus. *kochaya*, 1. To contract, MBh. 1, 2843. 2. To diminish, Bhartṛ. 2, 37.—Cf. Lat. quic in conquinisco, conquexi, cûlus for cuc + lus; κύκλος; Goth. hauh; N.H.G. hucke in huckeback, etc.

कुञ्चन *kuńch* + *ana*, n. Shrinking, Suçr. 1, 251, 16.

कुञ्चिका *kuńchikâ*, i.e. *kuńch* + *aka*, f. A key, Bhartṛ. 1, 62.

† कुञ्ज् *KUŃJ*, i. 1, Par. To make any inarticulate sound.—Cf. *kûj*.

कुञ्ज *kuńja*, m. 1. A place overgrown with creeping plants, a bower, Megh. 19. 2. A cavern, Râm. 4, 26, 6; Ragh. 9, 64.

कुञ्जर *kuńjara* (probably akin to the preceding), m. 1. An elephant, Pańch. i. d. 177. 2. Preeminent, Râm. 5, 2, 13; in this meaning it is generally the latter part of a compound, e. g. *kapi-*, m. A most excellent monkey (literally, an elephant among monkeys), Râm. 5, 3, 17. **3.** The name of a Nâga, or serpent, MBh. 1, 1560. **4.** The name of a prince, 3, 15597. **5.** The name of a mountain, Râm. 4, 41, 50.

1. **कुट्** *KUṬ*, i. 6, Par. To bend.

2. **कुट्** *KUṬ* (akin to *kṛit*, based on *kart*), i. 4, Par. To burst, Lass. 95, 15. † i. 10, *koṭaya*, To cut.—With the prepos. **अव** *ava*, To diminish, Suçr. 2, 175, 20.—With **प्र** *pra*, To divide, MBh. 1, 2842.

कुटज *kuṭa-ja* (vb. *jan*), m. A medicinal plant, Wrightia antidysenterica, Megh. 4.

कुटिक *kuṭ+ika*, I. adj. Crooked, MBh. 3, 13454. II. f. *kâ*, The name of a river, Râm. 2, 71, 15 (Gorr. 2, 73, 13, reads *kuṭilâ*).

कुटिकोष्टिका *kuṭikoshṭikâ*, f. The name of a river, Râm. 2, 71, 10.

कुटिल *kuṭ+ila*, I. adj., f. *lâ*, **1.** Crooked, Râm. 1, 44, 25. **2.** Crisped, Bhâg. P. 3, 33, 14. **3.** Frowning, Râm. 5, 89, 2. **4.** Deceitful, Pañch. i. d. 73; cf. *a-kuṭila*, adj. Candid, Pañch. i. d. 142. II. f. *lâ*, The name of a river, Râm. 2, 73, 13, Gorr. (cf. *kuṭika*); 4, 40, 20.

कुटिलक *kuṭila+ka*, I. adj. Crisped, Pañch. i. d. 225. II. f. *kuṭilikâ*, A kind of motion on the stage, Vikr. 62, 17.

कुटी *kuṭ+î*, f. **1.** A hut, Man. 11, 72. **2.** A vessel serving for fumigation, Suçr. 2, 33, 18. — **Comp.** *Açva-*, f. a stable, Pañch. 254, 22. *Parṇa-*, f. a hut made of leaves, Râm. 2, 92, 12. *Bhramatkuṭî*, i.e. *bhramant-*, f. a sort of umbrella.

कुटीचक *kuṭî-chak+a*, m. A class of religious mendicants, Bhâg. P. 3, 12, 43.

कुटीर *kuṭî+ra*, n. **1.** A hut, Git. 1, 27. **2.** Sexual intercourse, Bhartṛ. 3, 66.

कुटीरक *kuṭîra + ka*, n. A hut, Amar. 48.—**Comp.** *Tṛiṇa-*, a hut made of grass, Pañch. 34, 9.

† **कुटुम्ब्** *KUṬUMB*, i. 10 (rather a denom. derived from the next), Âtm. To support a family.

कुटुम्ब *kuṭumba*, n. **1.** Household, Çâk. d. 95. **2.** Family, Man. 11, 22. **3.** Family goods, Man. 9, 199.—**Comp.** *Vijaya-ratha-kuṭumba*, adj. taking care of Vijaya's chariot as a father would a household, Bhâg. P. 1, 9, 39.

कुटुम्बक *kuṭumba+ka*, n. Family, Hit. i. d. 64.

कुटुम्बिक *kuṭumbika*, i.e. *kuṭumba+ika*, adj. Taking care of one's family, MBh. 13, 4401.

कुटुम्बिन् *kuṭumbin*, i.e. *kuṭumba+in*, m. **1.** A householder, Man. 3, 80; f. *inî*, The wife of a householder, MBh. 3, 13660. **2.** A kinsman, Pañch. 96, 4. **3.** A cultivator of the soil, Râjat. 5, 468.—**Comp.** *Ratha-*, m. a charioteer, Râm. 6, 89, 19.

कुट्ट् *KUṬṬ* (a form of *kṛit*, based on *kart*), I. i. 10, Par. **1.** † To cut. **2.** To cut in a defective manner, Suçr. 1, 361, 19. **3.** † To censure. **4.** To multiply. II. † i. 10, Âtm., v.r. of *kûṭ*. —With the prepos. **वि** *vi*, Par. To cut off, MBh. 13, 3305.

कुट्ट *kuṭṭ+a*, adj., f. *ṭî*, **1.** Latter part of compound words, e.g. *açmakuṭṭa*, i.e. *açman-*, adj. Breaking with a stone, Man. 6, 17. **2.** A multiplier.—**Comp.** *Kâshṭha-*, m. the woodpecker, Picus Bengalensis, Pañch. 157, 4. *Tâmra-*,

m. a coppersmith, Râm. 2, 90, 25 Gorr. (thus to be read instead of *-kuṭa*).

कुट्टक *kuṭṭa + ka*, **1.** adj. = *kuṭṭa* 1. Yâjń. 3, 49. **2.** = *kuṭṭa* 2.

कुट्टनी *kuṭṭanî*, and **कुट्टिनी** *kuṭṭinî*, f. A procuress or bawd, Hit. i. d. 9; Prab. 14, 4.

कुट्टिम *kuṭṭima* (cf. *kuṭṭ*), I. adj., f. *mâ*, Plastered with small stones, Râm. 2, 80, 13. II. m. and n. A floor or ground smoothed and plastered, MBh. 14, 2522; 1, 6964; Mâlav. 21, d. 27.—Comp. *Vastra-*, n. 1. an umbrella. 2. a tent.

कुड्मल *kuṭ + mala*, m. and n. **1.** An opening bud, Mṛichchh. 10, 10. **2.** Opening, Râm. 4, 38, 40.

कुठार *kuṭhâra*, m. (and f. *rî*), I. An axe, Râm. 2, 35, 41. II. m. The name of a Nâga or serpent, MBh. 1, 2156.

कुठारिक *kuṭhârika*, i.e. *kuṭhâra + ika*, I. m. A wood-cutter, Râjat. 5, 310. II. f. *kâ*, A small axe, Bhartṛ. 3, 23. A lancet, Suçr. 1, 26, 13.

† **कुड्** *KUḌ*, i. 6, Par. **1.** To act as a child. **2.** To eat. **3.** To heap. **4.** To dive (?).

कुडव *kuḍava*, m. A measure of grain, etc., described as a vessel four fingers wide and as many deep, containing twelve handfuls; the fourth part of a Prastha, MBh. 14, 2722.

कुड्मल *kuḍmala* (cf. *kuṭmala*), I. m. An opening bud, Ṛit. 2, 25. II. adj. Opening, MBh. 4, 393. III. n. A kind of hell, Man. 4, 89.

कुड्मलित *kuḍmalita*, i.e. *kuḍmala + ita*, adj. Covered with opening buds, Amar. 70.

कुड्य *kuḍya*, n. A wall, Yâjń. 2, 223.

† **कुण्** *KUṆ*, i. 6, Par. **1.** To sound. **2.** To cherish; to support (or to pain). i. 10, Par. *kuṇaya*, **1.** To address. **2.** To converse with. **3.** To invite.—Cf. *kvaṇ*.

कुणप *kuṇapa*, I. m. and n. **1.** A dead body, carrion, Man. 12, 71. II. m. **2.** A spear, MBh. 14, 142.

कुणि *kuṇi* (probably a form of *kush + ni*, cf. *kûṇ*), m. **1.** A cripple with a crooked or withered arm, MBh. 3, 1270. **2.** The name of a prince, Bhâg. P. 9, 24, 13.

† **कुण्ट्** *KUṆṬ*, i. 1, Par. To maim (? v.r.).

कुण्ठ् *KUṆṬH*, i. 1, Par. **1.** † To be maimed. **2.** † To be lazy. † i. 10, Par. To cover (? v.r.). *kuṇṭhita*, **1.** Blunt, Kumâras. 2, 20. **2.** Powerless, Râjat. 5, 138.—Comp. *A-*, adj. sharp, Ragh. 1, 19.—With the prep. **वि** *vi*, *vikuṇṭhita*, Blunted, Ragh. 5, 44.

कुण्ठ *kuṇṭh + a*, adj. Blunt, Râm. 3, 32, 16.—Comp. *A-*, adj. sharp, Bhâg. P. 1, 19, 31.

कुण्ठक *kuṇṭha + ka*, m. pl. The name of a people, MBh. 6, 370.

† **कुण्ड्** *KUṆḌ*, i. 1, Par. To maim (?). i. 1, Âtm. To heat. i. 10, Par. To preserve.

कुण्ड *kuṇḍa*, I. m., f. *ḍî*, and n. A pitcher, a jar, a water pot, MBh. 3, 14311. II. m. and n. A basin of water, MBh. 13, 4816; Râm. 4, 26, 4. III. n. **1.** A hole in the ground for receiving and preserving consecrated fire, MBh. 3, 8216. **2.** A vessel for holding coals, Râm. 5, 10, 16. IV. m. **1.** A son of an adulteress born before the death of the husband, Man. 3, 156; 174. **2.** The name of a Nâga or serpent, MBh. 1, 4828. **3.** A name of Çiva, MBh. 12, 10358.—**Comp.** *Amṛita-*, n. the vessel containing the *amṛita*, or beverage of immortality. *Homa-*, n. a hole in the ground for receiving the fire for an oblation.

कुण्डक *kuṇḍa + ka*, **1.** A jar, Kathâs. 4, 47. **2.** m. A proper name, MBh. 1, 6983.

कुण्डल *kuṇḍala*, **I.** m. and n. **1.** A ring, Bhâg. P. 5, 23, 3. **2.** An ear-ring, Bhartṛ. 2, 63. **II.** m. The name of a Nâga, MBh. 1, 2154. **III.** f. *lâ*, A proper name, Mârk. P. 21, 34.—When the latter part of a comp. adj., the f. is *lâ*, e.g. *çaila-*, adj., f. *lâ*, Surrounded by mountains, MBh. 3, 10943. *sa-*, adj. With earrings.

कुण्डलिन् *kuṇḍalin*, i.e. *kuṇḍala + in*, adj., f. *nî*, Having earrings, MBh. 1, 7005.

कुण्डाशिन् *kuṇḍâçin*, i.e. *kuṇḍa -âçin*, **I.** adj. One who eats food offered by the son of an adulteress, Man. 3, 158. **II.** m. **1.** The name of a Nâga or serpent. **2.** A proper name, MBh. 1, 4553.

कुण्डिन् *kuṇḍin*, i.e. *kuṇḍa + in*, **I.** adj., f. *nî*, Carrying a water pot, MBh. 3, 16016. **II.** m. A horse, MBh. 2, 2061 (?).

कुण्डिन *kuṇḍina*, **I.** m. A proper name, MBh. 1, 3747. **II.** n. The name of a city, Nal. 21, 2.

कुतप *ku-tap + a*, m. and n. **1.** A blanket made of the hair of the mountain goat, Man. 3, 234. **2.** The eighth portion of the day, about noon, MBh. 13, 6040.

कुतस् *kutas*, i.e. *ka + va + tas* (cf. *kim* and *ku*), adv. **1.** =Abl. of *kim*, Lass. 13, 14. **2.** From what place, Hiḍ. 2, 24. **3.** Whence, Râm. 1, 14, 36. **4.** Whither, Bhâg. P. 8, 19, 34. **5.** Why, Râm. 3, 1, 12. **6.** How, Brâhmaṇ. 1, 28. **7.** How much less? Indr. 1, 17. **8.** With following *api*, From some, Pańch. 229, 1; from somewhere. **9.** With *na* and following *chana*, From no quarter whatever, Man. 6, 40. **10.** With following *chid*, From any, Daçak. in Chr. 179, 7; from anywhere, Pańch. 239, 5.—**Comp.** *A-*, adv. from no quarter, Pańch. 68, 25.

कुतुक *kutuka*, n. Desire, Gît. i. 42.

कुतूहल *kutûhala*, n. **1.** Eagerness, Nal. 1, 16; abl. Eagerly. **2.** Curiosity, Nal. 13, 48. **3.** Desire, Lass. 67, 12. **4.** A surprising object, Pańch. 124, 9.

कुतूहलवन्त् *kutûhala + vant*, adj., f. *vatî*, Anxious, eager, Mâlav. 51, 7.

कुतूहलिन् *kutûhalin*, i.e. *kutûhala + in*, adj., f. *nî*. **1.** Eager, Ragh. 15, 65. **2.** Inquisitive, Man. 4, 63.

कुत्र *kutra*, i.e. *ka + va + tra* (cf. *kim* and *ku*), adv. **1.** Where, Râm. 5, 34, 21. **2.** Whither, Lass. 25, 5. **3.** *kutra*—*kva* are used to denote a great difference, Bhâg. P. 7, 9, 25. **4.** With following *api*, Somewhere, Mârk. P. 8, 120. **5.** With following *chid*, **a.** In some, Pańch. 256, 6. **b.** Somewhere, Râm. 5, 1, 5. With preceding *na*, Nowhere, MBh. 3, 10359; Pańch. 36, 22. **c.** *kutra chid*—*kutra chid*, In some cases—in others, Man. 9, 34. **6.** With preceding *yatra* and following *cha*, In whomsoever even, Bhâg. P. 8, 8, 22.—Cf. Goth. hvathro and hvar; Engl. whither; Lat. cur.

कुत्रत्य *kutra + tya*, adj. Where dwelling, Bhâg. P. 5, 10, 17.

कुत्स् *KUTS*, i. 10 (rather a denom.

derived from *kutas*), in epic poetry also i. 1, MBh. 2, 2298, Par. 1. To blame, MBh. 2, 2121. 2. To contemn, Man. 2, 54. *kutsita*, Contemptible, MBh. 13, 2222. *kutsya*, Blameable, Bhartṛ. 2, 12 (thus to be read).—With the prep. अभि *abhi*, To blame, Râm. 2, 75, 2.

कुत्स *kutsa*, m. The name of a Ṛishi, Chr. 296.

कुत्सन *kuts+ana*, n. Contempt, Man. 4, 163.

कुत्सा *kuts+â*, f. Blaming, MBh. 13, 6589; Blame, 2, 2235.

कुथ् *KUTH*, i. 4, Par. To stink. *kuthita*, Fetid, Suçr. 2, 115, 3.—Causal, *kothaya*, To cause to putrefy, Suçr. 1, 344, 4.—With the prep. प्र *pra*, To begin stinking, to turn putrid, *prakuthita*, Suçr. 1, 344, 5.

कुथ *kutha*, I. m., and f. *thâ*, and n. A painted woollen blanket, MBh. 2, 1894. II. m. A kind of grass, Poa cynosuroides, Râm. 2, 30, 14 (but Gorr. reads *kuça*, 2, 30, 16).

† कुद् *KUD*, i. 10, Par. To speak falsely, to lie (v.r.).

कुद्दाल *kuddâla*, m. and n. A kind of spade or hoe, MBh. 3, 8871.

कुनख *ku-nakha*, m. A disorder of the finger nails (cf. the next), Suçr. 1, 292, 9.

कुनखिन् *kunakhin*, i.e. *kunakha+in*, adj., f. *nî*, One who has whitlows on his nails, Man. 3, 153.

कुन्त *kunta*, m. A lance, Râm. 3, 28, 24.

कुन्तल *kuntala*, m. 1. Hair, Bhâg. P. 3, 28, 30. 2. pl. The name of a people, MBh. 6, 347.

कुन्ति *kunti*, m. I. m. 1. pl. The name of a people, MBh. 2, 590. 2. The king of the Kuntis, Bhâg. P. 9, 24, 30. 3. A proper name, Mârk. P. 2, 2. II. f. *tî*, One of Pâṇḍu's wives, MBh. 1, 3811.

† कुन्थ् *KUNTH*, i. 1, Par. 1. To hurt. 2. To afflict. ii. 9, *kuthnâ*, *nî*, 1. To embrace. 2. To afflict.

कुन्द *kunda*, I. m. and n. A kind of jasmine, Jasminum multiflorum, or pubescens, Megh. 48. II. m. 1. A name of Vishṇu, MBh. 13, 7036. 2. The name of a mountain, Bhâg. P. 5, 20, 10.

† कुन्द्र् *KUNDR*, i. 10, Par. To speak falsely, to lie.—Cf. *kud*.

1. कुप् *KUP*, i. 4, Par. Âtm. 1. To become excited, Suçr. 2, 184, 11. 2. To be angry, Man. 3, 229. With dat. gen. and acc., Of the person with whom one is angry, Pañch. 23, 22; Râm. 4, 19, 24; 1, 49, 7. *kupita*, Enraged, Man. 9, 313. With *upari* and gen. (enraged against us), Pañch. 73, 15. *a-kupya*, adj. Not liable to become angry, MBh. 15, 821. Caus. *kopaya*, 1. To excite, Suçr. 2, 204, 3. 2. To provoke, MBh. 2, 2140. Âtm. To provoke against one's own self, MBh. 2, 2187. Anomalous *kopayîta* for *kopayeta*, *kopishṭhâs* for *chûkupathâs*, *kopayâna* for *kopayamâna*, MBh. 1, 5790; 2, 2188; 3, 1956. 3. To be angry, Bhâg. P. 4, 5, 11.—With the prep. परि *pari*, 1. To be much excited, MBh. 1, 1186. 2. To be very angry, MBh. 13, 2101.—Caus. 1. To excite violently, MBh. 14, 469. 2. To provoke violently, MBh. 13, 7403.—With प्र *pra*, 1. To become agitated, Suçr. 2, 396, 4; MBh. 13, 14508. *prakupita*, Very angry, Pañch. 163, 5. *nâtiprakupita*, Rather indif-

ferent, Daçak. in Chr. 194, 11. Anomalous *prakupta*, Vikr. d. 130.—Caus. 1. To excite, MBh. 14, 465. 2. To provoke, Man. 9, 313.—With सम् *sam*, To become angry, MBh. 3, 1093.—Caus. To provoke, MBh. 4, 1845.—Cf. Lat. cupio=*kupyâmi.*

† 2. कुप् *KUP*, i. 10, Par. To speak or shine.

कुप्य *kup+ya*, I. n. (and ऽकुप्यक -*kupya+ka* as latter part of a comp.), Any metal except gold and silver, Man. 7, 96. II. m. A proper name, Râjat. 6, 264.

कुब्ज *kubja*, i.e. *kubh-ja* (vb. *jan*, cf. *kumbha*), adj., f. *jâ*. 1. Hump-backed, Pańch. 261, 12. 2. Crooked, Pańch. ii. d. 74.

कुब्जक *kubja+ka*, I. adj. Hump-backed, Pańch. v. d. 77. II. m. An aquatic plant, Trapa bispinosa, Man. 8, 247.

† कुमार् *KUMÂR*, i. 10 (rather a denom. derived from the next), Par. To play as a child.

कुमार *kumâra*, i.e. *ku-mṛi+a* (vb. *mṛi* in its original signification, To be weak), I. m. 1. A child (ved.). 2. A boy, Man. 7, 152. 3. A youth, Ragh. 3, 40. 4. When compounded, often: Young, as latter part, Çâk. 27, 15; Ragh. 3, 40; as former part, Man. 3, 159, From early youth. 5. A young prince, Ragh. 12, 11. 6. A name of Skanda, the god of war, Suçr. 2, 394, 10. 7. The name of a people, MBh. 2, 1870. II. f. *rî*. 1. A girl, Man. 3, 54. 2. A proper name, MBh. 1, 3796. 3. The name of a river, MBh. 6, 343.—Comp. *Râjakumâra*, i.e. *râjan-*, m. a prince, Lass. 7, 2. *Sanatk°*, i.e. *sanad-*, m. one of the four sons of Brahman, and eldest of the progenitors of mankind. *Su-*, I. adj. 1. soft, smooth. 2. youthful. 3. delicate. II. m., and f. *râ*, names of several plants.

कुमारक *kumâra+ka*, I. m. 1. A boy, Çâk. 50, 1. 2. A youth, Bhâg. P. 3, 3, 24. 3. The name of a Nâga or serpent, MBh. 1, 2154. II. f. *rikâ*, A girl, Pańch. 184, 4.

कुमारत्व *kumâra+tva*, n. Youth, Ragh. 17, 30.

कुमारसू *kumâra-sû*, m. A name of Agni, MBh. 2, 1148.

† कुमाल् *KUMÂL*=*kumâr* (v.r.).

कुमुद् *ku-mud*, n. The esculent white water-lily, Nymphæa esculenta, Bhâg. P. 3, 23, 38.

कुमुद *ku-mud+a*, I. m. and n. The white esculent water-lily, Nymphæa esculenta, Pańch. 50, 10. II. m. The name of a Nâga or serpent, MBh. 1, 1560; of a celestial being, Bhâg. P. 7, 8, 39; of a monkey, Râm. 4, 39, 37; of a mountain, Bhâg. P. 5, 16, 12; of a man, Râjat. 5, 422.

कुमुदिनी *kumudinî*, i.e. *kumuda+in+î*, f. A group of lotus flowers, Pańch. i. d. 152.

कुमुद्वन्त् *kumud+vant*, I. adj., f. *vatî*, Abounding in lotusses, Ragh. 4, 19. II. f. *vatî*. 1. A group of lotus flowers, Çâk. d. 65. 2. A plant, Menyanthes indica, Suçr. 2, 251, 18. 3. A proper name, Ragh. 16, 85.

† कुम्प् *KUMP*, i. 10, Par., v.r. of *kumb*, i. 10.

† कुम्ब् *KUMB*, i. 1, and i. 10 (cf. the last and the next), To cover.

† कुम्भ् *KUMBH*, i. 10, Par., v.r. of *kumb*.—Cf. the last and the next.

कुम्भ *kumbh+a* (the vb. *kumbh*,

kubh, from which this noun is derived, is lost in the corresponding signification, but cf. *kubja*, κυφός, κύφων, κῦφος; Engl. hump; O.H.G. hofar; Lat. cŭbitus, the elbow, lying, etc., cŭbare, concumbere, etc.; and at the end of this article. From these and other instances, we may infer that the original signification of the vb. *kubh* was 'to be crooked'), **I.** m., and f. *bhî*. **1.** A pot, Man. 11, 186; MBh. 18, 84. **2.** A measure of grain, equal to twenty droṇas, Man. 8, 320; 4, 7. **II.** m. **1.** dual, The two frontal globes of an elephant, which swell in the rutting season, Pańch. i. d. 351. **2.** The paramour of a harlot, Çṛiṅgârat. 9. **3.** The name of a Dânava, MBh. 1, 2527; of a Râkshasa, Râm. 5, 79, 15.—Comp. *Agni-*, m. a fire pot, MBh. 13, 5490 (he will get [in hell] a fire pot, in order to be burnt therein; cf. *kumbhî-pâka*). *Âma-*, m. an unburnt earthen pot, Pańch. iii. d. 13. *Udakumbha*, i. e. *udan-*, m. a water pot, Man. 2, 182. *Kucha-*, m. a bosom like the frontal globes of an elephant, Çṛiṅgârat. 9 (v.r.). *Tapta-*, m. the name of a hell, Mârk. P. 12, 34. *Bhadra-*, m. a golden jar filled with water from a holy place. *Vâta-*, m. the part of an elephant's forehead below the frontal globes. *Çata-*, I. m. the name of a mountain. II. n. gold.—When latter part of a comp. adj. the fem. is *bhâ*, e.g. *vâri-pûrita-kumbha*, adj., f. *bhâ*, Bearing jars filled with water, Kathâs. 18, 339. —Cf. κῦφος, a vessel, κύφελλον, κυψέλη, κύβος, κύβιτον, κύβη, κύμβος, κύμβαχος, etc.; Goth. hups; O.H.G. huf; A.S. hipe; O.H.G. hufila, 'a cheek,' hûfo and hauf, a multitude, heap; cf. supra.

कुम्भक *kumbha+ka*, **I.** m. A religious exercise, closing the nostrils and mouth so as to suspend breathing, Vedântas. in Chr. 217, 18. **II.** f. *bhikâ*, A small pot, Kathâs. 6, 41.

कुम्भकार *kumbha-kâra*, m. A potter, Pańch. 217, 20.

कुम्भकारिका *kumbhakârikâ*, i. e. *kumbha-kâraka*, f. The wife of a potter, Kathâs. 21, 134.

कुम्भिल *kumbhila* (akin to *kumbha*), m. A thief, Çâk. 73, 2 (Prâkṛ.).

कुम्भीर *kumbhîra* (akin to *kumbha*), m. A crocodile, MBh. 13, 5457.

† **कुर्** *KUR*, i. 6, Par. To sound.

कुरङ्ग *kuraṅga*, **I.** m. An antelope, Pańch. 114, 18. **II.** f. *gî*, A female antelope, Gît. 9, 11. **III.** m. The name of a mountain, Bhâg. P. 5, 16, 27.

कुरङ्गाय *KURAṄGÂYA*, a denominative derived from the last by *ya*, Âtm. To turn an antelope.

कुरर *kurara* (onomatop.), **I.** m. An osprey, Râm. 3, 15, 6. **II.** f. *rî*, A female osprey, MBh. 1, 908. **III.** m. The name of a mountain, Bhâg. P. 5, 16, 27.

कुरव *kurava*, m. The name of a plant; see the next.

कुरवक *kurava+ka*, **I.** m. **1.** A crimson species of amaranth. **2.** A purple sort of Barleria, Ṛit. 6, 18. **II.** n. The flower of these plants, Ṛit 6, 31.

कुरु *kuru*, m. **1.** pl. The name of a people, Man. 8, 92. **2.** The progenitor of the Kurus, MBh. 1, 4346.

कुरुवक *kuruvaka*=*kuravaka*, Râm. 3, 79, 36.

कुरुविन्द *kuruvinda*, m. **1.** The name of several plants, a kind of barley, Suçr. 1, 197, 1. **2.** A ruby, Çiç. 9, 8.

कुर्कुट *kurkuṭa*, m. Rubbish (?), Pańch. iii. d. 118.

कुर्कुर *kurkura* (onomatop.), also कुक्कुर *kukkura and* कुकुर *kukura*, m. A dog, Pańch. ii. d. 97; Hit. 50, 3. *kukura*, also, The proper name of a prince, MBh. 13, 7679; and a people, Râm. 4, 41, 14.

कुर्द् *KURD*, i. 1, *kûrda*, Par. and Âtm. **1.** To hop, Hariv. 8398. **2.** † To play.—Caus. of the frequent. *chokûrdaya*, To invite to hop, Hariv. 8403 (*chukûrdayadbhiḥ*, read *chokûrd°*).—With the prep. अति *ati*, To hop briskly, Hariv. 8404.—With उद् *ud*, To jump aloft, Pańch. 124, 7.—With प्र *pra*, To jump on, Pańch. 118, 15.

कुर्पासक *kurpâsa + ka*, m. A bodice, Ṛit. 4, 16.

† कुल् *KUL*, i. 1, Par. **1.** To accumulate. **2.** To be of kin.

कुल *kula*, n. **1.** A herd, Râm. 4, 40, 24; a flock, Ṛit. 1, 23; Pańch. 82, 20. **2.** A multitude, Bhâg. P. 1, 9, 33. **3.** A caste, Bhâg. P. 9, 9, 43. **4.** Family, Man. 2, 34. **5.** A house, Man. 7, 82. **6.** A grange, holding as much land as can be tilled by two ploughs, each drawn by six bulls, Man. 7, 119. **7.** Noble lineage, Man. 7, 54. **8.** An inspector of causes, Man. 8, 169 (? Kull.).—**Comp.** *Anurûpa-*, adj., f. *lâ*, being of a suitable family, Râm. 3, 35, 67. *Uchchaiḥkula*, i. e. *uchchais-*, n. high rank, Çâk. d. 92. *Utkula-*, i.e. *ud-*, adj., f. *lâ*, degenerate, Çâk. d. 123. *Go-*, n. 1. a herd of kine, Râm. 1, 9, 60. 2. the name of a temple, Râjat. 5, 23. *Daṇḍa-deva-*, n. a temple of the god of punishment, perhaps Yama, or a court of justice, Pańch. 128, 25. *Dushkula*, i.e. *dus-*, I. n. a base family, Man. 2, 238. II. adj. sprung from a base family, Bhartṛ. 1, 89. *Deva-*, n. a temple, Mṛichchh. 30, 15. *Nishkula*, i.e. *nis-*, adj., f. *lâ*, having no kindred, Man. 8, 28; with *kṛi*, to exterminate one's family, Râm. 4, 26, 14. *Nîcha-*, n. a low family, Mṛichchh. 83, 8. *Râjakula*, i.e. *râjan-*, I. n. 1. the court of a king, Daçak. in Chr. 183, 18. 2. a court of justice, Pańch. 96, 20. 3. a royal race. II. m. a prince. *Vâgdevî-*, i.e. *vâch-devî-*, n. science, Râjat. 5, 158. *Sa-*, adj. 1. having a family. 2. belonging to a family.

कुलक *kula + ka*, n. A multitude, Bhâg. P. 5, 7, 11.

कुलज *kula-ja* (vb. *jan*), adj. m. A person of high birth, Man. 8, 179.—**Comp.** *A-*, adj. a person of base birth, Pańch. i. d. 466.

कुलटा *kulaṭâ*, f. An unchaste woman, Pańch. 37, 11.

कुलतस् *kula + tas*, adv. According to one's rank, Chr. 52, 10.

कुलत्थ *kulattha*, probably *kula-stha* (vb. *sthâ*), m. **1.** A kind of vetch, Dolichos uniflorus, MBh. 13, 5468. **2.** pl. The name of a people, MBh. 6, 373.

कुलंधर *kulaṁdhara*, i.e. *kula + m -dhṛi + a*, adj. Preserving a family, Bhâg. P. 1, 13, 15.

कुलपालिका *kulapâlikâ*, i.e. *kula -pâla + ka*, f. A proper name, Daçak. in Chr. 188, 24.

कुलंपुन *kulaṁpuna*, i. e. *kula + m -pû + na* (or rather mutilated *-punant*, ptcple. pres. of *pû*), **I.** n. The name of a Tîrtha, MBh. 3, 6074. **II.** f. *nâ*, The name of a river, 13, 7646.

कुलंभर *kulaṁbhara*, i.e. *kula + m -bhṛi + a*, adj. Nourishing a family, MBh. 13, 4427.

कुलवन्त् *kula+vant*, adj., f. *vatí*, Belonging to a high family, Kathâs. 21, 103.

कुलाय *kulâya*, n. and m. A nest, Pańch. 94, 16.

कुलाल *kulâla*, m. A potter, Pańch. 218, 11.

कुलिक *kulika*, i.e. *kula+ika*, m. **1.** A kinsman, Yâjń. 2, 233. **2.** The name of a king of the Nâgas or serpents, MBh. 1, 2549.

कुलिङ्ग *kulińga*, I. m. **1.** A kind of mouse, Suçr. 2, 278, 3. **2.** The fork-tailed shrike, Suçr. 1, 201, 18. **3.** A proper name, MBh. 1, 2239. II. f. *gâ*, The name of a city, Râm. 2, 68, 16.

कुलिन्द *kulinda*, m. **1.** pl. The name of a people, MBh. 2, 590. **2.** Its prince, MBh. 3, 12350.

कुलिश *ku-liç+a* (perhaps rather *kliç+a*), m. and n. **1.** An axe, MBh. 3, 810. **2.** The thunderbolt of Indra, Bhartṛ. 2, 29.—Comp. *Nakha-*, thunderbolt-like nails, Pańch. 16, 4.

कुलीन *kulîna*, i.e. *kula+îna*, adj., f. *nâ*. **1.** Being of a good family, Man. 7, 210. **2.** Of noble breed, Râm. 5, 12, 31. **3.** Latter part of a comp. adj. Belonging to a race or family of; the aff. *îna* belongs to the whole comp., e.g. *tad-*, adj. Belonging to the same (i.e. his) race, Chr. 25, 53. *mahârâja-*, adj., f. *nâ*, Belonging to a race of great kings, Râm. 2, 88, 3. *a-*, adj. Sprung from a low family, Böhtl. Ind. Spr. 404. *dushkulîna*, i.e. *dus-kula+îna*, adj. Sprung from a low family, Râm. 3, 23, 15. *satkulîna*, i.e. *sant-kula+îna* (vb. *as*), adj. Well born, nobly descended.

कुलीनत्व *kulîna+tva*, n. Noble birth, Bhartṛ. 1, 61.

कुलीर *kulîra*, probably borrowed from κόλουρος, m. (and n.), A crab, Pańch. 265, 9; the sign of the zodiac, Cancer, Râm. 1, 19, 8.

कुलीरक *kulîra+ka*, m. A little crab, Pańch. 50, 11.

ऽकुलेय *-kuleya*, i.e. *kula+eya*, in *tatkuleya*, i.e. *tad-kula+eya*, adj. Belonging to his family, MBh. 1, 6804.

कुल्माष *kulmâsha*, I. m. Sour gruel, Bhâg. P. 5, 9, 12. II. f. *shî*, The name of a river.

कुल्य *kulya*, i.e. *kula+ya*, adj., f. *yâ*, Referring or belonging to a family, Bhâg. P. 7, 6, 12; Bhartṛ. 3, 24.—Comp. *Sa-*, m. 1. A distant kinsman, Man. 9, 187. 2. A kinsman in general.

कुल्या *kulyâ*, f. **1.** A rivulet, a canal, MBh. 3, 10408. **2.** The name of a river, MBh. 13, 1742.—Comp. *Ṛishi-*, f. 1. a holy river, MBh. 2, 1041. 2. the name of a river, MBh. 3, 8026. 3. a proper name, Bhâg. P. 5, 15, 6. *Deva-*, f. a proper name, Bhâg. P. 5, 15, 5.

कुल्याय *KULYÂYA*, a denomin. derived from the last by *ya*, Âtm. To become a rivulet, Bhartṛ. 2, 78.

कुवल *kuvala*, n. A water lily; see *kuvaleçaya*.

कुवलय *kuvalaya*, I. n. A water lily, Megh. 34. II. m. and n. The terrestrial globe (i. e. 3. *ku-valaya*), Bhâg. P. 5, 16, 5; 7.

कुवलयित *kuvalayita*, i.e. *kuvalaya+ita*, adj. Adorned with water lilies, Ragh. 11, 93.

कुवलयेशता *kuvalayeçatâ*, i.e. *kuvalaya-îça+tâ*, f. Dominion over the terrestrial globe, Râjat. 4, 372.

कुवलेशय *kuvaleçaya*, i.e. *kuvala+*

i-çî + a, m. A name of Vishṇu, MBh. 13, 7012.

कुविन्द *kuvinda*, m. A weaver.

कुवेर *kuvera*, probably for *kuvârya*, i.e. *ku-vṛi + ya*, m. The god of wealth, Man. 7, 42.

† कुश् *KUÇ*, v.r.; see *kus*.

कुश *kuça*, I. m. and n. The sacrificial grass, Poa cynosuroides, Man. 2, 43. II. m. 1. A proper name, Râm. 1, 34, 1. 2. One of the great dvîpas or divisions of the universe, Bhâg. P. 5, 1, 32.

कुशल *kuçala* (perhaps for *ku-çara*, and akin to *çaraṇa*), I. adj., f. *lâ*. 1. Happy, Bhag. 18, 10. 2. Healthy, Râm. 2, 70, 12. 3. Expert, Pańch. v. d. 33; skilful, Nal. 19, 19; 20; with loc., Man. 7, 190; gen., Yâjń. 2, 181; infin., MBh. 1, 53. II. *lam*, adv. Well, Bhâg. P. 1, 14, 29; mildly, Man. 6, 48. III. m. The name of a people, MBh. 6, 359. IV. n. 1. Well-being, Râm. 1, 52, 5. 2. Happiness, Pańch. 192, 23; prosperity (of devotion), Man. 2, 127. 3. Salutation, Râm. 1, 73, 8.—Instr. *lena*, adverbially, Cheerfully, Râm. 2, 34, 22.—Comp. *A-*, adj. unlucky, Bhag. 18, 21; Râm. 2, 64, 44. *Vaitâna-*, adj. Knowing the sacred ordinances, Man. 11, 37. *Çastra-*, adj. expert in arms. *Samudra-yâna-*, adj. well acquainted with sea-voyages and journeys by land, Man. 8, 157. *Sarvârtha-*, i.e. *sarva -artha-*, adj. expert in all affairs, Nal. 8, 4. *Svâdhîna-*, i.e. *sva-adhîna-*, adj. having prosperity in one's own power, Çâk. 64, 23.

कुशलता *kuçala + tâ*, f. Cleverness, Man. 12, 73.

कुशलिन् *kuçalin*, i.e. *kuçala + in*, adj., f. *nî*. 1. Prosperous, Nal. 2, 16. 2. Safe and sound, Râm. 3, 69, 14.

कुशवन्त् *kuça + vant*, I. adj., f. *vatî*, Abounding in Kuça grass, MBh. 3, 10533. II. f. *vatî*, The name of a city, MBh. 3, 11792.

कुशाम्ब *kuçâmba*, m. A proper name, MBh. 1, 2363.

कुशिक *kuçika*, m. A proper name, Râm. 1, 23, 11. pl. His descendants, MBh. 1, 3723.

कुशिन् *kuçin*, i.e. *kuça + in*, adj., f. *nî*, Holding Kuça grass, MBh. 13, 973.

कुशीद *kuçîda*; see *kusîda*.

कुशीलव *ku-çîla + va* (*va* is mutilated *vant*), 1. m. An actor, Man. 3, 155. 2. du. *Kuça* and *Lava*, the sons of Râma, Râm. 1, 4, 2.

कुशूल *kuçûla*, m. A granary, Hit. 66, 19; Man. 4, 7.

कुशेशय *kuçeçaya*, i.e. *kuça + i-çî + a*, I. adj. Dwelling in Kuça grass (viz. fire), MBh. 13, 1698. II. n. A water lily, Ragh. 18, 3.

कुष् *KUSH* (akin to *kṛish*, and based on *karsh*), ii. 9, *kushṇâ*, *ṇî*, Par. (also i. 6, Bhâg. P. 3, 16, 10), 1. To tear, Bhâg. P. 3, 16, 10. 2. † To draw out. —With the prep. अभि *abhi*, To pull, Suçr. 2, 145, 2.—With निस् *nis*, To tear out (i. 6), Bhâg. P. 5, 26, 19; *nishkushita*, Torn out, Ragh. 7, 47.

कुष्ठ *kushṭha*, m. and n. 1. A plant, Costus speciosus, Râm. 2, 94, 23. 2. i.e. *kush + tha*, Leprosy, Bhartṛ. 1, 89.

कुष्ठित *kushṭhita*, i.e. *kushṭha + ita*, adj., f. *tâ*, and कुष्ठिन् *kushṭhin*, i.e. *kushṭha + in*, adj., f. *nî*, Subject to leprosy, Suçr. 1, 270, 21; Man. 3, 7.

† कुस् *KUS*, also कुश् *KUÇ*, i.

4, Par. To embrace.—Cf. κυνέω for κυσ-νέω, ep. fut. κύσ-σω, etc.—O.H.G. chus, kussian; A.S. coss, cyssan, belong rather to *jush*.

कुसीद *kusida*, probably *ku-sad+a* (from the base of the pres. *sîda*), n. Usury, Pañch. i. d. 12; with *ç* for *s*: *kuçîda*, Man. 8, 410.

कुसुम *ku-suma*, probably *ku-smi+a*, n. A flower, Man. 11, 70.—Comp. *A-*, adj. flowerless, Kir. 5, 10.

कुसुममय *kusuma+maya*, adj., f. *yî*, Consisting of flowers, Prab. 7, 14.

कुसुमशरत्व *kusuma-çara+tva*, n. Having flowers instead of arrows, Çâk. d. 54.

कुसुमित *kusumita*, i.e. *kusuma+ita*, adj., f. *tâ*, Blossoming, Râm. 2, 96, 15.

कुसुम्भ *kusumbha*, probably *s* for *ç* and *ku-çumbh+a*, I. m. and n. Safflower, Carthamus tinctorius, Çiç. 9, 14. II. m. 1. A student's water-pot. 2. The name of a mountain, Bhâg. P. 5, 16, 27.

कुसुम्भवन्त् *kusumbha+vant*, adj. Bearing a water-pot, Man. 6, 52.

† **कुस्म्** *KUSM*, i. 10 (rather a denomin. derived from *ku-smaya*), Âtm. 1. To smile. 2. To see mentally, to imagine.

कुह् *KUH*, i. 10, Âtm. To surprise, to deceive (cf. the next).

कुहक *kuh+aka* (*kuh* probably = κεύθω), I. adj., f. *kâ*, and sbst. Deceiving, a cheat, MBh. 3, 14718; a juggler, Bhâg. P. 1, 15, 21. II. m. 1. A kind of frog, Suçr. 2, 290, 6. 2. The name of a king of the Nâgas or serpents, Bhâg. P. 5, 24, 29. III. n. and f. *kâ*, Juggling, Hit. iv. d. 101; MBh. 5, 5461.—Comp. *A-*, m. one who is no deceiver, Suçr. 2, 290, 6.

कुहर *kuh+ara* (cf. the last), I. n. 1. A cavern, Bhartr̥. 3, 29. 2. A cavity, Prab. 3, 15. 3. The interior, Bhâg. P. 3, 28, 33. 4. Coition, Daçak. in Chr. 196, 22. II. m. The name of a serpent, MBh. 1, 2701.

कुहु *kuhu*, The cry of the cuckoo, MBh. 15, 724.

कुहुकुहाय *KUHUKUHÂYA* (onomatop.?), Âtm. To show surprise, MBh. 3, 14129.

कुहू *kuhû*, 1. *kuh+û* (cf. *kuhaka*), f. The new moon; probably that part of the day of the new moon when the moon is completely waned, MBh. 3, 14129. 2. The name of a river, Bhâg. P. 5, 20, 10. 3. The cry of the cuckoo, Gît. 1, 47.

कू *KÛ*, and **कु** *KU*, ii. 2, Par., i. 1 and 6, Âtm., and as v.r. of *knû*, ii. 9, Par. Âtm. To cry. Frequent. *kokûya*, cf. κωκύω; cf. *âkûta*.

कूज् *KÛJ* (onomatop., from the cry of the cuckoo, cf. κόκκυξ, κόκκυγος; O.H.G. gauch; A.S. gaec), i. 1, Par. (Âtm. see *ni*), To make any inarticulate sound: 1. To cry, as a bird, MBh. 3, 9926. To coo, Râm. 2, 52, 2. 2. To buzz, R̥it. 6, 34, v.r. 3. To rustle, Ragh. 2, 12. 4. To moan, Râm. 3, 32, 33. 5. To fill with one of these sounds, Râm. 3, 78, 27. *kûjita*, n. 1. Inarticulate sound, Ragh. 9, 26. 2. Chirping, Bhâg. P. 4, 6, 12.—With the prep. **अनु** *anu*, To rival in chirping, Râm. 3, 79, 24; in singing, 2, 96, 13; in moaning, MBh. 3, 14144.—With **अभि** *abhi*, To buzz, Râm. 3, 79, 6.—With **आ** *â*, To sing, as a bird, Suçr. 2, 503, 13.—

With उद् *ud,* To utter a monotonous sound, Kathâs. 10, 130. — With उप *upa,* To fill with a sound, MBh. 3, 5212.—With नि *ni,* 1. To chirp, Râm. 3, 7, 4. 2. To fill with chirping, Bhâg. P. 3, 23, 20.—With निस् *nis,* To utter inarticulate sounds, Râm. 2, 95, 11.—With परि *pari,* To buzz round about, Sâh. D. 55, 20.—With प्रति *prati,* To answer by an inarticulate sound, Râm. 2, 56, 9.—With वि *vi,* To cry, Râm. 3, 76, 7.

कूज *kûj+a,* m. Croaking of the bowels, Suçr. 2, 514, 1.—Comp. *A-,* adj. not murmuring, MBh. 1, 4116. *Nishkûja,* i.e. *nis-,* adj. silent, Râm. 2, 59, 10.

कूजन *kûj+ana,* n. Croaking of the bowels, Suçr. 2, 402, 12.

कूजिन् *kûjin,* i.e. *kûja+in,* adj., f. *nî,* Subject to croaking of the bowels, Suçr. 2, 428, 13.

† **कूट्** *KÛṬ,* i. 10, Par. 1. To burn. 2. To sorrow. 3. To advise.—i. 10, Âtm. 1. To be foul. 2. To avoid giving. 3. To despond.

कूट *kûṭa,* I. m. and n. 1. The head, MBh. 16, 110. 2. Top, Râm. 6, 95, 24. 3. The peak or summit of a mountain, MBh. 1, 1172. 4. Chief, Bhâg. P. 2, 9, 19. 5. A multitude, a heap, Râm. 1, 13, 15. 6. A hammer, Bhâg. P. 4, 25, 6. 7. A trap, Râm. 4, 17, 6. 8. An enigma; *vâchaḥ kûṭa,* enigmatic speech, Bhâg. P. 6, 5, 29. II. adj. 1. Untrue, false, Yâjń. 1, 80; 2, 241 (viz. coin). 2. Insidious, Man. 7, 90 (concealed in wood, Kull.; cf. *kûṭa-khaḍga*). — Comp. *A-,* adj. 1. open, honest, Yâjń. 1, 323. 2. genuine (viz. coin), 2, 241. *Aksha-,*. n. a trap by means of dice, MBh. 3, 1266. *Akshi-,* n. the prominence over the eye, Yâjń. 3, 96. *Âmra-,* m., *Gṛidhra-, Chitra-,* m. names of mountains, Megh. 17; Hit. 18, 6; Râm. 1, 1, 30. *Tri-,* I. adj. having three elevations, MBh. 12, 6170. II. m. the name of several mountains, MBh. 2, 1484. *Nishkûṭa,* i.e. *nis-,* adj. devoid of fraud, free from danger, Râm. 2, 84, 16. *Brahmakûṭa,* i.e. *brahman-,* adj. pretending falsely to be a Brâhmaṇa, MBh. 13, 4526. *Ratna-,* m. a mountain in the Dekhan. *Vamrî-,* n. an ant-hill. *Hamsa-,* m. the hump on the Indian ox. *Hima-,* m. winter. *Hemakûṭa,* i.e. *heman-,* m. a range of mountains.

कूटक *kûṭa+ka,* I. adj. False, Yâjń. 2, 241. II. m. The name of a mountain, Bhâg. P. 5, 19, 16.

कूटकारक *kûṭa-kâraka,* m. A false witness, Man. 3, 158.

कूटकृत् *kûṭa-kṛi+t,* m. A forger, Yâjń. 2, 70.

कूटज *kûṭa-ja=kuṭaja,* Râm. 4, 29, 10.

कूटशस् *kûṭa+ças,* adv. By heaps, Arj. 9, 5.

कूटस्थ *kûṭa-stha* (vb. *sthâ*), adj. 1. Having attained the summit, Bhag. 6, 8; chief, Bhâg. P. 3, 5, 49. 2. Universally and perpetually the same, Bhâg. P. 2, 5, 17.—Comp. *Strî-ratna -kûṭa-stha,* adj. surrounded by a multitude of most beautiful women, Bhâg. P. 1, 11, 36.

† **कूड्** *KÛḌ,* i. 6, Par. 1. To eat. 2. To become firm.—Cf. 2. *kûl.*

कूण् *KÛṆ* (derived from *kushṇâ,* the base of the present of *kush*), i. 10, Par., Âtm. To contract; *kûṇita,* Suçr. 1, 362, 1.

† **कूप्** *KÛP,* i. 10, Par. To be weak.

कूप *kûpa,* m. 1. A pit, MBh. 1, 716. 2. A well, Man. 4, 202.—Comp. *Andha-,*

m. a pit-fall, a pit the opening of which is overgrown, Kathâs. 4, 120. *Romakûpa*, i.e. *roman-*, m. a pore of the skin.

कूपकार *kûpa-kâra*, m. A well-digger, Râm. 2, 80, 3.

कूर्च *kûrcha*, m. and n. **1.** A bunch of grass, Hariv. 7816; cf. Kathâs. 24, 96. **2.** Designation of some puffed up parts of the human body, e. g. the palms and balls of the foot, Suçr. 1, 338, 13.

कूर्चक *kûrcha+ka*, m. A brush, Suçr. 1, 101, 17.

कूर्चकिन् *kûrchakin*, i.e. *kûrchaka+in*, adj., f. *nî*, Puffy, Suçr. 1, 260, 9.

कूर्दन *kûrdana*, i.e. *kurd+ana*, n. Leaping, Pańch. 122, 5.

कूर्पर *kûrpara*, m. The elbow, Daçak. in Chr. 200, 2.

कूर्पासक *kûrpâsa+ka*, m. A bodice, Ṛit. 5, 8, v. l.—Cf. *kurpâsaka*.

कूर्म *kûrma*, m. **1.** A tortoise, Râm. 4, 16, 32. **2.** One of the five vital airs of the body, Vedântas. in Chr. 207, 15. **3.** The name of a king of the Nâgas or serpents, MBh. 1, 2549.

† 1. **कूल्** *KÛL*, i. 1, Par. To hinder.

2. **कूल्** *KÛL* (*kûḍ*), i. 10, Par. To singe, Suçr. 2, 435, 20.—With the prep. **अव** *ava*, To singe, Suçr. 2, 350, 18.

कूल *kûla*, n. **1.** A slope (ved.). **2.** A bank, Man. 6, 78.—Comp. *Dakshiṇa-*, adj., f. *lâ*, the bank of which is turned toward the south, Bhâg. P. 1, 19, 17. *Prâkkûla*, i. e. *prâńch-*, adj., f. *lâ*, turned toward the east, Man. 2, 75.

कूलंकष *kûlaṁkasha*, i.e. *kûla+m-kash+a*, adj. Rapid, Çâk. d. 117.

कूलमुद्रुज *kûla+m-ud-ruj+a*, adj. Hollowing out a bank, Ragh. 4, 22.

कूलिनी *kûlinî*, i.e. *kûla+in+î*, f. A river, Râjat. 5, 68.

कूवर *kûvara*, m. and n. The pole of a carriage, MBh. 3, 14601.

कूश्माण्ड *kûshmâṇḍa*, I. m. A kind of imp, Yâjń. 1, 284. **II.** m., and f. *ḍî*, The name of certain holy texts, Man. 8, 106; Yâjń. 3, 304.

1. **कृ** *KṚI* (originally *skṛi*; cf. *ava-*, *upa-*, *pari-*, *sam-*, *abhi-sam-*, *upa-sam-*, *prati-sam-*, and *koçaskṛit*), ii. 8, Par., Âtm., *karomi* (in epic poetry also *kurmi*, MBh. 3, 10943); ved. ii. 5, *kṛiṇomi*; ii. 2, e.g. *karshi*; i. 1, *karasi*. **1.** To make, Chr. 293, 3=Rigv. i. 88, 3 (*kṛiṇavante*, ved. conjunct.); Pańch. i. d. 436; Man. 2, 154; Râm. 1, 1, 59. **2.** To do, Râm. 1, 9, 10. **3.** To perform, Chr. 293, 4=Rigv. i. 88, 4 (*kṛiṇvantaḥ*); Man. 1, 65 (one's natural functions); Râm. 3, 53, 11 (an order); 1, 2, 2 (to show respect); Pańch. 82, 14 (to show pride). **4.** To tell, Râm. 1, 2, 34. **5.** To compose, Râm. 1, 3, 38. **6.** To appoint, Man. 7, 78; 9, 127. **7.** To sacrifice, Man. 3, 210. **8.** To act for or against a person; with the gen. of the person, MBh. 3, 2160; with the loc., Râm. 2, 64, 61. **9.** To assume, Man. 7, 10. **10.** To prepare, MBh. 13, 2794; to cook, Man. 9, 219. **11.** To cultivate, Yâjń. 2, 158; to till, Man. 10, 114. **12.** With nouns designing sounds, speech, To utter, MBh. 3, 11718. **13.** With nouns designing time, To pass, MBh. 15, 6; to wait, 1, 2294; with *chiram*, To delay, Hid. 4, 13. **14.** With nouns denoting mind, To give one's heart to, Man. 12, 118; to resolve, Chr. 11, 11; Râm. 1, 9, 55. **15.** With *astrâṇi*, To practise, MBh. 3, 11824; with *udakam* or *salilam*, To make the oblation of water to a deceased one, Man. 5, 188;

Râm. 1, 44, 49; with *kanyâm*, To contaminate, Man. 8, 367; with *kâryam*, To put up with, Pańch. iv. 28; with *daṇḍam*, To inflict a punishment, Lass. 14, 14; with *dârân*, To give a wife in marriage, Râm. 1, 77, 26; with *nâma*, To give a name, Man. 5, 70; with *paççhât*, To surpass, Ragh. 17, 18; with *punar*, To undo, Man. 8, 154; with *bhaṅgam*, To break, Pańch. 8, 17; with *bhiyam*, To fear, Râm. 1, 22, 14 Gorr.; with *vasuṁdharâm*, To wander over, Râm. 4, 46, 14; with *vahis*, To exclude, Man. 2, 103; to expel; with *vinâ*, To deprive, Nal. 13, 25; with *çramam*, To apply diligence, Man. 2, 168; with *sneham*, To think of the love, Râm. 1, 21, 14. **16.** With the instr., To do with, *kiṁ karishyati saṁsargaiḥ*, Of what use will be conjunction, Châṇ. 106, in Monatsb. d. Berl. Ak. d. Wiss., 1864, 413; To use, Man. 10, 91; with *manasâ*, To mind, MBh. 1, 7051; with *hṛidayena*, To love, Mṛichchh. 73, 7. **17.** To be of use, with gen., Böhtl. Ind. Spr. 2436. **18.** With the loc., To put on, MBh. 1, 1883; with *manasi*, To mind, Râm. 2, 64, 8; with *hṛidaye*, To mind, Châṇ. 92, in Monatsber. d. Berl. Ak. d. Wiss. 1864, 413; with *hṛidi*, To remember, Râjat. 5, 313; with *vaçe*, To subdue, Man. 2, 100. **19.** With the infin., To begin, Râm. 2, 6, 10.—Ptcple. of the pf. pass. *kṛita*, I. very often as former part of comp. words, and as n. **1.** Well done, MBh. 1, 1615. **2.** Well, Râm. 3, 3, 16. **3.** Away with, with instr., or *saha* and instr., Mṛichchh. 108, 5. **II.** n. **1.** Doing, Man. 7, 197. **2.** A benefit, Pańch. i. d. 427. **3.** The name of one of the dice, MBh. 4, 1578. **4.** The name of the first age of the world, Man. 1, 69. **III.** m. A proper name, MBh. 13, 4356. **IV.** Instr. *kṛitena*, and loc. *kṛite*, On account of, Râm. 1, 76, 6; 1, 45, 45.—**Comp.** *Akṛita* see separately. *Dushkṛita*, i.e. *dus-*, I. adj. 1. wicked. Man. 11, 229. 2. unreasonable, MBh. 2, 1400. II. n. sin, Man. 3, 191. *Brahmâñjalikṛita*, i.e. *brahman-añjali-kṛita*, adj., an anomalous comp., having made scriptural homage, Man. 2, 70. *Viçva-*, adj. made by Viçvakarman (?), Chr. 38, 12. *Saha-*, adj. assisted, Bhâshâp. 65. *Su-*, I. adj. 1. done well. 2. treated with kindness. 3. virtuous, pious. 4. fortunate. II. n. 1. a virtuous act, Man. 3, 37. 2. kindness. 3. virtue. 4. fortune. *Svayam-*, adj. 1. self-formed. 2. Done by, to, or for one's self. *Hâhâ-*, adj. filled with the uproar of a battle, Chr. 32, 25.—Ptcple. of the fut. pass., *kartavya*, n. A work, Râm. 1, 34, 32. **Comp.** *Tad-*, n. suitable action, Râjat. 6, 269. *Kârya* and *kṛitya* see separately.—Causal, *kâraya*, **1.** To cause to be performed, Man. 2, 30; to cause to be cultivated, Yâjń. 2, 158; to cause to be put, Man. 8, 251; to cause to be treated, Râm. 2, 58, 16. **2.** To order to make, Man. 7, 16; to order to prepare, Pańch. 129, 9; to order to practise, Man. 8, 410. **3.** To make, Hit. d. 71. *kârita*, Caused, Man. 4, 118. *kâritâ vṛiddhiḥ*, An exacted interest, caused by risk, Man. 8, 153. *kârayitavya*, **1.** To be caused to perform, Râm. 2, 14, 16. **2.** To be procured, Pańch. 24, 21. —Desiderative, *chikîrsha* (in epic poetry Âtm., Nal. 3, 14), **1.** To desire to do, Râm. 2, 35, 11; to desire to perform, Man. 11, 192. **2.** To desire to establish, Râjat. 5, 461. *chikîrshita*, **1.** Desired to be performed, Man. 4, 254. **2.** n. Intention, Man. 7, 202.—*kṛi*, combined and compounded: With the adv.

अग्निसात् *agni + sât*, To burn, Râjat. 5, 226.—With *aṅga*, which becomes **अङ्गी** *aṅgî*, **1.** To put up with, Pańch. i. d. 192; to submit, Râjat. 5, 177. **2.** To subdue, Amar. 52. **3.** To take to heart, Pańch. 236, 4. **4.** To promise, Bhartṛ. 2, 69.—With the prepos. **अति** *ati*, *ati-*

kṛita, Excessive, MBh. 3, 10054; n. Excess, Râm. 5, 25, 21.—With the noun *adhara,* which becomes अधरी *adharî,* To overcome, Çâk. d. 16, v.r.—With the prep. अधि *adhi,* 1. To put at the head, Bhâg. P. 1, 9, 37. 2. To appoint, Yâjń. 2, 30. 3. Pass. To get entitled, Bhâg. P. 5, 10, 16. 4. With loc., To be at the head, to inspect, MBh. 4, 241. *adhikṛita,* Best, Pańch. iii. d. 67. Comp. *Dharma-,* m. a judge, Pańch. 41, 16.—Absolutive, *adhikṛitya,* Referring to, Çâk. 4, 5.—With अनु *anu,* 1. To do afterward, Amar. 50. 2. To back, Pańch. iii. d. 270. 3. To imitate, Man. 2, 199. 4. To repay, with the acc., Bhâg. P. 3, 14, 20. 5. To bring in harmony, Bhâg. P. 7, 7, 36. Caus. To cause to imitate, Bhâg. P. 4, 29, 17.—With अप *apa,* 1. To remove, MBh. 3, 10492. 2. To injure, Râm. 4, 16, 19; with the gen. of the person, Râm. 2, 38, 5; with the acc., MBh. 3, 14835. *apakṛita,* n. Injury, Pańch. i. d. 317. —With अभि *abhi,* To make (*nivâsam,* to settle), Sund. 2, 26. Desider. *raṇam,* To desire to fight, MBh. 4, 1660.—With the noun *abhyantara,* which becomes अभ्यन्तरी *abhyantarî,* 1. To initiate, Râm. 6, 40, 14. 2. To make intimate, Pańch. i. d. 290.—With अलम् *alam,* To adorn, Râm. 1, 73, 19.—With अभ्यलम् *abhi-alam,* To adorn, Râm. 3, 53, 36.—With उपालम् *upa-alam,* To adorn, Pańch. 159, 19.—With समलम् *sam-alam,* 1. To adorn, MBh, 1, 4941. 2. To violate, with gen., Man. 8, 16.—With स्वलम् *su-alam,* To adorn beautifully, Chr. 60, 35.—With the prep. अव *ava,* the initial is kept in *niravaskṛita,* i.e. *nis-,* Pure, MBh. 12, 13201.

—With the prep. आ *â,* Caus. 1. To ask, Râm. 2, 13, 2. 2. To call, Pańch. 24, 13; *âhâraṇîya,* To be called. 3. To produce, Vedântas. in Chr. 215, 6. Desider. To desire to perform, Daçak. in Chr. 200, 24.—With the prepositions अपा *apa-â,* To remove, MBh. 1, 5680. *ṛiṇam,* To pay, Man. 6, 35.—With उपा *upa-â,* 1. To bring near, MBh. 3, 3098. 2. To deliver, Nal. 25, 16. 3. To grant, MBh. 3, 15965. 4. To gain, MBh. 3, 10278. 5. To describe, Bhâg. P. 3, 6, 35. 6. To perform a preparation for a sacred work, Man. 4, 95. *an-upâkṛita,* adj. Not hallowed by holy texts, Man. 5, 7.—With समुपा *sam-upa-â,* To satisfy (?), MBh. 1, 7765.—With निरा *nis-â,* 1. To remove, Râm. 5, 13, 31. 2. To disown, Chr. 8, 27; MBh. 13, 4753. 3. To disapprove, Vedântas. in Chr. 215, 17. 4. To undo, MBh. 1, 7666.—With व्या *vi-â,* To explain, Râm. 5, 56, 5. *a-vyâkṛita,* adj. Undivided, Bhâg. P. 3, 11, 37.—With the noun *âkula,* which becomes आकुली *âkulî,* To trouble, Pańch. v. d. 25; Râm. 4, 41, 29.—With the adv. आत्मसात् *âtmasât,* i.e. *âtman + sât,* 1. To put in one's self, Yâjń. 3, 54; cf. Man. 6, 25. 2. To subdue, Bhartṛ. 3, 34.—With the adv. आविस् *âvis,* To make manifest, Sâh. D. 15, 20; to show, 60, 17. *âvishkṛita,* Publicly known, Man. 11, 226. *an-âvishkṛita,* adj. Not public, ib.—With the noun *âharaṇa,* which becomes आहरणी *âharaṇî,* To make a present, Ragh. 7, 29.—With the noun *unmanas,* which becomes उन्मनी *unmanî,* To agitate, Prab. 62, 3.—With the prep. उप *upa,* 1. To confer,

Man. 2, 149. **2.** To offer, Man. 2, 245. **3.** To serve, Pańch. i. d. 95; with the gen. of the person, Pańch. i. d. 398. **4.** To confer a benefit, Man. 8, 394; with the gen. of the person, Râm. 4, 38, 47. **5.** To honour, Râjat. 5, 311. **6.** To set out on, with the dat., Râm. 1, 37, 5 Schl. (Gorr. v.r.). The initial is kept in *upaskṛita*, **1.** Possessed of, having, Bhâg. P. 1, 11, 28. **2.** Prepared, MBh. 1, 778. **3.** Adorned, Bhartṛ. 2, 12. **4.** Benefitted, MBh. 13, 5893. **Comp.** *An-upaskṛita*, adj. 1. uncultivated, MBh. 13, 3335. 2. not ornamented, Man. 5, 112. 3. untainted, Man. 3, 257. 4. blameless, Man. 7, 98. *nirupaskṛita*, i. e. *nis-*, adj. 1. unaccomplished, MBh. 12, 9768. 2. plain, 12, 9079.—With the prepositions प्रत्युप *prati-upa*, To repay, Pańch. i. d. 95 v.r.—With the noun *upahâra*, which becomes उपहारी *upahârî*, To offer, with gen., Kathâs. 10, 141.—With the noun *uras*, which becomes उरी *urî*, To promise, to offer, Ragh. 15, 70.—With the noun *ushṇa*, which becomes उष्णी *ushṇî*, To warm, Mṛichchh. 50, 1.—With ऊरी *ûrî*, To grant, Hit. iii. d. 96.—With the numeral *eka*, which becomes एकी *ekî*, To join, Râm. 5, 13, 58.—With the noun *aushadha*, which becomes औषधी *aushadhî*, To change into a medicine, Mṛichchh. 121, 13.—With the noun *kad-arth* + *a*, which becomes कदर्थी *kadarthî*, To contemn, MBh. 3, 11381.—With the noun *kapila*, which becomes कपिली *kapilî*, To make tawny, MBh. 3, 16351.—With the noun *karada*, which becomes करदी *karadî*, To make tributary, MBh. 1, 4462.—With the noun *kara*, which becomes करी *karî*, To offer as tribute, Kathâs. 19, 114.—With the noun *kalusha*, which becomes कलुषी *kalushî*, To trouble, Râm. 3, 22, 14; 5, 57, 5.—With the noun *kashâya*, which becomes कषायी *kashâyî*, To redden, Râm. 6, 33, 17.—With कात् *kât*, an old abl. sing. of *kim*, To contemn, Bhâg. P. 5, 7, 11.—With the noun *kuṇḍala*, which becomes कुण्डली *kuṇḍalî* in *kuṇḍalî-kṛita*, adj. **1.** Ring-streaked, Nal. 14, 3. **2.** Moving circularly, Suçr. 2, 523, 16.—With the comp. *kṛita-artha*, which becomes कृतार्थी *kṛitârthî*, To satisfy, Lass. 83, 13.—With the noun *kṛiça*, becoming कृशी *kṛiçî*, To make poor, Mṛichchh. 19, 13.—With the noun *koshṭhaka*, which becomes कोष्ठकी *koshṭhakî*, To surround, MBh. 14, 2230.—With the noun *khaṇḍa*, which becomes खण्डी *khaṇḍî*, To cut to pieces, Pańch. 262, 16.—With the noun *khala*, which becomes खली *khalî*, To abuse, Mṛichchh. 33, 24.—With the noun *khila*, becoming खिली *khilî*, **1.** To lay waste, Ragh. 11, 14. **2.** To deprive of any strength, Mârk. P. 9, 8.—With *gaṇḍûsha*, becoming गण्डूषी *gaṇḍûshî*, to use as water for rinsing the mouth, Bhâg. P. 9, 15, 3.—With *goshpada*, becoming गोष्पदी *goshpadî*, To change into a pool, Râm. 5, 31, 62.—With *grâsa*, becoming ग्रासी *grâsî*, To devour, Kathâs. 9, 57.—With *chakra*, becoming चक्री *chakrî*, To make circular, Kumâras. 3, 70.—With *chaṇḍa*, becoming चण्डी *chaṇḍî*, To provoke, Mâlav. 44, 5.—With चमत् *chamat*,

Caus. To cause to be surprised, Kathâs. 26, 225.—With *chitta*, becoming चित्ती *chittî*, To make something the object of thinking, Bhâg. P. 4, 1, 28.—With *chitra*, becoming चित्री *chitrî*, To change into a picture, Çâk. d. 148.—With *chihna*, becoming चिह्नी *chihnî*, To mark, MBh. 13, 826.—With *chûrṇa*, becoming चूर्णी *chûrṇî*, To crush, Râm. 5, 54, 7.—With *jaṭila*, becoming जटिली *jaṭilî*, To interweave, Pañch. 223, 2.—With *jaṭhara*, becoming जठरी *jaṭharî*, To shut in one's self, Bhâg. P. 3, 9, 20.—With *jaḍa*, becoming जडी *jaḍî*, **1.** To stiffen, Râm. 6, 6, 1. **2.** To benumb, Râm. 5, 33, 5. **3.** To make stupid, Bhâg. P. 6, 3, 25.—With *jarjara*, becoming जर्जरी *jarjarî*, To beat to pieces, Râm. 6, 83, 54.—With *tanu*, becoming तनू *tanû*, To diminish, to abandon, Ragh. 6, 80.—With *tâmra*, becoming ताम्री *tâmrî*, To redden, MBh. 7, 8458.—With the adv. तिरस् *tiras*, **1.** To remove, Bhâg. P. 3, 2, 18. **2.** To cover, Man. 4, 49. **3.** To surpass, Pañch. 118, 13. **4.** To conquer, Hit. iii. d. 8. **5.** To contemn, Bhâg. P. 1, 18, 48. *a-tiraskṛita*, adj. Greatest, Pañch. 7, 10.—With the noun *tîrtha*, which becomes तीर्थी *tîrthî*, To hallow, Bhâg. P. 1, 13, 9.—With *tuchchha*, becoming तुच्छी *tuchchhî*, To despise, Bhâg. P. 5, 10, 25.—With *tṛiṇa*, becoming तृणी *tṛiṇî*, To value like a grass-blade, MBh. 1, 7062.—With the pron. त्वम् *tvam* (see *yushmad*), To thou somebody, as an insult, Yâjñ. 3, 292.—With the noun *dakshiṇa*, which becomes दक्षिणी *dakshiṇî*, To walk around somebody keeping the right side towards him, Bhâg. P. 3, 24, 41.—With *dâsa*, becoming दासी *dâsî*, To enslave somebody, Kathâs. 22, 84. To subdue, Chr. 94, 30.—With *divasa*, becoming दिवसी *divasî*, To turn into day, Mṛichchh. 59, 5.—With *dîrgha*, becoming दीर्घी *dîrghî*. **1.** To extend, Kumâras. 3, 26. **2.** To carry far, Megh. 32.—With *duḥkha*, becoming दुःखा *duḥkhâ*, To afflict, Çiç. 2, 11.—With *dûra*, becoming दूरी *dûrî*, **1.** To remove, Prab. 90, 15. **2.** To surpass, Çâk. d. 16.—With *dṛiḍha*, becoming दृढी *dṛiḍhî*, To fasten, Prab. 43, 14.—With *dvi-guṇa*, becoming द्विगुणी *dviguṇî*, To double, Çiç. 1, 63.—With the adv. द्विजातिसात् *dvi-jâti+sât*, To offer to Brâhmaṇas, Râjat. 5, 120.—With the interj. धिक् *dhik*, **1.** To reproach, MBh. 12, 1422. **2.** To show contempt, Râm. 4, 9, 8.—With the noun *dhvaja*, becoming ध्वजी *dhvajî*, To use as a means of protection, Hit. ii. d. 95.—With *nagna*, becoming नग्नी *nagnî*, To make somebody a naked mendicant, Bhartṛ. 1, 64.—With नमस् *namas*, *namas-kṛi*, **1.** To salute, Man. 11, 110. **2.** To adore, MBh. 3, 2160; with dat. and acc.—With *nava*, becoming नवी *navî*, **1.** To renew, Ragh. 16, 38. **2.** To refresh, Çâk. 62, 12.—With the prep. नि *ni*, *nikṛita*, **1.** Humbled, Râm. 1, 56, 22. **2.** Dejected, Nal. 14, 15. **3.** Base, Râm. 5, 23, 6; n. Mortification, Bhartṛ. 2, 30, v.r. *nikartavya* in *tair asmâkam nikartavyam*, We must be treated ill by them, MBh.

3, 1406.—With विनि *vi-ni,* 1. To injure, MBh. 3, 14036. 2. To defraud, Man. 9, 213.—With the noun *nimitta,* becoming निमित्ती *nimitti,* 1. To point out as cause, Râjat. 3, 89. 2. To use as means, Daçak. in Chr. 184, 14.—With *nis-dhana,* becoming निर्धनी *nirdhanî,* To make poor, Daçak. in Chr. 194, 7.—With the prep. निस् *nis,* 1. To remove, Dev. 1, 31. 2. To prepare, Chr. 294, 1 = Rigv. i. 92, 1. *nishkrita,* n. Expiation, Bhâg. P. 1, 19, 2. *a-nishkṛita,* adj. Not expiated, Man. 11, 53.—With the noun *nis-pattra,* which becomes निष्पत्त्रा *nishpattrâ,* To wound, e.g. a deer, with an arrow in such a manner that its feathered part juts out on the other side, Daçak. 196, 1.—With *nis-spand + a,* becoming निष्पन्दी *nishpandî,* To render motionless, Mṛichchh. 85, 1.—With न्यक् *nyak,* acc. sing. n. of *nyañch,* To insult, Râjat. 5, 436.—With *nyâsa,* becoming न्यासी, To deliver in trust, Râjat. 5, 182.—With *pañchan-çikhâ,* becoming पञ्चशिखी *pañchaçikhî,* To make somebody an ascetic, Bhartṛ. 1, 64.—With *pañchan,* becoming पञ्ची *pañchî,* To make fivefold, so as to contain the five elements, Vedântas. in Chr. 206, 19.—With the adv. परसात् *para + sât,* To give in marriage, Böhtl. Ind. Spr. 931.—With *parâñch-mukha,* becoming पराङ्मुखी *parâṅmukhî,* To put to flight, MBh. 6, 5500.—With the prep. परि *pari,* To surround, MBh. 13, 5044. The initial *s* changed to *sh* is preserved in *parishkṛita.* 1. Adorned, Râm. 3, 11, 4. 2. Prepared; *su-par°,* Well prepared, 4, 437; *kâla-par°,* Seasonable, Râm. 5, 25, 35.—With the noun *parusha,* becoming परुषी *parushî,* 1. To soil. 2. To use roughly.—With the compound noun *para-upakaraṇa,* becoming परोपकरणी *paropakaraṇî,* To make somebody the instrument of another, Hit. ii. d. 23.—With *parvata,* becoming पर्वती *parvatî,* To exalt, Bhartṛ. 2, 71.—With *pavitra,* becoming पवित्री *pavitrî,* To purify.—With *paçu,* becoming पशू *paçû,* 1. To change into a beast. 2. To destine for immolation.—With *pâtra,* becoming पात्री *pâtrî,* 1. To make something an object worthy of (e.g. interest), Megh. 48. 2. To honour, Çâk. d. 116.—With the adv. पुरस् *puras, puras-kṛi,* 1. To place in front, Râjat. 5, 327. 2. To lead, Chr. 20, 24. 3. To appoint, MBh. 4, 242. 4. To show, Râjat. 5, 328. 5. To regard, Râm. 5, 90, 30. 6. To prefer, Kathâs. 29, 105. 7. To honour, Çâk. 18, 18. 8. To use as pretext, Daçak. in Chr. 189, 2. *puraskṛita,* 1. Attended by. 2. Provided with.—With the noun *pulaka,* becoming पुलकी *pulakî, pulakî-kṛita,* Having the hairs of the body erect, Bhâg. P. 3, 15, 25.—With the imitative sound पूत् *pût,* To blow, Pañch. 93, 4.—With पेशी *peçî,* and पेषी *peshî,* To cut to pieces, Râm. 2, 105, 33 Gorr.—With the prep. प्र *pra,* 1. To make, Man. 8, 239. 2. To cause, Pañch. i. d. 276; with infin., Chr. 296, 8 = Rigv. i. 112, 8. 3. To do, Pañch. 4, 37. 4. To perform, MBh. 3, 12142. 5. To appoint, Man. 7, 60. 6. With *kanyâm,* To pollute, Man. 8, 370; with *dârân,* To marry, MBh. 1, 1844; with *buddhim,* To resolve,

Nal. 3, 25; with *manas*, To apply one's heart to, Man. 7, 12. *prakṛita*, 1. Accomplished, Kathâs. 4, 1. 2. Mentioned, Yâjń. 1, 243.—With विप्र *vi-pra*, To injure, Râm. 3, 1, 20.—With संप्र *sam-pra*, To make, Râm. 6, 82, 182; to perform, MBh. 1, 2387.—With the noun *prakaṭa*, which becomes प्रकटी *prakaṭi*, To make manifest, Bhartṛ. 2, 64.—With *praguṇa*, which becomes प्रगुणी *praguṇi*, To put up, Pańch. 157, 23; to array, 218, 7; to lay (as traps), 114, 6.—With the prep. प्रति *prati*, 1. To repay, Râm. 3, 38, 22; with the person in the gen., Râm. 3, 65, 14; in the dat., MBh. 1, 840; loc., MBh. 13, 4764. 2. To resist, with the acc. of an object, MBh. 1, 5656; gen. of a person, Râm. 6, 88, 34. 3. To cure, MBh. 1, 4027. 4. To repair, Man. 9, 285. *pratikṛita*, n. 1. Requital, Râm. 6, 91, 10. 2. Resistance, Ragh. 12, 94. **Comp.** *Kṛita-pratikṛita*, n. 1. assault and resistance, MBh. 4, 351. 2. requital for an assault, Râm. 6, 91, 10. Desider. To desire to repay, MBh. 3, 1282.—With the noun *prativachana*, which becomes प्रतिवचनी *prativachani*, To answer, Çâk. d. 85.—With *pradakshiṇa*, which becomes प्रदक्षिणी *pradakshiṇi*, To walk round some one, keeping the right side towards him, Çâk. p. 51, 17.—With *pramâṇa*, becoming प्रमाणी *pramâṇi*, 1. To mete out to, Bhartṛ. 2, 90. 2. To obey, Çâk. 78, 19. 3. To prove.—With the adv. प्रादुस् *prâdus*, To make visible, to show, Chr. 34, 12. *agnim*, To kindle, Man. 4, 104.—With the imitative sound फुत् *phut*, or फूत् *phût*, To boil, to show indignation, to foam, Pańch. 237, 14.—With the noun *bhasman*, becoming भस्मी *bhasmi*, To reduce to ashes.—With *manda*, becoming मन्दी *mandi*, To diminish, Çâk. 5, 13.—With *malina*, becoming मलिनी *malini*, To soil. *malini-karaṇiya*, n. An action which causes defilement, Mân. 11, 125.—With *mekhalâ*, which becomes मेखली *mekhali*, To put on the sacrificial string, MBh. 13, 973.—With *rakta-paṭa* (vb. *rańj*), becoming रक्तपटी *raktapaṭi*, To change into one who wears a red cloth, i.e. into an ascetic, Pańch. iv. d. 36.—With *rikta*, ptcple. pf. pass. of *rich*, becoming रिक्ती *rikti*, To steal, Pańch. 89, 2.—With *laksha*, becoming लक्षी *lakshi*, To aim at, Çâk. 104, 21.—With *vandî*, becoming वन्दी *vandi*, To take prisoner, Vikr. d. 3.—With *vaça*, becoming वशी *vaçi*, To subdue, Pańch, 13, 3.—With वशे *vaçe*, loc. of *vaça*, To subdue, Râm. 3, 55, 7.—With वषट् *vashaṭ*, To accompany with the exclamation *vashaṭ*, Man. 2, 106.—With the prep. वि *vi*, 1. To change, MBh. 13, 1513; Man. 1, 76. 2. To disfigure, Man. 9, 288. 3. To blind, MBh. 3, 8881. 4. To develop, Man. 1, 75. 5. To create, MBh. 14, 1497. 6. To adorn, MBh. 1, 1429. 7. To move to and fro, Râm. 3, 74, 18. 8. To destroy, MBh. 3, 1150. 9. To become alienated, Man. 9, 15. 10. To infest each other, MBh. 1, 7670. Caus. To cause to change, Hit. 75, 11.—With the noun *vikacha*, becoming विकची *vikachi*, To open, Bhartṛ. 2, 65.—With *vi-nigaḍa*, becoming विनिगडी *vinigaḍi*, To unfetter, Daçak. in Chr. 198, 8.—With *vi-manas*, becoming विमनी *vi-*

manî in *vimanî-kṛita*, **1.** Sad. **2.** Offended. **3.** Altered in mind.—With *vi-varṇa-maṇi*, becoming विवर्णमणी *vivarṇamaṇî*, To make jewels discoloured, Çâk. d. 61.—With *vi-rajas*, becoming विरजी *virajî* in *virajî-kṛita*, **1.** Freed from dust. **2.** Freed from passion.—With *vishaya*, becoming विषयी *vishayî*, To make something the object of thought, Vedântas. in Chr. 215, 23.—With *vyâkula*, becoming व्याकुली *vyâkulî*, To trouble, Pańch. 63, 8.—With *çithila*, becoming शिथिली *çithilî*, To make languid, Ṛit. 6, 24. — With *çîrshan-avaçesha*, becoming शीर्षावशेषी *çîrshâvaçeshî*, To leave only the head undestroyed, Bhartṛ. 2, 27. — With *çûnya*, becoming शून्यी *çûnyî*, To make empty, to leave, Pańch. 23, 18. — With *saṁkrama*, becoming संक्रमी *saṁkramî*, To use as means, Daçak. in Chr. 196, 17 (by means of her).—With *sajja*, becoming सज्जी *sajjî*, To prepare, Pańch. 62, 25.—With सत् *sat*, acc. n. s. of *sant*, ptcple. pres. of *as*, **1.** To adorn, Man. 3, 96. **2.** To welcome, to receive hospitably, Râm. 3, 53, 25. **3.** To honour, Pańch. 26, 21. *satkṛita*, **1.** Done rightly. **2.** Worshipped. **3.** Respected. **4.** Welcomed. n. **1.** Virtue. **2.** Hospitality. **3.** Food, Man. 3, 264.—Comp. *A-satkṛita*, adj. wicked, Nal. 24, 31. *Su-*, n. Excellent hospitality, Chr. 59, 18. —With *sa-nâtha*, becoming सनाथी *sanâthi*, To make possessed of a protector, Çâk. 28, 14.—With *sa-patra*, which becomes सपत्रा *sapatrâ*, To wound, e.g. a deer, with an arrow in such a manner that the feathered part enters in its body, Daçak. 196, 1.—With the prep. सम् *sam*, becoming *saṁkṛi*, and, by keeping the initial *s*, *saṁskṛi*, **1.** To unite, Mṛichchh. 137, 20. **2.** To prepare, Râm. 3, 53, 5. **3.** To hallow; *a-saṁskṛita*, Not hallowed, Man. 5, 56. **4.** To hallow by the investment of the sacrificial cord, to invest, Ragh. 15, 31; Man. 8, 412; *a-saṁskṛita*, Not invested, Man. 2, 39; to hallow by giving in marriage, Man. 9, 173; *a-saṁskṛita*, Unmarried, Pańch. iii. d. 218; to hallow by solemn obsequies, MBh. 13, 7777. **5.** To adorn, Çiç. 9, 25.—Causal, **1.** To cause to perform, MBh. 1, 4379. **2.** To cause to be invested, MBh. 2, 1594. **3.** To cause to be solemnly buried, MBh. 1, 4936. **4.** To make, MBh. 4, 2281.—With अभिसम् *abhi-sam*, *abhisaṁskṛi*, To hallow, MBh. 3, 8224.—With उपसम् *upa-sam*, *upasaṁskṛi*, **1.** To prepare, MBh. 1, 7203. **2.** To adorn, Suçr. 2, 76, 9.—With प्रतिसम् *prati-sam*, *pratisaṁskṛi*, **1.** To repair, Man. 9, 279. **2.** To unite, Suçr. 2, 77, 2.—With the noun *sam-ṛiddha* (vb. *ṛidh*), becoming समृद्धी *samṛiddhî*, To make wealthy, Daçak. in Chr. 194, 2.—With *sâchi*, becoming साची *sâchî*, To turn aside, Mâlav. d. 73.—With *sâra*, becoming सारी *sârî*, To make hard, Çâk. d. 54. —With *su-gupta*, becoming सुगुप्ती *suguptî*, To guard well, Pańch. 208, 21. —With *sthira*, becoming स्थिरी *sthirî*, To strengthen, Çâk. 53, 23.—With *sphîta*, becoming स्फीती *sphîtî*, To augment, Râm. 2, 65, 26.—With *sva*, becoming स्वी *svî*, **1.** To appropriate, Daçak. in Chr. 186, 4. **2.** To win, 180, 19. **3.** To assent to, Râjat. 5, 436.

svîkṛita, 1. Agreed. 2. Promised.—Cf. Lat. creare with the causal *kâra-yâmi,* whose first *a* originally was also short, as may be inferred from the comparison of the kindred languages.

2. कृ *KṚI* ; see 2. *kṛî.*

कृकर *kṛi-kara* (*kṛi* is an imitative sound), m. 1. A kind of partridge, Râm. 4, 50, 12. 2. One of the five vital airs, that which assists in digestion, Vedântas. in Chr. 207, 16.

कृकलास *kṛikalâsa,* m. A lizard, a chameleon, MBh. 13, 3455.

कृकलासक *kṛikalâsa* + *ka,* m. A lizard, a chameleon, MBh. 13, 736 (?).

कृकवाकु *kṛikavâku,* i.e. *kṛika* (an imitative sound) -*vach* + *u,* m. 1. A cock, Bhartṛ. suppl. 21. 2. A peacock, Râm. 2, 28, 10.

कृकाटिका *kṛikâṭikâ,* f. The joint of the neck, Suçr. 1, 345, 11. .

कृकालिका *kṛikâlikâ,* f. A certain bird, Pańch. 167, 25.

कृच्छ्र *kṛichchhra* (probably from an old pres. base *kṛichchha* of the vb. *kṛish*; cf. e.g. *ish,* pr. base *ichchha*), I. adj., f. *râ.* 1. Painful, Râm. 3, 74, 29. 2. Difficult, Râm. 3, 46, 16. 3. Dangerous, Suçr. 1, 131, 4. 4. Wicked, Man. 6, 78. 5. Miserable, MBh. 3, 15388. II. n. and m. 1. Pain, Bhâg. P. 9, 24, 35. 2. Difficulty, Râm. 3, 68, 53. 3. Distress, Bhartṛ. 2, 23. 4. Penance, Man. 4, 222. III. acc. *ram,* adverbially, Miserably, Râm. 4, 22, 7. Instr. *reṇa,* adv. With difficulty, Pańch. 137, 25 ; with much ado, Pańch. 40, 10. Abl. *rât,* adv. With difficulty, Râm. 3, 73, 11.—Comp. *Ati-,* m. 1. a very severe penance, described Man. 11, 213. 2. *Na ati-kṛichchhrât,* easily, MBh. 1, 1442. *Kṛi-chchhrâtikṛichchhra,* i. e. *kṛichchhra* -*ati-,* m. 1. du. a common and a very severe penance, Man. 11, 208. 2. a particular penance, Yâjń. 3, 321. *Artha-kṛichchhra,* n. a difficult question, Nal. 15, 3. *Tapta-,* m. and n. a kind of penance, Man. 11, 214. *Dharma-,* a moral difficulty, a situation in which it is difficult to act rightly, Nal. 24, 18. *Parṇa-,* m. a kind of penance. *Prâṇa-,* danger of life. *Saumya-,* n. a kind of penance.

कृच्छ्रता *kṛichchhra* + *tâ,* f. Dangerousness, Suçr. 2, 138, 20.

† कृड् *KṚIḌ,* v.r. of *kûḍ.*

† कृण्व् *KṚIṆV,* ii. 5 (base of the pres. *kṛiṇu*), Par. 1. To do (see 1. *kṛi* ii. 5, ved.). 2. To injure (see 2. *kṛî*).

1. कृत् *KṚIT,* i. 6, Par. (in epic poetry also Âtm., MBh. 3, 17212 ; and i. 1, MBh. 3, 11383), base of the pres., etc., *kṛinta.* 1. To cut, MBh. 1, 3641. 2. To cut off, Râm. 3, 75, 4. 3. To cut down, Pańch. 250, 6. 4. To cut out, Man. 4, 172 ; to extract, Man. 8, 12. 5. To kill, MBh. 1, 5593.—Caus. To cut, Pańch. 143, 13.—With the prepositions समधि *sam-adhi,* To cut in addition, MBh. 3, 13294.—With अनु *anu,* To cut one by one, MBh. 13, 2906. —With अव *ava,* 1. To cut off, Suçr. 2, 237, 15. 2. To destroy, MBh. 1, 6810. —Caus. To order a gash to be made on, Man. 8, 281.—With उद् *ud,* 1. To cut out, 11, 104 (105). 2. To pull out, Bhâg. P. 4, 5, 2. 3. To cut to pieces, Ragh. 12, 49.—With नि *ni,* To cut down, Râm. 3, 33, 36.—With विनि *vi-ni,* To cut off, Râm. 3, 31, 48.—With निस् *nis,* 1. To cut out, to separate, MBh. 3, 8846. 2. To cut down, 1, 2835. —With परि *pari,* 1. To cut wholly,

Râm. 6, 39, 21. 2. To exclude, Man. 4, 219.—With प्र *pra*, To cut to pieces, MBh. 3, 11383 (i. 1).—With वि *vi*, 1. To rend, Râm. 3, 56, 39. 2. To divide, Nal. 10, 17 (i. 1). Caus. To rend, Pañch. 91, 5.—With सम्, To cut in pieces, Râm. 3, 25, 6.—Cf. Lat. curtus; Goth. giltha, grinda-, dis-skreitan; κερσ in ἀκερσεκόμης, and *kartrikâ*.

2. कृत् *KṚIT*, ii. 7. 1. To spin, (ved.). 2. † To surround.

3. ऽकृत् *-kṛit*, i. e. 1. *kṛi*+*t*, latter part of comp. adj. 1. Making, e.g. *kshetrakarmakṛit*, i.e. *kshetra-karman-*, m. A husbandman, Kathâs. 20, 11; *chitra-*, m. A painter, Kathâs. 5, 28; *janmakṛit*, i.e. *janman-*, m. A father, Bhâg. P. 3, 13, 7; *dina-* and *divasa-*, m. The sun, MBh. 3, 192; 7, 2935; *su-kṛita-*, Performing virtuous acts, Man. 3, 37. 2. Causing, *sarva-bhûta-*, Causing, or the cause of, all beings, Man. 1, 18; *anta-*, 1. adj. causing death, Râm. 3, 67, 19; 2. death, 5, 23, 17. 3. Agent of all actions signified by the vb. 1. *kṛi*, e.g. *bahu-patnî-*, Marrying many wives, Brâhmaṇ. 2, 34.

कृतक 1. *kṛi*+*ta*+*ka*, I. adj. 1. Adopted, MBh. 13, 2630. 2. Feigned, Pañch. 188, 5. 3. False, MBh. 13, 2607. II. m. A proper name, Bhâg. P. 9, 24, 47. III. *kam*, acc. sing. n., adv. Feignedly, Çiç. 9, 83.—Comp. *A-*, adj. 1. unwrought, MBh. 1, 7364. 2. plain, Ragh. 18, 51. *Putra-*, adj. an adopted child, Çâk. d. 89.

कृतकृत्यता *kṛita-kṛitya*+*tâ*, f. Happiness, Man. 4, 17.

कृतघ्न *kṛita*+*ghna*, adj., f. *nâ*, Who returns evil for good, Man. 4, 214.

कृतघ्नता *kṛitaghna*+*tâ*, f., and कृतघ्नत्व *kṛitaghna*+*tva*, n. Returning evil for good, ingratitude, Pañch. 214, 5; Mârk. P. 15, 39.

कृतज्ञ *kṛita-jña*, adj., f. *ñâ*, Grateful, Man. 7, 209.

कृतज्ञता *kṛitajña*+*tâ*, f. Gratitude, Râm. 5, 35, 16.

कृतहस्तता *kṛita-hasta*+*tâ*, f. Skilfulness in archery, MBh. 4, 1976.

कृतार्थता *kṛitârthatâ*, i.e. *kṛita-artha*+*tâ*, f. Satisfaction, Ragh. 8, 3.

कृतास्त्रता *kṛitâstratâ*, i.e. *kṛita-astra*+*tâ*, f. Skilfulness in the use of missile weapons, MBh. 1, 5156.

कृति *kṛi*+*ti*, I. f. 1. Making, Pañch. 91, 3. 2. Action, Bhâshâp. 145. 3. A literary work, Mâlav. 3, 13. 4. Hurt, Dev. 5, 11 (?). II. m. and f. Proper names, MBh. 2, 320; Bhâg. P. 6, 18, 13.—Comp. *Chala-*, adj. fickle, Pañch. 109, 12. *Dushkṛiti*, i.e. *dus-*, m. a sinner, Man. 3, 230. *Su-*, f. 1. kindness. 2. virtue. 3. the practice of religious austerities.

कृतिन् *kṛitin*, i.e. *kṛita*+*in*, I. adj., f. *nî*. 1. Wise, Bhartṛ. 2, 16. 2. Clever, MBh. 3, 8278. 3. Satisfied, Ragh. 3, 51. II. m. A proper name, Bhâg. P. 9, 22, 5.—Comp. *Dushkṛitin*, i.e. *dus-kṛita*+*in*, m. a sinner, Man. 12, 16. *Su-*, adj. 1. benevolent, 2. virtuous, pious. 3. fortunate. 4. wise, learned.

कृतिमन्त् *kṛiti*+*mant*, adj., f. *matî* in *nânâ-deça-*, Administering, governing different countries, MBh. 14, 1776.

कृतिसाध्यत्व *kṛiti-sâdhya* + *tva*, n. Being accomplishable by action, Bhâshâp. 145.

कृत्ति *kṛit*+*ti*, f. A hide.—Cf. *vâsas*.

कृत्तिका *kṛittikâ*, f., generally pl.

The third of the lunar mansions, MBh. 1, 2588.

कृत्नु *kṛi-tnu*, adj. Clever, Chr. 295, 10=Rigv. i. 92, 10.

कृत्य *kṛi+tya*, I. ptcple. of the fut. pass. of *kṛi*. 1. To be done or performed, Râm. 3, 60, 27. 2. Seducible, bribable, Râjat. 5, 247. II. n. 1. Right, Pańch. i. d. 309. 2. Need, with instr., e.g. *na me jîvitena kṛityam*, I do not want (or wish) to live, Mṛichchh. 154, 3. 3. Duty, Man. 2, 237. 4. Service, Çâk. d. 193. *guṇa-kṛitye niyojitâ*, is used to serve as a string, Kumâras. 4, 15. 5. Business, Râm. 3, 47, 15. 6. motive, Râm. 6, 33, 18. III. f. *yâ*. 1. Causing, Man. 11, 67. 2. Act, Man. 11, 125. 3. Charm, witchery, Man. 9, 290.—Comp. *A-*, n. wrong, Pańch. i. d. 309; 128, 12. *Abhyupetârtha-*, i. e. *abhi-upa-ita-artha-*, adj. one who has undertaken to perform a business, Megh. 39. *Artha-*, n. a useful act, Râm. 4, 38, 43. *Asat-*, i.e. *a-sant-* (vb. 1. *as*), adj. one who has acted wickedly, Râjat. 5, 300. See *Ku-*. *Kṛita-*, I. n. 1. what has been done and what must be done. 2. fulfilled intention, MBh. 4, 882. II. adj., f. *yâ*, satisfied, Râm. 1, 1, 84. *Gṛiha-*, n. domestic affairs, Râjat. 5, 166. *Bhûti-*, n. any ceremony of a festive character, as marriage, Man. 8, 393. *Çighra-*, adj., f. *yâ*, what must be done quickly, Pańch. iii. d. 232.

कृत्यका *kṛitya+kâ*, f. A witch, Nal. 13, 29.

कृत्यवन्त् *kṛitya+vant*, adj., f. *vatî*, Occupied.

कृत्रिम *kṛi+trima*, I. adj., f. *mâ*. 1. Factitious, the reverse of what is natural, Pańch. 110, 16. 2. Feigned, Daçak. in Chr. 192, 5 (cf. *ârti*). 3. Adopted, Man. 9, 169. 4. False, Yâjń. 2, 247. II. m. An adopted son, Man. 9, 159.—Comp. *A-*, adj. Candid, Hit. i. d. 199.

ऽकृत्वस् *-kṛi+tvas*, adv. forming multiplicative numerals from numerals and other words, e.g. *sahasra-*, adv. A thousand times, Man. 2, 79. *tâvatkṛitvas*, i.e. *tâvant-*, adv. So many times, Man 5, 38.

कृत्स्न *kṛitsna*, adj. 1. Whole, Man. 1, 105. 2. All, Râm. 4, 43, 64.

कृत्स्नशस् *kṛitsna+ças*, adv. Completely, Man. 7, 215.

कृन्तन *kṛintana*, i. e. *kṛit+ana*, n. Cutting, Bhâg. P. 6, 2, 46.

कृप् *KṚIP*, i. 10, Par. *kṛipaya*, 1. To pity, Bhâg. P. 8, 7, 40. 2. † To be weak.—Cf. *krap*.

कृप *kṛipa*, m., and f. *pî*, Proper names, MBh. 1, 2436.

कृपण *kṛipaṇa*, i.e. *kṛip+ana*, I. adj., f. *ṇâ*. 1. Miserable, Râm. 4, 21, 19. 2. Lamenting, Megh. 5. 3. Avaricious, Hit. i. d. 152. II. n. Misery, MBh. 2, 2348. III. *ṇam*, acc. sing. n., adv. Miserably, Pańch. iii. d. 183.—Comp. *Sa-kṛipaṇa*, adj. miserable, Çântiç. 4, 4.

कृपणत्व *kṛipaṇa+tva*, n. Wretchedness, MBh. 2, 1361.

कृपा *kṛip+â*, f. Compassion, MBh. 2, 2294. *kṛipâm̐ kṛi*, To have compassion, Draup. 9, 22.—Comp. *Sa-kṛipa + m*, adv. compassionately, Çântiç. 4, 19.

कृपाण *kṛipâṇa*, i.e. *kṛip* (cf. Lat. carpo, discerpo) + *âna*, m. A sword, Daçak. in Chr. 187, 4.

कृपाय *KṚIPÂYA*, a denomin. derived from *kṛipâ* by *ya*, Âtm. To pity, MBh. 13, 2330; *kṛipâyîta*, anomal. for °*yeta*, 1, 5597. *kṛipâyita*, n. Lamentation, MBh, 3, 337.—With the prep. अनु *anu*, To pity, MBh. 3, 329.

कृपालु *kṛipâ+lu*, adj. Compassionate, Daçak. in Chr. 179, 17; 187, 9.

कृपावन्त् *kṛipâ+vant*, adj., f. *vatî*, Compassionate, Kumâras. 5, 26.

कृमि *kṛimi*, also **क्रिमि** *krimi*, i.e. *hvṛi+mi*, I. m. A worm, an insect in general, Man. 1, 40; Suçr. 2, 509, 11 sqq. II. m. and f. Proper names, Hariv. 2002; 1675.—Cf. Lat. vermis; Goth. vaurms; ἕλμινς.

कृमिक *kṛimi+ka*, m. A small worm, MBh. 1, 1800.

कृमिज *kṛimi-ja* (vb. *jan*), adj. Produced by a worm, Pañch. i. d. 107.

कृमिल *kṛimi+la*, adj., f. *lâ*, Wormy, Suçr. 1, 191, 7.

कृश् *KṚIÇ*, i. 4, Par. **1.** To become thin (ved.). **2.** To make thin.—Caus. *karçaya*, To cause to become thin, Suçr. 2, 196, 6. *karçita*, Emaciated, Râm. 1, 54, 2.—With the prep. वि *vi*, Caus. To cause to become thin, Bhâg. P. 1, 16, 25.—Cf. κολέκ+ανος, κολόκανος, κολοσσός for κολοκjος; Lat. gracilis.

कृश *kṛiç+a*, adj., f. *çâ*. **1.** Thin, emaciated, Suçr. 1, 53, 17. **2.** Weak, Hit. i. d. 196; Man. 7, 208. **3.** Poor, Man. 4, 184.—Comp. *A-*, adj. great, Kir. 5, 52. *Ati-*, adj. very thin, Râm. 5, 10, 17.

कृशता *kṛiça+tâ*, f., and **कृशत्व** *kṛiça+tva*, n. Meagerness, MBh. 2, 1933; Pañch. i. d. 301.

कृशानु *kṛiç+ânu*, m. **1.** A name of fire, Bhartṛ. 2, 67. **2.** A proper name, Chr. 297, 21=Rigv. i. 112, 21.

कृशाश्व *kṛiçâçva*, i.e. *kṛiça-açva*, m. A proper name, Râm. 1, 23, 12.

कृष् *KṚISH*, i. 1, Par. (in epic poetry also Âtm., e.g. MBh. 1, 6289), **1.** To draw, MBh. 1, 6468; Ragh. 9, 27 (an arrow to the ear). **2.** To draw (a bow), Ragh. 5, 20. **3.** To drag along, MBh. 1, 6001. **4.** To lead, Chr. 54, 14 (Âtm.). **5.** To bear, MBh. 13, 4580. **6.** To tear, MBh. 1, 5992. **7.** To allure, Lass. 85, 2. **8.** To subdue, Man. 2, 215. **9.** To attain, MBh. 3, 66. **10.** i. 1, Par., and i. 6, Par., Âtm., To draw furrows, to plough, Râm. 3, 4, 12 (i. 1); Yâjñ. 2, 150 (i. 6, *kṛishâṇa*, anom. instead of *kṛishamâṇa*). **11.** To walk, MBh. 3, 16021. *kṛishṭa*, **1.** Drawn, Çâk. d. 131. **2.** Ploughed, Pañch. i. d. 53.—Comp. *Indra-*, adj. growing without culture, MBh. 2, 1831. *Phâla-*, n. 1. tilled ground, Man. 4, 46. 2. produced by cultivation, 6, 16.—Absol. *kṛishya*, instead of *kṛishṭvâ*, Chr. 40, 10.—Caus. *harshaya*, **1.** To drag, Mṛichchh. 16, 25. **2.** To pluck out, MBh. 3, 2307. **3.** To distress, Man. 2, 24. **4.** To oppress, Man. 7, 111.—All the following are inflected after i. 1: With the prep. अनु *anu*, To drag after one's self, Râm. 1, 54, 1 (Âtm.).—Caus. *anukarshita*, Occupied, MBh. 13, 7281.—With अप *apa*, **1.** To draw away, MBh. 3, 10615; Râm. 6, 72, 68 (Âtm.). **2.** To remove, Râm. 5, 71, 5. **3.** To deduct, Suçr. 2, 40, 8. **4.** To put aside, Nal. 17, 33. **5.** To draw (a bow), MBh. 4, 1909. **6.** To humble, MBh. 13, 2186. *apakṛishṭa*, **1.** Lost, Nal. 9, 33. **2.** Inferior, Man. 5, 163.—Causal, To remove, MBh. 1, 6205.—With व्यप *vi-apa*, **1.** To drag away, Râm. 6, 88, 2. **2.** To cast off, MBh. 1, 5104. **3.** To remove, Nal. 24, 41. **4.** To atone, Man. 11, 210.—With अभि *abhi*, To subdue, MBh. 3, 15064.—With अव *ava*, **1.** To draw away, Çâk. d. 173.

2. To cast off, MBh. 13, 5007 (reflective pass.). 3. To remove, MBh. 2, 207. 4. To draw down, Suçr. 2, 291, 1. *avakṛishta*, Inferior, Man. 8, 177.—With व्यव *vi-ava*, To alienate, MBh. 13, 1642. —With आ *â*, 1. To draw near, Hit. i. d. 102. 2. To draw (a sword), Mṛichchh. 132, 5; (a bow) Çâk. d. 54. 3. To draw on, Çâk. 5, 5. 4. To drag along, Çâk. d. 32. 5. To allure, Hit. 41, 14. 6. To cast off, MBh. 2, 2291. 7. To draw out, Lass. 22, 7. 8. To take from, Hit. pr. d. 8; to withdraw, Râjat. 5, 69.—Caus. To draw near, Ṛit. 5, 11; to fetch, Pañch. 32, 17.—With अपा *apa-â*, To remove, Râm. 2, 17, 9. —With व्यपा *vi-apa-â*, To remove, MBh. 2, 2290.—With पर्या *pari-â*, To drag about, MBh. 18, 9.—With व्या, 1. To cast off, Râm. 5, 54, 15. 2. To remove, Prab. 37, 7.—With समा *sam-â*, 1. To drag near, MBh. 3, 10494; to fetch, Amar. 76. 2. To take out (with abl.), Pañch. 40, 16.—Caus. To carry along, Pañch. 74, 23.—With उद् *ud*, 1. To raise, Bhâg. P. 5, 6, 10 (pass. to rise). 2. To take out, MBh. 1, 7869. 3. To cast off, MBh. 2, 1810. 4. To draw (a bow), MBh. 4, 1635. *utkṛishṭa*, 1. Excessive, Râm. 3, 41, 5. 2. Superior, Man. 5, 163. 3. Distinguished, Man. 3, 132.—With समुद् *sam-ud*, To raise, MBh. 1, 3613.—With उप *upa*, To draw near, Bhâg. P. 7, 9, 22.—With समुप *sam-upa*, To draw near, Râm. 2, 89, 10.—With नि *ni*, To sink into (a river), MBh. 1, 3616. *nikṛishṭa*, Low, base, MBh. 1, 3067. n. Vicinity, Suçr. 1, 94, 4.—With संनि *sam-ni*; *saṁnikṛishṭa*, Near, Râm. 3, 21, 5. n. Vicinity, Çâk. 23, 23. °*ṭam*, adv. Near, Kumâras. 3, 2.—With निस् *nis*, 1. To draw out, MBh. 3, 16763. 2. To tear, Bhâg. P. 5, 26, 21; to dissolve, Râjat. 6, 272.—Caus. To destroy, Bhâg. P. 6, 5, 19.—With परा *parâ*, 1. To draw away, MBh. 2, 2227. 2. To blame, MBh. 13, 2102.—With परि *pari*, 1. To drag about, Râm. 2, 97, 30. 2. To carry about with one, MBh. 17, 104. 3. To lead, Râm. 6, 2, 28.—Caus. To torment, Râm. 1, 8, 13.—With प्र *pra*, 1. To drag away, MBh. 3, 12787. 2. To draw (a bow), MBh. 4, 1959. 3. To agitate, Râm. 5, 70, 11. 4. To lead, Râm. 6, 2, 44. *prakṛishṭa*, 1. Long, Nal. 12, 111. 2. Well to do, Man. 7, 170. 3. Excellent, Pañch, 191, 16. 4. Violent, Daçak. in Chr. 185, 4.—With विप्र *vi-pra*, To conquer, MBh. 1, 7197. *viprakṛishṭa*, Distant, Pañch. 127, 17.—With वि *vi*, 1. To draw (a bow), Râm. 3, 34, 8; (an arrow) Râm. 6, 70, 39. 2. To drag about, Râm. 2, 78, 16. 3. To draw out, Bhartṛ. 1, 84 (to catch). 4. To withdraw, Râjat. 5, 90. *vikṛishṭa*, Long, Râm. 2, 68, 21.—With सम् *sam*, To drag along, Râm. 5, 63, 19.—Cf. Lat. ac-cerso.

कृषक *kṛish + aka*, m. A husbandman, Châṇ. 90.

कृषि *kṛish + i* (कृषी *kṛishî*, MBh. 1, 7207), f. 1. Ploughing, Lass. 76, 18. 2. Agriculture, Man. 1, 90.

कृषीवल *kṛishî + vala*, m. A husbandman, Man. 9, 38.

कृष्टज *kṛishṭa-ja*, adj. Cultivated, Man. 11, 144 (145).

कृष्ण *kṛishṇa*, i. e. *kṛish + na* (the origin of the signification is dubious). I. adj., f. *ṇâ*. 1. Black, or dark blue, Râm. 3, 55, 5. 2. With or without *paksha*, m. The dark half of a month, from the full moon to that of the new moon, Man. 1, 66; 6, 20. **II.** m. **1.** *Kṛishṇa*, The most celebrated incarnation of Vishṇu, MBh. 14, 1589. **2.** The black antelope, Bhâg. P. 3, 10, 20. **III.** f. *ṇâ*. **1.** A name of Durgâ, MBh. 4, 184. **2.** The name of several plants, Suçr. 1, 162, 16.—Comp. *Ati-*, adj. very black, Pańch. 104, 15.

कृष्णता *kṛishṇa* + *tâ*, f., and **कृष्णत्व** *kṛishṇa* + *tva*, n. Blackness, Suçr. 1, 33, 20; MBh. 1, 4236.

कृष्णल *kṛishṇa* + *la*, m. and n. The berry of the plant Guńja, used as a weight; a coin of this weight, Man. 8, 215.

ऽकृष्णलक -*kṛishṇala* + *ka*, substitute for the last when latter part of a comp. adj., *pańchakṛishṇalaka*, i. e. *pańchan-*, Comprising five *kṛishṇalas*, Man. 8, 134.

कृष्णाजिनिन् *kṛishṇâjinin*, i.e. *kṛishṇa-ajina* + *in*, adj., f. *nî*, Covered with the hide of the black antelope, MBh. 14, 2113.

कृष्णाय *KṚISHṆÂYA*, a denom. derived from *kṛishṇa* by *ya*, Âtm. To blacken, Hit. i. d. 74.

कृष्णायस् *kṛishṇâyas*, i. e. *kṛishṇa-ayas*, and **कृष्णायस** *kṛishṇâyas* + *a*, n. Iron.

कृसर *kṛisara*, m. A dish consisting of sesamum and grain, Man. 5, 7.

1. **कृ** *KṚÎ*, i. 6, *kira*, Par. **1.** To pour out, Amar. 11. **2.** To cast, MBh. 14, 1898. **3.** To cover, Râm. 5, 42, 10. *kîrṇa*, **1.** Scattered, Râm. 5, 16, 17. **2.** Dishevelled, Daçak. in Chr. 179, 15. **3.** Covered, Pańch. i. d. 239.—With the prepositions **व्यति** *vi-ati*, To scatter, MBh. 4, 830.—With **अनु** *anu*, To cover, MBh. 1, 4340.—With **अप** *apa*, which forms also *apaskira*, Âtm. To rake (as a bird for pleasure), Uttararâmach. p. 31, 1.—With **अभि** *abhi*, To cover, MBh. 13, 2655.—With **अव** *ava*, **1.** To diffuse, Man. 6, 48. **2.** To cast off, MBh. 2, 2289. **3.** To leave, MBh. 1, 3057. **4.** To cover, Râm. 2, 43, 13. Âtm. and reflect. pass., **1.** To spread, MBh. 3, 12306. **2.** To vanish, Bhâg. P. 7, 15, 19.—With **अन्वव** *anu-ava*, To scatter about, Yâjń. 1, 230. Caus. To cause to be scattered about, MBh. 13, 4291 (read *kârayet*).—With **अभ्यव** *abhi-ava*, To cover, Râm. 2, 33, 19.—With **पर्यव** *pari-ava*, To cover round about, MBh. 3, 13596.—With **समव** *sam-ava*, To cover, Bhâg. P. 8, 18, 10.—With **आ** *â*, *âkîrṇa*, **1.** Crowded, Arj. 6, 7. **2.** Frequented, Man. 6, 51. **3.** Confused, Râjat. 5, 321.—With **अपा** *apa-â*, To repudiate, MBh. 1, 2851.—With **अवा** *ava-â*, To cover, Râm. 2, 42, 14 Gorr. (Schl. v.r.).—With **व्या** *vi-â*, *vyâkîrṇa*, Dishevelled, Pańch. i. d. 207.—With **समा** *sam-â*, To cover, Râm. 1, 6, 24.—With **उद्** *ud*, **1.** To throw up, Râm. 6, 90, 26. **2.** To dig up, MBh. 1, 5813. **3.** To engrave, Vikr. d. 43.—With **समुद्** *sam-ud*, To pierce, Ragh. 1, 4.—With **उप** *upa*, To cover, MBh. 3, 11886.—With **विनि** *vi-ni*, **1.** To cast down, Râm. 6, 8, 19. **2.** To leave, Kumâras. 4, 6. **3.** *vinikîrṇa*, Crowded, Râm. 4, 41, 33.—With **संनि** *sam-ni*, *saṁnikîrṇa*, Stretched out, Megh. 87.—With **परा** *parâ*, To leave, Râm. 4, 1369.—With **परि** *pari*, **1.** To

surround, MBh. 4, 585. **2.** To deliver, Ragh. 18. 32.—With प्र *pra*, To scatter, Râm. 2, 76, 15. **2.** To spring up, Râm. 1, 9, 19. **3.** Pass. (anom. *kiryet*, with the termination of the Par.), To vanish, MBh. 3, 14767. *prakîrṇa*, **1.** Dishevelled, MBh. 3, 11755. **2.** Squandered, Lass. 74, 17. **3.** Public, MBh. 13, 6735.—With विप्र *vi-pra*, *viprakîrṇa*, **1.** Scattered, Râm. 5, 14, 53. **2.** Dishevelled, MBh. 3, 401. **3.** Extended, MBh. 3, 730.—With प्रतिस् *pratis*, instead of प्रति *prati*, To injure (cf. 2. *kṛî*), Çiç. 1, 47.—With वि *vi*, **1.** To scatter, Hit. 9, 14. **2.** To cover, Man. 3, 234. **3.** To blame, Râm. 2, 12, 73. *vikîrṇa*, **1.** Dishevelled, Kumâras. 4, 4. **2.** Split, Râm. 3, 34, 25.—With प्रवि *pra-vi*, To scatter, MBh. 4, 298.—With सम् *sam*, **1.** To mix, MBh. 13, 6232. **2.** To confound, MBh. 3, 13736. *saṁkîrṇa*, **1.** Crowded, MBh. 1, 7675. **2.** Mixed, Man. 1, 116. **3.** Impure, Yâjń. 3, 310. — Cf. *kal*, *çakṛit*; and Lat. cribrum, cerno, procerus; κρίνω.

† 2. कॄ *KṚÎ*, also कृ *KṚI*, ii. 5 and 9, Par., Âtm. To injure, to kill.—Cf. 1. *kṛî* with *pratis*.

† 3. कॄ *KṚÎ*, i. 10, Âtm. To know (? v.r.).

कॄत् *KṚÎT*, i. 10, *kîrtaya* (rather a denomin. derived from *kîrti*), Par. (in epic poetry also Âtm. MBh. 1, 1549), **1.** To celebrate, Man. 3, 221. **2.** To propound, Man. 10, 131. **3.** To pronounce, Man. 2, 124. **4.** To say, Man. 2, 203. **5.** To call, Man. 10, 19. Anom. ptcple. of the pres. Âtm. *kîrtayâna*, MBh. 13, 7661.—With the prep. अनु *anu*, **1.** To mention, Râm. 1, 14, 22. **2.** To repeat, Bhâg. P. 8, 4, 15. **3.** To proclaim, MBh. 3, 13259. **4.** To propound, MBh. 2, 994.—With समभि *sam-abhi*, To tell, MBh. 14, 2066.—With उद् *ud*, To glorify, Ragh. 10, 33.—With परि *pari*, **1.** To proclaim, Man. 11, 122. **2.** To propound, MBh. 13, 12802. **3.** To glorify, MBh. 13, 7160. **4.** To pronounce, Man. 1, 92.—With संपरि *sam-pari*, To particularise, Suçr. 2, 268, 21.—With प्र *pra*, **1.** To propound, Man. 2, 95. **2.** To call, Man. 2, 21. **3.** To approve, Pańch. iv. d. 37.—With संप्र *sam-pra*, **1.** To mention, MBh. 13, 4926. **2.** To pronounce, Bhag. 18, 4.—With सम् *sam*, **1.** To celebrate, Man. 3, 221. **2.** To proclaim, Râm. 4, 59, 3. **3.** To mention, Chr. 13, 4.

कॢप् *KḶIP*, i. 1, *kalpa*, Âtm. **1.** To prosper, Man. 4, 15. **2.** To be fit, to be qualified for; with the loc. Râm. 2, 62, 26 Gorr.; 5, 37, 30; with the dat. Man. 3, 266; to become qualified, Man. 7, 22; Megh. 56 (*prâptaye*, to attain). **3.** To fall to one's lot, Bhâg. P. 3, 16, 12. **4.** To serve (with the dat.), Man. 8, 353. **5.** To resolve upon, Pańch. 150, 24. **6.** To create, Bhâg. P. 3, 7, 25. *kḷipta*, **1.** Well arranged. MBh. 3, 790. **2.** Fixed, Man. 3, 69. **3.** Made, Bhâg. P. 6, 10, 32.—Comp. *Kshura-*, adj, shaved, Kathâs. 12, 168.—Caus., *kalpaya*, Par., Âtm. **1.** To put in suitable order. *kalpita*, Fixed in proportion, Yâjń. 2, 244. *prathama-kalpita*, put at the head, Man. 9, 166. **2.** To make fit for something, MBh. 3, 9912. **3.** To approve, Râm. 2, 61, 17. **4.** To show, MBh. 1, 58. **6.** To design, Râm. 2, 52, 100; to determine, Man. 7, 125; Daçak. in Chr. 189, 1. **7.** To consider, Râm. 2, 23, 33. **8.** To form, Ragh. 8, 46; Bhâg. P. 8, 9, 26; to make, Râm. 2, 98, 29; MBh. 1, 700 (*vṛittim*, To live on, with the instr.). **9.** To create, Man. 5, 28; Bhâg. P. 2, 5, 42.—With the prep. अनु *anu*, Caus., *çraddhâm*, To give faith, Râm. 5, 56, 15. *anukalpita*, Accompanied, MBh. 13, 2150.—With समनु *sam-anu*, Caus., To assume, MBh. 3, 9964.—With अभि *abhi*, Caus., To arrange, Râm. 2, 54, 17.—With अव *ava*, To be fit (with the dat.), Bhâg. P. 6, 7, 18.—With उप *upa*, **1.** To be suitable, Bhâg. P. 6, 18, 42. **2.** To serve, Râm. 5, 25, 21. *upakḷipta*, **1.** Prepared for use, Man. 8, 333; prepared, MBh. 1, 4098. **2.** Produced, Bhâg. P. 5, 16, 2.—Caus. **1.** To prepare, Râm. 1, 12, 29. **2.** To fit out, MBh. 1, 4098. **3.** To design for (with the dat.), Yâjń. 1, 109. **4.** To place, Bhâg. P. 5, 23, 5; 1, 9, 32. **5.** To communicate, Bhâg. P. 5, 3, 9.—With समुप *sam-upa*, Caus. To prepare, Râm. 2, 50, 29.—With परि *pari*, *parikḷipta*, Existing, MBh. 13, 2831. Caus. **1.** To decide, Man. 12, 110. **2.** To determine, MBh. 13, 2689. **3.** To perform, Yâjń. 1, 346. **4.** To make, Kathâs. 15, 173; Man. 9, 152 (*daçadhâ*, To distribute into ten parts). **5.** To invite, MBh. 13, 1596.—With प्र *pra*, *prakḷipta*, Prepared, Kathâs. 18, 366. Caus. **1.** To prepare, 3, 264. **2.** To further, Râm. 2, 31, 24. **3.** To allot, Man. 7, 135. **4.** To establish, Man. 8, 46. **5.** To design, Bhâg. P. 4, 18, 20. **6.** To make, Nal. 25, 5; Amar. 73 (*açru*, To shed tears).—With संप्र *sam-pra*, Caus. To ordain, MBh. 3, 14110.—With वि *vi*, **1.** To change, MBh. 3, 697. **2.** To be doubtful, Pańch. i. d. 385; to doubt, Pańch. i. d. 87. Caus. **1.** To prepare in a different way, Bhâg. P. 5, 26, 38. **2.** To devise, Çâk. d. 51. **3.** To doubt, Prab. 106, 7. **4.** To presume, Pańch. iv. d. 62.—With सम् *sam*, To desire; *a-saṁkḷipta*, Not desired, MBh. 14, 1277. Caus. **1.** To desire, Man. 2, 5. **2.** To determine, MBh. 14, 4349. **3.** To fancy, Daçak. in Chr. 197, 1. **4.** To perform obsequies, Râm. 2, 72, 53.—With उपसम् *upa-sam*, *upasaṁkḷipta*, Put on, Bhâg. P. 4, 9, 54. Caus. To place, MBh. 16, 199.—Cf. Lat. corpus.

क्लृप्ति *kḷip* + *ti*, f. Causing, Râjat. 5, 463.—Comp. *Yathâ-kḷipti*, adv. in a suitable way, Râm. 2, 80, 15.

केकय *kekaya*, I. m. **1.** pl. The name of a people, MBh. 6, 356. **2.** Their prince, Râm. 2, 35, 21. **II.** f. *yî*, One of the wives of Daçaratha, Râm. 2, 70, 20.

केका *kekâ* (an imitative sound), f. The cry of the peacock, MBh. 15, 724.

केकिन् *kekin*, i.e. *kekâ* + *in*, m. A peacock, Bhartṛ. 1, 44.

केत् *KET*, i. 10, Par., see *kit*.

केत *keta*, i.e. *kit* + *a*, m. **1.** Desire (ved.). **2.** An abode, Bhâg. P. 2, 7, 12. **3.** An image, 1, 16, 34.

केतक *keta* + *ka*, m. The name of a tree, Pandanus odoratissimus, Râm. 2, 94, 6.

केतन *ketana*, i.e. *kit* + *ana*, n. **1.** Invitation, Man. 4, 110. **2.** An abode, MBh. 3, 13396. **3.** A place, Kathâs. 26, 44. **4.** A sign, MBh. 14, 2430.—Comp. *Kapi-*, m. a name of Arjuna (having as sign a monkey), MBh. 14, 2457. *Jhasha-*, *makara-*, and *mîna-* (having as sign a fish), m. the god of love, Bhartṛ. 1, 64.

केतु *ketu*, i.e. *kit* + *u*, m. **1.** A sign by which an object may be recognised,

Chr. 289, 3=Rigv. i. 50, 3; Chr. 294, 1=Rigv. i. 92, 1; Râm. 2, 54, 5. **2.** A banner, MBh. 4, 2068. **3.** Chief, Râm. 4, 28, 18. **4.** A meteor, Man. 1, 38. **5.** The mythological name of the descending node, represented as a headless demon, Râm. 3, 35, 52.—Comp. *Agni-*, m. the name of a Râkshasa. *Tâla-*, m. (having as banner the palmyra tree), epithet of Bhîshma, MBh. 5, 5081. *Dhûma-*, m. 1. fire, MBh. 1, 4162. 2. a meteor, MBh. 6, 80. *Dhṛishṭa-*, m. a proper name, MBh. 1, 231. *Makara-*, m. the god of love.—Cf. Goth. haidus; A.S. had.

केतुमन्त् *ketu+mant*, m. **1.** The name of a Dânava, or demon, MBh. 1, 2532. **2.** The name of a palace, Hariv. 8989.

केदार *kedâra*, m. A cultivated field, Man. 9, 44; particularly a watered one, Râm. 3, 22, 18; Râjat. 5, 112.—Comp. *Eka-*, adj. having the same fields, Man. 9, 38.

† **केप्** *KEP*, i. 1, Âtm. **1.** To tremble. **2.** To go.—Cf. *kamp* and *gep*.

केयूर *keyûra*, m. and n. A bracelet worn on the upper arm, Bhartṛ. 2, 16; Râjat. 5, 358.

केयूरिन् *keyûrin*, i.e. *keyûra+in*, adj., f. *iṇî*, Wearing a bracelet, Mârk. P. 23, 102.

केरल *kerala*, m. **1.** pl. The name of a people, Râm. 2, 82, 7. **2.** Their king, MBh. 3, 15250.

† **केल्** *KEL*, i. 1, Par. **1.** To shake. **2.** To go.

केलि *keli*, m. and f. **1.** Amorous sport, Man. 8, 357. **2.** Sport, Gît. 7, 11.—Comp. *Vâta-*, m. 1. Whisper. 2. the marks of finger nails on the lover's person. *Hemak°*, i.e. *heman-*, m. fire.

† **केव्** *KEV*, i. 1, Âtm. To serve. —Cf. *khev*, *sev*.

केवल *kevala*, i.e. *eke* (old loc. sing. of *eka*) +*vala*, **I.** adj., f. *lâ* (ved. *lî*). **1.** Exclusively proper; *vikshasva yad rûpaṁ mama kevalam*, Look what shape is proper only to me, Râm. 5, 35, 52; Bhâg. P. 6, 4, 26. **2.** Mere, Man. 2, 199; nothing but, 3, 118. **3.** Alone, only, Pańch. v. d. 12. **4.** United, i.e. entire, MBh. 13, 2686; whole, 4, 1485; all, Man. 2, 95. **II.** *lam*, adv. **1.** Only, Pańch. 31, 7. **2.** Entirely (?), Râm. 2, 87, 23; *na kevalam—api*, Not only, but also, Râjat. 5, 443. **III.** n. The knowledge of the unity of all the universe. **IV.** m. The name of a prince, Bhâg. P. 9, 2, 30. **V.** f. *lî*, The name of a locality, MBh. 3, 15245.

केवलिन् *kevalin*, i.e. *kevala+in*, m. One who possesses the knowledge of the universal unity, Bhâg. P. 4, 25, 39.

केश *keça*, m. **1.** Hair, Hit. i. d. 102. **2.** A lion's mane, Sch. ad Çâk. 6.—Comp. adj. end in the fem. in *çâ* or *çî*. *Ańjana-*, adj., f. *çî*, having manes as smooth as ointment, MBh. 1, 8008. *Bhûta-*, m., and f. *çî*, root of sweet flag. *Miçra-keçî*, f. an Apsaras. *Mukta-* (vb. *much*), adj., f. *çî*, one whose hair is loose, Man. 7, 91; MBh. 1, 782. *Muńja-*, m. Vishṇu. *vi-*, **I.** adj., f. *çî*, bald. **II.** f. *çî*, a small braid or dress of hair, tied up severally and then collected into the larger braid. *Vyomak°*, i.e. *vyoman-*, m. Çiva. *Vi-kirṇa-* (vb. *kṛî*), and *vi-galita-*, adj., fem. *çâ*, with dishevelled hair, Kumâras. 5, 68. *Çukla-*, adj. hoary-haired. *Su-*, adj., f. *çî*, having beautiful hair, Râm. 3, 52, 35.

केशर *keça+ra*, also **केसर** *kesara*, **I.** n. A lion's or horse's mane, Pańch. i. d. 207. **II.** m. and n. The filament of a lotus, or of any vegetable, Çiç. 9,

47 (with *s*). **III.** m. The name of several plants, Mesua ferrea, Mimusops elengi, Bottleria tinctoria; their flower, n., Râm. 2, 96, 6.—**Comp.** *Karâla-*, m. a proper name, Pańch. 214, 13. *Nâga-*, m. a tree, Mesua Roxburghii, Wight. Râm. 6, 96, 7.

केशरि *keçari* (i.e. mutilated *keçarin*, q. cf.), m. A proper name, Râm. 4, 33, 14.

केशरिन् *keçarin*, i.e. *keçara* + *in*, also **केसरिन्** *kesarin*, **I.** adj., f. *iṇî*, Having a mane, MBh. 1, 8286. **II.** m. **1.** A lion, Bhartṛ. 2, 22. **2.** A proper name, Râm. 4, 39, 26.—**Comp.** *Purusha-*, m. a name of Vishṇu in his fourth incarnation (half man, half lion).

केशव *keça* + *va* (*va* for *vant*), m. **1.** A name of Vishṇu, Râm. 1, 45, 31. **2.** A proper name, Pańch. iii. d. 270.—**Comp.** *Go-pâla-*, m. the name of an idol of Kṛishṇa set up by Gopâlavarman, Râjat. 5, 243.

केशवत्व *keçava* + *tva*, n. State of Vishṇu, MBh. 13, 1361.

केशवन्त् *keça* + *vant*, adj., f. *vatî*, Long-haired, Mârk. P. 8, 121.

केशाकेशि *keçâkeçi*, i.e. *keça-keça* + *i*, adv. In mutual grasping of hair, Yâjń. 2, 283; in closest proximity, MBh. 4, 1056.

केशान्तिक *keçântika*, i.e. *keça-anta* + *ika*, adj. Reaching to one's hair, Man. 2, 46.

केशिन् *keçin*, i.e. *keça* + *in*, **I.** m. The name of an Asura or demon, etc., MBh. 1, 2531; Bhâg. P. 9, 24, 47. **II.** f. *inî*, The name of an Apsaras, etc., MBh. 1, 2558; Râm. 1, 39, 3.—**Comp.** *Dhâmakeçin*, i.e. *dhâman-keça* + *in*, adj. having rays instead of hair, MBh. 3, 193. *Muńja-*, m. Vishṇu.

केसर *kesara*, and **केसरिन्** *kesarin*; see **केशर** *keçara*, **केशरिन्** *keçarin*.

कै *KAI*, i. 1, Par. To sound (ved.).

कैकय *kaikaya* = *kekaya*, and *kaikeya*, q. cf., MBh. 1, 2647; 3, 2009; f. *yî* = *kaikeyî*, Râm. i. 1, 21.

कैकेय *kaikeya*, a syncope of *kaikayeya*, i.e. *kekaya* + *eya*, patron. **I.** m. **1.** A descendant of Kekaya, a king of the Kekayas, MBh. 3, 462. **2.** pl. The people of the Kekayas, Râm. 4, 43, 11. **II.** f. *yî*, One of the wives of Daçaratha, Râm. 1, 1, 24.

कैंकर्य *kaiṁkarya*, i.e. *kiṁkara* + *ya*, n. Service, Bhâg. P. 3, 2, 22.

कैटभ *kaiṭabha*, m. The name of an Asura or demon, MBh. 3, 498.

कैतक *kaitaka*, i.e. *ketaka* + *a*, adj. Produced from the tree Pandanus odoratissimus, Ragh. 4, 55.

कैतव *kaitava*, i.e. *kitava* + *a*, **I.** n. **1.** A stake, MBh. 2, 2163. **2.** Gambling, Nal. 26, 10. **3.** Deceit, Bhartṛ. 2, 44. **II.** m. Patron. designation of Ulûka, MBh. 1, 7002.

कैतवक *kaitava* + *ka*, n. Game of hazard, MBh. 2, 2060.

कैरव *kairava*, n. The white esculent water-lily, Bhartṛ. 2, 65.

कैरात *kairâta*, i.e. *kirâta* + *a*, **I.** adj. Referring to the Kirâtas, MBh. 1, 320. **II.** m. A prince of the Kirâtas, MBh. 2, 1869.

कैरातक *kairâta* + *ka*, adj., f. *kî*, Belonging to the Kirâtas, MBh. 2, 1867.

कैलास *kailâsa*, also **कैलाश** *kailâça* (probably akin to *kila*), m. The name of a mountain, the residence of Kuvera, MBh. 3, 503; Râm. 3, 54, 5.

कैवर्त *kaivarta*, m. **1.** A fisherman, Man. 8, 260. **2.** A mixed tribe; the son of a Nishâda by an Âyogavî woman, Man. 10, 34.

कैवर्तक *kaivarta+ka*, m. A fisherman, Râm. 2, 83, 15.

कैवल्य *kaivalya*, i.e. *kevala+ya*, n. **1.** Complete absorption in the thought of the universal unity, absolute happiness, Vedântas. in Chr. 219, 13; MBh. 13, 1073. **2.** Totality, Bhâg. P. 3. 11, 2.

कैशव *kaiçava*, i.e. *keçava+a*, adj. Belonging to Keçava, Ragh. 17, 29.

कैशिक *kaiçika*, m. The name of a tribe, MBh. 2, 585.

कैशोर *kaiçora*, i.e. *kiçora+a*, n. Youth, Bhâg. P. 3, 28, 17.

कोक *koka*, m. **1.** A wolf, Râm. 5, 26, 9. **2.** The cuckoo (ved.). **3.** The ruddy goose, Gît. 5, 17.—Cf. Lat. cuculus.

कोकनद *kokanada*, I. n. The red lotus, Gît. 10, 5. **II.** m. pl. The name of a people, MBh. 2, 1026.

कोकिल *kokila*, i.e. *koka+ila*, m. **1.** The Indian cuckoo, Râm. 2, 52, 2. f. *lâ*, The female cuckoo, Bhartṛ. 1, 34. **2.** A kind of mouse, Suçr. 2, 274, 4. **3.** A poisonous insect, Suçr. 2, 288, 7.—Comp. *Puṁs-*, m. the male cuckoo, Ṛit. 6, 14.

कोङ्क *koṅka*, m. The name of a people, Bhâg. P. 5, 6, 8.

कोङ्कण *koṅkaṇa*, m. The name of a people, Daçak. 193, 11.

कोंकार *koṁ-kâra*, m. The sound *kom*, Pañch. 158, 7.

कोच *kocha*, i.e. *kuch+a*, m. Shrinking, Suçr. 1, 269. 1.

कोटर *koṭara* (cf. vb. *kuṭ*), m. and n. **1.** The hollow of a tree, Pañch. 104, 7. **2.** A cavity, Râjat. 5, 439.

कोटरस्थ *koṭara-stha* (vb. *sthâ*) adj. Being in the interior, Böhtl. Ind. Spr. 547.

कोटि and **टी** *koṭî*, i.e. *kuṭ+i*, f. **1.** A point, Pañch. 120, 23. **2.** Eminence, MBh. 3, 542 (*pramâṇa-koṭi*, extraordinary tallness). **3.** Ten millions, Man. 6, 63.

कोटिक *koṭika*, m. **1.** A worm, Jaṭâdh. in ÇKD.; f. *kâ*, *mânusha-koṭikâ*, A worm-like woman, Pañch. 44, 25. **2.** A kind of frog, Suçr. 2, 290, 7. **3.** A proper name, MBh. 3, 15586.

कोटिकाश्य *koṭikâçya*, and **कोटिकास्य** *koṭikâsya* (better), i.e. *koṭika-âsya*, m. The name of a prince, Draup. 1, 12; MBh. 3, 15593.

कोटिपाल *koṭipâla*, Lass. 13, 11; read *koṭṭapâla*.

कोटिमन्त् *koṭi+mant*, adj., f. *matî*, Pointed, Çâk. d. 185.

कोटिशस् *koṭi+ças*, adv. By ten millions, Sund. 3, 14.

कोट्ट *koṭṭa* (a dialect. form of *koshṭha*), n. A strong-hold, Pañch. 237, 15.

कोट्टवी *koṭṭavî*, f. A naked woman, Râjat. 5, 439.

कोठ *koṭha* (a dialect. form of *kushṭha*), m. A species of leprosy, Suçr. 1, 156, 3.

कोण *koṇa* (perhaps a dialect. form of *karṇa*), m. **1.** A corner, Pañch. 258, 8. **2.** An angle, MBh. 14, 2035. **3.** An instrument for sounding a lute,

Râm. 2, 71, 26.—Comp. *Sûtra-*, m. A kind of drum.

कोथ *kotha*, i.e. *kuth* + *a*, m. **1.** Putrefaction, Suçr. 1, 41, 19. **2.** Gangrene, Suçr. 1, 92, 4.

कोदण्ड *ko-daṇḍa* (*ko*=*kas*, nom. sing. of *kim*; cf. *ku-*), n. (and m.), A bow, Bhartṛ. 1, 97.

कोद्रव *ko-drava* (cf. the last), m. A species of grain eaten by the poorer people, Paspalum scrobiculatum, Lin., Bhartṛ. 2, 98.

कोप *kopa*, i.e. *kup* + *a*, m. **1.** Morbose excitement, Suçr. 1, 5, 8. **2.** Wrath, Pańch. i. d. 139. *kopań kṛi*, To be angry, Pańch. 162, 25.—Comp. *Antaḥkopa*, i. e. *antar-*, m. inward anger. *Krîḍâ-*, m. feigned anger, Amar. 12. *Mithyâ-*, m. feigned anger, Lass. 9, 11. *Mṛiga-*, m. rage at animals, Pańch. 56, 2. *Sa-kopa*, adj., f. *pâ*, enraged, Pańch. iii. d. 27. *Sa-kopa* + *m*, adv. angrily, Pańch. 38, 11.

कोपन *kopana*, i. e. *kup* + *ana*, I. adj., f. *nâ*. **1.** Passionate, wrathful, Râm. 1, 34, 22. **2.** Irritating, Suçr. 1, 177, 15. II. m. The name of an Asura or demon, Hariv. 2284. III. n. **1.** Excitement, MBh. 14, 466. **2.** Provocation, MBh. 13, 2426.—Comp. *A-*, adj. not inclined to wrath, Lass. 40, 9.

कोपयिष्णु *kopayishṇu*, i. e. *kup*, Caus., + *ishṇu*, adj. Provoking, MBh. 1, 6836.

कोपिन् *kopin*, i.e. *kopa* + *in*, adj., f. *nî*. **1.** Wrathful, Râm. 3, 16, 29.—**2.** When latter part of a comp. word, Irritating, Suçr. 1, 199, 15.

कोमल *ko-mala* (cf. *kodrava*, *kumâra*, and vb. *mlai*), adj., f. *lâ*, Soft, bland; Bhartṛ. 2, 56; 1, 97.

कोयष्टि *ko-yashṭi* (see the last), and **कोयष्टिक** *koyashṭi* + *ka*, m. A kind of bird, Man. 5, 13; MBh. 13, 2835.

कोर *kora*, m. **1.** A flexible joint (as of the fingers). **2.** A bud.

कोरक *kora* + *ka*, m. and n. A bud, Râm. 2, 59, 8; Bhâshâp. 165.

कोरदूष *kora-dûsha*, and **कोरदूषक** *koradûsha* + *ka*, m. = *kodrava*, Suçr. 2, 64, 1; MBh. 3, 13027.

कोल *kola*, I. m. **1.** A hog, Yâjń. 3, 273. **2.** A kind of weapon, Dev. 1, 4; 5 (?). II. n. The fruit of the jujube, Zizyphus jujuba, Suçr. 1, 25, 6.

कोलाहल *kolâhala*, I. m. n. **1.** A great and confused noise, Râm. 6, 8, 45. **2.** Screaming, Daçak. in Chr. 183, 13. **3.** A shout, Râjat. 5, 361. II. m. The name of a mountain, MBh. 1, 2367 sqq.

कोविद *ko-vid* + *a*, cf. *koyashṭi*, adj., f. *dâ*, Knowing, Man. 7, 26; MBh. 3, 1287 (with gen.); skilful, Râm. 2, 80, 5 (with loc.).

कोविदार *kovidâra*, i. e. *ko-vi-dṛî* + *a* (cf. the last), m. A species of ebony, Bauhinia variegata, Lin., Râm. 2, 84, 3.

कोश *koça*, also **कोष** *kosha*, m. and n. **1.** A coop, denoting a cloud (ved.), Chr. 293, 2=Rigv. i. 87, 2; Chr. 297, 11 =i. 112, 11. **2.** A sheath, Râm. 3, 18, 39 (with *sh*). **3.** A bud, Ragh. 13, 29. **4.** A shell, Mârk. P. 11, 6. **5.** The womb, Suçr. 1, 120, 12. **6.** A testicle, Suçr. 1, 290, 4. **7.** An egg, Bhâg. P. 2, 8, 16. **8.** An abode, Vedântas. in Chr. 204, 22; Bhâg. P. 2, 1, 34. **9.** A store-room, Râm. 2, 63, 7; a treasury, Man. 8, 38; 1, 99. **10.** Treasure, Nal. 26, 19. **11.** A cocoon, Yâjń. 3, 147. **12.** As latter part of comp. words, A ball, e.g. *netra-*, The eyeball, Râm. 3, 79, 28. **13.** A sacred draught, employed in a judicial trial by ordeal, Yâjń. 2, 95. **14.** Oath, Râjat. 5, 325. **15.** A kind of bandage, Suçr. 1, 65, 17.—Comp. *A-kosha,* adj. unsheathed, MBh. 4, 321. *Annamaya-,* m. the gross body, Vedântas. in Chr. 209, 12. *Jâti-,* n. and m. nutmeg, Suçr. 1, 215, 5. *Dharma-,* m. the treasury of duties, Man. 1, 99. *Madhu-,* m. the boneycomb or hive. *Vi-,* adj. unsheathed, Nal. 10, 18. *Vishâṇa-kosha,* m. the hollow of a horn.

कोशकार *koça-kâra,* also **कोषऽ** *kosha-,* m. **1.** A maker of sheaths, etc., Râm. 4, 40, 26. **2.** The silk-worm, Bhâg. P. 6, 1, 52. **3.** A kind of sugar cane, Suçr. 1, 187, 6.

कोशकारक *koça-kâraka,* m. The silk-worm, Yâjń. 3, 147.

कोशल *koçala,* see *kosala.*

कोशवत् *koça + vat,* adv. Like a cocoon, Vedântas. in Chr. 204, 21; cf. Bhâg. P. 6, 1, 52.

कोशवन्त् *koça + vant,* I. adj., f. *vatî,* Wealthy, MBh. 1, 5808. II. *vatî,* f. A certain plant, Suçr. 2, 107, 12.

कोशस्कृत् *koçaskṛit,* i.e. *koça-*1. *kṛi* + *t,* m. The silk-worm, Bhâg. P. 7, 6, 13.

कोष *kosha,* see *koça.*

कोष्ठ *koshṭha,* I. m. The stomach, MBh. 14, 570. II. m. and n. **1.** A granary. **2.** A store-room, MBh. 2, 201. III. n. A wall, Bhâg. P. 4, 28, 56.

कोष्ण *koshṇa,* i.e. *kâ-ushṇa,* adj., f. *ṇâ,* Moderately warm, tepid, Ragh. 1, 84.

कोसल *kosala,* also **कोशल** *koçala,* I. m. The name of a country and its inhabitants, Râm. 1, 5, 5; MBh. 6, 347. II. f. *lâ,* A name of its capital, Ayodhyâ, MBh. 3, 8152.

कौक्षेय *kauksheya,* i.e. *kukshi + eya,* and **कौक्षेयक** *kaukshaya + ka,* m. A sword, Daçak. in Chr. 186, 10.

कौङ्कण *kauṅkaṇa,* i.e. *koṅkaṇa + a,* m. pl. The name of a people, MBh. 6, 367.

कौञ्जर *kauñjara,* i.e. *kuñjara + a,* adj., f. *rî,* Belonging to an elephant, MBh. 13, 5580.

कौटसाक्ष्य *kauṭasâkshya,* i.e. *kûṭa -sâkshin + ya,* n. Fraudulent testimony, Man. 8, 117.

कौटिल्य *kauṭilya,* i.e. *kuṭila + ya,* n. **1.** Crispness (as of hair), Pańch. i. d. 205. **2.** Deceitfulness, Pańch. 99, 9.

कौटुम्ब *kauṭumba,* i.e. *kuṭumba + a,* n. Affinity, Râjat. 5, 395, in Chr. p. 278, see n.

कौटुम्बिक *kauṭumbika,* i.e. *kuṭumba + ika,* I. adj. Constituting a family, Bhâg. P. 5, 14, 3. II. m. The father of a family, Bhâg. P. 4, 28, 12.

कौणप *kauṇapa,* i.e. *kuṇapa + a.* **1.** A Râkshasa or demon (devouring corpses), MBh. 1, 6450. **2.** The name of a Nâga or serpent, MBh. 1, 2147.

कौण्डिन्य *kauṇḍinya,* i.e. *kuṇḍinî* (a proper name), *+ ya,* metron. MBh. 2, 111.

कौण्डिल्य *kauṇḍilya,* Hit. 123, 15, read *kauṇḍinya.*

कौतुक *kautuka,* i.e. *kutuka + a,* n. **1.** Eagerness, Râjat. 5, 359; desire, Pańch. 128, 18. **2.** Pleasure, Lass. 43, 11. **3.** Happiness, Pańch. iv. d. 35. **4.** An interesting spectacle, Kathâs. 6, 65. **5.** A festival, Bhartṛ. 3, 15; Mâlav. 64, 6. **6.** Marriage, Bhâg. P. 4, 3, 13. **7.** The marriage string, Daçak. in Chr. 201, 4. — Comp. *Kriḍâ-,* n. feigned curiosity, Kathâs. 18, 135. *Vi-*, adj. incurious, indifferent.

कौतूहल *kautûhala*, i.e. *kutûhala* + *a*, n. **1.** Eagerness, Nal. 1, 16. **2.** Curiosity, Râm. 3, 15, 8; 1, 1, 7. **3.** Desire, Sâv. 4, 26.

कौत्स *kautsa*, i.e. *kutsa* + *a*, **1.** adj. Used by Kutsa, Man. 11, 249. **2.** patron. MBh. 13, 6270.

कौनख्य *kaunakhya*, i.e. *kunakhin* + *ya*, n. Having whitlows on one's nails, Man. 11, 49.

कौन्तेय *kaunteya*, i.e. *kuntî* + *eya*, metronym., m. A son of Kuntî, Nal. 1, 17.

कौन्द *kaunda*, i.e. *kunda* + *a*, adj., f. *dî*, Belonging to, or made of, jasmine, Amar. 54; Vikr. d. 23.

कौपीन *kaupîna*, i.e. *kûpa* + *îna*, n. **1.** The pudenda, MBh. 1, 3638. **2.** A cloth worn over them, Daçak. in Chr. 185, 3.

कौपीनवन्त् *kaupîna* + *vant*, adj. Wearing only a cloth over the pudenda, Häberl. Chr. 487.

कौमार *kaumâra*, i.e. *kumâra* + *a*, I. adj., f. *rî*, **1.** Referring to abstinence, MBh. 3, 8527. **2.** Married as virgin (κουρίδιη), Râm. 2, 30, 8. **3.** Referring to the god of war, MBh. 3, 4086. **II.** f. *rî*, The energy of the god of war, one of the seven mothers, Dev. 8, 16. **III.** n. **1.** Childhood, Man. 9, 3. **2.** Chastity, MBh. 13, 5853.

कौमारक *kaumâra* + *ka*, n. Childhood, Mârk. P. 11, 20.

कौमारराज्य *kaumârarâjya*, i.e. *kumâra-râjan* + *ya*, n. Condition of a prince royal, Râm. 2, 58, 20.

कौमारिक *kaumârika*, i.e. *kumârî* + *ika*, m. The father of daughters, MBh. 1, 4054.

कौमुद *kaumuda*, i.e. *kumuda* + *a*, I. m. The month Kârttika, Oct.-Nov., MBh. 13, 3370. **II.** f. *di*, **1.** Moonlight, Bhartṛ. 1, 38. **2.** The day of full moon in the month Kârttika, MBh. 13, 6182.

कौमोदकी *kaumodakî*, i.e. *ku-modaka* + *î*, f. The club of Vishṇu, or Kṛishṇa, MBh. 1, 8200.

कौरव *kaurava*, i.e. *kuru* + *a*, adj., f. *vî*. **1.** Belonging to the Kurus, Megh. 49; consisting of Kurus, MBh. 1, 5457. **2.** patron. A descendant of Kuru, Nal. 14, 26; MBh. 1, 5457.—**Comp.** When latter part of an adj. the fem. ends in *vâ*, *Nishkaurava*, i.e. *nis-*, adj., f. *vâ*, deprived of Kauravas, MBh. 1, 7961.

कौरवेय *kauraveya*, i.e. *kuru* + *eya*, patron. A descendant of Kuru, MBh. 1, 5689.

कौरव्य *kauravya*, i.e. *kuru* + *ya*, **I.** m. **1.** A descendant of Kuru, MBh. 14, 2521. **2.** The name of a Nâga or serpent, MBh. 1, 5558. **II.** adj. Belonging to the Kurus, MBh. 14, 2484.

कौर्म *kaurma*, i. e. *kûrma* + *a*, adj. Peculiar to a tortoise, Pañch. iii. d. 20.

कौल *kaula*, i.e. *kula* + *a*, adj., f. *lî*, Peculiar to a tribe, Râm. 4, 28, 9.

कौलिक *kaulika*, i.e. probably *kula* + *ika*, m. **1.** A weaver, Pañch. 35, 15. **2.** A heretic, Pañch. iv. d. 12.

कौलीन *kaulîna*, i. e. *kula* + *îna*, **I.** adj., f. *nâ*, Peculiar to high birth, Râm. 5, 87, 12. **II.** n. Gossip, Çâk. 79, 12; rumour, Megh. 111.

कौलीन्य *kaulînya*, i.e. *kulîna* + *ya*, n. Nobleness, Pañch. 71, 14.

कौवेर *kauvera*, i.e. *kuvera* + *a*, adj., f. *rî*, Referring, or peculiar, or referable, to Kuvera, MBh. 2, 2578; with *diç*, The northern quarter or point of the compass, Râm. 4, 60, 15.

कौश *kauça*, i.e. **1.** *kuça*+*a*, adj., f. *çî*, Made of Kuça grass, MBh. 3, 10036. **2.** *koça*+*a*, adj. Silken, Bhâg. P. 3, 4, 7.

कौशल *kauçala*, i.e. *kuçala*+*a*, n. **1.** Well-being, MBh. 4, 486. **2.** Prosperity, prosperous event, Râm. 6, 86, 43. **3.** Cleverness, Bhag. 2, 50.

कौशल्य *kauçalya*, i.e. *kuçala*+*ya*, n. Well-being, Râm. 5, 31, 26.

1. कौशिक *kauçika*, i.e. *kuçika*+*a*, I. adj. and patronym. Descending from Kuçika, MBh. 13, 2719; Râm. 1, 35, 20. II. m. An owl, Pańch. 157, 21. III. f. *kî*, **1.** The name of a river, Râm. 4, 40, 19. **2.** A proper name, Mâlav. 12, 4.

2. कौशिक *kauçika*, i.e. *koçâ*+*ika*, I. adj. **1.** Sheathed, MBh. 3, 11461. **2.** Silken, MBh. 3, 1002. II. n. Silken cloth, MBh. 13, 5502.

कौशीलव्य *kauçîlavya*, i.e. *kuçîlava*+*ya*, n. Profession of an actor, Man. 11, 65.

कौशेय *kauçeya*, i.e. *koça*+*eya*, also कौषेय *kausheya*, I. adj. Silken, Râm. 2, 32, 16. II. n. Silken stuff, Man. 5, 120.

कौश्य *kauçya*, i.e. *kuça*+*ya*, adj. Made of Kuça grass, MBh. 15, 739.

कौषेय *kausheya*; see *kauçeya*.

कौष्ठ्य *kaushṭhya*, i.e. *koshṭha*+*ya*, adj. Being in the stomach, Yâjń. 3, 95.

कौसल्य *kausalya*, i.e. *kosala*+*ya*, I. adj. Belonging to the Kosalas, Bhâg. P. 6, 15, 15. II. *yâ*, f. The mother of Râma, Râm. 1, 1, 17.

कौसीद *kausîda*, i.e. *kusîda*+*a*, adj., f. *dî*, Proceeding from a loan, Man. 8, 143.

कौसुमायुध *kausumâyudha*, i.e. *kusuma-âyudha*+*a*, adj. Referring to the god of love, Lass. 20, 19.

कौस्तुभ *kaustubha*, i.e. *ku-stubh*+*a*, m. and n. A jewel worn by Vishṇu, Râm. 1, 45, 39.—Comp. *Sa-kirîṭa-kaustubha*, adj. with a diadem and the jewel of Vishṇu, Pańch. 44, 15.

† क्नंस् *KNAṄS*, i. 1, and 10, Par. To speak or to shine (? v.r.).

† क्नथ् *KNATH*, i. 1, Par. To hurt, to kill.

† क्नस् *KNAS*, i. 4, Par. **1.** To be crooked. **2.** To shine.—Cf. perhaps κνημός, κνήμη.

† क्नू *KNÛ*, or क्नु *KNU*, ii. 9, Par. and Âtm. To sound.—Cf. perhaps κνύζω, κινυρός.

क्नूय् *KNÛY*, i. 1, Âtm. **1.** To be wet. **2.** † To sound. **3.** † To stink.—Caus. *knopaya*, To make wet, Çiç. 10, 49.

† क्मर् *KMAR*, i. 1, Par. To be crooked.—Cf. perhaps καμάρα, etc.; Lat. camera.

क्रकच *krakacha* (base *krak*, an imitative sound), m. and n. A saw, MBh. 3, 882.

क्रकर *krakara* (based on an imitative sound), m. A sort of partridge, Perdix sylvatica, Suçr. 1, 73, 1.

क्रतु *kratu*, i.e. *kram*+*tu*, m. **1.** Power (ved.), Chr. 291, 13=Rigv. i. 64, 13. **2.** Sacrifice, Man. 7, 79. **3.** The name of one of the seven Ṛishis, Man. 1, 35.—Comp. *Vara-*, m. Indra. *Çata-*, I. adj. honoured by a hundred sacrifices (ἑκατομβαῖος), Chr. 298, 23=Rigv. i. 112, 23. II. m. a name of Indra, Pańch. i. d. 188.—Cf. κρατύς, κράτος, κάρτος, κραταῖος, etc.; Gradivus, Goth. hardu (*d*, not *th*, on account of the aff. *tu* being based on *tva*).

† क्रथ् *KRATH*, i. 1 and 10, To kill, to hurt. i. 10, To amuse.

क्रथ *kratha*, m. **1.** The name of a people, MBh. 2, 585. **2.** A proper name, MBh. 1, 2697. **3.** The name of an Asura or demon, MBh. 1, 2665.

क्रथन *krathana*, I. n. Slaughter, Prab. 5, 10. II. m. The name of an Asura or demon, MBh. 1, 1488; a monkey, Râm. 4, 63, 4, etc.

क्रथनक *krathana+ka*, m. A proper name, Pañch. 68, 12.

क्रद् *KRAD*, see *krand*.

क्रन्द् *KRAND*, i. 1, Par., Âtm., and † क्रद् *KRAD*, i. 1, Âtm. **1.** To roar (ved.). **2.** To cry miserably, MBh. 1, 6201. **3.** To implore, Mârk. P. 15, 68. —Caus. To cause to cry, Suçr. 2, 382, 13; cf. *kad*.—With the prep. आ *â*, **1.** To implore, MBh. 3, 11461. **2.** To cry miserably, MBh. 3, 2388. *â-krandita*, n. Crying, Vikr. 5, 5. Caus. To cause to cry, Bhâg. P. 3, 14, 38.—With समा *sam-â*, To cry miserably, MBh. 15, 1073.—With वि *vi*, *vi-krandita*, n. Lamenting, Râm. 2, 59, 30.—Cf. κέλαδος, etc., κάλανδρος, κρήνη (for κραδ-νη), κρουνός.

क्रन्दन *krand+ana*, n. Lamenting, Pañch. 213, 2.

क्रप् *KRAP*, or † कृप् *KṚIP*, † कप् *KAP*, i. 1, Âtm. **1.** To compassionate; ved. to desire, and base of the pres. *kṛip*. **2.** † To go.

क्रम् *KRAM*, i. 1, *krâma* (in epic poetry also *krama*, e.g. Râm. 5, 3, 73)

Par., Âtm. † i. 4, Par. **1.** To step, to walk, Râm. 5, 1, 45. **2.** To step through, MBh. 3, 485. **3.** To go to (with acc.), Râm. 4, 8, 4. **4.** To attain, Ragh. 14, 17. **5.** To undertake, Bhaṭṭ. 9, 23. **6.** To commit, Bhâg. P. 3, 16, 2. **7.** Âtm. To succeed, Râm. 4, 44, 121. **8.** Âtm. To prevail, MBh. 13, 3918. **9.** To overtop, Ragh. 1, 14. *krânta*, n. A step, Man. 12, 121. Frequent. *chaṅkram* and *chaṅkramya*, **1.** To roam, MBh. 5, 707; to go astray, MBh. 1, 716; anomal. ptcple. of the pres. *chaṅkramamâṇa*, MBh. 1, 7917.—With the prep. अति *ati*, **1.** To cross, Râm. 3, 60, 18; Man. 5, 76; absol. *atikramya*, Beyond, Râm. 4, 40, 34. **2.** To escape, Râm. 2, 9, 24. **3.** To let pass away, Râm. 6, 88, 20. **4.** To surpass, Man. 8, 151; MBh. 14, 86. **5.** To supersede, MBh. 14, 1810. **6.** To trespass, Râm. 2, 9, 22. **7.** To neglect, Man. 9, 78. **8.** To withdraw, Râm. 1, 9, 11. **9.** To become deprived (with abl.), Man. 9, 93. *atikrânta*, **1.** Passed, Pañch. i. d. 378. **2.** Excessive, MBh. 3, 657. *an-atikrânta*, adj. Not exceeded, Râjat. 5, 228. *an-atikramaṇîya*, adj. Unavoidable, Hit. iv. d. 72. Caus. *ati-kramaya*, **1.** To let pass away, Râm. 4, 26, 24. **2.** To disregard, Râm. 6, 16, 67.—With अत्यति *ati-ati*, To compress (in sexual intercourse), MBh. 1, 4883.—With अभ्यति *abhi-ati*, **1.** To pass, Râm. 2, 70, 26. **2.** To avoid, MBh. 14, 1551. **3.** To trespass, MBh. 1, 199.—With व्यति *vi-ati*, **1.** To pass, Râm. 2, 14, 29. **2.** To stride through, MBh. 13, 4897. **3.** To trespass, Pañch. i. d. 65. **4.** To pass away, Râm. 1, 63, 9. **5.** To surpass, Râm. 5, 43, 5. *vyatikrânta*, n. Fault, Râm. 5, 84, 11.—With समति, **1.** To pass, MBh. 3, 2851; Lass. 10, 1. **2.** To step out, Râm. 6, 31, 2. **3.** To let pass away, Râm. 5, 56,

79 (absol. *samatikramya*, After). **4.** To disregard, Râm. 2, 30, 33. **5.** To lose, MBh. 1, 7786.—With अधि *adhi*, To ascend to, MBh. 3, 1777.—With अनु *anu*, **1.** To follow, MBh. 3, 356. **2.** To particularise, Bhâg. P. 2, 6, 45. **3.** To make a table of contents, Bhâg. P. 1, 7, 8. *anukrânta*, **1.** Followed, Râm. 5, 47, 6. **2.** Following, Râm. 2, 30, 41.—With समनु *sam-anu*, To pass completely, Bhâg. P. 3, 30, 35.—With अप *apa*, **1.** To go away, MBh. 1, 177. **2.** To leave (with abl.), Râm. 4, 30, 21. **3.** To pass away, Bhâg. P. 3, 11, 33.—With व्यप *vi-apa*, To withdraw, Râm. 2, 87, 21.—With अभि *abhi*, **1.** To approach, MBh. 3, 8613. **2.** To enter, Râm. 4, 47, 3. **3.** To set out, Râm. 1, 77, 18.—With समभि *sam-abhi*, To approach, MBh. 3, 2389.—With अव *ava*, To withdraw, Mṛichchh. (Calc. ed.) 210, 21.—With आ *â*, **1.** To approach, Bhartṛ. 1, 69. **2.** To step on, Man. 4, 130. **3.** To step in, Râm. 5, 81, 22. **4.** To begin, Râm. 3, 4, 5. **5.** To seize, MBh. 1, 5936. **6.** To conquer, Mârk. P. 18, 26. **7.** To repose on, Râm. 1, 57, 28. **8.** Âtm., To rise, Ragh. 5, 71; to ascend, MBh. 1, 4076. *â-krânta*, **1.** Burdened, Mṛichchh. 115, 5. **2.** Full of, Bhartṛ. 3, 9; abounding with, Man. 4, 61.—Causal, To cause to step in, Kumâras. 6, 52.—With अध्या *adhi-â*, **1.** To assault, MBh. 3, 13827. **2.** To occupy, Çâk. d. 47.—With अन्वा *anu-â*, To visit one by one, Bhâg. P. 3, 1, 17.—With अपा *apa-â*, To withdraw, MBh. 13, 3717.—With उपा *upa-â*, To assail, MBh. 3, 11123.—With समुपा *sam-upa-â*, To attain, Râm. 1, 41, 21.—

With निरा *nis-â*, To step out, MBh. 1, 4292.—With समा *sam-â*, **1.** To step on, MBh. 1, 355. **2.** To assail, Pañch. iii. d. 18. **3.** To occupy, Ragh. 4, 4. *samâkrânta*, **1.** Burdened, Râm. 4, 15, 25; filled, Râm. 5, 20, 2. **2.** Performed, Râm. 1, 44, 54. **3.** Captive, Kathâs. 10, 193.—With उद् *ud*, **1.** To step out, Râm. 3, 9, 35. **2.** To leave, MBh. 13, 1828. **3.** To omit, MBh. 14, 1812. **4.** To neglect, MBh. 3, 1180. *utkrânta*, Left, Kathâs. 4, 2. *utkramaṇîya*, What ought to be removed, MBh. 3, 8226.—With अत्युद् *ati-ud*, To excel, MBh. 13, 1628.—With व्युद् *vi-ud*, **1.** To leave, MBh. 14, 1319. **2.** To neglect, MBh. 13, 4768.—With समुद् *sam-ud*, To neglect, MBh. 1, 4835.—With उप *upa*, **1.** To approach, MBh. 1, 6787. **2.** To assail, MBh. 13, 6716. **3.** To walk, Râm. 5, 1, 46. **4.** To treat, MBh. 2, 678. *upâyopakrânta*, adj. Treated with (the suitable) means, Daçak. in Chr. 196, 11; cf. 198, 1 (tortured). **5.** To physic, Daçak. in Chr. 187, 13; to cure, Suçr. 1, 31, 1. **6.** To seize, MBh. 3, 14984. **7.** To perform, Yâjñ. 3, 200. **8.** To dispose, MBh. 1, 4131. **9.** To begin, Râm. 2, 103, 6.—With समुप *sam-upa*, **1.** To approach, Râm. 2, 78, 14. **2.** To begin, MBh. 13, 4222.—With निस् *nis*, To go forth, to leave, MBh. 1, 4445; in dramatic language, Exit, exeunt, Çâk. 4, 20.—Caus. **1.** To cause to step out or to leave, Râm. 4, 9, 24. **2.** To deliver, Daçak. in Chr. 200, 7.—With अभिनिस् *abhi-nis*, **1.** To step out and near, Râm. 4, 25, 21. **2.** To leave (with abl.), Man. 6, 41.—With उपनिस् *upa-nis*, To leave (with abl.), MBh. 2, 1070.—With विनिस् *vi-nis*, To step out,

MBh. 3, 10273.—With परा *parâ*, **1.** To turn, MBh. 3, 15772. **2.** To put forth one's strength, Man. 7, 106; with *parasparam*, To rival each other, Chr. 25, 59.—With परि *pari*, **1.** To walk about, MBh. 3, 13878. **2.** To walk round (with acc.), Râm. 1, 73, 36. **3.** To walk through, Bhâg. P. 6, 13, 30. **4.** To overtake, Râm. 5, 3, 42. *pari-krânta*, n. Trace, Râm. 3, 68, 46.—Comp. *Tri-*, m. epitheton of a true Brâhmaṇa, MBh. 13, 6455 (perhaps: Who has been thrice victorious, viz. in *tapas*, *dama*, and *niyama*; cf. MBh. 12, 13566 and 13567). Frequent. *Pari-chaṅkram*, To turn round continually, Bhâg. P. 5, 23, 3.—With अनुपरि *anu-pari*, **1.** To visit one after another, MBh. 3, 10414. **2.** To visit in due order, Bhâg. P. 5, 1, 30. **3.** To survey one after another, Man. 7, 123.—With विपरि *vi-pari* in *viparikrânta*, Powerful, Râm. 4, 22, 16.—With संपरि *sam-pari*, To walk round (with acc.), Pańch. iii. d. 172; to visit, MBh. 1, 12.—With प्र *pra*, **1.** To walk on, Suçr. 1, 256, 14. **2.** To pass, Râm. 5, 3, 73. **3.** Âtm., To act, MBh. 13, 5573. **4.** Âtm., To begin, Râm. 5, 1, 34; in epic poetry also Par., Dev. 2, 48. *prakrânta*, n. The outset of a journey, Yâjń. 2, 198.—With संप्र *sam-pra*, Âtm., To begin, Râm. 6, 91, 10.—With प्रति *prati*, To return, MBh. 3, 15689.—With वि *vi*, **1.** Âtm., To walk along, Râm. 4, 58, 24; also Par., Râm. 2, 25, 33. **2.** Âtm., To walk through, Râm. 5, 2, 40. **3.** Âtm., To enter, Bhâg. P. 2, 6, 20. **4.** Âtm., To proceed, MBh. 2, 196. **5.** To assail, Râm. 6, 100, 8. **6.** To overcome, MBh. 3, 1611 (*akramat*); Âtm., Pańch. 79, 2. *vikrânta*, **1.** Courageous, Râm. 3, 4, 31. **2.** Preeminent, MBh. 14, 69. m. **1.** A hero. **2.** A lion. n. **1.** Gait, Râm. 3, 25, 13. **2.** Valour.—Comp. *Bhîma-*, m. a lion. *Su-*, I. m. a hero. II. n. heroism.—With निर्वि *nis-vi*, To come forth, MBh. 1, 3244.—With सम् *sam*, **1.** To walk along, MBh. 3, 1755 (*saṁ-kraman*). **2.** To walk through, Râm. 3, 76, 5. **3.** To turn to, Râm. 2, 96, 25. Caus. *sam-kramaya* and *sam-krâmaya*, **1.** To lead, Ragh. 13, 3. **2.** To transfer, MBh. 1, 3462. **3.** To ascribe (with loc.), Mṛichchh. 131, 2. **4.** To conquer, Râm. 6, 1, 41. **5.** To agree, Chr. 58, 8, Âtm.—With उपसम् *upa-sam*, To approach, Daçak. in Chr. 200, 19.—With प्रतिसम् *prati-sam*, To cease, Âtm., Bhâg. P. 3, 9, 9. Caus. *krâmaya*, To cause to return, Bhâg. P. 4, 25, 50.—Cf. *kratu*, κρέμαμαι, κρεμάννυμι for κρεμανjυμι, denomin., κρημνός, etc., κρείων, κρέων (cf. ved. *krâvan*, i.e. *kram* + *van*), κραιαίνω for κραϝανjω, denomin., κραίνω, ἀκράαντος for ἀ-κραϝαν + τος, ἄκραντος, κραντήρ, etc.; κραδαίνω for κραδανjω, denom. from κραμ + δαν for κραμ + tvan, κραδεύω, κραδάω, κράδη, etc., κλάδος, etc.; Lat. gradus, based on gram + tva, gradior, etc.; Goth. hramjan, hlamma, haldan, grids; O.H.G. scrîtan; A.S. scrîdhan.

क्रम *kram* + *a*, m. **1.** A step, MBh. 3, 11178. **2.** A foot, MBh. 3, 14316. **3.** A posture for assailing, Pańch. 197, 24; a bound, 229, 20. **4.** Strength, see comp. **5.** Regular order, Man. 8, 24; succession, Pańch. i. d. 83. **6.** Course, Pańch. iii. d. 240 **7.** Method, Hit. 68, 21. **8.** Way, Râm. 2, 26, 20. **9.** A sacred precept, Mârk. P. 23, 112. **10.** Intention, Kathâs. 18, 380; Hit. 39, 5. **11.** instr. *krameṇa*, **a.** By degrees, Pańch. 209, 24; **b.** In order, Man. 2, 173; **c.** Afterwards, Pańch. 221, 9. **12.** abl. *kramât*, In order, Man. 10, 28. **13.**

The name of a country=Kramavattu, Râjat. 5, 87.—Comp. *A-*, m. an unsuitable method, Bhartṛ. 1, 28. *Kâla-*, m. destiny, Pańch. iii. d. 240. *Madhu-*, m. 1. tippling. 2. the honeycomb. *Yathâ-krama+m*, adv. in due order, Man. 3, 2. *Çaikshya-guṇa-krama*, adj. possessing practice, talent, and strength, MBh. 1, 7023. *Samâksharapadakrama*, i. e. *sama-akshara-pada-krama*, adj. containing a succession of (metrical) feet of the same number of syllables, Râm. 1, 3, 58 Gorr.

क्रमण *kramaṇa*, i.e. *kram+ana*, n. 1. Walking, Mṛichchh. 50, 15. 2. Passing, MBh. 3, 16254.

क्रमतस् *krama+tas*, adv. By degrees, Çiç. 9, 29.

क्रमवत्तु *kramavattu* (a dialect. form of *krama-varta*, Râjat. 3, 227), m. The name of a country, Râjat. 4, 39.

क्रमशस् *krama+ças*, adv. 1. By degrees, Pańch. ii. d. 37. 2. In order, Man. 1, 68.

क्रमिक *kramika*, i.e. *krama+ika*, adj. Proceeding conformably to the sacred precepts, MBh. 2, 166.

क्रमेल *kramela*, m. A camel, Pańch. 89, 6.

क्रय *kraya*, i.e. *krî+a*, m. 1. Purchase, Man. 8, 201. 2. Purchased objects, 8, 209.

क्रयविक्रयिन् *krayavikrayin*, i. e. *kraya-vikraya+in*, adj. He who buys and he who sells, Man. 5, 51. He who buys and sells, Yajń. 2, 262.

क्रयाणक *krayâṇaka*, i.e. *krî+âna+ka*, adj. Marketable, Lass. 23, 13.

क्रयिक *krayika*, i.e. *krî+in+ka*, adj. Buying, MBh. 13, 5633.

क्रव्य *kravya*, n. Raw flesh, Bhâg. P. 4, 18, 24.—Cf. κρέας, base κρεατ; Lat. caro, base caron; Goth. hraiv.—Cf. also *krûra*.

क्रव्याद् *kravyâd*, i.e. *kravya-ad*, adj. Devouring raw flesh, Râm. 6, 16, 5.—Comp. *A-*, adj. not carnivorous, Yâjń. 3, 272.

क्रव्याद *kravyâda*, i.e. *kravya-âda*, adj., f. *dâ*, Devouring raw flesh, MBh. 1, 932.—Comp. *A-*, adj. not carnivorous, Man. 11, 137.

क्रशय *KRAÇAYA*, a denomin. derived from *kṛiça*, To make meager, Çiç. 9, 61.

क्राकचिक *krâkachika*, i.e. *krakacha+ika*, m. A sawyer, Râm. 2, 38, 14.

क्रिया *kriyâ*, i.e. *kṛi+yâ*, f. 1. Performance, Man. 9, 298. 2. Action, Pańch. 63, 9; an act, Yâjń. 2, 23. 3. Use, Pańch. i. d. 430. 4. Business, Man. 8, 154. 5. A literary work, Vikr. d. 2. 6. Physical treatment, Suçr. 1, 5, 10. 7. An act of piety, Man. 2, 80. 8. A religious ceremony, Man. 5, 84. 9. Obsequies, Râm. 6, 96, 10. 10. A proper name, MBh. 1, 2578.—Comp. *Agni-*, f. a religious act performed by means of fire, as burning of a corpse. *Atithi-*, f. hospitality, Râm. 1, 25, 19. *Udaka-*, f. pouring water in honour of a deceased one, Man. 5, 69. *Kṛita-kriya*, adj. one who has performed a religious ceremony, e.g. the funeral rites, Man. 5, 99. *Kautuka-kriyâ*, f. the nuptial ceremonics, Ragh. 11, 53. *Chitra-*, f. painting, MBh. 4, 1360. *Jala-*=*udaka-*, Râm. 1, 42, 15. *Dâra-*, f. marriage, Chr. 3, 8. *Dharma-*, f. observance of duties, Man. 12, 31. *Nishkriya*, i.e. *nis-*, adj. 1. inactive, Bhâshâp. 85. 2. one who does not perform his religious duties, Man. 11, 18. *Nirahaṁkriyâ*, i.e. *nis-aham-*, I. f. want of selfishness, Bhâg. P. 3, 29, 18. II. *-kriya*, adj. impersonal, 3, 27, 14. *Laghu-*, f. a trifle, *bahvârambhe laghukriyâ*, Much ado about nothing, Chân. 91, in Montasber. Berl. Ak. Hist. Phil. 1864, 413. *Vaça-*, f. 1. subduing by drugs, charms, etc. 2. the drugs, etc., so used. *Vikarmakriyâ*, i.e. *vikarman-*, f. 1. vicious conduct, Man. 9, 226. 2. illegal act. *Sa-kriya*, adj. one who observes his religious duties, Lass. 42, 2. *Hina-* (vb. *hâ*), adj. one who neglects his religious duties, Man. 3, 7.

क्रियावन्त् *kriyâ+vant*, adj., f. *vatî*. **1.** One who performs actions, Hit. i. d. 162. **2.** One who performs his religious duties, Râm. 2, 106, 10.—**Comp.** *Turaga-kriyâ+vant*, adj. skilful in managing horses, Lass. 70, 9.

क्री *KRÎ*, ii. 9, Par., Âtm.; *krînâ*, *ṇî*, base of the pres. etc. To buy, Man. 9, 74. *kretavya* and *kreya*, Purchasable, MBh. 13, 2450; Râjat. 5, 270.—With the prep. **आ** *â*, To buy, Daçak. 80, 4. —With **उप** *upa*, To buy, Hit. 115, 3. —With **परि** *pari*, To hire, MBh. 1, 4672.—With **वि** *vi*, To sell, Man. 10, 90. *vikrîta*, n. Sale, Man. 8, 165.—Desider. *vi-chikrîsha*, Atm. To desire to sell, Daçak. in Chr. 191, 6.—With **सम्** *sam*, To buy, MBh. 1, 6219.

क्रीड् *KRÎḌ*, i. 1, Par. (in epic poetry also Âtm.), To play, Râm. 4, 24, 39; with acc. *dyûtam̃ krîḍ*, To play (with dice), Mṛichchh. 30, 18; with instr. Man. 4, 74; Pańch. i. d. 201; Âtm. Râm. 3, 67, 6. *krîḍita*, n. Play, Râm. 5, 13, 23. *krîḍanîya*, n. A plaything, MBh. 13, 4206.—Caus. *krîḍaya*, To cause to play, MBh. 1, 6440.—With the prepositions **समा** *sam-â*, To play, MBh. 13, 659.—With **उप** *upa*, To surround playing (with acc.), MBh. 13, 3832.—With **प्र** *pra*, Âtm. To play, MBh. 3, 14882.—With **वि** *vi*, **1.** To play, MBh. 3, 11099. **2.** To act as if jesting, Râm. 3, 569. **3.** To treat like a plaything, Bhâg. P. 6, 2, 37.—With **सम्** *sam*, Âtm. To play, Râm. 1, 9, 14; Par., MBh. 1, 7651.—With **परिसम्** *pari-sam*, To jest, to indulge in amusements, Râm. 4, 30, 16.

क्रीडन *krîḍ+ana*, n. Play, Râm. 1, 9, 14.—**Comp.** *Udaka-*, n. playing in the water, MBh. 1, 4996.

क्रीडनक *krîḍana+ka*, m. (and n.) A plaything, Çâk. 105, 10; Bhâg. P. 3, 2, 30.

क्रीडनकता *krîḍanaka+tâ*, f. The character of a plaything, Bhâg. P. 5, 26, 32 (*tayâ*, instr. Like a plaything).

क्रीडनीयक *krîḍanîya+ka*, n. A doll, Kathâs. 12, 74.

क्रीडा *krîḍ+â*, f. **1.** Play, Râm. 3, 39, 17; jest, Gît. 9, 10. **2.** Amusement, Râjat. 5, 338.—**Comp.** *Jala-*, f. playing in the water, Pańch. 53, 1. *Toya-*, f. playing in the water, Megh. 34. *Vapra-*, f. butting at a bank or hillock, as of an elephant or bull.

क्रीडामय *krîḍâ+maya*, adj., f. *yî*, Consisting of dalliance, MBh. 14, 1486.

क्रीडितृ *krîḍitṛi*, i.e. *krîḍ+tṛi*, m. A gambler, Bhâg. P. 1, 13, 40.

क्रीतक *krîta+ka* (vb. *krî*), adj. Acquired by purchase, Man. 9, 174.

क्रीळि *krîḷi*, i.e. *krîḍ+i* (ved.), adj. Playing, Chr. 293, 3=Rigv. i. 87, 3.

† **क्रुञ्च्** *KRUŃCH*, i. 1, Par. **1.** To be crooked. **2.** To curve. **3.** To move crookedly. **4.** To become small.

5. To make small.—Cf. perhaps O.H.G. kriuchan.

† क्रुड् *KRUḌ*, i. 6, Par. To sink.

क्रुध् *KRUDH*, i. 4, Par. To be wrathful, Man. 6, 48. *kruddha*, Enraged, Pañch. iii. d. 75. *ati-kruddha*, adj. Much enraged, Râm. 3, 53, 55. *parama-*, adj. Very much enraged, Râm. 1, 51, 19. *su-*, adj. Much enraged, Râm. 3, 51, 19. *krodhanîya*, What may provoke to anger, Râm. 2, 41, 3. —Caus., *krodhaya*, To make angry, Râm. 2, 9, 21.—With the prep. अभि *abhi*, To be enraged at (with acc.), Vikr. 36, 2.—With समभि *sam-abhi*, To be angry, MBh. 3, 8738.—With प्रति *prati*, To be angry in turn against (with acc.), Man. 6, 48.—With सम् *sam*, To be angry, MBh. 3, 14828. *saṁ-kruddha*, Wrathful, Râm. 1, 55, 6.—With अभिसम् *abhi-sam*, To be enraged at (with acc.), MBh. 4, 1572.—With प्रतिसम् *prati-sam*, To be enraged against, MBh. 1. 5983.—Cf. Lat. crudus, crudelis; see also *krûra*.

क्रुध् *krudh*, f. Wrath, Kathâs. 18, 282.

† क्रुन्थ् *KRUNTH*, v.r. of *kunth*, ii. 9.

क्रुश् *KRUÇ*, i. 1. Par. (in epic poetry also Âtm., Râm. 1, 60, 19), To cry, Râm. 1, 54, 7; 2, 56, 9. *krushṭa*, One who reviles (?), MBh. 13, 2135.—With अनु *anu*, Caus. *kroçaya*, To pity, MBh. 13, 285.—With अभि *abhi*, **1.** To cry at, MBh. 4, 359. **2.** To bewail, Râm. 4, 24, 22.—With आ *â*, **1.** To cry, Bhartṛ. 3, 87. **2.** To revile, Man. 6, 48. *âkrushṭa*, n. Scream, Suçr. 1, 108, 17.—With प्रत्या *prati-â*, To revile in turn, MBh. 3, 1091.—With व्या *vi-â*, To lament, Râm. 3, 68, 22.—With उद् *ud*, **1.** To cry out, Râm. 6, 36, 60. **2.** To cry to (with acc.), MBh. 1, 7748.—With समुद् *sam-ud*, To cry out, Râm. 6, 111, 29.—With परि *pari*, To lament, Râm. 2, 65, 22.—With प्र *pra*, **1.** To cry out, MBh. 2, 2695. **2.** To call, MBh. 3, 2363.—With वि *vi*, To call aloud, MBh. 1, 7633. **2.** To call, MBh. 2, 2229. **3.** To resound, Râm. 6, 92, 69. *vikrushṭa*, Offensive, Man. 4, 176; n. **1.** Scream, Râm. 3, 30, 29. **2.** A cry for help, Yâjñ. 2, 234.—With सम् *sam*, To cry all together, MBh. 2, 1553.—With अभिसम् *abhi-sam*, To call to, Râm. 2, 100, 36.—Akin to *kruç*, but not its true reflex, are κραυγή, κρωγμός, etc.; Goth. hrukjan; Lat. lugeo.

क्रूर *krûra*, adj. **1.** Sore (ved.). **2.** Cruel, Hiḍ. 4, 31. **3.** Harsh, Râm. 3, 64, 2. **4.** Formidable, Pañch. iii. d. 75. **5.** Hard, Çâk. d. 37.—Comp. *A-*, adj. soft, Man. 2, 33. *Danta-krûra+m*, adv. (he seized) in a terrible way with the teeth, MBh. 7, 2431.—Cf. probably Lat. crusta; κρύος, etc., κρυσταίνω; see *krudh*.

क्रूरकर्मकृत् *krûrakarmakṛit*, i. e. *krûra-karman-kṛi+t*, adj. m. A cruel beast, Man. 12, 58.

क्रूरता *krûra+tâ*, f. Cruelty, Man. 10, 58.

क्रेतृ *kretṛi*, i.e. *krî+tṛi*, m. A purchaser, Yâjñ. 2, 253.

क्रोड *kroḍa*, I. m. and f. *ḍâ*. **1.** The breast, Râm. 6, 82, 10; Mṛichchh. 34, 14 (the bosom used to keep money in). **2.** The interior, Hit. 80, 14. II. m. A hog, Pañch. 120, 9.

क्रोध ***krodha,*** i.e. ***krudh + a,*** I. m. **1.** Anger, Man. 1, 25. **2.** A proper name, MBh. 1, 2543. **II.** f. ***dhâ,*** A proper name, MBh. 1, 2520.—Comp. *A-*, m. freedom from wrath, Man. 3, 235. *Sa-*, adj., f. ***dhâ,*** wrathful, Chr. 57, 28.

क्रोधन ***krodhana,*** i.e. ***krudh + ana,*** I. adj., f. ***nâ,*** Passionate, Râm. 2, 70, 10; Yâjń. 1, 333. **II.** n. Anger.—Comp. *A-*, adj. free from wrath, Man. 3, 192. *Sa-*, adj. enraged, Râm. 5, 85, 3.

क्रोधालु ***krodhâlu,*** i.e. ***krodha + âlu,*** adj. Passionate, Suçr. 2, 533, 8.

क्रोश ***kroça,*** i. e. ***kruç + a,*** m. **1.** Cry (ved.). **2.** A measure of distance, containing 4,000 cubits, Râm. 2, 90, 1.

क्रोष्टु ***kroshṭu,*** i.e. ***kruç + tu,*** the base of most cases is **क्रोष्टृ** ***kroshṭṛi,*** i.e. ***kruç + tṛi,*** m., f. ***trî,*** A jackal, Draup. 1, 17.

क्रोष्टुक ***kroshṭu + ka,*** m., f. ***kî,*** A jackal, MBh. 13, 6342; Râm. 3, 20, 22.

क्रौञ्च ***krauńcha,*** I. m., f. ***chî,*** A kind of heron, or curlew, Man. 11, 134; Râm. 2, 76, 21. **II.** m. **1.** The name of a mountain, Râm. 4, 44, 32. **2.** One of the Dvîpas, or principal divisions of the world, Bhâg. P. 5, 1, 32. **3.** The name of a demon.

क्रौर्य ***kraurya,*** i. e. ***krûra + ya,*** n. Cruelty, Man. 12, 33 (Jones: Detraction).

क्लथ् ***KLATH,*** i. 1, Par. To kill or hurt.

† **क्लद्** ***KLAD,*** see ***kland.***

† **क्लन्द्** ***KLAND,*** i. 1, Par. **1.** To call. **2.** To weep. i. 1, Âtm. (v.r. ***klad***), **1.** To be confused. **2.** To confound.—Cf. ***krand.***

† **क्लप्** ***KLAP,*** i. 10, Par. To speak (? v.r.).—Cf. perhaps Lat. crepare; O.H.G. hrôfan; A.S. hreopan; Goth. hrôpjan (=***klâpaya***).

क्लम् ***KLAM,*** i. 1 and 4, ***klâma*** and ***klâmya,*** Par. To be fatigued, exhausted. ***klânta,*** **1.** Fatigued, Râm. 2, 42, 19. **2.** Exhausted, Ragh. 2. 13. **3.** Withered, Çâk. d. 66. **4.** Thin, Çâk. d. 58.—With the prep. **परि** ***pari, pari-klânta,*** Much exhausted, MBh. 1, 5893.—With **वि**, Âtm. To despond, Çiç. 15, 127.

क्लम ***klam + a,*** m. **1.** Fatigue, Arj. 4, 47. **2.** Languor, Râm. 5, 49, 10.—Comp. *Gata-*, adj. f. ***mâ,*** recreated, Nal. 11, 1.

क्लव् ***KLAV,*** i. 1, Âtm. To fear.—With prep. **वि** ***vi,*** To fear.

क्लान्ति ***klânti,*** i. e. ***klam + ti,*** f. Languor, Bhartṛ. 1, 36.

क्लिद् ***KLID,*** i. 4, ***klidya,*** Par. To become wet, Suçr. 2, 23, 12. ***klinna,*** **1.** Wet, Râm. 1, 42, 20. **2.** Filled with tears. **3.** Compassionate, Bhâg. P. 4, 3, 10. Caus. ***kledaya,*** To make wet, Bhag. 2, 23.—With the prep. **समा** ***sam-â, samâklinna,*** Wet with tears, MBh. 3, 13472.—With **परि** ***pari, pariklinna,*** Completely wet, Râm. 4, 6, 16.—With **प्र** ***pra,*** Âtm. To become wet, Suçr. 1, 297, 17. ***praklinna,*** Wet, Râm. 3, 22, 21. Caus. To moisten, Suçr. 1, 68, 4.—With **वि** ***vi, viklinna,*** Thoroughly wet, MBh. 1, 5412.—With **सम्** ***sam, samklinna,*** Wet, Mṛichchh. 92, 7.—Cf. perhaps κλύδιος, κλύζω; Goth. hlûtrs, etc.

† **क्लिन्द्** ***KLIND,*** i. 1, Par., Âtm. To bewail.—Cf. ***krand.***

क्लिश् *KLIÇ*, ii. 9, *kliçnâ, kliçnî*, Par., and i. 4, *kliçya*, Âtm. (also Par. Man. 8, 169), **1.** To torment. MBh. 2, 2351; Ragh. 13, 73. **2.** i. 4. To suffer distress, MBh. 2, 2255, Man. 8, 169. *klishṭa*, **1.** Afflicted, Çâk. d. 58, Râm. 3, 58, 15. **2.** Hurt, Râm. 3, 58, 12. **3.** Wasted, Suçr. 2, 157. **4.** Painful, Pańch. i. d. 12. *ṭam*, adv. Miserably, Bhâg. P. 1, 9, 12.—Comp. *A-*, adj. 1. without pain, MBh. 3, 1706. 2. unhurt, Râm. 6, 103, 4. 3. firm, Râm. 1, 34, 1. 4. reliable, Râm. 1, 38, 6.—Caus. *kleçaya*, To torment, Râm. 5, 27, 33.—With उद् *ud*, To become uneasy, Suçr. 1, 331, 21. Caus. To stir, Suçr. 2, 184, 18.—With समुद् *sam-ud*, To become uneasy, Suçr. 2, 348, 18.—With परि *pari*, **1.** To torment, Râm. 5, 58, 21. **2.** i. 4, To suffer distress, Râm. 5, 25, 32; Par. MBh. 3, 578. *pariklishṭa*, Much pained, Râm. 3, 52, 41. *ṭam*, adv. With pain, Bhag. 17, 21. *a-*, adv. With cheerfulness, MBh. 3, 108.—With वि *vi*, *viklishṭa*, Violated, Ram. 4, 17, 15.—With सम् *sam*, To torment, Râm. 2, 22, 14. *saṁklishṭa*, Bruised, Suçr. 2, 16, 17.—Cf. *kṛiç* and *liç*.

† **क्लीब्** *KLÎB* and **क्लीव्** *KLÎV*, i. 1. Âtm. **1.** To behave like an eunuch; to be timorous.

क्लीब *klîba*, or **क्लीव** *klîva*, adj. **1.** Deprived of virility; m. An eunuch, Man. 3, 150. **2.** Timorous; m. A coward, MBh. 1, 5142. **3.** Neuter.—Comp. *A-*, adj. manly, Râm. 1, 28, 1.

क्लीबता *klîba+tâ*, f. and **क्लीबत्व** *klîba-twa*, n. **1.** Want of virility, Suçr. 1, 366, 8.—Comp. *A-*, f. manly behaviour, Ragh. 8, 83.

† **क्लु** *KLU*, i. 1, Âtm. To move (?).

क्लेद *kleda*, i.e. *klid+a*, m. Humidity, Râm. 5, 12, 42.

क्लेदन *kledana*, i.e. *klid+ana*, **I.** adj. Moistening, Suçr. 1, 76, 19. **II.** n. Moistening, Bhâg. P. 3, 26, 43.

† **क्लेश्** *KLEÇ*, i. 1, Âtm. **1.** To speak. **2.** To impede. **3.** To hurt.

क्लेश *kleça*, i.e. *kliç+a*, m. Pain, Man. 2, 227.—Comp. *A-*, m. want of bodily pain, Man. 4, 3; abl. *çât*, without any effort, Pańch. ii. d. 9. *Garbha-*, m. pains in labour, Mârk. P. 22, 45.

ऽक्लेशिन् *-kleçin*, i.e. *kliç+in*, adj., f. *nî*, Hurting, Megh. 88.

क्लेष्टृ *kleshṭṛi*, i.e. *kliç+tṛi*, m. Causing pain, MBh. 3, 1076.

क्लैब्य *klaibya*, or **क्लैव्य** *klaivya*, i.e. *klîba*, or *klîva*, *+ya*, n. **1.** Want of virility, Hit. i. d. 129. **2.** Timidity, Râm. 3, 19, 5. **3.** Weakness, Ragh. 12, 86.

क्लोमन् *kloman*, m. and n. The right lobe of the lungs, Suçr. 2, 446, 19. If identical with πλεύμων, Lat. pulmon, Sanskrit *k* stands for *p*; cf. *kshiv*.

क्व *kva*, i.e. *ka+va* (cf. *i+va*), from *kim*, adv. **1.** =loc. sing. of *kim*. In whom, Man. 10, 66. **2.** Where, Râm. 5, 34, 21. **3.** Whither, Pańch. 36, 21. **4.** *kva—kva* denotes the greatest difference: *kva vayaṁ kva parokshamanmatho mṛigaçâvaiḥ samam edhito janaḥ*, What communion could there be between me and a girl grown up among young fawns and disinclined to love? Çâk. d. 51. **5.** How much less, Râm. 1, 67, 10. **6.** With following *api*, Somewhere, Hit. pr. d. 17; Pańch. 96, 5; with *na*, Nowhere, Nal. 16, 6. **7.** With *na—cha*, Not anywhere, Bhâg. P. 4, 29, 64. **8.** With *na—cha na*, Nowhere, MBh. 14, 650. **9.** With following *chid*, **a.** In some,

Pańch. 118, 14. **b.** Somewhere, Lass. 6, 17; Kathâs. 4, 131; **c.** With *na*, or another negative particle, Nowhere, Man. 2, 56; Râm. 3, 60, 5. **d.** *kva chid—kva chid*, Here and there, Râm. 2, 100, 6; *kva chid—kva chid*, Here—there, Kathâs. 6, 26; 27; now—now, Râm. 3, 50, 7; with *na*, Never, Man. 2, 180. **e.** Some time, Nal. 14, 6. **10.** With preceding *yatra*, **a.** and following *api*, or *cha*, or *vâ*, Wherever, Bhartṛ. 3, 91; Bhâg. P. 8, 12, 34; 1, 17, 36; **b.** and following *cha na*, Wherever, Brâhmaṇ. 3, 12; whenever, Bhag. P. 5, 21, 9.

क्वण् *KVAṆ*, i. 1, Par. **1.** To sound, Ṛit. 3, 26. **2.** To buzz, Vikr. d. 103. *kvaṇita*, n. Sound, Ragh. 7, 83.—Caus. To cause to sound, Bhâg. P. 3, 15, 21.

क्वथ् *KVATH*, i. 1, Par. To boil, Man. 6, 20.—Caus. *kvâthaya*, The same, Mârk. P. 12, 26.—With उद् *ud*, To boil out, Suçr. 2, 418, 10. Caus. The same, 2, 432, 15.—With निस् *nis*, Caus. To boil down, Suçr. 2, 80, 16.—Cf. perhaps κότος, etc.

क्वथन *kvath + ana*, n. Boiling, Suçr. 1, 171, 5.

क्वाथ *kvâtha*, i.e. *kvath + a*, m. A decoction, Suçr. 2, 85, 10.

† **क्वेल्** *KVEL*, i. 1, Par. To shake (? v. r.; see *kshvel*).

† **क्षज्** *KSHAJ*, or **क्षञ्ज्** *KSHAŃJ*, i. 1, Âtm. **1.** To go. **2.** To give. i. 10, Par. To live in distress.

क्षण् *KSHAṆ*, ii. 8, *kshaṇu* (probably for original *kshe-ṇu*, cf. *kshi*); Par., Âtm. To wound, Kumâras. 5, 24. Ptcple. of the pf. pass. *kshata*, **1.** Wounded, Ragh. 3, 53. **2.** Destroyed, Ṛit. 1, 2. **3.** Violated, Yâjń. 1, 67. n. A wound, Suçr. 2, 19, 1. **Comp.** *A-*, f. A virgin, Yâjń. 2, 130. m. pl. or n. sing. Fried grain, Pańch. 158, 4.—With the prep. परि *pari*, *parikshata*, **1.** Wounded, Man. 4, 122. **2.** Hurt, Çâk. d. 72. *ati-pari-kshata*, Grievously wounded, Man. 7, 98.—With वि *vi*, *vikshata*, Hurt, MBh. 2, 1816. *vikshata* in *apa-vikshata*, adj. Unhurt, Çâk. 63, 3 Ch.—With अभिवि *abhi-vi*, *abhivikshata*, Hurt, Râm. 5, 16, 21.—With परिवि *pari-vi*, *parivikshata*, Wounded, MBh. 1, 6906.—Cf. κταν in ἔκτανον, κτόνος, κτείνω, etc.; κτείς, κτενός, etc.; κτηδών, i.e. κταν + *tvan*, ἀσκεθής, καίνω, κατακονά, ξαίνω, ξάντης, etc.; φθόνος, etc; perhaps Goth. skath, skathjan, skanda.

क्षण *kshaṇa* (probably for *îkshaṇa*, i.e. *îksh + ana*), m. and n. **1.** A moment, Nal. 5, 1. **2.** A measure of time=4 minutes, Bhâg. P. 3, 11, 7. **3.** Leisure, Mâlav. 8, 9. **4.** Opportunity, MBh. 4, 666. **5.** A festival, Bhâg. P. 3, 3, 21. **6.** Loc. *ṇe* and abl. *ṇât*, **a.** In an instant, Râm. 2, 42, 44; Man. 11, 246; **b.** After a moment, Nal. 2, 3; Râm. 3, 50, 5. **7.** *kshaṇekshaṇe*, Every moment, Râjat. 5, 165.—**Comp.** *Kim-*, adj. one who disregards a moment, Hit. ii. d. 87. *Kṛita-*, adj., f. *ṇâ*, expecting impatiently, MBh. 1, 778. *Tatkshaṇam*, i.e. *tad-kshaṇa + m*, and °*ṇât*, adv. instantly, Pańch. 69, 20; Râm. 1, 55, 4. *Vastu-kshaṇât* (abl.), when there is given an opportunity, Râjat. 5, 378. *Sa-*, adj. being at leisure, Bhâg. P. 1, 1, 21. *Svayaṁvara-kṛita-*, adj. having fixed the moment for the choosing a husband.

क्षणदा *kshaṇadâ*, i.e. *kshaṇa-da* (vb. *dâ*), f. Night, Râm. 2, 50, 7.

क्षणदाकर *kshaṇadâ-kara*, m. The moon, Çiç. 9, 70.

क्षणदाचर *kshaṇadâ-chara*, m. A Râkshasa, or demon, Râm. 3, 35, 4.

क्षणन *kshaṇ+ana*, n. Hurting, Suçr. 1, 31, 4.

क्षणिक *kshaṇika*, i.e. *kshaṇa+ika*, adj. Momentary, Hit. i. d. 60.

क्षणिन् *kshaṇin*, i.e. *kshaṇa+in*, adj. Being at leisure, MBh. 2, 558.

क्षतज *kshata-jâ* (vb. *kshaṇ* and *jan*), I. adj. Caused by wounding, Suçr. 2, 503, 5. II. n. Blood, Râm. 2, 94, 5.

क्षति *kshati*, i.e. *kshaṇ+ti*, f. 1. Hurting, MBh. 3, 12180. 2. Destroying, Çâk. d. 39. 3. Harm, MBh. 4, 101.

क्षत्तृ *kshattṛi*, m. 1. i.e. *kshad+tṛi*, A carver (ved.). 2. A door-keeper, MBh. 4, 2215. 3. A charioteer. 4. The son of a Çûdra man and a Kshatriyâ woman, Man. 10, 12.

क्षत्र *kshatra*, i.e. *kshi+atra*, I. n. 1. Dominion (ved.). 2. The second, or military caste, Man. 9, 322; its dignity, Bhâg. P. 3, 6, 31. II. m. A man of the military caste, Man. 3, 23.—Comp. *A-* and *Nis-*, adj. without the military caste, Man. 9, 322; Bhâg. P. 1, 3, 22.

क्षत्रबन्धुवत् *kshatra-bandhu + vat*, adv. Like a man of the military caste, Chr. 23, 28.

क्षत्रिय *kshatriya*, i.e. *kshatra+iya*, I. m. A man of the military caste, Man. 10, 4. II. f. *yâ*, A woman of the military caste, Man. 3, 44.—Comp. *Niḥkshatriya*, i.e. *nis-*, adj., f. *yâ*, devoid of Kshatriyas, MBh. 1, 2459.

क्षत्रियत्व *kshatriya+tva*, n. The dignity of a Kshatriya, MBh. 3, 13975.

क्षत्रियब्रुव *kshatriyabruva*, i.e. *kshatriya-brû+a*, m. A wicked Kshatriya, MBh. 13, 3565.

क्षद् *KSHAD*, i. 1, Âtm. To carve, to slaughter.—Cf. *σφάζω*, etc., *σχάζω*, *shkad*, and *khaḍga*.

क्षन्तृ *kshantṛi*, i.e. *ksham+tṛi*, m. One who endures, patient, MBh. 13, 4873.

1. **क्षप्** *KSHAP* (originally Caus. of 3. *kshi*), i. 1, Par., Âtm. To fast, MBh. 3, 13405.—With the prep. **सम्** *sam*, The same, MBh. 13, 5149.

2. **क्षप्** *KSHAP*, i. 10, Par. To throw, Pañch. 56, 2.—Cf. *kship*.

3. **क्षप्** see *kshapâ*, f. Night, Chr. 290, 8=Rigv. i. 64, 8.

क्षपण *kshapaṇa*, i.e. *kshap* and 3. *kshi*, Caus., + *ana*, I. n. 1. Fasting, Man. 4, 222. 2. Destroying, MBh. 2, 523. II. A Buddhistic mendicant; see *bhû*. III. adj. Destroying, Bhâg. P. 4, 7, 32.

क्षपणक *kshapaṇa+ka*, m. A religious, especially a Buddhistic, mendicant, MBh. 1, 789; Daçak. in Chr. 184, 6.

क्षपा *kshapâ*, i.e. 3. *kshi*, Caus., + *a*, f. Night, Râm, 2, 25, 9.—Cf. probably Lat. crepusculum.

क्षपाचर *kshapâ-chara*, m. A Râkshasa, or demon, Chr. 62, 53.

क्षम् *KSHAM*, i. 1, Âtm. (in epic poetry also Par.) and i. 4, † *kshâmya*, Par. (*kshamya*, Âtm., Bhâg. P. 6, 3, 30), 1. To endure, Râm. 4, 21, 23. 2. To have patience, Râm. 4, 26, 25. 3. To pardon, Râm. 2, 23, 11. 4. To permit, Râm. 2, 64, 37. 5. To be able, Çiç. 9, 65. *kshânta*, Patient, Man. 5, 158; n. Patience, Râm. 1, 34, 32. Caus. *kshamaya*, 1. To beg one's pardon for something (with two acc., literally, To cause somebody to endure something), MBh. 3, 3017. 2. To endure patiently,

Râm. 5, 49, 11.—With the prep. सम् *sam*, To indulge MBh. 2, 1389.—Cf. κομίζω, etc.

क्षम *ksham* + *a*, I. adj., f. *mâ*. 1. Enduring, Draup. 6, 4. 2. Endurable, Çâk. d. 123. 3. Able, Pańch. v. d. 30. 4. Favourable, Râm. 2, 35, 31. 5. Useful, Man. 7, 208. 6. Suitable, MBh. 14, 703. II. f. *mâ*, 1. Patience, forbearance, Râm. 1, 1, 19. 2. The earth, Râjat. 5, 334.—Comp. *Âyati-*, adj. useful in future time, Man. 7, 208. *Upabhoga-*, adj. abounding in enjoyment, Çâk. 4, 4. *Kâlântara-*, i.e. *kâla-antara-*, adj. suffering delay, Mâlav. 28, 8. *Dṛishṭi-*, adj. worth to be looked on, Vikr. d. 84. *Deça-kâla-*, adj. in accordance with place and time, Râm. 5, 49, 1. *Vana-vâsa-*, adj. suitable to a sojourn in a forest, Râm. 2, 30, 42.—Cf. χαμά + θεν χθαμαλός, etc., and ved. *ksham* = χθών.

क्षमवन्त् *kshama* + *vant*, adj. Knowing what is suitable (?), Râm. 5, 89, 68.

क्षमापय *KSHAMÂPAYA*, a denomin. derived from *kshamâ*, Par., Âtm. To beg one's pardon, Bhâg. P. 9, 4, 71.—Cf. *ksham*, Causal.

क्षमावन्त् *kshamâ* + *vant*, adj. Patient, forbearing, Râm. 1, 34, 32.

क्षमिन् *kshamin*, i.e. *kshama* + *in*, adj. Patient, forbearing, Yâjń. 2, 200.

† क्षम्प् *KSHAMP*, i. 1, and 10, Par. To endure.—Cf. *ksham*.

क्षय *kshaya*, i.e. 1. and 3. *kshi* + *a*, m. 1. An abode, MBh. 1, 2510. 2. Decrease, Man. 3, 122. 3. Diminution of price, Yâjń. 2, 258. 4. Loss, Brâhmaṇ. 2, 20. 5. End, Râm. 6, 105, 14. 6. Destruction, Hiḍ. 4, 84. 7. Consumption, phthisis, Suçr. 2, 445, 6.—Comp. *Dina-*, m. evening, Kâm. Nîtis. 7, 57. *Dhana-*, m. loss of wealth, Pańch. 234, 7. *Sarva-duḥkha-*, m. final emancipation. *Sva-kula-*, m. a fish.

क्षयंकर *kshayaṁkara*, i.e. *kshaya* + *m-kara*, adj., f. *rî*, Causing destruction, MBh. 4, 180.

क्षयरोगित्व *kshayarogitva*, i.e. *kshayarogin* + *tva*, n. Consumption, phthisis, Man. 11, 49.

क्षयरोगिन् *kshayarogin*, i.e. *kshaya-roga* + *in*, adj., f. *iṇî*, Phthisical, Yâjń. 3, 209.

क्षयिन् *kshayin*, i. e. 3. *kshi* and *kshaya* + *in*, adj., f. *iṇî*. 1. Decreasing, Bhartṛ. 2, 50. 2. Phthisical, Man. 3, 7.

क्षयिष्णु *kshayishṇu*, i. e. 3. *kshi* + *ishṇu*, adj. 1. Destroying, Bhâg. P. 6, 16, 41. 2. Perishable, 7, 7, 40.

क्षय्य *kshayya*, i.e. *kshaya* + *ya*, adj. 1. Subject to phthisis, Man. 3, 7. 2. Perishable.—Comp. *A-*, adj. imperishable, Man. 4, 156.

क्षर् *KSHAR*, i. 1, Par. (in epic poetry also Âtm.). 1. To stream, Râm. 5, 42, 8. 2. To pass away, Man. 2, 84. 3. To lose (with abl.), MBh. 13, 4716. 4. To let escape, to yield, Chr. 297, 11 = Rigv. i. 112, 11; MBh. 13, 3720.—With the prep. वि *vi*, To dissolve, MBh. 14, 2184.—Cf. Lat. scortum (cf. *mih*); Goth. hôrs.

क्षर *kshar* + *a*, adj., f. *râ*, Perishable, MBh. 2, 433; see *akshara*.

क्षरक *kshar* + *aka*, adj., f. *rikâ*, Effusing, Dev. 11, 12.

† 1. क्षल् *KSHAL*, i. 1, Par. To shake; to move.

2. क्षल् *KSHAL*, i. 10, *kshâlaya*, Par. (properly Causal of *kshar*), 1. To make clean, Kathâs. 25, 52; to purify, Prab. 94, 7. 2. To remove, Râjat. 5,

59.—With the prep. प्र *pra*, **1.** To wash, Pańch. 245, 7. **2.** To remove, MBh. 1, 7510.—With अभिप्र *abhi-pra*, To cleanse, Vikr. 78, 6.—With वि *vi*, To wash away, Ragh. 5, 44.

क्षवथु *kshavathu*, i.e. *kshu* + *athu*, m. Sneezing, catarrh, Suçr. 1, 39, 1.

क्षात्र *kshâtra*, i.e. *kshatra* + *a*, I. adj., f. *rî*, Peculiar to the military caste, Râm. 1, 54, 14. II. n. **1.** The military caste, MBh. 3, 5097. **2.** Royal dignity, Râm. 5, 84, 10.

क्षान्ति *kshânti*, i.e. *ksham* + *ti*, f. Patience, forbearance, Man. 5, 107.

क्षान्तिमन्त् *kshânti* + *mant*, adj., f. *matî*, Forbearing, Râjat. 5, 4.

क्षाम *kshâma*, see *kshai*.

क्षार *kshâra*, i.e. *kshar* + *a*, I. adj., f. *râ*, Salty, Pańch. 61, 11. II. m. **1.** A burning corrosive substance, either soda or potash, Râm. 2, 73, 3. **2.** Treacle, Bhâg. P. 7, 4, 17.—Comp. *Yava-*, m. saltpetre.

क्षारय *KSHÂRAYA*, a denomin. derived from the last, Par. **1.** To torment by corrosive substances, Mârk. P. 8, 142. **2.** To defame, MBh. 2, 238. —With the prep. आ *â*, To defame, Man. 8, 275.

क्षालन *kshâlana*, i.e. *kshal* + *ana*, n. Washing, Pańch. ii. d. 61.

1. क्षि *KSHI*, i. 6, *kshiya* (ved. ii. 2), Par. **1.** To dwell (ved.). 2. † To go. —With the prep. आ *â*, ii. 2, To acquire, Chr. 291, 13=Rigv. i. 64, 13. Cf. κτι in ἐΰκτιτος, ἐϋκτίμενος, κτίζω; perhaps Lat. civis, etc., so-cius, cf. *sakhi*.

2. क्षि *KSHI*, i. 1, *kshaya*, Par. To possess; to rule (with gen.), Chr. 296, 3=Rigv. i. 112, 3.—Cf. κτάομαι, κτέανον, κτέαρ, κτῆνος.

3. क्षि *KSHI*, ii. 9, *kshiṇâ*, *kshiṇi*, ii. 5, *kshiṇu*, i. 1, *kshaya*, Par. **1.** To destroy, Ragh. 2, 40. **2.** To hurt, MBh. 3, 1355. **3.** To oppress, Man. 9, 315.—Pass. *kshîya*, **1.** To decrease, Bhâg. P. 5, 22, 9. **2.** To become exhausted, Pańch. i. d. 181. **3.** To disappear, Bhartṛ. 2, 16.—Ptcple. of the pf. pass., I. *kshîṇa*, **1.** Decreased, Çâk. d. 133; Bhartṛ. 2, 88. **2.** Thin, Çâk. d. 58, v. r. **3.** Exhausted, Hit. 1, 66; Pańch. i. d. 244; iv. d. 16 (of hunger). Feeble, Châṇ. 99, in Montasb. d. Berl. Ak. Hist. Phil. 1864, 413. **4.** Finished, Kathâs. 5, 128. **5.** Perished, MBh. 2, 972. II. *kshita*. Comp. *A-kshita*, adj., not decayed, inexhaustible, Chr. 290, 6=Rigv. i. 64, 6.—Causal, I. *kshapaya*, **1.** To destroy, MBh. 3, 15163. **2.** To emaciate, Man. 5, 157. **3.** To pass away, MBh. 14, 2720. II. *kshayaya* in *kshayita*, **1.** Destroyed, Megh. 54. **2.** Atoned, Bhag. 4, 30 (v.r. *kshapita*). —Ptcple. of the fut. pass., *kshayayitavya*, To be destroyed, Râm. 6, 17, 4. —With the prep. अनु *anu*, pass., To disappear by degrees, Bhâg. P. 5, 14, 21.—With अप *apa* in *apakshita*, Exhausted, Bhâg. P. 3, 11, 32.—With उप *upa* in *upakshiṇa*, Disappeared, Sâh. D. 17, 2.—With परि *pari*, To destroy, Bhâg. P. 3, 8, 20. Pass., To become poor, Hit. ii. d. 91, v.r. *parikshiṇa*, **1.** Diminished, Kathâs. 25, 140. **2.** Weakened, Man. 7, 172. **3.** Indigent, Man. 8, 170. — With प्र *pra*, pass., To perish, MBh. 2, 1468. *prakshiṇa*, **1.** Destroyed, Bhâg. P. 6, 7, 23. **2.** Atoned, Vedântas. in Chr.

203, 21.—With वि *vi*, in *vikshita*, Miserable, Râm. 3, 79, 46.—With सम् *sam*, pass., To become exhausted, Bhartṛ. 3, 44.—Caus. **1.** *kshapaya*, To cause to fall off, Suçr. 2, 134, 3. **2.** Ptcple. pf. pass., *kshayita*, Vanished, Râm. 2, 48, 29. Cf. κτίννυμι (probably for κτεινυμι and original κτεισνυμι, cf. *ksheshṇu*, Vop. 26, 44), ψίω; Lat. sitis, properly, exhaustion by thirst.

† क्षिण् *KSHIṆ*, ii. 8, *kshiṇu* (cf. 3. *kshi*), Par., Âtm., To hurt, to kill.

ऽक्षित् -2. *kshi*+*t*, Ruling, e.g. *pṛithivî*-, m. A king, Nal. 5, 4. *mahî*-, m. The same, Chr. 5, 25.

क्षिति 1. *kshi*+*ti*, f. **1.** An abode, Bhâg. P. 4, 9, 5. **2.** The earth, Bhartṛ. 3, 5. **3.** Land, Râjat. 5, 109.

क्षितिज *kshiti-ja* (vb. *jan*) **I.** adj. Sprung from the earth, Suçr. 1, 224, 9. **II.** m. A tree, Râm. 6, 76, 2.

क्षितिधर *kshiti-dhara*, m. A mountain, Bhartṛ. 2, 10.

क्षितिभृत् *kshiti-bhṛi*+*t*, m. **1.** A mountain, Ṛit. 6, 25. **2.** A king, Bhartṛ. 3, 59, v.r.

क्षितिरुह् *kshiti-ruh*, m. A tree, Bhartṛ. 3, 28.

क्षितिवृत्तिमन्त् *kshiti-vṛitti*+*mant*, adj. Patient, like the earth, Bhâg. P. 4, 16, 7.

क्षिप् *KSHIP*, i. 6, Par., Âtm. (i. 4, Âtm. only in a grammatical poem). **1.** To throw, Pańch. 210, 17; MBh. 1, 1126 (*kshipyatas*, pass., instead of *kshipyamâṇasya*); (of arrows), MBh. 3, 1018. **2.** To move quickly, Mṛichchh. 9, 19. **3.** To impel, Râm. 3, 58, 21. **4.** To pour, Yâjń. 1, 230. **5.** To disdain, Bhâg. P. 3, 15, 17. **6.** To slander, Man. 8, 312. **7.** To destroy, Bhâg. P. 6, 1, 14.—Comp. partcple. of the pf. pass., *tiryakkshipta*, i.e. *tiryańch*-, adj. (One part of the bones of a joint) being turned outward, Suçr. 1, 300, 8. Caus. To cause to be thrown, Kathâs. 13, 160.—With the prep. अति *ati*, *ati-kshipta*, Dislocated, Suçr. 1, 300, 8.—With अधि *adhi*, **1.** To offend, Man. 4, 185. **2.** To humble, to surpass, Bhâg. P. 3, 28, 30. **3.** To prevent (a disease), Suçr. 2, 337, 8.—With अप *apa*, To remove, Râm. 3, 1, 24.—With अव *ava*, **1.** To cast down, MBh. 1, 1126. **2.** To cast off, Râm. 2, 37, 7. **3.** To slander, MBh. 2, 1337. **4.** To tender, to grant, MBh. 13, 3030.—With समव *sam-ava*, To repel, MBh. 3, 15662.—With आ *â*, **1.** To cast on, Pańch. 263, 20. **2.** To hit, Râm. 6, 78, 5. **3.** To pull, MBh. 4, 750. **4.** To rob, Vikr. d. 143. **5.** To throw down, Bhâg. P. 6, 12, 28. **6.** To expel, MBh. 3, 539. **7.** To set up, Kathâs. 18, 121. **8.** To put in, MBh. 3, 3094. **9.** To neglect, MBh. 3, 16117. **10.** To insult, Man. 4, 141. Caus. To cause to be overthrown, MBh. 3, 15733.—With पर्या *pari-â*, To twine, Kumâras. 7, 14.—With व्या *vi-â*, **1.** To put on, MBh. 3, 566. **2.** To discharge, to shoot off. **3.** To hit, MBh. 1, 1402. *vyâkshipta*, Agitated, Râm. 6, 91, 3.—With समा *sam-â*, **1.** To accumulate, MBh. 1, 156. **2.** To repel, MBh. 3, 15662. **3.** To move violently, MBh. 3, 117. **4.** To expel, MBh. 2, 1019. **5.** To pull down, Râm. 3, 56, 50. **6.** To destroy, MBh. 1, 1253. **7.** To insult, MBh. 1, 1677.—With उद् *ud*, **1.** To throw up, Man. 3, 90. **2.** To raise, MBh. 3, 11187; Pańch. 187, 21. **3.** To cast off, Bhâg. P. 4, 23, 17.—With समुद् *sam-ud*, **1.** To throw up, MBh.

3, 436. 2. To lift up, MBh. 3, 11519. 3. To expel, MBh. 3, 13972. 4. To loosen, Râm. 5, 56, 140. 5. To destroy, Râm. 5, 3, 69.—With उप *upa*, 1. To cast on, Sâh. D. 66, 5. 2. To set, Bhâg. P. 5, 20, 34. 3. To insult, Râm. 5, 11, 11. 4. To hint, Daçak. in Chr. 192, 6.—With नि *ni*, 1. To throw down, Râm. 3, 33, 20. 2. To put down, Yâjń. 1, 103. 3. To encamp, Râm. 2, 91, 5. 4. To put, Yâjń. 1, 327. 5. To pour, Pańch. 174, 14. 6. To dispense, Man. 7, 101. 7. To intrust, Man. 7, 59. 8. To establish, Râm. 2, 51, 17. 9. To cast off, MBh. 3, 14115. 10. To repel, Hit. 91, 11. Caus. To cause to be drawn up, Ragh. 7, 62.—With उपनि *upa-ni*, To put down, Man. 3, 224.—With प्रतिनि *prati-ni*, To put down again, MBh. 3, 15184.—With विनि *vi-ni*, 1. To throw down, Râm. 5, 11, 12. 2. To put down, Yâjń. 1, 231. 3. To intrust, MBh. 1, 3545. 4. To appoint, MBh. 3, 10403.—With निस् *nis*, 1. To put down, Râm. 1, 38, 21. 2. To put in, MBh. 3, 14314.—With विनिस् *vi-nis*, 1. To inlay with, MBh. 13, 1444. 2. To direct, MBh. 3, 14293.—With परा *parâ*, *parâkshipta*, 1. Robbed, Bhâg. P. 5, 24, 18. 2. Enraptured, Bhâg. 5, 2, 18.—With परि *pari*, 1. To overlay, Râm. 2, 32, 35. 2. To surround, Râm. 3, 61, 31. 3. To embrace, Râm. 2, 30, 2. 4. To fetter, Râm. 2, 72, 38. 5. To put in, MBh. 1, 4205. *sûryâtapa-parikshipta*, Darted upon by the rays of the sun.—With प्र *pra*, 1. To cast, MBh. 3, 707. 2. To put, Mṛichchh. 50, 1. Caus. To order to be put, MBh. 1, 5008.—With संप्र *sam-pra*, To cast, MBh. 13, 4609.—With प्रति *prati*, 1. To cast in, MBh. 1, 7068.—With वि *vi*, 1. To cast in different directions, Chr. 34, 10. 2. To disperse, MBh. 1, 7022. 3. To extend, MBh. 14, 1161. 4. To let go (the string of a bow, MBh. 3, 15690; or the bow, Râm. 3, 70, 2, i.e. to shoot).—With सम् *sam*, 1. To heap, Ragh. 1, 52. 2. To destroy, Râm. 3, 43, 42. 3. To constrain, Râm. 2, 40, 39. 4. To diminish, Man. 7, 34. 5. To abridge, MBh. 1, 51.—With अभिसम् *abhi-sam*, To contract, MBh. 5, 283; *abhisaṁkshipta*, Thrown at, MBh. 1, 5368.—With परिसम्, To surround, Râm. 5, 29, 20.

क्षिप्तचित्तता *kshipta-chitta* + *tâ*, f. Absence of mind, MBh. 2, 241.

क्षिप्र *kship* + *ra*, I. adj., f. *râ*, Quick, Man, 7, 179. Comparat. *kshepîyaṁs*, superl. *kshepishṭha*. II. *ram*, adv. Quickly, Râm. 1, 52, 21. III. *rât*, adv. Directly, Kathâs. 18, 280.

क्षिल्लिका *kshillikâ*, f. A proper name, Râjat. 5, 289.

† क्षिव् *KSHIV*, i. 1 and 4, *kshîvya*, Par. To spit.—If identical with Goth. speiwan, AS. spiwan, Lat. spuo, πτύω, Sskr. *k* stands for *p*, see *kloman*.—Cf. *shṭhiv*.

† क्षी *KSHÎ* = 3. *kshi*, v.r.

क्षीज् *KSHÎJ*, i. 1, Par. To sound inarticulately, to groan.

क्षीण *kshîṇa*, see 3. *kshi*.

क्षीणता *kshîṇa* + *tâ*, f. Being damaged, Mṛichchh. 47, 3.

क्षीब् *KSHÎB*, and क्षीब *kshîba*, = *kshîv*, *kshîva*, q. cf.

क्षीर *kshîra*, Milk, Man. 5, 8.

क्षीरप *kshîra-pa* (vb. 1. *pâ*), m. **1.** Drinking milk, MBh. 13, 646. **2.** A nurse-child, Suçr. 1, 129, 1.

क्षीरमय *kshîra+maya*, adj., f. *yî*, Consisting of milk, represented by milk, Bhâg. P. 4, 18, 9.

क्षीरय *KSHÎRAYA*, a denomin. derived from *kshîra*, Par. To become like milk, Lass. 12, 19.

क्षीरिन् *kshîrin*, i.e. *kshîra+in*, I. adj., f. *iṇî*, Abounding in milk, Yâjń. 1, 204; Man. 8, 246. II. m. A certain tree, Suçr. 1, 133, 16. III. f. *iṇî*, A name of several plants, Suçr. 2, 67, 17.

क्षीव् *KSHÎV*, i. 1, Par. To spit; cf. *kshiv* and *shṭhiv*.—With प्र *pra*, *prakshîvita*, Intoxicated.

क्षीव *kshîv+a*, adj., f. *vâ*, Intoxicated, Râm. 5, 60, 12.

क्षीवता *kshîva+tâ*, f. Intoxication, Kathâs. 13, 10.

क्षु *KSHU*, ii. 2, Par. To sneeze, Man. 5, 145; Çiç. 9, 83. *kshuta*, **1.** One who has sneezed, MBh. 13, 7584. **2.** On which a person has sneezed, MBh. 13, 1577. n. Sneezing, Yâjń. 1, 196.—With the prep. अव *ava*, *ava-kshuta*, On which a person has sneezed, Man. 4, 213.—Akin to *kshiv*, q. cf.

क्षुण्ण *kshuṇṇa*, see *kshud*.

क्षुत्पिपासित *kshutpipâsita*, i. e. *kshudh-pipâsâ+ita*, adj. Tormented with hunger and thirst, Man. 8, 93.

क्षुद् *KSHUD*, ii. 7, *kshuṇad*, *kshund*, Par., Âtm. To pound.—Ptcple. of the pf. pass., *kshuṇṇa*, **1.** Pounded, Pańch. 160, 3. **2.** Scattered, MBh. 3, 678. **3.** Exercised, Suçr. 2, 139, 12.—Comp. *A-kshuṇṇa*, adj. unbroken, Râm. 1, 8, 9.—Caus. To grind, Suçr. 2, 66, 13.—With the prep. अव *ava*, To grind, Suçr. 1, 163, 13.—With प्र *pra*, *pra-kshuṇṇa*, metaph., urged on, Pańch. ii. d. 150.—With वि *vi*, *vikshuṇṇa*, Pounded, Dev. 3, 25.—With सम् *sam*, To stamp, Râm. 2, 80, 10.—Cf. *khud*, probably Lat. cudere, incus.

क्षुद्र *kshud+ra*, adj., f. *râ*. **1.** Small, Râm. 3, 33, 21. **2.** Mean, Pańch. iii. d. 89. Comparat. *kshodîyaṁs*, superl. *kshodishṭha*.—Comp. *A-*, adj. Lofty, Pańch. iii. d. 69; MBh. 2, 152.

क्षुद्रक *kshudra+ka*, I. adj. **1.** Very little (young), Man. 8, 297. **2.** Short (of breath), Suçr. 2, 497, 7. II. m. **1.** pl. The name of a people, MBh. 2, 1871. **2.** The name of a prince, Bhâg. P. 9, 12, 14.

क्षुद्रंचर *kshudraṁchara*, i.e. *kshu-dra+m-chara*, adj. Pursuing small things, Bhâg. P. 4, 29, 53.

क्षुध् *KSHUDH*, i. 4, *kshudhya*, Par. To be hungry; *kshudhita*, Hungry, Râm. 3, 16, 24.

क्षुध् *kshudh*, f. Hunger, Man. 7, 134.

क्षुधा *kshudh+â*, f. Hunger, Pańch. 86, 4.

क्षुधालु *kshudhâ+lu*, adj. Hungry, Pańch. 88, 21.

क्षुप *kshupa*, m. **1.** A shrub, Yâjń. 2, 229. **2.** The name of a king, MBh. 14, 66. **3.** The name of a mountain, Hariv. 8950.—Cf. O.H.G. scubo, scubil.

क्षुब्धता *kshubdha+tâ* (vb. *kshubh*), f. Commotion, Bhartṛ. 3, 94.

क्षुभ् *KSHUBH*, i. 1, Âtm.; i. 4,

kshubhya, Par. (also Âtm.); ii. 9, *kshubhnâ, kshubhnî*, Par. To become agitated, Râm. 2, 34, 45. *kshubdha* and *kshubhita*, 1. Agitated, Suçr. 2, 147, 19; Râm. 1, 65, 12. 2. Shaken, Vikr. d. 115. 3. Trembling, Râm. 5, 36, 77. *a-kshobhya*, comp. participle of the fut. pass. 1. Unshakeable, Râm. 2, 18, 6. 2. Undisturbable, Râm. 2, 12, 86.—Caus. 1. To agitate, Râm. 1, 1, 77. 2. To shake, Râm. 5, 54, 12. 3. To impel, MBh. 13, 7256. 4. To throw in confusion, Man. 8, 418. 5. To trouble, Mârk. P. 1, 40 (Âtm.).—With the prep. प्र *pra*, To become agitated, Râm. 6, 87, 15; confused, Man. 9, 254.—Caus. To excite, Suçr. 2, 247, 10.—With संप्र *sam-pra*, To become confused, Râm. 6, 78, 24.—With वि *vi*, To become agitated, Bhâg. P. 7, 8, 32.—Caus. 1. To agitate, MBh. 1, 1216; 7283 (Âtm.). 2. To put in disorder, MBh. 1, 5484.—With सम् *sam*, To become agitated, Pañch. 163, 1.—Cf. A.S. be-scufan, contrudere; O.H.G. sciuban, A.S. sceofan; but their labial is not the regular substitute for Sskr. *bh*.

क्षुमा *kshumâ*, f. A sort of flax.

† क्षुर् *KSHUR*, i. 6, Par. 1. To cut. 2. To scratch. 3. To make furrows.

क्षुर *kshur* + *a*, m. A razor, Man. 9, 292.—Cf. ξυρόν, etc.

क्षुरप्र *kshura-pra* (cf. *khura*), m. A kind of arrow, one with a horse-shoe head, MBh. 4, 1732; Pañch. 38, 2 (a knife ?)

क्षुरिका *kshurikâ*, i.e. *kshura* + *ka*, f. A dagger, Râjat. 5, 437.

क्षुल्ल *kshulla* (a form of *kshudra*, with *l* for *r* and assimilation), adj. Small, Bhâg. P. 3, 5, 10.

क्षुल्लक *kshulla* + *ka*, adj., f. *kâ*, Small, Bhâg. P. 4, 30, 29.

क्षेत्र *kshetra*, i.e. 1. 2. *kshi* + *tra*, n. 1. Landed property, Bhâg. P. 9, 6, 37. 2. A field, Man. 10, 114. 3. Place, Lass. 17. 2. 4. Extent, Yâjń. 2, 156. 5. A wife, Man. 9, 33; MBh. 1, 4661. 6. The body, Bhag. 13, 1.—Comp. *A*-, n. a barren field, Man. 10, 71. *Karmakshetra*, i.e. *karman*-, n. the seat of sacred works, Bhâg. P. 5, 17, 11. *Kuru*-, I. n. the name of a country, Man. 2, 19; II. m. pl. the name of its inhabitants, Man. 7, 193. *Dharma*-, n. a plain in the north-west of India, Bhag. 1, 1. *Raṇa*-, n. a field of battle, Chr. 25, 57. *Sura-îçvarî*-, n. the name of a district, Râjat. 5, 37.

क्षेत्रज *kshetra-ja* (vb. *jan*), and

क्षेत्रजात *kshetra-jâta*, m. A wife's son by a kinsman or a person duly appointed to beget issue to the husband, Man. 9, 159; Yâjń. 2, 128.

क्षेत्रज्ञ *kshetra-jńâ* (vb. *jńâ*), I. adj. f. *jńâ*, Conversant with (with gen.), MBh. 1, 3653. II. m. The soul, Man. 8, 96.

क्षेत्रता *kshetra* + *tâ*, f. Residence, Kathâs. 3, 3.

क्षेत्रवित्तपता *kshetravittapatâ*, i.e. *kshetra-vid-tapa* + *tâ*, f. Illuminating the soul, Bhâg. P. 4, 22, 37.

क्षेत्रिक *kshetrika*, i.e. *kshetra* + *ika*, 1. m. The owner of a field, Man. 8, 241. 2. A husband, Man. 9, 145.

क्षेत्रिन् *kshetrin*, i.e. *kshetra* + *in*, m. 1. The owner of a field, Man. 9, 51. 2. A husband, Man. 9, 132.—Comp. *A*-, 1. one who has no property in a field, Man. 9, 41. 2. one who has no marital property in a woman, Man. 9, 51.

क्षेप *kshepa*, i.e. *kship + a*, m. **1.** Throwing, moving, Râm. 4, 62, 12. **2.** Abuse, Yâjń. 2, 204. **3.** A nosegay, Megh. 48.—**Comp.** *Kâla-*, m. delay, Pańch. 43, 22. *A-kâlakshepa + m*, adv. directly, Çâk. Ch. 91, 8. *paṭâkshepa*, i.e. *paṭa-a-kshepa*, m. not drawing away the curtain (?). *Apaṭi-kshepa*, m. tossing up the curtain; the instr. *eṇa* denotes (in theatrical language) abrupt entrance on the stage, Mṛichchh. 29, 17. *Bhrû-*, m. 1. a graceful motion of the eyebrows, Indr. 5, 7; 2. a frown. *Sa-dṛishṭi-kshepa + m*, adv. glancing to somebody, Çâk. 12, 7.

क्षेपण *kshepaṇa*, i.e. *kship + ana*, I. n. **1.** Striking (?), MBh. 4, 352. **2.** Letting go (the string of a bow). **3.** Expelling, MBh. 3, 13272. **4.** Suspension, MBh 4, 119. **5.** A sling, Bhâg. P. 3, 19, 18. **II.** fem. *ṇî*, A sling, or other missile weapon, Râm. 6, 7, 24.

क्षेपिष्ठ *kshepishṭha*, and **क्षेपीयंस्** *kshepîyaṁs*, see *kshipra*.

क्षेप्तृ *ksheptṛi*, i.e. *kship + tṛi*, m. A slinger, Râm. 4, 9, 84.

क्षेम *kshema*, i.e. 1. or 2. *kshi + ma*, I. adj., f. *mâ*. **1.** Safe, dangerless, MBh. 3, 488. **2.** Prosperous, MBh. 3, 15976. **II.** m. and n. **1.** Safety, Man. 2, 127. **2.** Well-being, Râm. 3, 44, 15. **3.** Happiness, Bhâg. P. 2, 6, 18. **4.** Fortune, wealth, MBh. 13, 3081. **5.** instr. *meṇa*, adverbially, Peacefully, Mṛichchh. 110, 8; happily, Pańch. i. d. 162; also *kshemais*, MBh. 13, 1519. **III.** m. **1.** *kshema*, safety, happiness, personified, Bhâg. P. 4, 1, 51. **2.** The name of a prince, MBh. 1, 2701. **IV.** f. *mâ*, The name of an Apsaras, MBh. 1, 4818. **V.** n. The name of one of the divisions of the continent, Bhâg. P. 5, 20, 3.—**Comp.** *Yoga-*, n. **1.** Security, Man. 8, 230. **2.** Expenses for securing goods (properly, for securing a business), Man. 7, 127. **3.** What serves for giving security of business (family priests and spiritual counsellors), Man. 9, 219.—Cf. Goth. haims; A.S. ham.

क्षेमंकर *kshemaṁkara*, i.e. *kshema + m-kara*, m. The name of a king, Draup. 2, 7.

क्षेमिन् *kshemin*, i.e. *kshema + in*, adj., f. *iṇî*, Safe, Nal. 12, 121.

क्षेम्य *kshemya*, i.e. *kshema + ya*, I. adj., f. *yâ*. **1.** Salubrious, Man. 7, 212. **2.** Secure, MBh. 14, 1691. **II.** m. The name of several princes, Hariv. 1592, etc.

† **क्षेव्** *KSHEV*, i. 1, Par. = *kshiv*, v.r.

क्षै *KSHAI*, i. 1, *kshâya*, Par. = 3. *kshi*; ptcple. of the pf. pass. *kshâma*, **1.** Dried up, Pańch. 20, 25. **2.** Emaciated, Ṛit. 6, 28. **3.** Slender, Megh. 80. **4.** Weak, Râjat. 5, 219. **5.** Little, Megh. 78, v.r.

क्षैण्य *kshaiṇya*, i.e. *kshîṇa + ya*, n. Ruin, Râjat. 5, 262.

क्षैत्रपत्य *kshaitrapatya*, i.e. *kshetra-pati + ya*, n. Estate, Chr. 297, 13 = Rigv. i. 112, 13.

† **क्षोट्** *KSHOṬ*, i. 10, Par. To cast.

क्षोणि and **क्षोणी** *kshoṇî*, f. The earth, Bhâg. P. 4, 21, 35; Râm. 1, 42, 23 Gorr.

क्षोणीमय *kshoṇî + maya*, adj. Containing the earth, Bhâg. P. 2, 7, 12.

क्षोद *kshoda*, i.e. *kshud + a*, m. Pulverised substance, flour, Râm. 2, 104, 12.

क्षोदस् *kshodas*, i.e. *kshud + as*, n. Stream, Chr. 259, 12 = Rigv. i. 92, 12; Chr. 297, 12 = Rigv. i. 112, 12.

क्षोदिष्ठ *kshodishṭha*, and **क्षोदीयंस्** *kshodîyaṁs*, see *kshudra*.

क्षोभ *kshobha,* i.e. *kshubh+a,* m. Agitation, MBh. 1, 1214; Çâk. d. 158.

क्षोभण *kshobhaṇa,* i.e. *kshubh+ana,* adj. Shaking, Râm. 3, 36, 10.

क्षौणी *kshauṇî=kshoṇi,* Bhâg. P. 3, 14, 3.

क्षौद्र *kshaudra,* i.e. *kshudra+a,* I. m. 1. The name of a tree, Michelia champaka, MBh. 3, 11569. 2. The name of a mixed caste, the offspring of a Vaideha man and a Mâgadhî woman, MBh. 13, 2584. II. n. Honey, Man. 10, 88.

क्षौम *kshauma,* i.e. *kshumâ+a,* I. adj., f. *mî.* 1. Made of flax, Man. 2, 41. 2. Made of linseed-oil, Suçr. 1, 182, 20. II. (m. and n.) A linen garment, Râm. 5, 45, 4. III. n. Linseed, Suçr. 2, 364, 8.

क्षौर *kshaura,* i.e. *kshura+a,* n. Shaving, Hit. 101, 6.

क्षौरपव्य *kshaurapavya,* i.e. *kshura-pavi+ya,* adj. made of razors and thunderbolts, Bhâg. P. 6, 5, 8.

क्ष्णु *KSHṆU* (a syncope of 3. *kshi+ṇu*) ii. 2, Par. To sharpen.—Cf. Goth. hnuto.

क्ष्मा *kshmâ,* a syncope of *ksham+â,* f. The earth, Bhartṛ. 2, 69.

क्ष्माप *kshmâ-pa* (vb. 2. *pâ*), m. A king, Râjat. 5, 314.

क्ष्माभुज् *kshmâ-bhuj,* m. A king, Râjat. 5, 50.

क्ष्माभृत् *kshmâ-bhṛi+t,* m. A mountain, Pañch. i. d. 171.

क्ष्माय् *KSHMÂY,* i. 1, Âtm. To tremble.

† **क्ष्मील्** *KSHMÎL* (cf. *çmîl, smîl, mîl* and *mish*), i. 1, Par. To twinkle, to close the eyelids.

क्ष्रौम् *kshraum,* A mystical exclamation, Bhâg. P. 5, 18, 3.

1. **क्ष्विड्** *KSHVIḌ,* i. 1, Par. To sound inarticulately: 1. To hum (?), Râm. 4, 45, 8. 2. To gnash the teeth, Man. 4, 64.—Caus. *kshveḍaya,* to make a noise, MBh. 3, 12379. *kshveḍita,* n. Noise, MBh. 1, 2820.—With the prep. आ *â, âkshveḍita,* Groaning (?), Râm. 6, 35. 2.—With प्र *pra,* 1. To whiz, MBh. 4, 1686. 2. To groan, Râm. 6, 17, 32.—Cf. *kshvel.*

† 2. **क्ष्विड्** *KSHVIḌ* (cf. *kshvid*), i. 1, Âtm. 1. To be unctuous. 2. To exude.

क्ष्विद् *KSHVID,* i. 1, Par. = 1. *kshviḍ.* † i. 1, Âtm., and i. 4, Par. = 2. *kshviḍ.* —Cf. *svid.*

क्ष्वेड *kshveḍa,* I. m. Poison, Sâyaṇa and Rigv. i. 117, 16. II. f. *ḍâ,* A bamboo rod.—Comp. *Sthûla-kshveḍa,* m. an arrow.

क्ष्वेडन *kshveḍana,* i.e. 1. *kshviḍ+ana,* n. An inarticulate sound (of sighing), MBh. 3, 12388.

क्ष्वेल् *KSHVEL* (originally = 1. *kshviḍ*), i. 1, Par. (To be noisy), To jump, to play, Râm. 5, 10, 13. *kshvelita,* m. and n., and *kshvelya,* n. Play, Bhâg. P. 8, 9, 11; 5, 1, 29.

क्ष्वेलिका *kshvelikâ,* i.e. *kshvel+aka,* f. Play, Bhâg. P. 5, 8, 18.

ख *KH.*

ख *kha* (vb. *khan*), n. 1. A cavity of the human body, as mouth, nose, etc., Man. 12, 120. 2. A wound, Man. 9, 45. 3. The subtile æther, Man. 12, 120. 4. Sky, Râm. 1, 19, 10.

† खक्ख् *KHAKKH*, see *kakh.*

खग *kha-ga*, I. adj. Moving, existing, in the sky, MBh. 3, 12257. II. m. **1.** A bird, Râm. 3, 20, 36. **2.** Wind, MBh. 3, 14616.

खच् *KHACH* (probably for *kshach*; cf. *khañj* and Lat. scatere), i. 1 (and † ii. 9), Par. **1.** To spring up, Kathâs. 23, 88. **2.** To appear, Lass. 73, 13. **3.** † To bind. *khachita*, **1.** Crowded, Çâk. d. 170, v.r. **2.** Inlaid, Megh. 36.—With the prep. उद् *ud*, *utkhachita*, Mixed, Ragh. 13, 54.

खचर *kha-chara*, I. adj. Moving, existing, in the sky, MBh. 3, 12205. II. m. A bird, Râm. 4, 68, 15.

† खज् *KHAJ*, i. 1, Par. To churn (properly, to move to and fro; cf. *khañj*).

खज *khaj+a*, m. and. f. *jâ*, A churning stick, Suçr. 2, 88, 3; MBh. 4, 231.

खञ्ज् *KHAÑJ* (probably for *kshañj*; cf. *khach*, σκάζω, and A.S. scanca), i. 1, Par. To limp, Suçr. 1, 256, 14.—Cf. O.H.G. hinkan.

खञ्ज *khañj+a*, adj., f. *jâ*, Lame, Man. 3, 242.

खञ्जन *khañj+ana*, m. A wag-tail, Çriñgârat. 4.

खञ्जरीट *khañjarîṭa*, and खञ्जरीटक *khañjarîṭa+ka*, m. A wag-tail, Yâjñ. 1, 174; Man. 5, 14.

† खट् *KHAṬ*, i. 1, Par. To desire.

खट *khaṭa*, Lass. 58, 9, read *shaṭka*.

खटकामुख *khaṭakâmukha*, A certain posture of the hand, Amar. 1.

खटखटाय *KHAṬAKHAṬÂYA*, a denominative derived from *khaṭakhaṭâ* (a reduplicated imitative sound) by *ya*, Âtm. To hiss, Mṛichchh. 2, 11.

खटिका *khaṭikâ*, f. Chalk, Prab. 63, 8.

† खट्ट् *KHAṬṬ*, i. 10, Par. To cover.

खट्वा *khaṭvâ*, f. A bedstead, Pañch. 187, 5.

खट्वाङ्गिन् *khaṭvâñgin*, i.e. *khaṭvâ-añga+in*, adj., Bearing a part of a bed, or a so-called weapon of Çiva (?), Man. 11, 105.

† खड् *KHAḌ*, i. 10, Par. To divide, to break.

खड्ग *khaḍga* (probably from *kshad*, q.v.; cf. *khañj* and φάσγανον) m. **1.** A sword, Râm. 1, 1, 41. **2.** A rhinoceros, Man. 3, 272.—**Comp.** *Kûṭa-*, m. a sword-cane, Râm. 6, 80, 4. *Sa-*, adj., f. *gâ*, with a sword, Râjat. 5, 385.

खड्गवन्त् *khaḍga + vant*, adj., f. *vatî*, Armed with a sword, MBh. 3, 10963.

खड्गिन् *khaḍgin*, i.e. *khaḍga+in*, I. adj., f. *inî*, Armed with a sword, Râm. 5, 10, 22. II. m. A rhinoceros, Râm. 1, 26, 14.

खणखणाय *KHAṆAKHAṆÂYA*, a denomin. derived from *khaṇakhaṇâ* (a reduplicated imitative sound) by *ya*, Âtm. To rustle, Bhâg. P. 5, 2, 5.

खण्ड् *KHAṆḌ*, I. † i. 1, Âtm. II. i. 10, Par. (rather a denomin. derived from the next), **1.** To cut to pieces, Pañch. 47, 5. **2.** To break, Vikr. d. 19. **3.** To bite, Pañch. 46, 1. **4.** To destroy, Hit. ii. d. 107. **5.** To cause to cease, to satisfy, Râjat. 5, 281. **6.** To trouble,

Râm. 3, 14, 14. *khaṇḍita*, Afflicted, Megh. 40.—With the prep. वि *vi*, **1.** To dismember, Pańch. iv. d. 60. **2.** To trouble, Bhâg. P. 4, 25, 30.

खण्ड *khaṇḍa*, m. and n. **1.** Breaking up, Râm. 2, 105, 3. (The sense is: You alone are able to avert this breaking up of the kingdom, [which is] like a bridge broken by a great torrent of water, etc.). **2.** A piece. **3.** A part. **4.** The section of a work. **5.** A group, Sâv. 5, 108. **6.** A multitude.—**Comp.** *A-*, adj., f. *ḍâ*, entire, Çâk. d. 43. *Karpûra-*, m. a group of camphor trees, Bhartr̥. 2, 98. *Padminî-*, n. a multitude of lotusses. *Çata-*, n. gold. *Çrî-*, m. and n. sandal wood.

खण्डक *khaṇḍa*+*ka*, A piece, Kathâs. 24, 121.

खण्डन *khaṇḍ* + *ana*, I. adj., Destroying, Gît. 10, 8. II. n. **1.** Hurting, Pańch. 45, 11. **2.** Violation, Pańch. 46, 3. **3.** Deceiving, baffling, Hit. ii. d. 58.

खण्डशस् *khaṇḍa* + *ças*, adv. In pieces, Râm. 3, 31, 39.

खद् *KHAD*, i. 1, Par. **1.** To be firm. **2.** † To kill.

खदिर *khad* + *ira*, m. A tree, Acacia catechu, the resin of which is used in medicine, Râm. 3, 21, 22; Suçr. 2, 76, 12.

खदिरमय *khadira-maya*, adj., f. *yî*, Made of Khadira-wood, Pańch. 237, 3.

खद्योत *kha-dyota*, I. m. A fire-fly, Râm. 6, 19, 28. II. f. *tâ*, The same, denoting an eye, Bhâg. P. 4, 25, 47.

खन् *KHAN*, i. 1, Par., Âtm. **1.** To dig, Man. 2, 218. **2.** To dig up, MBh. 14, 1716. **3.** To pierce, Bhartr̥. 2, 76; Pańch. ii. d. 96. **4.** To inter, MBh. 13, 3089.—Ptcple. of the pf. pass., *khâta*, n. **1.** A ditch, Hit. iii. d. 57; **2.** A pit, Pańch. v. d. 26.—**Comp.** *Deva-*, n. a natural pond (not artificial) Man. 4, 203.—Caus. *khânaya*, To cause to be dug, Râm. 2, 110, 25.—With the prep. अभि *abhi*, To dig up, Râm. 1, 41, 24. With उद् *ud*, **1.** To dig out, Kathâs. 20, 143. **2.** To dig up, Megh. 53. **3.** To pull out, Râjat. 5, 221. **4.** To eradicate, Pańch. 187, 18; to destroy, Râjat. 5, 149. *utkhâta*, n. A pit, Çâk. d. 192, v.r.—With प्रोद् *pra-ud*, **1.** To dig up, Râm. 1, 40, 14. **2.** To eradicate, Mr̥ichchh. 178, 1.—With समुद् *sam-ud*, To eradicate, Prab. 5, 12.—With नि *ni*, **1.** To bury, MBh. 1, 3616. **2.** To dig in, Ragh. 6, 38. **3.** To infix, Râm. 3, 8, 7. **4.** To dig up, Bhâg. P. 5, 19, 29.—Caus. *nikhânita*, Infixed, Suçr. 2, 456, 19.—With परि *pari*, *parikhâta*, m. Track, Bhâg. P. 5, 16, 2.—Cf. Lat. canalis.

खनक *khan* + *aka*, m. A digger, Râm. 2, 80, 1.

खनन *khan*+*ana*, n. Digging, Daçak. in Chr. 197, 21.

खनि *khan*+*i*, f. A mine, Ragh. 17, 66.

खनितृ *khan*+*itr̥i*, m. A digger, Hit. ii. d. 45.

खनित्र *khan*+*itra*, n. A spade, Man. 2, 218.

खनित्रक *khanitra*+*ka*, n. A small spade, Pańch. 122, 9.

खमूर्तिमन्त् *kha-mûrti*+*mant*, adj., f. *matî*, Having an ætherial form, Man. 2, 82.

† **खम्ब्** *KHAMB*, i. 1, Par. To go (? v.r.)

खर *khara*, **I.** adj. **1.** Solid, Suçr. 2, 176, 12. **2.** Pointed (?), Râm. 6, 87, 3. **3.** Sharp, Suçr. 1, 76, 14. **4.** Hoarse, Râm. 3, 28, 42. **5.** Hot, Chât. 7. **II.** *ram*, adv. Hoarsely, Râm. 3, 29, 9. **III.** m. **1.** An ass, Man. 2, 201. **2.** A proper name, Râm. 1, 1, 45.—**Comp.** *Ati-*, adj., very loud, Râm, 3, 30, 3.—Cf. the reduplicated κάρχαρος καρχαλέος, καρχαρίας.

खर्खोद्वेदिन् *kharkhodavedin*, i.e. *kharkhoda-veda* + *in*, adj. Versed in the art of Kharkhoda, i.e. in sorcery, Râjat. 5, 238.

खर्ज् *KHARJ*, i. 1, Par. **1.** To creak (ved.). **2.** † To worship. **3.** † To pain. **4.** † To cleanse.—Cf. O.H.G. krachjan, krachôn.

खर्जूर *kharjûra*, m. and f. *rî*, A tree, Phœnix sylvestris.—**Comp.** *Piṇḍa-*, m. and f. *rî*, A sort of date tree.

† **खर्द्** *KHARD*, i. 1, Par. To bite.

† **खर्ब्** *KHARB*, i. 1, Par. To go.

खर्ब *kharba*, see *kharva*.

† **खर्व्** *KHARV*, i. 1, Par. To be haughty.—Cf. *garv*.

खर्व *kharva* and **खर्ब** *kharba*, n. A very great number, 10,000,000,000, or 1 with 37 zeros, a quadrillion, Râm. 6, 4, 59.

खर्वट *kharvaṭa*, m. and n. A market or country town, Bhâg. P. 1, 6, 11.

† **खल्** *KHAL*, i. 1, Par. **1.** To totter. **2** To gather.—Cf. *skhal*.

खल *khala*, **I.** m. and n. A threshing-floor, Man. 11, 17. **II.** m. An oil-cake, Pańch. ii. d. 53. **III.** m. and f. *lâ*, **1.** Mischievous, Pańch, i. d. 443. **2.** Vile, Hit. ii. 43.

खलखलाय *KHALAKHALÂYA*, Âtm. To fluctuate (?), Châṇ. 72 in Monatsb. Berl. Ak. Hist. Phil. 1864, 411.

खलति *khalati*, adj. Baldheaded, Suçr. 1, 316, 8.

खलि *khali*, m. An oil-cake ; in *tila-khali*, Bhartṛ. 2, 98 (cf. Chr. p. 309), The deposit of oil prepared from sesamum.—Cf. *khala*.

खलिन *khalina*, i.e. *khala* + *ina*, adj. Covered with oil-cakes (?), MBh. 13, 7288.

खलीकार *khalîkâra*, i.e. *khala*, or *khali-kṛi* + *a*, m., and **खलीकृति** *khalîkṛiti*, i.e. *khala* or *khali-kṛi* + *ti*. f. Abuse, Kathâs. 12, 175 ; 13, 157.

खलीन *khalîna*, m. and n. The bit of a bridle, MBh. 1, 7343 ; (borrowed from the Greek χαλινός).

खलु *khalu*, a particle. **1.** Indeed, Râm. 3, 35, 32 ; Yâjń. 2, 64. **2.** Only, Râm. 2, 63, 37. **3.** With preceding *na*, Not at all, Râm. 1, 74, 21. **4.** It lays a stress on an interrogation, Çâk. 32, 11. **5.** *khalu kṛitvâ*, Enough of this, do it no more, Pâṇ. 3, 4, 18.

खल्ल् *KHALL*, i. 1, Âtm. To totter, to be loose, Suçr. 1, 301, 8.—Cf. *skhal*.

खल्ल *khalla*, m. A bag, Suçr. 2, 364, 4.

खल्वाट *khalvâṭa*, adj. Baldheaded, Bhartṛ. 2, 86.—Cf. *khalati*, and Lat. calvus.

† **खव्** *KHAV*, ii. 9, *khaunâ* (others, *khunâ*), Par., v.r. of *khach*.

खश *khaça*, **I.** m. **1.** pl. The name of a people, Man. 10, 47. **2.** The son of an outcast Kshatriya, Man. 10, 22 (written with *s* instead of *ç*). **II.** f. *çâ* (and *sâ*), A proper name, Hariv. 169; 11521.

खशरीरिन् *khaçarîrin*, i.e. *kha-ça-*

rira + in, adj., f. *iṇî*, Having an ætherial form, Man. 4, 243.

† खष् *KHASH*, i. 1, Par. To hurt.

खस *khasa*, खसा *khasâ*, see *khaça*.

खाण्डव *khâṇḍava*, i. e. *khaṇḍ + u + a*, m. **1.** Sweetmeats, Râm. 1, 53, 4. **2.** The name of a forest, MBh. 1, 316.

खाण्डवायन *khâṇḍavâyana*, i. e. *khaṇḍu*, or *khâṇḍava + âyana*, m. pl. A tribe of Brâhmaṇas, MBh. 3, 10208.

खाण्डविक *khâṇḍavika*, i.e. *khâṇḍava + ika*, m. A confectioner, MBh. 15, 19.

खातक *khâta + ka* (vb. *khan*), n. A pit, Bhâg. P. 6, 12, 22.

खाद् *KHÂD*, i. 1, Par. (in epic poetry also Âtm., MBh. 1, 5580), **1.** To eat, Man. 5, 53; *prishṭha-mâṁsam*, To be a backbiter, Hit. i. d. 76. **2.** To gnaw, Suçr. 1, 63, 16. *khâdya*, Eatable, Pañch. 61, 13.—Caus. **1.** To let devour, Man. 8, 371. **2.** To devour, MBh. 3, 2435.—With the prep. सम् *sam*, To devour, Mṛichchh. 176, 1.

खादक *khâd + aka*, m. One who eats, Man. 5, 51.

खादन *khâd + ana*, n. Food, Râm. 2, 50, 31.

खादि *khâdi*, m. A ring (ved.).—Comp. *Su-*, adj. beautifully adorned, Chr. 293, 6 = Rigv. i. 87, 6.

ऽखादिन् *-khâd + in*, adj. Biting, Man. 4, 71.

खादिर *khâdira*, i. e. *khadira + a*, adj., f. *rî*, Made of Khadira-wood, Man. 2, 45.

खाधूया *khâdhûyâ*, f. The name of an Agrahâra, Râjat. 5, 23.

खारी *khârî*, f. A measure of grain, containing 16 droṇas, or about three bushels, Pañch. iv. d. 27.

खार्कार *khâr* (an imitative sound) *-kâra*, m. Bray, Bhâg. P. 3, 17, 11.

खालित्य *khâlitya* (probably for *khâlatya*, ved., i. e. *khalati + ya*), n. Baldness, Suçr. 1, 129, 8.

† खिट् *KHIṬ*, i. 1, Par. **1.** To be terrified. **2.** To terrify.

खिद् *KHID*, i. 6, *khinda*, Par.; i. 4, and ii. 7, *khinad*, *khind*, Âtm. (i. 4, also Par. Bhâg. P. 3, 4, 16). **1.** To be afflicted, Râm. 2, 39, 7. **2.** To be subdued, Hit. ii. d. 134. **3.** To despair, Râm. 3, 49, 57. Ptcple. of the pf. pass. *khinna*, **1.** Tired, Man. 7, 141. **2.** Exhausted, Bhartṛ. 1, 47. **3.** Desponding, Râm. 3, 69, 5. Caus. To distress, Mṛichchh. 143, 14. *khedita*, Relaxed, Râm. 5, 13, 47.—With the prep. परि *pari*, To be afflicted, Bhâg. P. 3, 9, 23 (i. 4, Par.). *parikhinna*, Tired, Râm. 4, 51, 3. Caus. To afflict, Bhâg. P. 1, 17, 7.—Cf. probably κίνδυνος.

खिल *khila* (perhaps for 3. *kshi + la*; cf. *khaḍga*), m. and n. **1.** Waste or unploughed land (ved.). **2.** A powerless subject, Bhâg. P. 6, 4, 49. **3.** Remainder, Bhâg. P. 6, 4, 15. **4.** A supplement, MBh. 1, 357.—**Comp.** *A-*, adj., f. *lâ*. 1. entire, Man. 1, 59. 2. all, Man. 1, 144. °*lena*, instr. entirely, Man. 1, 107.

† खु *khu*, i, 1, Âtm. To sound.

† खुज् *KHUJ*, i. 1, Par. To steal.

† खुड् *KHUḌ*, i. 10, Par. To break in pieces (v.r. of *khuṇḍ*, and of *thuḍ*).

† खुण्ड् *KHUṆḌ*, i. 1, Âtm. and i. 10, Par. To break in pieces.

खुड् *KHUD*, i. 6, Par. To push, ved. (probably for *kshud*, q.v.; cf. *khila*).

† **खुर्** *KHUR* (=*kshur*, cf. *khud*), i. 6, Par. **1.** To cut. **2.** To break.

खुर *khura* (for *kshura*, cf. *kshura-pra*), m. A hoof, Çâk. d. 31.—Comp. *Açva-*, a horse's hoof, Pańch. 252, 23.

खुरक *khura + ka*, m. A kind of dancing, Vikr. 59, 4.

† **खुर्द्** *KHURD*, i. 1, *khûrda*, Âtm. To play.—Cf. *kurd*.

खेचर *khechara*, i.e. *kha + i-chara*, I. adj., f. *rî*, Moving in the sky, Râm. 6, 107, 25. II. m. **1.** A bird, Nal. 20, 1. **2.** A Gandharva, MBh. 3, 14887. III. f. *rî*, A name of Durgâ, MBh. 4, 186.

खेचरत्व *khechara + tva*, n. The faculty of flying, Kathâs. 3, 49.

† **खेट्** *KHEṬ*, i. 10, Âtm. To eat.

खेट *kheṭa*, m. A village, MBh. 3, 13220.

खेटक *kheṭaka*, m. A shield, MBh. 4, 181.

† **खेड्** *KHEḌ*, i. 10, Âtm. To eat (v.r. of *kheṭ*).

खेद *kheda*, i.e. *khid + a*, m. **1.** Fatigue, Râm. 4, 49, 14. **2.** Faintness, Megh. 90. **3.** Affliction, Pańch. i. d. 225.

खेल् *KHEL*, i. 1, Par. **1.** To move to and fro, Râm. 5, 55, 26 (to dance?).—Caus. To put in motion, to turn, Pańch. 221, 12.

खेल *khel + a*, I. adj. Moving from one side to the other, swinging, moving gently, MBh. 1, 7043; Vikr. d. 95. II. °*lam*, adv. Moving gently, Râm. 2, 60, 19. — Comp. *Sa-khela + m*, adv. moving gently, MBh. 2, 2536.

खेलन *khel + ana*, n. Moving to and fro, Gît. 1, 40.

खेलि *khel + i*, f. Play, Gît. 11, 30.

† **खेव्** *KHEV*, i. 1, Âtm. To serve. —Cf. *kev*, *sev*.

खै *KHAI*, i. 1, *khâya*, Par. † **1.** To be firm. † **2.** To hurt. **3.** To dig.—Cf. *khan*.

† **खोट्** *KHOṬ*, i. 1, Par. To be lame; cf. *khoḍ*, *khor*, *khol*. i. 10, Par. v.r. of *kshoṭ*.

† **खोड्** *KHOḌ*, i. 1, Par. To be lame. i. 10, Par. v.r. of *kshoṭ*.

† **खोर्** *KHOR*, i. 1, Par. To be lame.—Cf. *khoṭ*.

† **खोल्** *KHOL*, i. 1, Par. To be lame.—Perhaps cf. χωλός, etc.

ख्या *KHYÂ*, ii. 2, Par.—Pass. To be known, MBh. 3, 8384. *khyâta*, Known, Râm. 3, 22, 32.—Caus. *khyâpaya*, **1.** To proclaim, MBh. 5, 7403. **2.** To report, MBh. 3, 15697. **3.** To praise, Râm. 3, 27, 19.—With the prep. **अभि** *abhi*, *abhikhyâta*, Known, MBh. 13, 4644.—Caus. To proclaim, Man. 9, 262.—With **आ** *â*, **1.** To report, MBh. 1, 26. **2.** To announce, Râm. 2, 34, 1. **3.** To name, Man. 4, 6.—Comp. ptcple. of the fut. pass., *an-â-khyeya*, **1.** Not to be reported, Pańch. 19, 16. **2.** unutterable, Bhartṛ. 1, 51.—Caus. To proclaim, MBh. 1, 7485.—With **उपा** *upa-â*, To report, Bhâg. P. 2, 9, 45.—With **प्रत्या** *prati-â*, **1.** To repudiate, Râm. 3, 54, 21. **2.** To recant, Daçak. in Chr. 192, 13. **3.** To surpass, Mâlav. d. 40.—With **व्या** *vi-â*, To explain, MBh. 1, 53.—With **समा** *sam-â*, **1.** To reckon up, Arj. 5, 11. **2.** To add,

Man. 7, 156. 3. To report, MBh. 3, 11915.—With परि *pari*, *parikhyâta*, 1. Known, MBh. 1, 874. 2. Famed, Râm. 3, 62, 2. 3. Named, Râm. 5, 2, 4. —With प्र *pra*, 1. To report, Bhâg. P. 1, 5, 40. Pass. To shine, Râm. 5, 18, 4. *prakhyâta*, 1. Acknowledged, Man. 8, 399. 2. Renowned, Râm. 3, 23, 39. —Caus. To make generally known, Kathâs. 1, 61.—With वि *vi*, *vikhyâta*, 1. Generally known, Yâjń. 3, 301. 2. Renowned, Râm. 3, 55, 16. 3. Named, Râm. 1, 57, 10.—Caus. To proclaim, Man. 11, 83.—With अभिवि *abhi-vi*, *abhivikhyâta*, 1. Renowned, Râm. 4, 1, 22. 2. Named, MBh. 1, 2644.—With प्रवि *pra-vi*, *pravikhyâta*, 1. Renowned, MBh. 1, 2543. 2. Named, Mârk. P. 1, 26.—With सम् *sam*, 1. To sum up, MBh. 3, 2822. 2. To calculate, Râm. 2, 40, 15. *saṁkhyâta*, n. Number, Bhâg. P. 6, 14, 3.—Comp. ptcple. of the fut. pass., *A-saṁkhyeya*, adj. uncountable, Râm. 1, 1, 91.—With अभिसम् *abhi-sam*, To reckon up, Râm. 4, 47, 4; 6, 1, 5.—With परिसम् *pari-sam*, To add together, Man. 1, 71. —With प्रसम् *pra-sam*, 1. To number, MBh. 1, 2547.—Cf. Goth. gôds (=*khyâta*; the original signification of the vb. is probably 'to shine'); A.S. gôd; ἀ-γαθός, where ἀ=Sscrt. *sa*.

ख्याति *khyâ+ti*, f. 1. Fame, celebrity, Man. 12, 36; personified, Bhâg. P. 3, 24, 22. 2. Name, MBh. 1, 3180. 3. Knowledge, Yogas. 2, 26.—Comp. *Su-*, f. fame.

ख्यातिमन्त् *khyâti+mant*, adj. f. *matî*, Renowned, Kathâs. 17, 34.

ऽख्यापक *-khyâpaka*, i.e. *khyâ*, Caus., *+aka*, adj. Foreboding, Suçr. 1, 127, 12.

ख्यापन *khyâpana*, i.e. *khyâ*, Caus., *+ana*, n. 1. Report, Chr. 55, 2. 2. Confession, Man. 11, 227. 3. Making renowned, Râjat. 5, 160.

ग *G*.

1. ऽग *-ga* (vb. *gam*), latter part of comp. words. 1. Moving, going, e.g. *çighra-*, adj. Going quickly, Râm. 3, 31, 3. 2. Being, e.g. *kûpa-ga*, adj. Being in a pit, Kathâs. 4, 128. 3. Referring to, e.g. *râghavânuja-*, adj. Referring to the younger brother of Râma, Râm. 6, 70, 59.

2. ऽग *-ga* (vb. *gai*), latter part of comp. words. Singing.—Cf. *chhandoga*.

गगण *gagaṇa*, and गगन *gagana*, n. The sky.

गगणेचर *gagaṇechara*, and गगनेचर *gaganechara*, i.e. *gagaṇa* or *gagana+i-chara*, I. adj. Moving in the sky, Bhâg. P. 6, 17, 1; Râm. 3, 39, 6. II. m. A bird, MBh. 1, 1317 (with n.).

गगनचर *gagana-chara*, m. A bird, MBh. 1, 1339.

† गग्घ् *GAGGH*, i. 1, Par. =*kakh*, q. cf. (v.r.).

गङ्गदत्त *gaṅgadatta*, i.e. *gaṅgâ-datta* (the *â* of the first part is shortened; cf. the vb. *dâ*), m. A proper name, Pańch. iv. d. 16.

गङ्गा *gaṅgâ* (from **gaṅgam* for *jaṅgam*, frequentat. of *gam*), f. The river Ganges, supposed to exist also in the sky and in the lower regions, Râm. 1, 44, 14.—Comp. *Vyomagaṅgâ*, i.e. *Vyoman-*, f. the supposed Ganges of the sky. *Pâtâla-*, f. that of the lower regions.

गज् *GAJ*, † i. 1, Par. To be drunk. i. 1 and i. 10, Par. To roar.

गज *gaja*, for original *garj+a*, I. m. An elephant, Man. 8, 296. II. f. *jî*, A female elephant, Bhâg. P. 4, 6, 26.—Comp. *Aranya-*, m. a wild elephant, 219, 15. *Âçâ-*, m. an elephant, supposed to support a quarter of the world, Râm. 1, 43, 7 Gorr. *Diggaja*, i.e. *diç-*, and *diçâ-*, m. the same, Râm. 5, 3, 13; 1, 41, 13. *Mahâ-*, m. a great elephant, Pańch. 69, 1. *Vana-*, m. a wild elephant, Pańch. 80, 6. *Sura-*, m. Indra's elephant =Airâvata, q. cf. Kir. 5, 47. When latter part of a comp. adj. the fem. ends in *jâ*, e.g. *sa-gaja*, adj., f. *jâ*, With elephants, Râm. 2, 57, 7.

गजदन्तमय *gaja-danta+maya*, adj., f. *yî*, Made of ivory, Râm. 5, 27, 11.

गजपुष्पमय *gaja-pushpa* (cf. the next) *+maya*, adj., f. *yî*, Wreathen of flowers called *gajapushpî*, Râm. 4, 12, 45.

गजपुष्पी *gajapushpî*, i.e. *gaja-pushpa+î*, f. The name of a flower, Râm. 4, 12, 46.

गजवन्त् *gaja+vant*, adj., f. *vatî*, Provided with elephants, Ragh. 9, 10.

† गञ्ज् *GAŃJ*, i. 1, Par. To sound.

गञ्ज *gańja*, m. and n. A treasury, Râjat. 4, 588.

गञ्जन *gańjana*, adj. Surpassing, Gît. 10, 7.

गञ्जवर *gańjavara*, m. A treasurer, Râjat. 5, 176.

गञ्जाकिनी *gańjâkinî* (? perhaps *gṛiń°*), f. A preparation of hemp (?), Lass. 95, 8.

† गड् *GAḌ*, i. 1, Par. To drop (cf. *gal*); i. 10, *gaḍaya*, Par. To cover.

गण् *GAṆ*, i. 10 (rather a denomin. derived from the next), *gaṇaya*, Par. (also Âtm., Bhâg. P. 4, 7, 29). **1.** To number, MBh. 3, 2618. **2.** To value, MBh. 2, 1552. **3.** To impute, Bhartṛ. 2, 44. **4.** To regard, Pańch. 258, 21. *gaṇita*, Reckoned, MBh. 13, 4439; calculated, Lass, 37, 8. n. Arithmetic, MBh. 1, 293.—With the prep. अधि *adhi*, To praise, Bhâg. P. 1, 5, 21.—With अव *ava*, To disregard, to neglect, Pańch. 239, 2.—With परि *pari*, **1.** To count over, Suçr. 1, 334, 8 (*pariganya*, instead of the regular *pariganayya*). **2.** To consider, Megh. 5. *a-pariganita*, adj. Innumerable, Bhâg. P. 6, 9, 35.—With प्र *pra*, To calculate, MBh. 1, 6808.—With वि *vi*, **1.** To number, Râm. 3, 53, 11. **2.** To consider, Râm. 3, 44, 31. **3.** To disregard, Pańch. iii. d. 40.

गण *gaṇa*, m. **1.** A multitude, Râm. 5, 91, 1. **2.** A class, Man. 1, 22. **3.** Troops of inferior deities, considered as Çiva's attendants, and under the especial superintendence of Gaṇeça, Râm. 5, 89, 7. **4.** A community, Yâjń. 2, 187. **5.** A contemptible association, Man. 4, 209. **6.** A body of troops consisting of 3 gulmas: i.e. 27 chariots, 27 elephants, 81 horses, and 135 foot, MBh. 1, 291. **7.** A foot of a verse, Çrut. 5, Br.—Comp. *Târâ-*, m. a multitude of stars, Böhtl. Ind. Spr. 2743. *Trastarakshogaṇa*, i.e. *trasta-rakshas-*, adj., f. *ṇâ*, with terrified troops of Râkshasas, Râm. 5, 51, 1. *Sendragaṇa*, i.e. *sa-indra-*, adj. with the attendants of Indra, Chr. 25, 61. *Hari-*, m. **1.** a troop of horse, Râjat. 5, 142. **2.** a proper name, ib.

गणक *gaṇ+aka*, m. **1.** A calculator, MBh, 15, 417. **2.** An astrologer, Râm. 1, 12, 7.

गणत्व *gaṇa* + *tva*, n. The condition of an attendant of Çiva, Kathâs. 7, 110.

गणदीक्षिन् *gaṇadîkshin*, i.e. *gaṇa -dîkshâ* + *in*, adj. m. A priest who officiates for a community, Yâjń. 1, 161.

गणन *gaṇ* + *ana*, n. and f. *nâ*. **1.** Counting, Pańch. pr. d. 7. **2.** Calculation, settlement, Râjat. 5, 237. **3.** Annumerating, Ragh. 8, 94. **4.** Consideration, Daçak. in Chr. 188, 9. **5.** Regard, Râjat. 5, 308.

गणशस् *gaṇa* + *ças*, adv. By troops, Daçak. in. Chr. 183, 14.

गणश्री *gaṇaçrî*, i.e. *gaṇa-çri*, adj. United in troops, Chr. 290, 9=Rigv. i. 64, 9.

गणिका *gaṇikâ*, i.e. *gaṇa* + *ka*, f. A harlot, Man. 4, 209.

गणिन् *gaṇin*, i.e. *gaṇa* + *in*, adj. Having troops.—Comp. *Çragaṇin*, i.e. *çvan-gaṇa* + *in*, adj. having packs of hounds, Ragh. 9, 53.

गणेय *gaṇ* + *eya*, an anomal. participle of the fut. pass. of *gaṇ* (f. *yî*), Numerable; in *a-*, adj. Innumerable, MBh. 8, 2554.

गणेश *gaṇeça*, i.e. *gaṇa-îça*, m. **1.** A name of Çiva, MBh. 3, 1629. **2.** Ganeça, the son of Çiva and Pârvatî, god of wisdom, MBh. 1, 74.

† **गण्ड्** *GAṆḌ*, i. 1, Par. To be a cheek; cf. the next, and MBh. 13, 4499.

गण्ड *gaṇḍa*, I. m. **1.** A cheek, Megh. 27. **2.** A boil, Suçr. 1, 283, 8. **3.** A bronchocele, Suçr. 1, 288, 15. II. f. *ḍâ*, A proper name, MBh. 13, 4417. —Comp. *Gala-*, m. 1. throat and cheek, MBh. 2, 902. 2. bronchocele, Lass. 94, 8.

गण्डक *gaṇḍaka*, I. m. A name of the inhabitants of Videha, derived from the river Gaṇḍakî, MBh. 2, 1062. II. f. *kî*, The name of a river, MBh. 2, 794. —Comp. *Sûtra-gaṇḍikâ*, f. a stick used in spinning thread.

गण्डु *gaṇḍu* (akin to *gaṇḍa*), m. and f. A pillow, Pańch. 126, 2.

गण्डूष *gaṇḍûsha* (akin to *gaṇḍa*), m. and f. *shâ*. **1.** A mouthful, Daçak. in Chr. 194, 5 (of honey); MBh. 8, 2051 (of onions). **2.** A mouthful of water for rinsing the mouth with, Bhâg. P. 9, 15, 3. **3.** The tip of an elephant's trunk, Kumâras. 3, 37.

गतागत *gatâgata*, i.e. *gata-â-gata* (vb. *gam*), n. **1.** Going and coming, Kathâs. 3, 69. **2.** The flight of a bird backward and forward, MBh. 8, 1902.

गति *gati*, i.e. *gam* + *ti*, f. **1.** Going, Yâjń. 3, 170. **2.** Motion, Yâjń. 1, 250; Râm. 2, 60, 12. **3.** Course, Râm. 1, 3, 2. **4.** Flight, Râm. 5, 76, 7. **5.** The transmigration of the souls, Man. 6, 61. **6.** Gait, Man. 2, 199. **7.** Attainment, Bhag. 2, 43. **8.** Way, Brâhmaṇ. 1, 35; with *parâ*, The last way, i.e. death, Brâhmaṇ. 2, 22. **9.** A means of success, Kathâs. 18, 89. **10.** A stratagem, Râm. 6, 92, 6. **11.** Refuge, Man. 8, 84 (*kâ gatis*, in dramas, 'how can it be helped?') **12.** Condition, Bhag. 4, 17. **13.** Happiness, MBh. 3, 17389. **14.** Basis, Man. 1, 110.—Comp. *A-*, f. want of success, Vikr. 26, 3. *Adhogati*, i.e. *adhas-*, I. f. 1. going downwards, Pańch. i. d. 166. 2. going to hell, Man. 3, 17. II. adj. 1. going downwards, Râm. 6, 20, 26. 2. going to hell, Man. 8, 309. *A-vi-hata-* (vb. *han*), adj. whose course is irresistible, Megh. 10. *Âkâça-*, adj. rising to the sky, Pańch. 48, 7. *Âtmagati*, i.e. *âtman-*, f. one's own way; instr. *tyâ*, by one's own power, Çâk.

104, 14. *Ûrdhva-*, I. f. going onwards, Suçr. 1, 151, 12. II. adj. rising, Râm. 1, 2, 40. *Kâma-*, adj. going as one lists, Ragh. 13, 76. *Krishṇa-*, m. fire, MBh. 13, 4071. *Gagaṇa-*, adj. moving in the sky, Megh. 47. *Dus-*, f. 1. distress, Prab. 49, 9. 2. hell, MBh. 12, 5593. *Daiva-*, f. the run of fate, Râm. 6, 94, 26. *Sadâ-*, m. 1. the sun. 2. wind. 3. the Supreme Spirit.—Cf. βάσις.

गतिमन्त् *gati-mant*, adj., f. *matî*. **1.** Having the power of motion, Hariv. 11794. **2.** Fistulous, Suçr. 2, 7, 2.

1. **गद्** *GAD*, i. 1, Par. (in epic poetry also Âtm., MBh. 13, 1138), **1.** To recite, MBh. 3, 2642. **2.** To speak, Râm. 4, 5, 31; to speak to, with acc. of the person and of the object, Râm. 2, 36, 1. *gadita*, Reckoned up, MBh. 3, 13425. n. Speech, Çâk. d. 81, v.r.—Comp. *A-*, adj. uncommanded, Çiç. 9, 57.—Ptcple. of the fut. pass., *gadya*, n. A prosaic composition, MBh. 3, 966. Desid. *jigadisha*, To desire to speak, MBh. 12, 1604.—With the prep. **नि** *ni*, **1.** To declare, MBh. 1, 4223. **2.** To speak, Râm. 2, 40, 10. Pass. To be named, MBh. 1, 5308. *nigadita*, n. Speech, Bhâg. P. 8, 21, 5.—With **प्रति** *prati*, To answer, MBh. 13, 5887.—With **वि** *vi*, *vigadita*, Spread, Râm. 2, 35, 15. — Cf. Goth. quithan; Engl. quoth; perhaps also βάζω (cf. *gadgada*).

† 2. **गद्** *GAD*, i. 10, Par. To thunder.

गद *gada*, I. m. i.e. 1. *gad* + *a*, **1.** Speech, a spell, MBh. 1, 1787. **2.** Disease, Çringârat. 14. **3.** The younger brother of Krishṇa, MBh. 1, 7992. II. f. *dâ*, A club, Râm. 5, 80, 4.—Comp. *A-gada*, I. adj. healthy, Man. 8, 107. II. m. 1. a medicament, Man. 7, 218. 2. health, 11, 237.

गदिन् *gadin*, i.e. *gadâ* + *in*, adj. Having a club, Bhag. 11, 17.

गद्गद *gadgada*, i.e. reduplicated 1. *gad* + *a*, adj., f. *dâ*, Faltering, Suçr. 2, 254, 10; Râm. 3, 3, 13.—Comp. *Sa-gadgada* + *m*, adv. in a faltering voice, Pañch. 43, 16. *Haṁsa-*, f. *dâ*, a woman speaking pleasantly.—Cf. βαμβαίνω and βυβάζω, frequent. of βαδ = 1. *gad*.

गन्तृ *gantṛi*, i.e. *gam* + *tṛi*, m., f. *trî*, n. **1.** One who goes, MBh. 13, 7173. **2.** Able to go, Nal. 24, 38. **3.** Undergoing, Yâjñ. 3, 10.—Cf. Lat. in-ventor.

† **गन्ध्** *GANDH*, i. 10, Âtm. **1.** To injure. **2.** To move. **3.** To ask.

गन्ध *gandha*, m. **1.** Smell, odour, Hiḍ. 2, 12. **2.** A perfume, Man. 2, 177. **3.** A name of Çiva, MBh. 12, 10378.—Comp. *Dus-*, adj. stinking, Hariv. 2947. *Nis-*, adj. wanting fragrance, Böhtl. Ind. Spr. 2637. *Pûti-*, I. adj., having an offensive smell. II. m. a stench, Man. 4, 107. III. n. sulphur. *Matsya-*, adj., f. *dhâ*, smelling of fishes, MBh. 1, 2398. *Yojana-*, f. *dhâ*, 1. musk. 2. a name of Sîtâ and Satyavatî. *Sa-*, I. adj. fragrant. II. m. a kinsman. *Su-*, I. adj. sweet-smelling. II. m. 1. fragrance. 2. sulphur. III. f. *dhâ*, 1. the name of several plants. 2. a proper name. IV. n. the name of several plants.

गन्धकालिका *gandhakâlikâ*, i. e. *gandha-kâlî* + *ka*, f. A proper name, MBh. 1, 3801.

गन्धप *gandha-pa*, m. A class of Pitṛis or Manes, MBh. 13, 1372.

गन्धमादन *gandhamâdana*, i.e. *gandha-mad*, Caus., + *ana*, m. **1.** The name of a mountain, Râm. 2, 54, 28. **2.** A name of Râvaṇa, MBh. 2, 410. **3.** The name of a monkey, Râm. 1, 16, 13.

गन्धर्व *gandharva*, and र्ब *rba*, I. m. A Gandharva: in epic poetry the Gandharvas are demigods inhabiting Indra's heaven, and serving as celestial musicians, MBh. 1, 4806. II. f. *vî*. 1. A female Gandharva, Bhâg. P. 4, 29, 21. 2. A mythological person, Râm. 3, 20, 28; 29.—Comp. *Sa-*, f. *bâ*, with the Gandharba, Vikr. 13, 19. *Deva-*, m. a celestial Gandharva, Râm. 1, 75, 28 Gorr.

गन्धवन्त् *gandha+vant*, I. adj., f. *vatî*, Fragrant, Râm. 6, 112, 84. II. f. *vatî*, 1. A name of Vyâsa's mother, MBh. 1, 2411. 2. The name of a river, Megh. 34.

गन्धवह *gandha-vaha*, I. adj., f. *hâ*, Conveying fragrance, Bhâg. P. 2, 10, 20. II. m. The wind, Çâk. d. 101.

गन्धार *gandhâra*, m. pl. The name of a people, MBh. 1, 2440.

ऽगन्धि *-gandhi*, A substitute for *gandha*, when the latter part of a comp., e.g. *utpala-*, adj. Smelling like lotus flowers, Râm. 5, 5, 12. *ud-*, adj. Fragrant, Ragh. 16, 47. *tri-su-*, n. The three perfumes, Suçr. 2, 483, 9. *dus-*, adj. Having no agreeable smell, Man. 6, 76. *puṇya-*, adj. Having a fragrant smell, Chr. 34, 6. *pûti-*, adj. Stinking, MBh. 2, 2138. *vi-*, adj. Having a disagreeable smell, Bhartṛ. 2, 9. *su-*, I. adj. 1. Fragrant. 2. Virtuous. II. m. 1. A perfume. 2. A fragrant sort of mango. III. n. The name of several plants.

ऽगन्धिक *-gandhi+ka*, latter part of a comp. 1. Smelling, 2. Having only the smell of, e.g. *bhrâtṛi-*, adj. Being a brother only nominally, not really, MBh. 3, 16111.—Comp. *Tri-su-*, n. the three perfumes, Suçr. 2, 493, 21.

गन्धिन् *gandhin*, i.e. *gandha+in*, adj., f. *nî*, Fragrant, MBh. 14, 1398.—Comp. *Su-*, adj. smelling agreeably, Arj. 4, 51.

गभस्ति *gabhasti*, m. and f. 1. An arm, Chr. 290, 10=Rigv. i. 64, 10. 2. A ray of light, Râm. 4, 27, 3.

गभस्तिमन्त् *gabhasti+mant*, I. adj., f. *matî*, Radiant, MBh. 2, 443. II. m. The sun, Ragh. 3, 37.

गभीर *gabhîra* (from a lost vb. *gabh*, A.S. geapan) and गम्भीर *gambhîra*, I. adj., f. *râ*, 1. Deep, Râm. 1, 5, 10; dwelling in the depth, Pañch. v. d. 10. 2. Thick, impervious, Râm. 3, 53, 22. 3. Deep-toned, Râm. 3, 30, 27. 4. Unfathomable, Bhâg. P. 9, 14, 14. II. m. *gabhîra*, A proper name, Bhâg. P. 9, 17, 10. III. f. *gambhîrâ*, The name of a river, Megh. 41.—Cf. *βαφ* in *βάπτω*, and *gahana*.

गम् *GAM*, i. 1, *gachchha*, Par. (in poetry also Âtm., Râm. 5, 1, 41). 1. To go, Man. 4, 47. 2. To move, Hit. i. d. 84; Râm. 3, 52, 12. 3. To go to (with acc.), MBh. 1, 5746; *vanena vanam̃ gatvâ*, Going from one forest to another, Râm. 1, 1, 30; *avanim̃ jânubhyâm*, To fall upon one's knees, MBh. 13, 935; *dharanim̃ mûrdhnâ*, To bow one's head to the ground, Râm. 3, 11, 6; *eno gachchhati kartâram*, An evil deed recoils on him who committed it, Man. 8, 19; with the loc., Pañch. 129, 4; with the dat., MBh. 3, 453; with *prati*, Nal. 26, 1. 4. To turn to (with acc.), Nal. 5, 33. 5. To pass, Râm. 2, 75, 54; *kâle gachchhati*, In the long run, Kathâs. 18, 129. 6. To know carnally (with the acc.), Man. 8, 376 (Atm.); Yâjñ. 2, 289. 7. To undergo (cf. *i.*) *çûdratvam*, To become a Çûdra, Man. 2, 168; *ânṛiṇyam*, To become quit of a debt, Man. 9, 229; *nâçam*, To become extinct, Man. 8, 17; *sam̃khyânam*, To be numbered, Man. 3, 66. 8. To perceive, MBh. 3, 2108. 9. With

गम्

doshena, and the acc. of a person, To accuse somebody, Râm. 4, 21, 3.—Ptcple. of the pf. pass. *gata* (cf. *βατός*) **1.** Gone, Nal. 21, 29, (26). **2.** Trodden, Râm. 2, 52, 53. **3.** Spread, Draup. 7, 10. **4.** Dead, MBh. 5, 472. **5.** Passed, Râm. 1, 63, 12. **6.** As former part of a comp. adj., often: Disappeared, deprived of, e.g. *gata-asu,* adj. Dead, Bhag. 2, 11; *gata-chetana,* adj. Senseless, Nal. 9, 20. **7.** Sprung up (with abl.), Kathâs. 2, 11; come, Râm. 6, 8, 15. **8.** Come to (with acc.), *dṛik-patham,* i.e. *dṛiç-patha,* Come in sight, Vikr. d. 95; with the loc., Bhag. 15, 4. **9.** Turned, Râm. 1, 2, 30; with *prati,* Râm. 3, 49, 12. **10.** Being, Râm. 2, 100, 20. *âpad-,* adj. Being in distress, Bhartṛ. 2, 64. *kaṇṭha-,* adj. Being at the throat, Râm, 4, 26, 3; being in the throat, Suçr. 1, 306, 14; Pańch. i. d. 329. *antar-gata-,* adj. Remaining in the throat, Pańch. 265, 10. *tathâ-,* adj. Being in this state, MBh. 3, 3014. **11.** Belonging, Râm. 5, 91, 24. **12.** Undergone (with acc.), e.g. *anayam,* Fallen into distress, Man. 10, 95. **13.** Referring to, Çâk. 71, 18. *âtmagatam,* i. e. *âtman-gata + m,* adv. Speaking aside, in dramatic language, Çâk. 13, 8. **14.** n. Going, MBh. 4, 297.—Comp. *Tad-,* adj. 1. turned on him, her, it, that, Râm. 1, 2, 30. 2. only turned, Lass. 32, 12. *Tiryaggata,* i.e. *Tiryańch-,* adj. a quadruped, Râm. 2, 35, 17. *Dus-,* adj. distressed, Bhartṛ. 2, 46. *Dhûrgata,* i.e. *dhur-,* adj. being at the head, MBh. 1, 2826. *Payas-,* n. ceasing of water, Böhtl. Ind. Spr. 1610. *Manas-,* desired, Chr. 20, 18. *Yathâ-gata + m,* adv., (returning in the same manner) as one came. *Vayas-,* I. adj. old. II. n. the end of youth, Böhtl. Ind. Spr. 1610. *Sarva-,* adj. omnipresent. *Su-,* m. a Buddha.—Ptcple. of the fut. pass. *gamya,* **1.** Accessible, Pańch. iii. d. 46. **2.** Lascivious, Daçak. 62, 1. **3.** Conceivable, Man. 12, 122. **4.** Suitable (?) Yâjń. 1, 64.—Comp. *A-,* adj., f. *yâ,* unaccessible, unapproachable, unattainable. *Gamanîya,* accessible, Man. 7, 174.—Caus. *gamaya,* **1.** To cause to go, MBh. 18, 95. **2.** To send, Daçak. in Chr. 201, 13. **3.** To cause to undergo, MBh. 5, 12; *kshayam,* To ruin, MBh. 13, 12. **3.** To pass, Pańch. ii. d. 161. **4.** To grant, MBh. 14, 179. **5.** To explain, MBh. 3, 11290.—With the prep. अति *ati,* To pass away, Râm. 2, 77, 1.—With उपाति *upa-ati,* To cross, Râm. 2, 68, 15.—With व्यति *vi-ati,* To pass, MBh. 3, 11937.—With अधि *adhi,* **1.** To go, Râm. 6, 107, 16. **2.** To enter, Man. 3, 250. **3.** To attain, Râm. 4, 51, 36. **4.** To surround, Gît. 11, 7. **5.** To accomplish, Mâlav. d. 9. **6.** To feel, Râm. 3, 53, 33. **7.** To acquire, Man. 9, 204. **8.** To choose, Man. 9, 91. **9.** To espouse, Man. 9, 70. **10.** To study, Man. 12, 109. **11.** To read, MBh. 13, 5027. *adhigata,* also in the sense of the active, **1.** Having attained, Çâk. 59, 14, v.r. **2.** Having perused, Pańch. 223, 4.—Comp. ptcple. of the fut. pass., *an-adhigamanîya,* adj. Unattainable, Pańch. 203, 10.—With समधि *sam-adhi,* **1.** To approach, Râm. 2, 84, 5. **2.** To acquire, Man. 8, 416. **3.** To study, Man. 4, 20.—With अनु *anu,* **1.** To follow, Râm. 3, 15, 1. **2.** To approach (with acc.), MBh. 13, 1487. **3.** To visit, Râm. 2, 48, 10. **4.** To cover from behind, Kir. 5, 2. **5.** To imitate, Ragh. 16, 13. *anugata,* **1.** Accompanied, Râm. 1, 1, 17. **2.** Conformable, Pańch. 218, 8; also in the sense of the active, Following, Man. 9, 267.—With समनु *sam-anu,* **1.** To follow, Râm. 3, 66, 17. **2.** To pursue, to penetrate, MBh. 11, 125. —With अन्तर् *antar* in *antargata,* **1.**

Gone into, Râm. 6, 93, 2. **2.** Being in, Râm. 6, 100, 1. **3.** Interior, Man. 8, 25. **4.** Concealed, Çâk. d. 161. **5.** Destroyed, Bhag. 7, 28.—With अप *apa,* To go off, MBh. 7, 2087; to leave (with abl.) MBh. 13, 4284.—With व्यप *vi-apa,* To go away, MBh. 13, 7421. —With अभि *abhi,* **1.** To advance, Man. 2, 196. **2.** To approach, Man. 1, 1. **3.** To approach carnally, Yâjń. 2, 205. **4.** To visit, Man. 4, 153. **5.** To meet, MBh. 3, 2978. **6.** To undergo; *nidrâm,* To fall asleep, Râm. 5, 68, 3. *abhigamya,* Accessible, Ragh. 1, 16. Caus. To explain, MBh. 1, 1295.—With समभि *sam-abhi,* To approach, Râm. 3, 9, 16. — With अव *ava,* **1.** To enter into, MBh. 5, 740. **2.** To inquire, Çâk. 8, 22, v.r. **3.** To perceive, Hit. i. d. 92. **4.** To understand, Çâk. 21, 17. **5.** To guess, Çâk. 15, 4. **6.** To take for, Râm. 6, 101, 7. **7.** with *doshena,* To accuse, Râm. 2, 92, 29. Caus. **1.** To cause to experience, Mâlav. 14, 2. **2.** To let know, Daçak. 113, 3. — With प्रत्यव *prati-ava,* To know one by one, MBh. 11, 90.—With समव *sam-ava,* To know completely, Bhâg. P. 5, 13, 25. — With अस्तम् *asta+m* (cf. *asta*), To set (as the sun), Hit. 17, 20.—With आ *â,* **1.** To approach, Râm. 1, 2, 26. **2.** With *saha,* To meet with, Nal. 16, 34. **3.** To return, Lass. 30, 7. **4.** To undergo. *viçvâsam,* To take confidence, Pańch. 34, 15. *ânṛiṇyam,* To become quit of a debt, Râm. 3, 27, 13. *dâsatvam,* To become enslaved, Nal. 26, 21. *pańchatvam,* To die, Kathâs. 2, 32. *âgata,* **1.** Come, Nal. 3, 3. **2.** Having attained, Daçak. 2, 58. **3.** Devolved, Pańch. 16, 11. **4.** Gained, Man. 4, 226. **5.** Happened, MBh. 3, 2555. **6.** As former part of comp. words often: Possessed of; *âgata-manyu,* adj. Moved with resentment, Man. 2, 152.—**Comp.** *Tiryakpratimukha-,* i.e. *tiryańch-pratimukha-,* adj. overturned or running against anything, Man. 8, 291. *Su-,* n. welcome, salutation.—Caus. **1.** To cause to approach, Gît. 12, 3. **2.** To teach, Çiç. 9, 79. **3.** To learn, MBh. 5, 132.—With अध्या *adhi-â,* To find, MBh. 1, 3984. — With अन्वा *anu-â,* To follow, MBh. 1, 1917. *anvâgata,* also in the sense of an active, Following, MBh. 6, 2809.—With अभ्या *abhi-â,* **1.** To approach, MBh. 3, 10979. **2.** To undergo; *chintâm,* To become thoughtful, Râm. 3, 4, 20. *abhyâgata,* Come, Sâv. 7, 8; a guest, Hit. i. d. 54.—With समभ्या *sam-abhi-â, samabhyâgata,* Approached, Pańch. 205, 9.—With उपा *upa-â,* **1.** To approach, Nal. 7, 12. **2.** To appear, Râm. 4, 51, 40. **3.** To come to one's share, Hit. 268, 1. **4.** To return, Kathâs. 18, 400. **5.** To undergo; *dosham,* Yâjń. 2, 256; *pańchatvam,* To die, Pańch. 120, 13.—With समुपा *sam-upa-â,* **1.** To approach, MBh. 3, 2192. **2.** To befall, Yâjń. 2, 53. **3.** To undergo; *chintâm,* To become thoughtful, Râm. 2, 29, 22. —With पर्या *pari-â,* **1.** To approach all together, MBh. 4, 1146. **2.** To finish, Râm. 3, 35, 9. **3.** To subdue, MBh. 1, 4567. *paryâgata punar,* Recovered, MBh. 13, 3496.—With प्रत्या *prati-â,* **1.** To return, Râm. 4, 33, 22. **2.** To recover, Vikr. 8, 1, v.r.—With संप्रत्या *sam-prati-â,* To return, MBh. 13, 2193. —With समा *sam-â,* **1.** To meet, to assemble, Râm. 4, 28, 31; Man. 7 148. *samâgamya*, collectively, Man. 8, 408. **2.** To unite, Râm. 4, 44, 78; carnally, MBh. 3, 17097. **3.** To approach, Râm. 1, 32, 7.—Caus. To unite, Vikr. d. 34.—With **अभिसमा** *abhi-sam-â*, **1.** To approach, MBh. 11, 445.—With **उद्** *ud*, **1.** To rise, Ṛit. 1, 10, v.r.; Pañch. 47, 18. **2.** To open, Vikr. d. 107. **3.** To go out, Ragh. 7, 16 (uttered); Râm. 2, 48, 1 (vanished). **4.** To spread, Ragh. 18, 19. *udgamanîya*, see separately.—With **अभ्युद्** *abhi-ud*, To advance toward, MBh. 1, 3572. *abhyudgata*, **1.** Elevated. **2.** Risen. **3.** Approached.—With **प्रोद्** *pra-ud*, To project, Kathâs. 26, 9.—With **प्रत्युद्** *prati-ud*, To advance toward, Man. 2, 196.—With **समुद्** *sam-ud*, To come out, Ṛit. 1, 7.—With **उप** *upa*, **1.** To approach, Râm. 3, 4, 32; with *adharmeṇa*, To treat ill, MBh. 8, 2082. **2.** To undergo; *pratikûlatâm*, To become hostile, Çiç. 9, 6. *upagata*, **1.** Enchased, MBh. 12, 1545. **2.** Granted, Man. 2, 160. **3.** n. A receipt, Yâjñ. 2, 93. —Caus. To cause to approach, Daçak. 137, 18.—Desid. *upa-jigamisha*, To desire to walk, Bhâg. P. 5, 24, 26.—With **अभ्युप** *abhi-upa*, **1.** To approach, Pañch. 189, 24. **2.** To go to, Çiç. 9, 13. **3.** To attain, Râm. 5, 67, 10. **4.** To resign one's self (to somebody), Daçak. in Chr. 191, 12. **5.** To assent, Daçak. in Chr. 201, 8. **6.** To admit, to grant, Çâk. 69, 22.—Caus. To persuade to assent, Daçak. in Chr. 193, 12.—With **समुप** *sam-upa*, **1.** To approach, MBh. 1, 7718. **2.** To undergo; *pañchatvaṁ samupâgamat* (perhaps *sam-upa-â-agamat*), To die, Kathâs. 5, 122.—With **नि** *ni*, To undergo; *çântim*, To become pacified, Bhag. 9, 31.—With **निस्** *nis*, **1.** To go out, to come out, to depart from (with abl.), Mârk. P. 22, 47; Suçr. 1, 298, 1; Çâk. d. 131; Man. 9, 83. **2.** To undergo, MBh. 3, 15399 (*preshyatâm*, To become a servant). *nirgata*, Disappeared; *nirgata-viçaṅka*, adj. Fearless, Pañch. 124, 12.—With **अभिनिस्** *abhi-nis*, To depart from, Râm. 1, 9, 13.—With **विनिस्** *vi-nis*, **1.** To go out, to leave (with abl. and gen.), Râm. 5, 84, 10; 4, 22, 39. **2.** To depart, Pañch. 48, 13. **3.** To be beside one's self, Bhâg. P. 1, 18, 30. *vinirgata*, **1.** Stretched forth, Ṛit. 1, 21. **2.** Free from, Man. 8, 65.—With **संनिस्** *sam-nis*, To depart, Râm. 5, 42, 5.—With **परा** *parâ*, *parâgata*, Covered, Çiç. 6, 2.—With **परि** *pari*, **1.** To walk round, Râm. 2, 55, 24. **2.** To wander over, Sâv. 6, 3. **3.** To surround, Râm. 6, 15, 5. **4.** To spread everywhere, Çâk. d. 194. **5.** To die, Bhartṛ. 3, 49. **6.** To undergo, e. g. *çântim*, To become pacified, MBh. 2, 1761. *parigata*, **1.** Possessed of, Pañch. i. d. 55. **2.** Known, Çâk. 95, 20. Caus. To pass, Ragh. 8, 91.—With **प्र** *pra*, To advance, Râm. 1, 9, 30.—With **विप्र** *vi-pra*, To separate, MBh. 1, 7372.—With **प्रति** *prati*, **1.** To advance towards, MBh. 3, 10908. **2.** To return, Daçak. in Chr. 192, 17; Chr. 66, 12, read *prati gatâm*.—With **वि** *vi*, **1.** To pass, MBh. 14, 1912. **2.** To disappear, Man. 3, 259. *vigata*, **1.** As former part of comp. adj., Disappeared. -*asu*, adj. Lifeless, MBh. 7, 1420. **2.** Deceased, Man. 5, 75. **3.** Sunk down, base, Bhâg. P. 5, 1, 36.—With **सम्** *sam*, generally Âtm. **1.** To assemble, Râm. 3, 35, 97. **2.** To meet, Nal. 12,

29; Râjat. 5, 97; MBh. 1, 5989. **3.** To unite, Arj. 3, 1; carnally, MBh. 3, 17085. **4.** To shrivel, MBh. 1, 3471. **5.** To accord, Vedântas. in Chr. 213, 17. **6.** To undergo, *viçrambham*, To take confidence, Bhâg. P. 5, 6, 2. *saṁgata*, Seasonable, Râm. 2, 95, 14. n. **1.** Meeting, MBh. 3, 14044. **2.** Union, Çâk. d. 120; Vikr. d. 162; connection, Man. 3, 140. **3.** Friendship, Râm. 5, 94, 21. *a-saṁgata*, adj. Unfit, Böhtl. Ind. Spr. 404. Anom. absol., *saṁgatvâ*, MBh. 13, 456.—Caus. **1.** To unite, Vikr. d. 143. **2.** To lead to (with two acc.), Hit. pr. 55. **3.** To transfer on (with loc.), Ragh. 12, 104. **4.** To offer, MBh. 5, 4841.—With अभिसम् *abhi-sam*, **1.** To approach, Râm. 4, 1, 9. **2.** To unite, Râm. 2, 36, 8. **3.** To advance towards, Bhâg. P. 1, 13, 5.—With उपसम् *upa-sam*, **1.** To unite, MBh. 1, 6897. **2.** To approach, Bhag. 1, 2. **3.** To undergo, MBh. 13, 5697 (*samatâm*, To become alike).—With सह *saha*, To accompany, Râm. 4, 8, 26.—Cf. Lat. venio for vemio (=*gam*, i. 4); *βαίνω* for *βαμjω*, *βασκο* = *yachchha*; Goth. *gaggan*, an old frequent., cf. the Sskr. frequent. *jaṅgam*; also Goth. gatvo, qviman; A.S. cuman; see also *gati*, *gantṛi*, and *gâ*.

गम *gam + a*, I. latter part of comp. words, f. *mâ*, Going, e.g. *kha-*, **1.** adj. Moving in the sky, MBh. 3, 820. **2.** m. A bird, Nal. 1, 24. **3.** m. A proper name, MBh. 1, 995. II. m. **1.** Way, Chaurap. 44. **2.** Carnal approaching, Man. 11, 54.—Comp. *A-*, 1. adj. inaccessible, MBh. 3, 8247. 2. m. a tree. *Durgama*, i.e. *dus-*, adj., f. *mâ*, 1. difficult to be passed (as a way), Râm. 5, 74, 31. 2. difficult to be crossed, MBh. 1, 2924. 3. difficult to be attained, Râm. 6, 67, 10. 4. difficult in general, MBh. 13, 7535. *Paksha-*, adj. flying, Râm. 3, 56, 45. *Su-*, adj. 1. accessible. 2. easy, MBh. 13, 7535. 3. plain, intelligible.

गमन *gam + ana*, n. **1.** Gait, Çṛiṅgârat. 7. **2.** Going, Râm. 1, 9, 40. **3.** Going to, Râm. 1, 3, 16. **4.** Coming, Hiḍ. 4, 27 (? read *âgamanam*). **5.** Carnal approach, Râm. 3, 13, 6. **6.** Undergoing, e.g. *pañchatva-*, Death, Râm. 5, 15, 78. **7.** Way, Râm. 3, 68, 50.—Comp. *Adhogamana*, i.e. *adhas-*, n. descending, Râjat. 5, 310. *Anta-*, n. 1. accomplishing, Pañch. iii. d. 130. 2. dying. *Antarâ-*, n. passing between, Man. 4, 126. *Asta-*, n. setting (of the sun), MBh. 1, 6058. *Saha-*, n. 1. accompanying. 2. a woman's burning herself with her deceased husband.

ऽगमनीय *gamanîya*, i.e. *gamana + îya*, adj. Relating to carnal approach, Man. 11, 102.

† गम्ब् *GAMB*, i. 1, Par. To go.

गम्भीर *gambhîra*, see *gabhîra*.

गय *gaya*, I. m. **1.** The name of a Ṛishi, Râm. 2, 107, 11. **2.** pl. The name of a people, MBh. 2, 1827. **3.** The name of a mountain, MBh. 3, 8304. II. f. *yâ*. **1.** The name of a holy place, MBh. 3, 8075. **2.** The name of a river, MBh. 1, 7818.

गर *gara*, i.e. 2. *gṛî + a*, m. **1.** A fluid (ved.). **2.** m. and n. Poison, Râm. 2, 110, 24.—Comp. *Bhû-*, n. Poison.

गरद *gara + da* (vb. *dâ*), m. A giver of poison, Man. 3, 158.

गरल *garala* (cf. *gara*), m. Poison, Pañch. 63, 7.

गरिमन् *gariman*, i.e. *guru + iman* (cf. *guru*), m. Heaviness, Çiç. 9, 49. **2.** The magical faculty of making one's self as heavy as one lists, Lass. 3, 18.

3. Dignity, Pańch. i. d. 36. 4. A most venerable person, Bhâg. P. 4, 5, 21.

गरिष्ठ *garishṭha*, superl., and गरीयंस् *garîyaṁs*, comparat. of *guru*, q. cf.

गरीयस्त्व *garîyastva*, i.e. *garîyaṁs* + *tva*, n. Great importance, MBh. 1, 5080.

गरुड *garuḍa*, for **garutra*, i.e. probably, *gal* + *tṛi* + *a* = Lat. volucer, m. 1. The sovereign of the feathered race and vehicle of Vishṇu, MBh. 1, 1092. 2. The name of a battle-array, Man. 7, 187.

गरुत् *garut* (vb. *gal*), m. A wing.—Comp. *Çveta-*, m. A goose.

गरुत्मन्त् *garut* + *mant*, m. A name of Garuḍa, MBh. 1, 1510.

गर्ग *garga*, I. m. The name of an old Ṛishi, MBh. 9, 2132, and other persons. II. f. *gâ*, A proper name, Râjat. 5, 250.

गर्गर *gar-gar* + *a* (vb. 2.*gṛi*, reduplicated, + *a*), m. 1. A whirlpool (ved.). 2. A churn, MBh. 12, 2783.—Cf. Lat. gurges.

गर्ज् *GARJ*, i. 1, Par. To roar, Pańch. 9, 8. *garjita*, n. 1. Roaring, MBh. 3, 12137. 2. Thunder, Megh. 35. —With अनु *anu*, To roar after, MBh. 7, 1714. *anugarjita*, n. The echo of a roar, Kumâras. 6, 40.—With अभि *abhi*, To roar at, MBh. 7, 5484. *abhigarjita*, n. A wild challenging roar, Râm. 4, 14, 1.—With समभि *sam-abhi*, To roar at, MBh. 5, 5635.—With परि *pari*, To roar, Râm. 1, 28, 17 (*garjatîm*, anom. instead of *garjantîm*, on account of the metre).—With प्र *pra*, To begin to roar, MBh. 1, 1419.—With प्रति *prati*, To roar at, MBh. 5, 2048.—With वि *vi*, To roar, MBh. 6, 610.—With सम् *sam*, To roar at, MBh. 7, 5908.—Cf. probably γοργός, Γοργώ.

गर्जन *garj* + *ana*, n. Roaring, Hit. 34, 21.

गर्त *garta* (probably 2.*gṛi*), m., f. *tâ*, and n. 1. A hole, MBh. 1, 1034; Pańch. 81, 22; MBh. 7, 4953. 2. A ditch, Man. 4, 47; 203.

† गर्द् *GARD*, i. 1, and 10, Par. To sound.

गर्दभ *gardabha*, I. m. An ass, Man. 8, 298. II. f. *bhî*. 1. A she ass, MBh. 13, 1827. 2. An insect, a kind of beetle living in cow-dung, Suçr. 2, 288, 3,

गर्ध् *GARDH*, i. 10, Par. To desire. —Cf. *gṛidh*.

ऽगर्धिन् *-gardhin*, i.e. *gṛidh* + *in*, adj., f. *nî*, Latter part of comp. words, Desiring, greedy, Man. 4, 28.

† गर्ब् *GARB*, i. 1, Par. To go.—Cf. *garv*.

गर्भ *garbha*, i.e. *grabh* (ved. = *grah*) + *a*, m. 1. The womb, Pańch. Pr. 8. 2. The interior, MBh. 9, 2741. 3. A fœtus or embryo, Bhag. 3, 38. 4. A sprout, Râm. 5, 28, 6. 5. Conception, Man. 2, 36. 5. As former part of comp. words it has often the second signification; cf. *garbha-gṛiha*. As latter part of comp. adj. Holding in one's interior, containing; e.g. *çuka-*, adj. Containing parrots, Çâk. d. 14. *sneha-*, adj. Containing oil, MBh. 12, 13414.—Comp. *Gṛihîta-* (vb. *grah*), adj., f. *bhâ*, pregnant, Suçr. 1, 321, 16. *Jâra-*, adj., f. *bhâ*, Pregnant by an adulterer, not. ad Hit. Pr. d. 38; 39. *Deva-*, m. The child of a god, MBh. 3, 17161. *Mati-*, adj. full of understanding, Çiç. 9, 62. *Ratna-*, I. m. Kuvera. II. f. *bhâ*, the earth. *Çamî-*, m. 1. a Brâhmaṇa. 2. fire. *Sa-*, m. a brother by the same father and mother. *Sura-*, m. the child of a god, Hiḍ. 4, 27. *Soma-*, m. Vishṇu. *Sravadgarbhâ*, i.e. *sravant -garbha* (vb. *sru*), f. a woman or cow miscarrying by accident. *Sva-*, m. one's own fœtus, Râm. 3, 49, 49. *Hima-*, adj. laden with cold, Çâk. d. 54. *Hiraṇya-*, m. Brahman.—Cf. δελφύς, ἀδελφειός, ἀδελφεός, ἀδελφός; βρέφος; Goth. kalbo; A.S. calf.

गर्भवती *garbhavatî*, i.e. *garbha+vant+î*, f. A pregnant female, MBh. 3, 10667.

गर्भस्थ *garbha-stha* (vb. *sthâ*), adj. 1. Being in the womb, Pañch. ii. d. 82. 2. Being in the interior, MBh. 7, 3110.

गर्भास्राव *garbâsrâva*, i.e. *garbha -â-sru+a*, m. Abortion, Suçr. 1, 175, 7. —Cf. *garbha-srâva*.

गर्भिन् *garbhin*, i.e. *garbha + in*, adj., f. *iṇî*, Pregnant, Man. 9, 173.

गर्भेश्वरता *garbheçvaratâ*, i.e. *garbha-îçvara+tâ*, f. Hereditary dominion, Râjat. 5, 198.

† **गर्व्** *GARV*, or **गर्ब्** *GARB*, i. 1, Par. and i. 10, Âtm. To be proud.

गर्व *gar+va* (cf. *guru*), m. Pride, Pañch. 26, 2.—Comp. *Dhana-*, m. a proper name, Daçak. in Chr. 191, 23. *Sa-*, adj. proud; *°vam*, adv. haughtily, Râm. 3, 32, 2.

गर्वाय *GARVÂYA*, a denomin. derived from *garva* by *ya*, Âtm. To behave haughtily, Prab. 24, 7.

गर्वित *garvita*, i.e. *garva+ita*, adj., f. *tâ*, Proud, Râm. 1, 7, 6.—Comp. *Pari-*, adj. very proud, Châṇ. 94 in Berl. Monatsb. 1864, 413.

गर्ह् *GARH* (probably akin to *grah*), i. 1, Âtm. and Par.; i. 10, Par. Âtm. 1. To blame, Râm. 2, 75, 19; MBh. 5 648; 1, 5731; 3, 526. 2. To loathe, Man. 11, 229. *garhita*, 1. Contemned, Man. 10, 39. 2. Blameable, Râm. 3, 51, 23. 3. Prejudicial, Lass. 16, 15. 4. with abl., Worse, MBh. 3, 1040.—Comp. *A-*, adj. f. *tâ*, 1. unblamed, respected, Man. 9, 109. 2. unblameable, Man. 4, 3.—*garhya*, contemptible, Man. 5, 149.—With the prep. **अव** *ava*, *avagarhita*, Contemned, Râm. 2, 21, 19.—With **नि** *ni*, To despise, MBh. 13, 5892.—With **परि** *pari*, To blame much, Râm. 2, 106, 10.—With **प्रति** *prati*, *pratigarhita*, Blamed, Râm. 6, 103, 15 (perhaps *prati* must be separated, and signifies Concerning).—With **वि** *vi*, To blame, Râm. 6, 8, 3. *vigarhita*, 1. Blemished, Man. 9, 72. 2. Contemptible, Man. 3, 167.

गर्हण *garhaṇa*, i.e. *garh+ana*, n. and f. *ṇâ*, Blame, MBh. 12, 9153; Man. 2, 80.

गर्हा *garh+â*, f. Blame, Pañch. i. d. 192.

ऽगर्हिन् *-garh+in*, adj. Blaming, Bhâg. P. 4, 4, 18.

1. **गल्** *GAL*, (akin to *gur*, cf. *ud -gur*), i. 1, Par. 1. To drop, to distil, Kathâs. 11, 57. 2. To fall, Çiç. 9, 75. 3. To disappear, Bhartṛ. 1, 69.—Caus. *gâlaya*, 1. To percolate, Daçak. 156, 2. 2. To sift, Suçr. 1, 165, 18. 3. To dilute, Suçr. 1, 166, 6.—With the prep. **अव** *ava*, To fall off, Çiç. 8, 34.—With **आ** *â*, To fall, Râm. 5, 13, 34.—With **समा** *sam-â*, To tumble down, MBh. 1, 1409.—With **उद्** *ud*, To burst forth, Bhâg. P. 1, 10, 14.—With **निस्** *nis*, *nirgalita*, Distilling, Ragh. 5, 17.—With **परि** *pari*, *parigalita*, 1.

Tumbled down, MBh. 1, 1183. **2.** Sunk in, Pańch. 8, 17.—With वि *vi*, **1.** To distil, Prab. 79, 16. **2.** To fall off, Amar. 36. **3.** To disappear, Kathâs. 7, 75. *vigalita*, **1.** Drained by distilling, MBh. 1, 1182. **2.** Liquefied, dissolved, Kathâs. 18, 78; Gît. 1, 31. **3.** Tumbled down, MBh. 4, 826. **4.** Unwieldy, Bhartṛ. 3, 74.—Cf. *garuḍa*, and Lat. volare (concerning the signification, cf. *pat*), βάλλω (Causal).

† 2. गल् *GAL*, i. 10, Atm. To distil; see 1.*gal*.

† 3. गल् *GAL*, i. 1, Par. To eat. —Cf. 2.*gṛî*.

गल *gala*, i.e. 2.*gṛî*+*a*, m. The throat, Pańch. 249, 1.—Cf. Lat. gula; O.H.G. kela; A.S. ceolr, etc.

गलितक *galita*+*ka* (vb. 1. *gal*), m. A kind of dance, Vikr. 68, 14.

गल्भ् *GALBH* (akin to *grabh*, see *grah*), i. 1, Âtm. To be bold.—With the prep. प्र *pra*, To behave resolutely, Çiç. 10, 18.

गल्ल *galla* (probably a dialectical form of *gaṇḍa*), m. The cheek, Pańch. 125, 9.

गल्वर्क *galvarka*, m. Crystal (?), Râm. 3, 48, 12.

† गल्ह् *GALH*, i. 1, Atm.=*garh*.

गव *gava*, i.e. *go*+*a*, a substitute for *go* in comp. words, e.g. *gavârha*, i.e. *gava-arha*, adj. Worth a bull, MBh. 2, 828. *gavârthe*, i.e. *gava-arthe*, adv. For preserving a cow, Man. 10, 62. *ashṭagava*, i.e. *ashṭan-*, adj. Drawn by eight oxen, MBh. 8, 799. *strî-gavî*, f. a milch cow.

गवय *gavaya* (akin to *go*), m. **1.** A species of ox, Bos gavæus, Pańch. 53, 10. **2.** The name of a monkey, Râm. 4, 25, 33.

गवाक्ष *gavâksha*, i.e. *gava-aksha*, m. **1.** An air-hole, a round window, a bull's eye, Râm. 3, 61, 13. **2.** (m. ?) The name of a sea, Râjat. 5, 423. **3.** The name of a monkey, Râm. 4, 25, 33.

गवाक्षक *gavâksha*+*ka*, m.=*gavâksha* **1.**

गविष्ठ *gavishṭha*, m. **1.** The sun, Bhâg. P. 1, 10, 36. **2.** The name of a Dânava, MBh. 1, 2538.

गवेष् *GAVESH*, i.e. *gava-ish*, i. 1, Âtm.; i. 10, Par. To search, Ṛit. 1, 21; Kathâs. 24, 230.

गवेषण *gaveshaṇa*, i.e. *gavesh*+*ana*, n. Search, Kathâs. 21, 85.

गवेषिन् *gavesh*+*in*, adj. Searching, MBh. 3, 10896.

गव्य *gavya*, i.e. *go*+*ya*, I. adj., f. *yâ*, **1.** Produced by a cow. **2.** Consisting of milk. **II.** n. Milk.—**Comp.** *Pańchagavya*, i.e. *pańchan-*, n. the five pure things produced by the cow, Man. 11, 165.

गव्यूति *gavyûti*, i.e. *go-yu*+*ti*, f. **1.** Pasture-ground (ved.). **2.** A measure = 4000 daṇḍa = 2 kroças, Râm. 6, 33, 13.

† गह् *GAH*, i. 10, *gahaya*, Par. To strive, to penetrate.

गहन *gahana*, i.e. *gabh* (cf. *gabhîra*, and *gâh*)+*ana*, I. adj., f. *nâ*. **1.** Deep, Bhartṛ. 3, 11. **2.** Impervious, Râm. 2, 85, 4. **3.** Impenetrable, Pańch. i. d. 317. **II.** n. **1.** A thicket, Râm. 4, 48, 2. **2.** Impenetrability, obscurity, MBh. 11, 125. **3.** Multitude, Râm. 1, 35, 16.

गहनत्व *gahana + tva*, n. Impenetrability, MBh. 2, 2355.

गहनवन्त् *gahana + vant*, adj., f. *vati*, Full of thickets, Râm. 4, 48, 6.

गह्वर *gah + vara* (cf. *gahana*), I. adj., f. *râ* and *rî*, Impenetrable, Bhâg. P. 5, 14, 4. II. n. **1.** A thicket, MBh. 4, 727. **2.** An enigma, MBh. 13, 1388.

गह्वरित *gahvarita*, i.e. *gahvara + ita*, adj. Lying in one's hiding-place, MBh. 2, 2294.

गा *GÂ*, † i. 1. Âtm.; ved. ii. 2 and 3, *jigâ* (in classic writings only the Aor. Par. Âtm.). **1.** To go, Bhâg. P. 1, 13, 1. **2.** To come, Bhâg. P. 3, 18, 27. **3.** To undergo (cf. *gam*); *harsham*, To become glad, Râm. 5, 91, 25. Desider. *jigîsha*, To desire to go, Bhâg. P. 2, 10, 25.—With the prep. अति *ati*, **1.** To cross, Râm. 2, 52, 75. **2.** To pass, Arj. 4, 62. **3.** To die, Râm. 2, 72, 29. **4.** To escape, Bhâg. P. 4, 21, 56. **5.** To subdue, Bhâg. P. 9, 20, 27. **6.** To neglect, MBh. 5, 4212. —With व्यति *vi-ati*, To pass, Ragh. 6, 52.—With अधि *adhi*, **1.** To undergo; *çramam*, To become tired, Bhâg. P. 4, 26, 10. **2.** To think of, Nal. 10, 16. **3.** usually Âtm., To study, to learn, to read, MBh. 1, 5106; 13, 121; Man. 1, 59; Bhâg. P. 9, 22, 23.—With अनु *anu*, To follow, MBh. 3, 2303.—With समनु *sam-anu*, To follow, MBh. 5, 432.—With अभि *abhi*, **1.** To go to, Râm. 1, 63, 3. **2.** To approach, Râm. 1, 20, 2. **3.** To undergo, to attain, MBh. 3, 16625.—With आ *â*, **1.** To approach, MBh. 1, 3573. **2.** To befall, MBh. 3, 1355.—With अभ्या *abhi-â*, **1.** To approach, Bhâg. P. 9, 21, 10. **2.** To befall, MBh. 3, 1120. **3.** To resolve (with infin.), Man. 10, 108.—With समभ्या *sam-abhi-â*, To approach, MBh. 1, 5328. **2.** To befall, MBh. 2, 2597.—With उपा *upa-â*, To approach, Kathâs. 5, 68.—With पर्या, To expire, MBh. 12, 8157.—With नि *ni*, To nestle, MBh. 6, 1886.—With निस् *nis*, To go out, Kathâs. 18, 83.—With परि *pari*, **1.** To move round, Râm. 2, 96, 45. **2.** To befall, MBh. 1, 3647. **3.** To mistake, to know not, Bhâg. P. 2, 6, 35. —With अनुपरि *anu-pari*, To walk over, MBh. 12, 8081.—With प्र *pra*, To proceed, MBh. 6, 2212.—With प्रति *prati*, To return, Bhâg. P. 4, 20, 37.—With सम् *sam*, To go to, Bhâg. P. 9, 24, 66.—Cf. βιβα, βιβάς, βιβάω, ἔβην (= *agâm*), perhaps Lat. navi-gare.

गाङ्ग *gâṅga*, i.e. *gaṅgâ + a*, I. adj., f. *gî*. **1.** Belonging to the Gaṅgâ, MBh. 7, 2215. II. n. The name of a kind of rain-water (ascribed to the celestial Gaṅgâ), Suçr. 1, 170, 2.

गाङ्गेय *gâṅgeya*, i.e. *gaṅgâ + eya*, I. adj. **1.** Belonging to the Gaṅgâ, MBh. 3, 165. **2.** Being near the Gaṅgâ, Râm. 6, 4, 2. II. m. metronym. A son of the Gaṅgâ, MBh. 1, 94.

गाढ *gâḍha*, see *gâh*.

गाढत्व *gâḍha + tva*, n. **1.** Depth. **2.** Intensity, Daçak. 102, 3.

गाणपत्य *gâṇapatya*, i.e. *gaṇa-pati + ya*, n. Dominion over the inferior deities, or the condition of Gaṇeça, MBh. 3, 4093.

गाण्डिव *gâṇḍiva*, or गाण्डीव *gâṇḍ-*

iva (cf. the next), m. and n. The bow of Arjuna, MBh. 3, 228; 1, 8177.

गाण्डीमय *gâṇḍî + maya*, adj. Made of gâṇḍî (a plant?), MBh. 5, 3540.

गाण्डीव *gâṇḍîva*, see *gâṇḍiva*.

गाण्डीविन् *gâṇḍîvin*, i. e. *gâṇḍîva + in*, m. A name of Arjuna, MBh. 13, 6898.

गातु *gâ + tu* (ved.), m. Motion, course (of life), Chr. 297, 16 = Rigv. i. 112, 16.

† **गात्र्** *GÂTR*, i. 10, Par. To loosen.

गात्र *gâ + tra*, n. **1.** A limb, Man. 2, 209. **2.** The body, Man. 4, 122.—Comp. *Româñchita-*, adj., f. *râ*, with horripilation of the body, Pañch. 128, 21. *Vara-*, adj., f. *râ*, having a beautiful body, Mṛichchh. 10, 21.—Cf. *βάθρον*, although of different signification.

गात्रक *gâtra + ka*, n. The body, Vikr. d. 79.

गात्ररुह *gâtra-ruha*, n. The hair of the body, Bhâg. P. 2, 3, 24.

गाथा *gâthâ*, i.e. *gai + tha*, f. A song, a verse, Indr. 2, 28; Man. 9, 42.

गाथिका *gâthikâ*, i.e. *gâthâ + ka*, f. A song, Yâjñ. 1, 45.

गाथिन् *gâthin*, i.e. *gâthâ + in*, m. **1.** A singer, MBh. 2, 1450. **2.** The father of Viçvâmitra (ved.).

गाध् *GÂDH*, i. 1, Âtm. **1.** To stand. **2.** † To desire. **3.** † To heap together.

गाध *gâdha*, i.e. *gâdh* (probably = *gâh*) + *a*, I. adj., f. *dhâ*, Shallow (properly, Wherein one may get a footing), Râm. 5, 94, 6. II. n. and m. Bottom, MBh. 7, 91; Râm. 5, 94, 12.—**Comp.** *A-*, adj., 1. bottomless, Râm. 5, 74, 17. 2. unfathomable, MBh. 5, 897. *Dus-*, adj., unfathomable, Suçr. 2, 302, 15.—Cf. Lat. vădum, vâdere.

गाधि *gâdhi* (for *gâdhin*, q. cf.) m. The father of Viçvâmitra, Râm. 1, 35, 3.

गाधिज *gâdhi-ja* (vb. *jan*) m. A name of Viçvâmitra, Man. 7, 42.

गाधिन् *gâdhin* (for ved. *gâthin*) m. The father of Viçvâmitra, Râm. 1, 20, 5.

गाधेय *gâdheya*, i. e. *gâdhi + eya*, patron., f. *yî*, Offspring of Gâdhi, Râm. 1, 52, 19; MBh. 13, 242.

गान *gâna*, i.e. *gai + na*, n. A song, Çiç. 9, 54.

गान्धर्व *gândharva*, i.e. *gandharva + a*, I. adj., f. *vî*. **1.** Referable or belonging to the Gandharvas, MBh. 7, 6348; Râm. 1, 29, 15. **2.** m. viz. *vivâha*, A form of marriage, that which requires only mutual agreement, Man. 3, 21. **3.** Musical, MBh. 3, 8421. **4.** Possessed by the Gandharvas, Suçr. 1, 332, 21. II. n. Music and dance, MBh. 13, 1427.—**Comp.** *Yuddha-* (vb. *yudh*), n. a battle like the dance of the Gandharvas, Râm. 6, 28, 26.

गान्धार *gândhâra*, i. e. I. *gândhâri + a*, **1.** m. A prince of the Gândhâris. **2.** f. *rî*, A princess of the Gândhâris, MBh. 1, 3790. II. m. pl. The name of a people, MBh. 6, 361. III. m. The third note of the scale, MBh. 4, 515.

गान्धारि *gândhâri*, **1.** m. pl. The name of a people, MBh. 8, 2135. **2.** i.e. *gândhârî + i*, metronym. The son of Gândhârî, MBh. 2, 1791.

गान्धिक *gândhika*, i. e. *gandha +*

ika, I. m. A vendor of perfumes, Sâh. D. 35, 11. II. n. Perfumes, Pañch. 7, 17.

ऽगामिक *-gâmika*, i.e. *gâmin+ka*, adj. Leading to, Râm. 6, 106, 7.

ऽगामिन् *-gâmin*, i.e. *gam+in*, adj., f. *nî*. **1.** Going, moving, Hit. Pr. 40; *haṁsa-vâraṇa-*, Walking like a phenicopteros, or like a young elephant, Man. 3, 10. **2.** Approaching carnally, Yâjń. 2, 234. **3.** Attaining, Râm. 5, 21, 19. **4.** Devolving on, Yâjń. 2, 145. **5.** Turning, directed to, Bhag. 8, 8. **6.** Referring to, MBh. 2, 26.—Comp. *Agra-*, adj. going at the head, Râm. 5, 41, 2. *Anta-*, adj. going to death. *Ṛitu-*, adj. approaching one's wife at the due time, Bhâg. P. 7, 12, 11. *Kubja-*, adj. going astray, Pañch. ii. d. 5.

गाम्भीर्य *gâmbhîrya*, i. e. *gambhîra+ya*, n. **1.** Depth, Râm. 1, 1, 18. **2.** Dignity, Ragh. 3, 32.

गाय *gâya*, i.e. *gai+a*, n. A song, Yâjń. 3, 112. In *uttama-*, adj. Bhâg. P. 3, 12, 21, and *uru-*, adj. 2, 3, 20, perhaps *gâ+a*, Walking, or praise.

गायक *gâyaka*, i.e. *gai+aka*, m. A singer, Râm. 2, 65, 2.

गायत्र *gâyatra*, i.e. *gai+atra*, I. m. and n. A song (ved.). II. f. *trî*. **1.** A certain metre, MBh. 6, 172. **2.** A sacred verse from the Vedas: this is usually personified and considered as a goddess, MBh. 3, 13432.

गायत्रिन् *gâyatrin*, i.e. *gâyatra+in*, m. A singer, MBh. 12, 10352.

गायन *gâyana*, i.e. *gai+ana*, I. m. A public singer, Man. 4, 210. II. n. A song, Bhâg. P. 7, 9, 43.

गारुड *gâruḍa* i.e. *garuḍa+a*, I. adj. **1.** Referable to Garuḍa, Râm. 6, 86, 3. **2.** Having the form of Garuḍa, Râm. 6, 6, 11. II. n. An emerald, Ragh. 13, 53.

गारुत्मत *gârutmata*, i.e. *garutmant+a*, adj. Referable to Garuḍa, Ragh. 16, 77.

गार्ग्य *gârgya*, i.e. *garga+ya*, **1.** patronym., f. *gî*, Offspring of Garga, Râm. 2, 32, 28; Hariv. 10243 (a surname of Durgâ). **2.** The name of a tribe, MBh. 7, 396.

गार्त्समद *gârtsamada*, i.e. *gṛitsamada+a*, adj. Referring to Gṛitsamada, MBh. 13, 2006.

गार्दभ *gârdabha*, i.e. *gardabha+a*, adj. Referring, or belonging to, or proceeding from, an ass, MBh. 8, 2051.

गार्द्धपत्र *gârddhapatra*, see the next.

गार्धपत्र *gârdhapatra* (read **गार्ध्रपत्र** *gârdhrapatra*, i.e. *gṛidhra-patra+a*), m. An arrow, MBh. 4, 1331.

गार्धराजित *gârdharâjita* (read **गार्ध्रवाजित** *gârdhravâjita*, i.e. *gṛidhra-vâja+ita*, cf. *gṛidhravâjita*), m. An arrow, MBh. 3, 12230.

गार्धवासस् *gârdhavâsas* (read **गार्ध्रवासस्** *gârdhravâsas*, i. e. *gṛidhra+a-vâsas*), m. An arrow, MBh. 3, 1350.

गार्भ *gârbha*, i.e. *garbha+a*, adj. **1.** Born of a womb, Bhâg. P. 3, 7, 27. **2.** Referring to pregnancy, Man. 2, 27.

गार्भिक *gârbhika*, i.e. *garbha+ika*, adj. Referable to the womb, Man. 2, 27.

गार्हपत्य *gârhapatya*, i.e. *gṛiha-pati+ya*, I. adj. and m. (viz. *agni*), A sacred fire perpetually maintained by a householder, Man. 2, 132. II. m. pl. The name of a class of Pitṛis or Manes, MBh. 2, 462.

गार्हमेध *gârhamedha*, i.e. *gṛiha*

-medha + a, adj. Befitting a householder, Bhâg. P. 5, 11, 2.

गार्हस्थ्य *gârhasthya*, i.e. *griha-stha + ya*, I. adj. Befitting the householder, MBh. 9, 2854. II. n. 1. Condition of a householder, Râm. 2, 106, 21. 2. Household, MBh. 14, 162. 3. Abode, Bhâg. P. 3, 33, 15.

गालव *gâlava*, m. The name of a saint, MBh. 1, 331.

गालवि *gâlavi*, i.e. *gâlava + i*, patronym., m. A son of Gâlava, MBh. 9, 2995.

गालि *gâli*, i.e, *gal + i*, f. An execration, Bhartṛ. 3, 99.

गालिमन्त् *gâli + mant*, adj. Using execrations, Bhartṛ. 3, 99.

गालोडय *GÂLOḌAYA*, a denomin. (akin to the Caus. of *gal*), Âtm. To examine.

गाह् *GÂH* (akin to *gabh* in *gabhîra* and *gâdh* in *gâdha*), i. 1, Âtm. (in epic poetry also Par., MBh. 13, 3795). With acc. and loc. 1. To dive into, Râm. 3, 76, 33. 2. To enter, Râm. 2, 52, 95.—Ptcple. of the pf. pass. I. *gâhita*, with the sense of the act., MBh. 3, 8772. II. *gâḍha*, 1. Used for bathing in, Ragh. 9, 72. 2. Accessible, open, Bhâg. P. 4, 29, 40. 3. Fast, tight, Râm. 4, 15, 20. 4. Vehement, Amar. 36; Megh. 81. *ḍham*, adv. 1. Strongly, fast, Mârk. P. 16, 25; Râm. 2, 31, 2. 2. Vehemently, Râm. 1, 9, 47. 3. Heavily, Chr. 35, 7. 4. Much, Râm. 2, 57, 3.—Comp. *Dus-gâḍha*, unfathomable, Hariv. 17484.—With the prep. **अव** *ava* (sometimes *va* without its initial), 1. To dive into, Râm. 1, 2, 8. 2. To bathe, MBh. 3, 8649. 3. To betake one's self, Vikr. 62, 15. *avagâhita* and *avagâḍha*, Used for bathing in, MBh. 3, 8230; 8236. *avagâḍha*, 1. Immersed, Râm. 2, 59, 28. 2. Deeply impressed, Çâk. d. 56. 3. Vanished, MBh. 4, 2238. 4. Stagnating, Suçr. 1, 353, 3.—Caus. 1. To let bathe, Suçr. 2, 192, 11. 2. To bathe, Suçr. 2, 550, 11. —With **व्यव** *vi-ava*, 1. To dive, MBh. 1, 7285. 2. To break in, MBh. 4, 1984. 3. To sink down, to begin (as nightfall), MBh. 3, 16820.—With **उद्** *ud* in *udgâḍha*, Excessive, Prab. 67, 9.—With **उप** *upa*, To break in, Râm. 6, 31, 29.—With **संप्र** *sam-pra*, To dive into, MBh. 14, 1392.—With **वि** *vi*, 1. To dive into, Râm. 2, 48, 8. 2. To enter, Ragh. 14, 30. 3. To betake one's self to, MBh. 3, 11343. 4. To fall (as night; see *vi-ava*), MBh. 5, 7246. *vigâḍha*, 1. Bathed, Râm. 5, 7, 39. 2. Used for bathing, Râm. 5, 74, 31. 3. Having penetrated, MBh. 4, 2072. 4. Fallen (as night; see *vi-ava*), MBh. 3, 1821. 5. Having taken place, MBh. 5, 2776. 6. Much, exceeding. — Comp. ptcple. of the fut. pass., *durvigâhya*, i.e. *dus-*, adj. 1. Difficult to be sounded, MBh. 13, 1840. 2. Difficult to be passed, Hariv. 13670. 3. Difficult to be accomplished, Râm. 5, 51, 23.—With **प्रवि** *pra-vi*, To enter, Ram. 6, 16, 2.—Cf. βυθός, βῆσσα for βηθ-ια, βένθος.

गाहन *gâh + ana*, n. Bathing, Daçak. 145, 14.

गिर् *gir* (vb. 1. *gṛî*), f. 1. Voice, Yâjń. 1, 71. 2. Speech, Nal. 1, 26 (25). 3. A word, Nal. 11, 6.

ऽगिर *-gira*, A substitute for *giri*, when latter part of a comp. adv., e.g. *anu-gira + m*, Along the mountain, Ragh. 13, 49.

गिरय *GIRAYA*, a denomin. derived from *gir*, or perhaps an anomalous Caus. of 1. *gṛî*, Par.—With the prep. उद् *ud*, To utter, Pañch. 221, 13.

गिरि *giri* (for original *gara*; cf. Slav. gora, ὄρος, probably from *gur* for *gar*), m. **1.** A mountain, Râm. 1, 2, 29. **2.** A name of the numeral eight, Çrutab. 38.—**Comp.** *Antar-*, m. land lying in the midst of mountains, MBh. 2, 1012. *Asta-*, m. the mountain behind which the sun is supposed to set, Çiç. 9, 1. *Kâñchana-*, m. a name of Meru, Bhâg. P. 5, 16, 28. *Kula-*, m. a principal mountain, Bhâg. P. 5, 16, 7. *Tushâra-*, m. the Himâlaya, MBh. 13, 836. *Deva-*, *dhûmra-*, *râma-*, m. names of mountains. *Vahirgiri*, i.e. *vahis-*, m. land lying beyond a mountain, MBh. 2, 1012. *Svar-* and *svargi(n)-*, m. the mountain Sumeru.

गिरिचर *giri-chara*, adj. Living in mountains, wild, Çâk. d. 37.

गिरिज *giri-ja* (vb. *jan*), **I.** adj. Produced in mountains. **II.** f. *jâ*, A name of Çiva's wife Umâ, Bhâg. P. 1, 15, 12.

गिरित्र *giri-tra* (vb. *trâ*), m. A name of Çiva, Bhâg. P. 2, 1, 35.

गिरिव्रज *girivraja*, m. The name of the capital of Magadha, Râm. 1, 34, 7.

गिरिश *giri-ça* (vb. *çî*), m. A name of Çiva, MBh. 3, 1622.

गिरिसारमय *giri-sâra+maya*, adj. f. *yî*, Of iron, Râm. 6, 78, 19.

गीतक *gîta+ka* (vb. *gai*), n. A song, Yâjñ. 3, 113.

गीति *gîti*, i.e. *gai+ti*, f. Song, singing, Çâk. 59, 11.

गीतिका *gîti+kâ*, f. A little song, MBh. 3, 8173.

गीर्वाण *gîrvâṇa* (probably from ved. *gîrvan* for *gîrvant*, i.e. *gir+vant*), m. Deity, Bhâg. P. 3, 16, 32.

1. गु *GU*, i. 1, Âtm. To sound.—Cf. γοᾶν, Goth. gaunôn.

† 2. गु *GU* (v.r. *GÛ*), i. 6, Par. To void excrement.

3. ऽगु *-gu* (vb. *gam*), Going.—Cf. *adhrigu*.

4. ऽगु *-gu*, a substitute for *go* when latter part of comp. adj., e.g. *çata-*, adj. Possessing a hundred cows, Man. 11, 14.

गुग्गुलु *guggulu*, m. and n. A fragrant gum resin, Bdellium, MBh. 13, 3736.

गुच्छ *guchchha*, m. **1.** A shrub, Man. 1, 48. **2.** A cluster of blossoms, Gît. 11, 11.—**Comp.** *Romaguchchha*, i.e. *roman-*, n. a sort of whisk.

गुच्छक *guchchha+ka*, m. A cluster of blossoms, Mâlav. 38, 2.

† गुज् *GUJ*, i. 6, Par. To buzz.—Cf. the next.

गुञ्ज् *GUÑJ*, i. 1, Par. To buzz, Ṛit. 6, 14. *guñjita*, n. Buzzing.—Cf. γογγύζω (Frequentat.).

गुञ्जा *guñjâ*, f. A small shrub, Abrus precatorius, Lin., bearing a berry which forms the smallest of the jeweller's weights, Pañch. 93, 3.

गुटिका *guṭikâ*, f. **1.** A ball, Mṛichchh. 79, 2. **2.** A pearl, Ragh. 5, 70.

† गुड् *GUḌ*, i. 6, Par. To defend.

गुड *guḍa*, m. **1.** A ball, MBh. 7, 9212. **2.** Molasses, Man. 8, 326.—**Comp.** *Ayoguḍa*, i.e. *ayas-*, m. an iron ball, Man. 3, 133—Cf. *gola*.

गुडक *guḍa + ka*, m. A ball, MBh. 3, 643.

गुडाकेश *guḍâkeça*, i.e. *gūḍa-keça*, with lengthened final of the first part, m. A surname of Arjuna, MBh. 3, 1905.

गुण् *GUṆ*, i. 10, *guṇaya* (rather a denomin. derived from the next), Par. **1.** To multiply. *guṇita*, Multiplied, MBh. 3, 7030; Megh. 109. **Comp.** *Dvi-*, adj. double, Kir. 5, 46. **2.** † To invite.

गुण *guṇa* (for *gush + na*, from *gush* in ved. *gush-p*; cf. *push* and *push-p*), m. **1.** A string, Ragh. 2, 83. **2.** A bow-string, Râm. 3, 33, 16. **3.** A lute-string, Çiç. 4, 57. **4.** Time; *daça guṇâs*, Ten times, Man. 2, 85; in this signification it is almost always the latter part of a comp. adj. and preceded by numerals, e.g. *ashṭaguṇa*, i.e. *ashṭan-*, Eight-fold, Man. 8, 400. *dvi-*, **a.** Two-fold, double, Châṇ. 78. **b.** Twice as many, MBh. 3, 14316. **c.** Folded, Yâjñ. 1, 232. With an abl., As many times more as are denoted by the numeral, e.g. *mûlyât pañchaguṇa*, i.e. *pañchan-*, Five times the value, Man. 8, 289; *tvattaḥ çataguṇo bale*, A hundred times stronger than thou, Râm. 6, 95, 11; also comparat., e.g. *dviguṇatara*, Doubled, Pañch. 57, 15. **5.** Species, MBh. 12, 6847. **6.** A subordinate element. **7.** An accompanying dish, Man. 3, 226. **8.** Quality of a subject, Man. 3, 36; 1, 76–78. **9.** The three fundamental qualities: *sattva*, *rajas*, and *tamas*, Man. 12, 24. **10.** A good quality, virtue, Man. 9, 141; excellence, Ragh. 3, 30; gain, Pañch. ii. d. 21. **11.** Excess, MBh. 3, 14746. **12.** One of the six expedients in government, Man. 7, 160. — **Comp.** *A-*, m. a bad property, Man. 3, 22. *Ati-*, adj. extraordinary, Râm. 4, 41, 79. *Dhanus-*, a bow-string, Ṛit. 6, 1 (read *-mâlam* and *-guṇam*). *Tathâ-*, adj. having such qualities, Râm. 2, 22, 19. *Tri-*, I. m. pl. the three principal qualities, Bhâg. P. 4, 24, 28. II. adj. 1. consisting of three strings, Kumâras. 5, 10. 2. three times as many, Man. 5, 137. *Nis-*, adj., f. *ṇâ*, 1. without a string, Mṛichchh. 131 17. 2. without qualities, MBh. 1, 2432. 3. devoid of virtue, Râm. 2, 33, 11. *Muktâ-*, m. a string of pearls, Megh. 47. *Vi-*, adj. 1. void of all qualities. 2. void of distinguishing qualities, Çiç. 9, 12. 3. worthless, bad. 4. imperfect, Man. 10, 97 (imperfectly performed). *Viveka-vi-*, adj. contrary to reason, unreasonable, Râjat. 5, 352. *Viçesha-*, m. a special quality, Bhâshâp. 26, 89; 90. *Çruti-vishaya-*, adj. having as its special property that which is the object of hearing, i.e. sound, epithet of the ether, Çâk. d. 1. *Sa-*, adj. endowed with qualities, Vedântas. in Chr. 202, 18.

गुणज्ञ *guṇa-jña* (vb. *jñâ*), m. A friend of virtue, Bhartṛ. 2, 33.

गुणतस् *guṇa-tas*, adv. **1.** Concerning good qualities, Man. 11, 185. **2.** Conformably to the three fundamental qualities (see *guṇa* **9**), Bhag. 18, 29.

गुणता *guṇa + tâ*, f. **1.** Being subordinate, Bhâg. P. 3, 26, 39 (see *guṇa* **6**). **2.** Excellence, MBh. 3, 11236.

गुणत्व *guṇa + tva*, n. **1.** The state of being a string, Hit. i. d. 30. **2.** Excellence, Suçr. 1, 184, 10.

गुणन *guṇ + ana*, n. Exalting, Gît. 7, 29.

गुणमय *guṇa + maya*, adj., f. *yî*. **1.** Consisting of virtues, MBh. 1, 6546. **2.** Referable to the three fundamental qualities, MBh. 14, 1327.

गुणवत्ता *guṇavattâ*, i.e. *guṇavant*

+ *tâ*, f. Possession of virtues, MBh. 14, 86.

गुणवन्त् *guṇa+vant*, adj., f. *vatî*. **1.** Possessing good qualities, Râm. 3, 11, 16. **2.** Excellent, Nal. 1, 30. Compar. *vattara*, More excellent, Man. 5, 113. Superl. Most distinguished, Yâjń. 2, 78.—Comp. *A-*, adj. bad, Bhartṛ. 2, 97.

गुणिता *guṇitâ*, i. e. *guṇin+tâ*, f. Possession of virtues, Hit. Pr. 36.

गुणिन् *guṇin*, i.e. *guṇa+in*, adj., f. *nî*. **1.** Possessing qualities or attributes, i.e. being a subject, Bhâg. P. 2, 8, 14. **2.** Possessing good qualities, virtuous, Man. 8, 73. **3.** Knowing the qualities, Mârk. P. 27, 9.—Comp. *Su-*, adj. virtuous, Bhartṛ. 2, 54.

गुण्ठ् *GUṆṬH*, i. 10, Par. **1.** To cover, MBh. 7, 2734. **2.** To ensnare, 6, 819.—With the prep. **अव** *ava*, To cover, Man. 4, 49.

गुण्ठन *guṇṭh+ana*, n. Covering, Prab. 30, 17 (v.r.)

† **गुण्ड्** *GUṆḌ*, i. 10, Par. **1.** To cover. **2.** To pound. **3.** To preserve.

गुण्डन *guṇḍ+ana*, n.=*guṇṭhana*, Prab. 30, 17.

† **गुद्** *GUD*, i. 1. Âtm. To play.

गुद *guda*, m. and n. The anus, Man. 8, 283.

† **गुध्** *GUDH*, i. 4, Par. To cover. ii. 9, Par. To be angry. i. 1, Âtm. To play (v.r.)

† **गुन्द्र्** *GUNDR*, i. 10, Par. To lie, to speak falsely.

1. **गुप्** *GUP*, Par. Base of the present, etc., *gopâya* (*gopa*, Gît. 6, 12), Par.; and *gopaya*, Par. Âtm. (old Causals of *guh*; cf. *ruh*). **1.** To guard, to protect, *gopâyati*, MBh. 6, 472; *gopayasva*, 5, 350; *jugopa*, 6, 3897. **2.** To keep in memory, Gît. 6, 12 (*gopatas*, ptcple. of the pres.). **3.** To conceal, Râjat. 5, 222; Pańch. ii. d. 106. **4.** † *gopaya*, To speak.—Ptcple. of the pf. pass., *gopita* and *gupta*, Guarded, MBh. 1, 5090; Man. 7, 76. *gupta* +*m*. adv. Privately, Kathâs. 5, 40.—Comp. *Deva-*, m. a proper name, Râjat. 5, 436. *Nâbhi-*, the name of a division of the world, Bhâg. P. 5, 20, 15. *Parva*(*n*)- and *Vishṇu-*, m. proper names. *Su-gupta*, adj. well concealed, Lass. 15, 3. °*tam*, adv. privily, Pańch. 231, 17.—Ptcple. of the fut. pass. **1.** *goptavya* and *gopya*, To be guarded, MBh. 12, 3449; 12, 1481. **2.** *gopya*, To be concealed, Pańch. i. d. 113. **3.** *gopanîya*, To be prevented, MBh. 12, 5399.—Caus. *gopâyaya*, To guard, MBh. 3, 10835.—Desider. *jugupsa*, Âtm. (in epic poetry also Par. Râm. 2, 69, 20). **1.** To disdain, Man. 6, 58. **2.** To be offended, MBh. 1, 6375.—Ptcple. of the pf. pass., *jugupsita*, **1.** Abominated, MBh. 3, 1288. **2.** Contemned, Man. 4, 209. n. 1. An abominable act, Bhâg. P. 1, 5, 15. 2. Abominableness, 1, 7, 42. — Comp. *A-jugupsita*, being reverenced, Man. 3, 209. —With the prep. **अनु** *anu*, *anugupta*, Guarded, MBh. 3, 8436. *tam*, adv. Privately, MBh. 3, 251.—With **अभि** *abhi*, *abhigupta*, Protected, MBh. 1, 7989. —With **उप** *upa*, *upagupta*, Concealed, Bhâg. P. 4, 16, 10. — With **परि** *pari*, *gopâya*, To guard, Bhâg. P. 5, 2, 1.—Desider. To be on one's guard (with abl.), MBh. 12, 3136.—With **प्र** *pra*, *gopaya*, To guard, Pańch. i. d. 348.—With **सम्** *sam*, *saṁgupta*, **1.** Protected, MBh. 13, 248.

2. Concealed, MBh. 13, 514. **Comp.** *Su-*, adj. well guarded, MBh. 5, 900.—With अभिसम् *abhi-sam*, *abhisaṁ-gupta*, Guarded, MBh. 3, 274.

2. गुप् *GUP*, i. 4, Par. To be confused or disturbed.

ऽगुप् *-gup*, adj. Guarding, MBh. 13, 7000.

गुप्ति *gup+ti*, f. **1.** Guarding, protecting, Râm. 2, 51, 3. **2.** Defences, Râm. 6, 12, 16. **3.** Concealing.—**Comp.** *Ratha-*, f. an apparatus encompassing a war-chariot, to secure it from being injured by weapons or collision. *Su-*, f. secrecy, Hit. iv. d. 51 (closeness).

गुफ् *GUPH* and गुम्फ् *GUMPH* (from ved. *gushp*; cf. *guṇa*), i. 6, Par. To string together. *guphita*, Tied, clinging, Lass. 66, 9.

गुर् *GUR*, i. 6, Âtm. (also Par. Man. 4, 169), and i. 10, *goraya*, Âtm.; also गूर् *GÛR*, i. 10, Âtm. To make an effort.—With the prep. अव *ava*, To assault, Man. 4, 169.—With उद् *ud*, ptcple. of the pf. pass., *udgûrṇa*, Raised, Yâjñ. 2, 215.

गुरु *gur+u* (for original, *gar-u*; cf. compar. *gar+îyaṁs*, βαρύ), I. adj., f. *gurvî*, **1.** Heavy, MBh. 3, 885. **2.** Great, Bhartṛ. 2, 50; large, Pañch. 51, 8. **3.** Violent, Vikr. d. 6. **4.** Weighty, Brâhmaṇ. 2, 6; important, Man. 9, 52. **5.** Dear, MBh. 1, 2749. **6.** Venerable, Man. 2, 133. **II.** m. and f. A father or mother, a husband, or any venerable male or female relation, Râm. 1, 22, 20; Sâv. 4, 22; Sund. 4, 15. **III.** m. **1.** A spiritual teacher, Man. 2, 142. **2.** An object of veneration Böhtl. Ind. Spr. 868. Compar. **1.** *gurutara*, Heavier, MBh. 3, 13292; fem. *tarâ*, MBh. 1, 3267 (*tarî*, Indr. 5, 41, is to be changed to *tarâ*, according to the Calc. ed. 3, 1857). **2.** *garîyaṁs*, Very heavy, Râm. 6, 82, 43. **3.** Preferable, Böhtl. Ind. Spr. 910. Superl. *gurutama*, *garishṭha*.—**Comp.** *Ati-*, adj. exceedingly heavy, Ṛit. 6, 31. Compar. *atigarîyaṁs*, too dear, Daçak. in Chr. 188, 2. *Indra-*, m. Indra's teacher, Çâk. 101, 11. *Gaurî-*, m. a name of the Himâlaya, Çâk. d. 144. *Jagat-*, m. a name of Brahman, Vishṇu, Çiva, Râma, Râm. 3, 6, 18. *Sura-*, m. Bṛihaspati, the teacher of the gods.—Cf. βαρύς, etc. ἐπι-ζαρέω; Lat. gravis; Goth. kaurs, kauritha; A.S. caru, Engl. care.

गुरुक *guru+ka*, adj. A little heavy, MBh. 3, 11477.

गुरुतल्पग *guru-talpa-ga*, m. A violator of the bed of his guru, i.e. his father or teacher, Man. 9, 63.

गुरुतल्पिन् *gurutalpin*, i.e. *guru-talpa+in*, m. A violator of the bed of his guru, i.e. his father or teacher, Man. 11, 103.

गुरुता *guru+tâ*, f. **1.** Heaviness, Çâk. d. 35. **2.** Molestation, Râm. 2, 27, 22. **3.** Importance, Çiç. 9, 22. **4.** The condition of a teacher, Kathâs. 19, 75.

गुरुत्व *guru+tva*, n. **1.** Heaviness, Pañch. 247, 13. **2.** Dignity, Ragh. 10, 65. **3.** The condition of a teacher, Chr. 22, 21.

गुरुत्वक *gurutva+ka*, n. Heaviness, Bhâshâp. 4.

गुरुलघुता *guru-laghu+tâ*, f. The condition of being wealthy or poor, Bhartṛ. 2, 37.

गुरुवत् *guru+vat*, adv. Like a preceptor, Man. 2, 208.

गुर्जर *gurjara*, m. The name of a country, Guzarat, Pañch. 229, 2.

† गुर्द् *GURD*, or गूर्द् *GÛRD*, i. 1, *gûrda*, Âtm. To play.

† गुर्व् *GURV*, i. 1, *gûrva*, Par. To endeavour.—Cf. *gur*.

गुर्विणी *gurviṇî* (a dialect. fem. of *guru*), f. A pregnant woman, MBh. 14, 1843.

गुल्फ *gulpha*, m. The ancle, Râm. 6, 23, 12.—Comp. *Uchcha-*, adj., f. *phâ*, having high ancles, MBh. 4, 253.

गुल्म *gulma*, m. and n. 1. A shrub, MBh. 13, 2992. 2. A body of troops, consisting of 9 elephants, 9 chariots, 27 horses, and 45 foot, Man. 9, 266. 3. A morbose swelling in the belly, Kathâs. 15, 14.—Comp. *Nis-*, adj., f. *mâ*, free from bushes, MBh. 1, 5320. *Vâta-*, m. 1. a gale. 2. acute gout. *Vâyu-*, m. a whirlpool.

गुह् *GUH*, i. 1, *gûha*, Par. and Âtm. 1. To conceal, Man. 7, 105; ptcple. of the pf. pass., *gûḍha*, 1. Secret, Man. 7, 186. 2. Disguised, Man. 9, 261. *ḍham*, adv. Privately, Daçak. in Chr. 191, 13. *ḍhe*, loc. adv. Secretly, Man. 9, 170.—Comp. *Mantra-*, m. a spy. *Sa-gûḍha + m*, adv. secretly, privily, Daçak. in Chr. 201, 6.—Ptcple. of the fut. pass., *guhya*, 1. To be concealed, Man. 11, 265. 2. Hidden, MBh. 3, 173. 3. Mysterious, Bhag. 18, 63. *yam*, adv. Solitarily, MBh. 12, 902. n. 1. A secret, MBh. 13, 5876; a mystery, Man. 12, 117. 2. Pudendum, Suçr. 1, 116, 7.—Comp. *Deva-guhya*, n. a mystery known only to the gods, Râm. 5, 27, 33.—With the prep. अप *apa*, 1. To cover, MBh. 5, 7246. 2. To embrace, Pañch. iii. d. 191.—With उप *upa*, To embrace; *upagûḍha*, n. An embrace, Megh. 95.—With समुप *sam-upa*, To embrace, Chaurap. 6.—With नि *ni*, 1. To cover, Bhâg. P. 4, 25, 24. 2. To conceal, Pañch. 36, 20. *nigûḍha + tara*, Well-concealed, Pañch. 46, 7. *nigûḍha + m*, adv. Privately, Kathâs. 5, 65.—With विनि *vi-ni*, To conceal, Râm. 5, 20, 6.—With वि *vi*, *vigûḍha*, 1. Concealed, Man. 9, 260. 2. Scarcely perceivable, Bhâg. P. 5, 5, 31. 3. Blamed.—Cf. *kuhaka*.

गुह *guh + a*, m. 1. A name of Skanda, the god of war, MBh. 13, 4093. 2. A name of Çiva, MBh. 13, 1263. 3. pl. The name of a people, MBh. 12, 7559.

गुहा *guh + â*, f. 1. A cave, Râm. 1, 6, 20. 2. The heart, Bhâg. P. 2, 9, 24; cf. Çvet. Up. 3, 20.

गुह्यक *guhya + ka* (vb. *guh*), m. A class of demigods attendant upon Kuvera, Man. 12, 47.

गुह्यमय *guhya + maya*, adj. in *sarva-*, Comprehending all mysteries, MBh. 1, 5431.

गू *GÛ*, see 2. *gu*.

गूढत्व *gûḍha + tva* (vb. *guh*), n. Secretness, MBh. 1, 82.

† गूर् *GÛR*, i. 4, Âtm. To injure.—Cf. *gur*.

गूर्द् *GÛRD*, see *gurd*.

गूहन *gûhana*, i. e. *guh + ana*, n. Concealment, MBh. 11, 820.

गृ *GṚI*, i. 1, Par. To sprinkle.

† गृज् *GṚIJ*, and गृञ्ज् *GṚIÑJ*, i. 1, Par. To roar.—Cf. *garj*.

गृञ्जन *gṛiñj + ana*, and गृञ्जनक *gṛiñjana + ka*, m. Garlic, Man. 5, 5.

गृत्समद *gṛitsa-mada* (the first part is a vedic word), m. The name of a Ṛishi, MBh. 13, 1314.

गृद्धिन् *griddhin,* i. e. *griddha + in* (vb. *gridh*), adj. **1.** Greedy, MBh. 1, 2948. **2.** Loving, MBh. 13, 1876.

गृध् *GRIDH,* i. 4, *gridhya,* Par. To be greedy, Bhâg. P. 3, 3, 4 ; with loc., MBh. 3, 225 ; with acc., MBh. 4, 276. *griddha,* Greedy, MBh. 5, 811.—With the prep. **अनु** *anu,* To be greedy for (with loc.), MBh. 12, 372.—With **प्रति** *prati,* To be greedy for, (with acc.), MBh. 14, 847.—Cf. ἀγρήθετο; probably Goth. gredon, to hunger ; gredus, gredags ; λιμός ; see *gridhra.*

गृध्न *gridh + na,* MBh. 13, 5640, Greedy, is probably to be changed to *gridhnu.*

गृध्निनी *gridhninî,* Râm. 2, 79, 12, is to be changed to *griddhinî.*

गृध्नु *gridh + nu,* adj. Greedy, Megh. 9.—**Comp.** *A-,* adj. liberal, Ragh. 1, 21.

गृध्या *gridh + yâ,* f. Greediness, MBh. 13, 5590.

गृध्र *gridh + ra,* **I.** adj. Greedy, Pañch. i. d. 203. **II.** m. A vulture, Râm. 3, 20, 19. **III.** f. *rî,* A female vulture, Yâjñ. 3, 256.—Cf. Lat. vultur.

गृध्रवाजित *gridhravâjita,* i.e. *gridhravâja + ita,* m. An arrow, MBh. 14, 2454.

गृध्राण *gridhrâṇa* (akin to *gridhra*), adj. Full of desires, Bhâg. P. 5, 17, 13.

गृष्टि *grishṭi,* f. A cow that has had one calf, MBh. 13, 4919.

गृष्ट्या *grishṭyâ* (cf. the last), adj. f. (A cow) that has had but one calf, MBh. 13, 4427.

गृह् *GRIH,* see *grah.*

ऽगृह् *-grih* (vb. *grah*), adj. Seizing, Çiç. 9, 55.

गृह *griha,* i.e. *grah + a,* **1.** m. (sing. and pl. and) n. A house, Man. 9, 89 ; 4, 250 ; 4, 202. **2.** m. pl. Family, Bhâg. P. 3, 2, 7. **3.** (m. pl. and) n. A wife, Pañch. iii. d. 152.—**Comp.** When latter part of a comp. adj., the fem. ends in *hâ* or *hî,* e.g. *A-vi-chhinna-antara-griha,* adj., f. *hâ,* of which the houses are not separated by an intermediate space, Râm. 1, 5, 9. *Su-griha,* adj., f. *hî,* having a beautiful abode, Pañch. i. d. 435. *Antar-,* n. the inner apartments of a house, Râm. 2, 4, 3. *Kârâ-,* n. a prison, Bhartr. 3, 21. *Kula-,* n. a respectable house, Rit. 6, 21. *Koça-,* n. a treasury, Râm. 2, 39, 16. *Kriḍâ-,* n. a house for amusement, Râm. 3, 39, 16. *Garbha-,* n. 1. the inner apartments of a house, Daçak. in Chr. 201, 14. 2. the sanctuary of a temple, Kathâs. 7, 8. *Chitra-,* m. a picture-gallery (?), Râm. 5, 14, 65. *Chhatra-,* n. an apartment for guarding the royal parasol, MBh. 5, 3544. *Jatu-,* n. a house painted and filled with lac and other combustible substances, MBh. 1, 313. *Deva-,* n. a temple, Râm. 5, 49, 16. *Devî-,* n. 1. a temple of Durgâ. 2. the apartment of a queen, Kâm. Nîtis. 7, 50. *Devî-garbha-,* n. a temple of Durgâ, Kathâs. 3, 39. *Dhârâ-* and *Yantra-dhârâ-,* n. a bathing room with flowing water, Bhartr. 1, 38 ; Megh. 62. *Niçâ-,* n. a sleeping room, Râm. 5, 14, 65. *Bhoga-,* n. the inner apartment, the harem. *Yantra-,* n. 1. an oil-mill. 2. a manufactory. *Latâ-,* n. an arbour, Kir. 5, 5. *Vastra-,* n. a tent. *Vâsa-,* n. a sleeping room. *Çânti-,* n. a private apartment near the place of a sacrifice. *Çiras-,* n. a room on the top of a house.

गृहक *griha + ka* in *sâra-bhâṇḍa-,* n. A store-house, Mâlav. 44, 1.

गृहगोधिका *grihagodhikâ,* i.e. *gri-*

ha-godhâ + ka, f. A small lizard, Suçr. 2, 252, 12.

गृहगोलक *gṛihagolaka*, m. A small lizard, Mârk. P. 15, 24.—Cf. the last.

गृहज *gṛiha-ja*, adj. Born in the house, Man. 8, 415.

गृहपालाय *GṚIHAPALÂYA*, a denomin. derived from *gṛiha-pâla* by *ya*, Âtm. To resemble a house-dog, Bhâg. P. 7, 15, 18.

गृहबलिभुज् *gṛiha-bali-bhuj*, m. A sparrow; according to others, The Ardea nivea, and A crow.

गृहमेधिन् *gṛihamedhin*, i.e. *gṛiha -medha + in*, I. m. A householder, or a Brâhmaṇa who, after having finished his studies, performs the duties of the father of a family, Man. 3, 69. II. f. *nî*, The wife of such a householder, Bhâg. P. 4, 26, 13.

गृहवन्त् *gṛiha + vant*, adj., f. *vatî*, Possessing a house, Pańch. ii. d. 15.

गृहसंवेशक *gṛihasaṁveçaka*, i. e. *gṛiha-sam-viç + aka*, m. One who builds houses for gain, Man. 3, 163.

गृहस्थ *gṛiha-stha*, I. adj. Being in a house, Arj. 2, 16. II. m. A householder, or a Brâhmaṇa, who performs the duties of the father of a family, Man. 3, 68. III. f. *sthâ*, The wife of such a householder, Lass. 17, 19.

गृहिन् *gṛihin*, i.e. *gṛiha + in*. I. m. A householder (see the last), Man. 2, 232. II. f. *iṇî*, The wife of a householder, Pańch. iii. d. 152.

गृहेज्ञानिन् *gṛihejńânin*, i.e. *gṛiha + i-jńâna + in*, adj. Foolish, MBh. 13, 4576.

गृहेरुह *gṛiheruha*, i.e. *gṛiha + i-ruha*, adj. Growing in the house, MBh. 13, 6070.

गृह्य *gṛihya*, i.e. *gṛiha + ya*, I. adj., f. *yâ*, Domestic, Man. 3, 84. II. m. A dependent, a servant, Daçak. in Chr. 191, 20.

1. गॄ *GṚÎ*, ii. 9, *gṛiṇâ*, *gṛiṇî*, Par. (also Âtm.); i. 6, Âtm. see under *sam-*. 1. To call, MBh. 7, 1754. 2. To expose, Bhâg. P. 1, 4, 9. 3. To praise, Chr. 287, 4 = Rigv. i. 48, 4; Chr. 291, 12 = Rigv. i. 64, 12 (*gṛiṇîmasi*, ved. for °*mas*).—With the prep. अनु *anu*, To repeat, Bhâg. P. 7, 9, 18.—With अभि *abhi*, 1. To praise, Bhâg. P. 3, 21, 12. 2. To approve, Chr. 288, 14 = Rigv. i. 48, 14.—With प्र *pra*, To praise, Bhâg. P. 1, 5, 10.—With सम् *sam*, 1. To praise, Bhâg. P. 3, 14, 45. 2. i. 6, *gira*, Âtm. (Daçak. in Chr. 190, 24, Par., *sam agirat* is probably to be changed to *agirata*), To agree with (with instr.), Chr. 191, 9; 190, 24 (*âçayena*, She has taken a resolution).—Cf. Lat. garrire and gannire, both for garnire = Sskr. *gṛiṇâ*, for original *garṇâ*; ἀγ-γέλλω for ἀνα-γέλνω, γῆρυς; O.H.G. queran, to moan, and kerran, garrire, challôn; O.N. kalla.

2. गॄ *GṚÎ*, i. 6, *gira* and *gila*, Par. (in epic poetry also Âtm., MBh. 5, 1760). 1. To devour, MBh. 5, 1760; 2, 2193. 2. To eject, MBh. 12, 12872. Ptcple. of the pf. pass. *gîrṇa gilita*, Devoured, Bhâg. P. 9, 10, 13 (Vetâlapańchav. MS.).—With the prep. उद् *ud*, To vomit, to eject, Râm. 4, 48, 22; MBh. 1, 712. *udgîrṇa*, Caused, Gît. 1, 36.—With उप *upa*, To gulp down, Suçr. 2, 237, 8.—With नि *ni*, To swallow up, MBh. 1, 8238.—With निस् *nis*, To vomit, Râm. 3, 35, 62.—Cf. γάρον, γαργαρεών, derived from a frequent. γαργαρίζω, βιβρώσκω, βρῶμα, βορά, etc.; Lat. gurgulio, vorare (cf. *gargara* and

gala); O.H.G. giri, adj. and f., gerôn; Goth. gairns, O.H.G. gern, A.S. georn, O.H.G. girida, giridi.

† 3. गॄ *GṚÎ*, i. 10, *gâraya*, Âtm. To know; to make known.

† गेप् *GEP*, i. 1, Âtm. To tremble, to move.—Cf. *kep*.

† गेव् *GEV*, i. 1, Âtm. To serve.—Cf. *kev*.

† गेष् *GESH*, i. 1, Âtm. To search.—Cf. *gavesh*.

गेह *geha* (probably a dialect. form of *garha*, the original form of *gṛiha*), n. **1.** A house, Man. 2, 184. **2.** An edifice, Râjat. 5, 37 (a temple).—**Comp.** *Jatu-*, n. a house painted and filled with lac and other combustible substances, MBh. 5, 1987.

गेहिन् *gehin*, i.e. *geha*+*in*, **I.** m. A householder (cf. *gṛihin*). **II.** f. *inî*, The wife of a householder, Megh. 75.

गै *GAI*, i. 1, *gâya* (in epic poetry *gânti*, instead of *gâyanti*, from the original form of the vb. *gâ*), Par. (in epic poetry also Âtm., Râm. 1, 62, 20). **1.** To sing, Man. 4, 64. **2.** To teach, Bhâg. P. 4, 21, 40 (3 pl. Aor. *agus*).—Ptcple. of the pf. pass. *gîta*, Sung, Çâk. 4, 11. n. A song, Arj. 4, 10.—**Comp.** *Upâṅga-gîta*, n. a kind of song (perhaps of lascivious purport), Râjat. 5, 381. *Bhagavadgîtâ*, i.e. *bhagavant-*, f. the name of an episode of the Mahâbhârata.—Ptcple. of the fut. pass. *geya*, n. A song, Indr. 5, 27.—Caus. *gâpaya*, **1.** To cause to sing, Kathâs. 12, 31. **2.** To cause to praise, Bhâg. P. 6, 17, 3. Frequent. *jegîya*, To sing aloud, MBh. 12, 12200.—With the prep. अनु *anu*, **1.** To sing in harmony with (with acc.), Gît. 1, 39. **2.** To accompany with singing, MBh. 1, 7913. **3.** To sing, Bhâg. P. 6, 1, 60. Pass. *anu-gîya*, To be spoken of in songs, MBh. 12, 4211.—With अभि *abhi*, To sing, Râm. 1, 4, 24. *abhigîta*, Filled with song, Râm. 6, 15, 11.—With अव *ava*, in *avagîta*, Detested, Kir. 2, 7.—With उद् *ud*, **1.** To sing, Bhâg. P. 7, 4, 39. **2.** To celebrate by song, Ragh. 2, 12. *udgîta*, Filled with song, MBh. 3, 1533. n. song, MBh. 1, 6569.—With प्रोद् *pra-ud*, To begin to sing, Prab. 80, 3.—With उप *upa*, **1.** To sing before somebody (with the acc. of the pson.), MBh. 1, 4809; *upagîyant*, anomalous ptcple. of the pres. pass. MBh. 15, 883. **2.** To fill with song, MBh. 3, 11606. **3.** To celebrate by song, Râm. 4, 44, 57. **4.** To sing, Bhâg. P. 5, 14, 41. *upagîta* Singing in the vicinity, Çiç. 4, 57.—With नि *ni*, *nigîta*, Chanted, Man. 9, 19.—With परि *pari*, To sing round a person, MBh. 6, 75. **2.** To celebrate by song, MBh. 13, 4095.—With प्र *pra*, To sing, Râm. 1, 4, 31. *pragîta*, **1.** Filled with song, Râm. 1, 9, 17. **2.** Singing, Kathâs. 16, 85.—With संप्र *sam-pra*, To sing, MBh. 8, 1836.—With वि *vi*, *vigîta*, **1.** Inconsistent, contradictory, Man. 8, 53. **2.** Abused. **3.** Ill sung (i.e. *gîta*, with *vi*).—With सम् *sam*, To celebrate by song, Bhâg. P. 3, 22, 23. *saṁgîta*, n. **1.** A concert, Megh. 57. **2.** Science of music and dancing, Lass. 67, 5.

गैरिक *gairika*, i. e. *giri*+*ika*, n. Red chalk, Râm. 5, 83, 12.—**Comp.** *Kâñchana-*, n. a sort of ochre, Suçr. 2, 275, 19. *Svarṇa-*, n. golden ochre.

गो *go*, **I.** m. **1.** A bull; f. A cow, Man. 3, 141; pl. Bulls and cows, cattle,

Man. 4, 72. **2.** m. pl. Rays of light, Râjat. 5, 1. **II.** f. The earth, Râm. 1, 41, 18. **III.** m. and f. Water, Bhâg. P. 1, 10, 36. **IV.** f. Speech, Ragh. 5, 12. **V.** The deity of speech, MBh. 5, 4149. **VI.** m. The name of a Ṛishi, MBh. 2, 381. **VII.** f. A proper name, Bhâg. P. 9, 21, 25.—Cf. βοῦς, γαῖος, Γη-ρύων; Lat. bos, ceva; OHG. kô; AS. cû; probably also γαῖα, γῆ, δῆ, Δημήτηρ; Goth. gavi, gauja.

गोऽग्र *go-agra*, adj. Preceded by cows, Chr. 294, 7 = Rigv. i. 92, 7.

गोऽर्णस् *go-arṇas*, n. A drove of cows, Chr. 297, 18 = Rigv. i. 112, 18 (the clouds).

गोघ्न *go-ghna*, m. One who has killed a cow, Man. 11, 108.

गोचर *go-chara*, m. **1.** Pasture ground; in *adbhuta-*, adj. Having excellent pasture ground, Râm. 4, 44, 80. **2.** Stay, abode; used only as latter part of comp. adj., e.g. *vana-*, Inhabiting woods, Man. 8, 259; *âkâça-*, Moving in the air, Râm. 5, 3, 35. *çarîrântara-*, Being in the body, Râm. 6, 101, 30; *yauvana-*, Being in one's youth, MBh. 1, 3168. **3.** Reach, province; *hartur yâti na gocharam*, Comes not within the reach of a robber, i.e. cannot be robbed, Bhartṛ. 2, 49; *vâṇa-*, m. The reach of an arrow-shot, MBh. 1, 2833; *a-vâń-manasa-*, adj. Within the reach neither of speech nor thought, Vedântas. in Chr. 202, 3. **4.** The range of the eyes, MBh. 7, 5616. **5.** An object of sense, as sound, shape, etc., Bhag. 13, 5. **6.** An object of devotion, MBh. 13, 4349.—**Comp.** *Lochana-*, I. m. the range of the eyes, horizon, Pańch.v.d. 82. II. adj. accessible to the eyes, Bhartṛ. 1, 74. *A-lochana-*, adj. 1. inaccessible, Pańch. 106, 13. 2. unknown, Lass. 94, 7.

गोजाविधनधान्यतस् *gojâvidhanadhânyatas*, i.e. *go-aja-avi-dhana-dhânya + tas*, adv. By wealth consisting in kine, goats, sheep, money, and grain, Man. 3, 6.

गोणी *goṇî*, f. A sack, Daçak. 30, 20 (read *goṇîç cha*).

गोतम *gotama*, m. The name of a Ṛishi, MBh. 13, 4490.

गोत्र *go-tra* (vb. *trâ*), **I.** n. **1.** A cow-house (ved.). **2.** Family, race, Pańch. 130, 21; Man. 9, 149. **3.** The family name, MBh. 13, 548. **4.** Name, Çâk. d. 132. **II.** m. A mountain, Bhâg. P. 2, 6, 9.—**Comp.** *Sa-*, I. adj. being of the same family, Man. 9, 190. II. m. a distant kinsman. III. n. a family, a race.

गोत्रक *gotra + ka*, n. Family, Yâjń. 2, 85.

गोत्रज *gotra-ja*, adj. Belonging to the same family, Yâjń. 2, 135.

गोत्रभिद् *gotra + bhid*, m. A name of Indra, Çiç. 9, 80 (at the same time: Destroyer of names).

गोत्रवन्त् *gotra-vant*, adj., f. *vatî*, Belonging to a distinguished family, Râm. 2, 93, 24.

गोत्व *go-tva*, n. The condition of a cow, Mârk. P. 15, 34.

गोदावरी *godâvarî*, i.e. *go-dâvan + î*, f. The name of a river, Râm. 3, 19, 19.

गोधा *godhâ*, f. **1.** A leathern guard worn by archers on the left arm to prevent its being injured by the bowstring, Râm. 2, 100, 22. **2.** A kind of lizard, Man. 5, 18.—**Comp.** *Kṛishṇa-*, f. a certain poisonous insect, Suçr. 2, 288, 9.

गोधूम *go-dhûma*, m., usually pl., Wheat, Man. 5, 25.

गोधूमक *godhûma+ka*, m. A kind of snake, Suçr. 2, 265, 17.

गोप *go-pa* (vb. 2.*pâ*), I. m. **1.** A cowherd, Man. 8, 231. **2.** A preserver, MBh. 13, 1375. **3.** A name of Kṛishṇa, MBh. 12, 1438. **II.** f. *pî*, A cowherd's wife, Hit. 64, 7; a milk-maid, Gît. 2, 21.—**Comp.** When latter part of a comp. adj. the fem. ends in *pâ*, e.g. *A-gopa*, adj., f. *pâ*, without a cowherd, MBh. 1, 3213.

गोपन *gopana*, i.e. *gup+ana*, n. and f. *nâ*, Protection, MBh. 6, 2230; 12, 11907.

गोपय *GOPAYA*, and **गोपाय** *GOPÂYA*, see *gup*.

गोपायन *gopâyana*, i.e. *gopâya+ana*, I. adj. Protecting, MBh. 6, 3131. II. n. Protection, Hariv. 2142.

गोपायितृ *gopâyitṛi*, i.e. *gopâya+tṛi*, m. A protector, MBh. 12, 2726.

गोप्तृ *goptṛi*, i.e. *gup+tṛi*, m., f. *trî*, and n. **1.** A protector, Man. 7, 14; MBh. 13, 1842; Bhâg. P. 7, 10, 28. **2.** One who conceals, Yâjń. 1, 310.—**Comp.** *Chakra-*, m. du. Two men who take care of the wheels of a chariot, MBh. 7, 1627.

† **गोम्** *GOM*, i. 10, *gomaya* (rather for *gomayaya*, and a denomin. derived from *gomaya*), Par. To smear with cowdung.

गोमन्त् *go+mant*, I. adj., f. *matî*, **1.** Possessing cows, Chr. 295, 14=Rigv. i. 92, 14; Chr. 287, 2=Rigv. i. 48, 2 (*gomatis*, ved. for *gomatyas*). **2.** Abounding in cows, Chr. 292, 3=Rigv. i. 86, 3. **II.** f. *matî*, **1.** The name of a river, the modern Goomti, MBh. 3, 8051. **2.** The name of a vedic hymn, MBh. 13, 3844.

गोमय *go+maya*, m. and n. Cowdung, Man. 3, 206.

गोमयाय *GOMAYÂYA*, a denomin. derived from *gomaya*, by the aff. *ya*, Âtm. To taste like cowdung, Hit. iii. d. 56.

गोमायु *gomâyu*, i.e. *go*-2. *mâ+u*, m. A jackal, Man. 4, 115.

गोमिन् *go+min*, m. The owner of cattle, Yâjń. 2, 161.

गोरक्ष *go-raksha*, and **गोरक्ष्य** *gorakshya*, i.e. *goraksha+ya*, n. Attendance on cattle, keeping cattle, Man. 10, 8; 116.

गोल *gola* (cf. *guḍa*) m. A ball, Bhâg. P. 5, 20, 30; of the Kadamba's flower, Mâlat. p. 116.—Cf. *guḍa*.—**Comp.** *Bhû-*, m. the terrestrial globe.

गोलक *gola+ka*, m. **1.** A ball, as the Kadamba's round flower, Bhâshâp. p. 165 (v. r.); *bhû-*, m. The earth, Bhâg. P. 5, 16, 4. **2.** A widow's bastard, Man. 3, 156; 174.

गोलोमतस् *golomatas*, i. e. *go-loman+tas*, adv. From cow's hair, Pańch. i. d. 107.

गोविन्द *govinda*, i.e. *go-vid+a*, m. **1.** A name of Kṛishṇa, MBh. 5, 2572. **2.** The name of a mountain, MBh. 6, 460.—**Comp.** *Gîta-*, m. title of an idyllic drama.

गोविषाणिक *govishâṇika*, i.e. *go-vishâṇa+ika*, m. A kind of trumpet, MBh. 9, 2676.

गोषुयुध् *goshuyudh*, i.e. *go+su-yudh*, adj. Contending for cattle, Chr. 297, 22=Rigv. i. 112, 22.

† **गोष्ठ्** *GOSHṬH*, i. 1, Âtm. To assemble (probably better *goshṭh*; cf. the next.)

गोष्ठ *goshṭha*, i.e. *go-stha*, I. m. and n. **1.** A pasture ground, a cow-pen, Man. 11, 108; MBh. 1, 7338. **2.** A stable, Man. 4, 58. **3.** Stay, abode, MBh. 3, 12341; *simha-*, a lion's den, Draup. 4, 9. **4.** Family, Man. 3, 254. **5.** A name of Çiva, MBh. 14, 198. **II.** f. *shṭhî*, **1.** An assembly, MBh. 4, 891. **2.** Fellowship, MBh. 6, 3321. **3.** Conversation, Bhartṛ. 1, 35; Pañch. 31, 4. **4.** A kind of drama, Sâh. D. 541.—Comp. *Pañchavîra-*, i.e. *pañchan-vîra*, m. or n., perhaps an assembly-room named The five heroes, i.e. The five sons of Pâṇḍu, Daçak. in Chr. 190, 8.

गोष्ठि *goshṭhi*, probably for *goshṭhî* (see *goshṭha*), MBh. 5, 1536.

गोष्ठिक *goshṭhika*, i.e. *goshṭhî* + *ika*, adj. Referring to a company, Pañch. i. d. 14.

गोष्ठेशय *goshṭheçaya*, i.e. *goshṭha* + *i-çî* + *a*, adj. Sleeping in a cow-pen, Yâjñ. 3, 263.

गोष्पद *goshpada*, i.e. *go* + *as-pada*, n. **1.** The impression of a cow's foot, MBh. i. 1444. **2.** A puddle not larger than a cow's foot, Râm. 6, 69, 16.—Comp. *Samyuga-*, n. a most insignificant struggle, MBh. 7, 4724.

गोसंख्यातृ *gosamkhyâtṛi*, i.e. *go-sam-khyâ* + *tṛi*, m. A cow herd, MBh. 4, 67.

गौड *gauḍa*, i.e. *guḍa* + *a*, I. adj. Distilled from molasses, MBh. 8, 2050. **II.** f. *ḍî*, Rum, or spirit distilled from molasses, Man. 11, 94. **III.** n. pl. Sweetmeats, Râm. 1, 53, 4. **IV.** m. and n. The name of a country, modern Gaur; m. pl. Its inhabitants, Prab. 22, 13.

गौण *gauṇa*, i.e. *guṇa* + *a*, adj., f. *ṇî*. **1.** Named from a quality, MBh. 13, 4501. **2.** Subordinate, MBh. 12, 6798.

गौणिक *gauṇika*, i.e. *guṇa-ika*, adj., f. *kî*, Depending on the three fundamental qualities, Man. 12, 41.

गौतम *gautama*, i. e. *gotama* + *a*, patron., f. *mî*, A descendant of Gotama, and proper name, MBh. 9, 273; Çâk. 27, 23; MBh. 13, 17.

गौर *gaura*, I. adj., f. *rî*, White, yellow, pale red, Megh. 53; Râm. 5, 14, 30. **II.** m. **1.** A kind of buffalo, Bos gaurus, Bhâg. P. 3, 10, 21. **2.** White mustard, as a measure, Yâjñ. 1, 362. **III.** f. *rî*, **1.** Turmeric, Suçr. 1, 59, 11. **2.** A young girl prior to menstruation, Pañch. iii. d. 213. **3.** The wife of Çiva, Megh. 51. **4.** The wife of Varuṇa, MBh. 5, 3968. **5.** The name of a river, MBh. 6, 333. **IV.** n. Saffron, Chaur. 10.

गौरव *gaurava*, i.e. *guru* + *a*, I. adj. Relating to the spiritual teacher, Bhâg. P. 1, 7, 46. **II.** n. **1.** Heaviness, Râm. 3, 4, 26. **2.** Importance, Râm. 4, 16, 47. **3.** Dignity, Man. 2, 145. **4.** Respect, Pañch. 265, 4.—Comp. *Nis-*, adj., f. *vâ*, devoid of respect, Râjat. 1, 73. °*vam*, adv. condescendingly, 5, 17.

गौरिक *gaurika*, i.e. *gaura* + *ika*, m. White mustard (?), Suçr. 2, 119, 6.

गौल्मिक *gaulmika*, i.e. *gulma* + *ika*, adj. Belonging to a gulma (q. cf.), or a certain division of an army, MBh. 10, 359.

1. **ग्रथ्** *GRATH*, and **ग्रन्थ्** *GRANTH*, ii. 9, *grathnâ*, *nî*, Par. † i. 1 and 10, *grantha*, *granthaya*, *grâthaya* (?), *grathaya* (see *ud*), Par. † i. 1 (?), *gratha*, Par. Âtm. **1.** To connect, MBh. 4, 262 (*granth*). **2.** To compose, Prab. 101, 8.—Ptcple. of the pf. pass., *grathita*, **1.** Tied, MBh. 3, 10052. **2.** Tied together, joined, Çâk. d. 167. Tied in order, Çâk. 3, 12. **3.** Strung, Râm. 6, 84, 25. **4.** Studded,

Ragh. 16, 13. **5.** Tied together strongly, MBh. 12, 2901. **6.** Obdurate, Suçr. 1, 303, 8. **7.** Stopped, Suçr. 2, 501, 10. n. A tubercular abscess, Suçr. 1, 298, 7.—With the prep. उद् *ud*, **1.** *granth*, To tie up, MBh. 4, 1419. **2.** *grathaya*, To untie, Bhâg. P. 4, 22, 39. *udgrathita*, **1.** Tied up, Ragh. 2, 8. **2.** Wreathed, MBh. 3, 10066.—With समुद् *sam-ud*, *grath*, or *granth*, To tie up, MBh. 4, 244.—With वि *vi*, *vigrathita*, **1.** Bound up, Suçr. 1, 18, 3. **2.** Tubercular, Suçr. 1, 286, 18. **3.** Clotted, Suçr. 1, 176, 20. **4.** Hindered, Suçr. 2, 190, 6.—Cf. probably γρόνθος.

† 2. ग्रथ् *GRATH*, and ग्रन्थ् *GRANTH*, i. 1, Âtm. To be crooked, to be wicked.

ग्रन्थ *granth* + *a*, m. **1.** A literary composition, a book, Râm. 2, 108, 16; MBh. 12, 11340. **2.** Wealth, Pańch. i. d. 12.—Comp. *Tarka-*, m. a compendium of logic, Suçr. 2, 360, 13. *Nis-*, adj. free from every worldly tie or interest, Bhâg. P. 1, 7, 10.

ग्रन्थि *granth* + *i*, m. **1.** A tie, a knot, Man. 2, 43. **2.** A joint, Megh. 95. **3.** Swelling, MBh. 12, 9121.—Comp. *Suvarṇa-*, m. a knot made for keeping gold, Pańch. 134, 12. *Mâna-*, m. 1. pride, 2. fault. *Vastra-*, m. the string by which the lower garments are fastened above the hips.

ग्रन्थिक *granthika*, i.e. *grantha* + *ika*, **I.** m. **1.** An astrologer, MBh. 14, 2039. **2.** A name of Nakula, the fourth son of Pâṇḍu, MBh. 4, 63. **3.** A disease of the ear, Suçr. 1, 59, 4. **II.** n. The root of long pepper, Suçr. 2, 208, 21.

ग्रन्थिन् *granthin*, i.e. *grantha* + *in*, m. One who has read many books, Man. 12, 103.

ग्रन्थिमन्त् *granthi* + *mant*, adj., f. *matî*, Intwined, Kumâras. 3, 46.

ग्रस् *GRAS* (akin to 2. *gṛî*), i. 1, and † 10, Par. and Âtm. **1.** To seize with the mouth, MBh. 3, 2383. **2.** To seize, Yâjń. 3, 245; to devour, MBh. 3, 13829.—Comp. ptcple. of the pf. pass., *vâta-grasta*, m. **1.** Epileptic. **2.** Rheumatic. *vâyu-grasta*, Frantic, Daçak. in Chr. 200, 9. Ptcple. of the fut. pass., *grasya*, Eatable, MBh. 5, 1107.—With the prep. उप *upa*, To swallow, MBh. 2, 2693.—With प्र *pra*, To swallow, MBh. 1, 1153.—Cf. perhaps γράω, γάγγραινα from a frequent., λάμος, λαιμός, λαμία, λάρυγξ.

ग्रसन *gras* + *ana*, n. **1.** Swallowing, Suçr. 2, 267, 13. **2.** The jaws, Bhâg. P. 3, 13, 35.

ग्रसिष्णु *gras* + *ishṇu*, adj. Wont to swallow, Bhag. 13, 16.

ग्रस्ति *gras* + *ti*, f. Swallowing, Prab. 103, 12.

ग्रस्तृ *gras* + *tṛi*, m. A devourer, Hariv. 12465.

ग्रह् *GRAH* (for original *grabh*, preserved in the Vedas), ii. 9, *gṛihṇâ*, *ṇî*, **1.** To take, to seize, Man. 11, 100; 8, 283; *pâṇim*, To marry, Pańch. 130, 6. **2.** To marry, Bhâg. P. 9, 24, 38. **3.** To hold, Kathâs. 4, 32. **4.** To bear, Pańch. 226, 20. **5.** To catch, MBh. 3, 2090. **6.** To captivate, Râm. 2, 39, 23. **7.** To gain, Châṇ. 22. **8.** To rob, Râm. 4, 53, 25. **9.** To receive, Man. 3, 51. **10.** With *garbham*, To become pregnant, MBh. 1, 4490. **11.** To assume, to adopt, Râjat. 5, 228. **12.** To buy, Râm. 1, 61, 21. **13.** To obtain by entreaties, Râm. 1, 39, 13. **14.** To gather, Çâk. 48, 20. **15.** To put on, Man. 8, 256. **16.** To undergo,

MBh. 13, 6024. **17.** To pronounce, Man. 5, 157. **18.** To perceive, Man. 8, 26. **19.** To trace out, Çâk. 23, 11. **20.** To learn, Râm. 1, 24, 12; to understand, Pańch. i. d. 49; with *anyathâ*, To mistake, Mâlav. d. 19; *paramârthena*, To take in earnest, Çâk. d. 51. **21.** To approve, Mṛichchh. 145, 24. **22.** To follow, Bhâg. P. 3, 16, 23. — Comp. ptcple. of the pf. pass., *su-gṛihîta*, **1.** Held fast or firmly, **2.** Taken auspiciously.—Ptcple. of the fut. pass. I. *grahaṇîya*, Worth being taken to heart, MBh. 5, 2575. II. *grâhya*, **1.** Perceivable, Râm. 3, 22, 20; Man. 1, 7. **2.** To be regarded, Hit. i. d. 20. **3.** Agreeable, Daçak. in Chr. 180, 12. III. *gṛihîtavya*, sometimes instead of *grahîtavya*, e.g. MBh. 4, 1481.—Absol. *gṛihîtva*, Holding, i.e. with; *dârakaṁ gṛihîtva*, With the child, Mṛichchh. 94, 14; in epic poetry often *gṛihya*, instead of *gṛihîtva*, Râm. 1, 31, 24. Causal *grâhaya*, **1.** To cause to take, Ragh. 17, 3. **2.** To hand over to, Daçak. in Chr. 197, 4. **3.** To cause to be apprehended, Daçak. in Chr. 193, 15. **4.** To let choose, Râjat. 5, 102. **5.** To teach, Man. 1, 58; with *âtmânam*, To investigate, MBh. 3, 16267. **6.** *grâhita*, Occupied, Râm. 1, 7, 14 Gorr. —Desider. *jighṛiksha*, **1.** To be about to seize, MBh. 1, 5482. **2.** To be about to rob, Bhâg. P. 1, 17, 25. **3.** To desire to perceive, Bhâg. P. 4, 29, 4. —With the prep. अनु *anu*, **1.** To rob afterwards, MBh. 4, 996. **2.** To support, Bhâg. P. 5, 23, 3. **3.** To receive friendly, to favour, MBh. 1, 3158; 3, 1666; with instr. MBh. 2, 205. **4.** To show the favor of commanding, Daçak. in Chr. 189, 22. *anugrahita*, Râm. 1, 7, 15, is very questionable (Gorr. v.r.); if correct, it would be *anugraha* + *ita*; I propose *anugṛihîta*, Favoured.—With समनु *sam-anu*, To dress, MBh. 8, 205.—With अप *apa*, To tear off, MBh. 14, 250.—With अभि *abhi*, To seize. Daçak. in Chr. 201, 3. **2.** To accept, MBh. 3, 1705; to receive, MBh. 3, 16430. **3.** To put forth (as flowers), Bhâg. P. 3, 29, 41. **4.** To put together, Bhâg. P. 1, 19, 12. Caus. *abhigrâhita*, Caught, Daçak. 115, 4.—With अव *ava*, **1.** To divide, Suçr. 1, 101, 13. **2.** To resist.—Comp. ptcple. of the fut. pass., *dus-ava-grâhya*, Hard to be attained, Bhâg. P. 7, 1, 19.—Absolut. *avagṛihya*, By violence, Çiç. 5, 49.—With प्रत्यव *prati-ava*, To rescind, Râm. 2, 20, 15 Gorr.—With आ *â*, To pull, Çâk. 6, 15, v.r.—With उपा *upa-â*, To embrace, Râm. 2, 95, 9 Gorr. — With उद् *ud*, To raise, Megh. 8. Caus. **1.** To cause to be paid, Yâjń. 2, 200. **2.** To explain, Çiç. 2, 75.—With उप *upa*, **1.** To put under, Râm. 5, 13, 52. **2.** To support, Sâv. 5, 62. **3.** To seize, Râm. 5, 36, 77. **4.** To provide, Man. 7, 184. **5.** To undergo, Pańch. i. d. 415. **6.** To cherish, MBh. 12, 2506. **7.** To approve, MBh. 12, 6977. *upagṛihîtum*, Hit. ii. d. 3, is to be changed to *upagûhitum*.—With नि *ni*, **1.** To close (the eyes), Mṛichchh. 35, 19. **2.** To stop, MBh. 3, 10769. **3.** To seize, Râm. 3, 30, 34. **4.** To hold, Ragh. 2, 33. **5.** To apprehend, Man. 8, 184. **6.** To restrain, Man. 8, 310. **7.** To chastise, Hit. 67, 13. **8.** To subdue, Çâk. 16, 12. Caus. To cause to be apprehended, Daçak. in Chr. 194, 17.—With विनि *vi-ni*, **1.** To seize, MBh. 1, 4980. **2.** To stop, MBh. 3, 12170. **3.** With संनि *sam-ni*, **1.** To subdue, MBh. 3, 14357. **2.** To seize, MBh. 2, 2528.—

With परि *pari,* **1.** To embrace, MBh. 1, 4983. **2.** To wrap, MBh. 4, 215. **3.** To put on, MBh. 13, 2594. **4.** To put round, Râm. 3, 57, 27. **5.** To surround, MBh. 3, 14919; absol. *parigṛihya sarasvatîm,* Along the river Sarasvatî, Chr. 20, 24. **6.** To turn, MBh. 7, 1169; to overturn, 1170. **7.** To catch, MBh. 3, 11725. **8.** To seize, Ragh. 7, 18; absol. *parigṛihya,* with, Râm. 3, 62, 35. **9.** To accept, Çâk. 28, 10; to receive, Man. 9, 171; to treat kindly, MBh. 1, 6269. **10.** To undergo, Mâlav. d. 71. **11.** To marry, Çâk. d. 115. **12.** To support, Mâlav. d. 12. **13.** To follow, Man. 8, 73. **14.** To surpass, Man. 2, 151.—With संपरि *sam-pari,* **1.** To accept, Râm. 2, 112, 29; to receive, MBh. 4, 2143. **2.** To embrace, MBh. 12, 2663.—With प्र *pra,* **1.** To stretch forth, Râm. 3, 24, 25. **2.** To seize, Râm. 3, 21, 9; to take, Bhâg. P. 3, 5, 16; to touch, Râm. 2, 99, 7; absol. *pragṛihya,* with, MBh. 13, 173. **3.** To stop, Çâk. 6, 15. **4.** To favour, MBh. 4, 122. MBh. 13, 4435, *pragrâhitum,* To receive, has the same signification as *pragrahîtum,* and is probably to be changed to it, else it is an anomalous infin. of the causal for °*grâhayitum.*—With प्रतिप्र *prati-pra,* To receive again, MBh. 12, 6978.—With संप्र *sam-pra,* **1.** To seize, Râm. 6, 76, 9. **2.** To accept kindly, MBh. 12, 4643. —With प्रति *prati,* **1.** To seize, Mâlav. 47, 15. **2.** To receive, Man. 6, 28; to receive kindly, MBh. 3, 1774; to accept, Man. 4, 247. **3.** To approve, Râm. 3, 72, 1. **4.** To collect, MBh. 4, 2211. **5.** To occupy, Râm. 4, 26, 4. **6.** To assail, MBh. 3, 12225 (*agṛihṇam,* instead of *agṛihṇâm,* cf. *vi*). **7.** To eclipse, Râm. 3, 29, 4. **8.** To marry, Man. 9, 72.—Comp. ptcple. of the fut. pass., *a-pratigrâhya,* Not permitted to be accepted, Man. 11, 253. Caus. To offer, Çâk. d. 116.—With संप्रति *sam-prati,* To receive kindly, MBh. 13, 3863.—With वि *vi,* **1.** To quarrel, MBh. 12, 2705. **2.** To wage war, Man. 7, 183; against (with acc.), MBh. 15, 220. **3.** To assault, MBh. 3, 1226 (*agṛihṇam,* cf. *prati*). **4.** To seize, MBh. 4, 2086. **5.** To receive kindly, MBh. 3, 12274. **6.** To perceive, Bhâg. P. 3, 32, 24. *vigṛihîta,* **1.** Opposed, prevented. **2.** Encountered (as in fight). Caus. To cause to wage war against, Daçak. 193, 1.—With सम् *sam,* **1.** To collect, Râm. 1, 17, 15. **2.** To seize, Râm. 3, 48, 9. **3.** To catch, Râm. 7, 5235. **4.** To govern, Man. 7, 113. **5.** To unstring (a bow), MBh. 3, 16065. **6.** To constrain, Man. 8, 48. **7.** To accept, Bhâg. P. 3, 24, 12. **8.** To receive kindly, Hit. 91, 11. **9.** To marry, Bhâg. P. 9, 24, 36. **10.** To pronounce, Bhâg. P. 6, 2, 13. Caus. To impart, Bhâg. P. 3, 31, 18. Desider. **1.** To strive to collect, MBh. 3, 1356. **2.** To desire to marry, Daçak. 172, 8.—With अनुसम् *anu-sam,* **1.** To salute humbly, touching one's feet, MBh. 12, 3850. **2.** To favour, Râm. 6, 104, 31.—With उपसम् *upa-sam,* **1.** To seize, Man. 3, 224; to touch, MBh. 1, 5529. **2.** To salute, Man. 2, 132. **3.** To undergo, MBh. 12, 8791. **4.** To receive, MBh. 1, 8192; to receive kindly, Pańch. 187, 25. **5.** To gain, Daçak. in Chr. 191, 15.—With प्रतिसम् *prati-sam,* To receive, Râm. 1, 76, 4.—With सह *saha,* To take along with, Kathâs. 15, 88.—Cf. with the original *grabh,* O.H.G. kraft; A.S. craft; Goth. greipan, A.S. grîpan, cf. *garbha* and *labh.* With *grah,* cf.

δραχ in δράσσω, δραχμή, etc.; βρόχος, βρόχω, βρόχθος, etc.; perhaps also βραχίων; Lat. grex, congrego, brachium, etc. The *h* is dropped in gremium, gerere (for gerhere), and probably in gratus.

ग्रह *grah + a*, I. Latter part of comp. adj. **1.** Seizing, Bhâg. P. 3, 15, 35. **2.** Gathering, Bhâg. P. 8, 6, 23. II. m. **1.** A seizure of the sun or moon by Râhu, i.e. an eclipse, Bhartṛ. 2, 87. **2.** A planet, Man. 1, 24, 7. **3.** The five planets, Mars, Mercury, Jupiter, Venus, and Saturn, combined with Râhu, Ketu, sun and moon, making nine; it denotes the numeral Nine, Çrutib. 35. **4.** An imp, Suçr. 2, 382, 4. **5.** A crocodile, or shark, Râm. 4, 44, 47. **6.** Booty, MBh. 3, 11461. **7.** A draught, Bhâg. P. 4, 13, 30. **8.** A vessel, Man. 5, 116. **9.** The place where a bow is held when strung, MBh. 4, 1351. **10.** Gripe, Pańch. i. d. 237. **11.** Theft, Man. 9, 277. **12.** Receipt, Man. 8, 180. **13.** Mention, Man. 8, 271; Râjat. 5, 361. **14.** Perception, Bhâshâp. 58; understanding, Bhâg. P. 7, 14, 11. **15.** An organ of perception, Bhâg. P. 4, 7, 31. **16.** Tenacity, perseverance, Kathâs. 24, 156; Pańch. i. d. 291 (where *grâhas* must be changed to *grahas*).—Comp. *A-*, m. refusal, Râjat. 5, 441. *Ańkuça-*, m. a mohout, or elephant's driver, MBh. 3, 978. *Kuńjara-*, m. a hunter of elephants, Râm. 2, 91, 55. *Keça-*, m. laying hold of one's hair, Man. 4, 83. *Dus-*, I. m. a wicked imp, Kathâs. 17, 130. II. adj. 1. Difficult to be conquered, Ragh. 17, 52. 2. Difficult to be performed, MBh. 12, 775. *Deva-*, m. suffering from a certain kind of frenzy, MBh. 3, 14501. *Dhanus-*, m. 1. an archer, Râm. 2, 44, 18. 2. Archery, MBh. 12, 7662. *Nava-*, adj. lately caught, Râm. 2, 58, 2. *Nâmajâti-*, i.e. *nâman-jâti-* m. mentioning name and classes, Man. 8, 271. *Pâṇi-*, m. marriage. *Çabda-*, m. 1. The ear. 2. Catching sound. *Sûtra-*, adj. holding a thread. *Sûrya-*, m. 1. the sun. 2. an eclipse of the sun. 3. Ketu and Râhu. 4. the bottom of a water jar. *Hrada-*, m. a crocodile.

ग्रहण *grahaṇa*, i.e. *grah + ana*, I. adj. Seizing, Hariv. 2734. II. n. **1.** Taking, seizure, Mṛichchh. 147, 1. **2.** Captivity, Râm. 1, 1, 73. **3.** An eclipse (cf. *graha*, II. 1), Çringârat. 6. **4.** Receiving, Râm. 1, 24, 18. **5.** Buying, Pańch. 229, 2. **6.** Putting on, MBh. 2, 840. **7.** Undergoing, Pańch. 34, 9. **8.** Protection, Bhâg. P. 3, 1, 44. **9.** Pronouncing, Man. 6, 67. **10.** Perception, MBh. 14, 1197. **11.** Study, Man. 2, 173.—Comp. *Keça-*, n. laying hold of one's hair, Megh. 51; with *â*, even to laying hold, etc., i.e. to the utmost, Râm. 3, 46, 2. *Chakshus-*, n. weakness of the eyes, Suçr. 2, 267, 21. *Dâra-*, n. marrying, MBh. 1, 1044. *Dûra-*, n. the faculty of seizing distant objects, Bhâg. P. 5, 5, 35. *Pâṇi-*, n. marriage.

ग्रहणी *grahaṇî*, i.e. *grahaṇa + î*, f. An organ of the belly, Suçr. 2, 443, 12.

ग्रहत्व *graha + tva*, n. The condition of a planet, Bhâg. P. 5, 24, 1.

ग्रहमय *graha + maya*, adj., f. *yî*, Resembling a planet, Bhartṛ. 1, 16.

ग्रहिल *grahila*, i.e. *graha + ila*, adj. **1.** Assuming, Sâh. D. 24, 13. **2.** Frantic, Çukas. 15 (14).

ग्रहीतृ *grahîtṛi*, i.e. *grah + tṛi*, I. m. f. *trî*, and n. Apprehending, Man. 1, 15. II. m. **1.** A purchaser, Pańch. i. d. 15. **2.** A debtor, Man. 8, 166. — Comp. *Pâṇi-*, m, a husband, MBh. 13, 2423.

† **ग्राम्** *GRÂM*, i. 10 (rather a de-

nomin. derived from the next), Par. To invite, see *çrâm*.

ग्राम *grâma*, i.e. *grah + ma*, m. **1.** A village, Man. 4, 107 (n. Râm. 2, 57, 4). **2.** A villager, Man. 8, 258 (? perhaps is to be read *grâmasâm°*). **3.** As latter part of a comp. word, A multitude, Nal. 4. 10. **4.** A scale in music, Mârk. P. 23, 52.—**Comp.** *Indriya-*, m. all the senses, Man. 2, 100. *Guṇa-*, m. a multitude of good qualities, Bhartṛ. 3, 23. *Tri-grâmî*, f. the name of a locality, Râjat. 5, 97. *Daçagrâmî*, i.e. *daçan-*, f. a district of ten villages, MBh. 12, 3263. *Sâla-*, m. a stone, a species of ammonite worshipped by the Vaishṇavas.

ग्रामक *grâma + ka*, m. **1.** A village, MBh. 5, 1466. **2.** A fictitious name, Bhâg. P. 4, 25, 52.

ग्रामणी *grâmaṇî*, i.e. *grâma-nî*, m. **1.** The chief of a community, MBh. 1, 4798 (*grâmaṇi*, on account of the metre, MBh. 7, 1125 ; 4099). **2.** A chief, MBh. 12, 4798. **3.** A proper name, Râm. 4, 41, 61.

ग्रामणीत्व *grâmaṇî + tva*, n. The dignity of a chief, MBh. 12, 4861.

ग्रामवन्त् *grâma + vant*, adj., f. *vatî*, Crowded with villages, MBh. 8, 4570.

ग्रामान्तीय *grâmântîya*, i.e. *grâma -anta + îya*, adj. Near a village, Man. 8, 240.

ग्रामिक *grâmika*, i.e. *grâma + ika*, m. The chief of a village, Man. 7, 116.

ग्रामिन् *grâmin*, i.e. *grâma + in*, m. A peasant, Bhâg. P. 4, 29, 14.

ऽग्रामी *-grâmî*, see *grâma*.

ग्रामीण *grâmîṇa*, i.e. *grâma + îna*, adj., f. *ṇâ*, Inhabiting a village, a peasant, Bhartṛ. 1, 89.—**Comp.** *Eka-*. i.e. *ekagrâma + îna*, adj. living in the same village, Man. 3, 103.

ग्रामीयक *grâmîyaka*, i.e. *grâma + îya + ka*, adj. Belonging to a community, Man. 8, 254.

ग्रामेय *grâmeya*, i.e. *grâma + eya*, m. A villager, MBh. 12, 3264.

ग्राम्य *grâmya*, i.e *grâma + ya*, **I.** adj. **1.** Referring to villages, Man. 7, 120. **2.** Prepared in villages, MBh. 1, 3637. **3.** Inhabiting a village, Yâjń. 2, 166. **4.** Coarse, sensual, Râm. 3, 37, 3. **5.** Living in towns, Man. 11, 199 ; tame, Pańch. 68, 14. **6.** Cultivated, MBh. 1, 6658. **II.** n. Sensuality, MBh. 2, 2270.—**Comp.** *A-*, adj. town-made.

ग्रावन् *grâvan*, m. A stone, a rock, Bhartṛ, 3, 29.—**Comp.** *Nikasha-*, m. a touchstone, Hit. i. d. 204.—Cf. probably λᾶας, λεύς ; Lat. lapis (cf. ovis, opilio).

ग्रास *grâsa*, i.e. *gras + a*, m. **1.** A mouthful, Man. 3, 133 ; a morsel, Pańch. 221, 21. **2.** Food, Man. 8, 339. **3.** Swallowing, Bhartṛ. 2, 22.

ग्राह *grâha*, i.e. *grah + a*, **I.** adj., f. *hî*, **1.** Taking, Yâjń. 2, 51. **2.** Robbing, Râm. 4, 41, 38. **II.** m. **1.** A shark, Pańch. i. d. 420. f. *hî*, A female shark, Râm. 6, 82, 73. **2.** Seizing, seizure ; e. g. *pâṇi-*, Taking the hand at marriage. **3.** A fit, a disease, MBh. 6, 5680 (read *ûru-*). **4.** Enterprise, Bhag. 17, 19.—**Comp.** *Jîva-grâha + m* (absol. of *grah*), combined with *grah*, to take somebody prisoner alive, MBh. 3, 14918. *Dhanus-*, m. an archer, MBh. 3, 1430. *Pâṇi-*, m. a husband. *Pârshṇi-*, m. a supporting prince (perhaps, rather, a dangerous prince), Man. 7, 207. *Vandi-*, m. a housebreaker. *Sûtra-*, adj. taking a thread.

ग्राहक *grâhaka,* i.e. *grah + aka,* I. adj. **1.** Apprehending, MBh. 3, 13932. **2.** Convincing, Râm. 4, 38, 18. m. **1.** A purchaser, Pańch. 7, 16. **2.** A policeman, Yâjń. 2, 266.

ग्राहवन्त् *grâha + vant,* adj., f. *vatî,* Containing sharks, Râm. 5, 72, 12.—**Comp.** *Bhîma-,* i.e. *bhîmagrâha + vant,* adj. containing fearful sharks, Chr. 47, 37. *Râga-grâha + vant,* containing love instead of sharks, Bhartṛ. 3, 11.

ग्राहिन् *grâhin,* i.e. *grah + in,* adj., f. *iṇî,* **1.** Seizing, robbing, Râm. 5, 8, 6. **2.** Gaining, Râm. 3, 72, 1. **3.** Catching, Kathâs. 25, 49. **4.** Gathering, Sâh. D. 11, 12. **5.** Choosing, Mârk. P. 27, 28. **6.** Spying, Çâk. 24, 7. **7.** Holding, Bhartṛ. 3, 67. **8.** Containing, Daçak. in Chr. 189, 11. **9.** Charming, Râm. 5, 44, 8. **10.** Obstructing, Suçr. 1, 178, 10.—**Comp.** *Guṇa-,* m. acknowledging another's virtues, Lass. 34, 7. *Pallava-,* adj. shooting forth too luxuriantly (or twig-picking, superficial), Hit. i. d. 131. *Vachana-,* adj. compliant. *Vinaya-,* adj. compliant, governable.

ग्रीवा *grîvâ,* f. The neck, Man. 8, 283.—**Comp.** *Açva-grîva,* m. the name of a demon. *Ud-grîva,* adj., f. *vâ,* with raised neck, Râjat. 5, 359. *Kambu-,* I. adj., f. *vâ,* having a neck marked with three lines like a shell, and considered to be indicative of exalted fortune, Râm. 1, 1, 11. II. m. a proper name, Pańch. 76, 7. *Chitra-grîva,* m. a proper name, Pańch. 105, 6. *Daçagrîva,* i.e. *daçan-,* adj. 1. an epithet of Râvaṇa, Râm. 1, 16, 18. 2. the name of a demon, MBh. 2, 367. *Nishka-grîva,* adj. wearing a golden ornament on the neck, Bhâg. P. 3, 23, 31. *Nîla-grîva,* adj. with a blue neck (epithet of Çiva), MBh. 3, 1625. *Mahâ-grîva,* m. a camel. *Vakra-,* m. a camel. *Su-,* I. adj. handsome-necked. II. m. 1. a goose. 2. a hero. 3. a sort of weapon. 4. one of Kṛishṇa's horses. 5. a proper name. 6. Indra. 7. Çiva. 8. a serpent of the lower regions. 9. the name of a mountain. *Haya-,* m. a demon.

ग्रीष्म *grîshma,* m. The hot season, comprehending about June and July, Man. 3, 261.

† **ग्रुच्** *GRUCH,* i. 1, Par. To steal.

ग्रैव *graiva,* i.e. *grîvâ + a,* n. A neck-ornament, Ragh. 4, 48.

ग्रैवेय *graiveya,* i.e. *grîvâ + eya,* n. A chain for the neck, Râm. 1, 53, 17.

ग्रैवेयक *graiveya + ka,* m. and n. A chain for the neck, Daçak. in Chr. 188, 16; a neck-ornament, Dev. 2, 26.

ग्रैष्म *graishma,* i.e. *grîshma + a,* adj., f. *mî,* Referring to the hot season, Bhâg. P. 5, 9, 5.

ग्लपन *glapana,* i.e. *glai,* Caus., + *ana,* n. Relaxation, Suçr. 1, 151, 15.

† **ग्लस्** *GLAS=gras.*

ग्लह् *GLAH,* i. 1, Âtm. **1.** To play with dice, MBh. 8, 4404. **2.** To win, 7, 6538. **3.** † *=grah* (v.r.).

ग्लह *glah + a,* m. **1.** A gambler, MBh. 2, 2037. **2.** A stake, MBh. 2, 2409 Daçak. in Chr. 188, 22. **3.** A die, MBh 8, 3756. **4.** A dice-box, MBh. 2, 1986 **5.** Playing with dice, MBh. 5, 1898 **6.** Aim, MBh. 8, 4402.

ग्लानि *glâni,* i.e. *glai + ni,* f. 1 Lassitude, MBh. 1, 8142. **2.** Inertness Man. 1, 53.

ग्लुच् *GLUCH,* i. 1, Par. To steal

† **ग्लुञ्च्** *GLUŃCH,* i. 1, Par. T go.

† **ग्लेप्** *GLEP* (akin to *glai*), i. 1

Âtm. **1.** To be poor. **2.** To tremble. **3.** To move.

† ग्लेव् *GLEV*, i. 1, Âtm. To serve.

† ग्लेष *GLESH* (? v.r.), i. 1, Âtm. To search.

ग्लै *GLAI* (akin to *gal*), i. 1, *glâya* (in epic poetry *glâti* instead of *glâyati*, e.g. MBh. 3, 13730; cf. *gai*), Par. (in epic poetry also Âtm., MBh. 3, 16713). **1.** To become exhausted, MBh. 5, 7178. **2.** To decrease, MBh. 12, 7513. **3.** To repine, Man. 3, 98. Ptcple. of the pf. pass. *glâna*, **1.** Sad, MBh. 15, 132. **2.** Wearied, MBh. 3, 14109, n. Exhaustion, MBh. 13, 3519. Caus. *glâpaya* and *glapaya*, **1.** To macerate, Vikr. d. 54. **2.** To injure, Râjat. 1, 334. **3.** To pain, distress, MBh. 5, 1100 (*glapet*, instead of *glapayet*, cf. *gup*); 13, 4694 (Âtm.)—With the prep. परि *pari*, *pariglâna*, Exhausted, MBh. 7, 8898.—With अभिपरि *abhi-pari*, *abhipariglâna*, The same, MBh. 1, 4489.—With वि *vi*, Caus. *glâpaya*, To afflict, Bhâg. P. 3, 2, 22.—Cf. probably O.H.G. kleini, akin to *glâna*.

घ *GH.*

घ *gha*, usually *ghâ* (old instr. of a pronomin. base = Lat. ho, in ho-c, etc.), part., ved. Indeed, Chr. 287, 5 = Rigv. i. 48, 5; Chr. 297, 19 = Rigv. i. 112, 19. —Cf. *γέ*, *ha*.

† घंष् *GHAṂSH*, and घंस् *GHAṂS*, i 1, Âtm. **1.** To render handsome. **2.** To sprinkle, v.r.

† घग्घ् *GHAGGH*, and घघ् *GHAGH*, i. 1, Par. To laugh.—Cf. *gagh*.

घट् *GHAṬ* (akin partly to *han*, partly to *ghaṭṭ*), i. 1, Âtm. (also Par., MBh. 3, 14703), **1.** To endeavour, MBh. 3, 1581. **2.** To work, MBh. 5, 256. **3.** To take place, Çiç. 9, 44. **4.** To be possible, Bhâg. P. 7, 10, 3. **5.** To fall into, Lass. 18, 8 (one's hand). **6.** To be joined, Mâlat. p. 38, 9.—Comp. ptcple. of the pf. pass. *A-ghaṭita*, adj. impossible, Bhâg. P. 6, 16, 44. *Su-*, adj. **1.** well joined. **2.** well-contrived or managed.—Caus. **I.** *ghaṭaya*, **1.** To join, Pańch. 40, 12. **2.** To put on, Gît. 12, 26. **3.** To fetch, Bhartṛ. 3, 18. **4.** To make, Pańch. 44, 16; to perform, Râjat. 4, 364. **5.** To endeavour, MBh. 3, 14702. **6.** To touch, MBh. 4, 637. **II.**, also i. 10, Par. *ghâṭaya*, **1.** (cf. *ud*, *pari*), To injure. **2.** † To shine or speak.—With the prep. व्या *vi-â*, *vyâghaṭita*, Returned (?), Lass. 22, 9.—With उद् *ud*, Caus. *ghâṭaya*, **1.** To open, Mṛichchh. 80, 7. **2.** To discover (as a secret), Pańch. 184, 16. **3.** To begin, Hit. iv. d. 2. **4.** To tickle, Suçr. 2, 370, 2. Ptcple. of the pf. pass. **1.** *udghâṭita*, Râjat. 2, 100. **2.** *udghaṭita*, Kûmar. 7, 53.—With परि *pari*, Caus. *ghâṭaya*, To strike, to sound, Mṛichchh. 11, 4 (v.r.).—With वि *vi*, **1.** To burst, to crumble down, Prab. 8, 11. **2.** To become interrupted, Hit. iv. d. 2. Caus. *ghaṭaya*, **1.** To tear, Prab. 116, 3. **2.** To ruin, Hit. ii. d. 157.—With सम् *sam*, To assemble, Râjat. 6, 242. Caus. *ghaṭaya*, **1.** To strike, to sound, Râm, 2, 71, 26. **2.** To collect, Râjat. 5, 326.

घट *ghaṭ+a*, m. **I.** adj. Active, Pańch. ii. d. 74. **II.** m. **1.** A jar, Man. 11, 183 (184). **2.** The Aquarius of the zodiac, Mârk. P. 12, 22 (change *ghaṭî* to *ghaṭaḥ*). **III.** f. *ṭâ*, **1.** A multitude, Bhâg. P. 3, 17, 6. **2.** A troop of elephants assembled for martial purposes,

Râjat. 1, 369. **IV.** f. *ṭi*, A jar, Prab. 22, 18.—**Comp.** *Dus-*, adj. difficult, Râjat. 4, 364.

घटक *ghaṭ+aka*, adj. Striving, Bhartṛ. 2, 66.

घटन *ghaṭ+ana*, n. and f. *nâ*, **1.** Striving, Pañch. i. d. 175. **2.** Exertion, Çântiç. 2, 20. **3.** Junction, Vikr. 34, v.r.; Kathâs. 24, 231. **4.** Composition, Lass. 68, 12.

घटिका *ghaṭikâ*, i.e. *ghaṭi+ka*, f. **1.** A jar, Pañch. i. d. 206; a bucket, Mṛichchh. 178, 7. **2.** A *muhûrta*, or thirtieth part of a day and night, Bhâg. P. 5, 21, 4.

घट्ट् *GHAṬṬ* (probably a denominative derived from a dialectical form of *ghṛishṭa*, vb. *ghṛish*, based on the original *gharshṭa*), i. 1, Âtm. and i. 10 Par., *ghaṭṭaya*, **1.** To slip over, to touch, Suçr. 2, 28, 4. **2.** To stir, MBh. 7, 7742. **3.** To shake, MBh. 7, 9401. **4.** To churn, Suçr. 2, 88, 19.—With **अव** *ava*, *ghaṭṭaya*, **1.** To push away, Râm. 5, 15, 10. **2.** To touch, MBh. 11, 462. **3.** To besmear, Suçr. 1, 42, 17. **4.** To churn; Suçr. 1, 33, 4. *avaghaṭṭita*, n. Butting at each other, Hariv. 4720.—With **परि** *pari*, *ghaṭṭaya*, To rub, Çiç. 9, 64.—With **वि** *vi*, *ghaṭṭaya*, To open, MBh. 2, 1674. *vighaṭṭita*, **1.** Dispersed, Bhartṛ. 3, 36. **2.** Churned, Suçr. 1, 32, 19. **3.** Shaken, Kumâras. 1, 9. **4.** Hurt, Suçr. 1, 71, 18. **5.** Severed, Ṛit. 3, 8. **6.** Disclosed, MBh. 4, 1494.—With **सम्** *sam*, *ghaṭṭ*, To grind, Râm. 6, 68, 30. *ghaṭṭaya*, **1.** To rub, Ragh. 6, 73. **2.** To stir, MBh. 7, 8584. **3.** To collect, MBh. 7, 3512.

घट्टन *ghaṭṭ+ana*, n. **1.** Scratching, Râm. 6, 98, 25. **2.** Touching, Hariv. 14581. **3.** Churning, Mârk. P. 12, 38.

घट्टितृ *ghaṭṭ-itṛi*, m. One who strives, MBh. 3, 5890.

† **घण्** *GHAṆ*, ii. 8, Par., Âtm. To shine (v.r.)

† **घण्ट्** *GHAṆṬ*, i. 1, and 10, Par. To shine, or speak.

घण्ट *ghaṇṭa* (akin to *han*), **I.** adj., f. *ṭi*, Sounding (?), MBh. 12, 10377; 4, 188. **II.** f. *ṭâ*, A bell, Man. 10, 33.

घण्टावन्त् *ghaṇṭâ+vant*, adj., f. *vatî*, Having a bell or bells, Bhâg. P. 8, 11, 30.

घण्टिन् *ghaṇṭin*, i.e. *ghaṇṭâ+in*, adj. Having bells (?), MBh. 12, 10377.

घन *ghana*, i.e. *han+a*, **I.** adj., f. *nâ*, **1.** Firm, hard, Bhartṛ. 1, 17. **2.** Without interstices, Suçr. 1, 29, 8. **3.** Uninterrupted, Pañch. iii. d. 237. **4.** Dense, Pañch. iii. d. 188; 129, 8. **5.** As latter part of a compound adj., sometimes Full, Ragh. 8, 90. **6.** Dusk, Bhâg. P. 4, 5, 3. **7.** Deep (as a sound), MBh. 1, 6680; Râjat. 5, 377. **8.** Whole, Upak. 24. **II.** m. **1.** A solid mass, substance, Vedântas. in Chr. 211, 9. **2.** A heap, Râm. 5, 16, 55. **3.** A cloud, Megh. 20.—**Comp.** *Sa-*, adj. dense, Pañch. 141, 16. *Stamba-*, m. 1. a small hoe for weeding. 2. A sickle. 3. A basket for the heads of wild rice.

घनता *ghana+tâ*, f. Solidity, Çiç. 9, 64 (°*tâm nayati çravaṇam*, She makes her ear solid, i.e. she fills up its opening so that no empty space remains).

घनाघन *ghanâghana* (from *ghanâghan*, an old frequent. of *han*, by the aff. *a*), **I.** adj., f. *nâ*, Warlike, MBh. 8, 697. **II.** m. A rainy cloud, Bhâg. P. 5, 24, 7.

† **घम्ब्** *GHAMB*, i. 1, Âtm. To move.

घर्घर *gharghara* (based on an imitative sonnd), m. An inarticulate sound, rattling, Râjat. 2, 99 ; gurgling, Kathâs. 25, 66 (perhaps adj.).

घर्घरित *ghargharita*, i.e. *gharghara* + *ita*, n. Grunting, Bhâg. P. 3, 13, 25.

† **घर्ब्** *GHARB*, i. 1, Par. To move.

घर्म *gharma*, i.e. *ghṛi* + *ma*, m. 1. Heat, Pańch. 80, 7. 2. The hot season, Râm. 1, 63, 24.—Cf. θερμός; Lat. formus (Fest.), fermentum; O.H.G. waram; A.S. wearm; and *ghṛi*.

घर्ष *gharsha*, i. e. *ghṛish* + *a*, m. Dashing together, Râm. 2, 54, 6.

घर्षण *gharshaṇa*, i.e. *ghṛish* + *ana*, n. Grinding, rubbing into, Suçr. 2, 329, 6.

घस् *GHAS*, ii. 2, Par. and † i. 1, Par. To devour.—Desider. *jighatsa*, To desire to devour, MBh. 2, 1485.—Cf. Lat. gânea, ganeo; perhaps Goth. gasts; A.S. gest.

घस *ghas* + *a*, m. The name of a Râkshasa, Râm. 5, 12, 12.

घस्मर *ghasmara*, i.e. *ghas* + *man* + *a*, adj. Voracious, MBh. 8, 1856.

घाटिका *ghâṭikâ*, Pańch. 209, 24; 211, 24; 212, 4 = *ghaṭikâ*, which is probably to be read.

घाण्टिक *ghâṇṭika*, i.e. *ghaṇṭâ* + *ika*, m. A bard who sings in honour of the gods, and rings a bell before their images, MBh. 13, 6028.

घात *ghât* + *a*, i.e. *han*, Caus., + *a*, I. Latter part of comp. adj., Killing. II. m. 1. A stroke, Râm. 6, 98, 23. 2. A shot, Chr. 35, 4. 3. Killing, Pańch. i. d. 321. 4. Sacking, Man. 9, 274. 5. Spoiling, Yâjń. 2, 159.—**Comp.** *Danta-*, m. 1. bite, Sâh. D. 25, 12. 2. a proper name, Lass. 8, 10. *Viçvâsa-*, m. perfidy, treachery, Pańch. 101, 25. *Sa-mûla-*, m. utter destruction or eradication.

घातक *ghâtaka*, i. e. *han*, Caus., + *aka*, adj. and s., f. *kî*. 1. A murderer, Man. 5, 51; Lass. 12, 12. 2. Destroying, MBh. 3, 1277.—**Comp.** *Viçvâsa-*, m. a traitor, Pańch. 52, 15.

घातन *ghâtana*, i.e. *han*, Caus., + *ana*, I. n. Killing, MBh. 2, 1558. II. f. *nî*, A club, Râm. 6, 37, 54.

घातिन् *ghâtin*, i.e. *han*, Caus., + *in*, adj. and s., f. *nî*. 1. Killing, MBh. 3, 17198; a murderer, Man. 8, 89. 2. Destroying, MBh. 3, 63.—**Comp.** *Atmaghâtin*, i.e. *âtman-*, m. a felo-de-se, Yâjń. 3, 21. *Kâla-*, adj. killing slowly, Suçr. 2, 252, 19. *Grâma-*, adj. sacking a village, MBh. 12, 1213. *Pitṛi-*, m. a parricide, Râjat. 5, 448. *Viçvâsa-*, adj. perfidious, MBh. 3, 625.

घार्तिक *ghârtika*, i.e. *ghṛita* + *ika*, m. A cake fried with clarified butter, Pańch. 194, 6.

घास *ghâsa*, i.e. *ghas* + *a*, m. Food, Pańch. 215, 1.—**Comp.** *Açva-*, m. 1. food for horses, Râjat. 3, 489. 2. Pasture-ground for horses, Kathâs. 15, 124.

† **घिण्ण्** *GHIṆṆ* (a dialectical form of *gṛihṇ* from *gṛihṇâ*, vb. *grah*; cf. *ghṛiṇṇ*), i. 1, Âtm. To take.

† **घु** *GHU*, i. 1, Âtm. To sound.

† **घुंष्** *GHUṀSH*, i. 1, Âtm. To render beautiful.—Cf. *ghaṁsh*.

घुट् *GHUṬ*, i. 6, Par. 1. To resist. 2 To protect (v.r.). i. 1, Âtm. To return. —With the prep. **अव** *ava*, *avaghoṭita*, Covered, MBh. 3, 13155.—With **व्या** *vi-â*, To turn, Pańch. 36, 17.

† घुड् *GHUḌ*, i. 6, Par. **1.** To hinder. **2.** To protect, v.r.

† घुण् *GHUṆ* (a dialectical form of *ghûrṇ*), i. 1, Âtm., i. 6, Par. To whirl.

घुण *ghuṇa*, m. A wood-worm, Suçr. 1, 29, 5.

† घुण्ण् *GHUṆṆ* (like *ghiṇṇ*, a dialectical form of *gṛihṇ*, vb. *grah*), i. 1, Âtm. To take.

† घुर् *GHUR*, i. 6, Par. **1.** To be frightful. **2.** To sound.

घुरघुराय *GHURAGHURÂYA* (a denomin. based on an imitative sound), Âtm. To rattle in the throat, Bhâg. P. 3, 30, 17.

घुर्घुराय *GHURGHURÂYA* (a denomin. based on an imitative sound), Âtm. To whistle, Suçr. 1, 104, 1.

घुष् *GHUSH*, i. 1, Par. (Âtm. Râm. 5, 56, 139), To proclaim, Râm. 1. 1. 4, 10, 12. Ptcple. of the pf. pass., *ghushṭa*, **1.** Loud, MBh. 13, 4557. **2.** Resounding, Hariv. 1125. **3.** Offered, Man. 4, 209. Caus. *ghoshaya*, To proclaim, Râm. 5, 49, 13.—With the prep. अव *ava*, To proclaim, Hariv. 3522. *avaghushṭa*, **1.** Summoned, Râm. 3, 47, 9. **2.** Resounding, MBh. 13, 522. **3.** Offered, MBh. 13, 1576.—With आ *â*, To proclaim, MBh. 3, 647.—With व्या *vi-â*, *vyâghushṭa*, Loud sounding, MBh. 12, 3637. Caus. To proclaim loud, Hariv. 10542.—With उद् *ud*, To cry, MBh. 12, 5349. *udghushṭa*, Resounding, Râm. 3, 79, 45. Caus. **1.** To cause to be sounded loud, Râjat. 3, 5. **2.** To proclaim, Mṛichchh. 169, 8.—With प्रोद् *pra-ud*, *prodghushṭa*, Resounding, MBh. 3, 2512. Caus. To proclaim, Râjat. 1, 285.—With उप *upa*, *upaghushṭa*, Resounding, Bhâg. P. 3, 28, 28.—With प्र *pra*, Caus. To proclaim, MBh. 12, 2645.—With वि *vi*, To proclaim, Man. 8, 233. *vighushṭa*, Resounding, Râm. 3, 12, 14.—With उद्वि *ud-vi*, Caus. To proclaim, Bhâg. P. 9, 24, 66.—With सम् *sam*, *saṁghushṭa*, **1.** Sounding, Hariv. 3715. **2.** Resounding, Râm. 2, 31, 4. **3.** Offered, Yâjn. 1, 168.—With परिसम् *pari-sam*, *parisaṁghushṭa*, Resounding, MBh. 3, 2406.

† घूर् *GHÛR*, i. 4, Âtm. **1.** To kill. **2.** To become old.

घूर्ण् *GHÛRṆ*, (a dialectical form of *hvṛiṇ* in *hvṛiṇâ*, ii. 9, of *hvṛi*, based on the original *hvarṇâ*), i. 6, Par ; i. 1, Âtm. **1.** To reel, MBh. 10, 802. **2.** To move to and fro, MBh. 1, 2133. **3.** To roll (as the eye), Prab. 6, 5. **4.** To be uncertain, MBh. 1, 2061. Caus. *ghûrṇaya*, **1.** To roll, Bhartṛ. 1, 88.—With अव *ava*, To roll, Daçak. in Chr. 194, 12. *avaghûrṇita*, Cast down, MBh. 9, 3239.—With आ *â*, To wave, Mṛichchh. 85, 16. *âghûrṇita*, **1.** Shaken, Dev. 12, 26. **2.** Rolling, Bhâg. P. 6, 1, 59.—With व्या *vi-â*, To flutter, MBh. 7, 7301. *vyâghûrṇita*, **1.** Shaken, MBh. 5, 7191. **2.** Tottering, MBh. 2, 1673.—With परि *pari*, To be agitated, MBh. 1, 2089.—With वि *vi*, To stagger, MBh. 11, 522 ; to shake, 3, 11141. *vighûrṇita*, Revolved, Bhâg. P. 3, 19, 3.

घूर्ण *ghûrṇ + a*, adj., f. *ṇâ*, Vacillating, Bhâg. P. 7, 2, 2. **2.** Shaken, Bhâg. P. 9, 10, 17.—Comp. *Timira-* (corr. perhaps *timire-*), adj. staggering in dimness, Châṇ. 70, Berl. Monatsb.

1864, 411. *Mahâ-*, f. *ṇâ*, Spirituous liquor.

घूर्णन *ghûrṇ + ana*, n. and f. *ṇâ*, Trembling oscillation, Gît. 9, 11.

1. घृ *GHṚI*, i. 1, ii. 3, *jighṛi*, and i. 10, Par. To sprinkle.—Cf. *ghṛita* separately.

† 2. घृ *ghṛi*, ii. 3, *jighṛi*, Par. To shine.—Cf. χλιαίνω, etc.; θέρος, θέρω, θάλπω; Lat. fervor, fornax, and *gharma*.

† 3. घृ *GHṚI*, i. 10, Par. To cover.

† घृण् *GHṚIṆ*, ii. 8, *ghṛiṇu*, and *gharṇu*, Par. To shine.—Cf. 2. *ghṛi*.

घृणा *ghṛiṇâ*, i.e. probably 2. *ghṛi + ṇa*, f. **1.** Compassion, Râm. 1, 27, 16. **2.** Contempt, Naish. 1, 20.—Comp. *Nirghṛiṇa*, i.e. *nis-*, adj., f. *ṇâ*, cruel, Râm. 1, 32, 20. *Sa-nis-*, adj. The same, 1, 61, 20, Gorr.

घृणालु *ghṛiṇâ + lu*, adj. Compassionate, Bhâg. P. 4, 22, 43.

घृणि *ghṛiṇi* (akin to *ghṛiṇâ*), adj. Disagreeable, Hariv. 3588.

घृणित्व *ghṛiṇitva*, i.e. *ghṛiṇin + tva*, n. Compassion, MBh. 3, 1119.

घृणिन् *ghṛiṇin*, i.e. *ghṛiṇâ + in*, adj., f. *nî*, Compassionate, Pańch. i. d. 472.—Comp. *A-*, adj. Not despising, MBh. 1, 6374.

† घृण्ण् *GHṚIṆṆ* (a dialectical form of *griḥṇ*, vb. *grah*, cf. *ghiṇṇ*), i. 1, Âtm. To take.

घृत *ghṛi + ta* (properly ptcple. of the pf. pass. of 1. *ghṛi*), n. **1.** Clarified butter, or butter which has been boiled gently and allowed to cool, Man. 11, 134. **2.** (ved.) Rain, Chr. 291, 3 = Rigv. i. 85, 3.

घृतवन्त् *ghṛita + vant*, adj., f. *vatî*, Abundant in butter, Chr. 290, 6 = Rigv. i. 64, 6.

घृताची *ghṛitâchî*, i.e. *ghṛita-ańch + î*, f. The name of an Apsaras, MBh. 1, 4821.

घृतिन् *ghṛitin*, i.e. *ghṛita + in*, adj., f. *nî*, Containing ghṛita, MBh. 13, 1840.

घृष् *GHṚISH*, i. 1, Par. To grind, Pańch. i. d. 160. *ghṛishṭa*, **1.** Pounded, Pańch. iii. d. 240. **2.** Scratched, Hariv. 12175. **3.** Rubbed into, Suçr. 2, 278, 7. Caus. *gharshita*, Crumbled, Râm. 3, 79, 31.—With the prep. अव *ava*, To rub off, Pańch. i. d. 337. Caus. **1.** The same, Suçr. 1, 344, 6. **2.** To rub into, 1, 46, 12.—With उद् *ud*, **1.** To rub out, Ragh. 17, 28. **2.** To strike, Râjat. 2, 99.—With नि *ni*, To grind, MBh. 8, 1797. *nighṛishṭa*, Subdued, MBh. 12, 7318.—With निस् *nis*, To rub, Râm. 2, 96, 18.—With परि *pari*, To grind, Hariv. 5362.—With प्र *pra*, To rub into, Suçr. 2, 193, 3.—With संप्र *sam-pra*, The same, Suçr. 2, 67, 2.—With वि *vi*, *vighṛishṭa*, **1.** Ground. **2.** Sore, 2, 129, 6.—With सम् *sam*, **1.** To rub, Bhâg. P. 4, 6, 30; MBh. 1, 1133 (*ghṛishya*, pass. with the terminations of the Par.). **2.** To rival, Ragh. 19, 36.—Cf. χρίω, χρῖσμα, etc., χρίμπτω; Lat. frio, frico; O.H.G. and A.S., hrinan, to touch.

घृषु *ghṛishu*, i.e. ved. *ghṛish = hṛish + u*, adj. Brisk, Chr. 291, 12 = Rigv. i. 64, 12.

घृष्वि *ghṛishvi*, i. e. ved. *ghṛish = hṛish + vi*, adj. Brisk, Chr. 291, 1 = Rigv. i. 85, 1.

घोटक *ghoṭaka*, m. A horse, Pańch. 254, 23.

घोणा *ghoṇâ* (a dialectical form of *ghrâṇâ*), f. 1. The nose, Mṛichchh. 35, 10. 2. The nostrils of a horse, MBh. 6, 3390. 3. A beak, MBh. 10, 38.

घोण्टा *ghoṇṭâ*, f. The betel-nut tree, Suçr. 2, 103, 16.

घोर *ghora*, I. adj., f. *râ*. 1. Horrible, dreadful, Râm. 3, 8, 12. 2. Violent, Suçr. 1, 35, 7. II. m. 1. A name of Çiva, MBh. 12, 10375. 2. A proper name, MBh. 13, 4148. III. n. A horrible act, Râm. 1, 58, 8.—Comp. *Su-*, adj. terrific, hideous.—Cf. probably Goth. gaurs, sad.

घोरत्व *ghora+tva*, n. Horribleness, MBh. 3, 13781.

घोष *ghosha*, i.e. *ghush+a*, m. 1. Sound, Man. 7, 225; roar, Râm. 2, 66, 10; language, Râm. 3, 52, 20. 2. A station of herdsmen, MBh. 2, 215. 3. A name of Çiva, MBh. 12, 10386.—Comp. *Dama-*, m. a proper name, MBh. 1, 7029. *Nandi-*, m. shout, MBh. 13, 5288. *Mahâ-*, n. a market. *Simha-*, m. a proper name, Daçak. in Chr. 199, 20. *Sukha-puṇyâha-*, i.e. *sukha-puṇya-aha-*, m. the proclamation of a happy holiday. *Strî-*, m. day-break.

घोषक *ghoshaka*, i.e. *ghush+aka*, m. A bell-man, Kathâs. 24, 60.

घोषण *ghoshaṇa*, i.e. *ghush+ana*, I. adj. Causing to sound, Bhâg. P. 4, 5, 6. II. n., and f. *ṇâ*, Proclaiming, Râm. 5, 58, 18; Daçak. in Chr. 183, 5.

घोषवन्त् *ghosha+vant*, I. adj. *vatî*, Sounding, MBh. 2, 65; roaring, MBh. 6, 578. II. f. *vatî*, A kind of lute (?), Kathâs. 12, 32.

घोषिन् *ghoshin*, i.e. *ghosha+in*, adj., f. *iṇî*, Sounding, MBh. 5, 3348.

ऽघ्न *-ghna*, i.e. *han+a*, Latter part of comp. adj. and s., f. *ni* (*nâ*, MBh. 13, 2397), 1. Striking, Man. 8, 386. 2. Killing, a murderer, Man. 9, 232. 3. Destroying, Man. 8, 127; Râm. 2, 35, 6. 4. Removing, Man. 7, 218.

घ्रा *GHRÂ*, i. 1, *jighra* (ep. ii. 2, *ghrâti*, MBh. 14, 668), Par. (in epic poetry also Âtm., MBh. 1, 7982). 1. To smell, Man. 2, 98. 2. To sniff at, Râm. 2, 26, 35. 3. To perceive, Bhâg. P. 1, 3, 36. 4. To kiss (or, rather, To smell as a token of affection; see Wilson, Hindu Dr. vol. i. p. 45 n.), MBh. 9, 2940. Anomalous ptcple. of the pres. *jighrâṇa*, MBh. 1, 5781. Ptcple. of the pf. pass. *ghrâta*, also in the sense of an act, Having scented. Ptcple. of the fut. pass. 1. *ghrâtavya*, n. Smell, Bhartṛ. 1, 7. 2. *ghreya*, n. Smell, MBh. 2, 200. Comp. *A-*, adj. unfit to be smelt, Man, 11, 67. Anomalous absolut. *jighritvâ*, Hariv. 7059.—With the prep. **अव** *ava*, 1. To smell, Man. 3, 218. 2. To kiss, Râm. 2, 20, 21.—With **आ** *â*, 1. To smell, Man. 11, 149. 2. To kiss, Râm. 2, 70, 16.—Ptcple. of the pf. pass. *âghrâta*, in active sense, Hariv. 4478.—With **उपा** *upa-â*, 1. To smell, MBh. 3, 14504. 2. To kiss, Râm. 1, 4, 9.—With **समुपा** *sam-upa-â*, To kiss, Râm. 2, 72, 4.—With **समा** *sam-â*, 1. To smell, Râm. 5, 23, 32. 2. To kiss, Râm. 2, 72, 4.—With **उप** *upa*, 1. To smell, MBh. 5, 4059; to smell at, Man. 4, 209. 2. To kiss, Râm. 2, 72, 30.—With **समुप** *sam-upa*, To kiss, Râm. 4, 22, 1.—With **परि** *pari*, To kiss all over, MBh. 11, 616.—With **वि** *vi*, 1. To trace, Bhâg. P. 3, 13, 28. 2. To smell, Bhâg. P. 3. 2, 18.—Cf. *βρῶμος* and *ghrâṇa*; perhaps also Lat. frâgro.

घ्राण *ghrâṇa*, i.e. *ghrâ*+*na*, I. m. **1.** Smelling, Bhâg. P. 2, 1, 29. **II.** n. and f. *ṇâ*, The nose, MBh. 1, 6074.—Cf. ῥίν, ῥίς.

घ्राणज *ghrâṇa-ja*, adj. Produced by the nose, Bhâshâp. 51.

घ्राति *ghrâ*+*ti*, f. Smelling, Man. 11, 67 (68).

घ्रातृ *ghrâ-tṛi*, m. One who smells, MBh. 14, 619.

ङ *Ṅ*.

† ङु *ṄU*, i. 1, Âtm. To sound.

च *CH*.

च *cha*, I. A copulative particle, And. Where two things are to be joined, it is, **1.** Repeated, *cha—cha* (like τε—τε, Lat. que—que), As well—As, and, *saṁjîvayati châjasraṁ pramâpayati châvyayaḥ*, That immutable power revivifies as well as destroys in eternal succession, Man. 1, 57; *daça châshṭau cha*, Ten and eight, Man. 1, 64. **2.** Dropped in the first place; this is the general use, Hit. i. d. 33. **3.** Dropped, but not often, in the second place, e.g. *pretya cheha*, In the next world and in this, Man. 3, 20. Where more than two things are to be joined, some have the conjunction, while others are without it, e.g. *karṇau charma cha bâlâṁç cha vastiṁ snâyuṁ cha rochanâm*, (let him carry) their ears, their hides, their tails, the skin below their navels, their tendons, and the liquor exuding from their foreheads, Man. 8, 234. **II.** When followed by *vâ*, Either, Man. 12, 89; when preceded by *vâ*, Or, Nal. 14, 8. **III.** Even, Çâk. 6, 5; and even, Hiḍ. i. 26. **IV.** Just, Ragh. 12, 45. **V.** But, Hit. Pr. d. 12. **VI.** If, Bhartṛ. 2, 45.—Cf. τε; Lat. que; Goth. -h, e.g. in sa-h, 'and he.'

चक् *CHAK*, i. 1, Par., Âtm. **1.** † To be satisfied. **2.** † To resist. **3.** To shine. *chakita*, **1.** Frightened, Bhartṛ. 3, 10. **2.** Timid, Bhâg. P. 5, 8, 18. n. Being frightened, Mṛichchh. 86, 20.—With the prep. उद् *ud*, To see, Bhâg. P. 6, 16, 48.—With प्र *pra*, *prachakita*, Frightened, Pañch. i. d. 420.

चकास् *CHAKÂS* (cf. *kâç*), ii. 2, Par. To shine, Bhâg. P. 5, 24, 9 (with *ç* instead of *s*, Bhâg. P. 3, 19, 14).

चकोर *chakora*, m. The Greek partridge, Perdix rufa, MBh. 3, 936.

† चक्क् *CHAKK*, i. 10, Par. To give pain.

चक्नस *chaknasa*, Lass. 4, 17, is to be changed to *chakra-saṁ(kulam)*.

चक्र *chakra*, I. n. **1.** A wheel, Man. 8, 291. **2.** A potter's wheel, Yâjñ. 3, 146. **3.** A discus, or sharp circular missile weapon, especially of Vishṇu, Râm. 1, 29, 6. **4.** An oil-press, Man. 4, 84. **5.** A circle, Râjat. 5, 230. **6.** A form of military array, a circular position. **7.** An astrological or mystical figure, Râjat. 5, 55 (*mâtṛi-*). **8.** A multitude, Râm. 6, 75, 39. **9.** An army, MBh. 5, 1939. **10.** Dominion, Bhâg. P. 9, 20, 32. **II.** m. **1.** The ruddy goose, Anas casarca, MBh. 9, 443. **2.** The name of a people, MBh. 6, 352. **3.** A proper name, MBh. 1, 2147. **4.** The name of a mountain, Bhâg. P. 5, 20, 15.—Comp. *Eka-*, I. adj., f. *râ*, protected by one sovereign, Bhâg. P. 3, 1, 20. II. m. a proper name, MBh. 1, 2533. III. f. *kâ*, the name of a town, MBh. 1, 382. *Kâla-*, I. n. the wheel of ever-revolving time, MBh. 4, 1607.

II. m. the sun, MBh. 3, 151. *Dik-chakra,* i.e. *diç-,* n. the real horizon, Lass. 74, 1. *Dharma-,* n. the law, MBh. 2, 456. *Para-,* n. the host of the enemy, MBh. 1, 6209. *Mâtṛi-* (see 7). *Râçi-,* n. the zodiac. *Hiraṇya-,* adj. having golden wheels, Chr. 294, 5=Rigv. i. 88, 5.

चक्रक *chakra+ka,* m. **1.** A kind of snake, Suçr. 2, 265, 17. **2.** A proper name, MBh. 13, 253.

चक्रधर *chakra-dhara,* I. adj. **1.** Bearing a wheel, Pańch. 242, 15. **2.** Bearing a discus. II. m. **1.** A name of Vishṇu (wielding the discus) Mṛichchh. 76, 13. **2.** A sovereign, MBh. 3, 8221. **3.** A snake, Râjat. 1, 261.

चक्रबाल *chakra-bâla,* and **चक्रवाल** *chakra-vâla* (cf. *vâlaka,* A finger-ring). I. (m. or n.) A ring, MBh. 1, 7021. II. m. A range of mountains supposed to encircle the earth, and to be the limit of light and darkness. III. n. **1.** A circle, Bhâg. P. 5, 18, 14. **2.** A group, Bhartṛ. 2, 65.—Comp. *Daṇḍa-,* m. 1. the name of a fabulous weapon, Râm. 1, 29, 5. 2. A division of an army, Mâlav. 9, 10. *Diç-,* n. the horizon, Lass. 74, 1. 2. A compass-card, Varâh. Bṛih. S. 86, 99. *Sa-mâtṛi-,* adj. surrounded by the divine mothers, Râjat. 5, 55.

चक्रवर्तिता *chakravartitâ,* and **चक्रवर्तित्व** *chakravartitva,* i.e. *chakra-vartin +tâ,* f., or *+tva,* n. Sovereign dominion, Daçak. 185, ult.; Hariv. 8815.

चक्रवाक *chakravâka,* i.e. *chakra* (based on an imitative sound)-*vach+a,* I. m. The ruddy goose, Anas casarea Gm., Râm. 3, 20, 20. II. f. *kî,* Its female, Megh. 81.

चक्रवाकिन् *chakravâkin,* i.e. *chakravâka+in,* adj., f. *nî,* Crowded with ruddy geese, Ragh. 15, 30.

चक्रवाल *chakravâla,* see *chakra-bâla.*

चक्राङ्किता *chakrâṅkitâ,* i.e. *chakra-aṅkitâ* (vb. *aṅk*), f. The name of a plant (?), Pańch. 157, 23.

चक्राङ्ग *chakrâṅga,* i.e. *chakra-aṅga,* m. A goose, MBh. 8, 1895; Man. 5, 12.

चक्रिका *chakrikâ,* i.e. *chakra+ka,* f. **1.** A troop, Râjat. 4, 376. **2.** Artifice, Râjat. 5, 279.

चक्रिन् *chakrin,* i.e. *chakra+in,* I. adj. Driving in a carriage, Man. 2, 138. II. m. **1.** A name of Vishṇu, Bhag. 11, 17. **2.** A name of Çiva, MBh. 13, 745. **3.** An oil-grinder, Yâjń. 1, 141.

चच् *CHAKSH* (akin to *akshi*), ii. 2, Âtm. (in epic poetry also Par., MBh. 3, 601), **1.** To see, Bhâg. P. 5, 7, 13. **2.** To perceive, Bhâg. P. 1, 18, 25. **3.** To say, MBh. 8, 3384 (Par.).—With the prep. **अभि** *abhi,* **1.** To look at, Chr. 294, 9=Rigv. i. 92, 9 (*abhichakshyâ,* absol. with lengthened final); Bhâg. P. 4, 3, 18. **2.** To address, Bhâg. P. 3, 13, 5. **3.** To name, Bhâg. P. 3, 12, 51.—With **आ** *â,* **1.** To declare, Man. 4, 81. **2.** To address, Daçak. in Chr. 189, 2. **3.** To name, Bhâg. P. 5, 22, 6.—With **अभ्या** *abhi-â,* **1.** To look at, Bhâg. P. 1, 9, 11. **2.** To speak, Bhâg. P. 8, 5, 14.—With **प्रत्या** *prati-â,* **1.** To decline, MBh. 12, 6676. **2.** To repulse, Daçak. in Chr. 181, 6. **3.** To answer (with acc. of the person), Bhâg. P. 3, 15, 11.—With **समा** *sam-â,* To report, Bhâg. P. 1, 4, 13.—With **परि** *pari,*

1. To overlook, Bhâg. P. 4, 14, 33. 2. To report, MBh. 1, 1025. 3. To mention, admit, MBh. 12, 294. 4. To call, Man. 2, 171. 5. To answer (with acc.), Bhâg. P. 1, 17, 21. — With प्र *pra*, 1. To report, MBh. 1, 8331. 2. To declare, Man. 4, 102. 3. To call, Man. 2, 59.—With संप्र *sam-pra*, To explain, Suçr. 1, 37, 13. — With प्रति *prati*, 1. To perceive, Bhâg. P. 3, 9, 32. 2. To expect, Bhâg. P. 9, 4, 41.—With वि *vi*, 1. To see clearly, Bhâg. P. 3, 11, 17. 2. To explain, MBh. 1, 2199. With प्रवि *pra-vi*, To call, MBh. 12, 11466.—With सम् *sam*, 1. To look at, Bhâg. P. 3, 19, 8. 2. To consider, Râm. 2, 1, 27. 3. To report, MBh. 6, 253.—Cf. παπταίνω (properly a denominative of a lost noun, *παπταν = ved. *chakshan*), also ὀπιπτεύω, ὀπίπης; probably Goth. saihvan, A.S. sean; Goth. siuns (for organ. sihvni + s); O.H.G. sagên, A.S. saegan, etc.

चचस् *chaksh + as*, n. The eye, Chr. 295, 11 = Rigv. i. 92, 11. 2. Guidance, Chr. 293, 5 = Rigv. i. 87, 5. Comp. *Viçva-*, adj. all-seeing, Chr. 289, 2 = Rigv. i. 50, 2.

ऽचतुष *-chakshusha*, i.e. *chakshus + a*, A substitute for *chakshus*, when latter part of a comp. adj., e.g. *sa-*, adj. Seeing, MBh. 1, 6818.

चतुष्मत्ता *chakshushmattâ*, i.e. *chakshushmant + tâ*, f. The faculty of seeing, Ragh. 4, 13.

चतुष्मन्त् *chakshushmant*, i.e. *chakshus + mant*, adj., f. *matî*. 1. Seeing, MBh. 1, 737. 2. Having eyes, Bhâg. P. 3, 23, 19.

चतुष्य *chakshushya*, i.e. *chakshus + ya*, adj., f. *yâ*. 1. Fit for the eyes, MBh. 13, 3423. 2. Agreeable to the eyes, Râjat. 3, 493.

चतुस् *chaksh + us*, n. The eye, Indr. 4, 1.—Comp. *A-*, adj. blind, Pańch. i. d. 393. *Ghrâṇa-*, adj. using his nose instead of his eye, blind, MBh. 8, 3443. *Châra-*, adj. seeing by means of spies, Man. 9, 256. *Jana-*, n. the eye of all creatures, i.e. the sun, Hariv. 8050. *Jńâna-*, n. intellect, Man. 2, 8. *Divya-*, I. n. a divine, i.e. a prophetic eye, Daçak. in Chr. 179, 7. II. adj. having a divine eye, Ragh. 3, 45. *Dharma-*, adj. loving justice, Râm. 2, 111, 22. *Naya-*, n. the eye of prudence, Râm. 1, 7, 11. *Nis-*, adj. blind, MBh. 12, 10523. *Mukta-* (vb. *much*), I. adj. with one's eyes opened. II. m. a lion. *Sa-*, adj. seeing.

† चघ् *CHAGH*, ii. 5, Par. To kill.

चङ्क्रमण *chańkramaṇa*, i.e. *chańkram* (frequent. of *kram*) + *ana*, n. Going, walking, Pańch. 209, 1.

चञ्च् *CHAŃCH* (akin to *chal*, cf. *chańchala*), i. 1, Par. 1. To hop, to dance, Gît. 4, 8. 2. To move, Bhartṛ. 3, 1.

चञ्चल *chańchal + a* (frequent. of *chal*), adj., f. *lâ*. 1. Moving to and fro, unsteady, MBh. 8, 3920.; Pańch. 204, 1. 2. Fickle, Kathâs. 7, 57.

चञ्चलत्व *chańchala + tva*, n. Unsteadiness, Bhag. 6, 33.

चञ्चु *chańchu*, f. The beak, Pańch. i. d. 28.—Comp. *Vâda-*, m. a jester, Bhartṛ. 3, 57 (read *vâda-* instead of *vâdi*, and probably *chuńchavaḥ* instead of *chańchavaḥ*, cf. Pâṇ. 5, 2, 26; cf. Schol.).

चञ्चुता *chańchu + tâ*, f. Cleverness, Râjat. 5, 304.

चञ्चुरी *chańchur + î* (frequent. of

char), adj. Continually doing, MBh. 13, 1220.

चट् *CHAṬ* (a dialectical form of *chart*, vb. *chṛit*), i. 1, Par. 1. † To rain. 2. † To cover. 3. To separate, Pańch. 121, 1. i. 10 (rather Causal), *châṭaya*, 1. To separate. 2. † To kill.—With the prep. उद् *ud*, To disappear, Bhâg. P. 5, 9, 18. Caus. To drive out, Bhâg. P. 2, 7, 28.

चटक *chaṭaka*, m. A sparrow, Pańch. 80, 5. f. *kâ*, A hen-sparrow, Pańch. 80, 10.—Comp. *Mṛiga-indra-*, m. A hawk.

चटचटाऽ *chaṭachaṭâ-*, (an imitative sound), Clashing, MBh. 1, 7110; roaring, 3, 10980.

चटचटाय *CHAṬACHAṬÂYA* (a denomin. derived from the preceding by *ya*), Âtm. To crackle, Suçr. 2, 245, 20.

चटुल *chaṭula*, adj. 1. Unsteady, Ragh. 9, 58. 2. Inconstant, Amar. 71. 3. Beautiful, Gît. 10, 9.

† चण् *CHAṆ*, i. 1, Par. 1. To give (or to go, to kill). 2. To sound, v.r.

चण *chaṇa*, and चणक *chaṇa + ka*, m. Chick-pea, MBh. 13, 5468; Pańch. i. d. 148.

† चण्ड् *CHAṆḌ*, i. 1 and 10 (rather a denomin. derived from the next), Âtm. To be angry.

चण्ड *chaṇḍa* (a dialectical form of *chand + ra*), I. adj., f. *ḍî*. 1. Flaming, Bhâg. P. 7, 8, 20; hot, e.g. in *chaṇḍâṁçu*, i.e. *chaṇḍa-aṁçu*, m. The sun (properly, Having hot rays), Râjat. 4, 401. 2. Violent, MBh. 1, 1493; Bhartṛ. 2, 47. 3. Passionate, Ragh. 2, 49. 4. Wrathful, Râm. 2, 70, 10 (*ḍî*). 5. Cruel, MBh. 1, 6752. II. °*ḍam*, adv. Passionately, Mâlav. d. 56. III. m. 1. A name of Çiva, MBh. 12, 10358. 2. A name of Skanda, MBh. 3, 14631. 3. A proper name, Hariv. 12937. IV. f. *ḍâ*. 1. A name of Durgâ, MBh. 6, 797. 2. A name of several plants, Suçr. 1, 139, 9. V. f. *ḍî*, A name of Durgâ, MBh. 6, 797.—Comp. *Ati-*, adj. very passionate, Râjat. 5, 380.

चण्डत्व *chaṇḍa + tva*, n. Passionateness, Sâh. D. 176.

चण्डाल *chaṇḍâla* (akin to *chaṇḍa*), m. A man of the lowest of the mixed tribes, Man. 5, 131; 10, 12; f. *lâ*, A woman of that tribe, Man. 11, 175.

चण्डालता *chaṇḍâla + tâ*, f., and

चण्डालत्व *chaṇḍâla + tva*, n. The condition of a Chaṇḍâla, Râm. 1, 58, 9; 8.

चण्डिका *chaṇḍikâ*, i.e. *chaṇḍî + ka*, f. A name of Durgâ, Kathâs. 25, 86.

चण्डिमन् *chaṇḍiman*, i.e. *chaṇḍa + iman*, m. Cruelty and heat, Râjat. 6, 298.

चत् *CHAT*, i. 1, Par., Âtm. 1. To abscond (ved.). 2. † To ask.

चतसृ *chatasṛi*, see *chatur*.

चतुःसन *chatuḥsana*, i.e. *chatur-sana*, adj. Containing the four sons of Brahman, of whom the names begin with *sana*, Bhâg. P. 2, 7, 5, viz. *Sanaka, Sananda, Sanâtana, Sanatkumâra*.

चतुर् *chatur* (for *chatvar*), f. *chatasṛi*, numeral, Four, Chr. 28, 21; msc. instead of the fem. Râm. 4, 39, 33.—Cf. τέττυρες for τέτϝαρες; Lat. quatuor; Goth. fidvôr; A.S. feower.

चतुर *chatura*, I. adj., f. *râ*. 1. Dexterous, Pańch. 161, 2. 2. Ingenious, Pańch. 158, 9. 3. Charming, Ragh. 8, 94. 4. Quick, Râjat. 3, 176; °*ram*, adv. 188. II. n. Cleverness, Amar. 20.

चतुरक *chatura + ka*, m. 1. A proper name, Pańch. 87, 4. **2.** f. *rikâ*, A proper name, Kathâs. 6, 53.

चतुरता *chatura + tâ*, f. Shrewdness, Bhartṛ. 1, 71.

चतुरन्त *chatur-anta*, I. adj. Epithet of the earth, denoting: Whole (verbally, with its four ends, i.e. north, east, etc.), MBh. 1, 2801. II. f. *tâ*, The earth, Ragh. 10, 86.

चतुरस्रक *chatur-asra + ka*, m. and comp. *ardha-*, *dvi-*, m. The names of different postures, Vikr. 64.

चतुर्थ *chatur + tha*, I. ordin. number, f. *thî*, Fourth, Chr. 12. II. n. A fourth part, MBh. 1, 1822 —Cf. τέταρτος; Lat. quartus; O.H.G. fiordo; A.S. feordh.

चतुर्थक *chaturtha + ka*, adj. Returning every fourth day (as fever), Hariv. 10555.

चतुर्दश *chaturdaça*, i.e. *chaturdaçan + a*, I. ord. number, f. *çî*, Fourteenth, Râm. 2, 112, 25. II. f. *çî*, The fourteenth day of the half of a lunar month, Man. 4, 113.

चतुर्दशधा *chaturdaçadhâ*, i.e. *chaturdaçan + dhâ*, adv. Fourteen-fold, Bhâg. P. 5, 26, 38.

चतुर्दशन् *chatur-daçan*, numeral, Fourteen, Râjat. 5, 442.

चतुर्दशम *chaturdaçama*, i.e. *chaturdaçan + ma*, ordin. numb., f. *mî*, Fourteenth, Bhâg. P. 8, 13, 34.

चतुर्दिशम् *chatur-diç + a + m*, adv. To the four quarters or points of the compass, Bhâg. P. 5, 17, 5.

चतुर्धा *chatur + dhâ*, adv. **1.** In four parts; Vedântas. in Chr. 208, 19. **2.** Four-fold, MBh. 9, 2487.

चतुर्युज् *chatur-yuj*, adj. Drawn by four horses, Râm. 1, 53, 18.

चतुर्वर्णमय *chatur-varṇa + maya*, adj., f. *yî*, Consisting of the four castes, Ragh. 10, 23.

चतुर्विंशतिक *chatur-viṁçati + ka*, adj. Consisting of twenty-four, Bhâg. P. 3, 26, 11.

चतुष्क *chatushka*, i.e. *chatur + ka*, I. adj. with *çatam*, Four in the hundred, Man. 8, 142. II. n. **1.** A collection of four things, Man. 7, 50. **2.** A hall supported by four columns, Kumâras. 5, 68.

चतुष्कर्णता *chatushkarṇatâ*, i.e. *chatur-karṇa + tâ*, f. Confidence, Pańch. 66, 3.

चतुष्किका *chatushkikâ*, i.e. *chatushka + ka*, f. A collection of four things, Râjat. 5, 369.

ऽचतुष्किन् *-chatushkin*, i.e. *chatushka + in*, adj. Having four, MBh. 12, 13340.

चतुष्टय *chatushṭaya*, i.e. *chatur + taya*, I. adj., f. *yî*. **1.** Of four different sorts, MBh. 12, 11965. **2.** Being four, Bhâg. P. 3, 15, 28. II. n. A collection of four things, Man. 8, 180.

चतुष्टोम *chatushṭoma*, i.e. *chatur-stoma*, n. A stoma, or sacrifice, consisting of four parts, Râm. 1, 13, 43.

चतुष्पथ *chatushpatha*, i.e. *chatur-patha*, m. and n. A place where four roads meet, Man. 4, 131.

चतुष्पद् *chatushpad*, see *chatushpâd*.

चतुष्पद *chatushpada*, i.e. *chatur-pada*, I. adj., f. *dâ*. **1.** Having four legs, MBh. 3, 10661. **2.** Consisting of four pâdas, or verses, Mâlav. 19, 11. II. m. A quadruped, Bhâg. P. 6, 4, 9. III. n. A stanza of four pâdas (see I. 2), Mâlav. 16, 18.

चतुष्पाद् *chatushpâd*, i.e. *chatur-pâd*. The base of the weakest cases is *-pad*, I. adj., f. *-padî*, but n. *-pâd* and *pad*, 1. Having four legs, Chr. 288, 3= Rigv. i. 49, 3; Man. 1, 81. 2. Having four steps, MBh. 12, 8838. 3. Consisting of four parts, MBh. 5, 5352. II. m. A quadruped, MBh. 12, 5697.—Cf. τετράπους; Lat. quadrupes; A.S. feower-fed.

चतुष्पाद *chatushpâda*, i.e. *chatur-pâda*, I. adj., f. *dî*. 1. Having four legs, Râm. 5, 17, 30. 2. Having four parts, MBh. 3, 1459. II. m. A quadruped, Yâjń. 2, 298.

चतुस् *chatus*, i.e. *chatur*+*s*, adv. Four times, Chân. 71.—Cf. Lat. quater.

चत्वर *chatvar*+*a* (cf. *chatur*), n. and m. 1. A place where many (literally, four) roads meet; in the name of one of the mothers, *Chatvara-vâsinî*, MBh. 9, 2630 (dwelling on cross-roads, cf. *chatushpatha-niketâ*, MBh. 9, 2643; *chatushpatha-ratâ*, 2645, names of other mothers bearing the same signification; cf. Hecate trivia); a square, MBh. 3, 655. 2. A courtyard, Bhâg. P. 4, 9, 57.

चत्वारिंश *chatvâriṁça*, ordin. numb. (from *chatvâriṁçat*), f. *çî*, Fortieth, e.g. *eka-*, Forty-first, MBh. adhy. *ashṭa-chatvâriṁça*, i.e. *ashṭan-*, Forty-eighth, Râm. 3, 48. *tri-*, Forty-third, MBh. 4, chap. 43. *chatuçchatvâriṁça*, i.e. *chatur-*, Forty-fourth, MBh. adhy. *dvâ-*, and *dvi-*, Forty-second, ib. 1, adhy. 42; 2, adhy. 42. *navan-*, Forty-ninth, Râm. 6, 49.

चत्वारिंशत् *chatvâriṁçat*, i.e. *chatvâri-daçanti* (originally pl. n., cf. τεσσαράκοντα, Lat. quadraginta, but in Sanskrit it has become fem.), f. Forty, Râm. 5, 6, 19.—Comp. *Dvâ-*, forty-two, MBh. 12, adhy. 142.

चत्वारिंशति *chatvâriṁçati* (cf. the last), f. Forty, Râjat. 3, 475.

† **चद्** *CHAD*, i. 1, Par., Âtm. To beg.

चन *cha-na*, A particle used after derivatives of the interrogative pronoun *kim*, in order to make them indefinite; see *katham*, *kadâ*, *kim*, *kutas*, *kva*.—Cf. Goth. -hun, e.g. hvar-hun, whenever.

चन्द् *CHAND* (for original *çchand*; cf. the ved. frequent. *chaniçchand*, ved. *çchandra*, Rigv. 3, 31, 15; and some comp. words, e.g. *puru-çchandra*), i. 1, Par. To shine.—Cf. ξανθός, ξουθός, σπινθήρ; Lat. candere, accendo, scintilla, etc.

चन्दन *chand*+*ana*, I. m. and n. 1. Sandal, the tree, Râm. 3, 76, 3; the wood, Pańch. i. d. 47; the unctuous preparations of the wood, Pańch. v. d. 18. II. m. A proper name, Râm. 4, 41, 3. III. f. *nî*, The name of a river, Râm. 4, 40, 20.—Comp. *Ku-*, n. red-sanders, Pterocarpus santalinus. *Hari-*, I. m. and n. 1. A yellow and fragrant sort of sandal-wood. 2. a tree of paradise. II. n. 1. saffron. 2. moonlight. 3. the farina of the lotus. 4. the person of a beloved one.

चन्दनिन् *chandanin*, i.e. *chandana*+*in*, adj. Smeared over with the unctuous preparation of sandal, MBh. 13, 1249.

चन्द्र *chand*+*ra*, m. 1. The moon, MBh. 11, 220. 2. A moon-like spot, Bhâg. P. 4, 15, 7. 3. A proper name, MBh. 1, 2667. 4. The name of a mountain, Râm. 6, 26, 6.—Comp. *Ardha-*, see separately. *Pûrṇa-*, m. the full of the moon, Râm. 3, 53, 44. *Râma-*,

m. the second of the three renowned Râmas, the son of Daçaratha, and hero of the Râmâyaṇa. *Çarachchandra,* i.e. *çarad-,* m. the autumnal moon.

चन्द्रक *chandra + ka,* f. *rikâ.* **I.** A substitute for *chandra* when latter part of comp. adj. Mâlav. d. 82; Râm. 5, 42, 3. **II.** m. **1.** The eye in a peacock's tail, Râjat. 1, 260. **2.** A proper name, Râjat. 2, 16. **III.** f. *rikâ.* **1.** Moonlight, Çiç. 9, 28. **2.** A proper name, Mâlav. 50, 6.

चन्द्रकान्त *chandra + kânta,* (vb. *kam*), **I.** adj. Graceful, like the moon, Çrut. 23. **II.** m. A fabulous gem, supposed to be formed of the congealed rays of the moon, Pañch. i. d. 88.

चन्द्रमस् *chandramas,* i.e. *chandra -mâsa,* m. The moon, Nal. 17, 6.

चन्द्रवन्त् *chandra + vant,* **I.** adj., f. *vatî,* Moonlit, Ghaṭ. 2. **II.** f. *vatî,* A proper name, Pañch. 127, 22.

चन्द्रिका *chandrikâ,* see *chandraka.*

† **चप्** *CHAP,* i. 1. Par. To soothe. i. 10, Par. **1.** To grind. **2.** To deceive.

चपल *chapala* (i.e. *kamp + ala*) adj., f. *lâ.* **1.** Trembling, unsteady, Ragh. 11, 8; Hit. i. d. 46. **2.** Giddy, inconsiderate, Matsyop. 72; MBh. 3, 13848. **3.** Swift, Hariv. 4104; °*lam,* adv. Quickly, Daçak. in Chr. 200, 2. **4.** Wanton, Râm. 3, 51, 33.

चपलक *chapala + ka,* adj. Inconsiderate, Hariv. 4546.

चपलता *chapala + tâ,* f. Fickleness, Hit. 49, 15.

चम् *CHAM,* i. 1; ii. 5, Par. To sip. —With the prep. **आ** *â,* base of the pres. etc., *châma,* **1.** To sip water, Râm. 2, 52, 73. **2.** To rinse one's mouth, i.e. to make one's ablution, Man. 2, 61. **3.** To swallow figuratively, MBh. 5, 2978 (the horses swallowed the way, i.e. finished it very quickly). Ptcple. of the pf. pass. *â-chânta,* in active sense, One who has rinsed his mouth, Man. 3, 251. Ptcple. of the fut. pass., *â-chamanîya,* n. Water for rinsing the mouth with, MBh. 3, 13662. Causal, *châmaya,* To cause to sip, Man. 5, 241.—With **पर्या** *pari-â, paryâchânta* (viz. *anna,* food), One who has rinsed his mouth too early (without waiting the end of a meal), Man. 4, 212.—With **समा** *sam-â,* To make one's ablution, MBh. 13, 5063.

चमत्कार *chamat-kâra* (the latter part is *kâra,* the former questionable), n. Surprise, Prab. 76, 15.

चमर *chamara,* **I.** m. Bos grunniens, Râm. 3, 49, 24. **II.** m. and n. The tail of the Bos grunniens, used to whisk off insects, flies, etc.; one of the insignia of royalty, MBh. 2, 1861; Vikr. d. 76.

चमस *cham + asa,* m. and n. A drinking vessel, Man. 5, 116.

चमू *chamû,* f. An army, Râm. 1, 74, 16, consisting of 729 elephants, 729 chariots, 2187 horses, and 3645 foot, MBh. 1, 292.

† **चम्प्** *CHAMP,* i. 10, Par. To go, v.r.

चम्पक *champaka,* **I.** m. A tree, Michelia champaca, Lin., Râm. 1, 17, 35. **II.** f. *kâ.* The name of a town, Hit. 27, 10.—**Comp.** *Çita-,* m. 1. a lamp. 2. a mirror.

चम्पकवती *champakavatî,* i.e. *champaka + vant + î,* f. **1.** The name of a forest, Hit. 17, 13. **2.** The name of a town, 27, 10, v.r.

चम्पा *champâ*, f. The name of a town, Râm. 1, 17, 35.

† **चम्ब्** *CHAMB*, i. 1, Par. To go.

† **चय्** *CHAY*, i. 1, Âtm. To go.

चय *chaya*, i.e. *chi+a*, m. **1.** A heap, Mârk. P. 21, 86. **2.** A mass, MBh. 3, 16426. **3.** A multitude, Chaurap. 34. **4.** Arranged fuel, Hariv. 2161. **5.** A mound of earth, a rampart, Râm. 5, 9, 15.—Comp. *Agni-*, m. a funeral pile, Râm. 3, 9, 35.

चयन *chayana*, i.e. *chi+ana*, n. Arranged fuel, Draup. 2, 7.

चर् *CHAR* (for original *çchar*, cf. *âçcharya*), i. 1, Par. (in epic poetry also Âtm., MBh. 3, 12655), **1.** To move, Râm. 4, 51, 8. **2.** To go, MBh. 1, 3071. **3.** To graze, Man. 2, 23; with acc., Hit. 81, 15. **4.** To go through, over, along (with acc.), Man. 2, 185; 9, 238; Hariv. 3632. **5.** To behave, to live, Man. 5, 90. **6.** To act, MBh. 14, 534; *vishamam*, To deal unjustly, Man. 9, 287. **7.** To make, to perform, Man. 3, 30; 11, 53; *virâdam*, To contest, Man. 8, 8; *Indravratam*, To act like Indra, Man. 9, 304; *tejovrittam*, To emulate the power and acts, Man. 9, 303. **8.** To treat, *tapasâ . . . indriyagrâmam*, To mortify one's flesh, MBh. 14, 544. **9.** To spy, Râm. 6, 6, 16.—Ptcple. of the pf. pass. I. *charita*, n. **1.** Going, Suçr. 1, 21, 17. **2.** Doing, acting, Hit. i. d. 76; adventures in *daçakumâra-*, i.e. *daçan-*, The adventures of the ten princes, Daçak. in Chr. 179, 2. Comp. *Dus-*, n. sin, Man. 11, 48. *Su-*, I. adj. 1. well-conducted. 2. well-managed. II. n. 1. good action, Bhartṛ. 2, 58. 2. good-conduct. II. *chîrṇa*, Performed, MBh. 15, 91.—Ptcple. of the fut. pass. I. *charitavya*; II. *chartavya*, MBh. 13, 5134. III. *charya*, see separately.—Absol., I. *charitvâ*; II. *chartvâ*, MBh. 5, 3790; III. *chîrtvâ*, MBh. 13, 495.—Infin. I. *charitum*; II. *chartum*, Râm. 3, 14, 15.—Caus. *châraya*, **1.** To cause to graze, Hariv. 3548. **2.** To cause to wander, MBh. 3, 1498. **3.** To send out, MBh. 12, 2705. **4.** To expel, MBh. 12, 12944. **5.** To cause to perform, Man. 11, 176. **6.** To permit to hold a culpable intercourse, Man. 8, 362. **7.** To cause to be spied, MBh. 3, 10030.—Frequent. *chañchûrya*, **1.** To rove, MBh. 1, 7910. **2.** To wander over (with acc.), Hariv. 3726. Anomalous ptcple. of the pres. *chañchûryant*, Hariv. 3602.—With **अति** *ati*, **1.** To over-step, Hariv. 12790. **2.** To trespass, Bhâg. P. 5, 10, 8. **3.** To offend (one's husband by committing adultery, one's parents by disobedience), MBh. 12, 8387.—With **व्यति** *vi-ati*, To offend somebody, Râm. 6, 101, 11.—With **अनु** *anu*, **1.** To ramble through, Râm. 1, 59, 19. **2.** To follow, MBh. 4, 652. **3.** To act, MBh. 3, 1303. *anucharita*, n. Doing, history, Bhâg. P. 5, 6, 10. Caus. To cause to be marched through, Man. 9, 266.—With **अन्तर्** *antar*, To move in the midst, MBh. 3, 2989.—With **अप** *apa*, **1.** To trespass, MBh. 12, 9566. **2.** To offend, Mârk. P. 13, 13. *apacharita*, n. Sin, Çâk. d. 106.—With **अभि** *abhi*, **1.** To offend, Man. 9, 102. **2.** To use witchcraft, Bhâg. P. 3, 19, 13. **3.** To occupy, to possess, Râm. 1, 34, 10.—With **व्यभि** *vi-abhi*, **1.** To offend, MBh. 1, 3234. **2.** To fail, Bhâg. P. 4, 18, 5. **3.** To surpass, Kir. 5, 34.—With **अव** *ava*, Caus. To apply, Suçr. 2, 8, 12.—With **अभ्यव** *abhi-ava*, Caus. To send out, MBh. 12, 3779.—With

आ *â*, **1.** To frequent, Râm. 3, 57, 11. **2.** To live, Man. 11, 180. **3.** To act, Man. 2, 110. **4.** To treat, Man. 8, 102. **5.** To perform, Man. 5, 156; to make, MBh. 4, 117. **6.** To act according to custom, Çâk. 108, 22. *âcharita*, n. **1.** Behaviour, Bhâg. P. 3, 14, 26. **2.** Acting desperately, in order to excite compassion (as killing wife and cattle, and sitting before some-one's door till he complies with what is wished for), Man. 8, 49. *âchîrṇa*, Eaten.—With **अध्या** *adhi-â*, To occupy, Man. 2, 119 (*çayyâsane 'dhyâcharite çreyasâ*, A couch or chair being occupied by a superior).—With **अन्वा** *anu-â*, To imitate, Bhâg. P. 5, 4, 6.—With **अभ्या** *abhi-â*, To practise, MBh. 12, 9719.—With **समुदा** *sam-ud-â*, **1.** To treat, MBh. 12, 1203 (read *samud°* instead of *sadud°*). **2.** To perform, MBh. 13, 3968.—With **उपा** *upa-â*, **1.** To serve, MBh. 2, 408. **2.** To treat, MBh. 18, 95.—With **समुपा** *sam-upa-â*, **1.** To treat, Suçr. 1, 47, 4. **2.** To practise, MBh. 3, 10572.—With **समा** *sam-â*, **1.** To walk, Daçak. in Chr. 185, 9. **2.** To act, Pañch. i. d. 78. **3.** To perform, Man. 11, 231. **4.** With *dûrâd*, To remove far from, Man. 4, 151. *samâchîrṇa*, Committed, MBh. 8, 1281.—With **अनुसमा** *anu-sam-â*, To perform, Bhâg. P. 4, 22, 53.—With **उद्** *ud*, **1.** To rise, MBh. 3, 10088. **2.** To fly back (as a bow), Bhâg. P. 2, 7, 25. **3.** To void one's excrements, Man. 4, 49. **4.** To utter, to pronounce, MBh. 5, 917. **5.** To leave, Naish. 5, 48 (Âtm.). **6.** To offend, MBh. 16, 43. *uchcharita*, n. Excrements, Bhâg. P. 5, 5, 32. Caus. To utter, to pronounce, MBh. 1, 966.—With **प्रोद्** *pra-ud*, To pronounce, Hariv. 14694. Caus. To cause to sound, Pañch. 21, 3.—With **प्रत्युद्** *prati-ud*, Caus. To excite, MBh. 8, 3553.—With **व्युद्** *vi-ud*, **1.** To offend (Âtm.). **2.** To have culpable intercourse (with instr.), MBh. 3, 12868.—With **उप** *upa*, **1.** To approach, Râm. 5, 64, 5. **2.** To serve, Man. 4, 254; to attend, Daçak. in Chr. 199, 21; to honour, Man. 3, 193. **3.** To treat, Pañch. 43, 10. **4.** pass. To be used metaphorically (with loc.), Bhâg. P. 3, 11, 37. *upachîrṇa*, Attended, Bhâg. P. 3, 23, 38.—With **दुस्** *dus*, To treat ill, to deceive, Râm. 3, 2, 25.—With **निस्** *nis*, **1.** To come out, MBh. 1, 8235. **2.** To appear, MBh. 6, 4543. **3.** To proceed, MBh. 5, 4929.—With **विनिस्** *vi-nis*, To proceed, MBh. 4, 1322.—With **परि** *pari*, **1.** To go round, Râm. 5, 52, 5. **2.** To serve, Man. 2, 243; to attend, Râm. 1, 46, 11. **3.** To honour.—With **प्र** *pra*, **1.** To proceed, to appear, MBh. 6, 2189; Râm. 1, 35, 18. **2.** To succeed, Bhâg. P. 5, 3, 2. **3.** To visit, Râm. 2, 55, 5. **4.** To walk, Prab. 33, 10. **5.** To circulate, Râm. 1, 2, 40. **6.** To act, Man. 9, 284. **7.** To perform, Man. 10, 100. Caus. To cause to graze, Hariv. 785.—With **संप्र** *sam-pra*, To advance, Râm. 6, 16, 105.—With **प्रति** *prati*, Caus. To diffuse, MBh. 12, 12742.—With **वि** *vi*, **1.** To go in different directions, Hid. 2, 31; to rove, MBh. 3, 2486. **2.** To wander through, MBh. 1, 3931 (Âtm.). **3.** To live lasciviously, Man. 9, 20. **4.** To fail, Bhâg. P. 9, 1, 15. **5.** To act, Pañch. 26, 3. **6.** To live, Man. 4, 18; 9, 302 (to live virtuously); with instr., To converse with, Bhâg. P. 4, 28, 52. **7.** To make, to perform, Hariv. 10148. *vicharita*, n. Roving, Nal. 24, 43.

vichîrṇa, 1. Wandered through, Râm. 3, 73, 25. 2. Performed, Pańch. i. d. 307. Caus. 1. To cause to run, Arj. 6, 17. 2. To cause to go round, Râm. 4, 13, 44 ; *buddhim*, To reflect, Râm. 1, 41, 9. 3. To seduce, Râm. 1, 49, 6. 4. To consider, Man. 7, 178. 5. To doubt, Râm. 1, 23, 19. 6. To hesitate, Râm. 5, 35, 25 ; to decide, MBh. 4, 235. *vichârita*, n. 1. Consideration, Sâv. 3, 13. 2. Scruple, Mṛichchh. 9, 5. —Comp. *A-*, adj. Requiring no hesitation, Man. 8, 295. — Comp. absol. *A-vichârya*, without having considered, Râm. 3, 51, 21.—With अनुवि *anu-vi*, To walk through, Daçak. in Chr. 201, 13.—With प्रवि *pra-vi*, 1. To advance, MBh. 7, 1451. 2. To wander through, MBh. 10, 732. Caus. To consider duly, Pańch. iii. d. 116.—With अनुसंवि *anu-sam-vi*, To wander through one by one, MBh. 3, 10288. —With सम् *sam* (Âtm. when joined with an instrumental), 1. To come together, to join, Gît. 2, 2 ; to collect, Hariv. 10758 ; to converse with, Pańch. i. d. 335. 2. To wander, MBh. 12, 6669. 2. To descend, Kumâras. 1, 6. 3. To wander through, Râm. 6, 83, 20. 4. To move, to live, Bhartṛ. 1, 89. 5. To pass over to somebody, Pańch. 186, 24. 6. To practise, Bhâg. P. 1, 16, 33. Caus. 1. To put in motion, Hit. 65, 13. 2. To let go, Râjat. 5, 195. 3. To cause to wander over, Bhâg. P. 8, 14, 5. 4. To lead, Çâk. d. 102. 5. To transfer, MBh. 1, 3169.—With अनुसम् *anu-sam*, 1. To wander through, MBh. 3, 1366. 2. To rove, MBh. 1, 3606. 3. To visit one by one, MBh. 12, 7002. Caus. To cause to change to, MBh. 12, 11208 (*anusaṁchârya tân*, Having been changed to those). — With प्रतिसम् *prati-sam*, To meet, MBh. 12, 11022.—Cf. *chal*, κολ in βου-κόλος, δύσ-κολος (=*duçchara*, i.e. *dus-chara*), κόρος, κορέννυμι (based on κορενjυμι) ; Lat. colere, in-quilinus.

चर *char+a*, I. adj., f. *rî*. 1. Moveable, Man. 7, 15. 2. Latter part of comp. adj. a. Moving, Râm. 3, 9, 10. b. Practising, Man. 4, 196. II. m. A spy, Man. 7, 122.—Comp. *A-*, adj., 1. immoveable, Man. 5, 29. 2. not to be trodden, Hariv. 12302. *Anta-*, adj. going to the end (of the earth), Râm. 4, 40, 3. *Antaḥpura-*, i.e. *antar-pura-*, m. an attendant in a gynaeceum, Pańch. i. d. 61. *Araṇya-*, 1. adj. living in a forest, Pańch. 135, 23. 2. m. a wild beast, Pańch. 215, 6. *Eka-*, adj., f. *râ*, solitary, Man. 5, 17. *Ku-*, m. a fixed star, MBh. 14, 1070. *Kûla-*, adj. living near the banks of rivers, Suçr. 1, 204, 9. *Toya-*, m. an aquatic animal, MBh. 3, 17135. *Divâ-*, adj. walking by day, Man. 3, 90. *Duçchara*, i.e. *dus-*, adj., f. *râ*. 1. difficult to be passed, Râm. 3, 26, 7 ; MBh. 14, 2369. 2. difficult to be performed, MBh. 12, 656. *Su-duçchara*, very difficult, Man. 1, 34 (cf. δύσκολος). *Dhârântara-*, i.e. *dhârâ-antara-*, adj. moving among clouds, Râm. 2, 105, 38 Gorr. *Niçâ-*, 1. adj. wandering at night, Râm. 1, 36, 18. 2. m. a demon, a Râkshasa, Râm. 3, 54, 27. 3. f. *rî*, a female demon, 5, 25, 34. *Vyomachara*, i.e. *vyoman-*, adj. passing through the air. *Saha-*, I. adj., f. *rî*. 1. going with. 2. united, Pańch. 43, 4. II. m. 1. a companion, 2. a surety. III. m. and f. *rî*, yellow Barleria. IV. f. *rî*. 1. female acquaintance. 2. a wife.

चरण *charaṇa*, i.e. *char+ana*, I. m. A foot soldier, Hariv. 5957. II. m. and n. 1. A foot, Man. 9, 277. 2. A verse, Çrut. 22. 3. A school, MBh. 12, 6369. III. n. 1. Fixed observances, good conduct, MBh. 13, 3044. 2. Practice, Râm. 1, 31, 2.—**Comp.** *Tapas-*, n. mortification, Arj. 4, 22.

चरम *charama* (cf. *chara* and *chira*), adj., f. *mâ*, Last, Bhâg. P. 3, 4, 12. °*mam*, adv. At last, Man. 2, 194.

चरमशैर्षिक *charamaçairshika*, i.e. *charama-çîrshan* + *ika*, adj., f. *kî*, Of which the head-board is turned to the west, MBh. 13, 462.

चराचर *charâchara*, i.e. *chara-achara*, adj. Moveable and immoveable, Râm. 4, 15, 8.

चरितार्थ *charitârtha*, i.e. *charita-artha*, adj. **1.** Having obtained one's object, Çâk. 111, 12. **2.** Effected.

चरितार्थता *charitârtha* + *tâ*, f. Attainment of one's object, Çâk. 61, 18.

चरितार्थत्व *charitârtha* + *tva*, n. Condition of being effected, Bhâshâp. 113 (separatedness is not to be explained by mere mutual negation).

चरितार्थय *CHARITÂRTHAYA* (a denomin. derived from *charitârtha* by *aya*), Par. To let somebody attain his object, Naish. 9, 49.

चरित्र *char* + *itra*, n. **1.** Ancient usages, Man. 9, 7. **2.** Conduct, Râm. 5, 51, 17.—**Comp.** *Vi-chitra-*, adj., f. *trâ*, behaving in a surprising way, Pańch. iv. d. 57.

चरिष्णु *char-ishṇu*, adj. Moveable, belonging to the animal world, Man. 1, 56.

चरु *charu*, m. **1.** A caldron, Man. 5, 117. **2.** An oblation to the gods, chiefly of milk and butter, Man. 6, 11.

चर्च् *CHARCH*, i. 1 and 6, Par. **1.** † To abuse. **2.** † To menace. **3.** † To injure. i. 10, Par., Âtm. **1.** To repeat. **2.** † To study.

चर्चरिका *charcharikâ*, i. e. *charcharî* + *ka*, f. A kind of gesture, Vikr. 55, 20.

चर्चरी *charcharî* (*charchar* is probably an old frequent. of *char*), f. A kind of song, Vikr. 55, 15.

चर्चा *charchâ*, f. **1.** Cleaning the person with fragrant unguents, Gît. 9, 10. **2.** Smearing, anointing. **3.** Applying, practice, Râjat. 5, 303.

चर्चित *charchita*, i.e. *charchâ* + *ita*, adj. **1.** Anointed, MBh. 2, 2371. **2.** Smeared, Pańch. 123, 14.—**Comp.** *Vi-*, adj., anointed, smeared, Ṛit. 6, 12.

† **चर्ब्** *CHARB*, i. 1, Par. To go.

चर्मकार *charmakâra*, i.e. *charman-kâra*, m. A shoemaker, Man. 2, 36.

चर्मन् *charman*, n. **1.** Skin, Bhâg. P. 3, 6, 16. **2.** Hide, Man. 2, 41. **3.** A shield, Râm. 5, 73, 17.—**Comp.** *Gala-*, n. the throat, Suçr. 2, 215, 15. *Go-*, n. the hide of a cow, MBh. 13, 1228. *Dus-*, adj. suffering from a cutaneous disease, Yâjń. 3, 209.—Cf. perhaps πάλμη.

चर्ममय *charmamaya*, i.e. *charman* + *maya*, adj., f. *yî*, Made of leather, Man. 2, 157.—**Comp.** *Vyâghracharmamaya*, i.e. *Vyâghra-charman* + *maya*, covered by a sheath made of the hide of a tiger, MBh. 6, 1787.

चर्मवन्त् *charmavant*, i.e. *charman* + *vant*, adj., f. *vatî*, Covered by a hide, MBh. 3, 643.

चर्मावकर्तिन् *charmâvakartin*, i.e. *charman-ava-kṛit* + *in*, m. A leather-cutter, Man. 4, 218.

चर्मावकर्त्तृ *charmâvakarttṛi*, i. e. *charman-ava-kṛit* + *tṛi*, m. A leather-cutter, MBh. 12, 1321.

चर्मिन् *charmin*, i.e. *charman + in*, m. A shield-bearer, MBh. 3, 756.

चर्य *charya*, I. ptcple. of the fut. pass. of *char*, To be practised, Man. 3, 1. II. f. *yâ*. **1.** Roaming, MBh. 8, 2099. **2.** Visiting, Bhâg. P. 9, 16, 1. **3.** Going, Râm. 1, 19, 19. **4.** Observance, Man. 1, 111. **5.** Practising, occupation, Râm. 1, 40, 6. **6.** Conduct, Man. 6, 32. III. n. **1.** Going, MBh. 8, 4215. **2.** Practising.—Comp. *Ku-charyâ*, f. bad conduct, Man. 9, 17. *Tapaçcharyâ*, i.e. *Tapas-*, f. mortification, MBh. 7, 1280. *Deva-charyâ*, f. worship of the gods, MBh. 3, 11045. *Dharma-*, f. observance of the law, Kumâras. 7, 83. *Paçu-*, f. acting like beasts, Bhâg. P. 5, 26, 23. *Brahma-charya*, i.e. *Brahman-*, I. n. 1. studentship, the order of a religious student. 2. pious austerity, Man. 5, 160. 3. chastity, Vedântas. in Chr. 217, 15. II. *Brahmacharya*, m. a religious student. *Sa-brahmacharya*, n. studying together. *Ratha-charyâ*, f. a chariot-exercise. *Vrata-*, I. f. observance of religious vows, Chr. 42, 11. II. *vrata-charya*, m. a student in theology, Man. 1, 111.

चर्व् *CHARV* (akin to *char*), i. 1, and 10, Par. **1.** To chew, to bite, Pańch. 259, 8. **2.** To bite to pieces, Dev. 7, 10. **3.** To taste, Sâh. D. 27, 11.—Cf. *chûrṇ*, *chûrṇa*, τείρω, τρύω; Lat. terere, triticum, etc.

चर्वण *charvaṇa*, i.e. *charv + ana*, n. **1.** Chewing. **2.** Tasting, Sâh. D. 30, 17; also fem. *ṇâ*, 30, 2. **3.** Food. Bhâg. P. 3, 13, 35.—Comp. *Punaḥpunaçcharvita-*, i.e. *punar-punar-charvita-*, adj. chewing repeatedly what has been chewed already, Bhâg. P. 7, 5, 30.

चर्षणि *charshaṇi* (vb. *char*), pl. Men, Chr. 292, 5 = Rigv. i. 86, 5.—Comp. *Viçva-*, adj. active, strenuous in everything, Chr. 291, 14 = Rigv. i. 64, 14.

1. **चल्** *CHAL* (akin to *char*), i. 1, Par. (sometimes also Âtm.), **1.** To tremble, MBh. 2, 1589. **2.** To move, Hariv. 5591; to go, Bhâg. P. 3, 30, 23. **3.** To go away, MBh. 1, 6546. **4.** To become troubled, Pańch. i. d. 448. **5.** To swerve (with the abl.), Man. 7, 15 (*svadharmân na chalanti*, They do not swerve from their duty). *chalita*, **1.** Shaking, Râm. 3, 57, 23; trembling, MBh. 3, 10065. **2.** Gone away, Arj. 4, 39. **3.** Troubled, Râm. 5, 30, 13. **4.** Damaged, Pańch. iv. d. 30.—Ptcple. of the fut. pass. *chalitavya*, Râm. 3, 49, 14, *na chalitavyaṁ te*, You must not leave this place.—Caus. I. *chalaya*, **1.** To put in motion, Bhâg. P. 3, 15, 37; to stir, Çâk. d. 158. **2.** To trouble, to excite, Ṛit. 3, 10. **3.** To turn off, Mṛichchh. 147, 9. II. *châlaya*, **1.** To shake, Râm. 3, 7, 10; to move, MBh. 3, 11185. **2.** To cause to waver, Râm. 6, 73, 20. **3.** To drive onwards, MBh. 1, 5743. **4.** To drive away, Hariv. 2697. **5.** To put to flight, MBh. 7, 222. **6.** To trouble, Vedântas. in Chr. 218, 7. Anomalous ptcple. of the pres. Âtm. *châlayâna*, MBh. 3, 11095. Ptcple. of the fut. pass. Not to be turned off, Bhâg. P. 2, 17, 17.—Comp. *A-*, adj., immoveable, MBh. 13, 2161.—With the prep. **आ** *â*, Caus. *châlaya*, **1.** To cause to tremble, Hariv. 3036. **2.** To push away, MBh. 12, 5814.—With **उद्** *ud*, **1.** To depart, Çâk. d. 28. **2.** To rise, Bhâg. P. 6, 7, 8. **3.** To unbind, Hariv. 2886. **4.** To set out, Daçak. in Chr., 184, 6.—With **समुद्** *sam-ud*, To set out together, Daçak. in Chr. 188, 15. —With **परि** *pari*, To move, Sâh. D. 67, 12. Caus. *châlaya*, To turn round,

MBh. 12, 6870.—With प्र *pra*, 1. To tremble, Râm. 3, 29, 13. 2. To advance, Bhâg. P. 7, 2, 23. 3. To move, Pañch. 87, 17. 4. To set out, Pañch. 104, 14. 5. To become troubled, MBh. 12, 2736. 6. To swerve, MBh. 3, 11249. Caus. *chalaya*, To move, Amar. 58. *châlaya*, 1. To cause to tremble, Râm. 5, 38, 34. 2. To stir up, Pañch. 262, 20.—With वि *vi*, 1. To waver, Râm. 3, 57, 23. 2. To depart, Hariv. 4113. 3. To move, MBh. 3, 2614. 4. To fall down, Gît. 5, 10. 5. To become troubled, Hariv. 9948. 6. To swerve, Man. 7, 28. Caus. *châlaya*, 1. To cause to tremble, Râm. 1, 16, 23. 2. To make unsteady, Man. 7, 13 ; to rescind, 8, 167. 3. To trouble, Râm. 5, 32, 37. 4. To turn off, Bhâg. P. 9, 8, 15.—With प्रवि *pra-vi*, 1. To tremble, MBh. 1, 1184. 2. To become unsteady, Hariv. 1, 11126. 3. To deviate, Bhartṛ. 2, 81. Caus. *châlaya*, To cause to tremble, Hariv. 6226.—With सम् *sam*, 1. To tremble, Râm. 6, 75, 34. 2. To move, Râm. 2, 90, 4 (*âsanât*, To start up from one's seat). Caus. *châlaya*, 1. To cause to tremble, Hariv. 13211. 2. To put in motion, Çâk. d. 69. 3. To drive away, MBh. 10, 627.

† 2. चल् *CHAL*, i. 6, Par. To sport.

† 3. चल् *CHAL*, i. 10, Par. To foster, v.r.

चल *chal+a*, adj., f. *lâ*. 1. Trembling, Ragh. 3, 68. 2. Loose, Suçr. 1, 303, 18. 3. Troubled, Suçr. 1, 146, 16. 4. Fickle, Nal. 19, 6.—**Comp.** see *Achala*. *Nis-*, adj. 1. immoveable, Bhartṛ. 2, 69. 2. steady, Bhag. 2, 58. *Vi-nis-*, adj. immoveable, firm. *Vi-*, adj. 1. moving to and fro, unsteady. 2. conceited. *A-vi-*, adj. immoveable.

चलचित्तता *chala-chitta+tâ*, f. Fickleness, Hit. i. d. 91.

चलत्व *chala+tva*, n. Trembling, Megh. 94.

चलन *chal+ana*, n. 1. Trembling, Pañch. ii. d. 174. 2. Moving, MBh. 12, 3708. 3. Swerving, MBh. 3, 1319.—**Comp.** *Bhûmi-*, n. an earthquake, Man. 4, 105.

चलाचल *chalâchal+a* (derived from an old frequent. of *chal*), adj. 1. Moving to and fro, Râm. 5, 42, 11. 2. Unsteady, MBh. 5, 2758.

† चष् *CHASH*, i. 1, Par. To kill. i. 1, Par., Âtm. To eat.

चषक *chashaka*, m. and n. A drinking vessel, Ragh. 7, 46.

चषाल *chashâla*, m. and n. A ring on the top of a sacrificial post, MBh. 7, 2266.

† चह् *CHAH*, i. 1 and 10 (v.r.), Par. To deceive.

चाक्र *châkra*, i.e. *chakra + a*, adj. Performed with a discus, Hariv. 5648.

चाक्रिक *châkrika*, i.e. *chakra+ika*, m. 1. An oil grinder, Râjat. 6, 272 (at the same time, A partisan). 2. A bellman, Hariv. 9047. 3. A partisan, Râjat. 5, 267.

चाक्षुष *châkshusa*, i.e. *chakshus+a*, I. adj., f. *shî*. 1. Peculiar to the eye, e.g. *shî vidyâ*, The magic faculty of seeing every object, MBh. 1, 6478. 2. Perceptible by the eye, Suçr. 1, 153, 5. 3. Referring to Manu Châkshusha, Bhâg. P. 4, 30, 49. II. m. The name of the sixth Manu, Man. 1, 62.

चाट *châṭa*, m. A rogue, Böhtl. Ind. Spr. 907.

चाटु *châṭu*, m. and n. Pleasing, flattering discourse, Ṛit. 6, 14.

चाटुकार *châṭu-kâra*, m. A flatterer, Râjat. 5, 351.

चाणक्य *châṇakya*, I. m. A proper name, Pańch. 253, 12. II. adj. Composed by Châṇakya, Châṇ. 1.

चाण्डाल *châṇḍâla*, i.e. *chaṇḍâla* + *a*, m., f. *lî*; =*chaṇḍâla*, An outcast, Man. 3, 239; 8, 373.—Comp. *Brâhmaṇa-*, m. The son of a Çûdra man and Brâhmaṇî woman, Man. 9, 87.

चातक *châtaka*, m. A kind of cuckoo, Cuculus melanoleucus, supposed to drink only drops of rain, Bhartṛ. 2, 89.

चातुःसागरिक *châṭuḥsâgarika*, i.e. *chatur-sâgara* + *ika*, adj., f. *kî*, Directed to the four seas, Râm. 4, 16, 43.

चातुराश्रमिक *châturâçramika*, i.e. *chatur-âçrama* + *ika*, and चातुराश्रमिन् *châturâçramin*, i.e. *chatur-âçrama* + *a* + *in*, adj. Being in one of the four orders of brahmanical life, MBh. 14, 972; 7, 2757.

चातुराश्रम्य *châturâçramya*, i. e. *chatur-âçrama* + *ya*, n. The four orders of brahmanical life, MBh. 3, 11244.

चातुर्मास्य *châturmâsya*, i.e. *chatur-mâsa* + *ya*, n. The name of sacrifices which ought to be offered every four months, Man. 6, 10.

चातुर्य *châturya*, i.e. *chatura* + *ya*, n. Charm, beauty, Râm. 1, 6, 13.

चातुर्वर्ण्य *châturvarṇya*, i. e. *chatur-varṇa* + *ya*, n. The four castes, Man. 10, 30.

चातुर्विद्य *châturvidya*, i.e. *chatur-vidyâ* + *a*, I. adj. Conversant in the four Vedas, Râjat. 5, 158. II. n. The four Vedas, MBh. 12, 1574.

चातुर्वैद्य *châturvaidya*, i.e. *chatur-vidyâ* + *a*, adj. Conversant in the four Vedas, MBh. 5, 4741.

चातुर्होत्र *châturhotra*, i.e. *chatur hotṛi* + *a*, I. adj. Performed by the four principal priests, Bhâg. P. 1, 4, 19. II. n. 1. A sacrifice performed by the four principal priests, Bhâg. P. 5, 7, 5. 2. The functions of the four principal priests, Bhâg. P. 2, 6, 24. 3. The four principal priests, Bhâg. P. 4, 24, 37.

चान्द्रमस *chândramasa*, i.e. *chandramas* + *a*, adj., f. *sî*, Lunar, belonging to the moon, Bhag. 8, 25.

चान्द्रव्रतिक *chândravratika*, i. e. *chandra-vrata* + *ika*, adj. Having the character of the moon, Man. 9, 309.

चान्द्रायण *chândrâyaṇa*, i.e. *chandra-ayana* + *a*, n. A religious or expiatory observance regulated by the moon's age; diminishing the daily consumption of food by one mouthful every day for the dark half of the month, and increasing it in like manner during the light half, Man. 11, 216; Vedântas. in Chr. 202, 17.—Comp. *Yati-*, n. a species of this penance, Man. 11, 218. *Çiçu-*, n. another species of this penance, Man. 11, 219.

चाप *châpa* (probably from the Caus. of *chi*), m. and n. A bow, Man. 7, 192.—Comp. *Indra-*, m. the rainbow, Megh. 65. *Mahendra-*, i. e. *mahâ-indra-*, m. the same, Râjat. 5, 381. *Kusuma-*, *pushpa-*, m. a name of the god of love, Ragh. 9, 33; Kathâs. 14, 29. *Sa-sura-châpa* + *m*, adv. with Indra's bow, Kir. 5, 12. *Skandha-*, m. a sort of yoke for carrying burthens.

चापल *châpala*, i.e. *chapala* + *a*, n.

1. Quickness, Bhâg. P. 8, 12, 20. 2. Unsteadiness, Râjat. 5, 377.

चापल्य *châpalya,* i.e. *chapala + ya,* n. Unsteadiness, Pańch. iv. d. 81.—Comp. *Ati-*, n. great quickness, Pańch. 62, 12. *Pâṇi-*, n. fidgeting with the hands.

चापिन् *châpin,* i.e. *châpa + in,* m. An archer, MBh. 12, 10406.

चामर *châmara,* i.e. *chamara + a,* n. The tail of the Bos grunniens, used to whisk off flies, and one of the insignia of royalty, Râjat. 5, 449; Megh. 36. Used also as an ornament on the heads of horses, Çâk. d. 8.

चामीकर *châmîkara,* n. Gold, Râm. 3, 26, 6.

चामुण्डा *châmuṇḍâ,* f. A name of Durgâ, Mâlat. 81, 6.

चाय् *CHÂY,* i. 1, Par., Âtm. To worship.—With the prep. नि *ni,* To worship, Daçak, 174, 5.—Cf. *chi.*

चार *châra,* i.e. *char + a,* m. 1. A spy, Râjat. 5, 81. 2. Going, motion, Vikr. d. 140. 3. Course, Râm. 2, 66, 23. 4. Occupation with, MBh. 5, 1410. —Comp. *Pâda-*, m. 1. going on foot. 2. walking, Megh. 61. *Saha-*, m. the concomitance of the major and middle term, Bhâshâp. 136.

चारक *châraka,* i.e. *char + aka,* I. adj. Acting, Râm. 3, 66, 18. II. m. 1. A spy, MBh. 2, 172. 2. A prison, Daçak. in Chr. 195, 11. III. f. *rikâ,* A servant-girl, Kathâs. 14, 65. *prachchhanna-* (vb. *chad*), adj. Acting fraudulently, Râm. 3, 66, 18.

चारण *châraṇa,* i.e. *charaṇa + a,* m. 1. A strolling player, Man. 12, 44. 2. A panegyrist of the gods, Chr. 24, 46. 3. A spy, Bhâg. P. 4, 16, 12.

चारणत्व *châraṇa + tva,* n. Scenic art, Râjat. 5, 418.

चारणैकमय *châraṇaikamaya,* i.e. *châraṇa-eka + maya,* adj., f. *yî,* Full of panegyrists only, Kathâs. 23, 85.

चारित्र *châritra,* i.e. *charitra + a,* n. 1. Peculiar observance, praiseworthy observance, Râm. 6, 88, 11. 2. Conduct, Râm. 3, 59, 15. 3. Good conduct, Râm. 1, 1, 3.—Comp. *Dus-*, adj. wicked-lived, MBh. 12, 2359. *Dushṭa-* adj., f. *râ,* ill-behaving, Pańch. iv. d. 55.

चारित्र्य *châritrya,* i.e. *charitra + ya,* n. 1. Conduct, MBh. 12, 12357. 2. Good conduct, virtue, Mṛichchh. 147, 9.

चारिन् *chârin,* i.e. *char + in,* I. adj., f. *iṇî.* 1. Moveable, MBh. 7, 372. 2. As latter part of comp. words: a. Going, Bhâg. P. 6, 4, 9. b. Moving, Hiḍ. 4, 4. c. Roaming, Pańch. 69, 1. d. Living, Râm. 3, 15, 6. e. Acting, *prachchhanna-* (vb. *chad*), Acting fraudulently, Râm. 3, 51, 26. f. Observing, Râm. 3, 53, 21. g. Feeding on, Suçr. 1, 208, 12. II. m. A foot-soldier, MBh. 6, 3545.—Comp. *Eka-*, adj. solitary, MBh. 1, 6928; f. *riṇî,* a faithful wife, Daçak. in Chr. 180, 20; Râjat. 5, 8. *Kâma-*, adj. 1. moving where one lists, Chr. 58, 4. 2. self-willed, independent, Râm. 3, 52, 38. 3. Desirous, MBh. 13, 2265. *Kha-*, adj. moving in the sky, MBh. 3, 14635. *Gûḍha-* (vb. *guh*), adj. going disguised, Yâjń. 2, 268. *Chitta-*, adj., f. *iṇî,* compliant, MBh. 3, 14668. *Jala-*, m. an aquatic animal, MBh. 3, 11577. *Dus-*, adj. wicked-lived, Kathâs. 23, 8. *Dushṭa-*, m. a sinner, MBh. 4, 97. *Dharma-*, adj. virtuous, Râm. 3, 2, 19. *Pâda-*, I. adj. going on foot, Bhâg. P. 6, 4, 9. II. m. a foot-soldier. *Brah-machârin* i.e. *brahman-*,

m. 1. a religious student. 2. chaste, Man. 4, 128. *Saṁgha-*, m. a fish. *Saha-*, m., f. *iṇî*, and n., a companion, an attendant. *Svachchhanda-*, i.e. *sva -chhanda-*, adj., f. *iṇî*, a harlot, Çâk. 69, 9 (Prâkṛ.).

चारु *chàru* (akin to *char* in *charv*, cf. *chûrṇa*, properly: Delicate, cf. *τέρην, τείρω*), adj., f. *rvî*. **1.** Agreeable, Pañch. 256, 14. **2.** Beautiful, Râm. 1, 63, 6.—Comp. *Sa-*, adj. very beautiful. —Cf. *καλός*.

चारुता *chàru+tâ*, f. Beauty, Kumarâs. 3, 7.

चार्मिक *chârmika* i.e. *charman+ika*, adj. Leathern, Man. 8, 289.

चार्य *chârya*, m. The son of a Vrâtya, or outcaste Vaiçya, Man. 10, 23.

चार्वाक *chârvâka* i.e. *chàru-vach+a*, m. The name of a philosopher holding materialistic and heterodox principles, Vedântas. in Chr. 210, 16.

चालन *châlana*, i.e. *chal*, Caus., + *ana*, n. **1.** Motion, Bhâg. P. 3, 26, 37. **2.** Shaking, MBh. 16, 267.

चाष *châsha*, m. The blue jay, Coracias indica, Man. 11, 131.

1. चि *CHI*, ii. 5, *chinu*, Par. Âtm. **1.** To arrange, MBh. 12, 10745. **2.** To heap, Bhâg. P. 4, 28, 15. **3.** To collect, to gather, MBh. 1, 7719. **4.** To cover, Arj. 9, 9. *chita*, Full, Râm. 3, 68, 12. *chitâ*, see separately.—Caus. *châyaya* and *châpaya*. † 1, 10, *chayaya* and *chapaya*, To heap, to collect.—With the prep. अप *apa*, **1.** To gather, Râm. 2, 100, 5. **2.** To diminish, Mârk. P. 29, 8; *apachita*, fallen off, Çâk. d. 37. **3.** To deprive, MBh. 3, 1319.—With अव *ava*, To gather, Pañch. 93, 4.—With आ *â*, **1.** To heap on, Bhâg. P. 4, 29, 78. **2.** To cover, Râm. 6, 20, 23.—With अवा *ava-â*, To heap on, MBh. 12, 5952.—With समा *sam-â*, **1.** To heap, Hariv. 14815. **2.** To cover, MBh. 7, 7242.—With उद् *ud*, To gather, Kathâs. 22, 109.—With समुद् *sam-ud*, To arrange, MBh. 2, 2087 (anomalous absolut. *samuchchitya*).—With उप *upa*, **1.** To collect, to augment, MBh. 5, 473. **2.** To cover, MBh. 3, 11962. *chîya*, pass. To increase, Bhartṛ. 2, 84; to profit, Man. 8, 169. *upachita*, **1.** Well-fed, MBh. 13, 4460. **2.** Prosperous, Ragh. 17, 54. **3.** Loaded, Man. 6, 41. **4.** Endowed, Ram. 3, 41, 19.—With नि *ni*, **1.** To pile up, MBh. 12, 2099. **2.** To erect, MBh. 14, 2635. **3.** To cover, Râm. 6, 32, 24. **4.** To fill, MBh. 3, 650. **5.** To stagnate, Suçr. 1, 92, 19.—With संनि *sam-ni*, To stagnate, Suçr. 2, 430, 15.—With परि *pari*, **1.** To collect, Râjat. 4, 354. **2.** To augment, Bhâg. P. 5, 7, 11. **3.** To fill, Bhâg. P. 4, 9, 13.—With प्र *pra*, **1.** To gather, Hariv. 5237. **2.** To cut, MBh. 5, 1865. **3.** pass. To increase, MBh. 14, 509. **4.** To cover, MBh. 12, 1702.—With संप्र *sam-pra*, To cease gathering, MBh. 12, 5952.—With वि *vi*, **1.** To select, MBh. 5 1111. **2.** To pick out, Dev. 2, 67 (anomalous *vichinvati*, instead of *noti*).—With संवि *sam-vi*, To segregate, Râm. 5, 85, 18.—With सम् *sam*, **1.** To heap up, Râm. 1, 13, 30. **2.** To collect, Man. 6, 15. *saṁchita*, **1.** Dense, Râm. 5, 59, 13. **2.** Provided, MBh. 6, 3327. —With परिसम् *pari-sam*, To collect, Sâh. D. 73, 12.—Cf. Lat. capio= Caus. *chapayâmi*, capulus, capistrum;

perhaps also κώπη and Goth. hafjan, hafan, hafts; A.S. hebban, thu hefest; Engl. to heave.

2. चि *CHI*, ii. 5, *chinu*, Par., Âtm. **1.** To search, Kathâs. 26, 136. **2.** To search through, MBh. 3, 2659.—With the prep. अप *apa*, *apachita*, **1.** Honoured, MBh. 3, 10835. **2.** Invited, Bhâg. P. 5, 3, 9. n. Honour, MBh. 9, 3620,—With अव *ava*, To honour, MBh. 3, 10676.—With निस् *nis*, **1.** To know thoroughly, Râjat. 5, 124. **2.** To decide, Râm. 2, 1, 26. *niçchita*, n. Resolution, Râm. 5, 15, 57. *niçchita* + *m*, adv. Certainly, Pańch. 223, 7.—**Comp.** *A-niçchita*, wavering, Pańch. iii. d. 261. *Su-*, adj. 1. ascertained. 2. approved.—With अभिनिस् *abhi-nis*, To decide, MBh. 3, 1086; 12, 10635.—With विनिस् *vi-nis*, **1.** To consider, Man. 7, 59. **2.** To decide, Bhag. 13, 4.—With परि *pari*, **1.** To search, Râm. 4, 47, 1. **2.** To familiarise one's self with something, Ragh. 8, 18. *parichita*, Familiar, Çâk. d. 107; acquainted, Hariv. 8615.—Caus. *châyaya*, To search, Häberl. Anth. 432, 13.—With वि *vi*, **1.** To discern, Pańch. i. d. 42. **2.** To make discernible, Râm. 5, 11, 1. **3.** To search, Râm. 3, 68, 9. **4.** To examine, MBh. 5, 6088. — With प्रवि *pra-vi*, To search, Râm. 4, 48, 23. *pravichita*, Tested, MBh. 7, 4440. — With सम् *sam*, To think, Râjat. 6, 32 (? probably it is to be read *sam̃chintya*).—Cf. *ki*, *chây*, and ved. *chi*, i. 1, Âtm. To punish; τίνω, τίνυμι, τίω, τίμη; Lat. timeo.

चिकित्सक *chikitsaka*, i. e. *chikitsa* desiderat. of *kit*, + *aka*, m. A physician, Man. 9, 284.

चिकित्सन *chikitsana*, i. e. *chikitsa* (see the last), + *ana*, n. Remedying, MBh. 4, 63.

चिकित्सा *chikitsâ*, i.e. *chikitsa* (see *chikitsaka*), + *â*, f. The practice of medicine, curing, Râm. 6, 71, 26.—**Comp.** *Dus-chikitsa*, adj. difficult to be cured, Bhâg. P. 4, 30, 38.

चिकीर्षा *chikîrshâ*, i. e. *chikîrsha*, desiderat. of *kṛi*, + *â*, f. The desire to perform, Râm. 5, 36, 7.

चिकीर्षु *chikîrshu*, i.e. *chikîrsha* (see the last), + *u*, adj. **1.** Desiring to make, to perform, MBh 7, 881. **2.** Desiring to practise, MBh. 8, 1965.

चिकुर *chikura*, m. **1.** Hair, Gît. 7, 23. **2.** A proper name, MBh. 5, 3640.

† चिक्क् *CHIKK*, i. 10, Par. To give pain, v.r.—Cf. *chakk*.

चिक्कण *chikkaṇa*, adj. Smooth, slippery, MBh. 12, 6854; 14, 1416 (thus to be read instead of *chikvaṇa*); Suçr. 2, 176, 14.

चिक्रीडिषा *chikrîḍishâ*, i.e. *chikrîḍisha*, desiderat. of *krîḍ*, + *a*, f. The desire to play, Bhâg. P. 3, 7, 3.

चिखादिषु *chikhâdishu*, i.e. *chikhâdisha*, desider. of *khâd*, + *u*, adj. Desiring to devour, MBh. 10, 483.

चिच्छित्सु *chichchhitsu*, i. e. *chichchhitsa*, desider. of *chid*, + *u*, adj. Desiring to chop off, MBh. 7, 6001.

† चिट् *CHIṬ*, i. 1, Par. To send off.

1. चित् *CHIT* (akin to 2. *chi*), i. 1. Par. To perceive, Chr. 295, 12=Rigv. i. 92, 12.—Caus. and i. 10, Âtm. *chetaya*, **1.** To perceive, MBh. 12, 9890 (Âtm.). **2.** To get consciousness, MBh.

1, 3616 (Âtm.). **3.** To think, MBh. 18, 74 (Par.); Bhâg. P. 1, 8, 9 (Âtm.). **4.** To cause to think, Bhâg. P. 8, 1, 9 (Âtm.). **5.** To know, MBh. 3, 14877 (Par.). Anomalous ptcple. of the pres. Âtm. *chetayâna*, Sensible, Râm. 2, 109, 7.

2. **चित्** *chit*, f. Soul (as distinguished from *chitta*), Vedântas. in Chr. 215, 6; Sânkhya Aph. 1, 146.

3. **चित्** *chit*, see *chid*.

चिता *chitâ*, i.e. *chita*, ptcple. of the pf. pass. of 1. *chi*, f. A funeral pile, Râjat. 5, 226.

चिति *chi* + *ti*, f. **1.** A heap, Bhâg. P. 4, 28, 50. **2.** Wood raised for burning, Man. 4, 46. **3.** An altar, Bhâg. P. 3, 13, 36. **4.** Intellect, Dev. 5, 36.

चितिका *chitikâ*, i.e. *chitâ* + *ka*, f. A funeral pile, Pańch. iii. d. 135.

चित्कार *chit-kâra* (the first part is an imitative sound), m. Scream; braying of an ass, Hit. ii. d. 30, v.r.

चित्कारवन्त् *chitkâra* + *vant*, adj., f. *vatî*, Accompanied by shouts, Mâlat. 1, 5, v.r.

चित्त 1. *chit* + *ta*, n. **1.** Thought, Bhag. 16, 16. **2.** Intellect, Vedânt. in Chr. 207, 2. **3.** Will, Çâk. Ch. 32, 3. **4.** The mind, Râm. 3, 55, 19. **5.** The heart, Pańch. 140, 17.—**Comp.** *Anya-*, adj. thinking of some one or something else, Pańch. 225, 23. *Eka-*, I. n. 1. thought directed to one object only, Prab. 8, 5. 2. unanimity, Râm. 2, 40, 35. II. adj. 1. thinking only of one object; in *tad-*, thinking of him only, Hit. 39, 2. 2. unanimous, Hit. 14, 3. *Chala-*, I. n. fickleness, Man. 9, 15. II. adj. unsteady, Râm. 3, 1, 32. *Pramoha-*, adj., f. *tâ*, bewildered in mind.

चित्ति 1. *chit* + *ti*, f. Thought, Bhâg. P. 5, 18, 18.—**Comp.** *Pûrva-*, f. 1. first thought. 2. the name of an Apsaras.

चित्य 1. *chi* + *tyâ*, I. n. A tomb, Râm. 1, 58, 10. **II.** f. A layer.—**Comp.** *Chatuçchitya*, i.e. *chatur-*, adj. supported on four layers, MBh. 14, 2643.

चित्र् *CHITR*, i. 10 (rather a denomin. derived from the next), Par. **1.** To colour with various colours, Hit. i. d. 171. **2.** To adorn, MBh. 12, 988. **3.** † To see a wonderful sight.—With the prep. **वि** *vi*, *vichitrita* (rather *vi-chitra* + *ita*), **1.** Spotted, Râm. 3, 49, 35. **2.** Coloured with various colours, Chr. 34, 10. **3.** Wonderful.

चित्र 1. *chit* + *ra*, I. adj. **1.** Visible (ved.). **2.** Clear, shining, Chr. 293, 2 = Rigv. i. 88, 2. **3.** Variegated, Chr. 2, 21. **4.** Spotted, Râm. 3, 48, 12. **5.** Various, Man. 9, 248. **6.** Fluctuating, Râm. 3, 52, 15. **7.** Wonderful, Râm. 3, 35, 4. **8.** Surprised, Râjat. 5, 2. **9.** Uncommon, rigorous, Daçak. in Chr. 193, 4; adv. in a rigorous manner, ib. 198, 3. **II.** f. *trâ*, The name of a lunar mansion, Spica virginis, Râm. 3, 23, 11. **III.** n. **1.** A surprising appearance, Çâk. 110, 17; wonder, Râm. 3, 51, 26. **2.** A spot, MBh. 13, 2605. **3.** A picture, MBh. 13, 7692. **4.** Painting, Râm. 2, 90, 23 Gorr.—**Comp.** *Vi-*, I. adj. 1. variegated, spotted. 2. painted. 3. handsome. 4. surprising. II. n. 1. variegated (the colour). 2. surprise. 3. speech implying apparently the reverse of the intended object. *Sa-*, adj. 1. painted, Hariv. 4532. 2. containing pictures, Megh. 65.

चित्रक *chitra* + *ka*, I. m. The Cheeta, or small hunting leopard, Pańch. 72, 11. **II.** n. **1.** A sectarial mark, made on the forehead, Hariv. 7074. **2.** A mode of fighting, Hariv. 15979. **3.** The name of a forest, Hariv. 8952.

चित्रकार *chitra-kâra*, m. A painter, MBh. 5, 5025.

चित्रग *chitra-ga*, and **चित्रगत** *chitra-gata* (vb. *gam.*), adj., f. *gâ*, *tâ*, Painted, Kathâs. 5, 31; MBh. 6, 1662.

चित्रगुप्त *chitra-gupta*, m. Yama's registrar, who records the vices and virtues of mankind, MBh. 13, 5924.

चित्रधा *chitra-dhâ*, adv. Manifold, Bhâg. P. 3, 13, 20.

चित्रबर्हिन् *chitrabarhin*, i.e. *chitra-barha* + *in*, adj., f. *iṇi*, Having a variegated tail, MBh. 13, 4206.

चित्रवन्त् *chitra* + *vant*, adj., f. *vati*, Adorned with pictures, Ragh. 14, 25.

चित्रस्थ *chitra-stha*, adj. Painted, Kathâs. 6, 120.

चित्रामघ *chitrâmagha*, i.e. *chitra-magha*, with lengthened final of the former part, adj., f. *ghâ*, Having splendid treasures, Chr. 288, 10 = Rigv. i. 48, 10.

चित्रीय *CHITRÎYA*, a denomin. derived from *chitra* by *ya*, Âtm. **1.** To be surprised, Kathâs. 6, 50. **2.** To cause surprise, Daçak. 177, 13.

चिद् *chid* (properly acc. n. of a lost indefinite pronoun *chi* = *τι*; Lat. qui + s), a particle giving to the preceding word an indefinite signification: Any, Chr. 292, 5 = Rigv. i. 86, 5; Chr. 290, 3 = Rigv. i. 64, 3. All, Chr. 288, 3 = Rigv. i. 49, 3. In classic language it is only used after derivatives of the interrogative pronouns *kim*, and *jâtu*, and gives them an indefinite signification; cf. *katham*, *kadâ*, *kim*, *kutas*, *kva*, and *jâtu*.—Cf. Lat. -que (= Oscan -pid) in quando-que = *kadâ chid*, (qui)-cumque = *kam chid*.

चिदात्मन् *chidâtman*, i.e. *chit-âtman*, m. He whose essence is intelligence; the pure soul, Prab. 114, 19.

चिन्त् *CHINT* (akin to *chit* and *chi*), i. 10 and † i. 1, Par. (also Âtm., Râm. 5, 67, 10), **1.** To think, Lass. 36, 8. To think of, with the acc., Pańch. i. d. 100; with the dat., Hariv. 5976; with the loc., Bhâg. P. 5, 19, 14; with *prati* and acc., MBh. 3, 1714. **2.** To reflect, Râm. 1, 8, 2. **3.** To mind, MBh. 3, 2399. **4.** To regard, Râm. 5, 77, 11. **5.** To devise, Hit. 13, 19. Anomalous ptcple. of the pres., *chintayâna*, Pańch. 209, 6. *chintita*, n. **1.** Thought, Matsyop. 37. **2.** Design, Râm. 1, 70, 7. **3.** Care, Lass. 74, 17.—Comp. *A-*, adj. unexpected, Pańch. ii. d. 3.—Ptcple. of the fut. pass. **1.** Comp. *a-chintaniya*, Not to be thought of, Pańch. iii. d. 221. **2.** *chintya*, n. Necessity of minding something, Bhâg. P. 7, 5, 49. Comp. *A-*, adj. incomprehensible, Man. 1, 3. *Dus-*, adj. difficult to be penetrated, MBh. 7, 433.—With the prep. **अनु** *anu*, **1.** To think, to think of, Hariv. 9216. **2.** To reflect, Râm. 1, 15, 23. **3.** To remember, MBh. 3, 2642. **4.** To consider, Râm. 6, 21, 35.—With **समनु** *sam-anu*, **1.** To remember, MBh. 3, 9952. **2.** To consider, MBh. 12, 12393.—With **अभि** *abhi*, To ponder, MBh. 13, 4341.—With **निस्** *nis*, *a-niçchintya*, adj. Unfathomable, Râm. 5, 81, 6.—With **परि** *pari*, **1.** To reflect, MBh. 4, 1534. **2.** To remember, Râm. 5, 34, 23. **3.** To consider, MBh. 14, 568. **4.** To devise, Râm. 1, 9, 2.—With **संपरि** *sam-pari*, To devise, Râm. 6, 22, 10.—With **प्र** *pra*, **1.** To reflect, Râm. 4, 8, 8. **2.** To consider, MBh. 3, 12231. **3.** To devise, MBh. 3, 8820.—With विप्र *vi-pra,* To remember, MBh. 8, 4230.—With प्रति *prati,* 1. To remember, Râm. 5, 28, 11. 2. To consider again, Böhtl. Ind. Spr. 2977.—With वि *vi,* 1. To reflect, Pañch. 23, 10. 2. To consider, MBh. 1, 5190. 3. To care, Bhâg. P. 7, 2, 38. 4. To devise, Pañch. 92, 6. 5. To find out, MBh. 3, 1445.—Comp. ptcple. of the fut. pass. *durvichintya,* i.e. *dus-,* adj. Difficult to be penetrated, MBh. 12, 4628.—With प्रवि *pra-vi,* To think of (with acc.), Râm. 5, 66, 33.—With सम् *sam,* 1. To reflect, Râm. 5, 1, 86. 2. To consider, Pañch. 255, 3. 3. To design, Bhâg. P. 5, 7, 1. Comp. ptcple. of the fut. pass. *dus-sañchintya,* adj. Hardly to be imagined, Râjat, 6, 61.—With अनुसम् *anu-sam,* To reflect, MBh. 14, 59.—With अभिसम् *abhi-sam,* To remember, MBh. 7, 5551.

5चिन्तक *-chint + aka,* latter part of comp. words, Thinking of, caring, e.g. MBh. 1, 7777.—Comp. *Kârya-,* m. a superintendent of all affairs, Yâjñ. 2, 191. *Daiva-,* m. an astrologer, MBh. 12, 4454. *Sarvârtha-,* i.e. *sarva-artha-,* m. a superintendent of all affairs, Man. 7, 121. *Sthâna-,* m. a quartermaster, Pañch. 156, 22.

चिन्तन *chint+ana,* n. 1. Thinking, Man. 12, 5. 2. Way of thinking, Râjat. 5, 200.

चिन्ता *chint+â,* f. 1. Thinking, Bhâshâp. 65. 2. Thought, Râjat. 5, 11. 3. Care, Pañch. i. d. 226.—Comp. *An-anya-chinta,* adj. having one's thoughts fixed on one only object, Râm. 5, 57, 8. *Niçchinta,* i.e. *nis-,* adj. 1. free from thought, MBh. 14, 1307. 2. Careless, Hariv. 10302.

चिन्तामय *chintâ+maya,* adj., f. *yî.* 1. Appearing as thought, Bhâg. P. 2, 2, 12. 2. Produced by thinking, Râm. 2, 85, 16.

चिन्मात्र *chinmâtra,* i.e. *chit-mâtra,* n. Pure intelligence, Bhâg. P. 4, 7, 26.

चिर *chira* (i.e. probably *char+a,* cf. *charama*), I. adj., f. *râ.* 1. Long, Hariv. 9942. 2. Olden, Bhâg. P. 3, 2, 21. II. n. Delay, Râm. 4, 5, 27. III. The acc. *ram,* instr. *reṇa,* dat. *râya,* abl. *rât,* gen. *rasya,* and loc. *re,* are used adverbially: *ram,* A long time, Man. 4, 60. *reṇa,* After a long time, Sâv. 5, 84; from a long time back, Prab. 29, 14. *râya,* A long time, Ragh. 14, 59; after a long time, at last, Pañch. 231, 21; too late, MBh. 5, 780; for a long time, MBh. 13, 392. *rât,* After a long time, Pañch. ii. d. 63; at last, Râm. 4, 27, 17; from a long time back, Hit. 17, 14. *rasya,* After a long time, at last, Râm. 2, 54, 20.—When former part of a comp. word these adverbs drop their terminations, and appear in the form of the base *chira,* e.g. Râm. 1, 42, 1. Comp. *A-,* adj. short, Râm. 5, 37, 21; the acc. *ram,* instr. *reṇa,* and abl. *rât,* are used adverbially: In a short time, Draup. 5, 20; Man. 7, 134; Râm. 1, 70, 34. As former part of comp. words it signifies often, Just, Man. 3, 280. *Na-,* adj. not long, MBh. 1, 3860; °*ram,* adv. a short time, Râm. 2, 94, 14 Gorr. °*reṇa, râya,* and *rât,* adv. soon, MBh. 1, 7487; 833; Râm. 5, 89, 28. *Mâchira,* see separately. *Su-chira+m,* adv. a very long time, Râjat, 5, 9.

चिरकार *chira-kâra,* चिरकारि *chirakâri,* i.e. *chira-kṛi+i,* चिरकारिक *chirakârika,* i.e. *chirakâra+ika,* and चिरकारिन् *chira-kârin,* adj. Slow, tardy, MBh. 12, 9482; 9539; 9483; 9485.

चिरकारिता *chirakâritâ*, and चिरकारित्व *chirakâritva*, i.e. *chira-kârin* + *tâ*, f., or *tva*, n. Slowness, MBh. 12, 9524; 9489.

चिरकालत्व *chira-kâla* + *tva*, n. A long interval, Pańch. 115, 18.

चिरंतन *chiraṁtana*, i.e. *chira* + *m* + *tana*, adj. **1.** Old, Pańch. 228, 11. **2.** Hereditary, Pańch. 16, 1.

चिरय *CHIRAYA* (a denominative derived from *chira* by *aya*), Par. To tarry, Pańch. 52, 12.

चिराय *CHIRÂYA* (a denomin. derived from *chira* by *ya*), Par., Âtm. To tarry, Pańch. 257, 1.

† चिरि *CHIRI*, ii. 5, *chiriṇu*, Par. To hurt.

चिर्भटिका *chirbhaṭikâ*, i.e. *chirbhaṭî* + *ka*, and चिर्भटी *chirbhaṭî*, f. A kind of cucumber, Cucumis utilissimus, Pańch. 30, 7; 248, 12.

† चिल् *CHIL*, i. 6, Par. To put on clothes.

† चिल्ल् *CHILL*, i. 1, Par. **1.** To be loose. **2.** To indicate one's meaning (?).

चिल्लक *chillaka*, m. or f. *kâ*, A certain animal, MBh. 7, 1320.

चिल्लिका *chillikâ*, i.e. *chilli* + *ka*, m. and चिल्ली *chillî*, f. A kind of vegetable, Daçak. 169, 19; Suçr. 1, 220, 21.

चिवुक *chivuka*, n. The chin, Yâjń. 3, 98.

चिह्न *chihna* (probably for *chikhna*, from a reduplicated form of *khan* by the aff. *a*), n. **1.** A mark of any kind, Râm. 4, 12, 44. **2.** Insignia, Ragh. 2, 7. **3.** An attribute, Bhâg. P. 4, 15, 9. **4.** A sign, Pańch. i. d. 193. **5.** Character, Bhâg. P. 3, 32, 35.

चिह्नय *CHIHNAYA* (a denomin. derived from the last by *aya*), Par. To mark, Man. 8, 352.—With the prep. अभि *abhi*, To mark, Râm. 4, 42, 12.—With उपरि *upari*, *uparichihnita*, Signed above, Yâjń. 1, 318.—With परि *pari*, **1.** To mark, MBh. 3, 12445. **2.** To sign, Yâjń. 2, 93.

† चीक् *CHÎK*, i. 1 and 10, Par. To suffer.

चीचीकुची and चीचीकूची *chîchîkûchî*, a word imitative of the chirping of birds, Râm. 6, 11, 42; MBh. 16, 38.

चीत्कार *chît-kâra*, m. Noise, MBh. 7, 6666.—Cf. *chitkâra*.

चीत्कारवन्त् *chîtkâravant*, adj., f. *vatî*, Accompanied by noise, Mâlat. 1, 8.—Cf. *chitkâravant*.

चीन *chîna*, m. **1.** pl. The name of a people, Man. 10, 44. **2.** A sort of cloth, Suçr. 1, 65, 14.—Comp. *Apara-*, m. pl. the western Chînas, Râm. 4, 44, 14.

चीनक *chîna* + *ka*, m. The name of a people = Chîna, MBh. 8, 236.

† चीब् *CHÎB*, see *chîv*.

† चीभ् *CHÎBH*, v.r. of *bîbh*, q. cf.

† चीय् *CHÎY*, v.r. of *chîv*.

चीर *chîra* (perhaps a syncope of *chîvara*), n. **1.** Bark, Râm. 5, 31, 22; a vesture of bark, Man. 6, 6. **2.** A rag, Kathâs. 4, 48; also fem. *râ*, Râjat. 4, 573. **3.** A cloth, Râm. 2, 37, 10 (*kuça-*, A cloth of Kuça grass).

चीरिन् *chîrin*, i.e. *chîra* + *in*, adj. Covered with bark or rags, MBh. 3, 1002.

चीरी *chîrî* (based on an imitative sound; cf. the next), f. A cricket, Yâjń. 3, 215.

चीरीवाक *chîrîvâka*, i.e. *chîri-vach* + *a*, m. A cricket, Man. 12, 63.

चीर्ण *chîrṇa*, ptcple. of the pf. pass. of *char*, q. cf.

† **चीव्** *CHÎV*, or *chîb*, or *chîy*, i. 1, Par., Âtm. **1.** To take. **2.** To cover. *chîv*, i. 10, Par. To shine (or speak).

चीवर *chîvara* (perhaps from 1. *chi* by the affixes *van* + *a*), n. The tattered dress of a Buddhist mendicant, MBh. 1, 3638; or of any mendicant, Daçak. in Chr. 191, 15.

चुकोपयिषु *chukopayishu*, i.e. *chukopayisha*, desiderative of the Causal of *kup*, + *u*, adj. Desiring to make wrathful, MBh. 8, 1793.

† **चुक्क्** *CHUKK*, i. 10, Par. To give pain.—Cf. *chakk*.

चुक्र *chukra*, m. A kind of vinegar, made of fruits, Suçr. 2, 365, 17.

चुक्षोभयिषु *chukshobhayishu*, i.e. *chukshobhayisha*, desider. of the Causal of *kshubh*, + *u*, adj. Desiring to cause to waver, Man. 7, 1142.

चुचू *chuchchû*, f. A sort of vegetable, Suçr. 1, 219, 19.

चुच्य् *CHUCHY*, v.r. of *çuchy*.

चुञ्चु *chuńchu*, I. m. The name of a mixed class, Man. 10, 48. II. as latter part of comp. words, Renowned, known; see *chańchu*.

† **चुट्** *CHUṬ*, i. 6 and 10, Par. To cut. i. 1 and 10, Par. To become small (cf. *chuṭṭ*, of which it is a v.r.).

† **चुट्ट्** *CHUṬṬ*, i. 10, Par. To become small (probably a dialectical form of a denomin. derived from *kshudra*).

† **चुड्** *CHUḌ*, or **बुड्** *BUḌ*, i. 6, Par. To cover.

† **चुड्ड्** *CHUḌḌ*, i. 1, Par. To dally, to wanton (or to guess, to act).

† **चुण्** *CHUṆ*, i. 6, Par. To cut, v.r.

† **चुण्ट्** *CHUṆṬ*, i. 1 and 10, Par. To cut. i. 1, Par. To become small.—Cf. *chuṭ*.

चुण्टा *chuṇṭâ* and *ṭi*, f. A well, Suçr. 1, 169, 12.

† **चुण्ठ्** *CHUṆṬH*, i. 10, Par. To hurt, v.r.

† **चुण्ड्** *CHUṆḌ*, i. 1, Par. To become small (cf. *chuṭ*). i. 10, Par. To cut.

† **चुत्** *CHUT*, v.r. of *chyut*.

चुद् *CHUD* (for primitive *çchud*, cf. *chyu*), in the Vedas, i. 1, Par., Âtm. To speed. In classical language, i. 10, Par. (also Âtm. MBh. 13, 578), or rather Caus. **1.** To push on, Arj. 4, 37. **2.** To impel, MBh. 1, 5986. **3.** To order, Draup. 8, 1. **4.** To ask, MBh. 13, 578. **5.** To ordain, Man. 2, 165. **6.** To mention, Man. 3, 26. **7.** To lay a stress upon, Çiç. 9, 16 (*na chodyam adas*, It is not to be wondered at). Ptcple. of the fut. pass. *chodya*, n. A question, MBh. 5, 1653.—With the prep. **अभि** *abhi*, Caus. **1.** To impel, Chr. 4, 17. **2.** To order, Râjat. 3, 67. **3.** To announce, MBh. 3, 11396. **4.** To inquire, MBh. 1, 2913.—With **परि** *pari*, Caus. **1.** To wield, Hariv. 15892. **2.** To impel, MBh. 14, 2387.—With **प्र** *pra*, Caus. **1.** To push on, MBh. 3, 12095. **2.** To impel, Râm. 3, 28, 42. **3.** To command, Man. 2, 291. **4.**

To ask, Man. 4, 248. **5.** To proclaim, Man. 3, 228.—With **अभिप्र** *abhi-pra*, Caus. To impel, MBh. 1, 575.—With **संप्र** *sam-pra*, Caus. **1.** To wield, MBh. 7, 559. **2.** To push on, to impel, MBh. 3, 12109; 1, 4875. **3.** To invite, Râm. 1, 4, 32.—With **प्रति** *prati*, Caus. To push on, to impel, Râm. 3, 28, 40. *pratichodita*, One who has turned himself against (with the acc.), Râm. 4, 61, 48.—With **सम्** *sam*, Caus. **1.** To wield, MBh. 3, 12238. **2.** To push on, to impel, MBh. 3, 756; Râm. 2, 40, 40. **3.** To further, Râm. 6, 95, 59.—Cf. Goth. skiutan; A.S. sceótan; O.H.G. sciozan; probably *σπεύδειν*; Lat. studere; perhaps Goth. giutan; A.S. geotan.—Cf. *chyu*.

† **चुन्द्** *CHUND*, see *bund*.

1. **चुप्** *CHUP*, i. 1, Par. To move, MBh. 3, 10648.

2. **चुप्** *CHUP*, see *chhup*.

1. **चुम्ब्** *CHUMB*, i. 1, and 10, Par. (i. 1, Âtm., Pańch. iv. d. 7), To kiss Ṛit. 6, 14. Caus. To cause to be kissed, Daçak. 49, 9.—With **परि** *pari*, to kiss warmly, Amar. 77. *parichumbita*, Close-surrounded, Chaurap. 14.

† 2. **चुम्ब्** *CHUMB*, i. 10, Par. To hurt.

चुम्बक 1.*chumb*+*aka*, m. A loadstone, Prab. 108, 13.

चुम्बन *chumb*+*ana*, n. **1.** Kissing, Pańch. 263, 5. **2.** Kiss, Râjat. 5, 383.

चुम्बिन् *chumb*+*in*, adj. Kissing, Chaurap. 17.

चुर् *CHUR*, i. 10, *choraya*, † i. 1, Par. **1.** To steal, Man. 8, 333. **2.** To steal from, Hariv. 11146.—Cf. *chora*.

† **चुल्** *CHUL*, i. 10, Par. **1.** To rise. **2.** To let down, v.r.

† **चुलुम्प्** *CHULUMP*, i. 1, Par. **1.** To rock. **2.** To break (?).

† **चुल्ल्** *CHULL*, i. 1, Par. To dally, to wanton (or, to guess, to act), v.r.—Cf. *chuḍḍ*.

चुल्ली *chullî*, f. A fire-place, Man. 3, 63.

चूचुक *chûchuka* (cf. *chûsh*), n. **1.** A nipple, Suçr. 1, 349, 17. **2.** The breast, Râm. 6, 23, 13.

चूड *chûḍa*, I. m. or n. The ceremony of cutting the hair. II. f. *ḍâ*. **1.** A single lock of hair left on the crown of the head at the ceremony of tonsure. **2.** The hair. **3.** The ceremony of cutting the hair.—Comp. *Kṛita-chûḍa*, adj. one whose head has been shorn, Man. 5, 58. *Chandra-*, m. a name of Çiva. *Tâmra-*, I. adj. having a red cock's comb. II. m. 1. a cock. 2. a proper name. *Pańchachûḍa*, i.e. *pańchan-*, I. adj. having five tufts of hair. II. f. *ḍâ*, the name of an Apsaras. *Pushkara-*, m. the name of one of the four elephants who are supposed to support the world, Bhâg. P. 5, 20, 39. *Svarṇa-*, m. 1. a cock. 2. the blue jay.

ऽचूडक *-chûḍaka*, A substitute for *-chûḍâ*, when the latter part of a comp. adj., e.g. *nirvṛitta-*, i.e. *nis-* (vb. *vṛit*), adj. One whose head has been shorn, Man. 5, 67.

चूडाल *chûḍâ*+*la*, adj., f. *lâ*, Having a tuft of hair on the crown of the head, MBh. 10, 288.

† **चूण्** *CHÛṆ*, i. 10, Par. To contract.

चूत *chûta*, m. The mango, Mangifera indica, Râm. 3, 79, 17.

† **चूर्** *CHÛR*, i. 4, Âtm. To burn.

चूर्ण् *CHÛRN*, i, 10 (rather a denomin. derived from the next), Par. **1.** To grind, Suçr. 2, 56, 3. **2.** To crush, MBh. 3, 12133.—With the prep. **अव** *ava*, **1.** To powder, to cover with a ground substance, Suçr. 1, 46, 14; MBh. 8, 456. **2.** To cover, MBh. 2, 813.—With **विनि** *vi-ni*, To crush, MBh. 8, 4665.—With **वि** *vi*, **1.** To grind, MBh. 1, 4773. **2.** To crush, Râm. 6, 87, 23.—With **सम्** *sam*, **1.** To grind, Suçr. 1, 162, 19. **2.** To crush, MBh. 7, 1394; Râjat. 5, 411.

चूर्ण *chûrṇa* (an old ptcple. pf. pass. akin to *charv*), m. and n. Any pulverulent or minute division of substance. **1.** Flour, Pańch. 121, 11. **2.** Dust, MBh. 3, 10972. **3.** Powder, MBh. 6, 5764. **4.** Aromatic powder, Megh. 69. —**Comp.** *Yoga-*, m. or n. magical powder, Daçak. in Chr. 186, 10. *Râga-*, m. 1. a name of Kâma. 2. red lead. 3. the red powder thrown over one another by the Hindus, at the festival called Holi.

चूर्णक *chûrṇa + ka*, n. Aromatic powder, Suçr. 2, 392, 11.

चूर्णता *chûrṇa + tâ*, f. State of powder, Râjat. 5, 16.

चूर्णशस् *chûrṇa + ças*, adv. Into powder, MBh. 1, 3225.

चूर्णिका *chûrṇikâ*, i.e. *chûrṇa + ka*, f. A sort of pastry, Lass. 11, 20.

चूलिन् *chûlin*, i.e. *chûḍâ + in*, **1.** adj. Having a crest, Hariv. 2495; 4440. **2.** m. A proper name, Râm. 1, 34, 38.

चूष् *CHÛSH*, i. 1. Par. **1.** To suck. **2.** pass. To fester (of wounds), Suçr. 1, 103, 17. Ptcple. of the fut. pass. *chûshya*, To be sucked, Pańch. 61, 13. Caus. To suck up, Suçr. 2, 33, 16.—With the prep **सम्** *sam*, pass. To boil up, Suçr. 2, 486, 10.—Cf. probably Lat. sûgere, succus; A.S. súcan; O.H.G. sûgan (cf. *chaksh*).

चृत् *CHṚIT*, i. 6, Par. **1.** To connect together. **2.** To kill.—Cf. *chhṛid*.

† **चृप्** *CHṚIP*, i. 1, and 10, Par. To light, v.r.

चेट *cheṭa*, m., f. *ṭî*, A slave, a servant, Kâthas. 6, 127; Râm. 2, 91, 62.

चेटक *cheṭa + ka*, m., f. *ṭikâ*, A slave, a servant, Bhartṛ. 1, 91; Kathâs. 4, 51.

चेतन *chetana*, i.e. 1. *chit + ana*, I. m. A sentient being, Megh. 5. II. f. *nâ*. **1.** Consciousness, Bhâg. P. 4, 21, 34. **2.** Recollection, Pańch. 35, 11. (°*nâm labdhvâ*, After having recovered his senses). **3.** Intellect, Man. 9, 67. **Comp.** *A-*, adj., f. *nâ*. 1. insensible, Bhartṛ. 2, 30. 2. unconscious of one's self, Nal. 13, 35. *Nis-*, adj. 1. unreasonable, Râm. 2, 41, 6. 2. unconscious of one's self, Pańch. 146, 12. *Vi-*, adj. unconscious, senseless, lifeless. *Sa-*, adj. recovering one's senses, Pańch. 43, 10.

चेतनावन्त् *chetanâ + vant*, adj., f. *vati*. **1.** Sentient, MBh. 14, 529. **2.** Discreet, MBh. 12, 2449.

चेतयितृ *chetayitṛi*, i.e. 1. *chit*, Caus., + *tṛi*, m. A perceiver, MBh. 12, 7693.

चेतस् *chetas*, i.e. 1. *chit + as*, n. **1.** Intellect, Nal. 11, 24. **2.** Consciousness, MBh. 7, 6935.—**Comp.** *A-*, adj. unconscious of one's self, Chr. 31, 16. *Dushṭa-*, adj. malevolent, Man. 3, 225.

Nis, adj. senseless, Râm. 2, 77, 12. *Manda-*, adj. fainting, Chr. 29, 35. *Vi-*, adj. 1. stupid. 2. perplexed, unhappy. *Vyâkula-*, adj. bewildered. *Sa-*, adj. intelligent, Bhâshâp. 144.

चेतिष्ठ *chetishṭha*, superl. of 1.*chit*+*tṛi*, adj. Wisest, Lass. 101, 3=Rigv. vii. 16, 1.

चेतोमन्त् *chetomant*, i.e. *chetas*+*mant*, adj. Living, MBh. 3, 8676.

चेद् *ched*, i.e. *cha-id*, a particle. 1. Even, MBh. 1, 2403. 2. If, Man. 7, 25. 3. With preceding *no* it forms usually a short sentence, which must be completed by the preceding words, e.g. *bhavatâ maunavratena sthâtavyam no chet tava kâshṭhât pâto bhavishyati*, You must be silent, if not you will fall from the stick, Pańch. 76, 20. 4. With preceding *na* sometimes, That not, Râm. 5, 80, 24. 5. With preceding *iti* and following *na*, viz. *iti chen na*, a common form of concluding an opponent's objection, and proceeding to answer it. —Cf. probably *καί*.

चेदि *chedi*, m. pl. The name of a people, Nal. 6, 7.

† **चेल्** *CHEL*, i. 1, Par. To move. —Cf. *chal*.

चेल *chela*, n. Cloth, Man. 11, 166; raiment, Man. 4, 216.—Comp. *Ku-*, n. coarse vesture, Man. 6, 44. *Sa-*, adj. clothed.

चेल्ल् *CHELL*, v.r. of *chel*.

चेष्ट् *CHESHṬ*, i. 1, Par., Âtm. 1. To struggle, to move in convulsions, MBh. 3, 2542. 2. To stir, Matsyop. 22. 3. To strive, MBh. 6, 3642. 4. To perform, MBh. 13, 4676. 5. To act, Bhag. 3, 13. 6. To frequent, Ragh. 9, 51. Ptcple of the pf. pass. *cheshṭita*, n. 1. Motion, gesture, Man. 8, 25. 2. Action, Man. 2, 4. Comp. *Dus-*, n. acting perversely, Bhartṛ. 1, 72. Caus. Par. and Âtm. 1. To cause to move, MBh. 3, 13981. 2. To impel, Râm. 6, 94, 24.—With the prep. **अति** *ati*, To strive too much, Hit. i. d. 170.—With **आ** *â*, To perform, Daçak. in Chr. 197, 1.—With **परि** *pari*, To welter, Râm. 4, 19, 32.—With **वि** *vi*, 1. To stretch, MBh. 7, 3168. 2. To struggle against, Draup. 9, 3. 3. To move in convulsions, Râm. 2, 77, 20. 4. To surround, Hariv. 10200. 5. To move, Râm. 3, 54, 10. 6. To struggle, Râm. 2, 66, 21. 7. To act, Man. 8, 334. *vicheshṭita*, n. 1. Action, Pańch. 95, 16. 2. Evil or malicious act (i.e. *cheshṭita*, with *vi*).—With **सम्** *sam*, 1. To shrink up, MBh. 7, 3168. 2. To crowd together (from fear), MBh. 5, 1855. 3. To strive, MBh. 3, 2923.

चेष्ट *cheshṭ*+*a*, I. n. and f. *ṭâ*. 1. Motion, Kathâs. 23, 84. 2. Gesture, Man. 7, 63; 8, 26. 3. Action, Hariv. 5939; Man. 4, 63. II. f. *ṭâ*, Acting, activity, Man. 1, 65. Comp. *Karmacheshṭâ*, i.e. *karman-*, f. 1. acting, business, Man. 1, 66. 2. action, Nal. 23, 18 (16, read *karmacheshṭâbhi°*). 3. exertion, Râm. 2, 64, 11. *Niçcheshṭa*, i.e. *nis-*, adj. deprived of motion, Râm. 2, 45, 31. *Sa-*, I. adj. making effort, active. II. m. the mango, Mangifera indica.

चेष्टन *cheshṭ*+*ana*, n. Motion, Man. 12, 120.

चेष्टयितृ *cheshṭayitṛi*, i. e. *cheshṭ*, Caus., +*tri*, m. The being who causes motion, MBh. 12, 1181.

चेष्टावन्त् *cheshṭâ*+*vant*, adj., f. *vatî*, Moveable, Suçr. 1, 340, 3.

चैतन्य *chaitanya*, i.e. *chetana*+*ya*, n. 1. Intellect, Yâjń. 3, 81. 2. Consciousness, Vedântas. in Chr. 204, 18. 3. Soul, spirit, MBh. 14, 529.

चैत्त *chaitta*, i.e. *chitta+a*, adj. Belonging to the dominion of thought, Vedântas. in Chr. 209, 22.

चैत्य *chaitya*, I. probably *chiti+ya*, m. The individual soul, Bhâg. P. 3, 26, 61. II. *chitâ+ya*, m. and n. 1. A tomb, MBh. 12, 914. 2. An altar, Râm. 1, 13, 30. 3. A religious building, Râm. 5, 17, 20. 4. A sacred tree; a religious fig-tree growing in a village, or near it, and held in veneration by the villagers, Hiḍ. 1, 40.—Comp. *Grâma-*, m. a sacred tree growing in a village, Megh. 24.

चैत्र *chaitra*, i.e. *chitra* and *chitrâ+a*, I. adj. 1. Made of a tree called chitra, MBh. 7, 76. II. m. The name of a month, March—April, Man. 7, 182. III. f. *trî*, The day of the full-moon in this month, MBh. 12, 3691.

चैत्ररथ *chaitraratha*, i.e. *chitra-ratha+a*, I. adj. Treating of the Gandharva Chitraratha, MBh. 1, 313. II. patron. m. and f. *thî*, A descendant of Chitraratha, MBh. 1, 3740; Hariv. 712. III. n. The name of a forest, Râm. 1, 28, 37.

चैल *chaila*, cf. *chela*, n. 1. Cloth, Man. 5, 119. 2. Raiment, Man. 5, 103.

चैलधाव *chaila-dhâv+a*, m. A washer, Yâjń. 1, 164.

चैलाशक *chailâçaka*, i. e. *chaila-âçaka* (vb. *aç+aka*), m. The name of a demon, Man. 12, 72.

चोक्ष *choksha* (cf. *chauksha*), adj. Clean, pure, Man. 3, 207; MBh. 12, 2708.

चोदक *chodaka*, i.e. *chud + aka*, adj. Impelling, calling, MBh. 13, 71.

चोदन *chodana*, i.e. *chud+ana*, n. and f. *nâ*. 1. Inciting, invitation, MBh. 13, 41; Bhag. 18, 18. 2. Command, Man. 2, 35.

चोदयितृ *chodayitṛi*, i. e. *chud*, Caus., *+tṛi*, m., f. *trî*, n. Inciting, an inciter, Kumâras. 3, 21.

चोर *chora*, i.e. *chur + a*, m. A thief, Chr. 53, 1.—Cf. φώρ; Lat. fur.

चोरितक *chorita + ka* (vb. *chur*), n. A stolen object, Daçak. in Chr. 195, 15.

चोल *chola*, and चोलक *chola + ka*, m. pl. The name of a people, Râm. 4, 41, 18; Kathâs. 19, 95.

चोष *chosha* (cf. *chûsh*), m. Burning (of diseases), Suçr. 1, 37, 2.

चोष्य *choshya* (cf. *chûsh*, of which it is an anomalous ptcle. fut. pass.), adj. What is to be sucked, Râm. 1, 52, 4.

चौक्ष *chauksha*, i.e. *chukshâ* (Washing? Grammar.)*+a*, adj. Clean, MBh. 12, 4315.

चौक्ष्य *chaukshya*=the last, MBh. 12, 7049.

चौड *chauḍa*, i.e. *chûḍâ+a*, n. The ceremony of cutting the hair, Man. 2, 27.

चौर *chaura*, i. e. *churâ*, Theft (Grammar.) *+a*, m. 1. A thief, Man. 4, 118. 2. The robber of a heart; in the title, *chaura-pańchâçikâ*, The fifty strophes of a robber of a heart.—Comp. *Bhitti-* and *Vandi-*, m. a house-breaker. *Strî-*, m. a libertine.

चौरिका *chaurikâ*,, i.e. *chaura+ka*, f. 1. Theft, Pańch. v. d. 41. 2. Fraud, Pańch. 199, 9.

चौर्य *chaurya*, i.e. *chaura+ya*, n.

1. Theft, Man. 9, 276. 2. Fraud, Hariv. 15163. 3. Stealth, Pańch. i. d. 190 (*chaurya-rata*, literally, enjoyment of love by stealth, i.e. adultery).

चौर्यक *chaurya + ka*, n. Theft, MBh. 12, 8501.

चौल *chaula*, i.e. *chûḍâ + a*, n. The ceremony of cutting the hair, Ragh. 3, 28.

च्यवन *chyavana*, i.e. *chyu + ana*, I. m. The name of a Ṛishi, MBh. 1, 870. II. n. 1. Motion, Suçr. 1, 48, 12. 2. Loss, Bhâg. P. 8, 20, 5.

च्यावन *chyâvana*, i.e. *chyu*, Caus., + *ana*, I. adj. Felling, MBh. 8, 1506. II. n. Expelling, Hariv. 1512.

1. **च्यु** *CHYU* (for original *çchyu*, cf. *çchyut*), i. 1, Âtm. (in epic poetry also Par.), 1. To move (ved.). 2. To depart, Râm. 2, 72, 5. 3. To fly, Râm. 3, 33, 16. 4. (with abl.), To swerve, MBh. 2, 2357; Man. 7, 98 (*asmâd dharmân na chyaveta kshatriyaḥ*, From this law a king must never depart). 5. To become deprived, to lose (with the abl.), Man. 3, 140. 6. To fall, Râm. 5, 13, 31. 7. To perish, Man. 12, 96.—Comp. ptcple. of the pf. pass. *a-chyuta*, I. adj. 1. Unshakeable, Chr. 291, 4=Rigv. i. 85, 4; firm, MBh. 1, 7770. 2. Imperishable, Chr. 51, 18. II. m. A name of Vishṇu, Vedântas. in Chr. 209, 20.—Caus. *chyâvaya*, 1. To expel, MBh. 3, 15920. 2. To cause to fall, MBh. 13, 324. 3. To deprive (with two acc.), Râm. 2, 53, 7.—With the prep. **परि** *pari*, 1. To fly, MBh. 7, 5220. 2. To swerve, Râm. 4, 16, 20. 3. To become deprived, to lose, Râm. 4, 16, 8. 4. To escape, Mârk. P. 15, 38. 5. To come down, MBh. 3, 11614. 6. To surround, MBh. 7, 6449.—With **प्र** *pra*, 1. To depart, Man. 9, 273. 2. To proceed, Râm. 4, 44, 47. 3. To fall, Râm. 2, 91, 21. 4. To become deprived, Râm. 3, 53, 22. *a-prachyuta*, adj. Not swerving, Man. 12, 116. Caus. 1. To shake, Chr. 290, 6=Rigv. i. 64, 3. 2 To expel, Pańch. 86, 13. 3. To cause to fall, MBh. 7, 1717.—With **वि** *vi*, 1. To fall asunder, Bhâg. P. 8, 12, 21; to split, Râm. 3, 35, 53. 2. To depart, Man. 9, 273. *a-vichyuta*, Unperishable, Yâjń. 1, 212. °*tam*, adv. Faultless, Yâjń. 3, 112.—With **सम्** *sam*, Caus. To remove, MBh. 7, 7515.—Cf. σεύω, ἔσσευον, etc., Goth. skevjan, skura, vinthi-skauro; A.S. scur, Engl. shower; O.H.G. spuon; A.S. spëovan; O.H.G. spua + t, spuatôn; A.S. spaedan; see *chud*; χέω; Lat. jacere (Causal=*chyâvaya*.)

† 2. **च्यु** *CHYU*, i. 10, Par. To laugh.

च्युत् *CHYUT* (cf. *chyu* and *çchyut*), i. 1, Par. To drop.

च्युति *chyu + ti*, f. 1. Departing, MBh. 1, 4169. 2. Not doing one's duty, Bhartṛ. suppl. 10. 3. Perishing, Kumâras. 3, 10. 4. Flowing out, Pańch. i. d. 371. 5. Fall, Bhartṛ. 3, 32.—Comp. *Garbha-*, f. abortion, Hit. Pr. 36.

† **च्युस्** *CHYUS*, i. 10, Par. 1. To laugh. 2. To leave.

छ *CHH.*

छगल *chhagala*, m. A goat, Suçr. 1, 203, 19. f. *lî*, A she-goat.

छटा *chhaṭâ*, f. 1. A lump, a mass, Kathâs. 25, 274. 2. An assemblage, a multitude, Çiç. 1, 47. 3. Light, splendour, Prab. 65, 10.

छत्त्र *chhattra*, i.e. *chhad + tra*, usually written **छत्र** *chhatra*, I. n. A parasol,

Man. 2, 178; one of the insignia of a king, Râjat. 5, 18. II. f. *râ*, The name of a plant, Suçr. 2, 170, 2.—Comp. *Ahichchhattra*, i.e. *ahi-*, m. the name of a people.—Cf. Lat. castrum.

छत्रधारत्व *chhattra-dhâra + tva*, n. The office of bearing the royal parasol, Pañch. 63, 23.

छत्रवन्त् *chhattra + vant*, **1.** adj., f. *vatî*, Having a parasol, Suçr. 1, 30, 2. **2.** f. *vatî*, The name of a town or country, MBh. 1, 6348.

छत्राक *chhattrâka*, i.e. *chhatra + âka*, n. A mushroom, Man. 5, 19.

छत्रिन् *chhattrin*, i.e. *chhattra + in*, adj., f. *iṇî*, Having a parasol, Râm. 1, 31, 16.

1. **छद्** *CHHAD*, i. 10, *chhâdaya*, Par. (in epic poetry also Âtm. Râm. 4, 58, 7); † i. 1, Par. **1.** To cover, MBh. 1, 8245. **2.** To conceal, Râm. 5, 90, 16. **3.** To eclipse, Pañch. i. d. 319. Anomalous ptcple. of the pres. Âtm. *chhâdayâna*, MBh. 6, 2430. Ptcple. of the pf. pass. **1.** *chhâdita*, Kathâs. 17, 44. **2.** *chhanna*, Râm. 1, 74, 16; °*nam*, adv. Secretly, Daçak. in Chr. 197, 10; tacitly, Man. 9, 98; n. A hiding-place, Hariv. 8686.—With the prep. **समभि** *sam-abhi*, To cover, MBh. 12, 255.—With **अव** *ava*, **1.** To cover, MBh. 1, 5421. **2.** To leave unlighted, Bhâg. P. 5, 1, 30. *avachchhanna*, Filled, MBh. 12, 5835.—With **समव** *sam-ava*, **1.** To cover, Hariv. 6444. **2.** To obscure, MBh. 6, 94.—With **आ** *â*, **1.** To cover, Râm. 1, 13, 29. **2.** To obscure, MBh. 4, 1853. **3.** To clothe, Man. 3, 27. **4.** To put on, MBh. 2, 789. **5.** To conceal, Hit. 22, 1.—With **समा** *sam-â*, **1.** To cover, MBh. 3, 12179. **2.** To veil, MBh. 3, 15670.—With **उद्** *ud*, To unclothe, Râm. 2, 91, 51.—With **उप** *upa*, **1.** To cover, MBh. 1, 5005. **2.** To conceal, Man. 8, 249.—With **परि** *pari*, **1.** To cover, Pañch. 144, 23. **2.** To disguise, Râm. 1, 9, 9.—With **प्र** *pra*, **1.** To cover, MBh. 2, 2626. **2.** To obscure, MBh. 1, 4416. **3.** To conceal, Chr. 51, 5. **4.** To disguise, Man. 4, 198. *prachchhanna*, Secret, Man. 5, 107. °*nam*, adv. **1.** Privately, Man. 9, 228. Comp. *Su-*, adj. well-concealed, Daçak. in Chr. 190, 3.—With **प्रति** *prati*, **1.** To cover, Pañch. 224, 4. **2.** To endow, MBh. 3, 1268. **3.** To obscure, MBh. 7, 6129. **4.** To disguise, Râm. 3, 51, 27.—With **सम्** *sam*, **1.** To cover, Râm. 2, 93, 3. **2.** To obscure, MBh. 1, 8235. **3.** To conceal, MBh. 13, 2606.—Cf. Goth. skadus, shadow; σκήνη (for σκαδ-νη), σκότος, which show that the primitive form of *chhad* was *skad*; cf. also Lat. castrum, and *chhâyâ*.

† 2. **छद्** *CHHAD*, i. 1, Par. To make strong.

ऽछद् *-chhad*, Latter part of comp. adj. Covering.

छद *chhad + a*, m. A cover, Mṛichchh. 15, 19. **2.** A leaf, Pañch. ii. d. 2.—Comp. *Uttara-*, 1. a cover, MBh. 13, 746. 2. a coverlet, Daçak. in Chr. 199, 6. *Ghana-*, adj. covered by clouds, Bhâg. P. 7, 8, 27. *Tanu-*, 1. adj. covering the body, Râm. 4, 63, 2. 2. m. a coat of mail, MBh. 12, 4424. *Danta-* and *daçana-*, m. a lip, Ṛit. 4, 12; Râm. 5, 45, 5. *Dus-*, adj. ill-covering, Râm. 2, 32, 31. *Rada-* and *radana-*, m. a lip. *Sita-*, m. a goose.

छदन *chhad + ana*, n. **1.** Covering, a cover, Râm. 2, 56, 32. **2.** A wing,

MBh. 3, 11595. **3.** A leaf, Suçr. 1, 305, 16.

छदि *chhad + i,* The cover of a carriage, Bhâg. P. 3, 21, 18.

छदिस् *chhad + is,* n. A roof, Kathâs. 2, 49.

छद्मन् *chhad + man,* n. **1.** Disguise, Râm. 3, 53, 28. **2.** Hypocrisy, Râm. 4, 16, 16. **3.** Fraud, Man. 4, 199. **4.** Pretext, Megh. 76.—**Comp.** *Kûṭa-*, m. a rogue, Pańch. i. d. 390.

ऽछद्मिन् *-chhadmin,* i. e. *chhadman + in,* adj. Latter part of comp. adj. Disguised as, MBh. 3, 16957.

छनच्छन् *chhanachchhan,* i.e. repeated *chhanat* before *iti,* A word imitative of the sound of falling drops, Amar. 89.

छन्द् *CHHAND,* i. 1 and 10, Par. (ved. also *chhadaya,* Par., Âtm.).—i. 1. **1.** To appear (ved.). **2.** To please.—i. 10, or rather Caus. **1.** To wait on, Râm. 2, 97, 1; Chr. 48, 8. **2.** To present (especially with *vareṇa*), Râm. 6, 4, 43. —With the prep. **अव** *ava,* i. 1, To desire, MBh. 12, 7378.—With **उप** *upa,* Caus. **1.** To wait on, Ragh. 5, 58. **2.** To seduce, Prab. 101, 10.—With **सम्** *sam,* To wait on, to present, MBh. 3, 13507. — Cf. Lat. spons, spontis for spond + ti, spondĕo, σπένδειν.

छन्द *chhand + a,* **I.** adj. Flattering, Chr. 294, 6 = Rigv. i. 92, 6. **II.** m. **1.** Appearance, Hariv. 8359. **2.** Wish, Râm. 2, 9, 7. **3.** Will, Yâjń. 2, 195. **4.** Self-help, Man. 8, 176. **5.** Power, MBh. 12, 1820.—**Comp.** *A-*, m. unwillingness, Hariv. 8557 (against the will). *Para-*, m. dependence, Bhâg. P. 3, 31, 25. *Sva-*, I. m. 1. one's own will, Hit. i. d. 62. 2. independence, Ram. 1, 34, 28. II. adj. 1. independent, Râm. 1, 36, 17. 2. following one's own will, Hit. ii. d. 135. 3. spontaneous. 4. uncultivated. III. °*dam,* adv. by one's own will, Yâjń. 2, 234.

छन्दतस् *chhanda + tas,* adv. By one's own will, Yâjń. 3, 203.

छन्दस् *chhand + as,* n. **1.** Pleasure, MBh. 12, 7376. **2.** A holy hymn, MBh. 5, 1224. **3.** The Vedas, MBh. 12, 12933. **4.** Poetical metre, Bhag. 10, 35. **5.** Metrics, Pańch. ii. d. 34.—**Comp.** *Niç-chhandas,* i.e. *nis-*, adj. where the Vedas are not studied, Man. 3, 7.

छन्दस्कृत *chhandas-kṛita* (vb. *kṛi*), n. The metrical part of the Vedas, Man. 4, 100.

छन्दोग *chhandoga,* i.e. *chhandas -ga* (vb. *gai*), m. A chanter of the Sâma-Veda, Man. 3, 145.

छन्दोमय *chhandomaya,* i.e. *chhandas + maya,* adj., f. *yî,* Having the Vedas as one's substance, Bhâg. P. 2, 7, 11.

† **छम्** *CHHAM,* i. 1, Par. To eat.

छमच्छमित *chhamachchhamita,* n. i.e. repeated *chhamat,* an imitative sound, + *ita,* n. Crackling, Mârk. P. 8, 112.

† **छम्प्** *CHHAMP,* i, 10, Par. To go.

छर्द् *CHHARD,* i. 10, Par. To vomit, see *chhṛid.*

छर्दि *chhardi,* i. e. *chhṛid + i,* f. Nausea, vomiting, Suçr. 1, 108, 18.

छर्दिस् *chhardis,* n. A secure habitation, Chr. 288, 15 = Rigv. i. 64, 15.

छल *chhala* (cf. vb. *skhal*), **1.** Fraud, Râm. 4, 57, 10. **2.** Artful management,

Man. 8, 49. **3.** Pretext, Çiç. 9, 48. **4.** Intention, Mârk. P. 25, 10.

छलक *chhalaka* (cf. vb. *skhal*), adj. sbst. Deceiving, a deceiver, Hariv. 11476.

छलन *chhalana* (cf. vb. *skhal*), n. Deceiving, MBh. 6, 28.

छलय *CHHALAYA* (a denominative derived from *chhala*), Par. To deceive, MBh. 3, 15560. Anomalous infinitive, *chhalitum*, Râm. 6, 86, 13.

छलिक *chhalika*, n. A kind of song, Mâlav. 16, 18.

छवि *chhavi* (cf. vb. *sku*), f. **1.** Hide, skin, Hariv. 15709. **2.** Colour, Ṛit. 6, 20. **3.** Beauty, Ragh. 9, 34. **4.** Splendour, Çiç. 9, 3.—Cf. Goth. skauns, gutha-skaunei; A.S. sceone.

† **छष्** *CHHASH* (v.r. *kaç* and *kash*), i. 1, Par., Âtm. To kill, to hurt.

छाग *chhâga* (cf. *chhagala*), I. m. A goat, Man. 3, 269. II. adj. Produced from a goat, or a she-goat.—Comp. *Vana-*, m. 1. a wild goat. 2. a hog, Yâjn. 1, 257.

छागमय *chhâga+maya*, adj., f. *yî*, Resembling a goat, MBh. 3, 14399.

छागल *chhâgala*, i.e. *chhagala+a*, I. adj. Produced from a goat, or a she-goat, Suçr. 2, 12, 18. II. m. A goat, Râm. 6, 19, 42.

छात्त्र *chhâttra*, i.e. *chhattra+a*, I. m. A pupil, Pañch. 34, 25. II. n. A kind of honey, Suçr. 1, 185, 1.

छात्त्रता *chhâttra+tâ*, f. Apprenticeship. °*tâṁ vraj*, To become a pupil, Pañch. 33, 7.

छादन *chhâdana*, i.e. *chhad+ana*. n. **1.** Covering, raiment, MBh. 1, 3685. **2.** A means of concealing, Bhartṛ. 2, 7.

छाद्मिक *chhâdmika*, i.e. *chhadman+ika*, adj. Fraudulent, Man. 4, 195.

छान्दस *chhândasa*, i.e. *chhandas+a*, adj. **1.** Referring, or referable, to the Vedas (vedic), Hariv. 12284. **2.** Conversant with the Vedas, Kathâs. 18, 108.

छान्दोग्य *chhândogya* i.e. *chhandoga+ya*, n. The name of a Brâhmaṇa and Upanishad, belonging to the vedic literature, Vedântas. in Chr. 216, 5.

छाय *chhâya*, I. m. Shadowing, MBh. 12, 10374. II. f. *yâ*. **1.** Shade, Râm. 2, 45, 23; Man. 4, 51. **2.** Reflected image, Man. 5, 133. **3.** Reflected light, splendour, Megh. 36. **4.** Colour, Vikr. d. 146. **5.** When latter part of a comp. subst. noun, it becomes very often neuter, e.g. Ragh. 12, 50; Man. 3, 274 (*prâkchhâye* [i.e. *prâñch-*] *kuñjarasya*, When the shadow of an elephant falls to the east).—Comp. *Eka-*, adj. quite dark, MBh. 4, 1878. *Vi-*, I. adj. shadowless. II. n. the shadow of a flock of birds. *Vṛiksha-*, I. f. *yâ*, the shadow of a single tree. II. n. the shade of many trees.—Cf. σκιά.

छायावन्त् *chhâyâ+vant*, adj., f. *vatî*, Shadowy, Râm. 2, 94, 10.

छालिक्य *chhâlikya*, i.e. *chhalika+ya*, n. A kind of song, Hariv. 8449.

छिद् *CHHID*, ii. 7, Par., Âtm. **1.** To cut, Man. 4, 69. **2.** To lop off, Man. 9, 276. **3.** To wound, Man. 3, 33. **4.** To break, Man. 9, 276. **5.** To interrupt, Hariv. 16258. **6.** To destroy, Râm. 3, 70, 20. **7.** To remove, MBh. 1, 6890. With *ṛiṇam*, To discharge, Râjat. 6, 16. Comp. ptcple. of the pf. pass. *duçchhinna*, i.e. *dus-*, adj. Cut out, or extracted wrongly, MBh. 12, 5307 (a thorn). Comp. ptcple. of the fut. pass. *a-chchhedya*, adj. Not to be cut down, MBh. 1, 93. Caus. and i. 10, *chhedaya*, **1.** To lop off, MBh. 7, 5954. **2.** To order to be lopped off, Man. 8, 283.—With the prep. अव *ava*, *avachchhinna*, Confined, Vedântas. in Chr. 205, 13 ; *an-avachchhinna*, adj. Unbounded, Bhartṛ. 2, 1.—With व्यव *vi-ava*, **1.** To cut off, MBh. 7, 1166. **2.** To separate, Bhâg. P. 4, 29, 45. **3.** To resolve, Bhâg. P. 1, 19, 7. *a-vyavachchhinna*, adj. Uninterrupted, Hariv. 3580.—With आ *â*, **1.** To pull off, MBh. 12, 9377. **2.** To cut, MBh. 1, 5936. **3.** To break, Bhâg. P. 3, 21, 18. **4.** To remove, MBh. 3, 11710. **5.** To tear away, Pańch. 222, 4. **6.** To rob, MBh. 4, 2147. **7.** To draw, Daçak. 117, 4. **8.** To disregard, Râm. 2, 24, 33.—With अवा *ava-â*, To deliver, Vikr. d. 15.—With उपा *upa-â*, To snatch away, Bhâg. P. 5, 14, 24.—With समा *sam-â*, To snatch away, Râm. 6, 8, 17.—With उद् *ud*, **1.** To root out, MBh. 7, 139 ; to exterminate, MBh. 1, 6811. **2.** To cut off, Mâlat. 151, 6. **3.** To stop, MBh. 1, 4891. **4.** pass. To be deficient, Man. 3, 101.—Comp. ptcple. of the fut. pass. *duruchchhedya*, i.e. *dus-*, adj. Difficult to be exterminated, Prab. 93, 12. *sukhochchhedya*, i.e. *sukha-*, adj. To be exterminated easily, Pańch. iii. d. 25. Caus. or i. 10, To exterminate, Pańch. 55, 12. — With व्युद् *vi-ud*, pass., with the terminations of the Par. (i.e. i. 4), **1.** To become extinct, MBh. 12, 3923. **2.** To cease, MBh. 1, 6188. *a-vyuchchhinna*, adj. Uninterrupted, Vikr. d. 110.—With समुद् *sam-ud*, To exterminate, Pańch. iii. d. 57.—With परि *pari*, **1.** To cut off, MBh. 3, 2593. **2.** To wound, Râm. 3, 32, 26. **3.** To limit, Ragh. 6, 77. **4.** To weigh duly, Pańch. 161, 24. **5.** To be assured, Ragh. 15, 51. *parichchhinna*, Limited, small, Vedântas. in Chr. 206, 1. *a-parichchhedya*, adj. Boundless, Ragh. 10, 29.—With विपरि *vi-pari*, To destroy completely, MBh. 5, 4513.—With प्र *pra*, **1.** To cut, Râm. 2, 87, 9 Gorr. **2.** To cut to pieces, Hariv. 13580. **3.** To withdraw, MBh. 12, 9770. Caus. To order to be lopped off, MBh. 12, 686.—With संप्र *sam-pra*, To cut to pieces, Hariv. 13613.—With प्रति *prati*, To retort by cutting to pieces, MBh. 7, 4848.—With वि *vi*, **1.** To tear asunder, Hariv. 8530. **2.** To interrupt, Bhartṛ. 1, 95 ; Daçak. in Chr. 179, 16 (*a-vichchhinna -pâtam*, Without rising again). **3.** To separate, Vedântas. in Chr. 217, 20.—With सम् *sam*, **1.** To cut, MBh. 1, 2242. **2.** To cut to pieces, MBh. 5, 2909. **3.** To cut off, MBh. 7, 7918. **4.** To pierce, MBh. 4, 2004. **4.** To destroy, to remove, Bhag. 4, 11. **5.** To decide (a question), Bhâg. P. 4, 29, 52. —Cf. σκίδνημι, κίδναμαι, σκοῖδος, κοῖδος, σκινδάλαμος σκεδάννυμι (for σκειδαvjυμι), σχίζω, σχίδη, σχίνδαλμος, σχέδη, etc. ; Lat. scindo, caedo (Causal) ; Goth. skaidan ; A.S. sceádan ; O.H.G. sceit, etc.

ऽछिद् *-chhid*, latter part of comp. adj. **1.** Cutting, piercing, e.g. MBh. 7, 4656 ; Râm. 5, 37, 10. **2.** Destroying, MBh. 5, 1809. **3.** Removing, Bhâg. P. 4, 8, 23.—Comp. *Duçchid*, i.e. *dus-*, difficult to be destroyed, Kâm. Nîtis. 14, 68.

छिदुर *chhid + ura*, adj., f. *râ*, What may be torn easily, Ragh. 16, 62.

† छिद्र् *CHHIDR*, i. 10 (rather a denomin. derived from the next), Par. To perforate.

छिद्र *chhid+ra*, I. adj., f. *râ*, Perforated, Râm. 1, 73, 20. **II.** n. **1.** A gap, Man. 8, 239. **2.** A defect, Pańch. 40, 12. **3.** An opening, Suçr. 1, 54, 16; an entry, Bhâg. P. 5, 6, 4. **4.** A weak point, Pańch. i. d. 366; a vulnerable part, Man. 7, 105.—**Comp.** *A-chchhidra*, I. n. uninterruptedness, Râm. 4, 43, 25. II. adj. 1. unhurt, Râm. 6, 23, 16. 2. uninterrupted, Râm. 1, 40, 10. *Niçchhidra*, i.e. *nis-*, adj. without holes, and without weak points, Böhtl. Ind. Spr. 122.

छिद्रता *chhidra+tâ*, f. The quality of giving space, MBh. 12, 9137.

छिद्रदातृत्व *chhidra-dâtṛi+tva*, n. The quality of giving space, Bhâg. P. 3, 26, 34.

छिद्रात्मन् *chhidrâtman*, i.e. *chhidra-âtman*, m. One who shows his weak points, MBh. 12, 11345.

छिद्रिन् *chhidrin*, i.e. *chhidra+in*, adj. Hollow, Suçr. 1, 304, 21.

छुच्छुन्दर *chuchchhundara*, and °रि *ri*, m. The musk rat, Suçr. 2, 279, 4; Man. 12, 65.

† छुट् *CHHUṬ*, i. 6 and 10, Par. To cut, v.r.

† छुड् *CHHUḌ*, i. 6, Par. To cover, v.r.

† छुप् *CHHUP*, or चुप् *CHUP*, i. 6, Par. To touch.

छुर् *CHHUR* (a form of *kshur*), To cut. Caus. *chhoraya* and *chhuraya*, To inlay with, Kathâs. 24, 1.—With the prep. आ *â*, Caus. To scratch, Kathâs. 17, 33.—With वि *vi*, Caus. **1.** To inlay with, Kumâras. 1, 56. **2.** To paint, Vikr. d. 136. **3.** To cover, Chaurap. 12.

छुरिका *chhurikâ* (a form of *kshurikâ*), f. A knife, Kathâs. 12, 21.

छूरिका *chhûrikâ*, f. The nostril, Man. 8, 325.

छृद् *CHHṚID*, ii. 7, Par., Âtm. **1.** † To shine. **2.** To vomit. **3.** † To play. *CHHṚID*, or छृत् *CHHṚIT*, or छृप् *CHHṚIP*, i. 1 and 10, † To kindle.—Caus. To vomit, MBh. 5, 3493 (3492).—With the prep. प्र *pra*, Caus. To vomit, Suçr. 1, 276, 14.—Cf. σκόρδον and σκόροδον, perhaps also σκορδινέομαι and σκορδύλος, κορδύλος, etc.; Goth. spai-skuldrs; Lat. screare.

† छृप् *CHHṚIP*, see the last.

छेत्तृ *chhettri*, i. e. *chhid+tṛi*, m. **1.** A wood-cutter, Hit. i. d. 52. **2.** One who removes, Hit. i. d. 23.

छेद *chheda*, i. e. *chhid+a*, I. adj. One who cuts away, Man. 9, 44. **II.** m. **1.** A slice, a piece, Ragh. 12, 100; Megh. 11. **2.** Cutting, Pańch. 108, 11. **3.** Cutting off, Man. 8, 368. **4.** Destruction, MBh. 13, 1637. **5.** Dissipation, Çâk. d. 38. **6.** Ceasing, Vikr. d. 76. **7.** Want, Çâk. 91, 12. **8.** Limit, Yâjń. 1, 319.—**Comp.** *Bhakti-*, m. certain streaks on the forehead, nose, cheeks, breast, and arms, which denote a follower of Vishṇu. *Sa-*, adj. interrupted, Lass. 21, 1. *Sthâṇu-*, m. one who cuts away the trunks of trees, Man. 9, 44.

छेदन *chhedana*, i.e. *chhid+ana*, I. adj. **1.** Cutting, destroying, MBh. 1, 1498. **II.** m. **1.** Cutting, Man. 12, 75. **2.** Lopping off, Man. 8, 280. **3.** Removing, MBh. 3, 12700.

छेदिन् *chhedin*, i.e. *chhid+in*, adj. **1.** One who splits, Man. 4, 71. **2.** Removing, Çâk. 35, 15.

छो *CHHO*, i. 4, *chhya*, Par. To cut. — With the prep. प्र *pra*, Caus. To scarify, *prachchhita*, Suçr. 2, 247, 19; cf. 1, 33, 18 (*pra-chchhayitvâ*, sic !)

† छ्यु *CHHYU*, i. 1, Par. To go.

ज *J.*

ऽज *-ja* (vb. *jan*), latter part of comp. words, m., f. *jâ*, and n. **1.** Born, son, daughter, e.g. *gûḍha-* (vb. *guh*), Born secretly. m. A son of concealed birth, Yâjń. 2, 129. *dhṛitarâshṭra-jâ*, f. A daughter of Dhṛitarâshṭra, MBh. 14, 2285. *âtmaja*, i.e. *âtman-*, A son, Hit. 41, 21. *jaghanya-*, adj. Youngest, MBh. 1, 804. *deha-*, m. A son, Bhâg. P. 3, 20, 3. *pûrva-*, m. pl. Ancestors, Daçak. in Chr. 185, 7. **2.** Produced, Man. 1, 87; Bhâshâp. 62. **3.** Caused, Nal. 4, 13.— Cf. also *dharma-*, **I.** adj. Begotten from a sense of duty, Man. 9, 107. **II.** m. Son of Dharma, a name of Arjuna, Bhâg. P. 3, 3, 16.

† जंस् *JAṀS*, i. 10 (and 1?) Par. To protect, to deliver.

1. जक्ष् *JAKSH* (i.e. *jaghas*, vb. *ghas* reduplicated), ii. 2, Par. **1.** To eat, Bhâg. P. 4, 17, 23. **2.** To be hungry, Bhâg. P. 2, 10, 17. Ptcple. of the pf. pass. *jagdha*, Man. 5, 125.—With the prep. वि *vi*, To devour, MBh. 11, 479.

2. जक्ष् *JAKSH* (i.e. *jahas*, vb. *has* reduplicated), ii. 2, Par. To laugh.

जगत् *jagat* (i.e. an old ptcple. of the pres. of vb. *gam*, ii. 3), **I.** adj. Moveable, MBh. 12, 12465. **II.** n. **1.** Race of men, Man. 7, 22. **2.** The world, Man. 1, 52; dual, *jagatî*, Heaven and earth, Kir. 5, 20. **III.** f. *tî*. **1.** The earth, Man. 1, 100. **2.** The world, Râm. 2, 69, 11. **3.** The name of a metre, Bhâg. P. 3, 12, 45.—**Comp.** *A-jagat*, adj. immoveable, MBh. 12, 12465. *Tri-jagat*, n. the three worlds, heaven, earth, and the lower regions, Lass. 5, 1.

जगदायु *jagadâyu*, and जगदायुस् *jagadâyus*, i.e. *jagat-*, m. Containing the life of the world, MBh. 3, 11193; 12, 13569.

जगन्मय *jaganmaya*, i. e. *jagat+maya*, adj. Containing the universe, Hariv. 3762.

जगल *jagala*, probably a reduplicated form of 2. *gṛî*, *+a*, m. An intoxicating beverage, Suçr. 1, 189, 13.

जग्धि *jagdhi*, i.e. *jaksh+ti*, f. **1.** Eating, Man. 5, 31. **2.** Food, Man. 3, 115.

जग्मि *jagmi*, i.e. reduplicated *gam*, *+i*, adj. Hastening, Chr. 292, 8= Rigv. i. 85, 8.

जघन *jaghana*, i.e. reduplicated *han* *+a*, n. and m. **1.** The pudenda, Hariv. 8625. **2.** The buttocks, Râm. 5, 18, 11. **3.** The rear-guard of an army, MBh. 3, 16284.—Cf. *κοχώνη*.

जघनिन् *jaghanin*, i.e. *jaghana+in*, adj., f. *nî*, Having large buttocks, Hariv. 9547.

जघन्य *jaghanya*, i.e. *jaghana+ya*, adj., f. *yâ*. **1.** Last, MBh. 3, 1366. **2.** Late, MBh. 12, 4794. **3.** Shortest, Suçr. 1, 125, 5. **4.** Indifferent, Suçr. 1, 95, 14. **5.** Lowest, Man. 8, 270; Pańch. iii. d. 218. **6.** Comparat. *jaghanyatara*, Lower, MBh. 14, 1137. **7.** °*yam*, adv. At last, MBh. 3, 905. **8.** loc. *ye*, adverbially, At last, MBh. 3, 1303; Behind, Hariv. 3087.

जघन्यतस् *jaghanya + tas*, adv. At last, Râm. 5, 40, 5.

† जङ्क्ष् *JAṄKSH*, v.r. of *kshaṅj*.

जङ्गम *jaṅgam + a* (frequentat. of *gam*), adj., f. *mâ*. **1.** Moveable, Man. 1, 41; patrolling, Man. 9, 266. **2.** Living, MBh. 1, 5019.

जङ्गमत्व *jaṅgama + tva*, n. Mobility, MBh. 14, 654.

जङ्गल *jaṅgal + a* (frequentat. of *gal*? cf. *glai*), adj. Dry, desert.

जङ्घा *jaṅghâ*, i.e. reduplicated *han + a*, fem. The leg, Suçr. 1, 348, 15.—**Comp.** *Tâla-*, 1. adj. long-legged, Râm. 5, 12, 35. **2.** m. The name of a people, Râm. 1, 70, 28. *Su-*, adj., f. *ghâ*, having a beautiful leg, Çrut. 21.

जङ्घाल *jaṅghâ + la*, m. A rapid walker, Suçr. 1, 200, 6.

† जज् *JAJ*, i. 1, Par. To fight.

जञ्ज् *JAÑJ*, i. 1, Par. To fight (?).

† जट् *JAṬ*, i. 1, Par. To be entangled.

जट *jaṭa*, I. m. = f. (see II.), Hariv. 9551. **II.** f. *ṭâ*, **1.** The hair matted, as worn by the god Çiva and by ascetics; the long hair occasionally clotted together and brought over the head, so as to project like a horn from the forehead, or allowed to fall carelessly over the back and shoulders, Man. 6, 6. **2.** A braid, MBh 3, 16137.—**Comp.** *Tri-jaṭa*, I. adj. wearing three braids, MBh. 3, 16137. II. m. 1. a name of Çiva, 12, 10357. 2. a proper name, Râm. 2, 32, 28. III. f. *ṭâ*, a proper name, Râm. 3, 41, 34. *Çikhâ-*, adj. one who wears a lock of hair in a knot on the top of the head, Man. 2, 219.

जटाजिनिन् *jaṭâjinin*, i. e. *jaṭâ-ajina + in*, adj. Wearing matted hair and the hide of an antelope, MBh. 1, 4917.

जटायु *jaṭâyu* and जटायुस् *jaṭâyus*, m. A fabulous vulture, Râm. 1, 1, 51.

जटाल *jaṭâ + la*, and जटालक *jaṭâla + ka*, adj., f. *lâ*, *ikâ*, Wearing matted hair, Hariv. 10594; Mârk. P. 8, 176.

जटिन् *jaṭin*, i.e. *jaṭâ + in*, adj. Wearing matted hair, Man. 11, 92.

जटिल *jaṭila*, i.e. *jaṭâ + ila*, I. adj., f. *lâ*. **1.** Having matted or entangled hair, Man. 2, 219; MBh. 3, 16257. **2.** Entangled, Bhâg. P. 3, 33, 14. II. f. *lâ*. **1.** A proper name, MBh. 1, 7265. **2.** The name of several plants, e.g. Suçr. 1, 71, 16.

जटिलीभाव *jaṭilibhâva*, i.e. *jaṭila-bhû + a*, m. Clotting, Suçr. 1, 272, 2.

जठर *jaṭhara*, I. adj., f. *râ*. **1.** Hard, Çântiç. 4, 13. **2.** Old, Çiç. 4, 29 (?). II. m. **1.** The belly, Pañch. i. d. 27. **2.** The womb, Bhâg. P. 3, 33, 4. **3.** The interior, Râm. 3, 41, 26.—Cf. probably Lat. venter, γαστήρ, Goth. qvithra and in-kiltho.

जड *jaḍa* (probably for original *jala*, to which the Grammar. give the same signification; Lat. gĕlu gelidus; Goth. kald; A.S. ceald; cf. *jala*), adj. **1.** Cold, Pañch. i. d. 353. **2.** Rigid, immoveable, Râm. 6, 6, 1. **3.** Material, irrational, Vedântas. in Chr. 215, 22. **4.** Dimmed, Çâk. d. 81. **5.** Unfeeling, apathetic, Bhâg. P. 2, 7, 10. **6.** Stupid, Bhâg. P. 5, 9, 8. **7.** Dumb, Man. 2, 110. —**Comp.** *A-jaḍa*, m. not an idiot, Man. 8, 148.

जडता *jaḍa + ṭâ*, f. **1.** Apathy,

Sâh. D. 175. **2.** Stupidity, Mârk. P. 10, 33.

जडत्व *jaḍa+tva*, n. Stupidity, Râjat. 6, 26.

जडिमन् *jaḍiman*, i.e. *jaḍa+iman*, m. Stupidity, Râjat. 4, 110.

जतु *jatu*, m. Lac, the red animal dye, MBh. 1, 5725.—Comp. *Çilâ-*, n. 1. bitumen. 2. red chalk.

जत्रु *jatru*, m. and n. The collar-bone, MBh. 3, 713.

जन् *JAN*, ii. 3, Par.; i. 4, *jâya*, Âtm. (ved. also i. 1, Par.), I. Transitive, **1.** To bring forth, MBh. 1, 2770. **2.** To produce, Bhâg. 5, 7, 12. **II.** Intransitive, i. 4, Âtm. (in epic poetry also Par., MBh. 12, 7751). **1.** To be born, Man. 3, 39. **2.** To be produced, Man. 3, 76. **3.** To be caused, MBh. 3, 16748. **4.** To grow, Man. 9, 38. **5.** To be born again (by transmigration of the soul), Hit. Pr. 13. **6.** To fall to one's share, Pańch. ii. d. 3. **7.** To become, MBh. 3, 4083. **8.** To be, Çrut. 19, 25. **9.** To take place, Lass. 11, 5. —Ptcple. of the pf. act. *jajńivaṁs* and *jâtavant*, Born, Bhâg. P. 4, 23, 2; Chr. 24, 40; of the pass. *jâta*, **1.** Born, Râm. 1, 1, 26. **2.** Old, MBh. 8, 3389. **3.** Grown, Man. 9, 40. **4.** Sprung up, Râm. 1, 9, 27. **5.** Happened, Hit. 9, 7. **6.** Become, Çâk. d. 60. **7.** As former part of a comp. adj. very often, Having, e.g. *jâta-danta*, adj. Having teeth, Man. 5, 70. The same signification it has also sometimes as latter part, e.g. *danta-jâta*, adj. Having teeth, Man. 5, 58. **8.** m. A son, Pańch. i. d. 32. **9.** n. **a.** Class, MBh. 15, 215; **b.** Kind, MBh. 13, 7241; **c.** A multitude of objects of the same genus, MBh. 4, 143; 12, 1500.—Comp. *A-jâta*, see separately. *Eka-*, adj. 1. having the same father, Man. 9, 148. 2. having the same parents, Man. 9, 182. *Kula-*, adj. descending from a noble family, Râm. 1, 71, 2. *Chira-*, adj. old, MBh. 3, 13334. *Dus-*, 1. miserable, MBh. 12, 8120. 2. wicked, Râjat. 1, 356. *Yathâ-*, adj. foolish, a fool. *Su-*, adj. of high birth, Chr. 293, 3=Rigv. i. 88, 3. *Janya*, see separately.—Caus. *janaya* (also Âtm., MBh. 1, 3104; Hit. i. d. 133), **1.** To beget, Man. 3, 17. **2.** To bring forth, Man. 9, 172. **3.** To produce, Man. 12, 119. **4.** To cause, Pańch. v. d. 47.—With the prep. **अति** *ati*, *atijâta*, Superior by birth (to the parents), Pańch. i. d. 442.—With **अधि** *adhi*, To be born, Ragh. 18, 23.—With **अनु** *anu*, **1.** To be born afterwards, Man. 9, 134. **2.** To be born similar to (with the acc.), Ragh. 6, 78. *anujâta*, **1.** Similar by birth (to his parents), Pańch. i. d. 442. **2.** After teething (?) Man. 5, 58.—With **समनु** *sam-anu*, To be born similar to (with the acc.), Râm. 2, 35, 26.—With **अप** *apa*, *apajâta*, Inferior (to his parents), Pańch. i. d. 442.—With **अभि** *abhi*, **1.** To be born (predestinated) to, Bhag. 16, 3; with *mahîm*, To be born to rule the earth, MBh. 5, 4342. **2.** To be born, Man. 2, 147. **3.** To be produced, Bhag. 2, 62. **4.** To be born again (by transmigration of the soul), Bhag. 6, 41. **5.** To spring up again, MBh. 1, 3514. **6.** To become, Râm. 4, 44, 77. *abhijâta*, **1.** Inherited, MBh. 5, 1357. **2.** Of noble family, Râm, 5, 11, 21. **3.** Well-bred, Bhartṛ. 2, 48.—With **समभि** *sam-abhi*, To spring up, Râm. 1, 39, 24. —With **अव** *ava*, Caus. To bring forth, Hit. Pr. n. d. 12, 13.—With **आ** *â*, **1.** To be born again, Man. 2, 249. **2.** To be produced, Bhâg. P. 2, 10, 17.

—With उप *upa*, **1.** To be added, MBh. 4, 1608. **2.** To be born, Man. 1, 45. **3.** To spring up, Man. 12, 73. **4.** To appear, Daçak. in Chr. 194, 15. **5.** To be born again, Bhag. 14, 2. **6.** To be, Hit. i. d. 115. *upajâta*, as former part of comp. adj., Having, Hit. 42, 6. Caus. To cause, Prab. 29, 15.—With समुप *sam-upa*, **1.** To spring up, Râm. 2, 75, 41. **2.** To be born again, MBh. 13, 6722; cf. *abhiniveça*. Caus. To produce, Ṛit. 2, 28.—With प्र *pra*, **1.** To bring forth, Chr. 50, 14. **2.** To be born, Man. 10, 9. **3.** To be produced, Hit. i. d. 24. **4.** To be born again, MBh. 13, 5509. **5.** To propagate, Man. 10, 64. *prajâtâ*, f. A woman who has borne a child, MBh. 1, 3046.—With अपप्र *apa-pra*, To abort, Suçr. 2, 398, 21. *apaprajâtâ*, f. A woman who has miscarried, Suçr. 2, 398, 21.—With संप्र *sam-pra*, **1.** To spring up, Pañch. i. d. 69. **2.** To appear, Râm. 6, 90, 32. **3.** To exist, Pañch. i. d. 452. **4.** To be born again, MBh. 13, 5459.—With प्रति *prati*, To spring up anew, MBh. 6, 2651.—With वि *vi*, **1.** To bring forth, Râm. 1, 70, 35. **2.** To be born, Râm. 1, 16, 20. **3.** To spring up, Râm. 1, 68, 8. **4.** To be changed to, to become, MBh. 5, 7368. *vijâta*, Base born, of mixed origin (rather *jâta* with *vi*); f. *tâ*, The mother of children, a matron. —With सम् *sam*, **1.** To bring forth, Râm. 3, 20, 27. **2.** To be born, Râm. 1, 70, 27. **3.** To grow, Nal. 24, 52. **4.** To be produced, MBh. 3, 17684. **5.** To rise, Man. 8, 172. **6.** To happen, Râjat. 5, 180. **7.** To become, Pañch. 32, 9. **8.** To pass, Pañch. 242, 14. *saṁjâta*, as former part of comp. adj. often, Having, Kathâs. 4, 26. Caus. **1.** To beget, MBh. 1, 3135. **2.** To bring forth, Râm. 3, 20, 13. **3.** To build, MBh. 1, 4995. **4.** To produce, Pañch. 188, 10. **5.** To cause, Râm. 2, 95, 5.—With अभिसम् *abhi-sam*, To be produced, Hariv. 13778.—With प्रतिसम् *prati-sam*, To be produced, Râm. 2, 22, 7.—Cf. γίγνομαι, γένεσις, γονή, γνήσιος, τηλύ-γετος, νη-γάτεος, νεο-γνός, γυνή, etc.; Lat. gigno, genus, germen (cf. *janman*); Goth. keinan, us-kijan, niu-klahs, kuni, qvino; A.S. cyn; O.H.G. kind, A. S. cild; see *janaka*.

जन *jan-a*, m. **1.** Creature, MBh. 3, 1204. **2.** Man collectively, men, Râm. 1, 6, 7; Man. 4, 108; with *âyudhiya*, Armed men, 7, 222; crowd, Râm. 6, 101, 33. **3.** Man, individually, a person, Draup. 3, 5; Man. 11, 241. **4.** This person, Nal. 10, 10. **5.** With the msc. of the pronoun *idam*, I, Çâk. 85, 16. **6.** The name of a division of the world, the residence of deified mortals, Bhâg. P. 3, 11, 31. **7.** It is often used as latter part of comp. words, especially in signification **2** and **3**; e.g. *preshya-*, m. The whole set of menial servants, Man. 7, 125; *çiçu-*, m. sing. pl. Children, Pañch. 95, 17; *dâsa-*, m. A slave, Vikr. d. 54.—Comp. *A-*, adj. deserted, Râm. 2, 92, 10. *Antaḥpura-*, i.e. *antar -pura-*, m. the women of a gyneceum, Râm. 1, 10, 33. *A-sajjana*, i.e. *-sant -jana*, m. a wicked person, Râm. 2, 39, 28. *Kula-*, m. a person of a noble family, Mṛichchh. 120, 4. *Guru-*, m. a venerable person, as one's parents or spiritual teacher, Bhartṛ. 2, 19. *Grâma -bâla-*, m. young peasants, Lass. 11, 7. *Chapalâ-*, m. an unsteady woman, and the goddess of fortune, Çiç. 9, 16. *Tiryagjana*, i.e. *tiryañch-*, m. an animal, Bhâg. P. 2, 7, 46. *Dâsa-*, m. the household servants, Daçak. in Chr. 182, 3. *Dus-*, m. a mischief-making person,

Man. 9, 13. *Pańchajana*, i.e. *pańchan-*, I. m. 1. the five higher classes of beings (gods, men, Gandharvas with the Apsaras, serpents, and manes). 2. mankind. 3. the name of a demon, and of others. II. f. *ní*, a proper name. *Puṇya-*, m. pl. a kind of good demon. *Pṛithagjana*, i.e. *pṛithak-*, m. 1. low people, Man. 7, 137. 2. an ignorant man. 3. a sinner, a wicked man. 4. pl. children of one father by different mothers. *Paura-*, m. a citizen. *Mahâ-*, m. 1. a preeminent man, a virtuous man. 2. a merchant. *Vi-*, adj. lonely, private; loc. °*ne*, privately, Pańch. 58, 8. *Viçva-*, m. all men, mankind. *Su-*, m. 1. a virtuous man. 2. a benevolent one. 3. the charioteer of Indra. *Sva-*, m. 1. a kinsman. 2. family, Bhartṛ. 2, 19; Daçak. in Chr. 186, 24.

जनक *jan + aka*, I. adj. Causing, MBh. 4, 1456. II. m. **1.** A father, Pańch. v. d. 19. **2.** A producer, Bhâshâp. 44. **3.** A proper name, Râm. 1, 1, 26.—Comp. *Yamunâ-*, m. the sun. —Cf. O.H.G. kuning; A.S. eyning, king; ϝάναξ.

जनकता *janaka + tâ*, f. **1.** Causing, Sâh. D. 2, 5. **2.** Paternity, Kathâs. 17, 57.

जनता *jana + tâ*, f. **1.** Mankind, Bhâg. P. 5, 10, 8. **2.** Household servants, Bhâg. P. 1, 6, 24. **3.** Subjects, Kathâs. 18, 23.—Comp. *Su-*, f. 1. goodness. 2. benevolence. **3.** a number of respectable persons.

जनन *jan + ana*, I. adj., f. *ní*, **1.** Bringing forth, Man. 9, 81. **2.** Causing, MBh. 1, 1183. II. f. *ní*, A mother, Daçak. in Chr. 179, 20. III. n. **1.** Child-birth, Man. 5, 61. **2.** Producing, production, Râm. 1, 23, 17. **3.** Existence, Çâk. d. 99.—Comp. see *Ku-*. *Strî -jananî*, a woman who brings forth only daughters, Man. 9, 81.

जनयितृ *janayitṛi*, i.e. *jan*, Caus., + *tṛi*, I. m. **1.** A progenitor, Râm. 2, 111, 11. **2.** A father, Man. 9, 142. II. f. *trî*, A mother, Râjat. 3, 108.

जनयिष्णु *janayishṇu*, i.e. *jan*, Caus., + *ishṇu*, m. A progenitor, MBh. 9, 2222.

जनस् *jan + as*, n. indecl. One of the seven worlds beyond the *maharloka*, Vedântas. in Chr. 209, 1.

जनि *jan + i*, f. **1.** A woman, Chr. 291, 1 = Rigv. i. 85, 1. **2.** Birth-place, Hariv. 11979.

जनितृ *janitṛi*, i.e. *jan + tṛi*, I. m. A father, Pańch. i. d. 9. II. f. *trî*, A mother, MBh. 3, 10498.—Cf. Lat. genitor, genitrix; γενετήρ, γενέτωρ, γενέτειρα.

जनित्र *janitra*, i.e. *janitṛi + a*, n. Birth-place, MBh. 5, 2580.—Cf. γενέθλη.

जनिष्य *janishya* (mutilated *janishyant*, ptcple. of the fut. Par.), adj. Future, Râm. 3, 66, 14.

जन्तु *jan + tu*, m. **1.** A creature, Man. 3, 77. **2.** A man, Man. 4, 240. **3.** A proper name, Bhâg. P. 9, 22, 1.—Comp. *Karkaṭî-*, m. the offspring of a crab, Châṇ. 56 in Berl. Monatsb. *Jala-*, m. an aquatic animal, Hit. i. d. 187.

जन्तुमन्त् *jantu + mant*, adj. Full of reptiles, Mârk. P. 32, 19.

जन्मन् *jan + man*, n. **1.** Birth, Man. 1, 42. **2.** Production, Râm. 3, 20, 31. **3.** Sowing, planting, Kumâras. 5, 60. **4.** Appearance, Yâjń. 3, 23. **5.** Existence, Man. 5, 38. **6.** A father, Çâk. d. 177. **7.** Creature, Chr. 289, 7 = Rigv. i. 50, 7. **8.** Manner, Chr. 293, 5 = Rigv. i. 87, 5.—Comp. *Agra-*, m. a Brâhmaṇa, Man. 2, 20. *Antya-*, adj. of the lowest tribe, Man. 10, 110. *Ambhoja-*,

m. a name of Brahman, Lass. 66, 3. *Âtmajanman*, i.e. *âtman-*, I. n. the birth of a son, Kumâras. 6, 28. II. m. a son, Ragh. 1, 33. *Ûru*, m. = *Aurva*, Mâlav. 71, d. 92. See *Ku-*. *Kumbha-*, m. a name of Agastya, Ragh. 12, 31. *Chitta-*, m. the god of love, Daçak. 106, 13. *Dvi-*, m. a man of either of the three first classes, especially a Brâhmaṇa (cf. *dvija*), Man. 2, 26; Râjat. 4, 105. *Punar-*, n. Palingenesia (by transmigration of the soul), Bhag. 8, 15. *Pûrva-*, I. n. a former existence. II. m. an elder brother. *Brahmajanman*, i.e. *brahman-*, n. 1. second or spiritual birth, Man. 2, 146. 2. investiture. *Vi-*, I. adj. born by a paramour (ÇKD). II. m. the son of an outcaste Vaiçya, Man. 10, 23. *Çara-*, m. Kârtikeya, the god of war. *Saṁkalpa-*, m. Kâma. *Saroj°*, i.e. *saras-*, n. a lotus.—Cf. Lat. germen; O.H.G. chîmo.

जन्मान्तर *janmântara*, i.e. *janman -antara*, n. **1.** A preceding existence, MBh. 3, 2564. **2.** A future existence, Pańch. ii. d. 185.

जन्मान्तरीय *janmântarîya*, i.e. *janmântara + îya*, adj. Performed in a preceding existence, Râjat. 6, 85.

जन्मिन् *janmin*, i.e. *janman + in*, m. A creature, Pańch. i. d. 119.

जन्य *janya*, **A.** ptcple. of the fut. pass. of *jan*, **1.** To be born, Bhâshâp. 44. **2.** Produced, Bhâshâp. 110. **3.** n. The body, Bhâg. P. 1, 9, 31. **B.** i.e. *jana + ya*, I. m. The friend of a bridegroom, MBh. 1, 7203. II. f. *yâ*, A bridesmaid, Ragh. 6, 30. III. n. War, combat, MBh. 5, 3195.

जप् *JAP* (a form of *jalp*), i. 1, Par. (also Âtm., MBh. 13, 750). **1.** To speak low, to murmur (prayers), Man. 2, 78. **2.** To pray to in a low voice, MBh. 13, 750. **3.** To invoke murmuring, Bhâg. P. 4, 7, 29.—Ptcple. of the future pass. *japya* and *jâpya*, n. A low prayer, Man. 2, 87; Bhâg. P. 8, 3, 1.—With the prep. अनु *anu*, To pray low afterwards, Bhâg. P. 5, 18, 29. — With अभि *abhi*, To charm, Râm. 2, 25, 36.—With उप *upa*, **1.** To whisper to, Râm. 1, 9, 38. **2.** To bring over to one's party, Man. 7, 197.—With प्र *pra*, To recite in a low tone, MBh. 3, 13432.—With सम् *sam*, To report, MBh. 4, 111.

जप *jap + a*, m. **1.** Muttering prayers, Man. 3, 74. **2.** A prayer, Râm. 1, 25, 3.

जपन *jap + ana*, n. Muttering prayers, MBh. 12, 7157.

जपा *japâ*, f. The China rose, Kir. 5, 8; Çiç. 9, 8.

जपिन् *jap + in*, adj. Muttering prayers, Yâjń. 3, 286.

जबा *jabâ*, Megh. 37 = *javâ*, q. cf.

जभ् *JABH*, and जम्भ् *JAMBH*, i. 1, Âtm. **1.** To gape, to yawn. **2.** To destroy, Bhâg. P. 3, 20, 26.—Caus. and i. 10, *jambhaya*, Par. To destroy; cf. *yabh*.—Cf. A.S. geapan, to gape; and see *gabhîra*.

जम् *JAM*, i. 1, Par. To eat. Frequent. To chew, anomal. *jâjam*, MBh. 13, 4495.

जमदग्नि *jamadagni*, m. The name of a Ṛishi, MBh. 1, 2611.

जम्बाल *jambâla*, m. Mud, Râjat. 5, 94.—Comp. *Sa-*, adj. Muddy.

जम्बु *jambu*, and जम्बू *jambû*, f. **1.**

A fruit tree, the rose apple, Eugenia jambu, MBh. 1, 7587; Pańch. 205, 5. **2.** The name of a division of the world, comprising India (cf. *dvîpa*),-Bhâg. P. 5, 1, 32. **3.** The name of a fabulous river, Bhâg. P. 5, 20, 2.—**Comp.** *Bhû-jambû*, f. 1. wheat. 2. the fruit of the Flacourtia sapida.

जम्बुक *jambuka*, m. A jackal, Pańch. 35, 2. f. *kâ*, A female jackal, Pańch. iv. d. 64.

जम्बूल *jambûla*, m. A fragrant plant, Pandanus odoratissimus, Hariv. 5371.

जम्भ् *JAMBH*, see *jabh* and *yabh*.

जम्भ *jambha*, i.e. *jabh* + *a*, **I.** m., f. *bhâ*, and n. **1.** The jaws, the teeth, a tooth (ved.). **2.** Cracking, explaining, MBh. 5, 2474. **II.** m. A proper name. —Cf. γαμφηλαί, γόμφιος; A.S. geaflas.

जम्भक *jambh* + *aka*, **I.** adj. **1.** Bruising, Râm. 1, 30, 9. **2.** Cracking, explaining, MBh. 5, 2470. **II.** m. **1.** The name of certain demons, Râm. 1, 31, 4 Gorr. **2.** The name of a spell, Râm. 1, 31, 9.

जम्भन *jambh* + *ana*, adj., f. *nî*, Bruising, MBh. 6, 807.

जय *jaya*, i.e. *ji* + *a*, **I.** latter part of comp. adj. Conquering. **II.** m. **1.** Victory, Man. 7, 183. **2.** Conquest, Bhâg. P. 5, 19, 22. **3.** Resigning, resignation, Bhâg. P. 3, 28, 5. **4.** A name of the sun, MBh. 3, 154. **5.** A proper name, Bhâg. P. 8, 13, 22. **III.** f. *yâ*, A name of Durgâ, MBh. 4, 194.—**Comp.** *A-*, m. defeat, Bhag. 2, 38. *Kakubjaya*, i.e. *kakubh-*, m. the conquest of the world, Râjat. 5, 139. *Dus-*, I. adj., f. *yâ*, difficult to be conquered, Râm. 6, 75, 51. II. m. 1. the name of a race of demons, Çâk. 95, 4. 2. a proper name, Râm. 3, 29, 30. *Su-dus-*, adj. very difficult to be overcome. *Rakka-*, f. *yâ*, the name of an idol, Râjat. 5, 425.

जयन्त *jayanta*, i.e. *jayant*, ptcple. pres. of *ji*, + *a*, I. m. A proper name, Çâk. d. 161. **II.** f. *tî*. **1.** The name of a river, MBh. 3, 5089. **2.** The name of a country, Râjat. 8, 655.

जयवन्त् *jaya* + *vant*, adj. Victorious, MBh. 6, 154.

जयितृ *jayitṛi*, i.e. *ji* + *tṛi*, m., f. *trî*, and n. Victorious, MBh. 12, 3753.

जयिन् *jayin*, i.e. *ji* + *in*, adj. and sbst. **1.** Conquering, a conqueror, Bhâg. P. 3, 31, 38. **2.** Victorious, MBh. 9, 1676. **3.** The winning party in a law-suit, Yâjń. 2, 79.

जयिष्णु *jayishṇu* i.e. *ji* + *ishṇu*, adj. Victorious, MBh. 7, 1480.

जरठ *jaraṭha* (vb. *jṛî*), adj. Old, Bhâg. P. 6, 1, 25.

जरण *jaraṇa*, i.e. *jṛî* + *ana*, adj. **1.** Old (ved.). **2.** Digestive, Suçr. 1, 155, 16.

जरतिका *jaratikâ*, i.e. *jaratî* (fem. of the ptcple. pres. of *jṛî*) + *ka*, f. A contemptible old woman, Daçak. in Chr. 194, 20.

जरद्गव *jaradgava*, i.e. *jarant-gava* (vb. *jṛî*), m. **1.** An old ox, Pańch. ii. d. 169. **2.** A proper name, Hit. i. d. 49.

जरस् *jaras*, i.e. *jṛî* + *as*, and **जरा** *jarâ*, i.e. *jṛî* + *â*; *jaras* is optionally the base of the cases of which the terminations begin with a vowel, f. **1.** Old age, Man. 6, 62; Daçak. in Chr. 189, 13; Bhâg. P. 3, 2, 3. **2.** Digestion, Râm. 3, 53, 59. **3.** A proper name, MBh. 2, 715.—**Comp.** *A-jara*, adj. ever young, Chr. 290, 3 = Rigv. i.

64, 3. *A-jaras*, adj. not to be worn out by use, MBh. 13, 5862.

ऽजरस *-jaras+a*, a substitute for *jaras*, when the latter part of a comp. adv., also of the adj. *vitajanmajarasa*, i.e. *vi-ita-janman-jarasa*, Not subject to birth or old age, Kir. 5, 22.

जरायु *jarâyu*, i.e. *jarâ+yu*, n. m. f. The after-birth, Bhâg. P. 3, 31, 4.

जरायुज *jarâyu-ja*, adj., f. *jâ*, Born from the womb, as man and other animals, Man. 1, 43.

जरावन्त् *jarâ-vant*, adj., f. *vati*, Old, Hariv. 1621.

† जर्च् *JARCH*, also जर्छ् *JARCHH*, v.r., i. 1 and 6, Par. **1.** To speak. **2.** To abuse.

जर्ज् *JARJ*, † i. 1 and 6, Par. **1.** To speak. **2.** To abuse, v.r.—Ptcple. of the pf. pass. *jarjita*, Mangled, Pańch. 160, 4; cf. *jarjarita*, which is perhaps to be read.

जर्जर *jarjara*, i.e. reduplicated *jṛî+a*, adj. **1.** Decayed, Lass. 7, 9. **2.** Ragged, Mṛichchh. 49, 11. **3.** Broken, Pańch. 117, 6. **4.** Crushed, MBh. 3, 16049. **5.** Torn asunder, disunited, Râjat. 2, 152.

जर्जरत्व *jarjara+tva*, n. Decay, Mṛichchh. 65, 17.

जर्जरित *jarjarita*, i.e. *jarjara+ita*, adj. **1.** Mangled, Hariv. 4676. **2.** Weakened, MBh. 3, 10353.

† जर्झ् *JARJH*, v.r. of *jarch*.

† जर्त्स् *JARTS*, i. 1, Par. **1.** To speak. **2.** To abuse. **3.** To protect.

1. † जल् *JAL*, i. 1, Par. **1.** To be wealthy, or to cover; or to be blunt, or sharp. i. 10, *jâlaya*, To cover.

2. जल् *JAL* (a denomin. derived from the next), Par. To turn into water, Çatr. 14, 81.

जल *jala* (cf. *jaḍa*), I. n. **1.** Water, Man. 4, 46. **2.** A fragrant plant, Suçr. 2, 275, 19. II. f. *lâ*, The name of a river, MBh. 3, 10556.—**Comp.** *Ati-*, adj., f. *lâ*, abounding in water, Râm. 4, 44, 64. *Gandha-*, f. *lâ*, fragrant water, Bhâg. P. 1, 11, 15. *Netra-*, n. tears, Râm. 5, 25, 55. *Rajanî-*, n. frost, hoarfrost, dew. *Sa-*, adj. humid, Megh. 23.

जलचर *jala-chara*, n. An aquatic animal, Pańch. 50, 7.

जलज *jala-ja*, I. adj., f. *jâ*. **1.** Water-born, Hariv. 3621. **2.** Existing in water, MBh. 2, 94. II. m. **1.** An aquatic animal, Râm. 5, 5, 30. **2.** A fish, Râm. 2, 61, 22. **3.** A shell, Hariv. 10936. III. n. A lotus, MBh. 2, 1813.

जलजकुसुमयोनि *jalaja-kusuma-yoni*, m. A name of Brahman, MBh. 8, 4647.

जलद *jala-da*, m. **1.** A cloud, Kir. 5, 48. **2.** The name of a *varsha*, or division of the known continent, MBh. 6, 425.

जलधर *jala-dhara*, m. A cloud, Bhâshâp. 1.

जलधि *jaladhi*, i.e. *jala-dhâ* (cf. *nidhi*), m. The ocean, Çiç. 9, 31.

जलमय *jala + maya*, adj., f. *yî*, Consisting of water, Kathâs. 2, 10.

जलमुच् *jala-much*, m. A cloud, Megh. 70.

जलवन्त् *jala+vant*, adj., f. *vatî*, Abounding in water, MBh. 12, 3694.

जलस्थाय *jalasthâya*, *jala-sthâ+a*, m. A pond, MBh. 12, 4893.

जलाय *JALÂYA* (a denomin. derived from *jala*), Âtm. To turn into water, Bhartṛ. 2, 78.

जलाशय *jalâçaya*, I. i.e. *jala-â-çî+a*, adj. Reposing in water, MBh. 3, 11123. II. for *jaḍa-âçaya* (which is perhaps to be read), adj. Stupid, Kathâs. 6, 58. III. i.e. *jala-âçaya*, m. 1. A reservoir of water, Hariv. 3820. 2. A pond, Man. 4, 129. 3. A sea, Vedântas. in Chr. 204, 15.

जलाश्रय *jalâçraya*, i.e. *jala-âçraya*, m. A pond, Pańch. 76, 6.

जलूका *jalûkâ*, i.e. anomal. for *jala-oka*, f. A leech.—Comp. *Tṛiṇa-*, f. a caterpillar, Bhâg. P. 4, 29, 76.

जलेचर *jalechara*, i. e. *jala* + *i-chara*, I. adj., f. *rî*, Living in water, Râm. 4, 50, 18. II. m. An aquatic animal, Râm. 4, 51, 39. III. f. *rî*, The female of an aquatic animal, MBh. 1, 7852.

जलेशय *jaleçaya*, i.e. *jala+i-çî+a*, I. adj. Living in water, MBh. 1, 1365. II. m. Epithet of Vishṇu, Hariv. 14348.

जलौक *jalauka*, i.e. *jala-oka*, m. and f. *kâ*, A leech, Suçr. 1, 112, 6; 1, 39, 14.

जलौकस् *jalaukas*, i. e. *jala-okas*, 1. adj. and sbst. Living in water, an aquatic animal, MBh. 13, 2650. 2. f. A leech, Suçr. 1, 28, 10.

जल्प् *JALP*, (akin to, or rather old Causal of, 1. *gṛî*), i. 1, Par. (in epic poetry also Âtm., Hariv. 1173), 1. To speak, Pańch. 35, 10. 2. To speak with or of (with the acc.), Lass. 41, 18; MBh. 4, 864. *jalpita*, n. Talk, Pańch. 133, 5.—With the prep. अनु *anu*, To speak afterwards, Bhâg. P. 4, 25, 58.—With अभि *abhi*, 1. To address, Râm. 4, 2, 16. 2. To accompany by words, MBh. 12, 3189. 3. To advise, MBh. 7, 3033. 4. To determine, MBh. 4, 711.—With उप *upa*, *upajalpita*, n. Talk, Râm. 2, 60, 14.—With परि *pari*, 1. To prate, MBh. 5, 1125. 2. To speak of (with the acc.), Hariv. 11301. —With प्र *pra*, 1. To speak, Pańch. i. d. 300. 2. To chatter, Pańch. i. d. 437. 3. To proclaim, MBh. 13, 3686. *Prajalpita*, Having begun to speak, Kumâras. 1, 46; n. Words, Hiḍ. 1, 22. —With प्रति *prati*, To answer, Râm. 3, 75, 2.—With वि *vi*, To utter, Çâk. d. 51.—With सम् *sam*, 1. To converse, Râm. 1, 74, 20. 2. To speak, Râm. 5, 89, 21. *sańjalpita*, n. Words, Bhâg. P. 1, 15, 18.

जल्प *jalp+a*, m. and n. 1. Words, Bhâg. P. 1, 7, 17. 2. Prate, MBh. 1, 566.

जल्पक *jalp+aka*, adj. sbst. Chattering, a chatterer, Bhartṛ. 2, 48.

जल्पन *jalp+ana*, n. Speaking, Pańch. i. d. 193.

जल्पितृ *jalp* + *itṛi*, m., f. *trî*, n. Speaking, Râm. 5, 36, 63.

जल्पिन् *jalp+in*, adj., f. *nî*, Speaking, MBh. 5, 2038.

जव *java*, i.e. *jû+a*, I. m. Quickness, Chr. 297, 21=Rigv. i. 112, 21; MBh. 3, 10891. II. f. *javâ*=*japâ*, The China rose, Râm. 5, 3, 48.—Comp. *Ati-*, m. excessive quickness, Pańch. ii. d. 86. *Manojava*, i. e. *manas-*, I. adj. 1. swift as thought. 2. quick in thought, 3. fatherly, parental. II. m. Vishṇu. *Mahâ-*, adj. very fleet.

जवन *javana*, i.e. *jû+ana*, I. adj., f. *nî*, Quick, Kir. 5, 7. II. n. Quickness, MBh. 4, 1414.

जवस् *javas*, i.e. *jû + as*, n. Speed, velocity.—Comp. *Su-*, adj. quick.

जवनिका *javanikâ* (=*yavanikâ*), f. A curtain, Hariv. 4648.

जविन् *javin*, i.e. *jû + in*, adj. Swift, Yâjń. 2, 109.

† **जष्** *JASH*, i. 1, Par. To kill; to wound, v.r.

जस् *JAS*, i. 1, Âtm. (ved); i. 4, Par. 1. To be exhausted, Chr. 296, 6 = Rigv. i. 112, 6, 2. i. 4, Par. † To liberate. 3. i. 1 (?) and 10, or Caus., *jâsaya*, To kill, to strike, † to slight.—With the prep. उद् *ud*, Caus. or i. 10, To root out (with gen.), Ciç. 1, 37.—Cf. Goth. qvistjan.

जह्नु *jahnu*, m. The name of a king who adopted the river Gangâ as his daughter, Râm. 1, 44, 35.

जागर *jâgara*, i.e. *jâgṛi + a*, m. 1. Waking, Daçak. in Chr. 192, 3. 2. A vision, Yâjń. 3, 172.

जागरण *jâgaraṇa*, i.e. *jâgṛi + ana*, n. Waking, Pańch. 27, 9.

जागरिष्णु *jâgarishṇu*, i.e. *jâgṛi + ishṇu*, adj. Wakeful, Suçr. 1, 121, 16.

जागरूक *jâgarûka*, i.e. *jâgṛi + ûka*, adj. Watchful, Ragh. 14, 85.

जागृ *JÂGṚI*, ii. 2, Par. (in epic poetry also i. 1, *jâgara*, MBh. 12, 7823; anomalous *jâgṛimi*, 12, 6518), 1. To wake, Râm. 2, 63, 4. 2. To watch over (with the loc.), Ragh. 8, 23; with the acc., Chaurap. 35. 3. To be roused, Hit. 50, 14. Ptcple. of the pres. *jâgrat*, n. Waking, Vedântas. in Chr. 208, 13. Anomalous ptcple. of the pres. Âtm., *jâgramâṇa*, MBh. 13, 1274. Ptcple. of the pf. pass., *jâgarita*, One who has waked, Suçr. 1, 357, 18. n. Waking, Suçr. 1, 330, 8; Vedântas. in Chr. 209, 22. *jâgaritavant*, One who has waked, Suçr. 1, 330, 8. Ptcple. of the fut. pass., *jâgartavya*, n. Necessity of waking, MBh. 1, 5925; anomalous *jâgṛitavya*, MBh. 13, 2746.—Caus. *jâgaraya*, To rouse, Hit. 50, 4; ved. Aor. sing. 3, *ajîgar*, Chr. 294, 6 = Rigv. i. 92, 6.—With the prep. अनु *anu*, To wake near to somebody, Râm. 2, 50, 36. —With प्र *pra*, To lie in wait (with the gen.), MBh. 9, 1463.—Cf. ἐγείρω, ἔγρομαι; perhaps also Lat. vigil, vigilare; and Goth. vakan; A.S. wácian; O.H.G. wachar, A.S. waccor.

जाघनी *jâghanî*, i.e. *jaghana + a + î*, f. The tail, MBh. 12, 5375; Man. 10, 108.

जाङ्गल *jâṅgala*, i.e. *jaṅgala + a*, I. adj. 1. Dry, even and productive (country), Man. 7, 69. 2. Existing in such a country, Suçr. 1, 184, 12. 3. Belonging to game which lives in such a country, Suçr. 1, 72, 2. II. n. Game, Suçr. 2, 342, 21. III. m. pl. The name of a people, MBh. 5, 2127.—Comp. *Kuru-*, 1. n. the name of a country, Râm. 2, 68, 13. 2. m. pl. the name of its inhabitants, MBh. 3, 356.

जाटासुरि *jâṭâsuri*, i.e. *jaṭâsura* (the name of a demon), *+ i*, patronym., MBh. 7, 7856.

जाठर *jâṭhara*, i.e. *jaṭhara + a*, I. adj., f. *rî*, 1. Of the belly, Mârk. P. 2, 37. 2. With *agni*, a. The digestive power, Suçr. 1, 128, 18. b. Hunger, Pańch. ii. d. 193. II. m. A child, Bhâg. P. 3, 14, 38.

जाड्य *jâḍya*, i.e. *jaḍa + ya*, n. 1. Want of sensation, Vedântas. in Chr. 206, 17. 2. Stupidity, Bhartṛ. 2, 20.

जातक *jâta + ka*, (vb. *jan*) I. m. A

son, Man. 9, 143 (in *jâra-*, Begotten by an adulterer). **II.** n. **1.** A ceremony on the birth of a child, MBb. 1, 949. **2.** Astrological calculation of a nativity, Bhâg. P. 1, 12, 13.

जातरूपमय *jâta-rûpa + maya*, adj., f. *yî*, Golden, Râm. 3, 48, 13.

जातवेदस् *jâta-vedas*, and **जातवेद** *jâtaveda* (Bhâg. P. 5, 7, 13), m. **1.** The producer of wealth (?), Chr. 289, 1 = Rigv. i. 50, 1. **2.** Fire, Bhâg. P. 5, 10, 5.

जातवेदसी *jâtavedasî*, i.e. *jâtavedas + a + î*, f. A name of Durgâ, MBh. 6, 802.

जाति *jâti*, i.e. *jan + ti*, f. **1.** Birth, Man. 2, 148. **2.** Existence, life, Man. 4, 148. **3.** State, Man. 3, 15. **4.** Tribe, Man. 1, 118. **5.** Kind, genus, MBh. 4, 45; Pañch. 203, 3. **6.** Species, Man. 1, 48. **7.** Also **जाती** *jâtî*, Great flowered jasmine, Hariv. 7891. **जाती** *jâtî*, also The nutmeg-tree, Suçr. 1, 132, 20; nutmeg.—**Comp.** *A-jâti*, f. another sort, Yâjñ. 2, 246. *Eka-*, 1. adj. having only one birth, Man. 10, 4. 2. belonging to the same kind, Suçr. 2, 289, 12. II. m. a Çûdra, Man. 8, 270. *Dus-*, 1. f. misfortune, Mâlav. d. 86. 2. adj. wicked, MBh. 5, 1944. *Dvi-*, m. a man of either of the three first classes, especially a Brâhmaṇa (cf. *dvija*), Man. 10, 4; Bhâg. P. 6, 11, 15. *Pûrva-*, f. a former existence, Kathâs. 27, 82. *Mṛiga-*, f. pl. the deer species, Draup. 4, 16. *Sa-*, adj. being of the same class, Man. 9, 87. *Hîna-* (vb. *hâ*), adj. being of the lowest class, Man. 3, 15; degraded, outcaste.—Cf. Lat. gens; A.S. cynd; Engl. kind.

जातिमन्त् *jâti + mant*, adj., f. *matî*, High-born, Râm. 2, 75, 21 Gorr.

जातिस्मरता *jâti-smara + tâ*, f., and **जातिस्मरत्व** *jâti-smara + tva*, n. Remembrance of a former existence, MBh. 3, 160; 8107.

जाती *jâtî*, see *jâti* **7.**

ऽजातीय *-jâtîya*, i.e. *jâti + îya*, adj. Belonging to a caste, Man. 11, 162; or kind, Pañch. 190. 21; or genus, Pañch. 76, 8.—**Comp.** *Dus-*, wicked, Hariv. 4239. *Vi-*, adj. 1. of mixed origin. 2. of a different cast. 3. of a different kind, dissimilar. *Sa-*, adj. 1. of the same tribe. 2. of the same species. 3. like. *Samâna-*, adj. of the same caste or species. *Sva-*, adj. of one's own tribe, caste, species, &c.

जातु *jâtu*, i.e. *jan + tu*, adv. **1.** Ever, MBh. 5, 7071. **2.** Perhaps, MBh. 12, 6739. **3.** Once, Kathâs. 6, 89. **4.** With preceding *na*, Never, Man. 2, 94. **5.** With preceding *na*, and following *chid*, Nevermore, never, MBh. 1, 1936.

जातुष *jâtusha*, i.e. *jatus* (= *jatu*) + *a*, adj., f. *shî*, Made of lac, Pañch. i. d. 120; painted with lac, MBh. 1, 151.

जात्य *jâtya*, i.e. *jâti + ya*, adj. **1.** Belonging to a tribe, Râm. 2, 50, 18. **2.** Belonging to a family, Man. 10, 5. **3.** Of a noble race, Râm. 2, 45, 14. **4.** True, Râm. 2, 9, 40. *sva-*, adj. Belonging to one's own species, Pañch. 71, 11.

जानकी *jânakî*, i.e. *janaka + a + î*, patron. The daughter of Janaka, i.e. Sîtâ, Râm. 3, 51, 6.

जानपद *jânapada*, i.e. *jana-pada + a*, I. m. An inhabitant of a country, a subject, Yâjñ. 2, 36. **II.** adj. **1.** Living in the country, Râm. 2, 50, 4. **2.** Referring to districts, Man. 8, 41.—**Comp.** *Paura-*, m. The inhabitants of the town and of the country, MBh. 1, 2828.

जानपदिक *jânapadika*, i.e. *jana-*

pada + *ika*, adj. Concerning a realm, MBh. 11, 71.

जानार्दन *jânârdana*, i.e. *janârdana* + *a*, patronym. A descendant of Janârdana, MBh. 3, 723.

ऽजानि *-jâni*, i.e. *jan* + *i*, latter part of comp. adj. Wife, e.g. *an-anya-*, Having no other wife, Ragh. 15, 61. *vitta-*, adj. Having married (vb. *vid*), Chr. 297, 15 = Rigv. i. 112, 15.—Cf. Goth. quens, A.S. cwen, Engl. queen.

जानु *jânu* (for original *janvant*), n. and m. The knee, Suçr. 1, 348, 16.—Comp. *Antar-*, adj. and adv. Having (the hands) between the knees, Yâjń. 1, 18. *Indra-*, m. A proper name, Râm. 4, 39, 33. *Jânu-vi-*, n. Joining and disjoining the legs, a mode of fighting. *Saṁhata-* (vb. *han*), adj. knock-kneed.—Cf. γόνυ γούνατος (for γόνϝατος); Lat. genu; Goth. kniu; A.S. cneow.

जाप *jâpa*, i.e. *jap* + *a*, m. A prayer, Râm. 1, 31, 31.—Comp. *Karṇa-*, m. Tale-bearing, Pańch. i. d. 337.

जापक *jâpaka*, i.e. *jap* + *aka*, adj. **1.** Muttering prayers, MBh. 12, 7153. **2.** Produced by prayer, MBh. 12, 7249.

जापिन् *jâpin*, i.e. *jap* + *in*, adj. Reciting in a low tone, Yâjń. 3, 304.

जामदग्नेय *jâmadagneya*, i.e. *jamadagni* + *eya*, patron. A descendant of Jamadagni, Râm. 1, 74, 17.

जामदग्न्य *jâmadagnya*, i.e. *jamadagni* + *ya*, I. adj. Referring to Jamadagni, MBh. 1, 332. II. patron. A descendant of Jamadagni, Râm. 1, 74, 23.

जामा *jâmâ* (from **jam* = γαμ in γαμέω, an older form of *yam*, by the aff. *a*; cf. the next), f. A daughter-in-law, MBh. 13, 2474.

जामातृ *jâmâtṛi* (from **jam*, cf. the last and *yâmâtṛi*, by the aff. *tṛi*), m. A son-in-law, Râm. 1, 8, 26.—Cf. γαμβρός for γαμρός; Lat. gener for gem + ros.

जामातृक *jâmâtṛi* + *ka*, adj. Belonging to a son-in-law, Pańch. 46, 19.

जामातृत्व *jâmâtṛi* + *tva*, n. Condition of being a son-in-law, Pańch. 48, 23.

जामि *jâmi* (from **jam*, cf. *jâmâ*, but in the signification which appears in Lat. gem-ini and Sskt. *yama*, Twin, a pair), I. adj. and sbst. Brother and sister; related (ved.). II. also **जामी** *jâmî*, f. **1.** A female relation, Man. 3, 57. **2.** A sister, Yâjń. 1, 157.

जामित्र *jâmitra*, The seventh house in Astrology, Kumâras. 7, 1.

जाम्बव *jâmbava*, i.e. I. *jambu* + *a*, **1.** adj. Coming from the Jambu-tree, Suçr. 1, 190, 5. **2.** n. The fruit of the Jambu-tree, 1, 73, 17. II. = *jâmbavant*, A proper name, Râm. 5, 1, 57.

जाम्बवन्त् *jâmbavant*, m. A proper name, Râm. 4, 25, 33. f. *vatî*, A proper name, MBh. 3, 670.

जाम्बुक *jâmbuka*, i.e. *jambuka* + *a*, adj. Proceeding from a jackal, MBh. 12, 5779.

जाम्बुनद and **जाम्बूनद** *jâmbûnada*, i.e. *jambû-nadî* + *a*, I. adj. Coming from the river Jambu, epithet of a peculiar kind of gold, MBh. 6, 279. II. n. Gold, Râm. 3, 49, 9. III. adj., f. *dî*, Golden, Râm. 5, 7, 19. IV. m. **1.** A proper name, MBh. 1, 3745. **2.** The name of a mountain, MBh. 3, 10835. V. f. *dî*, The name of a river, MBh. 6, 338. VI. n. **1.** A golden ornament, Çiç. 4, 66. **2.** The name of a sea, MBh. 5, 3843.

जाम्बुनदमय and **जाम्बूनदमय**

jâmbûnada + maya, adj., f. *yî*, Golden, Pańch. 175, 8.

जायन्तेय *jâyanteya*, i.e. *jayantî + eya*, metronym. A son of Jayantî, Bhâg. P. 5, 4, 12.

जाया *jâyâ*, i. e. *jan + yâ*, f. A spouse, Man. 9, 8.—Cf. Lat. gaja.

जायात्व *jâyâ + tva*, n. The condition of a *jâyâ*, the name *jâyâ*, Man. 9, 8.

ऽजायिन् *-jâyin*, i. e. *ji + in*, adj. Conquering, MBh. 3, 1383.

जार *jâra*, i.e. *jṛî + a*, m. 1. A lover, Chr. 295, 11=Rigv. i. 92, 11. 2. A paramour, an adulterer, Yâjń. 2, 301.

जारज *jâra-ja*, m. A son begotten by an adulteress, Pańch. Pr. 6.

जारता *jâra + tâ*, f. Adultery, Daçak. in Chr. 182, 10.

जारासंधि *jârâsaṁdhi*, i. e. *jarâsaṁdha*, a proper name, *+ i*, patronym. A descendant of Jarâsaṁdha, MBh. 2, 966.

जारूथी *jârûthî*, f. The name of a river, Râm. 6, 109, 50.

जारूथ्य *jârûthya*, m. A kind of sacrifice, Râm. 6, 113, 10.

जार्यक *jâryaka*, m. A certain animal, Râjat. 5, 321.

जाल *jâla*, n. 1. A net, Pańch. 78, 14. 2. A coat of mail, MBh. 6, 725. 3. A lattice, Râm. 3, 61, 13. 4. A window, Man. 8, 132. 5. A dense multitude, Râm. 1, 28, 23. 6. A web-membrane between the fingers, Çâk. d. 175. 7. A disease of the eye, Suçr. 2, 311, 6. 8. Magic, illusion, Kathâs. 24, 199.—Comp. *Indra-*, n. 1. magic, Kathâs. 22, 12. 2. illusion, Vedântas. in Chr. 218, 20. 3. the name of a weapon, MBh. 3, 14995. *Dhvânta-*, n. deep darkness, Daçak. in Chr. 187, 18. *Muktâ-*, n. a string of pearls, Megh. 64. *Vindu-*, n. coloured marks on an elephant's face or trunk.

जालक *jâla + ka*, I. n. 1. A net, Pańch. iii. d. 179. 2. (m ?) A window, Çiç. 9, 39. 3. A bud, Megh. 96. II. m. The name of a tree, Bhâg. P. 8, 2, 18. III. f. *likâ*. 1. A net. 2. A coat of mail, Râm. 3, 28, 26.

जालपाद *jâla-pâda*, m. A web-footed bird, Man. 5, 13.

जालपादभुज *jâla-pâda-bhuja*, adj. Having a web-membrane on the feet and the hands, MBh. 12, 13339.

जालवन्त् *jâla + vant*, adj., f. *vatî*. 1. Having a net, Suçr. 1, 87, 16. 2. Covered with a coat of mail, MBh. 6, 747.

जाल्म *jâlma*, m. and f. *mî*. 1. Wicked, Vikr. 5, 14. 2. Contemptible, MBh. 5, 4518.

जाल्मक *jâlma + ka*, adj. Wicked, MBh. 7, 9023.

जाल्य *jâlya*, i.e. *jâla + ya*, adj. Exposed to nets, MBh. 12, 10417.

जाह्नव *jâhnava*, i.e. *jahnu + a*, patron. A descendant of Jahnu, Bhâg. P. 9, 22, 9. f. *vî*, A name of the Gańgâ, Kir. 5, 15.

जाह्नवीय *jâhnavîya*, i.e. *jâhnavî + îya*, adj. Belonging to the Gańgâ, MBh. 13, 1857.

जि *JI* (akin to *jyâ*, q. cf.), i. 1, Par. (in epic poetry also Âtm., MBh. 3, 15193). red. pf. *jigâya*; ptcple. *jigivâṅs*, etc. 1. To overpower, to conquer, Pańch. i. d. 375; Man. 4, 181. 2. To be victorious, Çâk. 23, 11. 3. To win,

MBh. 3, 2229. 4. To win something from somebody (with two accs.), Daçak. in Chr. 186, 3. 5. To restrain, Man. 7, 22. 6. To excel, MBh. 2, 2577. Anomal. potent. *jayyât*, MBh. 4, 1604. Anomal. pf. *parâ-jayâm âsa*, Hariv. 13946. Anomal. Aor. *ajaishṭa*, MBh. 1, 6378. Anomal. fut. *jayishyasi*, Râm. 1, 29, 3. Anomal. potent. of the pass. *jîyeyam*, MBh. 7, 2702. Comp. ptcple. of the pf. pass. *a-jita*, 1. adj. Unsubdued. 2. m. Vishṇu. Comp. ptcple. of the fut. pass., 1. *a-jeya*, and 2. *a-jayya*, adj. Unconquerable, Chr. 44, 6; Râm. 2, 11, 7. Caus. *jâpaya*; anomal. Aor. *ajîjayat*, MBh. 7, 2280; see *vi*. Desid. *jigîsha*, Par. and Âtm. To desire to conquer, MBh. 2, 1140; Pañch. i. d. 409.—With the prep. अनु *anu*, To subdue, MBh. 12, 3124. Desid. To desire to subdue, MBh. 5, 1274.—With अभि *abhi*, *abhijita*, m. The leading star of the twenty-second Nakshatra, or lunar asterism. Desid. 1. To desire to gain, MBh. 12, 8465. 2. To assail, Suçr. 1, 122, 3.—With अव *ava*, 1. To extort, MBh. 1, 7765. *avajitya*, Forcibly, Man. 11, 80. 2. To conquer, MBh. 4, 1118. — With निस् *nis*, 1. To overcome in play, MBh. 3, 2589. 2. To conquer, MBh. 1, 7658. 3. To gain, *nirjita*, run up, Man. 8, 154.—With अभिनिस् *abhi-nis*, To overpower, MBh. 14, 2220.—With परिनिस् *pari-nis*, To conquer, MBh. 4, 2251.—With प्रतिनिस् *prati-nis*, To rescind, Râm. 2, 26, 22.—With विनिस् *vi-nis*, 1. To overpower, Man. 11, 205. 2. To conquer, MBh. 3, 1883. —With परा *parâ*, Âtm. (in epic poetry also Par., MBh. 2, 2141), 1. To succumb, to be defeated, MBh. 4, 1604 (anomal. potent. *jayyât*). 2. To lose, MBh. 2, 2141. 3. To overpower, Râm. 3, 36, 13; to defeat in a law suit, Yâjń. 2, 75; *parâjita*, Condemned (by law), Man. 8, 58; to defeat in play, MBh. 2, 2171. *A-parâ-jita*, m. A poisonous insect, Suçr. 2, 289, 14. f. *tâ*, The north-eastern quarter, Man. 6, 31.—With परि *pari*, To overpower, MBh. 5, 712. —With प्र *pra*, To overpower, MBh. 7, 70.—With प्रति *prati*, To defeat (in game), MBh. 7, 1357. Desid. To desire to conquer, MBh. 7, 4376.—With वि *vi*, Âtm. (also Par., e.g. Man. 2, 232), 1. To be victorious, Pañch. 184, 1. 2. To conquer, MBh. 2, 992. 3. To defeat (in play), Nal. 26, 22. 4. To overcome; in *vijitâsana*, i. e. *vijita-âsana*, adj. Indifferent concerning one's seat, Bhâg. P. 3, 28, 8. Caus. To conquer (anomal. Aor. *ajîjayat*), MBh. 7, 2280. Desid. To desire to conquer, Hariv. 8828. — Cf. Goth. ga-geigan (Frequent.).

जिगमिषु *jigamishu*, i.e. *jigamisha*, desid. of *gam*, + *u*, adj. Being about to go, Râm. 2, 21, 63.

जिगीषा *jigîshâ*, i.e. *jigîsha*, desid. of *ji*, + *a*, f. 1. Wish to overcome, Chr. 31, 20. 2. Wish to win, Kathâs. 21, 81. 3. Wish to attain, MBh. 3, 13360. 4. Emulation, Chr. 28, 19. — Comp. *Guru-jigîsha*, adj. wishing to surpass, emulating the venerable, Kathâs. 21, 81.

जिगीषु *jigîshu*, i.e. *jigîsha* (see the last), + *u*, adj. 1. Desiring to conquer, MBh. 1, 6845. 2. Desiring to excel, Râm. 1, 13, 21. 3. Ambitious, Kathâs. 4, 126.

जिगीषुता *jigîshu* + *tâ*, f. Emulation, Kathâs. 18, 85.

जिघांसा *jighâṁsâ*, i. e. *jighâṁsa*,

desider. of *han*, + *a*, f. **1.** Intention to kill, Man. 11, 206. **2.** Intention to destroy, Bhâg. P. 4, 19, 24.

जिघांसिन् *jighâṁsin*, i.e. *jighâṁsa* (see the last), + *in*, adj. Desiring to kill, Râm. 6, 77, 27.

जिघांसु *jighâṁsu*, i.e. *jighâṁsa* (see the last), + *u*, adj. **1.** Desiring to kill, Bhâg. P. 7, 1, 41. **2.** Desiring to detroy, Suçr. 1, 71, 4.

जिघृक्षा *jighṛikshâ*, i.e. *jighṛiksha*, desider. of *grah*, + *a*, f. Desire to seize, MBh. 7, 794.

जिजीविषा *jijîvishâ*, i.e. *jijîvisha*, desider. of *jîv*, + *a*, f. Desire to live, MBh. 8, 1790.

जिजीविषु *jijîvishu*, i.e. *jijîvisha* (see the last), + *u*, adj. Wishing to live, Man. 4, 27.

जिज्ञासन *jijńâsana*, i.e. *jijńâsa*, desider. of *jńâ*, + *ana*, n. Wish to know, examination, Kathâs. 5, 136.

जिज्ञासा *jijńâsâ*, i.e. *jijńâsa* (see the last), + *a*, f. **1.** Wish to know, Râm. 1, 50, 23. **2.** Wish to test, Râm. 4, 8, 6. **3.** Examination, MBh. 2, 1158.

ऽजित् *-ji* + *t*, latter part of comp. words, Victorious, conquering, e.g. *kaiṭabha-*, m. A name of Vishṇu (slayer of the demon Kaiṭabha), Çiç. 9, 30. *yuddha-*, adj. Victorious in battle, Draup. 9, 11. *svar-*, The name of a kind of sacrifice, Man. 11, 74.

जिन *ji* + *na*, n. A name of Buddha, Pańch. 236, 8.

जिन्व् *JINV* (originally *ji* + *nu*, ii. 5; cf. γάνυμαι for γα + νυμαι; akin to *div*, *jîv*, and *jû*), i. 1, Par. **1.** To be brisk (ved.). **2.** To further (ved.). **3.** To help, Chr. 296, 1; 6; 9=Rigv. i. 112, 1; 6; 9. **4.** To love, Chr. 290, 8 =Rigv. i. 64, 8. † i. 10, To speak (? v.r.)

† **जिम्** *JIM*, i. 1, Par. To eat, v.r.

† **जिरि** *JIRI*, ii. 5, *jiriṇu*, Par. To hurt.

† **जिष्** *JISH*, i. 1, Par. To sprinkle.

जिष्णु *jishṇu*, i.e. *ji* + *snu*, **I.** adj. **1.** Overpowering, MBh. 6, 5352. **2.** Victorious, Râjat. 5, 136. **3.** Excelling, Bhartṛ. 1, 5. **II.** m. **1.** A name of Vishṇu, MBh. 5, 2571. **2.** Of Arjuna, MBh. 3, 425.—Comp. *Sa-*, adj. with Arjuna.

जिहासा *jihâsâ*, i.e. *jihâsa*, desider. of *hâ*, + *a*, f. Wish to resign, Bhâg. P. 5, 5, 11.

जिहासु *jihâsu*, i.e. *jihâsa* (see the last), + *u*, adj. Wishing to resign, Bhâg. P. 5, 6, 6.

जिहीर्षा *jihîrshâ*, i.e. *jihîrsha*, desider. of *hṛi*, + *a*, f. **1.** Wish to take, to seize, Bhâg. P. 1, 7, 25. **3.** Wish to remove, Bhâg. P. 3, 1, 43.

जिहीर्षु *jihîrshu*, i.e. *jihîrsha* (see the last), + *u*, adj. **1.** Wishing to fetch, to rob, Daç. 1, 36; MBh. 7, 8980. **2.** Wishing to remove, Râjat. 5, 401.

जिह्म *jihma* (probably akin to *hvṛi*, for primitive *jihvṛi*, i.e. redupl. *hvṛi*, + *a*), adj., f. *mâ*. **1.** Oblique, Chr. 292, 11 =Rigv. i. 85, 11. **2.** Squinting, Suçr. 2, 349, 3. **3.** Crooked, fallacious, Râm. 5, 89, 69. **4.** °*mam*, adv. Astray, MBh, 5, 7361.—**Comp.** *A-*, I. adj. candid, Yajń. 1, 123. II. m. a fish. *Vi-*, adj. 1. crooked. 2. dishonest.

जिह्मग *jihma-ga*, m. A snake, MBh. 1, 982.

जिह्मता *jihma* + *tâ*, f. Falsehood, Râm. 2, 43, 2.

जिह्मित *jihmita*, i.e. *jihma* + *ita*, adj. Crooked, Mṛichchh. 143, 22.

जिह्व *jihva*, i.e. *jihve* (a redupl. form of *hve*, for primitive *dhve*), + *a*, I. m. and f. *vâ*, The tongue, Hariv. 6326; Man. 2, 90.—Comp. *Adhi-*, m. a tumour on the tongue. *Dirgha-*, m. the name of a Dânava, MBh. 1, 2538. f. *vâ*, the name of a female Râkshasa, Râm. 1, 28, 18 Gorr. *Dvi-*, I. adj. 1. having two tongues, MBh. 1, 1543. 2. treacherous, Pañch. i. d. 74. II. m. a snake, Râm. 2, 42, 2 Gorr. *Saptaj°*, i.e. *saptan-*, m. Agni. *Sthira-*, m. a fish.—Cf. Lat. lingua for dingua; Goth. tuggo (based on an older redupl. *duhva*; cf. vedic *juhû*); A.S. tunge.

ऽजिह्वक *-jihva* + *ka*, a substitute for *jihvâ* when the latter part of comp. adj., e.g. *a-*, adj., f. *kâ*, Without a tongue, MBh. 3, 16137.

जीन *jîna*, I. ptcple. pf. pass. of *jyâ*. II. n. A leathern pouch, Man. 11, 138.

जीमूत *jîmûta* (probably akin to *jihma*, for *jihma* + *vant* + *a*), m. A cloud, Râm. 2, 92, 32. 2. A name of the sun, MBh. 3, 152.

जीर् *jîra* (akin to *ji* in *jinv*, and *jî* in *jîv*), I. adj., f. *râ*, Driving, Chr. 287, 3 = Rigv. i. 48, 3. II. m. Cumin seed.

जीरक *jîra* + *ka*, m. Cumin seed, Suçr. 1, 218, 1.

जीर्णता *jîrṇa* + *tâ* (cf. *jṛî*), f. Frailty, Mṛichchh. 48, 16.

जीव् *JÎV*, i. 1, Par. (also Âtm., MBh. 1, 5913). 1. To live, Man. 2, 235. 2. To return to life, Bhâg. P. 4, 6, 51. 3. To maintain one's self, Man. 10, 112; with the instr. 3, 152; with the loc. MBh. 5, 1059. Comp. ptcple. of the pres. *a-jîvant*, Unable to subsist, Man. 10, 81. Ptcple. of the pf. pass. *jîvita*, 1. Living, Ragh. 12, 75. 2. Revived, Pañch. 221, 8. 3. Enlivened, Râm. 5, 66, 24. n. 1. Life, Man. 6, 45. 2. Livelihood, Hit. i. d. 85. Comp. *A-*, n. death. *An-apekshita-* (vb. *îksh*), adj. regardless of life, Kathâs. 18, 374. *Sa-*, adj. still living, Râjat. 5, 58. *Hata-* (vb. *han*), I. adj. desponding. II. n. despair.—Ptcple. of the fut. pass. I. *jîvya*, n. Life, Hariv. 14376. II. *jîvitavya*, n. 1. Possibility of living, Pañch. 76, 13. 2. Life, Pañch. 221, 6. III. *jîvanîya*, n. Epithet of milk; perhaps, Just milked, still warm, Suçr. 1, 175, 14.—Caus. I. *jîvaya* (in epic poetry also Âtm., MBh. 3, 16230), 1. To revive, MBh. 1, 1995. 2. To let live, MBh. 3, 870. 3. To bring up, MBh. 1, 6152. II. *jîvâpaya*, To revive, Lass. 18, 8.—Desid. *jijîvisha*, 1. To wish to live, MBh. 4, 615. 2. To gain one's livelihood, Man. 10, 121.—With the prep. अनु *anu*, To imitate the life of (with the acc.), Ragh. 19, 15. 2. To live in conformance with, Râm. 6, 5, 7. 3. To live for (with the acc.) MBh. 8, 3388. 4. To maintain one's self by (with the acc.) Râm. 5, 2, 35. Caus. *jîvaya*, To revive, Daçak. in Chr. 187, 9.—With आ *â*, 1. To maintain one's self by (with the acc.), MBh. 5, 4536. 2. To use, Yâjñ. 2, 67.—With उद् *ud*, To return to life, MBh. 12, 5675.—With अभ्युद् *abhi-ud*, To live as chief, MBh. 5, 4538.—With प्रत्युद् *prati-ud*, To return to life, Kathâs. 10, 97. Caus. To revive, Pañch. 244, 2.—With उप *upa*, 1. To maintain one's self by (with the acc.), Man. 9, 105. 2. To apply to one's own use, Man. 3, 52. 3. To gain, Man. 4, 200. 4. To practise, Bhâg. P. 7, 13, 7. *upajîvya*, That by which one maintains one's self, Yâjñ. 2, 227. n. Livelihood, Râm. 2, 37, 25.

—With वि *vi*, To return to life, MBh. 1, 2002.—With सम् *sam*, 1. To live, MBh. 3, 3054. 2. To return to life, Draup. 9, 4. Caus. *jîvaya*, 1. To animate, Man. 1, 57. 2. To revive, Râm. 4, 51, 20. 3. To preserve, Râjat. 2, 28.

—With प्रतिसम् *prati-sam*, To return to life, Râm. 5, 28, 16.—Cf. βίος, βίοτος (=*jîvatha*), βείομαι, βιόμεσθα, etc.; Lat. vivo; Goth. qvivs; A.S. cwic; Goth. ga-qvivjan, etc.

जीव *jîv+a*, I. adj. 1. Living, MBh. 13, 31. 2. Causing life, Bhâg. P. 9, 21, 13. II. m. and n. 1. Creature, MBh. 13, 13828. 2. Life, Râm. 5, 3, 74. III. m. The individual soul, Vedântas. in Chr. 207, 6.—Comp. *Dus-*, I. adj. difficult to live, Râm. 2, 57, 20. II. n. hard life, Râm. 2, 105, 5. *Nis-*, I. death, Kathâs. 17, 15. II. adj., f. *vâ*, lifeless, dead, MBh. 7, 1954. *Su-*, n. easy life, Râm. 2, 105, 5.—Cf. βίος; Lat. vivus; Goth. qvivs.

जीवक *jîv+aka*, I. latter part of comp. adj. Maintaining one's self by, MBh. 13, 6455. II. m. A medicinal plant, considered as one of the eight principal drugs, Suçr. 1, 59, 16. III. f. *vikâ*, 1. Life, Man. 4, 11. 2. A means of subsistence, Man. 10, 76; Bhâg. P. 7, 13, 7.—Comp. *Ranga-*, m. 1. a painter. 2. an actor.

जीवजीवक *jîvajîvaka*, m. A kind of bird, Man. 12, 66.

जीवंजीव *jîvamjîva*, i.e. *jîva+m-jîva*, and जीवंजीविक *jîvamjîvika*, i.e. *jîva+m-jîva+ika*, m. A kind of pheasant, MBh. 3, 8702.

जीवथ *jîv+atha*, m. Life.—Cf. βίοτος.

जीवन *jîv+ana*, I. adj., f. *nî*, Animating, enlivening, MBh. 1, 3241. II. n. Life, Râm. 4, 19, 19. 2. Subsistence, Man. 11, 76. 3. A means of subsistence, MBh. 3, 13724. 4. Revivification, Râm. 6, 105.—Comp. *A-*, n. death, Râm. 2, 38, 7. *Dâsa-*, adj. living by slavish work, Man. 10, 32. *Dharma-*, adj. subsisting by the performance of religious works, Man. 9, 273. *Mṛiga-*, m. a hunter, Nal. 11, 28.

जीवनता *jîvana+tâ*, f. Conduct, Lass. 88, 15.

जीवन्ती *jîvantî*, i.e. *jîvant*, ptcple. pres. of *jîv*, +*a*+*î*, f. A vegetable and medicinal plant, MBh. 2, 98.

जीवमय *jîva + maya*, adj., f. *yî*, Living, Bhâg. P. 9, 9, 24.

जीवल *jîvala*, m. A proper name, Nal. 15, 7.

जीववन्त् *jîva+vant*, adj., f. *vatî*, Living, MBh. 8, 4930.

जीवातु *jîv+âtu* (m. and n.?), Life, Mṛichchh. 172, 2.

जीविन् *jîv+in*, I. adj., f. *nî*. 1. Living, Man. 9, 246. 2. Subsisting on, Râm. 1, 9, 61; especially latter part of comp. words, e.g. *kṛishi-*, adj. Supporting one's self by tillage, Man. 3, 165. II. m. A living being, Pañch. 68, 15.—Comp. *Dirgha-*, adj. long-lived, Man. 9, 246. *Buddhi-*, adj. intelligent. *Jala-*, and *matsya-*, m. a fisher, MBh. 12, 7427; 1, 1339. *Çyena-*, m. one who lives by training hawks, a falconer, Man. 3, 164. *Saṁgha-*, m. a hired labourer. *Saṁchâra-*, adj. living in distress. *Surâ-*, m. a distiller.

जु *JU*, see *jû* and *chhyu*.

जुगुपिषु *jugupishu*, i.e. *jugupisha*, desider. of *gup*, +*u*, adj. Desiring to protect, MBh. 8, 1737.

जुगुप्सा *jugupsâ*, i.e. *jugupsa*, desider. of *gup* (q. cf.), + *â*, f. Aversion, MBh. 14, 1733.—Comp. *A-jugupsa*, adj. having no aversion, MBh. 13, 3077.

† **जुङ्** *JUṄG*, i. 1, Par. To abandon.

† **जुञ्च्** *JUŃCH*, i. 1 and 10, Par. To speak (?).

† I. **जुट्** *JUṬ*, or **जुड्** *JUḌ*, i, 6. Par. To bind. II. **जुड्** *JUḌ*, or **जुन्** *JUN*, i. 6, Par. To go. III. **जुड्** *JUḌ*, i. 10, Par. To send.

† **जुत्** *JUT* (=*jyut*, q. cf.), i. 1, Âtm. To shine.

† **जुन्** *JUN*, see *juḍ* II.

जुर्व् *JURV*, i. 1, *jûrva*, Par. **1.** To hurt. **2.** ved. To burn.

† **जुल्** *JUL* (akin to *jṛî*), i. 10, Par. To grind.

1. **जुष्** *JUSH*, i. 6, Âtm. (also Par., Hariv. 7430). **1.** To be pleased, Mârk. P. 31, 49. **2.** To enjoy, MBh. 2, 1718. **3.** To like, MBh. 3, 12732. **4.** To undergo, Bhâg. P. 8, 7, 20. **5.** To frequent, MBh. 3, 2464. **6.** To befall, MBh. 3, 11081. *jushṭa*, **1.** Loved, Chr. 293, 1= Rigv. i. 87, 1. **2.** Endowed, Bhâg. P. 1, 19, 20. Caus. *joshaya*, To agree, MBh. 14, 1289.—With the prep. **अभि** *abhi*, To frequent, MBh. 5, 1040.—With **अव** *ava*, To visit, MBh. 13, 645.—With **समा** *sam-â*, To resolve upon, Hariv. 7431 (precat. Par., or ii. 2, potent.).—With **निस्** *nis*, *nirjushṭa*, Frequented, Bhâg. P. 4, 6, 21.—With **प्र** *pra*, *prajushṭa*, Strongly attached to, Man. 2, 96.—With **सम्** *sam*, *saṁjushṭa*, Frequented, MBh. 13, 646.—Cf. Lat. gustus, gustare; γεύω; Goth. kiusan, A.S. ceosan, also cyssan; Goth. kukjan, cf. with ved. *juj*; cf. *kus*.

2. **जुष्** *jush*, adj. **1.** Loving, attached to, Bhâg. P. 7, 6, 25; especially as latter part of comp. words, e.g. Bhâg. P. 4, 9, 36. **2.** Visiting, Bhâg. P. 2, 7, 25.

3. **जुष्** *JUSH*, i. 1 and 10, Par. **1.** † To reason or to hurt. **2.** To satisfy.—Cf. 1. *jush*.

जुहोति *juhoti*, i.e. 3. sing. of the pres. of *hu*, A technical expression for those sacrifices which are denoted by the term *juhoti*, Man. 2, 84, *juhoti-yajati-kriyâ*, sacrifices denoted by the terms *juhoti* and *yajati*.

जू *JÛ*, ii. 9, *junâ*, *nî*, Par. (in the native collection of roots, *ju*, i. 1, Âtm.), **1.** To push on (ved.). **2.** To impel.—With the prep. **प्र** *pra*, To push on, to impel. Ptcple. pf. pass. *prajavita*, Râm. 3, 33, 27; Hariv. 10848.—Cf. probably Lat. gavi in gaudeo, gavisus sum; γηθέω, ἀγανός.

जूट *jûṭa*, m. The matted hair of Çiva (cf. *jaṭâ*), Mâlat. 1, 13.—Comp. *Jaṭâ-jûṭa*, the same, Kathâs. 25, 231.

जूर् *JÛR* (akin to *jṛî*), i. 4, Âtm. **1.** To grow old (appearing in the Veda in the form *jur*, i. 6, and i. 4, *jûrya*, Par.). **2.** † To hurt. **3.** To be angry.

† **जूष्** *JÛSH*, i. 1, Par. To hurt.

† **जृ** *JṚI*, i. 1, Par. To subdue (?).

† **जृभ्** *JṚIBH*, i. 1, Âtm. =*jṛimbh* (?)

जृम्भ् *JṚIMBH*, i. 1, Âtm. **1.** To yawn, Man. 4, 43. **2.** To open, Kathâs. 25, 238. **3.** To snap backwards (of a bow), MBh. 5, 1909. **4.** To cause to snap backwards, Râm. 3, 30, 28. **5.** To spread, Hariv. 2556. **6.** To increase, Bhartṛ. 3, 4. **7.** To arise, Râjat. 5, 363. **8.** To revive, to take courage, Râjat. 6, 283; to feel at ease, Hariv. 12073. Ptcple. of the pf. pass. *jṛimbhita*, n. **1.** Yawning, Suçr. 1, 363, 15. **2.** Appearance, Kathâs. 26, 89. Causal, *jṛimbhaya*, To cause to gape, Hariv. 10632.—With the prep. **अभि** *abhi*, To gape at, Râm. 6, 2, 18. —With **उद्** *ud*, **1.** To open wide, Bhâg. P. 1, 6, 16. **2.** To arise, Prab. 10, 2.—With **समुद्** *sam-ud*, **1.** To spread, Mṛichchh. 84, 24. **2.** To endeavour, Bhartṛ. 2, 6.—With **प्र** *pra*, To begin to yawn, MBh. 3, 11138.—With **वि** *vi*, **1.** To gape, Râm. 5, 3, 4. **2.** To open, Bhâg. P. 3, 9, 25. **3.** To spread, Sâh. D. 71, 10; to increase, Vikr. 41, 15. **4.** To snap backwards, MBh. 8, 3984. **5.** To rise, Râm. 5, 2, 34. **6.** To appear, Bhâg. P. 3, 33, 15. *vijṛimbhita*, **1.** Yawning, Hariv. 10635. **2.** Expanded, blossomed. **3.** Sported, wantoned. n. **1.** Wish. **2.** Pastime, sport.—With **सम्** *sam*, To appear, Râjat. 6, 229.

जृम्भ *jṛimbh + a*, I. m. and f. *bhâ*, and n. **1.** Yawning, Suçr. 1, 98, 11. **2.** Opening, as a flower, Mâlat. 148, 8. II. m. A kind of animal, Râm. 2, 35, 18.

जृम्भक *jṛimbh + aka*, I. m. **1.** The name of certain demons, MBh. 3, 14548. **2.** The name of a spell, producing drowsiness, Râm. 1, 30, 7. II. f. *bhikâ*, Yawning, MBh. 5, 282. III. n. Swelling, Lass. 17, 4.

जृम्भण *jṛimbhaṇa*, i.e. *jṛimbh + ana*, I. adj. Causing to gape, Râm. 1, 56, 7. II. n. **1.** Yawning, Vedântas. in Chr. 207, 16. **2.** Opening, as a flower, Bhartṛ. 1, 24. **3.** Stretching, Ṛit. 6, 9.

जॄ *JṜÎ*, i. 1, Par., i. 4, Par. (also Âtm., MBh. 13, 367). † ii. 9, *jṛiṇâ, ṇî*, Par. **1.** To grow old, MBh. 3, 13860. **2.** To be digested, Suçr. 1, 70, 18.—Ptcple. of the pres. *jarant*, f. *rati*, Old, Râjat. 6, 172. Ptcple. of the pf. pass. *jîrṇa*, **1.** Old, decayed, Bhâg. P. 1, 13, 22; Râm. 3, 11, 9. **2.** Tumbled down, Man. 4, 46. **3.** Rotten, MBh. 3, 678. **4.** Faded, Çâk. d. 170. **5.** Destroyed, MBh. 3, 1939. n. Old age, Râjat. 3, 316. **Comp.** *A-*, n. indigestion, Man. 4, 121. Caus. and i. 10, **I.** *jaraya*, To cause to wax old, Chr. 287, 5=Rigv. i. 48, 5; Chr. 295, 10=Rigv. 1, 92, 10; MBh. 7, 5967 (Âtm.). **2.** To consume, Bhâg. P. 3, 25, 33. **3.** To overpower, MBh. 3, 1939. **4.** To digest, Râm. 5, 84, 12. **II.** † *jâraya*.—With the prep. **निस्** *nis*, To grind, Bhâg. P. 6, 12, 29. —With **परि** *pari*, **1.** To wear out, MBh. 4, 332. **2.** To fade, Suçr. 1, 224, 20. **3.** To wax old, MBh. 1, 5139. **4.** To be digested, Suçr. 2, 178, 14.—With **प्र** *pra*, To be digested, Suçr. 1, 239, 1. —Cf. γέρων (=*jarant*) γεραιός, γραῦς, γραΐς, γῆρας, γῦρις, γίγαρτον, γαργαλίζω γαγγαλίζω; Lat. granum; Goth. kaurn, ga-krôtôn; O.H.G. korn, kern; Goth. qvairnu; A.S. cweorn, cwyrn.

जेतुकाम *jetukâma*, i.e. *jetum*, infin. of *ji*, *-kâma*, adj. Desiring victory, Râm. 1, 63, 15.

जेतृ *jetṛi*, i.e. *ji + tṛi*, m., f. *trî*, and n. **1.** Conquering, a conqueror, Râm. 3, 38, 13. **2.** A winner in a game, Yâjń. 2, 200.

† **जेष्** *JESH*, i. 1, Âtm. To go.

† **जेह्** *JEH* (an old frequentat. of

hâ), i. 1, Âtm. **1.** To gape (ved.). **2.** † To endeavour.

† जै *JAI* (akin to *jyâ*), i. 1, Par. To wane.

जैत्र *jaitra*, i.e. *jetṛi* + *a*, adj., f. *rî*, Victorious, MBh. 2, 490.

जैमिनि *jaimini*, m. The name of a philosopher, the founder of the Pûrva Mîmânsâ school, Pańch. ii. d. 34.

जैमूत *jaimûta*, i.e. *jîmûta*, a proper name, + *a*, adj. Relating to Jîmûta, MBh. 5, 3845.

जैवातृक *jaivâtṛika*, i.e. *jîv* + *â* + *tṛi* + *ka*, adj. Long-lived, one who may live long, Daçak. 95, 12.

जैह्म्य *jaihmya*, i.e. *jihma* + *ya*, n. Cheating, Man. 11, 67.

जैह्व्य *jaihvya*, i.e. *jihva* + *ya*, n. Delight of the tongue, Bhâg. P. 7, 6, 13.

जोष *josha*, i.e. *jush* + *a*, m. Satisfaction (ved.). °*am*, adv. Silently, MBh. 2, 2431.

जोषण *joshaṇa*, i.e. *jush* + *ana*, n. Pleasure, Bhâg. P. 3, 25, 25.

ज्ञ *jńa* (vb. *jńâ*), adj., f. *ńâ*. **1.** Knowing, MBh. 12, 12028; particularly as latter part of comp. words, e.g. Man. 4, 102. **2.** Intelligent, Bhâg. P. 7, 8, 11. —**Comp.** *A*-, adj. 1. ignorant, Bhartṛ. 2, 3. 2. unreasonable, Pańch. ii. d. 3. 3. foolish, Mṛichchh. 24, 5. *Manojńa*, i.e. *manas*-, adj. beautiful, Lass. 53, 2. *Sarva*-, adj. omniscient, Bhartṛ. 2, 8.— Cf. Lat. beni-gnus, mali-gnus.

ज्ञता *jńa* + *tâ*, f. **1.** Knowledge, Yâjń. 3, 142. When latter part of comp. words, *tâ* is the aff. of the comp., e.g. *haya-jńa* + *tâ*, Knowledge of horses and their management, Nal. 19, 26.

ज्ञप्ति *jńapti*, i.e. *jńâ*, Caus., + *ti*, f. Comprehension, knowing, Kathâs. 25, 57.

ज्ञंमन्य *jńaṁmanya*, i. e. *jńa* + *m*, -*man* + *ya*, adj. Thinking one's self intelligent, Râjat. 3, 491.

ज्ञा *JŃÂ*, ii. 9, *jânâ*, *nî*, Par. Âtm. **1.** To know, Man. 2, 123; MBh. 3, 2154 (with the gen.). **2.** To be intelligent, Man. 2, 110. **3.** To recognise, Megh. 64; Bhag. 5, 29. **4.** To search, Râm. 3, 51, 1; to investigate, MBh. 4, 962; to learn, Pańch. 4, 17. **5.** To consider, Man. 8, 71; 2, 23. **6.** To perceive, Râm. 1, 42, 1. Anomalous 3 sing. pres. *jânate*, MBh. 13, 5204; 1 pl. *jânîma*, 3, 15591; 2 pl. *jânatha*, 2, 842; 2 pl. imptve. *jânata*, 2, 2397; 2 sing. impf. Âtm. *jânithâs*, 14, 1641; ptcple of the pres. Âtm. *jânamâna*, 3, 1413.—Ptcple. of the pf. pass. *jńâta*, **1.** Known, Mṛichchh. 2, 8. **2.** Thought, Pańch. i. d. 123. **Comp.** *A*-, without knowing, unknowingly, Man. 4, 140; 11, 155.— Ptcple. of the fut. pass. **1.** *jńâtavya*, Perceptible, Hariv. 11143. **2.** *dus-jńeya*, adj. Hard to be discerned, Man. 6, 73. Caus. *jńâpaya* and *jńapaya*, **1.** To declare, MBh. 2, 558. **2.** To teach, MBh. 14, 415. **3.** To report, MBh. 1, 5864. **4.** To address, MBh. 3, 8762. Ptcple of the pf. pass. *jńâpita* and *jńapta*. Desider. *jijńâsa*, **1.** To desire to know, Râm. 2, 35, 19. **2.** To search, to inquire, Bhâg. P. 2, 9, 35. **3.** To get certainty, Kathâs. 22, 84.—With the prep. अनु *anu*, **1.** To grant, Bhâg. P. 3, 13, 14. **2.** To promise, Daçak. in Chr. 186, 19. **3.** To permit, give leave, Mâlav. 16, 11; Râm. 2, 52, 44. **4.** To pardon, MBh. 1, 7772. **5.** To repent, Râm. 2, 42, 8. **6.** To dismiss, Man. 3, 251. **7.** To take leave, Râm. 2, 37, 4 (with the acc.). **8.** To beg, Râm. 2, 21, 25. **9.** To favour, MBh. 3, 11631. Caus. **1.** To ask permission, Man. 4, 122. **2.** To take leave (with the acc.), Râm. 2, 71, 13.—With अभ्यनु *abhi-anu*, **1.** To approve, Man. 2, 1. **2.** To permit, Man. 3, 243. **3.** To dismiss, Râm. 1, 2, 3. **4.** To take leave, Râm. 3, 12, 7. **5.** To favour, Râm. 3, 36, 19. Caus. To take leave, MBh. 1, 6619.—With प्रत्यभ्यनु *prati-abhi-anu*, To dismiss, MBh. 12, 13928.—With प्रत्यनु *prati-anu*, To spurn, Râm. 2, 87, 16.—With समनु *sam-anu*, **1.** To approve, MBh. 3, 14824. **2.** To pardon, Râm. 2, 39, 38. **3.** To empower, MBh. 3, 14815; to allow, MBh. 3, 1850. **4.** To dismiss, MBh. 5, 5974. **5.** To favour, MBh. 13, 3603. Caus. **1.** To beg, MBh. 1, 6340. **2.** To beg permission, Râm. 2, 40, 2. **3.** To take leave (with the acc.), Râm. 1, 74, 6. **4.** To salute, MBh. 1, 6423.—With अभि *abhi*, **1.** To recognise, MBh. 3, 2201. **2.** To perceive, Bhâg. P. 4, 19, 26. **3.** To know, Râm. 6, 94, 15; MBh. 3, 13339. **4.** To think, MBh. 1, 3337. **5.** To approve, MBh. 13, 5871. **6.** To acknowledge, MBh. 1, 3060.—With प्रत्यभि *prati-abhi*, **1.** To recognise, Prab. 24, 16. **2.** To recover, Kathâs. 18, 175.—With समभि *sam-abhi*, To recognise, MBh. 3, 2945.—With अव *ava*, To despise, Bhag. 9, 11. *avajñâta*, Accompanied with contempt, Bhag. 17, 22.—With आ *â*, To perceive, MBh. 3, 448; to learn, Râm. 1, 9, 61. Caus. **1.** To command, MBh. 2, 2567 (Âtm.); with that which is commanded in the dat., e.g. *svagṛihâya*, To command to go home, Pañch. 242, 24.—With समा *sam-â*, **1.** To recognise, MBh. 4, 1736. **2.** To learn, Lass. 18, 13. **3.** To know, MBh. 3, 680. Caus. To command, Mṛichchh. 66, 23.

—With उप *upa*, desider. To spy, MBh. 13, 3016.—With समुप *sam-upa*, To perceive, to learn, MBh. 12, 5241.—With परि *pari*, **1.** To recognise, Râm. 6, 8, 3. **2.** To learn, MBh. 7, 467. **3.** To know, Pañch. 99, 8. **4.** To know exactly, Vikr. 5, 14. Comp. ptcple. of the pf. pass. *ku-pari-jñâta*, adj. Imperfectly known, Pañch. v. d. 1.—Comp. ptcple. of the fut. pass. *a-pari-jñeya*, adj. Incomprehensible, Bhâg. P. 8, 12, 36.—With प्र *pra*, **1.** To discern, Bhag. 18, 31. **2.** To know, Bhag. 11, 31. *prajñâta*, Renowned, Man. 4, 39. *a-prajñâta*, adj. Imperceptible, Man. 1, 5.—With संप्र *sam-pra*, **1.** To discern, MBh. 12, 1872. **2.** To know exactly, MBh. 12, 2319.—With प्रति *prati* (according to the Grammar. Âtm., except in the seventh signification), **1.** To admit, Man. 8, 139. **2.** To promise (with the acc. and dat. of the promised object), Râm. 2, 109, 24; MBh. 1, 7234; with the gen. of the person to which something is promised, Man. 9, 99; with the dat., MBh. 3, 2135; with the loc., Râm. 1, 75, 7. **3.** To confirm, Sâv. 1, 16. **4.** To affirm, MBh. 2, 842. **5.** To recognise, MBh. 1, 2089. **6.** To perceive, Hariv. 1036. **7.** To remember sorrowfully, MBh. 12, 8438 (Âtm. against the rule).—With संप्रति *sam-prati*, To promise, MBh. 7, 2652.—With वि *vi*, **1.** To distinguish, Man. 2, 212. **2.** To know exactly, Man. 5, 121; to know, MBh. 9, 2666. **3.** To inquire, Pañch. 45, 24. **4.** To learn, Pañch. i. d. 430. **5.** To perceive, Râm. 3, 51, 1. **6.** To consider, Man. 9, 32. **7.** To explain, Bhâg. P. 3, 25, 30. **8.** To become learned, Man. 4, 20. Comp. ptcple. of the pres. adj. *a-vijânant*, Inconsiderate, Chr. 15, 5. Comp. ptcple of the pf. pass. *a-vijńâta*, adj. **1.** Unknown, Man. 4, 129. **2.** Unperceived, Bhâg. P. 1, 13, 16. Comp. ptcple. of the fut. pass. *dus-vijńeya*, adj. Difficult to be conceived, MBh. 13, 724. Comp. absol. *a-vijńâya*, Without knowing exactly, Pańch. 57, 3. Caus. **1.** To declare, Pańch. 152, 5. **2.** To speak, Râm. 5, 90, 17. **3.** To address, Pańch. 69, 12. **4.** To impart (with acc. of the person and of the object), Râjat. 3, 241. Desid. To wish to learn, Bhâg. P. 5, 16, 2.—With अभिवि *abhi-vi*, **1.** To learn, MBh. 1, 1565. **2.** To perceive, Râm. 2, 101, 1.—With प्रवि *pra-vi*, To know exactly, Suçr. 1, 342, 3.—With संवि *sam-vi*, To advise, MBh. 12, 2451. Caus. To recite, Râjat. 3, 180.—With सम् *sam*, Âtm. **1.** To allot, Bhâg. P. 9, 16, 34. **2.** To understand, Râm. 2, 35, 17. Caus. **1.** To satisfy, MBh. 12, 12567. **2.** To quiet an animal destinated to be sacrificed, MBh. 14, 2645. **3.** To speak in signs, Mṛichchh. 30, 15. **4.** To command, Hariv. 7056 (*saṁjńapan* instead of *-jńapayan*).—Cf. γιγνώσκω, γνῶσις, ἄγνοια, νοῦς, etc.; Lat. nosco, cf. co-gnosco, gnarus, narro; Goth. kunnan, kunths, kunthi; O.H.G. knajan; A.S. cnáwan.

ज्ञा *jńâ*, for *âjnâ* after *e* and *o*, MBh. 1, 3168; 3, 16303.

ज्ञाति *jńâti*, i.e. *jan*+*â*+*ti*, m. A paternal relation, Man. 2, 132.—Comp. *A-*, m. one who is not a paternal kinsman, Man. 5, 103. *Nis-*, adj. being without kinsmen, MBh. 8, 280. *Sva-*, I. f. kindred. II. m. a kinsman.—Cf. Goth. knôds; Lat. co-gnatus, natio; γνήσιος.

ज्ञातित्व *jńâti*+*tva*, n. Consanguinity, Man. 11, 172.

ज्ञातृ *jńâ*+*tṛi*, m., f. *tri*, n. **1.** One who knows, MBh. 13, 7173. **2.** A witness, Man. 8, 57, v.r.—Cf. Lat. co-gnitor.

ज्ञान *jńâna*, i.e. *jńâ*+*ana*, n. **1.** Knowledge, Man. 2, 13. **2.** Superior knowledge, Bhag. 3, 3. **3.** Consciousness, MBh. 1, 5827. **4.** Intention, Man. 11, 145.—**Comp.** *A-*, I. n. 1. ignorance, Pańch. ii. d. 34. 2. inadvertence, Man. 11, 145. Abl. *°nât*, without one's knowledge, Man. 8, 243. II. adj., f. *nâ*, ignorant. *Âtmajnâna*, i.e. *âtman-*, n. the knowledge of the universal soul, Man. 12, 85. *Dus-*, adj. difficult to be known, MBh. 12, 4026.

ज्ञानद *jńâna-da*, m. One who can impart knowledge, Man. 2, 109.

ज्ञानमय *jńâna*+*maya*, adj., f. *yî*, Containing knowledge, Man. 2, 7.

ज्ञानवन्त् *jńâna*+*vant*, adj., f. *vatî*. **1.** Knowing, Vedântas. in Chr. 218, 20. **2.** Endowed with superior knowledge, Râm. 6, 102, 7.

ऽज्ञानिक *-jńânika*, i.e. *jńâna*+*ika*, =*jńâna*, as latter part of a comp. adj. in *pra-nashṭa-* (vb. *naç*), adj. Without knowledge, Suçr. 1, 8, 14.

ज्ञानित्व *jńânitva*, i.e. *jńânin*+*tva*, n. Fortune-telling, Kathâs. 19, 75.

ज्ञानिन् *jńânin*, i.e. *jńâna*+*in*, I. adj., f. *nî*, One who understands fully, Man. 12, 103; learned, Râm. 1, 8, 13. II. m. An astrologer, a fortune-teller, Râm. 6, 23, 4.

ज्ञापक *jńâpaka*, i.e. *jnâ*, Caus., +*aka*, I. m. **1.** A teacher, Bhâg. P. 9, 6, 10. **2.** A master of requests, Pańch. 156, 18 (thus to be read instead of *nâyaka*). II. n. A precept, Râjat, 1, 5; a rule, MBh. 1, 5846.

ज्ञापन *jnâpana*, i.e. *jnâ*, Caus., + *ana*, n. Notifying, Râjat. 4, 180.

ज्ञु *-jńu,* a substitute for *jânu* in some comp. words, (cf. ved. *jńu-bâdh, ûrdhva-jńu*), *pra-jńu,* adj. Having the knees far apart.—Cf. πρόχνυ.

ज्ञेयत्व *jńeya + tva* (vb. *jńâ*), n. Capability of being known, Bhâshâp. 12.

ज्या *JYA,* ii. 9, *jinâ, nî,* Par. i. 4, *jîya,* Âtm. ved. **1.** To overpower (ved.). **2.** To be overpowered (*jîya,* ved.). **3.** † To decay, to become old. *jîna,* see separately.—Cf. βία (=ved. *jyâ*), βιάω, etc., probably also βῑνέω.

ज्या *jyâ,* f. A bow-string, MBh. 1, 8193.—Comp. *Sa-jya,* adj. strung.—Cf. βιός.

ज्याय *JYAYA,* a denominat. derived from the last Âtm. To represent a bow-string, Daçak. 2, 15.

ज्यायंस् *jyâ + yaṁs,* comparat. of *praçasya* and *vṛiddha,* f. *jyâyasî,* **1.** More powerful (ved.). **2.** Stronger, MBh. 9, 3247. **3.** Superior, Man. 3, 137. **4.** m. A master, Man. 8, 167. **5.** Elder, Man. 2, 139.

ज्यायिष्ठ *jyâyishṭha,* anomal. superl. of *praçasya* (cf. *jyeshṭha*), Best, MBh. 7, 3701.

† ज्यु *JYU,* i. 1, Âtm. To go, v.r.

ज्युत् *JYUT* (=*dyut,* q. cf.), i. 1, Âtm. v.r., and † i. 1, Par. v.r., To shine, Indr. 1, 32, v.r.—Caus. *jyotaya,* To illuminate, Indr. 1, 30, v.r.

ज्युतिमन्त् *jyuti + mant* (=*dyuti,* i.e. *div + ti*), adj., f. *matî,* Shining, Indr. 1, 33, v.r.

ज्येष्ठ *jyeshṭha,* i.e. *jyâ + ishṭha,* **I.** superl. of *praçasya* and *vṛiddha* (cf. *jyâyaṁs*), f. *ṭhâ,* **1.** Most excellent, Man. 9, 123. **2.** Eldest, Man. 9, 126; Daçak. in Chr. 184, 12. **II.** m. **1.** An elder brother, Man. 4, 184. **2.** =*jyaishṭha,* The name of a month, Râjat. 1, 220. **III.** f. *ṭhâ.* **1.** The name of a lunar station, Râm. 6, 86, 43. **2.** Misfortune, Bhâg. P. 1, 17, 32.—Comp. *A-,* adj. forfeiting one's primogeniture, Man. 9, 213. *Yathâ-jyeshṭha + m,* adv. according to (their) rank, Pańch. 198, 10.

ज्येष्ठतर *jyeshṭha + tara,* comparat. One of the elder ones, Pańch. 243, 18.

ज्येष्ठता *jyeshṭha + tâ,* f. **1.** Superiority, Hariv. 7164. **2.** Primogeniture, Man. 9, 134.

ज्येष्ठत्व *jyeshṭha + tva,* n. Primogeniture, MBh. 1, 8372.

ज्यैष्ठ *jyaishṭha,* i.e. *jyeshṭhâ + a,* m. The name of a month, May—June, Man. 8, 245.

ज्यैष्ठिनेय *jyaishṭhineya,* i.e. *jyeshṭha + in + î + eya,* adj. Borne by the eldest wife of a father, MBh. 2, 1934.

ज्यैष्ठ्य *jyaishṭhya,* i.e. *jyeshṭha + ya,* n. **1.** Precedence, Man. 9, 85. **2.** Primogeniture, Man. 1, 93.

† ज्यो *JYO,* i. 1. Âtm. **1.** To restrain. **2.** To vow. **3.** To instruct (?).

ज्योतिरीश *jyotirîça,* or ज्योतिरीश्वर *jyotirîçvara,* i.e. *jyotis-îça,* or *-îçvara,* m. The name of the author of the Dhûrtasamâgama, Lass. 68, 15; 67, 11.

ज्योतिर्मय *jyotirmaya,* i.e. *jyotis + maya,* adj., f. *yî,* Consisting of light, Ragh. 15, 59.

ज्योतिष *jyotisha,* i.e. *jyotis + a,* **I.** m. A kind of spell, Râm. 1, 30, 6. **II.** n. Astronomical science, MBh. 12, 13136.

ज्योतिष्क *jyotishka,* i.e. *jyotis + ka,* n. **1.** The name of a shining weapon of Arjuna's, MBh. 7, 1325. **2.** The name of the summit of Meru, MBh. 12, 10212.

ज्योतिष्टोम *jyotishṭoma*, i.e. *jyotis-stoma*, m. One of the great sacrifices in which especially the juice of the Soma is offered, Râm. 1, 13, 45.

ज्योतिस् *jyotis*, i.e. *jyut + is*, n. Light, Chr. 289, 10 = Rigv. i. 50, 10; Man. 1, 77. **2.** pl. The stars. Man. 1, 38. **3.** Intelligence, Bhag. 13, 17.—Comp. *Antar-*, adj. one whose light (i.e. thought) is fixed on his soul (not on external pleasures), Bhag. 5, 24. *Sa-*, adj., n. the time during which the sun or the stars give light, Man. 5, 82 (viz., when a king dies at day-time the impurity lasts till sunset, when he dies at night till the disappearance of the stars).

ज्योतीरथ *jyotîratha*, i.e. *jyotis-ratha*, I. m. A kind of snake, Suçr. 2, 265, 20. II. f. *thâ*, The name of a river, MBh. 6, 334.

ज्योतीरस *jyotîrasa*, i.e. *jyotis-rasa*, m. A kind of jewel, Râm. 2, 94, 6.

ज्योत्स्ना *jyotsnâ*, i.e. *jyut + sna*, f. **1.** Moonlight, Bhâg. P. 4, 28, 34. **2.** Light, Bhâg. P. 3, 28, 21 (pl.) **3.** The name of a body of Brahman, Bhâg. P. 3, 20, 39.

ज्योत्स्नावन्त् *jyotsnâ + vant*, adj., f. *vatî*. **1.** Moonlight (night), Ragh. 6, 34. **2.** Shining, Bhâg. P. 4, 21, 26.

1. **ज्रि** *JRI*, i. 1, Par. **1.** † To conquer. **2.** To go (ved.).

2. † **ज्रि** *JRI*, and **ज्री** *JRÎ*, i. 1, ii. 9, *jriṇâ*, *ṇi*, and i. 10, *jrâyaya*, Par. To grow old, v.r.—Cf. *jṛî*.

ज्वर् *JVAR* (cf. *jval*), i. 1, Par. To be feverish, Suçr. 2, 84, 13 (pass.). Caus. *jvaraya*, To cause to be feverish.—With the prep. **सम्** *sam*, To be afflicted, MBh. 3, 13743.—With **अनुसम्** *anu-sam*, **1.** To afflict, MBh. 5, 1607. **2.** To envy, MBh. 5, 1605.—With **अभिसम्** *abhi-sam*, To envy, MBh. 5, 1615.

ज्वर *jvar + a*, I. adj. Excited, MBh. 13, 3464, II. m. **1.** Fever, MBh. 12, 10255. **2.** Sorrow, Râm. 1, 18, 11.—Comp. *Gata-*, adj., f. *râ*, without sorrow, Râm. 6, 98, 7. *Jîrṇa-* (vb. *jṛî*), m. a lingering fever, Suçr. 1, 175, 5. *Jîrṇâmaya-*, i.e. *jîrṇa-âmaya-*, m. the same, Kathâs. 17, 36. *Dâha-*, m. a burning fever, Kathâs. 5, 122; Daçak. in Chr. 192, 4. *Maithuna-*, m. wantonness, MBh. 13, 1516. *Ratha-*, m. a crow.

ज्वरित *jvarita*, i.e. *jvara + ita*, adj., f. *tâ*, Feverish, Suçr. 2, 409, 7.

ज्वरिन् *jvarin*, i.e. *jvara + in*, adj., f. *iṇî*, Feverish, Suçr. 1, 34, 20.

ज्वल् *JVAL* (= *jvar*), i. 1, Par. (in epic poetry also Âtm., Hariv. 7914), **1.** To blaze, MBh. 1, 3687 (Âtm.). **2.** To shine, Suçr. 1, 113, 16. **3.** To burn, Pañch. 98, 1. **4.** To be consumed by fire, Bhâg. P. 9, 6, 23. **5.** To be red hot, Man. 8, 271. Ptcple. of the pf. pass. *jvalita*, **1.** Flaming, Pañch. i. d. 37; Indr. 1, 6. **2.** Shining, Râm. 3, 50, 18. **3.** Burnt. Chr. 24, 40 (*tṛiṇeshu jvalitam̃ tvayâ*, You have burnt up only grass, i.e. You have fought only with insignificant men). Caus. *jvâlaya* and *jvalaya*, after prep. only the latter (also *jvâlaya*, e.g. MBh. 3, 17078), **1.** To kindle, Râm. 2, 52, 99. **2.** To illuminate, Kir. 5, 14. *agni-jvalita*, Blazing with fire, Man. 7, 90. Frequent. *jâjval* and *jâjvalya*, **1.** To burn violently, MBh. 12. 11597. **2.** To flame violently, Râm. 4, 38, 15. **3.** To be very brilliant, Râm. 6, 19, 49.—With the prep. **अभि** *abhi*, To shine, MBh. 3, 10335. Frequent. To blaze powerfully, Kâm. Nitis. 15, 8.—With उद् *ud*, To flash up, Râm. 5, 93, 15. Caus. To kindle, Râjat. 3, 176.—With प्रोद् *pra-ud*, To shine brightly, Hariv. 15696.—With समुद् *sam-ud*, The same, MBh. 8, 1715. —With प्र *pra*, **1.** To begin to blaze, Râm. 3, 18, 32. **2.** To begin to burn, MBh. 1, 1770. **3.** To become wrathful, Râm. 2, 21, 53. **4.** To blaze brightly, Daçak. in Chr. 198, 15. *prajvalita*, **1.** Burning, Chr. 33, 5. **2.** Shining, Hariv. 9746. **3.** Flaming, Pańch. 55, 10. n. Blazing, Hariv. 3293. Caus. To kindle, Râm. 2, 47, 8.—With अभिप्र *abhi-pra*, To become inflamed, MBh. 6, 4188.—With संप्र *sam-pra*, The same, Râm. 6, 96, 17; Hariv. 6475. Caus. To kindle, MBh. 13, 7776.—With प्रति *prati*, To shine, MBh. 7, 7437.—With अभिवि *abhi-vi*, To shine towards, Bhag. 11, 28.—With सम् *sam*, To blaze, MBh. 9, 222. Caus. To kindle, MBh. 3, 16882. —Cf. O.H.G. quelan, A.S. cwellan; Goth. vulan, A.S. wellian, Lat. bullire, O.H.G. quellan, cf. A.S. weall (a well); ζῆλος (cf. *anu-sam-jvar*, and *abhi-sam-jvar*), probably also ζάλη, ζαλαίνω.

ज्वल *jval + a*, adj. f. *lâ*, Flaming, Hiḍ. 2, 7.

ज्वलन *jval + ana*, I. adj. Shining, MBh. 3, 12239. II. m. **1.** Fire, Man. 10, 103. **2.** Caustic potash, Suçr. 2, 125, 17. III. n. Shining (and fire), Çiç. 9, 13.

ज्वाल *jvâla*, i.e. *jval + a*, m. and f. *lâ*, Flame, MBh. 3, 14132; Ragh. 15, 16.—Comp. *Saptaj°*, i.e. *saptan-*, m. Agni. *Hemaj°*, i.e. *heman-*, m. fire.

ज्वालिन् *jvâlin*, i.e. *jvâla + in*, adj. Flaming, MBh. 13, 1171.

झ *JH.*

झंकार *jhaṁkâra*, i.e. *jham*, an imitative sound, *-kâra*, m. Humming, Bhâg. P. 8, 8, 43.

झंकारित *jhaṁkârita*, i.e. *jham-kârita* (ptcple. pf. pass. of the Caus. of *kṛi*; cf. the last), n. Humming, Bhartṛ. 1, 97.

झञ्झा *jhańjhâ*, i.e. probably a reduplicated form of *jham* (cf. *jhaṁkâra*), f. A sharp clanging sound, Amar, 48.

झट् *JHAṬ*, i. 1, Par. To be entangled; cf. *jaṭ*.—With the prep. उद् *ud*, *ujjhaṭita*, Confused, Râjat. 1, 116.

झटिति *jhaṭiti*, i.e. *jhaṭat* (?), probably based on an imitative sound, *-iti*, adv. Instantly, in a moment, Bhartṛ. i. 69; on a sudden, Daçak. in Chr. 186, 15.

झणझण *jhaṇajhaṇa*, a reduplicated form of the imitative sound *jhaṇat* (cf. *jhaṇatkâra*), Tinkling, Kathâs. 25, 222.

झणत्कार *jhaṇat-kâra* (see the last), m. Tinkling, Prab, 40, 6, v.r.

झनज्झना *jhanajjhanâ*, a reduplicated form of an imitative sound *jhanat* (cf. *jhaṇatkâra* ?). The sound caused by the flapping of an elephant's ear, Kâm. Nîtis. 1, 45.

† झम् *JHAM*, i. 1, Par. To eat. —Cf. *jam*.

झम्प *jhampa*, m. Jumping, Hit. 63, 15.

झरी *jharî* (probably a form of a

derivative from *kshar*), f. A waterfall, Prab. 73, 1.

† झर्च् *JHARCH*, झर्छ् *JHARCHH*, झर्झ् *JHARJH*, i. 1, and 6, Par. **1.** To explain. **2.** To menace. **3.** To hurt.

झर्झर *jharjhara*, i.e. *jharjhar*, a reduplicated form of an imitative sound, + *a*, m. and f. *rî*, A kind of drum, MBh. 6, 4463; Râm. 6, 99, 23 (but Sch., A flute); Hariv. 13212.

झर्झरिन् *jharjharin*, i.e. *jharjhara* + *in*, adj. Provided with a drum, MBh. 12, 10406.

झलज्झला *jhalajjhalâ*, i.e. a reduplicated form of *jhalat*, an imitative sound, and aff. *a*, f. The sounding of falling drops, Amar. 9, v. r.

झल्ल *jhalla*, m. A prize-fighter, considered as the son of an outcaste Kshatriya, MBh. 2, 102; Man. 10, 22.

† झष् *JHASH*, i. 1, Par., Âtm. **1.** To take. **2.** To cover. i. 1, Par. To hurt.

झष *jhasha*, m. **1.** A fish, MBh. 1, 8316. **2.** The sign Pisces.

झिल्लि *jhilli*, झिल्लिका *jhilli* + *kâ*, and झिल्ली *jhillî*, f. A cricket, Hariv. 3497; Râm. 1, 26, 13; Bhâg. P. 5, 13, 5.

झिल्लीक *jhillî* + *ka*, m. A cricket, MBh. 1, 2849.

† झूष् *JHÛSH*, v.r. for *jûsh*.

† झॄ *JHṚÎ*, i. 4, *jhîrya*; ii. 9, *jhṛiṇâ*, *ṇî*, m. To grow old, v.r.—Cf. *jṛî*.

झोड *jhoḍa*, m. The betel-nut tree.

झौलिक *jhaulika*, i.e. *jhoḍa* + *ika*, A little pouch containing betel, Dhûrtas. 95, 8.

† झ्यु *JHYU*, i. 1, Par. To go, v.r.

ट *Ṭ*.

टक्कदेश *ṭakka-deça*, m. The land of the Ṭakkas, Râjat. 5, 150.

टक्कर *ṭakkara*, A kind of musical sound (?), or a drum, Râjat. 5, 417. —Cf. *karoṭika*.

टङ्क् *ṬAṄK*, i. 1 (?), and 10, Par. **1.** † To bind. **2.** To cover (ved.).—With the prep. वि *vi*, *vitaṅkita*, **1.** Marked, Bhâg. P. 1, 16, 36. **2.** Loaded, Bhâg. P. 4, 4, 5.

टङ्क *ṭaṅka*, I. m. and n. **1.** A hatchet, Hariv. 5009. **2.** Slope, Bhaṭṭ. 1, 8 (Sch.). II. m. **1.** A weight equal to 4 mâshas, Lass. 29, 4. **2.** (and n ?) A coin, Hit. 98, 11.

टङ्कवन्त् *ṭaṅka* + *vant*, adj., f. *vatî*, Sloping, Râm. 3, 55, 44.

टंकार *ṭaṁkâra*, i.e. *ṭam*, an imitative sound, *-kâra*, m. Howling, Bhâg. P. 3, 17, 9; sound, Râjat. 5, 417 (?).

टंकारित *ṭaṁkârita*, i.e. *ṭam-kârita* (ptcple. pf. pass. of the Caus. of *kṛi*; cf. the last), m. Humming, Bhartṛ 1, 97, v.r.

† टल् *ṬAL*, i. 1, Par. To be confused, v.r.

टांकार *ṭâṁkâra*, v.l. for *taṁkâra*, Râjat. 5, 417.

टांकृत *ṭâṁkṛita*, i.e. *ṭâm-kṛita* (vb. *kṛi*), Sound, Râjat. 2, 99.

† टिक् *ṬIK*, i. 1, Par. To go.

टिट्टिभ *ṭiṭṭibha,* **1.** m. A bird, Parra jacuna, or goensis, Pañch. 74, 17. **2.** f. *bhî,* Its female, Râm. 2, 8, 43 Gorr.

† **टिप्** *ṬIP,* i. 10, Par. To cast, v.r.

टीक् *ṬÎK,* i. 1, Âtm. To go.

टीका *ṭîkâ,* f. A commentary.

टौक् *ṬAUK* (a form of *trauk*), i. 1, Âtm. To go, to approach, v. r.—Cf. *ḍhauk,* with *upa.*

† **ट्वल्** *ṬVAL,* i. 1, Par. To be confused, v.r.—Cf. *ḍval.*

ठ *ṬH.*

ठक्कुर *ṭhakkura,* m. A deity, a honorary title, Râjat. 7, 536.

ड *Ḍ.*

† **डप्** *ḌAP,* i. 10, *ḍâpaya,* Âtm. To collect.

डम् *ḌAM,* i. 1 or 6, Par. To sound, Prab. 55, 6.

डमरिन् *ḍamarin* and **डमरु** *ḍamaru,* m. A kind of drum, Bhâg. P. 8, 10, 7; Prab. 55, 6.

† **डम्प्** *ḌAMP,* v.r. for *ḍap.*

डम्ब् *ḌAMB,* i. 10, Par. To cast. —With the prep. **वि** *vi,* **1.** To imitate, Ragh. 4, 17. **2.** To simulate, Hariv. 8406. **3.** To deride, to sneer, Hariv. 1. **4.** To deceive, Bhartṛ. 1, 21. *viḍambita,* Low, poor, distressed.

डम्बर *ḍambara,* **I.** adj. **1.** Renowned, Mâlat. 3, 8, Lass. *vâch* - m. Graceful and eloquent language. **II.** m. **1.** A proper name, MBh. 9, 2541. **2.** A mass, assemblage (as of blossoms), Mâlat. 48, last l., 148, 8; (of clouds), Mahâvîr. 99, 17; Böhtl. Ind. Spr. 37.

डम्भ् *ḌAMBH,* v.r. of *ḍap.*

डाकिनी *ḍâkinî* (probably a form of *çâkinî*), f. A kind of female demon, Kathâs. 18, 147.

डाकिनीत्व *ḍâkinî + tva,* n. The character of a Ḍâkinî, Daçak. 164, 17.

डांकृति *ḍâṁkṛiti,* i.e. *ḍâm,* an imitative sound, *-kṛiti,* f. Sound, Prab. 55, 6.—Cf. *tâṁkṛita.*

डामर *ḍâmara,* **1.** m. An object causing surprise, Gît. 12, 23. **2.** The name of a people, Râjat. 5, 51.

डिण्डिम *ḍiṇḍima,* m. A kind of drum, Râm. 5, 13, 49,

† **डिप्** *ḌIP,* **डिम्प्** *ḌIMP,* i, 10, Âtm. To collect. **डिप्** *ḌIP,* i. 4; 6 and 10, Par., and **डिम्ब्** *ḌIMB,* i. 10, Âtm. To cast.

डिम्ब *ḍimba,* m. **1.** An affray, conflict, MBh. 1, 1219; a battle without king, i.e. after the king has been slain (?), Man. 5, 95. **2.** An egg or ball, Mâlat. 148, 8.

† **डिम्भ्** *ḌIMBH,* i, 10, Âtm. To collect.

डिम्भ *ḍimbha,* m. and f. *bhâ,* A child, Çâk. p. 103, 11 (Prâkṛ.).

डी *ḌÎ* (akin to 1. *ḍi,* q. cf.), i. 1 and 4, Âtm. To fly. Ptcple. of the pf. pass. *ḍîna,* n. Flying, the flight of a bird, MBh. 8, 1899.—With the prep.

अति *ati, atiḍîna*, n. Flying over, MBh. 8, 1900.—With अभि *abhi, abhiḍîna*, n. Flying towards, MBh. 8, 1900.—With अव *ava, avaḍîna*, n. Flying down, MBh. 8, 1899.—With उद् *ud*, To fly up, Pańch. 106, 1. *uḍḍîna*, Flown up, MBh. 7, 776. n. 1. Flying up, MBh. 8, 1899. 2. The flight of a bird, Pańch. 114, 25.—With प्रोद् *pra-ud*, To fly up and away, Mṛichchh. 84, 22. *proḍḍîna*, Flown up and away, Râm. 4, 63, 24.—With नि *ni, niḍîna*, n. Flying down, MBh. 8, 1899.—With परा *parâ, parâḍîna*, n. Flying away, MBh. 8, 1900.—With परि *pari, pariḍîna*, n. Flying round, MBh. 8, 1900.—With प्र *pra, praḍîna*, Flown forth, Râm. 6, 83, 26; n. Flying forward, MBh. 8, 1899.—With वि *vi, viḍîna*, n. Flying apart, MBh. 8, 1900.—With सम् *sam, saṁḍîna*, n. Flying together, MBh. 8, 1899.—With अवसम् *ava-sam, avasaṁḍîna*, n. Flying down together, MBh. 8, 1901.

डीनक *ḍîna+ka* (vb. *ḍî*) in *ḍîna-ḍînaka*, A kind of flying, MBh. 8, 1900.

डुण्डुभ *ḍuṇḍubha*, m. A kind of lizard, Amphisbæna, MBh. 1, 984.—Cf. *duṇḍubha*.

डोम्ब *ḍomba*, m. A man of a low caste, who gains his livelihood by singing and dancing, Râjat. 5, 353.

डौण्डुभ *ḍauṇḍubha*. i.e. *ḍuṇḍubha + a*, n. The body of a ḍuṇḍubha, MBh. 1, 1006.

ड्वल् *ḌVAL*, Caus. *ḍvâlaya*, with the prep. आ *â*, To mix (ved.).

ढ *ḌH*.

ढक्क *ḍhakka*, 1. m. A kind of sacred edifice (?), Râjat. 5, 305. 2. f. *kâ*, A large drum, Râjat. 6, 133.

ढौक् *ḌHAUK* (a form of *trauk*), i. 1, Âtm. To approach, Çâk. 63, 14 Ch. Caus. 1. To offer, Râjat. 445. 2. To procure, Kathâs. 26, 7.—With the prep. उप *upa*, Caus. 1. To offer, Hit. 67, 20, v.r. *upa ṭaukayâmaḥ*. 2. To perform, Pańch. 158, 4.

ढौकन *ḍhauk+ana*, n. Bestowing, Râjat. 6, 166.

त *T*.

तंस् *TAṀS*, i. 1 and 10, Par. 1. To shake (ved.). 2. † To adorn.

तक् *TAK*, 1. ii. 2, Par. Âtm. ved. To start. 2. † i. 1, Par. To laugh, or to endure.

तक्र *takra*, i.e. *tańch+ra* n. Buttermilk mixed with water, Man. 8, 326.

तक्ष् *TAKSH*, i. 1, Par. (also Âtm.), and ii. 5, *takshṇu*, Par. 1. To slice (wood), MBh. 5, 4161. 2. To cut to pieces, to wound, MBh. 3, 1585. 3. To prepare, to form (ved.). 4. † To cover with a hide.—With the prep. अनु *anu*, To sharpen, Chr. 292, 3 = Rigv. i. 86, 3.—With सम् *sam*, To cut to pieces, to wound, MBh. 6, 3725.—Cf. Lat. tignum; O.H.G. dehsa (an axe), dîhsila, A.S. thixl, thisl; Lat. temo, and probably O.H.G. dahs (a badger); *τάσσω*; see *takshan*.

तक्षक *taksh+aka* m. A cutter, a wood-cutter, Râm. 2, 80, 2.

तक्षण *takshaṇa*, i.e. *taksh+ana*, n. Planing, Man. 5, 115.

तक्षन् *taksh+an*, m. A carpenter, Man. 4, 210 (read *takshṇo vâ*).—Cf. τέκτων.

तक्षशिला *takshaçilâ*, f. The name of a town, Τάξιλα, Râm. 4, 43, 23.

तगर *tagara*, n. An ornamental plant, Tabernæmontana coronaria, and an aromatic powder made of it, MBh. 13, 5042.

† **तङ्क्** *TAṄK*, i. 1, Par. To live in distress.

† **तङ्ग्** *TAṄG*, i. 1, Par. **1.** To go. **2.** To stumble. **3.** To shake.

तज्ज्ञ *tajjña*, i.e. *tad-jña*, m. **1.** Knowing that, a connoisseur, Bhâg. P. 3, 11, 20. **2.** Versed in, Hariv. 8427.

तञ्च् *TAÑCH*, **1.** ii. 7, *tanach*, *tañch*, Par. To contract.—With the prep. **आ** *â* and **अभ्या** *abhi-â*, To curdle (ved.). **2.** † i. 1, Par. To go.

तञ्ज् *TAÑJ*, v.r. of 1. *tañch*.

तट् *TAṬ*, i. 1 or 6, Par. To groan (ved.). † i. 1. To rise; i. 10, *tâṭaya*, Par. v.r. of 1. *taḍ*.

तट *taṭa*, I. m. **1.** Slope, MBh. 1, 1567. **2.** Horizon, Kathâs. 26, 26. **II.** m. and f. *ṭî*, and n. **1.** A bank, MBh. 13, 1334. **2.** Often without a special signification as latter part of a comp. whose former part denotes a portion of the human body, e.g. *adhara-*, The lips, Gît. 4, 23; *kaṭi-*, The hip, Indr. 2, 32; *kaṇṭha-*, The throat, Râjat. 5, 1; *jaghana-*, The buttocks, Bhartṛ. 1, 49; *lalâṭa-*, The forehead, Çiç. 9, 28; *çravaṇa-*, The ear, Ṛit. 5, 13; *stana-*, The bosom, Amar. 21.—**Comp.** *A-*, adj. steep, Çâk. d. 137. *Diç-*, m. the end of the horizon, Râjat. 3, 253. *Vidruma-*, adj. f. *tâ*, having banks of coral, Bhâg. P. 3, 15, 22.

तटस्थ *taṭa-stha*, adj. Indifferent, Mâlat. 7, 10.

तटाक *taṭâ+ka*, cf. *taṭa*, m. and n. A pond, Râm. 2, 68, 19.

तटिनी *taṭinî*, i.e. *taṭa+in+î*, f. A river, Râjat. 3, 339.—**Comp.** *A-mara-*, f. a name of the Gaṅgâ, Bhartṛ. 3, 87.

तट्य *taṭya*, i.e. *taṭa+ya*, adj. Dwelling on slopes, MBh. 12, 10381.

1. **तड्** *TAḌ* (a form of *tṛid*, based on the original form *tard*), i. 10, *tâḍaya* (anom. pf. *tatâḍa*, Bhâg. P. 6, 12, 1), Par. **1.** To strike, Man. 4, 169. **2.** To chastise, Man. 4, 164. **3.** To wound, MBh. 1, 5302. **4.** Pass. To beat, Suçr. 1, 265, 15. **5.** To play a musical instrument, Varâh. Bṛih. S. 45, 61.—With the prep. **अभि** *abhi*, **1.** To strike, MBh. 7, 531. **2.** To wound, Râm. 2, 36, 13.—With **आ** *â*, To strike, Pañch. 235, 23.—With **परि** *pari*, To touch, Kathâs. 6, 114.—With **प्र** *pra*, To strike, MBh. 8, 4693.—With **प्रति** *prati*, To strike in one's turn, MBh. 13, 4562.—With **वि** *vi*, **1.** To cast, Pañch. 263, 8. **2.** To wound, MBh. 8, 1067.—With **सम्** *sam*, To strike, MBh. 7, 3401.

† 2. **तड्** *TAḌ*, i. 10, *tâḍaya*, Par. To shine, or speak.

तडाक *taḍâka*, m. and n. A pond.—Cf. *taṭâka*.

तडाकिन् *taḍâkin*, i.e. *taḍâka+in*, adj., f. *nî*, Provided with ponds, MBh. 3, 16088.

तडाग *taḍâga*, m. and n. A pond, Man. 4, 203.—Cf. *taḍâka*.

तडागवन्त् *taḍâga+vant*, adj., f.

vati, Provided with ponds, MBh. 13, 2973.

तडित् *tad+it,* f. Lightning, Kir. 5, 46.—Comp. *Sendrâyudha-,* i.e. *sa-indra-âyudha,* adj. with a rainbow and lightning.

तडित्वन्त् *tadit+vant,* adj. 1. Containing lightnings, Kir. 5, 4. 2. Flashing, Vikr. d. 14.

तडिन्मय *tadinmaya,* i.e. *tadit+maya,* adj. Resembling lightning, Kumâras. 5, 25.

† **तण्ड्** *TAND* (akin to *tad*), i. 1, Âtm. To strike. .

तण्डुल *tand+ula,* m. Grain after threshing and winnowing, especially rice, Pańch. 104, 20; Râm. 3, 76, 24.

तत *tata,* m. The father, Bhâg. P. 9, 4, 1.

ततस् *ta+tas* (cf. *tad*), adv. 1. = the abl. of *tad,* Man. 4, 82; with preceding *yatas,* Indiscriminately (literally, From whomsoever), Man. 4, 15. 2. From that place, Sâv. 5, 78. *yatas-yatas—tatas-tatas,* Wherever—from that place, Bhâg. P. 7, 15, 13. 3. Thither, Râm. 1, 44, 34. *yatas-yatas—tatas-tatas,* Wherever—thither, Çâk. d. 23. 4. *tatas-tatas,* Everywhere, Râm. 1, 35, 18. 5. *itas-tatas,,* From here and there, Râm. 6, 96, 2; here and there, 3, 61, 16. 6. *yatas-tatas,* From wherever, Pańch. i. d. 6. 7. Afterwards, then, Man. 2, 60. 8. Therefore, MBh. 12, 13626.

ततामह *tatâmaha,* i.e. *tata-mahant,* m. A grandfather, Bhâg. P. 6, 9, 40.

तति *tati,* i.e. *tan+ti,* f. A troop, Çâk. d. 39.

तत्त्व *tattva* (often *tatva*), i.e. *tad+tva,* 1. The very essence, Man. 4, 92; Bhag. 18, 1. 2. Truth, Çâk. d. 22. 3. A principle (especially the 25 of the Sânkhya philosophy), Râm. 3, 53, 42. Instr. *tvena,* 1. Truly, Râm. 1, 48, 13. 2. Thoroughly, Man. 7, 68.—Comp. *Nis-,* adj. not contained in the principles, MBh. 12, 11480. *Yathâ-tattva+m.* adv. truly, Chr. 17, 22. *Sa-,* I. adj. knowing the real essence, Vedântas. in Chr. 219, 3. II. n. natural property, nature.

तत्त्वतस् *tattva+tas,* adv. 1. According to the principles, Man. 8, 229. 2. Truly, Man. 8, 32. 3. From the bottom, Man. 7, 10.

तत्त्ववन्त् *tattva+vant,* adj. Possessing the principles or reality, MBh. 12, 11480.

तत्र *ta+tra* (cf. *tad*), adv. I.=the loc. of *tad,* 1. In that, Man. 3, 60. 2. *tatra-tatra,* On that continually, Nal. 5, 9. 3. On account of that, Nal. 18, 10. 4. *yatra-tatra,* For every trifle, MBh. 13, 514. II. There, Man. 7, 146. III. Thither, Nal. 7, 1. IV. *tatra-tatra,* Here and there, Man. 7, 81. V. *yatra-tatra,* Indiscriminately (literally, Wherever), MBh. 13, 3686. VI. Thereby, Man. 8, 34. VII. Then, Man. 8, 238.

तत्रत्य *tatra+tya,* adj. Being there, Bhâg. P. 3, 31, 6.

तत्व *tatva,* see *tattva.*

तथा *ta+thâ* (see *tad*), adv. 1. So, correl. to *yathâ,* As, Man. 3, 258; correl. to *iva,* Man. 3, 181. 2. Thus, in that manner, Man. 1, 4. 3. *yathâ-tathâ,* By all means, Man. 4, 17. 4. *yathâ-yathâ—tathâ-tathâ,* As far — so far, Man. 4, 20; in proportion, 8, 285; the more—the more, Nal. 8, 14. 5. Yes, Râm. 1, 2, 22. 6. So, in an oath, correl. to *yathâ,* e.g. *yathâ nânyaṁ varaṁ dhyâyâmi kaṁ chana tvâm ṛite—tathâ mûrdhânam â labhe,* I touch my head, in token that I have not thought of any bridegroom beside thee, Chr. 7, 16. **7.** Also, and, Man. 1, 24.—**Comp.** *Yathâ-tatha+m*, adv. Properly, suitably. *A-yathâ-tatha+m*, adv. without fruit, Man. 3, 240. *Vi-tatha*, adj. false, Man. 8, 118; with *kṛi*, To annul, 9, 73. °*tham*, adv. Falsely, 8, 94. *a-vitatha*, I. adj. true. II. n. truth.

तथाविधेय *tathâvidheya*, i.e. *tathâ-vidha+eya* (see *vidhâ*), adj. Being thus, MBh. 4, 246.

तथ्य *tathya*, i.e. *tathâ+ya*, I. adj. True, MBh. 7, 2136. II. n. Truth, Râm. 2, 34, 23. III. instr. *yena*, Truly, MBh. 8, 274.

तथ्यतस् *tathya+tas*, adv. Truly, Râjat. 1, 325.

तद् *tad*, except the nom. sing. m. and f., the base of the m. and n. and most derivatives is *ta*, of the f. *tâ*; the nom. sing. m. is *sas*, f. *sâ*. I. third personal pronoun, **1.** He, she, it, that, Man. 2, 234; 8, 11. **2.** Combined with the pronouns of the first, second, and third persons, Here, MBh. 1, 6415; 5, 5957; Hiḍ. 1, 38. **3.** Combined with the relative pronoun, a. Without a special signification, MBh. 7, 427. b. Every one, MBh. 13, 1674; whoever, Böhtl. Ind. Spr. 2429. c. with *vâ*, This or that, Man. 12, 68. **4.** Repeated, This and that, Man. 12, 74; with following *eva*, The same, Râm. 3, 50, 28. **5.** *yad-yad—tad-tad*, Whatever, that, Man. 4, 159. II. n. The universe, Râm. 6, 102, 25. III. acc. sing. n. *tad*, adverbially, **1.** Then, Pańch. 48, 3. **2.** Therefore, Man. 9, 41. IV. instr. *tena*, **1.** Thus, Man. 4, 178. **2.** Therefore, Man. 7, 36. V. abl. *tasmât*, Therefore, Man. 1, 108.—Cf. ὁ, ἡ, τό; Lat. te, ta, tud in iste, etc.; Goth. sa, so, thata; A.S. se, seo, thaet.

तदा *ta+dâ*, see *tad*, adv. **1.** Then, Nal. 1. 25; at that time, Man. 1, 52. **2.** From that time, MBh. 13, 2231.

तदात्व *tadâ+tva*, n. Present time, Man. 7, 163.

तदानीम् *tadânîm*, i.e. *tadâ+na+î+m*, adv. Then, at that time, Draup. 6, 10.

तदीय *tad+îya*, adj. **1.** Belonging, or referring, or proper, to him, her, it, that, Râm. 4, 21, 35; Pańch. i. d. 224. Vedântas. in Chr. 202, 8. **2.** Such, Kathâs. 3, 47.

तद्वत् *tad+vat*, adv. **1.** Thus, Pańch. ii. d. 62. **2.** Thus also, Pańch. i. d. 254. **3.** And, Kathâs. 6, 48.

तद्वत्ता *tadvat+tâ*, f. Harmony, Vedântas. in Chr. 202, 8.

तद्वन्त् *tad+vant*, adj., f. *vatî*, Possessed of that (i.e. the previously mentioned *udbhûta-rûpa*), Bhâshâp. 53.

1. तन् *TAN*, ii. 8, *tanu*, Par., Âtm. **1.** To draw (a bow), MBh. 4, 141. **2.** To spread, Bhag. 2, 17. **3.** To cover, Çiç. 9, 23. **4.** To propagate, Hariv. 2386. **5.** To augment, Çâk. d. 19. **6.** To direct, Nalod. 1, 20. **7.** To arrange, Man. 4, 205. **8.** To cause (pleasure or pain), Ragh. 3, 25; Bhâg. P. 1, 18, 37. **9.** To speak, Daçak. 7 ult. Pass. *tanya*, and *tâya*; ptcple. *tata*.—With the prep. अति *ati*, *atitata*, Very haughty, Çiç. 19, 3.—With अधि *adhi*, To cover, Râm. 5, 12, 33.—With अनु *anu*, **1.** To augment, MBh. 12, 4816. **2.** To maintain, MBh. 3, 12681.—With अव *ava*, **1.** To descend, *avatata*, Descending, Hariv. 3621. **2.** To cover, MBh. 6, 2066.——With आ *â*, **1.** with *padam*, To get a footing, Bhartṛ. 1, 32. **2.** To stretch, MBh. 5, 4164; to draw, Ragh.

1, 19. **3.** To effuse, Çâk. d. 193. **4.** To grant, Bhâg. P. 5, 24, 22. **5.** To cause, Bhartṛ. 1, 50. **6.** To arrange, Bhartṛ. 1, 36.—With समा *sam-â*, To procure, Râjat. 4, 247. *samâtata*, Violent, MBh. 8, 4205.—With प्र *pra*, **1.** To spread, Suçr. 1, 354, 5. **2.** To show, Çiç. 2, 30. **3.** To cover, Râm. 3, 76, 25. **4.** To begin (a sacrifice), MBh. 12, 9613. **5.** To cause, Râjat. 2, 78.—With वि *vi*, **1.** To spread out, MBh. 1, 1335. **2.** To stretch out, Mṛichchh. 143, 21. **3.** To draw, MBh. 1, 5290. **4.** To cover, Râm. 3, 33, 13. **5.** To arrange (a sacrifice), Man. 3, 28. **6.** To show, Râm. 4, 9, 89. *vitata*, **1.** Large, Bhâg. P. 5, 16, 7. **2.** Powerful, Râjat. 5, 22.—With आवि *â-vi*, To illuminate, Bhâg. P. 5, 20, 37. —With प्रवि *pra-vi*, *pravitata*, **1.** Large, Megh. 104. **2.** Begun, MBh. 5, 5317.—With सम् *sam*, **1.** To cover, Râm. 6, 21, 1. **2.** To fill up, Bhâg. P. 8, 23, 14. **3.** To expand, Bhâg. P. 1, 3, 37. *saṁtata*, **1.** Uninterrupted, Lass. 96, 9. **2.** Eternal. **3.** Extended. **4.** Much. °*tam*, adv. Eternally. Caus. *tânaya*, To cause to be performed, Bhâg. P. 4, 7, 16.—With अनुसम् *anu-sam*, **1.** To spread, Bhag. 15, 2. **2.** To cover, Râm. 5, 16, 8.—With अभिसम् *abhi-sam*, To cover, Hariv. 4986. —Cf. τάνυμαι, ἔκ-τατος (=*tata*), τιταίνω (for τιταɴjω), τείνω (for τεɴjω), ἐπιτηδές (for ταν + tvas); Lat. tenere, tendere, ostendere (for obs-), tenus, etc.; O.H.G. danjan; A.S. thenian; see also *tanu*.

2. तन् *TAN* (akin to *stan*), i. 4, Par. To sound (ved.).—Cf. τόνος; Lat. tonare; O.H.G. donar; A.S. thunor.

† 3. तन् *TAN* (or वन् *VAN*), i. 1 and 10, *tânaya*, Par. **1.** To believe. **2.** To assist (or to afflict, or to be afflicted). **3.** To sound (cf. 2. *tan*). **4.** With prepositions, To stretch (cf. 1. *tan*).

तनय *tanaya* (vb. 1. *tan*, anomal. Caus. + *a*), **I.** adj. Continuing a family, Chr. 291, 14=Rigv. i. 64, 14. **II.** m. **1.** A son. **2.** du. A son and a daughter. **III.** f. *yâ*, A daughter.—Comp. See *Ku-*. *Pavana-*, m. Hanumant, the son of the wind. *Râdhâ-*, m. Karṇa. *Sûrya-*, I. m. 1. Karṇa. 2. Sugrîva. II. f. *yâ*, the Yamunâ river.

तनु *tan + u*, **I.** adj., f. *nu* and *nvî*, **1.** Thin, Râm. 2, 8, 42 Gorr. **2.** Delicate, Nal. 12, 106. **3.** Moderate (in quantity and size), Man. 3, 10. **4.** Small, MBh. 3, 1747. Comparat. *tanîyaṁs*, Râjat. 3, 223, and *tanutara*, Amar. 3. Superl. *tanishṭha* and *tanutama*. **II.** f. *nu* and *nû*, **1.** The body, Man. 2, 28; Râm. 1, 16, 5. **2.** A person, Man. 4, 184. **3.** One's own self, Hariv. 2386. **III.** f. *nvî*, A slender woman, Bhartṛ. 1, 71.—Comp. *A-*, adj. large, MBh. 3, 6028. *Ardha-*, f. half a body. *Vâmana-*, adj. dwarf-bodied. *Su-*, I. adj. very delicate. II. f. a woman.—Cf. Lat. tenuis; O.H.G. dunni, A.S. thyn; ταvεῖα (=*tanvî*), ταναός for ταναϝός (cf. ταναύπους), i.e. ταvυ + o.

तनुक *tanu + ka*, adj. Small, Suçr. 1, 296, 12.

तनुज *tanu-ja*, m. A son, Pañch. v. d. 22.

तनुता *tanu + tâ*, f. **1.** Smallness, meagerness, Râm. 5, 19, 22; Megh. 83. **2.** in *kalabha-*, Condition of having the body of a young elephant, Megh. 79.—Comp. *Su-*, f. Great meagerness, Lass. 72, 10.

तनुत्र *tanu-tra* (vb. *trâ*), n. A coat of mail, MBh. 4, 1009.

तनुत्रवन्त् *tanutra* + *vant,* adj. Covered with a coat of mail, Râm. 6, 76. 21.

तनुत्व *tanu* + *tva,* n. Smallness, delicateness, MBh. 13, 541.

तनुस् *tan* + *us,* n. The body, Râm. 5, 93, 23.

तनूज *tanû-ja* (see *tanu*), I. m. A son, Râm. 2, 43, 20. II. f. *jâ,* A daughter, Chr. 52, 10.

तनूनपात् *tanû-napât,* m. Fire, or its deity, Hit. ii. d. 66 (read *-pâto*).

तन्तु *tan* + *tu,* m. **1.** A thread, MBh. 1, 806; epithet of the supreme deity, Being the thread, Bhâg. P. 8, 16, 31. **2.** A cobweb, Vedântas. in Chr. 206, 13. **3.** A filament, Bhartṛ. 2, 6. **4.** Series, Bhâg. P. 8, 13, 36. **5.** Propagation of a family, race, MBh. 8, 3393; 3, 15363 (on whom depends the propagation). **6.** Issue, Man. 9, 203.—**Comp.** *Âçâ-,* m. A thread of hope, Mâlat. 151, 6. *Tṛishṇâ-,* m. the thread of desire, MBh. 12, 7877. *Nis-,* adj. without offspring, MBh. 12, 6225. *Prajâ-,* m. race, Bhâg. P. 1, 12, 15. *Saptat°,* i.e. *saptan-,* m. a sacrifice. *Sûtra-,* m. a thread.

तन्तुक *tantu* + *ka,* **1.** a substitute for *tantu,* as latter part of a comp. adj., A string, Bhartṛ. 1, 95. **2.** m. A kind of snake, Suçr. 2, 265, 13.

तन्तुवाय *tantuvâya,* i.e. *tantu-ve* + *a,* m. A weaver, Man. 8, 397.

तन्त्र् *TANTR,* i. 10 (rather a denomin. derived from the following word), Par. **1.** To perform in a regular succession, MBh. 12, 7814. **2.** Âtm. To maintain a family, to govern, Çâk. d. 102, v.r.

तन्त्र *tan* + *tra,* I. n. **1.** A warp, MBh. 1, 806. **2.** A series, propagation, offspring, MBh. 13, 2567. **3.** A system, a totality, Bhâg. P. 3, 144; order, MBh. 1, 4171. **4.** The order of ceremonies, a ritual, Bhâg. P. 2, 6, 25. **5.** Necessary or indispensable act, or provision, Râm. 3, 61, 28; 2, 7, 19 Gorr. **6.** Main point, MBh. 14, 612; essence, Bhâg. P. 3, 30, 10; principle, MBh. 12, 7663. **7.** Rule, Yâjñ. 1, 228. **8.** Science, Bhâg. P. 3, 7, 30. **9.** A religious or scientific work, a literary work in general, Bhâg. P. 1, 3, 8; 9, 21, 6; Râm. 4, 17, 15. **10.** Part of a work, Suçr. 1, 3, 13; Pañch. pr. d. 3. **11.** A class of mystical and magical writings, treating particularly of spells, charms, etc. **12.** Spell, Pañch. i. d. 80. **13.** An army. **II.** f. *rî* (nom. sing. *tantris*), **1.** A string, Man. 4, 38; of a bow, MBh. 12, 4375; of a musical instrument, Megh. 84. **2.** Music of a string-instrument, Bhâg. P. 1, 6, 39.—**Comp.** *A-tantrî,* adj. n. *tri,* without strings, Râm. 2, 39, 29. *Âtmatantra,* i. e. *âtman-,* adj. independent, MBh. 13, 4399. *Ku-tantrî,* f. the tail, MBh. 12, 5355. *Pañchatantra,* i.e. *pañchan-,* n. Five books, the title of a work. *Para-tantra,* adj. dependent upon another, MBh. 13, 15. *Su-tantrî,* adj., n. *tri,* Melodious, Ṛit. 1, 3. *Sva-tantra,* adj. 1. independent. 2. of age. *A-sva-tantra,* adj. dependent, not of age, Daçak. in Chr. 180, 17.

तन्त्रक *tantra* + *ka,* a substitute for *tantra,* as latter part of comp. words, e.g. *pañchatantraka,* i.e. *pañchan-,* n. The five books, title of a work.

तन्त्रवाय *tantra* + *vâya,* cf. *tantuvâya,* m. A weaver, Râm. 2, 90, 15 Gorr.

तन्त्रि *tantri,* **1.** for *tantrî* (see *tantra*), Râm. 6, 28, 26. **2.** for *tandri,* MBh. 13, 6538 (ought to be corrected; also

तन्त्रित *tantrita,* sometimes for *tandrita,* e.g. MBh. 12, 12713).

तन्त्रिन् *tantrin,* i.e. *tantra + in,* m. A soldier, Râjat. 5, 248.

तन्त्री *tantrî,* see *tantra.*

तन्द् *TAND,* i. 1 (or 6), Âtm. To slacken (ved.).

तन्द्रा *tandrâ,* i.e. *tand + ra,* f. **1.** Lassitude, Suçr. 1, 13, 8. **2.** Want of energy, MBh. 14, 874; Hit. i. d. 29.

तन्द्रालु *tandrâ + lu,* adj. Weary, Suçr. 2, 403, 4.

तन्द्रि *tand + ri,* I. m. or n. Fatigue, Bhâg. P. 3, 20, 40. II. f. *rî,* The same, Râm. 2, 80, 24 Gorr. — **Comp.** *A-tandrî,* and *nis-tandri,* adj. unwearied, indefatigable, MBh. 12, 12585, Râm. 2, 1, 18.

तन्द्रिता *tandritâ,* i.e. *tandrin + tâ,* Lassitude, MBh. 12, 10512.

तन्द्रिन् *tandrin,* i.e. *tandrâ + in,* adj., f. *iṇî,* Lazy, MBh. 12, 7740.—**Comp.** *A-,* adj. 1. without remissness, Man. 3, 279. 2. unwearied.

तन्मय *tanmaya,* i.e. *tad + maya,* adj. Having the essence of him, her, it, that, MBh. 3, 1143.

तन्मयता *tanmaya + tâ,* f. and

तन्मयत्व *tanmaya + tva,* n. Identity with him, her, it, that, Bhâg. P. 1, 2, 2; MBh. 5, 1622.

तन्मात्र *tanmâtra,* i.e. *tad-mâtra,* I. n. **1.** That only, Pańch. i. d. 284. **2.** An atom, or rudimentary element, Vedântas. in Chr. 206, 19. **II.** adj. Consisting of atoms, Bhâg. P. 3, 10, 15.

तन्मात्रता *tanmâtra + tâ,* f. and

तन्मात्रत्व *tanmâtra + tva,* n. The condition of being an atom, or rudimentary principle, Mârk. P. 45, 46, Bhâg. P. 3, 26, 33.

1. तप् *TAP,* i. 1. Par. (also Âtm. MBh. 1, 8414), i. 4, Âtm. or pass. (also Par. MBh. 1, 3165). **I.** i. 1, **1.** To warm, to heat, Râm. 1, 14, 17. **2.** To be warm, MBh. 2, 1333. **3.** To shine, Çâk. d. 111; to illuminate, Bhag. 11, 19. **4.** To burn up, to consume, Bhâg. P. 7, 3, 4. **5.** To give pain, MBh. 1, 3323. **II.** i. 1, and i. 4, or pass., **1.** To suffer pain, MBh. 8, 1794; MBh. 1, 6217; 1, 3165, **2.** To mortify one's flesh, Râm. 1, 58, 1, and 4 Gorr.; usually with *tapas,* To do penance, Man. 2, 167; 166. **III.** i. 4, To become warm, Lass. 12, 19 (with the termination of the Par.). Ptcple. of the pf. pass. *tapta,* **1.** Hot, Man. 8, 272. **2.** Molten, Varâh. Bṛih. S. 6, 13. **3.** also *tapita,* Refined, MBh. 3, 1722; Hariv. 13035. Ptcple. of the fut. pass. *tapanîya,* n. Gold, Râm. 6, 70, 41. *tapya,* Doing religious penance, MBh. 12, 10381 (cf. 13, 750). Caus. and i. 10, Par. and Âtm., *tâpaya,* Par. **1.** To warm, to heat, MBh. 12, 5536; to burn, Râm. 6, 11, 44. **2.** To torment, Râm. 5, 32, 36; by mortification, Chr. 46, 23. **3.** To mortify one's flesh, MBh. 3. 8199. Anomal. ptcple. of the pres. Âtm. *tâpayâna,* MBh. 15, 855. Frequentat. *tâtapya,* To suffer violent pain, Râm. 1, 11, 8.—With the prep. अति *ati,* i. 1, To heat excessively, Râm. 3, 12, 8. *atitapta,* Very afflicted, Râm. 3, 66, 26. Caus. To heat excessively, MBh. 14, 506.—With अनु *anu,* i. 4, or pass. To suffer pain, MBh. 3, 13720. i. 1, and 4, **1.** To repent, MBh. 5, 1822; Râm. 2, 42, 11. **2.** To grieve, to long for (with the acc.), MBh. 11, 182; 7, 2195. *anutapta,* Hot, Suçr. 2, 181, 14. Caus. To cause to grieve, Ragh. 8, 88.—With समनु *sam-anu,* i. 4, or pass. To re-

pent, MBh. 13, 5335. — With अभि *abhi*, i. 4, or pass., To suffer pain, Râm. 2, 62, 5; Kathâs. 21, 72-; MBh. 7, 6555 (with the termination of the Par.). *abhitapta*, 1. Heated, Bhâg. P. 3, 6, 11. 2. Illuminated, Ṛit. 4, 14. 3. Tormented, MBh. 6, 5771. Caus. To torment, MBh. 7, 1417.—With अव *ava*, Caus. To illuminate, MBh. 5, 7162.—With आ *â*, i. 4, or pass. 1. To suffer pain, Bhâg. P. 3, 31, 13. 2. To mortify one's flesh, Bhâg. P. 2, 9, 8. *âtapta*, Refined, Hariv. 15769.—With *ud*, i. 1, To torment, Çic. 9, 67; to afflict, Râjat. 3, 183; *uttapta*, Nealed, purged by fire, Râjat. 4, 368; *uttapta tâmra*, Pure copper. Caus. To warm, MBh. 12, 11884. —With उप *upa*, i. 4, or pass. To become hot, MBh. 3, 71; to suffer pain, Suçr. 1, 21, 16. *upatapta*, Hot, Râm. 2, 59, 9. Caus. To torment, to mortify, MBh. 3, 10708. — With समुप *sam-upa*, i. 4, or pass. To suffer pain, MBh. 2, 856.—With निस् *nis*, of which the *s* becomes *sh*, i. 1, To purify, MBh. 7, 9458. *nishṭapta*, 1. Singed, MBh. 1, 8215. 2. Warmed, MBh. 13, 1796. 3. Roasted, Râm. 2, 97, 2. 4. Refined, MBh. 6, 228.—With विनिस् *vi-nis*, *vinishṭapta*, Well roasted, Râm. 3, 76, 10.—With परि *pari*, i. 1, 1. To set on fire, Râm. 3, 35, 15. 2. i. 1, and i. 4, or pass. To suffer pain, Râm. 2, 66, 7; MBh. 3, 9916; 14, 1070 (with the termination of the Par.). 3. i. 4, or pass. To mortify one's flesh, MBh. 1, 4784. Caus. To torment, Râm. 5, 86, 9.—With विपरि *vi-pari*, i. 4, or pass. To suffer much pain, Râm. 2, 19, 3, Gorr.—With पश्चात् *paçchât*, i. 4, or pass. To repent, MBh. 8, 1795.—With प्र *pra*, i. 1, To heat, Bhag. 11, 30; to burn, MBh. 3, 881; to roast, Râm. 2, 91, 65. 2. To shine, MBh. 13, 2125. 3. To illuminate, Bhâg. P. 5, 1, 30. 4. To suffer pain, Râm. 2, 12, 1. 5. To mortify one's flesh, Râm. 1, 67, 8. 6. To torment, MBh. 6, 5567. i. 4, or pass. To suffer pain, Bhâg. P. 5, 18, 21. Caus. 1. To warm, Man. 4, 53; to heat, Mârk. P. 14, 60. 2. To illuminate, Râm. 4, 60, 16. 3. To set on fire. 4. To torment, MBh. 4, 550; 6, 3103. Anomalous *pratâpitâ* (fut. i) instead of *pratâpayitâ*, MBh. 8, 1971.—With अभिप्र *abhi-pra*, *abhipratapta*, 1. Dried, Suçr. 1, 158, 12. 2. Tormented, Râm. 2, 21, 54.—With संप्र *sam-pra*, *sampratapta*, Suffering, Suçr. 1, 70, 17.—With प्रवि *pra-vi*, *pravitapta*, Tormented, Kâm. Nîtis. 15, 9.—With सम् *sam*, i. 1, To repent, MBh. 7, 4731. i. 4, or pass. 1. To suffer pain, Bhartṛ. 2, 84. 2. To mortify one's flesh, Râm. 1, 63, 26. *saṁtapta*, 1. Heated, Râm. 4, 44, 26. 2. Molten, Varâh. Bṛih. S. 32, 10. 3. Dried, Râm. 2, 85, 17. 4. Tormented, Ṛit. 1, 27. 5. *saṁtapta-vakshas*, Short-breathed. Suçr. 2, 447, 7. Caus. 1. To warm, Hit. i. d. 81. 2. To burn, MBh. 1, 1270. 3. To set on fire, MBh. 13, 3998. 4. To torment by heat, Bhartṛ. 2, 86; to torment, Pañch. iii. d. 244.—With अतिसम् *ati-sam*, *atisaṁtapta*, Much afflicted, Râm. 3, 68, 15.—With अभिसम् *abhi-sam*, *abhisaṁtapta*, Tormented, Râm. 4, 57, 13.—With परिसम् *pari-sam*, To suffer pain, Râm. 4, 21, 11. —Cf. τέφρα, Τέμπεα; Lat. tepeo; probably A.S. thâfian (to suffer, to allow), concerning the signification cf. Sskr. *ksham*.

† 2. तप् *TAP*, i. 4, Âtm. To govern.

तप *tap+a*, I. adj. 1. Illuminating. 2. Tormenting, e.g. *paraṁtapa*. II. m. 1. Heat, Pańch. 121, 13. 2. The hot season, Çiç. 1, 66. 3. Penance, Hariv. 15434.—Comp. *Su-*, adj. having accomplished great religious austerity.

तपन *tap+ana*, I. adj. 1. Warming, shining, Râm. 6, 79, 57. 2. Tormenting, MBh. 12, 10381. II. m. 1. The sun, Râm. 1, 16, 11. 2. The name of a hell, Man. 4, 89.

तपनीयमय *tapaníya+maya* (vb. *tap*), adj., f. *yí*, Golden, MBh. 7, 4389.

तपस् *tap+as*, n. 1. Fire, Man. 6, 23. 2. Penance, mortification, religious austerity, devotion, Man. 1, 33. 3. The name of a month, January—February, Suçr. 1, 19, 8.—Comp. *A-*, adj. one who does not practise austerities, Man. 4, 190. *Dírgha-*, adj. practising long-lasting austerities, Râm. 1, 59, 11 Gorr. *Pańchatapas*, i.e. *pańchan-*, adj. sitting exposed to five fires, i.e. four blazing around him with the sun above, Man. 6, 23. *Mahâ-*, or *su-tapas*, adj. one who has practised great religious austerities, Chr. 39, 4. *Su-mahâ-*, adj. one who has practised very great religious austerities, Chr. 11, 23.

1. **तपस्य** *TAPASYA*, a denominat. derived from *tapas* by *ya*, Par. To mortify one's flesh, Bhag. 9, 27; Kir. 5, 49.

2. **तपस्य** *tapas+ya*, I. m. The name of a month, February—March, Suçr. 1, 19, 8. II. n. Religious penance, MBh. 13, 445.

तपस्विता *tapasvitâ*, i.e. *tapasvin+tâ*, f. Religious penance, MBh. 13, 2896.

तपस्विन् *tapas+vin*, I. adj. 1. Distressed, Bhâg. P. 1, 9, 48. 2. Devout, Man. 4, 162. II. m. An ascetic, one engaged in the practice of rigorous and devout penance, Bhag. 6, 46.—Comp. *Ati-*, exceedingly devout, Chr. 25, 60.—See *Ku-*.

तपिष्णु *tap+ishṇu*, adj. Burning, MBh. 12, 11726.

तपीयंस् *tap+iyaṁs*, comparat. of *tapasvin*, A most rigorous ascetic, Bhâg. P. 2, 9, 8.

तपोमय *tapomaya*, i.e. *tapas+maya*, adj., f. *yí*. 1. Consisting in religious penance, Bhâg. P. 2, 4, 19. 2. Devout.

तपोवन्त् *tapovant*, i.e. anomalous, *tapas+vant*, adj. Practising religious austerities, devout, MBh. 12, 8548.

तप्तृ *tap+tṛi*, m. One who heats, MBh. 1, 8414.

तम् *TAM*, i. 4, *tâmya*, Par. (also Âtm., Râm. 2, 63, 50), 1. To become breathless, Suçr. 1, 120, 16. 2. To breathe with difficulty, Râjat. 5, 344. 3. To become exhausted, Râm. 2, 52, 25. 4. To be distressed, Amar. 7. 5. To become staring, immoveable, Amar. 8. 6. To choke (ved.). 7. † To desire. Ptcple. of the pf. pass. *tânta*, Distressed, Kathâs. 24, 65. Caus. *tamaya*.—With the prep. **आ** *â*, To become breathless, Râm. 2, 63, 50.—With **उद्** *ud*, 1. To become breathless, Râm. 2, 65, 45 Gorr. 2. To be distressed, Râjat. 6, 124.—With **नि** *ni* in *nitânta*, Excessive, much, Pańch. i. d. 139. °*ta+m*, adv. Much, excessively, Râjat. 4, 634; violently, Bhâg. P. 4, 8, 15.—With **परि** *pari*, To gasp. Suçr. 2, 447, 7.—**प्र** *pra*, 1. To become breathless, Suçr. 1, 121, 1. 2. To become exhausted, MBh. 12, 12241. 3. To be beside one's self, Râm. 2, 12, 105.—With **सम्** *sam*,

To become exhausted, Git. 4, 21.—Cf. probably Lat. temere, con-tumax, temetum, abs-temius perhaps O.H.G. damf, damfjan, an old Causal (to choke).

तम *tama* =*ishṭatama* in Kirât. 2, 13.

तमक *tam+aka*, m. A kind of asthma, Suçr. 1, 159, 12.

तमस् *tam+as*, n. **1.** Darkness, Hit. pr. 16. **2.** The gloom of hell, Man. 4, 242. **3.** The name of a hell, Mârk. P. 12, 10. **4.** =Râhu, or the personified ascending node, Râm. 2, 63, 2. **5.** One of the three guṇas, or qualities incident to creation, the property of darkness, whence proceed folly, ignorance, stupidity, worldly delusion, etc., Man. 12, 24. Comp. *Dîrgha-*, m. The name of a Ṛishi, MBh. 2, 293.—Cf. O.H.G. demar; A.S. dim, thystre; Lat. tenebrae.

तमस *tamas+a*, I. n. a substitute for *tamas*, when the latter part of a comp. word, e.g. *sam-*, n. Intense darkness, Çiç. 9, 22. II. f. *sâ*, The name of a river, Râm. 1, 2, 4.

ऽतमस्क *-tamas+ka*, a substitute for *tamas*, when latter part of a comp. adj., Bhâg. P. 7, 1, 11. *nis-*, adj. Free from darkness, Çâk. d. 165.

तमस्विन् *tamas+vin*, I. adj. f. *nî*, Dark. II. f. *nî*, Night, MBh. 4, 732.

तमाल *tamâla*, i.e. *tam+a+âla*, m. The name of a dark-coloured tree, Xanthochymus pictorius Roxb., Râm. 3, 21, 14.

तमालक *tamâla+ka*, m. and n.= *tamâla*, Râm. 2, 91, 48.

तमिस्र *tamisra*, i.e. *tamas+ra*, I. n. Darkness, a dark night, MBh. 4, 710. II. f. *râ*, A night without moon or star, Ragh. 5, 13.—Comp. *A-*, adj. without darkness, Çiç. 9, 12.

तमी *tamî*, i.e. *tam+a+î*, f. Night, Çiç. 9, 23.

तमोघ्न *tamoghna*, i.e. *tamas-ghna*, m. The sun, MBh. 3, 193.

तमोनुद् *tamonud*, i.e. *tamas-nud*, I. adj. Removing darkness, MBh. 13, 7298. II. m. Light, *nashṭa-* (vb. *naç*), adj. Dark, Râm. 5, 32, 23.

तमोनुद *tamonuda*, i.e. *tamas-nud +a*, I. adj., f. *dâ*, Removing darkness, Man. 1, 6. II. m. **1.** The sun, MBh. 3, 11892. **2.** The moon, Ragh. 3, 33.

तमोपह *tamopaha*, i.e. *tamas-apa -ha* (vb. *han*), adj. Removing darkness, Kir. 5, 22.

तमोभूत *tamobhûta*, i.e. *tamas-bhûta* (vb. *bhû*), adj. **1.** Dark, involved in darkness, Man. 1, 5. **2.** Foolish, Man. 12, 115.

तमोमय *tamomaya*, i.e. *tamas+ maya*, I. adj., f. *yî*. **1.** Consisting of darkness, Bhâg. P. 3, 22, 19. **2.** Involved in darkness, Râjat. 4, 583. II. m. Wrath, Mârk. P. 47, 15.

तमोवन्त् *tamovant*, i. e. anomal. *tamas+vant*, adj., f. *vatî*, Dark, Râm. 4, 44, 115.

† **तम्ब्** *TAMB*, i. 1, Par. To go.

तय् *TAY* (originally an anomal. pass. of *tan*, cf. *tây*), i. 1, Âtm. **1.** To go. **2.** † To preserve.

तर *tara*, i.e. *tṛî+a*, I. adj. Conquering, MBh. 12, 10380. II. m. **1.** Passage, crossing, Man. 8, 407. **2.** Freight, Man. 8, 406. **3.** A certain spell for banishing demons, Râm. 1, 30, 4.—Comp. *Dus-*, adj., f. *râ*. 1. hard to be crossed or traversed, Râm. 2, 28, 9; Man. 4, 242. 2. hard to be overcome, Râm. 3, 2, 46. 3. irresistible, Bhâg. P. 3, 16, 32.

A-su-, adj. hard to be surmounted, Kir. 5, 18.

तरक्षु *tarakshu*, m. A hyena, Râm. 2, 94, 7.

तरङ्ग् *TARAṄG*, a denomin. derived from the next, Par. To move to and fro, Gît. 2, 8.

तरङ्ग *taraṅga*, i.e. *tara* + *m* + *ga*, m. 1. A wave, Pańch. 263, 20; signifying a section of a book, Kathâs. 2. The gallop of a horse, Gît. 12, 20. 3. Moving to and fro, Hariv. 4298.—Comp. *Ud-*, adj. with high waves, Ragh. 7, 33.

तरङ्गित *taraṅgita*, i.e. *taraṅga* + *ita*, I. adj. 1. Wavy, MBh. 6, 3851. 2. Overflowing, Kathâs. 18, 223. II. n. Moving to and fro, Gît. 3, 13.

तरङ्गिन् *taraṅgin*, i.e. *taraṅga* + *in*, I. adj., f. *iṇî*. 1. Wavy, Râm. 2, 71, 2. 2. Unsteady, Gît. 5, 19. II. f. *iṇî*, A river, Bhartṛ. 3, 65.—Comp. *râjataraṅgiṇî*, i.e. *râjan-*, f. title of a historical poem.

तरण *taraṇa*, i.e. *tṛî* + *ana*, n. 1. Passing over, crossing, Râm. 6, 11, 4. 2. Overcoming, MBh. 1, 6054.—Comp. *Dus-*, adj., f. *ṇî*, difficult to be crossed, MBh. 8, 3905. *Pratipa-*, n. crossing over (literally, crossing against the stream), Vikr. d. 24 (read *uhyamânasya*, instead of *udyamânasya*, which would be the ptcple. pres. pass. of *und*; cf. Lenz. App. cr.).

तरणि *taraṇi*, i.e. *tṛî* + *ani*, I. adj., f. *ṇî*, Overcoming, Hariv. 14078. II. m. 1. The sun, Bhâg. P. 5, 1, 30. 2. (? or f.), A boat, Prab. 83, 10.

तरत्समन्दीय *taratsamandîya*, i.e. *tarat sa mandî* + *iya*, n. A hymn of the Rigveda (9, 58), beginning *tarat sa mandî*, Man. 11, 253.

तरल *tarala*, i.e. *tṛî* + *ala*, I. adj., f. *lâ*. 1. Trembling, tremulous, MBh. 1, 1234; 4, 269. 2. Sparkling, Çâk. d. 25. 3. Fickle, Râjat. 3, 515. II. m. The central gem of a necklace, MBh. 8, 4913. III. f. *lâ*, Spirituous liquor, Varâh. Bṛih. S. 75, 12.

तरलता *tarala* + *tâ*, f. Sprightliness, Pańch. i. d. 205.

तरलय *TARALAYA*, a denomin. derived from *tarala*, Par. 1. To cause to tremble, Amar. 87. 2. To move to and fro, Gît. 12, 15.

तरस् *taras*, i.e. *tṛî* + *as*, 1. Speed (ved.). 2. Energy, Râm. 5, 77, 18. 3. Strength, Ragh. 11, 77. Instr. °*sâ*, adv. Speedily, Hiḍ. 4, 2.

तरस्विन् *taras* + *vin*, adj., f. *nî*. 1. Swift, energetic, Bhâg. P. 8, 20, 31; MBh. 1, 2546. 2. Bold, Çâk. 90, 19.

तराम् + *tarâm*, acc. sing. f. of the aff. *tara*, is joined to indeclinables, i.e. verbs and adverbs in the signification of a comparative, Pańch. i. d. 368.

तरि and तरी *tarî*, i.e. *tṛî* + *ĭ*, f. A boat, MBh. 1, 4014; 4228.

तरिक *tarika*, i.e. *tara* + *ika*, m. A ferry-man, Yâjń. 2, 263.

तरित्र *taritra*, i.e. *tṛî* + *tra*, n. A boat, MBh. 5, 2436.

तरु *taru*, i.e. *tṛî* + *u* (for original *tar* + *van*), m. A tree, Râm. 6, 82, 115.—Comp. *Kalpa-*, m. a fabulous tree fulfilling all wishes, Pańch. v. d. 8. *Chhâyâ-*, m. a shady tree, Megh. 1. *Prati-*, adv. at every tree. *Çikhâ-*, m. a lampstand.—Cf. perhaps Lat. termes.

तरुण *taruṇa*, i.e. *tṛî* + *van* + *a* (cf. the last), I. adj., f. *ṇî*. 1. Young, MBh. 4, 1108. 2. Fresh, Suçr. 1, 191, 8. 3. Vivid, Bhartṛ. 3, 86. 4. Beginning,

Suçr. 2, 52, 16. II. m. A young man, Pañch. i. d. 11. III. f. ṇî, A young woman, Râm. 3, 59, 1 ; Daçak. in Chr. 186, 22. IV. n. Cartilage, Suçr. 1, 35, 1.—Cf. τέρην, τέρεινα.

तरुणाय *TARUṆÂYA*, a denomin. derived from the last by *ya*, Âtm. **1.** To become young, Hariv. 4745. **2.** To remain young, Pañch. v. d. 15.

तरुता *taru+tâ*, f. Condition of a tree, being a tree, Mârk. P. 31, 9.

तर्क् *TARK*, i. 10, Par. (in epic poetry also Âtm., Hariv. 11402), **1.** To suppose, Râm. 5, 18, 22. **2.** To utter one's supposition, Çâk. 83, 5, v. r. **3.** To find out, Kathâs. 26, 18 ; Nal. 11, 36. **4.** To reflect, MBh. 3, 1723. **5.** To bear in mind, MBh. 5, 1895. **6.** To intend, MBh. 3, 1894. **7.** † To shine or speak. Ptcple. of the pf. pass. *tarkita*, n. Supposition, Hariv. 9467. *a-*, adj. Unexpected, Hariv. 4467. Ptcple. of the fut. pass. *tarkaṇîya*, To be suspected, MBh. 5, 1093. Comp. *A-tarkya*, and *nis-*, adj. incomprehensible, Bhâg. P. 3, 33, 3 ; MBh. 12, 11299.—With the prep. अनु *anu*, **1.** To suppose, Bhâg. P. 1, 18, 32. **2.** To bear in mind, MBh. 3, 1722.—With परि *pari*, To reflect, Râm. 5, 30, 18. *a-paritarkita*, adj. **1.** Not examined, Râm. 2, 109, 16. **2.** Unexpected, Hariv. 4500.—With प्र *pra*, To search, to investigate, MBh. 12, 6687. *a-pratarkya*, adj. Undiscoverable by reason, inconceivable, Man. 1, 5.—With संप्र *sam-pra*, To think, Hariv. 13804.—With वि *vi*, **1.** To suppose, Pañch. 35, 5. **2.** To guess, MBh. 1, 3571. **3.** To take for, Suçr. 1, 298, 17. **4.** To reflect, Râm. 5, 35, 39. **5.** To infer, Kathâs. 7, 67. *a-vitarkita*, adj. Not anticipated, Râm. 2, 69, 21. *durvitarkya*, i.e. *dus-*, adj. Hard to be imagined, Bhâg. P. 7, 10, 53.—With संवि *sam-vi*, To reflect, MBh. 4, 234.—With सम् *sam*, To take for, MBh. 1, 6540.— Cf. ἀ-τρεκής, probably also ἄ-τρακτος (cf. *tarku*) ; Lat. torquere, torcular, torques, torvus ; O.H.G. drajan, N.G. drehen.

तर्क *tark+a*, I. m. **1.** Supposition, Râm. 5, 71, 12. **2.** Consideration, Pañch. iii. d. 258. **3.** Logical reasoning, logic, Man. 12, 106 ; MBh. 2, 453. **4.** A philosophical system, Prab. 86, 14. II. f. *kâ*, Logical reasoning, MBh. 4, 892.—Comp. *Ku-*, and *Dus-*, m. wrong reasoning, Bhâg. P. 5, 13, 22 ; 6, 9, 35.

तर्कक *tarka+ka*, adj. Poor (?), MBh. 12, 1537.

तर्किन् *tarkin*, adj., f. *iṇî*. **1.** i.e. *tark+in*, Supposing, Çâk. 103, 19. **2.** i.e. *tarka+in*, Skilled in speculation, Man. 12, 111.

तर्कु *tark+u*, m. (?), A spindle.

तर्कुट *tark+uṭa*, I. n. Spinning. II. f. *ṭî*, A distaff, a spindle.—Comp. *Sûtra-*, f. *ṭî*, A distaff, a spindle.

तर्ज् *TARJ*, i. 1, Par. (in epic poetry also Âtm., MBh. 7, 6131), **1.** To menace, Râm. 2, 96, 26. **2.** To blame, MBh. 8, 1543. Caus. and i. 10, Âtm. **1.** To menace, Ragh. 12, 41. **2.** To blame, Hariv. 11166. **3.** To terrify, Râm. 6, 98, 31. **4.** To ridicule, MBh. 5, 2485. *tarjita*, n. Menacing, Râm. 5, 66, 22.—With अभि *abhi*, **1.** To menace, Râm. 3, 55, 32. **2.** To blame, Ṛit. 5, 6, v.r.—With समभि *sam-abhi*, The same, MBh. 7, 7176.—With परि *pari*, To menace, Râm. 5, 42, 9.—With वि *vi*, **1.** To menace, Bhâg. P. 8, 11, 30. **2.** To blame, Ṛit. 5, 6.—With सम् *sam*, 1. To menace, Râm. 3, 68, 43. 2. To blame, Râm. 4, 61, 26.—Cf. A.S. threagan (to chide); O.H.G. drawjan, N.G. drohen.

तर्जन *tarj+ana*, I. n. 1. Menacing, Daçak. in Chr. 195, 20. 2. Blaming, Râm. 5, 66, 3. 3. Terrifying, MBh. 3, 12569. II. f. *nâ*, Menacing, Sâh. D. 66, 11. III. f. *ní*, The forefinger, Kathâs. 17, 88.

तर्णक *tarṇaka*, probably akin to *taruṇa*, m. A calf, Râjat. 5, 431.

तर्द् *TARD*, i. 1, Par. To kill; see *tṛid*.

तर्पण *tarpaṇa*, i.e. *tṛip+ana*, n. 1. Satisfaction given or received, Kathâs. 26, 236; MBh, 14, 673. 2. An oblation to the deities or Manes, Yâjñ. 1, 46; Man. 3, 70. 3. Pleasing, Bhâg. P. 3, 1, 27. 4. A sweetmeat (?), MBh. 18, 269. —Comp. *Apa-*, n. fasting (in sickness). *Ghrâṇa-tarpaṇa*, 1. adj. smelling sweetly, Hariv. 3710. 2. n. perfume, Râm. 2, 94, 14. *Pitṛi-*, n. oblation to the Manes, Man. 2, 176.

† तर्ब् *TARB*, i. 1, Par. To go.

तर्ष *tarsha*, i.e. *tṛish+a*, m. Thirst, desire, MBh. 12, 4296.

तर्षण *tarshaṇa*, i.e. *tṛish+ana*, n. Desiring, Bhâg. P. 3, 25, 7.

ऽतर्षुल *-tarshula*, i.e. *tṛish+ula*, in *a-tarshula+m*, adv. Without desire, MBh. 12, 7762.

तर्हि *ta+rhi*, see *tad* (probably for *tatra-hi*), adv. 1. At that time, Bhâg. P. 1, 8, 12. 2. Then, therefore, Bhâg. P. 3, 9, 32.

† तल् *TAL*, i. 1 and 10. To fulfil a vow.

तल *tala*, m. and n. 1. Surface, MBh. 3, 2412. 2. Bottom, Râm. 5, 13, 11. 3. Without a special signification, as latter part of many comp. words, e.g. *nabhas-tala=nabhas*, Heaven, Bhâg. P. 2, 1, 27. 4. The palm, Arj. 3, 40; often compounded with a word denoting hand, e.g. *pâṇi-tala*, MBh. 13, 5013. 5. Sole of the foot, Râm. 5, 13, 47; usually compounded with a word signifying foot, e.g. *pâda-tala*, MBh. 13, 7444. 6. That which is under or below anything, under, Hit. 43, 21; Mṛichchh. 34, 11; Man. 2, 59 (*aṅgushṭhamûlasya tale*, Under the root of the thumb). 7. (also f. *lâ*), A leathern fence worn by archers on the left arm, MBh. 6, 621 (*tala-baddha=baddhatala*, Having put on a leathern fence, etc., cf. *talatra*), Râm. 2, 87, 23.—Comp. *A-*, n. the name of a hell, Vedântas. in Chr. 209, 2. *Adhas-*, m. or n. that which is under anything, Pañch. 187, 5. *Kara-*, m. or n. the palm, Râm. 2, 66, 17. *Talâtala*, i.e. *tala-a-tala*, n. the name of a hell, Vedântas. in Chr. 209, 2. *Pâda-*, n. the sole of the foot. *Bhû-*, n. the earth, Pañch. 43, 7. *Mahâ-*, n. the name of a hell, Vedântas. in Chr. 209, 2. *Mahi-*, m. or n. the earth, Râm. 3, 52, 36. *Rasâ-*, n. 1. the lowest of the seven hells, Vedântas. in Chr. 209, 2. 2. the lower regions, Bhartṛ. 2, 32. *Vaṭa-*, under a fig-tree, Pañch. 9, 23. *Vi-*, n. one of the seven hells. *Vṛiksha-*, n. the foot of a tree. *Çilâ-*, n. the surface of a stone. *Su-*, m. one of the hells. *Hasta-*, m. 1. the palm of the hand. 2. the hand. 3. the tip of an elephant's trunk.

तलतस् *tala+tas*, adv. From the bottom, Çiç. 9, 20.

तलत्र *tala+tra* (vb. *trâ*), n. A leathern fence worn by archers on the left arm, MBh. 6, 1673.—Comp. *Sa-*, adj. with leathern fences, MBh. 8, 616.

तलिन् *talin*, i.e. *tala+in*, adj., f. *ní*,

Wearing the leathern fence of the archers (see *tala*, 7), MBh. 5, 5367.

तल्प *talpa*, m. and n. 1. A bed, Man. 3, 3. 2. A turret, MBh. 1, 7577. —Comp. *Guru-*, m. one who violates the bed of his guru, i.e. of his father or teacher, Man. 9, 237.

तल्पक *talpa*+*ka*, m. One who makes beds, Kâm. Nîtis. 12, 45.

तल्पज *talpa-ja*, adj. Brought forth in the marriage-bed, Man. 9, 167.

तवस् *tavas*, i.e. *tu*+*as*, adj. Strong, Chr. 291, 12=Rigv. i. 64, 12.—Comp. *Sva-*, adj. possessed of own or innate strength, Chr. 290, 7=Rigv. i. 64, 7.

तविषी *tavishî*, i.e. *tavas*+*a*+*î*, f. Strength, Chr. 290, 5=Rigv. i. 64, 5.

† **तस्** *TAS*, i. 4, Par. 1. To wane, 2. To cast, v.r. 3. To cast aloft.

तस्कर *tas-kara* (probably for *atas-*), m. A thief, Man. 4, 133.

तस्करता *taskara* + *tâ*, f., and

तस्करत्व *taskara* + *tva*, n. Theft, Ragh. 1, 27; Daçak. in Chr. 193, 15.

तस्थु *tasthu* (from *tasthus*, the weak form of the ptcple. pf. Par. of *sthâ*), adj. Immoveable, Bhâg. P. 7, 7, 23.

ताड *tâḍa*, i.e. *taḍ*+*a*, adj. Striking, Man. 10, 33.

ताडन *tâḍana*, i.e. *taḍ*+*ana*, I. adj., f. *nâ*, Striking, Râm. 1, 30, 17 Gorr. II. n. (The act of) striking, Yâjń. 1, 151.

ताडयितृ *tâḍayitṛi*, i.e. *taḍ*+*tṛi*, m. One who strikes, Yâjń. 2, 203.

ताडाग *tâḍâga*, i.e. *taḍâga*+*a*, adj. Being in ponds, Suçr. 1, 170, 11.

ताण्डव *tâṇḍava*, m. and n. Frantic dancing, Chaurap. 7; Râjat. 5, 380.

ताण्डवित *tâṇḍavita*, i.e. *tâṇḍava*+*ita*, adj. Dancing, fluttering, Prab. 21, 10; frowning, 85, 15.

तात *tâta*, m. 1. voc. sing. Dear; a caressing word used by parents addresssing their children, MBh. 1, 4728; by teachers addressing their pupils, Râm. 1, 2, 7; by children addressing their fathers, MBh. 1, 6796. 2. A father, Râm. 2, 53, 10.—Cf. *tata*.

तात्कर्म्य *tâtkarmya*, i.e. *tad-karman*+*ya*, n. Homogeneousness of occupation, Sâh. D. 13, 15.

तात्कालिक *tâtkâlika*, i.e. *tad-kâla*+*ika*, adj. 1. Lasting a time of equal length, MBh. 12, 12785. 2. Instantly appearing.

तात्पर्य *tâtparya*, i.e. *tad-para*+*ya*, n. 1. Purport, Bhâshâp. 83. 2. Aim, Bhartṛ. Suppl. 19. 3. Object, Vedântas. in Chr. 203, 24.

तादात्म्य *tâdâtmya*, i.e. *tad-âtman*+*ya*, n. Identity, Bhâg. P. 5, 1, 27.

तादृक्ष *tâdṛiksha*, i.e. *tad-dṛiç*+*sa*, adj. Such one, Râjat. 4, 242.

तादृश् *tâdṛiç*, i.e. *tad-dṛiç*, adj. 1. Such one, Râjat. 5, 425. 2. Equal, Pańch. 38, 15; 19.—Cf. Lat. talis, and see the next.

तादृश *tâdṛiça*, i.e. *tad-dṛiç*+*a*, adj., f. *çî*. 1. Such like, Daçak. in Chr. 185, 13. 2. Such one, Man. 5, 34. 3. Equal, Bhâg. P. 4, 27, 14. 5. With preceding *yâdṛiça*, Indiscriminate, Pańch. i. d. 435; compounded, MBh. 13, 5847.—Cf. τηλίκος.

तान *tâna*, i.e. *tan*+*a*, m. 1. A thread, Suçr. 1, 93, 17. 2. A musical tone, MBh. 2, 133.—Comp. *Eka-*, 1. adj. turning one's attention wholly upon an object, Bhâg. P. 7, 9, 8. 2. m. attention directed only to one object, Bhâg. P. 4, 20, 27. – Cf. τόνος.

तानव *tânava*, i.e. *tanu* + *a*, n. 1. Meagerness, Râjat. 4, 25. 2. Smallness, Bhartṛ. 1, 36.

तान्तव *tântava*, i.e. *tantu* + *a*, n. Woven cloth, Man. 9, 329. — Comp. *Çaṇa-*, adj., f. *vî*, woven of hemp, Man. 2, 42.

तान्त्र *tântra*, i.e. *tantrî* + *a*, n. Instrumental music, Râm. 1, 3, 70 Gorr.

तान्त्रिक *tântrika*, i.e. *tantra* + *ika*, I. m. One versed in a system, Bhâshâp. 148. II. adj. Taught in a work of the Tantra-class, Bhâg. P. 8, 6, 9.

ताप *tâpa*, i.e. *tap* + *a*, m. 1. Heat, Man. 12, 76. 2. Pain, MBh. 1, 4405. 3. Sorrow, Râm. 2, 22, 10.—Comp. *Paçchât-*, m. repentance.

तापत्य *tâpatya*, i.e. *tapatî*, a proper name, + *ya*, 1. adj. Relating to Tapatî, MBh. 1, 387. 2. metronym. A descendant of Tapatî, MBh. 1, 6505.

तापन *tâpana*, i.e. *tap*, Caus., + *ana*, I. adj., f. *nî*, Tormenting, MBh. 1, 1178. II. m. The sun, MBh. 5, 1739. III. n. 1. Heating, Suçr. 1, 151, 13. 2. Mortifying, MBh. 13, 1098. 3. The name of a hell, Yâjń. 3, 224.

तापनीय *tâpanîya*, i.e. *tapanîya* (vb. *tap*) + *a*, adj. Golden, MBh. 1, 8188.

तापस *tâpasa*, i.e. *tapas* + *a*, I. adj., f. *sî*. 1. Performing penance, a practiser of religious austerities, an ascetic, Man. 6, 27; MBh. 1, 3006. 2. Referring to religious penance, Râm. 2, 52, 5 Gorr. II. m. A sort of sugar-cane, Suçr. 1, 186, 15.—Comp. *Kapaṭa-*, m. a feigned ascetic, Kathâs. 24, 208. *Ku-*, m. and f., *sî*, a wicked ascetic, Kathâs. 13, 141.

तापस्य *tâpasya*, i.e. *tâpasa* + *ya*, n. The condition of an ascetic, Man. 1, 114; Chr. 45, 10.

तापिच्छ *tâpichchha*, m. A tree, Xanthochymus pictorius Roxb., Gît. 11, 11.

तामरस *tâmarasa*, I. n. A lotus, Râm. 3, 76, 14. II. f. *sî*, A pond full of lotus flowers, MBh. 4, 220.

तामस *tâmasa*, i.e. *tamas* + *a*, I. adj., f. *sî*. 1. Belonging to the dark *guṇa*, or quality, MBh. 12, 33. 2. Immersed in darkness, Man. 12, 40. 3. Referring to the Manu Tâmasa (see II.), Bhâg. P. 8, 1, 28. II. m. The name of a Manu, Man. 1, 62. III. f. *sî*, Night, Râjat. 1, 137.

तामिस्र *tâmisra*, i.e. *tamisra* + *a*, I. adj. With and without *paksha*, The dark half of the month, from full-moon to new-moon, MBh. 3, 11813. II. m. 1. Wrath, MBh. 14, 1019. 2. The name of a hell, Man. 4, 88.—Comp. *Andha-*, n. the name of a hell, Man. 4, 88.

ताम्बूल *tâmbûla*, n. and f. *lî*, Betel, Piper betel, Lin. Suçr. 1, 223, 2; Bhartṛ. 1, 48.—Comp. *Vâsa-*, n. betel mixed with fragrant substances, Daçak. 88, n. 2 Wils.

ताम्बूलिक *tâmbûlika*, i.e. *tâmbûla* + *ika*, m. A seller of betel, Râm. 2, 90, 23 Gorr.

ताम्र *tâmra* (vb. *tam*, cf. *tamas*), I. adj. 1. f. *râ*, Of a coppery-red colour, Râm. 2, 34, 13. 2. f. *rî*, Of copper, Râm. 3, 21, 17. II. n. 1. Copper, Man. 5, 114. 2. A sort of sandal, Râm. 2, 83, 17.

ताम्रक *tâmra+ka*, n. Copper, Yâjń. 1, 296.

ताम्रकुट *tâmra+kuṭa*, see *kuṭṭa*.

ताम्रत्व *tâmra+tva*, n. Coppery-red (the colour), Râm. 5, 85, 2.

ताम्रमय *tâmra+maya*, adj., f. *yî*, Coppery, Pańch. 241, 10.

ताम्रिक *tâmrika*, i.e. *tâmra+ika*, adj. Of copper, Man. 8, 136.

† **ताय्** *TÂY*, i. 1, Âtm. (properly pass. of *tan*), **1.** To spread. **2.** To protest.

तार *târa*, A. i.e. *tṛî+a*, I. adj. **1.** Saving, MBh. 13, 6986. **2.** Piercing, Mṛichchh. 44, 10; °*ra+m*, adv. Sounding loud, 92, 13. **II.** m. and n. A shrill loud sound, MBh. 7, 6737. **III.** m. **1.** A pearl, Gît. 11, 25. **2.** A proper name, Râm. 1, 3, 24. **B.** (for original *stâra*, cf. 3.*stṛi*), **I.** (m.), f. *râ* (and n.), **1.** A star, Râm. 1, 35, 16. **2.** The pupil of the eye, Ṛit. 6, 31. **II.** f. *râ*, **1.** A certain meteor, perhaps a shooting-star, Varâh. Bṛih. S. 32, 1. **C.** f. *râ*. **1.** The knowledge which arises from reasoning in regard to the principles, the conditions of intellect, the elemental creation, Tattvas. 41 Ball. **2.** The name of deities, MBh. 5, 3972; of a monkey, Râm. 1, 1, 67. **D.** n. Silver, Bhâg. P. 4, 6, 27.—Comp. *Dus-*, adj. difficult to be crossed or overcome, MBh. 6, 2337; Bhâg. P. 6, 14, 26.

तारक *târaka*, I. i.e. *tṛî+aka*, adj., f. *rikâ*, **1.** Bringing over, Râm. 2, 97, 23 Gorr. **2.** Saving, Prab. 25, 17. **II.** m. A proper name, MBh. 6, 4249. **III.** f. *rakâ*, and n. **1.** A star (see *târa* B.), Bhâg. P. 2, 5, 11; MBh. 5, 5390. **2.** The pupil of the eye, Râm. 3, 52, 34.

तारकामय *târakâ+maya* (*târakâ* =*târâ*, proper name), adj., f. *yî*, On account of Târâ, MBh. 2, 939.

तारकित *târakita*, i.e. *târakâ+ita*, adj. Starry, bestarred, Daçak. in Chr. 179, 14.

तारण *târaṇa*, i.e. *tṛî+ana*, I. adj., f. *ṇî*, Saving, Hariv. 7022. **II.** n. **1.** Crossing, passing over, Mṛichchh. 146, 25. **2.** Overcoming, MBh. 4, 135. **3.** Saving, MBh. 1, 1050. **4.** An implement of sacrifice (?), MBh. 14, 2668.

तारणेय *târaṇeya*, patronym. MBh. 1, 6363.

तारतम्य *târatamya*, i.e. *tara-tama*, the affixes of the comparative and superlative, *+ya*, n. More or less, proportion, Bhâg. P. 5, 26, 2. **2.** State or condition, Mṛichchh. 157, 20.

तारिक *târika*, i.e. *tṛî+ika*, n. Toll for passage, Man. 8, 407.

तारिन् *târin*, i.e. *tṛî+in*, adj., f. *iṇî*, Saving, MBh. 6, 797.

तारुण्य *târuṇya*, i.e. *taruṇa+ya*, n. Youth, Pańch. i. d. 196.

तार्किक *târkika*, i.e. *tarka+ika*, m. A dialectician, Vedântas. in Chr. 211, 6.

तार्क्ष *târksha*, m. **1.** A kind of bird, Suçr. 1, 334, 11. **2.** A kind of plant, 2, 498, 19. **3.** A name of Kaçyapa, Bhâg. P. 6, 6, 2. **4.** erroneously instead of *târkshya*, e.g. Hariv. 6966.

तार्क्ष्य *târkshya*, I. m. **1.** A fabulous being, sometimes fancied as a horse, sometimes as a bird, MBh. 1, 2548, identical with Garuḍa, Hariv. 7460. **2.** A bird (?), Suçr. 2, 162, 4. **3.** A kind of antidote, Suçr. 2, 275, 21. **II.** n. A certain medicine, Suçr. 2, 69, 13.

तार्ण *târṇa*, i.e. *tṛiṇa+a*, adj. Made of grass, MBh. 1, 996.

तार्तीय *târtîya*, i.e. *tṛitîya* + *a*, adj. **1.** Belonging to the third, Bhâg. P. 3, 6, 29. **2.** Third, 8, 19, 34.

ताल *tâla*, I. m. **1.** The palmyra tree, or fan palm, Borassus flabelliformis, Râm. 1, 1, 64; used as banner, MBh. 6, 1811. **2.** Slapping or clapping the hands together, Megh. 77; often compounded with a word denoting hand, MBh. 13, 1397. **3.** Slapping together in general, Ragh. 9, 71. **4.** Musical measure, Pańch. v. d. 43; MBh. 13, 995. **5.** A sort of cymbal, Pańch. 20, 8. II. n. The fruit of the palmyra tree, Hariv. 3711. III. f. *lî*, The name of a tree, Corypha taliera Roxb., Râm. 4, 43, 6.—Comp. *Apara-*, m. the name of a country, Râm. 2, 68, 12. *Eka-tâla*, adj. endowed with one tree, Ragh. 15, 23. *Kâṁsya-*, m. a cymbal, Râjat. 5, 464. *Tala-*, m. slapping the hands together, MBh. 3, 12379. *Manas-*, m. the lion of Durgâ. *Su-rata-* (see *ram*), f. *lî*, 1. a female messenger, a go-between. 2. a chaplet.

तालावचरण *tâlâvacharaṇa*, i.e. *tâla-ava-char* + *ana*, m. A dancer, Râjat. 3, 335.

तालिक *tâlika*, i.e. *tâla* + *ika*, I. m. Slapping the hands together, Pańch. ii. d. 137. II. f. *kâ*, The palm, Hariv. 9920.

तालिन् *tâlin*, i.e. *tâla* + *in*, adj. Provided with cymbals, MBh. 13, 1172.

तालीयक *tâlîyaka*, i.e. *tâla* + *îya* + *ka*, A cymbal, Râm. 5, 13, 54.

तालु *tâlu*, n. and m. and **तालूषक** *tâlûshaka*, The palate, Ṛit. 1, 11; MBh. 14, 568; Yâjń. 3, 87.

तावक *tâvaka*, i.e. *tava*, gen. sing. of *yushmad*, + *aka*, possess. pron., f. *kî*, Thine, Râm. 3, 13, 15.

तावद्धा *tâvaddhâ*, i.e. *tâvant* + *dhâ*, adv. So many times, Ragh. 12, 45, Calc.

तावन्त् *tâvant*, i.e. *tad* + *vant*, I. adj., correl. of *yâvant*, Man. 8, 155; of *yathâ*, Nal. 20, 24. **1.** So much, Man. 9, 249. **2.** So long, Man. 1, 72. **3.** Just so many, Man. 1, 64. **4.** So manifold, Ragh. 12, 45 (v.r.). **5.** Compounded with numerals, As much, e.g. *dvis-*, Twice as much, MBh. 4, 289. II. °*vat*, acc. ntr., adv. **A.** combined with a correlative, **1.** So much, Râm. 1, 73, 21. **2.** So long, Man. 2, 235; combined with *yâvat na*, As long as not, Till, Hit. pr. 39; sometimes also without *na*, Man. 8, 27. **3.** In that time, then, Lass. 5, 11. **B.** Without a correlative, **1.** Meanwhile, MBh. 13, 2727. **2.** For a while, Man. 4, 174. **3.** At first, Hit. 45, 1. **4.** Just, Daçak. in Chr. 188, 22. **5.** With *mâ*, Not for heaven's sake, Çâk. 66, 22. **6.** With *na*, Not yet, MBh. 1, 1273; not at all, Râm. 6, 5, 4. **7.** Indeed, Râm. 5, 49, 2. **8.** Even, Râm. 5, 49, 27. **9.** Only, Man. 3, 53.—Comp. *Dvis-*, twice as much, Hariv. 6927.—Cf. τῆμος=*tâvat*, also τέως, ταῦς, τηΰσιος (=*tâvat* + *ya*); Lat. tantus (for tâvant + o).

तास्कर्य *tâskarya*, i.e. *taskara* + *ya*, n. Theft, Man. 9, 222.

† **तिक्** *TIK*, i. 1, Âtm. To go. ii. 5, Par. **1.** To go. **2.** To assail. **3.** To seek to injure. **4.** To challenge.

तिक्तक *tikta* + *ka* (vb. *tij*), I. adj. Bitter, Suçr. 1, 215, 21. II. m. or n. An object of bitter taste, Suçr. 2, 136, 2. III. m. The name of several plants; Trichosanthes dioica Roxb., etc. — Comp. *Kaṭu-*, m. the name of two plants, Gentiana cherayta Roxb., Cannabis sativa, Lin.; (Râm. 2, 28, 21, Gorr., Pungent or disagreeable Trichosanthes).

† **तिग्** *TIG*, ii. 5 = *tik*, ii. 5.

तिग्म *tigma*, i.e. *tij* + *ma*, adj., f. *mâ*. **1.** Sharp, MBh. 6, 3187. **2.** Hot, Râm. 4, 44, 26. **3.** Passionate, MBh. 13, 1161.

तिग्मग *tigma* + *ga*, adj. Flying swiftly, Râm. 3, 34, 16.

† **तिघ्** *TIGH*, ii. 5, Par. To kill, —Cf. *stigh*.

तिङ्गुद *tiṅguda*, Nal. 12, 3, read *tinduka*.

तिज् *TIJ*, i. 1, Par., Âtm. To be sharp (ved.). Ptcple. of the pf. pass. *tikta*, Bitter, Pañch. 61, 11. Caus. *tejaya*, **1.** To sharpen, MBh. 5, 7169. **2.** To stir up, Râm. 3, 31, 36. Comp. ptcple. of the pf. pass. *su-tejita*, adj. Well-pointed, Chr. 30, 7. Desider. *titiksha*, Âtm. (also Par., MBh. 1, 3560), To endure, to suffer, Man. 6, 47.—With the prep. **उद्** *ud*, Caus. To stir up, Kathâs. 18, 91.—With **सम्** *sam*, Caus. To stir up, MBh. 5, 2742.—Cf. probably στίζω, στίγμα, etc.; Lat. stimulus for stig + mulus, instigo, instinguere; Goth. stiggqvan; A.S. stician, to sting; *tij* has lost the initial *s*, as *târa* **B.**, and others.

तितउ *titaü* (i.e. probably reduplicated *tan* + *u*, cf. τιταίνω for τιτανjω), m. A sieve, Châṇ. 108 in Berl. Monatsb.

तितिक्षा *titikshâ*, i.e. *titiksha*, desider. of *tij*, + *â*, f. **1.** Suffering, Vedântas. in Chr. 203, 17; Bhâg. P. 4, 22, 24. **2.** Patience, Bhâg. P. 1, 16, 27.

तितिक्षु *titikshu*, i.e. *titiksha*, see the last, + *u*, adj. Patient, Bhâg. P. 1, 12, 22.

तितीर्षु *titîrshu*, i.e. *titîrsha*, desider. of *tṛî*, + *u*, adj. **1.** Desiring to cross, Râm. 2, 52, 68. **2.** Desiring to attain, MBh. 1, 4647.

तित्तिर *tittira*, and **तित्तिरि** *tittiri* (based on an imitative sound), m. The francoline partridge, MBh. 5, 267; Man. 11, 134.

तित्तिरिक *tittiri* + *ka*, m. The francoline partridge, MBh. 9, 2587.

तिथि *tithi*, m. and f., also *tithî*, f. A lunar day, $\frac{1}{30}$ of a whole lunation, Man. 2, 30; MBh. 13, 4238.—Comp. *Dus-*, an inauspicious lunar day, MBh. 12, 6735.

तिनिश *tiniça*, m. A tree, Dalbergia ougeinensis Roxb., Râm. 3, 17, 7.

तिन्दुक *tinduka*, m. and f. *kî*, A tree, Diospyros embryopteris Pers., Râm. 2, 94, 8; Suçr. 2, 25, 2.

† **तिप्** *TIP*, i. 1, Par. To drop.

तिम् *TIM*, i. 4, Par. To become wet, Hit. 79, 5 Seramp. Ptcple. of the pf. pass. *timita*, Unmoved, Râm. 5, 1, 26.—Cf. *stim*.

तिमि *tim* + *i*, m. **1.** A large fish, MBh. 1, 1222. **2.** A whale, Ragh. 13, 10. **3.** A fish in general, Kathâs. 5, 24.

तिमिंगिल *timiṅgila*, i.e. *timi* + *m* -2 *gṛî* + *a*, m. **1.** A large fabulous fish, MBh. 1, 1208. **2.** The name of a people and their prince, MBh. 2, 1172.—Comp. *Timi-*, m. a large fabulous fish, MBh. 3, 12081.

तिमिर *timira* (akin to *tamas*, perhaps for original *tam* + *ira*), **I.** adj., f. *râ*, Dark, Râm. 6, 16, 104. **II.** m. and n. **1.** Darkness, Râm. 2, 28, 18. **2.** A class of diseases of the eye, Suçr. 1, 32, 4. **3.** A certain plant, Varâh. Bṛih. S. 54, 11. **III.** n. The name of a town, Râm. 4, 40, 26.—Comp. *Nis-*, and *vi-*, adj. clear, MBh. 12, 6817; Indr. 1, 3.

तिमिरय *TIMIRAYA*, a denomin.

derived from the last, Par. To darken, Hit. 103, 10.

तिमिश *timiça*, probably to be corrected to *tiniça*, Râm. 2, 94, 8.

तिमीर *timîra*, m. A certain tree, Râm. 3, 21, 19.

तिरय *TIRAYA*, a denomin. derived from *tiras*, Par. **1.** To stop, Mâlat. 21, 6. **2.** To restrain, to conquer, Prab. 41, 3.

तिरश्च् *tiraçch*, see *tiryañch*.

तिरश्चीन *tiraçchîna*, i.e. *tiras-añch* + *îna*, adj. Oblique, awry, Bhâg. P. 3, 18, 15.—Comp. *Â*-, adv. a little athwart, Daçak. in Chr. 198, 23.

तिरस् *tiras* (for original *taras*), i.e. *tṛî* + *as*, **1.** adv. Awry, Mârk. P. 17, 3. **2.** prepos. Over, through, etc. (ved.); see *kṛi*, *dhâ*, and *bhû*.—Cf. Lat. trans.

तिरस्कर *tiras-kara*, adj., f. *rî*, Surpassing, Bhâg. P. 1, 10, 27.

तिरस्करिन् *tiraskarin*, i.e. *tiras* -*kṛi* + *in*, I. m. A curtain, Râm. 2, 15, 20. II. f. *iṇî*. **1.** The same, Mâlav. d. 22. **2.** A hiding veil, Vikr. 27, 8.

तिरस्कार *tiras-kâra*, m. Abuse, Hit. 13, 14.

तिरस्क्रिया *tiras-kṛiyâ*, f. Disrespect, Pañch. i. d. 37.

तिरीट *tirîṭa* (perhaps for original *tirîtra*, i.e. *tṛî* + *tra*), **1.** n. A diadem. **2.** m. A tree, Symplocos racemosa Roxb.

तिरीटक *tirîṭa* + *ka*, m. A kind of bird, Râm. 3, 78, 23.

तिरोधान *tirodhâna*, i.e. *tiras* -*dhâna*, n. Disappearance, Bhâg. P. 3, 20, 44.

तिरोभवितृ *tirobhavitṛi*, i.e. *tiras* -*bhavitṛi*, m. f. *trî*, n. Disappearing, Bhâg. P. 3, 27, 23.

तिरोहय *TIROHAYA*, a denominative derived from a lost *tirodha* (see *dhâ* with *tiras*), with *h* for *dh*, To conceal, Chr. 52, 19.

तिरोहितता *tirohitatâ*, i.e. *tiras* -*hita* (vb. *dhâ*) + *tâ*, f. Disappearance, Kathâs. 21, 145.

तिर्यक्ता *tiryaktâ*, i.e. *tiryañch* + *tâ*, f. and **तिर्यक्त्व** *tiryaktva*, i.e. *tiryañch* + *tva*, n. The nature of beasts, Râjat. 3, 448; Man. 12, 40.

तिर्यग *tiryaga*, on account of the metre for *tiryagga*, i.e. *tiryañch-ga*, m. A quadruped, MBh. 13, 5755.

तिर्यगीक्ष *tiryagîksha*, i.e. *tiryañch* -*îksh* + *a*, adj. Looking at sideways, MBh. 12, 6575.

तिर्यग्ग *tiryagga*, i.e. *tiryañch-ga*, adj. **1.** Moving crookedly, Râm. 2, 12, 6 Gorr. **2.** Moving horizontally, Suçr. 1, 43, 7.

तिर्यग्ज *tiryagja*, i.e. *tiryañch-ja*, adj. Brought forth by animals, Man. 10, 72.

तिर्यग्योन *tiryagyona*, i.e. *tiryañch* -*yoni* + *a*, m. An animal, Man. 7, 149, v.r.

तिर्यञ्च् *tiryañch*, i. e. *tiras-añch* (the final *s* is dropped, as often, and *a* is changed to *î*, as before *as*, *kṛi*, *bhû*, cf. *viçvadryañch*, *samyañch*). I. adj., f. *tiraçchî*, i.e. *tiras-añch* + *î*, Horizontal (ved.). II. acc. sing. n. °*yak*, adv. **1.** Over, Man. 8, 291 (cf. *â-gam*). **2.** Horizontally, MBh. 2, 1396. **3.** Sideways, Râm. 2, 23, 5. III. m. and n. **1.** An animal, Bhâg. P. 1, 2, 34. **2.** An amphibious animal, Man. 5, 40.

— Cf. Goth. thairh, thairko; A.S. thurh.

1. तिल् *TIL*, i. 6 and 10, Par. To be greasy.

† 2. तिल् *TIL*, i. 1, Par. To go.

तिल *tila*, m. **1.** Sesame, a plant, Sesamum indicum, Lin., Man. 3, 210. **2.** Its seed, which gives a good oil, Pańch. ii. d. 68. **3.** A very small piece, Râjat. 4, 328.

तिलक *tila + ka*, m. (and n.). **1.** The name of a tree, Râm. 2, 91, 48. **2.** A freckle, a mole, Kathâs. 5, 32. **3.** A mark made on the forehead and between the eyebrows, either as an ornament or as a sectarial distinction, Râm. 3, 22, 8. **4.** Ornament, Râjat. 1, 47.

तिलकित *tilakita*, i.e. *tilaka + ita*, adj. Adorned, Râjat. 2, 10.

तिलपर्णिक *tilaparṇika*, i. e. *tilaparṇî + ka*, I. f. *kâ*, Red sanders, Pterocarpus santalinus, Lin., Suçr. 1, 215, 5. II. n. *ka*, Its wood, 2, 285, 10.

तिलपर्णी *tilaparṇî*, i.e. *tila-parṇa + î*, f. Red sanders (see the last), Suçr. 1, 146, 3.

तिलपीड *tila-pîḍ + a*, m. An oil-grinder, MBh. 12, 6481.

तिलशस् *tila + ças*, adv. (Broken) to pieces as small as seeds of sesame, Râm. 3, 35, 81.

तिलोत्तमा *tilottamâ*, i.e. *tila-uttama*, f. The name of an Apsaras, Daçak. in Chr. 182, 8.

† तिल्ल् *TILL*, i. 1, Par. To go, v.r. for *til*.

तिल्वक *tilvaka*, m. A tree, Symplocos racemosa Roxb., Suçr. 1, 32, 15.

तिष्य *tishya*, I. m. **1.** The name of a Nakshatra, or lunar mansion, containing three stars, of which one is δ Cancri, MBh. 3, 13099. II. n. The Kali yuga, i.e. fourth or present age, MBh. 6, 387.

तिसृ *tisṛi*, see *tri*.

† तीक् *TÎK*, i. 1, Âtm. To go, see *tik*.

तीक्ष्ण *tîkshṇa*, i.e. *tij + sna*, I. adj., f. *ṇâ*, **1.** Sharp, Râm. 1, 44, 22. **2.** Hot, Ṛit. 1, 18; flashing, Râm. 5, 29, 14. **3.** Energetic, Chr. 49, 14. **4.** Of a pungent taste, Bhag. 17, 9. **5.** Harsh, Man. 7, 140. **6.** Subtle, Çiç. 2, 109. II. n. Harsh speech, Râm. 2, 35, 23.— Comp. *Su-*, adj. very sharp, Ṛit. 6, 27.

तीक्ष्णता *tîkshṇa + tâ*, f. Sharpness, Râm. 3, 19, 7.

† तीम् *TÎM*, i. 4, Par. = *tim*.

तीर् *TÎR*, i. 10 (rather a denomin. derived from the next), Par. To get through or over, to finish, to settle, Man. 9, 233.

तीर *tîra* (for original *târa*), i.e. *tṛî + â*, n. A shore, a bank, Man. 3, 207.

तीरज *tîra-ja*, I. adj. Grown on a shore, MBh. 5, 2052. II. m. A tree grown on a shore, Râm. 2, 91, 31.

तीर्थ *tîrtha*, i.e. *tṛî + tha*, m. and n. **1.** Stairs of a landing-place, a descent, Bhâg. P. 9, 19, 4. **2.** A bathing-place, Râm. 1, 2, 6. **3.** A place of pilgrimage, Man. 8, 356; Râjat. 5, 304. **4.** A holy place, Man. 11, 196. **5.** The right or holy moment, Bhâg. P. 7, 8, 44; 1, 12, 14. **6.** Opportunity, Bhâg. P. 3, 19, 4. **7.** Instruction, Kir. 2, 3. **8.** A sacred preceptor, MBh. 5, 4212. **9.** Certain lines or parts of the hand, Man. 2, 58. **10.** A venerable object, Bhâg. P. 4, 20, 4. **11.** A venerable person, MBh. 13,

5856; Daçak. in Chr. 182, 20. **12.** Certain persons of a king's court, MBh. 2, 171; *tirthatama*, see separately.—Comp. *Apsaras-*, n. the name of a locality. *Dus-*, adj., f. *thâ*, difficult to be crossed, Chr. 47, 36. *Sa-*, m. a fellow student. *Soma-*, n. a place of pilgrimage in the west of India.

तीर्थक *tirtha+ka*, I. adj. Holy, Bhâg. P. 1, 19, 32. **II.** m. A Brâhmaṇa.

तीर्थंकर *tirtha-kara*, I. adj. Saving, MBh. 13, 7023. **II.** m. A Brâhmaṇa.

तीर्थतम *tîrtha+tama*, n. **1.** A holier place of pilgrimage, MBh. 3, 7018. **2.** A holiest object of veneration, Bhâg. P. 5, 24, 19.

तीर्थवन्त् *tirtha+vant*, adj., f. *vati*, Abounding in holy bathing-places, Râm. 3, 68, 31.

तीर्थीकरण *tirthîkaraṇa*, i.e. *tirtha-kṛi+ana*, adj. Hallowing, Bhâg. P. 5, 18, 7.

† **तीव्** *TÎV*, i. 1, Par. To become fat.—Cf. *tu*.

तीव्र *tivra*, probably *tij+van+a*, (with *r* for *n*, cf. *tigma* and *tikshṇa*), adj., f. *râ*. **1.** Sharp, Bhartṛ. 2, 77. **2.** Hot, Bhartṛ. 3, 19; flashing, Râm. 3, 62, 11. **3.** Violent, MBh. 7, 6893; deep (of darkness), Arj. 8, 13. **4.** Bad, MBh. 1, 3097.

तीव्रता *tivra+tâ*, f. Heat; in *a-*, moderate temperature, Râjat. 1, 41.

1. **तु** *TU*, ii. 2, Par. **1.** To be powerful (ved.). **2.** † To increase. **3.** † To go. **4.** † To hurt.—Cf. τύλος; Lat. tumor, tumere, tumulus, tuber, tueri, totus; Goth. thiuda, thiuth, thiuthjan; A.S. theod, people.

2. **तु** *tu*, a particle (akin to *tva*, a ved. pron., Some, one, another, etc.). **1.** But, Man. 1, 109. **2.** Preceded by *api*, But rather, Daçak. in Chr. 184, 17; by *kim*, Nevertheless, MBh. 1, 1916. **3.** Or, Man. 11, 201. **4.** And, Man. 2, 22. **5.** *tu—tu*, Indeed—but, Hit. i. d. 32. **6.** Often without a special signification, Man. 7, 95. **7.** Sometimes erroneously for *nu*, Brâhmaṇ. 3, 17 (where the Calc. ed. has *nu*).—Cf. perhaps *rol*.

तुखार *tukhâra*, m. pl. The name of a people, Râm. 4, 44, 14; also written **तुषार** *tushâra*, Râm. 1, 56, 3 Gorr.

तुगा *tugâ* and **तुगाक्षीरी** *tugâ-kshîri*, f. The manna of bambus, Suçr. 2, 504, 7; 1, 140, 9.

तुङ्ग *tuṅga*, i.e. *tuñj+a*. I. adj., f. *gâ*, Prominent, Bhâg. P. 1, 19, 27; high, Bhartṛ. 2, 77. **II.** m. **1.** A mountain, Râm. 4, 44, 20. **2.** Culmination, Varâh. Bṛih. 1, 13. **3.** Height, Bhâg. P. 3, 3, 1. **4.** A tree, Bottleria tinctoria Roxb., Suçr. 2, 78, 19. **5.** A proper name, Râjat. 6, 318.

तुङ्गक *tuṅga+ka*, n. The name of a holy forest, MBh. 3, 8195.

तुङ्गिन् *tuṅgin*, i.e. *tuṅga+in*, adj., f. *nî*, Lofty, Pañch. ii. d. 149.

तुच्छ *tuchchha*, adj. Void, vain, Prab. 76, 12.

तुच्छय *TUCHCHHAYA*, a denomin. derived from the last by *aya*, Par. To make poor, Mṛichchh. 178, 4.

तुज् *TUJ*, and **तुञ्ज्** *TUÑJ*, † i. 1, Par.; ved., i. 6 (and *tuñj*, once i. 1) Par., Âtm. **1.** To strike, to push. **2.** *tuñj*, † To protect, or to be strong. i. 10, *tojaya* and *tuñjaya*, **1.** † To be strong. **2.** To strike. **3.** To abide. **4.** To give, or to take.

तुञ्जीन *tuñjina*, m. A proper name, Râjat. 5, 277.

† तुट् *TUṬ*, i. 6, Par. To quarrel.

† तुड् *TUḌ* (a form of *tṛid*, based on *tard*), i. 1 and 6, Par. To split (v. r. to procure, to destroy).

† तुड्ड् *TUḌḌ*, i. 1, Par. To disregard.

तुण् *TUṆ*, i. 6, Par. To curve, to bend.

तुण्ड् *TUṆḌ*, i. 1, Âtm. To split. —With the prep. उद् *ud*, To jut out, Suçr. 1, 100, 12 (probably a denomin. derived from the following word).

तुण्ड *tuṇḍa*, a form of *tund*+*ra*, n. **1.** Beak, MBh. 1, 1474. **2.** Snout, Bhâg. P. 3, 13, 31. **3.** The name of a Râkshasa or demon, MBh. 3, 16372.—Comp. *Kaṅka-*, m. the name of a Râkshasa or demon, Râm. 6, 84, 13. *Siṁha-*, m. a kind of fish, Man. 5, 16.

† तुत्थ् *TUTTH*, i. 10 (rather a denomin. derived from the next), Par. To cover.

तुत्थ *tuttha*, n. Blue vitriol, Suçr. 2, 13, 2.

तुद् *TUD*, i. 6, Par. Âtm. **1.** To strike, Râm. 2, 36, 14. **2.** To sting, Bhâg. P. 3, 31, 27. Ptcple. of the pf. pass. *tunna*.—With the prep. आ *â*, To push on, Man. 4, 68. *âtodya*, n. A musical instrument, Kathâs. 23, 83.—With निस् *nis*, To sting, Suçr. 1, 61, 18.—With परि *pari*, To stamp to pieces, MBh. 5, 2747.—With प्र *pra*, To strike, MBh. 8, 4187. Caus. *todaya*, To push on, MBh. 13, 2795.—With वि *vi*, **1.** To sting, Yâjń. 3, 53. **2.** To strike, MBh. 8, 2729. **3.** To scratch, Râm. 5, 68, 7.—With सम् *sam*, To sting, MBh. 9, 3067.—Cf. *tund*, Lat. tundo, tussis; Τυδεύς Τυνδαρεύς; the initial *s* in Goth. stautan is original and dropped in Sskt., etc.; A.S. a-stintan, to blunt.

तुन्द् *TUND*, **1.** =*tud*, ved. **2.** † i. 1, Par. To be active, v.r. of *trand*.

तुन्नवाय *tunna-vâya*, i.e. *tunna* (vb. *tud*), *-ve*+*a*, m. A tailor, Man. 4, 214.

† तुप् *TUP*, and † तुफ् *TUPH*, तुम्प् *TUMP*, † तुम्फ् *TUMPH*, i. 1, and 6, Par. To hurt. *tump*, i. 10, v.r. of *tumb*.—Cf. τύπτω, τυπή, τύμπανον; Lat. stupeo; see *tud*, and cf. *stump*, in the Gaṇa pâraskarâdi.

तुभ् *TUBH*, † i. 1, Âtm. and † i. 4, Par., ii. 9, Par. To kill, to hurt.—Cf. *stubh*.

तुमुल *tumula*, and sometimes तुमल *tumala* (probably vb. *tu*), I. adj., f. *lâ*, **1.** Noisy, Râm. 1, 26, 6; *tumala*, MBh. 7, 6670. **2.** Tumultuous, Hariv. 9609. **3.** Excited, Daçak. in Chr. 188, 23. II. n. **1.** Tumultuous combat, melée, MBh. 2, 2688. **2.** Tumult, MBh. 6, 1642; *tumala*, 7, 6661.—Cf. Lat. tumultus.

तुम्प् *TUMP*, and † तुम्फ् *TUMPH*, see *tup*.

† तुम्ब् *TUMB*, i. 1, Par. To torment. i. 10, To be invisible, v.r.

तुम्ब *tumba*, m. and f. *bî*, A long gourd, Lagenaria vulgaris, Râm. 1, 39, 7 Ser.; Suçr. 1, 183, 17.

तुम्बुरु *tumburu*, I. m. The name of a Gandharva, Râm. 3, 8, 12. II. n. The fruit of Diospyros embryopteris Pers., Suçr. 2, 43, 2.

तुर् *TUR*, i. 6, Par., Atm.; ii. 3, Par. To hasten (ved.).—Cf. *tûr*, *tṛî*, and *tvar*.

तुर् *tur*, adj. Hastening, a warrior, Chr. 296, 4=Rig. i. 112, 4.

तुरग *tur+a-ga*, **1.** m. A horse, Pañch. i. d. 314. **2.** f. *gi*, A mare, Çatr. 14, 112.

तुरंग *turañga*, i.e. *tur+a+m-ga*, m. A horse, Pañch. i. d. 314.

तुरंगम *turañgama*, i.e. *tur+a+m-gam+a*, **1.** m. A horse, Râm. 2, 45, 14. **2.** f. *mi*, A mare, MBh. 4, 254.

तुरायण *turâyaṇa*, n. The name of a certain sacrifice or vow, MBh. 13, 4940.

तुरासाह् *turâsâh*, i.e. *tura-sah*, in the nomin. voc. sing., and dat. abl. du. and pl., and loc. pl., *s* becomes *sh*, e.g. nom. sing. तुराषाट् *turâshâṭ*, m. A name of Indra, Bhâg. P. 8, 11, 26; of Vishṇu, Hariv. 14114.

तुरीय *turîya*, i.e. *chatur+îya* (the intermediate form was probably *kturîya*), **1.** ord. number, fem. *yâ*, Fourth, Bhâg. P. 5, 10, 3. **2.** adj. and n. Fourth part, a quarter, Man. 11, 126; 4, 202. **3.** n. The fourth state of the student of the Vedânta philosophy, Vedântas. in Chr. 205, 19.

तुरीयक *turîya+ka*, adj. Fourth part, Yâjñ. 2, 124.

तुरुष्क *turushka*, m. **1.** The name of a people, Râjat. 5, 152. **2.** Olibanum, the resin of the Boswellia serrata Stackh.

तुर्य *turya*, i. e. *chatur + ya* (see *turîya*), **1.** ord. number, Fourth, Bhâg. P. 4, 3, 9. **2.** n. A quarter, Bhâg. P. 6, 9, 8.

तुर्व् *TURV*, i. 1, *tûrva*, Par. **1.** To overcome (ved.). **2.** † To hurt.

तुर्वसु *turvasu*, m. A proper name, MBh. 1, 3159.

तुर्वीति *turvîti*, m. A proper name, Chr. 298, 23=Rigv. i. 112, 23.

तुल् *TUL* (akin to *tṛî*), i. 10, *tolaya* and *tulaya*, Par. (also Âtm. Râm. 4, 9, 100), † i. 1, Par. **1.** To lift, Râm. 3, 4, 44. **2.** To weigh, MBh. 3, 10588. **3.** To ponder, MBh. 12, 2394. **4.** To suspect, Mṛichchh. 33, 5. **5.** To compare, Bhâg. P. 5, 5, 23. **6.** To equal, Megh. 65. **7.** To attain, Ragh. 13, 75.—With the prep. आ *â*, To lift, Râm. 1, 34, 10 Gorr.—With सम् *sam*, To weigh together, MBh. 13, 2607.—Cf. Lat. tollo, tuli, latum (for tlatum); ταλάω, τάλας, τλῆσις, τάνταλος (Frequent.), ἀντλέω (for ταντλέω, Frequent.), ὄτλος, τέλος (office), τέλλω, ἐντολή, τόλμα, τάλαντον; Goth. thulan; A.S. tholian, thyldian, athylgian.

तुलन *tul + ana*, n. **1.** Lifting, Mṛichchh. 146, 25. **2.** Taxing, 50, 16.

तुलसिका *tulasikâ*, i. e. *tulasî+ka*, and तुलसी *tulasî*, f. A small shrub, held in veneration by the Hindus, holy basil, Bhâg. P. 3, 15, 19; 1, 19, 6.

तुला *tul+â*, f. **1.** A balance, Man. 8, 403. **2.** Weight, MBh. 3, 10385. **3.** The beam of a balance, MBh. 12, 9350. **4.** Equality, Ragh. 19, 50; Megh. 93. **5.** The sign of the zodiac, Libra, Pañch. i. d. 375. **6.** A measure or weight of gold and silver=100 palas, MBh. 14, 1929.—Comp. *A-tula*, adj., f. *lâ*, incomparable, Râm. 5, 13, 19. *Kûṭa-*, f. a wrong balance, Pañch. 7, 15.

तुल्य *tulya*, i.e. *tulâ+ya*, adj., f. *yâ*, **1.** Equal, Brâhmaṇ. 1, 31; with the gen. Râm. 1, 7, 17; and the instr. Man. 4, 86. **2.** Indifferent, Bhâg. P. 1, 5, 24. **3.** Being of the same class, Man. 8, 364. **4.** °*yam*, adv. Equally, Râm. 6, 90, 31.—Comp. *Mâsa-*, adj., f.

yâ, equal to the number of mouths, Man. 5, 66. *Çarira-*, adj. dear as one's person.

तुल्यता *tulya + tâ*, f. and **तुल्यत्व** *tulya + tva*, n. Equality, Râm. 1, 4, 7 Gorr.; Prab. 27, 14.

तुल्यशस् *tulya + ças*, adv. In equal parts, Suçr. 2, 327, 13.

तुवर *tuvara*, i.e. *tu-van + a*, with *r* for *n*, adj. Astringent, Suçr. 1, 179, 5.

तुविद्युम्न *tuvi-dyumna* (*tuvi* is *tu + i*, ved. Much), adj. Wealthy, Chr. 293, 3 = Rigv. i. 88, 3.

तुश् *TUÇ*, i. 1, Âtm. To sprinkle (ved.).

तुष् *TUSH*, i. 4, Par. (in epic poetry also Âtm., or refl. pass., Bhâg. P. 1, 5, 8). **1.** To be calmed (properly, to be silent, cf. *tûshṇîm*), MBh. 3, 1109. **2.** To be satisfied, Man. 2, 228. **3.** To be content, Hit. i. d. 134. **4.** To be pleased, Man. 3, 207; with the gen., MBh. 1, 8361; with the dat., Kathâs. 24, 195; with the instr., MBh. 4, 291; with the loc., Pañch. iii. d. 155. **5.** To satisfy, MBh. 1, 4198. Ptcple. of the pf. pass. *tushṭa*, Content, satisfied, pleased, MBh. 4, 291. Ptcple. of the fut. pass. *tushya*, Easily to be satisfied, Hariv. 14882. Caus. **1.** To appease, MBh. 5, 7391. **2.** To satisfy, Mârk. P. 26, 37. **3.** To gladden, Pañch. 38, 3. Anomalous absolutive, *toshya*, MBh. 1, 160.—With the prep. **परि** *pari*, **1.** To be completely satisfied, Bhâg. P. 6, 18, 67; Râm. 2, 2, 33. **2.** To be much pleased, Bhartṛ. 2, 2. Caus. **1.** To satisfy completely, Râm. 6, 104, 28. **2.** To flatter, Pañch. 38, 22. —With **प्र** *pra*, Caus. To satisfy, Bhâg. P. 4, 30, 1.—With **संप्र** *sam-pra*, To be content, MBh. 12, 6283.—With **सम्** *sam*, **1.** To be calmed, Bhartṛ. 3, 4. **2.** To be satisfied, content, MBh. 13, 220. Ptcple. of the pf. pass. *saṁtushṭa*, Easy to be satisfied, Böhtl. Ind. Spr. 277. **Comp.** *A-*, adj. unsatiable, ib. *Dus -saṁtushṭa*, adj. discontented, Hit. i. d. 22. *Su-*, easily satisfied, Pañch. i. d. 31. Caus. **1.** To appease, Pañch. 101, 11. **2.** To please, to gladden, MBh. 3, 13685. —Cf. Lat. taceo; Goth. thahan.

तुष *tusha*, m. The husk of grain, especially rice, Man. 4, 78.

तुषार *tush + âra*, **I.** adj., f. *râ*, Cold, Naish. 3, 93. **II.** m. **1.** Mist, MBh. 9, 3632. **2.** Thin rain, Ragh. 2, 13. **3.** Dew, Çâk. d. 115. **4.** Hoar frost, Ṛit. 4, 1. **5.** Snow, Megh. 53. **6.** see *tukhâra*.

तुषित *tushita* (originally ptcple. of the pf. pass. of *tush*), **I.** m. **1.** pl. A class of subordinate deities, MBh. 13, 1371. **2.** Epithet of Vishṇu, MBh. 12, 12864. **II.** f. *tâ*, A proper name, Bhâg. P. 8, 1, 21.

तुष्टि *tushṭi*, i.e. *tush + ti*, f. Satisfaction, Man. 2, 6.

† **तुस्** *TUS*, i. 1, Par. To sound.

† **तुह्** *TUH*, i. 1, Par. To hurt, to give pain.

तुहिन *tuhina* (cf. *tushâra*), n. **1.** Mist, Prab. 13, 13. **2.** Dew, Ṛit. 4, 7. **3.** Snow, Râjat. 2, 18.

† **तूड्** *TÛḌ*, i. 1, Par. To split. —Cf. *tuḍ*.

† **तूण्** *TÛṆ*, i. 10, Par. To shrink. i. 10, Âtm. To fill.

तूण *tûṇa*, and **तूणि** *tûṇi*, **I.** m. and f. *ṇî*, A quiver, Hariv. 15940; Râm. 1, 48, 3; 2, 31, 30. **II.** f. *ṇî*, A disease of the nerves, Suçr. 1, 232, 8.—**Comp.** *Pûrṇa-*, adj. full quivered.

तूणवन्त् *tûṇa + vant*, adj., f. *vatî*, Provided with a quiver, MBh. 3, 8486.

तूणिन् *tûṇin*, i.e. *tûṇa+in*, adj. Provided with quivers, Râm. 6, 76, 21.

तूणीर *tûṇî+ra* (see *tûṇa*), m. and n. A quiver, MBh. 7, 1271; MBh. 6, 2288.

तूणीरवन्त् *tûṇîra+vant*, adj., f. *vatî*, Provided with a quiver, Hariv. 15154.

† तूर् *TÛR*, i. 4, Âtm. 1. To go quick. 2. To hurt, see *tur*.

तूर् *tûr*, f. Swiftness, Bhâg. P. 2, 7, 37.

तूर्य *tûrya*, I. =*turya*, Râjat. 2, 91. II. m. and n. Any musical instrument, Man. 7, 225.

तूर्यमय *tûrya+maya*, adj., f. *yî*, MusicalK·ıthâs. 23, 84.

† तूल् *TÛL*, i. 1 and 10, To weigh (cf. *tul*). i. 10, Âtm.=*tûṇ*.

तूल *tûla*, m. and n. Cotton, MBh. 1, 6740.—Comp. *Haṁsa-*, down, Daçak. in Chr. 198, 17.

तूलक *tûla+ka*, n. Cotton, Bhâshâp. 112.

तूलिका *tûlikâ*, i. e. *tûla + ka*, f. 1. A pencil, Kumâras. 1, 22. 2. A mattress filled with cotton, Kathâs. 26, 78.

तूवरक *tûvara+ka* (*tûvara*=ved. *tûpara*, Without horns, beardless, an eunuch), adj. Unmanly, MBh. 5, 5470.

† तूष् *TÛSH*, i. 1, Par. To be satisfied; see *tush*.

तूष्णीक *tûshṇîka*, i.e. *tûshṇîm+ka*, adj. Taciturn, Râm. 2, 117, 3 Gorr. °*kam*, adv. Silently, Râm. 5, 1, 97.

तूष्णीम् *tûshṇîm*, i.e. *tush+na+î+m*, adv. Silently, MBh. 12, 3839; Man. 8, 147.

तूष्णींभाव *tûshṇîṁbhâva*, i.e. *tûshṇîm-bhâva*, m. Silence, MBh. 12, 3840.

† तृंह् *TṚIṀH*, i. 6, *ṭṛiha*, Par. To hurt; see *tṛih*.

† तृक्ष् *TṚIKSH*, i. 1, Par. To go.

तृच *tṛicha*, i.e. *tri-ṛich+a*, m. and n. Three verses, Chr. 294, l. 5.

तृण् *TṚIN*, or तृन् *TṚIN*, ii. 8, Par. To eat, Skandap. Kâçikh. 3, 49.

तृण *tṛiṇa*, i.e. *tṛi+ṇa* (cf. *taru*), n. (and m.). 1. Grass, any gramineous plant, Man. 1, 48; Hit. i. d. 144; Râm. 2, 21, 26; Man. 4, 166. 2. A grass-blade, Pañch. i. d. 190.—Cf. perhaps O.H.G. dorn, A.S. thorn.

तृणक *tṛiṇa+ka*, n. A worthless grass-blade, MBh. 1, 3666.

तृणपीड *tṛiṇa-pîḍ+a*, n. A mode of close-fighting, MBh. 2, 909.

तृणमय *tṛiṇa+maya*, adj., f. *yî*, Made of grass, MBh. 1, 5554.

तृणवन्त् *tṛiṇa+vant*, adj., f. *vatî*, Abounding in grass, MBh. 12, 3694.

तृणाङ्कु *tṛiṇâṅku*, m. The name of a Ṛishi, Râm. 4, 41, 62.

तृतीय *tṛitîya*, i.e. *tri+tîya*, f. *yâ*. 1. ordinal number, Third, Man. 2, 35. 2. adj. A third part, Man. 6, 33. 3. °*yam*, adv. Thirdly, Man. 8, 129.—Cf. Goth. thridja; A.S. thridda; Lat. tertius; τρίτος.

तृतीयक *tṛitîya+ka*, adj. Tertian, Suçr. 2, 405, 14.

तृतीयिन् *tṛitîyin*, i.e. *tṛitîya+in*, adj., f. *nî*. 1. Being of the third rank. 2. Entitled to a third part.

तृद् *TṚID*, ii. 7, Par., Âtm. 1. To cleave (ved.). 2. To kill, to destroy,

Hariv. 7621. **3.** † To disregard (or, to eat).

तृन् *TṚIN*, see *tṛiṇ*.

तृप् *TṚIP* (i. 1, Par., MBh. 14, 1040), i. 4, Par. (in epic poetry also Âtm., MBh. 3, 1781), † i. 6, Par, ii. 5, *tṛipnu* (ved. *tṛipṇu*), Par., and तृम्प् *TṚIMP*, i. 6, Par. **1.** To become satiate, Kathâs. 26, 237. **2.** To be satisfied, Man. 3, 267. **3.** To enjoy, Man. 4, 251. With gen. instr. and loc., MBh. 3, 336; Hit. ii. d. 164; MBh. 4, 2320. **4.** † To kindle. Ptcple. of the pf. pass. *tṛipta*, Satisfied, Bhartṛ. 2, 82; MBh. 3, 2247. Caus. *tarpaya*, Par. (and Âtm., MBh. 12, 5542), **1.** To satisfy, Kathâs. 26, 237; Chr. 292, 11 = Rigv. i. 85, 11; Man. 3, 283. **2.** To gladden, to exhilarate, Bhâg. P. 7, 2, 8. **3.** † To kindle. Anomalous ptcple. of the pres. Âtm. *tarpayâna* (with *n* instead of *ṇ*), MBh. 14, 291.—With the prep. अति *ati*, To become satisfied, Bhâg. P. 8, 5, 13.—With अनु *anu*, To be satisfied after (with abl.), MBh. 13, 1922.—With अप *apa*, Caus. To cause to hunger, Suçr. 2, 43, 1.—With अभि *abhi*, **1.** To be satisfied, MBh. 5, 3604. **2.** To enjoy, Bhâg. P. 3, 5, 1. Caus. To satisfy, Râm. 1, 54, 5 Gorr.—With परि *pari*, Caus. To satisfy completely, MBh. 3, 8537.—With प्र *pra*, Caus. To satisfy, Pańch. 217, 6.—With वि *vi*, To be satisfied, Bhâg. P. 1, 1, 19; Râm. 4, 35, 9.—With सम् *sam*, Caus. To satisfy, MBh. 3, 946.—Cf. τέρπω; Lat. torpor, torpere; Goth. tharf (primitively 'to satisfy,' then 'to be of use,' cf. O.H.G. bidarbi; and finally 'to be necessary'), thrafstjan; A.S. thearf; O.H.G. trôstjan.

तृप्ति *tṛip + ti*, f. **1.** Satiating, Bhag. 10, 18. **2.** Satisfaction, Man. 3, 271. **3.** Disgust, Suçr. 1, 90, 11.—**Comp.** *Ati-*, f. over-satisfaction, Yâjń. 1, 114.

† तृफ् *TṚIPH* and तृम्फ् *TṚIMPH*, i. 6, Par. = *tṛip*.

तृम्प् *TṚIMP* and † तृम्फ् *TṚIMPH*, see *tṛip*, *tṛiph*.

1. तृष् *TṚISH*, i. 4, Par. To thirst. Ptcple. of the pf. pass. *tṛishita*. **1.** Thirsty, MBh. 3, 101. **2.** Desirous, Râm. 2, 104, 1. **3.** Greedy, Ṛit. 1, 18. —Cf. O.H.G. durst, A.S. thurst; Goth. thaursjan, thairsan, thaursus; A.S. thyrr; τέρσομαι, τυρσός, τρασιά; Lat. torrere.

2. तृष् *tṛish*, f. Thirst, MBh. 14, 1605. —**Comp.** *Mṛiga-*, f. mirage. *Sa-*, adj. 1. thirsty. 2. greedy.

तृषा *tṛish + â*, f. **1.** Thirst, Pańch. 81, 22. **2.** Desire, Hit. i. d. 133.—**Comp.** *Mṛiga-*, f. mirage.

तृष्णज् *tṛishṇaj*, i.e. *tṛish + na-ja*, adj. Thirsty, Chr. 289, 11 = Rigv. i. 85, 11.

तृष्णा *tṛishṇâ*, i.e. *tṛish + na*, f. **1.** Thirst, Man. 8, 67. **2.** Desire, Bhartṛ. 2, 70.—**Comp.** *Ati-*, f. excess of covetousness, Man. 7, 139. *Ati-tṛishṇa*, adj. very thirsty, Ragh. 2, 69. *Mṛiga-*, f. mirage. *Vi-*, adj. free from desire. *Sa-tṛishṇa + m*, adv. with desire, Çâk. d. 59.

तृष्णालु *tṛishṇâ + lu*, adj. Very thirsty, Suçr. 2, 383, 19.

तृह् *TṚIH*, ii. 7, *tṛiṇeh*, *tṛiṁh*, Par. To crush (ved.).

तॄ *tṝ*, i. 1, Par. (sometimes also Âtm., MBh. 1, 6184). **1.** To pass over, Man. 4, 194; to cross, Man. 4, 77. **2.** To hasten, Çâk. d. 8, v.r. **3.** To accomplish, Râm. 6, 100, 14. **4.** To fulfil,

Râm. 2, 25, 41. **5.** To overcome, MBh. 2, 669. **6.** To conquer, Râm. 2, 53, 26. **7.** To be saved, MBh. 14, 44. **8.** To save, MBh. 1, 8369. Ptcple. of the pf. pass. *tîrṇa*, **1.** Passed over, Prab. 92, 15. **2.** Having passed over, Râm. 2, 55, 22; 5, 15, 23. Comp. *Dus-*, adj., f. *ṇâ*, 1. difficult to be crossed, MBh. 5, 7368. 2. impenetrable, Râm. 5, 76, 10. Ptcple of the fut. pass. *tartavya*, MBh. 7, 4706. *târya*, n. Toll at a ferry, Man. 8, 405. Infin. *taritum*, Râm. 4, 44, 77; *tarîtum*, Râm. 5, 74, 18; *tartum*, MBh. 1, 6142. Caus. *târaya*, **1.** To bring over, MBh. 1, 5853. **2.** To save, MBh. 5, 1470; to release, Man. 4, 228. Desider. *titîrsha*, To desire to pass over, Bhâg. P. 4, 22, 40.—With the prep. अति *ati*, **1.** To cross, Bhâg. P. 6, 9, 21. **2.** To attain, Hit. iv. d. 85; Bhâg. P. 5, 13, 20. **3.** To overcome, MBh. 12, 4053. Desider. To desire to overcome, Bhâg. P. 1, 2, 3.—With व्यति *vi-ati*, To overcome, Bhag. 2, 52.—With अनु *anu*, pass. *tîrya*, To lay down, MBh. 7, 8721.—With अभि *abhi*, To attain, MBh. 7, 280.—With अव *ava*, **1.** To descend, Râm. 2, 45, 17; used especially of deities who descend from heaven to be born as men, MBh. 1, 2509. **2.** To betake one's-self, MBh. 3, 10015. **3.** To overcome, Kathâs. 24, 194. Caus. **1.** To cause to descend, MBh. 1, 4327; 3, 9917; to lead down, Râm. 2, 103, 23; to lead to, MBh. 5, 4395. **2.** To take off, Râm. 4, 19, 29. **3.** To introduce, Râjat. 5, 32. **4.** To perform, Râjat. 2, 58.—With समव *sam-ava*, Caus. To cause to descend, MBh. 1, 4326.—With उद् *ud*, **1.** To get out, MBh. 3, 211; to get out of water, MBh. 1, 6750. **2.** To descend, Lass. 5, 7. **3.** To pass over, MBh. 2, 795. **4.** To overcome, Hariv. 14227. **5.** To abandon, MBh. 3, 2042. *uttîrṇa*, Learned, MBh. 4, 1408. Caus. **1.** To fetch out, Râm. 4, 52, 15. **2.** To vomit, Man. 11, 160. **3.** To save, to deliver, MBh. 3, 8306; Râm. 1, 43, 4 Gorr. **4.** To cause to descend, Pańch. 187, 13. **5.** To take off, Lass. 22, 3. **6.** To bring over, Pańch. 226, 15. Desider. To wish to cross, MBh. 15, 1878.—With प्रोद् *pra-ud*, To pass over, Râjat. 3, 71.—With प्रत्युद् *prati-ud*, **1.** To get again out (as from water), Râm. 2, 111, 37. **2.** To betake one's-self, Râm. 2, 103, 28.—With समुद् *sam-ud*, **1.** To get out, Yâjń. 3, 7. **2.** To be saved, MBh. 13, 6676. **3.** To pass over, Râjat. 3, 344.—With निस् *nis*, **1.** To be saved, MBh. 3, 15561. **2.** To pass over, Bhartṛ. 3, 5. **3.** To pass, MBh. 13, 5155. **4.** To accomplish, Lass. 4, 2. **5.** To overcome, MBh. 12, 1566. **6.** To expiate, Bhâg. P. 3, 16, 30. **7.** To settle, Yâjń. 2, 9. Caus. To release, Man. 3, 98. Desider. To desire to pass over, Bhâg. P. 1, 1, 22.—With प्र *pra*, **1.** To pass over, MBh. 4, 1546. **2.** To propagate, MBh. 3, 8149. Caus. **1.** To extend, MBh. 3, 8647. **2.** To persuade, Kathâs. 26, 243. **3.** To deceive, Mṛichchh. 82, 2.—With विप्र *vi-pra*, To deceive, Çatr. 10, 121.—With वि *vi*, **1.** To cross, Ragh. 6, 77. **2.** To grant, MBh. 1, 4498; to favour with (with acc.), Pańch. 127, 21; to allow, MBh. 3, 1681. **3.** To give (as medicine), Suçr. 2, 337, 9. **4.** To give away, Bhartṛ. 3, 86. **5.** To perform, Bhâg. P. 3, 15, 24; to fight (a battle), Râjat. 5, 135. **6.** To produce, Kir. 5, 31.—With सम् *sam*, To cross, MBh. 1, 5887. **2.** To overcome, MBh. 12, 11161. **3.** To attain, Râm. 5, 35, 5. **4.** To be saved, Râjat. 4, 528. **5.** To save, MBh. 13, 4155. Caus. **1.** To bring over, Râm. 2, 89, 8. **2.** To save, Man. 9, 139. **3.** To persuade, MBh. 14, 2310. **4.** To deceive, Kâm. Nîtis. 14, 4. — Cf. *τερέω τέρετρον τορός, τόρος τορέω, τορεύω, τιτράω, τετραίνω, τρῆμα, τρῦμα, τιτρώσκω, τρῶμα, τέρμα, τέλος* (end), *τέλλω* (to rise), *τηρέω* (Causal), *τρῡτάνη* (i.e. *ταρ + ῡταν + ο*, cf. ved. *tarûtṛi* and *tul*), etc.; Lat. terminus; cf. *tul, trâ*.

† तेज् *TEJ*, i. 1, Par. To protect.

तेजन *tejana*, i.e. *tij + ana*, n. **1.** Kindling, Suçr. 2, 140, 10. **2.** A point, MBh. 6, 3187. **3.** A bambu.—**Comp.** *Agni-jvalita-*, adj. the points of which are blazing with fire, Man. 7, 90.

तेजस् *tejas*, i.e. *tij + as*, n. **1.** Sharpness (ved.). **2.** Splendour, Bhag. 10, 30. **3.** Flame, Man. 11, 246. **4.** Light, MBh. 2, 1395; Çâk. d. 77 (the sun and the moon). **5.** Beauty, Daçak. in Chr. 180, 3. **6.** Strength, Man. 9, 321. **7.** Violence, MBh. 3, 1031. **8.** Dignity, Man. 9, 303; glory, Man. 7, 5. **9.** A venerable person or object, MBh. 13, 5017; a renowned person, Chr. 24, 40. **10.** Semen virile, Râm. 1, 37, 11. — **Comp.** *A-mita-* (vb. *mâ*), adj. of boundless splendour. *Tigma-*, adj. 1. very sharp, Râm. 4, 7, 21. 2. very violent, MBh. 13, 184. *Nis-*, adj. devoid of energy, MBh. 10, 124. *Mahâ-*, I adj. 1. very bright. 2. very vigorous. II. m. 1. fire. 2. a name of the god of war. 3. a demigod. *Brahmatejas*, i.e. *brahman-*, n. Brahmanical virtue. *Mâṁsa-*, n. marrow or serum of the flesh. *Samâna-*, adj. equal in glory. *Su-*, adj. 1. sharp-edged. 2. very bright. 3. potent.

ऽतेजस *-tejas + a*, a substitute for *tejas* when latter part of a compound word, e.g. MBh. 3, 8681.

तेजस्काम *tejas-kâma*, adj. One who desires manly strength, Man. 4, 44.

तेजस्त्व *tejas + tva*, n. The essence of light, Bhâg. P. 3, 26, 39.

तेजस्विता *tejasvitâ*, i.e. *tejasvin + tâ*, f. Energy, MBh. 3, 10755.

तेजस्वित्व *tejasvitva*, i.e. *tejasvin + tva*, n. Splendour, Chr. 34, 7.

तेजस्विन् *tejas + vin*, adj., f. *nî*. **1.** Bright, Man. 9, 318. **2.** Strong, Sund. 1, 2. **3.** Awful, glorious, Man. 9, 310.

तेजोमय *tejomaya*, i.e. *tejas + maya*, adj., f. *yî*, Consisting of light, Man. 6, 39. —**Comp.** *Sarva-*, adj. containing every kind of power, Man. 7, 11. *Brahma-tejomaya*, i.e. *brahman-tejas + maya*, adj. having a holy splendour, Man. 7, 14.

† तेप् *TEP*, i. 1, Âtm. To drop.—Cf. *tip*.

† तेव् *TEV*, i. 1, Âtm. To play; cf. *div, dev*.

तैक्ष्ण्य *taikshṇya*, i. e. *tîkshṇa + ya*, n. **1.** Sharpness, Çâk. 32, 5, v. r. **2.** Severity, Man. 4, 163.

तैजस *taijasa*, i.e. *tejas + a*, adj., f. *sî*. **1.** Produced by fire, Bhâg. P. 7, 2, 42. **2.** Made of brilliant metals, Man. 5, 111.

तैतिल *taitila*, m. Deity, Daçak. 176, 15.

तैत्तिर *taittira*, i.e. *tittiri + a*, adj. Produced from partridges, Râm. 2, 100, 63 Gorr.

तैत्तिरिक *taittirika*, i.e. *tittiri + ika*, m. One who keeps partridges, Râm. 2, 90, 13 Gorr.

तैन्दुक *tainduka*, i.e. *tinduka + a*, adj., f. *kî*, Of the tree Tiuduka, Suçr. 2, 431, 13.

तैमिर *taimira*, i.e. *timira + a*, adj. adj. Combined with *roga*, A disease of the eyes, Suçr. 2, 86, 2.

तैमिरिक *taimirika*, i.e. *timira* + *ika*, adj. Suffering from the *timira*-disease, Suçr. 2, 186, 5.

तैर्थिक *tairthika*, i.e. *tîrtha* + *ika*, adj. 1. Coming from holy places, MBh. 3, 8085. 2. Frequenting holy places, an ascetic, Prab. 25, 19. 3. Holy (?), MBh. 13, 6066.

तैर्यग्योन *tairyagyona*, i.e. *tiryañch-yoni* + *a*, m. An animal, Man. 7, 150.

तैर्यग्योन्य *tairyagyonya*, i.e. *tiryañch-yoni* + *ya*, I. m. An animal, MBh. 5, 3506. II. adj. Referring to animals, Mârk. P. 47, 33.

तैल *taila*, i.e. *tila* + *a*, n. 1. Oil, Yâjñ. 1, 283. 2. Incense, Varâh. Bṛih. S. 76, 4.—Comp. *Gandha*-, n. oil prepared with perfumes, Râm. 4, 24, 16. *Tila*-, n. oil prepared from sesamum, Suçr. 1, 80, 6.

तैलपक *tailapaka*, i.e. *taila-pa* + *ka* (vb. 1. *pâ*), m. An oil-drinking beetle, a cockroach, Man. 12, 63.

तैलपर्णिक *tailaparṇika*, i.e. *tila-parṇa* + *ika*, m. A kind of sandal, Hariv. 12680.

तैलपायिका *tailapâyikâ*, i.e. *taila-pâyin* + *ka*, f. A kind of beetle (see *tailapaka*), MBh. 14, 5069.

तैलपायिन् *tailapâyin*, i.e. *taila*-1. *pâ* + *in*, m. 1. A kind of beetle (cf. *tailapaka*), Yâjñ. 3, 211. 2. A sword (?), MBh. 7, 6713.

तैलिक *tailika*, i.e. *taila* + *ika*, m. An oil-grinder, Man. 3, 158.

तैल्वक *tailvaka*, i.e. *tilvaka* + *a*, adj. Prepared from the Tilvaka tree, Suçr. 2, 324, 15.

तोक *toka*, I. n. 1. Offspring, Chr. 291, 14 = Rigv. i. 64, 14. 2. Child, Bhâg. P. 2, 7, 27. II. m. in *varâha-toka*, A young boar, Bhâg. P. 3, 13, 18.—Cf. ved. *tuch*, Offspring; *tvaksh*, *τέκνον* (= A.S. thegn, thegen, O.H.G. degan, servus), *τίκτω*, *ἔτεκον*, *τοκάς*; probably Goth. thius, thivi; A.S. theowa-man.

तोक्म *tokma* (akin to *toka*), m. Green barley, Bhâg. P. 4, 21, 2.

† **तोड्** *TOḌ*, i. 1, Âtm. To despise.

तोत्त्र *tottra*, written also **तोत्र** *totra*, i.e. *tud* + *tra*, n. 1. A goad for driving cattle, MBh. 6, 1674. 2. A stick with a sharp iron head for guiding an elephant, Râm. 2, 40, 41.

तोद *toda*, i.e. *tud* + *a*, m. 1. Stinging, Bhâg. P. 3, 18, 6. 2. A sting, Suçr. 1, 34, 16.

तोदन *todana*, i.e. *tud* + *ana*, I. n. Stinging, Suçr. 1, 5, 8. II. m. The name of a tree, and (n.) its fruit, Suçr. 1, 211, 12; 20.

तोमर *tomara* (perhaps *tud* + *man* + *a*, with *r* for *n*). 1. m. and n. A javelin, Râm. 2, 74, 31. 2. m. pl. The name of a people, MBh. 6, 377.

तोमराण *tomarâṇa*, m. A proper name, Râjat. 5, 232.

तोय *toya*, n. (perhaps from vb. *tu*), Water, Man. 8, 409; with *kṛi*, To pour water in honour of a deceased, MBh. 18, 32.—Comp. *Antastoya*, i.e. *antar*-, adj. containing water, Megh. 65. *Nis*-, adj. devoid of water, Râm. 4, 48, 8.

तोयद *toya-da*, m. A cloud, Râm. 5, 40, 10.

तोयधि *toyadhi*, i.e. *toya-dhâ* (cf. *nidhi*), in *kshîra*-, m. The sea of milk, Râm. 6, 26, 6.

तोयमय *toya* + *maya*, adj., f. *yî*, Consisting of water, MBh. 7, 9608.

तोयमुच् *toya-much*, m. A cloud, Râm. 3, 79, 4.

तोयवन्त् *toya + vant*, adj., f. *vatî*, Surrounded by water, MBh. 12, 3696.

तोरण *toraṇa*, n. (and m.), **1.** An arch, Pañch. 192, 16. **2.** A gate, Râm. 1, 6, 26.—**Comp.** *Ud-*, adj., f. *ṇâ*, adorned with erected arches, Ragh. 14, 10. *Kautuka-*, n. an arch erected at festivals, Bhâg. P. 1, 11, 14.

तोलक *tolaka*, i.e. *tul + aka*, m. and n. A weight = 2 *çâṇas*, Râjat. 4, 201.

तोलन *tolana*, i.e. *tul + ana*, n. Weighing, Hit. 140, 1; balancing, Râm. 1, 67, 10.

तोष *tosha*, i.e. *tush + a*, m. Satisfaction, pleasure, MBh. 13, 1285.—**Comp.** *Dus-*, adj. difficult to be satisfied, MBh. 12, 4166.

तोषण *toshaṇa*, i.e. *tush + ana*, adj., f. *aṇî*. **1.** Satisfying, MBh. 2, 678. **2.** Appeasing, Bhâg. P. 1, 2, 13.

ऽतोषिन् *-toshin*, i.e. *tush + in*, latter part of comp. adj., f. *iṇî*. **1.** Content, MBh. 13, 3030. **2.** Liking, Hariv. 15267. **3.** Gladdening, Râm. 4, 37, 31.

तौर्यत्रिक *taurya-trika*, i. e. *tûrya-trika + a*, n. Singing, instrumental music and dancing, Man. 7, 47.

तौषार *taushâra*, i.e. *tushâra + a*, adj. Produced by snow, Suçr. 1, 170, 1.

त्मन् *tman*, see *âtman*.

त्यक्तुकाम *tyaktukâma*, i.e. *tyaktum-kâma* (vb. *tyaj*), adj. Wishing to leave, Nal. 9, 13.

त्यक्तृ *tyaktṛi*, i.e. *tyaj + tṛi*, m, f. *trî*, n. One who resigns, or sacrifices, MBh. 7, 378.

त्यज् *TYAJ*, i. 1, Par. (also Âtm., Râm. 5, 80, 30). **1.** To leave, to abandon, MBh. 5, 5994; Nal. 24, 35. To throw away, Châṇ. 108, in Berl. Monatsb. **2.** To disown, Çâk. d. 122. **3.** To expose, Bhâg. P. 9, 24, 35. **4.** To give, MBh. 5, 2348. **5.** To resign, Man. 2, 95; with *prâṇân, çvâsam, jîvitam*, To sacrifice one's life, Râm. 3, 55, 24; to risk one's life, MBh. 5, 7204. **6.** To neglect, Hit. ii. d. 39. Caus. *tyâjaya*, **1.** To cause to abandon, to rob, Megh. 94. **2.** To expel, Kathâs. 20, 126. **3.** To cause to be disregarded, Ragh. 6, 56.—With the prep. **समभि** *sam-abhi*, **1.** To resign, MBh. 12, 269. **2.** To risk, MBh. 6, 158.—With **निस्** *nis*, To expel, Râm. 4, 46, 8.—With **परि** *pari*, **1.** To abandon, Hit. 25, 19. **2.** To disown, Man. 9, 175. **3.** To resign, Man. 4, 176; with *deham*, To die, Bhâg. P. 1, 15, 49. **4.** To disregard, to leave out, Vedântas. in Chr. 208, 19. **5.** pass. with instr. To lose, Hit. i. d. 128. Ptcple. of the pf. pass. *parityakta*, **1.** Deserted, Man. 12, 21. **2.** Robbed, Hit. i. d. 31. **3.** Left, wanting, Châṇ. 101, in Berl. Monatsb. Caus. To rob (with two accus.), Râm. 4, 19, 35.—With **संपरि** *sam-pari*, **1.** To abandon, Râm. 3, 54, 5. **2.** To risk, Râm. 6, 29, 15.—With **सम्** *sam*, To abandon, Pañch. i. d. 168. **2.** To shun, Man. 4, 131; Bhartṛ. 1, 80. **3.** To resign, Bhâg. P. 6, 10, 7. **4.** To except, Râjat. 3, 343. *saṁtyakta*, Robbed, Varâh. Bṛih. S. 67, 70. Caus. To rob (with two accus.), MBh. 7, 8991.—With **अभिसम्** *abhi-sam*, To leave, MBh. 6, 2232.

ऽत्यज् *-tyaj*, latter part of comp. adj. Abandonding, resigning, giving away, Bhâg. P. 8, 20, 9.—**Comp.** *Tanu-*, adj. 1. dying, Ragh. 1, 8. 2. risking one's life, MBh. 4, 2354.

त्यद् *tyad*, i.e. *ta-yad*, see *tad*; except the nom. sing. m. and f., the base of the m. and n. is *tya*, of the fem. *tyâ*; the nom. sing. msc. is *syas*, *f. syâ*; pronoun of the third person, That, Chr. 289, 1=Rigv. i. 50, 1.—Cf. Goth. si; O.H.G siu.

त्याग *tyâga*, i.e. *tyaj+a*, m. **1.** Abandoning, Man. 10, 111; Pańch. 261, 6; forsaking, Man. 8, 389; resigning, Râm. 4, 7, 9. **2.** Giving away, Böhtl. Ind. Spr. 499; liberality, Daçak. in Chr. 180, 16; prodigality, Böhtl. Ind. Spr. 1260. **3.** Secretion, MBh. 14, 630. —**Comp.** *Âtmatyâga*, i.e. *âtman-*, m. 1. loss of conscience, Suçr. 1, 192, 6. 2. suicide, Daçak. in Chr. 189, 9. *Tanu-*, m. risking one's life, Râm. 2, 40, 6. *Deha-*, m. dying, death, Man. 10, 62. *Sthâna-*, m. leaving one's place, Böhtl. Ind. Spr. 3348.

त्यागमय *tyâga+maya*, adj., f. *yî*, Consisting in donation, Kathâs. 23, 84.

त्यागिता *tyâgitâ*, i.e. *tyâgin+tâ*, f. Liberality, Hit. i. d. 89.

त्यागिन् *tyâgin*, i.e. *tyaj+in*, adj., f. *nî*. **1.** Deserting, Man. 3, 245; disowning, Çâk. d. 125; resigning, Bhag. 18, 11; with *âtmanas*, killing one's self, Man. 5, 89. **2.** Liberal, Pańch. iii. d. 259.—**Comp.** *Âtmatyâgin*, i.e. *âtman-*, m. a suicide, Yâjń. 3, 6.

त्याजक *tyâjaka*, i.e. *tyaj+aka*, adj. Abandoning, Yâjń. 2, 198.

ऽत्र *-tra* (vb. *trâ*), latter part of comp. words, Protecting, cf. e. g. *tanutra*.

† **त्रंस्** *TRAṂS*, i. 1 and 10, Par. To speak or shine.

† **त्रख्** *TRAKH*, i. 1, Par. To go.

† **त्रङ्क्** *TRAṄK*, i. 1, Âtm. To go.

† **त्रङ्ख्** *TRAṄKH*, and **त्रङ्ग्** *TRAṄG* (v.r.), i. 1, Par. To go.

† **त्रन्द्** *TRAND*, i. 1, Par. To be active.

त्रप् *TRAP*, i. 1, Âtm. (also Par. Râm. 2, 57, 28), To be embarrassed, to be ashamed, Râjat. 3, 94. Caus. *trâpaya*, To make ashamed, Çântiç. 14, 15. — With the prep. **अप** *apa*, **1.** To turn away on account of shame, MBh. 12, 3491. **2.** To be ashamed, MBh. 3, 110.—With **व्यप** *vi-apa*, **1.** To turn away on account of shame, MBh. 2, 433. **2.** To be ashamed, Râm. 3, 59, 3. —Cf. τρέπω; Lat. turpis, probably also trepidus (cf. ved. *tṛipra*, hastening), and perhaps Goth. dreiban; A.S. drîfan (Caus.).

त्रप *trap+a*, m., and f. *pâ*, Shame, Pańch. 84, 8; MBh. 2, 2239.—**Comp.** *A-trapa* and *nis-*, adj., f. *pâ*, Shameless, Pańch. i. d. 472; MBh. 5, 1458.

त्रपु *trap+u*, n. Tin, Man. 5, 114.

त्रपुस *trapusa*, n. Cucumber, the fruit of the *trapusî*, Suçr. 1, 29, 2.

त्रपुसी *trapusî*, f. A sort of cucumber, Suçr. 2, 481, 12.

त्रय *traya*, i.e. *tri+a*, I, adj., *f. yî*, Threefold, Man. 1, 23. **II.** f. *yî*, **1.** The three Vedas, Man. 4, 125. **2.** Triad, Râjat. 5, 143 (*çata-*, Three hundreds). **III.** n. Triad, Daçak. in Chr. 197, 17. —**Comp.** *Agni-*, n. The three holy fires, Râm. 3, 12, 3.

त्रयस्ऽ *trayas-*, nom. pl. m. of *tri*, Former part of compounded numerals, Three, e. g. *trayastriṃçat*, Thirty-three; *trayaçchatvâriṃçat*, Forty-three; *trayahpańchâçat*, Fifty-three.

त्रयीमय *trayî+maya* (see *traya*),

adj., f. *yî*, Consisting of the three Vedas, Bhâg. P. 3, 13, 40.

त्रयोदश *trayodaça*, i.e. *trayodaçan* + *a*, **1.** ordinal number, f. *çî*, Thirteenth, Râm. 2, 77, 22. **2.** f. *çî*, The thirteenth day of the lunar fortnight, Man. 3, 273.

त्रयोदशधा *trayodaçadhâ*, i.e. *trayodaçan* + *dhâ*, adv. Thirteen-fold, Râjat. 5, 173.

त्रयोदशन् *trayodaçan*, i.e. *trayas-daçan*, numeral, Thirteen, Man. 9, 129. —Comp. *Ardha-*, Thirteen and a half, Yâjń. 2, 165.—Cf. τρις-καί-δεκα, for τρεῖς- ; Lat. tredecim for tres-decem.

त्रयोदशिक *trayodaçika*, i.e. *trayodaçî* (see *trayodaça*) + *ika*, adj. Performed on the thirteenth day of the lunar fortnight, Râm. 2, 86, 1 Gorr.

त्रयोविंशतिक *trayoviṁçatika*, i.e. *trayas-viṁçati* + *ka*, adj. Consisting of twenty-three, Bhâg. P. 3, 6, 4.

1. त्रस् *TRAS*, i. 1 and 4, Par. (in epic poetry also Âtm., Bhâg. P. 1, 17, 20), To tremble, to be afraid, MBh. 7, 1402 ; 6, 20. *trasta*, Trembling, MBh. 3, 1431 ; fearful, Râm. 1, 49, 1 ; MBh. 4, 841. Comp. *A-trasta*, adj. intrepid, Ragh. 1, 21. Caus. *trâsaya*, To frighten, Râm. 2, 43, 3 ; anomalous ptcple. of the pres. Âtm. *trâsayâna*, MBh. 6, 2141. Ptcple. of the fut. pass. *trâsanîya*, Terrible, Hariv. 2430.—With the prep. अप *apa*, To retire in fear, MBh. 12, 2526.—With अव *ava*, *avatrasta*, Frightened, Hariv. 2520.—With उद् *ud*, *uttrasta*, Frightened, Râjat. 5, 148. Caus. To frighten, Hariv, 3377.—With परि *pari*, *paritrasta*, Trembling, Hariv. 10127 ; frightened, Râm. 3, 54, 7.—With वि *vi*, To tremble, to be afraid, MBh. 3, 8663. *vitrasta*, Frightened, MBh. 1, 5964. Comp. *A-vitrasta*, adj. intrepid, MBh. 1, 5496. Caus. To frighten, to alarm, MBh. 3, 698 ; Man. 7, 196.—With सम् *sam*, To be afraid, MBh. 7, 103. *saṁtrasta*, Frightened, MBh. 6, 2640. Comp. *Su-saṁtrasta*, adj. very frightened, Râm. 3, 55, 29. Caus. To frighten, Pańch. i. d. 212.—With अभिसम् *abhi-sam*, *abhisaṁtrasta*, Frightened, Râm. 2, 9, 6 Gorr.—Cf. *trâsa*, τρέω (for τρεσjω), τρέστης, ταρταρίζω, τρήρων (for τρεσρων), Goth. thlahsjan ; Lat. terrere (for tersere, tresere) ; cf. *tarala*, *tṛî*, *tur*, *trap* ; τρέμω, Lat. tremo, probably tristis, τάρβος, ταράσσω, θάλασσα, and many other words.

† 2. त्रस् *TRAS*, i. 10, Par. To hold, or to take, or to prevent.

त्रस *tras* + *a*, n. (moving) Living creatures, Matsyop. 29.

त्रसदस्यु *trasadasyu* (cf. *tras* and *dasyu*), m. A proper name, Chr. 297, 14 = Rigv. i. 112, 14.

त्रसरेणु *trasa-reṇu*, m. **1.** A small mote visible in a sunbeam, Man. 8, 132. **2.** A compound atom in the Vaiçeshika philosophy (said by some to be composed of three *paramâṇus*, by others of three *dvyaṇukas*), Brahmavaiv. P. 4, 96, 49.

त्रस्नु *tras* + *nu*, adj. Timid, Râjat. 5, 415.—Comp. *A-*, adj. intrepid, Ragh. 14, 47. *An-ati-*, adj. confident, Daçak. in Chr. 196, 14.

त्रा *TRÂ*, ii. 2, Par. Âtm., and त्रै *TRAI*, i. 1, *trâya* (i.e. properly *trâ*, i. 4), Âtm. To protect, to preserve (with the abl.), MBh. 2, 2606.—With the prep. परि *pari*, To protect, MBh. 13, 3600 ; *paritrâta*, Râm. 6. 6, 10.—With सम् *sam*, To protect, MBh. 1, 6819.—Akin to *tṛî*, and for original *tar* + *â*.

त्राण *trâṇa*, i. e. *trâ+ana*, n. 1. Shelter, Man. 11, 113. 2. Protection, MBh. 3, 13284. — Comp. *Aṅguli-* = *aṅgulitra*, q. cf. *Tanu-*, n. a coat of mail, Râm. 2, 31, 25 Gorr. *Tala-*, n. a leathern fence worn by archers on the left arm, MBh. 3, 1501. *Pâda-*, n. a shoe.

त्रातृ *trâtṛi*, i. e. *trâ+tṛi*, m. A preserver, a protector, MBh. 1, 8421.— Comp. *Makha-*, m. Râma, the son of Daçaratha, and second incarnation of Vishṇu.

त्रामन् *trâman*, i. e. *trâ+man*, n. Protection.—Comp. *Su-*, m. Indra (cf. *sûtrâman*).

त्रास *trâsa*, i. e. *tras + a*, I. adj. Moveable, MBh. 7, 9476. II. m. 1. Fear, terror, Râm. 3, 50, 17. 2. Frightening, Hit. 27, 15.—Comp. *Jala-*, m. hydrophobia, Suçr. 2, 282, 3.

त्रासन *trâsana*, i. e. *tras*, Caus., + *ana*, I. adj., f. *nî*, Frightening, Râm. 3, 7, 8. II. n. 1. Frightening, MBh. 4, 1706. 2. Fright, Bhâg. P. 4, 10, 28.

त्रासिन् *trâsin*, i.e. *trâsa+in*, adj., f. *nî*, Afraid, MBh. 12, 5904.—Comp. *Jala-*, adj. suffering from hydrophobia, Suçr. 2, 282, 4.

त्रि *tri*, numeral, f. *tisṛi*, Three, Man. 2, 229.

त्रिंश *triṁça*, i e. curtailed *triṁçat*, ordin. number, f. *çî*, Thirtieth.—Comp. *Chatustriṁça*, i. e. *chatur-*, Thirty-fourth, Râm. 1, 30; 34. *Dvâ-*, thirty-second. *Pañchatriṁça*, i.e. *pañchan-*, thirty-fifth.

त्रिंशत् *triṁçat*, i. e. *tri-dacant*, numeral, f. adj. and sbst., Thirty, MBh. 6, 5409; Râjat. 1, 286.—Comp. *Dvâ-*, thirty-two, Râm. 1, 43, 5. *Shaṭ-triṁçat*, i.e. *shash-*, thirty-six, Râjat. 5, 117.

त्रिंशत्क *triṁçat + ka*, n. An assemblage of thirty, Kâm. Nîtis, 8, 37.

त्रिंशत्तम *triṁçat + tama*, ordin. number, f. *mî*, Thirtieth, MBh. 12, chapter 30.

त्रिक *tri+ka*, I. adj. 1. Forming a triad, Suçr. 1, 158, 2. 2. (suppl. *çata*), Three per cent. Man. 8, 142. 3. (A place) where three roads meet, Hariv. 6501. II. n. 1. A triad, MBh. 12, 7954. 2. The chine-bone, Ragh. 6, 16. 3. The hip, Pañch. i. d. 205.

त्रिगर्त *trigarta*, m. pl. The name of a people, MBh. 2, 1026.

† त्रिङ्ख् *TRIṄKH*, i. 1, Par. To go; see *trakh*.

त्रिचतुर *tri-chatur+a*, pl. Three or four, Daçak. in Chr. 187, 3.

त्रिणाचिकेत *triṇâchiketa*, i. e. *tri-nâchiketa*, m. One who practises a certain vow prescribed in a part of the Yâjurveda, Man. 3, 185.

त्रित *trita*, m. The name of a deity, MBh. 1, 2112.

त्रितय *tri+taya*, n. A triad, MBh. 13, 5415.

त्रित्व *tri+tva*, n. A triad, MBh. 14, 2617.

त्रिदश *tridaça* (i.e. *tri-daçan*), I. adj. pl. Thirty, MBh. 1, 4445. II. m. A name of the thirty-three gods, a deity, MBh. 3, 8162. III. n. Heaven, MBh. 13, 3327.

त्रिदशत्व *tridaça+tva*, n. Divine nature, Ragh. 18, 30.

त्रिधा *tri + dhâ*, adv. Threefold, MBh. 13, 6467; in three places, 1, 8013;

in three parts, MBh. 5, 7206. — Cf. τρίχα, τρίχθα.

त्रिपुरेशाद्रि *tripureçâdri*, i. e. *tri-pura-îça-adri*, m. The name of a locality, Râjat. 5, 123.

त्रिरसक *tri-rasa + ka*, n. A spirituous liquor, Çiç. 9, 10; in Sâh. D. 66, 1, v.r. of *tri-saraka*.

त्रिवर्षीय *trivarshîya*, i.e. *tri-varsha + îya*, adj. Designed for three years, MBh. 13, 4467.

त्रिवृत् *tri-vṛit*, I. adj. Triple, Man. 11, 263. **2.** A peculiar mode of reciting the eleventh hymn of the ninth maṇḍala of the Rigv., Man. 11, 74. **II.** m. A triple string, Man. 2, 43. **III.** f. Ipomœa turpethum R. Br., Suçr. 2, 35, 9.

त्रिवृता *trivṛitâ*, i.e. *tri-vṛit + a*, f. = *trivṛit* III., Suçr. 1, 132, 17.

त्रिशङ्कु *tri-çaṅku*, m. The name of a king, Hariv. 730.

त्रिषवण *trishavaṇa*, i.e. *tri-savana*, n. The three daily ablutions, Man. 6, 24.

त्रिष्टुभ् *trishṭubh*, i.e. *tri-stubh*, f. A kind of metre, Bhâg. P. 3, 12, 45.

त्रिस् *tri + s*, adv. **1.** Thrice, Man. 2, 60. **2.** At three places, MBh. 1, 5885.—Cf. τρίς; Lat. ter.

त्रिसुपर्ण *tri-su-parṇa*, and त्रिसुपर्णक *trisuparṇa + ka*, adj. One conversant with a part of the Vedas called *trisuparṇa*, Man. 3, 185; Yâjń. 1, 219.

त्रिसुवर्चक *tri-su-varcha + ka* (cf. *varchas*), adj. Having a threefold splendour (?), MBh. 3, 14156.

त्रिसौपर्ण *trisauparṇa*, i. e. *tri-su-parṇa + a*, adj. Epithet of a certain religious study, MBh. 12, 13567.

त्रुट् *TRUṬ*, i. 4 and 6, Par. To burst asunder, Bhartṛ. 1, 95; Hit. 15, 20. *truṭita*, Burst, Pańch. 121, 2. Caus. To tear asunder, to break, Pańch. 146, 24. † i. 10, Âtm. To cut.

त्रुटि *truṭ + i*, f. **1.** A moment as measure of time, MBh. 1, 1292. **2.** Small cardamoms, Suçr. 2, 505, 1.

त्रुटिशस् *truṭi +ças*, adv. By moments called *truṭi*, MBh. 5, 3732.

† त्रुप् *TRUP*, त्रुफ् *TRUPH*, त्रुम्प् *TRUMP*, and त्रुम्फ् *TRUMPH*, i. 1, Par. To hurt. — Cf. perhaps θρύπτω, τρύφος, etc., and τρυπάω.

त्रेता *tretâ* (i.e. probably *traya + tâ*), f. **1.** A triad, MBh. 14, 2759. **2.** The three sacred fires, MBh. 5, 1559. **3.** A die, or the side of a die, which has three points, Mṛichchh. 33, 9. **4.** The name of the second *yuga*, or age, Man. 9, 201.—**Comp.** *Agni-*, f. the three sacred fires, Man. 2, 231.

त्रै *TRAI*, see *trâ*.

त्रैकालिक *traikâlika*, i.e. *tri-kâla + ika*, adj. Referring to the three times, past, present, and future, MBh. 12, 13033.

त्रैकाल्य *traikâlya*, i.e. *tri-kâla + ya*, n. **1.** The three times, past, present, and future, MBh. 12, 1690. **2.** Morning, noon, and evening, Yâjń. 3, 308. **3.** A triad (?), Hariv. 7446.

त्रैगर्त *traigarta*, i.e. *trigarta + a* (and त्रैगर्तक *traigarta + ka*), **I.** adj. Proper to the Trigartas, MBh. 4, 1117. **II.** m. **1.** A prince of the Trigartas, MBh. 4, 1070. **2.** pl. = Trigarta. **III.** f. *tî*, A princess of the Trigartas, MBh. 1, 3788.

त्रैगुण्य *traiguṇya*, i.e. *tri-guṇa + ya*, n. The three original qualities, Bhag. 2, 45.

त्रैदशिक *traidaçika*, i.e. *tridaça* + *ika*, adj. Referring to the *tridaças*, Man. 2, 58.

त्रैध *traidha*, i.e. *tridhâ* + *a*, adj. Triple; acc. sing. n. °*dham*, adv. In three different manners, MBh. 3, 1233.

त्रैपुर *traipura*, i.e. *tri-purâ* or *rî* + *a*, m. **1.** pl. The inhabitants of Tripurâ and Tripurî, i.e. the Chedis, Hariv. 7443; MBh. 6, 3855. **2.** A prince of the Chedis.

त्रैपुरुष *traipurusha*, i.e. *tri-purusha* + *a*, adj. Comprising three generations, MBh. 13, 4322.

त्रैफल *traiphala*, i.e. *tri-phalâ* + *a*, adj. Coming from the three myrobalans, Suçr. 2, 45, 7.

त्रैमासिक *traimâsika*, *tri-mâsa* + *ika*, adj. Three months old, Bhâg. P. 2, 7, 27.

त्रैयम्बक *traiyambaka*, i.e. *tryambaka* + *a*, adj. Referring or dedicated to Tryambaka, MBh. 7, 169.

त्रैलिङ्ग *trailiṅga*, i.e. *tri-liṅga* + *a*, adj. Being of three genders, MBh. 12, 11353.

त्रैलोक *trailoka*, i.e. *tri-loka* + *a*, m. A name of Indra, MBh. 12, 10106.

त्रैलोक्य *trailokya*, i.e. *tri-loka* + *ya*, n. The three worlds, Man. 11, 236.

त्रैवर्गिक *traivargika*, i.e. *tri-varga* + *ika*, adj., f. *kî*, Referring, attached to the three classes of ends, viz. virtue, pleasure, and interest, Bhâg. P. 2, 4, 4; 3, 32, 18.

त्रैवर्ग्य *traivargya*, i.e. *tri-varga* + *ya*, adj. Belonging to the three classes of ends, viz. virtue, pleasure, and interest, Bhâg. P. 4, 22, 35.

त्रैवार्षिक *traivârshika*, i.e. *tri-varsha* + *ika*, adj. Sufficient for three years, Man. 11, 7.

त्रैविक्रम *traivikrama*, i.e. *tri-vikrama* + *a*, I. adj. Belonging to Vishṇu, Ragh. 7, 32. **II.** n. Going three steps, Hariv. 3168.

त्रैविद्य *traividya*, i.e. *tri-vidyâ* + *a*, I. n. **1.** The three Vedas, Man. 2, 28. **2.** An assemblage of Brâhmaṇas skilled in the three Vedas, Yâjñ. 1, 9. **II.** adj. Skilled in the three Vedas, Man. 12, 111.

त्रैविध्य *traividhya*, i.e. *tri-vidha* + *ya* (cf. *vidhâ*), n. Triplicity, Bhâshâp. 12.

त्रैविष्टप *traivishṭapa* and **त्रैविष्टपेय** *traivishṭapeya*, i.e. *tri-vishṭapa* + *a* and *eya*, m. A god, Bhâg. P. 1, 11, 8; 8, 8, 19.

त्रैवृत *traivṛita*, i.e. *tri-vṛit* + *a*, adj. Coming from the plant Ipomœa turpethum, Suçr. 2, 378, 11.

त्रैवेदिक *traivedika*, i.e. *tri-veda* + *ika*, adj. Relating to the three Vedas, Man. 3, 1.

त्रैशङ्कव *traiçaṅkava*, i.e. *tri-çaṅku* + *a*, patronym. A descendant of Triçaṅku, Hariv. 755.

त्रैशीर्ष *traiçîrsha*, i.e. *tri-çîrshan* + *a*, adj., f. *shâ*, Referring to Triçîrshan, MBh. 5, 335.

त्रैस्रोतस *traisrotasa*, i.e. *tri-srotas* + *a*, adj. Belonging to the Gaṅgâ, Ragh. 16, 34.

त्रोटक *troṭaka*, n. A kind of drama, Vikr. 3, 8.

† **त्रौक्** *TRAUK*, i. 1, Âtm. To go, to move.

त्र्यम्बक *tryambaka*, i.e. *tri-ambaka*, m. Epithet of Rudra-Çiva, MBh. 2, 403.

त्र्यहैहिक *tryahaihika,* see *aihika.*

त्वक्ष् *TVAKSH,* i. 1, Par. **1.** To produce, to work (ved.). **2.** † To pare. **3.** † To cover.—Cf. *taksh, toka*; τύκος, τεύχω, τέχνη.

त्वग्दोषिन् *tvagdoshin,* i.e. *tvach -dosha + in,* adj., f. *iṇî,* Suffering from a cutaneous disease, MBh. 5, 5056.

त्वंकार *tvaṁkâra,* i.e. *tvam* (nom. sing. of *yushmad*) *-kâra,* m. Saying thou, as an insult, Man. 11, 204.

त्वङ्ग् *TVAṄG,* i. 1, Par. To gallop, Kathâs. 18, 7.

† 1. त्वच् *TVACH,* i. 6, Par. To cover.

2. त्वच् *tvach,* f. **1.** Skin, Man. 2, 90. **2.** Hide, Râm. 3, 49, 9. **3.** Bark, Ragh. 2, 37.

त्वच *tvach + a,* **I.** a substitute for *tvach,* when latter part of a comp. adj., e.g. *mṛidu-,* Having a tender skin, Hariv. 10425. **II.** n. Cinnamon, Râm. 3, 39, 22.

† त्वञ्च् *TVAÑCH,* i. 1, Par. **1.** To go. **2.** To contract.—Cf. *tañch.*

त्वद् *tvad,* substitute for the sing. of the pronoun of the second person when former part of a comp. word, and in many derivatives (cf. *yushmad*), e.g. *tvad-vidha* (see *vidhâ*), adj. Resembling thee, Râm. 2, 23, 7. *tvad-kṛita,* Made by thee, Râm. 1, 2, 40.

त्वदीय *tvad + îya,* possess. pron. Thine, Râm. 1, 45, 24.

त्वन्मय *tvanmaya,* i.e. *tvad + maya,* adj., f. *yî,* Consisting of thee, Hariv. 2585.

त्वर् *TVAR,* i. 1, Âtm. (in epic poetry also Par., Râm. 2, 19, 16), To make haste, Râm. 3, 78, 20. Ptcple. of the pf. pass. **I.** *tvarita,* **1.** Hastening, Râm. 1, 67, 24. **2.** Swift, Pañch. iii. d. 102. °*tam,* adv. Swiftly, Râm. 1, 42, 23. **II.** *tûrṇa,* °*ṇam,* adv. Quickly, Pañch. 167, 16. Ptcple. of the fut. pass. *tvaraṇîya,* Where there needs haste, MBh. 7, 5842. Caus. *tvaraya,* To cause to hasten, MBh. 7, 1584.—With the prep. अति *ati,* To hasten very much, MBh. 12, 5003.—With अभि *abhi,* To make haste, Râm. 6, 33, 4.—With प्र *pra,* To hasten, MBh. 6, 3776.—With सम् *sam,* To make haste, Râm. 2, 30, 43. Caus. To cause to hasten, MBh. 7, 955.—Cf. *tur*; *tṛî,* θόρνυμι, θοῦρος, θρώσκω; Lat. red-am-truare, probably ἀ-θύρω, τύρβη, Lat. turba, θόρυβος; probably A.S. a-thwerian (to move, or to shake together).

त्वरा *tvar + â,* f. Haste, Râm. 2, 46, 27.—Comp. *A-,* f. absence of precipitate haste, Man. 3, 235. *Sa-tvara,* adj. hastening, Chr. 28, 18; quick. °*ram,* adv. Quickly, Pañch. 46, 1.

त्वरावन्त् *tvarâ + vant,* adj., f. *vatî,* Quick, MBh. 3, 16207.

त्वष्टि *tvashṭi,* i.e. *tvaksh + ti,* f. The profession of a carpenter, Man. 10, 48.

त्वष्टृ *tvashṭṛi,* i.e. *tvaksh + tṛi,* m. **1.** A carpenter (ved.). **2.** The name of a deity, the artist of the gods, Chr. 292, 9 = Rigv. i. 85, 9; MBh. 4, 1178.

त्वादृश् *tvâdṛiç,* i.e. *tvad-dṛiç,* adj. Resembling thee, Bhâg. P. 1, 17, 12.

त्वादृश *tvâdṛiça,* i.e. *tvad-dṛiç + a,* adj., f. *çî,* Resembling thee, Râm. 4, 16, 31.

त्वाष्ट्र *tvâshṭra,* i. e. *tvashṭṛi + a,* **I.** adj. Referring to or made by Tvashṭṛi, Râm. 1, 29, 19. **II.** m. The name of an Asura or demon, MBh. 5, 504 = Vṛitra,

Bhâg. P. 6, 9, 17. III. f. *ri*, The daughter of Tvashṭṛi, and wife of Sûrya, MBh. 1, 2599. IV. n. The power of Tvashṭṛi, Bhâg. P. 8, 11, 35.

1. **त्विष्** *TVISH*, i. 1, Par., Âtm. **1.** To be excited (ved.). **2.** To shine.

2. **त्विष्** *tvish*, f. **1.** Light, Daçak in Chr. 195, 23. **2.** Splendour, Arj. 10, 65.

त्वेषसंदृश् *tveshasaṁdṛiç*, i.e. *tvesha* (ved.) *-sam-dṛiç* adj. Of a splendid aspect, Chr. 292, 8=Rigv. i. 85, 8.

त्सर् *TSAR*, i. 1, Par. To sneak, to steal upon (ved.).

त्सरु *tsaru*, m. The hilt of a sword, MBh. 10, 461.

त्सारुक *tsâruka*, i.e. *tsaru*+*ka*, adj. Skilled in sword-fight, MBh. 1, 5271.

थ *TH*.

थक्कियक *thakkiyaka*, m. A proper name, Râjat. 4, 493.

† **थुड्** *THUḌ*, i. 6, Par. To cover.

† **थुर्व्** *THURV*, i. 1, *thûrva*, Par. To hurt.

द *D*.

ऽद *-da*, latter part of compound words, I. (vb. 1. *dâ*), Giving, e. g. *açva-*, adj. Giving a horse, Man. 4, 231. *go-*, **1.** adj. Giving cattle, Man. 4, 231. **2.** f. *dâ*, The name of a river, Ragh. 13, 35 (*anu-goda*+*m*, compounded adverb, Along the Godâ). *janmada*, i.e. *janman-*, m. A father, Çâk. d. 177, v.r. *sahasra-*, adj. Giving, or one who has given, a thousand (cows), Man. 3, 186. II. (vb. 2. *dâ*), **1.** Destroying, cf. e.g. *anala-*, adj. Quenching fire. *mâna-*, adj. Destroying arrogance (or from I. pride-inspiring), Chr. 38, 15. III. (vb. 3. *dâ*), Binding; cf. *aṅgada*.

1. **दंश्** *DAṀÇ* (in epic poetry also **दश्** *daç*, MBh. 1, 1605), i. 1, *daça*, Par. (in epic poetry also Âtm., MBh. 1, 1798), To bite, MBh. 1, 843. Ptcple. of the pf. pass. *dashṭa*, Man. 11, 199. **2.** † To see (cf. *daṁs*, the Prâkṛit form of *dṛiç*). Caus. To cause to be bitten, MBh. 1, 2243. i. 10, Âtm. **1.** † To bite. **2.** † To see. Frequent. Caus. *dandaçaya*, To cause to be bitten violently, Daçak. 11, 14.—With the prep. **आ** *â*, To bite, MBh. 11, 638.—With **निस्** *nis*, To bite through, MBh. 6, 1798.—With **परि** *pari*, To bite violently, Bhâg. P. 3, 19, 27.—With **वि** *vi*, **1.** To bite through, MBh. 1, 3362. **2.** To wedge in, Suçr. 1, 101, 5.—With **सम्** *sam*, **1.** To bite, Bhâg. P. 6, 2, 15. **2.** To press together, MBh. 1, 6274; to crush, Çâk. d. 66. *saṁdashṭa*, **1.** Bound, Çâk. d. 170. **2.** Tight, Ragh. 16, 65.—Cf. δάκνω, δάκος, ὀδαγμός, ὀδάζω, ὀδακτάζω, ὀδαξέω, etc., δάκρυ; Lat. lacruma, perhaps lacero; Goth. tagr, A.S. taeher; O.H.G. zanga, A.S. taug; O.H.G. zangar, mordacitas.

† 2. **दंश्** *DAṀÇ*, i. 1 and 10. To speak or shine; cf. *daṁs* and the last.

दंश *daṁç*+*a*, m. **1.** Biting, Gît. 10, 11. **2.** Bite, Mâlav. 47, 4. **3.** A tooth, Bhâg. P. 5, 13, 3. **4.** A gad-fly, Man. 12, 62. **5.** A coat of mail, Bhâg. P. 3, 18, 9. **6.** A proper name, MBh. 12, 93.—**Comp.** *Vṛika-*, m. a dog. *Vṛisha-daṁç*+*a*, m. a cat.

दंशक *daṁç*+*aka*, I. adj. Biting. II. m. A gadfly.—Comp. *Sa-*, I. adj. having teeth. II. m. a crab.

दंशन *daṁç + ana*, n. **1.** Biting, MBh. 14, 754. **2.** Coat of mail, 8, 2848.

दंशित *daṁçita*, i.e. *daṁça + ita*, adj. **1.** Mailed, Bhâg. P. 6, 8, 33; armed, Bhâg. P. 9, 1, 24. **2.** Protected, MBh. 7, 4202. **3.** Close together, MBh. 4, 1329.—**Comp.** *Su-*, adj. Very close, Chr. 32, 22.

दंष्ट्र *daṁshṭra*, i.e. *daṁç + tra*, n. and f. *râ*, A tusk, a large tooth, Râm. 4, 39, 11; Pańch. 55, 15.—**Comp.** *Ayas-*, adj. with iron teeth, Chr. 294, 5 = Rigv. i. 88, 5. *Tikshṇa-*, adj. having sharp teeth, Hiḍ. 2, 7. *Pushpa-*, m. the name of a demon. *Sthira-*, m. 1. A snake. 2. Vishṇu in the boar avatâra.

दंष्ट्रिन् *daṁshṭrin*, i.e. *daṁshṭra + in*, m. Any animal having teeth, Man. 5, 29.

† **दंश्** *DAṀS* (cf. *daṁç* and the Prâkṛit form of *dṛiç*), and **दस्** *DAS*, i. 1, Par. and i. 10, Âtm. **1.** To bite. **2.** To see. **दंस्** *DAṀS*, i. 1 (?) and 10, Par. To speak or to shine.

दंसस् *daṁsas*, n. A work, an action (ved.).—**Comp.** *Su-*, adj. performing splendid actions, Chr. 291, 1 = Rigv. i. 85, 1.

† **दंह्** *DAṀH*, i. 10. To shine, to burn.—Cf. *dah*.

दकोदर *dakodara*, i.e. *daka* (for *udaka*), *-udara*, n. A dropsical belly, Suçr. 1, 92, 16.

दक्ष् *DAKSH*, i. 1, Par. ved. To act in a satisfying manner. Âtm. **1.** To be strong, Lass. 101, 15 (read *dakshate*) = Rigv. vii. 16, 6, ved. **2.** † To increase. **3.** To act quickly. **4.** To go or move. **5.** † To hurt.

दक्ष *daksh + a*, I. adj., f. *shâ*. **1.** Clever, able, Man. 7, 61; 5, 150. **2.** Suitable, Bhâg. P. 4, 6, 44. **II.** m. One of the Prajâpatis, sons of Brahman, Man. 9, 128; MBh. 1, 2574.—Cf. *dakshiṇa*; δεξιός, δεξιτερός; Lat. dexter; Goth. taihsvs, O.H.G. zeso.

दक्षता *daksha + tâ*, f. Cleverness, Sâh. D. 90.

दक्षिण *dakshiṇa*, i.e. *daksh + ina*, **I.** adj., f. *ṇâ*. **1.** Clever, Çatr. 14, 56. **2.** Right (not left), Râm. 2, 52, 86; with *pari-i*, To walk round a person or thing, keeping the right hand towards them, Bhâg. P. 4, 12, 25; with *kṛi*, To show one's reverence in this manner, 1, 14, 13. **3.** South, southern, Man. 3, 258. **4.** Upright, honest, MBh. 4, 167. **II.** m. and n. **1.** The right side, Râm. 2, 92, 13. **2.** South, Nal. 9, 23. **III.** f. *ṇâ*. **1.** A good milch cow (ved.). **2.** Legitimate possession (?), Man. 8, 349. **3.** A present to Brâhmaṇas, as a sacrificial fee, Man. 8, 207. **4.** Fee, MBh. 5, 3779. **5.** Gift, Man. 3, 141. **IV.** *dakshiṇena*, instr. adv. **1.** Southward, Bhâg. P. 5, 17, 9. **2.** To the right hand, 5, 21, 8. — **Comp.** *A-dakshiṇa*, adj. 1. left, Râm. 6, 29, 10. 2. foolish, 3, 24, 13. 3. devoid of presents, Pańch. ii. d. 101. *A-bhaya-dakshiṇâ*, f. promise of security, Man. 4, 247. *Pûrva-*, adj. south-eastern, Mârk. P. 58, 19. *Prâṇa-dakshiṇâ*, f. with *dâ*, to give one his life, Pańch. 231, 20. *Bhûri-dakshiṇa*, adj. one who makes large presents to Brâhmaṇas upon solemn or sacrificial occasions, Nal. 12, 14. *Sa-dakshiṇa*, adj. accompanied by presents, Râjat. 5, 285.

दक्षिणतस् *dakshiṇa + tas*, adv. **1.** To the right hand, MBh. 3, 14549. **2.** Southward, Man. 3, 91.

दक्षिणा *dakshiṇâ* (old instr. sing. of *dakshiṇa*), adv. To the right hand, southward.—Cf. *dakshiṇa*.

दक्षिणावन्त् *dakshiṇâ + vant*, adj., f. *vatî*, Abounding in presents, MBh. 1, 128.

दक्षिणीय *dakshiṇîya*, i.e. *dakshiṇâ + îya*, adj. Worthy to be honored with presents, Hariv. 2780.

दग्धृ *dagdhṛi*, i.e. *dah + tṛi*, m. f. *dhrî*, n. Consuming by fire, Mâlav. d. 92.

दघ् *DAGH*, i. 4, Par. To attain (ved.). ii. 5, Par. To hurt; to protect. —Cf. ταχύς, δέχομαι; Goth. tekan (to take); Lat. tango.

ऽदघ्न *-dagh + na*, latter part of comp. adj. Reaching to, e.g. *stana-*, to the breast, Hariv. 8324. *açva-*, adj. Of a horse's height, Râm. 1, 13, 28 Gorr.

† **दङ्घ्** *DAṄGH*, i. 1, Par. **1.** To quit. **2.** To protect.

दच्छद *dachhchada*, i.e. *dant-chhada*, m. The lip, Bhâg. P. 3, 12, 26.

दण्ड् *DAṆḌ*, i. 10 (rather a denomin. derived from the next), Par. **1.** To chastise, to punish, Man. 8, 132. **2.** To amerce (with two accus.), 9, 234. Ptcple. of the fut. pass., *daṇḍya*, Guilty, Man. 7, 20.—Comp. *A-daṇḍya*, 1. not to be punished, Man. 8, 335. 2. innocent, 8, 128.

दण्ड *daṇḍa* (a form of *dantra*, i.e. *dam + tra*), m. and n. **1.** A staff, Man. 8, 280. **2.** Often compounded with preceding words signifying arm, thigh, trunk, e.g. *bâhu-*, An arm as hard as a staff, Daçak. in Chr. 201, 11. **3.** A stem, MBh. 2, 2390. **4.** A handle, MBh. 2, 38. **4.** The staff of a banner, MBh. 2, 2079. **5.** m. A long measure, a pole of four cubits, Mârk. P. 49, 39. **6.** A staff as symbol of royal power, the sceptre of justice, etc., MBh. 12, 4482 sqq. **7.** Symbol of energetic power, Man. 7, 102 (*nityam udyatadaṇḍa*, Ever with raised staff, i.e. ever ready to use violence); military power, Man. 7, 101; force of arms, 7, 107. **8.** Violence, Man. 8, 72. **9.** An army, Man. 9, 294. **10.** Punishment of all kind, corporal and amercement, Man. 7, 22; 8, 274; personified, Mârk. P. 50, 26. **11.** The name of an attendant of the sun, MBh. 3, 198. **12.** A proper name, MBh. 1, 2681.—Comp. *Ud-*, adj. with raised staff, Hit. ii. d. 28; stem, Ragh. 16, 46; arm, Prab. 81, 13. *Khara-*, n. A lotus, Bhâg. P. 4, 6, 29. *Tri-*, n. 1. the three staves of a religious mendicant joined together, MBh. 12, 12007. 2. three kinds of self-command (in thought, word, and deed), Man. 12, 11. *Dhana-*, m. an amercement, Man. 8, 129. *Dhik-*, m. a harsh reproof, Man. 8, 129. *Manas-*, m. control over the mind. *Mahâ-*, m. heavy punishment, Chr. 61, 40. *Râjanirdhûta-*, i.e. *râjan-nis-* (vb. *dhû*), adj. punished by the king, Man. 8, 318. *Vâgdaṇḍa*, i.e. *vâch-*, m. 1. reprimand, Man. 8, 129. 2. restraint, or control of speech. *Vâṇa-*, m. a weaver's loom. *Vîṇâ-*, the neck of a lute.

दण्डक *daṇḍa + ka*, m. and n. **1.** The staff of a banner, MBh. 7, 1569. **2.** also f. *kâ*, The name of a great forest in the Dekhan, Râm. 1, 1, 39; Mahâv. 65, 11. **3.** m. pl. The name of the inhabitants of this locality, and of the locality itself, MBh. 13, 7223; Râm. 2, 21, 63. **4.** m. A proper name, Hariv. 637.—Comp. *Tri-*, n. the three staves of a religious mendicant, MBh. 12, 11870.

दण्डन *daṇḍ + ana*, n. Chastising, Kâm. Nîtis. 13, 53.

दण्डपाशक *daṇḍa-pâça + ka*, A policeman (? perhaps *-pâçika*), Pañch. 129, 1.

दण्डवन्त् *daṇḍa + vant*, adj., f.

vati, One who has a great army, Kâm. Nîtis. 13, 37.

दण्डिक *dandika,* i.e. *danda+ika,* adj. One who chastises, MBh. 6, 439.

दण्डिन् *dandin,* i.e. *danda + in,* I. adj. Bearing a staff, Man. 6, 52. II. m. 1. Epithet of Yama, Kâm. Nîtis. 2, 36. 2. A proper name, MBh. 1, 2738.—Comp. *Tri-,* i. e. *tri-danda +in,* m. 1. an ascetic, Yâjń. 3, 85. 2. one who has command over the three seats of action (mind, speech, and body), Man. 12, 10.

दत्तक *datta+ka* (vb. *dâ*), adj., with *putra,* Given to be adopted as a son, Yâjń. 2, 130.

दत्ति *datti,* i.e. *dâ+ti* (from the reduplicated form *dad*), f. Offering, Ragh. 8, 85.

दत्रिम *datrima* (rather *dattrima,* i.e. *dad,* see *datti,* +*tra*+*ima*), adj. Received by donation, Man. 9, 141.

दद् *DAD* (proceeded from *dâ,* ii. 3; cf. ved. red. pf. *dadad+âte,* etc.), i. 1, Âtm. To give.

दद्रु *dadru,* i.e. a reduplicated form of *drî+u,* m. and f. *rû,* A kind of cutaneous eruption, Suçr. 1, 31, 17; 2, 66, 6.

दध् *DADH* (proceeded from *dhâ,* ii. 3), 1. To hold. 2. To give.

दधन् *dadhan,* see *dadhi.*

दधि *dadhi,* from a reduplicated form of *dhe,* n. (the base for many of the cases is *dadhan*), Curdled milk, Man. 2, 107.

दधीच *dadhîcha,* i.e. *dadhyańch+a,* also **दधीचि** *dadhîchi,* and **दध्यञ्च्** *dadhi-ańch,* m. The name of a Muni or sage (originally of the sun), MBh. 3, 8695; 12, 10288; Bhâg. P. 6, 11, 20.

दनु *danu,* m. and f. Proper names, Râm. 3, 75, 24; 2, 30, 12.

दनुज *danu-ja,* m. A Dânava or demon, Bhâg. P. 6, 9, 39.

दन्त् *dant* (probably ptcple. of the pres. of *ad*; cf. ὀδούς, ὀδόντος), 1. m., without nom. voc., acc. sing., and du., and nom. and voc. pl., A tooth, Bhâg. P. 3, 13, 39. 2. Often latter part of comp. words, e.g. *ubhayatodant,* i.e. *ubhayatas-,* adj. Having two rows of teeth, Man. 1, 39 (43, anomalous nom. pl.). *ekatas-,* adj. Having but one row of teeth, Man. 5, 18. *kara-pâda-,* m. A hand, a foot, or a tooth, Yâjń. 2, 219. *su-,* adj. f. *datî,* Having handsome teeth. —Cf. Lat. dens, and the next.

दन्त *dant+a,* I. m. and n. A tooth, Man. 4, 69; Râm. 6, 82, 28. II. f. *tî,* A medicinal plant, Croton polyandrum Roxb., Suçr. 1, 139, 18. III. When latter part of comp. adj., the fem. ends in *tâ,* Kathâs. 21, 29, and *tî,* MBh. 9, 2649. —Comp. *Îçâ-,* or *îshâ-,* adj. having tusks like the pole of a carriage (i.e. an elephant), Râm. 5, 12, 31; MBh. 2, 1877. *Chatur-,* m. the name of an elephant, Pańch. 159, 13. *Nâga-,* I. m. 1. ivory, MBh. 12, 3630. 2. a pin projecting from a wall, and used to hang things upon, Pańch. 116, 19. II. f. *tâ,* the name of an Apsaras, Râm. 2, 91, 17. III. f. *tî,* a plant, Tiaridium indicum Lehm., Suçr. 1, 138, 12. *Pushpa-,* I. m. 1. the name of a Gandharva and other beings. 2. du. the sun and the moon, Çatr. 14, 225. II. f. *tî,* the name of a female Râkshasa. III. n. the name of a temple. *Râjad°,* i.e. *râjan-,* m. an upper and fore-tooth, applied to the two middle ones. *Hastid°,* i.e. *hastin-,* I. m. a pin projecting from a wall, and used to hang things upon. II. n. ivory. —Cf. Goth. tunthus; A.S. todh.

ऽदन्तक *-danta+ka*, a substitute for *danta* when latter part of comp. words, e.g. *krimi-*, m. Caries of the teeth, Suçr. 1, 93, 4.—Comp. *Nâga-*, m. 1. ivory, Varâh. Brih. S. 52, 62. 2. a pin projecting from a wall, and used to hang things upon, Hit. 27, 12.

दन्तमय *danta+maya*, adj., f. *yî*, Of ivory, Man. 5, 121.

दन्तवेष्टक *danta-veshta+ka*, m. A tumour in the gum, Suçr. 1, 303, 9.

दन्तादन्ति *dantâdanti*, i. e. *danta-danta+i*, adv. Biting one another, MBh. 8, 2377.

दन्तिदन्तमय *dantidantamaya*, i.e. *dantin-danta+maya*, adj., f. *yî*, Of ivory, MBh. 8, 1021.

दन्तिन् *danta+in*, m. An elephant, Hit. i. d. 30.

दन्तिल *dantila*, m. A proper name, Pañch. 26, 11.

दन्तुर *dantura*, i.e. *danta+ura*, adj., f. *râ*, Having large or projecting teeth, Kathâs. 20, 108.

दन्तुरित *danturita*, i.e. *dantura+ita*, adj. Having projecting teeth, Gît. 1, 31.

दन्दशूक *dandaç* (Frequent. of *daṃç*), *+ûka*, I. adj. 1. Mordacious, MBh. 1, 1199. 2. Mischievous, MBh. 5, 1254. II. m. 1. A snake, Yâjñ. 3, 197. 2. A kind of snake, Bhâg. P. 6, 6, 27. 3. The name of a hell, 5, 26, 7.

† दन्व् *DANV*, i. 1, Par. To go.

दभ् *DABH*, and दम्भ् *DAMBH*, i. 1, *dabha*, ii. 5, *dabhnu*, Par. 1. To hurt (ved.). 2. To deceive. Comp. ptcple. of the fut. pass. *a-dâbhya*, Not to be checked, Bhâg. P. 4, 23, 4. † i. 10, *dâbhaya*, and *dambhaya*, Par. To send, to impel. † *dambhaya*, Âtm. To gather.—Cf. probably θάμβος, ἔταφον, τέθηπα; O H.G. tepjan or depjan.

दभीति *dabhîti*, m. A proper name, Chr. 298, 23=Rigv. i. 112, 23.

दभ्र *dabh+ra*, adj. Little, insignificant, Bhâg. P. 6, 7, 11.—Comp. *A-*, adj. Great, Bhâg. P. 8, 3, 19. Excellent, 1, 15, 15.

दम् *DAM*, i. 4, *dâmya*, Par. 1. To be tamed. 2. To tame, MBh. 7, 2379. Ptcple. of the pf. pass. *dânta*, Tamed, MBh. 3, 15704. m. 1. A steer, a young bullock, Râjat. 5, 432. 2. One who has subdued his passions, calm, Man. 4, 35. Comp. *Dus-*, adj. unruly, MBh. 13, 1534. Ptcple. of the fut. pass. *damya*, 1. To be tamed for labour, Man. 8, 146. 2. m. A steer, a young bullock, MBh. 12, 6590. Caus. *damaya*, 1. To subdue, MBh. 1, 2995. 2. To break, Râjat. 4, 265.—With the prep. उद् *ud*, To subdue, MBh. 12, 6596.—Cf. δάμνημι, δαμνάω, δαμάω (=ved. *damâyâmi*, Lat. domare), δμώς; Lat. damnare, damnum; Goth. ga-timan; O.H.G. zeman, zam; A.S. tam, tamian; Lat. densus, δασύς, etc., cf. *dampati*.

दम *dam+a*, m. 1. Self-command, Man. 4, 246. 2. A fine, Man. 9, 230. 3. Punishment, chastisement, Man. 9, 284; Bhâg. P. 2, 7, 20. 4. The name of a Rishi, MBh. 13, 1762.—Comp. *Dus-*, 1. adj. difficult to be tamed, MBh. 12, 3310. 2. m. a proper name, Hariv. 1951. *Su-*, adj. easy to be subdued.—Cf. *dampati*.

दमक *dam+aka*, adj. Taming, a tamer, Man. 3, 162.

दमन *dam+ana*, I. adj., f. *nî*, Subduing, Bhartṛ. 3, 47. II. n. **1.** Subduing, Bhartṛ. 2, 52. **2.** Chastising, Bhâg. P. 1, 17, 14. **III.** m. A proper name, Nal. 1, 6.—**Comp.** *Sarva-*, I. adj. all-subduing. II. m. Bharata, the son of Çakuntalâ.

दमनक *damana + ka*, m. A proper name, Pańch. 9, 19.

दमयन्ती *damayantî*, fem. of the pres. ptcple. of the Causal of *dam*, A proper name, Nal. 1, 9.

दमयितृ *damayitṛi*, i.e. *dam*, Caus., + *tṛi*, m. A chastiser, MBh. 13, 7041.

दमिन् *damin*, i.e. *dama + in*, adj. One who has subdued his passions, MBh. 3, 5016.—**Comp.** *Kâma-damin + î*, f. a proper name, Pańch. 185, 10.

दम्पति *dampati*, probably *dam̃s* (=δῶ and δες) *-pati* (=ποτης), m. The master of the house; dual *tî*, The master and the mistress; husband and wife, Man. 3, 116; a couple, Pańch. 225, 22. Cf. δεσπότης, δόμος (=ved. *dama*), δέμω; Lat. domus; Goth. timrjan; A.S. timber, timbrian.

दम्भ् *DAMBH*, see *dabh*.

दम्भ *dambh + a*, m. **1.** Deceit, Pańch. i. d. 222. **2.** Feigning, Râjat. 6, 195. **3.** Arrogance, Mârk. P. 34, 46.—**Comp.** *A-*, 1. m. sincerity, Râm. 2, 86, 2. 2. adj. sincere, Hariv. 4137. *Vîta-*, i.e. *vi-ita-*, adj. humble, not proud.

दम्भक *dambh + aka*, adj. Deluding, Man. 4, 195.

दम्भन *dambh + ana*, n. Deceit, Man. 4, 198.

दम्भिन् *dambhin*, i.e. *dambha + in*, m. A deceiver, Pańch. iv. d. 39.

दय् *DAY*, i. 1, Âtm. (also Par. Bhâg. P. 2, 7, 42). **1.** To allot (ved.). **2.** To have compassion, Daçak. in Chr. 187, 2; with the gen., 195, 10. **3.** To destroy (ved.). **4.** † To move. **5.** † To protect. Ptcple. of the pf. pass. *dayita*, Dear, Râm. 1, 1, 26. m. A lover, a husband, Çâk. 58, 7, Ch. f. *tâ*, A mistress, a woman, Çiç. 9, 70. Comp. *Samudra-*, f. *tâ*, a river. *Su-*, adj. very dear, Chr. 38, 11. — Cf. δαίομαι, δαίνυμι, δαΐς, 2. *dâ* and *de*.

दया *day + â*, f. Compassion, Bhag. 16, 2.—**Comp.** *A-daya + m*, adv. passionately, Vikr. d. 147. *Nirdaya*, i.e. *nis-*, adj., f. *yâ*. 1. unmerciful, cruel, Pańch. 176, 10. 2. passionate, Râjat. 5, 281. 3. not treated with affection, Man. 9, 239. °*yam*, adv. passionately, Hit. i. d. 102. *Bhûta-*, f. compassion for living creatures, MBh. 14, 2841. *Sa-*, adj. 1. compassionate. 2. benevolent. °*yam-*, adv. softly, Çâk. d. 72.

दयालु *dayâ + lu*, adj. Compassionate, Pańch. iii. d. 30.

दयालुत्व *dayâlu + tva*, n. Compassion, Kâm. Nîtis. 3, 34.

दयावन्त् *dayâ + vant*, adj., f. *vatî*, Compassionate, Bhâg. P. 8, 21, 12.

दर *dara*, i.e. **A.** *dṛî + a*, I. m., f. *rî*, and n. A cave, Râm. 2, 96, 4; MBh. 1, 4651. **II.** m. and n. **1.** Cavity, Bhartṛ. 3, 24. **2.** A shell, Bhâg. P. 1, 11, 1. **B.** *dṛi + a*, m. and n. Fear, MBh. 5, 4622. **C.** adj. and indecl., A little, Sâh. D. 41, 18; Gît. 1, 35.—**Comp.** *Sa-*, adj. fearful, afraid.

दरद् *darad* and **दरद** *darada*, m. **1.** The name of a people, Râjat. 5, 152; Man. 10, 44. **2.** *darada*, The king of the Daradas, Hariv. 4969.

दरिद्र *daridra*, (derived from an old frequentat. of *drâ*), adj., f. *râ*. **1.** Strolling (ved.). **2.** Poor, Man. 9, 230.

दरिद्रता *daridra + tâ*, f. and **दरिद्रत्व** *daridra + tva*, n. Poverty, Bhartṛ. 2, 87; Râjat. 2, 90.

दरिद्रा *DARIDRÂ*, see *drâ.*

दरी *darî*, see *dara.*

दरीवन्त् *darî + vant*, adj., f. *vatî*, Abounding in caves, Râm. 4, 49, 22.

दर्दर *dardar + a* (anomal. frequent. of *dṛî*), m. The name of a mountain, Râm. 2, 91, 24, v.r.

दर्दुर *dardur + a* (anomal. frequent. of *dṛî*), m. **1.** A frog, Man. 12, 64. **2.** A flute, Bhâg. P. 1, 10, 15. **3.** The name of a mountain, Râm, 5, 34, 7. **4.** A proper name, Bhâg. P. 2, 7, 34.—Comp. *Kûpa-*, m. A frog living in a well, Pańch. i. d. 21.

दर्प *darpa*, i.e. *dṛip + a*, m. Arrogance, Râm. 1, 56, 3; pride, Hit. 28, 2. —Comp. *Ati-*, 1. m. excessive arrogance, Châṇ. 50. 2. the name of a snake, Pańch. 170, 23. *Bhagna-* (vb. *bhańj*), adj. humbled. *Su-*, adj. lofty. *Sam-iddha-* (vb. *indh*), adj. inflamed with pride.

दर्पण *darpaṇa*, i.e. *dṛip + ana*, m. A mirror, Megh. 59.

दर्पिन् *darpin*, i.e. *darpa + in*, adj. Insolent, Hariv. 15606.

दर्भ *darbha*, i.e. *dṛibh + a*, m. **1.** Kuça, or sacrificial grass, Man. 3, 216. **2.** Another kind of grass, Suçr. 1, 137, 19.—Cf. O.H.G. zurft (zurba), A.S. turf.

दर्भमय *darbha + maya*, adj., f. *yî*, Made of Darbha grass, Bhâg. P. 4, 6, 37.

दर्वि and **दर्वी** *darvî*, i.e. *dṛi + vî*, **1.** A spoon, MBh. 2, 1945. **2.** The expanded hood of a snake (see the next). **3.** The name of a country, MBh. 6, 362.

दर्वीकर *darvî-kara*, m. A kind of snake, Daçak. in Chr. 187, 8.

दर्श *darça*, i.e. *dṛiç + a*, m. **1.** The new moon, Ragh. 18, 34. **2.** The day of the conjunction, Man. 3, 282.—Comp. *Âtmadarça*, i.e. *âtman-*, m. a mirror, Ragh. 7, 65. *Dus-*, adj., f. *çâ*, 1. difficult to be beheld, Bhag. 11, 52. 2. disgusting, MBh. 1, 3471. *Su-dus-*, adj. very difficult to be beheld.

दर्शक *darçaka*, i.e. **A.** *dṛiç + aka*, adj. **1.** Looking, seeing, a spectator, MBh. 13, 5907. **2.** Searching, MBh. 1, 5559. **B.** *dṛiç*, Causal, *+ aka*, adj. **1.** Showing, causing to be seen, Mṛichchh. 65, 4; Man. 8, 284. **2.** Explaining, Hit. Pr. d. 9, v.r. **C.** m. pl. The name of a people, MBh. 6, 361.—Comp. *Pâra-*, adj. showing the opposite bank or shore, Bhâg. P. 1, 13, 38.

दर्शत *darçata*, ved. ptcple. of the fut. pass. of *dṛiç*, Visible, Chr. 289, 4 = Rigv. i. 50, 4; Chr. 290, 9 = 1, 64, 9.—Cf. δυς-δέρκετος.

दर्शन *darçana*, i.e. *dṛiç + ana*, I. adj. **1.** Looking on, Ragh. 11, 93, v.r. **2.** Knowing, MBh. 13, 3254. **3.** Teaching, MBh. 1, 583. **II.** n. **1.** Seeing, Suçr. 2, 158, 10. *âditya-*, Exposure to the sun, Mṛichchh. 47, 5. **2.** Sight, MBh. 13, 961; Çâk. 18, 18; a vision, Râm. 5, 27, 8; a dream, Hariv. 1285. **3.** Adoration, Kathâs. 3, 8. **4.** Appearance, Man. 2, 101; with the vbs. *i* and *yâ*, To become visible, Bhâg. P. 1, 6, 34; with *dâ*, To show one's self, Gît. 3, 9. **5.** Review, Yâjń. 1, 328; inspection, Man. 8, 9. **6.** Knowledge, Man. 6, 74. **7.** Opinion, Kâm. Nîtis. 2, 6. **8.** Precept, MBh. 14, 2700. **9.** Doctrine, Bhâg. P. 1, 5, 8. **10.** A philosophical system, Lass. 29, 7. **11.**

Intention, Râm. 1, 58, 18. **12.** An eye, Çâk. d. 81. **13.** A mirror, Megh. 59, v.r. **14.** Showing, Lass. 87, 3. **15.** Producing, Yâjñ. 2, 170. **16.** abl. *darçanât*, From, Ragh. 12, 60. **III.** f. *nî*, Epithet of Durgâ, Hariv. 10238. —**Comp.** *A-*, I. n. 1. not seeing, Râm. 5, 53, 6. 2. neglect, Man. 10, 43. 3. disappearance, Râm. 3, 50, 11; with *gam*, to disappear, Pañch. 137, 21; with *nî*, to cause to disappear, Râm. 5, 22, 2. II. adj. invisible, Arj. 8, 28. *Achchhidra-*, i.e. *a-chhidra-*, adj., f. *nâ*, faultless, MBh. 6, 384. *Adbhuta-*, adj. wonderfully handsome, Nal. 12, 6. *An-ati-*, n. not seeing too often, Daçak. in Chr. 180, 5. *Âtmadarçana*, i.e. *âtman-*, n. seeing one's self, Yâjñ. 3, 157. *Tulya-*, adj. indifferent, Bhâg. P. 1, 5, 24. *Dâra-*, n. interview with a woman, Chân. 22, in Berl. Monatsb. *Dus-*, adj. 1. difficult to be seen, Bhâg. P. 3, 13, 34. 2. disgusting, Suçr. 1, 260, 1. *Dûra-*, adj. hardly to be seen, Bhâg. P. 1, 11, 8. *Pâra-*, adj. seeing the opposite bank or shore, Bhâg. P. 9, 4, 58. *Puṇya-*, adj. f. *nâ*, of beautiful aspect, beautiful. *Bhâla-*, n. red lead. *Su-*, I. adj. handsome. II. m. 1. The discus of Vishṇu. 2. a vulture. 3. Mount Meru.

दर्शयितुकाम *darçayitukâma*, i.e. *darçayitum*, inf. of the Causal of *driç*, *-kâma*, adj. Wishing to show, Vikr. 29, 19.

दर्शयितृ *darçayitṛi*, i.e. *driç*, Caus., + *tṛi*, m. One who shows, MBh. 6, 129.

दर्शिन् *darçin*, i.e. *dṛiç* + *in*, adj., f. *nî*. **1.** Looking; *sama-*, Looking indifferently on every object, Bhag. 5, 18. **2.** Knowing, Man. 3, 212; *divya-*, Knowing celestial things, MBh. 15, 566. **3.** Having seen, Kathâs. 25, 297. **4.** Showing, Râm. 2, 75, 12. **5.** Teaching, MBh. 1, 522.—**Comp.** *Chhidra-*, adj. perceiving weak points, Hariv. 1265. *Dîrgha-*, adj. far-seeing, provident, Pañch. 194, 5. *Dûra-*, far-seeing, wise, Râm. 5, 87, 20. *Deva-*, adj. frequenting the gods, Râm. 5, 30, 2. *Dvâra-*, m. a porter, Râm. 2, 41, 25 Gorr. *Vidhi-*, m. a priest whose business at a sacrifice is to see that everything is done according to the rule. *Sama-*, adj. impartial. *Sûkshma-*, adj. acute, intelligent.

दर्शिवंस् *darçivaṁs* (an anomalous ptcple. pf. act. of *dṛiç*), only nom. sing. *vân*, **1.** Having seen, MBh. 8, 1756. **2.** Knowing, 1, 6157.—**Comp.** *Dîrgha-*, provident, MBh. 5, 4380.

दल् *DAL* (akin to *dṛi*), i. 1, Par. To burst, Lass. 66, 15. Caus. *dâlaya*, To cause to burst, Suçr. 1, 262, 9. *dalita*, **1.** Burst, MBh. 8, 4633. **2.** Split, wounded, Prab. 87, 13. **3.** Destroyed, Prab. 116, 6. **4.** Visible, Prab. 40, 10. —With the prep. अव *ava*, To burst, Suçr. 2, 166, 6.—With उद् *ud*, Caus. To divide, MBh. 12, 7349.—With वि *vi*, **1.** To burst, Naish. 4, 88. **2.** To rend, Râm. 2, 87, 10 Gorr. *vidalita*, Crushed, Bhartṛ. 2, 77.—With सम् *sam*. *saṁdalita*, Pierced, Lass. 73, 12.—Cf. *dṛi*.

दल *dal* + *a*, I. n. A part, Suçr. 2, 357, 4 (*aṇḍa-*, an egg-shell; *veṇu-*, a small shoot of a cane, Man. 8, 299). **2.** A half, Suçr. 1, 25, 2. **3.** A leaf, Râm. 2, 46, 14. **II.** m. A proper name, MBh. 3, 13178.—**Comp.** *Dvi-*, adj. broken, Hariv. 15522.

दलन *dal* + *ana*, I. adj., f. *nî*, Tearing, Bhâg. P. 7, 10, 59. **II.** n. Breaking, crushing, Gît. 5, 2; Râjat. 3, 284.

दलशस् *dala* + *ças*, adv. In pieces, Kathâs. 19, 109.

दव *dava*, i.e. *du* + *a*, m. A forest conflagration, Bhâg. P. 8, 6, 13.

दविष्ठ *davishṭha*, superl. **दवीयंस्** *davîyaṁs*, comparat. of *dûra*, q.v.

दश *daça*, 1. instead of *daçan*, Ten, MBh. 3, 15649. 2. =*daçama* when latter part of a comp. numeral; cf. *ashṭâdaça, dvâdaça, tridaça. nava-daça,* i.e. *navan-*, f. *çî*, Nineteenth. *pañchadaça,* i.e. *pañchan-*, f. *çî*, 1. Fifteenth. 2. f. *çî*, The fifteenth day of a half month.

दशक *daçaka*, i.e. *daçan+ka*, adj. Containing ten, Man. 6, 92.—Comp. *Çata-*, ten per cent., Yâjñ. 2, 38.

दशत् *daçat*, f. (cf. *daçan*), An aggregate of ten, a decade, Man. 8, 231.

दशति *daçati* (cf. *daçan*), f. A hundred, MBh. 1, 1081.

दशधा *daçadhâ*, i.e. *daçan+dhâ*, adv. In ten parts, Man. 9, 152.

दशन् *daçan*, cardinal number, 1. Ten, MBh. 3, 10677. 2. Ten bad qualities, Hariv. 744.—Cf. δέκα; Goth. taihun and -tigu in tvaim-tigum; A.S. tên, -tig; Lat. decem; cf. *daça*.

दशन *daçana*, i.e. *daṁç+ana*, n. A tooth, Pañch. 52, 8; when latter part of a comp. adj., the fem. ends in *nâ*, Man. 3, 10.—Comp. *Vajra-*, m. a rat.

दशम *daçama*, i.e. *daçan+ma*, I. ordinal number, f. *mî*, Tenth, Chr. 47. 38. II. f. *mî*. 1. The tenth day of the half month, Man. 3, 276. 2. The tenth decade of human life, Man. 2, 137. III. n. A tenth part, Man. 8, 33.—Comp. *Trayo-*, Thirteenth, Bhâg. P. 1, 3, 17. *Drâ-*, twelfth, MBh. 1, 6597.—Cf. Lat. decimus.

दशमास्य *daçamâsya*, i.e. *daçan-mâsa+ya*, adj. Of ten months, Bhâg. P. 1, 12, 11.

दशमीस्थ *daçamî-stha* (cf. *daçama*), adj. Above ninety years old, Man. 2, 138.

दशलक्षणक *daçalakshaṇaka*, i.e. *daçan-lakshaṇa+ka*, adj. Ten-fold, Man. 6, 91.

दशा *daçâ*, i.e. *daṁç+a*, f. 1. The skirt, or the ends of a garment, Man. 3, 44; Mṛichchh. 26, 17. 2. The wick of a lamp, Bhartṛ. 3, 1. 3. Condition, state of life, Râm. 3, 75, 59. 4. State, Kathâs. 7, 113. 5. Period, age, Hit. 10, 19; Hariv. 4394.

दशार्ण *daçârṇa*, m. 1. pl. The name of a people, MBh. 1, 4449. 2. Their king, Chr. 60, 33.

दशार्णक *dacârṇaka*, read *dâç°*, Chr. 52, 10.

दशार्ह *daçârha*, 1. m. pl. The name of a people, MBh. 3, 769. 2. m. A proper name, Hariv. 1991. 3. A name of Krishṇa, MBh. 13, 7003.

दशिन् *daçin*, i.e. *daçan+in*, m. A lord of ten towns, Man. 7, 119.

दशेरक *daçeraka*, i.e. *daṁç+era+ka*, m. 1. A young camel, MBh. 8, 1852. 2. pl. The name of a people, MBh. 7, 397.

दशेश *daçeça*, i.e. *daçan-îça*, m. A lord of ten towns, Man. 7, 116.

दस् *DAS*, i. 4, Par. To become exhausted (ved.).

दस्यु *dasyu*, m. 1. A ruffian, a thief, Man. 7, 143. 2. The name of one of the mixed classes, Man. 5, 131.

दस्युसात् *dasyu+sât*, adv. In the hand of ruffians, MBh. 12, 2554.

दस्र *dasra*, adj. 1. Helping (?), Chr. 295, 16=Rigv. i. 92, 16. 2. The name of one of the Açvins, MBh. 1, 723.

दह् *DAH* (originally *dagh*), i. 1, Par. (in epic poetry also Âtm., Râm. 5, 33, 38; also i. 4, MBh. 4, 799), **1.** To consume by fire, MBh. 8, 116. **2.** To destroy, Man. 7, 9. **3.** To give pain, Pańch. pr. d. 4; Pass. To suffer pain, MBh. 3, 2483. **4.** Pass. To burn, MBh. 1, 8330. Passive, with the terminations of the Par., MBh. 1, 2061; 8210. Ptcple. of the pf. pass. *dagdha*, **1.** Consumed by fire, Man. 8, 189. **2.** Pained, Ṛit. 1, 10. **3.** Cunning, Daçak. in Chr. 193, 15. **4.** n. Cauterising, Suçr. 1, 33, 20. **Comp.** *Agni-*, 1. adj. burned with fire. 2. m. a class of Pitṛis or Manes, Man. 3, 199. *An-agni-*, m. another class of Pitṛis, Man. 3, 199. Caus. *dâhaya*, **1.** To cause to be burned, Man. 5, 167. **2.** To cause to be roasted, Hariv. 15523. Desider. *didhaksha* (also Âtm., Râm. 2, 12, 106), To wish to consume by fire, to be about to consume, MBh. 1, 1244; Râm. 1. 1. Frequent. **1.** *dandah, dandahya*, To destroy completely, Hariv. 8726; Çiç. 2, 11. **2.** *dandahya*, To be consumed completely by fire, Bhâg. P. 2, 2, 26; by grief, Pańch. 58, 2.—With the prep. **अति** *ati*, To burn excessively, Suçr. 2, 47, 19. **2.** To press hard, MBh. 6, 5238.—With **अनु** *anu*, To consume completely by fire, Râm. 2, 63, 41.—With **अप** *apa*, To burn away, MBh. 12, 7705.—With **अव** *ava*, To burn away, Suçr. 2, 35, 10.—With **उप** *upa*, To set on fire, MBh. 3, 546.—With **नि** *ni*, To consume by fire, MBh. 1, 4454.—With **निस्** *nis*, **1.** To consume by fire, Man. 11, 246. **2.** To destroy, Râm. 1, 54, 22. Caus. To order to set on fire, Râjat. 6, 171.—With **विनिस्** *vi-nis*, **1.** To consume by fire, MBh. 1, 5307. **2.** To destroy completely, MBh. 5, 5769.—With **परि** *pari*, To consume by fire, Suçr. 1, 155, 22. Pass. To burn, Bhâg. P. 2, 7, 20.—With **संपरि** *sam-pari*, i. 4, To be consumed by fire, MBh. 3, 10067.—With **प्र** *pra*, **1.** To consume by fire, MBh. 1, 2120. **2.** To destroy, Râm. 2, 24, 8. Pass. To be consumed by fire, MBh. 2, 2689.—With **संप्र** *sam-pra*, **1.** To consume by fire, MBh. 1, 5796. **2.** To destroy, 9, 3526.—With **प्रति** *prati*, i. 4, To be consumed by fire, MBh. 8, 2750.—With **वि** *vi*, **1.** To cauterise, Suçr. 1, 100, 21. **2.** To consume by fire, MBh. 8, 464. Pass. **1.** To be consumed by fire, Râm. 4, 60, 20. **2.** To burn (as a wound), Suçr. 1, 103, 19. **3.** To be consumed by grief, MBh. 12, 52. **4.** To puff one's self up, Râm. 2, 6, 12 Gorr. *vidagdha*, **1.** Inflamed, Suçr. 2, 5, 21. **2.** Digested, Suçr. 2, 110, 14; 118, 15. **3.** Corrupt, Suçr. 2, 369, 18. **4.** Clever, MBh. 4, 745. **5.** Well-bred, Vikr. 3, 12. **6.** Intriguing, Bhartṛ. 1, 97. **Comp.** *A-*, adj. uncultivated, foolish, Pańch. i. d. 180. *Dus-*, adj. 1. puffed up, Bhartṛ. 2, 3. 2. stupid, Prab. 27, 8.—With **सम्** *sam*, To destroy, Râm. 1, 77, 12 Gorr. Pass. **1.** To burn, Bhâg. P. 3, 30, 8. **2.** To grieve, Ragh. 14, 56 Calc. Caus. To cause to be consumed by fire, MBh. 1, 4954. Cf. probably τήγανον; Lat. lignum; O.H.G. tâht or dâht; perhaps Goth. dags, A.S. daeg.

दहन *dah* + *ana*, I. adj., f. *nî*, Consuming by fire, Hariv. 2522. **2.** Destroying, Bhartṛ. 1, 70. **II.** m. **1.** Fire, Bhartṛ. 2, 29. **2.** The deity of fire, MBh. 1, 8360. **3.** One of the

Rudras, MBh. 1, 2567. III. n. 1. Consuming by fire, Ragh. 8, 20. 2. Burning, Bhâshâp. 156.—Comp. *Dava-*, n. The fire of a forest conflagration, Bhâg. P. 5, 8, 22.

दहर *dahara*, and दह्र *dahra* (forms of *dabhra*), I. adj. 1. Small, subtile. II. The cavity of the heart, Bhâg. P. 3, 12, 44.

1. दा *DÂ*, ii. 3, Par., Âtm. 1. To give, Man. 3, 31. 2. To grant, to bestow, Hariv. 5709; Hit. pr. d. 2. 3. To marry, MBh. 1, 6526. 4. To sell, with the instr. of the price, Râm. 1, 53, 8. 5. To deliver, Man. 8, 234. 6. To return, Man. 8, 222. 7. To pay, Man. 8, 154. 8. With *talam*, or *talân*, To shake hands, Hariv. 15741; MBh. 3, 14819. 9. To offer, Man. 9, 136. 10. To communicate, to teach, Man. 2, 114. 11. With *âtmânam*, To sacrifice one's self, Kathâs. 22, 227. 12. With many words it has the signification of Doing, performing, Chaurap. 35; with *anuyâtrâm*, To accompany, Kathâs. 18, 197; with *tâlam*, To beat the time, MBh. 1, 5939. 13. To cause, Râm. 2, 53, 21. 14. To allow, MBh. 1, 1528 (with infin.). 15. To put, Mṛichchh. 139, 8; cf. *ardhachandra*. 16. With *çâram*, To draw, Daçak. in Chr. 185, 24. 17. With *argalam*, To bolt, Kathâs. 4, 60. 18. To turn, Kathâs. 16, 40; MBh. 12, 2526. 19. To add, Pańch. ii. d. 148.—Anomalous 1. sing. pr. par. *dadmi*, MBh. 12, 10466; 3. sing. *dadati*, 3, 13422; 3. pl. *dadanti*, 13, 3148; 3. sing. impf. *adadat*, 2, 1880; 2. sing. imptive. *dada*, 9, 2442; Âtm. *dadasva*, 1, 3482; cf. *dad*.—Ptcple. of the pf. pass. *datta*, m. 1. A given son, Man. 9, 159. 2. A proper name. 3. n. Giving, Bhâg. P. 1, 5, 22. Comp. *Svayam-*, adj. self-given. m. a child who has given himself to adoptive parents, Man. 9, 177. Comp. ptcple. of the fut. pass. *a-deya*, What ought not to be given, Chr. 57, 26. Comp. absol. *a-dattvâ*, Without being given, Râjat. 5, 195. Caus. *dâpaya*, 1. To cause to be given, Râm. 2, 32, 19. 2. To oblige to pay, Man. 7, 127. 3. To oblige to return, Yâjń. 2, 269. 4. To procure, Pańch. 26, 1. 5. To cause to be performed, Kathâs. 5, 112. 6. To cause to utter, Hariv. 15782. 7. To cause to be put on, MBh. 1, 5724. Desider. *ditsa*, To wish to give, MBh. 1, 5119.—With the prep. अनु *anu*, To leave (?), MBh. 7, 9499.—With अभि *abhi*, To give, MBh. 3, 13309.—With आ *â*, Âtm. (in epic poetry also Par., MBh. 2, 2637), 1. To take, Man. 4, 223. 2. To receive, Man. 2, 238; with *garbham*, To become pregnant, Draup. 5, 9 (and To rob). 3. To take away, Man. 7, 124. 4. To impair, Man. 4, 218. 5. To carry with one's self, Man. 9, 92. 6. To seize, MBh. 4, 1113. 7. To perceive, MBh. 14, 675. 8. To agree, Râm. 2, 90, 16. 9. To undergo, Bhâg. P. 2, 3, 15. Ptcple. of the pf. pass. I. *âtta*, 1. Seized, MBh. 6, 5592. 2. Robbed, Râm. 2, 61, 18. 3. Undertaken, Kathâs. 21, 142. II. *â-datta*, Taken away, Hariv. 11811. *âdeya*, 1. What ought to be received, Man. 8, 171. 2. To be approved, Râjat. 5, 274. *an-âdeya*, What ought not to be taken, ib. Absol. *âdâya*, very often With, Râm. 3, 42, 30. Desider. To be about to seize, Daçak. in Chr. 201, 11.—With अभ्या *abhi-â*, Âtm. (Par., Hariv. 14602), 1. To take away, MBh. 1, 3558. 2. To put on, Hariv. 13086. 3. To begin, MBh. 5, 3384.—With उदा *ud-â*, *udâtta*, Prominent, Râm. 2, 100, 10; Prab. 97, 1. m. The acute accent. n. An ornament (in rhetoric), Sâh. D. 752. Comp. *An-*, m. the grave accent.—With उपा *upa-â*, Âtm. 1. To receive,

MBh. 3, 8537. **2.** To acquire, Mârk. P. 21, 93. **3.** To take away, MBh. 3, 8599. **4.** To take, MBh. 3, 1553. **5.** To gather, Râm. 3, 13, 18. **6.** To assume, Bhâg. P. 1, 9, 10. **7.** To consider, MBh. 12, 427. **8.** To begin, Râm. 5, 81, 32. Absol. *upâdâya*, **1.** With, MBh. 3, 3028. **2.** Inclusively, Râm. 2, 92, 6. **3.** By means of, MBh. 4, 1775. Desider. To wish to acquire, Bhâg. P. 5, 14, 7 (Par.).—With अभ्युपा *abhi-upa-â*, To gather, MBh. 12, 167. —With समुपा *sam-upa-â*, **1.** To take, Râm. 2, 25, 25. **2.** To acquire, Mârk. P. 21, 95. **3.** To rob, MBh. 3, 11876. **4.** To collect, Râm. 2, 32, 35 Gorr. **4.** To put on, MBh. 1, 6974. — With पर्या *pari-â*, Âtm. **1.** To take off, Suçr. 2, 36, 2. **2.** To seize, MBh. 5, 1940. **3.** To learn, MBh. 12, 3256. — With प्रा *pra-â*, To deliver, MBh. 1, 4899.— With प्रत्या *prati-â*, Âtm. **1.** To get back, MBh. 12, 7415. **2.** To take back, to rescind, MBh. 1, 785.—With व्या *vi-â*, Par. **1.** To open wide, Hariv. 16003. **2.** To gape, Bhâg. P. 3, 16, 14. Ptcple. of the pf. pass. *vyâtta*, and anomalous *vyâdita*, Wide-opened, MBh. 3, 2024; 2, 946.—With समा *sam-â*, I. Par. **1.** To give, Hariv. 16367. **2.** To return, Bhâg. P. 9, 17, 15. II. Âtm. (also Par., Bhâg. P. 8, 10, 43), **1.** To take up, Man. 6, 4. **2.** To take away, Man. 3, 219. **3.** To seize, Râm. 3, 32, 5. **4.** To begin, MBh. 5, 26. **5.** To take to mind, Bhâg. P. 3, 23, 24.—With उद् *ud*, To snatch away, Bhâg. P. 3, 1, 39.—With उप *upa*, To give, Râm. 1, 50, 9 Gorr.—With कद् *kad*, To reproach, Bhâg. P. 7, 5, 28.—With परा *parâ*, To exclude, Bhâg. P. 4, 6, 5.—With परि *pari*, Par., Âtm. **1.** To deliver, Man. 9, 327. **2.** To grant, Bhâg. P. 3, 5, 50. Caus. To cause to be delivered, MBh. 15, 445.—With प्र *pra*, Par. (Âtm., Naish. 6, 95), **1.** To give, Man. 9, 118; to communicate, MBh. 1, 103. **2.** To grant, Râm. 1, 62, 26. **3.** To give in marriage, Man. 8, 204. **4.** To sell, Pañch. i. d. 17. **5.** To pay, Yâjń. 2, 90. **6.** To make good, Man. 8, 232. **7.** To put, Yâjń. 1, 236. Ptcple. of the pf. pass. *pratta* and *pradatta*, Given, etc., Pañch. 25, 4; 63, 22. **Comp.** *A-pratta*, adj. of which nothing is given away before (eating it), Bhâg. P. 5, 26, 18. Caus. **1.** To compel to return, Yâjń. 2, 270. **2.** To cause to put in, MBh. 1, 5723. Desider. To wish to give in marriage, Daçak. in Chr. 190, 6.—With प्रतिप्र *prati-pra*, To return, MBh. 5, 5525.— With संप्र *sam-pra*, **1.** To deliver, Râm. 2, 32, 23. **2.** To grant, MBh. 1, 3346. **3.** To give in marriage, Hariv. 11006 (p. 790). Caus. To order to be given, Râm. 2, 32, 16.—With प्रति *prati*, **1.** To return, Chr. 58, 6. **2.** To give, MBh. 7, 6976. Caus. To cause to repay, Yâjń. 2, 61.—With वि *vi*, To divide, Râm. 1, 13, 39 Gorr.—With सम् *sam*, To grant, MBh. 7, 2618.— Cf, δίδωμι, δωτήρ, δοτήρ, δάνος, δαπάνη (Caus.); Lat. dare.

2. दा *DÂ*, ii. 2 Par., and दो *DO*, i. 4, *dya*, Par. To cut. Ptcple. of the pf. pass. *dita*, Cut off, Bhâg. P. 6, 6, 23.—With the prep. अव *ava*, To cut off, Bhâg. P. 5, 26, 31.—With वि *vi*, To cut, to destroy, Hariv. 8435 (anomal. absolut. *vi-ditya*).—Cf. *day*; δαιτήρ, δασμός, δάπτω (Caus.), δεῖπνον; Lat. daps.

† 3. दा *DÂ*, i. 4, *dya*, To bind (ved.).—With the prep. सम् *sam*, ptcple. of the pf. pass. *saṁdita*, Tied, Hariv. 3674.—Cf. δίδημι, δέμα, δετός, perhaps also δέω, δεσμός.

दाक्ष *dâksha*, i.e. *daksha* + *a*, I. adj. Referring to Daksha, Hariv. 7444. II. m. or n. South, Man. 6, 10 (with *ayana*, The sacrifice ordained for the winter solstice).

दाक्षायण *dâkshâyaṇa*, i.e. *daksha* + *âyana*, I. patronym., f. *ṇî*, A descendant of Daksha, Bhâg. P. 6, 5, 2; Çâk. 101, 7. II. n. 1. The posterity of Daksha, Bhâg. P. 4, ch. 1. 2. Gold, or a gold ornament; see the next.

दाक्षायणिन् *dâkshâyaṇin*, i.e. *dâkshâyaṇa* + *in*, adj., f. *nî*, Wearing gold ornaments, Yâjñ. 1, 133.

दाक्षायण्य *dâkshâyaṇya*, i.e. *dâkshâyaṇî* + *ya*, m. The son of Dâkshâyaṇî, MBh. 13, 6831.

दाक्षिणात्य *dâkshiṇâtya*, i.e. *dakshiṇâ* + *tya* + *a*, I. adj. Southern, MBh. 1, 4690; Pañch. 3, 9. II. m. 1. pl. The nations of the south, Râm. 2, 82, 7. 2. The south, Hariv. 6200.

दाक्षिण्य *dâkshiṇya*, i.e. *dakshiṇa* + *ya*, n. 1. Politeness, Daçak. in Chr. 180, 17. 2. Kindness, Bhartṛ. 2, 19.

दाक्ष्य *dâkshya*, i.e. *daksha* + *ya*, n. Ability, skill, Man. 10, 124.

दाडिम *dâḍima*, m. The pomegranate tree (n. the fruit), Râm. 3, 7, 10.

दाढिका *dâḍhikâ* (a form of *daṁshṭrikâ*, i.e. *daṁshṭrâ* + *ka*), f. The beard, Man. 8, 283.

दाण्डिक *dâṇḍika*, i.e. *daṇḍa* + *ika*, adj., f. *kî*, Punishing; m. A chastiser, MBh. 12, 2135.

दातुकाम *dâtukâma*, i.e. *dâtum*, infin. of 1. *dâ*, -*kâma*, adj. Wishing to make a present, Pañch. ii. d. 110.

दातृ *dâ* + *tṛi*, m., f. *trî*, n. 1. A donor, a giver, Man. 11, 9; Râm. 4, 20, 4. 2. Giving in marriage, Man. 3, 172. 3. Communicating, Man. 2, 146. 4. A creditor, Man. 8, 161.—**Comp.** *A*-, m. 1. one who gives no present, Man. 11, 15. 2. one who is not obliged to pay, Man. 8, 161. *kshîra-dâtri*, f. yielding milk, MBh. 13, 4919.—Cf. δωτήρ; Lat. dator.

दातृता *dâtṛi* + *tâ*, f., and दातृत्व *dâtṛi* + *tva*, n. Liberality, Râjat. 3, 197; Hariv. 14414.

दात्यूह *dâtyûha*, m. A gallinule, Râm. 2, 56, 9.

दात्र 2. *dâ* + *tra*, n. A kind of sickle, Râm. 2, 87, 9 Gorr.

दाद *dâda*, i.e. *dad* + *a*, m. Oblation, MBh. 9, 2117.

† दान् *DÂN*, i. 1, Par., Âtm. i. 10, Par. To cut. Desider. *dîdâṁsa*, Par., Âtm. 1. To be straight. 2. To make straight.

दान *dâna*, i.e. 1. *dâ* + *ana*, n. 1. Giving, Man. 1, 90. 2. Gift, Man, 4, 233; 11, 2. 3. Liberality, Man. 1, 86. 4. Oblation, Man. 3, 211. 5. Giving in marriage, Man. 3, 27. 6. The fluid that flows from the temples of an elephant in rut, Pañch. i. d. 419.—**Comp.** *A*-, I. n. 1. non-payment, Man. 8, 5. 2. illiberality, Pañch. ii. d. 74. II. adj. illiberal; and, without the fluid which flows from the temples of an elephant in rut, Pañch. ii. d. 73. *Ati*-, n. excessive liberality, Châṇ. 50. *Âtman*-, n. sacrificing one's self, Kathâs. 22, 219.

Udaka-, n. Pouring water in honour of a deceased one, Prab. 98, 3. *Yoga-*, n. a fraudulent gift, Man. 8, 165. *Vṛithâ-*, unprofitable donation, gift to musicians, actresses, etc., Man. 8, 159. *Sa-*, adj. pouring out the fluid which flows from the temples of an elephant in rut, Kir. 5, 9. *Sadâ-*, I. n. liberality. II. m. 1. Indra's elephant. 2. an elephant in rut. 3. Gaṇeça.—Cf. Lat. donum.

दानतस् *dâna+tas*, adv. By liberality, Sâv. 2, 17.

दानव *dânava*, i.e. *dânu*, ved. (a demon; cf. also *danu*, *danuja*), +*a*, **1.** m. A demon, Man. 3, 201. **2.** adj., f. *vî*, Peculiar to the Dânavas, Arj. 10, 24.

दानवन्त् *dâna+vant*, adj., f. *vatî*, Liberal, MBh. 13, 5555.

दानवेय *dânaveya*, i.e. *dânu+eya* (see *dânava*), m. =Dânava, a demon, MBh. 8, 3692.

ऽदानिक *-dânika*, i.e. *-dâna+ika*, adj. Referring to a gift, e.g. *udaka-*, Referring to an oblation to deceased ancestors, MBh. 1, 589. *vara-*, Caused by the grant of a favour, Râm. 2, 115, 7 Gorr.

दानिन् *dânin*, i.e. *dâna+in*, adj., f. *nî*, Liberal, Bhâg. P. 7, 2, 10.

दान्त *dânta*, i.e. I. *danta+a*, adj. Of ivory, Râjat. 5, 12, 21. II. Ptcple. pf. pass. of *dam*, q.v.

दान्तिक *dântika*, i.e. *danta+ika*, adj. Of ivory, Râm. 3, 61, 13.

ऽदाम *-dâma*, a substitute for *dâman* when being latter part of a comp. word, n. A string, MBh. 6, 2447. *ud-dâma*, adj., f. *mâ*, Unrestrained, Râm. 2, 28, 21.

दामन् 3.*dâ+man*, n. A rope, MBh. 1, 6678. **2.** A string, Râm. 2, 78, 7. **3.** A garland, Megh. 89. **4.** A large bandage to support parts, Suçr. 1, 65, 17.—Comp. *Pushpa-dâman*, n. a garland, Çriṅgârat. 10.—Cf. *δέμα*, *κρή-δεμνον*.

दामनी *dâman+î*, f. A rope for tying cattle, Hariv. 3536.

ऽदामनीक *-dâmanî+ka=dâmanî* at the end of a comp. adj., Hariv. 4354.

दामोदर *dâmodara*, i. e. *dâman-udara*, m. **1.** A name of Kṛishṇa, MBh. 5, 2566. **2.** A proper name, Râjat. 1, 64.

दाम्पत्य *dâmpatya*, i.e. *dampati+ya*, n. Matrimonial bliss, Bhâg. P. 2, 3, 7.

दाम्भिक *dâmbhika*, i.e. *dambha+ika*, adj. **1.** Deceitful, Man. 12, 44. **2.** A cheat, Man. 3, 159. **3.** A hypocrite, Man. 4, 211.

दाय् *DAY*, i. 1, Âtm. (properly 1.*dâ*, i. 4, Âtm.), To give.—With the prep. **आ** *â*, To seize, MBh. 1, 7029.

दाय *dâya*, i.e. 1.*dâ+a*, m. **1.** A gift, MBh. 1, 6938. **2.** Separate property of a wife, Man. 9, 77. **3.** Delivering, Man. 8, 180. **4.** Inheritance, Man. 9, 217.—Comp. *Su-*, m. A special gift, as a nuptial present, &c.

दायक *dâyaka*, i.e. 1.*dâ+aka*, adj. Giving, Man. 9, 271; a giver, MBh. 3, 13245.—Comp. *Agni-*, m. An incendiary, Râm. 2, 79, 19 Gorr. *Tâmbûla-*, m. The betel-bearer of a prince, Kâm. Nîtis. 12, 46. *Visha-*, m. a poisoner, Râm. 2, 75, 38.

ऽदायकता *-dâyaka+tâ*, f. Giving, Daçak. in Chr. 180, 21.

दायाद *dâyâda*, i.e. *dâya-â-da*, m. **1.** A heir, Man. 8, 160. **2.** A son, a kinsman, Râm. 2, 110, 35; 1, 60, 2.—

Comp. *A-*, f. *dâ*, not being a heir, Man. 9, 158; 8, 160.

दायादवन्त् *dâyâda + vant*, adj. Having a heir, MBh. 1, 3180.

दायाद्य *dâyâdya*, i.e. *dâyâda + ya*, n. Inheritance, Man. 11, 184.

दायाद्यता *dâyâdya + tâ*, f. Affinity, MBh. 1, 7509.

ऽदायिन् *-dâyin*, i.e. 1. *dâ + in*, adj., f. *nî*. 1. Giving, Man. 3, 104. 2. Causing, Hariv. 15379.—Comp. *Udaka-*, m. a kinsman connected only by the oblations of water to the manes of common ancestors, Man. 5, 64. *Visha-*, m. a poisoner, Kâm. Nîtis. 7, 26.

दार *dâra*, i.e. *drî + a*, m. 1. A ploughed field, Man. 9, 38. 2. m. pl. and f. sing. *râ* (n., Pañch. i. d. 450, but see Böhtl. Ind. Spr. 2173, where v.r.), A wife, Man. 2, 217; 247; Bhâg. P. 7, 14, 11.—Comp. *A-*, adj. unmarried, Râm. 4, 18, 15. *Krita-*, adj. married, Man. 4, 1. *Dharma-*, m. pl. a legitimate wife, Râm. 3, 57, 9. *Putra-*, n. son and wife, Man. 4, 239. *Bhû-*, m. a hog.

1. दारक *dâraka*, i.e. *drî + aka*, I. adj., f. *rikâ*, Splitting, MBh. 7, 6871. II. f. *rikâ*, A chap, Suçr. 1, 292, 10.—Comp. *Loha-*, n. the name of a hell, Man. 4, 90.

2. दारक *dâraka*, m. 1. A son, Pañch. 100, 24. 2. A young animal, Bhâg. P. 5, 8, 17. 3. du. A boy and a girl, Brâhmaṇ. 2, 35.—Comp. *Bhartri-*, 1. m. a young prince, designated as successor. 2. f. *kâ*, a princess.

दारण *dâraṇa*, i.e. *drî + ana*, I. adj., f. *ṇî*. 1. Splitting, MBh. 6, 5594. 2. f. *ṇî*, Epithet of Durgâ, Hariv. 10246. II. n. 1. Bursting, Suçr. 1, 25, 17. 2. A means for opening, Suçr. 1, 132, 9.

दारव *dârava*, i.e. *dâru + a*, adj., f. *vî*. 1. Wooden, Man. 5, 115. 2. Produced from wood, MBh. 13, 4718.

दारिद्र *dâridra* (perhaps to be corrected to *dâridrya*), i.e. *daridra + a*, n. Poverty, Pañch. 95, 13.

दारिद्र्य *dâridrya*, i.e. *daridra + ya*, n. Poverty, indigence, Pañch. i. d. 12.

दारिन् *dârin*, i.e. *drî + in*, adj., f. *iṇî*, Splitting, MBh. 7, 3993.

दारी *dârî*, i.e. *drî + a + î*, f. A chap, Suçr. 1, 294, 20.

दारु *dâru*, i.e. *drî + vant=van=u*, n. 1. Wood, Pañch. i. d. 100. 2. A species of pine, Pinus deodora Roxb., Suçr. 1, 161, 10.—Comp. *Deva-*, n. A species of pine, Pinus deodora Roxb., Râm. 2, 76, 16.—Cf. δόρυ, δούρατα for δορϝατα, δορήϊος, etc.

दारुण *dâruṇa*, i.e. *dâru + na* (or rather *darvan + a*), I. adj., f. *ṇâ*. 1. Hard, Suçr. 1, 295, 10. 2. Sharp, 1, 130, 14. 3. Harsh, severe, Pañch. 53, 11. 4. Violent, MBh. 14, 442. 5. Painful, Man. 12, 78. 6. Terrible, Râm. 1, 56, 8. II. n. Severity, MBh. 13, 2144.—Comp. *Ati-*, and *Su-*, adj. very terrible, very hard, Chr. 33, 1; 47, 32.

दारुणता *dâruṇa + tâ*, f. Severity, Hariv. 4248.

दारुणाय *DÂRUṆÂYA*, a denomin. derived from *dâruṇa* by *ya*, Âtm. To prove unmerciful, Naish. 1, 80.

दारुमय *dâru + maya*, adj., f. *yî*, Wooden, Pañch. 48, 10.

दार्ढ्य *dârḍhya*, i.e. *driḍha + ya*, m. 1. Hardness, Suçr. 2, 136, 18. 2. Strength, Suçr. 1, 201, 14. 3. Stability, Râjat. 6, 173; Kâm. Nîtis. 1, 21. 4. Confirmation, Kull. ad Man. 3, 281.

दार्दुर *dârdura*, i. e. *dardura + a*, adj., f. *rî*, and दार्दुरिक *dârdurika*, i.e. *dardura + ika*, f. *kâ*, Referring to a frog, Hariv. 4162; Bhâg. P. 2, 3, 20.

दार्व *dârva*, i.e. *dâru + a* (anomal.), I. adj., f. *vî*, Wooden, Bhâg. P. 5, 12, 6. II. m. pl. The name of a people, MBh. 2, 1026. III. f. *vî*, The name of several plants, Curcuma zantorhiza, Suçr. 2, 23, 14, etc.

दार्वाघाट *dârvâghâṭa*, i. e. *dâru-âghâṭa = âghâta*, m. The woodpecker, MBh. 10, 268.

दार्श *dârça*, i.e. *darça + a*, m. The sacrifice to be performed at the conjunction of the moon, Man. 6, 9.

दालन *dâlana*, i. e. *dal + ana*, n. Crumbling off (of the teeth), Suçr. 2, 132, 12.

दालिम *dâlima = dâḍima*, Amar. 13.

दाल्भ्य *dâlbhya*, i. e. *dalbha*, the name of a Ṛishi, *+ ya*, patronym. A descendant of Dalbha, MBh. 2, 106.

दाव *dâva*, i. e. *du + a*, m. **1.** A forest conflagration, MBh. 3, 2608. **2.** A forest, MBh. 1, 8088.

दावदहनज्वालाकलापाय *DÂVA-DAHANAJVÂLÂKALÂPÂYA*, i. e. *dâva-dahana-jvâlâ-kalâpa + ya*, a denomin. Âtm. To resemble the stream of flames of a burning forest, Gît. 4, 10.

दाश् *DÂÇ*, i. 1, Par. **1.** To worship, Chr. 292, 6 = Rigv. i. 86, 6. **2.** To make oblations. **3.** To bestow. **4.** † ii. 5, Par. To hurt. Ptcple. of the pf. act. *dadâçivaṁs*, Chr. 297, 20 = Rigv. i. 112, 20, and *dâçvaṁs*, 292, 12 = Rigv. i. 85, 12. **1.** Pious. **2.** Bestowing, Bhâg. P. 8, 22, 23.

दाश *dâça*, written also दास *dâsa*, I. m. **1.** A fisherman, MBh. 1, 4012. **2.** A boatman, MBh. 1, 5875; Man. 8, 408 (with *s*). **3.** The son of a Nishâda by an Âgoyava-woman, Man. 10, 34 (with *s*). II. f. *çî*, A fisher-maid.

दाशरथ *dâçaratha*, i.e. I. *daçaratha*, a proper name, *+ a*. **1.** patronym. A descendant of Daçaratha, Râm. 5, 80, 23. **2.** adj. Belonging to Daçaratha, Hariv. 4167. II. *daçan-ratha + a*, adj. Ten carriages broad, MBh. 12, 242.

दाशरथि *dâçarathi*, i.e. *daçaratha*, see the last, *+ i*, patronym. A descendant of Daçaratha, Râm. 1, 3, 11; 6, 19, 67.

दाशार्णक *dâçârṇaka*, i.e. *daçârṇa + a + ka*, adj. *ṇikâ*, Referring to the Daçârṇas, e.g., with *nṛipa*, The king of the Daçârṇas, Chr. 52, 11; with *dhâtrî*, A female servant of this people, Chr. 52, 16.

दाशार्ह *dâçârha*, i.e. *daçârha + a*, **1.** adj., f. *hî*, Belonging to Kṛishṇa, MBh. 2, 84. **2.** m. A name of Kṛishṇa, MBh. 2, 1223. **3.** m. pl. Daçârhas, the people, MBh. 1, 7513.

दाशार्हक *dâçârha + ka*, m. pl. = Daçârhas, the people, Bhâg. P. 3, 1, 29.

दाशेय *dâçeya*, written also दासेय *dâseya*, i.e. *dâçî + eya*, m. and f. *yî*, The son, the daughter, of a fisher-woman, MBh. 1, 4015; Chr. 5, 1 (with *s*).

दाश्वंस् *dâçvaṁs*, see *dâç*.

दास *dâsa*, i.e. probably *dam + sa*, I. m. A slave, a servant, Man. 4, 253; 8, 416. II. f. *sî*, A female slave, a servant-maid, Man. 9, 48. Cf. *dâça*.—Comp. *A-*, m. not being a slave, Man. 10, 32. *Daṇḍa-*, m. one enslaved by punishment, Man. 8, 415. *Dâsî-*, n. sing. and m. pl. male and female slaves, MBh. 13, 2950; 2, 2510. *Bhakta-* (vb.

bhaj), m. a slave maintained in consideration of service, Man. 8, 415. *Çiva-*, m. a proper name.

दासत्व *dâsa+tva*, n. Condition of a slave, Râm. 4, 3, 12.

दासप्रवर्ग *dâsa-pra-varga*, adj. Comprising a crowd of slaves, Chr. 294, 8 =Rigv. i. 92, 8.

दासीत्व *dâsî+tva* (see *dâsa*), n. The condition of a female slave, MBh. 1, 1088.

दासेरक *dâseraka* (*s* probably erroneously for *ç*, cf. *daçeraka*), i.e. *daçeraka+a*, m. **1.** A camel, Pańch. 87, 8. **2.** pl. The name of a people, Varâh. Bṛih. S. 14, 26.

दास्य *dâsya*, i.e. *dâsa+ya*, n. **1.** Servitude, Daçak. in Chr. 183, 11. **2.** Service, Man. 8, 410.

दास्वन्त् *dâsvant* (vb. 1.*dâ*, cf. *bhâ* and *bhâs*), adj., f. *vatî*, Liberal, Chr. 287, 1=Rigv. i. 48, 1.

दाह *dâha*, i.e. *dah+a*, m. **1.** Burning, Man. 4, 115. **2.** Conflagration, Râm. 1, 3, 31. **3.** Cauterising, Suçr. 1, 47, 8. **4.** Feverish heat, Suçr. 1, 34, 16.—Comp. *Antar-*, m. inward heat, Râm. 2, 85, 17.

दाहक *dâhaka*, i.e. *dah+aka*, adj., f. *hikâ*, Setting on fire, an incendiary, Yâjń. 2, 282.

दाहन *dâhana*, i.e. *dah*, Caus. +*ana*, n. Causing to be consumed by fire, MBh. 1, 403.

दाहिन् *dâhin*, i.e. *dah+in*, adj., f. *nî*. **1.** Setting on fire, Man. 3, 158. **2.** Burning, Suçr. 2, 213, 16. **3.** Paining, Bhartṛ. 2, 97.

दिगम्बर *digambara*, i.e. *diç-ambara*, I. adj., f. *râ*, Naked, Pańch. v. d. 14. II. m. An ascetic, Prab. 46, 5.

दिगम्बरत्व *digambara+tva*, n. Nakedness, Kumâras. 5, 27.

दिति *diti*, f. One of the wives of Kaçyapa and mother of the Daityas, MBh. 1, 2520.

दितिज *diti-ja*, and दितिनन्दन *diti-nandana*, m. A Daitya or demon, MBh. 13, 971; Bhâg. P. 8, 10, 3.

दित्सा *ditsâ*, i.e. *ditsa*, desider. of 1.*dâ*, +*a*, f. Wish to give, Râjat. 3, 252.

दित्सु *ditsu*, i.e. *ditsa*, desider. of 1.*dâ*, +*u*, (and दिदित्सु *diditsu*, MBh. 5, 187), adj. Willing, ready to give, MBh. 1, 1733.—Comp. *A-*, adj. one who will not give, Man. 9, 118.

दिदृक्षा *didṛikshâ*, i.e. *didṛiksha*, desider. of *dṛiç*, +*a*, f. Wish to see, Kir. 5, 1.—Comp. *Jâta-gîta-didṛiksha*, adj., f. *shâ*, desirous to see the singer, Râjat. 5, 357.

दिदृक्षु *didṛikshu*, i.e. *didṛiksha*, desider. of *dṛiç*, +*u*, adj. **1.** Desirous to see, Chr. 35, 11. **2.** Desirous of inspecting, Man. 8, 1.

दिधक्षा *didhakshâ*, i.e. *didhaksha*, desider. of *dah*, +*a*, f. The desire to consume by fire, MBh. 1, 8363.

दिधक्षु *didhakshu*, i.e. *didhaksha*, desider. of *dah*, +*u*, adj. Desirous to consume by fire, MBh. 1, 8090; to destroy, Bhâg. P. 5, 26, 35.

दिधिषु *didhishu*, i.e. *didhisha*, old desider. of *dhâ*, +*u*, I. m. A husband, Bhâg. P. 9, 9, 34. II. f. *shû*, A widow married to the brother of her deceased husband, Man. 3, 173.—Comp. *Agre-didhishû*, f. a younger sister married before her elder one, Man. 3, 160.

दिन *dina*, i.e. *div+an+a*, m. and n. Day, Man. 11, 144.—**Comp.** *Adya-*, the present day, Pañch. 186, 23. *Dus-*, I. n. 1. a cloudy day, Hariv. 7856. 2. rain, rainy weather, Râm. 3, 73, 13. II. adj. clouded, Râm. 6, 90, 90. *Vâshpa-dus-dina*, adj. clouded by tears, Daçak. in Chr. 187, 16. *Hima-dus-*, n. wintry weather, winter. *Su-*, n. a fine day, fine weather.

† दिन्व् *DINV*, i. 1, Par. To please, to be pleased.—Cf. *jinv*.

† दिप् *DIP*, i. 1, Par. To drop, v.r. of *tip*.

† दिम्प् *DIMP*, and दिम्भ् *DIMBH*, i. 10, Âtm. To accumulate. *DIMBH*, i. 10, Par. To cast.

दिलीप *dilîpa*, m. The name of a king, and ancestor of Râma, Râm. 1, 43, 2.

1. दिव् *DIV*, i. 4, *dîvya*, Par. (in epic poetry also Âtm. MBh. 4, 533), **1.** To play at dice, MBh. 3, 2260. **2.** To play, Daçak. in Chr. 186, 2. **3.** With the instrumental and dat. of the stake, MBh. 2, 2061; 4, 533. **4.** To shine, Bhâg. P. 3, 20, 22. **5.** † To praise. **6.** † To be glad. **7.** † To be mad. **8.** † To be sleepy. **9.** † To desire. Ptcple. of the pf. pass. *dyûta*, n. **1.** Gaming with inanimate things, Man. 9, 221. **2.** Game at dice, Nal. 9, 2. **3.** Battle, MBh. 7, 1350. **4.** The prize of a combat, MBh. 7, 3996. **Comp.** *Dus-*, n. a wicked game, MBh. 4, 532. *Mushṭi-*, n. a kind of game, odd or even. Ptcple. of the fut. pass. *devitavya*, To be played at dice, MBh. 2, 2493. n. Game at dice, 5, 894.—With the prep. अति *ati*, To lose at play, MBh. 2, 2041.—With प्र *pra*, To play, MBh. 8, 4210.—Wth प्रति *prati*, To throw dice in one's turn, MBh. 5, 137.—With वि *vi*, To lose at play, MBh. 2, 2384.

2. दिव् *DIV*, i. 1 and 10, Par. † To pain. i. 10, Par. † To beg. i. 10, Âtm. To suffer pain.—With the prep. परि *pari*, i. 1, Par. and Âtm. (see *dev*), To lament, Hariv. 3687. Ptcple. of the pf. pass. *paridyûna*, Miserable, MBh. 5, 3175. Caus. and i. 10, Âtm. *devaya*, To lament, Râm. 2, 40, 37. Ptcple. of the pf. pass. *paridevita*, Miserable, MBh. 4, 807. n. Lamentation, MBh. 1, 6199.

3. दिव् *div*, the base of many cases is *dyu*, of the nom. and voc. sing. *dyo* (m. ved. and), f. **1.** Heaven, Man. 8, 86. **2.** Day, Varâh. Bṛih. S. 21, 8. **3.** Splendour, Bhâg. 3, 8, 23.—Cf. Ζεύς (=*dyaus*), Διός (=*divas*), ἔν-διος, πρώϊ-ζος, χθι-ζός, ἤδη (cf. *a-dya*, Lat. hodie), δήν, cf. Lat. jam, dum, du-dum, etc.; Lat. dies, Ju-piter, Jovis, etc.; O.H.G. zies-tac; A.S. tiwes daeg.

दिव 1.*div+a*, n. **1.** Heaven, MBh. 3, 11746.—Cf. *tri-*, n. Heaven (perhaps properly the third, the most holy heaven), Man. 9, 253.

दिवंगम *divaṁgama*, i.e. *diva+m-gama*, adj. **1.** Rising to heaven, MBh. 4, 1526. **2.** Leading to heaven, 3, 11135.

दिवस *divasa*, i.e. 1.*div+as+a*, m. and n. Day, Sâv. 4, 2.—**Comp.** *Ardha-*, m. noon, Râm. 1, 36, 6. *Dus-*, m. a cloudy day, Pañch. i. d. 189.

दिवस्पति *div+as-pati*, m. A name of Indra, Bhâg. P. 8, 13, 32.

दिवा *div+â*, originally instr. of *div*, adv. **1.** By day, Man. 4, 50.—Cf. Lat. diu, du-dum, and *divâtana*.

दिवातन *divâ + tana*, adj., f. *ni*, Diurnal, Kumâras. 4, 46. — Cf. Lat. diutinus.

दिवाशयता *divâ-çî + a + tâ*, f. Sleeping by day, Râjat. 5, 252.

दिविगत *div + i-gata* (vb. *gam*), adj. Being in heaven, Hariv. 5150.

दिविचारिन् *div + i-chârin*, adj. Celestial, Râm. 5, 2, 14.

दिविज *div + i-ja*, m. A deity, Bhâg. P. 5, 2, 6.

दिविषद् *divishad*, i.e. *div + i-sad*, m. A deity, Lass. 66, 3.

दिविष्टि *divishṭi*, i.e. *div-ishṭi*, f. Sacrifice, Chr. 288, 9 = Rigv. i. 48, 9.

दिविष्ठ *divishṭha*, i e. *div + i-stha*, and दिविस्थ *div + i-stha*, adj., f. *ṭhâ*, *thâ*, Dwelling in heaven, MBh. 1, 2340; Bhâg. P. 4, 23, 22.

दिविस्पृश् *div + i-spṛiç*, adj. Touching heaven, Nal. 12, 37.

दिविस्पृशन्त् *div + i-spṛiçant* (pres. ptcple. of *spṛiç*), Touching heaven, Bhâg. P. 7, 8, 22.

दिवोदास *divodâsa*, i. e. *div + as -dâsa*, m. A proper name, Chr. 297, 14 = Rigv. i. 112, 14.

दिवौकस *divaukasa*, i.e. *diva-okas + a*, m. A deity, Hariv. 11884.

दिव्य *div + ya*, I. adj., f. *yâ*. **1.** Celestial, Chr. 290, 3 = Rigv. i. 64, 3. **2.** Divine, Bhag. 11, 8 (prophetic). **3.** Magical, Bhartṛ. 2, 18. **4.** Brilliant, Râm. 1, 4, 26. II. n. **1.** An ordeal, Yâjń. 2, 22. **2.** Oath, Hit. 133, 3.—Cf. δῖος; Lat. divus.

दिव्यक *divya + ka*, m. A kind of snake, Suçr. 2, 265, 19.

दिव्यता *divya + tâ*, f. Divine nature, Kathâs. 6, 82.

1. दिश् *DIÇ*, i. 6, Par., Âtm. **1.** To show, to produce, Man. 8, 57. **2.** To denote, Râm. 3, 30, 14. **3.** To give, Ṛit. 6, 34. **4.** To command, Kir. 5, 28. Ptcple. of the pf. pass. *dishṭa*. **1.** Shown, Bhaṭṭik. 2, 32. **2.** Determined, MBh. 3, 8847; with *gati*, Death, Râm. 2, 30, 40. n. **1.** Command, Bhâg. P. 4, 28, 1. **2.** Fate, MBh. 14, 1551. Comp. *Pûrva-*, n. fate, Bhâg. P. 6, 17, 17. Caus. *deçaya*, **1.** To point out, Râm. 3, 78, 13. **2.** To order, MBh. 4, 670. **3.** To govern, Râm. 2, 61, 34 Gorr.—With the prep. अति *ati*, **1.** To assign to, Bhâg. P. 5, 1, 19. **2.** To promise, 4, 9, 26.—With अनु *anu*, To order, Râm. 6, 89, 21. Comp. ptcple. of the pf. pass. *ekânudishṭa*, i.e. *eka-*, n. obsequies to a single ancestor, Man. 4, 111.—With अप *apa*, **1.** To state, Man. 8, 54. **2.** To denounce, Daçak. in Chr. 193, 4. **3.** To pretend, Daçak. in Chr. 190, 19. —With व्यप *vi-apa*, **1.** To design, MBh. 3, 16189. **2.** To name, Bhâg. P. 5, 4, 9. **3.** To name falsely, Râm. 3, 54, 24. **4.** To pretend, MBh. 13, 1458.—With आ *â*, **1.** To aim at, MBh. 7, 1234. **2.** To assign to, Râm. 4, 41, 7. **3.** To mark, Bhâg. P. 6, 8, 7. **4.** To show, Bhâg. P. 8, 32, 5. **5.** To teach, Man. 4, 80. **6.** To design, Bhâg. P. 8, 22, 4. **7.** To order, prescribe, Râm. 5, 38, 19; Man. 11, 192 (193). **8.** To banish, Kathâs. 2, 19. **9.** To undertake, Râm. 2, 52, 65 (a vow). **10.** To try, MBh. 3, 11986. *âdishṭa*, n. Command, Lass. 67, 13. Caus. **1.** To point out, Mṛichchh. 138, 4.—With उपा *upa -â*, **1.** To assign to, MBh. 1, 7239. **2.** To declare, Bhâg. P. 1, 12, 29. **3.** To

order, Bhâg. P. 2, 9, 7.—With निरा *nis-â*, To pay, Man. 8, 162.—With प्रत्या *prati-â*, **1.** To prescribe, Bhâg. P. 2, 9, 22. **2.** To advise, Râm. 5, 81, 4. **3.** To report again, MBh. 3, 14717. **4.** To summon, Hit. 71, 16. **5.** To countermand, Vikr. 56, 1. **6.** To decline, Çâk. 73, 3. **7.** To overcome, MBh. 14, 2460.—With व्या *vi-â*, **1.** To assign to, MBh. 14, 1921. **2.** To teach, Prab. 107, 5. **3.** To order, MBh. 1, 7689. **4.** To declare, Mâlav. 69, 13 v.r.—With समा *sam-â*, **1.** To assign to, Man. 1, 91. **2.** To declare, Bhâg. P. 1, 16, 1. **3.** To teach, Kâm. Nîtis. 15, 2. **4.** To determine, Râm. 1, 8, 14. **5.** To order, Arj. 3, 10. Caus. To order, Pañch. 171, 8.—With प्रतिसमा *prati-sam-â*, **1.** To answer, Daçak. 124, 3. **2.** To order, Râm. 5, 24, 35.—With उद् *ud*, **1.** To point out, Râm. 2, 56, 4. **2.** To defy, Çâk. 94, 1. **3.** To predict, Çâk. 71, 11. **4.** To denote, Mârk. P. 26, 17. **5.** To teach, Bhartṛ. 2, 54. Comp. ptcple. of the pf. pass. *eka-uddishṭa*, n. Obsequies to a single ancestor, Man. 4, 110. Absol. *uddiçya*, **1.** Against, on, Râm. 3, 50, 17. **2.** To, Râm. 1, 33, 17; 3, 2, 14. **3.** For, Râm. 1, 13, 31. **4.** In remembrance of, Râjat. 5, 120. **5.** On account of, Kathâs. 2, 17. **6.** In the name of, Râm. 1, 80, 21 Gorr. **7.** Referring to, Bhartṛ. 1, 56. Repeated *uddiçyoddiçya*, To one (this)—to another (that), MBh. 15, 414.—With समुद् *sam-ud*, **1.** To mention, Man. 5, 17. **2.** To name, Varâh. Bṛih. S. 47, 52. Absol. *samuddiçya*, **1.** Against, on, MBh. 1, 4573. **2.** For, MBh. 4, 742; Râm. 2, 15, 34 Gorr. **3.** In remembrance of, MBh. 15, 1094. **4.** With regard to, MBh. 1, 489.—With उप *upa*, **1.** To point out, Râm. 2, 55, 2 Gorr. **2.** To teach, Chr. 22, 16. **3.** To advise, Hit. 57, 1. **4.** To mention, Man. 3, 14. **5.** To name, Bhâg. P. 5, 26, 9. **6.** To ordain, Man. 2, 190. **7.** To govern, Kumâras. 1, 2. Comp. ptcple. of the pf. pass. *Kâla-atyaya-upadishṭa*, Produced too late, the designation of an argument which, however plausible, is precluded by higher evidence, Bhâshâp. 70.—With प्रत्युप *prati-upa*, To teach in one's turn, Mâlav. d. 5.—With समुप *sam-upa*, **1.** To point out, MBh. 3, 2328. **2.** To assign to, Râm. 3, 45, 18.—With निस् *nis*, **1.** To point to, Çâk. 63, 15. **2.** To assign to, Râm. 1, 15, 18 Gorr. **3.** To declare, Man. 3, 199. **4.** To denounce, Daçak. in Chr. 197, 23. **5.** To determine, Bhâg. P. 7, 6, 22. **6.** To mention, Man. 7, 144; with *pariyaṇanayâ*, To number, Megh. 22. **7.** To order, Man. 11, 146. **8.** To advise, Hit. iii. d. 39. *a-nirdishṭa*, adj. Allowed (by the Veda), Man. 5, 11.—With अभिनिस् *abhi-nis*, **1.** To point to, Râm. 3, 63, 15. **2.** To determine, MBh. 12, 6991. **3.** To call, Man. 10, 20.—With विनिस् *vi-nis*, **1.** To direct, Bhâg. P. 6, 8, 8. **2.** To determine, Bhâg. P. 7, 11, 35. **3.** To declare, Yâjñ. 2, 111. **4.** To order, Râm. 5, 37, 32.—With परि *pari*, *paridishṭa*, Known, MBh. 3, 12497.—With प्र *pra*, **1.** To show, MBh. 3, 2209. **2.** To declare, Bhag. 8, 28. **3.** To ordain, MBh. 12, 7050. **4.** To impel, Râm. 3, 66, 9. **5.** To assign to, Râm. 1, 14, 13. **6.** To grant, MBh. 1, 6472 (i. 4, Par.). Caus. To impel, MBh. 3, 2727.—With अभिप्र *abhi-pra*, Caus. To impel, Râm. 2, 32, 6.—With प्रति *prati*, Caus. To teach, MBh. 12, 13943.—With सम् *sam*, **1.** To assign to, Râm. 1, 22, 29. **2.** To promise, Yâjń. 2, 232. **3.** To declare, MBh. 5, 7534. **4.** To order, Râm. 2, 52, 59. Caus. To invite to speak, MBh. 14, 458.—With प्रतिसम् *prati-sam*, **1.** To give an order in one's turn, Râm. 6, 98, 37. **2.** To give an order, MBh. 1, 748. —Cf. δείκνυμι, δείκελος, δίκη, δικεῖν, δίκτυον, δειδίσκομαι (frequent. with inchoat. σκ for δειδικ + σκ), δίσκος; Lat. in-dicare, ju-dex, dicere, perhaps dignus (but cf. *yaças*); Goth. teihan, A.S. tihian, tihhan, O.H.G. zeigôn; A.S. taecan; probably Goth. taikns, A.S. tácn, tácen, taecan'; O.H.G. zît (for zig + ti); A.S. tiid, tíd; O.H.G. zeinjan.

2. दिश् *diç*, f. **1.** A region, or quarter, or point of the compass, Pańch. ii. d. 64. **2.** pl. The parts of the earth, Sund. 2, 26. **3.** pl. Different directions, Râm. 1, 55, 22; 2, 106, 27; repeated *diço-diças* (The one) hither—(the other) thither, Pańch. 129, 20; also sing. (but with *sarvatas*), Nal. 16, 5. **4.** There are variously reckoned four, eight, or ten quarters of the world, Kathâs. 15, 137; Man. 1, 13; MBh. 1, 729. **5.** The number ten, Çrut. 36. **6.** A foreign country, Yâjń. 2, 254. **7.** The name of a river, MBh. 6, 327.—**Comp.** *Vi-*, f. an intermediate point of the compass.

ऽदिश *-diç + a*, a substitute for *diç* when latter part of comp. adv.; see *yathâdiçam*, *yathâbhîshṭadiçam*.

दिशा *diç + â*, f. A quarter or point of the compass, MBh. 4, 1716.

दिशोभाग *diçobhâga*, i.e. *diç + as -bhâga*, adj. One who betakes himself to his heels, Pańch. 232, 16.

दिष्टि *dishṭi*, i.e. *diç + ti*, f. used only in the instr. *dishṭyâ*, implying joy or auspiciousness, Thank heaven! Sâv. 6, 23.—Cf. *diç*.

दिह् *DIH*, ii. 2, Par., Âtm. To smear. Ptcple. of the pf. pass. *digdha*, **1.** Smeared, Man. 3, 132. **2.** Anointed, Râm. 3, 42, 39. m. A poisoned arrow, Man. 7, 90; Râm. 2, 114, 33 Gorr.—With the prep. आ *â*, *âdigdha*, **1.** Smeared, MBh. 6, 4384. **2.** Anointed, 7, 4386.—With उप *upa*, *upadigdha*, Overlaid, Suçr. 2, 376, 11.—With प्र *pra*, **1.** To smear, Bhag. 2, 5. **2.** To anoint, Suçr. 1, 42, 19.—With सम् *sam*, **1.** To smear, MBh. 8, 3161. **2.** To cover, Vikr. d. 43. Pass. To be dubious, Râm. 5, 18, 17. *saṁdigdha*, **1.** Poisoned (?), Daçak. in Chr. 197, 2. **2.** Indistinct, MBh. 1, 6565. **3.** Dubious, uncertain, Pańch. i. d. 196. **4.** Desponding, Râm. 1, 66, 25. *a-saṁdigdha + m*, adv. Undoubtedly, Pańch. 241, 8. *nis -saṁdigdha*, adj. Certain, MBh. 13, 3528. °*dham*, adv. Undoubtedly, MBh. 12, 7809.—Cf. τείχος, τοῖχος; Lat. tingere, θιγγάνω, Lat. fingo, figulus; O.H.G. ziagal; A.S. tigel, tigul; Goth. deigan, ga-dikis, daigs; A.S. díc, deag.

1. दी *DÎ* (cf. *ḍî*), i. 4, Par. To soar, to fly (ved.).—Cf. probably δίνη, δινέω, perhaps δίω, δίεμαι.

2. दी *DÎ*, anomal. ii. 3, *dîdî*, Par., Âtm. To shine (ved.).—Cf. δέαται, δέατο, probably also δῆλος.

3. दी *DÎ*, i. 4, Âtm. To waste, to go to ruin. Ptcple. of the pf. pass. *dîna*, **1.** Scanty (ved.). **2.** Afflicted, wretched, Man. 9, 238. **Comp.** *A-dîna*, joyful. *Paridîna*, much afflicted. *Sa -dîna + m*, adv. lamentably.

दीक्ष् *DÎKSH* (originally a desider. of *daksh*), i. 1, Âtm. **1.** To hallow one's self, to prepare one's self for a sacred act. **2.** † To be shaved. **3.** † To perform a sacrifice. **4.** † To initiate. 5. † To restrain one's self. 6. † To declare a vow. Ptcple. of the pf. pass. *dîkshita*, 1. Prepared for a sacrifice, Man. 8, 360. 2. Initiated, MBh. 13, 918. 3. Ready, MBh. 2, 2514. Caus. *dîkshaya*, 1. To initiate, Par. and Âtm., MBh. 14, 2110; 2, 1247. 2. To determine, MBh. 5, 5648.

दीक्षण *dîkshaṇa*, i.e. *dîksh + ana*, n. Consecration, MBh. 14, 2092.

दीक्षा *dîksh + â*, f. 1. Consecration, MBh. 1, 8135. 2. Undergoing religious observances, engaging in a course of austerities, Râm. 1, 32, 4. 3. Religious observances, Man. 6, 29. 4. Devotion, Bhâg. P. 4, 2, 29.—Comp. *Yathâ-dîksha + m*, adv. according to the religious observances, MBh. 14, 1270.

दीधिति *dîdhiti*, i.e. *dîdhî + ti*, f. 1. A ray of light, a sun or moonbeam, MBh. 3, 188; Prab. 94, 6. 2. Light, Pańch. i. d. 369; Mârk. P. 18, 19. 3. Splendour (?), Bhartṛ. 2, 22.—Comp. *Sita-* and *Hima-*, m. the moon, Çiç. 9, 29.

दीधी *DÎDHÎ* (akin to *dî*), ii. 2, Âtm. To shine (ved.).

दीनकम् *dîna + ka + m* (see 3. *dî*), adv. Miserably, Arj. 10, 64.

दीनार *dînâra* (borrowed from δηνάριον), m. A coin, Pańch. 174, 17.

दीप् *DÎP* (originally a Causal of *dî*), i. 4, Âtm. (in epic poetry also Par., MBh. 3, 13984). 1. To blaze, Râm. 5, 50, 5. 2. To shine, MBh. 5, 7322. *dîpta*, 1. Blazing, Bhag. 11, 17. 2. Hot, Man. 3, 133. 3. Radiant, MBh. 5, 7040. 4. Illuminated by the sun, opposite to the sun, inauspicious, Draup. 6, 3; Hariv. 9702. 5. Clear, MBh. 3, 16603. Caus. *dîpaya*, 1. To kindle, Bhag. 4, 27. 2. To excite, Çiç. 9, 42. 3. To illuminate, Kir. 5, 2. 4. To make illustrious, MBh. 5, 1069. Comp. ptcple. of the pf. pass. *adîpita*, Not illuminated, Kir. 5, 48. Frequent. *dedîpya* (Par., MBh. 7, 8138), 1. To be all in flame, MBh. 3, 15588. 2. To be very radiant, MBh. 3, 2146.—With the prep. अति *ati*, *atidîpta* (rather *dîpta* with *ati*), Blazing violently, Râm. 5, 50, 8.—With अभि *abhi*, To shine towards, Hariv. 7501.—With आ *â*, *âdîpta*, 1. Blazing, Ṛit. 6, 19. 2. Burning, MBh. 15, 1081. Caus. To kindle, Râm. 2, 89, 16.—With व्या *vi-â*, Caus. To illuminate completely, MBh. 7, 7296.—With उद् *ud*, Caus. 1. To kindle, Hariv. 5521. 2. To excite, Bhâg. P. 8, 7, 11. 3. To illuminate, Mârk. P. 49, 11.—With समुद् *sam-ud*, Caus. To inflame, Râm. 4, 26, 14.—With उप *upa*, Caus. To kindle, set on fire, MBh. 3, 10230; 1, 5828.—With परि *pari*, 1. To boil up, MBh. 12, 2036 (Par.). 2. To be completely radiant, MBh. 7, 2237.—With प्र *pra*, *pradîpta*, 1. Blazing, Râm. 1, 54, 22. 2. Kindled (as anger), MBh. 3, 2374. 3. Shining, Ṛit. 1, 27. 4. Illuminated, Vedântas. in Chr. 205, 9. Caus. 1. To set on fire, kindle, MBh. 1, 5600; 13, 4037. 2. To inflame, Râm. 3, 69, 21.—With संप्र *sam-pra*, *sampradîpta*, Blazing, Râm. 5, 52, 13. Caus. To kindle, MBh. 7, 7237.—With प्रति *prati*, *pratidîpta*, Flaming towards, Hariv. 13155.—With वि *vi*, To shine, MBh. 7, 7322; *vidîpta*, Shining, MBh. 12, 8332. Caus. 1. To illuminate, MBh. 8, 1488. 2. To inflame, Bhâg. P. 9, 4, 46.—With अभिवि *abhi-vi*, Caus. To set on fire, MBh. 14, 2033.—With सम् *sam*, To blaze, Hariv. 3539; *saṁdîpta*, 1. Burning, Bhartṛ.

3. 26. **2.** Flaming, MBh. 5, 7205. Caus. **1.** To kindle, set on fire, Pańch. 97, 25; MBh. 1, 8366. **2.** To excite, MBh. 5, 2801.

दीप *dîp + a*, m. A lamp, Bhâg. 6, 19.—**Comp.** *Nirvâṇa-*, m. an extinguished lamp, Böhtl. Ind. Spr. 1610. *Nṛipa-*, m. a king like a lamp, Pańch. i. d. 251.

दीपक *dîp + aka*, **I.** adj. **1.** Inflaming, Pańch. iii. d. 27. **2.** Illuminating, Pańch. 190, 2. **II.** m. A lamp, Bhartṛ. 1, 55. **III.** f. *pikâ*, A lamp, Daçak. in Chr. 187, 4.—**Comp.** *Çarvarî-*, m. the lamp of the night (epithet of the moon), Böhtl. Ind. Spr. 2968.

दीपन *dîp + ana*, **I.** adj., f. *nî*. **1.** Inflaming, MBh. 1, 8455. **2.** Exciting, Ṛit. 1, 3. **II.** n. **1.** Setting on fire, Pańch. 194, 12. **2.** Burning, Daçak. in Chr. 181, 21. **3.** Exciting, or promoting digestion, Suçr. 1, 152, 8.—**Comp.** *Anala-*, adj. promoting digestion, Suçr. 1, 200, 14.

दीपनीय *dîpanîya*, i. e. *dîpana + îya*, adj. Promoting digestion, Suçr. 1, 177, 17.

दीप्ति *dîp + ti*, f. Splendour, Râm. 1, 7, 18.—**Comp.** *Gṛiha-*, f. being the splendour of the house, Man. 9, 26.

दीप्तिमन्त् *dîpti + mant*, adj., f. *matî*, Radiant, Indr. 1, 35.

दीप्र *dîp + ra*, adj. Shining, Kathâs. 25, 135.

दीर्घ *dîrgha*, i.e. *dṛih* (for original *dargh*), + *a*, **I.** adj., f. *ghâ*, Long, applied either to space or time, Râm, 5, 17, 28; 3, 68, 36; °*gham*, adv. 2, 62, 3; comparat. *dîrghatara*, Pańch. 209, 1; and *drâghîyaṁs*; superl. *dîrghatama*, Bhâg. P. 7, 5, 44, and *drâghishṭha*. **II.** m. A long vessel, Man, 2, 33.—**Comp.** *Su-*, adj. very long.—Cf. δολιχός.

दीर्घता *dîrgha + tâ*, f., and **दीर्घत्व** *dîrgha + tva*, n. Length, Suçr. 1, 117, 18; Bhâg. P. 7, 7, 16.

दीर्घदर्शिता *dîrghadarçitâ*, i. e. *dîrgha-darçin + tâ*, and **दीर्घदर्शित्व** *dîrghadarçitva*, i.e. *dîrgha-darçin + tva*, n. Longsightedness, providence, Kâm. Nîtis. 8, 10; 4, 8.

दीर्घसंध्यत्व *dîrgha-saṁdhya + tva* (see *saṁdhyâ*), n. The continued repetition of the twilight prayer, Man. 4, 94.

दीर्घसूत्रता *dîrgha-sûtra + tâ*, f. Irresolution, dilatoriness, MBh. 2, 241.—**Comp.** *A-*, f. Resoluteness, Kâm. Nîtis. 8, 8.

दीर्घसूत्रिन् *dîrghasûtrin*, i.e. *dîrgha-sûtra + in*, adj. Irresolute, dilatory, Bhag. 18, 28.

दीर्घिका *dîrghikâ*, i.e. *dîrgha + ka*, f. An oblong pond, MBh. 1, 5004.—**Comp.** *Sura-*, f. the Gaṅgâ of heaven.

1. **दु** *DU*, ii. 5, Par. (also Âtm., MBh. 1, 3289), i. 4, *dûya*, Âtm. (in epic poetry also Par., MBh. 4, 591). **1.** To burn morally or figuratively, to be in pain, MBh. 3, 10069; Gît. 3, 9; MBh. 3, 1371. **2.** To burn, to afflict, Bhâg. P. 3, 14, 9. Ptcple. of the pf. pass. **1.** *dûna*, Suffering pain, Gît. 8, 7. **2.** *duta*, Tormented, Çiç. 6, 59.—With the prep. **आ** *â*, To grieve, MBh. 1, 3289 (ii. 5, Atm.).—With **परि** *pari*, **1.** To burn violently, MBh. 6, 5779. **2.** To suffer pain, Râm. 2, 35, 34.—With **प्र** *pra*, **1.** To be consumed by fire, MBh. 13, 1800 (i. 4). **2.** To torment, Suçr. 1, 18, 5 (ii. 5).—With **वि** *vi*, To suffer pain, MBh. 1, 3289 (ii. 5, Âtm.); 2171 (i. 4, Par.).—Cf. *dâ̆va*, δαύω, ἐδαυμένος, δαυλός, ἐαίω, ἐαΐς,

δᾳδίον, δᾳδόω, δαλός, δανός, etc., probably also δυή.

2. † दु *DU*, i. 1, Par. To go, to move.

† दुःख् *DUḤKH*, i. 10 (rather a denomin. derived from the next), Par. To give pain.

दुःख *duḥkha* (properly दुष्ख *dush-kha*), i.e. *dus-kha*, I. n. Pain, Man. 1, 26; Yâjń. 2, 218. Instr. °*khena*, With difficulty, Pańch. iii. d. 263. II. adj., f. *khâ*. 1. Painful, unpleasant, Hariv. 12661; Râm. 2, 28, 7. 2. Difficult, Bhag. 18, 8. °*kham*, adv. Scarcely, hardly, Râm. 2, 53, 6; Çâk. d. 172.—Comp. *A-*, adj. propitious, Râm. 4, 22, 2. *Antar-*, adj. afflicted, Kathâs. 18, 256. *Sama-*, adj. sympathising. *Su-dushkha*, adj. abounding in pain, Chr. 10, 8.

दुःखता *duḥkha* + *tâ*, f. Discomfort, Râm. 2, 27, 23.

दुःखाकर *duḥkhâkara*, i.e. *duḥkha -kara*, adj. Afflicting, Daçak. in Chr. 181, 10.

दुःखाय *DUḤKHÂYA*, a denomin. derived from *duḥkha* by *ya*, Âtm. To suffer pain, Mâlav. d. 78.

दुःखित *duḥkhita*, i.e. *duḥkha* + *ita*, adj. 1. Pained, Man. 9, 288. 2. Afflicted, Pańch. 43, 8.—Comp. *Ati-dush-khita*, adj. very afflicted, Râjat. 5, 246. *Su-*, adj. The same, Chr. 12, 24.

दुःखीय *DUḤKHÎYA*, a denomin. derived from *duḥkha* by *ya*, Par. To suffer pain, Hit. ii. d. 55.

दुःप् ° *duḥp*°, see *dushp*°.

दुःशोध *duḥçodha*, i.e. *dus-çudh* + *a*, adj. Difficult to be cleansed.

दुःसंपाद *duḥsampâda*, i.e. *dus-sam -pad* + *a*, adj. Difficult to be attained, Daçak. in Chr. 181, 11.

दुःसह *duḥsaha*, i.e. *dus-sah* + *a*, I. adj., f. *hâ*, Insupportable, Man. 12, 76. II. m. A proper name, MBh. 1, 2447. III. f. *hâ*, A name of Çrî, MBh. 12, 8154.

दुःस्थ *duḥstha*, i.e. *dus-stha*, adj., f. *thâ*. 1. Insecure, Bhâg. P. 1, 16, 35. 2. Miserable, 4, 11, 21.

दुकूल *dukûla*, I. m. A certain plant, Hariv. 12680. II. n. 1. Very fine cloth, Hariv. 7041. 2. A garment, Bhâshâp. 1.

ऽदुघ *-dugha*, i.e. *duh* + *a*, I. adj., f. *ghâ*, Milking, yielding, Bhâg. P. 1, 17, 3. II. f. *ghâ*, A milking cow, Bhâg. P. 4, 6, 44.—Comp. *Droṇa-*, adj., f. *ghâ*, a cow that yields a *droṇa* of milk, MBh. 12, 951.

दुण्डुभ *duṇḍubha*, m. A kind of lizard, MBh. 7, 6905.—Cf. *ḍuṇḍubha*.

दुधुक्षु *dudhukshu*, i.e. *dudhuksha*, desiderat. of *duh*, + *u*, adj. Wishing to milk, MBh. 7, 2409.

दुध्रकृत् *dudhrakṛit* (the first part is akin to *dhu*, the last is *kṛi* + *t*), adj. Impetuous, Chr. 290, 11 = Rigv. i. 64, 11.

दुन्दुभि *dundubhi*, perhaps *dundubh*, a dialectical form of a frequentat. of *tubh*, + *i*, I. m. and f. *bhî*, A kettle-drum, Râm. 2, 91, 25; MBh. 3, 786. II. m. A name of Krishṇa, MBh. 12, 1511.

दुरधिग *duradhiga*, i.e. *dus-adhi-ga*, adj. Hard to be attained, Bhâg. P. 3, 23, 8.

दुरन्त *duranta*, i.e. *dus-anta*, adj. Miserable, Chân. 97, in Berl. Monatsb. (in *daranta-devaḥ kimu sarvam âstâm*, [Ganeça] is an unhappy deity, how much more all [other creatures]! Enough).

दुरवाप *duravâpa*, i.e. *dus-ava-âp* + *a*, adj., f. *pâ*, Hard to be attained, MBh. 7, 727.

दुराचर *durâchara*, i.e. *dus-â-char* + *a*, adj., f. *râ*. 1. Hard to be practised, MBh. 12, 656. 2. Difficult to be cured, Suçr. 2, 361, 9.

दुरात्मता *durâtmatâ*, i.e. *dus-âtman* + *tâ*, f. Wickedness, MBh. 1, 2010.

दुरात्मवन्त् *durâtmavant*, i.e. *dus-âtman* + *vant*, adj., f. *vatî*, Wicked, MBh. 1, 2017.

दुराधर *durâdhara*, i.e. *dus-â-dhṛi* + *a*, adj. 1. Difficult to be attained, MBh. 1, 7302. 2. Irresistible, MBh. 8, 1523.

दुराधर्ष *durâdharsha*, i.e. *dus-â-dhṛish* + *a*, adj, f. *shâ*. 1. Difficult to be attacked, Râm. 1, 30, 2. 2. Dangerous, MBh. 1, 3381.

दुरानम *durânama*, i.e. *dus-â-nam* + *a*, adj. Hard to bend (as a bow), Râm. 1, 77, 15 Gorr.

दुराप *durâpa*, i.e. *dus-âp* + *a*, adj., f. *pâ*. 1. Hard to be attained, Man. 11, 238. 2. Hard to be overcome, MBh. 4, 909.

दुरापादन *durâpâdana*, *dus-â-pad*, Caus., +*ana*, adj. Hard to be brought about, Bhâg. P. 3, 23, 42.

दुरापूर *durâpûra*, i.e. *dus-â-pûr* + *a*, adj. Hard to be satisfied, Bhâg. P. 7, 6, 8.

दुरारिहन् *durârihan*, i.e. *dus-ari-han* (*â* on account of the metre), adj. Slaying the wicked enemies, MBh. 13, 7032.

दुरावार *durâvâra*, i.e. *dus-â-vṛi* + *a*, adj. 1. Difficult to be filled up, Râm. 2, 105, 23. 2. Difficult to be stopped, MBh. 7, 1480.

दुरासद *durâsada*, i.e. *dus-â-sad* + *a*, I. adj., f. *dâ*. 1. Difficult to be approached, Râm. 3, 69, 16. 2. Difficult to be met with, Râm. 1, 18, 2. II. m. A sword, MBh. 12, 6203.

दुरासह *durâsaha*, i.e. *dus-â-sah* + *a*, adj. Difficult to be accomplished, Arj. 10, 58.

दुरुत्सह *durutsaha*, i.e. *dus-ud-sah* + *a*, adj. 1. Difficult to be borne, MBh. 13, 4392. 2. Difficult to be resisted, MBh. 5, 3305.

दुरुपलक्ष *durupalaksha*, i.e. *dus-upa-laksh* + *a*, adj. Difficult to be perceived, Daçak. in Chr. 185, 18.

दुरोदर *durodara*, I. m. 1. A dice-player, MBh. 2, 2000. 2. A dice-box, MBh. 8, 3763. II. n. Game at dice, MBh. 2, 1978.

दुर्ग *durga*, i.e. *dus-ga*, I. adj., f. *gâ*. Almost impassable or inaccessible, Man. 4, 77; 7, 70. II. m. The name of an Asura, Hariv. 9426. III. f. *gâ*, The wife of Çiva, MBh. 4, 178. IV. n. (also m., Râm. 4, 47, 3), 1. A difficult passage, Bhâg. P. 6, 6, 6. 2. Distress, Man. 3, 98. 3. A strong-hold, Man. 7, 29.—Comp. *Giri-*, adj. Almost inaccessible on account of surrounding mountains, Man. 7, 70.

दुर्गतता *durgatatâ*, i.e. *dus-gata* + *tâ* (vb. *gam*), f. Misery, Pañch. i. d. 297.

दुर्गता *durga* + *tâ*, 1. Difficulty of being crossed, Râm. 4, 27, 16.

दुर्गाह्यत्व *durgâhyatva*, i.e *dus-gâhya* + *tva* (vb. *gâh*), n. Unfathomableness, Pañch. i. d. 317, v.r.

दुर्गृभीय *DURGṚIBHÎYA*, a denomin. derived from ved. *durgṛibhi*, i.e. *dus-grah* + *i*, by *ya*, Âtm. To be difficult to catch, Lass. 98, 12=Rigv. v. 9, 4.

दुर्जनाय *DURJANÂYA*, a denomin. derived from *dus-jana* by *ya*, Âtm. To become wicked, Pañch. i. d. 5.

दुर्जर *durjara*, i.e. *dus-jṛi* + *a*, adj.

1. Difficult to be digested, Suçr. 1, 179, 15. 2. Hard, Râjat. 5, 19.

दुर्दर्शता *durdarçatâ*, i.e. *dus-darça* + *tâ*, f. Loathesomeness; with *yâ*, To become disgusting, MBh. 8, 861.

दुर्दृश *durdṛiça*, i.e. *dus-dṛiç* + *a*, adj. 1. Difficult to be looked at, MBh. 7, 1470. 2. Difficult to be met with, MBh. 10, 83 (read *durdṛiçau*). 3. Disgusting, MBh. 1, 568.

दुर्दैववन्त् *durdaivavant*, i.e. *dus -daiva* + *vant*, adj., f. *vati*, Unhappy, Hit. 123, 16.

दुर्धर्षता *durdharshatâ*, i.e. *dus-dharsha* + *tâ*, f. Difficulty of being touched, MBh. 12, 9135.

दुर्धर्षत्व *durdharshatva*, i.e. *dus dharsha* + *tva*, n. Difficulty of being conquered, Bhâg. P. 9, 15, 18.

दुर्निरीक्ष *durnirîksha*, i.e. *dus-nis -îksh* + *a*, adj. 1. Difficult to be looked at or seen, MBh. 2, 947; Hariv. 6616.

दुर्बलता *durbalatâ*, i.e. *dus-bala* + *tâ*, f. Weakness, Pañch. 224, 2.

दुर्भगत्व *durbhagatva*, i.e. *dus-bhaga* + *tva*, n. Misfortune, Bhâg. P. 3, 7, 6.

दुर्भिद *durbhida*, i.e. *dus-bhid* + *a*, adj., f. *dâ*. 1. Difficult to be torn asunder, MBh. 7, 1514. 2. Difficult to be destroyed, Bhâg. P. 5, 19, 15.

दुर्मर *durmara*, *dus-mṛi* + *a*, I. adj. Not easily dying, MBh. 16, 153. II. n. A hard death, MBh. 14, 2364.

दुर्मरत्व *durmara* + *tva*, n. A hard death, MBh. 8, 21.

दुर्मर्ष *durmarsha*, i.e. *dus-mṛish* + *a*, I. adj., f. *shâ*. 1. Insupportable, Bhâg. P. 8, 11, 18. 2. Hostile, 6, 14, 43. II. m. A name of the demon Bali, 8, 10, 32.

दुर्मेधस्त्व *durmedhastva*, i.e. *dus -medhas* + *tva*, n. Foolishness, Suçr. 1, 313, 1.

दुर्योधन *duryodhana* (see the next), m. The eldest of the Kuru princes, MBh. 1, 2728.

दुर्योधनता *duryodhana* + *tâ*, i.e. *dus-yudh* + *ana* + *tâ*, f. Difficulty of being attacked, MBh. 4, 2103.

दुर्लभ *durlabha*, i.e. *dus-labh* + *a*, adj., f. *bhâ*. 1. Hard to be attained, Man. 4, 137. 2. Hard to be found, 7, 22. 3. Difficult to be saved, Râm. 3, 25, 28. 4. Difficult, MBh. 3, 1728.—Comp. *Su-*, adj. very difficult to be attained, Râm. 3, 53, 46.

दुर्ललितक *durlalitaka*, i.e. *dus-lalita* + *ka* (vb. *lal*), adj. Wayward, Çâk. 103, 4, v.r.

† दुर्व् *DURV*, i. 1, *dûrva*, Par. To hurt.

दुर्वच *durvacha*, i.e. *dus-vach* + *a*, adj. 1. Abusing, Râm. 2, 22, 18. 2. Difficult to be explained, MBh. 14, 570.

दुर्वस *durvasa*, i.e. *dus-vas* + *a*, adj. 1. Difficult to dwell, MBh. 4, 93. 2. Difficult to be passed (as time), MBh. 4, 7.

दुर्वार *durvâra*, and दुर्वारण *durvâraṇa*, i.e. *dus-vṛi* + *a* or *ana*, adj. Difficult to be stopped, irresistible, MBh. 7, 344; Hariv. 14004.

दुर्विद *durvida*, i.e. *dus-vid* + *a*, adj., f. *dâ*, Difficult to be known, MBh. 1, 5429.

दुर्विभाष *durvibhâsha*, i.e. *dus-vi -bhâsh* + *a*, n. Abuse, MBh. 2, 2187.

दुर्विवक्तृ *durvivaktṛi*, i.e. *dus-vi-vach* + *tṛi*, m. One who answers a question wrongly.

दुर्विश *durviça*, i.e. *dus-viç*+*a*, adj., f. *çâ*, Difficult to be trod upon, Râm. 6, 19, 16.

दुर्विषह *durvishaha*, i.e. *dus-vi-sah* +*a*, I. adj., f. *hâ*. **1.** Hard to be borne, insupportable, Bhâg. P. 3, 3, 14. **2.** Difficult to be performed, 8, 5, 46. II. m. A proper name, MBh. 1, 6981.

दुल् *DUL* (a form of *tul*), i. 10, Par. To raise, to swing, Bhartṛ. 3, 43. Ptcple. of the pf. pass. *dolita*, Made uncertain, Çatr. 14, 197.

दुवस्य *DUVASYA*, a denomin. derived from the ved. *duvas* by the aff. *ya*, Par. To honour, Chr. 297, 15= Rigv. i. 112, 15.

दुश्चरत्व *duçcharatva*, i.e. *dus-chara* + *tva*, n. Difficulty of practising, Râm. 5, 86, 14.

दुश्च्याव *duçchyâva*, i.e. *dus-chyu*, Caus., +*a*, adj. Difficult to be felled, MBh. 8, 1506.

दुष् *DUSH*, i. 4, Par. (in epic poetry also Âtm., perhaps to be read *dûshyate*, pass. of the Caus. MBh. 1, 2405), **1.** To be depraved, MBh. 1, 2405. **2.** To be defiled, Man. 9, 318. **3.** To be ruined, Kâm. Nîtis. 11, 36. **4.** To sin, Man. 5, 32. **5.** To be faulty, Suçr. 2, 214, 15. Ptcple. of the pf. pass. *dushṭa*, **1.** Corrupt, Yâjń. 2, 257. **2.** Painful, Pańch. 38, 11. **3.** Wicked, Pańch. 98, 22. **4.** Convicted, Man. 8, 373. **5.** Ill-affected against somebody (with gen.), Râm. 2, 92, 16 Gorr. **6.** n. Sin, Hariv. 7760. Comp. *A*-, adj. innocent. *Su*-, adj. guilty, Râm. 5, 91, 2. *Vâgd°*, i.e. *vâch*-, m. a rude speaker, Man. 3, 156; a defamer, 8, 345. Caus. *dûshaya*, **1.** To hurt, Man. 2, 47; with gen., Râm. 2, 74, 3. **2.** To lay waste, Man. 7, 195. **3.** To defile, Man. 5, 125; 8, 364. **4.** To demoralise, Râjat. 5, 6. **5.** To falsify, MBh. 13, 1683. **6.** To rescind, MBh. 12, 7256. **7.** To blame, MBh. 13, 1469. **8.** To abuse, MBh. 2, 2133. **9.** To accuse, Râm. 1, 59, 20. Ptcple. of the pf. pass. *dûshita*, Disgraced, Man. 10, 29; deprived of the marks of his order (?), Man. 6, 66 (Kull.). Comp. ptcple. of the fut. pass. *a-dûshya*, Not to be defiled, MBh. 12, 6072.—With the prep. **अनु** *anu*, To lose courage afterwards, MBh. 5, 4543.—With **अभि** *abhi*, *abhidushṭa*, Defiled, MBh. 13, 1573. Caus. To hurt, Dev. 8, 37.—With **उप** *upa*, To be depraved, Hariv. 11264.—With **प्र** *pra*, **1.** To grow worse (as a disease), Suçr. 1, 83, 16. **2.** To be defiled, MBh. 12, 1237. **3.** To act amiss, Man. 9, 74. *pradushṭa*, **1.** Wicked, MBh. 12, 4540. **2.** Blameable, 1, 3666. Caus. **1.** To defile, Ragh. 11, 25. **2.** To deprave, Râm. 3, 51, 5 (*pradûshita*). **3.** To blame, Râm. 1, 61, 21 Gorr.—With **अभिप्र** *abhi-pra*, Caus. To corrupt, Suçr. 1, 187, 17.—With **विप्र** *vi-pra*, *vipradushṭa*, Exceedingly wanton, Man. 11, 176.—With **संप्र** *sam-pra*, **1.** To grow worse (as a disease), Suçr. 1, 443, 15. **2.** To become wicked, MBh. 2, 2397. *sampradushṭa*, Defiled, Varâh. Bṛih. S. 12, 14.—With **प्रति** *prati*, Caus., *pratidûshita* in *bhâva*-, n. Disturbance of mind, Man. 4, 65.—With **वि** *vi*, Caus. **1.** To defile, Bhâg. P. 2, 2, 37. **2.** To offend, Mârk. P. 34, 47. **3.** To disgrace, Râm. 2, 78, 8 Gorr.—With **सम्** *sam*, To be defiled, MBh. 12, 4009. *saṁdushṭa*, **1.** Wicked, Râm. 3, 51, 27. **2.** Ill-affected against somebody, Râm. 2, 91, 11 Gorr. Caus. **1.** To corrupt, Suçr. 1, 286, 12. **2.** To defile, Râm. 6, 103, 19. **3.** To expose to shame, Kâm. Nîtis. 6, 13. *samdûshita,* Grown worse (as a disease), Suçr. 2, 413, 1.

दुष्कर *dushkara,* i.e. *dus-kara,* adj., f. *râ.* **1.** Difficult to be performed, Man. 7, 55. **2.** Difficult to be supported, Râm. 2, 32, 2. **3.** Difficult, MBh. 4, 52. **4.** With following *yadi,* Scarcely, Râm. 2, 73, 7.

दुष्कृत् *dushkṛit,* i.e. *dus-kṛit,* adj. subst. An offender, MBh. 12, 6548.

दुष्ख्° *dushkh°,* see *duḥkh°.*

दुष्टता *dushṭa + tâ,* f. and दुष्टत्व *dushṭa + tva,* n. Wickedness, Râm. 4, 1, 31; Pańch. 99, 9.

दुष्टर *dushṭara,* i.e. *dus-tṛî + a,* adj. Unconquerable, Chr. 291, 14 = Rigv. i. 64, 14.

दुष्टि *dushṭi,* i.e. *dush + ti,* f. Corruptness, Suçr. 1, 253, 6.

दुष्प्रज्ञत्व *dushprajńatva,* i.e. *dus-prajńa + tva,* n. Stupidity, Prab. 108, 10.

दुष्प्रतर *dushpratara,* i.e. *dus-pra-tṛî + a,* adj., f. *râ,* Difficult to be crossed.

दुष्प्रधर्ष *dushpradharsha* and दुष्प्रधर्षण *dushpradharshaṇa,* i.e. *dus-pra-dhṛish + a* or *ana,* adj., f. *shâ, ṇâ,* Difficult to be attacked, Râm. 6, 95, 12; 5, 72, 11.

दुष्प्रसह *dushprasaha,* i.e. *dus-pra-sah + a,* adj., f. *hâ.* **1.** Difficult to be supported, irresistible, Ragh. 3, 58. **2.** Terrible, MBh. 12, 3094.

दुष्प्रसाह *dushprasâha,* = the last, with *â* on account of the metre, Arj. 3, 55.

दुष्प्राप *dushprâpa,* i.e. *dus-pra-âp-a,* adj., f. *pâ,* Difficult to be attained, MBh. 4, 115.

दुष्प्रेक्ष *dushpreksha,* i.e. *dus-pra-îksh + a,* adj., f. *shâ,* Difficult to be looked at, Râm. 3, 17, 22.

दुष्मन्त *dushmanta,* or दुष्यन्त *dushyanta,* or दुष्वन्त *dushvanta,* m. The name of a prince, the husband of Çakuntalâ, MBh. 1, 2801; Hariv. 1701; Râm. 2, 116, 29 Gorr.

दुस् *dus* (cf. *dush*), a prefix implying: **1.** Bad, wicked, contemptible, e.g. *durvâch,* A bad speech, abuse (see *vâch*); *durjana,* A wicked person (see *jana*); *durbuddhi,* Having a contemptible intellect, i.e. stupid (see *buddhi*). **2.** Wrong, e.g. *dustarka* (see *tarka*). **3.** Inauspicious, e.g. *dustithi* (see *tithi*). **4.** Difficult, e.g. *dushpreksha.*—Cf. δυς; Goth. tus in tuz-verjan; O.H.G. zur-.

दुस्त्यज *dus-tyaj + a,* adj., f. *jâ,* Difficult to be abandoned or resigned, Bhâg. P. 2, 10, 48; MBh. 1, 3513.—Comp. *Su-,* to be risked very unwillingly, Chr. 33, 3.

1. दुह् *DUH* (originally *dugh,* cf. *dugha*), ii. 2, and i. 4. I. Par. **1.** To milk, Man. 8, 231; Bhâg. P. 4, 17, 7; to milk out (with two accs.), 4, 18, 18. **2.** To enjoy, Ragh. 1, 26. **3.** To practise from interested motives, MBh. 3, 1165. **4.** To draw something out of anything (with two accs.), MBh. 12, 3305; with acc. and abl., Man, 1, 23. II. Âtm. **1.** To yield milk or other desired objects, MBh. 1, 6658; 6657 (also i. 4, Par., Bhâg. P. 1, 14, 19). Anomal. 3 pl. of the red. pf. *dudûhus,* on account of the metre, Bhâg. P. 5, 15, 9. Ptcple. of the pf. pass. *dugdha,* **1.** Milked, Hariv. 79. **2.** Impoverished, Daçak. in Chr. 192, 16. **3.** Collected, Bhâg. P. 5, 14, 12. n. Milk. Bhartṛ. 2, 15. Comp. *Vitta-,* n. wealth like milk (as if it were milk), Pańch. i. d.

249. Caus. *dohaya*, **1.** To cause to yield milk or other desired objects, Bhâg. P. 4, 18, 15. **2.** To produce, Man. 2, 77. Desider. *dudhuksha*, To wish to milk or to enjoy, Bhartr̥. 2, 38.—With the prep. निस् *nis*, **1.** To milk out, to produce, MBh. 2, 76. **2.** To withdraw, Kathâs. 16, 83.—With सम् *sam*, To milk, to enjoy, MBh. 12, 4384 (i. 4. Par.)—Cf. Goth. tiuhan, A.S. teon, teoge, O.H.G. ziuhan; Lat. duco, O.H.G. ziug (gaziug), zaugjan, τεῦχος.

† 2. दुह् *DUH*, i. 1, Par. To give pain.

ऽदुह *-duh+a*, adj. Yielding (cf. *kâmaduha*).—**Comp.** *Dus-*, adj., f. *hâ*, difficult to be milked, MBh. 5, 1128.

दुहितृ *duhitṛi*, i.e. *duh+tṛi*, f. A daughter, Man. 2, 215. Anomal. acc. pl. *duhitaras*, Râm. 3, 20, 28.—Abstract. त्व *tva*, n. Râm. 1, 44, 38.—Cf. θυγάτηρ; Goth. dauhtar; A.S. dohtor.

दू *DÛ* = 1. *du*.

दूऽ *dû-*, for *dus*, before following *r*; cf. *dûrakshya* under *raksh*.

दूत *dûta*, I. m. A messenger, an envoy, Man. 3, 163.—**Comp.** *Megha-*, The Cloud-messenger, a poem by Kâlidâsa. II. f. *ti* and *tî*. **1.** A female messenger, Nal. 21, 35. **2.** A procuress, Lass. 8, 17; Vikr. d. 88.—**Comp.** *Praçna-dûti*, f. a riddle.

दूतक *dûta+ka*, I. m. A messenger, MBh. 3, 15438. II. f. *tikâ*. **1.** A procuress, Lass. 24, 14. **2.** A betrayer, Râjat. 6, 362.—**Comp.** *Yama-*, m. 1. a messenger of Yama. 2. a crow.

दूतत्व *dûta+tva*, n. Condition of an envoy, Pañch. 24, 5.

दूतीत्व *dûtî+tva*, f. Condition of a procuress, Lass. 44, 4.

दूत्य *dûtya*, i.e. *dûta+ya*, n., also f. *yâ*, A message, Hariv. 6180; Kathâs. 13, 132.

दूर *dûra*, adj., f. *râ*. **1.** Distant, remote, Kathâs. 16, 47. **2.** Long, MBh. 9, 1738. Comparat. *davîyaṁs*, Bhartr̥. 1, 68; superl. *davishṭha*, Râjat. 4, 365. Acc. °*ram*, adv. **1.** Far, Râm. 1, 1, 28. **2.** High, Hit. 27, 19. **3.** Deep, Hariv. 14084. **4.** In a high degree, Daçak. in Chr. 190, 7. Instr. °*reṇa*, adv. Far, Bhartr̥. 1, 80. Abl. °*rât*, adv. **1.** From afar, Man. 2, 186. **2.** Far from (with abl.), Man. 4, 151. **3.** In a remote degree, Man. 3, 130 (Kull.) Loc. °*re*. **1.** Far, Çâk. d. 9. **2.** Far away, MBh. 9, 1737. *dûratare*, Far from (with abl.), Man. 11, 128 (129).—**Comp.** *A-*, adj. near, Lass. 41, 7; abl. °*rât*, adv. near, Râm. 3, 50, 15; with gen., 2, 92, 17. *Ati-*, °*ram*, adv. very far, Pañch. 105, 4; °*reṇa* and °*re*, adv. the same, Pañch. 51, 15; Râm. 3, 17, 16. *Kiyad-dûra*, i.e. *kiyant-*, adj., acc. °*ram*, not very far, some little way, Pañch. 229, 20; loc. s. *re*, how far, Pañch. 52, 4. *Vi-*, I. adj. very far. II. m. the name of a mountain (*vidûrâdri* i.e. *vidûra-adri*). *A-vi-*, adj. not very far; °*rât*, adv. near, Râm. 3, 48, 19. *Su-*, adj. very distant; °*ram*, adv. in a very high degree, Daçak. in Chr. 183, 3.

दूरग *dûra-ga*, adj. Being far, Râjat. 5, 320.

दूरतस् *dûra+tas*, adv. **1.** From afar, Râm. 1, 48, 9. **2.** Aloof from, Man. 4, 73. **3.** Far, Râm. 3, 60, 31; Pañch. i. d. 9.—**Comp.** *A-*, adv. near, Râm. 3, 9, 24.

दूरत्व *dûra + tva*, n. Distance, Bhâshap. 130.

दूरूढत्व *dûrûḍhatva*, i.e. *dus-rûḍha*

+*tva* (vb. *ruh*), n. Bad cicatrisation, Suçr. 2, 12, 7.

दूरेचर *dûra* + *i-chara*, adj. Distant, Kâm. Nîtis. 8, 54.

दूरेयम *dûra* + *i-yama*, adj. One from whom the god of death is far removed, Bhâg. P. 3, 15, 25.

दूर्वा *dûrvâ*, f. A kind of millet-grass, Panicum dactylon, MBh. 3, 9984.

दूर्वावन्त् *dûrvâ* + *vant*, adj., f. *vatî*, Joined with dûrvâ grass, Kathâs. 7, 14.

ऽदूष -*dûsha*, i.e. *dush*, Caus., + *a*, latter part of comp. adj., Defiling; in *pankti-* (a company), MBh. 13, 4274.

दूषक *dûshaka*, i. e. *dush*, Caus., + *aka*, I. adj., f. *shikâ*. **1.** Defiling, MBh. 12, 1236 (sinful); one who defiles, Râm. 2, 75, 38. **2.** Disfiguring, Suçr. 1, 295, 19. **3.** Seducing, Man. 3, 164; 9, 232 (sowing dissensions, Kull.). **4.** Hurting, Hariv. 3206. **5.** Trespassing, Râm. 4, 37, 13. **II.** f. *shikâ*. **1.** Concretion on the eyes, Man. 5, 135. **2.** A kind of rice, Suçr. 1, 195, 8.

दूषण *dûshaṇa*, i. e. *dush*, Caus., + *ana*, I. adj., f. *ṇî*. **1.** Defiling, disgracing, Bhâg. P. 1, 17, 13. **2.** Hurting, Râm. 2, 109, 7. **II.** m. The name of a Râkshasa or demon, Râm. 1, 1, 45. **III.** f. *ṇâ*, The name of a deity, Bhâg. P. 5, 15, 13. **IV.** n. **1.** Defiling, Man. 9, 286; 11, 61. **2.** Hurting, Man. 7, 48 (unjust seizure). **3.** Seducing, Man. 2, 213. **4.** Calumuiating, Kathâs. 24, 227. **5.** Fault, Man. 9, 13; Bhartṛ. 2, 89.

दूषयितृ *dûshayitṛi*, i.e. *dush*, Caus., + *tṛi*, One who deflowers, Mârk. P. 31, 28.

दूषिन् *dûshin*, i.e. *dush*, Caus., + *in*, adj., f. *iṇî*, Polluting, MBh. 3, 11158.

1. दृ *DṚI*, i. 6, *driya*, Atm. (in epic poetry also Par., MBh. 13, 7411).—With the prep. आ *â*, **1.** To consider, Kâm. Nîtis. 5, 67. **2.** To respect, Man. 2, 234. Ptcple. of the pf. pass. *âdṛita*, **1.** Respectful, Râm. 5, 25, 56. **2.** Careful, Pañch. iii. d. 243. **Comp.** *An-*, acc. adv. without any regard, Râm. 1, 59, 8.—With अत्या *ati-â*, To regard carefully, Bhâg. P. 3, 16, 21. *Atyâdṛita*, **1.** Very respectful, Dev. 4, 15. **2.** Much cared for, Daçak. in Chr. 181, 19.—With समा *sam-â*, *samâdṛita*, Very respectful, Bhâg. P. 8, 21, 5.—Cf. probably A.S. dyre, deorling, perhaps also draed, dread.

† **2.** दृ *DṚI*, ii. 5, Par. To hurt.

† **3.** दृ *DṚI*, i. 1, and i. 10, Par. To fear.—Cf. *dṛî*.

दृंह् *DṚIṀH*, i. 1, and i. 4, Par., Âtm. To fasten (ved.). To be fastened (ved.). Ptcple. of the pf. pass. *dṛiḍha*, **1.** Hard, firm, Râm. 2, 56, 14; Hit. 21, 20; Hariv. 7329. **2.** Reliable, MBh. 2646. **3.** Violent, MBh. 13, 1972. **4.** Great, MBh. 1, 7636. Compar. *draḍhiyaṁs*, superl. *draḍhishṭha*. Acc. °*ḍham*, adv. **1.** Tightly, Prab. 12, 3. **2.** Much, Arj. 8, 1. **3.** Well, Mâlav. 11, 8. **4.** Incessantly, MBh. 4, 314. Ved. frequent. *dâdṛih*, To be excessively firm, Chr. 292, 10=Rigv. i. 85, 10.—Cf. τραχύς.

दृढ *dṛiḍha*, see *dṛiṁh*.

दृढता *dṛiḍha* + *tâ*, f. and दृढत्व *dṛiḍha* + *tva*, n. Firmness, Prab. 13, 17; Pañch. i. d. 120.

दृढीकरण *dṛiḍhîkaraṇa*, n. and

दृढीकार *dṛiḍhîkâra*, i.e. *dṛiḍha-kṛi* + *ana* or *a*, m. Confirmation, Râm. 2, 90, 21; MBh. 12, 7307.

दृति *dṛiti*, i.e. *dṛî+ti*, f. A leather bag for holding liquids, Man. 2, 99.—Cf. δέρω, δείρω, δέρμα; O.H.G. gi-zelt, pelles, zelt; A.S. teld, tentorium.

1. **दृप्** *DṚIP*, i. 4, Par. To be mad or extravagant, arrogant, Gît. 9, 11. *dṛipta*, **1.** Wild, Râm. 1, 15, 7. **2.** Arrogant, MBh. 1, 162. Compar. *dṛiptatara*, Excessively arrogant, Daçak. in Chr. 195, 12. Caus. *darpaya*, **1.** To make mad, Kathâs. 20, 64. **2.** To make arrogant or proud, Pańch. iii. d. 244. Ptcple. of the pf. pass. *darpita*, **1.** Wild, Bhartṛ. 3, 73. **2.** Proud, Man. 8, 371.—With the prep. **अति** *ati*, *atidṛipta* (rather *dṛipta* with *ati*), Excessively arrogant, Kathâs. 20, 65.—Cf. probably δόρπον, a banquet.

† 2. **दृप्** *DṚIP*, **दृफ्** *DṚIPH*, **दृम्फ्** *DṚIMPH*, i. 6, Par. To hurt.

† 3. **दृप्** *DṚIP*, i. 1 and 10, Par. To kindle.

दृफ् *DṚIPH*, see 2. *dṛip*.

1. **दृभ्** *DṚIBH*, i. 6, Par. and † i. 1 and 10, Par. To string, to bind.—With the prep. **सम्** *sam*, To compose, Naish. 9, 159.

† 2. **दृभ्** *DṚIBH*, i. 1 and 10, Par. To fear.

† **दृम्प्** *DṚIMP*, i. 10 Âtm. To collect.

दृम्फ् *DṚIMPH*, see 2. *dṛip*.

1. **दृश्** *DṚIÇ*, i. 1, *paçya* (for original *spaç+ya*. i. 4, forms the pres. impfct. imptive. and potent.), Par. (also Âtm., MBh. 1, 2896; 2830), **1.** To see, Râm. 2, 64, 59. **2.** To behold, look at, Man. 4, 44. **3.** To be a spectator, Man. 7, 92; to look on something (without being able to prevent it), Râm. 1, 54, 18. **4.** To wait on, Lass. 2, 14. **5.** To inspect, Man. 7, 120. **6.** To live to see, Râm. 1, 1, 88. **7.** To discover, Man. 8, 38. **8.** To search, MBh. 4, 1172. **9.** To learn, Râm. 1, 13, 7. **10.** To know, Râm. 1, 57, 20. **11.** To decide, Pańch. 165, 7. Passive also with the terminations of the Par., e.g. MBh. 2345. Comp. ptcple. of the pres. *a-dṛiçyant*, adj. **1.** Invisible, Sund. 2, 19. **2.** fem. *ntî*, A proper name, MBh. 1, 6757. Ptcple. of the pf. pass. *drishṭa*, **1.** Seen, etc. **2.** Treated, Pańch. 85, 1. **3.** Experienced, Râm. 3, 47, 18. **4.** Devised, Nal. 4, 19. **5.** Determined, MBh. 13, 11784. **6.** Declared, Man. 9, 249. **7.** Acknowledged, Man. 8, 3. Comp. *A-*, I. adj. 1. not seen before, Râm. 5, 43, 10. 2. unperceived, Man. 5, 127. 3. not approved, Man. 8, 153. II. n. fate, Bhâshâp. 160; Pańch. v. d. 27. See *Ku-*. *Dus-*, adj. unrighteously decided, Yâjń. 2, 305. *Su-*, adj. looked at eagerly, Râm. 1, 17, 23. Ptcple. of the fut. pass. I. *darçanîya*, **1.** Visible, Râm. 1, 67, 6. **2.** Beautiful, Pańch. iv. d. 40. Comp. *A-*, n. invisibility, Pańch. 138, 40. II. *dṛiçya*, **1.** Visible, Râm. 4, 40, 64. **2.** To be looked at, Bhartṛ. 1, 86. **3.** Worth to be looked at, Ragh. 6, 31. Comp. *A-*, adj. 1. invisible, Râm. 1, 17, 33. 2. ugly, Arj. 10, 66. III. *drashṭavya*, **1.** To be seen, etc., MBh. 13, 1404. **2.** Visible, Bhartṛ. 1, 7. Caus. *darçaya*, **1.** To cause to see, to show (with two accus., or acc. and gen., and acc. and dat.), Râm. 3, 61, 5; Man. 4, 59; Râm. 2, 31, 33. **2.** To point out, Çâk. 12, 19. **3.** To confess, Râjat. 5, 124. **4.** To produce, Man. 8, 158. **5.** To pay, 8, 155. **6.** To prove, 8, 225. **7.** To show one's self, MBh. 1, 4709 (Âtm.); 1, 6561 (Par.). Anomal. ptcple. of the pres. Âtm. *darçayâna*, MBh. 1, 17. Desider. *didṛiksha*, To wish to see, Bhâg. P. 4, 3, 11. Ptcple.

दृश्

of the pf. pass. *didṛikshita*, n. Wish to see, Bhâg. P. 3, 15, 31.—With the prep. अनु *anu*, 1. To look afterwards, Bhâg. P. 4, 25, 60. 2. To see, Man. 3, 176. 3. To look on, Bhâg. P. 3, 12, 23. 4. To regard, to honour, MBh. 15, 679. 5. To perceive, MBh. 6, 5456. 6. To know, Bhag. 13, 30. 7. To find, MBh. 9, 2986. Caus. 1. To show, Râm. 2, 49, 12. 2. To teach, Râm. 2, 100, 1.—With समनु *sam-anu*, 1. To look after, Bhâg. P. 5, 21, 9. 2. To consider, MBh. 1, 5037.—With व्यप *vi-apa*, pass. To be visible, MBh. 7, 8136.—With अभि *abhi*, 1. To look at, MBh. 3, 9982. 2. To regard, Râm. 2, 30, 2 Gorr. 3. To perceive, MBh. 1, 5002. Caus. 1. To show, MBh. 14, 2151. 2. To show one's self, MBh. 1, 7740.—With अव *ava*, To infer, Bhâg. P. 3, 27, 12.—With आ *â*, Caus. To show, Ragh. 4, 38.—With व्या *vi-â*, To see distinctly, Bhâg. P. 3, 17, 6.—With उद् *ud*, 1. To foresee, Megh. 23. 2. To perceive, Megh. 102. Caus. To show one's self, Vikr. 11, 6.—With उप *upa*, 1. To look on, MBh. 1, 8440. 2. To perceive, Bhâg. P. 4, 10, 13. Caus. 1. To show, Hit. 38, 15. 2. To pretend, Kathâs. 19, 75.—With नि *ni*, Caus. 1. To show, MBh. 12, 13222. 2. To point out, Çâk. 100, 9, v.r. 3. To enter, Râjat. 1, 18. 4. To teach, MBh. 12, 2154. 5. To appear to somebody (acc.), Hariv. 1559.—With संनि *sam-ni*, Caus. To show, Râm. 4, 63, 15.—With परि *pari*, 1. To look at, MBh. 12, 6576. 2. To frequent, MBh. 15, 1014. 3. To see, Râm. 2, 91, 2 Gorr. 4. To consider, Prab. 71, 6. 5. To search, MBh. 1, 6222. 6. To know, MBh. 3, 224.—With प्र *pra*, 1. To foresee, Bhag. 2, 8. 2. To be intelligent, MBh. 7, 1057. 3. To see before one's self, Râm. 1, 60, 27 Gorr. 4. To see, Man. 8, 85; pass. To appear, Brâhmaṇ. 2, 6. 5. To behold, Bhag. 11, 49. 6. To learn, MBh. 9, 1550. 7. To know, Râm. 5, 3, 63. 8. To judge, MBh. 3, 1082. Caus. 1. To show, Râm. 4, 27, 21. 2. To describe, Man. 10, 40. 3. To explain, Daçak. in Chr. 185, 10.—With संप्र *sam-pra*, 1. To see, MBh. 3, 15050; pass. To appear, Râm. 2, 52, 80 Gorr. 2. To perceive, Râm. 1, 3, 4. 3. To consider, MBh. 5, 795. 4. To know, Râm. 5, 70, 3. 5. To judge, MBh. 12, 410. Caus. 1. To show, MBh. 9, 3280. 2. To declare, MBh. 6, 571.—With प्रति *prati*, 1. To behold, MBh. 3, 12005; pass. To appear, MBh. 5, 4679. 2. To know, MBh. 5, 2021. 3. To experience, MBh. 12, 12548.—With वि *vi*, 1. To discern, to recognise, Bhâg. P. 6, 1, 48. 2. To perceive, Bhâg. P. 9, 8, 22; pass. To appear, Râm. 1, 13, 14 Gorr. Caus. 1. To show, MBh. 4, 1844. 2. To teach, Râm. 2, 29, 7.—With सम् *sam*, 1. To behold, Râm. 2, 54, 3; pass. To appear, Arj. 1, 3. 2. To recognise, Yâjñ. 3, 64. 3. To look on something (without preventing it), Man. 7, 143. 4. To review (soldiers), Man. 7, 222. 5. To regard, MBh. 2, 2623. 6. To consider, Man. 8, 10. Caus. 1. To show, MBh. 13, 3505. 2. To represent, Râjat. 6, 244. 3. To show one's self to somebody (acc.), MBh. 12, 12882.—With अनुसम् *anu-sam*, To ponder one by one, MBh. 12, 12024.—Cf. *spaça* and *spashṭa*; O.H.G. spehôn, to spy; Lat. species, conspicio, specto; σκέπτομαι, σκέψις, σκοπός, etc., δέρκω, ἔδρακον, δέδορκα, δράκος, ὑπόδραξ, ὑπόδρα, δράκων, etc.; O.H.G. zorht in auga-zorht (= *dṛiç + ta*, ptcple. of the pf. pass.), A.S. torht; O.H.G. zorhtjan, manifestare; also, with *f* for *h*, zorft, zorftjan; Goth. ga-tarhjan.

2. **दृश्** *dṛiç*, I. adj., latter part of comp. adj. **1.** Seeing, e.g. *sarva-*, Seeing everything, Bhâg. P. 4, 22, 9. **2.** Knowing, Bhâg. P. 8, 8, 34. **II.** f. **1.** Sight, Bhâg. P. 1, 4, 18. **2.** Perception, Bhâg. P. 2, 9, 5. **3.** The eye, Bhâg. P. 1, 11, 26.—**Comp.** *Divya-*, I. adj. knowing the celestial phenomena, Varâh. Bṛih. S. 5, 13. **II.** m. An astrologer, 54, 31. *Bhâla-*, m. Çiva. *Mṛiga-*, I. adj. having eyes like an antelope. II. f. a woman, Râjat. 5, 481. *Mṛigî-*, adj. having eyes like a female antelope, Râjat. 5, 375 (a woman). *Sama-*, adj. equable, Lass. 6, 16. *Su-*, I. adj. having beautiful eyes. II. f. a pretty woman.

दृशि *driç + i*, f. **1.** Intuition, Vedântas. in Chr. 217, 5. **2.** The eye, Bhâg. P. 5, 2, 11.

दृश्यत्व *dṛiçya + tva* (vb. *dṛiç*), n. Visibility, Bhâg. P. 1, 3, 31.

ऽदृश्वन् *-driç + van*, latter part of comp. adj. Conversant with, Kâm. Nîtis. 1, 7.

दृषद् *dṛishad*, f. A rock, a large stone, especially a mill-stone, Bhartṛ. 2, 77.

दृषद्वती *dṛishadvatî*, i.e. *dṛishad + vant + î*, f. **1.** The name of a river, Man. 2, 17. **2.** A proper name, Hariv. 1473.

दृष्टनष्टता *dṛishṭa-nashṭa + tâ* (vb. *dṛiç* and 2. *naç*), f. Disappearance after having been scarcely seen, Râjat. 4, 111.

दृष्टान्ततस् *dṛishṭântatas*, i.e. *dṛishṭa-anta + tas*. As a precedent, MBh. 13, 2506; 2, 70.

दृष्टि *dṛishṭi*, i.e. *dṛiç + ti*, f. **1.** Looking at, Râm. 5, 14, 57. **2.** Sight, Pańch. iii. d. 195. **3.** Intelligence, Bhâg. P. 1, 4, 5. **4.** The eye, Mṛichchh. 48, 23. **5.** The pupil of the eye, Suçr. 1, 126, 8.—**Comp.** *A-*, f. a look of displeasure. *Adhas-*, adj. with downcast eyes, Man. 4, 196. *Eka-*, f. the eye fixed on one point, Pańch. 252, 11.—Cf. *ku-*.

दृष्टिप *dṛishṭi-pa*, adj. Enjoying one's self only by the eyes, MBh. 13, 1372.

दृष्टिमन्त् *dṛishṭi + mant*, adj., f. *matî*, Wise, Kâm. Nîtis, 8, 38.

† **दृह्** *DṚIH*, i. 1, Par. To grow. Cf. τέρχνος, τρέχνος, probably Goth. tagl, θρίξ, τριχός.

दृ *DṚÎ*, ii. 9, *dṛiṇâ, ṇî*, † i. 1; i. 4, *dîrya*, Par. **1.** To burst, Hariv. 15177. **2.** To divide, to tear, MBh. 3, 16426; Bhâg. P. 2, 7, 1. Pass. (also with the termination of the Par., MBh. 6, 677), **1.** To burst, Râm. 2, 23, 35; MBh. 6, 677. **2.** To be scattered, Râm. 5, 58, 11. **3.** To fear, see *anu*. Ptcple. of the pf. pass. *dîrṇa*, **1.** Torn, Râm. 2, 39, 23 Gorr. **2.** Frightened, MBh. 6, 144. Caus. *dâraya*, **1.** To tear asunder, MBh. 4, 1456. **2.** To divide, Bhâg. P. 3, 13, 30. **3.** To open, Râm. 5, 80, 18. **4.** To frighten, Kâm. Nîtis, 8, 70. Anomal. ptcple. of the pres. *dârayâṇa*, MBh. 8, 907.—With the prep. **अनु** *anu*, pass. **1.** To separate (according to one's wish), MBh. 12, 1035. **2.** To be frightened (following an example set by another), MBh. 6, 144.—With **अव** *ava*, pass. To burst, Râm. 2, 77, 16. *avadîrṇa*, **1.** Open, Râm. 4, 50, 11. **2.** Frightened, MBh. 8, 1831. Caus. To tear asunder, Râm. 6, 4, 22.

With व्यव *vi-ava, vyavadîrṇa,* Torn, afflicted, Râm. 2, 72, 28.—With आ *â,* To tear asunder, Râm. 5, 56, 60.——With उद् *ud,* Daçak. in Chr. 185, 2, read *ud-îrṇa.* — With निस् *nis,* To tear, Bhâg. P. 7, 8, 45. Caus. **1.** To tear, Hariv. 5691. **2.** To cause to be dug up, Râjat. 4, 272.—With प्र *pra,* pass. To be scattered, MBh. 8, 4106. Caus. To scatter, MBh. 8, 4084.—With अभिप्र *abhi-pra,* pass. To be scattered, MBh. 8, 3976.—With वि *vi,* **1.** To tear, Râm. 3, 57, 24. Pass. **1.** To burst asunder, MBh. 1, 5347 **2.** To be torn, Râm. 2, 112, 15 Gorr. **3.** To be frightened, MBh. 7, 329. *vidîrṇa,* **1.** Torn, Kathâs. 20, 109. **2.** Broken, Bhâg. P. 8, 16, 26. **3.** Pierced, Ragh. 12, 51. **4.** Opened, Ragh, 7, 37. Caus. **1.** To tear, Râm. 3, 57, 24. **2.** To cleave, Râm. 3, 4, 17. **3.** To break open, Lass. 2, 10. **4.** To open, Ṛit. 1, 14. **5.** To scatter, Râm. 6, 36, 6.—Cf. *dal,* Goth. tairan ; A.S. téran, torn, tirian ; O.H.G. zala, A.S. tale, zâla, dolus, O.H.G. zalon, diripere ; A.S. tellan ; Lat. dolus ; δόλος, δηλέομαι, δῆρις.

† दे *DE,* i. 1, Âtm. To protect.—Cf. *day.*

देव् *DEV,* i. 1, Âtm. **1.** To play. **2.** To shine.—Cf. 1. 2. *div.*

देव *deva,* i. e. *div+a,* **I.** m. **1.** A deity, a god, Man. 3, 117. **2.** Indra, Râm. 1, 9, 56. **3.** A king, Kathâs. 4, 73. **II.** f. *vî.* **1.** A goddess, Nal. 12, 73. **2.** Sâvitrî, the wife of Brahman, MBh. 5, 3969. **3.** Durgâ, the wife of Çiva, MBh. 1, 2315. **4.** A queen, Pañch. i. d. 58.—**Comp.** *A-,* m. a mortal, Man. 9, 315. *Ati-,* m. a superior god, Hariv. 7583. *Devâtideva,* i.e. *deva-ati-,* m. a god surpassing all other gods, MBh. 15, 819. *Kâma-,* m. the god of love, Hariv. 270. *Kâvya-devî,* f. a proper name. *Kshiti-,* m. a king, Bhâg. P. 3, 1, 12. *Gṛiha-devî,* f. the deity of a house, MBh. 2, 730. *Jana-,* m. a king, MBh. 12, 7883. *Deva-,* m. the god of the gods, MBh. 1, 1628 ; = Çiva, Chr. 50, 5. *Nara-,* and *nṛi-,* m. a king, Man. 11, 82 ; Râm. 2, 1, 42 Gorr. *Pûrva-,* m. a primeval divinity, MBh. 5, 1921. *Bala-,* see s.v. *Bhûmi-,* m. a Brâhmaṇa, Man. 11, 82. *Mahâ-,* I. m. Çiva. II. f. *vî.* 1. Durgâ. 2. a queen, Chr. 50, 7. *Râma-,* m. a proper name. *Vasu-,* m. the father of Kṛishṇa. *Vâgdevî,* i.e. *vâch-,* f. the goddess of speech, i. e. Sarasvatî. *Vâma-,* m. Çiva. *Viçva-,* m. a deity of a particular class, see *viçva. Vîra-,* m. a proper name. *Su-devî,* f. a proper name, Chr. 297, 19 = Rigv. i, 112, 19.—Cf. θεός ; Lat. deus.

देवक *deva+ka,* **I.** A substitute for *deva* when latter part of a comp. adj., e.g. *sa-,* adj. With the gods, MBh. 2, 1396. **II.** m. **1.** A proper name, MBh. 1, 2704. **2.** pl. The inhabitants of one of the varshas, or divisions of the world, Bhâg. P. 5, 20, 22. **III.** f. *vikâ,* **1.** The name of a river, MBh. 3, 5044. **2.** A proper name, MBh. 1, 3828. **IV.** f. *vakî,* A proper name, MBh. 1, 2428.

देवता *deva+tâ,* f. The state or nature of a deity, MBh. 13, 308. **2.** A deity, Man. 2, 176. **3.** A sacred image, Man. 4, 130.—**Comp.** *Adhi-,* f. a supreme or tutelary deity, Ragh. 12, 17. *Abhishṭa-,* i. e. *abhi-ishṭa* (vb. *ish*), f. a tutelar deity, Pañch. 208, 14. *Kula-,* f. a chief deity, Kumâras. 7, 27. *Kshiti-,* f. a Brâhmaṇa, MBh. 13, 6451. *Kshetra-,* f. the deity of a field, Pañch. 174, 12. *Gṛiha-,* f. a household deity, a Lar, Mṛichchh. 8, 22. *Pati-,* adj, f. *tâ,* worshipping the husband like a deity. *Para-,* f. the supreme deity.

Pûrva-, f. a primeval divinity, Man. 3, 192. *Yama-*, f. the lunar asterism, Bharaṇî. *Yoni-*, f. the eleventh lunar asterism. *Vasu-*, f. the lunar asterism, Dhanishṭhâ. *Saubhâgya-*, f. a guardian deity, Çâk. 44, 3 (Prâkṛ.). *Sthali-*, f. a deity of a certain locality, Megh. 105.

देवत्रा *deva + trâ*, adv. Among the gods, Chr. 289, 10 = Rigv. i. 50, 10.

देवत्व *deva + tva*, n. The state of deities, Man. 12, 40.—Comp. *Nara-*, i.e. *nara-deva + tva*, n. royalty, Bhâg. P. 1, 3, 22.

देवदत्त *deva-datta* (vb. *dâ*), I. adj. Given by the gods, Man. 9, 95. II. m. **1.** The conch of Arjuna, Arj. 5, 24. **2.** One of the vital airs, that which is exhaled in yawning, Vedântas. in Chr. 207, 16. **3.** A proper name used to denote a person in general, Pańch. 36, 2; Vedântas. 213, 1.

देवदारुमय *deva-dâru + maya*, adj., f. *yî*, Made of Devadâru wood, Râm. 1, 13, 23 Gorr.

देवन *devana*, i.e. *div + ana*, n. Game at dice, MBh. 2, 2033.

देवमय *deva + maya*, adj., f. *yî*, Containing the gods, Hariv. 2798.

देवर *devara*, m. i.e. **1.** *devṛi + a*, A husband's brother, but especially his younger brother, Man. 3, 55. **2.** *div + ara*, A lover, Bhâg. P. 4, 26, 26.

देवलक *deva + la + ka*, m. A Brâhmaṇa of inferior order, who subsists upon the offerings made to the images which he attends, Man. 3, 152.

देवसात् *deva + sât*, adv. To a god or gods (e.g. turned), MBh. 7, 8687.

देवहू *devahû*, i.e. *deva-hve*, adj. Invoking the gods, a designation of the left ear, Bhâg. P. 4, 25, 51.

देवापि *devâpi*, m. The name of a Ṛishi or sage, MBh. 1, 3750.

देवितृ *devitṛi*, i.e. *div + tṛi*, m. **1.** A dice-player, MBh. 2, 2005. **2.** A gamester, MBh. 4, 496.

देविन् *devin*, i.e. *div + in*, adj. A dice-player, a gamester, MBh. 3, 15204; 5, 895.

देवीक *devî + ka* (see *deva*), A substitute for *devî* when latter part of a comp. adj., e.g. *sa-*, With the queen, Kathâs. 18, 23.

देवीत्व *devî + tva*, n. The dignity, **1.** of a goddess, Kathâs. 12, 163; **2.** of a queen, 17, 45.

देवृ *devṛi*, m. A husband's brother, but especially his younger brother.—Cf. δαήρ; Lat. levir; O.H.G. zeihur; A.S. tacur, tacor.

देवेशय *deveçaya*, i.e. *deva + i-çî + a*, adj. Reposing in a god, MBh. 12, 12864.

देश *deça*, i.e. *diç + a*, m. **1.** A place, Man. 2, 222. **2.** A part, a side, Kathâs. 18, 280. **3.** A country, Râm. 1, 61, 10. **4.** When latter part of comp. words, often without a special signification, e.g. *kaṇṭha-deça = kaṇṭha*, Kathâs. 17, 81; *nitamba-*, Ṛit. 1, 6; Râm. 1, 55, 3. Comp. *A-*, m. 1. an improper place, Hit. iv. d. 45. 2. a place which ought not to be touched, Man. 8, 358. *Eka-*, m. 1. one place, Pańch. 21, 13. 2. one part, Man. 2, 141. *Tanû-*, m. a part of the body, Bhâg. P. 7, 13, 12. *Diç-*, pl. a country in this or that direction, distant countries, Hit. 9, 4; cf. Râjat. 4, 417. *Para-*, m. a foreign country. *Pûrva-*, m. the eastern country, MBh. 2, 1856. *Madhya-*, m. the middle region, a part of India, Man. 2, 21. *Vi-*, m. 1. a foreign country, abroad. 2. any place away from home. *Sa-*, adj. 1. near. 2. of the same country or place.

देशक *deçaka,* i.e. *diç+aka,* adj. Showing, teaching, Mârk. P. 19, 17.

देशज *deça-ja,* and देशजात *deça-jâta* (vb. *jan*), adj. Of genuine descent, born in the country whence comes the best kind (e.g. of horses, or elephants), Hariv. 6927; Râm. 1, 54, 21 Gorr.

देशना *deçanâ, diç,* Caus., *+ana,* f. Instruction, doctrine, Çatr. 14, 74.

देशान्तरिन् *deçântarin,* i.e. *deça-antara+in,* adj. subst. m. Foreign, a foreigner, Çatr. 10, 135.

देशिक *deçika,* i.e. *deça+ika,* m. 1. A guide, MBh. 7, 143. 2. A teacher, 13, 6847.

देशिनी *deçinî,* i.e. *diç+in+î,* f. The index or forefinger, Yâjń. 1, 19.

देशीय *deçîya,* i.e. *deça+îya,* adj. 1. Belonging to a country or province. 2. Latter part of comp. adj. Bordering, being about, e.g. *pańcha(n)-varsha+ka-,* About five years old, MBh. 12, 1119.

देश्य *deçya,* i.e. *deça+ya,* 1. adj. subst. A witness, Man. 8, 52. 2. adj. Belonging to a country, Râjat. 3, 9. 3. adj. Of genuine descent, Râm. 2, 72, 23 Gorr. (cf. *deçaja*). 4. adj. Being almost, e.g. *çiçu-,* Being almost still a child, Râjat. 5, 220.—**Comp.** *A-,* adj. one who has not been present at a place, Man. 8, 53. *Tad-,* adj. being of the same country, MBh. 12, 6305. *Nânâ-,* adj. belonging to or coming from several countries, MBh. 1, 5221.

देष्टृ *deshṭṛi,* i.e. *diç+tṛi,* m. One who shows, Bhâg. P. 6, 7, 14.

देह *deha,* i.e. *dih+a,* m. and n. The body, Man. 6, 40.—**Comp.** *Ûrdhva-,* n. obsequies, Râm. 2, 90, 37 Gorr. *Pûrva-,* m. a former existence, Hariv. 9153.

देहंभर *dehambhara,* i.e. *deha+m-bhṛi+a,* adj. Minding only one's own body, Bhâg. P. 5, 26, 12.

देहली *dehalî,* i.e. *dih+ala+î,* f. The threshold of a door, or a raised terrace in front of it, Megh. 85.

देहवन्त् *deha+vant,* I. adj., f. *vatî.* 1. Embodied, Râm. 6, 90, 44. II. m. A living creature, Bhâg. P. 6, 1, 44.

देहिन् *dehin,* i.e. *deha+in,* I. adj. subst. Embodied, a creature having a body, Man. 1, 30. II. m. 1. A man, Bhartṛ. 2, 18. 2. The soul, Bhag. 2, 22.

दै *DAI,* i. 1, Par. To purify.—With the prep. अव *ava,* ptcple. of the pf. pass. *avadâta,* 1. Pure, Lass. 67, 3. 2. White or yellow, Sâv. 5, 8. 3. Dazzling white, MBh. 5, 1794.—With व्यव *vi-ava,* pass. To spread, shining with clear light, Daçak. 55, 3.

दैतेय *daiteya,* i.e. *diti+eya,* 1. m. An Asura or demon, Râm. 1, 45, 38. 2. adj., f. *yî,* Referring, belonging to the Asuras, MBh. 12, 7544.—**Comp.** *A-,* m. a god, Hariv. 11139.

दैत्य *daitya,* i.e. *diti+ya,* m. An Asura or demon, Man. 12, 48; Râm. 1, 30, 20 Gorr.

दैन्य *dainya,* i. e. *dîna* (see 3. *dî*) *+ya,* n. 1. Affliction, Râm. 6, 89, 17. 2. Humbleness, Bhartṛ. 2, 44. 3. Miserable state, Megh. 82.

दैर्घ्य *dairghya,* i.e. *dîrgha+ya,* n. Length, MBh. 6, 427.

दैव *daiva,* i.e. *deva+a,* I. adj., f. *vî.* 1. Divine, Man. 1, 67. 2. (with and without *vivâha*), m. One of the forms of marriage, the gift of a daughter at a sacrifice to the officiating priest, Man. 3, 21; 9, 196. 3. n. The part of the hand sacred to the gods (the tips of the fingers), Man. 2, 59. **4.** Royal, Râjat. 5, 205. II. n. **1.** Deity, Bhâg. P. 3, 16, 4. **2.** An oblation to the gods, Man. 3, 18. **3.** Divine power, destiny, fate, Man. 3, 166; Hit. pr. d. 32; Daçak. in Chr. 187, 15.—**Comp.** *Adhi-*, n. 1. the supreme deity, Bhag. 8, 4. 2. a tutelary deity, Çâk. 7, 10, v.r. *Kula-*, n. 1. the fortune of a family, Bhâg. P. 9, 5, 9. 2. the deity of a family, 9, 9, 43. *Dus-*, n. misfortune, Lass. 74, 19.

दैवक *daiva+ka*, a substitute for *daiva*, when latter part of a comp. adj. *sa-*, Together with the divine ones, MBh. 8, 1985.

दैवज्ञ *daiva-jña*, m. An astrologer, Râm. 2, 3, 18 Gorr.

दैवत *daivata*, i.e. *devatâ+a*, n. A deity, Man. 5, 41.—**Comp.** *Adhi-*, n. 1. the supreme deity, Bhag. 8, 4. 2. a tutelary deity, Çâk. 7, 10, v.r. *Ap-*, adj. having water for its divinity, glorifying the deity of water, Man. 8, 106. *Pitṛi-*, adj., f. *tî*, referring to the worship of the Manes.

दैवतस् *daiva+tas*, adv. By fate, Bhâg. P. 4, 7, 39.

दैवत्य *daivatya*, i.e. *devatâ + ya*, adj., f. *yâ*, Having as deity, sacred to, Man. 2, 189.

दैवयानेय *daivayâneya*, i. e. *devayânî*, a proper name, *+eya*, metronym. A son of Devayânî, MBh. 1, 3163.

दैवराज्य *daivarâjya*, i.e. *deva-râja +ya*, n. Dominion over the gods, MBh. 5, 522.

दैवराति *daivarâti*, i. e. *deva-râta*, a proper name, *+i*, patronym. A descendant of Devarâta, MBh. 12, 11546.

दैवहतक *daiva-hata+ka* (vb. *han*), I. adj. Struck by fate, Amar. 46. II. n. A shock of fortune, Prab. 89, 17.

दैविक *daivika*, i. e. *deva+ika*, I. adj. **1.** Divine, Man. 1, 65. **2.** Caused by the gods, Yâjń. 2, 113. II. n. An inevitable accident, Man. 8, 109; Yâjń. 2, 66.

दैविन् *daivin*, Lass. 27, 2 (read *devo*, for *daivî*).

दैशिक *daiçika*, i.e. *deça + ika*, I. adj. **1.** Referring to space, Bhâshâp. 120. **2.** Belonging to a country, Râjat. 6, 303. II. m. **1.** A guide, MBh. 1, 3599. **2.** A preceptor, MBh. 12, 12137.

दैहिक *daihika*, i.e. *deha+ika*, adj. Corporeal, Man. 5, 134.

दैह्य *daihya*, i.e. *deha+ya*, I. adj. Being in a body, Bhâg. P. 1, 4, 30. II. m. The soul, 6, 1, 42.

दो *DO*, see 2. *dâ*.

दोग्धृ *dogdhṛi*, i.e. *duh + tṛi*, I. m. **1.** One who milks, Man. 4, 67. **2.** One who performs something from interested motives, Bhâg. P. 3, 29, 32. II. f. *dhrî*. **1.** Yielding milk or other desirable objects, MBh. 1, 3934; 13, 3104. **2.** A milch cow, MBh. 7, 2410.

दोला *dolâ*, i.e. *dul+a*, f. **1.** A swing, Nal. 10, 27. **2.** A swinging hammock, a sort of litter, Ragh. 19, 44. **3.** Fluctuation, incertitude, MBh. 9, 3525.

दोलाय *DOLÂYA*, a denomin. derived from the last by *ya*, Âtm. To fluctuate, to be unsteady, Hit. iv. d. 53.

दोष *dosha*, i.e. *dush+a*, m. **1.** Defect, blemish, Hariv. 2108; Man. 8, 205. **2.** Fault, vice, MBh. 5, 1048 **3.** Damage, Yâjń. 2, 256. **4.** Sin, Man. 5, 3. **5.** Crime, Man. 9, 262. **6.** Reproach, Râm. 2, 101, 32 Gorr.; *dosheṇa* *yam,* To accuse, Chr. 16, 14. **7.** Detrimental operation, Kathâs. 13, 35. **8.** Effect, Râm. 3, 79, 25. **9.** Disorder of the humours of the body, or defect in the functions of bile, phlegm, and wind, Suçr. 2, 562, 4. **10.** The humours of the body, Daçak. in Chr. 180, 4. **11.** Evening, darkness, Bhâg. P. 6, 8, 19.—**Comp.** *Anna-,* m. an offence in diet, Man. 5, 4. *Karmadosha,* i.e. *karman-,* m. a sinful act, Man. 6, 101. *Grahaṇi-,* m. diarrhœa, Suçr. 1, 175, 6. *Dṛishṭa-,* adj. 1. an object of which the defects have been perceived, Hariv. 2108. 2. a heinous offender, Man. 8, 64. *Pâna-,* m. the fault of intoxication, Daçak. in Chr. 196, 3. *Vâgd°,* i.e. *vâch-,* m. 1. defamation. 2. ungrammatical speech. 3. uttering a disagreeable sound. *Svapna-,* m. Pollutio nocturna.—Cf. δειελός, δείλη.

दोषतस् *dosha + tas,* adv. **1.** Of a transgression (viz. to suspect), Nal. 23, 28. **2.** By the detrimental effect of something, Kathâs. 13, 33.

दोषन् *doshan,* see *dos.*

दोषल *dosha + la,* adj., f. *lâ,* Corrupt, Suçr. 1, 173, 18.

दोषवन्त् *dosha + vant,* adj., f. *vatî.* **1.** Blemished, Man. 8, 224. **2.** Deficient, MBh. 12, 8037. **3.** Guilty, MBh. 13, 57. **4.** Detrimental, Râm. 5, 90, 26.—**Comp.** *A-,* adj. innocent, Man. 8, 114 (*pûrvam̃pûrvam adoshavat,* every preceding object [in a series of things, which are reckoned up] may be received [by a Brâhmaṇa] with less offence than the following).

दोषा *doshâ,* an old instr. of *dosha,* adv. At night, Çiç. 4, 46.

दोषातन *doshâ + tana,* adj., f. *nî,* Nocturnal, at evening, Ragh. 13, 76.

दोषिन् *doshin,* i.e. *dosha + in,* adj. Becoming defiled, Mârk. P. 5, 31, 21.

दोस् *dos* (the base of many cases is *doshan*), n. The fore-arm, Râm, 3, 35, 78.

दोह *doha,* i.e. *duh + a,* m. **1.** Milking, Kumâras. 1, 2; profiting, Daçak. in Chr. 192, 19. **2.** Milk, Bhâg. P. 3, 17, 13. **3.** A milk pail, Bhâg. P. 4, 18, 27.—**Comp.** *Kâm̃sya-,* adj., f. *hâ,* yielding a brass pail of milk, MBh. 13, 3517.

दोहद *dohada* (a form of *daurhṛida;* cf. *dauhṛida*), m. and n. **1.** The desired object of a pregnant woman, Yâjń. 3, 79. **2.** The longing of pregnant women, Kathâs. 9, 46. **3.** Pregnancy, Ragh. 3, 6. **4.** Morbid desire, Pańch. 208, 19. **5.** Desire, Râm. 5, 25, 45. **6.** A kind of incense used as a manure, Pûrva Naish. i. 82.

दोहदिन् *dohadin,* i.e. *dohada + in,* adj., f. *nî,* Desirous, Kathâs. 22, 9.

दोहन *dohana,* i.e. *duh + ana,* I. adj., f. *nâ,* Yielding milk or other desirable objects, MBh. 12, 7295; Hariv. 5294. II. n. A milk vessel, Bhâg. P. 4, 17, 3.—**Comp.** *Go-,* n. the time necessary for milking a cow, Bhâg. P. 1, 19, 39.

दोहल *dohala = dohada,* Mâlav. 33, 8.

दोहिन् *dohin,* i.e. *duh + in,* adj., f. *nî,* Yielding desirable objects, Râm. 1, 54, 26 Gorr.

दौःशील्य *dauḥçîlya,* i.e. *dus-çîla + ya,* n. Wickedness, Râjat. 5, 290.

दौत्य *dautya,* i.e. *dûta + ya,* n. The state of a messenger, Hariv. 9799.

दौरात्म्य *daurâtmya,* i.e. *dus-âtman + ya,* n. Wickedness. Pańch. iv. d. 61.

दौर्गत्य *daurgatya*, i.e. *dus-gata* + *ya*, n. Distress, Pañch. ii. d. 99.

दौर्गन्ध्य *daurgandhya*, i. e. *dus-gandha* + *ya*, n. Disagreeable smell, MBh. 3, 15454.

दौर्जन्य *daurjanya*, i.e. *dus-jana* + *ya*, n. Wickedness, Hit. 85, 9.

दौर्बल *daurbala*, i.e. *dus-bala* + *a*, and **दौर्बल्य** *daurbalya*, i.e. *dus-bala* + *ya*, n. Weakness, Râm. 2, 43, 17; Pañch. 234, 17.

दौर्भाग्य *daurbhâgya*, i.e. *dus-bhaga* + *ya*, n. Misfortune, Hariv. 7120.

दौर्मनस्य *daurmanasya*, i. e. *dus-manas* + *ya*, n. Dejection, Pañch. 9, 23.

दौर्मन्त्र्य *daurmantrya*, i. e. *dus-mantra* + *ya*, n. Evil advice, Böhtl. Ind. Spr. 1260.

दौर्योधन *dauryodhana*, i. e. *dur-yodhana* + *a*, adj. Belonging to Duryodhana, MBh. 4, 1712.

दौर्योधनि *dauryodhani*, i. e. *dur-yodhana* + *i*, patronym. A descendant of Duryodhana, MBh. 6, 2367.

दौर्हृद *daurhṛida*, i.e. *dus-hṛid* + *a*, n. 1. Enmity, MBh. 5, 751. 2. The longing of pregnant women.

दौवारिक *dauvârika*, i.e. *dvâra* + *ika*, m. and f. *kî*, A warder, a porter, Pañch. 156, 16; Ragh. 6, 59.

दौश्चर्म्य *dauçcharmya*, i. e. *dus-charman* + *ya*, n. A deformity in the generative organs, Man. 11, 49.

दौश्चर्य *dauçcharya*, i.e. *dus-chara* + *ya*, n. Acting wickedly, Râm. 6, 103, 20.

दौष्कुल *daushkula*, i. e. *dus-kula* + *a*, and **दौष्कुलेय** *daushkuleya*, i.e. *dus-kula* + *eya*, adj. Sprung from a contemptible family, MBh. 12, 1330; Râm. 4, 6, 3.

दौष्कुल्य *daushkulya*, i.e. *dus-kula* + *ya*, I. adj. Sprung from a contemptible family, MBh. 3, 12629. II. n. Low extraction, Bhâg. P. 1, 18, 18.

दौष्मन्त *daushmanta*, and **दौष्मन्ति** *daushmanti*, i.e. *dushmanta* + *a* or *i*, patron. A son of Dushmanta, MBh. 7, 2377; 12, 938.

दौष्यन्त *daushyanta*, i.e. *dushyanta* + *a*, adj. Referring to Dushyanta, MBh. 1, 3805.

दौष्यन्ति *daushyanti*, i.e. *dushyanta* + *i*, patronym. A son of Dushyanta, Çâk. d. 95.

दौष्वन्ति *daushvanti*, i.e. *dushvanta* + *i*, patron. A son of Dushvanta, Râm. 2, 116, 30 Gorr.

दौहित्र *dauhitra*, i.e. *duhitṛi* + *a*, I. m. A daughter's son, Man. 3, 148. II. f. *trî*, A daughter's daughter, Râm. 6, 95, 36. III. m. A rhinoceros, Mârk. P. 32, 7.

दौहित्रक *dauhitra* + *ka*, adj. Referring to a daughter's son, MBh. 13, 2476.

दौहित्रवन्त् *dauhitra* + *vant*, adj. Having a daughter's son, MBh. 5, 3930.

दौहृद *dauhṛida* (a dialectical form of *daurhṛida*, q. cf.), n. 1. The longing of pregnant women, Suçr. 1, 89, 12. 2. Pregnancy, Suçr. 1, 322, 15.

दौहृदिनी *dauhṛidinî*, i.e. *dauhṛida* + *in* + *î*, adj. f. Pregnant, Suçr. 1, 322, 12.

द्यावापृथिवी *dyâvâ-pṛithivî*, ved. dual of *div* and *pṛithivî*, f., Heaven and earth, Chr. 296, 1 = Rigv. i. 112, 1.

द्यावापृथिव्य *dyâvâpṛithivya*, i. e.

dyâvâprithivî + *ya*, Referring to heaven and earth, Chr. 296, l. 1.

द्यावाभूमी *dyâvâ-bhûmî*, ved. dual of *div* and *bhûmi*, f. Heaven and earth, Bhâg. P. 5, 20, 43.

1. द्यु *DYU*, ii. 2, Par. To attack.—Cf. *div*.

2. द्यु *dyu*, the base of many cases and derivatives of 3. *div*, and its substitute when former part of a comp. word, e. g. *dyu-chara*, m. An inhabitant of the heaven, Hariv. 7497. *dyu-jaya*, m. Attainment of heaven, Bhâg. P. 5, 19, 22.

1. द्युत् *DYUT* (originally a denomin., probably of *dyuti*), i. 1, Âtm. (in epic poetry also Par., MBh. 12, 8129), To shine, MBh. 3, 1745. Caus. 1. To illuminate, MBh. 4, 2031. 2. To hint, Sâh. D. 20, 2.—With the prep. अभि *abhi*, Caus. To illuminate, Ragh. 6, 36.—With उद् *ud*, To beam, Hariv. 15701. Caus. 1. To illuminate, Prab. 86, 11. 2. To make glorious, Ragh. 10, 81.—With समुद् *sam-ud*, To shine, Prab. 115, 2.—With प्र *pra*, Caus. To illuminate, Prab. 116, 1.—With वि *vi*, 1. To flash, MBh. 3, 180. 2. To illuminate, MBh. 12, 8063. Caus. To illuminate, MBh. 1, 1240.

2. द्युत् *dyut*, f. Splendour, MBh. 1, 6406.

द्युति *dyuti*, i.e. 1. *div* + *ti*, f. 1. Splendour, Bhartṛ. 1, 66; Hit. pr. d. 41. 2. Dignity, i. d. 167. — **Comp.** *A-mita-* (vb. *mâ*), adj. of boundless splendour. *Gharma-*, m. the sun, Kir. 5, 41. *Tuhina-*, m. the moon, Çiç. 9, 30. *Mahâ-*, adj. supremely glorious, Man. 1, 87. *Hima-*, m. the moon, Çiç. 9, 12.

द्युतिमन्त् *dyuti* + *mant*, I. adj., f. *matî*. 1. Brilliant, Kir. 5, 8. 2. Dignified, Râm. 1, 1, 10. II. m. A proper name, MBh. 1, 3832.

द्युमन्त् 2. *dyu* + *mant*, adj., f. *matî*. 1. Brilliant, Bhâg. P. 3, 23, 29. 2. Brisk, Chr. 291, 14=Rigv. i. 64, 14.

द्युम्न *dyumna*, i.e. 2. *dyu* + *man* (for *mant*) + *a*, n. 1. Splendour, Chr. 287, 1=Rigv. i. 48, 1. 2. Strength, Chr. 288, 16=Rigv. i. 48, 16. 3. Wealth, Daçak. in Chr. 185, 12.—**Comp.** *Indra-* and *Dhrishṭa-*, m. proper names, MBh. 3, 491; 1, 2437.

द्युषद् *dyushad*, i.e. 2. *dyu-sad*, m. A god, Râjat. 1, 109.

द्यूतता *dyûta* + *tâ* (vb. 1. *div*), f. Gaming at dice, MBh. 12, 2519.

† द्यै *DYAI*, i. 1, Par. To treat contemptuously, or to disfigure.

द्यो *dyo* (gunated form of 2. *dyu*), 1. Base of some cases of 3. *div* (q. cf.). 2. A substitute for *div* as former part of a comp., MBh. 8, 4658; 12, 1799.

द्योत *dyota*, i.e. *dyut* + *a*, m. Light, lustre, Hariv. 2402; Râjat. 3, 46.—**Comp.** *Chintya-* (vb. *chint*), m. a class of deities, MBh. 13, 1373.

द्योतक *dyotaka*, i.e. *dyut* + *aka*, adj. Showing, explaining, Râjat. 3, 158.

द्योतन *dyotana*, i.e. *dyut* + *ana*, n. Illuminating, Bhâg. P. 3, 26, 40.

द्योतिन् *dyotin*, i.e. *dyut* + *in*, adj., f. *nî*, Shining, Megh. 18.

द्योतिस् *dyotis*, i.e. *djut* + *is*, n. Light, a star, Ragh. 13, 68.

द्रङ्ग *dranga*, m. A town, Çatr. 14, 181. — **Comp.** *Srava-*, m. a fair, a market.

द्रढिमन् *draḍhiman*, i. e. *dṛiḍha*

(see *drimh*) + *iman*, m. Firmness, Bhâg. P. 1, 13, 27.

द्रढिष्ठ *draḍhishṭha*, superl., द्रढीयंस् *draḍhiyaṁs*, comparat. of *dṛiḍha*, see *driṁh*.

द्रप्सिन् *drapsin*, i.e. *drapsa* (ved.) + *in*, adj. Distilling, Chr. 290, 2 = Rigv. i. 64, 2.—With *drapsa*, Drop; cf. perhaps δρόσος.

द्रम् *DRAM*, i. 1, Par. To run. —Cf. ἔδραμον, δραμοῦμαι, δρόμος; see *drâ*, *dru*.

द्रव *drava*, i.e. *dru* + *a*, I. adj. 1. Running (ved.). 2. Liquid, Hariv. 12333. 3. n. A liquid substance, Man. 5, 115. II. m. 1. Quick motion, Hariv. 11430. 2. Flight, 12567. 3. Fluidity, Bhâshâp. 29.—Comp. *Amṛita-*, adj., f. *vâ*, flowing with Amṛita (and medicaments), Çiç. 9, 36.

द्रवता *drava* + *tâ*, f. Wetness, Çiç. 9, 65.

द्रवत्व *drava* + *tva*, n. 1. Fluidity, Bhâshâp. 153 (°*tva* + *ka* in 30). 2. Fusibility, Hit. i. d. 87.

द्रविड *draviḍa*, m. 1. The name of a people, MBh. 14, 832. 2. The son of a Vrâtya or degraded Kshatriya, Man. 10, 22.

द्रविण *draviṇa* (akin to *dravya* and probably to 3. *dru*), I. n. 1. Wealth, Man. 7, 136. 2. Money, Râjat. 5, 167. 3. Strength, Râm. 1, 16, 15. II. m. 1. pl. Wealth, Bhâg. P. 5, 14, 12. 2. A proper name, MBh. 1, 2585. 3. The name of a mountain, Bhâg. P. 5, 20, 15. 4. The name of the inhabitants of a Varsha or division of the world, 5, 20, 22.

द्रविणवन्त् *draviṇa* + *vant*, adj. Strong, MBh. 5, 3889.

द्रव्य *dravya* (probably akin to 3. *dru*), n. 1. Object, thing, Man. 1, 113; 8, 34. 2. Substance, Bhâshâp. 1. 3. Property, Man. 4, 114. 4. A fit object.—Comp. *A-*, n. a worthless object, Hit. pr. d. 43; Mâlav. 14, 23. *Apa-*, n. any bad substance. *Nis-*, adj. 1. immaterial, MBh. 12, 11350. 2. poor, Râm. 5, 33, 31. *Sîtâ-*, n. pl. implements of husbandry, Man. 9, 293.

द्रव्यत्व *dravya* + *tva*, n. Substantiality, Bhâshâp. 23.

द्रव्यमय *dravya* + *maya*, adj., f. *yî*, Substantial, Bhâg. P. 4, 14, 21.

द्रव्यवन्त् *dravya* + *vant*, adj., f. *vatî*, Wealthy, Râm. 2, 49, 26 Gorr.

द्रष्टुकाम *drashṭukâma*, i.e. *drashṭum* (infinitive of *driç*) -*kâma*, adj. Desirous of seeing, Sund. 3, 25.

द्रष्टुशक्य *drashṭuçakya*, Indr. 2, 6, read *drashtuṁ çakya*, MBh. 3, 1761.

द्रष्टृ *drashṭṛi*, i.e. *driç* + *tṛi*, m. 1. One who sees, MBh. 3, 12623. 2. One who decides, Yâjń. 2, 202. 3. A judge, Mṛichchh. 137, 16.

द्रष्टृत्व *drashṭṛi* + *tva*, n. The faculty of seeing, Bhâg. P. 3, 31, 46.

1. द्रा *DRA*, ii. 2. Par. To run. Caus. *drâpaya*. Anomal. frequent. *daridrâ*, To be in distress, to be poor, Hit. ii. d. 2.—Cf. διδράσκω, ἔδραν, δραπέτης (from the Causal).

2. द्रा *DRÂ*, ii. 2, and द्रै *DRAI*, i. 1, *drâ* + *ya* (properly *drâ*, i. 4), Par. (also Âtm. Mṛichchh. 116, 10), To sleep. —With the prep. नि *ni*, To fall asleep, MBh. 13, 7568; 7418. Ptcple. of the pf. pass. *nidrâṇa*, Sleeping, Râjat. 2, 165.—Cf. O.H.G. traum; O.S. drôm. O.H.G. denomin. traumjan; O.S. drômjan, to dream; Lat. dormire (*a*

denomin based on dor + mo), δαρθάνω, ἔδαρθον and ἔδραθον (also a denomin. based on δαρ + tvan).

द्राक् *drâk*, i.e. 1. *drâ-ańch*, acc. sing. ntr. adv. Soon, instantly, Pańch. 4, 22.

द्राक्षा *drâkshâ*, f. **1.** A vine, Hariv. 6407. **2.** A grape, Gît. 12, 29.

† द्राख् *DRÂKH*, i. 1, Par. **1.** To become dry. **2.** To be sufficient; cf. *dhrâkh.*—Cf. probably O.H.G. trukan; A.S. drig, dryg, drí.

† द्राघ् *DRÂGH*, i. 1, Âtm. (probably a denomin. derived from *dîrgha*, comparat. *drâghîyaṁs*, etc.), **1.** To lengthen. **2.** To exert one's self, to be tired. **3.** To be able. **4.** To torment. **5.** To stroll.

द्राघय *DRÂGHAYA*, a denomin. derived from *dîrgha*, comparat. *drâghîyaṁs*, Par. **1.** To extend, Râjat. 4, 513. **2.** To lengthen, Bhaṭṭ. 18, 33. **3.** To tarry, Râm. 2, 109, 14 Gorr.

द्राघिष्ठ *drâghishṭha*, and द्राघीयंस् *drâghîyaṁs*, see *dîrgha*.

द्राड् *DRÂḌ*, i. 1, Âtm. To divide, to split.—With the prep. उद् *ud*, Caus. To split, Çatr. 14, 44 (perhaps faulty).

द्रावण *drâvaṇa*, i.e. *dru*, Caus., + *ana*, I. adj. Putting to flight, MBh. 8, 1523. II. n. Putting to flight, Hariv. 7583.

द्राविड *drâviḍa*, i.e. *draviḍa* + *a*, I. adj., f. *ḍî*, Belonging to the Draviḍas, MBh. 8, 454. II. m. pl. = Draviḍa, MBh. 1, 6683. III. f. *ḍî*, Cardamom, Suçr. 1, 142, 4.

† द्राह् *DRÂH*, i. 1, Âtm. **1.** To wake. **2.** To cast down.

1. द्रु *DRU* (akin to *dram*, 1. *drâ*), i. 1, Par. (also Âtm., MBh. 6, 4710), **1.** To run, MBh. 8, 3014. **2.** To attack, MBh. 1, 5478. **3.** To melt, Lass. 24, 7. Ptcple. of the pf. pass. *druta*, **1.** Swift, MBh. 13, 1839. **2.** Flown, Ṛit. 1, 20. **3.** Running away, Bhâg. P. 4, 17, 14. **4.** Molten, Çiç. 9, 9. °*tam*, adv. Instantly, Man. 9, 272. Comparat. *druta* + *tara* + *m*, adv. As quickly as possible, Pańch. 25, 15. Caus. *drâvaya*, To put to flight, MBh. 4, 1082. Anomal. ptcple. of the pres. Âtm. *drâvayâṇa*, MBh. 6, 5199.—With the prep. अनु *anu*, To pursue, Bhâg. P. 4, 19, 16. *anudruta*, **1.** Pursued, Ragh. 3, 38. **2.** Accompanied, Râm. 2, 65, 26. **3.** Pursuing, Bhâg. P. 3, 18, 7.—With समनु *sam-anu*, To pursue, MBh. 10, 657; to follow, 14, 636.—With अभि *abhi*, **1.** To run on, MBh. 1, 6000. **2.** To attack, Arj. 7, 1.—With समभि *sam-abhi*, **1.** To assail, MBh. 6, 1953. **2.** To infest, MBh. 18, 46. *samabhidruta* + *m*, adv. Quickly, 12, 6402.—With आ *â*, To hasten on, MBh. 3, 248.—With अन्वा *anu-â*, To pursue, Bhâg. P. 1, 7, 17.—With पर्या *pari-â*, To hasten on round about, Bhâg. P. 4, 5, 13.—With प्रा *pra-â*, **1.** To run away, MBh. 1, 2843. **2.** To escape, 1, 6127.—With संप्रा *sam-pra-â*, To run away, MBh. 9, 1675 (perhaps only *sam-pra*).—With प्रत्या *prati-â*, To assail, MBh. 7, 5292.—With समा *sam-â*, To assail, MBh. 2, 815.—With उप *upa*, To assail, Pańch. 147, 1. *upadruta*, **1.** Assailed, Hariv. 1151. **2.** Distressed, Râm. 2, 48, 22.—With प्रत्युप *prati-upa*, To rush on, Pańch. 226, 23.—With समुप *sam-upa*, **1.** To run on, MBh. 3, 10993. **2.** To assail, Râm. 4, 48, 29.—With परा

parâ, To run away, Bhâg. P. 1, 7, 18. —With प्र *pra,* 1. To press on, Arj. 6, 8. 2. To run away, MBh. 3, 8749. 3. To hasten to, Râm. 1, 20, 6. 4. To attain, Brâhmaṇ. 1, 19. *pradruta,* Run away, Râm. 2, 97, 9. Caus. To put to flight, MBh. 8, 2424.—With अभिप्र *abhi-pra,* To assail, MBh. 9, 398.—With विप्र *vi-pra,* 1. To run in different directions, to disperse, Râm. 2, 102, 1 Gorr. 2. To run away, MBh. 3, 861. *vipradruta,* Run away, MBh. 3, 675.—With संप्र *sam-pra,* To run away, MBh. 3, 239.—With प्रति *prati,* To run to, Bhaṭṭ. 6, 17.—With वि *vi,* 1. To run in different directions, MBh. 3, 2549. 2. To run away, MBh. 4, 163. 3. To burst, MBh. 13, 7472. *vidruta,* 1. Run in different directions, Sund. 4, 20. 2. Run away, Draup. 8, 35. 3. Burst, Man. 7, 3. 4. Dissolved, i.e. destroyed, Bhâg. P. 4, 30, 49. 5. Unsteady, Pañch. 203, 3. Caus. To put to flight, MBh. 1, 6680.—With अभिवि *abhi-vi,* 1. To assail, MBh. 6, 1776. 2. To run away, MBh. 6, 4614. —With प्रवि *pra-vi, pravidruta,* Run away, MBh. 7, 4865.—Cf. Lat. gruere in in-gruere, etc., and ruere; probably O.H.G. triufan, A.S. driopan (an old Causal); O.H.G. trofo; A.S. dropa; O.H.G. trauf, traufi.

2. द्रु *DRU,* ii. 5, Par. 1. To hurt. 2.† To repent, v.r.

3. द्रु *dru,* i.e. *dṛî+u,* I. m. and n. Wood, Man. 7, 131. II. m. A tree. —Cf. δρῦς, δρύτη, δροίτη; Goth. triu; A.S. tre, a tree.

† द्रुड् *DRUḌ,* i. 1 and 6, Par. To sink.

† द्रुण् *DRUṆ,* i. 6, Par. 1. To make crooked. 2. To go. 3. To hurt; cf. 2. *dru* and *drû.*

द्रुपद *drupada,* m. The name of a king, Man. 1, 2453.

द्रुम 3. *dru+ma,* m. 1. A tree, Man. 9, 255. 2. A proper name, MBh. 1, 227.—Comp. *Kalpa-,* m. a fabulous tree fulfilling all wishes, Daçak. in Chr. 184, 5. *Grâma-* and *chaitya-,* m. a sacred tree growing in a village or near it, and held in veneration by the villagers, Hiḍ. 1, 39. *Chhâyâ-,* m. a very shady tree, Çâk. d. 86. *Sa-parvata-vana-,* adj. with (its) mountains, forests, and trees, Chr. 40, 20.—Cf. δρῡμός, δρῡμά.

द्रुमवन्त् *druma-vant,* adj., f. *vatî,* Woody, MBh. 7, 782.

द्रुमाय *DRUMÂYA,* a denomin. derived from *druma* by *ya,* Âtm. To pass for a tree, Hit. i. d. 63.

1. द्रुह् *DRUH,* i. 4, Par. (in epic poetry also Âtm., Râm. 2, 75, 22), 1. To hurt, Râm. 2, 25, 17. 2. To seek to injure or to grieve, Man. 2, 144. With the dat., Bhâg. P. 4, 4, 15; with the gen., Râm. 2, 99, 23 Gorr.; with the loc., Bhâg. P. 4, 2, 21; and with the acc., MBh. 2, 2107. Ptcple. of the pf. pass. *drugdha,* Wished to be injured, Râjat. 5, 298. Comp. *A-drugdha,* adj. innocent, MBh. 5, 715.— With the prep. अभि *abhi,* 1. To hurt, Bhâg. P. 4, 20, 3. 2. To seek to hurt, Pañch. i. d. 270, with the dat. and acc. *abhidrugdha,* Seeking to injure, MBh. 5, 2160.—With वि *vi,* To insult, Bhâg. P. 3, 1, 41.—Cf. Goth. driugan (*d* instead of *t* on account of the following *r*), dulgs; O.H.G. triugan (see *droha*).

2. द्रुह् *druh,* 1. m. An injurer, MBh. 7, 6512. 2. Latter part of

adj., Injuring, having injured, e. g. *garbha-bhartṛi-*, f. A woman who has caused an abortion or stricken her husband, Man. 5, 90. *mitra-*, n. An injurer of his friend, Man. 3, 160.

द्रू *DRÛ*, ii. 9, Par. To go, to hurt. —Cf. 2. *dru.*

द्रेक् *DREK*, i. 1, Âtm. **1.** To sound. **2.** To increase (?). **3.** To show pride (?).—With the prep. प्र *pra*, To begin to neigh, Bhaṭṭ. 17, 8.

द्रै *DRAI*, see 2. *drâ.*

द्रोग्धृ *drogdhṛi*, i.e. *druh* + *tṛi*, m. An injurer, MBh. 5, 2124.

द्रोण *droṇa*, probably *dru* + *van*(*t*) + *a*, I. n. A wooden tub, MBh, 1, 5105. II. m. and n. **1.** A measure of capacity, = *âḍhaka*, Man. 7, 126. **2.** A cloud abounding in water, Mṛichchh. 163, 8. III. m. A proper name, the military preceptor of the Pâṇḍus and Kurus, MBh. 1, 2434. IV. f. *ṇî*. **1.** A wooden tub, Hariv. 3866. **2.** A valley, Bhâg. P. 4, 10, 5 ; Râjat. 5, 141. —Comp. *Saha-droṇa*, adj. with Droṇa. *Snâna-droṇî*, f. a bathing-tub, Râjat. 5, 46.

द्रोणमय *droṇa* + *maya*, adj. Full of Droṇas (*droṇa* III.), MBh. 7, 936.

द्रोह *droha*, i.e. *druh* + *a*, m. **1.** Injury, Pañch. 45, 25. **2.** Insidious wounding, Man. 7, 48. **3.** Perfidy, Râjat. 4, 410.—Comp. *A-*, n. 1. absence of injury, Man. 4, 2. 2. kindness, Sâv. 5, 34. *Nis-*, adj. 1. not hostile, Râjat. 1, 362. 2. innocent, 5, 208. 3. Well disposed, 6, 260.

द्रोहिन् *drohin*, i.e. I. *druh* + *in*, latter part of comp. adj. Injuring, Râm. 3, 16, 34. II. *droha* + *in*, adj. Perfidious, Râjat. 1, 162.

द्रौणायनि *drauṇâyani*, i.e. *droṇa* + *âyani*, and द्रौणि *drauṇi*, i.e. *droṇa* + *i*, patron. A son of Droṇa, MBh. 1, 7019 ; 4, 1150.

द्रौणिक *drauṇika*, i.e. *droṇa* + *ika*, I. adj., f. *kî*, Containing a Droṇa (see *droṇa* II.), e.g. *pañchadrauṇika*, i.e. *pañchan-droṇa* + *ika*, Containing five Droṇas, MBh. 2, 2091. II. (m. or n.), A field which may be sown with a Droṇa of grain, Kathâs. 3, 33.

द्रौपद *draupada*, i.e. *drupada* + *a*, patron., f. *dî*, The daughter of Drupada, the common wife of the five Pâṇḍu princes, MBh. 1, 2791.

द्रौपदेय *draupadeya*, i.e. *draupadî* + *eya*, metronym. A son of Draupadî, MBh. 1, 429.

द्वंद्व *dvaṁdva*, i.e. *dva* + *m-dva* (+ *m*, old sing. ntr. of *dvi*, twice repeated), n. A pair, a couple, Megh. 46. **2.** A pair of opposite things, as heat and cold, Man. 1, 26. **3.** Quarrel, contest, MBh. 12, 7557. **4.** A duel, MBh. 5, 7083. **5.** Doubt, MBh. 1, 1867. **6.** A class of comp. words, Bhag. 10, 33. Acc. sing. °*dvam*, and instr. °*dvena*, adv. Two by two, Hariv. 3754 ; Bhâg. P. 8, 10, 34. —Comp. *Nis-*, adj. 1. indifferent in regard to the opposite pairs, as pleasure and pain, etc. (cf. Vedântas. in Chr. 203, 17), Bhag. 2, 45. 2. independent, MBh. 12, 489. 3. free from jealousy, MBh. 3, 14734. 4. uncontested, MBh. 4, 889.

द्वंद्वचर *dvaṁdva-chara*, m. The ruddy goose, Anas casarca Gm., Ragh. 8, 55.

द्वंद्वशस् *dvaṁdva* + *ças*, adv. Two by two, Râm. 2, 103, 11 Gorr.

द्वंद्विन् *dvaṁdvin*, i. e. *dvaṁdva* + *in*, adj. Contradictory, Prab. 86, 14.

द्वय *dvaya*, i.e. *dvi* + *a*, I. adj., f. *yî*, Of two different sorts, Bhartṛ. 2, 25. II. n. 1. A pair, Yâjñ. 1, 59. 2. Two things, Bhartṛ. 1, 53. 3. Both, MBh. 12, 6552.—**Comp.** *A-*, adj. without a second, Vedântas. in Chr. 204, 10.—Cf. δοιός.

द्वाऽ *dvâ-* (old nom. du. of *dvi*), former part in comp. numerals, Two, e.g. *dvâ-chatvâriṁçat*, Forty-two.

द्वाःस्थ *dvâḥstha*, i. e. *dvâr-stha*, I. adj. Standing at the door, Râm. 2, 71, 30. II. m. A porter, Râm. 6, 8, 37.

द्वादश *dvâ-daça*, I. ordin. numb., f. *çî*, Twelfth, Man. 2, 36 ; 7, 120. II. f. *çî*, The twelfth day of the half-month, Kathâs. 26, 4.

द्वादशक *dvâdaça* + *ka*, adj. 1. Twelfth, MBh. 12, 11955. 2. Amounting to twelve, Man. 8, 268.

द्वादशधा *dvâdaçadhâ*, i.e. *dvâdaçan* + *dhâ*, adv. Twelve-fold, Bhâg. P. 5, 22, 3.

द्वादशन् *dvâ-daçan*, numeral, Twelve, Man. 5, 134. — Cf. δυώδεκα δώδεκα ; Lat. duodecim.

द्वादशिक *dvâdaçika*, i.e. *dvâdaçan* + *ika*, adj. Taking place on the twelfth day of the half-month, Râm. 2, 86, 1 Gorr.

द्वापर *dvâ-para*, n. 1. The die which is marked with two points, MBh. 4, 1578. 2 The third of the four *Yugas* or great periods, Man. 9, 301.

द्वार् *dvâr* (vb. *dvṛi*), f. 1. A door, a gate, Man. 3, 88. 2. Opportunity, Mṛichchh. 138, 1. 3. A means ; instr. *dvârâ*, as latter part of comp. words, By, Vedântas. in Chr. 218, 11.

द्वार *dvâra*, i.e. *dvṛi* + *a*, n. 1. A door, a gate, Man. 9, 289. 2. A way, MBh. 7, 1526. 3. A means, Bhâg. P. 3, 20, 1 ; instr. *dvâreṇa*, as latter part of comp. words, 1. By, Pañch. i. d. 52. 2. By means of, Pañch. 166, 17.—**Comp.** *A-*, n. any other entrance than the door, Man. 4, 73 ; not a door, MBh. 13, 4749. *Gaṅgâ-*, n. the locality where the Gaṅgâ, leaving the mountains, enters the plains. *Gala-*, n. the mouth. *Giri-*, n. a mountain-pass. *Paksha-*, n. a side-door. *Çakṛiddv°*, i.e *çakṛit-*, n. the anus. *Siṁha-*, n. a gate, especially the chief gate of a palace.—Cf. θύρα, θαιρός ; Lat. foras, foris, fores ; Goth. daur, A.S. duru, dyr.

द्वारक *dvâra* + *ka*, I. n. A gate, MBh. 12, 2639. II. f. *kâ*, The name of Kṛishṇa's residence, MBh. 1, 7899.

द्वारता *dvâra* + *tâ*, f. Access, Ragh. 11, 18.

द्वारवती *dvâravatî*, i.e. *dvâra* + *vant* + *î*, f. The name of Kṛishṇa's residence, Râm. 4, 43, 6.

द्वारस्थ *dvâra-stha*, I. adj., f. *thâ*, Standing at the door, Pañch. 193, 11. II. m. A porter, Pañch. 15, 25.

द्वारिक *dvârika*, i.e. *dvâra* + *ika*, and द्वारिन् *dvârin*, i.e. *dvâra* + *in*, m. A porter, Pañch. iii. d. 85 ; MBh. 1, 4906.

द्वि *dvi*, the base of the declension is *dva*, m. n ; *dvâ*, f. ; du. numeral, 1. Two. 2. Both, Râm. 6, 95, 44.—Cf. δύο, δυάκις, etc., δεύτερος, δί-πυλος, διά, δίζω ; Lat. duo, bi-farius, dubius, duellum, bellum, dis- ; Goth. tvai ; A.S. tvá, twi-, tweogan ; Goth. tveifljan, tvi-standan, dis-dailjan.

द्विक *dvi* + *ka*, I. adj. Increased by

two, Man. 8, 141 (two in the hundred). II. (n.) A pair, Râjat. 1, 56.

द्विगुणत्व *dvi-guṇa+tva,* n. Duplication, Amar. 6, 8.

द्विज *dvi-ja,* I. adj. Twice born. II. m. **1.** A man of either of the three first classes, as their initiation passes for a second birth, especially a Brâhmaṇa, Yâjn. 1, 39; Nal. 16, 1. **2.** A bird, Man. 5, 17. **3.** A tooth, Bhartṛ. 1, 12. —Comp. *A-*, adj. deprived of Brâhmaṇas, Man. 8, 22.

द्विजत्व *dvija-tva,* n. Condition or state of a Brâhmaṇa, Râjat. 4, 105.

द्विजातिसात् *dvi-jâti+sât,* adv. (A present) to the Brâhmaṇas, Râjat. 5, 120.

द्वित *dvita,* m. The name of a mythical person, MBh. 12, 13174.

द्वितय *dvi+taya,* I. adj. **1.** Involved in duality, Bhâg. P. 6, 15, 28. **2.** Both, Ragh. 8, 89. II. n. A pair, two, Bhâg. P. 5, 22, 14.

द्वितीय *dvi+tîya,* I. ordinal number, f. *yâ,* **1.** Second, Man. 2, 169. °*yam,* adv. A second time, again, Man. 11, 232. II. m. A companion, MBh. 13, 4899.—Comp. *A-*, adj. 1. quite alone, Kathâs. 24, 103. 2. incomparable, Râm. 4, 22, 2.

द्वितीयवन्त् *dvitîya + vant,* adj. Having a friend, MBh. 3, 17333.

द्वित्र *dvitra,* i.e. *dvi-tri+a,* m., f. *trâ,* n. pl. Two or three, Bhartṛ. 2, 90.

द्वित्रिचतुरम् *dvi-tri-chatur+a+m,* adv. Twice, or three or four times, Daçak. in Chr. 193, 8.

द्वित्व *dvi+tva,* n. The number Two, Bhâshâp. 88.

द्विधा *dvi+dhâ,* adv. **1.** In two parts, Man. 1, 12. **2.** Divided, Sâv. 4, 33. **3.** Of two kinds, Sâh. D. 8.—Cf. *δίχα, διχθά, δισσός.*

द्विप *dvi-pa* (1.*pâ*), m. An elephant (drinking twice, the elephant imbibing fluids by his trunk and thence conveying them to his mouth), Man. 7, 192.—Comp. *Gandha-*, m. a very strong kind of elephant, Vikr. d. 156. *Maru-*, m. a camel. *Sura-*, m. an elephant of the gods.

द्विपदिका *dvipadikâ,* i.e. *dvi-pada +ka,* f. A kind of song, Vikr. 51, 5.

द्विपायिन् *dvipâyin,* i.e. *dvi-* 1.*pâ+in,* m. An elephant (cf. *dvipa*), Râm. 3, 30, 26.

द्विमातृ *dvi-mâtṛi,* adj. Having two mothers (Sch., the measurer of the two worlds), Chr. 296, 4=Rigv. i. 112, 4.

द्विशस् *dvi+ças,* adv. Two by two, Suçr. 1, 152, 18.

1. **द्विष्** *DVISH,* ii. 2 (in epic poetry also i. 6, MBh. 2, 1934; 1943), Par. Âtm. **1.** To hate, MBh. 12, 8051. **2.** To show one's hatred, Man. 7, 12. **3.** To dislike, Bhag. 2, 57. Ptcple. of the pres. *dvishant,* m. A foe, Man. 3, 144. Ptcple. of the pf. pass. *dvishṭa,* **1.** Odious, Yâjn. 2, 304. **2.** Hostile, Hariv. 4673. Ptcple. of the fut. pass. *dveshya,* **1.** Disagreeable, MBh. 4. 120. **2.** Odious, Râm. 2, 21, 57. m. A foe, Man. 9, 307.—With **अनु** *anu,* To wreak one's anger upon one, Bhâg. P. 1, 18, 7.—With **प्र** *pra,* **1.** To dislike, Bhag. 16, 18. **2.** To hate, MBh. 14, 789. **3.** To show one's hatred, MBh. 12, 8397.—With **वि** *vi,* To dislike, Hariv. 8395. *vidvishant,* m. A foe, Bhartṛ. 3, 68. *vidvishṭa,* **1.** Odious, Man. 2, 57. **2.**

Being in contradiction to, Râm. 2, 116, 46 Gorr.—With सम् *sam*, *saṁdvishṭa*, Hated, MBh. 12, 53.—Cf. ὠδυσάμην, ὀδύσσομαι (frequent.), ὀδυσσάμενος, probably also δέδια, ἔδδεισα, δείδια, δείδοικα, δεῖος, δέος; δέαρ, δειδίσσομαι (frequent.), δεδίσσομαι, δειλός, δεινός, etc.; Lat. in -vīsus, dirus.

2. द्विष् *dvish*, I. latter part of comp. adj. Hating, Man. 3, 41. II. m. A foe, MBh. 4, 509.—Comp. *Pura-*, m. a name of Çiva, Bhâg. P. 4, 6, 8.

द्विस् *dvi+s*, adv. Twice, Man. 2, 60.—Cf. δίς; Lat. bis.

द्वीप *dvîpa*, i.e. *dvi-ap+a*, m. and n. 1. An island, Râm. 2, 25, 34. 2. Shelter, MBh. 2, 2118. 3. The name of the four, seven, or thirteen grand divisions of the terrestrial world, each of these being separated from the next by a different circumambient ocean, MBh. 6, 404.—Comp. *Kuça-*, m. one of the seven divisions of the terrestrial world, MBh. 13, 673. *Gaṇa-*, m. the name of an island (?), Râm. 4, 40, 33. *Jambû-*, m. the name of one of the seven divisions of the world, and implying the central division, or the known world; according to the Bauddhas, it is confined to India, MBh. 6, 207; Lalit. 27. *Jala-*, m. the name of an island, Râm. 4, 40, 33. *Nâga-*, m. the name of a division of the world, MBh. 6, 251.

द्वीपवन्त् *dvîpa+vant*, adj., f. *vatî*, Abounding in islands, MBh. 1, 2872.—Cf. *trayodaçadvîpavant* i.e. *trayodaçan-*, adj., f. *vatî*, Containing thirteen *dvîpas*, MBh. 3, 182. *saptan-*, adj. Containing seven *dvîpas*, Bhâg. P. 3, 21, 2.

द्वीपिन् *dvîpin*, i.e. *dvîpa+in*, m. An ounce or panther, Pañch. 63, 22.

† द्वृ *DVṚI*, i. 1, Par. 1. To stop. 2. To cover. 3. To disregard. 4. To appropriate.

द्वेधा *dvedhâ* i.e. *dvaya+dhâ*, adv. In two parts, MBh. 2, 930.

द्वेष *dvesha*, i.e. *dvish + a*, m. 1. Hatred, Man. 4, 163. 2. Abhorrence, repentance, Çâk. 66, 2. 4. Malignity, Man. 8, 225.

द्वेषण *dveshaṇa*, i.e. *dvish + ana*, I. m. An enemy, MBh. 12, 6278. II. n. Hatred against (with gen.), 5, 3263.

द्वेषस् *dveshas* i.e. *dvish + as*, n. Hatred, an enemy, Chr. 287, 8=Rigv. 1, 48, 8.

द्वेषिन् *dveshin*, i.e. *dvish+in*, I. adj. Disliking, Suçr. 1, 118, 14. II. m. A foe, Hariv. 1507.

द्वेषोयुत् *dveshoyut*, i.e. *dveshas-yu +t*, adj. Preventing hostility, Lass. 99, 1=Rigv. v. 9, 6.

द्वेष्टृ *dveshṭṛi*, i.e. *dvish+tṛi*, m. 1. One who dislikes, Suçr. 1, 121, 5. 2. A foe, MBh. 1, 1941.

द्वेष्यता *dveshya+tâ* (vb. *dvish*), f. Odiousness, Pañch. i. d. 147.

द्वैगुण्य *dvaiguṇya* i.e. *dvi-guṇa+ya*, n. Double the amount, Man. 8, 151.

द्वैजात *dvaijâta*, i.e. *dvi-jâti+a*, adj. Belonging to one of the three higher classes, Man. 8, 374.

द्वैत *dvaita*, i.e. *dvi + tâ + a*, n. Duality, Prab. 21, 8.—Comp. *A-*, n. being alone, Râm. 3, 3, 3.

द्वैतवन *dvaitavana*, i.e. *dvitavana+a + a*, adj. Referring to Dhvasan Dvaitavana, i.e. son of Dvitavana, MBh. 3, 928.

द्वैध *dvaidha*, i.e. *dvidhâ+a*, n. **1.** Duality, Man. 2, 14 (two texts). **2.** Difference, Man. 9, 32. **3.** Contradiction, Man. 8, 73. **4.** A contest, a personal conflict, MBh. 5, 5828. **5.** Duplicity, Pañch. iii. d. 62. **6.** Division of an army, Man. 7, 167.

द्वैधीभाव *dvaidhîbhâva*, i.e. *dvaidha-bhû+a*, m. **1.** Duality, MBh. 14, 809. **2.** Doubt, MBh. 7, 1211. **3.** Uncertainty, Çâk. 15, 11. **4.** Duplicity, Pañch. iii. d. 59. **5.** Division of an army, Man. 7, 160.

द्वैध्य *dvaidhya*, i.e. *dvidhâ+ya*, n. Duplicity.—**Comp.** *A-*, adj. sincere, Kâm. Nîtis. 4, 67.

द्वैपक्ष *dvaipaksha*, i.e. *dvi-paksha+a*, n. Two parties, MBh. 8, 4432.

द्वैपायन *dvaipâyana*, i.e. **1.** *dvîpa+âyana*, m. A name of Vyâsa, MBh. 1, 2416. **2.** *dvaipâyana+a*, adj. Referring to Vyâsa, MBh. 9, 1743.

द्वैमातुर *dvaimâtura*, i.e. *dvi-mâtṛi+a*, adj. **1.** Having different mothers, Râjat. 4, 355. **2.** Having another mother, 5, 22.

द्वैरथ *dvairatha*, i.e. *dvi-ratha+a*, I. adj. combined with *yuddha*, and subst. n. without *yuddha*, A single fight in chariots, Râm. 6, 86, 27; MBh. 4, 1061. II. m. An adversary, Bhâg. P. 7, 8, 34.

द्वैराज्य *dvairâjya*, i.e. *dvi-râjan+ya*, n. A dominion divided between two princes, Mâlav. 69, 17.

द्वैविध्य *dvaividhya*, i.e. *dvi-vidha+ya* (see *vidhâ*), n. **1.** Duality, twofold character, Bhâshâp. 141. **2.** Duplicity, MBh. 15, 236.

ध *DH.*

† **धक्क्** *DHAKK*, i. 10, Par. To destroy.

धट *dhaṭa* (probably a dialectical form of *dhartṛi*, based on the nom. sing. *dhartâ*), m. The scale of a balance, Mit. 140, 1, below.

† **धण्** *DHAṆ*, i. 1, Par. To sound.—Cf. *dhvan*.

1. **धन्** *DHAN* (cf. *dhanv*), i. 1, Par. **1.** To put in motion (ved.). **2.** † To bear or produce grains, etc. Caus. *dhanaya*, To put in motion, Chr. 293, 3=Rigv. i. 88, 3.

2. **धन्** *DHAN*, i. 1, Par. To sound.—Cf. *dhvan*.

धन *dhana*, n. **1.** Property of any description, chattels, Man. 8, 201. **2.** A gift, Man. 3, 138. **3.** Gold, money, Man. 3, 6; Râm. 1, 5, 5. **4.** Abundance in, Man. 2, 155. **5.** Cattle, Hariv. 3886.—**Comp.** *A-*, adj., f. *nâ*. 1. having no property, Man. 8, 416. 2. poor, Râm. 1, 15, 18. *Antar-*, n. an inward treasure, Bhartṛ. 2, 13. *Alam-*, adj. having a sufficient property, Man. 8, 162. *Alpa-*, adj. possessing little wealth, Man. 3, 66. *Kanyâ-*, n. dowry, Râm. 1, 74, 3. *Go-*, n. 1. property in cattle, MBh. 4, 1504. 2. a station of cowherds, Râm. 2, 32, 42 Gorr. *Tapodhana*, i.e. *tapas-*, adj., f. *nâ*. 1. devout; subst. m. an ascetic, Man. 11, 241. 2. Consisting in devotion, MBh. 13, 2727. *Nis-*, adj. poor, Bhartṛ. 2, 12. *Mahâ*, I. adj. 1. rich. 2. valuable. II. n. 1. (ved.) battle, Chr. 297, 17=Rigv. i. 112, 17. 2. gold. 3. incense. 4. costly raiment. 5. agriculture. *Vidyâ-*, n. property acquired by learning, Man. 9, 206. *Satya-*, adj. sincere, virtuous. *Su-*, m. a proper name. *Hṛita-* (vb. *hṛi*), adj. spoiled of wealth. —Cf. probably εὐ-θενής.

धनंजय *dhanaṁjaya, dhana+m-ji+a,* I. adj. Conquering booty, MBh. 9, 2665. II. m. 1. One of the five vital airs, that which is supposed to fatten, Vedântas. in Chr. 207, 16. 2. A name of Arjuna, MBh. 1, 2444. 3. One of the Nâgas or infernal serpents, MBh. 1, 1550. 4. A proper name, MBh. 2, 1238.

धनद् *dhana-da,* I. adj. Liberal, Kâm. Nîtis. 3, 23. II. m. A name of Kuvera, Râm. 3, 39, 20.

धनवन्त् *dhana+vant,* adj., f. *vatî,* Wealthy, Man. 3, 40.—Cf. probably Lat. dives.

धनसा *dhanasâ* i.e. *dhana-san,* Conquering booty, Chr. 296, 7=Rigv. i. 112, 7.

धनस्थ *dhana-stha,* adj. Wealthy, MBh. 12, 3331.

धनस्पृत् *dhana-spṛi+t,* adj. Conquering booty, Chr. 291, 14=Rigv. i. 64, 14.

धनाय *DHANÂYA,* a denomin. derived from *dhana* by *ya,* Par., Âtm. To be desirous of (with gen.), MBh. 5, 4510.

धनिक *dhanika* i.e. *dhana+ika,* I. adj. Wealthy, Pańch. 229, 1. II. m. A creditor, Man. 8, 47.

धनिन् *dhanin* i.e. *dhana+in,* I. adj., f. *nî,* Wealthy, Man. 8, 179. II. m. 1. A creditor, Man. 8, 61. 2. An owner, Man. 8, 147.

धनिष्ठा *dhanishṭhâ,* f. The name of a Nakshatra or lunar mansion, MBh. 13, 4266.

धनु *dhanu* (a curtailed form of *dhanus*), m. 1. A bow, Hit. pr. d. 22. 2. A measure of length, MBh. 8, 4224. —Comp. *Sa-*, adj. with a bow (in his hand).

ऽधनुष्क *-dhanushka,* i.e. *dhanus+ka,* a substitute for *dhanus* when latter part of a comp. adj., e.g. *sa-*, adj. Having a bow or bows, MBh. 2, 2699.

धनुष्मत्ता *dhanushmattâ* i.e. *dhanus+mant+tâ,* f. Archery, Bhartṛ. 1, 13 (thus to be read).

धनुष्मन्त् *dhanushmant* i.e. *dhanus+mant,* I. adj. Bearing a bow, Draup. 2, 8. II. m. An archer, Pańch. i. d. 219.—Comp. *Mahâ-*, m. a mighty archer.

धनुस् *dhanus* i.e. probably *han+vant* (akin to *dhanvan*), I. adj. Armed with a bow, MBh. 7, 9536. II. n. 1. A bow, Man. 3, 160. 2. A measure of length, Man. 8, 237. 3. The sign Sagittarius. 4. A desert, Man. 7, 70 (cf. *dhanvan*).—Comp. *Indra-* and *Sura-pati-*, n. the rainbow, Man. 1, 38; Megh. 73. *Pushpa-*, m. a name of the god of love, Çiç. 9, 41. *Sa-*, adj. armed with a bow.

धन्य *dhanya* i.e. *dhana+ya,* I. adj. 1. Bringing wealth, Man. 4, 19. 2. Auspicious, MBh. 8, 3606. 3. Fortunate, MBh. 13, 937. II. m. A kind of spell, Râm. 1, 31, 8 Gorr.

धन्यता *dhanya+tâ,* f. Fortunate condition, MBh. 3, 3078.

धन्यंमन्य *dhanyaṁmanya* i.e. *dhanya+m-man+ya,* adj. Thinking one's self fortunate, Daçak. in Chr. 196, 23.

धन्व् *DHANV* (akin to *dhan* and to *dhâv*), i. 1, Par. To run, to flow (ved.).

धन्व *dhanva* (a curtailed form of

dhanvan), n. A bow.—**Comp.** *Priya-*, adj. bow-loving, MBh. 7, 9536.

धन्वन् *dhanvan*, I. (a curtailed form of *dhanvant*, cf. *dhanus*), n. A bow; in the classic language almost always latter part of comp. adj. or sbst. derived from adjectives, e. g. *udyata-* (vb. *yam*), adj. With raised bow, Râm. 2, 91, 10 Gorr. *kusuma-*, *pushpa-*, m. Kâma, the god of love (properly, adj. Having a bow made of flowers), Prab. 72, 11. *gâṇḍîva-*, m. A name of Arjuna, Megh. 49. **II.** m. and n. A country scantily supplied with water, a desert, Man. 7, 70 (v.r.).—**Comp.** *Su-*, m. 1. an archer. 2. the son of an outcast Vaiçya, Man. 10, 23. 3. Viçvakarman, the artist of the gods.

धन्वन्तरि *dhanvantari*, m. **1.** A name of the sun, MBh. 3, 155. **2.** The physician of the gods, who was produced at the churning of the ocean, Bhâg. P. 2, 7, 31.

धन्वायन *dhanvâyana*, in *bhîma-dhanvâyanî*, f. Armed with frightful bows, MBh 5, 7633; probably to be changed to *-dhanvâyinî*, i. e. *bhîma-dhanvan+vin+î* (with *y* for *v*, VS. 16, 22).

धन्विन् *dhanvin*, i.e. *dhanvan+in*, I. adj. Armed with a bow, MBh. 4, 1639. **II.** m. **1.** An archer, Bhâg. P. 1, 12, 21. **2.** The sign Sagittarius, Varâh. Bṛih. S. 5, 41. **3.** A name of Çiva, MBh. 12, 10361. **4.** A proper name, Hariv. 429.

धम् *DHAM*, see *dhmâ*.

ऽधम *-dham+a* (vb. *dhmâ*), latter part of comp. adj., Blowing, melting.

धमनि and **नी** *dham+anî* (vb. *dhmâ*), f. A vein, MBh. 1, 5936.

धम्मिल्ल *dhammilla*, m. Braided and ornamented hair tied round the head, Râjat. 5, 356.

धर *dhara*, i.e. *dhṛi+a*, **I.** adj., f. *râ*. **1.** Bearing, especially latter part of comp. adj., e.g. Arj. 6, 10. **2.** Preserving, MBh. 6, 3005. **3.** Possessed of, Râm. 1, 9, 27. **4.** Observing, Pañch. 187, 12. **II.** m. The name of a *Vasu*, MBh. 1, 2582. **III.** f. *râ*, The earth, Man. 6, 26.—**Comp.** *Gadâ-*, m. a name of Kṛishṇa, Bhâg. P. 1, 8, 39. *Garbha-*, adj., f. *râ*, pregnant, MBh. 3, 12864. *Jagatî-*, m. a mountain, Kir. 5, 45. *Jaṭâ-*, 1. adj. wearing matted hair (cf. *jaṭâ*) Râm. 2, 86, 22; an ascetic, Daçak. in Chr. 189, 7. 2. epithet of Çiva, MBh. 3, 1625. *Toya-*, adj. containing water, Râm. 2, 93, 9. *Daṇḍa-*, I. adj. 1. having a mast, Râm. 2, 97, 17. 2. holding a rod as symbol of justice, chastising, Man. 9, 245; MBh. 12, 694. II. m. 1. a king, Ragh. 9, 3. 2. a judge, Daçak. 111, 12. 3. epithet of Yama, Râjat. 4, 655. *Daṇḍa-vrata-*, adj. punishing, Bhâg. P. 4, 13, 22. *Dus-*, adj., f. *râ*. 1. difficult to be borne, MBh. 5, 4403. 2. hard to be supported, Hariv. 8293. 3. hard to be managed, Man. 7, 28. 4. hard to be kept in remembrance, MBh. 13, 3618. *Dhanus-*, adj. sbst. armed with a bow, an archer, Man. 7, 74. *Dharaṇî-*, I. adj. holding the earth, MBh. 13, 6159. II. m. 1. a mountain, Râm. 6, 16, 4. 2. a king, Râjat. 3, 63. *Dharâ-*, I. adj. holding, supporting the earth, MBh. 13, 6860. II. m. a mountain, Râm. 3, 35, 24; *dhârâ-*, m. a cloud, MBh. 4, 2039. *Paksha-*, I. adj. Siding with, MBh. 1, 7507. II. m. a bird, Hariv. 11852. *Pâça-*, m. (holding a noose), a name of Varuṇa, Hariv. 4808. *Mâyâ-*, adj. fraudulent, Râm. 3, 49, 17. *Râja-mantra-*, i.e. *râjan-mantra-*, m. a king's counsellor, Hariv. 4137. *Hala-*, I. adj. holding a plough. II. m. Balarâma.

धरण *dharaṇa*, i.e. *dhṛi* + *ana*, I. adj., f. *ṇí*, Preserving, Hariv. 9643. II. f. *ṇí*, and **धरणि** *dharaṇi*, The earth, Râm. 2, 42, 2; 1, 44, 17. III. n. 1. Supporting, Kumâras. 1, 17. 2. Support, Hariv. 12823. 3. A weight of ten Palas, Man. 8, 135; 136.

धरणि *dharaṇi*, see the last (II.).

धरित्री *dharitrí*, i.e. *dhṛi* + *tṛi* + *í*, f. 1. A supporter, Hariv. 7419. 2. The earth, Bhartṛ. 2, 37.

धरिमन् *dhariman*, i.e. *dhṛi* + *iman*, m. Weight, Man. 8, 321.

धर्तृ *dhartṛi*, i.e. *dhṛi* + *tṛi*, m. A preserver, Lass. 98, 11=Rigv. v. 9, 3.

धर्म *dharma* (a curtailed form of *dharman*, q. cf.), m. and n. 1. Virtue, Hit. i. d. 59. 2. Merit, Bhâshâp. 160. 3. Right, Man. 1, 26. 4. Law, Man. 1, 114; 2, 12. 5. Duty, Man. 6, 92. 6. Justice, Man. 7, 18. 7. Character, quality, MBh. 12, 7850. 8. Resemblance, Râm. 2, 123, 14 Gorr. (*dharmât*, Like). 9. A sacrifice, MBh. 14, 2623. 10. Personified justice, Râm. 1, 1, 19. 11. =Yama, the judge of the dead, Hiḍ. 1, 34.—**Comp.** *A-*, m. 1. wrong, Man. 1, 26. 2. unjust way, Man. 2, 111. 3. demerit, Bhâshâp. 160. *Atithi-*, m. 1. the duty of hospitality, Pańch. 35, 17. 2. the character of a guest, Man. 3, 111. *Araṇya-*, m. the customs of beasts, Pańch. 31, 6. *Âpad-*, m. the duties and dispensations in time of distress, Man. 1, 116. *Kâla-*, m. death, Râm. 1, 43, 10. *Kula-*, m. the customs of families, Man. 1, 118. *Kûṭa-*, adj. where falsehood passes for right, Bhâg. P. 3, 30, 10. *Go-*, m. 1. law concerning cattle, MBh. 1, 4195. 2. public sexual intercourse. *Grâmya-*, 1. m. the customs of tame animals (or of persons living in a village?), Pańch. 31, 6. 2. public sexual intercourse. *Chhadman-*, m. hypocrisy, Râm. 4, 16, 21. *Jâti-*, m. the customs of tribes, Man. 1, 118. *Dus-*, adj. following bad customs, MBh. 3, 2066. *Paçu-*, m. 1. manner of treating cattle, Pańch. 34, 16. 2. a custom fit only for beasts, Man. 9, 66. *Pâṇi-*, m. the form of marriage, MBh. 1, 3379. *Yuddha-*, m. the law of war. *Viçesha-*, m. peculiar or different duty. *Satya-*, m. a proper name. *Sâkshât-*, m. the living law, Man. 2, 12 (cf. 2, 237). *Su-*, f. *mâ* and *mí*, a council of the gods. *Strí-*, m. 1. law concerning women, Man. 1, 114. 2. duty of women. 3. Menses. *Sva-*, m. 1. that which is due to somebody, one's right, Chr. 21, 8. 2. one's duty, Daçak. in Chr. 181, 4. 3. peculiar duty or occupation. 4. peculiarity.

धर्मतस् *dharma* + *tas*, adv. By right, Man. 1, 98.—**Comp.** *Putra-*, adv. by the ceremonies used on the birth of a son, Chr. 55, 20.

धर्मन् *dharman*, i.e. *dhṛi* + *man*, 1. n. in ved. language =*dharma*. 2. in the later language hardly ever used except as a substitute for *dharma*, when latter part of a comp. adj., e.g. *vidita-*, adj. Knowing one's duty, Çâk. 40, 4.—**Comp.** *Kâla-*, n. death, Hariv. 4761. *Kshatra-*, adj. fulfilling the duty of a warrior, Chr. 30, 37. *Manushya-*, m. Kuvera, the god of wealth. *Çabdâdi-*, i.e. *çabda-âdi-*, n. quality of sound, etc., Bhâg. P. 3, 32, 28. *Sa-*, adj. 1. equal in respect of duty, Man. 10, 41. 2. of the same caste, performing like duties. 3. of the same properties. 4. Like.

धर्ममय *dharma* + *maya*, adj. Consisting of virtue, MBh. 1, 109.

धर्मवन्त् *dharma* + *vant*, adj., f. *vatí*, Virtuous, Râm. 5, 3, 58.

धर्मस्थ *dharma-stha*, m. A judge, Man. 8, 57.

धर्मात्मता *dharmâtmatâ*, i.e. *dharma -âtman* + *tâ*, f. Justice, Râm. 4, 55, 2.

धर्माधिकरणिक *dharmâdhikaraṇika*, i.e. *dharma-adhikaraṇa* + *ika*, m. A judge, Pañch. 97, 18.

धर्मित्व *dharmitva*, i.e. *dharmin* + *tva*, n. Virtue, Kâm. Nîtis. 8, 11.

धर्मिन् *dharmin*, i.e. *dharma* + *in*, adj., f. *iṇî*. I. Virtuous, MBh. 7, 1663. II. Having special qualities, Hariv. 10948. III. Latter part of comp. adj. 1. Following the law of (Bhagavant), Bhâg. P. 4, 23, 10. 2. Bound by the law of (the twice born), Man. 10, 41. 3. Following the habits of (beasts), MBh. 1, 3480. 4. Having the nature of (perishableness), Ragh. 8, 10. 5. Having duties (to each other), MBh. 14, 708.—Comp. *Sa-*, I. adj. Observing the same customs or laws. II. f. *iṇî*, A wife wedded according to the ritual of the Vedas. *Strî-*, i.e. *strî-dharma* + *in*, f. *iṇî*, A woman during menstruation.

धर्मिष्ठ *dharmishṭha*, superl. of *dharmavant*, f. *ṭhâ*. 1. Performing all duties, Man. 3, 40. 2. Very virtuous, Bhâg. P. 9, 16, 15. 3. Completely harmonising with law, Râm. 2, 26, 1.—Comp. *A-*, adj. 1. unjust, Râm. 2, 23, 13. 2. very wicked, MBh. 1, 4579.

धर्मिष्ठता *dharmishṭha* + *tâ*, f. Supreme virtuousness, MBh. 1, 2987.

धर्म्य *dharmya*, i.e. *dharma* + *ya*, adj. 1. Conformable to law, legal, Man. 3, 22; 9, 111. 2. Loving justice, just, Râm. 2, 21, 49; 50. 3. Legitimate (as a wife), Râm. 3, 4, 7. 4. Latter part of comp. words, Having the quality of (that), Bhâg. P. 5, 14, 2.—Comp. *A-*, adj. 1. illegal, Man. 3, 25. 2. unjust, Râm. 1, 27, 18.

धर्ष *dharsha*, i.e. *dhṛish* + *a*, m. Arrogance, MBh. 1, 7040. — Comp. *Dus-*, adj. 1. difficult to be injured or attacked, Nal. 11, 36; Râm. 6, 16, 58. 2. dangerous, Hariv. 2327. 3. horrible, MBh. 14, 1849.

धर्षक *dharshaka*, i.e. *dhṛish* + *aka*, adj. Assailing, Hariv. 8844.

धर्षण *dharshaṇa*, i.e. *dhṛish* + *ana*, n. and f. *ṇâ*, Disrespect, contumely, abuse, Râm. 6, 38, 21; MBh. 1, 6502; Pañch. 255, 9.—Comp. *Dus-*, adj. difficult to be attacked, Râm. 4, 9, 55.

धर्षिन् *dharshin*, i. e. *dhṛish* + *in*, adj. Ill-treating, Hariv. 8213.

धव् *DHAV*, i. 1, Âtm. To run, (ved.).—Cf. θέω, θεύσομαι, θοός, βοη-θέω, νω-θής.

धव *dhava*, m. 1. A man, Pañch. ii. d. 109. 2. A husband, Bhâg. P. 1, 16, 20. 3. A lord, Hariv. 14952. 4. A shrub, Grislea tomentosa Roxb., Râm. 1, 26, 15.—Comp. *Menâ-*, m. Himâlaya, the personified mountain. *Vi-*, see s.v. *Sa-dhavâ*, f. a wife whose husband is living.

धवल *dhav* + *ala* (cf. 2. *dhâv*), adj., f. *lâ*. 1. Dazzling white, Kathâs. 25, 15.—Comp. *Ati-*, adj. very white, Daçak. in Chr. 199, 6.

धवलित *dhavalita*, i.e. *dhavala* + *ita*, adj. Made dazzling white, Bhartṛ. 3, 85. — Comp. *Sudhâ-*, adj. whitewashed, plastered.

धवलिमन् *dhavaliman*, i.e. *dhavala* + *iman*, m. White (the colour), Çiç. 4, 65.

धा *DHÂ*, ii. 3, Par., Âtm. 1. To put, MBh. 5, 1075; Hit. ii. d. 163; pass. To be contained, MBh. 12, 8933. 2. With *manas* or *matim*, often To resolve, Râm. 1, 9, 40, 11, 1; to fix the mind on, Man. 12, 23. 3. To grant, confer, Chr. 291, 14=Rigv. i. 64, 14 (ved. *dhattana* for *dhatta*), MBh. 7, 5267; Man. 1, 29. **4.** To generate, Bhâg. P. 9, 6, 38. **5.** To undertake, Râjat. 1, 295. **6.** To put on, Ṛit. 6, 13. **7.** To carry, bear, Ragh. 3, 1; Ṛit. 6, 16. **8.** To nourish, Chr. 295, 13= Rigv. i. 92, 13 (ved. *dhâmahe*, conj. of the Aor.). **9.** To preserve, Ragh. 1, 26. **10.** Âtm. To get, Bhâg. P. 1, 2, 23. **11.** Âtm. To undergo, Hariv. 531. **12.** Âtm. To show, Hit. pr. d. 41. Anomal. impf. *adadhan*, MBh. 3, 12706. Anomal. Aor. *dhîmahi* (ved.), Bhâg. P. 6, 16, 18. Anomal. (or rather false) ptcple. of the pf. Par. f. *dadhyushî* (for *dadhushî*), Râm. 2, 16, 20 (=2, 13, 19 Gorr., where v.r.). Ptcple. of the pres. pass. *dhîyamâna*, One whose mind is directed to, Hariv. 1854 (*a-dharme*, to injustice). Ptcple. of the pf. pass. **I.** *dhita* (ved. and) Hariv. 7799, Resolved. **II.** *hita*, **1.** Fit, suitable, Chr. 10, 5. **2.** Salutary, Man. 4, 35; most beneficial, Man. 7, 57. **3.** Wothy, Pañch. i. d. 358. **4.** Friendly, agreeable, Man. 2, 108. m. A friend, MBh. 12, 5471. n. **1.** Well-being, Râm. 3, 53, 12; also pl., Bhartṛ. 2, 65. **2.** A good, a benefit, Râjat. 5, 62. Comp. *A-hita*, I. adj. 1. bad, Man. 3, 20. 2. prejudicial, Râm. 3, 30, 2. II. m. An enemy, Bhag. 2, 36. III. n. injury, Râm. 5, 91, 2. *Hita-a-hita*, adj. 1. good and evil. 2. beneficial and disadvantageous. *Su-*, I. adj. 1. fit, right. 2. kind. 3. satiate. n., and f. *tâ*, one of the tongues of Agni. Ptcple. of the fut. pass. *dheya*, To be produced, MBh. 12, 13108.—With the prep. अधि *adhi*, Âtm. To conquer, Chr. 291, 2=Rigv. i. 85, 2.—With अन्तर् *antar*, **1.** To cover, MBh. 4, 1683. **2.** To cause to disappear, Bhâg. P. 6, 9, 35. **3.** To eclipse, MBh. 1, 5519. **4.** especially pass. To disappear, Bhâg. P. 3, 2, 11; MBh. 4, 1042. **5.** To receive in one's self, contain, Ragh. 15, 81; MBh. 12, 12747. *antarhita*, **1.** Covered, Râm. 2, 9, 18. **2.** Hidden, Çâk. 9, 18, v.r. **3.** Disappeared, Chr. 39, 19.—With अपि *api* and पि *pi*, **1.** To cover, MBh. 1, 5863; 4, 1453. **2.** To shut, MBh. 3, 12089. **3.** To make invisible, Vikr. d. 72. **4.** pass. To disappear, MBh. 12, 8932. **5.** To hinder, Râm. 5, 29, 16. Caus. To cause to shut, Bhâg. P. 2, 7, 29.—With अन्वपि *anu-api*, pass. To disappear after somebody (acc.), Bhâg. P. 3, 11, 28.—With अभि *abhi*, **1.** To invade, MBh. 2, 1090. **2.** Âtm. To take back, Bhâg. P. 3, 13, 30. **3.** To name, Bhâg. P. 3, 12, 10. **4.** To declare, Man. 1, 42. **5.** To speak, Râm. 2, 123, 15 Gorr. (with acc., Râm. 6, 12, 7). *abhihita*, Called, Man. 3, 141.—With प्रत्यभि *prati-abhi*, **1.** To take back, Bhâg. P. 3, 7, 4. **2.** To answer, 4, 3, 15. **3.** To approve, MBh. 5, 7459.—With समभि *sam-abhi*, To address, Kathâs. 25, 93.—With अव *ava*, **1.** To put, MBh. 1, 4503. **2.** To fix one's attention on something, Çântiç. 3, 11. *avahita*, **1.** Shut, Bhâg. P. 1, 2, 32. **2.** Attentive, Prab. 33, 2.—With अभ्यव *abhi-ava*, *abhyavahita*, Allayed, Râm. 2, 40, 33.—With व्यव *vi-ava*, To separate, Râm. 2, 114, 13 Gorr.; pass. To separate one's self, Çântiç. 3, 11. *vyavahita*, **1.** Stopped, Çâk. 71, 18. **2.** Covered, Çiç. 9, 26. **3.** Hostile, Bhâg. P. 1, 9, 36.—With संव्यव *sam-vi-ava*, *a-saṁvyavahita* + *m*, adv. Immediately, Bhâg. P. 5, 6, 6.—With आ *â*, usually Âtm. **1.** To put, Râm. 5, 31, 1. **2.** To generate, MBh. 3, 8639; 16637; to produce, Bhâg. P. 3. 5, 34; to perform, MBh. 3, 2600. **3.** To instil, MBh. 1, 6157. **4.**

To direct, MBh. 5, 4172. **5.** With *matim, manas, chittam,* often To resolve, Râm. 1, 18, 7. **6.** To employ, Çâk, 3, 13. **7.** To put on, Çâk. d. 36. **8.** To hold, Man. 11, 104. **9.** To pawn, Nârada in Mit. 268, 2. **10.** To confer, MBh. 1, 7735. **11.** Âtm. To receive, Râm. 4, 21, 17. **12.** Âtm. To get, Hariv. 9283 (to fall into a passion). Desiderat. *dhitsa,* To wish to transfer, MBh. 12, 3170.—With अत्या *ati-â, atyâhita,* Very disagreeable, Prab. 25, 3. n. Misfortune, MBh. 4, 861.—With अन्वा *anu-â, anvâhita,* Delivered for the purpose of being restored to the owner, Yâjñ. 2, 67. *anvâdheya,* see s.v.—With अभ्या *abhi-â,* To throw under, Man. 8, 372.—With उपा *upa-â,* **1.** To put on, Bhâg. P. 3, 13, 45. **2.** To render, Râm. 2, 35, 28. *upâhita,* Produced, Bhartṛ, 3, 80.—With प्रत्युपा *prati-upa-â,* Âtm. To recover, Bhâg. P. 8, 24, 61.—With समा *sam-â,* **1.** To arrange, Râm. 5, 17, 1; (fire), Râm. 3, 9, 33. **2.** To put on, Pañch. i. d. 371; Âtm., Hariv. 10725. **3.** To impose, MBh. 7, 4180. **4.** To put to, Hariv. 10482. **5.** Âtm. To conceive, MBh. 1, 4264. **6.** To intrust, MBh. 7, 4253. **7.** To establish, Ragh. 17, 8. **8.** To direct, Râm. 2, 93, 25. **9.** With *manas,* To resolve, Bhag. 17, 11. **10.** With *manas, dhiyam, âtmânam,* To collect one's thoughts, Bhâg. P. 6, 1, 62. **11.** Âtm. To devote one's self completely to (with acc.), Râm. 1, 38, 11. **12.** To hold together, MBh. 6, 146. **13.** To redress, MBh. 15, 194. **14.** To cause, Hariv. 8671. **15.** To make, 11075. **16.** Âtm. To appropriate, Râjat. 5, 167. **17.** Âtm. To undergo, Hariv. 3919 (To fall into a passion). *samâhita,* **1.** One who has fixed his mind only on one object, Man. 6, 43; 2, 53. **2.** Joined, Râm. 6, 7, 47. **3.** All, Hariv. 12209. **4.** Passed, MBh. 1, 6614. **5.** Like, Râm. 1, 1, 26. Desider. To wish that somebody may collect his thoughts, MBh. 12, 9586.—With अनुसमा *anu-sam-â, anusamâhita,* Collected, Râm. 2, 22, 14 (cf. *sam-â,* 10).—With अभिसमा *abhi-sam-â, abhisamâhita,* Joined, Râm. 5, 90, 31.—With उपसमा *upa-sam-â,* To arrange, Daçak. in Chr. 201, 9.—With प्रतिसमा *prati-sam-â,* **1.** To put on, MBh. 13, 266. **2.** To affix again, Daçak. in Chr. 196, 20. **3.** To redress, 182, 7.—With आविस् *âvis, âvirhita,* Manifested, Bhâg. P. 2, 7, 36.—With उप *upa,* **1.** To place under, Man. 4, 54. **2.** To place in, Bhâg. P. 5, 5, 31. **3.** To enchase, MBh. 5, 3382. **4.** To affix, Çâk. d. 18. **5.** To transfer, Ragh. 7, 68. **6.** To employ, Ragh. 3, 29. **7.** To cover, Bhâg. P. 5, 5, 6. **8.** To provide, MBh. 1, 2891. *upahita,* **1.** Ready, MBh. 13, 2286. **2.** Suborned, excited, MBh. 12, 4159. **3.** Joined, Suçr. 1, 88, 3. **4.** Suitable, Râm. 5, 69, 15. Ptcple. of the fut. pass. *upadhânîya,* n. A pillow, Pañch. 125, 9.—With तिरस् *tiras,* **1.** To hide, Bhâg. P. 2, 6, 40. **2.** Âtm. To disappear, Bhâg. P. 3, 7, 12. *tirohita,* **1.** Concealed, Man. 8, 203. **2.** Surpassed, Dev. 9, 20 (made unperceivable by a louder sound).—With नि *ni,* **1.** To lay down, Man. 5, 143. **2.** To bury, Man. 5, 68; to conceal, Man. 8, 38. **3.** To leave, Râm. 2, 136, 1 Gorr. **4.** To intrust, Râm. 1, 77, 24 Gorr. **5.** To transfer, Chr. 289, 12 = Rigv. i. 50, 12. **6.** To put, Ram. 2, 50, 21. **7.** To direct, Megh. 96, v.r. **8.** With *manas,* To resolve, Hariv. 534. **9.** With *manasi,*

To think, Hit. 87, 13. **10.** To make, Bhâg. P. 7, 8, 18. **11.** To restrain, Bhâg. P. 7, 5, 50. Caus. **1.** To cause to be detained, Man. 8, 30. **2.** To establish, Bhâg. P. 5, 20, 25.—With अन्तर्नि *antar-ni,* To put in, Kathâs. 12, 112.—With उपनि *upa-ni,* **1.** To bring on, Gît. 5, 2. **2.** To conceal, Man. 8, 37. **3.** To intrust, Man. 8, 196. —With उपरिनि *upari-ni, uparinihita,* Put on, Ṛit. 6, 30.—With प्रणि *pra-ni,* **1.** To put at the head, MBh. 7, 1527. **2.** To lay down, MBh. 4, 1437. **3.** To put on, Bhâg. P. 1, 15, 16. **4.** To put in, MBh. 12, 6617. **5.** To enchase, Hit. ii. d. 71. **6.** To stretch out, Megh. 105. **7.** To direct, Bhartṛ. 1, 51. **8.** With *manas, âtmânam,* sometimes To resolve, to think, Bhaṭṭ. 6, 142. **9.** To consider with intention, Râm. 4, 27, 21. **10.** To send out (spies), MBh. 7, 2651. **11.** To spy, Râm. 5, 90, 15. *praṇihita,* **1.** Intent, Râm. 2, 47, 21 Gorr. **2.** Cautious (?), Man. 9, 269. **3.** Before admitted, Man. 8, 54. *praṇidheya,* n. **1.** Employing. **2.** Sending out (of emissaries), MBh. 12, 2155. —With संप्रणि *sam-pra-ni,* **1.** To leave, MBh. 4, 1247. **2.** To disregard, 3, 13194.—With प्रतिनि *prati-ni,* To order, MBh. 1, 4505.—With विनि *vi-ni,* **1.** To lay down, MBh. 1, 2984. **2.** To put on, Bhartṛ. 3, 61. **3.** To direct, Mṛichchh. 143, 20. **4.** To put in, Gît. 11, 31.—With संनि *sam-ni,* **1.** To put together, to collect, MBh. 14, 290. **2.** To put in, Pañch. 265, 5. **3.** To direct, Ragh. 13, 44. **4.** pass. To be near, Bhâg. P. 5, 17, 14. *saṁnihita,* **1.** Near at hand, Man. 2, 205; MBh. 13, 454. **2.** Ready, Çâk. 17, 20. Caus. **1.** To bring near, Bhâg. P. 5, 18, 1. **2.** pass. To show one's self, Bhâg. P. 5, 7, 8.—With परि *pari,* **1.** Âtm. To put on, Râm. 2, 37, 7 Gorr. **2.** To put on a garment, Bhâg. P. 1, 4, 5. **3.** To surround, Râm. 4, 48, 18. **4.** To let wander (as one's eye), Hariv. 3743. *parihita,* **1.** Surrounding, Râm. 6, 37, 31. **2.** Clothed, Daçak. in. Chr. 186, 9. Caus. To cause to put on, Daçak. in Chr. 200, 7. Desid. To be about to put on, MBh. 5, 853.—With विपरि *vi-pari,* To change, Yâjñ. 1, 196.—With पि *pi,* see *api.*—With पुरस् *puras,* **1.** To put at the head, MBh. 3, 1973. **2.** To weigh, to ponder. **3.** To esteem, Ragh. 12, 43. *purohita,* m. The family priest of a prince who conducts all the ceremonies and sacrifices of the family, Chr. 21, 3.—With प्रति *prati,* To employ, Çatr. 14, 245. —With वि *vi,* **1.** To grant, Râm. 1, 8, 27. **2.** To procure, MBh. 13, 2209. **3.** To fix, ordain, Man. 2, 29. **4.** pass. To pass for, Man. 3, 118. **5.** To create, Ragh. 1, 29. **6.** To make, build, MBh. 5, 7130; Râjat. 5, 155; 25. **7.** To perform, Man. 8, 282. **8.** To cause, Râm. 3, 54, 27. **9.** To treat, Râm. 2, 38, 17. **10.** To put on, Pañch. 236, 8; Kathâs. 21, 3. **11.** To show, Bhartṛ. 1, 59. **12.** To appoint, Châṇ. 102. **13.** To put in, MBh. 3, 8850. **14.** To direct, Bhartṛ. 3, 36. **15.** To put aside, MBh. 4, 155. **16.** To despatch to different directions, Man. 7, 184. *su-vihita,* Well provided, Râm. 1, 13, 16. *strî-vidheya,* adj. Uxorious. Caus. To cause to be laid, Râm. 6, 96, 13. Desid. **1.** To wish to give, Bhâg. P. 1, 10, 22. **2.** To wish to perform, Hariv. 1311. **3.** To wish to render, Bhâg. P. 7, 3, 1. **4.** To wish to devise, Bhâg. P. 4, 6, 7. **5.** To pursue one's aim, MBh. 3, 13952. Desider. *vidhitsita,* n. Design, Bhâg. P. 1, 9, 16.—With अनुवि *anu-vi,* **1.** To assign to, MBh. 5, 1372. **2.** To cause afterwards, Çântiç, 1,

17. **3.** pass. To conform one's self to, MBh. 1, 4721. **4.** To perform in conformity with a command, Râm. 5, 95, 4.—With प्रवि *pra-vi,* **1.** To divide, Suçr. 2, 347, 7. **2.** To mind, Râm. 4, 14, 29. **3.** To join, Râjat. 5, 421. **4.** To dispose before, Lass. 44, 14.—With प्रतिवि *prati-vi,* **1.** To dispose, Râm. 2, 36, 2. **2.** To despatch, Râm. 5, 90, 14. **3.** To do against, Çâk. 29, 21.—With संवि *sam-vi,* **1.** To dispose, MBh. 3, 8806. **2.** To order, Hariv. 8663. **3.** To mind, MBh. 12, 4730. **4.** To act, Pañch. 12, 21. **5.** To render, Bhartṛ. 1. 66. **5.** To put on, MBh. 2, 1510.—With श्रत् *çrat,* To believe, Chr. 7, 20 (*açraddadhat,* anomalous impf. instead of *çrad-adadhât*).—With सम् *sam,* **1.** To put together, to combine, Bhâg. P. 4, 7, 8; to unite, Man. 7, 66. **2.** To make an agreement, Daçak. in Chr. 198, 1; Kâm. Nîtis. 9, 41. **3.** To contract, close, Suçr. 1, 47, 7. **4.** To comprehend, MBh. 14, 1148. **5.** To compose, Kâm. Nîtis. 9, 68. **6.** To collect, Bhâg. P. 9, 9, 42. **7.** To put on, MBh. 5, 2340. **8.** To put an arrow on a bow, Râm. 3, 4, 27. **9.** To direct, Ragh. 11, 69. **10.** To redress, Kâm. Nîtis, 13, 60. **11.** To inflict, Kir. 5, 51. **12.** To grant, Pañch. ii. d. 13. **13.** To assist, MBh. 5, 3406; Âtm. with instr. To employ, MBh. 4, 964 (*dadhâmahe* anomalous, or ved. instead of *dadhmahe*). **14.** Âtm. To be a match for, Pañch. i. d. 260. **15.** To approach, MBh. 3, 15726. *saṁhita,* **I.** as latter part of comp. words, **1.** Endowed with, MBh. 12, 207. **2.** Abounding in, Man. 9, 103. **3.** Accompanied by, Râm. 1, 32, 19. **4.** Referring to, Râm. 2, 103, 1. **5.** Conformable to, MBh. 4, 472. **6.** Caused by, MBh. 14, 527. **II.** f. *tâ,* The arrangement of a text, a collection, especially that of the Vedas, Chr. 135, 2; Man. 11, 77; 262. Comp. ptcple. of the fut. pass. *dus-saṁdheya,* adj. Difficult to be united, MBh. 5, 5827.—With अतिसम् *ati-sam,* **1.** To deceive, Çâk. 69, 23, v.r. **2.** To settle completely, Mahâv. 109, 1. *atisaṁdhita,* Deceived, Ram. 2, 7, 23.—With अनुसम् *anu-sam,* **1.** To search, Man. 12, 106. **2.** To collect, Hit. 125, 20. *anusaṁhita,* as latter part of a comp., Conformable to, MBh. 13, 5593.—With अभिसम् *abhi-sam,* **1.** To combine, Râm. 5, 36, 42; to unite, Kâm. Nîtis. 9, 64. **2.** To aim at, MBh. 6, 5563. **3.** To have in view, to think of, MBh. 12, 5471. **4.** To make an agreement, Man. 9, 52. **5.** To deceive, MBh. 12, 5116. **6.** To make subservient, Man. 7, 159. **7.** To gain over, Râm. 4, 54, 5. *abhisaṁdhita,* Deceived, MBh. 12, 5113. *abhisaṁhita,* as latter part of a comp., **1.** Endowed with, MBh. 12, 3087 (conversant with). **2.** Referring to, 12, 4793.—With समभिसम् *sam-abhi-sam,* **1.** To put in, MBh. 3, 10452. **2.** To resolve, MBh. 9, 818.—With उपसम् *upa-sam,* **1.** To impart, Kâm. Nîtis. 1, 13. **2.** To have in view, MBh. 4, 1483. *upasaṁhita,* **1.** Endowed, MBh. 12, 10732. **2.** Surrounded, MBh. 13, 5895. **3.** Conformable to, MBh. 1, 602.—With प्रसम् *pra-sam,* To put on, MBh. 6, 3910. — With प्रतिसम् *prati-sam,* **1.** To collect, Prab. 99, 14, v.r. **2.** To put on, MBh. 6, 3313. **3.** To direct to (acc.), MBh. 3, 1926. **4.** To return, Hariv. 9240; to restore, Bhâg. P. 1, 17, 42. **5.** To understand, Prab. 34, 19.——Cf. τίθημι, θεμός, θέμις, θέμεθλον, θής, θῆσσα, θᾶκος, θῶκος, τεθμός, θεσμός (for θε + τμος), etc.; Lat. -dere in con-dere and others, credo = *çraddadhâmi*; Goth.

-*deds* (deed); O.H.G. tôn; A.S. dón (to do), dema (a judge), dóm (judgment).

धातु *dhâ+tu,* m. 1. A primary or elementary substance, MBh. 12, 6821. 2. Any constituent part of the body (usually said to be three), MBh. 1, 3633. 3. An organ of sense, MBh. 12, 6842. 4. m. and n. A metal, Man. 6, 71. 5. A grammatical root, MBh. 3, 17110.—Comp. *Giri-*, m. the constituent parts of a mountain, as minerals, etc., Râm. 2, 63, 18. *Gairika-*, m. =*gairika,* q.v. Râm. 5, 5, 26. *Tri-*, adj. threefold, Chr. 292, 12=Rigv. i. 85, 12. *Mahâ-*, m. gold. *Rakta-*, m. 1. red chalk. 2. copper. *Çilâ-*, m. 1. chalk. 2. red chalk. *Saumya-*, m. phlegm.

धातुमत्ता *dhâtumattâ,* i.e. *dhâtumant+tâ,* f. Abundance in metals, Kumâras. 1, 4.

धातुमन्त् *dhâtu+mant,* adj., f. *matî.* 1. Having elements, Bhâg. P. 2, 8, 7. 2. Abounding in metals, Râm. 2, 94, 4.—Comp. *Gairika-dhâtu+mant,* adj. abounding in red chalk, MBh. 3, 826.

धातृ *dhâ+tṛi,* m. 1. The creator, Ragh. 13, 6. 2. A bearer, Hariv. 11851. 3. A preserver, MBh. 1, 1722. 4. One of the Âdityas, MBh. 1, 2523. 5. A name of Brahman, Man. 5, 30. 6. A son of Brahman, MBh. 1, 2614. 7. An adulterer, Daçak. 191, 11.—Comp. *Jagat-*, I. m. a name of Brahman. II. f. *dhâtri,* a name of Sarasvatî, Mârk. P. 23, 30.—Cf. Lat. con-ditor.

धात्री *dhâtrî,* i.e. *dhe+tṛi+î,* f. 1. A mother, Yâjn. 3, 82. 2. A nurse, Râm. 1, 40, 18 Gorr. 3. A waiting-woman, Chr. 52, 15. 4. The earth, MBh. 11, 215. 5. Emblica officinalis Gaertn., Myrobalane, Suçr. 1, 162, 10.

धात्रेयिका *dhâtreyikâ,* i.e. *dhâtrî+eya+ka,* f. A foster-sister, Draup. 6, 9.

धान *dhâ+ana,* f. *nî,* latter part of comp. words implying especially the place of the preceding notion, e.g. *jîva-dhânî,* f. The seat of living creatures, epithet of the earth, Bhâg. P. 3, 13, 30. *matsya-dhânî,* f. A fish-basket. *yama-dhânî,* f. The residence of the god of death, Bhartṛ. 3, 51. *yâtu-dhâna,* m. A Râkshasa or demon. *râja-dhâna,* n. and *-dhânî,* f. i.e. *râjan-*, A capital.

धाना *dhânâ,* i.e. probably *dhâ+anâ,* f. pl. Grain, Bhâg. P. 6, 15, 4.

धानुष्क *dhânushka,* i.e *dhanus+ka+a,* m. An archer, MBh. 6, 756.

धान्य *dhânya,* i.e. *dhânâ+ya,* n. Corn, Man. 2, 55.—Comp. *Ku-*, n. a kind of corn, Suçr. 1, 196, 21 sqq. *Dhana-*, n. a kind of spell, Râm. 1, 30, 7.

धान्यक *dhânya+ka,* 1. A substitute for *dhânya* in the latter part of a comp. word. *kumbhî-*, adj. Having vessels full of corn, Man. 4, 7 (sufficing for one year, Kull.). *kuçûla-*, adj. Having granaries full of corn (sufficing for three years, Kull.), ib. *bahu-*, adj. Abounding in corn, MBh. 2, 1187.

धान्यवन्त् *dhânya + vant,* adj., f. *vatî,* Having much corn, MBh. 12, 3526.

धान्वन *dhânvana,* i.e. *dhanvan+a,* adj. Situated in a desert, Kâm. Nîtis. 4, 59.

धान्वन्तर *dhânvantara* and धान्वन्तर्य *dhânvantarya,* i.e. *dhanvantari+a* or *ya,* adj. 1. Referring to Dhanvantari (the incarnation of Vishṇu as Dhanvantari), Bhâg. P. 1, 3, 17. 2. Sacred to the sun, MBh. 13, 4660.

धाम *dhâma* (akin to *dhâman*), m.

pl. The name of a class of superhuman beings, MBh. 13, 15446.

धामन् *dhâ + man*, n. **1.** An abode, MBh. 1, 3602. **2.** State, Prab. 17, 15. **3.** A host, Chr. 292, 11, and 293, 6 = Rigv. i. 85, 11 ; 87, 6. **4.** Dignity, Ragh. 11, 85. **5.** Light, splendour, Prab. 26, 8. — **Comp.** *A-gharma-*, m. the moon, Çiç. 9, 40. *Tri-*, I. adj. referring to the three worlds, MBh. 13, 7376. II. m. a name of Vishṇu, MBh. 12, 1508. *Ruchi-*, adj. the abode of whom is light, epithet of the sun, Çiç. 9, 13. *Çveta-*, m. 1. the moon. 2. camphor. 3. cuttle-fish bone. *Hariṇa-*, m. the moon, Râjat. 5, 482—Cf. θέμα ; A.S. -dóm, as affix of abstracts, properly 'state.'

धार *dhâra*, i.e. I. *dhṛi + a*, latter part of comp. words, Holding, bearing, e.g. *chhattra-*, m. The bearer of the royal parasol, Pańch. 156, 22 ; *daṇḍa-*, adj. Holding the staff, as symbol of judicature, Râjat. 4, 108. II. *dhârâ + a*. **1.** adj. Coming down in a shower, Suçr. 1, 170, 1. **2.** m. A shower, Hariv. 6333.—Cf. *dhârâ*.

धारक *dhâraka*, i.e. *dhṛi + aka*, I. latter part of comp. adj., Bearing, MBh. 1691. *nâmadhâraka*, i.e. *nâman-*, adj. Being something only nominally, not really, Pańch. ii. d. 91. II. m. A trunk or box (for keeping clothes), Suçr. 2, 55, 11.

धारण *dhâraṇa*, i.e. *dhṛi + ana*, I. adj., f. *ṇî*. **1.** Preserving, MBh. 12, 12751. **2.** Keeping in remembrance, Bhâg. P. 2, 7, 46. **3.** Having the shape, MBh. 13, 739. II. f. *ṇâ*. **1.** Bearing, MBh. 7, 1912. **2.** Supporting, Râm. 2, 109, 25 Gorr. **3.** Suppression, Bhâg. P. 4, 4, 26. **4.** Mental retention, MBh. 1, 1010. **5.** Keeping the mind collected, the breath suspended, and all natural wants restrained; steady immoveable abstraction, Vedântas. in Chr. 217, 19. **6.** A settled rule, Man. 4, 38. III. n. **1.** Holding, bearing, Kumâras. 7, 68 ; MBh. 3, 9946. **2.** Maintaining, Yâjń. 3, 174. **3.** Observance, Man. 10, 3. **4.** Mental retention, MBh. 15, 756. **5.** Possession, Man. 1, 93. **6.** Fixing one's mind on one object, Vedântas. in Chr. 217, 19. **7.** Restraining, or rather stopping, the senses, MBh. 3, 13939. **8.** Enduring, Râm. 1, 38, 16.—**Comp.** *Garbha-*, n. pregnancy, MBh. 3, 10449. *Chhattra-*, n. carrying an umbrella, Man. 2, 178. *Tulâ-*, n. weighing, Yâjń. 2, 100. *Daṇḍa-*, n. punishment, Râm. 4, 17, 34. *Deha-*, n. 1. bearing a body, MBh. 5, 3693. 2. life, MBh. 5, 7258. *Hasta-*, n. warding off a blow, resisting.

धारणक *dhâraṇa + ka*, I. latter part of comp. adj., Containing, MBh. 12, 6889. II. m. A debtor, Yâjń. 2, 36. —**Comp.** *A-*, adj. unsupportable.

धारणामय *dhâraṇâ + maya*, adj., f. *yî*, depending on abstraction, Bhâg. P. 4, 18, 20.

धारयितृ *dhârayitṛi*, i. e. *dhṛi*, Caus., + *tṛi*, m. **1.** One who bears, Râm. 1, 44, 23 Gorr. **2.** One who restrains, MBh. 5, 3391.

धारा *dhârâ* (akin to *dhâv*,), f. **1.** A torrent, MBh. 6, 5785. **2.** A river, Hariv. 8325. **3.** A shower, Mṛichchh. 76, 15. **4.** A drop, Mṛichchh. 91, 4 ; Bhartṛ. 2, 89. **5.** A multitude, Râm. 6, 88, 3. **6.** pl. A horse's pace, as the trot, canter, etc., Çiç. 5, 60. **7.** The sharp edge of a sword or any cutting instrument, Râm. 2, 23, 35. **8.** The circumference of a wheel, Ragh. 13, 15.—**Comp.** *Kshura-dhâra*, 1. adj. as sharp as a razor, MBh. 4, 168. 2. (m. or n.) a sharp instrument, MBh. 4, 2063. *Kṛita-dhâra*, adj. sharpened, MBh. 7, 3090. *Khara-dhâra*, adj.

having a rough or jagged edge, Suçr. 1, 27, 15. *Tiryagdhâra*, i. e. *tiryañch-*, adj. having sharp sides, MBh. 7, 1875. *Tîkshṇa-dhâra*, 1. adj. having a sharp edge, MBh. 1, 786. 2. m. a sword, MBh. 12, 6263.

धारावन्त् *dhârâ + vant*, adj., f. *vatî*, Edged, Kâm. Nîtis. 11, 48.

धारिन् *dhârin*, i.e. *dhṛi+in*, adj., f. *iṇî*. **1.** Bearing, MBh. 13, 4350. **2.** Having, Ragh. 12, 41. **3.** Knowing, Kâthas. 13, 20. **4.** Maintaining, MBh. 1, 2596. **5.** Keeping. *nyâsa-*, A depositary, Man. 8, 196. **6.** Retaining (what one has read), Man. 12, 103. **7.** Observing, Râm. 3, 1, 35.—Comp. *Kanthâ-*, adj. wearing a patched cloth, Bhartṛ. 2, 79. *Jaṭâ-*, adj. wearing matted hair (see *jaṭâ*), Bhâg. P. 4, 2, 29. *Daṇḍa-*, adj. chastising, Bhâg. P. 6, 3, 5. *Mantra-*, adj. sbst. a counsellor, MBh. 5, 926. *Viçva-*, I. adj., f. *iṇî*, all-sustaining. II. m. a deity. III. f. *iṇî*, the earth.

धार्तराष्ट्र *dhârtarâshṭra*, i. e. *dhṛitarâshṭra + a*, I. adj. f. *rî*. **1.** Referring, belonging to Dhṛitarâshṭra, MBh. 8, 376. **II.** patronym. A son of Dhṛitarâshṭra, MBh. 1, 2726. **III.** m. A sort of goose with black legs and bill, Hariv. 8585.

धार्म *dhârma*, i.e. *dharma + a*, adj., f. *mî*, Belonging to the god of justice, MBh. 1, 2426.

धार्मिक *dhârmika*, i.e. *dharma + ika*, adj., f. *kî*, Just, performing all duties, virtuous, Man. 2, 109.—Comp. *A-*, adj. 1. unobservant of one's duties, Man. 4, 61. 2. where the duties are neglected, Man. 4, 60.

धार्मिकता *dhârmika + tâ*, f. Justice, Kâm. Nîtis. 4, 8.

धार्ष्ट *dhârshṭa*, i.e. *dhṛishṭa + a*, patronym. Descending from Dhṛishṭa, Bhâg. P. 9, 2, 17.

1. धाव् *DHÂV* (cf. *dhav*, *dhanv*), i. 1, Par., Âtm. **1.** To flow, Hariv. 14516. **2.** To run, Man. 8, 314. **3.** To run to (acc.), MBh. 3, 2543. **4.** To move, Râjat. 4, 425. Ptcple. of the pf. pass. *dhâvita*, Beginning to run, Kathâs. 3, 52. Caus. *dhâvaya*, **1.** To cause to run, to push on, Pañch. 223, 12.—With the prep. अनु *anu*, **1.** To stream through, Suçr. 1, 43, 8. **2.** To spread over, Râm. 2, 109, 13 Gorr. **3.** To run after, Râm. 2, 25, 8 Gorr. **4.** To pursue, Bhâg. P. 4, 11, 20. **5.** To come to one's assistance (acc.), MBh. 3, 2384.—With समनु *sam-anu*, To pursue, MBh. 8, 4086.—With अन्तर् *antar*, To run among, Bhâg. P. 3, 32, 37.—With अप *apa*, To deviate, to vary, Man. 8, 54.—With अभि *abhi*, **1.** To run to (acc.), Râm. 4, 41, 24. **2.** To come to assistance, Man. 9, 274.—With प्रत्यभि *prati-abhi*, To run to (acc.), Râm. 2, 82, 13 Gorr.—With समभि *sam-abhi*, To run to, MBh. 6, 3119. **2.** To fly against, Râm. 6, 34, 23.—With व्यव *vi-ava*, **1.** To run away, MBh. 12, 10599. **2.** To separate, Râm. 2, 105, 25.—With आ *â*, To run near, to rush upon, Bhâg. P. 8, 10, 39.—With उपा *upa-â*, To run to (acc.), Bhâg. P. 7, 13, 28.—With समा *sam-â*, To run near, Hariv. 14566.—With उप *upa*, **1.** To run near, Râm. 1, 28, 16. **2.** To run to, Bhâg. P. 5, 14, 6. **3.** To fly for refuge to (acc.), Bhâg. P. 4, 7, 38.—With समुप *sam-upa*, To run near, MBh. 3, 2097.—With निस् *nis*, To run out, Hariv. 11020.—With

परि *pari,* **1.** To flow about, Chr. 47, 40. **2.** To stream through, Suçr. 1, 91, 5. **3.** To run about, Pañch. 62, 23. **4.** To drive about, MBh. 4, 302. **5.** With *mṛigayâm,* To hunt, Râm. 5, 30, 8. **6.** To run round, Bhâg. P. 5, 22, 2. **7.** To run through, Râm. 6, 11, 38. **8.** To pursue, Pañch. 106, 7. Caus. To surround, MBh. 14, 828.—With विपरि *vi-pari,* **1.** To run to and fro, Râm. 5, 36, 38. **2.** To run through, Hariv. 4105. —With प्र *pra,* **1.** To flow away, Suçr. 1, 81, 9. **2.** To run away, MBh. 3, 2548. **3.** To run, Man. 4, 38. **4.** To run to, MBh. 4, 428. **5.** To spread, MBh. 1, 6400. *pradhâvita,* Run away, Râm. 6, 79, 37.—With अनुप्र *anu-pra,* To pursue, Daçak. in Chr. 179, 16.—With विप्र *vi-pra,* To run asunder, MBh. 8, 3036.—With संप्र *sam-pra,* **1.** To run away, MBh. 5, 5148. **2.** To run to, Bhâg. P. 8, 7, 15.—With प्रति *prati,* To assail, Râm. 6, 13, 26.—With वि *vi,* To run through, Râm. 5, 16, 14. —With परिवि *pari-vi,* To run through, Râm. 5, 29, 22.—With सम् *sam,* **1.** To run together, MBh. 3, 8879. **2.** To assail, Hariv. 5617. **3.** To run to, MBh. 12, 10070.—Cf. *dhav.*

2. धाव् *DHÂV,* i. 1, Par. Âtm. **1.** To cleanse, to wash, Çiç. 17, 8. **2.** To rub into one's person, Suçr. 2, 344, 14. Ptcple. of the pf. pass. *dhauta,* **1.** Cleansed, washed, MBh. 1, 3641; Daçak. in Chr. 188, 22. **2.** Polished, MBh. 9, 1079. **3.** Resplendent, Kathâs. 11, 31. **4.** Pure, Çâk. d. 152. **5.** Washed away, Çṛingârat. 7. **6.** n. Washing, Châṇ. 76, in Berl. Monatsb. Caus. To wash, Man. 4, 65.—With the prep. निस् *nis,* **1.** *nirdhauta,* Washed away, Çiç. 8, 51. **2.** Cleansed, Ragh. 5, 70. —With प्र *pra,* Caus. To wash, MBh. 3, 14024.—With वि *vi,* To wash away, Çiç. 8, 50. *vidhauta,* Cleansed, Çiç. 8, 70.—Cf. O.H.G. tau; A.S. deaw.

धावक *dhâv+aka,* adj. **1.** Running, Râm. 2, 32, 22 Gorr. **2.** Washing, Râm. 2, 38, 13, v.r.

धावन *dhâv+ana,* n. **1.** An attack, Râjat. 1, 114. **2.** Rubbing, Man. 4, 152. **3.** Washing, Râm. 1, 9, 57 Gorr. —Comp. *Danta-,* n. 1. cleansing the teeth, Pañch. 47, 23. 2. a small piece of wood for cleansing the teeth, Râm. 2, 91, 68. *Manaḥçilâ-chandana-,* n. a preparation made of red arsenic and sandal, Râm. 6, 96, 3 Gorr.

धावितृ *dhâvitṛi,* i.e. 1. *dhâv+tri,* m. A runner, MBh. 11, 760.

धाविन् 1. *dhâv+in,* adj. Running, Kathâs. 22, 105.

† धि *DHI,* i. 6, Par. To hold (akin to *dhâ*).

ऽधि *-dhi* (vb. *dhâ,* form of an old ptcple. *dhant,* cf. *ûdhan, payodhas* and *payodhi*), latter part of comp. nouns, The receptacle for keeping that which the preceding part denotes; cf. e.g. *ambu-dhi.*

धिक् *dhik,* an interjection: **1.** of dissatisfaction, Fie, Brâhmaṇ. 1, 35. **2.** of reproach, Shame, Pañch. 38, 12. With nom., voc., acc. (Draup. 9, 21), gen. (Râm. 6, 95, 40).

धिक्कार *dhik-kâra,* m. Contempt, Bhâg. P. 4, 14, 12.

† धिक्ष् *DHIKSH* (properly a desiderat. of *dah*), i. 1, Âtm. **1.** To kindle. **2.** To be weary. **3.** To live.

धिग्वण *dhigvaṇa* (probably a dialectical form of *dhik-varṇa*), m. The son of a Brâhmaṇa and an Âyogava-woman, MBh. 10, 15.

धिन्व् *DHINV* (properly *dhi*, ii. 5), ii. 5, *dhinu*, Par. 1. To satisfy (ved.). 2. To please, Prab. 55, 7.

धियावसु *dhiyâvasu*, i. e. *dhî + â -vasu*, adj. Granting wealth on account of devotion, Chr. 291, 15=Rigv. i. 64, 15.

† धिष् *DHISH*, ii. 3, Par. To emit sound.

धिषण *dhishaṇa*, I. n. An abode, a seat, Bhâg. P. 3, 16, 33. II. f. *ṇâ*, 1. Intellect, Bhâg. P. 1, 15, 47. 2. The name of one of the wives of the gods, MBh. 9, 2516. 3. A proper name, Bhâg. P. 6, 6, 20.

धिष्ठ्य *dhishṭhya*, n. A seat, an abode, Bhâg. P. 4, 2, 6 (probably to be changed to *dhishṇya*).

धिष्ठ्यप *dhishṭhya-pa*, m. A cherisher of the world, Bhâg. P. 7, 8, 27.

धिष्ण्य *dhishṇya* (i.e. probably *dhâ +sna+ya*), I. m. A fireplace, Bhâg. P. 8, 15, 9. II. n. 1. An abode, a seat, Bhâg. P. 8, 3, 27 ; MBh. 3, 17090. 2. A meteor, MBh. 5, 7272.

† धी *DHÎ*, i. 4, Âtm. (properly pass. of *dhâ*), To hold, to disregard, or to accomplish.

धी *dhî*, (vb. *dhyai*), f. 1. Knowledge, Bhâshâp. 45 ; Man. 6, 92. 2. Intellect, mind, Man. 12, 122. 3. Devotion, Chr. 293, 4=Rigv. i. 88, 4.—Comp. *Udâra-*, adj. high-minded, Chr. 44, 6. Cf. *Ku-*. *Para-droha-karman-*, adj. injuring another in deed or in thought, Man. 2, 161. *Sâdhu-*, I. adj. well-disposed. II. f. a wife's or husband's mother. *Su-*, m. 1. an intelligent, wise man. 2. a teacher. *Sthita-*, adj. calm.

धीमन्त् *dhî+mant*, adj., f. *mati*, Sensible, wise, Man. 1, 102.

धीर *dhîra*, i.e. I. *dhṛi+a*, adj. 1. Lasting, Châṭ. 7. 2. Firm, resolute, Hariv. 3755 ; Bhartṛ. 2, 72 ; Hit. i. d. 167 ; courageous, Kâthas. 18, 297. 3. Solemn, grave, Bhartṛ. 2, 26. 4. Deep (as a sound), Ragh. 16, 13. II. *dhî + ra*, adj. Sensible, wise, MBh. 5, 1076 ; Râm. 3, 19, 13 ; Chr. 290, 1=Rigv. i. 64, 1.

धीरता *dhîra+tâ*, f. (and धीरत्व *dhîra+tva*, n.), 1. Firmness, Ragh. 8, 43. 2. Courage, Pañch. 129, 22.—Comp. *A-*, f. pusillanimity, Prab. 15, 8.

धीवर *dhîvara*, 1. m. A fisherman, MBh. 2, 784. 2. f. *rî*, A fisherman's wife, Kathâs. 26, 149.

धु *DHU*, see *dhû*.

धुक्ष् *DHUKSH*, i. 1, Âtm. 1. To kindle. 2. To be weary. 3. To live. —With the prep. सम् *sam*, 1. To animate, MBh. 13, 3677. 2. To inflame, Daçak. in Chr. 197, 10. Caus. To kindle, to animate, MBh. 1, 5628.

धुनि *dhuni*, i.e. *dhvan+i*, I. adj. 1. Roaring, Chr. 290, 5=Rigv. i. 64, 5. 2. f. also धुनी *dhunî*, A river, Bhâg. P. 8, 21, 4.—Comp. *Dyu-dhuni*, f. a name of the Gaṅgâ, Bhâg. P. 3, 23, 39.

धुन्धु *dhundhu*, m. The name of an Asura or demon, Hariv. 672.

धुर् *dhur* (vb. *dhṛi*), f. (m., MBh. 13, 2876). 1. A yoke, Mṛichchh. 63, 10. 2. A burthen, a load, MBh. 1, 741 ; 5, 2799. 3. The fore-part of the pole where the yoke is fixed, MBh. 3,

13310. 4. Place of honour, the head, Ragh. 14, 74.

धुर *dhura*, i.e. *dhṛi + a*, I. m. A yoke, MBh. 7, 3675. II. m. and f. धुरा *dhurâ*, A burthen, MBh. 13, 4879; Pañch. 26, 3.—Comp. *Agrya-dhurâ*, f. the fore-part of the pole, Pañch. 8, 16.

धुरंधर *dhuraṁdhara*, i.e. *dhur + am-dhara*, I. adj. 1. Able to bear a burthen, MBh. 3, 12724. 2. Bearing patiently a burthen, MBh. 5, 1077. 3. Helping, Hit. i. d. 181. II. m. 1. A beast of burthen, Pañch. ed. orn. i. d. 17. 2. A chief, MBh. 13, 6275. 3. pl. The name of a people, MBh. 6, 349. 4. The name of a Râkshasa or demon, Râm. 6, 32, 15.

धुरीण *dhurîṇa*, i.e. *dhur + îna*, m. A chief, Pañch. 187, 13.

धुर्य *dhur + ya* (sometimes written धूर्य *dhûrya*), I. adj. 1. Able to bear a burthen, MBh. 13, 3518. 2. Being at the head, MBh. 4, 1074. 3. Best, MBh. 3, 13309. II. m. A beast of burthen, Man. 4, 67. III. n. The fore-part of the pole, Râm. 6, 92, 7.—Comp. *Kula -dhurya*, I. adj. able to bear the burthen of a family, Ragh. 7, 68. II. m. the chief of a family, MBh. 3, 11826.

धुर्व् *DHURV* (akin to *dhvṛi*), i. 1, *dhûrva*, Par. 1. To bend (ved.). 2. To hurt.

धू *DHÛ* and धु *DHU*, ii, 5, *dhûnu*, ii. 9, *dhunâ, ni*, Par. Âtm., and i. 6, *dhuva*, Par. 1. To shake, Megh. 63. 2. To shake out, to remove, Bhâg. P. 2, 8, 5. 3. To blow (as wind), MBh. 3, 2733. 4. To shake off, MBh. 5, 1588. 5. To struggle, to resist, Pañch. i. d. 42. Anomal. potent. *dhunet*, MBh. 13, 5006. Pass. with the terminations of the Par., Sâv. 4, 29. Ptcple. of the pf. pass. *dhûta* and *dhuta*, 1. Shaken, Râm. 3, 58, 37; 5, 16, 17. 2. Removed, Râm. 1, 31, 13; 1, 29, 11 Gorr. Frequent. *dodhû* and *dodhûya*, 1. To shake violently, MBh. 12, 8564. 2. To move violently to and fro, MBh. 12, 8563. 3. To be shaken violently, Bhâg. P. 8, 24, 36. Caus. *dhûnaya*, To shake, MBh. 3, 444.—With the prep. अव *ava*, 1. To shake off, to remove, MBh. 3, 2033. 2. To refuse, Vikr. d. 130. *avadhûta*, 1. Cast off, Bhâg. P. 3, 1, 19. 2. Removed, dispersed, Bhâg. P. 7, 8, 32. 3. Disregarded, Vikr. d. 46. 4. Sent back, Daçak. in Chr. 183, 21. 5. One who has shaken off every terrestrial bond, an ascetic, Râjat. 1, 112. 6. Shaken, Man. 5, 125. 7. Struck, Râm. 6, 82, 62. 8. n. Thrusting off, MBh. 4, 352. Comp. *Vîrya-*, adj. surpassed in prowess. Caus. To shake, Man. 3, 229.—With व्यव *vi -ava*, 1. To shake off, to remove, Hariv. 11076. 2. To abuse, MBh. 2, 2231. *vyavadhûta*, Indifferent in regard of life, MBh. 6, 150.—With आ *â*, To shake, Ragh. 16, 36. *âdhûta*, 1. Shaken, Râm. 2, 104, 9 Gorr. 2. Troubled, Râm. 1, 65, 3.—With व्या *vi-â*, To move to and fro, Çâk. d. 22.—With समा *sam-â*, To shake, Râm. 1, 33, 18 Gorr.— With उद् *ud*, 1. To rouse, Râm. 1, 28, 14. 2. To shake, Râm. 2, 95, 8. 3. To blow, Ragh. 7, 45. 4. To raise, Râm. 6, 92, 60. 5. To shake off, Bhâg. P. 8, 10, 38. 6. To dash out, Hariv. 4315. *uddhûta* and *uddhuta*, Loud, Hariv. 4718; 9608. Comp. *Pâda -uddhûta*, n. Kicking with the foot, MBh. 4, 353.—With समुद् *sam-ud*, 1. To rouse, MBh. 1, 1336. 2. To shake, MBh. 1, 3846.—With नि *ni*,

To move to and fro, Hariv. 14650. (probably to be changed into *vi-*).—With निस् *nis*, To shake off, Râm. 2, 95, 10. **2.** To remove, Bhag. 5, 17. **3.** To disown, Yâjń. 2, 71. **4.** To shake, Hariv. 6238. **5.** To torment, Râm. 5, 2, 26. *nirdhûta*, Deprived, Hariv. 3531.—With विनिस् *vi-nis*, **1.** To shake off, Bhâg. P. 6, 5, 4. **2.** To expel, Râm. 6, 16, 89. **3.** To move to and fro, Râm. 2, 20, 4 Gorr.—With प्रविनिस् *pra-vi-nis*, To fling to, MBh. 12, 13417.—With परि *pari*, To shake to and fro, Bhâg. P. 3, 13, 33.—With प्र *pra*, To blow away=to destroy, MBh. 13, 1800.—With वि *vi*, **1.** To move to and fro, to shake, Râm. 2, 23, 4; MBh. 1, 7035. **2.** To blow, MBh. 2, 1132. **3.** To excite, Sâv. 4, 29 (anomal. ptcple. of the pres. pass. *vidhûyant*). **4.** To remove, Râm. 3, 30, 18. **5.** To disperse, Râm. 1, 54, 6. **6.** To drive away, Kathâs. 4, 108. **7.** To shake off, Man. 6, 85. Caus. To press hard, MBh. 12, 4301. —With प्रवि *pra-vi*, To drive away, Hariv. 10492.—Cf. *θύω, θυίω, θύνω, θυνάω, θύελλα, θυεία, θυΐα, θύσσω, αἰθύσσω, θυάω*; Lat. suffire, fimus; Iceland. dyja; perhaps Goth. dauns.

धूति *dhû+ti*, m. One who shakes, Chr. 290, 5=Rigv. i. 64, 5.

धूनन *dhûnana*, i.e. *dhû*, Caus., + *ana*, n. Shaking, Râjat. 6, 12.

धूप् *DHÛP*, i. 1, *dhûpâya*, and i. 10, *dhûpaya*, Par. **1.** To fumigate, Suçr. 1, 16, 9. **2.** To perfume, Râm. 1, 10, 30; Çiç. 4, 52. **3.** i. 10, Par. † To speak, or to shine.—With the prep. अव *ava*, To perfume, Râm. 2, 83, 16 Gorr.—With उप *upa*, To fumigate, Râm. 5, 14, 7. **2.** To fill with smoke, MBh, 1, 815.—With प्र *pra*, To perfume, MBh. 12, 1389.—Cf. *τύφω, θύψω, τῦφος, τυφεδανός*, etc.

धूप *dhûp+a*, m. **1.** Incense, Râm. 1, 5, 15. **2.** The aromatic vapour that proceeds from the burning of incense, Vikr. d. 43.—Comp. *Vṛika-*, and *Vṛiksha-*, m. 1. compounded perfume. 2. turpentine.

धूपक i.e. I. *dhûpa+ka*, A substitute for *dhûpa*, as latter part of comp. adj., e.g. *sa-dhûpaka*, Filled with incense, Râm. 1, 73, 20. **II.** *dhûp+aka*, m. A preparer of perfumes, Râm. 2, 83, 13.

धूपन *dhûp+ana*, n. **1.** Fumigation, Suçr. 1, 133, 12. **2.** Perfuming, MBh. 13, 4749. **3.** Perfume, incense, Man. 7, 219.—Comp. *Sûpa-*, n. assafœtida.

धूपिक *dhûpika*, i.e. *dhûpa+ika*, m. =*dhûpaka* II., Râm. 2, 90, 14 Gorr.

धूम *dhûma* (vb. *dhû*, or *dhmâ*), m. Smoke, Man. 4, 69.—Comp. *vi-*, adj. smokeless; loc. *°me*, at the time when there is no smoke in the kitchen, Man. 6, 56.—Cf. Lat. fumus; *θυμός* (originally breath), cf. *dhmâ*.

धूमक *dhûma+ka*, **I.** a substitute for *dhûma* as latter part of comp. adj., e.g. *sa-*, adj. Covered with smoke, Suçr. 2, 318, 7. **II.** f. *mikâ*, Smoke, Kathâs. 8, 28.

धूममय *dhûma+maya*, adj., f. *yî*, Consisting of vapours, MBh. 5, 4059.

धूमय *DHÛMAYA*, a denomin. derived from *dhûma* by *aya*, To cover with vapours, to eclipse, Râm. 5, 21, 9.—With the prep. प्र *pra*, *pradhûmita*, Covered with smoke, Ragh. 4, 2.

धूमवत्त्व *dhûmavattva*, i.e. *dhûma-*

vant + *tva*, n. Condition of having smoke, Bhâshâp. 75.

धूमवन्त् *dhûma* + *vant*, adj., f. *vati*, Smoking, Tarkasaṁgr. 29.

धूमाय *DHÛMÂYA*, a denomin. derived from *dhûma* by *ya*, Par., Atm. To smoke, MBh. 3, 1319. **2.** To be covered with smoke, Chr. 41, 21. Ptcple. of the pf. pass. *dhûmayita*, n. Smoking, MBh. 5, 4508. Caus. *dhûmâyaya*, To cause to be covered with smoke, MBh. 3, 1545.

धूम्र *dhûmra*, i.e. *dhûma* + *ra* (or rather an old *dhûman* + *a*, with *r* for *n*), **I.** adj., f. *râ*, **1.** Of a smoky colour. **2.** Black red, MBh. 1, 2033. **3.** Gray, Bhâg. P. 3, 14, 24. **4.** Obscured, Bhâg. P. 4, 29, 48. **II.** m. A proper name, Râm. 4, 33, 14. **III.** f. *râ*, A proper name, MBh. 1, 2583.

† धूर् *DHÛR*, i. 4, Âtm. **1.** To hurt. **2.** To move.

धूर्जटि *dhûrjati* (curtailed from *dhûrjaṭin*), and धूर्जटिन् *dhûrjaṭin*, i.e. *dhur-jaṭâ* + *in*, m. A name of Çiva, MBh. 7, 9621.

धूर्त *dhûrta* (properly ptcple. pf. pass. of *dhvṛi*), adj., f. *tâ*, Fraudulent, knavish, a rogue, Pañch, 33, 4. **2.** Gaming at dice, a gamester, Râm. 5, 13, 21.—Comp. *Aksha-*, m. A dice-player, Daçak. in Chr. 185, 17; 196, 5.

धूर्तक *dhûrta* + *ka*, m. **1.** A cheat, MBh. 5, 1519. **2.** The name of a Nâga or infernal serpent, MBh. 1, 2154.—Comp. *Mṛiga-*, m. A jackal.

धूर्तता *dhûrta* + *tâ*, f. Shrewdness, Bhartṛ. 2, 19.

धूलि *dhûli*, i.e. *dhû* + *li*, or perhaps *dhvaṁs* + *li*, f. Dust, Pañch. 215, 2.

† धूश् *DHÛÇ* (= *dhûsh*, q. cf.), i. 10, Par. To make splendid.

धूष् *DHÛSH* (perhaps a dialectical form of *dhṛish* for *hṛish*), i. 10, Par. To make splendid.—With the prep. उद् *ud*, *uddhûshita*, Having the hairs (of the body) standing on end (out of joy), embellished, Pañch. 190, 21.—With प्रोद् *pra-ud*, *proddhûshita*, Having the hairs standing on end (on account of chill), Pañch. 94, 4.

धूषरत्व *dhûsharatva*, read *dhûsaratva*, Lass. 72, 11.

† धूस् *DHÛS* (a dialectical form of *dhûsh*, q. cf.), i. 10, Par. To make splendid.

धूसर *dhûsara*, i.e. *dhvaṁs* + *ara*, **I.** adj., f. *râ*, Gray (like dust), Ragh. 5, 42. **II.** f. *râ*, A small shrub, Varâh. Bṛih. S. 76, 6.—**Comp.** *Krama-*, adj. having become by degrees gray (like dust), Ragh. 16, 17.

धूसरक *dhûsara* + *ka*, m. A proper name, Pañch. 214, 13.

धूसरत्व *dhûsara* + *tva*, n. Paleness, Lass. 72, 11 (see *dhûsharatva*).

धृ *DHṚI*, i. 1, Par., Âtm.; i. 6, *dhriya*, Âtm. (also Par., Hariv. 9693). **1.** To bear, to carry, Râm. 1, 38, 11 Gorr.; Man. 4, 66; with *garbham*, To be pregnant, MBh. 5, 7399; with *daṇḍam* and *damam*, To punish, Râm. 4, 17, 24; Bhâg. P. 1, 18, 41. **2.** To maintain, Râm. 2, 109, 46 Gorr.; with *âtmânam*, *jîvitam*, *prâṇân*, *çarîram*, *gâtram*, *deham*, To endure, or to continue to live, Râm. 6, 82, 119. **3.** To support, Man. 9, 311 (Âtm.). **4.** i. 4, and pass. To exist, Bhag. 7, 5; to live, Man. 3, 220; with the termination of the Par., MBh. 3, 11293. **5.** With *manas*, *matim*, *buddhim*, To direct one's attention to, MBh. 2, 541; to resolve, Hariv. 8261. **6.** With and without *tulayâ*, To weigh, MBh. 8, 10585; 1, 266. **7.** With *samaye*, To bring to an agreement, Pańch. 24, 25. **8.** With *antare*, To give as surety, to pledge, Pańch. 223, 24. **9.** To stop, MBh. 7, 619. **10.** To retain, Pańch. 55, 23. **11.** To resist, Pańch. ii. d. 150. **12.** To have, MBh. 2, 81. **13.** To keep, Hit. 68, 13. *dhṛita*, **1.** Carried, Çâk. d. 103. **2.** Worn, used, Man. 4, 66. **3.** Held, Lass. 7, 5. **4.** Weighed, Man. 8, 135 (*sama-dhṛita*, Of equal weight). **5.** Maintained, Bhâg. P. 3, 3, 17. **6.** Observed, Râm. 2, 18, 47 Gorr. **7.** Firm, MBh. 5, 7337. **8.** Kept, Pańch. 229, 6. **9.** Ready, MBh. 5, 1446; resolved, 2108. **10.** *dhṛitam*, adv. Slowly, solemnly, Pańch. 158, 2. **11.** n. A mode of fighting, Hariv. 15979. *dhṛitavant*, Resolved, Kathâs. 12, 49. Comp. ptcple. of the fut. pass. *çirodharaṇiya*, i.e. *çiras-*, adj. To be borne on the head, i.e. to be venerated, Lass. 67, 14. Caus. and i. 10, *dhâraya*, Par. Âtm. **1.** To bear, MBh. 13, 5007. **2.** With *daṇḍam*, To punish, Man. 11, 21. **3.** To hold, Râm. 1, 123, 14 Gorr. **4.** With *tulayâ*, To weigh, MBh. 3, 13293. **5.** To continue to live, Chr. 46, 21. **6.** To support, MBh. 14, 710. **7.** To keep, MBh. 3, 11980; to possess, Râm. 1, 26, 25; Man. 5, 96. **8.** To practise, Yâjń. 3, 201. **9.** With *âtmânam*, *manas*, To direct one's attention to, Yâjń. 3, 201. **10.** With and without *manasâ*, To keep in remembrance, MBh. 13, 4455; Bhâg. P. 4, 8, 75. **11.** With *çirasâ*, *mûrdhni*, To honour, Mṛichchh. 19, 3. **12.** To hold in, Çâk. 8, 11. **13.** To endure, Râm. 3, 35, 39. **14.** To contain, Hariv. 6567. **15.** To recover, Râm. 1, 48, 33. **16.** To assign to, Hariv. 2091. **17.** To owe to, MBh. 12, 7286. Anomal. potent. *dhârayita*, MBh. 13, 5007; anomal. ptcple. of the pres. Âtm. *dhârayâṇa*, 6, 4600. Ptcple. of the pf. pass. *dhârita*, **1.** Borne, MBh. 3, 11169. **2.** Maintained, Vikr. d. 38. Comp. ptcple. of the fut. pass. *a-dhârya*, **1.** Not to be borne, Râm. 4, 16, 31; Man. 3, 79. **2.** Not to be stemmed, MBh. 13, 2161. *dus-*, **1.** Difficult to be supported, MBh. 3, 9941. **2.** Difficult to be kept in remembrance, 13, 4483.—With the prep. अभि *abhi*, Caus. To endure, MBh. 6, 5063. With *prâṇân*, To continue to live, MBh. 3, 16221.—With अव *ava*, *avadhṛita*, Perceived, MBh. 13, 3544. Caus. **1.** To know exactly, Râjat. 3, 179. **2.** To consider, MBh. 14, 1977. **3.** To perceive, MBh. 3, 11210. **4.** (Caus. of the Caus.), To communicate, Kathâs. 14, 7. *avadhârya*, What ought to be considered, Bhartṛ. 2, 97. *an-avadhâraṇiya*, Not to be known exactly, Ragh. 13, 5.—With आ *â*, Caus. To keep, Râm. 4, 20, 16; to keep in remembrance, Kathâs. 2, 37.—With उद् *ud*, To draw out, Râm. 4, 22, 21.—With उप *upa*, **1.** To support, MBh. 4, 1765. **2.** To consider, MBh. 1, 7805. **3.** To perceive, Bhâg. P. 1, 8, 11.—With नि *ni*, Caus. To keep, Bhâg. P. 3, 2, 22.—With निस् *nis*, To verify, Çiç. 9, 20.—With परि *pari*, Caus. To bear, MBh. 3, 10907.—With प्र *pra*, To direct to; with *manas*, To resolve, MBh. 8, 4336. Caus. **1.** To inflict a punishment, MBh. 12, 9569. **2.** To keep in remembrance, 5, 4120. **3.** To reflect, 1, 3581.—With संप्र *sam-pra*, Caus. **1.** To deliver, MBh. 3, 11741. **2.** To direct; with *buddhim*, To resolve, 3, 8772. **3.** To consider, to reflect, Pańch. 8, 14.—With वि *vi*, To bear, Bhâg. P. 2, 7, 13. *vidhṛita*, **1.** Separated, MBh. 13, 7070. **2.** Spread, Chaurap. 16. **3.** Far from,

Hariv. 4253. **4.** Retained, stopped, Amar. 85. **5.** Borne, MBh. 14, 1654; with *çirasâ*, Borne on the head, and Honoured, Pańch. i. d. 94. **6.** Maintained, Bhartṛ. 3, 58. Comp. *A-vidhṛita*, unrestrained, MBh. 1, 243. Caus. **1.** To dispose, MBh. 1, 5549. **2.** To act, 12, 3809. **3.** To withhold, Râm. 2, 13, 3. **4.** To stop, MBh. 3, 676. **5.** To have, 9, 2476. **6.** To direct, with *manas*, Bhâg. P. 1, 9, 30. **7.** To protect, 7, 5, 7.—With सम् *sam*, To observe, Râm. 4, 29, 34. Caus. **1.** To hold, Pańch. i. d. 93. **2.** To bear, Râm. 2, 62, 15 Gorr. **3.** To possess, MBh. 1, 6383. **4.** To observe, Bhâg. P. 2, 1, 21. **5.** To direct, with *manas*, 2, 1, 38. **6.** To keep in remembrance, Pańch. v. d. 78. **7.** To restrain, Râm. 2, 21, 47; MBh. 6, 3397. **8.** To endure, Râm. 2, 63, 88; to sustain, Man. 3, 79. **9.** To exist, Mârk. P. 8, 52.—Cf. θράομαι, θρᾶνος, θρῆνυς, θέλω, ἐθέλω, θρόνος; Lat. firmus, fre + tus (partly based on *dhrâ* for *dhṛi*; cf. e.g. *pṛi* and *prâ*); probably A.S. dragan, dreogan; O.H.G. tragan.

ऽधृक् *-dhṛik*, latter part of comp. words, and only in the nom. sing. (probably a form of *dhṛi* + *t*), **1.** Bearing, Râm. 1, 6, 9. **2.** Sustaining, MBh. 12, 10432. **3.** Old, 3, 12597.—Comp. *Daṇḍa-*, adj. ruling, Bhâg. P. 4, 21, 12. *Deha-*, m. Air, wind, Suçr. 1, 250, 9.

† धृज् *DHṚIJ*, and धृञ्ज् *DHṚIŃJ*, i. 1, Par. To go.—Cf. *dhraj*.

ऽधृत् *-dhṛi* + *t*, latter part of comp. words, Bearing, Hariv. 6766.

धृतराष्ट्र *dhṛita-râshṭra*, m. **1.** The father of Duryodhana and uncle of the Pâṇḍu princes, MBh. 1, 95. **2.** A frequent proper name.

धृति *dhṛi* + *ti*, I. f. **1.** Holding, MBh. 7, 4540 (*dhṛitim̃ kṛi*, To keep ground). **2.** Steadiness, Nal. 6, 10. **3.** Content, Man. 10, 116. **4.** Satisfaction, Kir. 5, 35. **5.** personified, MBh. 1, 2794. II. m. **1.** The name of a deity, MBh. 13, 4355. **2.** A proper name.—Comp. *A-*, f. 1. uneasiness. 2. discontent, Man. 12, 33. *Kshmâ-*, m. a king and a mountain, Râjat. 5, 476. *Çata-*, m. 1. Indra. 2. Brahman.

धृतिमन्त् *dhṛiti* + *mant*, I. adj., f. *matî*. **1.** Firm, Man. 7, 210. **2.** Content, MBh. 13, 3054. II. m. **1.** A name of Agni, 3, 14188. **2.** A proper name. III. f. *matî*, The name of a river, 6, 339. IV. n. The name of a division of the world, 6, 454.

धृतिमय *dhṛiti* + *maya*, adj., f. *yî*, Consisting of content, MBh. 3, 13372.

धृष् *DHṚISH*, i. 1; ii. 5, Par. **1.** To be courageous, Bhaṭṭ. 17, 81. **2.** To dare, MBh. 1, 3573. **3.** pass. To be subdued, Pańch. 265, 8. Ptcple. of the pf. pass. *dhṛishṭa*. **1.** Bold, MBh. 5, 1831. **2.** Impudent, Bhartṛ. 2, 48; Daçak. in Chr. 198, 2. **3.** n. The name of a spell, Râm. 1, 30, 4. **4.** m. A proper name. Comp. *A-dhṛishṭa*, timid, Pańch. iii. d. 163. Ptcple. of the fut. pass. *dhṛishya*, To be attacked, MBh. 12, 8176. Comp. *A-dhṛishya*, 1. unassailable, MBh. 1, 5054. 2. unconquerable, Râm. 5, 42, 4. Caus. and i. 10. **1.** To lay hands on, to offend, MBh. 1, 2346. **2.** To hurt, Hariv. 3153. **3.** To violate, MBh. 5, 373. **4.** To overcome, 3, 2149. † **5.** To rain, v.r. *a-dharshita*, adj. Unassailable, Râm. 4, 15, 3. *dharshaṇîya*, To be conquered easily, MBh. 5, 1472. *a-*, adj. Unconquerable, Hariv. 4368.—With the prep. अभि *abhi*, Caus. To overpower, MBh. 14, 47.—With आ *â*, Comp. ptcple. of the fut. pass. *an-âdhṛishya*, Unassailable, Chr. 27, 11. Caus. **1.** To aggrieve, Yâjń. 2, 5. **2.** To provoke,

Hariv. 10295.—With उद् *ud*, Caus. To animate, MBh. 5, 2357.—With परि *pari*, To pounce upon, MBh. 14, 1684. —With प्र *pra*, **1.** To lay hands on, Râm. 3, 62, 18. **2.** To overcome, 5, 58, 15; to lay waste, 5, 63, 5. Comp. ptcple. of the fut. pass. *a-pradhṛishya*, adj. Unconquerable, Pańch. 161, 14. *dush-pradhṛishya*, i.e. *dus-*, adj. **1.** Unapproachable, MBh. 6, 612. **2.** Difficult to be overpowered, Râm. 6, 36, 24. Caus. **1.** To assail, Râm. 3, 14, 12. **2.** To violate, MBh. 13, 2291. **3.** To overcome, 13, 2890.—With संप्र *sam-pra*, Caus. To hurt, MBh. 12, 4998.—With वि *vi*, Caus. **1.** To violate, Hariv. 4616. **2.** To trouble, MBh. 12, 10541.—With सम् *sam*, Caus. To violate, Hariv. 9937. —Cf. *θάρσος*, *θράσος*, etc., *φάρυμος*, *φαρυνός*; Lat. fortis; Goth. ga-dars; O.H.G. gaturst; A.S. dear, thu dearst, thu dors + test, dyrstig, thrist, bold, etc.; to dare.

धृष्टत्व *dhṛishṭa* + *tva*, n. Impudence, Pańch. 27, 6.

धृष्णु *dhṛishṇu*, i.e. *dhṛish* + *nu*, I. adj. Courageous, bold, Chr. 294, 1 = Rigv. i. 92, 1; MBh. 14, 2098. II. m. A proper name, MBh. 1, 3140.

धृष्णुत्व *dhṛishṇu* + *tva*, n. Boldness, MBh. 1, 6406.

† **धॄ** *DHṚÎ*, ii. 9, *dhṛiṇâ*, Par. To grow old, v.r. (?).

धे *DHE*, i. 1, Par. **1.** To suck, to drink, MBh. 7, 2276; Man. 4, 59. **2.** To suck in, to absorb, Prab. 40, 5.

धेनु *dhe* + *nu*, f. **1.** A milch cow, one that has lately calved, Man. 11, 137. **2.** The earth, MBh. 13, 3165. **3.** Gift, MBh. 3, 12727; in this signification the word is used especially as latter part of comp. words, e.g. *tila-*, MBh. 13, 3286; *ghṛita-*, 3523, etc., which imply that sesame, ghee, etc., are given instead of a milch cow, a milch cow being the usual present given to a Brâhmaṇa.—**Comp.** *Asi-*, f. a knife; Daçak. in Chr. 198, 12. *Kâma-*, f. a cow that yields every wish, Kathâs. 17, 134. *Kshiti-*, f. the cow-like earth, Bhartṛ. 2, 38.

धेनुक *dhenu* + *ka*, I. m. The name of a demon, MBh. 5, 4410. II. f. *kâ*. **1.** A milch cow, 3, 13035. **2.** A present (cf. *dhenu* **3**), 3, 8065.

धैर्य *dhairya*, i.e. *dhîra* + *ya*, n. **1.** Gravity, Hariv. 8408. **2.** Firmness, constancy, MBh. 3, 17381; Râm. 2, 63, 47. **3.** Courage, Pańch. 21, 8.—**Comp.** *A-*, n. perturbation of mind, Man. 12, 32.

धैर्यवन्त् *dhairya* + *vant*, adj., f. *vatî*, Endowed with constancy, Râm. 4, 2, 6.

† **धोर्** *DHOR*, i. 1, Par. To be quick, to have a good pace.

धौन्धुमार *dhaundhumâra*, i. e. *dhundhu-mâra* + *a*, adj. Referring to Dhundhumâra, MBh. 1, 468.

ध्मा *DHMÂ*, i. 1, *dhama*, Par. **1.** To blow (as breath, wind), MBh. 14, 1732; Suçr. 1, 332, 11. **2.** To produce sound by blowing, MBh. 2, 1925. **3.** To excite fire by blowing, 2, 2483. **4.** To melt, Man. 6, 71. **5.** To throw, MBh. 5, 7209. Anomal. fut. *dhamishyanti*, Râm. 3, 62, 7. Pass. **1.** *dhmâya*, in epic poetry also with the terminations of the Par., MBh. 2, 1756. **2.** In epic poetry also *dhamya*, 3, 16825; also with the terminations of the Par. 14, 1738. Caus. *dhmâpaya*. Ptcple. of the pf. pass. *dhmâpita*, Turned to ashes, Suçr. 1, 46, 16.—With the prep. अप *apa*, To blow away, Râm. 1, 42, 26

Gorr.—With आ *â*, 1. To blow a wind instrument, Hariv. 15853. 2. To blow up; pass. To be filled with air, to swell, MBh. 12, 3555; Suçr. 1, 62, 1; also Par. 290, 10. Caus. To blow up, to cause to swell, Suçr. 1, 374, 5.—With अत्या *ati-â*, To gasp violently for breath, Suçr. 1, 38, 12.—With उपा *upa-â*, To blow a wind instrument, MBh. 7, 3096. —With समा *sam-â*, 1. To blow a wind instrument, MBh. 2, 1925. 2. To sound, Hariv. 15854.—With उप *upa*, To excite fire by blowing, Man. 4, 53. —With निस् *nis*, To blow out of something, Suçr. 1, 100, 5.—With प्र *pra*, 1. To blow away, i.e. to destroy, MBh. 2, 1028. 2. To blow into something, MBh. 14, 78. 3. To blow a wind instrument, MBh. 3, 789. Caus. To blow a wind instrument, MBh. 3, 633.—With वि *vi*, 1. To blow asunder, i.e. to disperse, MBh. 1, 5462; i.e. to destroy, Râm. 2, 80, 8.—Cf. θυμός, perhaps σμώνη, σμῶδιξ; O.H.G. tunst, perhaps A.S. dust.

† ध्माङ्क्ष् *DHMÂṄKSH*, i. 1, Par. 1. To crow. 2. To desire. — Cf. *dhrâṅksh*.

ध्यातृ *dhyâtṛi*, i.e. *dhyai* + *tṛi*, m. One who reflects, who meditates, Bhâg. P. 3, 28, 22.

ध्यान *dhyâna*, i.e. *dhyai*+*ana*, n. 1. Religious, pious meditation, Bhâg. P. 3, 12, 13; Bhag. 12, 12; Vedântas. in Chr. 217, 15. 2. Intuition, Râm. 1, 9, 64.

ध्यानवन्त् *dhyâna* + *vant*, adj., f. *vati*, Applying one's self to religious meditation, MBh. 12, 7170.

ध्यानिक *dhyânika*, i.e. *dhyâna*+*ika*, adj. Proceeding from pious meditation, Man. 6, 82.

ध्यानिन् *dhyânin*, i.e. *dhyâna*+*in*, adj., f. *nî*=*dhyânavant*, MBh. 13, 1016.

ध्याम *dhyâma*, n. A fragrant grass, Suçr. 1, 103, 16.

ध्यै *DHYAI* (probably akin to *adhi -YÂ*, but cf. also *didhî*, *didî*), i. 1, *dhyâya* (in epic poetry also *dhyâ*, ii. 2, e.g. *dhyâhi*, MBh. 3, 13210), Par. (in epic poetry also Âtm., MBh. 13, 1994). 1. To contemplate, MBh. 2, 2563. 2. To think of, 5, 47; to meditate on, 3, 224. Ptcple. of the pf. pass. *dhyâta*, Thought of, Bhartṛ. 3, 46.—With the prep. अनु *anu*, To meditate on, MBh. 1, 3464. 2. To think of, 12, 9666 (with gen.). 3. To reflect, Râm. 1, 2, 20 (*anudhyâtvâ*, instead of °*dhyâya*). *anudhyâta*, 1. Thought of, MBh. 7, 2180. 2. Absorbed in meditation, 12, 4678.—With समनु *sam-anu-*, 1. To think of, MBh. 13, 968. 2. To think, 12, 6644.—With अप *apa*, To disregard, MBh. 7, 2076. 2. To hurt, 3, 13656. — With समप *sam-apa*, To hurt, MBh. 3, 13655 (Âtm.).—With अभि *abhi*, 1. To desire, Yâjń. 3, 134. 2. To think of, Bhâg. P. 4, 8, 44. 3. To meditate, to be absorbed in meditation, Man. 1, 8. 4. To curse (?), MBh. 13, 2144 (*abhidhyâsus*, 4. Aor. without augment in the sense of an imperat., cf. 2143).—With समभि *sam-abhi*, To reflect, MBh. 5, 2217. 2. To desire, Suçr. 1, 323, 15. —With अव *ava*, To disregard, Bhâg. P. 5, 4, 9.—With आ *â*, 1. To wish that something may happen to another (gen.), MBh. 13, 4900. 2. To be absorbed in meditation, Bhâg. P. 9, 14, 43.—With समा *sam-â*, To meditate on, Hariv. 14823.—With उप *upa*, To think of, MBh. 1, 3847; (Hariv. 7453, read *apadhyâto*).—With नि *ni*, To be absorbed in meditation, Bhâg. P. 3, 15, 44. — With अभिनि *abhi-ni*, To attend to (acc.), Râm. 1, 28, 7.—With प्रणि *pra-ni*, To direct one's attention to (acc.), Bhâg. P. 1, 7, 8.—With निस् *nis*, **1.** To muse over (acc.), Râjat. 1, 279. **2.** To reflect, Râm. 6, 31, 2. — With परि *pari*, To muse, Râm. 2, 37, 13 Gorr. (*parî* on account of the metre).—With प्र *pra*, **1.** To reflect, MBh. 1, 7013. **2.** To think of (acc. and *prati*), Hariv. 10381. **3.** To devise, MBh. 5, 3882.—With संप्र *sam-pra*, To reflect, MBh. 3, 1411.—With प्रति *prati*, To devise, MBh. 5, 3880. —With सम् *sam*, To reflect, MBh. 2, 8. —Cf. θεάω.

ध्र *-dhra* for *dhara*, f. *dhrî*, latter part of comp. words, e.g. *mahî-dhra*, m. A mountain, Bhartṛ. 2, 10.

ध्रज् *DHRAJ*, and † ध्रञ्ज् *DHRAŃJ*, i. 1, Par. To glide (as wind, birds, etc.), ved.

† ध्रण् *DHRAṆ*, i. 1, Par. To sound.—Cf. *dhvan*; Goth. drunjus; θρῆνος, τενθρηδών (Frequent.), ἀνθρηδών; A.S. dran, a drone.

† ध्रस् *DHRAS*, ii. 9, and i. 10. Par. **1.** To glean. **2.** To cast upward. —Cf. *udhras*.

† ध्राख् *DHRÂKH*, i. 1, Par.= *drâkh*.

† ध्राघ् *DHRÂGH*, i. 1, Âtm.= *drâgh*.

† ध्राङ्क्ष् *DHRÂŃKSH*, i. 1, Par. **1.** To crow. **2.** To desire. — Cf. *dhmâńksh*, *dhvâńksh*.

† ध्राड् *DHRÂḌ*, i. 1, Âtm. To divide, to split.—Cf. *drâḍ*.

† ध्रिज् *DHRIJ*, i. 1, Par. To move.—Cf. *dhraj*.

ध्रु *DHRU*, i. 1 and 6, Par. **1.** To stand firm. **2.** To go. **3.** To know.

† ध्रुव् *DHRUV*, i. 6, Par. **1.** To stand firm. **2.** To go.

ध्रुव *dhruva* (akin to *dhṛi*), **I.** adj., f. *vâ*. **1.** Firm, stable, MBh. 1, 808; Râm. 1, 60, 17. **2.** Permanent, Nal. 6, 11. **3.** Fixed (as a day), MBh. 14, 1888. **4.** Certain, Man. 7, 169. **II.** m. The polar star, MBh. 8, 2105; personified as son of Uttânapâda and grandson of Manu, 13, 195. **2.** A name of Vishṇu, 12, 1510. **3.** The name of a Vasu, 1, 2528, and others. **III.** n. Permanence, Hariv. 3959. **IV.** adv. °*vam*, Certainly, Man. 12, 16.—**Comp.** *A-*, adj. 1. perishable, Râm. 3, 61, 34. 2. uncertain, 5, 37, 11.—Cf. O.H.G. ga-triuwi; Goth. triggvs; A.S. treowe, for-truwian; perhaps Lat. durus.

ध्रुवच्युत् *dhruva-chyu + t*, adj. Felling what is firm, Chr. 290, 11=Rigv. i. 64, 11.

† ध्रेक् *DHREK*, i. 1, Âtm.=*drek*.

† ध्रै *DHRAI*, i. 1, Par. To be satisfied.—Cf. perhaps τρέφω, θρέψις, τρόφις, ταρφύς (=Caus. *dhrâpaya*).

ध्वंस् *DHVAṀS*, base of the pass. and some other forms, *dhvas*, i. 1, Âtm. (also Par., MBh. 1, 3596). **1.** To fall to pieces, to perish, Bhaṭṭ. 14, 55. **2.** To go away, MBh. 3, 12525. Ptcple. of the pf. pass. *dhvasta*, **1.** Fallen, Râm. 3, 58, 38. **2.** Lost, 1, 58, 10. **3.** Hurt, 6, 20, 22. **4.** Disappeared, 5, 21, 12. **5.** Covered, MBh. 10, 662. Caus. *dhvaṁ-*

saya, **1.** To fell, Râm. 5, 63, 23. **2.** To destroy, Daçak. in Chr. 188, 18. **3.** To interrupt, Râm. 2, 60, 15.—With the prep. अप *apa,* **1.** To go away, Hariv. 720. **2.** To cause to go away, MBh. 1, 5596. *apadhvasta,* Reviled, miserable, Mṛichchh. 124, 3 (crazed, Wils.).—With अभि *abhi,* To attack, MBh. 5, 3230.—With उद् *ud,* Caus. To cover, MBh. 13, 4817.—With समुद् *sam-ud,* To cover, Râm. 2, 42, 10.—With उप *upa,* pass. To be attacked, Suçr. 1, 21, 14.—With विनि *vi-ni, vinidhvasta,* Destroyed, Râm. 2, 125, 13 Gorr.—With परि *pari, paridhvasta,* **1.** Destroyed, Râm. 2, 33, 18. **2.** Covered, 2, 41, 11 Gorr. — With प्र *pra, pradhvasta,* Perished, Bhartṛ. 3, 26. Caus. **1.** To cause to fall, MBh. 7, 1387. **2.** To destroy, 1529.—With प्रति *prati, pratidhvasta,* **1.** Afflicted, MBh. 12, 3606. **2.** Left (?), 3717.—With वि *vi,* To crumble down, MBh. 12, 7978. **2.** To disperse, 5, 5877. *vidhvasta,* **1.** Fallen, 3, 2668. **2.** Fallen to pieces, Râm. 2, 114, 6. **3.** Destroyed, MBh. 1, 7675. **4.** Whirled up, Râm. 6, 19, 12. Caus. **1.** To break to pieces, MBh. 1, 8282. **2.** To crush, 3, 16501. **3.** To destroy, Râm. 5, 26, 37. **4.** To hurt, 3, 53, 51. —With प्रवि *pra-vi, pravidhvasta,* **1.** Thrown away, Râm. 6, 22, 26. **2.** Struck, Hariv. 10627.—Cf. perhaps Lat. vastus, vastare; O.H.G. wôsti; A.S. weste; Goth. driusan; A.S. dreosan, dysi, dyselic, dysig, dysian.

ध्वंस *dhvaṁs + a,* m. **1.** Destruction, Prab. 82, 14. **2.** Loss, Pañch. i. d. 117.

ध्वंसन *dhvaṁs + ana,* I. adj. Destroying, MBh. 5, 5316. II. n. Destruction, Râm. 6, 38, 21.

ध्वंसिन् *dhvaṁs + in,* adj., f. *nî.* **1.** Perishing, Bhartṛ. 3, 35. **2.** Destroying, Hariv. 4627.

† ध्वज् *DHVAJ,* i. 1, Par. To go. —Cf. perhaps Lat. vagus, vagari.

ध्वज *dhvaja,* m. and n. **1.** A flag or banner, Râm. 2, 67, 26. **2.** A mark, a symbol, MBh. 1, 1511. **3.** A distiller's flag, Man. 4, 85. **4.** The penis, Suçr. 2, 114, 9.—**Comp.** *Ud-patâka-dhvaja,* adj. with raised flags and banners, Râjat. 5, 465. *Kapi-,* m. a name of Arjuna, Bhag. 1, 20. *Kuça-,* m. a proper name, Râm. 1, 71, 13. *Garuḍa-,* m. a name of Vishṇu, MBh. 2, 30. *Go-vṛisha-,* m. a name of Çiva, Arj. 3, 44. *Jvâlâ-,* m. fire, Râjat. 4, 41. *Tâla-,* m. 1. a name of Balarâma, MBh. 9, 2139. 2. the name of a mountain, Çatr. 1, 50. *Timi-,* epithet of the demon Çambara, Râm. 2, 8, 12 Gorr. *Dharma-,* 1. adj. one who displays the flag of virtue, a hypocrite, Bhâg. P. 3, 32, 39. 2. m. a proper name, 9, 13, 19. *Pâra-,* m. pl. standards come from an opposite shore (i.e. from Ceylon), Râjat. 3, 78. *Makara-,* m. the god of love. *Mahisha-,* m. Yama. *Vṛishabha-,* m. a name of Çiva, Chr. 48, 11. *Sîra-,* m. Janaka, Mahâv. 5, 9. *Surâ-,* n. a tavern flag. *Smara-,* I. m. 1. any musical instrument. 2. a fabulous fish, the makara. 3. the penis. II. f. *jâ,* bright moonlight. III. n. the vulva.

ध्वजवन्त् *dhvaja + vant,* I. adj. **1.** Adorned with flags, Râm. 1, 5, 17. **2.** Branded, Yâjñ. 3, 243. II. m. **1.** An ensign, MBh. 9, 3302. **2.** A distiller or seller of spirits, Râm. 4, 84.

ध्वजिक *dhvajika,* i.e. *dhvajin + ka,* adj. One who displays the flag of virtue, a hypocrite, Man. 13, 7594.

ध्वजिन् *dhvajin*, i.e. *dhvaja + in*, I. adj., f. *nî*, Furnished with, or bearing, a flag, Râm. 3, 28, 32; Man. 11, 92. II. m. 1. An ensign, MBh. 1, 7765. 2. A distiller or seller of spirits, Yâjń. 1, 141.—Comp. *Dharma-*, i. e. *dharma -dhvaja + in*, m. one who displays the flag of virtue, a hypocrite, Man. 4, 195.

† ध्वञ्ज् *DHVAŃJ*, i. 1, Par. = *dhvaj*.

† ध्वण् *DHVAṆ*, i. 1, Par. To sound.

1. ध्वन् *DHVAN*, Par. To cover one's self. Ptcple. of the pf. pass. *dhvânta*, n. Darkness, Râm. 2, 21, 53.

2. ध्वन् *DHVAN*, i. 1, Par. 1. To produce a sound, to roar, Ṛit. 1, 25. 2. To buzz, Râjat. 5, 315. Ptcple. of the pf. pass. *dhvanita*, n. 1. Sound, Megh. 43. 2. Thunder, Kir. 5, 12. Caus. and i. 10, *dhvânaya*, To cause to sound, to strike, Çatr. 14, 223.—With अभि *abhi*, To sound, to hiss, Çiç. 20, 13.—With प्र *pra*, To resound, 17, 31.—Cf. A.S. dynan, dyne.

ध्वनि *dhvan + i*, m. 1. Sound, Man. 4, 123. 2. Figurative style, Sâh. D. 5, 9.—Comp. *Siṁha-*, m. 1. the roar of a lion. 2. war-cry.

ध्वसन्ति *dhvasanti*, m. A proper name, Chr. 298, 23 = Rigv. i. 112, 23.

ध्वस्ति *dhvasti*, i.e. *dhvaṁs + ti*, f. One of the four states of a Yogin, that in which all the consequences of actions cease, Mârk. P. 39, 22.

† ध्वाङ्क्ष् *DHVÂŃKSH*, i. 1, Par. = *dhrâńksh*.

ध्वाङ्क्ष *dhvâńksha*, m. A crow, Brâhmaṇ. 2, 17.

ध्वान *dhvâna*, i. e. *dhvan + a*, m. Murmuring, sound, Prab. 73, 9.

ध्वान्त *dhvânta*, see 1. *dhvan*.

ध्वृ *DHVṚI*, i. 1. Par. To bend, to fell; cf. *hvṛi*. — Cf. probably A.S. thwer; O.H.G. dweran, gadwor, twarôn, dwerh; A.S. thweorh, thwir, thwur; Goth. dvals; A.S. dwelian, dol, dweorg, for-dwilman; θόλος, θάλαμος.

† ध्रण् *dhvraṇ*, i. 1, Par. = *dhraṇ*, v.r.

न *N*.

न *na*, a particle, 1. Not, MBh. 3, 362. 2. When repeated in the same sentence it implies a very strong affirmation, Absolutely, Arj. 10, 17. 3. Lest (with a potential), Râm. 2, 63, 41. 4. Often in the beginning of comp. words, e.g. *nâtidûra*, i.e. *na-ati-dûra*, adj. Not very distant, Hiḍ. 1, 51. 5. ved. Like, just as, Chr. 294, 5; 4 = Rigv. i. 92, 5; 4.—Cf. Goth. ne, nei; A.S. ná; O.H.G. ni; Lat. ne in nonne; νη-.

नंश् *naṁç*, see *naç*.

नकिंचन *nakiṁchana*, i. e. *na-kim -cha-na*, adj. Beggarly, MBh. 5, 4522.

नकिस् *na-ki + s* (the latter part is an old nom. sing. msc. of *ki*, cf. *kim* and Lat. quis), a particle, Not, never, Chr. 287, 6 = Rigv. i. 48, 6.

नकुल *nakula*, m. 1. The Bengal mungoose, Viverra ichneumon, MBh. 12, 444. 2. f. *lî*, Its female, 16, 41. 3. The name of the fourth of the five Pâṇḍu princes, 1, 2445.

† नक्क् *NAKK*, i. 10, Par. To kill, to annihilate.

नक्त *nakta*, I. n. 1. Night, Bhâg. P. 5, 22, 5. 2. Eating only by night, Yâjń. 3, 319. II. °*tam*, adv. By night, Man. 6, 19.—Cf. Lat. nox, noctu; Goth. nahts; A.S. naht, niht; νύξ.

नक्तंचर naktaṁchara, i.e. nakta+m-chara, m., f. rî, A goblin, a demon, Râm. 5, 11, 9; Kathâs. 25, 104.

नक्तंचर्या naktaṁcharyâ, i.e. nakta+m-charyâ, f. Wandering by night, MBh. 12, 10575.

नक्तंचारिन् naktaṁchârin, i.e. nakta+m-chârin, adj. Walking by night, Man. 3, 90.

नक्तंदिन naktaṁdina, i.e. nakta+m-dina, **1.** n. sing. Day and night, Mâlav. d. 88. **2.** °nam, adv. By day and by night, Pañch. 32, 25.

नक्तमाल naktamâla, m. A tree, Pongamia glabra Vent., Râm. 3, 79, 37.

नक्र nakra, m. A crocodile, Man. 1, 44.—Comp. vakra-, m. **1.** A parrot. **2.** A depraved man.

नक्ष् NAKSH, (akin to 1. naç), i. 1, Par. (also Âtm.), To approach, to attain.

नक्षत्र nakshatra, n. **1.** A star, Man. 1, 24. **2.** An asterism in the moon's path or lunar mansion; they are regarded as wives of the moon and daughters of Daksha, Hariv. 104; MBh. 13, 3256.

नक्षत्रिन् nakshatrin, i.e. nakshatra+in, adj. Epithet of Vishṇu (containing the stars ?), MBh. 13, 6996.

† नख् NAKH, i. 4 and i. 1, Par., and नङ्ख् NAṄKH, i. 1, Par. To go.

नख nakha, I. m. and n. A nail of a finger or of a toe, Man. 4, 35. II. n. and f. khî, A certain perfume.—Comp. Agra-, the point of a nail, Râm. 2, 9, 43. Pañchanakha, i.e. pañchan-, m. a beast having five claws, Man. 5, 17. Sûrpa-, f. khâ, the sister of Râvaṇa. Hastinakha-, i.e. hastin-, n. a sort of covered way, covering the access to the gate of a fort or town.—Cf. O.H.G. nagal; A.S. naegel; ὄνυξ, ὀνύχιον; Lat. ungula.

नखर nakha+ra, I. adj. Shaped like a claw, MBh. 6, 693. II. (m. or n.), **1.** A knife, 7, 1318. **2.** A finger-nail, a claw, Chaurap. 15; Pañch. 91, 5.

नखानखि nakhânakhi, i.e. nakha-nakha+i, adv. Scratching one another, MBh. 8, 2377.

नखायुधत्व nakhâyudha+tva, i.e. nakha-âyudha+tva, n. Being a beast using its nails or claws as its weapon, Pañch. 71, 11.

नखिन् nakhin, i.e. nakha+in, m. A beast with nails or claws, Châṇ. 27.

नग na-ga, I. adj. Immoveable, MBh. 12, 5730 (?). II. m. **1.** A mountain, Râm. 6, 83, 1. **2.** A tree, Man. 8, 330.

नगर naga+ra, n. and f. rî, A town, Man. 4, 107.—Comp. Antar-nagara, n. a palace, Râm. 5, 11, 26. Kâçi-nagara, n. the city of the Kâçis = Benares, Chr. 11, 11. Gandharva-nagara, n. 1. the city of the Gandharvas, MBh. 2, 1043. 2. the fata morgana, Bhâg. P. 5, 14, 5. Vidarbha-nagarî, f. the city of the Vidarbhas, Nal. 1, 23. Çâkhâ-, n. a suburb. Sva-, n. own or native town.

नगराय NAGARAYA, a denomin. derived from nagara by ya, Âtm. To look like a town, MBh. 9, 2162.

नगरीय nagarîya, i.e. nagara+îya, adj. Belonging to a town, Lass. 75, 19.

नगवन्त् naga+vant, adj., f. vatî, Abounding in trees, Râm. 5, 9, 6.

नग्न nagna, I. adj., f. nâ, Naked, Man. 4, 45. II. f. nâ, A girl before menstruation, Pañch. iii. d. 217.—Cf. Goth. naqvadei; A.S. nacud, nacod, genacian; Lat. nudus.

नग्नक *nagna+ka*, I. m. A naked mendicant, Pańch. 236, 4. II. f. *nikâ*, A girl before menstruation, Pańch. iii. d. 213.

नग्नजित् *nagna-ji+t*, I. m. The name of a prince, MBh. 1, 2439.

नग्नत्व *nagna+tva*, n. Nakedness, Hit. pr. d. 27.

नङ्ख् *NAŃKH*, see *nakh*.

† नज् *NAJ*, i. 6, Âtm. To be ashamed.

नट् *NAṬ* (a form of *nart*, vb. *nṛit*), i. 1, Par. **1.** To dance, Gît. 4, 9. **2.** To injure. Caus. and i. 10, **1.** To dance, to represent as an actor, to act, Çâk. 6, 11. **2.** † To fall. **3.** † To speak or shine. Ptcple. of the pf. pass. *nâṭita*, n. Representing, Çâk. 43, 4, v.r.

नट *naṭa* (a form of *narta*), **1.** m. A mime, MBh. 1, 6940. **2.** f. *ṭî*, An actress, Çâk. 3, 9. **3.** m. A tree, Calorantlies indica, Jonesia asoca, Râm. 5, 74, 4.—**Comp.** *Mahâ-*, m. Çiva.

नटता *naṭa+tâ*, f. The state of an actor, Hariv. 8692.

नटन *naṭ+ana*, n. Dancing, Pańch. iii. d. 237.

† नड् *NAḌ*, i. 10, Par. To fall.—Cf. *naṭ*.

नड *naḍa*, probably a form of *narta*, m. (and n.), Reed.—Cf. *nala*.

नड्वल *naḍvala*, i.e. *naḍa+vala*, n. A reed-bed, MBh. 5, 707.

नतमंहस् *natamaṁhas*, i.e. *na tam aṁhas*, The beginning of a holy text, Man. 11, 251.

नताङ्ग *natâṅga*, i.e. *nata-aṅga* (vb. *nam*), I. adj., f. *gî*, Bent. II. f. *gî*, A woman.

नति *nati*, i.e. *nam+ti*, f. **1.** A bow, a courtesy, Kathâs. 9, 18. **2.** Modest behaviour, Navar. 3 in Haeb. Anth. 2.

नद् *NAD* (probably a form of *nard*), i. 1, Par. (also Âtm. MBh. 2, 1925), To sound, to roar, MBh. 3, 2855. Frequently with the acc. of a noun expressing sound, e.g. *çabdam*, To utter a sound, MBh. 3, 15655. Caus. *nâdaya*, To cause to resound, to fill with noise, Râm. 1, 28, 5. Anomal. ptcple. of the pres. Âtm. *nâdayâna*, MBh. 6, 2269. *nâdita*, n. Sound, 1, 7650. Frequent. **1.** *nânad*, To roar, Chr. 290, 8=Rigv. i. 64, 8; MBh. 7, 882. **2.** *nânadya*, To make a great noise, 7, 887.—With the prep. अनु *anu*, To sound against (with acc.), Râm. 2, 111, 53 Gorr. (to rise to). Caus. To cause to resound, to fill with noise, MBh. 5, 5169.—With व्यनु *vi-anu*, Caus. To fill with noise, Bhag. 1, 19.—With अभि *abhi*, **1.** To sound against, Bhâg. P. 1, 2, 2 (to answer). **2.** To roar, Hariv. 11042 (p. 791). Caus. To fill with noise, 13859. *abhinâdita*, Re-echoed, 4582.—With आ *â*, Caus. To fill with noise, MBh. 3, 789.—With उद् *ud*, **1.** To roar, MBh. 7, 6814. **2.** To bray, Pańch. 248, 17.—With प्रोद् *pra-ud*, To roar, Hariv. 6754.—With समुद् *sam-ud*, To roar, Hariv. 13167.—With उप *upa*, Caus. To fill with noise, Râm. 2, 28, 10.—With नि *ni*, **1.** To resound, Pańch. 158, 5. **2.** To sing, Râm. 2, 65, 2. **3.** To cry, Ragh. 5, 75. Caus. To fill with noise, MBh. 1, 119. *ninâdita*, n. Sound, Râm. 1, 73, 36.—With परि *pari*, To cry aloud, MBh. 6, 3256.—With प्र *pra*, णद् *ṇad*, To begin to sound, to roar, MBh. 2, 1925; 3, 2859. *praṇadita*,

Buzzing, Çiç. 9, 71.—With विप्र *vi-pra,* Caus. To fill with noise, Râm. 5, 12, 45. —With संप्र *sam-pra,* To cry, Râm. 5, 1, 87. Caus. To fill with a cry, Râm. 4, 29, 15.—With प्रति *prati,* To answer with a cry, or with cries, Râm. 3, 24, 30; (with acc.) Râjat. 4, 285; MBh. 6, 4518. Caus. 1. To fill with cries, Hariv. 4179. 2. To cry aloud, MBh. 3, 14057.—With वि *vi,* 1. To resound, Râm. 4, 9, 44. 3. To cry, 3, 30, 6. 3. To roar, MBh. 1, 6002. 4. To cry round about somebody (acc.), 11, 599. 5. To fill with cries, Hariv. 8097. Caus. 1. To cause to sound, or to cry, Bhâg. P. 8, 8, 13; Ghaṭ. 10. 2. To fill with noise, MBh. 1, 1187. 3. To sound aloud, Râm. 6, 11, 23.—With अनुवि *anu-vi,* Caus. To fill completely with noise, Râm. 2, 103, 48.—With अभिवि *abhi-vi,* To cry aloud, Râm. 6, 37, 37.—With सम् *sam,* To roar, MBh. 7, 8127. Caus. 1. To cause to resound, MBh. 1, 2896. 2. To cry aloud, MBh. 7, 8386.

नद *nad + a,* I. m. A river, MBh. 1, 8730. A male river, Man. 6, 90. II. f. *dî,* A river, 3, 9; a female river, 6, 90.—Comp. *Giri-ṇadî,* i.e. *giri-nadî,* f. a mountain stream. *Deva-nadî,* f. A holy river, Man. 2, 19. *Dyu-nadî,* f. a name of the Gangâ. *Naga-nadî,* f. the name of a river. *Pañchanada,* i.e. *pañchan-,* I. n. 1. the country which is now called Panjâb. 2. the name of a river. II. m. 1. pl. the inhabitants of the Panjâb. 2. a proper name. *Mahâ-nadî,* f. a great river, Râjat. 5, 98; =Gangâ, Chr. 26, 70. *Svar-,* f. the Gangâ of heaven.

नदिका *nadikâ,* i.e. *nadî + ka,* f. See *ku-nadikâ,* s.v. *ku-*.

नदीज *nadî-ja,* I. Born near a river, epithet of horses, Râm. 1, 6, 24 Gorr. II. m. 1. Epithet of Bhîshma, the son of the Gangâ, MBh. 4, 1294. 2. Antimony, Suçr. 2, 340, 16.

नदीष्ण *nadîshṇa,* i.e. *nadî-sna* (vb. *snâ*), adj. Versed in, Ragh. 16, 75.—Comp. *Ati-,* Much versed in, Daçak. 180, 14.

ननु *na-nu,* a particle of interrogation. 1. Not (Lat. nonne), MBh. 13, 313. 2. with an imperat., Do, Çiç. 9, 61. 3. Then, Mṛichchh. 174, 12.

नन्द् *NAND* (probably for *nanad,* a reduplicated form of *nad*), i, 1, Par. (also Âtm., Râm. 2, 84, 4), To be pleased, Râm. 1, 10, 28. Caus. *nandaya,* To gladden, Râm. 4, 22, 6.—With the prep. अभि *abhi,* 1. To be pleased, Bhag. 2, 57. 2. To be pleased with (acc.), Man. 6, 45. 3. To desire, MBh. 13, 6655. 4. To salute, Pañch. 57, 18; with *na,* sometimes To receive unkindly, MBh. 14, 134. 5. To take leave from (acc.), MBh. 1, 5751. 6. To approve, Râm. 4, 10, 33; Çâk. d. 71. 7. To acknowledge, Man. 8, 54. 8. With *na,* sometimes To refuse, MBh. 5, 7505. Ptcple. of the fut. pass. *abhinandanîya, abhinandya,* To be rejoiced at, Çâk. 63, 18; 27, 6. Caus. To exhilarate, Râm. 2, 107, 10.—With प्रत्यभि *prati-abhi,* To return a salutation, MBh. 13, 7721. —With समभि *sam-abhi,* To congratulate, Kathâs. 21, 148.—With आ *â,* To be pleased, Gît. 11, 10. Caus. To gratify, Yâjñ. 1, 355.—With परि *pari,* Caus. To gratify very much, MBh. 15, 522.—With प्रति *prati,* 1. To salute, MBh. 5, 1806. 2. To salute in one's turn, Man. 7, 146. 3. To show one's satisfaction, MBh. 13, 426. 4. To favour, Kumâras. 7, 87. 5. To receive joyfully, MBh. 1, 7253. **6.** With *na,* To refuse, 3673. *a-prati-nandita,* Disowned, Bhâg. 4, 4, 8. Caus. To gratify, MBh. 3, 16444. — With **संप्रति** *sam-prati,* To welcome joyfully, 10, 475.—With **वि** *vi,* To be pleased, 3, 2607 (Âtm.).

नन्द *nand+a,* I. m. One of Yudhishṭhira's drums, MBh. 7, 1032. **2.** A name of Vishṇu, 13, 7005. **3.** A proper name (especially of the foster father of Kṛishṇa and Durgâ), 4, 179; 1, 2731. **4.** The name of a mountain, Bhâg. P. 5, 20, 21. II. f. *dâ.* **1.** A proper name, MBh. 1, 2597. **2.** The name of a river, 7818. III. f. *dî,* A tree, Cedrela toona Roxb., Suçr. 1, 219, 19.—Comp. *Sa-,* m. one of the four sons of Brahman. *Su-,* I. adj. delighting. II. f. *dâ,* 1. Umâ. 2. a woman. III. n. the club of Baladeva.

नन्दक *nand+aka,* I. adj. in *devatâ-stava-,* Gladdening the deities by praises, MBh. 13, 7662. II. m. **1.** The name of Kṛishṇa's sword, MBh. 5, 4427. **2.** A proper name, 1, 6983.

नन्दकिन् *nandakin,* i.e. *nandaka+in,* m. A name of Vishṇu (possessed of the sword *Nandaka*), MBh. 13, 7056.

नन्दन *nand+ana,* I. adj., f. *nâ,* Gladdening, MBh. 3, 11073. II. m. **1.** A son, Yâjń. 1, 274. **2.** Epithet of Vishṇu and Çiva, MBh. 13, 7005; 1189. **3.** A certain plant, Suçr. 2, 251, 19. **4.** A proper name, MBh. 9, 2540. **5.** The name of a mountain, Bhâg. P. 5, 20, 21. III. n. The pleasure-ground of the gods, especially of Indra, Indr. 2, 3.—Comp. *Arka-,* m. the planet Saturn, Pańch. i. d. 240. *Kâçyapa-,* m. pl. the children of Kâçyapa, a name of the gods, MBh. 13, 3330. *Kuru-,* m. a descendant of Kuru, Chr. 22, 18. *Kula-,* adj., f. *nâ,* being an honour to a family, Pańch. 187, 4. *Nalinî-,* n. a garden of Kuvera, Râm. 3, 36, 14. *Bhṛigu-,* m. the son of Bhṛigu, i.e. Paraçurâma. *Raghu-,* m. Râma.

नन्दनक *nandana+ka,* a substitute for *nandana* when latter part of a comp. word, MBh. 3, 10856.

नन्दि *nand+i,* I. m. **1.** Epithet of Vishṇu and Çiva, MBh. 13, 7015; 1189. **2.** A proper name, 13, 872. II. f. (and m. and n.) Joy, MBh. 5, 4600; personified, Bhâg. P. 6, 6, 6.

नन्दिन् *nand+in,* I. adj., f. *nî.* **1.** Liking, MBh. 6, 16. **2.** Gladdening, 13, 4708. II. m. **1.** A son, Mṛichchh. 47, 21. **2.** A proper name, MBh. 12, 10223. III. f. *nî,* **1.** A daughter, 14, 1841. **2.** The name of a fabulous cow, 1, 3923. **3.** A proper name, 9, 2623.

नपात् *na-pâ+t,* **नप्तृ** *naptṛi* (i.e. *na-pâ+tṛi*), I. m. **1.** A grandson, Man. 4, 173. **2.** A proper name, MBh. 13, 4362. II. f. **नप्ती** *naptî* (i.e. *na-pât+î*), A granddaughter, Chr. 289, 9=Rigv. i. 50, 9, where the horses are denoted as granddaughters of the chariot.—Cf. Lat. nepos, neptis; O.H.G. nefo; A.S. nefa; O.H.G. nift; Goth. nithjis, nithjo; ἀ-νεψιός.

नपुंस *na-puṁs+a,* m. An eunuch, MBh. 13, 901.

नपुंसक *napuṁsa+ka,* I. adj. **1.** Neither man nor woman. **2.** Of neuter gender. II. m. **1.** An eunuch, MBh. 4, 1190. **2.** A coward, Pańch. i. d. 364.

नप्ती *naptî* and **नप्तृ** *naptṛi,* see *napât.*

नभ् *NABH,* i. 1, Âtm. † i. 4, ii. 9, Par. **1.** To burst. **2.** To injure.

नभ *nabha,* m. A proper name, Hariv. 823.

नभग *nabhaga*, m. A proper name, Bhâg. P. 8, 13, 2.

नभःश्रित् *nabhaḥçrit*, i. e. *nabhas-çri+t*, adj. Reaching to, or attaining heaven.

नभश्चर *nabhaçchara*, i. e. *nabhas-chara*, I. adj. Moving in the sky, Râm. 3, 49, 45. II. m. A deity, Ragh. 18, 5.

नभस् *nabhas*, n. 1. Sky, atmosphere, Man. 4, 37. 2. du. Heaven and earth, MBh. 12, 13240. 3. Æther as one of the five elements, Bhâg. P. 3, 26, 12. 4. (n. and m.) The name of a month of the rainy season (July—August), Ragh. 12, 29.—Cf. νέφος, δνόφος, ἰο-δνεφής, γνόφος, νεφέλη; Lat. nubes, nebula; O.H.G. nibul; A.S. ge-nip, a cloud.

नभस्य *nabhas+ya*, m. The name of a month of the rainy season, Hariv. 8781.

नभस्वन्त् *nabhas´+vant*, 1. m. Wind, Ṛit. 2, 27. 2. f. *vatî*, A proper name, Bhâg. P. 4, 24, 5.

नम् *NAM*, i. 1, Par. (also Âtm., MBh. 3, 1200, especially when intransitive), 1. To bow to (with dat., gen. and acc.), Chr. 287, 8=Rigv. i. 48, 8 (*nânâma*, ved. pf. red.); Bhâg. P. 4, 9, 47; MBh. 10, 495; Hariv. 10235. 2. To bow, Bhartṛ. 3, 61. 3. To submit, Kâm. Nîtis. 8, 55. 4. To sink, Mṛichchh. 85, 11. 5. To bend, Suçr. 1, 254, 7. 6. † To sound. Ptcple. of the pf. pass. *nata*, 1. Inclined to (with acc. and gen.), Bhâg. P. 6, 9, 40. 2. Cast down, Pańch. 46, 5; Râjat. 5, 372 (read *ekâ natamukhî*). 3. Bent, curved, Râm. 2, 96, 15; crooked, Vikr. d. 95. 4. Sunk in (not prominent), Kumâras. 1, 38. **Comp.** *Tri-nata*, bent at three places (as a bow), Râm. 6, 20, 28. Ptcple. of the fut. pass. *namanîya*, To be bowed to, Bhâg. P. 3, 21, 21. Caus. *nâmaya*, 1. To cause to bow, Ragh. 8, 9. 2. To curve, bend, Pańch. i. d. 430; (as a bow), MBh. 3, 3039. 3. To cause to sink in, Hariv. 3754. Comp. ptcple. of the fut. pass. *a-nâmya*, adj. Not to be curved, or bent, Pańch. i. d. 430; MBh. 5, 1335.—With the prep. **अभि** *abhi*, To bow to, Indr. 2, 19.—With **अव** *ava*, 1. To bow, Bhâg. P. 5, 25, 4. 2. To stoop, MBh. 1, 5336 (anomal. red. pf. *nanâmire*). *avanata*, 1. Stooping, MBh. 3, 1776. 2. Bent, crooked, Râm. 2, 56, 7; Kumâras. 5, 86. 3. Sunk in (not prominent), Râm. 6, 23, 12. Caus. 1. To cause to bow, Hariv. 3586. 2. To bend (a bow), MBh. 8, 4606.—With **अभ्यव** *abhi-ava*, Caus. To bend downward, MBh. 3, 10062.—With **आ** *â*, 1. To bow, Râm. 2, 25, 38. 2. To bow to (acc.), Bhâg. P. 8, 23, 3. *ânata*, 1. Stooping, Hariv. 6344. 2. Stooping to (with acc.), Bhâg. P. 1, 2, 2. 3. Submissive, Man. 7, 69. 4. Bent, MBh. 1, 1667. Caus. 1. To bend downward, 5561. 2. To subdue, 4, 967. 3. To bend (a bow), 1, 7088.—With **उद्** *ud*, 1. To rise, Pańch. ii. d. 98. 2. To erect, to raise, Pańch. i. d. 407. *unnata*, 1. Erected, upright, Hit. 76, 6; raised, Draup. 5, 1. 2. High, Kir. 5, 15. 3. Sublime, Pańch. 24, 17. 4. Prominent, Mṛichchh. 144, 18. 5. Vaulted, Bhartṛ. 1, 41. Caus. To raise. Râm. 5, 30, 12.—With **अभ्युद्** *abhi-ud*, *abhyunnata*, Elevated, Çâk. d. 56.—With **समभ्युद्** *sam-abhi-ud*, *samabhyunnata*, Risen, Mṛichchh. 76, 20.—With **प्रोद्** *pra-ud*, *pronnata*, 1. Very elevated, Pańch. 118, 9. 2. Superior, i. d. 387. Caus. To erect, Bhâg. P. 8, 21, 3.—With **समुद्** *sam-ud*, *samunnata*,

नम्

1. Upright, Hit. 76, 6. **2.** High, Râjat. 5, 38. **3.** Sublime, Kâm. Nîtis. 1, 64. **4.** Prominent, Râm. 3, 52, 30. **5.** Vaulted, Amar. 51. Caus. To raise, Çâk. 40, 16.—With उप *upa*, **1.** To fall to one's share (with dat. and gen.), Bhâg. P. 5, 14, 14. **2.** To present one with (acc. of the person and instr. of the object), 6, 19, 16. *upanata*, **1.** One who has submitted to somebody, MBh. 1, 5623. **2.** Approached, Ragh. 10, 40. **3.** Near, Bhâg. P. 5, 26, 18. **4.** Due, 4, 27, 25.—With निस् *nis* णम् *ṇam*, *nirṇata*, Prominent, MBh. 7, 7894.—With परि *pari* णम् *ṇam*, **1.** To stoop (as an elephant about to strike with his tusks), Çiç. 18, 27. **2.** To turn aside, Bhartṛ. 1, 4. **3.** To change into (instr.), Kir. 13, 44. **4.** To be digested, Pañch. 232, 7. **5.** To grow old, Kir. 5, 37. *pariṇata*, **1.** Changed into (instr.), Megh. 46. **2.** Ripe, MBh. 5, 1109. **3.** Advanced, Pañch. 197, 18. m. An elephant stooping to strike with his tusks, Daçak. in Chr. 188, 17. Caus. **1.** To ripen, Hariv. 2957. **2.** To pass, MBh. 6, 3847. **3.** To stoop, MBh. 8, 1143.—With प्र *pra* णम् *ṇam*, **1.** To bow, Man. 2, 197. **2.** To bow to, Man. 8, 23. *praṇata*, **1.** Bowing, Man. 11, 195. **2.** Bowing to (with gen. and acc.), MBh. 4, 202; Râm. 1, 52, 1. Caus. **1.** To order to bow to, Kumâras. 7, 27. **2.** To bend, Mâlav. d. 47. **3.** To give respectfully, Amar. 82.—With अभिप्र *abhi-pra*, **1.** To bow, Râm. 1, 18, 5 Gorr. **2.** To bow to, 2, 100, 37 Gorr. *abhipraṇata*, 1, 70, 5 Gorr.—With संप्र *sam-pra*, To bow to, Râm. 2, 112, 23.—With वि *vi*, **1.** To bow, MBh. 3, 2920. **2.** To bend, Bhartṛ. 1, 66. *vinata*, **1.** Sunk down, drooping, Çâk. d. 58; cast down, Brâhmaṇ. 1, 13. **2.** Bent, Râm. 3, 50, 2. **3.** Stooping, Ghaṭ. 18. *f. tâ*, **1.** A sort of basket. **2.** The wife of Kaçyapa and mother of Aruṇa and Garuḍa. Caus. **1.** To bend down, MBh. 3, 15588. **2.** To bend, 4, 394; (a bow), 1, 5436. **3.** To incline, Amar. 81.—With सम् *sam*, **1.** To bow, Râm. 2, 72, 30. **2.** To bow to, MBh. 5, 1130. **3.** To submit to, Ragh. 18, 33. *saṁnata*, **1.** Bent, Râm. 3, 16, 5. **2.** Curved, Kumâras. 1, 34. **3.** Stooping, Indr. 1, 10. **4.** Bowed to, Bhâg. P. 7, 4, 32. Caus. **1.** To bend, MBh. 12, 10675. **2.** To cause to sink, Bhâg. P. 8, 18, 20.—Cf. νέμω; Goth. and A.S. niman (originally, to subdue); perhaps A.S. ge-nedhan (cf. *nata*).

नमस् *nam + as*, n. Bowing, adoration, Bhâg. P. 3, 13, 41; Râm. 1, 52, 17.

नमस्कर्तृ *namas-kartṛi*, m. One who adores (the gods), MBh. 13, 6706.

नमस्कार *namas-kâra*, m. and **नमस्क्रिया** *namas-kriyâ*, f. Adoration, Nal. 5, 16; MBh. 15, 954.—**Comp.** *Nis-namaskâra*, adj. 1. respecting nobody, Râm. 2, 24, 24. 2. respected by nobody, Man. 9, 239.

नमस्य *NAMASYA*, a denomin. derived from *namas* by *ya*, Par. (Âtm. MBh. 13, 5129). To adore, MBh. 2, 234.—With the prep. सम् *sam*, The same, Hariv. 7769.

नमस्य *namas + ya*, adj., or ptcple. of the fut. pass. of *namasya*, What ought to be adored, MBh. 13, 2142.

नमस्विन् *namas + vin*, adj. Respectful, Lass. 102, 7=Rigv. vii. 14, 1.

नमुचि *na-much + i*, m. The name of a demon subdued by Indra, MBh. 1, 2530.

† **नम्ब्** *NAMB*, i. 1, Par. To go, to move.

नम्र *nam+ra*, adj., f. *râ*. **1.** Bent, Bhartṛ. 2, 62. **2.** Bowed, Bhâg. P. 6, 17, 16. **3.** Crooked, Ṛit. 6, 10. **4.** Addicted, Kathâs. 17, 56.—Comp. *Vi-*, adj. 1. bent, bowed. 2. humble.

नम्रता *namra+tâ*, f. **1.** Bowing, Râjat. 5, 223. **2.** Respect, Bhartṛ. 2, 52. **3.** Humbleness, Böhtl. Ind. Spr. 15.

नम्रत्व *namra + tva*, n. Humility, Bhartṛ. 2, 59.

† **नय्** *NAY*, i. 1, Âtm. **1.** To go. **2.** To protect.—Cf. *nî*.

नय *naya*, i.e. *nî + a*, m. **1.** Leading, Râm. 2, 1, 21. **2.** Conduct, Hariv. 7346; way of life, Kathâs. 20, 191. **3.** Prudent conduct, Bhartṛ. 2, 19. **4.** Prudence, Bhâg. P. 3, 7, 9; Daçak. in Chr. 198, 6 (read *tvannaya evâtra bhûyân*, Thy prudence is here of greater weight). **5.** Policy, Man. 7, 159. **6.** Design, Pañch. i. d. 358. **7.** Philosophical system, Bhâshâp. 16. **8.** Prudent conduct personified as son of Dharma by Kriyâ, Mârk. P. 50, 26. **9.** A proper name, Hariv. 489.—Comp. cf. *Anaya*. *Apa-*, m. bad policy, Râm. 4, 40, 16. *Dus-* (written sometimes **दुर्णय** *durṇaya* instead of **दुर्नय** *durnaya*), m. bad conduct, MBh. 1, 4379. *Râja-naya*, i.e. *râjan-*, m. policy. *Su-*, m. 1. good conduct. 2. policy.

नयन *nayana*, i.e. *nî+ana*, n. **1.** Leading, MBh. 12, 458. **2.** Ruling, 1, 2580. **3.** Leading to, Çâk. 71, 14. **4.** Bringing, Pañch. 174, 19. **5.** The eye, Râm. 1, 59, 16.—Comp. *Tri-*, **त्रिणयन** *triṇayana* and *trinayana*, adj. having three eyes, epithet of Çiva, Megh. 53; MBh. 14, 207. *Vishama-*, m. Çiva. *Sâçru-*, i.e. *sa-açru-*, adj., f. *nâ*, the eyes filled with tears, Chr. 7, 21. *Su-*, I. m. a deer. II. f. *nâ*, a woman.

नयवन्त् *naya+vant*, adj., f. *vatî*. **1.** Versed in policy, Râm. 5, 81, 14. **2.** Prudent, Kir. 5, 20.

नर *nara*, i.e. *nṛi+a*, m. **1.** A man; pl. Men, Man. 1, 96. **2.** The Eternal, the divine imperishable spirit pervading the universe, Man. 1, 10. **3.** pl. Certain fabulous beings, MBh. 2, 396. **4.** A proper name, Bhâg. P. 8, 1, 27.—Cf. Lat. Nero, Neriene.

नरक *naraka*, m. **1.** Hell, the infernal regions, Man. 2, 116. **2.** The name of a demon, MBh. 1, 2537. **3.** The name of a country, MBh. 2, 578.—Comp. *Mahâ-*, m. the name of a hell, Man. 4, 83.

नरकाय *NARAKAYA*, a denomin. derived from *naraka* by the aff. *ya*, Âtm. To resemble hell, Mârk. P. 8, 117.

नरता *nara+tâ*, f. Human condition, Bhâg. P. 7, 14, 5.

ऽनर्त *-narta*, i. e. *nṛit + a*, adj. Dancing, MBh. 13, 1164.

नर्तक *nartaka*, i.e. *nṛit+aka*, I. m. **1.** A dancer, Râm. 1, 12, 7. **2.** A dancing-master, MBh. 4, 305. II. f. *kî*, A female dancer, Ragh. 19, 14. III. adj. Causing to dance, Sâh. D. 74, 17.—Comp. *Hariṇa-*, m. a Kiṃnara.

नर्तन *nartana*, i.e. *nṛit+ana*. I. m. A dancer, MBh. 4, 1217. II. n. Dancing, Man. 2, 178.

नर्तयितृ *nartayitṛi*, i.e. *nṛit*, Caus., + *tṛi*, m. A dancing-master, Mâlav. d. 24.

नर्द् *NARD*, i. 1, Par. (also Âtm., Hariv. 11936), To roar, MBh. 1, 4114.

Ptcple. of the pf. pass. *nardita*, **1.** n. Roaring, Râm. 4, 8, 38. **2.** m. The name of one of the dice, Mṛichchh. 33, 10. Frequent. *nânard*, To sound aloud, Hariv. 8064 (anomal. Âtm. *nânardamâna*).—With the prep. **अभि** *abhi*, To roar at, MBh. 6, 2738.—With **आ** *â*, *ânardita*, n. Roaring, Râm. 2, 42, 20.—With **प्रति** *prati*, **1.** To greet with roaring, crying, MBh. 8, 1806. **2.** To roar for, 12, 5777.—With **वि** *vi*, To roar, MBh. 8, 2468.—With **अनुवि** *anu-vi*, To answer with roaring, Hariv. 14559.

† **नर्ब्** *NARB*, i. 1, Par. =*namb*.

नर्मद *narmada*, i.e. *narman-da*, **1.** adj. Causing pleasure, Somad. Nal. 128. **2.** f. *dâ*, The name of a river, the modern Nerbudda, MBh. 2, 371; personified, 15, 550.

नर्मन् *narman*, probably *nard* + *man*, n. Jest, sport, MBh. 1, 1000.

नर्मय *NARMAYA*, a denomin. derived from *narman* by *aya*, Par. To exhilarate by jesting, Kâm. Nîtis. 7, 42.

नर्य *narya*, i.e. *nara* + *ya*, **1.** adj. Manly (ved.). **2.** A proper name (?), Chr. 296, 9 = Rigv. i. 112, 9.

† **नल्** *NAL*, i. 1, Par. To smell; to bind (?). i. 10, Par. To speak, or to shine.

नल *nala* (for *naḍa*, q. cf.), m. **1.** A kind of reed, Amphidonax karka Lindl., MBh. 6, 4898. **2.** A proper name, Hariv. 823; the hero of the episode Nala and Damayantî.

नलद *nalada*, **1.** n. (and f. *dâ*), The Indian spikenard, Nardostachys jatamansi, Suçr. 1, 140, 20. **2.** n. The root of the Andropogon muricatus, Kir. 5, 25.

नलिन *nalina*, i.e. *nala* + *ina*, **I.** n. A lotus flower, MBh. 7, 1299. **II.** f. *nî*, **1.** A lotus, Nelumbium speciosum, Bhartṛ. 2, 57. **2.** An assemblage of lotus flowers, Vikr. d. 5. **3.** A pond in which the lotus grows or may grow, Draup. 6, 2. **4.** A branch of the heavenly Ganges, Hariv. 3502. **5.** A mystical name of one of the nostrils, Bhâg. P. 4, 25, 48. **6.** A proper name, 9, 21, 30.

ऽनलिनीक *-nalinî* + *ka*, A substitute for *nalinî*, as latter part of a comp. adj., Bhâg. P. 5, 8, 22.

नल्व *nalva*, perhaps *nala* + *va*, cf. *naḍvala*, m. A furlong, a distance measured by four hundred (?) cubits, Râm. 6, 82, 71.

नव *nava* (akin to the particle *nu*, cf. *nûtana*), **I.** adj., f. *vâ*. **1.** New, Man. 11, 186. **2.** Fresh, Bhartṛ. 1, 7. **3.** Young, MBh. 4, 410. **3.** °*vam*, adv. Just, Mṛichchh. 108, 7. **II.** m. A proper name, Hariv. 1677.—**Comp.** *Punar-*, m. a finger-nail.—Cf. Lat. novus; νέος; Goth. nivjis; A.S. niwe, neow, niwa.

नवक *navaka*, i.e. **I.** *nava* + *ka*, adj. New, Vâsavad. 7, 3. **II.** *navan* + *ka*, **1.** adj. Consisting of nine, MBh. 3, 14389. **2.** n. Nine, Râm. 4, 39, 24.

नवकृत्वस् *navakṛitvas*, i.e. *navan* -*kṛitvas*, adv. Nine times, Vedântas. in Chr. 216, 9.

नवज *nava-ja*, adj. Just visible, MBh. 12, 8819.

नवत *navata*, i.e. *navati* + *a*, ordinal number, Ninetieth, Râjat. 5, 260.—**Comp.** *Ekona-*, i.e. *eka-ûna-*, eighty-ninth, 5, 258. *Eka-*, ninety-first, MBh. 1, adhy. 91. *Dvâ-* and *dvi-*, ninety-second, MBh. 8, adhy. 92. *Tri-*, ninety-third, MBh. 1, 93. *Chatur-*, ninety-fourth, 1, 94. *Saptan°*, i. e. *saptan-*, ninety-seventh. *Ashṭânavata*, i.e. *ashṭan-*, ninety-eighth, Râjat. 5, 287.

नवता *nava + tâ*, f. Freshness, Kumâras. 5, 86.

नवति *navati*, i.e. *navan + ti*, cardinal number, f. Ninety, Man. 3, 177.—**Comp.** *Dvi-*, ninety-two, MBh. 1, adhy. 192.

नवतितम *navati + tama*, ordinal number, Ninetieth, MBh. 1, adhy. 90. —**Comp.** *Eka-, dvi-, tri-, chatur-, pańchan-, shash-, saptan-, ashṭan-*, ninety-first, second, third, fourth, etc., Râm. 2, adhy. 91 sqq. *Navan-*, ninety-ninth, 6, adhy. 99.

नवत्व *nava + tva*, n. Newness, Râjat. 5, 19.

नवधा *navadhâ*, i.e. *navan + dhâ*, adv. Nine-fold, nine times, Bhâg. P. 3, 21, 29.

नवन् *navan*, cardinal number, adj. Nine, Man. 3, 269.—Cf. Goth. and O.H.G. niun; A.S. nigan; ἐννέα; Lat. novem.

नवन *navana*, i.e. *nu + ana*, n. Praising, Nalod. 1, 4.

नवनलिनदलाय *NAVANALINADALAYA*, a denomin. derived from *nava-nalina-dala* by *ya*, Âtm. To resemble the leaf of a fresh lotus flower, Bhâg. P. 5, 5, 31.

नवनीत *nava-nîta*, n. Fresh butter, Râm. 5, 12, 27.—**Comp.** *Samudra-*, n. 1. the beverage of the immortals. 2. the moon.

नवम *navama*, i.e. *navan + ma*, I. ordinal number, f. *mî*, Ninth. II. f. *mî*, The ninth day of a lunar half month, Lass. 16, 14.—Cf. Lat. nonus (for novimus).

नवमल्लिका *navamallikâ*, or **नवमालिका** *navamâlikâ*, f. Double jasmine, Jasminum sambac Ait., Çâk. d. 41; cf. v.r.

नवीन *navîna*, i.e. *nava + îna*, adj. New, Çatr. 1, 277.

नवीभाव *navîbhâva*, i.e. *nava-bhû + a*, m. Renovation, Kathâs. 14, 63.

नव्य *navya*, i.e. *nava + ya*, adj. New, Râjat. 5, 384.

नव्यवत् *navya + vat*, adv. Like new, Bhâg. P. 4, 30, 20 (ever new ?)

नव्यंस् *navyaṁs*, ved. comparat. of *nava*, Very new, Lass. 99, 5 = Rigv. iii. 62, 7.

1. **नश्** *NAÇ*, i. 1, Par. To attain (ved.).—Cf. Lat. nanciscor, and 2 *naç*.

2. **नश्** *NAÇ* (the base of many forms is *naṁç*), i. 4, Par. (also Âtm., Râm. 5, 27, 24, and i. 1, Par. and Âtm., MBh. 13, 3083; 7, 685.), **1.** To be lost, Man. 8, 32. **2.** To disappear, Man. 8, 247. **3.** To escape, MBh. 5, 2736. **4.** To go away, Râm. 5, 27, 24. **5.** To perish, Man. 4, 52. Ptcple. of the pf. pass. *nashṭa*, **1.** Lost, Çâk. d. 167. **2.** Invisible, Râm. 3, 50, 7; disappeared, MBh. 3, 2690. **3.** Destroyed, MBh. 1, 3147. **4.** Dead, Man. 8, 166. Caus. *nâçaya*, **1.** To cause to disappear, Râm. 1, 55, 20. **2.** To efface, Man. 11, 245. **3.** To destroy, Râm. 5, 63, 8; Man. 2, 55. **4.** To violate, Daçak. in Chr. 191, 10. **5.** To extinguish, Bhâg. P. 4, 5, 20. **6.** To lose, Pańch. i. d. 23. **7.** To disappear, MBh. 5, 862. —With the prep. **व्यप** *vi-apa*, Caus. To remove, MBh. 5, 7090.—With **अव** *ava*, To disappear, 4, 1728.—With **निस्** *nis*, *nirnashṭa*, Disappeared, Râjat.

1, 83.—With प्र *pra* प्रणश् *naç*, except where *ç* is changed to *sh*, e.g. *pranashṭa*, **1.** To be lost, Man. 8, 149. **2.** To disappear, Bhag. 1, 40. *pranashṭa* (sometimes erroneously *praṇashṭa*), **1.** Perished, Râjat. 5, 211. **2.** Disappeared, Man. 8, 30. **3.** Escaped, Pañch. 89, 20. Caus. **1.** To cause to disappear, MBh, 7, 327. **2.** To cause to be lost, Hit. iv. d. 9 (to leave unrewarded).—With विप्र *vi-pra*, **1.** To disappear, MBh. 3, 5027. **2.** To be lost, 13, 3212. *vipranashṭa*, **1.** Disappeared, MBh. 4, 877. **2.** Lost, 1, 4802.—With संप्र *sam-pra*, To be lost, MBh. 3, 13751. *sampranashṭa*, Disappeared, 2847. —With वि *vi*, **1.** To disappear, Man. 11, 263. **2.** To perish, 2, 163. *vinashṭa*, **1.** Lost, Mâlav. 9, 3. **2.** Utterly ruined or spoiled, Man. 7, 41 ; 2, 64. Caus. **1.** To destroy, 7, 19. **2.** To kill, Pañch. 71, 24. **3.** To perish (Aor.), Râm. 2, 110, 30. Desid. of the Caus. *vinâçayishita*, without reduplication ; read rather *ninâç°*, Sought to be destroyed, Daçak. 112, 3, below.—With अनुवि *anu-vi*, To perish afterward, or together with, MBh. 12, 3400.—With प्रवि *pra-vi*, To perish, Râm. 1, 56, 27 Gorr.—With सम् *sam*, *saṁnashṭa*, Perished, Râm. 5, 51, 13.—Cf. 1. *naç*, The original signification of 1. and 2. *naç*, has been probably, To hasten (cf. Lat. per-nix) ; then on the one side, To overtake, to attain (1. *naç*) ; on the other, To hasten out of view, to disappear, to vanish, to perish (2. *naç*).—Cf. νέκυς, νεκρός, etc. ; Lat. per-nicies, necare, nocere, ve-nenum (for ve-nec + num) ; Goth. naus (for nahu + s = νέκυς), navis.

नश्वर 2. *naç* + *vara*, adj., f. *rī*, Perishable, Kathâs. 19, 50.—Comp. *A-*, adj. imperishable, Bhartṛ. 3, 21.

नश्वरत्व *naçvara* + *tva*, n. Perishableness, Daçak. in. Chr. 185, 15.

नष्टि *nashṭi*, i.e. *naç* + *ti*, f. Ruin, Bhâg. P. 9, 10, 21.

नस् *NAS*, i. 1, Âtm. **1.** † To be crooked. **2.** To go to, to join (ved.).—Cf. νέομαι (? perhaps = ved. *nu*), νίσσομαι (for νεσjομαι), νόστος.

नस् *nas*, see *nâsâ* and *asmad*.

ऽनस *-nas* + *a*, a substitute for *nâsâ*, when latter part of a comp. adj., e.g. *unnasa*, i.e. *ud-*, adj. Having a prominent nose, Bhâg. P. 8, 8, 42. *go-*, **1.** m. A large kind of snake, Suçr. 2, 265, 12. **2.** f. *sâ*, The nose of a cow, 2, 171, 7. **3.** f. *sī*, A certain plant, 2, 170, 1. *vi-*, adj. Noseless. *su-*, adj. Handsome-nosed.

नस्तक *nas* + *ta* + *ka*, m. A hole bored through the bridge of the nose of cattle for draught, MBh. 12, 9377.

नस्ततस् *nas* + *ta* + *tas*, adv. Out of the nose, MBh. 4, 2227.

नस्तस् *nas* + *tas*, adv. **1.** Out of the nose, Bhâg. P. 2, 7, 11. **2.** In the nose, Suçr. 2, 297, 6.

नस्य *nas* + *ya*, n. **1.** A sternutatory, Suçr. 2, 235, 21. **2.** f. *yâ*, A nose-bridle.—Comp. *Chhinna-nasya*, adj. with broken nose-bridle, Yâjñ. 2, 299.

नस्योत *nasyota*, i.e. *nas* + *i-â-uta* (vb. *ve*), adj. **1.** Led by a string through the septum of the nose, MBh. 3, 1142.

नह् *NAH* (for original *nadh*), i. 4, Par., Âtm. (also i. 1 or 6, MBh. 1, 1460), **1.** To bind, Bhâg. P. 5, 14, 38. **2.** Âtm. To arm one's self, MBh. 4, 1016. Ptcple. of the pf. pass. *naddha*, **1.** Tied, Râm. 4, 12, 19. **2.** Bound, Râm. 5, 14, 15. **3.**

Covered, Hariv. 8799. 4. Joined, Râm. 4, 13, 13. 5. Laid in, MBh. 2, 1915.—With the prep. अप *apa*, To untie, MBh. 3, 13309.—With अपि *api*, or पि *pi*, 1. To fasten, MBh. 4, 301; 13, 2352. 2. To squeeze, Çâk. d. 18. 3. To cover, Râm. 5, 18, 4. *pinaddha*, Striped, MBh. 13, 976 (*indrâyudhapinaddhâṅga*, of which the body was adorned by a rainbow, viz. a cloud).—With अव *ava*, *avanaddha*, Covered, Man. 6, 76.—With आ *â*, Âtm. To be obstructed, Suçr. 2, 369, 10. *ânaddha*, 1. Bound, MBh. 6, 5525. 2. Obstructed, Suçr. 2, 373, 21. 3. Covered, 1, 22, 3.—With व्या *vi-â*, *vyânaddha*, Striped (cf. *api*), Hariv. 6884.—With उद् *ud*, 1. To press out, Suçr. 1, 301, 9. 2. To come out, MBh. 3, 11016 (p. 570). *unnaddha*, 1. Bound upward, Ragh. 18, 50. 2. Raised, Bhâg. P. 4, 11, 4. 3. Unfettered, 4, 27, 4. 4. Proud, 4, 14, 4. 5. Arrogant, 7, 10, 26.—With समुद् *sam-ud*, *samunnaddha*, 1. Unfettered, Bhâg. P. 4, 17, 33. 2. Pressed out, Suçr. 1, 280, 20. 3. Excessive, Bhâg. P. 1, 15, 3. 4. Conceited, MBh. 5, 1000. Comp. *A-*, adj. modest, 5, 1010.—With उप *upa*, *upanaddha*, Laid in, Bhâg. P. 8, 15, 6. Caus. To cause to be dressed (as a wound), Suçr. 2, 109, 18.—With परि *pari* णह् *ṇah*, 1. To span, MBh. 1, 1406. 2. To surround, Ṛit. 6, 25. *pariṇaddha*, Large, Ragh. 3, 34.—With पि *pi*, see *api*.—With सम् *sam*, 1. To fasten, Bhâg. P. 8, 12, 21. 2. To dress, MBh. 4, 1220. 3. To put on, MBh. 218, 7; 3, 14958. 4. To prepare for, Bhartṛ. 2, 6. *saṁnaddha*, 1. Tied together, Râjat. 4, 543. 2. Fastened, MBh. 15, 627. 3. Bordering, Râm. 1, 38, 21. 4. Armed, MBh. 2, 2463. 5. Accoutred, Hariv. 6402. 6. Ready, Râjat. 1, 77.—With अभिसम् *abhi-sam*, *abhisaṁnaddha*, Armed, MBh. 3, 14883.—Cf. Lat. nexus, nectere, nere, νέω, νήθω; O.H.G. nâhan, nâwan; Goth. nêthla; A.S. naedl; Goth. nehv, nehva, nehvis; A. S. neah, nearra, neahst.

नहि *na-hi*, adv. 1. For not (non enim), Man. 3, 168. 2. Not at all, Daçak. in Chr. 187, 23. 3. *na—nahi*, Certainly not, Panch. translation by Benfey, T. i. p. 465, n. 3.

नहुष *nahusha*, m. The name of an ancient king, Man. 7, 41; of a Nâga, etc.

नाक *nâka*, n. 1. Heaven, MBh. 13, 4882. 2. The mystical name of a weapon, MBh. 5, 3490.—Comp. *Tri-*, n. the three heavens, Bhâg. P. 6, 13, 16.

नाकपृष्ठ्य *nâkapṛishṭhya*, i.e. *nâka-pṛishṭha*+*ya*, adj. Being in the highest heaven, Râm. 3, 9, 26.

नाकिन् *nâkin*, i.e. *nâka*+*in*, m. A god, Bhâg. P. 7, 8, 36.

नाकुल *nâkula*, i.e. *nakula*+*a*, I. adj. Ichneumon-like, Suçr. 2, 305, 21. II. m. pl. The name of a people, MBh. 6, 2084. III. f. *lî*, The ichneumon plant, Suçr. 2, 297, 5.

नाकुलि *nâkuli*, i. e. *nakula* + *i*, patronym. A descendant of Nakula, MBh. 1, 2451.

नाग *nâga*, i.e. *naga*+*a*, I. m. 1. A serpent, especially the name of fabulous serpents, having a human face and inhabiting Pâtâla, or the infernal regions, Râm. 2, 25, 30; Man. 1, 37. 2. An elephant, Râm. 1, 6, 22. 3. A small tree, Mesua Roxburghii Wight., Suçr. 1, 171, 7. 4. One of the five vital airs,

Vedântas. in Chr. 207, 15. **5.** A proper name, Hariv. 11537, **6.** The name of a mountain, Bhâg. P. 5, 16, 27. **II.** f. *gî*, A female elephant, Suçr. 1, 178, 1. **III.** adj., f. *gî*. **1.** Consisting of serpents, MBh. 8, 2586. **2.** Produced from an elephant, Suçr. 1, 194, 1. **IV.** f. *gâ*, A proper name, Râjat. 7, 293.—**Comp.** *Diṅnâga*, i.e. *diç-*, m. an elephant supposed to support a quarter of the world, Megh. 14. *Çiçu-*, m. a kind of Râkshasa or demon, Râm. 3, 76, 28.

नागमय *nâga+maya*, adj., f. *yî*, Consisting in elephants, Hariv. 9379.

नागर *nâgara*, i.e. *nagara+a*, **I.** adj. **1.** Belonging to a town, MBh. 1, 5682; m. A citizen, Râm. 1, 17, 34. **2.** Referring to a town, MBh. 2, 256. **3.** Polite, Çâk. 94, 10 Ch. **II.** f. *rî*, A crafty woman, Haeb. Anth. 351, 16. **III.** n. Dry ginger, Suçr. 1, 161, 2.—**Comp.** *Deva-nâgarî*, f. the name of the character proper to Sanskrit.

नागरक *nâgara+ka*, m. The chief of a town, Çâk. 73, 1, v.r.

नागरिक *nâgarika*, i.e. *nagara+ika*, **I.** adj. Inhabiting a town, Sch. ad. Çâk. d. 51. **II.** m. **1.** A citizen, Vikr. 77, 12. **2.** Polite, Çâk. 60, 2. **2.** A superintendent of the police, Daçak. 195, 13.

नागवन्त् *nâga+vant*, adj., f. *vatî*, Consisting in elephants, MBh. 5, 5703.

नागिन् *nâgin*, i.e. *nâga+in*, adj. Surrounded by serpents, Hariv. 14844.

नाग्नजित *nâgnajita*, i.e. *nagnajit+a*, patronym. f. *tî*, A descendant of Nagnajit, Bhâg. P. 3, 3, 4.

नाटक *nâṭaka*, i.e. *naṭ+aka*, **I.** m. A mime, Râm. 1, 5, 18. **II.** n. A drama, Râm. 2, 69, 4.

नाटितक *nâṭita+ka* (vb. *naṭ*), n. A gesture, Çâk. 73, 4.

नाट्य *nâṭya*, i.e. *naṭa+ya*, n. **1.** The art of acting or dancing, scenic art, Bhâg. P. 4, 15, 19. **2.** Mimical representation, Mṛichchh. 88, 4. **3.** The attire of an actor, Bhâg. P. 1, 8, 19.

नाडिका *nâḍikâ*, i.e. *nâḍi+ka*, f. **1.** A measure of time, $\frac{1}{60}$ of a sideral day, an Indian hour, Bhâg. P. 3, 11, 3. **2.** A measure of length, half a daṇḍa, Mârk. P. 49, 39. **3.** An Indian clock, Kâm. Nîtis. 5, 51.

नाडी *nâḍî*, i.e. *naḍa+a+î*, also

नाडि *nâḍi* (Bhâg. P. 3, 5, 11), f. **1.** The stalk or culm of any plant. **2.** Any tubular organ of the body, as an artery, a vein, an intestine, etc., MBh. 3, 13974; Ragh. 10, 59 (the rays of the sun, supposed to be hollow). **3.** A fistulous sore, Suçr. 1, 284, 11. **4.** =*nâḍikâ* 1, Sûryas. 1, 12.—**Comp.** *Garbha-nâḍî*, f. the navel-string, Suçr. 1, 368, 13.

नाणक *nâṇaka*, n. A coin, Yâjń. 2, 240.

नाथ् *NÂTH*, and **नाध्** *NÂDH* (akin to *nam*), i. 1, Âtm. (also Par., MBh. 3, 12630). To beg, MBh. 12, 1365 (with gen. of the object, MBh. 3, 12630).

नाथ *nâth+a*, m. **1.** A protector, MBh. 2292. **2.** A master, a lord, Pańch. v. d. 90; Râm. 1, 76, 19. **3.** A husband, Ragh. 12, 75.—**Comp.** *A-*, adj., f. *thâ*, having no protector, helpless, Râm. 6, 23, 21. *Kâla-*, m. a name of Çiva, MBh. 12, 10368. *Ku-*, 1. m. a bad protector, Bhâg. P. 9, 14, 28. 2. adj. having a bad guide, 5, 14, 2. *Gaurî-*, m. a name of Çiva, Bhartṛ. 3, 87. *Chamû-*, m. a commander of an army, Bhâg. P. 4, 26, 3. *Jagat-eka-*,

m. monarch of the world, Ragh. 5, 23. *Jagannâtha*, i.e. *jagat-*, m. a name of Vishṇu or Kṛishṇa, MBh. 2, 779. *Jivita-*, m. a husband, Kumâras. 4, 3. *Dharma-*, m. a legitimate lord, Râm. 5, 33, 39. *Nakshatra-*, m. the moon, Hariv. 16033. *Nara-*, m. a king, Râm. 2, 68, 55 Gorr. *Nâki(n)-*, m. a name of Indra, Çatr. 2, 7. *Prajâ-*, m. a king, Râjat. 5, 191. *Prâṇa-*, m. a husband. *Bhûmi-*, m. a king, Lass. 14, 20. *Yadu-*, m. a name of Kṛishṇa. *Raghu-*, m. Râma. *Rajani-chaya-*, m. the moon, Hit. ii. d. 107. *Viçva-*, m. 1. a name of Çiva. 2. a proper name, Chr. p. 234, l. 6. *Sa-*, I. adj. endowed, Pañch. 76, 18. II. f. *thâ*, a woman whose husband is living.

नाथत्व *nâtha+tva*, n. The dignity of a protector, Râm. 2, 81, 2 Gorr.

नाथवन्त् *nâtha+vant*, adj., f. *vatî*. **1.** Having a protector, Râm. 1, 62, 12. **2.** Having a husband, 5, 37, 20.

नाथाय *NÂTHÂYA*, a denomin. derived from *nâtha* with *ya*, Par. To grant, Bhâg. P. 2, 9, 25.

नाथिन् *nâthin*, i.e. *nâtha+in*, adj., f. *nî*, Having a protector, Râm. 1, 78, 3 Gorr.

नाद *nâda*, i.e. *nad+a*, m. **1.** Roaring, Râm. 4, 29, 12. **2.** Sound, cry, MBh. 4, 1885; 14, 2694. **3.** A semicircle representing the nasal sound, Bhâg. P. 7, 15, 53.—**Comp.** *Bhîma-*, m. a lion. *Mahâ-*, m. 1. a loud cry. 2. an elephant. 3. a lion. 4. a camel. 5. the car. *Megha-*, m. 1. Varuṇa. 2. a son of Varuṇa. *Siṁha-*, m. war cry, Pañch. 5, 4 (signifying principal).

नादिन् *nâdin*, i.e. *nad* or *nâda+in*, I. adj., f. *nî*, Sounding, sounding aloud, Hariv. 8069; MBh. 2, 987. II. m. a proper name, Hariv. 12941.

नादेय *nâdeya*, i.e. *nadî+eya*, I. adj. **1.** Coming from a river, Suçr. 1, 170, 11. **2.** Aquatic, Râm. 4, 39, 12. II. n. A sort of salt, Suçr. 2, 326, 9.

नाध् *NÂDH*, see *nâth*.

नाना *nânâ*, adv. Different, Bhâg. P. 1, 2, 32. Often in the beginning of comp. words, Of different classes, Man. 9, 148; various, 257.

नानात्व *nânâ+tva*, n. **1.** Difference, MBh. 2, 137. **2.** Manifoldness, Bhâg. P. 2, 10, 13.

नान्दी *nândî*, i.e. *nand+a+î*, f. **1.** Joy, MBh. 4, 2189. **2.** A prayer at the opening of a drama, Mṛichchh. 1, 8.

नापित *nâpita*, based on the nom. sing. *snâpitâ*, i.e. *snâp*, curtailed Causal of *snâ*, *+tṛi*. **1.** m. A barber, Man. 4, 253. **2.** f. *tî*, The wife of a barber, Pañch. 37, 7.

नाभ *nâbha*, I. a substitute for *nâbhi*, when latter part of a comp. adj. or of a noun based on an adj., e.g. *abja-* and *padma-* (Having a lotus in his navel), m. A name of Vishṇu. *padma-nâbha* also, **1.** A proper name. **2.** A kind of spell. *su-*, adj. **1.** Having a handsome nave, MBh. 10, 625. **2.** Having a beautiful centre, Râm. 1, 33, 12. *kâla-*, m. The name of an Asura or demon and others. *kuça-*, m. A proper name, Râm. 1, 34, 3. *tri-*, m. A name of Vishṇu (holding the three worlds in his navel), Bhâg. P. 8, 17, 26. *dṛidha-*, m. The name of a spell, Râm. 1, 30, 5. *pushkara-*, m. A name of Vishṇu, Bhâg. P. 4, 6, 48. *vatsa-*, m. a particular poisonous tree. II. m. Epithet of Çiva, MBh. 12, 10364. III. A proper name, Bhâg. P. 9, 9, 16.

नाभाग *nâbhâga* (cf. *nabhaga*), m. A proper name, MBh. 1, 3140; Râm. 1, 70, 41.

नाभागि *nâbhâgi*, i.e. *nâbhâga+i*, patronym. A son of Nâbhâga, MBh. 12, 993.

नाभि *nâbhi* (*nabh + i* ?), f. (also **नाभी** *nâbhî*), and m. **1.** The navel, Man. 1, 92. **2.** The nave of a wheel, MBh. 1, 726. **3.** Centre, Bhâg. P. 5, 16, 7. **4.** Chief, Ragh. 18, 19. **5.** Musk, Megh. 53. **6.** (m. ?) The musk animal, Bhâg. P. 3, 21, 44. **7.** m. A proper name, 5, 2, 19.—**Comp.** *Ûrṇa-*, m. a spider, 2, 5, 5. *Chakra-*, f. the nave of a wheel, Suçr. 1, 354, 7. *Nis-*, adj. not reaching to the navel, Kumâras. 7, 7. *Mṛiga-*, m. musk. *Visa-*, m. a quantity of lotusses. *Vṛiddha-*, adj. corpulent. *Sa-*, I. adj. 1. uterine, Man. 9, 192. 2. like, resembling. 3. affectionate. II. m. 1. an uterine brother. 2. a paternal kinsman, Man. 5, 72. —Cf. A.S. nafu, nafela; ὀμφαλός; Lat. umbilicus.

नाभिक *nâbhi+ka*, a substitute for *nâbhi* at the end of comp. adj., MBh. 12, 8946.

नाभ्य *nâbhya*, i.e. *nâbhi+ya*, adj. **1.** Proceeding from the navel, Bhâg. P. 3, 4, 13. **3.** Epithet of Çiva, MBh. 12, 10364.—**Comp.** *Sa-*, m. a relation as far as the seventh degree, Man. 5, 84.

नाम *nâma*, see *nâman*.

नामक *nâmaka*, i.e. *nâman+ka*, a substitute for *nâman* at the end of comp. adj., f. *mikâ*, e.g. *chandra-saras-*, Called Chandrasaras, Pañch. 159, 20. *parvata-nâmikâ*, f. Having the name of a mountain, Man. 3, 9.

नामतस् *nâmatas*, i.e. *nâman+tas*, adv. **1.** = the abl. of *nâman*, Bhâg. P. 5, 12, 8. **2.** By name, together with the name, Man. 8, 255. **3.** With respect to the name, Çâk. 104, 22.

नामधेय *nâmadheya*, i.e. *nâman+dheya* (vb. *dhâ*), n. **1.** A name, Man. 2, 123. **2.** A title, Bhâg. P. 4, 22, 56. **3.** The ceremony of giving a name to a child, Man. 2, 30.—**Comp.** *Puṁnâmadheya*, i.e. *puṁs-*, m. one of the male sex, Râm. 5, 35, 43.

नामधेयतस् *nâmadheya+tas*, adv. By name, Râm. 4, 62, 10.

नामन् *nâman*, i.e. *jñâ + man*, I. n. **1.** A name, Man. 2, 128. **2.** Only the name (opposed to the reality), 157. II. acc. sing. *nâma*, adv. **1.** By name, Man. 3, 127. **2.** Indeed, of course, 8, 335. **3.** Perhaps, Râm. 2, 85, 18 Gorr. **4.** It is often preceded, **a.** by an interrogative pronoun, Then, Râm. 2, 15, 20 Gorr.; **b.** by *api*, Perhaps, 2, 97, 6 Gorr. Of course, Çâk. 93, 5, v. r.; would that; **c.** by *mâ*, Perhaps (I hope not), Mṛichchh. 54, 24; **d.** by *nanu*, Certainly, Râm. 4, 24, 37. **5.** With an imperative, No matter, Mṛichchh. 75,6.—**Comp.** when latter part of a comp. adj. the fem. ends *-nâmnî*, Man. 3, 9; or *-nâman*, Râm. 1, 6, 25; or *-nâmâ*, 2, 109, 47 Gorr. *A-*, adj. not named, not declared, Man, 12, 108. *Ushṭra-*, adj. called camel, Pañch. 68, 15. *Gṛihîta-* (vb. *grah*), adj. called, Nal. 12, 48. *Dus-*, n. hæmorrhoids, Suçr. 1, 177, 10. *Pitṛi-*, adj. called after his father's name, Châṇ. 79 in Berl. Monatsb. *Mâtṛi-*, adj. called after his mother's name, ib. *Çyâla-*, adj. called after the name of his brother-in-law, ib. *Su-*, adj., f. *mnî*, well-named, MBh. 1, 1053. *Strî-*, adj. having a female name, Chr. 63, 67.—Cf. Lat. nomen, co-gnomen, nam, quis-nam (cf. quem-nam = *kaṁ nâma*), nem-pe (cf. *nâma api*); ὄνομα (for ὀ + γνομα), ὀνομαίνω (for ὀνομαν + jω); Goth. namo; A.S. nama, nemnan.

नायक *nâyaka*, i.e. *nî+aka*, I. m. **1.** A guide, Râm. 2, 64, 33. **2.** A chief, Bhâg. P. 4, 7, 22. **3.** A general, Râm. 3, 33, 14. **4.** A husband, Bhâg. P. 4, 25, 20. **5.** A lover, Çâk. 15, 12. **6.** The central gem of a necklace, Vâsav. 17, 1. 7. A proper name, Râjat. 5, 158. II. f. *yikâ*, A mistress, Lass. 24, 17.—Comp. *A-*, adj., f. *kâ*, deprived of or wanting a guide, a commander, a ruler, Râm. 2, 14, 52; 79, 3. *Ku-nâyaka*, adj. having a bad guide, Bhâg. P. 5, 13, 2. *Kumudinî-*, m. the moon, Hit. 9, 5. *Gaṇa-*, m. 1. the chief of the retinue of a god, Bhâg. P. 5, 17, 3. 2. the god Gaṇeça, MBh. 1, 77. *Chakra-*, m. the chief of a division of an army, Râjat. 2, 106. *Daṇḍa-*, m. 1. a judge, Hit. 66, 6. 2. the commander of a division of an army, Râjat. 7, 969. *Bhûta-nâyikâ*, f. Durgâ.

नायकत्व *nâyaka-tva*, n. Chieftainship.

नार *nâra*, I. i.e. *nṛi* or *nara* + *a*, adj. Belonging to a man, Man. 5, 87. II. m. Water (cf. *nîra*, νηρός, Νηρεύς), Man. 1, 10. III. f. **नारी** *nârî*, i.e. *nṛi* + *î*, 1. A woman, Man. 1, 32. 2. A proper name, Bhâg. P. 5, 2, 22.—Comp. *Kula-nârî*, f. a virtuous woman, Hit. i. d. 196. *Divya-nârî*, f. an Apsaras, Râm. 2, 91, 19. *Prakâça-nârî*, f. a harlot, Mṛichchh. 46, 2.

नारक *nâraka*, i.e. *naraka* + *a*, I. adj., f. *kî*, Infernal, hellish, Bhâg. P. 3, 30, 30. II. m. 1. An inhabitant of the infernal regions, 2, 10, 41. 2. Hell.

नारकिन् *nârakin*, i.e. *nâraka* + *in*, m. An inhabitant of hell, Prab. 46, 3.

नारङ्ग *nâraṅga*, m. An orange tree, Suçr. 1, 209, 6.

नारद *nârada*, m. A Devarshi, i.e. a celestial Ṛishi; in epic poetry the messenger of the gods, MBh. 1, 2048.

नारसिंह *nârasiṁha*, i.e. *nara-siṁha* + *a*, adj., f. *hî*, Referring, belonging, etc., to Vishṇu in his incarnation as man-lion, MBh. 3, 15837.

नाराच *nârâcha* (perhaps *nara-añch* + *a*), m. A kind of arrow, MBh. 1, 5522.

नारायण *nârâyaṇa*, probably *nara* + *âyana*, I. m. 1. The first living being, identified with Vishṇu or Kṛishṇa, MBh. 7, 9447; Man. 1, 10. 2. A proper name, Bhâg. P. 6, 1, 24. II. adj. Referring, belonging to Nârâyaṇa, MBh. 1, 337. III. f. *ṇî*, patronym. name of Indrasenâ, MBh. 4, 651.

नारायणमय *nârâyaṇa* + *maya*. adj. Consisting of Nârâyaṇa, Bhâg. P. 6, 8, 4.

नारायणीय *nârâyaṇîya*, i.e. *nârâyaṇa* + *îya*, adj. Referring to Nârâyaṇa, MBh. 12, 13422.

नारिकेर *nârikera*, and **नारिकेल** *nârikela*, m. The cocoa-nut, Suçr. 2, 108, 9; Râm. 3, 39, 12.—Cf. *nâlikera*.

नारी *nârî*, see *nâra*.

नारीक *nârî* + *ka*, a substitute for *nârî* at the end of comp. adj., Râm. 2, 109, 22 Gorr.

नारीमय *nârî* + *maya*, adj., f. *yî*, Consisting in wives, Bhartṛ. 1, 98.

नाल *nâla*, i.e. *nala* + *a*, I. adj. Consisting of reed, Bhâg. P. 6, 11, 8. II. n. 1. A hollow or tubular stalk, especially the stalk of the water-lily, MBh. 2, 88. 2. A tubular vessel of the body, Prab. 55, 5. 3. A handle, MBh. 9, 909. III. f. *lâ*, The name of a river, MBh. 6, 339.—Comp. *Nâbhi-nâlâ*, f. the navel-string, Ragh. 5, 7. *Yantra-nâla*, n. a pipe (of a well), Mârk. P. 39, 43.

नालाय *NÂLÂYA*, a denomin. derived from *nâla* with *ya*, ptcple. of the pf. pass. *nâlâyita*, Representing the handle of an axe, Bhâg. P. 7, 5, 17.

नालिकेर *nâlikera*, and **नालिकेल** *nâlikela*, m. The cocoa-nut, Suçr. 2, 175, 2; 1, 213, 3.—Cf. *nârikela*.

नालिनी *nâlinî*, i.e. *nâla*+*in*+*î*, f. A mystical name of one of the nostrils, Bhâg. P. 4, 29, 11.

नालीक *nâlîka*, i.e. *nâla*+*ika*, m. A kind of arrow, Râm. 3, 31, 24.

नावनीत *nâvanîta*, i.e. *navanîta*+*a*, adj. Mild, Chr. 43, 29.

नाविक *nâvika*, i.e. *nau*+*ika*, m. The helmsman of a vessel, a pilot, Râm. 2, 52, 74.

नाव्य *nâvya*, i.e. *nau*+*ya*, adj. **1.** Navigable, Ragh. 4, 31. **2.** Accessible to a ship, MBh. 3, 10027.

नाश *nâça*, i.e. 2. *naç*+*a*, m. **1.** Loss, Bhartṛ. 2, 35. **2.** Disappearance, Râm. 2, 47, 13. **3.** Destruction, Yâjń. 1, 339. **4.** Death, 63.—**Comp.** *Artha-*, m. ruin of wealth, Chân. 80 in Berl. Monatsb. *Chitta-*, m. the vanishing of consciousness, Râm. 2, 64, 68. *Duḥsvapna-*, i.e. *dus-*, adj. Removing the dreams, Hariv. 8459.

नाशक *nâçaka*, i.e. 2. *naç*, Caus., +*aka*, adj. Destroying, MBh. 13, 1634. —**Comp.** *Kṛita-*, adj. ungrateful, Hit. iii. d. 126. *Vighna-*, m. Gaṇeça.

नाशन *nâçana*, i.e. 2. *naç*, Caus., +*ana*, I. adj., f. *nî.* **1.** Destroying, MBh. 13, 2194; Man. 8, 127. **2.** Removing, MBh. 2, 426. **II.** n. **1.** Destruction, Mârk. P. 24, 36. **2.** Removal, MBh. 7, 5120.—**Comp.** *Kṛita-pûrva-*, n. ungratefulness, Hit. 27, 16, n. *Bhûta-*, I. m. 1. marking nut plant, Semicarpus anacardium. 2. mustard. II. n. the Eleocarpus seed. *Matsya-*, m. an osprey.

नाशिन् *nâçin*, i.e. 2. *naç*, or *nâça*+*in*, adj., f. *nî.* **1.** Perishable, Prab. 100, 11. **2.** Removing, Hariv. 10239. **3.** Destroying, Râm. 6, 80, 32.—**Comp.** *A-*, adj. 1. not being lost, Man. 8, 185. 2. not perishing, Bhag. 2, 18.

नाष्टिक *nâshṭika*, i.e. *nashṭa* (vb. 2. *naç*) +*ika*, m. The former owner who has lost a chattel.

† नास् *NAS*, i. 1, Âtm. To sound.

नासत्य *nâsatya*, i.e. *na-a-satya*, I. m. du. A name of the Açvins, MBh. 12, 7583. **II.** adj. Referring to the Nâsatyas, 12, 13491.

नासा *nâsâ*, the base of some cases and derivatives is *nas*, f. The nose, Man. 8, 125.—**Comp.** *Karṇa-nâsâ*, f. the ears and the nose, Râm. 3, 24, 22. *Tiryagnâsa*, i.e. *tiryańch-*, adj. having a wry nose, 5, 17, 32. *Nâga-nâsâ*, f. the trunk of an elephant, 5, 22, 2. *Sthûla-nâsa*, m. a hog.—Cf. O.H.G. nasa; A.S. nase; Lat. nâsus, nâris.

नासिका *nâsikâ*, i.e. *nâsâ*+*ka*, f. **1.** A nostril, Bhâg. P. 5, 23, 6. **2.** du. The nose, 2, 10, 20. **3.** sing. The nose, Man. 2, 90. **4.** The trunk of an elephant, MBh, 13, 4900.—**Comp.** *Agra-*, f. the tip of the nose, Râm. 1, 28, 10. *Pûti-nâsika*, adj. having a stinking nose, Yâjń. 3, 211. *Rakta-nâsika*, m. an owl. *Sthûla-*, m. a hog.

नास्तिक *nâstika*, i. e. *na-asti* (vb. 1. *as*) +*ka*, m. An unbeliever, Man. 2, 11.

नास्तिकता *nâstika*+*tâ*, f. Infidelity, MBh. 12, 4539.

नास्तिक्य *nâstikya*, i.e. *nâstika*+*ya*. **1.** Disbelief, Man. 3, 65. **2.** Infidelity, 4, 163.

नास्य *nâsya*, i.e. *nâsâ*+*ya*, n. **1.** A nose-cord, Man. 8, 291. **2.** A multitude of noses (?), Hariv. 15996.

नाह *nâha*, i. e. *nah*+*a*, m. Obstruction, Suçr. 2, 369, 5.

नाहुष *nâhusha*, i. e. *nahusha*+*a*, patronym. A son of Nahusha, Râm. 3, 23, 24.

नि *ni*, preposition, Downward, into, backward. **1.** Combined and compounded with verbs and their derivatives (q. cf.). **2.** Compounded with nouns, and implying sometimes negation, Deprived of, without; cf. *niviḍa*, *niçabda* (in this signification it is curtailed from *nis*). Probably for primitive *ani*.—Cf. ἐνί, εἰν, ἐν; Lat. in; Goth. in, inn; A.S. in, nidhan, see *nitarâm*.

निंस् *NIṀS* (probably an old desider. of *nam*, for *ninaṁsa*), i. 1, Âtm. To touch, to kiss.

निःशेषता *niḥçeshatâ*, i.e. *nis-çesha* + *tâ*, f. Complete destruction, Pańch. 195, 9.

निःशेषय *NIḤÇESHAYA*, a denomin. derived from *nis-çesha* with *aya*, Par. **1.** To destroy completely, Prab. 6, 11; Pańch. 201, 23 (see Benfey's translation, n. 1210). **2.** To consume completely, Râm. 1, 65, 6.

निःश्रेणि *niḥçreṇi*, and **निःश्रेणी** *niḥçreṇî*, i.e. *nis-çri* + *nî*, f. A ladder, MBh. 12, 12058; 8838.

निःश्वास *niḥçvâsa*, i.e. *nis-çvas* + *a*, m. **1.** Breathing, Daçak. in Chr. 198, 22. **2.** Breath, Man. 3, 19. **3.** Sigh, Râm. 2, 24, 7.

निःसत्यता *niḥsatyatâ*, i.e. *nis-satya* + *tâ*, f. Lying disposition, Hit. i. d. 91.

निःसरण *niḥsaraṇa*, i.e. *nis-sṛi* + *ana*, n. **1.** Going forth or out, MBh. 12, 10061; Pańch. i. d. 458. **2.** A means against, MBh. 12, 7799.

निःसार *niḥsâra*, i.e. *nis-sṛi* + *a*, m. Coming out, MBh. 12, 10686.—Cf. *sâra*.

निःसारण *niḥsâraṇa*, i.e. *nis-sṛi* Caus., + *ana*, n. Turning out, Râjat. 7, 582.

निःस्रव *niḥsrava*, i.e. *nis-sru* + *a*, m. A surplus, Yâjń. 2, 251.

निःस्राव *niḥsrâva*, i.e. *nis-sru* + *a*, m. Expense, Kâm. Nîtis. 4, 62.

निःस्वन *niḥsvana*, i.e. *nis-svan* + *a*, m. Noise, MBh. 1, 119; sound, Râm. 3, 34, 34.—**Comp.** *Sâgara-ud-bhûta-*, adj. roaring like the ocean.

निकट *ni-kaṭa* (cf. *kaṭa*), **I.** adj., f. *ṭâ*, Near. **II.** n. Proximity, Kathâs. 3, 73.

निकर *nikara*, i. e. *ni-kṛi* + *a*, m. A flock or multitude, Gît. 11, 4; MBh. 15, 722.

निकर्तन *nikartana*, i.e. *ni-kṛit* + *ana*, n. Cutting down, MBh. 5, 894; cutting off, Râm. 3, 74, 32.

निकष *ni-kash* (for *karsh*, vb. *kṛish*), + *a*, **I.** m. **1.** The touchstone, Ragh. 17, 46. **2.** The test appearing on the touchstone, MBh. 12, 7471. **II.** f. *shâ*, A proper name, Râm. 5, adhy. 76.

निकषण *nikashaṇa*, i.e. *ni-kash* (for (*karsh*, vb. *kṛish*), + *ana*, n. A touchstone, Bhâg. P. 5, 19, 3.

निकषा *nikashâ*, an old instr. of *ni-kash* (for *karsh*, vb. *kṛish*), + *a*, prepos. with acc. Near, Hariv. 16038.

निकषाय *NIKASHÂYA*, i.e. a denomin. derived from *nikasha* with *ya*, Âtm. To serve as touchstone, Daçak. 1, 7.

निकाम *nikâma*, i.e. *ni-kam* + *a*, **I.** m. Desire. **II.** °*mam*, acc. adv. **1.** Willingly, Bhâg. P. 8, 2, 24. **2.** At one's own discretion, Pańch. i. d. 417.

निकामतस् *nikâma* + *tas*, adv. Willingly, Mârk. P. 49, 57.—**Comp.** *A-*, adv. unwillingly, Bhâg. P. 4, 28, 10.

निकाय *nikâya*, i.e. *ni-chi* + *a*, m. **1.** An assemblage, a class, Man. 1, 36.

2. A multitude, Bhâg. P. 4, 24, 25. 3. A house, a dwelling-place, Râm. 4, 44, 31.

निकार *nikâra*, i. e. *ni-kṛi + a*, m. 1. Humiliation, MBh. 1, 7081. 2. Abuse, 14, 1788.

निकाश *ni + kâç + a*. 1. m. Sight, Bhâg. P. 3, 16, 30. 2. Latter part of comp. adj., Similar, Râm. 3, 30, 18.

निकुञ्ज *ni-kuñja*, m. (and n.). A place overgrown with creepers, a thicket, MBh. 1, 3730.

निकुम्भ *ni-kumbha*, m. 1. A plant, Croton polyandrum, Hariv. 3843. 2. A proper name, 8002.

निकुम्भिल *nikumbhila*, m. or n. and f. *lâ*, A place of offering, Râm. 5, 25, 51 ; 6, 19, 39.

निकुरुम्ब *nikurumba*, n. A multitude, Gît. 11, 5.

निकुलीनिका *nikulînikâ*, probably *ni-kulîna + ka*, f. An inherited art, MBh. 8, 1902.

निकूल *ni-kûla*, adj. Standing at the bank (?), Râm. 2, 68, 16, v. r.

निकृति *ni-kṛi + ti*, I. f. 1. Dishonesty, MBh. 2, 2042. 2. Abuse, Bhartṛ. 2, 30. 3. A wicked person, MBh. 12, 6269. II. m. The name of a deity, Hariv. 11540.

निकृतिन् *nikṛitin*, i.e. *ni-kṛita + in* (vb. *kṛi*), adj. Wicked, MBh. 13, 5120 ; cf. the last.

निकृत्या *ni-kṛi + tyâ*, f. Dishonesty, MBh. 12, 9766.

निकृन्तन *nikṛintana*, i.e. *ni-kṛit + ana*, I. adj., f. *nî*, Destroying, Râm. 1, 30, 14 Gorr. II. m. The name of a hell, Mârk. P. 12, 15. III. n. 1. Cutting, MBh. 2, 2193. 2. Destruction, 3, 14438.

निकृष्टाशयता *nikṛishṭâçayatâ*, i. e. *ni-kṛishṭa + âçaya + tâ*, f. Base disposition of mind, Daçak. in Chr. 196, 7 (jealousy).

निकेत *niketa*, i. e. *ni-kit + a*, m. 1. A mansion, MBh. 3, 8358. 2. A countersign, 12541.—Comp. *A-*, adj. without a house, Man. 6, 25. *Chatushpatha-niketâ*, i.e. *chatur-patha-*, f. the name of a deity, MBh. 9, 2643.

निकेतन *niketana*, i.e. *ni-kit + ana*, n. 1. A mansion, Man. 11, 128. 2. A temple, Râjat. 5, 30.—Comp. *Vairochana-*, n. (The abode of Bali, i.e.) Pâtâla, the intermediate region between the earth and Naraka, over which part Bali presides. *Svapna-*, n. A bed-chamber.

निक्ष् *NIKSH*, i. 1, Par. 1. † To kiss. 2. To pierce.

निक्षेप *nikshepa*, i.e. *ni-kship + a*, m. 1. Casting on, Sâh. D. 18, 14. 2. A deposit, Man. 8, 4.

निक्षेपण *nikshepaṇa*, i.e. *ni-kship + ana*, n. Putting down, Kumâras. 1, 33. 2. A place for keeping something, Suçr. 1, 171, 18.

निक्षेप्तृ *nikshepṭṛi*, i. e. *ni-kship + tṛi*, m. A depositor, Man. 8, 181.

निखर्ब *ni-kharba*, n. A very great number, 100,000,000,000, or a billion, Râm. 6, 3, 45.

निखिल *nikhila*, probably for *niḥ-khila*, i.e. *nis-khila*, adj. Complete, entire, all, Man. 2, 8. Instr. °*lena*, adv. Completely, Râm. 4, 41, 74.

निगड *nigaḍa*, probably *ni-gal + a*, m. and n. 1. An iron chain for the feet, Mṛichchh. 97, 25. 2. A fetter, Bhâg. P. 6, 9, 40.

निगडन *nigaḍana*, i.e. *nigaḍaya +*

ana, n. Putting in irons, Daçak. in Chr. 198, 11.

निगडय *NIGAḌAYA*, a denomin. derived from *nigaḍa* with *aya*, To put in irons, Daçak. in Chr. 198, 1.

निगद् *ni-gad* + *a*, m. A prayer, Bhâg. P. 5, 3, 16.

निगम *ni-gam* + *a*, m. **1.** Holy writ, the Vedas, Man. 9, 19. **2.** A passage (of the Vedas), Chr. 9, 45. **3.** A precept, Bhâg. P. 1, 5, 39. **4.** A merchant, Râm. 2, 125, 10 Gorr.

निगमिन् *nigamin*, i.e. *nigama* + *in*, adj. Versed in the Vedas, Bhâg. P. 4, 22, 47.

निगादिन् *nigâdin*, i.e. *ni-gad* + *in*, adj. Reciting, Suçr. 2, 158, 12.

निगूहन *nigûhana*, i.e. *ni-guh* + *ana*, n. Hiding, MBh. 3, 1404.

निगृहीतृ *nigṛihîtṛi*, i.e. a false form for *ni-grah* + *itṛi*, m. **1.** One who lays hold on somebody, Daçak. in Chr. 200, 13. **2.** One who prevents somebody, Bhâg. P. 1, 12, 26.

निग्रह *ni-grah* + *a*, m. **1.** Seizing, Mṛichchh. 10, 21. **2.** Confinement, Bhâg. P. 8, 22, 21. **3.** Subduing, Man. 7, 175. **4.** Suppression, restraining, 6, 71; 302. **5.** Chastising, Kathâs. 18, 36. **6.** A name of Çiva, MBh. 13, 1179.—Comp. *Upastha-*, m. continence, Yâjń. 3, 314. *Dus-*, adj. difficult to be subdued, Bhag. 6, 35. *Su-*, adj. easily restrained.

निग्रहण *nigrahaṇa*, i.e. *ni-grah* + *ana*, I. adj. Suppressing, Suçr. 1, 155, 16. II. n. **1.** Suppression, Râm. 6, 99, 48. **2.** Punishment, MBh. 15, 230.

निघर्ष *nigharsha*, i.e. *ni-ghṛish* + *a*, m. **1.** Friction, Kir. 2, 5. **2.** Crushing, Böhtl. Ind. Spr. 341.

निघर्षण *nigharshaṇa*, i.e. *ni-ghṛish* + *ana*, n. Rubbing, MBh. 12, 12375.

निघात *nighâta*, i.e. *ni-han*, Caus., + *a*, m. Blow, stroke, Ragh. 11, 78.

निघातिन् *nighâtin*, i.e. *ni-han*, Caus., + *in*, adj. **1.** Killing, Hariv. 7026. **2.** Destroying, Arj. 7, 26.

निघ्न *nighna*, i.e. *ni-han* + *a*, I. adj. Dependent, Ragh. 14, 58. II. m. A proper name, Hariv. 818.—Comp. *Vâyu-*, adj. frantic, Daçak. in Chr. 200, 9.

निचय *nichaya*, i.e. *ni-chi* + *a*, m. **1.** Heaping, Râm. 2, 77, 22. **2.** Collection, MBh. 15, 205. **3.** Heap, multitude, 4, 30. **4.** Provision, 11, 48. **5.** The parts (of a whole), 15, 5416.

निचुल *nichula*, m. A tree, Barringtonia acutangula Gaertn., Râm. 3, 17, 7.

निचोल *nichola*, m. A cover, a wrapper, Râjat. 3, 169.

निच्छिवि *nichchhivi*, m. The name of a mixed class: the son of a Vrâtya Kshatriya, Man. 10, 22.

निज् *NIJ*, ii. 3, Par. Âtm. **1.** To cleanse, MBh. 7, 8531. **2.** † To nourish.—With the prep. **निस्** *nis*, *nirṇikta*, **1.** Sprinkled, Man. 5, 127. **2.** Polished, Bhâg. P. 3, 28, 27. **3.** Purified, MBh. 12, 9735. **4.** Cleared up, explained, Hariv. 11220.—With **परिनिस्** *pari-nis*, To wash, MBh. 5, 1399.—Cf. probably νίζω.

निज *ni-ja* (vb. *jan*), adj. Own, Man. 2, 50.

† **निञ्ज्** *NIŃJ*, ii. 2, Âtm. = *nij*.

नितम्ब *nitamba* (akin to *stamba*), m. **1.** du. The buttocks, Çâk. d. 35. **2.** The slope of a mountain, Râm. 4, 44, 34. **3.** A bank, MBh. 1, 4650.

नितम्बिन् *nitambin*, i.e. *nitamba* + *in*, adj., f. *nī*. **1.** Latter part of comp. adj. Having buttocks, e.g. *chāru-pīna-nitamba* + *in*, Having beautiful big buttocks, Mârk. P. 17, 20. **2.** Having beautiful buttocks, Mâlav. 24. **3.** Having beautiful slopes, Râjat. 2, 121.

नितराम् *ni* + *tarâm*, comparative of *ni*. **1.** Continually, Vedântas. in Chr. 203, 11. **2.** Excessively, Râm. 3, 1, 2. **3.** At all events, Bhartṛ. 1, 95.—Cf. A.S. nidher; O.H.G. nidar.

नित्य *ni* + *tya*, adj., f. *yâ*. **1.** Constant, perpetual, Man. 2, 206; 58 (*nityakâlam*, adv. At all times). **2.** Eternal, Man. 1, 11. **3.** Essential, regular, 11, 203; Vedântas. in Chr. 202, 11. 4. **4.** °*yam*, adv. Perpetually, constantly, Man. 1, 108.—**Comp.** *A*-, adj. 1. perishable, 6, 77. 2. occasional, 7, 199. 3. inconstant, Râm. 2, 4, 26; uncertain, 5, 29, 31. 4. °*yam*, adv. not perpetually, Man. 3, 102. *Âtmanitya*, i.e. *âtman*-, adj. best-beloved, MBh. 1, 6080. *Taponitya*, i.e. *tapas*-, adj. practising perpetually religious austerities, 14, 264.

नित्यता *nitya* + *tâ*, f. **1.** Perpetuity, Bhâshâp. 101. **2.** Perseverance, in *dharma-nitya* + *tâ*. MBh. 3, 12531. **3.** Necessity, Mârk. P. 30, 25.—**Comp.** *A*-, f. perishableness, Bhartṛ. 3, 80.

नित्यत्व *nitya* + *tva*, n. **1.** Perpetuity, eternity, Bhâg. P. 3, 27, 17. **2.** Perseverance, in *adhyâtmajnâna-nitya* + *tva*, Bhag. 13, 11.—**Comp.** *A*-, n. 1. transitoriness, Pânch. iii. d. 21. 2. fickleness, Râm. 4, 32, 7.

नित्यदा *nitya* + *dâ*, adv. Perpetually, Indr. 1, 29.

नित्यमय *nitya* + *maya*, adj., f. *yī*, Eternal, MBh. 12, 8948.

नित्यशस् *nitya* + *ças*, adv. Constantly, Man. 2, 96.

1. **निद्** *NID*, i. 1, Par. Âtm. (only ved. and very seldom), and **निन्द्** *NIND* (perhaps originally vb. *nad*, with the prep. *ni*), i. 1, Par. (in epic poetry also Âtm., MBh. 7, 2601), To blame, MBh. 2, 2275. *nindita*, **1.** Reprehended, Man. 3, 47. **2.** Reprehensible, 42. **3.** Despised, 3, 165. **4.** Forbidden, 11, 44. **5.** Inauspicious, 182. **Comp.** *A*-, adj. blameless, Man. 3, 42. *nindya*, 1. reprehensible, Man. 3, 42. 2. forbidden, 3, 50. 3. disgraceful, 11, 53. **Comp.** 1. *A-nindya*, adj. blameless, Man. 3, 42. 2. *A-nedya*, adj. blameless, Chr. 293, 4 = Rigv. i. 87, 4.—With the prep. **परि** *pari*, To blame violently, MBh. 5, 40.—With **प्रति** *prati*, To blame, 3, 15656.—With **वि** *vi*, To blame, 3, 13700.—Cf. ὄνειδος, etc., λοίδορος, etc.; Goth. ga-naitjan, naiteins; O.H.G. neizjan; A.S. naetan, naeting; probably also Goth. neith, A.S. nidh, ge-nidhle (hatred).

† 2. **निद्** *NID*, i. 1, Par. Âtm. To be near.

निदर्शक *nidarçaka*, i. e. *ni-dṛç* + *aka*, adj. **1.** Seeing, MBh. 12, 7472. **2.** Announcing, 3, 13086.

निदर्शन *nidarçana*, i. e. *ni-dṛç* + *ana*, I. adj., f. *nī*. **1.** Showing, Bhâg. P. 2, 5, 1. **2.** Announcing, Hariv. 12815. **3.** Teaching, Bhâg. P. 5, 18, 33. II. n. **1.** Seeing, sight, MBh. 9, 62. **2.** Evidence, Man. 11, 45. **3.** Example, 9, 20; MBh. 8, 1882. **4.** Foreboding, Hariv. 9885. **5.** Prognostic, MBh. 5, 1235. **6.** Symptom, 12, 11718.

निदर्शिन् *nidarçin*, i.e. *ni-dṛç* + *in*, adj., f. *nī*, Knowing, MBh. 14, 1406.

निदाघ *nidâgha*, i.e. *ni-dah* + *a*, m. The hot season, MBh. 3, 12539.

निदान *nidâna*, i.e. *ni-3.dâ* + *ana*, n.

1. A first cause, Ragh. 3, 1. 2. The causes of disease, Bhâg. P. 6, 1, 8.

निदिग्धिका *nidigdhikâ*, i. e. *ni-digdha* + *ka*, (vb. *dih*), f. A sort of prickly nightshade, Solanum Jacquini Willd., Suçr. 1, 377, 21.

निदिध्यासन *nididhyâsana*, i.e. *ni-didhyâsa*, desider. of *dhyai*, + *ana*, n. Profound meditation, Vedântas. in Chr. 216, 1.

निदिध्यासु *nididhyâsu*, i.e. *ni-didhyâsa*, desider. of *dhyai*, + *u*, adj. Desiring to meditate on, Bhâg. P. 2, 10, 30.

निदेश *nideça*, m., i.e. 1. *ni-diç* + *a*, Order, MBh. 12, 8929. 2. *ni-deça*, Neighbourhood, Man. 2, 197.

निद्रा *ni-2. drâ*, f. 1. Sleep, Râm. 4, 26, 9. 2. Sleepiness, Hiḍ. 1, 4.—Comp. *A-*, I. f. sleeplessness. II. adj. (*A-nidra*), sleepless, Râm. 2, 2, 4. *Ati-nidra*, adj. one who sleeps excessively, 6, 37, 48. *Apa-*, adj. 1. sleepless, Kir. 5, 26. 2. opened, Çiç. 9, 30. *Unnidra*, i.e. *ud-*, and *nirnidra*, i.e. *nis-*, adj. sleepless, Megh. 86 ; Râjat. 2, 98. *Yoga-nidrâ*, f. 1. absorption in profound meditation, Pańch. 125, 25. 2. light sleep, 25, 25. *Yogi(n)-*, f. light sleep, wakefulness. *Vi-*, adj. 1. sleepless. 2. blown, budded.

निद्रालु *nidrâ* + *lu*, adj. Sleepy, Pańch. v. d. 41.

निद्रालुत्व *nidrâlu* + *tva*, n. Sleepiness, Suçr. 1, 313, 1.

निद्रित *nidrita*, i.e. *nidrâ* + *ita*, adj. Sleeping, Râjat. 3, 504.

निधन *nidhana*, i.e. perhaps *ni-han* + *a*, n. 1. Conclusion, end, MBh. 1, 4512 ; Suçr. 1, 18, 19. 2. Annihilation, Bhartṛ. 2, 13. 3. Death, Man. 5, 40.

निधनता *nidhanatâ*, i.e. *ni-dhana* + *tâ*, f. Poverty, Hit. i. d. 128 (cf. *nirdhanatâ*).

निधान *nidhâna*, i.e. *ni-dhâ* + *ana*, n. (m., Râm. 5, 11, 4), 1. Putting aside, MBh. 4, 158. 2. A receptacle, a place or vessel in or on which anything is collected or deposited, Hariv. 2477. 3. A treasure, Man. 8, 36.—Comp. *Daṇḍa-*, n. clemency, MBh. 12, 6559.

निधि *nidhi*, i.e. *ni-dhâ* (cf. *dhi* and *payodhi*), m. 1. A receptacle, MBh. 1, 1124. 2. A treasure, Man. 7, 82.—Comp. *Ambu-* and *ambhas-*, m. the ocean, Lass. 44, 11. *Kalâ-*, m. the moon, Lass. 91, 15. *Jala-*, m. the ocean, Bhartṛ. 2, 78. *Tapas-*, m. a pious person, Ragh. 1, 56. *Tejas-*, m. a majestic person, Chr. 21, 2. *Payas-*, m. the ocean. *Çila-jńâna-*, m. a virtuous and learned person.

निधिप *nidhi-pa* (vb. 2. *pâ*), m. The guardian of a treasure, Man. 2, 115.

निधुवन *nidhuvana*, i. e. *ni-dhû* + *ana*, n. Sexual intercourse, Râjat. 5, 285.

निनद *ni-nad* + *a*, m. 1. Sound, cry, MBh. 3, 820. 2. Buzzing, 8702.—Comp. *Su-*, adj. sounding agreeably, Kir. 5, 27.

निनयन *ninayana*, i.e. *ni-nî* + *ana*, n. Performance, Man. 2, 172.

निनाद *ninâda*, i.e. *ni-nad* + *a*, m. Sound, cry, MBh. 5, 3138 ; Râm. 2, 34, 19.

निनादिन् *ninâdin*, i.e. *ninâda* + *in*, and *ni-nad* + *in*, adj., f. *nî*. 1. Sounding, Râm. 1, 20, 7. 2. Playing, Hariv. 2458. 3. Accompanied by the sound of, MBh. 5, 3139.

निनीषा *ninîshâ*, i.e. *ninîsha*, desider.

of *nî*, + *a*, f. Desire to carry, MBh. 8, 3445.

निनीषु *ninîshu*, i.e. *ninîsha*, desider. of *nî*, + *u*, adj. Wishing to bring, Man. 4, 244.

निन्द् *NIND*, see 1. *nid*.

निन्दक *nind* + *aka*, adj. subst. Blaming, defaming, Man. 2, 201; a scorner, 2, 11.

निन्दन *nind* + *ana*, n. Blame, Bhâg. P. 7, 1, 22.

निन्दा *nindâ*, i.e. *nind* + *a*, f. 1. Blame, Man. 8, 19. 2. Defamation, Man. 2, 200. 3. Scorn, Bhâg. P. 4, 21, 6.

निन्द्यता *nindya* + *tâ* (vb. *nind*), f. Infamy, Man. 5, 164.

† निन्व् *NINV*, or सिन्व् *SINV*, i. 1, Par. To wet, or to wait on.

निपतन *ni-pat* + *ana*, n. 1. Falling, MBh. 8, 1788. 2. Flying, 1895.

निपात *nipâta*, i.e. *ni-pat* + *a*, m. 1. Falling, Man. 11, 104. 2. Casting, 3, 241. 3. Death, 8, 185. 4. The opposite extremity, Bhâg. P. 5, 21, 9.—Comp. *Dhârâ-*, m. A sudden shower of rain, Pańch. 93, 2.

निपातक *nipâtaka*, *ni-pat*, Caus., + *aka* (m. or n.), Sin, MBh. 5, 4053.

निपातन *nipâtana*, i.e. *ni-pat*, Caus., + *ana*, I. adj. Destroying, MBh. 3, 1624. II. n. 1. Dropping, Râm. 6, 74, 24. 2. Putting on, Suçr. 1, 95, 17. 3. Touching, 290, 17. 4. Beating, Man. 11, 208. 5. Killing, 8, 298. 6. Flying down, hurrying down, Pańch. ii. d. 57. 7. Falling down, Yâjń. 1, 145.

निपातिन् *nipâtin*, i.e. *ni-pat* + *in*, adj., f. *nî*. 1. Falling down, Vikr. d. 153. 2. Flying on, Ragh. 9, 40. 3. Destroying, MBh. 7, 9462.

निपान *nipâna*, i.e. *ni*-1. *pâ* + *ana*, n. 1. Drinking, MBh. 13, 3439. 2. A pool, Man. 4, 201.—Comp. *A-*, n. thirst, Bhâg. P. 5, 26, 8.

निपानवन्त् *nipâna* + *vant*, adj., f. *vatî*, Abounding in pools, Ragh. 9, 53.

निपुण *nipuṇa*, i. e. probably *ni-push* + *na*, adj., f. *ṇâ*. 1. Perfect, Man. 5, 61. 2. Clever, Böhtl. Ind. Spr. 490. 3. Conversant, 57. °*ṇam*, adv. 1. Completely, Râm. 2, 96, 1 Gorr. 2. Carefully, 4, 44, 82. 3. In a delicate manner, Çâk. 59, 15.

निपुणतस् *nipuṇa* + *tas*, adv. Completely, MBh, 12, 10217.

निपुणता *nipuṇa* + *tâ*, f. 1. Cleverness, Bhartṛ. Suppl. 10. 2. Carefulness, Pańch. 181, 18.

निबन्ध *ni-bandh* + *a*, m. 1. Fastening, binding, Râm. 5, 42, 4. 2. Fetter, Bhâg. P. 6, 2, 46. 3. Root, MBh. 2, 2532. 4. Fixed property, Yâjń. 2, 121. 5. A literary work.

निबन्धन *ni-bandh* + *ana*, I. adj., f. *nî*, Binding, Bhâg. P. 3, 21, 54. II. f. *nî*, Fetter, MBh. 5, 771. III. n. 1. Binding, ligation, Man. 2, 27; making (a bridge), MBh. 3, 10725. 2. Bond, fetter, 12, 9680. 3. A receptacle, Râm. 2, 31, 28 Gorr. 4. Cause, motive, MBh. 1, 5141; Man. 9, 27. 5. Syntax, Kumâras. 7, 90.—Comp. *Artha-*, adj. having (its) cause in wealth, MBh. 1, 5141. *Strî-*, n. domestic duty.

निबन्धिन् *nibandhin*, i.e. *ni-bandh* + *in*, and *nibandha* + *in*, adj., f. *nî*. 1. Binding, MBh. 12, 6548. 2. Joined, 11, 89.

निबर्हण *nibarhaṇa*, and निवर्हण *nivarhaṇa*, i.e. *ni-barh*, or *varh* + *ana*, I. adj. 1. Destroying, Ram. 1, 1, 11,

2. Removing, Suçr. 1, 166, 11. **II.** n. Destruction, Râm. 1, 3, 30 Gorr.

ऽनिभ *-ni-bha* (vb. *bhâ*), latter part of comp. adj., f. *bhâ*. **1.** Like, resembling, Râm. 3, 49, 34. **2.** Pleonastically in *châru-nibha-ânana*, adj. Handsome-faced, Hariv. 11789.

निभीम *ni-bhî+ma*, adj. Terrible, Hariv. 13599.

निमज्जन *ni-majj+ana*, I. adj., f. *nî*, Absorbing, MBh. 7, 897. **II.** n. Diving, immersion, Râjat. 1, 127.

निमन्त्रक *ni-mantr+aka*, m. An inviter, MBh. 13, 2350.

निमन्त्रण *nimantraṇa*, i.e. *ni-mantr +ana*, n. Invitation, Yâjń. 2, 263.

निमय *nimaya*, i.e. *ni-me+a*, m. Barter, exchange, MBh. 12, 2923.

निमि *nimi*, m. A proper name, Man. 7, 41.

निमित्त *ni-mitta* (vb. *mâ*), n. **1.** Aim, mark, MBh. 5, 3480. **2.** Sign, omen, Man. 6, 50; Çâk. 8, 17. **3.** Cause, motive, Bhâg. P. 8, 20, 6. **4.** Instrumental cause, MBh. 3, 10743 (the cause on which the life of a prince was dependent, cf. 10744 and 10739). **5.** °*tam* acc., °*tena* instr., °*tâya* dat., adverbially, On account of, Râm. 2, 48, 28; 90, 12; 30, 1.—**Comp.** *A-*, adj. having no motive, Çâk. d. 176. acc. °*tam*, adv. without a cause, Çâk. d. 45. *Atonimitta+m*, i.e. *atas-*, adv. therefore, Nal. 9, 34. *Kim-*, adj. by what occasioned or caused, Bhâg. P. 9, 9, 19. acc. °*tam*, adv. why, Chr. 80, 47. *Kutonimitta*, i.e. *kutas-*, adj. by what caused, Râm. 2, 74, 17. *Dus-*, n. a bad omen, MBh. 2, 818.

निमित्ततस् *nimitta+tas*, adv. By a special cause, Suçr. 1, 91, 14.—**Comp.** *A-*, adv. without cause, Man. 4, 144.

निमिष् *ni-mish*, f. Twinkling of the eye.—**Comp.** *A-*, adj. sbst. a god (free from twinkling of the eyes), Bhâg. P. 5, 23, 8.

निमिष *ni-mish+a*, m. **1.** Twinkling of the eye, Râm. 6, 102, 25. **2.** A moment, 5, 56, 59. **3.** A proper name, MBh. 5, 3595.—**Comp.** *A-*, I. adj. not twinkling, having the eyes fixed, Indr. 5, 28; Râm. 3, 6, 14. II. m. a god (see the preceding).

निमीलन *ni-mîl+ana*, n. Shutting the eye-lids, Amar. 33.

निमीलिका *nimîlikâ*, i.e. *ni-mîl+aka*, f. Twinkling of the eye; in *gaja-*, Connivance, Râjat. 6, 73.

निमीलिन् *nimîlin*, i.e. *ni-mîl+â+in*, Having the eye-lids shut, Naish. 5, 71 (cf. Sch.).

निमेष *nimesha*, i.e. *ni-mish+a*, m. **1.** Twinkling of the eye, Nal. 5, 26. **2.** A moment, Râm. 3, 36, 19. **3.** A proper name, MBh. 1, 1489.—**Comp.** *A-*, I. m. absence of twinkling, Ragh. 3, 43. **II.** adj. open, Râm. 3, 63, 22. **III.** m. a god, Bhâg. P. 6, 10, 1 (see *nimish*).

निम्न *ni+mna* (i.e. *ni+man+a*), **I.** adj., f. *nâ*. **1.** Deep, Ṛit. 5, 12; with *na*, high, grand, Bhartṛ. 2, 36. **II.** n. Low ground, MBh. 2, 784.

निम्नगा *nimnagâ*, i.e. *nimna-ga* (vb. *gam*), f. A river, Man. 9, 22.—**Comp.** *Giri-*, f. A mountain-stream, Râm. 2, 97, 1.

निम्ब *nimba*, m. A tree, Azadirachta indica Juss., Râm. 2, 35, 14.

निम्लोच *nimlocha*, i.e. *ni-mluch+a*, m. Setting (of the sun), Bhâg. P. 3, 2, 7.

नियति *niyati*, i.e. *ni-yam+ti*, f. Destiny, Râm. 4, 24, 4.

नियन्तृ *niyantṛi*, i.e. *ni-yam* + *tṛi*, m. **1.** A restrainer, Râm. 2, 1, 30 Gorr. **2.** A ruler, Ragh. 15, 51. **3.** A charioteer, 1, 17.

नियन्तृत्व *niyantṛi* + *tva*, n. The faculty of restraining, Vedântas. in Chr. 204, 18.

नियन्त्रण *niyantraṇa*, i.e. *ni-yantr* + *ana*, n. Restraining, Râjat. 3, 515.

नियम *ni-yam* + *a*, m. **1.** Restraining, preventing, Man. 8, 122. **2.** Restriction, MBh. 1, 6452. **3.** Certainty, Pañch. ii. d. 53. **4.** Any religious observance voluntarily practised, as fasting, pilgrimage, Man. 4, 204.—**Comp.** *Sa-*, adj. being engaged in a religious observance, Kir. 5, 40.

नियमन *ni-yam* + *ana*, I. adj. Subduing, Hariv. 10684. II. n. **1.** Subduing, MBh. 3, 1075. **2.** Restriction, Râjat. 4, 137.

नियमवन्त् *niyama* + *vant*, adj., f. *vatî*. **1.** Practising religious observances, MBh. 1, 3839. **2.** Having the menses, Suçr. 1, 317, 9.

नियामक *niyâmaka*, i.e. *ni-yam* + *aka*, adj. Subduing, MBh. 3, 15812.

नियामकता *niyâmaka* + *tâ*, f. Exact determination, explanation, Bhâg. P. 5, 7, 6.

नियुत *ni-yuta* (vb. *yu*), n. A great number, one hundred thousand, or a million, and greater numbers, Bhâg. P. 5, 16, 5.

नियोक्तृ *niyoktṛi*, i.e. *ni-yuj* + *tṛi*, m. A ruler, Ragh. 2, 56.

नियोग *niyoga*, i.e. *ni-yuj* + *a*, m. **1.** Fastening, Hariv. 3537. **2.** Appointment, Mṛichchh. 101, 19. **3.** An order, a commission, Man. 1, 41; 9, 61; 65. **4.** °*ena*, instr. Certainly, Ragh. 17, 49.—**Comp.** *A-*, m. a disagreeable commission, Râm. 2, 68, 17 Gorr.

नियोगिन् *niyogin*, i.e. *niyoga* + *in*, m. A functionary, Hit. ii. d. 94.—**Comp.** *A-*, adj. not partaking of, Râjat. 5, 177.

नियोजन *niyojana*, i.e. *ni-yuj* + *ana*, n. An order, MBh. 12, 13926.

नियोधक *niyodhaka*, i.e. *ni-yudh* + *aka*, m. A pugilist, MBh. 1, 6940.

निरनुक्रोशता *niranukroçatâ*, i. e. *nis-anukroça* + *tâ*, f. Unmercifulness, Râm. 1, 61, 22 Gorr.

निरन्तर *nirantara*, i.e. *nis-antara*, adj., f. *râ*. **1.** Without any interstice, Çiç. 9, 66. **2.** Completely filled, Râm. 6, 112, 42. **3.** Continual, Râm. 5, 58, 8. **4.** Faithful, Pañch. ii. d. 190. °*ram*, adv. **1.** Tightly, Ṛit. 2, 11. **2.** Constantly, Râm. 3, 2, 11.

निरपराधता *niraparâdhatâ*, i. e. *nis-aparâdha* + *tâ*, f. Innocence, Lass. 26, 14.

निरपराधवन्त् *niraparâdhavant*, i.e. *nis-aparâdha* + *vant*, adj., f. *vatî*, Innocent, Râm. 2, 112, 7 Gorr.

निरय *niraya*, i.e. *nis-i* + *a*, m. Hell, Man. 6, 61.—**Comp.** *Tiryaññiraya*, i.e. *tiryañch-*, m. the hell of beasts, MBh. 3, 12626.

निरर्थक *nirarthaka*, i.e. *nis-artha* + *ka*, I. adj., f. *thakâ* and *thikâ*. **1.** Without attaining one's purpose, Râm. 5, 9, 26. **2.** Useless, MBh. 5, 1114. **3.** Unmeaning, MBh. 3, 12686. II. °*kam*, adv. In vain, Râm. 3, 35, 21.—**Abstr.** °**त्व** *nirarthaka* + *tva*, n. Mṛichchh. 90, 4.

निरर्थता *nirarthatâ*, i.e. *nis-artha*

+*tâ*, f. Senselessness, Mârk. P. 26, 16.

निरवद्यत्व *niravadyatva*, i. e. *nis-avadya+tva*, n. Blamelessness, Bhâg. P. 7, 8, 1.

निरवद्यवन्त् *niravadyavant*, i.e. *nis-avadya+vant*, adj., f. *vatî*, Blameless, MBh. 3, 1827.

निरवशेषतस् *niravaçeshatas*, i.e. *nis-avaçesha+tas*, adv. Completely, Râm. 1, 72, 36 Gorr.

निरवस्तार *niravastâra*, i.e. *nis-ava-stṛi+a*, adj. Uncovered, bare, Bhâg. P. 4, 26, 17.

निरसन *nirasana*, i. e. *nis-2. as+ana*, I. adj., f. *nî*. **1.** Spitting out, Suçr. 1, 349, 3. **2.** Removing, Bhâg. P. 5, 3, 12. II. n. **1.** Expulsion, MBh. 14, 73. **2.** Removal, Vedântas. in Chr. 215, 21.

निरहम् *niraham*, i. e. *nis-aham* (see *asmad*), adj. Devoid of selfishness, Bhâg. P. 5, 19, 4.

निराकरण *nirâkaraṇa*, i. e. *nis-â-kṛi+ana*, n. Repudiation, Çâk. 82, 10.

निराकरिष्णु *nirâkarishṇu*, i. e. *nis-â-kṛi+ishṇu*, adj. **1.** One who repudiates, Ragh. 14, 57. **2.** Seeking to remove from (abl.), Râjat. 5, 154.

निराकरिष्णुता *nirâkarishṇu+tâ*, f. Malevolence, Suçr. 1, 336, 8.

निराकर्तृ *nirâkartṛi*, i.e. *nis-â-kṛi+tṛi*, m. A contemner (of the gods, etc.), MBh. 12, 6101.

निराकृतिन् *nirakṛitin*, i. e. *nis-â-kṛita+in*, adj. Obstructing, avoiding, MBh. 12, 8682 (who exerts no activity, whether to attain or to avoid).

निराक्रिया *nirâkriyâ*, i.e. *nis-â-kṛi+a*, f. Expulsion, MBh. 7, 2956.

निराशक *nirâçaka*, i.e. *nis-âça* (see *âçâ*) +*ka*, adj. Desponding of (abl.), MBh. 8, 3761.

निराशत्व *nirâçatva*, i.e. *nis-âça* (see *âçâ*)+*tva*, and **निराशित्व** *nirâçitva*, i. e. *nirâçin* + *tva*, n. Hopelessness, Kâm. Nîtis. 14, 45; MBh. 3, 13994.

निराशिन् *nirâçin*, i.e. *nis-âçâ+in*, adj. Hopeless, MBh. 12, 12435.

निरीक्षक *nirîkshaka*, i.e. *nis-îksh+aka*, adj. **1.** Seeing, Bhâg, P. 6, 9, 44. **2.** Visiting, Râjat. 6, 94.

निरीक्षण *nirîkshaṇa*, i.e. *nis-îksh+ana*, I. adj. Regarding, Bhâg. P. 7, 15, 32. II. n. **1.** Look, 1, 9, 40. **2.** Regarding, Râm. 5, 14, 56.

निरीक्षा *nirîkshâ*, i.e. *nis-îksh+a*, f. Regarding, Râm. 1, 75, 14.

निरीक्षिन् *nirîkshin*, i.e. *nis-îksh+in*, adj., f. *iṇî*, Looking, Râm. 5, 86, 12.

निरीतिक *nirîtika*, i.e. *nis-îti+ka*, adj. Free from inauspiciousness, Râm. 1, 32, 24.

निरीहता *nirîhatâ*, i.e. *nis-îha* (see *îhâ*) +*tâ*, f. Indifference, MBh. 3, 95.

निरुक्ति *nirukti*, i.e. *nis-vach+ti*, f. **1.** Interpretation, Bhâg. P. 5, 11, 3. **2.** Etymological explanation, MBh. 1, 1656.

निरुत्साहता *nirutsâhatâ*, i.e. *nis-ut-sâha+tâ*, f. Cowardice, Pañch. 219, 18.

निरुपाख्य *nirupâkhya*, i.e. *nis-upa-â-khya* (vb. *khyâ*), adj. Invisible, MBh. 13, 1101.

निरुपाधिक *nirupâdhika*, i.e. *nis*

-*upâdhi* + *ka*, adj. Having no attributes, Bhâg. P. 8, 12, 8.

निरूष्मत्व *nirushmatva*, i.e. *nis-ushman* + *tva*, n. Coldness, MBh. 12, 11718.

निरूढि *nirûḍhi*, i.e. *nis-vah* + *ti*, f. Renown, Kir. 2, 6.

निरूपण *nirûpaṇa*, i.e. *ni-rûp* + *ana*, I. adj. Determining, Sâh. D. 8, 14. II. n. 1. Shape, MBh. 3, 2802. 2. Determining, Bhâg. P. 5, 3, 5.

निर्ऋति *nirṛiti*, i.e. *nis-ṛi* + *ti*, 1. m. Imprecation, Bhâg. P. 1, 19, 4. 2. f. A demigod, patroness of the southwest, Man. 11, 118.

निरोध *nirodha*, i.e. *ni-rudh* + *a*, m. 1. Confinement, imprisonment, Man. 8, 375. 2. Coercion, 6, 60. 3. Obstruction, MBh. 3, 11554. 4. Destruction, Hariv. 111. 5. Disappointment, Daçarûp. 1, 31.

निरोधक *nirodhaka*, i.e. *ni-rudh* + *aka*, adj. Obstructing, MBh. 4, 1166.

निरोधन *nirodhana*, i.e. *ni-rudh* + *ana*, I. adj. 1. Confining, Bhâg. P. 5, 26, 7. 2. Obstructing, Suçr. 2, 525, 1. II. n. 1. Imprisonment, Man. 8, 310. 2. Coercion, MBh. 3, 125. 3. Disappointment, Daçarûp. 1, 31.

निर्गम *nirgama*, i.e. *nis-gam* + *a*, m. 1. Going out, setting out, Râm. 4, 14, 8. 2. Vanishing, MBh. 3, 11892. 3. Issue, outlet, Râm. 1, 44, 11. 4. Export, Man. 8, 401. 5. A door, Bhâg. P. 6, 5, 7.

निर्गमन *nirgamana*, i.e. *nis-gam* + *ana*, n. Going out, MBh. 3, 14308.

निर्गुणता *nirguṇatâ*, i.e. *nis-guṇa* + *tâ*, f. and **निर्गुणत्व** *nirguṇatva*, i.e. *nis-guṇa* + *tva*, n. 1. Want of properties, Bhâg. P. 7, 11, 32; MBh. 12, 11350. 2. Want of good qualities, wickedness, 7, 4490; Böhtl. Ind. Spr. 109.

निर्ग्रन्थिक *nirgranthika*, i. e. *nis-grantha* + *ika*, m. An ascetic, Daçak. in Chr. 192, 18.

निर्घण्टक *nirghaṇṭaka*, probably a form of *nirgranthaka*, i.e. *nis-granth* + *aka* (properly, Singling out the words of a verse or sentence, and setting them up in their absolute form, by neglecting the rules of Sandhi, or euphonical connection), (m. or n.) A collection of words, MBh. 12, 13247.

निर्घर्षणक *nirgharshaṇaka*, i.e. *nis-ghṛish* + *ana* + *ka*, adj. Fit for picking one's teeth with, Hit. ii. d. 65.

निर्घात *nirghâta*, i.e. *nis-han*, Caus., + *a*, m. A gust of wind, a whirlwind, Man. 1, 38.—Comp. *Sa-*, adj. accompanied by whirlwinds, Chr. 36, 23.

निर्घृणता *nirghṛiṇatâ*, f. and **निर्घृणत्व** *nirghṛiṇatva*, n., i.e. *nis-ghṛiṇa* + *tâ*, or *tva* (cf. *ghṛiṇâ*), Unmercifulness, Bhartṛ. 2, 44; Mârk. P. 15, 40.

निर्घोष *nirghosha*, i.e. I. *nis-ghush* + *a*, m. Sound, Râm. 1, 10, 32. II. *nis-ghosha*, adj. Soundless, MBh. 14, 567.—Comp. *Mahâ-megha-ogha-*, adj. sounding like a multitude of large thunder-clouds.

निर्जय *nirjaya*, i.e. *nis-ji* + *a*, m. Conquest, Râjat. 3, 273; MBh. 7, 5317.

निर्जेतृ *nirjetṛi*, i.e. *nis-ji* + *tṛi*, m. A vanquisher, Râm. 6, 95, 28.

निर्झर *nirjhara*, probably a form of *nis-kshar* + *a*, m. (also n. Râm. 4, 13, 6), A cascade or torrent, Râm. 2, 28, 7; Bhâg. P. 6, 4, 41.

निर्झरिणी *nirjhariṇî*, i.e. *nirjhara* + *in* + *î*, f. A torrent, Kathâs. 17, 7.

निर्णय *nirṇaya*, i.e. *nis-nî* + *a*, m.

1. Removal, Man. 12, 112. 2. Decision, MBh. 13, 7535.

निर्णेक *nirṇeka,* i.e. *nis-nij+a,* m. Expiation, Man. 11, 139.

निर्णेजक *nirṇejaka,* i.e. *nis-nij + aka,* m. A washer, Man. 4, 219.

निर्णेजन *nirṇejana,* i.e. *nis-nij+ana,* n. Expiation, Man. 11, 189.

निर्दयत्व *nirdayatva,* i.e. *nis-daya + tva* (see *dayâ*), n. Cruelty, Böhtl. Ind. Spr. 109.

निर्दर *nirdara,* i.e. *nis-dṛi+a,* m. A cave, Râm. 2, 28, 7.

निर्दलन *nirdalana,* i.e. *nis-dal+ana,* n. Splitting, Râjat. 7, 1516.

निर्दश *nirdaça,* i.e. *nis-daçan,* adj. 1. Older than ten days, Bhâg. P. 9, 7, 9. 2. Having happened more than ten days ago, Man. 5, 77.—**Comp.** *A-*, adj. not out of, i.e. within, the ten days of impurity which follow a case of birth or death, Man. 5, 75 ; 4, 212 ([food] of a woman whose days are not elapsed).

निर्दातृ *nirdâtṛi,* i.e. *nis-2.dâ+tṛi,* m. A husbandman, Man. 7, 110.

निर्दुःखत्व *nirduḥkhatva,* i.e. *nis-duḥkha+tva,* n. Painlessness, Bhâshâp. 144.

निर्देश *nirdeça,* i.e. *nis-diç+a,* m. 1. Order, Man. 6, 45. 2. Description, Bhag. 17, 23. 3. Detail, Mâlav. 8, 15. —**Comp.** *A-*, m. want of detail. Instr. *anirdeçena,* Without entering into the particulars, MBh. 12, 4022.

निर्धनता *nirdhanatâ,* f. and **निर्धनत्व** *nirdhanatva,* n., i.e. *nis-dhana+tâ* or *tva,* Poverty, Mṛichchh. 15, 20 ; Pańch. ii. d. 107.

निर्नाथता *nirnâthatâ,* i.e. *nis-nâtha + tâ,* f. Want of protection, MBh. 3, 2566.

निर्नाशन *nirnâçana,* i.e. *nis-naç,* Caus., *+ana,* n. Removing, MBh. 12, 1039.

निर्निद्रता *nirnidratâ,* i.e. *nis-nidra + tâ* (cf. *nidrâ*), f. Sleeplessness, Râjat. 3, 525.

निर्बन्ध *nirbandha,* i.e. *nis-bandh+a,* m. 1. Insisting upon (loc.), Hariv. 10966. 2. Pertinacity, MBh. 13, 5034. 3. Perseverance, Bhâg. P. 7, 5, 42. 4. Accusing, Man. 11, 55.

निर्बन्धिन् *nirbandhin,* i.e. *nis-bandh+in,* adj. Insisting upon (loc.), MBh. 5, 4901.

निर्भर्त्सन *nirbhartsana,* i.e. *nis-bharts+ana,* n. and f. *nâ,* Menace, reproach, MBh. 3, 17051 ; Râjat. 1, 256.

निर्भेद *nirbheda,* i.e. *nis-bhid+a,* m. 1. Bursting, Râm. 1, 41, 4. 2. Dividing, Râm. 4, 11. 3. A channel, Hariv. 12017.—**Comp.** *A-*, m. not betraying, Daçak. in Chr. 198, 7.

निर्मत्स्यता *nirmatsyatâ,* i.e. *nis-matsya+tâ,* f. Having no fishes, Pańch. 78, 15.

निर्मथन *nirmathana,* i.e. *nis-math + ana,* n. 1. Rubbing together, Râm. 3, 75, 50. 2. Churning, Kâm. Nîtis. 13, 3.

निर्मम *nirmama,* i.e. *nis-mama* (gen. sing. of *asmad*), adj., f. *mâ,* Indifferent, MBh. 13, 5358 ; 6749.

निर्ममता *nirmama + tâ,* f. and **निर्ममत्व** *nirmama + tva,* n. Indifference, Böhtl. Ind. Spr. 411 ; Mârk. P. 39, 4.

निर्मलता *nirmalatâ,* f. and **निर्मलत्व** *nirmalatva,* n. i.e. *nis-mala + tâ* or *tva,* Purity, Hariv. 14775.

निर्माण *nirmâṇa*, i.e. *nis-mâ* + *ana*, n. **1.** Measure, Râm. 3, 42, 24 (in *a-vyakta-*, vb. *añj*, adj., Not full-grown). **2.** A part, 4, 44, 44. **3.** Forming, creating, Lass. 91, 13. **4.** Work, Râm. 4, 40, 54.

निर्मातृ *nirmâtṛi*, i.e. *nis-mâ* + *tṛi*, m. f. *trî*. **1.** Creator, MBh. 5, 3493. **2.** A builder, Râjat. 4, 315.

निर्माथिन् *nirmâthin*, i.e. *nis-math* + *in*, adj. Stamping to pieces, Râjat. 3, 284.

निर्मार्जन *nirmârjana*, i.e. *nis-mṛij* + *ana*, n. Sweeping, cleaning, MBh. 12, 10781.

निर्माल्य *nirmâlya*, i. e. *nis-mâlya* (=*mala* + *ya*), n. The remains of an offering to a deity, MBh. 1, 3061.

निर्मिति *nirmiti*, i.e. *nis-mâ* + *ti*, f. Creation, Râjat. 4, 204.

निर्मुक्ति *nirmukti*, i.e. *nis-much* + *ti*, f. Deliverance, Kathâs. 5, 131.

निर्मूलन *nirmûlana*, i.e. *nirmûlaya* + *ana*, n. Uprooting, Böhtl. Ind. Spr. 541.

निर्मूलय *NIRMÛLAYA*, a denomin. derived from *nis-mûla* with *aya*, Par. To uproot, Çântiç. 4, 7.

निर्मोक *nirmoka*, i.e. *nis-much* + *a*, m. **1.** A hide, MBh. 13, 6490. **2.** The slough of a snake, Râm. 2, 91, 12 Gorr. **3.** A proper name, Bhâg. P. 8, 13, 11.

निर्मोक्तृ *nirmoktṛi*, i.e. *nis-much* + *tṛi*, m. One who solves, MBh. 2, 635.

निर्मोक्ष *nirmoksha*, i.e. *nis-moksh* + *a*, m. Deliverance, removal of, MBh. 13, 60.

निर्मोचन *nirmochana*, i.e. *nis-much* + *ana*, n. Deliverance, MBh. 5, 1890.

निर्यशस्क *niryaçaska*, i.e. *nis-yaças* + *ka*, adj. Inglorious, MBh. 3, 8499.

निर्याण *niryâṇa*, i.e. *nis-yâ* + *ana*, n. **1.** Setting out, MBh. 1, 333. **2.** Vanishing, Râjat. 3, 261. **3.** Death, MBh. 15, 1050. **4.** The outer corner of an elephant's eye, Çiç. 5, 41. **5.** A rope for binding a calf's feet, 12, 41.

निर्यातक *niryâtaka*, i. e. *nis-yat*, Caus., + *aka*, adj. Removing, Man. 3, 166.

निर्यातन *niryâtana*, i. e. *nis-yat*, Caus., + *ana*, n. Returning, delivering, Râm. 1, 3, 27 Gorr. — **Comp.** *Vaira-*, n. revenge, requital of an injury, Pañch. 89, 19.

निर्यापण *niryâpaṇa*, i. e. *nis-yâ*, Caus., + *ana*, n. Expulsion, Bhâg. P. 1, 7, 57.

निर्यास *niryâsa*, i.e. *nis-yas* + *a*, m. (and n.). **1.** Exudations of trees, gum, resin, etc., Man. 5, 6. **2.** Exudation, Hariv. 4747.

निर्यूह *niryûha* (probably for *nir-vyûha*, by dropping *v*), m. **1.** A crest, Hariv. 5502. **2.** An ornament, Râm. 5, 9, 58 (pinnacles?); MBh. 5, 573 (the crest of a helmet?). **3.** A door, Hariv. 5021. **4.** Extracted juice, Râm. 2, 100, 64 Gorr.

निर्वचन *nirvachana*, i.e. I. *nis-vach* + *ana*, n. **1.** A proverb, MBh. 1, 4359. **2.** Etymological explanation, 5, 2561. II. *nis-vachana*, adj. **1.** Silent. **2.** Blameless, MBh. 3, 13389. °*nam*, adv. Silently, Kumâras. 7, 19.

निर्वपण *nirvapaṇa*, i. e. *nis-vap* + *ana*, n. **1.** Offering, especially to the Manes, Man. 3, 248. **2.** Gift, Bhâg. P. 5, 12, 12.

निर्वर्तक *nirvartaka*, i.e. *nis-vṛit*, Caus.

+*aka,* Producing, causing, Bhâg. P. 5, 20, 18.

निर्वर्तिन् *nirvartin,* i.e. *nis-vṛit,* Caus. +*in,* adj. **1.** Uncivil, Kathâs. 26, 58. **2.** Performing, Çâk. 68, 13 (read *nirvart°*).

निर्वाण *nirvâṇa,* i.e. *nis-vâ*+*ana,* n. **1.** Becoming extinguished, MBh. 4, 716. **2.** Final emancipation, MBh. 14, 543. **3.** Union with God, Bhâg. P. 4, 6, 39. **4.** Complete satisfaction, MBh. 3, 10438. **5.** Pleasure, Mârk. P. 20, 13.

निर्वाद *nirvâda,* i.e. *nis-vad*+*a,* m. Blame, MBh. 5, 4618.

निर्वाप *nirvâpa,* i.e. *nis-vap*+*a,* m. **1.** Strewing, giving, Râm. 2, 91, 72. **2.** Offering, especially to the Manes, 2, 103, 28. **3.** Gift, Pańch. 239, 6.

निर्वापण *nirvâpaṇa,* i.e. I. *nis-vap,* Caus., +*ana,* **1.** Casting in, Suçr. 1, 171, 6. **2.** Sowing, Pańch. 85, 17. **II.** *nis-vâ,* Caus., +*ana,* n. **1.** Extinguishing, Mṛichchh. 49, 18. **2.** Cooling, Çâk. 31, 9. **3.** Amusing, 33, 2, v. r.

निर्वापयितृ *nirvâpayitṛi,* i.e. *nis-vâ,* Caus., +*tṛi,* m. One who allays, Çâk. d. 60.

निर्वास *nirvâsa,* i.e. *nis-vas*+*a,* m. Leaving one's home, MBh. 1, 2238.

निर्वासन *nirvâsana,* i. e. *nis-vas,* Caus., +*ana,* n. **1.** Expulsion, MBh. 5, 3168. **2.** Killing, Râjat. 6, 215.

निर्वाह *nirvâha,* i.e. *nis-vah*+*a,* m. Accomplishing, completion, Bhartṛ. 2, 69.

निर्विकल्पक *nirvikalpaka,* i. e. *nis-vikalpa*+*ka,* adj. Free from differences, Vedântas. in Chr. 217, 9.

निर्विकारवन्त् *nirvikâravant,* i. e. *nis-vikâra* + *vant,* adj. Unchanged, MBh. 12, 2332.

निर्विवरता *nirvivaratâ,* i. e. *nis-vivara*+*tâ,* f. Want of interstice, and, Want of enmity, Çiç. 9, 44.

निर्विवेकत्व *nirvivekatva,* i. e. *nis-viveka* + *tva,* n. Inconsiderateness, Kathâs. 5, 25.

निर्विशेषत्व *nirviçeshatva,* i. e. *nis-viçesha*+*tva,* n. Want of distinction, MBh. 14, 999.

निर्विशेषवन्त् *nirviçeshavant,* i. e. *nis-viçesha*+*vant,* adj. Indistinguished, MBh. 12, 7516.

निर्वृति *nirvṛiti,* i.e. *nis-vṛi*+*ti,* f. **1.** Tranquillity, MBh. 12, 4114. **2.** Happiness, Bhartṛ. 3, 71. **3.** Pleasure, Ragh. 12, 65.—Comp. *Pari-,* f. complete liberation of the soul from the body and exemption from future transmigration.

निर्वृत्ति *nirvṛitti,* i.e. *nis-vṛit*+*ti,* f. **1.** Completion, Man. 12, 1. **2.** Fruit, 4, 23. **3.** Impropriety, Hit. 110, 20, v. r. **4.** Sometimes erroneously for *nirvṛiti* and *nivṛitti.*

निर्वेद *nirveda,* i.e. *nis-vid*+*a,* m. **1.** Disgust, MBh. 11, 144. **2.** Loathsomeness, Pańch. ed. orn. 63, 21. **3.** Self-disparagement, humility, Sâh. D. 64, 8. **4.** Indifference, Bhâg. P. 1, 13, 25. **5.** Desperation, Râm. 1, 55, 10.—Comp. *A-,* m. self-confidence, courage, Râm. 5, 15, 5. *Sa-nirveda*+*m,* adv. desperately, Daçak. in Chr. 179, 14.

निर्वेदवन्त् *nirveda*+*vant,* adj. Full of disgust (with worldly concerns), Pańch. iii. d. 188.

निर्वेश *nirveça,* i.e. *nis-viç*+*a,* m. **1.** Returning payment, Râm. 3, 33, 25. **2.** Expiation, Bhâg. P. 5, 26, 18.

निर्व्याकुलता *nirvyâkulatâ,* i.e. *nis*

-*vyâkula* + *tâ*, f. Freedom from trouble, Pańch. 195, 5.

निर्व्याजता *nirvyâjatâ*, i.e. *nis-vyâja* + *tâ*, f. Candour, Bhartṛ. 2, 80.

निर्व्यूह *nirvyûha*, i.e. *nis-vi-ûh* + *a*, m. 1. Pinnacle (?), MBh. 3, 11700. 2. Crest, 7, 3166.

निर्हरण *nirharaṇa*, i.e. *nis-hṛi* + *ana*, n. 1. Rooting up, Bhâg. P. 7, 7, 28. 2. Removal, 6, 3, 24. 3. Carrying a corpse to the funeral pyre, Râm. 2, 80, 20.

निर्हाद *nirhâda*, i.e. *nis-had* + *a*, m. 1. Evacuation, Varâh. Bṛih. S. 85, 63. 2. Excrements, MBh. 3, 17249.

निर्हार *nirhâra*, i.e. *nis-hṛi* + *a*, m. 1. Carrying a corpse to the funeral pyre, Bhâg. P. 7, 2, 35. 2. A hoard, Man. 9, 199. 3. Rooting up, destruction, Bhâg. P. 3, 29, 10. 4. Evacuation of excrements, MBh. 13, 1796.

निर्हारक *nirhâraka*, i.e. *nis-hṛi* + *aka*, adj. Carrying (a corpse) to the funeral pyre, Man. 3, 166, ed. Calc.

निर्हारिन् *nirhârin*, i.e. *nis-hṛi* + *in*, adj. Diffusively fragrant, MBh. 12, 6848.

निर्हृति *nirhṛiti*, i.e. *nis-hṛi* + *ti*, f. Removal, Kâm. Nîtis. 13, 55.

निर्ह्राद *nirhrâda*, i.e. *nis-hrad* + *a*, m. Sound, Bhâg. P. 3, 17, 8.

निर्ह्रादिन् *nirhrâdin*, i.e. *nirhrâda* + *in*, adj. Resounding, Megh. 57.

† **निल्** *NIL*, i. 6, Par. To be impenetrable.

निलय *nilaya*, i.e. *ni-lî* + *a*, m. A dwelling-place, a nest, a house, Râm. 2, 46, 3; 25, 45.

निलयन *nilayana*, i.e. *ni-lî* + *ana*, n. 1. Settling, Suçr. 1, 118, 5. 2. A dwelling-place, Râm. 2, 28, 20.

निवपन *ni-vap* + *ana*, n. An offering to the Manes, Çâk. d. 152.

निवर्तक *nivartaka*, i.e. *ni-vṛit*, Caus., + *aka*, adj., f. *tikâ*. 1. Turning back, flying, Hariv. 5048. 2. Causing to cease, removing, Bhâshâp. 136.

निवर्तन *nivartana*, i.e. *ni-vṛit* + *ana*, I. adj. Disappearing, MBh. 6, 2427. II. n. 1. Return, Râm. 6, 92, 4. 2. Ceasing, MBh. 1, 8388. 3. Abstaining from (abl.), 1, 373. 4. Inactivity, Kâm. Nîtis. 1, 28. 5. Bringing back, Amar. 84. 6. Turning off from (abl.), Vedântas. in Chr. 203, 15.

निवर्तिन् *nivartin*, i.e. *ni-vṛit* + *in*, adj., f. *nî*. 1. Turning back, Râm. 2, 105, 29. 2. Flying, showing the heels, 1, 6, 20. 3. Returning, Böhtl. Ind. Spr. 788. 4. Leaving, MBh. 13, 2653. 5. Abstaining from, 12, 10386. 6. Allowing to return, Hariv. 4836.

निवर्हण *nivarhaṇa*, see *nibarhaṇa*.

निवसन *ni-vas* + *ana*, n. 1. Putting on, Râm. 2, 37, 13 Gorr. 2. Cloth, Ragh. 19, 41.

निवह *ni-vah* + *a*, m. A multitude, Pańch. v.d. 8.

निवात *ni-vâta*, I. adj., f. *tâ*, Protected against the wind, not windy, Hariv. 3947. II. n. 1. A place inaccessible to the wind, MBh. 2, 1218. 2. Calm, Kumâras. 3, 48. III. m. An impenetrable coat of mail.

निवाप *nivâpa*, i.e. *ni-vap* + *a*, m. 1. Seed, corn, MBh. 13, 4350. 2. Offering to the Manes, 12, 6996.

निवापक *nivâpaka*, i.e. *ni-vap* + *aka*, m. A sower, Râm. 2, 90, 20 Gorr.

निवारक *nivâraka*, i.e. *ni-vṛi + aka*, adj. Able to keep off, MBh. 8, 1276.

निवारण *nivâraṇa*, i.e. *ni-vṛi + ana*, I. adj. Keeping off, MBh. 3, 12454. II. n. 1. Keeping off, Râm. 2, 23, 40. 2. Preventing, MBh. 2, 2002. 3. Prohibition, Bhâg. P. 1, 5, 15.

निवास् *NIVÂS*, i. 10 (rather a denomin. derived from *nivâsa*), Par. To put on.

निवास *nivâsa*, i.e. *ni-vas + a*, m. 1. Dwelling, Râm. 3, 55, 22. 2. Passing the night, Hariv. 9700. 3. An abode, a house, Bhâg. P. 1, 11, 27. 4. Night-quarters, Râm. 2, 55, 33. 5. Cloth, Hariv. 10679.—Comp. *Kva-*, adj. where dwelling, MBh. 1, 7114.

निवासन *nivâsana*, i.e. *ni-vas + ana*, n. 1. Sojourn, Râm. 1, 3, 10 Gorr. 2. Passing (as time), 1, 3, 18 Gorr.

निवासिन् *nivâsin*, i.e. *ni-vas + in*, I. adj. 1. Dwelling, Râm. 1, 9, 36. 2. *nivâsa + in*, Latter part of comp. adj. Clothed, covered, MBh. 7, 9532. II. n. An inhabitant, Man. 5, 11.

निविड *niviḍa*, probably *ni-vila*, I. adj., f. *ḍâ*. 1. Without interstices, Mâlav. d. 24. 2. Dense, Bhâg. P. 5, 2, 4. 3. Firm, Kathâs. 5, 140. II. m. The name of a mountain, MBh. 6, 140.

निवीतिन् *nivîtin*, i.e. *ni-vîta + in* (vb. *vye*), adj. Wearing the sacred cord fastened on one's neck, Man. 2, 63.

निवृत्ति *ni-vṛit + ti*, f. 1. Return, MBh. 5, 7469. 2. Disappearance, 6, 5775. 3. Cessation, Çâk. 112, 16. 4. Abstinence, Man. 5, 56. 5. Abstaining from acting, inactivity, Bhag. 16, 7; Bhâshâp. 148.

निवेदन *nivedana*, i.e. *ni-vid*, Caus., + *ana*, I. adj. Announcing, Hariv. 9289. II. n. 1. Making known, Sâv. 3, 5. 2. Announcement, Böhtl. Ind. Spr. 417. 3. Offering, MBh. 2, 1361.

निवेदयिषु *nivedayishu*, i.e. *ni-vedayisha* (desider. of the Caus. of *vid*, without reduplication), + *u*, adj. Wishing to report (acc.), MBh. 3, 1543.

निवेदिन् *nivedin*, i.e. *ni-vid*, Caus., + *in*, adj., f. *nî*, Reporting, announcing, Râm. 1, 70, 5 Gorr.; Varâh. Bṛih. S. 85, 58.

निवेश *niveça*, i.e. *ni-viç + a*, m. 1. Settling, Hariv. 3520. 2. Encamping, 4999. 3. A residence, MBh. 1, 7781. 4. A camp, 5, 173. 5. Marriage, 1, 1051. 6. Foundation, Râm. 1, 34, 5. 7. Impression, mark, Çâk. d. 142, v.r.

निवेशन *niveçana*, i.e. *ni-viç + ana*, I. adj. Entering, Hariv. 15005. II. m. A proper name, 9195. III. n. 1. Sitting down, Râm. 6, 85. 2. Encamping, MBh. 14, 1901. 3. Marriage, Bhâg. P. 3, 7, 31. 4. A dwelling-place, a residence, Indr. 3, 2. 5. A camp, MBh. 5, 680. —Comp. *Antar-*, n. the interior of a palace, Man. 7, 62.

निवेशवन्त् *niveça + vant*, adj. Lying on, Kumâras. 7, 7.

निवेशिन् *niveçin*, i.e. *niveça + in*, adj., f. *nî*. 1. Lying near, Kathâs. 25, 74. 2. Being in, Vikr. d. 41.

† **निश्** *NIÇ*, i. 1, Par. To meditate profoundly.

निश् *niç*, probably curtailed *niçâ*, f. Night, Man. 9, 60.—Comp. *Dyu-*, f. day and night, Man. 4, 25. *Mahâ-*, f. the middle of the night, 4, 129.

ऽनिश *-niça* (cf. *niçâ*), in *a-niça + m*, adv. (Without rest) continually, Çiç. 9, 61. *ahar-niça*, n. A whole day, comprising a day and a night, Man. 1,

74. *divâ-niça+m*, adv. Day and night, Man. 7, 44. *niçâ-niça+m*, adv. Constantly, MBh. 3, 12343.

निशठ *ni-çaṭha*, I. adj. Candid, Bhâg. P. 6, 7, 15. II. m. A proper name, MBh. 1, 7915.

निशब्द *ni-çabda*, adj. Silent, Kir. 8, 35.

निशा *niçâ*, probably from *ni-çî*, (cf. *niçîtha*), f. 1. Night, Man. 11, 223. 2. A dream, MBh. 5, 7252. 3. Turmeric, Curcuma, Suçr. 2, 208, 14.—Comp. *Mahâ-*, f. midnight.

निशाकर *niçâ-kara*, m. The moon, Pañch. ii. d. 20.

निशीथ *ni-çî+tha*, m. 1. Midnight, Ṛit. 1, 3. 2. Night, Ragh. 3, 15.

निश्चय *niçchaya*, i.e. *nis-chi+a*, m. 1. Ascertainment, Man. 10, 1. 2. Firm conviction, Râm. 3, 29, 19. 3. Certainty, Nal. 19, 8. 4. instr. °*yena*, and abl. °*yât*, Certainly, Lass. 10, 5; Hariv. 14125. 5. Inquiry, Man. 8, 94. 6. Decision, Râm. 1, 8, 22. 7. Regard, MBh. 12, 2218. 8. Resolution, design, Pañch. 77, 13; Bhag. 17, 6.—Comp. *Eka-*, I. m. a common resolution, Sund. 1, 7. II. adj. having taken the same resolution, 1, 4.

निश्चयिन् *niçchayin* in *kṛita-niçchaya+in*, adj. Resolved, Pañch. ii. d. 149.

निश्रम *ni-çram+a*, m. Practice, MBh. 2, 132.

† निष् *NISH*, i. 1, Par. To sprinkle.

निषङ्ग *nishañga*, i.e. *ni-sañj+a*, m. A quiver, MBh. 4, 1693.

निषङ्गिन् *nishañgin*, i.e. *nishañga+in*, I. adj. Having a quiver, MBh. 4, 1639. II. m. A proper name, 1, 2738.

निषदन *nishadana*, i.e. *ni-sad+ana* n. Seat, Bhâg. P. 5, 14, 7.

निषध *nishadha*, m. 1. The name of a mountain, MBh. 3, 12917. 2. pl. The name of a people and their country, Nal. 1, 3. 3. A proper name, MBh. 1, 3745.

निषाद *nishâda*, i.e. *ni-sad+a*, m. 1. A name used to designate aboriginal tribes of India, who are described as fishermen, hunters, and robbers, and are considered as degraded tribes, viz. as the offspring of a Brâhmaṇa by a Çûdra woman, Man. 10, 8. 2. The first of the seven musical notes, MBh. 14, 1419.

निषादिन् *nishâdin*, i.e. *ni-sad+in*, I. adj. 1. Sitting, Ragh. 4, 20. 2. Lying, 1, 52. II. m. An elephant driver, Çiç. 5, 41.

निषिद्धि *nishiddhi*, i.e. *ni-sidh+ti*, f. Prohibition, Daçak. in Chr. 192, 5.

निषूदन *nishûdana*, see *nisûdana*.

निषेक *nisheka*, i.e. *ni-sich+a*, m. 1. Sprinkling, Ṛit. 1, 28. 2. Distilling, Ragh. 8, 38. 3. Impregnation, Man. 2, 16. 4. The ceremony performed on conception, 26. 5. Water for washing, Man. 4, 151 (according to another, Seminal impurity).

निषेचन *nishechana*, i.e. *ni-sich+ana*, n. Watering, Bhâg. P. 4, 31, 14.

निषेचितृ *nishechitṛi*, i.e. *ni-sich+tṛi*, m. Instiller, MBh. 3, 154.

निषेद्धृ *nisheddhṛi*, i.e. *ni-sidh+tṛi*, m. One who restrains or prevents, MBh. 7, 7826.

निषेध *nishedha*, i.e. *ni-sidh+a*, m. Keeping off, Râjat. 3, 1. 2. Prohibition, Kathâs. 1, 50. 3. Negation, Çâk. 106, 10, v.r.

निषेधक *nishedhaka*, i.e. *ni-sidh+*

aka, adj. Forbidding, Mârk. P. 14, 47.

निषेधिन् *nishedhin*, i.e. *nishedha + in*, adj. Surpassing, Ragh. 9, 42.

निषेव *nisheva*, i.e. *ni-sev + a*, I. adj. Practising; in *hrî-*, adj. Modest, MBh. 1, 3682. II. f. *vâ*. 1. Practice, Bhâg. P. 7, 15, 24. 2. Adoration, 7, 4, 24.

निषेवक *nishevaka*, i.e. *ni-sev + aka*, adj. 1. Frequenting, Bhâg. P. 1, 13, 56. 2. Practising; in *hrî-*, Modest, MBh. 4, 927. 3. Enjoying, Bhâg. P. 4, 7, 44.

निषेवण *nishevaṇa*, i.e. *ni-sev + ana*, n. 1. Visiting, Bhâg. P. 1, 2, 16. 2. Practice, MBh. 3, 13797. 3. Using, Râjat. 1, 228. 4. Living in, Suçr. 2, 304, 18. 5. Familiarity with, Man. 11, 66. 6. Adoration, Bhâg. P. 3, 4, 15.

निषेवितृ *nishevitṛi*, i.e. *ni-sev + tṛi*, m. One who enjoys, MBh. 12, 8920.

निषेविन् *nishevin*, i.e. *ni-sev + in*, adj. 1. Practising, Hariv. 11682. 2. Enjoying, Râm. 2, 37, 2 Gorr.—**Comp.** *Hrî-*, adj. modest, 3, 22, 30.

† निष्क् *NISHK*, i. 10 (rather a denomin. derived from *nishka*), Âtm. To weigh.

निष्क *nishka*, m. and n. 1. An ornament of the neck or breast, Hariv. 13892; Râm. 3, 9, 12. 2. A weight of gold, applied, however, to different quantities, Man. 8, 137. II. f. *kâ*, A measure of length, Mârk. P. 49, 37.

निष्कर्ष *nishkarsha*, i.e. *nis-kṛish + a*, m. 1. Drawing out, MBh. 12, 7318. 2. The essence of anything, Man. 4, 125. Abl. °*shât*, Principally, MBh. 13, 2241.

निष्कर्षण *nishkarshaṇa*, i. e. *nis-kṛish + aṇa*, n. 1. Drawing out, Ragh. 12, 97. 2. Putting off, 7, 63.

निष्कलत्व *nishkalatva*, i.e. *nis-kala + tva* (see *kalâ*), n. Condition of being undivided, MBh. 13, 779.

निष्काश *nishkâça* (wrong spelling), and निष्कास *nishkâsa*, i.e. *nis-kas + a*, m. Issue, Râm. 4, 52, 8.

निष्किंचन *nishkiñchana*, i. e. *nis-kim-cha-na*, adj., f. *nâ*, Poor, Bhâg. P. 2, 9, 6.

निष्किंचनत्व *nishkiñchana + tva*, n. Poverty, MBh. 13, 5359.

निष्कुट *nishkuṭa*, I. m. and n. A grove, MBh. 3, 14676. II. m. The name of a country (?), 2, 1037.

निष्कुलता *nishkulatâ*, i.e. *nis-kula + tâ*, f. Loss of one's family, Pańch. 233, 1.

निष्कृति *nishkṛiti*, i.e. *nis-kṛi + ti*, I. f. 1. Expiation, Man. 3, 19. 2. Compensation, 8, 150. 3. Personified, Bhâg. P. 4, 8, 3. II. m. A name of Agni, MBh. 3, 14143.

निष्कोषण *nishkoshaṇa*, i. e. *nis-kush + ana*, n. Drawing out, Suçr. 1, 87, 4.

निष्कोषणक *nishkoshaṇa + ka*, adj. Fit for picking, Pańch. i. d. 81.

निष्क्रम *nishkrama*, i.e. *nis-kram + a*, m. Going out, Yâjń. 1, 12.

निष्क्रमण *nishkramaṇa*, i. e. *nis-kram + ana*, n. Going out, Man. 2, 54; leaving (with abl.), Pańch. 37, 23; 193, 9, where erroneously °*krâm*°.

निष्क्रय *nishkraya*, i.e. *nis-krî + a*, m. 1. Redeeming, Yâjń. 2, 182. 2. Price, Hariv. 7697. 3. Reward, Râm. 1, 13, 51.

निष्क्रयण *nishkrayaṇa*, i.e. *nis-krî + ana*, n. Redeeming, Mṛichchh. 50, 11.

निष्क्रियता *nishkriyatâ*, i.e. *nis-kriya*

+*tâ* (see *kriyâ*), f. Neglect, MBh. 3, 17379.

निष्क्रियात्मता *nishkriyâtmatâ*, i.e. *nis-kriyâ-âtman* + *tâ*, f. Habitual neglect of prescribed duties, Man. 10, 58.

निष्टानक *nishṭânaka*, i.e. *nis-stan* + *aka*, I. m. **1.** Roar, MBh. 2, 2693. **2.** Murmur, 6, 1932. II. adj. Causing to cry, Râm. 6, 74, 41.

निष्ठ *nishṭha*, i.e. *ni-*, and probably also *nis*, *-stha* (vb. *sthâ*), I. adj., f. *ṭhâ*. **1.** Being on, Râjat. 5, 123. **2.** Grounded on, Man. 12, 95. **3.** Intent on, Man. 3, 134. II. f. *ṭhâ*, **1.** Basis, Bhag. 3, 3. **2.** Certain knowledge, MBh. 14, 626. **3.** Accomplishment, Man. 8, 227. **4.** End, catastrophe, Çâk. d. 78 n. **5.** Death, MBh. 13, 3151.

निष्ठान *nishṭhâna*, probably *ni-* or *nis*, *-sthâ* + *ana*, n. Sauce, condiment, Râm. 2, 91, 66.

निष्ठान्त *nishṭhânta*, i.e. *nishṭhâ-anta*, m. End, MBh. 11, 305.

निष्ठावन्त् *nishṭhâ* + *vant*, adj. Possessed of complete knowledge, Râm. 5, 11, 15.

निष्ठीवन *nishṭhîvana*, i.e. *nis-shṭhîv* + *ana*, n. Spitting out, MBh. 12, 2038.

निष्ठुर *nishṭhura*, adj., f. *râ*, Harsh, contumelious, coarse, Hit. iii. d. 101.

निष्ठुरता *nishṭhura* + *tâ*, f. **1.** Harshness, Man. 10, 58. **2.** Coarseness, Böhtl. Ind. Spr. 275.

निष्ण *nishṇa*, i.e. *ni-sna* (vb. *snâ*), adj. Clever, Râm. 3, 17, 29.

निष्पतिष्णु *nishpatishṇu*, i.e. *nis-pat* + *ishṇu*, adj. Hastening out, MBh. 12, 9040.

निष्पत्ति *nishpatti*, i.e. *nis-pad* + *ti*, f. Condition of being brought about, Râm. 2, 42, 9 Gorr. (*phala-*, The ripening of fruits).

निष्पत्त्रय *NISHPATRAYA*, a denomin. derived from *nis-patra* with *aya*, Par. To make leafless, MBh. 1, 7076.

निष्पन्द *nishpanda*, i.e. *nis-spanda*, adj. Motionless, Râm. 1, 36, 15 Gorr.

निष्पाव *nishpâva*, i.e. *nis-pû* + *a*, m. A sort of pulse, Dolichos sinensis Lin.; and pulse in general, MBh. 13, 5498.

निष्पेष *nishpesha*, i.e. *nis-pish* + *a*, m. **1.** Striking, Râm. 2, 20, 39 Gorr. **2.** The sound produced by striking, clashing, Râm. 3, 31, 42. — **Comp.** *Vajra-*, m. a clap of thunder.

निष्पेषण *nishpeshaṇa*, i.e. *nis-pish* + *ana*, n. Clashing, MBh. 7, 241.

निष्प्रतिग्रहता *nishpratigrahatâ*, i.e. *nis-pratigraha* + *tâ*, f. Not taking presents, Kâm. Nîtis. 2, 29.

निष्प्रभावता *nishprabhâvatâ*, i. e. *nis-prabhâva* + *tâ*, f. Powerlessness, Kathâs. 22, 38.

निष्यन्द *nishyanda*, see *nisyanda*.

निस् *nis*, adv. (ved.), and preposition, Outward, out, forth. I. Combined and compounded with verbs and their derivatives. II. Compounded with nouns, and implying: **1.** Out of, e.g. *nirvana*, Being out of a forest, MBh. 5, 863. **2.** Negation, No, without, e.g. *niranukroça*, **1.** m. No compassion = mercilessness, Râm. 4, 19, 21. **2.** adj. Without mercy = merciless, 2, 34, 11 Gorr. *nirjîva*, **1.** m. Death, Kathâs. 17, 15. **2.** adj. Without life, MBh. 7, 1954.

निसर्ग *nisarga*, i.e. *ni-sṛij* + *a*, m. **1.** Evacuation of excrements, MBh. 12, 7951. **2.** Giving away, Man. 8, 143. **3.** Grant, Hariv. 10033. **4.** Creation,

Hariv. 543. 5. The natural state, peculiar character, Kathâs. 20, 31.

निसर्गज *nisarga-ja,* adj. Innate, Man. 8, 414.

निसूदक *ni-sûd+aka,* m. A killer, Yâjń, 3, 251.—Comp. *Krauńcha-*, m. a name of the god of war, MBh. 3, 8138.

निसूदन *ni-sûd+ana,* and **निषूदन** *nishûdana* (against Gramm.), m. A destroyer, MBh. 3, 12013.

निसृष्टार्थ *nisṛishṭârtha,* i. e. *ni sṛishṭa-artha* (vb. *sṛij*), m. An envoy.

निस्तार *nistâra,* i.e. *nis-tṛî+a,* m. 1. Crossing, passing over a sea, Bhartṛ. 1, 68. 2. Payment, Hit. 99, 18.

निस्तारण *nistâraṇa, nis-tṛî,* Caus., +*ana,* n. Overcoming, Bhâg. P. 5, 17, 24.

निस्तोद *nistoda,* i.e. *nis-tud+a.* m. and **निस्तोदन** *nistodana,* i.e. *nis-tud* +*ana,* n. Pricking, Suçr. 1, 252, 8; 251, 13.

निस्त्रिंश *nistṛiṁça,* i.e. curtailed from *nis-tṛiṁçat,* I. m. A sword, MBh. 1, 5380. II. adj. Merciless, Pańch. 264, 7. —Comp. *Baddha-*, adj. girt with a falchion.

निस्पन्द *ni-spand+a,* m. Motion, MBh. 12, 12704.

निस्यन्द *nisyanda,* and **निष्यन्द** *nishyanda,* i. e. *ni-syand+a,* I. adj. Trickling, Ragh. 3, 41. II. m. 1. Trickling, drops, Râm. 2, 94, 13. 2. Discharge, Suçr. 1, 121, 9. 3. figuratively, Uttering, Hariv. 4092.

निस्यन्दिन् *ni-syand + in,* adj. Streaming down, Çâk. 99, 16.

निस्रव and **निस्राव** *nisrâva,* i.e. *ni -sru+a,* m. A torrent, MBh. 11, 161; Hariv. 5364.

निस्वन and **निस्वान** *nisvǎna,* i.e. *ni -svan+a,* m. Sound, Man. 4, 106; MBh. 7, 9569.

निहन् *ni-han,* m. A destroyer, MBh. 3, 740.

निहन्तृ *ni-han+tṛi,* m. 1. A killer, Man. 5, 51. 2. One who removes, Vikr. d. 48. 3. One who prevents, Suçr. 1, 308, 12.

निह्नव *nihnava,* i.e. *ni-hnu+a,* m. 1. Denial, Yâjń. 2, 11. 2. Concealment, 267. 3. Secrecy, MBh. 9376. 4. Distrust, 5, 1362. 5. Expiation, Man. 9, 21.

निह्नुति *ni-hnu+ti,* f. Concealment, Amar. 8.

निह्राद *ni-hrâd+a,* m. Sound, Ragh. 1, 41.

नी *NÎ,* i. 1, Par., Âtm. 1. To conduct, to guide, Râm. 1, 9, 55. 2. To lead away, Râm. 1, 54, 8. 3. To lead to (acc., dat.), Man. 6, 88; MBh. 2, 2480; Râm. 5, 58, 21. 4. To put a person or an object into a certain state or condition (with acc. and loc.), e.g. *vaçam,* To subdue, Ragh. 8, 19; *âdhânam,* To give in pledge, Yâjń. 2, 247; *paritosham,* To gladden, Pańch. 34, 12; *sâkshyam,* To admit as a witness, Man. 8, 197; *çûdratâm,* To degrade to the state of a Çûdra, 3, 15. With an adv. *bhasmasât,* To turn into ashes, Pańch. 38, 18. 5. With *daṇḍam,* To inflict a punishment, Man. 7, 30. 6. To carry, Râm. 2, 83, 22 Gorr. 7. To carry away, 5, 35, 35; to take away, Chaṇ. 5, in Berl. Monatsb. 8. To bring to (acc.), Matsyop. 14. 9. To pass (as time), Hit. 37, 20. 10. To trace, Man. 8, 44. 11. To ascertain, 245. Anomal. potent. *nayîta*; pf. *nayâmâsa*; fut. *nayitâ, nayishyati*;

ptcple. of the fut. pass. *nayitavya*; and infin. *nayitum*, in epic poetry. Comp. ptcple. of the pf. pass. *durnîta*, i.e. *dus-*, n. A foolish, a wicked action, Hariv. 7402; Pañch. ii. d. 21 (read *durnitam*). *su-*, I. adj., **1.** Well-behaved. **2.** Politic. II. n. **1.** Good conduct. **2.** Policy. Caus. *nâyaya*, To cause to be carried, Man. 5, 104. Desider. *ninisha*, **1.** To wish to carry, MBh. 7, 2617. **2.** To wish to trace, 11, 303. Frequent. *nenîya*, To rule, 12, 8989.—With the prep. अनु *anu*, **1.** To communicate, 1, 6481. **2.** To beg, 3528. **3.** To reconcile, Vikr. d. 61.—With पर्यनु *pari-anu*, To entreat urgently, Râm. 6, 112, 10.—With प्रत्यनु *prati-anu*, **1.** To induce somebody to yield, MBh. 12, 150. **2.** To deny, 1, 736.—With अप *apa*, **1.** To lead away, 1, 530. **2.** To remove, Man. 3, 242. **3.** To rob, Râm. 3, 54, 26. **4.** To put off, MBh. 7, 8192. **5.** To deny, Kull. ad. Man. 8, 53. *apanîta*, **1.** What has swerved from, Râm. 3, 55, 40. **2.** Performed wrongly, MBh. 5, 1499. n. Foolish or wicked behaviour, 6, 585; Râm. 3, 66, 24. Desider. To wish to remove, Prab. 108, 18.—With व्यप *vi-apa*, **1.** To lead away, Râm. 2, 66, 13. **2.** To remove, 2, 10, 37. **3.** To put off, MBh. 5, 4687. **4.** To abandon, Bhâg. P. 5, 10, 15. Caus. To cause to be removed, MBh. 7, 1290.—With अभि *abhi*, **1.** To bring on, conduct to, 5, 4759; 12, 3691. **2.** To mimic, Çâk. 31, 8. **3.** To represent, Prab. 2, 19. *abhinîta*, **1.** Fit, Râm. 4, 28, 13. **2.** Trained, MBh. 6, 1765. **3.** Prudent, Râm. 4, 28, 13.—With आ *â*, **1.** To lead on, MBh. 3, 271. **2.** To bring, Man. 3, 210. **3.** To take upon, MBh. 3, 2946. **4.** To bring back, Râm. 1, 40, 9. **5.** To sacrifice, MBh. 1, 3773. **6.** To allot, Ragh. 15, 24. **7.** To put a person or an object into a certain state or condition, e.g. *vaçam*, To reduce to submission, Man. 7, 107; *vidhvaṁsam*, To destroy, Mârk. P. 14, 65. Caus. To cause to be carried, Râm. 1, 4, 25.—With अन्वा *anu-â*, To carry to, MBh. 7, 6343.—With समभ्या *sam-abhi-â*, To lead on, MBh. 3, 10656.—With उपा *upa-â*, **1.** To bring or conduct near, Bhag. P. 4, 7, 19; with acc., Râm. 1, 45, 32 Gorr. **2.** To cause, Râm. 6, 82, 3. **3.** To carry off, Bhâg. P. 9, 22, 23.—With समुपा *sam-upa-â*, To assemble, Râm. 1, 11, 7 Gorr.—With पर्या *pari-â*, **1.** To lead about, MBh. 2, 2685. **2.** To conduct, to put, 1, 5446.—With प्रत्या *prati-â*, **1.** To bring back, Râm. 5, 75, 18. **2.** To regain, Hariv. 9855. Desider. To wish to settle, MBh. 5, 1499.—With समा *sam-â*, **1.** To assemble, Râm. 1, 12, 27 Gorr. **2.** To unite, Çâk. d. 112. **3.** To accumulate, MBh. 13, 5872. **4.** To bring on, 1, 7334. **5.** To bring home, 2, 1035. **6.** To offer (a sacrifice), 14, 362. Caus. **1.** To convoke, 17, 15. **2.** To cause to be brought together, Râm. 4, 24, 14. **3.** To cause to be brought near, MBh. 1, 4538.—With उद् *ud*, **1.** To bring upwards, 3, 17330. **2.** To raise, Bhâg. P. 4, 3, 10. **3.** To lead out (abl.), to (acc. and loc.), 2, 2, 21; MBh. 12, 6105. **4.** To lead aside, MBh. 3, 1438. **5.** To conduct away, 12, 9561. **6.** To lead in different directions, Bhâg. P. 7, 2, 21. **7.** To trace out, MBh. 3, 12444.—With प्रोद् *pra-ud*, To raise, Bhâg. P. 3, 18, 2.—With समुद् *sam-ud*, To raise, 3, 13, 6.—With उप *upa*, **1.** To bring on, MBh. 13, 3668. **2.** To inform, Râm.

3, 60, 36. **3.** To offer, Man. 3, 225. **4.** To bring about, Gît. 1, 46. **5.** To put a person or an object into a certain state or condition, Râm. 5, 87, 26. **6.** To bring, Çâk. 31, 6. **7.** To lead away, Râm. 5, 35, 3. **8.** To lead, Bhâg. P. 7, 5, 31. **9.** To admit as pupil, to gird with the sacrificial cord, Man. 2, 69. *upanîta,* Girt with the characteristic string, 2, 49. Caus. To cause to be admitted as pupil, or to be girt with the sacrificial string, Man. 11, 191.—With **समुप** *sam-upa,* **1.** To bring on, MBh. 1, 4319. **2.** With *mantram,* To consult, Râm. 5, 86, 18. **3.** To cause, Hariv. 10532. **4.** To take along with one's self, MBh. 2, 1036.—With **नि** *ni,* **1.** To bring near, Yâjń. 3, 295. **2.** To bring to (acc.), Bhâg. P. 2, 2, 16. **3.** To incline, 1, 8, 31. **4.** To pour out, 1, 8, 2. **5.** To perform, 4, 6, 50.—With **निस्** *nis,* **निर्णी** *nir ṇî,* **1.** To settle, Râm. 5, 85, 11, **2.** To devise, Daçak. in Chr. 194, 19. **3.** To trace out, to investigate, Râjat. 6, 27. **4.** To decide, MBh. 13, 7735.—With **विनिस्** *vi-nis,* To settle completely, Bhâg. P. 6, 2, 20.—With **परि** *pari* **णी** *ṇî,* **1.** To lead (a bride) round (the fire), MBh. 1, 7340 (anomal. *pariṇayâm âsa*). **2.** To marry, Pańch. 261, 8. **3.** To investigate, Man. 7, 122. *su-pariṇîta,* Well performed, MBh. 3, 13739. Caus. To spend (one's time), MBh. 10, 36.—With **प्र** *pra* **णी** *ṇî,* **1.** To lead, Râm. 6, 7, 19. **2.** To direct, Bhâg. P. 3, 13, 5. **3.** To show, Bhâg. P. 3, 9, 11. **4.** To bring on, Pańch. iii. d. 1. **5.** To cast, MBh. 6, 3796. **6.** To remove, 3453. **7.** with *daṇḍam,* To inflict a punishment, Man. 7, 20. **8.** To put into a state or condition, Bhâg. P. 7, 8, 8. **9.** To perform, 3, 21, 32. **10.** To apply, MBh. 12, 452. **11.** To establish, 13, 2542. **12.** To compose, 1, 591. **13.** To show one's love, to love, 2, 1288.—With **विप्र** *vi-pra,* **1.** To direct, 12, 3891. **2.** To expire, 3560.—With **संप्र** *sam-pra,* **1.** To collect, 2, 2126. **2.** with *daṇḍam,* To inflict a punishment, Man. 7, 16. **3.** To compose, MBh. 1, 561.—With **प्रति** *prati,* **1.** To lead back, Râm. 2, 99, 25 Gorr.—With **वि** *vi,* **1.** To remove, Râm. 3, 62, 79. **2.** To spread, 49, 29. **3.** To govern (as horses), MBh. 4, 599. **4.** To train, Man. 4, 68. **5.** To instruct, MBh. 3, 12585. **6.** To pass away, Gît. 8, 1. **7.** To perform, MBh. 13, 2201. *vinîta* (Well bred), **1.** Demure, Man. 4, 196. **2.** Modest, Man. 7, 39. **Comp.** *A-,* adj. 1. untrained, Man. 4, 67. 2. naughty, Râm. 3, 45, 11; *Durvinîta* i.e. *dus-,* adj. Naughty; subst. a miscreant, Pańch. v. d. 17.—With **अभिवि** *abhi-vi,* To instruct well, Râm. 6, 11, 10.—With **संवि** *sam-vi,* To remove, MBh. 12, 3176.—With **सम्** *sam,* **1.** To bring together, Man. 3, 244. **2.** To arrange, Bhâg. P. 4, 7, 48. **3.** To pay, Man. 9, 107. **4.** To direct, Bhâg. P. 6, 10, 11. **5.** To bring on, MBh. 1, 7412.—With **अभिसम्** *abhi-sam,* To conduct, MBh. 12, 6566.

नीकाश *nikâça,* i. e. *ni-kâç+a.* Latter part of comp. adj., f. *çâ,* Like, resembling, MBh. 3, 12552.

नीच *nîcha,* i.e. *ni-ańch+a,* adj., f. *châ.* **1.** Low, Man. 2, 198. **2.** Short, Yâjń. 1, 131. **3.** Deep, Pańch. i. d. 225. **4.** Base, mean, Râm. 3, 35, 35. **5.** °*chais,* instr. pl., adv. **1.** Below, Megh. 43. **2.** Low-bowing, MBh. 1, 3287. **3.** Little, Ragh. 3, 43. **4.** Humbly, Kâm. Nîtis. 7, 42. **5.** Softly, Amar. 67.—**Comp.** *Uchcha-,* adj. manifold, MBh. 14, 427. *Mahâ-,* m. a washerman.

नीचक *ni-cha + ka*, adj., f. *chikâ*, Soft, MBh. 3, 11018.

नीचता *nicha+tâ*, f. Inferiority, MBh. 3, 10635.

नीचीन *nichina*, i.e. *ni-anch + ina*, adj. 1. Downward, cast down, Bhâg. P. 8, 22, 14. 2. Flowing down, 5, 16, 25.

नीड *niḍa*, i.e. probably *ni-sad + a*, m. 1. A nest, Râm. 2, 96, 28. 2. A den, 4, 43, 17. 3. The seat, or the inner room of a chariot, 5, 40, 14.—Comp. *Eka-*, adj. having only one seat, Bhâg. P. 4, 26, 2. *Sa-*, adj. near.—Cf. A.S. nest; Lat. nidus.

नीडक *niḍa + ka*, (m.) A nest, MBh. 12, 9297.

नीति *ni + ti*, f. 1. Guidance. 2. Moral behaviour, Sâh. D. 489. 3. Prudent behaviour, MBh. 1, 7612. 4. Prudence, Yâjń. 1, 316. 5. A prudent counsel, Ragh. 12, 69. 6. Policy, Man. 7, 177. 7. Relation, support, MBh. 3, 1292. — Comp. *A-*, f. a foolish trick, Pańch. 143, 25. *Daṇḍa-*, f. the science of criminal justice, Man. 7, 43. *Râja-nîti*, i.e. *râjan-*, f. regal polity, rules of conduct and government for a king. *Su-*, f. 1. good behaviour, good manners. 2. good policy, Daçak. in Chr. 196, 1.

नीतिमन्त् *niti + mant*, adj. One who knows the rules of a moral and prudent behaviour, Râm. 1, 1, 11.

नीथ *nî + tha*, m. Guiding.—Comp. *Su-*, adj. righteous.

नीप *nipa*, i.e. *ni-ap + a*, I. adj. Deep, Kathâs. 27, 8. II. m. 1. The Cadamba tree (Nauclea Cadamba). 2. A proper name, MBh. 2, 333.

नीर *nira* (cf. *nâra*, probably *snâ + ra*), n. Water, MBh. 3, 10078.—Comp. *Kshira-*, n. water with milk, Lass. 12, 18.

नीरज I. *nira-ja*, m. and n. A lotus in general, Kathâs. 4, 6. II. = *nirajas* (q. cf.), Free from dust, MBh. 12, 3822.

नीरजस् *nirajas*, i.e. *nis-rajas*, and

नीरजस्क *nirajas + ka*, adj. 1. Free from dust, Râm. 2, 87, 21 Gorr.; 4, 44, 86. 2. Devoid of passions, 4, 44, 41; Prab. 117, 18 v.r.

नीरद *nira-da*, m. A cloud, Râm. 6, 66, 28.

नीररुह *nira-ruha*, m. A lotus, Chr. 241, 71 = Çiç. 9, 71.

नीराजन *nirâjana*, i. e. *nis-râj*, Caus., *+ana*, n. and f. *nâ*, Lustration of arms, a military and religious ceremony, Pańch. 158, 4.

नीरोग्यता *nirogyatâ*, i.e. *nis-roga + ya + tâ* (but perhaps an error for *nirogatâ*), f. Health, healing, Pańch. 217, 24.

† **नील्** *NÎL*, i. 1 (rather a denomin. derived from *nila*), Par. 1. To be blue. 2. To make or dye blue.

नील *nila*, i.e. *niç + la*, I. adj., f. *lâ* and *li*, Black or dark-blue, Man. 11, 136. II. m. 1. A proper name, MBh. 1, 2697. 2. The name of a mountain, 6, 198. III. f. *li*, 1. The indigo plant, Man. 10, 89. 2. A proper name, MBh. 1, 3722. IV. n. Indigo, the dye, Yâjń. 3, 38.—Comp. *Â-*, adj. blackish, Kir. 5, 31. *Indra-*, m. a sapphire, Megh. 47. *Kâṁsya-*, m. the name of a monkey, Râm. 4, 39, 23. *Mahâ-*, m. 1. the sapphire. 2. one of the Nâgas. *Râja(n)-*, n. the emerald.—Cf. Lat. niger for nigro = *niç + ra*.

नीलजा *nîlajâ*, i.e. *nîla-ja*, f. The river Vitastâ, Râjat. 5, 91.

नीलता *nîla* + *tâ*, f. Dark-blue colour, Kâm. Nîtis. 7, 16.

नीलिमन् *nîliman*, i.e. *nîla* + *iman*, m. Blackness, Gît. 8, 3.

† **नीव्** *NÎV*, i. 1, Par. To become corpulent.

नीवार *nîvâra*, I. m. Rice growing wild, Râm. 2, 28, 21 Gorr. II. f. *râ*, The name of a river, MBh. 6, 328.

नीवि and **नीवी** *nîvî*, f. A cloth worn round a woman's waist, Yâjń. 2, 284.—Comp. *Toya-nîvî*, adj. surrounded by the ocean, Bhâg. P. 1, 15, 38.

नीहार *nîhâra*, m. Fog, Hiḍ. 4, 40.

नीहारकर *nîhâra-kara*, m. The moon, Daçak. 7, 3, below.

1. **नु** *nu*, and **नू** *nû*, ved. (perhaps akin to *nava*, cf. *nûtana*), a particle, **1.** Now (ved.). **2.** A particle of interrogation in two or more interrogative sentences succeeding each other, Çâk. d. 137. **3.** Preceded by interrogatives, MBh. 5, 6003. **4.** *nu—nu*, Either . . . or, Râm. 2, 72, 27; *nu—nu—nu* . . . or . . . or, Kir. 5. 1. **5.** A part. of affirmation, Indeed, Chr. 291, 13=Rigv. i. 64, 13.—Cf. νύ; Goth. nu; A.S. nu; νῦν, Lat. nunc (i.e. num-ce=νῦν κεν); Goth. nuh.

2. **नु** *NU*, ii. 2, and *nu*, or **नू** *NÛ*, i. 6, *nuva*, Par., and ved. i. 1, Âtm. **1.** To shout (ved.). **2.** To praise, Bhâg. P. 3, 23, 39.—With the prep. **परि** *pari*, **णु** *ṇu*, To praise, 1, 8, 44.—With **प्र** *pra*, **णु** *ṇu*, To praise, 3, 21, 22.

† **नुड्** *NUḌ*, i. 6, Par. To kill.

नुति *nu* + *ti*, f. Praise, Bhartṛ. 2, 59 v.r.

नुद् *NUD*, i. 6, Par., Âtm. (ii. 2, Hariv. 7442). **1.** To push on, Megh. 9. **2.** To push away, to remove, MBh. 3, 12707; 4, 1819. Ptcple. of the pf. pass. *nutta*, *nunna*, *nûta*, and in epic poetry also *nudita*, MBh. 1, 6670. Caus. *nodaya*, **1.** To push on, MBh. 9, 1005. **2.** To incite, Râm. 5, 46, 12.—With the prep. **अप** *apa*, **1.** To drive away, Bhâg. P. 1, 16, 35. **2.** To remove, MBh. 14, 1858.—With **व्यप** *vi-apa*, To remove, 11, 24.—With **अभि** *abhi*, To strike, 14, 1718. Caus. To order, 1478.—With **अव** *ava*, Caus. **1.** To induce to drive away (two acc.), 7, 3069.—With **अपा** *apa-â*, (probably *apa* with lengthened final), **1.** To drive away, 7, 8691. **2.** To remove, 3, 16973. **3.** To expiate, Man. 6, 95.—With **व्यपा** *vi-apa-â* (see *apâ*), To remove, MBh. 4, 1319.—With **उपा** *upa-â* (?), **1.** To drive away, 7, 1771. **2.** To remove, 268. **3.** To bruise, 6, 5619.—With **उप** *upa*, To drive near, Çiç. 4, 68.—With **निस्** *nis*, **निर्णुद्** *nir ṇud*, **1.** To reject, Man. 4, 250. **2.** To remove, MBh. 12, 7126.—With **अभिनिस्** To remove, 12, 10728.—With **परा** *parâ*, **णुद्** *ṇud*, To remove, Bhâg. P. 3, 7, 7.—With **प्र** *pra*, **णुद्** *ṇud*, **1.** To drive away, MBh. 4, 1660. **2.** To remove, Râm. 3, 78, 8. **3.** To push on, MBh. 3, 12096. **4.** To stir, Râm. 5, 3, 38. Caus. *praṇodita*, Agitated, Pańch. 165, 10.—With **अतिप्र** *ati-pra*, To press hard, Daçak. in Chr. 193, 14.—With **अनुप्र** *anu-pra*, To put to flight, Râm. 6, 7,

36.—With संप्र *sam-pra,* **1.** To urge, MBh. 3, 377. **2.** To remove, 5, 745.—With वि *vi,* **1.** To strike, to wound, 6, 4846. **2.** To play (as a guitar), Bhâg. P. 4, 8, 38. Caus. **1.** To remove, Çiç. 4, 60. **2.** To spend (as a night), MBh. 3, 46. **3.** To exhilarate, Böhtl. Ind. Spr. 135.—With अभिवि *abhi-vi,* Caus. To exhilarate, MBh. 12, 898.—With सम् *sam,* **1.** To collect, 6, 777. **2.** To push on, Nal. 20, 42. **3.** To find, Râm. 5, 1, 92.—Cf. A.S. nydian (to compel), a-nydan (to repel); Goth. niutan, A.S. niótan (originally, to further), not, use, perhaps *νύσσα.*

ऽनुद् *-nud,* latter part of a comp. adj., Removing, Kir. 5, 28.

ऽनुद *-nud+a,* Removing, Râm. 2, 91, 24.

नू *nû,* see *nu,* **1. 2.**

नूतन *nû+tana* (1.*nu,* cf. *nava*), adj., f. *nâ,* **1.** New, Râjat. 5, 7. **2.** Fresh, young, Kathâs. 24, 228. **3.** Strange, Hit. 77, 7.

नूतनय *NÛTANAYA,* a denomin. derived from *nûtana* with *aya,* Par. To renew, Bhâg. P. 3, 8, 1.

नूत्न *nûtna,* i.e. *nû+tana* (q. cf.), adj., f. *tnâ,* **1.** New, Bhâg. P. 8, 9, 10. **2.** Fresh, young, 6, 1, 35.

नूनभाव *nûnabhâva,* i. e. *nûnam -bhâva,* abl. °*vât,* adv. Indeed, MBh. 3, 59.

नूनम् *nûnam* (1. *nu* and the pronoun *na,* acc.), adv. Surely, Râm. 3, 51, 27.

नूपुर *nûpura,* m. and n. An ornament for the ancles or toes, Râm. 3, 58, 32.

नूपुरवन्त् *nûpura + vant,* adj., f. *vati,* Adorned with an ornament for the feet, Amar. 52.

नृ *nṛi,* m. A man; pl. Men, mankind, Man. 3, 81. Superlat. *nṛitama,* Most manly, Chr. 293, 1=Rigv. i. 87, 1.

नृत् *NṚIT,* i. 4, Par. (in poetry also Âtm., MBh. 7, 2913), **1.** To dance, Man. 4, 64. **2.** To represent (as actor), Hariv. 8496. Ptcple. of the pf. pass. *nṛitta,* n. Dancing, Kathâs. 9, 40. Ptcple. of the fut. pass. *nṛitya,* n. Dancing, acting, Megh. 37. Caus. *nartaya,* To cause to dance, MBh. 4, 307. Ptcple. of the pf. pass. *nartita,* n. Dancing, 7, 177. Frequent. *narînṛit* and *narînṛitya,* To dance to and fro, Lass. 84, 9; 67, 7.—With the prep. अनु *anu,* **1.** To dance after (acc.), Râm. 3, 79, 15. **2.** To dance before somebody (acc.), MBh. 9, 2468.—With आ *â,* Caus. To cause to move softly, Amar. 32. — With उप *upa,* **1.** To dance before somebody (acc.), Râm. 6 92, 71. **2.** To mock somebody by dancing before him (acc.), MBh. 9, 3315. Ptcple. of the fut. pass. *upanṛitya,* used to be danced in, Râm. 3, 6, 3.—With परि *pari,* To dance round somebody (acc.), MBh. 2, 2532.—With प्र *pra,* **1.** To dance forward, Râm. 1, 45, 26 Gorr. **2.** To begin to dance, MBh. 3, 6087 (read *pranṛittavân*). **3.** To dance, Ṛit. 2, 14. **4.** To mock somebody by dancing before him (acc.), MBh. 8, 4250. *pranṛitta,* Having begun to dance, dancing, MBh. 3, 1844.—With संप्र *sam-pra,* To begin to dance, 3, 6093.—With प्रति *prati,* To mock somebody in one's turn by dancing, (acc.), 8, 4251.

नृतू *nṛit+û*, m. A dancer, a mime, Chr. 294, 4=Rigv. i. 92, 4.

नृत्तमय *nṛitta + maya* (vb. *nṛit*), adj. Consisting of dancing, Kathâs. 28, 84.

नृप *nṛi-pa* (vb. 2.*pâ*), A prince, a king, Man. 2, 139.—Comp. *Dus-*, m. a wicked king, Râjat. 5, 416.

नृपत्व *nṛipa + tva*, n. Sovereignty, Hariv. 4891.

नृवन्त् *nṛi+vant*, adj. Manly, Chr. 294, 7=Rigv. i. 92, 7.

नृशंस *nṛi-çam̃s+a*, adj. **1.** Malicious, mischievous, Man. 3, 41. **2.** Base, MBh. 13, 513.—Comp. *A-*, adj. mild, Râm. 2, 62, 7. *Su-*, very mischievous.

नृशंसता *nṛiçam̃sa+tâ*, f. Mischievousness, baseness, Kathâs. 26, 192.—Comp. *A-*, f. mildness, Râm. 3, 58, 42.

नृशंसवन्त् *nṛiçam̃sa + vant*, adj. Mischievous, MBh. 4, 925.

नृशंस्य *nṛiçam̃sya*, i.e. *nṛiçam̃sa+ya*, I. adj. Mischievous, MBh. 13, 3011. II. n. Mischievousness, 3, 494.

नृषद् *nṛishad*, i.e. *nṛi-sad*, f. Understanding, Bhâg. P. 5, 7, 13 (Sch.).

नृषाच् *nṛishâch*, i.e. *nṛi-sach*, adj. Benevolent to men, Chr. 290, 9=Rigv. i. 64, 9.

नृषाह्य *nṛishâhya*, i.e. *nṛi-sah+ya*, n. Battle, Chr. 297, 22=Rigv. i. 112, 22.

† **नॄ** *NṜÎ*, ii. 9, *nṛiṇâ*, Par. To lead.

नेजक *nejaka*, i.e. *nij+aka*, m. A washerman, Man. 8, 396.

नेजन *nejana*, i.e. *nij + ana*, n. Washing, MBh. 7, 8530.

नेतृ *netṛi*, i.e. *nî+tṛi*, m., f. *tri*, and n. **1.** One who guides or leads, Man. 7, 17. **2.** One who leads to, MBh. 3, 954. **3.** With *daṇḍasya*, One who inflicts punishment, Man. 7, 25. **4.** The hero of a drama, Sâh. D. 64.

नेत्र *netṛa*, i.e. *nî+tra*, I. A substitute for *netṛi* when latter part of a comp. adj., e.g. *bhavannetra*, i. e. *bhavant-*, Having thee as commander, MBh. 7, 3702. II. n. **1.** The eye, Man. 4, 44. **2.** The string of a churning rope, MBh. 1, 1124.—Comp. *A-yugma-*, and *tri-*, m. a name of Çiva, Kumâras. 3, 51; MBh. 12, 10357. *Sahasra-*, adj. possessed of a thousand eyes. *Pari-*, I. m. an owl. II. n. the white lotus.

नेद् *NED*, i. 1, Par. **1.** To blame (cf. *nid*). **2.** † To be near.

नेदिष्ठ *nedishṭha*, superl. (from *neda* for *naddha*, ptcple. of the pf. pass. of *nah*; cf. Goth. nehva; A.S. neah), Very near, nearest.

नेदीयंस् *nediyam̃s*, comparat. of the last (q. cf.), Nearer, as near as possible, Râjat. 4, 31.

नेपथ्य *nepathya*, n. **1.** Ornament, attire, Ragh. 6, 6. **2.** The attire of an actor, Çâk. 3, 6. **3.** The tiring room of a stage, the part behind the scenes, Çâk. 8, 20.

नेमि *nemi*, i.e. *nam* (with *e* instead of being reduplicated), *+i*, f. **1.** The circumference of a wheel, MBh. 3, 15489. **2.** Circumference, e.g. *samudra-nemi*, adj. Surrounded by the ocean, MBh. 1, 1585. **3.** Edge, Bhâg. P. 3, 19, 14.—Comp. *A-rishṭa-*, m. a proper name, 3, 20, 9. *Kâla-*, 1. f. the name of a weapon, Hariv. 2640. **2.** m. the name of a demon, Çâk. 95, 4.

† **नेष्** *NESH*, i. 1. Âtm. To go.

नैःश्रेयस *naiḥçreyasa,* i.e. *nis-çreyas* + *a,* I. adj., f. *sî,* Leading to future beatitude, Man. 9, 334. II. n. The name of a fabulous forest, Bhâg. P. 3, 15, 16.

नैःश्रेयसिक *naiḥçreyasika,* i.e. *naiḥçreyasa* + *ika,* adj. Leading to future beatitude, Man. 12, 88.

नैःस्नेह्य *naiḥsnehya,* i.e. *nis-sneha* + *ya,* n. Want of affection, Man. 9, 15 (read *naiḥsn°* instead of *naisn°*).

नैक *naika,* i.e. *na-eka,* adj., f. *kâ.* 1. Many a, Mârk. P. 28, 29. 2. pl. Many, Nal. 12, 109. 3. Manifold, Daçak. in Chr. 198, 15. 4. Including several matters, Yâjń. 2, 20.

नैकधा *naika* + *dhâ* (or rather *na -ekadhâ*), adv. 1. In many parts, Râm. 6, 77, 12. 2. To many directions, Bhâg. P. 4, 5, 18.

नैकशस् *naika* + *ças* (or rather *na -ekaças*), adv. Repeatedly, Râm. 3, 36, 21.

नैकशस्त्रमय *naika-çastra* + *maya,* adj. Consisting of many missiles, Râm. 6, 91, 20.

नैकृतिक *naikṛitika,* i.e. *nikṛiti* + *ka,* adj. Fallacious, Man. 4, 196 (read *naikṛi°,* instead of *naishkṛi°*).

नैगम *naigama,* i.e. *nigama* + *a,* I. adj. Referring to the Vedas (vedic), Bhâg. P. 3, 7, 38. II. m. 1. A means, MBh. 12, 3685. 2. A trader, Yâjń. 2, 192.

नैत्यक *naityaka,* and **नैत्यिक** *naityika,* i.e. *nitya* + *ka* or *ika,* adj. What must be done constantly or regularly (opposed to *naimittika*), Man. 2, 105; 8, 86.

नैदाघ *naidâgha,* and **नैदाघिक** *naidâghika,* i.e. *nidâgha* + *a,* or *ika,* adj. Belonging to the hot season, Bhâg. P. 3, 14, 48.

नैदेशिक *naideçika,* i.e. *nideça* + *ika,* m. A servant.

नैधन *naidhana,* i.e. *nidhana* + *a,* adj. 1. Referring to death, Hariv. 4900. 2. Perishable, 2194.

नैपुण *naipuṇa,* i.e. *nipuṇa* + *a,* n. 1. Dexterity, MBh. 13, 1378. 2. Skill, experience, Râjat. 4, 354. 3. Strictness, Man. 10, 85. 4. Completion, Bhâg. P. 3, 25, 14.

नैपुण्य *naipuṇya,* i.e. *nipuṇa* + *ya,* n. 1. Cleverness, Sâv. 3, 21. 2. Artfulness, Pańch. 121, 16. 3. Exactness, Râm. 3, 75, 70. 4. Completion, Man. 4, 107.

नैमित्तिक *naimittika,* i.e. *nimitta* + *ika,* adj. 1. Occasional, Daçak. in Chr. 180, 21. 2. Dependent on an external cause.

नैमिष *naimisha,* n. The name of a forest.

नैमिषीय *naimishîya,* i.e. *naimisha* + *îya,* adj. Referring to the Naimisha forest, MBh. 9, 2161.

नैमिषेय *naimisheya,* i.e. *naimisha* + *eya,* adj. Living in the Naimisha forest.

नैयमिक *naiyamika,* i.e. *niyama* + *ika,* adj. Conformable to a (religious) precept, Bhâg. P. 5, 8, 1.

नैयायिक *naiyâyika,* i.e. *nyâya* + *ika,* m. A logician, a follower of the Nyâya philosophy.

नैरन्तर्य *nairantarya,* i.e. *nis-antara* + *ya,* Absence of interruption.

नैरर्थ्य *nairarthya,* i.e. *nis-artha* + *ya,* n. Senselessness.

नैराश्य *nairâçya*, i. e. *nis-âça + ya* (cf. *âçâ*), n. Hopelessness.

नैरुक्त *nairukta*, i. e. *nirukti + a*, I. adj. Explained etymologically MBh. 13, 4485. II. m. One who is conversant with etymological interpretation, Man. 12, 111.

नैर्ऋत *nairṛita*, i.e. *nirṛiti + a*, I. adj., f. *tî*. 1. Southwestern, Man. 11, 104. II. m. 1. A son of Nirṛiti, i.e. a Râkshasa or demon, Ragh. 12, 43. 2. pl. The name of a people. III. adj. Belonging to the Râkshasas or demons, MBh. 12, 6132. IV. f. *tî*, A name of Durgâ, Dev. 5, 9.

नैर्गुण्य *nairguṇya*, i.e. *nis-guṇa + ya*, I. n. 1. Freedom from qualities, Bhâg. P. 1, 15, 31. 2. Want of good qualities, MBh. 2, 674. II. adj. Not having any relation to qualities, Bhâg. P. 3, 32, 32.

नैर्घृण्य *nairghṛiṇya*, i. e. *nis-ghriṇa + ya* (see *ghṛiṇâ*), n. Cruelty, Mâlav. 69, 10.

नैर्मल्य *nairmalya*, i.e. *nis-mala + ya*, n. Purity, MBh. 7, 9264.

नैर्लज्ज्य *nairlajjya*, i.e. *nis-lajja + ya* (see *lajjâ*), n. Impudence.

नैल्य *nailya*, i.e. *nîla + ya*, n. Dark-blue (the colour).

नैविड्य *naiviḍya*, i.e. *niviḍa + ya*, n. Denseness.

नैश *naiça*, i.e. *niçâ + a*, adj., f. *çî*, Nocturnal, Man. 2, 102.

नैशाकर *naiçâkara*, i.e. *niçâkara + a*, m. Caused by the moon.

नैशिक *naiçika*, i.e. *niçâ + ika*, adj., f. *kî*, Obtained in one night, Man. 5, 67.

नैश्चिन्त्य *naiçchintya*, i.e. *nis-chinta + ya* (see *chintâ*), n. Freedom from care, Bhartṛ. 3, 92.

नैषध *naishadha*, i.e. *nishadha + a*, I. m. 1. A prince of the Nishadhas, a designation of Nala. 2. pl. = Nishadhas (the people). II. n. The name of a poem treating of Nala.

नैषाद *naishâda*, i.e. *nishâda + a*, 1. adj. Belonging to the Nishâdas. 2. m. pl. Nishâdas (the people).

नैषादि *naishâdi*, i.e. *nishâda + i*, m. A prince of the Nishâdas.

नैष्कर्म्य *naishkarmya*, i.e. *nis-karman + ya*, n. Abandoning action, inactivity.

नैष्कृतिक *naishkṛitika*, see *naikṛitika*.

नैष्ठिक *naishṭhika*, i.e. *nishṭhâ + ika*, I. adj., f. *kî*. 1. Final, MBh. 17, 21. 2. Decided, Râm. 6, 21, 28. 3. Accomplished, MBh. 13, 758. II. m. A Brâhmana who remains always in the condition of a religious student, observing the vow of chastity.

नैष्ठुर्य *naishṭhurya*, i.e. *nishṭhura + ya*, n. Coarseness, Hit. i. d. 91.

नैष्फल्य *naishphalya*, i.e. *nis-phala + ya*, n. Want of fruit or effect.

नैसर्गिक *naisargika*, i.e. *nisarga + ika*, adj., f. *kî*, Innate, Böhtl. Ind. Spr. 660.

नैस्नेह्य *naisnehya*, see *naiḥsnehya*.

नो *no*, i.e. *na-u*, a particle. 1. Nor, Suçr. 2, 461, 18. 2. Not, Pañch. i. d. 97.

नोदन *nodana*, i.e. *nud + ana*, n. Removing, Bhâg. P. 3, 26, 43.

नोदिन् *nodin*, i.e. *nud + in*, adj., f. *nî*, Removing.

नोधस् *nodhas*, m. The name of a Ṛishi.

नोधा *nodhâ* (= *navadhâ*), adv. In nine parts, Bhâg. P. 3, 23, 47.

नौ *nau*, I. see *asmad*. II. probably *snâ+va*, f. A ship, a boat.—Cf. *ναῦς*; Lat. navis; O.H.G. nacho, A.S. naca.

नौक *nau+ka*, I. a substitute for *nau* when latter part of a comp. adj., e.g. *bhinna-* (vb. *bhid*), adj. Wrecked. II. f. *kâ*, A small vessel, a boat, Râm. 1, 9, 7.

न्यक्कार *nyakkâra*, i.e. *nyañch-kâra*, m. **1.** Humiliation. **2.** Disregard.

न्यग्भावयितृ *nyagbhâvayitṛi*, i. e. *nyañch-bhû*, Caus., *+tṛi*, m., f. *trî*, n. One who humbles, Daçak, 180, 13.

न्यग्रोध *nyagrodha*, i.e. *nyañch-ruh +a*, m. **1.** The Indian fig-tree, Ficus indica, Man. 8, 246. **2.** A proper name.

न्यङ्कु *nyañku* (probably *ni-añch+u*), m. A kind of antelope.

न्यञ्च् *nyañch*, i.e. *ni-añch*, I. adj., f. *nichî*, Downward. II. *nyak*, acc. n. adv., Humbly, MBh. 5, 1426; see *hṛi*.

न्यन्त *nyanta*, i.e. *ni-anta* (m. or n.). Proximity, Râm. 2, 68, 12.

न्यर्बुद *nyarbuda*, i.e. *ni-arbuda*, n. A hundred millions.

न्याय *nyâya*, i.e. *ni-i+a*, m. **1.** Rule. **2.** Method, manner, Man. 8, 310; Daçak. in Chr. 193, 13. **3.** Suitable manner, propriety, Man. 5, 140. **4.** A lawful act, 189, 15. **5.** A lawsuit, Pañch. 97, 2. **6.** Judgment, iii. d. 89. **7.** A syllogism, Prab. 111, 8. **8.** The Nyâya doctrine, consisting principally in logic.—**Comp.** *A-*, m. an unlawful act, Daçak. in Chr. 189, 15; acc. n. °*yam*, adv. improperly, Râm. 3, 51, 34. *Yathâ-nyâya+m*, adv. suitably, duly, Man. 3, 190.

न्यायवन्त् *nyâya+vant*, adj. Behaving properly, Râm. 5, 11, 15.

न्याय्य *nyâyya*, i.e. *nyâya+ya*, adj. **1.** Fit. **2.** Right, Man. 2, 152. **3.** Just, 9, 202. **4.** An infinitive governed by *nyâyya* has sometimes the signification of a passive, Râm. 2, 21, 3 Gorr.

न्यास *nyâsa*, i.e. *ni-* 2. *as+a*, m. **1.** Planting (as the foot), Râm. 5, 31, 60. **2.** Striking in, seizing with, Ragh. 12, 73. **3.** Seizing with one's claws, MBh. 12, 552. **4.** Putting on, Kathâs. 8, 15. **5.** Writing down, Böhtl. Ind. Spr. 170. **6.** Laying aside, Vikr. 87, 2; Bhag. 18, 2. **7.** A deposit, Yâjñ. 2, 67.—**Comp.** *Charaṇa-*, m. trace of a foot, Megh. 56.

न्यासिन् *nyâsin*, i.e. *nyâsa+in*, adj. subst. One who has abandoned all worldly concerns, Bhâg. P. 4, 30, 36.

न्युब्ज *nyubja*, i.e. *ni-ubja*, adj. One who lies on his face, MBh. 5, 7244.

न्यून *nyûna*, i.e. *ni-ûna*, adj., f. *nâ*. **1.** Defective, Bhâg. P. 1, 16, 21. **2.** Wanting, MBh. 3, 4057; *artha-*, Poor. **3.** Smaller, Yâjñ. 2, 116; less, Man. 8, 203. **4.** Low, MBh. 13, 6616. **5.** Inferior, MBh. 1, 5592.

न्यूनता *nyûna+tâ*, f. Inferiority, MBh. 8, 774.

प *P.*

ऽप *-pa*, latter part of a comp. adj. or subst. derived from adj. I. (vb. 1. *pâ*), Drinking, cf. *pâda-pa*, properly, Drinking by means of the foot, i.e. a tree. II. (vb. 2. *pâ*), **1.** Guarding, e.g. *dvâra-pa*, m. properly, Guarding a door, i.e. a doorkeeper. **2.** Ruling, e.g. *kshiti-pa*, m. properly, Ruling the earth, =a king; *daçapa*, i.e. *daçan -pa*, m. A governor of ten villages.

† **पंश्** *PAÑÇ*, and **पंस्** *PAÑS*, i. 1 and 10, Par. To destroy.

पक्कण *pakkaṇa*, m. The hut of a Châṇḍâla, or one of the outcast tribes, Kâçîkh. 12, 16.

पक्ति *pakti*, i.e. *pach* + *ti*, f. **1.** Cooking, Man. 9, 11. **2.** Digestion, 12, 120. **3.** Ripening, development, MBh. 12, 9745 (read *pakti* instead of *pañkti*). **4.** Dignity, Suçr. 1, 51, 20.

पक्तृ *paktṛi*, i.e. *pach* + *tṛi*, m., f. *tri*, and n. **1.** Cooking, a cook, MBh. 12, 10935. **2.** Promoting digestion, Suçr. 1, 189, 13.

पक्व *pakva*, i.e. *pach* + *va*. It is used as ptcple. of the pf. pass. of *pach*, f. *vâ*. **1.** Cooked, Man. 4, 223. **2.** Baked (as a brick, a pot), Yâjñ. 1, 197. **3.** Mature, Hit. i. d. 144. **4.** Grey (as hair), Lass. Anth. 80, 17. **5.** Accomplished, perfect. **6.** On the eve of decay, Bhâg. P. 4, 28, 38.—Comp. *A-*, adj. 1. uncooked. 2. unbaked (as a pot). 3. indigested. 4. immature. 5. imperfect, MBh. 12, 8440. *An-ati-pakva*, adj. rather immature (figuratively), Daçak. in Chr. 195, 13. *Kâla-*, adj. matured by time, Man. 6, 17.—Cf. πέπων (from which we may infer that *pakva* is curtailed *pakvan*), πεπανός, with ρ for ν, πέπειρος, curtailed in δρυπεπής, δρύπεψ.

पक्वण *pakvaṇa*, =*pakkaṇa*, MBh. 12, 5330.

पक्वापक्वा *pakvâpakvâ*, a sound imitative of the cry of birds.

† **पक्ष्** *PAKSH*, i. 1 and 10, Par. To seize; cf. *paç*.

पक्ष *paksha*, m. **1.** A wing; also n., Mârk. P. 9, 15. **2.** The feathers of an arrow. **3.** A flank, a side, Ragh. 5, 72. **4.** Half. **5.** The half of a lunar month, comprising fifteen days, Man. 1, 66. **6.** Party, Râm. 2, 18, 13 Gorr. (he who sides with Bharata). **7.** A partisan, Vikr. d. 16. **8.** A friend, Hariv. 3013. **9.** A class, a host, a troop, MBh. 13, 3315; Hariv. 7124. **10.** Place, condition, Râm. 6, 99, 32. **11.** Alternative, Ragh. 4, 10. **12.** Opinion, MBh. 2, 2266. **13.** The subject of an inference, Bhâshâp. 67.—Comp. *A-jâta-* (vb. *jan.*), adj. having not yet wings, Râm. 5, 11, 23. *Kâka-*, m. the side locks of the head of boys and youths, Râm. 1, 21, 9. *Kṛishṇa-*, m. the dark half of the month, the fifteen days during which the moon is in the wane, Man. 3, 276. *Keça-*, m. a tuft of hair, MBh. 4, 1114. *Tri-* (m. or n.), three fortnights, Man. 8, 58. *Pûrva-*, m. 1. the first half of a lunar month, Man. 3, 278. 2. the opponent's proposition, a primâ facie assertion. 3. action at law, Yâjñ. 2, 17. *Bhûmi-*, m. a swift horse. *Mahâ-*, adj. having a great family, Man. 8, 179. *Vi-*, I. adj. opposed, inimical. II. m. 1. an enemy, Pañch. 171, 10. 2. an opponent, a disputant. 3. a negative instance (*sâdhyâbhâvavân*), Bhâshâp. 72; one in which the major term is not found. *Çatru-*, m. an enemy, Hit. 53, 7, M.M. *Çukla-*, m. the light half of the month, from new to full moon. *Sa-*, I. adj. 1. winged. 2. having a side or party. II. m. a similar instance, one in which the major term is found (*sâdhyavân*), Bhâshâp. 72. III. m. a partisan. *Sva-*, m. a friend, Pañch. iii. d. 55.—Cf. perhaps παξ in ἅπαξ.

पक्षक *paksha* + *ka*, I. m. A side, Çiç. 11, 7. II. A substitute for *paksha* when latter part of a comp. adj.

पक्षगम *paksha-gama*, and **पक्षंगम** *pakshaṁgama*, i.e. *paksha* + *m-gama*, Moving by means of wings, flying, Râm. 5, 56, 45; 4, 43, 15.

पक्षता *paksha* + *tâ*, f. Alliance, MBh. 2, 2665.

पक्षति *paksha* + *ti*, f. The root of a wing, Râjat. 1, 374.

पक्षवन्त् *paksha* + *vant*, adj., f. *vati*. 1. Winged, Râm. 4, 63, 5. 2. Of a noble extraction, MBh. 13, 2965.

पक्षशस् *paksha* + *ças*, adv. By, or for, fortnights, MBh. 13, 5659.

पक्षि *pakshi*, i.e. curtailed *pakshin*, m. A bird, MBh. 12, 9306.

पक्षिन् *pakshin*, i.e. *paksha* + *in*, I. adj., f. *iṇî*. 1. Winged (figuratively). 2. Siding with; in *kṛishṇa-paksha* + *in*, Hariv. 4559. 3. fem. with *râtri* (a night), accompanied by the foregoing and following day, Man. 4, 97. II. m. 1. A bird, Man. 1, 44. 2. A name of Çiva, MBh. 13, 1183.—Comp. *Jala-*, m. a water-fowl, Pañch. 159, 19.—Cf. Goth. fugl; A.S. fugul.

पक्षिमृगता *pakshimṛigatâ*, i.e. *pakshin-mṛiga* + *tâ*, f. The form of a bird or beast, Man. 12, 9.

पक्षीय *pakshîya*, *paksha* + *îya*, in *kṛishṇa-paksha* + *îya*, adj. Siding with Kṛishṇa, Hariv. 3748.

पक्ष्मन् *pakshman* (akin to *paksha*), n. An eye-lash, Suçr. 1, 115, 10.—Comp. *Ud-*, adj. whose eye-lids are elevated, Çâk. d. 90.

पक्ष्मल *pakshmala*, i.e. *pakshman* + *a*, with *l* for *n*, adj. 1. Having long eye-lashes, Kathâs. 18, 14. 2. Hairy, Çiç. 4, 61.

पङ्क *paṅka*, m. Mud, mire, clay, Man. 4, 191. 2. Ointment, Ṛit. 1, 6; Râm. 3, 53, 57 (mire and ointment).

पङ्कज *paṅka-ja*, 1. m. A lotus flower, Çâk. d. 124. 2. f. *jî*, A name of Durgâ, MBh. 4, 188.—Comp. *Sa-*, adj., f. *jâ*, abounding in lotus flowers, Râm. 3, 68, 18.

पङ्कवन्त् *paṅka* + *vant*, adj., f. *vati*, Muddy, Râm. 2, 28, 9 (15 Gorr.).

पङ्किन् *paṅkin*, i.e. *paṅka* + *in*, latter part of comp. adj. Muddy, MBh. 3, 2959. *mâṁsa-çoṇita-paṅka* + *in*, Filled instead of mire with flesh and blood, MBh. 8, 2551.

पङ्किल *paṅkila*, i.e. *paṅka* + *ila*, adj., f. *lâ*, Muddy, MBh. 8, 4005.

पङ्केरुह *paṅkeruha*, i.e. *paṅka* + *i* *-ruh* + *a*, m. A lotus flower, Bhâg. P. 7, 15, 61.

पङ्क्ति and **पङ्क्ती** *paṅktî* (akin to *pañchan*), f. The number five, πεντάς, *smara-bâṇa-*, The five arrows of the god of love, Râjat. 3, 525. 2. A sort of metre, consisting of four times ten syllables. 3. The number ten, Ragh. 12, 99. 4. A line, a row, Pañch. 182, 16. 5. A multitude, a flock, Mârk. P. 43, 9. 6. A company, Man. 3, 183.—Comp. *Pada-*, a line of footsteps, Çâk. d. 56.

पङ्गु *paṅgu*, perhaps anomal. comp. *apa-aṅga* + *u*, adj., f. *gû* and *gvî*, Lame, Suçr. 1, 89, 11.

पङ्गुक *paṅgu* + *ka*, adj. Lame, MBh. 2, 2135.

पङ्गुता *paṅgu* + *tâ*, f. Lameness, Man. 11, 51.

पङ्गुल *paṅgu* + *la*, 1. adj. Lame. 2. Lameness, Suçr. 1, 360, 12.

1. **पच्** *PACH*, i. 1, Par. Âtm. 1. To cook, to bake, Man. 3, 118. 2. To roast, 7, 20. 3. pass. To be inflamed, 9, 231. 4. To melt, Hariv. 5525. 5.

To digest, Suçr. 1, 78, 5. **6.** To ripen. Ragh. 11, 50 (figurat.). **7.** To conduct something to its end, Râm. 6, 8, 16. Comp. ptcple. of the present Âtm. *a-pachamâna*, adj. One who does not prepare food for himself, a religious mendicant, Man. 4, 32. Anomalous *pachâna*, MBh. 3, 13239. Pass. with the termination of the Par., 5, 3792. Ptcple. of the pf. pass. *pakva* (see s. v.). Comp. ptcple. of the fut. pass. *kṛishṭa-pachya*, adj. Sown or ripening after ploughing, cultivated, Bhâg. P. 7, 12, 18. Caus. *pâchaya*, **1.** To cause to be dressed, MBh. 3, 104. **2.** To cure, Suçr. 1, 155, 20. Frequent. *pâpach* and *pâpachya*, **1.** To roast, Bhâg. P. 3, 24, 27. **2.** To burn violently (figur., to be much afflicted), 4, 3, 21.—With the prep. अनु *anu*, To ripen softly, 8, 5, 35.—With अभि *abhi*, To boil up, Suçr. 1, 149, 11.—With उद् *ud*, To heat, Suçr. 2, 67, 2.—With परि *pari*, **1.** To cook, Pańch. 199, 10. **2.** To roast, Hariv. 6079. **3.** To mature, Hariv. 4875. **4.** To conduct something to its end, MBh. 12, 8306. Caus. To mature by cooking, Suçr. 1, 230, 15.—With प्र *pra*, To use to cook, Râm. 3, 76, 24. — With अभिप्र *abhi-pra*, To develope, Suçr. 1, 322, 6.—With वि *vi*, **1.** To dissolve by cooking, Suçr. 1, 32, 20. **2.** To roast, MBh. 13, 6122. **3.** To digest, MBh. 14, 570. **4.** To ripen, Ragh. 17, 53. Caus. To dissolve by cooking. — Cf. Lat. coquere (for poquere by assimilation), culina (for cuclina); *πέπτω*, *πέσσω*, *πόπανον*, probably also *ὀπτός*, and *ἕψω*, *ἕψημα*, *ἑφθός*.

† 2. पच् *PACH* and पञ्च् *PAŃCH*, i. 1, Âtm. (Par.), To make evident. *pańch*, i. 10, Par. **1.** To state fully. **2.** To spread.

ऽपच *-pach + a*, latter part of comp. adj. Cooking, baking, roasting.

पचन *pach + ana*, n. **1.** Cooking, Suçr. 1, 31, 13. **2.** Ripening, Bhâg. P. 3, 26, 40. **3.** Becoming entirely cooked, MBh. 9, 2780. **4.** A frying-pan, Suçr. 2, 158, 1.

पञ्च् *PAŃCH*, see 2. *pach*.

ऽपञ्च *-pańcha* (see *pańchan*); in *chatuḥpańcha*, i.e. *chatur-*, adj. Four or five, Râjat. 6, 326.

पञ्चक *pańchaka*, i.e. *pańchan + ka*, I. adj. **1.** Consisting of five, Man. 2, 92. **2.** With *çata*, Five in the hundred, Man. 8, 139. II. n. **1.** The number five, *πεντάς*; *çata-*, Five hundred, Pańch. 134, 16. **2.** A collection of five, Bhâg. P. 3, 11, 15.—Comp. *Pańchap°*, i.e. *pańchan-*, n. the twenty-five (principles of the Sâńkhya philosophy), Râm. 3, 53, 42.

पञ्चकृत्वस् *pańchakṛitvas*, i.e. *pańchan-kṛitvas*, adv. Five times, Suçr. 1, 365, 9.

पञ्चता *pańchatâ*, i.e. *pańchan + tâ*, f. **1.** Quintuple amount, Man. 8, 151. **2.** Death (properly, Solution of the body into its five elements), Kathâs. 10, 127.

पञ्चत्व *pańchatva*, i. e. *pańchan + tva*, n. **1.** The five elements, Bhâg. P. 1, 15, 41. **2.** Death (see *pańchatâ*), Hariv. 1139.

पञ्चदशधा *pańchadaçadhâ*, i. e. *pańchadaçan + dhâ*, adv. In fifteen parts, Mârk. P. 78, 20.

पञ्चदशन् *pańchadaçan*, i.e. *pańchan-daçan*, numer. adj. Fifteen, Man. 10, 31.

पञ्चदशाह्निक *pañchadaçâhika,* i.e. *pañchadaçan-aha+ika,* adj. Lasting fifteen days, Yâjń. 3, 323.

पञ्चधा *pañchadhâ,* i.e. *pañchan+dhâ,* adv. In five parts, five-fold, Yâjń. 3, 9.

पञ्चन् *pañchan,* numer. adj. Five, Man. 2, 43.

पञ्चपुष्पमय *pañchapushpamaya,* i.e. *pañchan-pushpa + maya,* adj., f. *yî,* Consisting of five flowers, Kathâs. 34, 232.

पञ्चम *pañchama,* i.e. *pañchan+ma,* I. ordinal number, f. *mî,* Fifth, Man. 2, 37, II. acc. n. *mam,* adv. Fifthly, Man. 8, 125. III. with *aṁça,* A fifth part, Man. 9, 164. IV. m. 1. One of the seven musical notes, originally the fifth, afterwards the seventh, MBh. 14, 1419. 2. One of the modes of music, Gît. 10, 13. V. f. *mî.* 1. The fifth day of the half month, Hariv. 10241. 2. The name of a river, MBh. 6, 333.—Comp. *Ardha-,* adj. four and a half, Man. 4, 95.

पञ्चमक *pañchama+ka,* adj. Fifth, Çrut. 29.

पञ्चमय *panchamaya,* i.e. *pañchan+maya,* adj., f. *yî,* Consisting of five (elements), Mârk. P. 37, 39.

पञ्चवट *pañchavaṭa,* i.e. *pañchan-vaṭa,* n. and f. *ṭî,* The name of a locality near the Godâvarî, Râm. 1, 3, 18 (13 Gorr.).

पञ्चवर्षीय *pañchavarshîya,* i.e. *pañchan-varsha+îya,* adj. Five years old, Çatr. 14, 137.

पञ्चविंशक *pañchaviṁçaka,* i.e. *pañchan-viṁça+ka,* adj. 1. Twenty-fifth, Bhâg. P. 3, 26, 15. 2. Twenty-five (years old), Râm. iii. p. 469.

पञ्चविंशतिका *pañchaviṁçatikâ,* i.e. *pañchan-viṁçati+ka,* fem.; in *vetâla-,* Twenty-five tales of a Vetâla; the title of a work.

पञ्चशस् *pañchaças,* i.e. *pañchan+ças,* adv. Five by five, Bhâg. P. 3, 10, 13.

पञ्चष *pañchasha,* i.e. *pañchan-shash,* adj. Five or six, Râjat. 5, 333.

पञ्चा *pañch+â,* f. Spreading; in *chañchatpañcha,* i.e. *chañchant-,* adj. Shaking in all its parts, Utt. Râmach. 120, 3 (v.r.).

पञ्चाग्नित्व *pañchâgnitva,* i.e. *pañchan-agni+tva,* n. An aggregate of five fires (or passions), Kathâs. 28, 32.

पञ्चाल *pañchâla,* m. 1. pl. The name of a people and their country, Man. 2, 19. 2. A prince of the Pañchâlas, MBh. 12, 13262.

पञ्चालक *pañchâla+ka,* I. adj. Referring to the Pañchâlas; with *râjan,* A prince of the Pañchâlas, MBh. 5, 7504 (perhaps to be changed to *pâñchâlaka*). II. m. 1. pl.=The Pañchâlas, Bhâg. P. 9, 22, 3. 2. A certain poisonous insect, Suçr. 2, 288, 3.

पञ्चाश *pañchâça* (cf. *pañchâçat*), ordinal number, fem. *çî,* Fiftieth, Chr. 73, 3.—Comp. *Eka-,* fifty-first, Chr. 76, 21. *Dvâ-* and *dvi-,* fifty-second, Râm. 4, 52; Chr. 81, 9. *Tri-,* fifty-third. *Chatuḥpañchâça,* i. e. *chatur-,* fifty-fourth. *Pañchapañchâça,* i. e. *pañchan-,* fifty-fifth.

पञ्चाशत् *panchâçat,* i. e. *pañchâ-daçanti* (cf. *chatvâriṁçat*), numeral, f. Fifty, Man. 8, 297.—Comp. *Dvâ-* and *dvi-,* fifty-two, Hariv. 13076; MBh. 2, 52. *Chatuḥpañchâçat,* i. e. *chatur-,*fifty-four.—Cf. πεντήκοντα; Lat. quinquâginta.

पञ्चाशति *pañchâçati*, i.e. *pañchâ-daçanti* (see the preceding), numeral, f. Fifty, Râjat. 5, 71 (*â* is perhaps only a mistake; when shortened, we have *pañchaçatî*, Five hundred).

पञ्चाशत्क *pañchâçat + ka*, adj. Fifty years old, Kâm. Nîtis. 7, 44.

पञ्चाशत्तम *pañchâçat + tama*, ordinal number, f. *mî*, Fiftieth, MBh. 9, 50.—Comp. *Eka-*, fifty-first. *Tri-*, fifty-third.

पञ्चाशद्धा *pañchâçaddhâ*, i.e. *pañchâçat + dhâ*, adv. In fifty parts, Râm. 1, 48, 1 Gorr.

पञ्जर *pañjara*, n. **1.** A cage, MBh. 12, 3061. **2.** A skeleton, Prab. 71, 1. (Probably akin to *paj* in vedic *pajra*, *pâjas*; cf. πήγνυμι, πάγη; Lat. pango).

पञ्जरक *pañjara + ka*, m. or n. A cage, Pañch. iii. d. 143.

पट् *PAṬ*, † i. 1, Par. To go, to move. i. 10, *pâṭaya*, **1.** † To speak, or to shine. **2.** To split, to divide, MBh. 3, 16747; 882. **3.** To break, to breach, Mṛichchh. 47, 16. **4.** To tear, Kathâs. 20, 21. **5.** To pluck out, 28, 21. **6.** To cause to be torn up, Yâjñ. 2, 94. † **7.** i. 10, *paṭaya*, To string, to surround. —With the prep. **अव** *ava*, *pâṭaya*, To split, Suçr. 1, 32, 12.—With **आ** *â*, *pâṭaya*, To split, Suçr. 2, 22, 19.—With **उद्** *ud*, *pâṭaya*, **1.** To tear out, Man. 4, 69. **2.** To slit up, Râjat. 5, 432. **3.** To open, Pañch. 222, 5. **4.** To destroy, Râm. 6, 88, 19. **5.** To remove, 6, 37, 87. **6.** To dethrone, Râjat. 5, 298.—With **समुद्** *sam-ud*, *pâṭaya*, **1.** To tear out, Râm. 5, 39, 23. **2.** To draw out, Dev. 2, 20. **3.** To dethrone, Râjat. 5, 286.—With **विनि** *vi-ni*, *pâṭaya*, To split, Bhâg. P. 2, 7, 16.—With **वि** *vi*, *pâṭaya*, **1.** To split, MBh. 12, 591. **2.** To tear, Hariv. 4310. **3.** To uproot, Râjat. 5, 477. **4.** To open, 3, 482 (to bring on).

पट *paṭa* (probably for *patra*), m. and f. *ṭî*, and n. **1.** Woven cloth, MBh. 1, 806. **2.** Cloth, Râm. 5, 49, 5. **3.** A piece of cloth, MBh. 1, 4376. **4.** Garment, 5421. **5.** (cf. *paṭṭa*), A table, a plate (for painting and writing), Yâjñ. 1, 297. **6.** f. *ṭî*, The curtain of a stage.—Comp. *Ûrṇa-*, m. a spider, Bhâg. P. 4, 6, 43. *Kâṇḍa-*, m. a curtain, Daçak. 122, 6. *Ku-*, I. m. and n. a plain garment, Bhâg. P. 5, 9, 11. II. m. the name of a Dânava or demon, MBh. 1, 2534. *Chitra-*, m. or n. a picture, Kathâs. 5, 30. *Dhvaja-*, m. a flag, a standard, Vikr. d. 4. *Prachchhada-*, and *prachchhâdana-*, m. a cover, a blanket, Pañch. 62, 10. *Mukha-*, m. or n. a veil, Megh. 63. *Srastottara-*, i. e. *srasta-uttara-* (vb. *sraṁs*), adj. with the upper garment loose.

पटच्चर *paṭachchara*, i.e. *paṭat* (from *paṭ*, an imitative sound, perhaps of sneaking) *-chara*, I. m. **1.** A thief, MBh. 1, 6996. **2.** pl. The name of a people, MBh. 2, 590. **II.** n. Old cloth.

पटभाक्ष *paṭabhâksha*, m. or n. An implement for looking, or spying, Daçak. 71, 4.

पटल *paṭala*, I. n. **1.** A roof. **2.** A coverture, a veil, Prab. 116, 15. **3.** A film over the eyes, Suçr. 2, 277, 4. **4.** A heap, a multitude, MBh. 12, 4249. **II.** m. and n. A section of a book. —Comp. *Aksha-*, n. a court of justice, Râjat. 6, 287. *Abhra-*, n. the covering (of the sky) by clouds. *Nîla-*, n. a dark film over the eyes, Pañch. 262, 22.

पटलक *paṭala + ka* (m. or n.). A heap, Kathâs. 43, 27.

पटह *paṭa-ha* (vb. *han*), m. (and n.). A drum, a kettle-drum, Pańch. 261, 13. —Comp. *Yaças-*, m. a drum.

पटि *paṭi* (for *paṭl*, cf. *paṭa*), f. A kind of cloth, Pańch. 236, 25.

पटु *paṭ + u*, I. adj., f. *ṭu* and *ṭvî*, comparat. *paṭiyaṁs*, superl. *paṭishṭha*. 1. Sharp, Çântiç. 4, 16. 2. Hot, Râm. 6, 11, 44. 3. Clear (of sound), Hariv. 3554. 4. Violent, Hariv. 3823. 5. Clever, dexterous, skilful, Ragh. 9, 46. II. m. pl. The name of a people, Mârk. P. 57, 54.

पटुता *paṭu + tâ*, f.; in *vâkpaṭutâ*, i.e. *vâch-*, Eloquence, Bhartṛ. 2, 53.

पटुत्व *paṭu + tva*, n. 1. Keenness, Bâlab. 3. 2. Cleverness, Çâk. d. 118. — Comp. *A-*, n. want of cleverness, awkwardness, Vedântas. in Chr. 218, 17.

पटोल *paṭola*, A kind of cucumber; Trichosanthes dioeca, Roxb. m. The plant. n. The fruit, Pańch. i. d. 423.

पट्ट *paṭṭa*, probably for *patra*, m. 1. A table, a plate, for painting, Hariv. 9988. 2. A patent, a document, Yâjń. 1, 317. 3. A seat, a chair, MBh. 2, 90. 4. A bandage, a ligature, Suçr. 1, 15, 3. 5. A stripe, MBh. 13, 3456. 6. A frontlet, a diadem, a turban or cloth, etc., for that purpose, Kathâs. 14, 33. 7. (cf. *paṭa*) Cloth, Pańch. 251, 16. 8. A proper name.—Comp. *Aṁçu-*, n. a sort of cloth, Man. 5, 120. *Chitra-*, a picture, Hariv. 10069. *China-*, a sort of cloth, Kathâs. 43, 89. *Tâmra-*, m. a copper-plate, Yâjń. 1, 318. *Râjapaṭṭa*, i.e. *râjan-*, m. 1. a kind of gem, Utt. Râmach. 129, 1. 2. a tiara. *Lalâṭa-*, the forehead, Pańch. 35, 2. *Vaktra-*, m. a bag containing corn tied round a horse's head. *Vîra-*, m. war accoutrement (?), Râjat. 5, 332. *Çilâ-*, m. 1. a rocky seat, Râm. 2, 105, 6 Gorr. 2. a flat stone for grinding condiments.

पट्टक *paṭṭa + ka*, I. m. 1. A document, Râjat. 5, 396. 2. A bandage, Kathâs. 28, 159. 3. A frontlet, Kathâs. 13, 190. II. f. *ṭikâ*, 1. A ribbon, Bhâg. P. 3, 23, 14. 2. Cloth used for a turban, Râjat. 4, 575.—Comp. *Çilâ-*, m. a rocky seat, Mâlav. 31, 21.

पट्टज *paṭṭa-ja* (vb. *jan*), n. A sort of cloth, MBh. 2, 1347.

पट्टव *paṭṭa + va* (?). A sort of cloth, Râjat. 5, 161 (probably corr. *paṭṭaja*).

पट्टिश *paṭṭiça*, m. A spear with a sharp edge, Râm. 1, 54, 22.

पट्टिशिन् *paṭṭiçin*, i.e. *paṭṭiça + in*, adj. Armed with a paṭṭiça, Hariv. 15114.

पठ् *PAṬH* (probably a denomin. derived from *pashṭa* for *spashṭa*; cf. *paçya* for *spaçya*), i. 1, Par. (in epic poetry also Âtm.) 1. To speak distinctly, to recite, MBh. 2, 1154. 2. To invoke, Hariv. 12561. 3. To read, to study, Man. 4, 98. 4. To mention, MBh. 3, 1483. 5. To declare, Suçr. 2, 260, 16. 6. To learn from (abl.), Bhâg. P. 9, 22, 37. Caus. *pâṭhaya*, 1. To teach one to talk, Hit. Pr. d. 43. 2. To teach one to read, Bhâg. P. 7, 5, 2. 3. To cause to read, Pańch. 5, 11. 4. To teach, Bhâg. P. 7, 5, 2. Frequent. *pâpaṭhya*, To recite repeatedly, Kathâs. 37, 73.—With the prep. अनु *anu*, To say after one, to repeat, Bhâg. P. 7, 5, 3. —With अभि *abhi*, *abhipaṭhita*, Called, named, Suçr. 2, 310, 18.—With परि *pari*, 1. To mention, MBh. 1, 2020. 2. To declare, 3, 14192.—With प्र *pra*, To recite loudly, Hariv. 9591.—With सम्

sam, To read, Man. 4, 98. Comp. ptcple. of the fut. pass. of the Caus. *a-sampâṭhya*, One with whom nobody is allowed to read (or to pray), Man. 9, 238.

पठक *paṭh + aka*, m. A reader, MBh. 3, 17395.

पठन *paṭh + ana*, n. **1.** Reciting, Mârk. P. 51, 26. **2.** Reading, Böhtl. Ind. Spr. 664.

पठर्वन् *paṭharvan*, m. A proper name, Chr. 297, 17=Rigv. i. 112, 17.

1. **पण्** *PAṆ* (for original *par + ṇâ*, ii. 9 of *par*; cf. πέρνημι; O.H.G. feil), i. 1, Âtm. (in epic poetry also Par.), **1.** To buy, MBh. 13, 4564. **2.** To play, MBh. 3, 3047. **3.** To stake (at play), to bet, MBh. 2, 2144. **4.** To stake on, 9, 3258. **5.** To risk. Ptcple. of the pf. pass. *paṇita*, Betting, 1, 1225. n. A bet, 1226. Ptcple. of the fut. pass. *paṇya*, Saleable, Man. 8, 398. n. Ware, 5, 129. Comp. *Kara-*, n. ware offered as tribute, MBh. 2, 1052. *Masi-*, m. a scribe. *Yathâpaṇya + m*, adv. according to the value, Man. 8, 398.—With the prep. **वि** *vi*, **1.** To sell, Pańch. i. d. 88. **2.** To bet, MBh. 1. 1191.

2. † **पण्** *PAṆ* (akin to 1. *paṇ*), i. 1, Âtm., and **पणाय** *paṇ + âya*, Par. To praise, to honour.

पण *paṇ + a*, m. **1.** Play, MBh. 3, 2261. **2.** Playing for, MBh. 3, 2299. **3.** A bet, a stake (at play), MBh. 5, 1203. **4.** A cast (at play), MBh. 3, 3035. **5.** Wages or hire, reward, Kathâs. 18, 386; expense (of an expedition), Kâm. Nîtis. 9, 13–15. **6.** A coin of a certain weight, Man. 7, 126.—Comp. *Ardha-*, m. half a paṇa (see **6**), Man. 8, 404. *Dâsa-*, playing for slavery (the loser becoming the slave of the winner), MBh. 5, 5518.

पणव *paṇava* (probably for *praṇava*), m. A kind of drum, Bhag. 1, 13.

पणविन् *paṇavin*, i.e. *paṇava + in*, adj. Having a drum, MBh. 13, 1172.

ऽपणिक *-paṇika*, i.e. *paṇa + ika*; in *pańchâçat-*, adj. Consisting of fifty paṇas (see *paṇa* **6**), Yâjń. 2, 233.

पणितृ *paṇitṛi*, i,e. *paṇ + tṛi*, m. A trader, Naish. 2, 92.

† **पण्ड्** *PAṆḌ*, i. 1, Âtm. To go, to move. i. 10, Par. To heap together. i. 1 and 10, Par. To annihilate (v.r.).

पण्डक *paṇḍaka* (proceeded from *paṇḍraka*), m. A eunuch, Yâjń. 3, 273.

पण्डित *paṇḍita*, I. adj. Learned, wise, Bhartṛ. 2, 14; shrewd, Pańch. i. d. 334; skilled, Râjat. 5, 164. **II.** m. A scholar, a wise man, MBh. 5, 990.

पण्डितक *paṇḍita + ka*, m. **1.** A learned man, MBh. 12, 6736. **2.** A proper name, MBh. 1, 2736.

पण्डितता *paṇḍita + tâ*, f. and

पण्डितत्व *paṇḍita + tva*, n. Knowledge, wisdom, Bhartṛ. 2, 88 (*a-*, Foolishness), Mṛichchh. 17, 12.

पण्ड्रक *paṇḍraka* (perhaps *spand + ra + ka*), m. A eunuch, Mârk. P. 34, 82.

पण्यपतित्व *paṇya-pati + tva*, n. State of a great merchant, Râm. 1, 1, 96.

1. **पत्** *PAT*, i. 1, Par. (in epic poetry also Âtm.), **1.** To fly, Bhâg. P. 3, 6, 39. **2.** To descend, to set, MBh. 6, 480. **3.** To fall down, Bhâg. P. 3, 15, 35. **4.** To alight, Böhtl. Ind. Spr. 349. **5.** To fall, Man. 5, 141; figuratively, Bhartṛ. Suppl. 14. **6.** To be deprived of one's caste or rank, Man.

3, 16. **7.** To fall on, MBh. 3, 2199. **8.** To devolve upon, Râm. 2, 22, 20. **9.** To happen, Pańch. 232, 25. Ptcple. of the pres. *patant*, m. A bird, Ragh. 13, 19. Ptcple. of the pf. pass. *patita*, Sprung from, Böhtl. Ind. Spr. 240. n. Flying, MBh. 8, 1910. Comp. *Sâvitrî*-, m. a man of the three first classes, not invested at the proper time with the sacrificial cord, Man. 2, 39.—Ptcple. of the fut. pass., **1.** *pataniya*, n. A degrading crime, Yâjń. 3, 298. **2.** *patitavya*, n. Going to hell, MBh. 12, 3668. Caus. *pâtaya*, **1.** To cause to descend, Hit. iv. d. 74. **2.** To cause to fall down, Râm. 1, 74, 13. **3.** To dash out, Bhâg. P. 4, 5, 21. **4.** To throw, Râm. 6, 82, 93. **5.** To inflict, Man. 8, 126. **6.** To shed, MBh. 7, 4912. **7.** To cause to enter, Vikr. d. 56. **8.** To set (fire to), Pańch. iii. d. 166. **9.** To direct, Râm. 4, 7, 11. **10.** To ruin, 6, 94, 19. **11.** To cause to sin, Çâk. d. 117. **12.** To throw one's self, MBh. 1, 6752.—With the prep. **अति** *ati*, To neglect. Comp. ptcple. of the fut. pass. *an-atipâtya*, Not to be neglected, Çâk. 60, 17. Caus. **1.** To deprive something of its effect, Suçr. 1, 146, 12. **2.** To kill, 2, 266, 13.—With **अनु** *anu*, **1.** To fly along or in, Bhâg. P. 3, 11, 5. **2.** To follow, Çâk. d. 7. Caus. To cause somebody to fall down with one's self, Râm. 2, 75, 4 Gorr.—With **अभि** *abhi*, **1.** To fly near, to run near, especially with the intention of assailing, MBh. 3, 550. **2.** To fall down to (acc.), Arj. 10, 30. **3** To be shed, MBh. 7, 6287. **4.** To overtake, MBh. 8, 1910. Caus. **1.** To cast on somebody (acc.), Hariv. 13902. **2.** To cast down, MBh. 6, 1684.—With **समभि** *sam-abhi*, To assail, Râm. 5, 41, 34.—With **अव** *ava*, **1.** To fly down, Prab. 66, 14. **2.** To jump down, Hariv. 15949. **3.** To fall down, Râm. 2, 28, 12. *keça-kîṭa-avapatita*, On which lice have fallen, MBh. 13, 1577. Caus. To throw down, Kathâs. 25, 42.—With **आ** *â*, **1.** To fly near, to run near, especially with the intention of assailing, MBh. 1, 5965. **2.** To fall down, Râjat. 3, 202. **3.** To appear unexpectedly, MBh. 3, 2564. **4.** To strike unexpectedly, Râm. 2, 62, 16. **5.** To befall, 6, 100, 5. **6.** To come to one's share, Kathâs. 20, 213. **7.** To happen. Caus. **1.** To throw down, Bhâg. P. 7, 8, 29. **2.** To kill, Hariv. 5598. **3.** To shed, Man. 3, 229. —With **अभ्या** *abhi-â*, **1.** To run near, MBh. 4, 807. **2.** To assail, 4, 1041.—With **पर्या** *pari-â*, To run away, MBh. 8, 4964.—With **समा** *sam-â*, **1.** To fly near, MBh. 5, 7213. **2.** To hasten near. **3.** To assail. **4.** To obtain, MBh. 1, 7213. **5.** To have sexual intercourse, MBh. 1, 2461.—With **उद्** *ud*, **1.** To fly upwards, MBh. 1, 1335. **2.** To jump upwards, to start up, 1, 6019. **3.** To hasten out of (with abl.), MBh. 12, 5224. **4.** To come out, 6, 5785. **5.** To be set up (as a cry), MBh. 1, 6111. —With **अनूद्** *anu-ud*, To start up, to get up after somebody (acc.), Râm. 5, 64, 24.—With **अभ्युद्** *abhi-ud*, **1.** To fly upwards to (acc.), Kathâs. 22, 144. **2.** To start up, Hariv. 4114.—With **समुद्** *sam-ud*, **1.** To fly up together, MBh. 3, 2093. **2.** To start up together, 1, 7005. **3.** To assail, Böhtl. Ind. Spr. 315. **4.** To ascend, Râm. 5, 74, 35. **5.** To rush out of, MBh. 7, 4656. **6.** To gush out of, Hariv. 7068. *samutpatita*, **1.** Springing upwards, Pańch. ed. orn. i. d. 108. **2.** Sprung up, MBh. 1, 3320. **3.** Disappeared, Pańch i. d. 212.—With **उप** *upa*, To hasten to, Bhâg. P. 7, 2, 31.—With **नि** *ni*, **1.** To fly down, MBh.

1, 2094. **2.** To descend, Hariv. 9611. **3.** To fall down, MBh. 13, 1501. **4.** To tumble down, Râm. 5, 18, 7. **5.** To assail, MBh. 4, 1572. **6.** To rush in, Böhtl. Ind. Spr. 1170. **7.** To empty one's self into, Ragh. 10, 27. **8.** To fall on, MBh. 1, 7708. **9.** To fall into, Bhartṛ. 2, 82. **10.** To take place, Man. 9, 47. Caus. **1.** To cause to fall down, to cause a stick to fall on somebody, i.e. to smite somebody, Man. 4, 146. **2.** To cast down, Bhâg. P. 3, 3, 1. **3.** To cast, Ragh. 5, 217. **4.** To drop, Kathâs. 2, 10. **5.** To inlay with, MBh. 4, 1325. **6.** To spit out, Böhtl. Ind. Spr. 438. **7.** To direct to, Mârk. P. 61, 41. **8.** To kill, MBh. 14, 98. **9.** To levy (as tribute) from (abl.), MBh. 12, 3313. **10.** To set up as anomalous (in grammar). — With अभिनि *abhi-ni*, Caus. To throw down, MBh. 8, 3040. —With प्रणि *pra-ni*, **1.** To fall prostrate, Man. 11, 205. **2.** To bow respectfully to (acc. dat. and loc.), MBh. 4, 2131. Caus. To induce to fall prostrate, Mâlav. 39, 16.—With विनि *vi-ni*, **1.** To fly down, Ṛit. 4, 18. **2.** To fall headlong, Hariv. 3650. **3.** To attack suddenly, Kathâs. 22, 62. **4.** To fall in, Kathâs. 3, 33. Caus. **1.** To cause to fall down, Mârk. P. 75, 55. **2.** To chop off, MBh. 1, 5279. **3.** To inflict, Râm. 2, 75, 14 Gorr. **4.** To kill, Man. 11, 127. **5.** To ruin, Râm. 6, 94, 23.—With संनि *sam-ni*, **1.** To fly down, MBh. 5, 2462. **2.** To descend, Râm. 5, 62, 10. **3.** To perish, MBh. 7, 434. **4.** To assemble, to meet, MBh. 3, 14899. **5.** To appear, MBh. 12, 6676. Caus. **1.** To cause to fall down, MBh. 7, 7488. **2.** To shoot, Râm. 5, 42, 8. **3.** To cause to assemble, to convoke, MBh. 3, 2162.—With निस् *nis*, **1.** To fly out of (abl.), Çâk. d. 166. **2.** To rush out, Arj. 10, 62. **3.** To come out, MBh. 14, 1836. **4.** To depart from, Man. 8, 55. **5.** To spring from, 12, 15. **6.** To fly away. Caus. To ruin, Râm. 2, 75, 15.—With अभिनिस् *abhi-nis*, To rush out, MBh. 6, 2434. — With विनिस् *vi-nis*, **1.** To fly out, MBh. 5, 269. **2.** To rush out, Râm. 4, 19, 4. **3.** To fall out, Râm. 3, 31, 19. **4.** To run away, Man. 7, 106.—With परा *parâ*, **1.** To fly away, Bhâg. P. 3, 20, 24. **2.** To fail, Utt. Râmach. 117, 8. —With परि *pari*, **1.** To fly about, MBh. 1, 1391. **2.** To run about, 8, 707. **3.** To jump down, 7, 757. **4.** To assail, Arj. 8, 30. **5.** To fall, MBh. 3, 2791. Caus. **1.** To shoot down, MBh. 6, 2687. **2.** To shoot off, 6, 1852. **3.** To throw in, Mṛichchh. 155, 8.—With प्र *pra*, **1.** To fly away, MBh. 5, 1753. **2.** To fly, Hariv. 8266. **3.** To run away, MBh. 7, 676. **4.** To fall down, MBh. 3, 16038. **5.** To strike, MBh. 4, 1788. **6.** To fall into, MBh. 2, 2159. **7.** To be deprived (abl.), 14, 2737. Caus. **1.** To put to flight, MBh. 1, 7632. **2.** To pursue, 13, 2047.—With प्रति *prati*, To hasten to meet, 4, 2110.—With वि *vi*, Caus. **1.** To discharge (arrows), MBh. 4, 1862. **2.** To kill, MBh. 7, 6149.—With सम् *sam*, **1.** To meet, Indr. 1, 36. **2.** To fly to (acc.), Hariv. 12684. **3.** To hasten to, Râm. 5, 36, 43. **4.** To obtain, MBh. 12, 6737. **5.** To fly, 4, 1776. **6.** To walk, Râm. 2, 125, 20 Gorr. **7.** To fly down, MBh. 6, 3789. **8.** To fall down, 1, 1387. **9.** To happen, Hariv. 11739. Caus. **1.** To throw, Râm. 6, 18, 50. **2.** To throw down, Bhâg. P. 5, 26, 28.—With अभिसम् *abhi-sam*, **1.** To hasten to, Râm. 5, 60, 16. **2.** To assail, Hariv. 12545. 3. To fly about, MBh. 7, 7295.—Cf. πέταμαι, πέτομαι, πέταλον, ποτή, ποτάομαι, ὑπερ-πωτάομαι, ἴπταμαι, ἰθυπτίων, πτῆμα; Lat. penna (i.e. pet + na); O.H.G. fedara; cf. *patra*; also πίπτω (i.e. reduplicat. πετ), ἔπεσον, ἔπιτνον, πτῶμα, πότμος; Lat. petere, impetrare, etc.

2. **पत्** *PAT* (probably a denomin. derived from *pati*), i. 4, Âtm. To be powerful, to possess.—Cf. Lat. potiri.

पतग 1. *pat* + *a-ga* (vb. *gam*), m. 1. A winged animal, Man. 7, 23. 2. A bird, Bhâg. P. 2, 7, 16.

पतंग *patam̃ga*, i.e. 1. *pat* + *a* + *m-ga* (vb. *gam*), I. m. 1. A bird, Pańch. ed. orn. 57, 6. 2. A small grasshopper which is attracted by a light, MBh. 9, 152. 3. The sun, Bhâg. P. 2, 1, 30. 4. A playing-ball, Bhâg. P. 3, 20, 36. 5. A name of Kṛishṇa, MBh. 12, 1510. 6. The name of a caste in Plakshadvîpa, Bhâg. P. 5, 20, 4. 7. The name of a mountain, 5, 16, 20. 8. The name of a village. II. f. *gî*, A proper name, Bhâg. P. 6, 6, 21.

पतंगम *patam̃gama*, i.e. *pat* + *a* + *m -gam* + *a*, m. A small grasshopper, Bhâg. P. 7, 8, 24.

पतंगिका *patam̃gikâ*, i.e. *patam̃ga* + *ika*, f. A small bird, MBh. 1, 4332.

पतत्र *pat* + *atra*, n. 1. A wing. 2. A feather, Bhâg. P. 8, 11, 34.

पतत्रि *patatri* (i.e. curtailed *patatrin*), m. 1. A bird, MBh. 1, 1455. 2. m. A proper name, 8, 2263.

पतत्रिन् *patatrin*, i.e. *patatra* + *in*, I. adj. Winged. II. m. 1. A bird, Man. 4, 208. 2. A horse, Râm. 1, 13, 36. 3. An arrow, MBh. 3, 16430.

पतन 1. *pat* + *ana*, I. m. The name of a Râkshasa or demon, MBh. 3, 16365. II. n. 1. Falling, MBh. 5, 7187. 2. Hanging down, becoming slack, Böhtl. Ind. Spr. 422. 3. Ruin, 704. 4. Death, MBh. 2, 1636. 5. Throwing one's self, Böhtl. Ind. Spr. 902 (at one's feet).

पताका *patâkâ*, i.e. 1. *pat* + *âka*, f. 1. A flag or banner, MBh. 3, 3014. 2. A certain great number, MBh. 13, 5234. 3. An episode in a drama, Daçar. 1, 13, 33.—Comp. *Sa-patâka*, adj. with a banner.

पताकिन् *patâkin*, i.e. *patâkâ* + *in*, I. adj., f. *nî*. 1. Adorned with flags (as with flags, Vikr. d. 137). 2. Bearing a flag, MBh. 3, 646. II. m. 1. A colour-bearer. 2. A flag, Hariv. 8991. 3. A proper name. III. f. *nî*, An army.

पति *pati*, i.e. 2. *pâ* + *ti* (for original *pâ* + *tan*, cf. *patnî*). 1. A master, an owner. 2. A governor, a lord, Man. 7, 115. 3. A husband, MBh. 1, 4199. 4. When latter part of a comp. adj. the fem. is left unchanged, e. g. *jîvat -pati*, i.e. *jîvant-* (vb. *jîv*), f. A woman whose husband is alive, Râm. 2, 24, 8 Gorr.—Comp. *A-*, adj. unmarried, Râm. 1, 34, 44. *Anna-*, m. a name of Çiva, Râjat. 5, 72. *Ap-*, m. a name of Varuṇa, the regent of the waters, Man. 3, 87. *Ambu-*, m. the ocean, Pańch. i. d. 316. *Artha-*, m. 1. a king, Pańch. i. d. 84. 2. a judge, iii. d. 89. 3. a proper name. *Avani-* and *avanî-*, m. a king, ib. 28, 20; Kathâs. 24, 12. *Açva-*, m. a proper name. *Uḍu-*, m. the moon, Çiç. 9, 32. *Umâ-*, m. a name of Çiva, Chr. 48, 7. *Urvî-* (see *uru*), m. a king, Râjat. 5, 380. *Oshadhi-*, m. 1. the moon, Çiç. 9, 36. 2. a physician, ib. *Oshadhî-*, m. the moon, MBh. 3, 137. *Kula-*, m. the chief of a family, MBh. 1, 1. *Kratu-*, m. the performer of a sacrifice, Bhâg. P. 4, 19, 29. *Kshiti-*, and *Kshmâ-*, m. a king, Pańch. ii. d. 22; Râjat. 5, 59. *Gaṇa-*, and *Gaṇanâ-*, m.

a name of Gaṇeça, Pańch. i. d. 175; Râjat. 5, 26. *Griha-*, m. a householder, Pańch. i. d. 410. *Go-*, m. 1. a bull, Râm. 3, 51, 4. 2. the sun, Bhâg. P. 1, 12, 10. 3. a name of Kṛishṇa (properly the cow-herd κατ'ἐξοχήν), MBh. 13, 7002. 4. a name of Varuṇa, Çiva, and others. *Gaurî-*, m. a name of Çiva, Kathâs. 22, 16. *Graha-*, m. 1. the sun. 2. the moon. *Chamû-*, m. the commander of an army. *Jagat-*, m. a name of Çiva and Vishṇu. *Jagatî-* (see *jagat*), m. a king, Râm. 1, 12, 36. *Târâ-*, m. 1. the moon. 2. a proper name. *Tridaça-*, m. a name of Indra. *Dâna-*, m. a liberal man, Sâv. 1, 3. *Dina-*, m. the sun, Bhartṛ. 2, 69. *Deva-* and *Daivata-*, m. a name of Indra. *Dvâra-*, m. a doorkeeper, a chamberlain, MBh. 3, 10623. *Nada-nadî-*, m. a name of the Sindhu. *Nidhi-*, m. 1. a name of Kuvera. 2. a proper name. *Nṛi-*, m. a king. *Paçu-*, m. a name of Çiva. *Pitṛi-*, m. 1. a name of Yama (lord of the Manes). 2. pl. the Manes and the lords of the creatures, Bhâg. P. 7, 4, 6. *Prajâ-*, m. 1. lord of the creatures, Vikr. d. 9. 2. a name of the supreme deity, Brahman, Pańch. i. d. 188. 3. a king. 4. a father. *Prâṇa-*, m. 1. a husband. 2. the heart, Draup. 6, 4. *Phaṇipati*, i.e. *phaṇin-*, m. the king of the serpents, Bhartṛ. 2, 77. *Bhavânî-*, m. a name of Çiva, Kir. 5, 21. *Bhâṇḍa-*, m. a merchant, Pańch. 26, 25. *Nânâ-bhâṇḍa-*, m. a great merchant, 26, 11. *Bhû-*, m. a king, Pańch. i. d. 262. *Bhûmi-*, m. the same. *Bhṛigu-* (also *bhṛigûṇâm*), the chief of the descendants of Bhṛigu, a name of Paraçurâma, Megh. 68. *Bhoga-*, m. 1. a viceroy, a governor. 2. a person having possession or usufruct. *Mahî-*, m. a king, Chr. 47, 32. *Mṛiga-*, m. a lion. *Raghu-*, m. Râma. *Rati-*, m. a name of the god of love, Çiç. 9, 66. *Çachî-*, m. a name of Çiva, Daçak. in Chr. 182, 10. *Çâlva-*, m. the king of the Çâlvas, Chr. 18, 34. *Çri-*, m. 1. Vishṇu. 2. a king. *Sabhâ-*, m. 1. the president of an assembly. 2. the keeper of a gaming-house. *Sindhu-*, m. the lord of Sindh, i.e. Jayadratha. *Senâ-*, m. 1. the general of an army, Çâk. 24, 6. 2. Kârttikeya. *Svarga-*, m. Indra.—Cf. Lat. potis, δεσ-πότης, πόσις; Goth. faths; cf. *patnî*.

पतिंवरा *patiṁvarâ*, i.e. *pati* + *m* -*vṛi* + *a*, adj. One who chooses her husband herself, Ragh. 6, 10.

ऽपतिक -*pati* + *ka*, A substitute for *pati* when latter part of a comp. adj., Man. 9, 68 (*pra-mita-*, f. a widow).

पतित्व *pati* + *tva*, m. Matrimony, marriage, MBh. 3, 2140.

पतिधर्मतस् *pati-dharma* + *tas*, adv. = abl. of *pati-dharma*, m. The duty to a husband, Chr. 48, 2.

पतिधर्मवती *patidharmavatî*, i. e. *pati-dharma* + *vant* + *î*, adj., f. Fulfilling the duties of a wife, MBh. 4, 279.

पतिन् *patin*=*pati*, MBh. 12, 8883.

पतिवत्नी *pativatnî*, i.e. *pati* + *vant* + *î* (by metathesis *pativatnî*, instead of the later *pativatî*), f. A married woman, Ragh. 15, 35.

पत्तङ्ग *pattañga* (for *patrâñga*, q. cf.), (n. and) m. Red sanders, Suçr. 1, 46, 13.

पत्तन *pattana*, i.e. *pad* + *tana* (cf. Lat. op-pidum), n. A town, Mâlav. 13, 15.

पत्ति *patti*, i.e. *pad* + *ti* (probably for *tan*, see *pati*), m. 1. A pedestrian. 2. A foot-soldier, MBh. 5, 5164. 3. The name of a people.

पत्त्र *pattra*, see *patra*.

पत्नि *patni*, see *patnî.*

पत्नी *patnî*, and sometimes पत्नि *patni*, i.e. *patan* (see *pati*) + *î*, f. A wife, Man. 2, 129.—Comp. *Eka-*, f. 1. only one wife, Bhâg. P. 9, 10, 53. 2. the wife of one man only, a chaste wife, Man. 5, 158. 3. pl. the several wives of one husband, Man. 9, 183. *Guru-*, f. a mother-in-law, 9, 57. *Deva-*, f. the wife of a god, Kathâs. 16, 6. *Dharma-*, f. a lawful wife, Man. 3, 262. *Sa-*, f. a wife whose husband has other wives, Chr. 55, 2; Pańch. i. d. 318.—Cf. πότνια, δέσ-ποινα.

ऽपत्नीक *-patnî + ka*, a substitute for *patnî* when latter part of a comp. adj., e.g. *bahu-*, Having many wives, Çâk. 90, 21.

पत्नीत्व *patnî + tva*, n. Matrimony, Mârk. P. 50, 14.

पत्र *pat + ra*, n. (perhaps *pat + tra*, but cf. O.H.G. fedara; A.S. feher; and πτερόν for πετρόν). 1. The wing of a bird. 2. The feather of an arrow, Râm. 3, 35, 87. 3. A vehicle in general, as a horse, a camel, a car, Man. 9, 219. 4. A leaf, Man. 4, 49. 5. The leaf of the Laurus cassia (?). 6. A leaf prepared for writing on, paper, Çâk. 81, 2. 7. A letter, Çâk. 90, 8. 8. A document, Pańch. i. d. 451. 9. A thin piece of metal, Suçr. 2, 74, 21. 10. Lines and signs painted in the faces by means of musk and other fragrant substances, Ragh. 13, 55.—Comp. *Arka-*, m. Calotropis gigantea; n. its leaf. *Kańka-*, I. n. the feather of a heron, Râm. 4, 7, 22. II. m. an arrow, Râm. 6, 28, 4. *Kara-*, n. a saw, Hit. 49, 11. *Trakpatra*, i. e. *tvach-*, n. woody cassia. *Danta-*, n. a kind of ear-ring. *Nishpatra*, i.e. *nis-*, adj. leafless. *Bhûrja-*, m. a kind of birch. *Yuga-*, m. mountain ebony. *Çata-*, I. n. a lotus flower, Râm. 2, 60, 15 Gorr. II. m. 1. a peacock. 2. a parrot. 3. a woodpecker. 4. the Indian crane. III. f. *râ*, a woman. *Satp°*, i.e. *sant-* (ptcple. pres. of 1. *as*), n. the new leaf of a waterlily. *Svachchha-*, i.e. *su-achchha-*, n. talc.—Cf. supra O.H.G. fedara; πτερόν, also πτέρις, πτίλον, πτίλος, and πέτρος (cf. *patrin* 3; in the old poetical language clouds and rocks are identified, and the clouds considered as wings of the mountains).

पत्रक *patra + ka*, 1. A substitute for *patra* when latter part of a comp. adj., f. *trikâ*. 2. f. *trikâ*, A document, a letter, Çâk. 90, 16. — Comp. *Karṇa-patraka*, m. the lobe of the ear, Yâjń. 3, 96. *Yuga-*, m. mountain ebony.

पत्राङ्ग *patrânga*, i.e. *patra-anga*, n. Red sanders.

पत्रिन् *patrin*, i.e. *patra + in*, I. adj., f. *iṇî*. 1. Winged, Hariv. 5470. 2. Feathered, MBh. 3, 709. II. m. 1. A bird, Çâk. 78, 19. 2. An arrow, Kathâs. 33, 203. 3. A mountain.—Comp. *Kańka-*, m. an arrow, MBh. 4, 1804. *Pushpa-*, adj. having flowers for arrows, Kumâras. 4, 29.

1. पथ् *PATH*, i. 1, Par. To go. † i. 10, *pâthaya*, To throw (v. r.).

2. पथ् *path*, see *pathin*.

पथ *patha*, 1. m. Way, reach, Râm. 3, 56, 3. 2. Latter part of comp. words = *pathin*, A way, a road. *a-*, m. A wrong way. *apatya-*, m. The vulva. *ardha-*, m. The half of a way. *ârya-*, m. The road of the honourable ones. *uttarâ-* and *udakpatha*, i.e. *udańch-*, m. The northern country. *kusîda-*, m. An usurious way, Man. 8, 152. *jala-*, m. A sea voyage. *tri-*, n. Heaven, earth, and the infernal regions. *dakshiṇâ-*, m. The southern country. *darçana-*, m. Sight. *dikpatha*, i.e. *diç-*, m. The road of the country, Râjat. 5,

341. *dṛikpatha*, i.e. *dṛiç-*, m. Sight, Vikr. d. 95. *dharma-*, m. The road of virtue. *dhûma-*, m. A sacrifice, Bhâg. P. 4, 4, 10. *nakshatra-*, m. The starred heaven. *nayana-*, m. Sight, Vedântas. in Chr. 206, 1. *pâshaṇḍa-*, m. The way of the heretics, Daçak. in Chr. 185, 6. *baṇikpatha*, i. e. *baṇij-*, m. Trade, Man. 1, 90. *romarâji-*, i.e. *roman-râji-* (m.), A line of hair extending to the navel; in *tanuromarâjipatha*, The waist, Çiç. 9, 22. *vi-*, m. A bad road. *çrî-*, m. A highway. *satp°*, i.e. *sant-* (ptcple. pres. of 1. *as*), m. **1.** A good road. **2.** Correct conduct. *su-*, **I.** adj. Having good roads, Lass. 97, 2 (*thâ*, ved. for *thâni*). **II.** m. **1.** A good road. **2.** Good conduct.—Cf. πάτος; A.S. padh.

पथिक *pathika*, i.e. *patha + ika*, m. A traveller, Pańch. 245, 4.

पथिन् *pathin*, for *panthan* (cf. *paripanthin*), which is the base of some cases, the bases of some others is *path*, the nom. and voc. sing. *panthâs*, m. **1.** A road, a way, Megh. 28. **2.** The name of a hell, Man. 4, 90. — **Comp.** *Ardha-*, m. the half of a way, Pańch. 134, 17. *Dharma-*, m. the road of virtue. *Saha-*, m. a fellow-traveller, Râm. 3, 53, 3. — Cf. Lat. pons, pontis, and perhaps ponto, pontonis.

पथ्य *pathya*, i.e. *patha + ya*, **I.** adj., f. *yâ*, Furthering, Böhtl. Ind. Spr. 448. Fit, suitable, salutary, Pańch. 69, 17. **II.** f. *yâ*, Yellow myrobalan, Terminalia chebula. — **Comp.** *A-*, adj. unfit, unwholesome, Yâjń. 3, 65.

1. **पद्** *PAD*, i. 4, Âtm. (in epic poetry also Par.), **1.** To fall (ved.). **2.** To go to (acc.), MBh. 1, 4288. **3.** To obtain, MBh. 9, 2847. **4.** To observe, 7, 16. Caus. *pâdaya*; i. 10, †*padaya*, To go.—With the prep. **अनु** *anu*, **1.** To follow, MBh. 1, 6710. **2.** To court, MBh. 1, 4180. **3.** To resort to, Râm. 2, 45, 4. **4.** To fall down, MBh. 7, 3361. **5.** To find out, Bhâg. P. 4, 17, 12. **6.** To be deprived of, to lose (with abl.), MBh. 12, 4653. — With **समनु** *sam-anu*, To obtain, Hariv. 11210.—With **अभि** *abhi*, **1.** To come near, to approach, MBh. 1, 8105. **2.** To come to (acc. and loc.), 13, 4375. **3.** To worship, Çiç. 9, 27. **4.** To come to one's assistance (acc.), MBh. 6, 4043; to assist, 1, 1981. **5.** To seize, to catch, Râm. 5, 41, 24. **6.** To assail, MBh. 8, 3047. **7.** To attain, Man. 1, 30. **8.** To accept, Râm. 2, 36, 12. **9.** To apply one's self to, Râm. 2, 63, 1.—With **समभि** *sam-abhi*, **1.** To come to, to attain, MBh. 1, 5515. **2.** To come on, MBh. 3, 12539. **3.** To answer, 10441.—With **अव** *ava*, **1.** To fall down. Comp. ptcple. of the pf. pass. *keça-kîṭa-avapanna*, On which lice have fallen, Man. 4, 207.—With **आ** *â*, **1.** To come near, Bhâg. P. 5, 8, 25. **2.** To enter, Râm. 6, 16, 21. **3.** To fall into, Man. 10, 104. **4.** To undergo, Prab. 33, 8. **5.** To become unfortunate, Râm. 2, 53, 13. **6.** To be, Mâlav. 14, 23. Ptcple. of the pf. pass. *âpanna*, **1.** Unfortunate. **2.** Having obtained, Bhag. 9, 16, 37. **3.** Obtained, Râm. 2, 43, 31 Gorr. Caus. **1.** To put somebody into a certain state or condition; *mṛityum âpâdita*, Killed, Râm. 2, 73, 5. **2.** To ruin somebody, Vikr. 33, 2. **3.** To procure, MBh. 1, 7873. **4.** To produce, to cause, Râm. 2, 74, 5. **5.** To make, to change into, Daçak. 183, 2. — With **प्रत्या** *prati-â*, To return. *pratyâpanna*, Returned, Bhâg. P. 8, 11, 48.—With **व्या** *vi-â*, To perish, MBh. 7, 3008.

Vyâpanna, **1.** Fallen into disorder. **2.** Spoiled. **3.** Failed, Suçr. 1, 21, 9. **4.** Dead. **Comp.** *A-,* alive, Megh. 10. Caus. **1.** To injure, Suçr. 1, 21, 11. **2.** To ruin, to destroy, MBh. 1, 1607. **3.** To kill, Pańch. 22, 15. — With समा *sam-â,* **1.** To assail, MBh. 5, 2002. **2.** To undergo, MBh. 13, 411; to begin, Râm. 6, 92, 4. *Samâpanna,* **1.** Come. **2.** Endowed with, MBh. 2, 2588.—With अभिसमा *ahbi-sam-â,* To undergo, to begin, Râm. 2, 12, 1.—With उद् *ud,* **1.** To spring up, to rise, Man. 1, 70. **2.** To be brought forth, 9, 170. **3.** To become, 4, 228. *Utpanna,* **1.** Brought forth. **2.** Complete, Yâjń. 2, 157. **3.** Ready, MBh. 12, 4913. *gûḍhotpanna,* i.e. *gûḍha-* (vb. *guh*), Secretly born, i.e. one whose father is unknown, Man. 9, 159. Caus. **1.** To produce, Pańch. 132, 4; to bring forth, Man. 9, 175. **2.** To cause to be shed, Man. 4, 167. **3.** To procure, 2, 148.—With प्रोद् *pra-ud, protpanna,* Developed, Bhâg. P. 6, 5, 4.—With प्रत्युद् *prati-ud, pratyutpanna,* **1.** Present, MBh. 12, 8278. **2.** Ready, Çâk. 67, 23.—With व्युद् *vi-ud,* To become clear in (its) etymological relation, Çiç. 10, 23. *Vyutpanna,* Learned, versed, Bhartṛ. Suppl. 18. Caus. **1.** To produce, to cause, Bhâg. P. 3, 15, 33. **2.** To explain etymologically. — With समुद् *sam-ud,* (समु *sam-u,* MBh. 12, 946, on account of the metre, see Caus.), **1.** To spring up, to arise, Pańch. iii. d. 214. **2.** To be brought forth, Man. 10, 66. **3.** To come, Râm. 2, 29, 11. Caus. **1.** To produce, Mârk. P. 17, 6. **2.** To cause, Râjat. 5, 6. **3.** To expect, MBh. 12, 4912 (*samupâdayet*). — With उप *upa,* **1.** To come to, Pańch. 9, 5. **2.** To attain (acc. and dat.), Bhag. 13, 18. **3.** To undergo, Râm. 2, 72, 50. **4.** To take place, Man. 9, 121. **5.** To appear, Mârk. P. 49, 4. **6.** To be suitable, Çâk. 15, 6. **7.** To spring up, MBh. 14, 455. *Upapanna,* **1.** Present. **2.** Suitable. **3.** Endowed, provided with. **Comp.** *An-,* unnatural, Çâk. 111, 1. Caus. **1.** To induce to get, Râm. 5, 57, 12. **2.** To give, Man. 9, 73. **3.** To accomplish, Râm. 2, 50, 10 Gorr. **4.** To make suitable, to prepare, Man. 9, 36. **5.** To provide with. **6.** To make, to declare, Prab. 111, 17. **7.** To select, Man. 3, 206. **8.** To argue, Râm. 5, 18, 22. —With अभ्युप *abhi-upa,* **1.** To come to one's assistance, MBh. 10, 608. **2.** To come for receiving assistance, Râm. 3, 14, 7. **3.** To provide with, MBh. 2, 187. *Abhyupapanna,* **1.** Sprung up; in *-vatsala,* adj. Affectionate, Mṛichchh. 108, 5. **2.** Admitted. — With समुप *sam-upa,* To be accomplished, MBh. 2, 779. Caus. To prepare, Râm. 5, 14, 45.—With निस् *nis,* निष्पद् *nishpad,* **1.** To spring up, to arise. **2.** To ripen, Man. 9, 247. *Nishpanna,* **1.** Sprung up, Râm. 5, 2, 32. **2.** Descended, Râm. 1, 6, 23. **3.** Accomplished, Râjat. 4, 234. **4.** Ready. Caus. **1.** To cause to ripen, Kathâs. 20, 87. **2.** To accomplish, Bhâg. P. 4, 22, 43. **3.** To prepare, Lass. Anth. 17, 17. **4.** To perform, Râjat. 5, 21.—With प्र *pra,* **1.** To enter, Man. 4, 77. **2.** To begin, 4, 60. **3.** To attain, Bhâg. P. 3, 6, 22. **4.** To come to, Ragh. 12, 68. **5.** To come for receiving assistance, Râm. 1, 57, 16. **6.** To embrace (the doctrine of Jina), Râjat. 1, 102. **7.** To fall down, MBh. 1, 1183. **8.** To undergo, Yâjń. 1, 132. **9.** To be going on, to succeed, MBh. 13, 3527. **10.** To admit, Yâjń. 2, 40. **11.** *prapanna,* Provided, Çâk. d. 1. Desider. *pra-pitsa,* To be about to begin, Daçak.

114, 10.—With अनुप्र *anu-pra*, **1.** To enter one after another, MBh. 3, 16772. **2.** To enter, Suçr. 1, 258, 7. **3.** To appear, MBh. 13, 7363. **4.** To follow, Bhag. 9, 21. **5.** To comply with (acc.), Râm. 5, 28, 5.—With अभिप्र *abhi-pra*, **1.** To hasten to, MBh. 1, 1182. **2.** To begin, MBh. 3, 1209. **3.** *abhiprapanna*, Come for assistance, Daçak. in Chr. 179, 20.—With संप्र *sam-pra*, **1.** To set out on, to begin, Hariv. 5289. **2.** To enter, Bhâg. P. 3, 24, 2. **3.** To turn to somebody, especially for assistance, Hariv. 11685. **4.** To succeed, Pańch. ii. d. 137. **5.** *samprapanna*, Endowed, Chaurap. 43.—With प्रति *prati*, **1.** To go to, to enter, Râm. 2, 33, 21. **2.** To come to, MBh. 1, 5918. **3.** To return, Man. 6, 74. **4.** To obtain, Man. 7, 40. **5.** To receive, Râm. 1, 39, 15 Gorr. **6.** To recover, Man. 2, 120. **7.** To perceive, Böhtl. Ind. Spr. 57. **8.** To learn, MBh. 5, 6027. **9.** To consider. **10.** To comply with, Pańch. 129, 4. **11.** To avow, Çâk. d. 119. **12.** To promise, Kathâs. 1, 45. **13.** To give, Râm. 2, 1, 8. **14.** To act, MBh. 1, 1936. **15.** To perform, MBh. 2, 1420. **16.** To make, MBh. 4, 703. **17.** To restore, Man. 8, 183. **18.** *pratipanna*, Offered, Mâlav. d. 48; admitted; acting; conversant with, MBh. 2, 1949. Caus. **1.** To lead to, MBh. 3, 2852. **2.** To procure, MBh. 1, 3417. **3.** To bestow on, Man. 11, 4. **4.** To deliver, 9, 190. **5.** To install, Râm. 1, 1, 68. **6.** To cause, Râm. 4, 22, 20. **7.** To prepare. **8.** To teach, Man. 8, 391. **9.** To consider, Pańch, 169, 22.—With विप्रति *vi-prati*, **1.** To go in different directions. **2.** To waver, MBh. 5, 4276. **3.** *vipratipanna*, Opposite, Râm. 2, 109, 1.—With संप्रति *sam-prati*, **1.** To attain, Suçr. 1, 267, 13. **2.** To approach, MBh. 14, 946. **3.** To befall, Pańch. ed. orn. i. d. 164. **4.** To recover, Râm. 3, 73, 16. **5.** To receive, Hariv. 12201. **6.** To agree, MBh. 5, 2706. **7.** To consider, Kumâras. 5, 37. **8.** To perform, MBh. 13, 3629. Caus. To grant, MBh. 3, 12759.—With वि *vi*, **1.** Not to turn out well, Râm. 2, 23, 18. **2.** To perish, Râm. 2, 64, 68. **3.** To miscarry. **4.** *vipanna*, Weakened, unfortunate. Caus. To kill, Râjat. 2, 79.—With सम् *sam*, **1.** To succeed, MBh. 14, 154. **2.** To amount to (acc.), Hariv. 15082. **3.** To become, MBh. 1, 2995. **4.** To be brought forth, MBh. 1, 3143. **5.** To get, to obtain (with instr., loc., and acc.), Mâlav. d. 52; Bhag. 13, 30; Râm. 3, 54, 12. *Sampanna*, **1.** Endowed with. **2.** Accomplished. **3.** Conversant with. n. Sweetmeats (?), Pańch. iv. d. 81. Caus. **1.** To convey, to procure, MBh. 13, 2867. **2.** To cause to succeed, to bring about, Bhartṛ. 2, 59. **3.** To perform, Daçak. in Chr. 196, 14. **4.** To prepare, Râm. 3, 28, 27. **5.** To complete, Bhâg. P. 1, 16, 35. **6.** To turn into, Kathâs. 37, 114. **7.** To endow with, MBh. 6, 2304. **8.** To attain, Râm. 5, 3, 40.—With अभिसम् *abhi-sam*, *abhisampanna*, Composed, Utt. Râmach. 135, 6.—With उपसम् *upa-sam*, To attain, MBh. 11, 363. *Upasampanna*, **1.** Conversant with. **2.** Endowed with. **3.** Diseased, Man. 5, 81. Caus. To convey, to procure.—Cf. 3.*pad*; πηδάω, ὀπαδός; perhaps Goth. finthan; A.S. findan; the anomalous reflex of Sskr. *d* may have been caused by *n*.

† 2. पद् *PAD*, see *bad*.

3. पद् and पाद् *pâd*, i.e. *pad*, m. A foot, Man. 4, 207; 6, 46. — **Comp.** *A-pad*, and *-pâd*, adj., f. *-pâd* and *-padî*, having no feet. *Eka-pad* and *-pâd*, 1. adj. having one foot only,

Bhâg. P. 1, 16, 21. 2. m. a name of Çiva, and of a Dânava or demon, MBh. 13, 7031; 1, 2533. 3. f. *-padî*, a foot-path, 4, 246. *Chatushpâd*, i.e. *chatur-*, the base of many cases is *-pad*, 1. adj., f. *-padî*, four-footed. 2. m. a quadruped, MBh. 12, 5697. 3. adj. consisting of four parts, 5, 5352. *Tîrtha-pad*, adj. one whose feet are holy and hallowing, Bhâg. P. 3, 1, 17. 2. *Tri-pad* and *-pâd*, adj., f. *pâd* and *padî*, having three feet. *Dvi-pad* and *-pâd*, f. *pâd* and *padî*, I. adj. having two feet. II. m. a man, MBh. 1, 257. III. n. mankind. *Sahasra-pâd*, adj. thousand-footed.—Cf. πούς, ποδός, πέδη, πέδιλον, πέζα, πεζός; Lat. pes, pedis, tripudiare, repudiare, impedire; see *pada*.

पद् 1. *pad* + *a*, I. n. **1.** A step, Man. 8, 227. **2.** A footstep, Çâk. d. 190. **3.** A trace, Râm. 5, 5, 1. **4.** A mark, a sign, MBh. 3, 12474. **5.** Place, Arj. 4, 39 (*padât padam*, A step from the place). **6.** Abode, Kathâs. 26, 241. **7.** Home. **8.** An office, Pañch. 103, 3; dignity, Man. 12, 125. **9.** Object, thing, Lass. Anth. 43, 9. **10.** Cause, Hit. iv. d. 97. **11.** Pretext. **12.** A square of a chess-board, Râm. 1, 5, 12. **13.** A foot; with *kṛi*, a. To put one's foot on, Yâjñ. 3, 13. b. To possess one's self of, Böhtl. Ind. Spr. 528. c. To put one's confidence in, Çâk, 47, 6 (Prâkṛ.) **14.** A verse, Mâlav. d. 77. **15.** A word, Râm. 1, 9, 24. **16.** A kind of reading the Veda (every word separately, without applying the rules of Sandhi). II. m. A ray of light.—**Comp.** *A-*, I. n. a wrong place, Kathâs. 26, 23. II. adj. wanting feet, Pañch. 211, 6. *Âçrama-*, n. 1. a hermitage. 2. one of the three or four orders of the religious life of a Brâhmaṇa. *Eka-*, I. adj. 1. having one foot. 2. consisting of one word. II. m. pl. The name of a people. III. loc. *de*, adv. on a sudden, Kathâs. 22, 203. *Kshetra-*, n. a district which is consecrated to a deity, Bhâg. P. 9, 4, 20. *Chitra-*, adj. divided in several parts, 1, 5, 10. *Jana-*, m. 1. country, Râm. 1, 5, 5. 2. pl. and sing. people, Yâjñ. 1, 360. *Tri-*, adj., f. *dâ*, 1. having three feet. 2. having three verses. *Druta-*, (vb. *dru*) °*pada* + *m*, adv. hastily. *Dvi-*, m. a man, Bhâg. P. 4, 31, 22. *Pañchapada*, i.e. *pañchan-*, 1. adj., f. *dâ*, consisting of five verses 2. f. *dî*, five steps, Pañch. ii. d. 123. *Bhâdra-*, 1. m. the month Bhâdra. 2. f. *dâ*, a name common to the twenty-sixth and twenty-seventh lunar asterisms. *Bhû-*, 1. m. a tree. 2. f. *dî*, Arabian jasmine. *Vishṇu-*, I. n. 1. the sky. 2. the sea of milk. 3. a lotus. II. f. *dî*, the Ganges.—Cf. πέδον; Lat. oppidum.

पदक *pada* + *ka*, n. **1.** A step, MBh. 13, 2789. **2.** An office, Râjat. 5, 29.

पदवी *padavî*, i.e. *pada* + *va* + *î*, f. **1.** A road, a way, Draup. 6, 9. **2.** An office, Pañch. 13, 4.—**Comp.** *Ghana-*, f. the sky. *Viveka-*, f. reflexion, Kathâs. 33, 81. *Smaraṇa-*, f. death, Bhartṛ. 3, 49. *Hâsya-*, f. with *yâ*, To expose one's self to ridicule, Pañch. 252, 5.

पदशस् *pada-ças*, adv. By degrees, Râm. 2, 87, 15 Gorr.

पदस्थ *pada-stha* (vb. *sthâ*), **1.** A pedestrian, Râm. 2, 101, 36 Gorr. **2.** Fitting an office. **3.** Taking the place of, Râm. 4, 18, 13.

पदात *padâta*, i.e. *pada-at* + *a*, m. A pedestrian, a foot-soldier, Hariv. 5914.

पदाति *padâti*, i.e. *pada-at* + *i*, m. **1.** A pedestrian, a foot-soldier, Râm. 1, 55, 4. **2.** A proper name.

पदातिन् *padâtin*, i.e. I. *padâta* + *in*, adj., f. *nî*, Consisting of foot-soldiers, MBh. 5, 5703. **II.** *pada-at* +

in, m. A foot-soldier, Râm. 2, 40, 40.

पदातीय *padâtîya*, i.e. *padâti* + *îya*, m. A foot-soldier, MBh. 7, 7598.

पदान्तर *padântara*, i.e. *pada-antara*, n. The interval of a step. *padântare*, Having made a step, Çâk. 12, 6.—Comp. *A-padântara* + *m*, adv. immediately after, MBh. 2, 1766.

पदार्थ *padârtha*, i.e. *pada-artha*, m. **1.** The meaning of a word, Nyâya S. 2, 131. **2.** Substance, thing, Bhâg. P. 3, 11, 2. **3.** A category, Bhâshâp. 1.

पदी *padî*, see 3. *pad* and *pada*.

पद्धति *paddhati*, i.e. *pad-han* + *ti*, f. **1.** A way, a path, Ragh. 11, 87. **2.** A guide, designation of a class of literary compositions.—Comp. *Pâda-*, f. a line of footsteps, Pañch. 35, 18.

पद्म *padma* (curtailed *pad* + *mant*), I. m. and n. **1.** A lotus flower, MBh. 1, 5412. **2.** Ornament, Râm. 6, 10, 19. **3.** Moles or marks on the body, 5, 32, 11. **4.** A spot, 3, 48, 12. **5.** Coloured marks on the face and trunk of an elephant. **6.** A lotus-like form of array, Man. 7, 188. **7.** A particular sitting posture when absorbed in meditation, Vedântas. in Chr. 217, 17. **8.** One of Kuvera's treasures, MBh. 2, 418. **9.** A large number, 1000 billions, 2, 2143. **10.** A certain fragrant plant. II. m. **1.** A kind of snake, Suçr. 2, 265, 8. **2.** The name of a Nâga. **3.** A proper name. III. f. *mâ*, **1.** A name of Çrî, Man. 7, 11. **2.** The name of two plants, Clerodendrum siphonanthus, and Hibiscus mutabilis. **3.** A proper name.—Comp. *Abhi-*, adj. 1. adorned with lotus-like spots. 2. beautiful in every part of the body, Johns. Sel. 46, 74. *Bhrâtṛi-padma-vana*, n. a group of lotus-like brothers. *Mahâ-*, I. m. 1. one of the Nâgas. 2. one of Kuvera's treasures. 3. a Kiṁnara, or attendant on Kuvera. 4. a large number, one hundred thousand millions, MBh. 2, 2143. 5. the name of a lake, Râjat. 5, 68; 103. II. n. the white lotus. *Sa-*, adj. provided with lotus flowers, Râm. 3, 52, 39.

पद्मक *padma* + *ka*, m. **1.** An army arrayed in the form of a lotus flower, MBh. 7, 2674. **2.** A certain tree and its wood; m. and n. Costus speciosus or arabicus. **3.** A proper name.

पद्मज *padma-ja* (vb. *jan*), m. A name of Brahman, Bhâg. P. 8, 16, 24.

पद्मभव *padmabhava*, i.e. *padma-bhû* + *a*, **1.** adj. Sprung up from a lotus flower. **2.** A name of Brahman, Bhâg. P. 8, 21, 3.

पद्ममय *padma* + *maya*, adj., f. *yî*, Consisting of lotus flowers, Hariv. 9435.

पद्मरागमय *padma-râga* + *maya*, adj., f. *yî*, Consisting of rubies, MBh. 5, 3577.

पद्मवन्त् *padma* + *vant*, adj., f. *vatî*, Abounding in lotus flowers, Hariv. 3838.

पद्मशस् *padma* + *ças*, adv. By hundred thousand millions, MBh. 1, 233.

पद्मावती *padmâvatî*, i.e. *padma* + *vant* + *î*, f. **1.** A surname of Lakshmî, Gît. 1, 2. **2.** A proper name.

पद्मिन् *padmin*, i.e. *padma* + *in*, I. adj., f. *nî*, Having coloured marks, etc. (see *padma* 5), MBh. 2, 2075. II. m. An elephant. III. f. *nî*, **1.** A lotus, Nelumbium speciosum, MBh. 1, 7228. **2.** A multitude of lotusses, Râm. 2, 52, 98; a lake abounding in them, MBh. 13, 4471. **3.** A woman of the first of the four classes into which the sex is distinguished. **4.** A sort of witchcraft, Mârk. P. 64, 15.

पद्मेशय *padmeçaya,* i.e. *padma+i-çi+a,* adj. Sleeping in a lotus flower, Hariv. 14119.

पद्य *padya,* i.e. *pada+ya,* n. A verse, Häberl. Anth. 529, 1.

पद्वन्त् *pad+vant,* adj., f. *vatî.* 1. Having feet. 2. Running.—Cf. Lat. pedes, peditis.

पन् *PAN* (cf. *paṇ*), i. 1, Âtm.; base of the pres. *panâya,* Par. and Âtm. i. 10 *panaya,* To praise, Chr. 293, 3=Rigv. i. 87, 3.

पनस *panasa,* m. 1. The bread fruit or Jaka tree, Artocarpus integrifolia Lin. 2. A kind of snake, Suçr. 2, 265, 12. 3. A proper name.

† **पन्थ्** *PANTH,* i. 1 and 10, Par. To go.

पन्थन् *panthan,* **पन्थास्** *panthâs,* see *pathin.*

पन्नग *pannaga,* i.e. *pad-na-ga,* m. 1. A snake, Nal. 14, 8. 2. A snake-shaped demon.—Comp. *Sa-pannaga,* adj. with the snake-shaped demons, Râm. 3, 54, 3.

पम्पा *pampâ,* f. The name of a river.

† **पम्ब्** *PAMB,* i. 1, Par. To go.

पयस् *payas* (akin to 1.*pâ,* cf. also *pî*), n. 1. Juice. 2. Water, Bhartṛ. 2, 29. 3. Milk, Man. 2, 107.—Comp. *Apa-,* adj. without water, Kirât. 5, 12. *Gharma-,* n. sweat, Çiç. 9, 35.

पयस्वल *payas+vala,* adj., f *lâ,* Abounding in milk, Hariv. 3798.

पयस्विन् *payas+vin,* I. adj., f. *nî,* Abounding in milk, Man. 11, 137. II. f. *nî,* A cow with abundance of milk, MBh. 13, 703.

पयोद *payoda,* i.e. *payas-da,* I. m. 1. A cloud, Çâk. d. 75. 2. A proper name. II. f. *dâ,* A proper name.

पयोधर *payodhara,* i. e. *payas-dhara,* m. 1. A cloud, Râjat. 4, 365. 2. A woman's breast, Ṛit. 1, 6. 3. An udder, Ragh. 2, 3.

पयोधस् *payodhas,* i. e. *payas-dhant* (vb. *dhâ,* cf. *ûdhan* and *payodhi*), m. 1. The ocean. 2. A cloud.

पयोधि *payodhi,* i.e. *payas-dhi,* m. The ocean, Kathâs. 22, 205.

पयोमुच् *payomuch,* i. e. *payas-much,* 1. adj. Yielding milk, MBh. 13, 3754. 2. m. A cloud, 9, 1506.

पयोवृध् *payovṛidh,* i. e. *payas-vṛidh,* adj. Superabounding with water, Chr. 290, 11=Rigv. i. 64, 11.

पयोष्णी *payoshṇî,* i.e. an anomal. comp. *payas-ushṇa+î,* f. The name of a river.

पर *para,* i.e. perhaps *apa+ra,* or 1.*pṛi+a,* I. adj., f. *râ.* 1. Distant. 2. Opposite, ulterior, Râm. 1, 11, 19 Gorr. 3. Being beyond, Man. 7, 158. 4. Exceeding, MBh. 1, 7975; left or remaining, Kathâs. 39, 16. 5. Highest, longest, Bhâg. P. 3, 11, 12. 6. Ancient, Man. 9, 99. 7. Pre-eminent, superior, higher, Man. 2, 83. 8. Distinguished, greatest, Man. 1, 106. 9. Intent, Râm. 5, 24, 13. 10. Subsequent, following, Man. 3, 37. 11. Different, Prab. 114, 8; other, Râm. 6, 9, 12. 12. Inimical, enemy, Man. 7, 94. II. *param,* adv. 1. With abl., a. Beyond, Ragh. 1, 17. b. After, Man. 2, 122. 2. With preceding *atas,* a. Further from hence, Nal. 9, 23. b. After that, Man. 8, 129. c. Next, 9, 56. 3. Excessively, Râm. 6, 5, 14. 4. Completely, Mâlav. 4,

19. **5.** Rather, MBh. 13, 4857. **6.** Most willingly, Böhtl. Ind. Spr. 406. **7.** At the most, 993. **8.** With preceding *yadi,* Perhaps, Kathâs. 42, 19. **9.** Only, 40, 8. **10.** But, Pañch. 243, 14. **III.** *pareṇa,* **1.** with acc. Beyond; *pareṇâsmân paraihi,* Pass by us, MBh. 1, 8414. **2.** Afterwards, Man. 8, 30. **3.** With abl. After, MBh. 12, 842. **IV.** *pare,* adv. Afterwards, 12, 2880. **V.** m. and n. The universal soul, Bhag. 3, 19. **VI.** n. Culmen, highest degree, MBh. 1, 2025. **VII.** m. **1.** A descendant, Pañch. iii. d. 216. **2.** A proper name. **3.** The name of the palace of Mitravindâ, Hariv. 8986. **VIII.** f. *râ,* The name of a river. **IX.** When latter part of a comp. it implies often, **1.** Intent on, e.g. *çaucha-,* adj. Intent on purity, Man. 3, 192. **2.** Absorbed in, e.g. *chintâ-,* adj. Thoughtful. **3.** Affected with, e.g. *karuṇâ-,* adj. Compassionate.—**Comp.** *Tatpara,* i.e. *tad-,* 1. subsequent to that. 2. intent only on that. 3. completely devoted to. *Daiva-,* m. a fatalist, Kâm. Nîtis, 9, 36. *Mâna-,* adj., f. *râ,* arrogant, proud, Çiç. 9, 57. *Vigraha-,* adj. fighting, Pañch. 117, 9.—Cf. πέραν, πέρην, πέρα, πέρηθεν, περαίτερος, etc., περαῖος, πέρας, πεῖρας, ἄπειρος, ἀπειρέσιος, etc.; Lat. perendie, i.e. pere-m + die; see also *pṛi.*

परकीय *parakîya,* i.e. *para + ka + îya,* adj. **1.** Belonging to another, Çâk. d. 97. **2.** Hostile, Kâm. Nîtis. 8, 70.

परज *para-ja,* m. A stranger.

परतस् *para + tas,* adv. **1.** =abl. of *para,* e.g. *paratas-paras,* Higher than the highest, Kumâras. 2, 14; *svakât parato vâ gehât,* From his own house or that of another, Bhâg. P. 1, 13, 25. **2.** Further, Râm. 2, 15, 5 Gorr. **3.** With abl. **a.** After, Yâjñ. 2, 173. **b.** Over, Bhag. 3, 42.

परता *para + tâ,* f. **1.** Absoluteness, Bhâshâp. 7. **2.** Highest degree, Râjat. 5, 377.—**Comp.** *Tad-para + tâ,* f. intentness, Hit. iv. d. 96.

परत्र *para + tra,* adv. In the other world, Man. 3, 275. **परत्राय** *paratrâya,* To the other world, MBh. 13, 7688.

परत्व *para + tva,* n. **1.** Condition of being more extensive (as a genus), Bhâshâp. 7; comprehensive. **2.** Length of distance and time, Bhâshâp. 120.

परदारिन् *paradârin,* i. e. *para-dâra + in,* m. An adulterer, Râm. 3, 57, 20.

परंतप *paraṁtapa,* i. e. *para + m-tap + a,* adj. subst. Vexing the foe, Bhag. 4, 2. A conqueror.

परपुष्ट *para-pushṭa* (vb. *push*), m. The Cocila or Indian cuckoo, Râm. 3, 78, 29. f. *ṭâ,* Its female.

परभागता *para-bhâga + tâ,* f. Excellence, supremacy, Ragh. 5, 70.

परभृत *para-bhṛita* (vb. *bhṛi*), m. The Cocila or Indian cuckoo, Çâk. d. 85.

परम *para + ma,* **I.** superl. of *para,* f. *mâ.* **1.** Most excellent, Man. 1, 108; best, 4, 14. **2.** Highest, Man. 9, 319. **3.** Extreme, 8, 302. **4.** Worst, Brâhmaṇav. 1, 15. **5.** With *chetas,* All (the heart), Râm. 2, 34, 36. **6.** With an abl. it has the signification of the comparat., More excellent, superior, worse; *ko nyo sti paramaḥ çivât,* Who is higher than Çiva, MBh. 13, 793. **II.** *paramam,* adv. Yes, MBh. 3, 17056. Very well, Johns. Sel. 37, 20. **III.** When latter part of a comp adj. it implies sometimes, **1.** Amounting at the most to, MBh. 2, 2080. **2.** Consisting principally of, 5, 1143. **3.** Occupied only with, Man. 6, 96.

परमक *parama+ka*, adj., f. *ikâ*, 1. Most excellent, best, Râm. 4, 35, 13. 2. Highest, MBh. 3, 13695. 3. Extreme, Chr. 35, 12.

परमतस् *parama+tas*, adv. Still worse, Bhartr̥. 3, 6.

परमाणुता *paramâṇutâ*, i.e. *parama-aṇu+tâ*, f. 1. The condition of an atom, Ragh. 15, 22. 2. An infinitely short moment, Bhâg. P. 3, 11, 4.

परमार्थतस् *paramârthatas*, i.e. *parama-artha+tas*, adv. In the true sense of the word, Vedântas. in Chr. 218, 19; Pañch. i. d. 152.

परमेष्ठिन् *parameshṭhin*, i.e. *parama+i-sthin* (vb. *sthâ*), 1. m. The supreme being, a name of Brahman, Çiva, etc. 2. m. A proper name.

परंपर *paraṁpara*, i. e. *para+m-para*, I. adj. Successive, one after another, Suçr. 1, 105, 3. II. f. *râ*, 1. An uninterrupted succession, a chain, Pañch. 251, 9. 2. A continuous lineage, MBh. 3, 13621.—Comp. *Karṇa-*, f. rumour, Pañch. 130, 8.

परवत् *para+vat*, adv. Like a stranger, Kathâs. 27, 185.

परवत्ता *paravattâ*, i.e. *paravant+tâ*, f. Obedience, Vikr. d. 155.

परवन्त् *para+vant*, adj., f. *vatî*. 1. Depending on another, Çâk. d. 53. 2. Deprived of strength, Utt. Râmach. 80, 11. 3. Ready to obey, MBh. 13, 2731.—Comp. *A-dharma-*, i. e. *a-dharma-para+vant*, adj. become a prey to injustice, Râm. 5, 45, 17.

परवश्यता *para-vaçya+tâ*, f. Dependence on another, Râm. 5, 26, 18.

परवाच्यता *para-vâchya+tâ* (vb. *vach*), f. Condition of being an object of censure to others, MBh. 6, 4476.

परशु *paraçu*, i. e. *para-*, compounded with a derivative of *ço*, m. An axe, a hatchet, Râm. 1, 74, 18.—Cf. πέλεκυς.

परश्वध *paraçvadha* (cf. the last), m. An axe, a hatchet, Râm. 6, 27, 25.

परश्वधिन् *paraçvadhin*, i.e. *paraçvadha+in*, adj. Provided with an axe, MBh. 5, 6099.

परस् *paras* (akin to *para*), adv. and prep. 1. Beyond. 2. After. 3. More than. 4. Without.—Comp. *Pararajas*, i.e. *paras-rajas*, adj. untouched by passion, Utt. Râmach. 120, 10.

परसात् *para+sât*, adv. Into the hands of another, Böhtl. Ind. Spr. 931.

परस्तात् *paras-tât* (old abl. of *tad*), adv. and prep. with the gen. 1. Beyond, Bhag. 8, 9. 2. Higher, Mâlav. d. 1. 3. Further on. 4. Afterward, Bhâg. P. 4, 9, 20.

परस्पर *para+s-para*, I. adj. (sing. and without nom. sing.), 1. Each other, mutual, Bhag. 3, 11. 2. One with another, MBh. 12, 2420 (nom. pl.). II. *ram*, adv. 1. Each other, mutually, Man. 9, 62. 2. To one after another, Bhâg. P. 1, 8, 9.

परस्परतस् *paraspara+tas*, adv. One by another, mutually, Nal, 5, 34.

परा *parâ*, old instr. sing. of *para*, inseparable preposition combined and compounded with verbs and their derivatives (immediately with a noun in *parâsu*), Away, over, on, inverted, wrong, back, sideward.—Cf. παρά, πάλιν; Lat. per, e.g. in per-dere, perfidus (cf. *pari*); Goth. fair- and fra-; A.S. for.

पराक *parâka*, i.e. *parâñch* + *a*, m. A sort of penance, fasting for twelve days and nights, Man. 11, 215.

पराक्रम *parâ-kram* + *a*, m. **1.** Prowess, Böhtl. Ind. Spr. 498. **2.** Exertion, Râm. 6, 37, 49. **3.** Strength, valour, Man. 7, 11. **4.** Power, Râm. 1, 75, 17.

पराक्रमवन्त् *parâkrama* + *vant*, adj., f. *vatî*, Endowed with courage, or power, Mârk. P. 21, 92.

पराक्रमिन् *parâkramin*, i.e. *parâ-kram* + *in*, adj., f. *iṇî*, Exerting one's power, MBh. 6, 1915.

पराक्रान्तृ *parâkrântṛi*, i.e. *parâ-kram* + *tṛi*, m. Exerting one's power, MBh. 6, 1945.

पराग *parâga*, i.e. probably *upa* or *apa-râga*, m. The pollen or farina of a flower, Bhartṛ. 1, 39.

पराङ्मुखता *parâṅmukhatâ*, i.e. *parâñch-mukha* + *tâ*, f. Condition of having averted one's face, Böhtl. Ind. Spr. 530.

पराङ्मुखत्व *parâṅmukhatva*, i.e. *parâñch-mukha* + *tva*, n. The same figuratively, Aversion, Ragh. 18, 13.

पराचीन *parâchîna*, i.e. *parâñch* + *îna*, adj. **1.** Turned away, Suçr. 1, 100, 12. **2.** Not minding, MBh. 12, 8159. **3.** Being beyond, Bhâg. P. 5, 20, 30.

पराजय *parâjaya*, i.e. *parâ-ji* + *a*, m. **1.** Being deprived of, loss (with abl.), MBh. 3, 2565. **2.** Losing at play, 2, 2170; at a law-suit, Pañch. 167, 5. **3.** Defeat, Man. 7, 199. **4.** Conquering, victory, MBh. 1, 5514.

पराजिष्णु *parâjishṇu*, i.e. *parâ-ji* + *snu*, adj. Victorious, MBh. 10, 632.

पराञ्च् *parâñch*, i.e. *parâ-añch*, adj., f. *âchî*. **1.** Turned away, Bhâg. P. 4, 11, 10. **2.** Distant, 5, 5, 31.

पराधीनता *parâdhînatâ*, i.e. *para-adhîna* + *tâ*, f. Dependence, Mṛichchh. 137, 11.

परापरता *parâparatâ*, i.e. *para-apara* + *tâ*, f. and **त्व** *tva*, n. **1.** The condition of being both a genus and a species, Bhâshâp. 8. **2.** Priority and posteriority, 24.

पराभव *parâbhava*, i.e. *parâ-bhû* + *a*, m. **1.** Disappearance, Râm. 4, 29, 24. **2.** Defeat, Mârk. P. 18, 28. **3.** Mortification, humiliation, MBh. 4, 464; Pañch. pr. d. 11. **4.** Disregard, Lass. Anth. 43, 9.

पराभाव *parâbhâva*, i.e. *parâ-bhû* + *a*, m. Defeat, Arj. 10, 45.

पराभूति *parâ-bhû* + *ti*, f. **1.** Defeat, Bhâg. P. 2, 6, 9. **2.** Humiliation, Böhtl. Ind. Spr. 146.

परामर्श *parâmarça*, i,e, *parâ-mṛiç* + *a*, m. **1.** Pulling, MBh. 7, 1399. **2.** Drawing (as a bow), Râm. 1, 76, 17. **3.** Injuring, 3, 7, 30. **4.** Assailing, MBh. 3, 15060. **5.** Consideration, reflexion, MBh. 7, 4188. **6.** Knowledge of the minor premiss in its connection with the major, Bhâshâp. 67.

परायण *parâyaṇa*, i.e. *para-ayana*, I. n. **1.** Chief, principal, MBh. 1, 1624. **2.** with *kṛi*, To do one's utmost, 6, 3929. II. adj. **1.** Principal, 4, 2269. **2.** Adhering (with accus.), Râm. 1, 7, 9. **3.** Connected with (gen.), MBh. 7, 8252 (leading to victory). III. When latter part of a comp. adj. it implies, **1.** Wholly occupied with, Man. 4, 10,

2. Intent on, MBh. 3, 2482. 3. Affected by, Nal. 23, 1.

परायणवन्त् *parâyaṇa + vant*, adj., f. *vatî*, Most elevated, MBh. 1, 8055.

परार्ध *parârdha* i.e. *para-ardha*, I. m. 1. The ulterior part, MBh. 2, 1864. 2. The other part, Böhtl. Ind. Spr. 382. II. m. and n. 1. The number 100,000,000,000,000,000. 2. Fifty years of Brahman (half his supposed æon), Bhâg. P. 3, 11, 33. III. (inexactly), instead of *parârdhya*, adj. Most excellent, most beautiful, MBh. 4, 2188.

परार्ध्य *parârdhya*, i.e. *parârdha + ya*, I. adj., f. *yâ*, Most excellent, most beautiful, best, MBh. 1, 6962; with abl. More excellent than, Ragh. 10, 65. II. n. 1. An infinite number. 2. A maximum. III. as latter part of comp. adj. 1. Amounting to an infinite number. 2. Amounting at the most to.

परावर *parâvara*, i.e. *para-avara*, I. adj. 1. Far and near, MBh. 12, 8336. 2. Ancestors and descendants, Man. 1, 105. 3. All-comprising, Vedântas. in Chr. 218, 15. 4. Every succeeding one, Bhâg. P. 3, 5, 36. II. n. That which is far and near, i.e. 1. The universe, MBh. 1, 23. 2. Totality, Sâv. 6, 34.

परावरत्व *parâvara + tva*, n. Condition of being superior or inferior, Bhâg. P. 7, 9, 27.

परावर्तन *parâvartana*, i.e. *parâ -vṛit + ana*, n. Turning, MBh. 9, 3193.

परावृज् *parâvṛij*, adj. Humbled, miserable (?), Chr. 296, 8 = Rigv. i. 112, 8.

परावृत्ति *parâ-vṛit + ti*, f. Turning, Hariv. 3138.

पराशर *parâçara*, m. A proper name.

परासु *parâsu*, i.e. *parâ-asu*, adj. 1. Dying, Suçr. 1, 114, 15. 2. Dead, MBh. 1, 3835.

परासुता *parâsu + tâ*, f. and परासुत्व *parâsu + tva*, n. Apathy, MBh. 5, 715.

परि *pari*, and often परी *parî* (akin to *para*), I. adv. Round, all round. II. prep. 1. with acc. About, against, to, over. 2. with abl. From, out, except, after, Man. 3, 119 (?); on account, according. III. combined and compounded with verbs and their derivatives, Round, all round. IV. compounded with nouns, Round about, full, quite, excessively.—Cf. περί; Lat. per, e.g. in per-idoneus (cf. *parâ*).

परिकम्पिन् *pari-kamp + in*, adj. Trembling violently, Utt. Râmach. 80, 16.

परिकर *parikara*, i.e. *pari-kṛi + a*, m. 1. Retinue, dependents, MBh. 10, 274. 2. Preparation, commencement, Kathâs. 26, 200. 3. Effort, Utt. Râmach. 125, 2. 4. Judgment, Râjat. 5, 481. 5. A girth, Hariv. 3652.—Comp. *Sa-*, adj. With (one's) dependents, Pańch. 81, 22.

परिकर्मन् *parikarman*, i.e. *pari -kṛi + man*, I. m. A servant. II. n. 1. Adoration, Bhâg. P. 2, 9, 29. 2. Personal decoration, dressing, painting, or perfuming the body, Kumâras. 4, 19. 3. Preparation, Kathâs. 22, 101.

परिकर्मय *PARIKARMAYA*, a denomin. derived from *parikarman* with *aya*, Par. To adorn, Gît. 12, 21.

परिकर्मिन् *parikarmin*, i.e. *parikarman + in*. m. A servant, Suçr. 1, 15, 4.

परिकर्ष *parikarsha*, m. and परिकर्षण

parikarshaṇa, n. i.e. *pari-kṛish* + *a* or *ana*, Dragging about, MBh. 2, 2615.

परिकर्षिन् *parikarshin*, i. e. *pari -kṛish*, Caus., + *in*, adj. Carrying about (to every place), Râm. 5, 3, 42.

परिकल्पना *parikalpanâ*, i.e. *pari -kḷip*, Caus., + *ana*, f. Assuming (a form), Râm. 5, 41, 13.

परिकीर्तन *parikîrtana*, i.e. *pari -kṛit* + *ana*, n. **1.** Proclaiming. **2.** Stating, Chr. 14, 27.

परिकोप *pari-kopa*, m. Violent anger, Pańch. i. d. 139.

परिक्रम *pari-kram* + *a*, m. **1.** Walking for pleasure. **2.** Walking round, MBh. 4, 1701. **3.** Succession, Man. 3, 214 (see Lois.).

परिक्रय *parikraya*, i.e. *pari-krî* + *a*, m. Peace purchased with money, Hit. iv. d. 120.

परिक्रान्ति *parikrânti*, i.e. *pari-kram* + *ti*, f. Circumrotation, Bhâg. P. 4, 29, 21.

परिक्रिया *parikriyâ*, i.e. *pari-kṛi* + *yâ*, f. Attention to.—**Comp.** *Agni-*, f. attention to the sacred fire, Man. 2, 67.

परिक्लेद *parikleda*, i.e. *pari-klid* + *a*, m. Wetness, MBh. 12, 9192.

परिक्लेदिन् *parikledin*, i. e. *pari -klid* + *in*, adj. Moistening, Suçr. 2, 309, 7.

परिक्लेश *parikleça*, i.e. *pari-kliç* + *a*, m. Hardship, fatigue, MBh. 1, 745; Kathâs, 46, 102.

परिक्लेष्टृ *parikleshṭṛi*, i.e. *pari-kliç* + *tṛi*, m. A tormentor, MBh. 3, 15783.

परिक्षय *parikshaya*, i.e. *pari-kshi* + *a*, m. **1.** Vanishing, MBh. 1, 1884. **2.** Ceasing, Râm. 2, 17, 36 Gorr. **3.** Failure, Man. 9, 59. **4.** Ruin, Pańch. iii. d. 229.

परिक्षित् and परीक्षित् *parîkshit*, i.e. *pari-kshi* + *t*, m. The name of a king.

परिक्षेप *parikshepa*, i.e. *pari-kship* + *a*, m. **1.** Moving to and fro, Hariv. 10384. **2.** Surrounding, Râm. 5, 50, 14. **3.** Being surrounded, Ragh. 12, 66.

परिखा *parikhâ*, i.e. *pari-kha* (vb. *khan*), f. A moat, a ditch surrounding a fort or town, Man. 7, 196.—**Comp.** *Khâta-gambhîra-parikha*, adj., f. *khâ*, possessed of deep-dug moats, Râm. 3, 53, 36.

परिखेद *parikheda*, i.e. *pari-khid* + *a*, m. **1.** Fatigue, MBh. 13, 2662. **2.** Exhaustion, Ṛit. 1, 27.

परिगणना *pari-gaṇ* + *anâ*, f. Enumeration, Megh. 22.

परिगर्हण *parigarhaṇa*, i. e. *pari -garh* + *ana*, n. Censure, MBh. 12, 4543.

परिग्रह *pari-grah* + *a*, m. **1.** Embracing, Pańch. iv. d. 7. **2.** Putting on, Ragh. 18, 37. **3.** Number, Man. 10, 124. **4.** Seizing, Ragh. 9, 46; taking, Utt. Râmach. 67, 1. **5.** Selecting, Mâlav. 14, 23. **6.** Accepting, Bhâg. P. 3, 28, 4. **7.** Possession, Râm. 5, 43, 6. **8.** Property, MBh. 3, 13995. **9.** Admission, Man. 11, 196. **10.** Marrying, marriage, Man. 9, 326. **11.** A wife, 9, 42. **12.** A husband, Râm. 1, 46, 26 Gorr. **13.** Undertaking, committing, Man. 12, 32. **14.** Honouring, Râm. 2, 70, 20 Gorr. **15.** Grace, favour, 4, 23, 5. **16.** Dominion, Mârk. P. 53, 8. **17.** Claim, Hariv. 7264. **18.** Dependents, Yâjń. 3, 57; retinue; family, Pańch. i. d. 175. **19.** An abode, Hariv.

8909. **20.** Root, origin, MBh. 3, 1292.—**Comp.** *Dushparigraha*, i.e. *dus-pari-grah* + *a*, adj. difficult to be maintained, Pańch. i. d. 77. *Nishp°*, i. e. *nis-*, adj. having no property, MBh. 1, 4600.

परिग्रहत्व *parigraha* + *tva*, n. in *mad-*, Condition of being one's wife, Daçak. in Chr. 194, 15.

परिग्रहण *parigrahaṇa*, i. e. *pari-grah* + *ana*, n. Putting on, Prab. 3, 18.

परिग्रहमय *parigraha* + *maya*, adj., f. *yî*, Consisting in a family, Prab. 77, 8.

परिग्रहवन्त् *parigraha* + *vant*, adj. f. *vatî*, Having property, MBh. 12, 196.

परिग्रहिन् *parigrahin*, i. e. *pari-graha* + *in*, adj. Attached to (worldly) property, Mârk. P. 47, 30.

परिग्रहीतृ *pari-grah* + *itṛi*, m. A husband, Çâk. d. 97.

परिघ *pari-gha* (vb. *han*), m. **1.** An iron bar for shutting a gate, Suçr. 2, 92, 12. **2.** An iron club, or a bludgeon mounted with iron, MBh. 1, 1174. **3.** A line of clouds covering partially the rising or setting sun, 5, 4855. **4.** The gate of a palace, Râm. 2, 72, 1 Gorr. **5.** A proper name.

परिघट्टन *pari-ghaṭṭ* + *ana*, n. A stirring up, MBh. 3, 17403.

परिघातिन् *parighâtin*, i.e. *pari-han*, Caus., + *in*, adj. Trespassing. Râm. 5, 62, 6.

परिचतुर्दशन् *pari-chatur-daçan*, and **परिचतुर्दश** *pari-chatur-daça*, adj. Full fourteen, MBh. 2, 95; 3, 11.

परिचय *parichaya*, i.e. *pari-chi* + *a*, m. **1.** Knowledge, Suçr. 1, 28, 17. **2.** Trial, Çâk. 59, 4 (Prâkṛ.). **3.** Acquaintance, familiarity, Kathâs. 9, 9. **4.** Accumulation.

परिचयवन्त् *parichaya* + *vant*, adj. (Endowed with accumulation or collection, i.e.) All, finished, Mâlav. d. 55.

परिचर *pari-char* + *a*, m. An attendant, Suçr. 1, 124, 5.—Cf. περίπολος.

परिचरण *paricharaṇa*, i. e. *pari-char* + *ana*, n. Attention to, MBh. 12. 6991.

परिचर्या *pari-char* + *yâ*, f. **1.** Attendance, Bhag. 18, 44. **2.** Adoration, Bhâg. P. 3, 15, 32.

परिचर्यावन्त् *paricharyâ* + *vant*, adj. f. *vatî*, Respected, MBh. 12, 3711.

परिचार *parichâra*, i.e. *pari-char* + *a*, m. **1.** Attendance, homage, MBh. 4, 374. **2.** A walking-place, 4, 892. **3.** An attendant, 7, 1261.

परिचारक *parichâraka*, i.e. *pari-char* + *aka*, I. adj. Attending, Râm. 2, 84, 9 Gorr. **II.** m. An attendant, a servant, Man. 7, 217. **III.** f. *rikâ*, A female servant, Râm. 1, 46, 24 Gorr.

परिचारण *parichâraṇa*, i.e. *pari-char* + *ana*, m. Attendance, MBh. 13, 6464.

परिचारिक *parichârika*, i.e. *pari-chârin* + *ka*, m. A servant, MBh. 13, 6028.

परिचारिन् *parichârin*, i.e. *pari-char* + *in*, I. adj., f. *iṇî*. **1.** Moveable, MBh. 12, 8070. **2.** Attending on, Hariv. 403. **3.** Doing homage. **II.** m. An attendant, MBh. 1, 6296.

परिचिति *pari-chi-ti*, f. Acquaintance, Böhtl. Ind. Spr. 698.

परिचिन्तक *pari-chint* + *aka*, m. Meditating on, MBh. 11, 160.

परिचुम्बन *pari-chumb + ana*, n. Kissing passionately, Chaurap. 47.

परिच्छद् *parichchhad*, i.e. *pari -chhad*, in the comp. adj. *senâ-*, Provided with an army, Ragh. 1, 19.

परिच्छद *parichchhada*, i.e. *pari -chhad + a*, m. **1.** A cover, a covering, MBh. 2, 798. **2.** Domestic implements, Man. 11, 76. **3.** Implements in general, 6, 3. **4.** Necessaries for travelling, 8, 405. **5.** Retinue, train, Sâv. 3, 16. **6.** When latter part of a comp. adj. it implies often, Provided with, Bhâg. P. 7, 7, 5.—**Comp.** *Agni-*, m. the implements used in oblations to fire, Man. 6, 4. *Sa-*, adj. with, or attended by, a retinue, Râm. 2, 36, 24.

परिच्छेद *parichchheda*, i. e. *pari -chhid + a*, m. **1.** Separation. **2.** Exact discrimination, Kâm. Nîtis. 11, 33. **3.** Determination. **4.** Decision, Çâk. d. 106. **5.** A chapter (of a book).—**Comp.** *Bhâshâ-*, m. title of a philosophical work; definition of (the categories of) speech.

परिजन *pari-jana*, m. **1.** Surrounding company, court attendants, Râm. 2, 77, 14 Gorr. **2.** A servant, Böhtl. Ind. Spr. 731.

परिज्ञप्ति *pariǰńapti*, i.e. *pari-jńâ*, Caus., + *ti*, f. Conversation, Kathâs. 21, 128.

परिज्ञातृ *pari-jńâ + tṛi*, m. One who knows, Bhag. 18, 18.

परिज्ञान *pariǰńâna*, i.e. *pari-jńâ + ana*, n. Learning, Yâjń. 1, 317; knowledge, Râm. 4, 13, 14.

परिज्मन् *parijman*, i.e. *pari-gam + an*, adj. Walking round, Chr. 296, 4. = Rigv. i. 112, 4 (the sun; Sch. the wind.)

परिज्रि *pari-jri*, adj. Hastening about, Chr. 290, 5 = Rigv. i. 64, 5.

परिणति *pariṇati*, i.e. *pari-nam + ti*, f. **1.** Transmutation, Pańch. 97, 18. **2.** Ripening, Megh. 24. **3.** Consequence, effect, Kathâs. 22, 82. **4.** End, Böhtl. Ind. Spr. 343.

परिणमयितृ *pariṇamayitṛi*, i. e. *pari-nam*, Caus., + *tṛi*, m. One who causes something to bow, Megh. 43.

परिणय *pariṇaya*, i.e. *pari-nî + a*, m. Marriage, (properly, conducting the bride round the sacred fire), Kathâs. 33, 82.

परिणाम *pariṇâma*, i.e. *pari-nam + a*, m. **1.** Transformation, change, Prab. 27, 12. **2.** Digestion, Suçr. 1, 245, 10. **3.** Consequence, Vikr. 65, 20. **4.** Termination, end, Çâk. d. 3.

परिणामक *pariṇâmaka*, i. e. *pari -nam*, Caus., + *aka*, adj. Causing to change, Hariv. 3357.

परिणायक *pariṇâyaka*, i.e. *pari-nî + aka*, m. **1.** A guide, Râm. 2, 64, 4. **2.** A husband, Çiç. 9, 73.

परिणाह and **परीणाह** *pariṇâha*, i.e. *pari-nah + a*, m. **1.** Circumference, MBh. 6, 276. **2.** Width, Çâk. d. 18. **3.** Breadth, Yâjń. 2, 167.

परिणाहवन्त् *pariṇâha + vant*, adj., f. *vatî*, Big, Vikr. d. 6.

परिणाहिन् *pariṇâhin*, i.e. *pari-ṇâha + in*, adj. **1.** Big, large, Hariv. 12174. **2.** Having the circumference of, e. g. *mattebhakumbha-*, i. e. *matta -ibha-kumbha-pariṇâha + in*, Having the circumference of the globes of an elephant in rut, Pańch. i. d. 224.

परिणिनंसु *pariṇinaṁsu*, i. e. *pari -ninaṁsa*, desider. of *nam*, + *u*, adj.

Being about to strike with his tusks (viz. an elephant), Çiç. 5, 34.

परिणेतृ *pariṇetṛi*, i.e. *pari-nî + tṛi*, m. A husband (cf. *pariṇaya*), Çâk. d. 114.

परितर्कण *paritarkaṇa*, i. e. *pari -tark + ana*, n. Consideration, MBh. 13, 7553.

परितर्पण *paritarpaṇa*, i. e. *pari -tṛip + ana*, adj. Satisfying, Bhâg. P. 9, 21, 10; delighting, Utt. Râmach. 58, 3.

परितस् *pari + tas*, I. adv. All around, Ṛit. 2, 7; from every part, in every direction. II. prep. with acc. and gen., Round, MBh. 4, 11.

परिताप and **परीताप** *parîtâpa*, i. e. *pari-tap + a*, m. 1. Heat, warmth, Ṛit. 1, 22. 2. Sorrow, pain, Böhtl. Ind. Spr. 196.

परितापिन् *paritâpin*, i.e. *pari-tap + in*, and *paritâpa + in*, adj., f. *nî*. 1. Causing much pain or sorrow, Böhtl. Ind. Spr. 263. 2. Very hot, Kâm. Nîtis. 7, 34.

परितोष and **परीतोष** *parîtosha*, i.e. *pari-tush + a*, m. Satisfaction, Man. 4, 161; gratification, pleasure, Böhtl. Ind. Spr. 856.—Comp. *A-*, adj., f. *shâ*, not satisfied. *Sa-paritosha + m*, adv. very pleased.

परितोषण *paritoshaṇa*, i. e. *pari -tush + ana*, I. adj. Satisfying, who or what satisfies, Bhâg. P. 1, 5, 35. II. n. Satisfying, 4, 30, 40.

परितोषयितृ *paritoshayitṛi*, i. e. *pari-tush*, Caus., *+ tṛi*, m., f. *trî*, and n. Who or what satisfies, Çiç. 16, 28.

परितोषवन्त् *paritosha + vant*, adj., f. *vatî*, Satisfied, Kathâs. 33, 179.

परितोषिन् i.e. *paritosha + in*, adj., f. *iṇî*, Satisfied, Kathâs. 17, 161.

परित्यक्तृ *parityaktṛi*, i.e. *pari-tyaj + tṛi*, m., f. *trî*, and n. A forsaker, Man. 3, 157.

परित्यज् *pari-tyaj*, adj. Forsaking, MBh. 7, 706.

परित्याग *parityâga*, i.e. *pari-tyaj + a*, m. 1. Abandoning, Nal. 10, 10. 2. Repudiation, Chr. 7, 12. 3. Neglect, Chr. 22, 25. 4. Resigning, Mṛichchh. 166, 11. 5. Sacrifice, Böhtl. Ind. Spr. 364.

परित्यागिन् *parityâgin*, i. e. *pari -tyaj + in*, adj., f. *nî*. 1. Abandoning, Râm. 1, 79, 32 Gorr. 2. Resigning, Bhag. 12, 17.

परित्राण *paritrâṇa*, i.e. *pari-trâ + ana*, n. 1. Protection, Man. 8, 349. 2. Defence, MBh. 1, 1012. 3. Shelter, 7, 2526. 4. Abstaining from, MBh. 13, 6227.

परित्रातृ *pari-trâ + tṛi*, m. A protector, Râm. 2, 40, 5 Gorr.

परित्रास *paritrâsa*, i.e. *pari-tras + a*, m. Fright, fear, Râm. 2, 67, 11 Gorr.

परिदंशित *pari-daṁçita*, adj. Armed cap-a-pie, MBh. 1, 5407.

परिदर *paridara*, i.e. *pari-dṛî + a*, m. A disease of the jaw, Suçr. 1, 303, 10.

परिदाह and **परीदाह** *parîdâha*, i.e. *pari-dah + a*, m. 1. Burning, Suçr. 1, 38, 14. 2. Pain, sorrow, MBh. 12, 10511.

परिदेव *parideva*, m. and **परिदेवन** *paridevana*, n. and fem. *nâ*, i.e. *pari*

-2. *div* + *a*, or *ana*, Lamentation, MBh. 7, 3014; Kathâs. 50, 134; Yâjń. 3, 9.

परिदेविन् *paridevin*, i.e. *pari*-2. *div* + *in*, adj., f. *nî*, Lamenting, Çâk. 70, 12.

परिद्रष्टृ *paridrashṭṛi*, i.e. *pari-dṛiç* + *tṛi*, m., f. *trî*, and n. A perceiver, MBh. 12, 7107.

परिधर्षण *paridharshaṇa*, i.e. *pari -dhṛish* + *ana*, n. Abuse, MBh. 14, 1028.

परिधान and **परीधान** *parîdhâna*, i.e. *pari-dhâ* + *ana*, n. **1.** Putting on, dressing, Pańch. 226, 16. **2.** A garment, Pańch. v. d. 21. **3.** A lower garment, Nal. 9, 314.

परिधारण *paridhâraṇa*, i.e. *pari -dhṛi* + *ana*, n. Suffering, indulging, MBh. 12, 5750.

परिधि *pari-dhi* (vb. *dhâ*), m. **1.** That by which something is bordered, Bhâg. P. 1, 10, 3 (the ocean). **2.** An anthelia, a halo, Bhâg. P. 3, 17, 8 **3.** The horizon, 8, 15, 10. **4.** Circumference. **5.** Pieces of fresh wood, surrounding the sacrificial fire, MBh. 5, 4795. **6.** A proper name.

परिधूसर *pari-dhûsara*, adj. Quite grey, Çâk. d. 180.

परिध्वंस *pari-dhvaṁs* + *a*, m. **1.** Distress, Nal. 10, 9. **2.** Failure, Hit. ii. d. 118. **3.** Loss of caste, Man. 10, 61.

परिध्वंसिन् *paridhvaṁsin*, i.e. *pa-ri-dhvaṁs* + *in*, adj. Destroying. Kâm. Nîtis. 2, 40.

परिनिष्ठा i.e. *pari-nishṭhâ* (see *nish-ṭha*), f. **1.** Complete accomplishment, MBh. 3, 2815. **2.** Complete knowledge, Bhâg. P. 2, 1, 6.

परिपक्व *pari-pakva*, adj. **1.** Fully baked. **2.** Quite ripe, MBh. 5, 4220. **3.** Decaying, Suçr. 1, 44, 20.

परिपतन *pari-pat* + *ana*, m. Flying about, hovering, Çâk. 88, 11.

परिपन्थक *paripanthaka*, i.e. *pari -pathin* + *aka*, m. An enemy, Râjat. 4, 27 (cf. *paripanthin* and *paripanthika*).

परिपन्थय *PARIPANTHAYA*, a denomin. derived from *paripanthin* with *aya*, To resist (with acc.), Râjat. 4, 261.

परिपन्थिक *paripanthika*, i. e. *pari -panthin* + *ka*, m. An enemy, MBh. 10, 753.

परिपन्थिन् *paripanthin*, i.e. *pari -pathin* + *in*, m. and f. *nî*, An opposer, an enemy, Man. 7, 107.

परिपाक and **परीपाक** *parîpâka*, i. e. *pari-pach* + *a*, m. **1.** Becoming fully cooked. **2.** Digestion, Vedântas. in Chr. 207, 13. **3.** Ripening, Çiç. 4, 48. **4.** Consequence, effect, Böhtl. Ind. Spr. 1429. **5.** Experience, Naish. 5, 20.

परिपाचन *paripâchana*, i.e. *pari -pach*, Caus., + *ana*, adj. Maturing by cooking or ripening, Suçr. 2, 408, 13.

परिपाटल *pari-pâṭala*, adj. Pale-red, Çiç. 13, 42.

परिपाठ *paripâṭha*, i.e. *pari-paṭh* + *a*, m. Complete enumeration; *ṭhena*, instr. Completely, MBh. 12, 9259.

परिपाण्डु *pari-pâṇḍu*, adj. Very pale, Ṛit. 1, 17.

परिपार्श्व *pari-pârçva*, adj. Being at one's side, at the side, near, MBh. 8, 1499.

परिपार्श्वतस् *paripârçva* + *tas*, adv. with gen. At the side of, at both sides of, MBh. 7, 7307.

परिपालक *paripâlaka*, i.e. *pari*-2. *pâ* Caus., + *aka*, adj. Guarding, protecting, maintaining.—Comp. *Pṛithivî*-, m. a king, a prince, Mârk. P. 67, 5.

परिपालन *paripâlana*, i.e. *pari*-2. *pâ*, Caus., + *ana*, n. 1. Nurture, Man. 9, 27. 2. Protection, Râjat. 5, 481. 3. Maintaining, keeping, Râm. 6, 85, 9.

परिपीडन *pari-piḍ* + *ana*, n. 1. Squeezing out, Suçr. 2, 35, 14. 2. Prejudicing, Kâm. Nîtis. 14, 55.

परिपीडा *pari-piḍ* + *â*, f. Tormenting, Râm. 2, 19, 13 Gorr.

परिपुटन *pari-puṭ* + *ana*, n. Peeling off, Suçr. 1, 62, 4.

परिपुटनवन्त् *pariputana* + *vant*, adj., f. *vatî*, Peeling off, Suçr. 1, 57, 11.

परिपुष्टता *pari-pushṭa* + *tâ* (vb. *push*), f. Being nourished, feeding on, Yâjń. 3, 241.

परिपूरक *pari-pûr* + *aka*, adj. Fulfilling, Böhtl. Ind. Spr. 1255.

परिपूरण *paripûraṇa*, i.e. *pari-pûr* + *ana*, n. Filling, Çiç. 4, 61.

परिपोट *paripoṭa*, i.e. *pari-puṭ* + *a*, and **परिपोटक** *paripoṭa* + *ka*, m. Peeling off, a disease of the ear, Suçr. 2, 149, 10.

परिपोटन *paripoṭana*, i. e. *pari -puṭ* + *ana*, n. Peeling off, Suçr. 1, 251, 13.

परिपोटवन्त् *paripoṭa* + *vant*, adj. Peeling off, Suçr. 2, 149, 13.

परिपोषक *pariposhaka*, i. e. *pari -push*, Caus., + *aka*, adj. Furthering, Râjat. 6, 296.

परिपोषण *pariposhaṇa*, i. e. *pari -push*, Caus., + *ana*, n. Furthering, Bhâg. P. 7, 11, 23.

परिप्रश्न *paripraçna*, i. e. *pari -prachh* + *na*, n. Inquiring, Bhâg. P. 2, 1, 63.

परिप्राप्ति *pariprâpti*, i. e. *pari-pra -âp* + *ti*, f. Obtaining, Râm. 1, 67, 8 Gorr.

परिप्रेप्सु *pariprepsu*, i. e. *pari-pra -îpsa*, desider. of *âp*, + *u*, adj. Searching, desiring, Nal. 18, 11.

परिप्रेष्य *paripreshya*, i. e. *pari -pra-ish*, Caus., + *ya*, m. A servant, MBh. 4, 32.

परिप्लव *pariplava*, i.e. *pari-plu* + *a*, I. adj. Running to and fro, Çiç. 14, 68. II. m. 1. A ship, a boat, Râm. 1, 45, 13 Gorr. 2. A proper name.

परिप्लाव्य *pariplâvya*, i.e. *pari-plu* + *a* + *ya*, adj. Running (water), MBh. 3, 5055.

परिबर्ह *pari-barh* + *a*, and **परिवर्ह** *pari-varh* + *a*, m. 1. A suitable attire, trim, retinue, Draup. 1, 7. 2. A suitable furniture, Râm. 2, 83, 26.

परिबर्हण *paribarhaṇa* and **परिवर्हण** *parivarhaṇa*, i.e. *pari-bṛih*, or *vṛih* + *ana*, and *pari-barh*, or *varh* + *ana*, n. 1. Adoration, Bhâg. P. 5, 5, 27. 2. Trim, attire, MBh. 12, 7005.

परिबर्हवन्त् *paribarha* + *vant*, adj., f. *vatî*, Provided with a suitable furniture, Ragh. 14, 15.

परिबाधा *pari-bâdh* + *â*, f. Fatigue, Çâk. d. 70.

परिबृंहण *paribṛiṁhaṇa*, and **परिवृंहण** *parivṛiṁhaṇa*, i.e. *pari-bṛiṁh*, or *vṛiṁh* + *aṇa*, n. 1. Prosperity, Bhâg. P. 5, 1, 7. 2. Supplement, Man. 12, 109.

परिभक्षण *paribhakshaṇa*, i.e. *pari-bhaksh+ana*, n. Devouring, MBh. 1, 2617.

परिभर्त्सन *pari-bharts + ana*, n. Menace, Râm. 5, 37, 25.

परिभव *paribhava*, i.e. *pari-bhû+a*, m. **1.** Disrespect, humiliation, contumely, MBh. 3, 1520. **2.** Disregard, MBh. 13, 3864.

परिभवन *paribhavana*, i. e. *pari-bhû+ana*, n. Disrespect, Mâlav. 14, 2.

परिभाव *paribhâva*, i.e. *pari-bhû+a*, m. Contumely, Pańch. 56, 8.

परिभावन *paribhâvana*, i. e. *pari-bhû+ana*, I. n. Union, MBh. 12, 7145 (*a* is lengthened on account of the metre). II. f. *nâ*, Thought, Utt. Râmach. 95, 4.

परिभाविन् *paribhâvin*, i. e. *pari-bhû+in*, adj., f. *nî*, One who or what slights, Çâk. 44, 12.

परिभाषण *paribhâshaṇa*, i.e. *pari-bhâsh+ana*, I. adj. Speaking much, Râm. 5, 93, 6. II. n. Reproof, Man. 9, 283.

परिभाषा *pari-bhâsh + â*, f. **1.** Speech, MBh. 13, 7417. **2.** A general maxim.

परिभाषिन *pari-bhâsh + in*, adj., f. *iṇî*, Speaking, Râm. 3, 35, 60.

परिभूति *pari-bhû+ti*, f. Disrespect, Böhtl. Ind. Spr. 1249.

परिभूषण *paribhûshaṇa*, i.e. *pari-bhûsh+ana*, m. A peace bought by the cession of all the revenues of a country, Kâm. Nîtis. 9, 18.

परिभोक्तृ *paribhoktṛi*, i.e. *pari-bhuj+tṛi*, m. **1.** One who uses another's goods without his leave, Man. 2, 201. **2.** One who enjoys.

परिभोग *paribhoga*, i.e. *pari-bhuj+a*, m. Enjoyment, especially sexual intercourse, Ragh. 4, 45.

परिभ्रंश *pari-bhraṁç+a*, m. Escaping, Hariv. 5285.

परिभ्रंशन *pari-bhraṁç + ana*, n. Loss, Pańch. iii. d. 268 (with abl.).

परिभ्रम *pari-bhram+a*, m. Speaking what is nothing to the purpose, Mṛichchh. 1, 9.

परिभ्रमण *paribhramaṇa*, i.e. *pari-bhram+ana*, n. **1.** Turning, revolving (as of wheels), Bhâg. P. 5, 8, 6. **2.** Circumference.

परिमण्डल *pari-maṇḍala*, I. n. Circumference, MBh. 12, 7696. II. adj., f. *lâ*, Round, circular, globular, MBh. 6, 188. III. m. A poisonous kind of gnat.

परिमण्डलता *parimaṇḍala+tâ*, f. Circularity, Suçr. 1, 268, 18.

परिमण्डलित *parimaṇḍalita*, i. e. *parimaṇḍala+ita*, adj. Made round, Kir. 5, 42.

परिमन्थर *pari-manthara*, adj. Very slow, Çiç. 9, 78.

परिमन्द *pari-manda*, **1.** adj. Very faint, Çiç. 9, 8. **2.** adv. Very little, 9, 27.

परिमन्दता *parimanda + tâ*, f. Tiredness, Çiç. 9, 39.

परिमर्द *parimarda*, i.e. *pari-mṛid+a*, m. **1.** Wearing out, MBh. 12, 2185. **2.** Destruction, 2, 1030.

परिमर्श *parimarça*, i.e. *pari-mṛiç+a*, m. Examination, MBh. 12, 4370.

परिमल *pari-mala*, m. **1.** Fragrance, Bhartṛ. 1, 33. **2.** A fragrant substance, Pańch. 47, 8. **3.** Sexual intercourse, Kir. 10, 1.

परिमाण and **परीमाण** *parîmâṇa,* i.e. *pari-mâ + ana,* n. **1.** Circumference, Böhtl. Ind. Spr. 461. **2.** Measure, Hariv. 1033. **3.** Weight, Pañch. ii. d. 84. **4.** Length of time, MBh. 3, 1407. **5.** Number, MBh. 11, 763.

परिमाणक *parimâṇa+ka,* n. Quantity, Bhâshâp. 94.

परिमाणतस् *parimâṇa+tas,* adv. In weight, Man. 8, 133.

परिमार्गण *parimârgaṇa,* i.e. *pari-mârg+ana,* n. Tracing, searching, Râm. 3, 78, 19.

परिमार्गिन् *pari-mârg + in,* adj. Pursuing, MBh. 13, 5355.

परिमिति *parimiti,* i.e. *pari-mâ+ti,* f. Quantity, Bhâshâp. 3.

परिमिलन *pari-mil+ana,* n. Touch, Ratnâv. 40, 11.

परिमुग्धता *pari-mugdha+tâ* (vb. *muh*), f. Gracefulness and silliness, Çiç. 9, 32.

परिमूढता *pari-mûḍha + tâ* (vb. *muh*), f. Trouble, Çiç. 9, 70.

परिमोक्ष *pari-moksh + a,* m. **1.** Setting free, Râm. 1, 45, 9 Gorr. **2.** Evacuation, Bhâg. P. 2, 6, 8. **3.** Escaping, MBh. 9, 3192.

परिमोक्षण *parimokshaṇa,* i.e. *pari-moksh+ana,* n. **1.** Liberation, Mṛichchh. 67, 19. **2.** Deliverance from (gen.), MBh. 12, 4846.

परिमोष *parimosha,* i.e. *pari-mush+a,* m. Theft, robbing, Ragh. 9, 62.

परिमोषक *parimoshaka,* i. e. *pari-mush+aka,* adj. Stealing, MBh. 3, 12850.

परिमोहन *parimohana,* i. e. *pari-muh+ana,* n. Infatuation, Chaurap. 38.

परिरक्षण *parirakshaṇa,* i. e. *pari-raksh+ana,* I. m. and f. *ṇî,* A protector, Hariv. 3272. II. n. **1.** Guarding, Man. 7, 2. **2.** Maintaining, Râjat. 4, 283. **3.** Preservation, MBh. 2, 673.—Comp. *A-*, n. betraying, 2, 242.

परिरक्षा *pari-raksh+â,* f. **1.** Protection, Man. 5, 94. **2.** Preservation, 10, 106.

परिरक्षितृ *pari-raksh+itṛi,* m. **1.** A guardian, MBh. 12, 1138. **2.** A protector, 4, 2274.

परिरक्षिन् *pari-raksh + in,* adj. Guarding, MBh. 1, 6969.

परिरम्भ *parirambha,* i.e. *pari-rabh+a,* m. Embrace, Prab. 9, 1.

परिरम्भण *parirambhaṇa,* i.e. *pari-rabh+ana,* n. Embracing, Gît. 1, 33; Utt. Râmach. 129, 3.

ऽपरिरम्भिन् *-parirambhin,* i.e. *-parirambha+in,* adj. Girt, Bhâg. P. 3, 28, 24.

परिरोध *parirodha,* i.e. *pari-rudh+a,* m. Resistance, Râjat. 2, 165.

परिलङ्घन *pari-laṅgh + ana,* n. Jumping to and fro, Râm. 4, 52, 16.

परिवत्सर *pari-vatsara,* m. **A** full year, Man. 1, 12. **2.** A year, MBh. 1, 3202.

परिवर्जक *parivarjaka,* i.e. *pari-vṛij+aka,* adj. Abstaining from, MBh. 13, 6648.

परिवर्जन *parivarjana,* i.e. *pari-vṛij+ana,* n. **1.** Careful abstaining from, Man. 5, 54. **2.** Avoiding, Râm. 6, 8, 14.

परिवर्त and **परीवर्त** *parîvarta,* i.e.

pari-vṛit + a, m. 1. Turning, Bhâg. P. 2, 7, 13. 2. Revolution, Çâk. d. 139; the end of a period. 3. Destruction of the world, Râm. 2, 76, 8. 4. Palingenesia, transmigration, Bhâg. P. 1, 3, 39. 5. Exchange, barter, Hariv. 3331. 6. An abode, Hariv. 3401. 7. A proper name.

परिवर्तक *parivartaka*, i.e. *pari-vṛit*, Caus., *+ aka*, I. adj. 1. Causing to revolve, MBh. 3, 13105. 2. Causing to flow back, Kathâs. 46, 143. II. m. A proper name.

परिवर्तन *pari-vartana*, i.e. *pari-vṛit + ana*, I. adj., f. *nî*, Causing to turn, Kathâs. 46, 118. II. n. 1. Turning. 2. Moving to and fro, Pańch. 188, 10. 3. Revolution, the end of a period, MBh. 1, 1254. 4. Exchange, barter, Kathâs. 12, 50.

परिवर्तिन् *parivartin*, i.e. *pari-vṛit + in*, adj. f. *nî*, 1. Turning. 2. Revolving, ever renewing one's self, Bhartṛ. 2, 24. 3. Standing, abiding, being, Râm. 6, 97, 11.—Comp. *A-*, adj. Never showing the heels, Chr. 7, 13.

परिवर्धन *parivardhana*, i.e. *pari -vṛidh + ana*, n. Augmenting, Man, 9, 331.

परिवर्ह *parivarha*, and **परिवर्हण** *parivarhaṇa*, see *paribarha*, and *paribarhaṇa*.

परिवाद and **परीवाद** *parîvâda*, i.e. *pari-vad + a*, m. Detraction, censure, Man. 2, 179; 201; 7, 47.

परिवादिन् *parivâdin*, i.e. *pari vad + in*, I. adj., f. *nî*, Slandering, blaming, MBh. 7, 2592. II. f. *nî*, A viṇâ or lute with seven strings, Ragh. 8, 35.

परिवार *parivâra*, i.e. *pari-vṛi + a*, m. 1. A cover, MBh. 8, 1474. 2. Retinue, Pańch. 12, 20 (figur.); Daçak, in Chr. 182, 20.

परिवारण *parivâraṇa*, i.e. *pari-vṛi + ana*, n. 1. A cover, MBh. 5, 2937. 2. Retinue, 1435. 3. Keeping off, 9, 3192.

परिवारवन्त् *parivâra + vant*, adj. Having a great retinue.

परिवास *parivâsa*, i.e. *pari-vas + a*, m. Sojourn, Man. 5, 124.

परिवाह and **परीवाह** *parîvâha*, i.e. *pari-vah + a*, m. 1. Overflowing, Ragh. 8, 73. 2. A water-course, or a drain to carry off excess of water, Râm. 2, 80, 11; Utt. Râmach. 73, 5 (*rî*).—Comp. *Sa-*, adj. brimfull, Çâk. 29, 5 (Prâkṛ.).

परिवाहिन् *parivâhin*, i.e. *parivâha + in*, adj., f. *iṇî*, Overflowing, swimming with, Çâk. 51, 10 (figuratively, Prâkṛ.).

परिविक्रयिन् *parivikrayin*, i.e. *pari -vi-krî + in*, adj. Trading, MBh. 12, 1213. — Comp. *Mâṁsa-*, m. a fleshmonger.

परिविक्षोभ *parivikshobha*, i.e. *pari -vi-kshubh + a*, m. Destroying, MBh. 14, 1240.

परिवित्ति *parivitti*, i.e. *pari-vid + ti*, m. An unmarried elder brother, the younger being married, Man. 3, 154.

परिवित्तिता *parivitti + tâ*, f. The marrying of a younger brother before his elder, Man. 11, 60.

परिविहार *parivihâra*, i.e. *pari-vi -hṛi + a*, m. Walking for pleasure.

परिवृंहण *parivṛiṁhaṇa*, see *paribṛiṁhaṇa*.

परिवृढ *parivṛiḍha*, i.e. ptcple. of the pf. pass. of *pari-vṛih*, m. A master, an owner.

परिवृत्ति *pari-vṛit + ti*, f. 1. Exchange, barter; instr. Alternately,

Bhâg. P. 4, 27, 14. **2.** Dwelling, MBh. 14, 525.

परिवृद्धि *parivṛiddhi,* i. e. *pari-vṛidh + ti,* f. Increase, Mṛichchh. 43, 19.

परिवेत्तृ *parivettṛi,* i.e. *pari-vid + tṛi,* m. A younger brother married before his elder, Man. 3, 171.

परिवेदक *parivedaka,* i.e. *pari-vid + aka,* m. A younger brother married before his elder, Yâjń. 3, 238.

परिवेदन *parivedana,* n., i.e. I. *pari-vid + ana,* The marrying of a younger brother before his elder, Man. 11, 60. II. *pari-vedana,* Complete knowledge, MBh. 14, 418.

परिवेश *pariveça,* **°वेशक** *-veçaka,* **°वेशन** *-veçana,* **°वेशवन्त्** *-veçavant,* see *parivesha, -shaka, -shaṇa, -shavant.*

परिवेष *parivesha* (and erroneously **परिवेश** *pariveça*), i.e. *pari-vish + a,* m. **1.** Surrounding; *kṛitâṅgarakshâ-,* Surrounded by a body-guard, Pańch. 258, 6. **2.** A circle, Ragh. 5, 74. **3.** A halo, 11, 59.

परिवेषक *pariveshaka* (and erroneously **परिवेशक** *pariveçaka*) i.e. *pari-vish + aka,* m. A waiter; one who serves up dinner.

परिवेषण *pariveshaṇa* (and erroneously **परिवेशन** *pariveçana*), i.e. *pari-vish + ana,* n. **1.** Serving up dinner. **2.** Circumference, MBh. 14, 1234. **3.** A halo.

परिवेषवन्त् *parivesha + vant* (and erroneously **परिवेशवन्त्** *pariveça-vant*), adj. Surrounded by a halo.

परिवेषिन् *pariveshin,* i.e. *parivesha + in,* adj. Surrounded by a halo.

परिवेष्टन *pari-vesht + ana,* n. **1.** A cover, MBh. 4, 1319. **2.** A bandage.

परिवेष्टृ *pariveshṭri,* i.e. *pari-vish + tṛi,* m. A waiter, MBh. 13, 1668.

परिव्यय *pari-vyaya,* m. Condiment. —Comp. *Sa-,* adj. with the condiments, Man. 7, 127.

परिव्रज्या *pari-vraj + yâ,* f. **1.** Strolling, Man. 10, 152. **2.** Religious wandering.

परिव्राज् *parivrâj,* i.e. *pari-vraj,* m. A (wandering) ascetic, Râm. 3, 52, 4; cf. Kâm. Nîtis. 2, 29, 31.

परिव्राजक *parivrâjaka,* i. e. *pari-vraj + aka,* f. *kâ* and *jikâ,* A religious mendicant, Pańch. 32, 23.

परिशङ्किन् *pari-çaṅk + in,* adj., f. *nî.* **1.** Fearing. **2.** Being fearful on account of, Bhâg. P. 3, 17, 2.

परिशीलन *pari-çîl + ana,* n. **1.** Frequent touch, Gît. 1, 27. **2.** Study.

परिशुद्धि *pariçuddhi,* i.e. *pari-çudh + ti,* f. **1.** Becoming quite pure, Utt. Râmach. 99, 10. **2.** Proving innocent, Kathâs. 5, 98.

परिशेष *pariçesha,* i.e. *pari-çish + a,* m. and n. **1.** Remains. **2.** Supplement, MBh. 12, 11739.

परिशेषण *pariçeshaṇa,* i.e. *pari-çish + ana,* n. Remains, Bhâg. P. 9, 4, 5.

परिशोधन *pariçodhana,* i. e. *pari-çudh + ana,* Purification, Utt. Râmach. 100, 1.

परिशोषिन् *pariçoshin,* i. e. *pari-çush + in,* adj. Falling off, Râjat. 2, 69.

परिश्रम and **परिश्राम** *pariçrâma,*

i.e. *pari-çram + a*, m. **1.** Fatigue, Sâv. 4, 21. **2.** Exertion, Ragh. 19, 15.

परिश्रव *pariçrava*, see *parisrava*.

परिषत्त्व *parishattva*, i.e. *parishad + tva*, n. A legal assembly, Man. 12, 144.

परिषद् *parishad*, i.e. *pari-sad*, f. An assembly, an audience, a congregation, Man. 12, 110; Utt. Râmach. 105, 5.

परिषेक *parisheka*, i.e. *pari-sich + a*, m. **1.** Sprinkling, pouring over water. **2.** A bath.

परिषेचन *parishechana*, i. e. *pari-sich + ana*, n. **1.** Sprinkling, pouring over water. **2.** Water for watering trees, MBh. 12, 9116.

परिष्कर *parishkara*, i. e. *pari-kṛi + a*, m. Ornament, MBh. 8, 1477.

परिष्कार *parishkâra*, i.e. *pari-kṛi + a*, m. **1.** Adorning, Lass. Anth. 94, 14. **2.** Ornament.

परिष्क्रिया *parishkriyâ*, i. e. *pari-kṛi + yâ*, f. **1.** Adorning. **2.** Attention to, Man. 2, 67 (ed. Calc.).

परिष्वङ्ग *parishvaṅga*, i. e. *pari-svañj + a*, m. **1.** Embrace, Pañch. ii. d. 61; Vikr. 71, 5. **2.** Touch.

परिस् *paris*, see *kṛi* with *pari*.

परिसंख्या *parisaṁkhyâ*, i. e. *pari-sam-khyâ*, **1.** Full number, totality, Man. 1, 72. **2.** Number. **3.** Full enumeration (leaving nothing unsaid).

परिसंख्यान *parisaṁkhyâna*, i. e. *pari-sam-khyâ + ana*, n. **1.** = the preceding 1, 2, 3. **2.** Just examination, Yâjñ. 3, 158.

परिसमूहन *pari-sam-ûh + ana*, n. Sweeping.

परिसर *parisara*, i.e. *pari-sṛi + a*, I. adj. Encompassing, Megh. 68. II. m. **1.** Border, Pañch. 25, 3. **2.** Proximity, Vikr. d. 119. **3.** Standing-place, Suçr. 2, 166, 21.—**Comp.** *Godâvarî-*, adj. being near the Godâvarî, Utt. Râmach. 56, 2.

परिसर्पण *parisarpaṇa*, i. e. *pari-sṛip + ana*, n. **1.** Creeping, Mṛichchh. 46, 13. **2.** Walking about. **3.** Running to and fro, Mṛichchh. 15, 20.

परिसर्पिन् *parisarpin*, i. e. *pari-sṛip + in*, adj. Moving about.

परिसान्त्वन *pari-sântv + ana*, n. Consoling, Utt. Râmach. 5, 9.

परिसाधन *pari-sâdh + ana*, n. **1.** Performing. **2.** Settling, Man. 8, 188.

परिस्कन्द *pari-skand + a*, m. A servant.

परिस्तर *paristara*, i.e. *pari-stṛi + a*, m. **1.** A layer. **2.** A cover (?), MBh. 5, 5246.

परिस्तोम *pari-stoma*, m. (n. MBh. 6, 2287), A cover, a bolster.

परिस्पन्द *pari-spand + a*, m. **1.** Motion, Bhâshâp. 122. **2.** Attention to, MBh. 13, 6438.

परिस्पर्धिन् *pari-spardh + in*, adj. Emulating.

परिस्यन्द *pari-syand + a*, m. Flow, stream (figuratively), Bhartṛ. 1, 6.

परिस्रव *parisrava*, i.e. *pari-sru + a*, m. **1.** A river, a torrent, MBh. 7, 6437. **2.** Birth (of a child), Râm. 1, 38, 26 (erroneously *pariçrava*).

परिहर्षण *pariharshaṇa*, i. e. *pari-hṛish*, Caus., + *ana*, adj., f. *ṇî*, Causing much pleasure, MBh. 9, 582.

परिहाटक *pari-hâṭaka*, n. A ring worn on the arms or legs, MBh. 4, 453.

परिहाणि *parihâṇi*, i.e. *pari-hâ + ni*, f. Decreasing.

परिहार and **परीहार** *parîhâra*, i.e. *pari-hṛi + a*, m. 1. Avoiding, MBh. 12, 848. 2. Escaping, Hariv. 577. 3. Abandoning, Vikr. 32, 15. 4. Removing. 5. Reserve, MBh. 13, 5116. 6. Concealment, Çâk. 39, 9 (ed. Will.). 7. Leaving out. 8. Largess, Man. 7, 201. 9. A space round a town or village left for pasture, Man. 8, 237.

परिहारिन् *parihârin*, i. e. *pari-hṛi + in*, adj. Avoiding.

परिहास and **परीहास** *parîhâsa*, i.e. *pari-has + a*, m. 1. Jest, Vikr. 13, 1; pleasantry, Nal. 11, 8. 2. Deriding, mocking, Pańch. iii. d. 261.

परीक्षक *parîkshaka*, i.e. *pari-îksh + aka*, m. An examiner, one who knows well, Pańch. i. d. 88.

परीक्षण *parîkshaṇa*, i.e. *pari-îksh + ana*, n. and f. *ṇâ*, Examination, Man. 1, 117.

परीक्षा *parîkshâ*, i.e. *pari-îksh + a*, f. Examination, test, Man. 9, 19.—Comp. *Nishparîksha*, i.e. *nis-*, adj. not examining.

परीक्षित् *parîkshit*, see *parikshit*.

परीक्षिन् *parîkshin*, i.e. *pari-îksh + in*, m. An examiner, Yâjń. 2, 241.

परीणाह *parîṇâha*, **परीताप** *parîtâpa*, **परीतोष** *parîtosha*, **परीदाह** *parîdâha*, **परीधान** *parîdhâna*, **परीपाक** *parîpâka*, see **परिण°** *pariṇâha*, etc., with *i*.

परीप्सा *parîpsâ*, i.e. *pari-îpsa*, desider. of *âp*, + *a*, f. Wish to obtain, to maintain, to preserve, Bhâg. P. 9, 4, 49.

परीप्सु *parîpsu*, i.e. *pari-îpsa*, desider. of *âp*, + *u*, adj. Wishing to maintain, to preserve, Bhâg. P. 1, 7, 18.

परीमाण *parîmâṇa*, **परीवर्त** *parîvarta*, **परीवाद** *parîvâda*, **परीवाह** *parîvâha*, **परीहार** *parîhâra*, **परीहास** *parîhâsa*, see **परिमा°** *parimâ°*, etc., with *i*.

परुत् *parut*, i.e. *para-vat* (a word occurring only in compounds, cf. *saṁvat*), adv., Last year.—Cf. πέρυσι, πέρυτις, ἔτος.

परुष *parusha*, i.e. *parus + a*, adj., f. *shâ*. 1. Knotty, huge, Vikr. d. 142. 2. Variegated, spotted. 3. Soiled, Râm. 2, 71, 34. 4. Rough, rugged, Râjat. 4, 308. 5. Harsh, MBh. 1, 7090. 6. Severe, Böhtl. Ind. Spr. 1314. 7. Coarse, Yâjń. 1, 309.

परुषित *parushita*, i.e. *parusha + ita*, adj., Used roughly, Hit. i. d. 81.

परुस् *parus*, i.e. *prî + vant* (cf. *parvan* and *parvata*), n. The knot or joint of a plant.—Comp. *Tri-*, m. a surname of Vishṇu.

परोक्ष *paroksha*, i.e. *paras-aksha*, I. adj., f. *shâ*. 1. Being beyond sight, invisible, imperceptible, Bhâg. P. 2, 1, 12. 2. Unknown, strange, Çâk. 108, 17. II. *ksham*, acc. and loc. *kshe*, 1. In one's absence, Man. 2, 199. 2. Imperceptibly, Pańch. 46, 7. 3. Surreptitiously, 112, 22. III. m. A proper name.—Comp. *A-*, I. adj. not imperceptible, Daçak. in Chr. 182, 24 (although not [quite] imperceptible, [nevertheless] perceivable only by one's self). II. *ksham*, adv. in one's view. Hence the denominative *aparokshaya*, to make visible, MBh. 1, 781.

परोक्षता *paroksha + tâ*, f. Obscurity, MBh. 3, 2820.

परोक्षत्व *paroksha+tva*, n. Want of perceptibility, Vedântas. in Chr. 213, 4.

परोपकारित्व *paropakâritva*, i. e. *para-upakârin + tva*, n. Supporting others, Bhartṛ. Suppl. 13.

पर्कटिन् *parkaṭin*, m., and **पर्कटी** *parkaṭî*, f. The waved-leaf fig tree, Ficus infectoria, Hit. 38, 10, M.M.

पर्जन्य *parjanya* (and incorrectly **पर्यन्य** *paryanya*), probably *sphurj*, for old *sparj*, *+ana+ya*, m. **1.** A rain-threatening cloud, Ragh. 17, 15. **2.** Rain, Bhag. 3, 14. **3.** The deity of rain.

† **पर्ण्** *PARṆ*, i. 10 (rather a denomin. derived from *parṇa*), Par. To be green.

पर्ण *parṇa*, perhaps *pṛî+na*, **I.** n. **1.** A wing. **2.** A feather, MBh. 1, 1517. **3.** A leaf, Nal. 16, 12. **II.** m. A tree, Butea frondosa Roxb. **III.** f. *ṇî*, An aquatic plant, Pistia stratiotes Lin. —Comp. *Açva-*, adj. having horses serving for wings, Chr. 293, 1=Rigv. i. 88, 1. *Ṛitu-*, m. a proper name, Nal. 8, 25. *Tâmra-parṇî*, f. 1. the name of a river. 2. the name of a town in Ceylon. *Çrî-*, I. n. 1. a lotus. 2. a tree, Premna spinosa. II. f. *ṇî*, the name of several plants. *Saptap°*, i. e. *saptan-*, I. adj. seven-leaved. II. m. a tree, Alstonia scholaris, Lass. Anth. 25, 14. III. n. a sort of sweetmeat. *Su-*, I. m. 1. Garuḍa. 2. a cock. II. f. *ṇâ* and *ṇî*, 1. a number of lotusses. 2. the mother of Garuḍa. *Tri-su-*, adj. conversant with hymns called trisuparṇa, Man. 3, 185. *Sûpa-*, f. *ṇî*, a sort of bean.—Cf. O.H.G. farn; A.S. fearn; perhaps Πάρνης, Παρνασός, Παρνασσός; perhaps Lat. penna (but cf. *pat*).

पर्णवन्त् *parṇa+vant*, adj., f. *vatî*, Abounding in leaves, Kathâs. 30, 10.

पर्णिन् *parṇin*, i.e. *parṇa+in*, **I.** m. A tree, MBh. 12, 5858. **II.** f. *inî*. **1.** A certain plant. **2.** The name of an Apsaras.

पर्णोटज *parṇoṭaja*, i. e. *parṇa-uṭaja*, n. A hut of leaves, Utt. Râmach. 46, 6.

† **पर्द्** *PARD*, i. 1, Âtm. To fart. —Cf. πέρδω, ἔπαρδον, πορδή; O.H.G. ferzan.

† **पर्ब्** *PARB*, i. 1, Par. To go, to move.

पर्यक् *paryak* (acc. sing. n. of *pari-añch*), adv. Round about.—Cf. πέριξ.

पर्यगु *paryagu*, see *pâramahaṁsya-pari*.

पर्यङ्क *paryaṅka*, i.e. *pari-aṅka*, m. **1.** A couch-bed, a bed, Pañch. i. d. 190. **2.** Sitting on one's legs in the oriental manner, Kumâras. 3, 45.

पर्यट *paryaṭa*, and comp. *apara-*, m. Names of peoples.

पर्यटन *paryaṭana*, i.e. *pari-aṭ+ana*, n. Wandering about, strolling, Pañch. 163, 22.

पर्यन्त *paryanta*, i.e. *pari-anta*, **I.** m. **1.** A boundary, MBh. 13, 5225. **2.** A skirt, Râm. 3, 55, 11. **3.** A border, Daçak. in Chr. 198, 17. **4.** End, Pañch. i. d. 141. **II.** adj., f. *tâ*, Surrounded by (its) boundary, Hariv. 9151 (with its last limits, viz. the earth.) —Comp. *A-*, and *nishparyanta*, i.e. *nis-*, adj., f. *tâ*, unbounded, boundless.

पर्यन्य *paryanya*, see *parjanya*.

पर्यय *paryaya*, i.e. *pari-i* + *a*, m. 1. Expiration (of a period), Man. 11, 27. 2. Loss (of time), Râm. 1, 24, 11. 3. Change, Man. 1, 30. 4. Confounding, MBh. 12, 449.

पर्ययण *paryayaṇa*, i.e. *pari-i* + *ana*, n. Walking round.

पर्यवसान *paryavasâna*, i.e. *pari-ava-so* + *ana*, n. Conclusion, end, Hit. 116, 20.

पर्यवसानिक *paryavasânika*, i.e. *paryavasâna* + *ika*, adj. Inclining towards (its) end, MBh. 12, 12953.

पर्यवसायिन् *paryavasâyin*, i. e. *pari-ava-so* + *in*, adj., f. *nî*, Ending, Utt. Râmach. 157, 7.

पर्यवस्कन्द *paryavaskanda*, i.e. *pari-ava-skand* + *a*, m. Jumping down, MBh. 6, 3319.

पर्यवस्थातृ *paryavasthâtṛi*, i.e. *pari-ava-sthâ* + *tṛi*, m. An adversary, MBh. 2, 880.

पर्यश्रु *paryaçru*, i.e. *pari-açru*, adj. Tearful, Chr. 5, 3.

पर्याकुलत्व *paryâkulatva*, i.e. *pari-âkula* + *tva*, n. Confusion, Kumâras. 2, 25.

पर्याण *paryâṇa*, i.e. *pari-yâ* + *ana*, n. A saddle.

पर्याप्ति *paryâpti*, i.e. *pari-âp* + *ti*, f. 1. Sufficiency, enough, Kathâs. 26, 199. 2. Dexterity, Kathâs. 26, 47.

पर्याय *paryâya*, i.e. *pari-i* + *a*, m. 1. Expiration (of time), Hariv. 4791. 2. Change, MBh. 6, 3745. 3. Regular order, return, 4, 612. 4. Repetition, Hariv. 9647. 5. Succession, Böhtl. Ind. Spr. 1424. 6. Turn, MBh. 13, 4755. 7. Manner. 8. A synonyme, Pańch. ii. d. 107. 9. *yeṇa*, instr. Alternately.

पर्यायशस् *paryâya* + *ças*, adv. 1. Periodically. 2. Seriatim, MBh. 13, 4755.

पर्यावर्त *paryâvarta*, i.e. *pari-â-vṛit* + *a*, m. Return, Bhâg. P. 6, 9, 38.

पर्यास *paryâsa*, i.e. *pari-2. as* + *a*, m. Rotation, Mârk. P. 54, 2.

पर्यासन *paryâsana*, i.e. *pari-2. as*, Caus., + *ana*, n. Revolution, MBh. 8, 4478.

पर्युक्षण *paryukshaṇa*, i.e. *pari-uksh* + *ana*, n. Sprinkling.

पर्युपासक *paryupâsaka*, i. e. *pari-upa-âs* + *aka*, m. One who honours or respects, Bhâg. P. 1, 12, 25.

पर्युपासन *paryupâsana*, i.e. *pari-upa-âs* + *ana*, n. Honouring somebody.

पर्युपासितृ *paryupâsitṛi*, i.e. *pari-upa-âs* + *tṛi*, m. One who honours, MBh. 2, 2436.

पर्येषण *paryeshaṇa*, i.e. *pari-ish* + *ana*, n. Investigating, searching, MBh. 3, 16213.

† **पर्व्** *PARV*, i. 1, Par. To fill.—Cf. *pṛi*.

ऽ**पर्व** -*parva*, a substitute for *parvan* as latter part of a comp. adj., f. *vâ*, e.g. *karkaça-*, One whose (fingers') joints are hard. *tri-*, Having three knots.

पर्वण *parvaṇa*, i.e. *parvan* + *a*, I. m. The name of a demon. II. f. *ṇî*. 1. The periodical change of the moon, MBh. 13, 6061. 2. A disease of the eye.—Comp. *Karma-parvaṇî*, i.e. *karman-*, adj., f. holding the links of (the chain) of works, Bhâg. P. 5, 17, 24.

पर्वत *parvata*, i.e. *parvant* (the original form of *parvan*) + *a*, m. 1. A mountain, Megh. 23. 2. A proper name.—Comp. *Agni-*, m. a volcano.

Amara-, and *Indra-*, m. names of mountains. *Uttara-*, m. the northern ridge of mountains. *Jambu-*, m. = *Jambu* **2.** *Varsha-*, m. A mountainous range supposed to separate the Varshas, or divisions of the globe, from each other.

पर्वतीय *parvatîya*, i.e. *parvata* + *îya*, adj. Referring to a mountain, growing on, ruling over, a mountain, Hariv. 2668.—**Comp.** *A-*, adj. situated in a plain, Râm. 4, 44, 106.

पर्वन् *parvan*, i.e. *prî* + *vant* (cf. *parus* and *parvata*), n. **1.** A knot, a joint in a cane or plant in general, Böhtl. Ind. Spr. 413. **2.** A joint of the body, Çâk. d. 80. **3.** A limb, Vikr. d. 112. **4.** A section, a division, especially of a book, MBh. i. ii. etc. **5.** The days of the four periodic changes of the moon, particularly the days of conjunction and opposition, Man. 3, 45. **6.** The sacrifice performed at these days. **7.** A festival.—**Comp.** *A-*, n. a day which is not *parvan* (see **5** and **7**). *Su-*, m. 1. a bamboo. 2. an arrow. 3. = **5** and **7**. 4. a deity. 5. smoke.

पर्विणी *parviṇî*, i.e. *parvan* + *in* + *î*, f. A festival, Râjat. 4, 242.

† **पर्ष्** *PARSH*, or **वर्ष्** *VARSH*, **स्पर्ष्** *SPARSH*, i. 1, Âtm. To grow wet.

पर्षद् *parshad* = *parishad* (q. cf.), f. An assembly, Bhâg. P. 3, 14, 23.

† **पल्** *PAL*, i. 1, Par. To go, to move. i. 10, *pâlaya*, see **2.** *pâ*.—Cf. πάλλω; Lat. pello (both Caus.); O.H.G. fallan; A.S. feallan.

पल *pala*, n. **1.** A weight = 4 karshas, Man. 8, 135. **2.** Flesh, Yâjń. 3, 215.—**Comp.** *Daça(n)-*, n. ten palas.

पलल *palala*, n. (and m.). **1.** Pounded sesamum, Hariv. 7362. **2.** Mire, mud, Râm. 5, 87, 26.

पलाण्डु *palâṇḍu*, m. and n. An onion, Man. 5, 5.

पलाय् *palây*, see vb. *i*, with the prep. *palâ*.

पलायन *palâyana*, i.e. *palâ* (for *parâ*) *-i* + *ana*, n. Flight, running away, Pańch. 63, 9.

पलायिन् *palâyin*, i.e. *palâ* (for *parâ*) *-i* + *in*, adj. Running away, showing the heels, MBh. 12, 3719.

पलाल *palâla*, I. m. and n. **1.** Straw, Man. 5, 122. **2.** The stalk of Sorghum. **II.** f. *lâ*, A proper name.

पलाश *palâça*, I. n. **1.** A leaf. **2.** Foliage, MBh. 3, 1400. **II.** m. A tree bearing red blossoms, Butea frondosa.—**Comp.** *Sa-*, adj., f. *çâ*, together with a Butea frondosa.

पलाशिन् *palâçin*, i.e. *palâça* + *in*, **I.** adj., f. *nî*, Leafy, MBh. 1, 1775. **II.** m. The name of a town. **III.** f. *nî*, The name of a river.

ऽपलिक *-palika*, i.e. *-pala* + *ika*, latter part of comp. adj. preceded by numerals, Weighing (so many) palas, Yâjń. 2, 105.

पलित *palita*, I. adj., f. *iknî* (and *tâ*), Grey, MBh. 7, 5089. **II.** n. Grey hair, Man. 6, 2.—Cf. πελιδνός, πελιός, πελός, πελλός, πολιός; Lat. pullus, pallidus, pallere; O.H.G. falw; A.S. fealo, falu, fealwe, falewe.

पलितिन् *palitin*, i.e. *palita* + *in*, adj. Grey-haired.

पल्पूल् *PALPÛL* (perhaps an old anomal. frequent. of *pal*; cf. *char*, *chańchûrya*, *phal pamphul*, *trî*, ved. *tartur*, etc.), i. 10, Par., ved. **1.** To tan. **2.** To cleanse. † पल्यूल् *PALYÛL,* and † पल्युल् *PALYUL,* † वल्यूल् *VALYÛL,* † वल्युल् *VALYUL,* i. 10, Par. **1.** To purify. **2.** To cut.

† पल्ल् *PALL,* i. 1, Par. To go, to move.

पल्लल *pallala,* see *palvala.*

पल्लव *pallava,* probably for original *parṇa + vant,* **1.** m. and n. A sprout, a shoot, Çâk. d. 34. **2.** m. pl. The name of a people. **3.** The red dye of lac; cf. *pallavita.*—**Comp.** *Aṁçuka-,* m. and. n. a scarf. *Kara-* and *pâṇi-,* m. and n. the fingers. *Sa-,* adj. together with shoots, Ṛit. 6, 16.

पल्लवय *PALLAVAYA,* a denomin. derived from *pallava* with *aya,* Par. **1.** To get new shoots, Häberl. Anth. 238, 6. **2.** To extend, Gît. 1, 4.

पल्लवित *pallavita,* i.e. *pallava + ita,* and पल्लविन् *pallavin,* i.e. *pallava + in* adj. **1.** Having young shoots, Kumâras. 3, 54. **2.** Possessing the red dye of lac, Vikr. d. 141 (*prabhâ-,* having its own radiance instead of the red dye).

पल्वल *palvala,* sometimes incorrectly पल्लल *pallala,* akin to *palita* (cf. O.H.G. falw), n. (and m.), A small pond, Pańch. 142, 13.—Cf. Lat. palus, πηλός, perhaps A.S. pol, pool.

† पव् *PAV,* i. 1, Âtm. To go (v.r.).

पव *pava,* i.e. *pû + a,* n. Cowdung.

पवन *pavana,* i.e. *pû + ana,* I. m. **1.** Wind, air, Çâk. d. 55. **2.** A potter's kiln, Böhtl. Ind. Spr. 117. **3.** A proper name. **II.** m. (or n.) The sacred fire.—**Comp.** *Danta-,* n. A small piece of wood for cleaning the teeth with.

पवमान *pavamâna* (properly ptcple. of the pres. Âtm. of *pû,* i. 1), m. **1.** Wind, Ragh. 8, 9. **2.** Agni, the deified fire. **3.** The moon.

पवि *pavi,* m. **1.** The iron band of a wheel (ved.). **2.** The thunderbolt of Indra, Çatr. 14, 219. Perhaps akin to Lat. pavire puvire; παίω, πταίω.

पवित्र *pavitra,* i.e. *pû + tra,* **I.** n. **1.** A means of purifying, Man. 11, 85. **2.** Sacrificial grass, Man. 2, 75. **3.** Prayer, Man. 11, 225. **II.** m. pl. The name of a class of deities. **III.** f. *trâ,* The name of a river. **IV.** adj., f. *trâ.* **1.** Purifying, Râm. 1, 1, 94. **2.** Pure, Man. 3, 235.—**Comp.** *A-,* adj. Impure, Pańch. 169, 17.

पवित्रक *pavitra + ka,* **I.** n. The vessel in which an Argha or oblation is presented (?), Yâjń. 1, 250. **II.** As latter part of comp. adj., a substitute for *pavitra.*—**Comp.** *Sa-,* adj. Containing sacrificial grass, Yâjń. 1, 230.

पवित्रता *pavitra + tâ,* f., and पवित्रत्व *pavitra + tva,* n. Purity, Utt. Râmach. 168, 14.

पवित्रय *PAVITRAYA,* a denomin. derived from *pavitra* with *aya,* Par. To purify.

पवित्रिन् *pavitrin,* i.e. *pavitra + in,* adj. **1.** Purifying, MBh. 1, 1543. **2.** Pure.

पश् *PAÇ,* i. 10 *pâçaya,* Par. To bind. *pâçita,* Bound, Hariv. 3536.—With the prep. अव *ava,* ptcple. of the pf. pass. *avapâçita,* Bound, Râm. 3, 59, 18; cf. *dṛiç,* and *spaç.*—Cf. probably Goth. fahan; A.S. fón with feng; O.H.G. fahan with fang, fôgjan;

A.S. fegan; Goth. fahjan; O.H.G. gafagjan; A.S. ge-fegan; Lat. pac in paciscor, dispesco for dis-pec + sco, compesco.

पशव्य *paçavya,* i.e. *paçu+ya,* adj. 1. Fit for cattle. 2. Brutish, Bhâg. P. 8, 5, 42, with *kâma,* sexual intercourse.

पशु *paç+u,* m. 1. Cattle (viz. neat-cattle, horses, goats, sheep, asses, and dogs), Man. 10, 48. 2. A beast, Böhtl. Ind. Spr. 304. 3. An animal to be immolated, Râm. 1, 61, 8.—Comp. *Ghṛita-,* m. the image of a beast formed with clarified butter, Man. 5, 37. *Deva-,* m. cattle consecrated to a deity. *Nara-,* and *purusha-,* m. a beast-like man. *Nṛi-,* m. a man destinated to be immolated. *Pishṭa-* (vb. *pish*), m. the image of a beast formed with dough, Man. 5, 37.—Cf. Goth. faihu; A.S. feoh; Lat. pecus, pecoris and pecudis; probably also πῶϋ.

पशुता *paçu+tâ,* f. 1. The condition of cattle, Man. 3, 104. 2. The condition of an animal destined to be immolated.

पशुत्व *paçu+tva,* n. 1. Bestiality, Prab. 59, 11. 2. The condition of an animal destined to be immolated.

पशुमन्त् *paçu+mant,* adj., f. *matî,* 1. Abounding in cattle, MBh. 2, 798. 2. Possessing many flocks, 4, 1162.

पशुमारक *paçu-mâra + ka,* adj. Accompanied by immolation of animals, Bhâg. P. 4, 27, 11.

पशुसमाम्नायिक *paçusamâmnâyika,* i.e. *paçu-samâmnâya+ika,* adj. Read of in the books on animal sacrifices, Utt. Râmach. 114, 3.

पश्चात् *paçchât,* abl. sing. of the ved. adj. *paçcha,* i.e. *apas* (=*apa*) *-añch+a* (cf. *tiraçchîna*), I. adv. 1. Behind, Man. 2, 196. 2. From behind, Böhtl. Ind. Spr. 1235. 3. After, afterwards, Man. 8, 164. 4. Backwards, Yâjñ. 2, 299. 5. Westward, Megh. 16. II. prep. with gen. and abl. After, Man. 3, 116.—Cf. probably Lat. postid-ea, post; akin is also pone for pos-ne, perhaps ὀπίσσω.

पश्चात्तापिन् *paçchâttâpin,* i.e. *paçchât-tâpa+in,* adj. Repenting, Yâjñ. 3, 221.

पश्चार्ध *paçchârdha,* i.e. *paçcha* (cf. *paçchât*) *-ardha,* m. Hind-part, Çâk. d. 7.

पश्चिम *paçchima,* i.e. *paçcha* (cf. *paçchât*) *+ima,* adj., f. *mâ.* 1. Hinder, last; with *saṁdhyâ,* The evening twilight, Man. 2, 101; with *kriyâ,* Obsequies. 2. Western, west, Man. 2, 22. —Comp. *A-,* adj. 1. last. 2. extreme. *Dakshiṇa-,* adj. south-western.

पश्चिमतस् *paçchima + tas,* adv. From behind, MBh. 4, 2108.

† **पष्** *PASH,* i. 1, Par. Âtm., v. r. of *spaç,* q. cf. i. 10, *pashaya,* Par. 1. To bind. 2. To hinder. 3. To touch. 4. To go (v.r. *paç*). i. 10, *pâshaya,* Par. To bind (v.r.).

† **पस्** *PAS,* i. 1, Par. Âtm. v.r. of *spaç,* q. cf. i. 10, Par. *pâsaya,* To bind (v.r.)

पह्लव *pahlava,* n. The name of a people, the Persians.

1. **पा** *PA,* i. 1, base of the pres. *piba, piva,* Par. (in epic poetry also Âtm.), 1. To drink, Man. 4, 63. 2. with *rajas,* To quaff dust, Man. 11, 110. 3. To enjoy, e.g. with *chakshushâ,* Megh. 16. 4. (figuratively) To swallow up, Pañch. iii. d. 233. Ptcple. of the pf. pass., *pîta,* 1. Drunk. 2. Enjoyed. 3. Swallowed up, squandered away, Râjat. 5,

421. 4. Having drunk, Kathâs. 39, 57. 5. Filled. Ptcple. of the fut. pass., *peya*, Drinkable. I. n. Drink, beverage, Pańch. 47, 8 (at the end of a comp. adj., *nânâ-prakâra-vastra-pushpa-bhakshya-peya*, Accompanied by garments, flowers, food, and drink of different kinds). II. f. *yâ*, Rice gruel. *pânîya*, Drinkable. n. 1. Beverage. 2. Water, Man. 8, 326. Comp. *A*-, adj. not drinkable. Caus. *pâyaya*, To cause to drink, MBh. 1, 192. Desider. *pipâsa*, To desire to drink, MBh. 7, 705. Ptcple. of the pf. pass., *pipâsita*, Thirsty, 3, 17247. Frequentat. *pepiya*, 1. To drink repeatedly or greedily. 2. To be drunk greedily (pass., probably to be corrected to *pepîyya*), Bhâg. P. 5, 8, 1; Hariv. 8798.—With the prep. अति *ati*, Caus. To cause to drink plenty of (acc.).—With अनु *anu*, 1. To drink after or afterwards, Ragh. 8, 67. 2. To drink of, Râm. 2, 104, 5 Gorr. —With अभि *abhi*, To drink of.—With आ *â*, 1. To drink up, Râm. 3, 55, 9. 2. To drink. 3. To imbibe (figuratively) with one's ears, Bhâg. P. 3, 13, 49. . Caus. To cause to imbibe, Bhâg. P. 1, 18, 12.— With समा *sam-â*, 1. To imbibe, Kâm. Nît. 12, 48. 2. To press, to impoverish, MBh. 12, 3307.—With नि *ni*, 1. To sip in, Râm. 2, 95, 18. 2. To drink. 3. To absorb, Bhâg. P. 3, 10, 6. Caus. To cause to sip in, Bhâg. P. 8, 2, 25. —With निस् *nis*, *nishpîta*, Dried up, Râm. 2, 62, 17 Gorr.—With परि *pari*, To drink up, Ṛit. 3, 6. *paripîta*, Imbibed.—With प्र *pra*, 1. To begin to drink. 2. To drink. 3. To enjoy, Râm. 2, 45, 5.—With सम् *sam*, Caus. To cause to drink, Bhâg. P. 5, 26, 26.— Cf. Lat. bibo, potare, poculum, etc.; *πέπωκα, πῶθι, ποτός, ποταμός, πίνω* (cf. *pinv*), *πιπίσκω, πιστός*.

2. पा *PÂ*, ii. 2, Par. 1. To guard, MBh. 14, 514. 2. To preserve, Bhâg. P. 1, 3, 15. 3. To beware of (with abl.), MBh. 1, 3417. 4. To govern. Caus. and *pal*, *pâl*, i. 10, *pâlaya* (properly, a denomin. derived from *pâla*), 1. To protect, Râm. 1, 45, 29. 2. To guard as guardian, Râjat. 5, 227. 3. To cherish, Mâl. 48, 19. 4. To govern, Pańch. i. d. 253. Comp. ptcple. of the pf. pass. *nidhi-pâlita*, m. A proper name. *vasu*-, m. A proper name.—With the prep. अनु *anu*, Caus. 1. To cause to be guarded, Man. 8, 27. 2. To observe, MBh. 2, 2509; to maintain, Hariv. 3762.—With समनु *sam-anu*, Caus. 1. To observe, MBh. 12, 476. 2. To keep, Râm. 2, 26, 27.—With अभि *abhi*, Caus. To assist, MBh. 3, 8472.—With समभि *sam-abhi*, Caus. To govern, Hariv. 5233.—With नि *ni*, To protect, Râm. 5, 81, 22. Caus. To govern, Râm. 1, 6, 29 Gorr.—With परि *pari*, 1. To protect, MBh. 1, 8413. 2. To maintain, Bhâg. P. 3, 1, 36. Caus. 1. To protect, to guard, to govern. 2. To maintain, to keep, Chr. 3, 5. 3. To expect, to wait, Râm. 2, 70, 13.—With प्र *pra*, To beware of (with abl.), Bhâg. P. 6, 8, 17. Caus. To protect.—With प्रति *prati*, Caus. 1. To protect, MBh. 1, 4080. 2. To maintain, to observe, 1, 3521. 3. To expect, to wait, Çâk. 9, 4. — With संप्रति *sam-prati*, Caus. To wait.—With सम् *sam*, 1. Caus. To protect, MBh. 12, 2667. 2. To maintain, to keep, MBh. 3, 15249. 3. To overcome, MBh.

4, 2321. 2.*pâ* is akin to 1.*pâ*; the link between the signification To drink and To protect is formed by the signification To nourish.—Cf. *πάομαι*, *πῶμα*, akin is also *πατέομαι*; Goth. fôdjan; A.S. foda; Lat. pasco, pabulum; *βόσκω*, *ποιμήν*.

पांशु *pâṁçu* and **पांशुल** *pâṁçula*, see *pâṁsu*, *pâṁsula*.

पांसन *pâṁsana*, latter part of comp. adj., f. *nî* (and *nâ*), Disgracing, Hiḍ. 1, 39.

पांसव *pâṁsava*, i.e. *pâṁsu*+*a*, adj. Consisting of dust, Bhâg. P. 3, 19, 18.

पांसु *pâṁsu*, and **पांशु** *pâṁçu*, m. **1.** Dust, Man. 4, 102. **2.** A particle of dust, Man. 4, 168.

पांसुक *pâṁsu*+*ka*, m., pl. Dust.

पांसुल *pâṁsu*+*la*, and **पांशुल** *pâṁçula*, adj. **1.** Dusty, covered with dust, Râm. 2, 43, 30 Gorr. **2.** Disgraced, Çâk. d. 125. **3.** Disgracing (?), Râm. 5, 88, 13.—**Comp.** *Vana-*, m. a hunter.

पाक *pâka*, i.e. *pach*+*a*, m. **1.** Cooking, baking, MBh. 3, 15551. **2.** Food, Man. 3, 104. **3.** Burning (as pots, bricks), 5, 122. **4.** Digestion. **5.** Ripening, maturing, Vikr. d. 90. **6.** The appearance of the consequences, e.g. of an action, Pañch. 129, 13. **7.** Fulfilling, accomplishment. **8.** Inflammation. **9.** The name of a demon.—**Comp.** *Karma*(*n*)-, m. the requital for actions done in a former existence, Pañch. i. d. 417. *Kiṁpâka*, i.e. *kim-*, m. a kind of cucumber; n. its fruit. *Kumbhî-*, m. sing. and pl. the name of a hell in which the wicked are baked like potters' vessels, Man. 12, 76. *Punaḥpâka*, i.e. *punar-*, m. repeated burning. *Puras-*, adj. of which the fulfilment is imminent on. *Havya-* (vb. *hu*), m. 1. an oblation dressed for the gods. **2.** the vessel it is prepared in.

पाकज *pâka-ja*, adj. Produced by maturing.—**Comp.** *A-*, adj. not produced by maturing.

पाकजत्व *pâkaja*+*tva*, n. Capability of being affected by contact with fire, Bhâshâp. 104.

पाकशासन *pâka-çâsana*, m. A name of Indra, Vikr. 89, 1 (chastiser of *Pâka*, see *pâka* **9**).

पाकशासनि *pâkaçâsani*, i.e. *pâka-çâsana*+*i*, patronym., m. A son of Indra, a surname of Arjuna, Johns. Sel. 17, 72.

पाकिन् *pâkin*, i.e. *pach*+*in*, latter part of comp. adj., f. *nî*, Maturing, being digested.

पाकिम *pâkima*, i.e. *pâka*+*ima*, adj. Prepared by cooking, baking, or evaporation (as salt).

पाक्य *pâkya*, i.e. *pâka*+*ya*, adj., n. A kind of salt.

पाक्षिक *pâkshika*, i.e. *paksha*+*ika*, adj., f. *kî*, Belonging to a fortnight, MBh. 14, 2513.

पाङ्क्तेय *pâṅkteya*, and **पाङ्क्त्य** *pâṅktya*, i.e. *paṅkti*+*eya* or *ya*, adj. Worthy to belong to a respectable society, Man. 3, 176.—**Comp.** *A-*, adj. inadmissible into society, Man. 3, 170.

पाचक *pâchaka*, i.e. *pach*+*aka*, I. adj., f. *chikâ*. **1.** Cooking, Böhtl. Ind. Spr. 1787. **2.** Effecting digestion. II. m., f. *chikâ*, A cook.

पाचन *pâchana*, i.e. *pach*+*ana*, I. adj. Digestive. II. n. **1.** A warm cataplasm. **2.** A digestive.

पाञ्चजन *pâñchajana*, i.e. *pañchan*

-jana + *a*, patronym., m. and f. *nî*, A son or daughter of Pańchajana.

पाञ्चजन्य *pâńchajanya*, i.e. *pańchan-jana* + *ya*, m. **1.** Kṛishṇa's conch, Bhag. 1, 15. **2.** The name of a part of Jambu-dvîpa.

पाञ्चदश्य *pâńchadaçya*, i.e. *pańcha-daçî* + *ya* (cf. *daça*), adj. Used at the fifteenth day of a half month, Bhâg. P. 6, 4, 27.

पाञ्चनख *pâńchanakha*, i.e. *pańchan-nakha* + *a*, adj. Made of the skin of an animal with five claws, MBh. 4, 1338.

पाञ्चनद *pâńchanada*, i.e. *pańchan-nada* + *a*, I. adj. Observed in Pańcha-nada, i.e. the Panjab. II. m. **1.** A prince of Pańchanada. **2.** pl. The inhabitants of Pańchanada.

पाञ्चभौतिक *pâńchabhautika*, i.e. *pańchan-bhûta* + *ika*, adj. Consisting of the five elements, Bhâg. P. 1, 6, 29.

पाञ्चयज्ञिक *pâńchayajńika*, i.e. *pańchan-yajńa* + *ika*, adj. Belonging to the five sacrifices, Man. 3, 83.

पाञ्चाल *pâńchâla*, i.e. *pańchâla* + *a*, I. adj., f. *lî*, Belonging to, referring to, ruling over, etc., the Pańchâlas. II. m. pl. The Pańchâlas. III. f. *lî*, A surname of Draupadî.

पाञ्चालक *pâńchâla* + *ka*, adj., f. *likâ*, Belonging to the Pańchâlas.

पाञ्चालेय *pâńchâleya*, i.e. *pańchâ-la* + *eya*, m. A prince of the Pańchâlas.

पाञ्चाल्य *pâńchâlya*, i.e. *pańchâla* + *ya*, I. adj. Belonging to the Pańchâlas. II. m. A prince of the Pańchâlas, Johns. Sel. 5, 26.

पाटक *pâṭaka*, i.e. *paṭ* + *aka*, m. One who divides, Hariv. 9767.

पाटच्चर *pâṭachchara*, i.e. *paṭach-chara* + *a*, m. A thief, a robber.

पाटन *pâṭana*, i.e. *paṭ* + *ana*, n. **1.** Ripping up, slitting up, Mârk. P. 14, 88. **2.** Opening, Böhtl. Ind. Spr. 1405.

पाटल *pâṭala*, I. adj., f. *lâ*. **1.** Of a pale red colour, Ragh. 7, 24. **2.** Pallid, Çâk. d. 182. II. m. **1.** Pale red, rose colour, Ragh. 4, 68. **2.** A kind of rice ripening in the rains. **3.** A proper name. **4.** The tree of trumpet flower, Bignonia suaveolens. III. f. *lâ*, The tree and its flower. IV. n. Its flower, Pańch. i. d. 152.—Comp. *Satâ-pâṭala*, m. the red mane of a lion, Râjat. 5, 332.

पाटलि *pâṭali*, I. m. and f., and

पाटली *pâṭalî*, f. **1.** Trumpet flower, Bignonia suaveolens. II. *pâṭalî*, f. **1.** The name of a tree. **2.** A proper name.

पाटलिमन् *pâṭaliman*, i.e. *pâṭala* + *iman*, m. Pale red, rose colour, Prab. 85, 2.

पाटव *pâṭava*, i.e. *paṭu* + *a*, n. **1.** Sharpness, energy. **2.** Cleverness, dexterity, Hit. pr. d. 2. **3.** Quickness, precipitation, Kathâs. 5, 89.

पाठ *pâṭha*, i.e. *paṭh* + *a*, m. **1.** Reading, recital, Kathâs. 2, 36. **2.** A text.—Comp. *Vandipâṭha*, i. e. *vandin-*, m. a panegyric, an eulogium.

पाठक *pâṭhaka*, i.e. *paṭh* + *aka*, m. **1.** A student, one who is conversant with a science, Pańch. 165, 2. **2.** A preceptor. — Comp. *Dharma-*, m. one who has applied himself most assiduously to the Dharmaçâstra, Man. 12, 111. *Nakshatra-*, m. an astrologer, Châṇ. 88 in Berl. Monatsb. *Madana-*, m. the Indian cuckoo. *Stuti-*, m. a panegyrist, a herald.

पाठवन्त् *pâṭha* + *vant*, adj. Learned.

पाठिन् *pâṭhin*, i.e. *pâṭha* + *in*, adj. **1.** Having studied, MBh. 5, 1668. **2.** Conversant with.

पाठीन *pâṭhîna*, m. A sort of fish, Silurus boalis Ham.

पाण *pâṇa*, i.e. *paṇ* + *a*, m. A stake (at a game), MBh. 2, 2037.

पाणि *pâṇi*, perhaps akin to *parṇa*, m. The hand, Man. 2, 63.—**Comp.** *A-rikta-* (vb. *rich*), adj. not empty-handed. *Chakra-*, m. a name of Vishṇu (holding a discus in one hand). *Daṇḍa-*, m. 1. a name of Yama. 2. a proper name. *Dhanushpâṇi*, i.e. *dhanus-*, adj. armed with a bow. *Rathâṅga*, i. e. *ratha-aṅga-* (= *chakra*), m. a name of Vishṇu. *Vajra-*, m. Indra. *Çârṅga-*, m. Vishṇu, Megh. 109.

पाणिक *pâṇi* + *ka*, **I.** m. A proper name. **II.** f. *kâ*, A kind of singing.

पाणिग्रहणिक *pâṇigrahaṇika*, i. e. *pâṇi-grahaṇa* + *ika*, **I.** adj. Nuptial, Man. 8, 226. **II.** n. A nuptial present, MBh. 1, 8015.

पाणिज *pâṇi-ja*, m. A finger-nail.

पाणिन् *pâṇin*, latter part of comp. adj. = *pâṇi*, e. g. *çastra-*, adj. Holding a weapon in one's hand. *çûla-*, adj. **I.** Wearing a lance, MBh. 3, 1622. **II.** m. pl. The name of a tribe.

पाणिनि *pâṇini*, m. The name of a great grammarian.

पाणिनीय *pâṇinîya*, i. e. *pâṇini* + *îya*, adj. Connected with, composed by, Pâṇini.

पाणिमन्त् *pâṇi* + *mant*, adj., f. *matî*, Having hands, MBh. 12, 6701.

पाण्डर *pâṇḍara*, akin to *pâṇḍu*, **I.** adj., f. *râ*, Pale, yellowish, white, Râm. 3, 2, 17 Gorr. **II.** m. **1.** The name of a mountain. **2.** The name of a Nâga or serpent.

पाण्डव *pâṇḍava*, i.e. *pâṇḍu* + *a*, **I.** patronym. A descendant of Pâṇḍu, viz. Yudhishṭhira and his four brothers. **II.** m. A partisan of the five Pâṇḍavas. **III.** adj., f. *vî*, Belonging to, connected with, the five Pâṇḍavas, MBh. 6, 3303.

पाण्डवीय *pâṇḍavîya*, i.e. *pâṇḍava* + *îya*, adj. Relating to the five Pâṇḍavas, MBh. 5, 123.

पाण्डवेय *pâṇḍaveya*, i.e. *pâṇḍu* + *eya*, **I.** patronym. A descendant of Pâṇḍu. **II.** m. A partisan of the Pâṇḍavas. **III.** adj. Belonging to, connected with, the five Pâṇḍavas (?), MBh. 8, 1634.

पाण्डित्य *pâṇḍitya*, i.e. *paṇḍita* + *ya*, n. **1.** Scholarship, learning, MBh. 5, 917. **2.** Wisdom, prudence, Böhtl. Ind. Spr. 1735.

पाण्डु *pâṇḍu*, **I.** adj. Pale, white, yellowish white, Çâk. d. 80. **II.** m. The name of a sovereign, father of Yudhishṭhira, and the other four Pâṇḍavas.—**Comp.** *Pushpa-*, m. a kind of snake. *Vi-*, adj. pale, Çiç. 9, 3.

पाण्डुक *pâṇḍu* + *ka*, m. The jaundice.

पाण्डुकिन् *pâṇḍukin*, i.e. *pâṇḍuka* + *in*, adj. Jaundiced.

पाण्डुता *pâṇḍu* + *tâ*, f., and **पाण्डुत्व** *pâṇḍu* + *tva*, n. Paleness, Megh. 66.

पाण्डुर *pâṇḍu* + *ra*, **I.** adj., f. *râ*, Of a yellowish white colour, white, pale, Bhâg. P. 8, 8, 8. **II.** m. a proper name.—**Comp.** *Â-*, adj. a little pale, Amar. 89. *Vi-*, adj. pale.

पाण्डुरता *pâṇḍura* + *tâ*, f. White colour, Pañch. 253, 2.

पाण्ड्य *pâṇḍya*, m. **1.** pl. The name

of a people and its country. **2.** A prince of the Pâṇḍyas. **3.** The name of a mountain.

पात *pâta,* i.e. *pat + a,* m. **1.** Flying, MBh. 8, 1898. **2.** Manner of flying, 3, 10646. **3.** Throwing one's self, Bhartṛ. 2, 77. **4.** Falling. **5.** A cast. **6.** A stroke. *khaḍga-,* A stroke with the sword, Kathâs. 27, 50. **7.** Case, Lass. 43, 3.—**Comp.** *Asṛikpâta,* i.e. *asṛij-,* m. drops of blood, Man. 8, 44. *Kûla-,* m. falling from the bank (of a river), Râm. 2, 103, 4. *Garbha-,* m. miscarriage. *Charaṇa-,* m. 1. laying one's self at another's feet, Pañch. 113, 2. 2. a kick, Hariv. 13607. *Dûra-,* I. m. flying far. II. adj. shooting from afar. *Dṛikpâta,* i.e. *dṛiç-,* and *dṛishṭi-,* m. a glance. *Dhârâ-,* m. a shower. *Paksha-,* m. 1. siding with somebody, MBh. 1, 5347. 2. partiality, Bhartṛ. 1, 54. *Vi-paksha-,* m. indifference. *Mahâ-,* adj. falling with great force (as an arrow). *Vartma(n)-,* m. aberration. *Vâṇa-,* m. an arrow-shot, as a measure of distance, Chr. 27, 12. *Vilochana-,* m. a glance.

पातक *pâtaka,* i.e. *pat,* Caus., + *aka,* m. and n. Sin, crime, Man. 8, 88.

पातकिन् *pâtakin,* i.e. *pâtaka + in,* adj., f. *nî,* Wicked, a criminal, Mṛichchh. 154, 24.—**Comp.** *Mahâ-,* adj. offending, or an offender, in the highest degree, Man. 9, 235.

पातङ्ग *pâtañga,* i.e. *patañga + a,* adj., f. *gî,* Peculiar to a grasshopper, Râjat. 8, 469.

पातन *pâtana,* i.e. *pat,* Caus., + *ana,* I. adj. *nî,* Cutting down, MBh. 1, 6560. II. n. Causing to fall, Man. 5, 130; with *daṇḍasya,* Chastising, Man. 7, 51; with *garbhasya,* Causing a miscarriage. —**Comp.** *Daṇḍa-,* n. chastising. *Dûra-,* n. throwing missiles from afar.

पाताल *pâtâla,* i.e. perhaps *pâta-âlaya,* n. **1.** One of the seven hells, Vedântas. in Chr. 209, 3. **2.** The regions under the earth, and the abode of the Nâgas or serpents.

पातिन् *pâtin,* i.e. *pat + in,* and *pâta + in,* adj. **1.** Flying, MBh. 8, 1911. **2.** Falling, Kathâs. 19, 29. **3.** Causing to fall.—**Comp.** *Eka-,* adj. fallen on a sudden, MBh. 1, 3032. *Daṇḍa-,* adj. inflicting punishment. *Dûra-,* adj. 1. flying far. 2. making wide ways. 3. Throwing missiles over a great distance. *Dûra-ishu-,* adj. shooting arrows over large distances. *Paksha-,* adj. siding with, partial, Mâlav. 13, 17. *Pṛishṭha-,* adj. following, Râjat. 6, 70.

पातुक *pâtuka,* i.e. *pat + uka,* adj. Disposed to fall, MBh. 12, 3444.

पातृ *pâ + tṛi,* m. **1.** One who drinks, MBh. 10, 287. **2.** A protector, Hariv. 14617.—Cf. Lat. pôtor, ποτήρ.

पात्य *pâtya,* i.e. *pati + ya,* n. Dominion, MBh. 12, 9517.

पात्र *pâ + tra,* I. n. **1.** A vessel in general, a plate, a cup, etc., Man. 5, 116. **2.** A receptacle, Kâm. Nîtis. 5, 90. **3.** The bed of a river, Râm. 2, 73, 2 Gorr. **4.** A person worthy of receiving gifts, Bhartṛ. 2, 80. **5.** A king's counsellor or minister, Râjat. 5, 304. **6.** The persons of a drama, Vikr. 3, 9. II. f. *trî.* **1.** A vessel, a plate, MBh. 1, 7215. **2.** A name of Durgâ.—**Comp.** *A-,* n. a person not worthy of receiving gifts, Bhag. 17, 22. *Uda(n)-,* n. a pot of water. *Upakroça-,* n. an object of blame, Daçak. in Chr. 192, 22. *Tâmra-,* n. a copper vessel. *Dâru-,* n. a wooden bowl. *Dûra-,* adj. having a wide bed (as a river). *Dhûpa-,* n. a box for keeping incense. *Piṇḍa-,* n. 1. the vessel in which cakes are offered to the Manes. 2. alms (properly, the pot for receiving food). *Pûrṇa-*, m. and n. 1. a full cup. 2. a measure of 256 handfulls of rice. *Prasâda-*, n. an object of favour. *Yâna-*, n. a ship, a boat, Pañch. 262, 3. *Viçvâsa-*, n. a confidential agent. *Su-*, n. 1. an earthen vessel. 2. a very fit or respectable person.—Cf. Goth. fôdr; perhaps Lat. patera.

पात्रता *pâtra + tâ*, f., and **पात्रत्व** *pâtra + tva*, n. **1.** Condition of being a receptacle, Böhtl. Ind. Spr. 1249. **2.** Condition of being worthy, Yâjñ. 1, 200; Hit. pr. d. 6, M.M.

पात्रय *PÂTRAYA*, a denomin. derived from *pâtra* with *aya*, Par. To use as drinking vessel, Böhtl. Ind. Spr. 1754.

पात्रिक *pâtrika*, i.e. *pâtra + ika*, n. and f. *kî*, A vessel, a cup, MBh. 12, 8327; Bhâg. P. 8, 18, 17.

पात्रिन् *pâtrin*, i.e. *pâtra + in*, adj. Having a vessel, Man. 6, 52.

पाथस् *pâ + thas*, n. Water, Kathâs. 27, 122.

पाथेय *pâtheya*, i.e. *pathin + eya*, n. Provisions for a journey, Vikr. d. 94. —Comp. *A-*, adj. without provisions for a journey.

पाथोज *pâthoja*, i.e. *pâthas-ja*, n. A lotus, Râjat. 4, 110.

पाथोधर *pâthodhara*, i.e. *pâthas-dhara*, m. A cloud, Râjat. 3, 202.

पाथोधि *pâthodhi*, i.e. *pâthas-dhâ* (see *payodhi*), m. The ocean, Râjat. 3, 68.

पाद् *pâd*, see 3. *pad*.

पाद *pâda*, i.e. 1. *pad + a*, m. **1.** A foot. **2.** The bottom (of a bag), Man. 2, 99. **3.** The foot of a mountain, Megh. 19. **4.** A hill at the foot of a mountain, Çâk. d. 145. **5.** The root of a tree. **6.** A ray, a beam, Pañch. i. d. 372. **7.** A quarter, Man. 8, 18. **8.** The fourth part of a çloka or strophe, Man. 2, 77. **9.** The quadrant of a circle.—**Comp.** *Adhaḥpâda*, i.e. *adhas-*, m. the sole of the feet, Pañch. 165, 16. *Ashṭa(n)-*, adj. having eight feet. *Eka-*, I. adj., f. *dâ*. 1. one-footed. 2. using only one foot. II. m. the name of a fabulous people. *Guru-*, m. the feet of a guru, i.e. of the parents or of the spiritual teacher, instead of *guru*, Bhartṛ. 2, 55. *Chandra-*, m. a moonbeam. *Jala-* (rather *jâla-*), m. a proper name. *Jâla-*, see s. v. *Deva-*, m. pl. the feet of a king, instead of a king, Pañch. 16, 6. *Dvi-*, adj., f. *dî*, biped. *Rakta-*, m. a parrot. *Çîrṇa-*, m. Yama (having shrivelled feet in consequence of a curse of his mother; cf. probably the devil with his horse's foot). *Sthûla-*, m. an elephant. *Haṁsa-*, I. m. vermilion. II. f. *dî*, a particular shrub.—Cf. Goth. fôtus; A.S. fôt.

पादक *pâda + ka*, a substitute for *pâda* when latter part of a comp. adj., f. *dikâ*, e.g. *tri-*, Three-footed, Râm. 5, 17, 30.

पादतस् *pâda + tas*, adv. **1.** Out of the feet, Man. 1, 31. **2.** At the foot (of one's bed), Man. 4, 54. **3.** =In the south-west, Man. 3, 89. **4.** By degrees (*hîna*, Each in succession is lower in rank than the preceding), Kâm. Nîtis. 12, 3.

पादप *pâda-pa* (vb. 1. *pâ*), m. A tree, Man. 8, 246.

पादभाज् *pâdabhâj*, i.e. *pâda-bhaj*, adj. Possessing a fourth part.

पादरक्ष *pâda-raksh + a*, m. A footguard, Draup. 8, 10.

पाद्वन्त् *pâda+vant*, adj., f. *vatî*, Possessed of feet, Râm. 2, 107, 19 Gorr.

पादशस् *pâda+ças*, adv. 1. Foot by foot, Man. 1, 82. 2. By a fourth, Man. 1, 83.

पादात *pâdâta*, i.e. *pâda-at+a*, I. m. A foot-soldier. II. n. Foot, infantry, MBh. 12, 3672.—Comp. *Sa-ratha-*, adj. with chariots and infantry.

पादान्त *pâdânta*, i.e. *pâda-anta*, m. End of the feet; loc. *te*, Near the feet, Böhtl. Ind. Spr. 752.

पादान्तर *pâdântara*, i.e. *pâda-antara*, n. The interval of a step; loc. *re*, After having made a step, Çâk. 16, 1, Chezy (cf. *padântara*).

पादिक *pâdika*, i.e. *pâda+ika*, adj. Amounting to a quarter, Man. 3, 1.—Comp. *Ardha-*, adj. Consisting in the loss of half of one foot, 8, 325.

पादिन् *pâdin*, i.e. *pâda+in*, adj. 1. Having feet. 2. Entitled to a fourth part or share, Man. 8, 210.

पादुका *pâdukâ*, i.e. *pad+u+ka*, f. A shoe, Râm. 2, 115, 20.—Comp. *Sa-pâduka*, adj. With sandals, Râm. 3, 52, 9.

पादुकृत् and पादूकृत् *pâdûkṛit*, i.e. *pad+u-kṛi+t*, m. A shoemaker.

पाद्म *pâdma*, i.e. *padma+a*, adj. Referring to, treating of, the lotus, Bhâg. P. 2, 10, 47.

पाद्य *pâdya*, i.e. *pâd* or *pâda+ya*, I. adj. Referring or belonging to the feet. II. n. Water for cleaning the feet, Indr. 3, 2.

पान *pâna*, i.e. 1.*pâ+ana*, n. 1. Drinking, Pańch. 184, 18. 2. Enjoying, Lass. 25, 11. 3. Beverage, Man. 3, 227. —Comp. *Vira-pâna* and *-pâṇa*, n. the drink of warriors, taken for refreshment or to elevate courage. *Saha-*, n. drinking together.

पानक *pâna+ka*, m. and n. Beverage, MBh. 15, 21.

पानिक *pâna+ika*, m. A seller of liquors, Râm. 2, 90, 16 Gorr.

पान्थ *pântha*, i.e. *panthan+a* (see *pathin*), m. A traveller, Pańch. 117, 10.

पान्नग *pânnaga*, i.e. *pannaga+a*, adj. Consisting of snakes, Hariv. 9387.

पाप *pâpa*, I. adj., f. *pâ* and *pî*, comparat. *pâpatara*, *pâpîyaṁs*, and *pâpîyastara*, MBh. 13, 2213; superl. *pâpatama*, *pâpishṭha*, *pâpishṭhatara*, MBh. 7, 8734, and *pâpishṭhatama*, Daçak. in Chr. 189, 9. 1. Wicked, sinful, Chr. 61, 46; 9, 43. 2. Inauspicious. 3. *pâpishṭhatama*, with abl., Worse, Daçak. in Chr. 189, 9. II. n 1. Wickedness, Râm. 3, 51, 36. 2. Evil, 3, 54, 27. 3. Crime, Pańch. i. d. 321. 4. Sin, Chr. 30, 37.—Comp. *A-*, adj. innocent. *Upa-*, n. a crime of the third degree, Yâjń. 3, 286. *Dhûta-* (vb. *dhû*), adj. free from sin. *Nishpâpa*, i.e. *nis-*, adj. the same. *Mahâ-*, n. a sin of the highest degree, Yâjń. 3, 286.—Cf. probably, Lat. pejor (for pepjor), pessimus, peccare, perhaps κακός, κακίων, κάκιστος.

पापक *pâpa+ka*, I. adj., f. *kî* and *pikâ*, Wicked, Indr. 5, 61. II. m. A rascal, MBh. 5, 1270. III. n. 1. Evil, 1, 3016. 2. Sin.

पापकृत् *pâpa-kṛi + t*, adj. sbst. Wicked, sinful, a villain, Râm. 3, 50, 22.

पापर्द्धि *pâparddhi*, i.e. *pâpa-ṛiddhi*, f. Hunting, Pańch. 120, 8.

पापलोक्य *pâpalokya*, i.e. *pâpa-loka+ya*, adj., f. *yâ*, Belonging to hell, infernal, MBh. 1, 3558.

पापहन् *pâpa-han*, adj. Destroying sin, Man. 7, 25.

पापिन् *pâpin*, i.e. *pâpa + in*, adj. Wicked, sinful, a sinner, Râjat. 5, 402.

पापिष्ठतम *pâpishṭha + tama*, see *pâpa*.

पापीय *pâpîya = pâpîyaṁs*, see *pâpa*, Worse, MBh. 2, 2123.

पापीयस्त्व *pâpîyastva*, i.e. *pâpîyaṁs + tva* (see *pâpa*), n. Sinfulness, Râjat. 5, 177.

पाप्मन् *pâpman*, i.e. *pâpa + man*, m. **1.** Evil. **2.** Sin, wickedness, Man. 11, 93.

पामन् *pâman*, n. and f. *mâ*, Cutaneous eruption, herpes, scab.

पामर *pâmara*, i.e. *pâman + a*, with *r* for *n*, adj. Base, wicked, Râjat. 5, 400.

पायना *pâyanâ*, i.e. 1.*pâ*, Caus. + *ana*, f. Causing to drink, moistening, Suçr. 1, 27, 19.

पायस *pâyasa*, i.e. *payas + a*, **I.** adj. Made of milk. **II.** m. and n. Food made of milk, Man. 3, 271.

पायिन् *pâyin*, i.e. 1.*pâ + in*, latter part of comp. adj. Drinking, Vikr. d. 121.

पायु *pâyu*, m. The anus, Man. 2, 91.

पार् *PÂR*, i. 10, see 1.*pṛi*, Caus.

पार *pâra*, i.e. 1.*pṛi + a*, **I.** m. and n. The further or opposite bank of a river or sea, Râm. 3, 54, 14 ; figuratively with gen. The totality of the object denoted by the gen., e.g. *tamasas*, The whole darkness, Chr. 294, 6 = Rigv. i. 92, 6. *kâraṇânâm*, All the tortures, Daçak. in Chr. 195, 16. **2.** End, Yâjñ. 1, 51. **II.** m. Quicksilver.—**Comp.** *A-*, adj., f. *râ*, boundless. *Dushpâra*, i.e. *dus-pṛi + a*, adj. 1. difficult to be sailed across. 2. difficult to be overcome. 3. difficult to be performed. *Dûra-*, I. adj. the opposite bank of which is very distant, broad. 2. difficult to be obtained. II. m. a broad river, difficult to be crossed. *Nishpâra*, i.e. *nis-*, adj. boundless.

पारक्य *pârakya*, i.e. *para + ka + ya*, adj. **1.** Belonging to another, Man. 10, 97. **2.** Hostile. m. An enemy, Hit. 109, 6.

पारग *pâra-ga*, adj. **1.** Crossing, MBh. 2, 2418. **2.** Intending to cross, 4, 451. **3.** Accomplishing, Râm. 3, 53, 8. **4.** Having studied, knowing, Pañch. 155, 4.—**Comp.** *Veda-*, adj. sbst. skilled in the Vedas, Chr. 60, 25.

पारग्रामिक *pâragrâmika*, i.e. *para-grâma + ika*, adj., f. *kî*, Hostile, Daçak. in Chr. 200, 24 (*pâragrâmikaṁ vidhim â chikîrsha*, To prepare for hostility).

पारजायिक *pârajâyika*, i.e. *para-jâyâ + ika*, adj. sbst. An adulterer, MBh. 12, 2512.

पारण *pâraṇa*, i.e. *pṛi + ana*, **I.** adj. Saving, Hariv. 7941. **II.** n. **1.** Fulfilling, MBh. 7, 2907. **2.** Reading, studying, MBh. 18, 212. **III.** n. and f. *ṇâ*, **1.** with and without *vrata*, Concluding a fast, eating or drinking after a fast, Kathâs. 21, 146. **2.** Breakfast, Kathâs. 23, 44.

पारत *pârata* (cf. *pâra*), m. Quicksilver, Kathâs. 37, 232.

पारतन्त्र्य *pâratantrya*, i.e. *para-antra + ya*, n. Dependence, MBh. 5, 1725.

पारत्रिक *pâratrika*, i.e. *paratra + ika*, adj. Relating to the next world.

पारत्र्य *pâratrya*, i.e. *paratra + ya*,

adj. Relating to the next world, Man. 2, 236.

पारद *pârada*, m. 1. Quicksilver (cf. *pârata*). 2. pl. The name of a people, the Parthians, Man. 10, 44.

पारदारिक *pâradârika*, i.e. *para-dâra+ika*, adj. sbst. Having sexual intercourse with another's wife, an adulterer, Kathâs. 19, 48.

पारदार्य *pâradârya*, i.e. *para-dâra+ya*, n. Adultery, Man. 11, 59.

पारदेश्य *pâradeçya*, i.e. *para-deça+ya*, adj. Belonging to, or coming from, a foreign country, Yâjń. 2, 252.

पारमहंस्य *pâramahamsya*, i.e. *parama-hamsa+ya*, I. adj. Relating to the *paramahamsas*, or religious men who have subdued all their senses by abstract meditation, Bhâg. P. 6, 5, 4. II. n. Most sublime asceticism or meditation (see the following).

पारमहंस्यपरि *pâramahamsya-pari*, adv. Relating to the most sublime meditation or speculation, Bhâg. P. 4, 21, 40.

पारमार्थिक *pâramârthika*, i.e. *parama-artha+ika*, adj. 1. Real. 2. Loving right, Pańch. i. d. 389.

पारमेश्वर *pârameçvara*, i.e. *parama-içvara + a*, adj. Referring to, coming from, the supreme lord, Çiva, etc., Kathâs. 6, 124.

पारमेष्ठ्य *pârameshṭhya*, i.e. *para-meshṭhin+ya*, I. adj. 1. Referring to the supreme lord, Brahman, etc., MBh. 1, 7682. 2. Referring to a king, Bhâg. P. 9, 10, 38 (n. the royal insignia). II. n. Highest position, 2, 2, 22.

पारम्पर्य *pâramparya*, i.e. *param-para+ya*, n. Hereditary succession, tradition, Man. 2, 18.

पारयिष्णु *pârayishṇu*, i. e. 1. *pṛi*, Caus, +*ishṇu*, adj. 1. Accomplishing. 2. Victorious, MBh. 12, 3749.

पारलोक्य *pâralokya*, i. e. *para-loka+ya*, adj. Referring to the next world, MBh. 5, 778.

पारलौकिक *pâralaukika*, i.e. *para-loka+ika*, adj. Referring to the next world, MBh. 3, 12616.

पारवर्ग्य *pâravargya*, i. e. *para-varga+ya*. Siding with the enemy, MBh. 2, 2131.

पारशव *pâraçava*, i. e. *paraçu+a*, I. m. and n. Iron. II. adj., f. *vî*, Of iron, MBh. 4, 1011. III. m. 1. pl. The name of a people (v.r. *pârasava*). 2. The son of a Çûdra woman by a Brâhmaṇa, Man. 9, 178. 3. A bastard, f. *vî* (*pârasava*, and *vî* with *s*), MBh. 1, 4361.

पारसव *pârasava*. See the last.

पारहंस्य *pârahamsya*, i. e. *para-hamsa + ya*, adj. Relating to an ascetic who has subdued all his senses (cf. *pâramahamsya*), Bhâg. P. 2, 7, 10.

पारापत *pârâpata*, and **पारावत** *pârâvata*, m. A pigeon, Vikr. d. 43; Pańch. 157, 3 (with *v*).

पारायण *pârâyaṇa*, i.e. *pâra-ayana*, n. 1. Study, Utt. Râmach. 34, 10. 2. Totality, MBh. 13, 2701; Utt. Râmach. 98, 4.

पारावत *pârâvata*, m. 1. See *pârâpata*. 2. A kind of snake. 3. A tree, Diospyros embryopteris Pers. (n. its fruit). 4. pl. A class of deities.

पारावर्य *pârâvarya*, i.e. *para-avara+ya*, n. Totality; instr. *yeṇa*, Completely, MBh. 11, 655.

पारावार *pârâvâra*, i.e. *pâra-avâra* (from *ava*, being on this side, Gramm.

ved.) **1.** The opposite bank or shore, and that on this side, MBh. 5, 1017. **2.** m. The sea.

पाराशर्य *pârâçarya*, i.e. *parâçara* + *ya*, patronym. A son of Parâçara, i.e. Vyâsa, Daçak. in Chr. 182, 12.

परिक्षित *pârikshita*, i.e. *parikshit* + *a*, patronym. A descendant of Parikshit, i.e. Janamejaya.

पारिजात *pârijâta*, i. e. *pari-jâta* (vb. *jan*), + *a*, m. **1.** A tree of paradise, Hariv. 7168. **2.** The coral tree, Erythrina indica Lam. **3.** A proper name.

पारिजातक *pârijâta* + *ka*, m. The same.

पारिजातमय *pârijâta* + *maya*, adj., f. *yî*, Made of the flowers of the tree of paradise, Kathâs. 15, 129.

पारिणाह्य *pâriṇâhya*, i.e. *pariṇâha* + *ya*, n. Household furniture and utensils, Man. 9, 11.

पारितोषिक *pâritoshika*, i.e. *paritosha* + *ika*, n. A gratuity, a reward, Mṛichchh. 82, 9.

पारिपन्थिक *pâripanthika*, i.e. *paripathin* + *ika*, m. A robber (MBh. 12, 12100 has *pâripânthika*).

पारिपार्श्व *pâripârçva*, i. e. *paripârçva* + *a*, n. Retinue, Hariv. 8664.

पारिपार्श्वक *pâripârçva* + *ka*, **1.** m. An attendant, MBh. 12, 4339. **2.** f. *vikâ*, A chambermaid, Mâlav. 47, 8.

पारिपार्श्विक *pâripârçvika*, i.e. *pâripârçva* + *ika*, m. An attendant, Mâlav. 3, 7.

पारिप्लव *pâriplava*, i.e. *pariplava* + *a*, I. adj., f. *vâ*. **1.** Swimming, Ragh. 16, 61. **2.** Moving to and fro, unsteady, Ragh. 3, 11. II. m. **1.** A ship, Râm. 1, 44, 20. **2.** A proper name.

पारिबर्ह *pâribarha*, and **पारिवर्ह** *pârivarha*, i.e. *paribarha* + *a*, m. **1.** Suitable furniture, Hariv. 9039. **2.** A proper name.

पारिभद्र *pâribhadra*, i. e. *pari-bhadra* + *a*, and **पारिभद्रक** *pâribhadra* + *ka*, m. The coral and other trees.

पारिमाण्डल्य *pârimâṇḍalya*, i. e. *parimaṇḍala* + *ya*, adj. Having the measure of an atom, Bhâshâp. 14.

पारिमाण्य *pârimâṇya*, i. e. *parimâṇa* + *ya*, n. Circumference, MBh. 12, 10055.

पारिवित्त्य *pârivittya*, i.e. *pari-vitta* (vb. *vid*), + *ya*, and **पारिवेत्त्र्य** *pârivettrya*, i. e. *parivettṛi* + *ya*, n. The condition of an elder brother who is unmarried while the younger is married, Yâjń. 3, 235.

पारिव्राजक *pârivrâjaka*, i.e. *parivrâjaka* + *a*, adj. Destined for a religious mendicant.

पारिषद *pârishada*, i.e *parishad* + *a*, I. adj. and sbst., Belonging, or one who belongs, to an assembly or council, Nal. 18, 4. II. m. **1.** A king's companion, Pańch. 156, 18. **2.** pl. The retinue of a god, Râm. 3, 35, 107. III. n. Partaking of an assembly, Bhâg. P. 1, 16, 17.

पारिषद्य *pârishadya*, i.e. *parishad* + *ya*, m. One who assists at an assembly, a spectator, Râjat. 5, 465.

पारिहार्य *pârihârya*, i.e. *parihâra* + *ya*, m. A bracelet, Râjat. 5, 358.

पारिहास्य *pârihâsya*, i.e. *parihâsa* + *ya*, n. Jest, Bhâg. P. 6, 2, 14.

पारी *pârî*, i.e. *pṛi* + *a* + *î*, f. A cup, Râjat. 5, 368.

पारीक्षित *pârikshita*, i.e. *parikshit* + *a*. **1.** adj. Referring to Parîkshit. **2.** Patronym., a descendant of Parîkshit.

पारीन्द्र *pârindra*, m. A lion, Böhtl. Ind. Spr. 1772.

पारुष्य *pârushya*, i.e. *parusha* + *ya*, n. **1.** Roughness, Suçr. 1, 267, 17 (of the skin). **2.** Squalor, Böhtl. Ind. Spr. 1472. **3.** Violence, either in word (*vâkpârushya*, Man. 8, 266), or deed (*daṇḍa-*, 278). **4.** Abuse, contumelious speech, Man. 12, 6.

पारेसिन्धु *pâresindhu*, i.e. *pâra* + *i-sindhu*, adv. Beyond the Indus, MBh. 2, 1831.

पारोक्ष *pâroksha*, i.e. *paroksha* + *a*, adj. Unintelligible, obscure, Bhâg. P. 5, 13, 26.

पारोक्ष्य *pârokshya*, i.e. *paroksha* + *ya*, I. adj. Invisible, Bhâg. P. 8, 22, 5. II. n. A mystery, 4, 28, 65.

पार्जन्य *pârjanya*, i.e. *parjanya* + *a*, adj. Belonging to Parjanya, MBh. 1, 5365.

पार्थ *pârtha*, i.e. *prithâ*, a proper name, + *a*, metronym. **1.** Offspring of Prithâ, a surname of Yudhishṭhira, Bhîmasena, and Arjuna. **2.** m. A proper name.

पार्थक्य *pârthakya*, i.e. *prithak* + *ya*, n. Severalty, individuality.

पार्थमय *pârtha* + *maya*, adj. Consisting of descendants of Prithâ, MBh. 8, 4847.

पार्थव *pârthava*, i.e. *prithu* + *a*, adj., f. *vî*, Belonging to Prithu, Bhâg. P. 1, 3, 14.

पार्थिव *pârthiva*, i.e. *prithivî* + *a*, I. adj., f. *vî*. **1.** Terrestrial, Chr. 290, 3 =Rigv. i. 64, 3 (*vâ* for *vâni*). **2.** Ruling or possessing the earth, Chr. 14, 17. **3.** Royal, fit for kings or princes, MBh. 5, 2187. II. m. **1.** An inhabitant of the earth. Râm. 2, 25, 20. **2.** A king, a prince. III. f. *vî*, Sîtâ.

पार्थिवता *pârthiva* + *tâ*, f., and

पार्थिवत्व *pârthiva* + *tva*, n. Royal dignity, MBh. 2, 1007; 1051.

पार्वण *pârvaṇa*, i.e. *parvan* + *a*, adj. **1.** Relating to the *parvan* (q. cf.) **2.** Increasing (as the moon), Kathâs. 35, 114. **3.** Full, Ragh. 11, 82.

पार्वत *pârvata*, i.e. *parvata* + *a*. I. adj., f. *tî*, Mountain, produced or consisting in mountains, etc., MBh. 1, 3654. II. f. *tî*. **1.** A name of Durgâ. **2.** The name of several plants.

पार्वतीय *pârvatîya*, i.e. *parvata* + *îya*, I. adj. Mountain, mountaineer, Draup. 8, 8. II. m. A certain prince ruling in the mountains, MBh. 1, 2692.

पार्वतेय *pârvateya*, i.e. *parvata* + *eya*, m. A certain prince ruling in the mountains, MBh. 1, 2666.

पार्वायनान्तीय *pârvâyanântîya*, i.e. *parvan-ayana-anta* + *îya*, adj. Occurring at the end of a Parvan (i.e. a half of the lunar month), or a solstice, Man. 4, 10 (Lois. *pârvâyaṇânt°*).

पार्श्व *pârçva*, i.e. *parçu* (ved. a rib), + *a*, n. and m. **1.** The part of the body below the armpit. **2.** A side, MBh. 13, 2749. **3.** = *pârshṇi* **3**, q. cf. **4.** Proximity. **5.** *ve*, loc. Near, Çâk. d. 9. **6.** *vam*, acc. Near to, Râjat. 5, 467.

पार्श्वक *pârçva* + *ka*, m. A rib, Yâjú. 3, 89.

पार्श्वग *pârçva-ga*, adj. An attendant, Râjat. 5, 56.—Comp. *Yuga-*, m. a young ox in training.

पार्श्वतस् *pârçva + tas*, adv. By or from the side of, Chr. 35, 11.

पार्श्वद *pârçva-da*, m. An attendant, MBh. 9, 2546.

पार्श्वस्थ *pârçva-stha*, adj. Staying near or at the side, Râm. 3, 40, 21.

पार्षत *pârshata*, i. e. *prishata* + *a*. I. patronym. f. *tî*, A descendant of Prishata, i.e. Drupada, Johns. Sel. 27, 20. II. adj. Of, or belonging to, the spotted deer, Man. 3, 269.

पार्षद् *pârshad* (cf. *pârshada*), m. pl. The retinue of a god, Bhâg. P. 3, 6, 29.

पार्षद *pârshada*, i.e. *parshad* + *a*, m. **1.** An attendant. **2.** Retinue, Hariv. 7252.

पार्ष्णि *pârshṇi*, m. and f., and

पार्ष्णी *pârshṇî* (Pañch. 200, 3), f. **1.** The heel, MBh. 7, 3179. **2.** The rear of an army, the back, Ragh. 4, 26. **3.** The extremities of the axletree to which are fastened the two outer horses of a carriage drawn by four horses in one line, MBh. 4, 1415. — Cf. Goth. fairzna; O.H.G. fersna; A.S. fiersna; Lat. compernes, pernix; πτέρνα.

पार्ष्णिग्रह *pârshṇi-graha*, adj. Seizing from behind, Bhag. 8, 2, 27.—**Comp.** *Dushpâr°*, i. e. *dus-*, adj. having a dangerous enemy in the rear, Kâm. Nîtis. 13, 72.

पार्ष्णिग्राह *pârshṇi-grâha*, m. An enemy in the rear, Man. 7, 207.—**Comp.** *Dushpâr°*, i. e. *dus-*, adj. having a dangerous enemy in the rear, Kâm. Nîtis. 13, 89.

पाल् *PÂL*, see 2.*pâ*, Caus.

पाल 2.*pâ* + *la*, m. One who guards or protects, Râm. 1, 42, 15 Gorr.—**Comp.** *Añka-*, f. *lî*, embrace. *Anta-*, m. 1. a guard of the frontiers. 2. a guard of the rear of an army. *Avani-*, m. a king, Bhag. 11, 26. *Udyâna-*, m. the inspector of a garden, a gardener. *Kalpa-*, m. 1. a protector of the holy precepts or institutes. 2. a distiller or seller of spirituous liquors, Râjat. 5, 205 (where *kalya-* is to be changed to *kalpa-*). *Koṭṭa-*, m. the governor of a fort. *Kshiti-*, m. a king, Ragh. 2, 51. *Kshetra-*, m. 1. a field-guard, Pañch. 224, 5. 2. the tutelary deity of a field, 174, 15. *Kshmâ-*, m. a king, Râjat. 5, 319. *Griha-*, m. 1. a castle-ward. 2. a dog, Bhâg. P. 1, 13, 21. *Go-*, I. m. 1. a cowherd, Man. 4, 251. 2. a king, Pañch. i. d. 249. 3. a proper name. II. f. *lî*, a proper name. *Chaitya-*, m. the watchman of a sanctuary. *Jagatî-*, m. a king, Hit. ii. d. 123. *Dikpâla*, i.e. *diç-*, and *diçâ-*, m. the guardian deity of a quarter of the world. *Dvâra-*, m. a door-keeper, a porter. *Dharma-*, m. 1. the guardian of law. 2. a proper name. *Paçu-*, m. 1. a herdsman. 2. pl. the name of a people. *Prajâ-*, *bhû-*, *bhûmi*, and *mahî-*, m. a king. *Bhoga-*, m. a groom. *Loka-*, see s.v. *Vi-*, adj. having no keeper, Man. 8, 240; unguarded. *Çiçu-*, m. the name of a king.

पालक *pâla* + *ka*, m. **1.** A guardian, Râjat. 5, 263. **2.** A protector, Mârk. P. 61, 66.—**Comp.** *Kula-pâlikâ*, f. a proper name, Daçak. in Chr. 188, 24. *Go-*, I. m. 1. a cowherd. 2. a proper name. II. f. *likâ*, the wife of a cowherd. *Daṇḍa-*, m. the chief of the police, Mṛichchh. 117, 19 v. l. — Cf. probably Lat. bubulcus (with *gopâlaka*).

पालन *pâl* + *ana*, i. e. *pâ*, Caus., + *ana*, I. adj., f. *nî*, Guarding, fostering, Mârk. P. 76, 23. II. n. **1.** Preserving, guarding, Man. 7, 88; nourishing. **2.** Maintaining, keeping, MBh. 1, 327.

पालयितृ *pâlayitṛi*, i.e. 2.*pâ*, Caus., +*tṛi*, m. A protector, MBh. 1, 2107.

पालाश *pâlâça*, i.e. *palâça*+*a*, adj., f. *çî*, Made of the wood of the Palâça-tree, Man. 2, 45.

पालि *pâli*, and **पाली** *pâlî*, f. **1.** The tip of the ear, Gît. 3, 13. **2.** The edge of a sword or any other cutting instrument. **3.** A line or row, Gît. 6, 10. **4.** A raised bank, a dike, Râjat. 5, 106 (*lî*). **5.** A boundary, a margin, Bhartṛ. 3, 24 (*lî*).—Comp. *Aṅka-pâlî*, f. embrace.

पालिन् *pâlin*, i.e. 2.*pâ*, Caus., +*in*, adj., f. *nî*, Protecting, Bhâg. P. 3, 21, 50.

पावक *pâvaka*, i.e. *pû*+*aka*, I. adj. **1.** Belonging to Agni, Utt. Râmach. 142, 12. **2.** Pure. II. m. **1.** Fire, or its deified personification, Man. 2, 187. **2.** A kind of Ṛishi. **3.** Name of several plants.

पावकि *pâvaki*, i.e. *pâvaka*+*i*, patronym., m. A son of fire, i.e. Kârttikeya.

पावन *pâvana*, i.e. *pû*+*ana*, I. adj., f. *nî*. **1.** Purifying, Man. 2, 26. **2.** Pure, Râm. 1, 27, 17. II. m. **1.** Fire. **2.** A proper name. III. f. *nî*, The name of a river. IV. n. **1.** Purifying, Man. 11, 85. **2.** A means of purifying, 11, 177.—Comp. *Paṅkti-*, adj. purifying a company.

पावमानी *pâvamânî*, i.e. *pavamâna* (vb. *pû*), +*a*+*î*, f. The name of hymns referring to the preparation of the *Soma*, Man. 5, 86.

पावर् *pâvara*, a corrupt form of *dvâpara*, The die which is marked with two points, Mṛichchh. 33, 9.

पाश *pâça*, i.e. *paç*+*a*, m. **1.** A tie, a string, a chain, a fetter, MBh. 1, 6749. **2.** A string for fastening tamed animals. **3.** A net or noose for catching birds, Hit. 21, 10. **4.** A noose as principal attribute of Varuṇa, Râm. 3, 54, 9 (cf. the Vedas).—Comp. *Karṇa-*, m. a handsome ear, Daçak. in Chr. 198, 24. *Kûṭa-*, m. a net for catching deer. *Keça-*, m. much or flowing hair, a tuft of hair, Vikr. d. 85. *Dharma-*, m. the noose of the god of justice. *Nâga-*, m. a special kind of noose. *Paçu-*, m. the fetter which enchains the soul, i.e. the external world, Prab. 59, 7. *Vi-*, adj. deprived of his noose, Râm. 3, 54, 97; unfettered.

पाशन *pâçana*, i.e. *paç*+*ana* (m. or n.), A noose, MBh. 7, 5923.

पाशभृत् *pâça-bhṛi*+*t*, m. (holding a noose), Varuṇa, Ragh. 2, 9.

पाशव *pâçava*, i.e. *paçu*+*a*, adj. **1.** Come from animals, animal, Nal. 23, 10. **2.** Used by animals, beastly, Lass. 11, 11.

पाशवन्त् *pâça*+*vant*, adj. Possessed of a noose, MBh. 7, 3136.

पाशिन् *pâçin*, i.e. *pâça*+*in*, I. adj. Having a noose, MBh. 8, 1998. II. m. **1.** Varuṇa. **2.** A proper name.

पाशुपत *pâçupata*, i.e. *paçu-pati*+*a*, I. adj., *f. tî*, Belonging or referring to Çiva. II. m. A follower or worshipper of Çiva in one of his forms as the supreme deity of the Hindu triad, Râjat. 5, 403.

पाशुपाल्य *pâçupâlya*, i.e. *paçu-pâla*+*ya*, n. The business of a grazier rearing and keeping cattle, Daçak. in Chr. 182, 20.

पाश्चात्त्य *pâçchâttya*, i.e. *paçchât*+

tya, adj. **1.** Last, posterior, Pańch. ed. orn. 49, 15. **2.** Western, Ragh. 4, 62.

पाषण्ड *pâshaṇḍa*, I. m. n. Heresy, Man. 5, 90. II. adj. Heretical, MBh. 12, 11284. III. m. A heretic, Prab. 21, 1.

पाषण्डिन् *pâshaṇḍin*, i.e. *pâshaṇḍa* + *in*, m. A heretic, Man. 4, 30.

पाषाण *pâshâṇa*, m. A stone, Yâjń. 2, 298.—Comp. *Kasha-*, and *Nikasha-*, m. a touchstone, Böhtl. Ind. Spr. 1940.

† 1. **पि** *PI*, i. 6, *piya*, Par. To go.

2. **पि** *pi*, sometimes for *api*.

† **पिंस्** *PIṂS*, i. 10 and 1, Par. To speak or to shine.

पिक *pika*, **1.** m. The Indian cuckoo, Cuculus indicus, Böhtl. Ind. Spr. 857. **2.** f. *kî*, The female. Probably for primitive *spi* + *ka*, cf. σπίζω.—Cf. Lat. picus, pîca; O.H.G. speh, speht; σίττη for σπίττη or ψίττη, σίττακος ψίττακος, φίττακ for σφίττα (the π is aspirated by the influence of the preceding σ), φιττάκη, βίττακος.

पिङ्ग *pińga*, i.e. *pińj* + *a*, adj., f. *gâ*. **1.** Of a tawny colour, Pańch. 182, 18. **2.** Yellow, Vikr. d. 157. **3.** Red, Hiḍ. 2, 2 (cf. *pińgâksha*).—Comp. *Eka-*, m. a name of Kuvera. *Çveta-*, m. a lion.

पिङ्गल *pińga* + *la*, I. adj., f. *lâ*. **1.** Of a tawny colour, brown, Ragh. 12, 71; yellowish. **2.** Red-eyed, Man. 3, 8 (Kull.). II. m. A proper name. III. f. *lâ*, A proper name.—Comp. *Kṛishṇa-*, adj., f. *lâ*, of a fuscous colour.

पिङ्गलिका *pińgalikâ*, i.e. *pingala* + *ka*, f. A kind of bee, Suçr. 2, 290, 17.

पिङ्गलित *pińgalita*, i.e. *pińgala* + *ita*, adj. Grown of a tawny colour, Kathâs. 21, 123.

पिङ्गाक्ष *pińgâksha*, i.e. *pińga-aksha*, I. adj., f. *kshî*, Red-eyed, Hiḍ. 2, 2. II. m. **1.** A monkey, Ram. 5, 5, 23. **2.** A proper name. III. f. *kshî*, The name of a deity.

पिचु *pichu*, m. **1.** Cotton, Suçr. 1, 60, 16. **2.** The name of an Asura.

पिचुमर्द *pichumarda*, see *-manda*.

पिचुल *pichu* + *la*, m. **1.** Tamarix indica. **2.** Cotton.

† **पिच्च्** *PICHCH*, i. 10, Par. **1.** To cut, to divide.—Cf. *pichh*.

पिच्छ *pichchha*, I. m. A tail. II. n. **1.** A feather of the tail, Pańch. 175, 9; especially of a peacock. **2.** A crest.

पिच्छिका *pichchhikâ*, i.e. *pichchha* + *ka*, f. A bunch of feathers of a peacock's tail, Kathâs. 30, 3.

पिच्छिल *pichchhila*, I. adj., f. *lâ*, Slimy, lubricous, Mârk. P. 10, 9. II. f. *lâ*, The name of several plants.—Cf. πίσσα, Lat. pix.

† **पिछ्** *PICHH*, i. 10, Par. To cut, to divide. i. 6, Par. **1.** To inflict pain. **2.** To obstruct, to hinder.—Cf. *michh*.

† 1. **पिञ्ज्** *PIŃJ*, ii. 2, Âtm. **1.** To dye or colour (probably *api-ańj*, cf. Lat. pingere). **2.** To join. **3.** To adore. **4.** To sound inarticulately. i. 10, Par. **1.** To kill or injure. **2.** To be strong. **3.** To give or take. **4.** To dwell.

† 2. **पिञ्ज्** *PIŃJ*, i. 10 and 1, Par. **1.** To speak or shine. **2.** To sound.

पिञ्ज *pińja*, adj. Disturbed.—Comp. *Utpińja*, i.e. *ud-*, Insurrection (?), Râjat. 3, 122.

पिञ्जर *pińj* + *ara*, I. adj., f. *râ*,

Yellow or tawny, reddish-yellow, Mṛichchh. 48, 11. II. n. Gold.—**Comp.** *Â-*, adj., f. *râ*, reddish, Ragh. 16, 51. *Pari-*, adj. brown-red, Kâm. Nîtis, 13, 14.

पिञ्जल *piñja + la* adj. Disturbed.

पिञ्जलक *piñjala + ka* in *utpiñjalaka*, i.e. *ud-*, adj. Full of disturbance, MBh. 7, 1048.

† **पिट्** *PIṬ*, i. 1, Par. 1. To sound. 2. To heap together.

पिट *piṭa*, I. m. A basket. II. n. A roof.

पिटक *piṭa + ka*, m., f. *kâ*, and n. 1. A basket, Hariv. 14578. 2. A boil. 3. An ornament on Indra's banner, MBh. 1, 2354.

† **पिठ्** *PIṬH*, i. 1, Par. 1. To hurt. 2. To feel pain.

पिठर *piṭhara* I. m. and f. *rî*, and n. A pot, Böhtl. Ind. Spr. 1782; a pan. II. m. 1. A kind of fire, Hariv. 10467. 2. The name of a Dânava.

पिठरक *piṭhara + ka*, A pot, Böhtl. Ind. Spr. 729.

पिडक *piḍaka*, m. (n.?). A small boil, a pimple.

पिण्ड् *PIṆḌ*, probably akin to *pish*, i. 1, Âtm., and i. 10, Par. 1. To accumulate. 2. To assemble. *piṇḍita*, 1. Gathered, Kathâs. 26, 283; collected, MBh. 10, 622; massy, solid, close. 2. Multiplied, MBh. 7, 4746. 3. Thick. —With **सम्** *sam*, To heap together, MBh. 10, 8310. *sampiṇḍita*, Clenched, united.

पिण्ड *piṇḍa*, probably akin to *pish*, I. m., f. *ḍî*, and n. 1. A lump, Pañch. 136, 2; a heap, a cluster, a quantity, Kathâs. 4, 81. 2. A ball, a globe, a little button, Bhâg. P. 5, 26, 19. II. m. n. 1. A mouthful, or roundish lump of food, Man. 11, 216. 2. Food. 3. Livelihood, means of living, MBh. 1, 4148. 4. Alms, Daçak. in Chr. 191, 15. 5. The body. 6. An object, Bhâshâp. 123. 7. An oblation to deceased ancestors, as a ball or lump of meat, or rice mixed up with milk, curds, flowers, etc., and offered to the manes at the several Çrâddhas by the nearest surviving relations; the funeral cake, Man. 3, 215. III. f. *ḍi*, A plant, Jonesia açoka, Daçak. in Chr. 185, 10; cf. 184, 7.—**Comp.** *Pṛithak-*, m. a relation who offers the oblations to the Manes separately, Man. 5, 78 (Kull.). *Saha-* (Man. 3, 248), and *sa-*, m. a kinsman, especially one connected by the offering of the funeral cake to either or all of the manes of the father, grandfather, and great-grandfather, and their wives respectively, as sprung from them in directly collateral lines; the relationship stops with every fourth person. The following are enumerated as *Sapiṇḍas*: the son, son's son, and son's grandson; widow, daughter, and daughter's son; the father, the mother, the brother, brother's son, and brother's grandson; father's daughter's son; paternal grandfather; paternal grandmother; paternal grandfather's brother, brother's son, and grandson; and lastly, the great-grandfather's daughter's son. Other enumerations extend the connection of Sapiṇḍas to seven persons, both in an ascending or descending line; cf. Man. 2, 247; 3, 247. *A-sapiṇḍa*, adj., f. *ḍâ*, Not descended from a relation within the sixth degree, Man. 3, 5.

पिण्डक *piṇḍa + ka*, I. m. and n. 1. A lump, Utt. Râmach. 114, 11. 2. A lump of food, Hariv. 14740. 3. The frontal globes of an elephant in rut, MBh. 1, 5471. II. f. *ḍikâ*, A fleshy part of the body, Yâjń. 3, 97; as the calf, MBh. 14, 2582.—**Comp.** *Bhinna-mastaka-piṇḍaka*, and *-piṇḍika* (from the fem. *piṇḍikâ*), adj. (an elephant) whose frontal globes are open, MBh. 1, 5471; 7, 4564.

पिण्डतस् *piṇḍa + tas*, adv. Of a lump, Hit. Pr. d. 33.

पिण्डत्व *piṇḍa + tva*, n. State of a mass, density; figuratively, Kathâs. 11, 44.

पिण्डद *piṇḍa-da*, adj., f. *dâ*. **1.** Who or what gives the funeral cake to deceased ancestors, Yâjń. 2, 132. **2.** Giving a mouthful of food, Bhartṛ. 2, 56.

पिण्डन *piṇḍ + ana*, n. Forming globes, taking a globular form (as water), Bhâg. P. 3, 26, 43.

पिण्डमय *piṇḍa + maya*, adj. Consisting of a lump (of clay), Mṛichchh. 47, 9.

पिण्डवत् *piṇḍa + vat*, adv. Like a ball.—**Comp.** *Ayas-*, Like a ball of iron, Vedântas. in Chr. 205, 21.

पिण्याक *piṇyâka* (probably from *pish*, cf. *puṇya*), m. **1.** The sediments of seed, etc., ground for oil, oil-cake, Man. 11, 92. **2.** Assafœtida.

पितापुत्र *pitâputra*, i.e. *pitṛi*, nom. sing., *+putra*, m. du. Father and son.

पितामह *pitâmaha*, i.e. *pitṛi*, nom. sing., *-maha* (for *mahant*), **I.** m. **1.** A paternal grandfather, Man. 3, 221. **2.** pl. Ancestors, Chr. 43, 21. **3.** A name of Brahman. **II.** f. *hî*, A paternal grandmother, Kathâs. 30, 25.—**Comp.** *Pûrva-*, m. an ancestor, Kathâs. 21, 20. *Loka-*, m. the great forefather of mankind.

पितु *pitu*, i.e. 1. *pâ + tu*, m. Drink. —Cf. Lat. potus.

पितृ *pitṛi*, i. e. 2. *pâ + tṛi*, m. (acc. pl. *pitaras*, MBh. 3, 12924), **1.** A father, Man. 2, 145. **2.** du. Mother and father, parents, Çâk. 109, 9. **3.** pl. **a.** Paternal ancestors, Man. 2, 159. **b.** The Manes, or the deceased and deified progenitors of mankind, Man. 3, 194, etc. — **Comp.** *An-eka-*, adj., descended from different fathers (viz. grandsons), Yâjń. 2, 120. *Ku-*, m. a wicked father. *Sva-*, m. pl. one's ancestors.—Cf. Lat. pater, πατήρ; Goth. fadar; A.S. faeder.

पितृक i. e. *pitṛi + ka*, **I.** adj. **1.** Paternal. **2.** Ancestral. **II.** A substitute for *pitṛi*, when latter part of comp. adj., Yâjń. 2, 120.

पितृत्व *pitṛi + tva*, n. Paternity, Böhtl. Ind. Spr. 966.

पितृपैतामह *pitri-paitâmaha*, **I.** adj., f. *hî*, Inherited by the father from the grandfather, Sâv. 7, 7. **II.** m. pl. Father and ancestors, Manes, Pańch. 89, 18.

पितृपैतामहिक *pitṛipaitâmahika*, i.e. *pitṛipaitâmaha + ika*, adj. Inherited by the father from the grandfather, Pańch. 78, 7.

पितृमन्त् *pitṛi + mant*, adj., f. *matî*. **1.** Having a father, MBh. 1, 6578. **2.** Accompanied by the Manes, Mârk. P. 31, 47.

पितृव्य *pitṛi + vya*, m. A paternal uncle, Man. 2, 130. — Cf. Lat. patruus; πατρυιός.

पितृष्वसृ *pitṛishvasṛi*, i. e. *pitṛi-svasṛi*, f. A father's sister, Man. 2, 131.

पितृष्वस्रीय *pitṛishvasrîya*, and **पितृस्वस्रीय** *pitṛisvasrîya*, i.e. *pitri-svasṛi + îya*, m., f. *yâ*, A paternal aunt's son or daughter, MBh. 1, 4382.

पितृहन् *pitṛi-han*, m. A parricide, Râjat. 5, 447.

पितृह्व *pitṛihû*, i.e. *pitṛi-hve*, f. The right ear, Bhâg. P. 4, 25, 50.

पित्त *pitta*, n. Bile, MBh. 6, 3736. — Comp. *Nâsâ-rakta-*, n. bleeding of the nose.

पित्र्य *pitrya*, i.e. *pitṛi+ya*, I. adj., f. *yâ*. **1.** Paternal, Man. 9, 92. **2.** Referring, devoted, to the Manes, 2, 59. II. n. **1.** Worship of the Manes. **2.** The lunar mansion Maghâ.

पिधान *pidhâna*, i.e. *api-dhâ+ana* (m.), n. **1.** Covering, shutting, Mâlav. d. 32. **2.** A lid, a covering, Mârk. P. 50, 89.

पिधानवन्त् *pidhâna+vant*, adj., f. *vatî*, Covered with a lid, Râjat. 5, 74.

पिधायकता *pidhâyakatâ*, i.e. *api-dhâ+aka+tâ*, f. The act of covering, Vedântas. in Chr. 206, 1.

पिनद्धक *pinaddhaka*, i.e. *api-naddha* (vb. *nah*) +*ka*, adj., f. *dhikâ*, Dressed, clothed, Hariv. 11164.

पिनाक *pinâka*, m. and n. **1.** A staff, MBh. 5, 5259. **2.** The bow of Çiva, 13, 849. **3.** The club of Çiva, 6, 2797.

पिनाकभृत् *pinâka-bhṛi+t*, m. A name of Çiva.

पिनाकि *pinâki*, i.e. curtailed *pinâkin*, m. A name of Çiva, MBh. 2, 1642.

पिनाकिन् *pinâkin*, i.e. *pinâka+in*, I. adj. Armed with a *pinâka* (a bow ?), MBh. 6, 684. II. m. A name of Çiva.

पिन्व् *PINV*, i. 1, Par. **1.** † To sprinkle, to wet. **2.** To cause to abound, Chr. 290, 6=Rigv. i. 64, 6. **3.** To cause to abound in milk, Chr. 296, 3=Rigv. i. 112, 3.

पिपतिषु *pipatishu*, i. e. *pipatisha*, desider. of *pat*, +*u*, adj. Being about to fall, MBh. 3, 15471.

पिपासा *pipâsâ*, i.e. *pipâsa*, desider. of 1. *pâ*, +*a*, f. Thirst, Nal. 10, 4.

पिपासावन्त् *pipâsâ + vant*, adj. Thirsty.

पिपासु *pipâsu*, i.e. *pipâsa*, desider. of 1. *pâ*, +*u*, adj. Thirsty, Râm. 5, 19, 5.

पिपील *pipîla* (perhaps redupl. *piḍ* +*a*), m. An ant, MBh. 5, 5668.

पिपीलक *pipîla+ka*, m., f. *likâ*, An ant, MBh. 13, 5476.

पिपीलिक *pipîlika*, i.e. *pipîla+ika*, I. m. An ant, MBh. 2, 1860. II. n. Gold carried by ants, MBh. 2, 1860 (cf. Herod. iii. 102).

पिप्पल *pippala*, I. m. The holy fig-tree, Ficus religiosa. II. f. *lî*, Long pepper. III. n. **1.** The fruit of the Ficus religiosa. **2.** Sensual enjoyment, Bhâg. P. 3, 4, 8.

पिप्रीषु *piprîshu*, i.e. *piprîsha*, desider. of *prî*, +*u*, adj. Wishing to delight, MBh. 7, 6855.

पिप्लु *piplu*, i.e. perhaps *api-plu*, m. A freckle, a mark, a mole, Nal. 17, 5.— Comp. *Mṛiga-*, m. The moon.

पियाल *piyâla*, for original *priyâla* (q. cf.), m. A tree, Buchanania latifolia Roxb. n. Its fruit.

† **पिल्** *PIL*, i. 10, Par. To throw, to cast.

पिलु and **पीलु** *pîlu*, m. A certain tree; cf. *pailava*.

पिव् *piv*, see 1. *pâ*.

पिश् *PIÇ*, i. 6, *pimça*, Par. **1.** To adorn. **2.** To form.—Cf. ποικίλος; Goth. failhu; O.H.G. fêh; A.S. faeger, fah, fag, fagian.

पिश *piç + a*, m. A deer, Chr. 290, 8 = Rigv. i. 64, 8.

पिशङ्ग *piçanga* (vb. *piç*), adj., f. *gî* and *gâ*, Of a tawny, or brown, or reddish colour, Kathâs. 1, 18.

पिशाच *piçâcha* (cf. *piçuna*), perhaps *piça-anch + a*, **1.** m. A fiend, a malevolent being, Man. 1, 37. **2.** f. *chî*, A female demon.—**Comp.** *Sa-*, adj. together with Piçâchas, Râm. 3, 53, 3.

पिशाचक *piçâcha + ka*, **1.** m. A fiend. **2.** f. *chikâ*, A female demon.—**Comp.** *Âçâ-piçâchikâ*, f. a demon like alluring and deceiving hope, Pańch. 252, 4.

पिशित *piç + ita* (cf. *piçanga*), n. Flesh, MBh. 4, 770.

पिशुन *piç + una*, I. adj., f. *nâ*. **1.** Malignant, mischievous, Pańch. i. d. 1. **2.** Betraying, Vikr. d. 32. **3.** Backbiting, Pańch. i. d. 339. **4.** Wicked, Böhtl. Ind. Spr. 300. **5.** Unkind, Hit. 56, 16. **6.** One who excites hopes and disappoints them (ÇKD. sub *râgâru*). **II.** m. **1.** A backbiter, Man. 4, 213. **2.** A spy, an informer, 3, 161. **III.** n. Sycophancy, MBh. 14, 1025.

पिशुनता *piçuna + tâ*, f. Backbiting, sycophancy, Bhartṛ. 2, 45.

पिशुनय *PIÇUNAYA*, a denomin. derived from *piçuna* with *aya*, Par. To betray, Çâk. d. 166.

पिष् *PISH*, ii. 7, *pinash*, *pimsh*, Par. **1.** To grind, to pound, MBh. 4, 632. **2.** To bruise, to destroy (with gen.), Çiç. 1, 40. In epic poetry anomal. imperf. *apimshat*, potent. *pisheyam*. Ptcple. of the pf. pass. *pishṭa*, n. The flour or meal of anything that is ground. *na pinashṭi pishṭam*, He does not grind flour, i.e. he does no useless work, Bhâg. P. 5, 10, 24. Caus. *peshaya*, To grind, to pound, MBh. 1, 3223. † i. 10, Par. **1.** To injure. **2.** To be strong. **3.** To dwell. **4.** To give, or take.—With the prep. **अव** *ava*, To grind.—With **उद्** *ud*, To bruise, MBh. 3, 457.—With **निस्** *nis*, **1.** To grind, to bruise, to crush, MBh. 2, 2377. **2.** To rub together, MBh. 1, 5922 (the hands); 4, 465 (to gnash the teeth). Caus. To destroy, Prab. 36, 11, v. r.—With **विनिस्** *vi-nis*, **1.** To bruise, Hiḍ. 4, 35. **2.** To rub together, Râm. 3, 55, 1.—With **परि** *pari*, To strike, Râm. 3, 51, 30.—With **प्र** *pra*, To crush, Pańch. ed. orn. i. d. 266.—With **प्रति** *prati*, **1.** To bruise, to destroy in one's turn, MBh. 12, 5206. **2.** To grind, to bruise, MBh. 4, 361. **3.** To rub together, 1, 2004.—With **सम्** *sam*, To bruise, to destroy, Râm, 1, 45, 48.—Cf. Lat. pinso, pistor, pistillum, pistrinum, pistura, pîla, pîlum, pîlus; πτίσσω, πτίσμα, πίσος, πίσσος.

पिष्टप *pishṭapa*, n. and m. A world, a division of the universe, Man. 4, 231.—**Comp.** *Tri-*, n. the mansion of Indra.

पिष्टमय *pishṭa + maya* (vb. *pish*), adj., f. *yî*. **1.** Made of flour, MBh. 13, 5499. **2.** Mixed with flour, MBh. 13, 6228.

पिस् *PIS*, i, 4, † i. 1, and **पेस्** *PES*, i. 1, Par. To go. † i. 10, Par. *pesaya*, **1.** To go. **2.** To injure or hurt. **3.** To be strong. **4.** To give or take. **5.** To dwell.—Cf. *pish*.

पिस्पृक्षु *pispṛikshu*, i. e. *pispṛiksha*,

desider. of *spriç*, + *u*, adj. Being about to touch (viz. water, i.e.) to make one's ablution, MBh. 12, 8338.

पी *Pî*, i. 4, Âtm. (originally pass. of 1. *pâ*), To drink.—With the prep. आ *â*, To drink, MBh. 3, 13611.

पीठ *pîṭha* n. and m. **1.** A stool, a seat, a chair, MBh. 5, 1399; a bench. **2.** A base or pedestal, Râjat. 2, 126. **3.** The seat of a deity, an altar, Râjat. 5, 46; 473. **4.** A kind of ornament, Hariv. 8063.—**Comp.** *Pâda-*, m. a footstool, Vikr. d. 60. *Pûga-*, n. a spitting pot. *Bhadra-*, a throne, Vikr. 87, 13. *Rañga-*, n. a place for dancing, Daçak. in Chr. 190, 10.

पीठक *pîṭha*+*ka*, I. m. and n. **1.** A chair, a bench. **2.** A saddle (?), MBh. 1, 3486. II. f. *ṭhikâ*. **1.** A bench. **2.** The section of a literary work, Daçak. 48, 7.

पीठग *pîṭha-ga*, adj. Lame (moving by means of a small car), MBh. 3, 871.

पीठमर्द *pîṭhamarda*, i.e. *pîṭha-mṛid* + *a*, I. adj. **1.** Mounted on horses (?), MBh. 4, 674. **2.** Very impudent, Daçak. in Chr. 180, 13 (?). II. m. **1.** The companion of a hero. **2.** A dancing master of courtesans.

पीठसर्प *pîṭha-sṛip* + *a*, adj. sbst. Lame, a cripple (cf. *pîṭhaga*), MBh. 3, 1397.

पीड् *pîḍ* (perhaps akin to *pish*), Âtm. To be squeezed (ved.) Caus. or i. 10, Par. **1.** To squeeze, Bhartṛ. 2, 5. **2.** To give pain, to afflict, Man. 5, 50. **3.** To oppress, Chr. 30, 38. **4.** To cover, Daçak. in Chr. 186, 14. **5.** To hurt, MBh. 1, 7798. **6.** To remove, Man. 1, 51. **7.** To eclipse (in astrology).—With the prep. अभि *abhi*, Caus. To press hard, Râm. 1, 68, 20 Gorr. *abhipîḍita*, **1.** Trodden, Bhâg. P. 7, 8, 38 **2.** Afflicted, MBh. 3, 2490. **3.** Oppressed, Chr. 40, 19.—With समभि *sam-abhi*, Caus. To crush, Hariv. 2936. —With अव *ava*, Caus. **1.** To press down, MBh. 1, 6292. **2.** To strike down, MBh. 14, 1944. **3.** To oppose, 4, 1455. *avapîḍita*, Pressed, Mârk. P. 37, 18.—With आ *â*, Caus. **1.** To press hard, to give pain, MBh. 3, 12121. **2.** To oppress. *âpîḍita*, Adorned, MBh. 3, 2501 (rather *âpîḍa* + *ita*).—With उद् *ud*, Caus. **1.** To press on, Kumâras. 1, 40. **2.** To tuck up, MBh. 3, 426. **3.** To squeeze out, Suçr. 2, 47, 5.—With उप *upa*, Caus. **1.** To afflict, Man. 8, 67. **2.** To lay waste, Man. 7, 195. **3.** To eclipse, Râm. 5, 73, 57.—With नि *ni*, Caus. **1.** To press, Râm. 2, 25, 42 Gorr. **2.** To impress, Râm. 1, 44, 1. **3.** To embrace, Ragh. 2, 23. **4.** To torment, MBh. 2, 6106. **5.** with *daṇḍena*, To punish, to correct, Man. 7, 23. **6.** with *dantais* and *dantân*, To gnash the teeth, Pañch. 249, 7; 259, 10.—With अभिनि *abhi-ni*, Caus. **1.** To squeeze, MBh. 3, 14759. **2.** To torment, 1, 7009. —With उपनि *upa-ni*, Caus. To oppress, Chr. 58, 1.—With निस् *nis*, Caus. **1.** To squeeze out, Pañch. i. d. 161 (read *nishpî°* instead of *nipî°*, also i. d. 209). **2.** To squeeze hard, MBh. 8, 1256; to compress, Râjat. 5, 88; to knock at (the door), Râm. 4, 9, 61.—With परि *pari*, Caus. **1.** To press, to compress, Suçr. 1, 16, 6. **2.** To embrace, Hit. 65, 12. **3.** To torment violently, Pañch. 88, 4.—With प्र *pra*, Caus. **1.** To press, MBh. 6, 3907. **2.** To press hard, to oppress, MBh. 1, 5892. **3.** To torment violently, Lass.

54, 5.—With अभिप्र *abhi-pra,* To oppress, Râm. 2, 22, 23.—With प्रति *prati,* Caus. **1.** To press, Râm. 5, 62, 11. **2.** To press hard, MBh. 4, 980.—With सम् *sam,* Caus. **1.** To compress, Chaurap. 3. **2.** To press hard, to torment, Râm. 4, 21, 37. **3.** To restrain, MBh. 13, 5893.

पीडन *piḍ+ana,* n. **1.** Pressing, squeezing, Râm. 5, 15, 29. **2.** Inflicting pain, distressing, 2, 22, 16.—**Comp.** *Graha-,* n. pain, distress caused by an eclipse, Bhartṛ. 2, 87.

पीडा *piḍ+â,* f. **1.** Pain, anguish, suffering, Böhtl. Ind. Spr. 753. **2.** Infraction, Daçak. in Chr. 182, 14.—**Comp.** *Graha-,* f. pain, distress caused by an eclipse, Dev. 12, 15.

पीत *pîta,* adj., f. *tâ,* Of a yellow colour, Râm. 2, 94, 5.—**Comp.** *Â-,* adj. yellowish, Râm. 2, 76, 4.

पीतक *pîta+ka,* I. adj., f. *tikâ,* Of a yellow colour, Râm. 6, 82, 60. **II.** f. *tikâ,* Saffron.

पीतता *pîta + tâ,* f. Yellowness, yellow (the colour), Bhâshâp. 127.

पीति *pîti,* i.e. 1.*pâ+ti,* f. Drinking, a drink.—**Comp.** *Sa-,* f. drinking together. *Soma-,* f. drinking the Soma juice, Chr. 288, 12=Rigv. i. 48, 12.

पीथ *pîtha,* i.e. 1.*pâ+tha,* **I.** m. A drink. **II.** n. Water.—**Comp.** *Go -pîtha,* i.e. 2.*pâ+tha,* m. protection, Bhâg. P. 4, 22, 55.

पीथिन् i.e. *pîtha+in*; in *koça-pîthin,* adj. Squandering away the treasury, Râjat. 5, 422; *soma-,* m. Drinking the Soma juice, Utt. Râmach. 7, 6.

पीनता *pîna+tâ* (vb. *pyai*), f. Fatness, Böhtl. Ind. Spr. 2735.

पीनस *pînasa,* probably *api-nas* (=*nâsâ*), +*a,* m. **1.** Cold affecting the nose. **2.** Catarrh, cough.

पीयूष् *PÎYÛSH,* a denomin. derived from *pîyûsha,* Par. To turn into nectar, Çatr. 14, 81.

पीयूष *pîyûsha,* probably *pîvas* (ved. grease, cf. *pîvan*), +*a,* **1.** n. The food or beverage of the gods, nectar, Böhtl. Ind. Spr. 838. **2.** m. and n. The milk of a cow during the first seven days after calving.

पीयूषवर्षाय *PÎYÛSHAVARSHÂYA,* a denomin. derived from *pîyûsha -varsha* with *ya,* Âtm. To turn into a shower of nectar, Bhartṛ. 2, 78.

† **पील्** *PÎL,* i. 1, Par. **1.** To impede, to obstruct. **2.** To become stupid.

पीलु *pîlu,* perhaps *pish+lu,* m. **1.** An elephant. **2.** An arrow. **3.** A tree, Careya arborea Roxb. n. Its fruit.

† **पीव्** *PÎV,* i. 1, Par. To be fat or corpulent.

पीवन् *pîvan,* i.e. probably *pyai* (or *pî, pâ*)+*van,* cf. the next, **I.** adj., f. ved. *varî.* **1.** Fat, large. **2.** Strong. **II.** f. *varî,* A proper name.—Cf. πίων, πίειρα, Πιερία (=*pîvarî*), πῖαρ, etc.; Lat. pinguis, pĭgere, pĭger.—Cf. *pyai.*

पीवन्त् *pîvant,* original form of the last, Fat, MBh. 1, 700.

पीवर *pîvara,* i.e. *pîvan+a,* with *r* instead of *n,* adj., f. *râ* and *rî.* **1.** Fat, large, MBh. 5, 5437. **2.** Dense, Daçak. in Chr. 186, 14.

पीवरत्व *pîvara+tva,* n. Largeness, heaviness, Lass. 72, 10 (of deep sighs).

पुंवत् *puṁvat,* i.e. *puṁs+vat,* adv.

1. As a man, Ragh. 6, 20. **2.** As on the birth of a male, Chr. 51, 19.

पुंश्चली *puṁçchali*, i.e. *puṁç-chal+a+i*, adj. and sbst., f. A harlot, an unchaste woman, Man. 4, 211.

पुंश्चलीय *puṁçchalîya*, i. e. *puṁç-chali+iya*, m. The son of a harlot, Böhtl. Ind. Spr. 1536.

1. **पुंस्** *PUṀS*, i. 10, Par. To grind.

2. **पुंस्** *puṁs*, i.e. probably *api-man+t*, the base of some cases is *pumâṁs*, *pum*, the nom. sing. *pumân*, voc. sing. *puman*, m. **1.** A man or male, Man. 2, 29. **2.** A servant, Bhâg. P. 3, 15, 38. **3.** The soul, 7, 1, 11.—**Comp.** *A-* and *na-*, m. an eunuch. *Su-puṁs+î*, f. (a woman) having a good husband. *Strî-*, m. one who has been changed from a female into a male, Chr. 50, 5.

पुंसवन *puṁsavana*, i.e. *puṁs-savana*, adj. **1.** Causing the birth of a male child, Bhâg. P. 9, 6, 28. **2.** n. with or without *vrata*, A religious and domestic festival, held on the mother's perceiving the first signs of a living conception, Bhâg. P. 6, 19, 1. **II.** n. Fœtus, 5, 24, 15.

पुंस्त्व *puṁs+tva*, n. Virility, manhood, Yâjń. 1, 55.—**Comp.** *A-*, n. being an eunuch, Indr. 5, 58.

पुक्कश *pukkaça*, and **पुक्कस** *pukkasa*, m. A mixed tribe; the offspring of a Nishâda by a Çûdra female, Man. 10, 18. f. *çî*, *sî*, A female of this tribe, Man. 10, 38.

पुक्कस *pukhasa*, see the last.

पुङ्ख *puṅkha*, m. The lower part of an arrow, containing the feathers and the shaft, Çâk. d. 10.

पुङ्खित *puṅkhita*, i.e. *puṅkha+ita*, adj. Endowed with the *puṅkha* (see the last), Böhtl. Ind. Spr. 774.

पुङ्गव *puṅgava*, i.e. *puṁs-gava*, **1.** m. A bull Hariv. 3796. **2.** As latter part of comp. words, Excellent, e. g. *gaja-*, m. A pre-eminent elephant, Bhartr. 2, 26. *nara-*, m. An excellent warrior, Chr. 21, 12.

पुच्छ *puchchha*, m. and n. **1.** A tail, Draup. 5, 8. **2.** The hinder part, MBh. 7, 206.—**Comp.** *Kâla-*, m. a certain animal. *Go-*, 1. m. and n. a cow's tail. 2. m. a kind of monkey. *Dadhi-*, m. a proper name. *Hasta-*, n. the hand below the wrist.—Cf. probably πυγή, perhaps πύματος.

† **पुछ्** *puchh*, v.r. of *yuchh*.

पुञ्ज *puñja*, m. **1.** A heap, a mass, MBh. 3, 9957. **2.** A quantity, Mark. P. 8, 82.

पुञ्जय *PUÑJAYA*, a denomin. derived from the last with *aya*, To heap. *puñjita*, Heaped, Utt. Râmach, 126, 2; put together, Râjat. 3, 19.

पुञ्जशस् *puñja+ças*, adv. In heaps, MBh. 2, 1860.

पुट् *PUṬ*, i. 6, Par. † To embrace. † i. 1, Par. To grind, to pound (v.r.). † i. 10, *puṭaya*, Par. To fasten, to bind together. † i. 10, *poṭaya*, Par. **1.** To speak or shine. **2.** To reduce to powder, to grind. **3.** To be small.—With the prep. **परि** *pari*, pass. To peel, to lose the skin, Suçr. 1, 302, 14.

पुट *puṭa*, m., f. *ṭî*, and n. **1.** A concavity. **2.** A cup or concavity made of a leaf folded or doubled, MBh. 9, 2827. **3.** A shallow cup or receptacle, as the hollow of the hand, Pañch. 44, 24. **4.** A vessel, or basket made of leaves, Man. 6, 28. **5.** A cover, a covering, Utt. Râmach. 50, 8. **6.** A cloth worn to cover the privities. **II.** m. A horse's hoof.—**Comp.** *Adhara-* and *oshṭha-*, m. or n. the cup-like lips, Çṛingârat. 7; Çâk. d. 182 (in a comp. adj. having pale-red cup-like lips). *Kṛita-añjali-*, adj. putting the hands together, Râm. 1, 9, 62. *Nayana-*, an eyelid. *Nâsâ-*, m. the nostril. *Paksha-*, m. a wing. *Bhâṇḍa-*, m. a barber. *Mûtra-*, n. the lower belly.

पुटक *puṭa + ka*, n. and f. *ṭikâ* (Pañch. 265, 5), **1.** A concavity. **2.** A bag or vessel or concavity made of a leaf doubled over in a funnel-like shape, Râjat. 1, 213.—**Comp.** *Ghrâṇa-*, m. the nostril.

† **पुट्ट्** *PUṬṬ*, i. 10, Par. To be small.

† **पुड्** *PUḌ*, also **बुड्** *BUḌ*, and **मुड्** *MUḌ*, i. 6, Par. To emit, to leave. —Cf. 2. *muṭ*.

† **पुण्** *PUṆ*, i. 6, Par. To be pure or virtuous, to do a pious or holy act. —Cf. *pûl*.

† **पुण्ट्** *PUṆṬ* (?), i. 10, Par. To speak or shine.

† **पुण्ड्** *PUṆḌ*, see 2. *muṭ* and *muṇḍ*.

पुण्डरीक *puṇḍarîka*, **I.** n. **1.** The white lotus flower. **2.** A lotus in general, Râm. 2, 95, 3 Gorr. **II.** m. **1.** A kind of sacrifice, MBh. 3, 1133. **2.** A kind of rice. **3.** A kind of leprosy. **4.** The elephant of the south-east quarter, Ragh. 18, 7.

पुण्डरीयक *puṇḍarîyaka*, m. The name of a divine being, MBh. 13, 4359.

पुण्ड्र *puṇḍra*, m. **1.** pl. The name of a people and their country, the greater part of Bengal and part of Behar. **2.** A kind of sugar-cane. **3.** (and n.), A mark or line made on the forehead with sandal.—**Comp.** *Tri-*, n. three horizontal marks made across the forehead, especially by the followers of Çiva.

पुण्ड्रक *puṇḍra + ka*, m. **1.** The name of a people=Puṇḍra, Man. 10, 44. **2.** A sort of sugar-cane.—**Comp.** *Kṛita-tri-*, adj. provided with the three horizontal marks (see the last), Hariv. 15426.

पुण्य *puṇya*, probably from *push*, **I.** adj., f. *yâ*. **1.** Beautiful, Nal. 12, 37. **2.** Pure, Man. 9, 186; virtuous, Man. 2, 106. **3.** Fragrant, Chr. 37, 6. **4.** Producing bliss, propitious, Man. 2, 30. **5.** Holy; festival, Daçak. in Chr. 180, 5. **II.** n. **1.** Virtue, Indr. 2, 4. **2.** A good or meritorious act, Râjat. 5, 72. **3.** Happiness.

पुण्यक *puṇya + ka*, n. **1.** A festival, MBh. 15, 407. **2.** A ceremony performed by a woman in order to keep the love of her husband and to get a son, 1, 817. **3.** The observance of this ceremony, 1, 760. **4.** The presents given to the woman on this occasion, Hariv. 7654 (m., corr. perhaps *idaṁ* for *imaṁ*).

पुण्यकृत् *puṇya-kṛi + t*, adj. Virtuous, pious, Bhag. 6, 41.

पुण्यता *puṇya + tâ*, f., and **पुण्यत्व** *puṇya + tva*, n. Purity, holiness, MBh. 1, 557.

पुण्यदुह् *puṇya-duh*, adj. Yielding bliss, MBh. 7, 2181.

पुण्यभरित *puṇyabharita*, i.e. *puṇya-bhara + ita*, adj. Abounding in holiness or bliss, Çatr. 1, 297.

पुण्यवन्त् *puṇya + vant*, adj., f. *vatî*. **1.** Virtuous, Mârk. P. 20, 23. **2.** Well-fated, Hit. 14, 21; with abl. Happier, Hit. i. d. 38, M.M.

पुण्याह *puṇyâha*, i.e. *puṇya + aha*,

n. A good or happy day; with *vâchaya,* To wish somebody a happy day, MBh. 2, 1240.

पुत् *put,* A hell (to which the childless are condemned), Man. 9, 138.

पुत्तिका *puttikâ,* f. **1.** A termite, Man. 4, 238. **2.** A kind of bee.

पुत्र *putra,* perhaps *pû* + *tra,* I. m. **1.** A son, Man. 9, 138. **2.** du. Two sons. **3.** A son and a daughter, Nal. 23, 26. **4.** pl. Children, young ones, MBh. 12, 3306. **II.** f. *trî,* A daughter, Pańch. 190, 1.—**Comp.** *A-,* adj., f. *râ,* sonless. *Ârya-,* m. the son of an Ârya, used to denote: 1. a prince, Râm. 6, 8, 38. 2. the son of an elder brother, 2, 23, 26. 3. a husband (by his wife), 3, 49, 9. *Kula-,* m. the son of a respectable family. *Gâdhi-,* m. the son of Gâdhi, i.e. Viçvâmitra. *Taruṇa-,* adj., f. *râ,* having young ones, Râm. 3, 53, 51. *Jîva-,* adj. one of whom a son or children are alive. *Dâsyâs-* (gen. sing. of *dâsî,* see *dâsa*), m. the son of a female slave, a contemptible person. *Dharâ-,* m. the planet Mars. *Nanda-putrî,* f. a name of Durgâ. *Niçâ-,* m. pl. a class of demons. *Pâṭali-,* n. the name of a town, the Palibothra of the ancients. *Marut-,* m. Bhîmasena, the second of the Pâṇḍavas. *Râjaputra,* i.e. *râjan-,* I. m. 1. the son of a king. 2. a man of the military tribe. 3. a soldier. 4. the planet Mercury. II. f. *trî.* 1. a princess. 2. a woman of the Kshatriya tribe. 3. a kind of brass. 4. the musk shrew. *Lakshmî-,* m. 1. Kâma. 2. a horse. *Çilâ-,* m. a muller or roller for grinding condiments on a flat stone. *Sa-,* adj. together with (his) son, Râjat. 5, 42. *Satp°,* i.e. *sant-,* adj. having sons living, Man. 9, 154. *Sûrya-,* I. m. 1. Varuṇa. 2. Saturn, Pańch. i. d. 238. 3. Yama. II. f. *rî.* 1. lightning. 2. the Yamunâ river.

पुत्रक *putra* + *ka,* I. m. A son, Man. 2, 151. **II.** f. *trikâ* and *trakâ.* **1.** A daughter, Pańch. 190, 2. **2.** A daughter appointed to raise issue for her father, Man. 9, 127. **3.** A doll, Böhtl. Ind. Spr. 635.—**Comp.** *A-,* adj. sonless. *Kṛitrima-,* m. and f. *trikâ,* a doll. *Pâṭali-,* n. the name of a town, the Palibothra of the ancients. *Muni-,* m. a wagtail. *Vastra-putrikâ,* f. a doll.

पुत्रता *putra* + *tâ,* f., and पुत्रत्व *putra* + *tva,* n. The state of a son, Râm. 1, 20, 1 Gorr.

पुत्रवत् *putra* + *vat,* adv. As on the birth of a son, Chr. 50, 16.

पुत्रवन्त् *putra* + *vant,* adj., f. *vatî,* Having a son or sons, or children, Man. 9, 182.

पुत्रिन् *putrin,* i.e. *putra* + *in,* adj., f. *iṇî,* The same, Man. 9, 182; Vikr. d. 152.—**Comp.** *Sa-,* adj. with one's sons, Hariv. 11842.

पुत्रिय *putriya,* i.e. *putra* + *iya,* adj., f. *yâ,* Referring to a son, procuring a son, Râm. 1, 15, 2 Gorr.

पुत्रीय *putrîya,* i.e. *putra* + *iya,* adj., f. *yâ,* Relating to a son or child, procuring a son, Râm. 1, 14, 1 Gorr.

1. पुथ् *PUTH,* i. 4, Par. To hurt, to kill.—Caus. *pothaya.* **1.** To kill, MBh. 4, 727. **2.** To bruise, 4, 643. **3.** To overpower (sound), Kathâs. 34, 257. *pothita,* Annihilated, MBh. 4, 795.—With the prep. अभि *abhi,* Caus. To crush, Hariv. 3347.—With अव *ava,* Caus. The same, Hariv. 5611.—With आ *â,* Caus. The same.—With नि *ni,* Caus. To strike down, Hariv. 4525.—With प्र *pra,* Caus. To push on, Râm. 6, 25, 7.—With वि *vi,* Caus. To bruise,

Dev. 2, 57.—With सम् *sam*, The same, MBh. 7, 1935.

† 2. पुथ् *PUTH*, i. 10, Par. To speak or shine.

पुद्गल *pudgala*, I. adj., f. *lâ*, Beautiful, Mârk. P. 99, 57. II. m. 1. The body, Hit. i. d. 41 (read *pudgale*). 2. The soul. 3. Çiva.

पुनर् *punar*, adv. 1. Back, Chr. 8, 27. 2. Again, Man. 2, 120. 3. In an opposite way, Pañch. 263, 15. 4. But, Nal. 17, 15; on the contrary. 5. Nevertheless, Böhtl. Ind. Spr. 1964. 6. With preceding *kim*, a. How much more, Böhtl. Ind. Spr. 504. b. How much less, Pañch. i. d. 452.—Comp. *Punaḥ-punar*, i.e. *punar-*, adv. 1. repeatedly, Man. 1, 28. 2. again and again, Utt. Râmach. 82, 12; every day, Chr. 295, 10=Rigv. i. 92, 10.

पुनरर्थिता *punararthitâ*, i.e. *punar-arthin+tâ*, f. Renewed begging, Bhâg. P. 5, 19, 27.

पुनरुक्ति *punar-ukti*, f. 1. Tautology. 2. A useless word, Böhtl. Ind. Spr. 462.

पुनर्भू *punar-bhû*, I. adj., n. *bhu*, Reborn, regenerated. II. f. A virgin widow remarried, Yâjñ. 1, 67.

† पुन्थ् *PUNTH*, i. 1, Par. 1. To hurt. 2. To give pain. 3. To suffer pain.

पुन्नाग *punnâga*, m. 1. i.e. *puṁs-nâga*, A pre-eminent man. 2. A white elephant. 3. A tree, from the flowers of which is prepared a yellowish dye, Rottleria tinctoria. 4. A white lotus. 5. Nutmeg.

पुन्नामन् *punnâman*, i.e. 1. *puṁs-nâman*, adj. Having a male name. 2. *put-nâman*, adj. called *put* (q. cf.), Man. 9, 318.

पुप्पुट *pupputa*, m. The name of a disease, a swelling at the palate or the teeth.

पुप्फुस *pupphusa*, and फुप्फुस *phupphusa*, m. The lungs.—Cf. φῦσα, φυσάω, etc.

पुम् *pum*, and पुमांस् *pumâṁs*, see *puṁs*.

1. पुर् *pur* (probably vb. *pṛî*), f. 1. A town, Bhâg. P. 6, 6, 12. 2. The body, 2, 10, 28.—Comp. *Tri-*, f. pl. three forts.

† 2. पुर् *PUR*, i. 6, Par. To go at the head.

पुर *pura*, i.e. probably *pṛî+a*, I. n. 1. A fortified town, Man. 7, 70. 2. A town, 8, 386. 3. The town, κατ' ἐξοχήν, i.e. Pâṭaliputra. 4. An abode, Bhâg. P. 5, 11, 9. 5. An upper story. 6. The body, Bhâg. P. 5, 11, 5. 7. A kind of Cyperus. 8. Skin. II. m. 1. A sort of resin, Bdellium. 2. The name of a demon. III. f. *râ*, A perfume. IV. f. *rî* (also *ri*). 1. A town, Megh. 31. 2. The body, Bhâg. P. 2, 10, 28.—Comp. *Aṅga-purî*, f. the capital of the Aṅgas. *Amara-pura*, n. and *-purî*, f. the residence of the gods. *Avanti-*, n. the name of a town. *Kanyâ-pura*, n. a gynæceum. *Kâñchana-pura*, n. the name of a town. *Kâçi-purî*, f. the capital of the Kâçis, i. e. Benares. *Kumârî-pura*, n. a gynæceum. *Kusuma-pura*, n. a surname of Pâṭaliputra. *Gaja-pura*, n. a name of Hâstinapura. *Gandharva-pura*, n. a mirage, Bhâg. P. 5, 13, 3. *Go-*, n. 1. a town-gate, Râm. 5, 27, 20. 2. a gate in general, Kir. 5, 5. *Pâṇḍara-dvâra-go-*, adj. f. *râ*, having white doors and town-gates, Râm. 5, 9, 58. *Tri-pura*, I. n. three forts. II. m. the name of a demon. III. f. *râ.* 1. the name of a town. 2. a form of Durgâ. IV. f. *rî,* the name of a town. *Daça(n)-pura,* n. the name of a country. *Deva-pura,* n. the residence of Indra. *Nâga-pura,* n. a name of Hâstinapura. *Pañcha(n)-pura,* n., *parihâsu-pura,* n., and *phala-pura,* n., names of towns. *Mahâ-purî,* f. a great town. *Rukma-,* n. the name of a fabulous town, Pañch. 84, 7. *Çâkhâ-,* n. a suburb. *Çûra-,* n. the name of a town. *Hiraṇya-,* n. the town of the Asuras, Arj. 10, 13.—Cf. πόλις, πτόλις, perhaps also πύργος.

पुरःसर *puraḥsara,* i.e. *puras-sṛi + a,* adj., f. *rî,* and sbst. 1. One who goes first or before, Bhâg. P. 4, 25, 27; a leader, a preceder, MBh. 4, 630; Çâk. d. 77. 2. When latter part of a comp. adj. the fem. ends in *râ,* Preceded by, attended with, with; e.g. *priya-âkhyâna-,* adj. Preceded by agreeable news, i.e. with agreeable news, Râm. 1, 10, 31 Gorr. 3. *ram,* adv. Preceded by, with; e. g. *praṇipâta-puraḥsaram,* With a prostration, Mârk. P. 77, 30 (laying herself at his feet); after, Pañch. 16, 4.

पुरग *puraga,* i.e. probably *puras-ga,* adj. Inclined to, Mârk. P. 64, 3.

पुरजित् *pura-ji + t,* m. 1. A name of Çiva. 2. A proper name.

पुरंजन *puraṁjana,* i. e. *pura + m-jan + a,* I. m. The soul, personified as a king, Bhâg. P. 4, 25, 9 sqq. II. f. *nî,* The intellect, personified as his queen.

पुरंजय *puraṁjaya,* i.e. *pura + m-ji + a,* m. A proper name.—Comp. *Para-,* adj. conquering the enemy's towns, Nal. 20, 1.

पुरट *puraṭa,* n. Gold, Bhâg. P. 3, 15, 29.

पुरतस् *pura + tas* (cf. *purâ*), adv. 1. Before, in front (with gen.), Râm. 2, 39, 6. 2. Forward, Vikr. 65, 7.

पुरंदर *puraṁdara,* i. e. *pura + m-dṛî + a,* m. Destroyer of castles, a name of Indra.

पुरंधि *puraṁdhi,* I. f. Understanding, wisdom. II. adj. Intelligent.

पुरंध्रि and **पुरंध्री** *puraṁdhrî,* i. e. *pura + m-dhṛi + î,* and the final shortened, f. A respectable matron, Ragh. 7, 25.

पुरश्चरणता *puraçcharaṇatâ,* i. e. *puras-charaṇa + tâ,* f. Preparation, MBh. 12, 13206.

पुरस् *pura + s* (cf. *purâ*), I. adv. 1. Forward. 2. Before, in front, in presence, Çâk. 29, 1; Pañch. i. d. 135. 3. First, Çâk. d. 33. 4. Eastward, from the east, MBh. 7, 2349. II. prep. with the gen., Before, Megh. 3.—Comp. *Dakshiṇatas-puras,* adv. south-eastward, MBh. 2, 1120.—Cf. πάρος, πρόσθε, πρόσθιος, etc., perhaps πρες, in πρέσβυς.

पुरस्कार *puras-kâra,* m. 1. Preference, Mâlav. 19, 6. 2. Deference, Râm. 1, 80, 11 Gorr. 3. As latter part of comp. adj. Preceded by, joined with; e.g. *surâ-sava-,* adj. Together with spirituous liquors, MBh. 13, 4737.

पुरस्क्रिया *puras-kriyâ,* f. Deference, Ragh. 4, 87.

पुरस्तात् *puras-tât* (*tât,* an old abl. of *tad*), I. adv. 1. Before, in front, Bhag. 11, 40. 2. First, preceding, Râm. 2, 80, 5. 3. Forward, Vikr. 31, 4. 4. Formerly, MBh. 1, 735. 5. Eastward, in the east, from the east, Megh. 15. II. prep. with gen. and abl. Before, Hit. 8, 15.

पुरा *purâ* (old instrum. sing. of a

base *pura*, for *para*, cf. *puras*; *u* is changed to *a* by the influence of the preceding *p*), I. adv. **1.** Formerly, Man. 1, 119. **2.** Of old, Böhtl. Ind. Spr. 1231. **3.** With *na*, Never, MBh. 9, 1806. **4.** First. **5.** Soon. II. prep. with abl., Before, Arj. 4, 20. — Cf. πάροι (old loc.) in πάροιθε, παροίτερος, πάλαι (old dat.), παλαιός, etc.; perhaps also πέλας, with πλησίος, etc.; Goth. faura and faur; A.S. for, fora-, fore-; Lat. por-, e.g. in por-tendere, and probably also prō-.

पुराण *purâṇa*, i.e. *purâ* + *na*, I. adj., f. (*ṇâ* and) *ṇî*. **1.** Primeval, Man. 5, 23. **2.** Old, ancient, Mâlav. 4, 2. **3.** Aged, Vikr. d. 9; worn out. II. n. A tale of past ages; old history, legends; a sacred work treating for the most part of the creation, the destruction and renovation of worlds, the genealogy of gods, etc. There are eighteen acknowledged Purâṇas. III. m. A coin of a certain weight, Man. 8, 136.— Comp. *nishpurâṇa*, i.e. *nis-*, adj. New, unheard of.

पुरातन *purâ* + *tana*, I. adj., f. *nî*, Old, ancient, Man. 3, 213. II. n. An old tale, Râm. 1, 45, 13.—Cf. Lat. (regarding the form) prôtenus.

पुरारति *purârâti*, and **पुरारि** *purâri*, i.e. *pura-arâti* and *-ari*, m. Names of Çiva.

पुराविद् *purâ-vid*, adj. Knowing the past.

पुरि *puri*, and **पुरी** *purî*, see *pura*.

पुरीतत् *purîtat*, probably *pur* + *i* *tan* + *t*, n. **1.** An entrail near the heart. **2.** The entrails in general, Daçak. in Chr. 188, 17.

पुरीष *purîsha* (akin to *prî*), I. n. **1.** Fæces, excrements, Man. 5, 138. **2.** The remains of food (in a pot), Bhâg. P. 5, 9, 12. II. f. *shî* (perhaps f. of *purîshya*), The name of a religious ceremony, 3, 12, 40.

पुरीषण *purîshaṇa*, i.e. *purîshaya* (a denomin. derived from *purîsha* with the aff. *aya*) + *ana*, n. **1.** Evacuation of excrements. **2.** Fæces.

पुरीषधान *purîsha-dhâna*, n. The strait-gut, Yâjñ. 3, 94.

पुरीषम *purîshama* (akin to *purîsha*), m. The black kidneybean.

पुरीष्य *purîshya*, adj. Epithet of fire.—Cf. *purîsha*, f.

पुरु *puru*, in the Veda also *pûru*, i.e. *prî* + *u*, I. adj., f. *purvî*. **1.** Much, many. **2.** Exceeding. adv. Very, exceedingly. II. also *pûru*, m. The name of an old prince, Çâk. 7, 4.—Cf. πολύ; Goth. filu; A.S. fela, feala; comparat. πλεῖον; Lat. plus.

पुरुकुत्स *puru-kutsa*, m. A proper name.

पुरुदंशक *puru-daṁç* + *aka*, m. A goose.

पुरुदंशस् *puru-daṁç* + *as*, m., nom. sing. *çâ*, A name of Indra.

पुरुधा *puru* + *dhâ*, adv. Manifold.

पुरुष *purusha*, and sometimes *pûrusha*, I. m. **1.** A man generally or individually, a male, mankind, Man. 1, 32. **2.** Punishment personified, Man. 7, 17. **3.** An attendant, a functionary, 8, 43. **4.** The first man, Hariv. 51. **5.** The soul, Yâjñ. 3, 194. **6.** The universal soul, the supreme Being, Mârk. P. 26, 21; Man. 1, 11. **7.** A principle, Man. 1, 19. **8.** A tree, Rottleria tinctoria. **9.** A proper name. II. f. *shî*, A female, Bhâg. P. 5, 24, 17. III. n. (?). A name of the mountain Meru. — Comp.

A-drishṭa- (vb. *driç*), adj. (viz. *saṁdhi*), a kind of alliance where one party alone settles for the other, on the condition that the enemy has to disburse the expenses of the expedition, Hit. iv. d. 117. *Antara-pûrusha*, m. the soul, Man. 8, 85. *Âdi-purusha*, m. the first man. *Upari-*, m. a rider, Daçak. in Chr. 188, 16. *Eka-*, I. m. the one universal soul, Vikr. d. 1. II. adj. consisting only of one person. *Kiṁ-purusha*, i.e. *kim-*, m. 1. a class of horse-faced beings belonging to the suite of Kuvera, Kumâras. 1, 11. 2. one of the portions into which the world is divided. *Kula-*, m. a polite man. *Gûḍha-* (vb. *guh*), m. a spy. *Tulâ-*, m. 1. a person weighed in a balance, i.e. a present of gold or other precious things of equal weight. 2. the name of a penance. *Dharmâdhi-kâripurusha*, i.e. *dharma-adhi-kârin-*, m. a judge. *Nishpurusha*, i.e. *nis-*, adj. 1. not having produced male children, Man. 3, 7. 2. devoid of men. *Prakṛiti-*, m. a minister, Megh. 5. *Pramâṇa-*, m. an arbitrator, Hit. 116, 12. *Mûla-*, m. the last male of a race. *Rakshika-*, m. a policeman, Daçak. in Chr. 199, 24. *Râja(n)-*, m. 1. a servant of the king. 2. A guard, a watchman. *Satpurusha*, i.e. *sant-*, m. an honest man.

पुरुषक *purusha + ka*, n. Rearing as a horse, standing like a man on two feet, Çiç. 5, 56.

पुरुषकार *purusha-kâra*, m. 1. Any act of man, care, Man. 8, 232. 2. The exertion of man (opposite to fate), Yâjñ. 1, 348. 3. A proper name.

पुरुषता *purusha + tâ*, f., and **पुरुषत्व** *purusha + tva*, n. Manhood, MBh. 13, 552.

पुरुषन्ति *purushanti*, m. A proper name, Chr. 298, 23 = Rigv. 1, 112, 23.

पुरुषशीर्षक *purusha-çîrsha + ka* (m. n. ?), The name of a thief's instrument, Daçak. 71, 1.

पुरुषादत्व *purushâdatva*, i.e. *purusha-âda + tva*, n. State or condition of a man-eater, or demon, MBh. 13, 326.

पुरुषान्तर *purushântara*, i.e. *purusha-antara*, I. n. A following generation, Mârk. P. 118, 31. II. m. 1. Man (opposed to deities), Vikr. d. 35. 2. A treaty by which is stipulated that the affairs of the one shall be settled by warriors selected from both parties, Kâm. Nîtis. 9, 13.

पुरुषाय *PURUSHÂYA*, a denomin. derived from *purusha* with *ya*, Âtm. To behave like a man, MBh. 12, 8102.

पुरूरवस् *purûravas*, m. The name of a king.

पुरूवसु *purûvasu*, i.e. *puru-vasu*, adj. Abounding in riches.

पुरोग *puroga*, and **पुरोगम** *purogama*, i.e. *puras-ga* and *-gama*, I. adj. 1. Going before, preceding, Nal. 4, 20. 2. Chief, Ragh. 6, 55. II. m. A leader, MBh. 3, 2522. — Comp. *Agni-purogama*, adj. led by Agni, Nal. 5, 34. *Prîti-puroga*, adj. accompanied by love, friendly, MBh. 12, 10935. *Yudhishṭhira-purogama*, adj. having Yudishṭhira as leader, led on by Yudhishṭhira.

पुरोजन्मता *purojanmatâ*, i.e. *puras-janman + tâ*, f. Priority of birth, Ragh. 16, 1.

पुरोडाश *puroḍâça*, i.e. *puras-dâç + a*, m. 1. A kind of cake made of rice meal, offered in oblations to the gods, Man. 6, 11. **2.** An oblation to deities, Man. 5, 23.

पुरोडाशीय *puroḍâçîya*, i.e. *puroḍâça + îya*, adj., f. *yâ*, Relating to the sacrificial cakes.

पुरोध *purodha = purodhas*, MBh. 3, 10635.

पुरोधस् *purodhas*, i.e. *puras* and vb. *dhâ*, m. The family or domestic priest of a prince, Çâk. 71, 18.

पुरोधिका *purodhikâ* (probably *puras-dhâ + ikâ*), f. A favourite wife, Hariv. 7817.

पुरोहित *purohita*, see *dhâ* with *puras*.

† **पुर्व्**, **पूर्व्** *PÛRV*, and **पूर्ब्** *PÛRB*, i. 1, Par. To fill (cf. *pṛî*). i. 10, Par. To dwell.

† **पुल्** *PUL*, i. 1, and 6, and 10, Par. To be great or large, to be lofty or high.

पुल *pula*, I. adj. Extensive. II. m. Erection of the hairs of the body, considered as proof of exquisite delight.

पुलक *pula + ka*, m. **1.** Erection of the hairs of the body, considered as occasioned by pleasure, Vikr. d. 57. **2.** Flaw or defect in a gem. **3.** A ball of bread and sweetmeats with which elephants are fed. **4.** An insect of any class affecting animals whether externally or internally. **5.** A kind of esculent plant, MBh. 13, 4363.—Comp. *Vi-*, adj. free from horripilation.

पुलकय *PULAKAYA*, a denomin. derived from *pulaka* with *aya*, Par. To have or feel one's hairs of the body erect by pleasure, Gît. 11, 10. Ptcple. of the pf. pass. *pulakita*, rather *pulaka + ita*, adj. Having the hairs of the body erect, Hit. 16, 11.

पुलस्त्य *pulastya*, i.e. *puras + tya*, m. The name of one of the seven Ṛishis and mental sons of Brahman, Râm. 3, 53, 31.

पुलह *pulaha*, m. The name of one of the seven Ṛishis and mental sons of Brahman, Man. 1, 35.

पुलाक *pulâka*, m. and n. **1.** Shrivelled, or blighted, or empty grain. **2.** Bad grain, Man. 10, 125. **3.** A lump of boiled rice. **4.** Abridgement. **5.** Celerity.

पुलिन *pulina*, m. and n. **1.** An alluvial formation, a small island, MBh. 4, 395. **2.** The bank of a river, Pañch. 226, 19.

पुलिन्द *pulinda*, m. **1.** pl. The name of a barbarian tribe. **2.** One belonging to this tribe, Pañch. 120, 8. **3.** A prince of the Pulindas, MBh. 2, 119.

पुलिन्दक *pulinda + ka*, m. **1.** The name of a people. **2.** A proper name.

पुलोम *puloma*, I. m. = *puloman*, Râm. 4, 39, 7. II. f. *mâ*, The wife of Kaçyapa (Vishṇu. P. 148).

पुलोमजा *pulomajâ*, i. e. *puloman -ja*. f. Çachî, the wife of Indra.

पुलोमन् *puloman*, m. The name of an Asura (ÇKD.), or Dânava (VP. 147), father-in-law of Indra, by whom he was slain.

पुष् *PUSH*, ii. 9, Par. **1.** To nourish, MBh. 3, 13639. **2.** To cherish, Pañch. 238, 7. **3.** To manage, Bhartṛ. 2, 38. **4.** To augment, Râjat. 5, 159. i. 4, Par. **1.** To thrive, to prosper, Chr. 291, 13 = Rigv. i. 64, 13. **2.** To enjoy, Ragh. 18, 32. **3.** To possess, Ragh. 16, 58. **4.** To exhibit, Man. 9, 37. **5.** To unfold, Çâk. d. 18. **6.** To support, to maintain, Râm. 4, 61, 24. Ptcple. of the pf. pass. *pushṭa*, **1.** Nourished. **2.** Well-fed, strong, Chr. 4, 18. **3.** Eminent, Man. 4, 231. **4.** Loud, Hariv. 14063. **Comp.** *A-pushṭa*, adj. deficient, Sâh. d. 7, 19. *Anya-*, m. the Indian cuckoo. *Bali-*, m. a crow. Caus. To cause to be nourished, Çâk. 107, 7. Caus. or i. 10, Par. **1.** To nourish, Lass. 99, 3 = Rigv. v. 9, 7. To cherish, Böhtl. Ind. Spr. 1890. Cf. **2.** *vyush.* —With the prep. **अति** *ati*, *atipushṭa*, Very strong, Pañch. iii. d. 8. **Comp.** *Na-*, adj. rather insignificant, paltry, Daçak. in Chr. 184, 14.—With **परि** *pari*, *paripushṭa*, **1.** Cherished. **2.** Abounding in. Caus. **1.** To cause to be cherished or managed, Bhartṛ. 2, 38. **2.** To cherish, Böhtl. Ind. Spr. 2602.—With **प्र** *pra*, To nourish, Bhâg. P. 5, 26, 10.—With **वि** *vi*, *vipushṭa*, Ill-fed, low, Pañch. i. d. 313 (rather *pushṭa*, with *vi*).—With **सम्** *sam*, ii. 9, To increase, Bhartṛ. 2, 13.

पुष *push* + *a*, in *graha-*, m. The sun (nourishing the planets by its light). f. *shâ*, The name of a plant.

पुष्कर *pushkara* (probably *push-kṛi* + *a*). I. n. **1.** Water. **2.** The sky, heaven, Böhtl. Ind. Spr. 1770. **3.** The blue lotus flower, MBh. 1, 4704. **4.** The tip of an elephant's trunk, Pañch. 80, 8. **5.** The skin of a drum, Ragh. 17, 11. **6.** A drug, Costus speciosus. **7.** The name of a celebrated place of pilgrimage. **8.** The blade of a sword. **9.** The sheath of a sword. **10.** (also m.), One of the seven great Dvîpas, or divisions of the world. **11.** An arrow. **12.** The art or science of dancing. **13.** War, battle. **14.** Intoxication. **15.** A cage. **16.** A part. II. m. **1.** A pond or lake. **2.** A drum, a kettle-drum, Megh. 67. **3.** One of the principal clouds, that which occasions dearth. **4.** The Indian crane. **5.** A sort of snake. **6.** A proper name.—**Comp.** *Tri-*, pl. three holy ponds, Ragh. 18, 30.

पुष्कराय *PUSHKARÂYA*, a denomin. derived from *pushkara* with *ya*, Âtm. To represent a drum, Daçarûp. 1.

पुष्करावती *pushkarâvatî*, i.e. *pushkara* + *vant* + *î*, f. The name of a town.

पुष्करावर्तक *pushkarâvartaka*, i.e. *pushkara-âvarta* + *ka*, m. A certain kind of cloud, Megh. 6.

पुष्करिन् *pushkarin*, i.e. *pushkara* + *in*, I. adj., f. *iṇî*, Abounding in lotus flowers, Râm. 3, 76, 5. II. m. An elephant. III. f. *iṇî*, A pool where the lotus does or may grow, Arj. 4, 50.

पुष्कल *pushkala* (= *pushkara*, with *l* for *r*), I. adj., f. *lâ*. **1.** Excellent, Man. 8, 81; best. **2.** Good, salutary. **3.** Much, Râm. 1, 71, 2 Gorr.; many, Bhag. 11, 21; with following *na*, More than, Man. 3, 129. **4.** Complete. **5.** Loud, MBh. 7, 578. II. m. A kind of drum, MBh. 6, 1631. III. n. **1.** A certain measure. **2.** Alms to the extent of four mouthfuls of food. **3.** The name of a holy place. **4.** A proper name. —**Comp.** *Su-*, adj. Very copious, MBh. 9, 2146.

पुष्कलक *pushkala* + *ka*, m. **1.** The musk deer. **2.** A pin, a bolt. **3.** A Bauddha mendicant.

पुष्कलावती = *pushkarâvatî.*

पुष्टि *pushṭi*, i. e. *push* + *ti*, f. **1.** Thriving, increase, Pañch. 215, 2. **2.** Vegetation, Man. 9, 37. **3.** Prosperity, Pañch. i. d. 246. **4.** Nourishment,

Man. 2, 32. **5.** One of the divine mothers.

पुष्टिका *pushṭi + kâ*, f. An oyster.

पुष्टिद *pushṭi + da*, I. adj. Yielding prosperity, Hariv. 833. II. m. A class of Manes, Mârk. P. 96, 45. III. f. *dâ*, The name of a plant, Physalis flexuosa Lin.

पुष्प् *PUSHP* (rather an anomal. denomin. derived from *pushpa*), i. 4, Par. To flower, to blossom, Hariv. 12799 (also i. 1, Mâlatîm. 153, 5; Hariv. 7874). Ptcple. of the pf. pass. *pushpita* (rather *pushpa + ita*), Flowered, in flower. f. *tâ*, A woman during menstruation. **Comp.** *Su-*, adj. blossoming beautifully, Râm. 3, 55, 45. *Suvarṇa-*, adj. having gold instead of flowers, Pañch. i. d. 51 (but cf. Böhtl. Ind. Spr. 3284).

पुष्प *push + pa*, I. n. **1.** A flower, Nal. 13, 3. **2.** The menses, Mârk. P. 51, 42. **3.** The vehicle or car of Kuvera. **4.** A disease of the eyes, albugo. **5.** A topaz, Râm. 2, 94, 6 (cf. *pushpa-râga*). II. m. A proper name. III. f. *pâ*, The capital of Karṇa. —Comp. *A-*, adj., f. *pâ*, without flowers. *Abhra-*, n. 1. water. 2. a flower in the air, i. e. anything non-existent. 3. the ratan, Calamus rotang. *Kha-*, n. a sky-flower, a nonentity. *Gandha-*, I. n. a fragrant flower. II. m. the name of several plants. *Jîva-*, I. n. 1. the flower of life, denoting a certain plant and the head. 2. the name of two plants. II. f. *pâ*, the name of a plant. *Darbha-*, m. 1. a kind of snake. 2. a certain insect. *Nâga-*, m. the name of several plants. *Bhâṇḍa-*, m. a sort of snake. *Lakshmî-*, m. a ruby. *Visha-*, n. the blue lotus. *Vîja-*, n. 1. common citron. 2. a thorny plant, Vangueria spinosa. *Çaṅkha-pushpî*, f. a sort of grass, Andropogon aciculatum, Man. 11, 147. *Sa-*, adj. endowed with blossoms, Ṛit. 6, 2. *Su-*, m., f. *pâ*, and n. the name of several plants. *Sûtra-*, m. the cotton plant.

पुष्पक *pushpa + ka*, I. m. A kind of snake, Suçr. 2, 265, 20. II. n. **1.** The chariot of Kuvera, Râm. 3, 36, 15. **2.** A bracelet of diamonds or jewels. **3.** A cup or vessel of iron. **4.** Green vitriol.

पुष्पध *pushpa-dha*, m. The offspring of an outcaste Brâhmaṇa, Man. 10, 21.

पुष्पंधय *pushpaṁdhaya*, i.e. *pushpa + m-dhe + a*, m. A bee.

पुष्पमय *pushpamaya*, adj., f. *yî*, Consisting of flowers, Râm. 5, 5, 17.

पुष्पलिह् *pushpa-lih*, m. A bee.

पुष्पवत् *pushpa + vat*, adv. Like a flower or flowers, Böhtl. Ind. Spr. 1876.

पुष्पवन्त् *pushpa + vant*, I. adj., f. *vatî*, Having flowers, MBh. 6, 529. II. m. **1.** A proper name. **2.** du. The sun and the moon. III. f. *vatî*. **1.** A woman during menstruation. **2.** A proper name.

पुष्पाकर *pushpâkara*, i.e. *pushpa -âkara*, adj. Abounding in flowers, Vikr. d. 9 (with *mâsa*, i.e. Spring).

पुष्पिन् *pushpin*, i.e. *pushpa + in*, adj., f. *iṇî*, Bearing flowers, blossoming, Man. 1, 47.

पुष्पेषु *pushpeshu*, i.e. *pushpa-ishu*, m. Kâma, the god of love (properly, Having flowers for arrows.)

पुष्य *push + ya*, m. **1.** The eighth lunar asterism. **2.** The name of a month, Dec.—Jan. **3.** The fourth age, Kaliyuga.

पुस् *PUS*, see *vyush*.

† **पुस्त्** *PUST*, i. 10, Par. I. To bind. II. (also **बुस्त्** *BUST*), i. 10, Par. 1. To respect. 2. To disregard.

पुस्त *pusta*, I. m. and n. A book. II. n. Working in clay, modelling, Kathâs. 34, 172.

पुस्तक *pusta+ka*, m. and n. A book, a manuscript, Pańch. 127, 2.

पुस्तमय *pusta+maya*, adj., f. *yî*, Wrought in clay, modelled, Suçr. 1, 29, 9.

पू *PÛ*, ii. 9, *punâ*, *punî*, Par. Âtm. i. 1, Âtm. (Par. Bhag. 10, 31); i. 4, Âtm., properly Passive. To purify, Man. 1, 105; to make pure, 8, 311. Ptcple. of the pf. pass. *pûta*, 1. Purified, pure. 2. Cleaned. 3. Threshed, winnowed. 4. Foul smelling, stinking (cf. *pûti* and *pûy*). n. Truth. Comp. *A-*, adj. impure. *Çastra-*, adj. purified by arms, absolved from guilt by dying in the field of battle. Caus. *pâvaya*, To cause to be purified, to purify, Man. 3, 183. Ptcple. of the pf. pass. *pâvita*, Purified, 2, 75.—With the prep. **निस्** *nis*, *nish-pû*, To purify, Bhâg. P. 6, 1, 18.—With **परि** *pari*, *paripûta*, 1. Purified completely, Mṛichchh. 159, 2. 2. Threshed (winnowed ?), Man. 8, 331.—With **वि** *vi*, To purify, MBh. 2, 1150.—Cf. Lat. purus, pŭtus, putare (cf. the vedic use of *pû*), pius, ex-piare, piaculum, punio, poena; ποινή, ἄποινα, νηποινῆ; Goth. fon (fire, cf. *pâvaka*), probably for favan; with *r* for *n*, O.H.G. fiur; A.S. fyr, πῦρ, πυρός.

पूग *pûga*, I. m. 1. A heap, Arj. 3, 32. 2. A multitude, MBh. 5, 1085. pl. A number of persons, Man. 3, 152. 3. The betel-nut tree (Areca faufel). II. n. The fruit of the last.—Comp. *Kâla-*, m. lapse of long time, MBh. 2, 1329.

पूज् *PÛJ*, i. 10, Par. (also Âtm., Hit. ii. d. 36, and in epic poetry, i. 1, MBh. 3, 1005). 1. To honour, to reverence, MBh. 1, 6038; Pańch. i. d. 146 (Âtm.). 2. To regard, Yâjń. 2, 14. Ptcple. of the pf. pass. Anomalous potential *pûjayita*, MBh. 3, 1070). *pûjita*, 1. Frequented, Arj. 4, 55. 2. Recommended. 3. Acknowledged, Böhtl. Ind. Spr. 3174. 4. Endowed, Râm. 2, 26, 16. Comp. *Su-pûjita*, adj. much honoured, Chr. 62, 52. —With the prep. **अनु** *anu*, To honour one after the other, Râm. 2, 99, 9 Gorr. —With **अभि** *abhi*, 1. To honour, Râm. 1, 1, 83. 2. To value highly, MBh. 1, 17. 3. To approve, Râm. 2, 76, 12. *abhipûjita*, 1. Offered after humble reverences, Man. 6, 58 (?). 2. Agreeable, Râm. 1, 52, 23.—With **समभि** *sam-abhi*, To honour, MBh. 4, 98.—With **परि** *pari*, To honour much, Çiç. 1, 14. —With **संपरि** *sam-pari*, The same, MBh. 13, 2110.—With **प्र** *pra*, 1. To honour especially, Pańch. i. d. 164; MBh. 6, 3790 (*prapûjire* without reduplication; probably it is to be changed to *pupûjire*); 13, 914. 2. To approve, MBh. 8, 3244.—With **संप्र** *sam-pra*, To show honour, Hariv. 16223. —With **प्रति** *prati*, 1. To return a salutation, Râm. 1, 26, 4. 2. To salute in one's turn, Man. 1, 1. 3. To approve, Râm. 1, 11, 10. 4. To honour, Man. 3, 58.—With **संप्रति** *sam-prati*, To honour, to salute with reverence, Râm. 2, 70, 6.—With **सम्** *sam*, 1. To honour, Man. 2, 210. 2. To esteem highly, MBh. 3, 1110.—With **अभिसम्** *abhi-sam*, To honour, MBh. 1, 6376.

पूजक *pûj+aka*, adj., f. *jikâ*, Worshipping, MBh. 2, 454; honouring, a worshipper.

पूजन *pûj+ana,* I. n. Honouring, worshipping, Man. 4, 152. II. f. *nî,* The name of a female bird (in a legend).—Comp. *Atithi-pûjana,* n. receiving guests with honour, Man. 3, 70.

पूजयितृ *pûjayitṛi,* i.e. *pûj,* Caus., + *tṛi,* m., f. *trî,* and n. Worshipping, a worshipper, MBh. 13, 7517.

पूजा *pûj + â,* f., Worshipping, honouring, respect, adoration, Kathâs. 4, 43; Vikr. 45, 18.—Comp. *Agra-,* f. first oblation. *Atithi-,* f. receiving guests with honour. *Tyakta-pûja* (vb. *tyaj*), adj. abandoning the worship, Râjat. 5, 53.

पूज्यता *pûjya+tâ* (vb. *pûj*), f., and

पूज्यत्व *pûjya+tva,* n. Venerableness, MBh. 2, 1386.

† **पूण्** *PÛṆ,* see *pûl.*

पूत् *pût,* a sound imitative of blowing, Pañch. 93, 4.

पूतना *pûtanâ,* f. 1. Yellow myrobalan, Terminalia Chebula. 2. The name of a female demon causing a certain disease of children, and killed by Kṛishṇa.

पूति *pûti,* A. i.e. *pû+ti,* f. 1. Purification. B. i.e. *pûy+ti,* I. adj. Putrid, stinking, MBh. 12, 3606. II. n. 1. Pus, matter. 2. Civet.—Cf. Lat. putidus; see *pûy.*

पूतिक *pûti+ka,* I. adj. Putrid, stinking, MBh. 4, 173. II. m. Grey bonduc, Guilandina Bonduc Lin. III. f. *kâ,* A civet or pole-cat.

पूतित्व *pûti+tva,* n. Stinking.

पूतिवक्त्रता *pûti-vaktra+tâ,* f. Condition of having stinking breath, Man. 11, 50.

पूत्यण्ड *pûtyaṇḍa,* i.e. *pûti-aṇḍa,* m. A kind of insect, cf. Böhtl. Ind. Spr. 1808.

पूप *pûpa,* m. A cake, Râm. 1, 54, 3 Gorr.

पूपालिक *pûpâlika,* i.e. *pûpa + âla + ika,* m., and f. *kâ,* A cake, Suçr. 2, 511, 14; 155, 7.

पूय् *PÛY,* i. 1, Âtm. 1. To become putrid, to stink. 2. To putrefy. 3. To be dissolved. *pûta,* see *pû.*—Cf. Goth. fûls, and A.S. fúl; πύϊον, πῦον, πῦος, πυόω, etc., πύθω, πυθεδών, etc.; Lat. pŭter, putris, putrescere, pŭdere, repudium, repudiare, probably also fœtor, etc.

पूय *pûy+a,* m. and n. Pus, matter, Man. 3, 180.—Cf. πύϊον, πῦον, πῦος; Lat. pus.

पूयन *pûy+ana,* n. Pus, discharge from a wound.

पूयभुज् *pûya-bhuj,* adj. Eating purulent carcasses, Man. 12, 72.

पूयोद *pûya-uda* (cf. *udaka*), m. The name of a hell, Bhâg. P. 5, 26, 7.

पूर् *PÛR,* see *pṛî.*

पूर *pûr+a,* m. 1. Filling, Bhâg. P. 6, 9, 7. 2. A large quantity of water, Ragh. 3, 17. 3. A cake, Râm. 2, 100, 64 Gorr. 4. Drawing in breath through the nose, a religious practice, Bhâg. P. 3, 28, 9. 5. The healing or cleansing of ulcers.—Comp. *A-pûra,* adj. not to be satisfied, unquenchable, Bhâg. P. 7, 13, 23. *Ati-,* m. large stream, Utt. Râmach. 68, 12. *Karṇa-,* m. 1. an ornament of the ear, Utt. Râmach. 62, 13. 2. the name of several plants. *Kâma-,* adj. Fulfilling wishes. *Ghṛita-,*

m. a sweetmeat composed of flour, butter, etc. *Jala-*, m. a bed full of water. *Dushpûra*, adj., f. *râ*, difficult to be filled or satisfied. *Pâṇi-*, adj. filling the hand, Yâjń. 3, 320. *Phala-*, m. common citron. *Su-*, I. adj. easy to be filled, Pańch. i. d. 31. II. m. a sort of lime or citron.

पूरक *pûr+aka*, I. adj. 1. Filling. 2. Filling up, Man. 9, 289. 3. Satisfying, MBh. 1, 75. II. m. 1. Closing the right nostril, and drawing up air through the left, a religious observance, Vedântas. in Chr. 217, 17. 2. A citron (Citrus medica). 3. The final obsequial cake.—Comp. *Phala-*, m. a citron.

पूरण *pûraṇa*, i.e. *pûr+ana*, I. adj., f. *ṇî*, Filling, Hariv. 7441. II. n. Act of filling, Ragh. 9, 73; completing, satisfying, Mâlav. d. 73. 2. Drawing (a bow), MBh. 16, 271. III. m. 1. A dyke. 2. The ocean.—Comp. *Gartâ-*, n. Filling up a hole, Pańch. 96, 20.

पूरयितृ *pûrayitṛi*, i.e. *pûr*, i. 10, +*tṛi*, m., f. *trî*, n. One who fills up, who satisfies.

पूरिक *pûrika*, i.e. *pûra+ika*, m., and f. *kâ*, A sort of cake, MBh. 7, 2309.

ऽपूरिन् *-pûr+in*, adj. Filling, MBh. 8, 4669.

पूरु *pûru*, **पूरुष** *pûrusha*, see *puru*, *purusha*.

पूर्णक *pûrṇa+ka* (vb. *pṛî*), I. adj. Filled, full, MBh. 7, 2199. II. m. 1. A certain tree, Râm. 3, 79, 38. 2. The blue jay. III. f. *ṇikâ*, A sort of bird.

पूर्णता *pûrṇa + tâ* (vb. *pṛî*), f. Plenty, Megh. 20.

पूर्णत्व *pûrṇa + tva* (vb. *pṛî*), n. Being full of, Kathâs. 16, 46.

पूर्णपात्रमय *pûrṇa-pâtra+maya* (cf. *pâtra*), adj., f. *yî*. 1. Consisting in a *pûrṇa-pâtra*, MBh. 12, 2306. 2. Concerning full cups, Kathâs. 23, 84 (? Brockh., Consisting in a poem).

पूर्णमा *pûrṇamâ*, and **पूर्णिमा** *pûrṇimâ*, i.e. *pûrṇa* and curtailed *mâsa*, f. The night or day of full moon, Râjat. 5, 156; Pańch. 74, 22.

पूर्ब् *PÛRB*, see *purv*.

पूर्ब *pûrba*, see *pûrva*.

पूर्भिद्य *pûrbhidya*, i.e. *pur-bhid+ya* n. The destruction of castles, war, Chr. 297, 14=Rigv. i. 112, 14.

पूर्व् *PÛRV*, see *purv*.

पूर्व *pûrva*, i.e. *pura+va* (see *purâ*), also *pûrba*, adj., f. *vâ* (*bâ*). 1. Fore, Çâk. d. 37. 2. Former, prior, Böhtl. Ind. Spr. 905. 3. First, Man. 1, 10. 4. Lowest, Man. 8, 120. 5. Eastern, Man. 2, 22. II. adv. *vam*. 1. Before, Chr. 3, 2; first, Pańch. 51, 18. 2. Formerly, Chr. 16, 20. 3. Immemorially, Man. 9, 87. III. *pûrveṇa*, instr. adv. To the east, Râm. 2, 70, 11. IV. An ancestor, Pańch. iii. d. 216; Man. 3, 220. V. f. *vâ*, The east.—Comp. *A-*, adj. 1. new, Pańch. ii. d. 16; unknown, 68, 13. 2. incomparable. *A-dṛishṭa-* (vb. *dṛiç*), I. adj. not seen before, Râm. 5, 54, 3. *Adya-*, adv. till to-day, Râm. 1, 32, 8. *An-âmaya-praçna-*, adv. after having inquired for a person's health. *Anya-*, f. *vâ*, a woman previously promised to one and married to another. *A-bodha-*, adv. without having perceived before, Çâk. d. 99. *Aham-*, adj. desiring to be the first, Râm. 2, 12, 92. *Tri-abda-*, adv. less than three years, Man. 2, 134. *Dakshiṇa-*, adj., f. *vâ*, south-eastern. *Para-*, f. a woman formerly married, having belonged formerly to another man, Chr. 6, 8. *Pûrva-pûrva*, I. adj. every preceding one. II. m. pl. ancestors, MBh. 3, 12408. *Bhûta-*, adj. prior; *°vam*, adv. formerly. *A-bhûta-*, adj. not having existed before. *Mṛidu-*, adj. mild, friendly. adv. mildly, gently at first, Râm. 2, 1, 8. *Yathâ-pûrvam*, adv. 1. as before, Pañch. 36, 18. 2. formerly. 3. in order or succession. *Sakhi-*, adj. more excellent than a friend, MBh. 1, 5142. *Strî-*, one who has been before a wife. *Smita-*, adv. smiling first.—Cf. *pûrvedyus*.

पूर्वक *pûrva + ka*, I. adj., f. *vikâ*. 1. Prior, before, preceding, MBh. 12, 13697. 2. First, Râm. 1, 70, 21. 3. As latter part of comp. adj. often, Accompanied by, Man. 2, 78. II. *kam*, adv. 1. With, Man. 2, 128. 2. Conformable to, 2, 173. III. m. An ancestor, Hariv. 5176.—Comp. *An-anya-pûrvikâ*, f. a woman who had no other husband before, Yâjñ. 1, 52. *Aham-pûrvikâ*, f. emulation for precedence, Kir. 14, 32. *Dârikâ-dâna-*, adj. preceded by the gift of a daughter, Hit. iv. d. 109. *Sâmânya-pratipatti-pûrvam*, adv. after an elevation equal (with the other wives), Çâk. d. 92. *Strî-*, adj. one who has been before a woman, MBh. 5, 5940.

पूर्वग *pûrva-ga*, adj. Preceding, Râjat. 1, 18.

पूर्वज *pûrva-ja*, I. adj., f. *jâ*. 1. Born or produced before, formerly, Man. 9, 31. 2. Eldest, Bhâg. P. 9, 2, 2. II. m. 1. An elder brother, Man. 2, 226. 2. pl. Ancestors, Daçak. in Chr. 185, 7.

पूर्वतन *pûrva + tana*, adj. Former, older.

पूर्वतस् *pûrva + tas*, adv. 1. To the east, MBh. 9, 2361. 2. First, Bhâg. P. 9, 9, 32.

पूर्वत्र *pûrva + tra*=loc. of *pûrva*; with *janmani*, In a former existence, Kathâs. 18, 131.

पूर्वदेहिक *pûrvadehika*, i.e. *pûrva-deha + ika*, adj. Done in a former existence, MBh. 12, 12151.

पूर्ववत् *pûrva + vat*, adv. As before, Man. 11, 213.

पूर्वथा *pûrva + thâ*, adv. As before, Chr. 294, 2=Rigv. i. 92, 2.

पूर्ववर्तिता *pûrvavartitâ*, i.e. *pûrva-vartin + tâ*, f. Priority, Bhâshâp. 15.

पूर्वविद् *pûrva-vid*, adj. Knowing former times, Man. 9, 44.

पूर्वाह्ण *pûrvâhṇa*, i.e. *pûrva-ahan + a*, m. The forenoon, Man. 4, 96.

पूर्वाह्णिक *pûrvâhṇika*, i.e. *pûrvâhṇa + ika*, f. *kî*, Belonging to the forenoon, in the forenoon, MBh. 13, 1573.

पूर्विक in *strî-*, i. e. *strî-pûrva + ika*, adj. One who has been at first a female, Chr. 63, 67.

पूर्विन् *pûrvin*, adj., f. *iṇî*, Done by ancestors.—Comp. *A-pûrvin*, adj. doing what has not been done by the ancestors, MBh. 12, 10796; *strîpûrvin*, see s. v.

पूर्वेद्युस् *pûrvedyus*, i. e. *pûrva + i-div + as*, adv. 1. A former day, yesterday, Man. 3, 187. 2. The morning.—Cf. *prâtar* and πρώϊ-ζος, πρώϊζα.

पूर्वोत्पन्नत्व *pûrvotpannatva*, i. e. *pûrva-ud-panna* (vb. *pad*), *+ tva*, n. Condition of anterior existence, Bhâshâp. 122.

† **पूल्** *PÛL*, i. 1, Par. To accumulate. i. 10 (or **पूण्** *pûṇ*, or **पुण्** *puṇ*), Par. To accumulate.

† **पूष्** *PÛSH*, i. 1, Par. To nourish.—Cf. *push*.

पूषन् *pûshan*, i.e. *push + an*, m. 1.

The name of a vedic deity. **2.** One of the Âdityas, MBh. 1, 2523. **3.** The sun, Böhtl. Ind. Spr. 461.

1. पृ *PṚI*, ii. 3, *pipṛi* (*pipṛi*, Bhâg. P. 7, 9, 41), Par. † ii. 9, *pṛiṇâ*, *ṇî*, Par. **1.** To bring over (ved.). **2.** To protect, Bhâg. P. 7, 9, 41. (**3.** To fill, see *prî*). Caus. and *pâr*, i. 10, *pâraya*, **1.** To accomplish, Râm. 2, 55, 19. **2.** To keep one's ground, MBh. 9, 1074. **3.** To live, Man. 9, 178. **4.** To be able, Bhâg. P. 5, 10, 4. — With the prep. अति *ati*, To maintain, Bhâg. P. 3, 18, 12. Caus. To save from (abl.), 3, 25, 40.— Cf. *para* and πείρω, πεῖρα, πόρος, πορεύς, ἄπορος, ἀπορέω, πορίζω, πορσύνω, πορθμός, παρών, πειράτης, πεπαρεῖν; Lat. par, peritus, ex-pertus, ex-perior, parere, partus, parare, portus, porta, portare; Goth. farjan; O.H.G. and A.S. faran; O.H.G. furt; A.S. fyrd.

2. पृ *PṚI*, i. 6, *priya*, Âtm. To be busy or active.—With the prep. आ *â*, ptcple. of the pf. pass. *âpṛita*, Occupied, Bhâg. P. 3, 9, 10.—With व्या *vi-â*, To be busy, occupied with. *vyâpṛita*, Occupied, Râm. 2, 39, 14; affected with, Lass. 94, 10. Caus. To occupy, Ragh. 6, 19.—Cf. πέρ-νημι (see *paṇ*), περνάω, πιπράσκω, ἔμπορος, πόρνος, νη (cf. *paṇya-strî*), ἐμπολάω, πωλέω, πρίαμαι (old pass.); O.H.G. feil, feili.

3. पृ *PṚI*, ii. 5, *pṛiṇu*, Par. To be pleased with.—With the prep. आ *â*, To be attached to, Bhâg. P. 5, 5, 4 (cf. *prî*).

पृक्ति *pṛikti*, i.e. *pṛich* + *ti*, f. Contact.

पृच् *PṚICH*, ii. 7, Par., and ii. 2, Âtm., and पृञ्च् *PṚIŃCH*, ii. 2, Âtm. **1.** To mix. **2.** To unite, Râjat. 4, 1. **3.** To fill, MBh. 1, 3659. Ptcple. of the pf. pass. *pṛikta*, **1.** Touched. **2.** Touching.—With the prep. अनु *anu*, *anupṛikta*, Mixed.—With सम् *sam*, *sampṛikta*, **1.** Mixed. **2.** United, Man. 9, 322; near to, Vikr. d. 142.—Cf. probably πλέκω, πόρκος; Lat. plicare, plecto; Goth. flahta; O.H.G. flehtan; also A.S. folgian.

पृच्छक *pṛichchhaka*, i.e. *prachh* + *aka*, adj. Inquiring, Böhtl. Ind. Spr. 1819.

पृच्छा *pṛichchhâ*, i.e. *prachh* + *a*, f. Asking a question, inquiring, Çâk. 104, 23 v.r.; question, Pańch. i. d. 438.

† पृज् *PṚIJ*, and पृञ्ज् *PṚIŃJ*, ii. 2, Âtm. v.r. of *pṛich*, ii. 2, and *pṛińch*, and of *pińj*.

† पृञ्च् *PṚIŃCH*, see *pṛich*; पृञ्ज् *PṚINJ*, see *pṛij*.

† पृड् *PṚIḌ*, i. 6, Par. To delight.

पृण् *PṚIṆ*, i. 6, To fill.—Cf. *prî*.

पृत् *pṛit*, see *pṛitanâ*.

पृतना *pṛitanâ*, f., the base of many cases is *pṛit*. **1.** Battle, Chr. 291, 14 = Rigv. i. 64, 14. **2.** An army, MBh. 1, 291.

पृतनानी *pṛitanâ-nî*, m. The commander of an army, MBh. 7, 1464.

पृतन्या *pṛitanyâ*, i. e. *pṛitanâ* + *ya*, f. An army, Bhâg. P. 8, 15, 23.

† पृथ् *PṚITH*, or प्रथ् *PRATH*, i. 10, Par. To throw or cast, to extend (cf. *prath*).

पृथक् *pṛithak*, I. adv. Separately, severally, Draup. 6, 1. II. prep. (with acc., instr., abl.), Without, except.—Comp. *Pṛithak-pṛithak*, separately, Man. 3, 26.—Cf. Lat. pars, partis, privus, privare; perhaps φάρσος.

पृथक्त्व *pṛithak* + *tva*, n. **1.** Individuality, Bhag. 9, 15. 2. Separation, Bhâg. P. 2, 10, 28; separateness. *prithaktvena*, Singly, one by one, MBh. 14, 1058. 3. Severality, Bhâshâp. 88.

पृथा *prithâ*, f. Kunti, one of the wives of Pandu.

पृथि *prithi*, m. A proper name, Chr. 297, 15=Rigv. i. 112, 15.

पृथिवी *prithivî*, i.e. *prithvî*, f. of *prithu*. 1. The earth personified, Man. 2, 225. 2. Earth as an element, Prab. 27, 19.

पृथिवींजय *prithivîṁjaya*, i.e. *prithivî + m-ji + a*, m. A prince, MBh. 2, 364.

पृथिवीभुज् *prithivî-bhuj*, m. A king, Vikr. d. 110.

पृथिवीमय *prithivî + maya*, adj., f. *yî*, Earthen, MBh. 12, 1452.

पृथिवीरुह *prithivî-ruh + a*, m. A plant, a tree, Hariv. 11445.

पृथु *prithu*, i.e. *prath + u*, I. adj., f. *thu* and *thvî*, comparat. *prithutara* and *prathîyas*, superl. *prithutama* and *prathishtha*, Large, great, Megh. 47. II. m. The name of a king and of others. III. f. *thvî*, The earth, Pañch. i. d. 51. IV. f. *thu* and *thvî*, A pungent seed, Nigella Indica.—Cf. Goth. braids; A.S. brád; πλατύς; Lat. lātus.

पृथुक *prithuka*, perhaps *prath + uka*, I. m. 1. Rice or grain flattened. 2. A child, a boy, Çiç. 3, 30. 3. The young of any animal. II. f. *kâ*, A girl.—Cf. probably πόρταξ, πόρτις, perhaps παρθένος.

पृथुता *prithu + tâ*, f., and **पृथुत्व** *prithu + tva*, n. Largeness, greatness.

पृथुल *prithu + la*, adj., f. *lâ*, Large, great, Çiç. 10, 65.

पृथ्वीदण्डपालता *prithvî-danda-pâla + tâ*, f. The office of a chief of the police, Mṛichchh. 177, 19.

पृदाकु *pridâku* (vb. *pard* ?) m., f. *kû*. 1. A snake, MBh. 3, 12190. 2. A scorpion. 3. A tiger. 4. A leopard. 5. An elephant. 6. A tree.

पृश्नि *priçni*, I. adj. 1. Of variegated colour. 2. Delicate, feeble. 3. Thin, small, short. II. m. 1. A proper name. 2. A tribe of Ṛishis. III. f. 1. A ray of light. 2. The mother of the Maruts. 3. A kind of fruit. *priçnî*, Pistia stratistes Lin.

पृश्निगु *priçnigu*, i.e. *priçni-go*, m. A proper name, Chr. 296, 7=Rigv. i. 112, 7.

पृश्निमातृ *priçni-mâtri*, adj. Brought forth by Priçni, epithet of the Maruts, Chr. 291, 2=Rigv. i. 85, 2.

† **पृष्** *PRISH*, (akin to *prush*), i. 1, Par. 1. To sprinkle. 2. To hurt. 3. To vex. 4. To give.

पृषत *prishata*, i.e. *prishant + a*, I. adj. Speckled. II. m. 1. A drop, Râm. 3, 32, 4. 2. A spot. 3. The porcine deer, 2, 93, 2. 3. The father of Drupada, Chr. 51, 7.

पृषत्क *prishatka*, i.e. *prishant + ka*, m. An arrow, Râm. 3, 18, 47.

पृषदश्व *prishadaçva*, i.e. *prishant + açva*, I. adj. Riding on antelopes, epithet of the Maruts, Chr. 293, 4=Rigv. i. 87, 4. II. m. 1. The God of air, or wind divinely personified. 2. A proper name.

पृषदाज्य *prishadâjya*, i.e. *prishant-âjya*, n. Clarified butter mixed with curds, forming an oblation, Râm. 6, 96, 12.

पृषद्वल *prishadvala,* i.e. *prishant+vala,* m. The vehicle of the god of wind (cf. *prishadaçva*).

पृषन्त् *prishant* (properly, ptcple. pres. of *prish*), I. adj., f. *ati,* Speckled (ved.). II. n. A drop of water, Hariv. 3586. III. m. The porcine deer, Râm. 3, 76, 12. IV. f. *shati,* Its female, MBh. 7, 27.

पृषन्ति *prishant+i,* m. A drop of water.

पृषाकरा *prishâkarâ,* i.e. probably *prisha,* for *prishant, -âkara,* f. A small stone, used as weight.

पृषोदर *prishodara,* i.e. probably *prisha,* for *prishant, -udara,* adj. Having the belly speckled.

पृषोद्यान *prishodyâna,* i.e. probably *prisha,* for *prishant, -udyâna,* n. A small garden.

पृष्ठ *prishṭha,* perhaps *pra-stha,* n. 1. The back, Man. 4, 72; with *dâ,* To incline deeply, Râjat. 4, 135. 2. The rear, the hinder-part of anything. *shṭhe* and *shṭhena,* from behind, Mârk. P. 23, 5; Vikr. 47, 12. 3. The surface or superficies, Man. 7, 147; terrace, Vikr. 38, 11.—Comp. *Kâṇḍa-,* 1. m. a soldier, MBh. 13, 1593. 2. the husband of a Vaiçya female. 3. the bow of Karṇa. *Giri-,* n. the top of a mountain. *Tri-,* n. the highest heaven, Bhâg. P. 1, 19, 23. *Loha-,* m. a heron. *Harmya-,* n. the upper room of a palace, Vikr. 38, 11.

पृष्ठक *prishṭha+ka,* n. The back. *prishṭhake kri,* To postpone, Böhtl. Ind. Spr. 138 v.r.

पृष्ठतस् *prishṭha+tas,* adv. and prep. (with the gen.). 1. Behind, at the back of, Râm. 2, 30, 11; with *gam,* To follow, Pañch. 9, 1; to pursue, 172, 17. 2. On the back, Man. 8, 300. 3. Backward, Râm. 5, 49, 33. 4. Secretly, MBh. 13, 5046. 5. With *kri,* To postpone, to renounce, MBh. 1, 6694.

पृष्ठमांसादन *prishṭhamâmsâdana,* i.e. *prishṭha-mâmsa-ad+ana,* n. Backbiting.

पृष्ठानुग *prishṭhânuga,* i.e. *prishṭha-anuga,* adj. Following, Böhtl. Ind. Spr. 2493.

पृष्ठ्य *prishṭhya,* i.e. *prishṭha+ya,* m., f. A pack-horse or riding-horse, MBh. 1, 8011.

पॄ *PṚÎ,* ii. 9, *priṇâ, priṇî,* Par. (whence a new verb **पृण्** *PṚIṆ,* i. 6, Par. Âtm.); hither also **पृ** *PṚI,* ii. 3, and **पूर्** *PÛR,* i. 4, Âtm. (properly passive; in epic poetry also Par. and ii. 2). 1. To fill. 2. To collect, Bhâg. P. 3, 32, 1. 3. To satisfy. 4. *pûr,* i. 4, Âtm., To be filled, Böhtl. Ind. Spr. 945. Ptcple. of the pf. pass. I. *pûrṇa,* 1. Filled, full, Nal. 23, 11. 2. Complete, entire, Râm. 1, 54, 12. 3. Satisfied, Râm. 1, 10, 34. 4. Strong, able. 5. Selfish. Comp. *Â-karṇa-,* adj. drawn to the ear (as the string of a bow), MBh. 4, 1096. *Kalâ-,* 1. adj. equal to the sixteenth part of, MBh. 4, 1299. 2. m. the moon. *Vija-,* m. common citron, or a large kind of lime. II. *pûrta,* 1. Filled, Bhâg. P. 3, 24, 32; full. 2. Complete; with *dharma-,* An act of pious liberality (see n.). 3. Covered. n. An act of pious liberality, as digging a well, etc., Man. 4, 226. Caus. and **पॄ** *PṚÎ,* i. 10, *pâraya,* Par. and **पूर्** *PÛR,* i. 10, *pûraya,* Par. Âtm. 1. To fill, Hariv. 6456. 2. To intensify (a sound), MBh. 10, 412. 3. To blow (a wind instrument), Râm. 6, 37, 39. 4. To draw (a bow), 1, 34, 10 Gorr. 5. To draw (an arrow to the ear), 6, 79, 16. 6. To fulfil, Böhtl. Ind. Spr. 587. **7.** To cover, 6, 86, 36. Comp. ptcple. of the fut. pass. *a-pûrya,* adj. Not to be satisfied, insatiable, MBh. 12, 514.—With the prep. अति *ati,* i. 4, To swell, to rise, MBh. 6, 4783 (Par.).—With अनु *anu, pûraya,* To accomplish, Gît. 1, 25.—With अभि *abhi,* i. 4, To be filled, MBh. 12, 6502. *abhipûrṇa,* Full, full of. *pûraya,* **1.** To fill, Râm. 5, 56, 111. **2.** To load, Kathâs. 44, 47. **3.** To cover, MBh. 6, 1721. **4.** To present with, Hariv. 6556. — With समभि *sam-abhi, pûraya,* To fill, MBh. 3, 10723.—With अव *ava, ava-pûrṇa,* Full of, Hariv. 11993.—With आ *â,* i. 4, **1.** To be filled, MBh. 1, 1302. **2.** To increase, Kathâs. 27, 8. **3.** To abound, Hit. ii. d. 72. *âpûrṇa,* Satisfied, MBh. 14, 627. *pûraya,* **1.** To fill, Bhag. 11, 30. **2.** To blow (a wind instrument), Râm. 6, 75, 11. **3.** To cover, Râm. 3, 32, 15.—With समा *sam-â,* i. 4, To be filled, MBh. 1, 2472. *samâpûrṇa,* Complete, entire. *pûraya,* To draw (a bow), Râm. 1, 34, 9 Gorr.—With निस् *nis, nishpûrta,* Poured out, MBh. 7, 2239.—With परि *pari,* i. 4, To be filled, Râjat. 4, 109. *paripûrṇa,* **1.** Full, filled. **2.** Covered. **3.** Satisfied. **4.** Wealthy, Pańch. v. d. 10. **5.** Being at the summit of (his) power, i. d. 370. **6.** Very intelligent, Râm. 3, 52, 52. *pûraya,* **1.** To fill, MBh. 5, 7523. **2.** To complete, to enjoy entirely, Gît. 2, 16.—With संपरि *sam-pari, sampariपûrṇa,* **1.** Filled. **2.** Accomplished, MBh. 3, 15641.—With पि *pi,* instead of *api,* ii. 3, To fulfil, Bhâg. P. 4, 19, 38.—With प्र *pra,* i. 4, To be filled, Hit. i. d. 62. *pûraya,* **1.** To fill. **2.** To cause to grow wealthy, Mṛichchh. 178, 4. — With अभिप्र *abhi-pra,* i. 4, To be filled, MBh. 15, 678.—With प्रति *prati, pratipûrṇa,* Full, full of, Hariv. 5654. *pûraya,* **1.** To fill, MBh. 14, 2122. **2.** To satisfy, MBh. 13, 4442.—With सम् *sam, sampûrṇa,* **1.** Full, full of, Râm. 6, 96, 12. **2.** Plentiful, Böhtl. Ind. Spr. 779. **3.** Fulfilled, Çâk. 106, 3; complete, Man. 1, 109. *pûraya,* **1.** To fill, Kathâs. 2, 83. **2.** To satisfy, 22, 12. — Cf. πίμπλημι and *prâ*; Goth. and A.S. full =*pûrṇa*; Goth. fulljan; A.S. fyllan; Lat. multus = *pûrta* + *s*; Lat. populus.

पेचक *pechaka,* **I.** m. **1.** An owl, Râm. 6, 27, 31. **2.** The root of an elephant's tail. **3.** A bed. **4.** A louse. **5.** A cloud. **II.** f. *chikâ,* A kind of owl, Râm. l. l.

पेट *peṭa,* m., and f. *ṭâ* and *ṭi.* A basket, bag, Pańch. 126, 2; 127, 1.

पेटक *peṭa+ka* **I.** m. and n. (?), A basket for holding clothes, books, etc., Vikr. 78, 7. **II.** f. *ṭikâ,* A box, Daçak. in Chr. 197, 4. **III.** n. Multitude, Kathâs. 34, 209.

पेडा *peḍâ,* f. A basket.

पेण् *PEṆ,* see *paiṇ.*

पेत्व *petva,* i.e. *pî+tva,* n. **1.** Nectar. **2.** Clarified butter.

पेब् *PEB,* see *pev.*

पेयूष *peyûsha* (=*pîyûsha,* q. cf.), m. and n. **1.** The milk of a cow which has calved within seven days, Man. 5, 6. **2.** Fresh butter. **3.** Nectar.

पेरा *perâ,* f. A musical instrument.

पेरु *peru,* m. **1.** The ocean. **2.** The sun. **3.** Fire.

† पेल् *PEL*, i. 1, Par. To go, to move.

पेलव *pelava*, adj., f. *vâ*. **1.** Delicate, Çâk. d. 70 (too delicate). **2.** Thin, slender. **3.** Soft, tender, Kathâs. 21, 97.—Comp. *Pari-*, I. adj. 1. very small. 2. very delicate. II. n. a fragrant grass, Cyperus rotundus.

† पेव् *PEV*, and प्लेव् *PLEV*, and पेब् *PEB*, i. 1, Âtm. To serve, to attend on.

पेशल *peçala*, i.e. *piç* + *ala*, I. adj., f. *lâ*. **1.** Beautiful, Megh. 75. **2.** Soft, tender, Böhtl. Ind. Spr. 650. **3.** Dexterous, 889. **4.** Crafty. **II.** n. Beauty, Bhâg. P. 1, 10, 30.—Comp. *Ati-*, adj. very crafty, Hit. ii. d. 109. — Cf. ποικίλος.

पेशस् *peças*, i.e. *piç* + *as*, n. An ornament, Chr. 294, 4=Rigv. i. 92, 4.—Comp. *Viçva-*, adj. containing all that is beautiful, Chr. 288, 16=Rigv. i. 48, 16. *Su-*, adj. very splendid, Chr. 288, 13=Rigv. i. 48, 13.

पेशस्कृत् *peças-kṛi* + *t*, m. I. The hand, Bhâg. P. 4, 25, 54. II. A kind of insect, 7, 1, 27.

पेशिका *peçikâ*, i.e. *peçî* + *ka*, f. The peel of a fruit.

पेशी *peçî* (cf. *piçita*), f. **1.** A ball or piece of flesh or meat, MBh. 1, 4494. **2.** The fœtus directly after conception, 12, 11968. **3.** A muscle, Yâjń. 3, 100. **4.** The peel of a fruit. **5.** A kind of drum, MBh. 6, 1535. **6.** An egg.

† पेष् *PESH*, or येष् *YESH*, i. 1, Âtm. To exert one's self.

पेष *pesha*, i.e. *pish* + *a*, m. Grinding, Bhâg. P. 5, 10, 14.

पेषक *peshaka*, i.e. *pish* + *aka*, adj., f. *shikâ*, One who grinds, Hariv. 8394.

पेषण *peshaṇa*, i.e. *pish* + *ana*, n. **1.** Grinding, Mârk. P. 14, 87 (with *yâ*, To be ground). **2.** A threshing floor.

पेषणि and णी *peshaṇi*, i.e. *peshaṇa* + *î*, and the final shortened., f. A grindstone, Man. 3, 68. — Comp. *Yantra-peshaṇi*, f. A hand-mill.

पेषाक *peshâka*, i.e. *pish* + *âka*, m. A grindstone.

† पेस् *PES*, see *pis*.

† पै *PAI*, i. 1., Par. To dry or wither.

पैङ्गल्य *paiṅgalya*, i.e. *piṅgala* + *ya*, n. Tawny, the colour, Suçr. 1, 335, 5.

पैच्छिल्य *paichchhilya*, i.e. *pichchhila* + *ya*, n. Sliminess, Suçr. 1, 154, 15.

पैजवन *paijavana*, i.e. *pijavana* + *a*, patronym., m. A son of Pijavana, Man. 7, 41 (thus to be read).

पैञ्जूष *paiṅjûsha*, m. The ear.

पैठर *paiṭhara*, i.e. *piṭhara* + *a*, adj. Boiled in a pot, Râm. 2, 100, 63 Gorr.

† पैण् *PAIṆ*, पेण् *PEṆ*, लैण् *LAIṆ*, प्रैण् *PRAIṆ*, i. 1, Par. **1.** To go. **2.** To embrace. **3.** To send, or to pound.

पैण्डिन्य *paiṇḍinya*, i.e. *piṇḍa* + *in* + *ya*, n. Living upon alms.

पैतामह *paitâmaha*, i.e. *pitâmaha* + *a*, I. adj. **1.** Belonging or relating to the grandfather, inherited from him, Râjat. 1, 76. **2.** Belonging or relating to Brahman, Râm. 5, 44, 16. **II.** m. **1.** pl. Ancestors, Pańch. 89, 18. **2.** The son of Brahman, MBh. 1, 2581.

पैतृक *paitṛika*, i.e. *pitṛi* + *ka*, adj., f.

ki. **1.** Paternal, Man. 9, 104. **2.** Ancestral. **3.** Relating to the Manes, Râjat. 6, 87.

पैतृयज्ञिय *paitṛiyajñiya,* i.e. *pitṛi-yajña + iya,* adj. Referring to the sacrifice offered to the Manes, Man. 3, 282.

पैतृष्वसेय *paitṛishvaseya* and **पैतृष्वस्रीय** *paitṛishvasrîya,* i.e. *pitṛi-svasṛi + eya* and *îya,* I. adj., f. *yî,* Descended from a paternal aunt, Man. 11, 171. II. m. A paternal aunt's son, Bhâg. P. 1, 19, 35. III. f. *eyî,* and *îyâ,* The daughter of a paternal aunt.

पैत्त *paitta,* and **पैत्तिक** *paittika,* i.e. *pitta + a,* and *ika,* adj., f. *tî, kî,* Bilious, biliary, Suçr. 1, 10, 21.

पैत्र *paitra,* i.e. *pitṛi + a,* I. adj. Relating to the Manes, MBh. 7, 9466. II. n. The part of the hand between the thumb and forefinger.

पैत्रिक *paitrika,* i.e. *pitṛi + ika,* adj., f. *kî,* Paternal, ancestral, Man. 8, 415.

पैत्र्य *paitrya,* i.e. *pitṛi + ya,* adj., f. *rî,* Relating to the Manes, Suçr. 1, 106, 5.

पैनाक *painâka,* i.e. *pinâkin + a,* adj. Belonging to, or proceeding from, Çiva, Râm. 1, 30, 11 Gorr.

पैप्पल *paippala,* i.e. *pippala + a,* adj. Made of the wood of the holy fig-tree, Utt. Râmach. 106, 2.

पैयवन *paiyavana,* incorrectly instead of *paijavana.*

पैल *paila,* i.e. *pîlâ + a,* metronym., m. A proper name.

पैलगर्ग *paila-garga,* m. A proper name, Chr. 46, 28.

पैलव *pailava,* i.e. *pîlu + a,* adj. Made of the tree *pîlu* (Jones=*veṇu,* A bamboo), Man. 2, 45.

पैशल्य *paiçalya,* i.e. *peçala + ya,* n. Mildness, MBh. 1, 5155.

पैशाच *paiçâcha,* i.e. *piçâcha + a,* I. adj., f. *chî.* **1.** Relating to a Piçâcha, or kind of demon, Râm. 1, 29, 17; demon-like. **2.** (with *vivâha*), A mode of marriage, the ravishment of a girl by her lover, Man. 3, 21. II. A Piçâcha, or kind of demon, MBh. 13, 1397.

पैशुन *paiçuna,* i. e. *piçuna + a,* n. Tale-bearing, backbiting, Man. 11, 55.

पैशुन्य *paiçunya,* i.e. *piçuna + ya,* n. **1.** Espionage, backbiting, Man. 12, 6; Pañch. i. d. 115. **2.** Wickedness.

पैष्ट *paishṭa,* i. e. *pishṭa + a* (vb. *pish*), I. adj., f. *ṭî.* **1.** Made of meal. II. f. *ṭî,* Spirituous liquor extracted from bruised rice, Man. 11, 94.

पैष्टिक *paishṭika,* i. e. *pishṭa + ika,* adj. Made of meal, Suçr. 1, 235, 2.

पोगण्ड *pogaṇḍa,* adj. **1.** Not full grown, young, a boy. **2.** Having a defective member.

पोट *poṭa,* I. m. **1.** The foundation of a house. **2.** Uniting, mixing. II. f. *ṭâ.* **1.** A hermaphrodite. **2.** A female servant.

पोत *pota,* I. m. **1.** The young of any animal, Hariv. 3705; used also of plants, e.g. *druma-pota,* m. A young tree, Hariv. 3478. **2.** An elephant of ten years old. **3.** A vessel, a ship, Hariv. 3530. **4.** The site of a house. **5.** Cloth.

पोतक *pota + ka,* I. m. **1.** The young of any animal, used also of plants, Râm. 3, 67, 6; e.g. *chûta-,* A young mango, Daçak. in Chr. 179, 9. **2.** The foundation of a house. II. f. *tikâ* and *taki*, A potherb, Basella lucida. III. f. *taki*, A bird, Turdus macrourus.

पोतृ *potṛi*, i.e. *pû + tṛi*, m. One of the officiating priests at a sacrifice.

पोत्र *potra*, n. 1. The snout of a hog, Ṛit. 1, 17. 2. The share of a plough.

पोत्रिन् *potrin*, i.e. *potra + in*, m. A hog.

पोष *posha*, i.e. *push + a*, m. 1. Thriving, prosperity. 2. Nourishing, cherishing, Bhâg. P. 3, 30, 33.—Comp. *Paratas-*, adj. nourished by another, 3, 33, 28.

पोषक *poshaka*, i.e. *push + aka*, m. 1. One who nourishes, MBh. 2, 2123. 2. A breeder, a keeper, Man. 3, 162.—Comp. *Vṛitti-*, m. subsisting on, Mârk. P. 50, 77.

पोषण *poshaṇa*, i.e. *push + ana*, n. Nourishing, cherishing, breeding, MBh. 3, 11300.

पोषयित्नु *poshayitnu*, i.e. *push*, Caus., + *itnu*, adj. Nourishing.

पोषिन् *poshin*, i.e. *push + in*, adj., f. *shiṇî*, Nourishing, cherishing, Kathâs. 14, 51.

पोष्टृ *poshṭṛi*, i.e. *push + tṛi*, m. A nourisher, one who brings up, Mârk. P. 99, 47.

पौंश्चलीय *pauṁçchalîya*, i.e. *puṁç-chalî + îya*, adj. Relating to harlots, Râjat. 4, 662.

पौंश्चल्य *pauṁçchalya*, i.e. *puṁç-chalî + ya*, n. Female incontinence, Man. 9, 15.

पौंस्न *pauṁsna*, i.e. *puṁs + na*, I. adj., f. *nî*, Human, Bhâg. P. 3, 15, 45. II. n. Manhood, 4, 26, 26.

पौगण्ड *paugaṇḍa*, i.e. *pogaṇḍa + a*, I. adj. Proper to boys, boyish, Bhâg. P. 3, 31, 28. II. n. Boyhood.

पौगण्डक *paugaṇḍa + ka*, n. Boyhood, Bhâg. P. 10, 12, 37.

पौण्डरीक *pauṇḍarîka*, i.e. *puṇḍa-rîka + a*, m. A certain Soma sacrifice, lasting eleven days, MBh. 13, 4934.

पौण्ड्र *pauṇḍra*, i.e. *puṇḍra + a*, m. 1. pl. The name of a people. 2. Their prince. 3. A sort of sugar-cane (cf. *puṇḍra*). 4. Bhîshma's conch, Bhag. 1, 15.

पौण्ड्रक *pauṇḍra + ka*, m. pl. 1. The name of a people, Man. 10, 44. 2. Their king. 3. A sort of sugar-cane, Suçr. 1, 186, 14 (cf. *puṇḍra*).

पौतिनासिक्य *pautinâsikya*, i. e. *pûti-nâsikâ + ya*, n. Fœtor of the nostrils, Man. 11, 50.

पौत्तिक *pauttika*, i.e. *puttikâ + a*, n. The honey of the puttikâ, Suçr. 1, 185, 1.

पौत्र *pautra*, i.e. *putra + a*, I. adj. Relating to sons or children, Râm. 1, 35, 1. II. m. A grandson, Man. 9, 133. III. f. *trî*, A granddaughter Kathâs. 10, 39.—Comp. *Putra-*, n. sons and grandsons, Man. 3, 200.

पौत्रिन् *pautrin*, i.e. *pautra + in*, adj. Having a grandson, Man. 9, 136.—Comp. *Putra-*, adj. having sons and grandsons, Sâv. 5, 57.

पौनःपुन्य *paunaḥpunya*, i. e. *punar-punar + ya*, n. Repetition, Vedântas. in Chr. 216, 8.

पौनरुक्त्य *paunaruktya*, i.e. *punar-ukta* (vb. *vach*) + *ya*, n. 1. Repetition, Ragh. 12, 40. 2. Tautology.

पौनर्भव *paunarbhava*, i.e. *punarbhû + a*, I. adj. Connected with a twice married woman, Man. 9, 176. **II.** m. The son of a twice married woman, Man. 3, 155.

पौर *paura*, i.e. *pura* + *a*, adj., f. *rî*, abst. Relating to or produced in a town, citizen, Çâk. 18, 9; Utt. Râmach. 74, 6.

पौरंजन *pauraṁjana*, i.e. *puraṁjana* + *a*, patronym. Descended from Puraṁjana, Bhâg. P. 4, 27, 9.

पौरंदर *pauraṁdara*, i.e. *puraṁdara* + *a*, adj. Belonging or relating to Purandara, i.e. Indra, MBh. 1, 4477.

पौरव *paurava*, i.e. *puru* + *a*, patronym., f. *vî*. **1.** Descended from Puru, MBh. 1, 3180. **2.** m. pl. The race of Puru, Çâk. d. 49. **3.** m. pl. The name of a people.—**Comp.** *A*-, adj. deprived of descendants of Puru, Hariv. 11081.

पौरस्त्य *paurastya*, i.e. *puras* + *tya*, adj. **1.** Prior, first. **2.** Eastern, Bhâg. P. 4, 25, 46.

पौराण *paurâṇa*, i.e. *purâṇa* + *a*, adj., f. *ṇî*. **1.** Relating to past ages, ancient, MBh. 1, 543. **2.** Deep-rooted, Chr. 24, 38.

पौराणिक *paurâṇika*, i.e. *purâṇa* + *ika*, adj., f. *kî*. **1.** Relating to past ages, old, Prab. 13, 5. **2.** Conversant with the events of former times, MBh. 1, 851.

पौरिक *paurika*, i.e. *pura* + *ika*, m. **1.** Citizen, Mârk. P. 120, 18. **2.** pl. The name of a people. **3.** The name of a prince.

पौरुष *paurusha*, i.e. *purusha* + *a*, **I.** adj., f. *shî*. **1.** Manly, MBh. 12, 718. **2.** Human, Bhâg. P. 4, 27, 26. **3.** Sacred to Purusha; epithet of a holy text, Man. 11, 251. **4.** Having the measure of a man with both arms elevated and the fingers extended. **II.** m. The load which a man may bear, Man. 8, 404 (Kull. ? perhaps a full grown man). **III.** n. **1.** Manhood, manliness, MBh. 13, 542. **2.** Action of men, Bhartṛ. 2, 85; man's work, Râm. 1, 58, 22. **3.** Strength, vigour, Man. 7, 102. **4.** Membrum virile.—**Comp.** *Daiva-antar-ita*-, adj. whose energy is checked by fate, Pañch. ii. d. 140. *Nis*-, adj. devoid of manliness.

पौरुषाद *paurushâda*, i.e. *purusha-âda* + *a*, adj. Proper to man-eaters, Hariv. 3815.

पौरुषिक *paurushika*, i.e. *purusha* + *ika*, m. A worshipper of Purusha.

पौरुषेय *paurusheya*, i.e. *purusha* + *eya*, adj., f. *yî*, Made by, derived from, relating to men, MBh. 5, 2645.

पौरुष्य *paurushya*, i.e. *purusha* + *ya*, n. Manhood, manliness, Mârk. P. 125, 10.

पौरुहूत *pauruhûta*, i.e. *puru-hûta* (vb. *hve*) + *a*, adj. Belonging to Indra, Çâk. d. 48.

पौरूरवस *paurûravasa*, i.e. *purûravas* + *a*, adj. Relating, proper to Purûravas, MBh. 8, 1866.

पौरोगव *paurogava*, i.e. *puras-go* + *a*, m. Overseer or superintendent of a princely kitchen, MBh. 4, 28.

पौरोडाश *paurodâça*, i.e. *purodâça* + *a*, m. A prayer recited on making an oblation of clarified butter.

पौरोधस *paurodhasa*, i.e. *purodhas* + *a*, n. The office of a family priest, Bhâg. P. 6, 7, 36.

पौरोभाग्य *paurobhâgya*, i.e. *puras-bhâgin* + *ya*, n. Envy, Çâk. 89, 5.

पौरोहित *paurohita*, i.e. *puras-hita* (vb. *dhâ*, with *puras*), adj., f. *tî*,

Conformable to, proceeding from a family priest, Mârk. P. 126, 18.

पौरोहित्य *paurohitya*, i.e. *puras-hita* (vb. *dhâ*, with *puras*), + *ya*, n. The office of a family priest, MBh. 1, 675.

पौर्णमास *paurṇamâsa*, i.e. *pûrṇa* (vb. *prî*), -*mâsa* + *a*, I. adj., f. *sî*, In which the moon is full (a night), Nal. 16, 14. II. m. and n. A ceremony performed at the full of the moon, Man. 4, 25. III. n. Day of full moon, MBh. 13, 7386. IV. f. *sî*, Day or night of full moon, Man. 4, 113. V. m. patronym. A proper name.

पौर्णमास्य *paurṇamâsya*, i.e. *paurṇamâsî* + *ya*, n. The sacrifice performed at the full of the moon, MBh. 3, 14135.

पौर्त *paurta*, i.e. *pûrta* (vb. *prî*), + *a*, n. A meritorious work, MBh. 14, 1031.

पौर्तिक *paurtika*, i.e. *pûrta* (vb. *prî*), + *ika*, adj. Relating to or connected with meritorious works, Man. 3, 178; 4, 227.

पौर्वदेहिक *paurvadehika*, i.e. *pûrva-deha* + *ika*, adj. 1. Belonging or relating to a former existence, Yâjń. 1, 348. 2. Done in a former existence, MBh. 12, 6758.

पौर्वाह्णिक *paurvâhṇika*, i.e. *pûrvâhṇa* + *ika*, adj., f. *kî*, Belonging or relating to, or produced in the forepart of the day, Sâv. 7, 1.

पौर्विक *paurvika*, i.e. *pûrva* + *ika*, adj., f. *kî*, Former, Man. 4, 148; previous, old; f. *kî*, A female ancestor, MBh. 1, 6632.

पौलस्त्य *paulastya*, i.e. *pulastya* + *a*, patronym., f. *tî*, Descended from Pulastya; epithet of Kuvera, Râvaṇa, etc., Utt. Râmach. 83, 2.

पौलोम *pauloma*, i.e. *puloman*, and *pulomâ* + *a*, 1. adj. Relating to, treating of, Pulomâ, MBh. 1, 312. 2. patronym., f. *mî*, Descended from Puloman; f. The wife of Indra, Vikr. d. 152. 3. m. pl. A class of demons, MBh. 1, 460.

पौष *pausha*, i.e. *pushya* + *a*, I. adj., f. *shî*, Relating to the time when the moon is in the asterism Pushya, Ragh. 18, 31. II. m. The name of a month, Dec.—Jan. III. f. *shî*, Day or night of full moon in the month Pausha.

पौष्कर *paushkara*, i.e. *pushkara* + *a*, I. adj., f. *rî*. 1. Relating to the blue lotus. 2. Consisting of its flowers, Hariv. 9437. 3. Relating to the Costus speciosus. II. n. The fruit of the Costus speciosus.

पौष्करक *paushkara* + *ka*, adj. Consisting in a lotus flower, Hariv. 11557.

पौष्कल *paushkala*, i.e. *pushkala* + *a*, m. A kind of grain, Mârk. P. 32, 9.

पौष्कल्य *paushkalya*, i.e. *pushkala* + *ya*, n. Full-growth, complete developement. Bhâg. P. 4, 29, 72.

पौष्टिक *paushṭika*, i.e. *pushṭi* + *ika*, adj., f. *kî*. 1. Relating to or furthering increase, Kâm. Nîtis. 4, 32. 2. Furthering, MBh. 13, 7134.

पौष्प *paushpa*, i.e. *pushpa* + *a*, adj., f. *pî*, Coming from flowers, made of flowers, Vikr. d. 38; Râm. 4, 41, 26.

पौष्य *paushya*, i.e. *pushya* + *ya*, I. adj. Relating to the asterism Pushya, MBh. 1, 7333. II. m. The name of a prince. III. adj. Relating to the prince Paushya, MBh. 1, 312.

प्याय् *PYÂY*, see *pyai*.

† **प्युष्** *PYUSH*, and **प्युस्** *PYUS*, see 1. 2. and 3. *vyush*.

प्यै *PYAI*, and प्याय् *PYAY* (developed out of vedic *pî*), i. 1, Âtm. To be exuberant, to increase. Ptcple. of the pf. pass. **I.** *pyâna.* **II.** *pîna*, Fat, bulky, corpulent, Râm. 1, 1, 13. **III.** *pyâyita.*—With the prep. आ *â*, **1.** To increase, MBh. 14, 989. **2.** To cause to prosper, 5, 508. *âpîna*, Full, abounding in milk, MBh. 1, 3934. n. An udder, Ragh. 2, 18. Caus. *pyâyaya*, **1.** To augment, MBh. 3, 13542. **2.** To nourish, Lass. 59, 14. **3.** To refresh, Megh. 45. **5.** To encourage, MBh. 12, 10148. *âpyâyita*, Fattened, strengthened, Pańch. 9, 4.—With समा *sam-â*, To increase. Caus. To refresh, to animate, MBh. 3, 8725.—Akin are probably A.S. faett, O.H.G feizt.

प्र *pra*, prep. **1.** Before. **2.** Forward. **3.** Away. **4.** Pre-eminent. **5.** Excessive. **6.** Beginning. **I.** Combined and compounded with verbs and derivatives. **II.** Compounded with nouns.—Cf. πρό; Lat. prŏ, e.g. in pronepos; Goth. frums; A.S. form; see *pranaptṛi* and *purâ*.

प्रकट् *PRAKAṬ*, a denomin. derived from *prakaṭa*, Par. To appear, Hariv. 15789.

प्रकट *pra-kaṭa* (probably a form of *kṛita*, based on **karta*), **I.** adj., f. *ṭâ*, Displayed, unfolded, manifest, Mârk. P. 105, 7; discovering one's self, Kathâs. 12, 190. **II.** m. A proper name.

प्रकटन *prakaṭana*, i.e. *prakaṭaya* + *ana*, n. Making visible.

प्रकटय *PRAKAṬAYA*, a denomin. derived from *prakaṭa* with *aya*, Par. **1.** To make visible, Çiç. 9, 40. **2.** To show, Bhartṛ. 1, 50. *prakaṭita*, **1.** Manifested. **2.** Apparent; *prakaṭita-hata-a-çesha-tamas*, adj. Having evidently destroyed all darkness, Böhtl. Ind. Spr. 1723. **3.** Opened.

प्रकम्प *pra-kamp* + *a*, m. **1.** Shaking, trembling, Böhtl. Ind. Spr. 2216. **2.** Violent motion, Chr. 33, 33.—Comp. *A-*, adj. unshaken, Râjat. 5, 57. *Dushprakampa*, i.e. *dus-*, adj. difficult to be shaken. *Nishpra°*, i.e. *nis-*, 1. adj. motionless. 2. one of the seven Ṛishis of the thirteenth period.

प्रकम्पन *pra-kamp* + *ana*. **I.** adj. Causing to tremble. **II.** m. **1.** Wind, **2.** A hell. **III.** n. Violent motion, great trembling, shaking, MBh. 12, 3840.

प्रकम्पिन् *pra-kamp* + *in*, adj. Trembling, Utt. Râmach. 80, 16; moving to and fro, Mârk. P. 109, 42.

प्रकर *prakara*, i.e. *pra-kṛî* + *a*, **I.** m. **1.** A heap, a quantity, plenty, Çâk. d. 136. **2.** Aid. **3.** Custom, use. **II.** n. Aloe-wood. **III.** f. *rî.* **1.** A kind of song, Yâjń. 3, 113. **2.** A short interlude in a drama.

प्रकरण *prakaraṇa*, i.e. *pra-kṛi* + *ana*, **I.** n. **1.** Treating, expounding. **2.** A chapter. **3.** Subject, Kathâs. 6, 111. **4.** Opportunity, occasion, MBh. 12, 768. **5.** Relation, Hariv. 3982. **6.** A kind of dramatic poem, Çâk. p. 4, 12. **7.** Treating with respect. **8.** Doing much or well. **II.** f. *ṇî*, A kind of drama.

प्रकर्तृ *prakartṛi*, i.e. *pra-kṛi* + *tṛi*, m. One who causes, MBh, 9, 3054.

प्रकर्ष *prakarsha*, i.e. *pra-kṛish* + *a*, m. **1.** Excellence, Râjat. 5, 381. **2.** Superiority, MBh. 1, 6076. **3.** Intensity, Kathâs. 17, 170. **4.** Length, MBh. 13, 2933.

प्रकर्षण *prakarshaṇa*, i.e. *pra-kṛish* + *ana*, **I.** m. One who troubles, MBh.

8, 1971. **II.** n. **1.** Drawing off, MBh. 1, 7309. **2.** Length, Suçr. 1, 270, 4. **3.** Realising by the use of a pledge more than the interest of a loan. **4.** Bridle (?), MBh. 7, 6446.

प्रकर्षिन् *prakarshin*, adj., i.e. I. *pra-kṛish + in*, Drawing forth, MBh. 6, 2524. II. *prakarsha + in*, Pre-eminent, Hariv. 6404.

प्रकल्पना *prakalpanâ*, i.e. *pra-kḷip*, Caus., *+ana*, f. Allotting, allotment, Man. 8, 211.

प्रकाण्ड *pra-kâṇḍa*, m. and n. **1.** The stem of a tree. **2.** As latter part of comp. word, Excellent, e.g. *mantri-prakâṇḍa*, i.e. *mantrin-*, m. An excellent minister, Râjat. 6, 260; cf. Utt. Râmach. 145, 3.

प्रकाम *pra-kâma*. I. m. Pleasure, Râm. 3, 2, 8. **II.** acc. *mam*, adv. **1.** Willingly, Pańch. 191, 16. **2.** According to one's wish, MBh. 4, 401. **3.** Sufficiently, 7, 2767. **4.** Indeed, Böhtl. Ind. Spr. 3098.

प्रकामतस् *prakâma + tas*, adv. With great delight, Hiḍ. 2, 14.

प्रकार *prakâra*, i.e. *pra-kṛi + a*, m. **1.** Kind, MBh. 1, 7412; species, Ṛit. 1, 2. **2.** Speciality, Bhâshâp. 134. **3.** Way, manner, Pańch. 199, 20.

प्रकारता *prakâra + tâ*, f. Speciality, Bhâshâp. 135.

प्रकालन *prakâlana*, i. e. *pra-kal*, Caus., *+ana*, I. adj. Driving on, MBh. 1, 2585. II. m. The name of a Nâga or serpent.

प्रकाश *pra-kâç + a*, I. adj., f. *çâ*. **1.** Clear, bright, MBh. 3, 12156. **2.** Open, manifest, visible, Râm. 6, 75, 14. **3.** Generally known, Daçak. in Chr. 193, 2. **4.** As latter part of comp. adj. Resembling, like, MBh. 3, 914. **II.** *çam*, adv. **1.** Openly, publicly, Man. 8, 193. **2.** (in dramatic language), Aloud, Çâk. 13, 15. **III.** m. **1.** Lustre, splendour, light, Böhtl. Ind. Spr. 2132. **2.** Manifestation. **3.** Publicity. **4.** Renown, Hariv. 5224. **5.** The open air, Çâk. 46, 7. **6.** Loc. *çe*, In presence, MBh. 12, 8579. **IV.** n. White, or bell metal. —**Comp.** *A-*, I. adj. 1. obscure, dark, Râm. 2, 125, 2 Gorr. 2. concealed, Man. 8, 251. II. *çam*, adv. secretly. *Ati-*, adj. generally known. *Dushpr°*, i.e. *dus-*, adj. dark. *Nishpr°*, i.e. *nis-*, adj. lightless. *Su-*, adj. 1. very visible, Man. 8, 245. 2. manifest. 3. public.

प्रकाशक *pra-kâç + aka*, I. adj., f. *çikâ*. **1.** Clear, bright, Bhag. 14, 6. **2.** Renowned, Râjat. 4, 79. **3.** What makes open or apparent, illuminating, MBh. 14, 1066. **II.** m. The illuminator, the sun, Kathâs. 18, 18.

प्रकाशता *prakâça + tâ*, f. **1.** Brightness, shining, Böhtl. Ind. Spr. 1941. **2.** Renown, Nal. 26, 38.

प्रकाशत्व *prakâça + tva*, n. **1.** Brightness. **2.** Appearance. **3.** Renown, MBh. 13, 4730.

प्रकाशन *pra-kâç + ana*, I. m. f. n. One who or what illuminates, epithet of Vishṇu, MBh. 13, 6978. II. n. **1.** Illuminating. **2.** Making manifest, making known, Pańch. 238, 23. **3.** Showing publicly, Daçak. in Chr. 180, 11.

प्रकाशात्मकत्व *prakâçâtmakatva*, i. e. *prakâça-âtmaka + tva*, n. Condition of having the nature of light, Vedântas. in Chr. 207, 4.

प्रकाशिता *prakâçitâ*, f., and **प्रकाशित्व** *prakâçitva*, n., i.e. *prakâçin + tâ*, or *tva*, Clearness, light, MBh. 12, 6228; 1, 3576.

प्रकाशिन् *prakâçin*, i. e. *pra-kâç*, and *prakâça*, *+ in*, adj. **1.** Clear, bright,

MBh. 1, 1434. **2.** Making visible, Böhtl. Ind. Spr. 3120.

प्रकाशीकरण *prakâçîkaraṇa,* i. e. *prakâça-kṛi + ana,* n. Illuminating, Râm. 2, 15, 18 Gorr.

प्रकाश्य *prakâçya,* **I.** ptcple. fut. pass. of the Caus. of *pra-kâç,* To be illuminated, to be manifested. **II.** incorrectly, instead of *prâkâçya* (q. cf.), e.g. MBh. 8, 1960.

प्रकाश्यता *prakâçya + tâ,* f. Publicity, Râjat. 3, 317.

प्रकिरण *prakiraṇa,* i.e. *pra-kṛi + ana,* n. Strewing, scattering, Mârk. P. 31, 8.

प्रकीर्णक *pra-kîrṇa + ka* (vb. *kṛî*), n. The tail of the Bos grunniens, used as a fan and as an ornament of horses (m.), MBh. 7, 1575.

प्रकीर्तन *prakîrtana,* i.e. *pra-kṛit + ana,* n. Reciting, praising, Mârk. P. 19, 13.

प्रकीर्त्ति *prakîrtti, pra-kṛit + ti,* f. Praise, Bhag. 11, 36.

प्रकुञ्च *pra-kuñch + a,* m. A measure of quantity, about a handful.

प्रकृति *pra-kṛi + ti,* f. **1.** The original or natural state of anything, Pañch. ii. d. 95 (by birth); Vikr. 8, 2; Hit. ii. d. 131; Ragh. 5, 54. **2.** Nature, Bhag. 3, 33; *prakṛityâ,* properly, Pañch. 218, 11. **3.** With *tṛitîyâ,* 'the third nature,' i.e. an eunuch's nature. **4.** A radical form or predicament of being, as illusion, intelligence, etc. **5.** The eight elements, from which all is produced, Bhag. 7, 4. **6.** Cause, the original source, Çâk. d. 1. **7.** The requisites of royal administration, Man. 9, 294. **8.** The chief objects of royal consideration, Man. 7, 156. **9.** Business, affairs, Man. 8, 161. **10.** The minister of a king, 9, 232. **11.** Subjects, people, Man. 7, 175.—**Comp.** *Dushprakṛiti,* i. e. *dus-,* adj. wicked, base.

प्रकृतिज *prakṛiti-ja,* adj. Innate, Bhag. 3, 5.

प्रकृतिमन्त् *prakṛiti + mant,* adj., f. *mati,* Original, natural, MBh. 3, 16003.

प्रकृतिस्थ *prakṛiti-stha,* adj. **1.** Natural, genuine. **2.** Bare, stripped of everything, Daçak. in Chr. 185, 10. **3.** Recovered, 195, 21.

प्रकृष्टत्व *pra-kṛishṭa* (vb. *kṛish*), + *tva,* m. Eminence, superiority, Hit. iv. d. 111.

प्रकोथ *prakotha,* i.e. *pra-kuth + a,* m. Putridity.

प्रकोप *prakopa,* i.e. *pra-kup + a,* m. Effervescence, emotion, wrath, Man. 7, 24.

प्रकोपण *prakopaṇa,* and **प्रकोपन** *prakopana,* i.e. *pra-kup,* Caus., + *ana,* **I.** adj., f. *ṇî* or *nî,* Irritating, who or what irritates. **II.** n. **1.** Irritating. **2.** Provoking, MBh. 1, 2440.

प्रकोपितृ *prakopitṛi,* i. e. *pra-kup,* Caus., + *tṛi* (anomal.), m. One who irritates, MBh. 12, 4855.

प्रकोष्ठ *pra-koshṭha,* m. **1.** The fore-arm, Çâk. d. 133. **2.** and °*ṭa + ka,* The room near the gate of a palace, Kumâras. 15, 6.

प्रक्रम *pra-kram + a,* m. **1.** Proceeding. **2.** Beginning, Kathâs. 18, 63 (*prâchi-,* Beginning from the east). **3.** Opportunity. **4.** Proportion, Vedântas. in Chr. 206, 18.

प्रक्रमण *prakramaṇa,* i.e. *pra-kram + ana,* n. Proceeding, Ragh. 7, 21.

प्रक्रिया *pra-kriyâ,* f. **1.** Manner, way, MBh. 14, 2304. **2.** Rite, observance, Hariv. 2306. **3.** Elevation,

MBh. 12, 4170. 4. Dignity. 5. Insignia (of rank), Gît. 12, 27.

प्रक्लेद *prakleda*, i.e. *pra-klid + a*, m. Being wet, MBh. 12, 9093.

प्रक्लेदन *prakledana*, i.e. *pra-klid + ana*, adj. Making wet, Suçr. 1, 247, 6.

प्रक्लेदवन्त् *prakleda + vant*, **प्रक्लेदिन्** *prakledin*, i.e. *pra-kleda + in*, adj., f. *vatî*, *inî*, Making wet, Suçr. 2, 291, 7.

प्रक्वण and **प्रक्वाण** *pra-kvaṇ + a*, m. The sound of the vîṇâ or lute.

प्रक्षय *prakshaya*, i.e. *pra-kshi + a*, m. Destruction, ruin, Arj. 7, 16.

प्रक्षालक *prakshâlaka*, i.e. *pra-kshal + aka*, adj. Who or what washes, Râm. 2, 32, 21 Gorr.—Comp. *Sadyas-*, m. one who cleans (corn) immediately (for use), i.e. who does not store corn, Man. 6, 18.

प्रक्षालन *prakshâlana*, i.e. *pra-kshal + ana*, I. adj. One who performs frequent ablutions, Râm. 1, 52, 26 Gorr. II. n. 1. Cleaning, bathing, washing away, Pańch. ii. d. 167. 2. A means of cleaning, water for washing with, Yâjń. 1, 229.

प्रक्षेप *prakshepa*, i.e. *pra-kship + a*, m. 1. Throwing. 2. Throwing on, Man. 5, 125. 3. The box for a carriage (?), Bhâg. P. 4, 29, 19.

प्रक्षेपण *prakshepaṇa*, i.e. *pra-kship + ana*, n. Throwing on, pouring on. —Comp. *Argha-*, n. fixing the prices, Yâjń. 2, 261.

प्रक्षोभण *prakshobhaṇa*, i. e. *pra-kshubh + ana*, n. Agitating, Prab. 61, 16.

प्रक्ष्वेडा *prakshveḍâ*. i.e. *pra-kshviḍ + a*, f. An inarticulate sound, grumbling, MBh. 9, 1038.

प्रखल *pra-khala*, m. A very wicked person, Mṛichchh. 168, 14.

प्रख्य *pra-khya* (vb. *khyâ*), I. adj. Clear, MBh. 12, 7447. II. Latter part of comp. adj. 1. Looking, MBh. 13, 547. 2. Like, resembling, MBh. 1, 1236.

प्रख्याति *pra-khyâ + ti*, f. Perceptibility. — Comp. *A-*, f. *aprakhyâtim*, with *i* or *gâ*, To disappear, MBh. 3, 860.

प्रख्यान *prakhyâna* i.e. *pra-khyâ + ana*, m. Making known, report, Râm. i. 71, title.

प्रख्यापन *prakhyâpana*, i. e. *pra -khyâ*, Caus., *+ ana*, n. 1. Publishing, Daçak. in Chr. 180, 12. 2. Report.

प्रगण्ड *pragaṇḍa*, I. m. The upper arm. II. f. *ḍî*, A wall or rampart, MBh. 12, 2638.

प्रगर्जन *pra-garj + ana*, n. Roaring, roar.—Comp. *Siṁha-*, adj. roaring like a lion, MBh. 5, 5119.

प्रगल्भ *pra-galbh + a*, adj., f. *bhâ*, 1. Bold, confident, MBh. 12, 2592. 2. Prompt, courageous, Ragh. 2, 41. 3. Brave, Böhtl. Ind. Spr. 1921; eminent. 4. Impudent, MBh. 12, 4210.—Comp. *A-*, adj. irresolute, disheartened, Bhartṛ. 2, 48.

पगल्भता *pragalbha + tâ*, f. Boldness, Kumâras. 6, 32.

प्रगातृ *pragâtṛi*, i.e. *pra-gai + tṛi*, m. A singer, MBh. 3, 14856.

प्रगामिन् *pragâmin*, i.e. *pra-gam + in*, adj. Being about to depart, Râm. 2, 31, 9.

प्रगायिन् *pragâyin*, i.e. *pra-gai + in*, adj. Singing, Hariv. 12006.

प्रगुण *pra-guṇa*, adj. **1.** Straight; °*ṇî kṛi*, To put in order, to array, Pañch. 218, 7; to arrange, 114, 6. **2.** Honest, upright.

प्रगुणित *praguṇita*, i.e *praguṇa*+*ita*, adj. Made straight or even, Pañch. 207, 23 (?).

प्रगुणिन् *praguṇin*, i.e. *pra-guṇa*+*in*, adj. Honest, friendly (?), MBh. 12, 1052.

प्रगे *prage*, i.e. *pra-ga*+*i* (vb. *gam*), adv. In the morning, at the break of day, Man. 6, 6.—**Comp.** *Ati-*, adv. too early, Man. 4, 62.

प्रगेतन *prage*+*tana*, adj., f. *nî*. **1.** Relating to the morning. **2.** To be performed in the morning, Daçak. in Chr. 188, 22.

प्रगेनिश *prage-niça* (cf. *niçâ*), and

प्रगेशय *prage-çi*+*a*, m. Sleeping in the morning, MBh. 12, 8369; 8396.

प्रग्रह *pra-grah*+*a*, m. **1.** Stretching out, MBh. 13, 6374. **2.** Taking, seizing, Hariv. 15103. **3.** An arm. **4.** A ray of light. **5.** Favour, kindness, MBh. 13, 6709. **6.** Confinement, captivity. **7.** A prisoner, a captive. **8.** Restraining. **9.** A rein, a rope, MBh. 7, 9567; 13, 3456. **10.** The string suspending a balance.

प्रग्रहण *pragrahaṇa*, i.e. *pra-grah*+*ana*, n. **1.** Seizing, MBh. 5, 1229. **2.** Restraining, MBh. 12, 1991.

प्रग्रहवन्त् *pragraha*+*vant*, adj. **1.** Holding, MBh. 12, 1780. **2.** Kind, Râm. 2, 1, 11.

प्रघण *praghaṇa*, i.e. *pra-han*+*a*, m. **1.** (also **प्रघन** and **प्रघान** *praghâna*, and **प्रघाण** *praghâṇa*), A terrace before a house. **2.** A copper pot. **3.** An iron club.

प्रचण्ड *pra-chaṇḍa*, I. adj., f. *ḍâ*. **1.** Excessively violent, Mṛichchh. 2, 12. **2.** Passionate, wrathful, Râm. 6, 36, 83. **3.** Terrible, MBh. 3, 15701. **II.** m. The name of a Dânava or demon.

प्रचण्डता *prachaṇḍa*+*tâ*, f. Boldness, Utt. Râmach. 133, 16.

प्रचय *prachaya*, i.e. *pra-chi*+*a*, m. **1.** Gathering, Bhâshâp. 111. **2.** A heap, a quantity, Ṛit. 5, 1; Kir. 5, 48.

प्रचर *pra-char*+*a*, m. **1.** A road. **2.** pl. The name of a people, Râm. 4, 44 12 (v.r.).

प्रचल *pra-chal*+*a*, adj. Trembling, MBh. 1, 1379.

प्रचलन *pra-chal*+*ana*, n. **1.** Trembling. **2.** Moving to and fro, rocking (on the knees), Pañch. 252, 22. **3.** Fleeing, flight, Pañch. iii. d. 128.

प्रचलाक *pra-chal*+*âka*, m. **1.** Shooting with arrows. **2.** A snake. **3.** A peacock's tail.

प्रचलाकिन् *prachalâkin*, i.e. *prachalâka*+*in*, m. **1.** A snake. **2.** A peacock, Utt. Râmach. 49, 11.

प्रचलायित *prachalâyita*, i. e. a ptcple. pf. pass. of *prachala*+*ya* (denomin.), adj. and n. Nodding with the head when sleeping, Râjat. 1, 371.

प्रचार *prachâra*, i.e. *pra-char*+*a*, m. **1.** Proceeding, Râm. 5, 32, 8. **2.** Going, Pañch. 31, 3. **3.** Pasture ground, Man. 9, 219. **4.** Conduct, Man. 7, 153. **5.** Appearance, Prab. 10, 8.—**Comp.** *Nishpr°*, i.e. *nis-*, adj. not moving, MBh. 13, 270. 2. fixed on one point, 12, 7810 (viz. *manas*).

प्रचारिन् *prachârin*, i.e. *pra-char*

+in, adj. **1.** Proceeding, appearing, MBh. 12, 7480. **2.** Behaving, MBh. 12, 1783.

प्रचालन *prachâlana*, i.e. *pra-chal*, Caus., *+ana*, n. Stirring, stir, Pańch. 248, 7.

प्रचिकीर्षु *prachikîrshu*, i. e. *pra-chikîrsha*, desider. of *kṛi*, *+u*, adj. Wishing to requite, Bhâg. P. 4, 10, 10.

प्रचुर *prachura*, adj., f. *râ*. **1.** Much, many, Pańch. 141, 18. **2.** Frequent, Bhâg. P. 5, 13, 21. **3.** Abounding in, 1, 18, 43.

प्रचुरत्व *prachura + tva*, n. **1.** Plenty, Hariv. 11143. **2.** Abounding in, Vedântas. in Chr. 204, 21.

प्रचेतस् *pra-chetas*, I. adj. Wise, intelligent. II. m. **1.** A name of Varuṇa. **2.** The name of a Ṛishi. **3.** (also *prachetas+a*), m. pl. The ten sons of Prachînavarhis. **4.** The name of a king.

प्रचेतस *prachetas+a*, see the last.

प्रचोद *prachoda*, i.e. *pra-chud+a*, m. Inciting.

प्रचोदन *prachodana*, i.e. *pra-chud+ana*, n. Inciting, directing, order, MBh. 5, 73.

प्रचोदिन् *prachodin*, i.e. *pra-chud+in*, f. *nî*, Driving.—Comp. *Guṇa-chakra-*, adj. driving the wheel, i.e. possessed of all virtues, Böhtl. Ind. Spr. 1155.

प्रच्छद *prachchhada*, i.e. *pra-chhad+a*, m. A cover, a blanket, Ragh. 19, 22.

प्रच्छर्दन *prachchhardana*, i.e. *pra-chhṛid+ana*, n. **1.** Vomiting, emitting. **2.** An emetic.

प्रच्छर्दिका *prachchhardikâ*, i.e. *pra-chhṛid+aka*, f. Vomiting.

प्रच्छादक *prachchhâdaka*, i.e. *pra-chhad+aka*, adj. Covering.

प्रच्छादन *prachchhâdana*, i.e. *pra-chhad+ana*, I. adj. Covering, Nal. 17, 10. II. n. **1.** Concealment, Pańch. 188, 13. **2.** An upper or outer garment.

प्रच्छान *prachchhâna*, i. e. *pra-chho+ana*, n. Cupping.

प्रच्छाय *prachchhâya*, i.e. *pra* and *chhâyâ*, n. Dense shadow, Çâk. d. 3.

प्रच्यवन *prachyavana*, i.e. *pra-chyu+ana*, n. **1.** Departing, withdrawing. **2.** (with abl.), Loss, MBh. 4, 646.

प्रच्युति *pra+chyu+ti*, f. Loss.

प्रछ् *PRACHH*, i. 6, *pṛichchha*, Par. (in poetry also Âtm., Man. 2, 152). **1.** To ask, Man. 8, 88. **2.** To ask about (with two accus.), Daçak. in Chr. 179, 18. Anomal. condit. 2. sing. *aprâkshyas*, Vedântas. in Chr. 216, 15.—With the prep. **अनु** *anu*, To ask about, Râm. 2, 57, 29.—With **अभ्यनु** *abhi-anu*, The same, MBh. 13, 2169.—With **समनु** *sam-anu*, The same, MBh. 2, 2142.—With **अभि** *abhi*, The same, MBh. 3, 13339.—With **आ** *â*, Âtm. (in epic poetry also Par.). **1.** To take leave of one (acc.), Râm. 2, 31, 28. **2.** To ask, Bhâg. P. 3, 7, 36 (ved.). Ptcple. of the fut. pass. *âpṛichhya*, Praiseworthy, Chr. 291, 13=Rigv. i. 64, 13.—With **उपा** *upa-â*, To take leave of one, Râm. 3, 5, 18.—With **समा** *sam-â*, The same, Râm. 2, 31, 27 Gorr.—With **उप** *upa*, To ask, MBh. 12, 12272.—With **परि** *pari*, **1.** To ask, Man. 11, 195. **2.** To ask about, MBh. 1, 6311.—With **संपरि** *sam-pari*, To ask, MBh. 14, 576.—With

प्रति *prati,* **1.** To ask, Kathâs. 26, 121. **2.** To ask about, Râm. 1, 8, 18.—With वि *vi,* To ask, Bhâg. P. 2, 4, 25.—With सम् *sam,* Âtm. **1.** To ask, Lass. 41, 10. **2.** To ask about, MBh. 15, 6.—With उपसम् *upa-sam,* To ask, MBh. 5, 2658.—Cf. Lat. procus, procax, precor, prex, probably posco, postulare, perhaps suf-fragari, rogare, flagitare; Goth. fragan, fraihnan; A.S. fregnan.

प्रजन *pra-jan + a,* **I.** m. and n. **1.** Impregnating, Man. 9, 61. **2.** Impregnation, MBh. 14, 1127. **3.** The season for a cow's taking the bull. **4.** Bringing forth. Man. 9, 96. **II.** m. A progenitor, Bhâg. P. 8, 5, 34.

प्रजनन *pra-jan + ana,* n. **1.** Generating, Bhâg. P. 4, 1, 28. **2.** Children, 9, 14, 45.

प्रजल्प *pra-jalp + a,* m. Prattle.

प्रजल्पन *pra-jalp + ana,* n. Speaking, Pańch. 85, 21.

प्रजवन *pra-javana,* adj. Very quick, Utt. Râmach. 119, 4.

प्रजविन् *prajavin,* i.e. *pra-jû + in,* adj. Quick, Utt. Râmach. 48, 2.

प्रजस् *prajas,* i.e. *pra* and vb. *jan,* a substitute for *prajâ* when latter part of comp. adj.; e.g. *a-,* Having no progeny, Yâjń. 2, 144. *bahu-,* Having a numerous progeny.

प्रजा *prajâ,* i.e. *pra* and vb. *jan,* f. **1.** Progeny, offspring, Man. 3, 42. **2.** Creature, Man. 3, 76. **3.** Subjects, people, 1, 89.—**Comp.** *A-praja,* I. adj., f. *jâ.* 1. not bringing forth, MBh. 1, 4491. 2. childless, Pańch. ii. d. 101. II. f. *jâ,* a female who has not borne (a child), Man. 9, 161. *Sakṛit-praja,* m. a crow.

प्रजागर *prajâgara,* i.e. *pra-jâgṛi + a,* **I.** m. **1.** One who wakes, MBh. 13, 7051. **2.** A guardian, Bhâg. P. 4, 27, 15. **3.** The act of waking, watching, MBh. 1, 330. **4.** Taking care, Râjat. 5, 317. **5.** Awaking, being roused, Kâm. Nîtis. 7, 58. **II.** f. *râ,* The name of an Apsaras.

प्रजागरण *prajâgaraṇa,* i.e. *pra-jâgṛi + ana,* n. Sleeplessness.

प्रजाति *prajâti,* i.e. *pra-jan + ti,* f. Generating, Bhâg. P. 2, 6, 7.

प्रजापाल्य *prajâpâlya,* i.e. *prajâ-pâla + ya,* n. The office of a king, Râm. 2, 23, 26.

प्रजायिनी *prajâyinî, pra-jan + in + î,* f. **1.** Being about to bring forth. **2.** Bringing forth, MBh. 13, 4229. **3.** A mother, Nal. 13, 67.

प्रजावन्त् *prajâ + vant,* **I.** adj., f. *vatî,* Having progeny, abounding in progeny, Chr. 294, 7 = Rigv. i. 92, 7. **II.** f. *vatî.* **1.** Pregnant, Bhâg. P. 9, 8, 3. **2.** A mother, Mârk. P. 125, 7. **3.** A brother's wife, Ragh. 14, 45.

प्रजिहीर्षु *prajihîrshu,* i.e. *pra-jihîrsha,* desider. of *hṛi, + u,* adj. Being about to strike, Râjat. 3, 510.

प्रजीवन *pra-jîv + ana,* n. Livelihood, subsistence, Man. 9, 163.

प्रज्ञ *pra-jńa,* **I.** adj. **1.** (vb. *jńâ*), Intelligent. **2.** i.e. *pra-jânu,* Bandy-legged, having the knees far apart. **II.** f. *jńâ,* Understanding, wisdom, Pańch. i. d. 475; knowledge, Man. 4, 41.—**Comp.** *Dîrgha-prajńa,* adj. having a far-seeing understanding. *Dushprajńa,* i.e. *dus-,* adj. foolish. *Sthita-,* adj. calm.

प्रज्ञप्ति *prajńapti,* i.e. *pra-jńâ,* Caus., *+ ti,* f. **1.** Teaching, Bhâg. P. 3, 25, 1. **2.** A certain magical art, Kathâs. 30, 6.

प्रज्ञान *pra-jñâ + ana*, n. 1. Knowledge, wisdom, MBh. 3, 12693. 2. A mark, 5, 992.—Comp. *Dushprajñâna*, i.e. *dus-*, n. foolishness.

प्रज्ञामय *prajñâ + maya*, adj., f. *yî*, Made of, consisting in intelligence, MBh. 12, 8630.

प्रज्ञावन्त् *prajñâ + vant*, adj., f. *vatî*, Wise, intelligent, Pañch. 132, 10.

प्रज्ञु *prajñu*, i.e. *pra-jânu*, adj. Bandy-legged.—Cf. *πρόχνυ*.

प्रज्वार *prajvâra*, i.e. *pra-jvar + a*, m. The heat of the fever, Bhâg. P. 4, 27, 30.

प्रणति *praṇati*, i.e. *pra-nam + ti*, f. Salutation, reverence, Râjat. 5, 145.

प्रणय *praṇaya*, i.e. *pra-nî + a*, m. 1. Guidance, MBh. 12, 3934. 2. Affection, Böhtl. Ind. Spr. 364; friendly or fond regard, love, Vikr. d. 34. 3. Confidence, familiarity, Bhag. 11, 41. 4. Desire, MBh. 13, 224.—Comp. *A-*, m. want of affection. *Ati-*, m. exceeding love. *Nishpraṇaya*, i.e. *nis-*, adj. cold, Utt. Râmach. 70, 5. *Sa-*, I. adj. affectionate, friendly. II. *yam*, adv. 1. affectionately, Chr. 44, 32. 2. confidently, Kathâs. 46, 191.

प्रणयन *praṇayana*, i.e. *pra-nî + ana*, n. 1. Performing, practising, MBh. 1, 7593. 2. Sentencing, Man. 8, 277. 3. Adducing.

प्रणयवन्त् *praṇaya + vant*, adj., f. *vatî*. 1. Attached to, loving, Çâk. d. 143. 2. Confident, MBh. 12, 13929.

प्रणयिता *praṇayitâ*, i.e. *praṇayin + tâ*, f. Desire, Böhtl. Ind. Spr. 396.—Comp. *Pâṇi-*, f. condition of being taken as wife, Râjat. 3, 390 (cf. *pâṇi-praṇayin + î*).

प्रणयिन् *praṇayin*, i.e. *praṇaya + in*, I. adj., f. *inî*. 1. Affectionate, attached to, Böhtl. Ind. Spr. 1762. 2. Beloved, Bhâg. P. 9, 10, 8. II. m. 1. A friend, Vikr. d. 94; a favourite, Böhtl. Ind. Spr. 1903. 2. A husband or lover, Megh. 40. III. f. *inî*, A wife or mistress, Prab. 100, 3.—Comp. *Pâṇi-praṇayinî*, f. a wife, Râjat. 3, 307.

प्रणव *praṇava*, i.e. *pra-nu + a*, m. 1. The holy syllable *om*, Man. 2, 74. 2. A small tabor.

प्रणवक *praṇava + ka*, a substitute for *praṇava* when latter part of a comp. adj. *sa-vyâhṛiti-praṇavaka*, With the holy words and the syllable *om*, Man. 11, 248.

प्रणाद *pranâda*, i.e. *pra-nad + a*, m. 1. A loud noise, MBh. 4, 1684; a shout. 2. Neighing, MBh. 6, 137. 3. Roar, Râm. 6, 79, 10. 4. Tingling in the ear.

प्रणाम *praṇâma*, i.e. *pra-nam + a*, m. 1. Bowing, a bow, MBh. 1, 5384. 2. Prostration, Daçak. in Chr. 194, 8. 3. Respectful salutation, Pañch. 91, 3. —Comp. *Sa-praṇâma + m*, adv. with a bow, Çâk. 7, 8.

प्रणामिन् *praṇâmin*, i.e. *pra-nam + in*, adj. Bowing, worshipping, Böhtl. Ind. Spr. 558.

प्रणायक *praṇâyaka*, i.e. *pra-nî + aka*, m. A commander, MBh. 10, 54.

प्रणाली *praṇâlî*, i.e. *pra-nâḍî*, f. A channel from a pond, a watercourse, Mṛichchh. 158, 26.

प्रणाश *praṇâça*, i.e. *pra-naç + a*, m. 1. Disappearance, loss, Pañch. 5, 10. 2. Death, 87, 19.

प्रणाशन *praṇâçana*, i.e. *pra-naç*, Caus., *+ ana*, I. adj., f. *nî*, Destroying, removing, MBh. 1, 354. **II.** n. Destroying, destruction, Ragh. 3, 60.

प्रणाशिन् *praṇâçin*, i. e. *pra-naç*, Caus., + *in*, adj. Destroying, removing, MBh. 3, 6054.

प्रणिधान *praṇidhâna*, i. e. *pra-ni-dhâ* + *ana*, n. **1.** Putting on, employing. **2.** Respectful behaviour, attendance to, MBh. 3, 17016. **3.** Profound meditation, Vedântas. in Chr. 217, 6. **4.** Prayer.

प्रणिधि *praṇidhi*, i.e. *pra-ni-dhâ* (cf. *nidhi*), m. **1.** Spying, MBh. 12, 2155. **2.** Sending out (of emissaries), Râm. 1, 4, 103 Gorr. **3.** Request. **4.** A spy, an emissary, Man. 7, 153. **5.** A follower.

प्रणिपतन *praṇipatana*, i. e. *pra-ni-pat* + *ana*, n. Prostration, Böhtl. Ind. Spr. 1720.

प्रणिपात *praṇipâta*, i.e. *pra-ni-pat* + *a*, m. **1.** Prostration, Böhtl. Ind. Spr. 442; Vikr. 34, 4. **2.** Submission, Ragh. 4, 64.

प्रणिपातिन् *praṇipâtin*, i.e. *pra-ni-pat* + *in*, adj. Falling at another's feet, submitting one's self, MBh. 5, 2654.

प्रणुद् *praṇud*, i.e. *pra-nud*, adj. **1.** Forcing away, MBh. 3, 720. **2.** Removing, MBh. 9, 390.

प्रणुद *praṇuda*, i. e. *pra-nud* + *a*, Forcing away, Hariv. 7420.

प्रणेतृ *praṇetṛi*, i.e. *pra-nî* + *tṛi*, m. **1.** A leader, MBh. 2, 264. **2.** A creator, MBh. 1, 7277. **3.** An author, 13, 7166.

प्रतति *pratati*, i.e. *pra-tan* + *ti*, f. **1.** Spreading. **2.** A creeper.

प्रतन *pra* + *tana*, adj., f. *nî*, Old.—Cf. probably πρύτανις; cf. *purâtana*.

प्रतनु *pra-tanu*, adj. **1.** Very thin, Megh. 104. **2.** Very delicate, Böhtl. Ind. Spr. 3322. **3.** Very small, Megh. 30; indifferent, Çâk. d. 138.

प्रतनुक *pratanu* + *ka*, adj. Very delicate.

प्रतपन *pra-tap* + *ana*, n. Warming, MBh. 1, 3576.

प्रतर *pratara* i.e. *pra-tṛî* + *a*, m. Crossing over.—**Comp.** *Dushpr°*, i.e. *dus-*, adj., f. *râ*, difficult to be crossed over, Râm. 2, 71, 9.

प्रतरण *pratarana*, i. e. *pra-tṛî* + *ana*, n. Crossing over, MBh. 4, 199.

प्रतर्क *pra-tark* + *a*, m. Supposition, MBh. 1, 7180.—**Comp.** *Su-*, m. great understanding, 5, 3062.

प्रतर्कण *pratarkaṇa*, i.e. *pra-tark* + *ana*, n. Judging.

प्रतवस् *pra-tavas*, adj. Very strong, Chr. 293, 1 = Rigv. i. 87, 1.

प्रतान *pratâna*, i.e. *pra-tan* + *a*, m. **1.** A tendril, Çâk. d. 170. **2.** A plant having tendrils, a climber, Man. 1, 48. **3.** Spreading, Kathâs. 35, 153.

प्रतानवन्त् *pratâna* + *vant*, adj., f. *vatî*. **1.** Having tendrils, Suçr. 1, 4, 17. **2.** Spread, 1, 308, 16.

प्रताप *pratâpa*, i.e. *pra-tap* + *a*, m. **1.** Heat, Ragh. 4, 12. **2.** Splendour, Böhtl. Ind. Spr. 131. **3.** Majesty, dignity, Kâm. Nîtis. 8, 12.—**Comp.** *Nish-pratâpa*, i.e. *nis-*, adj. base, Pańch. ii. d. 97.

प्रतापन *pratâpana*, i. e. *pra-tap*, Caus., + *ana*, **I.** adj. Distressing, inflicting pain, Râm. 3, 53, 29. **II.** m. A hell. **III.** n. Burning, MBh. 13, 3302.

प्रतापवन्त् *pratâpa* + *vant*, **I.** adj. Majestic, Bhag. 1, 12. **II.** m. A proper name, MBh. 9, 2567.

प्रतापिन् *pratâpin*, i. e. *pra-tap*, Caus., +*in*, and *pratâpa*+*in*, adj. **1.** Burning, MBh. 9, 1334; distressing, 3, 1685. **2.** Shining, majestic, 13, 2149.

प्रताम्र *pra-tâmra*, adj. Very red, Çâk. d. 133.

प्रतार *pratâra*, i.e. *pra-tṛi*+*a*, m. Crossing over, Râm. 1, 3, 33.

प्रतारक *pratâraka*, i. e. *pra-tṛi*+*aka*, adj. Cheating, Böhtl. Ind. Spr. 3328.

प्रतारण *pratârana*, i.e. *pra-tṛi*+*ana*, n. **1.** Crossing over, Râm. 1, 3, 28 Gorr. **2.** and f. *ṇâ*, Cheating, fraud.

प्रति *pra*+*ti*, **I.** preposition with acc. and abl. **1.** Towards, to, against, Man. 4, 52. **2.** In proportion to, compared with, Kathâs. 45, 400; Utt. Râmach. 116, 14. **3.** Near, Râm. 2, 83, 19. **4.** On, MBh. 3, 15745. **5.** About; *phâlgunaṁ vâtha chaitraṁ vâ mâsau prati*, 'About the month of Phâlguna or Chaitra,' Man. 7, 182. **6.** For, as compensation (with abl.); *asmât kapotât prati*, 'For this pigeon,' MBh. 3, 13287. **7.** Concerning; *simâṁ prati samutpanne vivâde*, 'If a contest arises concerning a boundary,' Man. 8, 245; with respect to, in regard of. **8.** According; *dharmaṁ prati*, 'By law,' Man. 8, 55; *mâṁ prati*, 'According to my opinion,' Mâlav. d. 50. **9.** In every, each by each; *yajñaṁ prati*, 'In every sacrifice,' Yâjñ. 1, 110. **II.** Combined and compounded with verbs and their derivatives, in the same significations as in I., and besides in the signification Back, returning, again. **III.** Compounded with nouns, in the significations of I., and 'equally.' In comp. adv. we find it with a distributive signification, 'Each by each,' 'every,' e.g. *prati-gṛiha*+*m*, adv. In every house. **IV.** With following *uta*, On the contrary.—Cf. *προτί*, *πρός*; Lat. red, e.g. in red-dere, red-ire, and re, e.g. in re-ferre.

प्रतिकर *pratikara*, i.e. *prati-kṛi*+*a*, **I.** adj., f. *rî*, Counteracting, Suçr. 2, 270, 6. **II.** m. Compensation, Râjat. 5, 169 (read *râjâpratikareṇa*, i. e. *râjâ apratikareṇa*, 'Without compensation').

प्रतिकर्कश *prati-karkaça*, adj., f. *çâ*, Equally hard, of the same hardness as, Mṛichchh. 91, 6.

प्रतिकर्तृ *pratikartṛi*, i.e. *prati-kṛi*+*tṛi*, m. **1.** One who requites, Hariv. 11170. **2.** One who opposes.

प्रतिकर्म *pratikarma*, i.e. *prati-karman*, adv. In every work, MBh. 12, 2963.

प्रतिकर्मन् *prati-karman*, n. **1.** Dress, personal embellishment, Çiç. 5, 27. **2.** Requital, MBh. 4, 1841. **3.** Redress, opposing.—Comp. *A-*, adj. obedient, Râm. 1, 75, 22.

प्रतिकाङ्क्षिन् *prati-kâṅksh*+*in*, adj. Desiring, Hariv. 5557.

प्रतिकामिनी *prati-kâmin*+*i*, f. A female rival, Çiç. 9, 35.

प्रतिकाय *prati-kâya*, m. **1.** An effigy. **2.** A target for archers to practice at.

प्रतिकार and **प्रतीकार** *pratîkâra*, i. e. *prati-kṛi*+*a*, m. **1.** Obviating, Böhtl. Ind. Spr. 370. **2.** Remedying, help, Hit. 85, 6, M.M.; help against, alleviation, Vikr. 20, 9. **3.** A remedy, Man. 10, 185. **4.** Requital, Râm. 4, 27, 20. **5.** A kind of peace or alliance, concluded in the hope that the one part will requite services received from the other, Hit. iv. d. 113, 114.—Comp. *A-pratîkâra*, adj. 1. irremediable. 2.

Nishpratikâra + m, i.e. *nis-*, adv. without any trouble, MBh. 1, 8250.

प्रतिकारिन् *pratikârin*, i.e. *prati-kṛi + in*, adj. Counteracting, obviating.

प्रतिकाश and **प्रतीकाश** *pratîkâça*, i.e. *prati-kâç + a*, adj. Like, resembling, Utt. Râmach. 50, 8 (*ti*).

प्रतिकितव *prati-kitava*, m. An adversary at play, Daçak. in Chr. 185, 24.

प्रतिकुञ्जर *prati-kuñjara*, m. A hostile elephant, MBh. 9, 3217.

प्रतिकूल *prati-kûla*, I. adj., f. *lâ*. **1.** Contrary, Hariv. 11261; disagreeable, Pañch. iii. d. 104. **2.** Contradictory, Râm. 3, 30, 14. **3.** Hostile, Man. 9, 80; *pratikûleshu sthita*, Refractory, 9, 275. **4.** Disastrous, Çâk. 7, 16. **5.** Perverse, MBh. 13, 3403. II. *pratikûlam*, adv. **1.** Contrary, Râm. 6, 90, 26. **2.** Inversely, Man. 10, 31.

प्रतिकूलकृत् *pratikûla-kṛi + t*, adj. Opposing, making opposition, in *a-*, Râm. 2, 52, 10 Gorr.; not opposing.

प्रतिकूलतस् *pratikûla + tas*, adv. In contradiction, MBh. 12, 8805.

प्रतिकूलता *pratikûla + tâ*, f. **1.** Opposition, Kathâs. 31, 85. **2.** Hostility, Böhtl. Ind. Spr. 1841.

प्रतिकूलदैवता *pratikûla-daiva + tâ*, f. Hostility of fate, Pañch. 192, 21.

प्रतिकूलय *PRATIKÛLAYA*, a denomin. derived from *pratikûla* with *aya*, Par. To oppose, Râm. 2, 52, 70.

प्रतिकूलवन्त् *pratikûla + vant*, adj. Refractory, MBh. 10, 124.

प्रतिकृति *prati-kṛi + ti*, f. **1.** An image, Çâk. 90, 2. **2.** Resistance, Hariv. 4211.

प्रतिकोप *pratikopa*, i.e. *prati-kup + a*, m. Wrath, anger, MBh. 4, 1929.

प्रतिक्रिया *prati-kriyâ*, f. **1.** Counteracting, keeping off, Râm. 6, 1, 5. **2.** A fence, Râjat. 5, 92. **3.** Remedying, help, Kathâs. 31, 75; Utt. Râmach. 73, 5. **4.** Care, MBh. 12, 2187. **5.** Requital, Kathâs. 4, 124.—**Comp.** *An-anya-pratikriya*, adj. having no other help, Böhtl. Ind. Spr. 1949. *Nishpratikriya*, i.e. *nis-*, adj. irremediable.

प्रतिक्रूर *prati-krûra*, adj. Returning cruelty, in *a-*, MBh. 12, 9974; not returning cruelty.

प्रतिक्षणम् *prati-kshaṇa + m*, adv. Every moment, continually, Hit. 59, 17; 97, 15.

प्रतिक्षेप *pratikshepa*, m., and **प्रतिक्षेपण** *pratikshepaṇa*, n., i.e. *prati-kship + a* or *ana*, Contest, contesting, MBh. 7, 3958; Prab. 87, 1.

प्रतिगज *prati-gaja*, m. A hostile elephant, MBh. 1, 7092.

प्रतिगमन *prati-gam + ana*, n. Returning, Ram. 1, 17, title.

प्रतिगर्जना *prati-garj + anâ*, f. Answering roar, MBh. 5, 5526.

प्रतिगृहीतृ *pratigṛihîtṛi*, sometimes incorrectly instead of *pratigrahitṛi*, q. cf.

प्रतिग्रह *prati-grah + a*, m. **1.** Acceptance, Man. 1, 88. **2.** A present, Çâk. 17, 5. **3.** Friendly reception, MBh. 1, 7556. **4.** Favour, Râm. 1, 62, 29 Gorr. **5.** Hearing, MBh. 3, 8373. **6.** A receiver, Râm. 1, 69, 14. **7.** A spitting pot. **8.** The reserve of an army.

प्रतिग्रहण *prati-grahaṇa*, i.e. *prati-grah + ana*, n. Receiving, reception, Râm. 1, 45, 35.

प्रतिग्रहिन् *prati-grah + in*, m. A receiver, MBh, 12, 1333.

प्रतिग्रहीतृ *prati-grah + itṛi*, m. A receiver, Man. 3, 143.

प्रतिग्राह *pratigrâha*, i.e. *prati-grah + a*, m. A spitting pot.

प्रतिग्राहक *pratigrâhaka*, i.e. *prati -grah + aka*, adj. Receiving presents. Mṛichchh. 49, 21.

प्रतिग्राहिन् *pratigrâhin*, i.e. *prati grah + in*, adj. Receiving presents, in *a-*, MBh. 4, 544; not receiving presents.

प्रतिघ *pratigha*, i.e. *prati* and vb. *han*, m. **1.** Opposing, resistance. **2.** Rage. **3.** Fainting.—Comp. *A-*, adj. 1. what cannot be warded off, Man. 12, 28. 2. irresistible, MBh. 2, 143. *Nish-pratigha*, i.e. *nis-*, adj. not hindered, Ragh. 8, 77.

प्रतिघात and **प्रतीघात** *pratighâta*, i.e. *prati-han*, Caus., *+ a*, m. **1.** Repulse, MBh. 5, 2650. **2.** Warding off a blow, 4, 2118. **3.** Preventing, 1, 1592. **4.** Resistance, 7, 1373.

प्रतिघातक *pratighâtaka*, i.e. *prati -han*, Caus., *+ aka*, adj., f. *ikâ*, Troubling, MBh. 3, 9972.—Comp. *A-*, adj. without an opposer, MBh. 5, 1274.

प्रतिघातन *pratighâtana*, i.e. *prati -han*, Caus., *+ ana*, n. **1.** Repulsing, Arj. 4, 26. **2.** Killing.

प्रतिघातिन् *pratighâtin*, i.e. *prati -han*, Caus., *+ in*, adj., f. *ní*. **1.** Repelling, repulsing, Daçak, 62, 5. **2.** Injuring, Kâm. Nîtis. 14, 5.

प्रतिघ्न *pratighna*, i.e. *prati-han + a*, n. The body.

प्रतिचक्र *prati-chakra*, n. An equal discus. *a-pratichakra*, adj. Having an unrivalled discus, Hariv. 10709.

प्रतिचक्षण *pratichakshaṇa*, i.e. *prati -chaksh + ana*, n. Making visible, Bhâg. P. 4, 1, 55.

प्रतिचन्द्र *prati-chandra*, m. A mock moon, Râm. 5, 74, 29.

प्रतिचिकीर्षा *pratichikîrshâ*, i.e. *prati -chikîrsha*, desider. of *kṛi*, *+ a*, f. Wish to requite, Bhâg. P. 9, 9, 20.

प्रतिचिकीर्षु *pratichikîrshu*, i.e. *prati -chikîrsha*, desider. of *kṛi*, *+ u*, adj. Wishing to requite.

प्रतिच्छन्द *pratichchhanda*, i.e. *prati -chhanda*, m. An image, Râjat. 3, 77.

प्रतिच्छाया *pratichchhâyâ*, i.e. *prati -chhâyâ*, f. An image, Hariv. 8758.

प्रतिजागर *pratijâgara*, i.e. *prati -jâgṛi + a*, m. Watchfulness, attention.

प्रतिजागरण *pratijâgaraṇa*, i. e. *prati-jâgṛi + ana*, n. Watching, Mârk. P. 99, 14.

प्रतिजिह्वा *prati-jihvâ*, f. The uvula or soft palate.

प्रतिजीवन *prati-jîv + ana*, n. Resuscitation, Râm. 1, 4, 131 Gorr.

प्रतिज्ञा *prati-jñâ*, f. **1.** Promise, Râm. 4, 13, 31. **2.** Assent, Râm. 1, 4, 40 Gorr. **3.** Agreement, MBh. 4, 177. **4.** Assertion, Çâk. 23, 12 v.r.

प्रतितर *pratitara*, i.e. *prati-tṛî + a*, m. A sailor, Suçr. 1, 123, 13.

प्रतित्र्यहम् *pratitryaham*, i.e. *prati -tri-aha + m*, adv. Ever for three days successively, Man. 11, 214.

प्रतिदर्शन *pratidarçana*, i.e. *prati -dṛiç + ana*, n. **1.** Seeing, perceiving, Râm. 5, 14, 65. **2.** Sight, MBh. 7, 3214.

प्रतिदान *pratidâna*, i.e. *prati-dâ + ana*, n. **1.** The return (of a deposit).

2. Barter. 3. Giving in return for, a present made in return, Daçak. in Chr. 188, 3.

प्रतिदारण *pratidârana*, i.e. *prati-drî+ana*, n. Battle.

प्रतिदिनम् *prati-dina + m*, adv. Day by day, Çâk. d. 104.

प्रतिदिवसम् *prati-divasa+m*, adv. Day by day, Pañch. 183, 25.

प्रतिदिशम् *prati-diç+a+m*, adv. From every quarter, all around, Megh. 59.

प्रतिदृशम् *prati-driç+a+m*, adv. In every eye, Bhâg. P. 1, 9, 42.

प्रतिदेशम् *prati-deça+m*, adv. In every country, Râjat. 4, 533.

प्रतिद्रुह् *prati-druh*, adj. Seeking to injure in one's turn, Bhâg. P. 4, 2, 21.

प्रतिद्वंद्व *prati-dvamdva*, m. An adversary, a rival.—Comp. *A-*, adj. 1. without an adversary, unopposed, Râm. 2, 107, 8. 2. unconquerable, 5, 22, 19. *Nishpratidvandva*, i.e. *nis-*, adj. having no adversary, MBh. 7, 9265.

प्रतिद्वंद्विन् *prati-dvamdvin*, m. 1. An adversary, Ragh. 7, 34. 2. One who rivals, Çâk. d. 80.—Comp. *A-*, adj. having no adversary, no rival, MBh. 5, 1897.

प्रतिद्वारम् *prati-dvâra+m*, adv. At every door, Bhâg. P. 4, 9, 55.

प्रतिद्विरद *prati-dvi-rada* (see *rada*), m. An opposite, a hostile elephant, MBh. 5, 4823.

प्रतिधावन *prati-dhâv+ana*, n. Assailing, MBh. 8, 3398.

प्रतिध्वनि *pratidhvani*, and **प्रतिध्वान** *pratidhvâna* (Böhtl. Ind. Spr. 2754), i.e. *prati-dhvan+i* or *a*, m. Echo.

प्रतिनप्तृ *prati-naptri*, m. A great-grandson.

प्रतिनव *prati-nava*, adj. New, young, fresh, recent, Megh. 37.

प्रतिनाग *prati-nâga*, m. A hostile elephant, MBh. 8, 498.

प्रतिनाद *pratinâda*, i. e. *prati-nad +a*, m. Echo.

प्रतिनिधि *pratinidhi*, i. e. *prati-ni-dhâ* (see *nidhi*), m. 1. A substitute, Man. 9, 180. 2. An image, likeness, Ragh. 5, 63.

प्रतिनिपात *pratinipâta*, i.e. *prati-ni-pat+a*, m. Falling down, MBh. 7, 8591.

प्रतिनिवर्तन *pratinivartana*, i.e. *prati-ni-vrit*, + *ana* n. Turning back, return, Râm. 5, 1, 81.

प्रतिनिवारण *pratinivârana*, i. e. *prati-ni-vri + ana*, n. Keeping off, Bhâg. P. 5, 14, 34.

प्रतिनिशम् *prati-niça+m* (*niçâ*), adv. Every night, Kathâs. 3, 69.

प्रतिपक्ष *prati-paksha*, m. 1. Opposite part, MBh. 8, 4409. 2. Opposition. 3. An opponent, an adversary, Pañch. ed. orn. 56, 10.—Comp. *Satpratipaksha*, i.e. *sant-* (ptcple. pres. of 1. *as*), m. a contradictory premiss.

प्रतिपक्षता *pratipaksha+tâ*, f. Opposition, obstacle, Bhâg. P. 5, 8, 24.

प्रतिपक्षवादित्व *pratipakshavâditva*, i.e. *pratipaksha-vâdin+tva*, n. Double-dealing, deceitful talk, Mâlav. 57, 19.

प्रतिपक्षित *pratipaksha+ita*, adj., f. *tâ*, Nullified by a contradictory premiss (one of the five kinds of fallacious middle-term), Bhâshâp. 70.

प्रतिपत्ति *pratipatti*, i.e. *prati-pad* + *ti*, f. **1.** Obtaining, acquirement, Böhtl. Ind. Spr. 2801. **2.** Perception, 1747. **3.** Knowledge, Ragh. 8, 4. **4.** Acknowledgment, Böhtl. Ind. Spr. 2159. **5.** Admitting, Yâjñ. 2, 283. **6.** Proceeding, acting, MBh. 13, 2461. **7.** A means, Mâlav. 48, 6. **8.** Respectful behaviour, honouring, worshipping, Pañch. 117, 12; MBh. 7, 7467. **9.** Giving, Böhtl. Ind. Spr. 2659. **10.** Causing, Kâm. Nîtis. 1, 40. **11.** Confidence.

प्रतिपत्तिमन्त् *pratipatti* + *mant*, adj., f. *matî*, Intelligent, Râm. 2, 1, 13 Gorr.

प्रतिपथम् *prati-patha* + *m*, adv. Along the way, straight-way (?), Râjat. 5, 88.

प्रतिपद् *prati-pad*, f. **1.** The first day of a lunar fortnight, the first of the moon's increase or wane, especially that of its increase, Râm. 2, 122, 28 Gorr. **2.** Understanding.

प्रतिपदम् *prati-pada* + *m*, adv. **1.** At every step, Kathâs. 19, 84. **2.** Everywhere, 23, 79. **3.** Place for place, at their several places, Prab. 44, 9 (Sch.).

प्रतिपाण *pratipâṇa*, i.e. *prati-paṇ* + *a*, m. **1.** A counter-pledge, the thing staked against another, Nal. 9, 2. **2.** Revenge at play, Nal. 26, 7.

प्रतिपात्रम् *prati-pâtra-m*, adv. Every actor, Çâk. 3, 13.

प्रतिपादक *pratipâdaka*, i.e. *prati-pad*, Caus., + *aka*, adj. Illustrating, explanatory, Vedântas. in Chr. 204, 1. —Comp. *A-*, adj. not forwarding, MBh. 12, 1212.

प्रतिपादन *pratipâdana*, i.e. *prati-pad*, Caus., + *ana*, n. **1.** Causing to attain, Râm. 6, 69, 33. **2.** Bringing back, 3, 76, 1. **3.** Giving back, returning, MBh. 3, 13349. **4.** Producing, Vedântas. in Chr. 215, 16. **5.** Repetition, Vedântas. in Chr. 216, 8. **6.** Giving, gift, donation, Daçak. in Chr. 182, 20. **7.** Teaching. **8.** Beginning, MBh. 12, 5332.

प्रतिपादपम् *prati-pâdapa* + *m*, adv. Tree for tree, in every tree, Vikr. 21, 3.

प्रतिप्रणाम *pratipraṇâma*, i.e. *prati-pra-nam* + *a*, m. Saluting in one's turn, Râjat. 5, 223.

प्रतिप्रयाण *pratiprayâṇa*, i.e. *prati-pra-yâ* + *ana*, n. Return.

प्रतिप्रसव *prati-prasava*, m. Precept for an act which under other circumstances is forbidden.

प्रतिफल *prati-phal* + *a*, and **प्रतिफलन** *prati-phal* + *ana*, n. **1.** A reflection, a reflected image, Ânandal. 62. **2.** A requital.

प्रतिबन्ध *prati-bandh* + *a*, m. **1.** Obstacle, Mâlav. 10, d. 9; Çâk. 23, 13. **2.** Blocking up, Hariv. 5512. **3.** Connection.

प्रतिबन्धक *prati-bandh* + *aka*, I. adj. Impeding, obstructing, Bhâshâp. 146. II. m. A branch. III. At the end of comp. adj. = *pratibandha*.

प्रतिबन्धवन्त् *pratibandha* + *vant*, adj. Beset with obstacles, difficult to be obtained, Mâlav. 28, 8.

प्रतिबन्धिता *pratibandhitâ*, i.e. *prati-bandh* + *in* + *tâ*, f. State of checking, impeding, Vikr. 84, 14.

प्रतिबल *prati-bala*, adj. **1.** Able, adequate, Râm. 4, 9, 52. **2.** Of equal strength, Hiḍ. 3, 8.—Comp. *A-*, adj. of incomparable strength, Râm. 6, 70, 55.

प्रतिबिम्ब *pratibimba*, or **प्रतिविम्ब** *prativimba*, n. A reflection, Çiç. 9, 18; a reflected image, Hit. 68, 9; an image.

प्रतिबिम्बित *pratibimbita*, i.e. *prati-bimba + ita*, adj. Reflected, Vedântas. in Chr. 215, 10.

प्रतिबोध *pratibodha*, i.e. *prati-budh + a*, m. **1.** Waking, awaking. **2.** Instructing, admonishing, Lass. 38, 13. **3.** Knowledge, Bhâg. P. 2, 7, 47.

प्रतिबोधन *pratibodhana*, i.e. *prati-budh + ana*, I. adj. Awakening, Bhâg. P. 3, 8, 14. II. n. **1.** Awaking, MBh. 12, 901. **2.** Awakening, Râm. 6, 37, 38. **3.** Instructing, Bhâg. P. 8, 24, 53.

प्रतिबोधवन्त् *pratibodha + vant*, adj., f. *vatî*, Possessed of understanding, Çâk. d. 118.

प्रतिभय *prati-bhaya*, adj. Terrible, Pañch. ii. d. 178.

प्रतिभा *prati-bhâ*, f. **1.** Light. **2.** Understanding, Daçak. in Chr. 194, 15; Matsyop. 52 (corr. *pratibhâsya*).—**Comp.** *Utpanna-*, i.e. *ud-panna-* (vb. *pad*), adj., f. *bhâ*, alert in mind, Pañch. 199, 11. *Nishpr°*, i.e. *nis-*, adj., f. *bhâ*, deprived of splendour, Hariv. 4422.

प्रतिभाग *prati-bhâga*, m. A small daily present, Man. 8, 307.

प्रतिभान *pratibhâna*, i.e. *prati-bhâ + ana*, n. Understanding, Hariv. 1219.

प्रतिभानवन्त् *pratibhâna + vant*, adj., f. *vatî*, Endowed with presence of mind, Hit. iii. d. 19, M.M.; Indr. 4, 8.

प्रतिभावन्त् *pratibhâ + vant*, adj., f. *vatî*, Endowed with presence of mind, Kathâs. 4, 31.

प्रतिभास *prati-bhâsa*, m. Reflection, Vedântas. in Chr. 219, 14.

प्रतिभू *prati-bhû*, m. A surety, a sponsor, Pañch. 88, 11; Man. 7, 17.

प्रतिमा *prati-mâ*, f., and **प्रतिमान** *pratimâna*, i.e. *prati-mâ + ana*, n. **1.** A resemblance, a figure, Hit. ii. d. 149. **2.** An idol, Man. 9, 285. **3.** The part of an elephant's head between the tusks.—**Comp.** *A-pratima*, adj., f. *mâ*, incomparable, Pañch. iii. d. 240. *Devatâ-pratimâ*, f. Image of a deity. *Pushpita-palâça-*, adj. Resembling a Butea frondosa full of flowers, Pañch. 91, 7.

प्रतिमुख *prati-mukha*, I. adj. Being in front, Râm. 6, 90, 11. II. *°kham*, adv. **1.** In front, Megh. 18, n. **2.** Against, Man. 8, 291.

प्रतियातन *pratiyâtana*, i. e. *prati-yat + ana*. I. n. Requital, MBh. 8, 4635. II. f. *nâ*, An image, Ragh. 16, 17.

प्रतियोग *prati-yoga*, m. **1.** Opposition. **2.** Existing as the counterpart of anything, Kathâs. 19, 84 (an antidote).

प्रतियोगिन् *pratiyogin*, i.e. *prati-yuj + in*, and *pratiyoga + in*, I. adj., f. *nî*. **1.** Who or what impedes. **2.** Connected. II. m. **1.** An opponent. **2.** A counterpart. **3.** Any thing or object depending upon another and not existing without it. **4.** The counter-entity of a negation, i.e. that thing of which there is a negation. (Cf. *a-*, adj., Bhâshâp. 68; the meaning is, that in a true *vyâpti* the middle term is always found with the major, and this latter cannot be incapable of being found where the middle term is, i.e. in the minor term.)

प्रतियोद्धृ *pratiyoddhṛi*, i.e. *prati-yudh + tṛi*, m. Able to oppose, Sund. 4, 3.

प्रतिरव *prati-rava*, i.e. *prati-ru + a*, m. **1.** Echo, Pañch. 193, 23. **2.** Answering aloud, quarrel, 183, 6.

प्रतिरात्रम् *prati-râtra + m*, adv. Every night, Hit. 90, 10, M. M.

प्रतिरूप *prati-rûpa*, I. adj. Suitable, Utt. Râmach. 130, 14. II. n. A picture. —Comp. *A*-, adj., f. *pâ*. 1. incomparable, Râm. 3, 52, 6. 2. unsuitable, 3, 51, 32.

ऽप्रतिरूपक *-pratirûpa+ka*, latter part of comp. adj., f. *pikâ*, Resembling, counterfeiting, Man. 11, 9; Çâk. 16, 12.

प्रतिरोद्धृ *pratiroddhṛi*, i.e. *prati -rudh+tṛi*, m., f. *dhri*, and n. 1. Who or what hinders, opposes, an opposer, Man. 3, 153. 2. One who recovers, Man. 11, 80.

प्रतिरोध *pratirodha*, i.e. *prati-rudh +a*, m. 1. Impediment, opposition. 2. Siege, blockade.

प्रतिरोधक *pratirodhaka*, i.e. *prati -rudh+aka*, m. 1. An opponent. 2. A thief, Mâlav. d. 85.

प्रतिरोधन *pratirodhana*, i.e. *prati -rudh+ana*, n. Hindering, obstructing, Man. 9, 93.

प्रतिरोधिन् *pratirodhin*, i.e. *prati -rudh+in*, I. adj., f. *nî*, Impeding. II. m. 1. An opponent. 2. A thief.

प्रतिलम्भ *pratilambha*, i.e. *prati -labh+a*, m. Obtaining, Lass. 89, 2.

प्रतिलोम *pratiloma*, i.e. *prati-loman*, adj., f. *mâ*. 1. Inverted, contrary to the natural order (regarding the intermixture of castes, where the mother is of a higher caste than the father), Man. 10, 25. 2. Left. 3. Low, vile.

प्रतिलोमज *pratiloma-ja*, adj. Born in the inverse order of the castes (cf. *pratiloma*), Man. 10, 25.

प्रतिलोमतस् *pratiloma+tas*, adv. Against the grain, invertedly, Pañch. iii. d. 230; because the order of the castes was inverted, Man. 10, 68.

प्रतिवचन and **प्रतिवचस्** *prati-vach +ana* or *as*, n. An answer, Vikr. 58, 16; Pañch. 117, 15.

प्रतिवसथ *prati-vas+atha*, m. A village.

प्रतिवाक्य *prati-vâkya*, n. An answer, Nal. 22. 4.

प्रतिवात *prati-vâta*, m. The wind that blows in front. *te*, loc. To the leeward, Man. 3, 203. *tam*, adv. Against the wind, Pañch. iii. d. 22.

प्रतिवारण *prativâraṇa*, i.e. *prati -vṛi+ana*, I. adj. Keeping off, MBh. 12, 6165. II. n. Keeping off, Chr. 32, 31. —Comp. *Dushpr°*, i.e. *dus*-, adj. difficult to be kept off, Râm. 3, 31, 49.

प्रतिवासिन् *prativâsin*, i.e. *prati-vas +in*, adj., f. *nî*, Neighbouring, a neighbour.

प्रतिविधान *prat͏ividhâna*, i.e. *prati -vi-dhâ + ana*, n. 1. Arrangement against something, prevention, Pañch. 148, 20; help, 260, 24. 2. Arrangement. 3. Subsidiary ceremony.

प्रतिविम्ब *prativimba*, see *pratibimba*.

प्रतिवेश *prativeça*, m., and **प्रतिवेश्मन्** *prativeçman*, n. i.e. *prati-viç+a* or *man*. A neighbouring house or neighbourhood, Pañch. ap. Weber. Ind. St. iii. 372, 2 (*man*).

प्रतिवेशिन् *prativeçin*, i.e. *prativeça +in*, adj., f. *nî*, Neighbouring, a neighbour, Lass. 76, 6.

प्रतिव्यूह *prati-vyûha*, m. 1. Arraying an army against an enemy, MBh. 6, 2073. 2. A multitude, Hariv. 3605.

प्रतिशब्द *prati-çabda*, m. Echo, Pañch. 57, 15.

प्रतिशम *prati-çam + a*, m. Cessation, deliverance, Chr. 57, 30.

प्रतिश्या *pratiçyâ*, f., and **प्रतिश्याय** *pratiçyâya*, m., i.e. *prati-çyai*, without aff., and with aff. *a*, Catarrh.

प्रतिश्रय *pratiçraya*, i.e. *prati-çri + a*, m. **1.** Assistance. MBh. 3, 8828. **2.** An asylum, Pañch. i. d. 282. **3.** Habitation, Nal. 24, 6; Man. 10, 36 (*vahis-grâma-*, adj. Living without the town). **4.** A house.

प्रतिश्रव *pratiçrava*, i.e. *prati-çru + a*, m. **1.** A promise, Râjat. 5, 132. **2.** An assent.

प्रतिश्रवण *pratiçravaṇa*, i.e. *prati-çru + ana*, n. **1.** Promising. **2.** Listening to, Man. 2, 195.

प्रतिश्रुत् *prati-çru + t*, f. **1.** Echo, Ragh. 13, 40. **2.** Promise.

प्रतिषेद्धृ *pratisheddhṛi*, i.e. *prati-sidh + tṛi*, m., f. *dhrî*, n. Who or what keeps off, opposes, prevents, Râm. 1, 22, 9 Gorr.

प्रतिषेध *pratishedha*, i.e. *prati-sidh + a*, m. **1.** Keeping off, Man. 9, 266. **2.** Avoiding, Utt. Râmach. 125, 4. **3.** Prohibition, Vedântas. in Chr. 215, 16.

प्रतिषेधन *pratishedhana*, i.e. *prati-sidh + ana*, n. **1.** Keeping off, preventing, Chr. 56, 13. **2.** Prohibition, Man. 10, 126.

प्रतिष्क *pratishka*, probably curtailed *pratishkaça*, m. An emissary.

प्रतिष्कश *pratishkaça* (*prati* and akin to *kâç*), m. **1.** A spy, an emissary. **2.** A companion. **3.** A leader. **4.** A leather thong, a whip (cf. *kaça*).

प्रतिष्टम्भ *pratishṭambha*, i.e. *prati-stambh + a*, m. Obstacle, impediment.

प्रतिष्ठा *pratishṭhâ*, i.e. *prati-sthâ*, f. **1.** Place, Bhag. 14, 27. **2.** A firm standing, staying, Bhag. 2, 70. **3.** Quiet, Vikr. d. 42. **4.** The earth. **5.** Accomplishment, completion. **6.** Fame, celebrity, Râjat. 5, 28; Utt. Râmach. 131, 7. **7.** Pre-eminence, MBh. 12, 6690. **8.** Erecting the image of a deity, Râjat. 1, 124.—Comp. *A-pratishṭha*, adj. 1. without stability, Bhag. 16, 8. 2. perishable. *Janmapratishṭhâ*, i.e. *janman-*, f. a mother, Çâk. 83, 8. *Su-*, I. f. 1. erection (as of a temple), consecration. 2. fame. II. adj., f. *ṭhâ*, famous, Nal. 12, 66.

प्रतिष्ठान *pratishṭhâna*, i.e. *prati-sthâ + ana*, n. **1.** A firm standing, Johns. Sel. 93, 50. **2.** Base, Râm. 1, 5, 12 Gorr. **3.** The name of a town.

प्रतिसंहार *pratisaṁhâra*, i.e. *prati-sam-hṛi + a*, m. **1.** Taking back, MBh. 10, 698. **2.** Resigning, 12, 7161.

प्रतिसंधान *pratisaṁdhâna*, i.e. *prati-sam-dhâ + ana*, n. **1.** Joining again, a remedy, Daçak. in Chr. 189, 10. **2.** Suppressing of feeling for a time. **3.** Praise.

प्रतिसमाधान *pratisamâdhâna*, i.e. *prati-sam-â-dhâ + ana*, n. A remedy.

प्रतिसर *pratisara*, i.e. *prati-sṛi + a*, I. m. f. n. A servant, dependent. II. m. **1.** The rear of an army. **2.** A garland. **3.** A bracelet, Kir. 5, 33. **4.** A string worn round the hand at nuptials, Daçak. in Chr. 201, 5. **5.** Ornament.

प्रतिसर्ग *prati-sarga*, m. **1.** Secondary creation, or the creation of the world by Brahman and other divine beings. **2.** The portion of a Purâṇa which treats of the destruction and renovation of the world.

प्रतिसान्धानिक *pratisândhânika*, i.e. *pratisaṁdhâna + ika*, m. A bard.

प्रतिसारण *pratisâraṇa*, i.e. *prati*

-sri, Caus., *+ana*, n. 1. Repelling. 2. Applying remedies to a wound.

प्रतिसूर्य *prati-sûrya*, and प्रतिसूर्यक *prati-sûrya+ka*, m. 1. A mock sun, Varâh. Bṛih. S. 3, 37; 36, 1. 2. A lizard, Utt. Râmach. 43, 7 (*ka*).

प्रतिस्कन्ध *prati-skandha*, Hit. iv. d. 122, read *skandha-skandha*, q. cf.

प्रतिस्पन्दन *prati-spand+ana*, n. Throbbing, vibration.

प्रतिस्पर्धा *prati-spardhâ*, f. Emulation.

प्रतिहति *pratihati*, i.e. *prati-han+ti*, f. 1. Repulse, rebound, Çiç. 9, 49. 2. Disappointment.

प्रतिहरण *pratiharaṇa*, i.e. *prati-hṛi+ana*, n. Avoiding.

प्रतिहस्त *prati-hasta*, and प्रतिहस्तक *prati-hasta+ka*, m. A substitute, Hit. ii. d. 32.

प्रतिहस्तिन् *pratihastin*, m. The keeper of a neighbouring brothel (?perhaps, a rival), Daçak. in Chr. 180, 22.

प्रतिहार and प्रतीहार *pratîhâra*, i.e. *prati-hṛi+a*, I. m. 1. A door. 2. A door-keeper, Hit. 89, 2 (*î*); a chamberlain, Kathâs. 18, 194 (*î*). 3. A juggler. II. f. *rî*, A female door-keeper, Utt. Râmach. 25, 1.

प्रतीक *pratîka*, i. e. *pratyañch+a*, m. I. adj. 1. Contrary. 2. Inverted. II. m. 1. A limb. 2. A part.—Comp. *Su-*, I. adj., f. *kâ*. 1. handsome-faced, Chr. 294, 6=Rigv. i. 92, 6. 2. handsome. II. m. 1. Çiva. 2. Kâma. 3. the elephant of the south-east (?) quarter.

प्रतीकार *pratîkâra*, and प्रतीकाश *pratîkâça*, see *pratik°*.

प्रतीक्षा *pratîkshâ*, i.e. *prati-îksh+a*, f. 1. Looking to. 2. Regard. 3. Expectation.

प्रतीक्षिन् *pratîkshin*, i.e. *prati-îksh+in*, adj., f. *iṇî*, Waiting for, Râjat. 5, 405; expecting, Nal. 17, 28.

प्रतीघात *pratîghâta*, see *pratigh°*.

प्रतीचीन *pratîchîna*, and प्रतीच्य *pratîchya*, i.e. *pratyañch+îna*, or *ya*, adj. Western, Râm. 2, 82, 7 (*chya*).

प्रतीच्छक *pratîchchhaka*, i.e. *prati-ish* (cf. the base of the pres. *ichchha*), *+aka*, m. A receiver, Man. 4, 194.

प्रतीति *pratîti*, i.e. *prati-i+ti*, f. 1. Knowledge, Bhâshâp. 113. 2. Conviction, Çâk. d. 190. 3. Notoriety.—Comp. *A-*, f. the not being understood, Vedântas. in Chr. 214, 8.

प्रतीनाह *pratînâha*, i.e. *prati-nah+a*, m. Obstruction; in *nâsâ-*, m. Obstruction of the nose, Suçr. 2, 370, 8.

प्रतीप *pratîpa*, i.e. *prati-âp+a*, adj., f. *pâ*. 1. Backward. 2. Retrograde, Pañch. iii. d. 7. 3. Contradictory, opposite, Böhtl. Ind. Spr. 396. 4. Refractory, Hit. ii. d. 173; disobedient. 5. Adverse, Man. 4, 206; against the stream, Vikr. d. 24.—Comp. *Nishpr°*, i.e. *nis-*, adj. going straight forward, unconcerned, MBh. 4, 933.

प्रतीमान *pratîmâna*, i.e. *prati-mâ+ana*, n. A measure for gold, etc. (gold-weights, etc.), Man. 8, 403.

प्रतीहार *pratîhâra*, see *pratih°*.

प्रतीहारता *pratîhâra+tâ*, f., and

प्रतीहारत्व *pratîhâra+tva*, n. The office of a door-keeper or chamberlain, Pañch. 63, 23; Râjat. 5, 151.

प्रतुद *pra-tud+a*, m. A bird of

game, one that kills with his beak, Man. 5, 13.

प्रतुष्टिद *pratushṭida*, i.e. *pra-tushṭi-da* (vb. *dâ*), adj. Giving pleasure, Pańch. i. d. 285.

प्रतोद *pratoda*, i.e. *pra-tud+a*, m. A goad, Daçak. in Chr. 188, 16; Man. 8, 44.

प्रतोली *pratolî*, f. A high street, Râm. 2, 87, 22 Gorr.

प्रत्त *pratta*, i.e. *pra-datta*, vb. *dâ*.

प्रत्न *pra+tna*, adj., f. *nâ*, Old.

प्रत्यक्ष *pratyaksha*, i.e. *prati-aksha*, I. adj., f. *kshâ*. **1.** Being before one's eyes, visible, Utt. Râmach. 43, 9; Hit. iii. d. 24. **2.** Present. **3.** Perceptible, evident, Hit. 85, 21 (°*kshî-kṛita*, made evident). **II.** *ksham*, adv. In the presence, Pańch. 216, 3; publicly, iii. d. 93. **III.** instr. *ksheṇa*, At sight, Hit. i. d. 98, M.M.; evidently, Hit. 106, 12. **IV.** n. **1.** Perception, Bhâshâp. 51. **2.** Superintendence, Man. 9, 27.—**Comp.** *A-*, adj. 1. not seen by one's own eyes, Man. 8, 95. 2. unknown, Râm. 4, 9, 102.

प्रत्यक्षता *pratyaksha+tâ*, f. Visibility, Pańch. 256, 10 (°*tayâ*, visibly).

प्रत्यक्षय *PRATYAKSHAYA*, a denomin. derived from *pratyaksha* with *aya*, To make visible, Mâlav. 20, 3.

प्रत्यग्र *pratyagra*, i.e. *prati-agra*, adj. New, fresh, Vikr. d. 51.

प्रत्यङ्ग *pratyańga*, i.e. *prati-ańga*, I. n. A minor member of the body, as the chin, nose, etc. **II.** *gam*, adv. **1.** Limb by limb, Pańch. 183, 21. **2.** Each part, Man. 8, 208.

प्रत्यञ्च् *pratyańch*, i.e. *prati-ańch*, I. adj., f. *tîchî*. **1.** Proceeding to, Chr. 289, 5=Rigv. i. 50, 5. **2.** Behind, following in time or place. **3.** West, western. **4.** Inward, Vedântas. in Chr. 212, 24; 17; 211, 22; 210, 12. **II.** *yak*, adv. with abl. **1.** Behind, following in time or place. **2.** To the west, Man. 2, 21. **III.** f. *tîchî*, The west quarter, Draup. 3, 7.

प्रत्यनन्तर *pratyanantara*, i.e. *prati-an-antara*, adj. Next, Man. 10, 81. m. The next heir, Man. 8, 185.

प्रत्यनीक *pratyanîka*, i.e. *prati-anî-ka*, I. adj. sbst. Hostile, an enemy, Bhâg. P. 5, 24, 30. **II.** n. **1.** A hostile army, MBh. 7, 1986. **2.** Enmity, 6, 571.

प्रत्यन्तर *pratyantara*, i.e. *prati-an-tara*, adj. Near, Utt. Râmach. 53, 5 (is it to be changed to *pratyanantarî* ? cf. *pratyanantara*).

प्रत्यभिज्ञा *pratyabhijńâ*, f., and

प्रत्यभिज्ञान *pratyabhijńâna*, n., i.e. *prati-abhi-jńâ*, without aff. and with *ana*, Recognition Bhâshâp. 159 (*jńâ*).

प्रत्यभिवाद *pratyabhivâda*, i.e. *prati+abhi-vad+a*, m. **1.** Returning a salute. **2.** The benediction of a teacher.

प्रत्यय *pratyaya*, i.e. *prati-i+a*, m. **1.** Knowledge, Utt. Râmach. 162, 6. **2.** Ascertainment, certainty, proof, Pańch. iii. d. 91; 64, 12. **3.** Decisive sentence, Pańch. 165, 4. **4.** Usage, practice. **5.** Truth, belief, Utt. Râmach. 116, 1; confidence, Kathâs. 49, 122; dependence on (loc.), Pańch. i. d. 373. **6.** Oath, ordeal, Man. 8, 178. **7.** Instrument, means of agency. **8.** A helpmate.—**Comp.** *A-*, I. m. mistrust, Pańch. i. d. 204. II. adj. not confiding, Çâk. d. 2.

प्रत्ययित *pratyayita*, i.e. *pratyaya+ita*, adj. Trusted, trusting, Pańch. 216, 23.

प्रत्ययिन् *pratyayin*, i.e. *pratyaya* + *in*, adj. Trustworthy, Râm. 6, 5, 18.

प्रत्यर्थिन् *pratyarthin*, i. e. *prati-arthin*, m. A defendant, Man. 8, 71.

ऽप्रत्यवभास *-pratyavabhâsa*, i. e. *prati-ava-bhâs* + *a*, in *âkasmika-*, adj., f. *sâ*, Appearing on a sudden, Utt. Râmach. 36, 5.

प्रत्यवमर्श *pratyavamarça*, i.e. *prati-ava-mṛiç* + *a*, m. Meditation on, Bhâg. P. 5, 1, 39.

प्रत्यवमर्ष *pratyavamarsha*, i.e. *prati-ava-mṛish* + *a*, m. Return and continuation, Hariv. 1203.

प्रत्यवर *pratyavara*, i.e. *prati-avara*, adj. Lower, less valued, Man. 10, 109.

प्रत्यवसान *pratyavasâna*, i.e. *prati-ava-so* + *ana*, n. Eating, Pâṇ. 1, 4, 52.

प्रत्यवाय *pratyavâya*, i.e. *prati-ava-i* + *a*, m. **1.** Decrease, Bhag. 2, 40. **2.** Disappearance. **3.** Disappointment, Daçak. in Chr. 188, 10. **4.** Reverse, contrary course, Man. 4, 245. **5.** Disadvantage, Prab. 12, 13. **6.** Sin, Vedântas. in Chr. 202, 15.

प्रत्यवेक्षा *pratyavekshâ*, i.e. *prati-ava-iksh* + *a*, f. **1.** Attention, Râjat. 5, 168 ('having directed his mind to stealing,' read *mushe* instead of *mukhe*). **2.** Management, 180.

प्रत्यहम् *pratyaham*, i. e. *prati-aha* + *m*, adv. Day by day, Pañch. 191, 14.

प्रत्याख्यान *pratyâkhyâna*, i.e. *prati-â-khyâ* + *ana*, n. **1.** Rejection. **2.** Refusing, Hit. i. d. 12, M.M.; denial. **3.** Reproach.

प्रत्यादर्श *pratyâdarça*, i.e. *prati-â-dṛiç* + *a*, m. An image, Pañch. iii. d. 176.

प्रत्यादेश *pratyâdeça*, i. e. *prati-â-diç* + *a*, m. **1.** Rejection, repudiation, Çâk. d. 183. **2.** Refusal, abstemiousness, Megh. 93. **3.** Eclipsing, Daçak. 138, 3. **4.** Prevention, Man. 8, 344. **5.** Informing.

प्रत्यानयन *pratyânayana*, i.e. *prati-â-nî* + *ana*, n. Bringing back, Vikr. 5, 11.

प्रत्याशा *pratyâçâ*, i.e. *prati-âçâ*, f. **1.** Desire (ÇKD.), Daçak. 195, 18. **2.** Hope, expectation, Vikr. 40, 17 (*sa-pratyâça* + *m*, Full of expectation).

प्रत्यासर and **प्रत्यासार** *pratyâsâra*, i.e. *prati-â-sṛi* + *a*, m. The rear of an army.

प्रत्याहरण *pratyâharaṇa*, n., and

प्रत्याहार *pratyâhâra*, m., i.e. *prati-â-hṛi* + *ana* or *a*. **1.** Taking back. **2.** Recovering, Vikr. 11, 15. **3.** Restraining the organs of sense, Vedântas. in Chr. 217, 18; Man. 6, 72. **4.** Withholding.

प्रत्युत्क्रम *pratyutkrama*, m., and

प्रत्युत्क्रान्ति *pratyutkrânti*, f., i.e. *prati-ud-kram* + *a* or *ti*. **1.** Beginning. **2.** Effort. **3.** Setting out to assail an enemy. **4.** Declaration of war.

प्रत्युत्तर *pratyuttara*, i. e. *prati-uttara*, n. **1.** A reply to an answer. **2.** An answer, Hit. 64, 14.

प्रत्युत्थान *pratyutthâna*, i.e. *prati-ud-sthâ* + *ana*, n. Rising from a seat as a mark of respect, Pañch. 117, 11.

प्रत्युद्गम *pratyudgama*, m., and **प्रत्युद्गमन** *pratyudgamana*, n., i. e. *prati-ud-gam* + *a* or *ana*. **1.** Rising from a seat as a mark of respect. **2.** Going to meet.

प्रत्युद्धरण *pratyuddharaṇa*, i. e. *prati-ud-hṛi* + *ana*, n. Recovering, reobtaining.

प्रत्युपकार *pratyupakâra*, i.e. *prati-upa-kṛi+a*, m. **1.** Service in return, Pańch. 207, 17. **2.** Requital, Râjat. 5, 190.—**Comp.** *Punaḥpr°*, i.e. *punar-*, m. requital, Pańch. i. d. 384.

प्रत्युपमान *pratyupamâna*, i.e. *prati-upamâna*, n. A counter-comparison, Vikr. d. 22 (*upamânasyâpi*, of every comparison, i.e. incomparable).

प्रत्युष and **प्रत्यूष** *pratyûsha*, i.e. *prati-ushas*, m. Morning, dawn, Pańch. 40, 13 (*u*); 27, 5 (*û*).

प्रत्यूषस् *pratyûshas*, i.e. *prati-ushas*, n. Morning, dawn, Lass. 57, 9.

प्रत्यूह *pratyûha*, *prati-ûh+a*, m. Obstacle, Hit. ii. d. 13.

प्रत्येकम् *pratyekam*, i.e. *prati-eka+m*, adv. One by one, Prab. 44, 9.

प्रत्वक्षस् *pra-tvakshas* (ved.), adj. Possessed of great energy, Chr. 293, 1 = Rigv. i. 87, 1.

प्रथ् *PRATH*, i. 1, Âtm. **1.** To be extended, to spread, Chr. 295, 12 = Rigv. i. 92, 12 (ved. ptcple. of the pres. *prathâna*). **2.** To be unfolded, Râjat. 5, 366. **3.** To be famous, Râm. 2, 61, 2. Caus. *prathaya*, **1.** To extend, Bhartṛ. 2, 37. **2.** To show, Kir. 5, 3. **3.** (and i. 10 *prâthaya* ?) To praise, Râm. 1, 4, 1; cf. *pṛith*. Ptcple. of the pf. pass. *prathita*, Renowned, Râm. 3, 53, 12.—With the prep. **वि** *vi*, *viprathita*, Spread, MBh. 2, 2667. Caus. To praise, MBh. 3, 10277.—Cf. probably Lat. interpretari, perhaps Goth. frathjan.

प्रथम *pra + tha + ma*, **I.** ordinal number, f. *mâ*. **1.** First, Hit. 77, 1, M.M.; prior, Vikr. 14, 6. **2.** Chief, excellent, Çâk. 99, 23. **II.** *mam*, adv. **1.** First, Vikr. d. 132. **2.** Previously, Vikr. d. 58.

प्रथमतस् *prathama + tas*, adv. First, Bhâshâp. 78.

प्रथा *prath + â*, f. Fame, celebrity, Râjat. 5, 179.

प्रथिति *prathiti*, i.e. *prath + ti*, f. Celebrity, renown.

प्रथिमन् *prathiman*, i.e. *pṛithu + iman*, m. Greatness, Ragh. 18, 48.

प्रथिष्ठ *prathishṭha*, **प्रथीयंस्** *prathiyaṁs*, see *pṛithu*.

प्रथुक *prathuka* (cf. *pṛithuka*), m. The young of any animal.

प्रद *pra-da* (vb. *dâ*), **I.** adj. sbst. Giving, Vikr. d. 9; a giver, Râjat. 5, 162. **II.** f. *dâ*, A gift.—**Comp.** *Puṇya-*, adj. meritorious, Hariv. 351.

प्रदक्षिण *pra-dakshiṇa*, **I.** adj., f. *ṇâ*, Being at the right hand, Man. 4, 39. **II.** m., f. *ṇâ*, and n. Reverential salutation by circumambulating a person or object, keeping the right side towards them, Pańch. 236, 8. **III.** *ṇam*, adv. **1.** From left to right, Man. 2, 48. **2.** Proceeding from the east in a southern direction, 3, 87.—**Comp.** *Abhi-pradakshi-ṇam*, adv. From left to right, Râm. 1, 15, 16.

प्रदक्षिणसव्य *pra-dakshiṇa-savya*, adj. Having the right hand next to the left of the adversary (watching for an opportunity of striking a blow at the unguarded side).

प्रदर *pradara*, i.e. *pra-dṛî + a*, m. **1.** Scattering, MBh. 12, 3715 (an army). **2.** A cleft, Utt. Râmach. 43, 6. **3.** Fracture. **4.** An arrow.

प्रदर्शक *pradarçaka*, i.e. *pra-dṛiç + aka*, m. A teacher, MBh. 2, 1452.

प्रदल *pradala* (= *pradara*), m. An arrow.

प्रदातृ *pra-dâ+tṛi*, m. A giver, Râjat. 5, 182.

प्रदान *pradâna*, i.e. *pra-dâ+ana*, n. 1. Giving, Daçak. in Chr. 180, 17. 2. Gift, Pańch. 184, 2; delivery 101, 11. 3. Giving in marriage, marriage, Çâk. d. 26.—Comp. *Avaskanda-*, n. Giving the opportunity of being surprised, Pańch. iii. d. 37.

प्रदायिन् *pradâyin*, i.e. *pra-dâ+in*, adj. sbst. Giving, a giver, Man. 3, 175.

प्रदिश् *pra-diç*, f. Intermediate point of the compass, or half-quarter, as north-east, Matsyop. 43.

प्रदीप *pra-dîp+a*, m. 1. A lamp, Hit. i. d. 167, M.M. 2. Splendour, Çâk. 7, 4.

प्रदीपन *pra-dîp+ana*, I. adj. Inflaming, Suçr. 1, 177, 10. II. m. A kind of poison. III. n. Kindling, Râm. 5, 49.

प्रदीप्ति *pra-dîp+ti*, f. Light, lustre, splendour.

प्रदीप्तिमन्त् *pradîpti+mant*, adj., f. *mati*, Radiant, luminous, Johns. Sel. 94, 54.

प्रदेश *pradeça*, i.e. *pra-diç+a*, m. 1. A place, Pańch. 118, 14; part, 134, 20 (*pṛishṭha-pradeçe*, from behind). 2. A country, Pańch. 159, 21. 3. A foreign country. 4. A short span, measured from the tip of the thumb to that of the forefinger.

प्रदेशन *pradeçana*, i.e. *pra-diç+ana*, I. n. 1. A present. 2. A bribe. II. f. *nî*, The forefinger.

प्रदेशस्थ *pradeça-stha*, adj. Situated in a district, Râjat. 5, 39.

प्रदेशिनी *pradeçinî*, i.e. *pra-diç+in+î*, f. The forefinger, Râjat. 5, 206.

प्रदेह *pradeha*, i.e. *pra-dih+a*, m. Unguent, unction, Suçr. 1, 42, 19.

प्रदोष *pra-dosha*, m. 1. Offence. 2. Evening, the first part of the night, Pańch. 186, 3.—Comp. *Grahaṇî-*, m. Diarrhœa, Suçr. 2, 186, 2.

प्रद्युम्न *pra-dyumna*, m. The god of love.

प्रद्योत *pra-dyota*, m. 1. A ray of light. 2. Light.

प्रधन *pra-dhana* (see *nidhana*), n. 1. Tearing, destroying, Megh. 49; destruction, Utt. Râmach. 119, 7. 2. War, battle.

प्रधान *pradhâna*, i.e. *pra-dhâ+ana*, I. n. 1. Nature, MBh. 13, 1009. 2. The Supreme God. 3. Intellect. 4. Chief, Hit. 49, 18; principal (only sing.), excellent, Pańch. 156, 15. 5. The first companion of a king, his minister, his confidant, etc. II. adj. Chief, principal, Pańch. i. d. 324; Hit. 60, 22; Bhartṛ. 2, 99.—Comp. *A-*, adj. not principal, not minister, subordinate, inferior, Hit. 51, 22. *Tad-*, adj. having her (viz. his wife) as chief, i.e. performed principally with her assistance, Man. 3, 18. *Dharma-*, adj. loving justice, Man. 4, 243. *Nishpr°*, i.e. *nis-*, adj. deprived of one's chief, Râm. 2, 111, 16 Gorr. *Yathâ-pradhâna+m*, adv. according to their chiefs, represented by their chiefs, Johns. Sel. 46, 73. *Viçuddha-sattva-*, adj., f. *nâ*, having the nature of pure goodness, Vedântas. in Chr. 204, 17.

प्रधानतस् *pradhâna+tas*, adv. According to superiority, Man. 9, 150.

प्रधानता *pradhâna+tâ*, f. 1. Condition of a thing's nature, latter part of comp. words; e.g. *sva-pradhâna+tâ*, The character of one's own nature, Vedântas. in Chr. 206, 12. 2. Supremacy, excellence, Râm. 3, 49, 12. **3.** Ministership, Hit. 52, 1.—**Comp.** *A-pradhâna* + *tâ*, f. the condition of not being minister, ib.

प्रधि *pradhi*, i.e. *pra-dhâ* (cf. *nidhi*), m. The periphery of a wheel.

प्रध्यान *pradhyâna*, i.e. *pra-dhyai* + *ana*, n. **1.** Thinking. **2.** Thought, Johns. Sel. 92, 43.

प्रनप्तृ *pra-naptṛi*, m. A great grandson.—Cf. Lat. prŏnepos.

प्रनिघातन *pranighâtana*, i.e. *pra-ni-han*, Caus., + *ana*, n. Killing, slaughter.

प्रपञ्च *prapañcha*, m. **1.** Extent. **2.** Developement, analysis, Bhâshâp. 126. **3.** Prolixity. **4.** Heap. **5.** Error. **6.** Delusion, deceit, Pańch. 256, 1.

प्रपद *pra-pada*, n. The point of the foot, the tip of the toes, Draup. 5, 7.

प्रपलायन *pra-palâyana*, n. Flight, Pańch. i. d. 362.

प्रपा *pra-pâ*, f. A cistern, Man. 8, 319.

प्रपाठक *prapâṭhaka*, i.e. *pra-paṭh* + *a* + *ka*, m. A chapter, Vedântas. in Chr. 216, 5.

प्रपाणि *pra-pâṇi*, m. The palm of the hand.

प्रपात *pra-pâta*, m. **1.** A precipice, Çâk. d. 137. **2.** A bank, Ragh. 2, 26. **3.** A cascade. **4.** Flying forward, Pańch. ii. d. 57. **5.** Hastening away, Kathâs. 43, 264. **6.** Throwing one's self, Pańch. iii. d. 234.—**Comp.** *Giri-*, m. a precipice. *Jala-*, m. A cascade, Râm. 2, 94, 13.

प्रपावन *prapâ-vana*, n. A grove.

प्रपितामह *pra-pitâmaha*, I. m. **1.** A paternal great-grandfather, Bhag. 11, 39. **2.** pl. Ancestors, Utt. Râmach. 15, 5. **3.** A name of Brahman. **II.** f. *hî*, A paternal great-grandmother.—**Comp.** *Vṛiddha-*, I. m. a paternal great-great-grandfather. II. f. *hî*, a paternal great-great-grandmother.

प्रपित्सु *prapitsu*, i.e. *pra-pitsa*, desider. of *pat*, + *u*, adj. Being about to descend, to alight, Çiç. 9, 1.

प्रपूरण *prapûraṇa*, i.e. *pra-pûr* + *ana* (see *pṛi*), n. The drawing of a bowstring, Râm. 1, 60, 10 Gorr.

प्रपौत्र *pra-pautra*, **1.** and °त्रक *tra* + *ka*, m. A great-grandson, Kathâs. 9, 7; Yâjń. 1, 78. **2.** f. *trî*, A great-granddaughter.

प्रबन्ध *pra-bandh* + *a*, m. **1.** Uninterrupted connexion. **2.** Continuous application, Hit. 47, 3, M.M.; or action. **3.** A connected narrative, composition, Utt. Râmach. 112, 5. **4.** A literary production, Mâlav. 3, 2 bel.—**Comp.** *Ati-*, m. Uninterruptedness, Ragh. 3, 58. *Kapaṭa-*, m. A fraudulent design, Hit. 21, 13. *Drishṭa-rasa-*, adj. one who has seen dramas, Vikr. 3, 7.

प्रबल *pra-bala*, I. adj., f. *lâ*. **1.** Prevailing, Hiḍ. 4, 46; strong, Ṛit. 1, 24; powerful. **2.** Violent, Vikr. d. 81. **3.** Much, Râjat, 5, 68. **II.** m. A sprout.

प्रबाल *pra-bâla*, m. and n. **1.** Coral, Râm. 3, 49, 4. **2.** A sprout, Bhâg. P. 4, 25, 18. **3.** A new leaf. **4.** The bridge of a lute, through which the strings are drawn.

प्रबोध *prabodha*, i.e. *pra-budh* + *a*, m. **1.** Waking, Hit. iii. d. 142; vigilance. **2.** Awaking either from sleep or ignorance, Pańch, 37, 20. **3.** Knowledge, intellect. **4.** Awakening, Râm. 6, 37, 38.

प्रबोधन *prabodhana*, i.e. *pra-budh*, Caus., + *ana*, n. **1.** Awakening, Pańch.

4, 13; recalling to life, Utt. Râmach. 160, 10. **2.** Instructing, Pańch. 4, 15.

प्रभञ्जन *pra-bhańj + ana*, I. adj. Breaking down. II. m. Air or wind, Hit. ii. d. 84.

प्रभव *prabhava*, i.e. *pra-bhû + a*, m. **1.** Generative cause, the root of existence, origin, Draup. 2, 5; Bhag. 7, 6. **2.** The father. **3.** The mother. **4.** The place of receiving existence, birth-place. **5.** Birth. **6.** Strength, superiority.—Comp. *Antara-*, m. a mixed class produced by the intermixture of different castes, Man. 1, 2. *Prâńch-puṇya-*, adj. caused by the merits of a former existence, Pańch. iii. d. 187. *Vidveshipr°*, i.e. *vidveshin-*, adj. proceeding from an enemy, Pańch. i. d. 425. *Sparça-maṇi-*, n. gold.

प्रभवितृ *prabhavitṛi*, i.e. *pra-bhû + tṛi*, m. A mighty one, Bhartṛ. 2, 80.

प्रभविष्णु *prabhavishṇu*, i.e. *pra-bhû + ishṇu*, I. adj. Mighty, pre-eminent, Bhag. 13, 16. II. m. A master, a lord, Çâk. 24, 6.

प्रभा *pra-bhâ*, f. **1.** Light, Râm. 3, 53, 47. **2.** Radiance, Böhtl. Ind. Spr. 1155; splendour, Vikr. d. 125.—Comp. *A-chira-prabhâ*, f. lightning, Vikr. d. 137. *Âtmaprabha*, i.e. *âtman-*, adj. enlightened by themselves, Indr. 1, 37. *Nishprabha*, i.e. *nis-*, adj., f. *bhâ*, deprived of light or radiance, MBh. 1, 29. *Mahâtama prabhâ*, i.e. *mahâ-tama-* (for *tamas*), f. the lowermost hell. *Samaprabha*, adj., f. *bhâ*, of equal splendour, Lass. 51, 8. *Su-*, adj. splendid.

प्रभाकर *prabhâ-kara*, m. **1.** The sun. **2.** The moon. **3.** Fire. **4.** A proper name=Kumârilasvâmin.

प्रभाव *prabhâva*, i.e. *pra-bhû + a*, m. **1.** Power, Vikr. 73, 4; Pańch, 29, 20. **2.** Celestial power, Vikr. d. 30. **3.** Dignity. **4.** Majesty. **5.** Magnanimity, high spirit, Pańch. 29, 15, (*gata-*, adj. humbled).—Comp. *Kiṁprabhâva*, i.e. *kim-*, adj. possessed of how large a power, Pańch. 258, 13. *Tathâ-*, adj. possessed of such a power.

ऽप्रभावत्व *-prabhâva + tva*, in *alpa-*, n. Small ability, Hit. iv. d. 35.

प्रभावन्त् *prabhâ + vant*, adj., f. *vati*, Luminous, splendid, Pańch. i. d. 82.

प्रभु *pra-bhu* (vb. *bhû*), I. adj., f. *bhvî* and *bhu*. **1.** Strong. **2.** Able; with gen., Man. 11, 30; with inf., Mâlav. d. 9. **3.** Eternal, Sund. 1, 19. II. m. **1.** A master, a lord, Vikr. 12, 8; Bhartṛ. 2, 12; a husband, Çṛiṅgârat. 2. **2.** A name of Vishṇu, cf. Johns. Sel. 51, 111. **3.** Sound.—Comp. *A-*, adj. unable. *Kim-*, m. A bad master, Hit. ii. d. 31 (read *kiṁprabhu*). *Champaka-*, m. a proper name. *Jagat-*, m. the lord of the world.

प्रभुता *prabhu + tâ*, f. Power, Çâk. d. 122; supremacy, sovereignty, tyranny, Vikr. d. 89; *sva-prabhutayâ*, arbitrarily, Pańch. 26, 3.

प्रभुत्व *prabhu + tva*, n. Sovereignty, Pańch. 63, 17; power, Hit. Pr. d. 11, M.M.—Comp. *A-*, n. weakness, Pańch. 69, 4.

प्रभूतता *pra-bhûta + tâ*, f., and **प्रभूतत्व** *pra-bhûta + tva*, n. Plenty, Pańch. 171, 2.

प्रभूष्णु *prabhûshṇu*, i.e. *pra-bhû + snu*, adj. Strong.

प्रभृति *pra-bhṛi + ti* (originally, Beginning), ind. with abl. Beginning and continuing from, since, Pańch. 264, 5; Man. 9, 68. It is usually the latter part of comp. nouns implying, And those of the same kind (as the former part), the remainder, others, etc.; e.g. *bṛihaspati-*, m. The planet Jupiter and the other planets, Bhartṛ. 2, 27, cf. Pańch. 157, 4.—**Comp.** *Adya-*, adv. from to-day, Chr. 61, 48. *Tatas-*, adv. from that time, Hit. 57, 7, M.M.

प्रभेद *prabheda*, i. e. *pra-bhid+a*, m. 1. Division, cutting through, Bhartṛ. 3, 23. 2. Difference, Bhâshâp. 51. 3. Kind, Daçak. in Chr. 185, 22.

प्रभ्रष्टक *pra-bhrashṭa + ka* (vb. *bhraṁç*), n. A chaplet of flowers suspended from the middle lock of hair.

प्रमथ *pra-math+a*, I. m. 1. A horse. 2. An attendant on Çiva, MBh. 13, 983. II. f. *thâ*, Terminalia chebula.

प्रमथन *pra-math+ana*, I. adj., f. *nî*, Paining, MBh. 1, 2793. II. n. 1. Killing. 2. Paining.

प्रमद *pra-mad+a*, I. adj., f. *dâ*. 1. Mad, intoxicated. 2. Impassioned. II. m. Joy. III. f. A handsome woman, a woman, Bhâg. P. 4, 25, 20; Pańch. iii. d. 271.

प्रमय *pramaya*, i.e. *pra-mî+a*, m. Death, Râjat. 4, 708.

प्रमा *pra-mâ*, f. True perception, true knowledge, Bhâshâp. 125.—**Comp.** *A-*, f. wrong knowledge, Bhâshâp. 125, 126.

प्रमाण *pramâṇa*, i.e. *pra-mâ+ana*, n. 1. Measure, Pańch, i. d. 371; a scale, Hit. i. d. 12, M.M.; analogy, Hit. 110, 12; quantity, power, Pańch. 75, 22. 2. Authority. 3. Decision, a decider, Çâk. 61, 8; Pańch. 30, 18; 34, 10. 4. A work of sacred authority. 5. Proof, Pańch. iii. d. 93; evidence. 6. Cause. 7. Principal. 8. A title of Vishṇu.—**Comp.** *Ati-*, adj. of exceeding largeness, Râm. 5, 54, 17. *Anu-*, adj. suitable, Suçr. 2, 7, 14.

प्रमाणतस् *pramâṇa+tas*, adv. 1. With respect to measure, Man. 2, 46. 2. Agreeably to measure. 3. According to authority.

प्रमाणय *PRAMÂNAYA*, a denomin. derived from *pramâṇa* with *aya*, Par. 1. To receive as authority, Hit. i. d. 9, M.M. 2. To prove, Râjat. 5, 205.

प्रमातामह *pra-mâtâmaha*, 1. m. A maternal great-grandfather. 2. f. *hî*, A maternal great-grandmother.—**Comp.** *Vṛiddha-*, I. m. a maternal great-great-grandfather. II. f. *hî*, a maternal great-great-grandmother.

प्रमातृ *pra-mâ+tṛi*, m. One who knows well, an authority, Vedântas. in Chr. 202, 13.

प्रमात्व *pramâ+tva*, n. The state of true knowledge, Bhâshâp. 135.

प्रमाथ *pramâtha*, i.e. *pra-math+a*, m. 1. Paining, torturing. 2. Violence. 3. Carrying off forcibly (ÇKD.), Draup.; title. 4. Killing, Utt. Râmach. 120, 8.

प्रमाथिन् *pramâthin*, i.e. *pra-math +in*, adj., f. *nî*. 1. Agitating, MBh. 12, 9040. 2. Afflicting, torturing, ib. 3, 16435. 3. Killing, destroying, a destroyer, Chr. 34, 12.

प्रमाद *pramâda*, i.e. *pra-mad+a*, m. 1. Intoxication. 2. Insanity, distraction, Utt. Râmach. 51, 5. 3. Inadvertence, carelessness, Pańch. iii. d. 243. 4. Distress, Utt. Râmach. 61, 3. —**Comp.** *A-*, I. m. carefulness, Râm. 2, 85, 14. II. adj. careful, 3, 49, 13.

प्रमादिका *pramâdikâ*, i.e. *pramâdin +ka*, f. A deflowered girl.

प्रमादिन् *pramâdin*, i.e. *pramâda +in*, adj., f. *nî*. 1. Intoxicated. 2. Insane. 3. Careless, Pańch. i. d. 20; imprudent, Vikr. 30, 14; Hit. ii. d. 173. —**Comp.** *A-*, adj. careful, vigilant, Man. 2, 115.

प्रमापण *pramâpaṇa*, i.e. A. *pra-mî*, Caus., + *ana*, I. adj. Killing, Yâjń. 2, 279. II. n. 1. Killing. 2. Slaughter, Man. 11, 140. B. *pra-me*, Caus., + *ana*, n. Change, MBh. 12, 13252.

प्रमिति *pramiti*, i.e. *pra-mâ* + *ti*, f. 1. Measure. 2. True knowledge.

प्रमीला *pra-mîl* + *â*, f. Lassitude.

प्रमुख *pra-mukha*, adj., f. *khâ*. I. adj. 1. First, Utt. Râmach. 34, 6. 2. Chief, Hit. iii. d. 83. 3. Best. II. n. Mouth, Johns. Sel. 15, 55 (cf. p. 39, n.). III. *khe*, loc., adverbially. 1. In presence, Çâk. d. 181. 2. In front, Chr. 30, 5. IV. *khatas*, adv. At the head, Johns. Sel. 9, 13.

प्रमोक्ष *pra-moksha*, m. The liberation of the soul from the body and exemption from transmigration, eternal happiness, Brâhmaṇ. 2, 26.

प्रमोचन *pramochana*, i.e. *pra-much* + *ana*, I. adj., f. *nî*, Liberating, MBh. 3, 8031. II. n. Liberating.

प्रमोद *pramoda*, i.e. *pra-mud* + *a*, m. 1. Hilarity, Man. 3, 61; joy, Vikr. d. 153. 2. Fragrance, Bhâg. P. 2, 6, 2.

प्रमोदन *pramodana*, i.e. *pra-mud* + *ana*, n. Hilarity, Lass. 87, 8 (*sa-pra-modana* + *m*, adv. Cheerfully).

प्रमोह *pramoha*, i.e. *pra-muh* + *a*, m. 1. Fascination. 2. Fainting, insensibility, Utt. Râmach. 23, 6. 3. Confusion, Draup. 6, 20 (*-chitta*, adj. bewildered in mind).

प्रम्लोचा *pramlochâ*, i.e. *pra-mluch* + *a*, f. One of theAsparas, Lass. 50, 18.

प्रयज्यु *pra-yaj* + *yu*, adj. To be worshipped especially, Chr. 292, 7 = Rigv. i. 86, 7.

प्रयत्न *pra-yatna*, m. 1. Persevering exertion, effort, Vikr. d. 143. 2. Great care, Man. 3, 79. 3. Difficulty, Çâk. 5, 11 (scarcely). 4. Articulation of sound, Pâṇ. 1, 1, 9.—Comp. *A-*, adj. not solicitous, Man. 6, 26. *Nishprayatna*, i.e. *nis-*, adj. abstaining from any exertion, Hariv. 2514.

प्रयत्नतस् *prayatna* + *tas*, adv. With great care, Man. 3, 123.

प्रयत्नवन्त् *prayatna* + *vant*, adj., f. *vati*, Taking great care, Pańch. iii. d. 44.

प्रयस् *prayas*, i.e. *prî* + *as*, n. Sacrifice, Chr. 292, 7 = Rigv. i. 86, 7.

प्रयाग *prayâga*, i.e. *pra-yaj* + *a*, m. 1. Sacrifice. 2. A celebrated place of pilgrimage, the confluence of the Gangâ and Yamunâ, Chr. 46, 27.

प्रयाण *prayâṇa*, i.e. *pra-yâ* + *ana*, n. 1. Going forth, march, Pańch. 8, 19. 2. Going, Hit. iv. d. 80. 3. Attack, Pańch. 232, 16; invasion.

प्रयास *prayâsa*, i.e. *pra-yas* + *a*, m. 1. Labour, fatigue, Utt. Râmach. 34, 11. 2. Effort, Pańch. 82, 9.

प्रयुक्ति *prayukti*, i.e. *pra-yuj* + *ti*, f. Object, Utt. Râmach. 124, 1.

प्रयुत *pra-yuta* (vb. *yu*), n. A million, Chr. 33, 35.

प्रयोक्तृ *prayoktṛi*, i.e. *pra-yuj* + *tṛi*, m. 1. Creator, Utt. Râmach. 89, 2. 2. A mime, Ragh. 19, 36.

प्रयोग *prayoga*, i.e. *pra-yuj* + *a*, m. 1. Throwing missiles, Arj. 5, 6. 2. Application, employment, Pańch. i. d. 205; use, Çiç. 9, 79. 3. Example, comparison. 4. Lending money at interest, Man. 10, 115. 5. Appointing. 6. Ceremonial form, course of proceeding. 7. Device, contrivance. 8. Act, action, practice, Daçak. in Chr. 180, 10. 9. Dramatic performance, Vikr. d. 36.

10. Affair, matter. **11.** Cause, motive, occasion, object. **12.** Consequence, result. **13.** Magic, magical rites.—**Comp.** *Artha-*, m. lending money, Chāṇ. 22 in Berl. Monatsb. 1864, 408. *Vidhi-*, m. acting in conformity to a rule. *Su-*, m. 1. approximation. 2. dexterity, expertness.

प्रयोगतस् *prayoga + tas*, adv. **1.** By employing, Hit. iii. d. 60. **2.** According to. **3.** Actually.

प्रयोजक *prayojaka*, i.e. *pra-yuj + aka*, **I.** adj. Who or what causes. **II.** m. **1.** An author, Yâjń. 1, 5. **2.** A creditor, 2, 62.

प्रयोजन *prayojana*, i.e. *pra-yuj + ana*, n. **1.** Cause, Vikr. 80, 11; motive, Pańch. 107, 10. **2.** Purpose, design, Pańch. 58, 2; 240, 15. **3.** Use, Pańch. 5, 5; need, Hit. 54, 20; profit, Pańch. 88, 10; interest, 114, 22. **4.** Means of attaining, Man. 7, 100.—**Comp.** *A-*, and *nis-*, adj. 1. not induced by motives, MBh. 13, 2025 (*nishp°*). 2. useless, Hit. 105, 19 (*nishp°*). *Samâna-artha-*, adj. depending on equal interests, Hit. iv. d. 110 (read *°naḥ*, cf. Kâm. Nîtis. 4, 7).

प्ररक्षण *prarakshaṇa*, i.e. *pra-raksh + ana*, n. Guarding, Pańch. iii. d. 35.

प्ररोह *praroha*, i.e. *pra-ruh + a*, m. A shoot, Vikr. d. 157; a branch, Pańch. 259, 1.

प्ररोहिन् *prarohin*, i.e. *pra-ruh + in*, adj., f. *iṇî*, Sprouting, Man. 1, 46.

प्रलपन *pra-lap + ana*, n. Prattling, speaking, Pańch. 163, 14.

प्रलम्ब *pra-lamb + a*, **I.** adj. **1.** Hanging down, pendulous, Lass. 4, 19. **2.** Prominent, Johns. Sel. 55, 142. **3.** Dilatory, slow. **II.** n. **1.** Hanging on or from. **2.** The new shoot or bud of a creeping plant. **3.** A branch. **4.** A garland of flowers worn round the neck. **5.** The name of a demon killed by Balarâma.

प्रलम्भ *pralambha*, i.e. *pra-labh + a*, m. **1.** Obtaining, Râm. 5, 68, 43. **2.** Fraud. —**Comp.** *Su-*, adj. easy of attainment.

प्रलय *pralaya*, i.e. *pra-lî + a*, m. **1.** Dissolution, **2.** Destruction, Utt. Râmach. 83, 10; Hit. ii. d. 175. **3.** End, Pańch. 265, 11. **4.** Death. **5.** The destruction of the world, Hit. 47, 18.—**Comp.** *Mahâ-*, m. 1. a destruction of the world occurring after every period of 4,320,000,000 years. 2. a total destruction of the universe.

प्रलाप *pralâpa*, i.e. *pra-lap + a*, m. **1.** Prattlement, useless speech, Utt. Râmach. 84, 1. **2.** Lamentation, Utt. Râmach. 73, 6; Pańch. 213, 2.—**Comp.** *Su-*, m. eloquence.

प्रलापिन् *pralâpin*, i.e. *pra-lap + in*, adj. Prattling, Nal. 26, 16.

प्रलीनता *pra-lîna + tâ* (vb. *lî*), f. **1.** Destruction. **2.** The end of the universe.

प्रलोठन *pralothana*, i.e. *pra-luṭh + ana*, n. **1.** Rolling on the ground. **2.** Tossing (as of the ocean).

प्रलोभ *pralobha*, i.e. *pra-lubh + a*, m. **1.** Allurement, Bhâg. P. 2, 7, 37. **2.** Greediness, Pańch. i. d. 462.

प्रलोभन *pralobhana*, i.e. *pra-lubh*, Caus., *+ ana*, n. **1.** Allurement, Sund. 3, 20. **2.** Seducing.

प्रवक्तृ *pravaktṛi*, i.e. *pra-vach + tṛi*, m. A teacher, a propounder, Man. 3, 186; 4, 162.—**Comp.** *A-*, m. one who does not instruct, Pańch. iii. d. 71.

प्रवचन *pra-vach + ana*, n. **1.** Eloquence, Hit. ii. d. 26. **2.** Teaching. **3.** A holy treatise, Man. 3, 184.

प्रवण *pravaṇa* (akin to *prahva*), I.

adj. **1.** Declining. **2.** Bent. **3.** Curved. **4.** Inclined to, Kathâs. 3, 54; Lass. 77, 3; endowed with. **5.** Swift, Ṛit. 1, 24 v.r. **6.** Ready (with infin.), MBh. 1, 2187. **II.** m. A place where four roads meet.—**Comp.** *Dakshiṇâ-*, adj. with a declivity towards the south, Man. 3, 206.

प्रवपण *pravapaṇa*, i.e. *pra-vap+ana*, n. Sowing.

प्रवयण *pravayaṇa*, i.e. *pra-vî+ana*, n. A goad.

प्रवयस् *pra-vayas*, **I.** adj. Aged, Utt. Râmach. 106, 6. **II.** m. An old man, Ragh. 8, 18.

प्रवर *pravara*, i.e. *pra-vara*, **I.** adj., f. *râ*, Best, Indr. 5, 20; exalted, Pañch. 3, 10; Man. 3, 167; chief, Man. 9, 67. **II.** m. **1.** A Muni who contributes to the credit of a particular family (*gotra*). **2.** One of the forty-nine gotras, as opposed to the eight principal, Âçval. S. ap. M. Müller, Anc. Sskr. Lit. 380. n. 1.; cf. Weber, Berl. Handschriften, p. 59, 60; Kusumâñj. 3, 19. **III.** n. A family.—**Comp.** *Çaṅkha-*, m. or n. an excellent conch, Chr. 25, 60.

प्रवर्ग *pra-varga*, m. Sacrificial fire.

प्रवर्ग्य *pravargya*, i.e. *pravarga+ya*, m. A very holy sacrifice, Bhâg. P. 5, 3, 2; MBh. 3, 13027.

प्रवर्तक *pravartaka*, i.e. *pra-vṛit+aka*, **I.** adj. **1.** Inciting, stimulating. **2.** One who causes. **II.** m. **1.** An instigator, Man. 12, 4. **2.** An author, a founder, Bhâg. P. 9, 17, 4; Hariv. 4135. **III.** n. The entrance of the first person of the drama at the close of the introduction.

प्रवर्तन *pravartana*, i.e. *pra-vṛit+ana*, n. **1.** Going forward, Râm. 6, 92, 4. **2.** Engaging in, Man. 11, 63. **3.** Beginning. **4.** Activity. **5.** Stimulating, Daçak. in Chr. 194, 6. **6.** Directing. **7.** Informing. **8.** Revolving.—**Comp.** *A-*, n. abstaining from (with loc.), Hit. i. d. 20.

प्रवर्तिन् *pravartin*, i.e. *pra-vṛit+in*, adj., f. *nî*, Acting, moving, in *pratikûla-*, adj. Acting and moving in a contrary or perverse way, Chr. 94, 10.

प्रवर्ष *pravarsha*, i.e. *pra-vṛish+a*, adj. Raining fast, Pañch. 93, 2.

प्रवर्षण *pravarshaṇa*, i.e. *pra-vṛish+ana*, adj. Raining, MBh. 3, 10012.

प्रवर्ह *pravarha*, i.e. *pra-vṛih+a*, adj. Chief, principal.

प्रवलाकिन् *pravalâkin*, m. **1.** A snake. **2.** A peacock.

प्रवसन *pra-vas+ana*, n. Sojourn abroad, Hit. i. d. 113, M.M.

प्रवह *pra-vah+a*, m. Wind.

प्रवहण *pravahaṇa*, i.e. *pra-vah+ana*, n. A covered car, a litter or carriage for women, Daçak. in Chr. 183, 4.

प्रवह्लि *pravahli*, and **प्रवह्लिका** *pravahli+kâ*, f. A riddle.

प्रवाणी *pravâṇî*, i.e. *pra-ve+na+î*, f. A weaver's shuttle.—**Comp.** *Nish-pravâṇi*, i.e. *nis-*, adj. Quite new, Daçak. 62, 1 bel.

प्रवात *pra-vâta*, m. **1.** A breeze, Çâk. 32, 16; Kathâs. 20, 223.

प्रवाद *pravâda*, i.e. *pra-vad+a*, m. **1.** Rumour, report, Hit. 19, 4, M.M. **2.** A proverb, Pañch. 174, 1. **3.** Speaking, discourse.—**Comp.** *Loka-*, m. common report or saying, Lass. 12, 13.

प्रवापिन् *pravâpin*, i.e. *pra-vap+in*, m. A sower, one who sows seed, Man. 9, 49.

प्रवास *pravâsa*, i.e. *pra-vas+a*, m. **1.** Living away from home, a temporary foreign residence, Vikr. 61, 17 (cf. *manasa*); far away, d. 135. **2.** A journey, Utt. Râmach. 34, 11.

प्रवासन *pravâsana*, i.e. *pra-vas*, Caus., *+ana*, n. **1.** Banishment, Man. 7, 125. **2.** Killing.

प्रवासिन् *pravâsin*, i.e. *pra-vas+in*. **1.** adj. sbst. Living away from home, Hit. i. d. 138, M.M. (*chira-*, long exiled). **2.** A traveller, Ṛit. 6, 28.

प्रवाह *pravâha*, i.e. *pra-vah+a*, m. **1.** Stream, Vikr. d. 49. **2.** A torrent, Pańch. 38, 20. **3.** A pond. **4.** A swift horse. **5.** Occupation, Vedântas. in Chr. 216, 24.—Comp. *Vâri-*, m. a cascade.

प्रवाहक *pravâhaka*, i.e. *pra-vah+aka*, I. adj. Who or what carries well. II. m. A demon. III. f. *hikâ*, Diarrhœa.

प्रविख्याति *pra-vi-khyâ+ti*, f. Celebrity.

प्रविदारण *pravidârana*, i.e. *pra-vi-dṛi+ana*, n. **1.** Tearing. **2.** Bursting. **3.** War, battle. **4.** Tumult.

प्रविभाग *pravibhâga*, i. e. *pra-vi-bhaj+a*, m. **1.** Division, Man. 1, 66. **2.** A part, Utt. Râmach. 110, 18.

प्रविवाद *pra-vivâda*, m. Quarrel, Lass. 18, 18.

प्रविश्लेष *praviçlesha*, i.e. *pra-vi-çlish+a*, m. Separation.

प्रवीण *pra-vîṇa* (cf. *vîṇâ*), adj. Skilful, clever, Lass. 39, 3.

प्रवीणता *pravîṇa+tâ*, f. Cleverness, Hit. Pr. d. 41, M.M.

प्रवीर *pra-vîra*, I. adj. Excellent, bravest, Hit. iii. d. 70. II. m. **1.** A hero, Utt. Râmach. 122, 4. **2.** A chief, Râm. 3, 49, 57.

प्रवृत्ति *pra-vṛit+ti*, f. **1.** Action, Hit. 17, 5 (engaging); occupation, doing, Man. 5, 31; Daçak. 186, 13; activity, Bhâshâp. 148. **2.** Perseverance. **3.** Practice, Daçak. in Chr. 182, 10. **4.** Tidings, Vikr. 57, 18; report, d. 102; utterance, Çâk. d. 21; Ragh. 12, 60. **5.** Continuous flow, Vikr. d, 110. **6.** The juice that exudes from an elephant's temples when in rut.—Comp. *Dushpr°*, i.e. *dus-*, f. ill-tidings, Ragh. 12, 51. *Sneha-*, f. love, Çâk. d. 92; 58, 4.

प्रवृद्धि *pravṛiddhi*, i.e. *pra-vṛidh+ti*, f. **1.** Growing, Ragh. 13, 71. **2.** Elevation, prosperity, Râjat. 5, 388.

प्रवेक *praveka*, i.e. *pra-vich+a*, adj. Chief, principal.—Comp. *Maṇi-*, most excellent jewels, Râm. 3, 52, 24.

प्रवेणी *praveṇî*, see *veṇi*.

प्रवेदिन् *pravedin*, i.e. *pra-vid+in*, adj. Well-knowing, Man. 9, 267.

प्रवेपन *pra-vep+ana*, n. Shaking, trembling.

प्रवेरित *praverita*, i.e. *pra-va* (for *ava*), *-îrita* (vb. *îr*), ptcple. pf. pass. Thrown, Lass. ed. 2, p. 115.

प्रवेश *praveça*, i.e. *pra-viç+a*, m. **1.** Entering, Pańch. 33, 6. **2.** Entrance, Vikr. 20, 8. **3.** Intentness on an object. —Comp. *Dushpr°*, i.e. *dus-*, adj., f. *çâ*, difficult to be entered, Râm. 3, 6, 2.

प्रवेशक *praveçaka*, i. e. *pra-viç+aka*, I. adj. Who or what enters. II. m. An interlude, Çâk. 76, 10.

प्रवेशन *praveçana*, i. e. *pra-viç+ana*, n. **1.** Entering, entrance. **2.** The principal door of a house. — Comp. *Agni-*, n. ascending a funeral pile, Kathâs. 18, 270.

प्रवेष्ट *praveshṭa*, m. **1.** An arm. **2.** The fleshy part on the back of an elephant.

प्रवेष्टृत्व *praveshṭritva*, i.e. *pra-viç* + *tṛi* + *tva*, n. Condition of one who enters, Vedântas. in Chr. 209, 14.

प्रव्रज्या *pra-vraj* + *yâ*, f. **1.** Emigrating, Râm. 6, 8, 27. **2.** Wandering about as a religious mendicant, Chr. 10 8; Man. 5, 89 (in a dress not authorised by the Vedas, cf. Kull.).

प्रव्राजन *pravrâjana*, i.e. *pra-vraj*, Caus., + *ana*, n. Banishment, Râm. 3, 53, 6.

प्रशंसन *pra-çaṁs* + *ana*, n. Praising, Vedântas. in Chr. 216, 14.

प्रशंसा *pra-çaṁs* + *â*, f. Praise, applause, Man. 10, 127; Daçak. in Chr. 186, 5.

प्रशत्वन् *praçatvan*, i.e. *pra-çad* + *tvan*, I. m. The ocean. II. f. *varî*, A river.

प्रशम *pra-çam* + *a*, m. **1.** Quiet, end, Pañch. iii. d. 3, 21. **2.** Tranquillising, removing, Çiç. 9, 87.

प्रशमन *pra-çam* + *ana*, n. **1.** Tranquillising, pacifying, Daçak. in Chr. 194, 4. **2.** Securing, Man. 7, 56. **3.** Killing.

प्रशस्ति *praçasti*, i.e. *pra-çaṁs* + *ti*, f. Praise, Lass. 98, 16 = Rigv. v. 9, 6; Utt. Râmach. 156, 12.

प्रशाखा *pra-çâkhâ*, and **प्रशाखिका** *praçâkhikâ*, i.e. *praçâkhâ* + *ka*, f. A small branch or twig, Râm. 5, 29, 21; Nal. 20, 11.

प्रशान्ति *praçânti*, i.e. *pra-çam* + *ti*, f. **1.** Calm, tranquillity, moral or physical, Pañch. 123, 21. **2.** Removal, iii. d. 120.

प्रशासन *pra-çâs* + *ana*, n. **1.** Governing. **2.** Dominion, Chr. 296, 3 = Rigv. i. 112, 3.

प्रशासितृ *pra-çâs* + *itṛi*, m. A governor, master, Pañch. v. d. 52.

प्रशास्तृ *pra-çâs* + *tṛi*, m. **1.** A king, Nal. 12, 51. **2.** A governor. **3.** A kind of priest, Pañch. 156, 17.

प्रश्चोतन *pra-çchut* + *ana*, n. Sprinkling, Utt. Râmach. 58, 1.

प्रश्न *praçna*, i.e. *prachh* + *na*, m. A question, Pañch. 149, 4.—**Comp.** *Kuçala-*, m. Inquiring after another's welfare, Utt. Râmach. 70, 6; Lass. 10, 20.

प्रश्रय *praçraya*, i.e. *pra-çri* + *a*, m. **1.** Affection, love, Pañch. ii. d. 2. **2.** Affectionate behaviour. **3.** Civility, modesty, Indr. 2, 21. **4.** Respect, Utt. Râmach. 152, 4.—**Comp.** *Sa-praçraya* + *m*, adv. affectionately, Pañch. 25, 25; 33, 12.

प्रश्लथ *pra-çlath* + *a*, adj. Flaccid.

प्रष्ठ *prashṭha*, i.e. *pra-stha*, I. adj. One who goes first. II. m. A leader.

† **प्रस्** *PRAS*, i. 1, Âtm. **1.** To extend. **2.** To bring forth (?).

प्रसक्ति *prasakti*, i.e. *pra-sañj* + *ti*, f. **1.** Connexion. **2.** Attachment. **3.** Perseverance, activity, Kir. 5, 50. **4.** Energy. **5.** Practicableness, Râjat. 6, 154.—**Comp.** *A-*, f. absence of attachment, Man. 1, 89. *Ati-*, f. excessive attachment, Man. 4, 16.

प्रसंख्यान *prasaṁkhyâna*, i.e. *pra-sam-khyâ* + *ana*, n. Meditation, Kumâras. 3, 40.

प्रसङ्ग *prasaṅga*, i.e. *pra-sañj* + *a*, m. **1.** Association, union, Pañch. i. d. 218. **2.** Attachment, Man. 2, 93; 4, 186;

illicit gratification, Man. 9, 5; 4, 15 (an art which pleases the senses). **3.** Connected reasoning. **4.** Conjuncture, occasion, Pańch. 117, 10; time, Râjat. 5, 276. **5.** Insertion, introduction.—**Comp.** *Ati-*, m. 1. excessive attachment, Pańch. i. d. 201. 2. asserting too much, Utt. Râmach. 135, 11. *Kathâ-*, m. conversation, Hit. 61, 7, M.M. *Dharma-dosha-*, m. a sinful attachment to duty, Râm. 2, 23, 6. *Vidhi-*, m. application of, or acting upon, a rule.

प्रसङ्गवन्त् *prasańga + vant*, adj., f. *vatî*, Occasional, Daçak. in Chr. 180, 11.

प्रसङ्गिन् *prasańgin*, i.e. *prasańga + in*, adj. **1.** Attached to, Ṛit. 6, 1. **2.** Occasional. **3.** Subordinate, MBh. 5, 1442.

प्रसभम् *pra-sabha + m* (probably vb. *sah*), adv. **1.** Forcibly, Böhtl. Ind. Spr. 1917; Vikr. d. 19; violently, Çâk. d. 5. **2.** Exceedingly, importunately, Johns. Sel. 5, 28.

प्रसर *prasara*, i.e. *pra-sṛi + a*, **I.** adj. Who or what proceeds. **II.** m. **1.** Going forward, Çâk. d. 28. **2.** Spreading. **3.** A multitude. **4.** Battle. **5.** An iron arrow. **6.** Space, room, Hit. i. d. 185, M.M.; Megh. 93. **7.** Occasion. **8.** Affectionate solicitation.

प्रसरण *prasaraṇa*. i.e. *pra-sṛi + ana*, n., and f. *ṇî* and *ṇi*. **1.** Going forth. **2.** Spreading over the country to forage.

प्रसव *prasava*, i.e. *pra-sû + a*, m. **1.** Bringing forth, Pańch. 75, 23; being in labour, 228, 14. **2.** Offspring, Man. 3, 22; 9, 55. **3.** Blossom. **4.** Fruit, Utt. Râmach. 44, 11.

प्रसवितृ *prasavitṛi*, i.e. *pra-sû + tṛi*. **I.** m. **1.** A father. **2.** Forefather, Utt. Râmach. 53, 1. **II.** f. *trî*, A mother.

प्रसह *pra-sah + a*, m. A beast or bird of prey.

प्रसहन *pra-sah + ana*, **I.** m. A beast or bird of prey. **II.** n. **1.** Enduring. **2.** Overcoming. **3.** Embrace.

प्रसाद *prasâda*, i.e. *pra-sad + a*, m. **1.** Clearness, Vikr. d. 8. **2.** Perspicuity. **3.** Calmness (of mind), Vikr. d. 147. **4.** Favour, Vikr. d. 54. **5.** Kind behaviour, Böhtl. Ind. Spr. 1372.—**Comp.** *Dushprasâda*, i.e. *dus-*, adj. difficult to be pacified, MBh. 1, 1679. *Dṛishṭi-*, m. favour of looking at, Hit. 88, 6, M.M. *Sa-*, adj. propitious, Pańch. 85, 4. *Su-*, I. adj. kind. II. m. Çiva.

प्रसादक *prasâdaka*, i.e. *pra-sad*, Caus., *+ aka*, adj. **1.** Making clear, purifying, Man. 6, 67. **2.** Exhilarating, Râm. 3, 55, 36.

प्रसादन *prasâdana*, i.e. *pra-sad*, Caus., *+ ana*, **I.** n. **1.** Cleaning. **2.** Exhilarating, Indr. 2, 31. **II.** f. *nâ*, Worship.—**Comp.** *Dushpr°*, i.e. *dus-*, adj. difficult to be pacified, Bhâg. P. 4, 9, 34.

प्रसाधन *pra-sâdh + ana*, **I.** n. **1.** Dressing, Man. 10, 32; 2, 211 (decking the hair). **2.** Dress, embellishment, accomplishment, Vikr. d. 22. **3.** Accomplishing, adorning, Mâlav. 62, 23; anointing the body, Man. 7, 220; 4, 152. **II.** m., f. *nî*, and n. A comb.—**Comp.** *Dushpr°*, i.e. *dus-*, adj. difficult to be dealt with, MBh. 11, 222.

प्रसार *prasâra*, i.e. *pra-sṛi + a*, m. **1.** Going about, spreading. **2.** Going to forage.

प्रसारण *prasâraṇa*, i.e. *pra-sṛi*, Caus., *+ ana*, **I.** n. Extending, Bhâshâp. 5. **II.** f. *ṇî*. **1.** Surrounding an enemy. **2.** The dispersion of an army for collecting forage.

प्रसारिन् *prasârin*, i.e. *pra-sṛi + in*,

adj., f. *iṇî*. 1. Breaking forth, Çâk. d. 61. 2. Going along. 3. Spreading.

प्रसिद्धि *prasiddhi*, i.e. *pra-sidh + ti*, f. 1. Accomplishment, Man. 4, 3. 2. Ornament. 3. Fame. 4. Notoriety. 5. Name, Hit. 83, 8.

प्रसू *pra-sû*, f. 1. A mother, Çiç. 9, 14. 2. A mare. 3. A spreading creeper. 4. The plantain.—Comp. *Masi-*, f. an inkstand.

प्रसूति *pra-sû + ti*, f. 1. Bringing forth (as young). 2. Birth, Man. 4, 84 (*a-râjanya-prasûti + tas*, from one who is not born in the Kshatriya caste); springing up, Daçak. in Chr. 182, 4. 3. Offspring, Man. 9, 6; Vikr. 78, 21; Pańch. 74, 25.

प्रसूतिका *prasûtikâ*, i.e. *pra-sûta + ka*, f. A woman who has had a child, or who has been recently delivered.

प्रसृति *pra-sṛi + ti*, f. 1. The palm of the hand hollowed. 2. A handful, Bhartṛ. 2, 57.

प्रसेक *praseka*, i.e. *pra-sich + a*, m. 1. Sprinkling. 2. Oozing, dropping, Ṛit. 3, 6.

प्रस्कण्व *praskaṇva*, m. The name of a Vedic poet, Chr. 287, l. 3.

प्रस्तर *prastara*, i.e. *pra-stṛî + a*, m. 1. A handful or bundle of Kuça grass used at sacrifices. 2. A plain, level, Râm. 3, 79, 5; Man. 2, 204. 3. A stone or rock, Utt. Râmach. 71, 2.

प्रस्तार *prastâra*, i.e. *pra-stṛî + a*, m. 1. A bed. 2. A thicket or wood, overgrown with grass.

प्रस्ताव *prastâva*, i.e. *pra-stu + a*, m. 1. An introductory eulogium, introduction, Hit. 13, 4, M.M. 2. Beginning, Çâk. 101, 9. 3. Opportunity, Hit. 52, 16; Pańch. 158, 19 (loc. opportunely). 4. Turn, Pańch. 55, 16. 5. Treating a subject, Pańch. ii. d. 176. 6. A chapter. 7. Report. Hit. 120, 11.

प्रस्तावना *prastâvanâ*, i.e. *pra-stu*, Caus., *+ ana*, f. 1. Causing to be praised, Daçak. in Chr. 180, 14. 2. A dramatic prelude, prologue, Vikr. 4, 8. 3. Commencement.

प्रस्थ *pra-stha* (vb. *sthâ*), I. adj. 1. Who goes on a journey. 2. Expanding. 3. Solid. II. m. and n. 1. Table-land on the top of a mountain, Sund. 4, 6. 2. A measure of quantity.—Comp. *Indra-*, n. (m.), the name of a town. *Udaya-*, the table-land on the top of the mountain, behind which the sun rises, Daçak. in Chr. 184, 4. *Khâṇḍava-*, m. the name of a town. *Hima-*, m. the Himâlaya mountains.

प्रस्थान *prasthâna*, i.e. *pra-sthâ + ana*, n. 1. Departing, Megh. 42. 2. March of an assailant.—Comp. *Mahâ-*, n. Death, Hariv. 11070.

प्रस्थानिक *prasthânika*, Sund. 2, 2; read *prâsth°*, q. cf.

प्रस्थायिन् *prasthâyin*, i.e. *pra-sthâ + in*, adj. Preparing to go, or to depart.

प्रस्नव *prasnava*, i.e. *pra-snu + a*, m. Dropping, stream, Vikr. d. 150 (v.r., cf. *prasnuta-stana*); Utt. Râmach. 153, 3.

प्रस्फोटन *prasphoṭana*, i.e. *pra-sphuṭ + ana*, n. 1. Expanding, opening. 2. Striking. 3. Winnowing corn. 4. A winnowing basket.

प्रस्रव *prasrava*, i.e. *pra-sru + a*, m. 1. Oozing, dropping, Johns. Sel. 14, 47: Vikr. d. 150 (v.r. *prasnava*, q. cf.). 2. The flowing of milk, Man. 5, 130. 3. Urine, MBh. 1, 6683.

प्रस्रवण *prasravaṇa*, i.e. *pra-sru + ana*, I. n. 1. Washing away of rocks.

2. Oozing, Nal. 13, 7. 3. A cascade Man. 4, 203 (Kull.); spring, Indr. 1, 25; 27. 4. A pool of water, formed by dripping of springs. 5. A pure stream, Johns. Sel. 9, 9. 6. Sweat, perspiration. II. m. The name of a range of mountains, Râm. 3, 55, 44.

प्रस्राव *prasrâva*, i.e. *pra-sru + a*, m. 1. Flowing, dropping. 2. Urine.

प्रस्वाप *prasvâpa*, i.e. *pra-svap + a*, I. adj. Epithet of a weapon (causing to sleep), Chr. 38, 12. II. m. Falling asleep, Bhâg. P. 6, 16, 56.

प्रस्वेद *prasveda*, i.e. *pra-svid + a*, m. Excessive perspiration, Lass. 28, 12.

प्रहर *prahara*, i.e. *pra-hṛi + a*, m., and **प्रहरक** *prahara + ka*, A watch, or a division comprising about three hours, Lass. 29, 9; Pańch. 237, 3.

प्रहरण *praharaṇa*, i.e. *pra-hṛi + ana*, n. 1. Striking, pecking, Pańch. 146, 14; biting, 147, 2. 2. A weapon, Hariv. 13745.

प्रहर्तृ *prahartṛi*, i.e. *pra-hṛi + tṛi*, m., f. *trî*, and n. 1. One who strikes, a combatant, a shooter, Vikr. 78, 13. 2. One who attacks, Pańch. 149, 14.

प्रहर्ष *praharsha*, i.e. *pra-hṛish + a*, m. Joy, Bhâg. P. 5, 7, 11; merriness, Sund. 1, 29; Vikr. 58, 17.

प्रहसन *pra-has + ana*, n. 1. Hearty laughter, laughter, Utt. Râmach. 91, 7. 2. Mirth. 3. Scoffing, sarcasm, Hit. i. d. 107. 4. A comedy, Lass. 67, 12.

प्रहाणि *prahâṇi*, i.e. *pra-hâ + ni*, f. Disappearance, Mârk. P. 58, 68.

प्रहार *prahâra*, i.e. *pra-hṛi + a*, m. 1. Striking, Pańch. 245, 12; pecking, Hit. 107, 19; killing. 2. A stroke, Man. 4, 83; a shot (of an arrow), Pańch. 141, 10; a kick, 215, 21.—Comp. *Tala-*, m. a stroke with the palm of the hand or claw, Pańch. 215, 21. *Pâda-*, m. a kick, Râm. 4, 9, 22.

प्रहारिन् *prahârin*, i.e. *pra-hṛi + in*, adj. sbst. Striking, a warrior, a hero, Mâlav. 69, 5.

प्रहास *prahâsa*, i.e. *pra-has + a*, m. 1. Loud laughter. 2. An actor. 3. Çiva.

प्रहि *prahi*, m. A well.

प्रहेला *pra-hel + â*, f. Wantonness, carelessness, Pańch. ii. d. 48 (°*layâ*, with a jump (?), cf. *helâ*).

प्रहेलि *pra-hel + i*, f. An enigma, a riddle.

प्रह्लाद *pra-hlâd + a*, m. 1. Joy, pleasure. 2. The name of a Daitya, Arj. 8, 20.

प्रह्लादन *pra-hlâd + ana*, adj., f. *nî*, Rejoicing, refreshing, MBh. 14, 2045.

प्रह्व *prahva*, probably curtailed *pra-hvara*, i.e. *pra-hvṛi + a*, adj. 1. Bowed, stooping, Arj. 1, 5. 2. Intent upon. 3. Propitious, Kathâs. 46, 127.

प्रा *PRÂ* (akin to *pṛi* for *par + â*), ii. 2, Par. To fill. Ptcple. of the pf. pass. *prâṇa*, Full.—Cf. πλῆμα, πλήρης, πληρότης, πλήθω, πλῆθος, πλέθρον, πλοῦτος, etc.; Lat plenus (=*prâṇa*), implere, etc., plebes.

प्रांशु *prâñçu*, adj. 1. Tall, Johns. Sel. 15, 53; lofty, Ragh. 15, 19. 2. Long, Çâk. d. 49.—Comp. *Ati-*, adj. very tall, Prab. 21, 10.

प्राक् *prâk*, see *prâńch*.

प्राकषिक *prâkashika*, i.e. *pra-â-kash + ika*, m. A dancer, one who gets his livelihood from the wives of others.

प्राकाम्य *prâkâmya*, i.e. *prakâma* + *ya*, n. The faculty to perform what one lists, a magical power, Lass. 3, 19.

प्राकार *prâkâra*, i.e. *pra-kṛi* + *a* + *a*, m. An inclosure, a surrounding wall, Pańch. iii. d. 48; Daçak. in Chr. 197, 17; Man. 9, 289.

प्राकाश्य *prâkâçya*, i.e. *prakâça* + *ya*, n. 1. Clearness, brightness. 2. Celebrity, Pańch. i. d. 107.

प्राकृत *prâkṛita*, i.e. *prakṛiti* + *a*, I. adj., f. *tî*. 1. Natural. 2. Material. 3. Low, Man. 8, 336. 4. Common, Pańch. 25, 2. II. n. A peculiar dialect, or rather some peculiar dialects akin to the Sanskrit language used particularly in dramatic compositions.—Comp. *Ati*-, adj. supernatural, Vedântas. in Chr. 210, 13.

प्राक्तन *prâktana*, i.e. *prâńch* + *tana*, adj., f. *nî*. 1. Old. 2. Prior, former, Pańch. iii. d. 160.

प्रागभाव *prâgabhâva*, i.e. *prâk-a-bhâva*, m. The non-existence (of any effect) previous to production, Bhâshâp. 11.

प्रागल्भ्य *prâgalbhya*, i.e. *pragalbha* + *ya*, n. 1. Confidence, boldness. 2. Arrogance. 3. Pride, Lass. 67, 17. 4. Rank, proficiency, Pańch. 31, 5; 112, 19.

प्राघुण (a dialectical form of *prâghûrṇa*, see the next), m. A guest, Pańch. iii. d. 122.

प्राघूर्णक *prâghûrṇaka* (Pańch. 117, 10), and **प्राघूर्णिक** *prâghûrṇika* (ÇKD.), i.e. *pra-ghûrṇ* + *a* + *ka* or *ika* (cf. *prâghuṇa*), m. A guest.

प्राङ्गण *prâṅgaṇa*, n. 1. A sort of drum. 2. and **प्राङ्गन** *prâṅgana*, (i.e. *pra-aṅgana*), A court, Hit. 50, 3.

प्राङ्गनतस् *prâṅgana-tas*, (see the last), adv. Near the court, Râjat. 5, 40.

प्राचीन *prâchîna*, i.e. *prâńch* + *îna*, adj. 1. Former, old. 2. Eastern, east. 3. Left, not right, Man. 2, 63 (Kull.).

प्राचुर्य *prâchurya*, i.e. *prachura* + *ya*, n. Plenty, Pańch. 253, 22.

प्राचेतस *prâchetasa*, i.e. *prachetas* + *a*, patronym. A descendant of Prachetas, i.e. 1. Vâlmîki, Utt. Râmach. 34, 10. 2. The ten sons of Prâchînavarhis

प्राच्य *prâchya*, i.e. *prâńch* + *ya*, adj. Eastern, Mârk. P. 57, 42.

प्राछ् *prâchh* (vb. *prachh*), m. An inquirer, see *prâḍvivâka*.

प्राजक *prâjaka*, i.e. *pra-aj* + *aka*, m. A driver, Man. 8, 293; 294.

प्राजापत्य *prâjâpatya*, i. e. *prajâpati* + *ya*, I. adj. 1. Coming from, belonging to, Prajâpati, Chr. 38, 12; Pańch. i. d. 239. 2. Belonging to the Prajâpatis, Man. 4, 182. 3. With and without *vidhi*, a form of marriage, Man. 3, 30. 4. With or without *krichchhra*, A sort of penance, Man. 11, 105; 211.

प्राज्ञ *prâjńa*, i.e. *prajńâ* + *a*, I. adj. Wise, Pańch. i. d. 129. II. m. A learned man, Man. 2, 123. III. f. *jńâ*, Knowledge. IV. f. *jńî* and *jńâ*, A clever woman.

प्राज्य *prâjya* (vb. *aj*), adj. 1. Much, Çâk. d. 193. 2. Lofty, Râjat. 5, 347.

प्राञ्च् *prâńch*, i.e. *pra-ańch*, I. adj., f. *âchî*. 1. Former, Pańch. 49, 1; prior. 2. Before, in front. 3. Eastern, east. II. *prâk* (acc. sing. n.), adv. 1. First. 2. Before, Râjat. 5, 45; 338; formerly, Pańch. 217, 3. 3. In front, Utt. Râmach. 56, 11 (so that she cannot see); Hit. i. d. 80, M.M. 4. Past. 5.

Eastern. **6.** At dawn. **III.** f. *âchî*, The east, Draup. 3, 7.

प्राञ्जल *prâñjala*, adj. **1.** Straight. **2.** Honest, upright.

प्राञ्जलता *prâñjala + tâ*, f. Straightness, Pañch. 263, 10.

प्राञ्जलि *prâñjali*, i.e. *pra-añjali*, adj. Putting the hands together to the forehead, as a mark of respect, Vikr. 45, 18.

प्राड्विवाक *prâḍvivâka*, i.e. *prâchh-vi-vach + a*, m. A judge, Man. 8, 79; 181; 9, 234.

प्राण *prâṇa*, i.e. *pra-an + a*, m. **1.** Breath, Vikr. d. 1. **2.** Air, wind. **3.** A vital organ, Man. 4, 143. **4.** One of the five vital airs, Vedântas. in Chr. 207, 9. **5.** The Supreme Spirit, ib. 208, 3. **6.** A name of Brahman. **7.** pl. Life, Hit. i. d. 11, M.M.—**Comp.** *Ati-prâṇa + m*, adv. more than life, Pañch. 220, 24. *Kṛichchhra-*, adj. supporting life with difficulty, Râm. 4, 9, 30. *Gata-*, adj. dead. *Nishpr°*, i.e. *nis-*, adj. 1. dead. 2. exhausted. *Pati-*, adj., f. *ṇâ*, living in, or for, one's husband, Pañch. iii. d. 151. *Mahâ-*, m. a raven. *Yashṭi-*, adj. out of breath, Johns. Sel. 21, 105. —Cf. probably *φρήν, φρένες, φρόνιμος, φρόντις, φρονέω*.

प्राणथ *prâṇatha*, i.e. *pra-an + atha*, adj. Strong, powerful.

प्राणन *prâṇana*, i.e. *pra-an + ana*, I. n. Breathing, Chr. 288, 10 = Rigv. i. 48, 10. II. m. The throat.

प्राणन्त *prâṇant + a* (vb. *an*), I. m. Wind. II. f. *tî*, Hiccough.

प्राणमय *prâṇa + maya*, adj., f. *yî*, Consisting in breath or life.

प्राणवन्त् *prâṇa + vant*, adj., f. *vatî*, Endowed with life, Çâk. d. 1.

प्राणिन् *prâṇin*, i.e. *prâṇa + in*, adj. sbst., f. *nî*, Living, a living being, Man. 4, 117, Pañch. iii. d. 140.—**Comp.** *A-*, adj. inanimate, Man. 4, 117.

प्राणीत्य *prâṇîtya*, i.e. *pra-nîta + ya*, n. Debt (or *prâmitya*).

प्रातर् *prâtar*, i.e. a curtailed case of *prâ* (probably akin to *purâ=pra*) + *tara*, adv. In the morning, at dawn, Kathâs. 22, 100; early, Hit. 15, 2, M.M. Doubled, *prâtaḥprâtar*, adv. Every morning, Daçak. in Chr. 189, 17.—With *prâ* cf. O.H.G. frô, fruo; *πρωΐ*; see *pûrvedyus*.

प्रातिभाव्य *prâtibhâvya*, i.e. *prati-bhû + ya*, n. Surety, Man. 8, 159.—**Comp.** *Darçana-*, n. Surety for appearing, 8, 160.

प्रातिलोम्य *prâtilomya*, i.e. *prati-loma + ya*, n. Inverted order, Man. 10, 13.

प्रातिवेश्य *prâtiveçya*, i.e. *prativeça + ya*, and **प्रातिवेश्यक** *prâtiveçya + ka*, m. A next-door neighbour, a neighbour, Man. 8, 392; Pañch. 164, 14.

प्रातिस्विक *prâtisvika*, i.e. *prati-sva + ika*, adj. Own, peculiar.

प्राथमकल्पिक *prâthamakalpika*, i.e. *prathama-kalpa + ika*, m. **1.** One who has begun the perusal of the Veda. **2.** A student.

प्राथमिक *prâthamika*, i.e. *prathama + ika*, adj. First, initial, Vedântas. in Chr. 208, 18.

प्रादुर्भाव *prâdurbhâva*, i.e. *prâdus-bhû + a*, m. Appearance, manifestation.

प्रादुष्य *prâdushya*, i.e. *prâdus + ya*, n. Manifestation, appearance.

प्रादुस् *prâdus*, adv. and prep.

combined and compounded with verbs and their derivatives. **1.** Arising, coming to light. **2.** Visible, manifestly. **3.** Existent.

प्रादेश *prâdeça*, i.e. *pradeça* + *a*, m. **1.** The span of the thumb and forefinger. **2.** Place.

प्रादेशन *prâdeçana*, i.e. *pra-â-diç* + *ana*, n. Offering.

प्रादेशिक *prâdeçika*, i.e. *pradeça* + *ika*, adj. Limited, Bhâshâp. 98.

प्राधनिक *prâdhanika*, i.e. *pradhana* + *ika* (n. ?), A weapon, Bhâg. P. 3, 8, 31.

प्राधान्य *prâdhânya*, i.e. *pradhâna* + *ya*, n. Prevalence, supremacy, Hit. ii. d. 75 (*tad-*, abl. When these rule).

प्राध्व adj. **1.** *prâdhva*, i.e. *pra-adran*, Being on a journey. **2.** Bent. **3.** Inclined, friendly (ÇKD.).

प्रान्त *prânta*, i.e. *pra-anta*, m. **1.** Edge. **2.** Border, cheek, Utt. Râmach. 14, 4. **3.** End, Vikr. d. 4; Pańch. 197, 21.

प्रान्तर *prântara*, i.e. *pra-antara*, n. **1.** A long unshaded lonesome road, Hit. 121, 2. **2.** A forest, Hit. 85, 3. **3.** A hollow tree.

ऽप्राप् *-prâp*, i.e. *pra-âp*, adj. Obtaining, Megh. 45 (*kuvalaya-dala-*, Else adorned with lotus leaves).

प्रापण *prâpaṇa*, i.e. *pra-âp* + *ana*, n. Attainment, Man. 2, 95.—**Comp.** *Dushpr°*, i.e. *dus-*, adj. difficult to be attained, Bhâg. P. 8, 3, 18.

प्रापणिक *prâpaṇika*, i.e. *pra-â-paṇ* + *ika*, m. A trader, a merchant.

प्राप्तव्यमर्थ *prâptavya* + *m-artha*, m. A surname, proceeded from its owner saying ever *prâptavyam artham*, etc., Pańch. 130, 15; cf. 127, 21.

प्राप्ति *prâpti*, i.e. *pra-âp* + *ti*, f. **1.** Coming, taking place, Pańch. 119, 5 (*kutas te brâhmaṇa-bhojana-*, Whence can you afford to entertain a Brâhmaṇa ?). **2.** Taking possession, obtaining, Kathâs. 4, 105; Bhâshâp. 114. **3.** The power of obtaining every thing, one of the eight superhuman faculties, Lass. 3, 19. **4.** Obtaining by actions done in a former existence, Pańch. ii. d. 132. **5.** Gain, Hit. 101, 10. **6.** Fortune, MBh. 14, 1337. **7.** Successful termination of a plot.—**Comp.** *A-*, f. 1. non-attainment. 2. not taking place. 3. not being justified. *Akarmaprâpti*, i.e. *a-karman-*, f. acquisition without being deserved by actions done in a former existence, Pańch. 132, 17. *Yathâ-*, adj. as justified, suitable, Hit. 100, 5 (cf. *prâpta*, i.e. *pra-âpta*, proper, right; perhaps with Schlegel, corr. *yathâprâpti*, adv.).

प्राबल्य *prâbalya*, i.e. *prabala* + *ya*, n. **1.** Predominance, Vedântas. in Chr. 211, 20. **2.** Power.

प्राबोधक *prâbodhaka*, or **प्राबोधिक** *prâbodhika* (vv. rr.), i.e. *prabodha* + *ka* or *ika*, m. Dawn.

प्राभवत्य *prâbhavatya*, i.e. *pra-bhavant* (vb. *bhû*), + *ya*, n. Authority, Man. 8, 412.

प्राभाकर *prâbhâkara*, i.e. *prabhâkara* + *a*, m. pl. The followers of Prabhâkara, one of the sects of the Pûrva Mîmânsâ school, Vedântas. in Chr. 211, 6.

प्राभातिक *prâbhâtika*, i.e. *pra-bhâta* (vb. *bhâ*), + *ika*, adj. Matutinal, Pańch. i. d. 353.

प्राभृत *prâbhṛita*, i.e. *pra-bhṛita* + *a*, n. A present, an offering, Kathâs. 22, 97.

प्रामाणिक *prâmâṇika*, i.e. *pramâṇa* + *ika*, I. adj. **1.** Proceeding from some evidence. **2.** Being of authority. II. m. **1.** A chief. **2.** A learned man.

प्रामाण्य *prâmâṇya*, i.e. *pramâṇa* + *ya*, n. **1.** Proof, Bhâshâp. 139. **2.** Authority.—Comp. *A-*, n. want of authority, irrelevancy, Vedântas. in Chr. 208, 20.

प्रामाण्यतस् *prâmâṇya* + *tas*, adv. According to (the) authority, Man. 2, 8.

प्रामोदिक *prâmodika*, i.e. *pramoda* + *ika*, adj. Affording pleasure, Utt. Râmach. 152, 8.

1. **प्राय** *prâya*, i.e. *prâ* + *a* or *ya* (cf. *prâyas*), or *pra-i* + *a*, I. adj. Exceeding, much, abundant, Pañch. 163, 23 (or a Bahuvr.) II. m. **1.** Quantity, plenty, Man. 7, 69. **2.** A banquet, a feast, Man. 3, 264 (?). **3.** *yeṇa*, instr. a. Generally, Bhartṛ. 2, 57. b. How much more, Ṛit. 6, 23. c. Likely, Hit. 16, 6, M.M. **4.** As latter part of comp. adj. a. Almost; e.g. *gata-*, adj. Almost past, MBh. 4, 376. *sam-â-gata-*, Almost approached, very near, Hit. 97, 14. b. Like, resembling; e.g. *amṛita-*, Like nectar, Pañch. 206, 6; 194, 21.—Comp. *Pra-siddha-kshatriya-*, adj. consisting for the most part of renowned Kshatriyas, Hit. iii. d. 87. *Priya-*, adj. very kind. *Supta-jana-*, adj. almost everybody being asleep, Johns. Sel. 60, 188. *Hiṁsâ-*, adj., f. *yâ*, abundant in injury (to living beings), Man. 10, 83.

2. **प्राय** *prâya*, i.e. *pra-i* + *a*, I. m. **1.** Death. **2.** Fasting to death, Pañch. 50, 15. **3.** Age. II. n. Sin.

प्रायण *prâyaṇa*, i.e. *pra-i* + *ana*, n. Death, Man. 9, 323.

प्रायशस् 1. *prâya* + *ças*, adv. Usually, for the most part, Hit. i. d. 201, M.M.; Man. 12, 20.

प्रायश्चित्त *prâyaçchitta*, i.e. *prâyas-chitta*, n. **1.** Penance, Man. 2, 221; Pañch. i. d. 307. **2.** Expiation, Man. 9, 236; Pañch. 207, 17. **3.** Punishment, Hit. ii. d. 172.

प्रायश्चित्तीय *PRÂYAÇCHITTÎYA*, a denomin. derived from *prâyaçchitta* with *ya*, Âtm. To be obliged to perform an expiatory penance, Man. 11, 44.

प्रायश्चित्तीयता *prâyaçchittîyatâ*, i.e. *prayaschitta* + *îya* + *tâ*, f. Condition of one who is obliged to perform a penance, Man. 11, 47.

प्रायस् *prâyas* (probably acc. sing. n. of an old comparat. of *puru* = πλεῖον, Lat. plus), adv. **1.** Frequently, Pañch. iv. d. 7; commonly, v. d. 19. **2.** Probably, MBh. 12, 4989.

प्रारब्धि *prârabdhi*, i.e. *pra-â-rabh* + *ti*, f. **1.** Beginning. **2.** A rope for binding an elephant.

प्रारम्भ *prârambha*, i.e. *pra-â-rabh* + *a*, m. Beginning, Daçak. in Chr. 191, 19.

प्रार्थक *prârthaka*, i.e. *pra-arth* + *aka*, adj. One who sues for, woos, Böhtl. Ind. Spr. 1448.

प्रार्थन *prârthana*, i.e. *pra-arth* + *ana*, n., and f. *nâ*. **1.** Asking, Pañch. 169, 7; demand, Pañch. 5, 5. **2.** Desire, wish, Vikr. 50, 5; wishing for, Çâk. 15, 11.—Comp. *Â-lambita-*, adj. one whose desire is supported, Vikr. d. 38 (*añjasâ abhibhavitum*, to be attained quickly, i.e. one who may hope to attain his desire quickly). *Sa-phala-*, adj. one who has attained his desire, Vikr. d. 27.

प्रार्थयितृ *prârthayitṛi*, i.e. *pra-arth*, i. 10, + *tṛi*, m. **1.** One who solicits,

Hit. i. d. 115, M.M. **2.** A wooer, Çâk. 21, 6.

प्रालम्ब *prâlamba*, i.e. *pra-â-lamb* + *a*, n. A garland hanging down from the neck to the breast, Ragh. 6, 14.

प्रालेय *prâleya*, i.e. *pralaya* + *a* (anomal.), n. Snow, hail, Pańch. i. d. 353 (cf. *leça*).

प्रालेय *PRÂLEYA*, a denomin. derived from *prâleya*, Par. To play the part of hail, Lass. 67, 16.

प्रावरण *prâvaraṇa*, i.e. *pra-â-vṛi* + *ana*, n. **1.** An upper garment, Pańch. 97, 18 (*dhauta-*, adj. Dressed in a white garment); Râjat. 4, 669. **2.** Any covering. — Comp. *Karṇa-*, 1. adj., f. *ṇâ*, using the ears as a cloak, Râm. 5, 17, 34. 2. m. pl. the name of a fabulous people, MBh. 2, 1170.

प्रावार *prâvâra*, i.e. *pra-â-vṛi* + *a*, m. **1.** An upper garment, a garment, MBh. 2, 1733. **2.** A cover, MBh. 3, 181.

प्रावितृ *prâvitṛi*, i.e. *pra-av* + *tṛi*, m. A protector, Chr. 293, 4 = Rigv. i. 87, 4.

प्रावीण्य *prâvîṇya*, i.e. *pravîṇa* + *ya*, n. Skilfulness, accurate knowledge, Utt. Râmach. 110, 14.

प्रावृति *pra-â-vṛi* + *ti*, f. An inclosure, a fence.

प्रावृष् *prâvṛish*, i.e. *pra-vṛish*, and

प्रावृषा *prâvṛishâ*, i.e. *pra-vṛish* + *a*, f. The rainy season, the months Çrâvaṇa and Bhâdra, about July and August, Hiḍ. 2, 1; Pańch. 118, 22 (*sh*); Megh. 113 (*shâ*).

प्रावृषेण्य *prâvṛisheṇya*, i. e. *prâvṛish* + *enya*, **I.** adj. **1.** Referring to the rainy season, Vikr. 56, 9; Böhtl. Ind. Spr. 1915 (a cloud). **2.** Produced in the rains. **3.** Much. **II.** m. The Kadamba tree.

प्रावेण्य *prâveṇya*, i.e. *pra-veṇî* + *ya*, n. A texture made of hairs, Râm. 3, 49, 44.

प्रावेशिक *prâveçika*, i.e. *praveça* + *ika*, adj., f. *kî*, Referring to the entrance, Vikr. 51, 3 (cf. Sch. ad ed. Calc. p. 76).

प्राव्रज्य *prâvrajya*, i.e. *pravrajyâ* + *a*, n. Wandering as a religious mendicant, Chr. 9, 42.

ऽप्राश् *-prâç* (vb. *prachh*, cf. *prâchh*), adj. Asking; in *çabda-prâç*, adj. Inquiring after (the meaning of) a word.

प्राश *prâça*, i.e. *pra-* 2. *aç* + *a*, m. Eating, Man. 11, 143.—Comp. *Dhûma-*, adj. feeding only on smoke, MBh. 13, 646.

प्राशन *prâçana*, i.e. *pra-* 2. *aç* + *ana*, n. **1.** Causing to eat, Man. 2, 29. **2.** Eating, Man. 5, 144.—Comp. *Anna-*, n. the first feeding of a child with rice, a religious ceremony taking place in the sixth month after his birth, Man. 2, 34.

प्राशित्र *prâçitra*, *pra-* 2. *aç* + *tra*, n. The part of a sacrifice to be eaten by a Brâhmaṇa (Bhâg. P. 3, 13, 35, the vessel containing the part of the Brâhmaṇa, Burnouf).

प्राश्निक *prâçnika*, i.e. *praçna* + *ika*, m. **1.** An inquirer. **2.** An examiner, Mâlav. 11, 23.

प्रास *prâsa*, i.e. *pra-* 2. *as* + *a*, m. A bearded dart, MBh. 7, 559.

प्रासक *prâsaka*, i.e. *pra-* 2. *as* + *a*, m, A die, dice.

प्रासङ्ग *prâsańga*, i.e. *pra-â-sańj* + *a*, m. A yoke for cattle, MBh. 13, 3270.

प्रासङ्गिक *prâsańgika*, i.e. *prasańga*

+ *ika*, adj., f. *kî*. **1.** Belonging to any connexion, connected, Utt. Râmach. 37, 17. **2.** Inherent. **3.** Incidental, episodical, Râjat. 5, 67.

प्रासङ्ग्य *prâsangya*, i.e. *prâsanga* + *ya*, adj. Yoked.

प्रासाद *prâsâda*, i.e. *pra-(â-?) sad* + *a*, m. **1.** A palace, Pańch. 256, 3. **2.** A temple, Pańch. 10, 8; Râm. 5, 38, 27.

प्रासिक *prâsika*, i.e. *prâsa* + *ika*, adj. Armed with a spear.

प्रास्थानिक *prâsthânika*, i.e. *prasthâna* + *ika*, adj. Referring to a journey, Râm. 2, 25, 16 Gorr.

प्राहुण *prâhuṇa*, (a form of *prâghuṇa*), m. A guest, Kathâs. 45, 269; 311.

प्राहुणक *prâhuṇa* + *ka*, f. *ṇikâ*, A guest, Kathâs. 45, 267; 272.

प्राह्णेतन *prâhṇetana*, i.e. *pra-ahna* + *i* + *tana*, adj., f. *nî*, Belonging to the forenoon, matutinal.

प्रिय *priya*, i.e. *prî* + *a*, I. adj., f. *yâ*, comparat. *priyatara* and *preyaṁs*, superl. *priyatama* and *preshṭha*, Beloved, dear, Pańch. i. d. 205; agreeable, Çâk. 112, 15. *preyaṁs*, Much beloved, Kathâs. 26, 283; Lass. 68, 4. II. m. **1.** A husband, Bhâg. P. 4, 3, 6. **2.** A lover, Pańch. i. d. 205. **3.** A sort of deer. **4.** A sort of drug. III. f. A wife or mistress. IV. n. **1.** Love, Râjat. 5, 47; sake, Chr. 22, 18. **2.** A service, Vikr. 11, 18.—Comp. *A-*, I. adj. unkind, offensive, Man. 5, 156. II. m. an enemy, Man. 6, 62. *Putra-*, m. a kind of bird, MBh. 3, 9927. *Prâṇa-*, adj. as dear as life, Lass. 8, 11. *Ati-prâṇa-*, adj. dearer than life, Pańch. 220, 24. *Priyâpriya*, i.e. *priya-a-*, adj. agreeable and disagreeable, Hit. i. d. 11. *Maru-*, m. a camel. *Yavana-*, m. black pepper. *Raṇa-*, 1. adj. warlike. 2. m. a hawk. *Ramâ-*, n. the lotus. *Ravi-*, n. 1. the red lotus. 2. copper. *Vana-*, m. the Indian cuckoo. *Vi-*, I. adj. disagreeable, Râjat. 5, 210. II. n. offence, transgression, Râm. 3, 55, 17; hostility, Pańch. i. d. 409. *Sarva-*, adj. 1. generally beloved. 2. generally friendly, loving all. *Su-*, adj. agreeable. *Sura-*, m. Indra. *Vṛihaspati-su-rata-* (vb. *ram*), f. *yâ*, a proper name. *Sneha-*, m. a lamp. *Haya-*, m. barley. *Hari-*, I. m. 1. Çiva. 2. a foot. 3. armour. II. f. *yâ*, Lakshmî.—Cf. φίλος, φιλίων; Lat. filius.

प्रियंवद *priyaṁvada*, i.e. *priya* + *m* -*vad* + *a*, I. adj. **1.** Speaking what is agreeable, Hit. iii. d. 103. **2.** Sweet speaking, Indr. 4, 11. II. m. A proper name, Ragh. 3, 53. III. f. *dâ*, A proper name, Çâk. 10, 15.

प्रियक *priya* + *ka*, m. **1.** The name of several plants. **2.** A kind of deer. **3.** A bee. **4.** A certain bird, MBh. 3, 11576.

प्रियकार *priya-kâra*, and **प्रियंकर** *priyaṁkara*, i.e. *priya* + *m-kara*, adj. **1.** Acting kindly, Sund. 1, 5. **2.** Amiable.

प्रियकृत् *priya-kṛi* + *t*, adj. sbst. Doing a kindness, a friend, Johns. Sel. 18, 80.

प्रियंकर *priyaṁkara*, see *priyakâra*.

प्रियंगु *priyaṁgu*, m. **1.** A medicinal plant and perfume. **2.** Panick seed, Panicum italicum. **3.** Black mustard seed. **4.** Long pepper.

प्रियता *priya* + *tâ*, f. **1.** Being beloved, Man. 5. 50. **2.** Love, Râjat. 5, 351.

प्रियाल *priyâla* (akin to *priya*), m. A tree, commonly Piyal.

प्री *PRÎ*, ii. 9, *priṇâ*, *priṇî*, and i. 1: † i. 10, Par. Âtm. **1.** To please, to delight, Bhartṛ. 2, 71; Râjat. 5, 280. **2.** † To love. Pass. and i. 4, Âtm. (properly pass.), **1.** To be pleased, MBh. 1, 1070; with the termination of the Par., MBh. 3, 15025 (and loc.). **2.** To be satisfied, to assent, Daçak. in Chr. 193, 19. **3.** To love, Râm. 6, 10, 23. Ptcple. of the pf. pass. I. *prîta*. **1.** Beloved, Râm. 3, 49, 11. **2.** Pleased, delighted, Daçak. in Chr. 186, 21. **3.** Satisfied, Chr. 28, 17. **4.** Kind. II. *prîṇa*. Comp. *Su-prîta*, adj. well pleased, very happy, Johns. Sel. 5, 24. Caus. *prîṇaya* (properly a denomin. derived from *prîṇa*), To delight, MBh. 1, 6414. *prîṇita*, Pleased, Pańch. 198, 21.—With the prep. सम् *sam*, i. 4, Âtm. To be pleased, Râm. 2, 45, 22 Gorr. (=Schl. 2, 48, 18, where erroneously *priyeta* with short *i*).—Cf. ἐφιλάμην, *priya* and *prîti*; Goth. frijon, frijônds, friathva, freis; A.S. fréfrian, freónd, freo, frio, frige, fridh.

प्रीति *prî+ti*, f. **1.** Joy, Pańch. ii. d. 71; gratification, Hit. i. d. 96, M.M. **2.** Love, Pańch. i. d. 317; Kathâs. 99, 100. **3.** Peaceable way, Pańch. i. d. 421. **4.** The wife of Kâma, or Cupid. —Comp. *Nirupama-rasa*, i.e. *nis-upama-rasa-*, f. unparalleled delight, Bhartṛ. 2, 9 (thus to be read).—Cf. A.S. fridh, fredho; O.H.G. fridu.

प्रीतिमन्त् *prîti+mant*, adj., f. *matî*. **1.** Affectionate, Lass. 66, 1. **2.** Joyful, Chr. 60, 30. **3.** Content, voluntary, Chr. 6, 7.

प्रु *PRU*, i. 1, Âtm. To go.

प्रुष् *PRUSH*, i. 1, Par. (i.e. probably *pra-ush*), To burn, to consume by fire. ii. 9 (i.e. probably *pra-uksh*), *prushṇâ*, *prushṇi*, Par. **1.** To sprinkle. **2.** † To be wet. **3.** † To fill.—Cf. perhaps περι-φλύω.

प्रुष्व *prush+va*, I. m. **1.** The rainy season. **2.** The sun. II. f. *vâ*, A drop of water.

प्रुष्वाय *PRUSHVÂYA*, a denomin. derived from *prushvâ* with *ya*, Âtm. To dribble.

प्रेक्षक *prekshaka*, i.e. *pra-îksh+aka*, adj., f. *ikâ*, and sbst. Looking at, a spectator, Chr. 26, 63; Utt. Râmach. 162, 2.

प्रेक्षण *prekshaṇa*, i.e. *pra-îksh+ana*, I. n., and f. *ṇâ*, Seeing, looking at, Böhtl. Ind. Spr. 1212; looking wantonly, Man. 2, 179. **2.** Seeing, visiting, Çâk. 18, 16 (Prâkṛ.). II. n. **1.** The eye. **2.** A public spectacle, Man. 9, 264. —Comp. *Tiryak-* (see *tiryańch*), adj. looking sideways, Bhâg. P. 5, 26, 36.

प्रेक्षा *prekshâ*, i.e. *pra-îksh+a*, f. **1.** Seeing, Johns. Sel. 9, 11. **2.** Seeing a play or entertainment of dancing, etc., Man. 9, 48. **3.** Any public spectacle. **4.** Consideration, Hariv. 6462; intellect.

प्रेक्षावन्त् *prekshâ+vant*, adj., f. *vatî*, Intelligent.

प्रेक्षिन् *prekshin*, i.e. *pra-îksh+in*, adj., f. *iṇî*, Seeing, Râm. 3, 52, 13.—Comp. *Tiryak-* (see *tiryańch*), adj. looking sideways, MBh. 2, 2164.

प्रेङ्खा *preṅkhâ*, i.e. *pra-iṅkh+a*, f. **1.** A swing, a hammock. **2.** Dancing. **3.** A horse's pace.

प्रेङ्खोल् *PREṄKHOL*, i. 10 (properly a denomin. akin to *pra-iṅkh*), To swing, Pańch. rec. orn. *preṅkholita*, Swung.

प्रेङ्खोलन *preṅkhol+ana*, n. A swing, a hammock.

प्रेणि *preṇi*, i.e. *prî+ni*, m. One who delights by praises, Chr. 296, 10=Rigv. i. 112, 10.

प्रेप्सु *prepsu,* i.e. *pra-îpsa,* desider. of *âp,* + *u,* adj. Desirous of obtaining, desiring, Man. 5, 46.

प्रेमन् *preman,* i.e. I. *prî* + *man* (and *priya* + *iman*), n., Lass. 56, 16, and m. Love, Megh. 45; kindness, Böhtl. Ind. Spr. 187; 3337. II. m. 1. A name of Indra. 2. Wind.—Comp. *Sthita-*, m. a faithful friend. *Prakrishṭa-*, f. *mâ*, exceedingly loving, Utt. Râmach. 53, 4.

प्रेयंस् *preyaṁs,* see *priya.*

प्रेरण *preraṇa,* i.e. *pra-îr* + *ana,* I. n. 1. Sending, directing. 2. Ordering. 3. Passion. II. f. *ṇâ,* Instigation, Hit. 88, 4; Râjat. 5, 478.

प्रेर्त्वन् *prertvan,* i.e. *pra-îr* + *tvan,* I. m. The ocean. II. f. *varî,* A river.

† **प्रेष्** *PRESH* (? or **ह्रेष्** *hresh*), i. 1, Âtm. To go.

प्रेषण *preshaṇa,* i.e. *pra-*1. *ish* + *ana,* n. Sending, despatching, Daçak. in Chr. 196, 7; errand, Lass. 30, 8.

प्रेष्ठ *preshṭha,* see *priya.*

प्रेष्य *preshya,* i.e. *pra-*1. *ish,* Caus., + *ya,* m. A servant, Chr. 52, 17; a slave, Man. 3, 9.—Comp. *Grâma-*, m. the public servant of a town, MBh. 12, 2359; cf. Man. 3, 153.

प्रेष्यता i.e. *preshya* + *tâ,* f. Slavery, service, Man. 12, 70; Pañch. iii. d. 239.

प्रैण् *PRAIṆ,* see *paiṇ.*

प्रैष *praisha,* i.e. *pra-*1. 2. *ish* + *a.* 1. Order. 2. Sorrow. 3. Frenzy.

प्रैष्य *praishya,* i.e. *preshya* + *a,* I. m., f. *yâ,* A servant. II. n. Condition of a servant, Man. 2, 32.

प्रोक्षण *prokshaṇa,* i.e. *pra-uksh* + *ana,* n. 1. Sprinkling with water, Man. 5, 115. 2. Immolation of victims.

प्रोच्चण्ड *prochchaṇḍa,* i.e. *pra-ud-chaṇḍa,* adj. Horrible, Utt. Râmach. 43, 4.

प्रोच्चैस् *prochchais,* i.e. *pra-uchchais* (cf. *uchcha*), adv. Very loud, Pañch. 78, 6.

प्रोज्झन *projjhana,* i.e. *pra-ujjh* + *ana,* n. Leaving.

प्रोत्कट *protkaṭa,* i.e. *pra-utkaṭa,* adj. Favourite (?), Pañch. 156, 19.

प्रोत्कर्ष *protkarsha,* i.e. *pra-utkarsha,* m. Pre-eminence, Utt. Râmach. 134, 1.

प्रोत्साहन *protsâhana,* i.e. *pra-ud-sah,* Caus., + *ana,* n. Instigating, Daçak. in Chr. 180, 23.

प्रोथ् *PROTH,* i. 1, Par. Âtm. 1. To neigh, to snort. 2. To be able (cf. *protha*).

प्रोथ *protha,* i.e. I. *proth* + *a* (perhaps *pra-ud-stha,* vb. *sthâ*; in this case the vb. *proth* would be an old denomin., but cf. N.H.G. prusten), m. and n. The nose of a horse, Nal. 13, 20; of a hog, Arj. 3, 19. II. (for *prottha,* i.e. *pra-ud-stha*), adj. 1. Travelling, a traveller. 2. Notorious. 3. Fixed. III. m. 1. The loins or hips. 2. The womb.

प्रोष्ठपद *proshṭhapada,* m. The month Bhâdra, August—September.

प्रोष्ण *proshṇa,* i.e. *pra-ushṇa,* adj. Very hot, Pañch. iii. d. 204.

प्रोह *proha,* i.e. *pra-ûh* + *a,* I. adj. 1. Skilful. 2. A reasoner. II. m. 1. An elephant's foot. 2. A joint.

प्रौढ *prauḍha,* see *pra-vah.*

प्रौढि *prauḍhi,* f., i.e. I. *pra-vah* + *ti.* 1. Increase, Kathâs. 14, 63. 2. Elevation, Kathâs. 21, 103 (in speech). 3. Enterprize, confident or audacious exertion. II. *pra-ûh + ti*, Investigation, discussion.

प्रौष्ठपद *praushṭhapada*, i.e. *proshṭhapada + a*. **1.** m. The month Bhâdra, August—September. **2.** f. *dî*, Full moon in Bhâdra, Man. 4, 95.

† **प्लक्ष्** *PLAKSH*, v.r. of *bhaksh*.

प्लक्ष *plaksha*, m. **1.** The holy fig-tree, Ficus religiosa, Nal. 12, 4. **2.** The waved-leaf fig-tree, Ficus infectoria. **3.** Another tree, Hibiscus populneoides. **4.** One of the seven Dvîpas or divisions of the world. **5.** A side door.

† **प्लब्** *PLAB*, and **प्लव्** *PLAV*, i. 1, Âtm. To go; cf. *plu*.

प्लव *plava*, i.e. *plu + a*, I. adj. Leaping, jumping. II. m. **1.** Jumping. **2.** Swimming, Bhartṛ. i. 19 (cf. Böhtl. Roth. Sskr. Wörterbuch. s.v. *pulakay*). **3.** A raft, a boat, Pañch. ii. d. 42. **4.** A frog. **5.** A monkey. **6.** A sort of duck, Man. 5, 12. **7.** A declivity or shelving ground. **8.** A sort of basket or snare for catching fish.—Comp. *Açma(n)*-, m. a boat of stone, Man. 4, 190. See *Ku-. Marut-*, m. a lion.—Cf πλόος.

प्लवक *plavaka*, i.e. *plu + aka*, m. A tumbler, a man who walks on the edge of a sword, etc.

प्लवग *plava-ga* (vb. *gam*), m. **1.** A monkey, Râm. 5, 58, 13. **2.** A frog.

प्लवंग *plavaṁga*, i.e. *plava + m-ga* (vb. *gam*), m. **1.** A monkey. **2.** A deer.

प्लवंगम *plavaṁgama*, i.e. *plava + m -gam + a*, m. **1.** A monkey, Man. 7, 72; Utt. Râmach. 3, 4. **2.** A frog.

प्लवन *plavana*, i.e. *plu + ana*, n. **1.** Jumping. **2.** Swimming. **3.** Inclining, MBh. 12, 1454.—Comp. *Kuça-*, n. the name of a holy place, MBh. 3, 8179.

† **प्लिह्** *PLIH*, i. 1, Âtm. To go.

प्लिहन् and **प्लीहन्** *plîhan*, m., and **प्लीहा** *plihâ* (ÇKD.), f. **1.** The spleen, Yâjñ. 3, 94 (*î*). **2.** Its disease.—Cf. σπλήν, probably σπλάγχνα; Lat. lien.

† **प्ली** *PLÎ*, or **ल्वी** *LVÎ*, ii. 9, *plinâ, plini, lvinâ, lvini*, Par. To go.

प्लीहन् *plîhan* and **प्लीहा** *plîhâ*, see *plihan*.

प्लु *PLU*, i. 1, Âtm. **1.** To swim, Râm. 2, 69, 9. **2.** To navigate, MBh. 3, 12782. **3.** To fly, 3, 11767. **4.** To jump, Çâk. d. 7; Râm. 5, 2, 34 (*plavant*, ptcple. of the pres. Par., perhaps A monkey). **5.** To jump over (with acc.), Râm. 1, 1, 70. **6.** To blow, MBh. 3, 11070. Ptcple. of the pf. pass. *pluta*. **1.** Bathed, Chr. 46, 25; wet, Pañch. 206, 24. **2.** Jumped. **3.** Lengthened to three moras, Man. 2, 125. n. **1.** Leaping, Utt. Râmach. 117, 12. **2.** Bounding, Lass. 27, 1; capering, one of a horse's paces. Frequent. *poplûya*, To swim swiftly, Râm. 2, 95, 10. Caus. *plâvaya*, **1.** To inundate, Râjat. 5, 269. **2.** To sprinkle, Pañch. 208, 12. **3.** Âtm. To bathe, Râm. 1, 44, 56. **4.** To cause to stagger. *plâvita*, Moistened, Pañch. 122, 24; covered (with blood), 237, 17. —With the prep. **अभि** *abhi, abhipluta*, **1.** Overflowed. **2.** Attacked, Hit. iv. d. 87 (v.r. Böhtl. Ind. Spr. 936). **3.** Labouring, Man. 4, 41.—With **समभि** *sam-abhi*, To cover, MBh. 3, 2016. *samabhipluta*, Overwhelmed, labouring, Man. 4, 42.—With **अव** *ava*, To spring down, MBh. 4, 1260. **2.** To deviate, 2, 1452.—With **आ** *â*, **1.** To bathe, Man. 5, 77. **2.** To wash, MBh. 3, 8514. **3.** To swim near, 3, 12098. **4.** To leap on, Johns. Sel. 31, 50. *âpluta*, **1.** Bathed, Johns. Sel. 41, 49. **2.** Wetted, Pańch. 238, 23; 160, 4 (covered, viz. with blood). **3.** Covered, MBh, 3, 10693. m. An initiated householder. n. Bathing. Caus. **1.** To cause to bathe, MBh. 1, 7334. **2.** Âtm. To bathe (*gâtrâṇi*, one's own limbs), Chr. 46, 29. **3.** To sprinkle, Man. 3, 244. **4.** To inundate, Man. 11, 97. **5.** To cause to move, to excite, Râm. 1, 16, 24.—With समा *sam-â*, *samâpluta*, **1.** Drenched, drowned. **2.** Filled, MBh. 3, 2172.—With उद् *ud*, **1.** To leap up, Pańch. 117, 1. **2.** To spring on, Man. 8, 236. *utpluta*, Jumped upon, approached suddenly.—With उप *upa*, *upapluta*, **1.** Wet. **2.** Covered, Râm. 2, 7, 16. **3.** Assailed, Man. 4, 118. **4.** Distressed, MBh. 3, 2025. **5.** Eclipsed. **6.** Marked by prodigies.—With परि *pari*, To fluctuate, throb, Utt. Râmach. 171, 5. *paripluta*, **1.** Circumfused, Chr. 30, 37. **2.** Bathed. **3.** Immersed.—With अभिपरि *abhi-pari*, *abhipari-pluta*, **1.** Overflowed. **2.** Filled, Râm. 1, 73, 27. **3.** Agitated, Chr. 17, 29.—With वि *vi*, To fluctuate, Hit. iii. d. 2. *vipluta*, **1.** Immersed, Râjat. 5, 20. **2.** Mixed. **3.** Having had sexual intercourse, Man. 8, 377. **4.** Interrupted, Chr. 7, 21; troubled, Chr. 35, 7. **5.** Depraved, false, Utt. Râmach. 104, 7. **6.** Devastated, destroyed, Bhâg. P. 2, 6, 40. Comp. *A*-, adj. uninterrupted, without intermission, Man. 2, 249. *Bhaya*-, adj. panic-struck. Caus. to divulge, to profane, Man 11, 198.—With सम् *sam*, **1.** To flow together, Utt. Râmach. 97, 14. **2.** To fluctuate, Utt. Râmach. 155, 9. *sampluta*, Overspread, Johns. Sel. 60, 188. Caus. To inundate, Râm. 1, 44, 35.—Cf. πλέω, πλεύσομαι, πλύνω, πύελος, probably λούω; Lat. pluere, plorare, fluere, probably lavare; O.H.G. flawjan, fluz; A.S. fleot; O.H.G. fliuzan; A.S. fleowan, aet-flowan, fleotan; O.H.G. flot; A.S. flód, also fleógan, fliógan, and fleón, flión.

झुक्षि *plukshi* (cf. 1. *plush*), m. Fire.

1\. झुष् *PLUSH*, i. 1 and 4, Par. To burn (cf. *prush*). *plushṭa*, Râm. 2, 79, 20; Utt. Râmach. 15, 5.—With उद् *ud*, To consume with fire; *utplushṭa*, Ṛit. 1, 22.

2\. झुष् *PLUSH*, ii. 9, Par. **1.** † To be wet. **2.** † To sprinkle. **3.** † To fill. **4.** To burn (cf. *prush*).

† झुस् *PLUS*, i. 4, Par. **1.** To burn. **2.** To share.

† झेव् *PLEV*, see *pev*.

झोष *plosha*, i.e. *plush* + *a*, m. Burning, Râjat. 4, 316.

प्सा *PSÂ* (sprung from *bhas* + *â* by dropping *a*), ii. 2, Par. To eat. Ptcple. of the pf. pass. *psâta*, Eaten.—Cf. ὄψον.

प्सान *psâna*, i.e. *psâ* + *ana*, n. Eating.

फ *PH.*

फक्क् *PHAKK*, i. 1, Par. **1.** † To creep, to move slowly. **2.** † To act wrongly.

फक्किका *phakkikâ*, f. **1.** An assertion to be proved. **2.** A sophism. **3.** Fraud.

फट् *phaṭ*, A mystical syllable, Bhâg. P. 6, 8, 8.

फट *phaṭa* (probably *sphaṭ* + *a*), I. m., and f. *ṭâ*, The expanded hood or neck of the cobra di capello, or snake, Pañch. iii. d. 83; i. d. 229. II. f. *ṭâ*. **1.** A tooth. **2.** A cheat.

फण् *PHAṆ*, i. 1, Par. To go. Caus. *phâṇaya*, **1.** To cause to go. **2.** To produce easily (cf. *phâṇṭa*).

फण *phaṇa*, m., and f. *ṇâ*, The expanded hood or neck of the cobra di capello, or snake in general, Pañch. i. d. 107; Çâk. d. 158; Bhartṛ. 2, 28 (*ṇâ*). —Comp. *Avâkph°*, i.e. *avâñch-*, adj. with downcast neck, Ṛit. 1, 13 v.r. *Go-phaṇâ*, f. a concave bandage for the chin, nose, etc., Suçr. 1, 65, 18.

फणभृत् *phaṇa-bhṛi+t*, **फणवन्त्** *phaṇa+vant*, and **फणिन्** *phaṇin*, i.e. *phaṇa+in*, m. A snake, Kir. 5, 11 (*°bhṛit*); 27 (*vant*); Pañch. i. d. 175 (*°ṇin*).

फण्ड *phaṇḍa*, m. The belly.

फर्फरीक *pharpharîka*, I. m. The palm of the hand with the fingers extended. II. n. **1.** Sweetness. **2.** A shoot.

फल् *PHAL* (sprung from original *spar*, cf. *sphar*, *sphur*), i. 1, Par. **1.** To burst, MBh. 3, 1654. **2.** To disappear (as if by bursting), MBh. 13, 7472. **3.** To produce, Hit. ii. d. 132. **4.** To bear fruit, figuratively, Man. 1, 84; to fall to one's share, Hit. 54, 18; to befall, Hit. iii. d. 21 (*sâdhushu*, the good ones). **5.** To be fruitful, Bhartṛ. 2, 38. **6.** To be useful, 2, 98. **7.** Impersonal pass. *phalitam* (supply *asti*), Fruit is borne, produced, Hit. 21, 13. **8.** † To go. Ptcple. of the pf. pass. I. *phalita* (or *phala+ita*), **1.** Fruitful, bearing fruit, Hit. 47, 3, M.M. **2.** Successful, Daçak. in Chr. 196, 1. **II.** *phulla* (instead of *phal+na*), **1.** Blown, expanded as a flower, Ṛit. 6, 6; Pañch. i. d. 152. **2.** Opened (as the eyes, with pleasure), smiling. — With **उद्** *ud*, *utphulla*, **1.** Blown, as a flower, Kir. 5, 39. **2.** Expanded (as the eyes, with fear), Râm. 3, 50, 15; (with surprise, with joy), Hit. 51, 10, M.M.; Indr. 2, 26. Caus. *phâlaya*, To open, MBh. 1, 5977. — With **प्रोद्** *pra-ud*, *protphulla*, Blown, as a flower, Ṛit. 6, 34.—With **प्र** *pra*, *praphulla*, **1.** Blown, as a flower, Ṛit. 6, 1. **2.** Smiling. **3.** Shining. **4.** Glad.—With **प्रति** *prati*, To bound against, to be reflected, Çiç. 9, 37. *pratiphalita*, **1.** Reflected. **2.** Requited.—Cf. probably ὄφελος, ὀφέλλω; Lat. flos; A.S. blowan; Goth. bloma; A.S. bloma, blostma.

फल *phal+a*, n. **1.** Fruit, Utt. Râmach. 33, 8. **2.** Revenue, Hit. iv. d. 121. **3.** Consequence, Chr. 9, 43. **4.** Result, Hit. iv. d. 98 (*saṁkhyâ-mâtram*, consisting only in the number, i.e. by reckoning four you have nothing but the number, really there is only one). **5.** Fulfilment of an omen, Çâk. d. 15. **6.** Gain, Bhartṛ. 2, 18. **7.** Reward. **8.** A shield. **9.** The blade of a sword or knife, the head of an arrow, Daçak. 197, 2 (?). **10.** A ploughshare. — Comp. *A-*, adj., f. *lâ*. 1. Without fruit, Râm. 4, 59, 12. 2. unproductive, Man. 2, 158; figurat. 234. 3. unprofitable, prejudicial, Daçak. in Chr. 185, 8. *Karma(n)-*, n. retribution for actions, Man. 11, 231. *Kṛishṭa-*, n. the value of the crop, Yâjñ. 2, 158. *Kshîṇa-* (vb. *kshi*), adj. fruitless, Pañch. ii. d. 102. *Tri-*, I. adj., f. *lâ*, endowed with three fruits, Kâm. Nîtis. 8, 42. II. f. *lâ*, the three myrobalans. *Nishph°*, i.e. *nis-*, adj., f. *lâ*. 1. without fruit, Râm. 4, 48, 6. 2. fruitless, useless, Man. 3, 144. 3. unproductive, Pañch. 174, 19. 4. irrelevant. *Puṇya-*, n. reward of virtue or meritorious works

Man. 3, 95. *Puraḥph°*, i.e. *puras-*, adj. of which the fruit is coming on. *Marut-*, n. hail. *Mahâ-*, I. n. a great fruit, Bhartṛ. 2, 86. II. m. a fruit-tree, Aegle marmelos. III. f. *lâ*, a bitter gourd. *Manda-*, adj., f. *lâ*, bearing scanty fruit, Lass. 35, 20. *Muktâ-*, n. 1. a pearl, Pañch. pr. d. 9. 2. camphor. *Yathâ-phala+m*, when bearing fruit, Pañch. i. d. 246. *Vi-*, adj. vain, fruitless, useless, Böhtl. Ind. Spr. 1395. *Çâri-*, n. a chequered cloth or table for playing draughts. *Çrî-*, 1. m. a fruit-tree, Aegle marmelos. 2. (n.) the fruit of the Vilva, Man. 5, 120. *Sa-*, adj. 1. bearing fruit, Hit. i. d. 10, M.M.; rewarded, Vikr. 10, 9; fulfilled, Vikr. d. 27. 2. yielding a profit. 3. blessed, Râjat. 5, 373. *Su-*, I. adj. bearing good fruit. II. m., and f. *lâ*, the name of several plants.

फलक *phala+ka*, I. (m. and) n. **1.** A board, Man. 8, 396. **2.** A bench, Man. 2, 204 (Kull.). **3.** A layer, a base, Megh. 77 (at the end of a comp. adj., f. *kâ*, Having a base of crystal). **4.** Surface, Bhartṛ. 2, 28. **5.** A shield. **6.** A leaf for writing on, Daçak. in Chr. 199, 13 (? a small table). **7.** The bone of the forehead. II. n. **1.** The buttocks. **2.** The receptacle of the seed = core; in *gaṇḍa-*, a core-like, or core-representing cheek, Çiç. 9, 47 (at the end of a comp. adj. Having cheeks instead of cores).—Comp. *Chitra-*, n. a table with a likeness, a picture, Çâk. 85, 17. *Çilâ-*, n. a layer or table of stone.

फलपाकान्त *phalapâkânta*, i.e. *phala-pâka+anta*, I. adj., f. *tâ*, Perishing when the fruit is mature, Man. 1, 46. II. f. *tâ*, An annual plant.

फलमुद्गरिका *phalamudgarikâ*, i.e. *phala-mudgara+ka*, f. A sort of date.

फलवन्त् *phala+vant*, adj. *vatî*, Bearing fruit, Man. 1, 47; fruitful, Hit. pr. 43, M.M.

फलस *phala-sa*, m. The jack or bread-fruit-tree.

फलिन् *phalin*, i.e. *phala+in*, I. adj., f. *nî*, Having fruits, Châṇ. 21 in Berl. Monatsb. 1864, 408; bearing fruit, Man. 1, 47. II. m. A tree, MBh. 14, 498. III. f. *nî*. **1.** = Priyañgu. **2.** A potherb, Echites dichotoma. **3.** A flower, Celosia cristata.

फलिन *phalin+a*, adj. Bearing fruit.

फल्क *phalka*, adj., explained by *viçodhitâṅka*, which may be *viçodhita-aṅka*, or *çodhita-aṅka* with *vi*.—Cf. perhaps φολκός.

फल्गु *phalgu*, i.e. *sphurj+a*, I. adj. **1.** Pithless, sapless. **2.** Vain, worthless, Pañch. pr. d. 10. **3.** Weak, Hit. iii. d. 79. II. f. **1.** The opposite-leaved fig-tree. **2.** The spring season. **3.** Falsehood.

फल्गुता *phalgu+tâ*, f., and **फल्गुत्व** *phalgu+tva*, n. Vainness, Bhartṛ. 2, 9.—Cf. *sâraphalgutva*.

फल्गुन *phalgu+na*, I. m. **1.** The month Phâlguna. **2.** A name of Arjuna. II. f. *nî*, du. or pl. The eleventh and twelfth lunar asterisms, distinguished as former, *pûrva*, and latter, *uttara*; see *phâlguna*.

फल्गुनक *phalguna+ka*, m. **1.** Name of a people, Mârk. P. 58, 36. **2.** A proper name, Râjat. 5, 472.

फल्य *phalya*, i.e. *phala+ya*, n. A flower.

फाण्ट *phâṇṭa*, i.e. *phaṇ*, Caus., + *ta*, I. ptcple. of the pf. pass. of the causal of *phaṇ*, Readily or easily prepared. II. m. Diluted decoction. III. n. The first particles of butter that are prepared by churning.

फाण्ड *phâṇḍa* (cf. *phaṇḍa*), n. The belly.

फाल *phâla*, i.e. *phal* + *a*, I. m. n. The share of a plough, Man. 4, 46; 6, 16. II. m. A name of Çiva and Balarâma.

फाल्गुन *phâlguna*, i.e. *phalguna* + *a*, I. m. 1. A month, February—March, Râjat. 5, 221. 2. A name of Arjuna, Johns. Sel. 13, 43. 3. A sort of tree, Pentaptera arjuna. II. f. *nî*. 1. The day of full moon in the month Phâlguna. 2. The name of the eleventh and twelfth lunar asterisms, distinguished by the epithet former, *pûrva*, and latter, *uttara*.

फुट *phuṭa*, probably *sphuṭ* + *a*, m., f. *ṭâ*, and n. The expanded hood or neck of a snake, Pańch. 174, 11 (*ṭa*).

फुत् *phut*, indecl. 1. The expression of disregard. 2. Imitative sound, implying the boiling of water, etc. (see *kṛi*, and cf. *phût*).

फुत्कार *phut-kâra*, I. adj. Disdainful, arrogant. II. m. The sound of bubbling (see *phûtkâra*).

फुप्फुस *phupphusa*, see *pupphusa*.

† **फुल्** *PHULL* (cf. *phal*), i. 1, Par. To blossom.

फूत् *phût*=*phut*, 1. Imitative sound of blowing, Böhtl. Ind. Spr. 1184. 2. Crying aloud, expression of indignation, anger, Pańch. 35, 11; 82, 18; 193, 11; Vetâlap. xviii. MS. (see *kṛi*).

फूत्कर्तुमनस् *phûtkartumanas*, i.e. *phût-kartum-manas*, adj. Intending to cry aloud, to rage, Pańch. 40, 19.

फूत्कार *phût-kâra*, m. 1. Blowing, hissing, Kathâs. 22, 183. 2. Crying aloud, 13, 59.

फेन *phena*, probably akin to *sphây*, m. 1. Froth, foam, Vikr. d. 115. 2. Moisture, Man. 3, 19. 3. Vapour. 4. Cuttle-fish bone.—Comp. *A*-, adj. not frothy, Man. 2, 61.—Cf. A.S. fam, foeman; Lat. spuma.

फेनल *phena* + *la*, **फेनवन्त्** *phena* + *vant*, adj., f. *vatî*, Frothy, foamy, Arj. 6, 2 (*vant*).

फेनाय *PHENÂYA*, a denomin. derived from *phena* with *ya* (Par.), Âtm. To froth, to foam, MBh. 6, 101.

फेनिन् *phenin*, i.e. *phena* + *in*, **फेनिल** *phenila*, i.e. *phena* + *ila*, adj. Frothy, foamy, Hiḍ. 2, 11 (*nin*); Ragh. 13, 2 (*nila*).

फेर *phera*, and **फेरु** *pheru*, m. A jackal.

फेरव *pherava*, i.e. *pheru* + *a*, I. adj. 1. Fraudulent. 2. Malicious. II. m. 1. A jackal, Mâlat. 79, 17. 2. A Râkshasa, Kathâs. 47, 53.

फेरु *pheru*, see *phera*.

† **फेल्** *PHEL*, i. 1, Par. To go.

फेल *phela*, n., **फेला** *phelâ*, f., **फेलि** and **फेली** *phelî*, **फेलिका** *pheli* + *kâ*, f. Orts, leavings of a meal, or droppings from the mouth.

ब *B*.

† **बंह्** *BAṂH*, or **वंह्** *VAṂH* (cf. *bṛih*), i. 1, Âtm. To grow or increase.

बंहिष्ठ *baṃhishṭha*, **बंहीयंस्** *baṃhîyaṃs*, see *bahula*.

बकुल *bakula*, see *vakula*.

बट् *BAṬ*, see *vaṭ*; **बठ्** *BAṬH*, see *vaṭh*.

बडवा *baḍavâ* and *vaḍavâ*, f. 1. A

mare, Pańch. 252, 16; Utt. Râmach. 123, 1. **2.** The nymph Açvinî, or the personified asterism which is designated by a horse's head, Daçak. in Chr. 182, 11. **3.** A female slave, Râjat. 5, 280 (cf. *-anala*).

बण् *BAṆ*, see *vaṇ*.

बणिग्वह *baṇigvaha*, i.e. *baṇij-vah + a*, n. A camel.

बणिज् *baṇij*, and **वणिज्** *vaṇij*, i.e. *paṇi* (ved. A merchant), *-ja* (vb. *jan*), m. A merchant, Hit. 62, 9, M.M.—Comp. *Pota-*, m. a seafaring merchant, Hit. 63, 11.

बणिज्य *baṇij + ya*, n., and f. *yâ*, Trade, traffic (probably erroneously for *bâṇijya*, q. cf.).

† **बद्** *BAD*, **पद्** *PAD*, **बन्द्** *BAND*, i. 1, Par. To be steady or firm.

बदर *badara*, I. m., and f. *rî* (and *vadarî*), The jujube, Zizyphus jujuba or scandens, Nal. 12, 5 (*v*). II. m. The seed of the cotton pod. III. f. *râ* and *rî*, Cotton. IV. f. *râ*. **1.** A plant, Mimosa octandra. **2.** A medicinal drug. V. n. **1.** The fruit of the jujube. **2.** The pod of the cotton.—Cf. *vadarî*.

बदरिका *badarikâ* (?), i.e. *badarî + ka* (see the last), f. The jujube, Hit. i. d. 93, M.M.

बध् *BADH*, **1.** See *han*. **2.** See *bandh*. **3.** See *bîbhatsa*.

बध *badha*, **बधक** *badhaka*, see *vadha*, *vadhaka*.

बधत्र 1. *badh + atra*, n. A weapon.

बधिर *badhira*, probably *bandh + ira*, adj. Deaf, Pańch. v. d. 84.

बधिरता *badhira + tâ*, f. Deafness, Böhtl. Ind. Spr. 831.

बधूयु *badhûyu*, see *vadhûyu*.

बध्य *badhya*, see *han*.

बध्यता *badhya + tâ*, see *vadhyatâ*.

बध्र *badhra*, I. n. Lead. II. (i.e. *bandh + ra*), f. *rî*, A thong, MBh. 1, 1406.

बन् *BAN*, see *van*.

बन्ध् *BANDH*, ii. 9, *badhnâ*, *badhnî*, Par. (in epic poetry also Âtm., Chr. 27, 2). **1.** To bind, Daçak. in Chr. 194, 14; with *añjalim*, to put one's hands together, etc. (see *añjali*, 3), Vikr. 58, 12; *setunâ Gaṅgâm*, To bridge over the Ganges, MBh. 3, 10727; to overpower, Pańch. i. d. 128; to preclude, Pańch. i. d. 350. **2.** To fasten, Matsyop. 47. **3.** To bind on, MBh. 3, 12066. **4.** To put on, Râm. 2, 37, 12; Âtm., Chr. 27, 2. **5.** To fix on (as the inclination), Man. 5, 47. **6.** To catch, Hit. i. d. 46. **7.** To gain, get, Vikr. d. 27 (*dhṛitim*, satisfaction). **8.** To bear (as fruit), Ragh. 12, 69. **9.** To punish, Hit. ii. d. 63. Ptcple. of the pf. pass. *baddha*, **1.** Bound. **2.** Fixed, Vikr. 54, 4; firmly rooted, Râjat. 5, 377. **3.** Directed, Pańch. i. d. 350. **4.** Got, Vikr. d. 26. **5.** Inlaid, Megh. 77. **6.** Checked, suppressed, Utt. Râmach. 125, 1; Daçak. in. Chr. 187, 10. **7.** Withheld. **Comp.** *A-*, adj. inept. Nal. 26, 16. Comp. ptcple. fut. pass. *A-badhya*, adj. what may not be checked, Pańch. i. d. 413. Caus. *bandhaya*, **1.** To cause to be bound, endowed, Ragh. 12, 7. **2.** To cause to be embanked, Râjat. 5, 90. i. 10, and † **बध्** *BADH*, i. 10, To bind, Râm. 2, 84, 4.—With the prep. **अनु** *anu*, **1.** To unite, Râm. 1, 72, 8.

2. To hold together, Hit. i. d. 94, M.M. **3.** To set on, Utt. Râmach. 82, 12 (Premachandra Tark°, to confound). **4.** To continue, MBh. 3, 2562. **5.** To follow, Çâk. 101, 20. *anubaddha*, **1.** Bound to. **2.** Connected, Daçak. in Chr. 181, 1 (*-artha*, adj. Wealthy). **3.** Pressed, Mâlav. 44, 14.—With अपि *api*, *apibaddha*, Connected, fastened.—With आ *â*, **1.** To fasten, Râm. 2, 96, 31. **2.** To put on, Râm. 3, 50, 3. *âbaddha*, **1.** Bound on, Kir. 5, 33 (*-vepathu*, adj. Trembling). **2.** Joined, Râjat. 5, 92; Daçak. in Chr. 199, 14. **3.** Put on, Megh. 9.—With नि *ni*, **1.** To fasten, Pańch. 135, 5; MBh. 3, 10030; to fix, Vikr. d. 118. **2.** To fetter, Man. 6, 74. **3.** To impose, Vikr. d. 36. **4.** To catch, Pańch. 105, 9; and, To gain, i. d. 18. **5.** To gain, i. d. 18. **6.** To record, Man. 8, 255. **7.** To destroy, MBh. 4, 982. *nibaddha*, **1.** Bound, Utt. Râmach. 143, 2 (covered). **2.** Connected, Man. 4, 155; made, Pańch. 211, 5. **3.** Fixed upon. **4.** Checked. **5.** Restricted. **Comp.** *A-*, adj. not called upon as witness, Man. 8, 76 (Kull.).—With उपनि *upa-ni*, *upanibaddha*, Composed, Utt. Râmach. 162, 13.—With निस् *nis*, *nirbaddha*, Pressed hard, Daçak. in Chr. 193, 3. Ptcple. of the fut. pass. *nirbandhanîya*, n. Quarrel (?), Hariv. 7267.—With परि *pari*, *paribaddha*, Obstructed, Râm. 2, 58, 11.—With प्र *pra*, To bind, Pańch. iii. d. 269. *prabaddha*, Bound, fastened, Pańch. 89, 10.—With प्रति *prati*, **1.** To disclaim, Daçak. in Chr. 190, 6. **2.** To obstruct, Ragh. 1, 80 (79). **3.** To enchase, Pańch. i. d. 85. *pratibaddha*, **1.** Obstructed. **2.** Opposed. **3.** Set, inlaid, bestudded, Çiç. 9, 8. **4.** Bound, connected with, Hit. iii. d. 128.—With सम् *sam*, *sambaddha*, **1.** Connected with. **2.** Endowed with. **3.** Bound. **Comp.** *A-*, adj. 1. one who has received no mandate, being without authority, Man. 8, 163. 2. unconnected. 3. incoherent. 4. inept, Çâk. d. 16.—With अनुसम् *anu-sam*, *anusambaddha*, Accompanied, Johns. Sel. 23, 123.—Cf. Goth. and A.S. bindan; A.S. bonda, baend, baest; Goth. fastan; O.H.G. fasti; A.S. faest; Lat. patibulum (cf. *rudhira*), pendĕre pendêre, pondus, etc., probably filum, funis (for fid + lum, fud-nis); mani-festus; πεῖσμα (for πενθ + ματ), πενθερός.

बन्ध *bandh + a*, m. **1.** Binding, Pańch. 248, 12; laying (snares), Pańch. 114, 11. **2.** Holding in fetters, Man. 8, 310. **3.** The body. **4.** Building, Râjat. 5, 114. **5.** Forming, 344. **6.** Agreement, Daçak. in Chr. 183, 19; union, Pańch. 60, 19. **7.** A tie, Vikr. d. 85; fetter, knot, Hit. i. d. 49, M.M. **8.** A pledge, a deposit.—**Comp.** *Ańka-*, m. branding with a dishonouring mark, Yâjń. 2, 294. *Artha-*, m. a text, Çâk. d. 164. *Lalita-artha-*, adj. composed in verses treating of love, Vikr. d. 32. *Açva-bandh + a*, m. a groom, Râm. 2, 91, 55. *Âçâ-*, m. 1. confidence, Megh. 10. 2. a spider's web, ib. *Âsana-*, m. sitting down, Ragh. 2, 6. *Keça-*, m. a hair fillet, Bhâg. P. 8, 12, 28. *Daçabandha*, i.e. *daçan-*, m. a fine amounting to the tenth part, Man. 8, 107. *Paçu-*, m. immolation of an animal, MBh. 3, 184. *Pâṇi-*, m. union of the hands (as in marriage), MBh. 12, 9516. *Pâda-*, m. a chain for the feet, MBh. 8, 2586. *Pâça-*, m. a net or noose, Hit. i. d. 44. *Maṇi-*, m. the wrist. *Râga-*, m. true connection of the râgas, Mâlav. d. 29. *Vatsa-*, adj., f. *dhâ*, anxious for (her) calf, Brâhmaṇav. 1, 12. *Su-*, I.

adj. well-secured. II. m. Sesamum. *Setu-*, m. 1. a dike, Râjat. 5, 92. 2. the ridge of rocks between the Coromandel coast and Ceylon.

बन्धक *bandh+aka*, I. n. **1.** Binding. **2.** Barter. II. m. A pledge. III. f. *kî*. **1.** An unchaste woman, Pańch. i. d. 197. **2.** A barren woman. **3.** A she elephant.—**Comp.** *Nâga-*, m. an elephant-hunter. *Pâça-*, m. a bird-catcher, Pańch. iii. d. 224.

बन्धन *bandh+ana*, I. n. **1.** Binding, Pańch. ii. d. 20; Hit. iii. d. 21 (of the ocean, by a bridge), fastening, Hit. i. d. 29, M.M.; catching, Pańch. 114, 6. **2.** Confining, Hit. 34, 3, M.M. (*jâla-*, by a net). **3.** A prison, Man. 9, 288. **4.** A rope for tying cattle. II. m., f. *nâ* or *nî*, and n. The instrument of tying, holding together, Utt. Râmach, 40, 12; tie, Pańch. v. d. 19; string, Hit. 77, 1, M.M. (*snâyu-*, made of a sinew); a rope, a thread, Pańch. iv. d. 78; a chain, snare, Pańch. ii. d. 19; stem, Utt. Râmach. 53, 15.—**Comp.** *Nau-*, n. the name of the highest top of the Himâlaya, Matsyop. 49. *Pâça-*, I. n. a snare, Bhâg. P. 9, 16, 31. II. adj. caught in a snare, Kathâs. 13, 105. *Maṇi-*, n. the wrist, Çâk. d. 61. *Lalita-pada-*, n. a composition in verses treating of love, Çâk. 36, 16 (Prâkṛ.). *Sa-avaçesha-*, adj. still bound, Pańch. 109, 17. *Sâmarthya-*, adj. cemented by power, Johns. Sel. 5, 30.

बन्धमय *bandhamaya*, see *çloka-bandhamaya*.

ऽबन्धिन् *-bandhin*, i.e. *bandh*, and *bandha+in*, adj., f. *nî*, Fettered, Vikr. d. 147. *matsya-*, m. A fisher, Pańch. 247, 8.

बन्धु *bandh+u*, m. **1.** A kinsman, Pańch. iii. d. 182. **2.** Kindred, Man. 2, 136; 3, 148 (maternal cousin, Kull.). **3.** A friend, Hit. i. d. 30, M.M.—**Comp.** *A-*, adj. having no friends, Pańch. i. d. 393. *Kshatra-*, m. 1. a Kshatriya, Man. 2, 38. 2. a mere, a base Kshatriya, Bhâg. P. 1, 16, 23. *Brahmabandhu*, i.e. *brahman-*, m. 1. a Brâhmaṇa. 2. a base Brâhmaṇa, a term of abuse, Mâlav. 39, 13; 58, 2. *Râjanya-*, m. a Kshatriya, Man. 2, 65. *Vasanta-*, m. the god of love, Daçak. in Chr. 199, 11.

बन्धुर *bandhura* (partly vb. *bandh*), I. adj. **1.** Uneven, undulating, Ragh. 13, 47. **2.** Bent, Daçak. in Chr. 198, 23. **3.** Pleasing, handsome, Çâk. d. 140. **4.** Deaf. **5.** Injurious. II. m. **1.** A goose. **2.** A crane. III. f. *râ*, A prostitute. IV. n. **1.** A diadem. **2.** The dregs of oil. —**Comp.** *A-*, adj. straight, Utt. Râmach. 154, 8.—Cf. *vandhura* and A.S. bendan.

बन्धूर *bandhûra*, adj. **1.** Bent. **2.** Handsome (cf. the last).

बन्ध्य *bandhya*, i.e. *bandh+ya*, I. adj., f. *yâ*. **1.** Barren, Hit. pr. d. 15, M.M. **2.** Confined. II. f. *yâ*. **1.** A childless woman. **2.** A barren cow.—**Comp.** *A-*, adj. 1. fruitful, Megh. 11, s.v.; having a result, not vain, Vikr. d. 21. 2. happy, Vikr. d. 10.

बभ्र् *BABHR* (sprung from *babhram*, i.e. reduplicated *bhram*), or **वभ्र्** *VABHR*, i. 1, Par. To go, to go astray, Hit. 82, 13.

बभ्रु *babhru*, I. adj. **1.** Large. **2.** Tawny. **3.** Bald-headed through disease. II. m. **1.** Vishṇu, Çiva, fire. **2.** A large ichneumon. III. n. **1.** A tawny or brown colour. **2.** Any object of that colour; e.g. a tawny (red-) haired man, Man. 4, 130.—Cf. O.H.G. brûn.

बभ्रुश *babhru+ça*, adj. Tawny.

बम्ब् *BAMB*, see *barb*.

बर्जह *barjaha*, m. or n. An udder, Chr. 294, 4=Rigv. i. 92, 4.

† बर्ब् *BARB*, बम्ब् *BAMB*, मर्ब् *MARB*, and मम्ब् *MAMB*, i. 1, Par. To go.

बर्बर *barbara* (borrowed from the Greek *βάρβαρος*, cf. *varvara*), m. A blockhead, Hit. 50, 8.

बर्ह् *BARH*, or वर्ह् *VARH*, i. 1, Âtm. † 1. To be pre-eminent. † 2. To speak. 3. To kill. † 4. To give, or to cover. i. 10, † 1. To speak. 2. To kill, to hurt.—With the prep. नि *ni*, i. 10, To destroy, to remove, Çiç. 1, 29.—Cf. *varh*, *valh*.

बर्ह *barha*, and वर्ह *varha*, m. and n. 1. A peacock's tail, Megh. 15, 45. 2. A leaf. 3. Retinue.—Comp. *Chitra-*, 1. m. a peacock, MBh. 2, 2103. 2. a proper name, 5, 3597.

बर्हिण *barhiṇa*, and वर्हिण *varhiṇa*, i.e. *barhin* + *a*, m. A peacock, Vikr. d. 43.

बर्हिन् *barhin*, and वर्हिन् *varhin*, i.e. *barha* + *in*, m. A peacock, Draup. 8, 11.—Comp. *Chitra-*, adj. having a variegated peacock's tail, MBh. 13, 4206.

बर्हिषद् *barhishad*, i.e. *barhis-sad*, m. The name of a class of Pitṛis, Man. 3, 196.

बर्हिस् *barhis*, or वर्हिस् *varhis*, I. n. A layer, a seat of sacred grass, Chr. 291, 6=Rigv. i. 85, 6. II. m. and n. 1. Sacrificial grass. 2. Sacrifice, Bhâg. P. 4, 6, 5. III. m. 1. Fire. 2. Lustre.

† बल् *BAL*, i. 1, Par. 1. To live. 2. To hoard grain. i. 10, Par. I. *bâlaya* (Caus.), To nourish. II. *balaya*, To live.—Cf. *bhal*.

बल *bala*, I. m. 1. Baladeva. 2. A crow, Chr. 24, 45. 3. A demon. II. n. 1. Strength, Hit. i. d. 191, M.M.; power, Pańch. 44, 14. 2. An army, Hit. iv. d. 32. 3. Bulkiness. 4. The body. 5. Rigour, violence; abl. *balât*, Forcibly, Vikr. 33, 2 (as if it was your intention); without, or against one's will, Chr. 77, 11; Pańch. 27, 10. III. f. *lâ*, A plant, Sida cordifolia.—Comp. *A-*, I. n. weakness, Râm. 1, 7, 12. II. adj., f. *lâ*, weak, Pańch. i. d. 387. III. m. a proper name. IV. f. *lâ*, a woman, Megh. 2. *Balâbala*, i.e. *bala-a-bala*, n. strength and weakness, Hit. iii. d. 8. *Ati-*, I. adj., excessively strong, Râm. 3, 20, 37. II. m. a proper name. III. f. *lâ*. 1. the name of a spell, Râm. 1, 24, 12. 2. a plant, Sida cordifolia. 3. a proper name. *A-mogha-*, adj. of unfailing power. *Kim-*, adj. possessed of what a power, Bhâg. P. 7, 8, 7. *Tuṅga-*, m. a proper name. *Durbala*, i.e. *dus-*, adj., f. *lâ*. 1. weak, feeble, Pańch. i. d. 128. 2. without a prepuce, Man. 3, 151 (?). *Nâga-*, 1. m. a name of Bhîmasena. 2. f. *lâ*, a shrub, Uraria lagopodioides. *Pari-dus-*, adj. very weak, Râm. 3, 63, 5. *Mahâ-*, I. adj. very strong, powerful, Hit. 89, 22. II. m. air, wind. III. n. lead. IV. f. *lâ*, a sort of Sida with yellow flowers, S. rhombifolia. *Yathâ-bala* + *m*, adv. to the utmost of one's power, Johns. Sel. 48, 84. *Vṛihadb°*, i.e. *vṛihant-*, m. a proper name. *Sa-*, adj. 1. powerful, strong, Pańch. i. d. 267. 2. with (his) army, Chr. 54, 16. *Su-mahâ-*, adj. very strong, Chr. 54, 14.

बलदेव *baladeva*, m. 1. Air, wind. 2. The elder brother of Kṛishṇa.

बलभिद् *bala-bhid*, m. Indra (the slayer of *Bala*), Bhartṛ. 2, 85.

बलय *balaya*, see *valaya*.

बलवन्त् *bala+vant*, adj., f. *vatî*, comparat. *balîyaṁs*, superl. *balishṭha*, strong, Daçak. in Chr. 185, 5; powerful, Chr. 35, 7; heavy, Vikr. 50, 8. *balîyaṁs*, Stronger, Pańch. iii. d. 7; *balîyas+tara*, much stronger, Böhtl. Ind. Spr. 191. *balavat*, acc. sing. n., adv. **1.** Much, Vikr. 7, 9. **2.** Well, Çâk. d. 2.

बलाक *balâka*, see *valâka*.

बलाकिन् *balâkin*, i.e. *balâka+in*, I. adj. Having cranes, Ragh. 11, 15. II. m. A proper name, Johns. Sel. 42, 58.

बलात्कार *balâtkâra*, i.e. *bala+at* (abl. of *bala*), *-kâra*, m. Violence, Çâk. d. 173; Lass. 24, 19.

बलाहक *balâhaka*, also **वला°** *valâ°*, m. **1.** A cloud, MBh. 1, 1289; Çiç. 4, 54. **2.** A mountain. **3.** A Nâga. **4.** A demon, Draup. 2, 13.

बलि *bali* (also *vali*), I. m. **1.** A religious offering, Pańch. 199, 13. **2.** Presentation of food to all created beings; it consists in throwing a small parcel of the offering into the open air, Hit. ii. d. 41. **3.** Fragments of food left at an oblation, or a meal, Pańch. 114, 5. **4.** The sacrifice of an animal, sacrifice in general, Lass. 31, 7. **5.** An animal, or one which is fit for an oblation. **6.** Tax, royal revenue, Man. 7, 80; 9, 254; Pańch. 130, 17. **7.** The handle of a fly-flapper, Megh. 36. **8.** A king of the Daityas, also *Mahâbali*, Johns. Sel. 95, 65; Pańch. iii. d. 268. II. f., also *balî*, and *vali*. **1.** A wrinkle. **2.** The fold of skin upon the upper part of the belly, especially in females, Man. 6, 2; MBh. 1, 3467 (*î*). **3.** The ridge of a thatch.—Comp. *Gṛiha-bali*, m. a domestic sacrifice, Man. 3, 265. *Tri-balî*, or *-valî*, f. three folds of skin on the abdomen, Bhartṛ. 1, 80. *Sa-bali*, I. adj. endowed with (royal) revenues, Pańch. 130, 17. II. m. evening twilight. *Sa-pushpa-*, adj. filled with offerings, surrounded by flowers, Vikr. d. 43.

बलिन् *balin*, i.e. *bala+in*, I. adj., f. *nî*, Strong, Pańch. i. d. 128. II. m. **1.** A bull. **2.** A camel. **3.** A hog. **4.** A name of Balarâma. **5.** A sort of pulse, Phaseolus radiatus. **6.** A sort of jasmine. III. f. *nî*, Sida cordifolia.

बलिन *bali+na*, and **बलिभ** *bali+bha*, adj. Wrinkled, shrivelled.

बलिष्ठ *balishṭha*, and **बलीयंस्** *balîyaṁs*, see *balavant*.

बलीयस्त्व *balîyastva*, i.e. *balîyaṁs+tva*, n. **1.** State of being very powerful, Hit. iv. d. 42. **2.** Excessive strength, Hit. iv. d. 125.

बलीवर्द *balîvarda*, m. An ox (cf. *balin*), Pańch. i. d. 311.

बलीवर्ध *balîvardha*, Hit. 57, 17 (corr. *balîvarda*).

† **बल्ह्** *BALH*, or **वल्ह्** *VALH*, i. 1, Âtm. **1.** To speak. **2.** To hurt. **3.** To give, or to cover. i. 10, Par. To speak, to shine.—Cf. *barh* and *valh*.

बष् *BASH*, see *vash*.

बस् *BAS*, see 3. *vas*.

बहिस् *bahis*, see *vahis*.

बहु *bahu*, adj., f. *hu* and *hvî*, comparat. *bahu+tara*, Utt. Râmach. 13, 13, and *bhûyaṁs*, i.e. *bahu+îyams*, superl. *bhûyishṭha*, i. e. *bhûyaṁs+tha*. **1.** Much, Hit. 82, 5, M.M.; many, Hit. ii. d. 35. **2.** Large, great. **3.** *bahunâ*, with *kim*, In short, Vedântas. in Chr. 219, 10. Comparat. I. *bhûyaṁs*. **1.**

More, largest, Utt. Râmach. 89, 4. **2.** Greater part, Çâk. d. 7. **3.** Stronger, Vikr. 65, 12. **4.** More important, Daçak. in Chr. 198, 6. *yas*, acc. sing. n., adv. **1.** Repeatedly. **2.** Again, Pańch. i. d. 184; Vikr. d. 94. **3.** With following *api*, Again, Pańch. 24, 12; anew, Râjat. 5, 296. **4.** Doubled, *bhûyobhûyas*, Repeatedly, Pańch. 37, 25. *bhûyasâ*, instr. sing. n. Generally, Utt. Râmach. 128, 1. II. *bahutara*+*m*, adv. with following *stokam*, More than, Çâk. d. 7. Superl. *bhûyishṭha*, **1.** Very rich, Çâk. 3, 11. **2.** Very many. **3.** Almost all, Vikr. d. 8. adv. °*ṭham*, For the greatest part, Utt. Râmach. 114, 2.—Comp. *A-bhûyishṭha*, adj. scanty, Hit. iii. d. 108. *Samâpta-bhûyishṭha*, adj. having the greater part finished. *Su-bahu*, adj. very much, Chr. 28, 19.

बहुक *bahuka*, m. **1.** A crab. **2.** The digger of a tank.

बहुकुसुमित *bahukusumita*, i.e. *bahu-kusuma*+*ita*, adj. Full of blossoms, Vikr. d. 27.

बहुतस् *bahu*+*tas*, adv. From or by much, or many.

बहुतिथ *bahu*+*titha*, adj., f. *thî*. **1.** Manifold, manieth. **2.** Very long, Nal. 13, 2. **3.** °*tham*, adv. A very long time, Chr. 57, 23.

बहुत्र *bahu*+*tra*, adv. In many ways.

बहुत्व *bahu*+*tva*, n. **1.** Multitude, Böhtl. Ind. Spr. 997. **2.** Majority, Man. 8, 73.

बहुधनत्व *bahu-dhana*+*tva*, n. Wealth, Çâk. 90, 20.

बहुधा *bahu*+*dhâ*, adv. **1.** In many ways, Ṛit. 6, 10. **2.** Manifoldly, Chr. 33, 4; Pańch. iii. d. 74.

बहुपत्नीकृत् *bahu-patnî-kṛi*+*t*, adj. One who marries many wives, Brâhmaṇav. 2, 34.

बहुल *bahu*+*la*, I. adj., f. *lâ*, comparat. *baṁhiyaṁs*, superl. *baṁhishṭha*. **1.** Manifold. **2.** Much, Bhartṛ. 2, 29; numerous, Pańch. ii. d. 8; abundant, Utt. Râmach. 24, 13; exceeding, ib. 69, 2 (thus to be read). **3.** Abounding in, Man. 4, 60; Hit. i. d. 183, M.M.; Chr. 47, 41. **4.** Variously applicable (a rule). **5.** Black, Ragh. 11, 15. II. m. **1.** Agni. **2.** The dark half of a month. III. f. *lâ*, pl. The Pleiades. IV. n. The sky.

बहुशस् *bahu*+*ças*, adv. **1.** Abundantly, Pańch. iii. d. 183. **2.** Repeatedly, Çâk. d. 22; Vikr. d. 115.

† **बाड्** *BÂḌ*, or **वाड्** *VÂḌ*, i. 1, Âtm. To bathe, to dive and emerge.

बाडव *bâḍava* (also *vâḍava*), i.e. *baḍavâ*+*a*, I. m. **1.** A Brâhmaṇa. **2.** Submarine fire, Pańch. iv. d. 26. II. n. A stud.

बाण *bâṇa*, see *vâṇa*.

बाणिजिक *bâṇijika*, i.e. *baṇij*+*ika*, m. A trader, Man. 3, 181.

बाणिज्य *bâṇijya*, i.e. *baṇij*+*ya*, n. Trade, Hit. 46, 14 (°*yena*, for traffic).

बादर *bâdara*, i.e. *badarâ*+*a*, I. adj. Made of cotton. II. m. The cotton plant.

बाध् *BÂDH*, or **वाध्** *VÂDH* (akin to *badh*, see *han*), i. 1, Âtm. **1.** To repel, Chr. 294, 5=Rigv. i. 92, 5. **2.** To oppose. **3.** To remove, Vedântas. in Chr. 215, 7. **4.** To annoy, Hit. 57, 5; to grieve, Man. 10, 129; Pańch. 31, 10; pass. To suffer, ii. d. 95. **5.** To torment, Böhtl. Ind. Spr. 2220 (=Hit. ii. d. 102, but cf. l. l.). **6.** To damage, Daçak. in Chr. 182, 7. Ptcple. of the pf. pass. *bâdhita*, **1.** Obstructed. **2.** Pained. **3.** Self-refuted, contradictory, Daçak. in Chr. 182, 7. Caus. To annoy, Râm. 1, 14, 15.—With अधि *adhi*, To annoy, MBh. 1, 5693.—With अनु *anu*, To pain, Râjat. 5, 442.—With अप *apa*, To repel, Chr. 291, 3=Rigv. i. 85, 3.—With आ *â*, To restrain, Çâk. Chezy. 58, 10.—With परि *pari*, To annoy, MBh. 3, 8743; to importune, Çâk. d. 184.—With प्र *pra*, **1.** To repel, MBh. 2, 1648. **2.** To throw down, Pañch. i. d. 183. **3.** To destroy, i. d. 455. **4.** To annoy, Râm. 2, 53, 15.—With प्रति *prati*, **1.** To repel, Râm. 2, 52, 46. **2.** To restrain, MBh. 3, 1081.

बाध *bâdh+a*, or वाध *vâdha*, **I.** m. **1.** Opposing. **2.** Being precluded by superior evidence (one of the five forms of fallacious middle term), Bhâshâp. 77. **3.** Annoyance. **4.** Damage, Yâjñ. 2, 156. **5.** Danger, Böhtl. Ind. Spr. 3136. **II.** f. *dhâ*. **1.** Refutation. **2.** Annoyance, affliction, pain, Gît. 1, 26.—**Comp.** *A-bâdha*, adj. 1. Not harassed, Nal. 12, 104 (by fear). 2. and *Abâdha+ka*, free, Kathâs. 26, 80. *Para-loka-*, f. loss of paradise, Pañch. 167, 8 (cf. my transl.). *Prâṇa-bâdha*, m. extreme peril. *Madana-*, f. pain of love, Vikr. 41, 15. *Sa-*, adj. 1. painful. 2. oppressive.

बाधन *bâdh+ana*, n. **1.** Opposing. **2.** Refutation, Vedântas. in Chr. 218, 11. **3.** Pain.

बाधितत्व *bâdhita+tva*, n. Condition of being contradicted, refuted, Vedântas. in Chr. 211, 21.

बान्धकिनेय *bândhakineya*, i.e. *bandhakî+in+eya*, m. A bastard.

बान्धव *bândhava*, i.e. *bandhu+a*, m. **1.** A relation, a kinsman, Pañch. iii. d. 141; Hit. i. d. 71, M.M.; Man. 4, 179 (a maternal relation, Kull.). **2.** A friend, Hit. i. d. 72, M.M.—**Comp.** *A-*, adj. without kinsmen or friends, Râjat. 5, 23; 220. *Hata-* (vb. *han*), adj. without relations, Chûṇ. 6 in Berl. Monatsb. 1864, p. 407.

बाल *bâla*, **I.** adj. **1.** Young, Vikr. d. 26. **2.** Ignorant, Pañch. 169, 16. **II.** m., and f. *lâ*. **1.** A child (till sixteen years of age), Pañch. iv. d. 41; 219, 3; a foolish boy, Pañch. iv. d. 62. **2.** A colt. **3.** A five years' old elephant. **4.** A tail, Man. 8, 234. **5.** An elephant's or horse's tail, Râjat. 5, 386. **6.** Hair. **III.** m. and n. A perfume, Andropogon schoenanthus. **IV.** f. *lâ*. **1.** A woman, Lass. 59, 10. **2.** Small cardamoms. **V.** f. *lî*, A sort of earring.—**Comp.** *Dus-*, Man. 3, 151 v.r. The signification is questionable; Medâtithi gives, bald-pated, or red-haired, or without a prepuce.

बालक *bâla+ka*, **I.** m. **1.** A boy, a child, Pañch. 238, 20; a young one, 49, 18; young, Pañch. i. d. 372 (just risen, viz. the sun). **2.** A foot. **3.** The tail of a horse or elephant. **4.** A finger ring. **5.** A perfume. **II.** f. *likâ*. **1.** A female infant. **2.** A woman, Pañch. iv. d. 62. **3.** Sand (perhaps erroneously for *bâluka*).

बालखिल्य *bâla-khilya* (ved.), m. A divine personage of the size of the thumb, sixty thousand of whom were produced from the hair of Brahman's body, MBh. 13, 442; Sund. 3, 5.

बालधि *bâladhi*, i.e. *bâla-dhâ* (see *nidhi*), m. A hairy tail, Man. 4, 67.—**Comp.** *Vakra-*, m. a dog.

बालि *bâli*, and बालिन् *bâlin*, i.e. *bâla+in*, m. A monkey, the son of Indra.

बालिश *bâliça*, derived from *bâla*,

I. adj. **1.** Young. **2.** Ignorant, foolish, Man. 3, 176; Pañch. i. d. 338. **3.** Careless. II. n. A pillow.—Comp. *A-*, adj. wise, Hit. iv. d. 18.

बालिशता *bâliça+tâ*, f. Childishness, foolishness, Utt. Râmach. 147, 14.

बालिश्य *bâliçya*, i.e. *bâliça+ya*, n. **1.** Youth. **2.** Folly, Daçak. in Chr. 193, 8. **3.** Thoughtlessness.

बालुक *bâluka*, cf. *bâla*, I. m. A drug and perfume. II. f. *kâ*. **1.** Sand, Man. 8, 250; 12, 76; Pañch. 105, 8. **2.** Powder, Daçak. in Chr. 199, 13. **3.** Camphor. **4.** and °की *kî*, also **बालुङ्की** *bâluṅkî*, **बालुङ्गिका** *bâluṅgikâ*, **बालुङ्गी** *bâluṅgî*, A sort of cucumber.—Comp. *Tapta-bâluka*, adj. covered with hot sand, Bhâg. P. 3, 30, 23. *Rakta-bâluka*, n. red lead.

बालेय *bâleya*, i.e. *bâla+eya*, I. adj. **1.** Fit for a child. **2.** Soft. II. m. **1.** An ass. **2.** A demon.

बाल्य *bâlya*, i.e. *bâla+ya*, n. **1.** Childhood, Pañch. 219, 14. **2.** Youth, Utt. Râmach. 15, 1. **3.** Foolishness, Draup. 5, 6.

बाष्प *bâshpa*, see *vâshpa*.

बाह् *BÂH*, see *vâh*.

बाह *bâha*, I. m., and f. *hâ*, The arm. II. m. A horse (vb. *vah*).

बाहु *bâhu*, m. The arm, Vikr. d. 50.—Comp. *Ud-*, and *Ûrdhva-*, adj. having the arms lifted up, Ragh. 1, 3; Pañch. 165, 16. *Chatur-*, 1. adj. having four arms, Pañch. 251, 24. 2. m. Vishṇu, Bhâg. P. 8, 17, 4; Çiva. *Dîrgha-*, 1. adj. long-armed, Râm. 3, 74, 20. 2. m. a proper name. *Pṛithu-*, adj. lusty-armed. *Mahâ-*, and *su-mahâ-*, adj. having long arms. *Su-*, I. adj. powerful, Chr. 3, 2; very powerful, 39, 7; epithet of Râvaṇa, Utt. Râmach. 103, 2. II. m. a proper name, Johns. Sel. 27, 9.—Cf. πῆχυς.

बाहुक *bâhu+ka*, I. adj. Servile, a servant. II. m. **1.** A monkey. **2.** also **वाहुक** *vâhuka*, The name of Nala after his change of form, Nal. 15, 2.

बाहुगुण्य *bâhuguṇya*, i.e. *bahu-guṇa+ya*, n. Excess, Man. 7, 71 (instr. *yena*, Exceedingly).

बाहुमय *bâhu+maya*, adj., f. *yî*, Made with the arms.

बाहुल *bâhula*, I. i.e. *bahula+a*, m. **1.** Fire. **2.** The month Kârttika. II. i.e. *bâhu+la*, n. Mail worn on the arms.

बाहुल्य *bâhulya*, i.e. *bahula+ya*, n. Plenty, Hit. 47, 5, M.M.

बाह्य *bâhya*, see *vâhya*.

† **बिट्** *BIṬ*, **विट्** *VIṬ*, **विड्** *VIḌ*, and **हिट्** *HIṬ*, i. 1, Par. To curse, to swear.

† **बिन्द्** *BIND*, or **भिन्द्** *BHIND*, i. 1, Par. To divide; cf. *bhid*.

बिम्ब *bimba*, or *vimba*, I. m. and n. **1.** The disk of the sun or moon, Pañch. 162, 23. **2.** A reflected form, an image, Megh. 48. **3.** Reflection, Utt. Râmach. 35, 18. **4.** The gourd of the Momordica monadelpha. II. n., and f. *bâ* or *bî*, A cucurbitaceous plant with red fruit, Momordica monadelpha, Pañch. i. d. 225.—Comp. *Abhi-arka-bimba+m*, adv. towards the orb of the sun, Çâk. d. 170. *Indu-*, n. or m. the disk of the moon, Vikr. d. 34. *Nitamba-*, n. the rounding of the buttocks, Ṛit. 6, 5. *Ratha-aṅga-çroṇi-vimba*, adj., f. *bâ*, having buttocks like the part (half) of a wheel, i.e. semicircular, Vikr. d. 100. *Hasta-*, n. perfuming the person.

बिम्बित *bimbita*, i.e. *bimba* + *ita*, also *vimbita*, adj. **1.** Reflected, Râjat. 5, 343. **2.** Pictured.—Comp. *Prati-*, adj. reflected, Utt. Râmach. 109, 5; Lass. 73, 14.

बिम्बोष्ठ *bimboshṭha*, and **बिम्बौष्ठ** *bimbaushṭha*, or *vimb°*, i.e. *bimba-oshṭha*, I. m. A bimba-like lip, i.e. red as the Bimba fruit, Kathâs. 4, 8 (corr. p. 146 A, 2 bel.). II. adj., f. *ṭhâ* and *ṭhî*, Having lips like the Bimba fruit, red-lipped.

† **बिल्** *BIL*, i. 6, Par., and i. 10, Par., also **भिल्** *BHIL*, To break, to divide; cf. *bhid*.

बिल *bila*, see *vila*.

† **बिश्** *BIÇ*, and **बेश्** *BEÇ*, i. 6, Par. To go (?).

† **बिस्** *BIS*, i. 4, Par. To throw or cast.

बीज *bîja*, see *vîja*.

† **बीभ्** *BÎBH*, or **चीभ्** *CHÎBH*, i. 1, Âtm. To boast.

1. **बीभत्स** *BÎBHATSA*, an anomal. desider. probably of *bâdh*, Âtm. To be angry, to detest, Utt. Râmach. 6, 6 (with abl.).

2. **बीभत्स** *bîbhatsa*, i.e. *bîbhatsa* + *a*, I. m. Disgust, abhorrence. II. adj. **1.** Loathing, detesting. **2.** Loathful, Utt. Râmach. 99, 9; Pańch. iii. d. 112. **3.** Mischievous, cruel. **4.** Envious.—Comp. *Ati-*, I. m. grudge, envy, Râm. 3, 1, 21. II. adj. exceedingly loathful, cruel, Utt. Râmach. 29, 2.

बीभत्सु *bîbhatsu*, i.e. *bîbhatsa* + *u*, adj. Envious, emulous, Arj. 3, 1 (read *bîbh°*).

बुक्क् *BUKK*, i. 1 and † 10, Par. **1.** To sound, to bark, Pańch. rec. orn. **2.** † i. 10, To give pain.

बुक्क *bukka*, I. m. A goat. II. m., f. *kâ* and *kî*, and n. The heart.

बुङ्ग् *BUṄG*, see *vuṅg*.

† **बुट्** *BUṬ*, i. 10 and 1, Par. To kill.

बुड् *BUḌ*, see *chuḍ* and *puḍ*.

बुद् *BUD*, see *bund*.

बुद्धि *buddhi*, i.e. *budh* + *ti*, f. **1.** Understanding, Bhâshâp. 50; Vedântas. in Chr. 206, 24; Pańch. 81, 5. **2.** Reflexion, Râm. 3, 48, 14. **3.** Intellect, Pańch. i. d. 219. **4.** Mind, Pańch. i. d. 87; Chr. 5, 8. **5.** Thought, Râm. 3, 48, 14; intention, Pańch. v. d. 83. **6.** Knowledge, Bhâshâp. 165. **7.** Opinion, Hit. 81, 14 (*vyâghra-*, mistaking him for a tiger). **8.** Presence of mind, Pańch. ii. d. 6.—Comp. *A-*, I. f. foolishness, Râm. 4, 1, 23. II. adj. foolish, Man. 3, 104. *Ati-manushya-*, adj. having a more than human intellect, Johns. Sel. 54, 139. *Apekshâ-*, f. that operation of the mind by which we count things one by one, which produces *dvitva*, etc., Bhâshâp. 106. See *Ku*. *Kṛita-*, adj. 1. one who knows his duty, Man. 1, 97. 2. resolved, Vikr. 86, 19. *Kshudra-*, m. a proper name. *Durb°*, i.e. *dus-*, I. f. foolishness, MBh. 5, 4890. II. adj. perverse, foolish, MBh. 4, 416; Hiḍ. 1, 45. *Dushṭa-* (vb. *dush*), adj. ill-minded, Pańch. 22, 11. *Droha-*, I. adj. treacherous, Pańch. 58, 8. II. f. treachery, 58, 21. *Dharma-*, I. adj. virtuous. II. m. a proper name. *Nirb°*, i.e. *nis-*, adj. deprived of reason, Hit. i. d. 133, M.M. *Pâpa-*, 1. adj. evil-minded. 2. m. a proper name. *Bheda-*, f. distinction, Bhâg.

P. 3, 16, 10. *Manda-*, adj. stupid. *Su-manda-*, adj. very disheartened, Chr. 41, 8. *Mahâ-*, adj. endowed with much intellect, Pańch. 4, 22; very sensible (ironically, Chr. 6, 7). *Vikṛita-*, adj. ill-minded, Hit. 73, 18. *Vita-viruddha-*, i.e. *vi-ita-vi-ruddha-* (vb. *rudh*), adj. peaceable. *Su-*, adj. intelligent, wise. —Cf. πύστις.

बुद्धितस् *buddhi+tas*, adv. **1.**=abl. of *buddhi*, Bhâshâp. 121. **2.** By the mind, Râm. 6, 95, 54.

बुद्धिमन्त् *buddhi + mant*, adj., f. *mati*, Endowed with understanding, Man. 1, 96; intelligent, Pańch. iii. d. 40; wise, Pańch. i. d. 219.

बुद्बुद *budbuda*, m. A bubble, Utt. Râmach. 88, 3; Pańch. 203, 6.

बुध् *BUDH*, i. 1, Par. Âtm., i. 4, Âtm. (in epic poetry also Par., MBh. 1, 5053); originally, To fathom, to penetrate (cf. ved. *budh+na*, Depth, ground; A.S. bytne, botm; βυθός; Lat. fundus). **1.** To understand, Hit. i. d. 92 (pass.). **2.** To know, MBh. 1, 5148 (i. 4). **3.** To think, Hit. i. d. 3. **4.** To perceive, MBh. 3, 2893 (i. 4); Lass. 55, 12 (Âtm.); 14 (Par.). **5.** To admonish, Pańch. i. d. 176; (*boddhavya*, in the sense of *bodhayitavya*). **6.** i. 4, To recover one's senses, Bhaṭṭ. 15, 57. **7.** i. 4, To awake, Râm. 1, 46, 19; pass., Pańch. 183, 2; Çiç. 9, 24. Ptcple. of the pf. pass. *buddha*, **1.** Known, understood. **2.** Knowing, Vedântas. in Chr. 215, 5. m. **1.** A sage. **2.** The founder of the Bauddha religion. Comp. *A-*, adj. foolish. Comp. ptcple. of the fut. pass. *Açva-budhya*, adj. cognoscible, distinguished by horses, Chr. 294, 7=Rigv. i. 92, 7. Caus. *bodhaya*, **1.** To cause to know (with two acc.), to inform, MBh. 2, 2506. **2.** To advise, 3, 12774. **3.** To admonish, 1, 5785. **4.** To awaken, Pańch. i. d. 351; MBh. 1, 5959. **5.** To expand (as a flower), Çâk. d. 124. *bodhita*, Brought to consciousness, Daçak. in Chr. 194, 14.—With the prep. **अनु** *anu*, i. 4, Âtm. **1.** To learn, MBh. 3, 14779. **2.** To know, Daçak. in Chr. 197, 17. **3.** To remember, MBh. 1, 4874. **4.** To awake, 1, 5024. Caus. To cause to remember, Çâk. 4, 16. *anubodhita*, Informed or convinced by reflection.—With **अव** *ava*, i. 4, Âtm. **1.** To know, MBh. 2, 1371. **2.** To perceive, Man. 8, 53. **3.** To awake, Râm. 2, 72, 50, ed. Ser. Caus. To inform, MBh. 1, 5811. —With **समव** *sam-ava*, i. 4, Âtm. To know, to perceive, Râm. 2, 9, 31.—With **नि** *ni*, i. 1, **1.** To learn, Man. 1, 119. **2.** To hear, MBh. 3, 311. **3.** To know, 3, 2443.—With **प्र** *pra*, **1.** i. 1, To awaken, MBh. 3, 10635. **2.** i. 4, To awake, Hit. iii. d. 142; Kathâs. 3, 65. *prabuddha*, **1.** Wise, Pańch. 4, 22. **2.** Wakened, awakened, Utt. Râmach. 36, 12; awake, Hit. 14, 7, M.M. **3.** Expanded. Caus. **1.** To cause to know, to inform, to admonish, Pańch. 121, 10; Ragh. 3, 68; to instruct, Hit. i. d. 53, M.M. **2.** To awaken, Râm. 2, 56, 1. *prabodhita*, **1.** Instructed. **2.** Aroused.—With **विप्र** *vi-pra*, *viprabuddha*, Awakened, aroused, Megh. 110.—With **प्रति** *prati*, i. 4, To awake, Man. 1, 74. *pratibuddha*, **1.** Known. **2.** Wakened, awake. **3.** Exalted. Caus. **1.** To inform, Ragh. 1, 75. **2.** To admonish, to instruct, Pańch. 87, 24. **3.** To charge one with, Râm. 2, 52, 35. **4.** To awaken, Çâk. d. 143. *pratibodhita*, **1.** Instructed. **2.** Awakened.—With **वि** *vi*, i. 4, To awake, MBh. 2, 162. *vibuddha*, **1.** Awake. **2.** Opened (as a flower), Mâlav. d. 60. Caus. **1.** To awaken. **2.** To instruct, Daçak. 181, 17.—With

सम् *sam*, i. 4, **1.** To know, MBh. 1, 2498. **2.** To be wise, 2, 2187 (Par.). Caus. **1.** To cause to agree, Pańch. 101, 11. **2.** To exhort, Pańch. 84, 1; to admonish, Pańch. 103, 2. **3.** With *parasparam*, To come to an explanation with each other, Pańch. 101, 11. **4.** To ask, MBh. 1, 3521.—With **प्रतिसम्** *prati-sam*, *pratisaṁbuddha*, Recovered, MBh. 3, 12519.—Cf. πυθμήν, πυνθάνομαι, πεύθομαι; Lat. puteus (cf. *rudhira* and *bandh*), putare; Goth. biudan; A.S. beodan, boda, bodian, bodare, and look to the beginning of this article.

बुध *budh* + *a*, **I.** adj. Wise, Pańch. i. d. 427. **II.** m. **1.** Budha, the son of the moon and regent of the planet Mercury. **2.** A proper name, Vikr. d, 159.—**Comp.** *A-*, adj. foolish, Hit. ii. d. 23; Râjat. 5, 380. *Durb°*, i.e. *dus-*, adj. foolish, MBh. 11, 166.

बुधान *budhâna* (properly a ptcple. pres. of *budh*, following ii. 2), m. A spiritual guide or teacher.

बुध्न *budh* + *na*, m. **1.** The root of a tree. **2.** Çiva; see *budh*.—Cf. probably A.S. bytne, the bottom of a ship.

बुन्द् *BUND*, or † **चुन्द्** *CHUND*, also † **बुद्** *BUD*, **बुन्ध्** *BUNDH*, i. 1, Par. Âtm. **1.** To perceive. † **2.** To reflect.

† **बुन्ध्** *BUNDH*, i. 10, Par. To bind; cf. *bund*.

बुभुक्षा *bubhukshâ*, i.e. *bubhuksha*, desider. of *bhuj*, + *a*, f. Desire of eating, Hit. 77, 1, M.M.; Hunger, Pańch. 114, 4.

बुभुक्षित *bubhukshita*, i.e. *bubhukshâ* + *ita*, adj. Hungry, starving, Pańch. 114, 5.

बुभुक्षु *bubhukshu*, i.e. *bubhuksha*, desider. of *bhuj*, + *u*, adj. Wishing to eat.

बुभुत्सा *bubhutsâ*, i.e. *bubhutsa*, desider. of *budh*, + *a*, f. Wishing to know.

बुभुत्सु *bubhutsu*, i.e. *bubhutsa*, desider. of *budh*, + *u*, adj. Desirous of knowing, Daçak. in Chr. 179, 8.

† **बुल्** *BUL*, i. 10, Par. To sink, to dive.

बुलि *buli*, f. The vulva.

बुस् *BUS*, i. 4, Par. **1.** To effund. † **2.** To distribute (cf. 2. *vyush*).

बुस्त् *BUST*, see *pust*.

बृंह् *BṚIṀH*, and **बृह्** *BṚIH*, see *vṛiṁh*, *vṛih*.

बृहन्त् *bṛihant*, and **वृहन्त्** *vṛihant* (originally ptcple. pres. of *bṛih*), **I.** adj., f. *hatî*. **1.** Large, great, Pańch. 175, 9. **2.** Much. **II.** f. *atî*. **1.** A wrapper, a mantle. **2.** A reservoir, a place containing water. **3.** A large lute. **4.** The name of two plants.—Cf. probably Goth. bairgahei; A.S. beorh, beorg.

बृहस्पति *bṛih* + *as-pati*, and **वृहस्पति** *vṛihaspati*, m. **1.** A deity, originally The lord of prayer, Daçak. in Chr. 182, 12. **2.** The regent of the planet Jupiter and preceptor of the gods, Bhartṛ. 2, 27. **3.** The name of a saint and lawgiver, Pańch. i. d. 111.

बॄ *BṚÎ*, see *vṛî*; **बेश्** *BEÇ*, see *biç*; and **बेह्** *BEH*, see *veh*.

बोध *bodha*, i.e. *budh* + *a*, m. **1.** Knowledge, Bhâshâp. 140. **2.** Intellect, wisdom. **3.** Arousing.—**Comp.** *A-*, **I.** m. stupidity, Bhartṛ. 3, 2. **II.**

adj. ignorant, Chân. 35 in Berl. Monatsb. 1864, 409. *Âtmabodha*, i.e. *âtman-*, I. m. knowledge of the universal soul, Häberl. Anth. 489. II. adj. endowed with the knowledge of the universal soul, Bhartṛ. 1, 62. *Durb°*, i.e. *dus-*, adj. difficult to be understood, or penetrated, Râm. 4, 17, 6; Bhâg. P. 4, 22, 58. *Su-*, I. adj. 1. easily taught. 2. of easy apprehension. II. m. 1. waking. 2. knowledge.

बोधक *bodhaka*, i.e. *budh*, Caus., + *aka*, I. adj. Causing to know, Vedântas. in Chr. 204, 1. II. m. 1. A teacher. 2. A spy.

बोधन *bodhana*, i.e. *budh* + *ana*, I. n., and f. *nî*. 1. Knowledge, Ragh. 9, 49. 2. Teaching. 3. Arousing, Çiç. 9, 24. II. n. Burning incense. III. m. The planet Mercury.

बोधि *bodhi*, i.e. *budh* + *i*, I. adj. Wise, learned. II. m. 1. Intellect. 2. The holy fig-tree.

बौद्ध *bauddha*, i.e. *buddha* + *a*, m. A follower of the Bauddha religion, Vedântas. in Chr. 211, 4.

बौध *baudha*, i.e. *budha* + *a*, patronym. A son of Budha=Purûravas.

ब्युस् *BYUS*, see 2. *vyush*.

ब्रण् *BRAṆ*, see *vraṇ*.

ब्रध्न *bradhna*, perhaps *vṛidh* + *na*, m. 1. The root of a tree. 2. A son. 3. The body. 4. The sun, Man. 4, 231. 5. Çiva, Brahman.

ऽब्रह्मक *-brahmaka*, i.e. *brahman* + *ka*, at the end of a comp. adj. instead of *brahman*, in *sa-*, adj. With Brahman, Utt. Râmach. 174, 3.

ब्रह्मघातक *brahmaghâtaka*, i. e. *brahman-ghâtaka*, and **ब्रह्मघ्न** *brahmaghna*, i.e. *brahman-ghna*, m. The slayer of a Brâhmaṇa, Pańch. ii. d. 115; iv. d. 11.

ब्रह्मघोष *brahmaghosha*, i.e. *brahman-ghosha*, m. The word of Brahman, the Vedas, Utt. Râmach. 145, 6.

ब्रह्मण्य *brahmaṇya*, i.e. *brahman* + *ya*, adj. 1. Relating or connected with Brahman or a Brâhmaṇa; fit for a Brâhmaṇa. 2. Pious, Nal. 1, 3.—Comp. *A-*, I. adj. 1. not fit for a Brâhmaṇa. 2. hostile to the Brâhmaṇas. II. n. 1. wickedness, a wicked act, Pańch. 101, 1. 2. an exclamation of distress, alas! woe! Pańch. 82, 18; murder, Kathâs. 4, 111.

ब्रह्मत्व *brahmatva*, i.e. *brahman* + *tva*, n. 1. Identification with, or state of, Brahman, MBh. 13, 1361. 2. Godhead. 3. The rank of a Brâhmaṇa, Johns. Sel. 23, 118.

ब्रह्मद *brahmada*, and **ब्रह्मदातृ** i.e. *brahman-da* (vb. *dâ*), or *-dâtṛi*, m. A spiritual teacher, Man. 2, 146.

ब्रह्मदायहर *brahmadâyahara*, i.e. *brahman-dâya-hṛi* + *a*, adj. One who receives the gift of holy science, Man. 3, 2.

ब्रह्मन् *brahman*, probably *bṛih* + *man*, I. n. Prayer, Chr. 293, 4=Rigv. i. 88, 4. 2. The practice of austere devotion. 3. Chastity, Çâk. 14, 12. 4. The Vedas or scripture, Man. 1, 23. 5. The Brâhmaṇas, or theological part of the Veda, Man. 4, 100. 6. Holy knowledge. 7. The brahmanical caste, Man. 9, 320. 8. The divine cause and essence of the world, the unknown God. II. m. 1. A Brâhmaṇa, a priest (originally possessed of, or performing, powerful prayer), Chr. 15, 5. 2. Brahman, the first deity of the Hindu triad, and the operative creator of the world, Man. 1, 9; 50; Utt. Râmach. 36, 12 (*vâgâtman*, i.e. *vâch-*, adj. whose soul is speech).—**Comp.** *A-*, adj. without Brâhmaṇas, Man. 9, 322. *Mahâ-*, m. a great, mighty Brâhmaṇa, Chr. 20, 18. *Çabda-*, n. holy writ, Veda, Utt. Râmach. 37, 3; cf. 36, 11. *Su-*, adj. endowed with beautiful prayers, Lass. 101, 6=Rigv. vii. 16, 2.

ब्रह्मयोनिस्थ *brahmayonistha*, i.e. *brahman-yoni-stha*, adj. Intent on the means of attaining holy knowledge, Man. 10, 74.

ब्रह्मवर्चस *brahmavarchasa*, i. e. *brahman-varchas+a*, n. **1.** Holiness, Man. 2, 37; 4, 94. **2.** The superhuman power of a Brâhmaṇa, Çâk. 81, 16 (ironically).

ब्रह्मवित्त्व *brahmavittva*, i.e. *brahmavid+tva*, n. The state of one who knows the nature of the Supreme Spirit, Vedântas. in Chr. 219, 5.

ब्रह्मविद् *brahmavid*, i.e. *brahman-vid*, m. One who knows the Supreme Spirit; a wise one.

ब्रह्माञ्जलिकृत *brahmâñjalikṛita*, i.e. *brahman-añjali-kṛita*, adj. Having joined together the hands, as token of homage, Man. 2, 70; cf. 71.

ब्रह्माधिगमिक *brahmâdhigamika*, i.e. *brahman-adhigama+ika*, adj. Proceeding from the study of the scripture, Man. 2, 164.

ब्रह्मोज्झता *brahmojjhatâ*, i. e. *brahman-ujjh+a+tâ*, f. Neglecting or forgetting the Veda, Man. 11, 56.

ब्रह्मोद्य *brahmodya*, i.e. *brahman-vad+ya*, adj., f. *yâ*, Speaking or treating of holy knowledge, Man. 3, 231.

ब्राह्म *brâhma*, i.e. *brahman+a*, I. adj., f. *mî*. **1.** Relating to the Brâhmaṇas, brahmanical, Johns. Sel. 33, 67; deposited with the sacerdotal class, Man. 7, 82. **2.** Relating to holy knowledge. **3.** Relating to study, scriptural, Man. 3, 157. **4.** Prescribed by the Veda, 7, 2. **5.** Relating to Brahman, 1, 68. **6.** Fit for a divine state, 2, 28. **7.** Epithet of a weapon, Chr. 40, 15. **8.** also sbst. m. The name of the first nuptial form, Man. 3, 27, and 21. **9.** Relating, sacred to Brâhmî, the goddess of speech, 4, 92. **II.** m. Nârada, the son of Brahman. **III.** f. *mî*. **1.** A wife espoused according to the Brâhma form, Man. 3, 37. **2.** The goddess of speech, the wife of Brahman. **3.** The moon plant (Asclepias acida). **IV.** n. The part of the hand under the root of the thumb.

ब्राह्मण *brâhmaṇa*, i.e. *brahman+a*, I. adj., f. *ṇî*, Relating to, becoming a Brâhmaṇa, brahmanical, Johns. Sel. 38, 27. **II.** m. A Brâhmaṇa, a man of the first caste, Pañch. 220, 24. **III.** f. *ṇî*. **1.** A woman of the brahmanical tribe. **2.** The wife of a Brâhmaṇa, Pañch. 118, 25. **IV.** n. **1.** An assemblage of Brâhmaṇas. **2.** The theological portion of the Vedas, Pâṇ. 2, 3, 60, Sch.—**Comp.** *A-*, 1. m. one who is not a Brâhmaṇa, Man. 2, 241. 2. adj. without Brâhmaṇas. *Go-*, a cow and a Brâhmaṇa, Man. 5, 95.

ब्राह्मणब्रुव *brâhmaṇabruva*, i. e. *brâhmaṇa-brû+a*, m. A wicked Brâhmaṇa, Man. 7, 85; Chr. 24, 38 (read *-bruva* instead of *-bruvam*).

ब्राह्मण्य *brâhmaṇya*, i.e. *brâhmaṇa* (or *brahman*), *+ya*, I. m. The planet Saturn. **II.** n. Brahmanhood, priestly character, Man. 11, 97; the dignity of a Brâhmaṇa, Pañch. i. d. 76—**Comp.**

Sva-brâhmaṇyâ, f. a sort of text, Man. 9, 126.

ब्राह्म्य *brâhmya*, i.e. *brahman* or *brâhma*, + *ya*, I. adj. with and without *huta*, n. One of the five sacraments, the worship or veneration of Brâhmaṇas, Man. 3, 73, 74. II. n. Astonishment.

ब्रू *BRÛ*, ii. 2, Par. Âtm., used only in the pres., imperf., imperat., and potent. All other forms are supplied by *vach*, and the redupl. pf., partly also by 1. *ah*. **1.** To speak, Man. 1, 1. **2.** To speak to, with dat. and acc., 1, 60. **3.** To answer, 8, 94. **4.** With *anyathâ*, To decide wrongly, to give a wrong sentence (in a law suit), Pańch. iii. d. 108. In epic poetry, anomal. 1. sing. present, *brûmi*, Râm. 2, 19, 4; imperf. *abruvam*, even in Daçak. in Chr. 185, 11.—With the prep. अति *ati*, To abuse, MBh. 3, 15640.—With अनु *anu*, To pronounce, MBh. 1, 176.—With प्र *pra*, **1.** To declare, MBh. 1, 838. **2.** To recite, Man. 10, 1. **3.** To tell, MBh. 3, 16678. **4.** To speak, 3, 10487.—With प्रति *prati*, To answer, MBh. 3, 2737.—With वि *vi*, **1.** To explain, MBh. 1, 4245. **2.** To speak at variance, Man. 8, 194. **3.** To say what is false, 8, 13; to declare falsely, 8, 75. **4.** To decide unjustly, 8, 390. **5.** To speak, MBh. 3, 2990.

ब्ली *BLÎ* (ved.), व्ली *VLÎ*, ii. 9, *blinâ*, *vlinâ*, *nî*, ved. *blînâ*, *vlînâ*, *nî*, Par. **1.** To select. **2.** † To hold. **3.** † To maintain. **4.** † To go.

भ *BH*.

भ *bha* (vb. *bhâ*), I. n. **1.** A star, Bhâg. P. 3, 17, 14. **2.** A lunar asterism. **3.** A planet. II. m. A name of the planet Venus. III. f. *bhâ*, see s.v.

भक्त *bhakta*, i.e. ptcple. pf. pass. of *bhaj* (in the signification To cook, cf. also *bhaksh*), n. **1.** Food, Man. 9, 271. **2.** Boiled rice. **3.** A meal, Man. 11, 16.—Comp. *Eka-*, n. eating only once a day, MBh. 13, 5146. *Chaturtha-*, n. eating only the fourth meal (leaving out three), i.e. eating only every second day, MBh. 13, 5145; cf. *bhaj*.

भक्तकर *bhakta-kara*, m. Factitious incense.

भक्ति *bhakti*, i.e. *bhaj* and *bhańj* + *ti*, **1.** Worship, Vikr. d. 1; service. **2.** Devotion, Hit. iii. d. 65. **3.** Attachment, Pańch. i. d. 326. **4.** Faith, Pańch. 71, 4; belief, Çâṇḍilyas. ed. Ballantyne, 76 sqq. **5.** Fracture, breaking, Megh. 61. **6.** In *bhakti-chheda*, Megh. 19, see *chheda*.—Comp. *Kshetra-*, f. partition of a field, Pâṇ. 5, 1, 46, Sch. *Dṛigbhakti*, i.e. *driç-*, f. a side look, an amorous look, Lass. 66, 11.

भक्तिभाज् *bhaktibhâj*, i.e. *bhakti-bhaj*, adj. Devout, Pańch. 236, 20.

भक्तिमन्त् *bhakti* + *mant*, adj., f. *tî*, Devoted, faithful, Pańch. pr. d. 5.

भक्ष् *BHAKSH*, akin to *bhaj* and *bhańj*, i. 1, Par. Âtm., and i. 10, Par. (in epic poetry also Âtm.), **1.** To devour, Man. 5, 50. **2.** To eat, MBh. 3, 1741. **3.** To enjoy, Pańch. 137, 20. **4.** To bite, Pańch. 62, 23; Kathâs. 4, 69. Ptcple. of the fut. pass. *bhakshya*, Eatable, allowed to be eaten, Man. 1, 113. n. **1.** Food, Pańch. 199, 13. **2.** Dainty food, Man. 9, 268; 3, 227. Comp. *A-*, adj. unfit, or not allowed, to be eaten, Man. 1, 113. *Sarva-*, adj. 1. eating anything (a child). 2. omnivorous. Desider. of i. 10, *bibhakshayisha*, To desire to devour, MBh. 1, 5951.—With

सम् *sam*, To devour, MBh. 3, 422.—Cf. φαγεῖν, perhaps φακός, φάσηλος; Lat. fames, perhaps bacca.

भक्ष *bhaksh + a*, I. m., f. *shâ*, and n. (Pańch. rec. orn.), Eating food, Pańch. 53, 23. II. latter part of comp. adj. Devouring, Man. 9, 314 v.r.—Comp. *Vâyu-*, I. adj., f. *shâ*. 1. feeding on air, Johns. Sel. 51, 1. 2. fasting, Chr. 46, 20. II. m. 1. an ascetic. 2. a snake. *Sarva-*, I. adj. omnivorous, eating all things, Hit. ii. d. 173. II. f. *shâ*, a female goat.

भक्षक *bhaksh + aka*, I. adj. **1.** Voracious. **2.** Eating, feeding on, Hit. 75, 8. **3.** A feeder, Hit. i. d. 54, M.M. II. f. *shikâ*, A meal.

भक्षण *bhakshaṇa*, i.e. *bhaksh + ana*, n. **1.** Eating, Pańch. 114, 10; being eaten, 88, 25. **2.** Enjoying, Vedântas. in Chr. 219, 4.—Comp. *Vâyu-*, n. fasting.

ऽभक्षिन् *-bhaksh + in*, adj. Eating; in *sarva-*, adj. Eating all kinds of food, Pańch. i. d. 472.

भग *bhaga*, i.e. *bhaj* and *bhańj + a*, I. m. **1.** The sun. **2.** Çiva. II. n. **1.** Divine power. **2.** Fortune. **3.** Virtue. **4.** Beauty. **5.** Pudendum muliebre, Râjat. 5, 282.—Comp. *Durbh°*, i.e. *dus-*, adj., f. *gâ*. 1. difficult to be obtained, Râjat. 4, 113. 2. unfortunate, Hit. i. d. 17, M.M. *Su-*, I. adj., f. *gâ*. 1. fortunate, Chr. 287, 7 = Rigv. i. 48, 7. 2. beautiful, Vikr. d. 123; lovely, Çâk. d. 3; charming, d. 57. 3. beloved, amiable, Man. 2, 129. II. m. 1. the Açoka tree. 2. the Champaca, Michelia champaka. III. f. *gâ*. 1. a favourite woman. 2. a respectable mother. 3. the name of several plants. IV. n. fortune, Daçak. in Chr. 184, 19.—Cf. Goth. ga-bigs.

भगदत्त *bhaga-datta* (vb. *dâ*), m. A proper name.

भगनेत्र *bhaga-netra*, m. The name of a demon, Johns. Sel. 97, 80.

भगवन्त् *bhaga + vant*, I. adj., f. *vatî*, Adorable, Man. 1, 6; Vikr. 31, 18; 85, 21; respectable, worshipful (used in address), Chr. 17, 27; Pańch. 80, 13. II. f. *vatî*, A name of Gaurî.

भगाल *bhagâla*, n. The human skull.

भगालिन् *bhagâlin*, i.e. *bhagâla + in*, m. A name of Çiva.

भगिनी *bhaginî*, i.e. *bhaga + in + î*, f. **1.** A sister, Pańch. 214, 25; 222, 9. **2.** A woman in general.—Comp. *Dharma-*, f. 1. a woman on whom the rank of a sister is bestowed, Kathâs. 4, 96; cf. Pańch. 222, 9. 2. a Bauddha nun, Mṛichchh. 134, 22.

भगीरथ *bhagîratha*, m. A king whose austerities brought Gańgâ, the river, from heaven; called her father, Râm. 1, 44, 8 sqq. Gorr.; Utt. Râmach. 167, 10; Chr. 24, 47.

भगोस् *bhagos*, an old voc. sing. of *bhagavant*, indecl. A particle used as respectful address.

भङ्क्तृ *bhańktṛi*, i.e. *bhańj + tṛi*, m., f. *trî*, and n. Breaking, one who breaks down, Man. 9, 289.

भङ्ग *bhańga*, i.e. *bhańj + a*, I. m. **1.** Breaking, Pańch. iii. d. 16. **2.** A fissure, a broken piece, Vikr. d. 107 (a branch). **3.** Interruption, Pańch. 8, 19; obstacle, Vikr. 12, 17. **4.** Repudiation. **5.** Defeat, discomfiture, destruction, Hit. 100, 3; ruin, Lass. 76, 18. **6.** Disappointment, neglect, Hit. ii. d. 52. **7.** Fear, Pańch. 219, 18; iv. d. 43. **8.** Curving, Çâk. d. 7;

knitting (the brow), Utt. Râmach. 138, 3. **9.** Fraud. **10.** A wave. **11.** A water-course. **12.** Disease. II. f. *gâ*, Hemp.—**Comp.** *Asu-*, m. danger of life, Bhartṛ. 2, 61. *Utsâha-*, m. destroying, breaking one's courage, Hit. 94, 13. *Gṛiha-*, m. loss of a wife, Pańch. 225, 17 (cf. iii. d. 152). *Daṇḍa-*, m. hinderance of punishment, Bhâg. P. 6, 3, 2. *Danta-*, m. splitting, breaking of teeth, Pańch. i. d. 418. *Durbh°*, i.e. *dus-*, adj. difficult to be loosened, Hariv. 1138. *Patra-*, m., and f. *gî*, strokes and lines drawn on the face with fragrant pigments of sandal, musk, etc., Böhtl. Ind. Spr. 622 (*ga*). *Pushpa-*, m. treading on flowers, Nal. 25, 7 (Sch.). *Pṛishṭha-*, m. a sort of fighting, MBh. 2, 908. *Pota-*, m. shipwreck, Böhtl. Ind. Spr. 1072. *Praṇaya-*, m. faithlessness, Vikr. d. 118. *Bhrû-*, m. a frown, Vikr. d. 115; Râjat. 5, 398. *Sa-bhrû-bhaṅga+m*, adv. knitting the brows, Çâk. 16, 17. *Sâra-*, I. adj. void of pith, substance, strength. II. m. destroying vigour. *Hitâ-*, m. breaking of a dike, Man. 9, 274.

भङ्गि and **भङ्गी** *bhaṅgî*, i.e. *bhańj+a+i*, f. **1.** Fracture. **2.** Separation, interval, Lass. 83, 1; step, degree, Ragh. 13, 69. **3.** Incurvation, Lass. 87, 16. **4.** Current, Râjat. 2, 131. **5.** figurat. Modesty, Kathâs. 21, 103. **6.** Fraud, pretext, Kathâs. 3, 53. **7.** A wave, Ragh. 16, 36.—**Comp.** *Putra-*, see s.v. *bhaṅga*.

भङ्गिन् *bhaṅgin*, i.e. *bhaṅga+in*, adj., f. *nî*, Frail, perishable, Lass. 42, 18; Bhartṛ. 2, 88 (*kshaṇa-*, in a moment; v., and better r.).

भङ्गुर *bhaṅgura*, i.e. *bhańj+ura*, I. adj. **1.** Crooked, Bhartṛ. 3, 36. **2.** Frail, perishable, Pańch. 165, 17; vanishing, Hit. i. d. 186, M.M. **3.** Fraudulent, Lass. 84, 9. II. m. The bend of a river.—**Comp.** *A-*, adj. 1. unbroken. 2. undisturbed, Râjat. 5, 4.

भङ्ग्य *bhaṅgya*, i.e. *bhaṅgâ+ya*, n. A field of hemp.

भज् *BHAJ*, i. 1, Par. Âtm. **1.** To divide, Man. 9, 104. **2.** To obtain as one's share, to obtain, Man. 10, 59 (Âtm.); to get, Çâk. d. 167; Pańch. 69, 4 (Par.). **3.** To take, MBh. 4, 237 (Âtm.); to embrace, Çâk. d. 107 (Âtm.); to love, Lass. 44, 7. **4.** To go to, Râm. 1, 16, 28; with *diças*, To run away, MBh. 3, 11113. **5.** To take possession of, Man. 1, 28. **6.** To possess, to have, Man. 5, 148. **7.** To enjoy carnally, to love, Man. 9, 70. **8.** To make advances, Man. 8, 365. **9.** To serve, to worship, MBh. 3, 16004. **10.** Âtm. To favour, Pańch. i. d. 41. **11.** To practise, Man. 4, 204. Ptcple. of the pf. pass. *bhakta*, **1.** Attached, devoted, Hit. ii. d. 74; believing; *tad-*, believing in him, Râmatap. Up. 1, 94. **2.** Served. **3.** Dressed, cooked. m. A follower, a votary; cf. also s. v. *bhakta*. **Comp.** *Eka-*, adj. kept by one master, Man. 8, 363. *Sûrya-*, I. adj. worshipping the sun. II. m. a flower, Pentapetes phoenicea. Caus., with *diças*, To put one to flight, Bhaṭṭ. 17, 80. † i. 10, Par. **1.** To give. **2.** To dress, or cook.—With the prep. निस् *nis*, To exclude, Man. 9, 207.—With प्रति *prati*, To return to (acc.), Daçak. in Chr. 193, 5 (anomal. *bhajishyati*).—With वि *vi*, **1.** To distribute, to divide, Man. 9, 164. **2.** To put up severally, Vikr. d. 43. **3.** To distinguish, Râm. 2, 67, 31. *vibhakta*, Attached, Çâk. d. 107; Vikr. d. 160.—With प्रवि *pra-vi*, To divide, MBh. 3, 16147. *pravibhakta*, **1.** Formerly distributed, Çâk. d. 165. **2.** Divided, Man. 8, 166.—With संवि *sam*

-*vi*, **1.** To make one partake of something, Râjat. 5, 109. **2.** To divide, Pańch. 217, 12. *saṁvibhakta*, Divided, parted. Caus. To cause to be divided, MBh. 3, 12683.—Cf. perhaps Lat. famulus, familia; Goth. anda-bahti, and bahtjan; also φώγω, φώγνυμι, and A.S. bacan; O.H.G. bachan (but see *pach*).

भजन *bhaj+ana*, n. **1.** Sharing. **2.** Possession. **3.** Service, adoration.

भञ्ज् *BHAŃJ*, ii. 7, *bhanaj*, *bhańj*, Par. **1.** To split, Râm. 1, 67, 17. **2.** To break, Pańch. i. d. 148; to destroy, MBh. 3, 10990. Ptcple. of the pf. pass. *bhagna*. **1.** Broken, Pańch. 36, 12; torn. **2.** Defeated, Bhartṛ. 2, 85; Râjat. 5, 340. **3.** Disheartened, Chr. 5, 23; Pańch. iv. d. 43. **4.** Disappointed, Bhartṛ. 2, 82. **5.** Extinct, Man. 8, 148. **6.** Disregarded, humbled; † i. 10, Par. To speak, to shine.—With the prep. अव *ava*, To break down, MBh. 1, 7081.—With नि *ni*, To break, Bhaṭṭ. 15, 117.—With विनिस् *vi-nis*, *vinirbhagna*, Broken down, MBh. 3, 12477.—With प्र *pra*, To break down, MBh. 3, 11121. The original form has been probably *bhrańj*.—Cf. Lat. frango; Goth. brikan; A.S. bracan, brecan; ῥαγή, ῥήγνυμι, ῥηγμίν.

भञ्जन *bhańj+ana*, n. **1.** Breaking, destroying. **2.** Afflicting.

† भट् *BHAṬ*, i. 1, Par. **1.** To hire. **2.** To nourish. **3.** To speak. Caus. of 1. 2. *bhâṭaya*, of 3. *bhaṭaya*.

भट *bhaṭa* (a form of *bhṛita*, based on *bharta*), m. **1.** A soldier. **2.** An outcaste of a particular tribe. **3.** A goblin.—Comp. *Châra-*, m. a soldier, Bhartṛ. 1, 91. *Bhû-*, m. a proper name. *Mahâ-*, m. a great warrior, Bhâg. P. 4, 25, 27. *Vâr-*, m. an alligator. *Su-*, m. a warrior (cf. *bhaṭṭa*), Pańch. iii. d. 48. *Sva-*, m. 1. one's own soldier, Hit. 104, 17. 2. a life-guardian (?), Hit. iii. d. 72.

भट्ट *bhaṭṭa* (a dialectical form based on *bhartâ*, nom. sing. of *bhartṛi*), m. **1.** A philosopher, a learned man, Râjat. 5, 66. **2.** An enemy. **3.** Authority. **4.** Best.—**Comp.** *Su-*, m. a very learned man, or perhaps rather a distinguished warrior. Lass. 29, 1 (in the latter case read *subhaṭa*, see *bhaṭa*).

भट्टार *bhaṭṭâra* (probably a dialectical form sprung from *bhartṛi*, and based on *bhartâram*, etc.), adj. Venerable.

भट्टारक *bhaṭṭâra+ka*, **I.** adj., f. *rikâ*, Venerable, Lass. 13, 18. **II.** m. **1.** Sir, Mâlav. 28, 4. **2.** The sun (?), Hit. 48, 3, M.M. **III.** f. *rikâ*, Lady, tutelar deity, Lass. 31, 6.

भडिल *bhaḍila*, m. **1.** An attendant. **2.** A hero.

भण् *BHAṆ* (a dialectical form based on *bhâsh+ṇâ*, i.e. *bhâsh* ii. 9), i. 1, Par. To speak, Lass. 21, 3. *bhaṇita*, Spoken, Pańch. 128, 5; sounded.—With प्रति *prati*, To answer, Bhaṭṭ. 4, 38. *pratibhaṇita*, Answered.

† भण्ट् *BHAṆṬ*, i. 10, Par. To deceive.

† भण्ड् *BHAṆḌ*, i. 1, Âtm. **1.** To upbraid; to reprove. **2.** To jest. **3.** To deride. **4.** To speak. i. 10 or 1, Par. To be, and to make fortunate; to do an auspicious act.

भण्डन *bhaṇḍana*, n. **1.** Armour. **2.** Battle. **3.** Evil.

भण्डि and भण्डी *bhaṇḍî*, f. **1.** A wave. **2.** A plant, Rubia manjith Roxb.—Comp. *Tri-bhaṇḍî*, f. a plant,

Convolvulus turpethum, Suçr. 1, 161, 21; 2, 70, 1.

भण्डिल *bhaṇḍila* (probably a dialectical form, akin to *bhadra*), I. adj. **1.** Fortunate. **2.** A messenger. II. m. A tree, Mimosa sirisha.

भदन्त *bhadanta*, m. A Bauddha mendicant.

भदाक *bhadâka* (cf. *bhand*), adj. Auspicious.

भद्र *bhad+ra* (cf. *bhand*), I. adj., f. *râ*. **1.** Excellent, best, Vikr. 27, 10; Pańch. 146, 17. **2.** Worthy, dear, Daçak. in Chr. 185, 11. **3.** Pious. **4.** Happy, Vikr. d. 163; propitious, Hit. 22, 5, M.M. **5.** Comparat. *bhadratara*, Better, Hit. 80, 5. II. *bhadra+m*, adv. Well, happy. III. n. **1.** Prosperity, Pańch. iii. d. 191; hail, Hit. 83, 10, M.M. **2.** Happiness, Böhtl. Ind. Spr. 1212. **3.** (with the dat. of the second person), A polite address, especially accompanying an advice, an objection, or expression of a different opinion; if you please, Râm. 3, 53, 2; Chr. 12, 3; 10, 5; with all respect for you, Chr. 11, 13; I beg your pardon, Râm. 3, 52, 37. **4.** Gold. **5.** Iron or steel. **6.** A fragrant grass, Cyperus, Ṛit. 1, 17 v.r. IV. m. **1.** Çiva. **2.** A wagtail. **3.** A bull. **4.** A heap. **5.** A fortune-teller, an impostor, Man. 9, 258. V. f. *râ*. **1.** The Ganges of heaven. **2.** A name of the second, seventh, and twelfth days of the lunar fortnight.—**Comp.** *A-*, adj. distressed, Bhâg. P. 4, 30, 28. *Chatur-*, n. sing. four good things, Hit. i. d. 158, M.M. *Tuńga-*, 1. m. an elephant in rut. 2. f. *râ*, a river in Mysore, Bhâg. P. 5, 19, 18. *Bala-*, I. m. 1. Baladeva. 2. Ananta, the great serpent. 3. a strong man. II. f. *râ*, a young girl. *Maṇi-*, m. a name of Kuvera, Nal. 12, 130. *Sarvatobh°*, i.e. *sarvatas-*, I. adj. everywhere auspicious. II. m. and n. a temple or palace of a square form, with an entrance opposite to each point of the compass. III. m. 1. the carriage of Vishṇu. 2. a form of military array. 3. a bambu. 4. the Nimb tree. IV. f. *drâ*. 1. an actress. 2. the name of two plants. *Râma-*, m. (auspicious Râma), a surname of Râma, Utt. Râmach. 38, 9. *Su-*, I. adj. propitious, fortunate, Ṛit. 1, 17 v.r. II. m. Vishṇu. III. f. *râ*, The sister of *Jagannâtha*.—Cf. Goth. bats, bat+izo, bat+ista; A.S. bet; O.H.G. baz; Goth. ga-bat+non, bot+a, bot+jan; A.S. bót; Lat. fastus (for fad-tus), fastigium, fastidium, festivus (but festus belongs rather to *bhâsh*).

भद्रक *bhadra+ka*, adj., f. *rikâ*. **1.** Beautiful, agreeable. **2.** Respectable, worthy, Daçak. in Chr. 195, 1. **3.** Good, Man. 9, 226.

भद्रंकर *bhadraṁkara*, i.e. *bhadra +m-kara*, adj., f. *rî*, Propitious.

† भन्द् *BHAND*, i. 1, Âtm. **1.** To be fortunate. **2.** To make fortunate. **3.** To worship. **4.** To be excellent. **5.** To be glad. **6.** To exhilarate. **7.** To shine. i. 10, Par. To make fortunate; cf. *bhadra*.

भय *bhaya*, i.e. *bhî+a*, n. **1.** Fear, Pańch. v. d. 67. **2.** Fright, Pańch. 242, 21. **3.** Danger, Pańch. ii. d. 14.—**Comp.** *A-*, I. n. 1. safety, Hit. i. d. 104, M.M. 2. protection from danger, Man. 4, 247. 3. the name of a Dvîpa, or division of the world. 4. a fragrant grass, Andropogon muricatum. II. adj., f. *yâ*, fearless, Bhartṛ. 3, 32. III. m. 1. epithet of Çiva. 2. a proper name. IV. f. *yâ*, a plant, Terminalia citrina, Suçr. 1, 139, 14. *Akutobhaya*, i.e. *a-kutas-*, adj. having nothing to fear from any part, Pańch. 107, 2. *A-jâta-*, adj. fearless, Pañch. i. d. 352. *Apa-*, adj. fearless, Ragh. 3, 51. *Nirbh°*, i.e. *nis-*, I. adj., f. *yâ*. 1. fearless, Pañch. 111, 25. 2. free from danger, Man. 9, 255. II. m. a proper name. *Bhaṅga-*, Pañch. i. d. 357 (*bhaṅgabhayâd divaḥ*, from fear that (else) heaven would break down). *Vîta-*, i.e. *vi-ita-*, adj. fearless. *Sa-*, adj. fearful, Pañch. 45, 8. *°yam*, adv. with fear, Hit. 85, 3, M.M.

भयंकर *bhayaṁkara*, i.e. *bhaya + m -kara*, adj., f. *rî*, Terrific, Hit. i. d. 88, M.M.; formidable, Pañch. iii. d. 83.

भयद *bhaya-da* (vb. *dâ*), adj. Terrific, Pañch. i. d. 350.

भयानक *bhayânaka*, properly an old anomal. ptcple. pres. Âtm. of *bhî*, viz. *bhayâna + ka*, I. adj. Frightful, formidable, Bhag. 11, 27; Utt. Râmach. 43, 12. II. m. **1.** The sentiment of terror, as excited by poetical composition. **2.** A tiger. **3.** Râhu.

भर *bhara*, i.e. *bhṛi + a*, I. m. **1.** A load, Lass. 88, 2; Vikr. d. 42; 52; with *bhuvas*, *ἄχθος ἀρούρας*, i.e. a dead mass. **2.** With *kṛi*, To make a load, to support one's self, Hit. 47, 3. **3.** Plenty, Çiç. 9, 47. **4.** Much, excessive, Bhartṛ. 2, 68. **5.** A measure of value of two thousand Palas. II. adj. Who or what supports.—**Comp.** *Ati-*, m. excessive heaviness, Çiç. 9, 73. *Apa -hṛita-*, adj., unburthened, Vikr. d. 42. *Durbh°*, i.e. *dus-*, adj., f. *râ*, 1. difficult to be borne, Bhâg. P. 3, 9, 8. 2. difficult to be maintained, Pañch. iii. d. 168. *Nirbh°*, i.e. *nis-*, I. adj., f. *râ*. 1. excessive, violent, ardent, Böhtl. Ind. Spr. 396. 2. deep (as sleep), Hit. 85, 8. 3. latter part of comp. adj. full of, Pañch. 259, 3; Kathâs. 6, 126. II. *°ram*, adv. much, excessively, Hit. 86, 8; 10; Hit. 59, 2 (deeply). *Su-*, adj. 1. heavily burthened. 2. heavy, Chr. 296, 2 = Rigv. i. 112, 2. 3. f. *râ*, perhaps a proper name, Chr. 297, 20 = Rigv. i. 112, 20 (Sch. nourishing, viz. food).—Cf. Lat. -fer; A.S. -bora.

भरट *bharaṭa*, m. A potter.

भरण *bharaṇa*, i.e. *bhṛi + ana*, I. n. **1.** Bearing, Pañch. 257, 23; supporting, Çâk. d. 192. **2.** Nourishing, Hit. ii. d. 42. **3.** Wages, hire. II. f. *ṇî*. **1.** The name of the second lunar asterism. **2.** A creeper, commonly Ghoshâ.

भरण्ड *bharaṇḍa* (vb. *bhṛi*), m. A master, a lord.

भरण्य *bharaṇya* (for *bharaṇîya*, ptcple. of the fut. pass. of *bhṛi*), n. Wages, hire.

भरत *bharata*, i.e. *bharant*, ptcple. pres. of *bhṛi*, + *a* (cf. Çâk. d. 192), m. **1.** The name of several princes, and of a sage, the inventor of dramatic composition, Vikr. d. 36; Utt. Râmach. 111, 4. **2.** pl. The descendants of Bharata, Chr. 3, 1. **3.** An actor, a mime.

भरथ *bharatha*, m. A deity presiding over one of the regions.

भरद्वाज *bharadvâja*, i.e. *bharant*, ptcple. pres. of *bhṛi*, *-vâja*, m. The name of a Muni, Johns. Sel., 1, 1.

भरित *bharita*, i.e. *bhara + ita*, adj. Filled, MBh. 2, 2061.

भरिमन् or **भरीमन्** *bharîman* (vb. *bhṛi*, or *bhara*, + *iman*), m. A household, a family.

भरु *bharu*, i.e. *bhṛi + u*, m. **1.** Gold. **2.** A lord. **3.** Çiva. **4.** Vishṇu.

भरुज *bharu-ja*, m. A small sort of jackal.

भरुटक *bharuṭaka* (vb. *bhṛi*), n. Fried meat.

भर्ग *bharga*, i.e. *bhrâj*, or *bhṛij*, + *a*, m. Çiva.

भर्गस् *bhargas*, i.e. *bhrâj*, or *bhṛij*, +*as*, n. **1.** Light, Lass. 99, 11=Rigv. iii. 62, 10. **2.** A name of Brahman.—Cf. A.S. baelch, superbia.

भर्तृ *bhartṛi*, i.e. *bhṛi*+*tṛi*, I. m., f. *trî*, and n. **1.** One who contains, Çiç. 9, 17. **2.** A cherisher, Bhag. 9, 18. **3.** A protector. II. m. **1.** A lord, Vikr. d. 36; master, d. 155. **2.** A commander, Man. 7, 94. **3.** A husband, Hit. i. d. 196, M.M.—**Comp.** *Kanyâ-*, m. epithet of the god of war, MBh. 3, 14633. *Gaṇa-*, m. epithet of Çiva, Kir. 5, 42. *Jagatî-*, *bhû-*, *mahî-*, m. a king, Râm. 2, 103, 17; Râjat. 5, 69, 23. *Paçu-*, m. epithet of Çiva, MBh. 13, 620. *Ruchi-*, m. bearer of light and cherisher of love, Çiç. 9, 17. *Svarga-*, m. Indra.

ऽभर्तृक *-bhartṛi*+*ka*, latter part of comp. words, which are, or were originally adj.; e.g. *proshita-* (ptcple. of the pf. pass. of *pra-vas*), f. *kâ*, A woman whose husband is absent, Ṛit. 6, 9. *sa-*, f. *kâ*, A woman whose husband is alive.

भर्तृघ्नत्व *bhartṛi-ghna*+*tva*, n. Injuring one's master, MBh. 2, 2123.

भर्तृत्व *bhartṛi*+*tva*, n. Husbandship, Kathâs. 26, 148.

भर्तृमन्त् *bhartṛi* + *mant*, adj., f. *matî*, Married, Çâk. d. 114.

भर्तृहरि *bhartṛi-hari*, m. The name of a prince and poet.

भर्त्स् *BHARTS*, i. 10, Âtm. (also Par.). **1.** To menace, Daçak. in Chr. 195, 14. **2.** To blame, to abuse, MBh. 4, 357. Ptcple. of the pf. pass. *bhartsita*, Blamed, Pañch. i. d. 170. n. Menace, Daçak. in Chr. 185, 21.—With the prep. **अभि** *abhi*, To menace, Râm. 1, 28, 13. *abhibhartsita*, Terrified, MBh. 3, 10921. —With **अव** *ava*, To deter, Chr. 26, 66 (read °*bharts-ayat*). —With **नि** *ni*, To menace, Pañch. 220, 2 (probably corr. *nirbh*°).—With **निस्** *nis*, **1.** To menace, Pañch. 84, 18; MBh. 1, 4190. **2.** To blame, Utt. Râmach. 174, 6; Chr. 60, 32. **3.** To abuse, Hit. 64, 22.—With **अभि-निस्** *abhi-nis*, To blame, Râm. 2, 78, 19.—With **परि** *pari*, To menace, MBh. 3, 16008.—With **सम्** *sam*, To reproach, to blame, Râm. 2, 75, 16.

भर्त्सन *bharts*+*ana*, n. **1.** Threat. **2.** Reproach, curse.

भर्ब् *BHARB*, **भर्भ्** *BHARBH*, see *bharv*.

भर्मन् *bharman*, i.e. *bhṛi*+*man*, n. **1.** Wages, hire. **2.** Gold. **3.** A coin, a piece of money. **4.** The navel.—**Comp.** *Garbha-*, n. cherishing of a child, Ragh. 3, 12.

भर्व् *BHARV*, and † **भर्भ्** *BHARBH*, or † **भर्ब्** *BHARB*, i. 1, Par. **1.** To injure (ved.). **2.** † To eat.—With the second signification and the form *bharb* cf. φέρβω, φορβή; Lat. herba; with the first and *bharv* Goth. balvjan.

भल् *BHAL*, and **बल्** *BAL*, † i. 1, Âtm. **1.** To describe. **2.** To kill, to hurt. **3.** To give. i. 10, Âtm. **1.** To describe, to see, to behold (ved.); with the prep. *ni*, Chhand. Up. 452; and Prâkṛ. with *nis*, Mâlav. 5, 0. **2.** † To throw up.—With the prep. **सम्** *sam*, To bear, Naish. 6, 76.

† **भल्ल्** *BHALL*, i. 1, Âtm. **1.** To describe. **2.** To kill. **3.** To give.

भल्ल *bhalla*, I. m. A bear. II. m. and n. A kind of arrow, Chr. 29, 27. III. f. *lî*. 1. An arrow with a crescent-shaped head. 2. The marking nut plant, Semicarpus Anacardium.

भल्लक *bhalla + ka*, भल्लुक and भल्लूक *bhallûka*, m. A bear, Utt. Râmach. 45, 1 (*lû*).

भल्लातक *bhallâtaka* (cf. *bhalla*), m., and f. *kî*, The marking nut plant, Lass. 52, 15.

भव *bhava*, i.e. *bhû + a*, m. 1. Being, existing, Sâv. 3, 10. 2. Birth, Çâk. d. 186; Megh. 46 (at the end of a comp. adj.). 3. Origin, Ragh. 3, 14 (at the end of a comp. adj. Arising; *tvad-viyoga-*, Arising from absence from thee, Vikr. d. 133). 4. The place or means of being. 5. Welfare. 6. Excellence, Pańch. v. d. 12. 7. The world, Hit. iii. d. 140. 8. A god. 9. Çiva, Kir. 5, 29; Rudra, Bhâg. P. 4, 6, 5.—Comp. *A-*, m. 1. non-existence, Sâv. 3, 10. 2. cessation of existence, Râm. 3, 69, 9. *Araṇya-*, adj. growing in a forest, without culture, Pańch. ii. d. 93. *Âtmabhava*, i.e. *âtman-*, I. m. the existence of one's self, Nal. 5, 37. II. adj. attracted by one's self, Râm. 2, 64, 69. *Âdi-*, adj. who is the first being, Ragh. 13, 8. *Durvâgbh°*, i.e. *dus-vâch-*, m. abusing, MBh. 13, 2258. *Punarbh°*, i.e. *punar-*, m. regeneration, MBh. 1, 251; transmigration, Çâk. d. 194. *Maghâ-*, m. the planet Venus.

भवदीय *bhavadîya*, i.e. *bhavant + îya*, adj. Thine, yours, Pańch. 135, 8.

भवन *bhavana*, i.e. *bhû + ana*, n. 1. Nature. 2. A dwelling, house, Pańch. ii. d. 17; a palace, Pańch. iii. d. 236. 3. A temple, Râjat. 5, 100.—Comp. *Garbha-*, n. a sanctuary, Mâlat. 13, 3 (below). *Deva-*, n. a temple, Kathâs. 6, 75. *Devî-*, n. a temple of Durgâ, Kathâs. 18, 170.

भवन्त् *bhavant*, properly ptcple. pres. of *bhû*, m., and f. *atî*, Lord, lady, used as respectful term of address instead of the second personal pronoun, Thou, You, Vikr. 9, 6; Pańch. 107, 8; but taking the verb in the third person, Pańch. 109, 1; pl., Vikr. 3, 9; f., 9, 6; pl., 5, 6.—Comp. *Atra-*, adj., f. *atî*, respectable, Kir. 11, 18. II. m., f. *atî*, used to denote in a respectful manner third persons who are present, Çâk. 16, 20. *Tatra-*, m., f. *atî*, used to denote in a respectful manner persons who are absent, Çâk. 9, 12.—Cf. φώς, φωτός.

भवन्त *bhavant + a*, m. Time.

भवादृश् *bhavâdriç*, and भवादृश *bhavâdriça*, i.e. *bhavant-driç* or *driç + a*, adj. Like you, your like, Pańch. ii. d. 185; Hit. iii. d. 15.

भवानी *bhavânî*, i.e. *bhava + î*, f. The wife of Çiva, Kir. 5, 29.

भवितव्यता *bhavitavya + tâ* (vb. *bhû*), f. 1. Necessity of coming into existence, of taking place, Pańch. ii. d. 11; 133. 2. Fate, Vikr. 36, 1.

भवितृ *bhavitri*, i.e. *bhû + tri*, m., f. *trî*, and n. 1. Actually being. 2. Being about to become. 3. Well-being.

भविल *bhavila*, i.e. *bhû + ila*, adj. Future.

भविष्य *bhavishya*, curtailed *bhavishyant*, ptcple. fut. of *bhû*, adj., f. *yâ*, Future, Pańch. i. d. 103.—Comp. *Yad-*, m. a proper name, Pańch. 77, 9.

भष् *BHASH*, i. 1, Par. (in epic poetry also Âtm., MBh. 2, 1425). 1. To bark, MBh. 1, 5249. 2. To bark at, to reproach malevolently, to rail, 3, 15641; cf. *bhâsh*.

भष *bhash+a*, m. A dog. f. *shî*, A bitch.

भषक *bhasha+ka*, m. A dog.

भस् *BHAS*, ii. 3, Par. **1.** To eat. **2.** To shine. † **3.** To blame. *bhasita*, see s.v.; cf. *psâ* and *bhâ*.

भसद् *bhasad*, f. **1.** Pudendum muliebre. **2.** The sun. **3.** A month.

भसन्त *bhasanta*, m. Time.

भसित *bhasita*, n. Ashes.

भस्त्रका *bhastrakâ*, see *bhastrâkâ*.

भस्त्रा *bhastrâ*, f. **1.** A bellows, Pańch. iii. d. 97. **2.** A bag, Pańch. 265, 8.

भस्त्राका *bhastrâkâ*, **भस्त्रका** *bhastrakâ*, **भस्त्रिका** *bhastrikâ*, i.e. *bhastrâ+ka* or *ika*, f. **1.** A bellows. **2.** *bhastrikâ*, A bag, Daçak. in Chr. 189, 2 (*charma-ratna-*, a most wonderful leather bag).

भस्मक *bhasmaka*, n. **1.** A disease of the eyes, indistinctness of vision. **2.** (i.e. *bhas + man + ka*), Morbid appetite with general decay.

भस्मन् *bhasman* (cf. *bhasita*), n. Ashes, Hit. ii. d. 163.

भस्मसात् *bhasmasât*, i.e. *bhasman +sât*, adv. Completely into ashes; with *nî* and *kṛi*, To reduce to ashes, Pańch. 38, 18; 186, 14; Utt. Râmach. 74, 3.

भस्मी *bhasmî*, see *kṛi* and *bhû*.

1. **भा** *BHÂ*, ii. 2, Par. **1.** To shine, Kir. 5, 20. **2.** To appear, Râjat. 5, 94. Ptcple. of the pf. pass. *bhâta*, Bright. n. Morning.—With the prep. **अभि** *abhi*, To shine from every part, Ghaṭ. 10.—With **अव** *ava*, To shine, MBh. 3, 10094.—With **आ** *â*, **1.** To shine forth, Chr. 288, 9=Rigv. i. 48, 9. **2.** To illuminate, Chr. 289, 4=Rigv. i. 50, 4. **3.** To shine, Râm. i. 15, 19. **4.** To appear, Vikr. d. 142; MBh. 3, 13701.—With **उद्** *ud*, To shine forth, Man. 1, 7.—With **निस्** *nis*, **1.** To shine forth, Man. 5, 44. **2.** To proceed, Man. 2, 10.—With **प्र** *pra*, **1.** To begin to shine, Râm. 1, 45, 5. **2.** To shine forth, MBh. 3, 10054. *prabhâta*, Begun to become clear, Râm. 2, 6, 10. n. Daybreak, morning, Pańch. 246, 16; loc. *te*, tomorrow, 119, 1. **Comp.** *Tatpr°*, i.e. *tad-*, loc. the following morning, Lass. 12, 1. *Su-*, adj. enlightened.—With **संप्र** *sam-pra*, To appear, MBh. 3, 10055.—With **प्रति** *prati*, **1.** To shine, Ghaṭ. 15. **2.** To appear, Vikr. d. 23; Chr. 41, 23. **3.** To please, Pańch. 78, 12; 151, 1; Vikr. 43, 17 (with acc.)—With **संप्रति** *sam-prati*, To appear, MBh. 1, 8095.—With **वि** *vi*, **1.** To shine, Vikr. d. 44; Chr. 294, 6=Rigv. i. 92, 6. **2.** To appear, Lass. 75, 2. *vibhâta*, Become manifest, Vedântas. in Chr. 217, 5. n. Daybreak.—Cf. φῶς, φωτός, φανός, φαλός, ἐμφατικός, ἀμφαδόν, probably, φοῖβος (for φοβ+ιος, from the Caus. *bhâpaya*), φάος (for φαϝος), φαέθω, φαίνω (for φαϝέσνω), φαίδιμος, etc.; Lat. focus, februus (from the Causal).

2. **भा** *bhâ*, I. f. **1.** Light. **2.** Splendour. II. m. The sun.

भाग *bhâga*, i.e. *bhaj+a*, m. **1.** A portion, part, Pańch. i. d. 447; side, Vikr. d. 26; Utt. Râmach. 42, 12. **2.** Fortune, fate, Utt. Râmach. 38, 9. **3.** A division of time, the 30th part of a zodiacal sign. **4.** A degree, the 360th part of the circumference of a great circle.—**Comp.** *A-*, adj. deprived of one's share, Man. 9, 213. *Agra-*, m. fore or top part, Çâk. 141, 10 Chezy. *Adhobh°*, i.e. *adhas-*, m. 1. the lower part, Daçak. in Chr. 198, 18; Pańch. 76, 23 (under). 2. the lower part of the body, Suçr. 1, 208, 7. *Ardha-*, m. 1. half, Kumâras. 5, 50. 2. a part, Ragh. 7, 42. *Açîti-*, m. an 80th part, Man. 8, 140. *Chatur-*, m. a 4th part, Man. 8, 176. *Tri-*, m. a 3rd part, Hariv. 8887. *Dâya-*, m. partition of heritage, Man. 9, 103. *Digbh°*, i.e. *diç-*, m. region, quarter, Pańch. 106, 22. *Nimna-*, m. a deep place, Râm. 2, 80, 9. *Para-*, m. 1. supremacy, Pańch. i. d. 375. 2. highest degree, Kathâs. 1, 47 (cf. *divya-mânusha.*) *Pâda-*, f. a fourth part, MBh. 2, 204. *Purobhâga*, i.e. *puras-*, I. m. 1. obtrusiveness, Hariv. 7338. 2. envy, Mâlav. d. 19. II. adj., f. *gâ*, obtrusive, Çâk. 70, 14. *Mahâ-*, adj. 1. eminent. 2. virtuous in a high degree, Chr. 9, 41; 24, 47; Utt. Râmach. 38, 8. *Yajńa-*, m. a deity, Çâk. d. 186. *Çesha-*, m. the remaining or last part. *Shaḍbhâga*, i.e. *shash-*, m. a sixth part, Pańch. i. d. 391.

भागधेय *bhâga-dheya* (vb. *dhâ*), I. m. **1.** A heir. **2.** Royal revenue. **II.** n. **1.** Portion, Man. 3, 245. **2.** Fate, fortune, happiness, Vikr. 55, 10.

भागशस् *bhâga+ças*, adv. Part for part, MBh. 2, 211; Man. 12, 22 (Jones: In the order of their natural distribution.)

भागिन् *bhâgin*, i.e. *bhaj* and *bhâga +in*, I. adj., f. *nî*. **1.** Who or what shares. **2.** One who partakes, Man. 3, 143; Pańch. 16, 2. **3.** Undergoing, suffering, Pańch. 29, 9; 68, 23. **4.** An owner, Man. 9, 48. **5.** Consisting of parts. **II.** m. A co-heir. **III.** f. *nî*, Co-heiress.—**Comp.** *Duḥkha-*, adj. suffering pain, Hit. i. d. 24, M.M. *Dharma-*, adj., f. *nî*, virtuous, Hit. iii. d. 25. *Purobhâgin*, i.e. *puras-* (cf. *purobhâga* under *bhâga*), adj., f. *giṇî*, 1. obtrusive, Çâk. 70, 14 v. r. 2. envious, censorious, Râjat. 6, 83. *Manda-*, adj. unhappy, Utt. Râmach. 79, 11.

भागिनेय *bhâgineya*, i.e. *bhaginî+eya*, I. m. A sister's son, Pańch. 231, 20. II. *yî*, A sister's daughter.

भागीरथी *bhâgîrathî*, i.e. *bhagîratha+a+î*, f. The Ganges, Hit. 3, 3, M.M.

भाग्य *bhâgya*, i.e. *bhâga+ya*, n. **1.** Merit and demerit acquired in former existences, fate, fortune, Vikr. 63, 19. **2.** Merit, Bhartṛ. 2, 94. **3.** Happiness, Hit. pr. d. 5, M.M. **4.** instr. *yena*, Happily, Hit. 17, 4, M.M. **5.** Sensual pleasure, Râjat. 5, 385.—**Comp.** *A-*, adj. unfortunate, Pańch. 197, 23. *Para-* n. another's property, Hit. i. d. 24, M.M. *Manda-*, adj. unhappy, Vikr. 32, 8. *Mahâ-*, n. great luck, happiness, Sâv. 1, 1; Man. 11, 244 (Jones: Transcendent excellence).

भाग्यवन्त् *bhâgya+vant*, adj. **1.** Abounding in merits. **2.** Happy, Pańch. 201, 7.

भाङ्गासुरि *bhâṅgâsuri*, m. A proper name, Nal. 19, 11.

भाङ्गीन *bhâṅgîna*, i.e. *bhaṅgâ+îna*, n. A field of hemp.

1. †**भाज्** *BHÂJ*, i. 10, Par. To divide; cf. *bhaj*.

2. **ऽभाज्** *-bhâj*, (vb. *bhaj*), latter part of comp. adj. One who possesses or obtains; e.g. *ardha-* adj. Obtaining or entitled to a half, Man. 8, 239.

nṛipa-mâna-, Obtaining royal honour, Man. 2, 139. *vibhâga-*, m. Entitled to a portion of a property already distributed, as a son born after the distribution of his father's property. *viyoga-*, adj. Suffering separation, cf. also Pańch. i. d. 196; 147, 12.

भाजन *bhâjana*, *bhaj + ana*, n. **1.** Any vessel, as a pot or cup, Hit. pr. d. 8, M.M.; figuratively, Pańch. ii. d. 194 (a vessel of love and confidence, a person on whom one may depend). **2.** A fit person. **3.** Sharing.—**Comp.** *Dîpa-* n. a lamp, Daçak. in Chr. 186, 11.

भाजनत्व *bhâjana + tva*, n. Condition of being a vessel, i.e. a fit object, Mâlav. d. 83.

भाटक *bhâṭaka*, i.e. probably *bhaṭa + ka*, m. Price, wages.

भाट्ट *bhâṭṭa*, i.e. *bhaṭṭa + a*, m. A follower of Kumârila Bhaṭṭa, Vedântas. in Chr. 211, 9.

भाण्ड *bhâṇḍa*, n. **1.** Any vessel, a pot, a cup, Pańch. 96, 18; Hit. 85, 14. **2.** Any implement or utensil, Sâv. 3, 1. **3.** The capital, principal of a merchant. **4.** Goods, wares, Pańch. 7, 17 (*deça-antara-bhâṇḍa-ânayana*, n. Exporting wares to foreign countries), i. d. 19. **5.** An ornament, Daçak. in Chr. 187, 2. **6.** Any musical instrument, Man. 10, 49. **7.** The bed of a river.—**Comp.** *Kshura-*, n. a razor-case, Hit. 64, 20. *Bhinna-* (vb. *bhid*), n. 1. a potsherd. 2. a broken vessel. *Mahâ-*, n. a great vessel, Pańch. 62, 25. *Sâra-*, n. 1. a natural vessel, as the bag or skin in which musk is sold. 2. a bale of goods, Pańch. 8, 14. 3. implements, Mâlav. 44, 1 (Prâkṛ.)

भाण्डायन *bhâṇḍâyana*, n. A proper name, Utt. Râmach. 91, 8.

भाण्डिक *bhâṇḍika*, i.e. *bhâṇḍa + ika*, m. A musician.

भाण्डिल *bhâṇḍila*, i.e. *bhâṇḍa + ila*, m. A barber.

भातु *bhâ + tu*, m. The sun.

भाद्र *bhâdra*, i.e. *bhadra + a*, m. The name of a month, August—September.

भाद्रमातुर *bhâdramâtura*, i. e. *bhadra-mâtṛi + a*, m. The son of a virtuous wife.

भान *bhâna*, i.e. *bhâ + ana*, n. **1.** Appearance, Vedântas. in Chr. 217, 3. **2.** Perception, Bhâshâp. 65.—Cf. φανός.

भानतस् *bhâna + tas*, adv. In consequence of the appearance, Vedântas. in Chr. 202, 5.

भानवन्त् *bhâna + vant*, adj. Endowed with the appearance, Vedântas. in Chr. 217, 3.

भानु *bhâ + nu*, I. m. **1.** A ray of light, Chr. 288, 9 = Rigv. i. 48, 9. **2.** Light. **3.** The sun, Pańch. 134, 17. **4.** A sovereign, a master. **II.** f. A handsome woman.—**Comp.** *Chitra-*, I. adj. resplendent, Chr. 290, 7 = Rigv. i. 64, 7. II. m. fire, MBh. 1, 2036. *Vṛihad-bhânu*, i.e. *vṛihant-*, m. a name of Agni. *Svar-*, m. Râhu, the ascending node, Chr. 36, 23.

भानुमन्त् *bhânu + mant*, adj., f. *matî*. **1.** Luminous, splendid. **2.** Beautiful, Draup. 7, 2.

भाम् *BHÂM* (rather a denomin. derived from *bhâma*), i. 1, Âtm., and i. 10, Par. To be angry or wrathful.

भाम *bhâ + ma*, I. m. **1.** Light. **2.** The sun. **3.** Passion, wrath. **4.** A sister's husband. **II.** f. *mâ*. A passionate woman.—Cf. probably A.S. beam, a sun-beam, beamian, to shine (cf. the last).

भामिन् *bhâmin,* i.e. *bhâma + in,* I. adj., f. *nî,* Passionate, Ragh. 8, 28. II. f. *nî,* A passionate woman, often used, as a term of endearment, in the same sense as *mânini.*

भार *bhâra,* i.e. *bhṛi+a,* m. 1. Carrying burthens, Pańch. i. d. 312. 2. Weight, a burthen, Pańch. 52, 4; figurat., Pańch. 31, 3 (of government); v. d. 4. 3. A great weight, Pańch. 99, 25. 4. A weight of gold equal to two thousand Palas. 5. A yoke.—Comp. *Ati-*, m. 1. a too great burthen, Pańch. i. d. 22. 2. a proper name. *Kâshṭha-*, m. a load of wood, Hariv. 4356. *Garbha-*, m. the burthen of being with child, Kathâs. 26, 216. *Varha-*, m. 1. the circumference of a peacock's tail, Megh. 102. 2. the tuft of a peacock's feathers at the shaft of a lance or the handle of a club.

भारक *bhâra+ka,* m. A load, Man. 11, 133.

भारण्ड *bhâraṇḍa,* **भारुण्ड** *bhâruṇḍa,* **भेरण्ड** *bheraṇḍa* (m.), The name of a fabulous bird, see Pańch. 263, 19; cf. my translation, 535, n. 1437. f. *ḍî,* Its female, Pańch. 264, 4.

भारत *bhârata,* i.e. *bharata+a,* I. patronym. A descendant of Bharata, Hit. iv. d. 86. II. m. 1. An actor. 2. A name of fire. III. f. *tî.* 1. Speech, Chr. 53, 1. 2. Dramatic recitation. 3. The goddess of speech, Pańch. ii. d. 16. 4. A quail. IV. n. 1. India proper. 2. A great epic poem, also **महाभारत** *mahâ-*, n.

भारद्वाज *bhâradvâja,* i.e. *bharadvâja+a,* I. patronym., m. 1. Epithet of Droṇa. 2. One of the seven Ṛishis. 3. Agastya. 4. The son of Vṛihaspati. II. m. A skylark, Pańch. 157, Wild cotton. IV. n. A bone.

भारव *bhârava,* n. A bowstring.

भारवि *bhâravi,* m. The name of a poet, Chr. 170, 1.

भारि *bhâri,* m. A lion.

भरिक *bhârika,* i.e. *bhâra+ika,* m. A porter, Râjat. 5, 204 (treasurer; cf. 176 and my Chr. p. 315, n. ad 176. I propose to read *bhaurika*).

भारिन् *bhârin,* i.e. *bhâra+in,* m. A porter, Man. 2, 138; Kathâs. 22, 96.

भारुण्ड *bhâruṇḍa,* see *bhâraṇḍa.*

भार्गव *bhârgava,* i.e. *bhṛigu + a,* patronym. I. m. 1. A descendant of Bhṛigu. 2. Epithet of Paraçurâma, Johns. Sel. 4, 22; Utt. Râmach. 13, 10. 3. A name of Çukra, regent of Venus. 4. An archer. 5. An elephant. 6. A proper name, Johns. Sel. 60, 189. II. f. *vî.* 1. Pârvatî. 2. Lakshmî. 3. Bent grass, Panicum dactylon.

भार्या *bhâryâ,* properly ptcple. fut. pass. of *bhṛi,* f. A wife, Pańch. 137, 9.—Comp. *Ku-*, I. f. a wicked wife, Mârk. P. 21, 73. II. *Ku-bhârya,* adj. having a wicked wife, Bhâg. P. 6, 5, 15. *Sa-bhârya,* adj. with (his) wife, Râm. 3, 55, 42.

भार्याट *bhâryâṭa,* m. A man who lets out his wife for prostitution.

भार्यात्व *bhâryâ+tva,* f. State of a female, Man. 12, 69.

भाल *bhâla,* m. 1. The forehead, Bhartṛ. 2, 48. 2. i.e. *bhâ+la,* Lustre.

भालु *bhâ+lu,* m. The sun.

भालूक *bhâlûka*, m. A bear (cf. *bhallaka*).

भाव *bhâva*, i.e. *bhû* + *a*, m. **1.** State, Hit. pr. d. 28, M.M.; Vikr. d. 115 (*nadî-bhâvena pariṇata*, changed into a river). **2.** Property, Pańch. iv. d. 62; nature, Nal. 10, 15. **3.** Meaning, Man. 2, 124. **4.** Purpose, Man. 4, 234; intention, Vikr. d. 102 (Sch.). **5.** Mind, Pańch. i. d. 317; heart, Râm. 3, 24, 11; Chr. 18, 35. **6.** Emotion, passion, as an object of poetry, Daçak. in Chr. 190, 11; (of music? Pańch. v. d. 44); love, Vikr. d. 72; Lass. 58, 16 (read *kurvantyâ bhâva*°). **7.** Gesture. **8.** Corporeal expression of amorous sentiments. **9.** A being. **10.** Substance, Bhâshâp. 13; thing, object, Utt. Râmach. 74, 9. **11.** The world. **12.** Superhuman power. **13.** The Supreme Being, Man. 4, 234. **14.** A learned man. **15.** Venerable, master, Vikr. 3, 11.—Comp. *A*-, m. 1. absence, Man. 8. 259; Hit. i. d. 118, M.M. 2. nonexistence; *abhâva* + *tas*, adv. in consequence of the non-existence, Bhâshâp. 113. 3. death, Kathâs. 18, 270. 4. destruction, Râm. 5, 27, 6. *A-badhya*-, adj. state of being inviolable, Hit. iii. d. 63. *Âdhâra-â-dheya*- (vb. *dhâ*), m. state or relation of the receptacle and the object received, Hit. iii. d. 12 (instr. because it [viz. the mirror] can receive [reflect] only in proportion to its greatness). *Ârya*-, m. honest behaviour, Râm. 1, 1, 35. *Eka*-, I. m. 1. same state, Hit. ii. d. 151. 2. simplicity (opposite to duplicity), candour, Pańch. iii. d. 61. II. adj. unchanged, MBh. 13, 3677. *Kanyâ*-, m. virginity, MBh. 1, 2405. *Kṛita*-, adj. resolute, Râm. 6, 70, 12. *Tanu*-, m. scantiness, Çâk. d. 167. *Dâsa*-, m. slavery, Draup. 9, 16. *Durnîta*-, i.e. *dus*-, m. foolish behaviour, Chr. 8, 32. *Dûra*-, m. distance, Megh. 47. *Droha*-, m. malignance, Man. 9, 17. *Dvandva*-, m. discord, Ṛit. 1, 27. *Punar*-, m. regeneration, Prab. 108, 1. *Pṛithagbhâva*, i.e. *pṛithak*-, m. 1. separateness. 2. difference. *Prâpta*-, i.e. *pra-âpta*, I. adj. 1. of a good disposition. 2. wise. 3. handsome. II. m. a bullock. *Bâla*-, m. youth, Pańch. 182, 12, *Vṛiddha*-, m. old age, Pańch. 50, 8. *Sadbhâva*, i.e. *sant*-, m. 1. the property of being, entity. 2. truth, Lass. 57, 7. 3. the property of goodness, kindness, Megh. 18, n. 4. honesty, Hit. iv. d. 103. 5. merit, Böhtl. Ind. Spr. 1880; a pure or holy disposition. 6. amiability. *Sarva*-, m. one's whole being, Hit. ii. d. 33. *Sâdhu*-, m. goodness, Brâhmaṇav. 1, 4. *Sva*-, m. 1. nature, natural disposition, Râm. 3, 51, 33; Hit. i. d. 19, M.M. 2. purpose, Johns. Sel. 46, 76, *Strî-sva*-, m. 1. female nature. 2. an eunuch, attendant on women. *Sthâyibh*°, i.e. *sthâyin*-, m. 1. fixed condition. 2. A passion or feeling, as object of poetical description, viz. desire, mirth, etc.

भावज *bhâva-ja*, m. Love, Kâma.

भावतस् *bhâva* + *tas*, in *jńâti*-, adv. By being a relation, Hit. ii. d. 92.

भावत्क *bhâvatka*, i.e. *bhavant* + *ka*, adj., f. *kî*, Thine.

भावन *bhâvana*, i.e. *bhû*, Caus., + *ana*, I. m. **1.** A creator, Utt. Râmach. 36, 11. **2.** A founder. **II.** n., and f. *nâ*. **1.** Causing to be. **2.** Mental perception, Bhâshâp. 31; Pańch. v. d. 91 (cf. Böhtl. Ind. Spr. 2119; the success of an advice, etc., depends on the manner in which it is mentally received, faithfully believed, etc.). **3.** Recollection, Utt. Râmach. 25, 13. **4.** Imagination, Vedântas. in Chr. 206, 6. **5.** Meditation, Bhag. 2, 66. **6.** Observing. **7.** Decorating with flowers, etc.

— **Comp.** *Nyagbhâvana,* i.e. *nyańch-,* n. 1. contempt. 2. humbling. *Viçesha-,* f. reflecting on, or perceiving, differences.

भावित्र *bhâvitra* (vb. *bhû*), n. The universe.

भाविन् *bhâvin,* adj., f. *nî,* i.e. **I.** *bhû* + *in,* Future, Vikr. 87, 1; what will be, Daçak. in. Chr, 186, 24; what will fall at one's share, Pańch. iv. d. 73. **II.** *bhâ* + *vin.* **1.** Beautiful, Râm. 3, 53, 39. **2.** f. *nî,* A distinguished woman, a wanton woman.—**Comp.** *Avaçyabh°,* i.e. *avaçyam-,* adj. what will be inevitably, Brâhmaṇav. 2, 2. *Tathâ-,* adj. destined to become really, Çâk. 111, 20. *Punar-,* adj. possible to be undone, Chr. 22, 20.

भावुक *bhâvuka,* i.e. *bhû* + *uka,* **I.** adj. **1.** Actually being. **2.** Happy. **3.** Latter part of comp. adj. Becoming. **II.** m. A sister's husband. **III.** n. Happiness. See *çubhambh°.*

भाष् *BHÂSH,* i. 1, Âtm. (in epic poetry also Par., Chr. 27, 1). **1.** To speak, Man. 8, 216. **2.** To speak to (acc.), Râm. 2, 78, 19. **3.** To address, MBh. 3, 2747. **4.** To describe, Man. 4, 255. *bhâshita,* n. Speech, Pańch. i. d. 356. **Comp.** *Su-,* I. adj. 1. well spoken. 2. and n. well discoursing, Pańch. 31, 4; ii. d. 177. II. n. 1. eloquence. 2. a good advice (?), Man. 2, 239.—With the prep. **अनु** *anu,* **1.** To speak distinctly, Man. 3, 30. **2.** To confess, Man. 11, 228.—With **अप** *apa,* To revile, Kumâras. 5, 83.—With **अभि** *abhi,* **1.** To address, Man. 2, 128. **2.** To speak to (with instr.), Man. 4, 57. **3.** To declare loudly, Man. 11, 103.—With **समभि** *sam-abhi,* To converse, MBh. 3, 12697. —With **आ** *â,* **1.** To address, MBh. 1, 74. **2.** To speak, Böhtl. Ind. Spr. 396. **3.** To exclaim, Dev. 2, 36.—With **व्या** *vi-â,* To address, MBh. 3, 15169. Comp. ptcple. *duḥkha-vyâbhâshita,* adj. Difficult to be pronounced, MBh. 13, 4485. —With **समा** *sam-â,* To address, MBh. 1, 4198.—With **परि** *pari,* **1.** To declare, Utt. Râmach. 130, 5. **2.** To persuade, MBh. 1, 4287.—With **प्र** *pra,* **1.** To speak, Râm. 3, 51, 25. **2.** To address, MBh. 3, 2599. *prabhâshita,* n. Speech, Nal. 8, 11.—With **संप्र** *sam-pra,* To speak, MBh. 5, 41.—With **प्रति** *prati,* **1.** To answer, MBh. 3, 2524. **2.** To address, Râm. 1, 8, 29; Pańch. 193, 13.—With **सम्** *sam,* **1.** To converse, Chr. 56, 18; to converse with (instr.), Man. 8, 55. **2.** To have sexual intercourse with, Hit. 64, 12 (with acc.). **3.** To greet, Hit. 14, 20. **4.** To speak. MBh. 1, 5190; to say, Hit. 57, 6 (read *sambhâshate.* The sense is: It is true he is anxious, else he would not have said to me, etc.). *bhâsh* is probably akin to *bhâ.*—Cf. Lat. fastus, nefastus, nefarius, festus, feriæ, hariolus, fas, nefas, fari; φημί, φάσις, φατός, φήμη, φωνή; akin are φθέγγομαι, φθέγμα (but cf. *bhańj,* i. 10); A.S. bannan, abannan.

भाषण *bhâshaṇa,* i.e. *bhâsh* + *ana,* n. Speech, Lass. 8, 8.

भाषा *bhâsh* + *â,* f. **1.** Speech, Chr. 220, l. 1. **2.** Language, Pańch. i. d. 445. **3.** Vernacular speech, Lass. 39, 11; MBh. 2, 2040. **4.** Speech exposing the plaint in a law-suit, Lass. 90, 3; Pańch. 167, 6 (?).—**Comp.** *Deça-bhâshâ,* f. the language of a country, MBh. 9, 2605. *Vi-bhâshâ,* indecl. alternatively, either of two ways, optionally.

भाषिन् *bhâsh* + *in,* adj., f. *shiṇî,* Speaking, Pańch. 184, 4; Râjat. 5, 61.—

Comp. *Dus-*, adj. abusing, MBh. 5, 751. *Pûrva-*, adj. speaking first, making advances, Râm. 2, 1, 7 Gorr. *Mṛidu-*, adj. speaking sweetly, Vikr. d. 88.

1. भास् *BHÂS* (akin to *bhâ*, probably a denomin.), i. 1, Âtm. (in epic poetry also Par., MBh. 1, 4852). **1.** To shine, MBh. 3, 12299. **2.** To appear, Vedântas. in Chr. 217, 4. Caus. **1.** To illuminate, Bhagav. 15, 6. **2.** To make evident, Vedântas. in Chr. 215, 22. —With the prep. अव *ava*, **1.** To shine, Râm. 1, 35, 16. **2.** To appear, Vedântas. in Chr. 212, 12. Caus. To illuminate, Çiç. 9, 37.—With आ *â*, To shine, MBh. 2, 1313.—With उद् *ud*, Caus. **1.** To beautify, Ragh. 7, 16. **2.** To honour, Bhartṛ. 2, 49.—With नि *ni*, To seem likely.—With प्र *pra*, **1.** To shine, MBh. 3, 17090. **2.** To seem likely. Caus. To illuminate, MBh. 1, 6532.—With प्रति *prati*, To reflect, Vedântas. in Chr. 204, 15.—With वि *vi*, **1.** To shine agreeably, Râm. 2, 30, 10. **2.** To shine, Böhtl. Ind. Spr. 88; 595.

2. भास् *bhâs*, f. **1.** Light, Ṛit. 6, 33. **2.** A ray of light, Râjat. 5, 343. **3.** Splendour, Pañch. i. d. 213. **4.** Image, Bhâg. P. 6, 9, 38. **5.** Wish.—Comp. *A-chira-*, f. lightning, Çâk. d. 166. *Çaçâṅka-*, adj. shining like the moon, Ṛit. 6, 3.

भास *bhâs + a*, I. m., and f. *sâ*, Light. II. m. **1.** A vulture, Man. 11, 135; Pañch. 157, 3 (?). **2.** A cock. **3.** A sort of water-fowl. **4.** A station of cowherds.—Comp. *Padma-*, m. a name of Vishṇu, Hariv. 14119. *Pûshabhâsâ*, i.e. *pûshan-*, f. The capital of Indra.

भासक *bhâs + aka*, adj. Making evident, Vedântas. in Chr. 211, 22.

भासता *bhâsa + tâ*, f. Condition of a vulture, Man. 11, 25.

भासन्त *bhâsant + a* (vb. *bhâs*), I. adj. **1.** Shining. **2.** Beautiful. II. m. **1.** The sun. **2.** The moon. **3.** A kind of water-fowl.

भासिन् *bhâs + in*, adj. Shining, Hariv. 985.

भासुर *bhâsura* (=*bhâsvara*), I. adj. Shining, Bhartṛ. 2, 27. II. m. **1.** Crystal. **2.** A hero.

भासुरक *bhâsura + ka*, m. A proper name, Pañch. 53, 17.

भासुरत्व *bhâsura + tva*, n. Splendour, Mâlav. d. 12.

भास्कर *bhâs-kara*, I. adj. Resplendent. II. m. **1.** The sun, Pañch. 190, 4. **2.** Fire. **3.** A hero. III. n. Gold.

भास्यत्व *bhâsya + tva* (vb. *bhâs*), n. Condition of appearing, Vedântas. in Chr. 211, 19.

भास्वन्त् *bhâs + vant*, I. adj., f. *vatî*, Shining, Man. 1, 77; radiant, Chr. 294, 7=Rigv. i. 92, 7. II. m. **1.** Light. **2.** The sun, Pañch. iii. d. 77. **3.** A hero. III. f. *vatî*, The city of the sun.

भास्वर *bhâsvara*, i.e. *bhâsvan* (curtailed °*vant*), + *a* (with *r* for *n*), I. adj. Shining, Bhâshâp. 40; radiant. II. m. **1.** The sun. **2.** A day.

भिक्ष् *BHIKSH* (for *bibhaksh*, desider. of *bhaj*), i. 1, Âtm. (in epic poetry also Par., MBh. 3, 16986). **1.** To beg, Man. 2, 184. **2.** To solicit from, Man. 2, 50 (acc.); 11, 24 (abl.). **3.** † To obtain. **4.** † To fail of obtaining. **5.** † To be distressed. **6.** † To solicit anything through covetousness (?).

भिक्षा *bhiksh + â*, f. **1.** Begging,

Pańch. 116, 17. **2.** Alms, Pańch. 116, 19. **3.** Begged food, Man. 2, 50. **4.** Hire. **5.** Service.—**Comp.** *Durbhiksha*, i.e. *dus-*, n. **1.** Famine, Pańch. 114, 4. **2.** Want of provisions, Hiḍ. iii. d. 108. *Subhiksha*, i.e. *su-*, n. abundance of food, Râjat. 5, 116; Pańch. iv. d. 82.

भिक्षाक *bhikshâ + ka*, m., and f. *kî*, A mendicant, Râjat. 6, 166.

भिक्षु *bhiksh + u*, m. **1.** A mendicant; one who subsists only upon alms, Pańch. v. d. 55. **2.** A religious mendicant, Hit. iii. d. 104.—**Comp.** *Çveta-*, a sort of mendicant, Pańch. iii. d. 73.

भिक्षुक *bhikshu + ka*, m., and f. *kî*, A beggar, Daçak. in Chr. 180, 14.—**Comp.** *Dharma-*, m. a virtuous mendicant, Man. 11, 2. *Çâkya-*, f. *kî*, a Bauddha nun, Daçak. in Chr. 191, 16.

भिण्ड I. m. A shrub. II. f. *dâ*, A kind of shrub (ÇKD.), Pańch. i. d. 108.

भित्त *bhitta*, i.e. *bhid + ta*, n. A part.

भित्ति *bhitti*, i.e. *bhid + ti*, f. **1.** Breaking. **2.** A thing broken or divided. **3.** A fissure, Bhartṛ. 2, 31. **4.** A fragment, Kir. 5, 8. **5.** A defect. **6.** Opportunity. **7.** An asylum. **8.** A wall of earth or masonry, Daçak. in Chr. 197, 17; Mâlav. 50, 6. **9.** A place, Çiç. 9, 75.—**Comp.** *Sudhâ-* f. a plastered wall, Daçak. in Chr. 199, 18.

भित्तिका *bhitti + kâ*, f. **1.** A wall. **2.** A small house-lizard.

1. **भिद्** *BHID*, ii. 7, *bhinad*, *bhind*, Par. Âtm. **1.** To break, Râm. 2, 80, 17; to destroy, Pańch. i. d. 112. **2.** To tear up, Pańch. 230, 16. **3.** To pierce, Râm. 3, 50, 18; pass. to be afflicted, Pańch. i. d. 436. **4.** To divide, Pańch. i. d. 115; to disjoin, Man. 7, 66. **5.** To betray, 7, 50. **6.** Pass. To differ, Çiç. 9, 46. **7.** Pass. To split, Chânḍ. 21 in Berl. Monatsb. 1864, 408. Ptcple. of the pf. pass. *bhinna*, **1.** Broken, split, cloven, Râjat. 5, 260. **2.** Divided, Râjat. 5, 176. **3.** Disunited, Hit. iv. d. 39 (*dâna-*, on account of gifts). **4.** Distinguished, other, different (*dinasya pûrvârdhaparârdhabhinnachhâyâ*, the shade of the day different in the morning and in the afternoon, Pańch. ii. d. 38). **5.** Separated, detached, without (also as former part of comp. adj.), Pańch. i. d. 212; Megh. 82; Bhâshâp. 133. **6.** Blown, opened. **7.** Performed with great strides, Vikr. d. 80 (*bhinna-gati*, adj. Going quickly, cf. *gati-bheda*). **8.** Neglected, deviated from. **9.** Connected, joined, mixed, Megh. 60. m. A flaw in a jewel. n. **1.** A bit, a portion. **2.** (in arithmetic), A fraction. **Comp.** *A-*, adj. 1. unhurt, Ragh. 17, 12. 2. undivided. 3. not different, unchanged, Çâk. d. 14; equal, identical, Prab. 9, 8. Ptcple. of the fut. pass. I. *bhedya*. **Comp.** *A-bhedya*, adj. 1. impenetrable, Râm. 6, 79, 65. 2. indestructible. n. a diamond. *Durbh°*, i.e. *dus-*, adj. difficult to be broken or divided, Hit. i. d. 91, M.M. *Suchi-*, 1. to be pierced by a needle. 2. palpable. 3. very dense (viz. darkness), Hit. 98, 22. II. *bhidya*, m. a river. Caus. *bhedaya*, **1.** To divide, to cleave, Râm. 1, 16, 23. **2.** To perplex, Râm. 1, 64, 7. **3.** To disunite, MBh. 1, 7399. **4.** To remove, to overcome, MBh. 1, 5592.—With the prep. **अति** *ati*, *atibhinna* in *nâtibhinna*, Wholly like, Çâk. 27, 18.—With **अनु** *anu*, To break afterward, MBh. 2, 2483.—With **उद्** *ud*, **1.** To divide, to pierce through, Vedântas. in Chr. 209, 7. **2.** Pass. To break forth, Daçak. in Chr. 199, 5. *udbhinna*, **1.** Opened, burst, Ragh. 13, 21. **2.** Budded. **3.** Destroyed, Lass. 64, 1.—With **प्रोद्** *pra-ud*, *prodbhinna*, **1.**

Breaking forth, Çâk. 128, 18 Chezy. **2.** Standing erect, Böhtl. Ind. Spr. 830.—With निस् *nis*, **1.** To divide, to cleave, Râm. 3, 55, 10; to open, Vikr. d. 41. **2.** To break down, Daçak. in Chr. 201, 1. **3.** To put out (one's eyes), MBh. 3, 10328. **4.** To pierce, Vikr. d. 144; Râm. 2, 35, 4. **5.** To destroy, Hit. ii. d. 21. **6.** To betray, to divulge, Daçak. in Chr. 193, 8. *nirbhinna*, **1.** Pierced, Vikr. d. 150. **2.** Undistinguished, equal (rather *bhinna* with *nis*). Ptcple. of the fut. pass. *nirbhedya*, **1.** Not disappointed, Râm. 6, 91, 26. **2.** Without fissures, Kâm. Nîtis. 11, 66 (rather *bhedya* with *nis*). — With विनिस् *vi-nis*, To cleave, MBh. 3, 8551.—With प्र *pra*, *prabhinna*, **1.** Pierced, Sund. 2, 20. **2.** Well cut, detached, Johns. Sel. 54, 134; severed. m. A furious elephant (cf. Johns. l. l.). — With प्रति *prati*, **1.** To disown, Çiç. 9, 58. **2.** To pierce, Draup. 6, 15. **3.** To reproach, Ragh. 19, 22. **4.** To betray, Daçak. in Chr. 199, 22. *pratibhinna*, **1.** Pierced. **2.** Separated.—With वि *vi*, **1.** To cleave, Chr. 292, 10 =Rigv. i. 85, 10. **2.** To pierce, MBh. 3, 709. *vibhinna*, **1.** Pierced, wounded. **2.** Broken. **3.** Scattered, moved to and fro, Vikr. d. 85. **4.** Mixed, Kir. 5, 34. **5.** Various. **6.** Disappointed. **7.** Bewildered. Caus. To alienate, Râm. 2, 7, 18.—With सम् *sam*, *sambhinna*, **1.** Divided. **2.** Shaken. **3.** Combined, united. — Cf. Lat. findo, finis (for fid + nis); Goth. beitan; A.S. bitan (with batan, Caus. to cause to bite, to bait); Goth. baitar; A. S. biter; O. H. G. biz, bizzo, fiza, etc.; φείδομαι, φιτρός (for φιδ + τρος), and probably φῖμός (for φιδ-μός).

2. भिद् *bhid*, I. adj. Who or what breaks, divides, destroys; cf. *balabhid*. II. f. **1.** Difference, kind. **2.** Breaking, dividing.—**Comp.** *Yamunâ-*, m. Baladeva.

भिदक *bhid + aka*, I. m. A sword. II. n. Indra's thunderbolt.

भिदा *bhid + â*, f. **1.** Tearing, cleaving, Kir. 5, 43. **2.** Coriander.

भिदि *bhid + i*, m., भिदिर *bhid + ira*, n., भिदु *bhid + u*, m., and भिद्र *bhid + ra*, n. Indra's thunderbolt.

भिदुर *bhid + ura*, I. adj. Brittle. II. n. Thunderbolt; Pañch. i. d. 241 corr. *piṭhara*, see my translation.

भिन्द् *BHIND*, see *bind*.

भिन्नक *bhinna + ka* (vb. *bhid*), m. **1.** A Bauddha. **2.** A musical mode, Vikr. 56, 17.

भिन्नदेशत्व *bhinna-deça + tva*, n. Condition of being widely distant, Çâk. d. 50.

भिन्नवृत्तिता *bhinna-vṛitti + tâ*, f. Omission of prescribed acts, Man. 12, 33.

भिया *bhiyâ*, i.e. *bhî + a*, f. Fear.

भिल् *BHIL*, see *bil*.

भिल्ल *bhilla*, m. A barbarian of a particular tribe.

भिषग्जित *bhishagjita*, i.e. *bhishaj + jita* (vb. *ji*), n. A medicament.

भिषज् *bhishaj*, i.e. *abhi-sañj*, m. A physician, Pañch. 156, 21.

1. भी *BHÎ*, ii. 3; i. 1, ved. (and † i. 10 ?), Par. (ved., and in epic poetry also Âtm., Chr. 292, 8=Rigv. i. 85, 8; MBh. 3, 16289). **1.** To fear, Râm. 1,

59, 2. **2.** To be afraid of, with abl., Man. 4, 191; with gen., Râm. 1, 1, 4; with acc., Lass. 51, 7. Anomal. aor. sing. 2. *bhais*, Chr. 36, 16. Ptcple. of the pf. pass. *bhîta*, Frightened, Pańch. i. d. 364; fearful, Chr. 19, 14; timid, Chr. 54, 11; afraid of, Châṇ. 96 in Berl. Monatsb. 1864, 413. n. Fear. Comp. *A-*, adj. fearless, Râm. 2, 60, 7. *Divâ-*, m. 1. an owl, Kumâras. 1, 12. 2. a thief. 3. any flower, the petals of which close in the daytime. *Mahâ-*, 1. adj. very timid. 2. f. *tâ*, a sort of sensitive plant, Mimosa pudica. *Su-*, adj. much afraid, Pańch. i. d. 20. Caus. **1.** *bhâyaya*. **2.** *bhâpaya*, Âtm. **3.** *bhîshaya*, Âtm. (in epic poetry also Par., MBh. 1, 185), To terrify, MBh. 8, 1791. *bhîshita*, Terrified, Daçak. in Chr. 193, 15.—With the prep. निस् *nis*, *nirbhîta*, adj. fearless, Râm. 2, 27, 17 (rather *bhîta*, n. Fear, with *nis*).—With प्र *pra*, To fear in a high degree, Bhaṭṭ. 6, 2. (वि *vi*, in *vi-bhîta*, adj. Fearless, is compounded rather with *bhîta*.)—Cf. φέβομαι, φόβος (φεβ=*bhâp* in the Caus. *bhâpaya*), and probably φάψ; O.H.G. bibên; A.S. bifian, beofian (old frequent.).

2. भी *bhî*, f. Fear, Pańch. i. d. 125.—Comp. *A-*, and *apa-*, adj. fearless, Râm. 5, 14, 12; Draup. 8, 19.

भीति *bhî+ti*, f. **1.** Fear, Bhartṛ. 2, 72; Hit. ii. d. 54 (*dosha-*, of committing faults). **2.** Trembling.—Comp. *Divâ-*, m. an owl.

भीम *bhî+ma*, I. adj. **1.** Fearful, horrid, Râm. 3, 50, 27; Bhartṛ. 2, 72. **2.** Terrifying, Utt. Râmach. 139, 10. II. m. **1.** Çiva. **2.** One of the five Pâṇḍu princes. III. f. *mâ*. **1.** Durgâ. **2.** A whip. IV. n. **1.** Horror. **2.** Danger.—Comp. *Mahâ-*, 1. a name of Çântanu. 2. one of Çiva's chamberlains.

भीमसेन *bhîmasena* (cf. *senâ*), m. The second of the five Pâṇḍu princes.

भीरु *bhî+ru*, I. adj., f. *ru* or *rû*, Timid, Pańch. iii. d. 25. II. m. **1.** A jackal. **2.** A tiger. III. f. *ru* or *rû*. **1.** A timid woman, Vikr. d. 5. **2.** A plant, Asparagus racemosa. **3.** A sort of prickly nightshade. **4.** A centipede. **5.** A goat.—Comp. *A-*, 1. adj. fearless, Man. 7, 190. 2. f. *rû*, a plant, Asparagus racemosa, Suçr. 2, 223, 10. *Adhyavasâya-*, adj. afraid of exertion, Hit. i. d. 167, M.M.

भीरुक *bhîru+ka*, I. adj. **1.** Afraid, Çâk. 30, 6 (Prâkṛ.). **2.** Timid, a coward, Hit. iv. d. 30. **3.** Formidable. II. m. An owl.

भीरुता *bhîru+tâ*, f. Fear, timidity. Hit. i. d. 118, M.M.; Vikr. d. 102.

भीरुत्व *bhîru+tva*, n. **1.** Fear, timidity, Pańch. i. d. 118; 205. **2.** The nature of a tiger, Pańch. i. d. 205 (at the same time in the first signification).

भीरुमय *bhîru+maya*, adj., f. *yî*, Terrible, Hit. 116, 8.

भीलु *bhî+lu*, and भीलुक *bhîlu+ka*, adj. Timid, Hit. iv. d. 30 (*ka*).

भीषण *bhîshaṇa*, i.e. *bhî*, Caus., +*ana*, I. adj., f. *ṇâ*. **1.** Horrible, Pańch. 174, 11. **2.** Awful, Utt. Râmach. 42, 8. II. m. **1.** The sentiment of horror, as the object of poetical composition. **2.** The olibanum tree, Boswellia thurifera. **3.** Çiva. III. n. **1.** Horror, the property that excites fear. **2.** An object of horror, Man. 3, 9.—Comp. *Ati-*, adj. very terrific, Hit. ii. d. 158.

भीषा *bhîshâ*, i.e. *bhî*, Caus., +*a*, f. Terrifying, intimidation, Man. 8, 264.

भीष्म *bhîshma*, i.e. *bhî*, Caus., +*ma*, I. adj. Frightful, terrific. II. n. Horror.

III. m. **1.** The sentiment of horror, as the object of poetical composition. **2.** Çiva. **3.** An imp, a goblin. **4.** The grand-uncle of the Pâṇḍus, son of the Gaṅgâ, Chr. 19, 5.—**Comp.** *Mahâ-*, m. a name of Çântanu.

भीष्मक *bhishma+ka*, m. The contemptible Bhîshma, Chr. 6, 6.

भुक्ति *bhukti*, i.e. 2.*bhuj+ti*, f. **1.** Eating, Pańch. 138, 2. **2.** Food, Râjat. 5, 170. **3.** Fruition. **4.** Possession, Man. 8, 252; Pańch. iii. d. 93; iv. d. 76 (but cf. also Böhtl. Ind. Spr. 125).

1. **भुज्** *BHUJ*, i. 6, Par. **1.** To bend, to make crooked. **2.** Pass. To incline one's self, Hit. iv. d. 28. Ptcple. of the pf. pass. *bhugna*, **1.** Bent, crooked. **2.** Bending, stooping. **Comp.** *Â-*, adj. slightly inflexed, Daçak. in Chr. 198, 21.—With the prep. **अव** *ava*, *avabhugna*, Crooked, MBh. 1, 5891.—Cf. Goth. biugan; A.S. bigan, búgan; O.H.G. baug; A.S. beág, beagrian; O.H.G. bogo; A.S. bóga; O.H.G. elin-bogo; A.S. elnboga, elboga; O.H.G. buoc, bûh; φεύγειν, φυγή; Lat. fugio, fuga; cf. A.S. bi-bugan, To flee away.

2. **भुज्** (akin to the preceding; cf. *bhaj* and *bhańj*), ii. 7, *bhunaj*, *bhuńj*, Par. Âtm. **1.** To eat and drink, Man. 2, 53; Nal. 13, 68; Râm. 3, 53, 7. **2.** To enjoy (regularly, Âtm.), MBh. 3, 2167. **3.** To endure, Megh. 1. **4.** To govern, to possess (regularly, Par.), Man. 7, 148 (Âtm.). Ptcple. of the pf. pass. *bhukta*, **1.** Eaten. **2.** Possessed, Pańch. iii. d. 93. **3.** Eating, having eaten, Pańch. iv. d. 75; n. Food. **Comp.** *Ku-*, n. bad food, Lass. 3, 9. Ptcple. of the fut. pass. **I.** *bhogya*, To be enjoyed, Pańch. i. d. 133. n. **1.** Enjoyment, Çâk. d. 47. **2.** Wealth. **3.** Grain. f. *yâ*, A whore. **Comp.** *A-*, I. adj. what cannot be enjoyed. II. n. absence of enjoyment, Megh. 111. *Su-*, adj. to be enjoyed easily, Pańch. iv. d. 84. **II.** *bhojya*, To be eaten, edible. n. **1.** Food, meal, Hit. 76, 7, M.M.; milky messes, Man. 3, 227 (Kull.). **2.** Gratification, Man. 9, 268. **Comp.** *A-*, adj. 1. prohibited as food, Pańch. 121, 16. 2. a person whose food must not be eaten, Man. 4, 221. *Ku-*, n. bad food, Châṇ. 30 in Berl. Monatsb. 1864, 409. Desider. *bubhuksha*, **1.** To wish to eat, MBh. 1, 8087. **2.** To wish to govern, or to possess, 1, 5667. Caus. I. *bhojaya*, To cause to eat, to invite, to give food, Man. 3, 106; 151; 8, 392; to treat, to entertain, Pańch. 26, 20. II. *bhuńjâpaya*, To cause to eat, Lass. 12, 4.—With the prep. **अधि** *adhi*, To dispose of, Hit. 130, 4.—With **अनु** *anu*, To receive the reward of, Man. 4, 240; Pańch. 259, 15.—With **उप** *upa*, **1.** To eat, to drink, Râm. 2, 30, 16; Ragh. 1, 68 (67). **2.** To enjoy, Hit. i. d. 112, M.M. **3.** To have a reward of, Man. 12, 8. **4.** To appropriate, 4, 202. Ptcple. of the fut. pass. **I.** *upabhogya*, To be enjoyed, what may be eaten, Pańch. 86, 23. n. An object of enjoyment, MBh. 1, 2346. **II.** *upabhojya*, Edible, serving for food, MBh. 14, 2552.—With **परि** *pari*, **1.** To eat, Mṛichchh. 297, 12 (Calc.). **2.** To enjoy, Kir. 5, 5.—With **प्र** *pra*, To govern, Chr. 287, 5=Rigv. i. 48, 5.—With **सम्** *sam*, To enjoy, Hit. ii. d. 167; Râjat. 5, 283. *a-sambhojya*, m. One with whom nobody is allowed to eat, Man. 9, 238. Caus. *bhojaya*, To cause to eat, to treat, MBh. 3, 12672.—Cf. Lat. fungi; Goth. bugjan; A.S. bycgan, to buy (originally, to possess one's self of something); Goth. biuhts, biuhti. As *bhrańj* for *bhańj*, the original form was probably *bhruńj*, cf. Lat. frux, frugis, fruor, fructus, frustum, frustra,

frutex; Goth. bruks, brûkjan; O.H.G. brûhan; A.S. brúcan, bryce.

3. ऽभुज् 2. *-bhuj*, latter part of comp. nouns. **1.** Eating, e.g. *çesha-*, adj. Eating the rest, Man. 3, 117. **2.** Enjoying, governing; e.g. *kshiti-*, m. A king, Bhartṛ. 3, 78. *kshiti-lava-*, m. A small prince, Bhartṛ. 3, 100. *kshmâ-*, *go-*, *jagati-*, m. A king, Râjat. 5, 50; 6; 2, 44. *deha-*, m. Epithet of Çiva, MBh. 13, 1067. *dharâ-*, *pṛithivî-*, m. A king, Râjat. 2, 7. *bali-*, m. A crow. *bhû-*, *bhûmî-*, *mahî-*, m. A king, Bhartṛ. 2, 47; Çṛiṅgârat. 5; Râjat. 5, 11.

भुज 1. *bhuj + a*, m., and f. *jâ*. **1.** The arm, Pañch. 215, 7. **2.** The hand, Hiḍ. 1, 2. **3.** The proboscis of an elephant, Draup. 8. 21. **4.** A bending.—Comp. *Ûrmi-*, m. an arm-like wave, i.e. a wave instead of an arm, Çiç. 9, 38. *Chatur-*, I. four arms, Bhâg. P. 6, 1, 35. II. adj., f. *jâ*, having four arms, 4, 12, 20. III. m. the name of a Dânava, Hariv. 12934. *Mahâ-*, adj. having great, powerful arms, Râm. 3, 55, 4; Indr. 5, 55.

भुजग 1. *bhuj + a-ga*, m. A snake, Kir. 5, 4. f. *gî*, A female snake, Böhtl. Ind. Spr. 1156.

भुजंग *bhujaṁga*, 1. *bhuj + a + m-ga*, I. m. **1.** A snake, Bhartṛ. 2, 4; Vikr. 25, 20. **2.** A catamite, Daçak. in Chr. 191, 10. II. f. *gî*, A female snake.

भुजंगम *bhujaṁgama*, i.e. 1. *bhuj + a + m-gam + a*, m. A snake, Pañch. 174, 11; Bhartṛ. 2, 87.

भुजाकण्ट *bhujâ-kaṇṭa* (cf. *kaṇṭaka*), m. A finger-nail.

भुजान्तर *bhujântara*, i.e. *bhuja-antara*, n. The breast, Vikr. d. 112 (*alpa-*, adj., f. *râ*, Having a small chest).

भुजि 2. *bhuj + i*, m. Fire.

भुजिष्य *bhuj + ishya*, I. m., and f. *yâ*, A servant, Nal. 13, 55. II. m. **1.** An independent man. **2.** A string worn round the wrist. III. f. *yâ*, A harlot.

भुज्यु 2. *bhuj + yu*, m. **1.** Eating. **2.** A vessel (?). **3.** A proper name, Chr. 296, 6 = Rigv. i. 112, 6.

भुञ्जापय *bhuñjâpaya*, see 2. *bhuj*.

† भुण्ड् *BHUṆḌ*, and हुण्ड् *HUṆḌ*, i. 1, Âtm. **1.** To support. **2.** To select. **3.** To take.

भुरण्य *BHURAṆYA* (a ved. denomin. from ved. *bhuraṇa*, based on *bhur* = Lat. fur-ere), Par. To be active, Chr. 289, 6 = Rigv. i. 50, 6.

भुरिज् *bhurij*, f. The earth.

भुवन *bhuvana*, i.e. *bhû + ana*, n. **1.** A being, Chr. 290, 3 = Rigv. i. 64, 3; creature, Chr. 292, 8 = Rigv. i. 85, 8. **2.** The world, Hit. i. d. 32, M.M. **3.** Man, mankind. **4.** Heaven. **5.** Water.—Comp. *Tri-*, n. the three worlds, heaven, sky, and earth; or heaven, earth, and the lower regions, Bhartṛ. 1, 98.

भुवन्यु *bhuvanyu* (akin to *bhuvana*), m. **1.** A master, a lord. **2.** The sun.

भुवर्लोक *bhuvarloka*, i.e. *bhuvas-loka*, m. The space between the earth and the sun.

भुवस् *bhuvas*, i.e. *bhû + as*, indecl. The sky, the atmosphere, Man. 2, 76; Vedântas. in Chr. 209, 1.

भुविस् *bhuvis* (vb. *bhû*), m. (?) The ocean.

भुशुण्डी *bhuçuṇḍî*, f. A weapon, apparently a kind of fire-arms, MBh. 3, 643.

1. भू *BHÛ*, i. 1, Par. Âtm. **1.** To

become, Man. 1, 9; with *anyathâ*, To be changed, to fail, Pańch. 187, 1; *na jâtu anyathâ*, To be unalterable, Chr. 50, 6. **2.** To spring up, Bhag. 14, 17. **3.** To be, MBh. 2, 150; auxiliary verb, Râm. 1, 41, 3; with *agre*, To precede, Pańch. 215, 13. **4.** To behave, Pańch. iii. d. 61. **5.** To take place, Pańch. 4, 15; to be possible, Pańch. 33, 6; to be asked, Man. 12, 108. **6.** With dat. To serve to, to cause; e.g. *vinâçâya*, Causes destruction, MBh. 3, 12812; *sańgamâya*, To unite, Vikr. d. 129. **7.** With gen. To belong to; e.g. *dhanaṁ bhavishyati me*, I shall have wealth; to fall to one's share, Hit. iii. d. 104; to befall, Hit. pr. d. 28, M.M. **8.** With loc. To be occupied with, MBh. 5, 205; Pańch. iii. d. 258 (*bhavishyant*, Who will be occupied, i.e. who begins). **9.** To live, to exist, MBh. 3, 2372. **10.** With *na*, To perish, Pańch. 164, 13; MBh. 1, 2781. **11.** With *punar*, To marry a second time, Man. 9, 175. **12.** To obtain (with acc.), MBh. 1, 5366. **13.** Impersonal pass. with instr., literally, It is existed by=exists; e. g. *yair eva bhûmipâlair bhavishyate*, literally, 'by whom will be existed kings,' i.e. 'who were to be kings,' Râjat. 5, 418. **14.** *bhavatu*, imperat. 3. sing. **a.** May be, but, Çâk. 64, 8. **b.** Stop, Çâk. 12, 12. **c.** Well, Vikr. 4, 2. **d.** No matter, Çâk. 7, 17; 9, 18. ved. conjunctive of the aor. *bhuvat*, Lass. 99, 3=Rigv. v. 9, 7. Ptcple. of the pf. pass. *bhûta*. **1.** Been, become, Arj. 3, 28; Pańch. ii. d. 2 (*bhû-târa-bhûto 'parah*, Become, or being, a second Saviour of the world). **2.** Being, Pańch. i. d. 324; consisting of, Hit. 114, 22 (*çaktu-* perhaps to be read *çaktu-pûrṇaḥ*). **3.** Gone, past, former, Pańch. iii. d. 136. **4.** Proper, right. **5.** True. m. and n. **1.** A malignant spirit, Chr. 37, 2. **2.** A living being, a creature, Man. 1, 50; 95; 2, 159; Pańch. iii. d. 136. m. **1.** A son, a child. **2.** A demigod of a particular kind. **3.** Çiva. n. An element, Vedântas. in Chr. 206, 19; Bhâshâp. 28; five *Bhûtas* are enumerated: earth, fire, water, air, and æther. **Comp.** *Âtmabhûta*, i. e. *âtman-*, adj. true to himself, Man. 7, 217. *Ittham-*, adj. so natured, Pańch. 31, 17 (read as one word). *Evam-*, adj. such, Hit. 10, 7, M.M.; 84, 14. *Tîrtha-*, adj. hallowed, MBh. 13, 1725. *Divâ-*, adj. become as clear as the day, MBh. 14, 1757. *Mahâ-*, n. a primary element, as earth, etc., Man. 1, 6. *Vahirbhûta*, i.e. *vahis*, adj. produced. *Sadbh°*, i.e. *sant-* (ptcple. pres. of 1. *as*), adj. true. Ptcple. of the fut. pass. **I.** *bhavitavya*, What is or ought to be, Chr. 50, 8; 58, 2; used as impersonal pass., Çâk. 22, 17, *bhavitavyaṁ tvayâ sahâyena mama*, You must become my helpmate; *avahitais bhavadbhiḥ*, You must be attentive, Vikr. 3, 9; *asmâbhis tathâ bhavitavyam*, We will fare thus, Hit. 16, 7, M.M. **II.** *bhavya*. **1.** What is or ought to be, Sâv. 5, 47. **2.** Being. **3.** Good, pleasant, Pańch. 215, 6; Lass. 92, 8; profitable, Pańch. 228, 24; proper, Pańch. 138, 11. **4.** True. m. A tree, Averhoa Carambola, Lass. 52, 12. f. *yâ*, A name of Umâ. n. **1.** Fruit. **2.** Existence. **Comp.** *A-*, adj. 1. what is or ought not to be, Pańch. 91, 6. 2. unhappy. 3. deceitful. 4. wicked, Râm. 3, 52, 14. **III.** *bhâvya*, **1.** What must or ought to be, Râm. 3, 49, 13; Bhartṛ. 2, 91; Pańch. 88, 19. **2.** To be investigated (from the Caus.). **Comp.** *A-*, adj. what is not to be, or not predestined to be, Bhartṛ. 2, 91. *Durbh°*, i.e. *dus-*, adj. difficult to be imagined, Mârk. P. 10, 7 (from the Caus.). Desider. *bubhûsha*. **1.** To wish to be or to live, MBh. 4. 678. **2.** To wish to obtain, to choose, MBh. 1, 7068. Caus. *bhâvaya*. **1.** To cause to exist, to produce, MBh. 1, 8419. **2.** To support, MBh. 3, 8763. **3.** To make manifest, Man. 8, 60. **4.** (i. 10), To (imagine, to) reflect, to consider, Râm. 2, 67, 20; Pańch. iii. d. 63; Râjat. 5, 125 (*bhâvita-âtman*, adj. One who reflects about the universal soul). **5.** (i. 10), To obtain, Râm. 1, 44, 48. **6.** (i. 10), † To purify. **7.** (i. 10), † To mix. *bhâvita*, **1.** Animated. **2.** Occupied with. **3.** Imagined. **4.** Acknowledged. **5.** Feigned, Daçak. in Chr. 187, 6. **6.** Obtained. **7.** Mixed. **8.** Infused. **9.** Perfumed.—With the prep. **अति** *ati*, To surpass, MBh. 3, 10731.—With the noun *a-darçana*, becoming **अदर्शनी** *adarçanî*, To become invisible, Pańch. 34, 24; 106, 20.—With *adhara*, becoming **अधरी** *adharî*, *adharîbhûta*, Put down, i.e. admitted, Yâjń. 2, 17 (cf. Roer, transl. n.).—With the prep. **अधि** *adhi*, *adhibhûta*, n. The Supreme Being, Bhag. 8, 4.—With **अनु** *anu*, **1.** To be present at (acc.), Nal. 5, 40. **2.** To feel, Man. 12, 17; Vikr. d. 110. **3.** To suffer, Daçak. in Chr. 195, 19. **4.** To enjoy, Pańch. 38, 5. **5.** To learn, Daçak. in Chr. 185, 23. **6.** To perceive, MBh. 3, 2112. Comp. ptcple. of the pf. pass. *an-anubhûta*, adj. Not perceived, Hit. 47, 18. —With **समनु** *sam-anu*, **1.** To enjoy together, Lass. 6, 4. **2.** To perceive, Ragh. 9, 48.—With *anu-guṇa*, becoming **अनुगुणी** *anuguṇî*, To increase in proportion (to the obstacle), Vikr. d. 49 (cf. *çataguṇî bhû*).—With **अन्तर्** *antar*, To be comprised in, Man. 12, 87. —With the noun *andha*, becoming **अन्धी** *andhî*, To become blind, Pańch. 200, 1. —With the prep. **अभि** *abhi*, **1.** To attain, Vikr. d. 38. **2.** To assail, Bhag. 1, 40. **3.** To overpower, Man. 7, 179. **4.** To surpass, Man. 7, 5. **5.** To spread over (acc.), MBh. 3, 10592. *abhibhûta*, **1.** Overpowered, Pańch. 169, 21; Vedântas. in Chr. 215, 11. **2.** Aggrieved, Pańch. 80, 10. **3.** Perplexed.—With **आ** *â*, To exist, to live, MBh. 1, 3608.— With the noun *âkula*, becoming **आकुली** *âkulî*, To be perplexed, Çâk. 29, 23. —With the indecl. **आविस्** *âvis*, To become visible. *âvirbhûta*, Appeared, Utt. Râmach. 100, 14; become visible, Vikr. d. 8; 78, 20.—With the prep. **उद्** *ud*, To spring up, to arise, Râjat. 5, 216. *udbhûta*, **1.** Born, produced. **2.** Proceeded, Ṛit. 1, 24. **3.** Lofty. **4.** Visible, present. **5.** Proportionate, Bhâshâp. 53; 54. Caus. **1.** To cause to exist, Bhaṭṭ. 17, 8. **2.** To bring to consciousness, Vedântas. in Chr. 206, 9. **3.** To apply, Ragh. 2, 62. *udbhâvita*, **1.** Neglected. **2.** Said.—With **प्रोद्** *pra-ud*, *prodbhûta*, **1.** Breaking forth, Lass. 11, 12. **2.** Proceeding, come, Pańch. i. d. 18.—With **समुद्** *sam-ud*, To spring up, to arise, Pańch. 42, 1. *samudbhûta*, Born, produced, Pańch. i. d. 392; 42, 1.—With the numeral *eka*, becoming **एकी** *ekî*, To unite, MBh. 1, 919—With *eka-chitta*, becoming **एकचित्ती** *ekachittî*, and *eka-mati*, becoming **एकमती** *ekamatî*, To become unanimous, Hit. 27, 3, M.M.; Pańch. 175, 19.—With *kaṭhora*, becoming **कठोरी** *kaṭhorî*, *kaṭhorîbhûta*, Grown sharp, hot, Utt. Râmach. 40, 9.—With *kuṇḍala*, becoming **कुण्डली** *kuṇḍalî*, To ringle, Bhâg. P. 5. 23, 5.—With *kshapaṇa*, becoming **क्षपणी** *kshapaṇî*, To become a Bauddha mendicant, Daçak. in Chr.

192, 16.—With *khila*, becoming खिली *khilî, khilîbhûta*, **1.** Wasted, impervious, Kumâras. 2, 45. **2.** Vanished, Çâk. d. 149.—With *guṇa*, becoming गुणी *guṇî, guṇîbhûta*, **1.** Made secondary, MBh. 2, 670. **2.** Become an ornament, Kâvyapr. 48, 7. **3.** Invested with attributes. **4.** Varied. **5.** Having a certain force or application (as a word) [gunated].—With *gochara*, becoming गोचरी *gocharî*, To become visible, Utt. Râmach. 155, 1.—With *ghana*, becoming घनी *ghanî, ghanîbhûta*, Thickened, become thick, Râm. 3, 5, 8. —With *chûrṇa*, becoming चूर्णी *chûrṇî*, To turn into dust, to be pounded, Vikr. d. 4.—With *chaura*, becoming चौरी To become a thief, Bhâg. P. 4, 18, 7. —With *jarjara*, becoming जर्जरी *jarjarî, jarjarîbhûta*, Decayed, Lass. 7, 9.—With *jhaṇajhaṇâ*, becoming झणझणी *jhaṇajhaṇî, -bhûta*, Rattling, MBh. 6, 738.—With तरुणी *taruṇî*, To become marriageable, Daçak. in Chr. 186, 22. —With the indecl. तिरस् *tiras*, To disappear, Bhâg. P. 9, 4, 53. Caus. To remove, Râm. 1, 44, 9.—With *tîvra*, becoming तीव्री *tîvrî, -bhûta*, Heavy, Râjat. 6, 99.—With तूष्णीम् *tûshṇîm*, To become silent, Pañch. 193, 12. *tûshṇîmbhûta*, Silent, MBh. 1, 7951.—With the noun *dûra*, becoming दूरी *dûrî*, To retire, Pañch. 19, 14 (*sarvair dûrîbhûtam*, All retired).—With *dṛiḍha*, becoming दृढी *dṛiḍhî*, To become strong, Pañch. iii. d. 258.—With *drava*, becoming द्रवी *dravî, dravîbhûta*, **1.** Become liquid, Mârk. P. 12, 38. **2.** Melted, Utt. Râmach. 60, 5.—With *dvaṁdva*, becoming द्वंद्वी *dvaṁdvî, -bhûta*, Engaged in close fight, MBh. 7, 3577.—With *dvaidha*, becoming द्वैधी *dvaidhî*, To become divided, Çâk. d. 50.—With *nava*, becoming नवी *navî*, To be renewed, Ragh. 12, 56.—With *nikaṭa*, becoming निकटी *nikaṭî, -bhûta*, Approached, Kathâs. 19, 87.—With *niḥsva*, i.e. *nis-sva*, becoming निःस्वी *niḥsvî*, To become poor, Daçak. in Chr. 193, 5.—With *nirâça*, i.e. *nis-* (cf. *âçâ*), becoming निराशी *nirâçî*, To become hopeless, Pañch. 21, 15.—With the prep. परा *parâ*, To perish, MBh. 1, 4167. *parâbhûta*, **1.** Defeated, Pañch. 151, 11. **2.** Humbled, treated with contempt, Pañch. 82, 7.—With the noun *parâñmukha*, i.e. *parâñch-mukha*, becoming पराङ्मुखी *parâñmukhî*, **1.** To turn away, to turn the back, Lass. 24, 20. **2.** To be disinclined, Mâlav. 68, 8. *parâñmukhîbhûta*, Being adverse, Pañch. 121, 16.—With the prep. परि *pari*, To despise, MBh. 3, 1025. **2.** To grieve, Pañch. 47, 2. **3.** To injure, Böhtl. Ind. Spr. 2375. Caus. To make known, Utt. Râmach. 177, 6.—With संपरि *sam-pari*, To despise, MBh. 3, 13230. —With the noun *paryutsuka*, becoming पर्युत्सुकी *paryutsukî*, To become very sad, Çâk. d. 99.—With *pâtra*, becoming पात्री *pâtrî*, To become a worthy person, MBh. 4, 1513.—With the prep. प्र *pra*, **1.** To spring up, Hit. i. d. 26, M.M.; to proceed, Hit. 13, 8; to rise, pr. 47, M.M. **2.** To be brought forth, MBh. 3, 17164. **3.** To appear, Megh. 15. **4.** To become prevalent, Hit. i. d. 86, M.M.; to be powerful. *pra bhavati + tarâm*, It is most powerful, Vikr. d. 156; with *na*, to be powerless, Pańch. 52, 5. **5.** To prevail over, Man. 5, 2; Böhtl. Ind. Spr. 814; to be master of (with gen.), Hit. i. d. 193, M.M. **6.** To be able, to serve (with inf. and dat.), Hit. i. d. 96, M.M.; Vikr. d. 9; 55; Ragh. 8, 44. *prabhûta*, **1.** Large, Pańch. 47, 25; much, Pańch. 69, 8; long, 4, 17. **2.** Abounding in, distinguished, Daçak. in Chr. 180, 15. **3.** Comparat. Very large, Pańch. 95, 24. **4.** Superl. Highest, Daçak. in Chr. 180, 15.—With *prakaṭa*, becoming प्रकटी *prakaṭi*, To become visible, Çiç. 9, 23; known, Pańch. 223, 19.—With *prachura*, becoming प्रचुरी *prachurî*, To increase, Çiç. 9, 20.—With *praṇayin*, becoming प्रणयी *praṇayi*, To become affectionate or attached to, Suçr. 1, 236, 17.—With *praṇidhi*, becoming प्रणिधी *praṇidhi*, To become a spy, Pańch. 172, 6.—With *pratyantara* (see s. v.), becoming प्रत्यन्तरी *pratyantarî*, To be near, Utt. Râmach. 53, 5.—With *preman-râçi*, becoming प्रेमराशी *premarâçî*, To become a heap, (a great) store of love, Megh. 111.—With प्रादुस् *prâdus*, To become manifest or visible, to appear, Pańch. 235, 22.—With बन्धकी *bandhakî*, To become a harlot, Râjat. 5, 466.—With *bahula*, becoming बहुली *bahulî*, To be multiplied, Pańch. ii. d. 187; *bahulîbhûta*, Generally known, Çâk. 79, 11.—With *bhasman*, becoming भस्मी *bhasmî*, To become mere ashes, Man. 4, 188; Pańch. iii. d. 155. *bhasmîbhûta*, Mere ashes, i.e. wholly worthless, Man. 3, 97.—With *bhṛitya*, becoming भृत्यी *bhṛityî*, To become a servant, Râjat. 5, 51.—With *manda*, becoming मन्दी *mandî*, *-bhûta*, Become slack or dull, tired, Johns. Sel. 15, 58.—With *malina*, becoming मलिनी *malinî*, To become soiled, Çâk. d. 176.—With *rahas*, becoming रही *rahî*, *rahîbhûta*, Solitary, alone.—With *râçi*, becoming राशी *râçî*, *-bhûta*, Heaped, Râjat. 5, 190.—With *vaça*, becoming वशी *vaçî*, *-bhûta*, Subject to another's will.—With the prep. वि *vi*, Caus. **1.** To trace out, Man. 8, 25. **2.** To observe, Çiç. 9, 81. **3.** To perceive, Vikr. 31, 6; Pańch. 198, 1; v. d. 7; to feel, Vikr. d. 132; to recognise, Vikr. 54, 12; pass. to appear, Pańch. 45, 13. **4.** To prove, Man. 8, 56. **5.** To decide, Pańch. 210, 10. *vibhâvita*, **1.** Seen, perceived, Vikr. d. 96 (*vibhâvita-chadeça*, That with whom is seen a part of a stolen object). **2.** Judged. **3.** Conceived. **4.** Established. **5.** Put right, Daçak. in Chr. 192, 14 (?). Comp. *A-*, 1. unobserved, Man. 7, 147. 2. not perceived, Çiç. 9, 40. Comp. ptcple. of the fut. pass. *a-vibhârya*, not to be perceived, Çiç. 9, 12. *Durv°*, i.e. *dus-*, difficult to be understood, Râm. 2, 24, 33.—With *vi-phala*, becoming विफली *viphalî*, To become fruitless, Pańch. 174, 12.—With *vi-shama*, i.e. *vi-sama*, becoming विषमी *vishamî*, To stumble, Çâk. d. 90.—With *vishaya*, becoming विषयी *vishayî*, To become the province, property, Pańch. 25, 9.—With *vaira*, becoming वैरी *vairî*, To be changed into hate, Çâk. d. 120.—With *vyakta* (vb. *vi-añj*), becoming व्यक्ती *vyaktî*, To become visible, Râjat. 5, 240.—With *vyâkula*, becoming व्याकुली *vyâkulî*, To become perplexed, Pańch. 46, 1 (*bhûtvâ*, against gramm.), anxious, Pańch. 142, 3.—With *çata-guṇa*, becoming शतगुणी *çataguṇî*, *-bhûta*, Become a hundred times as many, or stronger, Vikr. d. 49, v.r.—With *çithila*, becoming शिथिली *çithilî*, To become loosened, to slacken, Hit. iv. d. 79.—With *çiçira*, becoming शिशिरी *çiçirî*, To become cool, Utt. Râmach. 158, 10.—With *çuchi*, becoming शुची *çuchî*, To become pure, to purify one's self, Pańch. 221, 7.—With *çûdra*, becoming शूद्री *çûdrî*, To become a Çûdra, Man. 10, 92.—With *çyâma*, becoming श्यामी *çyâmî*, To become dark blue, Kir. 5, 37.—With *çreṇî*, becoming श्रेणी *çreṇî*, *çreṇî-bhûta*, Formed in lines, Megh. 22.—With *sajja*, becoming सज्जी *sajjî*, **1.** To be accoutred, Hit. 59, 9 (*sajjîbhûya*, in full decoration). **2.** To be ready, Hit. 76, 20.—With the prep. सम् *sam*, **1.** To be together, MBh. 1, 5658; to unite, Hit. 107, 19. **2.** To be composed, Man. 1, 27. **3.** To accrue, Man. 8, 255; Pańch. 192, 3. **4.** To meet with (instr.), Daçak. in Chr. 201, 6. **5.** To have sexual intercourse with (instr.), MBh. 1, 4398. **6.** To become, Chr. 63, 64. **7.** To spring up, to arise, to proceed, Vedântas. in Chr. 206, 17. **8.** To be engendered, Johns. Sel. 1, 2; to be born, Râm. 1, 43, 2. **9.** To take place, Chr. 39, 2; to happen, Hit. 17, 4, M.M. **10.** To be, Hit. 97, 17; to exist, Hit. 130, 12. **11.** To be adequate, Lass. 76, 16. **12.** To be able to exist, Matsyop. 12. **13.** To be able, Çiç. 1, 27. **14.** To be possible, Hit. 99, 6. *sambhûta*, **1.** Combined with. **2.** Adequate. **3.** Born. Caus. **1.** To cause to be with, to meet, MBh. 3, 1982. **2.** To cause to get, to deliver, Pańch. 84, 17; Ragh. 16, 40. **3.** To confide to, MBh. 1, 2088. **4.** To cause to exist, MBh. 1, 1425. **5.** To cause to recover, Utt. Râmach. 78, 13. **6.** To nourish, Man. 2, 142. **7.** To preserve, MBh. 1, 1343. **8.** To appoint, Pańch. ii. d. 25. **9.** To make, MBh. 3, 13316. **10.** To manifest, to show, Daçak. in Chr. 188, 12. **11.** To prove, Mâlav. 21, 17. **12.** To think, to represent, Çâk. 21, 6; to take for, Pańch. 78, 18. **13.** With *anyathâ*, To misunderstand, Çâk. 17, 5. **14.** To consider, Pańch. iii. d. 208; Ragh. 6, 42. **15.** To believe, Pańch. 111, 10. **16.** To honour, Bhartṛ. 2, 27; Utt. Râmach. 47, 14. **17.** To expect, Pańch. iv. d. 81. *sambhâvita*, **1.** Adequate, suited. **2.** Possible. **3.** Considered, reflected. **4.** Satisfied. Ptcple. of the fut. pass. *sambhâvya*, Suitable, Pańch. 117, 11. **Comp.** *A-*, adj. impossible, Pańch. 30, 8; v. d. 59.—With *su-varṇa*, becoming सुवर्णी *suvarṇî*, To turn into gold, Pańch. 192, 2.—With *stambha*, becoming स्तम्भी *stambhî*, To become a post, Hit. i. d. 29, M.M.—With *sthira*, becoming स्थिरी *sthirî*, To be calm, Lass. 43, 17.—With *sphâra*, becoming स्फारी *spharî*, To become large, to spread, Häberl. Anth. 217, 8; Pańch. v. d. 22; Mṛichchh. 49, 6 (to show a hidden property in a magical way, by becoming large, or by throbbing).—Cf. φύω, φύλη, φώς, φωτός (cf. *bhavant*), probably φῖτυ, φιτύω, perhaps πρές-βυς; Lat. fio, fui, facio (causal), fecundus, fetus, fetare, perhaps femur, femen; O.H.G. pim, pis, etc.; A.S. beón, beó, bist, etc.; Goth. ga-bauan; O.H.G. bûwan, bûan, pu, bûr; A.S. búan, bur; O.H.G. bûari.

2. भू *bhû*, f. **1.** The earth, Pańch. iii. 77. **2.** pl. Landed property, land,

Hit. iv. d. 121. 3. Ground, Megh. 65 (at the end of a comp. adj.). 4. Site, place, Kir. 5, 5. 5. Sacrificial fire. 6. Nom. sing. *bhûs*, indecl. 1. Earth, Man. 2, 76. 2. Hell. —Comp. *Pâna-*, f. a drinking-room, Kathâs. 21, 10. *Malla-*, f. an arena for athletic contests. *Parichita-*, adj. of which the places are known, Utt. Râmach. 42, 11.

भूक *bhûka*, I. m. Darkness. II. n. 1. A hole. 2. The head of a fountain. 3. Time.

भूकल *bhûkala*, m. A restive horse.

भूक्षित् *bhû-kshit*, m. A hog.

भूचर *bhû-chara*, adj. Moving on the ground, Pañch. 114, 21.

भूतघ्न *bhûta-ghna*, I. m. 1. A camel. 2. Garlic. II. f. *ghnî*, Holy basil.

भूति *bhû+ti*, f. 1. State of being. 2. Production, birth. 3. Prosperity, Pañch. iii. d. 131; personified, Râm. 3, 52, 27. 4. Wealth, Man. 3, 59. 5. Power, dignity. 6. Superhuman power, as attainable by the practice of austere and magical rites. 7. The rut of elephants. 8. A decoration of elephants, consisting in many-coloured stripes, Megh. 19 (Sch.; read *maṇḍanam* and *gajamaṇḍanam* instead of *maṇḍalam*). 9. Ashes. 10. Fried meat. — Comp. *Ranga-* f. the day of full moon in the month Âçvina. *Viyadbh°*, i.e. *viyat-*, f. darkness.—Cf. φύσις.

भूत्तम *bhûttama*, i.e. *bhû-uttama*, n. Gold.

भूधर *bhû-dhara*, m. 1. A mountain, Pañch. 157, 25. 2. A kind of chemical or medicinal apparatus; a sand-bath in which a covered crucible is placed, and the fire is lighted above as well as below it.

भूध्र *bhûdhra*, i.e. *bhû-dhṛi+a*, m. A mountain.

भूप *bhû-pa* (vb. 2. *pâ*), m. A king, prince, Daçak. in Chr. 193, 22.

भूभुज् *bhû-bhuj*, m. A king, Pañch. iii. d. 86.

भूभृत् *bhû-bhṛi+t*, m. 1. A king, Râjat, 5, 46. 2. A mountain, Pañch. i. d. 372.—Comp. *Kula-*, m. a principal mountain, Ragh. 17, 78.

भूमन् I. i.e. *bhû+man*, n. The earth, Chr. 291, 5=Rigv. i. 85, 5. II. i.e. *bahu+iman*, m. Multitude, majority, Râjat. 5, 165.—Cf. Lat. hŭmus, hŭmilis.

भूमय *bhû+maya*, I. adj., f. *yî*, Made or consisting of earth. II. f. *yî*, A name of *Chhâyâ*, or shadow personified, the wife of the sun.

भूमि *bhûmi* (also *bhûmî*, i.e. *bhû+ma+î*, cf. I. *bhûman*), f. 1. The earth, Pañch. 165, 16. 2. Land, estate, Pañch. iii. d. 92; domain (where one governs or works), Bhâg. P. 5, 11, 9. 3. Place, Pañch. 161, 13; site.—Comp. *A-*, f. 1. anything but earth. 2. an unsuitable place, Çâk. 101, 19. 3. no object for, Çâk. 97, 9 (exceeding). *Ati-*, f. highest degree, Amar. 80; Utt. Râmach. 82, 7. *Antar-*, f. the interior of the earth, Arj. 10, 27; Sund. 2, 8. *Karma(n)-*, f. the land of holy works, Âryâvarta, or the central part of India, Râm. 2, 109, 28. *Janma(n)-*, f. home, Pañch. v. d. 25. *Pâna-*, f. a drinking-room, Râm. 5, 14, 39. *Malla-*, f. an arena for athletic contests. *Badhya-* (vb. *vadh*), f. place of execution, Hit. 63, 6. *Ranga-*, f. 1. a field of battle, Pañch. 35, 3. 2. an arena, Johns. Sel. 9, 11. 3. a stage, a place where dancing, etc., is exhibited. *Vâsa-*, f. a dwelling-place, Hit. 38, 2, M.M. *Viçvâsa-*, f. a person worthy of confidence, Hit. 18, 7, M.M. *Saṁketa-*, f. place of assignation, Lass. 24, 15. *Sthâna-*, f. dwelling-place, a palace (?), Lass. 28, 10. *Sneha-*, f. one worthy of love, Mâlat. 83, 11. *Siddha-*, f. the country in which the Siddhas live, Pañch. 242, 5.

भूमिका *bhûmi + kâ*, f. **1.** Change of costume in order to represent a different character on the stage. **2.** Decorating images, temples, gateways, etc. **3.** A story; *grihoparibhûmikâyâm âruḍhaḥ*, He mounted to the upper story of the house, Çukas. cod. Petersb. p. 31, b. **4.** A preface to a book.—Comp. *Chatur-bhûmika*, adj. having four stories, Pañch. 228, 11. *Sapta(n)-*, adj. having seven stories, 44, 28.

भूमिज *bhûmi-ja*, I. adj. Born on the earth. II. m. **1.** The planet Mars. **2.** Hell. III. f. *jâ*, Sîtâ, the wife of Râma.

भूमिष्ठ *bhûmishṭha*, i.e. *bhûmi-stha*, adj. Standing or staying on the earth, Chr. 27, 1.

भूमिस्पृश् *bhûmi-spṛiç*, m. **1.** A man, mankind. **2.** A Vaiçya. **3.** A thief, one who creeps along the ground to carry off his plunder. **4.** A blind man. **5.** A cripple.

भूय *bhû + ya*, n. State.—Comp. *Brahma(n)-*, n. identification with Brahman, ultimate happiness, Man. 1, 98, 12, 102. *Râja(n)-*, n. royalty.

भूयंस् *bhûyaṁs*, see *bahu*.

भूयस्त्व *bhûyastva*, i.e. *bhûyaṁs + tva*, n. State of being more or greater, Bhâshâp. 131.

भूयिष्ठ *bhûyishṭha*, see *bahu*.

भूरि *bhûri* (probably *bahu-rai*, n., i.e. *bahu-ri*), I. adj. Much, Pañch. i. d. 23; many, Râjat. 5, 215; Kathâs. 22, 96. II. adv. **1.** Much, exceeding, Pañch. i. d. 213; Bhartṛ. 2, 62. **2.** Frequently, repeatedly, Chr. 287, 2 = Rigv. i. 48, 2. III. m. **1.** Brahman. **2.** Vishṇu. **3.** Çiva. **4.** A day. IV. n. Gold.

भूर्ज *bhûrja*, m. A kind of birch; its leaf or bark used for writing on, Vikr. 30, 11.—Cf. probably O.H.G. bircha; A.S. byrc, birce.

भूर्णि *bhûrṇi*, i.e. *bhṛi + ni*, f. The earth.

भूर्लोक *bhû + s-loka*, m. The earth.

भूष् *BHÛSH*, i. 1 and 10, Par. To decorate, to adorn, Man. 3, 55.—With the prep. **वि** *vi*, The same, Chr. 296, 4 = Rigv. i. 112, 4; Bhartṛ. 2, 16; Pañch. 256, 3.

भूषण *bhûshaṇa*, i.e. *bhûsh + ana*, n. Ornament, Hit. ii. d. 71; 171.—Comp. *Para-*, adj., Hit. iv. d. 121; false reading for *pari-*, q. cf. *Maṅgala-mâtra-*, adj., f. *ṇâ*, only adorned with turmeric, Vikr. d. 53.

भूषा *bhûsh + â*, f. Adorning, ornament, Râm. 3, 49, 27.

भूष्णु *bhûshṇu*, i.e. *bhû + snu*, adj. **1.** Being. **2.** Being well. **3.** One who desires bliss, Man. 4, 135.

भूस्तृण *bhû + s-tṛiṇa* (?), n. A fragrant grass, Andropogon schaenanthus, Man. 6, 14.

भृ *BHṚI*, i. 1, and ii. 3, *bibhṛi*, Par. Âtm. **1.** To bear, to hold, Vikr. d. 140; Chr. 16, 17. **2.** To wear, Man. 6, 6. **3.** Âtm. To gain, Chr. 291, 13 = Rigv. i. 64, 13. **4.** To possess, MBh. 3, 2583; to have, 2, 57. **5.** To form,

Râjat. 5, 332. **6.** To nourish, to maintain, Daçak. in Chr. 188, 5. **7.** i. 1, Âtm. To hire, Nal. 15, 4. **8.** To support, Man. 9, 95. **9.** To fill, Hit. 2, 34. Ptcple. of the pf. pass. *bhṛita.* **1.** Hired. **2.** Having, being possessed of. **3.** Filled. m. A servant. **Comp.** *A-*, adj. not paid, Man. 8, 231. *Kshîra-*, adj. paid with milk, ib. *Bhṛitya*, see s. v.—With the prep. अति *ati*, *atibhṛita* (rather *bhṛita* with *ati*), **1.** Carefully protected. **2.** Filled, Kir. 5, 20.—With आ *â*, To bring near, to bestow, Lass. 99, 2= Rigv. v. 9, 7.—With नि *ni*, *nibhṛita*, **1.** Modest, humble; *°tam*, humbly, Pańch. 162, 24. **2.** Unmoved, Çâk. d. 8. **3.** Hidden, Pańch. 46, 13; 193, 7. **4.** *°tam*, adv. Hidden, Pańch. 105, 4; secretly, Man. 9, 263. **5.** *°tam*, adv. with *vi-dhâ*, To make hidden, to shut, Pańch. 186, 8. **6.** Lonely, solitary, Megh. 83; *°tam* with *kṛi*, To dismiss all but one, Hit. 56, 19. **Comp.** *A-*, adj. immodest, bold, Megh. 69. *Su-*, adj. very lonely. *°tam*, adv. 1. secretly, Hit. 86, 6. 2. privately, Hit. 73, 16 (in a very low voice?).—With प्र *pra*, To offer, Chr. 291, 1.—With सम् *sam*, **1.** To bring together, Râm. 1, 11, 13. **2.** To accomplish, Vikr. 85, 17; d. 157. **3.** To nourish, Râm. 1, 52, 8. *sambhṛita*, **1.** Collected, all, Vikr. d. 38. **2.** Gained, got. **3.** Composed, Hit. iv. d. 68. **4.** Filled. **5.** Nourished, Hit. iii. d. 125 (but cf. Böhtl. Ind. Spr. 3272). **6.** Brought, put, Megh. 44.—Cf. φέρω, φόρτος, φορμός, φωριαμός, φάρετρα, φᾶρος, δί-φρος, δι-φθέρα; Lat. fero; Goth. bairan; A.S. beran; Goth. barms; A.S. bearm; Goth. barn; A.S. bearn; byrdhen; Goth. briggan; A.S. bringan.

† भ्रंश् *BHṚIṂÇ*, i. 1 and 10, Par. To speak, to shine.

भृकुंश *bhṛikuñça*, and भृकुंस *bhṛikuñsa*, भ्रकुंश and °स *bhrakuñça* and *°sa*, and भ्रुकुंश and °स *bhrukuñça*, *°sa*, and भ्रूकुंश, °स *bhrûkuñça*, *°sa*, m. A male actor in female apparel.

भृकुटि *bhṛikuṭi*, see *bhrûkuṭi.*

† भृक्ष् *BHṚIKSH*, v. r. of *bhaksh.*

भृगु *bhṛigu*, m. **1.** The name of a Muni, Chr. 17, 29. **2.** Jamadagni. **3.** Çiva. **4.** Çukra. **5.** A cliff, a precipice. **6.** Table-land. **7.** pl. The descendants of Bhṛigu.

भृङ्ग *bhṛiṅga*, probably *bhram-ga*, I. m., and f. *gî* (Kathâs. 22, 103). **1.** A large bee, Ragh. 8, 52. **2.** A wasp. **3.** The fork-tailed shrike, Lanius cærulescens, Ṛit. 6, 24 (cf. Lass. 52, 18). **4.** A golden vase. **5.** A libertine. **II.** n. **1.** A plant, Woody cassia. **2.** Another, Verbesina prostrata Roxb.

भृङ्गक *bhṛiṅga+ka*, m. A bird, a sort of shrike.

भृङ्गार *bhṛiṅgâra* (cf. *bhṛiṅga*), I. m. A golden vase. **II.** n. Gold. **III.** f. *rî*, A cricket.

† भृज् *BHṚIJ*, i. 1, Âtm. To parch, to fry; cf. *bhrajj.*

भृज्जन *bhṛijjana*, i.e. *brajj+ana*, n. A frying-pan.

† भृड् *BHṚIḌ*, i. 6, Par. To dive.

ऽभृत् *-bhṛi+t*, latter part of comp. nouns, Bearing, nourishing, protecting; e.g. *a-pâtra-*, adj. Supporting unworthy ones, Hit. ii. d. 147. *gadâ-*, m. **1.** A mace-bearer. **2.** A name of Kṛishṇa,

Bhâg. P. 1, 13, 9. *chakra-*, m. Vishṇu, Râjat. 1, 38. *tanu-*, m. **1.** A living creature. **2.** A man, mankind, Bhartṛ. 3, 36. *tapobhṛit*, i.e. *tapas-*, m. An ascetic, Hariv. 4849. *deha-*, m. **1.** A living creature. **2.** A man, mankind, Bhâg. P. 7, 7, 46. **3.** Epithet of Çiva, MBh. 13, 1067. *dharaṇî-*, m. **1.** A king. **2.** A mountain. *dharâ-*, m. A mountain, Arj. 7, 27. *dharma-*, **1.** m. Supporter of right, an epithet of kings, MBh. 1, 4766. **2.** m. A proper name. *nava-çaçi(n)-*, Bearing the young moon, epithet of Çiva, Megh. 44. *prâṇa-*, adj. Living, a living creature, Hit. i. d. 111, M.M.; a man, mankind. *bhû-*, see s.v.

भृतक *bhṛita+ka* (see *bhṛi*), **1.** m. A servant, Man. 6, 45. **2.** (n.) Wages, Man. 3, 156 (or 'Hired').—**Comp.** *Madhyama-*, m. a husbandman.

भृति *bhṛi+ti*, f. **1.** Nourishment, Hit. ii. d. 32. **2.** Wages, hire, Man. 8, 231. **3.** Service, Nal, 8, 25. **4.** Capital, principal.—**Comp.** *Piṇḍa-*, f. livelihood, Râm. 2, 26, 37 Gorr. *Sudhâ-*, m. 1. sacrifice. 2. the moon. *Hala-*, f. agriculture.—Cf. Lat. fors; A.S. beordh.

भृत्य *bhṛitya*, I. ptcple. fut. pass. of *bhṛi*, To be nourished. II. m. A servant, Pańch. 175, 16; i. d. 325. **III.** f. *yâ*, Hire.—**Comp.** *Ku-* and *kim-*, m. a wicked servant, Pańch. 83, 18; Hit. ii. d. 31 (read *kiṁbhṛitya*). *Kumâra-bhṛityâ*, f. the fostering of a child, Ragh. 3, 12. *Protkaṭa-*, m. a favourite, Pańch. 156, 19. *Mûla-*, m. an old servant, Hit. ii. d. 129.

भृत्यता *bhṛitya+tâ*, f., and **भृत्यत्व** *bhṛitya+tva*, n. Servitude, service, dependence, Pańch. 24, 11; Hit. ii. d. 37.

भृमि *bhṛimi*, i.e. *bhram+i*, m. A whirlwind.

† **भृश्** *BHṚIÇ*, i. 4, Par. To fall; cf. *bhruṁç*.

भृश *bhṛiça* (perhaps akin to *bhraṁç*), I. adj., comparat. *bhraçiyaṁs*, superl. *bhraçishṭha*, Much, exceeding. II. °*çam*, adv. **1.** Much, Pańch. iii. d. 188. **2.** Exceedingly, violently, Pańch. iii. d. 183. **3.** Superiority, better. **4.** Repeatedly, often, Pańch. iii. d. 13. **5.** Beautifully. **6.** Quickly, Chr. 7, 13; 25, 15. **7.** In the beginning of comp. *bhṛiça-*, e.g. Chr. 31, 16.—**Comp.** *Su-*, adj. much, exceeding. °*çam*, adv. much, excessively.

भृशता *bhṛiça + tâ*, f. Violence, Ragh. 11, 58.

भृष्टि *bhṛishṭi*, f., i.e. *bhrajj+ti*, **1.** Frying. **2.** A lonely garden.—**Comp.** *Sahasra-*, adj. having a thousand points (vb. *hṛish+ti*), Chr. 292, 9= Rigv. i. 85, 9.

† **भॄ** *BHṜÎ*, ii. 9, *bhṛiṇâ*, *bhṛiṇî*, Par. **1.** To blame. **2.** To bear (cf. *bhṛi*). **3.** To fry. **4.** To bend, to be crooked.

भेक *bheka* (vb. *bhî*), I. m. **1.** A frog, Pańch. 81, 13. **2.** A cloud. II. f. *kî*, The female frog, or a small frog.

भेड *bheḍa*, m. A ram.

भेत्तृ *bhettṛi*, i.e. *bhid+tṛi*, I. m., f. *trî*, and n. Who or what divides, breaks, etc. II. m. **1.** One who breaks down, Man. 9, 289. **2.** A separator, divider. **3.** One who wounds, Man. 8, 284. **4.** A traitor.

भेद *bheda*, i.e. *bhid+a*, m. **1.** Breaking, Vikr. d. 26. **2.** Dividing, division, Pańch. 248, 19. **3.** Separating, Pańch. 156, 19; separation, Hit. pr. d. 9, M.M. **4.** A chasm, a fissure, a cleft, Vikr. 69, 8; a wound, Hit. ii. d. 138 (and betrayal). **5.** Creating divisions,

Man. 7, 198. 6. Disunion, Pañch. iv. d. 74. 7. Betrayal, Pañch. 65, 19. 8. Difference, Pañch. 199, 20. 9. Kind, Hit. iv. d. 124.—Comp. *A-*, m. undividedness, Hit. iii. d. 79. *Anyonya-*, m. separation from each other, Hit. 76, 12. *Gati-*, m. going with great strides, Çâk. 93, 12. *Granthi-*, m. a cutpurse, Man. 9, 277. *Durbh°*, i.e. *dus-*, adj. difficult to be separated or divided, Pañch. ii. d. 36. *Svara-*, m. difference of voice, Pañch. 37, 25; 199, 20 (different, changed voice).

भेदक *bhedaka*, i.e. *bhid + aka*, m. 1. One who breaks, Man. 8, 284 (*asthi-*). 2. One who breaks open, 9, 280. 3. One who scratches, 8, 284 (*tvach-*). 4. One who diverts (watercourses), Man. 3, 163. 5. A mischief-maker.—Comp. *Gaṇḍa-*, m. a cutpurse, Çâk. 74, 14 (Prâkṛ.).

भेदतस् *bheda + tas*, adv. According to the difference, Bhag. 18, 19.

भेदन *bhedana*, i.e. *bhid + ana*, n. 1. Dividing. 2. Piercing, Man. 9, 286.—Comp. *Puṭa-*, n. a town, MBh. 1, 3978.

भेदिन् *bhedin*, i.e. *bhid + in*, adj., f. *nî*. 1. Dividing, breaking, Man. 8, 218. 2. Wounding, Hit. iv. d. 82.—Comp. *Marma(n)-*, adj. piercing the vitals, fatal, Chr. 29, 33. *Vṛiksha-*, m. 1. a carpenter's chisel. 2. a hatchet.

भेरण्ड *bheraṇḍa*, see *bhâraṇḍa*.

भेरि and **भेरी** *bherî*, f. A kettle-drum, Pañch. 20, 7; Bhag. 1, 13.

भेरुण्ड *bheruṇḍa*, I. (vb. *bhî*), adj. Formidable. II. m. A form of Çiva. III. f. *ḍâ*, One of the Yakshiṇîs or female attendants on Durgâ. IV. n. (vb. *bhṛi*), Conception.

भेल *bhela*, i.e. *bhî + la*, I. adj. 1. Timid. 2. Ignorant. 3. Tall. II. m. 1. A raft. 2. The name of a Muni.

† **भेष्** *BHESH*, i. 1, Par. Âtm. 1. To fear (cf. *bhî*, Caus.). 2. To go (?).

भेषज *bheshaja*, i.e. *bhishaj + a* (anomal.), n. 1. A medicine, a drug, a remedy, Pañch. ii. d. 59; Nal. 9, 30. 2. Help (against, gen.), Pañch. 184, 19. 3. A kind of fennel, Nigella indica.

भैक्ष *bhaiksha*, and **भैक्ष्य** *bhaikshya*, i.e. *bhikshâ + a* or *ya*, n. 1. Begging, Man. 2, 48 (*ksha*); Lass. 76, 4 (*ya*). 2. Living by alms, Pañch. i. d. 312 (*ya*). 3. What is collected by begging, alms, food, Man. 5, 129 (*ya*).

भैमी *bhaimî*, i.e. *bhîma* (a proper name), *+ a + î*, patronym., f. Damayantî, daughter of Bhîma, Nal. 1, 12.

भैरव *bhairava*, i.e. *bhîru + a*, I. adj. 1. Formidable, horrid, Râm. 3, 50, 21. 2. Miserable, Râjat. 5, 408. II. m. 1. Çiva, Râjat. 5, 55. 2. The name of a river. 3. A musical mode. III. f. *vî*, Durgâ. IV. n. Horror.

भैषज *bhaishaja*, i.e. *bhishaj + a*, I. n. A medicament. II. m. (? ÇKD. n.), A sort of quail.

भैषज्य *bhaishajya*, i.e. *bhishaj + ya*, I. n. A medicament, a drug, Hit. i. d. 110, M.M.; a remedy. II. m. The descendant of a physician.

भो *bho*, curtailed *bhos*, A vocative particle (properly, Sir!), O! Pañch. 44, 14; Ho! there! Pañch. 161, 17; also repeated, *bhobho*, Ho! ho! Pañch. 35, 12; 161, 15.

भोक्तुकाम *bhoktukâma*, i.e. *bhoktum* (vb. 2. *bhuj*), *-kâma*, adj. Wishing to eat, Hiḍ. 3, 17.

भोक्तृ *bhoktṛi*, i.e. 2.*bhuj*+*tṛi*, I. m., f. *trî*, and n. One who eats, Hit. i. d. 53, M.M.; or enjoys, Çâk. d. 43; Vedântas. in Chr. 211, 5. II. m. 1. An adverse possessor, Man. 8, 148. 2. A husband.

भोक्तृत्व *bhoktṛi*+*tva*, n. 1. Enjoyment, perception, Bhag. 13, 20. 2. Possession.

भोग *bhoga*, i.e. 1. and 2.*bhuj*+*a*, m. 1. A snake's body, Utt. Râmach. 43, 4. 2. A snake. 3. A snake's expanded hood, Pańch. 53, 6. 4. An army in column. 5. Nourishing, cherishing, food, Bhag. 2, 5. 6. Pleasure, Râm. 3, 53, 3. 7. Enjoyment, Bhartṛ. 2, 35; Pańch. ii. d. 131; feasting, Hit. ii. d. 99. 8. Adverse enjoyment (usufruct), Man. 8, 149. 9. Possession. 10. Wealth. 11. Hire. 12. The hire of dancing girls. — Comp. *Kâma-*, m. sensual enjoyment, Râm. 3, 37, 2. *Nâga-*, m. a kind of snake, Râm. 5, 74, 31. *Nirbh°*, i.e. *nis-*, adj. not attached to pleasure, MBh. 12, 2332.

भोगकर *bhoga-kara*, adj., f. *rî*, Affording enjoyment, Bhartṛ. 2, 17.

भोगवन्त् *bhoga*+*vant*, I. adj., f. *vatî*. 1. Having enjoyment. 2. Delightful. II. m. 1. A snake. 2. Dancing. 3. Singing. III. f. *vatî*, 1. The capital of the snakes, Bhâg. P. 4, 25, 15. 2. The Gaṅgâ of the lower regions.

भोगार्ह *bhogârha*, i.e. *bhoga-arha*, n. Wealth.

भोगिक *bhogika*, i.e. *bhoga*+*ika*, n. A groom.

भोगिन् *bhogin*, i.e. *bhoga*+*in*, I. adj., f. *nî*. 1. Enjoying. 2. Abounding in enjoyments, Bhag. 16, 14. 3. Having enjoyments and an expanded hood, Pańch. i. d. 73. II. m. 1. A snake, Bhartṛ. 2, 82. 2. A king, Hit. iii. d. 58. 3. The head man of a village. 4. A barber. 5. A person who accumulates money for a particular expenditure. III. f. *nî*. 1. The capital of the serpents. 2. A royal concubine. —Comp. *Kṛishṇa-*, m. a sort of black snake, Gît. 6, 12.

भोज *bhoja*, i.e. *bhuj*+*a*, m. 1. A cowherd. 2. The name of a country. 3. The name of a king, Johns. Sel. 19, 91.

भोजन *bhojana*, i.e. 2.*bhuj*+*ana*, n. 1. Enjoying, Pańch. 61, 22. 2. Eating, Pańch. 245, 22. 3. Food, Pańch. 138, 2.—Comp. *A-*, n. abstaining from food, Man. 11, 166. *Ati-*, n. excessive eating, Man. 2, 57. *Eka-*, n. 1. eating once a day, MBh. 13, 5161. 2. eating in company, MBh. 13, 6238. *Kṛimi-*, I. adj. one who feeds upon worms, Bhâg. P. 5, 26, 18. II. m. the name of a hell, Bhâg. P. 5, 26, 7. *Mlechchha-*, I. m. wheat. II. n. half-ripe barley. *Saha-*, n. eating with somebody, Lass. 18, 2.

भोजस् *bhojas*, i.e. 2.*bhuj*+*as* in *viçva-*, adj. Yielding all the enjoyments, Lass. 101, 5=Rigv. vii. 16, 2.

भोजिन् *bhojin*, i.e. 2.*bhuj*+*in*, adj. One who eats, Man. 4, 212.—Comp. *Gṛiha-*, m. a house-mate, Râjat. 5, 402. *Bhujaṅga-*, m. the boa constrictor. *Çashpa-*, adj. sbst. a beast feeding on grass, Pańch. 25, 6.

भोज्यता *bhojya*+*tâ* (vb. 2.*bhuj*), f. Condition of being eaten, Pańch. 193, 21.

भोलि *bholi*, m. A camel.

भोस् *bhos*, an old voc. sing. of *bhavant*. 1. A vocative particle, Man. 2, 124; Ho! there! repeated, *bhobhos*,

O! Hit. 10, 6, MM. **2.** An interrogative particle, Vikr. 85, 20. **3.** Interj. of grief, Oh! Hit. 71, 3, M.M.

भौजङ्ग *bhaujaṅga*, i.e. *bhujaṁga* + *a*, adj., f. *gî*, Like a snake, Pańch. iii. d. 18.

भौत *bhauta*, i.e. *bhûta* + *a* (vb. *bhû*), I. adj. **1.** Relating to spirits, Man. 3, 70. **2.** Demoniac. **3.** Elemental. **4.** Relating to existing beings. II. m. **1.** An attendant upon idols. **2.** A worshipper of sprites.

भौतिक *bhautika*, i.e. *bhûta* + *iha* (vb. *bhû*), I. adj. **1.** Relating or appertaining to spirits, Man. 3, 174. **2.** Elemental. **3.** Existing. II. m. Çiva.

भौम *bhauma*, i.e. *bhûmi* + *a*, I. adj. **1.** Relating to the earth, rising from the ground, Man. 11, 155. **2.** Terrestrial. **3.** Relating to the planet Mars, Lass. 16, 16. II. m. **1.** The planet Mars, Pańch. 50, 20. **2.** Hell. III. f. *mî*, A name of Sîtâ.—Comp. *Antar-*, adj. being or living in the interior of the earth, Râm. 1, 42, 3. *Bahu-*, adj. having many stories. *Sapta(n)-*, adj. having seven stories, Râm. 5, 10, 11 (? cf. my translation of the Pańch. n. 208, and *bhûmikâ*).

भौरिक *bhaurika*, i.e. *bhûri* + *ika*, m. The superintendent of gold in a royal treasury (cf. *bhârika*).

भ्यस् *BHYAS*, i. 1, Âtm. To fear, to tremble (cf. *bhî*).

भ्रंश् *BHRAṀÇ*, and (erroneously)

भ्रंस् *BHRAṀS*, i. 4, *bhraçya* (cf. *bhraç*), *bhrasya*, Par. (also Âtm., e.g. Pańch. iv. d. 39), and † i. 1, Par. Âtm. **1.** To fall, Sund. 1, 15; to fall down, Pańch, i. d. 146. **2.** To be lost, Râm. 3, 54, 20. **3.** To run away, to flee from (abl.), Bhaṭṭ. 14, 105. **4.** To be deprived (with abl.), Man. 7, 111; Pańch. iv. d. 39 (with *s* and Âtm.). Ptcple. of the pf. pass. *bhrashṭa*. **1.** Fallen, Hit. i. d. 168 (*sthâna-*, adj. Having lost their rank). **2.** Lost. **3.** Deprived of, Bhag. 6, 11. **4.** Deviated, Pańch. 228, 14. **5.** Fallen from virtue, wicked. Comp. *Bhaya-*, adj. put to flight. Caus. *bhraṁçaya*. **1.** To expel, MBh. 3, 8759. **2.** To deprive, MBh. 3, 1571. *bhraṁçita*, Deprived, Chr. 48, 2.—With the prep. **अप** *apa*, *apabhrashṭa*, Corrupted (as speech), Kathâs. 17, 41.—With **परि** *pari*, To be deprived (with abl.), Hit. i. d. 128. *paribhrashṭa*, **1.** Fallen, Pańch. 188, 15. **2.** Degraded. **3.** Deprived of (instr.), Pańch. iii. d. 55; Man. 10, 20. **4.** Lost, Nal. 18, 10.—With **प्र** *pra*, **1.** To fall, Ragh. 14, 54 (Calc.). **2.** To be deprived, Mṛichchh. 14, 12 (Calc.). *prabhrashṭa*, **1.** Fallen, dropping, fallen off. **2.** Broken. Caus. To throw down from (abl.), Ragh. 13, 36 (Calc.). *prabhraṁçita*, Expelled, MBh. 3, 601.—With **वि** *vi*, *vibhrashṭa*, **1.** Broken off, or from. **2.** Fallen. **3.** Separated. **4.** Deprived, MBh. 3, 3. **5.** Lost. Caus. To deprive, Chr. 21, 6.—Cf. A.S. hreósan and reosan, To fall; Goth. ur-risan; A.S. arisan, To rise; Goth. us-hrisjan and af-hrisjan (Caus.), To cast off.

भ्रंश *bhraṁç* + *a*, m. **1.** Falling. **2.** Declining from a height, or from propriety, ruin, Bhag. 2, 63. **3.** Falling off, Megh. 2. **4.** Abandoning, dropping, Pańch. iii. d. 246; desertion, Pańch. 145, 10. **5.** Losing, Pańch. 68, 22; loss, Râjat. 5, 307; Hit. iii. d. 5 (*sthâna-bhraṁçaṁ yayuḥ*, They did lose their nest).—Comp. *Jâti-*, m. Loss of caste, Man. 11, 67.

भ्रंशिन् *bhraṁç*+*in*, **भ्रंसिन्** *bhraṁs*+*in*, adj., f. *nī*. **1.** Falling, Megh. 30; Çâk. d. 7. **2.** Causing to fall (*sva-artha-*, injuring, or detrimental to, our interest), Pañch. 248, 18.—**Comp.** *A-*, adj. not falling, durable, Pañch. iii. d. 18.

भ्रंस् *BHRAṀS*, **भ्रंसिन्** *bhraṁsin*, see *bhraṁç*, *bhraṁçin*.

भ्रकुंश and **°स** *bhrakuṁça*, *°sa*, see *bhṛikuṁça*.

भ्रकुटि *bhrakuṭi*, see *bhrûkuṭi*.

† **भ्रक्ष्** *BHRAKSH*, v.r. of *bhaksh*.

भ्रज्ज् *BHRAJJ*, i. 6, *bhṛijja*, Par. Âtm. To boil or fry, Bhaṭṭ. 14, 86; the base of many forms is *bharj*. Ptcple. of the pf. pass. *bhṛishṭa*. **Comp.** *Tila-*, n. fried grains of sesame, MBh. 13, 5025.—Cf. Lat. frigere, frictus, frixus (=*bhṛikta*, see *bhṛij*); φρύγω; O.H.G. briuwan; A.S. briwan; and O.N. brugga, To brew.

† **भ्रण्** *BHRAṆ*, i. 1, Par. To sound (cf. *bhram* and *raṇ*).

भ्रभङ्ग *bhrabhaṅga*, m. A frown (cf. *bhrû-bhaṅga*, s.v. *bhaṅga*, and *bhrakuṁça*, *bhrakuṭi*).

भ्रम् *BHRAM*, i. 1 and 4, *bhrâmya*, Par. (in epic poetry also Âtm., MBh. 3, 12228), originally, The flying about and humming of insects. **1.** To turn round, to move circularly, to whirl, Pañch. v. d. 20. **2.** † To be unsteady or unfixed. **3.** To stray, to roam, to wander, Pañch. 43, 4; i. d. 446; to go astray, Pañch. v. d. 68 (Âtm.). **4.** To wander over (acc.), MBh. 1, 5184. **5.** To surround, Râjat. 5, 146. **6.** To mistake. **7.** † To be ignorant. Ptcple. of the pf. pass. *bhrânta*. **1.** Being wandered over (with acc.), Bhartṛ. 3, 4. **2.** Running, Arj. 4, 38; rolling, Chr. 35, 2. **3.** Whirled. **4.** Confused, Râm. 3, 55, 36. **5.** Blundering. n. Roaming, Bhartṛ. 2, 11. Caus. *bhramaya* (in epic poetry also *bhrâmaya*, also Pañch. 263, 8, or i. 4, Âtm.). **1.** To turn round, Bhag. 18, 61; to whirl, MBh. 2, 762. **2.** To move to and fro (without getting a way of egress), Râm. 1, 44, 12. **3.** To agitate, Utt. Râmach. 23, 8.—With the prep. **उद्** *ud*, **1.** To jump out of (abl.), Draup. 8, 19. **2.** To be beside one's self, Daçak. in Chr. 183, 17 (read *udbhramya*). *udbhrânta*, **1.** Flying upward, Râm. 6, 83, 26. **2.** Whirled on, thrown up, Hit. iii. d. 140. **3.** Whirling on, Utt. Râmach. 138, 4. **4.** Bewildered, Pañch. 141, 4.—With **परि** *pari*, **1.** To walk round about, Pañch. 230, 16. **2.** To roam about, Hit. 76, 6, M.M.; Pañch. 21, 1. **3.** To fly round about, Pañch. 148, 10.—With **वि** *vi*, To rove, Nalod. 3, 26. **2.** To wander over, MBh. 3, 2648. **3.** † To play, to wanton. *vibhrânta*, **1.** Agitated, Bhag. 16, 16. **2.** Hurried. **Comp.** *A-*, adj. not playing (?), unmoved, Daçak. in Chr. 199, 5.—With **सम्** *sam*, *saṁbhrânta*, Agitated, confused, Utt. Râmach. 50, 3; troubled, Çâk. 12, 17. **Comp.** *A-*, adj. fearless, Utt. Râmach. 44, 7. *Su-saṁbhrânta*, adj. greatly bewildered. — Cf. *bhramara*; Lat. fremere; O.H.G. breman; A.S. bremman; O.H.G. bremo, briosa; N.G. brausen; πεμφρηδών, φριμάσσομαι, βρέμω, βροντή, βαϐράζω, βαϐραδών, etc.

भ्रम *bhram*+*a*, m. **1.** Whirling, going round, Râjat. 5, 363. **2.** Straying, roaming. **3.** Error, Bhâshâp. 133. **4.** A whirlpool. **5.** A watercourse. **6.** A potter's wheel.

भ्रमण *bhramaṇa*, i.e. *bhram*+*ana*,

I. n. 1. Whirling, turning round, Bhâshâp. 6. 2. Giddiness, Lass. 17, 5. 3. Wandering, Vikr. 23, 11. II. f. *ṇî*, A sort of game performed by women for the amusement of a lover or husband.

भ्रमर *bhram* + *ara*, I. m. 1. A (large black) bee, Vikr. 64, 1. 2. A lover, a gallant. II. n. Epilepsy.

भ्रमि *bhram* + *i*, f. 1. Going round, turning about, Utt. Râmach. 66, 4. 2. A lathe, Kâçikh. 17, 117.

भ्रश् *BHRAÇ*, i. 4, Par. To fall, impersonal pass., Çiç. 9, 73 (it was fallen by the mirror=the mirror fell); cf. *bhraṁç*.

भ्रष्टाधिकारत्व *bhrashṭâdhikâratva*, i. e. *bhrashṭa-adhikâra* + *tva* (vb. *bhraṁç*), n. Loss of office, Pańch. 22, 11.

भ्राज् *BHRÂJ* (probably *abhi-râj*), i. 1, Âtm. (in ved. and epic poetry also Par., MBh. 4, 219). 1. To shine, to beam, Chr. 289, 3=Rigv. i. 50, 3 (Par.). Caus. To illuminate, MBh. 3, 15579.—With the prep. वि *vi*, To shine brilliantly, Chr. 291, 4=Rigv. i. 85, 4; Râm. 3, 52, 25.—Cf. *bhṛij*; Lat. flagrare, flamma (for flagma), flamen, fulgur, fulgere, fulmen, fulvus, etc.; Goth. bairhts; A.S. bearht, beorht; O.H.G. beraht, blanch, blich, blichan; φλέγω, φλόξ; probably also A.S. blác, blaecan, blícan.

भ्राजदृष्टि *bhrâjadṛishṭi*, i.e. *bhrâjant-ṛishṭi*, adj. Having shining swords (i.e. lightnings), Chr. 290, 11=Rigv. i. 64, 11.

भ्राजिष्णु *bhrâj* + *ishṇu*, adj. Splendid, elegant.

भ्रातृ *bhrâtṛi*, i.e. *bhṛi* + *â* + *tṛi*, m. 1. A brother, Chr. 3, 5; du. *tarau*, Brother and sister. 2. A friend, Megh. 10.—Comp. *Durbh°*, i.e. *dus-*, m. A wicked brother, MBh. 3, 996. *Dharma-*, m. an associate dwelling in the same religious retreat, Yâjń. 2, 137. *Sa-* or *saha-*, adj. with a brother, or with brethren, Johns. Sel. 54, 139.—Cf. Lat. frater; φράτηρ and φρατήρ, φατρία, etc.; Goth. brothar; A.S. bródhor.

भ्रातृव्य *bhrâtṛi* + *vya*, m. 1. A brother's son. 2. An enemy.—Cf. Lat. fratrūelis.

भ्रात्रीय *bhrâtrîya*, i.e. *bhrâtṛi* + *îya*, I. adj. Fraternal. II. m. A brother's son.

भ्रान्ति *bhrânti*, i.e. *bhram* + *ti*, f. 1. Going round, whirling, rolling, Vikr. d. 4. 2. Wandering. 3. Error, Bṛihaspati ap. Cowell, Kuçumâńjali, transl. p. 65, n. †; Pańch. 50, 10 (*kumuda-bhrântiṁ janayati matsyânâm*, Causes the fishes to mistake him for a lotus-flower). *chandana-*, instr. Mistaking (it) for a sandal tree, Utt. Râmach. 29, 8.

भ्रामक *bhrâmaka*, i.e. *bhram*, Caus., + *aka*, I. adj. Causing to whirl. II. m. 1. A cheat. 2. A jackal. 3. The sun-flower. 4. A sort of loadstone.

भ्रामर *bhrâmara*, i.e. *bhramara* + *a*, I. m. A sort of loadstone. II. f. *rî*. 1. Pârvatî. 2. A female attendant on Durgâ. III. n. 1. Honey. 2. Whirling round. 3. Epilepsy. 4. A kind of dancing. 5. A village.

भ्रामरिन् *bhrâmarin*, i.e. *bhrâmara* + *in*, adj., f. *iṇî*. 1. Made of honey. 2. Whirling. 3. Epileptic, Man. 3, 161.

भ्राश् *BHRÂÇ*, and † **भ्रास्** *BHRÂS*, † **भ्लाश्** *BHLÂÇ*, and † **भ्लास्** *BHLÂS*, i. 1 and 4, Âtm. To shine; cf. *bhrâj*.

भ्राष्ट्र *bhrâshṭra,* i.e. *bhrâj + tra* (cf. *bhṛij*), I. m. (and n.), A frying-pan, Pańch. i. d. 148. II. n. Æther.

भ्रास् *BHRÂS,* see *bhrâç.*

† भ्री *BHRÎ,* ii. 9, Par. 1. To fear. 2. To bear, to nourish; cf. *bhṛi* and *bhṛî.*

भ्रुकुंश and °स *bhrukuṁça* and °*sa,* see *bhṛikuṁça.*

भ्रुकुटि *bhrukuṭi,* see *bhrûkuṭi.*

† भ्रुड् *BHRUḌ,* i. 6, Par. 1. To cover. 2. To collect.

भ्रुभङ्ग *bhrubhaṅga* = *bhrû-bhaṅga,* see *bhaṅga.*

ऽभ्रुव *-bhruva,* i.e. *bhrû + a,* a substitute for *bhrû* when latter part of comp. adj.; e.g. *su-nâsâ-akshi-bhruva,* Endowed with handsome noses, eyes, and eyebrows, Nal. 5, 6.

भ्रू *bhrû,* f. An eyebrow, Râm. 3, 52, 28.—Comp. *A-sita-,* adj. having black eyebrows, Çiç. 9, 71. *Nata-* (vb. *nam*), adj. having arched brows, Vikr. d. 95. *Sam-hata-,* adj. knitting the brows. *Su-bhrû,* I. adj. having fine brows, Vikr. d. 13. II. and *Su-bhru,* f. a woman, Lass. 90, 15 (*û*); Sund. 4, 12 (*ŭ*).—Cf. ὀφρύς; O.H.G. brâwa; A.S. braew; Lat. frons, frontis.

भ्रूकुंश and °स *bhrûkuṁça* and °*sa,* see *bhṛikuṁça.*

भ्रूकुटि and टी *bhrû-kuṭi,* or भ्रुकुटि, टी *bhrukuṭi,* or भ्रकुटि *bhrakuṭi,* and भृकुटि, टी *bhṛikuṭi,* f. A frown, MBh. 1, 4601 (*bhrû-*); 7, 762 (*bhru-*); Pańch. 220, 1 (*bhṛi°*).

† भ्रूण् *BHRÛṆ,* i. 10, Âtm. 1. To hope. 2. To wish. 3. To fear.

भ्रूण *bhrûṇa,* m. The embryo (cf. *bhrûṇahan*).

भ्रूणघ्न *bhrûṇa-ghna,* adj., f. *ghnî,* One who occasions or procures abortion.

भ्रूणहन् *bhrûṇa-han,* adj., f. *ghnî,* One who occasions or produces abortion, Man. 4, 208; 8, 317 (Jones: At the first place as if he had read *brahmaghnâ,* the killer of a priest; at the second, *the killer of a priest* or destroyer of an embryo).

† भ्रेज् *BHREJ,* i. 1, Âtm. To shine; cf. *bhrâj.*

† भ्रेष् *BHRESH,* i. 1, Par. and Âtm. 1. To go, to move. 2. To fear. 3. To be wrathful (cf. *hresh*).

भ्रेष *bhresha,* m. 1. Deviation from rectitude (cf. *bhraṁça*). 2. Loss. 3. Going.

† भ्लक्ष् *BHLAKSH,* v. r. of *bhaksh.*

भ्लाश् *BHLÂÇ,* and भ्लास् *BHLÂS,* see *bhrâç.*

† भ्लेष् *BHLESH,* i. 1, Par. Âtm. 1. To go. 2. To fear.

म *M.*

मंह् *MAṀH,* i. 1, Âtm. 1. To increase. 2. To give (ved.). i. 10 and 1, Par. † To speak, to shine. Frequent. ved. *mâmah,* To grant, Chr. 298, 25 = Rigv. i. 112, 25.

मंहना *maṁhanâ,* f. Liberality, Lass. 98, 2 (read *maṁhanâ*) = Rigv. vi. 64, 5.

मकर *makara,* I. m. 1. A marine

monster confounded usually with the crocodile and shark, but properly a fabulous animal, Johns. Sel. 28, 27; Pańch. 51, 9; iv. d. 1. **2.** One of the signs of the zodiac. **3.** A form of marching an army, Man. 7, 187. **4.** One of Kuvera's treasures. **II.** f. *rî,* The wife of the marine monster called *makara,* Pańch. 206, 14.

मकरन्द *makaranda,* **I.** m. **1.** The nectar of a flower, Prab. 79, 16. **2.** A kind of jasmine. **II.** m. The filament of a lotus.

मकुर *makura,* **मकुल** *makula,* see *mukura, mukula.*

मकुष्ठ *makushṭha,* **I.** adj. Going slowly. **II.** m. A sort of rice.

मक्क् *MAKK,* see *mask.*

मक्कोल *makkola,* m. Chalk.

† **मक्ष्** *MAKSH,* see *mraksh.*

मक्ष *maksha,* m. **1.** Hypocrisy. **2.** Wrath. **3.** Multitude.

मक्षिका and **मक्षीका** *makshikâ,* f. A fly, Râm. 3, 53, 59.—**Comp.** *Nirmakshika,* i.e. *nis-,* adj. free from flies, untroubled, Çâk. 24, 18 (Prâkṛ.). *Madhu-,* f. a bee.—Cf. Lat. musca; O.H.G. mucca; A.S. micge; O.N. my; μυῖα.

मक्षु and **॰क्षू** *makshû* (properly loc. pl.), adv. Quickly, Chr. 291, 15= Rigv. i. 64, 15.—Cf. Lat. mox.

† **मख्** *MAKH,* and **मङ्ख्** *MAŃKH,* i. 1, Par. To go.

मख *makha,* m. **1.** A warrior, Chr. 290, 11=Rigv. i. 64, 11. **2.** Sacrifice, oblation, Draup. 2, 10.—**Comp.** *Su-,* adj. probably well fighting, a powerful warrior, Chr. 291, 5=Rigv. i. 85, 5.—Cf. μάχομαι, μάχαιρα, μάκελον, μαῖμαξ (from a frequent.), μαιμάκτης, μαιμακτήρια; Lat. macellum, mactare, mucro, maceria; A.S. méce; O.N. moekir.

† **मङ्ख्** *MAŃKH,* see *makh.*

मगध *magadha,* **I.** m. **1.** The name of a country, Hit. 36, 10, M.M. **2.** An inhabitant of that country. **3.** A bard. **II.** f. *dhâ,* Long pepper.

मघ *magha* (cf. *mah*), **I.** n. **1.** Power, wealth (ved.). **2.** A kind of flower. **II.** m. **1.** One of the Dvîpas or divisions of the universe. **2.** Pleasure. **III.** f. *ghâ* (usually pl.), The tenth lunar asterism, Man. 3, 273; Sund. 2, 2. **IV.** f. *ghâ* or *ghî,* A sort of grain.

मघवन् *maghavan,* a curtailed form of the next. **I.** adj., f. *ghonî,* Wealthy, Chr. 287, 2=Rigv. i. 48, 2. **II.** m. Indra, Vikr. 86, 19.

मघवन्त् *magha + vant,* **I.** adj. Wealthy. m. A sacrificer, Chr. 291, 14 =Rigv. i. 64, 14. **II.** m. Indra, Vikr. 88, 21.

मङ्क् *MAŃK,* i. 1, Âtm. **1.** To go, Bhaṭṭ. 14, 10. †**2.** To adorn.

मङ्कुर *mańkura,* m. A mirror; cf. *mukura.*

मङ्क्तृ *mańktṛi,* i.e. *majj + tṛi,* m., f. *trî,* and n. **1.** Bathing or drowning. **2.** Cleaning by immersion.

मङ्क्षु *mańkshu,* ind. (=*makshu*), **1.** Quickly, instantly. **2.** Much, exceedingly.

मङ्क्षुण *mańkshuṇa,* n. Armour for the thighs or legs.

† **मङ्ग्** i. 1, Par. To go.

मङ्ग *mańga,* m. The head of a boat.

मङ्गल *mañgala*, I. adj. Lucky, propitious, Man. 2, 34; brave, Pańch. 8, 15. II. m. and n. 1. Prosperity, welfare, Ṛit. 6, 34; bliss, Utt. Râmach. 89, 4. 2. Rejoicing, a festival, Pańch. 129, 17; solemnity, Vikr. d. 43 (*sandhyâ-*, Evening service). 3. Blessing, Dâçak. in Chr. 201, 10; Sund. 2, 4; prayer, ib. 188, 22. III. m. 1. The planet Mars. 2. Burnt offering on various occasions of rejoicing. IV. f. *lâ*. 1. Umâ, the wife of Çiva. 2. A sort of bent grass, Panicum dactylon. V. n. Turmeric, Vikr. d. 53 (Sch.).—Comp. *A-*, I. adj. inauspicious, Daçak. in Chr. 186, 23. II. n. ill luck, Kumâras. 5, 65; evil omen, Çâk. 63, 13. III. m. the castor-oil plant, Ricinus communis. *Kautuka-*, n. a solemn ceremony, Pańch. 129, 17. *Pâna-*, n. a banquet, Kathâs. 36, 67. *Sarva-*, f. *lâ*, Durgâ, Hit. 99, 8. *Su-*, adj. very fortunate or auspicious.

मङ्गल्य *mañgalya*, i.e. *mañgala* + *ya*, I. adj., f. *yâ*. 1. Auspicious, conferring happiness, Utt. Râmach. 99, 1. 2. Beautiful. 3. Pious, pure, implying holiness, Man. 2, 31. II. m. 1. The holy fig-tree, Ficus religiosa. 2. A sort of pulse or lentils. III. n. 1. Sour curds. 2. Sandal. 3. Red lead. 4. Gold. 5. Water brought from various holy places for the consecration of a king. IV. f. *yâ*. The name of several plants, Agallochum, etc.

मङ्गिनी *mañginî*, i.e. *mañga* + *in* + *î*, f. A boat.

† मङ्घ् *MAÑGH*, i. 1, Par. To adorn. i. 1, Âtm. 1. To go. 2. To begin moving. 3. To begin. 4. To move swiftly. 5. To blame. 6. To cheat.

† मच् *MACH*, मञ्च् *MAÑCH*, मुच् *MUCH*, and मुञ्च् *MUŃCH*, 1. To cheat, to be wicked. 2. To boast, to be vain. 3. To pound.

मचर्च्छिका *macharchhikâ*, f. Excellence.

मज्ज् *MAJJ* (probably *mad-jan*; cf. *madgu* and Lat. mergere; the Indian grammarians write *masj*), i. 6, Par. (in epic poetry also Âtm., MBh. 2, 605). The base of many forms is *mañj*. 1. To dive, Bhartṛ. 2, 91. 2. To bathe, MBh. 1, 5299. 3. To sink, Vikr. d. 133; to perish in water, Râm. 1, 1, 89. 4. To sink into, MBh. 1, 3717 (loc.); Man. 4, 81 (acc.). 5. To be plunged, Man. 10, 91. 6. To become disheartened, MBh. 1, 5631. Ptcple. of the pf. pass. *magna*, 1. Plunged, Hit. i. d. 4, M.M.; dived, immersed, Râm. 3, 52, 19. 2. Sunk, Daçak. in Chr. 197, 6; drowned, Chr. 17, 27. Caus. 1. To cause to plunge, MBh. 1, 3908. 2. To overwhelm, Râm. 2, 77, 13.—With the prep. उद् *ud*, 1. To emerge, Çâk. d. 167. 2. Pass. impers. To rise, Çiç. 9, 30. Caus. To force up, Man. 8, 115.—With नि *ni*, 1. To bathe, Man. 5, 73. 2. To submerge, to sink under, Man. 4, 194; Hit. ii. d. 145. 3. To disappear, MBh. 2, 1504. 4. To cause to sink (into hell), MBh. 1, 4156. *nimagna*, 1. Plunged in, immersed, Râjat. 5, 85. 2. Sunk in (not prominent), Vikr. d. 80; Râjat. 5, 74; slender, d. 129. 3. Covered, Daçak. in Chr. 199, 6. Caus. 1. To cause to dive under water, Man. 8, 114. 2. To cause to be submerged, MBh. 3, 16612.—With प्र *pra*, *pramagna*, Immersed, drowned.

मज्जकृत् *majjakṛit*, i.e. *majjan-kṛi* + *t*, n. A bone.

मज्जन् *majjan* (perhaps for original *marjan*; cf. O.H.G. marag; A.S. mearh, mearg, merg), m. **1.** The marrow of the bones and flesh. **2.** The pith or sap of trees.

मज्जा *majjâ* (cf. the last), f. The marrow of the bones and flesh, Pańch. i. d. 191, cf. my translation, n. 171.—Comp. *Nirmajja*, i.e. *nis-*, adj. marrowless, Hariv. 14533.

मज्जन *majj+ana*, n. **1.** Immersion. **2.** Bathing. **3.** Drowning, Pańch. i. d. 34.

मज्जूषा *majjûshâ=mańjûshâ.*

मज्मन् *majman*, n. Strength, Chr. 290, 3=Rigv. i. 64, 3.—Cf. Lat. magmentum.

मञ्च् *MAŃCH*, i. 1, Âtm. †**1.** To hold. †**2.** To grow high or tall. †**3.** To adore. †**4.** To shine. Cf. *mach* and *mluńch.*—With the prep. निस् *nis*, To purify, Naish. 7, 43. Cf. *mṛij.*

मञ्च *mańcha*, m. **1.** A bedstead. **2.** A scaffold, Johns. Sel. 9, 12. **3.** A chair, Ragh. 6, 1.

मञ्ज् *MAŃJ*, see *mârj* (Lass. 74, 4, read *majjat*).

मञ्जर *mańjara*, n., and f. *rî*, **1.** A pearl. **2.** A creeper.

मञ्जरि and मञ्जरी *mańjarî*, f. **1.** =*mańjara*, Râm. 6, 15, 7 (pearl). **2.** A shoot, sprout, Vikr. d. 26, 76 (*mańjari-châmara*, A fan-like sprout).—Comp. *Kâma-*, *Madana-*, and *Râga-mańjarî*, f. proper names. *Lobha-mańjarî*, f. used instead of *Kâmamańjarî*, Daçak. in Chr. 192, 21 (the pearl of covetousness.)

मञ्जरीपिञ्जरित *mańjaripińjarita*, i.e. *mańjarî-pińjara+ita*, adj. Adorned with pearls and gold, Daçak. in Chr. 199, 1.

मञ्जा *mańjâ*, f., मञ्जि *mańji*, m., and मञ्जी *mańjî*, f. A creeper.

मञ्जिका *mańji+kâ*, f. A harlot.

मञ्जिष्ठा *mańjishṭhâ*, properly superl. of *mańju*, f. Bengal madder, Rubia manjith Roxb.

मञ्जीर *mańjîra*, I. m. and n. An ornament for the feet. II. m. A post round which passes the string that works the stick of a churn.

मञ्जु *mańju* (based on *mańj*, a form of *mṛij*), adj. Beautiful, Vikr. 60, 12.

मञ्जुल *mańju+la*, I. adj. Beautiful. II. m. A gallinule. III. n. **1.** A bower. **2.** A watercourse.

मञ्जूषा *mańjûsha*, f. **1.** A basket, Kathâs. 4, 74. **2.** A receptacle, Râm. 1, 67, 4.

† मठ् *MAṬH*, i. 1, Par. **1.** To inhabit. **2.** To grind. **3.** To go.

मठ *maṭha*, m. **1.** A school. **2.** A building inhabited by ascetics, a cloister, a college, Pańch. 116, 18. **3.** A temple. **4.** A carriage.—Comp. *Gopâla-*, *Chakra-*, *Çûra-*, m. colleges called 'that of *Gopâla*,' 'that of *Chakra(-varman)*,' 'of *Çûra*,' Râjat. 5, 243; 403; 39.

मठर *maṭhara*, I. adj. Intoxicated. II. m. The name of a saint.

मडव *maḍava*, or मडवराज्य *maḍava-râjya*, n. The name of a district in Kashmir, Râjat. 5, 84; 302; 446.

मड्डु *maḍḍu*, m. A sort of drum.

मण् *MAṆ*, i. 1, Par. To sound, to murmur. Ptcple. of the pf. pass. *maṇita*, Nalod. 2, 60. n. A murmuring sound.

मणि *maṇi*, m. and f., and मणी *maṇi*, f. **1.** A precious stone, a jewel, Vikr. d. 40. **2.** A pearl, Vikr. d. 51. **3.** Fleshy processes hanging from the neck of a goat. **4.** A waterpot.—**Comp.** *Indu-* and *Chandra-*, m. a fabulous stone, moon-stone, Çiç. 9, 35; Râjat. 3, 296; Utt. Râmach. 23, 2. *Kâcha-*, m. crystal, Hit. pr. d. 44, M.M. *Chintâ-*, m. a fabulous gem, the possessor of which may get all he wishes for, Hariv. 8702. *Chûḍâ-*, m. a jewel worn in a crest or diadem, Hit. i. d. 211, M.M. (*chandra-ardha-*, adj. having the crescent for his crest-jewel). *Jatu-*, m. a mole, Suçr. 1, 92, 3. *Masi-*, m. an inkstand. *Latâ-*, m. coral. *Vi-mala-*, m. crystal. *Çikhâ-*, m. a jewel worn on the head, Vikr. d. 129. *Çuchi-*, m. the same. *Sarpa-*, m. the snake-stone, or carbuncle, a jewel said to be found in the head of a snake. *Sita-*, m. crystal, Megh. 67. *Sûrya-*, m. 1. the sun-stone. 2. a tree, Hibiscus phœniceus. *Sparça-*, m. the philosopher's stone, converting everything it touches to gold.

मणिक *maṇi + ka*, I. m. A precious stone, a jewel. II. n. A small waterpot, Pârask. in Journ. of the German Oriental Society, ix. xxi. n. 4.

मणिकार *maṇi-kâra*, m. A jeweller.

मणिमय *maṇi-maya*, adj., f. *yî*, Consisting of jewels, Megh. 65.—**Comp.** *Sita-maṇi + maya*, adj. made of crystal, Megh. 67.

मणीचक *maṇichaka*, m. **1.** The kingfisher. **2.** The moon-stone, a fabulous stone.

मणीवक *maṇivaka*, n. A flower.

† मण्ठ् *MAṆṬH*, i. 1, Âtm. To remember with regret.

मण्ड् *MAṆḌ* (akin to *mad*, *mand*, probably a denomin. based on a lost signification of *mandra*), † i. 1, Âtm. **1.** To dress. **2.** To divide. † i. 1, Par. To adorn one's self. i. 10, Par. (in epic poetry also Âtm., MBh. 1, 7572), **1.** To adorn, Pañch. 255, 16. **2.** † To exhilarate. Ptcple. of the pf. pass. *maṇḍita*, Adorned, Chr. 29, 31; Pañch. 51, 15. **Comp.** *A-*, adj. not adorned, Nal. 16, 17.

मण्ड *maṇḍ + a*, I. m. **1.** Ornament. **2.** The castor-oil tree, Palma christi. II. m. (and n.). **1.** Scum, Utt. Râmach. 90, 7. **2.** Pith. **3.** The head, Lass. 4, 18. III. f. *ḍâ*. **1.** Spirituous liquor. **2.** Emblic myrobalan.—**Comp.** *Dadhi-*, m. Whey, Bhâg. P. 5, 1, 34.

मण्डक *maṇḍa + ka*, m. A kind of pastry, Pañch. 245, 24 (see my translation, n. 1387).

मण्डन *maṇḍ + ana*, n. **1.** Dressing, Pañch. 116, 21 (of the idols). **2.** Ornament, Vikr. d. 157.

मण्डप *maṇḍa-pa* (vb. *pâ*), m. (and n.). **1.** A shed or hall erected on festival occasions, as marriages, and adorned with flowers, Pañch. 129, 17. **2.** An open temple. **3.** A bower, Megh. 76.—**Comp.** *Adhikaraṇa-*, a court of justice, Mṛichchh. 138, 4. *Keli-*, m. and n. a pleasure-house, Çântiç. 1, 5. *Garbha-*, m. the haram, Kathâs. 26, 77. *Paṭa-*, m. and n. a tent, Ragh. 5, 73. *Latâ-*, m. or n. an arbour, Çâk. 32, 19.

मण्डपिका *maṇḍapikâ*, i.e. *maṇḍapa + ka*, f. A small shop, Hit. 115, 1, 9.

मण्डयन्त *maṇḍayant + a* (vb. *maṇḍ*), m. An ornament.

मण्डल *maṇḍala*, I. m. **1.** A sort of sacrifice. **2.** A kind of snake. **3.** A dog. II. f. *lî*. **1.** A circle, Utt. Râmach. 66, 4. **2.** Walking round, Sund. 3, 22; 24. **3.** Bent grass. **4.** A nest, Daçak. 151, 6. III. n. (and m.). **1.** A circle, Vikr. d. 140; Pañch. 230, 18; a globe, a ball, Pañch. 157, 25. **2.** The disk of the sun or moon, Pañch. 160, 23. **3.** The halo round the sun. **4.** A wheel, Utt. Râmach. 141, 3. **5.** A heap, a multitude, Pañch. iii. d. 224; Ṛit. 1, 10 (at the end of a comp. adj.); a troop, Râjat. 5, 379. **6.** A district, a province, Râjat. 5, 146; an empire, ib. 155, 262. **7.** Surrounding countries, Man. 7, 154. **8.** A form of array, an army drawn up in a circle, Pañch. 9, 14. **9.** Twelve great empires, into which the whole of India is said to have been divided in old times. **10.** A sort of leprosy with circular spots. **11.** A sort of mystical diagram, Hit. 59, 22; Lass. 13, 18 (?). **12.** A sort of perfume, Lass. 20, 20 (? corr. perhaps *maṇḍana*, cf. *maṇḍana* and *gaja-maṇḍana*, s.v. *bhûti*).—**Comp.** *Âdarça-*, 1. the reflection of a mirror, Kir. 5, 41. 2. a kind of snake, Suçr. 2, 265, 11. *Âçrama-*, n. the dwelling-place of anchorites, Nal. 12, 64. *Kshmâ-tala-*, m. or n. the terrestrial globe, earth, Lass. 68, 14. *Tri-maṇḍalâ*, f. a poisonous kind of spider, Suçr. 2, 269, 12. *Diṅ-maṇḍala*, i. e. *diç-*, n. 1. all the quarters of the world, Bhartṛ. 3, 71. 2. the compass-card. *Prakṛiti-*, n. the whole empire, Ragh. 9, 2. *Raṅga-*, n. the circuit of an assembled throng. *Sûrya-*, m. or n. the disk of the sun, Sâv. 7, 1. *Stana-*, n. the balls of the female bosom, Ṛit. 1, 8; Lass. 80, 15.

मण्डलय *MAṆḌALAYA*, a denomin. derived from the preceding; with **परि** *pari*, in the ptcple. pf. pass. *parimaṇḍalita*, Turned round, Kir. 5. 42.

मण्डलिन् *maṇḍalin*, i.e. *maṇḍala* + *in*, m. **1.** A snake. **2.** A cat.

मण्डूक *maṇḍûka*, I. m. **1.** A frog, Pañch. 197, 21. **2.** A flower, Bignonia indica. II. f. *kî*, A female frog.—**Comp.** *Kûpa-*, m. a frog in a well, applied to a person of no enterprise, one who never leaves his home, Hit. 82, 2.

मण्डूर *maṇḍûra*, m. and n. Rust of iron.

मत् *mat*, see 2. *mad*.

मतंग *matam̃ga*, i.e. *mata* (vb. *man*), + *m-ga*, m. **1.** A cloud. **2.** An elephant, Hiḍ. 1, 13. **3.** A proper name, Utt. Râmach. 19, 14.

मतंगज *matam̃ga-ja*, m. An elephant, Mâlav. 32, 6; Kir. 5, 47.

मतल्लिका *matallikâ*, f. Excellence.

मति *mati*, i.e. *man* + *ti*, f. **1.** Mind, Pañch. iii. d. 76. **2.** Understanding, Pañch. 251, 6; intelligence, Hit. pr. d. 42. **3.** Thought, Pañch. iii. d. 258; resolution, Pañch. 216, 14. **4.** Hymn, Chr. 292, 2 = Rigv. i. 86, 2. **5.** Perception, Bhâshâp. 126. **6.** Opinion, Chr. 13, 13. **7.** Advice. **8.** Wish. **9.** Recollection. **10.** Respect. **11.** A pot-herb.—**Comp.** *A-*, f. 1. not knowing (instr. unknowingly), Man. 4, 222. 2. glimmer, image, Chr. 290, 9 = Rigv. i. 64, 9. *Eka-*, I. f. direction of the mind on one object, Bhâg. P. 4, 8, 21. II. adj. unanimous, MBh. 12, 12723. See *Ku-*. *Kṛita-*, adj. resolved, MBh. 13, 2211. *Durm°*, i.e. *dus-*, adj. 1. foolish, Hit. ii. d. 48. 2. wicked, Man. 11, 30. *Nindita-* (vb. *nind*), adj. base-minded, Hit. i. d. 152, M.M. *Nirahammati*, i.e. *nis-aham-*, adj. free from selfishness, Bhâg. P. 4, 22, 52. *Pratyut-*

panna-, i.e. *prati-ud-panna* (vb. *pad*), adj. ready-minded, Çâk. 67, 23. *Bahu-*, f. estimation. *Manda-*, adj. foolish, Pañch. 229, 12. *Mahâ-*, adj. high-minded, Chr. 6, 4. *Yathâ-mati*, adv. according to one's understanding or intellect, Vedântas. in Chr. 202, 4. *Vi-*, f. 1. difference of opinion. 2. dislike, aversion. *Vidyamâna-* (vb. *vid*), adj. having understanding, Pañch. i. d. 86. *Vipula-*, adj. endowed with great understanding, Pañch. i. d. 410. *Vṛithâ-*, adj. foolish, MBh. 2, 865. *Su-*, I. f. kindness. II. adj. very wise, Pañch. 25, 13.—Cf. Lat. mens, mentis, mentio, mentiri, mendax; Goth. ga-munds, môds; A.S. mod, ge-mynd; μῆτις (ved. *-mâtî*), μοῦσα, i.e. μαν+τια (=ved. *mati*, hymn).

मतिमन्त् *mati-mant*, adj., f. *matî*, Sensible, intelligent, wise, Pañch. ii. d. 20; Hit. i. d. 127, M.M.

मत्क *matka*, **1.** i.e. 2. *mad+ka*, adj. Mine. **2.** m. A bug.

मत्कुण *matkuṇa*, **1.** A bug (cf. *matka*), Pañch. iii. d. 105. **2.** A flea. **3.** An elephant without tusks. **4.** A beardless man. **5.** A buffalo. **6.** Armour for the thighs or legs. **6.** A cocoa-nut.

मत्य *matya*, n. The handle of a sickle.

मत्सर *matsara*, probably 2.*mad-sṛi* +*a*, I. adj. **1.** Envious, hostile, Utt. Râmach. 133, 13. **2.** Niggardly. **3.** Wicked. II. m. **1.** Envy, Çiç. 9, 63; Man. 3, 231. **2.** Jealousy, Mâlav. 55, 8. **3.** Anger, passion. III. f. *râ*, A gnat.—Comp. *Nirm°*, i.e. *nis-* and *vi-*, adj. free from envy, passion, Lass. 85, 9 (*nis-*); 49, 10 (*vi-*). *Vîta-*, i.e. *vi-ita-* (vb. *i*), adj. free from envy, Indr. 4, 8. *Sa-*, adj. envious.

मत्सरिन् *matsarin*, i.e. *matsara+in*, adj., f. *iṇî*. **1.** Envious, Man. 2, 201. **2.** Wicked.

मत्स्य *matsya*, i.e. 1. *mad+sya*, **1.** m. A fish, Man. 1, 39. **2.** A particular fish, probably the *Saphari*. **3.** A name of Vishṇu. **4.** The name of a country, Man. 2, 19; 7, 193.—Comp. *Pâka-*, m. 1. a particular fish, Suçr. 1, 206, 17. 2. a poisonous kind of insect, ib. 2, 288, 3.

मत्स्यक *matsya+ka*, m. A fish, Matsyop. 35.

मत्स्यण्डी *matsyaṇḍî*, and **मत्स्यण्डिका** *matsyaṇḍikâ*, i.e. *matsyaṇḍî+ka*, f. The juice of the sugar-cane, unrefined, Mâlav. 30, 19.

मत्स्याद *matsyâda*, i.e. *matsya-ad+a*, adj. Feeding on fishes, Pañch. 50, 14.

मथ् *MATH*, † i. 1, Par., **मन्थ्** *MANTH*, ii. 9, *mathnâ*, *mathnî*, Par. (in epic poetry also Âtm., MBh. 1, 1120), and † i. 1, Par., and † **मान्थ्** *mânth*, i. 1, Par. **1.** To churn, Kir. 5, 30. **2.** To produce by churning. **3.** To agitate (mentally), MBh, 1, 3330. **4.** To crush, Pañch. 162, 18; to hurt, to kill. Ptcple. of the pf. pass. *mathita*. **1.** Churned. **2.** Stirred. **3.** Distressed, Megh. 81 (faded). **4.** Agitated, Pañch. i. d. 247. **5.** Destroyed, MBh. 1, 7669.—With the prep. **आ** *â*, To agitate, Râm. 2, 26, 2.—With **उद्** *ud*, **1.** To agitate, MBh. 3, 14227. **2.** To cut off, MBh. 3, 10267. **3.** To kill, Pañch. ii. d. 34.—With **नि** *ni*, To annoy, to hurt, Râm. 3, 54, 28.—With **निस्** *nis*, **1.** To churn, to agitate, MBh. 1, 1120. **2.** To shake out, MBh. 1, 6547.—With **प्र** *pra*, **1.** To trample down, to bruise, MBh. 3, 16435. **2.** To annoy,

MBh. 1, 194. †3. To rob (ved.). 4. To cut off, MBh. 3, 10267. *pramathita*, 1. Well churned. 2. Trampled down. 3. Pained. n. Butter-milk without water. Absolut. *pramathya*, Forcibly, Brâhmaṇav. 2, 17. Caus. *mâthaya*, To annoy, MBh. 3, 8769. *pramâthita*, Ravished, violated, forcibly carried off. —With संप्र *sam-pra*, To agitate, MBh. 1, 4876.—With वि *vi*, To destroy, MBh. 3, 12258.—Cf. μάτος, ματεύω, μανθάνω, Προμηθεύς, μόθος, and see *mathin*.

मथन *math + ana*, n. Churning, Pańch. v. d. 28.—Comp. *Pura-*, m. the destroyer of Pura, a name of Çiva, Lass. 67, 6. *Madhu-*, m. the destroyer of Madhu, a name of Vishṇu, Lass. 71, 6; Bhâg. P. 6, 9, 38 (Burnouf, 'qui produis le nectar').

मथिन् *math + in*, the bases of some cases are *manthan* and *math*, m. 1. A churning-stick, MBh. 1, 1124. 2. The penis.—Cf. Lat. mentula.

मथुरा *mathurâ*, f. A district and city now called Muttra, Pańch. 8, 14.

1. **मद्** *MAD*, ved. i. 1, Par.; i. 4, *mâdya*, Par. (originally, to be wet). 1. To get drunk (ved.). 2. To be glad, to rejoice, Chr. 291, 1=Rigv. i. 85, 1; MBh. 1, 4688. Ptcple. of the pf. pass. *matta*. 1. Drunk, a drunkard, Man. 9, 78. 2. Intoxicated, Hit. iv. d. 55; with love, Ṛit. 6, 14; with pride, Daçak. in Chr. 193, 20. 3. Mad, Râm. 3, 55, 36; furious, Hit. i. d. 34, M.M.; being in rut (as an elephant), Râm. 3, 52, 46. 4. Pleased. m. 1. An elephant in rut. 2. A buffalo. 3. The Indian cuckoo. 4. The thorn apple. f. *tâ*, Vinous liquor. Comp. *Mṛita-*, m. a jackal. Caus. I. *mâdaya*. 1. To intoxicate. 2. To exhilarate, MBh. 3, 10678. i. 10, Âtm. To rejoice, Chr. 291, 6=Rigv. i. 85 6. II. *madaya*, 1. To exhilarate. 2. To be satisfied, MBh. 1, 4736. 3. † To doze, to be sluggish.—With अनु *anu* in *anumatta*, Cured from insanity, again sane, Daçak. in Chr, 200, 14.—With उद् *ud*, To be mad, MBh. 3, 14503. *unmatta*, 1. Drunk. 2. Insane, Râm. 3, 55, 8; furious, Hit. ii. d. 116; Utt. Râmach. 42, 16; a lunatic, Man. 3, 161; Pańch. iii. d. 67. m. The thorn apple. Caus. I. *mâdaya*, *unmâdita*, Caused to be mad, Daçak. in Chr. 180, 16. II. *madaya*, *unmadita*, The same, ib. 191, 18 (read °*mâd*°).—With प्र *pra*, 1. To stray from (with abl.). 2. To be negligent, careless, unguarded, Man. 2, 213. Comp. ptcple. pres. *a-pramâdyant*, Being careful, MBh. 12, 3996. *pramatta*, 1. Careless, Hit. ii. d. 104. 2. Intoxicated. 3. Insane, furious, Chr. 35, 6; being in rut, Pańch. 80, 6. 4. Addicted to gaming, Man. 9, 78. 5. Mad with desire, 4, 40. Comp. *A-*, adj. careful, watchful, Pańch. 88, 19.—With वि *vi*, *vimatta*, Ruttish, Kir. 5, 47. —With सम् *sam*, *sammatta*, Intoxicated with love, Sund. 4, 17; cf. 12; see *mand*.—Cf. Lat. madidus, madere, manare (for mad + no, denomin.); μαδός, μαδάω, μαδαρός; probably Goth. mats; A.S. maete; Goth. matjan; μασάομαι; Lat. mandere; A.S. maetan, To dream.

2. **मद्** *mad* (or *mat*, probably abl. sing. of *asmad*), former part of compounds and base of many derivatives, implying the singular of the pronoun of the first person; cf. e.g. *mad-vidha*, *madîya*.

मद 1. *mad + a*, I. m. 1. Intoxication, Chr. 292, 10=Rigv. i. 85, 10; Pańch. 202, 25. 2. Insanity, Pańch. iv. d. 68; rut of an elephant, 87, 16. 3. Pride, Hit. i. d. 175, M.M. 4. Joy, Ṛit. 6, 32; sensual enjoyment, Ṛit. 6, 12. 5. Passion, Râjat. 5, 214; love, Vikr. 59, 2.

6. Spirituous liquor. 7. The juice that flows from an elephant's temples when in rut, Pańch. i. d. 139. 8. Semen virile. 9. Musk. II. f. *dí*. 1. A drinking vessel. 2. An instrument for making furrows.—Comp. *Durm°*, i.e. *dus-*, I. m. insanity, Bhâg. P. 5, 12, 6. II. adj. 1. frantic, ib. 8, 2, 25. 2. desiring violently, MBh. 1, 2796; Chr. 23, 38 (*yuddha-*, battle). *Dhana-*, m. pride produced by wealth, Kathâs. 18, 129. *Nirm°*, i.e. *nis-*, adj. free from arrogance, MBh. 3, 8683. *Mahâ-*, m. an elephant in rut. *Mṛiga-*, m. musk, Kathâs. 22, 96. *Rati-madâ*, f. an Apsaras. *Viçva-madâ*, f. one of the seven tongues of fire. *Sa-*, adj. 1. intoxicated, Ṛit. 6, 27; delighted, Utt. Râmach. 44, 10. 2. furious, Bhartṛ. 2, 29. *Sadâ-*, adj. ever furious, Pańch. i. d. 48 (but cf. Böhtl. Ind. Spr. 1324). *Su-*, adj. very drunk, mad, or impassioned.

मदच्युत् *mada-chyu + t*, adj. Yielding intoxication or joy, Chr. 291, 7 = Rigv. i. 85, 7.

मदन 1. *mad + ana*, I. m. 1. Love, Vikr. 22, 8; Kâmadeva, the god of love, Vikr. d. 9. 2. The season of spring. 3. Thorn apple, Datura metel. 4. A bee. 5. Beeswax. II. f. *nâ* and *nî*, Spirituous liquor.—Comp. *Unmadana*, i.e. *ud-*, adj., f. *nâ*, inflamed with love, Kumâras. 5, 55.

मदमुच् *mada-much*, adj. Distilling juice, being in rut (viz. an elephant; cf. *mada*), Utt. Râmach. 62, 14.

मदयित्नु *madayitnu*, i.e. *mad*, Caus., + *itnu*, m. 1. A drunken man. 2. A distiller. 3. A cloud. 4. The god of love. 5. Spirituous liquor.

मदार 1. *mad + âra*, m. 1. An elephant. 2. A rogue. 3. A hog.

मदिर 1. *mad + ira*, I. m. A red species of Khayar, Mimosa catechu. II. f. *râ*. 1. Spirituous liquor, Man. 11, 148; wine, nectar, Megh. 76. 2. The wagtail.

मदिराक्षी *madirâkshî*, i.e. *madirâ-aksha + î*, f. A (fascinating) woman, Vikr. d. 105.

मदिरेक्षणी *madirekshaṇî*, i.e. *madirâ-ikshaṇa + î*, f. A fascinating woman, Vikr. d. 32; Çâk. d. 67.

मदिष्ठा *madishṭhâ*, f. of the superl. of *mada + vant*, Spirituous liquor.

मदीय 2. *mad + îya*, adj. Mine, Pańch. 191, 10.

मद्गु *madgu*, i.e. *majj + u* (see *majj*), m. 1. An aquatic bird, the diver, Lass. 50, 1. 2. An outcaste, the son of a Brâhmaṇa by a woman of the bard class. 3. A ship.—Comp. *Kâka-*, m. a kind of fowl, MBh. 13, 5520.—Cf. Lat. mergus.

मद्गुर *madgura*, i.e. *majj + ura* (see *majj*), m. A sort of fish.

मद्य *mad + ya*, n. Spirituous liquor, wine, Pańch. 35, 15.

मद्यप *madya-pa* (vb. 1. *pâ*), m. A drinker of intoxicating spirits, Man. 3, 159; a drunkard, Pańch. iv. d. 10.

मद्र *mad + ra*, I. m. 1. Joy. 2. The name of a country, Sâv. 1, 2. 3. A sovereign of that country. II. f. *râ*, The name of a river.

मद्वन् *mad + van*, m. Çiva.

मधु *madhu*, I. adj. Sweet, Chr. 291, 6 = Rigv. i. 85, 6; Megh. 67. II. m. 1. Liquorice. 2. A tree, Bassia latifolia. 3. The month Chaitra, March—April, Ṛit. 6, 24. 4. The season of spring, Mâlav. d. 26. 5. The name of a Daitya slain by Vishṇu; cf. *madhubhid*. III. n. 1. Honey, Hit. i. d. 81, M.M. 2. The nectar of flowers. 3. Milk. 4. Sugar. 5. Spirituous liquor from the blossoms of the Bassia latifolia, or wine, Megh. 93; Ragh. 4, 60. 6. Water.—Comp. *Tri-*, adj. one who knows or recites the three verses of the Rigveda, beginning with *madhu* (Rigv. i. 90, 6–8), Yâjń. 1, 219—Cf. μέθυ; O.H.G. medu, mito; A.S. medu, medo.

मधुक *madhu + ka*, I. adj. Sweet. II. m. A bard. III. m. and n. Liquorice. IV. n. Tin.

मधुकर *madhu-kara*, I. m. 1. A bee, Vikr. d. 105. 2. A lover. II. f. *rî*, A bee, Pańch. ii. d. 158.

मधुकरिका *madhukarikâ*, i.e. *madhukara + ka*, f. A proper name, Çâk. 77, 16 (Prâkṛ.).

मधुकृत् *madhu-kṛi + t*, and **मधुद्रु** *madhu-dru*, and **मधुप** *madhu-pa* (vb. 1.*pâ*), m. A bee, Pańch. i. d. 419 (*pa*).

मधुच्युत् *madhu-chyu + t*, adj. Distilling honey, Utt. Râmach. 69, 4.

मधुपर्क *madhu-pṛich + a*, m. A dish of curds, honey, and clarified butter, Man. 3, 119; Chr. 16, 19.

मधुभिद् *madhu-bhid*, m. Vishṇu (see *madhu*), Pańch. v. d. 28.

मधुमन्त् *madhu + mant*, adj., f. *matî*, Sweet, Chr. 296, 9 = Rigv. i. 112, 9.

मधुमय *madhu + maya*, adj., f. *yî*, Sweet, Hit. ii. d. 154; luscious.

मधुर *madhu + ra*, I. adj. 1. Sweet (figuratively), Pańch. ii. d. 65. 2. Agreeable, Pańch. 248, 11. 3. Tender, Daçak. in Chr. 201, 13. II. °*ram*, adv. Sweetly, in an agreeable manner, Chr. 17, 21. III. m. Sweetness. IV. f. *râ*. 1. Marrow. 2. The name of a town, Utt. Râmach. 176, 8. 3. The name of several plants. V. n. 1. Treacle. 2. Poison. 3. Tin.—Comp. *Vâṅmadhura*, i.e. *vâch-*, adj. sweet in speech, Hit. 74, 20.

मधुरता *madhura + tâ*, f. Sweetness, figurat., Pańch. v. d. 83; gracefulness, Pańch. v. d. 2.

मधुल *madhula* (for *madhura*), n. Spirituous liquor.

मधुलिह् *madhu-lih*, m. A bee, Vikr. d. 130.

मधूक *madhûka*, derived from *madhu*, m. A tree, Bassia latifolia, Kathâs. 7, 14.

मधूपघ्न *madhûpaghna*, i.e. *madhu-upaghna*, n. A name of the town Mathurâ.

मधूलक *madhûlaka*, derived from *madhu*, I. adj. Sweet. II. m. 1. Sweetness. 2. A sort of Bassia latifolia.

मध्य *ma + dhya* (*ma* is an old pronoun), I. adj. 1. Middle, Râjat. 5, 313. 2. Middle-sized, Man. 8, 134; of middle sort, Bhartṛ. 2, 73. 3. Intermediate; amongst. 4. Right, proper. 5. Low. II. m. and n. 1. The middle, Vikr. d. 6; the centre, abl. amongst, Pańch. 253, 14; at the end of comp. In, Pańch. 10, 5 (*nagara -madhya + m*, in the town). 2. The waist, Vikr. d. 129. III. m. Cessation, interval. IV. f. *yâ*. 1. A young woman, a girl arrived at puberty. 2. The middle finger. V. n. 1. A horse's flank. 2. A very large number.—Comp. *Tanu-*, adj., f. *yâ*, having a slender waist, Nal. 3, 13. *Bhuja-*, n. the breast, Ragh. 13, 73.—

Cf. Lat. medius; Goth. midja; A.S. midd, ge-midlian; Goth.-missô, missa-; A.S. mis-; O.H.G. missa, missi, mis-; μέσος.

मध्यग *madhya-ga*, adj. **1.** Who or what goes in the centre or amongst. **2.** Existing in, Pańch. iii. d. 205.—Comp. *Bahu-*, adj. belonging to many, Man. 9, 199.

मध्यतस् *madhya + tas*, adv. From or in the middle, Hiḍ. 1, 21.

मध्यन्दिन *madhyandina*, i.e. *madhya + m-dina*, n. Noon, Pańch. 82, 1.—Comp. *Ati-*, n. time too near the mid-day, Man. 4, 140.

मध्यम *madhya + ma*, **I.** adj. **1.** Middle, Vikr. d. 19. **2.** Of middle sort, Hit. ii. d. 69; of moderate strength. **3.** Middle born, neither the oldest nor youngest, Chr. 4, 11. **II.** m. and n. The waist, Nal. 1, 10. **III.** m. **1.** The fifth note of the Hindu gamut. **2.** One of the scales. **3.** The middle country (=*madhya-deça*). **4.** A sort of deer. **IV.** f. *mâ*, A girl arrived at puberty. **2.** The middle finger. **3.** A central blossom.—Comp. *Yava-*, a kind of penance, Man. 11, 217. *Su-*, adj. having a fine waist, Râm. 3, 52, 49.—Cf. A.S. medeme.

मध्यस्थ *madhya-stha*, **I.** adj. **1.** Middle. **2.** Living in the midst (of persons), Pańch. 191, 10. **3.** Neutral, Man. 9, 272. **4.** Impartial, Mâlav. 9, 2. **5.** Indifferent, Çâk. 63, 19. **II.** m. A mediator, a judge, Lass. 92, 3.

मध्येपृष्ठम् *madhyeprishṭham*, i. e. *madhya + i-prishṭha + m*, adv. On the back, Bhartṛ. 2, 28.

मध्वल *madhvala*, i.e. *madhu + vala* m. Tippling.

मध्वासवनिक *madhvâsavanika*, i.e. *madhu-â-su + ana + ika*, m. A distiller.

मध्विजा *madhvijâ*, probably *madhu + i-ja* (an anomal. loc.), f. Spirituous liquor.

मन् *MAN*, i. 4, and ii. 8, Âtm. (in epic poetry, and also elsewhere Par., e.g. Pańch. ii. d. 97). **1.** To think, Chr. 10, 3; 154, 16; Pańch. i. d. 126 (*samam vishamam eva cha manyate*, To consider even and odd, i.e. to make long reflections); with *anyathâ*, To doubt, Utt. Râmach. 104, 2. **2.** To wish, Vikr. 12, 9. **3.** To mind, MBh. 3, 2092; with *na*, To disregard, Johns. Sel. 53, 125. **4.** To believe, Râjat. 5, 255; Chr. 14, 27. **5.** To understand, Vedântas. in Chr. 215, 15. **6.** To know, Lass. 98, 7=Rigv. v. 9, 1; Daçak. in Chr. 183, 23. **7.** To mention, to declare, Chr. 296, 2=Rigv. i. 112, 2 (*mantave*, ved. infin. 'So many that even a loquacious man cannot reckon them up'). **8.** To take, to value, Pańch. ii. d. 97; i. d. 190; with *bahu*, To estimate highly, Râjat. 5, 276. **9.** *manye* is often inserted without syntactic connection. **a.** To strengthen an assertion, Lass. 72, 13. **b.** In order to give it a modest form, Daçak. in Chr. 182, 15. **c.** Ironically, Râm. 3, 51, 25. Ptcple. of the pf. pass. *mata*. **1.** Admitted, Bhâshâp. 57. **2.** Believed, held, Man. 1, 76. **3.** Understood, known. **4.** Desired, with gen., Chr. 15, 2; Kir. 5, 27. **5.** Respected, regarded. n. **1.** Purpose. **2.** Opinion, Indr. 3, 1. **3.** Doctrine, Pańch. 253, 12. **4.** Knowledge. **5.** Wish. **Comp.** *Bahu-*, adj. 1. thought much of, respected, Bhartṛ. 2, 59. 2. having many different opinions. *Sâdhu-*, adj. praised, Chr. 56, 12. *Su-*, adj. kindly disposed. Desider. **I.** † *mimanisha* and † *mimaṁsa*. **II.** Anomal. *mimâṁsa*, Âtm.

1. To consider, Man. 4, 224. **2.** To learn, MBh. 1, 3878. Comp. ptcple. of the fut. pass. *a-mîmâṁsya*, adj. Not to be questioned, Man. 2, 10. Caus., and *i.* 10, *mânaya*, **1.** To estimate highly, to honour, MBh. 3, 2424; also Âtm., Chr. 43, 23. **2.** To love, Râm. 1, 38, 8. **3.** Âtm. † **1.** To be proud. **2.** † To be stupid. Anomal. ptcple. of the pres. Âtm. in the signification of the Par. *mânayâna*, MBh. 3, 13111. *mânita*, Honoured, Chr. 28, 23. *mânya, mânanîya*, To be honoured, Bhartṛ. 2, 70; Râjat. 5, 337.—With the prep. अनु *anu*, **1.** To assent, Man. 9, 97. **2.** To approve, Râm. 2, 2, 13. **3.** With *na*, To disown, Ragh. 16, 85. **4.** To permit, Râm. 2, 21, 45. **5.** To pardon, Çâk. d. 116. *anumata*, **1.** Assented to, Man. 3, 4. **2.** Concurred with. **3.** Accepted, Daçak. in Chr. 184, 3. **4.** Agreeable. **5.** Beloved. n. Assent, Man. 5, 151; Vikr. d. 58. Caus. **1.** To cause to approve, Râm. 2, 2, 8. **2.** To honour, MBh. 3, 278. **3.** To cause to agree, to bring in analogy with, Daçak. in Chr. 188, 1.—With अभि *abhi*, **1.** To intend, Pañch. 15, 23. **2.** To desire, Man. 10, 95. **3.** To approve, MBh. 2, 1374. **4.** To believe, Bhaṭṭ. 5, 71. **5.** To consider, Pañch. iii. d. 154. **6.** To surpass, MBh. 3, 1388. *abhimata*, **1.** Wished. **2.** Assented to. **3.** Agreeable, Megh. 50. **4.** Beloved, Pañch. i. d. 80. n. Wish, Hit. 57, 5, M.M. **Comp.** *An-abhimata-*, adj. disagreeable, Hit. 15, 2, M.M. *Yathâ-abhimata+m*, adv. according to one's wish; how one lists, ad libitum, Pañch. 167, 24. — With अव *ava*, To despise, Man. 4, 135; Vikr. d. 30. **2.** To offend, Man. 8, 84. Caus. To despise, Man. 2, 50.—With अभ्यव *abhi-ava*, To disdain, Man. 4, 249.—With प्रति *prati*, Caus. To honour, Râm. 3, 53, 27.—With वि *vi*, *vimata*, **1.** Disliking. **2.** Disagreeing. m. An enemy (rather *mata* with *vi*). Caus. To disgrace, Çâk. d. 116. *vimânita*, Dishonoured, Pañch. i. d. 127.—With सम् *sam*, **1.** To think, Râm. 3, 52, 2. **2.** To resolve, Râm. 3, 53, 4. *saṁmata*, **1.** Assented to, approved; *açvapṛishṭhe saṁmata*, A good horseman, Râm. 1, 19, 19. **2.** Conformable. **3.** Like, resembling, Chr. 32, 23. **4.** Attached to. **5.** Beloved, Man. 3, 39; Pañch. i. d. 65. n. Opinion, Hit. 48, 1. **Comp.** *Su-*, adj. much approved, honoured, Chr. 49, 14. Caus. To honour, Râm. 2, 16, 15; Chr. 22, 26.—Cf. *mnâ, mati*; μένος, μέμονα, αὐτό-ματος (= *mata*), μάτην, μάταιος (not real, only imagined), μάντις, μαίνομαι, μῆνις, μαίομαι, μέμαα; Lat. monere, monstrum, monstrare, mentiri (cf. *mati*), mendax; Goth. munan, muns, munths (cf. *mantra*); A.S. manian, monian, ge-munan, mudh.

मनन *man+ana*, n. **1.** Minding, considering, Vedântas. in Chr. 216, 1; cf. 21. **2.** Understanding.

मनस् *man+as*, n. **1.** Mind, Chr. 3, 8; Man. 1, 104; considered as seat of perception (MBh. 14, 668), and passion, the heart, Vikr. d. 19; Bhâg. P. 5, 11, 9. **2.** The intellect, Vedântas. in Chr. 206, 24; power of mind, Chr. 27, 7. **3.** Purpose, Chr. 12, 23; Râjat. 5, 251.—**Comp.** *Anya-* (cf. *anyad*), adj. 1. one whose mind is directed to another, Râm. 5, 35, 2. 2. fickle-minded, Hit. i. d. 110, M.M. 3. absent. *Ud-*, see s.v. *unmanas*, and adde, sorry, Vikr. 30, 10. *Eka-*, adj. one whose mind is directed to one object, intent, Râm. 4, 4, 20. *Durm°*, i.e. *dus-*, 1. n. perversity of mind, Râm. 2, 31, 20. 2. adj. disheartened, sad, Bhâg. P. 1, 6,

19. *Dveshimanas,* i.e. *dveshin-,* adj. hostile, Hit. ii. d. 150. *Pra-,* adj. delighted, happy. *Prîti-,* adj. pleased in mind. *Mahâ-,* adj. high-minded, magnanimous, Râm. 3, 55, 52. *Vaktumanas,* see s.v. *Vi-,* adj. 1. sad, Utt. Râmach. 5, 9; heart-broken, Bhâg. P. 4, 25, 11. 2. perplexed. 3. changed in mind. 4. averse. 5. absent, thinking of something else. *Çankita-,* adj. timid, Panch. 104, 16. *Sa-,* adj. unanimous, Chr. 295, 16=Rigv. i. 92, 16. *Su-,* I. adj. satisfied, Lass. 54, 20. II. m. 1. a god. 2. a learned man. 3. a student of the Vedas. 4. wheat. 5. the name of two plants. II. m. n. and f. (the last only pl.), a flower, Man. 2, 182. III. f. *sî,* great flowered jasmine. *Su-sthita-,* adj. content, Hit. ii. d. 5.. *Sthira-,* adj. having a faithful mind or heart, Panch. 107, 11. —Cf. *μένος, δυσμένης* (=*dus-*), *εὐμενής* (=*su-*), and *mnâ.*

मनस *manas+a,* A substitute of *manas* as latter part of compounds; e.g. *pramatta-,* adj. Furious, Chr. 35, 6. *pravâsa-utsuka-,* adj., f. *sâ,* One whose mind is directed to his foreign residence, to the place to which he is about to depart, Vikr. 61, 17. *vân-manasa,* i.e. *vâch-,* I. n. sing. or du. Word and mind, Vedântas. in Chr. 202, 3. II. f. *sâ,* The goddess of the serpent race.

मनसिज *manas+i-ja,* I. adj. Mental. II. m. The god of love, Vikr. d. 12.

मनसिशय *manasiçaya,* i.e. *manas+i çî+a,* m. Love, Vikr. d. 49.

मनस्विता *manasvitâ,* i.e. *manasvin+tâ,* f. 1. Intelligence. 2. Hope.

मनस्विन् *manas+vin,* I. adj. 1. Intelligent, Panch. ii. d. 128; prudent, Vikr. d. 46. 2. Attentive. II. f. *nî,* A virtuous woman, Râm. 3, 55, 34.

मनाक् *manâk,* probably **mana-* (for *mâ+na,* ptcple. pf. pass. of *mâ*; cf. *μανός* and *μινυν* in *μίνυνθα, μινυ* in *μινύθω*; Lat. minu in minuo; Goth. mins, minz, minniza, minnists, which are also derived from *mâ*) *-anch,* adv. A little, Hit. ii. d. 138.—Comp. *A-,* adv. much.

मनाका *manâkâ,* f. A female elephant.

मनायु *manâyu,* i.e. **manâya,* a denomin. derived from *manas* with *ya,* +*u,* adj. Intelligent, Chr. 294, 9=Rigv. i. 92, 9.

मनीषा *man+îshâ,* f. 1. Intellect. 2. Hymn, Chr. 298, 24=Rigv. i. 112, 24.—Comp. *Ku-manîsha,* adj. stupid, Bhâg. P. 1, 3, 37.

मनीषित *manîshita,* i.e. *manîshâ+ita,* adj. 1. Cherished in mind, Chr. 18, 35. 2. Aimed at, desired, 12, 4.

मनीषिन् *manîshin,* i.e. *manîshâ+in,* adj., f. *inî,* Intelligent, wise, Man. 2, 14.—Comp. *Ku-,* adj. stupid, Bhâg. P. 4, 31, 21.

मनु *manu,* curtailed *manus,* q. cf. I. m. 1. A man. 2. Manu, the progenitor of mankind, Man. 1, 1; 36 (Chr. 297, 16=Rigv. i. 112, 16). II. f. *manâvî* and *manâyî,* The wife of Manu.

मनुज *manu-ja,* I. m. A man in general, Bhartr. 2, 98. II. f. *jâ,* A woman.—Comp. *Nis-,* adj. deserted, Bhâg. P. 1, 6, 16.

मनुष्य *manushya,* i.e. *manus+ya,* I. m. Man, a man, Panch. 255, 17; mankind, Man. 1, 39. II. f. *shî,* A woman.—Comp. *A-,* I. m. one who is not a man, Râm. 2, 93, 21. II. adj.

deserted. *Ati-*, adj. superhuman. *Durm°*, i.e. *dus-*, m. a wicked man, MBh. 8, 2117. *Nirm°*, i.e. *nis-*, adj. 1. deserted, Râm. 2, 18, 12 Gorr. 2. without a man (upon its back, viz. an elephant), MBh. 6, 3893.—Cf. O.H.G. mannisco; Goth. mannisks; A.S. mennesc, mennisc.

मनुष्यत्व *manushya + tva*, n. Condition of man, manhood, Man. 12, 40.

मनुस् *manus*, for original *manvant* (ptcple. pres. Par. of *man*, ii. 8), m. Man (ved.).—Cf. *manu*; German, mannus (Tacit. Germ. 2); Goth. man, manna; A.S. man, mann; Lat. mas, maris; Μίνως.

मनोगत *manogata*, i.e. *manas-gata* (vb. *gam*), I. adj. Seated in the mind. II. n. **1.** Thought. **2.** Wish, Chr. 20, 18.

मनोजू *manojû*, i.e. *manas-jû*, adj. Swift as thought, Chr. 291, 4 = Rigv. i. 85, 4.

मनोज्ञ *manojña*, i.e. *manas-jña*, I. adj. Beautiful, Ṛit. 6, 25. **II.** f. **1.** A princess. **2.** Red arsenic.

मनोभव *manobhava*, and **मनोभू** *manobhû*, i.e. *manas-bhû + a*, and *manas-bhû*, m. The god of love, Pañch. 128, 5 (*bhava*); Kathâs. 3, 62 (*bhû*).

मनोरम *manorama*, i.e. *manas-ram + a*, adj. Beautiful, Pañch. 127, 24.

मनोहर *manohara*, i.e. *manas-hṛi + a*, adj. Beautiful, charming, Vikr. d. 9; 119.—**Comp.** *Su-*, adj. very charming, Pañch. pr. d. 3.

मनोह्वा *manohvâ*, i.e. *manas-hve + a*, f. Red arsenic.

मन्तु *man + tu*, I. m. **1.** A man. **2.** A king. **3.** Offence. II. f. Intellect.—Comp. *Tri-*, adj. knowing the three worlds, i.e. all-wise, Chr. 296, 4 = Rigv. i. 112, 4.—Cf. μαντεύομαι.

मन्तूय *MANTÛYA*, a denomin. derived from *mantu* with *ya*, Par. To be offended or jealous, Bhaṭṭ. 5, 73.

मन्तृ *man + tṛi*, m. **1.** A wise man. **2.** An adviser.—Cf. Μέντωρ.

मन्त्र् *MANTR*, i. 10 (properly a denomin. derived from *mantra*), Âtm. (but often also Par.). † i. 1, Par. **1.** To take secret council with (with instr. and acc.), Man. 7, 146; Pañch. rec. orn. **2.** To deliberate, Râm. 2, 16, 15. **3.** To resolve, Hit. 129, 13. **4.** To speak, Hit. 64, 6 (Par.). Ptcple. of the pf. pass. *mantrita*, Advised. **Comp.** See *Ku-*. *Durm°*, i.e. *dus-*, I. adj. imprudently advised, MBh. 5, 4262. II. n. a bad advice, ib. 5, 2697. *Su-*, I. adj. 1. well deliberated, Hit. iii. d. 137. 2. well counselled. II. n. wise counsel.—With the prep. **अनु** *anu*, **1.** To accompany with spells or prayers, to consecrate by spells, to charm, Chr. 31, 12; Utt. Râmach. 39, 10. **2.** To dismiss, MBh. 3, 39.—With **अभि** *abhi*, To consecrate by blessings, Râm. 1, 24, 2; by spells, to charm, Draup. 8, 54.—With **आ** *â*, **1.** To address, Râm. 1, 1, 8. **2.** To salute, MBh. 3, 2243. **3.** To invite, Man. 3, 191; Pañch. 26, 20. **4.** To call, Utt. Râmach. 125, 9. **5.** To ask, MBh. 4, 64. **6.** To take leave (acc.), MBh. 3, 2295.—With **समा** *sam-â*, To address, MBh. 2, 42.—With **उप** *upa*, **1.** To address, Daçak. in Chr. 197, 10. **2.** To invite, Râm. 1, 46, 12. **3.** To take leave (acc.), Chr. 45, 11.—With **नि** *ni*, To invite, Man. 3, 187; to present with (with instr.) Pañch. iii. d. 139.—With **उपनि** *upa*

-ni, 1. To invite, Râm. 3, 52, 51. 2. To consecrate, MBh. 3, 15959.—With संनि *sam-ni*, To invite, MBh. 3, 2112.—With परि *pari*, To consecrate, to charm, Arj. 7, 18.—With सम् *sam*, 1. To take council with (instr.), Pañch. 25, 13; Chr. 53, 6. 2. To deliberate, Man. 7, 216. 3. To reflect, Pañch. 25, 14. 4. To salute, MBh. 1, 5454.—Cf. probably Goth. mathljan; see *mantra*.

मन्त्र *man + tra*, m. 1. That part of the Veda which comprises the hymns, Madhusûdana in Weber, Ind. St. i. 14. 2. A holy text, Vikr. 87, 10; Pañch. 189, 24. 3. A mystical verse or incantation, charm, Pañch. i. d. 73. 4. Prayer, Vikr. 32, 16. 5. A formula sacred to any individual deity. 6. Advice, Hit. 54, 14; secret consultation, Pañch. i. d. 61 (*mantraṁ sam-â-char*, To intrigue). 7. A design, Hit. i. d. 128, M.M.—Comp. *A-*, adj. 1. not accompanied by holy texts, Man. 3, 121. 2. excluded from the use of the Veda, 9, 18. *Âkṛishṭi-*. m. a charm having the power of attraction, Hit. i. d. 96, M.M. See *Ku-*. *Durm°*, i.e. *dus-*, m. bad advice, Bhartṛ. 2, 34. *Nirm°*, i.e. *nis-*, adj. unaccompanied by holy texts, MBh. 1, 2980. *Visha-*, m. a snake-catcher.—Cf. probably Goth. mathl, mathleins.

मन्त्रज्ञ *mantra-jña*, m. 1. A spy. 2. A priest.—Comp. *Su-*, adj. well versed in holy texts, Johns. Sel. 10, 20.

मन्त्रण *mantraṇa*, i.e. *mantr + ana*, n., and f. *ṇâ*, Advising.

मन्त्रतस् *mantra + tas*, adv. 1.=abl. of *mantra*, Man. 3, 65. 2. Advisedly, deliberately.

मन्त्रवन्त् *mantra + vant*, I. adj., f. *vatî*. 1. Accompanied with holy texts, Man. 2, 29. 2. Entitled to use the Vedas. 3. Initiated. II. *°vat*, adv. With holy verses, hallowed by holy texts, Man. 2, 64.

मन्त्रविद् *mantra-vid*, I. adj. 1. Conversant with the Vedas, Johns. Sel. 42, 51. 2. Conversant with charms, Daçak. in Chr. 187, 9. II. m. 1. A spy. 2. A counsellor, Chr. 55, 6. 3. A priest.—Comp. *A-*, adj. unacquainted with holy texts, unlearned, Man. 3, 133.

मन्त्रिक *mantrika*, i.e. *mantra + ika*, m. One who is conversant with charms, Lass. 17, 8.

मन्त्रिता *mantritâ*, f., and मन्त्रित्व *mantritva*, n., i.e. *mantrin + tâ* or *tva*, The state or office of a counsellor, ministership, Hit. 54, 14.—Comp. *Sa-mantritva*, n. assent, Râjat. 5, 248.

मन्त्रिन् *mantrin*, i.e. *mantra + in*, m. A counsellor, Pañch. i. d. 428 (*a-sant-*, adj. Having wicked counsellors).—Comp. *Durm°*, i.e. *dus-*, m. a bad counsellor, Pañch. iii. d. 244. *Pradhâna-*, m. the prime minister, Lass. 35, 6. *Mahâ-*, m. the prime minister, Hit. 97, 16.

मन्त्रिवत् *mantrivat*, i.e. *mantrin + vat*, adv. Like a counsellor, Râjat. 5, 389.

मन्थ् *MANTH*, see *math*.

मन्थ *mantha*, curtailed *manthan* (see *mathin*), m. 1. A churning-stick. 2. The sun. 3. Churning, Utt. Râmach. 172, 12. 4. Stirring, Ragh. 3, 10. 5. Killing.—Comp. *Maṇi-*, n. rock-salt.

मन्थज *mantha-ja*, n. Butter.

मन्थन *manth + ana*, I. n. 1. Churning, MBh. 1, 1141. Agitating. II. f. *nî*, A churn. — Comp. *Amṛita-*, n. production of the Amṛita, the beverage of the gods, by churning, MBh. vol. i. p. 41, l. 2.

मन्थर *manth+ara,* I. adj. **1.** Slow, Daçak. in Chr. 182, 2. **2.** Torpid, Ragh. 19, 21. **3.** Large. **4.** Crooked. **5.** Stupid. **6.** Low. **II.** m. **1.** A treasure. **2.** Fruit. **3.** An obstacle. **4.** A churning-stick. **5.** A proper name, Hit. 58, 7, M.M. **III.** n. Safflower.

मन्थरु *manth+aru,* m. The wind from a whisk.

मन्थान *manthâna* (vb. *manth*), m. A churning-stick, Râm. 1, 45, 19.

मन्थिन् *manth + in,* I. adj. **1.** Churning. **2.** Afflicting. II. f. *nî,* A churn.—Comp. *Ûrdhva-*, adj. chaste (cf. *mathin*), Bhâg. P. 5, 3, 20.

मन्द् *MAND* (from *mad*), i. 1, Âtm. **1.** † To get drunk. **2.** To rejoice. **3.** To praise. **4.** To sleep. † **5.** To languish. † **6.** To move slowly. † **7.** To shine.—Cf. probably Lat. mundus; O.H.G. mandjan, to rejoice.

मन्द *manda,* I. adj. **1.** Slow, Çṛingârat. 7. **2.** Stupid, Chr. 8, 31. **3.** Unlucky. **4.** Little, Hit. 58, 13. **5.** Low (as a tone), Râm. 3, 55, 36 (adv.); Pańch. 173, 1. **6.** Doubled, *mandammandam*, adv. Very slowly, Pańch. 90, 21. **II.** m. **1.** A name of Saturn. **2.** A name of Yama.—Comp. *Pichu-*, m. a tree, Azadirachta indica A. Juss. (also, but erroneously, *pichumarda*), Çiç. 5, 66.

मन्दगतित्व *manda-gati + tva,* n. Property of moving slowly, Pańch. 142, 11.

मन्दत्व *manda + tva,* n. Foolishness, Pańch. ii. d. 179.

मन्दन *mand+ana,* n. Praise.

मन्दभाग्यता *manda-bhâgya+tâ,* f. Misfortune, Pańch. 227, 20.

मन्दर *mandara* (cf. *manthara,* and vb. *mand*), I. adj. **1.** Slow. **2.** Large. **II.** m. **1.** The name of a fabulous mountain with which the ocean was churned, MBh. 1, 1112; Kir. 5, 30. **2.** The mandara tree, one of the trees of paradise. **3.** The paradise. **4.** A mirror.

मन्दसान *mandasâna* (vb. *mand*), m. **1.** A name of Agni. **2.** Life. **3.** Sleep.

मन्दाक *mandâka,* n. A current, a stream.

मन्दाकिनी *mandâkinî,* i.e. *mandâka+in,* f. The Ganges of heaven, Utt. Râmach. 158, 3.

मन्दाय *MANDÂYA,* a denomin. derived from *manda* with *ya,* Âtm. To go tardily, to delay, Vikr. d. 56; Megh. 39.

मन्दार *mandâra* (vb. *mand*), m. **1.** One of the five trees in Indra's paradise, Vikr. d. 6, 127; Megh. 73. **2.** The coral tree, Erythrina fulgens, Megh. 68. **3.** Swallow-wort, Asclepias gigantea.—Comp. *Kṛita-*, m. A proper name, Râjat. 5, 35.

मन्दारवती *mandâravatî,* i.e. *mandâra+vant+î,* f. A proper name, Lass. 16, 6.

मन्दारु *mandâru,* m. The coral tree, Erythrina fulgens (see *mandâra*).

मन्दिर *mandira,* I. m. **1.** The sea. **2.** The back of the knee. **II.** f. *râ,* A stable. **III.** f. *râ,* and n. A house, Hit. ii. d. 126 (n.); a palace, Vikr. 35, 2; Kathâs. 26, 283 (f.). **IV.** n. **1.** A town. **2.** A temple.—Comp. *Avaskara-*, n. the privy, Râjat. 5, 406. *Keli-*, n. A pleasure-house, Chaurap. 23. *Jala*

-yantra-, n. a summer-house erected in the midst of water or on the bank of a river, Ṛit. 1, 2.

मन्दुरा *mandurâ*, f. A stable for horses, Weber, Ind. St. iii. 370, 14.

मन्द्र *mandra*, m. **1.** A deep, hollow, or low tone, or sound, Megh. 97 (read *mandra-*); Vikr. 65, 11 (adj. ?). **2.** A sort of drum.—Comp. *Â-*, adj. Grumbling, Megh. 35 (read *âmandr°*).

मन्धातृ *mandhâtṛi*, m. A proper name, Chr. 297, 13=Rigv. i. 112, 13.

मन्मथ *manmatha* (frequent. of *manth* + *a*), m. **1.** A name of the god of love, Pañch. 216, 17. **2.** Love, Ṛit. 1, 27. **3.** The elephant or wood-apple.

मन्मय *manmaya*, i.e. 2.*mad* + *maya*, adj. Full of me, attached to me, Bhag. 4, 10.

ऽमन्य *-man* + *ya*, latter part of comp. adj. Thinking one's self; e.g. *jña* + *m-manya*, adj. Thinking one's self a wise man, Râjat. 3, 491.

मन्या *manyâ*, f. The tendon forming the nape of the neck.

मन्यु *man* + *yu*, m. **1.** Anger, Utt. Râmach. 83, 11; fury, Pañch. 59, 16. **2.** Sorrow, grief, Chr. 7, 21; Utt. Râmach. 94, 14. **3.** Distress. **4.** A sacrifice.—Comp. *Abhi-*, m. a proper name. *Ahi-*, adj. furious like snakes, Chr. 290, 8=Rigv. i. 64, 8. *Vita-*, i.e. *vi-ita-* (vb. *i*), adj. exempt from sorrow or anger, Brâhmaṇav. 1, 6. *Sa-*, I. adj. 1. angry. 2. sorrowful. II. m. Çiva.—Cf. μῆνις.

मन्युमन्त् *manyu* + *mant*, adj., f. *mati*, **1.** Angry. **2.** Sorrowful.

मन्वन्तर *manvantara*, i.e. *manu-antara*, n. The period of a Manu, equal to seventy-one ages of the gods, Man. 1, 79; Utt. Râmach. 19, 7; fourteen *Manvantaras* constitute a *Kalpa*.

† मभ्र् *MABHR*, i. 1, Par. To go.

ममता *mamatâ*, i.e. *mama*, gen. sing. of *asmad*, + *tâ*, f. **1.** Selfishness. **2.** Pride.

ममत्व *mama* + *tva* (cf. the last), n. Arrogance, Lass. 85, 11.

मम्ब् *MAMB*, see *barb*.

† मय् *MAY*, i. 1, Âtm. To go.—Cf. perhaps Lat. meare; see *mi*.

मय *maya*, m. **1.** A camel. **2.** A mule.

मयु *mayu*, m. The name of a class of attendants on Kuvera.

मयूख *mayûkha*, m. **1.** A ray of light, Pañch. i. d. 92. **2.** Light, splendour, Ṛit. 6, 29. **3.** Beauty.—Comp. *Unm°*, i.e. *ud-*, adj. radiant, Ragh. 16, 69. *Çita-*, m. 1. the moon. 2. camphor.

मयूर *mayûra*, I. m. **1.** A peacock, Hit. i. d. 178, M.M. **2.** The name of a flower and of a plant. II. f. *rî*, A peahen, Utt. Râmach. 55, 8.

मयोभू *mayobhû*, i.e. *mayas* (ved. Enjoyment), *-bhû*, adj. Yielding enjoyment, Chr. 295, 18=Rigv. i. 92, 18.

मरक *maraka*, i.e. *mṛi* + *aka*, m. Epidemic disease.

मरकत *marakata*, and मरक्त *marakta*, n. An emerald, Bhâg. P. 4, 25, 15 (*°kata*); Pañch. 9, 5 (*°kata*).

मरण *maraṇa*, i.e. *mṛi* + *ana*, n. **1.** Dying, Râm. 3, 48, 1. **2.** Death, Pañch. 128, 7.—Comp. *Â-maraṇa* + *m*, adv. till death, Hit. i. d. 187, M.M. (*âmaraṇa-anta*, adj. ending only at death).

Saha-, n. a widow's burning herself with her deceased husband.

मरणज *maraṇa-ja*, adj. Produced by death, Pańch. v. d. 24.

मरत *marata*, i.e. *mṛi* + *ata*, m. Death.

मराल *marâla*, I. adj. Soft. II. m. 1. A sort of goose. 2. A duck. 3. A cloud. 4. A grove. 5. Lamp-black used as collyrium.

मरिच and मरीच *marîcha*, n. Pepper.

मरीचि *marîchi* (also °*chî*, f., Râm. 1, 56, 18). I. m. and f. A ray of light, Vikr. d. 47. II. m. 1. One of the Prajâpatis, Man. 1, 58; first of the Pitṛis, 3, 194. 2. A proper name, Daçak. in Chr. 179, 7.

मरीचिका *marîchi* + *kâ*, f. The mirage.

मरीचिप *marîchi-pa* (vb. 1.*pâ*), m. A kind of genius, Sund. 3, 5.

मरु *maru*, i.e. *mṛi* + *u*, m. 1. A desert, Hit. i. d. 10, M.M.; Bhâg. P. 6, 8, 36. 2. A mountain. 3. The name of a country.—Cf. probably A.S. mór.

मरुत् *marut* (vb. *mṛi* ?), I. m. 1. pl. The deities of wind, Vikr. d. 36. 2. Wind, Pańch. i. d. 353. 3. Air, Bhâshâp. 2. II. n. A sort of perfume.

मरुत *marut* + *a*, m. Wind.

मरुत्त *marutta*, m. The name of a fabulous king, MBh. 14, 226; Vishṇu P. 352.

मरुत्वन्त् *marut* + *vant*, m. 1. Indra, Vikr. d. 15. 2. The monkey Hanumant. 3. A cloud.

मरुल *marula*, m. A sort of duck.

मरूक *marûka*, m. A sort of deer.

मरोल *marola*, m. A marine monster.

मर्क *marka* (vb. *mṛi*), m. 1. A body. 2. The vital breath which pervades the body. 3. A monkey. 4. An imp, Stenzler, in Journ. of the German Oriental Society, vii. 531, 16.

मर्कट *marka* + *ṭa*, m. 1. A monkey, Man. 12, 67; Pańch. 118, 12. 2. A spider. 3. A large crane, Ardea argala. 4. A kind of venom.

मर्करा *markarâ*, f. 1. A chasm, a hole. 2. A vessel. 3. A barren woman.

मर्च् *MARCH*, see *mârj*.

मर्जू *marjû*, i.e. *mṛij* + *u*, I. m. 1. A washerman. 2. A catamite. II. f. Cleansing, cleanliness.

मर्त *marta* (old ptcple. pf. pass. of *mṛi*), m. A mortal, a man, Chr. 291, 13 = Rigv. i. 64, 13.—Cf. μορτός, βροτός; Lat. mortuus, mortalis.

मर्त्य *martya*, i.e. *marta* + *ya*, I. m. 1. A mortal, a man, Pańch. ii. d. 89. 2. The earth. II. f. *yâ*, A woman. III. n. The body, Bhâg. P. 3, 33, 32.—Comp. *A-*, 1. adj. immortal, Ragh. 7, 50. 2. m. a deity.

मर्द *marda*, i.e. *mṛid* + *a*, m. Grinding, pounding, MBh. 1, 1121.

मर्दन *mardana*, i.e. *mṛid* + *ana*, n. 1. Rubbing, Pańch. 238, 7. 2. Touching, Çṛingârat. 14. 3. Grinding, Hit. iii. d. 76.—Comp. *Ari-*, m. 1. a destroyer of enemies, Draup. 6, 14 2. a proper name, Hariv. 1917. *Sarva-kshatriya-*, m. the destroyer of all the military class, Johns. Sel. 3, 16.

मर्दल *mardala*, m. A sort of drum.

मर्दिन् *mardin*, i.e. *mṛid* + *in*, adj., f. *nî*, Grinding; in *mahisha-mardinî*, f.

Durgâ. *loshṭa-*, adj. Who or what breaks clods of earth, Man. 4, 71.

मर्ब् *MARB*, see *barb*.

मर्मज्ञ *marmajña*, i.e. *marman-jña*, I. adj. One who knows another's weak points, Pańch. i. d. 278. II. m. A learned and intelligent man, Hit. 92, 5.

मर्मन् *marman*, i.e. *mṛi* + *man*, n. 1. A vital member or organ, Böhtl. Ind. Spr. 1586. 2. A joint of a limb, Hit. iv. d. 82. 3. A weak point, Hit. iii. d. 59. 4. A secret, Pańch. iii. d. 200. 5. Design, Hit. iii. d. 19. 6. Truth.—Comp. *Antar-*, n. the heart, Utt. Râmach. 128, 5. *Çirom°*, i.e. *çiras-*, m. a hog.—Cf. Lat. membrum.

मर्ममय *marmamaya*, i.e. *marman* + *maya*, adj., f. *yî*, Containing (their) secrets, Pańch. 184, 22.

मर्मर *marmara* (a reduplicated form based on an imitative sound), m. The rustling sound of cloth, or dry leaves, Ragh. 6, 57 (at the end of a comp. adj.); of the wind, Râjat. 2, 165 (roaring).—Cf. Lat. murmurare; O.H.G. murmuron; μόρμορος, μορμύρω, etc.

मर्मरीक *marmarîka*, m. A low, a wicked man.

मर्मविद् *marmavid*, and **मर्मवेदिन्** *marmavedin*, i.e. *marman-vid*, or *-vedin*, m. A learned and intelligent man.

मर्मस्पृश् *marmaspṛiç*, i.e. *marman -spṛiç*, adj. Giving pain.

मर्य *marya*, i.e. *mṛi* + *ya*, I. m. (ved.), A man, a warrior, Chr. 290, 2 = Rigv. i. 64, 2; a husband. II. f. *yâ*, A boundary. —With I. cf. perhaps Lat. maritus.

मर्यादा *maryâdâ*, i.e. *maryâ-da* (vb. *dâ*), f. 1. A landmark, Mân. 9, 291. 2. A boundary, limit, Pańch. i. d. 65. 3. Continuance in the right way, rectitude. — Comp. *A-maryâdo*, adj. not keeping within the right way, Pańch. i. d. 158; unrestrained, unruly. *Agni-sâkshika-*, adj. one who is married in presence of the sacred fire, Hit. i. d. 191. *An-apa-îkshita-*, adj. regardless of the limits (drawn by the holy scriptures), Man. 8, 309. *Durm°*, i.e. *dus -maryâda*, adj. wicked, Utt. Râmach. 113, 4. *Nirm°*, i.e. *nis-*, I adj. 1. boundless. 2. unruly. 3. sinful, impious, Pańch. 152, 7. 4. confused, Râm. 3, 69, 19. II. n. confusion, MBh. 4, 1052; a sort of battle, Hariv. 15978. *Bhinna-* (vb. *bhid*). adj. unbounded, unrestrained, Utt. Râmach. 137, 3. *Sa-*, adj. 1. bounded. 2. near. 3. correct in conduct.

मर्यादिन् *maryâdin*, i.e. *maryâdâ* + *in*, adj. not trespassing one's boundary, Lass. 1, 12.

† **मर्व्** *MARV*, i. 1, Par. To fill; cf. *mârj*.

मर्ष *marsha*, i.e. *mṛish* + *a*, m. Endurance. — Comp. *A-*, m. 1. impatience, inability to endure, Utt. Râmach. 134, 1; indignation, Johns. Sel. 5, 27. 2. passion, wrath, Râm. 6, 100, 3. *Nis-a-*, adj. devoid of energy, MBh. 5, 2896. *Sâmarsha*, i.e. *sa-a-*, adj. full of passion, wrathful, Râm. 6, 91, 6. *°sham*, adv. angrily, Mṛichchh. 19, 17.

मर्षण *marshaṇa*, i.e. *mrish* + *ana*, n. Enduring.—Comp. *A-*, adj. impatient, unable to endure, Nal. 12, 54; wrathful, Hiḍ. 4, 54 (*ati-a-*). *Agha-*, n. the name of a holy text, Man. 11, 260. *Durm°*, i.e. *dus-*, I. adj. difficult to be endured, or to be managed, Râm. 6, 3, 33. II. m. a proper name.

† **मल्** *MAL*, **मल्ल्** *MALL*, i. 1, Âtm., and **मल्** *MAL*, i. 10, *malaya*, or *malâpaya*, Par. To hold.

मल *mala,* I. adj. **1.** Dirty. **2.** Niggardly. **II.** (m. and) n. **1.** Dirt, filth, Daçak. in Chr. 184, 9. **2.** Sediment, dregs. **3.** Filthy refuse, Man. 11, 93. **4.** Excretion of the body, as fæces, etc., Man. 5, 132. **5.** Sin, Man. 2, 102. **6.** Defilement, Man. 11, 70. **7.** Rust. **8.** Camphor. **9.** Cuttle fishbone.—Comp. *A-*, adj., f. *lâ*, pure, Pańch. ii. d. 182; white, Vikr. d. 157. *Kâṁsya-*, n. verdigris, Suçr. 2, 237, 18. *Nirm°*, i.e. *nis-*, adj., f. *lâ*. 1. stainless, Hit. i. d. 47, M.M. 2. pure, Hit. ii. d. 134; clear, Pańch. 248, 5. 3. bright, Johns. Sel. 12, 33. *Bahu-*, m. lead. *Vi-*, I. adj. 1. clean, spotless, Chr. 40, 12. 2. pure, Pańch. v. d. 36; Çiç. 9, 13. 3. clear, Pańch. iii. d. 147 = day, Chr. 37, 31. 4. transparent. 5. white. 6. beautiful. II. n. silvergilt. *Çânta-*, adj. exempt from soil, literally and figuratively. *Sa-*, I. adj. 1. dirty. 2. sinful. II. n. fæces, ordure.—Cf. μέλας (cf. *malina*), μόρον, μάρμαρος, μαρμαίρω; A.S. smere, smerian, smerwian, smyrian.

मलपङ्किन् *malapańkin*, i.e. *mala-pańka + in*, adj. Covered with mud and dirt, Chr. 46, 20.

मलमल्लक *mala-malla + ka*, n. A piece of cloth worn over the privities, Daçak. in Chr. 184, 24.

मलय *malaya*, m. **1.** A mountainous range in the Dekhan, Lass. 38, 17; Vikr. d. 25. **2.** The country lying along this range, Malabar. **3.** A garden. **4.** The garden of Indra.

मलयज *malaya-ja*, m. and n. Sandalwood, Böhtl. Ind. Spr. 3322; Vikr. d. 51.

मलाका *malâkâ*, i.e. *mala + âka*, f. **1.** A lewd woman. **2.** A female messenger. **3.** A female elephant.

मलिन *malina*, i.e. *mala + in + a*, I. adj. **1.** Dirty, Pańch. iii. d. 178; soiled, Hit. ii. d. 39. **2.** Black, Çiç. 9, 18; obscure, ib. 23; obscured, Hit. i. d. 27, M.M. **3.** Sinful. **4.** Bad. **II.** n. **1.** Fault. **2.** Buttermilk.—Comp. *A-*, adj. pure, Bhartṛ. 3, 100.

मलिनत्व *malina + tva*, n. Blackness, Châṇ. 76 in Berl. Monatsb. 1864, 412.

मलिम्लुच *malimluch + a* (from an anomal. frequent. of *mluch*), m. **1.** A thief. **2.** The intercalary lunar month. **3.** Fire. **4.** Wind. **5.** An imp.

मलीमस *malîmasa* (cf. *mala*), adj. **1.** Dirty, Hit. ii. d. 148; stained, Ragh. 2, 53. **2.** Wicked.

मल्ल् *MALL*, see *mal*.

मल्ल *malla*, I. adj. **1.** Strong. **2.** Excellent. **II.** m. **1.** A wrestler; the son of an outcaste Kshatriya, Man. 10, 22; 12, 45. **2.** A cup. **3.** The hemicranium. **4.** The residue of an oblation. **III.** f. *lâ*. **1.** A woman. **2.** Arabian jasmine.—Comp. *Hastimalla*, i.e. *hastin-*, m. 1. the elephant of Indra. 2. *Gaṇeça*. 3. a chief of the Nâgas, or serpents.

मल्लक *malla + ka*, I. m. **1.** A tooth. **2.** A leaf to wrap up something, or a cup, Mṛichchh. 126, 9 v.r.; cf. Wilson, Hind. Th. i. 2 ed. 134, n., and Stenzler, n. II. m., and f. *likâ*, An oil vessel.

मल्लघटी *mallaghaṭi*, f. A kind of dancing, Vikr. 62, 19.

मल्लि and **मल्ली** *mallî*, f. Arabian jasmine, Jasminum zambac, Lass. 67, 7 (*li*).—Comp. *Madhu-mallî*, f. double jasmine. *Rańga-mallî*, f. a lute.

मल्लिक *mallika*, I. m. **1.** A sort of goose with brown legs and bill, Utt. Râmach. 20, 4 (rather *mallikâkhya*).

2. A shuttle. 3. The month Mâgha. II. f. *kâ* (i.e. *malli* + *ka*). 1. Arabian jasmine, Ṛit. 6, 6. 2. A goblet. 3. A river. 4. See *mallaka*.

† **मव्** *MAV*, and **मव्य्** *MAVY*, i. 1, Par. To bind, see *mû*.

† **मश्** *MAÇ*, **मिश्** *MIÇ*, i. 1, Par. 1. To sound. 2. To be angry.

मशक *maçaka* (akin to *makshikâ*, q. cf.), m. 1. A gnat, a musquito, Hit. i. d. 80, M.M.; Pańch. iii. d. 98. 2. A kind of cutaneous eruption. 3. A leather water-bag. — Comp. *Daṁça-*, m. a biting gnat, Man. 1, 40.

मशहरी *maçaharî* (*maça*[=*maçaka*]-*hṛi* + *a* + *î*), f. Curtains to keep off musquitoes.

मशुन *maçuna* (perhaps a form of *mahâ-çvan* + *a*), m. A dog.

† **मष्** *MASH* (and **मुष्** *MUSH*), i. 1, Par. To kill, to hurt.

मषि m., and **मषी** f. *mashî*, and **मसि** m., **मसी** f. *masî*, 1. Ink, Kathâs. 4, 69 (*shî*); also in Pehlewi *masi*, Haug, in Journ. of the German Oriental Society, xix. 305; if it was originally the juice of the cuttle-fish, which the Romans also used for writing, it may be akin to Zend. *maçyo* = Sskr. *matsya*. 2. The stalk of the Nyctanthes tristis.

मष्क् *MASHK*, see *mask*.

मस् *MAS* (cf. *mâ*), i. 4, Par. To mete, to measure. Ptcple. pf. pass. *masta*.—Cf. perhaps μεστός.

मसार *masâra*, m. A sapphire, Râm. 3, 48, 12 (? cf. Böhtl. s.v. *galvarka*).

मसि, मसी *masî*, see *mashi*.

मसिन *masina*, adj. Well ground.

मसुर and **मसूर** *masûra*, 1. m., and f. *râ*, A sort of lentil, Ervum hirsutum, Suçr. 1, 24, 9; 26, 1 (?). 2. f. *râ*, A harlot.

मसूरिका *masûrikâ*, i.e. *masûra* + *ka*, f. A procuress.

मसृण *masṛiṇa*, I. adj. 1. Soft, Utt. Râmach. 24, 14. 2. Unctuous, shining, ib. 107, 6. II. f. *ṇâ*, Linseed.

मसृणित *masṛiṇita*, i.e. *masṛiṇa* + *ita*, adj. Polished, Utt. Râmach. 129, 1.

† **मस्क्** *MASK*, **मष्क्** *MASHK*, and **मक्क्** *MAKK*, i. 1, Âtm. To go.

मस्कर *maskara*, m. A bambu.

मस्करिन् *maskara* + *in*, m. 1. A religious mendicant, Lass. 76, 15. 2. The moon.

मस्त *masta* (perhaps vb. *man*), n. The head, Lass. 70, 2 (at the end of a comp. adj.); cf. *mas*.

मस्तक *masta* + *ka*, m. n. 1. The head, Pańch. 246, 14. 2. The top, the summit, Man. 4, 47; Pańch. 262, 17.—Comp. *Madhu-*, n. a sweetmeat made of flour, honey, oil, and butter (cf. *mastu*).

मस्तिष्क *mastishka* (akin to *masta*), n. The brain, Lass. 4, 17; Hariv. 4740.

मस्तु *mastu*, n. Whey.

मस्तुलुङ्ग and **मस्तुलुङ्गक** *mastuluṅga* and °*ga* + *ka*, m. The brain.

मह् *MAH*, i. 1, and i. 10, Par. To adore, to honour, Pańch. ii. d. 72; Kir. 5, 24. The original form was *magh* and the original signification 'To be great, powerful.'—Cf. *magha*, *mahant*, and Goth. and A.S. magan; Goth. magu, mavi, mahts; A.S. maeht, meaht, miht; Goth. mahteig; O.H.G. magan, great, heavy; A.S. maegn, meagn, strength; Goth. magus, a boy; A.S. mag, maeg, maegen, macian; Goth. magaths; A.S. maegdh; O.H.G. machôn; A.S. macian; *μόγος*, *μόχθος*, *μόλις* (for *μόγλοις*), *μέγαρον* (cf. O.H.G. ga-mah; N.G. Gemach), *μηχανή*, *μηχανάομαι*; Lat. magnus, mactus.

मह *mah + a*, I. adj., f. *hî*, Great, Chr. 288, 14=Rigv. i. 88, 14. **II.** m. **1.** Light. **2.** A festival. **3.** A sacrifice. **4.** A buffalo. **III.** f. *hâ*, A cow. **IV.** f. *hî*. **1.** The earth, Utt. Râmach. 172, 13 (as deity); Daçak. in Chr. 179, 6; landed property, Pańch. i. d. 322. **2.** A cow. **3.** Name of a river.—**Comp.** *Dhanurmaha*, i.e. *dhanus-*, m. a festival at the consecration of a bow, Hariv. 4391.—Cf. Μαῖα, Μαιάς.

महत्त्व *mahattva*, i.e. *mahant + tva*, n. Greatness, Pańch. iii. d. 254; finite magnitude (as found in the *trasareṇu*), Bhâshâp. 57.

महन्त् *mahant* (properly ptcple. pres. of *mah*); the bases of all cases, except the sing. voc. msc., are *mahânt* and *mahat*; ved. *mahâm* instead of *mahântam*, Chr. 297, 14=Rigv. i. 112, 14. **I.** adj. **1.** Great, large, Vikr. 11, 18. **2.** Pre-eminent, Hit. pr. d. 28, M.M. **3.** Much, many. **4.** Excellent, Nal. 2, 25. **II.** adv. *hat*, Exceedingly, much, Utt. Râmach. 42, 2. **III.** m. The intellectual principle, Sâṅkhyak. 3, 22; Man. 12, 14. **IV.** n. **1.** Greatness, infinity, Bhâshâp. 25. **2.** Kingdom. **V.** f. *atî*, The lute of Nârada.—**Comp.** *Vi-*, adj. exceedingly tall, Indr. 1, 33. *Su-*, adj. 1. very great, Chr. 12, 26; very tall, Râm. 3, 55, 1. 2. very important, Nal. 8, 2. 3. abundant.—Cf. *μέγας*, *μεγάλου*, etc., *μείζων*, *μέγεθος*, *μεγαίρω*, *μάλα*, *μᾶλλον*, *μῆκος*, *μακρός*, *μάκαρες*; Lat. magis, major, majus, maximus, magister, Majus; Goth. mikils; A.S. meagol, micel, micyl, etc.; comparat. Goth. mais; A.S. ma, mae; superl. Goth. maist; A.S. maest, maegeste.

महर् *mahar*, and **महर्लोक** *mahar-loka* (*mahar* for *mahan*, akin to *mahant*, or anomal. for *mahas*), m. The abode of the saints who survive a destruction of the world; it is said to be situated above the polar star, Weber, Ind. St. ii. 178; cf. 213; Vedântas. in Chr. 209, 1 (*mahar*).

महर्द्धि *maharddhi*, i.e. *mahâ-ṛiddhi*, adj. Very perfect, Râjat. 5, 33.

महर्षि *maharshi*, i.e. *mahâ-ṛishi*, m. A sage of a pre-eminent class, Man. 1, 34.

महस् *mah + as*, n. **1.** Light, lustre, Utt. Râmach. 15, 5; Lass. 97, 6=Rigv. vi. 64, 2. **2.** A festival. **3.** A sacrifice. —**Comp.** *Piyûsha-*, m. the moon. *Mitra-*, adj. having a friendly light or lustre, Chr. 289, 11=Rigv. i. 50, 11. *Vi-*, adj. very resplendent, Chr. 292, 1 =Rigv. i. 86, 1.

महस *mahasa*, n. Knowledge.

महाऽ *mahâ-*, a substitute for *mahant*, when former part of compounds of the Bahuvrîhi and Karmadhâraya classes; e.g. *mahâ-râja*, m. A great king, Chr. 3, 4. *mahâ-durga*, adj. Very difficult to be crossed, Pańch. 123, 17. *mahâ-tapas*, adj. Practising great austerities, Chr. 9, 39.

महात्यागमय *mahâ-tyâga + maya*, adj., f. *yî*, Consisting in great liberality, Kathâs. 23, 84.

महानस *mahânasa*, n. A kitchen, Pańch. 253, 14.

महायशस्क *mahâ-yaças + ka*, adj. Illustrious.

महाराजिक *mahârâjika*, i.e. *mahâ -râja + ika*, m. A kind of demigod.

महावस *mahâ-vasa* (vb. *vas*), m. The Gangetic porpoise.

महासाहसिकता *mahâ-sâhasika + tâ*, f. Great boldness, Pańch. 129, 22.

महि *mah + i*, ved. adj. Great.

महिका *mahikâ*, f. Frost.

महित्वन *mahi + tvana*, ved. n. Greatness, Chr. 291, 7=Rigv. i. 85, 7.

महिमन् *mahiman*, i.e. *mahant + iman*, m. Greatness, Hit. ii. d. 2; majesty, Vikr. d. 5; exaltation, Utt. Râmach. 42, 2.—**Comp.** *A-kṛita-tyâga-*, adj. not having practised the greatness (i.e. great virtue) of liberality, Pańch. ii. d. 72. *A-mogha-*, adj. possessing a greatness which is not devoid of effect.

महिला *mahilâ*, f. **1.** A woman, Hit. iv. d. 54. **2.** A plant=*priyańgu*.

महिष *mah + isha* (cf. *maha*), **I.** m. **1.** A buffalo, Hit. i. d. 86, M.M. **2.** The emblem and vehicle of Yama. **II.** f. *shî*. **1.** The female buffalo, Pańch. ii. d. 53; 252, 15. **2.** A queen, Utt. Râmach. 159, 9; Pańch. 27, 6.—**Comp.** *Agra-*, f. the first of a king's wives, Râm. 5, 22, 16.

मही *mahî*, see *maha*.

महीक्षित् *mahî-kshi + t*, m. A king, Chr. 3, 23.

महीधर, महीध्र *mahî-dhara*, and *mahîdra*, i.e. *mahî-dhṛi + a*, m. A mountain, Bhartṛ. 2, 10 (*dhra*).—**Comp.** *Sa -mahî-dhara*, adj. mountainous, Hit. iii. d. 73.

महीप *mahî-pa* (vb. 2. *pâ*), m. A king, Pańch. i. d. 127.

महीभुज् *mahî-bhuj*, m. A king, Hit. iii. d. 99.

महीभृत् *mahî-bhṛi + t*, m. **1.** A mountain; in *meru-*, The mountain called Meru, Kir. 5, 1. **2.** A king, Pańch. iii. d. 63.

महीमय *mahî + maya*, adj., f. *yî*, Made of earth, earthen.

महीय *MAHÎYA*, a denomin. derived from *maha*, Âtm. (Par., Râm. 6, 82, 44). **1.** To be honoured, Man. 4, 260; pass. *mahiyya*, The same, Bhaṭṭ. 2, 38. **2.** To be exalted, Çâk. d. 194.

महीरुह् *mahî-ruh*, and **महीरुह** *mahî-ruh + a*, m. A tree, Kir. 5, 10 (*-ruh*); Bhâshâp. 1 (*saṁsâra-mahîruha*, The tree-like world).

महेला *mahelâ*, f. A woman (cf. *mahilâ*).

1. **मा** *MÂ*, ii. 2, Par., ii. 3, *mimâ*, *mimî*, and † i. 4, Âtm. **1.** To mete, to measure, Chr. 289, 7=Rigv. i. 50, 7. **2.** with *na*, To surmount, Çiç. 1, 23. Ptcple. of the pf. pass. *mita*. **1.** Moderate, little, Pańch. i. d. 98 (in few words); iii. d. 156. **2.** Scattered. **3.** Known. **Comp.** *A-*, adj. immeasurable, measureless, Pańch. iii. d. 156. Ptcple. of the fut. pass. *meya*, Measurable. **Comp.** *A-*, adj. immeasurable, Chr. 37, 29. Caus. *mâpaya*. **1.** To cause to be measured, to get measured, MBh. 1, 2024. **2.** To get prepared, 14, 2521.—With **अनु** *anu*, **1.** To infer, to conclude, MBh, 3, 12470; Böhtl. Ind. Spr. 610 (*karmânumeya*, i.e. *karman-*, To be found out by one's actions, cf. Hit. iv. d. 100, where *kâryân°*, to be inferred from the effects); also pass. (*miya*), in the signification of the active, MBh.

1, 7043 (regularly, Kir. 5, 47). **2.** To reconcile, MBh. 3, 286.—With उप *upa*, **1.** To admeasure, to give, Chr. 294, 7 = Rigv. i. 92, 7. **2.** To compare, Chaurap. 43 (anomal. infin. *-mitum*). *upamita*, Like, Bhartṛ. 3, 17. *upameya*, Comparable, Megh. 53.—With नि *ni*; comp. ptcple. pf. pass. *dus-nimita*, adj. Put down badly, Ragh. 7, 10. *nimeya*, Measurable, MBh. 13, 2676.—With निस् *nis*, **1.** To build, Râm. 1, 5, 6. **2.** To create, Man. 1, 13; Vikr. d. 9. **3.** To cause, Pańch. v. d. 67. **4.** To make, Hit. 48, 2, M.M.; MBh. 1, 2026. **5.** To form, Man. 1, 21; to compose, Hit. i. d. 46, M.M.—With अभिनिस् *abhi-nis*, To create, Kir. 5, 3.—With विनिस् *vi-nis*, **1.** To create, Nal. 17, 7. **2.** To prepare, Râm. 1, 13, 45.—With परि *pari*, *parimita*, **1.** Limited, Bhartṛ. 3, 50. **2.** Moderate, Râm. 3, 55, 20. **3.** Measured. **4.** Regulated. **5.** Joined. *parimeya*, Measurable, few, Râjat. 4, 414. **Comp.** *A-*, immeasurable, MBh. 1, 2455.—With प्र *pra*, To understand, Hit. 74, 7. *pramita*, **1.** Measured. **2.** Known. Comp. ptcple. of the fut. pass. *a-prameya*, adj. Unfathomable, Man. 1, 3.—With प्रति *prati*, To compare, Râjat. 5, 482.—With सम् *sam*, *sam̃mita*, **1.** Like, resembling. **2.** Of equal measure, conformable, Sâv. 5, 30. **3.** Reaching to, Man. 2, 46. **4.** Measured. **Comp.** *Mṛityu-*, adj. death-like, Chr. 35, 6. *Veda-*, adj. made up of the Vedas, Johns. Sel. 94, 53.—Cf. μάρις, μανός, μέτρον, ἄ-μοτον, μοτόν, μίτος, μῖμος, μιμέομαι, μάτιον, μόδιος, μέδιμνος, μέδομαι, μῆδος; Lat. im-mânis, metior (a denomin. of an old ptcple. pres., cf. mensus), mētare, manus, materia, maturus, imitari, mos, modus, meditari; O.H.G. mez; O.N. met; Goth. mitan; A.S. metan, maedhian.

2. मा *MÂ*, ii. 3, *mimâ*, *mimî*, Âtm. (ved. Par.). To sound, to roar.

3. मा *mâ*, indecl. A prohibitive particle. **1.** No, with imperat., also with imperf. and aor., which then drop their augment, Vikr. d. 110; in epic poetry it is sometimes retained, Chr. 6, 9; also Utt. Râmach. 36, 7. **2.** With following *sma*, The same, Chr. 41, 4; 42, 10. **3.** Doubled, *mâmâ*, In no way, Chr. 26, 66; Vikr. 12, 1.—Cf. μή; perhaps Lat. ne.

मांस *mâm̃sa*, the base of many cases is optionally मांस् *mâm̃s*, n. Flesh, Pańch. iii. d. 139; meat.—**Comp.** *Adhi-*, m. Fleshy excrescences on the eye, Suçr. 2, 310, 9. *Danta-*, n. the gums, Suçr. 1, 125, 9. *Nirm°*, i.e. *nis-*, adj. fleshless, Hit. ii. d. 39. *Pûti-*, n. dead or decayed flesh. *Prishṭha-*, n. the flesh of the back; with *khâd*, *bhaksh*, to assail from behind, Hit. i. d. 80, M.M. *Mahâ-*, n. man's flesh, Kathâs. 20, 191. *Vṛithâ-*, n. flesh which has not been sacrificed, Man. 4, 213; 5, 34 (read *vṛithâmâm̃sâni* in one word).

मांसज *mâm̃sa-ja*, n. Marrow, or serum of the flesh.

मांसत्व *mâm̃sa* + *tva*, n. The true etymology of *mâm̃sa*, Man. 5, 55.

मांसमय *mâm̃sa* + *maya*, adj., f. *yî*, Of flesh, MBh. 1, 4495.

मांसल *mâm̃sa* + *la*, adj. Strong, Utt. Râmach. 154, 9.

मांसाद *mâm̃sâda*, i.e. *mâmsa-ad* + *a*, and मांसाशिन् *mâm̃sâçin*, i. e. *mâm̃sa-* 2. *aç* + *in*, adj. Feeding on flesh, Pańch. 59, 10; 60, 7.

मांसिक *mâṁsika*, i.e. *mâmsa + ika*, m. A vendor of flesh or meat.

माकन्दी *mâkandî*, f. The name of a town, Johns. Sel. 33, 65.

माकरन्द *mâkaranda*, i.e. *makaranda + a*, adj. Consisting of the nectar of flowers, Utt. Râmach. 154, 6.

माक्षिक *mâkshika*, i.e. *makshikâ + a*, n. 1. Honey. 2. A peculiar mineral substance.

माक्षिकज *mâkshika-ja*, n. Bees-wax.

मागध *mâgadha*, i.e. *magadha + a*, I. adj. Belonging to, or produced in, Magadha, Ragh. 1, 57. II. m. 1. pl. The inhabitants of Magadha. 2. A bard, Johns. Sel. 37, 16. 3. The son of a Vaiçya by a Kshatriya woman, Man. 10, 11. 4. Cumin-seed. III. f. *dhî*. 1. One of the Prakṛita dialects. 2. A kind of jasmine, Jasminum auriculatum. 3. Long pepper. 4. A sort of cardamoms. 5. Refined sugar.

माघ *mâgha*, m. 1. A month, January—February, Pañch. 169, 6. 2. The name of a poet.

माघवत *mâghavata*, i.e. *maghavant + a*, adj. Belonging to Indra, Utt. Râmach. 124, 11 (*-châpa*, the rainbow).

माघवन *mâghavana*, i.e. *maghavan + a*, adj., f. *nî*, Ruled by Indra, Çiç. 9, 25.

† **माङ्क्ष्** *MÂṄKSH*, i. 1, Par. To desire.

माङ्गलिक *mâṅgalika*, i.e. *maṅgala + ika*, I. adj. Propitious. II. f. *kâ*, A proper name, Daçak. in Chr. 196, 16.

माङ्गल्य *mâṅgalya*, i.e. *maṅgala + ya*, I. adj. Portending good fortune, Çâk. d. 80. II. n. 1. Prosperity. 2. Festivity, festival, Utt. Râmach. 154, 9.

माचल *mâ-chal + a* (probably a noun formed from *mâ chala*, 'Do not stir'), m. 1. A crocodile. 2. A robber. 3. Sickness.

माचिर *mâ-chira*, adj. Short, Chân. 44 in Berl. Monatsb. 1864, 410; °*ram*, adv. Without delay, quickly, Chr. 19, 5; 57, 24.

माञ्जिष्ठ *mâñjishṭha*, i.e. *mañjishṭhâ + a*, I. adj. Of a red colour, Râm. 2, 94. 5. II. n. Red colour.

माञ्जिष्ठिक *mâñjishṭhika*, i.e. *mañjishṭhâ + ika*, adj. Dyed with Bengal madder, red, Utt. Râmach. 106, 1.

माठर *mâṭhara*, m. 1. One of the sun's attendants. 2. Vyâsa. 3. A distiller.

माठव्य *mâṭhavya*, m. A proper name, Çâk. 23, 12.

माड् *MÂḌ*, see *mâh*.

माणव *mâṇava* (=*mânava*, q. cf.), m. 1. A child. 2. A man, in a contemptuous sense. 3. A necklace of sixteen strings.

माणवक *mâṇava + ka*, m. A proper name, Vikr. 44, 12.

माणिका *mâṇikâ* (akin to *maṇi*), f. A weight of eight Palas.

माणिक्य *mâṇikya*, i.e. *maṇi + ka + ya*, I. n. A ruby, Pañch. 207, 23. II. f. *yâ*, A house-lizard.

माणिमन्थ *mâṇimantha*, i.e. *maṇi -mantha + a*, n. Sea-salt.

माण्डलिक *mâṇḍalika*, i.e. *maṇḍala*

+*ika*, m. The superintendent of a district or province.

माण्डव्य *mâṇḍavya*, i.e. *maṇḍu*, A proper name, + *ya*, patronym., m. A proper name, Chr. 46, 28.

मातङ्ग *mâtaṅga*, i.e. *matam̃ga* + *a*, I. m. **1.** An outcaste, Râjat. 5, 6. **2.** A barbarian. **3.** An elephant, Hit. ii. d. 63. **4.** The sacred fig-tree, Ficus religiosa. II. f. *gî*, Pârvatî.

मातरिश्वन् *mâtariçvan*, i.e. *mâtṛi* +*i-çvan* (vb. *çvi*), m. Air, wind, Chr. 27, 4; Kir. 5, 36; Daçak. in Chr. 200, 12.

मातलि *mâtali*, m. The charioteer of Indra, Çâk. 94, 14.

मातापितृ *mâtâ-pitṛi* (*mâtâ*, nom. sing. of *mâtṛi*), m. du. Mother and father, Man. 3, 157.

मातामह *mâtâ-maha* (*mâtâ*, nom. sing. of *mâtṛi*), **1.** m. A maternal grandfather, Vikr. d. 101. **2.** f. *hî*, A maternal grandmother, Râjat. 5, 289.

मातुल *mâtula*, i.e. *matṛi* + *a*, I. m. A maternal uncle, Râjat. 5, 292; Pañch. 215, 10. II. f. *lâ*, *lî*, and *lânî*, The wife of a maternal uncle. III. f. *lânî*, Hemp, Cannabis sativa.

मातुलक *mâtula* + *ka*, m. Dear uncle, Pañch. 52, 11.

मातृ *mâ* + *tṛi*, f. **1.** A mother, Pañch. ii. d. 190. **2.** A divine mother, the personified energy of a deity, Pañch. pr. d. 1; MBh. 9, 2619 sqq. **3.** The wife of a Brâhmaṇa. **4.** The earth. **5.** A cow. **6.** Space, æther. —**Comp.** *Go-*, adj. having a cow as mother, Chr. 291, 3=Rigv. i. 85, 3. *Jaganmâtṛi*, i.e. *jagat-*, f. epithet of: 1. Durgâ, Hariv. 10276; 2. Lakshmî, Mârk. P. 18, 32. *Nâga-*, f. the mother of the serpents, epithet of Surasâ, Râm. 5, 6, 2. *Raṅga-*, f. 1. a bawd. 2. lac, the animal dye. *Vi-*, f. a step-mother. *Veda-*, f. source of the Veda, epithet of the Gâyatrî, a vedic prayer. *Çâṇḍili-*, f. a matron descended from Çaṇḍila, Pañch. 122, 1.—Cf. Lat. mater; μήτηρ; A.S. móder.

मातृक *mâtṛi* + *ka*, I. adj. Maternal, Man. 9, 92. II. f. *kâ*. **1.** A mother. **2.** A nurse, Daçak. in Chr. 181, 3. **3.** A goddess. **4.** The alphabet.—**Comp.** *Deva-mâtṛi* + *ka*, adj. deprived of any water but rain, MBh. 2, 211. *Raṅga-*, f. lac, the animal dye.

मातृवत् *mâtṛi* + *vat*, adv. As a mother, as with a mother, Man. 2, 133; as on a mother, Hit. i. d. 13, M.M.

मातृष्वसृ *mâtṛishvasṛi*, i.e. *mâtṛi* -*svasṛi*, f. A mother's sister.

मातृष्वसेय *mâtṛishvaseya*, and **मातृष्वस्रीय** *mâtṛishvasrîya*, i.e. *mâtṛi-shvasṛi* + *eya*, or *îya*, **1.** m. A mother's sister's son. **2.** f. *seyî*, *srîyâ*, A mother's sister's daughter.

मात्र *mâ* + *tra*, I. f. *trâ*. **1.** Measure, Hit. 121, 5 (distance). **2.** Quantity, Pañch. 32, 24; 226, 14 (*dravya-*, f. All things of value). **3.** Wealth, substance, Pañch. 34, 13. **4.** Requisite, Pañch. 265, 5 (luggage); material. **5.** A little, a trifle, Pañch. i. d. 46; an atom, Man. 1, 27; an element, Bhag. 2, 14 (also n., Bhâg. P. 5, 11, 9). **6.** A moment. **7.** A short vowel. **8.** Quantity in metre, Pañch. v. d. 43. **9.** An ear-ring. II. n. **1.** The totality, the whole, Vedântas. in Chr. 202, 17. **2.** As latter part of comp. words (Being limited), alone, only, Châṇ. 70 in Berl. Monatsb. 1864, 411 (cf. comp.). **3.** As latter part of compounds, often almost without any signification ; cf. e.g. *artha-mâtra.* — Comp. *Aksha-*, n. a moment, Arj. 8, 4. *Angula-*, n. only the breadth of a thumb, Pańch. 124, 16. *Ati-*, adj. excessive, much, overstepping the boundaries, Râm. 2, 12, 108. *°ra + m*, adv. exceedingly, Râm. 2, 93, 18. *Artha-*, f. *râ*, and n. money, Pańch. 132, 25. and 33, 5. *Âtma(n)-*, f. *râ*, the developments of themselves, Man. 1, 16 (Kull.). *Etâvanmâtra*, i.e. *etâvant-*, adj. so great, Pańch. 108, 14. *Kiyanmâtra*, i.e. *kiyant-*, adj. of little importance, Pańch. 47, 4. *Kroça-*, adj. having the measure of a kroça, ib. i. d. 447. *Kshaṇa-mâtra + m*, adv. a moment, Vikr. 7, 1. *Jâta-*, adj., f. *râ*, just born, immediately after one's birth or beginning, Daçak. in Chr. 186, 18; Pańch. i. d. 264. *Jâti-*, n. nothing but birth, Man. 8, 20. *Jiva-*, n. germ alone, Pańch. 200, 12 (with *na*, not even a germ). *Tanmâtra*, see s. v. *Tâla-mâtra + m*, adv. only a moment, Râm. 3, 50, 19. *Tâvanmâtra*, i.e. *tâvant-*, adj., f. *î*, so much, Bhâg. P. 4, 8, 29. *Darçana-*, n. seeing only, Pańch. 128, 21. *Dhyâta* (vb. *dhyai*)-, n. only thought of, immediately after having been thought of, Kathâs. 5, 45. *Naga-*, adj. large as mountains, Arj. 8, 1. *Nâma(n)-*, I. n. nothing but the name, only the name, Pańch. iii. d. 78. II. adj bearing only the name of something (not being it really), Pańch. i. d. 87; ii. d. 93. *Padâti-*, m. a mere foot soldier, Râjat. 5, 424. *Pâpa-kshaya-* (n.), entire destruction (or expiation) of sins, Vedântas. in Chr. 202, 17. *Prâṇa-dhâraṇa-*, adj., f. *râ*, only sufficing for bare subsistence, Pańch. 236, 21. *Bali-*, n. even the offering called *bali*, Pańch. 114, 5. *Mahâ-*, I. m. 1. a king's minister. 2. an elephant driver, or breaker, Man. 9, 259. 3. superintendent of the elephants. 4. a man of wealth and consequence. II. f. *trî*. 1. the wife of an officer of state. 2. the wife of a spiritual teacher. *Mûrta-*, n. only corporeal, Bhâshâp. 157. *Mûrti-*, f. a minute substantial portion, Man. 1, 19. *Yuga-* (n.?), scarcely, Sâv. 4, 10. *Varsha-*, n. one year only, Pańch. 134, 15. *Vânmâtra*, i.e. *vâch-*, n. speech only, Pańch. ii. d. 13. *Rûpa-*, n. only beauty, Daçak. in Chr. 181, 4. *Vârttâ-*, (n.), a superficial knowledge, Daçak. in Chr. 180, 8. *Vitta-*, f. *râ*, wealth, Pańch. 32, 24. *Çabda-*, n. mere sound, sound only, Pańch. 20, 20. *Çarira-*, n. the mere person, body only. *Samâdhâna-*, n. only religious contemplation, Daçak. in Chr. 182, 5. *Samkshepa-*, n. only an abridgement, Pańch. 4, 17. *Smṛita-*, adj. only remembered, Pańch. 48, 8 (without being called, but only in consequence of being thought of). *Hastimâtra*, i.e. *hastin-*, adj. as great as an elephant, Pańch. i. d. 373.—Cf. *μέτρον*.

ऽमात्रक *-mâtra + ka*, a substitute for *mâtra*, when latter part of a comp. adj.; e.g. *angushṭha-*, adj. As long as a thumb, Nal. 14, 9. *stanya-tyâga-*, adj. In which (viz. age), one is just weaned, Utt. Râmach. 34, 16.

मात्सर *mâtsara*, i.e. *matsara + a*, adj. Envious.

मात्सर्य *mâtsarya*, i.e. *matsara + ya*, n. 1. Envy, Hit. i. d. 194, M.M. 2. Malice.—Comp. *Dus-*, n. wicked envy, Bhartṛ. 3, 31.

मात्स्यक *mâtsyaka*, i.e. *matsya + ka*, adj. Relating to a fish, Matsyop. 58.

माथ *mâtha*, i.e. *math + a*, m. 1. Churning. 2. A road.

माद *mâda*, i.e. *mad + a*, m. 1. Intoxication. 2. Joy. 3. Pride.

मादन *mâdana*, i.e. *mad*, Caus., + *ana*, n. 1. Delighting. 2. Cloves.

मादृश् *mâdṛiç*, and मादृश *mâdṛiça*, i.e. 2. *mad-dṛiç* and *dṛiç* + *a*, adj. Like me, Lass. 41, 17 (*dṛiç*); Utt. Râmach. 42, 15 (*ça*).

माद्य *mâdya*, Daçak. in Chr. 183, 3, but I prefer correcting *mândya*.

माद्रवती *mâdravatî*, i.e. *madra* + *a* + *vant* + *î*, f. The wife of Paṇḍu, and mother of the two youngest Pâṇḍava princes, Draup. 8, 17.

माद्री *mâdrî*, i.e. *madra* + *a* + *î*, f. The wife of Paṇḍu, and mother of the two youngest Pâṇḍava princes.

माद्रेय *mâdreya*, i.e. *mâdrî* + *eya*, m. A son of Mâdrî, i.e. Nakula or Sahadeva, Johns. Sel. 27, 25.

माधव *mâdhava*, i.e. *madhu* + *a*, I. adj. 1. Made of honey. 2. Belonging to the spring, Vikr. d. 23 (cf. Sch.). II. m. 1. Vishṇu, Pañch. i. d. 238. 2. The month Vaiçâkha. 3. Spring. III. f. *vî*. 1. Sugar, clayed or candied. 2. Spirituous liquor. 3. Durgâ. 4. A large creeper, Gaertnera racemosa, Megh. 76. 5. A bawd. IV. n. Sweetness.—Comp. *Latâ-mâdhavî*, f. Gaertnera racemosa, Çâk. d. 58.

माधवसेनाराजन् *mâdhava-senâ-râjan*, m. A proper name, Daçak. in Chr. 191, 2.

माधुपर्किक *mâdhuparkika*, i.e. *madhuparka* + *ika*, adj. Presented as a token of respect to a guest, Man. 9, 206.

माधुमत *mâdhumata*, m. pl. The people of Kashmir.

माधुर *mâdhura*, i.e. *madhura* + *a*, I. n. Arabian jasmine. II. f. *rî*, Spirituous liquor; see *mâdhurya*.

माधुर्य *mâdhurya*, i.e. *madhura* + *ya*, n., and f. *rî*. 1. Sweetness, Bhartṛ. 2, 6. 2. Gracefulness, Daçak. in Chr. 180, 14.—Comp. *Bhrûkshepâlâpa-*, i.e. *bhrû-kshepa-âlâpa-*, n. the gracefulness of the motion of one's brows and speech, Indr. 5, 7.

माधूक *mâdhûka* (from *madhu* and *madhûka*), adj. 1. Sweet-voiced, Man. 10, 33. 2. Made of the Bassia tree.

माध्य *mâdhya*, i. e. *madhya* + *a*, adj., f. *yâ*, and माध्यम *mâdhyama*, i.e. *madhyama* + *a*, adj., f. *mî*, Middle.

माध्यस्थ *mâdhyastha*, i.e. *madhyastha* + *a*, n. 1. Middle state. 2. Indifference to earthly objects, Man. 4, 257.

माध्यस्थ्य *mâdhyasthya*, i.e. *madhyastha* + *ya*, n. 1. Mediation. 2. Office of an arbiter, Lass 92, 4.

माध्वक *mâdhvaka*, i.e. *madhu* + *a* + *ka* (anomal.), n. Spirit distilled from the flowers of the Bassia.

माध्वी *mâdhvî*, i.e. *madhu* + *a* + *î* (anomal.), f. 1. Spirituous liquor distilled from the flowers of the Bassia, Man. 11, 94. 2. A sort of fish.

माध्वीक *mâdhvî* + *ka*, n. 1. Spirituous liquor made from the Bassia. 2. Wine.

मान् *MÂN*, i. 10 (properly Caus. of *man*, q. cf.), and † i. 1, Par. To honour.

मान *mâna*, I. m., i.e. *mân* + *a*. 1. Self-confidence, Pañch. v. d. 3. 2. Pride, Pañch. iii. d. 13. 3. Arrogance, Pañch. iii. d. 108; female caprice, indignation, anger, Vikr. 37, 8. 4. Honour, Pañch. 16, 4; i. d. 251. 5. Taking. 6. An agent. 7. A blockhead. 8. A barbarian. II. i.e. *mâ* + *ana*, n. 1. Measuring, Bhâshâp. 108. 2. Measure in general, Pañch. 7, 16 (*kûṭa-tulâ-*, With a wrong balance). 3. A particular measure, the fourth part of a *khârî*. **4.** The computation of the duration of a year.—**Comp.** *Ati-*, m. arrogance, Châṇ. 50. *A-bhagna-mâna* + *m*, adv. without injury to one's honour, Hit. ii. d. 41. *Nirm°*, i.e. *nis-*, adj. free from pride, Bhartṛ. 3, 95. *Praṇaya-*, m. lovers' quarrels. *Bahu-*, m. reverence, respect, Vikr. d. 2. *Mâsa-*, m. a year. *Sa-bahu-mâna* + *m*, adv. with great reverence, Pańch. 130, 16.

मानद् *mâna-da* (vb. *dâ*), adj. **1.** Inspiring pride; a respectful address, used only in the voc. sing. m., Chr. 38, 15; Böhtl. Ind. Spr. 830.

मानधानिका *mânadhânika*, f. A cucumber.

मानयितृ *mânayitṛi*, i.e. *man*, Caus., + *tṛi*, m. One who honours, Indr. 4, 9.

मानव *mânava*, i.e. *manu* + *a*, **I.** adj. **1.** Human, Utt. Râmach. 53, 1. **2.** Declared by Manu, Chr. 135, l. 2. **II.** m. **1.** A man, Pańch. iii. d. 61; mankind, Chr. 8, 33. **2.** A boy. **III.** f. *vî*. **1.** A woman. **2.** A daughter of the first Manu.—**Comp.** *Kapaṭa-*, m. under the disguise of a man, Bhâg. P. 1, 1, 20. *Daṇḍa-*, m. a man bearing a staff, a Brâhmaṇa, Râm. 2, 32, 18.

मानवन्त् *mâna* + *vant*, adj., f. *vatî*. **1.** Proud. **2.** Angry, Çiç. 9, 84.

मानव्य *mânavya*, i.e. *mânava* + *ya*, n. A multitude of boys (and of men).

मानस *mânasa*, i.e. *manas* + *a*, **I.** adj., f. *sî*, Mental, Man. 2, 85; Vikr. d. 30. **II.** n. **1.** The mind, the seat of reasoning and feeling, Pańch. v. 12; Bhâshâp. 33; Hit. i. d. 140, M.M.; Pańch. iii. d. 45 (*bhaya-saṁtrasta-*, adj. Having one's mind terrified by fear); iii. d. 180 (*çoka-saṁtapta-*, burned by grief). **2.** The name of a lake, Vikr. d. 93. **III.** f. *sî*, A goddess of the Jainas.—**Comp.** *Anya-*, adj., f. *sâ*, being in love with another, Chr. 14, 22. *An-anya-*, adj. intent only on one object, Indr. 5, 4. *Pûrṇa-* (see vb. *pṛî*), adj. satisfied, Râm. 3, 75, 25. *Hṛishṭa-* (vb. *hṛish*), adj. glad, happy, Johns. Sel. 14, 48.

ऽमानिक *-mânika*, i.e. *mânin* + *ka*, in *paṇḍita-*, adj. Fancying one's self a learned man, MBh. 12, 6738.

मानिन् *mânin*, i.e. *mâna* + *in*, and *man* + *in*, **I.** adj., f. *nî*. **1.** Proud, Ragh. 13, 38. **2.** When latter part of a comp., Who thinks or fancies (cf. comp.). **II.** f. *nî*. **1.** A woman, especially one indignant towards her lover, Vikr. d. 118. **2.** A plant, commonly *Priyańgu*. —**Comp.** *A-*, adj. not proud. *Ati-*, adj. very proud, Râm. 3, 34, 17. *A-stena-*, adj. pretending to have committed no theft, Man. 8, 197. *Dhṛishṭa-*, adj. arrogant, Râm. 2, 96, 43. *Paṇḍita-*, adj. fancying one's self a learned man, MBh. 4, 113. *Purusha-*, adj. fancying one's self a hero, MBh. 5, 6094. *Prâjńa-*, adj. fancying one's self a learned man. *Çûra-*, adj. one who thinks himself a hero, a boaster, Hit. iv. d. 2. *Su-bhaga-*, adj. fancying one's self fortunate, Daçak. in Chr. 195, 12.

मानुष *mânusha*, i.e. *manus* (q. cf.), + *a*, **I.** adj., f. *shî*. **1.** Human, Râm. 3, 53, 3; 54, 17. **2.** Relating to mankind, Man. 4, 124. **II.** m. A man, Pańch. 61, 10. **III.** f. *shî*, A woman, Nal. 13, 55. **IV.** n. Human effort, Chr. 56, 16 (*daivaṁ mânushopetam*, Fate combined with human effort).—**Comp.** *A-*, I. adj., f. *shî*. 1. not human. 2. inhuman. II. m. not a man, any other than a man, Man. 9, 284. *Ati-*, adj. superhuman, Chr. 46, 19. *Divya-*, m. a demigod, Kathâs. 1, 47 (*ekântasukhino devâ manushyâ nityaduḥkhinaḥ; di-*

vyamânushacheshṭâ tu parabhôgena hâriṇi. vidyâdharâṇâm̃ charitam ata *te varṇayâmy aham;* The gods are ever happy, men ever unhappy; [but] the doing of the demigods is charming in the highest degree. Therefore, I shall tell you the adventures of Vidyâdharas).

मानुष्य *mânushya,* i.e. *mânusha + ya,* I. adj. Human, Nal. 19, 28. II. n. The state of a man.

मानुष्यक *mânushya + ka,* n. A multitude of men.

मान्त्रिक *mântrika,* i.e. *mantra + ika,* m. A sorcerer, Râjat. 5, 102.

† **मान्थ्** *MANTH* (?), i. 1, Par. To hurt (see *math*).

मान्द्य *mândya,* i.e. *manda + ya,* n. 1. Indisposition, sickness. 2. Stupidity, torpor, Vedântas. in Chr. 218, 17. 3. Slowness, languishing (and stupidity), Pańch. i. d. 205. — **Comp.** *A-,* n. activity.

मान्धातृ *mândhâtṛi,* m. A proper name, Pańch. iii. d. 270.

मान्मथ *mânmatha,* i.e. *manmatha + a,* adj. Caused by love, Prab. 41, 4.

मापत्य *mâpatya* (probably from the Caus. of *me*), m. The god of love.

मापन *mâpana,* i.e. *mâ,* Caus., *+ ana,* n. A balance.

माम *mâma,* i.e. *mama,* gen. sing. of *asmad, + a,* adj. Mine, Pańch. 98, 13; dear, 50, 12; 16; 51, 13; 23; 52, 4, etc.

मामक *mâmaka,* i.e. *mama,* gen. sing. of *asmad, + ka,* I. adj., f. *kî* and *mikâ,* Mine, Bhag. 1, 1. II. m. 1. A mother's brother. 2. A niggard.

मामकीन *mâmakîna,* i.e. *mâmaka + îna,* adj. Mine.

माय *mâya,* i.e. *man + ya,* I. m. 1. A juggler. 2. An Asura. II. f. 1. Understanding. 2. Fraud, deceit, Man. 7, 104; Hit. i. d. 194, M.M. 3. Trick in negotiation, diplomacy, Pańch. i. d. 404 (*yo mâyâm̃ kurute mûdhaḥ prâṇatyâge dhanâdishu,* The fool who uses tricks about wealth, etc., his life being in danger). 4. Wickedness. 5. Illusion, unreality, Vedântas. in Chr. 205, 2. 6. Magical power, Kathâs. 25, 274. 7. Compassion. 8. The wife of a juggler.—**Comp.** *A-,* f. honesty, truth, Hit. ii. d. 33. *Deva-,* f. a phantom created by a god, Bhâg. P. 2, 7, 42. *Bahu-,* adj. Very wicked, Pańch. i. d. 364. *Su-,* adj. abounding in tricks (?), Chr. 293, 1 = Rigv. i. 88, 1.

मायाद *mâyâ-da* (vb. *dâ*), m. A crocodile.

मायाधर *mâyâ-dhara,* adj. Deceitful, disguised, Râm. 3, 49, 17.

मायामय *mâyâ + maya,* adj., f. *yî,* 1. Illusive, Râm. 3, 49, 31. 2. Magical, Indr. 1, 7; Râm. 3, 55, 31.

मायावन्त् *mâyâ + vant,* I. adj., f. *vatî,* Deceitful, illusory, unreal. II. m. A name of Kansa. III. f. *vatî,* The wife of Kâma.

मायायिन् *mâyâyin,* and **मायाविन्** *mâyâvin,* i.e. *mâyâ + vin,* I. adj. 1. Deceitful, using tricks, Râm. 3, 49, 47 (*vin*). 2. Illusory, unreal. II. m. 1. A juggler. 2. A cat.

मायिक *mâyika,* i.e. *mâyâ + ika,* m. A juggler.

मायिन् *mâyin,* i.e. *mâyâ + in,* I. adj. 1. Wise, Chr. 290, 7 = Rigv. i. 64, 7. 2. Deceptive. II. m. 1. A juggler. 2. A cheat. 3. Agni, Vishṇu, Brahman.—**Comp.** *A-,* adj. void of deceit. *Durm°,* i.e. *dus-,* adj. using tricks, Bhâg. P. 8, 11, 6.

मायु *mâyu,* **I.** m. Bile. **II.** i.e. **2.** *mâ + u,* Sounding, crying, at the end of comp. words ; ved. *gomâyu* see s.v.

मायूर *mâyûra,* i.e. *mayûra + a,* **I.** adj., f. *rî.* **1.** Belonging to, or coming from, peacocks, Râm. 2, 100, 63 Gorr.; agreeable to peacocks, Mâlav. d. 20. **2.** Made of its feathers. **II.** n. A flock of peacocks.

मार *mâra,* i.e. *mṛi + a,* **I.** m. **1.** Dying. **2.** Death. **3.** Killing, Hit. 18, 3, M.M. **4.** Obstruction. **5.** The god of love. **II.** f. *rî.* **1.** Plague. **2.** A name of Chaṇḍî or Durgâ.—Comp. *A-,* m. not dying, Râjat. 5, 64. *Dhundhu-,* m. a proper name and surname, Râm. 1, 72, 21 Gorr ; MBh. 3, 13486. *Paçu-,* m. the manner of killing a beast, MBh. 3, 370. *Mahâ-mârî,* f. a name of Durgâ, Dev. 12, 7. *Çiçu-,* m. 1. the Gangetic porpoise, Pańch. 51, 9. 2. the heavenly porpoise, or collection of the stars and planets ; north-west, Johns. Sel. 40, 36. 3. a name of Vishṇu.

मारक *mâraka,* i.e. *mṛi,* Caus., + *aka,* m. **1.** A slayer. **2.** A hawk. **3.** Plague. —Comp. *Paçu-mâra + ka,* adj. accompanied by sacrificing beasts, Bhâg. P. 4, 27, 11.

मारकत *mârakata,* i.e. *marakata + a,* adj., f. *tî,* Emerald-like, Hit. pr. d. 41, M.M.

मारण *mâraṇa,* i.e. *mṛi,* Caus. + *ana,* n. **1.** Killing. **2.** Being killed, Man. 5, 38.

मारि *mâri* (vb. *mṛi*), f. **1.** Killing. **2.** Plague.

ऽमारिन् *-mârin,* i.e. *mṛi + in* in *pûrva-,* adj., f. *iṇî,* Dying before, Man. 5, 167.

मारिष *mârisha* (for *mârsha,* q. cf.), **I.** m. A venerable person (in dramatic language), Vikr. 3, 6. **II.** f. *shâ,* The mother of Daksha, Lass. 59, 15.

मारीच *mârîcha,* i.e. *marîchi + a,* m. The name of a Muni, Çâk. 100, 8 ; of a Râkshasa, Râm. 3, 48, 2.—Comp. *Saha-,* adj. With Mârîcha, Râm. 3, 48, 8.

मारुत *mâruta,* i.e. *marut + a,* **I.** adj. **1.** Belonging to the Maruts, Chr. 293, 6 = Rigv. i. 87, 6. **2.** Consisting of the Maruts, Chr. 291, 12 = Rigv. i. 64, 12. **II.** m. **1.** A Marut. **2.** Wind, Pańch. iii. d. 56. **3.** Vital air, Lass. 17, 6 (*ûrdhva-,* m. Pressing upwards). **III.** n. Burnt offering on conception.—Comp. *Ati-,* m. strong wind, Yâjń. 1, 149. *Paçchânmâruta,* i.e. *paçchât-,* m. wind blowing from behind, Ragh. 7, 51. *Puromâruta,* i.e. *puras-,* m. wind blowing in front, ib.

मारुति *mâruti,* i.e. *marut + i,* patronym., m. **1.** Hanumant. **2.** Bhîmasena.

मार्कण्डेय *mârkaṇḍeya,* m. The name of a Muni.

मार्ग् *MÂRG* (properly a denomin. derived from *mârga*), i. 1 and 10, Par. (in epic poetry also i. 1, Âtm.). **1.** To trace out, to search, Johns. Sel. 93, 50 ; Pańch. ii. d. 130. i. 10, † **2.** To purify. † **3.** To adorn. † **4.** To go.—With the prep. **परि** *pari,* **1.** To search, MBh. 3, 10975. **2.** To beg for, 14948.

मार्ग *mârga,* i.e. **A.** *mṛij + a* (originally, the tracing out of game by a sporting dog), m. **1.** Search. **2.** Musk. **3.** Trace, Vikr. 57, 12. **4.** A road, Pańch. 122, 6 ; Vikr. 19, 18 ; way, Pańch. 98, 22 ; figuratively, Pańch. 167, 22 ; use, Lass. 20, 18 ; title of law, Man. 8, 3 ; mode, Johns. Sel. 11, 28. **5.** The anus. **B.** *mṛiga + a,* **I.** adj.

Coming from deer, Râm. 2, 100, 63 Gorr. II. m. 1. The name of a month, November—December. 2. The constellation Mṛigaçîrsha. — Comp. *Ambara-chara-*, m. the road of the birds, Pańch. i. d. 350. *Ardha-*, m. mid-way, Vikr. d. 3. *Âhâra-niḥsaraṇa-*, m. the anus, Pańch. i. d. 458. *Unm°*, i.e. *ud-*, m. wrong way, Hit. 4. 2, M.M. *Karma(n)-*, m. an opening in walls, etc., serving as a way for thieves, Mṛichchh. 64, 12. *Kula-*, m. the road of honesty, Lass. 40, 6. *Kṛita-*, adj. made accessible, Vikr. d. 21. *Tri-*, I. the three worlds, Râm. 1, 45, 40 Gorr. II. f. *gî*, three roads. *Deva-*, m. the penis and the anus, Râm. 5, 61, 4, 6; Pańch. ed. orn. 55, 9. *Nakshatra-*, m. the road of the stars, Indr. 2, 12. *Râja(n)-*, m. a royal or main road, Pańch. 129, 16.

मार्गण *mârgaṇa*, i.e. *mârg + ana*, I. adj. Begging, a beggar. II. m. 1. A solicitor. 2. An arrow, Chr. 34, 15. III. n. 1. Searching, Hit. iv. d. 71. 2. Begging.

मार्गणता *mârgaṇa + tâ*, f. The nature of an arrow, Vikr. d. 144.

मार्गव *mârga + va*, m. The son of a Nishâda by an Ayogava female, Man. 10, 34.

मार्गशिर *mârgaçira*, and मार्गशीर्ष *mârgaçîrsha* (cf. *mârga*, and *çiras*, and *çîrsha*), m. The name of a month, November—December, Bhag. 10, 35 (*-çîrsha*).

मार्गिक *mârgika*, i.e. *mṛiga* and *mârga*, *+ika*, m. 1. A hunter. 2. A traveller.

मार्ज् *MÂRJ* (cf. *mṛij*), † मञ्ज् *MAŃJ*, † मर्च् *MARCH*, † मर्व् *MARV*, i. 10, Par. 1. † To cleanse. 2. † To sound.

मार्ज *mârja*, i.e. *mṛij + a*, m. 1. Cleaning. 2. A washerman. 3. Vishṇu.

मार्जन *mârjana*, i.e. *mṛij + ana*, I. n., and f. *nî*. 1. Cleaning. 2. Rubbing, Man. 5, 116. 3. Cleaning the person by wiping, bathing, or rubbing it with unguents. II. f. *nâ*, The sound of a drum, Mâlav. d. 20. III. f. *nî*, A brush, Pańch. ii. d. 108.

मार्जार *mârjâra*, i.e. *mṛij + âra*, m., and f. *rî*. 1. The common cat, Pańch. 110, 23. 2. The pole-cat. — Comp. *Araṇya-*, m. a wild cat, Pańch 165, 14.

मार्जारक *mârjâraka*, i.e. *mṛij + âra + ka*, m. A peacock.

मार्जारीय *mârjârîya*, i.e. *mârjâra + îya*, and मार्जालीय *mârjâlîya* (with *l* for *r*), m. 1. A cat. 2. A Çûdra. 3. Cleaning the body.

मार्तण्ड *mârtaṇḍa*, i.e. *mṛitaṇḍa + a*, m. 1. The sun, Utt. Râmach. 140, 9; Râjat. 5, 153. 2. A hog.

मार्त्तिक *mârttika*, i.e. *mṛittikâ + a*, I. adj. Earthen. II. m. A lid, a cover.

मार्त्य *mârtya*, i.e. *mṛita + ya* (adj. or sbst. n.), Mortal, the mortal part, Bhâg. P. 3, 33, 32.

मार्दङ्ग *mârdańga*, i.e. *mṛidańga + a*, I. m. A drummer. II. n. A town.

मार्दव *mârdava*, i.e. *mṛidu + a*, n. Softness, Chr. 57, 24; Bhartṛ. 1, 5.— Comp. *Su-*, n. beautiful softness, Pańch. iv. d. 62.

मार्ष *mârsha*, i.e. *marsha + a*, m. A

venerable man (in dramatic language), Sch. ad Vikr. ed. Bollensen, p. 142.

मार्ष्टि *mârshṭi*, i.e. *mṛij* + *ti*, f. 1. Cleaning. 2. Cleaning the person by bathing, etc.; cf. *mârjana*.

माल *mâla*, I. m. 1. A name of a barbarous tribe, Lass. 38, 14. 2. The name of a country, Megh. 16. 3. Vishṇu. II. i.e. *mala* + *a*, f. *lâ*. 1. A line. 2. A garland, a necklace, Hit. i. d. 174, M.M. (*dhṛita-kanaka-mâla*, adj. Bearing a gold necklace). 3. A chaplet of flowers. 4. A rosary. 5. A chain, Pańch. 255, 19. III. n. A field.—Comp. *Aksha-*, f. *lâ*, 1. a rosary, Dev. 2, 23. 2. a name of Arundhatî, the wife of Vaçishṭha, Man. 9, 23. *Ketu-*, I. m. 1. pl. the name of a people, Hariv. 8227. 2. the name of a *varsha* or division of the earth, Bhâg. P. 5, 2, 19. II. f. *lâ*, the name of a holy place, MBh. 3, 8368. *Nakshatra-*, f. *lâ*, 1. a group of stars, Râm. 1, 60, 21. 2. all the lunar mansions. 3. a string of twenty-seven pearls. *Nara-*, f. *lâ*, a chaplet of human skulls, Dev. 7, 6. *Vana-*, f. *lâ*, the chaplet worn by Kṛishṇa. *Vandana-*, f. *lâ*, the ornamented arch of a gateway (cf. *mâlaka*). *Varṇa-*, f. *lâ*, the alphabet. *Haṁsa-*, f. *lâ*, 1. a duck. 2. a flight of wild geese. *Hema-*, f. *lâ*, the wife of Yama.

ऽमालक *-mâla* + *ka*, at the end of comp. adj., f. *likâ*; e.g. *akshara-*, Consisting of a line of letters, Pańch. ii. d. 183. *baddha-vandana-*, adj. Having fastened garlands of salutation, Pańch. 207, 24 (but cf. *vandana-mâlâ*, s.v. *mâla*).

मालती *mâlatî*, f. 1. A bud. 2. A young woman. 3. Moonlight. 4. Night. 5. A river. 6. Great-flowered jasmine, Jasminum grandiflorum, Megh. 96; Ṛit. 2, 25.

मालव *mâlava*, m. The province of Malva, Hit. 113, 19.

मालाकार *mâlâ-kâra*, m., f. *rî*, A flower-seller, a gardener, Pańch. i. d. 394; Lass. 24, 8.

मालिक *mâlika*, i.e. *mâlâ* + *ika*, I. adj. Relating to a garland. II. m. 1. A flower-gatherer, Pańch. v. d. 55 (cf. Pańch. 156, 20). 2. A painter. 3. A sort of bird. III. f. *kâ*. 1. A garland of flowers, Pańch. 236, 16. 2. A multitude, Hit. iii. d. 89. 3. A necklace. 4. A daughter. 5. A palace. 6. A spirituous liquor. 7. Double jasmine. — Comp. *Vandana-*, f. *kâ*, the ornamented arch of a gateway; cf. *mâlaka*.

मालित *mâlita*, i.e. *mâlâ* + *ita*, Surrounded, Lass. 4, 18.

मालिन् *mâlin*, i.e. *mâlâ* + *in*, I. m. A florist. II. f. *nî*. 1. A female vendor of flowers. 2. A name of Durgâ. 3. The Ganges of heaven. 4. A plant, Hedysarum alhagi. 5. A shrub, Echites caryophyllata. III. As latter part of compounds, very often adj., f. *nî*, Wearing a garland or chaplet of, cf. comp.—Comp. *Aṁçu-*, m. the sun, Ṛit. 1, 28. *Aksha-* (cf. *aksha-mâlâ*), m. a name of Çiva, MBh. 12, 10374. *Ûrmi-*, I. adj. adorned with a chaplet of waves, Râm. 2, 113, 21. II. m. the sea, Ragh. 5, 61. *Kapâla-*, adj. wearing a string of skulls, MBh. 14, 202. *Gaṇḍa-*, adj. sbst. one who has the erysipelas, Man. 3, 161. *Jâlaka-*, adj., f. *nî*, adorned with a necklace in the form of a net, Bhâg. P. 8, 20, 17. *Nagara-*, adj. garlanded with cities, Johns. Sel. 4, 19. *Padma-*, m. the name of a Râkshasa, Râm. 6, 7, 33. f. epithet of Çrî, MBh. 12, 8353 (adorned with a string of lotus flowers). *Pura-*, f. *nî*, the name of a river, MBh. 6, 329.

Marichi-, I. adj. surrounded by a circle of rays, Hit. 38, 1, M.M. II. m. the sun. *Vana-*, m. Kṛishṇa. *Vichi-*, m. the ocean. *Hema-*, adj. adorned with a chaplet of gold, Râm. 3, 50, 20.

मालिन्य *mâlinya*, i.e. *malina*+*ya*, n. Blackness, Böhtl. Ind. Spr. 1915 (*mâlinyam̃ ho doshaḥ*, What an object of blame is the blackness! i. e. the blackness is no object of blame).

मालूर *mâlûra*, m. A fruit-tree, Aegle marmelos, Lass. 86, 6 (Prâkṛ.).

माल्य *mâlya*, i.e. *mâlâ*+*ya*, I. adj. Fit for a garland. II. n. **1.** A flower, Johns. Sel. 40, 38. **2.** A garland, Pańch. 199, 19. **3.** A chaplet, Man. 2, 177.—Comp. *Gandha-*, n. an agreeably smelling wreath, Pańch. 182, 10.

माल्यगुणाय *MÂLYAGUṆÂYA*, a denomin. derived from *mâlya-guṇa* with *ya*, Âtm. To become a garland, Bhartṛ. 2, 78.

माल्यवन्त् *mâlya*+*vant*, I. m. The name of a mountainous range. II. f. *vatî*, The name of a river.

माष *mâsha*, m. **1.** A sort of kidney bean, Phaseolus radiatus, Man. 3, 267. **2.** A goldsmith's weight, Man. 8, 134. **3.** A fool. **4.** A cutaneous disease.—Comp. *Mahâ-*, m. a sort of bean, Dolichos catjang.

माषक *mâsha*+*ka*, m. A weight of gold and of silver, Man. 8, 135.

ऽमाषिक *-mâshika*, i.e. *mâsha*+*ika*, latter part of comp. adj. Amounting to mâshas; e.g. *pańcha(n)-*, Amounting to five mâshas, Man. 8, 298.

माषीण *mâshîṇa*, and **माष्य** *mâshya*, i.e. *mâsha*+*îna*, or *ya*, n. A field of kidney beans.

मास् *mâs* (=*mâsa*, q. cf.), m. **1.** The moon. **2.** A month. — Comp. *Pushpa-*, m. spring (the season), Râm. 3, 79, 16.

मास *mâsa*, (sprung from *mânt*, ptcple. pres. of *mâ*); the base of many cases is optionally *mâs*, m. A month, Pańch. 169, 6.—Comp. *Ardha-*, m. half a month, a fortnight, Man. 4, 25. *Garbha-*, m. a month of pregnancy, Kathâs. 26, 146. *Pushpa-*, m. spring (the season), Râm. 3, 79, 39. *Pûrṇa-*, m. 1. the full of the moon. 2. a monthly sacrifice performed on the day of full moon.—Cf. μήν; Lat. mensis; Goth. mêna; A.S. mona; Goth. mênôths; A.S. monadh.

मासज्ञ *mâsa-jńa*, m. A gallinule.

मासर *mâsara*, m. The scum of boiled rice.

मासशस् *mâsa*+*ças*, adv. For months, MBh. 13, 5659.

मासानुमासिक *mâsânumâsika*, i.e. *mâsa-anu-mâsa*+*ika*, adj. Performed from month to month, Man. 3, 122.

मासावधिक *mâsâvadhika*, i.e. *mâsa-avadhi*+*ka*, adj. Having as limit a month, taking place after a month, Daçak. in Chr. 189, 1.

मासिक *mâsika*, I. adj., f. *kî*. **1.** Monthly, Man. 3, 123; 5, 140. **2.** Payable in a month. **3.** Hired by the month. **4.** Lasting for a month. **5.** Happening at the end of a month. II. n. An obsequial sacrifice performed every day of the new moon.—Comp. *Ashṭamâsika*, i.e. *ashṭan-*, f. *kî*, lasting eight months, Chr. 47, 36. *Shaṇmâsika*, i.e. *shash-*, adj. happening every sixth month, Pańch. 252, 14.

मासुरि *mâsuri*, f. A beard.

मासूर *mâsûra*, i. e. *masûra*+*a*,

adj., *f. rî,* Consisting, made of lentils or pulse.

† माह् *MÂH* (माड् *MÂḌ*) i. 1, Par. Âtm. To mete, to measure.

माहाकुल *mâhâkula,* i.e. *mahâ-kula* + *a,* adj. Of a respectable family.

माहात्मिक *mâhâtmika,* i.e. *mahâ-âtman+ika,* adj. 1. Majestic, Man. 5, 94. 2. Of great honour. 3. Glorious.

माहात्म्य *mâhâtmya,* i.e. *mahâ-âtman+ya,* n. 1. Majesty, might, Utt. Râmach. 96, 3; Pańch. 48, 18; ii. d. 52. 2. The peculiar efficacy or virtue of a deity or sacred shrine. 3. A work giving an account of the merits of any holy object, Dev. title.

माहित्र *mâhitra,* (n.), The name of a holy text, Man. 11, 249.

माहिर *mâhira,* m. Indra.

माहिष *mâhisha,* i.e. *mahisha+a,* adj., f. *shî,* Belonging to, or coming from, a buffalo (flesh, milk, etc.), Çârńg. 82, 219.

माहिषिक *mâhishika,* i.e. *mahisha+ika,* m. A keeper of buffaloes, Man. 3, 166.

माहिष्य *mâhishya,* i.e. *mahisha+ya,* m. The offspring of a Kshatriya father and a Vaiçya mother.

माहेन्द्र *mâhendra,* i.e. *mahâ-indra+a,* adj. Relating to Indra.

माहेयी *mâheyî,* i.e. *mahî+eya+î,* f. A cow.

मि *MI,* ii. 5, Par. Âtm. To throw.

† मिछ् *MICHH,* पिछ् *PICHH,* i. 6, Par. 1. To inflict pain. 2. To obstruct.

† मिञ्ज् *MIŃJ* (?), i. 10, Par. To speak. To shine.

मितद्रु *mita* (vb. *mâ*), *-dru,* m. The ocean.

मितंपच *mitampacha,* i.e. *mita* (vb. *mâ*), + *m-pach+a,* adj. Niggardly, a niggard, Hit. i. d. 154, M.M.

मिति *miti,* i.e. *mâ+ti,* f. 1. Measuring. 2. Determining. 3. Knowledge.

मित्त्र *mittra,* commonly written मित्र *mitra,* i.e. *mid+tra,* I. m. 1. A vedic deity, Chr. 298, 25 = Rigv. i. 112, 25. 2. The sun, Pańch. ii. d. 75. II. n. 1. A friend, Râm. 3, 51, 9. 2. An ally. — Comp. *A-,* m., and f. *râ,* an enemy, Râm. 3, 51, 9. *Ku-,* n. a treacherous friend, Pańch. iii. d. 61. *Nis-a-,* 1. adj. free from enemies, Râm. 2, 18, 7 Gorr. 2. m. a proper name. *Dhana-* and *Puru-,* m. proper names. *Sa-,* adj. with (his) friends, Chr. 54, 16. *Su-,* f. *trâ,* one of the wives of Daçaratha.

मित्त्रता *mittra+tâ,* f., and मित्त्रत्व *mittra+tva,* n. Friendship, Pańch. ii. d. 32; iii. d. 1.

मित्त्रयु *mittra+yu,* I. adj. Acquiring friends. II. m. A person acquainted with the ways and manners of mankind (?).

मित्त्रवन्त् *mittra+vant,* adj., f. *vatî,* One who has friends, Pańch. ii. d. 26.

मिथ् *MITH,* मिध् *MIDH* (see *medh*), † मिद् *MID,* † मेद् *MED,* i. 1, Par. Âtm. † 1. To understand. 2. To hurt. 3. To rival (ved.). Caus. *medhaya,* To further, MBh. 13, 7510.

मिथस् *mith+as,* adv. 1. Mutually, reciprocally, with each other, Pańch. 125, 10; from each other, Pańch. 42, 22.

2. Privately, Man. 8, 195 (Daçak. in Chr. 192, 20, read *pârthivam̃ mitho*).

मिथिला *mithilâ*, f. The name of a town.

मिथुन *mith* + *una* (for + *vana*), I. n. 1. A couple, Utt. Râmach. 36, 8. 2. Copulation. 3. Union. II. m. The sign of the zodiac, Gemini.—Comp. *Go-*, n. a bull and a cow, Man. 3, 29.

मिथ्या *mithyâ* (vb. *mith*), adv. Falsely, Pañch. 7, 16; untruly, feigned, Lass. 9, 11; wrong, Pañch. 206, 11; what does not concern one, Pañch. 9, 24; in vain, Sâv. 6, 14.

मिद् *MID*, i. 1, Âtm., i. 4, *medya*, Par., and i. 10, Par., also † **मिन्द्** *MIND*, i. 10, Par. 1. To be unctuous. 2. † To liquefy. † 3. To love. 4. To rejoice (ved.).—With **प्र** *pra*, Caus. *pramedita*, Made unctuous; greasy. See *mith*.—Cf. *μειδάω*.

† **मिध्** *MIDH*, see *mith*.

† **मिन्द्** *MIND*, see *mid*.

† **मिन्व्** *MINV*, i. 1, Par. 1. To sprinkle. 2. To gratify by service.

मिल् *MIL* (probably an old denomin. based on a noun derived from *miçla* (=*miçra*), changed to *milla*), i. 6, Par. Âtm. 1. To associate, Pañch. 220, 13. 2. To be connected, 229, 11 (*pṛishṭha âgatya militaḥ*, Was the last). 3. To meet, Hit. 83, 6, M.M. 4. To assemble, Pañch. 53, 20; Râjat. 5, 465. Ptcple. pf. pass. *milita*, Mixed (covered), Pañch. 122, 11.—With **परि** *pari*, *parimilita*, Penetrated, filled, Çiç. 11, 23.—With **सम्** *sam*, *sam̃milita*, Collected, Pañch. 229, 5.

† **मिश्** *MIÇ*, see *maç*.

मिश्र् *MIÇR*, and † **मिस्र्** *MISR*, i. 10 (rather a denomin. derived from *miçra*), Par. To mix, Çâk. d. 30. *miçrita*, 1. Mixed, Pañch. 215, 2. 2. Respected (i.e. *miçra* + *ita*, cf. *miçra*).—With the prep. **वि** *vi*, To put in disorder, MBh. 1, 3282.

मिश्र *miçra*, i.e. *miç* (perhaps for *miksh*, desider. of *mih*, without red., cf. *mih* with *sam*), + *ra*, I. adj. Mixed, Böhtl. Ind. Spr. 187; Pañch. 9, 4; Utt. Râmach. 42, 11. II. n. Mixing. III. m. 1. An elephant. 2. A respectable person, Sir, Lass. 95, 9; in this sense it is a common affix to nouns, Vikr. 3, 12, and proper names, Lass. 89, 6.—Comp. *Ârya-*, m. pl. a respectable person, Râm. 2, 82, 18; Prab. 25, 2.—Cf. Lat. miscere; O.H.G. miscjan; A.S. miscan; *μίσγω*, *μίγνυμι*.

मिश्रक *miçra* + *ka*, I. m. 1. A mixer. 2. An adulterator of commodities, a mixer of bad wares with good ones, Man. 11, 50. II. n. A grove of paradise.

1. **मिष्** *MISH* (probably for *miksh*, and akin to *mih*), i. 1, Par. To sprinkle. Ptcple. of the pf. pass. *mishṭa*. 1. Sprinkled. 2. Sweet, Pañch. 119, 7. n. A fine dish, Böhtl. Ind. Spr. 1787; sweetmeat.

2. **मिष्** *MISH*, i. 6, Par. (properly To wink, to contract the eyelids, cf. *mil*, *kshmil*, *çmil*, *smil*, and *smi*). 1. To look at angrily, Chr. 4, 16 (*harâmi mishatâm̃ vas*, I shall take [her] while you are looking on angrily, i.e. in spite of you). 2. † To contend, to resist.—With the prep. **उद्** *ud*, 1. To open one's eyes, Bhag. 5, 9; Kumâras. 5, 25. 2. To flash, Daçak. in Chr. 186, 16.—With **प्रत्युद्** *prati-ud*, To break forth, Daçak. in Chr. 184, 4.—With **नि** *ni*,

To shut one's eyes, to wink, MBh. 3, 10649.—Cf. Lat. miser; *μῖσος*, probably also *μύω*, cf. *ὄμματα συμ-μεμυκότα*, *ἀναμεμυκότα*; Lat. micare.

मिष *mish + a*, I. m. Emulation. II. n. Fraud.

† **मिस्** *MIS*, i. 4, Par. To go.

मिस्र् *MISR*, see *miçr*.

मिह् *MIH* (for original *migh*), i. 1, Par. **1.** To sprinkle. **2.** To urine, Chr. 290, 6=Rigv. i. 64, 6; Man. 4, 52. Ptcple. of the pf. Par. *miḍhvaṁs* (ved.), also before vowels, *miḷh°* for *miḍh°*, One who effuses or gives, Lass. 100, 1 =Rigv. vii. 15, 1. Ptcple. of the pf. pass. *miḍha*. Comp. *Puru-*, m. a proper name.—With the prep. प्र *pra*, *pramiḍha*, **1.** Passed, as urine. **2.** Thick.—With सम् *sam*, **1.** To sprinkle, to give, Chr. 288, 16=Rigv. i. 48, 16. (*mimikshva*, imperat., ii. 3, Âtm. or anomal. desider.). Desider. *mimiksha*, To wish to mix, to unite one's self, Chr. 293, 6=Rigv. i. 87, 6 (*mimikshire*, anomal. pf. red.).—Cf. Lat. mingere, mejere; A.S. mígan; Goth. maihstus; A.S. meox, miox, mist; *ὀμίχλη*, *ὀμιχεῖν*, *μοιχός*, *μιαίνω*, *μιαρός*.

मिहिर *mihira*, m. **1.** i.e. *mih + ira*, A cloud. **2.** (borrowed from the Persian language), The sun. **3.** The moon. **4.** Wind. **5.** A proper name.

मिहिलारोप्य *mihilâropya*, n. The name of a town, Pańch. 3, 9.

1. **मी** *MÎ*, ii. 9, *minâ*, *mini*, and ved. *minâ*, *mini*, Par. To hurt. Comp. ptcple. pres. *a-minant*, Not hurting, Chr. 295, 12=Rigv. i. 92, 12. i. 4, Âtm. To perish.—With the prep. आ *â*, ii. 9, To hurt, to scrape off, Chr. 295, 10=Rigv. i. 92, 10.—With प्र *pra*, ii. 9, **1.** To diminish, Chr. 295, 11=Rigv. i. 92, 11. **2.** To surmount, to surpass. i. 4, To perish. *pramîta*, Deceased, Man. 3, 245. Caus. *mâpaya*, To cause to perish, Man. 1, 57; to kill, 8, 295.—Cf. Lat. prō-mĭnere, e-minere, minere, prō-minare, e-minus, co-minus, minari.

2. † **मी** *MÎ*, i. 1 and 10, Par. To go, see *me*.—Cf. Lat. meare and movere (causal).

मीन *mîna* (probably vb. *mih*), m. **1.** A fish, Pańch. ii. d. 3. **2.** The sign of the zodiac, Pisces.

† **मीम्** *MÎM*, i. 1, Par. **1.** To go. **2.** To sound (cf. 2. *mâ*).

मीमांस *MÎMÂṀSA*, see *man*.

मीमांसक *mîmâṁsaka*, i.e. *mîmâṁsâ + aka*, m. A follower of the Pûrva-Mîmâṁsâ philosophy.

मीमांसा *mîmâṁsâ*, i.e. *mîmâṁsa + a*, f. Two of the philosophical systems of the Hindus, distinguished as *pûrva* and *uttara*.

मीमांसाकृत् *mîmâṁsâ-kṛi + t*, m. The author of the Pûrva-Mîmâṁsâ philosophy, Jaimini, Pańch. ii. d. 34.

मीर *mîra* (vb. *mih*), m. The ocean.

मील् *MÎL* (originally a denomin. based on a noun derived from *mish* by an affix, with initial *l*), i. 1, Par. **1.** To wink, to contract the eyelids, to close the eyes, Gît. 10, 16. **2.** To be closed of itself (viz. the eyes), Bhaṭṭ. 14, 54. **3.** To be collected, Utt. Râmach. 126, 5 (with v.r.). Comp. ptcple. pf. pass. *ishanmîlita*, i.e. *îshat-* adj. Closed a little, Lass. 13, 7. Caus. *mîlaya*, To close (viz. one's eyes), *lochane mîlayitvâ*, Like a moment, Megh. 109.—With the prep. अभि *abhi*, To close (viz. one's eyes), Râj. t. 5, 348.—With आ *â*, To close (viz. one's eyes), Daçak. in Chr. 199, 4. —With उद् *ud*, 1. To open one's eyes, MBh. 3, 11155. 2. To be opened of itself (as one's eyes), Bhaṭṭ. 16, 8. 3. To open, Gît. 1, 36; (one's eyes), Vikr. d. 5. 4. To show, Daçak. in Chr. 187, 23. 5. To hang down (as curls), Utt. Râmach. 14, 4. Caus. To open (viz. one's eyes), MBh. 2, 2630. —With प्रोद् *pra-ud*, To open one's eyes, Gît. 4, 19.—With समुद् *sam-ud*, To open of itself, to spring up, Bhartṛ. 2, 78.—With नि *ni*, 1. To close (viz. one's eyes), Çiç. 9, 11; Vikr. 7, 5; Pańch. 165, 15. 2. To fall asleep, Man. 1, 52. 3. To be covered, Râjat. 5, 481. Caus. 1. To cause to shut the eyes, to kill, Pańch. iii. d. 269. 2. To close, Ṛit. 6, 26.—With विनि *vi-ni*, To close the eyes, Bhaṭṭ. 11, 9. — With प्र *pra*, To close the eyes, Gît. 4, 19.—With सम् *sam*, 1. To close (viz. the eyes), Ragh. 3, 26 (Calc.). 2. To close (as flowers), Çâk. 45, 4 Chezy. Caus. 1. To cause to shut the eyes, to make insensible, Utt. Râmach. 23, 7. 2. To close, Ragh. 13, 10 (Calc.).

† मीव् *MÎV*, i. 1, Par. To grow corpulent.

मीवर *mîvara* (probably from vb. *mih*), adj., f. *rî*, Mischievous.

मीवा *mîvâ* (perhaps from vb. *mih*), f. The worm of the intestines, ascarides, etc.

मुक्‌ *muku* (vb. 2. *much*), m. Liberation.

मुकुट *mukuṭa*, I. n. A crest, a diadem, Pańch. 3, 10. II. (vb. 2. *much*, cf. *muchuṭi*), f. *ṭi*, Snapping the fingers.—Comp. *Pratâpa-*, m. a proper name, Lass. 5, 20.

मुकुन्द *mukunda*, m. 1. A precious gem. 2. Quicksilver. 3. One of Kuvera's treasures. 4. A name of Vishṇu, Bhâg. P. 4, 9, 36. 5. Gum olibanum.

मुकुर *mukura* (also मकुर *makura*), m. 1. A looking-glass, Çiç. 9, 73 (*mu°*). 2. The stick of a potter's wheel. 3. A bud. 4. A tree, Mimusops elengi. 5. Arabian jasmine.

मुकुल *mukula* (also मकुल *makula*), m. and n. 1. An opening bud, Ragh. 9, 27 (*mu°*); Utt. Râmach. 14, 5 (*daçana-mu°*, bud-like teeth). 2. The body. 3. The soul.

मुकुलित *mukulita*, i.e. *mukula* + *ita*, adj. 1. Half closed (as a bud). 2. Half shut (as the eye), Vikr. 47, 19.

मुक्तक *mukta* + *ka* (vb. *much*), n. Any missile weapon.

मुक्ता *muktâ* (f. of the ptcple. pf. pass. of *much*), f. A pearl, Vikr. d. 153. —Comp. *Çańkha-*, f. Shells and pearls, Râm. 3, 49, 36.

मुक्ताकण *muktâ-kaṇa*, m. A proper name, Râjat. 5, 34.

मुक्ताकारता *muktâkâratâ*, i.e. *muktâ-âkâra* + *tâ*, The form of a pearl, Bhartṛ. 2, 57.

मुक्ति *mukti*, i.e. 2. *much* + *ti*, f. 1. Leaving off, Bhartṛ. 2, 52. 2. Deliverance, release (*muktim̃ prâpnumaḥ*, We shall be released), Pańch. 106, 1; ii. d. 44. 3. The delivery of the soul from the body, and exemption from further transmigration, final beatitude.

मुख *mukha*, I. n. 1. The mouth,

Pańch. 258, 16. 2. The face, Pańch. 238, 23. 3. Front, Draup. 8, 8. 4. Entrance, Utt. Râmach. 15, 19; the entrance to a house. 5. An aperture, Çiç. 9, 2. 6. Commencement, Pańch. 29, 16; Chr. 8, 33. 7. A means. 8. Sound. II. m. The beak of a bird.—Comp. *Ańguli-*, n. the tip of the finger, Çiç. 9, 64. *Aja-mukhî*, f. the name of a female Râkshasa, Râm. 5, 25, 49. *Adhom°*, i.e. *adhas-*, adj., f. *khî*. 1. looking downwards, Pańch. 84, 7. 2. turned downwards, Râm. 5, 26, 20. *Abhi-*, see s.v. *Ayom°*, i.e. *ayas-*, adj. iron-pointed, Râm. 3, 53, 53. *Avâńm°*, i.e. *avâńch-*, adj. looking downwards, Râm. 4, 32, 1. *Açru-*, adj., f. *khî*, the face covered with tears, Râm. 2, 59, 14. *Açva-*, adj., f. *khî*, having a horse's head, a Kimnara, Râm. 4, 44, 38. *Udańmukha*, i.e. *udańch-*, adj. facing the north, Man. 2, 52. *Unm°*, i.e. *ud-*, adj., f. *khî*. 1. with the face turned upward, Vikr. 61, 17. 2. directed to, towards, Pańch. 141, 17. 3. desiring, Vikr. d. 26 (*bheda-*, desiring, or ready (cf. 5.), to break out of its bud). 4. intending, Râjat. 5, 259. 5. near to, Ragh. 3, 12. 6. expecting, Râm. 5, 55, 35. *Ûlkâ-*, m. 1. the name of a goblin, Man. 12, 71. 2. a proper name, Râm. 6, 3, 48. *Ûrdhva-*, adj. of which the aperture is turned upward; turned upward, Kumâras. 1, 16. *Ṛitu-*, n. the commencement, or first day of a season, Râm. 2, 105, 23. *Eka-*, adj. having one as (head) chief, or superintendent, Yâjń. 2, 202. *Kańka-*, adj. heron-mouthed, Râm. 6, 79, 69. *Kathâ-*, n. introduction to a tale, Pańch. 5, 16. *Kâla-*, m. 1. a kind of monkey, Râm. 6, 3, 35. 2. the name of a fabulous people, MBh. 2, 1171. *Kâlikâ-*, m. a Râkshasa, Râm. 3, 29, 30. *Kravya-*, m. a proper name, Pańch. 87, 4. *Go-*, m. 1. a proper name, MBh. 5, 3574. 2. a certain musical instrument, Bhâg. P. 1, 10, 15. *Chatur-*, (n.) I. four faces, Kumâras. 2, 17. II. adj. 1. having four faces, epithet of Brahman, Râm. 1, 2, 26; Vishṇu, Ragh. 10, 23; Çiva, Sund. 3, 28; and a Dânava, Hariv. 12934. 2. having four points, Hariv. 10630. *Jaya-sthala-*, adj. looking like trophies, Râjat. 5, 121. *Jyotirmukha*, i.e. *jyotis-*, m. a proper name, Râm. 6, 6, 26. *Jvâlâ-*, f. *khî*, a place where subterraneous fires break forth. *Dakshiṇâ-*, adj., f. *khî*, turned to the south, Man. 2, 52. *Dakshiṇâ-abhi-*, adj. the same, Man. 4, 50. *Dadhi-*, m. 1. a kind of snake, Suçr. 2, 265, 8. 2. a proper name, Râm. 5, 1, 39. *Darî-*, I. n. 1. a mouth resembling a cave, MBh. 7, 6437, a. 2. the aperture of a cave, ib. b. 3. a cave representing a mouth, Ragh. 13, 47. II. m. a proper name, Râm. 4, 39, 32. *Daça(n)-*, I. n. pl. ten faces, Bhâg. P. 9, 10, 23. II. adj. having ten faces, epithet of Râvaṇa, Megh. 59. *Dińm°*, i.e. *diç-*, n. any part of the heavens, Daçak. in Chr. 180, 12. *Durm°*, i.e. *dus-*, I. adj., f. *khî*. 1. hideous, Bhartṛ. 1, 89. 2. foul-mouthed, scurrilous, ib. 2, 59. II. m. a proper name, MBh. 2, 116. *Dûta-*, adj. speaking by means of ambassadors, Pańch. 161, 20. *Nandî-*, m. 1. epithet of Çiva, MBh. 12, 10428. 2. a kind of water-fowl, Suçr. 1, 205, 13. 3. a kind of rice, ib. 1, 196, 2. *Nândî-*, I. adj. 1. with *pitṛi*, a class of Manes, Yâjń. 1, 249. 2. with or without *çrâddha*, n. an oblation to that class of Manes, Mârk. P. 34, 105. II. f. *khî*, a sort of corn, Suçr. 1, 197, 1. *Niçâ-*, n. the commencement of night, Hariv. 4122. *Payas-*, adj. having milk on (its) surface, Hit. i. d. 76, M.M. *Parâń-mukha*, i.e. *parâńch-*, I. adj., f. *khî*. 1. having the face averted, Pańch. 181, 15. 2. averse, Pańch. i. d. 405; disinclined, Vikr. d. 102 (*pravṛitti-*, to give a report). 3. regardless, Mârk. P. 22, 44. II. m. a spell or charm spoken over weapons, Râm. 1, 31, 5 Gorr. *Pari-*

vritta-ardha-, adj., f. *khî*, having turned half her face, Vikr. d. 17. *Pûrva-paçchânmukha*, i. e. *pûrva-paçchât-*, adj., f. *khî*, running to the east and west, Râm. 2, 12, 6 Gorr. *Prâṅmukha*, i.e. *prâñch-*, adj. facing the east, Sund. 3, 23. *Phaṇi(n)-*, a kind of spade, Daçak. in Chr. 186, 10. *Baḍavâ-*, m. submarine fire. *Bali-* and *balî-*, m. a monkey. *Bhṛikuṭi-*, adj. knitting the brow, Sund. 4, 14. *Sa-bhṛikuṭi-*, adj. with a frowning face. *Mahâ-*, m. a crocodile. *Mâtṛi-*, m. a fool. *Mlech-chha-*, n. copper. *Vi-*, adj. 1. with averted face, Hit. i. d. 189, M.M. 2. averted, Böhtl. Ind. Spr. 814. 3. averse, disinclined, Pañch. ii. d. 86; iv. d. 5. *Çâstra-vi-*, adj. disinclined to learning, Pañch. 3, 13. *Vinâçonmukha*, i.e. *vi-nâça-ud-*, adj. mature (near) to decay. *Çaṅkha-*, m. an alligator. *Çata-*, I. (n.), a hundred shapes, Bhartṛ. 2, 10. II. adj. having a hundred issues, Pañch. ii. d. 14; having a hundred shapes, in a hundred ways, Bhartṛ. 2, 10 v. r. *Çilî-*, m. 1. a bee, Çiç. 9, 41. 2. an arrow, ib.; MBh. 6, 3910. 3. a fool. 4. war. *Shaṇm°*, i.e. *shash-*, m. a proper name, Râjat. 6, 319 (Calc.). *Sa-kala-indu-* (cf. *kalâ*), adj., f. *khî*, having a face like the full moon, Vikr. d. 28. *Sam-*, adj. 1. being in front, Pañch. iv. d. 12 (cf. Böhtl. Ind. Spr. 2753); facing, in front of, Pañch. 104, 15. 2. encountering, Pañch. 240, 13. 3. directed towards, Pañch. 104, 17. 4. propitious, Pañch. v. d. 77 (n. 1424 of my transl.). *Sarvatomukha*, i.e. *sarvatas-*, I. adj., f. *khî*. 1. facing every quarter, i.e. to every quarter (of the world), Sund. 2, 13. 2. complete, unrestrained, Çâk. d. 122. II. m. 1. Brahman. 2. a Brâhmaṇa. 3. soul, spirit. 4. paradise. III. n. 1. sky. 2. water. *Su-*, I. n. a beautiful mouth, Pañch. i. d. 202. II. adj., f. *khâ* and *khî*. 1. handsome-faced. 2. pleasing, propitious, Lass. 55, 20. III. m. 1. a teacher. 2. a proper name, Man. 7, 41. IV. n. the scratch of a finger-nail. *Sûchi-*, I. m. a bird. II. f. *khî*, a female bird, Pañch. i. d. 437. III. n. a diamond. *Senâ-*, n. 1. a division of an army. 2. a mound or covered way before a city gate. *Stana-*, m. a nipple. *Svasti-*, m. 1. a letter. 2. a Brâhmaṇa, a panegyrist.

मुखज *mukha-ja*, m. A Brâhmaṇa.

मुखतस् *mukha + tas*, adv. From the mouth, Nal. 11, 28.

मुखबाहूरुपज्ज *mukhabâhûrupajja*, i.e. *mukha-bâhu-ûru-pad-ja*, adj. Born from the mouth, the arms, the thighs, and the feet, Man. 1, 87.

मुखर *mukha + ra*, I. adj. 1. Foul-mouthed, speaking harshly or scurrilously, Bhartṛ. 2, 61. 2. Rallying. 3. Resounding, Lass. 69, 5; noisy, Utt. Râmach. 16, 9; Megh. 38. II. m. 1. A leader, Hit. i. d. 28, M.M. 2. A conch-shell.—Comp. *Unmukhara-*, i.e. *ud-*, adj. sounding loudly, Prab. 78, 3.

मुखरता *mukhara + tâ*, f. 1. Talkativeness, Kir. 5, 16. 2. Garrulity, Bhartṛ. 2, 44.

मुखरित *mukharita*, i.e. *mukhara + ita*, adj. Sounding, ringing, Râjat. 5, 482.

मुख्य *mukhya*, i.e. *mukha + ya*, I. adj. 1. Being in, or belonging to, the face. 2. Fallen from the mouth, Man. 5, 141. 3. Chief, principal, Pañch. 158, 2; Hit. 83, 18; Daçak. in Chr. 183, 14; 189, 14. II. n. A principal rite or ordinance.—Comp. *Dvi-ja-*, and *Dvi-jâti-*, m. A Brâhmaṇa, MBh. 5, 7279; Man. 3, 286. *Vâra-mukhyâ*, f. the head of a set of harlots, Bhâg. P. 9, 10, 38; Daçak. in Chr. 183, 14.

मुख्यता *mukhya + tâ*, f. Pre-eminence.

मुख्यशस् *mukhya + ças*, adv. Principally, Nal. 8, 21.

मुग्धता *mugdha + tâ*, f., and **मुग्धत्व** *mugdha + tva*, n. (vb. *muh*). **1.** Loveliness, charm, Vikr. d. 26. **2.** Simplicity. **3.** Stupidity.

† 1. **मुच्** *MUCH*, see *mach*.

2. **मुच्** *MUCH*, i. 6, *muńcha*, Par. Âtm. **1.** To let loose, Pańch. 32, 25; ii. d. 123 (to go); to loosen, Vikr. 13, 10. **2.** To dismiss, Pańch. 128, 25. **3.** To release from (with abl. and instr.), MBh. 1, 5641; Man. 11, 228. **4.** To leave, to abandon, Vikr. 5, 11; Pańch. 57, 10; with *deham*, To die, Hit. iii. d. 31. **5.** To take away, MBh. 3, 2982. **6.** To lose, Râm. 1, 25, 14. **7.** To give up, Man. 8, 150; to sacrifice, Utt. Râmach. 27, 10. **8.** To cast, Chr. 32, 29; Megh. 85. **9.** To effuse, Ṛit. 6, 28. **10.** To shed, Râm. 2, 37, 15; Chr. 34, 15. **11.** To spit out, Kir. 5, 38. **12.** To void, MBh. 3, 11115. **13.** To utter, Pańch. 57, 14; Kathâs. 18, 154; Megh. 55. **14.** To put on, Bhaṭṭ. 14, 95. Pass. (has in epic poetry sometimes the terminations of the Par., e.g. MBh. 3, 1695). **1.** To deliver one's self, to escape, MBh. 1, 656 (with acc., perhaps i. 4). **2.** To deviate from, to abandon (abl.), Pańch. i. d. 302. Ptcple. of the pf. pass. *mukta*. **1.** What has been let loose, shot, Pańch. i. d. 219; darted, Hit. i. d. 193, M.M.; spit out, Kir. 5, 38; Man. 3, 225; Pańch. 253, 1 (given). **2.** Liberated from corporeal existence, finally happy. **3.** Deprived, Hit. iii. d. 127. **4.** Open, Hit. iii. d. 121 (*mukta-hasta*, Liberal). n. The spirit released from corporeal existence. *muktâ*, see s.v. Comp. *A-*, adj. not lost, Pańch. 174, 25. *Jîvanm°*, i.e. *jîvant-*, m. one who has obtained final beatitude during his life, Vedântas. in Chr. 218, 10. Absol. *muktvâ*, Except, Pańch. 44, 11; 73, 19. Desider. *mumuksha*. **1.** To wish to cast, Ragh. 2, 42 (Calc.). **2.** To desire final beatitude, MBh. 3, 167 (cf. *moksha*). Caus. **1.** To cause, or to order, to be liberated, Pańch. 192, 16; Daçak. in Chr. 192, 18. **2.** To cause to shed (tears), Megh. 91. i. 10, Par. **1.** To let loose, to release, Pańch. in Weber, Ind. St. iii. 373, 6; Hit. 52, 2, M.M. **2.** To redeem from (abl.), Man. 3, 37. **3.** † To delight.—With the prep. **अव** *ava*, **1.** To unyoke, MBh. 3, 2870. **2.** To take off, MBh. 2, 2520.—With **आ** *â*, To put on, MBh. 1, 4095; Mâlav. 37, 19. *âmukta*, **1.** Dressed. **2.** Loosed. **3.** Cast, discharged.—With **उद्** *ud*, To let loose, Daçak. in Chr. 187, 2; to liberate, Pańch. 38, 21. Caus., or i. 10, To set free, Pańch. 87, 20.—With **निस्** *nis*, pass. refl., with acc., To abandon, Râjat. 5, 125. *nirmukta*, **1.** Let loose, Chr. 34, 12. **2.** Liberated, MBh. 1, 6197. **3.** Separated. m. A snake who has lately cast his skin.—With **अभिनिस्** *abhi-nis*, *abhinirmukta*, Darted (surprised) by the setting sun (cf. *mluch*), Man. 2, 221 (Weber reads *abhinimrukta*, Journ. of the German Oriental Society, xiv. 756).—With **विनिस्** *vi-nis*, *vinirmukta*, **1.** Left, Nal. 13, 21. **2.** Liberated. **3.** Exempt. **4.** Separated, MBh. 3, 2552.—With **परि** *pari*, *parimukta*, Liberated, MBh. 1, 4659.—With **प्र** *pra*, **1.** To throw, Chr. 44, 4. **2.** To throw out, to vomit, MBh. 1, 7628. **3.** To utter, MBh. 3, 2542. **4.** To produce, Râm. 2, 91, 26. **5.** To remove, MBh. 3, 10819. **6.** To loosen, MBh. 2, 2325. **7.** To release, Man. 4, 181. **8.** To put on, Râm. 2, 9,

39.—With विप्र *vi-pra*, To liberate, to release, MBh. 3, 11800. *vipramukta*, Liberated from (instr.), MBh. 1, 6771. —With प्रति *prati*, **1.** To bind, MBh. 2, 2323. **2.** To let loose again, to return, Pańch. iv. d. 1. **3.** To restore, to return, Ragh. 16, 59 (Calc.). **4.** Pass. To be freed from, Man. 10, 118. *pratimukta*, **1.** Clothed, armed. **2.** Thrown mutually, or at one another. **3.** Loosed, or liberated repeatedly. Caus., or i. 10, To save, MBh. 1, 5812.—With वि *vi*, **1.** To separate, Vikr. d. 129. **2.** To let loose, Çâk. 5, 15. **3.** With *garbham*, To lay eggs, Pańch. 75, 9. **4.** To set free, Pańch. 41, 22. **5.** Pass. To liberate one's self, to escape from (abl.), MBh. 2, 882. **6.** To take off, MBh. 1, 4095. **7.** To lose, MBh. 3, 315. **8.** Pass. To be released or deprived, Man. 2, 79; Hit. i. d. 65, M.M. **9.** To abandon, Hit. iv. d. 38; MBh. 3, 12381; to leave, Utt. Râmach. 4, 3; 67, 5. **10.** Pass. To obtain final beatitude, Vedântas. in Chr. 219, 15; 216, 13. **11.** To effuse, MBh. 1, 3317. **12.** To shed, Râm. 2, 59, 5. **13.** To throw, MBh. 4, 1866; Utt. Râmach. 163, 10. **14.** To utter, Chr. 41, 8; Râjat. 5, 408. **15.** To assume, Man. 1, 56. *vimukta*, **1.** Loosed. **2.** Thrown, hurled. **3.** Quitted, lost, i.e. without, Râm. 3, 51, 33. **4.** Issued, let loose from. Caus., or i. 10, **1.** To liberate, MBh. 3, 2435. **2.** To relieve, Man. 11, 112. **3.** To avoid, Râm. 5, 42, 11.—With प्रवि *pra-vi*, To abandon, MBh. 3, 15602.—With सम् *sam*, To shed, MBh. 3, 10236.—Cf. Lat. mucus, e-mungere; *μυκτήρ, ἀπομυκτίζω, μύξα*.

ऽमुच् *-much*, adj. Letting loose; e.g. *ambu-*, *jala-*, q. cf.

मुचिर 2.*much*+*ira*, adj. Liberal, a donor.

मुचुटी 2.*much*+*uṭi*, f. **1.** Snapping the fingers. **2.** The fist.

मुछ् *MUCHH*, v.r. of *yuchh*.

† **मुज्** *MUJ*, **मुञ्ज्** *MUŃJ* (others, **मृज्** *MṚIJ*, **मृञ्ज्** *MṚIŃJ*), i. 1, Par. To sound. *muj*, *muńj*, i. 10, Par. **1.** To sound. **2.** To cleanse (cf. *mṛij*).

† **मुञ्च्** *MUŃCH*, see *mach* and *mruńch*.

मुञ्चक *muńchaka* (vb. 2.*much*), m. The testicle.

† **मुञ्ज्** *MUŃJ*, see *muj*.

मुञ्ज *muńja*, m. **1.** A sort of grass, Saccharum munja, from the fibres of which the string is prepared to form the thread worn by the Brâhmaṇas, Man. 2, 43. **2.** The brahmanical girdle. **3.** An arrow.

† 1. **मुट्** *MUṬ* (cf. *mṛid*), i. 6, Par. **1.** To rub, to grind. **2.** To rebuke. i. 10, Par. To rub, to grind.

† 2. **मुट्** *MUṬ*, **मुण्ट्** *MUṆṬ*, **मुड्** *MUḌ*, **मुण्ड्** *MUṆḌ* (cf. *mṛiḍ* and 1.*muṇḍ*), **पुड्** *PUḌ*, **पुण्ड्** *PUṆḌ*, i. 1, Par. To rub, to grind.

मुड् *MUḌ*, see *puḍ* and 2.*muṭ*.

† **मुण्** *MUṆ*, i. 6, Par. To promise.

मुण्ट् *MUṆṬ*, see 2.*muṭ*.

† **मुण्ठ्** *MUṆṬH*, i. 1, Âtm. To run away (or to protect).

† 1. **मुण्ड्** *MUṆḌ*, i. 1, Par. **1.** To shave. **2.** To grind or pound; see 2.*muṭ*.

† 2. मुण्ड् *MUṆḌ*, i. 1, Âtm. 1. To be pure. 2. To sink.

मुण्ड *muṇḍa* (probably a form of a noun derived from *mṛid*, based on the original form *mard*), I. adj. 1. Shaved, bald, having no hair on the head, Man. 2, 219. 2. Low, mean. II. m. and n. 1. The head, Daçak. in Chr. 183, 6; Hit. iii. d. 89. 2. The forehead. III. m. 1. A bald-pate. 2. A barber. 3. Râhu. 4. The name of a Daitya. IV. f. *ḍâ*, Bengal madder, Rubia manjith. —Comp. *Daṇḍimuṇḍa*, i.e. *daṇḍin-*, m. a name of Çiva (bearing a staff and having his head shorn), MBh. 12, 10358.

मुण्डय *MUṆḌAYA*, a denomin. derived from *muṇḍa*, Par. To shave, Pańch. 223, 8. Ptcple. of the pf. pass. *muṇḍita*, Shaven, bald, shorn, Pańch. iv. d. 36; 49.

मुण्डिन् *muṇḍin*, i.e. *muṇḍaya* + *in*, m. A barber.

1. मुद् *MUD*, i. 1, Âtm. (in epic poetry also Par., Râm. 1, 46, 17), To be delighted, to rejoice, Man. 2, 232. Ptcple. of the pf. pass. *mudita*, Delighted, Pańch. i. d. 458; Chr. 14, 24. n. Pleasure. Caus. To exhilarate (also Âtm.), Bhaṭṭ. 7, 171.—With the prep. अनु *anu*, 1. To approve, to permit, MBh. 2, 1787. 2. To rejoice, MBh. 3, 11535. Caus. To celebrate, Chr. 55, 3. *anumodita*, Agreed, Utt. Râmach. 38, 18.—With अभ्यनु *abhi-anu*, To dismiss, MBh. 1, 4447.—With प्र *pra*, To be delighted, Râm. 1, 1, 84. *pramudita*, Pleased, happy, Pańch. 238, 23. Caus. To exhilarate, Man. 3, 61. *pramodita*, Happy. m. A name of Kuvera.—With प्रति *prati*, To expect with delight, MBh. 1, 6781.

2. मुद् *MUD*, i. 10, Par. To mix.

3. मुद् 1. *mud*, f. 1. Pleasure, joy, Pańch. 159, 20; Kir. 5, 25. 2. Intoxication. 3. A wife.—Comp. *Krîḍâ-*, f. the pleasure of love, Gît. 9, 10.

मुदा 1. *mud* + *â*, f. Joy, pleasure, Chr. 13, 19; 35, 10.

मुदिर 1. *mud* + *ira*, m. 1. A cloud. 2. A lover.

मुद्ग *mudga*, m. 1. A sort of kidney bean, Phaseolus mungo, Lass. 79, 15. 2. A cover.

मुद्गर *mudgara*, m. 1. A carpenter's hammer. 2. A mace, Râm, 3, 54, 10; Sund. 2, 3. 3. A staff armed with iron, used for breaking clods of earth. 4. A sort of flower.—Comp. *Kûṭa-*, m. a hidden mace, MBh. 13, 150.

मुद्रा *mudrâ*, f. 1. A seal, a signet, Pańch. iv. d. 36 (*strî-*, woman who is, as it were, the seal, i.e. the order, viz. of the god of love). 2. A seal-ring. 3. A stamp, figurat., a form, Utt. Râmach. 155, 3. 4. A mode of intertwining the fingers during religious worship, Daçak. in Chr. 187, 12.—Comp. *Añguli-*, f. a seal-ring, Çâk. d. 135, v.r. *Tarka-*, f. a particular intertwining of the fingers, Bhâg. P. 4, 6, 38. *Nâma(n)-*, f. a seal-ring with the name of the possessor, Çâk. 17, 4. *Pâda-*, f. 1. impression of a footstep, Râjat. 4, 669. 2. trace, ib. 4, 103. *Vi-mudra*, adj. 1. unsealed. 2. blown, budded. *Sa-mudra*, adj. sealed, Yâjń. 2, 247.

मुद्रिका *mudrikâ*, i.e. *mudrâ* + *ka*, f. = *mudrâ*.—Comp. *Añguli-*, f. a seal-ring.

मुद्रित *mudrita*, i.e. *mudrâ* + *ita*, adj. 1. Sealed. 2. Stamped, marked, Daçak. in Chr. 197, 3; written, Hit. iv. d. 10. 3. Sealed up, contracted. 4. Unblown (as a flower).

मुधा *mudhâ*, probably from *muh* (cf. the ptcple. pf. pass. *mûḍha*), adv. In vain, Hit. iii. d. 139.

मुनि *muni*, i.e. *man* + *i* (*u* for *a*, by the influence of the preceding labial), I. m. **1.** A holy sage, endowed with divine inspiration, Vikr. d. 3. **2.** An ascetic, Pańch. 34, 13. **3.** The saint Agastya, Vyâsa, Kir. 5, 49. **4.** The name of two plants. II. f. *nî*, A female saint.—Comp. *Mahâ-*, I. m. 1. a great Muni, Chr. 15, 29; Râm. 3, 49, 50 (epithet of Agastya.) 2. the saint Agastya. 3. epithet of Paraçurâma, Chr. 19, 12, and of Vyâsa. 4. time. II. n. Coriander.

मुमुक्षु *mumukshu*, i.e. *mumuksha*, desider. of *much*, + *u*, I. adj. **1.** Desiring to dart (viz. arrows), Ragh. 9, 58. **2.** Anxious for liberation from mundane existence or final beatitude, Vedântas. in Chr. 203, 22; Vikr. d. 1. II. m. A sage abstracted from all human passion.

मुमुक्षुत्व *mumukshu* + *tva*, n. Condition of one who is anxious for final beatitude; wishing for final beatitude, Vedântas. in Chr. 203, 7.

मुमूर्षा *mumûrshâ*, i.e. *mumûrsha*, desider. of *mṛi*, + *a*, f. Desire to die, MBh. 1, 1899.

मुमूर्षु *mumûrshu*, i.e. *mumûrsha*, desider. of *mṛi*, + *u*, adj. Being about to die, Hit. 64, 8; Râjat. 5, 218; 411.

† **मुर्** *MUR*, i. 6, To circle, to surround.—Cf. perhaps Lat. mūrus.

मुर *mura*, m. The name of a Daitya killed by Vishṇu.

मुरज *muraja*, I. m. A small drum, Mâlav. d. 21. II. f. *jâ*. **1.** A large drum, Kumâras. 6, 40. **2.** The wife of Kuvera.

मुरला *muralâ*, f. The Narmadâ river, Utt. Râmach. 50, 2.

मुरली *muralî*, f. A flute.

मुरलीधर *muralî-dhara*, m. Kṛishṇa.

मुर्छ् *MURCHH* (akin to *mṛi* and *mlai*), i. 1, *mûrchha*, Par. **1.** To be faint, to lose consciousness, Râm. 2, 34, 17. **2.** To increase, to grow vehement, Ragh. 12, 57 (Calc.). **3.** To be frequent, Çâk. 66, 4. **4.** To fill, 6, 9 (Calc.). **5.** To be a match for, 2, 34 (Calc.); to be powerful, Çâk. d. 191 (to appear in a looking-glass). Ptcple. of the pf. pass. *mûrchhita*. **1.** Fainted, Vikr. 54, 17; insensible, Râm. 2, 34, 17. **2.** Stupid. **3.** Intoxicated, MBh, 3, 1864. **4.** Infatuated, Chr. 37, 27; bewildered, Lass. 7, 10. **5.** Increased, grown. **6.** Tall. Comp. *Krodha-*, adj. overpowered by wrath, Indr. 5, 48.—With the prep. **अभि** *abhi*, *abhimûrchhita*, Intoxicated, infatuated, MBh. 1, 7794.—With **वि** *vi*, *vimûrchhita*, Wrapped (Stenzler), Yâjń. 3, 75.—With **सम्** *sam*, **1.** To increase, Kir. 5, 41. **2.** To be powerful, Ragh. 16, 64 (Calc.). Caus. To cause to faint, Utt. Râmach. 47, 2.—Cf. Goth. untila-malsks, foolish.

मुर्मुर *murmura*, m. **1.** A fire of chaff. **2.** The god of love. **3.** A horse of the sun.

† **मुर्व्** *MURV*, i. 1, *mûrva*, Par. To bind, to tie.

मुल् *MUL*, see 2. *mûl*.

मुशल *muçala*, **मुषल** *mush* + *ala* (see *mus*), and **मुसल** *mus* + *ala*, I. m. n. A pestle, a club, Arj. 10, 5 (*sh*). II. f. *lî*, A house-lizard.—Comp. *Kaṅkâla-mu-*

shala, m. or n. a kind of weapon, Râm. 1, 30, 13 Gorr.; 57, 12 Gorr. *Chakra -mushala*, adj. performed with the disk and club, Hariv. 5346. *Danta-mushala*, m. or n. a pestle-like tusk, Pańch. 69, 1. Cf. *musala*.

1. मुष् *MUSH*, ii. 9, *mushṇâ*, *mushṇí*, and i. 6 (MBh. 3, 13047; Lass. 35, 16), Par. To steal, Daçak. in Chr. 189, 22; to rob, to plunder, Râjat. 5, 268; to captivate, Nal. 5, 7. Ptcple. of the pf. pass. *mushita*. **1.** Stolen. **2.** Robbed, plundered, Daçak. in Chr. 194, 1. **3.** Deprived of, free from, Hit. 42, 12.—With परि *pari*, To rob, to plunder, MBh. 3, 13030.—With प्र *pra*, To rob, Bhaṭṭ. 17, 60. See *mash*, *mus*, and *mûsh*.

2. मुष् *mush*, I. f. Stealing, Râjat. 5, 168 (read *mushe* instead of *mukhe*, 'Having turned his mind on stealing.') II. Latter part of comp. adj. Stealing, robbing; e. g. *dhṛiti-*, adj. Stealing, destroying constancy, Hit. i. d. 193, M.M. *netra-*, adj. Captivating the eyes, MBh. 3, 1720. *çrî-*, Having stolen, i.e. possessed of the beauty, Megh. 48.

मुषल *mushala*, see *muçala* and *musala*.

मुषल्य *mushalya*, see *musalya*.

मुषितक *mushita*+*ka* (vb. *mush*), n. Stolen objects, Daçak. in Chr. 188, 14.

मुष्क *mushka*, m. **1.** i.e. *mush*+*ka*, A thief. **2.** A testicle, the scrotum, Hit. 76, 1, M.M.; 49, 14. **3.** A heap, a multitude. **4.** The name of a plant.

मुष्कर *mushka*+*ra*, m. A man with large testicles.

मुष्टि *mushṭi*, m. and f. **1.** The fist, Râm. 3, 15, 17; Pańch. i. d. 203. **2.** A handful, Pańch. 215, 1. **3.** The handle of a sword.—Cf. perhaps A.S. fyst.

मुष्टिक *mushṭika*, m. A goldsmith.

मुष्टिता *mushṭi*+*tâ*, in *dṛiḍha-* (vb. *dṛiṁh*), f. Firmness of grasp, Johns. Sel. 12, 30.

मुष्टिंधय *mushṭiṁdhaya*, i.e. *mushṭi* +*m-dhe*+*a*, m. A child.

मुस् *MUS*, or मुष् *MUSH*, i. 4, Par. To break to pieces.

मुसल *mus*+*ala*, also मुषल *mush*+*ala* (see *mus*), n. **1.** A pestle, Man. 3, 88 (*s*). **2.** A club. Cf. *muçala*.

मुसलिन् *musalin*, i.e. *musala*+*in*, m. A name of Baladeva.

मुसल्य *musalya*, and मुषल्य *mushalya*, i.e. *musala*+*ya*, adj. Deserving death by pounding with a pestle.

† मुस्त् *MUST*, i. 10, Par. To accumulate.

मुस्त *musta*, m., and f. *tâ*, A fragrant grass, Cyperus rotundus, Çâk. d. 39 (*tâ*).—Comp. *Sa-bhadra-musta*, adj. full of Cyperus rotundus (cf. *bhadra -mustaka*), Ṛit. i, 17 (but v. r. *su -bhadra-*, containing very auspicious Cyperus rotundus).

मुस्तक *musta*+*ka*, I. m. and n. A fragrant grass, Cyperus rotundus. II. n. A sort of poison.—Comp. *Bhadra-*, n. =*musta*, q. cf.

मुस्तु *mustu*, m. The fist (cf. *mushṭi*).

मुस्र *musra*, n. A tear.

मुह् *MUH*, i. 4, Par. **1.** To be faint, to lose consciousness, Chr. 32, 24. **2.** To be disturbed (in mind), to be perplexed, Bhag. 2, 13. **3.** To fail, Hit. iii. d. 54. Ptcple. of the pf. pass. I. *mûḍha*. **1.** Perplexed, confused, Çiç.

9, 77. **2.** Foolish, stupid, Nal. 6, 12; 18, 10. **3.** Deceived. **4.** Ignorant, unlearned, Pańch. 243, 18. m. **1.** A fool, Vikr. 32, 15. **2.** A sluggard. **II.** *mugdha.* **1.** Stupid, Pańch. 166, 25. **2.** Being in love, Çâk. d. 36. **3.** Innocent, d. 24. **4.** Simple. **5.** Beautiful, lovely, Utt. Râmach. 14, 5. **Comp.** *A-mûḍha,* adj. 1. not perplexed, bold. 2. wise. *Dinmûḍha,* i.e. *diç-,* adj. one who has lost the points of the compass, and cannot tell the east from the west, Râm. 3, 60, 3. *Mahâ-mûḍha,* adj. very foolish, a great fool, Pańch. 38, 12. *Ati-mugdha,* being much in love, Daçak. in Chr. 197, 2. Frequent. *momuhya,* To be much disturbed, MBh. 4, 801. Caus. *mohaya,* **1.** To perplex, MBh. 1, 5457. **2.** To infatuate, Hit. i. d. 179, M.M.; Râm. 3, 55, 22; *mohita,* Infatuated, Hit. i. d. 25, M.M. **3.** To stupefy, Man. 11, 96. *mohita,* **1.** Puzzled, Utt. Râmach. 36, 8. **2.** Beguiled, Nal. 8, 16.—With the prep. व्या *vi-â,* Caus. To disturb, to perplex, Pańch. 129, 8. *vyâmohita,* Infatuated, Pańch. 199, 1.—With उद् *ud, unmugdha,* Disturbed, Siddh. K. 16, 6.—With परि *pari,* Caus., Âtm. To perplex, MBh. 1, 3571. *parimûḍha,* Bewildered, Utt. Râmach. 23, 7.—With प्र *pra,* I. *pramûḍha.* **1.** Fainted, Utt. Râmach. 160, 10. **2.** Disturbed, perplexed, Matsyop. 54. **3.** Foolish, stupid, a fool. **II.** *pramugdha,* Fainted, Utt. Râmach. 164, 17. Caus. To perturb, Draup. 6, 21. *pramohita,* Insensible.—With विप्र *vi-pra,* To be disturbed, Bhag. 2, 72. Caus. To perplex, MBh. 1, 5978.—With वि *vi,* I. *vimûḍha.* **1.** Bewildered, Utt. Râmach. 101, 1. **2.** Beguiled. **3.** Foolish. m. A kind of divine being (i.e. *mûḍha* with *vi,* Wise), Sund. 3, 5. **II.** *vimugdha,* Bewildered, Hit. 91, 9, M.M.; absorbed. Caus. **1.** To disturb, Bhag. 3, 40. **2.** To infatuate, Râjat. 5, 378. *vimohita,* Bewitched, Kathâs. 25, 274.—With सम् *sam,* To be disturbed, MBh. 3, 10978. I. *sammûḍha.* **1.** Bewildered. **2.** Stupefied. **3.** Foolish, Hit. iv. d. 71. **4.** Produced rapidly. **5.** Heaped. **6.** Broken. **II.** *sammugdha.* **1.** Fascinated. **2.** Stupefied, Utt. Râmach. 171, 5. **3.** Beautiful. Caus. **1.** To perplex, MBh. 2, 1949. **2.** To infatuate, Pańch. i. d. 210.

मुहिर *muh+ira,* I. adj. Foolish. II. m. Love, the god of love.

मुहुर् *muhur,* probably *muh+u+trâ,* adv. **1.** A moment, Râm. 3, 50, 10 (cf. *muhûrta* and Râm. 3, 50, 6). **2.** Repeatedly, Vikr. d. 6. Doubled, *muhur-muhur,* adv. Repeatedly, Ṛit. 6, 9.

मुहूर्त *muhûrta,* i.e. *muhur+ta,* I. m. and n. **1.** A moment, Râm. 3, 50, 6; some time, Vikr. 40, 4 (*param muhûrtât,* After some time, not yet). **2.** The thirtieth part of a day and night, or forty-eight minutes. II. m. An astrologer.—**Comp.** *Durmuhûrta,* i.e. *dus-,* n. an inauspicious hour, MBh. 12, 6735.

मुहेर *muh+era,* m. A fool.

† मू *MŪ,* i. 1, Âtm. To bind; see *mav.*

मूक *mûka,* I. adj. Dumb, Pańch. i. d. 71. II. m. **1.** A fish. **2.** A poor man. **3.** A Daitya.—Cf. Lat. mūtus.

मूढता *mûḍha+tâ* (vb. *muh*), f., and

मूढत्व *mûḍha+tva,* n. Foolishness, Pańch. 123, 13; 228, 3.

मूढवत् *mûḍha+vat* (vb. *muh*), adv. Like a fool, Chr. 8, 30.

मूत्र् *MŪTR* (properly a denomin.

derived from *mûtra*), i. 10, Par. To urine.—With the prep. अव *ava*, To urine on somebody, Man. 8, 282.

मूत्र *mûtra* (vb. *mih* and aff. *tra*), n. Urine, piss, Pańch. 121, 15.

मूत्रित *mûtrita*, i.e. *mûtra + ita*, adj. Soiled with urine.

मूर्ख *mûrkha*, i.e. *murchh + a*, m. A fool, a blockhead, Vikr. 33, 2.

मूर्खता *mûrkha + tâ*, f., मूर्खत्व *mûrkha + tva*, n., and मूर्खिमन् *mûrkhiman*, i.e. *mûrkha + iman*, m. Stupidity, Pańch. iii. d. 246; 127, 14.

मूर्छता *mûrchhatâ*, i.e. *murchh + a + tâ*, f. Denseness, Vikr. d. 48.

मूर्छन *mûrchhana*, i.e. *murchh + ana*, I. n. Modulation, Râm. 1, 4, 11. II. f. *nâ*. 1. A melody, Megh. 84. 2. A tone as placed in its scale, the seventh part of a scale, Lass. 39, 9; Pańch. iii. d. 43.

मूर्छा *mûrchh + a*, f. Fainting, loss of consciousness, Utt. Râmach. 58, 7; Pańch. 35, 10 (instr. by fainting, i.e. fainted).

मूर्छाल *mûrchhâ + la*, adj. Fainted.

मूर्त *mûrta* (akin to *mûrti*), adj., f. *tâ*. 1. Solid, material, corporeal, Bhâshâp. 86; 157; Utt. Râmach. 60, 7. 2. Embodied, incarnate, Çâk. d. 32; Kathâs. 3, 62.—Comp. *A*-, adj. incorporeal, Bhâshâp. 87; Kathâs. 20, 70.

मूर्तत्व *mûrta + tva*, n. Corporality, Bhâshâp. 24.

मूर्ति *mûrti*, probably better *mûrtti*, i.e. *mṛid + ti*, cf. Man. 12, 120. 1. Matter, substance, Man. 1, 17; hard substances, Man. 12, 120 (Jones: the terrene parts of the human body). 2. Figure, form, Bhartṛ. 2, 1; Pańch. ii. d. 169. 3. Body, Râjat. 5, 364. 4. Incarnation, Man. 1, 98. 5. Image, Man. 2, 225. 6. Beauty, Pańch. ii. d. 107. —Comp. *Ashṭa(n)*-, m. a name of Çiva, Çiç. 14, 18. *Tapas*-, I. f. incarnation of devotion, Râm. 1, 31, 11. II. m. a proper name, Bhâg. P. 8, 13, 29. *Tejas*-, adj. consisting entirely of light, Man. 3, 93. *Tri*-, adj. having three forms, Kumâras. 2, 4.—Cf. perhaps βρέτας and μορφή.

मूर्तितस् *mûrti + tas*, adv. = abl. sing. of *mûrti*, Man. 1, 55.

मूर्तिमन्त् *mûrti + mant*, adj., f. *matî*. 1. Having shape or substance, embodied, Utt. Râmach. 13, 4. 2. Incarnate, Hit. 100, 2; Çâk. d. 112. —Comp. *Viçva*-, adj. taking all forms, omnipresent, Vishṇu, Johns. Sel. 90, 31.

मूर्धज *mûrdhaja*, i.e. *mûrdhan-ja*, m. Hair, the hair of the head, Çâk. d. 29.

मूर्धन् *mûrdhan*, m. The head, Pańch. 184, 10.—Comp. *Raṇa*-, m. battle, Chr. 59, 21. *Tri*-, m. instead of *Triçiras* (see -*çiras*), the name of a Râkshasa, Utt. Râmach. 42, 14.

मूर्धन्य *mûrdhan + ya*, adj. Cerebral (rather lingual).

मूर्ध्वन् *mûrdhvan*, m. The head.

मूर्वा *mûrvâ*, f. A sort of creeper, Sanseviera zeylanica, from the fibres of which are made bowstrings and the girdle of the Kshatriyas.

† 1. मूल् *MÛL* (cf. *mûla*), i. 1, Par. (and Âtm.), To stand, to be rooted, or firm.

2. मूल् *MÛL*, also † मुल् *MUL*, i. 10 (rather a denomin. derived from

mûla), To plant.—With the prep. उद् *ud*, 1. To uproot, Hit. ii. d. 84. 2. To destroy, Vikr. d. 25. — With समुद् *sam-ud*, 1. To uproot, Hit. iii. d. 49. 2. To exterminate, Râjat. 5, 214.—With निस् *nis*, To destroy, Çântiç. 4, 7.

मूल *mûla* (vb. *mah*), I. n. 1. The root of a tree, Vikr. 41; root (figuratively), Pańch. ii. d. 23. 2. An eatable root, Utt. Râmach. 33, 8. 3. The lowest part, Megh. 77. 4. Origin. 5. Cause, Utt. Râmach. 5, 1. 6. The vendor, Man. 8, 202. 7. Commencement; *â mûlât*, From its beginning, Kathâs. 22, 98. 8. Capital, principal. 9. The original text of any work, as opposed to its comment. 10. Own. 11. One's own kingdom, Man. 7, 184. 12. Near, proximate. 13. The root of the Arum campanulatum. II. m. and n. The nineteenth lunar asterism, Lass. 16, 18. III. f. *lî* (cf. *muçalî*, s.v. *muçala*), A small house-lizard.—Comp. *Unmûla*, i.e. *ud-*, adj., f. *lâ*, uprooted, Râm. 4, 19, 11. *Jyeshṭhâ-*, m. the month Jyaishṭha, MBh. 13, 4609. *Tapas-*, I. adj. having its cause in devotion, Man. 11, 234. II. m. a proper name. *Danta-*, n. the root of a tooth, Suçr. 1, 303, 9. *Dhana-*, adj. rooted, founded, in wealth, Hit. i. d. 121, M.M. *Dharma-*, n. the roots of law, Man. 2, 6. *Nirmûla*, i.e. *nis-*, adj., f. *lâ*, without any root, MBh. 5, 2747. *Pâda-*, n. 1. the sole of the foot, Pańch. i. d. 161 (*pâdamûle ni pâtyate*, the dye is smeared on the sole of the foot, and the lover is caused to fall down before his mistress). 2. the root of the foot, tarsus, Bhâg. P. 2, 1, 26; a polite designation of a person, Râm. 1, 54, 16. 3. the foot of a mountain, Kathâs. 1, 27. *Baddha* (vb. *bandh*)-, adj. firmly rooted, Pańch. 232, 18. *Vismaya-harsha-*, adj. caused by astonishment and joy, Daçak. in Chr. 183, 12. *Sa-mûla+m*, adj. with the root, completely, Pańch. i. d. 339.

मूलक *mûla+ka*, I. m. A sort of poison. II. n. 1. An esculent root, Man. 8, 341. 2. The radish, Raphanus sativus. 3. A sort of yam.—Comp. *Mastaka-*, n. the neck.

मूलखानक *mûlakhânaka*, i.e. *mûla-khan+aka*, m. A digger for roots, Man. 8, 260.

मूलहरत्व *mûlaharatva*, i.e. *mûla-hṛi+a+tva*, n. Complete ruin, Daçak. in Chr. 189, 4.

मूलिक *mûlika*, i.e. *mûla+ika*, I. adj. Radical, primary. II. m. A devotee. III. f. *kâ*, A multitude of roots (?), Pańch. 157, 24.

मूल्य *mûlya*, i.e. *mûla+ya*, I. n. 1. The original price, Man. 8, 144. 2. Price, Pańch. ii. d. 61. 3. Wages. 4. An article purchased. II. adj. 1. Purchasable. 2. To be bought for a fair or just price.—Comp. *Bahu-* and *Mahâ-*, adj. costly. *Bahu-svarṇa-laksha-*, adj. worth many hundred thousand gold coins, Kathâs. 22, 97.

† मूष् *MÛSH*, मुष् *MUSH*, i. 1, Par. To steal (cf. *mush*).

मूष *mûsha*, I. m. A rat, a mouse, Pańch. 190, 21. II. f. *shâ* and *shî*. 1. A female mouse. 2. A crucible.—Cf. μῦς; Lat. mus; O.H.G. and A.S. mûs.

मूषिक *mûshika*, i.e. *mûsha+ika*, I. m., f. *kâ*, A mouse, a rat, Pańch. 190, 19; 22. II. m. 1. A thief. 2. A tree, Mimosa çirisha. 3. The name of a country.

मूषिकाञ्चन *mûshikâńchana,* i.e. *mûshika-ańch* + *ana,* m. Gaṇeça.

मृ *MṚI,* i. 6, *mriya,* Âtm. (properly pass. refl.), in the pf. fut. and condit. Par. (in epic poetry and Châṇ. 109 in Berl. Monatsb. 1864, 414, also in other forms, MBh. 1, 6189), To die, Râm. 3, 50, 21. Ptcple. of the pf. pass. *mṛita.* **1.** Dead, Chr. 39, 17. **2.** Calcined, reduced (as metals). n. **1.** Death. **2.** Solicited alms, Man. 4, 4. *jîvanmṛita,* i.e. *jîvant-,* adj. Living and dead (at the same time), Bhâg. P. 5, 10, 8. Desider. *mumûrsha,* To be about to die, Hariv. 4737; Râjat. 5, 13. Caus. *mâraya,* To kill, MBh. 1, 7276 (also Âtm. 13, 1926); Pańch. 229, 22.—With **अनु** *anu,* To die after, Râm. 2, 12, 84.—With **प्र** *pra, pramṛita,* **1.** Dead. **2.** Concealed. n. Tillage, Man. 4, 4.—Cf. Lat. morior; A.S. uta-maeran; Goth. maurthr; A.S. mórdher, myrdhra, a-myrdran, mordh, and see *marta,* and *amṛita,* and *mṛidh.*

मृक्ष् *MṚIKSH,* see *mraksh.*

मृग् *MṚIG,* † i. 4, Par. i. 10, *mṛigaya* (properly a denomin. derived from *mṛiga*), Âtm. (in epic poetry also Par., MBh. 1, 5897), To hunt, to search, Vikr. 32, 16; MBh. 1, 5644; with *antar,* inwardly, i.e. in the mind, Vikr. d. 1. Anomal. ptcple. pres. *mṛigayâṇa,* MBh. 3, 2745.

मृग *mṛiga,* i.e. *mṛij* + *a* (cf. *mârga*), I. m. **1.** Hunting, Draup. 6, 4. **2.** Investigation. **3.** Asking. **4.** A deer, Hit. pr. d. 36, M.M.; an antelope. **5.** Game, Bhartṛ. 2, 51. **6.** An animal in general, Chr. 290, 7 = Rigv. i. 64, 7. **7.** A kind of elephant. **8.** The fifth lunar constellation. **9.** Musk. II. f. *gî,* A female deer or antelope, a doe, Vikr. d. 121.—Comp. *Îhâ-,* m. a wolf, Râm. 6, 79, 70. *Kṛishṇa-,* m. the black antelope, Çâk. d. 144. *Krîḍâ-,* m. a deer for playing with, Râm. 5, 20, 12. *Gaura-,* m. a kind of buffalo, Bos gaurus, Bhâg. P. 8, 10, 9. *Chitra-,* m. the spotted antelope, Râm. 5, 20, 11. *Târâ-,* m. the fifth lunar constellation, Râm. 3, 49, 45. *Mahâ-,* m. an elephant. *Mahî-,* m. a terrestrial deer, Râm. 3, 49, 45. *Mâyâ-,* m. seeming a deer, not being one really, Râm. 3, 49, 21. *Çâkhâ-,* m. 1. a monkey, Pańch. 94, 3. 2. a squirrel. *Çâlâ-,* m. a jackal, Râm. 3, 52, 45. *Hemamṛiga,* i.e. *hema-,* or *heman-,* m. a golden deer, Hit. i. d. 27, M.M.

मृगणा *mṛigaṇâ,* i.e. *mṛig* + *ana,* f. Searching.

मृगतृष्णिका *mṛigatṛishṇikâ,* i.e. *mṛiga-tṛishṇâ* + *ka,* f. Mirage.

मृगधर *mṛiga-dhara,* m. The moon, Çiç. 9, 34.

मृगनाभिजा *mṛiganâbhijâ,* i.e. *mṛiga-nâbhi-ja* (vb. *jan*), f. Musk.

मृगया *mṛigayâ,* i.e. *mṛig,* i. 10, + *a,* f. Chase, hunting, Râm. 3, 49, 18.

मृगयु *mṛigayu,* i.e. *mṛig,* i. 10, + *u,* m. **1.** A hunter, Man. 4, 212; Bhâg. P. 4, 17, 14. **2.** A jackal. **3.** Brahman.

मृगरोमज *mṛigaromaja,* i.e. *mṛiga-roman-ja,* adj. Woollen.

मृगव्य *mṛiga* + *vya,* n. Chase, hunting.

मृगादन *mṛigâdana,* i.e. *mṛiga-ad* + *ana,* m. **1.** A leopard. **2.** A hyæna.

मृगाविध् *mṛigâvidh,* i.e. *mṛiga-â-vyadh,* m. A hunter.

मृगावती *mṛigâvatî,* i.e. *mṛiga* + *vant* + *i,* f. A proper name, Râjat. 5, 283.

मृगेन्द्रता *mṛigendratâ,* i.e. *mṛiga*

-*indra* + *tâ*, f. Dominion over the beasts, Pańch. i. d. 25.

1. मृज् *MṚIJ* (akin to *mṛi*), ii. 2, *mârj*, *mṛij*, Par. (in epic poetry also Âtm., MBh. 4, 722). **1.** To wipe, MBh. 4, 722. **2.** To rub, to stroke, Râm. 1, 64, 7. **3.** To cleanse, MBh. 3, 2577. **4.** To sweep or to cast on somebody, Man. 8, 317. Ptcple. of the pf. pass. *mṛishṭa*. **1.** Rubbed, touched. **2.** Sprinkled. **3.** Cleansed. **4.** Pure, Nal. 12, 36. **Comp.** *Su-mṛishṭa*, adj. very fine, Pańch. 113, 8; very delicate, i. d. 303. Caus., and i. 10, *mârjaya*, Par. To wipe away, Bhartṛ. 2, 89. *mârjita*, Bright, Râjat. 5, 369.—With the prep. अप *apa*, To remove, Man. 2, 27.—With अव *ava*, **1.** To sweep away, to destroy, MBh. 1, 5487. **2.** To (rub away, to) wash, to moisten, Utt. Râmach. 153, 3.—With आ *â*, To wipe, MBh. 2, 2224. *âmṛishṭa*, Rubbed at, Çâk. d. 161.—With नि *ni*, To wipe, Man. 4, 216. Desider. *mimṛiksha*, To flash down, Chr. 290, 4 = Rigv. i. 64, 4 (ved. red. pf.).—With निस् *nis*, To wipe, Lass. 59, 11.—With परि *pari*, **1.** To wipe, MBh. 3, 584. **2.** To touch, Çâk. 83, 7.—With प्र *pra*, **1.** To wipe, Man. 2, 60. **2.** To rub, to stroke, MBh. 3, 1778. **3.** To remove, Ragh. 6, 41; 44. **4.** To destroy, Bhartṛ. 2, 75. *pramṛishṭa*, **1.** Rubbed. **2.** Polished, bright, Mâlav. d. 24; clear.—With वि *vi*, **1.** To wipe, Sâv. 5, 96. **2.** To rub, to stroke, MBh. 3, 16849.—With सम् *sam*, **1.** To sweep together, Râjat. 5, 74. **2.** To cleanse, Chr. 61, 38. **3.** To purify, MBh. 2, 2186.—Cf. ἀμέργω, ὀμόργνυμι, ὄμοργμα, ἀμέλγω, γλάγος (for μλάγος, by assimilation), γάλα, γάλακτος (for original μλακτο, ptcple. of the pf. pass.); Lat. mulgere, mulier, lac (for mlac), margo; Goth. miluks; A.S. meoluc, meolc, melcan; Goth. marka; A.S. mearc, mearcian, ge-mearc.

2. मृज् *MṚIJ*, see *muj*.

मृज *mṛija*, I. m. A musical instrument. II. *jâ* (1. *mṛij* + *a*), f. Cleaning.

मृञ्ज् *MṚIŃJ*, see *muj*.

मृड् *MṚIḌ* (for original *mṛiḍḍh*, i.e. *mṛish-dhâ*, cf. Zend. *marezhdâ* and *merezhdika*), i. 6, and ii. 9, *mṛiḍṇâ*, *mṛiḍṇî*, Par. **1.** To pardon (ved.). **2.** To exhilarate, to delight (ved.).

मृड *mṛiḍ* + *a*, m. Çiva. f. *ḍâ*, *ḍi*, Durgâ.

मृडङ्कण *mṛiḍaṅkaṇa*, m. A child.

मृण् *MṚIṆ* (developed out of *mṛi* + *nâ*, see *mṛi*), i. 6, Par. To kill.—Cf. μάρναμαι.

मृणाल *mṛiṇâla*, I. m. and n. The stalk of a lotus, Vikr. d. 19. II. m., and f. *lî*, A small fibre of a lotus, Vikr. d. 54 (°*la*); Utt. Râmach. 15, 16 (°*lî*).

मृणालवन्त् *mṛiṇâla* + *vant*, adj., f. *vatî*, Possessing fibres, Çâk. 31, 7.

मृणालिन् *mṛiṇâlin*, i.e. *mṛiṇâla* + *in*, I. m. A lotus. II. f. *nî*, A place where lotus flowers grow.

मृण्मय *mṛiṇmaya*, and better मृन्मय *mṛinmaya* (Man. 5, 122), i.e. *mṛid* + *maya*, adj., f. *yî*, Made of earth or clay, earthen, Vedântas. in Chr. 216, 18.

मृतक *mṛita* (vb. *mṛi*), + *ka*, n. A dead body, Lass. 4, 11.

मृतण्ड *mṛitaṇḍa*, m. The father of the sun.

मृतवत् *mṛita+vat* (vb. *mṛi*), adv. Like one dead, Hit. 91, 16.

मृति *mṛi+ti*, f. Death.—Cf. Lat. mors, mortis.

मृत्तिका *mṛittikâ* (derived from *mṛid*), f. **1.** Earth, Vedântas. in Chr. 216, 18; clay (?), Chr. 57, 22. **2.** A fragrant earth. **3.** Fresh earth, Man. 2, 182.—Comp. *Pâṇḍu-mṛittika*, adj. having a white ground, Râm. 2, 71, 19; chalk-like, ib. 91, 41. *Pûti-mṛittika*, m. the name of a hell, Man. 4, 89.

मृत्पिण्डतस् *mṛitpiṇḍatas*, i.e. *mṛid-piṇḍa+tas*, adv. Of a piece of clay, Hit. pr. d. 33.

मृत्यु *mṛityu* (vb. *mṛi*), **1.** m. f. Death, Pańch. iii. d. 14. **2.** m. Yama.—Comp. *Apa-*, m. sudden, or unnatural death, Pańch. 186, 24. *Pratyâsanna-* (vb. *sad*), adj. to whom death was imminent, Pańch. 10, 9. *Mahâ-*, m. Çiva. *Visha-*, m. a kind of pheasant.

मृत्युंजय *mṛityuñjaya*, i.e. *mṛityu+m-ji+a*, m. Çiva.

मृत्युभङ्गुरक *mṛityu-bhańgura+ka*, m. A drum beat on funeral occasions.

मृत्सा *mṛitsâ*, and **मृत्स्ना** *mṛitsnâ* (derived from *mṛid*), f. Good soil.

मृत्स्नाभाण्डक *mṛitsnâ-bhâṇḍa+ka*, n. An earthen vessel.

1. **मृद्** *MṚID* (akin to *mṛi*), ii. 9, *mṛidnâ, nî*, Par. (in epic poetry also Âtm., MBh. 3, 2937, and i. 1, Par., ib. 1, 4979). **1.** To rub, MBh. 3, 2937. **2.** To stroke, MBh. 4, 767. **3.** To grind, to pound, to reduce to dust, MBh. 3, 1349. **4.** To crush, to dash to pieces, Böhtl. Ind. Spr. 2149. **5.** To batter, Johns. Sel. 25, 5. **6.** To trample on, to tread under foot, Nal. 13, 39. *mṛidita*, Languid, Bhartṛ. 2, 36. Caus. *mardaya*, **1.** To rub, Hit. ii. d. 131. **2.** To tread under foot, to kill, MBh. 3, 11106 (anomal. ptcple. pres. Âtm. *mardayâna*). **3.** To break to pieces, Râm. 1, 1, 72.—With the prep. **अभि** *abhi*, To trample on, MBh. 1, 7750.—With **अव** *ava*, **1.** To rub, MBh. 4, 468. **2.** To break to pieces, 3, 16346. **3.** To trample on, Râm. 2, 93, 8. **4.** To destroy, MBh. 3, 10203.—With **आ** *â*, To grind to pieces, Râm. 2, 96, 20.—With **उप** *upa*, To kill, Naish. 5, 110.—With **परि** *pari*, **1.** To wipe off, Râm. 2, 77, 26. **2.** To surpass (i. 1, Par.), MBh. 1, 4979. *parimṛidita*, Rubbed, ground, Utt. Râmach. 15, 16 (trampled upon).—With **प्र** *pra*, To destroy, MBh. 3, 11676.—With **वि** *vi*, **1.** To rub to pieces, Râm. 2, 88, 8. **2.** To break, Man. 4, 70. **3.** To destroy, MBh. 1, 5504. Caus. To grind, Râm. 2, 88, 2.—With **सम्** *sam*, Caus. To rub, to clean, Pańch. 121, 13.—Cf. Lat. mordere; A.S. malt; O.H.G. malz; A.S. meltan, miltan; O.H.G. smelzan; A.S. smeortan; O.H.G. smerzan; A.S. smilt, smylt, smolt; ἀμέρδω, ἀμαλδύνω, μέλδω.

2. **मृद्** *mṛid*, f. **1.** Earth, Pańch. ii. d. 109; clay, Pańch. ii. d. 36. **2.** A piece of earth, Man. 5, 136. **3.** A fragrant earth.

मृदङ्ग *mṛidańga*, probably *mṛid+a+m-ga*, m. **1.** A tabour, Utt. Râmach. 154, 9; a small drum, Pańch. 20, 8. **2.** A sound. **3.** Bambu.

मृदर *mṛid+ara*, m. **1.** A hole. **2.** Disease.

मृदा *mṛid+â*, f. Earth, clay.—Cf. Goth. mulda; A.S. molde; probably Lat. merda.

मृदाकर *mṛidâ-kara*, m. The thunderbolt.

मृदिनी *mṛidinî*, i.e. *mṛid*, or *mṛidâ*, + *in* + *î*, f. Good soil.

मृदु *mṛid+u*, adj., f. *dvî* (Râm. 4, 2, 2), comparat. *mradiyaṁs*, superl. *mradishṭha*. **1.** Soft, Pańch. i. d. 303; iii. d. 253; Johns. Sel. 56, 153 (*-pûrvam*, adv. At first mildly). **2.** Mild, Vikr. d. 85. **3.** Weak, Hit. 81, 22. **4.** Blunt. **5.** Slow, Sâv. 4, 33.—Cf. Goth. and A.S. mild; Lat. mollis; probably βραδύς; Lat. bardus; ἀβλαδέως; Lat. blandus.

मृदुता *mṛidu+tâ*, f. Softness.

मृदुल *mṛidu+la*, I. adj. Soft. II. n. Water.

मृदुलोमक *mṛidulomaka*, i.e. *mṛidu-loman+ka*, m. A hare.

मृद्वीका *mṛidvî+kâ* (*mṛidu*, f.), f. A grape.—Comp. *Pṛithu-*, f. a broad-grape (?), MBh. 7, 2309.

मृध् *MṚIDH* (i.e. *mṛi-dhâ*), i. 1, Par. Âtm. **1.** To kill (ved.). **2.** † To be moist or wet.—Cf. probably (in spite of the anomal. correspondence), Goth. maurthr; A.S. mórdher, mórdhor; O.H.G. multjan; probably μαλθακός.

मृध *mṛidh+a*, n. War, battle, Chr. 19, 20.

मृन्मय *mṛinmaya*, see *mṛiṇmaya*.

मृन्मरु *mṛinmaru*, i.e. *mṛid-maru*, m. A stone.

मृश् *MṚIÇ* (often confounded with *mṛish*), i. 6, Par. (in epic poetry also Âtm., Râm. 2, 62, 18). **1.** To touch, to stroke. **2.** To think, to consider. —With the prep. अनु *anu*, To consider, Râm. 2, 11, 9.—With अव *ava*, Caus. To trouble, Bhâg. P. 4, 7, 48.—With आ *â*, **1.** To touch, Çiç. 9, 34. **2.** To destroy, Ragh. 9, 5 (Calc.). Comp. ptcple. pf. pass. *an-âmṛishṭa*, Untouched, Daçak. in Chr. 200, 1.—With पर्या *pari-â*, To overpower, MBh. 4, 164 (with *sh* instead of *ç*).—With परा *parâ*, **1.** To stroke, Utt. Râmach. 25, 14. **2.** To touch, Ragh. 3, 68 (Calc.). **3.** To seize, MBh. 4, 46. **4.** To seduce, Chr. 6, 7. **5.** To violate, Daçak. in Chr. 199, 11.—With परि *pari*, **1.** To stroke, Râm. 2, 10, 25. **2.** To seize, Râm. 2, 23, 5 (with *sh*). **3.** To consider, Râm. 1, 2, 20.—With वि *vi*, **1.** To stroke, Râm. 2, 20, 32. **2.** To inquire, MBh. 3, 2680 (with *sh.*) **3.** To examine, Mâlav. 11, 23. **4.** To reflect, Hit. 71, 2, M.M.; Bhâg. P. 6, 5, 10; Hit. iv. d. 97 (*vimṛiçya-kârin*, One who acts [only] after due reflection). *a-vimṛiçya*, Without reflecting, Pańch. 238, 25. **5.** To perceive, Bhaṭṭ. 3, 7. Caus. To examine, Pańch. i. d. 122.—With अनुवि *anu-vi*, To reflect, Daçak. in Chr. 181, 15.—Cf. Lat. mulcere, probably, mulcare.

1. मृष् *MṚISH* (often confounded with *mṛiç*), i. 4, and i. 10, and † i. 1, Par. Atm. **1.** To bear, to endure patiently, Man. 4, 217; Pańch. iii. d. 19; v. d. 67. **2.** To suffer, Utt. Râmach. 71, 8. **3.** To let, Daçak. in Chr. 199, 10. **4.** To pardon, Man. 8, 313. Comp. ptcple. of the pres. *a-mṛishyant*, *a-marshayant* (Johns. Sel. 54, 135), and *a-mṛishyamâṇa*, Enraged. Caus. To suffer, Hit. iii. d. 48. Comp. ptcple. of the pf. pass. *a-marshita*, adj. Impatient, angry, Râm. 4, 9, 13. *durmarshita*, i.e. *dus-*, adj. Incited, stirred up, MBh. 14, 2314.—With the prep. अव *ava*, To endure, Pańch. rec. orn.—With प्रत्यव

prati-ava, To endure reluctantly, Daçak. in Chr. 185, 5.—With वि *vi,* To neglect, MBh. 3, 15441.—Cf. Goth. marzjan (Caus.); O.H.G. marrjan; A.S. myrran.

2. † मृष् *MṚISH,* i. 1, Par. To sprinkle.

मृषा *mṛishâ* (an old instr. sing. of 1. *mṛish* + *a,* properly, 'With pardon,' 'I beg your pardon'), adv. **1.** Falsely, Man. 3, 53. **2.** Uselessly.—Comp. *A-,* adv. truly.

मृषार्थक *mṛishârthaka,* i.e. *mṛishâ -artha* + *ka,* n. An absurdity, an impossibility.

मृषोद्य *mṛishodya,* i.e. *mṛishâ-vad* + *ya,* I. adj. and sbst. Lying, a liar. II. n. Falsehood, Utt. Râmach. 104, 2.

मृष्टि *mṛishṭi,* i.e. *mṛij, mṛiç,* and *mṛish,* + *ti,* f. **1.** Cleaning. **2.** Preparing food, Man. 3, 255. **3.** Touching. **4.** Sprinkling.

† मॄ *MṚÎ,* ii. 9, *mṛiṇâ, ṇî,* Par. To kill (see *mṛiṇ*).

मे *ME,* i. 1, Âtm. To barter or to exchange. Caus. *mâpaya,* To cross over, MBh. 1, 5842 (anomal. ptcple. pres. Âtm. *mâpayâna*).—With the prep. नि *ni,* To barter, Man. 10, 94.—Cf. Goth. maithms; A.S. madhm; Goth. maidjan, ga-mains; A.S. maene, mán, gemaene; Lat. mūtuus, communis, munus; μοῖτος, ἀμείϐω (Caus. for ἀ-μεϐίω).

मेखला *mekhalâ,* f. **1.** A girdle, Ragh. 8, 63; Utt. Râmach. 106, 1. **2.** The sacrificial string, see *kṛi* with *mekhalâ.* **3.** A sword-belt. **4.** A sword-knot. **5.** The slope of a mountain, Megh. 12. **6.** The Narmadâ river.—Comp. *Maṇi-mekhala,* adj. surrounded by jewels, Ṛit. 6, 3.

मेखलिन् *mekhalin,* i.e. *mekhalâ* + *in,* adj. f. *nî,* Wearing a girdle, Pańch. iii. d. 237.

मेघ *megha,* i.e. *mih* + *a,* m. **1.** A cloud, Pańch. 163, 6. **2.** A demon. **3.** A fragrant grass.—Comp. *Gṛiha-,* m. a multitude of houses, Râm. 5, 10, 5.

मेघवत् *megha* + *vat,* adv. Like a cloud, Chr. 35, 9.

मेचक *mechaka,* I. adj. Black, Utt. Râmach. 149, 15; dark blue, Pańch. ed. orn. i. d. 63; Megh. 60. II. m. **1.** Black, or dark blue (the colour). **2.** The eye of a peacock's tail. **3.** A cloud. **4.** Smoke. III. m. and n. Darkness. IV. n. Antimony.

मेट् *MEṬ,* see *mleṭ.*

मेठ *meṭha,* मेण्ठ *meṇṭha,* and मेण्ड *meṇḍa,* m. An elephant-keeper.

मेड् *MEḌ,* see *mreḍ.*

मेढ्र *meḍhra,* i.e. *mih* + *tra,* n. **1.** The penis, Man. 8, 282. **2.** A ram.

मेथ् *METH,* and मेध् *MEDH,* i. 1, Par. **1.** To hurt (ved.). **2.** To understand. **3.** To associate (ved.). Caus. *medhaya,* To cause to understand, to know, MBh. 13, 7510.

मेथि *methi,* and मेधि *medhi,* m. The part of a threshing floor round which the cattle turn to tread out the corn.

मेद् *MED,* see *mith.*

मेद *meda,* m. **1.** Adeps, fat. **2.** The son of a Vaideha by a Kârâvara female, Man. 10, 36.

मेदस् *medas,* n. **1.** Marrow, Pańch. i. d. 123. **2.** The serous secretion that spreads amongst the muscular fibres. **3.** Morbid corpulency, Çâk. d. 38.—Cf. perhaps Lat. medulla.

मेदिनी *medinî* (probably =*mṛidinî*, and based on its original form *mardinî*, cf. *geha*, *vetana* ; or perhaps *meda* + *in* + *î*), f. **1.** The earth, Pańch. iii. d. 41 ; earth, Johns. Sel. 95, 67. **2.** A country, Châṇ. 45 in Berl. Monatsb. 1864, 410.

मेदुर *medura* (cf. *medas*), adj. **1.** Unctuous. **2.** Smooth. **3.** Soft. **4.** Thick, Utt. Râmach. 143, 2.

मेदुरित *medurita*, i.e. *medura* + *ita*, adj. Unctuous, abounding in water, Utt. Râmach. 16, 10.

मेध् *medh*, see *meth*.

मेध *medha* (i.e. *mah* and perhaps *dhâ*), I. m. (and ved., also n., Chr. 293, 3=Rigv. i. 88, 3), Sacrifice, l. l. II. f. *dhâ*, Understanding, Daçak. in Chr. 180, 4.—Comp. *Açva-*, *Turaga-*, *Turańgama-*, m. the sacrifice of a horse, Hit. iv. d. 129 ; Râm. 6, 104, 7 ; Ragh. 13, 61. *Gṛiha-*, I. m. a domestic sacrifice. II. adj. referring to the duties of a householder, Bhâg. P. 3, 22, 11. *Dus-*, adj., f. *dhâ*, stupid, Bhâg. P. 1, 4, 17. *Nara-*, *Nṛi-*, *Purusha-*, m. the sacrifice of a man, Râm. 1, 63, 6 Gorr. (*nara-*); Kathâs. 26, 238 (*purusha-*). *Pitṛi-*, m. oblation to the Manes, Man. 5, 65.

ऽमेधस् *-medhas*, a substitute for *medhâ*, when latter part of a comp. adj. ; e.g. *alpa-*, Having little understanding, Pańch. ii. d. 92. *dus-*, Stupid, Râm. 1, 25, 11. *parama-dus-*, adj. Most stupid, Pańch. 3, 12. *su-*, I. adj. Intelligent. II. m. Heart pea.

मेधाविन् *medhâ* + *vin*, adj., f. *nî*, Intelligent, Man. 2, 110 ; wise, Hit. ii. d. 20.—Comp. *Dus-*, adj. stupid, MBh. 12, 9486.

मेधि *medhi*, see *methi*.

मेधिर *medhira*, i.e. *medhâ* + *ira*, adj. Intelligent.

मेध्य *medhya*, i.e. *medha* + *ya*, adj. **1.** Fit for, belonging to, a sacrifice, Utt. Râmach. 39, 10. **2.** Pure, Man. 1, 92. —Comp. *A-*, I. adj. impure, Man. 4, 53. II. n. an impure substance, Man. 2, 239.

मेनका *menakâ*, i.e. *menâ* + *ka*, f. One of the courtesans of heaven, and wife to Himâlaya, Çiç. 9, 86 ; Çâk. 14, 23 (Prâkṛ.).

मेना *menâ*, f. One of the courtesans of heaven, and wife to Himâlaya, Râm. 1, 37, 15 Gorr.

मेनाद *me-nâda* (*me*, an imitative sound), m. **1.** A cat. **2.** A goat. **3.** A peacock.

† **मेप्** *MEP*, i. 1, Par. **1.** To go. **2.** To serve.

मेब् *MEB*, see *mev*.

मेरु *meru*, m. A fabulous mountain, Bhartṛ. 2, 41.—Comp. *Su-*, I. m.= Meru. II. adj. excellent.

मेल *mela*, i.e. *mil* + *a*, I. m., and f. *lâ*, Assemblage, meeting, Pańch. 245, 4 (*lâ*). II. f. *lâ*, Ink (borrowed from μέλας).

मेलक *mela* + *ka*, m. Assemblage, Hit. 72, 17.

† **मेव्** *MEV*, **मेब्** *MEB*, and **म्लेव्** *MLEV*, i. 1, Âtm. To serve.

मेष *mesha* (vb. *mih*, probably for *meksha*), I. m. **1.** A ram, Pańch. iii. d. 40. **2.** The sign *Aries*. II. f. *shî*, An ewe.

मेषिका *meshikâ*, i.e. *meshî* + *ka*, f. An ewe.

मेह *meha*, i.e. *mih* + *a*, m. **1.** Making water, Man. 4, 52. **2.** Urine. **3.** A ram.

मेहतस् *meha* + *tas*, adv. By making water, Man. 4, 52.

मेहन *mehana*, i.e. *mih* + *ana*, n. **1.** Membrum virile. **2.** Urine.

मैत्र *maitra*, properly *maittra*, i.e. *mittra* + *a* (see *mittra*), I. adj. **1.** Relating to a friend, friendly, Bhag. 12, 13. **2.** Given by a friend, Man. 9, 206. **3.** m. (viz. *saṁdhi*), Proceeding from friendship, the name of a kind of alliance, Hit. iv. d. 123. **II.** m. **1.** A friend to all creatures, Man. 2, 87. **2.** A Brâhmaṇa. **3.** The son of an outcaste Vaiçya, Man. 10, 23. **4.** The anus. **5.** Discharging of excrement, Man. 4, 152. **III.** n. **1.** Friendship, Pañch. ii. d. 47. **2.** The seventeenth lunar asterism. Cf. *maitrya*. — **Comp.** *Durmaitra*, i.e. *dus-*, adj. hostile, Bhâg. P. 7, 5, 27.

मैत्रक *maitra* + *ka*, n. Friendship, Utt. Râmach. 128, 2.

मैत्रता *maitra* + *tâ*, f. Friendship, Châṇ. 19 in Berl. Monatsb. 1864, 408.

मैत्राक्षज्योतिक *maitrâkshajyotika*, i.e. *maitra-aksha-jyoti* (instead of *jyotis*), + *ka*, m. The name of a demon, Man. 12, 72.

मैत्रावरुण and **मैत्रावरुणि** *maitrâvaruṇa*, or °*ṇi*, i. e. *mitrâvaruṇa* (*dvandva* comp. of *mitra* and *varuṇa*), + *a* or *i*, patronym., m. A son of Mitra and Varuṇa; a name of Vaçishṭha, Utt. Râmach. 9, 4, and of Agastya.

मैत्रेय *maitreya*, i.e. *mitra* + *eya* (cf. *mittra*). I. adj. Relating to a friend. II. m. **1.** The son of a Vaideha by an Ayogava female. **2.** A proper name.

मैत्रेयक *maitreya* + *ka*, m. **1.** The son of a Vaideha by an Ayogava female, Man. 10, 33. **2.** A crier or chaunter of the hours (this being probably the office of a Maitreyaka).

मैत्र्य *maitrya*, i.e. *mitra* + *ya* (cf. *mittra*), n., and f. *trî*, Friendship, Pañch. iv. d. 70 (n.); 243, 13, and 248, 2 (f.).

मैथिल *maithila*, i.e. *mithilâ* + *a*, I. adj., f. *lî*, Born in, referring to, Mithilâ, Utt. Râmach. 110, 13. **II.** m. The king of Mithilâ, Ram. 3, 53, 2. **III.** f. *lî*, A name of Sîtâ, ib. 3, 49, 55.

मैथुन *maithuna*, i.e. *mithuna* + *a*, I. adj. Worn at a time of sexual intercourse, Man. 4, 116. **II.** n. **1.** Sexual intercourse, Hit. pr. d. 25, M.M. **2.** Marriage, holy union, Man. 3, 5 (perhaps adj. Being in accordance with a legitimate marriage). **3.** Matrimony, Pañch. ii. d. 101. **4.** Union.

मैथुनिन् *maithunin*, i.e. *maithuna* + *in*, adj. sbst. One who has been connected with a woman, Man. 5, 144. —**Comp.** *Divâ-*, adj. having sexual intercourse by day, Mârk. P. 14, 74.

मैथुन्य *maithunya*, i.e. *maithuna* + *ya*, adj. Contracted for the purpose of amorous embraces, Man. 3, 32.

मैनाक *mainâka*, i.e. *menâ* + *ka* + *a*, m. The name of a mountain, Râm. 5, 49, 27.

मैन्द *mainda*, m. The name of a demon.

मैन्दहन् *mainda-han*, m. Vishṇu.

मैरेय *maireya*, n. A spirituous liquor, Râjat. 5, 368.

मो *mo*, i.e. *mâ-u*, But not, Chr. 289, 13 = Rigv. i. 50, 13.

मोक्तुकाम *moktukâma*, i.e. *moktum -kâma* (infin. of *much*), adj. Desiring to cast, Chr. 41, 22.

मोच् *MOKSH*, i, 10 (properly a denomin. derived from *moksha*), and † i. 1, Par. (in epic poetry also Âtm., MBh. 1, 5301). **1.** To release, to liberate, MBh. 1, 2084. **2.** † To cast. Comp. ptcple. of the pres. *a-mokshayant*, adj. Neglecting to liberate, Yâjń. 2, 300.—With the prep. परि *pari*, To release, to liberate, Weber, Ind. St. iii. 371, 4, below.—With वि *vi*, To release, to protect, MBh. 1, 7880.

मोक्ष *moksh + a* (*moksh* is an anomal. desider. of *much*), m. **1.** Untying, Pańch. 109, 9; Megh. 97. **2.** Liberation, Pańch. 109, 11; Chr. 4, 16. **3.** Liberation of the soul from the body and from further transmigration, final beatitude, Man. 1, 114; Pańch. ii. d. 127. **4.** Death. **5.** Acquittance of an obligation.

मोक्षक *moksh + aka*, adj. and sbst., m. **1.** One who sets at liberty, Man. 8, 342. **2.** A deliverer.

मोक्षण *mokshaṇa*, i.e. *moksh + ana*, n. **1.** Letting go (shedding of blood), Mâlav. d. 62. **2.** Liberation, Pańch. 143, 6. **3.** Squandering.—**Comp.** *Prâṇa-*, n. resigning life, suicide, Pańch. 110, 9.

मोघ *mogha*, i.e. *muh + a*, I. adj. **1.** Vain, useless, Sâv. 5, 49; Megh. 6; °*gham*, adv. In vain, Bhag. 3, 16. **2.** Left. **II.** m. A fence. **III.** f. *ghâ*, Trumpet-flower, Bignonia suaveolens. —**Comp.** *A-*, I. adj., f. *ghâ*, not vain, not going astray, unfailing, Vikr. d. 88; attaining one's aim, efficacious, Megh. 72. II. f. *ghâ*. 1. the name of a club, Râm. 1, 29, 12. 2. the name of several plants. 3. a proper name.

मोच *mocha* (vb. *much + a*), **I.** m. A tree, Hyperanthera morunga. **II.** f. *châ*. **1.** The silk cotton-tree. **2.** The plantain. **III.** n. Its fruit.

मोचक *mochaka*, i.e. **A.** *mocha + ka*, m. = *mocha*, **I, II.** **B.** *much + aka*, m. **1.** A devotee, free from worldly passion and desire. **2.** A liberator.

मोचन *mochana*, i.e. *much + ana*, n. Liberating, liberation, Daçak. in Chr. 198, 10; Lass. 39, 20.

मोटन *moṭana*, **I.** m. Wind. **II.** n. **1.** Pressing, strangulating, Lass. 43, 1. **2.** Grinding, reducing to dust.

मोण *moṇa*, m. **1.** Dried fruit. **2.** A crocodile. **3.** A fly. **4.** A basket for carrying snakes in.

मोद *moda*, i.e. *mud + a*, m. Joy, Utt. Râmach. 41, 15.

मोदक *modaka*, i.e. *mud + aka*, **I.** adj. Delighting. **II.** m. and n. A sort of sweetmeat, Pańch. i. d. 303; sweetmeats in general, Vikr. 45, 13.

मोष *mosha*, i.e. *mush + a*, m. **1.** Robbing, Daçak. in Chr. 186, 16. **2.** Robbery, Man. 9, 274.

मोषक *moshaka*, i.e. *mush + aka*, m. A thief.

मोषण *moshaṇa*, i.e. *mush + ana*, n. Stealing.

मोह *moha*, i.e. *muh + a*, m. **1.** Fainting, Vikr. 84, 10; loss of consciousness, Vikr. d. 8. **2.** Bewilderment, distraction, Daçak. in Chr. 192, 13; Ṛit. 6, 26. **3.** Weakness of intellect, Man. 3, 15. **4.** Ignorance, foolishness, infatuation, Pańch. i. d. 250; iii. d. 87. **5.** Error, Matsyop. 53.

मोहन *mohana*, i.e. *muh + ana*, **I.** adj., f. *nî*, Depriving of consciousness or understanding, infatuating, Utt. Râmach. 23, 13; Kathâs. 46, 110 (with *vidyâ*, A magical knowledge). **II.** m. One of the arrows of Kâma, Lass. 7, 3. **III.** n. Temptation, the overpowering of reason by sensual allurements.—Comp. *Kûṭa-*, m. epithet of Skanda, MBh. 3, 14632.

मोहिन् *mohin*, i.e. *muh* + *in*, I. adj., f. *nî*, Bewildering, infatuating, Bhag. 9, 12. II. f. *nî*, A kind of jasmine.

मौकुलि *maukuli*, m. A crow, Utt. Râmach. 48, 10.

मौक्तिक *mauktika*, i.e. *muktâ* + *ika*, n. A pearl, Pañch. iv. d. 78.—Comp. *Gaja-*, n. pearls which are supposed to be in the frontal globes of the elephant, Kir. 12, 41.

मौक्य *maukya*, i.e. *mûka* + *ya*, n. Dumbness, Man. 10, 51.

मौखर्य *maukharya*, i.e. *mukhara* + *ya*, n., and f. *rî*. 1. Defamation. 2. Scurrility.

मौख्य *maukhya*, i.e. *mukha* + *ya*, n. Pre-eminence.—Comp. *Grâma-*, Hit. 66, 6, probably an erroneous reading for *grâmamukhya*, chief of a village.

मौग्ध्य *maugdhya*, i.e. *mugdha* (vb. *muh*), + *ya*, n. Charm, beauty, Utt. Râmach. 107, 6.

मौञ्ज *mauñja*, i.e. *muñja* + *a*, I. adj., f. *jî*, Made of *muñja*, Man. 2, 42. II. f. *jî* (and मौञ्जि *mauñji*, Man. 2, 169, by metrical exigence), The girdle of a Brâhmaṇa, Man. 2, 27; Kumâras. 5, 10.

मौढ्य *mauḍhya*, i.e. *mûḍha* (vb. *muh*), + *ya*, n. Ignorance, folly.

मौण्ड्य *mauṇḍya*, i.e. *muṇḍa* + *ya*, n. 1. Baldness. 2. Shaving of the head, Man. 8, 370.

मौद्गलि *maudgali*, m. A crow.

मौन *mauna*, i. e. *muni* + *a*, n. Silence, taciturnity, Hit. i. d. 134, M.M.; Pañch. iv. d. 51. — Comp. *Chintâ-*, n. silent thinking, Vikr. d. 130.

मौनिन् *maunin*, i.e. *mauna* + *in*, I. adj., f. *nî*, Silent, Böhtl. Ind. Spr. 1677; Râjat. 5, 304. II. m. An ascetic.

मौरजिक *maurajika*, i.e. *muraja* + *ika*, m. A drummer.

मौर्ख्य *maurkhya*, i.e. *mûrkha* + *ya*, n. Stupidity, folly, Râjat. 5, 389.

मौर्य *maurya*, m. The name of an Indian dynasty.

मौर्यदत्त *maurya-datta* (vb. *dâ*), m. A proper name, Daçak. in Chr. 193, 17.

मौर्व *maurva*, i.e. *mûrva* + *a*, I. adj., f. *vî*, Made of *mûrva*, Man. 2, 42. II. f. *vî*, A bowstring, Çâk. d. 13.

मौल *maula*, i.e. *mûla* + *a*, adj. 1. Proceeding from a root. 2. Of pure blood, Hit. iii. d. 17. 3. Descended from those who had lived in a village when it was built, Man. 8, 259. 4. Born in the same district (of the same root), Man. 8, 62. 5. Hereditary, Man. 7, 54.

मौलि *mauli* (akin to *mûla*), m. and f. 1. A lock of hair on the crown of the head. 2. Hair ornamented and braided round the head. 3. A crown, diadem, Vikr. d. 60; Pañch. 230, 18. 4. The head, Lass. 66, 2; Hit. 72, 19 (*maulau nidhâya*, Obeying). — Comp. *Ardha-indu-*, adj. epithet of Çiva (wearing the crescent as diadem), Megh. 56. *Chakra-*, m. the name of a Râkshasa, Râm. 6, 69, 14. *Niçâkara-kalâ-*, adj. (wearing the crescent as diadem), epithet of Çiva, Kathâs. 4, 89.

मौलिक *mauli+ka* (scarcely *mûla* +*ika*), adj. Chief, best, Utt. Râmach. 51, 10.

मौलिन् *maulin,* i.e. *mauli + in,* adj. Endowed with a diadem, Sund. 1, 30.

मौली *maulî* (akin to *mûla*), f. The earth.

मौल्य *maulya,* i.e. *mûla+ya* (cf. *mûlya*), n. Price, Lass. 3, 4.

मौषल *maushala,* i.e. *mushala + a,* adj. Performed with a club, Hariv. 5648.

मौष्टा *maushṭâ,* i.e. *mushṭi+a,* f. Playing at fisticuffs.

मौहूर्त *mauhûrta,* and **मौहूर्तिक** *mauhûrtika,* i.e. *muhûrta + a,* or *ika,* m. An astrologer, Hit. 94, 9 (*tika*).

म्ना *MNÂ* (i.e. *man+â*), i. 1, *mana,* Par. 1. To fix in the memory by frequent repetition. 2. To remember, to praise (ved.).—With the prep. **आ** *â,* To repeat frequently, Bhaṭṭ. 17, 30. *âmnâtâ,* Recorded, Pañch. i. d. 408.—With **समा** *sam-â,* To prescribe, Utt. Râmach. 92, 6.—Cf. μιμνήσκω, μνῆμα, μνάομαι; Lat. meminisse. Cf. *man.*

म्रक्ष् † *MRAKSH,* **मृक्ष्** *MṚIKSH* (akin to *mṛij*), † **मक्ष्** *MAKSH,* i. 1, Par. To accumulate. † *mraksh, mṛiksh,* i. 10, Par. 1. To smear. 2. To speak incorrectly. 3. To accumulate. 4. To divide, to cut.—*Mṛiksh,* with **अभि** *abhi,* i. 10, To anoint, MBh. 13, 7426.

म्रक्ष *mraksh + a,* m. Concealment of one's vices.

म्रक्षण *mrakshaṇa,* i.e. *mraksh + ana,* n. Oil.

† **म्रद्** *MRAD* (cf. *mṛid*), i. 1, Âtm. To grind, to reduce to powder.

म्रदिष्ठ *mradishṭha,* **म्रदीयंस्** *mradiyaṁs,* see *mṛidu.*

म्रुच् *MRUCH,* i. 1, Par. To go.—With **नि** *ni,* and **अभिनि** *abhi-ni,* To set (as the sun), ved., Weber, Journ. of the German Oriental Society, xiv. 756, sqq.—Cf. *mluch.*

† **म्रुञ्च्** *MRUŃCH,* **म्लुञ्च्** *MLUŃCH,* **मञ्च्** *MAŃCH,* **मुञ्च्** *MUŃCH,* i. 1, Par. To go.

म्रेट् *MREṬ,* see *mleṭ.*

म्रेड् *MREḌ,* † **म्लेड्** *MLEḌ,* † **मेड्** *MEḌ,* i. 1, Par. To be mad.—With the prep. **आ** *â,* Caus. To repeat, MBh. 3, 10388.

† **म्लक्ष्** *MLAKSH* (?), i. 10, Par. To cut, to divide.

म्लानता *mlâna + tâ* (vb. *mlai*), Languor, Lass. 72, 11.

म्लानि *mlâni,* i.e. *mlai + ni,* f. 1. Fading, decay. 2. Languor. 3. Weariness.

म्लुच् *MLUCH,* i. 1, Par. To go.—With the prep. **नि** *ni,* 1. To set (as the sun), Bhâg. P. 5, 21, 9. 2. With acc. To surprise setting, Man. 2, 220.—With **अभिनि** *abhi-ni,* with acc. To surprise setting, Man. 2, 219.—Cf. *mruch.*

म्लुञ्च् *MLUŃCH,* see *mruñch.*

म्लेच्छ *mlechchha,* m. 1. A barbarian, Hit. iii. d. 62. 2. A sinner.

म्लेछ् *MLECHH,* i. 1 and 10, Par. 1. To speak barbarously, MBh. 2, 2040. † 2. To speak confusedly.

† ब्लेट् *MLEṬ*, ब्रेट् *MREṬ*, मेट् *MEṬ*, i. 1, Par. To be mad.

† ब्लेव् *MLEV*, see *mev*.

ब्लै *MLAI*, i. 1, Par. (in epic poetry, ii. 2, e.g. *mlânti*, MBh. 3, 15683). **1.** To fade, MBh. 3, 15455. **2.** To grow weary, Ragh. 11, 9 (Calc.). **3.** To be faint or languid, MBh. 1, 3391. Ptcple. of the pf. pass. *mlâna*. **1.** Withered, faded, Pañch. i. d. 88; Utt. Râmach. 23, 12. **2.** Languid, faint, Bhartṛ. 2, 82; Râjat. 5, 431. **3.** Foul, dirty. **Comp.** *A-*, adj. 1. not faded. 2. clear.—With परि *pari*, To fade away, to disappear, Pañch. cod. Berol. 144, a. *parimlâna*, **1.** Withered, Râm. 2, 59, 8. **2.** Faded, Ragh. 14, 50 (Calc.). **3.** Languid. **4.** Diminished. **5.** Soiled. n. **1.** Change of countenance by grief. **2.** Soil.—Cf. *βλάπτω* = Caus. *mlâpayâmi*, *μῶλυς*, *μωλυρός*.

य *Y*.

यकृत् *yakṛit*, the base of many cases is optionally यकन् *yakan*, n. The liver.—Cf. Lat. jecur; *ἧπαρ*, *ἥπατος*; perhaps also A.S. lifer.

† यक्ष् *YAKSH*, i, 10, Âtm. To worship, to honour (cf. *yaj*).

यक्ष *yaksha* (vb. *yaj*), **I.** m. **1.** A kind of demigod, attendant on Kuvera, Chr. 57, 21. **2.** Kuvera. **3.** The palace of Indra. **II.** f. *kshî*. **1.** A female *yaksha*, Râm. 3, 52, 35. **2.** The wife of Kuvera.

यक्षदर *yaksha-dara*, m. The name of a district, Râjat. 5, 87.

यक्षिणी *yakshiṇî*, i.e. *yaksha* + *in* + *î*, f. The wife of Kuvera.

यक्ष्म *yakshma*, and यक्ष्मन् *yakshman*, i.e. *jaksh* + *man*, m. Pulmonary consumption.—**Comp.** *Râjayakshman*, i.e. *râjan-*, m. the same.

यक्ष्मिन् *yakshmin*, i.e. *yakshman*, or *yakshma*, + *in*, adj., f. *iṇi*, and sbst. Phthisical, one who suffers from pulmonary consumption, Man. 3, 154.

यच्छ *yachchha*, see *yam*.

यज् *YAJ*, i. 1, Par. Âtm. (ved., also ii. 2, Lass. 101, 13 = Rigv. vii. 16, 5). **1.** To sacrifice, Man. 11, 87; with acc., Râm. 1, 31, 5; with instr., MBh. 1, 2473. **2.** To worship (the deities) by sacrifices, Man. 8, 105. **3.** To worship (the deities), Bhag. 9, 23. **4.** To inaugurate, Râm. 2, 56, 18. **5.** To give, Bhaṭṭ. 8, 49. *yajati*, see s.v. Ptcple. pres. Âtm. *yajamâna*, m. A person who institutes a sacrifice and pays the expense of it, Pañch. 169, 8; 182, 12. Pass. *ijya*, in epic poetry ptcple. pres. *ijyant*, MBh. 2, 1325. Pf. ptcple. *ishṭa*. Ptcple. of the fut. pass. *yâjya*, To be sacrificed. m. A sacrificer, Man. 8, 317. n. Presents for sacrificing. **Comp.** *A-*, m. one for whom it is not allowed to sacrifice, Man. 11, 59. Infin. *yashṭum*, in epic poetry anomal. *ijitum*, MBh. 2, 1230 (looks like an infin. of the redupl. pf.). Desider. *yiyaksha*, To wish to sacrifice, MBh. 2, 59. Caus. *yâjaya*, To perform a sacrifice for another, Man. 3, 151 (also Âtm., MBh. 1, 8123).—With the prep. सम् *sam*, To worship, Bhaṭṭ. 15, 96. Ptcple. of the fut. pass. (Caus. ?), *saṁyâjya*, n. Sacrificing, Man. 11, 59. **Comp.** *A-saṁyâjya*, adj. one with whom nobody is allowed to sacrifice, Man. 9, 238. Caus. To perform a sacrifice for another, MBh. 1, 6375.—Cf. *ἅγιος*, *ἁγίζω*, *ἁγνός*.

यजत *yaj* + *ata*, m. An officiating priest at a sacrifice.

यजति *yajati*, 3. sing. pres. of *yaj*. **1.**

A technical term for those sacrifices which are denoted by the word *yajati* (cf. *juhoti*), Man. 2, 84. **2.** m. A sacrifice (ÇKD.).

यजत्र *yaj + atra*, I. adj. Adorable, Lass. 102, 9 = Rigv. vii. 14, 2. II. m. A Brâhmaṇa who keeps a sacrificial fire. III. n. Maintenance of a sacrificial fire.

यजन *yaj + ana*, n. **1.** Sacrificing, Man. 1, 88. **2.** Worshipping.—**Comp.** *Deva-*, n. a place of offering to the deities, MBh. 5, 7354; Utt. Râmach. 10, 4.

यजि *yaj + i*, **1.** Sacrifice, Man. 10, 79. **2.** A sacrificer.

यजुस् *yaj + us*, n. The *Yajus*, one of the four Vedas, Man. 1, 23.

यज्ञ *yajńa*, i.e. *yaj + na*, m. A sacrifice, Man. 1, 22; 23.—**Comp.** *A-*, m. time when the sacrifice is over, Man. 3, 120. *Ṛishi-*, m. inaudible muttering of prayers, Man. 4, 21; cf. 3, 81. *Graha-*, m. a sacrifice offered to the planets, Yâjń. 1, 294. *Japa-*, murmuring prayers, Man. 2, 85. *Nâma(n)-*, m. a nominal sacrifice only (not real), Bhag. 16, 7. *Pańcha(n)-*, m. (pl.), the five great sacraments, Man. 3, 67. *Pâka-*, m. a domestic sacrifice, Man. 2, 86; 11, 118. *Prastâva-*, m. sacrifice-like treating of a subject, i.e. treating a subject where those who partake of it must propound and prove their views, as at sacrifices every one must give presents, Pańch. ii. d. 176. *Mahâ-*, m. an essential ceremony, a sacrament, Man. 1, 112; 2, 28. *Vidhi-*, m. a ceremonial act of worshipping, Man. 2, 85.

यज्ञवाहस् *yajńavâhas*, i.e. *yajńa-vah + as*, adj. sbst. Carryiug away the sacrifices, Chr. 292, 2 = Rigv. i. 86, 2.

यज्ञसेन *yajńa-sena* (cf. *senâ*), m. A name of Drupada, Chr. 55, 6.

याज्ञिय *yâjńiya*, i.e. *yajńa + iya*, I. adj. Suitable to a sacrifice, Man. 2, 23. II. m. The *dvâpara*, or third *yuga*.

यज्ञोपवीतवन्त् *yajńopavitavant*, i.e. *yajńa-upavita + vant* (vb. *vye*), adj. Invested with the sacred thread, Johns. Sel. 10, 18.

यज्यु *yajyu* (vb. *yaj*), m. An assistant priest at a sacrifice.

यज्वन् *yaj + van*, m. A sacrificer, Pańch. i. d. 333.—**Comp.** *A-*, m. one who performs no sacrifices, irreligious, Man. 11, 14; 20.

यज्विन् *yaj + vin*, m. A sacrificer, Bhâg. P. 5, 14, 39.

यत् *YAT* (an old denomin. based on a noun derived from *yam*, by an aff. with initial *t*), i. 1, Âtm. (ved., and in epic poetry also Par., MBh. 3, 2722). **1.** To exert one's self, Pańch. i. d. 284; Chr. 4, 16; to endeavour, Man. 11, 6; with infin., MBh. 1, 6360; with dat., Bhag. 7, 3; Vikr. 5, 11 (*yatishye sakhîpratyânayanâya*, I shall endeavour to bring back your friend); Pańch. i. d. 99 (*nâçâya*, to remove); loc., MBh. 3, 2727; gen., 1, 8085. **2.** With acc. To make, to produce, Râm. 3, 49, 56. Ptcple. of the pf. pass. I. *yatita*, Endeavoured, tried, MBh. 1, 6015. II. *yatta*. **1.** Exerting one's self, Chr. 18, 16. **2.** Watchful, Râm. 1, 32, 7. **3.** Resolved. Cf. *yam*. Caus. and i. 10, Par. *yâtaya*. **1.** To prepare, to cause to be shown, Mâlav. 74, 17. **2.** To distress, to torture, Bhâg. P. 5, 26, 31; also Âtm. with *âtmânam*, 5, 26, 18. **3.** Âtm. To be used, Râm. 2, 62, 26 Gorr. **4.** Âtm. To return, to requite, MBh. 3, 1383. **5.** To reprehend, to despise.—With the prep. **अधि** *adhi*, To put on, Chr. 290, 4 = Rigv. i. 64, 4.—With **आ** *â*, *âyatta*,

1. Depending on, Man. 7, 65. **2.** Docile, tractable, Hit. 54, 5. Comp. *An-*, adj. independent, Hit. ii. d. 21. *Para-*, adj. 1. depending on another, Pańch. i. d. 295, v.r. 2. ruled, Kathâs. 18, 381.—With अत्या *ati-â*, To exert one's self excessively, Daçak. in Chr. 182, 6.—With समा *sam-â*, *samâyatta*, Depending on, MBh. 3, 10484. — With निस् *nis*, Caus., or i. 10, **1.** To give back, to restore, Man. 11, 164. **2.** To requite, MBh. 2, 2660. **3.** To pardon, 1, 3018.—With प्रतिनिस् *prati-nis*, Caus., or i. 10, To give back, MBh. 3, 13183.—With प्र *pra*, **1.** To endeavour, Man. 7, 198. **2.** To apply to, Râm. 1, 58, 21. *prayatita*, Determined, Johns. Sel. 32, 61.—With प्रति *prati*, Caus., or i. 10, To requite, MBh. 3,14728.—With वि *vi*, Caus., or i. 10, To punish, MBh. 1, 3019.

यतम *yatama*, यतर् *yatara*, see *yad*.

यतस् *ya+tas* (*yad*), adv. **1.** Whence, Râm. 3, 53, 27; from any place, Man. 11, 17; Pańch. i. d. 6 (*yatas tatas*, from wherever, Chr. 19, 5). **2.** Since, Râm. 2, 7, 1. **3.** As, Hit. 127, 10. **4.** Because, Pańch. i. d. 402. **5.** That, Vikr. d. 118. **6.** For, Hit. 7, 2, M.M.; Daçak. in Chr. 194, 4. **7.** Where, Brâhmaṇav. 1, 20. **8.** Doubled, *yatoyatas*, Whencesoever.

1. यति *yati*, i.e. *yam+ti* (or perhaps rather a curtailed form of *yatin*), I. m. **1.** A sage of subdued passions, Hit. ii. d. 171. **2.** A religious mendicant, Râm. 3, 52, 26. II. f. **1.** (i.e. *yam+ti*), A pause (in music), Pańch. v. d. 44. **2.** also यती *yatî*, A widow.

2. यति *ya+ti* (*yad*), adj. As many.

यतिन् *yatin*, perhaps *yata+in* (vb. *yam*), I. m. One who has subdued his passions. II. f. *nî*, A widow.

यत्किंचिद *yatkiṁchida*, i.e. *yad-kim-chid+a*, The name of a holy text, Man. 11, 252.

यत्न *yat+na*, m. **1.** Effort, Pańch. ii. d. 133; 99 (*yatnât*, in spite of every effort), perseverance, energy, Man. 2, 88. **2.** Will, Bhâshâp. 4. **3.** Diligence, Chr. 51, 1. *yatnena*, Carefully, Pańch. 192, 12. **4.** °*nât*, Necessarily, Pańch. 176, 8.—Comp. *A-*, m. absence of hardship; instr. and abl. sing. without hardship, Man. 5, 47; easily, Pańch. 201, 16. *Sa-*, I. adj. endeavouring, Hit. 20, 8, M.M. II. °*nam*, adv. vigorously.

यत्नतस् *yatna+tas*, adv. **1.** Vigorously, strenuously, Bhartṛ. 2, 5. **2.** Carefully, Hit. i. d. 128, M.M.; Bhartṛ. 2, 97.—Comp. *A-*, adv. without hardship, Vedântas. in Chr. 219, 9.

यत्र *ya+tra* (*yad*), adv. **1.**=loc. of *yad*, Bhag. 8, 23. **2.** Where, in what place. **3.** Doubled, *yatrayatra*, Wherever, Hit. iii. d. 69. **4.** Because, Nal. 12, 7. **5.** That, Nal. 8, 17. **6.** With following *kutra*, In whatever, Hit. iv. d. 84 (cf. v.r. in Böhtl. Ind. Spr. 1225). **7.** With following *tatra*, Wherever, Chr. 8, 22.

यत्रत्य *yatra+tya*, adj. Where being, whose, Mâlat. 144, 17.

यथा *ya + thâ* (*yad*), adv. **1.** In which manner, like, as, Hit. pr. 38, M.M.; Chr. 8, 25; with following *tad evam*, As—just so, Vikr. 37, 7, 8. **2.** With following *tathâ*, In every way, Hit. ii. d. 138. **3.** As truly as (a form of asseveration), Chr. 7, 16 (literally: 'As truly I love nobody but thee, so truly I touch my head,' i.e. 'As I touch my head, so I love nobody but thee'). **4.** In order that, that, Chr. 12, 30. **5.** It is used often as introduction to a direct sentence, Çâk. 7, 1, bel. *jńâyate yathâyam âbhogas tapovanasyeti*, 'One perceives these are the environs of a forest of ascetics.' **6.** Doubled, *yathâyathâ*, In what proportion, Man. 4, 20. **7.** Very often it is the former part of comp. adv., of which the latter part has the form of an acc. sing. n.; they may be resolved by supplying 'is,' and generally translated by 'according to that which is implied by the latter part,' e.g. *yathâ-kâma + m*, literally, 'as is desire,' 'according to one's wish,' 'at pleasure, ad libitum,' Chr. 56, 17. *yathâ-yatha + m*, adv. Properly, suitably (ÇKD.).—Comp. *Tad-*, adv. namely, Pańch. 3, 10; 7, 15; for, Utt. Râmach. 35, 17.

यथाक्रमम् *yathâ-krama + m*, adv. In order, successively, Vikr. 66, 21.

यथादिशम् *yathâ-diç + a + m*, adv. In all directions, MBh. 5, 1753.

यथाभीष्टदिशम् *yathâbhishṭadiçam*, i.e. *yathâ-abhi-ishṭa-diç + a + m* (vb. *ish*), adv. In whatever direction one lists, Pańch. 63, 2.

यथार्थाक्षर *yathârthâkshara*, i.e. *yathâ-artha-akshara*, adj. Of which the letters imply the true sense, Vikr. d. 1.

यथावकाशम् *yathâvakâçam*, i. e. *yathâ-avakâça + m*, adv. When there is any opportunity, Hit. 102, 11.

यथार्हतस् *yathârhatas*, i.e. *yathâ-arha + tas*, adv. Justly, Man. 7, 16.

यथावत् *yathâ + vat*, adv. **1.** Exactly as it was, truly, Chr. 63, 63. **2.** According to law, Man. 2, 89. **3.** Accordingly, suitably, Nal. 6, 8.

यथेच्छकम् *yathechchhakam*, i. e. *yathâ-ichchha + ka + m*, and **यथेच्छम्** *yathechchham*, i.e. *yathâ-ichchha + m* (cf. *ichchhâ*), adv. As one lists, Pańch. 192, 13.

यथेष्टतस् *yatheshṭatas*, i.e. *yathâ ishṭa* (vb. *ish*), + *tas*, adv. According to will or inclination, Hiḍ. 2, 13.

यद् *yad*, **I.** Relative pronoun; the base of the cases and of most derivatives is *ya*, Who, which, what, Chr. 5, 8. **II.** Indefinite pronoun, Any, Chr. 23, 30. **III.** Doubled. **1.** In proportion, as each of which, Man. 1, 20. **2.** Whoever, whatever, Hit. pr. d. 34, M.M. **IV.** With following interr. pronoun (*kim*), Whoever, whatever, Pańch. i. d. 403. **V.** Two and more relatives may be combined with one verb; e.g. *yad yena yujyate*, What is fitting for something, Hit. i. d. 53, M.M.; *yo 'tti yasya yadâ mâṁsam*, When one eats the flesh of some (creature), Hit. i. d. 65, M.M. **VI.** *yad*, acc. sing. n., a particle. **1.** As, since, because, Hit. pr. d. 8, M.M.; wherefore. **2.** That, Hit. 41, 4, M.M. **3.** It is often used as introduction to a direct sentence, Pańch. 175, 13. *vadanti yad asmâkaṁ râjâ kiṁ karishyati*, 'They say: what will the king do to us?' 227, 7. **3.** With following *vâ*, Or, Râjat. 5, 441. **4.** With following *api*, Although, Pańch. i. d. 7. **VII.** *yena*, instr. sing. n., adv. **1.** In what manner, Man. 4, 178. **2.** Because, MBh. 3, 10631. **3.** As, Böhtl. Ind. Spr. 1212. **4.** That, Pańch. 84, 17. **VIII.** *yasmât*, abl. sing. n., adv. Because, Hit. iv. d. 88; Chr. 16, 11.—Cf. probably ὅς, ἥ, ὅ, ἵνα, εἵνε-κα (=*yena*); Goth. ja in jabai.

यदा *ya + dâ* (*yad*), adv. **1.** When, at what time, Hit. 98, 18. **2.** Doubled, Whenever, Bhag. 4, 7. **3.** With following *kadâ chid—na*, Nevermore, Hit. 58, 12.

यदि *yadi* (probably *yad + ya*, cf. *âdi*, *âdya*), adv. If, Pańch. 229, 13; with following *api*, Although, Böhtl. Ind. Spr. 2389; with following *vâ*, Or, Pańch. iii. d. 108.

यदु *yadu*, m. **1.** The name of a king, Çiç. 9, 38. **2.** The name of a country. **3.** pl. **a.** The name of a people. **b.** The descendants of Yadu, Johns. Sel. 46, 73.

यदृच्छा *yad-ṛichchh* + *â* (see vb. *ṛi*), f. Following one's own will or fancy; instr. °*chhayâ*, Pańch. iii. d. 2 (without being stopped); by itself, MBh. 12, 6676; as one lists, Bhâg. P. 4, 25, 20; by chance, accidentally, Vikr. d. 10; also *yadṛichcha-*, as former part of a comp., by itself, Bhag. 4, 22; Utt. Râmach. 127, 11 (*-saṁvada*, accidental meeting).

यद्वत् *yad*+*vat*, adv. In what manner, as, Pańch. ii. d. 62.

यन्तृ *yantṛi*, i.e. *yam* + *tṛi*, **I.** m., f. *tri*, and n. A person or thing that restrains. **II.** m. A charioteer, Man. 2, 88.—Comp. *Deha-*, m. a charioteer, i.e. subduer, of (his) body, i.e. of his senses, Lass. 53, 11.

यन्त्र् *YANTR*, † i. 10 (properly a denomin. derived from *yantra*), Par., and † i. 1, Par. To restrain. *yantrita*, **1.** Checked, restrained, Râm. 1, 40, 17. **2.** Bound, fettered, MBh. 3, 33. Comp. *A-*, adj. one who does not govern his passions, Man. 2, 118. *Su-*, adj. 1. well governed. 2. one who governs his passions completely, Man. 2, 118.—With the prep. **उप** *upa*, *upayantrita*, Solicited, Man. 11, 177.—With **नि** *ni*, *niyantrita*, **1.** Fastened, Utt. Râmach. 106, 1. **2.** Checked. **3.** Squeezed, Çâk. 9, 20 (Prâkṛ.). **4.** Ruled, Vedântas. in Chr. 209, 17. **5.** Fettered, Pańch. 142, 14. **6.** Embanked, Râjat. 5, 103.—With **सम्** *sam*, *saṁyantrita*, Stopped, Çâk. 100, 21.

यन्त्र *yantra*, i.e. *yam* + *tra*, n. **1.** An engine or machine in general, any implement, or apparatus, Man. 7, 75; Johns. Sel. 39, 30; Râjat. 5, 104. **2.** A thong, Man. 8, 292. **3.** A sort of vessel, Hit. iii. d. 52. **4.** A mystical diagram, Râmatap. Up. 1, 13. **5.** Restraining.—Comp. *Kodaṇḍa-*, n. a bow, Râjat. 5, 104. *Kûṭa-*, n. a trap for deer, birds, etc. *Gṛiha-*, n. an apparatus for raising flags on a house, Kumâras. 6, 41. *Ghaṭikâ-* (thus to be corrected, Pańch. 212, 4), and *Ghaṭî-*, n. the rope and bucket of a well, Mârk. P. 12, 20. *Jala-*, n. a machine for raising water, Hariv. 8425. *Tâla-*, n. 1. a small pair of pincers, Suçr. 1, 23, 16. 2. a lock. *Taila-*, n. an oil-mill, Bhâg. P. 5, 21, 13. *Toya-*, n. a clepsydra, Sûryas. 13, 21. *Dhârâ-*, n. a water-spout, Prab. 79, 11. *Dhvaja-*, n. an apparatus for planting the staff of a standard, Râm. 4, 13, 20. *Nâḍî-*, n. any tube-like apparatus, Suçr. 1, 23, 17. *Mahâ-*, n. any great mechanical work, Man. 11, 63. *Su-*, adj. with machines, Hit. iii. d. 52. *Sûtra-*, n. 1. a loom. 2. a shuttle. *Strî-*, n. a woman who works like an artificial machine, Pańch. i. d. 204. *Sva-mâyâ-*, adj. formed by his art, Kathâs. 29, 18.

यन्त्रक **1.** *yantr* + *aka*, m. An artisan, Râm. 2, 80, 1. **2.** *yantra* + *ka*, n. A lathe.—Comp. *Jala-*, n. an engine, Hariv. 8432.

यन्त्रण *yantraṇa*, i.e. *yantr* + *ana*, **I.** n. **1.** Binding. **2.** Restraining. **3.** Confining. **II.** f. *ṇâ*. **1.** Torturing, pain (ÇKD.), Mâlav. 46, 3. **2.** A means of fastening, Daçak. in Chr. 185, 5; Pańch. rec. orn. MS. Berol. 81, a., and Weber, Ind. St. iii. 372, 4, below (read *yantraṇayâ* instead of *yantrayâ*).—Comp. *Niryantraṇa*, i.e. *nis-*, adj. unrestrained, unobstructed, Böhtl. Ind.

Spr. 408. °*nam*, adv., Ṛit. 1, 9. *Mukha-*, n. the bit of a bridle.

† यभ् *YABH*, जभ् *JABH*, जम्भ् *JAMBH*, i. 1, Par. To lie with.

यम् *YAM* (akin to *dam*), i. 1, *yachchha*, Par. (in epic poetry also Âtm., MBh. 1, 5704). **1.** To tame, to restrain. **2.** To govern (as horses), MBh. 3, 751. **3.** To give, Man. 2, 55. Ptcple. of the pf. pass. *yata*, Restrained, governed, Hit. iii. d. 130; in epic poetry also *yatta*, MBh. 2, 2011 (maintained by the metre). **Comp.** *Vâgyata*, i.e. *vâch-*, adj. silent, taciturn, Man. 3, 236. Caus., and i. 10, *yămaya*. **1.** To restrain. **2.** † To give food. Ptcple. pf. pass. *yamita*, Restrained, Çâk. d. 29. **Comp.** *A-*, adj. not pared (as nails), Megh. 89. — With the prep. अधि *adhi*, To give, Chr. 292, 12 = Rigv. i. 85, 12.—With आ *â*, **1.** To stop, Bhaṭṭ. 6, 119. **2.** To suppress, Man. 11, 149. **3.** To draw, to bend (as a bow), Râm. 3, 50, 9; Johns. Sel. 50, 101. **4.** Âtm. To extend, Çâk. 73, 4, Ch. **5.** Âtm. To possess, Bhaṭṭ. 8, 46. *âyata*, Long, Pañch. ii. 8. **Comp.** *Pûrṇa-âyata*, adj. completely drawn (as a bow), Hariv. 13413. Comp. ptcple. of the fut. pass. *an-âyamya*, Not to be drawn, unpliant, MBh. 1, 6953. — With निरा *nis-â*, *nirâyata*, Contracted, Çâk. d. 8.—With व्या *vi-â*, **1.** Âtm. To exert one's power, MBh. 3, 12740. **2.** To fight, Mṛichchh. 202, 7; Âtm., Bhaṭṭ. 6, 119. **3.** To open wide one's eyes, Johns. Sel. 47, 76. *vyâyata*, Long. **2.** Excessive. **3.** Busy. **4.** Hard, firm. Caus. *yâmaya*, To use exercise, Man. 7, 216.—With उद् *ud*, **1.** To rise, Hit. 81, 4 (with infin., in order to kill). **2.** To lift up, Man. 4, 64. **3.** To brandish, Man. 5, 58. **4.** To govern (as horses), Chr. 36, 19. **5.** To offer, MBh. 1, 1853. **6.** To endeavour, MBh. 2, 2357. **7.** To study. *udyata*, **1.** Raised, Chr. 3, 1. **2.** Ready, Hit. 41, 4, M.M. **3.** Intending, Râjat. 5, 237. **4.** Trained. **5.** Active. **Comp.** *Samara-*, adj. ready for the combat.—With अभ्युद् *abhi-ud*, **1.** To raise, Mṛichchh. 171, 20. **2.** To offer, Man. 4, 247. *abhyudyata*, **1.** Lifted up, Mṛichchh. 327, 5 (Calc.). **2.** Rising, proceeding to act, Man. 4, 302.—With प्रोद् *pra-ud*, **1.** To lift up. *prodyata*, lifted, Pañch. 105, 19. **2.** To cast, Bhaṭṭ. 15, 60.—With समुद् *sam-ud*, **1.** To incite, to urge (as horses), MBh. 3, 756. **2.** To lift up, 1, 6278. **3.** To endeavour, Râm. 1, 14, 8. *samudyata*, Ready.—With उप *upa*, **1.** Âtm. To marry, Man. 3, 11 (Par., Man. 11, 172, v.r., see Lois.). **2.** To seize, Âtm., Bhaṭṭ. 1, 16; with *bhayam*, To fear, Bhaṭṭ. 7, 101.—With नि *ni*, **1.** To stop, to govern, MBh. 4, 1953. **2.** To direct, Chr. 295, 16 = Rigv. i. 92, 16. **3.** To curb, to restrain, Râm. 2, 122, 22; to hold in (the breath), Vikr. d. 1. **4.** To punish, Man. 9, 213. **5.** To bind, Râm. 2, 87, 23. **6.** To attain, Man. 2, 93. **7.** To assume, Man. 10, 93. **8.** To conceal, Man. 10, 59. *niyata*, **1.** Subdued, self-governed. **2.** Submissive, Sâv. 4, 11. **3.** Abstemious, Chr. 50, 9. **4.** Attentive. **5.** Fixed, Megh. 44. **6.** Certain, destined, Hit. i. d. 43, M.M.; right, i. d. 202, M.M. **7.** Constant, Man. 5, 44. **8.** Inevitable, Man. 8, 419; Utt. Râmach. 52, 12. °*tam*, adv. **1.** Forcibly, Ṛit. 6, 20. **2.** Inevitably, Bhartṛ. 2, 41. **3.** Constantly, always. **4.** Surely, Pañch. ii. d. 199. n. Elementary matter. Caus. To restrain, Çâk. 92, 19, Chezy. *niyamita*, **1.** Restrained. **2.**

Confined, Bhartṛ. 2, 93. 3. Prescribed. 4. Governed.—With प्रतिनि *prati-ni*, *pratiniyata*, Determined proportionally (in proportion to the acts done in a preceding existence), Bhartṛ. 2, 92; Daçak. in Chr. 187, 22.—With विनि *vi-ni*, To punish, Man. 9, 249.—With संनि *sam-ni*, To subdue, Man. 2, 93.—With प्र *pra*, 1. To offer, to deliver, Hit. 65, 15; to give, Man. 3, 223; Chr. 288, 15=Rigv. i. 48, 15 (*yachchhatât*, imperat. 2. sing.). 2. To give in marriage, Man. 9, 89. 3. To restore, Man. 8, 181; Pañch. 88, 14. 4. To pay, Man. 8, 158. *prayata*, Well restrained, keeping his organs controlled, Man. 2, 222.. 2. Submissive, Nal. 25, 2. 3. Careful, Man. 2, 183; intent on his devotion, 11, 158; zealous, Vikr. d. 43. 4. Pure, Man. 5, 145. Comp. *A-*, adj. impure, Man. 5, 142. — With प्रतिप्र *prati-pra*, To restore, Daçak. in Chr. 195, 14.—With संप्र *sam-pra*, 1. To give, Man. 11, 19. 2. To give in marriage, MBh. 3, 16661 (=Sâv. 2, 4, v. r. erroneous). — With वि *vi*, To give, Chr. 292, 12=Rigv. i. 85, 12 (*yanta*, 2. pl. imperat. aor. 1.).—With सम् 1. To constrain, Man. 8, 365. 2. To bind, MBh. 3, 1694. 3. To subdue, Man. 12, 11. 4. To govern (as horses), MBh. 3, 12110. *saṁyata*, Restrained, subdued, Nal. 1, 4; fettered. Comp. *Su-saṁyata*, adj. well composed, Man. 2, 193 (v.r.).—Cf. ἥμερος, ζημία, ἡνία, ὄμνυμι; Lat. jejunus, and probably jentare, fræna; Goth. aiths; A.S. adh, adhum; O.H.G. eidum.

यम *yam+a*, I. adj. sbst. Twin, one of a pair. du. The twins, Draup. 6, 29. II. m. 1. Restraining. 2. Taming of passion, Vedântas. in Chr. 217, 14. 3. Moral duty, Man. 4, 204. 4. Penance. 5. A festival. 6. Yama, the judge of the deceased ones, ruler of the infernal regions, Râm. 2, 54, 28; god of death, Pañch. 247, 8. 7. A crow. 8. A name of the planet Saturn. III. f. *mî*, The Yamunâ. IV. n. A pair.—Comp. *Kâla-anta+ka-*, m. Yama, as all-destroying time, Râm. 3, 32, 5.

यमक *yama+ka*, I. m. A religious observance. II. n. A poetical refinement, a species of alliteration.

यमज *yama+ja*, m. Twin, Draup. 3, 17; Utt. Râmach. 112, 3.

यमत्व *yama+tva*, n. The name Yama, Sâv. 5, 33.

यमन *yam+ana*, I. m. Yama. II. n. 1. Restraining, Râjat. 5, 114. 2. Binding. 3. Cessation.

यमल *yama+la*, I. n. A pair. II. f. *lî*, A sort of dress, a body and petticoat.

यमुना *yam+unâ* (or rather *yam+van+a*), f. The name of a river, Chr. 46, 19.

यमेरुका *yam+erukâ*, f. A metal plate or drum used to strike the hours.

ययाति *yayâti*, m. The name of a king, Çâk. d. 82.

ययि *yayi* (vb. *yâ*, red.), A cloud, Chr. 293, 2=Rigv. i. 87, 2.

ययिन् (vb. *yâ*, red., +*in*), *yayin*, m. Çiva.

ययी *yayî* (cf. *yayi*), m. A horse.

ययु *yayu* (vb. *yâ*, red., +*u*), m. 1. A horse. 2. A horse fit for sacrifice.

यर्हि *yarhi*, probably *yatra-hi*, adv. When.

यव *yava*, m. **1.** Barley, Hordeum hexastichon, Pańch. 224, 4. **2.** The measure of a barleycorn, equal to six mustard seeds. **3.** A natural line across the thumb, supposed to indicate good fortune. **4.** Velocity (vb. *jû*).—Comp. *Kâka-*, m. barren corn, Pańch. ii. d. 93. *Tri-*, adj. weighing three barleycorns, Man. 8, 134. — Cf. *ζεά*, *ζειά*, *εἶα*.

यवक *yava+ka*, m. Barley.

यवक्य *yavakya*, i.e. *yavaka+ya*, adj. Fit for producing barley.

यवज *yava-ja*, m. Saltpetre.

यवन *yavana*, I. adj. Swift (vb. *jû*). II. m. **1.** The name of a country. **2.** The name of a people (originally Greek, Ionian), Man. 10, 44. **3.** (vb. *jû*), Velocity. **4.** A swift horse. III. f. *nî*, A Yavana woman, Vikr. 77, 5.—Comp. *Kâla-*, m. the name of a prince of the Yavanas, Hariv. 1961.

यवनिका *yavanikâ*, i.e. *yavana+ka*, f. A curtain, Bhartṛ. 3, 51.

यवनेष्ट *yavaneshṭa*, i.e. *yavana-ishṭa* (vb. *ish*), n. Lead.

यवमय *yava+maya*, adj., f. *yî*, Made of or from barley.

यवस *yava+sa*, m. Pasture grass, Pańch. 182, 13.

यवागू *yavâgû* (from *yava*, and *gu* for *go*), f. Rice-gruel, Man. 11, 106; 6, 20.

यवान *yavâna* (vb. *jû*), adj. Swift.

यविष्ठ *yavishṭha*, **यवीयंस्** *yavîyaṁs*, see *yuvan*.

यव्य *yavya*, i.e. *yava+ya*, I. adj. Fit for producing barley. II. m. A month.

यशस् *yaças* (for original *daças*=Lat. decus, from a lost vb. *daç*, see below), I. n. **1.** Glory, Vikr. 11, 17; fame, Pańch. iii. d. 116 (pl.). **2.** Splendour. **3.** Praise. II. adj. Renowned, resplendent, Chr. 294, 8=Rigv. i. 92, 8; superl. *yaçastama*, Lass. 101, 9=Rigv. vii. 16, 4.—Comp. *A-*, n. disgrace, Pańch. ii. d. 116. *Ati-*, adj. much renowned; archaic acc. (cf. *srotas* and ved. forms) *-yaçâm*, for *yaçasam*, Nal. 8, 4 (Böhtl., Bopp. v.r.). *Apa-*, n. disgrace, Bhartṛ. 2, 45. *Prithu-*, I. adj. widely renowned, MBh. 7, 2783. II. a proper name. *Mahâ-*, adj. illustrious, Râm. 3, 55, 38. *Su-*, adj. renowned.—Cf. Lat. decere, docere; *δοκέω*, *δόξω*, *δόγμα*, *δοκεύω*, *διδάσκω*, *δάκτυλος*; probably A.S. ta, tah; O.H.G. zêha.

यशस्कर *yaças-kara*, I. adj., f. *rî*, Rendering famous, Hit. iii. d. 122. II. m. A proper name, Râjat. 5, 472.

यशस्य *yaças+ya*, adj. Bringing reputation, Man. 3, 106.—Comp. *A-*, adj. bringing disgrace, Râm. 5, 91, 12.

यशस्वन्त् *yaças+vant*, adj., f. *vatî*, and **यशस्विन्** *yaças+vin*, adj., f. *vinî*, Famous, Chr. 21, 6 (*vin*); Lass. 31, 13 (*vin*).

यष्टि *yashṭi*, I. m. and f. (and **यष्टी** *yashṭi*, f.), **1.** A staff, a stick, Pańch. 105, 19; 261, 12; Çiç. 9, 39; a perch, Vikr. d. 43; a stem, d. 44; support, Sâv. 5, 89. **2.** A palisade, Man. 9, 285. **3.** A club, Daçak. in Chr. 187, 4. **4.** A string, Vikr. d. 51. **5.** A necklace. **6.** Any creeping plant, Utt. Râmach. 81, 5. **7.** Liquorice. **8.** A shrub, Siphonanthus indica. II. m. **1.** A flag-staff. **2.** The arm and forearm.—Comp. *Ketu-*, m. a flag-staff, Ragh. 12, 103. *Gâtra-*, m. a delicate body; when latter part of comp. adj., the fem. ends in *î*, Ṛit. 6, 24. *Tulâ-*, the beam of a balance, Pańch. i. d. 166. *Dhvaja-*, f. a flag-staff, Râm. 5, 12, 38. *Bhâra-*, f. a yoke or pole for carrying burthens. *Vâsa-*, f. a column for a bird to perch on, Megh. 77. *Hâra-*, f. a necklace, Ṛit. 1, 8.

यष्टिक *yashṭi + ka*, I. m. A bird, the lapwing. II. f. *kâ*. **1.** A staff, a club. **2.** A necklace. **3.** A pond. **4.** Liquorice.

यष्टुकाम *yashṭukâma*, i.e. *yashṭum* (infin. of *yaj*), *-kâma*, adj. Desiring to sacrifice, Râm. 1, 57, 10.

यष्टृ *yashṭṛi*, i.e. *yaj + tṛi*, m. A sacrificer.

यस् *YAS* (akin to *yam*, for *yaṁs*), i. 4, and † 1, Par. To make strenuous and persevering exertion, to endeavour. —With the prep. **आ** *â*, **1.** To endeavour, Râm. 2, 14, 62. **2.** To be afflicted, Bhaṭṭ. 6, 69. *âyasta*, **1.** Pained, distressed, Râm. 2, 20, 8. **2.** Vexed, angry. **3.** Managed with difficulty. **4.** Hurt. **5.** Thrown. **6.** Sharpened. **7.** Strained, Pańch. v. d. 28. Caus. To torment, Mâlav. 32, 7 (Prâkṛ.). Comp. ptcple. of the pf. pass. *an-âyâsita*, Not practised, Pańch. i. d. 429 (rather *an-âyâsa + ita*).—With **प्र** *pra*, To endeavour, Naish. 1, 125. *prayasta*, Seasoned, dressed with condiments.

या *YÂ* (akin to *i*), ii. 2, Par. (in epic poetry also Âtm., Râm. 1, 33, 6). **1.** To go, Râm. 2, 72, 27; imperat. *yâtu*, Let it go, enough, Hit. 77, 9, M.M.; no matter, Hit. 128, 9. **2.** To go to (with acc.), MBh. 3, 2828; (with dat.), Hit. i. d. 153; (with two acc.), Râm. 3, 55, 48 (*sarvâṇi çaraṇaṁ yâmi*, All those I approach, or I implore, for help). **3.** To undergo, to obtain, to get, especially with abstract nouns; e.g. *kshayam*, To perish, MBh. 3, 8840; *reṇu-padavîm*, To become dust, Vikr. d. 4; *saṁparkam*, To be united, Vikr. d. 13; *prasâdam*, To become propitious, inclined to somebody, Pańch. 67, 8; *dveshyatâm*, To grow odious, Pańch. i. d. 317; *vilayam*, To be dissolved, Pańch. i. d. 425. **4.** To pass away, Pańch. iii. d. 97; Bhaṭṭ. 7, 89. Ptcple. of the pf. pass. *yâta*. **1.** Gone, Vikr. d. 72; went. **2.** Escaped, Hit. ii. d. 144. **3.** Obtained, got. n. Driving an elephant with a goad. Desider. *yiyâsa*, To desire to go, MBh. 3, 47. Caus. *yâpaya*, **1.** To remove, Ragh. 9, 27. **2.** To pass away (time), Pańch. 183, 24. **3.** To induce, Daçak. in Chr. 194, 4 (with dat. in the sense of an infin. 'Induced to abandon').—With the prep. **अति** *ati*, To pass, Râm. 2, 49, 3.—With **समति** *sam-ati*, To pass away, Râm. 1, 19, 1.—With **अधि** *adhi*, To escape, Bhaṭṭ. 8, 90.—With **अनु** *anu*, **1.** To follow, Man. 8, 17. **2.** To cut in succession, MBh. 4, 1727. *anuyâta*, **1.** Followed, accompanied, Daçak. in Chr. 190, 15. **2.** Practised.—With **समनु** To follow, MBh. 2, 1608.—With **अप** *apa*, **1.** To go away, Hit. iv. d. 81; MBh. 3, 15214; Chr. 57, 31 (I propose to read *purân*, i.e. *purât*). **2.** To run away, Draup. 8, 35. *apayâta*, Fallen from, Chr. 35, 3.—With **व्यप** *vi-apa*, **1.** To go away, MBh. 3, 739. **2.** To desist from (abl.), Chr. 42, 13. **3.** To pass away, Râm. 2, 49, 2.—With **अभि** *abhi*, To go near (acc.), Râm. 1, 25, 10. *abhiyâta*, Approaching, Indr. 2, 8.—With **समभि** *sam-abhi*, To go near at the same time, MBh. 1, 1338.—With **आ** *â*, **1.** To approach, Vikr. d. 121;

Pańch. i. d. 213. **2.** To come, Pańch. iii. d. 97; Râjat. 5, 31. **3.** With and without *punar*, To return, Râm. 1, 1, 75; Chr. 5, 23. **4.** To attain, Lass. 21, 2. **5.** To undergo, to obtain, Râjat. 5, 376; with *kshayam*, To be ruined, Pańch. v. d. 52; with *saṁkocham*, To be diminished, Pańch. i. d. 105; with *hetutâm*, To become the cause, Hit. i. d. 29, M.M.; with *tosham*, To be satisfied, Hit. ii. d. 149. *âyâta*, Come. n. Excess, Kir. 5, 23. **Comp.** *Krama-*, adj. descended from a succession, i.e. a long line of princes, Pańch. i. d. 83.—With अभ्या *abhi-â*, To approach, MBh. 3, 246.—With उपा *upa-â*, **1.** To approach, MBh. 3, 738. **2.** To undergo, to obtain, Râjat. 5, 126. *upâyâta*, n. Arrival, Draup. 4, 24.—With समुपा *sam-upa-â*, To approach, MBh. 4, 280.—With प्रत्या *prati-â*, To go towards, MBh. 4, 1698.—With समा *sam-â*, **1.** To meet with, Pańch. 46, 6; 245, 2 (*dvau panthânau samâyâtau*, They came to two roads). **2.** To approach, Pańch. 23, 10; Chr. 34, 6. **3.** To obtain, Pańch. i. d. 104. **4.** To come, Hit. pr. 33, 2; to arrive, Hit. 29, 6, M.M.—With उद् *ud*, To rise, Gît. 4, 19.—With प्रत्युद् *prati-ud*, To go to meet (a guest), Râm. 1, 20, 8. *pratyudyâta*, Saluted, welcomed, Megh. 23.—With उप *upa*, **1.** To go to (acc.), Râm. 2, 50, 15. **2.** To approach, Pańch. i. d. 44; Ragh. 9, 24 (Calc.). **3.** To undergo, to obtain, Man. 12, 69; with *prîtim*, To grow agreeable, Pańch. i. d. 317. **4.** To befall, Pańch. iii. d. 244.—With आोप *â-upa*, To come near to (acc.), Lass. 102, 11=Rigv. vii. 14, 3.—With उपोप *upa-upa*, To approach gradually, MBh. 3, 12358.—With प्रत्युप *prati-upa*, To return, MBh. 1, 8393.—With समुप *sam-upa*, To go, MBh. 3, 1912.—With प्रणि *pra-ni*, To proceed, Bhaṭṭ. 9, 100.—With निस् *nis*, To go out, or out of (abl.), Râm. 2, 76, 19.—With अभिनिस् *abhi-nis*, To go out, to depart, Râjat. 5, 218.—With परि *pari*, **1.** To go round, to circumambulate (as a token of respect), MBh. 1, 7205. **2.** To protect, Chr. 297, 13 (corr. *yâthaḥ*) = Rigv. i. 112, 13.—With प्र *pra*, **1.** To go forth, Hit. 84, 7 (*kaḥ pra yâtu*, Who shall go forth?); to proceed, MBh. 3, 2848. **2.** To proceed to (acc.), MBh. 3, 240. **3.** To rise to (acc.), Bhartṛ. 2, 91. **4.** To attain, Pańch. i. d. 186; to obtain, Pańch. iii. d. 262; with *asâdhyatâm* (i.e. *a-sâdh + ya + tâ*), To become unconquerable, Pańch. i. d. 245; with *parâbhavam*, To be spoiled, Pańch. i. d. 424. **5.** To proceed from, Râjat. 5, 374. **6.** To depart, Hit. i. d. 189, M.M.; Daçak. in Chr. 187, 15. **7.** To pass away, Kathâs. 4, 23. Comp. ptcple. pres. *a-prayânt*, adj. Not able to move away, Chr. 31, 16. *prayâta*, **1.** Gone away. **2.** Gone. **3.** Deceased. m. **1.** A lazy fellow. **2.** A name of Bhṛigu. Desider. To desire to proceed, Bhaṭṭ. 3, 25. Caus. *prayâpita*, Driven away.—With अभिप्र *abhi-pra*, To assail, MBh. 4, 1381.—With प्रतिप्र *prati-pra*, To return, MBh. 3, 10287.—With संप्र *sam-pra*, **1.** To proceed together, MBh. 1, 4645. **2.** To depart to (acc.), MBh. 3, 15082.—With प्रति *prati*, To return, Râm. 1, 66, 6.—With वि *vi*, **1.** To pervade (the heavens), and come, Chr. 287, 7=Rigv. i. 48, 7. **2.** To pierce, to destroy, Chr. 292, 10=Rigv. i. 86, 10. *viyâta*, Ill-behaved, impudent.—With

सम् *sam*, 1. To enter, MBh. 3, 6013. 2. To come, Lass. 34, 4. — With अनुसम् *anu-sam*, 1. To visit in succession, or one by one, MBh. 3, 10094. 2. To follow, Râm. 2, 79, 13.—Cf. perhaps some forms of *i*; e.g. *ἱέναι*; Lat. Janus, janua.

याग *yâga*, i.e. *yaj+a*, m. A sacrifice, Bhâshâp. 160.

याच् *yâch* (akin to *yâ*), i. 1, Par. Âtm. 1. To ask, Vikr. d. 41; to solicit, Daçak. in Chr. 195, 1. With the acc. of the object and of the person, Man. 3, 258; also with the abl. of the person, MBh. 1, 6197. 2. To offer, to tender. Ptcple. of the pf. pass. *yâchita*. 1. Importuned, Yâjń. 2, 238. 2. Requisite, necessary, Pańch. 182, 13. Comp. *A-*, adj. unasked, Man. 4, 5. *Ati-*, adj. asked too often, too much assailed with begging, Hit. ii. d. 164. Caus. *yâchaya*, To cause to be asked, Pańch. 25, 15; to be invited, Vikr. 37, 8.—With the prep. अभि *abhi*, To ask, to beg; with two acc., MBh. 3, 10586.—With उप *upa*, *upayâchita*, 1. Requested. 2. Offered to the deities to render them propitious. n. A vow, Pańch. ii. d. 50; a demand, Kathâs. 13, 166.—With प्र *pra*, 1. To beg, to solicit, Chr. 26, 65; with two acc., MBh. 3, 9950.— With संप्र *sam-pra*, The same, 3, 8696.—With सम् *sam*, The same, 3, 8837.—Cf. *αἰτέω*, and perhaps *ζητέω*.

याचक *yâch+aka*, adj. Asking, a beggar, Pańch. ii. d. 110.

याचनक *yâch+ana+ka*, adj. Begging importunately, Man. 3, 165.

याचना *yâch*, Caus., *+anâ*, f. Asking, soliciting, Ragh. 11, 78 (Calc. 77, where the Sch. takes it as n.).

याचितक *yâchita+ka* (vb. *yâch*), n. A borrowed thing.

याचिष्णुता *yâch + ishnu + tâ*, f. Habit of soliciting favours, Man. 12, 33.

याञ्ञा *yâchńâ*, i.e. *yâch+na*, f. Begging, Hit. i. d. 97, M.M.

याज *yâja*, i.e. *yaj+a*, m. Food.

याजक *yâjaka*, i.e. *yaj+aka*, m. 1. A sacrificer, Man. 3, 164. 2. A royal elephant. 3. A furious elephant.— Comp. *Grâma-*, m. one who sacrifices for a village, MBh. 3, 13355. *Nakshatra-grâma-*, adj. one who offers sacrifices to the asterims, MBh. 12, 2874.

याजन *yâjana*, i.e. *yaj*, Caus., *+ana*, n. Conducting a sacrifice, sacrificing, Man. 3, 65.

याजि *yâji*, i.e. *yaj+i*, m. An institutor of sacrifices, Man. 4, 33; 3, 148; anomal. du. *yâjyau*.

याजिन् *yâjin*, i.e. *yaj+in*, adj. 1. Sacrificing. 2. Worshipping, Bhag. 9, 34.—Comp. *Âtma(n)-*, adj. sacrificing one's self, Man. 12, 91. *Grâma-*, m. a common sacrificer, Man. 4, 205. *Soma-*, m. a sacrificer who drinks the Soma juice. *Havis-*, m. a priest.

याज्ञवल्क्य *yâjńavalkya*, m. The name of a saint, Utt. Râmach. 98, 4.

याज्ञसेनी *yâjńasenî*, i.e. *yajńâsena +a+î*, f. A name of Draupadî.

याज्ञिक *yâjńika*, i.e. *yajńa+ika*, m. 1. The institutor of a sacrifice. 2. Kuça grass.

याज्ञिक्य *yâjńikya*, i.e. *yâjńika+ya*, n. A sacrifice.

यातना *yâtanâ*, i.e. *yat*, Caus., *+ana*,

f. **1.** Pain, torment, Man. 6, 61; Bhâg. P. 7, 1, 41. **2.** Punishment. **3.** Requital, Pańch. 188, 3.

यातु *yâ + tu,* I. m. **1.** A traveller. **2.** Time. II. n. A Râkshasa, or demon.

यातृ *yâtṛi,* I. i.e. *yâ + tṛi,* m. A driver, Man. 8, 290. II. Perhaps *yam + tṛi,* f. A husband's brother's wife.

यात्रा *yâ + trâ,* f. **1.** Going, travelling. **2.** The march of an assailing force, an expedition, Man. 7, 160; 207; Pańch. iii. d. 35. **3.** Going on pilgrimage. **4.** The procession of idols, Hit. i. d. 113, M.M. **5.** A sort of dramatic entertainment. **6.** Passing away time. **7.** Practice, usage, conduct, Man. 9, 25; intercourse, Man. 11, 184. **8.** An expedient, support of life, Man. 4, 3.—Comp. *Tirtha-*, f. pilgrimage to holy places, Pańch. 117, 10. *Deva-*, f. 1. the procession of idols, Mâlav. 69, 13. 2. a sacred festival. *Deha-*, f. 1. death. 2. support of life, Bhâg. P. 4, 23, 20. *Prâṇa-*, f. support of life, Pańch. 52, 6. *Loka-*, f. 1. the way of the world, Mâlav. 68, 17. 2. worldly affairs, domestic affairs, Man. 9, 27. 3. traffic, intercourse, Hit. i. d. 104, M.M. 4. the life of the world, Bhâg. P. 3, 9, 20.

यात्रिक *yâtrika,* i.e. *yâtrâ + ika,* I. adj. **1.** Relating to a march or an enterprise, Man. 7, 184. **2.** Necessary for supporting life, Man. 6, 27. **3.** Usual. II. m. **1.** A traveller. **2.** A pilgrim. III. n. Provision for a march. —Comp. *Siddha-*, m. a pilgrim who seeks for the territory of the Siddhas, Pańch. 240, 16; cf. 242, 5.

याथातथ्य *yâthâtathya,* i.e. *yathâ -tatham* (see *tathâ*), *+ya,* n. Truth, Hit. iv. d. 102 (but cf. Böhtl. Ind. Spr. 2676).

याथात्म्य *yâthâtmya,* i.e. *yathâ-âtman + ya,* n. Character, Ragh. 10, 25.

यादव *yâdava,* i.e. *yadu + a,* I. m. **1.** A Yâdava, or descendant of Yadu. **2.** Kṛishṇa. II. f. *vî,* Durgâ. III. n. A stock of cattle.—Comp. *Niry°*, i.e. *nis-*, adj., f. *vâ,* free from Yâdavas, Hariv. 4558.

यादस् *yâdas,* n. Any aquatic animal, Kir. 5, 29.

यादृश् *yâdṛiç,* and **यादृश** *yâdṛiça,* i.e. *yad-driç* and *-dṛiç, + a,* adj. **1.** Which like, (*qualis*), Pańch. ii. d. 190. **2.** Which, what, Bhag. 13, 3 (*dṛiç*); Man. 1, 42; Pańch. i. d. 236; Hit. i. d. 205, M.M. **3.** With following *tâdṛiça,* Whoever, whatever, Pańch. i. d. 435.

यान *yâna,* i.e. *yâ + ana,* n. **1.** Going, Man. 4, 72; moving, Pańch. iii. d. 248. **2.** Marching, generally comprising as well: Retreating before an enemy (Pańch. iii. d. 34; cf. 35, and p. 153, 6, 7), as: Attacking an enemy (Pańch. iii. d. 35; Man. 7, 160). **3.** Any vehicle or form of conveyance, a carriage, Man. 2, 202. —Comp. *Âkâça-*, n. moving through the sky, Vikr. 22, 9. *Ushṭra-*, n. a vehicle drawn by camels, Man. 11, 201. *Khara-*, n. a vehicle drawn by asses, ib. *Go-*, n. a carriage drawn by oxen, Man. 11, 174. *Jala-*, n. a boat, Bhâg. P. 3, 14, 17. *Deva-*, I. adj., f. *nî,* leading to the gods, MBh. 3, 11000. II. n. 1. the road leading to the gods, Bhâg. P. 7, 15, 55. 2. the vehicle of a god. III. f. *nî,* the daughter of Çukra, MBh. 1, 3159. *Nara-*, n. 1. a carriage drawn by men, MBh. 12, 1383. 2. *-yâṇa* (with *ṇ*), riding on a man, Pańch. iii. d. 248. *Nârî-*, n. a carriage for women, Man. 3, 52. *Nau-*, n. navigation, Râjat. 1, 201. *Pitṛi-*, m. the way of the Manes, leading to the Manes, MBh. 12, 525, *Pṛishṭha-*, n. 1. going on horseback, riding, Suçr. 1, 258, 5. 2. a horse, Kâm. Nîtis. 7, 36 (at the end of a comp. adj.). *Çata-sahasra-*, n. a hundred thousand roads, Pañch. ii. d. 135. *Simha-*, f. *nâ*, Durgâ.

यापन *yâpana*, i.e. *yâ*, Caus., + *ana*, n., f. *nâ* (Kâm. Nîtis. 9, 1). **1.** Spending time. **2.** Staying. **3.** Rejection. **4.** Alleviating.—**Comp.** *Kâla-*, n. procrastination, Hit. ii. d. 58.

याम *yâma*, I. i.e. *yâ* + *ma*, m. Going, march, Chr. 293, 3=Rigv. i. 87, 3; Chr. 287, 4=Rigv. i. 48, 4 (approaching, rising). II. i.e. *yama* + *a*, adj., f. *mî*. **1.** Relating to Yama. **2.** Inflicted by Yama, Man. 12, 17. III. i.e. *yam* + *a*, m. **1.** Forbearance. **2.** Cessation. **3.** A watch of three hours, Man. 7, 145.—**Comp.** *A-vinoda-dîrgha-*, adj., f. *mâ*, endowed with long watches (i.e. seeming long) on account of offering no interesting pursuit, Vikr. d. 45. *Tri-*, I. adj., f. *mâ*, consisting of three watches, epithet of night, Râm. 2, 10, 7 Gorr. II. f. *mâ*, night, Vikr. d. 63. *Yâta-*, adj. (originally, flat, from having stood a night). 1. old, spoiled, Bhag. 17, 10. 2. used. 3. rejected.

यामन् *yâ* + *man*, n. Going, Chr. 291, 1=Rigv. i. 85, 1 (ved. loc. without termination).

यामन *yâmana*, Hiḍ. 1, 38, is a false reading (see MBh. 1, 5912).

यामल *yâmala*, i.e. *yamala* + *a*, n. A pair.

यामातृ *yâmâtṛi*, i.e. *yam* + *âtṛi* (cf. *jâmâtṛi*), and **यामातृक** *yâmâtṛi* + *ka* (Lass. 24, 18). m. A daughter's husband.—Cf. Lat. janitrix; εἰνατέρες; and O.H.G. eidum, A.S. adhum, derived from the same verb.

यामि and **यामी** *yâmi̋*, I. i.e. *yam* + *î*, f. **1.** A sister. **2.** A daughter-in-law, Man. 4, 180 (*mi*); 183 (*mî*). II. i.e. *yâma* + *î*, Night.

यामिक *yâmika*, i.e. *yâma* + *ika*, I. adj. One who announces the watches, Kathâs. 3, 63. II. f. *kâ*, Night.

यामिनी *yâminî*, i.e. *yâma* + *in* + *î*, f. Night, Daçak. in Chr. 188, 8; Kir. 5, 44.

यामी *yâmî*, see *yâmi*.

यामेय *yâmeya*, i.e. *yâmi* + *eya*, m. A sister's son.

याम्य *yâmya*, i.e. *yama* + *ya*, I. adj., f. *yâ*, Relating to Yama, Râm. 3, 54, 10 (with *diç*, The south); propounded by Yama, Man. 8, 173. II. m. **1.** Agastya. **2.** Sandal. III. f. *yâ*. **1.** The south. **2.** i.e. *yâma* + *ya*, f. Night.

यायजूक *yâyaj* + *ûka* (frequent. of *yaj*), m. A performer of frequent sacrifices.

ऽयायिन् *-yâyin*, i.e. *yâ* + *in*, adj. **1.** Going in; e.g. *nau-*, adj. sbst. Who or what goes in a boat, Man. 8, 409. **2.** Leading to, Utt. Râmach. 15, 10 (*chitrakûta-*, to the mount of Chitrakûta). **3.** *satata-*, adj. Taking place continually, Man. 1, 50. *samudra-*, adj. m. A navigator of the ocean, 3, 158.

याव *yâva*, I. *yava* + *a*, adj. Relating to barley. II. m. Lac, the red animal dye.

यावक *yâva* + *ka*, m. **1.** Half ripe barley. **2.** Barley-gruel. Man. 11, 125. **3.** Lac.—**Comp.** *Sa-*, adj., f. *vikâ*, painted with lac, Kir. 5, 40.

यावज्जीवम् *yavajjivam*, i.e. *yâvant-jîva* + *m*, adv. All one's life, Pañch. pr. d. 4.

यावतिथ *yâvatitha* (an old superl. of *yâvant*), adj. **1.** That which is as far as. **2.** In how many soever degrees advanced, Man. 1, 20.

यावदायुस् *yâvadâyus*, i.e. *yâvant*-*âyus*, adv. All one's life, Vikr. 87, 3.

यावन *yâvana*, i.e. *yavana* + *a*, I. adj. Relating to the Yavanas. II. n. Incense.

यावन्त् *yâvant*, i.e. *yad* + *vant*, I. adj., f. *vatî*, As much, as many, Hit. iv. d. 69 ; how much, Râjat. 5, 110 ; how many, Bhâg. P, 4, 25, 12. II. *vat*, acc. sing. n. adv. 1. As much as, as far as, Johns. Sel. 33, 66. 2. As many as. 3. As long as, Pańch. iii. d. 94 ; with preceding acc. of a word signifying a division of time, During ; e.g. *sakalâm̃ râtrim̃ yâvat*, During the whole night, Pańch. 117, 8 ; *varsham*, During a year, Pańch. ii. d. 66 ; with following *na*, Before, Vikr. 61, 10 ; Pańch. 61, 3. 4. Meanwhile, Çâk. 18, 22 ; Vikr. 3, 12. 5. As far as, unto, until, Râm. 3, 49, 13 ; with preceding acc., Hit. 111, 18 ; Pańch. 87, 20 ; cf. i. d. 132 ; even, 31, 17. 6. When, Hit. 85, 9 (with following *tâvat*, Then), Pańch. 48, 24 ; if, Pańch. 62, 1. 7. In order that, Vikr. d. 13 ; that, Chr. 18, 34. 8. With a verb it often expresses one's will ; e. g. *yâvat pratipâlayâmi*, I will wait, Vikr. 38, 5. 9. Often former part of comp. adverbs ; e.g. *yâvajjivam*, q. cf.

यावस *yâvasa*, i.e. *yavasa* + *a*, m. (n., Hit. iii. d. 53). 1. A heap of grass. 2. Provision, Hit. iii. d. 53.

याष्टीक *yâshṭîka*, i.e. *yashṭi* + *ka*, m. A warrior armed with a club.

यियक्षु *yiyakshu*, i.e. *yiyaksha*, desider. of *yaj*, + *u*, adj. Desirous of sacrificing, Ragh. 13, 3.

यियासु *yiyâsu*, i.e. *yiyâsa*, desider. of *yâ*, + *u*, adj. Wishing to go, Kir. 14, 32.

1. यु *YU*, ii. 2, Par., and ii. 9, *yunâ*, *yunî*, Par. Âtm. 1. To bind. 2. To join, to mix. 3. To separate (? cf. 2. *yu*). Ptcple of the pf. pass. *yuta*, 1. Joined, connected, Râm. 3, 52, 26. 2. United, Lass. 39, 19. 3. Attached to. 4. Endowed, full of, Nal. 12, 2 ; Chr. 13, 9 ; Hit. i. d. 152, M.M. (seized). Comp. *A*-, m. and n. a myriad, Man. 12, 113. *Go*-, 1. adj., f. *tâ*, full of cattle, Râm. 2, 49, 10. n. a cow-pen, MBh. 14, 1934.—With the prep. व्यति *vi-ati*, To mix, Bhaṭṭ. 8, 6.—With आ *â*, *âyuta*, Endowed, Nal. 12, 39.—With प्र *pra*, *prayuta*, Joined. n. A million.—With सम् *sam*, *sam̃yuta*, 1. Joined, mixed. 2. Heaped, Çâk. 69, 15. 3. Endowed, Sâv. 5, 33 ; Pańch. iii. d. 48. 4. Implying, Man. 2, 32. Comp. *Su*-, adj. well accompanied by, Lass. 50, 6.—Cf. Lat. juvare, jus (= ved. *yos*), jubere (Caus.) ; ζώννυμι (probably for ζωσνυμι), ζώνη, ζῶστρον.

2. यु *YU*, ii. 3, Par. To keep back. Caus., and i. 10, Âtm. † To despise. —With the prep. अप *apa*, ii. 3, To remove, Chr. 295, 11 = Rigv. i. 92, 11.

युक्तत्व *yukta* + *tva* (vb. *yuj*), n. Fitness, suitableness, Vedântas. in Chr. 214, 3.

युक्ति *yukti*, i.e. *yuj* + *ti*, f. 1. Union, connection. 2. Propriety, Pańch. iii. d. 163. 3. Suitable manner, Râjat. 5, 90. 4. Use, Pańch. 183, 22 ; Râjat. 5, 165. 5. Usage, traditionary law. 6. Inference, argument, Vedântas. in Chr. 211, 16 ; Hit. i. d. 96, M.M. 7. Probability, Yâjń. 2, 212. 8. Insertion of circumstances in written evidence, specification of place, time, etc. 9. Supplying an ellipsis.—Comp. *Sva*-, adj. self-harnessed, Chr. 289, 9 = Rigv. i. 50, 9.

युक्तितस् *yukti* + *tas*, adv. According to justice, Chr. 15. 8.

युग *yuga,* i.e. *yuj+a,* **I.** m. (in epic poetry also n., Chr. 34, 14), A yoke. **II.** n. **1.** A pair, a couple, Çiç. 9, 72 ; Nal. 14, 25. **2.** Age (ved.), Chr. 295, 11=Rigv. i. 92, 11. **3.** A lustre of five years. **4.** An age, a period, Man. 1, 71, sqq. ; one of the four Indian periods, called *Satya* (or *Kṛita*), *Treta, Dvâpara,* and *Kali,* Man. 1, 69.—Comp. *Ambara-,* n. upper and lower garments. *Kṛita-,* n. =*satya-yuga,* Man. 1, 85. *Go-,* a pair of oxen or beasts in general, Pańch. iii. d. 198 ; 182, 12. *Chatur-,* I. n. the aggregate of the four yugas, Man. 1, 71. II. adj. containing the four yugas, Ragh. 10, 23. *Tri-,* adj. appearing in three yugas, epithet of Kṛishṇa, Bhâg. P. 3, 24, 26. *Deva-* and *Dharma-,* n. the first age, MBh. 2, 421 ; Hariv. 761. *Pańcha(n)-,* n. the cycle of five years, MBh. 2, 455. *Mahâ-,* n. the aggregate of the four ages.—Cf. Lat. jugum ; Goth. juk ; A.S. ioc, iuc, geóc ; ζυγόν, ζυγός.

युगंधर *yugaṁdhara,* i.e. *yuga + m-dhṛi+a,* m. **1.** The pole of a carriage. **2.** The name of a mountain.

युगपद् *yuga-pad,* adv. **1.** At one time, Çiç. 9, 41. **2.** Together, Man. 1, 54.—Cf. perhaps A.S. geoc, rash, praeceps.

युगल *yuga+la,* n. A pair, Pańch. 184, 16.—Comp. *Kaṇṭha-niveçita-hasta-* (vb. *viç*), adj., f. *lâ,* with (both her) hands put to (her) neck, i.e. with her head leaning on her hands, Pańch. 226, 19. *Vastra-,* n. two garments, Pańch. 29, 16.

युगांशक *yugâṁçaka,* i.e. *guga-aṁ-ça+ka,* m. A year.

युग्म *yugma,* i.e. *yuj+ma,* **I.** adj., f. *mâ,* Even, Man. 3, 48. **II.** n. **1.** A pair, a couple, Utt. Râmach. 36, 4 (*-chârin,* du. Two going together). **2.** Mixing. **3.** Man. 8, 298, read *yugyam.*—Comp. *A-,* adj., f. *mâ,* odd, Man. 3, 48. *Vastra-,* n. two garments.

युग्मक *yugma+ka,* m. A couple, a pair, Lass. 16, 20.

युग्य *yugya,* i.e. *yuj+ya,* ptcple. of the fut. pass. of *yuj,* **I.** Fit to be yoked. **II.** m. A beast of burthen, Ragh. 5, 49. **III.** n. A carriage, Man. 8, 294.

† **युङ्ग्** *YUṄG,* i. 1, Par. To abandon.

युच्छ् *YUCHH* (akin to 2. *yu*), i. 1, Par. To be inattentive or negligent.

1. **युज्** *YUJ* (akin to 1. *yu*), ii. 7, *yunaj, yuńj,* Par. Âtm. i. 1, Par. **1.** To join, Chr. 290, 7=Rigv. i. 64, 7 (ved. *ayugdhvam,* ii. 2) ; MBh. 3, 2489. **2.** To connect, Draup. 4, 24. **3.** To endow, Râm. 1, 9, 68. **4.** To put to, Chr. 291, 4=Rigv. i. 85, 4 ; MBh. 1, 192. **5.** To direct, to throw, Chr. 41, 2 (anomal. *ayuńjam*). **6.** To fix one's mind in order to obtain union with the universal spirit, Bhâshâp. 64. **7.** To meditate, Bhâg. 6, 12. **8.** To appoint, MBh. 2, 1290. **9.** To employ, Man. 6, 12. Ptcple. of the pres. Âtm. *yuńjâna,* Suitable, MBh. 3, 15633. m. **1.** One who endeavours to obtain union with the universal soul, or one who is engaged in the religious exercise called *yoga,* Bhâshâp. 64. **2.** A charioteer. Pass., and i. 4, Âtm. (in epic poetry also with the terminations of the Par.). **1.** To be fit, becoming, Hit. iv. d. 11 ; Pańch. 61, 4 ; i. d. 283 (Par.). **2.** To be placed, Hit. iv. d. 76 (cf. Böhtl. Ind. Spr. 3265). **3.** To attach one's self to, Hit. iv. d. 65. **4.** To make one's self ready, Bhag. 2, 38. **5.** To unite one's self with, to attain, Man. 2, 78. **6.** To be obliged, Man. 7, 144. **7.** To meditate, Bhag. 2, 50. Ptcple. of the pf. pass. *yukta.* **1.** Joined.

2. Fit, Pańch. 69, 10. 3. Proved. 4. Endowed with, Hit. iv. d. 33 (*kâlena na*, Not endowed with, not seizing the right time; cf. Hit. iv. d. 47: *a-kâla-sainya-yukta*, Not possessed of an army at the right time). 5. Employed. 6. Occupied, Man. 3, 75. 7. Intent on, 8, 142. 8. Occupied in the performance of the Yoga. 9. A student, Man. 2, 223. 10. °*tam*, adv. Well, Vikr. 12, 6. 11. Comparat. *yuktatara*, One who is to the utmost on his guard, Man. 7, 186. m. The sage who has acquired union with the universal soul, Bhâshâp. 64. f. *tâ*, A plant, commonly Eláni. n. A measure of four cubits. **Comp.** *A-*, adj. 1. negligent, Râm. 3, 37, 7. 2. not used to, ib. 3, 37, 23. 3. unsuitable, Pańch. 170, 8. *Kshema-yukta+m*, adv. in a prosperous way, Râm. 1, 13, 10. *Tapas-*, adj. devout, Chr. 9, 41. *Vidhâna-*, adj. conformable to the sacred precepts, Chr. 51, 19. Ptcple. of the fut. pass. *yogya*. 1. Fit, Hit. ii. d. 73. 2. Suitable, Hit. i. d. 62, M.M. 3. Able, Râjat. 5, 249. 4. Clever. See s.v. **Comp.** *Artha-*, adj. profitable, Daçak. in Chr. 181, 6. Caus., and i. 10, Par. 1. To join, Hit. i. d. 53, M.M.; Râjat. 5, 104; to fix (a snare), Hit. 46, 9, M.M. 2. To achieve, Râjat. 5, 403. 3. To treat, Pańch. iv. d. 74. 4. To bring on, to instigate, Pańch. iv. d. 18. 5. To entangle, Pańch. ii. d. 125 (Âtm.). 6. To mix, Man. 7, 218. 7. To oblige, Chr. 18, 34. 8. To put to, Râm. 2, 82, 31. 9. To place, Hit. iii. d. 80. 10. To appoint, Râjat. 5, 129. 11. To throw, Chr. 33, 2. 12. To endow, Man. 1, 26; Vikr. d. 40. 13. To present with, to give, MBh. 1, 6477. 14. To return, Daçak. 185, 12. 15. Pass. To belong, MBh. 3, 12313. i. 10, Âtm. † To despise.—With the prep. अनु *anu*, ii. 7, Âtm. 1. To examine, Man. 8, 31. 2. To order, MBh. 4, 105. 3. To choose a husband, MBh. 3, 15633.—With अभि *abhi*, Âtm. 1. To prepare for, Daçak. in Chr. 190, 2. 2. To draw near, to attack, 200, 23. Pass. 1. To be accused, Man. 8, 183; to be asked (in lawsuit), Vikr. d. 96. 2. To be rebuked, Man. 8, 50. *abhiyukta*, 1. Diligent, Vedântas. in Chr. 217, 4; ever striving, Utt. Râmach. 73, 8. 2. Absorbed in meditation, Pańch. i. d. 345. 3. Attacked, assailed, Hit. iv. d. 24. 4. Hurt, Râm. 2, 10, 27. 5. Accused, prosecuted. Caus. To appoint, Pańch. 163, 15. — With आ *â*, Âtm. To put, MBh. 1, 7948. *âyukta*, m. Commissioned, an agent, a deputy, Bhaṭṭ. 8, 115.—With समुपा *sam-upa-â*, *samupâyukta*, Surrounded, MBh. 3, 10099. — With समा *sam-â*, *samâyukta*, 1. Connected, Man. 12, 28; united, Nal. 25, 8. 2. Surrounded, MBh. 3, 3017. 3. Gifted, endowed, Pańch. iii. d. 117; Hit. i. d. 174, M.M. Caus. To join, MBh. 1, 7200 (to string).—With उद् *ud*, *udyukta*, 1. Excited, Râm. 1, 1, 45. 2. Zealously active, Hit. iii. d. 112; Râjat. 5, 331. 3. Extended, Lass. 67, 1. Caus. To excite, to make ready, MBh. 5, 70.—With समुद् *sam-ud*, Caus. To order to act, Mâlav. 9, 16.—With उप *upa*, Âtm. 1. To meddle, MBh. 5, 992. 2. To employ for one's self, Man. 8, 40. 3. To enjoy, Megh. 13. 2. To consume, MBh. 3, 57. 4. To attach one's self to, MBh. 3, 15633. Pass. 1. To be suitable, Pańch. 155, 8; to be of use, Böhtl. Ind. Spr. 1915; to be necessary, Pańch. i. d. 372; *an-upayujyamâna*, Unable to be employed, quite weak, Utt. Râmach. 95, 1. 2. To employ for one's self, MBh. 3, 12739. 3. To be worth being regarded, Pańch. i. d. 37.

upayukta, **1.** Suitable, Hit. 98, 14 (*kim upayukto 'yam etad vartanam̃ grihṇâty athânupayukto vâ*, Whether he deserves so large a pay or not; literally, whether he receives so large a pay as a suitable person, or as an unsuitable). **2.** Touched by. **3.** Taken. **4.** Eaten. Comp. *An-*, adj. unworthy, Çâk. 97, 3. —With समुप *sam-upa*, To consume, MBh. 3, 1538.—With नि *ni*, Âtm. **1.** To place; to put to (as horses), Vikr. d. 155; to place at the head, Hit. iii. d. 128; to engage, Johns. Sel. 37, 19; to appoint, Man. 1, 28; Pańch. i. d. 82. **2.** To constrain, Chr. 10, 3; to coerce, Râm. 1, 1, 92; to harass, Man. 8, 186. **3.** To order, Râm. 1, 54, 16. **4.** To commit, Man. 9, 64. *niyukta*, **1.** Connected, Hit. i. d. 158, M.M. **2.** Fastened, Râm. 1, 13, 31. **3.** Placed, Hit. 81, 13. **4.** Ascertained. **5.** Engaged in. **6.** Commanded, Râm. 1, 14, 34. **7.** Appointed, Hit. 58, 17. **8.** Authorised, Man. 9, 58. **9.** Offered, Man. 5, 16. m. A functionary, Hit. ii. d. 105. Ptcple. of the fut. pass. *niyojya*. **1.** To be placed, Pańch. i. d. 82. **2.** To be ordered, MBh. 12, 12358. m. A servant, Çâk. d. 163. Comp. *A-niyogya*, and *a-niyojya*, adj. not suitable to be commanded, Râm. 2, 66, 7; MBh. 1. 3267. Caus. **1.** To order to be put, Hit. 46, 13. **2.** To fasten, Pańch. 135, 4; to bring (*sam̃dehe*, in danger), Pańch. 8, 21; to accustom, 31, 6. **3.** To endow, Pańch. 4, 25. **4.** To employ, Man. 9, 324; Pańch. i. d. 413; pass. To employ one's self, Pańch. v. d. 68. **5.** To appoint, to charge, Râm. 1, 38, 10. **6.** To direct, Man. 9, 68; to order, to refer (to an ordeal), Pańch. 97, 1. **7.** To coerce, Bhag. 3, 36. **8.** To offer, Pańch. 70, 3. **9.** To present with, Pańch. 4, 25. **10.** To perform, Man. 3, 204; to make, Pańch. 24, 5.—With विनि *vi-ni*, **1.** To appoint, to charge, MBh. 1, 4152. **2.** To use, Utt. Râmach. 148, 10; Lass. 95, 9. *viniyukta*, **1.** Separated, detached, loosed, Johns. Sel. 31, 46. **2.** Parted with. **3.** Appointed. **4.** Applied to. Caus. **1.** To appoint, Hit. iii. d. 54. **2.** To intrust, Man. 7, 226. —With संनि *sam-ni*, To appoint, MBh. 1, 2500. *sam̃niyukta*, **1.** Appointed. **2.** Attached to. Caus. **1.** To appoint, MBh. 1, 6912. **2.** To allot, Pańch. ii. d. 78.—With विनिस् *vi-nis*, To throw, Râm. 2, 23, 37.—With प्र *pra*, **1.** To put to, Chr. 291, 5 = Rigv. i. 85, 5. **2.** To put at the head, Bhaṭṭ. 3, 51. **3.** To join, Râm. 1, 17, 11. **4.** To employ, Man. 2, 159; Pańch. i. d. 39. **5.** To direct, Chr. 287, 4 = Rigv. i. 48, 4. **6.** To conduct, Mâlav. 45, 9. **7.** To throw, Chr. 31, 11. **8.** To give, Râm. 1, 13, 38. **9.** To lend, Man. 8, 146. **10.** To perform, Man. 2, 248. **11.** To represent, Mâlav. 3, 10. **12.** To behove, to be convenient (i. 4, Âtm., or Pass.), Pańch. 224, 24. *prayukta*, **1.** Connected with, Râm. 1, 17, 14. **2.** Closely united. **3.** Suitable, MBh. 1, 6845. **4.** Endowed with. **5.** Resulting from, Hit. ii. d. 59. **6.** Appointed, Râm. 3, 51, 27. **7.** Governed, Lass. 53, 10. **8.** Lent, Man. 8, 49. **9.** Done, Çâk. 95, 13. **10.** Lost in meditation. n. Cause. Comp. *Su-*, 1. closely connected. 2. well managed. Caus. **1.** To throw, Chr. 31, 7. **2.** To cause to be exhibited, Utt. Râmach. 111, 7. **3.** To show, Man. 3, 112. **4.** To receive, Man. 10, 117. Ptcple. of the fut. pass. *prayojya*. **1.** To be set to work. **2.** To be used. m. A servant. n. Capital, principal.—With विप्र *vi-pra*, **1.** To separate, Râm. 2, 53, 20. **2.** To deprive, MBh. 1, 6735.—With संप्र *sam-pra*, To connect, MBh. 1, 4475. *sam̃prayukta*, **1.** Joined. **2.** Connected with, holding any intercourse with, Man. 11, 179. **3.** Overtaken, reached. Caus. To connect, MBh. 3, 1153.—With वि *vi*, Âtm. **1.** To separate, MBh. 3, 10924. **2.** To abandon, Chr. 47, 35 (Par., perhaps it is to be changed to *mokshyasi*). Pass. To be deprived, Pańch. i. d. 340; to lose, Man. 7, 46; to violate, 5, 91. *a-viyukta*, adj. Not separated, Vikr. 78, 20. *a-viyojya*, Not to be deprived, Daçak. in Chr. 196, 12. Caus. To cause to leave, to break off from, Pańch. 31, 6. **2.** To deprive, Pańch. 30, 10; MBh. 3, 2851; to rob, 1, 6225.—With सम् *sam*, **1.** To unite, Man. 9, 22. **2.** To endow, MBh. 1, 6289; to endow with, Râm. 1, 1, 21. *saṁyukta*, **1.** Connected, Chr. 59, 22. **2.** Attached. **3.** Accompanied. **4.** Mixed. **5.** Endowed with, Man. 1, 109. Caus. **1.** To join, MBh. 3, 11762. **2.** To endow with, MBh. 1, 6474; Pańch. 244, 5; to present with, Pańch. 30, 12. **3.** To employ, MBh. 3, 816. **4.** Âtm. To meditate, Chr. 38, 13.—With विसम् *vi-sam*, *visaṁyukta*, Separated from, neglecting, Man. 2, 80.—Cf. Lat. jungere; ζεύγνυμι; A.S. geocan, geóce, help.—Cf. *yuga*.

2. युज् *yuj*, **I.** adj. Even, Man. 3, 277. **II.** m. **1.** A joiner. **2.** One who devotes his time to abstract speculation. **III.** (n.), A pair. **IV.** Latter part of comp. adj. Joined, which are (horses) put to, drawn by, Chr. 27, 7. *chatur-*, adj. Drawn by four horses, MBh. 1, 8005. *hari-*, adj. Drawn by (Indra's) horses, Arj. 4, 32.—Cf. Lat. -jux in conjux.

† युत् *YUT* (cf. *dyut*), i. 1, Âtm. To shine.

युतक *yuta + ka* (vb. *yu*), n. **1.** A pair. **2.** Alliance. **3.** Nuptial presents. **4.** A garment worn by women. **5.** The ends of a cloth. **6.** The edge of a winnowing basket. **7.** Doubt.

युद्धकारित्व *yuddhakâritva*, i.e. *yuddha-kârin + tva* (vb. *yudh*), n. Fighting, Hit. iii. d. 86.

युद्धमय *yuddha + maya* (see *yudh*), adj. Warlike, martial, Chr. 24, 41.

1. युध् *YUDH* (akin to 1. *yu*), i. 4, Âtm. (also Par., MBh. 1, 7119). **1.** To fight, to contend in battle, Man. 7, 89; impersonal pass., Hit. iii. d. 88. **2.** To oppose, Johns. Sel. 55, 145. *yuddha*, n. **1.** The use of arms, Man. 3, 162. **2.** War, battle, Pańch. 87, 15. **Comp.** *A-*, n. 1. absence of war, Chr, 56, 14 (instr. without war). 2. not fighting, Hit. ii. d. 160. *Kûṭa-*, I. n. 1. a fraudulent manner of fighting, Ragh. 17, 69. II. adj. fighting fraudulently, Râm. 1, 22, 7. *Dvandva-*, n. single combat, MBh. 7, 582. Comp. ptcple. of the fut. pass. *A-yodhya*, I. adj., f. *yâ*, not to be warred against, Râm. 6, 112, 47. II. f. *yâ*, the capital of Râma, the modern Oude, Râm. 1, 5, 1, sqq. Desider. *yuyutsa*, To desire to fight, MBh. 4, 1252. Caus. **1.** To cause to fight, Man. 7, 193. **2.** To defend, MBh. 3, 639. **3.** To oppose, MBh. 2, 2120; to be a match for, Man. 7, 74; Hit. iii. d. 50.—With the prep. आ *â*, To oppose, MBh. 3, 15645. Caus. **1.** The same, 3, 15054. **2.** To fight with, Utt. Râmach. 130, 5.—With प्रा *pra-â*, To fight, Çiç. 18, 32.—With नि *ni*, *niyuddha*, n. Fighting, particularly boxing, MBh. 1, 5340.—With प्र *pra*, *prayuddha*, n. War, battle. Desider. To desire to fight, MBh. 3, 15646.—With प्रति *prati*, To oppose, MBh. 1, 7103. Caus. The same, 1, 7116.—With सम् *sam*, The same, 1, 5477.

Caus. The same, 1, 7098.—Cf. ὑσμίνη, ὑσμίν (cf. *yudhma*).

2. युध् *yudh*, I. f. War, battle, Pańch. iii. d. 11. II. m. A warrior, Johns. Sel. 57, 165.

युधान *yudhâna* (ptcple. pres. of *yudh*, ii. 2), m. An enemy.

युधिश्रेष्ठ *yudh*+*i-çreshṭha*, adj. Pre-eminent in battle, Chr. 49, 1.

युधिष्ठिर *yudhishṭhira*, i.e. *yudh*+*i-sthira*, m. The elder of the five Pâṇḍavas, Pańch. ii. d. 4.

युध्म *yudh*+*ma*, m. 1. War, battle. 2. A bow. 3. An arrow. 4. A warrior.

ऽयुध्वन् i.e. *-yudh* + *van* in *saha-*, I. adj. Fighting with, or along with. II. m. A brother in arms.

युन्थ् *YUNTH*, v.r. of *punth*.

युप् *YUP*, i. 4, Par. To confuse, to trouble.

युयु *yuyu* (probably vb. *jû*), m. A horse.

युयुत्सा *yuyutsâ*, i.e. *yuyutsa*, desider. of *yudh*, + *a*, f. Eager desire for the combat, Chr. 24, 50.

युयुत्सु *yuyutsu*, i.e. *yuyutsa*, desider. of *yudh*, +*u*, I. adj. Eager for combat, Johns. Sel. 56, 150; pugnacious, Chr. 63, 66. II. A proper name, Johns. Sel. 24, 6.

युयुधि *yuyudh*+*i* (red. *yudh*), adj. Pugnacious, Chr. 292, 8=Rigv. i. 85, 8.

युवति *yuvati*, see *yuvan*.

युवन् *yuvan* (for *yavan*, cf. comparat. *yavîyaṁs*, *u* by the influence of *v*), I. adj., f. *vatî* and *yûnî*, comparat. *yavîyaṁs*, superl. *yavishṭha*, Young, Chr. 293, 4=Rigv. i. 87, 4. II. m. A young man, Ṛit. 6, 20. III. f. *vatî* or *yûnî*, A young woman, Bhartṛ. 2, 60; Pańch. 158. 3; Sâv. 2, 24.—Comp. *Vâra-yuvati*, f. a courtesan, Daçak. in Chr. 179, 14. *Sura-yuvati*, f. a celestial woman, Megh. 62.—Cf. juvenis, junior, Junius, junix, etc.; Goth. juggs; A.S. iong, iung, geong, geogudh.

युष्मद् *yushmad*, pronoun of the second person, Thou; the bases of the cases are *tva*, *tu*, *yuva*, *yu*, *yushma*, i.e. *yu*+*sma*, and *ta*, *va*. Ved. nom. du. *yuvam*, Chr. 295, 17=Rigv. i. 92, 17; gen., abl. *yuvos*, 296, 2=Rigv. i. 112, 2.—Cf. Lat. tu, te, vos; τούν, τύ, σύ, τέ, σέ, σφῶι, ὔμμες; Goth. thu, jus, izvis; A.S. thu, gyt, eow.

युष्मादृश् *yushmâdṛiç*, i.e. *yushmad-dṛiç*, adj. Like you, Lass. 76, 4.

यू *yû*, f. Pease soup (cf. *yûsha*).

यूक *yûka*, m., and f. *kâ*, A louse, Man. 1, 40; Pańch. iii. d. 105.

यूति *yûti*, i.e. *yu*+*ti*, f. Mixing.

यूथ *yûtha*, i.e. *yu*+*tha*, I. n. A multitude of birds or beasts, a herd, Vikr. d. 110; Pańch. 93, 1. II. f. *thî*, A kind of jasmine, Jasminum auriculatum.—Comp. *Niryûtha*, i.e. *nis-*, adj. separated from the herd, Râm. 3, 68, 27.

यूथप *yûtha-pa* (vb. 2. *pâ*), m. The leader of a herd, Pańch. 253, 16; Lass. 46, 4.

यूथशस् *yûtha*+*ças*, adv. In flocks, gregariously, Nal. 12, 9.

यूथिका *yûthikâ*, i.e. *yuthî* (see *yûtha*), +*ka*, f. A kind of jasmine, Vikr. d. 109; Ṛit. 2, 25.

यूप *yûpa*, I. m. and n. A sacrificial post, MBh. 7, 2266. II. m. A trophy.

† यूष् *YÛSH*, i. 1, Par. To hurt.

यूष *yûsha*, m. and n. Pease soup,

the water in which pulse of various kinds has been boiled.—Cf. Lat. jus; probably also ζωμός, ζύθος.

येष् *YESH*, see *pesh*.

योक्त्र *yoktra*, i.e. *yuj* + *tra*, n. The tie of the yoke of a plough; a halter, Man. 8, 292.

योक्त्राय *YOKTRAYA*, a denomin. derived from *yoktra*, To enclose, Hid. 4, 56.

योग *yoga*, i.e. *yuj* + *a*, m. **1.** Junction, Bhâshâp, 56; joining, union, Vikr. d. 23. **2.** Putting to (horses), Chr. 4, 17. **3.** Putting on armour. **4.** Armour. **5.** Connexion, Hit. i. d. 98, M.M. (*kathâ-*, Conversation). **6.** Result, Hit. iii. d. 140 (*puṇya-*, of merit), Man. 1, 41 (*tapas-*, force of devotion). **7.** Use, performance, Kir. 5, 52. **8.** Propriety, aptness, Utt. Râmach. 35, 13. **9.** Mode, Man. 9, 330; Nal. 15, 6. **10.** A rule, a precept. **11.** A means, an expedient, Brâhmaṇav. 1, 19; Hit. i. d. 201, M.M. (*a-daṇḍa-*, Except by means of punishment: *niyata-vishaya -vartî prâyaço 'daṇḍa-yogâj jagati para-vaçe 'smin durlabhaḥ sâdhu-vrittaḥ*, He who keeps in his appointed sphere (does so) generally by reason of punishment. In this dependent world it is hard to find one who acts of himself virtuously. **12.** A conveyance, a carriage. **13.** Fraud, Man. 8, 165. **14.** Wealth. **15.** Thing. **16.** Lucky conjuncture, Vikr. 38, 12. **17.** Religious and abstract meditation (properly union, viz. with the universal soul), Pańch. 165, 9. **18.** A system of philosophy, Bhag. 2, 39. **19.** The particular practice of devotion, by which union with God is supposed to be obtained. **20.** Magic, or the acquisition of supernatural powers; magical art, Böhtl. Ind. Spr. 1212. **21.** Death-like state of meditation, Kathâs. 4, 111. **22.** A spy. **23.** A violator of truth or confidence. **24.** The leading or principal star of a lunar mansion.—Comp. *A-*, m. unfitness, unsuitableness, impossibility, Vedântas. in Chr. 210, 23. *Ati-*, m. excess, Suçr. 2, 192, 8. *Artha-*, m. Concurrence of circumstances (as of cause and effect), Hit. ii. p. 2, 13, M.M. *Kathâ-*, m. conversation, MBh. 14, 377. *Karma(n)-*, m. business, Man. 10, 115. *Kâla-*, m. destiny, MBh. 3, 9919. *Krama-*, m. order, Man. 1, 42; regular succession, 2, 64. *Chûrṇa-*, m. a mixture of fragrant powders, MBh. 12, 2163. *Daṇḍa-*, m. punishment; cf. Hit. i. d. 201, M.M. (supra, s. **10.**). *Duryoga*, i.e. *dus-*, m. 1. wickedness, Utt. Râmach. 147, 14. 2. fraud, MBh. 1, 1316. *Daiva-*, m. contingency, fate, Pańch. i. d. 197. *Dhyâna-*, m. meditation, Man. 6, 73; 79. *Nakshatra-*, m. the moon's conjunction with the lunar mansions, MBh. 5, 1905. *Nidrâ-*, m. sleep-like absorption in meditation, Hariv. 2217. *Pûrṇa-* (vb. *prî*), m. a sort of fighting, MBh. 2, 910. *Bhakti-*, m. devotion, as shown by implicit faith in any divinity. *Yathâ-yoga* + *m*, adv. in due order, Man. 5, 92. *Vâsa-*, m. fragrant powder sprinkled on the cloth. *Vidhi-*, m. 1. combination for any act or rite. 2. the occurrence of predestined events, fate, Hit. i. d. 20, M.M. *Sâra-*, m. possession or application of the essence of any thing, Kir. 5, 52. *Strî-dharma-*, m. the laws concerning women, Man. 1, 114. *Sthâna-*, m. 1. assignment of suitable places. 2. the best mode of preserving articles, Man. 9, 332.

योगक्षेमकर *yoga-kshema-kara*, adj., f. *rî*, Maintaining and protecting.

योगज *yoga-ja*, adj. Produced by religious and abstract meditation, Bhâshâp. 62.

योगतस् *yoga* + *tas*, adv. **1.** Conjointly. **2.** Suitably. **3.** Conformably to the law, Man. 6, 9. **4.** Seasonably. **5.** Through religious austerities, devotion, Man. 2, 100.

योगस् *yogas,* i.e. *yuj + as,* n. **1.** Meditation, religious abstraction. **2.** The half of a lunar month.

योगिता *yogitâ,* i.e. *yogin + tâ,* f. Connection, Bhâshâp. 23.

योगिन् *yogin,* i.e. *yoga + in,* I. adj., f. *nî.* **1.** Being united, or endowed with, Bhâshâp. 27. **2.** Who or what joins. **3.** Possessed of superhuman power. II. m. **1.** A performer of the religious meditation called Yoga, Bhag. 6, 10. **2.** An ascetic, Pańch. i. d. 333. **3.** One who has acquired supernatural power, Hit. ii. d. 26. **4.** A magician, Pańch. 240, 12; Lass. 4, 9. III. f. *nî,* A female fiend.—**Comp.** *Kâla-,* i.e. *kâla-yoga + in,* m. a name of Çiva, MBh. 13, 1162. *Ku-,* m. a wicked Yogin, Bhâg. P. 1, 6, 22. *Nakshatra-,* adj. sbst. being connected with the lunar mansions, MBh. 1, 2581; its principal stars.

योग्य *yogya,* I. See *yuj.* II. n. **1.** A vehicle. **2.** A cake. **3.** A drug, commonly Riddhi. **4.** Sandal. III. f. *yâ,* Military exercise.—**Comp.** *Krita-,* adj. fighting perfectly, Johns. Sel. 12, 38.

योग्यता *yogya + tâ,* f., and **योग्यत्व** *yogya + tva,* n. Fitness, Pańch. 241, 6; Vedântas. in Chr. 207, 22 (*tva*); suitableness, consistency, Bhâshâp. 81 (*tâ*).

योजन *yojana,* i.e. *yuj + ana,* n. **1.** Joining. **2.** A means for inducing (the gods) to yoke (their horses and to come), Chr. 294, 5 = Rigv. i. 88, 5. **3.** A line, row, Chr. 294, 3 = Rigv. i. 92, 3. **4.** The Supreme Being. **5.** A measure of distance of about five or nine miles, Pańch. 226, 9.—**Comp.** *Â-yojana + m,* adv. the length of a Yojana, Johns. Sel. 41, 41. *Vâṇa-* n. a quiver, Pańch. MS. Berol. 139, 6. *Saptayojanî,* i.e. *saptan-yojana + î,* f. an extent of seven Yojanas, Râjat. 5, 103.

योजयितृ *yojayitṛi,* i.e. *yuj,* Caus., + *tṛi,* m., f. *trî,* n. **1.** Who or what joins. **2.** One who enchases, Hit. ii. d. 71.

योत्र *yotra,* i.e. *yu + tra,* n. = *yoktra.*

योद्धृ *yoddhṛi,* i.e. *yudh + tṛi,* m. A warrior, Pańch. 218, 7.

योध *yodha,* i.e. *yudh + a,* m. A warrior, Man. 7, 97.—**Comp.** *Vasanta-,* m. the god of love, Ṛit. 6, 1. *Hata-sarva-,* adj. with all the warriors killed.

योधिन् *yodhin,* i.e. *yudh + in,* adj. sbst. Fighting, Hit. iv. d. 48 (*kâla-,* at the right time); a warrior.—**Comp.** *Agra-,* m. a champion, Râm. 4, 21, 12. *Kûṭa-,* adj. fighting fraudulently, Râm. 6, 21, 21. *Gaja-,* adj. fighting mounted on an elephant, Chr. 4, 18. *Dvandva-,* adj. fighting in single combat, or by pairs, Bhâg. P. 8, 10, 26.

योनि *yoni,* i.e. *yu + ni,* m. f., and *nî,* f. **1.** The vulva, Suçr. 2, 397, 10; the womb, Pańch. 188, 5; 6. **2.** Place of birth, Hit. iv. d. 68. **3.** Origin, Man. 2, 25. **4.** A mine. **5.** Water.—**Comp.** *A-,* I. f. any but the natural part (the vulva), Man. 11, 173. II. adj. without beginning, Kumâras. 2, 9. *Antya-,* adj. of lowest birth, or race, Man. 8, 68. *Ambhoja-,* m. Brahman, Prab. 24, 1. *Eka-,* adj. of the same caste, Man. 9, 148. *Kumbha-,* m. epithet of Agastya, Ragh. 4, 21. *Chitta-,* m. love. *Jagat-,* m. a name of Çiva, MBh. 7, 9506. *Jîva-,* adj. containing life, Bhâg. P. 3, 9, 19. *Tiryagyoni,* i.e. *tiryańch-,* f. the womb of a brute animal, Man. 4, 200. *Dury°,* i.e. *dus-,* adj. of debased birth, Man. 10, 59. *Deva-,* adj. of divine origin, Dev.

5, 60. *Padma-*, m. epithet of Brahman, MBh. 7, 9427. *Pâpa-*, m. wicked, or low, birth, Man. 4, 166. *Purâ-*, adj. of old lineage, MBh. 3, 12705. *Vi-yonî*, f. the womb of beasts, Man. 12, 77. *Vi-hîna-* (vb. *hâ*), adj. base-born, brutish. *Çaila-sutâ-charaṇa-râga-*, adj. produced by the colour of the feet of Pârvatî, Vikr. d. 128. *Saṁkalpa-*, m. Kâmadeva. *Sva-*, I. adj. related by kin, Man. 2, 134; 206. II. f. 1. a sister, Man. 11, 170. 2. a near female relative.

योनितस् *yoni + tas*, adv. By blood, Man. 2, 129.

योषणा *yoshaṇâ*, i.e. *jush + an + a*, f. A woman, Lass. 99, 8=Rigv. iii. 62, 8.

योषा *yoshâ*, i.e. *jush + a*, f. A woman, Chr. 287, 5=Rigv. i. 48, 5; Chr. 295, 11=Rigv. i. 92, 11.—**Comp.** *Garbha-*, f. a pregnant woman, MBh. 13, 1846 (figurat.). *Deva-*, f. the wife of a god, MBh. 9, 2714.

योषित् *yoshit*, i.e. *jush + it* (for *joshant*, ptcple. pres.), f. A woman, Vikr. d. 40.—**Comp.** *Kula-*, f. a virtuous woman, Man. 3, 245. *Paṇya-*, and *Vâra-*, f. a harlot, Man. 9, 259 (*paṇya-*); Daçak. in Chr. 189, 4 (*vâra-*).

योषिता *yoshit + â*, f. A woman.

यौक्तिक *yauktika*, i.e. *yukti + ika*, I. adj. 1. Connective. 2. Deducible. 3. Usual. 4. Proper, right. II. m. An associate of one's amusements.

यौगक *yaugaka*, i.e. *yoga + ka*, adj. Relating to the religious practice called *yoga* (see s. v. *yoga*, 19.).]

यौगंधरायण *yaugaṁdharâyaṇa*, i.e. *yugaṁdhara + âyana*, m. A proper name, Kathâs. 15, 61.

यौगपद्य *gaugapadya*, i.e. *yugapad + ya*, n. Simultaneousness, Draup. 1, 4 [(at once).—**Comp.** *A-*, r. non-simultaneousness, Bhâshâp. 84.

यौगिक *yaugika*, i.e. *yoga + ika*, adj. 1. Usual. 2. Proper. 3. Relating to the religious practice called *yoga* (see s. v. *yoga*, 19.).

† **यौट्** *YAUṬ*, **यौड्** *YAUḌ*, i. 1, Par. To join (i.e. *jos-dhâ*, see *yu*, and cf. Zend. *yaozhdâ* and supra *mṛiḍ*).

यौतक *yautaka*, i.e. *yutaka + a*, n. 1. Appropriating, Man. 9, 214. 2. Property, Man. 9, 131 (a nuptial gift, presents made to a bride by her father or friends.).

यौधिष्ठिर *yaudhishṭhira*, i. e. *yudhishṭhira + a*, adj. Belonging to Yudhishṭhira, Johns. Sel. 96, 77.

यौन *yauna*, i.e. *yoni + a*, I. adj. 1. Relating to the womb, uterine. 2. Connubial, Man. 3, 157; 2, 40. II. (n.), Contracting affinity, Man, 11, 180.

यौवन *yauvana*, i.e. *yuvan + a*, I. adj. Juvenile, Châṇ. 49 in Berl. Monatsb. 1864, 410. II. n. 1. Youth, Vikr. d. 26; Pańch. 128, 2; manhood. 2. The age of marriageableness, Chr. 51, 4. 3. An assemblage of young women.—**Comp.** *Sthira-*, adj., f. *nâ*, possessed of eternal youth, Vikr. d. 109.

यौवनवन्त् *yauvana + vant*, adj., f. *vatî*, I. Youthful, Hit. 63, 2, M.M. II. and **यौवनस्थ** *yauvana-stha*, f. *thâ*, Marriageable, Lass. 23, 15; Pańch. 183, 25.

यौवराज्य *yauvarâjya*, i.e. *yuvan-râja + ya*, n. The dignity of an heir apparent, Daçak. in Chr. 197, 15; Vikr. d. 161.

यौष्माक *yaushmâka*, and **यौष्माकीन** *yaushmâkina*, i.e. *yushmad + ka + a*, or *îna*, adj. Yours.

र *R.*

1. रंह् *RAṀH* (akin to *laṅgh*, q. cf.), i. 1, Par. and † i. 10, Par. To go, to move, with speed. Caus. To impel to speed, Chr. 291, 5=Rigv. i. 85, 5.—Cf. perhaps τρέχω; Goth. thragjan; in this case the Sskr. word has dropped the initial.

2. † रंह् *RAṀH*, वंह् *VAṀH*, i. 10, Par. To speak, to shine.

रंहस् 1. *raṁh+as*, n. Speed, velocity, Ragh. 2, 34 (Calc.).—Comp. *Ati-*, adj. of excessive velocity, Çâk. d. 5. *Vâta-*, adj. swift as the wind, Indr. 1, 7.

† रक् *RAK*, लक् *LAK*, रग् *RAG*, लग् *LAG*, रघ् *RAGH*, i. 10, Par. **1.** To taste. **2.** To obtain.

रक्क *rakka*, m. A proper name, Râjat. 5, 423.

रक्तक *rakta+ka* (see *rañj*), m. **1.** Red garments, or cloth. **2.** A man affected with fondness or passion. **3.** A player. **4.** The name of several plants.

रक्तप *rakta-pa* (1. *pâ*, cf. *rañj.*), I. adj. Who or what drinks blood. II. m. A Râkshasa, or demon. III. f. *pâ*. **1.** A leech. **2.** A female fiend.

रक्तपायिन् *rakta-pâyin* (vb. *rañj.*), I. m. A bug. II. f. *nî*, A leech.

रक्तफेनज *rakta-phena-ja*, m. A part of the body, apparently intending the lungs.

रक्ष् *RAKSH* (perhaps a desider. of *rañj*, without reduplication), i. 1, Par. (in epic poetry also Âtm., MBh. 3, 8886). **1.** To preserve, Man. 7, 213; Pañch. i. d. 402 (Âtm.). **2.** To spare, Pañch. iii. d. 253. **3.** To guard, to keep, Vikr. 18, 6; Hit. i. d. 194, M.M. (with gen. in the sense of a dat.); to protect from (abl.), MBh. 3, 8762. **4.** To tend, to keep, Man. 9, 328. **5.** To govern, Man. 7, 36. Comp. ptcple. of the pf. pass. *su-rakshita*, Well guarded, Nal. 3, 10. *dharma-rakshitâ*, f. A proper name, Daçak. in Chr. 191, 14. Comp. ptcple. of the fut. pass. *dûrakshya*, i.e. *dus-*, adj. Difficult to be guarded, Mṛichchh. 65, 17. Caus. To protect, Pañch. 70, 13.—With the prep. अभि *abhi*, **1.** To assist, Bhag. 1, 10. **2.** To defend, to protect, MBh. 4, 161; Pañch. i. d. 395. **3.** To guard, MBh. 1, 5616. **4.** To command, Bhag. 1, 10. *abhirakshita*, Cultivated, Pañch. i. d. 254.—With आ *â*, comp. ptcple. of the fut. pass. *dus-â-rakshya+tama*, Most difficult to be protected, Râm. 2, 52, 66.—With परि *pari*, **1.** To preserve, MBh. 1, 6195. **2.** To protect, Pañch. 215, 7; MBh. 3, 14366. **3.** To restrain, Man. 9. 10. **4.** To govern, Man. 7, 142. **5.** To keep, Râm. 2, 96, 38. **6.** To conceal, MBh. 3, 14717.—With प्र *pra*, To save, Pañch. v. d. 89.—With सम् *sam*, **1.** To protect, Man. 7, 135; Pañch. iii. d. 9. **2.** To keep off, Râm. 1, 32, 2.—Cf. probably ἀρκέω, ἀλκτήρ ἀλαλκτήρ (frequent.), ἄλξις, ἀλέξω; Lat. arx; Goth. ga-rehsns.

रक्ष *raksh+a*, I. m. One who guards, Lass. 34, 8. II. m., and f. *kshâ*. **1.** Preserving, guarding, Pañch. 184, 8; protecting, protection, Pañch. 157, 7. **2.** (i.e. *rañj+ta*, cf. *raktâ*, s.v. *rañj*), Lac. III. f. *kshâ*. **1.** Ashes. **2.** A sort of bracelet, an amulet, Çâk. 105, 12 (Prakṛ.).—Comp. *Kshetra-*, m. a field-guard, Pañch. 248, 12. *Go-*, I. m. a cowherd. II. n. keeping cattle, MBh. 2, 525. *Chakra-*, m. two men who take care of the wheels of a chariot, MBh. 1, 5467. *Nagara-*, f. government of a town, Mṛichchh. 148, 5. *Pura-*, m. the watchman of a town, Daçak. 26, 1. *Senâ-*, m. a guard, a sentinel.

रक्षक *raksh + aka*, I. adj. Who or what protects, who tends, Man. 8, 102. II. m. A protector, a guardian, Hit. 91, 1, M.M.—Comp. *A-*, adj. imprudent, Pañch. 129, 5. *Aṅga-*, m. a life-guard, Pañch. 156, 22. *Go-*, adj. keeping cattle, Man. 8, 102. *Bhûmi-*, m. a swift horse. *Çasya-*, m. a watchman over a field of corn, Hit. 81, 15.

रक्षण *rakshaṇa*, i.e. *raksh + ana*, n. Preserving, protecting, Hit. 114, 7; Pañch. iv. d. 29.

रक्षपाल *raksha-pâla*, m. One who guards, Pañch. 217, 4; 232, 2; probably it is to be changed to *rakshâpâla*, cf. *rakshâpurusha*, Pañch. 229, 6, the same.

रक्षस् *raksh + as* (perhaps a kind of euphemism, cf. Εὐμενίδες, denoting the Ἐριννύες), n. A Râkshasa, or evil spirit, Vikr. 54, 5.

रक्षिक *rakshika*, i. e. *raksha + ika* (adj. or m. ?), A watchman, a policeman, Daçak. in Chr. 188, 18; 199, 24.

रक्षितृ *raksh + itṛi*, m. One who protects, Pañch. i. d. 391; a protector, a guard, Utt. Râmach. 39, 11.—Comp. *A-*, m. one who does not protect, Pañch. iii. d. 72.

रक्षिन् *raksh + in*, adj., f. *iṇî*, I. adj. Who or what guards, Vikr. d. 5. II. m. A policeman, Çâk. p. 73, 1.—Comp. *Nagara-*, *Nagarî-*, and *Pura-*, m. the watchman of a town, a policeman, Mṛichchh. 140, 17; MBh. 13, 6216; Kathâs. 13, 169. *Paçu-*, m. a herdsman, Man. 8, 238.

रक्ष्ण *rakshṇa*, i.e. *raksh + na*, m. Protection.

† **रख्** *RAKH*, **रङ्ख्** *RAṄKH*, **रिख्** *RIKH*, **रिङ्ख्** *RIṄKH*, i. 1, Par. To go, to move.

† **रग्** *RAG*, i. 1, Par. To suspect; cf. *rak*.

रघ् *RAGH*, see *rak*.

रघु *raghu*, i.e. *raṅgh + u*, I. adj. ved. = *laghu*. II. m. **1.** The name of a king, Utt. Râmach. 96, 3. **2.** pl., and often in comp. words, His descendants, Râm. 3, 49, 57; Megh. 12 (*raghu-pati* = Râma).

रघुपत्वन् *raghu-pat + van*, adj., f. *varî*, Flying swiftly, Chr. 291, 6 = Rigv. i. 85, 6.—With *-patvan*, cf. Lat. -piter, in acci-piter = ved. *âçu-patvan*.

रघुष्यद् *raghushyad*, i. e. *raghu-syand*, adj. Moving quickly, Chr. 290, 7 = Rigv. i. 64, 7.

रङ्क *raṅka*, adj. **1.** Niggardly. **2.** Slow. **3.** Indigent, poor, a beggar, Pañch. i. d. 12; 284.—Comp. *Raṇa-*, m. the part of an elephant's face between his tusks.

रङ्कु *raṅku*, m. A sort of deer, the spotted axis.

रङ्ख् *RAṄKH*, see *rakh*.

† **रङ्ग्** *RAṄG*, **रिङ्ग्** *RIṄG*, i. 1, Par. To go, to move.

रङ्ग *raṅga*, i.e. *rañj + a*, I. m. **1.** Colour, paint. **2.** The place where dancing or acting is exhibited, a stage, Çâk. 4, 12; Daçak. in Chr. 190, 10; a place for an assembly, Nal. 5, 3; 8. **3.**

A field of battle, Pańch. 35, 3. **4.** Dancing, acting, Çṛiñgârat. 17. **5.** A proper name, Râjat. 5, 353. **II.** n. Tin. —**Comp.** *Keli-*, m. a pleasure-ground, Lass. 87, 16. *Pûrva-*, m. the prelude to a drama, Çiç. 2, 8. *Râja(n)-*, n. silver. *Su-*, **I.** m. 1. bright colour. 2. the orange. II. f. *gâ*, crystal. III. n. 1. red sanders. 2. vermilion.

रङ्गज *rańga-ja*, n. Red lead.

रङ्गावतारक *rańgâvatâraka*, i.e. *rańga-ava-tṛî + aka*, m. A stage player, Man. 4, 215.

रङ्घ् *RAŃGH*, i. 1, Âtm. To go, to move swiftly (cf. *lańgh*), Bhaṭṭ. 14, 15. † i. 10, To speak, to shine.

रच् *RACH*, i. 10, *rachaya*, Par. **1.** To make mechanically, Megh. 75. **2.** To make, Râm. 2, 13, 12; Kathâs. 3, 66 (*gatâgatam*, literally a going and returning, i.e. looking on him and turning away her eye). **3.** To arrange, Gît. 5, 10. **4.** To compose, Pańch. 5, 11. **5.** To adorn, Megh. 67. **6.** To prepare, Bhartṛ. 2, 6. **7.** To string, Pańch. iii. d. 235. Ptcple. of the pf. pass. *rachita*, Written. Caus. *rachaya*, To cause to make, Utt. Râmach. 127, 14 (*mama hṛidayam̃ tasminn avadhânam̃ rachayati*, Causes my heart to fix itself only on him, i.e. fills it with love).—With the prep. **आ** *â*, *ârachita*, Put on, Daçak. in Chr. 183, 6.—With **वि** *vi*, *virachita*, **1.** Contrived, arranged, Pańch. 86, 18; Ragh. 5, 76. **2.** Made, Megh. 19. **3.** Ornamented. **4.** Composed, Megh. 84; written, Pańch. 103, 4.—Cf. Lat. locare; A.S. logian, To place; Lat. locus; A.S. loh.

रचना *rach + anâ*, f. **1.** Making, work, Lass. 83, 4; Kathâs. 26, 283 (*kanaka-*, f. Being made, built, of gold.) **2.** Orderly arrangement. **3.** Dressing of the hair. **4.** Stringing flowers. **5.** Suspending garlands. **6.** The arrangement of troops, Pańch. 9, 23. **7.** Composition, Râjat. 5, 380; literary composition.—**Comp.** *Kûṭa-*, f. a trap, Pańch. ii. d. 86. *Keça-*, f. dressing of the hair, Ṛit. 4, 15. *Paksha-*, f. winning friends, Daçak. in Chr. 185, 21. *Paṭa-*, f. art of making cloth, Pańch. 132, 24. *Vachana-*, f. eloquence, Pańch. 68, 5. *Vihita-durga-rachana*, adj. having ordered the building of a fortress, Pańch. 148, 7. *Vyûha-*, f. arrangement of troops, Pańch. 9, 22.

रज *raja* (see *rajas*), m. **1.** Dust, Hit. i. d. 152, M.M. **2.** The pollen of flowers. **3.** The menstrual excretion. **4.** The quality of passion.—**Comp.** *Ni-raja*, i.e. *nis-*, adj. 1. free from dust, MBh. 13, 3822. 2. free from passion, epithet of Çiva, ib. 13, 1261.

रजक *rajaka*, i.e. *rańj + aka*, **I.** m. **1.** A washerman, Hit. 50, 1. **2.** Cloth. **II.** f. *kî*. **1.** A washerman's wife. **2.** A woman in her courses at the third day, Lass. 10, 9.

रजत *rajata* (cf. *arjuna*, *rańj*, and *râj*), **I.** adj. White. **II.** n. **1.** White, the colour. **2.** Silver, Kir. 5, 41; Râjat. 5, 482. **3.** Gold. **4.** Ivory. **5.** Blood. **6.** A necklace. **7.** The name of the mountain Kailâsa. **8.** An asterism.—**Comp.** *Mahâ-*, n. gold.

रजन *rajana* i.e. *rańj + ana*, n. **1.** Colouring. **2.** Safflower.—**Comp.** *Mahâ-*, n. 1. safflower. 2. gold.

रजनि and **रजनी** *rajanî*, i.e. *rańj + anî*, f. **1.** Night, Pańch. 128, 11; 248, 5 (*nî*); Çṛiñgârat. 8 (*nî*). **2.** The indigo plant. **3.** Lac. **4.** Turmeric.

रजनिकर and **रजनीकर** *rajanî-kara*, m. The moon, Çiç. 9, 38 (*nî*).

रजनिचर and **रजनीचर** *rajanî*

-chara, I. adj. Wandering at night, Böhtl. Ind. Spr. 2583 (*nî*). II. m. 1. A Râkshasa, Râm. 3, 53, 61 (*nî*). 2. A thief.

रजनीकर *rajanîkara*, and **रजनीचर** *rajanîchara*, see s.v. *rajanî°*.

रजस् *rajas*, I. i.e. *rañj* + *as*, n. (the original signification was probably 'Dimness;' cf. *rajani* and Goth. riquis). 1. Sky, Chr. 289, 7=Rigv. i. 50, 7. 2. Dust, Man. 11, 110. 3. The pollen of a flower, Vikr. d. 26. 4. The menses, Man. 4, 41. II. i.e. perhaps *ṛij* + *as* (cf. ὄρεξις), n. The quality of passion, Vedântas. in Chr. 207, 8.—Comp. *A-*, adj. free from dust, Nal. 24, 42. *Nîrajas*, i.e. *nis-*, adj. 1. free from dust, Râm. 2, 87, 21 Gorr. 2. free from passion, Râm. 4, 44, 41. *Parorajas*, see s. v. *paras*. *Vi-*, I. adj. free from passion, Chr. 16, 17. II. f. a woman who has ceased to menstruate. *Sa-*, f. a woman during menstruation.—Cf. Goth. riquis.

ऽरजस्क *-rajas+ka*, a substitute for *rajas* when latter part of comp. adj.; e.g. *nîrajaska*, i.e. *nis-*, adj. 1. Free from dust, Râm. 4, 44, 86. 2. Free from passion, Prab. 117, 18, v.r. *vi-*, adj. Free from dust, Ragh. 10, 74.

रजस्तुर् *rajas-tur*, adj. Running over the sky (?), Chr. 291, 12=Rigv. i. 64, 12.

रजस्वल *rajas+vala*, I. m. A buffalo. II. f. *lâ*. 1. A woman who has already her courses, Pañch. iii. d. 219. 2. A woman in her courses, Man. 3, 239.

रजिष्ठ *rajishṭha*, **रजीयंस्** *râjîyaṁs*, see *ṛiju*.

रज्जु *rajju* (probably for original *srajyu*; cf. *sraj* and O.H.G. stricch, stric, stracchian; A.S. streccan; Lat. stringere), f. (m., Pañch. i. d. 376 erroneously, cf. my translation, n. 385). 1. A rope, Hit. ii. d. 131; a cord, Pañch. 76, 17. 2. A lock of braided hair.—Comp. *Karkaṭaka-*, f. a rope with a hook resembling the claw of a crab, Daçak. 71, 2. *Kâshṭha-*, f. a rope for tying bundles of sticks, Râm. 1, 4, 20. *Pâça-*, f. fetter, Kathâs. 18, 298.

रज्जुमात्रत्व *rajju-mâtra + tva*, n. Condition of being only a rope, Vedântas. in Chr. 211, 24.

रज्जुवाल *rajjuvâla*, m. A particular bird, Man. 5, 12.

रञ्ज् *RAÑJ*, † i. 1, *raja*, and i. 4, *rajya*, Par. Âtm. 1. To dye, to colour, Pañch. 132, 24. 2. To be attached (perhaps originally different and akin to *sraj*, see *rajju*, and *lag*). 3. † To go (cf. *ṛij*). The reflexive pass. takes also the terminations of the Par. 1. To attach one's self to, Pañch. v. d. 8. 2. To glow, Utt. Râmach. 138, 2. Ptcple. of the pf. pass. *rakta*. 1. Coloured. 2. Red, Vikr. d. 124; reddened, d. 136. 3. Agitated by passion, Man. 4, 64. 4. Fond, affected with love, Pañch. i. d. 155, 159; attached, Daçak. in Chr. 180, 20. 5. Pure. 6. Sporting. Comparat. *rakta + tara*, Very attached, Daçak. in Chr. 197, 19. *rakta*, m. Red, the colour. n. 1. Blood, Pañch. 60, 25. 2. Vermilion. 3. Minium. 4. Copper. 5. Saffron. f. *tâ*, 1. Lac. 2. The gunjâ plant, Abrus precatorius. 3. Bengal madder. Comp. *Â-*, adj. 1. reddish, Vikr. 78. 2. red, Pañch. 64, 15. *Jîva-*, n. the blood of the menses, Suçr. 1, 43, 19. *Su-*, adj. 1. well dyed. 2. deep red. 3. strongly impassioned. Caus. I. *rañjaya*. 1. To colour, Pañch. 132, 24. 2. To illuminate, Vikr. d. 60; MBh. 1, 6772. 3. To cause to be attached, to conciliate, Pañch. 113, 24;

Man. 7, 19. 4. † To worship. II. † *rajaya*, To hunt.—With the prep. अनु *anu*, i. 4, 1. To grow red and fond, Çiç. 9, 7. 2. To be attached, Bhag. 11, 36; Pańch. i. d. 335. 3. To love, Râm. 3, 55, 15. 4. To dally lasciviously with, Man. 3, 173. *anurakta*, 1. Fond, attached, Pańch. 32, 9; loving, Vikr. 59, 21; propitious, Hit. 53, 18. 2. Pleased. Caus. 1. To cause to be in love, to inspire with affection, Daçak. in Chr. 181, 22. 2. To conciliate, to win, Daçak. 196, 17.—With अप *apa*, *aparakta* (rather *rakta* with *apa*), Discoloured, blanched, Çâk. d. 133.—With अभि *abhi*, i. 4, To be rejoiced, Râm. 2, 67, 13. Caus. To colour, to illuminate, Râm. 1, 38, 21.—With उप *upa*, *uparakta*, 1. Eclipsed, Râm. 1, 55, 9. 2. Afflicted with pain or calamity. m. Râhu.—With वि *vi*, i. 4, To grow discoloured (viz. the hair), and disinclined (viz. the servants), Pańch. i. d. 94. 2. To grow alienated, Mṛichchh. 23, 5. *virakta*, 1. Disinclined, Bhartṛ. 2, 2. 2. Free from worldly passion, Pańch. 33, 16. 3. Impassioned. **Comp.** *A-virakta*, adj. faithful, Hit. iii. d. 87.—With सम् *sam*, i. 4, To grow red, MBh. 1, 6443. *saṁrakta*, 1. Red, MBh. 5, 273. 2. Inflamed. 3. Impassioned. — With अनुसम् *anu-sam*, *anusaṁrakta*, Attached, loving, with acc., Râm. 1, 17, 16.—Cf. ῥέζω, ῥέγος, ῥεγεύς, ῥήσσω, ῥῆγος, λέγνον; probably A.S. ge-regnian, to colour.

रञ्जक *rańj+aka*, I. m. 1. A dyer, Man. 4, 216. 2. A stimulus, an inciter of affection. II. n. Red sandal.

रञ्जन *rańj+ana*, I. m. (?), n. 1. Dyeing, colouring, Râjat. 5, 381. 2. Conciliating, befriending, Râjat. 5, 436 (at the end of a comp. adj.). 3. Exciting passion, delighting. II. n. Red sandal. III. f. *nî*, The indigo, and several other plants.—**Comp.** *Loka-*, n. gaining public confidence. *Strî-*, n. pan eaten with the betel-nut.

रट् *RAṬ*, i. 1, Par. To yell, Mṛichchh. 157, 10; to cry, Kathâs. 18, 109. i. 10, Par. † To speak (?).—With the prep. आ *â*, To call to, Çâk. 55, 5 (Prâkṛ.).

† रठ् *RAṬH*, i. 1, Par. To speak.

रण् *RAṆ* (developed out of *ramṇâ*, i.e. *ram*, ii. 9), i. 4, and i. 1, Par. i. 4, 1. To shout. 2. To rejoice, Chr. 292, 10 = Rigv. i. 85, 10. i. 1, To sound, Çiç. 1, 10. Ptcple. of the pf. pass. *raṇita*, Sounding, Lass. 21, 1. n. Sound. † i. 10, *raṇaya*, To go.—With the prep. नि *ni*, i. 4, To rejoice, Chr. 297, 18 = Rigv. i. 112, 18.

रण *raṇ+a*, I. m. 1. Noise. 2. The quill or bow of a lute. II. m. and n. War, battle, Pańch. 218, 16. Doubled, *raṇa-raṇa*, 1. m. A musquito. 2. n. Anxiety.—**Comp.** *Priya-*, adj. delighting in war. *Mahâ-*, great battle, Chr. 23, 33.

रणरणक *raṇa-raṇa + ka*, m. 1. Regret, care, Utt. Râmach. 25, 11. 2. Desire.

रण्डक *raṇḍaka*, m. A barren tree.

रण्डा *raṇḍâ*, f. 1. A widow, Pańch. i. d. 437 (as an abusive word, cf. the last). 2. A plant, Salvinia cucullata.

† रण्व् *RAṆV*, रम्ब् *RAMB*, रिण्व् *RIṆV*, रिम्ब् *RIMB*, i. 1, Par. To go.

रतर्द्धिक *ratarddhika*, i.e. *rata* (vb.

ram), *-riddhi*+*ka*, n. **1.** A day. **2.** Bathing for pleasure. **3.** The aggregate of eight auspicious objects.

रति *rati*, i.e. *ram*+*ti*, f. **1.** Pleasure, Çâk. d. 34; joy, Pańch. iii. d. 258; love, Pańch. 226, 1; the goddess of love, Râm. 3, 52, 27; Kathâs. 22, 104. **2.** Passion. **3.** Coition, Pańch. ii. d. 154; sexual intercourse, Pańch. iii. d. 116; enjoyment of love, Vikr. d. 85. **4.** A private part.—**Comp.** *Dharma-*, adj. fond of law or virtue, Ragh. 1, 23.

रती *ratî*=*rati*, Goddess of love, Nal. 16, 12 (on account of the metre).

रतू *ratû*, f. **1.** The Ganges of heaven. **2.** A woman who speaks the truth.

रत्न *ratna*, i.e. *ram*+*tna*, n. (m., MBh. 3, 13182). **1.** A jewel, a gem, Râm. 3, 49, 37; figurat., Pańch. ii. d. 194. **2.** A treasure, Böhtl. Ind. Spr. 985 (*vidyâ-*, Consisting in science). **3.** Anything the best of its kind; e.g. *pum̃ratna*, i.e. *pum̃s-*, n. An excellent man, Böhtl. Ind. Spr. 2706. *strî-*, An excellent woman, Vikr. d. 110; cf. *bhastrâkâ*. — **Comp.** *Sa-mauli-*, adj. with the crown jewel, Vikr. d. 144.

रत्नभाज् *ratnabhâj*, i.e. *ratna-bhaj*, adj. Acquiring jewels, Râm. 3, 49, 42.

रत्नद्रुममय *ratna-druma*+*maya*, adj., f. *yî*, Resembling corals, Arj. 10, 2.

रत्नसंघातमय *ratna-sam̃ghâta*+*maya*, adj., f. *yî*, Consisting of a heap of jewels, Sund. 3, 14.

रत्नि *ratni* (curtailed *aratni*), I. m. (and f.), A cubit measured from the elbow to the end of the closed fist. II. m. The closed fist.

रथ *ratha* (vb. *ṛi*), m. **1.** A car, Hit. pr. d. 32, M.M.; a war chariot, Chr. 4, 10. **2.** Any vehicle. **3.** A limb. **4.** A foot. **5.** The body.—**Comp.** *Ati-*, m. a pre-eminent warrior who fights in a chariot, Râm. 6, 4, 20. *Kîrti-* and *Kṛitti-*, m. a proper name, Râm. 1, 71, 9. *Krîḍâ-*, m. a carriage serving for excursions, MBh. 13, 2782. *Chitra-*, I. adj. having a brilliant chariot, Bhâg. P. 4, 10, 22. II. m. 1. the sun. 2. a proper name, MBh. 2, 407. III. f. *thâ*, the name of a river, 6, 341. *Daça(n)-*, and *daçapûrva-*, i.e. *daça(n)-pûrva-*, m. Daçaratha, the name of Râma's father, and of others, Râm. 1, 72, 31 Gorr.; Ragh. 8, 29. *Patra-*, m. a bird, Râm. 3, 25, 7. *Pushpa-*, or *pushya-*, m. a carriage for pleasure, Râm. 2, 26, 15 (*pushpa-*). *Bhîma-*, I. m. an Asura. II. f. *thî*. 1. the seventh night in the seventh month of the seventy-seventh year of a man, supposed to be the ordinary period of human life. 2. the name of a river. *Manoratha*, i.e. *manas-*, m. wish, desire, Vikr. 13, 20. *Samâgama-manoratha*, m. desire of union, Vikr. d. 30. *Marut-*, m. 1. a horse. 2. a car in which idols are carried. *Mahâ-*, m. 1. a great chariot, Râm. 3, 55, 32. 2. (having a great chariot), a hero, ib. 3, 53, 11. *Vishṇu-*, m. Garuḍa. *Sa-*, adj. with the carriage. *Ham̃sa-*, m. Brahman.—Cf. Lat. rota; A.S. and O.H.G. rad (probably borrowed); probably ῥέθος, Goth. lithus, A.S. lidh.

रथकट्या *rathakaṭyâ*, i.e. *ratha-kaṭa*+*ya* (cf. *kaṭa* and *nikaṭa*), f. A multitude of cars.

रथकर *ratha-kara*, m. A carpenter.

रथकार *ratha-kâra*, m. **1.** A carpenter, Pańch. 229, 8. **2.** A man sprung from a male of the *Mâhishya* and a female of the *Karaṇî* caste, by profession a coach-maker.

रथकारत्व *rathakâra*+*tva*, n. The business of a carpenter, Pańch. 228, 12.

रथगर्भक *ratha-garbha+ka*, m. A car or litter borne on men's shoulders.

रथतुर् *ratha-tur*, adj. Overpowering, i.e. drawing, the carriage, Chr. 293, 2=Rigv. i. 88, 2.

रथधूर्गत *rathadhûrgata*, i.e. *ratha-dhur-gata* (vb. *gam*), adj. Gone upon the pole of the chariot, Johns. Sel. 15, 53.

रथारथि *rathârathi*, i.e. *ratha-ratha+i*, adv. In mutual contact of the chariots, i.e. in closest fight, MBh. 4, 1056.

रथिक *rathika*, i.e. *ratha+ika*, m. The owner of, or rider in, a car.

रथिन् *rathin*, i.e. *ratha+in*, I. adj. Mounted on carriages, Râm. 3, 49, 18. II. m. **1.** The owner of, or rider in, a car, lord of chariots, Vikr. d. 100. **2.** A warrior who fights in a car, Draup. 2, 12; Utt. Râmach. 130, 4.—**Comp.** *A-*, m. one who is not lord of chariots, Johns. Sel. 6, 35.

रथिन *rathina*, and **रथिर** *rathira* i.e. *ratha+in+a*, and with *r* for *n*, m. The owner of, or rider in, a car.

रथ्य *rathya*, i.e. *ratha+ya*, I. m. A carriage horse. II. f. *yâ*. **1.** A multitude of cars, Râjat. 5, 241 (warriors?). **2.** A high street. **3.** A place where several roads meet. III. n. A wheel.

रद् *RAD*, i. 1, Par. **1.** To split, to divide. **2.** To dig.—Cf. probably Goth. lêtan, A.S. laetan (cf. the vedic use of *rad*); Lat. rādere, rōdere (cf. *rada*, *radana*), perhaps rădius.

रद *rad+a*, m. **1.** Splitting, Ghaṭ. 1. **2.** A tooth.—**Comp.** *Dvi-*, I. adj. having two teeth. II. m. an elephant, Râm. 4, 9, 62. *Vajra-*, m. a hog.

रदन *rad+ana*, m. A tooth.

रदिन् *radin*, i.e. *rada+in*, m. An elephant.

रध् *RADH*. i. 4, Par. **1.** To perish (ved.). **2.** To be at one's mercy, Chr. 289, 13=Rigv. i. 50, 13. **3.** To kill, to hurt. **4.** To be completed, finished, matured. Caus. *randhaya*, **1.** To give in one's power, Chr. 289, 13 =Rigv. i. 50, 13. **2.** To pain, to torment, Râm. 2, 81, 3. **3.** To destroy, Bhâg. P. 8, 21, 2.—Cf. A.S. rendan, To rend.

रन्तिदेव *rantideva*, m. **1.** A name of Vishṇu. **2.** The name of a king, Megh. 46 (cf. Vishṇu P. 481, n. 18). **3.** A dog.

रन्तु *rantu*, f. **1.** A road. **2.** A river.

रन्धन *randhana*, i.e. *radh*, Caus., *+ana*, **1.** Destroying, Bhâg. P. 4, 30, 28. **2.** Cooking, Pâṇ. ii. 1, 36, Sch.

रन्ध्र *randhra*, i.e. *radh*, Caus., *+ra*, n. **1.** A hole, a fissure, Pańch. ii. d. 42 (cf. also **3.**). **2.** A cavity, Çiç. 4, 61. **3.** A fault, a defect, a weak point, Pańch. 182, 2.—**Comp.** *Karṇa-*, m. n. the auditory passage, Bhâg. P. 3, 13, 35. *Nirandhra*, i.e. *nis-*, adj. without an interstice, Utt. Râmach. 143, 2.

रप् *RAP*, i. 1, Par. **1.** To speak. **2.** To praise (ved.). Cf. *lap*.

† **रफ्** *RAPH*, **रम्फ्** *RAMPH*, **रर्फ्** *RARPH*, i. 1, Par. **1.** To go. **2.** To kill.

रभ् *RABH* (originally =*grabh*, *labh*), i. 1, Âtm. (in epic poetry and Man. also Par., Man. 7, 59). **1.** † To desire vehemently. **2.** † To act inconsiderately. **3.** To seize, to take (ved.). —With the prep. **आ** *â*, To begin, Man.

7, 299. **2.** To act strenuously, Bhaṭṭ. 3, 7. Ptcple. of the pf. pass. *ârabdha.* **1.** Begun, done; *rahasy ârabdhâ kathâ,* A secret conversation, Vikr. d. 51. **2.** Having begun, MBh. 1, 7660. Absol. *ârabhya,* From, Hit. 91, 21.—With अन्वा *anu-â,* To get back, Râm. 2, 64, 60.—With अभ्या *abhi-â,* To begin, MBh. 3, 10724 (Par.).—With प्रा *pra-â,* To begin, Bhag. 18, 15; Pańch. iii. d. 130. *prârabdha,* n. An attempt, enterprise, Lass. 1, 6.—With समा *sam-â,* **1.** To begin, Râm. 1, 45, 13; to undertake, Hit. 44, 6, M.M. **2.** To try, MBh. 1, 2238. **3.** To treat, MBh. 3, 16298.—With परि *pari,* To embrace, Vikr. d. 147; MBh. 4, 514. Desider. *pari ripsa,* To desire to embrace, Ragh. 13, 32 (Calc.).—With सम् *sam, saṁrabdha,* **1.** Exasperated, enraged, Râm. 2, 55, 30. **2.** Agitated, overwhelmed, Nal. 13, 14. Comp. *Su-,* adj. 1. very enraged, Chr. 31, 20. 2. very agitated, Pańch. 238, 24.—With अभिसम् *abhi-sam, abhisaṁrabdha,* Enraged, Râm. 6, 3, 17.—Cf. Lat. rabies, robur (labor, see *labh*); probably ῥωβίδας, ῥώννυμι; Goth. arbaiths; A.S. earfedh, earfodh; Goth. liban; A.S. leofian, lifian, lybban; O.H.G. laba, labôn; perhaps A.S. a-refian, To bear, a-raefnan, To take away.

रभस् *rabh+as,* n. ved. **1.** Zeal (in *rabhas+vant,* zealous, Rigv. i. 9, 6). **2.** Strength, strengthening food, sacrifice, Rigv. i. 145, 3. See *rabh.*

रभस *rabhas+a,* I. adj. Joyful, Kir. 5, 1. II. m. **1.** Joy. **2.** Passion, rage, Daçak. in Chr. 194, 8. **3.** Speed, velocity, Çiç. 9, 72; abl. quickly, Râjat. 5, 190. **4.** Precipitation, Böhtl. Ind. Spr. 315. **5.** Regret, sorrow.—Comp. *Ati-,* m. (or adv. °*sa+m*), excessive precipitation, or, with excessive precipitation, Bhartṛ. 2, 97. *Ambhas-vindu-grahaṇa-,* adj. running, desirous to get drops of water, Megh. 22. *Sa-rabhasa+m,* adv. 1. quickly, Utt. Râmach. 144, 11. 2. passionately, Lass. 24, 15.

रम् *RAM,* i. 1, Âtm. (in poetry also Par., Man. 2, 223), in the Veda also ii. 9, Par. **1.** To rest, Man. 3, 251; to like to stay, Hit. ii. d. 128. **2.** To be delighted, Pańch. i. d. 429; to rejoice, Râm. 2, 34, 50; Vikr. 19, 1 (*raṁsyate bhavatâ,* impers. pass. You will be glad), 70, 21. **3.** To rejoice at, with loc., Daçak. in Chr. 181, 5 (to be in love); with instr., MBh. 3, 58. **4.** To have sexual intercourse with (instr.), Hit. 66, 7. **5.** To sport, Bhaṭṭ. 6, 15. Ptcple. of the pf. pass. *rata.* **1.** Beloved, Pańch. v. d. 53. **2.** Intent on, Man. 2, 235 (with loc.); occupied, Pańch. 27, 9. **3.** Inclined, Pańch. 203, 2. **4.** Satisfied, Pańch. 228, 10. n. **1.** Coition, copulation, Pańch. i. d. 224. **2.** A private part. Comp. *Deva-,* adj. devout, Pańch. 118, 22. *Nirmâṇa-,* m. the name of a class of deities, MBh. 13, 1372. *Su-,* I. adj. 1. playing, playful. 2. compassionate, tender. II. n. 1. coition, Hit. iii. 27. 2. sexual intercourse, love, Ṛit. 6, 1. *Vara-su-,* adj. very wanton, Hit. ii. d. 64. Ptcple. of the fut. pass. I. *rantavya,* To be rejoiced at, Mṛichchh. 62, 22. II. *ramaṇîya,* Pleasing, agreeable, Vikr. 37, 10; Hit. iv. d. 73 (*âpâta-,* in the beginning); beautiful, Vikr. 65, 18 (*viçesha-,* most beautiful). III. *ramya.* **1.** The same, Ṛit. 6, 2. **2.** m. The champaca, Michelia Champaca. **3.** f. *yâ.* a. Night. b. The name of a river. **4.** n. Semen virile. Comp. *Nis-âtapatra-,* adj. needing no parasol, i.e. cool, and therefore charming, a Karmadhâraya compound, Vikr. d. 73. Caus. *ramaya,* **1.** To exhilarate, MBh. 2, 305.

2. To be delighted, to rejoice, MBh. 3, 11379.—With the prep. अनु *anu*, *anurata*, 1. Fond of, attached to. 2. Beloved.—With अभि *abhi*, To be delighted, to rejoice, Râm. 2, 27, 18. *abhirata*, 1. Intent upon, Chr. 14, 26. 2. Pleased with. 3. Engaged in, Râm. 3, 49, 39. 4. Practising.—With अव *ava*, *avarata*, Stopped, ceased. Comp. *An-*, adj. uninterrupted, Vedântas. in Chr. 216, 21. °*tam*, adv. without stopping, Pańch. 93, 15; incessantly, Pańch. 145, 14.—With आ *â*, Par. 1. To repose, Bhaṭṭ. 3, 38. 2. To cease, Man. 2, 73. 3. To take pleasure, Man. 4, 175. *ârata*, Ceased, Kir. 5, 6.—With उपा *upa-â*, 1. To repose, MBh. 1, 6035. 2. To cease, Ragh. 16, 3 (Calc.). 3. To rejoice, to dally, MBh. 1, 4183.—With उप *upa*, Par. Âtm. 1. To cease, Chr. 30, 39; with the ptcple. of the pres. in the sense of the infin., Pańch. 53, 19 (*mṛigaçaçakâdîn vyâpâdayan nopa ra-râma*, He did not cease killing deer, hares, etc.). 2. To desist from, with abl., Daçak. in Chr. 181, 12. *uparata*, 1. Stopped, ceased. 2. Having ceased, Man. 5, 66. 3. Having desisted from, Bhaṭṭ. 2, 35. 4. Dead, Pańch. 98, 3 (he breathed out his last).—With व्युप *vi-upa*, *vyuparata*, Interrupted, stopped, Mṛichchh. 1, 2.—With नि *ni*, *nirata*, 1. Pleased, satisfied, Man. 3, 45. 2. Attached to (with loc.), loving, Utt. Râmach. 57, 5; faithful, Râm. 3, 48, 18. 3. Engaged in, practising, Nal. 6, 10 (*a-hiṁsâ-*, benevolence).—With परि *pari*, Par. To be delighted, Bhaṭṭ. 8, 53.—With वि *vi*, 1. To cease, Utt. Râmach. 17, 6; with the ptcple. of the pres. in the sense of the infin., Pańch. 93, 16. 2. To desist, Man. 4, 97. 3. To cease from, desist from (with abl.), Vikr. d. 39; Pańch. 161, 1. *virata*, Stopped, ceased, Çiç. 9, 12. Comp. *A-*, adj. 1. uninterrupted, Kir. 5, 6. 2. eternal.—With सम् *sam*, To rejoice, Bhaṭṭ. 19, 30.—Cf. O.H.G. râwa, ruowa (i.e. **ram* + *van*, cf. acc. sing. ruouun), râwên (denomin.), resti, rastjan; A. S. rest, restan; ἠρέμα, ṙω-λεμ + ής.

रम *ram* + *a*, I. adj. 1. Pleasing, Kir. 5, 20 (at the end of a comp.). 2. Dear. II. m. 1. A husband, a lover. 2. The deity of love. III. f. *mâ*. 1. A wife or a mistress, Pańch. i. d. 369 (?). 2. A name of Lakshmî, Pańch. 46, 8.—Comp. *Manas-*, see s.v. *manorama*.

रमक *ram* + *aka*, m. A lover, a gallant.

रमण *ramaṇa*, i.e. *ram* + *ana*, I. adj. Delighting, Bhâg. P. 5, 7, 11. II. m. 1. A husband, Megh. 85. 2. A lover, Vikr. d. 89; Pańch. i. d. 196; Çiç. 9, 60. 3. A name of Kâma. 4. An ass. III. f. *ṇî*, and *ṇâ*, A wife, a mistress. IV. n. 1. Sporting. 2. Dalliance, love, Megh. 38. 3. Coition. 4. The mons veneris.—Comp. *Para-*, m. a paramour, Pańch. i. d. 196.

रमणीयता *ramaṇîya* (vb. *ram*), + *tâ*, f. Agreeableness, charm, Utt. Râmach. 90, 4; Çâk. 82, 2 (Prâkṛ.).

रमणीयत्व *ramaṇîya* + *tva*, n. Agreeableness, charm, Çâk. 80, 7.

रमति *ram* + *ati*, m. 1. Love. 2. Paradise. 3. A crow. 4. Time.

रम्फ् *RAMPH*, see *raph*.

† रम्ब् *RAMB*, i. 1, Âtm. To sound. See *raṇv*.

† रम्भ् *RAMBH,* लम्भ् *LAMBH,* i. 1, Âtm. To sound.

रम्भ *rambha,* **A.** i.e. *rabh + a,* **I.** m. **1.** A bambu. **2.** The name of a monkey. **II.** f. *bhâ.* **1.** A plantain, Lass. 79, 16. **2.** The name of an Apsaras, Vikr. 87, 10. **3.** A name of Gaurî. **B.** (cf. *rambh*), f. *bhâ,* Lowing, as of a cow.—**Comp.** *Go-rambha,* m. a proper name, Pańch. 26, 22.

† रय् *RAY,* लय् *LAY,* i. 1, Âtm. To go.

रय *raya,* i.e. *ṛî + a,* m. **1.** The stream of a river, Hit. iii. d. 49. **2.** Speed, Megh. 20.—**Comp.** *Âçu-,* adj. impetuous, Bhâg. P. 5, 13, 3. *Çânta-* (vb. *çam*), adj. slackened in speed.

रयि *rayi,* m. Wealth (cf. *rai*), Chr. 288, 13=Rigv. i. 48, 13.

रयिष्ठ *rayishṭha,* superl. of *raya + vant,* **1.** Very fleet. **2.** m. A name of Kuvera, Agni or fire, and Brahman.

रर्फ् *RARPH,* see *raph.*

रल्लक *rallaka,* m. **1.** A blanket. **2.** An eyelash. **3.** A sort of deer, Çiç. 4, 61.

रव *rava,* i.e. *ru + a,* m. **1.** Sound, Mâlat. 79, 19 (at the end of a comp. adj.); cry, Indr. 1, 3; Râjat. 5, 346; 408. **2.** Talk, Böhtl. Ind. Spr. 1723, 3; Pańch. i. 30 (false r.; cf. my transl. and Böhtl. Ind. Spr. 2542).—**Comp.** *Kala-,* m. 1. a pleasing sound, Bhartṛ. 1, 35. 2. (properly, uttering a pleasing sound), a pigeon. 3. the Indian cuckoo. *Ghaṇṭâ-,* I. m. the sound of a bell, Pańch. 229, 15. II. f. *vâ,* crotolaria of various species. *Chaṇḍa-,* m. the name of a jackal, Pańch. 62, 21. *Nirava,* i.e. *nis-,* adj. noiseless, Ragh. 8, 57. *Bhîma-vega-,* m. a proper name (fearful in velocity and noise). *Madana-kâku-,* m. a pigeon. *Viṇa-,* f. *vâ,* a proper name, Pańch. 81, 5. *Çârṅga-,* m. a proper name.

रवण *ravaṇa,* partly *ru + ana,* **I.** adj. **1.** Sounding, crying. **2.** Sharp, hot. **3.** Unsteady. **4.** Jesting. **II.** m. **1.** The Indian cuckoo. **2.** A camel. **III.** n. Bell-metal.

रवथ *ravatha,* i. e. *ru + atha,* m. The Indian cuckoo.

रवि *ravi,* m. **1.** The sun, Pańch. 189, 23; Man. 1, 23. **2.** A proper name, Draup. 2, 21.

रशना *raçanâ,* see *rasana.*

रश्मि *raçmi* (i.e. *raç + mi*; with *raç* cf. probably Lat. laqueus, cf. *rasanâ*), m. **1.** A rein, Nal. 19, 22. **2.** A ray of light, Pańch. 162, 11. **3.** An eyelash. —**Comp.** *Ushṇa-* and *Tigma-,* m. the sun, Ragh. 5, 4; Çiç. 9, 11. *Çita-,* m. the moon, Çṛiṅgârat. 6. *Syûma-,* m. a proper name, Chr. 297, 16=Rigv. i. 112, 16.

1. रस् *RAS,* i. 1, Par. **1.** To sound, Gît. 10, 6. **2.** To roar, MBh. 3, 14602. **3.** To sing, Çiç. 6, 70. **4.** † To praise. Ptcple. of the pf. pass. *rasita,* Sounded. n. **1.** The rattling of thunder, Ghaṭ. 14. **2.** Sound. Cf. s.v. Frequent. *râras,* To cry loudly, Bhaṭṭ. 5, 96.—With the prep. अनु *anu, anurasita,* Accompanied by howling, Utt. Râmach. 45, 2.—With आ *â,* To lament, Nal. 1, 11. *ârasita,* n. Cry, Mâlav. d. 41. —With वि *vi,* To cry, Bhaṭṭ. 15, 42. —Cf. Goth. razda; O.H.G. rartjan; A.S. reordian; O.H.G. rerjan; A.S. rarian.

2. रस् *RAS,* i. 10, *rasaya* and *rasâ-*

paya (rather a denomin. derived from *rasa*), Par. **1.** To taste, Çiç. 10, 27. **2.** † To love. Desider. *rirasayisha*, To wish to taste, Çiç. 11, 11.

रस *rasa*, probably from *ram*, I. m. **1.** Taste (as sweet, salt), Pańch. 61, 11. **2.** Pleasure, Utt. Râmach. 146, 1; enjoyment, Çâk. d. 179; Pańch. ii. d. 175; charm, Pańch. iv. d. 62. **3.** Inclination, Hit. iii. d. 115 (*sâhasa-ekânta-rasa-anuvartin*, adj. One who follows only his inclination to inconsiderate haste); love, Utt. Râmach. 26, 2. **4.** Juice, Man. 2, 77; liquid, 3, 159; Çiç. 9, 46; a dish, Vikr. 19, 1. **5.** Essence, Hit. iv. d. 94 (*tad-*, Its best). **6.** Condiment, Hit. iii. d. 56. **7.** Water. **8.** The essential juice of the body, whence blood, etc., are supposed to be engendered. **9.** Semen virile. **10.** Poison. **11.** Gum myrrh. **12.** Quicksilver. **13.** A mineral substance, as sulphur, borax. **14.** Taste, sentiment, emotion, as an object of poetry, as love, terror, etc., Bhartṛ. 2, 21; Râm. 1, 4, 7; Pańch. v. d. 44 (? nine *rasas* of music). **15.** Affection of the mind, Utt. Râmach. 50, 8; passion, Vikr. d. 36; love, Vikr. d. 40. **II.** f. *sâ*. **1.** A river of the lower regions, Chr. 297, 12=Rigv. i. 112, 12. **2.** The tongue. **3.** The earth. **4.** A grape. **5.** The name of several plants.—**Comp.** *A-*, adj. tasteless, insipid. *Anu-*, m. a secondary flavour, Suçr. 1, 224, 13. *Anna-*, m. the essential properties of food, Nal. 5, 37 (the knowledge of them). *Amṛita-*, I. m. the amṛita essence, the drink of immortality, Bhartṛ. 3, 77 (*kâvya-*, poetical works which are like the essence of amṛita). II. adj., f. *sâ*, having an amṛita-like juice, Pańch. 248, 12. *Ikshu-*, m. the juice of the sugar-cane, Pańch. i. d. 411. *Eka-*, I. m. only pleasure, Râm. 1, 9, 3. II. adj., f. *sâ*. 1. pleased with one object only, ib. 2, 67, 20 (v. r. Gorr.). 2. unchanged, Utt. Râmach. 102, 3. *Kanaka-*, m. 1. melted gold, Çâk. 99, 15. 2. yellow orpiment. *Kâma-*, m. semination, MBh. 1, 3812. *Kshudra-*, m. honey, Bhâg. P. 5, 13, 10. *Gandha-*, m. myrrh, MBh. 5, 777. *Go-*, m. 1. milk, MBh. 5, 1143. 2. buttermilk. 3. coagulated milk. *Nirasa*, i.e. *nis-*, adj. 1. sapless, vain, Vikr. d. 30. 2. insipid, Bhartṛ. 3, 16. 3. merciless, Utt. Râmach. 117, 6. 4. charmless, Pańch. iv. d. 62. *Pishṭa* (vb. *pish*)-, m. water mixed with flour, MBh. 1, 5186. *Praṇipâta-*, m. the name of a spell, Râm. 1, 31, 5 Gorr. *Yaksha-*, m. spirituous liquor. *Yathâ-rasa + m*, adv. according to the sentiments, Mâlav. 20, 20. *Vi-*, I. adj. 1. insipid. 2. painful, Utt. Râmach. 157, 6. II. m. pain, Utt. Râmach. 18, 9. *Çṛiṅgâra-eka-*, adj. only pleased with love, Vikr. d. 9. *Sa-*, see s.v. *Siddha-*, I. adj. mineral, metallic. II. m. 1. quicksilver. 2. an alchymist. *Su-*, I. adj. 1. well-flavoured. 2. sweet. 3. elegant. II. m. a plant, Vitex trifolia. III. f. *sâ*, and n. 1. holy basil. 2. the name of several plants. IV. f. *sâ*, Durgâ. *Sva-*, m. 1. proper taste. 2. proper flavour. 3. expressed juice. 4. sediment of oil. *Svâdu-*, f. *sâ*, 1. the hog-plum. 2. a grape. 3. vinous liquor.

रसक *rasa + ka*, m. Stewed or boiled meat.

रसज *rasa-ja*, m. **1.** Any insect engendered by the fermentation of liquids. **3.** Molasses.

रसज्ञ *rasa-jña*, I. adj. Acquainted with tastes, sentiments, etc. **II.** m. **1.** An alchymist. **2.** A physician. **3.** A poet. **III.** f. *jñâ*, The tongue, Bhâshâp. 52; 101.

रसन *ras + ana*, I. n. **1.** Sounding, tinkling. **2.** Tasting, Bhâshâp. 39; Bhag. 15, 9. **II.** f. (written also *raçanâ*, and perhaps akin to *raçmi*, q. cf.). **1.** A woman's girdle, Vikr. d. 115. **2.** The tongue, Bhâshâp. 100.—Comp. *Nirasana*, i.e. *nis-rasana*, adj. without a girdle, Kir. 5, 11.

रसमय *rasa + maya*, adj., f. *yî*, Delightful, Utt. Râmach. 128, 1.

रसवन्त् *rasa + vant*, adj., f. *vatî*, **1.** Succulent, Bhartṛ. 3, 97. **2.** Agreeable, Vikr. d. 62. **3.** Endowed with the *rasas*, love, etc., Utt. Râmach. 111, 3.

रसायन *rasâyana*, perhaps *rasa-ayana*, I. n. **1.** Buttermilk. **2.** Poison. **3.** A medicine preventing old age and prolonging life, Pańch. ii. d. 80; elixir, Hit. i. d. 209, M.M. (*prîti-*, Elixir-like joy). **4.** Medicine, a remedy, Utt. Râmach. 24, 2. **5.** Alchymy, chemistry. II. m. **1.** An alchymist. **2.** Garuḍa. III. f. *nî*, A vessel conveying nutrition.

रसिक *rasika*, i.e. *rasa + ika*, I. adj. **1.** Having taste, flavoured. **2.** Tasteful, as a composition. **3.** Impassioned, inclined, Hit. 103, 3 (*sâhasa-eka-*, Inclined only to inconsiderate haste). II. m. **1.** A horse. **2.** An elephant. **3.** A libertine. III. f. *kâ* (cf. *rasana*). **1.** A woman's girdle. **2.** The tongue. **3.** Curds with sugar and spice. **4.** Molasses.

रसिकता *rasika + tâ*, f. Pleasure, Böhtl. Ind. Spr. 411.

रसित *rasita*, probably *rasa + ita*, adj. Gilded, plated.

रस्न *rasna*, n. A thing.

रस्य *rasya*, i.e. *rasa + ya*, I. adj. **1.** Savoury, Bhag. 17, 8. **2.** Juicy. II. n. Blood.

रह् *RAH* (for original *radh*), i. 1, and i. 10, *rahaya*, Par. To quit, to leave. Ptcple. of the pf. pass. *rahita*. **1.** Abandoned, Râm. 3, 52, 5. **2.** Deprived of, without, Râm. 1, 70, 35. n. Privacy; loc. sing. Privately, Chr. 37, 2.—With the prep. **वि** *vi*, **1.** To abandon, Râm. 3, 51, 17. **2.** With instr. To separate from, Vikr. d. 114. *virahita*, **1.** Abandoned, left, Çiç. 9, 75. **2.** Deprived of, without, Vikr. d. 33; Nal. 10, 23. Comp. *A-*, adj. 1. not separated, Vikr. 86, 11. 2. abounding in, Kir. 5, 52.—Cf. λανθάνω, ἔλαθον, ἀλήθης, probably ἔρημος; Lat. latere (cf. *rudhira*); also perhaps λόχος, λέχος (cf. *rahas*); Lat. lectum, legere; Goth. ligan, 'lagjan; A.S. leegan, licgan.

रहस् *rah + as*, I. n. **1.** Secrecy, Pańch. 253, 25; Chr. 5, 6; Vikr. d. 51 (loc., secretly). **2.** A secret, Râjat. 5, 317; a religious or mystic truth. **3.** A place of privacy, a hiding-place, solitude, Daçak. in Chr. 181, 23; Lass. 55, 15. **4.** Copulation, Pańch. i. d. 197 (but cf. Böhtl. Ind. Spr. 2366). **5.** A privity. II. adv. Secretly, privily, Pańch. 192, 23; Chr. 53, 22. Cf. *rah*.

रहःस्थ *rahaḥstha*, or **रहस्थ** *rahastha*, i. e. *rahas-stha*, adj. Being alone, Pańch. 45, 24.

रहस्य *rahas + ya*, I. adj. Secret, Man. 11, 247; concealed, 4, 144; mysterious. II. n. A secret, Pańch. 129, 2; a mystery, Lass. 20, 20. III. f. *yâ*, The name of a river.—Comp. *Deva-*, n. a secret of the gods, MBh. 15, 964. *Sa-*, adj. magical (as weapons), Utt. Râmach. 11, 3. *Sa-prayoga-*, adj. with the charms or spells for employing (the magic weapons), Johns. Sel. 4, 22.

रही *rahî*, A substitute for *rahas* before the derivatives of *kṛi* and *bhû*; cf. *bhû*.

रा *RÂ*, ii. 2, Par. (in the ved. also Âtm.), To give, Bhâg. P. 4, 27, 25. Ptcple. of the pf. pass. *râta*. Comp. *Kîrti-*, and *Kṛiti-*, m. a proper name,

Râm. 1, 71, 11.—Cf. ved. *râtam astu* with Lat. ratum esto and reor.

राका *râkâ*, f. **1.** Full moon, or the day of full moon, Sah. D. p. 323, 19. **2.** A girl in whom menstruation has commenced. **3.** Itch. **4.** The name of a river.

राक्षस *râkshasa*, i.e. *rakshas* + *a*, I. adj., f. *sî*. **1.** Belonging to a Râkshasa, demoniacal, Râm. 3, 48, 11; Lass. 18, 3. **2.** Infested by demons, Man. 3, 280. **3.** (see *vidhi*), A form of marriage, Man. 3, 33. **II.** m. An evil spirit, Pańch. 182, 22. **III.** f. *sî*. **1.** A female demon, Hiḍ. 2, 16. **2.** A large tusk. **3.** A sort of perfume.—**Comp.** *Jala-râkshasî*, f. a female demon of the water, MBh. 3, 16255. *Brahmarâkshasa*, i.e. *brahman-*, m. a demon of the brahmanical class, Man. 12, 60; Pańch. 182, 19. *Mânusha-*, m. a Râkshasa-like man, a Râkshasa in the shape of man, Bhartṛ. 2, 66. *Sadevâsura-*, i. e. *sa-deva-asura-*, adj. with the gods, Asuras, and Râkshasas, Chr. 41, 22.

† **राख्** *RÂKH*, **लाख्** *LÂKH*, i. 1, Par. **1.** To grow dry. **2.** To adorn. **3.** To suffice. **4.** To prevent.

राग *râga*, i.e. *rańj* + *a*, **I.** m. **1.** Colour, Pańch. 203, 5; Vikr. d. 26 (red colour). **2.** Being subdued by affections, MBh. 13, 12427; Ṛit. 6, 23. **3.** Affection, love, Pańch. iii. d. 266; Daçak. in Chr. 197, 6; desire, sorrow, joy, Râjat. 5, 382. **4.** Wrath, Pańch. 29, 17. **5.** Envy. **6.** Greediness. **7.** Passion, Hit. iv. d. 83 (*ni-vṛitta-*, adj. Free from passions). **8.** A mode of music, of which six are enumerated, Pańch. 248, 6. **9.** Harmony, Çâk. d. 5. **10.** A king. **II.** f. *gî*, A sort of grain, Eleusine corocana.—**Comp.** *Ańga-*, m. paint, unguent, powder for smearing and perfuming the body, Ṛit. 6, 12. *Apa-*, m. enmity, Man. 7, 154. *Kritrima-*, m. an artificial colour, Vikr. d. 40. *Padma-*, m. a ruby, Hit. pr. d. 44, M.M. *Pushpa-*, m. a topaz, Ragh. 18, 31. *Vi-*, m. 1. disinclination, hatred, Böhtl. Ind. Spr. 1156. 2. the absence of desire or passion, indifference, disregard of all sensual enjoyment, Vedântas. in Chr. 203, 6. *Vîta-*, i.e. *vi-ita-*, I. adj. 1. colourless. 2. exempt from passions, Hit. 42, 10, M.M. II. m. a sage. *Sa-*, adj. 1. coloured. 2. impassioned. *Haridrâ-*, adj. fickle, unsteady.

रागमञ्जरिका *râgamańjarikâ*, i.e. *râga-mańjarî* + *ka*, f. The wicked Râgamańjarî, Daçak. in Chr. 194, 21.

रागारु *râgâru*, adj. One who excites hopes and disappoints them.

रागिन् *râgin*, i.e. *râga* + *in*, **I.** adj., f. *iṇî*. **1.** Coloured. **2.** Red, Pańch. i. d. 225. **3.** Impassioned, agitated by affections, Bhag. 18, 27; given to passions, Hit. iv. d. 83. **4.** Loving, Çiç. 9, 38; being in love, Daçak. in Chr. 180, 23. **II.** m. **1.** A painter. **2.** A lover. **III.** f. *giṇî*. **1.** A shrewd and intriguing woman. **2.** A modification of a musical mode, personified as the wife of the Râga, Lass. 39, 10.—**Comp.** *Vi-* (properly, *virâga* + *in*, see *râga*), adj. void of passion.

† **राघ्** *RÂGH*, **लाघ्** *LÂGH*, i. 1, Âtm. To be able or equal to.

राघव *râghava*, i.e. *raghu* + *a*, patronym., m. (cf. *raghu*), **1.** A descendant of Raghu; a name of Râma, Râm. 3, 48, 8. **2.** A sort of fish. **3.** The ocean.

राङ्कव *râńkava*, i.e. *rańku* + *a*, adj. Made of the hair of the *rańku*, Râm. 3, 49, 15.

राङ्ग *râńga*, A proper name, Lass. 67, 2.

1. **राज्** *RÂJ*, i. 1, Par. Atm. **1.**

To shine, Vikr. d. 160; to beam, Râm. 1, 1, 32; Chr. 25, 52 (*râjatam*, anomal. instead of *râjantam*). **2.** ved. To govern (akin to *ṛij*, originally *raj*). Caus. *râjaya*, To illuminate. Ptcple. of the pf. pass. *râjita*. **1.** Illuminated. **2.** Adorned, Kir. 5, 9.—With अभि *abhi*, To shine, MBh. 3, 10960.—With उप *upa*, Caus. *uparâjita*, Illuminated, Pañch. v. d. 12.—With निस् *nis*, *nirâjita*, Shining, Utt. Râmach. 150, 12.—With परि *pari*, To be very resplendent, Râm. 3, 49, 3.—With वि *vi*, **1.** To shine forth, Pañch. v. d. 2. **2.** To shine, ib. i. d. 373; Râm. 3, 52, 25. Caus. To cause to beam, Râm. 2, 26, 2. *virâjita*, **1.** Illuminated, splendid, Kir. 5, 4; Nal. 5, 3. **2.** Manifested.—With अभिवि *abhi-vi*, To shine, to beam, Râm. 2, 26, 10.

2. राज् *râj*, latter part of comp. nouns, I. adj. Shining. II. curtailed for *râjan*, m. A king, Hiḍ. 1, 13.—Comp. *Araṇya-*, m. king of the forest, epithet of the lion and the tiger, Nal. 12, 13; 31. *Asura-*, m. king of the Asuras, epithet of the Asura Baka (see *vaka*), MBh. 1, 6208. *Indu-* and *Uḍu-*, m. the moon, Pañch. i. d. 104; Râm. 4, 5, 14. *Eka-*, 1. adj. only shining, Bhâg. P. 3, 5, 24. 2. m. an absolute king, ib. 1, 18, 5. *Kratu-*, m. the principal sacrifice, Man. 11, 260. *Giri-*, m. the king of the mountains, probably the Himâlaya, MBh. 6, 3419. *Tṛiṇa-*, m. the palmyra tree, Râm. 6, 91, 13. *Deva-*, m. epithet of Indra and Nahusha, Chr. 4, 20; MBh. 13, 4788. *Dharma-*, m. epithet of Yama, Yudhishṭhira, and of a king of the herons, Man. 7, 7; Draup. 8, 13; MBh. 12, 6350. *Nâga-*, m. the king of the serpents, Mârk. P. 23, 24. *Mṛiga-*, m. a lion, Çiç. 9, 18 (*patañga-*, m. the lion-like sun). *Yaksha-*, m. Kuvera. *Viçva-*, and in some cases, *viçvâ-*, m. an universal sovereign. *Sva-*, m. Brahman or Supreme Spirit.—Cf. Lat. rex.

ऽराज *-râja*, a substitute for *râjan*, when latter part of comp. words, m. A king.—Comp. *Amara-*, m. king of the gods, epithet of Indra. *Amara -çatru-*, m. epithet of Râvaṇa, Râm. 6, 35, 1. *Âdi-*, m. the first or primeval king, epithet of Manu and of a son of Kuru, Râm. 1, 6, 4; MBh. 1, 3741. *Ṛiksha-*, m. 1. the king of the bears, Râm. 6, 6, 12. 2. the king of the stars, epithet of the moon, Vikr. 39, 15. *Tṛiṇa-*, m. the palmyra tree, MBh. 4, 1309. *Deva-*, m. Indra, Râm. 6, 34, 10. *Dvija-* and *Nakshatra-*, m. the moon, Ragh. 5, 23; Râm. 5, 18, 17. *Dharma-*, m. epithet of Yama and Yudhishṭhira, MBh. 13, 3471; Hariv. 842. *Nada-*, the king of the rivers, i.e. the Sindhu, Çiç. 9, 30. *Nâga-*, 1. the king of the serpents, Kathâs. 22, 209. 2. a great elephant, MBh. 4, 1679. *Pitṛi-*, m. the king of the Manes, i.e. Yama, Sâv. 5, 14. *Bhujaga-*, m. the king of the snakes, epithet of Çesha. *Bhṛiñga-*, m. 1. a sort of bird (Lanius malabaricus), Lass. 52, 18. 2. the humble bee. 3. a sort of shrub. 4. a particular sacrifice. *Mahâ-*, m. 1. a sovereign, king, Vikr. 37, 9. 2. a finger-nail. *Mṛiga-*, m. a lion, Vikr. 70, 13. *Yaksha-*, m. Kuvera, Chr. 62, 52. *Yuvarâja*, i.e. *yuvan-*, m. a young prince, especially the heir apparent, Pañch. 156, 16. *Râjarâja*, i.e. *râjan-*, m. 1. an universal monarch, Kir. 5, 51. 2. Kuvera. 3. the moon. *Vighna-*, m. Gaṇeça. *Vimâna-*, m. the driver of a chariot (of the gods), Utt. Râmach. 55, 2. *Çaila-*, m. the king of the mountains, epithet of the Himâlaya, Megh. 51. *Sindhu-*, m. Jayadratha, the king of Sindh. *Sukha-*, m. a proper name, Râjat. 5, 206. *Sura-*, m. Indra, Râjat. 5, 157.

Saubha-, m. the king of the Saubhas, Chr. 18, 35.—Cf. Goth. reiks.

राजक *râjaka*, I. adj. **1.** *râj+aka*, Splendid. **2.** *râjan+ka*, A substitute for *râjan* when latter part of comp. adj.; e.g. *a-*, adj. Having no king, Man. 7, 3. **II.** m. A king. **III.** n. An assemblage of kings.—**Comp.** *Mahâ-*, and *mahâ-râjika*, m. a kind of demigod. *Sa-*, adj. together with the king, Böhtl. Ind. Spr. 519.

राजकीय *râjakîya*, i.e. *râjan+ka+îya*, adj. Royal, Lass. 13, 17; 31, 6.

राजघ *râjagha*, i.e. *râjan-han*, **I.** m. A king killer. **II.** adj. Sharp.

राजत *râjata*, i.e. *rajata+a*, **I.** adj. Made of silver, Man. 2, 202; Râjat. 5, 12. **II.** n. Silver (ÇKD.), Râm. 3, 49, 1.

राजतस् *râjatas*, i.e. *râjan+tas*, From a king, Man. 4, 33.

राजता *râjatâ*, i. e. *râjan+tâ*, f. Royalty, Hit. iii. d. 77.

राजन् *râj+an* (or rather *ṛij*, properly *raj*, *+an*, cf. Lat. rĕgere), **I.** m. **1.** A king, Chr. 3, 6. **2.** One of the Kshatriya caste, Man. 2, 32. **3.** A master. **4.** The moon. **5.** Indra. **6.** A Yaksha. **II.** f. *râjñî*. **1.** A queen, Chr. 54, 18; a princess, Chr. 18, 3. **2.** The wife of the sun.—**Comp.** *A-*, m. one who is not a king, Johns. Sel. 32, 61. *Kâçi-*, m. the king of Kâçi, Chr. 11, 19 (but *-râja*, 3, 9). *Dharma-râjan*, m. (cf. *râja*), Yudhishṭhira, MBh. 2, 146. *Nâga-*, m. (cf. *râja*), Nal. 14, 3.—Cf. Lat. rēgina (for regonia=*râjñî* for *râjan+yâ*), and perhaps Goth. raginon, see 2. *râj*, and *râja*.

राजन्य *râjan+ya*, m. **1.** A Kshatriya, a man of the military caste, Utt. Râmach. 152, 4; Chr. 37, 2. **2.** A name of Agni.—**Comp.** *A-*, m. one who is not a Kshatriya, Man. 4, 84.

राजन्यक *râjanya+ka*, n. A multitude of Kshatriyas.

राजन्वन्त् *râjan+vant*, adj., f. *vatî*, Possessing, or ruled by, a good king.

राजर्षि *râjarshi*, see *ṛishi*.

राजवत् *râjavat*, i.e. *râjan+vat*, adv. As towards the king, Pańch. i. d. 58.

राजवन्त् *râjavant*=*râjanvant*.

राजस *râjasa*, i.e. *rajas+a*, **I.** adj., f. *sî*. **1.** Belonging to the quality of passion, Man. 12, 32. **2.** Endowed with passion, 12, 40. **II.** f. *sî*, Durgâ.

राजसूय *râjasûya*, i.e. *râjan-su+ya*, m. A sacrifice performed by an universal monarch, attended by his tributary princes, Indr. 1, 15.

राजाय *RÂJÂYA*, a denomin. derived from *râjan* with *ya*, Âtm. To behave like a king, Hit. ii. d. 96.

राजि and **राजी** *râjî*, i.e. partly probably *ṛij* (properly *raj*, cf. Lat. di-vigere), *+î*, f. **1.** A row, a line, Pańch. i. d. 217; a stripe, Vikr. d. 78; a line parting the hair, Râm. 3, 52, 32. **2.** A continuous line.—**Comp.** *Nîla-râji*, f. a dark line, darkness, Ṛit. 1, 2 (at the end of a comp. adj.). *Vana-râj+i*, I. adj. embellishing a forest. II. f. a tree, Râm. 3, 52, 23; 55, 45; Draup. 1, 2.

राजिका f. I. *râji+kâ*, A line. **II.** A field. **III.** Black mustard, Sinapis racemosa, Pańch. 184, 18. Cf. *râjaka*.

राजीव *râjîva*, I. m. **1.** An elephant. **2.** A kind of deer. **3.** The Indian crane. **4.** A large fish, Cyprinus niloticus Buch., Man. 5, 16. **II.** n. A lotus, Chr. 50, 11; Indr. 4, 41.

राज्ञी *râjnî*, see *râjan.*

राज्य *râjya*, i.e. *râjan+ya*, n. 1. A government, Pañch. iii. d. 265. 2. A kingdom, Râm. 3, 53, 22; Pañch. 202, 19. 3. Exercise of sovereignty, Râjat. 5, 242. 4. Administration.—Comp. *Deva-*, n. the dominion over the gods, Râm. 6, 98, 19. *Pṛithivî-*, n. the sovereignty of the earth. *Mahâ-*, n. sovereignty, Chr. 3, 5. *Yuvarâjya-*, i.e. *yuvan-*, n. the dignity of heir apparent, Pañch. 130, 18. *Hṛita-*, adj. stripped of a kingdom.

राटि *râṭi*, f. War, battle.

राढा *râḍhâ* f. 1. Splendour. 2. The name of a country.

राति *râ+ti*, f. Gift, present, Lass. 99, 14=Rigv. iii. 62, 12.—Comp. *A-*, m. an enemy, Böhtl. Ind. Spr. 110. *Vâyasa-a-*, m. an owl.

ऽरात्र *-râtra*, a substitute for *râtri*, when latter part of comp. words; e.g. *ati-*, m. 1. The name of a part of the Jyotishṭoma, and of the Sattra sacrifices, Râm. 1, 13, 44; 45. 2. A proper name, Hariv. 72. *apara-*, m. The last watch of the night, Râm. 3, 22, 29. *ardha-*, m. Midnight, Man. 7, 151. *eka-*, I. m. A festival of one night's duration, MBh. 13, 4914. II. n. One night, Man. 3, 102. *chira-*, n. A long time, Man. 3, 266. *tri-*, n. sing. Three nights or days, Man. 4, 119; 5, 67. *daçarâtra*, i.e. *daçan-*, m. Ten days, Man. 5, 65. *pañchar°*, i.e. *pañchan-*, I. n. 1. Five nights or days, Man. 8, 402; 11, 147. 2. The sacred scripture of several Vaishṇava sects, MBh. 12, 7891. II. adj. Lasting five nights or days, MBh. 13, 4914. *pûrva-*, m. The first part of the night, MBh. 1, 6443. *vi-*, Deep night, Sâv. 6, 28 (cf. 5, 66). *saptar°*, i.e. *saptan-*, n. A period of seven nights, Man. 2, 187.

रात्रक *râtra+ka*, n.=*pañcharâtra*, see *râtra.*—Comp. *Pañcha(n)-*, adj. Lasting five nights, Pañch. ed. orn. 4, 17.

रात्रि and **रात्री** *râtrî*, probably *ram+tṛi+î*, f. Night, Hit. pr. d. 24, M.M.—Comp. *Kâla-*, f. 1. the last night of a Kalpa, in which the universe is destroyed by Kâla, Râm. 5, 47, 26. 2. Durgâ, Hariv. 3269. 3.=*bhîmarathî*, see *ratha.* *Yaksha-râtri*, f. the night of full moon in the month Kârttika. *Çiva-râtri*, f. a festival in honour of Çiva. *Çesha-râtri*, f. the last watch of the night.

रात्रिका *râtri+kâ*, f. Night, Râjat. 5, 482.—Comp. *Pañcha(n)-*, adj. epithet of Vishṇu (cf. *pañchan-râtra*), MBh. 12, 12864 (p. 818, l. 9, bel.).

रात्रिचर *râtri-chara*, and **रात्रिंचर** *râtriṁchara*, i.e. *râtri+m-chara*, m. A Râkshasa. *râtricharî*, f. A female Râkshasa.

रात्रिहिण्डक *râtri-hiṇḍ+aka*, m. A guard of the women's apartment.

राध् *RÂDH* (probably *râ-dhâ*), ii. 5, *râdhnu*, and i. 4, *râdhya*, Par. ved. 1. To make merciful or favourable (ii. 5). 2. To make agreeable (ii. 5). 3. To accomplish. 4. To be merciful, or favourable (i. 4). 5. To be accomplished or finished (i. 4). Ptcple. of the pf. pass. *râddha.* 1. Accomplished. 2. Perfect in mysterious or magical power, Bhâg. P. 3, 11, 17. 3. Cooked. Desider. 1. *riratsa*, 2. *ritsa*, To kill, to hurt, to destroy, Bhaṭṭ. 14, 19. —With the prep. अप *apa*, ii. 5, and i. 4, 1. To offend against, with gen., MBh. 1, 1889; to injure, Vikr. 5, 8. 2. To sin, MBh. 4, 1611. 3. To restrain, MBh. 3, 17005. *aparâddha*, 1. Sinned, Çâk. d. 57 (*na tu grîshmasyairaṁ* *subhagam aparâddhaṁ yuvatishu*, But when heat [sins against, i.e.] injures the girls, it is not so charming). **2.** Sinning, having sinned, guilty, Çâk. 110, 16 (with gen., against).—With अभि *abhi*, i. 4, To propitiate, Râm. 2, 30, 33.—With आ *â*, **1.** To accomplish, Daçak. in Chr. 197, 16 (pass.). Caus. **1**. To make favourable, to propitiate, Râm. 1, 17, 31. **2.** To conciliate, Hit. iv. d. 99; to win, Râm. 2, 60, 6. **3.** To worship, Vedântas. in Chr. 202, 6. **4.** To serve, Man. 10, 122; Pañch. 125, 12 (*kim anenârâdhitena*, For what purpose serve him?). **5.** To perform, Bhartṛ. 2, 96. *ârâdhita*, Pleased, Vikr. 85, 4. **Comp.** *Su-*, adj. caused to be very propitious, Böhtl. Ind. Spr. 2977. Comp. ptcple. of the fut. pass. *durârâdhya*, i. e. *dus-*, adj. difficult to be propitiated, or worshipped, or served, Bhartṛ. 3, 78; Bhâg. P. 4, 11, 11.—With उपा *upa-â*, Caus. To serve, Man. 10, 121.—With समा *sam-â*, Caus. **1.** To make favourable, to propitiate, MBh. 3, 10344. **2.** To satisfy, to get the approbation of, Utt. Râmach. 167, 6.—Cf. ἱλάσκομαι, ἵληθι, ἱλάομαι, etc. (for ἱλλαθ, instead of λιλαθ); cf. also ved. *iradhya*.

राध *râdh + a*, **I.** m. The month Vaiçâkha, April—May. **II.** f. *dhâ*. **1.** The sixteenth lunar asterism. **2.** The favourite mistress of Kṛishṇa, Pañch. 45, 2. **3.** The wife of the charioteer of Dhṛitarâshṭra, by whom Karṇa was fostered. **4.** Lightning. **5.** Emblic myrobalan.

राधन *râdh + ana*, **I.** n. **1.** Completing. **2.** Obtaining. **3.** Pleasure. **II.** f. *nâ*, Speaking.

राधस् *râdh + as*, n. Favour, bliss, wealth, Chr. 287, 2 = Rigv. i. 48, 2.

राधेय *râdheya*, i. e. *râdhâ + eya* (see *râdha*), metronym., m. Karṇa, Johns. Sel. 56, 155; Râjat. 5, 379.

राभस्य *râbhasya*, i.e. *rabhasa + a*, n. The state or condition of velocity, or of joy.

राम *râma*, i.e. *ram + a*, **I.** adj. **1.** Beautiful. **2.** Black. **3.** White. **II.** m. **1.** A proper name, particularly the hero of the Râmâyaṇa. **2.** A name of Varuṇa. **3.** A horse. **4.** A sort of deer. **III.** f. *mâ*, A beautiful female, Vikr. d. 114; Amar. 58.—**Comp.** *Paraçu-*, m. the first of the three renowned Râmas, the son of Jamadagni, Prab. 5, 5 (cf. Chr. 16, 17). *Bala-*, m. the third Râma, the half-brother of Kṛishṇa, MBh. 1, 7912. Cf. *râma-chandra*.

रामज *râma-ja*, m. A proper name.

रामायण *râmâyaṇa*, i.e. *râma-ayana* (or rather + *âyana*), n. The name of a renowned epic poem, Utt. Râmach. 110, 9.

राम्भ *râmbha*, i.e. *rambhă + a*, m. The bambu staff of a religious student.

राल *râla*, m. The resinous exudation of the Shorea robusta.

राव *râva*, i.e. *ru + a*, m. Sound, Hit. 92, 8.—**Comp.** *Dîrgha-*, m. the proper name of a jackal, Hit. 76, 6, M.M.

रावण *râvaṇa*, m. The king of the Râkshasas, the ravisher of Sîta, and destroyed by Râma, Râm. 3, 48, 2.

रावणि *râvaṇi*, i.e. *râvaṇa + i*, patronym., m. The eldest son of Râvaṇa.

राश् *RÂÇ*, v.r. for *râs*.

राशि *râçi*, m. **1.** A heap, a quantity, Pañch. 121, 11; 203, 7. **2.** A sign of the zodiac.—**Comp.** *Agni-*, m. a fireball, Râm. 4, 60, 17. *Ambu-* (Ragh. 6, 57), and *Lavaṇa-ambu-* (Vikr. d.

18), *Jala-* (Kathâs. 18, 2, but, plenty of water, Kir. 5, 19), *Payas-* (Hit. ii. d. 15), and *Vâri-* (Râjat. 5, 15), m. the ocean. *Brahma(n)-*, heap of holiness, Chr. 34, 15 (=Paraçurâma). *Yaças-*, m. greatness of glory, i.e. a glorious deed, Vikr. 11, 17.

राष्ट्र *râshṭra*, m. and n. I. i.e. *râj* + *tra*, **1.** A realm, empire, kingdom, Pańch. iii. d. 39 ; v. d. 64 (*kurâjântâni râshṭrâṇi*, Kingdoms find their end [i.e. are ruined] by wicked kings). **2.** An inhabited country, Lass. 76, 18. II. Any public calamity, as famine.—Comp. *Su-*, m. the name of a country, *Surat*, Râm. 3, 53, 56.

राष्ट्रिक *râshṭrika*, i.e. *râshṭra* + *ika*, adj.. sbst. Inhabiting, or an inhabitant of, a realm, Man. 10, 61.

राष्ट्रिय and **राष्ट्रीय** *râshṭrîya*, I. adj. Relating to a realm. II. (*râshtrîya*), m. A king's brother-in-law (in theatrical language), Mṛichchh. 66, 23 ; cf. Böhtl. ad Çâk. 73, 1.

रास् *RÂS* (cf. *ras*), i. 1, Âtm. (MBh. 8, 1941, Par.), To sound, to cry.—Cf. *râç*.

रास *râsa*, i.e. *ras* + *a*, m. **1.** Sound. **2.** Confused noise. **3.** Speech. **4.** A festival among the cowherds, including especially a circular dance. **5.** A chain. —Comp. *Dûrâsa*, i.e. *dus-*, m. disagreeable speech, Utt. Râmach. 44, 5.

रासभ *râsabha*, i.e. *ras* + *a* + *bha*, m. An ass, Pańch. iii. d. 118. f. *bhî*, A she-ass, Pańch. 215, 9.

रासेरस *râserasa*, m. I. i.e. *râsa* + *i-rasa*. **1.** =*râsa*. **2.** Mirth. **3.** A company, a party. II. (cf. *rasa*), Alchymy.

रासन *râsana*, m. =*rasa*, Pân. Sch. iv. 2, 92.

रास्ना *râsnâ*, f. A sort of perfume.

राहु *râhu*, i.e. *rah* + *u*, m. **1.** A Daitya to whom the eclipses are ascribed, Hit. i. d. 20, M.M. **2.** The ascending node.—Comp. *Sa-*, adj. seized by Râhu, i.e. eclipsed, Bhâg. P. 3, 17, 8.

1. **रि** *RI*, i. 6, *riya*, Par. To go.

2. **रि** *RI*, ii. 5, v. r. for *ṛi*, ii. 5, To hurt.

रिक्तक *rikta* + *ka* (vb. *rich*), adj. **1.** Void, empty. **2.** Unloaded, unburthened, Man. 8, 404.

रिक्थ *riktha*, i.e. *rich* + *tha*, n. **1.** An inheritance, Man. 9, 104. **2.** Property, Man. 8, 30. **3.** Wealth. **4.** Gold. —Comp. *Gotra-*, n. du. family and estate, Man. 9, 142.

रिक्थाद *rikthâda*, i.e. *riktha-â-da* (vb. *dâ*), m. An heir, a son, Bhâg. P. 2, 9, 40.

रिक्थिन् *rikthin*, i.e. *riktha* + *in*, I. adj. Wealthy. II. m. An heir, Man. 9, 162 (*eka-*, An heir of one man).

रिक्षा *rikshâ*, f. **1.** A nit. **2.** A mote in a sunbeam.

रिख् *RIKH*, **रिङ्ख्** *RIṄKH*, see *rakh*.

रिच् *RICH*, ii. 7, *riṇach*, *rińch*, Par. Âtm. **1.** To evacuate, to leave, pass., Vikr. d. 8 (being delivered). **2.** To separate, Bhaṭṭ. 6, 36. † i. 1, and i. 10, **1.** To join, to mix. **2.** To divide, to separate. Ptcple. of the pf. pass. *rikta*, **1.** Empty, Pańch. 89, 2. **2.** Unloaded. **3.** Purged. **4.** Free from, Ragh. 14, 85. **5.** Poor. Comp. *A-*, adj. filled, Mâlav. 45, 15. Ptcple. of i. 10, or Caus. *rechita*, **1.** Freed from. **2.** Purged.—With the prep. **अति** *ati*, pass. **1.** To surpass, with abl., Man. 4, 175 ; with acc., 2, 145 ; with instr., MBh. 3, 10588. **2.** To prevail, Man. 12, 25 ; to play the chief part, Hit.

i. d. 161, M.M. *atirikta*, Exceeding, Bhâshâp. 19; excessive.—With व्यति *vi-ati*, pass. To surpass, with abl., Ragh. 10, 31. *vyatirikta*, 1. Different, distinct, Vedântas. in Chr. 203, 14; 15. 2. Excepted. 3. Withdrawn.—With आ *â*; instead of *ârcchita* (Mixed?), Daçak. in Chr. 190, 15, I propose to read *ârachita* (Made).—With उद् *ud*, pass. To surpass, MBh. 1, 3070. *udrikta*, 1. Distinct. 2. Increased. adv. Surely, Chr. 20, 19 (perhaps, adj. and, Arrogant). *Udrechita*, Pre-eminent, Râjat. 5, 365. —With वि *vi*, *virikta*, Purged, Man. 5. 144.—Cf. Lat. licere, licitare, linquere; λείπω; Goth. af-lifnan; A.S. lyfan, be-lifan, laefan, To leave; also Goth. leihvan; A.S. laen, laenan.

† रिज् *RIJ*, i. 1, Par. To fry.

रिण्व् *RIṆV*, see *raṇv*.

रिपु *ripu*, probably *lip* + *u* (*r* for *l*, or rather the original sound), m. An enemy, Pañch. ii. d. 168. — Comp. *Krauñcha-*, m. a name of the god of war, Pañch. i. d. 175.

रिपुता *ripu* + *tâ*, f. Enmity, Hit. ii. d. 149.

रिप्र *rip* + *ra* (probably *lip* + *ra*, cf. *ripu*), adj. Vile, bad.

† रिफ् *RIPH* (ऋफ् *ṚIPH*, and रिह् *RIH*), i. 6, Par. 1. To say or to boast. 2. To fight. 3. To blame. 4. To hurt. 5. To give.

† रिम्फ् *RIMPH*, i. 6, Par. To hurt.

रिम्ब् *RIMB*, see *raṇv*.

रिरंसा *riraṁsâ*, i.e. *riraṁsa*, desider. of *ram*, + *a*, f. 1. Wish to sport, Nal. 1, 41. 2. Desire of enjoyment, Bhâg. P. 9, 14, 20.

रिरी *riri*, f. Pale brass, prince's metal.

रिश् *RIÇ* (cf. *liç*), i. 6, Par. To hurt.

रिशादस् *riçâdas*, probably *riç* + *a* -*ad* + *as*, adj. m. A destroyer of those who injure, Chr. 290, 5 = Rigv. i. 64, 5.

रिश्य *riç* + *ya*, m. A deer, see *ṛishya*.

रिष् *RISH*, i. 1 and 4, Par. 1. To kill, to hurt, MBh. 3, 13111. 2. To give offence, Man. 4, 178, Âtm. (Sch., but perhaps pass. To be hurt). 3. To be hurt (ved.). Ptcple. of the pf. pass. *rishṭa*. 1. Injured. 2. Unlucky. n. 1. Bad luck. 2. Destruction. 3. Sin. m. 1. A sword (cf. *ṛishṭi*). 2. The name of a demon.—Comp. *A-rishṭa*, see s.v.—Cf. probably ῥαίω, ῥαιστός; Lat. lædo.

रिष्टि *rishṭi*, I. f. m. A sword (cf. *ṛishṭi*). II. *rish* + *ti*, f. Bad luck.

रिष्व *rish* + *va*, adj. Injurious.

रिह् *RIH*, 1. See *riph*. 2. Ved. = *lih*. Frequent. *rerih*, ptcple. of the pres. Âtm. *rerihâṇa*, m. 1. Çiva. 2. An Asura or demon. 3. A thief.

1. री *RÎ*, ii. 9, *riṇâ*, *riṇî*, Par. 1. To go. 2. To howl. 3. To hurt.

2. री *RÎ*, i. 4, Âtm. To distil, to ooze, to drop.—With the prep. अनु *anu*, To drop after, to follow dropping, Chr. 291, 3 = Rigv. i. 85, 3.—Cf. Goth. and A.S. rinnan (based on ii. 5).

रीढक *rîḍhaka*, m. The backbone.

रीढा *rîḍhâ*, f. Disrespect.

रीति *rî* + *ti*, f. 1. Going. 2. Boundary. 3. Usage, manner, way, Lass. 2. ed. 2, 6. 4. Natural property. 5.

Oozing. 6. Brass, pale brass. 7. Calx of brass. 8. Rust of iron.

† रीव् *RÎV*, i. 1, Par. Âtm. To take.

1. रु *RU*, ii. 2, Par. 1. To sound, to make a particular sound, as birds, MBh. 1, 5898; bees, etc., to hum, Hit. i. d. 80, M.M. 2. To bray, MBh. 1, 4508. 3. To yelp, Man. 4, 113. 4. To yell, MBh. 4, 1463. Ptcple. of the pf. pass. *ruta*, n. 1. Any cry or noise, humming of bees, Bhaṭṭ. 2, 10. 2. The cry of birds, Lass. 52, 11. 3. Song, Çâk. d. 131. Frequent. *roru* and *rorûya*, To cry loudly, to yelp loudly, MBh. 1, 6112; 663. Caus. *râvaya*, To fill with a roar, MBh. 3, 15928.—With the prep. अभि *abhi*, *abhiruta*, 1. Sounded, filled with the sound of, MBh. 3, 1535. 2. Sounding. 3. Humming, Çiç. 9, 34. n. Sound, Râm. 1, 9, 17.—With आ *â*, To cry, Bhaṭṭ. 17, 24.—With वि *vi*, 1. To sound, Mṛichchh. 144, 2. 2. To yell, Pańch. 64, 4. 3. To lament, Vikr. d. 102; MBh. 3, 336. *viruta*, n. Tone, Çâk. d. 85; singing, Ṛit. 6, 33. Caus. To make a braying noise, Man. 4, 64.—With सम् *sam*, To cry, Bhaṭṭ. 17, 71.—Cf. ὠρύω (frequent.); Lat. raucus, rūmor; A.S. ryn.

†2. रु *RU*, i. 1, Âtm. 1. To go. 2. To hurt, or to be angry (?). 3. To speak.

† रुंश् *RUÑÇ*, i. 10 and 1, Par. To speak, to shine (?).

रुक्म *rukma*, i.e. *ruch*+*ma*, I. adj. Clear, bright. II. n. (ved. m., Chr. 293, 2=Rigv. i. 88, 2). 1. Gold. 2. Iron. III. m. A golden chain, Chr. 290, 4=Rigv. i. 64, 4.

रुक्मिन् *rukmin*, i.e. *rukma*+*in*, I. m. The name of a prince, slain by *Balarâma*. II. f. *minî*, A princess carried off and married by Kṛishṇa, Mâlav. d. 77; cf. Wilson, Hind. Theatr. 2. ed. 83, n.

रुक्ष and रूक्ष *rûksha*, adj. 1. Rugged, rough, difficult, Vikr. d. 61 (*rŭ*). 2. Harsh, unkind, Pańch. iv. d. 62 (*rû°*); uncouth, Pańch. v. d. 6 (*rŭ°*, but cf. Böhtl. Ind. Spr. 805); Bhartṛ. 2, 59 (*rŭ°*); cruel, Çâk. d. 191 (*rû°*). 3. Austere, Utt. Râmach. 42, 8 (*rŭ*).—Cf. A.S. rug, ruh, ruw; Engl. rough, rugged.

रुक्ष्म *rukshma*, Hard, fleshless (?), Râjat. 5, 433 (? perhaps to be changed to *ruksha*).

रुग्णता *rugna*+*tâ* (cf. *ruj*), f. 1. Sickness. 2. Crookedness.

1. रुच् *RUCH*, i. 1, Âtm. (in epic poetry also Par., MBh. 3, 468). 1. To shine, MBh. 1, 6613; Man. 4, 20. 2. To please, with dat., MBh. 1, 7550; Hit. ii. d. 49. 3. To be pleased, to approve, MBh, 1, 7444. Ptcple. of the pf. pass. *ruchita*. 1. Bright. 2. Sweet. 3. Pleased, MBh. 1, 7952. 4. Sharpened (as the appetite). 5. Digested. Ptcple. of the fut. pass. *ruchya*. 1. Beautiful. 2. Tonic, stomachic. m. A lover. n. A digestive. Caus. *rochaya*, Par. and Âtm. 1. To cause to like. 2. Âtm. To like, Man. 2, 243. 3. To choose, Râm. 1, 43, 1. 4. To resolve, Hariv. 6416.—With the prep. अति *ati*, To surpass by splendour, MBh. 3, 468.—With अनु *anu*, Caus. To desire, MBh. 3, 12679.—With अभि *abhi*, To please (with the dat. of the pers.), Vikr. 21, 11. *abhiruchita*, 1. Pleased. 2. Delighting, Johns. Sel. 93, 52. Caus. 1. To desire, to like, Râm. 2, 30, 27. 2. To be ready, Râm. 1, 36, 2.—With आ *â*, Caus. Âtm. To like, Râm. 2, 30, 28.—With प्रति *prati*, Caus. To

resolve, MBh. 3, 11546 (*prati* belongs perhaps to the noun, not to the vb.).—With वि *vi*, To shine, MBh. 3, 1754. —Cf. *loch*; Lat. lucere, lumen (cf. Goth. lauhmuni; A.S. leóma), luna; Goth. liuhath, liuhtjan; A.S. leoht, lioht, gelihtan, lócian; probably also O.H.G. liuchan, fovere, luchjan, lochon, mulcere; λευκός, λεύσσω, ἀμφι-λύκη, etc., λύχνος.

2. रुच् *ruch*, f. 1. Light, splendour, Kir. 5, 45; Çiç. 9, 23; Kir. 5, 43. 2. Beauty, Pańch. i. d. 152 (*smita-pâṭala-adhara-*, adj. Showing the beauty of smiling *pâṭala*-like lips). 3. Lightning. 4. Desire.—Comp. *Ghana-*, adj. of a cloud-like, i.e. dark, colour, Bhâg. P. 4, 5, 3. *Phaṇâ-maṇi-sahasra-*, f. the splendour of the thousand jewels of the serpent's hoods, Çiç. 9, 25. *Vistârita-varṇa-saṁkara-*, adj. shining brilliantly by the mixture of colours, and, being very desirous of the mixture of the castes, Râjat, 5, 377. *Çita-*, m. the moon, Çiç. 9, 25. *A-çita-*, m. the sun, Çiç. 9, 5.—Cf. Lat. lux.

रुचक *ruch + aka*, I. adj. Agreeable. 2. Sharp. 3. Tonic, stomachic. II. m. 1. An ornament of the neck and breast. 2. A tooth. 3. A pigeon. 4. The citron. III. n. 1. Any auspicious or fortunate object. 2. A garland, a chaplet. 3. A curl on a horse's neck. 4. A perfume, commonly *Rochanâ*. 5. Salt. 6. The fruit of the citron.

रुचि (and रुची), *ruch + ĭ*, f. 1. Light, Vikr. d. 48 (*chī*); splendour, 19, 9 (*chī*). 2. A ray of light. 3. Beauty, Bhâshâp. 1, a (at the end of a comp. adj.). 4. Appearance, Çiç. 9, 19 (at the end of a comp. adj.). 5. Wish, desire, Çiç. 9, 17; pleasure, Pâṇ. 1, 4, 33. 6. Passion. 7. Intent application to any object. 8. Hunger. 9. Taste, Pańch. iii. d. 259 (*chī*); pleasure, Râjat. 5, 1 (*chī*).—Comp. *Ushṇa-*, m. the sun, Çiç. 9, 1. *Daṇḍa-ruchi*, adj. inclined to severity, Pańch. 91, 18. *Pratigraha-*, adj. eager to take a gift, Man. 4, 190. *Mâṁsa-*, adj. liking flesh, Hit. 42, 7, M.M. *Viçesha-vikrama-*, adj. desiring to attack the pre-eminently powerful, Bhartṛ. 2, 27. *Saṁsarga-*, adj. liking intercourse (with), Pańch. iii. d. 259. *Sphurita-*, adj. having a trembling (glittering) splendour, Megh. 15. *Sva-*, adj. 1. wilful. 2. self-willed, uncontrolled.

रुचिता *ruchi + tâ*, f. Interest, interested motives, Man. 12, 32.

रुचिर *ruch + ira*, adj. 1. Beautiful, Râm. 3, 52, 16; 24; brilliant, Vikr. d. 76. 2. Agreeable, Pańch. 170, 6. 3. Sweet. 4. Stomachic.

रुचिष्य *ruch + ishya*, adj. Agreeable, pleasing.

1. रुज् *RUJ*, i. 6, Par. 1. To break, MBh. 3, 678. 2. To bend. 3. To pain, to afflict with disease. Ptcple. of the pf. pass. *rugṇa* (MBh. l. l.); also wrongly written *rugna*. 1. Broken. 2. Bent, crooked. 3. Injured. 4. Sick. Caus., and i. 10, † To hurt, to kill.—With the prep. अव *ava*, To break, MBh. 1, 5884. — With आ *â*, To break, MBh. 3, 423. —With समा *sam-â*, To break, MBh. 4, 1082.—With वि *vi*, To destroy, Çâk. d. 32, v.r.—Cf. perhaps ὀρύσσω, διωρυγή, probably λυγρός, λευγαλέος, λοιγός, λύγος; Lat. lues (cf. fruor from frug). See *romantha*.

2. रुज् *ruj*, f. 1. Pain, Man. 11, 67; Vikr. d. 30. 2. Sickness, Vikr. d. 51. 3. Effort, Megh. 27.—Comp. *Niruj*, i.e. *nis-*, adj. 1. free from pain, Suçr. 1, 289, 2. 2. healthy.

रुजस्कर *ruj + as-kara*, m. Producing pain, MBh. 3, 14144.

रुजा *ruj + â*, f. **1.** Sickness, Sâv. 5, 61; 81. **2.** Destruction. **3.** An ewe. —Comp. *A-ruja*, I. adj. 1. not breaking, Suçr. 2, 300, 14. 2. healthy, Bhartṛ. 3, 76. II. m. a proper name, Hariv. 14284. *Nîruja*, i.e. *nis-*, adj., f. *jâ*. 1. free from pain, Suçr. 1, 292, 14. 2. healthy, Hit. i. d. 14, M.M. *Sa-ruja*, adj. sick, Sâv. 5, 79. *Su-*, adj. the same.

रुजाय *RUJAYA*, a denomin. derived from *rujâ* with *ya*, Âtm. To be sick, Mâlav. 44, 7.

† **रुट्** *RUṬ*, i. 1, Âtm. **1.** To resist. **2.** To suffer pain. **3.** To shine. i. 10, **1.** To be angry. **2.** To shine, to speak (cf. *ruṭh*).

† **रुठ्** *RUṬH*, i. 1, Par. To strike, to fell. i. 1, Âtm. **1.** To resist. **2.** To suffer pain (cf. *ruṭ*).

† **रुण्ट्** *RUṆṬ*, **रुण्ड्** *RUṆḌ*, i. 1, Par. To steal.

† **रुण्ठ्** *RUṆṬH*, **लुण्ठ्** *LUṆṬH*, i. 1, Par. **1.** To go. **2.** To be idle. **3.** To be lame. **4.** To resist. **5.** To steal. See 2. *luṭh*.

रुण्ड् *RUṆḌ*, see *ruṇṭ*.

रुण्ड *ruṇḍa*, m. A headless body, retaining life and fighting, Utt. Râmach. 121, 6.

रुण्डिका *ruṇḍika* (cf. the last), f. **1.** A field of battle. **2.** Superhuman power.

रुद् *RUD*, ii. 2, Par. (in epic poetry also Âtm., Râm. 2, 52, 19, and i. 1, Chr. 24, 46). **1.** To weep, Vikr. 83, 12; Hit. 99, 3 (read *rudatî*); to cry, MBh. 2, 2616. **2.** To bewail, Bhaṭṭ. 5, 5. Ptcple. of the pf. pass. *rudita*. **1.** Wept. **2.** Weeping. n. Weeping, Daçak. in Chr. 184, 10. **Comp.** *Araṇya-*, n. complaining of one's griefs to a forest, i.e. without being heard, Amar. 76. Frequent. *rorud*, *rorudya*, To weep, to cry excessively, MBh. 3, 10192. Caus. *rodaya*, To cause to weep, Utt. Râmach. 85, 3.—With the prep. **अनु** *anu*, To weep, Nal. 3, 32.—With **उपा** *upa-â*, To bewail, Bhaṭṭ. 2, 4.—With **प्र** *pra*, **1.** To burst into tears, MBh. 3, 2919. **2.** To weep, to cry, Râm. 1, 17, 22. *pra-rudita*, **1.** Wept. **2.** Weeping, Brâhmaṇav. 3, 21. **3.** Beginning to weep, Vikr. d. 153.—With **वि** *vi*, To weep, Bhâg. P. 3, 17, 13. *virudita*, n. Weeping, Utt. Râmach. 73, 11.—Cf. Lat. rudere; O.H.G. riuzan; A.S. reotan; probably ὀρρωδέω (frequent., cf. *raudra*).

रुद्र *rud + ra*, I. adj. One who roars, Chr. 290, 3=Rigv. i. 64, 3. II. m. **1.** A name of Çiva as the god of the tempests, Pañch. pr. d. 1; Bhartṛ. 2, 93. **2.** A class of eleven demigods (personified roaring of the wind), Nal. 10, 24. **III.** f. *rudrâṇî*, Durgâ. Pâṇ. iv. 1, 49. **IV.** f. *drî*, A sort of lute.—Cf. perhaps λύρα.

रुद्राणी *rudrâṇî*, see the last.

रुध् *RUDH*, ii. 7, *ruṇadh*, *rundh*, Par. Âtm. (i. 4, see *anu*), **1.** To obstruct, MBh. 1, 2367; to check, Râm. 2, 63, 43; to stop, Vikr. d. 121; to obscure, 3, 55, 10. **2.** To keep off, Râm. 1, 28, 22. **3.** To confine, Man. 9, 12; to arrest, Vikr. d. 103. **4.** To bind, Bhartṛ. 2, 6. **5.** To hold, to support, Megh. 10. **6.** To besiege, MBh. 3, 638 (anomal. *arundhat*). Ptcple. of the pf. pass. *ruddha*. **1.** Obstructed, stopped, retained, Chr. 33, 33. **2.** Opposed. **3.** Shut, Daçak. in Chr. 187, 14 (separate, *ruddhâ dṛishṭiḥ*, 'His eye is shut'). **4.** Besieged. **5.** Surrounded. **6.** Secured, held, Çiç. 9, 75; taken possession of, Pañch. 227, 21. f. *dhâ*, A siege. Caus. To cause to be besieged, Ragh. 12, 71; epic anomal. *rundhaya*, To obstruct, pain, MBh. 3, 999.—With the prep. अनु *anu,* To retain, Man. 5, 63. i. 4, Âtm. (originally pass.; in epic poetry also with the terminations of the Par., MBh. 4, 492). **1.** (To comply with), to approve, MBh. 3, 13891. **2.** To obey, Utt. Râmach. 97, 7. **3.** To spare, MBh. 2, 926. **4.** To love, MBh. 3, 16194; Utt. Râmach. 66, 8; to caress, ib. 71, 1. *anuruddha,* **1.** Checked. **2.** Soothed.—With अव *ava,* **1.** To restrain, Râm. 2, 30, 9; to stop, Çâk. d. 35. **2.** To keep in order, Man. 8, 236. **3.** To besiege, Daçak. in Chr. 200, 23. *avaruddha,* **1.** Checked. **2.** Shut up, secluded, as in a haram. Frequent. *rorudh,* To offend, Râm. 2, 58, 20.—With आ *â,* To keep off, Bhaṭṭ. 17, 49. Caus. To obstruct, MBh. 1, 4188.—With उप *upa,* **1.** To obstruct, Man. 8, 348. **2.** To block up, Man. 7, 195. **3.** To molest, Çâk. 24, 8; to trouble, 18, 10. **4.** To obscure, Ragh. 7, 36. *uparuddha,* **1.** Obstructed. **2.** Covered. **3.** Favoured.—With नि *ni,* **1.** To obstruct, Hit. i. d. 154, M.M.; to stop, Çâk. d. 169. **2.** To restrain, MBh. 3, 13633. **3.** To confine, Man. 11, 176. **4.** To keep off, Bhag. 16, 20. *niruddha,* Obstructed (not able to work fitly), Pańch. ii. d. 164. Caus. To cause to be shut, Râjat. 5, 428.—With संनि *sam-ni,* To confine, Man. 9, 83. —With प्र *pra,* To keep back, MBh. 3, 16830.—With प्रति *prati,* **1.** To obstruct, MBh. 3, 12114; to stop, Chr. 43, 30. **2.** To make unable to move, Chr. 28, 21. **3.** To interrupt, to make imperfect, Man. 11, 11. **4.** To accuse unjustly, Man. 11, 88. *pratiruddha,* **1.** Impeded. **2.** Surrounded, blockaded. —With वि *vi,* **1.** To withhold, MBh. 2, 227. **2.** To obstruct, Ṛit. 6, 26; to check, Râm. 2, 36, 10. **3.** To combat, to quarrel with, Pańch. iii. d. 123; iv. d. 82. *viruddha,* **1.** Opposed, hindered. **2.** Prohibited, Man. 4, 15. **3.** Contrary, opposite, Çiç. 9, 62; Pańch. 131, 11; perverse, Pańch. 199, 4; °*dham,* Perversely, Pańch. i. d. 64. **4.** Inconsistent, incongruous, Bhâshâp. 70; Pańch. 130, 1. **5.** Hostile, Râjat. 5, 452; Pańch. 213, 20; disagreeable, Hit. 58, 18. **6.** Surrounded, blockaded, shut up, Pańch. iv. d. 78. **Comp.** 1. *A*-, adj. unobstructed, without obstacles, Vikr. 49, 16; untroubled, Pańch. i. d. 406. 2. friendly, kind, with gen., Lass. 2. ed. 45, 16. *Smṛiti*-, adj. contrary to law. Caus. To obstruct, MBh. 3, 360. *virodhita,* Fought with, Pańch. iii. d. 1.—With सम् *sam,* **1.** To obstruct, MBh. 3, 2541; to check, 2, 226. **2.** To refrain, MBh. 3, 13633. **3.** To fetter, Bhartṛ. 2, 14. *sańruddha,* **1.** Obstructed, Man. 8, 295. **2.** Attacked, 8, 235. **Comp.** *A*-, adj. unimpeded, Râjat. 5, 453. Caus. To cause to be embanked, 5, 106.—With अभिसम् *abhi-sam,* To keep off, Râm. 2, 14, 42.

ऽरुध् *-rudh,* adj. Impeding; e.g. *kara*-, adj. Impeding the hand, or rays, viz. of the sun, Megh. 40.

रुधिर *rudhira* (from a vb. *rudh,* lost in corresponding signification), n. **1.** Blood, Pańch. 123, 14. **2.** Saffron.—Cf. O.H.G. rôt; A.S. reád, roder; ἐρυθρός, ἐρεύθω, ῥούσιος; Lat. rutilus (for old ruthilus), rufus, ruber, robigo, etc.

† **रुप्** *RUP,* i. 4, Par. To confound (cf. *lup*).

रुमण्वन्त् *rumaṇvant,* i.e. *ruman* (=*lavaṇa*), + *vant,* m. The name of a mountain, Pâṇ. 8, 2, 12.

रुमा *rumâ,* f. **1.** The wife of a monkey. **2.** The name of a district.

रुम्र *rumra*, adj. **1.** Tawny. **2.** Beautiful (cf. *rumaṇvant* and *lavaṇa*).

रुरु *ruru*, m. A sort of deer, Draup. 4, 15.

रुवथ *ruvatha*, i.e. *ru*+*athu*, m. A dog.

† रुश् *RUÇ*, i. 6, Par. To hurt.

रुशन्त् *ruçant*, adj. I. Probably originally a ptcple. pres. of *ruch*, f. *çati*, Red, Chr. 288, 13=Rigv. i. 48, 13. II. Probably a ptcple. pres. of *rush*, Cursing, imprecative.

1. रुष् *RUSH* (akin to *ruksh* in *ruksha*), † i. 1 and 4, Par. † To hurt. † i. 4 and i. 10, Par. To be angry. Ptcple. of the pf. pass. *rushṭa* (Pańch. 223, 9; Çringârat. 7), *rushita* (Man. 9, 83), and *roshita*, Enraged. Caus. To irritate, Pańch. 163, 4. *roshita*, Irritated, Daçak. in Chr. 186, 16.—Cf. probably λύσσα, perhaps ἀλυσταίνω, ἀλυκταίνω, ἀλαλύκτημαι; Goth. in-rauhtjan.

2. रुष् *rush* (and रुषा *rush*+*â*), f. Wrath, anger, Pańch. iv. d. 61; Vikr. d. 80.—**Comp.** *Ati-rush*, adj. very furious, Pańch. ii. d. 34. *Sa-rush*, adj. angry, Pańch. i. d. 80 (cf. Böhtl. Ind. Spr. 3196).

रुह् *RUH* (originally *rudh*, cf. *nyagrodha*), i. 1, Par. (in epic poetry also Âtm.). **1.** To grow, Man. 9, 36. **2.** To be lost by growing, to cicatrize, to heal, Pańch. iii. d. 112 (but cf. Böhtl. Ind. Spr. 2647). **3.** Pass. with the terminat. of the Par. To be mounted, Johns. Sel. 11, 25. Ptcple. of the pf. pass. *rûḍha*, **1.** Grown, increased, much, Râjat. 5, 173. **2.** Budded, blown. **3.** Born, produced. **4.** Certain. **5.** Notorious, Daçak. in Chr. 193, 10. **6.** Traditional, conventional, applied especially to words of unknown origin, but of which the employment is familiar. **7.** Obscure, Çiç. 10, 23. **Comp.** *Dûrûḍha*, i.e. *dus-*, adj. badly cicatrized, Suçr. 1, 297, 7. *Su-*, adj. prominent. Caus. I. *rohaya*. II. *ropaya*. **1.** To plant, Râm. 2, 80, 7 (*ropaya*). **2.** To sow, MBh. 3, 13116 (*rohaya*).—With the prep. व्यति *vi-ati*, To obtain, MBh. 3, 13929. Caus. *ropaya*, To cover, MBh. 3, 601.—With अधि *adhi*, **1.** To ascend, to mount on, Vikr. d. 14; Râjat. 5, 217. **2.** To fly upward, Râm. 2, 95, 11. Caus. *ropaya*, **1.** To lift, Ragh. 11, 81. **2.** To give, Daçak. in Chr. 186, 21.—With व्यप *vi-apa*, Caus. *ropaya*, To deprive, MBh. 3, 1579.—With अभि *abhi*, To ascend, to mount, Râm. 1, 44, 5; Chr. 36, 17.—With अव *ava*, To descend, Râm. 2, 7, 11. Caus. I. *rohaya*, To order to descend, Ragh. 1, 54. **II.** *ropaya*, **1.** To take down, MBh. 4, 1318. **2.** To root up, Johns. Sel. 53, 123. **3.** To diminish, Man. 1, 82. **4.** Âtm. To alight from, Draup. 3, 8.—With प्रत्यव *prati-ava*, Caus. *ropaya*, To deprive, MBh. 4, 536.—With आ *â*, **1.** To mount, Râm. 3, 48, 5. **2.** To ascend to (with acc., MBh. 3, 1727. *ankam âruhya*, Having climbed into one's lap, Hit. ii. d. 166. **3.** With *saṁçayam*, To doubt, Hit. i. d. 6. **4.** With *pratijńâm*, To promise, MBh. 1, 2015. *ârûḍha*, **1.** Mounted, Man. 4, 120. **2.** Standing, Man. 7, 91. **3.** Elevated, Pańch. i. d. 225. **4.** Having reached, Pańch. 87, 14. **Comp.** *Haya-*, adj. mounted on horseback, Hit. iii. d. 85. *Ratha-*, adj. mounted on a chariot, Vikr. 5. 4. *Lekhya-*, adj. recorded. Caus. *ropaya*, **1.** To cause, to ascend, Chr. 4, 14; Âtm. To try to string, Johns. Sel. 49, 93. **2.** To lift up, Hit. ii. d. 44; on, Chr. 11, 21; to cast, Pańch. i. d. 273; with *tulâm*, To put in a balance, i.e. in danger, Pañch. i. d. 421. Absol. *âruhya,* Having encountered, Hit. i. d. 5, M.M. **3.** To put upon, Pañch. 41, 15. **4.** To draw (a bow), Utt. Râmach. 118, 1. **5.** To take to, Man. 3, 17. **6.** To cause to grow, to plant, Râjat. 5, 149. **7.** To transfer, Vedântas. in Chr. 210, 12.—With अत्या *ati-â, atyârudha,* Risen, Utt. Râmach. 147, 14.—With अध्या *adhi-â,* To mount, Daçak. in Chr. 188, 16. Caus. *ropaya,* **1.** To cause to ascend, Râm. 2, 55, 15. **2.** To elevate, Pañch. 24, 9.—With अन्वा *anu-â,* To ascend after, MBh. 2, 36.—With समन्वा *sam-anu-â,* The same, MBh. 1, 3818.—With उपा *upa-â,* **1.** To ascend, MBh. 2, 37. **2.** To obtain, Ragh. 17, 30 (Calc.).—With प्रा *pra-â,* To ascend, MBh. 3, 10594.—With प्रत्या *prati-â,* Caus. To cause to remount, Utt. Râmach. 133, 4.—With समा *sam-â,* **1.** To mount on, Pañch. 115, 3; Chr. 45, 12. **2.** To engage, Prab. 116, 9. *samârûdha,* Mounted, Pañch. 48, 10. Caus. *ropaya,* **1.** To cause to mount, Pañch. 44, 16; to lift up, 52, 2. **2.** To deposit, Man. 6, 38.—With उप *upa, uparûdha,* Undergone, Mûlav. 31, 13.—With प्र *pra,* **1.** To shoot up, Pañch. iii. d. 55. **2.** To grow, Man. 9, 14. **3.** To heal, Pañch. iii. d. 112. *prarûdha,* **1.** Grown long, Pañch. 182, 10. **2.** Rooted, fastened **3.** Born, produced. m. The belly.—With प्रति *prati,* Caus. *ropaya,* To reestablish, Ragh. 17, 42 (Calc.).—With वि *vi,* **1.** To grow, Çâk. d. 96. **2.** To spread, Bhag. 15, 3. *virûdha,* **1.** Budded, blown. **2.** Born. Caus. *ropaya,* To heal, Daçak. in Chr. 195, 21.—With सम् *sam,* To grow, Bhaṭṭ. 11, 5. *saṁrûdha,* **1.** Budded. **2.** Confident, Arj. 11, 1. Caus. To plant, to cause to get offspring, Çâk. 138, 1, Chezy.—Cf. Goth. liugan, jugga-lauths; A.S. leód, liód, probably λαός, βασι-λεύς.

रुह *ruh + a,* I. adj. **1.** Growing. **2.** Mounted. II. f. *hâ,* Bent grass.—Comp. *Jagatî-,* m. a tree, MBh. 7, 8098. *Jala-,* n. a lotus, ib. 1, 5005. *Tanû-,* I. m. a son, Çâtr. 10, 52. II. n. (and m.). 1. the hair of the body, Arj. 5, 3. 2. the wing of a bird, Varâh. Bṛih. S. 62, 1. *Tîra-,* I. adj. growing on the bank of a river, Râm. 2, 95, 4. II. m. a tree growing on the bank of a river, ib. 104, 4 Gorr. *Vîja-kâṇḍa-,* adj. springing from a seed, or from a slip, Man. 1, 48.

रुक्वन् *ruh + van,* m. A tree.

† **रूक्ष्** *RÛKSH,* i. 10 (rather a denomin. derived from *rûksha*), Par. To be harsh.

रूक्ष *rûksha,* see *ruksha.*

रूढि *rûdhi,* i.e. *ruh + ti.* **1.** Growing, Râjat. 5, 477. **2.** Birth. **3.** Notoriety. **4.** Traditional meaning of words as opposed to their etymological signification, Pan. i. 2, 55.

रूप् *RÛP,* i. 10 (rather a denomin. derived from *rûpa*), Par. **1.** To form, to represent in pantomime, Vikr. 6, 6; 12, 16; to notify by a gesture, Vikr. 47, 13. **2.** To feign, Vikr. 12, 17.—With the prep. नि *ni,* **1.** To perform, Man. 6, 38. **2.** To represent in pantomime, Çâk. 5, 16; Vikr. 29, 8. **3.** To look out, Vikr. 39, 5; to see, 78, 11; to perceive, Daçak. in Chr. 200, 10. **4.** To consider, to ponder, Hit. 10, 3. **5.** To investigate, Utt. Râmach. 39, 18; to examine, Hit. 99, 1. **6.** To search, Hit. 68, 14. **7.** To select, Pañch. 161, 10. **8.** To appoint, 8, 24; 184, 8. *nirûpita*, **1.** Seen. **2.** Discovered. **3.** Considered, Bhâshâp. 124. **4.** Ascertained, Bhâshâp. 107. **5.** Resolved, Pańch. 158, 18. **6.** Appointed. Comp. *Su-nirûpita*, adj. 1. well-considered, Pańch. iii. d. 74. 2. well-searched, Hit. 91, 1. 3. well-ascertained, Hit. 98, 15.—With वि *vi*, To disfigure, Hit. 65, 1. *virûpita*, Deformed, Man. 4, 67.

रूप *rûpa* (probably from *rûp*, an old form of *rop*, in *ropaya*, the Caus. of *ruh*), n. **1.** Natural state or condition. **2.** State, Pańch. 137, 19. **3.** Form, Vikr. d. 9; figure, Chr. 17, 28; kind, Pańch. 21, 25. **4.** Appearance. **5.** An image. **6.** Beauty, Pańch. iii. d. 239. **7.** Colour, Bhâshâp. 2. 99. **8.** A play, a dramatic poem.—Comp. *A-*, adj., f. *pâ*, disfigured, Râm. 2, 23, 43. *Ati-*, I. n. beauty, Lass. 37, 5. II. adj. beautiful, Râm. 3, 23, 16. *Anya-*, I. n. another shape, Kathâs. 13, 172. II. adj., f. *pâ*, having another shape, Kathâs. 12, 195. *An-eka-*, adj., f. *pâ*, having manifold forms, Hit. ii. d. 174. *Açva-*, adj. having the shape of a horse, Pańch. 258, 23. *Kâma-*, I. n. a shape changing as one lists, MBh. 1, 6077. II. adj., f. *pâ*, taking any or every shape at will, Megh. 6. III. m. sing. and pl. the name of a country, Ragh. 4, 83. *Kiṁrûpa*, i.e. *kim-*, adj. of what shape, Pańch. 258, 13. See *Ku-*. *Jâta-* (vb. *jan*), I. n. gold, Nal. 1, 19. II. adj. golden, MBh. 14, 190. *Tathâ-*, adj., f. *pâ*, having such a shape, Pańch. 44, 20. *Garbha-*, adj. child-like, Utt. Râmach. 168, 3. *Deça-*, n. suitableness, MBh. 12, 3961. *Nashṭa-*, adj. disappeared, MBh. 3, 2604. *Nânâ-*, I. n. pl. many shapes, Râm. 3, 1, 21 Gorr. II. adj. having many shapes, different, Man. 9, 38. *Padma-*, adj., f. *pâ*, having the colour of a lotus, MBh. 3, 14404. *Puṁrûpa*, i.e. *puṁs-*, n. the shape of a man, Kathâs. 39, 175. *Pûrva-*, I. n. symptom of occurring disease, Suçr. 1, 127, 12. II. adj., f. *pâ*, having its former shape, Lass. 72, 13. *Prâpta-*, adj. 1. handsome. 2. learned, wise. 3. suitable, Daçak. in Chr. 198, 5. *Bhavya-*, adj., f. *pâ*, good, Râm. 3, 52, 14. *Yukta-*, adj. suitable, Çâk. d. 12. *Vi-*, I. adj. 1. deformed, Pańch. i. d. 159. 2. unusual. 3. wicked, Pańch. 213, 23. II. n. 1. difference of nature. 2. deformity, Châṇ. 73 in Berl. Monatsb. 1864, 411; monstrous shape. III. f. *pâ*, the wife of Yama. *Viçva-*, I. adj. taking all forms, omnipresent. II. m. Vishṇu. *Sa-*, adj. like, resembling. *Saṁkalpa-*, adj. conformable to one's wish. *Sva-*, I. n. 1. one's own shape, Chr. 62, 51. 2. natural condition, nature, Pańch. 145, 16. 3. natural and obvious purpose. 4. kind. II. adj. 1. of like character, Vedântas. in Chr. 217, 5. 2. like, similar, suitable, Lass. 35, 12. 3. pleasing, Lass. 20, 11. 4. wise. *Âtmasvarûpa*, i.e. *âtman-sva-*, adj. true (just as it happened), Pańch. 43, 12. *Strî-sva-*, adj. having the body of a female, Chr. 61, 45. *Hṛishṭa-*, adj., f. *pâ*, having the hair of the body erect with pleasure, Chr. 60, 33.

रूपक *rûpa+ka*, n. **1.** Shape. **2.** A drama. **3.** A kind of coin (cf. *rûpya*), Pańch. 127, 8; 252, 13.—Comp. *Mahâ-*, n. a drama. *Vi-*, adj. 1. misshaped. 2. frightful, hideous, used as nickname, Daçak. in Chr. 184, 12.

रूपतस् *rûpa+tas*, adv. By shape, Nal. 19, 32.

रूपवन्त् *rûpa+vant*, adj., f. *vatî*, **1.** Having shape. **2.** Beautiful, Pańch. i. d. 159, Chr.—Comp. *Adhika-*, adj., f. *vatî*, most beautiful, Hit. 115, 5. *Strî-sva-*, adj. having the body of a female, Chr. 61, 42.

रूपिन् *rûpin*, i.e. *rûpa+in*, adj., f.

in̂, **1.** Having shape. **2.** Beautiful, Sâv. 1, 26.—**Comp.** When latter part of comp. words, *rûpa* generally belongs to the former part, and the aff. *in* to the comp. word. *A-*, adj. without shape, Râm. 1, 23, 15. *Anya-*, adj. having another shape, Kathâs. 16, 44. *Kun̂jara-*, adj. having the shape of an elephant, Sund. 2, 20. *Kshapaṇaka-*, adj. wearing the guise of a Bauddha mendicant, Pańch. 235, 10. *Tathâ-*, adj. having such a shape, MBh. 12, 7344. *Deva-*, adj. having a divine shape, Hiḍ. 2, 24. *Mṛiga-*, adj. having the shape of an antelope, Râm. 3, 49, 21. *Sâdhana-*, adj. having the form or character of expedients, Vedântas. in Chr. 219, 9. *Sva-*, adj. endowed with one's own form, Chr. 26, 64. *Strî-sva-*, adj. having the body of a female, Chr. 63, 67.

रूप्य *rûpya*, i.e. *rûpa*+*ya*, I. adj. Handsome, Pâṇ. v. 2, 120. II. n. **1.** Silver, Man. 4, 230. **2.** Wrought silver, Pâṇ. ib. **3.** Wrought gold.—**Comp.** *Sama-*, i.e. *samarûpa*+*ya*, adj. of like or same origin.

ऽरूप्यक *'-rûpya*+*ka*, in *suvarṇa-rûpya*+*ka*, adj. Abounding in gold and silver, Râm. 4, 40, 33.

रूप्यमय *rûpya*+*maya*, adj., f. *yî*, Consisting of silver, Pańch. 241, 16.

रूष् *RÛSH*, i. 1, Par. † To decorate. i. 10, Par. **1.** To tremble. **2.** To burst. Ptcple. of the pf. pass. *rûshita*. **1.** Adorned, Indr. 5, 8. **2.** Inlaid, covered, Râm. 4, 19, 32. **3.** Made rough or rugged. **4.** Pounded, reduced to dust.

रे *re*, A vocative particle, implying contempt or woe, Hit. 81, 21; Bhartṛ. 1, 68.

† रेक् *REK*, i. 1, Âtm. To suspect.

रेक *reka*, I. m., and f. *kâ*. **1.** Doubt. **2.** Fear. II. m. **1.** Loosening, purging (i.e. *rich*+*a*). **2.** An outcaste. **3.** A frog.

रेक्नस् *reknas*, i.e. *rich* + *nas*, n. Gold.

रेखा *rekhâ*, i.e. *likh*+*a*, f. **1.** A line, Pańch. ii. d. 183. **2.** Drawing, Çâk. d. 141. **3.** A stripe, Pańch. i. d. 209. **4.** A little, Pańch. ii. d. 148. **5.** Fraud. **6.** Fulness, satisfaction.—**Comp.** *Chandra-*, f. *khâ* the crescent, Râm. 5, 20, 3. *Patra-*, f. *khâ*, decorating the person by staining it with fragrant pigments of sandal, musk, etc., Ragh. 16, 67. *Sama-rekha*, adj. straight, Çâk. d. 9.—Cf. probably O.H.G. riga.

रेचक *rechaka*, i.e. *rich*+*aka*, I. adj. Purgative, aperient. II. m. **1.** A purgative. **2.** A proper name, Vikr. 76, 2 (but cf. Wilson, Spec. of the Theatre of the Hind. i. 2. ed. p. 260, n.). III. n. A purge. IV. m. or n. Exhalation, Bhâg. P. 3, 28, 9; a method of suppressing the breath, Vedântas. in Chr. 217, 17.

रेचन *rechana*, i.e. *rich*+*ana*, n., and f. *nâ*, **1.** Purging, looseness. **2.** Evacuating, Bhâshâp. 6.

रेज् *REJ*, i. 1, Âtm. **1.** To shine. **2.** Ved. To tremble.—With the prep. प्र *pra*, To tremble vehemently, Chr. 293, 3=Rigv. i. 87, 3.

† रेट् *REṬ*, i. 1, Par. Âtm. **1.** To speak. **2.** To ask.

रेणु *reṇu*, m. (and f.), Dust, Vikr. d. 4; Pańch. ii. d. 108.—**Comp.** *Trasa-*, see s. v. *Rakta-*, m. 1. red lead. 2. the blossom of the Butea frondosa. 3. a sort of cloth. 4. an angry man. *Sikatâ-*, m. a grain of sand, Pańch. ii. d. 62. *Su-* and *Hema-*, n. sorts of atom.

रेणुका *reṇu+kâ*, f. **1.** A sort of perfume and medicine. **2.** A sort of pulse, Ervum. **3.** The wife of *Jamadagni* and mother of *Paraçu-râma*, MBh. 3, 11072.

रेतस् *retas*, i.e. *rî+tas*, **1.** Semen virile, MBh. 13, 1160. **2.** Quicksilver. —**Comp.** *Ûrdhva-*, I. adj. chaste, MBh. 2, 470; Hariv. 949. II. m. a name of Çiva, MBh. 13, 1160. *Kumbha-*, I. n. semen virile contained in a jar, MBh. 13, 7372. II. m. a name of Agni, MBh. 3, 14139. *Vasu-*, m. fire, MBh. 1, 1021. *Vahni-*, m. Çiva. *Viçva-*, m. Brahman. *Hiraṇya-*, m. 1. fire, Daçak. in Chr. 181, 14. 2. the sun. 3. Çiva.

रेत्र *retra*, i.e. *rî+tra*, n. **1.** Semen virile. **2.** Nectar. **3.** Quicksilver.

† **रेप्** *REP*, i. 1, Âtm. **1.** To go. **2.** To sound.

रेप *repa*, i.e. *lip+a*, adj. **1.** Low. **2.** Niggardly. **3.** Cruel.

रेपस् *repas*, i.e. *lip+as*, n. Wrong or blameable action.—**Comp.** *Vi-*, adj. without blemish, faultless.

रेफ *repha*, I. adj. Contemptible, bad. II. m. The letter *R*.—**Comp.** *Dvi-*, m. A sort of bee (properly containing two *r*'s in its name *bhramara*), Hariv. 4585.

रेब् *REB*, see *rev*.

रेभ् *REBH*, i. 1, Âtm. **1.** To sound. **2.** Ved. Par. To praise.—Cf. *ῥοίβδην*, *ῥοῖβδος*, *ῥοιβδέω*.

रेभण *rebhaṇa*, i.e. *rebh+ana*, n. The lowing of kine.

† **रेव्** *REV*, **रेब्** *REB*, i. 1, Âtm. **1.** To go by leaps, to flow. **2.** To go.

रेवन्त् *revant*, i.e. *rayi+vant*, I. adj., f. *vatî*, Wealthy, Chr. 295, 14=Rigv. i. 92, 14. II. f. *vatî*. **1.** A cow. **2.** The last of the lunar asterisms. **3.** One of the *mâtṛis* or energies of the gods. **4.** The wife of *Bala-râma*, Megh. 50, cf. Vishṇu P. 439.

रेवन्त *revant+a*, m. The fifth Manu of the present Kalpa or period.

रेवा *revâ* (akin to *revant*), f. **1.** The *Narmadâ* river, Megh. 19. **2.** The wife of Kâma. **3.** The indigo plant.

† **रेष्** *RESH* (for *hresh*, q. cf.), i. 1, Âtm. **1.** To howl. **2.** To neigh.

रै *RAI*, i. 1, Par. To bark.—Cf. Lat. latrare.

रै *rai* (cf. *rayi*), m. **1.** Wealth, property, Chr. 287, 1=Rigv. i. 48, 1. **2.** Gold.—Cf. Lat. res.

रैत्य *raitya*, i.e. *rîti+ya*, adj. Brazen, made of brass.

रैवत *raivata*, i.e. *revant+a* (cf. *revanta*), m. **1.** The fifth Manu, Man. 1, 62. **2.** A name of Çiva. **3.** A Daitya. **4.** A mountain, the eastern part of the Vindhya range.

रैवतक *raivata+ka*, m. **1.** The mountain *Raivata*. **2.** A proper name.

रैवतिक *raivatika*, i.e. *revatî+ika* (cf. *revant*), m. A descendant of *Revatî*, Pâṇ. iv. 1, 146; iv. 3, 131.

रोक *roka*, i.e. *ruch+a*, I. m. **1.** Light. **2.** Buying with ready money. **II.** n. **1.** A hole. **2.** A boat. **3.** Moving.

रोग *roga*, i.e. *ruj+a*, I. m. **1.** Disease, Pañch. iii. d. 244. **2.** A sort of Costus, C. speciosus.—**Comp.** *A-*, I. m. health, Hit. i. d. 166, M.M. II. adj., f. *gâ*, healthy, Man. 1, 83. *Kshudroga*, i.e. *kshudh-*, m. hunger, Pañch. 70, 13. *Tṛishâ-*, m. a morbose thirst, MBh. 12, 11268. *Niroga*, i.e. *nis-*, adj.

healthy, Pańch. i. d. 134. *Pâṇḍu-*, m. the jaundice, Suçr. 1, 90, 11. *Pâpa-*, m. a disease considered as a punishment for sin, Man. 5, 164. *Sa-*, adj. sick. *Hṛid-*, m. 1. any disease of the heart. 2. heart-burn. 3. sorrow, Chr. 289, 11=Rigv. i. 50, 11.

रोगभाज् *rogabhâj*, i.e. *roga-bhaj*, adj. One who suffers from a disease, Pańch. i. d. 217.

रोगिता *rogitâ*, i.e. *rogin* + *tâ*, f. in *a-*, Health, Hit. pr. d. 19, M.M. *sa-*, f. Sickness, Hit. ii. d. 4.

रोगिन् *rogin*, i.e. *roga* + *in*, adj., f. *iṇî*, Sick, Man. 2, 138.—**Comp.** *A-*, adj. healthy, Hit. iii. d. 112. *Pâṇḍu-*, i.e. *pâṇḍu-roga* + *in*, adj. jaundiced, Suçr. 1, 45, 10. *Pâpa-*, i.e. *pâpa-roga* + *in*, adj. one who suffers from a disease considered as a punishment for sin, Man. 3, 159.

रोचक *rochaka*, i.e. *ruch* + *aka*, **1.** adj. What pleases, brightens. **II.** m. **1.** Hunger. **2.** A stomachic. **3.** A sort of onion. **4.** Plantain.—**Comp.** *A-*, I. adj. producing want of appetite, Suçr. 1, 207, 13. II. m. want of appetite, ib. 1, 169, 1.

रोचन *rochana*, i.e. *ruch* + *ana*, **I.** adj. **1.** Irradiating. **2.** Splendid. **3.** Pleasing. **4.** Sharpening (the appetite). **II.** m. **1.** A stomachic. **2.** The name of several plants. **III.** f. *nâ* and *nî*, A yellow pigment, supposed to be the concrete bile of the cow, or to be found in the head of the animal, Man. 8, 234. **IV.** f. *nâ*, An excellent woman. **V.** f. *nî*, Red arsenic, Pâṇ. iv. 2, 2. **VI.** n. The æther, Chr. 288, 1=Rigv. i. 49, 1. —**Comp.** *Go-rochanâ*, f. a yellow pigment, Pańch. i. d. 107=**III.** *Yoga-rochanâ*, f. a magical *rochanâ*, or unguent, which makes invisible and invulnerable, Mṛichchh. 47, 22–24. *Vaṁça-rochanâ*, f. Bambu manna.

रोचिष्णु *rochishṇu*, i.e. *ruch* + *ishṇu*, adj. Elegantly dressed, Pâṇ. iii. 2, 136.

रोचिस् *rochis*, i. e. *ruch* + *is*, n. Light, flame.—**Comp.** *Vasu-*, n. a religious ceremony in which the Vasus especially are worshipped.

† रोड् *ROḌ* (cf. *rush*), i. 1, Par. **1.** To be mad. **2.** and रौट् *RAUṬ*, रौड् *RAUḌ*, i. 1, Par. To despise.

रोदन *rodana*, i.e. *rud* + *ana*, n. **1.** Weeping, Lass. 30, 7. **2.** A tear, tears.

रोदस् *rodas*, i.e. *rud* + *as* (the seat of the roaring storm), n. Heaven. du. *sî*, and as former part of a comp. Heaven and earth, Vikr. d. 1; Chr. 46, 23; Nal. 3, 32.

रोध *rodha*, i.e. *rudh* + *a*, m. **1.** Obstruction, Kir. 5, 15. **2.** A bank, a shore. —**Comp.** *Prâṇa-*, m. danger of life, Hit. iv. d. 23 (but cf. Böhtl. Ind. Spr. 3136).

रोधन *rodhana*, i.e. *rudh* + *ana*, **I.** adj. That which obstructs. **II.** m. The planet Mercury. **III.** n. **1.** Obstructing. **2.** Besieging.

रोधस् *rodhas*, i. e. *rudh* + *as*, n. **1.** A bank, a shore, Vikr. d. 8. **2.** The brink of a well, Bhâg. P. 9, 19, 4. **3.** The flank, Bhâg. P. 3, 20, 29.

ऽरोधिन् *-rodhin*, i.e. *rudh* + *in*, adj. Stopping, Râjat. 5, 346; Çâk. d. 135.

रोध्र *rodhra*, i.e. **I.** *rudh* + *ra*, n. **1.** Sin. **2.** Offence. **II.** Probably akin to *rudhira*, m. A tree, the bark of which is used in dyeing, Ragh. 2, 29.

रोप् *rop*, see *ruh*.

रोप *ropa*, **I.** m. probably *ruh*, Caus., + *a*, An arrow. **II** i.e. *rup*=*lup* + *a*, Confusing. **III.** n. A hole.

रोपण *ropaṇa*, n. **I.** i.e. *ruh*, Caus.,

+*ana*. **1.** Planting. **2.** Raising. **3.** Placing. **4.** Cicatrizing. **5.** A healing application to sores. **II.** i.e. *rup*=*lup* +*ana*, Confusing.

रोपणाका *ropaṇâkâ*, f. A bird, Turdus salica, Chr. 289, 12=Rigv. i. 50, 12.

रोम *roma*, n. Water.

रोमन् *roman*, i.e. *ruh*+*man*, n. The hair of the body, Pańch. iii. d. 186. —Comp. *Ûrdhva-*, I. adj. one whose hairs are erect, Bhâg. P. 6, 1, 28. II. m. the name of a mountain, ib. 5, 20, 15. *Kâńchana-* and *Suvarṇa-*, adj. having gold-like wool, Râm. 3, 49, 4; (Pańch. 35, 1, i.e. a ram). *Stabdha-* (vb. *stambh*), m. a hog.

रोमन्थ *romantha*, probably a noun derived from *ruj*, and compounded with *manth*+*a*, m. **1.** Ruminating, Çâk. d. 39. **2.** Chewing, Râjat. 5, 364.—Cf. O.H.G. ita-ruchjan; A.S. roccettan; Lat. rūmen, ruminare (for rug-men), ructare; ἐρεύγομαι (old frequent.), ἐρυγγάνω, ὀρυγγάνω, etc.

रोमन्थाय *ROMANTHÂYA*, a denomin. derived from *romantha* with *ya*, Âtm. To ruminate, Pâṇ. iii. 1, 15.

रोमवन्त् *romavant*, i. e. *roman*+*vant*, adj., f. *vatî*, Hairy, woolly.

रोमश *romaça*, i.e. *roman*+*ça*, I. adj. **1.** Hairy, Man. 3, 7. **2.** Woolly. II. m. **1.** A ram. **2.** A hog.

रोमाञ्च *româńcha*, i.e. *roman-ańch* +*a*, m. Horripilation, considered as a sign of rapture, Pańch. ii. d. 175.

रोमाञ्चित *româńchita*, i.e. *româńcha*+*ita*, adj. **1.** Affected with horripilation, Utt. Râmach. 81, 4. **2.** Enraptured, Pańch. 128, 21.

रोष *rosha*, i.e. *rush*+*a*, m. Anger, wrath, Vikr. d. 144; Pańch. 174, 25.—Comp. *Vi-*, adj. angry, Draup. 9, 6. *Sa-*, adj. angry, Çiç. 9, 83. °*sham*, adv. angrily, Vikr. 55, 7.

रोषण *roshaṇa*, i.e. *rush*+*ana*, I. adj. Angry. II. m. **1.** Quicksilver. **2.** A touchstone.

रोषणता *roshaṇa*+*tâ*, f. Wrath, Çâk. d. 93.

रोह *roha*, i.e. *ruh*+*a*, m. **1.** A bud. **2.** Mounting, Râjat. 5, 15.

रोहक *rohaka*, i.e. *ruh*+*aka*, I. adj. Riding, mounted on any vehicle. **II.** m. A sort of goblin.

रोहण *rohaṇa*, i.e. *ruh*+*ana*, I. m. A mountain, Adam's peak in Ceylon, Pańch. MS. Berol., cf. Wilson in Trans. of the R.A.S. i. 169. II. n. **1.** Growing. **2.** Mounting. **3.** Semen virile.

रोहिण *rohiṇa*, i.e. *ruh*+*in*+*a*, I. m. **1.** The Indian fig-tree. **2.** A fragrant grass. II. n. A part of the forenoon. See *rohita*.

रोहित् *rohit*, probably akin to *rudhira*, *h* for *dh*, I. m. The sun. II. f. The female of the black antelope.

रोहित *rohita*, akin to *rudhira*, *h* for *dh*, I. adj., f. *tâ* and *iṇî*. **1.** Red. **2.** Coloured, Man. 1, 38. II. m. **1.** Red, the colour. **2.** A (kind of) deer, Utt. Râmach. 117, 4. **3.** A fish, Cyprinus rohita, Man. 5, 16. III. f. *iṇî*, also **रोहिणि** *rohiṇi*. **1.** The fourth lunar asterism, Vikr. 38, 12 (*ṇi*). **2.** The mother of *Bala-râma*. IV. f. *iṇî*. **1.** Lightning. **2.** A girl at the commencement of the menstruation, Pańch. iii. d. 213. **3.** A woman stained with red pigments. **4.** Inflammatory affection of the throat. **5.** A cow. **6.** Yellow myrobalan. **7.** Bengal madder. V. n. **1.** Blood. **2.** Safflower. **3.** The rainbow appearing in a straight form.

रोहिन् *rohin,* I. *ruh + in,* m. 1. The Indian fig-tree. 2. The holy fig-tree. II. (cf. *rohit*), A stag, Râm. 5, 36, 35 (but perhaps is to be read *rohin-mâṁsam,* i.e. *rohit-*).

रौक्म *raukma,* i.e. *rukma + a,* adj. Golden, Man. 4, 36.

रौक्ष्य *raukshya,* i.e. *rûksha + ya,* n. Roughness, hardness, Ragh. 5, 58.

रौचनिक *rauchanika,* i.e. *rochanâ + ika,* adj., f. *kî,* Yellowish, Kir. 5, 45 (cf. also Pâṇ. 4, 2, 2 Sch.).

रौच्य *rauchya,* m. An ascetic with a staff of Vilva wood.

रौट् *RAUṬ,* रौड् *RAUḌ,* see *roḍ.*

रौद्र *raudra,* i.e. *rudra + a,* I. adj., f. *drî.* 1. Relating to Rudra-Çiva, Arj. 3, 50; cf. 10, 42; descended from Rudra, Johns. Sel. 22, 117. 2. Formidable, Pańch. i. d. 116. 3. Irascible. 4. Acute. II. m. Heat. III. f. *rî,* The wife of Çiva.—Comp. *Ati-,* adj. exceedingly terrible, Pańch. 216, 9. *Soma-,* the name of a holy text (perhaps Rigv. vi. 74), Man. 11, 254.

रौद्रता *raudra + tâ,* f. Horribleness, Mâlat. 77, 7.

रौद्रीभाव *raudrîbhâva,* i.e. *raudra-bhû + a,* m. The character of Çiva, Johns. Sel. 93, 47.

रौप्य *raupya,* i.e. *rûpya + a,* I. adj. 1. Of silver, Man. 8, 135. 2. Like silver, Râm. 3, 48, 12. II. n. Silver, Bhâg. P. 4, 25, 14.

रौप्यमय *raupya + maya,* adj., f. *yî,* Made of silver, Râjat. 5, 46.

रौम *rauma,* and रौमक *rauma + ka,* n. A sort of salt (cf. *rumaṇvant*).

रौरव *raurava,* I. i.e. *ruru + a,* adj., f. *vî.* 1. Proceeding from the common deer (viz. flesh, etc.), Man. 2, 41; 3, 269; Utt. Râmach. 105, 11. 2. Unsteady. II. adj. 1. Formidable. 2. Dishonest. III. m. 1. The name of a hell, Man. 4, 88. 2. A savage.—Comp. *Mahâ-,* m. the name of a hell, Man. 4, 88.

रौहिण *rauhiṇa* (cf. *rohita*), n. Sandal wood, MBh. 1, 1381.

रौहिष *rauhisha* (cf. *rohit*), I. m. A sort of deer. II. f. *shî.* 1. A doe. 2. A creeper.

ल *L.*

लक् *LAK,* see *rak.*

लक्तक *laktaka,* n. 1. A rag, or rags. 2. i.e. *=rakta + ka* (vb. *rañj*), Lac, the animal dye.

लक्ष् *LAKSH* i. 10 (probably a denomin. derived from *laksha*), Par. and Âtm. 1. To mark, MBh. 3, 14852. 2. To see, Vikr. d. 8; to perceive, Çâk. 16, 20. Pass. To appear, Vikr. d. 53; MBh. 3, 2110. Ptcple. of the pf. pass. *lakshita,* Perceived, evident, Bhâg. P. 4, 25, 13. Comp. *A-,* adj. unobserved, Hit. 65, 10, M.M. *Su-lakshita,* adj. well-ascertained, Man. 8, 403. Ptcple. of the fut. pass. *lakshya.* 1. To be seen, visible, Vikr. d. 37; Daçak. in Chr. 198, 24. 2. Deserving to be regarded, Hit. iv. d. 14. 3. To be defined or described, Vedântas. in Chr. 210, 10. 4. Having attributes attached, Vedântas. in Chr. 212, 14; 23. n. 1. A mark. 2. A butt. 3. Aim, Utt. Râmach. 124, 8 (*baddha,* vb. *bandh,* adj. Having taken his aim); Megh. 72 (*kâmin-,* Aim, represented by lovers). 4. Object, Vedântas. in Chr. 205, 22. 5. A Lac, a hundred thousand, Hit. ii. d. 36. Comp. *A-,* adj. 1. invisible, Kathâs. 24, 8. 2. undistinguishable, unimportant, Kumâras. 5, 72. *Abhi-lak-*

shya + *m*, adv. to the aim, Râm. 2, 63, 22. *Durl°*, i.e. *dus-*, adj. difficult to be perceived, Bhâg. P. 7, 10, 53. *Yûpa-*, m. a bird. *Sthûla-*, adj. 1. = *sthûla-laksha* (see *laksha*). 2. aiming carelessly. Caus. **1.** To cause to be seen, to perform, to settle, Chr. 20, 17. **2.** To signify, Vedântas. in Chr. 204, 17.—With the prep. अभि *abhi*, *abhilakshita*, Marked.—With आ *â*, **1.** To see, to perceive, MBh. 2, 2403. **2.** To view, Daçak. in Chr. 186, 12. Pass. To appear, Çâk. d. 133. *âlakshya*, Çâk. d. 176, is *lakshya* with *â*, adj. Hardly visible.—With समा *sam-â*, **1.** To direct one's look to, Lass. 2. ed. 66, 17. **2.** To see, MBh. 1, 5249.—With उप *upa*, **1.** To see, to perceive, Vikr. 78, 21; MBh. 3, 2186. **2.** To suspect, Çâk. 15, 15. **3.** To consider, MBh. 3, 12188. **4.** Pass. To be probable, Râm. 2, 61, 11. *upalakshita*, Comprehended, understood. **Comp.** *An-*, adj. not perceived, Daçak. in Chr. 190, 15.—With समुप *sam-upa*, To see, to perceive, MBh. 2, 1557.—With निस् *nis*; *nirlakshya*, Kathâs. 6, 119, is *lakshya* with *nis*, adj. Imperceivable.—With वि *vi*, To perceive, Gît. 2, 19; to see, Pañch. 235, 25. *vilakshita*, **1.** Seen. **2.** Affected without a cause. **3.** Disappointed, Utt. Râmach. 148, 13; Johns. Sel. 52, 115 (rival). **4.** Unmarked (i.e. *lakshita* with *vi*, adj.).—With सम् *sam*, **1.** To perceive, MBh. 3, 16751. **2.** Pass. To appear, Vikr. d. 157. *saṁlakshita*, Distinguished. *saṁlakshya*, To be marked.—**Comp.** *Duḥs°*, i.e. *dus-*, adj. difficult to be perceived, Râjat. 6, 64.

लक्ष *laksha*, probably from *rañj*, and for original *rakta*, **I.** n. **1.** A mark, MBh. 3, 14852; Chaurap. 15. **2.** Aim, Ragh. 1, 61; Vikr. 54, 4 (? look, perhaps corr. *°lakshaṇaḥ*). **3.** Disguise, fraud. **II.** m., and f. *kshâ*, and n. (Pañch. 255, 23), A Lac, a hundred thousand, Pañch. 255, 23.—**Comp.** *Vi-*, adj. 1. unmarked. 2. having no characteristic property. 3. having a mark or character contrary to what is usual. 4. surprised. 5. (one who has missed his aim), ashamed, abashed, Pañch. 29, 15; embarrassed, Pañch. 147, 4. 6. with *kṛi*, becoming *vilakshî kṛi*, to scoff, to insult, Kathâs. 6, 126. *Sthûla-*, adj. 1. liberal, Indr. 4, 11. 2. wise. 3. remembering both benefits and offences.

लक्षण *lakshaṇa*, i.e. *laksh* + *ana*, **I.** n. **1.** Seeing, sight. **2.** A characteristic mark, Pañch. iii. d. 130; Bhartṛ. 2, 70; a spot. **3.** A holy mark, Hit. 99, 7; a lucky mark, Daçak. in Chr. 197, 11. **4.** Form, Bhâg. P. 5, 20, 38. **5.** A name, Pañch. iii. d. 35 (read *yâtrâlakshaṇam*, called *yâtrâ*). **6.** An indication, a definition, Man. 1, 112. **7.** Settlement, 8, 406. **8.** A symptom of actual disease. **II.** m. **1.** The Indian crane. **2.** A proper name. **III.** f. *ṇâ*. **1.** Metonymy, as distinguished from a word's literal meaning, Vedântas. in Chr. 212, 16; Bhâshâp. 81. Cf. *Sâhitya*, Darp. ii. **2.** The female of the Indian crane. **3.** A goose.—**Comp.** *A-*, I. n. a mark of ill fortune, Man. 4, 156. II. adj., f. *ṇâ*. 1. without distinguishing marks, Man. 1, 5. 2. inauspicious, Ragh. 14, 5. *Ajahallakshaṇâ*, i.e. *a-jahat-* (vb. 2. *hâ*), f. using a word in an elliptic meaning, without depriving it of its original signification; e.g. *çoṇa*, adj. 'of a chesnut colour,' in the sense of 'a horse of a chesnut colour,' Vedântas. in Chr. 214, 11. *Kṛita-*, adj. brandished, Man. 9, 239. *Ṛigyajuḥsâmalakshaṇa*, i.e. *ṛich-yajus-sâman-*, adj. named Ṛich, Yâjus, and Sâman, Man. 1, 23. *Jñâna-*, adj., f. *ṇâ*, one of the three transcendental perceptions, Bhâshâp. 62, cf. 64.

Dvi-, adj. of two kinds, Man. 7, 163. *Nirlakshaṇa*, i.e. *nis-*, adj. not distinguished, unimportant, Râm. 2, 118, 5 Gorr. *Râjalakshaṇa*, i.e. *râjan-*, n. 1. royal insignia. 2. any natural mark indicating royalty. *Lakshita-*, adj., f. *ṇâ*, in which are evident the marks (of a town), Bhâg. P. 4, 25, 13. *Vi-*, see s. v. *Viçesha-*, n. characteristic mark or sign. *Sâmânya-*, f. *ṇâ*, one of the three transcendental perceptions, Bhâshâp. 62, 63. *Su-*, I. adj. having auspicious marks, Râm. 3, 49, 57. II. n. determining. III. f. *ṇâ*, a proper name.

लक्षता *laksha+tâ*, f. Condition of being the aim, Daçak. in Chr. 184, 24.

लक्षितत्व *lakshita+tva* (vb. *laksh*, n. Condition of being hinted at, of being supplied, Vedântas. in Chr. 214, 15.

लक्ष्मण *lakshmaṇa*, i.e. *lakshman+a*, I. m. 1. The son of Daçaratha by Sumitrâ, Râm. 3, 50, 24. 2. The Indian crane, Arj. 9, 21. II. f. *ṇâ*, The female of the Indian crane. III. n. 1. A mark, a spot, Çiç. 9, 31 (and at the same time Lakshmaṇa). **Comp.** *Saha-*, adj. with Lakshmaṇa, Râm. 3, 52, 2. 2. A name.

लक्ष्मन् *laksh+man*, n. 1. A mark, Ragh. 19, 30; a spot, Çâk. d. 19. 2. Chief.

लक्ष्मी *lakshmî*, i.e. *lakshma* (i.e. curtailed *lakshman*), *+î*, f. (nom. sing. *mîs*). 1. The wife of Vishṇu, and goddess of prosperity, Râm. 3, 52, 26; Hit. pr. d. 31, M.M. 2. Prosperity, Bhartṛ. 2, 54. 3. Wealth, Bhartṛ. 2, 14; Râjat. 5, 18. 4. Beauty, splendour, Kir. 5, 39; Vikr. d. 23; Çâk. d. 19. 5. Royal power, Pañch. iii. d. 32; dominion, Râjat. 5, 136. 6. Superhuman power. 7. Sîta, the wife of Râma. 8. A pearl.—**Comp.** *A-*, f. bad luck, Râm. 3, 72, 25. *A-kṛiça-*, adj., n. *mi* (nom. sing. m., f. *mîs*), endowed with great prosperity, Kir. 5, 52. *Jaya-*, f. 1. Lakshmî, as deity of victory, Râjat. 5, 245. 2. a proper name, ib. 7, 124. *Mahâ-*, f. Sarasvatî. *Râjalakshmî*, i.e. *râjan-*, f. royal majesty, Vikr. d. 160.

॰लक्ष्मीक *-lakshmî+ka*, at the end of comp. adj.; e.g. *putra-sam-krânta-*, Having transferred the royal power to (their) sons, Utt. Râmach. 14, 15.

लक्ष्मीवन्त् *lakshmî+vant*, adj., f. *vatî*, 1. Fortunate. 2. Wealthy.

लक्ष्यता *lakshya+tâ* (see *laksh*), f. Visibility, Râjat. 5, 321.

† लख् *LAKH*, **लङ्ख्** *LAṄKH*, **लिङ्ख्** *LIṄKH*, i. 1, Par. To go, to move.

1. **लग्** *LAG*, i. 1, Par. 1. To adhere, Pañch. i. d. 340. 2. To attach one's self, Pañch. 245, 6. 3. To stick (in the throat), Çiç. 9, 69. 4. To pass away, to expire, Pañch. 185, 19. Ptcple. of the pf. pass. I. *lagna*. 1. Attached, Daçak. in Chr. 199, 13; impressed, Hit. pr. d. 8, M.M.; joined, Hit. 35, 12; following, Pañch. 106, 13; impending, 50, 18. 2. Left, Çâk. d. 32. 3. Intent on, occupied, being about, Pañch. 244, 6. 4. Auspicious, Hit. 89, 8, M.M. m. A bard. n. 1. The rising of a sign, its appearance above the horizon, Lass. 24, 8. 2. Auspicious time, Hit. 97, 13; cf. 94, 9. **Comp.** *Pâda-*, adj. being in the foot, Böhtl. Ind. Spr. 483. *Pṛishṭha-*, adj. m. one who follows, a partisan, Pañch. 125, 12. *Çubha-*, m. (?), an auspicious moment, Hit. 94, 9. *Hastâgra-*, i.e. *hasta-agra-*, adj., f. *nâ*, married, Pañch. 119, 6 (since I have been married to you). **II.** *lagita*. 1. Connected. 2. Obtained. 3. Entered, Hit. 129, 14.—With the prep. **अनु** *anu*, *anulagna*, Following, Lass. 30, 10.—With **अव** *ava*,

avalagna, **1.** Attached. **2.** m. and n. The waist, Çiç. 9, 49.—With वि *vi*, *vilagna*, **1.** Joined, attached, Çiç. 9, 20; clinging to, ib. 84; Pańch. 259, 2 (*tatraiva vilagnaḥ*, Took hold of it). **2.** Touching, Pańch. 186, 9. **3.** Tarried, Pańch. 207, 22. n. The waist.—With सम् *sam*, *samlagna*, Joined, adhering.—Cf. perhaps λήγω (but cf. *lańja* and *lańgûla*).

2. लग् *LAG*, see *rak*.

लगड *lagaḍa*, adj. Beautiful.

लगुड *laguḍa*, m. **1.** A stick, a staff, Hit. 51, 6, M.M. **2.** An iron club, a club, Hit. 101, 12.

लग्नक *lagna+ka* (vb. *lag*), m. A surety.

लघट् *laghaṭ*, and लघटि *laghaṭi*, m. Wind.

लघय *LAGHAYA*, a denomin. derived from *laghu*, Par. **1.** To make light, Kir. 5, 4. **2.** To alleviate, to soften, Vikr. d. 51.

लघिमन् *laghiman*, i. e. *laghu+iman*, m. **1.** Lightness, Bhaṭṭ. 3, 7. **2.** A supernatural faculty to make one's self as light as one lists, Lass. 3, 18. **3.** Diminutiveness. **4.** Insignificance.

लघु *laghu*, i.e. *lańgh+u*, I. adj., f. *ghu* and *ghvî*, comparat. *laghutara* and *laghîyams*, superl. *laghutama* and *laghishṭha*. **1.** Light, Pańch. 76, 18; easy, Pańch. 202, 4; *laghîyams*, Very light, Pańch. i. d. 119. **2.** Insignificant, Pańch. 68, 6; 172, 4 (innoxious). **3.** Quick, Pańch. 55, 11. **4.** Beautiful. **5.** Clean, Man. 2, 70. **6.** Little, Pańch. i. d. 301; small, Pańch. ii. d. 38; narrow, Pańch. 170, 24. **7.** Young, Pańch. 253, 13; younger, Pańch. 220, 3. **8.** Feeble, Man. 7, 209; Pańch. iii. d. 28. **9.** Mean, low, Châṇ. 68 in Berl. Monatsb. 1864, 411; living in a low position, Pańch. ii. d. 71. **10.** Vain, frivolous. **11.** Short, as a vowel, Çrut. 3. **12.** A way of flying (of birds), Pańch. ii. d. 57. **II.** acc. sing. n. *ghu*, adv. Quickly, Lass. 81, 13 (Prâkṛ.). **III.** f. *ghvî*. **1.** A delicate woman. **2.** A light carriage.—**Comp.** *A-*, adj. 1. heavy, Çiç. 9, 78. 2. powerful, ib. 9, 38. 3. long, as a vowel, Çrut. 44. *Pari-*, adj. 1. very small, Utt. Râmach. 107, 9. 2. very pure, Megh. 13. 3. very indifferent, Utt. Râmach. 100, 4.—Cf. ἐλαχύς, ἐλαφρός, λαγώς; Lat. lepus (for old lephus; cf. formus for old phormus, s.v. *gharma*, and *rudhira*, and *skandha*); Lat. levis; Goth. leihts; O.H.G. lîhti; A.S. lîht.

लघुता *laghu+tâ*, f. **1.** Lightness. **2.** Wantonness, Çiç. 9, 56. **3.** Meanness, insignificance. **4.** Disrespect, Pańch. i. d. 399.

लघुत्व *laghu+tva*, n. Disregard, Pańch. i. d. 156.

लघुविवरत्व *laghu-vivara+tva*, n. The opening being narrow, Pańch. 170, 25.

लङ्का *lańkâ*, f. **1.** The capital of Ceylon, Lass. 5, 3. **2.** Ceylon, Râm. 3, 53, 35; Pańch. iii. d. 268. **3.** The name of a *Çâkinî*, or evil spirit. **4.** An unchaste woman. **5.** A branch.

लङ्ख् *LAŃKH*, see *lakh*.

लङ्ग् *LAŃG*, i. 1, Par. **1.** To go. **2.** To go limpingly, to be lame.—With the prep. वि *vi*, Caus., Pańch. i. d. 369, To stop (? corr. perhaps *vilambayan*, delaying; cf. *vilambana* and my transl.).

लङ्ग *lańga* (vb. *lag*), m. **1.** Union. **2.** A lover, a gallant.

लङ्गक *lańga+ka*, m. A lover, a gallant.

लङ्गिमन् *laṅgiman* (vb. *lag*), (m.), Union, Lass. 67, 17.

लङ्गिममय *laṅgimamaya*, i.e. *laṅgiman* + *maya*, adj., f. *yî*, Fit to be joined, Lass. 83, 1.

लङ्गूल *laṅgûla* (vb. *lag*), n. The tail of an animal (cf. *lâṅgûla*).

लङ्घ् *LAṄGH*, i. 1, Par. † To diminish. i. 1, Par. Âtm. To ascend, Bhaṭṭ. 15, 32. i. 1, Âtm. † To fast. Caus., and i. 10, Par. **1.** To jump over, Megh. 55. **2.** To step over, MBh. 3, 11178; Man. 4, 38. **3.** To hinder, Pańch. ii. d. 113. **4.** To surpass, Ragh. 3, 48 (Calc.). **5.** To disregard, Man. 5, 151; Pańch. i. d. 37. **6.** To violate, Man. 8, 371. **7.** † To speak. **8.** † To shine. Comp. ptcple. of the fut. pass. **1.** *a-laṅghanîya*, adj. Not to be overtaken, unattainable, Çâk. d. 8. **2.** *durlaṅghya*, i.e. *dus-*, adj. Difficult to be set aside, Râjat. 5, 395.—With the prep. अभि *abhi*, i. 10, To stride over, Man. 4, 54.—With अव *ava*, i. 10, To stay, Ghaṭ. 7.—With उद् *ud*, i. 10, **1.** To pursue, Megh. 46. **2.** To neglect, Râjat. 5, 395. **3.** To violate, Daçak. in Chr. 181, 4. **4.** To injure, 191, 21. Comp. ptcple. of the fut. pass. *an-ullaṅghanîya*, adj. Not to be neglected, Pańch. 247, 19.—With परि *pari*, i. 10, To trespass, to leave, Pańch. iv. d. 75.—With वि *vi*, i. 10, **1.** To overstep, Kir. 5, 1. **2.** To violate, Ragh. 9, 74. **3.** To neglect, Ragh. 3, 4 (Calc.). —Cf. O.H.G. langên, ga-lingan, ga-langôn; Goth. laggs; A.S. lang, etc.; Lat. longus, languere, etc.; λαγγάζω, λογγάζω, λαγχάνω, λάχος, λόγχη, ἐλέγχω; probably also Goth. laikan, etc. The original signification of this vb. was probably, 'To overtake by jumping,' then, 'To attain.'

लङ्घन *laṅgh* + *ana*, n. **1.** Jumping over. **2.** Passing over, Daçak. in Chr. 183, 1. **3.** Coition, 182, 11. **4.** Exceeding, transgressing, Hit. 87, 1, M.M. (*pati-*, Injuring one's husband); disregarding, Brâhmaṇav. 2, 34 (of a former husband by marrying another); disdain, Vikr. 34, 4. **5.** Storming, capturing a fort, Hit. iii. d. 136. **6.** Going. **7.** One of a horse's paces, curvetting. **8.** Fasting, abstinence.

† लछ् *LACHH* (a form of *laksh*), and लाञ्छ् *LAŃCHH*, q. v. i. 1, Par. To mark.

1. लज् *LAJ*, see *lajj*.

† 2. लज् *LAJ*, and लञ्ज् *LAŃJ*, i. 1, Par. **1.** To fry. **2.** To calumniate, to blame.

† 3. लज् *LAJ*, and लञ्ज् *LAŃJ*, i. 10, Par. To appear, to shine.

† 4. लज् *LAJ*, i. 10, Par. To cover (v.r.).

लज्ज् *LAJJ* (akin to *rańj*, and for original *rajya*), and लज् *LAJ* (Bhaṭṭ. 14, 105), i. 6, Âtm. (also Par., Man. 12, 35), To be ashamed, Pańch. ii. d. 106; with the ptcple. pres. in the sense of the infin., Râm. 2, 12, 52; Pańch. 119, 6. (*bruvâṇo na lajjase*, You are not ashamed to speak). Ptcple. of the pf. pass. *lagna*, Ashamed.—With the prep. वि *vi*, To be ashamed, MBh. 3, 2217.—With सम् *sam*, The same, Râm. 2, 55, 16.

लज्जा *lajj* + *â*, f. **1.** Shame, Pańch. v. d. 10. **2.** Bashfulness, Pańch. v. d. 83. **3.** Modesty.—Comp. *Nirlajja*, i.e. *nis-*, and *Vi-*, adj., f. *jâ*, shameless, Pańch. i. d. 148. *Sa-*, adj., f. *jâ*. 1. ashamed. 2. bashful, Pańch. 45, 8; Daçak. in Chr. 182, 1. 3. modest, Hit. iii.

d. 64. °*jam*, acc. sing. n. adv. bashfully, Daçak. in Chr. 187, 19; Vikr. 22, 12.

लज्जावन्त् *lajjâ + vant*, adj., f. *vatî*, Bashful, modest, Nal. 3, 18.

लज्जित *lajjita*, i.e. *lajjâ + ita*, adj. Ashamed, bashful, Utt. Râmach. 158, 7.

† **लञ्ज्** *LAÑJ*, **लुञ्ज्** *LUÑJ*, i. 10, Par. **1.** To be strong. **2.** To injure. **3.** To dwell. **4.** To give. **5.** To speak, to shine. See 2., 3. *laj*.

लञ्ज *lañja*, I. m. **1.** A foot. **2.** The end of the lower garment, tucked into the waistband. **3.** A tail. II. f. *jâ*. **1.** An adulteress. **2.** Lakshmî. **3.** Sleep. See the next.

लञ्जिका *lañjikâ*, i.e. *lañjâ + ka*, f. A harlot.—Cf. perhaps λάγνος.

† **लट्** *LAṬ*, i. 1, Par. **1.** To be a child. **2.** To cry (cf. *raṭ*).

लटक *laṭaka*, m. A bad man.

लट्वा *laṭvâ*, f. **1.** A sparrow. **2.** A musical instrument (?). **3.** A game. **4.** A tree, a species of the *Karañja*.

† 1. **लड्** and **लाड्** *LÂḌ*, i. 10, *lâḍaya*, *lâḍâpaya*, Par. To throw up, to blame.

2. **लड्** *LAḌ*, Caus., or i. 10, Par. *laḍaya*, **1.** † To loll (the tongue). **2.** To stir with the tongue, Pañch. 229, 20 (but with *l* instead of *ḍ*). **3.** † To use the tongue. **4.** † To apprise, to show. **5.** † To throw out, to be thrown out. **6.** † To coagulate, to pain. **7.** † To suffer pain. The final *ḍ* seems to stand for *l* (cf. *lal*).—Perhaps cf. λάλος, λαλέω, λῆρος; N.H.G. lallen.

3. **लड्** *LAḌ*, see *lal*.

लड्डु *laḍḍu*, A class of sweetmeats, Lass. 2, ed. 59, 5.

लड्डुक *laḍḍu + ka*, m. n. A class of sweetmeats, Lass. 2. ed. 9, 11; 13; Brahmav. 3, 8, 53.

† **लण्ड्** *LAṆḌ* (see 1. *laḍ*), **उलण्ड्** *ULAṆḌ* (i.e. *ud-laṇḍ*), and **ओलण्ड्** *OLAṆḌ* (i.e. *ud-laṇḍ*, or *ava-laṇḍ*), i. 10, Par. To toss up.

लता *latâ*, f. **1.** A creeper, Kathâs. 22, 103. **2.** A plant, Pañch. i. d. 253. **3.** A branch, Vikr. d. 13. **4.** Thread. **5.** The name of several plants.—**Comp.** *Amṛita-*, f. a creeper yielding nectar, Bhartṛ. 1, 75. *Ud-patâka-bhuja-laṭa*, adj., f. *tâ*, having raised banners instead of creeper-like arms, Kathâs. 20, 22. *Kalpa-*, f. a creeper yielding all wishes (cf. *kalpa-taru*), Çâk. d. 164. *Nâga-*, f. a proper name, Râjat. 5, 359. *Bâhu-*, f. the creeper-like arms, Râjat. 5, 27. *Bhrû-*, f. the creeper-like eyebrow, Daçak. in Chr. 190, 15. *Bhû-*, and *Mahi-*, f. an earth-worm. *Muktâ-*, f. a pearl necklace. *Mohana-*, f. a fascinating plant, Lass. 82, 14 (Prâkṛ.). *Romalatâ*, i.e. *roman-*, f. a line of hair extending to the navel. *Taḍillatâ*, i.e. *taḍit-*, f. zigzag lightning, Kirât. 10, 19. *Vetra-*, f. a stick (of the doorkeeper), Pañch. 16, 1. *Sûrya-*, f. a plant, Cleome viscosa. *Soma-*, f. the Soma plant, Sarcostema viminalis.

लतिका *latikâ*, i.e. *latâ + ka*, f. A creeper.—**Comp.** *Aṅga-*, f. a creeper-like body, Utt. Râmach. 72, 12. *Amṛita-*, f. a creeper yielding nectar, Çrut. 35 (Brockhaus). *Bâhu-*, f. creeper-like arms, Çṛiṅgârat. 9.

लप् *LAP*, i. 1, Par. (in epic poetry also Âtm., Nal. 21, 16). **1.** To speak, Gît. 1, 41. **2.** To lament, Nal. 3, 27. Ptcple. of the pf. pass. *lapita*, n. Voice. Frequent. *lâlap*, *lâlapya*, To lament, MBh. 3, 10200. *lâlapya*, Par., MBh. 1, 968.—With the prep. **अप** *apa*, To deny,

Râm. 2, 75, 24.—With आ *â*, To address, MBh. 3, 15604. Caus. *lâpaya*, To ask, Pańch. i. d. 431; 242, 13.—With प्र *pra*, 1. To prattle, Çâk. 13, 14. 2. To speak, Pańch. 94, 12; to cry, Böhtl. Ind. Spr. 309. 3. To bewail, Pańch. 75, 25; MBh. 3, 1203. 4. To invoke, MBh. 2, 2339. *pralapita*, n. 1. Prattle, Pańch. 146, 1 (*vṛithâ-*, Useless words). 2. Lamentation, Pańch. 224, 16. Caus. To incite to speak, Mṛichchh. 86, 14.—With वि *vi*, 1. To wail, Hit. 44, 6, M.M.; MBh. 3, 1203. 2. To bewail, Râm. 1, 1, 52. 3. To speak, Johns. Sel. 51, 110.—With सम् *sam*, To converse, Daçak. in Chr. 179, 7. Caus. To cause to converse, to address, Hit. i. d. 77, M.M.—Cf. Lat. loqui; probably ὀλοφύρομαι (a denomin. based on an old frequent. ὀλοπ, and aff. *van*, with ρ for *v*.)

लपन *lap+ana*, n. 1. Speaking. 2. The mouth.

लभ् *LABH* (in epic poetry also लम्भ् *LAMBH*, MBh. 2, 1365, cf. Caus.), i. 1, Âtm. (in epic poetry also Par., Chr. 21, 8). 1. To obtain, to get, MBh. 1, 6839; Vikr. d. 42; to acquire, Hit. i. d. 47, M.M.; to enjoy, Vikr. d. 20; Kathâs. 26, 283 (*alabhata+tarâm*, Enjoyed in the highest degree). 2. With *garbham*, To become pregnant, Chr. 50, 10. 3. To approach, MBh. 1, 1756. 4. To undergo, to perform, Râjat. 5, 154. 5. Pass. To be contained, Bhâshâp. 6. 6. Pass. refl. To take, Râjat. 5, 108. Comp. ptcple. pres. Âtm. *a-labhamâna*, adj. Unable to catch, Hit. 121, 15. Ptcple. of the pf. pass. *labdha*, Got, obtained, Lass. 20, 7; Râjat. 5, 135. f. *dhâ*, A woman whose husband or lover is faithless. Desider. *lipsa*, To strive to obtain, Man. 7, 99; 8, 340; to long for, Hit. ii. d. 7. Comp. ptcple. pres. (Par.), *a-lipsant*, adj. Not desiring, Hit. ii. d. 8. Caus. *lambhaya*, To cause to obtain. 1. To bestow, MBh. 3, 16068; to give, Vikr. 47, 12. 2. To find out, Man. 8, 109. 3. To cause to suffer, MBh. 2, 1529. Ptcple. of the pf. pass. *lambhita*. 1. Procured, given. 2. Adapted. 3. Addressed. 4. Heightened, improved. 5. Cherished. 6. Gained. 7. Abused.—With the prep. अभि *abhi*, desider. To covet, MBh. 1, 2940.—With आ *â*, To touch, Man. 11, 202; 5, 87; Chr. 7, 16.—With उपा *upa-â*, 1. To reproach, Vikr. 63, 12; Çiç. 9, 60. 2. To reprove, Çâk. 59, 15. Caus. To blame, Pańch. 134, 24.—With समा *sam-â*, 1. To touch, to stroke, Râm. 1, 29, 45. 2. To rub, Râm. 2, 25, 35. —With उप *upa*, 1. To obtain, Râjat. 5, 297; to get, Vikr. d. 29. 2. With *garbham*, To become pregnant, Râm. 1, 25, 25. 3. To find, Vikr. 65, 19; Daçak. in Chr. 192, 10. 4. To perceive, Râm. 2, 65, 13; to feel, Vikr. 67, 4; to be told, Pańch. 172, 21. 5. To find out, Vikr. 57, 11; to ascertain, Çâk. 11, 16; Man. 7, 57. 5. To understand, MBh. 2, 769. — With प्रत्युप *prati-upa*, To recover, Vikr. d. 133.— With प्र *pra*, To deceive, MBh. 3, 2785. — With विप्र *vi-pra*, 1. To deceive, Hit. 92, 6; Chr. 53, 23. 2. To confound, Utt. Râmach. 155, 10. 3. To violate, MBh. 3, 223.—With प्रति *prati*, To recover, MBh. 1, 7882.— With वि *vi*, To occupy, Râjat. 5, 265. Cf. λάφυρον, λαμβάνω, εἴληφα, λαῖλαψ (based on a frequent.), probably λέβης, λίπτω. See *rabh*.

लभस *labh+asa*, m. A rope for tying a horse.

लम्पट *lampaṭa* (vb. *lap*, but cf. also *limpaṭa*), I. adj. Covetous, greedy, Pañch. 253, 18. II. m. A libertine, Lass. 83, 18 (Prâkṛ.).

लम्पटत्व *lampaṭa+tva*, n. Greediness, Bhartṛ. 3, 67.

लम्पाक *lampâka*, m. 1. A libertine (see the last). 2. The name of a country.

लम्ब् *LAMB*, i. 1, Âtm. (Par., Pañch. 107, 25). 1. To fall, MBh. 2, 2187. 2. To set (as the sun), Râm. 1, 33, 20. 3. To hang downwards, Pañch. v. d. 36. 4. † To sound. Ptcple. of the pres. *lambamâna*. 1. Depending, Pañch. 259, 7. 2. Being large or bulky, Pañch. 136, 1.—With the prep. **अव** *ava*, 1. To fall, MBh. 1, 1035; to descend, Hit. 25, 5, M.M. 2. To set, MBh. 4, 1040. 3. To rest upon, Lass. 5, 11. 4. To lean on, to be supported, MBh. 1, 8443. 5. To suspend, Pañch. 252, 10. 6. To support, to hold, Çâk. 86, 21; Vikr. 49, 16. 7. To take, Çâk. 108, 19. With *dhairyam*, a. To take courage, Hit. 13, 19. b. To keep firm, i.e. to yield not, Vikr. 34, 4. 8. To choose, Çâk. 70, 14. *avalambita*, 1. Hanging, Pañch. 116, 23. 2. Hanging with the head downwards, Lass. 15, 18. 3. Supported, Vikr. 7, 5. 4. Depended upon, Hit. i. d. 143, M.M. Caus. To support, Mâlav. 31, 2; to hold, 42, 6.—With **समव** *sam-ava*, To support, MBh. 3, 10988.—With **आ** *â*, 1. To lean on, to depend upon, Chr. 28, 16. 2. To support, MBh. 3, 10989. 3. To keep (*sthairyam̃ gṛihe*, To stay at home); Pañch. 225, 23. 4. To take, Ghaṭ. 22; to seize, Râjat. 5, 432. With *dhairyam*, To take courage, Pañch. 21, 8. With *dhṛitim*, To be untroubled, Kathâs. 22, 100. *âlambita*, 1. Hanging, Vikr. d. 140. 2. Laid on, Vikr. d. 125. *nâlambita*, i.e. *na-âlambita*, Unsupported, hopeless, Vikr. d. 38.—With **समा** *sam-â*, 1. To suspend, Pañch. 144, 23. 2. To maintain, Hit. i. d. 193, M.M. 3. To take, Mṛichchh. 55, 19. 4. To dwell, Hit. i. d. 211, M.M.—With **उद्** *ud*, *ullambita*, Hanging (between heaven and earth), Mṛichchh. 33, 19.—With **समुद्** *sam-ud*, *samullambita*, Hanging, 34, 2.—With **प्र** *pra*, *pralambita*, Hanging.—With **प्रति** *prati*, To suspend, Pañch. 98, 4.—With **वि** *vi*, To tarry, Çâk. 18, 21; Pañch. 84, 10. *a-vilambita*, adj. Without delay, Mâlav. 53, 13; Vikr. 79, 13. Caus. 1. To suspend, Pañch. 116, 19. 2. To delay, iii. d. 232.—With **प्रवि** *pra-vi*, Pañch. 98, 4; erroneous reading, see my transl. n. 480.—Cf. Lat. labi; A.S. limpian, ge-limp; Engl. To limp.

लम्ब *lamb+a*, I. adj, 1. Depending, Megh. 82, 88. 2. Long, Böhtl. Ind. Spr. 1210; Çâk. 87, 15 (Prâkṛ.). 3. Expanded, large, Hiḍ. 2, 3. 4. Spacious. II. m. 1. A bribe. 2. Moving a man at a sort of backgammon. III. f. *bâ*. 1. Lakshmî. 2. Durgâ. 3. A bitter gourd. —Comp. *Â-gaṇḍa-*, adj. hanging down to the cheeks, Megh. 88.

लम्बक *lamba+ka*, m. A section, Kathâs. 1, 8.

लम्बन *lamb+ana*, n. 1. Falling. 2. A long necklace reaching to the navel.

लम्बय *LAMBAYA*, a denomin. derived from *lamba*, Par. To extend, Ragh. 6, 75 (Calc.).

लम्बालकत्व *lambâlakatva*, i.e. *lamba-alaka+tva*, n. Hanging down of the curls, Megh. 82.

लम्बिन् *lamb+in*, adj. Depending,

Pañch. i. d. 160.—Comp. *A-*, adj. unsupported, Lass. 20, 20. *An-ati-*, adj. short, Mâlav. d. 82. *Pûrva-ardha-*, adj. inclining (his) fore-part, Megh. 52.

लम्बुषा *lamb + ushâ*, f. A necklace of seven strings.

लम्भ् *LAMBH*, see *rambh* and *labh*.

लम्भ *lambha*, i.e. *labh + a*, m. Gain, Vikr. 49, 16.

लम्भन *lambhana*, i.e. *labh + ana*, n. **1.** Gaining, getting. **2.** Causing to get, Daçak. in Chr. 180, 12. **3.** Abuse, reviling.

लय् *LAY*, see *ray*.

लय *laya*, i.e. *lî + a*, m. **1.** Adhering. **2.** A house. **3.** Sport. **4.** Equal time in music and dancing, Pañch. v. d. 43. **5.** Melting; *layam̃ yâ*, To melt away, to vanish, Pañch. v. d. 4. **6.** Dissolution, Vedântas. in Chr. 204, 23; 211, 7; destruction. **7.** Loss. **8.** A pause in music, Mâlav. 19, 11. **9.** Slackness of mind, Vedântas. in Chr. 217, 23.—Comp. *A-*, I. m. nondestruction, duration, Râm. 3, 71, 10. II. adj. without a fixed abode, Çiç. 4, 57.

† **लर्ब्** *LARB*, i. 1, Par. To go.

लल् *LAL*, and † **लड्** *LAḌ*, i. 1, Par. (in epic poetry, Âtm., Râm. 1, 9, 19). **1.** To sport, MBh. 3, 1741. **2.** To dally, Râm. 1, 9, 19. Ptcple. of the pf. pass. *lalita*. **1.** Dallying, wanton, Megh. 65. **2.** Beautiful, Utt. Râmach. 14, 6. **3.** Wished. n. **1.** Beauty, Râm. 1, 9, 16. **2.** Love of pleasure, love, Vikr. d. 32. **3.** Softness and delicacy of motion, Utt. Râmach. 14, 6. **4.** °*tam*, adv. Sweetly, Dev. 10, 27. Comp. *Durlalita*, i. e. *dus-* (cf. Caus. A.), I. adj. spoiled, Vikr. d. 27; wayward, Çâk. 103, 4. n. 1. ill habit, Hariv. 8539 (with *ati-*, excessive). 2. disfavour, Prab. 90, 15. *Su-*, adj. 1. sporting. 2. pleased, very delicate, Hit. 37, 4, M.M. 3. very beautiful, Ṛit. 1, 28; Bhartṛ. 3, 28. °*tam*, adv. delightedly, easily. Caus., and i. 10, Par. A. *lalaya*, † *laḍaya*, **1.** To exhilarate, Râm. 2, 43, 5. **2.** To nurse, to foster, to attend, Râm. 2, 47, 6; Pañch. 87, 11. B. *lâlaya*, **1.** To cherish, Pañch. i. d. 397. **2.** To spoil, Böhtl. Ind. Spr. 2664. i. 10, Âtm. † *lâḍaya*, To desire. *lâlita*, **1.** Desired. **2.** Cherished tenderly, Pañch. iii. d. 126. **3.** Loved, Râjat. 5, 6. **4.** Coaxed, Pañch. 87, 11 (or n. Joy; °*tena*, Joyfully ?). **5.** Seduced; cf. 2. *laḍ*.—With the prep. **उप** *upa*, Caus. *lâlaya*, **1.** To court, Mâlav. 29, 1. **2.** To fondle, Çâk. 104, 5.

ललज्जिह्व *lalajjihva*, i. e. *lalant -jihva* (see 2. *laḍ* and *jihvâ*), I. adj. Fierce, savage. II. m. **1.** A camel. **2.** A dog.

ललन *lalana*, i.e. *laḍ*, and *lal + ana*, I. m. **1.** A tree, Shorea robusta. **2.** A boy. II. f. *nâ*. **1.** A wanton woman, Indr. 5, 6. **2.** A woman in general, Bhâg. P. 4, 25, 27. III. n. **1.** Sport, pleasure. **2.** Lolling the tongue.

ललन्तिका *lalantikâ* (akin to *lal*), f. A necklace reaching to the navel.

ललाट *lalâṭa*, n. The forehead, Pañch. ii. d. 183; Vikr. 73, 8.—Comp. *Mahâ-*, adj. with a large forehead, Râm. 3, 55, 4.

ललाटंतप *lalâṭa + m-tap + a*, adj. Burning the forehead, Utt. Râmach. 153, 5; Mâlat. 12, 8.

ललाटिका *lalâṭikâ*, i.e. *lalâṭa + ka*, f. **1.** An ornament worn on the forehead, as a jewel. **2.** A mark made with sandal on the forehead, Pâṇ. iv. 3, 65.

ललाम *lalâma* (akin to *lal*), I. n.,

also ललामन् *lalâman*, **1.** A mark. **2.** A flag. **3.** An ornament, Çâk. 25, 4. **4.** A mane. **5.** A tail. **6.** A line. **7.** Majesty, dignity. **8.** Chief, principal, Daçak. in Chr. 184, 18. **II.** f. *mî*, An ornament worn in the ear.

ललामक *lalâma+ka*, n. A chaplet of flowers falling over the forehead, Pâṇ. iv. 4, 40.

ललितादित्य *lalitâditya*, i.e. *lalita-âditya*, m. A proper name, Râjat. 5, 69.

लल्लिय *lalliya*, m. A proper name, Râjat. 5, 154.

लव *lava*, i.e. *lû+a*, I. m. **1.** Cutting, Daçak. in Chr. 198, 17. **2.** Plucking, Nal. 2, 30. **3.** Reaping. **4.** Smallness, Bhartṛ. 3, 100; Vikr. d. 118 (*aparâdha-*, A very small fault); a little, Hit. iv. d. 76 (but cf. Böhtl. Ind. Spr. 3265); a piece, Vikr. d. 125; a drop, Kir. 5, 44. **5.** Hair, Ragh. 15, 32; wool, Man. 8, 151. **6.** A minute, and also a larger division of time. **7.** A kind of quail. **8.** One of Râma's sons, Utt. Râmach. 85, 8. **II.** n. **1.** The nutmeg. **2.** Cloves.—**Comp.** *Jñâna-* (m.), a smattering of knowledge, Bhartṛ. 2, 3.

लवक *lavaka*, i.e. *lû+aka*, adj. Who or what cuts, Pâṇ. iii. 1, 149.

लवंग *lavaṁga*, i.e. *lava+m-ga*, I. m. The clove tree, Myristica caryophyllata, Ragh. 6, 57. II. n. Cloves.

लवट *lavaṭa*, m. A proper name, Râjat. 5, 176.

लवण *lavaṇa*, for original *ravaṇa* cf. *rumaṇvant*, I. n. Salt, Pañch. 184, 9. **II.** m. **1.** Saltness, Hit. iii. d. 56. **2.** The sea of salt water. **3.** The name of a Râkshasa, Utt. Râmach. 176, 8. **III.** f. *ṇâ*. **1.** Light, beauty. **2.** The name of a river. **IV.** adj. **1.** Salt, saline, Pâṇ. iv. 4, 24. **2.** Charming, beautiful. — Comp. *A-kshâra-lavaṇa*, adj. 'not' containing artificial salt, Man. 3, 257.

लवन *lavana*, i.e. *lû+ana*, n. Cutting, reaping.

लवली *lavalî*, f. A kind of creeper, Vikr. d. 146.

लवशस् *lava+ças*, adv. In pieces.

लवाक *lavâka*, i.e. *lû+âka*, m. A sickle.

लवि *lavi*, i.e. *lû+i* (m.?), An iron instrument for cutting or cleaving.

लवित्र *lavitra*, i.e. *lû+tra*, n. A sickle, Pâṇ. iii. 2, 184.

लश् *LAÇ*, see 2. *las*.

लशुन *laçuna*, n. Garlic, Man. 5, 5.

लष् *LASH* (akin to 1. *las*, cf. *lâlasa*), i. 1 and 4, Par. To desire; cf. 2. *las*.—With the prep. अभि *abhi*, **1.** To desire, Vikr. 13, 20; to covet, Hit. 69, 5; MBh. 1, 6580. **2.** To take, Vikr. d. 107. *abhilashita*, n. Desire, Hit. 95, 4, M.M.—Cf. λῶ, λῆμα, λαρός, λωΐων, λίαν, λιλαίομαι, λήλαντος, probably λαμία, λάμος, λάρυγξ, λαιμός, λαίτμα, etc.; Lat. lascivus; Goth. luston, lustus; A.S. lust, lyst, lystan.

लष्व *lashva*, m. A dancer.

1. लस् *LAS*, i. 1, Par. **1.** To embrace. **2.** To sport or play. **3.** To shine, MBh. 3, 15533. Caus. *lâsaya*, To cause to sport, to move, Vikr. d. 23. — With the prep. उद् *ud*, **1.** To sport, Pañch. i. d. 152; Bhaṭṭ. 9, 86. **2.** To shine, Çiç. 20, 56. Caus. **1.** To cause to shine, Ṛit. 6, 8. **2.** To delight, Hit. 21, 15.—With प्रोद् *pra-ud*, To shine, Çiç. 2, 19.—With समुद् *sam-ud*, **1.** To break forth, Pañch. ii. d. 193. **2.** To

shine forth, Çiç. 8, 65. 3. To sport. *samullasita*, 1. Sportive. 2. Beautiful. —With वि *vi*, 1. To sport, to dally, Hit. 42, 9; with *uparî* in *upari-vi-lasant*, Flashing up, Megh. 48. 2. To play, to exhibit, Pañch. iii. d. 237. 3. To shine, Bhartṛ. 3, 23; 36 (to flash); Pañch. i. d. 461 (*yena vilasitam*, Who has lived in a brilliant style). *vilasita*, Sportive, wanton. n. 1. Wanton pastime. 2. Splendour, Kir. 5, 46; flashing, Vikr. d. 137. Comp. *Durvilasita*, i.e. *dus-*, n. A wicked trick, Prab. 104, 7.—With प्रवि *pra-vi*, To break forth, Lass. 24, 14.—Cf. probably Lat. ludo; see *lash*.

† 2. लस् *LAS*, लष् *LASH*, लश् *LAÇ*, i. 10, Par. To do anything skilfully.

लसिका *lasikâ*, f. Saliva, spittle.

लस्तक *lastaka*, perhaps *lasta+ka* (1. *las*, To embrace). m. The middle of a bow.

लहर *lahara*, The name of a district (Lahore), Râjat. 5, 51.

लहरि and लहरी *lahari*, *lahari*, f. A large wave, a wave, Böhtl. Ind. Spr. 814.—Comp. *Ânanda-*, f. title of a hymn.

ला *LÂ*, ii. 2, Par. To take, Bhaṭṭ. 15, 53.

लाक्षणिक *lâkshaṇika*, i.e. *lakshaṇa +ika*, adj., f. *kî*, Characteristic.

लाक्षा *lâkshâ*, i.e. *laksha=lakta* in *laktaka* (q. cf.), *+a*, f. Lac, the animal dye, Ṛit. 6, 13.—Comp. *Charaṇa-*, f. lac, with which the feet are dyed, Kir. 5, 23.

लाक्षिक *lâkshika*, adj. 1. i.e. *lâkshâ +ika*, Made of lac, dyed with lac, Pâṇ. iv. 2, 2. 2. i.e. *laksha+ika*, Relating to a large number or a Lac.

लाख् *LÂKH*, see *râkh*.

लागुडिक *lâguḍika*, i.e. *laguḍa+ika*, m. One who bears a club, a sentinel, Pañch. 230, 19.

लाघ् *LÂGH*, see *râgh*.

लाघव *lâghava*, i.e. *laghu+a*, n. 1. Lightness. 2. Undervaluing, a cause of undervaluing, Pañch. ii. d. 107; disgrace, iii. d. 113; contempt, Bhag. 2, 35. 3. Swiftness, Chr. 34, 7. 4. Readiness, Chr. 5, 23. 5. Dexterity, Johns. Sel. 11, 25. 6. Health. 7. Meanness, Hit. iii. d. 78; insignificance. 8. Frivolity. 9. Shortness (of a vowel), Çrut. 4.—Comp. *Guru-*, n. the relative weight, Man. 9, 229. *Hasta-*, n. light-handedness, readiness, cleverness, Pañch. 218, 17.

लाङ्गल *lâṅgala*, vb. *lag*, cf. *lâṅgula*, I. n. 1. The penis. 2. A plough, Bhartṛ. 2, 98. 3. The main beam of a house. 4. The palm tree. II. f. *lî*, The name of several plants.

लाङ्गलिन् *lâṅgalin*, i.e. *lâṅgala+in*, m. 1. A snake. 2. A name of *Balarâma*, Megh. 50 (armed with a plough).

लाङ्गुल and लाङ्गूल *lâṅgûla* (vb. *lag*, properly, To hang), n. A tail, Pañch. 259, 7 (*û*); Hit. i. d. 170, M.M. (*ŭ*).

† लाज् *LÂJ*, लाञ्ज् *LÂÑJ*, i. 1, Par. 1. To fry. 2. To blame.

लाज *lâja*, I. m. Grain wetted or sprinkled. II. f. *jâ*, or pl. m. Fried grain, Pañch. 158, 3; Chr. 57, 22.

लाञ्छ् *LÂÑCHH* (akin to *laksh*; cf. *lachh*), i. 1, Par. † 1. To mark. 2. To dress, Vikr. d. 53.

लाञ्छन *lâñchh+ana*, n. 1. A mark, Pañch. iii. d. 204. 2. A name, Utt. Râmach. 2, 4 (*çrî-kaṇṭha-pada-*, adj. Having as surname the word Çrî-kaṇṭha.)—Comp. *Mṛiga-*, m. the moon, Lass. 91, 8 (Prâkṛ.). *Çrî-vatsa-*, m. a name of Vishṇu. *Çaça-*, m. the moon, Pańch. iii. d. 204.

लाञ्ज् *LÂŃJ*, see *lâj*.

लाट *lâṭa*, m. **1.** Cloth. **2.** The name of a country.

लाड् *LÂḌ*, see 1. *laḍ*.

लाड *lâḍa*, m. A proper name, Râjat. 5, 226.

लाडन *lâḍana*, see *lâlana*.

† **लाभ्** *LÂBH*, i. 10, Par. To throw, to direct.

लाभ *lâbha*, i.e. *labh* + *a*, m. **1.** Acquirement, acquisition, Pańch. ii. d. 197. **2.** Gain, Man. 9, 331; Pańch. ii. d. 100. **3.** Enjoying, Pańch. 202, 10.—Comp. *A-*, m. 1. no possibility of getting, Man. 2, 42. 2. loss, Man. 11, 80. *Guṇa-a-*, m. the not taking effect, Suçr. 1, 131, 5. *Durlâbha*, i.e. *dus-*, adj. difficult to be got, MBh. 12, 11168. *Dvi-guṇa-*, m. (condition of) receiving something doubled, Pańch. 88, 9. *Lâbha-a-*, m. profit and loss, Man. 9, 331. *Siddhi-*, m. acquirement of success, i.e. applause, Daçak. in Chr. 190, 14.

ऽलाभिन् *-lâbhin*, i.e. *labh* + *in*, adj. in *parîkshâ-kshaṇa-*, adj. Getting the time of proving, Râjat. 5, 131.

लालक *lâlaka*, i.e. *lal*, Caus., + *aka*, adj., f. *likâ*, Seducing, Nal. 2, 28.

लालन *lâlana*, also *lâḍana*, Châṇ. 84 in Berl. Monatsb. 1864, 412, i.e. *lal*, Caus., + *ana*, n. **1.** Coaxing, Râjat. 5, 290. **2.** Spoiling, over-indulging, Pańch. i. d. 185.

लालस *lâlasa*, i.e. *lâlas*, frequent. of 1. *las*, but partly in the signification of *lash*, + *a*, m., and f. *sâ*. **1.** Ardent desire, Bhartṛ. 3, 36 (m.); Pańch. 81, 21 (at the end of a comp. adj. *çravaṇa-sukha-*, Ardently desiring the pleasure for his ears). **2.** Regret. **3.** Asking. **4.** The longing of a pregnant woman. **5.** Dalliance, MBh. 7, 3383 (?).—Comp. *Darçana-*, adj., f. *lâ*, ardently desiring to see, Nal. 12, 84. *Pati-*, adj., f. *sâ*, ardently longing for (her) husband, ib. 13, 1.

लाला *lâlâ* (akin to *li*), f. Saliva, spittle, Bhartṛ. 2, 9; Ṛit. 1, 5.

लालाटिक *lâlâṭika*, i.e. *lalâṭa* + *ika*, I. adj. **1.** Relating to the forehead, worn on it, etc. **2.** Contemplating the forehead. **3.** Relating to fate (which is supposed to be written on one's forehead). **4.** Low. **II.** m., and f. *kî*. **1.** An attentive servant. **2.** An idler.

लालाय *LÂLÂYA*, a denomin. derived from *lâlâ* with *ya*, Âtm. To secrete saliva continually, Pańch. iii. d. 195.

लालितक *lâlita* + *ka* (see *lal*, Caus.), m. A favourite, Râjat. 6, 166.

लालित्य *lâlitya*, i.e. *lalita* + *ya* (vb. *lal*), n. Loveliness.

लाव *lâva*, i.e. *lû* + *a*, I. adj. **1.** Cutting. **2.** Plucking, Ragh. 13, 43. **II.** m., and f. *vâ*, A sort of quail, Perdix chinensis, Râm. 3, 53, 57.—Comp. *Pushpa-*, 1. m. a garland-maker, a flower-seller. 2. f. *vî*, a female flower-gatherer, Megh. 27.

लावण *lâvaṇa*, i.e. *lavaṇa* + *a*, adj. **1.** Relating to salt. **2.** Salted.

लावणिक *lâvaṇika*, i.e. *lavaṇa* + *ika*, I. adj. **1.** Relating to salt. **2.** Salted. **3.** Beautiful. **II.** m. A salt merchant. **III.** n. A vessel holding salt.

लावण्य *lâvaṇya*, i.e. *lavaṇa* + *ya*, n. **1.** Saltness. **2.** Loveliness, charm, Hit. i. d. 136, M.M.; beauty, Lass. 2. ed. 19, 3.

लास *lâsa*, i.e. *las* + *a*, m. **1.** Dancing.

2. Dalliance. 3. Pea-water, pulse that has been lightly boiled.

लासक *lâsaka*, i.e. *las + aka*, I. m. 1. A dancer, an actor. 2. A peacock. II. f. *akâ* and *ikâ*, A dancing girl.

लास्य *lâsya*, i.e. *lâsa + ya*, I. m. A dancer. II. f. *yâ*, A female dancer. III. n. 1. Dancing. 2. Union of dance and music, Mârk. P. 68, 26. 3. The dance of the Indian dancing girls.

लिक्षा *likshâ*, f. 1. A nit, a young louse. 2. A poppy seed, considered as a measure of weight, Man. 8, 133.—Comp. *Yûkâ-liksha*, n. lice and nits.

लिख् *LIKH*, i. 6, Par. 1. To scratch, to pick, Hit. 43, 15. 2. To touch, Bhaṭṭ. 15, 22. 3. To write, Pańch. 5, 6; Râjat. 5, 396. 4. To delineate, MBh. 2, 731. Ptcple. of the pf. pass. *likhita*, Scarified. n. 1. Writing, scripture. 2. A book. Comp. *Chitra-*, adj. painted, Hit. 91, 6, M.M. (*-iva*, as if painted, i.e. motionless). Ptcple. of the fut. pass. *lekhya*, n. 1. A letter. 2. A written accusation. 3. A manuscript. 4. Drawing, Chr. 51, 1. Comp. *Dur-lekhya*, i.e. *dus-*, adj. illegibly written, Yâjń. 2, 91.—With the prep. अभि *abhi*, 1. To write on, Vikr. 25, 17. 2. To write, Lass. 91, 5. 3. To paint, Utt. Râmach. 9, 13.—With आ *â*, To delineate, Daçak. in Chr. 199, 14; Megh. 103. *âlekhya*, 1. To be written. 2. To be delineated. n. 1. Writing. 2. A painting, picture, Vikr. d. 29.—With व्या *vi-â*, To pierce, Kir. 5, 30.—With उद् *ud*, 1. To scratch up, MBh. 3, 374. 2. To polish, Çâk. d. 133. 3. To peck, Pańch. 146, 14 (see n.). 4. To slit open, Pańch. 91, 5. 5. To touch, MBh. 3, 2453.—With समुद् *sam-ud*, To strike, Kumâras. 1, 57.—With प्र *pra*, To scratch, to draw lines on (acc.), Man. 4, 55.—With वि *vi*, 1. To draw furrows on (acc.), Bhartṛ. 2, 98. 2. To strike, MBh. 3, 11953. 3. To peck, Hit. 93, 10, M.M. 4. To delineate, MBh. 3, 16670.

लिखन *likh + ana*, n. 1. Scratching, scarifying. 2. Writing. 3. A written document.

लिङ्ख् *LIŃKH*, see *lakh*.

लिगु *ligu*, I. m. 1. A fool. 2. A deer. 3. Part of the earth. II. n. The mind.

लिङ्ग् *LIŃG*, i. 1, Par. † To go. i. 10 (rather a denomin. derived from *lińga*), Par. To change a noun according to its gender.—With the prep. आ *â*, i. 1, Par. (in epic poetry also Âtm., Râm. 2, 64, 30), and i. 10, To embrace, Vikr. 71, 11; Mṛichchh. 91, 14; Pańch. 187, 6 (i. 10); Kathâs. 3, 65 (pf. red. *lilińga*). Ptcple. of the fut. pass. *âlińgya*, n. A small drum, Râm. 5, 13, 47.—With प्रत्या *prati-â*, i. 1, To return an embrace, Mṛichchh. 91, 15.—With समा *sam-â*, i. 1, 1. To embrace, Pańch. 27, 6; Mṛichchh. 91, 13. 2. To hold, Râm. 5, 13, 48; 53.—Cf. probably O.H.G. and A.S. hring; O.H.G. hringjan.

लिङ्ग *lińga*, n. 1. A mark, a sign, Nal. 5, 14. 2. A spot. 3. A religious mark, Man. 4, 200. 4. The penis. 5. The phallus, or Çiva under that emblem. 6. Nature, as the active power in creation. 7. The primary body, Vedântas. in Chr. 206, 11; cf. 21. 8. Gender. 9. The reason, or middle term, Bhâshâp. 66. 10. The order of the religious student. 11. Symptom of disease.—Comp. *Ṛitu-*, n. the peculiar marks of the seasons, Man. 1, 30. *Tri-*, I. adj. 1. possessed of the three qualities, Bhâg. P. 3, 20, 13. 2. having three genders (as an adj.). II. the name of a country. *Deva-*, n. an idol, Bhâg. P. 3, 17, 13. *Nirliṅga*, i.e. *nis-*, adj. without distinguishing marks, MBh. 5, 1610. *Puṁliṅga*, i.e. *puṁs-*, I. n. 1. manhood, MBh. 5, 7489. 2. the masculine gender. II. adj. having the marks of a male, MBh. 9, 3304. *Vishṇuliṅgî*, i.e. *vishṇu-liṅga* + *î*, f. a quail. *Strî-*, n. 1. the female organs, Chr. 58, 5. 2. the feminine gender.

लिङ्गस्थ *liṅga-stha*, m. A student in theology, Man. 8, 65.

लिङ्गालिका *liṅgâlikâ*, f. A small mouse or shrew.

लिङ्गिन् *liṅgin*, i.e. *liṅga* + *in*, **I.** adj., f. *nî*. **1.** Having marks, characterised. **2.** One who is entitled to wear religious marks, Man. 4, 200. **II.** m. **1.** An ascetic, Pańch. iv. d. 41. **2.** A religious student. **3.** A worshipper of Çiva. **4.** A hypocrite. **5.** An elephant. — **Comp.** *A-*, adj. and m. one who is not entitled to wear religious marks, Man. 4, 200. *Ârya-*, adj. one who wears the signs of an Ârya, Man. 9, 260. *Dvija-*, adj. one who wears the marks of a twice-born (i.e. one of the three first castes), Man. 9, 224. *Mârjâra-*, adj. one who has the nature of a cat, Man. 4, 197.

लिप् *LIP*, i. 6, *limpa*, Par. Âtm. **1.** To anoint, Bhaṭṭ. 14, 94. **2.** To smear, Hit. 21, 14. **3.** To stain (*lipyate doshena*, Incurs sin), Hit. ii. d. 118; to pollute, Man. 4, 201; 10, 104. **4.** To burn, Bhaṭṭ. 6, 22. Ptcple. of the pf. pass. *lipta*. **1.** Envenomed. **2.** Embraced. **3.** Defiled. **Comp.** *A-medhya-lipta*, adj. defiled (soiled with impurity), Man. 4, 56. Caus. To cause to be decorated, Râm. 2, 9, 40.—With the prep. **अनु** *anu*, **1.** To anoint, Daçak. in Chr. 183, 6. **2.** To smear, Çiç. 9, 15. *anulipta*, **1.** Smeared, Pańch. iii. d. 32. **2.** Anointed, Hit. 90, 8, M.M.; glistening, Çâk. d. 166. Caus. To cause to be anointed, Daçak. in Chr. 200, 7.—With **अव** *ava*, To smear, Lass. 9, 19. *avalipta*, Proud, arrogant, Man. 4, 79; Pańch. i. d. 341.—With **आ** *â*, **1.** To anoint, Utt. Râmach. 79, 1; Ṛit. 6, 12, v.r. **2.** To smear, Pańch. 171, 11.—With **समा** *sam-â*, To anoint, Bhaṭṭ. 17, 5.—With **उप** *upa*, To pollute, MBh. 2, 2625; Bhag. 13, 32. Caus. To let smear, Man. 3, 206. —With **वि** *vi*, **1.** To anoint, Bhaṭṭ. 3, 20. **2.** To smear, Lass. 9, 12. **3.** To pollute, Hit. 128, 12.—With **सम्** *sam*, To anoint, MBh. 1, 4950.—Cf. λίπος, λιπαρής, ἀ-λείφω, λισσός; Lat. limpidus, lippus; probably also liquidus, liquere, and O.H.G. salba, Goth. salbôn, A.S. sealf.

लिपि and **लिपी** *lip* + *î*, f. **1.** Anointing, smearing. **2.** Painting. **3.** Writing, Daçak. in Chr. 180, 7; the alphabet, Ragh. 18, 45. **4.** A written paper or book.

लिपिकर and **लिपिकार** *lipi-kâra*, m. **1.** A scribe. **2.** *-kara*, A plasterer, whitener, Râm. 1, 12, 6 Gorr.

लिप्तक *lipta* + *ka* (vb. *lip*), m. A poisoned arrow.

लिप्सा *lipsâ*, i.e. *lipsa*, desider. of *labh*, + *a*, f. Wish.

लिप्सु *lipsu*, i.e. *lipsa* (see the last), + *u*, adj. Desirous, greedy, Pańch. 5, 4.

लिम्पट *limpaṭa* (vb. *lip*, but cf. also *lampaṭa*), m. A lecher.

लिम्पक *limpâka*, m. **1.** The lime tree, Citrus acida. **2.** An ass.

लिश् *LIÇ*, i. 4, Âtm. To become small. † i. 6, Par. To go.—Cf. *kliç* and *kṛiç*; ὀλίγος, perhaps λίγδος.

लिह् *LIH*, ii. 2, Par. Âtm. To lick, Hit. i. d. 112, M.M. Ptcple. of the pf. pass. *liḍha*. **1.** Licked, Kir. 5, 38. **2.** Eaten. Ptcple. of the fut. pass. *lehya*, To be licked, Pańch. 61, 12. n. Food, Ragh. 5, 73. Frequent. *lelih*, *lelihya*, To lick repeatedly, MBh. 3, 10394. *lelih*, Âtm., Chr. 39, 5. Ptcple. of the pres. Âtm. *lelihâna*, m. **1.** A snake. **2.** A name of Çiva.—With the prep. **अव** *ava*, **1.** To lick here and there (figurat.), Lass. 2. ed. 79, 79. **2.** To lick up or off; to eat, Çâk. d. 7. **3.** To touch with the tongue, Man. 4, 203. *avaliḍha*, Devoured, destroyed, Kirâtârj. 13, 11. Frequent. To lick repeatedly, MBh. 1, 1181.—With **आ** *â*, To lick, to touch, Ragh. 10, 46. *âliḍha*, **1.** Eaten. **2.** Polished, Bhartṛ. 2, 36. n. An attitude in shooting, the right knee advanced, the left leg retracted, Kumâras. 3, 70.—With **प्रत्या** *prati-â*, *pratyâliḍha*, Eaten. n. An attitude in shooting, etc. = *âliḍha*, n.—With **परि** *pari*, To lick, to enjoy, Râm. 2, 61, 16. Frequent. To lick repeatedly, Pańch. 55, 7 (see my transl. n. 257).—With **सम्** *sam*, To lick, MBh. 3, 10653.—With **परिसम्** *pari-sam*, To lick, MBh. 3, 11500.—Cf. λείχω, λιχανός, λειχήν; Lat. lingere, pol-lex; Goth. bi-laigôn; A.S. liccian.

ऽलिह् *-lih*, latter part of comp. words, Licking.—Comp. *Rasanâ-*, m. a dog.

ली *LÎ* (the original signification is 'To be viscous,' then 'To be solvable'), i. 1 and 10, Par. To melt, to liquefy, to dissolve. ii. 9, *linâ*, *lini*, Par. **1.** To adhere. **2.** To obtain. i. 4, Âtm. (properly pass.), **1.** To be dissolved, to vanish, Böhtl. Ind. Spr. 450. **2.** To adhere or cling to. **3.** To dwell, to live, to haunt, MBh. 1, 4310. Ptcple. of the pf. pass. *lîna*. **1.** Melted, dissolved, Vedântas. in Chr. 219, 12. **2.** Effaced, wiped away, removed, Kir. 5, 26. **3.** Left. **4.** Embraced. **5.** Staying, Pańch. 187, 5; being situated, resting, Çâk. d. 144. **6.** Entered, Böhtl. Ind. Spr. 830.—With the prep. **अन्तर्** *antar*, *antarlîna*, Inherent, staying; haunting in the interior, Pańch. 109, 19; i. d. 420; Utt. Râmach. 56, 10; (not coming out), Pańch. 175, 24. Acc. sing. °*nam*, adv. Inwardly, Pańch. 185, 3.—With **अप** *apa*, Caus. *lâpaya*, Âtm. To deceive, Bhaṭṭ. 8, 44.—With **अभि** *abhi*, *abhilina*, Adhering, Megh. 37.—With **अव** *ava*, To cling to, Nal. 2, 46.—With **समव** *sam-ava*, i. 4, To be dissolved, Vedântas. in Chr. 219, 15.—With **आ** *â*, i. 4, To faint, MBh. 3, 2573.—With **नि** *ni*, i. 4, **1.** To alight, to settle, MBh. 3, 10560. **2.** To lie down, MBh. 3, 12091. **3.** To hide one's self, MBh. 3, 10978. *nilina*, **1.** Fused in or into. **2.** Transformed. **3.** Destroyed. **4.** Encompassed. **5.** Full.—With **संनि** *sam-ni*, i. 4, To lie down, MBh. 3, 13654.—With **प्र** *pra*, i. 4, **1.** To be dissolved or absorbed, Man. 1, 54. **2.** To die, Man. 4, 240. **3.** To unite intimately, Man. 12, 17. *pralina*, **1.** Destroyed. **2.** Unconscious, insensible.—With **संप्र** *sam-pra*, pass. To be destroyed, Hit. iii. d. 129.—With **वि** *vi*, i. 4, **1.** To alight, Çiç. 1, 12. **2.** To be dissolved, to vanish, Pańch. ii. d. 98; to become ineffectual, iii. d. 74. *vilina*, **1.** Liquefied, melted. **2.** Dissolved, Böhtl. Ind. Spr. 830; Lass. 11, 15. **3.** Disappeared. **4.** Imagined. **5.** United. **Comp.** *A-*, adj. living, Utt. Râmach. 168, 7. Caus. *vi-lâyaya*, *-lâpaya*, *-lînaya* (properly a denomin. derived from *vilîna*), *lâlaya* (also a denomin. from *lâlâ* with *vi*), To dissolve. *vilâyita*, Dissolved, Prab. 116, 8.—With प्रवि *pra-vi*, i. 4, To be dissolved, to vanish, Bhag. 4, 23. —With सम् *sam*, *saṁlîna*, **1.** Joined, put together, Pańch. 163, 6. **2.** Staying, MBh. 1, 7671. — Cf. Lat. līmus (borrowed O.H.G. lim; A.S. líme, and O.H.G. leim; A.S. lám), po-lîre, linere; λεῖμαξ.

लीनता *lîna* + *tâ* (vb. *lî*), f. Lying, Çâk. d. 167.

लीला *lîlâ* (akin to *las*), f. **1.** Play, sport, pastime, Pańch. 161, 15; *lîlayâ* (instr.), Sportively, Pańch. 229, 10; easily, without any effort, Pańch. 211, 12; Hit. 81, 18. **2.** Amorous or wanton sport, Pańch. iii. d. 237.—**Comp.** *Sa-lîla*, adj. wanton, sportive. *°lam*, adv. affectionately, Kir. 5, 33.

लीलावती *lîlâvatî*, i.e. *lîlâ* + *vant* + *î*, f. A wanton woman, Hit. i. d. 193, M.M.

लुच् *luch* (vb. *luńch*), f. **1.** Cutting off. **2.** Dropping.

लुञ्च् *LUŃCH*, i. 1, Par. **1.** To pull out, Bhaṭṭ. 15, 3. **2.** To pare, to peel, Pańch. 121, 13.—With the prep. अव *ava*, To pull off, MBh. 3, 10760.—With वि *vi*, To pull out, Bhaṭṭ. 18, 38. —Cf. probably O.H.G. liuhhan; A.S. lyccan, evellere; Lat. runcare.

लुञ्चक *luńch* + *aka*, adj. One who pulls out.—**Comp.** *Keça-*, adj. pulling out the hair, Prab. 54, 9.

लुञ्चन *luńch* + *ana*, n. Pulling out, Daçak. in Chr. 185, 3.

लुञ्ज् *LUŃJ*, see *lańj*.

1. लुट् *LUṬ*, i. 1 and 4, Par. **1.** To roll upon the ground, Bhaṭṭ. 3, 32 (cf. 3. *luṭh*). **2.** † To be connected with (?).

† 2. लुट् *LUṬ*, i. 1, Âtm. **1.** To resist. **2.** To suffer pain. **3.** To shine. i. 10, Par. To shine, to speak.—Cf. *ruṭ* and *lunṭh*.

† 1. लुठ् *LUṬH*, i. 1, Par. To knock down. i. 1, Âtm. **1.** To oppose. **2.** To suffer pain. **3.** To go.

2. लुठ् *LUṬH*, i. 10, Par., and लुण्ठ् *LUNṬH*, † रुण्ठ् *RUNṬH*, i. 1, Par. To rob. Ptcple. of the pf. pass. *lunṭhita*. **1.** Plundered, robbed, Râjat. 5, 345; 427. **2.** Peeled (?), Pańch. 121, 11 (cf. my transl. n. 790).—With the prep. निस् *nis*, *nirloṭhita*, Robbed, Râjat. 5, 159. Cf. *lunṭ*.

3. लुठ् *LUṬH*, i. 6, Par. **1.** To roll upon the ground, to welter, Hit. 123, 18. **2.** To roll down, Râjat. 5, 92. **3.** To move to and fro, Hit. ii. d. 67. **4.** To agitate, to touch, Bhâg. P. 1, 15, 18. Ptcple of the pf. pass. *luṭhita*, Rolling on the ground. m. A horse's rolling on the ground.—With the prep. निस् *nis*, *nirluṭhita*, Rolled down, Râjat. 5, 88.—With परि *pari*, To roll about, Daçak. 151, 5.—With प्र *pra*, To roll on the ground, Pańch. 254, 22. Caus. *praloṭhita*, Rolling, heaving, tossing.

लुठन *luṭh* + *ana*, n. **1.** A horse's rolling himself on the ground. **2.** Rolling on the ground with sorrow.

1. लुड् *LUḌ*, and लुल् *LUL*, i. 1,

Par. To agitate, to stir, to disturb. Ptcple. of the pf. pass. *lulita.* **1.** Agitated, Râm. 1, 42, 29. **2.** Shaken, Utt. Râmach. 140, 3. **3.** Heaving, panting, Utt. Râmach. 15, 15; Lass. 20, 20. **4.** Destroyed. Caus. *loḍaya,* To agitate, MBh. 1, 2833. Ptcple of the pf. pass. I. *loḍita,* Troubled, Râm. 2, 95, 18. II. *lolita,* Agitated, Çiç. 9, 4.—With the prep. अभि *abhi,* comp. ptcple. of the pf. pass. *an-abhi-lulita,* Without being touched, Çâk. d. 61.—With आ *â,* Caus. *loḍaya,* **1.** To trouble, MBh. 1, 7921; with *jâlais,* Pańch. 78, 14 (see my transl. n. 374, 'To fish out,' cf. *vi*). **2.** To mix, MBh. 4, 689.—With समा *sam-â,* Caus. *loḍaya,* **1.** To mix, MBh. 3, 11471. **2.** To reflect, Skandap. Kâçîkh. 10, 48. —With परि *pari,* Caus. *loḍaya,* To agitate, to disturb, MBh. 2, 389.—With वि *vi, vilulita,* **1.** Tremulous. **2.** Falling, shed fast (viz. tears), Utt. Râmach. 68, 12. Caus. *loḍaya,* **1.** To disturb, MBh. 2, 11604. **2.** To fish out, MBh. 12, 4901. —With सम् *sam,* Caus. *loḍaya,* To disturb, MBh. 1, 1477.

† 2. लुड् *LUḌ,* i. 6, Par. **1.** To adhere, to be attached. **2.** To cover.

लुण्ट् *LUṆṬ,* i. 1 and 10, Par. **1.** To plunder. **2.** † To disregard. **3.** To peel (cf. my transl. of the Pańch. n. 790).—With the prep. उद् *ud,* ptcple. of the pf. pass. *ulluṇṭita,* Sacked, Pańch. rec. orn. MS. Berol. 121, a. Cf. 2. *luṭh.*

लुण्ठ् *LUṆṬH,* see 2. *luṭh.*

† लुण्ड् *LUṆḌ,* i. 1 and 10, Par. To plunder.

लुण्डीकृत *luṇḍîkṛita,* i. e. *luṇḍ + a -kṛita,* adj. Ragged, Mṛichchh. 34, 11.

† लुन्थ् *LUNTH,* i. 1, Par. **1.** To hurt, to kill. **2.** To afflict. **3.** To suffer pain.

लुप् *LUP,* i. 1, *lumpa,* Par. Âtm. **1.** To break, to destroy, Hit. iv. d. 12; MBh. 1, 5560. **2.** To spoil, Vikr. 27, 2. Pass. **1.** To be violated, Man. 2, 189. **2.** To be lost, Man. 9, 211. † i. 4, Par. To disturb, to bewilder. Ptcple. of the pf. pass. *lupta.* **1.** Neglected, Bhag. 1, 42. **2.** Disturbed, Çṛiṅgârat. 7. **3.** Lost. n. Booty, plunder. Caus. *lopaya,* **1.** To cause to leave, to divert, Ragh. 12, 9 (Calc.). **2.** To let violate, Man. 8, 16.—With the prep. अव *ava,* To break forth, Man. 7, 106.—With आ *â,* Pass. To be troubled, to be clouded, Megh. 103.—With व्या *vi-â,* To remove, Megh. 71. Pass. To be divided, Lass. 20, 20.—With परि *pari,* To disturb, to diminish, Daçak. in Chr. 187, 4.—With प्र *pra,* pass. To be disturbed, MBh. 1, 7750.—With विप्र *vi-pra,* **1.** To rend in pieces, Man. 3, 225. **2.** To disturb, MBh. 2, 161.—With वि *vi,* **1.** To rend in pieces, Man. 3, 204. **2.** To disturb, Man. 2, 161. **3.** To extinguish, Lass. 2. ed. 97, 54. **4.** To become disfigured, Râm. 2, 60, 15 Gorr. *vilupta,* **1.** Cut off. **2.** Lost, Utt. Râmach. 72, 12. **3.** Interrupted, Pańch. ii. d. 2. **4.** Seized. Comp. *A-,* adj. undisturbed, Râjat. 5, 5. Caus. **1.** To disturb, MBh. 1, 7752. **2.** To extinguish, MBh. 1, 5233.—With प्रवि *pra-vi, pravilupta,* Lost, removed, fallen.—Cf. Lat. rumpere; A.S. reaf, reafian; O.H.G. raubôn; very probably also Goth. raupjan, to pull out; λύπη, probably Ὄλυμπος (præruptus, based on a frequent.).

लुब्धक *lubdha + ka* (vb. *lubh*), m.

1. A covetous or greedy man, Râjat. 5, 345. 2. A hunter, Pańch. 106, 7. 3. A libertine.

लुब्धता *lubdha* + *tâ* (vb. *lubh*), f. Greediness, Râjat. 5, 186.

लुभ् *LUBH*, i. 4, Par. To covet, to desire, Hit. i. d. 27, M.M. (with dat.). i. 6, Par. To bewilder, to perplex. Ptcple. of the pf. pass. *lubdha*. 1. Desiring, Hit. 16, 4, M.M. 2. Covetous, greedy, Daçak. in Chr. 190, 1. 3. Avaricious, Man. 4, 87. m. 1. A hunter, Râm. 2, 71, 35. 2. A lecher. **Comp.** *Ati-*, adj. excessively greedy, Hit. ii. 1 (envious). *Guṇa-*, adj., f. *dhâ*, loving excellent qualities, Hit. iv. d. 97. Ptcple. of the fut. pass. *lobhanîya*, Worthy to be desired, Çâk. d. 20. Superl. *lobhanîyatama*, Most worthy to be desired, Indr. 5, 14. Caus. 1. To cause to desire, to make greedy, Pańch. 256, 1. 2. To allure, Râm. 1, 8, 23. 3. To entice away, Râm. 3, 50, 6.—With the prep. **अनु** *anu*, Caus. To suffer to be allured, to long after, Râm. 3, 49, 38.—With **परि** *pari*, Caus. To allure, Mṛichchh. 127, 16 (anomal. *lobhase*).—With **प्र** *pra*, 1. To pollute, Man. 9, 20 (Âtm.). 2. To follow one's carnal desire, Pańch. 262, 9. Caus. To allure, MBh. 3, 10044.—With **वि** *vi*, To disturb. *vilubhita*, 1. Bewildered. 2. Shaken (by wind). Caus. 1. To allure, to seduce, Vikr. 8, 16; Daçak. in Chr. 191, 10. 2. To beguile, Râm. 2, 94, 1. 3. To enchant, Çâk. 81, 17.—Cf. Lat. lubet, libet, libido, līber, 'free' and 'son'; ἐλευθερός (based on an old frequent.); Goth. liubs, us-laubjan; A.S. leóf, lyfan, lufian, lóf, leaf, left.

† **लुम्ब्** *LUMB*, i. 1, Par. To torment. i. 10, Par. To torment, or to be invisible.

लुल् *LUL*, see 1. *luḍ*.

लुष् *LUSH*, see 2. *lûsh*.

लुषभ *lush* + *a* + *bha* (*lush* = vb. *rush*, cf. λύσσα), m. An elephant in rut.

† **लुह्** *LUH*, i. 1, Par. To covet (cf. *lubh*; *bh* is changed to *h*).

लू *LÛ*, ii. 9, *lunâ*, *lunî*, Par. Âtm. 1. To cut, to clip, MBh. 3, 15644. 2. To destroy, Çiç. 1, 51. Ptcple. of the pf. pass. *lûna*. 1. Cut, clipped, Pańch. i. d. 201; cut off. 2. Wounded, Hit. iv. d. 77. 3. Injured by biting, Hit. 58, 3.—With the prep. **विप्र** *vi-pra*, *vipralûna*, Severed, Utt. Râmach. 53, 15.—Cf. λύω, ἀπο-λαύω; Lat. lucrum, solvo; akin are also Goth. fra-liusan; A.S. leosan, lysan, leás, los.

लूता *lûtâ*, f. 1. A spider, Man. 12, 57; Vedântas. in Chr. 206, 13. 2. An ant.

लूनि *lû* + *ni*, f. (?), Rice.

लूम *lûma*, n. A tail.

† 1. **लूष्** *LÛSH*, i. 1, Par. To adorn. i. 10, Par. To hurt, to injure.

† 2. **लूष्** *LÛSH*, i. 10, and **लुष्** *LUSH*, i. 1, Par. To rob.

लेख *lekha*, i.e. *likh* + *a*, I. m. 1. A letter, Hit. 120, 10. 2. A god. II. f. *khâ*. 1. Writing. 2. A line, Daçak. in Chr. 194, 3; Bhartṛ. 2, 14; a stripe (of a cloud), Pańch. 203, 5; a stroke, Hit. pr. d. 1, M.M.; flashing (of lightning), Vikr. d. 76. 3. A mark, Kir. 5, 40. 4. Delineation.—**Comp.** *Indu-*, f. *khâ*, the crescent, Kir. 5, 44. *Chandra-*, I. m. the name of a Râkshasa, Râm. 6, 84, 12. II. f. *khâ*. 1. the crescent, ib. 5, 19, 21. 2. a proper name, Râjat. 1, 218. *Chitra-*, f. *khâ*, 1. an image, a picture, Gît. 10, 15. 2. name of an Apsaras, Vikr. 7, 5. *Patra-*, f. *khâ*, decorating the person by staining it with fragrant pigments of sandal, musk, etc., Hariv. 7078. *Sa-patra-lekha*, adj. decorated with fragrant pigments, Ṛit. 6. 7. *Çaçilekhâ*, i.e. *çaçin-*, f. 1. a digit of the moon. 2. the name of an Apsaras, Lass. 51, 13. *Hṛillekha*, i.e. *hṛid-*, m. 1. reasoning. 2. knowledge. 3. heartache.

लेखक *lekhaka*, i.e. *likh* + *aka*, m. A writer, Pañch. 237, 1.

लेखन *lekhana*, i.e. *likh* + *ana*, n. **1.** Scarifying. **2.** Writing, copying, Pañch. 237, 1; scripture. **3.** The bark of the Bhój tree and the leaf of the palm tree, used for writing on.

लेखनिक *lekhanika*, i.e. *lekhana* + *ika*, m. **1.** A letter-carrier. **2.** One who signs by proxy.

† **लेप्** *LEP*, i. 1, Âtm. **1.** To go. **2.** To serve (?).

लेप *lepa*, i.e. *lip* + *a*, m. **1.** Smearing, plastering, Böhtl. Ind. Spr. 748. **2.** Mortar, plaster, MBh. 1, 5724. **3.** Stain, spot. **4.** The wipings of the hand which has offered funeral oblations to three ancestors, these wipings being considered as an oblation to ancestors in the fourth, fifth, and sixth degrees. **5.** Food, Man. 3, 210.—**Comp.** *Nirlepa*, i.e. *nis-*, adj. free from spots, Man. 5, 112. *Piṇḍî-*, m. a kind of ointment, Kathâs. 28, 178. *Vajra-*, m. a kind of ointment (?), Pañch. iv. d. 10 (Böhtl. Ind. Spr. 2704, pitch); cf. Wilson, Th. of the Hind. 2. ed. ii. p. 55.

लेपक *lepaka*, i.e. *lip* + *aka*, m. A bricklayer, a plasterer.

लेपकर *lepa-kara*, m. A writer, Râm. 1, 12, 17.

लेपन *lepana*, i.e. *lip* + *ana*, n. **1.** Anointing, Lass. 11, 2. **2.** Smearing. **3.** Plastering, Chr. 57, 22; Râm. 2, 91, 41 (both at the end of comp. adj. Plastered with). **4.** Mortar, Man. 6, 76.—**Comp.** *Bhûmi-*, n. cow-dung.

ऽलेपिन् *-lepin*, i.e. *lepa* + *in*, adj. Having a plastering; in *prabhâ-*, adj. Covered with splendour, Vikr. d, 125.

लेप्यकृत् *lepya-kṛi* + *t* (vb. *lip*), m. A bricklayer, a plasterer.

लेप्यमयी *lepyamayî*, i. e. *lepya* + *maya* + *î* (vb. *lip*), f. A doll.

लेलिह *leliha*, i.e. *lih*, frequent., + *a*, m. **1.** A serpent, MBh. 1, 1318. **2.** A worm breeding in the stomach.

लेश *leça*, i.e. *liç* + *a*, m. **1.** Smallness. **2.** When latter part of compound words, often A little bit, little; e.g. Pañch. i. 353; MBh. 3, 1268; Çâk. d. 37.—**Comp.** *Açru-*, m. drops of tears, Megh. 105. *Prâleya-*, m. hailstone, Pañch. i. d. 353. *Sukha-*, m. insignificant pleasure, Bhâg. P. 6, 9, 38; Pañch. i. d. 203. *Sa-*, adj. entire, Kirât. 14, 2.

लेष्टु *leshṭu*, perhaps *liç* + *tu* (but cf. *loshṭa*, to which it seems to be akin), m. A clod of earth.

लेहन *lehana*, i.e. *lih* + *ana*, n. Licking, tasting with the tongue.

लैण् *LAIṆ*, see *paiṇ*.

लोक् *LOK*, i. 1, Âtm., and i. 10, Par. (probably a denomin. derived from *loka*), **1.** To see. **2.** i. 10, † To shine, to speak.—With the prep. **अव** *ava*, i. 1 and 10, **1.** To see, Hit. 15, 2, M.M.; to look, Hit. 85, 15; to regard, Vikr. 3, 6; to see to, Çâk. 3, 6; to watch, Pañch. 249, 4. **2.** To perceive, Vikr. 21, 3; Lass. 9, 16. **3.** To review (an army), Hit. 94, 8.—With **समव** *sam-ava*, i. 10, To inspect, Çâk. d. 13.—With **आ**

â, i. 1 and 10, **1.** To look out, MBh. 4, 250. **2.** To regard, Vikr. d. 81; to see, Pańch. i. d. 21; to inspect, to view, MBh. 3, 11024. **3.** To perceive, MBh. 2, 1817. **4.** To consider, Man. 8, 126. *sâlokita*, n. Look, eye, Mâlat. 16, 8.—With **समा** *sam-â*, **1.** To look at, MBh. 2, 775. **2.** To acknowledge, Pańch. pr. d. 3.—With **वि** *vi*, i. 10, To see, Vikr. 8, 17; to regard, 12, 20; Utt. Râmach. 47, 8. *vilokya*, **1.** Regarding, i.e. to, Vikr. 40, 1; to view, Râm. 1, 44, 19. **2.** To take a view of, Pańch. 46, 7. **3.** To look over, Man. 8, 239. **4.** To perceive, 2, 9. Ptcple. of the pf. pass. *vilokita*, n. Seeing, Çâk. d. 36.—With **प्रवि** *pra-vi*, To look forward, Râm. 1, 9, 59. Cf. *ruch*.

लोक *loha*, i.e. *loch*, or *ruch*, + *a* (with *l* for *r*, cf. *ruch*), m. **1.** Seeing, sight. **2.** The world, the universe, Chr. 34, 8. **3.** A world, a division of the universe, Vikr. 86, 8 (*madhyama*, The middle world, i.e. the earth). **4.** Man, mankind. **5.** Men, people, sing. and pl., Daçak. in Chr. 183, 13; Pańch. i. d. 19; 256, 24; Bhartṛ. 2, 52.—**Comp.** *A-*, m. ceasing of the world, Râm. 1, 37, 12. *Ańga-*, m. the name of a country, ib. 4, 43, 8. *Amara-*, m. the world of the immortals. *Indra-*, m. the world of Indra, Man. 4, 182. *Go-*, m. Kṛishṇa's heaven. *Gṛiha-*, m. the household servants, Hit. 88, 18 (read *tvadgṛiha°*). *Jana-*, m. the name of a world supposed to be situated over the *Maharloka*, Bhâg. P. 2, 5, 39. *Jîva-*, m. 1. the world of living beings, i.e. the earth, Pańch. 226, 6. 2. mankind, people, Pańch. i. d. 9. *Tapoloka*, i.e. *tapas-*, m. one of the supposed seven worlds, Bhâg. P. 2, 5, 39. *Tala-*, m. the lower regions, ib. 2, 6, 42. *Tri-*, I. (n.), and f. *kî*, the three worlds, MBh. 13, 1505; Râm. 3, 52, 22; Bhâg. P. 1, 5, 7. II. m. *°ka*, the inhabitants of the three worlds, ib. 3, 2, 13. *Nara-vîra-*, m. mankind, Hit. iv. d. 80. *Para-*, m. heaven, paradise, Pańch. 207, 21. *Paura-*, m. pl. citizens, Pańch, 48, 25. *Brahmaloka*, i.e. *brahman-*, m. the supposed eternal residence of the spirits of the pious, Sund. 4, 25; MBh. 12, 3996, in Chr. 94. *Lokâloka*, i.e. *loka-a-*, m. a mountainous belt bounding the world. *Vi-*, adj. solitary.

लोकपाल *loka-pâla*, m. **1.** A king. **2.** The name of certain divinities, guardians of the world, as Indra, Soma, etc.; cf. a list of them in Wilson's Specimens of the Theatre of the Hindus, i. 2. ed. 219, n. ad Vikr. d. 36.

लोकायत *lokâyata*, i.e. *loka-â-yata* (vb. *yam?*), n. The system of atheistical philosophy, taught by *Chârvâka*.

लोकायतिक *lokâyatika*, *lokâyata* + *ika*, m. A follower of the Chârvâka system (see the last).

1. **लोच्** *LOCH* (= *ruch*, the initial *r* is changed to *l*, as in the kindred languages, see *ruch*), i. 1, Âtm. To see.—With the prep. **आ** *â*, Caus. **1.** To behold, to perceive, MBh. 2, 617. **2.** To regard, Hit. ii. d. 91 (cf. Böhtl. Ind. Spr. 787). **3.** To consider, Vedântas. in Chr. 202, 8; to reflect, Hit. 14, 17. Comp. ptcple. of the pf. pass. *an-âlochita*, adj. Unconsidered, without due reflection, Pańch. 239, 4.—With **पर्या** *pari-â*, To ponder, Lass. 33, 2.—Cf. λεύσσω, s. v. *ruch*.

† 2. **लोच्** *LOCH*, i. 10, Par. To speak, to shine.

लोचक *loch* + *aka*, m. **1.** The pupil of the eye. **2.** A wrinkled or contracted eyebrow. **3.** Stibium. **4.** An ornament worn by women on the forehead. **5.** An ear-ring. **6.** The rejected slough of the snake. **7.** A lump of flesh.

लोचन *loch + ana*, n. The eye, Vikr. d. 56.—Comp. *Châru-*, adj., f. *nâ*, having beautiful eyes, Hariv. 8705. *Tri-*, adj. having three eyes; epithet and name of Çiva, Ragh. 3, 66. *Vâma-*, adj., f. *nâ*, having beautiful eyes, Hit. ii. d. 111. *Sthira-*, adj. with fixed gaze. *Hari-*, m. 1. a crab. 2. an owl.

लोट् *LOṬ*, see *loḍ*.

† **लोड्** *LOḌ*, **लौड्** *LAUḌ*, and **लोट्** *LOṬ*, i. 1, Par. To be mad; cf. *roḍ*.

लोत *lota*, m. **1.** A tear. **2.** A mark, a sign.

लोत्र *lotra* (a corruption of *loptra*), n. Stolen goods, booty.

लोध *lodha*, and **लोध्र** *lodhra*, m. A tree, the bark of which is used in dyeing, Symplocos racemosa, Çiç. 9, 46; cf. *rodhra*.

लोप *lopa*, i.e. *lup + a*, m. **1.** Cutting off. **2.** Omission, Man. 3, 63; Lass. 2. ed. 55, 73. **3.** Destruction, disappearance. **4.** Annulling, cancelling. **5.** Elision, Lass. 2. ed. 115.

लोपक *lopa + ka*, m. Violation, MBh. 1, 7772.

लोपन *lopana*, i. e. *lup+ana*, n. Violation, Man. 11, 61.

लोपाक *lopâka*, m. A jackal.

लोपापक *lopâpaka*, **1.** m. A jackal. **2.** f. *pikâ*, A female jackal.

लोपामुद्रा *lopâmudrâ*, f. The wife of Agastya, Utt. Râmach. 48, 1.

लोपाशक *lopâçaka*, **1.** m. A jackal. **2.** f. *çikâ*, A female jackal.

लोप्त्र *loptra*, i.e. *lup + tra*, n. Plunder, booty, MBh. 1, 4309.

लोभ *lobha*, i.e. *lubh + a*, m. Covetousness, Man. 2, 178; Pańch. ii. d. 168. — Comp. *A-*, m. absence of desire, contentment, Hit. i. d. 7, M.M. *Ati-*, m. too great covetousness, Pańch. v. d. 20.

लोभिन् *lobhin*, i.e. *lubh + in*, adj., f. *nî*, Desirous, covetous.

ऽलोम *-loma*, a substitute for *loman*, in *ati-*, adj., f. *mâ*, With too much hair, Man. 3, 8. *anu-*, I. adj. With the hair regular, Râm. 3, 49, 33. II. f. *mâ*, A wife of a caste inferior to that of the man, Yâjń. 2, 288. *prati-*, see s.v. *vi-*, I. adj. (f. *mî*), Against the grain, reverse, backward, contrary. II. m. **1.** Reverse order. **2.** A snake. **3.** A dog. **4.** Varuṇa. III. n. A water-wheel. *su-*, adj., f. *mâ*, Having beautiful hair, Râm. 3, 49, 33.

लोमन् *loman*, i.e. *ruh + man* (cf. *roman*), n. **1.** The hair of the body, Hit. iii. d. 29. **2.** Feather, Chr. 32, 30. —Comp. *Asi-*, m. the name of a demon, MBh. 1, 2531.

लोमपाद *lomapâda*, i. e. *loman -pâda*, m. The name of a king of Ańga, Lass. 2. ed. 58, 2.

लोमश *lomaça*, i.e. *loman + ça*, I. adj. **1.** Hairy, mixed with hair, Lass. 2. ed. 40, 24. **2.** Woollen. II. m. **1.** A ram. **2.** The name of a Ṛishi. III. f. *çâ*. **1.** A fox. **2.** A female divine being, an attendant on Durgâ. **3.** Green vitriol. **4.** The name of several plants. — Comp. *Haṁsa-*, n. sulphate of iron.

लोमालिका *lomâlikâ*, i.e. perhaps *loman-âli + ka*, f. A fox.

लोल *lola*, i. e. *lul + a*, I. adj. **1.** Shaking, tremulous, Hit. i. d. 152, M.M.;

trembling, Mâlat. 21, 8. **2.** Agitated, Ṛit. 6, 31. **3.** Unsteady, Bhartṛ. 3, 36. **4.** Desiring, Megh. 101; greedy, Râjat. 5, 376. **II.** f. *lâ.* **1.** The tongue. **2.** Lakshmî.—**Comp.** *Â-*, adj. trembling a little, Bhartṛ. 3, 48; Kir. 5, 41. *Mahâ-*, m. a crow.

लोलुप *lolup + a* (frequent. of *lup*), adj. **1.** Desirous, Çâk. d. 98 (Prâkṛ.); longing for, covetous, Pańch. iv. d. 12 (cf. Böhtl. Ind. Spr. 2753). **2.** Destroying, MBh. 1, 1970.

लोलुपता *lolupa + tâ*, f. Greediness, Bhartṛ. 3, 48.

लोलुभ *lolubh + a* (frequent. of *lubh*), adj. Covetous, greedy.

† **लोष्ट्** *LOSHṬ*, i. 1, Âtm. (cf. *loshṭa*), To gather into a heap.

लोष्ट *loshṭa* (for *loshṭra*, q.v.), **I.** m. and n. A clod, a lump of earth, Utt. Râmach. 117, 3; Man. 11, 263; 4, 49 (potsherd ?). **II.** n. Rust of iron.

लोष्टक *loshṭa + ka*, **1.** (m. and n.), A clod (of dust), Râm. 3, 37, 18. **2.** (n.), Spot, mark (of stripes), Mṛichchh. 34, 3.

लोष्टमय *loshṭa + maya*, adj., f. *yî*, Made of clay, Man. 8, 289.

लोष्टु *loshṭu* (a form of *loshṭra*, q. cf.; cf. *kroshṭu=kroshṭṛi*), m. A clod of earth.

लोष्ट्र *loshṭra*, n. A clod of earth, Vikr. 54, 6.

लोह *loha*, i.e. *luh*, instead of *rudh* (see *rudhira*), *+a*, **I.** m. and n. **1.** Iron, Man. 9, 321; Pańch. 100, 23 (cf. my transl.). **2.** Steel. **3.** Any metal, Hit. i. d. 92, M.M. **4.** A weapon. **5.** A fish-hook, Kâm. Nîtis. 1, 44. **6.** Blood. **7.** Aloe-wood. **II.** m. An iron-coloured kid, Man. 3, 272.—**Comp.** *Kṛishṇa-*, n. the loadstone, Suçr. 1, 142, 17. *Nîla-*, n. blue steel, Râm. 3, 53, 57. *Pańchaloha*, i.e. *pańchan-*, n. a metallic alloy containing five metals, copper, brass, tin, lead, and iron. *Mahâ-*, m. the loadstone. *Ravi-*, n. copper. *Sâra-*, n. steel.

लोहकार *loha-kâra*, m. A blacksmith, Pańch. iii. d. 97.

लोहज *loha-ja*, n. **1.** Bell-metal. **2.** Rust of iron.

लोहमय *loha + maya*, adj., f. *yî*, Made of iron.—**Comp.** *Sarva-*, adj. entirely of iron, Pańch. 122, 10.

लोहल *lohala*, **I.** adj. Speaking indistinctly. **II.** (akin to *loha*), m. The principal ring of a chain.

लोहित *lohita* (=*rohita*, q. cf.), **I.** adj., f. *tâ*, or *inî*, Red, Çâk. d. 29. **II.** m. **1.** Red, the colour. **2.** The planet Mars. **3.** A sort of deer. **4.** A snake. **5.** A form of array. **6.** A sort of fish, Cyprinus rohita. **7.** (m. ?). A kind of mineral, Pańch. i. d. 89. **III.** n. **1.** Blood, Man. 4, 56. **2.** War, battle. **3.** Red sanders. **4.** Saffron.—**Comp.** *Dhûmra-*, adj. of a grey-red colour, MBh. 13, 753. *Nîla-*, I. adj. blue-red, purple, of a purple colour, Çâk. d. 194. II. m. the name of one of the great periods called Kalpas.

लोहितक *lohita + ka*, **I.** adj. Red. **II.** m. **1.** A ruby. **2.** The planet Mars. **III.** n. Calx of brass.

लोहिताङ्ग *lohitâṅga*, i. e. *lohita -aṅga*, m. The planet Mars, Vikr. d. 142.

लोहिताय *LOHITÂYA*, a denomin. derived from *lohita* with *ya*, Par. (anomal.), To become red, Lass. 2. ed. 78, 71; 96, 49.

लौकायतिक *laukâyatika*, i.e. *lokâyata + ika*, m. An atheist.

लौकिक *laukika*, i.e. *loka + ika*, adj.,

f. *kî*, **1.** Relating to worldly things, Man. 2, 117; mundane (opposed to holy), Utt. Râmach. 8, 2. **2.** Usual, Man. 11, 184—**Comp.** *A-*, adj. 1. superhuman, Vikr. 19, 6; transcendental, Bhâshâp. 62. 2. not common. 3. rare. 4. vedic. *Jîva-*, adj. belonging to the human world, MBh. 12, 8495.

लौड् *LAUḌ*, see *loḍ*.

लौल्य *laulya*, i.e. *lola+ya*, n. **1.** Greediness, Pańch. 62, 21; desire, Ragh. 19, 19. **2.** Passion, Pańch. v. d. 61.—**Comp.** *A-*, adj. free from greediness, MBh. 1, 1506. *Ati-*, n. excessive greediness, Pańch. 247, 20. *Jihvâ-*, n. greediness of one's tongue, Pańch. 105, 8. *Manas-*, n. covetousness of mind, Hit. 87, 1.

लौह *lauha*, i.e. *loha*, I. adj. Made of iron, Johns. Sel. 15, 55 (?). **II.** m. Iron, Râm. 2, 59, 41. (Hit. ii. d. 38, read *loha*; cf. Böhtl. Ind. Spr. 2771.)

लौहित्य *lauhitya*, i.e. *lohita+ya*, n. Redness.

† **ल्पी** *LPÎ*, **ल्यी** *LYÎ*, **ल्वी** *LVÎ*, ii. 9, Par. To unite.

व *V.*

व *va*, adv. Like, as (=*iva*), MBh. 12, 6597; Ragh. 4, 42 (Calc.); Megh. 81.

वंश *vam̃ça*, I. m. **1.** A bambu, Hit. pr. d. 23, M.M.; a staff, Indr. 1, 8. **2.** Lineage, race, Bhartṛ. 2, 24; Vikr. d. 153; bambu (or tree in general), and race, Pańch. ii. d. 189. **3.** Multitude, Draup. 8, 5. **4.** The back-bone. **II.** m., and f. *çî*. **1.** A pipe, a flute, Ragh. 2, 12; Râjat. 5, 362 (m.). **2.** Bambu manna.—**Comp.** *A-*, m. a low race, Chân. 1, 80. *Âdi-*, m. a primary, a very old race, MBh. 1, 864. *Jarjara-*, m. an old bambu stick, Pańch. 117, 7. *Nâsâ-*, m. the bone of the nose, Pańch. 182, 16 (at the end of a comp. adj.). *Pṛishṭha-*, m. the back-bone, Suçr. 1, 350, 2. *Raghu-*, m. the race of Raghu. *Soma-*, m. 1. the lunar dynasty. 2. a name of Yudhishṭhira.

वंशज *vam̃ça-ja*, adj. **1.** Caused in (or to) one's tribe, Pańch. v. d. 67 (cf. Böhtl. Ind. Spr. 1323). **2.** Sprung from a good family.

वंशिक *vam̃çika*, I. adj. Relating to a family. **II.** n. Aloe.

वंश्य *vam̃çya*, i.e. *vam̃ça+ya*, I. adj. **1.** Belonging to a family, of the same family, Râjat. 5, 127. **2.** Of a good family. **II.** m. **1.** A son. Man. 1, 61. **2.** A kinsman. **3.** pl. Ancestors, Ragh. 1, 66. **4.** A pupil.—**Comp.** *Mahâ-*, adj. belonging to a very noble family, Râjat. 5, 337. *Viçuddha-*, i.e. *viçuddhavam̃ça + ya* (vb. *çudh*), adj. descended from a good family, Râjat. 5, 335.

वंह् *VAM̃H*, see *bam̃h* and 2. *ram̃h*.

वक *vaka*, m. **1.** A crane, Ardea nivea, Pańch. ii. d. 87. **2.** The name of a demon. **3.** Kuvera. **4.** An apparatus for subliming metals.

वकव्रतिक *vakavratika*, i.e. *vaka-vrata+ika*, adj. (acting like cranes), Hypocritic, Man. 4, 192.

वकुल *vakula*, I. m. A plant, Mimusops elengi, Ṛit. 2, 25 (*bakula*); Mâlav. (Weber, n. 73). **II.** f. *lî*, A sort of drug.

वकेरुका *vakerukâ*, f. **1.** (from *vaka*), A small crane. **2.** (vb. *vańk*), The branch of a tree, bent by the wind.

वकोट *vakoṭa* (from *vaka*), m. A crane.

वक्क् *VAKK*, see *vask*.

वक्तव्यता *vaktavya+tâ* (vb. *vach*),

f. **1.** The nature of what is to be said. **2.** Blame, Man. 8, 230.

वक्तुकाम *vaktukâma*, i. e. *vaktum -kâma* (vb. *vach*), adj. Desirous of speaking, wishing to say, Vikr. 30, 1.

वक्तुमनस् *vaktumanas*, i.e. *vaktum -manas* (vb. *vach*), adj. Being about to speak, Pañch. 77, 2.

वक्तृ *vaktṛi*, i.e. *vach + tṛi*, m., f. *tṛî*, and n. **1.** One who speaks, Bhâshâp. 83; a speaker, Hit. ii. d. 128. **2.** Talkative. **3.** Eloquent, Bhartṛ. 2, 33. **4.** Speaking truth. **5.** Wise. **6.** A teacher.—Cf. Lat. auctor (see the vedic significations).

वक्त्र *vaktra*, i.e. *vach + tra*, n. **1.** The mouth, Pañch. ii. d. 138; 264, 1. **2.** The face, Pañch. 158, 22. **3.** A verse. **4.** A sort of garment.—Comp. *Dadhi-*, m. the name of a monkey, Râm. 5, 60, 19. *Danta-*, m. a proper name, MBh. 1, 2698. *Daçavaktra*, i.e. *daçan-*, m. a certain spell, Râm. 1, 31, 6 Gorr. *Pañchavaktra*, i.e. *pañchan-*, I. adj. having five faces, Râm. 5, 68, 7. II. m. a name of Çiva, Lass. 66, 6. *Mahâ-*, adj. having a large mouth, Hiḍ. 2, 6.

वक्र *vakra*, i.e. *vañk + ra*, I. adj. **1.** Crooked, Pañch. iii. d. 75; bent, Çâk. d. 9; with *pathin*, a round-about way, Megh. 28. **2.** Indirect, evasive. **3.** Ambiguous, double-meaning, Kathâs. 17, 141. **4.** Fraudulent, Pañch. 44, 20; dishonest. **5.** Cruel. II. m. A name of the planets Saturn and Mars, and of Rudra. III. n. The bend of a river.—Comp. *Ashṭâ-*, m. a proper name, MBh. 3, 10599.

वक्रिम *vakrima*, i.e. *vakra + ima*, adj., f. *mâ*, Bent, Amar. 16.

वक्रोष्ठिका *vakroshṭhikâ*, i.e. *vakra -oshṭha + ka*, f. A gentle smile.

वक्ष् *VAKSH*, i. 1, Par. (ved., also Âtm.), **1.** To grow, to become tall, Chr. 290, 3=Rigv. i. 64, 3. **2.** † To be angry. Ptcple. pf. pass. *ukshita*, Grown up, Chr. 291, 2=Rigv. i. 85, 2.—Cf. 2. *vaj*, of which it is probably an old desider.; Goth. vahsjan; A.S. weaxan; αὔξω, αὐξάνω.

वक्षस् *vakshas*, n. The breast, Hit. iv. d. 130; the bosom, Pañch. 239, 4.—Probably for original *pakshas*, akin to *paksha* (cf. *piba*, *piva*, for original *pipâ*, *baṇij*, *vaṇij*, for *paṇi-j*); and cf. Lat. pectus.

वक्षोज *vakshoja*, i.e. *vakshas-ja*, n. The female breast. Sâh. Darp. 307, 7.

वक्षोरुह् *vakshoruh* (Lass. 66, 8), and

वक्षोरुह *vakshoruha*, i. e. *vakshas-ruh* and *ruh*, + *a*, m. The female breast.

† **वख्** *VAKH*, **वङ्ख्** *VAÑKH*, i. 1, Par. To go.

वग्नु *vagnu*, i.e. *vach + nu*, adj. Talkative.

वङ्क् *VAÑK*, i. 1, Par. **1.** To go tortuously. **2.** To be crooked.—Cf. Lat. vacillare, vacare (properly, 'To give way'), vacuus; O.H.G. waga, cuna, wagôn, moveri, waga; A. S. waeg, etc.; O. H. G. wank, wankôn; A. S. woh, wog, wó, a bending; wancol (perhaps to *vañg*), vacillans; probably ὄκνος.

वङ्क *vañk + a*, I. m. **1.** The bend of a river. **2.** Crookedness. **II.** f. *kâ*, The pommel of a saddle.

वङ्क्रि *vañk + ri*, I. n. A rib. **II.** f. **1.** The ribs of a building. **2.** A sort of musical instrument.

वङ्क्षण *vañkshaṇa*, m. The groin.

वङ्ख् *VAÑKH*, see *vakh*.

† **वङ्ग्** *VAÑG*, i. 1, Par. **1.** To go. **2.** To limp.—Cf. *vañk*.

वङ्ग *vaṅga*, I. m. **1.** Cotton. **2.** The name of a country, Bengal. **3.** Its inhabitants, Ragh. 4, 36. **II.** n. **1.** Lead. **2.** Tin.

वङ्गशुल्वज *vaṅga-çulva-ja*, n. Brass.

† **वङ्घ्** *VAṄGH*, i. 1, Âtm. **1.** To go. **2.** To blame. **3.** To begin moving. **4.** To begin. **5.** To move swiftly.

वच् *VACH*, ii. 2, Par. (also Âtm.), **1.** To speak, Draup. 6, 24 (*avochas*, aor. with augment after *mâ*); to say, with the acc. of the object and of the addressed person, Bhag. 2, 1. **2.** To describe, Chr. 34, 7. Pass. *uchya*, **1.** To be spoken of (*tat kim uchyate*, That needs not to be spoken of, i.e. that is of course the best), Pańch. 154, 24. **2.** To be told, Vikr. 81, 5; to be admonished, Pańch. 32, 11. **3.** To be called, Man. 1, 71. Ptcple. of the pf. pass. *ukta*, Addressed (*parushâṇi*, with hard words), Hit. iii. d. 25. n. **1.** A sentence, Pańch. 68, 1. **2.** Speech, Râjat. 5, 205. **Comp.** *An-*, adj. not uttered, Râm. 3, 14, 21. *Ardha-*, adj. half uttered; °*tena*, instr. without finishing one's speech, Vikr. 29, 19. *Durukta*, i.e. *dus-*, I. adj. 1. harshly spoken to, Pańch. i. d. 100. 2. injurious, MBh. 13, 4987. II. n. injurious speech, ib. 13, 501. *Punar-*, I. adj. 1. repeated, MBh. 5, 632. 2. useless, Vikr. 40, 2. II. n. 1. repetition, Vikr. d. 153 (a second string of pearls). 2. tautology. *Pratikûla-*, n. disagreeable speech, Böhtl. Ind. Spr. 1525. Ptcple. of the fut. pass. I. *vaktavya*. **1.** Fit or proper to be said. **2.** Reprehensible. **3.** One of bad fame, Man. 8, 66. **4.** Vile, low. **5.** Dependant, subject. n. **1.** A rule. **2.** Speaking, Pańch. 194, 23. **3.** Speech. **Comp.** *Bahu-*, adj. much to be praised, Râjat. 5, 67. **II.** *vachanîya*. **1.** To be spoken. **2.** To be noticed, censurable. n. Blame, Utt. Râmach. 28, 13. **III.** *vâchya*. **1.** Fit or proper to be spoken, Pańch. 83, 20. **2.** To be predicated of anything, Vedântas. in Chr. 210, 9; 212, 13. **3.** Blameable, Sâv. 1, 32. **4.** Contemptible, vile, outcaste. n. **1.** A predicate. **2.** Blame, Çâk. d. 112. **Comp.** *A-*, adj. 1. not to be spoken of, Râm. 5, 36, 81. 2. not to be addressed, Man. 2, 128. *Dus-*, adj. difficult to be spoken, harsh, Mârk. P. 8, 27. n. evil tidings, Râm. 5, 15, 42. Comp. absol. *an-uktvâ*, without being ordered, Râjat. 5, 62. Desider. *vivaksha*, To desire to speak, to say to, Chr. 57, 26. Caus. *vâchaya*. **1.** To order to recite, Râm. 2, 25, 28. **2.** To order to recite blessings, Râm. 2, 6, 7; Chr. 25, 51 (anomal. absol. *vâchya*). **3.** To read, Vikr. 26, 7.—With the prep.

अनु *anu*, To teach, Man. 11, 191. *anûchâna*, see s.v. Caus. To read, Çâk. 17, 4; Vikr. 26, 3.—With **अभि** *abhi*, To address, to say to (with two acc.), MBh. 2, 1998.—With **निस्** *nis*, **1.** To declare, MBh. 3, 1223; to explain, Vedântas. in Chr 204, 11. **2.** To speak, to put properly, Man. 8, 55. *nirukta*, Distinctly declared. n. **1.** Etymological explanation, MBh. 1, 266. **2.** The name of one of the Vedâṅgas (see *aṅga*), ib. 12, 13232.—With **प्र** *pra*, **1.** To begin to speak, Pańch. 77, 1. **2.** To explain, Man. 1, 103; to tell, Pańch. 116, 1. **3.** To say, Pańch. 4, 14; MBh. 2, 503. **4.** To address, Pańch. i. d. 64; Chr. 44, 5. *prokta*, **1.** Declared, Hit. iii. d. 74. **2.** Called, Man. 1, 10; Pańch. ii. d. 93. *pravachanîya*, **1.** To be well spoken. **2.** (m.), A good speaker.—With **संप्र** *sam-pra*, To explain comprehensively, Man. 8, 61.—With **प्रति** *prati*, To answer (with two acc.), Râm. 2, 68, 1. *pratyukta*, n. Answer, Megh. 112.—With **सम्** *sam*, To address, Pańch. 97, 12.—Cf. Lat. vocare, vox; O.H.G. ga-wahan, memorare; ἔπος, εἶπον (i.e. ἐϜέϜεπον and ϜεϜεπον), θεό-προπος, πέπρωται, ὄψ, ὄσσα.

वच *vach+a*, m. A parrot.

वचक्नु *vachaknu* (vb. *vach*), I. adj. Talkative, eloquent. II. m. A Brâhmaṇa.

वचन *vach+ana*, n. **1.** Speaking, Megh. 83 (at the end of a comp. adj., f. *nâ*). **2.** Speech, Pańch. 140, 16. **3.** Word, name, Megh. 29; Vikr. 37, 8; Chr. 12, 26. **4.** Order, Râm. 3, 48, 16. **5.** Sentence, Pańch. 158, 13; 164, 20. **6.** Rule.—**Comp.** *A-*, adj., f. *nâ*, speechless, Çâk. 12, 21. *Tathya-*, n. assertion, Pańch. 5, 1. *Priya-*, n. word of love, Vikr. d. 40. *Pratikûla-*, n. refractory speech, Pańch. 37, 3. *Viçesha-*, n. special or different text. *Su-*, n. eloquence.

वचनकर *vachana-kara*, in *a-*, adj. Not regarding advice, Hit. ii. c. 161, M.M.

वचनीयता *vachaniya + tâ* (vb. *vach*), f. **1.** Rumour, especially ill report. **2.** Blame, Hit. ii. d. 71.

वचनेस्थित *vachanesthita*, i.e. *vachana+i-sthita* (vb. *sthâ*), adj. Compliant, obedient.

वचस् *vach+as*, n. **1.** Speech, Pańch. iii. d. 113. **2.** Words, a word, Vikr. d. 50. **3.** Order, Chr. 12, 27. **4.** Sentence, Pańch. 167, 7. **5.** Voice, Ṛit. 6, 21.—**Comp.** *Durvachas*, i.e. *dus-*, 1. m. abuse, bad language, Ram. 5, 31, 16. 2. adj. one who uses bad language, ib. 2, 1, 18. *Sadvachas*, i. e. *sant* (vb. 1. *as*), n. agreeable speech, Ṛit. 6, 29. *Su-*, adj. speaking well or much.—Cf. ἔπος.

वचस *vachas+a*, adj. Talkative, eloquent, Chr. 296, 2=Rigv. i. 112, 2.

वचस्कर *vachas-kara*, adj. Compliant, obedient.

† 1. **वज्** *VAJ*, i. 1, Par. To go.—Cf. perhaps Lat. vagari.

2. **वज्** *VAJ*, i. 10, Par. **1.** (rather Caus. of a lost vb. *vaj*, probably 'To increase, to be strong;' cf. *vajra*, *ugra*, *ojas*), To strengthen, Lass. 99, 7=Rigv. iii. 62, 8. † **2.** To prepare the way. **3.** † (rather a denomin. derived from *vâja*), To trim or feather an arrow. **4.** † To go. — Cf. Lat. vegere and augere, probably vigor, vigere; ὑγιής; O.H.G. auhôn; A.S. eacan, see *vaksh*; probably also A. S. wacor, cf. Icel. vakr; A.S. wácian.

वज्र 2. *vaj+ra*, I. adj. **1.** Hard. **2.** Cross, forked. II. m. and n. **1.** Indra's thunderbolt, a thunderbolt, Bhartṛ. 2, 32; Hit. ii. d. 158. **2.** A diamond, Johns. Sel. 54, 136; Ragh. 1, 4; Râm. 3, 53, 59 (?). **3.** A form of array, Man. 7, 191. **4.** The blossom of the sesamum. **5.** n. Emblic myrobalan, Pańch. iv. d. 10 (?). **6.** Sour gruel. **7.** Harsh language. **8.** A child or pupil. III. f. *râ*, A plant, Menispermum cordifolium. IV. f. *râ* and *rî*, A species of Euphorbia. —Cf. O. H. G. weggi; A.S. waecg, wecg, cuneus, which probably was also the original signification of the Indian sbst.

वज्रकपाटमन्त् *vajra-kapâṭa + mant*, adj., f. *matî*, Having doors of diamond, Bhâg. P. 3, 23, 18.

वज्रकीलाय *VAJRAKÎLÂYA*, a denomin. derived from *vajra-kîla* with *ya*, Âtm. To act like a thunderbolt. Ptcple. of the pf. pass. *vajrakîlayita*, Struck as by thunderbolts, Utt. Râmach. 30, 2.

वज्रधर *vajra-dhara*, and **वज्रभृत्** *vajra-bhṛi+t*, m. Indra, Râm. 3, 53, 60; Lass. 2. ed. 76, 49.

वज्रमय *vajra + maya*, adj., f. *yî*, Hard, adamantine, Utt. Râmach. 164, 6.

वज्रिन् *vajrin*, i. e. *vajra+in*, m. Indra, Vikr. d. 5.

वञ्च् *VAŃCH*, i. 1, Par. (Âtm., see with *nis*), 1. To go, to go to, Bhaṭṭ. 14, 74. 2. To pass over, Bhaṭṭ. 7, 106. Caus. (properly, 'To cause to go astray'), 1. To avoid. 2. and i. 10, Âtm. (also Par., MBh. 1, 5794), To deceive, Pańch. 169, 1. Ptcple. of the fut. pass. *kim arthinâm vańchayitavyam asti*, 'Why must the poor ones be deceived?' Hit. i. d. 77, M.M.—With the prep. अभि *abhi*, Caus. To deceive, Chr. 59, 20.—With उप *upa*, Caus. To disappoint, Râm. 2, 52, 18.—With निस् *nis*, i. 1, Âtm. To deceive, Çṛiṅgârat. 10.—With परि *pari*, *parivańchita*, Deceived, Hit. iv. d. 101.—Cf. Lat. vafer; probably ἄτη, ἀτάω (cf. *vidhinâ vańchita*, Kumâras. 4, 10), ἀπάτη, ἀτάσθαλος, ἀτύζομαι.

वञ्चक *vańch+aka*, I. adj. Fraudulent. II. m. 1. A cheat, Lass. 87, 11; a rogue, Man. 9, 257. 2. A vile man. 3. A jackal. 4. A tame, or house ichneumon.

वञ्चथ *vańch+atha*, m. A rogue.

वञ्चन *vanch+ana*, n., and f. *nâ*, 1. Fraud, Kathâs. 3, 54. 2. Being cheated, Hit. i. d. 127, M.M. 3. Hallucination of mind, Râm. 2, 34, 37 (*nâ*).

वञ्चुक *vańch+uka*, adj. Crafty.

वञ्जुल *vańjula*, I. m. 1. The name of several plants, Utt. Râmach. 46, 1; Sâh. d. 19, 19. 2. A sort of bird. II. f. *lâ*, A cow that yields abundance of milk.

† **वट्** *VAṬ* (a form of *vṛit*, based on the original *vart*), i. 1, Par. To surround. i. 10, Par., also **बट्** *BAṬ*, *vaṭaya*, *baṭaya*, 1. To surround. 2. To tie. 3. To partition. i. 1, Par. or Caus. *vaṭaya*, To speak.

वट *vaṭa* (probably a dialectical form of **varta*, i.e. *vṛit+a*), I. m., and f. *ṭi*, A string, a rope. II. m. 1. The large Indian fig-tree, Ficus indica, Pańch. 104, 17. 2. A circle. 3. Equality in shape or dimension. 4. A small shell, a cowrie. 5. Pulse ground and fried with oil or butter.

वटक *vaṭa+ka*, I. m. 1. Pulse ground and fried in oil or butter. 2. A weight of eight *Mâshas*. II. f. *ṭikâ*, A pill, a bolus.

वटर *vaṭara*, m. 1. A cock. 2. A thief. 3. A rogue. 4. A turban (cf. *vaṭa*). 5. i.e. *vaṭa*, =**varta*, +*ka*, cf. *vaṭa*, A churning-stick. 6. A mat. 7. A fragrant grass, Cyperus.

वटाकर *vaṭâkara* (probably *vaṭa-âkara*, but see the next), m. A cord.

वटारक *vaṭâraka*, m. A cord, MBh. 3, 12776 (at the end of a comp. adj., f. *kâ*); cf. the last and *varâṭaka*.

वटारकमय *vaṭâraka+maya*, adj., f. *yi*, Made of a cord, MBh. 3, 12785.

वटि *vaṭi*, m. A sort of insect.

वटिभ *vaṭi+bha*, adj. Having or containing the insects called *vaṭi*.

वटु *vaṭu*, m. 1. A young Brâhmaṇa. 2. A pupil, Utt. Râmach. 104, 9; Prab. 22, 3. 3. A lad, a stripling, Kumâras. 5, 83. 4. A fool, Çâk. 30, 12. 5. A flower, Bignonia indica.

वटुक *vaṭu+ka*=*vaṭu*, 1. 3. 4.

† **वठ्** *VAṬH*, **बठ्** *BAṬH*, i. 1, Par. 1. To be large. 2. To be able.

वठर *vaṭhara*, m. A fool.

वडभि and **वडभी** *vaḍabhî*, or **वलभि** and **वलभी** *valabhî*, f. **1.** The wooden frame of a thatch, a roof, Megh. 39 (*ḍ*). **2.** A temporary building on the top of a palace, a turret, Mâlav. d. 33 (*valabhi*).

वडवा *vaḍavâ*, see *baḍavâ*.

वडा *vaḍâ*, f. Pulse ground and fried with oil or butter (cf. *vaṭa*).

वडिका *vaḍika*, i. e. *vaḍâ* + *ka*, f. Pulse ground and fried, Lass. 79, 14.

वडिश *vaḍiça*. n., and f. *çî*, A fish-hook, Bhartṛ. 1, 84.

वड्र *vaḍra*, adj. Large.

† **वण्** *VAṆ*, **बण्** *BAṆ*, i. 1, Par. To sound.

वणिज् *vaṇij*, see *baṇij*.

वण्ट् *VAṆṬ*, i. 1 and 10, To partition, Böhtl. Ind. Spr. 985.—Cf. *vaṇḍ*.

वण्ट *vaṇṭ* + *a*, m. **1.** A part. **2.** The handle of a sickle.

वण्टक *vaṇṭa* + *ka*, m. A part.—**Comp.** *Hṛid-*, m. the stomach.

वण्टन *vaṇṭ* + *ana*, n. Dividing, Châṇ. 5 in Berl. Monatsb. 1864, p. 407.

† **वण्ठ्** *VAṆṬH*, i. 1, Âtm. To go without a companion.

वण्ठ *vaṇṭha*, m. **1.** An unmarried man. **2.** A dwarf. **3.** A javelin.

वण्ठर *vaṇṭhara*, m. **1.** A rope for tying a goat. **2.** A dog's tail. **3.** The sheath that envelopes the young bambu.

वण्ठाल *vaṇṭhâla*, m. **1.** A mode of conflict, the contest of heroes. **2.** A boat. **3.** A hoe.

† **वण्ड्** *VAṆḌ*, i. 1, Âtm. **1.** To divide. **2.** To cover. i. 1 and 10, Par. To divide.—Cf. *vaṇṭ*.

वण्ड *vaṇḍa*, **I.** adj. (A person) whose hands have been cut off. **II.** f. *ḍâ*, An unchaste woman.

वत *vata* (perhaps curtailed *avata*, 2. pl. imperat. of *av*; cf. Prâkṛ. *avidhâ*, Sch. ad Çâk. 93, 11), indecl. An interjection implying, **1.** Sorrow, woe, Çâk. d. 152; Chr. 3, 37. **2.** Compassion. **3.** Pleasure. **4.** Surprise, Kâvya Prak. 80, 7. **5.** A vocative particle.

वतंस *vataṁsa*, i.e. *ava-taṁs* + *a*, m. **1.** An ear-ring. **2.** A crest.

वतोका *vatokâ*, i.e. *ava-toka*, f. A cow miscarrying from accident.

वत्स *vatsa*, **I.** (vb. 1. *vas*), m. **1.** A calf, Hit. i. d. 29, M.M. **2.** i. e. probably **vatas*, =Ϝέτος, + *a*, A year. **3.** The name of a Ṛishi, or saint, Man. 8, 116. **4.** pl. The name of a people and their country, Chr. 47, 41; 46, 24. **II.** m., and f. *sâ*, Child, Pañch. 169, 25; a term of endearment, Pañch. 130, 4; Vikr. 70, 10; Utt. Râmach. 8, 9. **III.** n. The breast.—**Comp.** *Çri-*, m. 1. Vishṇu. 2. a mark, usually said to be a curl of hair on the breast of Vishṇu or Kṛishṇa, represented by , Johns. Sel. 96, 74. 3. a hole in a wall for felonious purposes.—Cf. *vatsatara*.

वत्सतर *vatsata* + *ra*, **I.** m. A steer. **II.** f. *rî*, A heifer, Man. 11, 137.

वत्सर *vatsa* + *ra*, m. A year, Pañch. iii. d. 93.

वत्सल *vatsa* + *la*, **I.** adj., f. *lâ*, Affectionate, loving, Pañch. 222, 14; tender, Utt. Râmach. 48, 1. **II.** f. *lâ*, A cow anxious for her calf. **III.** n. Fondness.—**Comp.** *Vara-*, f. the wife of a father-in-law. *Sahaja-*, adj., f. *lâ*, of inborn fondness, Hit. 87, 12.

वत्सलता *vatsala + tâ*, f. **1.** Tenderness, Utt. Râmach. 35, 8. **2.** Love, Râjat. 5, 194.

वत्सलय *VATSALAYA*, a denomin. derived from *vatsala*, Par. To make tender towards children, Çâk. 102, 7.

वत्सीय *vatsîya*, i. e. *vatsa + îya*, **I.** adj. Fit for a calf. **II.** m. A cowherd.

वद् *VAD*, i. 1, Par. Âtm. **1.** To speak, to address (with the acc. of the object and the addressed person), MBh. 3, 1853. **2.** To speak of (with gen.), Pańch. 67, 22. **3.** To sound, to yell, MBh. 3, 15669. Ptcple. of the pf. pass. *udita*, **1.** Pronounced, Chân. 1 in Berl. Monatsb. 1864, 407. **2.** Addressed, Çiç. 9, 61. Comp. ptcple. of the fut. pass. *brahmodya*, i.e. *brahman-udya*, n. Reciting or explaining the Veda; *mṛishodya*, see s.v. *sukhodya*, i.e. *sukha-udya*, adj. To be uttered agreeably, Man. 2, 33. Caus. *vâdaya*, To cause to sound, Pańch. 229, 13; to play, Man. 4, 64. Comp. ptcple of the pf. pass. *jala-vâdita*, n. Water music, music performed by water, Hariv. 8426. Ptcple. of the fut. pass. *vâdya*, n. **1.** Sound, Ragh. 16, 64. **2.** Any musical instrument, Pańch. 129, 15; Daçak. in Chr. 180, 7 (instrumental music). Comp. *Jala-*, n. a musical instrument sounded by means of water, Hariv. 8427. *Parṇa-*, n. a musical instrument made of leaves, Hariv. 3477. † i. 10, Par. Âtm. **1.** To speak. **2.** To command.—With the prep. **अनु** *anu*, To speak similarly, to imitate another's voice or sound, Ragh. 5, 74 (Calc.).—With **अप** *apa*, To reprove, to insult, Man. 4, 236. Caus. To dissuade from, to reprove, MBh. 3, 1036. —With **अभि** *abhi*, **1.** To address, Man. 8, 356. **2.** To salute respectfully, MBh. 3, 15668. Caus. **1.** To greet respectfully, Man. 2, 117; Vikr. 81, 2; with *pâdayos*, To greet one by touching his feet, Man. 2, 212. **2.** To play, MBh. 3, 14386. — With **प्रत्यभि** *prati-abhi*, Caus. To return a salute, Mṛichchh. 34, 7.—With **आ** *â*, To salute by roaring, Chr. 290, 9=Rigv. i. 64, 9. —With **समा** *sam-â*, To speak, MBh. 3, 16148.—With **उप** *upa*, Âtm. **1.** To conciliate, Bhaṭṭ. 8, 28. **2.** To beg, Pańch. in Weber, Ind. St. 272, 22 (see my transl. n. 922). **3.** To allure.— With **परि** *pari*, To calumniate, MBh. 1, 3079.—With **प्र** *pra*, **1.** To converse, Pańch. 143, 21. **2.** To explain, Man. 5, 55. **3.** To declare, Hit. ii. d. 160. **4.** To call, Hit. ii. d. 41. **5.** To tell, MBh. 3, 2910. Caus. To play, MBh. 1, 5356.—With **विप्र** *vi-pra*, To disagree.—With **संप्र** *sam-pra*, Par. To accord. Âtm. To converse, Bhaṭṭ. 8, 28.—With **प्रति** *prati*, To answer, Daçak. in Chr. 181, 13.—With **वि** *vi*, Âtm. (also Par., Hit. iii. d. 32; Pańch. 183, 6). **1.** To dispute, to wrangle, Man. 3, 159. **2.** To contest, with acc., MBh. 2, 2390. — With **सम्** *sam*, To converse, Chr. 19, 8; Hit. 88, 13; iii. d. 36. Caus. **1.** To play, MBh. 1, 7056. **2.** To declare, Man. 8, 31.—With **विसम्** *vi-sam*, To break a promise, Man. 8, 219.—Cf. *αὐδή, αὐδάω*, perhaps *φράζω, φραδάω*; probably Lat. vas, vadis; perhaps O. H. G. far-wâzan; O. Saxon, for-wâtan, recusare.

वद *vad + a*, adj. Speaking, speaking well.—Cf. *vaçaṁvada*.

वदन *vad + ana*, n. The mouth, the face, Pańch. 185, 25.—Comp. *Maṁsa-piṇḍa-gṛihîta-*, adj., f. *nâ*, carrying in the mouth a piece of flesh, Pańch. 226, 20. *Su-*, adj., f. *nâ*, beautiful, Ṛit. 6, 20.

वदन्य *vadanya*, see *vadânya*.

वदरी *vadarî*, f. see *badara*, Matsyop. 3, and MBh. 3, 1637; questionable, probably = *badarî-çaila*, n. A part of the Himâlaya range, and a celebrated place of pilgrimage, cf. Johns. Sel. 90, n.

वदान्य *vadânya*, adj. I. i.e. *ava -dâna+ya* (also **वदन्य** *vadanya*), Munificent, liberal, Man. 4, 224. II. (from *vad*), 1. Speaking kindly. 2. Eloquent.

वदाल *vadâla*, m. A skeat-fish, Silurus boalis Ham.

वदावद *vadâvada* (an old frequent. of *vad+a*), adj. Speaking, able to speak well.

वध् *VADH*, see *han*.

वध *vadh+a* (also **बध** *badha*, probably better) m. 1. Killing, Man. 5, 39; murder, Pańch. i. d. 305. 2. Death, Man. 8, 104. 3. Corporal punishment, Man. 9, 291. 4. A stroke, 11, 100. 5. A whip, 8, 267. 6. Hurting, Man. 4, 165. 7. A killer, a slaughterer, Man. 5, 39.—Comp. *A-*, m. no slaughterer, Man. 5, 39. *Âtmavadha*, i.e. *âtman-*, m. suicide, MBh. 1, 6228. *Go-*, m. slaying a bull or a cow, Man. 11, 59. *Çiçu-pâla-*, m. the destruction of Çiçupâla, title of a poem. *Çuddha-* (vb. *çudh*), m. simple putting to death, i.e. in any ordinary way, Man. 9, 279 (*b*).

वधक *vadh+aka*, also *badhaka*, I. adj. Destructive, injurious. II. m. A murderer, Kathâs. 3, 43.

वधत्र *vadh+atra*, n. A weapon.

वधु *vadhu* (vb. *vah*, q. cf.), f. 1. A wife. 2. A son's wife (cf. *vadhû*).

वधुटी *vadhuṭî*, f. A son's wife.

वधू *vadhû*, also **बधू** *badhû* (vb. *vah*, q. cf.), f. 1. A woman, Kirât. 6, 45. 2. A wife, Hit. i. d. 192, M.M.; Râm. 3, 51, 14; 55, 29. 3. A wife recently married. 4. A son's wife, Sâv. 6, 9. 5. A female relation, Sund. 4, 16. 6. The name of several plants.—Comp. *Kula-*, f. a virtuous or respectable wife, Hit. i. d. 135, M.M. *Nava-*, f. a woman recently married, Ṛit. 6, 19. *Nâga-*, f. the female of an elephant, Râm. 2, 65, 24. *Preshya-*, f. a female servant, Draup. 6, 9. *Vâra-*, f. the head of a set of harlots. *Svar-*, *Svarga-*, and *Svargi(n)-*, f. an Apsaras.

वधूटी *vadhûṭî*, f. 1. A son's wife. 2. A young woman, living in her father's house, whether married or unmarried, Bhâshâp. 1, a.

वधूयु *vadhûyu*, i.e. *VADHÛYA*, ved., *+u*, adj. One who loves his wife, Lass. 99, 8 (where *badhûyu*) = Rigv. iii. 62, 8.

वध्यता *vadhya+tâ*, or **बध्यता** *badhya+tâ* (from *vadh*, see *han*), f. 1. Deserving death, Nal. 9, 8. 2. Destruction.

† 1. **वन्** *VAN*, i. 1, Par. 1. To sound. 2. To serve, to honour. Caus. *vanaya*, 1. To act. 2. To hurt, to kill. See 3. *tan*.—Cf. perhaps A.S. an-winnan, to fight against.

2. **वन्** *VAN*, ii. 8, Par. Âtm. (in the Vedas also i. 1; ii. 2, etc.). 1. To ask, to beg. 2. To accept, Chr. 288, 11 = Rigv. i. 48, 11. Ptcple. of the pf. pass. *vanita*, Solicited, begged. f. *tâ*, 1. A beloved woman, a mistress, Bhartṛ. 2, 36. 2. A woman in general, Vikr. d. 44. 3. A female bird, Kir. 6, 8. Comp. *Tridaça-*, f. *tâ*, the wife of a deity, Megh 59. *Sa-nâka -vanita*, adj. endowed with the celestial women (i.e. the Apsarases), Kir. 5, 27.

—Cf. 1. *van*, the vedic use, and Lat. Venus, venustas, venerari; O.H.G. wunna; A.S. wyn, ge-wenian; Goth. vêns; A.S. to-wenan; probably ὀνίνημι, ὀνήσω, ὄνειαρ.

वन *vana*, I. n., and f. *nî*, A forest, Vikr. d. 79 (*na*); Pańch. iii. d. 56 (*na*). II. n. **1.** Water. **2.** A cascade or fountain. **3.** A residence, Nal. 3, 22. **4.** A house. —**Comp.** *Asi-patra-*, n. the name of a hell, Man. 4, 90. *Chitra-*, n. the name of a forest, Hit. 14, 16. *Topovana*, i.e. *tapas-*, n. a place frequented by ascetics, a sacred grove, Hit. iv. d. 83. *Nirvaṇa*, i.e. *nis-*, adj. one who has left a forest, MBh. 5, 863 (°*vana*). *Paraçu-*, n. the name of a hell, MBh. 12, 12075. *Pitṛi-*, n. a cemetery, MBh. 11, 119. *Pramada-*, n. a royal garden, Vikr. 19, 18. *Mahâ-*, n. a large forest, Râm. 3, 55, 48.

वनचर *vana-chara*, m. **1.** A wild beast, Pańch. 255, 17. **2.** A forester, Kirât. 6, 29.

वनज *vana-ja*, I. adj. Wild. II m. **1.** An elephant. **2.** A fragrant grass, Cyperus rotundus. III. f. *jâ*, A sort of pulse. IV. n. A lotus, Ragh. 5, 73.

वनद *vana-da*, and **वनमुच्** *vana-much*, m. A cloud.

वनर *vanara* (from *vana*), m. A monkey.

वनस्थ *vana-stha*, I. adj. **1.** Being in a forest, Pańch. iii. d. 145. **2.** Living in a forest, Râm. 3, 48, 18. II. m. **1.** A deer. **2.** An ascetic.

वनस्पति *vanaspati*, i.e. *van* (=*vana*), + *as-pati*, m. **1.** A tree, Utt. Râmach. 15, 11. **2.** An ascetic.

वनाटु *vanâṭu*, i.e. *vana-aṭ* + *u*, m. A blue fly.

वनायु *vanâyu*, m. The name of a country, Ragh. 5, 73.

वनायुज *vanâyu-ja*, m. A horse of the Vanâyu breed.

वनार्चक *vanârchaka*, i.e. *vana-arch* + *aka*, m. A florist, a garland maker.

वनाहिर *vanâhira*, m. A hog.

वनि *van* + *i*, m. **1.** Fire or its deity. **2.** Desire, wish.

वनिन् *vanin*, i.e. *vana* + *in*, adj. Abounding in water, Chr. 291, 12 = Rigv. i. 64, 12.

वनीक *vanika*, and **वनीयक** *vaniyaka* (vb. *van*), m. A beggar.

वनेचर *vanechara*, i. e. *vana* + *i* -*chara*, I. adj. Who or what abides in a forest, Râm. 3, 51, 34. II. m. **1.** A forester, Kirât. 1, 1. **2.** A demon. **3.** A wild beast, Lass. 47, 10.

वन्द् *VAND* (akin to *vad*), i. 1, Âtm. **1.** To salute respectfully, Vikr. 8, 81, 11; MBh. 2, 23. **2.** To praise, Râm. 2, 16, 27. **3.** To venerate, Megh. 12. Comp. ptcple. of the fut. pass. *jagadvandya*, i.e. *jagat-*, adj. To be praised by mankind, epithet of Krishṇa, MBh. 2, 23. —With the prep. **अभि** *abhi*, To salute respectfully, Daçak. in Chr. 179, 15.—With **सम्** *sam*, The same, MBh. 1, 5420.

वन्दन *vand* + *ana*, I. m. A proper name, Chr. 296, 5 = Rigv. i. 112, 5. II. n. **1.** Salutation, Man. 2, 216. **2.** The mouth or face. III. f. *nâ*. **1.** Praise, Chr. 19, 6; praising especially the gods. **2.** Prayer, Vedântas. in Chr. 202, 16. IV. f. *nî*. **1.** Worship. **2.** Begging, asking. **3.** A drug for restoring the dead to life.—**Comp.** *Pâda-*, n. worship, reverence, Yâjń. 1, 83.

वन्दारु *vand* + *âru*, I. adj. **1.** Civil,

polite. **2.** Praising, worshipping, Lass. c7, 6. **II.** m. A bard.

वन्दि and **वन्दी** *vandî*, f. **1.** A woman in captivity, also a man, Bhaṭṭ. 8, 32; 63; Vikr. d. 3 (*vandî kṛi*, To make captive). **2.** A ladder or stairs.

वन्दिन् *vand+in*, m. **1.** A praiser, Pańch. 158, 2. **2.** An encomiast, Man. 3, 158; a bard, Vikr. d. 76.

वन्दीकार *vandî-kâra*, m. A house-breaker.

वन्द्र *vand+ra*, adj. Worshipping.

वन्धुर *vandhura*, m. The seat of a chariot, Chr. 290, 9=Rigv. i. 64, 9.

वन्य *vanya*, i.e. *vana+ya*, I. adj. Produced in, or by, a wood, Pańch. 216, 10; wild, Man. 6, 12. **II.** f. *yâ*. **1.** A multitude of groves. **2.** A quantity of water, a flood. **III.** n. Wild fruit, Râm. 3, 52, 51; 53, 24.

वन्र *van+ra*, m. **1.** A co-partner. **2.** A co-heir.

वप् *VAP*, i. 1, Par. Âtm. **I.** (properly Caus. of *vî*). **1.** To sow, MBh. 3, 1248; figurat., Man. 2, 113. **2.** To cast, MBh. 2, 2033. **3.** † To procreate. Pass. *upya*, Man. 9, 26. **II.** (properly a Caus. of *ve*), To weave. **III.** † To shave. Caus. *vâpaya*, To sow, MBh. 3, 13031.—With the prep. **अधि** *adhi*, To put on, Chr. 294, 4=Rigv. i. 92, 4. —With **आ** *â*, **1.** To sow, MBh. 3, 17341. **2.** To throw to, MBh. 3, 103. Caus. To arrange, to dress, MBh. 1, 819 (cf. with *vi*). — With **समा** *sam-â*, Caus. To cause to be sown, or thrown in, Lass. 2. ed. 72, 9.—With **नि** *ni*, **1.** To sow, MBh. 3, 17341. **2.** To offer, Man. 3, 216. — With **निस्** *nis*, **1.** To drop. Man. 3, 92. **2.** To sprinkle, Man. 3, 214. **3.** To offer, Man. 9, 140. **4.** To perform (a sacrifice), Man. 4, 10; 6, 38 (read *nirupya*). Caus. To disseminate, Pańch. 85, 20.—With **प्र** *pra*, **1.** To sow, MBh. 3, 15725. **2.** To cast, ib. 3, 1931.—With **प्रति** *prati*, To inlay, to stud, to adorn, Daçak. in Chr. 198, 16. *pratyupta*, Shut (?), Utt. Râmach. 87, 3. — With **वि** *vi*, *vyupta*, Disordered, dishevelled, Bhâg. P. 4, 2, 14.—Cf. ὀπυίω and οἴφω, οἰφέω; A.S. wíf; probably also ὅπλον; Goth. vêpn; A.S. waepen. Cf. *ve*.

वप *vapa*, i.e. I. *vap+a*, m. **1.** Sowing seed. **2.** Shaving. **II.** f. *pâ*. **1.** The mucous or glutinous secretion of the flesh or bones, marrow, Râm. 1, 13, 39. **2.** Fat, Man. 12, 63. **3.** Any hole or cavity.

वपन *vap+ana*, I. n. **1.** Sowing seed. **2.** Semen virile. **3.** Shaving, Man. 5, 140. **II.** f. *nî*, A barber's shop.

ऽवपुष *-vapusha*, i.e. *vapus+a*, at the end of comp. instead of *vapus*, in *varâha-*, n. The body of a hog, Johns. Sel. 94, 53.

वपुष्मन्त् *vapushmant*, i.e. *vapus+mant*, adj., f. *matî*, **1.** Having a body, corporeal, embodied, Kir. 2, 59; Lass. 2. ed. 76, 47. **2.** Beautiful, Sund. 3, 17.

वपुस् *vapus* (cf. *vapâ*), n. **1.** The body, Pańch. iii. d. 221. **2.** A handsome form or figure, Çâk. d. 16. **3.** Beauty, Chr. 290, 4=Rigv. i. 64, 4 (dat. in the sense of the infin. ' In order to be beautiful ').

वप्तृ *vap+tṛi*, I. m., f. *tṛî*, and n. **1.** Who or what sows. **2.** A husbandman, Man. 3, 142. **II.** m. **1.** A progenitor, a father. **2.** A poet.

वप्यटदेवी *vapyaṭa-devî*, f. A proper name, Râjat. 5, 281.

वप्र *vap+ra,* I. m. (and n.). 1. A field, Kir. 5, 36. 2. Dust, earth. 3. A mound, Megh. 2; a hillock. 4. The foundation of any building. 5. A shore or bank, Kir. 6, 8. 6. A rampart, MBh. 1, 5810. 7. The gate of a fortified city. II. m. A father. III. f. *ri,* An ant-hill. IV. n. Lead.

वप्रि *vap+ri,* m. (?), A field.

वभ्र् *VABHR,* see *babhr.*

वम् *VAM,* i. 1, Par. 1. To vomit, Man. 4, 121. 2. To spit out, Râm. 1, 28, 26. 3. To send forth, Utt. Râmach. 148, 8. Ptcple. of the pf. pass. *vânta.* 1. Vomited. 2. Effused, Megh. 20. 3. One who has vomited, Man. 5, 144. Comp. *Durvânta,* i.e. *dus-,* adj. one who has been wrongly treated with emetics, Suçr. 2, 191, 15. Caus. *vâmaya*; ptcple. of the pf. pass. *vamita,* Made to vomit. —With the prep. **उद्** *ud,* To spit out, to vomit, MBh. 3, 15729; figuratively, 3, 1931.—Cf. Lat. vomere; ἐμέω; Goth. vamm, macula, ana-vammjan; A.S. wemman, maculare.

वम *vam+a,* m., and f. *mî,* Vomiting.

वमथु *vam+athu,* m. 1. Vomiting. 2. Water ejected from an elephant's trunk.

वमन *vam+ana,* I. n. 1. Vomiting, Lass. 17, 4; taking, getting. Ragh. 15, 29. 2. An emetic. 3. Paining. II. f. *nî,* A leech.

वमि *vam+i,* I. m. 1. Fire. 2. A rogue. II. 1. Vomiting, Suçr. 2, 491, 21. 2. An emetic.

वम्र *vamra,* 1. m. A proper name, Chr. 297, 15=Rigv. i. 112, 15. 2. f. *râ* and *rî,* A small ant.

† **वय्** *VAY,* i. 1, Âtm. To go.

वयःस्थ *vayaḥstha,* and **वयस्थ** *vayastha,* i.e. *vayas-stha,* I. adj. 1. Young. 2. Mature, middle-aged, from sixteen to seventy. II. m. A contemporary, a friend. III. f. *sthâ.* 1. A woman's female friend. 2. The name of several plants.

वयस् *vayas,* n. 1. Youth, Pańch. i. d. 11. 2. Age, Vikr. d. 42; time of life, Pańch. iii. d. 221. 3. A bird, Pańch. i. d. 28.—Comp. *Gata-,* adj. old, Pańch. i. d. 11. *Pûrva-,* adj. Young, MBh. 1, 3196. *Sa-,* I. adj. contemporary. II. m. a contemporary, a friend. III. f. a woman's female friend, Çiç. 9, 53.

वयस्क *vayas+ka,* adj. 1. Relating to age. 2. A substitute for *vayas,* as latter part of comp. adj.; e.g. *abhinava-,* adj. Young, Hit. 50, 1. *samâna-,* adj. one who is of the same age.

वयस्थ *vayastha,* see *vayaḥstha.*

वयस्य *vayas+ya,* I. m. 1. A contemporary, Râm. 1, 12, 22. 2. A friend, Vikr. 11, 15. II. f. *yâ,* A woman's female friend, Nal. 4, 32.

वयुन *vayuna,* n. 1. The faculty of perceiving, consciousness, Chr. 294, 2; 6=Rigv. i. 92, 2; 6. 2. A temple, Bhâg. P. 3, 4, 30.

वयोतिग *vayotiga,* i.e. *vayas-ati-ga* (vb. *gam*), adj. m. A decrepit old man, Man. 7, 149.

वयोधस् *vayodhas,* i.e. *vayas-dhâ,* m. A young man.

वय्य *vayya,* m. A proper name, Chr. 296, 6=Rigv. i. 112, 6.

वर् *VAR,* see *vṛi.*

वर *vara* (erroneously **बर** *bara*), i.e. *vṛi+a,* I. adj., f. *râ.* 1. Better, Pańch. ii. d. 96. 2. Best, Indr. 5, 20; excellent, Vikr. d. 119; precious, Hit. i. d. 135, M.M.; beautiful, Râm. 3, 51,

37. 3. Eldest. II. acc. sing. *ram*, adv. Better, preferable, Pańch. pr. d. 4 (*a-jâta-mṛita-mûrkhebhyo mṛita-a -jâtau sutau varam*, If it is to be chosen between having a dead son, or no son, or a stupid one, it is better to have a dead one, or no son at all); with following *na*, Rather than, Bhartṛ. 2, 11; with following *na punar*, Better than, Pańch. 138, 19. *varam̐ vâ—mâ*, Rather than, Pańch. pr. d. 6. III. m. 1. Selecting. 2. Soliciting. 3. Wish, Râm. 3, 53, 8. 4. A boon, a blessing, Pańch. 135, 8; Hit. 116, 6; a favour, Râm. 3, 53, 6; a privilege, Daçak. in Chr. 193, 17. 5. One who solicits a girl for his wife, Sâv. 1, 28; a bridegroom, Pańch. 129, 15. 6. A son-in-law. 7. A husband, Lass. 2. ed. 35, 20. 8. A catamite. 9. A sparrow. 10. Surrounding. IV. f. *râ*. 1. A sort of perfume. 2. The three myrobalans. 3. A plant, Cissampelos hexandra. V. f. *rî*. 1. *Chhâyâ*, the wife of the sun. 2. Asparagus racemosus. VI. m. Saffron.—**Comp.** *Kâma-*, m. choosing what one lists, Bhâg. P. 9, 9, 45. *Datta-*, adj. 1. one to whom is given the permission to choose a boon, Râm. 1, 1, 22. 2. granted as a boon, ib. 6, 19, 61. *Dvija-*, m. a Brâhmaṇa, Kathâs. 25, 254. *Pika-*, m. an excellent cuckoo (and ascetic), Böhtl. Ind. Spr. 411. *Pura-*, n. an excellent town, Râjat. 5, 157. *Prâpta-*, adj., f. *râ*, abounding in blessings, Pańch. 252, 18. *Muni-*, m. the chief of the ascetics, Ṛit. 6, 30. *Raghu-*, m. Râma. *Vîra-*, m. a proper name, Lass. 28, 14. *Sarovara*, i. e. *saras-*, m. a lake. *Sarit-*, f. *râ*, the Gaṅgâ.—Cf. Goth. vaila; A.S. wel; O.H.G. wela; A.S. wela, felicitas; ἀρείων, ἄριστος, and see *vṛi*.

वरट *varaṭa*, I. m. A wasp. II. f. *ṭâ*, *ṭî*, and **वरला** *varalâ*. 1. A goose. 2. A wasp.

वरण *varaṇa*, i. e. *vṛi + ana*, I. m. 1. An enclosure raised on a mound of earth. 2. A causeway, a bridge. 3. A camel. 4. A tree, Capparis trifoliata, Kir. 5, 25. 5. Any tree. II. f. The name of a rivulet. III. n. 1. Selecting, choice, Johns. Sel. 53, 127. 2. Surrounding. 3. Screening, covering. 4. Nourishing.

वरण्ड *varaṇḍa* (vb. *vṛi*), m. 1. A portico. 2. The string of a fish-hook. 3. A pucket. 4. A multitude. 5. A heap of grass. 6. Pimples on the face.

वरण्डक *varaṇḍa + ka*, I. adj. 1. Large. 2. Fearful. 3. Niggardly. II. m. 1. A canopy on the back of an elephant. 2. A wall. 3. A ball. 4. Pimples on the face.

वरत्रा *varatrâ* (vb. *vṛi*), f. 1. A strap or string of leather, Pańch. 128, 9. 2. An elephant's or horse's leather girth.

वरद *vara-da*, I. adj. 1. Conferring a boon, or boons, Chr. 57, 26. 2. Propitious. II. f. 1. A girl. 2. The name of a river, Mâlav. d. 76.

वरप्रद *vara-pra-da*, I. adj. Conferring a boon. II. f. *dâ*, The wife of Agastya.

वरयितृ *varayitṛi*, i.e. *vṛi*, Caus., + *tṛi*, m. A husband.

वरल *varala*, m. A wasp; cf. *varaṭa*.

वराक *varâka*, i.e. *vṛi + aka*, I. adj., f. *kî*. 1. Poor, Pańch. 108, 13. 2. Low, vile, impure, Böhtl. Ind. Spr. 429; Daçak. in Chr. 186, 2; Pańch. 81, 18. 3. Unhappy, Pańch. 41, 5. II. m. 1. Çiva. 2. War, battle.

वराट *varâṭa*, m. 1. (akin to *varatrâ*, probably a dialect. form of it), A cord. 2. The small shell, called (*kaparda*) cowrie, and used as a coin, Pańch. i. d. 88.

वराटक *varâṭa+ka*, m , f. *ṭikâ* (and n.), **1.** A rope. **2.** The small shell, called cowrie, and used as a coin, Pańch. 135, 7. **3.** The seed vessel of the lotus. —**Comp.** *Kim-*, adj. despising a cowrie (a farthing), Hit. ii. d. 87.

वराण *varâṇa* (a ptcple. Âtm. of *vṛi*), m. Indra.

वरारक *varâraka*, n. A diamond.

वराह *varâha*, m. **1.** A hog, Pańch. 120, 14. **2.** Vishṇu, who assumed in his third *avatâra*, or descent, the shape of a boar, Utt. Râmach. 132, 6. **3.** A form of marching an army, Man. 7, 187. **4.** A mountain. **5.** A sort of measure. **6.** One of the smaller *Dvîpas*, or divisions of the world.—**Comp.** *Mahâ-* and *Yajńa-*, m. Vishṇu, Johns. Sel. 94, 55 (*yajńa-*).—Cf. Lat. verres.

वराहु *varâhu*, m. A hog, Chr. 294, 5=Rigv. i. 88, 5.—Cf. *varâha*.

वरिमन् *variman*, i. e. *uru+iman* (cf. the comparat. of *uru*, *varîyaṁs*), m. Extent, greatness.

वरिवस्य *VARIVASYA*, denomin. derived from the vedic noun *varivas* with *ya*, Par. To adore, Daçak. in Chr. 189, 23.

वरिवस्या *varivasyâ*, i.e. *varivasya+â*, f. Worship, service.

वरिष *varisha* (for *varsha*), m. n. A year, Lass. 2. ed. 54, 55 (? hypothet. r.).

वरिष्ठ *varishṭha*, and **वरीयंस्** *varîyaṁs*, see *uru*.

वरीवर्द *varîvarda=balîvarda*.

वरीषु *varîshu* (vb. *vṛi*), m. Kâma.

वरुण *varuṇa*, i.e. *vṛi+una*, I. m. **1.** In the Veda, the deity of the heavens, Chr. 289, 6=Rigv. i. 54, 6; in the later time, of the waters (originally those of the atmosphere), Râm. 3, 54, 9; the lord of punishment, Man. 9, 245; sovereign of the western quarter, Çiç. 9, 7. **2.** A name of the sun. **3.** Water, or the ocean. II. f. *varuṇânî*, The wife of Varuṇa.—Cf. Οὐρανός.

वरुत्र *varutra*, i.e. *vṛi+tra*, n. An upper garment.

वरूथ *varûtha* (vb. *vṛi*), I. m. A wooden fender round a carriage, to protect it from collision. II. n. **1.** Armour. **2.** Leather skin. **3.** A house.

वरूथिन् *varûthin*, i. e. *varûtha+in*, I. adj. Protected by fenders (cf. the last), Ragh. 9, 11. II. f. *nî*. **1.** An army, Chr. 54, 14. **2.** The name of an Apsaras, Indr. 2, 29.

वरेण्य *vareṇya* (properly an anomal. ptcple. of the fut. pass. of *vṛi*), adj. Superior, excellent, Lass. 99, 11=Rigv. iii. 62, 11.

वरोल *varola*, m. A wasp (cf. *varala*).

वर्कर *varkara*, m. **1.** Any young animal. **2.** A lamb. **3.** A goat. **4.** Sport, pastime.

वर्कराट *varkarâṭa*, m. **1.** A side glance. **2.** The marks of a lover's finger-nails on the bosom of a woman.

वर्ग *varga*, i.e. *vṛij+a*, m. **1.** A class (a multitude of similar things), Pańch. 33, 14. **2.** A troop, Pańch. 192, 23. **3.** A chapter. — **Comp.** *Âpta-*, m. friends, Mâlav. 67, 11. *Chatur-*, m. 1. any assemblage of four things, Hit. i. d. 8, M.M. 2. the four objects of human pursuit, viz. wealth, pleasure, virtue, and final beatitude, Râgh. 10, 23. *Tri-*, m. any assemblage of three things, e.g. wealth, pleasure, and virtue, Man. 2, 224; Daçak. in Chr. 181,

21; the three qualities of nature; viz. *satya*, truth; *rajas*, passion; and *tamas*, darkness; three conditions of a king, loss, gain, equality, MBh. 12, 2664; the three myrobalans. *Dâsa-*, m. all the servants, Man. 3, 246. *Pâtra-*, m. a troop of actors, Vikr. 3, 9. *Bandhu-*, m. relations, Pañch. i. d. 30. *Bhṛitya-* m. servants, ib. (cf. my transl. and Böhtl. Ind. Spr. 2542). *Rakshi(n)-*, m. a sentinel.—Cf. probably Lat. vulgus (or =*vraja*).

ऽवर्गिण *-vargiṇa*, in *mad-varga+ina*, adj. Connected with, or related to, me.

ऽवर्गीय *-vargîya*, in *sva-*, adj. Belonging to (thy) own fraction, Pañch. 212, 6.

वर्ग्य *vargya*, i.e. *varga+ya*, adj. Belonging to a class, Mâlat. 4, 6 (a mime).

† **वर्च्** *VARCH*, i. 1, Âtm. To shine.

वर्चस् *varchas*, I. n. **1.** Lustre, Râm. 3, 49, 4. **2.** Form, MBh. 1, 1076; Lass. 2. ed. 79, 80. **3.** Excrements. II. m. The son of Chandra.—Cf. *brahmavarchasa*.

वर्चस्क *varchas+ka*, m. and n. Ordure.

वर्चस्विन् *varchas+vin*, I. adj., f. *nî*, Bright, Nal. 12, 66. II. m. The moon.—**Comp.** *Brahman-*, i.e. *brahmavarchas+vin*, adj. illumined by the Vedas, Man. 3, 39.

वर्चित *varchita*, Pañch. 3, 10, read *charchita*.

वर्ज *varja*, i.e. *vṛij+a*, I. adj. **1.** Devoidof. **2.** Excepted. II. °*jam*, adv. Except, Utt. Râmach. 35, 10. III. m. **1.** Leaving. **2.** Excepting.—**Comp.** *Tṛicha-*, adj. except three verses, Chr. 294, l. 5. *Tvad-varja+m*, adv. except you, Pañch. 128, 22 (cf. my transl.). *Parvavarja+m*, i.e. *parvan-*, adj. except the forbidden days of the month, Man. 3, 45.

वर्जन *varjana*, i.e. *vṛij+ana*, n. **1.** Abandoning, leaving, Vedântas. in Chr. 202, 11. **2.** Desertion, Man. 5, 4. **3.** Avoiding, Man. 5, 26.

वर्ण् *VARṆ*, 1, 10 (rather a denomin. derived from *varṇa*), Par. **1.** To colour, Daçak. in Chr. 199, 13. **2.** To depict, to describe, Böhtl. Ind. Spr. 145; to explain, Vedântas. 207, 23. **3.** To praise, MBh. 2, 1226. **4.** † To illuminate. **5.** † To exert one's self. **6.** † To throw, or to grind.—With the prep. **अनु** *anu*, To expose, MBh. 4, 107.—With **उप** *upa*, **1.** The same, MBh. 3, 8732. **2.** To tell, Hit. 27, 8.—With **नि** *ni*, To regard, Daçak. in Chr. 187, 12 (probably to be changed to *nirvarṇya*).—With **निस्** *nis*, To regard, Çâk. 33, 13; to examine, Vikr. 10, 3. Comp. ptcple. of the fut. pass. *a-nirvarṇanîya*, adj. Not to be looked at, Çâk. 64, 8.—With **सम्** *sam*, **1.** To describe, MBh. 4, 106. **2.** To extol, MBh. 4, 121.

वर्ण *varṇa*, i.e. *vṛi+na*, I. m. **1.** Colour, Hit. iii. d. 33. **2.** Staining the body with coloured unguents. **3.** Coloured cloth thrown over the back of an elephant. **4.** Gold. **5.** Beauty. **6.** Theatrical dress or embellishment. **7.** Quality, property. **8.** Fame. **9.** Praise. **10.** A musical mode, Pañch. v. d. 44. **11.** The arrangement of a poem. **12.** A caste, Man. 1, 91; Hit. pr. 46, M.M. (*hîna-*, adj. One of a low caste); caste and colour at once, Râjat. 5, 377; class, tribe, kind. **13.** Religious observance. II. m. and n. **1.** Perfume for the person. **2.** Form, figure. **3.** Sort, kind. **4.** A letter of the alphabet, Bhâshâp. 163; Vikr. 78, 10. **5.** A syllable, Çrut. 19. **6.** The purity of gold, as ascertained by its streak on the touch-stone. III.

n. Saffron.—Comp. *A-*, m. reproach, blame, Ragh. 14, 38. *Agni-*, I. adj. 1. fire-coloured, Râm. 3, 58, 35. 2. boiling hot, Man. 11, 91. II. m. a proper name, Hariv. 828. *Eka-*, adj. 1. one-coloured, plain, MBh. 13, 3781. 2. identical, Bhâg. P. 8, 5, 29. 3. consisting in one caste only, MBh. 3, 13051. *Jyeshṭha-*, m. a Brâhmaṇa, MBh. 13, 6571. *Durvarṇa*, i.e. *dus-*, I. adj. of a bad colour, Bhâg. P. 3, 14, 45. II. n. silver. *Dhûmra-*, I. adj. grey-coloured, Râm. 4, 39, 28. II. m. 1. the name of a mountain, Hariv. 12856. 2. a proper name, ib. 1799. *Bhinna-*, adj. discoloured, pale, Megh. 82; cf. Pańch. i. d. 212 (*bhinna-svara-mukha-varṇa*, speechless and pale, or, 'with altered accents and complexion'). *Madhu-*, adj. sweet, like honey, Chr. 293, 2=Rigv. i. 87, 2. *Megha-*, adj. cloud-coloured, Indr. 5, 15. *Yathârha-*, i.e. *yathâ-arha-*, m. a spy. *Labdha-*, adj. learned, Ragh. 11, 2. *Vi-*, I. adj. 1. wanting colour, pale, Nal. 2, 2. 2. bad-coloured. 3. changing colour. 4. low. II. m. a man of a low caste. *Sa-*, I. adj. 1. like, resembling, Megh. 18. 2. of the same caste, kind, MBh. 2, 865. II. f. *ṇâ*, Chhâyâ, the wife of the sun. *Sama-*, I. adj. of the same colour, caste, etc. II. m. community of caste. *Su-*, I. adj. 1. of a good colour. 2. brilliant. 3. of a good tribe. II. n. 1. gold, Pańch. 191, 25. 2. wealth. III. m. and n. a weight of gold equal to sixteen Mâshas, i.e. about seventy-five grains Troy, Man. 8, 134; a sort of coin, Pańch. 134, 3. IV. m. 1. a sort of sacrifice. 2. a tree, Cassia fistula. V. f. *ṇâ*, the name of several plants. *Hiraṇya-*, f. *ṇâ*, a river.

वर्णक *varṇa+ka*, I. A substitute for *varṇa*, at the end of comp. adj., Daçak. in Chr. 184, 8 (*kṛipaṇa-*, Of a miserable complexion). II. m., and f. *kâ*, A paint, as indigo, orpiment, etc., Bhaṭṭ. 19, 16. III. m. and n. 1. Perfume for the person. 2. Sandal. IV. m. 1. A panegyrist. 2. A circle. V. f. *kâ*, Touch or purity of gold.—Comp. *Tri-*, n. the three myrobalans, Suçr. 1, 161, 5.

वर्णन *varṇ+ana*, I. n. 1. Colouring. 2. Describing, description, Chr. 235, l. 2; Daçak. in Chr. 185, 22; tale, Pańch. 187, 14. II. f. *nâ*. 1. Describing, description, Vikr. 19, 9 (*prati-avayava-*, A detailed description, limb for limb). 2. Praise, Lass. 2. ed. 81, 1.

वर्णाट *varṇâṭa*, m. 1. A painter. 2. A singer.

वर्णिक *varṇika*, i.e. *varṇa+ika*, I. m. A scribe. II. f. *kâ*. 1. A pen. 2. Ink. 3. Colour, Çâk. d. 142, v.r. 4. Attire, Prab. 3, 18, Mâlat. 4, 11.

वर्णिन् *varṇin*, I. adj., i.e. *varṇa+in*, f. *nî*, Belonging to a caste or tribe. II. m. 1. A painter. 2. A scribe. 3. A religious student, Ragh. 5, 19. 4. A man of either of the four castes. III. f. *nî*. 1. A woman. 2. Turmeric.—Comp. *Vara-varṇinî*, f. 1. an excellent woman, Râm. 3, 53, 30. 2. a virtuous woman, Chr. 47, 39. 3. Gaurî. 4. Lakshmî. 5. Sarasvatî. 6. turmeric. 7. lac. 8. a yellow pigment=*rochanâ*.

वर्तक *vartaka*, i.e. *vṛit+aka*, I. adj. Who is, or exists, or abides. II. m., and f. *takâ* and *tikâ* (Chr. 298, 6=Rigv. i. 112, 6), A quail, Hit. iii. d. 22; Mâlat. 135, 8. III. m. A horse's hoof. IV. n. A sort of mixed metal.—Cf. *vartikâ*.

वर्तजन्मन् *vartajanman*, i.e. *vṛit+a-janman*, m. A cloud.

वर्तन *vartana*, i.e. *vṛit+ana*, I. adj. Staying. II. m. A dwarf. III. f. *nî*, and n. 1. Staying, abiding, Utt. Râmach. 17, 2. 2. A road. 3. Grinding. 4. A ball. IV. n. 1. Turning. 2. A ball of cotton from which the threads are spun. 3. Occupation, Pańch. i. d.

12. **4.** Livelihood, Hit. 114, 2. **5.** Appointing, being appointed, Hit. 98, 8. **6.** Wages, Hit. i. d. 45, M.M. **7.** A soldier's pay, Hit. 98, 10; 99, 18. **8.** Colouring, Kir. 10, 42.

वर्तनि and **नी** *vartanî*, i.e. *vṛit+ana+î*, f. A road, Chr. 298, 18=Rigv. i. 112, 18.

वर्ति and **वर्ती** *vartî* (vb. *vṛit*), f. **1.** Perfume for the person. **2.** The wick of a lamp, Bhâg. P. 5, 11, 8 (*ti*). **3.** A line, a ruled line. **4.** A magic ball, Pańch. 241, 2 (*ti*), sqq. (?). **5.** The ends of a cloth. **6.** A sort of collyrium, Mâlat. 14, 14; Utt. Râmach. 24, 12 (*amṛita-varti*, consisting of nectar). **7.** A bougie.

वर्तिका *varti+kâ*, f. **1.** The wick of a lamp. **2.** Colour, Çâk. d. 142 (?). **3.** A pencil, Daçak. in Chr. 199, 13; Ragh. 19, 19; Mâlat. 21, 3.—Comp. *Yoga-*, f. a magic lamp (see *varti*), Daçak. in Chr. 186, 10.—Cf. *vartaka*.

वर्तिन् *vartin*, i.e. *vṛit+in*, adj., f. *ni*, **1.** Abiding, resting, Pańch. i. d. 224. **2.** Being, Hit. 65, 5, M.M.—Comp. *Uchchhâstra-*, i.e. *ud-çâstra-*, adj. one who transgresses the sacred precepts, Man. 4, 87. *Unmârga-*, i.e. *ud-mârga-*, adj. following evil courses, Râjat. 5, 209. *Guṇa-*, adj. pursuing the path of virtue, Râm. 2, 82, 18. *Guru-*, adj. one who behaves respectfully towards his parents and spiritual teacher, ib. 4, 35, 12. *Chakra-*, m., f. *inî*, 1. a sovereign of the world, MBh. 12, 808. 2. a sovereign, Kathâs. 1, 13. *Dûra-*, adj. being afar, Megh. 100. *Ati-dûra-*, adj. being far over, surpassing, Çâk. 146, 8, Chezy. *Nyâya-*, adj. well-behaving, Pańch. i. d. 393. *Pârçva-*, adj. being at the side, Ragh. 19, 4. *Purovartin*, i.e. *puras-*, adj. being before one's eyes, in one's presence, Vikr. d. 72. *Pratikûla-*, adj. troubling, Kumâras. 3, 24. *Vaça-*, adj. acting according to another's will, obedient. *Sama-*, m. Yama. *Hasta-*, adj. being in one's hand, Hit. iii. d. 85.

वर्तिष्णु *vartishṇu*, i.e. *vṛit+ishṇu*, adj. **1.** Abiding, being fixed. **2.** Facing an enemy, standing firm in battle. **3.** A circle.

वर्तिस् *vartis*, i.e. *vṛit+is*, n. A house, Chr. 295, 16=Rigv. i. 92, 16.

वर्तुल *vartula* (vb. *vṛit*), **I.** adj. Round, circular, Lass. 5, 10. **II.** m. **1.** A ball. **2.** A pea. **III.** f. *lâ*, A ball at the end of a spindle to assist its rotation.

वर्त्मन् *vartman*, i.e. *vṛit+man*, n. **1.** A road, Vikr. 13, 20; way, Hit. i. d. 197, M.M. (*pańka-*, A swamp-way). **2.** An eyelid.—Comp. *Âkâça-*, n. a way through the air, Hit. 111, 8 (instr. through the air). *Kṛishṇa-*, m. fire, Man. 2, 94. *Ghana-*, n., *Nabhas-*, n. the sky, Kir. 5, 17; 4, 29. *Râjavartman*, i.e. *râjan-*, n. a royal or main road.

वर्द्ध्र *varddhra* (also **वर्ध्र** *vardhra*, Pâṇ. iv. 3, 151), **I.** n., and f. *rî*, A leathern thong for securing a saddle. **II.** n. Leather.

वर्ध् *VARDH*, i. 10, Par. **1.** † To cut. **2.** To fill (rather Caus. of *vṛidh*).

वर्ध *vardha*, **I.** m. **1.** i.e. *vṛidh+a*, Increase. **2.** Cutting. **II.** n. Red lead.

वर्धक *vardhaka* (Râm. 1, 12, 7), and **वर्धकि** *vardhaki* (Râm. 2, 63, 2, ed. Seramp.), m. A carpenter.

वर्धन *vardhana*, i.e. **A.** *vṛidh+ana*, **I.** adj. **1.** Growing, increasing. **2.** Causing to increase, Nal. 3, 20. **II.** n. **1.** Growing, increasing. **2.** Causing to increase, Daçak. in Chr. 182, 19; Hit. ii. d. 58. **3.** Making powerful, Hit. iii. d. 3. **4.** Elevation, ii. d. 132. **B.** n. Cutting. **C.** f. *nî*. **1.** A small water-jar. 2. A brush.—Comp. *Kamala-*, m. the name of a king, Râjat. 5, 446. *Kula-*, adj. propagating a family, Râm. 1, 13, 46 (Brâhmaṇav. read °*dhanaḥ*). *Nandi-*, I. adj. causing joy, MBh. 5, 2937. II. m. 1. a son, Râm. 6, 112, 4. 2. a proper name, Bhâg. P. 9, 13, 14. *Nâbhi-*, n. the section of the navel-string, Man. 2, 29. *Puṇya-*, n. the name of a town, Lass. 21, 16. *Meru-*, m. a proper name, Râjat. 5, 366. *Ratna-*, *Çam̃kara-*, *Çambu-*, m. proper names, Râjat. 5, 40; 268; 300. *Vam̃ça-*, m. one by whom his race prospers, Vikr. 87, 20. *Varsha-*, n. increase of years, or causing increase of years (?), Utt. Râmach. 85, 7.

वर्धमानक *vardhamâna* + *ka* (vb. *vṛidh*), m. A lid, a cover.

वर्धापन *vardhâpana*, n. 1. Cutting, dividing. 2. i.e. *vardhâpaya* (anomal. Caus. of *vṛidh*), + *ana*; also °**नक** °*na* + *ka*, A festival on a birthday, Lass. ed. 18, 8; Pañch. ed. orn. 49, 16.

वर्धिन् *vardhin*, i.e. *vṛidh* + *in*, adj. 1. Growing, increasing. 2. Augmenting, Utt. Râmach. 170, 7; Chr. 51, 5.

वर्धिष्णु *vardhishṇu*, i. e. *vṛidh* + *ishṇu*, adj. 1. Growing, increasing. 2. Enlarging, expanding.

वर्पस् *varpas*, n. Form, figure.—Comp. *Ghora-*, adj. having a terrible figure, Chr. 292, 2 = Rigv. i. 64, 2.

वर्मन् *varman*, i.e. *vṛi* + *man*, n. Armour, mail, Râjat. 5, 195.—Comp. *Varman* may be added after all Kshatriya names, Colebr. Essays, i. 278; e.g. *Apahâra-*, *Avanti-*, *Kṛita-*, *Go-pâla-*, *Chakra-*, *Chaṇḍa-*, *Chandra-*, m. proper names, Daçak. in Chr. 179, 3; Râjat. 5, 2; MBh. 1, 562; Râjat. 5, 181; 287; Daçak. in Chr. 200, 23; MBh. 1, 2668. *Dharma-*, n. the armour or protection of the law, epithet of Kṛishṇa, Bhâg. P. 1, 1, 23. *Nirjita-*, i.e. *nis-jita*, *Çam̃kara-*, *Çûra-*, m. proper names, Râjat. 5, 251; 128; 22.

वर्मित *varmita*, i.e. *varman* + *ita*, and

वर्मिन् *varmin*, i.e. *varman* + *in* (MBh. 1, 7765), adj. Armed.

वर्वर *varvara*, I. (probably borrowed from *βάρβαρος*, cf. *barbara*), m. 1. A barbarian, an outcaste. 2. The country inhabited by barbarians. II. m. 1. Woolly or curly hair. 2. A sort of worm. 3. The clash of weapons. 4. A mode of dancing. III. f. *râ* and *rî*, A small bee. IV. n. Vermilion.

वर्वरीक *varvarîka*, i.e. *varvara* + *îka*, m. 1. Curly or woolly hair. 2. A name of Çiva.

वर्ष् *VARSH*, see *parsh*.

वर्ष *varsha*, i.e. *vṛish* + *a*, I. adj. at the end of a comp. Raining, Hit. ii. d. 147. II. m. and n. 1. Rain, Megh. 36; figurat., Chr. 39, 3 (a shower of arrows). 2. A cloud. 3. A year, Râm. 3, 53, 10 (n.); Pañch. 159, 14 (n.). 4. A division of the known continent, of which there are reckoned nine, Bhâg. P. 8, 9, 22. 5. India, also called *Bhârata-*. II. f. *shâ*. 1. pl. The rainy season, Man. 3, 173; Hit. 80, 15. 2. A sort of gramineous plant.—Comp. *A-*, m. drought, Râm. 3, 35, 28. *Ashṭavarsha*, i.e. *ashṭan-*, adj. eight years old, Man. 9, 94. *Tirovarsha*, i.e. *tiras-*, adj. protected against rain, MBh. 4, 171. *Dvâdaçavarsha*, i.e. *dvâdaçan-*, n. pl. twelve years, Pañch. i. d. 238 (perhaps two words). *Pra-*, m. raining fast, Pañch. 93, 2. *Çara-*, m. a shower of arrows, Chr. 4, 20.

वर्षकर *varsha-kara*, I. adj. Producing rain. II. m. A cloud. III. f. *rî*, A cricket.

वर्षण *varshaṇa*, i.e. *vṛish* + *ana*, n.

Raining.—Comp. *A-*, m. drought, Lass. 27, 2.

वर्षधर *varsha-dhara*, m. 1. A cloud. 2. An eunuch, Pañch. 43, 5; 53, 2.

वर्षवर *varsha-vara*, m. An eunuch, Mâlat. 16, 16.

वर्षाभू *varshâ-bhû* (see *varsha*), I. m. A frog. II. f. *bhû* and *bhvî*. 1. A she-frog. 2. Hog-weed.

वर्षिक *varshika*, i. e. *varsha + ika*, adj. Raining, rainy.

वर्षिन् *varshin*, i.e. *vṛish*, and *varsha*, *+in*, adj., f. *iṇî*, Raining, Böhtl. Ind. Spr. 1183.—Comp. *A-pâtra-*, adj. raining on (i.e. giving presents to) unworthy persons, Hit. iii. d. 101. *Abhishṭa-*, i. e. *abhi-ishṭa-varsha + in*, adj. yielding the wished-for rain, Böhtl. Ind. Spr. 1915. *Chitra-*, adj. raining in an extraordinary manner, Hariv. 11145. *Shashṭi-*, adj. sixty years old, Hiḍ. 1, 13.

वर्षिष्ठ *varshishṭha* (superl. of *vṛiddha*), 1. Oldest. 2. Very abundant, Chr. 293, 1=Rigv. i. 88, 1. वर्षीयंस् *varshiyaṁs* (its comparat.), Very aged, old, Daçak. in Chr. 200, 4 (properly from *varsha + vant*).

वर्षुक *varshuka* (vb. *vṛish*), adj. Rainy, Bhaṭṭ. 2, 37.

वर्षेज *varsheja*, i. e. *varsha + i-ja*, adj. Produced in the rains.

वर्ष्मन् *varshman*, n. 1. The body, Johns. Sel. 94, 54; Hiḍ. 2, 7 (at the end of a comp. adj. Having the body of a mass of clouds, i.e. as black as a big cloud). 2. Height. 3. A measure, largeness, Ragh. 4, 76; MBh. 1, 1443. 4. A handsome form.

वर्ह् *VARH*, बर्ह् *BARH*, i. 1, Âtm. To be pre-eminent. i. 10, To hurt, to kill.—With the prep. नि *ni*, i. 10, To destroy, Çiç. 1, 29; cf. *barh*.

वर्ह *varha*, see *barha*.

वर्हण *varhaṇa*, n. A leaf (cf. *barha*).

वर्हिण *varhiṇa*, see *barhiṇa*.

वर्हिन् *varhin*, see *barhin*.

वर्हिषद् *varhishad*, वर्हिस् *varhis*, see *bar°*.

वल् *VAL* (cf. *vṛi*), i. 1, Âtm. 1. To cover. 2. To be attached to, Nal. 3, 5. 3. To hasten, Çiç. 6, 38; Gît. 6, 3. 4. To move to and fro, Çiç. 6, 11; Vikr. 59, 20. 5. To increase, Gît. 1, 26. Ptcple. of the pf. pass. *valita*. 1. Surrounded. 2. Moved, Râjat. 5, 360; 481; moving, Mâlat. 16, 9; turned, 16, 19; Amar. 83. 3. Constrained. Caus. To cause to move, Çiç. 6, 3. Cf. s.v.—With the prep. अति *ati*, *an-ativalita*, see s.v. *valita*.—With वि *vi*, *vivalita*, Turned away, Amar. 44.—With सम् *sam*, *saṁvalita*, 1. Encompassed, Kir. 5, 48. 2. United, Mâlat. 73, 4. 3. Mixed Kir. 5, 38. 4. Possessed of.

वलक्ष *valaksha* = *ava-laksha*, adj. White.

वलन *val + ana*, n. 1. Turning, Amar. 19. 2. Agitation, 26.

वलन्तिका *valantikâ*, f. A musical mode, Vikr. 59, 15.

वलभि *valabhi*, see *vaḍabhi*.

वलय *val* (Caus., or i. 10), *+ a* (sometimes *balaya*), I. m. and n. 1. A bracelet, Pañch. iii. d. 235. 2. Circle, circumference, Çiç. 9, 8 (*diç-*, The universe). II. m. 1. An enclosure, Ragh. 13, 21. 2. Inflammation of the larynx. — Comp. *Aksha-sûtra-*, n. a rosary, Utt. Râmach.

106, 2. *Ku-*, see s.v. *Bhû-*, m. n. the terrestrial globe, Mârk. P. 20, 51. *Lekhâ-*, an encircling line, Vikr. d. 140. *Vratati-*, a creeper winding round like a bracelet, Çâk. d. 32.

वलयवन्त् *valaya + vant*, adj. Endowed with bracelets, Çâk. 32, 14 (*latâ-*, Endowed with bracelets consisting in creepers).

वलयित *valayita*, i.e. *valaya + ita*, adj. **1.** Surrounded, Böhtl. Ind. Spr. 2245. **2.** Whirling, Mâlat. 75, 21.

वलयिन् *valayin*, i.e. *valaya + in*, adj. in *jyotis-lekhâ-*, Endowed with circles formed by resplendent lines, Megh. 45.

वलाक *valâka*, I. m. A crane. II. f. *kâ* (also *balâkâ*, Man. 5, 14). **1.** The female crane, Megh. 9. **2.** A crane in general, Man. 11, 135. **3.** A flight of cranes. **4.** A mistress.

वलाहक *valâhaka*, and वलि *vali*, see *balâhaka*, *bali*.

वलित *valita*, i.e. *vali* or *bali*, + *ita*, adj., f. *tâ*, and वलिभ *vali + bha*, adj. Having wrinkles, Bhaṭṭ. 4, 16 (*valibha*).—Comp. *An-ativalita*, adj. almost free from wrinkles (cf. Amar. 47, Sch.), Daçak. in Chr. 198, 22.—Cf. *val*.

वलिश *valiça*, see *vaḍiça*.

वलीक *valika*, n. The edge of a roof.

वलूक *valûka*, m. **1.** A bird. **2.** (n.), The root of a lotus.

† वल्क् *VALK*, i. 10, Par. To speak.

वल्क *valka*, i.e. *vṛi + ka*, **1.** m. n. The bark of a tree, Kir. 1, 35. **2.** n. The scales of a fish.—Comp. *Danta-*, n. the enamel of the teeth, Suçr. 1, 305, 8.

वल्कल *valka + la*, m. and n. **1.** The bark of a tree, Pańch. 188, 13. **2.** A cloth made of bark, Pańch. v. d. 21.

वल्ग् *VALG*, i. 1, Par. **1.** To go by leaps, MBh. 3, 16123. **2.** To bounce, Bhartṛ. 3, 73. **3.** To gallop, Râjat. 5, 342. **4.** To move in different ways, Pańch. i. d. 71. **5.** To fluctuate, MBh. 3, 12080. Ptcple. of the pf. pass. *valgita*, n. **1.** Running, Lass. 2. ed. 50, 15. **2.** A horse's gallop.—With the prep. आ *â*, To run to, MBh. 4, 342. —With व्या *vi-â*, To gallop, Utt. Râmach. 119, 4.—With वि *vi*, To burst asunder, Mṛichchh. 85, 15.—With सम् *sam*, *saṁvalgita*, Overrun, resounding, Mâlat. 79, 16.—Cf. *valgu* and perhaps A.S. wlaence, pompa.

वल्गा *valg + â*, f. A bridle, Râjat. 5, 343.

वल्गु *valg + u*, I. adj. **1.** Handsome, Pańch. i. d. 202. **2.** Precious, Hit. iii. d. 70. II. adv. Beautifully, Pańch. i. d. 71. III. m. A goat.

वल्गुक *valgu + ka*, I. adj. Handsome. II. n. **1.** Sandal. **2.** A wood. **3.** Price.

वल्गुल *valgu + la*, I. m. The flying fox. II. f. *lâ*, A sort of bird.

वल्गुलिका *valgulikâ*, f. A cockroach.

† वल्भ् *VALBH*, i. 1, Âtm. To eat.

वल्भन *valbhana*, n. Eating, food.

वल्मिक *valmika*, m., वल्मिकि *valmiki*, m., and वल्मीक *valmîka*, m. and n., i.e. *valmî + ka*, An ant-hill, Man. 4, 46 (*mika*); Pańch. 170, 23 (*mîka*); Çâk. d. 170 (*mîka*).

वल्मी *valmî* (cf. *vamra*), f. An ant, Häberl. Anth. 238, 2.

वल्युल् and वल्यूल् *VALYÛL*, see *palpûl*.

† वल्ल् *VALL*, i. 1, Par. **1.** To go. **2.** To be covered.

वल्लकी *vallakî*, f. The Indian lute, Ṛit. 1, 8; Çiç. 4, 57.

वल्लभ *vallabha*, I. adj., f. *bhâ*. **1.** Beloved, Pańch. 169, 25; iv. d. 8; superl. °*bhatama*, dearest, Bhartṛ. 2, 78. **2.** Superintendent. **II.** m. **1.** A lover, a favourite, Pańch. 129, 7; Râjat. 5, 380. **2.** The chief herdsman. **3.** A horse with good marks. **III.** f. *bhâ*, A mistress, Râjat. 5, 6.—**Comp.** *Kuvera-*, m. a proper name, Daçak. in Chr. 186, 17. *Çri-*, m. a favourite of fortune, Böhtl. Ind. Spr. 1912.

वल्लभता *vallabha*+*tâ*, f. **1.** Love, Prab. 10, 8. **2.** State of a favourite, Pańch. ii. d. 75.—**Comp.** *Ati-*, f. excessive love, Pańch. 221, 5.

वल्लभत्व *vallabha* + *tva*, n. Love, Pańch. 228, 22.

वल्लरि and री *vallarî*, f. **1.** A creeping plant, Pańch. 229, 16 (*ri*). **2.** A compound pedicle.—**Comp.** *Alaka-*, f. pl. creeper-like curls, Amar. 58. *Visha-vallarî*, f. a poisonous creeper, Bhartṛ. 1, 75. *Soma-*, f. the Soma plant, Sarcostema viminalis.

वल्लव *vallava*, I. m. **1.** A cook. **2.** A herdsman, Nalod. 1, 2. **3.** A name of Bhîmasena. **II.** f. *vi*, A cowherdess, Kir. 4, 17.

वल्लि f. I., and वल्ली *vallî*, A creeper, Man. 1, 48 (*li*); Pańch. 229, 9; Bhartṛ. 3, 23 (*li*). **II.** *valli*, The earth. **III.** *li*, A plant, Ligusticum ajwaen.—**Comp.** *Nâga-vallî*, f. the betel plant, Piper betel, Çiç. 9, 65. *Sûrya-vallî*, f. a plant, Cleome viscosa.

वल्लीज *vallî-ja*, n. Pepper.

वल्लुर *vallura*, n. **1.** A thicket, a wood. **2.** An arbour, a bower. **3.** A place overrun with wild grass, an uncultivated field. **4.** A solitude, a wild. **5.** A place destitute of water, a desert. **6.** A field. **7.** A compound pedicle.

वल्लूर *vallûra*, I. (m., f. *râ*, and) n. **1.** Dried flesh, Man. 5, 13. **2.** Hog's flesh. **II.** n. (cf. the last). **1.** A thicket. **2.** A field overrun with grass. **3.** A desert.

वल्वज *valvaja*, m. A sort of coarse grass, Man. 2, 42.

वल्श *valça* (m. n. ?), A branch, Bhâg. P. 3, 8, 29.

† वल्ह् *VALH*, i. 1, Âtm. To be pre-eminent; cf. *balh* and *varh*.

वश् *VAÇ*, ii. 2 (*vaçmi*, *uçvas*), Par. To desire, to will, Çak. d. 179; Chr. 292, 10=Rigv. i. 86, 10.—Cf. ἑκών, ἀέκων, ἕκηλος, εὔκηλος.

वश *vaç*+*a*, I. adj. **1.** Willing. **2.** Tamed, overpowered, Pańch. 208, 13. **3.** Subdued by charms, fascinated. **II.** m. and n. Wish, desire. **III.** n. **1.** Will, authority, power, Râm. 3, 55, 18; Pańch. 38, 3. **2.** abl. °*çât*, at the end of a compound word, By means, Pańch. 32, 24; on account of, Vikr. d. 2; Pańch. 33, 6; 148, 10; 264, 23. **3.** Subjection, Pańch. iii. d. 10; 30; *vaçe kṛi*, To overpower, Râm. 3, 55, 7; submission, Pańch. iv. d. 60; *vaçe bhû*, To be subjected, to obey, Râm. 3, 55, 18. **4.** Birth. **IV.** m. **1.** The residence of harlots. **2.** A proper name, Chr. 296, 10=Rigv. i. 112, 10. **V.** f. *çâ*. **1.** A wife. **2.** A daughter. **3.** A husband's sister. **4.** A woman. **5.** A cow. **6.** A female elephant, Vikr. d. 110. **7.** A barren cow. **8.** A barren woman, Man. 8, 28.—**Comp.** *A-*, adj., f. *çâ*, 1. having no free will, unwilling, against one's wish, Râm. 2, 59, 4; powerless, Hit. iii. d. 133; without being able to resist, Râm. 4, 6, 12; Man. 5, 33. 2. unsubdued,

Hit. i. d. 17, M.M. 3. disobedient, Hit. ii. d. 173. °*çam*, adv. necessarily, Hit. ii. d. 75. *Aṅkuça-*, adj. obeying the goad of an elephant, Pańch. i. d. 373. *Âtmavaça*, i.e. *âtman-*, I. m. subjection to one's self, Hit. ii. d. 54, M.M. II. adj. independent, Man. 4, 159. *Karmavaça*, i.e. *karman-*, adj. dependent upon the acts performed in former existences, MBh. 13, 72. *Krodha-*, I. (m.), the power of wrath, Man. 2, 214. II. adj. 1. ruled by wrath, Bhâg. P. 5, 24, 29. 2. the name of several bad spirits. *Daiva-*, n. will of fate, Pańch. 160, 17; 174, 25. *Nidrâ-* (n.), sleep (literally, power of sleep), Pańch. 37, 7. *Para-*, adj. depending on another, Hit. i. d. 201, M.M. *Mantra-oshadhi-*, adj. to be overcome by charms and herbs, Böhtl. Ind. Spr. 3197. *Moha-* (n.), unconsciousness (literally, power of unconsciousness), Chr. 36, 21. *Vi-*, adj., f. *çâ* (deprived of will). 1. subject, subjected, Râm. 3, 55, 51; Hit. i. d. 171, M.M. (even against their will). 2. independent. 3. uncontrolled, unsubdued. 4. apprehensive of death, Bhartṛ. 2, 29. 5. desirous of death, having the soul free from worldly cares, dead, Ragh. 8, 81. *Sva-*, adj. self-controlled, ruled by one's free will, Hiḍ. 4, 4; independent, Vikr. d. 37.

वशंवदत्व *vaça + m-vad + a + tva*, n. Speaking compliantly, Ragh. 18, 12.

वशग *vaça + ga*, 1. adj. Obedient, subject, MBh. 3, 14687; Pańch. i. d. 155; 285. 2. f. *gâ*, An obedient wife.

वशतस् *vaça + tas*, adv. In consequence, or on account, of the power of, Bhartṛ. 2, 91.

वशता *vaça + tâ*, f. Subjection, Châṇ. 65 in Berl. Monatsb. 1864, 411.

वशि *vaç + i*, n. Subduing by magical means, bewitching.

वशिक *vaçika*, adj. Empty.

वशिता *vaçi + tâ*, f., **वशित्व** *vaçi + tva*, n., or *vaçin + tâ*, or *tva*, 1. Subduing by magical means, Lass. 3, 19 (*tva*). 2. Subjugation, dominion, Böhtl. Ind. Spr. 2977.

वशिन् *vaçin*, i.e. *vaça + in*, I. adj., f. *nî*, Subdued. II. m. One who has subdued his senses, a sage, Çâk. d. 47. III. f. *nî*. 1. A tree, Mimosa Sama Roxb. 2. A parasite plant.

वशिर *vaçira*, I. m. The name of several plants. II. n. Sea salt (cf. *vasuka*).

वशिष्ठ *vaçishṭha* (in the Vedas **वसिष्ठ** *vasishṭha*, properly superl. of *vasu*), m. The name of a Ṛishi, Man. 1, 35; Chr. 296, 9 = Rigv. i. 112, 9 (*s*).

वशीकरण *vaçîkaraṇa*, i.e. *vaça-kṛi + ana*, 1. Subduing in general, Pańch. i. d. 80. 2. Subduing by magical expedients.

वश्य *vaçya*, i.e. *vaça + ya*, I. adj., f. *yâ*. 1. Governable, able to be subdued, Pańch. iii. d. 128; subdued, Pańch. 156, 10; 23, 3; being in one's power, 146, 24. 2. Obedient, ib. 46, 20. II. m. A dependent, a slave. III. f. *yâ*, An obedient wife. IV. n. Cloves.—Comp. *A-vaçya + m*, see s. v. *Kâma-*, adj. subdued by love, MBh. 3, 11590.

ऽवश्यकता *-vaçyakatâ*, in *a-*, i.e. *a -vaçya + ka + tâ*, f. Necessity, Hit. 116, 10.

† **वष्** *VASH*, **बष्** *BASH*, i. 1, Par. To hurt or kill.

वषट् *vashaṭ* (probably for *vahshat*, ved. conj. aor. of *vah*), ind. An exclamation used on making an oblation to a deity with fire; cf. *kṛi*.

वषट्कार *vashaṭ-kâra*, m. Oblation with fire, Hariv. 11187.

वषट्कृति *vashaṭ-kṛiti*, f. Oblation with fire, Lass. 100, 11 = Rigv. vii. 11, 6.

† वष्क् *VASHK*, विष्क् *VISHK*, i. 10, Par. To see; see *vask*.

वष्क *vashka*, वष्कय *vashkaya*, and वस्कय *vaskaya*, i. e. 1. *vas* + *ka*, and *vas* + *ka* + *ya*, m. A one-year-old calf. —Cf. Lat. vacca.

वष्कयणी *vashkayaṇî*, वस्कयणी *vaskayaṇî*, and वष्कयिणी *vashkayiṇî* (i.e. *vashkaya* + *in* + *î*; cf. the last), f. A cow bearing many calves.

1. वस् *VAS*, i. 1, Par. (in epic poetry also Âtm., Râm. 2, 48, 21). **1.** To dwell, MBh. 1, 749; sometimes with *vâsam*, Man. 2, 242; Chr. 60, 30; to dwell with (with the loc.), Nal. 15, 7. **2.** To pass (the night), Râm. 1, 29, 1. **3.** To live, Hit. 127, 11 (*asmad-sevayâ*, as our servant). Pass. imps. *ushya*, Pańch. 30, 24 (*ushyatâm*, may it be lived). Ptcple. of the pf. pass. *ushita*. **1.** Dwelt, having dwelt, Chr. 11, 13. **2.** Remaining in or on. **3.** Stale. Anomal. ptcple. of the fut. pass. *vâstavya*, To be dwelt, Pańch. iii. d. 236. m. **1.** An inhabitant, a citizen, Pańch. 48, 25. **2.** A kinsman, a dependent. Comp. *Grâma-*, m. the inhabitant of a village, MBh. 12, 4803. Anomal. absol. *ushya*, Râm. 1, 48, 8. Caus. *vâsaya*, **1.** To cause to dwell, MBh. 4, 278; to lodge, Hit. 92, 19. **2.** To people, Hit. iii. d. 95. **3.** To receive hospitably, MBh. 3, 982. **4.** To let abide, MBh, 4, 5600. *vâsita*, Well peopled, Hit. iii. d. 95; see s. v. † i. 10, Par. *vasaya*, To dwell.—With the prep. अधि *adhi*, **1.** To inhabit, Râm. 1, 34, 46. **2.** To dwell, Utt. Râmach. 55, 16. Comp. ptcple. of the pf. pass. *samayâdhyushita*, see s.v.—With अनु *anu*, . **1.** To dwell with (with acc.), Râm. 2, 37, 26. **2.** To inhabit, Bhaṭṭ. 5, 75.—With अन्तर् *antar* (adv.), To dwell in, Çiç. 3, 9.—With आ *â*, **1.** To dwell with (with acc.), Râm. 2, 50, 2. **2.** To inhabit, MBh. 3, 8032. **3.** To have an adulterous connection with (acc.), Man. 8, 374. **4.** To dwell, MBh. 3, 2014. **5.** To undergo, to assume, Man. 3, 2. Caus. **1.** To receive, Râm. 2, 12, 101. **2.** To inhabit, MBh. 3, 12188.—With अध्या *adhi-â*, To inhabit, MBh. 1, 5512.—With समा *sam-â*, To inhabit, Râm. 2, 54, 41. Caus. To pitch, Hit. 84, 11, M.M. (*samâvâsita-kaṭaka*, adj. Having pitched his camp).—With उद् *ud*, Caus. To expel, Pańch. 47, 6.—With उप *upa*, **1.** To inhabit. **2.** To fast, Man. 2, 220. *uposhita*, **1.** Fasted. **2.** Who has fasted, Pańch. 199, 12. **3.** Fasting. n. Fast, Man. 5, 155. Caus. To cause to fast, to instruct to fast, Râm. 2, 5, 4.—With नि *ni*, **1.** To dwell, Pańch. 160, 23; Man. 2, 24. **2.** To pass (the night), MBh. 4, 276.—With अधिनि *adhi-ni*, To dwell near (with acc.), Bhartṛ. 3, 77.—With संनि *sam-ni*, To dwell, MBh. 3, 16777.—With निस् *nis*, To dwell abroad, MBh. 3, 915 (?). Caus. **1.** To expel, MBh. 2, 2644; Pańch. iii. d. 270. **2.** To banish, Utt. Râmach. 112, 6.—With परि *pari*, *paryushita*, **1.** One who has passed the night, Pańch. 40, 13. **2.** Stale, not fresh, Man. 4, 211; Pańch. ii. d. 102 (of a flower); Häberl. Anthol. 6, 4. **3.** Insipid, Nal. 12, 13; MBh. 3, 2856.—With प्र *pra*, **1.** To dwell abroad, Râm. 2, 36, 8. **2.** To order to dwell abroad, Râm. 2, 41, 6. *proshita*, **1.** Departed, Daçak. in Chr. 179, 11. **2.** Absent, being on a journey, Megh. 49. Caus. To send abroad, to banish, Man. 8, 123.—With विप्र *vi-pra*,

To dwell abroad, Man. 2, 132. *viproshita,* Having been abroad, Râm. 2, 103, 26. Caus. To banish, Man. 8, 219.—With प्रति *prati,* **1.** To dwell near, Hit. 110, 2. **2.** To dwell, Pañch. 32, 23.—With वि *vi,* **1.** To dwell, to pass, Râm. 1, 23, 23. **2.** To pass away, Pañch. 130, 7. Caus. **1.** To dismiss, MBh. 3, 8277. **2.** To banish, Man. 8, 123.—With सम् *sam,* **1.** To dwell, or to live with (with the acc.), Man. 11, 190. **2.** To cohabit (acc.), Man. 9, 77.—Cf. Goth. visan; A.S. wesan, ed-wist, werig; O.H.G. wesan and werên, wonên; A.S. wunian; Lat. Vesta, vestibulum, verna; ἄστυ, ἀστός, ἑστία, ὑπερ-ῷον, probably εὐνή, ἰαύω, αὐλή, αὖλις.

2. वस् *VAS* (the original form of *ush,* q. cf.), base of the present, *uchchha,* i. 6, Par. To shine, Chr. 287, 3 = Rigv. i. 48, 3 (*uchchhât,* conj. imperf., and *uvâsa,* pf. red.). Infin. *vastave,* ib. 287, 2 = Rigv. i. 48, 2.—With the prep. वि *vi, vyushṭa,* see separately.—Cf. Goth. uhtvo, see *ushas.*

3. वस् *VAS,* ii. 2, Âtm. **1.** To wear, as clothes, Man. 1, 101; 2, 41. **2.** To put on, Man. 4, 116.—With नि *ni,* To put on, Nal. 10, 29. Caus. To put on, MBh. 3, 2631.—With प्र *pra,* To put on, Râm. 2, 100, 30.—With प्रति *prati,* Caus. To dress, MBh. 2, 2502.—With वि *vi,* Caus. To put on, MBh. 2, 2520.—Cf. Goth. vasjan (to wear), vasti; A.S. werian; Lat. vestis; ἕννυμι, εἷμα (= ved. *vasman,* Rigv. iv. 13, 4), ἐσθής.

† 4. वस् *VAS,* i. 4, Par. To be unbending.

5. वस् *VAS,* i. 10, *vâsaya,* Par. **1.** † To love. **2.** To cut. **3.** † To take, or to offer, or to kill.

6. ५वस् 3. *-vas,* adj. Wearing, Ragh. 11, 16.

वसति and ती *vasatî* (vb. 1. *vas*), f. **1.** A dwelling-place, Vikr. d. 137 (*ti*); Pañch. 123, 16 (*ti,* at the end of a comp. adj.). **2.** A house, Nalod. 4, 29. **3.** (perhaps vb. 3. *vas*), Night, Sâv. 4, 5; figurat., Chr. 48, 4 (*ti*).—**Comp.** *Garbha-vasati,* f. the womb, Hariv. 3312. *Durvasati,* i.e. *dus-,* f. an uneasy dwelling, Ragh. 8, 93. *Ramaṇa-vasati,* f. the dwelling-place of the lover, Megh. 38.

वसन 1. 3. *vas* + *ana,* n. **1.** A dwelling. **2.** Covering. **3.** Cloth, Vikr. d. 115. **4.** Also f. *nâ,* An ornament worn by women round the loins.—**Comp.** *Su-,* adj., f. *nâ,* elegantly attired, Johns. Sel. 41, 49.—Cf. ἑανός.

वसन्त *vasanta,* m. **1.** The season of spring, Pañch. v. d. 4; personified, Lass. 2. ed. 51, 26. **2.** Diarrhœa. **3.** Small-pox.—**Comp.** *Su-,* m. the day of full moon in the month Chaitra, a festival in honour of Kâma.—Cf. ἔαρ; Lat. ver.

वसा *vasâ,* f. **1.** Marrow, Nalod. 3, 11; brain (*-chaṭâ,* the mass of the brain), Kathâs. 25, 274. **2.** Fat, adeps, Pañch. 253, 23. **3.** Oily exudation, Man. 5, 135.

वसि 3. *vas* + *i,* (m. f. ?), Clothes.

वसिष्ठ *vasishṭha,* m. The name of a Ṛishi; cf. *vaçishṭha.*

वसु *vasu,* I. adj. **1.** Sweet. **2.** Dry. II. m. **1.** A kind of demigod, Râm. 3, 52, 42; MBh. 1, 2582. **2.** A name of Agni. **3.** Çiva. **4.** Kuvera, Kir. 1, 18. **5.** The sun. **6.** A ray of light, Çiç. 9, 10 (at the end of a comp. adj.; cf. 2. *vas*). **7.** A rein. **8.** The tie of a yoke. **9.** A tree. **10.** The name of two plants. **11.** A kind of fish. **12.** A proper name, Lass. 2. ed. 67, 21. **III.** n. **1.** Wealth, Lass. 100, 8=Rigv. vii. 15, 4 (*vasvas*, ved. abl.); Nal. 5, 48; Daçak. in Chr. 184, 14. **2.** Gold, MBh. 3, 13472. **3.** A gem. **4.** Water. **5.** A sort of salt. **6.** A yellow kind of kidney bean.—Comp. *Punar-*, m. 1. the seventh of the lunar asterisms, Ragh. 11, 36. 2. a name of Vishṇu and Çiva, MBh. 12, 1511. *Purâ-*, m. a name of Bhîshma. *Mitrâvasu*, i.e. *mitra-*, m. a proper name, Çâk. 79, 2. *Vibhâ-*, m. 1. the sun, Lass. 2. ed. 78, 76. 2. the moon, Çriṅgârat. 2. 3. fire.—Cf. ἐΰς, ἐάων; cf. *vasna*.

वसुक *vasu+ka*, I. m. **1.** A tree, Sesbana grandiflora. **2.** A shrub, Asclepias gigantea. II. n. Sea salt (cf. *vaçira*).

वसुदेवभू *vasu-deva-bhû*, m. Kṛishṇa.

वसुधा *vasu-dhâ*, f. The earth, Vikr. d. 16.—Comp. *Kshetra-*, f. cultivated land, Râm. 3, 4, 17.

वसुधाधर *vasudhâ-dhṛi+a*, m. A mountain, Vikr. d. 16.

वसुधार *vasudhâra*, i.e. *vasu-dhṛi+a*, adj. Having wealth, Hit. ii. d. 102 (cf. Böhtl. Ind. Spr. 2220).

वसुंधरा *vasum̄dharâ*, i.e. *vasu+m-dhṛi+a*, f. The earth, Pañch. 101, 23.

वसुमन्त् *vasu+mant*, I. adj., f. *matî*, Wealthy, Johns. Sel. 6, 33. **II.** f. *matî*. **1.** The earth, Vikr. d. 79. **2.** A proper name.

वसूयु *vasûyu*, i.e. *vasûya*, a ved. denomin. derived from *vasu*, +*u*, adj. Desiring wealth, Chr. 289, 4=Rigv. i. 49, 4.

† वस्क *VASK*, वष्क् *VASHK*, वक्क् *VAKK*, i. 1, Âtm. To go.

वस्क *vaska*, m. Perseverance.

वस्कय *vaskaya*, and वस्कयणी *vaskayaṇî*, see *vashka*.

† वस्त् *VAST*, i. 1, Âtm. To torment.

वस्त *vasta*, I. m. A goat, Man. 11, 138. **II.** i.e. 1. *vas+ta*, n. A house.

वस्ति *vasti*, m. and f. **1.** The belly below the navel, Man. 8, 234. **2.** The bladder, Suçr. 2, 201, 12. **3.** A bag made of bladder. **4.** Abiding (vb. 1. *vas*). **5.** pl. The skirt of a cloth (vb. 3. *vas*).—Comp. *Indra-*, the calf (of the leg), Suçr. 1, 348, 16.

वस्तु 1. *vas+tu*, n. **1.** Natural disposition. **2.** Essence, the true object, Vedântas. in Chr. 204, 10; substance, wealth, Lass. 12, 14. **3.** Object, Bhartṛ. 2, 37; thing, Vedântas. in Chr. 204, 9; Pañch. 253, 19; means, Hit. i. d. 30, M.M. **4.** The object of love, Megh. 111. **5.** The subject of a poem or play, Vikr. 3, 8.—Comp. *A-*, n. the unreal, the nothing, Vedântas. in Chr. 204, 9, 10. *A-dvitîya-*, n. the substance besides which there is nothing else, Vedântas. in Chr. 216, 2. *Grathita-*, adj. composed, Vikr. 3, 8.

वस्तुतस् *vastu+tas*, adv. Essentially, in fact, Siddh. Mukt. 76, 4.

वस्तुता *vastu+tâ*, in *parihâsa-*, f. Condition of being the object of derision, Pañch. iii. d. 261.

वस्त्य 1. *vas+tya*, or *vasta+ya*, n. A house.

वस्त्र 3. *vas+tra*, n. m. Cloth, garment, Pañch. 29, 16; bed-linen, 62, 13. —Comp. *Antar-*, n. a lower garment, Kathâs. 4, 52. *Vi-*, adj. deprived of clothes, naked, Lass. 14, 7. *Snâna-*, n. a bathing cloth, Hit. ii. d. 102.

वस्न *vasna*, I. m. **1.** Price. **2.** Wages. II. n. **1.** Wealth. **2.** Abiding (vb. 1. *vas*). **3.** Substance, thing. **4.** Cloth (vb. 3. *vas*). **5.** Skin.—Cf. ὦνος (for ϝόςνος); Lat. venum (acc.), ven -dere. The vb. which is the base of *vasna* is probably also the base of *vasu* (q. cf.), ἐΰ, and ἐσθλός, ἐσλός.

वस्नसा *vasnasâ*, i.e. *ava-snasâ*, f. A tendon, a nerve.

वस्निक *vasnika*, i.e. *vasna*+*ika*, adj., f. *kî*, Living on, or getting, wages.

वस्वौकसारा *vasvaukasârâ*, i.e. probably *vasu-oka-sâra*, f. **1.** The capital of Kuvera, Ragh. 16, 10. **2.** That of Indra. **3.** The name of a lake.

वह् *VAH*, i. 1, Par. Âtm. (cf. 2. *ûh*). **1.** To draw, Indr. 1, 7. **2.** To carry, Vikr. d. 24. **3.** To bear, MBh. 1, 5888; 8169; Hit. i. d. 78, M.M.; iv. d. 59 (*mûrdhnâ*, on one's head, as token of reverence). **4.** To have, Pañch. 218, 5; to feel, Râjat. 5, 11. **5.** To carry away, Man. 8, 189; Lass. 98, 7=Rigv. v. 9, 1 (ved. *vakshi*, ii. 2). **6.** To bring, Râm. 1, 23, 7. **7.** Pass. To ride, MBh. 1, 5337. **8.** To take in matrimony, MBh. 1, 3377. **9.** To spit out, to vomit, Dev. 8, 45 (corr. perhaps *vam*, but cf. *ud*). **10.** To proceed, to move, MBh. 3, 2786. **11.** To flow, MBh. 3, 2936. **12.** To breathe, Gît. 5, 2. Ptcple. of the pf. pass. *ûḍha*, Taken in marriage, Chr. 55, 4. f. *ḍhâ*, A bride, a wife espoused according to the ritual. **Comp.** *An-*, f. *ḍhâ*, a concubine, Sâh. Darp. 36, 9. *Navoḍhâ*, i.e. *nava-*, f. a newly-married woman, Hit. i. d. 211, M.M. Ptcple. of the fut. pass. *vâhya*, To be carried. m. A beast of burthen, Man. 8, 151. n. A carriage. **Comp.** *Râjavâhya*, i.e. *râjan-*, m. a royal elephant. Caus. *vâhaya*, **1.** To cause to be brought, Ragh. 5, 32 (Calc.). **2.** Âtm. To cause to be conveyed, MBh. 1, 3153. **3.** Âtm. To travel, Râm. 2, 92, 13. **4.** Pass. To let one's self be employed as a vehicle, Pañch. 199, 4. **5.** To cause to move, to direct, MBh. 4, 1332. **6.** To cause something (a boat) to carry one's self, to ship in a boat, MBh. 1, 4014. **7.** To cause to take in matrimony, MBh. 1, 4287. **8.** To finish, Megh. 39. Ptcple. of the pf. pass. *vâhita*, n. A heavy burden. **Comp.** *Preta-*, adj. possessed by a spirit.—With the prep. **अति** *ati*, Caus. **1.** To pass (as time), Pañch. 185, 25. **2.** To suffer, Ragh. 13, 28 (Calc.).—With **अधि** *adhi*, *adhyûḍha*, Superseded by another wife, MBh. 2, 2332.—With **अप** *apa*, To carry away, MBh. 1, 2939. *apoḍha*, Left, Ragh. 11, 25. Caus. **1.** To cause to be carried away, Râm. 1, 1, 51. **2.** To cause to retreat, to remove, Pañch. 231, 5. **3.** To cause to be driven away, Daçak. in Chr. 184, 24. **4.** To carry away, Râm. 2, 45, 16. **5.** To ride away, Daçak. in Chr. 188, 19.—With **अभि** *abhi*, *abhivâhya*, see s.v.—With **आ** *â*, **1.** To bring near, Chr. 288, 9=Rigv. i. 48, 9; to bring, Man. 9, 5; Vikr. d. 48. **2.** To bring on, to effect, Vikr. d. 128; to produce, Daçak. in Chr. 182, 14. **3.** To come near, Chr. 288, 11=Rigv. i. 48, 11. Caus. To cause to be brought, MBh. 2, 2770.—With **उदा** *ud-â*, **1.** To convey near, MBh. 3, 15704. **2.** To carry away, Chr. 31, 15. **3.** To marry, MBh. 1, 8830.—With **उद्** *ud*, **1.** To bear on, Chr. 289, 1=Rigv. i. 50, 1. **2.** To lift up, Râm. 3, 55, 9; Pañch. v. d. 24. **3.** To bounce, Pañch. 141, 4. **4.** To bear, Hit. 127, 1; MBh. 1, 4272. **5.** To feel, Mâlat. 96, 4. **6.** To show, Vikr. d. 136. **7.** To carry away, Ragh. 7, 32. **8.** To marry, Man. 3, 8. **9.** To spit out, MBh. 3, 16129. Caus. **1.** To give in matrimony, Pańch. iii. d. 217. **2.** To ask in marriage, Pańch. 261, 5; to marry, Pańch. 181, 5. **3.** To suffer to be expelled, MBh. 1, 3801.—With समुद् *sam-ud*, **1.** To lift up, MBh. 2, 718. **2.** To marry, Râm. 2, 107, 3.—With उप *upa*, **1.** To convey near, MBh. 2, 2064. **2.** To bring about, MBh. 2, 2051. **3.** To bear, Râm. 2, 87, 23. *upoḍha*, **1.** Near. **2.** Collected, Çâk. d. 106; much, Vikr. d. 26; Daçak. in Chr. 194, 6. **3.** Married, Râm. 1, 13, 37. Ptcple. of the fut. pass. Caus. *upavâhya*, m. A king's elephant.—With समुप *sam-upa*, *samupoḍha*, Risen, Utt. Râmach. 131, 14.—With नि *ni*, **1.** To bring, Chr. 297, 19=Rigv. i. 112, 19. **2.** To support, Gît. 1, 16.—With निस् *nis*, To extricate one's self, Lass. 45, 3. Caus. **1.** To pass away, Pańch. 219, 14. **2.** To fulfil, Hit. 106, 4. **3.** To settle, Kathâs. 13, 86.—With प्र *pra*, Par. To draw, Râm. 2, 52, 43. *prauḍha*, **1.** Raised, lifted up. **2.** Forward (as the hand to seize anything). **3.** Confident, bold, Râjat. 5, 457. **4.** Arrogant. **5.** Impudent, Lass. 85, 10. **6.** Full-grown, Çṛiṅgârat. 1; full blowing, Megh. 26 (+ *tva*, n. Fertility [of imagination], Mâlat. 3, 20). **7.** Thick, heavy, dense (darkness, etc.), large, Râjat. 5, 476. **8.** Old. **9.** Married. **10.** Controverted. f. *ḍhâ*, A woman from thirty years of age to fifty-five. **Comp.** *A*-, adj. not bold, gentle, Râjat. 5, 458. *Ati*-, adj. full-blown, Hit. 86, 2, M.M. *An-ati*-, adj. just shot up, Megh. 77.—With अनुप्र *anu-pra*, To convey successively, MBh. 3, 13305.—With वि *vi*, To marry, MBh. 1, 3884. *vyûḍha*, **1.** Arrayed, Râjat. 5, 260. **2.** Compact. **3.** Large, Nal. 12, 13. Caus. **1.** To cause to marry, to grant sexual intercourse, Pańch. 129, 9. **2.** To marry, Lass. 23, 11. Comp. ptcple. fut. pass. *a-vivâhya*, adj. Not to be married, Pańch. iii. d. 218. *Pratijńâ*-, adj., f. *yâ*, To be married according to a vow (under a condition), Hit. 63, 19.—With निर्वि *nis-vi*, To expel, MBh. 1, 6257.—With सम् *sam*, **1.** To convey, Râm. 1, 67, 4. **2.** To bring near, MBh. 3, 13188. Caus. To agitate, Pańch. v. d. 14.—Cf. Lat. vehere, via, uxor (originally perhaps 'one who is about to marry,' a bride, which was perhaps also the original signification of *vadhû*), probably bajulus; Goth. ga-vigan; A.S. wegan; Goth. vigs; A.S. weg; O.H.G. wagan; A.S. waegen; ἄχθος, ὄχος, ὀχέω, ὀχεύω, αὐχήν (cf. *vaha*), ὀχλεύς; also A.S. weddian, To marry; cf. *vadhu*.

वह *vaha*, I. m. **1.** Bearing, conveying. **2.** Any vehicle, as a horse, a car. **3.** The shoulder of an ox. **4.** A road, a way. **5.** Any male river, a current (? Sâv. 4, 31, at the end of a comp. adj. rather, carrying purity, i.e. clear). **6.** Air, wind. **7.** A measure of four *Droṇas*. II. f. *hâ*, A river in general. **III.** Latter part of comp. words; e.g. *pushpa-gandha*-, adj. Bringing flowers and perfumes, Indr. 2, 9. *sarva-gandha*-, adj. Conveying all scents, Man. 1, 76. *durvaha*, i.e. *dus*-, adj., f. *hâ*, Difficult to be borne, Utt. Râmach. 41, 4; or carried, MBh. 12, 3047. *vârttâ*-, m. A chandler, a vendor of grain, oil, etc. *çlâghâ*-, adj., f. *hâ*, Earning praise, Böhtl. Ind. Spr. 1155. *su*-, I. adj. **1.** Bearing well. **2.** Patient. **3.** Easy to be borne. II. f. *hâ*. **1.** The Indian lute. **2.** The name of several plants. *huta*- (vb. *hu*), m. Agni or fire, Megh. 44; Ṛit. 1, 27.—Cf. ὄχος; Lat. via; Goth. vigs; O.H.G. wagan, see *vah*.

वहत *vahata*, i.e. *vahant+a* (vb. *vah*), m. **1.** An ox. **2.** A traveller.

वह्वति *vah + ati* (cf. the last), I. m. **1.** An ox. **2.** A friend. **3.** Air, wind. II. f. *ti*, A river.

वह्तु *vahatu* (vb. *vah*), m. An ox.

वह्न *vah + ana*, n. **1.** Bearing. **2.** Flowing. **3.** Any vehicle. **4.** A raft, a boat.

वहन्त *vahant + a* (vb. *vah*), m. Wind.

वहल *vahala*, I. adj. Hard, firm, compact, dense, Utt. Râmach. 44, 7; Çiç. 9, 16; 8 (*-anurâga*, dark-red). II. n. A raft.

वहित्र *vah + itra*, n. A boat, a vessel.

वहिस्चर *vahiçchara*, i.e. *vahis-chara*, I. adj. Going externally, out of somebody, Daçak. in Chr. 192, 2. II. m. A crab.

वहिष्करण *vahishkaraṇa*, i.e. *vahis-karaṇa*, n. Expelling.

वहिस् *vahis*, perhaps from *avadhi*, I. adv. **1.** Outwards, Pañch. i. d. 211; out, Hit. 29, 5, M.M.; with *bhû*, to go out, Pañch. 141, 19. **2.** Outside the door, Râjat. 5, 353 (i.e. expecting one's introduction to the king). **3.** In the open air, Râjat. 5, 275. **4.** Apart (from the multitude), Man. 2, 79. **5.** Except (viz. on his hair, Kull.), Man. 4, 72. II. prep. **1.** With a gen. a. Besides, Man. 10, 45. b. Outside, Daçak. 184, 7. **2.** With abl. Outside, Râjat. 5, 329.

वह्नि *vah + ni*, m. **1.** A sacrificer, Chr. 288, 11 = Rigv. i. 48, 11. **2.** Fire, Pañch. ii. d. 96; or its deity, Râm. 3, 53, 60. **3.** Digestion, appetite. **4.** Marking-nut plant. **5.** Lead-wort, Plumbago zeylanica.

वह्य *vah + ya*, I. n. **1.** A vehicle in general. **2.** A cart. II. f. *yâ*, The wife of a Muni.

1. **वा** *VA* (originally *av + â*, cf. *ἄημι*), ii. 2, Par. **1.** To blow (as the wind), Man. 4, 122; Pañch. i. d. 353. **2.** † To hurt. i. 4, *vâya* (gramm. **वै** *vai*, i. 1), Par. To become dry, to dry. Ptcple. **1.** *vâta*, Blown. **2.** *vâna*, Dry, dried (cf. both s.v.).—With the prep. **आ** *â*, To blow upon (with acc.), Kir. 5, 36.—With **निस्** *nis*, **1.** To cease blowing. **2.** To be extinguished, Çâk. 91, 11, Chezy. **3.** To be refreshed, Çiç. 1, 65. *nirvâta*, see under *vâta*. *nirvâṇa*, **1.** Extinguished, Hariv. 2391. **2.** Liberated from existence, MBh. 13, 2178. n. **1.** Being extinguished, expiring, MBh. 4, 716. **2.** Final beatitude, ib. 14, 543. **3.** Bliss, happiness, ib. 3, 10438; Çâk. 33, 2. **4.** Repose. Comp. *A-*, adj. not yet calm, still wild, Ragh. 1, 71. Caus. *vâpaya*, **1.** To extinguish, MBh. 1, 1608; to cool, Mâlat. 128, 15. **2.** To delight, Ragh. 9, 36 (Calc.).—With **परिनिस्** *pari-nis*, *a-parinirvâṇa*, adj. Not completely finished, Çâk. 39, 20.—With **प्र** *pra*, **1.** To blow vehemently, Pañch. 169, 6. **2.** To blow, Râm. 2, 71, 25. **3.** To smell, to yield a scent, MBh. 1, 6934. *pravâta*, Agitated by the wind, Kumâras. 1, 47. Caus. To dry, MBh. 1, 8431.—With **वि** *vi*, To blow, Ṛit. 6, 22. — With **सम्** *sam*, To blow at the same time, MBh. 4, 1288.—Cf. *ἄημι*, *ἄελλα*, *ἀήρ*, *μετέωρος*, *ἀείρω* (*ἀερjω* denomin., cf. *ἀέῤῥω*), *ἄρδην*, *ἀρτάω*, *ἀορτήρ*, *αἰωρέω*, *αὖρα*, probably *αὐλός*, *οὖρος*; *ἀϋτμήν* (= *âtman*), *ἀτμή*; probably Lat. vanus, vapor (from the Caus.); Goth. vaian; O.H.G. wadal; see also *vâta*.

2. **वा** *vâ*, A particle of, **1.** Comparison, As, Draup. 7, 15; Râm. 1, 10, 37. **2.** On the one side, Pañch. 43, 14

(*kshamyatâm̃ yad vâlpe kim api praṇaye nâtirekâd ayuktam̃ tad anushṭhitam̃ tava*, What on the one side must be indulged to a very feeble affection, that, done by thee, will not be unsuitable on account of the excess of thy love). **3.** Option, Or; *vâ—vâ*, Either—or, Hit. ii. d. 159; Chr. 9, 34; Hit. 73, 22 (*kim̃ vâ—na vâ*, Is it—or not). **4.** Doubt, Or if, but if, Pañch. 246, 21. **5.** Opposition, But, Chr. 10, 8; Hiḍ. 4, 2. **6.** Exception, Only. **7.** Asseveration, Indeed, even, Pañch. pr. d. 6. **8.** Conjunction, And. **9.** With preceding *atha* (cf. *atha*), or also, Hit. iii. d. 95; or, Pañch. 142, 5; or if, Pañch. 137, 20; or rather, Pañch. 82, 17; or, 90, 4; but, Pañch. 27, 1; 38, 17; certainly, Vikr. 70, 21.—Cf. Lat. ve; ἤ.

वांशिक *vâm̃çika*, i. e. *vam̃ça+ika*, m. A flute-piper.

वाक *vâka*, I. i.e. *vaka+a*, **1.** adj. Relating to a crane. **2.** n. A flight of cranes. **II.** i.e. *vach+a*, latter part of comp. words, Sounding, speaking, cf. *chakravâka, chîrîvâka*.—Comp. *Nis-*, m. a proper name, MBh. 12, 8901.

वाक्य *vâkya*, i. e. *vach+ya*, n. **1.** Speech, Böhtl. Ind. Spr. 2375; *mama vâkyât*, In my name, Pañch. 142, 24. **2.** A sentence, Pañch. 41, 17. **3.** A rule.—Comp. *Nirvâkya*, i.e. *nis-*, adj., f. *yâ*, speechless, Râm. 6, 98, 14. *Mahâ-*, n. a principal sentence, Vedântas. in Chr. 210, 9; 205, 21.

वाक्यतस् *vâkya+tas*, adv. Conformably to the saying, Pañch. i. d. 410.

वागर *vâgara*, m. **1.** A whetstone. **2.** A scholar. **3.** One desirous of final emancipation. **4.** A fearless one. **5.** Certainty. **6.** An obstacle. **7.** Submarine fire. **8.** A wolf.

वागारु *vâgâru*, adj. One who disappoints.

वागुरा *vâgurâ*, f. A net for deer and wild animals, a snare, Hit. ii. d. 144.

वागुरिक *vâgurâ+ika*, m. A hunter, Ragh. 9, 53.

वाग्गुद *vâgguda*, m. A sort of bird, Man. 12, 64.

वाग्घस्तवन्त् *vâgghastavant*, i. e. *vâch-hasta + vant*, adj. Possessed of speech and hands, Böhtl. Ind. Spr. 1106.

वाग्मित्व *vâgmitva*, i.e. *vâgmin+tva*, n. Eloquence, Râjat. 5, 474.

वाग्मिन् *vâgmin*, i.e. *vâch+min*, adj., f. *nî*, **1.** Talkative. **2.** Eloquent, Pañch. iii. d. 84.

वाघन्त् *vâghant* (probably ptcple. pres. of a lost vb. *vâgh*=Lat. vāgire; εὔχομαι) m. Praying, Chr. 294, 6=Rigv. i. 88, 6.

† **वाङ्क्ष्** *VÂṄKSH* (perhaps akin to the last), i. 1, Par. To wish.—Cf. O.H.G. wunsc, wunskian; A.S. wiscan.

वाङ्मय *vâṅmaya*, i.e. *vâch+maya*, I. adj., f. *yî*. **1.** Relating to speech, Bhag. 17, 15. **2.** Endowed with speech, Johns. Sel. 94, 53. **3.** Consisting of words, Ragh. 3, 28. **4.** Eloquent. **II.** n. Eloquence. **III.** f. *yî*, Sarasvatî.

वाच् *vâch* (vb. *vach*), f. **1.** Speaking, Böhtl. Ind. Spr. 2647. **2.** Speech, Pañch. iii. d. 112. **3.** A word, Râm. 3, 51, 20 (voice?). **4.** A phrase, a proverb. **5.** Sarasvatî. **6.** Voice, Chr. 44, 36.—**Comp.** *An-ṛita-*, adj. speaking an untruth, lying, Râm. 1, 6, 15. *A-bhaya-*, f. promise of safety, Hit. 59, 2. *A-mogha-*, adj. one whose speech is not idle. *Âpta-*, 1. f. the word of a trustworthy person, Ragh. 10, 29. 2. adj. worthy of trust, Çâk. d. 121. *Dur-vâch*, i.e. *dus-*, f. abuse, MBh. 1, 3076. *Dushṭa-*, m. a defamer, Man. 8, 386.

Nirvâch, i.e. *nis-*, adj. dumb, Bhâg. P. 4, 25, 54. *Pra-*, adj. eloquent. *Satya-*, I. adj. speaking truth, Râm. 3, 53, 12; Hit. 120, 15. II. m. 1. a Ṛishi. 2. a crow.

वाचंयम *vâchaṁyama*, i.e. *vâch* + *am-yam* + *a*, m. A sage practising rigid taciturnity.

वाचक *vâchaka*, i.e. *vach* + *aka*, I. adj. 1. Speaking. 2. Expressed by words, signifying, Vedântas. in Chr. 213, 2. II. m. 1. A word, a significant sound. 2. A speaker. 3. A messenger.

वाचन *vâchana*, i.e. *vach*, Caus., + *ana*, n. in *svasti-*, n. A preparatory religious rite in which the Brâhmaṇas invoke the blessings of the gods, etc., Vikr. 44, 14; Mâlav. 56, 1 (Prâkṛ.).

वाचनिक *vâchanika*, i.e. *vachana* + *ika*, adj. 1. Verbal. 2. Textual.

वाचस्पति *vâch* + *as-pati*, m. Vṛihaspati, preceptor of the gods, Pańch. pr. d. 2.

वाचस्पत्य *vâchaspatya*, i.e. *vâchaspati* + *ya*, adj. Declared by Vâchaspati, Hit. iii. d. 96.

वाचा *vâchâ*, i.e. *vâch* + *â*, f. 1. Speech, Vedântas. in Chr. 216, 18. 2. A holy word, Pańch. 221, 7 (oath).

वाचाट *vâchâṭa*, and **वाचाल** *vâchâla* (vb. *vach*), adj. 1. Talkative, Man. 3, 8 (*ṭ*). 2. Boasting, Megh. 92 (*l*).

वाचिक *vâch*, and *vâchâ*, + *ika*, I. adj. 1. Verbal. 2. Done by speech, Man. 12, 9. II. n. News, intelligence.—Comp. *Tri-*, adj. given by three holy words (by an oath), Pańch. 222, 16; 17. *Daṇḍa-*, i.e. *daṇḍavâch* + *ika*, adj. performed by deeds or words, Man. 8, 6.

वाच्यता *vâchya* + *tâ* (vb. *vach*), f. 1. Blame, Hit. iii. d. 127. 2. Ill repute. 3. The quality of being predicable.—Comp. *A-*, f. blame (cf. *a-vâchya*, s.v. *vach*), Kir. 11, 53.

वाज *vâja*, i.e. *vaj* + *a*, I. m. and n. A wing (see comp.). II. m. 1. Food, sacrificial food, Chr. 288, 11 = Rigv. i. 48, 11. 2. Battle, Chr. 291, 5 = Rigv. i. 85, 5. 3. Speed. 4. The feather of an arrow. 5. Sound. III. n. 1. Clarified butter. 2. Water. 3. Rice. 4. The acidulous mixture of ground meal and water left to ferment.—Comp. *Gṛidhra-*, adj. adorned with a vulture's feathers, MBh. 9, 1413. *Chitra-*, adj. adorned with variegated feathers, Bhâg. P. 4, 10, 11. *Patra-*, adj. endowed with feathers, Hariv. 13254.—Cf. perhaps Engl. wing.

वाजिन् *vâjin*, i.e. *vâja* + *in*, I. adj. Swift, Chr. 290, 6 = Rigv. i. 64, 6. II. m. 1. A sacrificer, Chr. 292, 3 = i. 86, 3. 2. A horse, Pańch. 218, 7; Râjat. 5, 143. 3. An arrow. 4. A bird. III. f. *nî*, A mare.—Comp. *Çveta-*, m. 1. the moon. 2. Arjuna.

वाजिन *vâjina* i.e. *vâja* + *in* + *a*, n. The scum of curdled milk, Hemach. 3, 495 (= 831, Böhtl.).

वाजिनीवन्त् *vâjin* + *î* + *vant*, adj., f. *vatî*, Possessed of sacrifices (?), Chr. 287, 6 = Rigv. i. 48, 6.

वाञ्छ् *VÂŃCHH* (a form of *vâńksh*, with *chh* for *ksh*), i. 1, Par. (also Âtm., Hit. i. d. 186, M.M.). 1. To wish, to desire, Hit. iii. d. 18. 2. To pursue (?), Pańch. i. d. 421. Ptcple. of the pf. pass. *vâńchhita*, n. Wish, Vikr. d. 28; Pańch. iii. d. 42.—With the prep. **अभि** *abhi*, 1. To wish, Hit. i. d. 161; Pańch. i. d. 134. 2. To long after, Hit. i. d. 165, M.M.—With **सम्** *sam*, To wish, Bhaṭṭ. 17, 53.—Cf. *vâńksh*.

वाञ्छन *vâńchh* + *ana*, n. Wishing.

वाञ्छा *vâñchh+â*, f. Wish, desire, Pañch. ii. d. 165.—Comp. *Sva-*, instr. ad libitum, Hit. ii. d. 91.

वाञ्छिन् *vâñchh+in*, I. adj., f. *nî*, Wishing, desirous. II. f. *nî*, A libidinous woman.

वाट *vâṭa*, i.e. *vaṭa+a*, I. adj. Made of the Indian fig-tree, Man. 2, 45. II. m., f. *ṭî*, and n. 1. An enclosure, Johns. Sel. 40, 36 ; a grove (?), Bhâg. P. 1, 6, 11 (*ṭî*). 2. A mud wall. 3. The groin. 4. A road. III. f. *ṭî*. 1. The site of a building. 2. A house.—Comp. *Govâṭa*, m. a cow-pen, Hariv. 3397. *Pushpa-vâṭî*, f. a flower-garden, Pañch. 221, 10 (erroneously *pushya-*). *Yajña-*, m. a place prepared and enclosed for a sacrifice, Johns. Sel. 95, 64. *Veça-vâṭa*, house and court, Daçak. in Chr. 192, 10. *Çmaçâna-*, m. a cemetery, Mâlat. 77, 7.

वाटधान *vâṭadhâna*, m. The son of an outcaste Brâhmaṇa by a female Brâhmaṇa, Man. 10, 21.

वाटिका *vâṭikâ*, i.e. *vâṭî+ka*, f. 1. The site of a house. 2. A garden, Pañch. 221, 10.—Comp. *Vṛiksha-*, f. an orchard, Çâk. 8, 21.

वाट्या *vâṭyâ*, f., and **वाट्याल** *vâṭyâ+la*, m., *lî*, f. A plant, Sida cordifolia, Lass. Pentap. p. 64, v. 10 (*la*) ; p. 66, v. 33 (*yâ*)=MBh. 8, 2034 ; 2059 (vv. rr.)

वाड् *VÂḌ*, see *bâḍ*.

वाडव *vâḍava*, see *bâḍava*.

वाढ *vâḍha* (cf. *vahala* and *bahu*), I. adj., comparat. *sâḍhiyaṁs*, superl. *sâḍhishṭha*. 1. Hard, firm ; *sâḍhiyaṁs*, firmest, Daçak. in Chr. 195, 19. 2. Much. II. acc. sing. *ḍham*, adv. 1. Much, excessively, Çiç. 9, 77. 2. Indeed, truly, Râm. 3, 51, 6 ; Çiç. 9, 51. 3. Well, very well, Pañch. 24, 11 ; yes, Daçak. in Chr. 192, 9.

वाण *vâṇa* (also **बाण** *bâṇa*), I. m. 1. (perhaps for *parṇa*), An arrow, Pañch. 128, 1. 2. Fire. 3. The udder of a cow. 4. A pipe, Chr. 292, 10=Rigv. i. 85, 10 (with *dhamantas*, playing the pipe, i.e. roaring). 5. Alone. 6. The name of an Asura. II. m., and f. *ṇâ*. 1. The feathered part of an arrow. 2. Blue Barleria, Kir. 4, 28 (*ṇâ*) ; 10, 24 (double meaning, also arrow).—Comp. *A-sama-*, *Kusuma-*, and *Pañcha(n)-*, m. Kâma (being armed with five arrows), Gît. 4, 6 ; Pañch. 128, 1 ; Megh. 104. *Dṛishṭi-*, m. an arrow-like look, Hit. i. d. 193, M.M. *Vâra-*, m. and n. an iron cuirass, or a thick quilted jacket, Ragh. 4, 55.

वाणमय *vâṇa+maya*, adj., f. *yî*, Consisting in arrows, Chr. 34, 9.

वाणासन *vâṇâsana*, i.e. *vâṇa-asana*, n. A bow, Çâk. 20, 15.

वाणि and **वाणी** *vâṇî* (vb. *ve*), f. 1. Weaving. 2. A weaver's loom.

वाणिज *vâṇija*, i.e. *vaṇij+a*, m. A merchant.

वाणिजिक *vâṇijika*, and **वाणिज्य** *vâṇijya*, see *bâṇ°*.

वाणिन् *vâṇin*, i.e. *vâṇa*, and *vâṇî*, *+in*, I. adj., f. *nî*. 1. Having an arrow or arrows, Arj. 5, 25 ; Râm. 3, 55, 12. 2. Speaking. II. f. *nî*. 1. An intriguing woman. 2. An intoxicated woman, literally and figuratively. 3. A dancing girl.

वाणी *vâṇî*, 1. Speech, Hit. i. d. 99, M.M. 2. Voice, Chr. 294, 6=Rigv. i. 88, 6 ; Pañch. 186, 17. 3. A literary production, Utt. Râmach. 177, 6. 4. *Sarasvatî*, the goddess of speech, Brahmav. 2, 78. See *vâṇi*.

वात् *VÂT*, i, 10 (rather a denomin. derived from *vâta*), Par. 1. To fan or ventilate. **2.** † To give pleasure in travelling. **3.** † To serve. **4.** † To go.

वात *vâta*, i.e. *vânt*, ptcple. pres. of *vâ*, + *a*, m. **1.** Air, wind, Vikr. d. 25; breeze, 67, 8. **2.** Rheumatism, gout, Çriñgârat. 14.—**Comp.** *A-*, (m. or n.), absence of wind, quiet, Lass. 97, 11 = Rigv. vi. 64, 4. *Anu-*, m. the windward side; °*te*, loc. to the windward, Man. 3, 203. *Nirvâta*, i.e. *nis-*, I. adj. 1. not windy, calm. 2. sheltered from the wind, Hit. 80, 20. II. m. absence of wind, Pañch. iii. d. 54. *Purovâta*, i.e. *puras-*, m. east wind, Vikr. d. 81. *Pûti-*, m. a fart, Bhâg. P. 5, 5, 30. *Prati-*, see s.v.—Cf. Lat. ventus; Goth. vinds; A.S. wind; O.H.G. wetar; A.S. weder (cf. *vâtara*); ἐτώσιος.

वातकिन् *vâta* + *ka* + *in*, adj. Rheumatic, gouty.

वातप्रमी *vâta-pra-mî*, m. and f. A swift antelope.

वातमज *vâta* + *m-aj* + *a*, m. A swift antelope, Bhaṭṭ. 2, 17.

वातर *vâta* + *ra*, adj. Windy, stormy. —Cf. Goth. vintrus; A.S. winter.

वातरूष *vâta-rûsh* + *a* (perhaps rather vb. *rush*), m. **1.** A gale. **2.** The rainbow. **3.** A bribe.

वातर्द्धि *vâtarddhi*, i.e. *vâta-ṛiddhi*, m. **1.** A sort of cup or vessel of wood, with an iron foot. **2.** A club.

वातल *vâta* + *la* (cf. *vâtara*), **I.** adj. **1.** Windy, stormy. **2.** Flatulent. **II.** m. **1.** Wind. **2.** A sort of pulse, Cicer arietinum. **III.** f. *lâ*, A morbid state of the uterus.—**Comp.** *A-*, adj. not causing flatulence, Suçr. 1, 221, 17.

वातापि *vâtâpi*, m. The name of an Asura devoured by Agastya, Râm. 3, 49, 49, sqq.; MBh. 3, 8619.

वातायन *vâtâyana*, i.e. *vâta-ayana*, I. n. **1.** A window, Pañch. 46, 11. **2.** A porch, a pavilion, Utt. Râmach. 22, 13. **II.** m. **1.** A horse. **2.** A proper name, Çâk. 81, 4.

वाति *vâti*, m. **1.** (vb. *vâ*), Air, wind. **2.** The sun. **3.** The moon.

वातिक *vâtika*, i.e. *vâta* + *ika*, **I.** adj. **1.** Produced by wind. **2.** Windy. **3.** Rheumatic. **4.** Mad, Sâh. Darp. 286, 14. **II.** n. Fever or inflammation, ascribed to a vitiated state of the aerial humour.

वातुल and **वातूल** *vâtûla* (from *vâta*), **I.** adj. **1.** Gouty. **2.** Mad (cf. the last), Hit. ii. d. 26 (*tŭ*); Râjat. 5, 83 (*tû*). **II.** m. A whirlwind.

वात्या *vâtyâ*, i.e. probably *vâta* + *ya*, f. A gale, a whirlwind, Kir. 5, 39; Râjat. 5, 477.

वात्सल्य *vâtsalya*, i.e. *vatsala* + *ya*, n. Tenderness, Pañch. 221, 1; Vikr. d. 147; love, Hit. ii. d. 4.

वात्स्यायन *vâtsyâyana*, i.e. *vâtsya*, patronym. of *vatsa*, + *âyana*, patronym., m. The name of a Muni, Pañch. 45, 9.

वाद *vâda*, i.e. *vad* + *a*, m. **1.** Speaking, Daçak. in Chr. 198, 11. **2.** Sound, Pañch. 248, 11; words, i. d. 475. **3.** Discussion, controversy, Man. 12, 46. **4.** Exposition of holy texts, Man. 6, 50. **5.** Demonstrated conclusion, result. **6.** Accusation. **7.** Report, Daçak. in Chr. 191, 19.—**Comp.** *Artha-*, m. praise, Vedântas. in Chr. 216, 14. *Âçîrvâda*, i.e. *âçis-*, m. a benediction, Pañch. 208, 7. *Itihâsa-*, m. a tale, Mâlat. 47, 1. *Uchchais-*, m. boasting, Utt. Râmach. 136, 2. *Dharma-*, m. a conversation concerning law or virtue, Râm. 5, 48, 4. *Paksha-*, m. uttering one's opinion, MBh. 7, 6009. *Pâṇi-*, n. clapping of the hands, Râm. 2, 65, 4. *Pratikûla-*, m. objection, in *a-*, adj. not opposing, MBh. 3, 10265. *Mithyâ-*, adj. speaking untruth, lying, Pańch. iii. d. 85. *Loka-*, m. rumour, Daçak. in Chr. 185, 14. *Viṇâ-*, m. a lutanist. *Sâma(n)-*, m. pl. words of conciliation, Pańch. iii. d. 27. *Hîna-* (vb. *hâ*), m. contradictory evidence, prevarication. *Hetu-*, m. disputation.

वादक *vâdaka*, i.e. *vad*, Caus., + *aka*, adj. sbst. **1.** A musician, Johns. Sel. 52, 116. **2.** A speaker.—Comp. *Pâṇi-*, m. one who makes a clapping of the hands, Râm. 2, 65, 4.

वादन *vâdana*, i.e. *vad*, Caus., + *ana*, n. Instrumental music, Man. 2, 178.

वादि *vâdi* (vb. *vad*), adj. **1.** Speaking. **2.** Wise.

वादित्र *vâditra*, i.e. *vad*, Caus., + *tra*, n. **1.** A musical instrument, Man. 4, 64. **2.** Instrumental music, Indr. 3, 9.

ऽवादित्व *-vâditva*, i.e. *vâdin* + *tva*, n. in *satya-*, Veracity, Hit. i. d. 98, M.M.

वादिन् *vâdin*, i.e. *vad* + *in*, I. adj. **1.** Speaking, Vikr. d. 118; Johns. Sel. 57, 164; a speaker, Bhartṛ. 3, 53. **2.** Asserting. **3.** Disputing, Bhartṛ. 3, 47. II. m. **1.** An expounder of the law. **2.** A plaintiff, Lass. 92, 2. **3.** Key-note. — Comp. *Artha-*, adj. speaking truth, Pańch. 161, 19; cf. Böhtl. Ind. Spr. 467. *Ahaṁvâdin*, i.e. *aham-* (see *asmad*), adj. self-conceited, Bhag. 18, 26. *Uttara-*, m. the defendant (in an action at law), Yâjń. 2, 17. *Ṛita-*, adj. speaking the truth, MBh. 13, 4402. *Dharma-*, adj. one who likes to speak of law or virtue, Pańch. 166, 14. *Paṇḍita-*, adj. pretending to be wise, Pańch. i. d. 437. *Pûrva-*, m. the plaintiff (in an action at law), Yâjń. 2, 17. *Pratikûla-*, adj. contradicting, opposing, MBh. 5, 1359. *Priya-*, adj. speaking agreeably, as one wishes, Pańch. ii. d. 171; Hit. pr. d. 19, M.M. *Brahmavâdin*, i.e. *brahman-*, m. 1. one who recites the Vedas, Man. 6, 39. 2. an expounder of the Vedas, Man. 2, 113. 3. a follower of the Vedânta system. *Mantra-*, adj. sbst. one who is conversant with charms, Pańch. 210, 17; 43, 10; Lass. 16, 12. *Mithyâ-*, adj., f. *nî*, lying, a liar, Pańch. 52, 14. *Satya-*, adj., f. *nî*, speaking truth, Pańch. 100, 23. *Hîna-* (vb. *hâ*), adj. (speaking deficiently), 1. dumb. 2. contradictory. 3. inadmissible (as evidence). 4. cast in law, Pańch. 166, 18.

वाध् *VADH*, **वाध** *vâdha*, see *bâdh*, *bâdha*.

वाधुक्य *vâdhukya*, i.e. *vadhû* + *ka* + *ya*, n. Marriage.

वाधू *vâdhû* (vb. *vah*, cf. *vadhu*), f. A boat, a vessel.

वान A. i.e. *vâ* + *na*, I. adj. Dry, Nalod. 2, 26. II. m., f. *nâ*, and n. Dry fruit. III. n. **1.** Moving. **2.** A heavy sea. **3.** A mat of straw. **4.** Living. **5.** A perfume. B. n. A hole in the wall of a house. C. i.e. *vana* + *a*, I. adj. Relating to a wood, a house. II. n. A number of woods, Nalod. 3, 6.

वानप्रस्थ *vânaprastha*, i.e. *vana-pra-stha* + *a*, m. **1.** The Brâhmaṇa of the third order, who lives in woods, a hermit, Man. 6, 87. **2.** The name of two particular trees.

वानर *vânara*, i.e. *vanara* + *a*, I. m., and f. *rî*, A monkey, Pańch. 203, 3; 206, 15. II. adj., f. *rî*, Belonging to a monkey, MBh. 13, 411.

वानस्पत्य *vânaspatya*, i.e. *vanaspati* + *ya*, I. adj. Belonging to a tree, Man. 8, 339. II. m. and n. (Râm. 6, 96, 13), A tree bearing fruits from blossoms, as the mango.

वानीर *vânîra*, m. A sort of cane, Calamus rotang, Megh. 42; Ragh. 13, 30.

वान्ताशिन् *vântâçin*, i.e. *vânta* (vb. *vam*) -*aç* + *in*, m. A foul-feeding demon, Man. 3, 109.

वान्ति *vânti*, i.e. *vam* + *ti*, f. Vomiting.

वान्या *vânyâ*, i.e. *vana*+*ya*, f. A multitude of groves.

वाप *vâpa*, i.e. *vap* + *a*, m. Shaving, shearing, Man. 11, 108.

वापक *vâpaka*, see *vâyaka*.

वापन *vâpana*, i. e. *vap* + *ana*, n. Shaving, shearing, Man. 11, 78.

वापि and **वापी** *vâpî*, f. A pond, Ṛit. 6, 3 (*pi*); Pañch. iii. d. 91 (*pî*); an oblong reservoir of water.—**Comp.** *Svar-vâpî*, f. the Gaṅgâ.

वाम *vâma*, **I.** adj. **1.** Left (not right), Râjat. 5, 97; Megh. 94. **2.** Reverse, adverse, Pañch. ii. d. 87; opposite, Çâk. d. 93 (those who act in an opposite way). **3.** Bad, wicked, crooked, Kir. 11, 24. **4.** Short. **5.** Beautiful, Pañch. i. d. 152. **II.** m. **1.** Çiva. **2.** Kâma. **3.** An udder. **4.** An animal. **5.** A snake. **III.** f. *mâ*. **1.** A woman. **2.** Gaurî. **3.** Lakshmî. **4.** Sarasvatî. **IV.** f. *mî*. **1.** A mare, Ragh. 5, 32. **2.** A she-ass. **3.** A young female elephant. **4.** The female of a jackal. **V.** n. Wealth, Chr. 287, 1 = Rigv. i. 48, 1.—Cf. O.H.G. winistar; A.S. wynstre.

वामक *vâma*+*ka*, **I.** adj. Left, Mâlat. 5, 7. **II.** n. A kind of gesture, Vikr. 59, 20.

वामत्व *vâma*+*tva*, n. Disfavour, Mâlat. 146, 10.

वामन *vâmana* (from *vâma*), **I.** adj. **1.** Dwarfish, Johns. Sel. 96, 79; a dwarf, Johns. Sel. 95, 63; Bhâg. P. 8, 19, title. **2.** Pressed flat or down, Böhtl. Ind. Spr. 830 (*vâmanî-kṛita*, Pressed down). **3.** Vile, low. **II.** m. **1.** A name of Vishṇu (on account of his *avatâra* in the shape of a dwarf, Bhâg. P. 8, 19). **2.** The elephant that supports the south quarter, Râm. 1, 6, 23. **III.** f. *nâ*, The name of an Apsaras, Lass. 2. ed. 50, 23. **IV.** f. *nî*, A female dwarf.

वामलूर *vâmalûra* (cf. *vamra*, *valmî*), m. An ant-hill.

वाय *vâya*, i.e. *ve* + *a*, m. Weaving. —**Comp.** *Tantu-*, *Tantra-*, m. 1. a weaver, Man. 8, 397; Râm. 2, 90, 15 Gorr. 2. a spider. *Tunna-* (vb. *tud*), m. a tailor, Man. 4, 214.

वायक *vâyaka*, **I.** m. A multitude. **II.** adj. Weaving, a weaver (? in *paṭṭikâ-*, A weaver of ribbons, Râm. 2, 90, 21 Gorr.; who has *vâpaka*, which Böhtl. changes in *vâyaka*).

वायन *vâyana*, n. Sweetmeats.

वायव *vâyava*, i.e. *vâyu* + *a*, **I.** adj. Windy. **II.** f. *vi*, The region of the wind, the north-west.

वायव्य *vâyavya*, i.e. *vâyu* + *ya*, adj. **1.** Relating to the wind, Arj. 3, 30. **2.** Coming from, belonging to, its deity, Vikr. d. 18; Utt. Râmach. 143, 5. **3.** Sacred to the deity of the wind. Chr. 31, 11.

वायस *vâyasa* (probably *vayas* + *a*, Long-lived), **I.** m. **1.** A crow, Pañch. 140, 16. **2.** Two plants. **II.** f. *sî*. **1.** A she-crow, Hit. 67, 13. **2.** A species of fig, Ficus oppositifolia. **3.** A vegetable, Solanum indicum. **III.** adj. **1.** (*vâyasa* + *a*), Used by crows (?), Bhâg. P. 1, 5, 10. **2.** (*vayas* + *a*), f. *sî*, Consisting of birds, Nalod. 1, 27.—**Comp.** *Nis-*, adj. deprived of crows, Pañch. 148, 12.

वायु *vâ* + *yu*, m. **1.** Air, wind, Pañch. 184, 11; its deity, Man. 1, 23. **2.** The air of the body. **3.** Morbid affection of the windy humour.—**Comp.** *Mahâ-*, m. air as element, Bhâshâp. 43.

वायुज *vâyu-ja* (literally, Produced by air), Pańch. 44, 15, name of a tree (? cf. my transl. n. 204).

वार् *vâr*, n. Water, Nalod. 3, 51.—Cf. *οὖρον*, *οὐρέω*, *οὐρία*, perhaps *ὑρτήρ*, *ὕρχη*; Lat. urina, urceus, urna.

वार *vâra*, I. m. **1.** A multitude, Daçak. in Chr. 190, 23; Râjat. 5, 342; a troop, ib. 453. **2.** A moment. **3.** Opportunity, time, Pańch. 256, 7. **4.** Turn, Hit. 67, 21. **5.** A day of the week, Hit. 48, 3 (*bhaṭṭâraka-*, Sunday). **6.** A gate. **7.** A name of Çiva. **II.** acc. *ram*, adv. doubled, *vâraṁvâram*, Repeatedly, Hit. 67, 12. **III.** instr. *reṇa*, adv. Frequently. **IV.** n. A vessel for holding spirituous liquor.—**Comp.** *Eka-vâra+m*, adv. 1. once, Pańch. 216, 2. 2. only once, Bhartṛ. 3, 16. 3. at once, Pańch. 174, 23. 4. suddenly. *Bahu-*, m. pl. many times, Bhaṭṭ. 3, 32. *Madhu-*, m. drinking repeatedly. *Ravi-*, m. Sunday. *Vâṇa-*, m. (vb. *vṛi*), 1. a cuirass. 2. armour. *Viçva-*, adj. (vb. *vṛi*), containing every boon, Chr. 288, 13=Rigv. i. 48, 13. *Soma-*, m. Monday.—Cf. *ἦρα*.

वारक *vâraka*, i.e. *vṛi+aka*, I. adj. Opposing, an agent of resistance. **II.** m. **1.** A horse's paces. **2.** A horse. **III.** n. **1.** The seat of pain. **2.** A sort of fragrant grass, Brahmav. 2, 50.

वारकिन् *vârakin*, i.e. *vâraka+in*, m. **1.** An enemy. **2.** The ocean. **3.** A horse with good marks. **4.** An ascetic.

वारङ्ग *vâranga*, m. The narrow end of a sword, sickle, etc., to which the handle is fastened.

वारटा *vâraṭâ*, i.e. *varaṭa+a*, f. A goose.

वारण *vâraṇa*, i.e. *vṛi+ana*, I. m. **1.** Armour. **2.** An elephant, Hit. ii. d. 28. **II.** n. **1.** Warding off, Bhartṛ. 2, 14. **2.** Resistance. **3.** Obstacle. **4.** Protecting.—**Comp.** *Atapa-*, *Ushṇa-*, n. a parasol, Ragh. 3, 70; Kumâras. 5, 52. *Digvâraṇa*, i.e. *diç-*, m. an elephant supposed to support a quarter of the world, MBh. 3, 9929. *Hasta-*, n. resisting an assault.

वारणावत *vâraṇâvata*, i.e. *vâraṇa+vant+a* (m. or n.), A name of Hastinâpura, Hiḍ. 1, 30.

वारला *vâralâ*, i.e. *varala+a*, f. **1.** A wasp. **2.** A goose (cf. *varaṭâ*).

वाराणसी *vârâṇasî*, f. The city Benares, Lass. 5, 20.

वाराह *vârâha*, i.e. *varâha+a*, I. adj. Relating to a boar, boarish, Johns. Sel. 93, 52. **II.** f. *hî*. **1.** A sow. **2.** The earth. **3.** One of the divine mothers. **4.** A measure. **5.** An esculent root, Dioscorea.

वारि *vâri*, I. (cf. *vâr*), n. Water, Pańch. ii. d. 149; fluidity, i. d. 139. **II.** f., also **वारी** *vârî*, **1.** A water-pot. **2.** (vb. *vṛi*), A hole for catching elephants. **3.** (vb. *vṛi*), A rope for fastening elephants. **III.** f. *ri*. **1.** A place where elephants are tied up. **2.** A captive. **3.** Sarasvatî.—**Comp.** *Kuça-*, n. water in which *kuça* grass is boiled, Man. 11, 148. *Kshârâmlodakavâri*, i.e. *kshâra-amla-udaka-*, n. pl. ashes, acids, and water, Man. 5, 114. *Chandana-*, n. water mixed with sandal, Râm. 3, 53, 57. *Netra-*, n. a tear, tears, Râm. 2, 111, 12 Gorr.

वारिज *vâri-ja*, I. adj. Produced in or by water. **II.** m. **1.** A conch-shell. **2.** Any bivalve shell. **III.** n. **1.** A lotus, Bhartṛ. 2, 46. **2.** Salt.

वारित्रा *vâri-trâ*, f. An umbrella.

वारिद *vâri-da* (vb. *dâ*), I. adj. Yielding water. II. m. A cloud, Utt. Râmach. 120, 14; Râjat. 5, 189.

वारिधर *vâri-dhara*, m. A cloud, Vikr. d. 73; Râjat. 5, 377.

वारिधि *vâridhi*, i.e. *vâri-dhâ* (cf. *nidhi*), m. The ocean, Kir. 1, 23.—Comp. *Kshîra-*, m. the sea of milk, Kathâs. 22, 188.

वारिरुह *vâri-ruh + a*, n. A lotus, Kir. 5, 13.

वारुण *vâruṇa*, i.e. *varuṇa + a*, I. adj., f. *ṇî*. 1. Relating, belonging to Varuṇa, MBh. 1, 1132; Man. 8, 82; 9, 308. 2. Sacred to Varuṇa, 8, 106. 3. Epithet of a weapon, Utt. Râmach. 142, 10; Chr. 31, 12. II. f. *ṇî*. 1. Any spirituous liquor, Man. 11, 146; Pańch. i. d. 194 (at the same time, The west). 2. The west, the region of Varuṇa, Pańch. i. d. 194. 3. The twenty-fifth lunar asterism. III. n. Water (ÇKD.).

वारुण्ड *vâruṇḍa*, I. m. The king of the serpents. II. m. and n. 1. A vessel for baling water out of a boat. 2. The rheum of the eyes. 3. The wax of the ear.

वार्कार्य *vâr-kârya* (vb. *kṛi*), adj., f. *yâ*, Effecting rain, Chr. 293, 4 = Rigv. i. 88, 4.

वार्क्ष *vârksha*, i.e. *vṛiksha + a*, I. adj. 1. Made of trees. 2. Consisting of trees, Man. 7, 70. II. m. A forest. III. f. *kshî*, A sort of Dryad.

वार्णिक *vârṇika*, i.e. *varṇa + ika*, m. A scribe.

वार्त्त *vârtta*, i.e. *vṛitti + a*, I. adj. 1. Well, healthy. 2. Following any business. II. m. 1. Health. 2. Chaff. III. f. *tâ*. 1. Abiding. 2. Livelihood, business, Man. 9, 326; 10, 80. 3. Agriculture and trade, Ragh. 16, 2. 4. Rumour, report, Hit. 93, 19. 5. News, tidings, Utt. Râmach. 151, 6; Pańch. 231, 21. 6. The egg-plant.—Comp. *Gala-*, adj. voracious, Pańch. iii. d. 95. *Durvârttâ*, i.e. *dus-*, f. bad tidings, Sch. ad Ragh. 12, 51. *Mithyâ-*, f. false report, Pańch. 51, 21. *Lubdhaka-*, f. speaking about the hunter, Pańch. 143, 24.

वार्त्तिक *vârttika*, and **वार्तिक** *vârtika*, i.e. *vârttâ* and *vṛitti*, + *ika*, I. adj. 1. Relating to news. 2. Commentatory, explaining (see IV.). II. m. 1. A man of the third caste (i.e. a husbandman or trader). 2. An envoy. III. f. (rather **वार्तिका** *vârtikâ*), A sort of quail (cf. *vartaka*). IV. n. A critical gloss, e.g. to Pâṇini's Grammar.

वार्त्रघ्न *vârtraghna*, i.e. *vṛitraghna + a*, patronym., m. (a son of Indra), Arjuna, Kir. 15, 1.

वार्दल *vâr-da + la* (vb. *dâ*, cf. *vârida*), n. A rainy day.

वार्द्धक *vârddhaka*, i.e. *vṛiddha + ka + a*, n. 1. A multitude of old men. 2. Old age, Pańch. 95, 16 (read *vârdhakabhâve*, but cf. also my transl. n. 466). 3. Infirmity of old age.

वार्द्धक्य *vârddhakya*, i.e. *vṛiddha + ka + ya*, n. Old age, Hit. i. d. 113, M.M.

वार्द्धक्षत्रि *vârddhakshatri*, i.e. *vṛiddha-kshatra + i*, patronym., m. A proper name, Draup. 1, 5.

वार्द्धुषि *vârddhushi* (probably rather *vârdhushi*, i. e. *vṛidh + ushi*, anomal., cf. ved. *aç + usha*), m. A usurer, Man. 3, 153; 180.

वार्द्धुषिक *vârddhushi + ka* (see the last), m. A usurer, Man. 8, 140.

वार्द्धुष्य *vârddhushya*, i.e. *vârddhushi* + *ya*, n. Usury, Man. 11, 61.

वार्द्ध्र *vârddhra*, i.e. *varddhra* + *a*, I. adj., f. *rî*, Leathern. II. n., and f. *rî*, A thong.

वार्द्ध्रीणस *vârddhrîṇasa*, i. e. *vârddhrî-nasa*, m. 1. A long-eared white goat, Man. 3, 271. 2. A rhinoceros.

वार्धि *vârdhi*, i.e. *vâr-dhâ* (cf. *nidhi*), m. The ocean, Pańch. i. d. 420 (*vârdhi* + *vat*, adv. Like the ocean).

वार्मण *vârmaṇa*, i.e. *varman* + *a*, n. A multitude of coats of mail.

वार्षिक *vârshika*, i. e. *varsha* and *varshâ*, + *ika*, adj., f. *kî*, 1. Belonging to a year. 2. Yearly, annual. 3. Lasting the whole year, Chr. 47, 36 (at the end of a comp. adj. Of which the water does not dry up in the hot season, viz. a river). 4. Belonging to the rainy season, Man. 9, 304; Draup. 8, 17. 5. Growing in the rainy season.—Comp. *Daçavârshika*, i.e. *daçan*-, adj., f. *kî*, 1. after the lapse of ten years, Yâjń. 2, 24. 2. having lasted ten years, Pańch. iii. d. 94. *Dvâdaça(n)*-, adj., f. *kî*, 1. twelve years old, Man. 9, 94. 2. lasting twelve years, 3, 271. *Ûna-dvi*-, adj. under the age of two years, Man. 5, 68.

वार्षिला *vârshilâ* (vb. *vṛish*), f. Hail.

वार्ष्णेय *vârshṇeya*, i.e. *vṛishṇi* + *eya*, patronym., m. A proper name, Nal. 9, 1.

वार्हस्पत *vârhaspata*, i.e. *vṛihaspati* + *a*, adj. 1. Sacred to Vṛihaspati. 2. Declared by Vṛihaspati, Pańch. 253, 12.

वार्हस्पत्य *vârhaspatya*, i. e. *vṛihaspati* + *ya*, n. Rules of conduct, ethics (Vṛihaspati being supposed to be the author of this science).

वालक *vâlaka*, i.e. *val* + *aka*, m. and n. 1. A bracelet. 2. (also f., ÇKD.), A finger-ring.

वालवितु *vâlavitu*, m. A proper name, Râjat. 5, 225.

वाल्क *vâlka*, i. e. *valka* + *a*, adj. Made of the bark of trees.

वाल्मीक *vâlmîka*, and **वाल्मीकि** *vâlmîki*, m. A proper name, the poet of the Râmâyaṇa.

वाव *vâva*, i. e. probably *vâ-eva* (Weber, Journ. of the German Oriental Society, ix. 2, 4); indecl., used in a question, Bhâg. P. 6, 9, 38.

वावदूक *vâvad* + *ûka* (frequent. of *vad*), adj. Eloquent.

वावृत् *VÂVṚIT*, **वृत्** *VṚIT*, i. 4, Âtm. (the first looks rather like an old frequent. of *vṛit*), To select, to love.

वाश् *VAÇ*, and **वास्** *VÂS*, i. 4, Âtm. (in epic poetry i. 1, Par. Âtm., MBh. 3, 10493; Nal. 11, 20; 1, 8433; also Mṛichchh. 143, 13), To cry, to howl, ll. ll. Ptcple. of the pf. pass. *vâçita*, n. The cry of birds or animals. f. *tâ*, 1. A woman. 2. A female elephant. Frequent. *vâvaçya*, To cry repeatedly, MBh. 6, 111.—With the prep. **उद्** *ud*, To bewail, Bhaṭṭ. 3, 32.

वाशि *vâçi*, m. Fire.

वाशी *vâç* + *î*, f. Roar, prayer (?), Chr. 293, 3 = Rigv. i. 88, 3.

वाशीमन्त् *vâçî* + *mant*, adj. Roaring, Chr. 293, 6 = Rigv. i. 87, 6.

वाशुरा *vâçurâ*, f. Night.

वाश्र *vâçra*, I. m. A day (cf. *vâsara*). II. n. 1. A dwelling. 2. A place where four roads meet. 3. Dung.

वाष्प *vâshpa* (and **वास्प** *vâspa*), I. m. n. 1. Vapour, Ragh. 13, 29; steam (cf. Pańch. 262, 21). **2.** A tear, Pańch. 160, 5. **3.** n. Iron. **II.** f. *pî*, A drug, commonly *Hingupatrî*.—**Comp.** *Antar-*, adj. with suppressed tears, Vikr. d. 78. *Ud-*, adj. shedding tears, Kathâs. 10, 208 (hence *udvâshpa + tva*, n. shedding tears, Vikr. d. 29). *Sa-vâshpa + m*, adv. with tears in his eyes, Pańch. 243, 4.—Cf. Lat. vappa, perhaps vāpor (cf. 1. *vâ*).

वाष्पाय *VÂSHPÂYA*, a denomin. derived from *vâshpa* with *ya*, Âtm. To shed tears, Vikr. d. 147; Mâlat. 102, 11.

वास् *VÂS*, i. 10 (rather a denomin. derived from *vâsa*), Par. (in epic poetry also Âtm., MBh. 3, 24), To introduce another quality, to perfume, Gît. 1, 35. Ptcple. of the pf. pass. *vâsita*. **1.** Made fragrant, Utt. Râmach. 63, 4. **2.** Filled with fragrance, Böhtl. Ind. Spr. 551; see s.v. **Comp.** *Su-*, adj. well perfumed, Ṛit. 1, 3.—With the prep. **अधि** *adhi*, To adorn, Vikr. d. 127.—Cf. *vâç*.

वास *vâsa*, i.e. 1. 3. *vas* and *vâs*, + *a*, **I.** m. **1.** Dwelling, Man. 2, 67; resting, Megh. 77; living, Pańch. i. d. 347; Hit. i. d. 113, M.M.; with *vas*, to dwell, to live (see s.v. 1. *vas*). **2.** A dwelling-place, Vikr. d. 43; a habitation, a house, Daçak. in Chr. 188, 12; Lass. 75, 10. **3.** Cloth, Kathâs. 3, 71. **4.** Perfuming, Vikr. d. 38; perfume, Çiç. 9, 52. **II.** m., and f. *sâ*, A plant, Justicia ganderusa.—**Comp.** *Udavâsa*, i.e. *udan-*, m. abiding in water, MBh. 13, 354. *Garbha-*, m. the womb, Man. 12, 78. *Gṛiha-*, m. 1. domestic life, Utt. Râmach. 27, 3. 2. living as householder, the second order of brahmanical life, MBh. 13, 2181. *Go-*, I. m. a cow-pen, ib. 2, 825. II. adj. covered with the skin of a bull or cow, ib. 8, 3650. *Jala-*, I. m. abiding in water, ib. 12, 9281. II. adj. one who abides in water, ib. 12, 9280. *Tapovâsa*, i.e. *tapas-*, m. a place where hermits live, Hariv. 5168. *Paṭa-*, m. perfumed powder, Gît. 1, 35. *Bhûta-*, m. Beleric myrobalan. *Markaṭa-*, m. a spider's web. *Yathâ-vâsa + m*, adv. as far as to one's own abode, home. *Reṇu-*, m. a bee. *Vâri-*, m. a distiller or dealer in spirituous liquors. *Çayanîya-* (vb. *çî*), m. a sleeping-room, Lass. 2. ed. 19, 22. *Sa-*, adj. 1. having a dwelling. 2. scented. *Su-*, m. 1. a pleasant dwelling. 2. an agreeable perfume.

वासन *vâsana*, i.e. 1. 3. *vas* and *vâs*, + *ana*, **I.** n. **1.** Abiding, abode. **2.** Any receptacle. **3.** A box, a basket. **4.** A water-jar. **5.** A particular posture. **6.** Knowledge. **7.** Steeping, infusing. **8.** Cloth. **9.** An envelope. **10.** Perfuming. **II.** f. *nâ*. **1.** An impression remaining unconsciously in the mind from past actions, etc., and, by the resulting merit or demerit, producing pleasure or pain, Bhâshâp. 162. Cf. Ballantyne, Yoga, ii. 12. **2.** Trust, confidence. **3.** Imagination, fancy, Vedântas. in Chr. 218, 1; 219, 2.—**Comp** *Go-*, I. adj. covered with the skin of a bull or cow, MBh. 2, 1825. II. m. a proper name, ib. 1, 3826. *Durvâsanâ*, i.e. *dus-*, f. a bad inclination, Prab. 109, 7. *Nirvâsana*, i.e. *nis-*, adj. deprived of imagination, Sâh. D. 26, 7; see s.v. *Vana-*, m. a polecat. *Sam-ud-chhinna-* (vb. *chhid*), adj. one in whom ignorance is extirpated, Prab. 50, 12.

वासनामयत्व *vâsanâ + maya + tva*, n. State of (or consisting in) imagination, Vedântas. in Chr. 208, 6.

वासन्त *vâsanta*, i.e. *vasanta + a*, **I.** adj. **1.** Vernal, growing in the spring, Man. 6, 11. **2.** Young, in the spring of life. **3.** Diligent in the performance of religious ceremonies. **II.** m. **1.** The Indian cuckoo. **2.** The southern wind. **3.** Any young animal. **4.** A camel. **5.** A catamite. **6.** The name of several plants. III. f. *ti.* 1. The name of a deity, Utt. Râmach. 37, 14; 46, 11. 2. A festival in honour of Kâma. 3. The name of several plants.

वासन्तक *vâsanta + ka,* adj. Vernal.

वासन्तिक *vâsantika,* i.e. *vasanta + ika,* I. adj. Vernal, Çâk. 78, 18. II. m. The buffoon in a drama.

वासर *vâsara* (vb. 2. *vas*), I. m. and n. A day, Pańch. ii. d. 99; Kathâs. 4, 23 (m.); Megh. 104 (n.). II. m. A kind of snake.

वासव *vâsava,* i.e. *vasu + a,* I. m. Indra, Chr. 22, 23. II. f. *vî,* The mother of Vyâsa. III. adj., f. *vî,* Belonging to Indra, Megh. 44.

वासस् *vâsas,* i.e. 3. *vas + as,* n. 1. Cloth, clothes, Hit. ii. d. 38. 2. Curtain, Râm. 1, 13, 29 (read *vâsobhiḥ*).—Comp. *Adhas-*, and *Antar-*, n. a lower garment, Utt. Râmach. 106, 1; Kathâs. 4, 52. *Uttara-*, n. an upper garment, Râm. 5, 18, 5. *Eka-*, adj. wearing only a single cloth, Man. 4, 45. *Kṛitti-*, adj. covered with a skin, MBh. 2, 1642. *Chira-*, I. adj. 1. covered with a cloth made of bark, Man. 11, 101. 2. covered with rags, Bhâg. P. 1, 15, 43. *Chîra-valkala-*, adj. covered with a cloth made of bark, Râm. 3, 55, 15. *Danta-* (n.), the lip, Kumâras. 5, 34. *Digvâsas,* i.e. *diç-*, adj. naked, Man. 11, 201. *Durvâsas,* i.e. *dus-*, 1. adj. poorly clothed, MBh. 13, 1176. 2. a proper name, ib. 1, 2768. *Nîla-*, 1. adj. covered with a blue cloth, Bhâg. P. 5, 25, 7. 2. m. the planet Saturn. *Sa-*, adj. clothed.

वासि *vâsi,* f. A carpenter's adze or chisel.

वासित *vâsita,* I. see *vas, vâs.* II. n. 1. Sound. 2. The cry of birds. 3. Knowledge. III. f. *tâ.* 1. A woman. 2. A female elephant, Johns. Sel. 12, 32; Ragh. 19, 11.

वासिन् *vâsin,* adj., f. *nî,* i.e. I. 1. *vas + in,* Inhabiting, Pańch. 129, 14. II. *vâsa + in,* Clothed, Johns. Sel. 59, 184; wearing clothes, Râm. 3, 52, 19; 25.—Comp. *Kâma-*, adj. abiding where one lists, Nal. 13, 55. *Grâma-*, adj. 1. dwelling in villages, Man. 7, 118. 2. tame, MBh. 6, 166. *Vana-*, I. adj. abiding in woods, wild, Hit. 88, 7, M.M. II. m. a hermit. *Sâmanta-*, adj. bordering, neighbouring, Man. 8, 258. *Su-*, I. adj. dwelling comfortably. II. f. *nî,* a bride residing in her father's house, Man. 3, 114. *Sva-*, f. a woman residing in her father's house.

वासिष्ठ *vâsishṭha,* i.e. *vasishṭha + a,* adj. 1. Composed by Vasishṭha, Man. 11, 249. 2. Explained by Vasishṭha.

वासु *vâsu,* m. Vishṇu; *vâsû,* see s.v.

वासुकि *vâsuki,* m. The serpent Vâsuki, sovereign of the snakes, Bhag. 10, 28.

वासुदेव *vâsudeva,* i.e. *vasu-deva + a,* m. Kṛishṇa or Vishṇu, Johns. Sel. 55, 140; Pańch. 44, 19.

वासुरा *vâsurâ,* f. I. probably *vâs + u + ra.* 1. A woman (cf. the next). 2. A female elephant. II. (vb. 1. *vas*). 1. Night. 2. The earth.

वासू *vâsû,* i.e. *vâs + u,* f. A young girl, Daçak. in Chr. 181, 24; 187, 14.

वास्त *vâsta,* i.e. *vasta + a,* adj. Made, derived, or coming, from goats, Man. 2, 41.

वास्तव *vâstava,* and **वास्तविक** i.e. *vastu + a,* or *ika,* adj. 1. Being anything in the true sense of the word; real, substantial. 2. Demonstrated.

वास्तव्य *vâstavya,* see 1. *vas.*

वास्तिक *vâstika,* i.e. *vasta + ika,* n. Goats, Râm. 2, 62, 2, ed. Seramp.

वास्तु *vâstu* (vb. 1. *vas*), m. and n. **1.** The site of a building, a building-place. **2.** Ground, Man. 3, 255. **3.** A house.—**Comp.** *Pura-*, n. a ground fit for building a town, Hariv. 6409. *Pṛishṭha-*, n. the upper room of a building, Man. 3, 91.

वास्तुक and **वास्तूक** *vâstûka*, n. A potherb, Lass. 79, 14 (*û*).

वास्तोस्पति *vâstospati* (*vâstos*, gen. of *vâstu*), m. The deity of the house (Man. 3, 89), a name of Indra.

वास्त्र *vâstra*, i. e. *vastra* + *a*, adj. Covered with cloth.

वास्प *vâspa*, see *vâshpa*.

वाह् *VÂH* (akin to *vah*), † **बाह्** *BAH*, i. 1, Âtm. (in epic poetry, Par., MBh. 1, 6639), To endeavour. Caus. *vâhaya*, To employ, Man. 3, 68; 4, 86. Ptcple. of the pf. pass. *vâhita*, Mystified, Pańch. 64, 7. —With the prep. **सम्** *sam*, To stroke, MBh. 3, 11005. Caus. The same, Çâk. d. 69.

वाह *vâha*, i.e. *vah* + *a*, m. **1.** Carrying, Hit. 81, 12 (*ati-bhâra-*, carrying too heavy burthens). **2.** A vehicle, a conveyance of any kind, a car, Arj. 1, 1. **3.** A horse, Arj. 4, 12. **4.** A carrier of burthens. **5.** The arm. **6.** A bull. **7.** A buffalo. **8.** Air, wind. **9.** A measure of capacity, nearly equal to a ton in freight.—**Comp.** *Ambu-*, m. a cloud, Daçak. in Chr. 201, 15. *Gandha-*, m. the wind, Gît. 1, 35. *Jala-*, I. adj. carrying water, MBh. 2, 301. II. m. a cloud. *Purusha-*, m. Garuḍa, the vehicle of Vishṇu, Bhâg. P. 5, 24, 29. *Bhâra-*, m. a porter. *Marudvâha*, i.e. *marut-*, m. smoke. *Râjavâha*, i.e. *râjan-*, m. a horse. *Vâyu-*, m. smoke. *Vâri-*, m. a cloud. *Çuka-*, m. Kâma. *Sâdhu-*, m. a well-trained horse. *Sârtha-*, m. 1. the leader of a caravan, Pańch. 9, 1. 2. a great merchant, Mṛichchh. 2, 3. 3. a merchant. *Skandha-*, m. an ox of burthen. *Havya-*, m. fire. *Hastivâha*, i.e. *hastin-*, m. a goad.

वाहक *vâhaka*, i.e. *vah* + *aka*, m. **1.** A horseman. **2.** A porter, Pańch. ii. d. 149; 156, 2.—**Comp.** *Jala-*, m. the water-bearer, a court officer, Pańch. 156, 21. *Tâmbula-*, m. the betel-bearer, a court officer, Pańch. 156, 21. *Ratha-*, m. the driver of a carriage, Nal. 22, 1. *Çiçu-*, m. a wild goat. *Skandha-*, m. an ox of burthen.

वाहन *vâhana*, i.e. *vah* + *ana*, n. **1.** Carrying, Pańch. 253, 13; bearing, 83, 19. **2.** Governing (of horses), Nal. 15, 2. **3.** A vehicle, Hit. 126, 16; Man. 7, 222; a chariot, Hit. iv. d. 62; a horse, Man. 5, 29; an elephant.—**Comp.** *Dvija-*, m, Vishṇu (having a bird, Garuḍa, as his vehicle), Hariv. 3982. *Nara-*, adj. drawn by men, epithet and name of Kuvera, MBh. 3, 8358. *Mahisha-*, m. Yama. *Megha-*, m. 1. Indra. 2. Çiva. 3. a proper name, Râjat. 5, 64. *Yama-*, m. a buffalo. *Vâri-*, m. a cloud. *Çâli-*, m. the name of a king. *Çikhi(n)-*, m. Kârttikeya, the god of war. *Çveta-*, m. 1. the moon. 2. Arjuna. *Hari-*, m. 1. Garuḍa. 2. Indra, Indr. 5, 54. *Havya-*, see s.v. *Hotra-*, m. a proper name.

वाहस *vâhasa* (vb. *vah*), m. The boa-constrictor.

वाहिक *vâhika* (vb. *vah*), m. **1.** A car. **2.** A large drum.—**Comp.** *Bhâra-*, I. adj. carrying burthens. II. m. a porter.

वाहिन् *vâhin*, i.e. *vah* and *vâha*, + *in*, I. adj. (at the end of comp. words), Bearing, Pańch. 79, 16; carrying, Çâk. d. 57. II. f. *nî*. **1.** An army, Hit. iii. d. 125. **2.** A body of forces, consisting of 81 elephants, 81 cars, 243 horse, and 405 foot. **3.** A river, Râm. 2, 66, 26, ed. Seramp.—**Comp.** *Daṇḍa-*, m. a policeman, Daçak. 160, 1, bel. *Nara-*, i.e. *naravâha + in*, adj. drawn by men, Nal. 17, 23. *Mala-*, adj. bringing stain, Hit. i. d. 47, M.M. *Lomavâhin*, i.e. *loman-*, adj. feathered (?), Chr. 32, 30. *Vega-*, adj. swift, Râjat. 5, 217. *Sâdhu-*, m. a well-trained horse.

वाहीक *vâhîka*, I. adj. **1.** (vb. *vah*), Bearing burthens. **2.** (i.e. *vahis + îka*), Outer. II. m. **1.** An ox. **2.** The name of a country.

वाहुक *vâhuka*, see *bâhuka*.

वाह्य *vâhya*, i.e. *vahis + ya*, adj. **1.** Outer, external, Vikr. 72, 5 (*sa-vâhya -antar-âtman*, Body and soul, the whole being); Pańch. 60, 7 (*tava vyavasâya -vâhyam̃ kutas teshâm̃ mâm̃sâdanam*, How will they be able to feed on flesh except by thy exertion?). **2.** Foreign, a foreigner, Pańch. i. d. 293. **3.** An outcaste, one of a low tribe, Man. 10, 28; 30. **4.** Abl. *yât*, From without, Pańch. 193, 14. Cf. *vah*.—Comp. *A-*, adj. inward, Ragh. 14, 50. *Loka-*, m. an outcaste.

वाह्यतस् *vâhya + tas*, adv. Externally, being out of (the water), Pańch. 255, 24.

वाह्लिक *vâhlika*, n. Saffron (cf. the next).

वाह्लीक *vâhlîka*, I. m. **1.** The name of a country, Balkh. **2.** A horse from Balkh. **3.** One of the principal *Gandharvas*. **4.** A proper name, Johns. Sel. 7, 2. II. n. **1.** Saffron. **2.** Assafœtida.

1. **वि** *vi*, i.e. *dvi*, prep. I. Combined and compounded with verbs and their derivatives. II. Compounded with nouns. It implies, **1.** Separation, cf. *viyoga*. **2.** Privation, cf. *vi-kacha*. **3.** Wrongness, cf. *vikarman*; baseness, cf. *vi -yonî*; opposition, cf. *vi-loma*. **4.** Difference, cf. *vilakshaṇa*. **5.** Spreading; falling in different directions, asunder, cf. *vi-kṛî*, e.g. *vi-kîrṇa-keça*. **6.** Manifoldness, much, cf. *vikarman*. —Cf. probably Lat. vi, in di-vi-dere.

2. **वि** *vi*, m., f. *vî*, **1.** A bird, Chr. 287, 6 = Rigv. i. 48, 6. **2.** The eye. **3.** Heaven. **4.** The region of the wind. —Comp. *Bahu-*, adj. containing many birds.—Cf. Lat. avis; αἰετός, οἰωνός, ᾤιον, ᾠόν; Lat. ovum; O.H.G. ei; A.S. aeg.

विंश *vim̃ça*, **1.** Ordinal number (cf. *vim̃çati*), m., f. *çî*, n. Twentieth, Chr. 55, l. 8; Bhâg. P. iii. 20. **2.** The twentieth part, Man. 8, 398.—Comp. *Ekona-*, i.e. *eka-ûna-*, or *Ûna-*, ord. num. nineteenth, Chr. 53, l. 11. *Eka-*, twenty-first, Chr. 57, 1, bel. *Dvâ-*, twenty-second, Man. 2, 38. *Trayovim̃ça*, i.e. *trayas-*, twenty-third, Kathâs. i. p. 378. *Chatur-*, twenty-fourth, ib. p. 405. *Pańchavim̃ça*, i.e. *pańchan-*, twenty-fifth, ib. p. 437. *Shaḍvim̃ça*, i.e. *shash-*, twenty-sixth, ib. p. 469, etc. *Trim̃çadvim̃ça*, i. e. *trim̃çat-*, comp. card. num. from twenty to thirty, Râjat. 5, 209.

विंशक *vim̃çaka*, i.e. *vim̃çati*, or *vim̃çat*, + *ka*, adj. Twenty, or an aggregate of twenty.—Comp. *Eka-*, ord. num. twenty-first, Man. 3, 37.

विंशत् *vim̃çat* (cf. *vim̃çati*), card. num. Twenty; in *eka-*, Twenty-one, Râm. 1, 13, 27. *pari-*, Full twenty, MBh. 11, 561.

विंशति *vim̃çati*, i.e. *dvi-daçant* (original form of *daçan*), + *i*, card. num. f. Twenty, Hit. iv. d. 33.—Comp. *Eka-*, f. twenty-one, Man. 4, 87. *Dvâ-*, f. twenty-two, MBh. 7, 1878. *Trayovim̃çati*, i.e. *trayas-*, f. twenty-three, Bhâg. P. 3, 6, 2. *Chatur-*, f. twenty-four. *Ashṭâvim̃çati*, i.e. *ashṭan-*, f.

twenty-eight, Yâjń. 1, 302.—Cf. Lat. viginti; Ϝίκατι, βείκατι, εἴκοσι.

विंशतितम *vimçati* + *tama*, ord. num., f. *mî*, Twentieth.—Comp. *Eka-*, twenty-first, Râm. iii. 21. *Dvâ-*, twenty-second, etc., Râm. iii. 22.

विंशतिम *vimçatima*, curtailed for *vimçatitama*, in *pańchavimçatima*, i.e. *pańchan-*, Twenty-fifth, MBh. 12, 11251.

विंशिन् *vimçin*, i.e. *vimça*, in the signification of *vimçati* (cf. *trimçat* -*vimça*), + *in*, m. **1.** Twenty. **2.** A lord of twenty towns, Man. 7, 119.

विक *vika*, n. The milk of a prolific cow.

विकङ्कत *vikańkata*, m. A small tree, Ragh. 11, 25.

विकच *vi-kacha*, see s.v. *kacha*.

विकट *vikaṭa*, I. adj. **1.** Large, Utt. Râmach. 118, 6. **2.** Large-toothed. **3.** Knitted (as the brows), Prab. 85, 15; formidable, Utt. Râmach. 150, 13; hideous. **4.** Obsolete, obscure. **5.** Changed in form or appearance. **6.** Beautiful. **7.** i.e. *vi-kaṭa*, Without a mat, Nal. 10, 6. II. n. A tumour. III. m. A proper name, Pańch. 76, 7.

विकत्थन *vi-katth* + *ana*, I. adj. **1.** Boastful. **2.** Praising ironically. **3.** Speaking idly. II. n. **1.** Boasting. **2.** Assigning anything to an unreal origin. **3.** Proclaiming, repeating. **4.** Praising. **5.** Irony.—Comp. *A-*, adj. not boasting, modest, Hit. iii. d. 101; Ragh. 14, 73. *Dus-*, adj. boasting in a disagreeable manner, Daçak. 102, 15.

विकत्था *vi-katth* + *â*, f. **1.** Boasting. **2.** Proclaiming. **3.** Praise. **4.** Ironical praise.

विकम्प *vi-kamp* + *a*, adj. **1.** Trembling. **2.** Unsteady. **3.** Shrinking from. **4.** Heaving.

विकरालता *vi-karâla* + *tâ*, f. Dreadfulness, Pańch. 218, 13.

विकर्तन *vikartana*, i.e. *vi-kṛit* + *ana*, m. **1.** A son who has usurped his father's kingdom. **2.** The sun, Utt. Râmach. 124, 2.

विकर्त्तृ *vikarttṛi*, i.e. *vi-kṛit* + *tṛi*, in *go-*, m. A butcher, MBh. 4, 36.

विकर्मकृत् *vikarmakṛit*, i.e. *vikarman-kṛi* + *t*, adj. **1.** One who does forbidden acts, Man. 8, 66. **2.** Busy in various ways.

विकर्मन् *vi-karman*, I. adj. Not acting, Lass. 2. ed. 68, 40. II. n. **1.** Unlawful act, Bhag. 4, 17. **2.** Fraud. **3.** Various business.

विकर्मस्थ *vikarmastha*, i.e. *vikarman* -*stha*, adj. **1.** One who has done an illegal or an immoral act, Man. 11, 192. **2.** Addicted to vice, 4, 30; 9, 214. **3.** Engaged in various business.

विकर्ष *vikarsha*, i.e. *vi-kṛish* + *a*, m. **1.** Pulling, pulling out. **2.** An arrow.

विकर्षण *vikarshaṇa*, i.e. *vi-kṛish* + *ana*, **1.** Pulling, Kir. 4, 15; drawing (of a bow), Kir. 3, 57. **2.** A throwing across, a cross-buttock, Johns. Sel. 58, 169.

विकल *vikala*, i.e. *vi-kalâ*, I. adj. **1.** Defective, Hit. i. d. 201, M.M. **2.** Wanting, failing, Pańch. v. d. 8; Hit. i. d. 200, M.M.; Çâk. d. 152. **3.** Decayed, Utt. Râmach. 68, 3; impaired. **4.** Confused (cf. *kala*), Lass. 54, 7; sorrowful, Utt. Râmach. 18, 1. II. f. *lâ* and *lî*, A woman in whom menstruation has ceased.—Comp. *A-*, adj. 1. unimpaired, Hit. i. d. 126, M.M. 2. excellent, Megh. 25; 35.

विकल्प *vikalpa*, i.e. *vi-klip* + *a*, m. **1.** Option, Daçak. in. Chr. 181, 20 (-*upahâra-karman*, Optional offerings, not prescribed); alternative, distinction, Vedântas. in Chr. 217, 2. **2.** Alternation, Mâlav. d. 29. **3.** Doubt, Pańch. i. d. 411; indecision, ib. 71, 20; hesitation, Ragh. 17, 49. **4.** Error, mistake. **5.** Ignorance.—**Comp.** *A-vikalpa*, adj. not tarrying, Pańch. 88, 6; *°pam*, adv. 1. in an undoubted (legal?) manner, Pańch. 45, 4. 2. without indecision, i.e. without any delay, Pańch. i. d. 59. *Daṇḍa-*, m. a discretional punishment, Man. 9, 228. *Nis-*, adj. allowing no alternative, Bhâshâp. 57. *°pam*, adv. without hesitation, Pańch. i. d. 59. *Sa-*, adj. admitting of an alternative, distinguishing, Vedântas. in Chr. 217, 1.

विकल्पक *vikalpa + ka*, a substitute for *vikalpa*, at the end of comp. adj. *nis-*, adj. Allowing no alternative, no distinction, Vedântas. in Chr. 217, 9; Bhâshâp. 134. *sa-*, adj. Admitting of an alternative, distinguishing, Vedântas. in Chr. 217, 1.

विकल्पिन् *vikalpin*, i.e. *vikalpa + in*, adj. Endowed with doubt or illusion, Ṛit. 6, 34, v.r. *nîlâçokavikalpikeçanikaraḥ*, 'Having plenty of hair, on account of an illusion caused by the black açoka,' i.e. his hair is represented by the black açoka.

विकस्वर *vi-kas + vara* (also **विकश्वर** *vikaçvara*, cf. *kas*), adj. Opening.

विकाङ्क्षा *vi-kâṅksh + â*, f. Hesitation, Râm. 2, 57, 18, ed. Seramp.

विकार *vikâra*, i.e. *vi-kṛi + a*, m. **1.** Change, Vedântas. in Chr. 216, 18; Utt. Râmach. 23, 7 (perturbation); Çâk. 13, 9 (passion), Mâlat. 14, 8. **2.** Change of form, Pańch. 257, 23. **3.** Change of mind, Çâk. 66, 4. **4.** Disease, Nalod. 2, 17; a wound, Pańch. 218, 13.—**Comp.** *Chitta-*, m. perturbation of mind, MBh. 18, 74. *Nis-*, adj. unchanged, MBh. 13, 2318. *Romavikâra*, i.e. *roman-*, m. horripilation (cf. *româńcha*).

विकारतस् *vikâra + tas*, adv. From the change, Hit. iii. d. 33.

विकारत्व *vikâra + tva*, n. The condition of transforming, transformation, Vedântas. in Chr. 209, 12.

विकारिन् *vikârin*, i.e. *vi-kṛi + in* and *vikâra, + in*, adj. **1.** Producing a change, Hit. ii. d. 98 (spoiling). **2.** Undergoing a change, Prab. 111, 17; falling in love, Mâlat. 11, 10.—**Comp.** *A-*, adj. faithful, Man. 7, 190.

विकाल *vi-kâla*, m. **1.** Twilight, Pańch. 258, 9. **2.** Afternoon (? cf. *vaikâlika*).

विकालक *vikâla + ka*, I. m. Twilight, evening. II. f. *likâ*, A sort of clepsydra which defines that period.

1. **विकाश** *vi-kâç + a*, m. **1.** Æther, heaven. **2.** Solitude, loneliness.

2. **विकाश** *vikâça*, and (better) **विकास** *vikâsa*, i.e. *vi-kas + a*, m. **1.** Opening, expanding, exhibition, Vikr. 35, 8 (*sa-dosha-*, A defective exhibition). **2.** Budding, blowing, Çiç. 9, 41 (*ç*, of flowers, and of the heart for falling in love); figuratively, Pańch. 187, 2. **3.** Display, splendid appearance, Çiç. 9, 53 (*ç*). **4.** Pleasure, enjoyment.—**Comp.** *Sa-*, adj. expanded, extensive.

विकाशक *vikâçaka*, better **विकासक** *vikâsaka*, i.e. *vi-kas*, Caus., *+ aka*, adj. Causing to expand, Lass. 90, 11.

विकाशन *vikâçana* (cf. 1. 2. *vikâça*), n. **1.** Manifestation. **2.** Expansion. **3.** Blowing of a flower. **4.** Causing to blow (again), Utt. Râmach. 23, 12.

विकाशिन् *vikâçin*, **विकाषिन्** *vikâshin*, and (better) **विकासिन्** *vikâsin*, i.e. *vi-kas + in*, adj. **1.** Expanding, developing itself, Bhartr. 3, 70; opening. **2.** Budding, blowing.

विकास, विकासिन् *vikâsa, vikâsin,* see *vikâça, çin.*

विकिर *vikira,* m. I. i.e. *vi-kṛî+a,* 1. A fallen fragment, what has been dropped, Man. 3, 245. 2. Scattering. 3. A well. II. A bird.

विकिरण *vikiraṇa,* i.e. *vi-kṛî+ana,* I. n. Scattering. II. m. Gigantic swallow-wort, Asclepias gigantea.

विकूजन *vi-kûj+ana,* n. Grumbling, in *antra-,* n. Grumbling of the bowels, Suçr. 2, 451, 7.

विकूणिका *vikûṇikâ,* f. The nose.

विकृति *vi-kṛi+ti,* f. 1. Change of any kind, Utt. Râmach. 133, 16 (wrath); of mind, Pańch. 58, 25. 2. Sickness. 3. Fear. 4. Spirituous liquor.

विकृतिमन्त् *vikṛiti+mant,* adj., f. *matî,* 1. Changed, wounded, Nalod. 2, 47. 2. Changeable, Çâk. d. 38.

विक्रम *vi-kram+a,* m. 1. A step, Johns. Sel. 95, 67; Çâk. d. 165. 2. Proceeding, Man. 3, 214 (v.r.). 3. Overpowering. 4. Great strength, Johns. Sel. 48, 82. 5. Strength, Hit. ii. d. 84 (with *kṛi,* To use one's strength). 6. Heroism, Vikr. 11, 12; Pańch. ii. d. 146; in the title of the drama, *vikramorvaçî,* i.e. *vikrama-urvaçî,* f. Urvaçî, gained by heroism. 7. A proper name.—Comp. *A-,* adj. weak, Kir. 2, 14. *Chaṇḍa-,* adj. possessed of fierce courage, Râm. 5, 39, 24. *Tulya-,* adj. fought with equal prowess, Hit. iii. d. 1. *Tri-,* I. n. three steps, Râm. 6, 79, 11. II. adj. and sbst. walking with three steps over the heaven, epithet of Vishṇu (as sun), Râm. 1, 32, 13 Gorr. *Satya-,* adj. having real valour.

विक्रमसेन *vikramasena* (cf. *senâ*), and

विक्रमादित्य *vikramâditya,* i.e. *vikrama-âditya,* m. Proper names, Lass. 15, 18 (corr. °*seneno*°); 1, 10.

विक्रमिन् *vikrama+in,* m. 1. A hero. 2. A lion.

विक्रय *vikraya,* i.e. *vi-krî+a,* m. Sale, selling, Pańch. 121, 21.—Comp. *Âtmavikraya,* i.e. *âtman-,* m. selling one's self, Man. 11, 59. *Kraya-,* m. buying and selling, traffic, 8, 401.

विक्रयिक *vikrayika,* i.e. *vikraya+ika,* adj. One who sells.

विक्रयिन् *vikrayin,* i.e. *vi-krî+in,* m. A vendor.—Comp. *Apatya-,* m. a seller of his offspring, Man. 3, 51. *Kratu-,* m. one who sells the reward of his sacrifice, Man. 4, 214. *Mâṅsa-,* m. a vendor of flesh, a term of reproach.

विक्रान्ति *vikrânti,* i.e. *vi-kram+ti,* f. 1. A horse's canter or gallop. 2. Great strength. 3. Prowess.

विक्रायक *vikrâyaka,* i.e. *vi-krî+aka,* m. A seller.

विक्रिया *vikriyâ,* i.e. *vi-kṛi+ya,* and *vi-kriyâ,* f. 1. Change, Pańch. i. d. 330; transformation, Çâk. p. 106, 1. 2. A dish prepared from (milk), Man. 5, 25. 3. Disease, Daçak. in Chr. 187, 7. 4. Mischief, Râm. 3, 49, 56.—Comp. *Bhûta-,* f. epilepsy, possession by evil spirits. *Sa-romavikriya,* i.e. *sa-roman-,* adj. affected with horripilation (as a sign of excessive pleasure), Vikr. d. 12.

विक्रेतृ *vikretṛi,* i.e. *vi-krî+tṛi,* m. A vendor.

विक्लव *viklava* (cf. *klav,* but this vb. is dubious; I should prefer a derivation from *klam*), adj. 1. Overcome with fear or agitation, confused, bewildered, Daçak. in Chr. 200, 16. 2. Disgusted, Çâk. 22, 5.—Comp. *A-,* adj. intrepid, MBh. 1, 2070.

विक्लेद *vikleda*, i.e. *vi-klid+a*, m. Dissolution, Bhâg. P. 3, 20, 41.

विक्षाव *vikshâva*, i.e. *vi-kshu+a*, m. 1. Cough. 2. Sound.

विक्षेप *vikshepa*, i.e. *vi-kship+a*, m. 1. Casting, or throwing away (*charaṇa-*, Casting asunder of the feet, i.e. striding, Vikr. 60, 14). 2. Dispatching. 3. Refuting an argument. 4. Confusion, perplexity, fear, proceeding from ignorance or error, Vedântas. in Chr. 205, 23; cf. 206, 8; 217, 24. 5. Looking about wildly. 6. Celestial latitude.—Comp. *Chitta-*, m. scattering, diversion of mind, Utt. Râmach. 52, 12. *Dṛishṭi-*, m. a leer, a side glance, Çâk. 16, 1, Chezy.

विक्षेपण *vikshepaṇa*, i.e. *vi-kship+ana*, n. 1. Scattering. 2. Throwing. 3. Dispatching. 4. Confusion, proceeding from ignorance or error, Vedântas. in Chr. 217, 24.

विख *vikha*, also **विखु** *vikhu*, **विख्य** *vikhya*, **विख्र** *vikhra*, and **विख्रु** *vikhru* (perhaps dialectical forms of *vigra*, q. cf.), adj. Noseless.

विख्याति *vi-khyâ+ti*, f. 1. Fame. 2. Notoriety.

विगणन *vi-gaṇ+ana*, n. Reckoning, computing.

विगम *vi-gam+a*, m. 1. Parting, withdrawing, Ṛit. 6, 22. 2. Separation.—Comp. *Divasa-*, m. the decline of the day, Megh. 77.

विगर्हण *vigarhaṇa*, i.e. *vi-garh+ana*, n. 1. Abusing. 2. Abuse, blame, Chr. 63, 70.

विगान *vigâna*, i.e. *vi-gai+ana*, n. 1. Blame. 2. Ill report.

विगाह *vi-gâh+a*, m. 1. Bathing. 2. Plunging into, literally and figuratively.—Comp. *Dus-*, I. adj. impenetrable, unfathomable, Pańch. i. d. 125. II. m. a proper name, MBh. 1, 4544.

विग्र *vigra* (perhaps anomal. *vi-agra*), adj. Noseless.

विग्रह *vi-grah+a*, I. m. and n. 1. War, battle, Pańch. 149, 14; Hit. pr. d. 9, M.M. 2. Opposition, encounter, quarrel, Bhartṛ. 2, 42. 3. Disfavour, Râjat. 5, 247. II. m. 1. Extension. 2. Shape, Kir. 5, 43. 3. The body, Râm. 5, 2, 15. 4. A portion.—Comp. *Â-vṛita-* (vb. *vṛi*), adj., f. *hâ*, whose body is covered, hidden, Vikr. d. 102. *Sa-*, adj. 1. embodied, living, Râjat. 5, 27. 2. meaning, importing.

विग्रहवन्त् *vigraha+vant*, adj., f. *vatî*, Embodied, incarnate, Sâv. 1, 22; Mâlav. d. 13; Sund. 3, 17.

विघटन *vi-ghaṭ+ana*, n. Destruction, Prab. 80, 6.

विघट्टना *vi-ghaṭṭ+anâ* f. Separation, Nalod. 4, 45.

विघट्टिन् *vi-ghaṭṭ+in*, adj., f. *nî*, Touching, Ragh. 16, 56.

विघस *vi-ghas+a*, m. 1. The residue of food offered to the gods, manes (Man. 3, 285), to a venerable guest, or a spiritual teacher. 2. Food, Utt. Râmach. 121, 7.

विघात *vighâta*, i.e. *vi-han*, Caus., *+a*, m. and n. 1. Prohibition. 2. Opposition. 3. Impediment, obstacle, Pańch. 42, 12. 4. Destruction, Sund. 1, 12; Pańch. 156, 23. 5. Abandoning, Pańch. 172, 25. 6. A blow, Vikr. 85, 19 (*dṛishṭi-*, Being dazzled).—Comp. *Danta-*, m. biting, bite, Ṛit. 4, 12.

विघातिन् *vighâtin*, i.e. *vi-han*, Caus., *+in*, adj. 1. Opposing, impeding. 2. Removing. 3. Killing.

विघोषण *vighoshaṇa*, i.e. *vi-ghush* + *ana*, n. Proclamation.

विघ्न *vighna*, i.e. *vi-han* + *a*, m. (n., Sund. 1, 12), **1.** Obstacle, Utt. Râmach. 35, 19; trouble, Çâk. d. 13. **2.** Impediment, Pańch. 168, 3.—**Comp.** *A-*, I. adj. free from obstacles, unobstructed, Çâk. 13, 23. II. n. absence of obstruction, Ragh. 1, 91; instr. °*nena*, without impediment, Râm. 4, 38, 8. *Apa-vighna* + *m*, adv. free from impediments, Ragh. 3, 38. *Kshaṇa-*, m. a delay of a moment, Vikr. d. 17.

ऽविघ्नक *-vighna* + *ka*, at the end of a comp. adj. Obstructing, impeding, Lass. 5, 3.

विघ्नवन्त् *vighna* + *vant*, adj., f. *vatî*, Obstructed by obstacles, Çâk. 41, 11.

विघ्नित *vighnita*, i.e. *vighna* + *ita*, adj. Obstructed, impeded, Pańch. 168, 7; Vikr. d. 49.

विच् ii. 7, *vinach*, *vińch*, † ii. 3, anomal. *vevich*, Par. Âtm. To separate, to deprive, Bhaṭṭ. 14, 103 (*vikta*, Lass. 2, 14, must be changed to *rikta*); cf. 2. *vij*.—With the prep. **वि** *vi*, **1.** To remove, MBh. 1, 6372. **2.** To change, MBh. 1, 7396. **3.** To decide, MBh. 2, 2244. Ptcple. of the pf. pass. *vivikta*. **1.** Separated. **2.** Solitary, Man. 2, 215; 3, 206; Pańch. 159, 21. **3.** Scattered, Chr. 29, 29 (perhaps it is to be changed to *nivishṭa*). **4.** Discriminated. **5.** Pure, Bhartṛ. 3, 62. **6.** Discriminative. **7.** Profound (as thought). **8.** Intent on. n. Loneliness, being alone, Vikr. 40, 5.—With **प्रवि** *pra-vi*, *pravivikta*, **1.** Separated, Vedântas. in Chr. 208, 13. **2.** Solitary, Râm. 2, 48, 59, ed. Seramp.—Cf. O.H.G. wîchan, A. S. wícan, recedere (perhaps rather to 2. *vij*); perhaps also O.H G. wehsal; A.S. wrixl; εἴκειν; Lat. vicis, invicem, vicissim, and vincere, i.e. to cause to cede.

विचक्षण *vichakshaṇa*, i.e. *vi-chaksh* + *ana*, adj. **1.** All-seeing, Chr. 289, 8 = Rigv. i. 112, 8; Chr. 296, 4 = Rigv. i. 112, 4. **2.** Discerning, knowing, Pańch. i. d. 59 (cf. Böhtl. Ind. Spr. 984); circumspect, wise, Bhag. 18, 2; clever.—**Comp.** *Kârya-*, adj. understanding to manage affairs, Pańch. i. d. 424 (cf. Böhtl. Ind. Spr. 3241). *Sańdhi-*, adj. knowing the different kinds of peace-making, Hit. iv. d. 107. *Su-*, adj. well-discerning, Hit. i. d. 21, M.M.

विचक्षस् *vi-chaksh* + *as*, m. A preceptor.

विचय *vichaya*, i. e. *vi-chi* + *a*, m. Search, Utt. Râmach. 15, 4; research.

विचयन *vichayana*, i.e. *vi-chi* + *ana*, n. Seeking, search.

विचर्षणि *vicharshaṇi* (*vi*, and vb. *char*), adj. Swift, Chr. 291, 12 = Rigv. i. 64, 12.

विचलन *vi-chal* + *ana*, n. **1.** Deviating from. **2.** Unsteadiness. **3.** Self-praise, conceit.

विचार *vichâra*, i.e. *vi-char* + *a*, m. **1.** Consideration, Hit. ii. d. 42; deliberation, Pańch. i. d. 417 (doubt). **2.** Discrimination, selection, Hit. 104, 7 (read *sârâsâravichâraḥ*). **3.** Discussion. **4.** Judging, Hit. ii. d. 72; judgment, Hit. 116, 10; decision. **5.** Prudence, Böhtl. Ind. Spr. 2891.—**Comp.** *A-vichâra* + *m*, adv. without long consideration, Daçak. in Chr. 188, 13. *Nis-*, adj. not reflecting, Râjat. 6, 323. °*ram*, adv. without long reflection, Râm. 2, 23, 10 Gorr. *Su-*, m. due consideration. *Svapna-*, m. interpretation of dreams.

विचारण *vichâraṇa*, i. e. *vi-char*,

Caus., + *ana*, I. n., and f. *ṇâ.* **1.** Deliberation, Hit. 51, 22; investigation, Prab. 100, 3. **2.** Hesitation, doubt, Nal. 13, 27. **II.** f. *ṇâ*, The Mîmâṁsâ system of philosophy.

विचारिन् *vichârin*, i.e. *vi-char* + *in*, adj., f. *iṇî*, **1.** Wandering, Chr. 46, 25. **2.** Discussing, judging. **3.** Lascivious, Châṇ. 29 in Berl. Monatsb. 1864, 408.—**Comp.** *Svapna-*, m. an interpreter of dreams.

विचाल *vichâla*, i.e. *vi-chal* + *a*, adj. Intervening, intermediate.

विचिकित्सा *vichikitsâ*, i.e. *vi-chikitsa*, desider. of *kit*, + *â*, f. Doubt, Mâlat. 42, 11. —**Comp.** *Nis-vichikitsa* + *m*, adv. without long reflecting, Kull. ad Man. 8, 417.

विचिति *vi-chi* + *ti*, f. Searching, Nalod. 4, 2.

विचित्रित *vichitrita*, see *chitr*; विचीर्ण *vichîrṇa*, see *char*.

विचेष्टा *vi-cheshṭ* + *â*, f. Behaviour.—**Comp.** *Dus-*, adj. ill-behaving, MBh. 12, 7033. *Nis-*, adj. motionless, Râm. 5, 44, 11.

विच्छन्द *vichchhanda*, and विच्छन्दक *vichchhanda* + *ka*, m. **1.** A palace. **2.** A temple.

विच्छर्दक *vichchhardaka*, m. **1.** A palace. **2.** A temple (cf. ved. *chhardis*).

विच्छायय *VICHCHHÂYAYA*, a denomin. derived from *vi-chhâya* (cf. *chhâyâ*), Par. To free from shadow, Häberl. in Anth. 224, 79.

विच्छित्ति *vichchhitti*, i.e. *vi-chid* + *ti*, f. **1.** Cutting, Bhartṛ. 3, 46. **2.** Dividing. **3.** Separation. **4.** Loss. **5.** The boundary of a house. **6.** Colouring the body with coloured unguents, Çâk. d. 164.

विच्छेद *vichchheda*, i.e. *vi-chid* + *a*, m. **1.** Cutting. **2.** Dividing, breaking, Kir. 7, 16. **3.** Separation, interruption, Vikr. 60, 5. **4.** A section, a chapter. **5.** Interval. **6.** Dissension.

विच्छेदन *vichchhedana*, i.e. *vi-chhid* + *ana*, n. Destruction, Pańch. ii. d. 165.

विच्युति *vi-chyu* + *ti*, f. Separation, Nal. 13, 34.—**Comp.** *Garbha-*, f. miscarriage, Suçr. 1, 278, 20. *Sańga-*, f. 1. disunion. 2. separation from worldly attachment.

† 1. विछ् *VICHH* (akin to *vî*), i. 6, *vichchhâya*, Par. To go, to approach. —Cf. οἰχνέω, οἴχομαι.

† 2. विछ् *VICHH*, i. 10, Par. To speak, to shine.

1. विज् *VIJ*, ii. 7, *vinaj*, *vinj*, Par. **1.** To tremble. **2.** To fear. Ptcple. of the pf. pass. *vigna*, Trembling, Ragh. 14, 88. Caus. *vejaya*, To terrify, Ragh. 8, 39.—With the prep. आ *â*, *âvigna*, Terrified, Arj. 6, 9.—With उद् *ud*, i. 6, Âtm. (in epic poetry also Par., MBh. 1, 5549; and i. 1, Âtm., MBh. 3, 2322). **1.** To tremble, to be agitated, MBh. 3, 2322. **2.** To suffer uneasiness, Man. 2, 161. **3.** To fear (with the abl. and gen.), Man. 2, 162; 7, 103; to abhor, Pańch. iii. d. 191; to be reckless of (with abl.), Mâlat. 51, 1. **4.** To terrify, MBh. 2, 178. *udvigna*, **1.** Terrified, Râm. 1, 9, 12. **2.** Afflicted, sorrowful, Hit. 4, 2, M.M.; Chr. 11, 14. **3.** Anxious. **Comp.** *An-*, adj. not afflicted, Bhag. 2, 56. Ptcple. of the fut. pass. *udvejanîya*. **1.** To be feared, Pańch. iii. d. 142; fearful, horrible. Caus. To terrify, MBh. 1, 8427. *udvejita*, **1.** Terrified, Pańch. 209, 23. **2.** Grieved, pained, Pańch. 222, 7. **3.** Caused to loathe, Daçak. in Chr. 181, 16; 185, 5.—With निरुद् *nis-ud*, *nirudvigna*, Fearless (rather *udvigna* with *nis*), Râm. 6, 16, 81.—With पर्युद् *pari-ud*, To suffer,

Râm. 2, 66, 9.—With समुद् *sam-ud*, *samudvigna*, Terrified, anxious, Lass. 50, 16. — With वि *vi*, *vivigna*, Agitated, stirred, Râjat. 5, 339.—With सम् *sam*, *saṁvigna*, Very frightened, MBh. 3, 2561.—Cf. probably ἀΐσσω; A.S. wicelian, vacillare, wince, A winch.

† 2. विज् *VIJ*, ii. 3, *vevij*, Par. Âtm. To be separate, to separate; cf. *vich*, at the end.

3. विज् *vij* (m.), A die, for playing with, Chr. 295, 10 = Rigv. i. 92, 10.

विजनन *vi-jan* + *ana*, n. Birth, delivery.

विजय *vijaya*, i.e. *vi-ji* + *a*, I. m. **1.** Victory, Pańch. iii. d. 11. **2.** Overpowering, Pańch. 168, 25. **3.** A name of Arjuna. **4.** Name of an auspicious hour, Râm. 1, 73, 1. **II.** f. *yâ*. **1.** Durgâ. **2.** The name of several plants.—**Comp.** *Digvijaya*, i.e. *diç-*, m. conquest of the whole earth, Hit. 84, 10, M.M.

विजयन्त *vi-jayant* + *a* (vb. *ji*), m. Indra.

विजयिन् *vijayin*, i.e. *vijaya* + *in*, **I.** adj. Victorious, Hit. iii. d. 84. **II.** m. Conqueror, Pańch. iii. d. 270.—**Comp.** *Samara-*, m. one who has been victorious in battle, Böhtl. Ind. Spr. 2087.

विजिगीष *vijigîsha*, i.e. *vi-jigîsha*, desider. of *ji*, + *a*, adj. Desirous of conquering, emulative.

विजिगीषा *vijigîshâ*, i.e. *vi-jigîsha* + *â* (see the last), f. Wish to surpass, emulation.

विजिगीषिन् *vijigîshin*, i.e. *vi-jigîsha* + *in* (see the last), adj. Desirous of victory, Johns. Sel. 56, 156.

विजिगीषु *vijigîshu*, i.e. *vi-jigîsha* + *u* (see the last), **I.** adj. **1.** One who wishes to conquer, Man. 7, 155; Pańch. iii. d. 36. **2.** Desirous to surpass. **II.** m. **1.** A warrior. **2.** An invader. **3.** A disputant.

विजिल *vijila*, and विजिविल *vijivila*, adj. Mixed with rice-water or gruel (sauces, etc.).

विजृम्भण *vijṛimbhaṇa*, i.e. *vi-jṛimbh* + *ana*, n. **1.** Yawning. **2.** Expanding, extending, Mâlat. 144, 20. **3.** Sport.

विजेतृ *vijetṛi*, i.e. *vi-ji* + *tṛi*, m., f. *tṛî*, n. **1.** A conqueror, Kir. 5, 34; Utt. Râmach. 62, 14. **2.** Victorious.

विज्जल *vijjala*, **I.** adj. = *vijila*. **II.** n. An arrow.

विज्ञ *vi-jńa*, adj. **1.** Knowing, Lass. 2. ed. 90, 44. **2.** Wise, Chân. 20 in Berl. Monatsb. 1864, 408; Hit. ii. d. 151 (but cf. Böhtl. Ind. Spr. 2042). **3.** Skilful.

विज्ञान *vijńâna*, i.e. *vi-jńâ* + *ana*, n. **1.** Knowledge, Hit. ii. d. 142. **2.** Learning. **3.** Wisdom, Hit. i. d. 167, M.M. **4.** Art, Çâk. d. 2. **5.** Music. **6.** Intelligence, Chr. 6, 9 (at the end of a comp. adj.). **7.** Distinction, Vedântas. in Chr. 207, 5. **8.** Business, employment.—**Comp.** *A-*, n. absence of knowledge; abl. *nât*, unknowingly, Man. 2, 220; on a sudden, Lass. 2. ed. 40, 22. *Su-*, adj. very wise, Pańch. iii. d. 117.

विज्ञापक *vijńâpaka*, i. e. *vi-jńâ*, Caus., + *aka*, **I.** adj. Who or what makes known. **II.** m. **1.** An informant. **2.** An instructor.

विज्ञापन *vijńâpana*, i.e. *vi-jńâ*, Caus., + *ana*, **I.** n. **1.** Teaching. **2.** Informing, representing. **II.** f. *nâ*, Information, Ragh. 17, 40.

विट् *VIṬ*, see *biṭ*.

विट *viṭa*, m. **1.** A catamite, a pathic, a voluptuary, Daçak. in Chr. 180, 13; Bhartṛ. 1, 49. **2.** A paramour, Pańch. 186, 1. **3.** An attendant on a dissolute character or courtezan, a bawd, Bhartṛ. 3, 57. **4.** A rogue, Râjat. 5, 202; 351. **5.** A rat. **6.** A branch and its shoot. **7.** The orange tree. **8.** The name of a mountain.

विटङ्क *viṭaṅka*, m. n. An aviary; the loftiest point, Mâlat. 166, 2 (Prâkṛ.).

विटप *viṭapa*, **I.** m. and n. **1.** The branch of a tree with its new sprout. **2.** A branch, Vikr. 59, 2; Bhâg. P. 4, 25, 18. **3.** A new shoot, Hit. iv. d. 101. **4.** A bush. **5.** A bunch, a cluster, a tuft. **6.** A thicket, Pańch. 184, 21. **7.** Spreading, expansion. **8.** The septum of the scrotum. **II.** m., i.e. *viṭa-pa*, The keeper of catamites. — **Comp.** *Namra-*, adj. the branches of which are bent down, Vikr. d. 27.

विटपशस् *viṭapa+ças*, adv. In branches, Bhâg. P. 2, 7, 36.

विटपिन् *viṭapin*, i.e. *viṭapa+in*, **I.** adj. Having branches, MBh. 1, 1775. **II.** m. **1.** A tree, Râjat. 5, 477. **2.** The large Indian fig-tree.

विट्चर *viṭchara*, i.e. *viç* (in the ved. signification, family, house), *-chara*, m. The tame or village hog (cf. *viḍvarâha*).

विट्पति *viṭpati*, i.e. *viç-pati*, **1.** A daughter's husband, Man. 3, 148. **2.** A head merchant.

विड् *VIḌ*, see *biṭ*.

विड *viḍa* (perhaps a dialectical form based on *vi-dra*, vb. 1. *drâ*), n. **1.** Factitious salt. **2.** A particular kind of fetid salt. **3.** A part, a bit.

विडङ्ग *viḍaṅga*, adj. Clever.

विडम्बन *vi-ḍamb+ana*, **I.** n. **1.** Imitation, copying, disguise, Bhartṛ 3, 23; Râjat. 5, 207. **2.** The supernatural assumption of a borrowed form. **3.** Afflicting, distressing. **4.** Frustrating. **5.** Vexation, Hit. 99, 18; mortification, Brahmav. 2, 79. **II.** f. *nâ*. **1.** Deceiving, fraud, Pańch. iv. d. 9; breach of faith, Pańch. 125, 25. **2.** Pain, distress, Pańch. 220, 14; Bhartṛ. 3, 23.

विडम्बिन् *vi-ḍamb+in*, adj., f. *nî*, Causing error, like, Utt. Râmach. 118, 6.

विडारक *viḍâra+ka* (see the next), m. A cat.

विडाल *viḍâla*, m. **1.** A cat, Râm. 3, 53, 57; Hit. 58, 7. **2.** The eyeball. —**Comp.** *Vana-*, m. a sort of wild cat.

विडालक 1. *viḍâla+ka*, **I.** m. **1.** A cat. **2.** Application of ointment to the external part of the eye. **II.** n. Yellow orpiment.

विडीनक *vi-ḍîna+ka* (vb. *ḍî*), n. Flying severally, MBh. 8, 1901.

विडौजस् *viḍaujas* (the last part is *ojas*), m. Indra, Çâk. d. 193; Ragh. 3, 59.

विड्वराह *viḍvarâha*, i.e. *viç-varâha* (cf. *viṭchara*), m. A tame hog, Man. 5, 14.

† **विण्ट्** *VIṆṬ*, **वुण्ट्** *VUṆṬ*, i. 10, Par. **1.** To kill. **2.** To decay.

वितंस and **वीतंस** *vitaṁsa*, i.e. *vi-taṁs+a*, m. A cage, a net, or any apparatus for confining birds or beasts.

वितण्डा *vitaṇḍâ*, f. **1.** Controversy. **2.** Criticism, Windischmann, Sancara, 96. **3.** A ladle. **4.** The name of two plants.

विततत्व *vi-tata+tva* (vb. *tan*), n. Largeness, Hariv. 12375.

वितति *vitati*, i.e. *vi-tan+ti*, f. **1.** Spreading. **2.** Quantity. **3.** A cluster, a clump, Kir. 12, 47.

वितरण *vitaraṇa*, i.e. *vi-tṛî+ana*, n. **1.** Passing, crossing. **2.** Gift, donation. **3.** Abandoning.

वितर्क *vi-tark+a*, m. **1.** Deliberation, Pańch. i. d. 226. **2.** Consideration.

Hit. iv. d. 96. **3.** Opinion, Johns. Sel. 55, 143; conjecture, Mâlat. 20, 3. **4.** Discussion, Prab. 116, 9. **5.** Doubt, Lass. 2. ed. 21, 1. **6.** A teacher in divine knowledge.—Comp. *Dus-*, adj. difficult to be considered or penetrated, Bhâg. P. 3, 20, 12. *Sa-vitarka* + *m*, adv. thoughtfully, Çâk. 33, 11.

वितर्कण *vitarkaṇa*, i.e. *vi-tark* + *ana*, n. **1.** Reasoning. **2.** Discussion. **3.** Doubt.

वितर्द्धि and **वितर्द्धी** *vitarddhî*, **1.** A terrace in the centre of a court-yard of a palace or temple. **2.** A seat, a bench.

वितस्ता *vitastâ*, f. The name of a river, Râjat. 5, 88; 271.

वितस्ति *vitasti*, i.e. *vi-taṁs* + *ti*, m. and f. A long span, measured by the extended thumb and little finger, Âçvalây. Gṛihyas. iv. 1, in Journ. of the German Oriental Society, ix. i. 8.

वितान *vitâna*, i.e. *vi-tan* + *a*, m. **I.** adj. **1.** Empty. **2.** Pithless. **3.** Stupid. **II.** m. and n. **1.** Spreading, expansion, Nalod. 2, 50. **2.** A heap, a quantity. **3.** A canopy, Vikr. d. 76; Bhartṛ. 3, 93; an awning, Johns. Sel. 40, 37; a cover, Ragh. 9, 50; a cushion, Böhtl. Ind. Spr. 2156. **4.** The hearth or hole in which the sacred fires are kept. **5.** Sacrifice, Nalod. 2, 50.

वितानाय *VITÂNÂYA*, a denomin. derived from *vitâna* with *ya*, Âtm. To turn a canopy, Mâlat. 148, 7 (pass. refl.).

† **वित्त्** *VITT*, i. 10, Par. To quit, to abandon, to give (cf. *vitta*, under *vid*).

वित्तक *vitta* + *ka* (vb. *vid*), Known, famous, Daçak. in Chr. 180, 12.

वित्तज *vitta-ja*, adj. Produced by wealth, Pañch. ii. d. 67.

वित्तवन्त् *vitta* + *vant* (vb. *vid*), adj. Wealthy, Pañch. 8, 3; ii. d. 124.

वित्ति *vitti*, i.e. *vid* + *ti*, f. **1.** Investigation. **2.** Probability, likelihood. **3.** Knowledge. **4.** Acquisition, gain.

वित्रप *vitrapa*, m. A proper name, Râjat. 5, 26.

वित्रास *vitrâsa*, i.e. *vi-tras* + *a*, m. Fear.

† **विथ्** *VITH*, **वेथ्** *VETH*, **विध्** *VIDH*, i. 1, Âtm. To beg.

विथुर *vithura*, I. probably *vyath* + *ura*, adj. Trembling, Chr. 293, 3 = Rigv. i. 87, 3. **II.** m. **1.** A Râkshasa. **2.** A thief.—Comp. *A-*, adj. fearless, Chr. 293, 1 = Rigv. i. 87, 1.

1. **विद्** *VID* (originally 'To see'), **A.** ii. 2, Par. (in epic poetry also Âtm., Râm. 1, 57, 5). **1.** To perceive, to feel, Ragh. 14, 56. **2.** To learn, MBh. 3, 16968. **3.** To find out, MBh. 1, 6040. **4.** To know, Man. 2, 126; imperat. *vidâṁ karotu*, He may know, Pañch. v. d. 23; ved. *vidâ* (the final lengthened), Chr. 292, 8 = Rigv. i. 86, 8. Âtm. ved. To be known, Chr. 293, 6 = Rigv. i. 87, 6 (*vidre*, ved. 3. pl. of the the pres.). **5.** To consider, Man. 2, 156; Pañch. iii. d. 231; to value, Hit. iv. d. 52; to take for, Bhag. 2, 19; also ii. 7, Bhaṭṭ. 6, 39. **6.** To ascertain, Man. 7, 135. **B.** i. 6, *vinda*, Par. Âtm. **1.** (To see =), to find, Hit. i. d. 199, M.M.; also ii. 7, MBh. 3, 15388. **2.** To obtain, MBh. 3, 6016. **3.** Âtm. (in epic poetry also Par., MBh. 1, 4090), To take in marriage, Man. 9, 69; to choose a bridegroom, Man. 9, 90. **C.** ii. 7, *vinad*, *vind*, Âtm. (in epic poetry also Par., MBh. 3, 8123). **1.** See **A. 5.** **2.** See **B. 1.** **3.** † To consider, to reason. **D.** i. 4, Âtm. (properly pass.). **1.** To be found, to happen, Man. 4, 49. **2.** To exist, Hit. i. d. 116, M.M.; Bhag. 4, 38. Ptcple. of the pres. *vidvaṁs*. **1.** Intelligent, wise, Hit. iii. d. 5. **2.**

Learned, Man. 4, 91 ; Hit. pr. d. 12, M.M. m. **1.** A sage, Bhartṛ. 2, 96. **2.** A scholar, Çâk. d. 2. **Comp.** *A*-, adj. sbst. ignorant, an ignorant man, Man. 4, 191 ; a fool, Man. 2, 214. *Veda*-, 1. adj. skilled in the Vedas, Chr. 12, 2. 2. m. a Brâhmaṇa learned in the Vedas. *Çastra*-, adj. skilled in arms. *Vidyamâna*, 1. existing, Pañch. 139, 4 ; being preserved, Pañch. i. d. 402. 2. real, actual. 3. being in one's possession. **Comp.** *A*-, adj. 1. non-existing, not being alive, Man. 2, 248. 2. not present, absent. 3. not being in one's possession, Man. 11, 116. Ptcple. of the pf. pass. **I.** *vidita*. **1.** Known (with gen.), Vikr. 63, 9. **2.** Promised. **3.** Informed. **4.** Represented. **5.** Who or what knows. m. A learned man, a sage. n. Information, representation. **Comp.** *A*-, adj. unknown. n. not knowing, Chr. 5, 6 (loc. *°te pituḥ*, without the knowledge of my father). **II.** *vitta*. **1.** Known. **2.** Notorious. **3.** Famous, Daçak. in Chr. 179, 20 ; Lass. 26, 18. **4.** Investigated, discussed, judged. **5.** Acquired, gained. n. **1.** Wealth, property, Johns. Sel. 3, 15 ; Pañch. 6, 7 ; iv. d. 30 ; money, Pañch. 237, 1. **2.** Substance, power, Pañch. i. d. 25 (but cf. Böhtl. Ind. Spr. 1544) ; thing. **III.** *vinna*. **1.** Known. **2.** Discussed, judged. **3.** Obtained, gained. **4.** Married. **5.** Placed, fixed. Comp. ptcple. of the fut. pass. *a-vedya*, adj. **1.** Not to be known, unascertainable, secret. **2.** Not to be married, Man. 10, 24. m. A calf. Desider. *vividisha*, To desire, to strive to know, Bhâg. P. 2, 9, 40 ; Vedântas. in Chr. 203, 1. Caus., and i. 10, Par. Âtm. *vedaya*. **1.** To teach, MBh. 3, 14048. **2.** To report, Man. 11, 31. **3.** To know, MBh. 2, 175. **4.** Âtm. To be perceived, to be sensible, Man. 12, 13. **5.** † To dwell, to inhabit. Comp. anomal. ptcple. of the pres. Âtm. *a-vedayâna*, adj. One who is not able to show, Man. 8, 32. — With the prep. अधि *adhi*, i. 6, To supersede (a wife), by taking in marriage another, Man. 9, 80. *adhivinna*, f. *nâ*, A superseded wife, 9, 83. —With अनु *anu*, i. 6, **1.** To find again, Pañch. ii. d. 134. **2.** To find out, to believe. Git. 4, 2. **3.** Atm. To take in marriage, MBh. 1, 5114.—With अभि *abhi*, i. 6, **1.** To obtain, MBh. 3, 1933. **2.** To follow, MBh. 3, 13698. —With आ *â*, Caus. **1.** To report, Râm. 1, 20, 5. **2.** To present, Vikr. 82, 18 ; Sâv. 3, 6.—With समा *sam-â*, Caus. To report, MBh. 2, 14.—With नि *ni*, Caus. **1.** To make known, to report, MBh. 3, 1689. **2.** To betray, MBh. 3, 11322. **3.** To pass one's self off as, Çâk. 13, 21. **4.** To present, Man. 2, 51. **5.** To offer as sacrifice, Pañch. 174, 16. **6.** To know, Pañch. 228, 4 (perhaps it is to be changed to *nividita*). *nivedya*, n. An oblation, Râjat. 5, 52. Comp. absol. *a-nivedya*, Without having reported it, Daçak. in Chr. 189, 19. Anomal. infin. *niveditum*, MBh. 2, 1723 (but Çâk. 60, 18, read *nivedayitum*). — With विनि *vi-ni*, Caus. To report, Râm. 1, 1, 72.—With संनि *sam-ni*, Caus. To report, MBh. 1, 3224.—With निस् *nis*, i. 4, Âtm. **1.** To be disgusted, Böhtl. Ind. Spr. 528 ; with one's self, MBh. 3, 14792. **2.** To resign, Bhâg. P. 1, 4, 12. *nirviṇṇa*, **1.** Disgusted with (gen.), Pañch. 51, 25 ; 137, 1 (instr.), Çâk. 20, 2 (Prâkṛ.). **2.** Despondent, Hit. i. d. 133, M.M. **3.** Emaciate with grief, decayed. **4.** Abused, degraded. **5.** Humble. **6.** Known.—With परि *pari*, i. 6, pass. To marry before one's elder brother, Man. 3, 172. *parivinna*, An unmarried elder brother whose junior is married. —With प्रति *prati*, ii. 7, To obtain,

MBh. 3, 8420. Caus. **1.** To make known, to report, Râm. 2, 45, 15. **2.** To deliver, Râm. 1, 2, 9.—With संप्रति *sam-prati*, Caus. To report, to tell, MBh. 1, 3627.—With सम् *sam*, ii. 2, Âtm. **1.** To know, to meditate, Bhaṭṭ. 8, 17. **2.** To teach, MBh. 1, 2114. *saṁ-vidita*, **1.** Known. **2.** Agreed, promised. n. Agreement, concurrence, Mâlav. 45, 17. *sva-saṁvedya*, **1.** To be known only by one's self, Daçak. in Chr. 182, 14. **2.** To be understood by themselves, Râjat. 5, 366. Caus. To perceive, Bhaṭṭ. 17, 63.—Cf. Lat. videre, vitrum; Goth. vitan; A.S. wítan; Goth. veitvods (=*vidvat*, *vidvaṁs*); A.S. wíta, gnarus, ge-wit, ge-wittig; O.H.G. weizian, To show; A.S. wisian, ge-wis; Goth. vitôth, in-veitan; A.S. witan, imputare, wite, poena, witnian, punire; O. H. G. wîzago, propheta, wîzagôn; A.S. wítegian; *ἴδον*, *εἶδον* (i.e. *ἔϝιδεν*), *ἴνδαλμα*, *ἀειδής*, *ἀϊδής*, *ἄϊστος*, *οἶδα* (=*veda*), *εἰδώς* (=*vidvân* [*s*]), *ἴδμων*, *ἵστωρ*, *ἱστορέω*, *ὕδνης*, *ὕδω*, *ὑδέω*, *ἀείδω* (cf. the Zend. use).

2. विद् *vid*, adj. Who or what knows; latter part of comp. nouns, *açva-*, adj. sbst. Conversant with the qualities of horses, epithet of Nala, Nal. 1, 1. *kṛitsna-*, adj. All-knowing, Bhartṛ. 3, 29. *kshetra-*, I. adj. Conversant with any object, Kumâras. 3, 50. **II.** m. The soul, Bhâg. P. 4, 22, 37.—Comp. *Chitrakarmavid*, i.e. *chitra-karman-*, adj. skilled in painting, Hit. ii. d. 109. *Jyotirvid*, i.e. *jyotis-*, adj. sbst. knowing the stars, an astrologer, Yâjñ. 1, 332. *Tad-*, adj. knowing that, Vikr. d. 40. *Dharma-*, adj. 1. acquainted with the law, Man. 2, 61. 2. virtuous, ib. 2, 245. *Sarva-dharma-*, adj. one who knows the whole of duty, Man. 8, 63. *Veda-*, adj. conversant with the Vedas, Chr. 13, 11.

विदग्धता *vidagdha + tâ* (vb. *dah*), f. **1.** Cleverness, Lass. 5, 18. **2.** Elegance, Mâlat. 2, 19. **3.** Shrewdness, sharpness, wit, Hit. ii. d. 166.

विदथ *vid + atha*, I. m. **1.** A wise or learned man. **2.** An ascetic, a devotee. II. n. Sacrifice, Chr. 290, 1 =Rigv. i. 64, 1; Chr. 291, 1=Rigv. i. 85, 1.—Cf. Goth. vitôth.

विदर *vidara*, i.e. *vi-dṛî + a*, I. m. Tearing, rending. II. n. A plant, Cactus indicus.

विदर्भ *vi-darbha*, m. **1.** The name of a country, Nal. 1, 5 (pl.); ib. 32 (sing.). **2.** The king of that country, Nal. 1, 32. **3.** Any dry or desert soil.

विदर्शिन् *vidarçin*, i.e. *vi-dṛiç + in*, adj., f. *nî*, Penetrating, Râm. 2, 116, 27 Gorr.

विदल *vidala*, i.e. *vi-dala* and *vi-dal + a*, I. adj. **1.** Opened, blown (as a flower). **2.** Rent. II. m. **1.** Dividing, separating. **2.** A cake. **3.** Mountain ebony, Bauhinia variegata. III. n. **1.** The cuttings or chips of any substance, a twig, Man. 9, 230. **2.** Split peas, Lass. 79, 15. **3.** Pomegranate bark. **4.** A basket made of split bambus.

विदलन *vi-dal + ana*, n. Tearing, rending, Pañch. i. d. 351.

विदा *vid + â*, f. Knowledge.

विदार *vidâra*, i.e. *vi-dṛî + a*, I. m. **1.** Tearing. **2.** Cutting, Bhartṛ. 2, 23. **3.** War, battle. **4.** The rising of a river above its banks, inundation. II. f. *rî*, The name of two plants.

विदारक *vidâraka*, i.e. *vi-dṛî + aka*, I. m. **1.** A render, a divider. **2.** A rock in the middle of a stream. **3.** A hole or pit for water, sunk in the middle of a dry river. II. f. *rikâ*, The name of a plant.

विदारण *vidârana*, i.e. *vi-drî + ana*, I. m. The name of a tree. II. n. 1. Tearing, breaking, Pańch. i. d. 418. 2. Killing. 3. Afflicting. III. n., and f. *nâ*, War, battle.

विदाहिन् *vidâhin*, i.e. *vi-dah + in*, adj. 1. Burning, hot, Bhag. 17, 9. 2. Pungent.

विदिशा *vidiçâ*, f. The name of a river and town, Pańch. iii. d. 240 (cf. Wils. Vishṇu P. 183, 52).

विदुर *vid + ura*, I. adj. Wise, knowing. II. m. 1. A learned or clever man. 2. An intriguer. 3. A proper name, Pańch. i. d. 176; Johns. Sel. 8, 2.

विदूर *vi-dûra*, I. m. The name of a mountain and city whence the lapis lazuli is brought. II. *vi-dûra + tas*, adv. Far, Mâlat. 61, 12.

विदूषक *vidûshaka*, i.e. *vi-dush*, Caus., + *aka*, I. adj. 1. Censorious, detracting. 2. Facetious, witty. II. m. 1. A jester, a buffoon. 2. (In dramatic language), The jocose companion of the principal person, Vikr. 15, 1. 3. A catamite, Daçak. in Chr. 180, 13.

विदूषण *vidûshaṇa*, i. e. *vi-dush*, Caus., + *ana*, n. 1. Censuring. 2. Abuse.

विदेशग *vi-deça-ga*, adj. Going in a foreign country, Pańch. v. d. 84.

विदेह *vi-deha*, I. adj. Without body. II. m. The king of Videhâ. III. f. *hâ*, The name of a district.

विद्या *vid + yâ*, f. 1. Knowledge, learning, Pańch. i. d. 446; 243, 19, sqq. 2. A magical pill or bolus, by putting which into the mouth, a person has the power of ascending to heaven. 3. Durgâ. 4. A tree, Premna spinosa.—Comp. *A-*, I. f. want of knowledge, ignorance. II. adj. unlearned, Man. 9, 205. *Âtmavidyâ*, i.e. *âtman-*, f. the knowledge of the Supreme Spirit, Man. 7, 43. *Adhyâtma-*, f. the same, Bhag. 10, 32. *Kṛita-*, adj. learned, Pańch. iv. d. 40. *Tarka-*, f. the science of reasoning or logic, Prab. 105, 8. *Dus-*, adj. unlearned, rude, Râjat. 1, 356. *Dhanus-*, f. knowledge of archery, Lass. 36, 18. *Nakshatra-*, f. astronomy, or rather astrology, Man. 6, 50. *Nis-*, adj. unlearned, Kâm. Nîtis. 5, 56. *Nîti-*, f. knowledge of correct conduct, Hit. pr. d. 2, M.M. *Sa-*, adj. 1. learned, Râjat. 5, 178. 2. wise. *Sadvidyâ*, i.e. *sant-* (vb. 1. *as*), f. good learning, Bhartṛ. 2, 45. *Sam-pûrṇa-* (vb. *prî*), adj. replete with knowledge.

विद्यातस् *vidyâ + tas*, adv. = abl. of *vidyâ*, Than learning (*buddhir uttamâ*, Understanding is better than learning), Pańch. v. d. 31.

विद्याधर *vidyâ-dhara*, I. m. A kind of demigod, Kathâs. 1, 13. II. f. *rî*, A female demigod of this kind, Hit. 63, 16.

विद्याधार *vidyâ-âdhâra*, m. The abode of knowledge, Mâlat. 41, 2.

विद्यावन्त् *vidyâ + vant*, adj., f. *vatî*, Learned, possessed of science, Pańch. i. d. 43; v. d. 9.

विद्युत् *vi-dyut*, f. Lightning, Vikr. d. 76.

विद्युत्वन्त् *vidyut + vant*, adj. Containing lightning, electrical, Megh. 65.

विद्युन्मन्त् *vidyunmant*, i.e. *vidyut + mant*, adj. Loaded with lightning, Chr. 293, 1 = Rigv. i. 88, 1.

विद्योतन *vidyotana*, i.e. *vi-dyut + ana*, adj. Illustrating, Lass. 67, 2.

विद्र *vidra*, i.e. *vi-drî + a*, n. 1. Piercing, perforating. 2. A hole, a chasm.

विद्रव *vidrava*, i.e. *vi-dru + a*, m. 1. Liquefaction. 2. Flowing out, oozing.

3. Flight, retreat. 4. Fear. 5. Censure, reproach. 6. Intellect.

विद्राव *vidrâva,* i.e. *vi-dru* + *a,* m. 1. Liquefaction. 2. Flight, retreat.

विद्रुम *vi-druma,* m. 1. Coral, Ṛit. 6, 16; Bhâg. P. 4, 25, 16. 2. A tree bearing precious gems. 3. A young sprout.

विद्वत्त्व *vidvattva,* i.e. *vidvaṅs* (ptcple. perf. or pres. of *vid*), + *tva,* n. Wisdom, Pañch. ii. d. 56.

विद्विष् *vi dvish,* m. An enemy, Hit. iii. d. 92.

विद्विष्टता *vi-dvishṭa* + *tâ* (vb. *dvish*), f. Hatred, Johns. Sel. 50, 102.

विद्वेष *vidvesha,* i.e. *vi-dvish* + *a,* m. 1. Enmity, Man. 2, 111; 8, 346. 2. Contempt, Bharata, 8, in Sch. ad Nalod. 2, 55.

विद्वेषण *vidveshaṇa,* i.e. *vi-dvish* + *ana,* n. Causing abhorrence, Nal. 9, 9.

विद्वेषिन् *vidveshin,* i.e *vidvesha* + *in,* I. adj., f. *iṇî,* Inimical. II. m. An enemy, Pañch. i. d. 425.

1. **विध्** *VIDH,* see *vith.*

2. **विध्** *VIDH,* i. 6 (developed out of *vi-dhâ* and *vyadh*), Par. 1. To dispose (ved.). 2. To perform (ved.). 3. To worship (ved.). 4. † To pierce.

विधनता *vi-dhana* + *tâ,* f. Poverty, Hit. i. d. 133, M.M.

विधवा *vidhavâ,* i.e. *vi-dhava,* f. A widow, Pañch. ii. d. 98.—**Comp.** *A-,* f. one who is not a widow, Megh. 97.—Cf. Lat. vidua, viduus; Goth. viduvo; A.S. wuduwe, and m. wuduwa; perhaps ἠίθεος.

विधा *vi-dhâ,* f. 1. Form. 2. Manner. 3. Act, action. 4. Thriving, prosperity. 5. Hire, wages. 6. Food of horses, elephants, etc. 7. (vb. *vyadh*), Piercing.—**Comp.** *An-eka-vidha,* adj. being of manifold kind, Pañch. 61, 10. *Ashṭa-vidha,* i.e. *ashṭan-,* adj. eight-fold, Man. 7, 154. *Asmad-,* adj. such as we, Râm. 4, 31, 6. *Evam-,* adj. of such kind, Vikr. d. 38; such, Pañch. 30, 10. *Kati-,* adj. how manifold, MBh. 13, 6278. *Guṇa-,* adj. possessed of the different qualities, MBh. 12, 11466. *Chatur-,* adj. quadruple, Man. 2, 12. *Tathâ-,* I. adj. so conditioned, Hit. 48, 8, M.M. II. °*dham,* adv. 1. thus, Nal. 7, 16. 2. in the same manner, Bhâshâp. 94. *Tad-,* adj. 1. proportioned to that, Man. 2, 112. 2. of that kind, Ragh. 2, 22. *Tâdṛigvidha,* i.e *tâdṛiç-,* adj. being in such a situation, Kathâs. 22, 231. *Tri-,* adj. of three kinds, Man. 1, 117; 7, 185. *Tvad-,* adj. such as you, Râm. 3, 2, 27. *Daça-vidha,* i.e. *daçan-,* adj. tenfold, of ten kinds, Bhâg. P. 3, 6, 9. *Dus-,* adj. 1. base, Râm. 2, 109, 30 Gorr. 2. poor. *Dri-,* adj. of two sorts, Man. 7, 162. *Navavidha,* i.e. *navan-,* adj. consisting of nine parts, Bhâg. P. 3, 10, 13. *Nânâ-,* adj. of various sorts, Man. 5, 110; manifold, Hit. 46, 14. *Pṛithagv*°, i.e. *pṛithak-,* adj. various, Man. 1, 40. *Bahu-,* adj. various, multiform. °*dham,* adv. in several directions, up and down, Vikr. 30, 17. *Mad-,* adj. such as I, Chr. 24, 40; Hit. iii. d. 100. *Yathâ-,* adj. of what sort, how like. *Vi-,* adj. various, of many sorts, Pañch. 192, 22; manifold, Vikr. d. 46. *Shaḍvidha-,* i.e. *shash-,* adj. of six sorts, Bhâshâp. 34. *Sa-,* adj. 1. of the same kind. 2. near, Mâlat. 7, 14. *Saptavidha,* i.e. *saptan-,* adj. sevenfold, Pañch. 7, 15. *Su-,* I. adj. 1. of a good kind. 2. in a good or easy way. II. °*dham,* adv. easily.

विधातृ *vi-dhâ* + *tṛi,* m., properly, Ruler. 1. Fate, Pañch. 138, 23. 2. Brahman, Lass. 91, 13; Bhartṛ. 2, 7, 15 (or fate). 3. Kâma. 4. A maker, Mâlat. 18, 7.—**Comp.** *Anâgata-,* m. 1.

a cautious person. 2. the proper name of a fish, Pańch. 77, 9.

विधान *vidhâna*, i.e. *vi-dhâ* + *ana*, n. **1.** Sending, ordering, arrangement, creation, Man. 1, 3; Ragh. 6, 11; disposition, Chr. 15, 6; Johns. Sel. 8, 5 (dat. in the sense of the infin.). **2.** Ordinance, Ragh. 8, 40; rule, precept, regulation, Man. 1, 112; 115. **3.** Form, mode, Sund. 1, 22; 26; manner. **4.** Action, especially the performance of religious acts, Chr. 56, 17. . **5.** Worship. **6.** Ceremony, Man. 3, 67. **7.** Means, expedient, Pańch. 258, 11. **8.** Gaining. **9.** Wealth. **10.** Act of hostility. **11.** Conflict of opposite feelings. **12.** An elephant's fodder.—**Comp.** *Tathâ-*, adj. following this mode, in this manner, Hit. 101, 12. *Puṁvat-*, n. ceremonies as on the birth of a male, Chr. 51, 19.

विधायिन् *vidhâyin*, i.e. *vi-dhâ* + *in*, adj. **1.** Establishing a rule or law, Lass. 2. ed. 89, 30. **2.** Placing, Râjat. 5, 295; fixing, securing. **3.** Building, Râjat. 5, 37. **4.** Causing, making, ib. 5, 255. **5.** Delivering, entrusting. — **Comp.** *Bhaya-*, adj. alarming, fearful.

विधि *vidhi*, i.e. *vi-dhâ* (cf. *nidhi*), m. **1.** Order, injunction, command, Bhâg. P. 8, 20, 27; Pańch. iii. d. 238 (*daiva-*, When destiny commands). **2.** Rule, Pańch. 117, 11; precept, Hit. i. d. 167, M.M.; 89, 6 (*na vidhiḥ*, Is not prescribed, cf. Hit. 94, 3; not just). **3.** A sacred precept. **4.** Ceremony, Man. 2, 67; Pańch. 158, 5. **5.** A text prescribing any particular act. **6.** A sacred work. **7.** Fate, Pańch. ii. d. 20. **8.** Creator, Brahmav. 2, 94; Brahman. **9.** A name of Vishṇu. **10.** Time. **11.** Kind, sort, manner, Pańch. 138, 15; Vikr. d. 72 (*ko yaṁ vidhiḥ*, How comes that to pass?). **12.** Act, action, Çiç. 9, 78; Pańch. 260, 17; Vikr. d. 9; creation, Kir. 7, 7. **13.** Behaviour, life, Man. 2, 16. **14.** Food for horses, elephants, etc.—**Comp.** *A-*, m. wrong way; instr. unjustly, Pańch. i. d. 421. *Karmavidhi*, i.e. *karman-*, m. rule of action, Man. 9, 325. *Kriyâ-*, m. rule of conduct, Man. 12, 87. *Chhadmavidhi*, i.e. *chhadman-*, m. disguise, Utt. Râmach. 17, 14. *Dus-*, m. ill fate, Kathâs. 21, 79. *Paribhava-*, m. humiliation, Böhtl. Ind. Spr. 1233. *Prasâdhana-*, m. embellishing, Vikr. d. 22. *Prâyaçchitta-*, m. rules for penance, Man. 1, 116. *Bhavadvidhi*, i.e. *bhavant-*, adj. thy manner (i.e. the same manner in which you are treated), Pańch. 215, 8. *Bheda-*, m. separation, Bhartṛ. 2, 15. *Mańgala-*, m. the ceremony of oblations, Daçak. in Chr. 180, 6. *Yathâ-*, adv. according to rule, Pańch. iii. d. 162. *Viçesha-*; m. 1. special rule or observance. 2. special form, Hit. 117, 19 (of a treaty). *Çṛińgâra-*, m. dress fit for amorous interviews, Pańch. 35, 15.

विधिज्ञ *vidhi-jńa*, adj. Knowing the rules, Pańch. ii. d. 130.

विधितस् *vidhi* + *tas*, adv. According to rule.

विधित्सा *vidhitsâ*, i.e. *vi-dhitsa*, desider. of *dhâ*, + *a*, f. Wish to do, desire, MBh. 12, 6603; design. — **Comp.** *Nirvidhitsa*, i.e. *nis-*, adj. free from desire, MBh. 3, 13953.

विधित्सु *vidhitsu*, i.e. *vi-dhitsa* (see the last), + *u*, adj. Wishing to do or make, Kir. 10, 17.

विधिवत् *vidhi* + *vat*, adv. Agreeably to rule, Vedântas. in Chr. 202, 10; Pańch. i. d. 347.

विधु *vidhu*, m. **1.** The moon, Man. 3, 127. **2.** Vishṇu. **3.** Brahman. **4.** A Râkshasa. **5.** An expiatory oblation. **6.** Camphor.

विधुति *vi-dhu* + *ti*, f. Shaking, trembling, trepidation, Mâlat. 1, 5.

विधुंतुद *vidhuṁtuda*, i.e. *vidhu+m -tud+a*, m. Râhu, the personified ascending node, Pańch. i. d. 370.

विधुर *vidhura*, i.e. *vyadh+ura*, I. adj. 1. Trembling, Çiç. 9, 77; agitated, Bhartṛ. 1, 37. 2. Bewildered, Utt. Râmach. 78, 1. 3. Adverse, Pańch. 42, 13; i. d. 220. 4. Separate from a mistress or lover, abandoned, Nalod. 3, 50; Megh. 113; Vikr. d. 102. II. n. 1. Agitation of mind. 2. Danger, Hit. 50, 8. 3. Separation.

विधुरता *vidhura+tâ*, f. Trembling, agitation, Lass. 72, 11.

विधुवन *vidhuvana*, i.e. *vi-dhû+ana*, n. Trembling.

विधूति *vi-dhû+ti*, f. 1. Shaking. 2. Agitation.

विधूनन *vidhûnana*, i.e. *vi-dhû*, Caus., +*ana*, Shaking (rather causing to shake).

विधेयज्ञ *vi-dheya-jña* (vb. *dhâ*), adj. One who knows what must be done, Pańch. i. d. 383.

विधेयता *vi-dheya+tâ* (vb. *dhâ*), f. 1. Necessary or proper act or conduct. 2. Fitness for enactment as a rule. 3. Submission, Kir. 11, 33.

विध्वंस *vi-dhvaṁs+a*, m. 1. Aversion. 2. Disrespect. 3. Offence, Kir. 3, 16. 4. Destruction.

विध्वंसिन् *vi-dhvaṁs+in*, adj. 1. Falling asunder, Hit. i. d. 48, M.M. 2. Destroying. 3. Hostile.—**Comp.** *A-*, adj. not laying aside, Dev. 1, 4.

विनद *vi-nad+a*, m. 1. Sound, noise. 2. A tree, Echites scholaris.

विनदिन् *vi-nad+in*, adj. Roaring, grumbling, Johns. Sel. 91, 34.

विनय *vinaya*, i.e. *vi-nî+a*, m. 1. Training, discipline, Ragh. 10, 80. 2. Good behaviour, Pańch. iii. d. 122. 3. Behaviour, Utt. Râmach. 109, 6. 4. Reverence, Lass. 2. ed. 35, 11. 5. Modesty, Pańch. i. d. 12.—**Comp.** *A-*, m. 1. want of modesty or propriety of conduct, Man. 7, 40. 2. wrong behaviour, Hit. ii. d. 135. *Dus-*, m. improper conduct, Pańch. 259, 15. *Sa-*, adj. well-behaved, modest, Ṛit. 6, 21. °*yam-*, adv. humbly, modestly, Pańch. 47, 1; Vikr. 86, 10; graciously, Hit. 12, 2, M.M.

विनयन *vinayana*, i.e. *vi-nî+ana*, I. adj. Removing, Megh. 53. II. n. Instruction, accomplishment, Daçak. in Chr. 180, 8.

विनयवन्त् *vinaya+vant*, adj., f. *vati*, Modest, well-behaved.—**Comp.** *A-*, adj. ill-behaved, Lass. 31, 18.

विनशन *vi-naç+ana*, n. 1. Destroying, destruction. 2. The name of a country, Man. 2, 21.

विनश्वर *vi-naç+vara*, adj. Perishable, Hit. i. d. 46, M.M.

विना *vinâ* (from *vi*), prep. Without, Pańch. i. d. 131; except (with acc., instr., and abl.), Vikr. d. 10; Hit. pr. d. 32, M.M.; Pańch. 250, 5; iii. d. 34 (*na yânaṁ vinâ pra çasyate*, Nothing but, i.e. only, marching is recommended).

विनायक *vinâyaka*, i.e. *vi-nî+aka*, I. m. 1. A spiritual teacher. 2. Gaṇeça, Lass. 1, 1. 3. Garuḍa. 4. An obstacle. II. f. *yikâ*, The wife of Garuḍa.

विनाश *vinâça*, i.e. *vi-naç+a*, m. 1. Perdition, Man. 3, 179; ruin, destruction, Pańch. 162, 12; death, Pańch. 175, 3; 184, 9 (with *upa yâ*, To die). 2. Removal, Pańch. 187, 7; disappearance; with *abhi-i*, To disappear, Pańch. v. d. 66. 3. Loss, Vikr. d. 85; Pańch. 145,

15.—**Comp.** *A-*, m. deliverance from ruin, Chr. 56, 15.

विनाशक *vinâçaka*, i.e. *vi-naç*, Caus., + *aka*, adj. sbst. Destroying, a destroyer, Lass. 4, 1.

विनाशन *vinâçana*, i.e. *vi-naç*, Caus., + *ana*, **I.** m. A destroyer, Nal. 12, 30 (at the end of a comp.). **II.** n. Destruction, Chr. 56, 19; Râm. 4, 19, 11.

विनाशिन् *vinâçin*, i. e. *vi-naç* and *vinâça*, + *in*, adj. **1.** Destroying, destructive. **2.** Perishing, Hit. iv. d. 126. **3.** Undergoing transformation, Man. 1, 27.—**Comp.** *A-*, adj. imperishable, Bhag. 2, 17.

विनाह and **वीनाह** *vînâha*, i.e. *vi-nah* + *a*, m. The top or cover of a well.

विनिग्रह *vi-ni-grah* + *a*, m. Restraining, subduing, Bhag. 13, 7.

विनिद्रत्व *vi-nidra* + *tva* (*nidrâ*), n. Waking, vigilance.

विनिपात *vinipâta*, i.e. *vi-ni-pat* + *a*, m. **1.** Falling, Bhartṛ. 2, 10; falling down, Pańch. 203, 2. **2.** Ruin, Çâk. 70, 1. **3.** Calamity, Man. 4, 146. **4.** Death, Man. 8, 185. **5.** Pain. **6.** Disrespect.

विनिमय *vinimaya*, i.e. *vi-ni-me* + *a*, m. **1.** Barter, exchange, Mâlav. d. 31; instr. alternately, Ragh. 1, 26. **2.** A pledge, a deposit.

विनिमेष *vinimesha*, i.e. *vi-ni-mish* + *a*, m. A wink, sign, Kir. 12, 26.

विनियोग *viniyoga*, i.e. *vi-ni-yuj* + *a*, m. **1.** Separation. **2.** Abandoning, Hit. 99, 13. **3.** Parting with anything in expectation of some advantage. **4.** Appointment to any office. **5.** Application to, or employment in, Hit. 98, 15.

विनिर्जय *vinirjaya*, i.e. *vi-nis-ji* + *a*, m. Victory.

विनिर्णय *vinirṇaya*, i.e. *vi-nis-nî* + *a*, **1.** Ascertainment, Kir. 2, 12. **2.** Settling, Man. 8, 300. **3.** Decision, 1, 114. **4.** A rule, 5, 110.

विनिर्बन्ध *vinirbandha*, i. e. *vi-nis-bandh* + *a*, m. Pertinacious pursuit, Lass. 2. ed. 77, 64.

विनिवृत्ति *vi-ni-vṛit* + *ti*, f. **1.** Stop, stopping, Man. 8, 368. **2.** Abstaining, Pańch. MS. Berol. 149, b.

विनिवेश *viniveça*, i.e. *vi-ni-viç* + *a*, m. An impression, Çâk. d. 142.

विनिश्चय *viniçchaya*, i.e. *vi-nis-chi* + *a*, m. **1.** Decision, Chr. 15, 6; resolution, Sâv. 3, 10. **2.** Certainty, Chr. 17, 31.—**Comp.** *Pâpa-*, adj. intending evil, Râm. 6, 81, 8. *Sva-dharma-artha-*, m. certainty concerning the objects of one's duty.

विनीतत्व *vi-nîta* + *tva* (vb. *nî*), n. Modesty, Hit. i. d. 118, M.M.

विनेतृ *vinetṛi*, i.e. *vi-nî* + *tṛi*, m. **1.** A guide. **2.** A teacher. **3.** A ruler. **4.** A chastiser, Râm. 3, 55, 37.

विनोद *vinoda*, i.e. *vi-nud* + *a*, m. **1.** Dismissing, removing, Utt. Râmach. 73. 10; Çâk. 13, 3 (Prâkṛ.). **2.** Play, pastime, entertainment, Hit. 13, 7, M.M.; Lass. 5, 15; sport, Pańch. 5, 6 (*sarasvati-*, The sport of the goddess of eloquence, i.e. literary practice). **3.** Pleasure, Pańch. 147, 14; happiness, Çâk. 86, 17. **4.** Interest, interesting pursuit, Vikr. d. 45. **5.** Eagerness.—**Comp.** *Nis-*, adj. without pastime, Megh. 86. *Vilapana-*, m. removing (viz. grief), by lamenting, Utt. Râmach. 73, 10.

विनोदन *vinodana*, i.e. *vi-nud* + *ana*, n. Play, pastime, enjoyment, Vikr. d. 38; Bhâg. P. 3, 16, 24.

विनोदिन् *vinodin*, i.e. *vi-nud+in*, adj. Removing, Çâk. d. 69.

विन्दु *vindu*, I. i.e. *vid+u*, adj. **1.** Intelligent. **2.** Liberal. **II.** m. **1.** A drop of any liquid, Pañch. 123, 14; Vikr. d. 80. **2.** A drop of water, taken as a measure. **3.** A spot. **4.** The bite or mark of a tooth. **5.** A mark of coloured paint on an elephant's face or trunk. **6.** A dot over a letter representing the *Anusvâra*. **7.** The part of the forehead between the eyebrows.—**Comp.** *Suvarṇa-* (m.), Vishṇu, Mâlat. 166, 16; the name of a holy place, Mâlat. 145, 6. *Hiraṇya-*, m. fire, MBh. 13, 1697.

विन्ध्य *vindhya*, I. m. **1.** The name of a mountainous range, Hit. 75, 11, M.M. **2.** A hunter. **II.** f. *yâ.* **1.** Small cardamoms. **2.** A fruit, Annona reticulata.—**Comp.** *Nis-*, f. *yâ*, the name of a river, Megh. 29.

विन्नप *vinnapa*, m. A proper name, Râjat. 5, 129.

विन्यास *vinyâsa*, i.e. *vi-ni-as+a*, m. **1.** Entrusting. **2.** A deposit. **3.** Orderly arrangement, Bhâg. P. 5, 20, 38. **4.** Assemblage, collection. **5.** Site, place. **6.** Receptacle.—**Comp.** *Akshara-*, m. writing, writ, Vikr. 25, 20.

विप् *VIP*, † **व्यप्** *VYAP*, i. 10, Par. To throw.—With the prep. **प्र** *pra*, To spend, Pañch. MS. Berol. 4, b (*pravepyamâno*, v. r. of *praveçyamâno*, Kos. ed. orn. 3, 14; cf. Götting. Gel. Anz. 1862, p. 1362).

विपक्त्रिम *vipaktrima*, i.e. *vi-pach+tṛi+ima*, adj. **1.** Ripened, Bhaṭṭ. 1, 10. **2.** Fulfilled.

विपक्षतस् *vi-paksha+tas*, adv. Inimically.

विपक्षता *vi-paksha+tâ*, f. **1.** Hostility. **2.** Opposition. **3.** Contradiction.

विपण *vi-paṇ + a*, m. **1.** Sale, Sund. 2, 23. **2.** Low traffic, Man. 3, 152; 10, 116.

विपणि *vi-paṇ+i*, (m. and) f., and *ṇî*, f. **1.** A shop. **2.** A market, Mâlav. 24, 21. **3.** The street of a market. **4.** An article for sale. **5.** Traffic, Hariv. 3809.

विपत्ति *vi-patti*, i.e. *vi-pad+ti*, f. **1.** Misfortune, Pañch. iii. d. 77. **2.** Failing, Böhtl. Ind. Spr. 263. **3.** Pain. **4.** Death, Bhartṛ. 2, 97.

विपद् *vi-pad*, and **विपदा** *vi-pad+â*, f. Calamity, misfortune, Pañch. i. d. 418 (°*pad*); Ragh. 18, 34 (°*pad*, death).

विपरिणाम *vipariṇâma*, i.e. *vi-pari-nam+a*, m. Change of state or form.

विपरिणामिन् *vipariṇâmin*, i.e. *vi-pari-nam + in*, adj. Undergoing or producing change of state or form.

विपरिवर्तन *viparivartana*, i.e. *vi-pari-vṛit+ana*, I. adj., f. *nî*, Causing to return, Kathâs. 46, 121 (with *vidyâ*, a magical knowledge producing that effect). **II.** n. Turning back.

विपरीतता *viparîtatâ*, i.e. *vi-pari-ita+tâ*, f. **1.** Reverse, that which is contrary, opposite to something, counterpart, Hit. ii. d. 43. **2.** Contrariety.

विपर्यय *viparyaya*, i.e. *vi-pari-i+a*, m. **1.** Change, Pañch. 37, 3. **2.** A morbid change, Man. 11, 48; failure of conception, 3, 49; cf. Râm. 1, 47, 3. **3.** Reverse, that which is contrary, opposite to something, Man. 4, 12; Kir. 11, 44; loc. *ye*, On the contrary, Râm. 2, 26, 34. **4.** Error. **5.** Trespass, Man. 8, 249. **6.** Overthrow, Man. 4, 171. **7.** Opposition, Vedântas. in Chr. 218, 12; contrariety. **8.** Perverseness of disposition. **9.** Hostility.—**Comp.** *Karmaviparyaya*, i.e. *karman-*, m. wrong doing, Hit. ii. d. 100. *Bhâgya-*, and *Vidhi-*, m. misfortune, Vikr. 68, 19; 69, 9.

विपर्यास *viparyâsa*, i.e. *vi-pari-as* + *a*, m. **1.** Reverse (cf. the two last), Utt. Râmach. 96, 15; interchange, ib. 47, 6 (*ghana-virala-bhâvaḥ kshiti-ruhâm yâto viparyâsam*, As for the trees, their state of being close together, or scanty, has interchanged, i.e. where there were before plenty of trees, there are at present few, and vice versâ). **2.** Error, mistake, Bhâshâp. 136; Pańch. 129, 5. **3.** Investing imaginary things with real attributes.

विपश्चित् *vipaçchit*, m. A learned man; prudent, wise, Pańch. i. d. 308; Hit. iii. d. 17.

विपाक *vipâka*, i.e. *vi-pach* + *a*, m. **1.** Cooking. **2.** Ripening, Kir. 4, 26; taking place, Utt. Râmach. 52, 5. **3.** The consequence of actions, Bhartṛ. 2, 97. **4.** Unexpected or improbable result. **5.** Distress, Utt. Râmach. 96, 14. **6.** Change of form or state. **7.** Flavour, taste, MBh. 1, 716. **8.** Digestion.—**Comp.** *Karmavipâka*, i.e. *karman-*, m. the ripening of actions, retribution, MBh. 4, 1405. *Daçâ-*, m. state, Mâlat. 149, 4. *Dus-*, adj. turning out destructive, Utt. Râmach. 29, 8. *Daiva-dus-*, m. cruelty (literally, the hard ripening) of fate, Utt. Râmach. 164, 4; Hit. 18, 7; Utt. Râmach. 27, 5.

विपाकिन् *vipâkin*, i.e. *vipâka* + *in*, adj. Followed, Mâlat. 83, 9.

विपाटन *vipâṭana*, i.e. *vi-paṭ* + *ana*, n. Spoliation, Râjat. 5, 264.

विपाठ *vipâṭha*, m. An arrow, MBh. 4, 168; 5, 1865.

विपादिका *vipâdikâ* (akin to *pâda*), f. **1.** A blister on the foot. **2.** A riddle.

विपाश् *vipâç* (curtailed *vipâçâ*), and **विपाशा** *vipâçâ*, i.e. *vi-pâça*, f. The name of a river, MBh. 1, 6750 (*çâ*).

विपिन *vipina*, n. A thicket, a forest, Lass. 2. ed. 41, 4; a grove, Vikr. 57, 18; Ragh. 4, 31.—**Comp.** *Ati-*, adj. very impenetrable, Kir. 5, 18.

विपुल *vipula* (cf. *pul*), I. adj., f. *lâ*. **1.** Large, great, Pańch. i. d. 18; v. d. 5; Bhartṛ. 2, 91, 99; Râm. 3, 54, 28. **2.** Broad. **3.** Deep. **II.** m. **1.** The mountain Meru. **2.** The Himâlaya mountain. **3.** A respectable man. **III.** f. *lâ*, The earth.—**Comp.** *Sa-*, adj. very spacious.

विपुलता *vipula* + *tâ*, f. Magnitude, Çâk. d. 9.

विप्र *vipra*, m. **1.** A poet, or singer of vedic hymns, Chr. 292, 11 and 3 = Rigv. i. 85, 11; 86, 3. **2.** A Brâhmaṇa, a priest, Kathâs. 4, 110; Pańch. 158, 2.

विप्रकर्ष *viprakarsha*, i.e. *vi-pra-kṛish* + *a*, m. Distance, Vikr. 66, 10.

विप्रकार *viprakâra*, i.e. *vi-pra-kṛi* + *a*, m. **1.** Opposition. **2.** Retaliation. **3.** Injury, abuse, Kir. 3, 55. **4.** Wickedness.

विप्रकारिन् *viprakârin*, i.e. *vi-pra-kṛi* + *in*, adj., f. *iṇî*, **1.** Opposing. **2.** Retaliating.

विप्रकृति *vi-pra-kṛi* + *ti*, f. **1.** Retaliation. **2.** Abuse.

विप्रतिकार *vipratikâra*, i. e. *vi-prati-kṛi* + *a*, m. **1.** Opposition. **2.** Reverse. **3.** Contradiction. **4.** Retaliation.

विप्रतिपत्ति *vipratipatti*, i.e. *vi-prati-pad* + *ti*, and *vi-pratipatti*, f. **1.** Mutual connexion with. **2.** Conversancy. **3.** Perplexity. **4.** Various acquirements. **5.** Difference. **6.** Opposition of interests. 7. Contest, dispute, Windischmann, Sancara, 93.

विप्रतीसार *vipratisâra*, i. e. *vi-prati-sṛi + a*, m. 1. Enmity, hate. 2. Rage. 3. Wickedness, evil action. 4. (also **विप्रतिसार** *vipratisâra*), Repentance.

विप्रयोग *viprayoga*, i.e. *vi-pra-yuj + a*, m. 1. Separation, Man. 9, 1; Pańch. ii. d. 184. 2. Disunion. 3. Quarrel. 4. Deserving.

विप्रलम्भ *vipralambha*, i.e. *vi-pra-labh + a*, m. 1. Deceiving, deceit, Ragh. 19, 18; Utt. Râmach. 82, 12; Daçak. in Chr. 182, 14; 185, 9. 2. Separation, Utt. Râmach. 82, 7 (*ati-bhûmi-gata-*, adj. Whose separation has reached the highest degree, i.e. who has suffered an exceedingly sorrowful separation). 3. Disunion. 4. Quarrel.

विप्रलम्भन *vipralambhana*, i.e. *vi-pra-labh + ana*, n. Deception, Daçak. in Chr. 184, 14.

विप्रलम्भिन् *vipralambhin*, i. e. *vi-pra-labh + in*, adj., f. *nî*, Deceiving, fallacious, Pańch. 203, 3.

विप्रलय *vipralaya*, i.e. *vi-pra-lî + a*, m. Dissolution, annihilation, Utt. Râmach. 143, 8.

विप्रलाप *vipralâpa*, i.e. *vi-pra-lap + a*, m. 1. Idle discourse, prattle. 2. Quarrel.

विप्रलुम्पक *vipralumpaka*, i.e. *vi-pra-lup + aka*, adj. Rapacious, Man. 8, 309.

विप्रवास *vipravâsa*, i.e. *vi-pra-vas + a*, m. Staying abroad.

विप्रवासन *vipravâsana*, i.e. *vi-pra-vas*, Caus., *+ ana*, n. 1. Banishment. 2. Residence abroad.

विप्रश्निका *vipraçnikâ*, i.e. *vi-praç-na + ka*, f. A female fortune-teller.

विप्रुष् *vi-prush*, f. A drop (of any fluid), Man. 5, 133; Pańch. 79, 16 (see my transl. n. 383).

विप्रुष्मन्त् *viprush + mant* (against grammar), adj., f. *matî*, Filled with drops, Bhâg. P. 4, 25, 18.

विप्लव *viplava*, i.e. *vi-plu + a*, m. 1. Spreading; with *gam*, To become known, Pańch. iii. d. 258. 2. Perplexity. 3. Calamity, disaster, Man. 8, 348. 4. Tumult, trouble, Hit. i. d. 72, M.M. 5. Predatory warfare. 6. Rapine, extortion. 7. Affray, scuffle, Râjat. 5, 420 (disturbance). 8. Terrifying an enemy by shouts and gestures. 9. Sin, wickedness, Râjat. 5, 19. — Comp. *Prâṇa-*, adj. depriving of life, Bhâg. P. 1, 18, 2.

विप्लवतस् *viplava + tas*, adv. In consequence of the calamity or disturbance, Râjat. 5, 471.

विप्लाव *viplâva*, i.e. *vi-plu + a*, m. 1. Inundating. 2. Devastating. 3. Causing disturbance. 4. A horse's gallop.

विफलता *vi-phala + tâ*, f., and

विफलत्व *vi-phala + tva*, n. Fruitlessness, Çiç. 9, 6 (*tva*); Pańch. 244, 8 (°*tâṁ nî*, To make fruitless).

विबन्धन *vi-bandh + ana*, in *paras-para-*, adj. Depending on each other, Pańch. i. d. 91.

विबुध *vi-budh + a*, m. 1. A god, Man. 12, 47. 2. A learned, a wise man, Pańch. ii. d. 47 (adj.); ii. d. 182. 3. The moon.

विभक्ति *vibhakti*, i.e. *vi-bhaj + ti*, f. 1. A partition, division, Man. 1, 24.

2. Part. 3. Inheritance. 4. An affix of declension, Pâṇ. i. 4, 104 ; v. 3, 1, sqq.

विभङ्ग *vibhaṅga,* i.e. *vi-bhañj + a,* m. 1. Breaking. 2. Fracture. 3. Stopping, Bhartṛ. 2, 60. 4. Bending, contracting (especially of the eye-brows). 5. Expression of features. 6. Division.—Comp. *Âçâ-,* adj. (with broken hope), hopeless, Hit. i. d. 189, M.M.

विभव *vibhava,* i.e. *vi-bhû + a,* m. 1. Power, Bhartṛ. 2, 40. 2. Supreme or superhuman power, Kir. 5, 21. 3. Wealth, Pañch. iii. d. 96. 4. Property. 5. Substance. 6. Thing, Pañch. iii. d. 167. 7. Magnanimity. 8. Emancipation from existence.—Comp. *Galita-,* adj. one who has spent his fortune (*arthishu,* on the poor), Bhartṛ. 2, 36.

विभवतस् *vibhava + tas,* adj. Agreeably to one's power or rank, to the royal majesty, Mâlav. 19, 1 ; Vikr. 30, 18.

विभा *vi-bhâ,* f. 1. Light. 2. Lustre, Nalod. 1, 48. 3. Beauty. 4. A ray of light.

विभाकर *vibhâ-kara,* m. 1. The sun, Sâh. Darp. p. 312, 2. 2. Fire.

विभाग *vibhâga,* i.e. *vi-bhaj + a,* m. 1. Dividing, Bhâshâp. 3 ; division, Vedântas. in Chr. 207, 23 ; Hit. 119, 18 ; arrangement, Daçak. in Chr. 198, 15. 2. Part, Pañch. 243, 20 ; 241, 7. 3. Distribution, Râjat. 5, 111. 4. Partition of inheritance, Man. 1, 115. 5. The share or portion of inheritance. —Comp. *Digvi°,* i.e. *diç-,* m. a quarter of the compass, direction, Vikr. 5, 14.

विभागतस् *vibhâga + tas,* adv. Proportionately.

विभागशस् *vibhâga + ças,* adv. Proportionately, part for part, Man. 12, 17 ; Bhag. 4, 13.

विभाव *vibhâva,* i.e. *vi-bhû + a,* m. 1. An acquaintance. 2. An excitant of the sentiments of poetical composition, Sâh. Darp. p. 31. 3. The affections or sentiments, as love, Sch. ad Nalod. 2, 8.

विभावक *vibhâvaka,* i. e. *vi-bhû,* Caus., *+ aka,* adj. Discussing, illustrating.

विभावन् I. *vibhâ + van,* adj., f. *vari,* Shining, 287, 1 = Rigv. i. 48, 1 ; Chr. 295, 14 = Rigv. i. 92, 14. II. *vi-bhâ + van,* f. *vari.* 1. Night, Râm. 2, 84, 18. 2. A harlot. 3. A bawd. 4. Turmeric.

विभावन *vibhâvana,* i. e. *vi-bhû + ana,* n. 1. Discussion. 2. Ascertaining, Vikr. 78, 10 (reading). 3. Perceiving distinctly, Man. 2, 101. 4. Conceiving, imagination.

विभावरी *vibhâvarî,* see *vibhâvan.*

विभाविन् *vibhâvin,* i.e. *vibhâva + in,* adj., f. *nî,* Exciting love, Nalod. 2, 8.

विभीतक *vi-bhîta + ka* (vb. *bhî*), m., f. (*kî*), A plant, Terminalia belerica, Lass. 52, 15 (m.).

विभीषण *vibhîshaṇa,* i. e. *vi-bhî,* Caus., *+ ana,* I. adj. Terrific, horrible, Hiḍ. 2, 4. II. m. The brother of Râvaṇa. III. f. *ṇâ,* and n. The property of exciting fear, terrifying, a means of terrifying, Draup. 5, 10 (n.).—Comp. *Su-,* adj. very terrible, Râm. 3, 55, 25.

विभीषिका *vibhîshikâ,* i. e. *vi-bhî,* Caus., *+ aka,* f. A means of terrifying, Utt. Râmach. 117, 1 ; Pañch. 160, 17.

विभु *vibhu,* i.e. *vi-bhû,* I. adj. 1. Omnipresent. 2. All-pervading, pervading, Bhâshâp. 50 ; 93. 3. Eternal. 4. Firm, solid. II. m. 1. A master, a lord, Pañch. 202, 10 ; Chr. 33, 2 ;

used particularly in addressing, Indr. 1, 39; Chr. 13, 15; 17, 27. **2.** One who is able (with infin.), Kir. 5, 43. **3.** Çiva. **4.** Brahman. **5.** Vishṇu. **6.** The soul. **7.** Time. **8.** Space. **9.** Æther. **10.** A servant.

विभुता *vibhu+tâ*, f., and **विभुत्व** *vibhu+tva*, n. Power, Çâk. d. 42 (*tva*).

विभूति *vi-bhû+ti*, f. **1.** Power, dignity, Pańch. 203, 1. **2.** Superhuman power, Hit. iii. d. 115. **3.** Ashes of cow-dung.

विभूतिमन्त् *vibhûti+mant*, adj., f. *matî*, **1.** Powerful. **2.** Superhuman, Bhag. 10, 41.

विभूषण *vibhûshaṇa*, i.e. *vi-bhûsh+ana*, n. Ornament, decoration, Pańch. ii. d. 168.

विभूषा *vi-bhûsh+â*, f. **1.** Light, lustre. **2.** Ornament.

विभेत्तृ *vibhettṛi*, i.e. *vi-bhid+tṛi*, m. A destroyer, Çâk. d. 163.

विभेद *vibheda*, i.e. *vi-bhid+a*, m. **1.** Dividing, Kir. 13, 1. **2.** Breaking, violating, Hit. iv. d. 124. **3.** Wounding. **4.** Bewildering. **5.** A separation. **6.** Distinction. **7.** Contradiction. **8.** Enmity.

विभ्रंश *vi-bhrañç+a*, m. A precipice, Bhâg. P. 8, 22, 5.

विभ्रंशिन् *vi-bhrañç+in*, adj. Falling, fallen, Megh. 68.

विभ्रम *vi-bhram+a*, m. **1.** Whirling, Hit. iii. d. 140; going round, Kathâs. 20, 223 (agitation); motion, Mâlat. 15, 12. **2.** Error, Utt. Râmach. 23, 3 (*hâra-*, adj. Producing the error of a necklace, i.e. like a necklace); Râjat. 5, 332 (*babhruḥ—saṭâ-pâṭala-vibhramam*, Could be mistaken for [i.e. were like] a Bignonia-like mane). **3.** Erroneous use, Man. 7, 24. **4.** Doubt. **5.** Play (of the eyes), Çâk. d. 23. **6.** Amorous actions, Pańch. i. d. 151; flurry, confusion, perturbation, Bhag. 2, 63. **7.** Enrapture, Mâlat. 155, 7. **8.** Beauty, Pańch. v. d. 3; grace, Utt. Râmach. 14, 6.—Comp. *Chitta-*, m. derangement, madness, MBh. 18, 74. *Drishṭi-*, m. amorous playing of the eyes, Çâk. d. 23. *Sa-*, adj. playing, looking amorously, Ṛit. 1, 12; 6, 23.

विभ्राज् *vi-bhrâj*, adj. **1.** Shining. **2.** Elegant, richly dressed.

विभ्रान्ति *vibhrânti*, i.e. *vi-bhram+ti*, f. **1.** Whirling, going round. **2.** Hurry, precipitation. **3.** Error. **4.** Confusion.

विमतिता *vi-mati+tâ*, f. Stupidity, Bhartṛ. 2, 44.

विमनस्क *vi-manas+ka*, adj. Sad, etc.=*vi-manas*, see *manas*.

विमय *vimaya*, i.e. *vi-me+a*, m. Barter, exchange.

विमर्द *vimarda*, i.e. *vi-mṛid+a*, m. **1.** Rubbing, Çâk. 105, 14 (rubbing against, or playing with, the young lion); Ṛit. 1, 20. **2.** The trituration of perfumes. **3.** Touch, contact, Daçak. in Chr. 182, 23; conjunction of the sun and moon, eclipse. **4.** Destroying, Hit. 50, 18. **5.** Killing. **6.** War, Vikr. 87, 1; battle, Utt. Râmach. 138, 5. **7.** Weariness, Chr. 42, 13; tediousness, Mṛichchh. 1, 9.

विमर्दक *vimardaka* (vb. *mṛid*), m. A proper name, Daçak. in Chr. 186, 7.

विमर्दन *vimardana*, i.e. *vi-mṛid+ana*, n. **1.** Rubbing, grinding. **2.** The trituration of perfumes. **3.** Conjunction of the sun and moon, eclipse. **4.** Destroying, killing.

विमर्दिन् *vimardin,* i.e. *vi-mṛid + in,* adj. Destroying, removing, Çâk. d. 69, v.r.

विमर्श *vimarça* (erroneously also **विमर्ष** *vimarsha,* e.g. Kathâs. 21, 25), i.e. *vi-mṛiç + a,* m. **1.** Investigation. **2.** Reasoning. **3.** Discussion, hesitation, Râm. 1, 20, 23.—Comp. *Nis-,* adj. devoid of reflection, Kathâs. 15, 39. *Sa-vimarça + m,* adv. thoughtfully, Çâk. 58, 4.

विमर्शन *vimarçana,* i.e. *vi-mṛiç + ana,* n. Investigating, discussing.

विमर्शिन् *vimarçin,* i.e. *vi-mṛiç + in,* adj. Thinking, deliberating.

विमर्ष *vimarsha,* i.e. *vi-mṛish + a,* m. **1.** Irritation, Chr. 60, 28. **2.** Displeasure. Cf. *vimarça.*

विमलता *vi-mala + tâ,* f. Clearness, Chr. 35, 1.

विमान *vi-mâna,* m. and n. **1.** A chariot of the gods, Vikr. 4, 1; Râm. 3, 48, 6. **2.** Any vehicle, Râm. 3, 54, 6. **3.** A horse. **4.** A palace, Megh. 64. **5.** (*vi-mâ + ana*), A measure.

विमानता *vimâna + tâ,* f. State of a chariot of the gods, Vikr. d. 137.

विमानना *vimânanâ,* i.e. *vi-man,* Caus., *+ ana,* f. Contempt, Böhtl. Ind. Spr. 159; Râjat. 5, 339.

विमानस्थ *vimâna-stha,* adj. Standing on a divine chariot, Pańch. iii. d. 184.

विमार्ग m. I. *vi-mârga.* **1.** A bad road, Lass. 2. ed. 68, 40. **2.** Evil conduct. II. i.e. *vi-mṛij + a,* A broom, a brush.

विमार्गण *vimârgaṇa,* i.e *vi-mârg + aṇa,* n. Seeking, Kir. 14, 9.

विमिश्र *vi-miçra,* adj. Mixed, MBh. 1, 1139.

विमुक्ति *vimukti,* i.e. *vi-much + ti,* f. **1.** Separation. **2.** Liberation, Böhtl. Ind. Spr. 191; remission, Man. 11, 232. **3.** Saving (one's life), Pańch. ii. d. 174. **4.** Final emancipation from future existence.

विमुखता *vi-mukha + tâ,* f. **1.** Turning away. **2.** Departure. **3.** Disinclination, opposition, Çâk. 66, 2.

विमोक्ष *vi-moksh + a,* m. **1.** Letting loose. **2.** Deliverance (from embarrassment), Chr. 54, 19. **3.** Dismissing unhurt, Man. 8, 316. **4.** Final emancipation, Bhag. 16, 5; Vedântas. in Chr. 217, 7.

विमोक्षण *vimokshaṇa,* i.e. *vi-moksh + ana,* n., and f. *ṇâ,* **1.** Untying, Pańch. 107, 24. **2.** Liberation, release, Johns. Sel. 97, l. 6; Pańch. ii. d. 191. **3.** Abandoning, Man. 2, 243; Pańch. 74, 20 (*aṇḍa-,* Laying eggs).

विमोचन *vimochana,* i.e. *vi-much + ana,* n. Liberating, Brâhmaṇav. 3, 13.

विमोहन *vimohana, vi-muh + ana,* n. Seducing, confounding the mind and exciting passions, Râjat. 5, 370.

विम्ब *vimba,* **विम्बित** *vimbita,* **विम्बोष्ठ** *vimboshṭha,* and **विम्बौष्ठ** *vimbaushṭha;* see *bimb°.*

वियत् *viyat* (perhaps *vi-yam + t*), n. Sky, heaven, Pańch. iii. d. 147.

वियम and **वियाम** *viyâma,* i. e. *vi -yam + a,* m. **1.** Restraint. **2.** Cessation. **3.** Pain.

वियोग *viyoga,* i.e. *vi-yuj + a,* m. **1.** Separation, Vikr. 29, 17 (with *saha,* Pańch. 30, 22). **2.** Disunion. **3.** Loss, Pańch. ii. d. 184; death, Hit. iv. d. 62. **4.** Absence, Megh. 78.—Comp. *A-,* m.

the not being deprived (with instr.), Daçak. in Chr. 193, 17. *Sadviyoga*, i.e. *sant-* (vb. 1.*as*), separation from the good, Kir. 5, 51.

वियोगिन् *viyogin*, i.e. *viyoga* + *in*, I. adj., f. *nî*. 1. Separated, Nalod. 2, 12. 2. Absent. II. m. The ruddy goose.

विरक्ति *virakti*, i.e. *vi-rañj* + *ti*, and *vi-rakti*, f. 1. Absence of affection. 2. Aversion, Pańch. 114, 1.

विरचन *vi-rach* + *ana*, n., and f. *nâ*, 1. Making, Vikr. d. 153 (read *muktâ-valî-virachanâ-punar-uktam*; cf. *vach* and Böhtl. Roth. s.v. *punarukta*). 2. Composing. 3. Embellishing. 4. Embellishment, Mâlat. 13, 20 (*nâ*).

विरञ्च *virańcha*, and **विरञ्चि** *virańchi* (perhaps *vi-rach* + *a* or *i*, but cf. *viriñchana*), m. Brahman. Çiç. 9, 9; MBh. 1, 1638 has *viriñchi*.

विरति *virati*, i.e. *vi-ram* + *ti*, and *vi-rati*, f. 1. Stop. 2. Cessation. 3. End, Bhartṛ. 1, 51. 4. Indifference, Vedântas. in Chr. 203, 11.

विरप्शिन् *virapçin*, adj. Shaking, tossing, Chr. 290, 10=Rigv. i. 64, 10.

विरम *vi-ram* + *a*, m. Cessation, sunset, Çiç. 9, 11.

विरल *virala* (perhaps *vila* + *la*), I. adj. 1. Fine, delicate, thin. 2. Little, Çiç. 9, 3; few, Râjat. 5, 56. 3. Loose, relaxed, Utt. Râmach. 14, 4. 4. Separated by an interval, wide. 5. Remote. 6. Single, Bhartṛ. 2, 33; rare, Prab. 10, 8; Pańch. i. d. 35; °*lam*, adv. Rarely, Hit. i. d. 32, M.M. II. n. Sour curds. —Comp. *A-*, adj. 1. coarse. 2. uninterrupted, Utt. Râmach. 69, 6. 3. close; °*lam*, adv. closely, Çâk. d. 55; fast, Mâlat. 60, 10. 4. dense, Utt. Râmach. 44, 6; plentiful, Mâlat. 14, 6. *Pra-*, adj. 1. very rare, very scanty, Pańch. 182, 16; 214, 22. 2. separate, apart.

विरलित *viralita*, i.e. *virala* + *ita*, in *a-viralita-kapola* + *m*, adv. With closely united cheeks, Utt. Râmach. 17, 4.

विरह *vi-rah* + *a*, m. 1. Separation, Megh. 12; Râjat. 5, 373; separation from (with instr.), Man. 5, 149. 2. Absence, Bhâshâp. 68; want, Hit. 127, 5. 3. Cessation, Vikr. d. 130. 4. Relinquishment.—Comp. *Prathama-*, loc. sing. immediately after the separation, Megh. 92.

विरहज *viraha-ja*, adj. Produced by separation, Vikr. d. 110.

विरहिन् *virahin*, i.e. *viraha* + *in*, I. adj. 1. Separate, Mâlat. 144, 3. 2. Absent from. II. f. *iṇî*. 1. A woman absent from her husband or lover. 2. Wages, hire.

विरागार्ह *virâgârha*, i.e. *vi-râga-arha* (see *râga*), adj. Fit for freedom from passion, free from passion.

विराज् *vi-râj*, m. 1. Splendour. 2. A man of the military class. 3. The name of the first progeny of Brahman, Man. 1, 32; 3, 195. 4. The consciousness which perceives collections or aggregates, Vedântas. in Chr. 209, 11.

विराट *virâṭa*, m. The name of a country.

विराद्धृ *virâddhṛi*, i.e. *vi-râdh* + *tṛi*, m., f. *dhri*, and n. 1. Thwarting, opposing. 2. Injuring. 3. Abusive.

विराध *vi-râdh* + *a*, m. 1. Prevention, opposition. 2. Vexation. 3. A Râkshasa, Utt. Râmach. 15, 19.

विराधन *vi-râdh* + *ana*, n. Pain.

विराम *virâma*, i.e. *vi-ram* + *a*, m.

1. Cessation, rest, Man. 2, 73; °*mam yâ*, To rest, Bhartṛ. 2, 72. **2.** End, Utt. Râmach. 63, 5. **3.** Pause.

विराव *virâva*, i. e. *vi-ru + a*, m. Sound.

विराविन् *virâvin*, i.e. *virâva + in*, adj. **1.** Shouting. **2.** Resounding, Râm. 1, 19, 12.

विरिञ्चन *viriñchana*, m. Brahman (cf. *viraṅcha*).

विरिब्ध *viribdha* (anomal. ptcple. pf. pass. of *vi rebh*), m. A tone, a note.

विरुक्मन्त् *virukmant*, i.e. *vi-ruch + mant*, adj. Splendid, Chr. 291, 3 = Rigv. i. 85, 3 (*mataḥ*, acc. pl. f. ved.).

विरुद्धता *vi-ruddha + tâ* (vb. *rudh*), f. **1.** Opposition, contrariety. **2.** Enmity. **3.** Incongruity, abominableness, Pañch. 260, 3.—Comp. *A-*, f. absence of abominableness, Pañch. 261, 6.

विरूपाक्ष *virûpâksha*, i. e. *vi-rûpa -aksha*, adj. Having deformed eyes; m. Çiva, Johns. Sel. 89, 25.

विरेक *vireka*, i.e. *vi-rich + a*, m., and

विरेचन *virechana*, i.e. *vi-rich + ana*, n. **1.** Purging. **2.** A purgative.

विरोक *viroka*, i.e. *vi-ruch + a*, I. m. A ray of light. II. n. A chasm.

विरोचन *virochana*, i.e. *vi-ruch + ana*, I. m. **1.** Fire. **2.** The sun. **3.** The moon. II. (n. ?), Light, lustre, Râjat. 5, 448.

विरोचिष्णु *virochishṇu*, i.e. *vi-ruch + ishṇu*, adj. **1.** Shining. **2.** Illuminating, making visible, Man. 1, 77.

विरोध *virodha*, i.e. *vi-rudh + a*, I. m. **1.** Hindrance, impediment. **2.** Restraint, check. **3.** Opposition, Pañch. 162, 14; Chr. 56, 16; contradiction, Vedântas. in Chr. 211, 18; Kusumâñj. 3, 8; i. d. 147. **4.** Inconsistency (in argument). **5.** Surrounding. **6.** Siege, blockade. **7.** Enmity, Utt. Râmach. 146, 1; Pañch. 148, 10. **8.** War. **9.** Calamity. II. f. *dhî*, Fixed rule, institute.—Comp. *Vachana-*, m. inconsistency of texts. *Smṛiti-*, m. 1. illegality. 2. disagreement between two or more codes of law.

विरोधन *virodhana*, i.e. *vi-rudh + ana*, n. **1.** Hindering. **2.** Opposition. **3.** Incongruity. **4.** Blockading. **5.** Provoking. **6.** Encountering or defying peril.—Comp. *A-*, adj. useful, Böhtl. Ind. Spr. 175.

विरोधिन् *virodhin*, i.e. *vi-rudh* and *virodha*, + *in*, I. adj. f. *nî*. **1.** Obstructive. **2.** Preventing, impeding, Man. 4, 17. **3.** Contradictory, inconsistent, Vikr. d. 162. **4.** Exclusive, Vedântas. in Chr. 204, 11. **5.** Besieging, blockading. **6.** Quarrelsome. II. m. An enemy, Lass. 2. ed. 88, 28.—Comp. *Deça -kâla-*, adj. acting contrary to place and time, Pañch. iii. d. 209.

विरोपण *viropaṇa*, i.e. *vi-ruh*, Caus., + *ana*, adj. Healing, Çâk. d. 89.

† **विल्** *VIL*, i. 6, Par. To cover, to conceal. i. 10, Par. To throw (cf. *pil*).

विल *vila*, or *bila*, I. m. One of Indra's horses. II. n. **1.** A chasm, a hole, Pañch. ii. d. 14; 107, 2 (of a mouse). **2.** A cave, a cavern, Pañch. 193, 15; Râm. 4, 9, 19.—Comp. *Ud-*, adj. being out of one's hole, Râm. 2, 33, 19. *Mahâ-*, n. 1. a cave. 2. sky, heaven. 3. the heart. 4. a water-jar. *Sthâlî-*, n. the interior or hollow of a pot.

विलक्षण *vilakshaṇa*, i.e. A. *vi-laksh* + *ana*, n. Seeing. B. i.e. *vi-lakshaṇa*, I. adj. Different, Bhâshâp. 113. II. n. State or condition for which no cause can be assigned, causeless state.

विलक्षत्व *vi-laksha* + *tva*, n. 1. Absence of mark or aim. 2. Absence of distinguishing property. 3. Surprise. 4. Shame.

विलङ्घन *vi-laṅgh* + *ana*, n. 1. Overstepping. 2. Striking against, Kir. 5, 29. 3. Offence, 13, 55.

विलङ्घिन् *vi-laṅgh* + *in*, adj. Transgressing, ascending to, Kathâs. 14, 13.

विलपन *vi-lap* + *ana*, n. 1. Lamenting, Utt. Râmach. 73, 10; Hit. 65, 20. 2. Chattering.

विलम्ब *vi-lamb* + *a*, m. 1. Falling. 2. Hanging down. 3. Slowness. 4. Delay, Râm. 3, 35, 35; Lass. 75, 10.—Comp. *A-* and *Mâ-*, acc. *bam*, adv. without delay, Pańch. 107, 25 (*mâ-*); Vikr. (Lenz.), 84, 12 (*a-*).

विलम्बन *vi-lamb* + *ana*, n. 1. Depending. 2. Delaying, delay, Hit. 99, 12.

विलम्बिन् *vi-lamb* + *in*, adj. 1. Hanging down, Çâk. d. 145. 2. Delaying.

विलम्भ *vilambha*, i.e. *vi-labh* + *a*, m. Liberality (cf. ÇKD.).

विलय *vilaya*, i.e. *vi-lî* + *a*, m. 1. Liquefaction, Çiç. 9, 17; *vilayaṁ gam*, To be dissolved, to end. 2. Death, Utt. Râmach. 172, 3. 3. Destruction, Bhartṛ. 2, 77. 4. Destruction of the world.—Comp. *Su-*, adj. easily fusible.

विलयन *vilayana*, i.e. *vi-lî* + *ana*, n. 1. Liquefying. 2. Attenuating. 3. Corroding. 4. Removing. 5. Destroying.

विलसन *vi-las* + *ana*, n. 1. Sporting, dallying, Daçak. in Chr. 199, 7. 2. Flashing, Megh. 39.

विलाप *vilâpa*, i.e. *vi-lap* + *a*, m. Lamentation, Lass. 30, 3.

विलास *vilâsa*, i.e. *vi-las* + *a*, m. 1. Sport, pastime, dalliance, merriness, Pańch. v. d. 83. 2. Coquetry, Çâk. d. 35. 3. Wantonness, Böhtl. Ind. Spr. 1610. 4. Charm, beauty, Utt. Râmach. 154, 3.—Comp. *Bhrû-*, m. amorous motion of the eyebrows, Megh. 93. *Sa-*, adj. amorous, wanton, Çiç. 9, 26; °*sam*, adv. by expressive looks, Mâlat. 15, 6.

विलासन *vilâsana*, i.e. *vi-las* + *ana*, n. Fascination, Indr. 5, 13 (perhaps corr. *vilasanais* with *ă*).

विलासवन्त् *vilâsa* + *vant*, adj., f. *vatî*, 1. Sportive, 2. A dallying, wanton woman, Ṛit. 1, 12.

विलासिन् *vilâsin*, i.e. *vilâsa* + *in*, I. adj., f. *nî*. 1. Sportive. 2. Dallying, wanton, Kir. 10, 41. II. m. 1. Vishṇu, Çiva, Kṛishṇa, Kâma. 2. The moon. 3. Fire. 4. A snake. 5. A sensualist. III. f. *nî*. 1. A woman, Râm. 3, 52, 23. 2. A harlot, Pańch. iii. d. 122. 3. The favourite mistress of a king (?), Pańch. 156, 23.—Comp. *Vâra-*, f. a harlot, Hit. iv. d. 130. *Sura-*, f. a courtesan of heaven, Lass. 82, 4.

विलेखन *vilekhana*, i.e. *vi-likh* + *ana*, n. 1. Digging. 2. Dividing. 3. Making furrows.

विलेखिन् *vilekhin*, i.e. *vi-likh* + *in*, adj. Scraping, touching, reaching, Johns. Sel. 40, 39.

विलेप *vilepa*, i.e. *vi-lip* + *a*, m. 1. Ointment. 2. Anointing. 3. Mortar, plaster.

विलेपन *vilepana*, i.e. *vi-lip + ana*, I. n. 1. Anointing the body with fragrant substances, Daçak. in Chr. 198, 8. 2. Ointment, Hit. i. d. 96, M.M. 3. Plastering. II. f. *nî*. 1. A woman adorned with perfumes. 2. Rice-gruel.

विलेपनिन् *vilepanin*, i.e. *vilepana + in*, in *a-*, adj. Deprived of ointments, Râm. 1, 6, 9.

विलेशय *vileçaya*, i.e. *vila + i-çî + a*, m. Any animal living in holes, as a snake, a rat, a hare.

विलोकन *vi-lok + ana*, n. 1. Seeing, regarding, Mâlat. 68, 5; sight, Kir. 5, 16. 2. Spying, Hit. iii. d. 35.

विलोचन *vi-loch + ana*, n. The eye, Kumâras. 5, 33; Vikr. d. 132.

विलोडन *viloḍana*, also **विलोलन** *vilolana*, i.e. *vi-luḍ* or *lul*, *+ ana*, n. 1. Agitating, stirring. 2. Rolling.

विलोप *vilopa*, i.e. *vi-lup + a*, m. Seizing, taking away, Hariv. 7267.

विलोपन *vilopana*, i.e. *vi-lup + ana*, n. 1. Destruction. 2. Deluding.

विलोभ *vilobha*, i.e. *vi-lubh + a*, m. Seduction.

विलोभन *vilobhana*, i.e. *vi-lubh + ana*, n. 1. Beguiling, Kir. 10, 17. 2. Seduction. 3. Praise.

विलोमित *vilomita*, i.e. *vi-loma + ita*, adj. Made disaffected, i.e. surpassed, and made reversed, Naish. 22, 47.

विलोल *vilola*, i.e. *vi-lul + a*, adj. 1. Shaking, trembling, Ṛit. 1, 14; 19. 2. Unsteady, fickle. 3. Rolling (as the eyes). 4. Tossing.

विल्व *vilva*, I. m. A fruit tree, Aegle marmelos, Bhartṛ. 2, 68. II. n. 1. Its fruit. 2. A measure, the same as the Pala.—**Comp.** *Chira-*, m. a tree, Pongamia glabra Vent., Râm. 3, 79, 34.

विवक्षा *vivakshâ*, i.e. *vivaksha*, desider. of *vach*, *+ a*, f. 1. Wish to speak. 2. Wish. 3. A question, MBh. 1, 7197.

विवध and **वीवध** *vîvadha*, probably *vi-vah + a*, m. 1. A road, Pañch. iii. d. 39 (*vi°*). 2. A yoke for carrying burthens. 3. A load. 4. Storing grain or hay, etc. 5. An ewer.—**Comp.** *Uduka-*, and *uda(n)-vîvadha-*, m. a yoke for carrying water, Pâṇ. 6, 3, 60.

विवधिक and **वीवधिक** *vîvadhika*, i.e. *vîvadha + ika*, m. A chandler.

विवर *vivara*, i.e. *vi-vṛi + a*, n. 1. Separation. 2. A hole, Hit. 28, 10, M.M.; a chasm, a fissure, Pañch. 10, 12; a breach, Man. 7, 105; an interval, Çâk. d. 166; space, Nalod. 2, 19. 3. A cave, Pañch. 241, 1. 4. A vulnerable part, MBh. 9, 3280. 5. A wound, Ragh. 11, 18. 6. Fault, defect.—**Comp.** *Karṇa-*, n. the auditory passage, Bhâg. P. 3, 15, 46. *Nâsâ-*, n. the nostril, ib. 3, 15, 18.

विवरण *vivaraṇa*, i.e. *vi-vṛi + ana*, n. 1. Uncovering. 2. Explanation. 3. A sentence, Brahmav. 2, 28. 4. Detailing.

विवर्त *vivarta*, i.e. *vi-vṛit + a*, m. 1. Going round, Lass. 74, 16; revolving. 2. Dancing. 3. Confounding of truth and falsehood, mistaking unreal objects and conceiving them to be what they are not, e.g. mirage for water, Vedântas. in Chr. 211, 24. 4. Object as unreal, opposed to Brahman, the only real essence, Utt. Râmach. 143, 8. 5. Modification, Utt. Râmach. 37, 3; 88, 2.

6. An assemblage, multitude, Mâlat. 24, 8.

विवर्तन *vivartana,* i.e. *vi-vṛit + ana,* n. 1. Going round, revolving. 2. Reverential salutation, Kir. 5, 40. 3. Turning round, overturning, Utt. Râmach. 102, 4. 4. Tossing to and fro, Çâk. d. 132. 5. Returning, Kir. 7, 11. 6. Passing in succession, Mâlat. 23, 14; as various hells, Man. 12, 75. 7. Being, abiding. 8. Causing to change, Mâlat. 71, 8.

विवर्तिन् *vivartin,* i.e. *vi-vṛit + in,* adj. Turning back, Çâk. d. 73; Kir. 5, 5.—Comp. *A-,* adj. not showing the heels, Sâv. 7, 12. *Pârçva-,* adj. living at the side, Kathâs. 19, 101.

विवर्धन *vivardhana,* i.e. *vi-vṛidh + ana,* I. adj. 1. Growing, Râm. 3, 49, 41. 2. Furthering, increasing, Man. 1, 106; Hit. ii. d. 57 (but cf. v.r. Böhtl. Ind. Spr. 1217). II. n. Increase.

विवस्वन्त् *vi- 2. vas + vant,* I. m. 1. The sun, Pañch. v. d. 37; Kir. 5, 48. 2. Aruṇa, the charioteer of the sun. 3. The seventh Manu (see *vaivasvata*). 4. A god. II. f. *vati,* The city of the sun.

विवाक *vivâka,* see *prâḍvivâka.*

विवाद *vivâda,* i.e. *vi-vad + a,* m. 1. Contesting, Çâk. 106, 10; contest, strife, Man. 4, 180; dispute, Pañch. i. d. 68. 2. Argument, Man. 11, 205. 3. A lawsuit, Pañch. iii. d. 92. 4. Sound, Ragh. 18, 42.—Comp. *A-,* m. accordance, Man. 8, 92. *Nis-,* adj. not contesting, agreeing with each other, MBh. 3, 305. *Çânta-* (vb. *çam*), adj, reconciled, appeased. *Sîmâ-,* m. a litigation respecting boundaries, Man. 8, 6.

विवादिन् *vivâdin,* i.e. *vivâda + in,* adj. and sbst. 1. Contending. 2. A party in a lawsuit, Man. 8, 69.

विवास *vivâsa,* i. e. I. *vi- 1. vas,* Caus., *+ a,* m. Banishment, Nal. 19, 6. II. *vi-vâsa,* adj. Without clothes, naked.

विवासन *vivâsana,* i. e. *vi- 1. vas,* Caus., *+ ana,* n. Banishment, banishing, Utt. Râmach. 41, 5.

विवाह *vivâha,* i.e. *vi-vah + a,* m. 1. Marriage, Pañch. 188, 22. 2. Nuptial form, Man. 3, 20. — Comp. see *Ku-. Dus-,* m. a bad form of marriage, Man. 3, 41.

ऽविवाहिन् *-vivâhin,* i.e. *vivâha + in,* in *a-,* adj. Such one who is forbidden to be allied by marriage, Man. 9, 238.

विविंशति *viviñçati,* m. A proper name.

विविक्तता *vi-vikta + tâ* (vb. *vich*), f. A free or empty space, Râjat. 5, 354.

विविक्षु *vivikshu,* i.e. *viviksha,* desider. of *viç, + u,* adj. Desiring to enter, Vikr. d. 24.

विवीत *vi-vîta* (vb. *vî,* substitute for *aj*), n. A pasture ground, Yâjñ. 2, 282.

विवृति *vi-vṛi + ti,* f. 1. Discovery, manifestation, Kir. 10, 19. 2. Explanation.

विवृत्ति *vi-vṛit + ti,* f. Turning round, rolling, whirling, tumbling.

विवृद्धि *vivṛiddhi,* i.e. *vi-vṛidh + ti,* f. Growth, increase, Man. 1, 31.

विवेक *viveka,* i.e. *vi-vich + a,* m. 1. Discrimination, Man. 1, 26; Pañch. i. d. 294. 2. Judgment, Bhartṛ. 2, 10. 3. Discussion, investigation. 4. True knowledge, Bhartṛ. 1, 89. 5. A reservoir.—Comp. *A-,* I. m. absence of discrimination or judgment, Hit. iv. d. 97.

II. adj. wanting discrimination, stupid, Hit. i. d. 135, M.M.

विवेकज्ञ *viveka-jña*, adj. Intelligent, Pañch. i. d. 431.

विवेकता *viveka + tâ*, in *a-*, f. Want of judgment, Hit. pr. d. 11, M.M. *nis-vivekatva*, see s.v. *nirvi°*.

विवेकिन् *vivekin*, i.e. *viveka + in*, adj. Judicious, discriminative, prudent, Pañch. 131, 19.—**Comp.** *A-*, adj. defective in judgment, unable to discriminate, Kathâs. 24, 225.

विवेक्तृ *vivektṛi*, i.e. *vi-vich + tṛi*, m. A wise man, Râjat. 5, 5.

विवेचन *vivechana*, i.e. *vi-vich + ana*, n. **1.** Discrimination. **2.** Decision, Man. 8, 21.

विवोढृ *vivoḍhṛi*, i.e. *vi-vah + tṛi*, m. **1.** A husband. **2.** A bridegroom.

विव्वोक *vivvoka*, m. Affectation of indifference, one of the feminine actions, tending to excite love, Sâh. Darp. 284, 20.

1. **विश्** *VIÇ*, i. 6, Par. (in epic poetry also Âtm., Râm. 2, 43, 6), **1.** To enter, Hit. ii. d. 48. **2.** To enter in (with acc.), Bhag. 11. 29. **3.** To pierce, Râjat. 5, 217. **4.** To begin, Râm. 1, 11, 20. **5.** To sit down, Râm. 2, 82, 2. Ptcple. of the pf. pass. *vishṭa*, Penetrated, pervaded. Ptcple. of the fut. pass. *veçya*, I. f. *yâ*, A harlot, Hit. i. d. 135, M.M. II. n. The habitation of harlots. **Comp.** *Svar-veçyâ*, f. an Apsaras. —With the prep. **अनु** *anu*, **1.** To enter after somebody, MBh. 1, 796. **2.** To enter, Pañch. 187, 25.—With **आ** *â*, **1.** To approach, Hit. i. d. 2, M.M. **2.** To enter, Man. 1, 29. **3.** To occupy, Chr. 35, 5. **4.** To proceed, Man. 1, 18. *âvishṭa*, **1.** Pierced, wounded, Râm. 3, 52, 20. **2.** Overpowered, affected with, Lass. 2. ed. 45, 18; possessed (by a demon, or by any sentiment), Pañch. 40, 18; Chr. 31, 15; 7, 21. **3.** Covered, Pañch. i. d. 73 (*kañchuka-*, by a coat of mail and by a snake's hide). **4.** Full of, Hit. 126, 17. Caus. *veçaya*, To cause to enter, Bhag. 8, 10.—With **अन्वा** *anu-â*, To enter, MBh. 1, 5389. —With **समुपा** *sam-upa-â*, **1.** To enter, Râm. 2, 85, 15. **2.** To begin, Râm. 1, 62, 22.—With **समा** *sam-â*, **1.** To enter at once, Man. 1, 56. **2.** To enter, MBh. 7272. **3.** To approach, Bhartṛ. 2, 81. **4.** To sit on, Man. 2, 119; Pañch. ii. d. 63. *samâvishṭa*, Endowed, Lass. 2, 2. Caus. **1.** To put on, MBh. 3, 9913. **2.** To commit, Pañch. i. d. 106.—With **उप** *upa*, **1.** To sit down, Vikr. 15, 5; Chr. 11, 17. **2.** To encamp, MBh. 3, 659. **3.** To enter, to occupy, MBh. 1, 5389. *upavishṭa*, **1.** Seated, Pañch. 68, 21; sitting, Daçak. in Chr. 184, 10; sitting quietly, Pañch. 53, 23; sitting down for performing, Pañch. 224, 15. **2.** Arrived, entered, Lass. 2. ed. 44, 3. **Comp.** *Bala-*, adj. endowed with, or possessed of, strength. Caus. **1.** To cause to sit down, Vikr. 28, 18 (corr. *veçayati*); to place, Man. 3, 208. **2.** To sit down, Pañch. 147, 6 (probably to be read, *upaviçya*).—With **उपोप** *upa-upa*, **1.** To sit near, (with the acc.), MBh. 3, 11777. **2.** To sit down, MBh. 1, 4914. *upopavishṭa*, **1.** Surrounded, Râm. 1, 4, 26. **2.** Sitting, MBh. 1, 6959.—With **प्रत्युप** *prati-upa*, To sit down opposite to, MBh. 2, 1156 (perhaps *prati* is to be separated, and preposition belonging to the preceding word).—With **समुप** *sam-upa*, To sit down, Vikr. 81, 4; MBh. 1, 8479. Caus. To cause to sit down, Hit. 6?, 5.—With **नि** *ni*, Âtm. (in epic

poetry also Par., MBh. 1, 6960). **1.** To enter, MBh. 1, 7566. **2.** To descend, MBh. 1, 7308. **3.** To sit down, Çiç. 1, 19. **4.** To lie down, Pańch. 205, 8. **5.** To marry, MBh. 1, 1852. **6.** To be intent on, Man. 2, 8. **7.** To return, MBh. 3, 1426 (probably is to be read *nirveçya*). *nivishṭa*, **1.** Situated on, Râm. 3, 53, 35. **2.** Arranged, Man. 9, 252. Caus. **1.** To cause to enter, Man. 4, 171. **2.** To place, Râm. 1, 18, 21. **3.** To lay the foundation of, Hariv. 6521. **4.** With *manas*, To apply one's mind to, Man. 6, 35. **5.** To draw, Çâk. d. 42. **6.** To cause to lie down, to encamp, Çâk. 18, 23. **7.** To cause to marry, MBh. 1, 7138; to unite to a match, Çâk. d. 95.—With अभिनि *abhi-ni*, **1.** To sit down, to settle in (with acc.), Pâṇ. 1, 4, 47; figurat., Bhaṭṭ. 8, 80. **2.** To be very set upon, Daçak. in Chr. 190, 21. *abhinivishṭa*, **1.** Endowed with, Ragh. 2, 75 (Calc.). **2.** Fixed, Mâlat. 19, 2. **3.** Determined. Caus. **1.** To place, Çiç. 1, 15. **2.** To build, Ragh. 15, 29. **3.** To cause to be very set upon, Mâlav. 28, 8.—With प्रत्यभिनि *prati-abhi-ni*, *pratyabhinivishṭa*, Pursuing pertinaciously, Mâlat. 88, 22. —With प्रतिनि *prati-ni*, *pratinivishṭa*, Obstinate, Bhartṛ. 2, 4.—With विनि *vi-ni*, Caus. **1.** To cause to enter, Râjat. 5, 318. **2.** To join (?), Râjat. 5, 39. **3.** To place, Râjat. 5, 445. **4.** To suspend, Pańch. i. d. 160.—With संनि *sam-ni*, *saṁnivishṭa*, Entered, seated, Bhag. 15, 15. Caus. **1.** To cause to enter, Man. 11, 202 (read *saṁniveçya*). **2.** To cause to lie down, MBh. 3, 665. **3.** To unite, to join, Man. 1, 16. **4.** To place, Vikr. 73, 8; Ragh. 12, 58 (Calc.). **5.** To put on, Ṛit. 1, 7. **6.** To contemplate, Man. 12, 120.—With निस् *nis*, **1.** To enjoy, Megh. 109. **2.** To return, to reward, MBh. 5, 4943. **3.** To embellish, Hariv. 7858.—With परि *pari*, see 2. *vish* with *pari*.—With प्र *pra*, **1.** To enter, Chr. 24, 50. **2.** To appear, Vikr. 71, 11. **3.** To begin, Râm. 1, 31, 28. *pravishṭa*, **1.** Entered, pass. and act., Çâk. d. 7; Râjat. 5, 13; 58. **2.** Entered upon, engaged in. Desider. *viviksha*, To wish to enter, MBh. 3, 10836. Caus. **1.** To cause to enter, Pańch. 256, 1; to let enter, 16, 2. **2.** To introduce (with two acc.), MBh. 1, 4427; as one's wife, Chr. 6, 8. **3.** To lay up, Man. 8, 38. *praveçita*, Called, or sent in.—With अनुप्र *anu-pra*, **1.** To enter after somebody, MBh. 1, 7800. **2.** To enter, Daçak. in Chr. 186, 13. **3.** To go through, Utt. Râmach. 37, 10. **4.** To follow, to accommodate one's self to, Pańch. i. d. 78 (cf. Hit. ii. d. 50). **5.** To cohabit with. MBh. 1, 4275.—With संप्र *sam-pra*, **1.** To enter, MBh. 1, 3303. **2.** To cohabit with, Man. 9, 8. —With सम् *sam*, **1.** To enter, MBh. 1, 6741. **2.** To lie down, MBh. 3, 13149; to go to rest, Man. 4, 55. **3.** To cohabit with, Man. 3, 48. Caus. To place, MBh. 1, 4274.—With अनुसम् *anu-sam*, To lie down after somebody, Ragh. 2, 24 (Calc.).—Cf. ἵκω, ἱκνέομαι; see 2. *viç* and *veça*.

2. विश् *viç*, I. m. **1.** A man of the mercantile caste, Chr. 4, 19 (the king may be called lord of the Vaiçyas, because the Brâhmaṇas are theoretically his superiors, the Kshatriyas his equals, and the Çûdras too base for being meant; but perhaps it has the following signification). **2.** A man in general. II. f. **1.** Family, tribe, Chr. 289, 5 = Rigv. i. 50, 5; Chr. 296, 3 = Rigv. i.

112, 3. 2. Entrance. 3. A daughter. —Cf. Goth. vaihts; A.S. wiht; O.H.G. ni-wiht, eo-wiht, neo-wiht.

विश *viça*, see *visa*.

विशङ्क I. *vi-çanka* (cf. *çankâ*), adj. Fearless; acc. *kam*, adv., Daçak. in Chr. 196, 3. II. *vi-çank* + *â*, f. Suspicion, Nal. 24, 41.—Comp. *A-*, adj. free from suspicion, fearless, Nal. 4, 12. *Nis-*, adj. fearless, Man. 7, 176 (Pañch. 123, 18 read also *nirv°*).

विशङ्कट *viçankaṭa* (Pâṇ. 5, 2, 28, nevertheless for original *vi-saṁkaṭa*), adj. Great, large, Bhaṭṭ. 2, 50; Mâlat. 78, 2 (with *s*); acc. *ṭam*, adv. Vehemently, Pañch. 46, 5.

विशद *viçada*, I. adj. 1. Of a white colour, Megh. 41; Çiç. 9, 26; Kir. 5, 12. 2. Clear, Böhtl. Ind. Spr. 3322. 3. Pure, Böhtl. Ind. Spr. 2680; spotless, Çâk. d. 97. 4. Evident. 5. Beautiful. II. m. White, the colour.

विशय *viçaya*, i.e. *vi-çî* + *a*, m. Doubt, uncertainty.

विशयिन् *viçayin*, i.e. *viçaya* + *in*, adj. Dubious.

विशर *viçara*, i.e. *vi-çṛî* + *a*, m. Killing.

विशसन *vi-ças* + *ana*, I. n. 1. Dissecting. 2. Killing, ruin, Utt. Râmach. 96, 5. II. m. A crooked sword.

विशसितृ *vi-ças* + *itṛi*, m., f. *tri*, and n. 1. Who or what dissects, Man. 5, 51. 2. Who or what kills.

विशाख I. *vi-çâkha* (cf. *çâkhâ*), adj. Branchless. II. m. 1. Kârttikeya. 2. An attitude in shooting, standing with the feet a span apart. 3. A solicitor, a beggar. 4. A spindle. III. f. *khâ*, The sixteenth lunar asterism, Lass. 16, 18.

विशातन *viçâtana*, i. e. *vi-çâtaya*, (Caus. of *çad*), + *ana*, adj., f. *nî*, Causing to fall asunder, Bhâg. P. 3, 14, 4.

विशाय *viçâya*, i.e. *vi-çî* + *a*, m. Sleeping and watching alternately.

विशारण *viçâraṇa*, i.e. *vi-çṛî* + *ana*, n. Killing.

विशारद *viçârada*, 1. Learned, wise. 2. Skilled, conversant with, Pañch. ii. d. 14; Chr. 5, 5. 3. Famous. 4. Bold, presuming.

विशाल *viçâla* (perhaps vb. *çri*), I. adj. 1. Great, large, Hit. 14, 4, M.M. 2. Broad. 3. Eminent, illustrious, Hit. pr. d. 39, M.M. II. m. A sort of deer. III. f. *lâ*. 1. The city Ougein, Megh. 31, and another town. 2. Bitter apple, Cucumis colocynthis.

विशालता *viçâla* + *tâ*, f. 1. Magnitude. 2. Breadth. 3. Distinction.

विशिख *vi-çikha* (probably from *çikhâ*), I. m. 1. An arrow, Chr. 34, 13; Râjat. 5, 221 (*utkhâyamâna-*, adj. While the arrow was drawn out). 2. An iron crow. II. f. *khâ*. 1. A sort of needle. 2. A spade. 3. A highway.—Comp. *Kaṭâksha-*, m. an arrow-like amorous look, Bhartṛ. 2, 76.

विशिप *viçipa*, n. A house.

विशिष्टता *vi-çishṭa* + *tâ* (vb. *çish*), f. 1. Excellence, distinction, Hit. pr. d. 42, M.M. 2. Individuality, having distinguishing properties. 3. Peculiarity, as of duty.

विशुद्धि *viçuddhi*, i.e. *vi-çudh* + *ti*, f. 1. Purity, Man. 5, 67; 9, 9. 2. Correctness. 3. Purifying, purification, Bhag. 6, 12; Utt. Râmach. 9, 17. 4. Sameness. 5. Removal of doubt.

विशेष *viçesha*, i.e. *vi-çish* + *a*, m. 1.

Difference, Pańch. 219, 14; at the end of comp. words, Different, e.g. *gati-*, m. Different ways, Pańch. 247, 11. *purusha-*, This or that man, Pańch. i. d. 124. **2.** Special property, Hit. pr. d. 25, M.M. **3.** A change for the better, Mâlav. 46, 9. **4.** Sort, kind, manner, Megh. 65; Hit. ii. d. 149; Pańch. 114, 25; a different object, Megh. 58. **5.** Excellence, superiority; *viçeshena*, Particularly, Pańch. 142, 15; 162, 9; at the end of comp. words, Excellent; e.g. *bhaksha-*, m. Excellent food, Pańch. 113, 9; 117, 2, cf. my transl. n. 767; Vikr. d. 142. **6.** A limb. **7.** A mark on the forehead with sandal. **8.** Speciality, characteristic marks, Lass. 13, 4 (*tapasvin-*, of an ascetic). **9.** Abl. *viçeshât*, Especially, Pańch. ii. d. 100; even more, just for that, Pańch. 109, 19.—**Comp.** *A-viçesha + m*, adv. without choosing, Arj. 3, 32. *Tapoviçesha*, i.e. *tapas-*, m. pl. various modes of devotion, Man. 2, 165. *Daçâ-*, m. a special condition, Hit. 78, 8, M.M. *Nis-*, I. m. want of difference, Hit. 113, 11. II. adj. 1. having no discrimination, Hit. ii. d. 68. 2. not different. 3. equal. 4. acc. *sham*, adv. a. without difference, Hit. 84, 5, M.M. b. alike, Hit. 128, 10. c. exceedingly, Utt. Râmach. 99, 6. *Prasâdhana-*, m. highest accomplishment, Vikr. d. 22. *Rasa-*, m. a more excellent juice, Pańch. ii. d. 37. *Sa-*, adj. 1. having discrimination, Hit. 55, 13. 2. having characteristic qualities. 3. extraordinary, Hit. 60, 6, M.M.

विशेषक *viçeshaka*, i. e. *vi-çish + aka*, I. adj. Discriminative, distinguishing. II. m. and n. **1.** An attribute, a predicate. **2.** A mark on the forehead made with sandal, etc., and worn either as an ornament, Mâlav. d. 40; Daçak. in Chr. 199, 4, or sectarial distinction. — **Comp.** *Patra-*, strokes and lines drawn on the face with fragrant pigments of sandal, musk, etc., Ragh. 3, 55. *Vi-pra-nashṭa-* (vb *naç*), adj., f. *kâ*, one whose discriminative faculty or perception has disappeared, Râm. 3, 55, 6. *Sa-*, adj. discriminated, having distinguishing properties, Bhâshâp. 1.

विशेषज्ञ *viçesha-jńa*, adj. **1.** Deeply learned, Hit. 129, 9; iv. d. 98. **2.** Wise, intelligent. — **Comp.** *A-*, adj. having no judgment, Hit. iii. d. 126.

विशेषण *viçeshaṇa*, i.e. *vi-çish + ana*, I. adj. **1.** Discriminative. **2.** Distinctive. **II.** n. **1.** Distinguishing, discriminating. **2.** An attribute, epithet, Vikr. 20, 3.—**Comp.** *Nis-*, adj. without attributes, Bhâg. P. 2, 10, 34. *Sa-*, adj. distinguished, characterised.

विशेषणता *viçeshaṇa + tâ*, f. The state of being a distinguishing mark, Bhâshâp. 60; cf. Kusumâńj. transl. pp. 13, 55, n.

विशेषणवन्त् *viçeshaṇa + vant*, adj., f. *vatî*, Having a distinguishing attribute, Bhâshâp. 131.

विशेषतस् *viçesha + tas*, adv. Especially, Hit. 80, 1, M.M.; particularly, Vikr. d. 62.—**Comp.** *Sa-*, adv. particularly, excellently.

विशेषवन्त् *viçesha + vant*, adj. **1.** Peculiar. **2.** Excellent. **3.** Superior, better, Johns. Sel. 17, 73.

विशेष्यक *viçeshya + ka* (vb. *çish*), latter part of a comp. adj. in *tadvadviçeshyaka*, i.e. *tadvant-*, Relating to an object possessing such an attribute, Bhâshâp. 134; cf. Kusumâńj. transl. 61, 1–6.

विशोधन *viçodhana*, i.e. *vi-çudh + ana*, I. n. **1.** Cleaning. **2.** Purifying,

Râm. 1, 26, 19. **3.** Expiation, Man. 11, 143; 156. **II.** f. *nî*, The capital of Brahman.

विशोधित्व *viçodhitva*, i.e *viçodhin + tva*, n. **1.** Cleaning. **2.** Purifying. **3.** Freeing from obstructions, clearing, Hit. iii. d. 86.

विशोधिन् *viçodhin*, i.e. *vi-çudh + in*, adj. **1.** Cleaning. **2.** Purifying. **3.** Clearing.

विशोषण *viçoshaṇa*, i.e. *vi-çush + ana*, **I.** adj. (?), Drying, Arj. 8, 8; the name of a weapon. **II.** n. Drying.—**Comp.** *Tâlu-*, n. the growing dry of the palate (by much speaking), MBh. 8, 4760.

विश्न *viçna*, i.e. *2. vichh + na*, m. Splendour, Pâṇ. iii. 3, 90; vi. 4, 19.

विश्पति *viç-pati*, m. Lord of the house, Lass. 100, 13 = Rigv. vii. 15, 7.

विश्पला *viçpalâ*, f. A proper name, Chr. 296, 10 = Rigv. i. 112, 10.

विश्रणन and **विश्राणन** *viçrâṇana*, i.e. *vi-çraṇ + ana*, n. Gift, donation, Ragh. 2, 54 (*â*).

विश्रम *vi-çram + a*, m. Rest, repose, quiet, Vikr. d. 42.

विश्रम्भ *vi-çrambh + a* (also **विस्रम्भ** *visrambha*), m. **1.** Trust, confidence, Pańch. i. d. 306; ii. d. 190. **2.** Affection, Hit. 46, 1, M.M. (*-âlâpa*, Affectionate talk). **3.** Sportive noise.

विश्रम्भिन् *viçrambhin*, i.e. *vi-çrambh*, and *viçrambha*, *+ in*, also **विस्रम्भिन्** *visrambhin*, adj. **1.** Trusting, confiding in. **2.** Trustworthy, MBh. 1, 5845 (*s*).

विश्रय *viçraya*, i.e. *vi-çri + a*, m. **1.** Abode, asylum. **2.** Dependence upon.

विश्रयिन् *viçrayin*, adj. **1.** Living or dwelling in. **2.** Depending on.

विश्रवस् *vi-çravas*, m. A proper name, Râm. 3, 53, 30.

विश्राणन *viçrâṇana*, see *viçraṇana*.

विश्रान्ति *viçrânti*, i.e. *vi-çram + ti*, f. Rest, repose, Vikr. d. 20; Kathâs. 22, 104 (*rates—vâsaveçmeva viçrântyai—âvayor abhavat*, literally, It was for us like the sleeping-room of the goddess of love for reposing in).

विश्राम *viçrâma*, i.e. *vi-çram + a*, m. **1.** Rest, repose, Pańch. 145, 9; Hit. i. d. 138, M.M. **2.** Stop, pause, Utt. Râmach. 103, 13.

विश्राव *viçrâva*, i.e. *vi-çru + a*, m., and **विश्रुति** *vi-çru + ti*, f. Fame, celebrity, notoriety.—**Comp.** *Loka-viçruti*, f. 1. fame. 2. unfounded rumour.

विश्लथ *vi-çlath + a*, adj. Relaxed, Ragh. 6, 73; languid.

विश्लेष *viçlesha*, i.e. *vi-çlish + a*, m. **1.** Separation, Pańch. 225, 18 (with *saha*); disunion. **2.** A chasm, Kathâs. 2, 49.—**Comp.** *Chitta-*, m. separation of the hearts, loss of friendship, Pańch. 225, 17 (with instr.).

विश्लेषिन् *viçleshin*, i.e. *vi-çlish + in*, adj. Falling, Ragh. 16, 67.

विश्व *viçva*, probably *vi-çri* (cf. the aor. of *çvi*, *a-çram*, and *çaçvant*), **I.** adj. **1.** All, every, Lass. 97, 2 = Rigv. vi. 64, 1; every one, Lass. 101, 4 = Rigv. vii. 16, 1; particularly former part of comp. words, cf. *viçva-karman*, *viçvakṛit*, etc. **2.** Whole. **3.** Universal. **II.** m. **1.** A term of the Vedânta philosophy, the faculty perceiving singleness, Vedântas. in Chr. 209, 13. **2.** pl. (*viçve*), A class of deities, Indr. 2, 13. **III.** n. The world, Çâk. d. 1. **IV.** (n. and) f. *râ*,

Dry ginger. V. f. *vâ*, A tree, a plant, Aconitum ferox.

विश्वकद्रु *viçva + ka-dru*, I. adj. Wicked. II. m. 1. A dog trained for the chase. 2. Sound.

विश्वकृत् *viçva-kri + t*, m. 1. The creator. 2. A son of Brahman, the artist of the gods (=*viçva-karman*), Sund. 3, 13, cf. 10.

विश्वजनीन *viçvajanîna*, **विश्वजनीय** *viçvajanîya*, and **विश्वजन्य** *viçvajanya*, i.e. *viçva-jana + îna*, or *îya*, or *ya*, adj. Good for all men, universally salutary, Man. 9, 31 (*-janya*).

विश्वजित् *viçva-ji + t*, I. adj. All-subduing. II. m. 1. A particular sacrifice, Man. 11, 74. 2. The noose of Varuṇa.

विश्वञ्च् *viçvañch*, A false writing for *vishvañch*, q. cf.

विश्वतस् *viçva + tas*, adv. Everywhere.

विश्वतुर् *viçva-tur*, adj. All-subduing, Chr. 288, 16=Rigv. i. 48, 16.

विश्वद्र्यञ्च् *viçvadryañch*, i.e. *viçva + tra-añch* (with *d* for *t*; cf. also *tiryañch*), adj., f. *drîchî*, Moving everywhere.

विश्वप्सन् *viçvapsan*, i.e. *viçva-bhas + an* (properly the curtailed ptcple. of the pres.), m. 1. A god. 2. Fire. 3. The sun. 4. The moon.

विश्वंभर *viçvam̃bhara*, i.e. *viçva + m -bhṛi + a*, I. adj. All-sustaining. II. m. 1. Vishṇu. 2. Indra. III. f. *râ*, The earth, Utt. Râmach. 7, 11.

विश्वसन *vi-çvas + ana*, n. Trusting, confiding in.

विश्वसनीयता i.e. *vi-çvasanîya + tâ* (vb. *çvas*), f. Inspiring confidence, Çâk. 27, 17.

विश्वसह *viçva-sah + a*, I. adj. All-enduring. II. f. 1. The earth. 2. One of the tongues of fire.

विश्वसुविद् *viçva-su-vid*, adj. Giving everything well, Chr. 287, 2=Rigv. i. 48, 2.

विश्वसृज् *viçva-sṛij* (nom. sing. *-sṛiṭ* and *sṛik*, MBh. 14, 7367), m. 1. The creator of the universe, MBh. l. l.; Çiç. 9, 80. 2. Brahman.

विश्वाची *viçvâchî*, i. e. *viçva-añch + î*, f. The name of an Apsaras, Lass. 2. ed. 50, 22.

विश्वामित्र *viçvâmitra*, i. e. *viçva -mitra*, m. The name of a Muni, Johns. Sel. 23, 118.

विश्वावसु *viçvâvasu*, i.e. *viçva-vasu*, m. 1. One of the Manus. 2. One of the Gandharvas, Indr. 2, 18.

विश्वास *viçvâsa*, i.e. *vi-çvas + a*, m. 1. Confidence, trust, Pañch. ii. d. 23. 2. Faith, Vikr. 71, 13. 3. Secret, Hit. 73, 16.—Comp. *A-*, m. 1. want of confidence, distrust, Pañch. i. d. 295. 2. treachery (?), Râm. 3, 52, 48. *°çam*, adv. without confiding, distrustfully, Pañch. iii. d. 59.

विश्वासन (or **ना** ?), *viçvâsana* (or *nâ*), i.e. *vi-çvas*, Caus., + *ana*, n. (or f.), Producing confidence, Pañch. 165, 15.

विश्वासिन् *viçvâsin*, i.e. *vi-çvas*, and *viçvâsa*, + *in*, adj., f. *nî*, 1. Trusting. 2. Trusty, honest.—Comp. *A-*, adj. mistrustful, Megh. 111.

विश्वासैकसार *viçvâsaikasâra*, i. e. *viçvâsa-eka-sâra*, m. A proper name, Râjat. 5, 44.

विश्वेभोजस् *viçvebhojas* (i.e. *viçva* and *bhojas*), m. A name of Indra, Matsyapurâṇa, see Aufrecht, Ujjvalad. p. 250, n.

† 1. विष् *VISH,* i. 1, Par. To sprinkle.

2. विष् *VISH,* ii. 3, *vevish,* Par. Âtm. To pervade, to embrace, etc. (ved.).—With the prep. परि *pari,* Caus. **1.** To present, to offer, Man. 3, 228; to offer food, MBh. 1, 7182 (where it is written with *ç* instead of *sh*). **2.** To wait on, Râm. 1, 13, 14.

† 3. विष् ii. 9, *vishṇâ, vishṇi,* Par. To separate.

4. विष् *vish,* f. Excrement, Man. 4, 48.—Comp. *Karṇa-,* f. ear-wax, Man. 5, 135.

विष *visha,* I. m. and n. Poison, Pañch. iii. d. 83 (n.). II. n. **1.** Water. **2.** See *visa.*—Comp. *Karṇa-,* n. poison sprinkled in one's ears (treacherous speech), Pañch. i. d. 338. *Dûshî-,* n. vegetable poison that has become old and diminished in strength, Suçr. 2, 254, 7. *Drishṭi-,* m. a snake, Kir. 14, 25. *Nis-,* adj., f. *shâ,* deprived of poison, Pañch. iii. d. 83. *Netra-,* adj. having poison in one's eyes, MBh. 2, 2140. *Mahâ-,* m. a small venomous snake, Râm. 3, 53, 55. *Lâlâ-,* m. an insect whose spittle is poison, as a spider.—Cf. Lat. virus; ἰός, ἰόν; Lat. viola (poison is connected with blue, cf. *visha-pushpa,* and Çiva's neck growing blue, by swallowing the poison churned out of the sea).

विषङ्ग *vishaṅga,* i.e. *vi-sañj + a,* m. Attachment.—Comp. *Nis-,* adj. indifferent, Bhâg. P. 4, 22, 51.

विषण्णता *vishaṇṇa + tâ* (vb. *sad*), f. Dejection, want of energy.

विषता *visha + tâ,* f. State of poison, Çiç. 9, 68.

विषद *visha-da,* I. adj. **1.** Giving poison. **2.** Shedding water. **II.** m. A cloud. **III.** n. Green vitriol.

विषदर्शनमृत्युक *visha-darçana-mṛityu + ka,* m. A kind of pheasant.

विषधर *vishadhara,* i.e. *visha-dhṛi + a,* I. adj. Venomous. **II.** m. A snake.

विषम *vishama,* i.e. *vi-sama,* I. adj., f. *mâ.* **1.** Unequal, different, Kir. 5, 40. **2.** Inconstant, Hit. ii. d. 104. **3.** Odd (in numbers), figurat., Pañch. i. d. 126. **4.** Unhappy, Hit. iv. d. 3. **5.** Unparalleled, unequalled, Daçak. in Chr. 199, 1. **6.** Uneven, Pañch. ii. d. 188; sloping, Vikr. 10, 9. **7.** Rough, Vikr. d. 49; Pañch. 188, 9. **8.** Difficult, painful, Bhartṛ. 2, 54; disagreeable, Pañch. i. d. 12. **9.** Frightful, Hit. iii. d. 133. **10.** Dishonest, wicked, Hiḍ. 1, 39; Hit. ii. d. 111. **11.** Partial, Man. 7, 27. **II.** n. **1.** Inequality. **2.** Oddness. **3.** Unevenness, Man. 1, 24 (uneven valleys, Jones). **4.** An inaccessible place, a precipice, Râm. 3, 51, 40; Pañch. 142, 6; a thicket, a pit, Man. 8, 232. **5.** Difficulty, pain, Pañch. v. d. 65; misfortune, Bhartṛ. 2, 95.—Comp. *Vâkya-vajra-,* adj. rough, coarse, by (using) thunderbolt-like words, Pañch. iii. d. 236 (cf. Böhtl. Ind. Spr. 2928).

विषमय *visha + maya,* adj., f. *yî* (Pañch. i. d. 211, *yâ,* but cf. Böhtl. Ind. Spr. 119, read *vishamayyo*), Poisonous.

विषमस्थ *vishama-stha,* adj. **1.** Standing unevenly. **2.** Being in difficulty or misfortune, Nal. 10, 1. **3.** Inaccessible, Pañch. i. d. 195. **4.** Safely posted.

विषमित *vishamita,* i.e. *vishama + ita,* adj. **1.** Made crooked, Kir. 10, 56. **2.** Made difficult to be walked on, Kir. 12, 50.

विषय *vishaya* (probably *vi-kshi* + *a*), m. **1.** A collection of villages. **2.** A country, Râjat. 5, 51; Pańch. 129, 14; a kingdom, Bhartṛ. 2, 12; Râm. 3, 54, 28 (*yama-*, The lower regions, death); a place, Çâk. 104, 14; Kir. 5, 38. **3.** Anything indigenous or peculiar to a province. **4.** Home, province, department, sphere, Vikr. 39, 14; Pańch. 4, 17 (*jîvitavya-*, Duration of life); Pańch. 227, 22 (application); element, that which is peculiarly known to those who occupy themselves with it or live therein. **5.** Horizon, sight, a place which may be looked over by somebody, reach, Man. 8, 148; Hit. 28, 3, M.M.; Megh. 35; 101. **6.** Anything perceivable by the senses, an object of sense, Man. 1, 15; Vikr. d. 9. **7.** An object in general, Bhâshâp. 36; *atra vishaye*, Concerning this object, Pańch. 114, 20; *dhanavishaye*, Concerning wealth, Pańch. 139, 3; *strîṇâm vishaye*, Concerning women, 27, 18; an object of art, Mâlav. d. 29. **8.** Worldly object, affair, business, enjoyment, etc., Pańch. iii. d. 244; sensual enjoyment, Hit. iii. d. 116. **9.** Aim, Çiç. 9, 40. **10.** A religious observance. **11.** Refuge, asylum. **12.** A lover, a husband.—**Comp.** *A-*, I. adj. unacquainted with worldly objects, Çâk. 55, 20. II. m. 1. not being an object, Mâlat. 17, 2. 2. invisibility, Hit. ii. d. 77. *An-anya-*, adj. having, or referring to, no other object, Vikr. d. 1. *Avakâça-*, adj., f. *yâ*, literally, having as its sphere space, room, i.e. demanding a place (which it cannot get because the heart is filled with pride, etc.), Pańch. iii. d. 264. *Chakshurvishaya*, i.e. *chakshus-*, m. sight, Man. 2, 298. *A-chakshus-*, adj. not distinguishable by one's eye, Man. 4, 77. *Guṇa-samudaya-avâpti-*, adj., f. *yâ*, having as its object the acquirement of a multitude of good qualities, Hit. i. d. 174, M.M. *Nis-*, I. m. no home, not being a dwelling-place, Hariv. 3654. II. adj. 1. having no home, banished, Râm. 3, 79, 47. 2. not attached to worldly objects, Bhâg. P. 2, 1, 19. *Nîti-*, m. sphere of prudent conduct, Pańch. 112, 19. *Palâyana-*, adj., f. *yâ*, having flight as its object, i.e. advising flight, Pańch. 247, 6. *Mitra-*, m. friendship, Pańch. 131, 11. *Yuvati-*, m. a woman, Megh. 80. *Çruti-*, m. 1. an object of hearing, i.e. sound, Çâk. d. 1. 2. an object of the Vedas. *Sva-*, m. one's own country, Hit. i. d. 170, M.M.

विषयायिन् *vishayâyin*, i.e. *vishaya* + *yin* (for *vin*), m. **1.** A king. **2.** An organ of sense. **3.** Kâma. **4.** A sensualist. **5.** A materialist. **6.** A man of business.

विषयिन् *vishayin*, i.e. *vishaya* + *in*, I. adj., f. *ṇî*. **1.** Attached to sensual objects, carnal, sensual, Hit. ii. d. 144; voluptuary, Çâk. 68, 14. **2.** Conversant with worldly occupations, Hit. 13, 7, M.M. II. m. **1.** A king. **2.** Kâma. **3.** A sensualist. **4.** A materialist. **5.** A man of business.

विषहर *vishahara*, i.e. *visha-hṛi* + *a*, I. adj. Removing venom. II. f. *râ* and *rî*, The goddess of the serpent race, the sister of Vâsuki.

विषा *vish* + *â*, I. f. Excrement, Amarak. II. ind. Intellect.

विषाण *vishâṇa*, i.e. *vi-so* + *ana*, m. (f. *ṇî*), and n. **1.** The horn of an animal, Bhartṛ. 2, 5; Pańch. i. d. 311. **2.** The tusks of an elephant or boar, Lass. 2. ed. 46, 24; Draup. 8, 21. **II.** f. *ṇî*, The name of two plants. **III.** n. Costus speciosus. — **Comp.** *Nis-*, adj. without tusks, MBh. 6, 4677. *Çaça-*, and *çaçaka-*, n. the horn of a hare;

anything improbable or extraordinary, Bhartṛ. 2, 5; 3, 99.

विषाणिन् *vishâṇin*, i.e. *vishâṇa* + *in*, I. adj. 1. Having horns, MBh. 6, 71. 2. Having huge tusks, Râm. 2, 52, 18, Seramp. II. m. 1. Any animal with horns. 2. A bull. 3. An elephant.

विषाद *vishâda*, i.e. *vi-sad* + *a*, m. 1. Lassitude, dejection, lowness of spirits, want of energy, fear, Draup. 8, 3; Chr. 40, 20; weakness, Mâlat. 35, 9. 2. Distress, affliction, sorrow, Vikr. 5, 11; Pañch. 221, 5. 3. Disappointment, despair, Hit. i. d. 32, M.M.—Comp. *A*-, adj. unwearied, Johns. Sel. 57, 160. *Sa-vishâda* + *m*, adv. afflicted, Pañch. 107, 19; sorrowful, Vikr. 30, 12.

विषादिन् *vishâdin*, i.e. *vishâda* + *in*, adj., f. *nî*, 1. Dejected, Bhag. 18, 23. 2. Sorrowful, Man. 6, 57.

विषाय *VISHAYA*, a denomin. derived from *visha* with *ya*, Âtm. To turn into poison, Bhartṛ. 1, 34.

विषु *vishu* (probably a loc. pl. of *dvi*, cf. *vi*), adv. 1. Equally, same, alike. 2. Many, various.

विषुव *vishuva*, **विषुवत्** *vishuvat*, i.e. *vishu* + *vant*, n. (*va*, by dropping the final *t*), The equinox, Hit. 114, 22 (*va*).

विष्क् *VISHK*, see *vashk*.

विष्कम्भ *vishkambha*, i.e. *vi-skambh* + *a*, m. 1. Obstacle, hindrance, resistance. 2. The bolt of a door. 3. A post, the roof-tree of a house. 4. Spreading. 5. A posture of the devotees, called *yogin*. 6. Act, doing anything. 7. The first of the twenty-seven astronomical periods called *Yogas*. 8. A prelude.

विष्कम्भक *vishkambha* + *ka*, m. A prelude, Vikr. 36, 14; Çâk. 31, 13.

विष्कम्भिन् *vishkambhin*, i.e. *vi-skambh* + *in*, I. adj. Obstructive, impeding. II. m. The bolt of a door.

विष्किर *vishkira*, i.e. *vi-kṛi* + *a*, m. 1. A bird, Utt. Râmach. 40, 13. 2. Tearing to pieces.—Comp. *Nakha*-, m. a bird wounding with strong talons, a bird of prey, Man. 5, 13. *Smera*-, m. a peacock.

विष्टप *vishṭapa* (cf. *pishṭapa*, and *piv* for *pi-pâ*, s.v. 1. *pâ*), m. and n. A world, Böhtl. Ind. Spr. 3288.—Comp. *Tri*-, n. the world of Indra, Yâjń. 3, 330.

विष्टम्भ *vishṭambha*, i.e. *vi-stambh* + *a*, m. 1. Obstacle. 2. Stopping. 3. Placing in or upon, planting (one's feet), Kir. 13, 16. 4. Paralysis, loss of motion.

विष्टम्भिन् *vishṭambhin*, i.e. *vi-stambh* + *in*, adj., f. *nî*, 1. Stopping. 2. Checking. 3. Making motionless.

विष्टर *vishṭara*, i.e. *vi-strî* + *a*, m. 1. A handful of Kuça or sacred grass, MBh. 3, 1881. 2. A seat made of twenty-five straws of Kuça grass tied up in a sheaf. 3. A layer, MBh. 15, 739; a bed. 4. A couch, a seat, Vikr. 86, 15. 5. The seat of a Brahman, either real or in effigy, as presiding at a sacrifice. 6. A tree.

विष्टा *vishṭâ*, (Pañch. 192, 16), and **विष्ठा** *vishṭhâ* (Man. 3, 180; 4, 220; 10, 91), f. Fæces, ordure (cf. 4. *vish*).—Comp. *Go-vishṭhâ*, f. cow-dung. *Mukha-vishṭhâ*, f. a cockroach.

विष्टि *vishṭi*, i.e. 2. *vish* + *ṭi*, I. adj. and sbst. Working, a workman. II. f. 1. Occupation, Chr. 294, 3 = Rigv. i. 92, 3; act, action. 2. Unpaid labour. 3. Hire, Râm. 2, 63, 55, Seramp. 4.

Sending, dispatching. 5. Sending to hell.

विष्ठल *vishṭhala*, i.e. *vi-sthala*, n. A place situated remote or apart.

विष्ठा *vishṭhâ*, see *vishṭâ*.

विष्णु *vishṇu*, i.e. 2. *vish* + *nu*, m. 1. Vishṇu, one of the three principal Indian deities, Chr. 291, 7 = Rigv. i. 85, 7; Pańch. 44, 16. 2. Agni. 3. One of the Vasus. 4. The name of an ancient law-giver. 5. A pious man.

विष्णुमय *vishṇu* + *maya*, adj., f. *yî*, Emanated from Vishṇu.

विष्पन्द *vishpanda*, i.e. *vi-spand* + *a*, m. Throbbing.

विष्फार *vishphâra*, i.e. *vi-sphar* + *a*, m. The twang of a bow (cf. *visphâra*).

विष्य *vishya*, i.e. *visha* + *ya*, adj. Deserving death by poison.

विष्यन्द *vishyanda*, i.e. *vi-syand* + *a*, m. Flowing, trickling.

विष्वचेण *vishvakshena*, and **विष्वक्सेन** *vishvaksena*, i. e. *vishvańch* -*sena* (see *senâ*), m. Vishṇu, Bhâg. P. 8, 13, 24 (*s*).

विष्वञ्च् *vishvańch*, i.e. *vishu-ańch*, I. adj., f. *shûchî*, Going everywhere, all-pervading, Bhâg. P. 2, 6, 20. II. acc. *vak*, adv. 1. Every way, everywhere, Pańch. ii. d. 2. 2. All about, Vedântas. in Chr. 207, 11.

विष्वणन *vishvaṇana*, n., and **विष्वाण** *vishvâṇa*, m., i.e. *vi-svan* + *ana*, or *a*, Eating, food.

† **विस्** *VIS*, i. 1, Par. To go.

विस *visa* (also *viça* and *visha*), probably curtailed *visara*, or *visala* (cf. both), i.e. *vi-sṛi* + *a*, n. The film or fibres of the stalk of the water-lily, Çâk. d. 66; Vikr. d. 94; MBh. 13, 4509; 12, 7877 (all with *s*).

विसंयोग *visaṁyoga*, i.e. *vi-sam-yuj* + *a*, m. Separation.

विसंवाद *visaṁvâda*, i.e. *vi-sam-vad* + *a*, m. 1. Contradiction, disagreement, Pańch. iii. d. 261; Mâlav. d. 23. 2. Disappointing, deceiving.

विसंवादिन् *visaṁvâdin*, i.e. *vi-sam* -*vad*, and *visaṁvâda*, + *in*, adj., f. *nî*, 1. Contradicting, disagreeing, Râjat. 5, 193. 2. Disputing. 3. Crafty, cunning. — **Comp.** *A*-, adj. incontestible, Daçak. in Chr. 197, 11.

विसंष्ठुल *visaṁshṭhula* (*vi*, *sam*, and vb. *sthâ*), adj. Unsteady, agitated, Kâvya Pr. 105, 1.

विसर *visara*, i.e. *vi-sṛi* + *a*, m. 1. Spreading, Kâvya Pr. 79, 9. 2. A multitude, Mâlat. 23, 14.

विसर्ग *visarga*, i.e. *vi-sṛij* + *a*, m. 1. Abandoning. 2. Final emancipation. 3. Departure. 4. Relinquishment. 5. Dismission, Chr. 9, 38. 6. Creation, Bhag. 8, 3. 7. Evacuation of excrement, Vedântas. in Chr. 209, 20. 8. Separation. 9. Donation. 10. Light, lustre. 11. The southern course of the sun.

विसर्जन *visarjana*, i.e. *vi-sṛij* + *ana*, n. 1. Relinquishing, Nal. 10, 15. 2. Sending away, dismissing, Chr. 9, 38. 3. Sending. 4. Donation, Lass. 80, 3 (Prâkṛ.). 5. Throwing the image of a deity in holy water, as the concluding rite of a festival.

विसर्प *visarpa*, i.e. *vi-sṛip* + *a*, m. 1. Spreading, Utt. Râmach. 23, 6. 2. Flying, gliding. 3. Going. 4. Unwished consequence of any act.

विसर्पण *visarpaṇa*, i.e. *vi-sṛip* + *ana*,

n. **1.** Spreading. **2.** Flying. **3.** Going gently.

विसर्पिन् *visarpin*, i.e. *vi-sṛip + in*, adj., f. *iṇî*, **1.** Spreading, Çiç. 9, 36; Vikr. d. 16 (*vasudhâdhara-handarâ-*, Spreading through the clefts of the mountains, viz. the echo); 67, 1. **2.** Gliding, going gently.—**Comp.** *Manda-*, adj. moving slowly, Pańch. i. d. 282 (a louse).

विसल *visala*, probably *vi-sṛi + a* (with *l* for *r*), m. A shoot, a sprout.

विसार *visâra*, i.e. *vi-sṛi + a*, **I.** m. **1.** Going smoothly, gliding. **2.** Expansion, Nalod. 1, 19. **3.** A fish. **II.** n. A wood. **III.** f. *rî*, The region of the winds.

विसारिन् *visârin*, i.e. *vi-sṛi + in*, **I.** adj., f. *iṇî*. **1.** Gliding, flowing. **2.** Spreading, Kir. 10, 11. **II.** m. A fish.

विसिनी *visinî*, i.e. *visa + in + î* (see *viça*), f. **1.** A lotus flower, Bhartṛ. 3, 7. **2.** An assemblage of lotus flowers, Mâlat. 51, 5.

विसूचिका *visûchikâ* (akin to *sûchi*), f. **1.** Spasmodic cholera, Pańch. 138, 8. **2.** Symptoms of disease.

विसूरण *visûraṇa*, i.e. *vi-* † *sûr + ana*, n., and f. *ṇâ*, Sorrow, Vikr. d. 82 (Prâkṛ.).

विसूरित *vi-* † *sûr + ita*, **I.** n. Repentance. **II.** f. *tâ*, A fever.

विसृत्वर *vi-sṛi + tvara*, adj. Going smoothly, gliding.

विसृमर *vi-sṛi + mara*, adj. Gliding.

विसृष्टि *visṛishṭi*, i.e. *vi-sṛij + ti*, f. **1.** Quitting. **2.** Leaving. **3.** Dismissing. **4.** Giving.

विस्त *vista*, m. A weight of gold, about half an ounce Troy.

विस्तर *vistara*, i.e. *vi-stṛî + a*, m. **1.** Spreading. **2.** Prolixity, Pańch. iii. d. 103. **3.** Detail; instr. °*reṇa*, Fully, at length, Chr. 9, 37; Sund. 1, 1. **4.** Abundance, Man. 6, 55; multitude, Hit. iii. d. 12. **5.** Assemblage, a large company, Man. 3, 125. **6.** A bed. **7.** A seat, Bhaṭṭ. 2, 26.—**Comp.** *Ati-*, m. excessive prolixity, Vikr. 3, 6 (*alam*, with instr., enough). *Sa-*, adj. with (its) detail, complete, Pańch. 114, 20. *Su-vistara + m*, adv. at large, Hit. 73, 15.

विस्तरतस् *vistara + tas*, adv. Fully, at length, Pańch. 181, 2.

विस्तरता *vistara + tâ*, f. Spreading, Kir. 5, 7.

विस्तरशस् *vistara + ças*, adv. Fully, at length, Man. 9, 250.

विस्तार *vistâra*, i.e. *vi-stṛî + a*, m. **1.** Spreading, extension, Megh. 18. **2.** Vastness. **3.** Length, Râm. 1, 40, 15. **4.** Detail, Yâjń. 3, 95. **5.** Breadth, amplitude. **6.** Amplification. **7.** The diameter of a circle. **8.** The branch of a tree with its new shoots.—**Comp.** *Ati-*, m. excessive extension, Pańch. 245, 24.

विस्तारिन् *vistârin*, i.e. *vistâra + in*, adj., f. *riṇî*, **1.** Extending, Utt. Râmach. 157, 16; large, Mâlat. 131, 10. **2.** Powerful, Mâlat. 81, 15.

विस्तीर्णता *vi-stîrṇa + tâ* (vb. *stṛî*), f. **1.** Extension, Hit. iii. d. 53. **2.** Vastness.

विस्तृति *vi-stṛi + ti*, f. **1.** Spreading, expansion. **2.** Breadth. **3.** The diameter of a circle.

विस्पष्ट *vi-spashṭa* (properly ptcple. of the pf. pass. of *spaç*, see *dṛiç*), adj. **1.** Apparent, evident. **2.** Plain, intelligible. **3.** °*ṭam*, adv. Evidently, Indr.

5, 39.—Comp. *A-*, 1. adj. not clear, obscure. 2. acc. *ṭam*, adv. without pronouncing well letters and accents, Man. 4, 99.

विस्फार *visphâra*, i.e. *vi-sphar* + *a*, m. The twang of a bow.

विस्फुलिङ्ग *vi-sphuliṅga*, m. **1.** A spark of fire, MBh. 1, 1431. **2.** A sort of poison.

विस्फूर्जथु *vi-sphûrjathu*, m. **1.** Rolling, Ragh. 13, 12. **2.** Thunder, ib. 14, 62.

विस्फोट *visphoṭa*, i.e. *vi-sphuṭ* + *a*, m., and f. *ṭâ*, **1.** Boil, pustule, Çâk. Sch. ad 20, 10. **2.** Small-pox.

विस्मय *vismaya*, i.e. *vi-smi* + *a*, m. **1.** Surprise, Vikr. 78, 5; wonder, Pańch. i. d. 459 (*bâlake ko tra vismayaḥ*, literally, What wonder concerning a little boy, i.e. how much more a little boy). **2.** Pride, Man. 4, 237. **3.** Doubt, uncertainty, Hit. 13, 19; perplexity, Hit. ii. d. 13.—Comp. *Sa-vismaya*, adj., f. *yâ*, 1. surprised, Pańch. 44, 24. 2. doubtful, Hit. 54, 18. 3. °*yam*, adv. surprised, Pańch. 76, 24.

विस्मयंगम *vismayaṁgama*, i.e. *vismaya* + *m-gam* + *a*, adj. Astonishing (with acc. *âtmânam*, thyself), Johns. Sel. 17, 73.

विस्मयिन् *vismayin*, i.e. *vismaya* + *in*, adj., f. *nî*, Astonished.

विस्मरण *vismaraṇa*, i.e. *vi-smṛi* + *ana*, n. Forgetting.

विस्मापन *vismâpana*, i.e. *vi-smi*, Caus., + *ana*, n. **1.** Causing surprise, Bhâg. P. 1, 15, 5. **2.** Illusion, deceit. **3.** Kâma. **4.** A magical or enchanted city, a city of the Gandharvas.

विस्मृति *vi-smṛi* + *ti*, f. Forgetting. Utt. Râmach. 122, 5.

विस्यन्द *vi-syand* + *a*, m. Flowing, trickling.

विस्र *visra*, n. A smell like that of raw meat, Çâk. 74, 10 (Prâkṛ.).

विस्रंस *vi-sraṁs* + *a*, m. **1.** Relaxation. **2.** Decay.

विस्रंसन *vi-sraṁs* + *ana*, n. **1.** Loosening, untying, Sâh. D. 113, 16. **2.** Falling. **3.** Flowing, dropping. **4.** A laxative.

विस्रम्भ *visrambha*, and **विस्रम्भिन्** *visrambhin*, see *viçr*°.

विस्रसा *visrasâ*, i.e. *vi-sraṁs* + *a*, f. Decrepitude.

विस्रावण *visrâvaṇa*, i.e. *vi-sru*, Caus., + *ana*, n. **1.** Causing to flow. **2.** Bleeding. **3.** Distilling. **4.** A spirit distilled from molasses.

विहग *viha-ga* (cf. *vihâ*), m. **1.** A bird, Pańch. ii. d. 21. **2.** A cloud. **3.** An arrow. **4.** The sun. **5.** The moon. **6.** A planet.

विहंग *vihaṁga*, i.e. *viha* + *m-ga* (see the last), I. adj. Flying, going swiftly. II. m. A bird, Pańch. 157, 20.—Comp. *Nis-*, adj. without birds, Hariv. 3489.

विहंगम *vihaṁgama*, i.e. *viha* + *m-gam* + *a* (see the last), I. m. A bird, Pańch. ii. d. 20. II. f. *mâ*, A pole or yoke for carrying burthens.

विहंगिका *vihaṁgikâ*, i.e. *vihaṁga*, in the signification of *vihaṁgamâ*, + *ka*, f. A pole or yoke for carrying burthens.

विहति *vihati*, i.e. I. *vi-han* + *ti*, f. **1.** Striking, killing. **2.** Defeat, Nalod. 1, 10; Kir. 10, 63. II. *vi-hati*, m. A friend.—Comp. *Praṇaya-*, f. denial.

विहनन *vi-han* + *ana*, m. **1.** Impediment. **2.** Killing, injuring. **3.** A bow for cleaning cotton.

विहर *vihara,* i.e. *vi-hṛi+a,* m. **1.** Separation. **2.** Absence. **3.** Exchanging, Böhtl. Ind. Spr. 920.

विहरण *viharaṇa,* i.e. *vi-hṛi+ana,* n. **1.** Taking off or away. **2.** Going about for pleasure or exercise, Pańch. 25, 10; roaming, Bhartṛ. 3, 92. **3.** Relaxation, pastime, pleasure, Pańch. 236, 18.

विहर्तृ *vihartṛi,* i.e. *vi-hṛi+tṛi,* m. One who robs, Draup. 8, 46.

विहसन *vi-has+ana,* n. Laughing gently.

विहा *vi-hâ,* indecl. Heaven, paradise.

विहायस् *vihâyas,* i.e. *vi-hâ+yas* (for *vas*), I. m. and n. **1.** The sky. **2.** The open air, Man. 2, 186. II. instr. *sâ,* adv. Through the air, Râm. 3, 54, 6. III. m. A bird.—Cf. χάος.

विहार *vihâra,* i.e. *vi-hṛi+a,* m. **1.** Wandering, going about, walking for pleasure, Râm. 3, 51, 20; Vedântas. in Chr. 219, 1. **2.** Sporting, Hit. 83, 4, M.M; pleasure, Daçak. in Chr. 182, 9; relaxation, Râm. 3, 49, 39. **3.** A Bauddha or Jaina convent, Pańch. 236, 8. **4.** A temple, Hit. 19, 10 (cf. *vihâra*). **5.** A palace, Mâlat. 8, 4. **6.** The shoulder. **7.** A sort of bird.—**Comp.** *Jayendra-,* i.e. *jaya-indra-,* m. a convent built by Jayendra, a king of Cashmere, Râjat. 5, 427. *Nis-,* adj. deprived of pleasure, Hariv. 11150. *Hiṁsâ-,* m. roaming with the intention to do mischief, Râm. 3, 51, 20.

विहारक *vihâra+ka* (or **विहारिक** *vihâra+ika* ?), adj., f. *rikâ,* Belonging to a Bauddha convent, Mâlat. 104, 9.

विहारवन्त् *vihâra + vant,* adj. Taking pleasure, liking, Man. 10, 9.

विहारिन् *vihârin,* i.e. *vi-hṛi* and *vihâra, +in,* adj., f. *iṇi,* **1.** Walking about, wandering, Hit. i. d. 20, M.M. **2.** Taking pleasure or relaxation, rejoicing one's self, Çâk. 17, 21; Pańch. 30, 25; ii. d. 21. **3.** Beautiful, Bhartṛ. 1, 17.

विहास *vihâsa,* i.e. *vi-has+a,* m. A gentle laugh.

विहिंसक *vi-hiṁs+aka,* adj. Injuring, Pańch. iii. d. 143.

विहित्रिम *vihitrima,* i.e. *vi-hita+rima* (vb. *dhâ*), adj. Done according to rule, Bhaṭṭ. 1, 13.

विहीनता *vi-hîna+tâ* (vb. *hâ*), f. Abandoning, Pańch. ii. d. 146.

विहृति *vi-hṛi+ti,* f. **1.** Opening. **2.** Pastime, pleasure, Nalod. 2, 38.

विहेठक *vi-heṭh+aka,* m. An injurer, a reviler, MBh. 1, 3076.

विहेठन *vi-heṭh+ana,* n. **1.** Hurting, killing. **2.** Rubbing, grinding. **3.** Afflicting. **4.** Affliction.

विह्वल *vi-hval+a,* adj. **1.** Agitated, Râm. 2, 48, 2; overcome with fear or agitation, Chr. 34, 8. **2.** Distressed, afflicted, Chr. 32, 28 (perhaps rather *savihvala,* in one word, full of emotion). **3.** Fused, liquid. **4.** Languishing, Lass. 2. ed. 60, 25. **5.** Desponding, Mâlat. 142, 5.—**Comp.** *A-,* adj. strong, Chr. 30, 2. *Pari-,* adj. very agitated, Râm. 2, 84, 6 Gorr.

विह्वलता *vihvala+tâ,* f. Agitation, anxiety.

1. **वी** *VÎ,* ii. 2, Par. (ved.), **1.** To go. **2.** To approach. **3.** To pervade, to obtain. **4.** To conceive, to grow pregnant. **5.** To desire, to love, Chr. 287, 6=Rigv. i. 48, 6. **6.** To eat, to enjoy. **7.** It is used as substitute for

the vb. *aj*, To drive, to move. **3.** To throw. Ptcple. of the pf. pass. *vîta*, Tranquil, quiet, tame. Caus. *vâyaya* and *vâpaya*, To cause to conceive (see *vap*).—Cf. οἴσω, οἴαξ, οἰήϊον; Lat. in-vîtus (Not liking), in-vitare, To invite.

2. वी *vî*, f. Going.

वीक *vîka*, i.e. *vi+ka*, m. **1.** A bird. **2.** Wind.

वीकाश *vîkâça*, i.e. *vi-kâç+a*, m. Æther, heaven.

वीक्ष *vîksha*, i.e. *vi-îksh+a*, I. m., and f. *kshâ*, Sight, seeing, investigation, Pańch. 62, 12 (f.). II. n. **1.** Surprise. **2.** A visible object.

वीक्षण *vîkshâṇa*, i.e. *vi-îksh+ana*, n. Sight, seeing.

वीङ्खा *vînkhâ*, i.e. *vi-inkh+a*, f. **1.** Moving. **2.** Dancing. **3.** One of a horse's paces. **4.** Cowach, Carpopogon pruriens.

वीचयन *vîchayana*, i.e. *vi-chi+ana*, n. Research, inquiry.

वीचि *vîchi* (m. and) f., also वीची *vîchî*, f. **1.** A wave, Hit. iii. d. 140 (*i*); Pańch. i. d. 209 (*î*). **2.** A ray of light. **3.** Small, little. **4.** Leisure. **5.** Pleasure.—Comp. *A-*, I. adj. waveless. II. m. a hell, Yâjń. 3, 224. *Mahâ-*, m. a hell, Man. 4, 89.

वीज् *VÎJ*, † i. 1, Âtm. To go. i. 10 (properly a denomin. derived from *vyaja*), Par. To fan, Mâlat. 63, 9; Chr. 25, 56.—With the prep. अनु *anu*, i. 10, To fan, MBh. 3, 1764.—With उद् *ud*, i. 10, To fan, MBh. 3, 1757.—With उप *upa*, i. 10, To fan, Çâk. 33, 6.

वीज *vîja*, also बीज *bîja*, i.e. probably *vi-ja* (vb. *jan*), n. **1.** Seed, germ, Çâk. 91, 14; Pańch. 51, 11; 200, 12. **2.** Semen virile. **3.** Receptacle, place of deposit. **4.** Marrow. **5.** Origin. **6.** Divine truth as the cause of being. **7.** The origin of the business of a drama. **8.** The mystical syllable which forms the essential part of the *mantra* of any deity. **9.** Algebra.—Comp. *A-*, I. n. bad grain, Man. 9, 291. II. adj. without manly strength, Man. 9, 79. *Agni-*, n. gold, Man. 5, 113. *Upta-* (vb. *vap*), adj., f. *jâ*, sown, Çâk. 91, 14. *Uçîra-*, m. the name of a mountain, Râm. 6, 3, 32; also *ushîra-*, with *sh* instead of *ç*, 4, 41, 46. *Nîti-*, n. a germ of intrigue, Pańch. 85, 20. *Maṇi-*, m. the pomegranate. *Mantra-*, n. seed-like deliberation, Hit. ii. d. 138. *Rańga-*, n. silver. *Sva-*, m. the soul. *Hara-*, n. quicksilver. *Hari-*, n. yellow orpiment.

वीजक *vîja+ka*, **1.** m. The common citron, Râm. 2, 69, 8, ed. Seramp. **2.** A substitute for *vîja*, as latter part of a comp. adj., e.g. *a-*, adj. Not sown, Man. 10, 71.

वीजन I. n. *vîj+ana*. **1.** Fanning, being fanned, Râjat. 5, 386. **2.** A fan. II. n. Thing. III. m. **1.** A sort of pheasant. **2.** The ruddy goose.

वीजवत् *vîja+vat*, adv. Like seed.

वीजवन्त् *vîja+vant*, adj., f. *vatî*, Who or what has seed.

वीजिन् *vîjin*, i.e. *vîja+in*, I. adj. **1.** Having seed. **2.** Having sown seed, Man. 9, 51; 52. II. m. A father, a progenitor.

वीज्य *vîjya*, i.e. *vîja+ya*, adj. **1.** Sprung from seed. **2.** Sprung from some family.—Comp. *Mahâ-*, n. the septum of the scrotum, and part of the perinæum.

वीटिका *viṭikâ*, f. 1. The betel plant. 2. The preparation of the Areca nut with spices, and enveloped in the leaf of the betel plant, Daçak. in Chr. 199, 17. 3. A tie, a fastening, Amar. 23.

वीणा *viṇâ*, f. The Indian lute, Hit. ii. d. 73.—Comp. *Danta-*, f. chattering of the teeth, Pańch. 94, 4. *Sûtra-*, f. a sort of lute.

वीणिन् *viṇin*, i.e. *viṇâ + in*, adj. Furnished with lutes, Megh. 46.

वीतंस *vitaṁsa*, see *vitaṁsa*.

वीतहव्य *vita-havya* (vb. *vi* and *hu*), m. A proper name, MBh. 13, 1943.

वीति *vi + ti*, I. f. 1. Going. 2. Engendering. 3. Eating, Lass. 101, 9 = Rigv. vii. 16, 4. 4. Cleaning. 5. Light, lustre. II. m. A horse.

वीथि and **वीथी** *vithi*, probably *vi-i + tha + i*, f. 1. A line, MBh. 13, 5261. 2. A road, Pańch. i. d. 189; Indr. 2, 12. 3. A stall, a shop, Çiç. 9, 32. 4. A terrace in front of a house. 5. A sort of drama.—Comp. *Aja-vithi*, f. the name of a part of the orbit of the moon, Yâjń. 3, 184. *Ghana-vithi-vithi*, f. the road of the clouds, as if they were shops, Çiç. 9, 32. *Nakshatra-vithi*, f. the orbit of the stars, MBh. 13, 521. *Nabhovithi*, i.e. *nabhas-*, f. the orbit of the sun, Bhâg. P. 5, 22, 6. *Nâga-vithi*, f. 1. a line formed by snakes, MBh. 13, 5261. 2. the name of a part of the orbit of the moon, Yâjń. 3, 187. 3. a proper name, Hariv. 148. *Sura-vithi*, f. the road of the gods, Indr. 2, 12.

वीथिका *vithi + kâ*, f. A hall, Utt. Râmach. 9, 13.

वीथी *vithi*, see *vithi*.

वीध्र *vidhra*, i.e. *vi-indh + ra*, adj. Clear, clean, pure.

वीनाह *vinâha*, see *vinâha*.

वीपा *vipâ*, f. Lightning.

वीप्सा *vipsâ*, i.e. *vi-ipsa*, desider. of *âp*, *+ a*, f. 1. Successive order, Pâṇ. viii. 1, 4. 2. Repetition.

वीर् *VÎR*, i. 10 (properly a denomin. derived from *vira*), Âtm. 1. To be valiant. 2. To show one's heroism.

वीर *vira*, i.e. *vṛi + a* (probably for original *vâra*), I. adj. 1. Heroic. 2. Strong. 3. Powerful. 4. Eminent. II. m. 1. A hero, Chr. 5, 1. 2. A brave man, Hit. i. d. 169, M.M. 3. A soldier, Râjat. 5, 134. 4. Heroism, as a *rasa* or poetical sentiment. 5. Fire. 6. Sacrificial fire (see *virahan*, *virojjha*, and *viropajivika*). 7. An actor. III. f. *râ*. 1. A matron, a wife and mother. 2. The plantain tree. 3. The name of several plants. 4. Spirituous liquor, or a particular kind of it. IV. n. The name of several plants. *viratara*, see s.v.—Comp. *A-*, and *nis-*, f. *râ*, a woman who has neither husband nor son, Man. 4, 213. *Eka-*, m. an unparalleled hero, MBh. 4, 1912. *Mahâ-*, m. 1. a hero. 2. a lion. 3. a white horse. 4. a sort of hawk. 5. Garuḍa. 6. Indra's thunderbolt. 7. Vishṇu. 8. Agni. 9. sacrificial fire. *Su-*, I. adj. abounding in heroes. II. m. pl. the name of a people, Draup. 8, 9. —Cf. Lat. vir; Goth. vair; A.S. wer; probably ἥρως, Ἥρα, Ἡρακλῆς, εἰρήν.

वीरजयन्तिका *virajayantikâ*, i. e. probably *vira-jayanta + ka*, f. 1. A war-dance. 2. War, battle.

वीरण *viraṇa*, I. n. A fragrant grass, Andropogon muricatum, Râm.

2, 80, 8. II. f. *ṇî*. **1.** A side-glance. **2.** A deep place.

वीरतर *vira+tara*, m. **1.** A distinguished hero, Lass. 48, 11. **2.** An arrow.

वीरता *vira+tâ*, f. Heroism.

वीरवन्त् *vîra + vant*, I. adj. **1.** Abounding in heroes, Chr. 291, 15= Rigv. i. 64, 15. **2.** Having a hero. II. f. *vatî*, A wife whose husband is living.

वीरहन् *vîra-han*, m. A Brâhmaṇa who has suffered the sacred domestic fire to become extinct.

वीरानक *virânaka*, The name of a town, Râjat. 5, 213.

वीराय *VÎRÂYA*, a denomin. derived from *vira* with *ya*, To show one's heroism, Utt. Râmach. 148, 3.

वीरिणी *viriṇî*, f. The name of a river, Matsyop. 5.

वीरुध् *virudh*, i.e. *vi-ruh*, f. **1.** A creeper. **2.** A plant which grows again when being cut, Man. 11, 142. **3.** A plant in general, Pañch. iii. d. 50; Vikr. d. 38. **4.** A branch and shoot, Utt. Râmach. 44, 10.—**Comp.** *Nis-*, adj. deprived of plants, Bhâg. P. 4, 30, 45.

वीरोज्झ *virojjha*, i.e. *vira-ujjh+a*, m. A Brahman who omits offering burnt offerings.

वीरोपजीविक *viropajivika*, i.e. *vira-upa-jiva+ika*, m. A Brâhmaṇa who claims presents on the merit of having preserved his sacrificial fire.

वीर्य *virya*, i.e. *vira+ya*, n. **1.** Strength, power, Chr. 23, 33; Vikr. d. 16. **2.** Fortitude, Chr. 4, 14. **3.** Heroism. **4.** Dignity **5.** Splendour. —**Comp.** *A-mogha-*, adj. 1. of unfailing virility. 2. of unfailing power. *Nis-*, adj. powerless, Hit. ii. d. 6. *Mahâ-*, I. adj. very strong, Râm. 3, 53, 12. II. m. Brahman. *Vi-chitra-*, m. a proper name, Chr. 3, 6. *Sama-*, adj. having equal strength, Hit. iv. d. 20. *Su-*, n. 1. great vigour. 2. abundance in heroes, Chr. 288, 12= Rigv. i. 48, 12 (cf. i. 40, 2).

वीर्यवन्त् *virya+vant*, adj. **1.** Strong, Man. 2, 114. **2.** Victorious.

वीवध *vivadha*, and **वीवधिक** *vivadhika*, see *vivadha, vivadhika*.

वीहार *vihâra*, i.e. *vi-hṛi+a* (cf. *vihâra*), m. A Bauddha or Jaina convent, a sanctuary, a temple, a holy place.

† **वुङ्ग्** *VUṄG*, **बुङ्ग्** *BUṄG*, i. 1, Par. To abandon.

वुण्ट् *VUṆṬ*, see *viṇṭ*.

वृ *VṚI*, and **वॄ** *VṚÎ*, i. 1. ii. 5, *vṛiṇu*, and ii. 9, *vṛiṇâ*, *vṛiṇî*, Par. Âtm (this verb comprehends perhaps two verbs which were originally different; the original signification of the one seems to be, 'To guard by covering,' that of the other, 'To choose'). **1.** To screen, to cover, MBh. 3, 10970. **2.** To conceal (ved.). **3.** To surround, MBh. 5, 164. **4.** To resist (ved.). **5.** To select, to choose, Râm. 2, 9, 25. **6.** To woo, MBh. 3, 16647. **7.** ii. 9, Âtm. To select for one's self, Ragh. 3, 6; to beg, Dev. 11, 36. **8.** To prefer, Râm. 2, 70, 12. Ptcple. of the pf. pass. *vṛita*. **1.** Agreed or assented to. **2.** Served. **3.** Affected by. **4.** Vitiated, spoiled. **Comp.** *Ûrdhva-*, adj. worn over the shoulder, Man. 2, 44. *Svayam-*, adj. chosen by one's self, Vikr. d. 101. Ptcple. of the fut. pass. *varya*, **1.** To be applied to for aid. **2.** To be yielded to or indulged.

3. Chief, principal (rather *vara + ya*), Bhâg. P. 1, 9, 41; Kir. 7, 20. m. Kâma. f. *yâ*, A girl choosing her own husband (rather *vara + ya*). **Comp.** *Arya-*, m. a respectable man of the third caste, Daçak. in Chr. 186, 17. Caus., and i. 10, I. *varaya*, Par. Âtm. **1.** To select, to choose, Hit. 116, 7; Râm. 1, 43, 17; in marriage, Chr. 52, 10. **2.** To beg (with two acc.), Râm. 1, 36, 16. **3.** To fall to one's share (acc.), Râm. 1, 65, 21. **II.** *vâraya*, Par. Âtm. **1.** To stop, Man. 8, 239. **2.** To hinder, Nal. 3, 24. **3.** To keep off. Ptcple. of the pf. pass. *vârita*, Prevented. **Comp.** *Dus-*, adj. kept off badly, MBh. 13, 267. Ptcple. of the fut. pass. I. *vârya*, Excellent. n. Sacrifice, Lass. 101, 13=Rigv. vii. 16, 5. **Comp.** *Dus-*, adj. 1. difficult to be kept off, irresistible, MBh. 12, 3661. 2. dangerous to be troubled, cf. MBh. 1, 1917 (+*tâ*, f. state of such one). **II.** *vâraṇiya*. **Comp.** *Dus-*, adj. irresistible, MBh. 8, 3629.—With the prep. अप *apa*, **1.** To open (ved.). **2.** To show, Ragh. 10, 7 (Calc.). Caus. *apavârita*, Screened, Mâlat. 93, 14. Absol. *apavârya* (in theatrical language), Aside, apart, Çâk. 28, 17.—With आ *â*, **1.** To cover, MBh. 1, 1296. **2.** To conceal, Ragh. 17, 61. **3.** To fill, Man. 2, 144. **4.** To comprehend, Bhag. 13, 13. **5.** To obstruct, Râm. 1, 26, 28. **6.** To choose, MBh. 1, 4738. **7.** To beg. *âvṛita*, **1.** Enclosed, surrounded, Man. 4, 73. **2.** Invested. **3.** Overspread. **4.** Covered, Hit. 80, 15. **5.** Filled, Chr. 293, 4=Rigv. i. 87, 4. **6.** Occupied, Râjat. 5, 235. m. A man of mixed origin, the son of a Brâhmaṇa by an Ugra woman, Man. 10, 15. Caus., and i. 10, **1.** To cover, Râm. 1, 32, 11. **2.** To conceal, MBh. 3, 2370. **3.** To keep off, MBh. 2, 2431.—With अपा *apa-â*, To uncover, MBh. 1, 1341; to open, Bhag. 2, 32.—With पर्या *pari-â*, *paryâvṛita*, Covered, Mâlat. 90, 7.—With प्रा *pra-â*, To put on, MBh. 1, 2033. *prâvṛita*, Covered, enclosed, encompassed. m., f. *tâ*, and n. A wrapper, a cloak, a veil.—With व्या *vi-â*, To stop, MBh. 3, 363.—With समा *sam-â*, **1.** To cover, MBh. 3, 2310. **2.** To shut, MBh. 1, 8343. **3.** To stop, MBh. 3, 10329. *samâvṛita*, **1.** Surrounded, encompassed, Râm. 3, 54, 15. **2.** Enclosed. **3.** Concealed, Chr. 32, 32.—With उद् *ud*, Caus., or i. 10, *varaya*, To ask, Râm. 2, 11, 9.—With नि *ni*, To surround, Chr. 296, 3=Rigv. i. 112, 3. *nivṛita*, m., f. *tâ*, and n. A wrapper, a cloak, a veil. Caus. **1.** To surround, MBh. 1, 4961. **2.** To protect, Chr. 42, 15. **3.** To stop, to hinder, MBh. 1, 8172. **4.** To draw back from (abl.), Bhartṛ. 2, 64. **5.** To withhold, Hit. iii. d. 10. **6.** To interdict, Pañch. 28, 19; Daçak. in Chr. 181, 7. **7.** To exclude, Man. 9, 221. *nivârita*, **1.** Opposed, Pañch. 247, 20. **2.** Stopped, Lass. 18, 1. *a-nivârya*, adj. Irresistible, Chr. 45, 7. *durnivârya*, i.e. *dus-*, adj. Difficult to be kept off, MBh. 12, 3770. —With विनि *vi-ni*, To keep off, MBh. 1, 1756. Caus., or i. 10, To obstruct, Mâlat. 11, 16.—With निस् *nis*, *nirvṛita*, **1.** Free from cares, Hit. 50, 6. **2.** Happy, satisfied, Man. 1, 54. **3.** Enraptured, Vikr. 71, 12. n. A house. **Comp.** *A-nirvṛita + m*, adv. cheerlessly, Hit. ii. d. 143.—With परि *pari*, To surround, Vikr. d. 44; MBh. 1, 3. *a-parivṛita*, adj. Unenclosed, Man. 8, 238. Caus., and i. 10, **1.** To surround, Pañch. ii. d. 23; Chr. 42, 9. **2.** To cover, Chr. 4, 20.—With संपरि *sam-pari*, Caus. To surround, MBh. 3, 10234.—With प्र *pra*, **1.** To cover, Bhaṭṭ. 9, 25. **2.** To put

on, MBh. 3, 2977. **3.** To choose, MBh. 3, 17186. Caus. **1.** To guard, MBh. 3, 10474. **2.** To expose for choice, Chr. 8, 31. **3.** To prefer, MBh. 3, 10810.—With प्रति *prati*, Caus., or i. 10, **1.** To keep off, MBh. 4, 1896. **2.** To oppose, Râm. 3, 49, 22. *a-prativârita*, adj. Not prohibited, Man. 8, 360.—With वि *vi*, **1.** To open, Chr. 294, 4=Rigv. i. 92, 4 (ved. *âvar*, aor.); MBh. 1, 6275. **2.** To disclose, Râjat. 5, 185; to reveal, MBh. 2, 6925. **3.** To woo, MBh. 1, 4413. *vivṛita*, **1.** Opened, Hit. 76, 6. **2.** Naked, MBh. 1, 2924. **3.** Expanded. **4.** Displayed, Man. 7, 102. **5.** Exposed, discovered. **6.** Explained, expounded. **Comp.** *A-*, adj. without showing a weak side, MBh. 1, 5559.—With सम् *sam*, **1.** To cover, Vikr. 47, 12; MBh. 2, 2623; to hide, Vikr. 43, 5. **2.** To secure, Man. 7, 102. **3.** To restrain, Bhaṭṭ. 9, 27. *saṁvṛita*, **1.** Covered, Hit. ii. d. 139. **2.** Concealed, Ragh. 7, 27. **3.** Surrounded, MBh. 3, 571. **4.** Closed. **5.** Compressed. **6.** Secured, Pańch. 91, 2. **7.** Attended, Johns. Sel, 59, 178. **Comp.** *A-* (m. or n.), the name of a hell, Man. 4, 81. *Su-*, adj. decently dressed, Man. 2, 193 (v.r.). Caus. To keep off, MBh. 3, 14994.—With अभिसम् *abhi-sam*, To cover, Chr. 36, 23 (imperf. without augment).—Cf. O.H.G. wara; A.S. ware, heed; O.H.G. wâr, verus; Goth. varjan; A.S. wreon, To cover; warian, werian, arcere; O.H.G. wari, depulsio; werna, A.S. wearne, obstaculum; O.H.G. warnôn, A.S. warnian, wearnian, cavere, prohibere; Goth. viljan, A.S. willan, velle; Goth. valjan, O.H.G. weljan, eligere; Lat. perhaps aperio, operio; probably velum, velare; verus, valeo, valor; velle; ἐρύω, ἀρνέομαι, ὄρομαι, ὥρα, εὑρίσκω; ἀρά, ἀρείων, ἄριστος, ἦρα, βούλομαι, βουλή, βελτίων, βέλτιστος.

1. वृंह् *VṚIṀH*, बृंह् *BṚIṀH*, i. 1, Par. **1.** To grow, to increase. **2.** To roar, Çiç. 17, 31 (Âtm.). Ptcple. of the pf. pass. *vṛiṁhita*. **1.** Increased. **2.** Cherished, MBh. 2, 2589. **3.** Nourished. n. The roar of elephants, Kir. 7, 39. Caus. To augment, MBh. 3, 11334.—With the prep. उप *upa*, Caus. To augment, Dev. 8, 8. *upavṛiṁhita*, **1.** Collected from. **2.** Possessed of, endowed with, Daçak. in Chr. 182, 6.—With समुप *sam-upa*, To augment, MBh. 1, 260.—Cf. *vṛih*; βράχω, βράζω, βράγχος, βρόγχος, βρόχθος, probably also βράσσω, and βρυχάομαι; ῥόχθος, ὀρεχθέω, ῥαχία, ῥέγχω, ῥόγχος, and probably ῥύγχος, ῥυζέω.

† 2. वृंह् *VṚIṀH*, बृंह् *BṚIṀH*, i. 10, Par. To speak, to shine.

वृंहण *vṛiṁhaṇa*, i.e. 1. *vṛiṁh* + *ana*, I. adj. Nourishing. II. m. A kind of sweetmeat.

† वृक् *VṚIK*, i. 1, Âtm. To take.

वृक *vṛika*, perhaps akin to *vraçch*, I. m. **1.** A wolf, Pańch. 19, 13. **2.** A crow. **3.** A jackal. **4.** Turpentine. **5.** Compounded perfume. **6.** A tree, Sesbana grandiflora. **II.** *f. kâ*, A plant, Cissampelos hexandra.—**Comp.** *A-*, adj. secure, Chr. 288, 15=Rigv. i. 48, 15. *Çâlâ-*, m. 1. a jackal, Draup. 6, 8. 2. a monkey. 3. a cat. 4. a dog. 5. a deer.—Cf. Goth. vulfs; A.S. wulf; λύκος; Lat. lupus.

वृकोदर *vṛikodara*, i.e. *vṛika-udara*, m. A name of Bhîma, Johns. Sel. 12, 31.

वृक्कक *vṛikkaka*, m. The kidney, Yâjń. 3, 94.

† वृक्ष् *VṚIKSH*, i. 1, Âtm. **1.** To select. **2.** To cover. **3.** To keep off.

वृक्ष *vṛiksha*, probably akin to *vṛih*,

m. A tree, Man. 1, 47; Pañch. iii. d. 107. —**Comp.** *Asi-patra-*, m. a fabulous tree in hell, Ragh. 14, 48. *Kalpa-*, m. a tree yielding all wishes (cf. *kalpataru*), Megh. 63; Vikr. d. 157. *Kshîra-*, m. the glomerous fig-tree, Ficus glomerata, Çâk. 54, 23. *Chaitya-*, m. a fig-tree growing in a holy place, Man. 9, 264. *Dîpa-*, m. the stand of a lamp, Râm. 2, 5, 18 Gorr.; a lamp on a stand, a lantern, MBh. 12, 7402. *Nis-*, adj. deprived of trees, MBh. 5, 338.

वृक्षक *vṛiksha+ka*, m. **1.** A tree. **2.** A particular tree, Wrightea antidysenterica.—**Comp.** *A-*, adj. deprived of trees, Râm. 4, 44, 35.

वृक्षभिद् *vṛiksha-bhid*, f. An axe.

वृक्षमय *vṛiksha+maya*, adj., f. *yî*, Abounding in trees.

† वृच् *VṚICH*, ii. 7, v.r. of *vṛij*, ii. 7.

वृज् *VṚIJ*, ii. 7, *vṛiṇaj*, *vṛiñj*, Par.; i. 1, Par. and (also वृञ्ज् *VṚIÑJ*), ii. 2, Âtm. (the original signification seems to be 'To bend'). **1.** To exclude, Man. 3, 152. **2.** To purify, Man. 9, 20. Ptcple of the pf. pass. *vṛikta*, Spread, Lass. 98, 8=Rigv. v. 9, 2. Caus., and i. 10, **1.** To deprive, Kâm. Nitis. 9, 15 (=Hit. iv. d. 118, where *varjita* corr. for *ûrjita*). **2.** To abandon, Râjat. 5, 312. **3.** To abstain, Man. 2, 177; MBh. 13, 5659. **4.** To shun, Man. 9, 246; to avoid, Pañch. i. d. 112. **5.** To spare, MBh. 3, 10583. *varjita*, **1.** Relinquished, Râm. 3, 51, 12; remnant, Pañch. 138, 2. **2.** Deprived of, without, Râm. 3, 52, 41; except, Hit. iv. d. 124. **3.** Given. Ptcple. of the fut. pass. *varjya*, To be excepted, left out. n. A point in each lunar mansion during the passage of the moon, in which no business should be begun. Absol. *varjayitvâ*, Except, Râm. 1, 14, 40.—With the prep. अप *apa*, Caus. To fulfil (a promise), Râm. 1, 44, 40.—With आ *â*, Caus. **1.** To bend, to incline, Vikr. 87, 15; Megh. 47; Çâk. 11, 9. **2.** To win one's affection, Daçak. in Chr. 183, 19. **3.** To pour out, Ragh. 1, 62. **4.** To offer, Ragh. 8, 26.—With परि *pari*, Caus. To avoid, Man. 3, 6. *parivarjita*, **1.** Abandoned. **2.** Deprived, Pañch. i. d. 311; devoid of, Man. 5, 154.—With वि *vi*, Caus. To avoid, Man. 2, 184. *vivarjita*, **1.** Left. **2.** Deprived of, Pañch. i. d. 40 (*sevâ-*, Not practising service); devoid of, Hit. iii. d. 16; Pañch. ii. d. 61 (*mûlya-*, Unpayable).—Cf. the ved. use of this vb., the two next words, and Lat. vergere; A.S. wealcan, To roll; probably also wrenc, Deceit (cf. *vṛijana*); O.H.G. wurgjan, strangulare; ἔργνυμι, ἔργω, εἴργω.

वृजन *vṛij+ana*, I. adj. Crooked. II. m. Curled hair. III. n. **1.** ved. Creature, Chr. 287, 5=Rigv. i. 48, 5. **2.** The atmosphere. **3.** Sin.

वृजिन *vṛij + ina*, I. adj. **1.** Crooked. **2.** Wicked. II. m. Curled hair. III. n. **1.** Sin, Râm. 6, 103, 10; Ragh. 14, 57; wickedness. **2.** Distress. **3.** Red leather.

वृञ्ज् *VṚIÑJ*, see *vṛij*.

वृण् *VṚIṆ*, † i. 8, *vṛiṇu*, *varṇu*, Par. Âtm. To eat. i. 6, Par. To exhilarate.—With वि *vi*, Caus. To exhilarate, Utt. Râmach. 152, 9.

1. वृत् *VṚIT*, i. 1, Âtm., and in the fut., condit., and aor., also Par. (in epic poetry also in other forms, MBh. 1, 4308; 4832; 3, 14683). The original signification was 'To turn,' Âtm. 'To turn one's self.' **1.** To be occupied, to occupy one's self, to act, Man. 2, 5; Vikr. 63, 13; *vyâjena*,

 वृत्

To act fraudulently, Pańch. 147, 15. **2.** To employ, Râm. 2, 82, 18. **3.** To behave, Man. 9, 108; Pańch. i. d. 90. **4.** To stay, Râm. 1, 18, 4; Hit. iii. d. 47 (*apakartari*, near to the man who has injured him). **5.** To be fixed, MBh. 3, 16715. **6.** To depend upon (loc.), Chr. 12, 25. **7.** To exist, Pańch. i. d. 174; 366. **8.** To be, Râm. 2, 67, 9; Vikr. 9, 5. With *upakâre*, To give assistance, Râm. 3, 75, 14. With *manasi*, To be thought, Çâk. 25, 22; Vikr. 30, 5. With *atitya*, i.e. *ati-i+tya*, and *mûrdhni*, To surpass, Çâk. 6, 5; Hit. i. d. 19, M.M. **9.** To take place, Man. 2, 15; Pańch. 74, 19; to come to pass, ib. 101, 1. **10.** To subsist, Man. 3, 77. **11.** To live, Utt. Râmach. 66, 1; Râm. 1, 8, 10. Ptcple. of the pres. *vartamâna*. **1.** Being present, Pańch. 48, 8; being inclined to (with loc.), Mâlat. 3, 10. **2.** Dwelling in. n. The present tense. Ptcple. of the pf. pass. *vṛitta*. **1.** Turned, Çâk. d. 64. **2.** Round, Bhâg. P. 4, 25, 24. **3.** Past, Hit. iv. d. 1; gone, been. **4.** Finished. **5.** Dead, Man. 9, 195. **6.** Done, performed. **7.** Having acted, Nal, 8, 13. **8.** Firm. **9.** Unimpaired, Man. 1, 6. **10.** Famous. **11.** Read, studied. n. **1.** A circle. **2.** Event, occurrence, Indr. 5, 52. **3.** Procedure. **4.** Practice, profession, means of gaining subsistence. **5.** Conduct, behaviour, Daçak. in Chr. 183, 6; Man. 7, 135; observance of enjoined practice in private or social life, Vikr. d. 147 (*ujjhita-dhairya-vṛitta+m*, adv. Without regard to my dignity); law, Ragh. 5, 33. **6.** Verse, metre. m. A tortoise. Comp. *Ârya-*, I. n. the conduct of an Ârya, laudable practice, Man. 4, 175. II. adj. one who behaves in a laudable manner, Man. 9, 253. *Iti-*, n. event. *Kalyâṇa-*, adj., f. *tâ*, well-behaved, Râm. 3, 53, 54. *Kâma-*, adj. debauched, Man. 5, 154. *Kim-*, adj. timid, afraid, Pańch. 9, 15. *Guru-*, adj. one who treats respectfully his parents and spiritual teacher, Râm. 4, 17, 36. *Chhandov°*, i.e. *chhandas-*, n. metre, MBh. 1, 28. *Tejov°*, i.e. *tejas-*, n. power and behaviour, Man. 9, 303. *Dus-*, I. n. 1. a bad action, Châṇ. 82 in Berl. Monatsb. 1864, 412. 2. bad conduct, MBh. 1, 100. II. adj. sbst. 1. ill-behaved, a wicked person, Yâjń. 1, 335. 2. unhappy, Hit. ii. d. 165. *A-dus-*, adj. unblameable, Râjat. 5, 293. *Ati-dus-*, adj. exceedingly wicked, Hit. 18, 4, M.M. *Purâ-*, I. adj. 1. done in times of yore. 2. lived in times of yore, MBh. 14, 2842. 3. referring to times of yore, ib. 3, 12602. II. n. 1. history, ib. 12, 2885. 2. any old or legendary event, Hit. iii. d. 105. *Pûrva-*, I. n. 1. a previous occurrence, Çâk. 71, 3. 2. previous behaviour, Mârk. P. 20, 41. II. adj. relating to a previous occurrence, Hariv. 2976. *Mańgalâdeça-*, i.e. *mańgala-âdeça-*, m. a fortune-teller, Man. 9, 258. *Yathâ-vṛitta+m*, adv. relating a thing as it happened, circumstantially, truly, Chr. 9, 37; 11, 22; 58, 11. *Veda-*, n. the doctrine of the Vedas. *Sadv°*, i.e. *sant-* (vb. 1. *as*), I. adj. 1. well-behaved. 2. virtuous. 3. well-rounded. II. n. good or amiable disposition. *Sâdhu-*, I. m. a virtuous person, Hit. i. d. 201, M.M. II. n. virtue. *Su-*, adj. 1. virtuous, good, Pańch. ii. d. 74. 2. handsomely round, Pańch. iv. d. 78; i. d. 303. 3. well-conditioned, Pańch. ii. d. 74. *Sva-*, n. 1. one's own occupation, Daçak. in Chr. 183, 6. 2. occupation, Pańch. i. d. 79, Caus. **1.** To turn, MBh. 1, 809. **2.** With *antar*, To mix, Mâlat. 153, 2. **3.** To pass (as time), MBh. 1, 7976. **4.** To sustain one's self, Man. 4, 10; Kir. 2, 18. **5.** To live, Râm. 2, 51, 12. **6.** To make, Chr. 292, 9 = Rigv. i. 85, 9; with *dyûtam*, To play, MBh. 2, 2507; with *açrûṇi*, To shed tears, MBh. 1, 4468; with *âkhyânam*, To tell, Râm. 1, 5, 4. **7**, To act, Hit.

iii. d. 111. Comp. ptcple. pf. pass. *su-vartita*, adj. Well made, Lass. 2. ed. 61, 38. i. 10, † To speak, to shine.—With the prep. अति *ati*, **1.** To overcome, MBh. 3, 16679. **2.** To surpass, MBh. 3, 10169. **3.** To pass (as a place), Râm. 2, 50, 10. **4.** To trespass, Lass. 2. ed. 71, 63; to neglect, to violate, MBh. 2, 693. **5.** To injure, to slight, Man. 5, 161. **6.** To avoid, Chr. 62, 57. **7.** To pass away (as time), Râm. 2, 51, 20; Pañch. 174, 9. **8.** To be delayed, Man. 2, 38. *ativṛitta*, **1.** Surpassing, Mâlat. 16, 1. **2.** Hastening on, Râm. 3, 50, 6.—With व्यति *vi-ati*, To pass (as time), Sâv. 4, 9.—With अधि *adhi*, To assail, Çâk. d. 23.—With अनु *anu*, **1.** To follow, Man. 6, 93. **2.** To resemble, MBh. 3, 15940. **3.** To seek, Man. 8, 175. **4.** To espy, Çâk. 23, 14. **5.** To wait on, to court, Daçak. in Chr. 196, 7. **6.** To take one's directions from, Râm. 4, 29, 29. **7.** To assent, MBh. 1, 1799. **8.** To obey, MBh. 3, 14683. **9.** To undergo, Sâv. 5, 46. *anuvṛitta*, Shown, Utt. Râmach. 167, 10. n. Obeying, Hit. iv. d. 102 (*chhandas-*, n. Accommodation to one's will). Caus. **1.** To cause to turn, Bhag. 3, 16. **2.** To perform, MBh. 4, 105.—With समनु *sam-anu*, To follow, Râm. 2, 14, 8.—With अप *apa*, **1.** To turn away from, Ragh. 6, 58 (Calc.). **2.** To return, MBh. 1, 1784. **3.** To be overturned, Man. 8, 293. *apavṛitta*, Reversed, Kir. 12, 49. Caus. To cause to turn away, Mâlat. 24, 15.—With व्यप *vi-apa*, To leave, Mâlat. 11, 15.—With अभि *abhi*, **1.** To turn to, Mâlat. 10, 10; to turn, Sund. 3, 29. **2.** To stretch to (with acc.), Utt. Râmach. 43, 2. **3.** To be imminent, Utt. Râmach. 52, 17. **4.** To approach, Râm. 3, 52, 15. **5.** To assail, MBh. 1, 4114. **6.** To exist, to be, Chr. 16, 13. *abhivṛitta*, Going towards.—With समभि *sam-abhi*, **1.** To approach, MBh. 1, 7261. **2.** To assail, Râm. 2, 28, 8. **3.** To pass (as time), Râm. 1, 8, 10.—With आ *â*, **1.** To advance, Man. 4, 172. **2.** To come, Ragh. 1, 52 (Calc.). **3.** To return, Man. 7, 82. *âvṛitya*, Having done (?), Man. 3, 214 (v., and probably erroneous reading). *âvṛitta*, **1.** Perused repeatedly, Utt. Râmach. 156, 14. **2.** Averted, Kir. 11, 51. Caus. **1.** To invert, MBh. 1, 2930. **2.** To cause to approach (*açrûṇi*, i.e. to shed tears), MBh. 3, 336. **3.** To fetch, Mâlat. 155, 3. **4.** To win, MBh. 5, 117. **5.** Âtm. To come, Draup. 6, 18.—With अपा *apa-â*, *apâvṛitta*, **1.** Reversed, turned to the contrary, Râm. 1, 12, 59. **2.** Turned away from, desisting from, MBh. 3, 4052. n. The rolling on the ground, of a horse.—With उपा *upa-â*, **1.** To approach, MBh. 1, 2318. **2.** To go round, Râm. 1, 33, 17. **3.** To turn away from, MBh. 3, 4084. **4.** To return, Çâk. 8, 14. *upâvṛitta*, Returned, Çâk. 46, 6. Caus. **1.** To cause to approach, Daçak. in Chr. 201, 7. **2.** To win to confidence, Mâlat. 128, 1. **3.** To lead back, Râm. 2, 19, 13.—With पर्या *pari-â*, To return, MBh. 3, 10074. —With प्रत्या *prati-â*, To return, Megh. 40. *pratyâvṛitta*, Returned, come back, Utt. Râmach. 21, 8.—With व्या *vi-â*, **1.** To turn away from, Vikr. d. 9. **2.** To be divided, Sâv. 5, 108. **3.** To return, Râjat. 5, 85. **4.** To perish, MBh. 3, 11259. *vyâvṛitta*, **1.** Rolled backwards. **2.** Removed, Vikr. d. 154; uncovered. **3.** Excluded, Pañch. 5, 5; Bhâshâp. 72. **4.** Encompassed, surrounded. **5.** Fenced. Caus. **1.** To throw down, MBh. 3, 12447.

2. To destroy, Ragh. 15, 7 (Calc.). **3.** To contrive (?), Daçak. in Chr. 197, 7. —With समा *sam-â*, To advance, Chr. 40, 10. *samâvṛitta*, **1.** Assembled, MBh. 3, 16282. **2.** Completed, MBh. 1, 3526. **3.** Returned, Man. 3, 4. m. A pupil who has completed his studies, Man. 8, 27.—With उद् *ud*, To surge, Ragh. 7, 56, Calc. (Stenzl. v. r.). *udvṛitta*, **1.** Raised, elevated. **2.** Exalted, prosperous. **3.** Unrestrained, ill-behaved, MBh. 1, 1718. **4.** Vomited. **5.** Left. Caus. To destroy, MBh. 3, 13680.—With उप *upa*, **1.** To approach, MBh. 1, 3850. **2.** To return, MBh. 1, 7821. *upavṛitta*, Recovered (?), Chr. 30, 2.—With नि *ni*, **1.** To return, Vikr. d. 3; Bhag. 15, 4; Hit. 71, 22 (*doshân*, i.e. *doshât*, *nivṛitya*, Having improved); to turn, Vikr. 66, 2. **2.** To recoil, Bhag. 2, 59. **3.** To abstain, Man. 5, 49. **4.** To refuse, MBh. 2, 1720. **5.** To escape (abl.), Bhag. 1, 39. **6.** To run away, Chr. 5, 23. **7.** To cease from (abl.), Râm. 2, 78, 24. **8.** To cease, Man. 10, 77. **9.** To set (as the sun), Sâv. 5, 73. **10.** To be withheld, Man. 11, 185. **11.** To be forbidden, Man. 5, 89. **12.** Not to take place, Man. 11, 151. **13.** To be reversed, Man. 8, 117. **14.** To be occupied with, MBh. 3, 2347. *nivṛitta*, **1.** Returned, returning, Râm. 3, 50, 28. **2.** Gone. **3.** Ceased, Daçak. in Chr. 183, 6. **4.** Finished, Râm. 2, 52, 28; vanished, 6, 22, 17. **5.** Completed. **6.** Whole, Chr. 36, 19. **7.** Desisting from any improper conduct. **8.** Abstained from, Utt. Râmach. 93, 2 (*-mâṅsa*, adj. One who abstains from eating meat). **9.** Abstaining, Hit. i. d. 63, M.M.; abstaining from worldly acts. **10.** Abstracted from this world, quiet, Man. 12, 88. **11.** Prohibited, MBh. 2, 1770. **Comp.** *Dus-*, adj. whence it is difficult to return, Râm. 4, 22, 36. Ptcple. of the fut. pass. I. *nivartanîya*. **1.** To be led back, Mâlav. 71, 1 (read *niv°*). **2.** To be stopped. **Comp.** *A-*, adj. not to be untied, firm, MBh. 1, 7330. **II.** *nivartitavya*, To be led back, MBh. 18, 55. Caus. **1.** To cause to return, Râm. 1, 1, 37. **2.** To cause to turn away from, Çâk. 19, 1. **3.** To persuade to desist from, Chr. 26, 71. **4.** To lead back, Râm. 2, 73, 22. **5.** To repel, Râm. 1, 58, 24; to avert, Çâk. d. 53. **6.** To unravel, Man. 9, 233. **7.** To deliver from, MBh. 2, 45. **8.** To restrain, Man. 6, 59. **9.** To accomplish, to perform, Râm. 1, 42, 25. *nivartayitavya*, To be restrained, to be hindered, Râm. 2, 21, 22 Gorr. *durnivartya*, i.e. *dus-*, adj. **1.** Difficult to be caused to turn, MBh. 6, 145. **2.** Whence it is difficult to return, ib. 13, 3504.—With अभिनि *abhi-ni*, To return, Mâlat. 13, 2.—With प्रतिनि *prati-ni*, **1.** To turn round, Pañch. 163, 3. **2.** To betake one's self to one's heels, Utt. Râmach. 122, 1. **3.** To return, Çâk. d. 28; Vikr. 5, 5. **4.** To turn away from, Hit. i. d. 62, M.M.—With विनि *vi-ni*, **1.** To return, MBh. 3, 8451. **2.** To turn away from, Bhag. 2, 59. **3.** To cease, Man. 5, 60; Pañch. i. d. 392. *vinivṛitta*, **1.** Stopped. **2.** Ended. **3.** Foiled. **4.** Refrained. **5.** Desisting. Caus. **1.** To lead back, Râm. 2, 82, 17. **2.** To recall, Mâlat. 169, 12. **3.** To annul, Man. 8, 165. *vinivartita*, Caused to turn away (as looks, caused to be cast down), Mâlav. d. 11.—With संनि *sam-ni*, To turn back, MBh. 3, 12231; to return, Râm. 2, 45, 2. Caus. To preclude, Man. 4, 16.—With निस् *nis*, **1.** To be accomplished, Man. 7, 61. **2.** Not to take place, Bhaṭṭ. 16, 6. *nirvṛitta*, Accomplished, Man. 9, 62; 5, 67 (shorn).

Caus. **1.** To finish, to accomplish, Man. 3, 122; Vikr. 87, 15; Bhâg. P. 6, 7, 36. **2.** To produce, Man. 1, 31.—With **विनिस्** *vi-nis, vinirvṛitta,* **1.** Produced. **2.** Occurring. **3.** Completed.—With **परा** *parâ,* **1.** To turn round, Çâk. 54, 7; to turn back, Hit. 89, 12, M.M. **2.** To return, Man. 3, 217. *parâvṛitta,* **1.** One who has turned his back, Man. 7, 93. **2.** Turned aside, Daçak. in Chr. 198, 24. **Comp.** *A-*, adj. not returned, Vikr. 55, 10.—With **परि** *pari,* **1.** To turn round, Vikr. 12, 18. **2.** To change, Vikr. d. 132 (*anyathâ,* into another object); to interchange, Hit. i. d. 172, M.M. **3.** To be whirled, Man. 4, 165. **4.** To hasten to and fro, MBh. 3, 12230. **5.** To roam about, Râm. 1, 9, 42. **6.** To become, Çâk. d. 172. **7.** To be, Râm. 2, 96, 17. *parivṛitta,* **1.** Returned, Mâlat. 164, 10. **2.** Ended, Lass. 2. ed. 55, 73. n. An embrace, Mâlat. 76, 10. Caus. **1.** To turn, Lass. 2. ed. 75, 41. **2.** To change, Man. 8, 154.—With **विपरि** *vi-pari,* **1.** To slide backwards and forwards, Man. 6, 22. **2.** To turn round, to revolve, Bhag. 9, 10. **3.** To roll on the ground, Râm. 2, 72, 26.—With **संपरि** *sam-pari,* To exist, to be, Râm. 2, 1, 24. Caus. To cause to turn, Râm. 2, 45, 33.—With **प्र** *pra,* **1.** To begin, Çâk. 4, 4; Vikr. d. 90. **2.** To proceed, MBh. 3, 2298; Megh. 106; Pañch. i. d. 6 (from, with abl.); i. d. 132 (*vâkye,* To follow, to obey the words). **3.** To go on well, Pañch. i. d. 93. **4.** To engage, Hit. 87, 1, M.M. **5.** To hold good, Râm. 2, 58, 20. **6.** To prosper, Man. 3, 61. **7.** To subsist, Man. 4, 3. **8.** To turn (*adharottaram,* Topsy-turvy), Man. 7, 21. **9.** To become, Pañch. 5, 13; Râm. 1, 35, 8. **10.** To behave, MBh. 3, 2414. **11.** To act, Çâk. d. 194. **12.** To take place, Pañch. 114, 18; MBh. 3, 1871. *pravṛitta,* **1.** Begun, Daçak. in Chr. 190, 9; beginning, Mâlat. 88, 11. **2.** Engaged in, Hit. 68, 13; occupied by. **3.** Doing, acting, Man. 3, 12. **4.** Active, Man. 12, 88. **5.** Coming, Mâlat. 91, 11. **6.** Fixed, settled. **7.** Undisputed. **Comp.** *A-*, adj. not having taken place, never done, Chr. 61, 48. Caus. **1.** To push forward, to direct, Utt. Râmach. 48, 5. **2.** To throw, Bhaṭṭ. 15, 90. **3.** To produce, Râjat. 5, 122; Râm. 2, 21, 35. **4.** To create, MBh. 3, 13932. **5.** To further, Râjat. 5, 175. **6.** To behave, Chr. 23, 30. *pravartita,* **1.** Caused to turn, Bhag. 3, 16. **2.** Instigated. **3.** Revolving, going round. **4.** Made, Mâlat. 13, 2. **5.** Made pure, Man. 11, 196. **6.** Informed.—With **अभिप्र** *abhi-pra,* To empty one's self into (as a river), Râm. 2, 54, 2. *abhipravṛitta,* **1.** Active, Bhag. 4, 20. **2.** Occurring.—With **संप्र** *sam-pra,* **1.** To begin, Çâk. d. 75. **2.** To assail, MBh. 3, 68. **3.** To be occupied, MBh. 3, 8737. **4.** To take place, MBh. 3, 13537. *saṁpravṛitta,* Being at hand, Bhag. 14, 22.—With **अभिसंप्र** *abhi-sam-pra,* Caus. To confound, Lass. 2. ed. 80, 82.—With **प्रति** *prati,* To accrue, Man. 1, 81 (v. r.).—With **वि** *vi,* **1.** To roll, to welter, Arj. 3, 19. **2.** To revolve, to return, Utt. Râmach. 143, 3. **3.** To assail, MBh. 3, 8438. **4.** To be, Mâlat. 24, 13. *vivṛitta,* **1.** Turned off, Çâk. d. 59. **2.** Whirling, Chr. 34, 9. Caus. To cause to alternate (i.e. to be born and to die), MBh. 1, 809. *vivartita,* Turned round, Çâk. d. 23.—With **सम्** *sam,* **1.** To be produced, Pañch. 38, 19. **2.** To be recalled, Utt. Râmach. 13, 1. **3.** To fall to one's lot, Vikr. 57, 2. **4.** To become, Nal. 17, 42; Pañch. 125, 24; Vikr. 65, 1 (*kritâhârakaḥ saṁvṛittaḥ,*

He has finished his meal). **5.** To exist, to be, MBh. 3, 14839. *samvṛitta*, **1.** Past, gone. **2.** Become, Pańch. 77, 12. **3.** Fallen to one's lot, ib. 41, 25. **4.** Taken place, 43, 3. **5.** Being. **6.** Possessed of. **7.** Pańch. i. d. 6, read *sambhṛitebhyaḥ* with Râm. 6, 62, 29. m. Varuṇa. Caus. To accomplish, Râm. 1, 15, 7.—Cf. Lat. vertere, versus; Goth. vairthan; A.S. weordhan; Goth. ana-vairths; A.S. ward, weard, wyrd; Goth. vaurstv.

2. **वृत्** *VṚIT*, see *vâvṛit*.

वृति *vṛi+ti*, f. **1.** Surrounding. **2.** An enclosure, a hedge, Man. 8, 239; Pańch. iii. d. 129; 248, 2. **3.** Hiding. **4.** Choosing. **5.** Soliciting.

वृतिंकर *vṛitimkara*, i.e. *vṛiti+m-kṛi+a*, I. adj. Surrounding. II. m. A plant, Flacoustia sapida Roxb.

वृत्ततस् *vṛitta+tas* (vb. *vṛit*), adv. Relating to observance or duty.

वृत्तवन्त् *vṛitta+vant*, adj. Well-conducted, discharging the duties of caste or calling.

वृत्तस्थ *vṛitta-stha*, adj. Discharging the duties of caste or calling.

वृत्तान्त *vṛittânta*, i.e. *vṛitta-anta*, m. (n., Pańch. 30, 22). **1.** Occurrence, Pańch. 38, 23; 130, 10; 130, 4 (*ko yam vṛittântaḥ*, What has come to pass here?). **2.** A tale or story, Hit. 65, 9. **3.** An ancient story, Man. 3, 14. **4.** Report, rumour. **5.** Tidings. **6.** Topics, subject. **7.** Leisure. **8.** Opportunity, Vikr. 37, 10. **9.** Sort, manner. **10.** Whole. **11.** Solitary.—**Comp.** *Sadvṛ°*, i.e. *sant-* (vb. 1. *as*), adj. having (heard) beautiful tales, Hit. 78, 3.

वृत्ति *vṛit+ti*, f. **1.** The circumference of a circle. **2.** Staying, being, abiding. **3.** State, Pańch. iii. d. 18 (*vaitasîm vṛittim â char*, To behave like a reed). **4.** Livelihood, Man. 2, 141; maintenance, 9, 74. **5.** An agent of activity, Bhâg. P. 5, 11, 9; activity, Vedântas. in Chr. 215, 13. **6.** Means of subsistence, Pańch. 6, 5; Man. 1, 113; wages, hire, Pańch. 229, 6. **7.** Behaviour, Man. 2, 206; Hit. iv. d. 100 (cf. Böhtl. Ind. Spr. 610). **8.** Respectful treatment, MBh. 12, 3996, in Chr. p. 94. **9.** Explanation, gloss. **10.** Style. **11.** Style of dramatic composition.—**Comp.** *A-*, f. want of means for subsistence, Man. 4, 223. *Anyathâ-*, adj. changed, agitated, Megh. 3. *A-vyâpya-*, f. (in logic) limited in space, as the special qualities of soul and æther, sc. knowledge, etc., and sound, Bhâshâp. 26. *Uńchha-*, m. a gleaner, Man. 8, 260. *Evam-*, adj. so conditioned, Böhtl. Ind. Spr. 212=Pańch. i. d. 93. *Garva-*, f. state of pride, female arrogance, Vikr. d. 53 (*vrata-apadeça-ujjhita-garva-vṛitti*, adj. having abandoned her pride under the pretext of a vow). *Chitta-*, f. 1. feeling, sentiments, Çâk. 4, 11; Ṛit. 6, 26. 2. thinking, thought, Vedântas. in Chr. 215, 9. *Jyeshṭha-*, adj. acting as an elder brother ought to act, Man. 9, 110. *A-jyeshṭha-*, adj. not acting as an elder brother ought, ib. *Tad-vṛitti*, adj. abiding in that, i.e. as *çabdatva* in *çabda*, Bhâshâp. 60, cf. 22. *Tamas-*, f. darkness, Vikr. d. 20. *Dus-*, f. 1. a bad action, Böhtl. Ind. Spr. 799. 2. distress, MBh. 13, 2389. *Dyûta-*, m. the keeper of a gaming house, Man. 3, 160. *Dhairya-*, adj. constant, Hit. ii. d. 66. *Patańga-*, adj. acting like a grasshopper (flying into a flame), Pańch. iii. d. 131. *Para-adhina-*, adj. dependent on another, Megh. 8. *Paroksha-*, I. f. unseen, unwitnessed behaviour, Böhtl. Ind. Spr. 610. II. adj. one whose behaviour is not witnessed by anybody, ib. *Pratikûla-*, adj. opposing, Bhâg. P. 3, 16, 6. *Bhâgya-*, f. state of fortune, fortune, Râjat. 5, 261.

Vaka-, adj. living like cranes, a hypocritical devotee, Man. 4, 30. *Vâgurâ-*, m. one who subsists by catching wild animals, Man. 10, 32. *Vaiçya-*, f. agriculture or trade. *Çîla-*, f. virtue, Pańch. ii. d. 154. *Çvavṛitti*, i.e. *çvan-*, f. 1. life of a dog, Pańch. i. d. 300 (cf. Böhtl. Ind. Spr. 3292). 2. servitude, service. *Sama-*, adj. equable, moderate. *Sâdhu-*, I. f. the institutes or moral and ritual observances of the Hindus. II. adj. virtuous, Bhartṛ. 2, 83. *Sva-*, adj. subsisting by one's own exertion, Chaṇ. 23 in Berl. Monatsb, 1864, 408.

वृत्तिता *vṛitti+tâ*, f., and **वृत्तित्व** *vṛitti+tva*, n. **1.** State of residing or being contained in, as the *hetu* in the *paksha*, Bhâshâp. 67 (*tva*). **2.** Profession, subsistence. — Comp. *An-â-yatta-vṛittitâ* (vb. *yat*), f. independence, Hit. ii. d. 21.

वृत्तिमन्त् *vṛitti+mant*, adj. Thinking, Lass. 2. ed. 88, 23.

वृत्र *vṛitra*, m. **1.** The name of a demon slain by Indra, Chr. 292, 9 = Rigv. i. 85, 9; Chr. 18, 41. **2.** An enemy. **3.** Darkness. **4.** A cloud. **5.** A mountain. **6.** Sound. **7.** A wheel.

वृत्रहन् *vṛitra-han*, m. Indra.

वृथा *vṛithâ*, i.e. *vara+thâ*, adv. **1.** Without pain (to one's own pleasure), Chr. 294, 6=Rigv. i. 88, 6. **2.** Without necessity, Man. 11, 144 (*vṛithâ-âlambha*, m. Cutting or plucking unnecessarily). **3.** In vain, Man. 4, 63; vain, Pańch. i. d. 62. **4.** Useless, fruitless, Pańch. iii. d. 31. **5.** Foolishly, Vikr. 55, 20, **6.** Wrongly, incorrectly, Çṛiṅgârat. 21. **7.** Without being sacrificed, Man. 5, 34; 4, 213.—Cf. ῥεῖα, βρᾶ, ῥᾷ, ῥᾴστος, ῥᾴδιος, etc.

वृथासंकरजात *vṛithâ-saṁkara-jâta* (vb. *jan*), adj. Born in vain (i.e. one who discharges not his duties), or by the mixture of different castes, Man. 5, 89.

वृधसान *vṛidhasâna* (vb. *vṛidh*), m. A man.

वृद्ध *vṛiddha*, I. ptcple. of the pf. pass. of *vṛidh*. **1.** Old, ancient, aged, Vikr. d. 43. Comparat. *jyâyaṁs*, and *varshîyaṁs*; superl. *jyeshṭha*, and *varshishṭha*, see s. v. **2.** Wise, learned. II. m. **1.** An old man. **2.** A sage, a respectable man, Daçak. in Chr. 201, 7. III. n. Benzoin.—Comp. *Kula-*, m. the senior of a tribe, Bhâg. P. 4, 9, 39. *Vayas-*, adj. very old, Chr. 13, 7. *Vidyâ-vayas-*, adj. high in science and age, Hit. 41, 3, M.M. *Sa-bâla-*, adj. with children and old men.—Cf. *vṛidh*.

वृद्धत्व *vṛiddha+tva*, m. Old age, Pańch. 226, 2.

वृद्धि *vṛiddhi*, i.e. *vṛidh+ti*, f. **1.** Increase, Pańch. 187, 7; augmentation, Böhtl. Ind.. Spr. 438. **2.** Prosperity, Bhartṛ. 2, 82; Pańch. i. d. 382. **3.** Wealth. **4.** Interest, Man. 8, 143; Pańch. 88, 14 (*dvi-guṇa-*, Consisting in doubling the lent amount); usury. **5.** Profit, gain, Man. 8, 401. **6.** Extension of power or revenue, Pańch. i. d. 264. **7.** A heap, a quantity, a multitude. **8.** Rise, ascending. **9.** The increase of the digits of the sun or moon. **10.** The eleventh of the astronomical *Yogas*, or the principal star of the eleventh lunar mansion. **11.** Cutting off. **12.** (In law), Forfeiture.—Comp. *Kâla-*, f. periodical, monthly interest, Man. 8, 153. *Kusîda-*, f. interest on money, Man. 8, 151. *Chakra-*, f. 1. interest agreed on the risk of safe carriage, Man. 8, 156. 2. interest upon interest, Man. 8, 153.

वृद्धिमन्त् *vṛiddhi+mant*, adj., f. *matî*, **1.** Augmented, increased, increasing, Pańch. ii. d. 38; Bhartṛ. 2, 50. **2.** Wealthy. **3.** Prosperous.

वृध् *VṚIDH* (i.e. *vi-ṛidh*), i. 1, Âtm.; in the aor., fut., and condit., also Par. (in epic poetry also in the remaining forms, MBh. 1, 7864), **1.** To grow, to increase, MBh. 1, 4865; Pańch. i. d. 408; iv. d. 66 (but cf. Böhtl. Ind. Spr. 781). **2.** To prosper, Chr. 298, 24=Rigv. i. 112, 24 (*vṛidhe*, ved. infin.); MBh. 3, 12268; with *dishṭyâ*, properly, to prosper by fortune: it is used as a mode of giving joy; *dishṭyâ vardhase*, I give you joy, Vikr. 8, 2; with the instr. of the object of gratulation, Vikr. 11, 11, I give you joy on account of. **3.** To last, Râjat. 5, 461. **4.** To augment, MBh. 1, 5540. Ptcple. of the pres. *vardhamâna*, m. **1.** A shallow earthen platter, used also as top to water-jars, a lid. **2.** A sort of riddle. **3.** A mystical figure. **4.** Vishṇu. **5.** The name of a district and city, Burdwan, Pańch. 134, 2 (f. *nâ*, Lass. 28, 9). **6.** The castor-oil tree. Ptcple. of the pf. pass. *vṛiddha* (see also s.v.). **1.** Grown up, Vikr. d. 148. **2.** Full-grown. **3.** Heaped. **4.** Large. Comp. *Tapov°*, i.e. *tapas-*, adj. abounding in austerities, pious, Chr. 48, 2. Caus. *vardhaya*, **1.** To augment, Man. 6, 23; Hit. ii. d. 88 (cf. Böhtl. Ind. Spr. 3228). **2.** To make powerful, Hit. iii. d. 3. **3.** To exalt, Man. 9, 109. *vardhita*, Filled, full, Man. 3, 224. i. 10, † To speak, to shine.—With the prep. अभि *abhi*, **1.** To increase, Man. 2, 94. **2.** To abound, Man. 3, 259.—With परि *pari*, **1.** To grow up, Pańch. i. d. 228. **2.** To increase, Râjat. 5, 194. Caus. To rear, Çâk. 100, 15.—With प्र *pra*, To increase, Man. 4, 42. *pravṛiddha*, **1.** Grown up, Râjat. 5, 8; full-grown. **2.** Expanded. **3.** Large, Râm. 3, 53, 15. **4.** Swollen. **5.** Deep. **6.** Violent, Ṛit. 1, 15. Comp. *Su-*, I. adj. full-grown. II. m. a proper name.—With अतिप्र *ati-pra*, *atipravṛiddha* (rather *pravṛiddha* with *ati*), One who behaves too arrogantly, Man. 9, 320.—With अभिप्र *abhi-pra*, Caus. To cause to prosper, MBh. 1, 4350.—With वि *vi*, **1.** To increase too much, Pańch. i. d. 201. **2.** To increase, MBh. 1, 2992; to grow, Pańch. i. d. 47. **3.** To prosper, MBh. 3, 16881. *vivṛiddha*, Very large, Pańch. i. d. 6.—With संवि *sam-vi*, To increase, MBh. 1, 4977.—With सम् *sam*, To grow up, Sâv. 2, 10. *saṁvṛiddha*, Increased, Râjat. 5, 382. Caus. **1.** To cause to grow, to plant, Pańch. i. d. 275. **2.** To augment, Vikr. d. 158; MBh. 2, 1601. **3.** To cherish, Râm. 1, 39, 18; to bring up, Pańch. 182, 13. **4.** To nourish, Hit. 58, 10, M. M. *saṁvardhita*, Cherished, brought up, Daçak. in Chr. 189, 4.—Cf. Goth. valdan; A.S. waldan, and at least as akin, Goth. vaurts, O.H.G. uurza; βραδινός, ῥαδινός, ῥίζα, βλαστός, βλασταίνω, βλωθρός (βλωθ =ved. *vrâdh* in *vrâdhant*); A.S. weald; ἄλσος.

वृधु *vṛidhu*, m. A proper name, Man. 10, 107.

वृन्त *vṛinta*, n. **1.** The nipple. **2.** The foot, stalk of a leaf or fruit, Mâlat. 16, 20. **3.** The stand of a water-jar.—**Comp.** *Tâla-*, n. a fan (properly a leaf of the palm-tree), Râm. 5, 20, 14. *Dirgha-*, m. a tree, Calosanthes indica Bl., Suçr. 2, 13, 21. *Stana-*, m. a nipple.

वृन्तिका *vṛintikâ*, i.e. *vṛinta*+*ka*, f. A small stalk, MBh. 1, 1443.

वृन्द *vṛinda*, I. adj. Many, all. **II.** n. **1.** A heap, Chr. 25, 62. **2.** A multitude, Pańch. 222, 23; Bhartṛ. 3, 47. **III.** f. *dâ*, Holy basil, Ocymum sanctum. —**Comp.** *Eka-*, m. a disease of the throat, Suçr. 1, 306, 15.

वृन्दार *vṛindâra*, i.e. *vṛinda* + *âra* (cf. the next), adj. Comparat. *vṛindiyaṁs*; superl. *vṛindishṭha*. **1.** Eminent. **2.** Beautiful, Lass. 2. ed. 88, 20.

वृन्दारक *vṛindâra* + *ka*, I. adj. **1.** Much, great. **2.** Excellent, chief, venerable, Bhaṭṭ. 2, 45. **3.** Handsome. II. m. **1.** The head of a crowd or herd. **2.** A deity.

ऽवृन्दिन् *-vṛindin*, in *açva-*, i.e. *-vṛinda* + *in*, adj. Consisting in a multitude of horses, MBh. 5, 5703.

वृन्दिष्ठ *vṛindishṭha*, **वृन्दीयंस्** *vṛindîyaṁs*, see *vṛindâra*.

† **वृश्** *VṚIÇ*, i. 4, Par. To choose, to select (cf. *vṛi*).

वृश्चिक *vṛiçchika* (vb. *vraçch*), m. **1.** A scorpion, Bhâg. P. 3, 30, 27. **2.** The sign Scorpio. **3.** A caterpillar. **4.** A crab. **5.** A centipede. **6.** A sort of beetle.—**Comp.** *Patra-*, m. a certain poisonous animal, Suçr. 2, 287, 19.

वृष् *VṚISH* (probably *vi-ṛish*, q. cf.), i. 1, Par. (in epic poetry also Âtm., MBh. 1, 5464), **1.** To rain, Râm. 1, 9, 56. **2.** To shed, MBh. 1, 1419. **3.** To moisten, Dev. 3, 2. **4.** † To hurt. **5.** † To weary. **6.** † To give. **7.** † To engender. **8.** † To have supreme power. Ptcple. of the pres. *varshant*, Rain, Man. 4, 38. Comp. ptcple. pf. pass. *a-vṛishṭa*, adj. Not having rained, Pañch. 51, 16. Caus. To induce to rain, MBh. 3, 9991. i. 10, Âtm. † **1.** To be possessed of generative power. **2.** To be powerful.—With the prep. **अभि** *abhi*, **1.** To shower on, Râm. 2, 67, 8; Vikr. 54, 6. **2.** To rain, MBh. 1, 4062; figuratively, Man. 9, 304. *abhivṛishṭa*, Rained on, extinguished by rain, Vikr. d. 125.—With **निस्** *nis*, *nirvṛishṭa*, Having done raining, Ragh. 4, 15 (Calc.).—With **प्र** *pra*, **1.** To begin to rain, Pañch. 169, 7. **2.** To rain, Naish. 22, 41. *pravṛishṭa*, One who has caused to rain, Utt. Râmach. 158, 6.—With **अभिप्र** *abhi-pra*, To rain fast, Man. 9, 304.— With **प्रति** *prati*, To assail, Chr. 34, 15.—With **वि** *vi*, To deluge with rain.—Cf. ἀπο-έρσει, etc.; ἕρση; akin is βρέχω.

वृष *vṛish* + *a*, I. m. **1.** A bull, Hit. 58, 16. **2.** The sign Taurus. **3.** A rat (as in *vṛisha-daṁçaka*, m. A cat, Sâh. D. 303, 6). **4.** As latter part of comp. nouns, Excellent, pre-eminent. II. f. *shî*, The seat of the religious student, made of Kuça grass (cf. Râm. 3, 49, 23), MBh. 13, 462. III. n. A peacock's tail.—**Comp.** *Kshmâ-*, m. a lord of the earth, Râjat. 5, 126. *Go-*, m. 1. the bull kept for impregnating cows, Man. 9, 150. 2. a bull, Pañch. i. d. 1. *Nis-*, adj. deprived of bulls, Hariv. 4108.

वृषक *vṛisha* + *ka*, m. A proper name.

वृषखादि *vṛishakhâdi*, i.e. *vṛishan-khâdi*, adj. Adorned or endowed with rain, Chr. 290, 10 = Rigv. i. 64, 10.

वृषण *vṛishaṇa*, i.e. *vṛish* + *ana*, m. The testicles or scrotum, Man. 8, 283; Pañch. 10, 12.—**Comp.** *Tîkshṇa-*, m. a proper name, Pañch. 135, 20.—Cf. as akin, ὄρχις.

वृषध्वज *vṛisha-dhvaja*, I. adj. Having as emblem a bull. II. m. Çiva, Johns. Sel. 89, 25; Kir. 13, 28.

वृषन् *vṛish* + *an*, m. I. adj. Raining, Chr. 290, 1 = Rigv. i. 64, 1. II. m. **1.** The dropping beverage, called Soma, Chr. 291, 7 = Rigv. i. 85, 7. **2.** A bull. **3.** A horse. **4.** A name of Indra, Ragh. 10, 53. **5.** Karṇa.

वृषभ *vṛisha-bha* (vb. *bhû*), I. m. **1.** A bull, Hit. i. d. 135, M.M. (*dushṭa-*, A malicious bull). **2.** The orifice of the ear. **3.** An elephant's ear. **4.** As latter part of comp. words, Pre-eminent, excellent. II. f. *bhî*, A widow.—Comp. *Go-*, m. a bull, MBh. 1, 3935. *Nara-vara-*, m. a most pre-eminent man, Pańch. i. d. 204.

वृषय *vṛishaya*, m. Refuge, shelter.

वृषल *vṛishala* (from *vṛish*), I. m. **1.** A horse. **2.** A Çûdra, Utt. Râmach. 40, 1, cf. 4. **3.** A man of the three first classes who, by neglecting his religious duties, has lost his caste. **4.** A sinner, Lass. Pentap. p. 70, v. 73. **5.** Garlic. II. f. *lî*. **1.** A Çûdra woman, Man. 3, 19; Pańch. iii. d. 218 (but cf. Kûçîkh. 40, 93). **2.** A woman during menstruation. **3.** A barren woman.

वृषलक *vṛishala+ka*, m. A poor Çûdra, Utt. Râmach. 42, 4.

वृषस्य *VṚISHASYA*, a denomin. derived from *vṛisha* with *sya*, Par. To be warm, to long for sexual intercourse, Ragh. 12, 34.

वृषाकपि *vṛishâkapi* (probably *vṛishan-kapi*), I. m. **1.** Vishṇu. **2.** Çiva. **3.** Agni. II. f. *pâyî*. **1.** Lakshmî. **2.** Gaurî. **3.** Swâhâ, the wife of Agni. **4.** Çachi, the wife of Indra.

वृष्टि *vṛishṭi*, i.e. *vṛish+ti*, f. Rain, Vikr. d. 154.—Comp. *A-*, f. drought, Pańch. 50, 18. *Prâjya-*, adj. sending plenty of rain, Çâk. d. 193. *Çilâ-*, f. hail.

वृष्णि *vṛishṇi*, i.e. *vṛish+ni*, I. adj. **1.** Passionate, angry. **2.** Heretical. II. m. **1.** A ram. **2.** Indra. **3.** Agni. **4.** Vishṇu. **5.** One of the descendants of Yadu, Bhag. 10, 37. **6.** The name of a class of Kshatriyas and Vaiçyas, Pańch. iii. d. 268. **7.** Air, wind. **8.** A ray of light.—Cf. ἀρν in ἀρνός, ἀρνειός, ῥήν, ἔρσαι, ἔριφος.

1. **वृह्** *VṚIH*, **बृह्** *BṚIH*, i. 6, Par. To make any effort, to raise.—With the prep. **उद्** *ud*, **1.** To raise, Bhaṭṭ. 17, 9. **2.** To pull out, MBh. 1, 7307. **3.** To draw forth, Man. 1, 14. *pari-vṛiḍha*, see separately.

† 2. **वृह्** *VṚIH*, i. 1, Par. **1.** To increase; cf. *vṛidh*. **2.** To roar; cf. *vṛimh*.

वृहतिका *vṛihatikâ*, i.e. *vṛihant+î+ka*, f. **1.** An upper garment, a mantle, a wrapper, Kir. 5, 45. **2.** A small sort of egg plant.

वृहन्त् *vṛihant*, see *bṛihant*.

वृहस्पति *vṛihaspati*, see *bṛihaspati*.

वॄ *VṚÎ*, † **बॄ** *BṚÎ*, ii. 9, Par. Âtm., see *vṛi*.

वे *VE*, i. 1, Par. Âtm. To weave, MBh, 1, 806.—With the prep. **आ** *â*, To warp, Bhâg. P. 9, 9, 7.—With **प्र** *pra*, To work in the woof, Bhâg. P. 9, 9, 7 ('Who is the warp and the weft of the universe'). Ptcple. of the pf. pass. *prota*, i.e. *pra-uta*. **1.** Sewn or stitched. **2.** Joined. **3.** Tied, strung. **4.** Set, inlaid. **5.** Pierced, Ragh. 9, 75. **6.** Put on (a spit), MBh. 1, 4316; impaled. n. Cloth. —Cf. ἤτριον, ἀθόνη; O.H.G. wât; A.S. waed, vestimentum; O.H.G. weban; A.S. wefan (=the regular Sskr. Caus., which would have been *vâpaya* or *văpaya*), waefels, weft; probably also ὀπέας, ἠπητής; akin at least is also ὑφή, ὑφαίνω; Lat. viere, vimen.

† **वेक्ष्** *VEKSH*, **व्लेक्ष्** *VLEKSH*, i. 10, Par. To see (cf. *ava-îksh*).

वेग *vega*, i.e. *vij+a*, m. **1.** Speed, Vikr. 6, 6; Pańch. ii. d. 174; 258, 21 (*vegâd vegam̃ gam*, To increase one's speed more and more). **2.** The flight of an arrow, Kir. 13, 24. **3.** Impetus, Bhâg. P. 5, 7, 11; breeze, Mâlat. 127, 12. **4.** Stream, Hit. iv. d. 59. **5.** Sudden impulse, inconsiderate haste, Pańch. i. d. 122. **6.** Energy. **7.** Strength, Râm. 5, 3, 42. **8.** Pleasure. **9.** Love. **10.** External indication of any internal effect, proceeding from passion, medicine, poison, etc., as convulsion, sweat, etc., Daçak. in Chr. 187, 16. **11.** Evacuation of natural excretions. **12.** Semen virile. —**Comp.** *Chaṇḍa-*, adj. possessed of violent speed or movement, Râm. 5, 74, 29. *Nis-*, adj. quiet, Râm. 1, 56, 9 Gorr. *Mahâ-*, I. adj. very swift, Chr. 29, 33. II. m. a monkey. *Visha-*, m. absorption of venom, as shown by some bodily changes, Daçak. in Chr. 187, 6. *Sa-vega+m*, adv. hastily, Pańch. 89, 13.

वेगतस् *vega+tas*, adv. Quickly.

वेगवन्त् *vega+vant*, adj., f. *vatî*, **1.** Swift, Râm. 3, 50, 5. **2.** Impetuous, Lass. 2. ed. 79, 77; 78.

वेगित *vegita*, i.e. *vega+ita*, adj. **1.** Quickened. **2.** Swift, MBh. 8, 3048.

वेगिता *vegitâ*, i. e. *vegin + tâ*, f. Speed.

वेगिन् *vegin*, i.e. *vega+in*, **I.** adj. Swift, Kir. 8, 39. **II.** m. **1.** A courier. **2.** A hawk. **III.** f. *nî*, A river, Râm. 2, 55, 6, ed. Seramp.

वेडा *veḍâ*, f. A boat.

वेण् *VEṆ*, see *ven*.

वेण *veṇa*, m. **1.** The son of a Vaideha by an Ambashṭha woman, Man. 10, 19. **2.** A proper name, 7, 41.—**Comp.** *Kṛishṇa-* and *Tuṅga-veṇâ*, f. names of rivers, MBh. 3, 8180; 14233.

वेणि I. and **वेणी** *veṇî* (vb. *vê*), **1.** Weaving. **2.** Unornamented and braided hair, as worn by widows and women whose husbands are absent, viz. twisted together in a single braid, Megh. 97 (*ṇi*); 18 (*ṇî*). **3.** A braid of hair in general, Râjat. 5, 449 (as royal ornament?). **4.** Assemblage of water, as the conflux of rivers. **II. वेणी** *veṇî*, f. **1.** An ewe. **2.** Stream.—**Comp.** *Eka-veṇî*, f. a single braid (as a token of mourning, Çâk. 106, 11. *Pushpa-veṇî*, f. 1. a chaplet, Râm. 3, 68, 41. 2. the name of a river. *Pra-veṇî*, f. 1. unornamented hair, as worn by widows or women in absence of their husbands, Ragh. 15, 30. 2. a coloured woollen cover, MBh. 15, 727.

वेणु *veṇu*, m. **1.** A bambu, Hit. iv. d. 26; reed, Pańch. iii. d. 57. **2.** A flute, a pipe, Brahmav. 2, 50. **3.** The name of a king.—**Comp.** *Tri-*, I. adj. epithet of a chariot, ornamented with three flags (?), Bhâg. P. 4, 26, 1. II. m. a part of a chariot, MBh. 7, 1626.

वेणुक *veṇu+ka*, n. A pike used for driving an elephant.

वेणुध्म *veṇu-dhma* (vb. *dhmâ*), m. The player on a flute or pipe.

वेतन *vetana* (probably a form of *vartana*, q. cf.), n. **1.** Hire, wages, Pańch. 22, 10; Nal. 15, 6. **2.** Livelihood, Hit. 88, 17. **3.** Silver.—**Comp.** *Ubhaya-*, adj. 1. accepting wages from his master and his master's enemy, Pańch. 22, 10. 2. living in two elements (water and land), Hit. 88, 17. *Kṛita-*, adj. hired, Yâjń. 2, 164. *Nis-*, adj. receiving no wages, Râjat. 5, 204.

ऽवेतनिन् *-vetanin*, i.e. *vetana+in*, adj. Receiving wages, in *kupya-vetana+in*, Receiving a very small pay, MBh. 3, 657.

वेतस *ve+tas+a*, m. The ratan,

Calamus rotang, Nal. 12, 112; Vâmanap. ap. Aufrecht, Ujjvalad. 251, n.—Cf. O.H.G. wida; A.S. widhig; Lat. vitex, vitis; *ἰτέα, οἶσος, οἶνος*.

वेतस्वन्त् *ve + tas + vant* (cf. the last), adj., f. *vatî*, Reedy, abounding in reeds.

वेताल *vetâla*, m. 1. i.e. *ava-ita-âlaya*, A sprite haunting cemeteries and animating dead bodies, Lass. 5, 13; Hit. 65, 12. 2. (for *vetra + âla*, cf. *vetradhara*), A door-keeper.

वेत्तृ *vettṛi*, i.e. *vid + tṛi*, I. m., f. *trî*, and n. 1. Knowing, understanding, acquainted with, Râm. 3, 53, 41. 2. Who obtains or acquires. II. m. 1. A sage. 2. A husband.

वेत्र *ve + tra*, I. m. A reed, a cane, the ratan, Nal. 12, 5. II. n. A staff, Pańch. 16, 1; the staff of a door-keeper, Ragh. 6, 26.

वेत्रधर *vetradhara*, i.e. *vetra-dhṛi + a*, 1. m., *f. râ*, A door-keeper, Ragh. 6, 82 (*râ*). 2. m. A mace-bearer, a staff-bearer.

वेत्रवती *vetravatî*, i.e. *vetra + vant + î*, f. 1. The name of a river, Megh. 25. 2. A proper name, Çâk. 61, 15 (or, a female door-keeper, cf. 16 and *vetrin*).

वेत्रिन् *vetrin*, i.e. *vetra + in*, m. A door-keeper.

वेथ् *VETH*, see *vith*.

वेद *veda*, i.e. *vid + a*, m. 1. Knowledge. 2. The generic name for the sacred writings of the Hindus, especially for the four collections called *Ṛigveda*, i.e. *Ṛich-*, *Yajurveda*, i.e. *Yajus-*, *Sâmaveda*, i.e. *Sâman-*, and *Atharvaveda*, i.e. *Atharvan-*, Man. 1, 21; Pańch. iii. d. 64; 205 (pl.); MBh. in Chr. 94, 2 (three Vedas, i.e. the three first).—Comp. *A-*, m. oblivion, Man. 5, 60. *Âyurveda*, i.e. *âyus-*, m. 1. the science of medicine, Suçr. 1, 1, 12. 2. the writings of authority on medicine, Hariv. 1539. *Kshatra-*, m. the Veda of the second caste (science of government, politics), Râm. 1, 65, 22. *Gandharva-*, m. the science of music. *Chatur-*, I. m. pl. 1. the four Vedas, Hariv. 14074. 2. a kind of Manes, MBh. 2, 463. II. adj. 1. containing the four Vedas, ib. 3, 13560. 2. conversant with the four Vedas, Hariv. 7993. *Tri-*, adj. conversant with the three (first) Vedas (i.e. the Ṛich, Yajus, and Sâman), Man. 2, 118. *Dus-*, adj. 1. difficult to be known, Râm. 4, 46, 2. 2. unlearned, MBh. 3, 13437. *Dhanurveda*, i.e. *dhanus-*, m. the knowledge of the bow, of archery, the title of a sacred work, Râm. 5, 32, 9; Johns. Sel. 57, 161 (with *sâkshât*, the embodied Dhanurveda). *Pari-*, m. complete knowledge, MBh. 3, 13462.

वेदन *vedana*, i.e. *vid + ana*, I. n., and f. *nâ*. 1. Perception, knowledge conveyed by the senses. 2. Knowledge. 3. Pain, Pańch. 146, 23 (*nâ*); agony, Pańch. 44, 2 (*nâ*). 4. Presenting. 5. The ceremony of holding the ends of a mantle, to be observed by a Çûdra female on her marriage with a man of either of the three first classes. II. n. Marrying, Man. 10, 24; marriage, 9, 65.—Comp. *Prasava-*, f. pains in labour, Pańch. 228, 14.

वेदविद् *veda-vid*, adj. and sbst. Versed in the Vedas, Chr. 27, 9.

वेदस् *vedas*, i.e. *vid + as*, I. m. The Vedas collectively. II. n. Wealth, Lass. 100, 5 = Rigv. vii. 15, 3.—Comp. *Viçva-*, adj. and sbst. one who knows all things, Chr. 290, 8 = Rigv. i. 64, 8; a sage. *Sarva-*, m. a man who, at the conclusion of the *viçvajit* sacrifice, divides all his property amongst the priests.

ऽवेदस *-vedas + a*, at the end of a comp. for *vedas*, in *sarva-*, **I.** n. All one's property, Man. 6, 38. **II.** adj. One who has given all his property at a sacred rite, Man. 11, 1, Calc. (v.r.).

वेदाङ्ग *vedâṅga*, i.e. *veda-aṅga*, m. A sacred science connected with the Vedas; six sciences come under this denomination, viz. pronunciation, grammar, prosody, explanation of obscure terms, description of religious rites, and astronomy, Vedântas. in Chr. 202, 10; Lass. 49, 7.

वेदान्त *vedânta*, i.e. *veda-anta*, m. **1.** The complete Veda, Man. 2, 160. **2.** A philosophical system based particularly on the Upanishads, Vedântas. in Chr. 202, sqq.; 203, 24. **3.** pl. Works concerning this philosophy, Vikr. d. 1.

वेदान्तग *vedânta-ga* (vb. *gam*),

वेदान्तज्ञ *vedânta-jña* (vb. *jñâ*), and

वेदान्तिन् *vedântin*, i.e. *vedânta + in*, m. A follower of the *Vedânta* philosophy.

वेदि I. and **वेदी** *vedi*, f. **1.** Ground prepared for sacrifice, an altar, Çâk. 31, 6; Nal. 1, 9; Râm. 1, 21, 5. **2.** A quadrangular spot in the court-yard of a temple or palace, usually furnished with a raised floor or seat, and covered with a roof supported by pillars, Bhâg. P. 4, 25, 16. **3.** A bench, ib. 3, 23, 17. **4.** A seal-ring. **II.** **वेदि** *vedi*, **1.** m. A teacher. **2.** f. Sarasvatî.—Comp. *Uttara-vedi*, f. the northern fire-place, MBh. 3, 7078. *Ud-vedi*, adj. furnished with an elevated altar, Ragh. 17, 9. *Vahis-vedi*, adv. on the outside of the sacred hearth, Man. 11, 3.

वेदिका *vedi + kâ*, f. **1.** Ground prepared for sacrificial ceremonies, a rude altar, Mâlav. 60, 3. **2.** A quadrangular open shed in the middle of a court-yard, erected for various purposes, and furnished with a seat, Pañch. 129, 17. **3.** A seat, Râm. 6, 75, 27.

वेदिजा *vedijâ*, i.e. *vedi-ja* (vb. *jan*), f. Draupadî.

वेदिन् *vedin*, i.e. *vid* and *veda*, + *in*, **I.** adj. **1.** Knowing, acquainted with, Man. 1, 97. **2.** Marrying, Man. 3, 16. **II.** m. **1.** Brahman. **2.** A learned Brâhmaṇa, a teacher. **III.** m. A plant, Cissampelos hexandra.—Comp. *Kanyâ-*, m. a son-in-law, Yâjñ. 1, 261. *Karuṇa-*, adj. compassionate, Râm. 3, 69, 7. *Gambhira-*, m. a restive elephant, Ragh. 4, 39. *Nîti-*, adj. knowing the rules of policy, Hit. 31, 8, M.M. *Purusha-antara-*, adj. knowing the heart of mankind, Vikr. 36, 10.

वेद्धृ *veddhṛi*, see *vyadh*.

वेध *vedha*, i.e. *vyadh + a*, m. **1.** Piercing, breaking through, Râjat. 5, 95. **2.** Perforation. **3.** Depth.

वेधक *vedhaka*, i.e. *vyadh + aka*, **I.** adj. **1.** Piercing, sharp. **2.** A perforator (of gems), Râm. 2, 64, 12, ed. Seramp. **II.** m. Camphor. **III.** n. Grain, rice in the ear.

वेधन *vedhana*, i.e. *vyadh + ana*, **I.** n. **1.** Piercing. **2.** Perforation. **3.** Depth. **II.** f. *nî*. **1.** An instrument used to pierce gems. **2.** An instrument for piercing an elephant's ear.—Comp. *Dṛiḍha-*, n. hitting with an arrow which remains in the wound, MBh. 7, 2635.

वेधस् *vedhas*, **I.** adj. sbst. m. Creating, Chr. 290, 1 = Rigv. i. 64, 1. **II.** m. **1.** The creator, Mâlat. 14, 4; Brahman, Bhartṛ. 3, 98. **2.** Vishṇu.

3. Çiva, Arj. 10, 50. 4. The sun. 5. A wise man, Çṛiṅgârat. 21 (v.r.).

वेधिन् i.e. *vyadh + in*, I. adj. Piercing, hitting, Lass. 36, 19. II. f. *nî*, A leech.—Comp. *Koṭi-*, adj. piercing the top, i.e. able to perform the most difficult task, Râjat. 1, 110. *Çabda-*, I. adj. an archer who is able to hit an object not seen but only heard, Râm. 2, 63, 10; °*dhitva*, n. its abstract, Râm. 1, 28, 22. II. m. a name of Arjuna. *Çîghra-*, m. a good archer.

वेन् *VEN*, † **वेण्** *VEṆ*, i. 1, Par. Âtm. 1. † To go. 2. † To know. 3. † To reflect. 4. † To discern. 5. † To hold or take a musical instrument. 6. † To play on a musical instrument. 7. † To take. 8. To praise (ved.). 9. To love, Chr. 292, 8=Rigv. i. 86, 8.—Cf. αἰνέω, αἶνη.

वेन *ven + a*, m. Brahman.

वेप् *VEP* (akin to *vi*, its old Caus.), i. 1, Âtm. (in epic poetry also Par., Indr. 5, 48), To shake, to tremble, Pañch. 94, 4; Daçak. in Chr. 201, 13.—With the prep. **उद्** *ud*, To tremble, Nal. 9, 26.—With **प्र** *pra*, To tremble, Râm. 2, 8, 8.—Cf. Lat. vibrare; O.H.G. weibôn, fluitare; weibjan.

वेपथु *vep + athu*, m. Trembling, Vikr. d. 147; Pañch. iii. d. 227; tremor.—Comp. *Ati-*, adj. trembling vehemently, Lass. 59, 5.

वेपथुभृत् *vepathu-bhṛi + t*, adj. Trembling, Çiç. 9, 73.

वेपथुमन्त् *vepathu + mant*, adj., f. *matî*, Trembling, Çâk. d. 22.—Comp. *Ati-*, adj. trembling vehemently, Çiç. 9, 77.

वेपन *vepana*, i.e. *vip* and *vep*, + *ana*, n. 1. Trembling (ÇKD.). 2. The shooting off of a bow, Râm. 1, 67, 10.

वेपस् *vep + as*, n. Trembling.

वेम *ve + ma*, m., and **वेमन्** *ve + man*, m. and n. A loom.—Comp. *Su-vema*, m. a good loom, MBh. 1, 806.

वेर *vera* (m. and) n. 1. The body. 2. Saffron. 3. The egg-plant.

1. **वेल्** *VEL*, see *vell*.

2. **वेल्** *VEL*, i. 10 (rather a denomin. derived from *velâ*), Par. To declare the time.

वेल *vela*, I. n. A grove. II. f. *lâ*. 1. Time, Pañch. 55, 6; 163, 20; loc. *lâyâm*, Seasonably. 2. Tide, Pañch. 75, 24; flow, current. 3. Sea-shore, Çiç. 9, 38 (at the end of a comp. adj.). 4. Boundary, Pañch. iii. d. 269. 5. Leisure, interval, opportunity. 6. Sudden death. 7. Sickness. 8. The gums. 9. Speech.—Comp. *Ati-vela + m*, adv. unseasonably, MBh. 2, 2187. *Anu-vela + m*, adv. continually, Ragh. 3, 5. *Ud-vela*, adj. breaking out of its shore, Kathâs. 18, 2. *Toya-velâ*, f. a bank, a shore, Hariv. 12014. *Mahâ-vela*, adj. of high tides, surgy, Johns. Sel. 13, 39.

वेल्ल् *VELL*, **वेल्** *VEL*, † **वेह्ल्** *VEHL*, i. 1, Par. 1. † To go. 2. *vell*, To shake, to tremble, Utt. Râmach. 121, 6. Ptcple. of the pf. pass. *vellita*. 1. Shaking. 2. Crooked, Daçak. in Chr. 198, 19.—With the prep. **अनु** *anu*, *anuvellita*, Lying crooked under, Daçak. in Chr. 198, 18. n. A bandage used in surgery, Suçr. 1, 65, 17.—With **उद्** *ud*, 1. *vell*, To abscond, Utt. Râmach. 48, 12. 2. *vel*, To struggle, Mâlat. 140, 3.—With **वि** *vi*, *vell*, To struggle, to tremble, Kathâs. 18, 174. Probably akin to Lat. volvo; εἴλω, ἑλύω, etc.; O.H.G. wuoljan; Goth. valvjan; A.S. willian, waeltan, etc. (cf. the next).

वेल्लन *vell + ana*, n. **1.** Rolling on the ground (as a horse). **2.** A sort of rolling-pin with which cakes, etc., are prepared. **3.** Going. **4.** Shaking.

वेवी *VEVÎ* (properly a frequent. of *vî*, q. cf.), ii. 2, Âtm. (ved. also Par., Rigv. iii. 55, 9), **1.** To go. **2.** To pervade. **3.** To conceive or become pregnant. **4.** To desire. **5.** To throw. **6.** To eat.

वेश *veça*, m. I. i.e. *viç + a*. **1.** Entrance. **2.** A house. **3.** A house of prostitutes, Man. 4, 84; Daçak. in Chr. 193, 13. II. also **वेष** *vesha*. **1.** Dress, apparel, Man. 4, 18, and 200 (*sh*); Pañch. 129, 17 (*sh*). **2.** Ornament, decoration. **3.** Disguise.—**Comp.** *Agni-*, m. a proper name, Johns. Sel. 1, 3. *Abhisaraṇa-*, adj., f. *çâ*, dressed in a garb fit for meeting one's lover, Vikr. 40, 17. *Ârya-*, adj. dressed like an Ârya, or a respectable man, Râm. 1, 7, 6. *Kapaṭa-yuvati-*, adj. under the disguise of a girl, Bhâg. P. 8, 12, 47. *Kṛita-*, adj. dressed, Gît. 11, 1. *Puṁ-veça*, i.e. *puṁs-*, adj. dressed like a man, Kathâs. 29, 108. *Çṛingâra-*, adj. dressed suitably for amorous enterprises, MBh, 5, 237. *Sa-*, adj. 1. near. 2. dressed, ornamented.—Cf. οἶκος; Lat. vicus; Goth. veihs; A.S. wic.

वेशक *veçaka*, i.e. *viç + aka*, I. adj. Who or what enters. II. m. A house. III. f. *çikâ*, Entrance.

वेशन्त *veçanta* (vb. *viç*), m. **1.** A small pond. **2.** Fire.

वेशिन् *veçin*, i.e. *veça + in*, adj. Assuming a particular dress or form.—**Comp.** *Sarva-*, i.e. *sarvaveça + in*, m. an actor, a dancer.

वेश्मन् *veçman*, i.e. *viç + man*, n. **1.** A house, Pañch. iii. d. 172; 218; an abode. **2.** A temple, Râjat. 5, 167.—**Comp.** *Krîḍâ-*, n. a house for amusement, Vikr. d. 41. *Jatu-*, m. a house, constructed of shell-lac, Johns. Sel. 55, 143. *Pâyu-kshâlana-*, n. a privy, Râjat. 4, 572. *Bandhana-*, n. a prison. *Vâsa-*, n. the inner part of a house, a sleeping-room, Kathâs. 22, 104. *Çmaçâna-*, m. 1. Çiva. 2. a ghost.

वेश्या *veçyâ*, see under *viç*.

वेष *vesha*, see *veça*.

वेष्ट् *VESHṬ*, i. 1, Âtm. To surround, to encompass, to twist about, MBh. 1, 1800. *veshṭita*, **1.** Dressed, Hit. pr. d. 40, M.M. **2.** Stopped, Hit. 106, 17. **3.** Secured from access. **4.** Enveloped, wrapped up, Man. 1, 49. Caus. **1.** To surround, MBh. 12, 12449. **2.** To twist about, MBh. 1, 1801. **3.** To invest, to blockade, Ragh. 11, 51; 52 (Calc.).—With the prep. **आ** *â*, To twist, Pañch. i. d. 376.—With **उद्** *ud*, To untwist, Megh. 89; MBh. 7, 3168 *udveshṭanti* is to be changed to *uchcheshṭanti*. Caus. To open, Mâlav. 70, 17.—With **उप** *upa*, *upaveshṭita*, Twined, Mṛichchh. 115, 13.—With **परि** *pari*, To surround, Pañch. 97, 25. *pariveshṭita*, **1.** Tied, Hit. ii. d. 131. **2.** Covered, veiled. Caus. To embrace, Pañch. i. d. 41.—With **प्र** *pra*, *praveshṭita*, Covered, MBh. 3, 10047.—With **सम्** *sam*, To surround one's self, to be surrounded, MBh. 12, 12449. Caus. **1.** To surround, to encompass, MBh. 3, 10264. **2.** To cover, MBh. 3, 12889.

वेष्ट *veshṭ + a*, m. **1.** Surrounding. **2.** An enclosure, a fence. **3.** A turban.

4. Resin. 5. Turpentine. — Comp. *Karṇa-*, m. 1. an ear-ring, Râm. 5, 19, 12. 2. a proper name, MBh. 1, 2696. *Danta-*, m. 1. the gum, the jaw, Yâjń. 3, 96. 2. a disease of the teeth, Suçr. 1, 93, 5. *Patra-*, m. a kind of ear-ring, Ragh. 16, 67.

वेष्टक *vesht+aka*, I. adj. Surrounding, a surrounder. II. m. 1. A wall, a fence. 2. A pumpkin gourd. III. n. 1. A turban. 2. Resin. 3. Turpentine.—Comp. *Danta-*, m. a disease of the teeth, Suçr. 1, 303, 9.

वेष्टन *vesht+ana*, n. 1. Surrounding, being worn, Râjat. 5, 343 (see *ullâsana*). 2. An envelope, Pańch. 147, 2. 3. A wall, a fence. 4. A turban, a diadem, Ragh. 1, 42 (cf. Sch. Calc. 43). 5. The outer ear, or the meatus auditorius and the concha. 6. An attitude in dancing, a particular disposition of the hands, also a crossing of the feet. 7. Bdellium.—Comp. *Ud-*, I. n. pressure, a pressing pain, Suçr. 1, 332, 2. II. adj. of which the band is loosened (as hair), Ragh. 7, 6.

वेष्प *veshpa*, m. Water (cf. *vâshpa*).

† **वेस्** *VES*, i. 1, Par. 1. To go. 2. To desire.

वेसर *vesara*, m. A mule.

वेसवार *vesavâra*, m. A condiment, as pepper, spice.

† **वेह्** *VEH*, **बेह्** *BEH*, i. 1, Âtm. To endeavour.

वेहत् *vehat*, probably *vi-han+t*, f. A cow miscarrying from taking the bull unseasonably.

वेह्ल् *VEHL*, see *vell*.

1. **वै** *VAI*, see 1. *vâ*.

2. **वै** *vai*, a particle, 1. So indeed, Pańch. ii. d. 26. 2. Just, Nal. 26, 5. 3. Although, Chr. 6, 6. 4. Granted, if, Hit. ii. d. 21 (but cf. Böhtl. Ind. Spr. 572). 5. Preceded by *tu*, But just, Man. 2, 22. 6. Preceded by *na*, Perhaps not, Lass. 27, 2.

वैकक्ष *vaikaksha*, i.e. *vi-kaksha+a*, n. 1. A garland worn over one shoulder and under the other. 2. An upper garment, a wrapper.

वैकक्षक *vaikaksha+ka*, n. =*vaikaksha*, 1.

वैकर्तन *vaikartana*, i.e. *vikartana* (The sun), *+a*, patronym. Son of the sun, i.e. Karṇa, Johns. Sel. 56, 154.

वैकल्प *vaikalpa*, i.e. *vikalpa + a*, n. in *artha-*, n. Perversion or disguise of fact, Man. 8, 95.

वैकल्पिक *vaikalpika*, i.e. *vikalpa +ika*, adj. 1. Alternative. 2. Doubtful, indeterminate.

वैकल्य *vaikalya* i.e. *vikala+ya*, n. 1. Lameness, imbecility, Pańch. i. d. 193; Hit. 121, 14; Pańch. 254, 9 (*buddhi-*, of understanding). 2. Deficiency, defect, want, Man. 10, 85; Pańch. i. d. 119. 3. Insufficiency, Pańch. 166, 16. 4. Non-existence. 5. Agitation.

वैकारिक *vaikârika*, i.e. *vikâra+ika*, I. adj. Modified, Bhâg. P. 2, 5, 30. II. m. A class of deities, ib.; MBh. 12, 13626.

वैकालिक *vaikâlika*, i.e. *vikâla+ika*, adj. Occurring in, or belonging to, the afternoon, Lass. 24, 18 (*kam*, adv.).

वैकुण्ठ *vaikuṇṭha* (partly properly patronym. from *vikuṇṭhâ*, The mother of Vishṇu, *+a*), I. m. 1. Vishṇu, Padmap. 2, 5. 2. Indra. II. n. 1. The paradise of Vishṇu, Pańch. 48, 3. 2. Talc.

वैकृत *vaikṛita*, i.e. *vikṛiti+a*, I. adj.

Changed. II. n. 1. Change, Râm. 1, 9, 45; Râjat. 5, 314. 2. Aversion.

वैक्लव्य *vaiklavya*, i.e. *viklava + ya*, n. Confusion, commotion, affliction, Nal. 23, 23; Çâk. d. 81; 111, 3 (at the end of a comp. adj., f. *yâ*); despair, Mâlat. 142, 7.—**Comp.** *Su-vaiklavya + m*, adv. despairingly, 164, 7.

वैखानस *vaikhânasa*, i.e. *vikhânasa* (a proper name), *+ a*, I. adj. Instituted by Vaikhânasa (with *vrata*, the life of an anchoret), Çâk. d. 26. II. m. An anchoret, Utt. Râmach. 16, 5; cf. 93, 5. III. f. *sî*, A vessel used for frying meat to be offered in sacrifice.

वैगुण्य *vaiguṇya*, i.e. *vi-guṇa + ya*, n. 1. Absence of qualities. 2. Contrariety of qualities. 3. Inferiority, badness, baseness, Man. 10, 68. 4. Unskilfulness, Man. 8, 293. 5. Fault, defect.

वैचक्षण्य *vaichakshaṇya*, i.e. *vichakshaṇa + ya*, n. Skill, cleverness, proficiency.—**Comp.** *Ati-*, n. excessive proficiency, Daçak. in Chr. 196, 6.

वैचित्र्य *vaichitrya*, i.e. *vi-chitra + ya*, n. 1. Variety, Hit. pr. d. 2, M.M. 2. Surprisingness, Mâlat. 16, 2; surprise, 36, 9. 3. Sorrow, Mâlat. 46, 12; despair, 66, 16.

वैजनन *vaijanana*, i.e. *vijanana + a*, m. The last month of uterine gestation.

वैजयन्त *vaijayanta*, i.e. *vijayanta + a*, I. m. 1. The banner of Indra, Indr. 1, 8. 2. A banner in general, Râm. 2, 97, 25 Gorr. 3. The palace of Indra. II. f. *ti*. 1. A flag, a banner, Hit. 63, 1, M.M. 2. A kind of garland. 3. The name of two trees.

वैजयन्तिक *vaijayantika*, I. i.e. *vaijayanta + ika*, adj. Bearing a flag, a flag-bearer. II. f. *kâ*, i.e. *vaijayantî + ka*, f. 1. A flag, Mâlat. 13, 19. 2. A string of pearls, Vikr. 12, 17 (Prâkṛ.; cf. Sch.).

वैजात्य *vaijâtya*, i.e. *vi-jâti + ya*, n. 1. Difference or deviation from ordinary conduct. 2. Looseness, wantonness. 3. Difference of species or caste. 4. Exclusion from caste.

वैजिक *vaijika*, i.e. *vîja + ika*, I. adj. 1. Seminal, relating to seed, to conception, Man. 2, 27. 2. Relating to sexual union, Man. 5, 63. II. m. A young shoot. III. n. 1. Origin, cause. 2. Soul, spirit. 3. Oil prepared from the Morunga.

वैडालव्रतिक *vaiḍâlavratika*, i.e. *viḍâla-vrata + ika*, adj. and sbst. Acting like a cat, hypocritical, Man. 4, 192; a hypocrite, 4, 30.

वैण *vaiṇa*, i.e. *veṇu + a* (anomal.), m. A cutter of bambu, a worker in bambu-work, Man. 4, 215 (v.r.).

वैणव *vaiṇava*, i.e. *veṇu + a*, I. adj., f. *vî*, Made of bambu, Man. 4, 36. II. m. 1. A bambu-staff. 2. A worker in bambu or wicker-work.

वैणविक *vaiṇavika*, i.e. *veṇu + ika*, m. A player on a flute.

वैणिक *vaiṇika*, i.e. *vîṇâ + ika*, m. A lutist.

वैणुक *vaiṇuka*, i.e. *veṇu + ka*, n. A bambu pike, headed with iron, used to drive an elephant.

वैण्य *vaiṇya*, i.e. *veṇa + ya*, patronym., m. The son of Veṇa, Pañch. iii. d. 269.

वैतंसिक *vaitaṁsika*, i.e. *vitaṁsa + ika*, m. A vendor of the flesh of beasts or birds, Govardhana, Âryâ Sapt. 154, b.—**Comp.** *Dyûta-*, m. vendors of beasts and birds for playing with, Râm. 2, 90, 28.

वैतनिक *vaitanika*, i.e. *vetana + ika*, adj., f. *kî*, sbst. 1. Living on wages.

2. A hireling, a labourer. **3.** A stipendiary.

वैतरणि and **णी** *vaitaraṇî*, i.e. *vi-taraṇa + î*, f. **1.** The river of hell, MBh. 18, 84 (*ṇî*). **2.** A proper name.

वैतस *vaitasa*, i.e. *vetasa + a*, I. adj., f. *sî*, Reed-like, Pańch. iii. d. 18. II. m. A sort of cane, Calamus fasciculatus.

वैतान *vaitâna*, i.e. *vitâna + a*, I. adj. **1.** Taken from the holy hearth, Çâk. d. 83. **2.** Sacrificial, sacred, Çâk. 43, 11, Chezy (v.r.). II. n. **1.** Oblation with fire. **2.** The sacred ordinances, Man. 11, 37.

वैतानिक *vaitânika*, i.e. *vitâna + ika*, I. adj. **1.** Performed with the three sacred fires, Man. 6, 9; 7, 78. **2.** Sacrificial, sacred, Çâk. 31, 11. II. n. Burnt offering, especially of clarified butter.

वैतालिक *vaitâlika*, m. I. i.e. *vitâla + ika*, A bard, whose principal duty is to awaken a chief at dawn with music and song, a singer, Çâk. 62, 1; MBh. 1, 6940. II. i.e. *vetâla + ika*, One who has a Vetâla for a familiar.

वैतृष्ण्य *vaitṛishṇya*, i.e. *vi-tṛishṇa* (see *tṛishṇâ*), *+ ya*, n. Quenching of the thirst, Man. 5, 128.

वैदग्ध *vaidagdha*, n., **वैदग्ध्य** *vaidagdhya*, n., and f. *dhî*, i.e. *vi-dagdha* (vb. *dah*), *+ a* or *ya*, **1.** Cleverness, skill, Bhartṛ. 2, 15 (*dha*); Lass. 91, 13 (*dhî*); Mâlat. 3, 20; 18, 7; 9 (*dhya*). **2.** Acuteness, intelligence, Mâlat. 129, 7. **3.** Cunning, craft.

वैदर्भ *vaidarbha*, A. i.e. *vidarbha + a*, I. m. The sovereign of Vidarbha, the father of Damayantî. II. f. *bhî*. **1.** Damayantî, Nal. 24, 50. **2.** Rukmiṇî. **3.** The wife of Agastya. **4.** The law of Vidarbha, by which cousins-german were allowed to intermarry in that country. B. i.e. *vi-dṛibh + a + a*, n. Crafty or indirect speech. — **Comp.** *Danta-*, m. the loosening of the teeth, Suçr. 1, 31, 19.

वैदल *vaidala*, I. i.e. *vidala + a*, adj. Made of cane, Man. 5, 119. II. m. **1.** A flat unleavened cake. **2.** Any leguminous vegetable or grain. III. n. A vessel of wicker-work, a basket made of reeds, Man. 6, 54.

वैदिक *vaidika*, i.e. *veda + ika*, I. adj., f. *kî*. **1.** Relating to the Vedas, Man. 2, 117. **2.** Scriptural, 2, 15. **3.** Recommended, ordained in the Vedas, 2, 2; 84; 8, 190. II. m. A Brâhmaṇa well versed in the Vedas.

वैदुष्य *vaidushya*, i.e. *vidvaṁs* (vb. *vid*), *+ ya*, n. Science, Râjat. 6, 290.

वैदूर्य *vaidûrya*, i.e. *vidûra + ya*, I. adj. Brought from Vidûra. II. n. A gem of a dark-blue colour, the lapis lazuli, Bhâg. P. 4, 25, 15; Râm. 3, 49, 2; 53, 15.

वैदूर्यमय *vaidûrya + maya*, adj., f. *yî*, Made of lapis lazuli, Bhartṛ. 2, 98.

वैदेशिक *vaideçika*, i.e. *vi-deça + ika*, adj. Foreigner, a foreigner, Pańch. 184, 4.

वैदेह *vaideha*, i.e. *videhâ + a*, I. m. **1.** The king of Videhâ, father of Sîtâ, Utt. Râmach. 93, 12. **2.** A trader by profession. **3.** The son of a Vaiçya by a Brâhmaṇa woman, Man. 10, 11. **4.** pl. Descendants of mixed castes, Lass. Pentap. 66, 31. **5.** An attendant on the women's apartments. II. f. *hî*. **1.** The wife of a trader. **2.** Sîtâ (the daughter of the king of Videhâ), Râm. 3, 49, 12; Utt. Râmach. 14, 9. **3.** Long pepper. **4.** A sort of pigment, called Rochanâ.

वैदेहक *vaideha+ka*, m. =*vaideha*, I., cf. Man. 10, 13 (=*vaideha*, 1. 2.).

वैद्य *vaidya*, i.e. *veda+ya*, I. adj. 1. Relating to the Vedas, Lass. Pentap. 67, 43. 2. Relating to medicine, medical. II. m. 1. A follower of the Vedas, or one conversant with the Vedas. 2. A learned man, Brâhmaṇav. 2, 1. 3. A physician, Pañch. iii. d. 67.—Comp. *Visha-*, m. a dealer in antidotes. *Svar-*, m. either of the Açvins, the physicians of the heaven.

वैद्यक *vaidya+ka*, m. A physician, Çringârat. 14.

वैद्याधर *vaidyâdhara*, i.e. *vidyâdhara+a*, adj. Belonging to the Vidyâdharas, Kathâs. 26, 241.

वैद्युत *vaidyuta*, i.e. *vidyut+a*, adj. Proceeded from lightning, Vikr. d. 154 (*agniḥ*, A flash of lightning); Utt. Râmach. 125, 11.

वैध *vaidha*, i.e. *vidhi+a*, adj. According to rule, ritual.

वैधर्म्य *vaidharmya*, i.e. *vi-dharma+ya*, n. 1. Irreligion, impropriety. 2. Difference of duty. 3. Difference, Bhâshâp. 28; Kusumâñj. 3, 9.

वैधव *vaidhava*, i.e. *vidhu+a*, patronym., m. The son of the moon, i.e. Budha, Vikr. d. 159.

वैधवेय *vaidhaveya*, i.e. *vidhavâ+eya*, m. The son of a widow, Çâk. 23, 14 (but read *vaidheya*).

वैधव्य *vaidhavya*, i.e. *vidhavâ+ya*, n. Widowhood, Böhtl. Ind. Spr. 450.—Comp. *A-*, adj., f. *yâ*, relating to non-widowhood, not to become a widow, Sâv. 4, 12. *Bâla-*, n. state of one who has become a widow already when a child, Böhtl. Ind. Spr. 450.

वैधात्र *vaidhâtra*, i.e. *vidhâtṛi+a*, patronym., m. Sanatkumâra, the son of Brahman.

वैधेय *vaidheya* (perhaps *dheya* [vb. *dhâ*], compounded with *vi* and aff. *a*), adj. Foolish, a fool, Vikr. 30, 14.

वैध्यत *vaidhyata*, m. Yama's doorkeeper.

वैनतेय *vainateya*, i.e. *vi-natâ*, A proper name, the wife of Kâçyapa (vb. *nam*), +*eya*, metronym., m. Garuḍa, Vikr. 6, 6.

वैनयिक *vainayika*, i.e. *vinaya+ika*, I. adj., f. *kî*. 1. Relating to morals or behaviour. 2. Enforcing proper conduct. 3. Magisterial, performed by the officers of criminal justice, Man. 7, 65. II. m. A war carriage.

वैनायक *vainâyaka*, i.e. *vinâyaka+a*, adj., f. *kî*, Referring to, or made by, Gaṇeça, Mâlat. 1, 5.

वैनाशिक *vainâçika*, i.e. *vinâça+ika*, m. 1. A dependent, a subject, a slave. 2. An astrologer. 3. A spider.

वैनीतक *vainîtaka*, i.e. *vi-nîta* (vb. *nî*), +*ka*, m. and n. A mediate conveyance, as a porter carrying a letter.

वैन्य *vainya*, i.e. *vena+ya*, patronym., m. 1. The king Pṛithu, the son of Vena (ÇKD.). 2. The name of a deity (?), Râjat. 5, 97; 99.

वैपरीत्य *vaiparîtya*, i.e. *vi-pari-ita* (vb. *i*), +*ya*, n. 1. Contrariety, opposition, reverse, Sâh. Darp. 12, 17. 2. Counterpart, Hit. ii. d. 133.

वैफल्य *vaiphalya*, i.e. *vi-phala+ya*, n. Uselessness, MBh. 13, 285.

वैभव *vaibhava*, i.e. *vibhava+a*, n. Power, greatness, Kir. 12, 3.

वैभ्राज *vaibhrâja*, i.e. *vi-bhrâj+a+a*, n. A garden of the gods.

वैमत्य *vaimatya*, i.e. *vi-mati + ya*, n. Dissension, Râjat. 5, 462.

वैमनस्य *vaimanasya*, i.e. *vi-manas + ya*, n. Sadness, heart-break, Çâk. 79, 23.

वैमल्य *vaimalya*, i.e. *vi-mala + ya*, n. Purity, cleanness, Râjat. 5, 15.

वैमात्र *vaimâtra*, i.e. *vi-mâtṛi + a*, I. adj. Born of a step-mother, Râm. 3. 53, 19. II. m. A step-mother's son. III. f. *trî*, A step-mother's daughter.

वैमात्रेय *vaimâtreya*, i.e. *vi-mâtṛi + eya*, I. m. A step-mother's son. II. f. *yi*, A half-sister, or one by a different mother.

वैमानिक *vaimânika*, i.e. *vimâna + ika*, adj. 1. Relating to a heavenly car. 2. Borne in chariots of the gods, Man. 12, 48. 3. A god, Râjat. 5, 370.

वैमूल्यतस् *vaimûlyatas*, i.e. *vi-mûla + ya + tas*, adv. By overcharging the price (?), Man. 9, 287 (v.r.).

वैमेय *vaimeya*, i.e. *vi-meya* (vb. *me*), + *a*, m. Barter, exchange.

वैयग्र्य *vaiyagrya*, i.e. *vyagra + ya*, n. Being engaged, Lass. 2. ed. 37, 16.

वैयर्थ्य *vaiyarthya*, i.e. *vi-artha + ya*, n. Uselessness, Vikr. 29, 18; unprofitableness.

वैयाकरण *vaiyâkaraṇa*, i.e. *vyâkaraṇa + a*, I. adj. Grammatical. II. m. A grammarian.—**Comp.** *Prathama-*, a first-rate grammarian, Pâṇ. 6, 2, 56, Sch.

वैयाघ्र *vaiyâghra*, i.e. *vyâghra + a*, adj. 1. Consisting of a tiger-skin, Chr. 25, 52. 2. Covered with a tiger-skin.

वैयात्य *vaiyâtya*, i.e. *vi-yâta* (vb. *yâ*), + *ya*, n. 1. Lasciviousness, Hit. iii. d. 7; Râjat. 5, 384. 2. Boldness.

वैयासकि *vaiyâsaki*, i.e. *vyâsa + ak + i* (or rather + *ka* + *i*), patronym., m. A son of Vyâsa, Bhâg. P. 2, 3, 13.

वैर *vaira*, i.e. *vîra + a*, n. 1. Heroism, prowess. 2. Enmity, Pańch. 66, 11.—**Comp.** *Nis-*, I. n. peaceableness, Bhâg. P. 3, 14, 45. II. adj. peaceable, MBh. 15, 882. III. *ram*, adv. being no enmity, Râm. 4, 20, 7.

वैरकृत् *vaira-kṛi + t*, m. An enemy, Pańch. ii. d. 121.

वैरङ्गिक *vairańgika*, i.e. *vi-rańga + ika*, m. An ascetic.

वैरागिक *vairâgika*, and **वैरागिन्** *vairâgin*, i.e. *vi-râga + ika*, and *in*, m. An ascetic.

वैराग्य *vairâgya*, i.e. *vi-râga + ya*, n. 1. Absence of worldly desire, Bhag. 6, 35 (devotion); Pańch. 50, 16. 2. Disaffection, Hit. iii. d. 90. 3. Sorrow, Pańch. 82, 13; 116, 11. 4. Despondency, 235, 11.—**Comp.** *Sa-vairâgya + m*, adv. sorrowfully, Pańch. 66, 20.

वैराग्यता *vairâgya + tâ*, f. Absence of worldly desire, Pańch. 50, 15 (devotion).

वैराज *vairâja*, i.e. *virâj + a*, adj. or m. (viz. *loka*), The name of certain worlds, Utt. Râmach. 41, 14.

वैराय *VAIRÂYA*, a denomin. derived from *vaira* with *ya*, Âtm. To fight, to behave inimically, Bhartṛ. 2, 27.

वैरिता *vairitâ*, i.e. *vairin + tâ*, f. Enmity, Pańch. iii. d. 114.

वैरिन् *vairin*, i.e. *vaira + in*, I. adj. 1. Heroic, Bhartṛ. 2, 32 (? Böhtl., as on an enemy). 2. Hostile, Megh. 100. II. m. 1. A hero. 2. An enemy, Pańch. ii. d. 121.—**Comp.** *Dṛiḍha-* (vb. *dṛiṁh*), m. a relentless foe, Johns. Sel.

60, 189. *Pûrva-*, adj. one who has first commenced hostilities, MBh. 6, 3745.

वैरूप्य *vairûpya*, i.e. *vi-rûpa + ya*, n. **1.** Deformity, Pańch. i. d. 466; Ragh. 12, 40. **2.** Difference of form.

वैरूप्यता *vairûpya + tâ*, f. Deformity, Nal. 19, 33.

वैरोचन *vairochana*, i.e. *virochana + a*, I. adj. Proceeding from the sun, Kir. 5, 46. II. patronym. **1.** The son of Agni. **2.** The son of the sun. **3.** Bali, son of Virochana, Johns. Sel. 30, 42.

वैरोचनि *vairochani*, i.e. *virochana + i*, patronym., m. **1.** The son of the sun. **2.** Bali, the son of Virochana, Arj. 8, 19.

वैलक्ष्य *vailakshya*, i.e. *vi-laksha + ya*, n. **1.** Absence of any characteristic. **2.** Contrariety, reverse. **3.** Contrary course to that which is usual or natural.—Comp. *Sa-*, adj. abashed, embarrassed, Râjat. 5, 60. °*yam*, adv. embarrassed, Vikr. 32, 10.

वैल्व *vailva*, i.e. *vilva + a*, I. adj. **1.** Relating to the *Vilva* tree. **2.** Made of its wood, Man. 2, 45. II. n. The fruit of the *Vilva* tree.

वैवधिक *vaivadhika*, i.e. *vivadha + ika*, m. A chandler, a vendor of grain, etc.

वैवर्ण्य *vaivarṇya*, i.e. *vi-varṇa + ya*, n. **1.** Change of colour, Pańch. i. d. 213. **2.** Deviation from tribe or caste. **3.** Difference.

वैवस्वत *vaivasvata*, i.e. *vivasvant + a*, patronym., m. **1.** Yama. **2.** The seventh Manu, Matsyop. 9 (cf. Man. 1, 62). **3.** One of the Rudras. **4.** The planet Saturn.

वैवाहिक *vaivâhika*, i.e. *vivâha + ika*, I. adj. Relating to marriage, nuptial, Man. 2, 67. II. m. (or perhaps *tam̃ tu* is to be changed to *tat tu*; then it would be n.), Wedding, Chr. 14, 21.

वैशम्पायन *vaiçampâyana*, m. The name of a Muni or sage, MBh. 1, 97; 107.

वैशस *vaiçasa*, i.e. *vi-ças + a + a*, n. **1.** Rending in pieces, Bhâg. P. 3, 30, 27. **2.** Slaughter, Utt. Râmach. 113, 6; Pańch. ed. orn. 36, 22; Bhâg. P. 4, 11, 10. **3.** Distress, Utt. Râmach. 160, 5. **4.** Hindrance.

वैशस्त्र *vaiçastra*, i.e. *vi-çastra + a*, n. The state of being defenceless.

वैशाख *vaiçâkha*, i.e. *viçâkhâ + a*, I. m. **1.** The name of a month, April—May, Râjat. 5, 260. **2.** A churning-stick. II. f. *khî*, The day of full moon in the month *Vaiçâkha*. III. n. An attitude in shooting, standing with the feet a span apart.

वैशिक *vaiçika*, i.e. probably *veçyâ + ika*, anomal., n. Arts of a courtesan, Lass. 2. ed. 59, 9.

वैशिष्ट्य *vaiçishṭya*, i. e. *vi-çishṭa* (vb. *çish*), *+ ya*, n. **1.** Endowment with. **2.** Distinction, difference, Vedântas. in Chr. 208, 22.

वैशेषिक *vaiçeshika*, i.e. *viçesha + ika*, I. adj. **1.** Characteristic, Bhâshâp. 43. **2.** Belonging to the Vaiçeshika doctrine (cf. II.), Bhâshâp. 104; 140. II. n. A peculiar philosophical system, the Vaiçeshika doctrine. III. m. A follower of the Vaiçeshika doctrine, Kusumâńj. 3, 8 (p. 29, 13, ed. Cowell).

वैशेष्य *vaiçeshya*, i.e. *viçesha + ya*, n. **1.** Specific or generic distinction. **2.** Superiority, Man. 9, 296.

वैश्य *vaiçya*, i.e. *viç + ya*, I. m. A

man of the third caste, Man. 1, 116; Hit. iv. d. 21. II. f. *yá*, A woman of the Vaiçya caste.

वैश्रवण *vaiçravaṇa*, m. Kuvera, Hit. ii. d. 91.

वैश्वदेव *vaiçvadeva*, i.e. *viçva-deva* + *a*, I. adj. 1. Relating to the Viçvadevas, Man. 4, 183; dedicated or sacred to them. 2. Relating to all divinities. II. n. Offering or sacrifice to all the divinities, Man. 3, 83, 84; Pañch. iv. d. 2.

वैश्वानर *vaiçvânara*, I. i.e. *viçva-nara* + *a*, adj. Relating to, fit for, etc., all men. II. m. 1. Agni, fire, Utt. Râmach. 174, 3; Pañch. 224, 21. 2. The general consciousness, Vedântas. in Chr. 209, 11. III. f. *rî*, A particular sacrifice, Man. 11, 27.

वैश्वासिक *vaiçvâsika*, i.e. *viçvâsa* + *ika*, adj. Trustworthy, Daçak. in Chr. 180, 10.

वैश्वी *vaiçvî*, i.e. *viçva* + *a* + *î*, f. The name of the twenty-first lunar mansion.

वैषम्य *vaishamya*, i.e. *vishama* + *ya*, n. 1. Inequality, unevenness. 2. Solitariness. 3. Difficulty. 4. Misery, distress, Nal. 9, 20.—Comp. *Ati-*, n. situation in a place of very difficult access, Hit. iii. d. 55.

वैष्टुत *vaishṭuta*, i.e. *vi-stuta* (vb. *stu*), + *a*, n. The ashes of a burnt offering.

वैष्ट्र *vaishṭra*, n. The world.

वैष्णव *vaishṇava*, i.e. *vishṇu* + *a*, I. adj., f. *vî*, Relating or belonging to Vishṇu, Johns. Sel. 95, 70; Râjat. 5, 125; Arj. 4, 30. II. m. A follower of Vishṇu, Râjat. 5, 43. III. f. *vî*. 1. One of the *Mâtṛis*, the personified energy of Vishṇu. 2. Durgâ. 3. A flower, Clitoria ternatea. 4. Sacred basil, Ocymum sanctum.

वैष्णवत्व *vaishṇava* + *tva*, n. Faith in Vishṇu, Râjat. 5, 124.

वैसारिण *vaisâriṇa*, i.e. *visârin* + *a*, m. A fish.

वैहायस *vaihâyasa*, i.e. *vihâyas* + *a*, adj. Being in the air, aërial, Pâraskara, Gr. S. ii. 2 in Journ. of the German Oriental Society, vii. 533, 23; suspended in the air, Johns. Sel. 39, 30.

वैहासिक *vaihâsika*, i.e. *vihâsa* + *ika*, m. A comic actor.

वोटा *voṭâ*, f. A female slave.

वोड्र *voḍra*, I. m. 1. The boa-constrictor. 2. A sort of fish. II. f. *rî*, The fourth part of a *Paṇa*.

वोढृ *voḍhṛi*, i.e. *vah* + *tṛi*, m. 1. A porter, one who carries or draws, Pañch. 8, 16. 2. A charioteer. 3. A bull. 4. A guide, a leader, Lass. 97, 10=Rigv. vi. 64, 3 (ved. *volhâ*, nom. sing.). 5. A bridegroom, Man. 8, 204. —Comp. *Dhûrvoḍhṛi*, i.e. *dhur-*, m. a beast of burthen, Pañch. ed. orn. 4, 7. —Cf. Lat. vector.

वोरुखान *vorukhâna*, m. A horse described as of red and white colour.

वोल्लासक *vollâsaka*, The name of a city, Râjat. 5, 224.

वोल्लाह *vollâha*, m. A horse with light mane and tail.

वोहित्थ *vohittha*, n. A vessel, a ship.

वौषट् *vaushaṭ* (=*vashaṭ*, q. cf.; *vashaṭ* has first become *voshaṭ* by the influence of the *v*, as in *voḍhṛi*, from *vah*, and then, as in Zend., *vaoshaṭ* =*vaushaṭ*).

व्यंसक *vyaṁsaka*, i.e. *vi-aṁs+aka*, m. A cheat, a rogue, a juggler.

व्यक्ति *vyakti*, i.e. *vi-añj+ti*, f. **1.** Distinctness, Çâk. d. 167. **2.** Individuality. **3.** An individual (opp. to *jâti*), Siddh. Mukt. 82, 10. **4.** Appearance, manifestation, Bhag. 7, 23; 10, 14; Megh. 12.—**Comp.** *A-sakala-*, adj. not being visible completely, Megh. 82.

व्यग्र *vyagra*, i.e. *vi-agra*, adj., f. *râ*, **1.** Bewildered, Hit. iii. d. 108 (*bhojana-*, by the care for provisions). **2.** Distracted. **3.** Agitated, Pañch. 200, 8. **4.** Engaged in, Vikr. 77, 4; occupied, Pañch. 121, 14; zealously occupied, Pañch. iii. d. 236; zealous, eager, Râjat. 5, 144.—**Comp.** *A-*, adj. 1. not distracted, Utt. Râmach. 52, 13; careful, Chr. 16, 19. 2. not disturbed, Lass. 2. ed. 39, 9; peaceable, Nal. 26, 20. 3. cool, deliberate, Draup. 9, 1; *ram*, adv. reckless, Mâlat. 78, 18.

व्यग्रता *vyagra+tâ*, f. Zealous occupation, Pañch. 252, 24.

व्यग्रत्व *vyagra+tva*, n. Perplexedness, confusion, Pañch. iii. d. 128.

व्यङ्ग *vyaṅga*, i.e. *vi-aṅga*, **I.** adj. **1.** Deformed, mutilated, MBh. 1, 1089. **2.** Lamed. **3.** Bodiless. **4.** Ill-arranged. **II.** m. **1.** A cripple. **2.** A frog. **3.** Discoloration of the face, dark spots on the cheek.—**Comp.** *A-*, adj. having no defect, Man. 3, 10; sound, Pañch. 184, 23.

व्यङ्गता *vyaṅga+tâ*, f. Mutilation, Pañch. i. d. 217.

व्यङ्गय *VYAṄGAYA*, a denomin. derived from *vyaṅga*, Par. To mutilate, Pañch. 38, 13; 40, 25.

व्यङ्गार *vyaṅgâra*, i.e. *vi-aṅgâra*, adj. Without charcoal. n. loc. *re*, At the time when the burning charcoal is extinguished, Man. 6, 56.

व्यच् *VYACH* (i.e. *vi-añch*), i. 6, *vicha*, Par. **1.** To surround, to encompass (ved.). **2.** † To deceive.

व्यज *vyaja*, i.e. *vi-aj+a*, m. A fan, Böhtl. Ind. Spr. 3322.

व्यजन *vyajana*, i.e. *vi-aj+ana*, n. A fan, Hit. ii. d. 155; Bhâg. P. 3, 23, 16. —**Comp.** *Bâla-*, n. a fly-flapper used as an emblem of princely rank (made of the bushy tail of the Bos grunniens), Johns. Sel. 21, 102.

व्यञ्जक *vyañjaka*, i.e. *vi-añj+aka*, **I.** adj. Clearly showing, Man. 2, 68. **II.** m. **1.** A mark. **2.** External indication of passion or feeling. **3.** Feeling, Mâlat. 154, 6.

व्यञ्जन *vyañjana*, i.e. *vi-añj+ana*, **I.** n. **1.** A mark, a sign, Hit. iii. d. 36; the marks of puberty (hairs of the body), Pañch. iii. d. 214 (pl.). **2.** Paraphernalia, insignia. **3.** A beard, Brâhmaṇav. 1, 28. **4.** A privy part, either male or female. **5.** Sauce, Râm. 1, 13, 15; condiment, Pañch. 52, 1. **6.** A consonant, Sâv. 5, 25. **II.** n., and f. *nâ*, Irony, sarcasm. **III.** f. *nâ*, The third power of a word, suggestion, Sâh. Darp. 16, 20.—**Comp.** *A-*, adj. *nâ*, without the marks of puberty, Pañch. iii. d. 213. *A-jâta-* (vb. *jan*), adj. beardless, Râm. 3, 42, 33. *Nis-*, adj. without condiment, MBh. 12, 3189. loc. *ne*, downrightly, Pañch. 218, 8.

व्यतिकर *vyatikara*, i.e. *vi-ati-kṛi+a*, **I.** adj. **1.** Reciprocal, or acting one with another. **2.** Pervading. **3.** Contiguous to. **II.** m. **1.** Reciprocity, exchange, Daçak. in Chr. 184, 16; interchange, Mâlat. 34, 11; reciprocal action, ib. 199, 16; relation, alternation, Utt. Râmach, 125, 11. **2.** Action in general, Pańch. 30, 8; 237, 22; 1 ... 3. Contact, Böhtl. Ind. Spr. 429; contiguity. 4. Opportunity, Pańch. 40, 18. 5. Mixture, Megh. 15; union, Utt. Râmach. 84, 2 (at the end of a comp. adj. 'united'); conflux, Ragh. 8, 94. 6. Misfortune, calamity, Pańch. 42, 5.—Comp. *Dṛishṭa-*, adj. one whose misfortune is evident, Hit. 110, 6. *Vârtâ-*, m. a report's going from one to another, i.e. a report going from one to another, Pańch. 130, 8.

व्यतिकरित *vyatikarita*, i.e. *vyatikara + ita*, adj. Pervaded, Mâlat. 40, 1.

व्यतिक्रम *vyatikrama*, i.e. *vi-ati-kram + a*, m. 1. Inverted or retrograde order, reverse, Kir. 11, 76. 2. Contrariety. 3. Misfortune. 4. Passing over or beyond, transgression, Man. 8, 244; Pańch. 46, 20. 5. Fault, Man. 8, 229; sin, Râm. 1, 8, 12. 6. Non-performance (as of contracts), 8, 5.

व्यतिरेक *vyatireka*, i.e. *vi-ati-rich + a*, m. 1. Separateness. 2. Negative inference, Bhâshâp. 141. 3. Interception, Mâlat. 140, 20. 4. Difference. 5. Dissimilitude of things compared in some respects to each other. 6. Exclusion, exception.

व्यतिलङ्घिन् *vyatilańghin*, i.e. *vi-ati-lańgh + a + in*, adj. Removed, Ragh. 6, 19.

व्यतिषङ्ग *vyatishańga*, i.e. *vi-ati-sańj + a*, m. 1. Mutual or reciprocal junction. 2. Fastening, tying together.

व्यतिहार and **व्यतीहार** *vyatîhâra*, i.e. *vi-ati-hṛi + a*, m. 1. Barter, exchange. 2. Exchange of blows or abuse.

व्यतीपात *vyatîpâta*, i.e. *vi-ati-pat + a*, m. 1. Disrespect. 2. A portent indicating calamity. 3. Great calamity. 4. Day of new moon, falling on a Sunday, and the moon being in certain mansions. 5. The seventeenth of the astrological Yogas.

व्यतीहार *vyatihâra*, see *vyatihâra*.

व्यत्यय *vyatyaya*, i.e. *vi-ati-i + a*, m. 1. Inverted or retrograde order. 2. Contrariety, reverse. 3. Interchange, Pâṇ. iii. 1, 85.

व्यत्यास *vyatyâsa*, i.e. *vi-ati-2. as + a*, m. 1. Inverted or retrograde order. 2. Reversed position. 3. Contrariety, reverse.

व्यथ् *VYATH*, i. 1, Âtm. (in epic poetry also Par., MBh. 4, 1453), 1. To tremble, MBh. 8, 4693. 2. To be disquieted or afflicted, MBh. 2, 1801. 3. To fear, MBh. 3, 717. 4. To suffer pain, ib. 8, 2675. 5. To dry (Sch.), Man. 7, 84. Ptcple. of the pf. pass. *vyathita*. 1. Alarmed, frightened, Râm. 3, 53, 61. 2. Afflicted, Ṛit. 6, 18. 3. Disturbed, Kir. 5, 11; Daçak. in Chr. 193, 1 (changed). 4. Pained, Pańch. 69, 2. Caus. 1. To make uneasy, Bhag. 2, 15; to afflict, Pańch. ii. d. 103. 2. To frighten, MBh. 3, 16418. 3. To lead away from, Bhaṭṭ. 10, 36.—With the prep. प्र *pra*, 1. To be afflicted, Râm. 2, 18, 41. 2. To be frightened, Bhag. 11, 20; to fear (or to tremble), with gen., MBh. 5, 4564. *pravyathita*, Very anxious, Daçak. in Chr. 194, 7.—With संप्र *sampra*, *sampravyathita*, Frightened, Râm. 1, 38, 16.—Cf. Goth. vithon, To shake; probably *ὄθη*, *ὄθομαι*, *ὠθέω*, *ἐνοσί-χθων*, *ἔνοσις*.

व्यथक *vyath + aka*, adj. 1. Inflicting pain. 2. Distressing, afflicting, Kir. 2, 4.

व्यथा *vyath + â*, f. 1. Alarm, fear, Utt. Râmach. 9, 6. 2. Distress, Pańch. 215, 19. 3. Pain, Pańch. iv. d. 19;

disease, Pańch. v. d. 66.—**Comp.** *A-vyatha*, adj. without pain, Daçak. in Chr. 186, 13. *Guru-*, adj. afflicted by heavy pains, Vikr. d. 50. *Nirvyatha*, i.e. *nis-*, adj. 1. quiet, MBh. 3, 13065. 2. free from pain, Râjat. 5, 61. *Sa-*, adj. 1. suffering pain, with distress, Hit. 113, 13. 2. sorrowful, Çiç. 9, 83.

व्यध् *VYADH*, i. 4, *vidhya*, Par. **1.** To pierce, Chr. 292, 9=Rigv. i. 86, 9 (ved. *vidhyatâ*, with lengthened final). **2.** To hit, Johns. Sel. 39, 31 (*veddhâ*, anomal. first fut.). **3.** To wave in triumph, Johns. Sel. 52, 115 (anomal. red. pf. *vivyadhus*). **4.** To pick, Pańch. 62, 9; to wound, Man. 8, 12. Ptcple. of the pf. pass. *viddha*. **1.** Wounded, Chr. 31, 16. **2.** Thrown, Man. 9, 43. **3.** Beaten, whipped. **4.** Opposed, impeded. **5.** Resembling, like. n. A wound, Böhtl. Ind. Spr. 2647. **Comp.** *Su-*, adj. deeply wounded, Ṛit. 6, 28. Anomal. infin. *veddhum* (from *vidh*, for *vyadh*, based on *vidhya*), MBh. 1, 5286.—With the prep. **अति** *ati*, *atividdha*, Pierced, transfixed, Râm. 2, 9, 51.—With **अनु** *anu*, To throw after (another), Man. 9, 43. *anuviddha*, **1.** Wounded, Ṛit. 1, 13. **2.** Obstructed, Çâk. d. 19; checked. **3.** Mixed, Mâlat. 15, 13. **4.** Ornamented, Megh. 66; variegated. **5.** Set (as a jewel). **6.** Full of, abounding.—With **अप** *apa*, **1.** To throw away, MBh. 3, 15686. **2.** To omit, to neglect, Man. 11, 4. *apaviddha*, **1.** Thrown away, Daçak. in Chr. 193, 21. **2.** Discarded, Kir. 5, 30 (by churning). **3.** (viz. *putra*, A son), who having been disowned by his parents, is adopted by another, Man. 9, 159. **4.** Contemptible. **5.** Disabled, broken, literally and figuratively.—With **व्यप** *vi-apa*, *vyapaviddha*, Rejected, MBh. 3, 15763.—With **आ** *â*, To throw, MBh. 3, 11511. *âviddha*, **1.** Thrown, Man. 9, 43. **2.** Pierced, wounded. **3.** Crooked, Vikr. d. 115. **4.** Disappointed. **5.** Stupid. **Comp.** *An-*, adj. 1. not bored, Çâk. d. 43. 2. unhurt, Suçr. 2, 32, 20.—With **व्या** *vi-â*, To vibrate, MBh. 3, 677. *vyâviddha*, Dishevelled, Daçak. in Chr. 199, 1.—With **समा** *sam-â*, To vibrate, Ragh. 26, 78 (Calc.).—With **उद्** *ud*, *udviddha*, Lofty, Lass. 2. ed. 72, 5.—With **निस्** *nis*, *nirviddha*, Wounded, Râm. 3, 50, 19.—With **परि** *pari*, To wound, MBh. 1, 4102.—With **प्र** *pra*, To throw away, Râm. 2, 63, 34.—With **विप्र** *vi-pra*, To strike, Ragh. 14, 54.—With **प्रति** *prati*, To wound, MBh. 3, 11960.—Cf. perhaps Ϝεθ in ἄεθλος.

व्यध्व *vyadhva*, i.e. *vi-adhvan*, m. A bad road.

व्यध *vyadh* + *a*, I. m. **1.** Piercing, Kâvya Pr. 100, 9. **2.** Striking. **II.** f. *dhâ*, Bleeding, Suçr. 1, 362, 5.

व्यन्तर *vyantara*, i.e. *vi-antara*, m. A deity (haunting in a tree), Pańch. 250, 2.

व्यप् *VYAP*, see *vip*.

व्यपत्रप *vyapatrapa*, i. e. *vi-apa-trapa*, adj. Shameless, Râm. 2, 68, 17, ed. Scramp.

व्यपदेश *vyapadeça*, i.e. *vi-apa-diç* + *a*, m. **1.** Information. **2.** Name, appellation, Bhâshâp. 46. **3.** Race, Çâk. 104, 6. **4.** Renown, Man. 7, 168. **5.** Pretext, Panch. iii. d. 79 (*mahatâm*, Pretending [the authority of] powerful men). **6.** Hint. **7.** Craft. **8.** Stratagem.

व्यपरोपण *vyaparopaṇa*, i.e. *vi-apa-ruh*, Caus., + *ana*, n. **1.** Extirpating, expelling. **2.** Cutting, Ragh. 3, 56.

व्यपाकृति *vyapâkṛiti*, i.e. *vi-apa-â-kṛi+ti*, n. Repelling, denial.

व्यपाय *vyapâya*, i.e. *vi-apa-i+a*, m. End, Ragh. 3, 3.

व्यपाश्रय *vyapâçraya*, i.e. *vi-apa-â-çri+a*, m. **1.** Taking refuge with, Bhag. 18, 56; relying upon. **2.** Expectation.

व्यपेक्षा *vyapekshâ*, i.e. *vi-apa-iksh+a*, f. **1.** Mutual connexion. **2.** Regard, Chr. 43, 24 (corr. thus); expectation.—**Comp.** *Nirvyapeksha*, i.e. *nis-*, adj. indifferent, Ragh. 14, 39. *Sa-*, adj. connected, Utt. Râmach. 146, 7.

व्यभिचार *vyabhichâra*, i.e. *vi-abhi-char+a*, m. **1.** Going astray, erring (literally and figurat.) **2.** The presence of the *hetu* without the *sâdhya*, Bhâshâp. 136. **3.** Following improper courses. **4.** Crime, vice, sin, Hit. iii. d. 16; MBh. 1, 912. **5.** Infidelity of a wife, Man. 10, 164.—**Comp.** *Sa-*, m. a too general middle term (as fire to prove smoke).

व्यभिचारतस् *vyabhichâra + tas*, adv. From the *vyabhichâra*, involved in the other supposition, Bhâshâp. 47.

व्यभिचारिता *vyabhichâritâ*, i.e. *vyabhichârin+tâ*, f. Error, Bhâshâp. 138.

व्यभिचारित्व *vyabhichâritva*, i.e. *vyabhichârin+tva*, n. Doubt.—**Comp.** *Svatva-*, n. doubt or uncertainty of ownership.

व्यभिचारिन् *vyabhichârin*, i.e. *vi-abhi-char* and *vyabhichâra+in*, **I.** adj., f. *iṇî*. **1.** Going astray, wanton, Hit. pr. d. 21, M.M. **2.** Doing what is improper. **II.** f. *iṇî*, A wanton woman, Böhtl. Ind. Spr. 507.—**Comp.** *A-*, adj. never failing, Çâk. 81, 9.

व्यभ्र *vyabhra*, i.e. *vi-abhra*, adj. Cloudless, Nal. 17, 11.

व्यय् *VYAY*, i. 1, Âtm. (a denomin. from *vyaya*), To squander away, Hit. ii. d. 91. Ptcple. of the pf. pass. *vyayita*, **1.** Expended, Hit. 98, 17. **2.** Dissipated, Hit. 60, 10. **3.** Fallen to decay. † i. 10, Par. To throw.

व्यय *vyaya*, i.e. *vi-i+a*, **I.** adj. Mutable, Man. 1, 19. **II.** m. **1.** Disappearance, loss, Lass. 59, 1; Pańch. i. d. 179; Mâlat. 70, 14 (risk). **2.** Destruction, Ragh. 5, 5; Daçak. in Chr. 181, 5 (detriment). **3.** Expenditure, expense, Man. 8, 287; Pańch. 138, 4. **4.** Squandering away, Lass. 75. 13. **5.** Misfortune, decline. — **Comp.** *A-*, adj. 1. immutable, Man. 1, 19. 2. eternal, Johns. Sel. 23, 118; Râjat. 5, 37. *Ati-*, m. spending too much, Hit. ii. d. 90. *Bhojana-*, m. expense for food, Hit. 98, 17. *Su-alpa-*, I. adj. suffering small expenses, Hit. 46, 8. II. m. a very small expense, Hit. iii. d. 130 (read *koshasval°*).

ऽव्ययिन् *-vyayin*, i.e. *vyaya+in*, adj. in *udaya-*, Mounting and falling, Hit. iii. d. 128.

व्यर्थ *vyartha*, i.e. *vi-artha*, adj. **1.** Useless, unprofitable, Pańch. i. d. 445; Hit. i. d. 129, M.M.; Pańch. 134, 14. **2.** Unmeaning.

व्यर्थता *vyartha+tâ*, f. **1.** Uselessness, with *yâ* or *gam*, To become useless, Pańch. 128, 1, 215, 22. **2.** Inoffensiveness, Pańch. 169, 14. **3.** Nonsense.

व्यलीक *vyalika* (cf. *alika*), **I.** adj. **1.** Disagreeable, offensive. **2.** Improper. **3.** Painful. **4.** Strange. **II.** m. A catamite. **III.** n. **1.** Any displeasing or improper act. **2.** Disagreeableness. **3.** Pain, grief, Çâk. d. 183; Pańch. i. d. 272. **4.** Fault, transgression, Çiç. 9, 85; Hit. ii. d. 125. **5.** Cheating, falsehood, Pańch. i. d. 136 (cf. Böhtl. Ind. Spr. 3208).—**Comp.**

Nis-, adj. 1. not offending, Bhâg. P. 1, 7, 49. 2. without pain, pleased, Râm. 2, 18, 53 Gorr; (given) with pleasure, MBh. 13, 5994. 3. *°kam*, adv. sincerely, Bhâg. P. 2, 7, 42; cf. *°ka + tas*, adv. the same, 3, 24, 12.

व्यवक्रोशन *vyavakroçana*, i. e. *vi-ava-kruç + ana*, n. **1.** Altercation. **2.** Abuse.

व्यवच्छेद *vyavachchheda*, i.e. *vi-ava-chhid + a*, m. **1.** Dividing. **2.** A division. **3.** Discrimination. **4.** Distinction, contrast. **5.** Letting fly an arrow, shooting. **6.** Cutting in pieces.

व्यवधा *vyavadhâ*, i.e. *vi-ava-dhâ*, f. **1.** A covering, a screen. **2.** Being covered, disappearance.

व्यवधान *vyavadhâna*, i. e. *vi-ava-dhâ + ana*, n. **1.** Intervening, Ragh. 13, 44. **2.** Separation, Çiç. 9, 51. **3.** Covering, a cover, Çâk. 92, 13 (Prâkṛ.). **4.** Being covered, disappearance.

व्यवधायक *vyavadhâyaka*, i. e. *vi-ava-dhâ + aka*, adj. **1.** Intervening. **2.** Separating. **3.** Screening, hiding.

व्यवधि *vyavadhi*, i.e. *vi-ava-dhâ* (cf. *nidhi*), m. Covering, or a covering.

व्यवसाय *vyavasâya*, i. e. *vi-ava-so + a*, m. **1.** Perseverance, Pańch. iii. d. 264; eagerness. **2.** Exertion, effort, Pańch. 215, 22; energy, Pańch. 134, 10; cf. 138, 7; i. d. 195 (*yeshâṁ vyavasâya-niçchayaḥ*, Who are resolved to endeavour). **3.** Following any business or profession. **4.** Resolve, determination, Brâhmaṇav. 2, 32. **5.** Obstinacy, Böhtl. Ind. Spr. 412. **6.** Plan, device, trick, Hit. ii. d. 113 (or, perseverance). **7.** Boasting.

व्यवसायिन् *vyavasâyin*, i. e. *vyavasâya + in*, adj. **1.** Persevering. **2.** Active, energetic, Hit. ii. d. 11; willing, Pańch. 134, 10; cf. 138, 7; undertaking, resolute, Pańch. i. d. 278. **3.** Engaged in business. **4.** Performing one's duty, Man. 12, 103. — **Comp.** *A-*, adj. not energetic, Hit. ii. d. 3.

व्यवस्था *vyavasthâ*, i.e. *vi-ava-sthâ*, f. **1.** Separating, placing remote or apart. **2.** Placing. **3.** Staying. **4.** State, course, Râjat. 5, 80. **5.** A decree, a written declaration of the law, decision, Râjat. 5, 461. **6.** An engagement, a contract.—**Comp.** *A-vyavastha*, adj. undecided, Ragh. 7, 51.

व्यवस्थापक *vyavasthâpaka*, i.e. *vi-ava-sthâ*, Caus., *+ aka*, adj. Deciding, Râjat. 6, 54 (*dus-*, adj. Deciding wrongly).

व्यवस्थापन *vyavasthâpana*, i.e. *vi-ava-sthâ*, Caus., *+ ana*, n. **1.** Placing apart. **2.** Placing. **3.** Fixing. **4.** Appointing. **5.** Deciding. **6.** Declaring.

व्यवस्थिति *vyavasthiti*, i. e. *vi-ava-sthâ + ti*, f. **1.** Constancy, perseverance, Bhag. 16, 1. **2.** Determining. **3.** Rule, Man. 10, 70. **4.** Extracting.

व्यवहर्तृ *vyavahartṛi*, i.e. *vi-ava-hṛi + tṛi*, I. m., f. *trî*, and n. **1.** Transacting business, engaged in affairs. **2.** Observing established usages. **II.** m. **1.** A judge. **2.** A litigant, a plaintiff. **3.** Partaker, associate.

व्यवहार *vyavahâra*, i.e. *vi-ava-hṛi + a*, m. **1.** Doing, performing, Bhâshâp. 105 (*gaṇana-*, Numbering); Lass. 76, 9; occupation, Çâk. 104, 23; action, Mâlat. 70, 6. **2.** Affair, Utt. Râmach. 127, 3 (*nâsya vyavahâro streshu*, He has nothing with weapons); Man. 8, 420. **3.** Profession, business, Pańch. i. d. 91. **4.** Pecuniary transaction, Man. 3, 64; usury, Pańch. i. d. 12. **5.** Petty traffic, Man. 7, 137; trade, Pańch. 7, 17. **6.** Usage, custom, Hit. 58, 18. **7.**

Conduct, Hit. i. d. 57; 70, M.M. **8.** Practice of the courts, or civil and criminal law, Man. 8, 148; judicial proceeding, Man. 8, 1. **9.** Administration of justice, Journ. of the German Oriental Society, vii. 528. **10.** Any acts cognisable in courts. **11.** An occurrence which must be inquired, an important affair, Pańch. 45, 13. **12.** Lawsuit, Pańch. 165, 4. **13.** A contract.—Comp. *Yathâ-vyavahâra + m*, adv. conformably to custom, Hit. 87, 15.

व्यवहारक *vyavahâraka* i.e. *vi-ava-hṛi + aka*, I. m. A trader, Pańch. 138, 15. II. f. *rikâ*. **1.** Usage. **2.** A brush.

व्यवहारज्ञ *vyavahâra-jńa*, m. A young man of age.

व्यवहारवन्त् *vyavahâra + vant*, adj. Occupied, working with, Man. 10, 37.

व्यवहारिक *vyavahârika*, i.e. *vyavahâra + ika*, adj. **1.** Customary. **2.** Relating to legal process. **3.** Litigant.

व्यवाय *vyavâya*, i.e. *vi-ava-i + a*, I. m. **1.** Copulation, Râjat. 5, 280. **2.** Intervening, interval. **3.** Covering, disappearance. II. n. Light, lustre.

व्यवायिन् *vyavâyin*, i.e. *vyavâya + in*, adj. sbst. Lecherous, a lecher.

व्यश्व *vyaçva*, i.e. *vi-açva*, adj. Having no horse, Chr. 297, 15 = Rigv. i. 112, 15.

व्यष्टि *vyashṭi*, i.e. *vi-aksh + ti*, f. Singleness, individuality, Vedântas. in Chr. 204, 13.

व्यसन *vyasana*, i.e. *vi-as + ana*, n. **1.** Calamity, misfortune, Vikr. 59, 1; Pańch. ii. d. 13; destruction, Mâlat. 154, 13; loss, Kir. 13, 15. **2.** Fate. **3.** Ill luck. **4.** Fruitless effort, Bhartṛ. 2, 96 (pl.). **5.** Inability, incompetence (see the next). **6.** Fault, vice, Man. 7, 45; Hit. pr. d. 48, M.M.; crime. **7.** Sin, Çâk. d. 38. **8.** Intent application or attachment to an object, Pańch. i. d. 314; diligence, Hit. i. d. 31, M.M. **9.** Individuality.—Comp. *Âyudha-*, n. destruction of weapons, Man. 7, 93. *Nau-*, n. shipwreck, Çâk. 90, 19. *Bala-*, n. defeat or rout of an army, Hit. iv. d. 32. *Mûla-*, n. execution for a crime (Sch.), Man. 10, 38.

व्यसनिता *vyasanitâ*, f., and **व्यसनित्व** *vyasanitva*, n., i.e. *vyasanin + tâ*, or *tva*, **1.** Wickedness, Râjat. 5, 255 (*tva*); Hit. 94, 3 (*tâ*, instr. Wrongly). **2.** Calamity.

व्यसनिन् *vyasanin*, i.e. *vyasana + in*, adj. **1.** Wicked, Pańch. v. d. 17; vicious, Man. 7, 53; Pańch. 163, 14; ruled by passions, Kathâs. 26, 199. **2.** Unfortunate, Böhtl. Ind. Spr. 814; being in distress, Hit. iii. d. 34; afflicted, Hit. iv. d. 44 (*durbhiksha-*, by the calamity of famine). **3.** Intent on, Bhartṛ. 2, 100. **4.** Occupied, Pańch. 192, 3.—Comp. *A-*, adj. not attached to wicked inclinations, Hit. iii. d. 16. *Mânotseka-parâkrama-*, i.e. *mâna-utseka-parâkrama-vyasana + in*, adj. endowed with pride, loftiness, prowess, and intent application, Pańch. iii. d. 264. *Sûta-*, i.e. *sûtavyasana + in*, adj. being distressed by the incompetence of the charioteer, Chr. 35, 7.

व्यसु *vyasu*, i.e. *vi-asu*, adj. Lifeless, Râjat. 5, 241.

व्याकरण *vyâkaraṇa*, i.e. *vi-â-kṛi + ana*, n. **1.** Explaining. **2.** Grammar, Pańch. 4, 14; ii. d. 34.—Comp. *Garbha-*, n. the development of the embryo, Suçr. 1, 325, 19. *Garbhiṇî-*, n. the development of pregnancy, Suçr. 1, 366, 16.

व्याकुल *vyâkula*, i.e. *vi-âkula*, adj. **1.** Confounded, bewildered, Pańch. 9, 13; 144, 4; Hit. iii. d. 110. **2.** Trembling, Utt. Râmach. 83, 5. **3.** Dimmed, Chr. 17, 25. **4.** Occupied, Megh. 83.

व्याकुलता *vyâkula* + *tâ*, f., and

व्याकुलत्व *vyâkula* + *tva*, n. Perplexity, Pańch. 143, 4 (*tâ*); agitation, 58, 3 (*tâ*); fear, ib. 76, 12 (*tva*).—**Comp.** *Nirvyâkulatâ*, see s. v.

व्याकुलय *VYÂKULAYA*, a denomin. derived from *vyâkula*, Par. To frighten, Pańch. 89, 14. Ptcple. of the pf. pass. *vyâkulita* (or *vyâkula* + *ita*), Agitated, alarmed, Pańch. 222, 8; perplexed, Pańch. 142, 14.

व्याकृति *vyâkṛiti*, i.e. *vi-â-kṛi* + *ti*, f. **1.** Explaining. **2.** Grammar. **3.** Change of form, development, Suçr. 1, 9, 10.

व्याकोश *vyâkoça*, and **व्याकोष** *vyâkosha*, i.e. *vi-â-koça*, adj. Budded.

व्याक्षेप *vyâkshepa*, i.e. *vi-â-kship* + *a*, m. Delay; in *a-*, m. Absence of delay, Ragh. 10, 6.

व्याख्या *vyâkhyâ*, i.e. *vi-â-khyâ*, f. Exposition, comment.

व्याख्यातृ *vyâkhyâtṛi*, i.e. *vi-â-khyâ* + *tṛi*, m. An expounder, Râjat. 5, 29.

व्याख्यान *vyâkhyâna*, i.e. *vi-â-khyâ* + *ana*, n. Explaining.

व्याघट्टन *vyaghaṭṭana*, i.e. *vi-â-ghaṭṭ* + *ana*, n. **1.** Rubbing. **2.** Churning.

व्याघात *vyâghâta*, i.e. *vi-â-han*, Caus., + *a*, m. **1.** Obstacle, Hit. ii. d. 4. **2.** Striking. **3.** Wounding, Indr. 5, 11. **4.** Destroying. **5.** The thirteenth of the astronomical Yogas.

व्याघ्र *vyâghra*, i.e. *vi-â-ghrâ*, **I.** m. **1.** A tiger, Pańch. 157, 25. **2.** As latter part of comp. words, Best, preeminent, e.g. *purusha-*, m. An eminent man (literally, A tiger-like man), Râm. 3, 53, 19. **II.** f. *ghrî*, The female of a tiger, Bhartṛ. 3, 39.—**Comp.** *Nis-*, adj. tigerless, Pańch. 231, 17.

व्याज *vyâja*, i.e. *vi-ańj* + *a*, m. **1.** Deceit, fraud, Böhtl. Ind. Spr. 396; Pańch. 147, 15. **2.** Disguise either of purpose or person. **3.** Appearance, Pańch. iii. d. 125; pretence, Daçak. in Chr. 186, 2. **4.** Means, Pańch. 75, 24; 118, 3. **5.** Wickedness.—**Comp.** *Nis-*, adj. upright, honest, Kathâs. 22, 146. °*jam*, adv. 1. honestly, Amar. 79. 2. exactly, Râjat. 4, 343. *Sa-vyâja*, adj. 1. cunning, pretending. 2. fraudulent. °*jam*, adv. cunningly, under a pretext, Çâk. 18, 21; Vikr. 12, 18.

व्याड *vyâḍa*, m. **1.** A snake. **2.** A beast of prey. **3.** A rogue. **4.** Indra (cf. *vyâla*).

व्याडि *vyâḍi*, m. The name of a grammarian, Kathâs. 4, 108.

व्यादान *vyâdâna*, i.e. *vi-â-dâ* + *ana*, n. Opening, setting ajar, Hit. 85, 8.

व्यादित *vyâdita*, see *dâ* with *vi-â*.

व्यादीर्घ *vyâdîrgha*, i.e. *vi-â-dîrgha*, adj. Long, Bhartṛ. 1, 86.

व्याध *vyâdha*, i.e. *vyadh* + *a*, m. **1.** A hunter, Pańch. 147, 11. **2.** A low or wicked man. — **Comp.** *Dharma-*, m. the pious hunter, epithet of a Brâhmaṇa re-born as hunter in consequence of a curse, MBh. 3, 13710. *Mṛiga-*, m. a hunter, Râjat. 5, 196.

व्याधाम *vyâdhâma*, i.e. *vi-â-dhmâ* + *a* (from *dham*), m. Indra's thunderbolt.

व्याधाय *VYÂDHÂYA*, a denomin. derived from *vyâdha* with *ya*, Âtm. To become a hunter, Çriṅgârat. 13.

व्याधि *vyâdhi,* i. e. *vyadh* + *i,* m. **1.** Pain, Mâlat. 69, 5. **2.** Sickness, Hit. i. d. 3, M.M.—**Comp.** *Nis-*, adj. healthy, MBh. 9, 2322.

व्याधित *vyâdhita,* i.e. *vyâdhi* + *ita,* adj. Afflicted with disease, Man. 4, 157; 8, 395; sick, Hit. i. d. 201, M M.

व्याधिन् *vyâdhin,* i.e. *vyâdha* + *in,* adj. Frequented by hunters, Nalod. 3, 35.

व्यान *vyâna,* i.e. *vi-an* + *a,* m. One of the five vital airs, that which is diffused throughout the body, Vedântas. in Chr. 207, 11.

व्यापक *vyâpaka,* i.e. *vi-âp* + *aka,* I. adj. **1.** Diffusive. **2.** Extensive. II. m. A pervading attribute, one always found where some other is found, Bhâshâp. 137.

व्यापकत्व *vyâpaka* + *tva,* n. **1.** Diffusion, pervadence. **2.** State of being more extensive, Bhâshâp. 9, cf. 142.

व्यापत्ति *vyâpatti,* i.e. *vi-â-pad* + *ti,* f. Ruin, Pańch. i. d. 316.

व्यापद् *vyâpad,* i.e. *vi-â-pad,* f. **1.** Calamity, Hit. 95, 1, M.M. (at the end of a comp. adj. *tyakta-*, vb. *tyaj,* Free from calamity). **2.** Derangement. **3.** Disease. **4.** Death, Megh. 111.—**Comp.** *Viraha-*, adj. (dying), vanishing by separation, Megh. 111.

व्यापाद *vyâpâda,* i.e. *vi-â-pad* + *a,* m. The wish or project to injure another person.

व्यापादन *vyâpâdana,* i.e. *vi-â-pad,* Caus., + *ana,* n. **1.** Killing, Pańch. 265, 16 (*sarpa-*, Being killed by the snake). **2.** Wishing to injure another person.

व्यापादनीयता *vyâpâdanîya* + *tâ* (vb. *pad*), f. Necessity of being killed, Pańch. 143, 25.

व्यापार *vyâpâra,* i.e. *vi-â-* 2. *pṛi* + *a,* m. **1.** Occupation, Vedântas. in Chr. 202, 18; doing, Pańch. 162, 8; business, 262, 7; Vikr. d. 58 (*vyâpâraṁ vrajasi çarîre,* You have to do with my body, i.e. you command over my body). **2.** Work, Çâk. d. 26; Bhâshâp. 58; 79. **3.** Affair, Pańch. 57, 8. **4.** Trade (cf. *vraj*), profession. **5.** Exercise, practice, exertion, Hit. pr. d. 43, M.M.; activity, Mâlat. 10, 11.—**Comp.** *A-* and *Mithyâ-*, m. occupation with things in which one is not concerned, Pańch. 9, 24 (*mithyâ-*), and i. d. 26 (*a-*). *Kim-*, adj. with what occupied, Çâk. Chezy, 150, 8. *Dṛigvyâpâra,* i.e. *dṛiç-*, m. play of the eyes, Râjat. 5, 366 (pl.). *Nis-*, I. m. absence of occupation, Utt. Râmach. 148, 13. II. adj. not occupied, Ragh. 15, 56. *Vâgvy°,* i.e. *vâch-*, m. conversation, Hit. 85, 21.

व्यापित्व *vyâpitva,* i.e. *vyâpin* + *tva,* n. The state of pervading, Vedântas. in Chr. 205, 3.

व्यापिन् *vyâpin,* i.e. *vi âp* + *in,* I. adj. **1.** Diffusive. **2.** Comprehensive. **3.** Pervading, Bhâshâp. 42. **4.** Filling, Kir. 5, 18. **5.** Extending to, Çâk. d. 170. II. m. The pervading property or power.

व्याप्ति *vyâpti,* i.e. *vi-âp* + *ti,* f. **1.** Pervading, Vedântas. in Chr. 215, 18. **2.** Universal permeation, omnipresence. **3.** Inherence, the inherent and essential presence of any thing or property in another, as heat in fire, oil in the sesamum seed. **4.** The relation of a subject (*vyâpta, vyâpya*) to a predicate (*vyâpaka*) in an universal proposition, Bhâshâp. 65; 67; 68; 136.

व्याप्तिमन्त् *vyâpti* + *mant,* adj., f.

mati, 1. Pervading, diffusive. 2. Pervaded, attended by, Man. 12, 26.

व्याप्यत्व *vyâpya+tva* (vb. *âp* with *vi*), n. 1. Capacity of being pervaded, or of obtaining, Vedântas. in Chr. 215, 15. 2. State of being less extensive, Bhâshâp. 9.

व्याम *vyâma*, i.e. *vi-yam+a*, m. 1. A fathom, or the space between the tips of the fingers of either hand when the arms are extended, Daçak. in Chr. 197, 17; MBh. 3, 10207. 2. Smoke.

व्यामर्ष *vyâmarsha*, i.e. *vi-â-mṛish +a*, m. 1. Erasure (vb. *mṛiç*?). 2. Impatience.

व्यामिश्र *vyâmiçra*, i.e. *vi-â-miçra* q. cf.), adj. Mixed, blended, confounded, Bhag. 3, 2.

व्यामोह *vyâmoha*, i.e. *vi-â-muh+a*, m. Error, foolishness, Prab. 76, 9.

व्यायतत्व *vyâyatatva*, i.e. *vi-â-yata* (vb. *yam*), *+tva*, n. Firmness, Çâk. d. 37.

व्यायाम *vyâyâma*, i.e. *vi-â-yam+a*, m. 1. Athletic exercise. 2. Exertion, fighting, Arj. 3, 40. 3. Manhood, manliness, MBh. 13, 542. 4. Occupation, business. 5. A difficulty. 6. Fatigue, labour, Sâv. 5, 2. 7. A fathom (see *vyâma*).

व्यायामिन् *vyâyâmin*, i.e. *vyâyâma+in*, adj. 1. Athletic. 2. Active. 3. Undergoing fatigue.

व्याल *vyâla*, I. adj. 1. Wicked, Kir. 17, 25. 2. Cruel. II. m. 1. A snake, Hit. iii. d. 30. 2. A beast of prey, Pañch. i. d. 420. 3. A vicious elephant, Bhartṛ. 2, 6. 4. A rogue. 5. A king. III. f. *lî*, A female snake, Chr. 22, 22.

व्यालग्राहिन् *vyâla-grâhin*, m. A serpent-catcher, Hit. iii. d. 30.

व्यालोल *vyâlola*, i.e. *vi-â-lul+a*, adj. Tremulous, shaking, Râjat. 5, 372. Cf. the next.

व्यालोलकुन्तलकलापवन्त् *vyâlola-kuntala-kalâpa+vant*, adj., f. *vati*, With dishevelled hair, Chaur. 7.

व्यावक्रोशी *vyâvakroçî*, i.e. *vi-â-ava -kruç+a+î*, f. Mutual imprecation.

व्यावभाषी *vyâvabhâshî*, i.e. *vi-â -ava-bhâsh+a+î*, f. Mutual abuse or imprecation.

व्यावर्त *vyâvarta*, i.e. *vi-â-vṛit+a*, m. 1. Going round, revolving. 2. Encompassing. 3. Choosing, appointing.

व्यावर्तकता *vyâvartakatâ*, i.e. *vi-â -vṛit+aka+tâ*, f. Excluding, Vedântas. in Chr. 213, 18.

व्यावर्तन *vyâvartana*, i.e. *vi-â-vṛit +ana*, n. 1. Rolling round. 2. A volute, Kir. 5, 30. 3. A band. 4. Encompassing.

व्यावहारिक *vyâvahârika*, i.e. *vyavahâra+ika*, I. adj. 1. Active, Vedântas. in Chr. 207, 6. 2. Usual, customary. 3. Judicial, relating to trials, Man. 8, 78. II. m. A counsellor, Râm. 2, 51, 13, ed. Seramp. (thus to be read). III. n. Use, Man. 8, 164.

व्यावृति *vyâvṛiti*, i.e. *vi-â-vṛi+ti*, f. 1. Covering, screening. 2. Exclusion, exception (? see the next).

व्यावृत्ति *vyâvṛitti*, i.e. *vi-â-vṛit+ti*, f. 1. Rolling back. 2. Surrounding, screening. 3. Rejection, exclusion, exception, Kumâras. 2, 27. 4. Choice. 5. Praise.

व्यास *vyâsa*, i.e. *vi-* 2. *as+a*, m. 1. Extension, diffusion. 2. Distinction, detail. 3. A sage, the supposed compiler of the Vedas and Purâṇas, Lass. 49, 2; Chr. 45, 17.

व्यासङ्ग *vyâsanga*, i.e. *vi-â-sanj + a*, m. **1.** Addition. **2.** Attachment, Bhartṛ. 1, 66; sitting on, Mâlat. 153, 4. **3.** Separation, detachment. **4.** Perplexity, confusion, Lass. 2. ed. 67, 22.

व्याहार *vyâhâra*, i.e. *vi-â-hṛi + a*, m. **1.** Voice, a word, speech, Utt. Râmach. 104, 5. **2.** Humorous speech, jest.

व्याहृति *vyâhṛiti*, i.e. *vi-â-hṛi + ti*, f. **1.** Voice, speech. **2.** A word. **3.** A mystical word, as *Om*, *Svar*, Man. 2, 78.

व्युच्छेत्तृ *vyuchchhettṛi*, i.e. *vi-ud-chhid + tṛi*, m., f. *trî*, and n. Who or what destroys.—Comp. *A-*, m. a protector, MBh. 12, 2901.

व्युति *vyuti*, i.e. *vi-ve + ti*, f. **1.** Weaving. **2.** Sewing.

व्युत्क्रम *vyutkrama*, i.e. *vi-ud-kram + a*, Inverted order, Vedântas. in Chr. 212, 7.

व्युत्थान *vyutthâna*, i.e. *vi-ud-sthâ + ana*, n. **1.** Completion of religious meditation, Vedântas. in Chr. 218, 16. **2.** Independence. **3.** Obstruction, hindering. **4.** Opposition, doing that which is prohibited.

व्युत्पत्ति *vyutpatti*, i.e. *vi-ud-pad + ti*, f. **1.** Conversancy with literature or science. **2.** Etymology.

व्युदास *vyudâsa*, i.e. *vi-ud- 2.as + a*, m. **1.** Throwing away, Nalod. 4, 14 (loss). **2.** Indifference to, disregard for.

व्युपदेश *vyupadeça*, i.e. *vi-upa-diç + a*, m. Pretext.

व्युपरम *vyuparama*, i.e. *vi-upa-ram + a*, m. Cessation, Utt. Râmach. 159, 6.

व्युपशम *vyupaçama*, i.e. *vi-upaçama*, m. Not ceasing (at the end of a comp. adj.), Mâlat. 86, 17.

† 1. व्युष् *VYUSH*, or प्युष् *PYUSH*, i. 4, Par. To burn (cf. *ush*).

† 2. व्युष् *VYUSH*, or प्युष् *PYUSH*, प्युस् *PYUS*, पुष् *PUSH*, ब्युस् *BYUS*, or बुस् *BUS*, i. 4, Par. To divide.

† 3. व्युष् *VYUSH*, or प्युष् *PYUSH*, पुस् *PUS*, i. 10, Par. To reject.

व्युष्ट *vyushṭa*, i.e. the ptcple. of the pf. pass. of *vi- 2.vas*, **I.** Dawned. **II.** n. **1.** Dawn. **2.** Day. **3.** Fruit.

व्युष्टि *vyushṭi*, i.e. *vi- 2.vas + ti*, f. **1.** Dawn, Chr. 287, 6 = Rigv. i. 48, 6. **2.** Fruit, consequence. **3.** Increase. **4.** Praise, Brâhmaṇav. 2, 22.

व्यूह *vyûha*, i.e. *vi-ûh + a*, m. **1.** Military array, Man. 7, 187. **2.** An army, Ragh. 7, 51; squadron, Man. 7, 188. **3.** A flock, a multitude, Nal. 12. 30. **4.** Logic. **5.** Making. **6.** The body.—Comp. *Garbha-*, m. a kind of array, MBh. 6, 3850; 3851. *Chakra-*, m. the array in a circle, ib. 7, 1441. *Daṇḍa-*, m. the array in line, Man. 7, 187. *Maṇḍala-*, m. the array in a circle, cf. Pañch. 9, 14.

व्यूहन *vyûhana*, i.e. *vi-ûh + ana*, n. **1.** Arraying. **2.** Structure of the body.

व्ये *VYE* (i.e. *vi-i*), i. 1, Par. Âtm. To cover. Ptcple. pf. pass. *vîta*, placed, bound, Vikr. d. 157.—With the prep. आ *â*, *ârîta*, Enveloped, Bhâg. P. 3, 31, 4.—With उप *upa*, *upavîta*, n. The cord worn by the three first classes of the Hindus over the left and under the right shoulder, Man. 2, 44. **Comp.** *Yajña-*, n. the sacrificial cord.—With नि *ni*, *nivîta*, n. The brahmanical thread suspended round the neck, in which manner it is worn on some occasions.—With परि *pari*, *parivîta*, **1.** Surrounded, Kir. 5, 42; invested. **2.** Covered, clothed, Ragh. 15, 77 (Calc.). **3.** Overspread, pervaded. n. The bow of Brahman. —With सम् *sam*, *saṁvîta*, **1.** Surrounded. **2.** Covered, Râm. 3, 50, 12. **3.** Clothed, Râm. 3, 52, 9. **4.** Adorned, Ram. 3, 52, 30. **Comp.** *Su-*, adj. well covered, Chr. 27, 4.—Cf. *ἱ* in *ἱμάτιον*.

व्योकार *vyo-kâra* (*vyo* is perhaps an imitative sound), m. A blacksmith.

व्योमन् *vyoman*, n. **1.** The sky, atmosphere, heaven, Pañch. ii. d. 21; Vikr. d. 20. **2.** Æther, Bhâshâp. 2. **3.** Water. **4.** A temple sacred to the sun.

व्योष *vyosha*, i.e. *vi-ush* + *a*, n. The aggregate of three spices, black pepper, long pepper, and dry ginger.

व्रज् *VRAJ*, i. 1, Par. (in epic poetry also Âtm., MBh. 1, 2263), **1.** To go, Man. 2, 56; Pañch. i. d. 129 (*viçvâse*, To trust). **2.** To proceed, Hit. iv. d. 75. **3.** To pass away (as time), Pañch. 117, 9; Megh. 104. **4.** To go to (with acc.), Pañch. i. d. 325; to approach, Bhag. 18, 66; to visit for adultery, Man. 8, 383. **5.** To obtain, Pañch. i. d. 246. **6.** To undergo; with abstracts, to become that which the corresponding concrete noun signifies, e.g. Pañch. 33, 7, *chhâtratâm*, to become a pupil; cf. Man. 3, 179; Çâk. d. 9; *nirvṛitim*, To grow happy, Vikr. d. 28. **7.** With *vyâpâram* and loc. To rule over, Vikr. d. 58. Ptcple. of the pf. pass. *vrajita*, Going. n. Roaming. **Comp.** *Dus-*, n. a bad manner of going, MBh. 3, 14669. *vrajyâ*, see s.v. Caus. To send. i. 10, Par. **1.** † To prepare, to adorn. **2.** † To go.—With the prep. अनु *anu*, **1.** To follow, Man. 11, 111; to pursue, Pañch. i. d. 314 (*saṅgam*, To attach one's self). **2.** To visit in successive order, MBh. 3, 8266. **3.** To perform, Man. 2, 241.—With समनु *sam-anu*, To follow, MBh. 2, 1606.—With आ *â*, **1.** To approach, Man. 2, 196. **2.** With *punar*, To return, MBh. 3, 10273. —With प्रत्या *prati-â*, To go to meet, Ragh. 1, 90.—With परि *pari*, **1.** To wander about as a mendicant, Man. 6, 33. **2.** To walk, MBh. 12, 5098. *parivrajyâ*, see s.v.—With प्र *pra*, **1.** To go away (from home), Man. 6, 39; cf. 34. **2.** To go in exile, Râm. 3, 53, 16. *pravrajita*, Gone away, Hit. 64, 4. m. A mendicant. f. *tâ*, A female devotee, Man. 8, 363. n. Wandering about as a mendicant, Chr. 10, 5. *pravrajyâ*, see s.v. Caus. To banish, MBh. 2, 2674.—With प्रति *prati*, To go near, Bhaṭṭ. 8, 96.—With उपसम् *upa-sam*, To go near, Man. 6, 51.—Cf. Goth. vrikan, persequi; A.S. wrecan; O.H.G. rehhan, wreh, exul; A.S. wraecca; probably Lat. ulciscor (or to *raksh* ?).

व्रज *vraj* + *a*, m. **1.** A road. **2.** A flock, a herd, Chr. 292, 3 = Rigv. i. 86, 3; a multitude, MBh. 6, 5441. **3.** A cow-pen, Chr. 294, 4 = Rigv. i. 92, 4. **4.** The name of a district about *Agra* and *Mathurâ*.—**Comp.** *Go-*, m. 1. pasture ground for cattle, Man. 4, 52. 2. a proper name, MBh. 9, 2568. *Netra-*, m. (pl.), all the eyes, Ragh. 6, 7.—Cf. perhaps Lat. vulgus (or =*varga*).

व्रजन *vraj + ana*, n. Going, roaming, Pańch. 116, 24; exile, Pańch. iii. d. 268.

व्रज्या I. *vraj + yâ*, f. **1.** March. **2.** Attack. **3.** Wandering about as a mendicant. **II.** *vraja + ya*, f. **1.** A flock, a class, a tribe. **2.** A theatre.

† **व्रञ्ज्** *VRAŃJ* (?), i. 1, Par. To go (cf. *vraj*).

व्रण् *VRAṆ*, † i. 1, Par. To sound. i. 10 (cf. the next), Par. To wound, *vraṇita* (rather *vraṇa + ita*), Wounded, Utt. Râmach. 94, 12.

व्रण *vraṇa*, n. **1.** A wound, Pańch. 170, 25. **2.** A fracture, Man. 2, 47. **3.** A boil, a tumour, Hit. ii. d. 101.—Comp. *A-*, adj. 1. without any fracture, Man. 2, 47. 2. without a wound or perceivable injury, Suçr. 2, 311, 13 (?). *A-kṛita-*, m. a proper name, Chr. 13, 11. *Nis-*, adj. 1. unwounded, MBh. 7, 2742. 2. without a fracture, Man. 6, 53. *Vi-stârita-bahu-*, (vb. *stṛi*), adj., f. *ṇâ*, having made many wounds, Pańch. 171, 3.—Cf. Lat. vulnus; οὐλή (i.e. Fολrη), ἄπ-ελος.

व्रणिन् *vraṇin*, i.e. *vraṇa + in*, adj. Having boils, sores, Bhartṛ. 1, 63.

व्रत *vrata* (an old ptcple. of the pf. pass. of *vṛi*), n. **1.** A (self-chosen) voluntary act, Chr. 43, 24; rule, Râm. 3, 53, 18; Bhartṛ. 2, 69. **2.** Action, doing, Man. 9, 304. **3.** Work, Chr. 295, 12 = Rigv. i. 92, 12. **4.** A devout act, Man. 2, 173; as fasting, continence, a vowed observance, a vow, Vikr. 37, 7; Pańch. 260, 13. **5.** Eating (cf. *payas-vrata*).—Comp. *A-*, adj. one who does not observe the rules of his order, Man. 3, 170. *Arka-*, n. levying taxes, drawing the wealth of the people, as the sun evaporates water, Man. 9, 305. *Asi-dhârâ-*, n. a vow to stand on the edge of a sword, Pańch. 196, 15. *Ârya-*, adj. one who observes the rules of the Âryas, or respectable men, MBh. 1, 7424. *Indu-*, n. a kind of vow, MBh. 13, 1797. *Indra-*, n. the duty of the king to distribute gratifications, Man. 9, 304. *Go-*, adj. continent, MBh. 5, 3560. *Gaurî-*, n. lasciviousness, Hit. 42, 2. *Daṇḍa-*, n. judicial power, Bhâg. P. 4, 13, 22. *Dṛiḍha-*, adj. 1. one who observes his vows, Man. 11, 81. 2. persevering in observing one's vow, Sund. 1, 10. 3. persisting in, Râm. 3, 52, 52. *Deva-*, adj. attached to the deities, pious, Bhâg. P. 1, 9, 1. *Dhṛita-*, adj. attached, faithful, Râm. 3, 2, 18. *Niyama-*, n. vow of penance, Pańch. 165, 9. *Nis-*, adj. one who does not observe the religious precepts, MBh. 12, 1335. *Pati-*, I. n. fidelity to one's husband, ib. 13, 165; Böhtl. Ind. Spr. 741. II. f. *tâ*, a faithful or virtuous woman, Pańch. iii. d. 151. *Payovrata*, i.e. *payas-*, I. n. the vow of living only on milk, Bhâg. P. 8, 16, 58. II. adj., f. *tâ*, nourished by milk alone, Man. 11, 144. *Brahmavrata*, i.e. *brahman-* (n.), chastity, Pańch. 187, 6. *Madhu-*, m. a bee. *Mahâ-*, adj., f. *tâ*, one who has undergone great austerities, Chr. 17, 27; 40, 15 (read *mahâvrataḥ*). *Mâruta-*, n. the duty of a king to trace out everything by means of spies, cf. Man. 9, 306. *Mauna-*, adj., f. *tâ*, holding one's tongue, Pańch. 94, 8. *Yata-* (vb. *yam*), adj. firm to an engagement or vow, Johns. Sel. 36, 12. *Yama-*, n. the duty of a king to punish offences without partiality, cf. Man. 9, 305. *Rahasya-*, n. the command of that mysterious power by which mystical weapons may be wielded. *Vipula-*, adj. of great devotion, Johns. Sel. 4, 17. *Sam-çita-* (vb. *çi*), adj. 1. one who has accomplished his vow, Man. 1, 104 (read *saṁçita* instead of *çaṁsita*). 2. faithful to a vow or obligation, Johns. Sel. 1, 1. *Satya-*, I. adj. veracious, honest, Râm. 3, 55, 38. II. m. a proper name, Pañch. iii. d. 270. *Su-*, I. adj. rigidly observing any religious vow or obligation, virtuous, Chr. 58, 6. II. f. *tâ*. 1. a virtuous wife. 2. a cow easily milked. 3. a proper name, Çâk. 102, 22 (Prâkṛ.). *Stuti-*, m. a bard, a herald.—Cf. probably ἑορτή.

व्रतति and **ती** *vratatî* (vb. *vṛit*), f. **1.** Spreading. **2.** A creeper, Çâk. d. 32.

व्रतस्थ *vrata-stha*, adj., f. *thâ*, Engaged in religious austerities, Chr. 47, 35.

ऽव्रतिक *-vratika*, i.e. *vrata+ika* in *vaka-*, adj. Acting like a crane, hypocritic, Man. 4, 192.

व्रतिन् *vratin*, i.e. *vrata+in*, I. adj. Engaged in a religious vow or obligation, pious, Pañch. i. d. 467. II. m. **1.** An employer of priests. **2.** An ascetic. **3.** A religious student, Man. 2, 189; 4, 91; 11, 121.—Comp. *Go-*, m. the name of a sort of anchorite, MBh. 5, 3559 (cf. *go-vrata*). *Deva-*, adj. worshipping the deities, MBh. 13, 3534 (cf. *deva-vrata*). *Mahâ-*, m. 1. a devotee, an ascetic (cf. *mahâ-vrata*). 2. a name of Çiva. *Vaka-*, adj. acting like a crane, hypocritic, Man. 4, 197.

व्रतीन *vratîna*, i.e. *vrata+îna*, m. A hired labourer, Bhaṭṭ. 4, 12.

व्रश्च् *VRAÇCH*, i. 6, *vṛiçcha*, Par. **1.** To tear. **2.** To cut, Bhaṭṭ. 9, 41. **3.** To wound. Ptcple. of the pf. pass. *vṛikṇa*, Broken, Bhaṭṭ. 12, 75.—Cf. ἕλκος, ῥάκος, λακίς, λακερός; Lat. lacerare, ulcus.

व्रश्चन *vraçch+ana*, I. m. A small saw or chisel. II. n. Cutting, wounding, Man. 5, 5.

व्राजि *vrâji*, i.e. *vraj+i*, f. (?), A whirlwind.

व्रात *vrâta*, probably *vrata+a*, I. m. **1.** The company and attendants at a marriage feast. **2.** An assemblage, a multitude, Bhâg. P. 4, 25, 19; Chr. 4, 19. **3.** The son of an outcaste. II. n. **1.** Bodily labour. **2.** Day labour.—Comp. *Vṛishavrâta*, i.e. *vṛishan-*, adj. abounding in drops of rain, Chr. 291, 4 = Rigv. i. 85, 4.

व्रात्य *vrâtya*, i.e. *vrâta+ya*, I. m. An outcaste, Man. 2, 39. II. f. *yâ*, The daughter of an outcaste, Man. 8, 373.

व्रात्यता *vrâtya+tâ*, f. The state of an outcaste, Man. 11, 62.

† **व्री** *VRÎ*, ii. 9, *vrîṇâ*, *vrîṇî*, Par. To choose. i. 4, Âtm. To be chosen.

व्रीड् *VRÎḌ*, i. 4, Par. **1.** To be, or grow bashful, Vikr. 8, 17. **2.** † To throw. Ptcple. of the pf. pass. *vrîḍita* (perhaps rather *vrîḍâ+ita*), Ashamed, modest, Chr. 56, 18.

व्रीड *vrîḍa* (m. and) f. *ḍâ*, **1.** Shame, Râjat. 5, 338. **2.** Bashfulness, Bhartṛ. 2, 18.—Comp. *Sa-*, adj., f. *ḍâ*, 1. ashamed, Chr. 61, 42. 2. bashful, Chr. 5, 4; Vikr. 10, 12. 3. modest. °*ḍam*, adv. 1. with shame, ashamed, Pañch. 208, 13. 2. bashfully, Vikr. 28, 14.

व्रीस् *VRÎS*, see *vrûs*.

व्रीहि *vrîhi* (probably derived from *vṛidh*), m. Rice, Pañch. 167, 1 (pl. grains of rice).

† **व्रुड्** *VRUḌ*, i. 6, Par. **1.** To cover. **2.** To heap. **3.** To sink.

व्रूष् *VRÛSH*, see the next.

† **व्रूस्** *VRÛS*, or **व्रूष्** *VRÛSH*,

कष् *KASH*, व्रीस् *VRÎS*, i. 10, Par. To hurt or kill.

व्रैहेय *vraiheya*, i.e. *vrîhi + eya*, adj. Fit for, or sown with, rice.

व्ली *VLÎ*, see *blî*.

व्लेक्ष् *VLEKSH*, see *veksh*.

श *Ç*.

शंयु *çaṁyu*, i. e. *çam + yu*, adj. Happy.

शंव *çaṁva*, i.e. *çam + va*, I. adj. Prosperous, happy, Bhaṭṭ. 4, 18. II. m. 1. Indra's thunderbolt. 2. The iron head of a pestle.

शंवर *çaṁvara*, n. Water (see *çambara*).

शंस् *ÇAṀS*, i. 1, Par. (in epic poetry also Âtm., MBh. 1, 7687), 1. To praise, MBh. 2, 2298; pass. *çasya*, Chr. 292, 4 = Rigv. i. 86, 4. 2. To report, Man. 7, 116; Râm. 3, 55, 16. 3. To say, Vikr. d. 105; MBh. 3, 2584. 4. † To be unhappy. 5. † To hurt. Ptcple. of the pf. pass. I. *çasta*. 1. Best, excellent. 2. Right, happy. n. 1. Happiness. 2. The body. II. *çaṁsita*. 1. Praised, Pañch. i. d. 195. 2. Said. 3. Wished. 4. Calumniated. 5. Certain. Man. 1, 104, read *saṁçita*. Comp. *A-çasta*, adj. 1. not praiseworthy, Râjat. 5, 13. 2. inauspicious, Lass. 16, 17. Ptcple. of the fut. pass. *çasya*. 1. Praiseworthy, Pañch. i. d. 248; excellent. 2. Desirable. n. 1. Good quality, merit. 2. Fruit (cf. *sasya*), Böhtl. Ind. Spr. 650. 3. Corn, Hit. 46, 6, M.M. Comp. *Nava-*, n. new grain, Man. 4, 26.—With the prep. अभि *abhi*, *abhiçasta*, 1. Accused, Man. 8, 373. 2. Defamed, Man. 4, 211. —With आ *â*, I. Par. 1. To report, Ragh. 1, 86. 2. To conciliate, Draup. 5, 12. II. Âtm. (in epic poetry also Par., MBh. 2, 1904). 1. To wish, MBh. 3, 17171. 2. To hope, Çâk. d. 48. 3. To fear, Bhâg. P. 1, 13, 31. 4. To believe, Râm. 2, 51, 14. *âçaṁsita*, Desired, Kir. 5, 52.—With समा *sam-â*, To desire, MBh. 1, 6920. —With प्र *pra*, 1. To praise, Man. 3, 230; anomal. *praçaṁsiyât*, Böhtl. Ind. Spr. 975 = Châṇ. 37 in Berl. Monastb. 1864, 409; absol. *praçasya*, Pañch. 98, 4. 2. To recommend, Man. 5, 127. 3. With *na*, To disapprove, to blame, Chr. 7, 12. 4. To esteem, Man. 7, 209. 5. To declare, Lass. 12, 18. *praçasta*, Good, Hit. iii. d. 74. Comp. *A-praçasta*, bad, inferior, Nalod. 20, 41. n. dirt, Man. 11, 255. Ptcple. of the fut. pass. *praçasya*, Good. Comparat. *jyâyaṁs* and *çreyâṁs*, superl. *jyeshṭha* and *çreshṭha*, see s. v.v.—With अभिप्र *abhi-pra*, To praise, MBh. 3, 11908.—Cf. Lat. censere, canere, Casmena, carmen, con-cinn + us; Goth. hazjan.

शंसा *çaṁs + â*, f. 1. Praise, Pañch. i. d. 80. 2. Speech. 3. Wish.

ऽशंसिन् *-çaṁs + in*, adj. 1. Announcing, Vikr. 60, 14; 65, 11. 2. Showing, Çiç. 9, 77.

शंस्त् *ÇAṀST*, see *sas*.

शंस्तृ *çaṁs + tṛi*, m. 1. A panegyrist. 2. A flatterer.

शक् *ÇAK*, ii. 9, *çaknu*, Par., and i. 4, *çakya*, Par. Âtm. 1. To endure, MBh. 3, 11277. 2. To be able, Râm. 1, 42, 21; with the infin., Man. 7, 6; with the ptcple. in the signification of the infin., *apûryâṁ pûrayann ichchhâm . . . . na çaknuyât*, He is not able to satisfy the insatiable desire, MBh. 12,

514. 3. Impers. pass. To be fit to be done, MBh. 1, 6678. 4. The pass. transfers its pass. signification to the infin. which it governs, e.g. *na çakyante niyantum*, Man. 2, 96 (They cannot be restrained); Hit. 11, 6, M.M. (*nîtim̃ grâhayitum̃ çakyante*, They are able to be taught good behaviour); with a ptcple. of the pass. of the Caus. instead of the infin., *na çakyate nivartyamânâ*, Chr. 46, 23 (She cannot be induced to return). Ptcple. of the pf. pass. I. *çaktu*. 1. Powerful, capable, Man. 2, 109. 2. Able, Vikr. d. 72; with the infin., Man. 9, 10; with the loc. in the sense of an infin., MBh. 3, 2263; Pańch. iv. d. 28. 3. Clever, Hit. ii. d. 74. 4. Diligent, attentive, intent. 5. Speaking civilly (cf. *çach*). **Comp.** *A*-, adj. powerless, Pańch. i. d. 362. II. *çakita*, Able, i.e. could; transfers its pass. signification to the infin. which it governs, e.g. *na çakitâ netum*, Râm. 1, 44, 53 (She could not be led). Ptcple. of the fut. pass. *çakya*. 1. Easy to be overpowered, Pańch. iii. d. 53. 2. Practicable, possible, Râm. 3, 53, 27; Chr. 8, 27. 3. Transfers its pass. signification to the infin. which it governs, e.g. *çakyâ rakshitum*, Man. 9, 10 (They can be guarded). 4. Superl. *çakyatama*, Most possible, Hit. iii. d. 115 (*na çakyatamâḥ samîhitum*, Are not at all to be aspired to). **Comp.** *A*-, adj. impossible, Hit. i. d. 89, M.M.; Chr. 57, 25. Anomal. desider. *çiksha*, Par. Âtm. To learn, Man. 2, 20. *çikshita*, 1. Instructed, Pańch. 94, 20. 2. Learned, Hit. ii. d. 154. 3. Disciplined. 4. Trained (as an animal). 5. Docile. 6. Modest, diffident. 7. Skilful, clever, conversant. Caus. of the desider. *çikshaya*, To teach, Man. 2, 69.—With the prep. अनु *anu*, *anuçikshita*, Learned (by imitation), Utt. Râmach. 63, 2. Caus. of the desider. To instruct, MBh. 1, 5761. — With अव *ava*, *avaçakya*, Possible, Chaurap. 43.—With अभि *abhi*, Caus. of the desider. To instruct, MBh. 1, 8033.—With आ *â*, desider. To impart, to grant, Chr. 297, 19=Rigv. i. 112, 19. — With उप *upa*, desider. To learn, MBh. 3, 1790.—Cf. Lat. queo (for quecjo), ne-queo (nequinont, for ne-quic+nont), conari; O.N. hagr, dexter, hagna, prodesse.

शक *çaka*, 1. m. pl. The name of a people, Man. 10, 44. 2. A particular caste. 3. An era, especially that of Çâlivâhana, commencing seventy-six or seventy-eight years after the Christian.

शकच *çakacha*, Râjat. 5, 176 (? perhaps to be corrected to *çakaja*, A man of Çaka, i.e. Scythic extraction, or a proper name).

शकट *çakaṭa*, probably for *çak*+*atra*, I. m., f. *ṭi*, and n. A cart, Hit. i. d. 89, M.M. (n.); Pańch. 8, 15 (*ṭâ*); Râm. 1, 33, 18 (*ṭî*); with *prâjâpatya*, name of an asterism, Pańch. i. d. 239 (*ṭâ*). II. m. 1. A cart-load. 2. A Daitya slain by Kṛishṇa. III. m. or n. 1. An implement for preparing grain, Man. 5, 117. 2. A form of marching an army, 7, 187. — **Comp.** *Rohiṇî*-, m. or n. an asterism, probably αεγδε Tauri, Pańch. 50, 20.

शकटार *çakaṭâra*, m. 1. A bird of prey (a vulture ?), Hit. ii. d. 97. 2. and शकटाल *çakaṭâla*, A proper name, Kathâs. 4, 104 (*l*).

शकटिका *çakaṭikâ*, i.e. *çakaṭî*+*ka*, f. A small cart.—**Comp.** *Mṛichchhakaṭikâ*, i.e. *mṛid*-, f. the cart made of clay, the toy-cart, title of a drama.

शकन् *çakan*, see *çakṛit*.

शकल *çakala* (a form of *çarkara* by

intermediate *çakkara, and with *l* for *r*, cf. *çarkarâ*), **I.** m. and n. A part, a portion, a piece, Utt. Râmach. 46, 19; Pańch. iii. d. 193 (194); 262, 25; a potsherd, Man. 6, 28. **II.** n. **1.** Skin. **2.** Bark. **3.** The scales of a fish. **4.** A kind of (black) pigment.

शकलिन् *çakalin*, i.e. *çakala + in*, m. A fish.

शकार *çakâra*, m. A silly brother-in-law of a king.

शकुन *çak + una* (or rather *çak + van + a*, cf. *çakunta*), **I.** m. A bird, Nal. 9, 12. **II.** n. An omen; **a.** auspicious, Lass. 43, 5; **b.** inauspicious, Pańch. 52, 11 (*kiṁ çakunakâraṅaṁ kiṁ chit saṁjâtam*, Has something come to pass caused by a bird, or by an inauspicious omen, i.e. has there happened a misfortune?).—**Comp.** *A-*, n. an inauspicious omen, Çiç. 9, 83.

शकुनि *çak + uni* (see the last), **I.** m. **1.** A bird, Pańch. iii. d. 140. **2.** The Indian kite, Falco cheela. **3.** A surname of the Açvins, MBh. 1, 723. **4.** A proper name, Indr. 3, 9. **II.** f. *ni*, A hen-sparrow. — Probably akin to O.N. haukr; Danish, hog; O.H.G. habuh; A.S. hafoc.

शकुन्त *çak + unta* (or rather *çak + vant + a*, cf. *çakuna*), m. **1.** A bird, Pańch. i. d. 155. **2.** The Indian vulture. **3.** The blue jay.

शकुन्तक *çakunta + ka*, m., f. *tikâ*, A bird, Utt. Râmach. 29, 4.

शकुन्तला *çakunta + lâ*, f. A proper name, Çâk. 3, 5.—**Comp.** *Abhijńâna-*, n. (suppl. *nâṭaka*, a drama), having as subject Çakuntalâ, recognised by a token of remembrance, Çâk. 3, 12.

शकुन्ति *çakunti* (cf. *çakunta*), m. A bird, Utt. Râmach. 69, 6.

शकुल *çakula*, m. A fish (cf. *çakalin*).

शकृत् *çakṛit*, and **सकृत्** *sakṛit* (for original *skṛit*, from the old form of the vb. *kṛî*), n., the base of some cases is *çakan*, Fæces, excrement, Man. 2, 182.—Cf. σκώρ, σκατός, σκέρ-βολος; A.S. scearn; perhaps Lat. stercus and cerda in su-cerda (rather to *çṛidh*?), etc.; and Goth. spai-skuldrs, Spittle.

शक्कर *çakkara*, and **शक्वर** *çakvara*, i.e. *çak + van + a* (with *r* for *n*), **I.** m. A bull. **II.** f. *rî*. **1.** A zone, a girdle. **2.** A woman of impure caste.

शक्ति *çak + ti*, f. **1.** Strength, Pańch. i. d. 265; with loc., Bhartṛ. 2, 60 (*âtmadamane*, in restraining or ruling one's self). **2.** Power, Hit. pr. d. 31, M.M. **3.** The active power of a deity personified as his wife (as *Gaurî* of *Çiva*, etc.), Kathâs. 3, 62 (of the god of love); eight particular goddesses, *Brâhmî*, etc., cf. Wilson, Hind. Th. 2. ed. ii. 52, n. ad Mâlat. 74, 5. **4.** Signification, Bhâshâp. 79. **5.** Allaying opposition. **6.** An iron spear or dart, MBh. 5, 5259; a sword, Mâlat. 82, 16.—**Comp.** *A-*, f. want of strength, Bhartṛ. 2, 44. *Ananta-*, *Amara-*, *Ugra-*, *Deva-*, *Bahu-*, m. proper names, Pańch. 3, 11, 12; 183, 20. *Âtmaçakti*, i.e. *âtman-*, f. one's own strength or power, Hit. pr. d. 31, M.M. *Yathâ-*, adv. to the utmost of one's power, Hit. ii. d. 51; Lass. 59, 1. *Rati-*, f. the faculty of enjoying love, Böhtl. Ind. Spr. 2077. *Çiva-*, m. a proper name, Râjat. 5, 131.

शक्तितस् *çakti + tas*, adv. According to power or ability, Pańch. 161, 24.

ऽशक्तिता *-çakti + tâ*, in *bhojana-*, f. The faculty of enjoying food, Chân. 40 in Berl. Monatsb. 1864, 409.

शक्तिधर *çakti-dhara*, m. A name of Skanda, the god of war.

शक्तिमन्त् *çakti + mant*, adj., f. *mati*, 1. Powerful, mighty, Pañch. iii. d. 14. 2. Able, ib. iii. d. 169. 3. Having gained a fortune or a competence, Man. 10, 98.

शक्तु *çaktu*, and सक्तु *saktu*, m. and n., according to some authorities only m. pl. (Pañch. 252, 10, with *s*), The flour of barley and other grain first fried and then ground, Hit. 114, 22 (*ç*). —Comp. *Dadhi-*, pl. fried meal mixed with curds, MBh. 13, 5049.

शक्नु *çak + nu* (cf. *çach*), adj. Speaking civilly.

शक्र *çak + ra*, m. 1. Indra, Râm. 3, 54, 8. 2. A king (?), Râm. 3, 49, 41 (cf. Gorr. n.). 3. The name of two trees, Pentaptera arjuna and Nerium antidysentericum. — Comp. *Ati-*, adj. exceeding Indra, Arj. 4, 41.

शक्ल *çak + la* (cf. *çach*), adj. Affable.

शक्वन् *çak + van*, I. m. An elephant. II. f. *vari*, A river. Cf. *çakkara*.

शक्वर *çakvara* (cf. *çakkara*), I. m. A bull. II. f. *ri*. 1. A finger-ring. 2. A zone. Cf. the last.

शङ्क् *ÇAṄK*, i. 1, Âtm. (in epic poetry also Par., Râm. 2, 90, 15), 1. To hesitate, to be uncertain, Râm. 3, 49, 16. 2. To doubt, MBh. 3, 16512. 3. To think probable, to believe, MBh. 4, 97; to think, Vikr. d. 55. 4. To distrust, to suspect, MBh. 3, 2327. 5. To fear, Vikr. 66, 10; MBh. 3, 2274. Ptcple. of the pf. pass. *çaṅkita*. 1. Suspicious, Pañch. 187, 4; alarmed, frightened, Râm. 3, 52, 48. 2. Being fearful of (with gen. and abl.), Pañch. 100, 9. 3. Doubtful, uncertain. 4. Weak, unsteady. Comp. *Nitya-*, adj. constantly suspicious, Hit. i. d. 24, M.M. Caus. To frighten, Mâlav. 44, 13.—With the prep. अति *ati*, 1. To suspect, Râm, 2, 52, 57. 2. To fear, Râm. 2, 22, 30.—With अभि *abhi*, 1. To be uncertain, Man. 8, 96. 2. To doubt, Matsyop. 34. *abhiçaṅkita*, 1. Suspecting, Chr. 14, 26. 2. Afraid, Mâlat. 143, 3.—With आ *â*, 1. To hesitate, Pañch. i. d. 437 (with ptcple. in the sense of an infin.). 2. To doubt, Çâk. 66, 19. 3. To think probable, Daçak. in Chr. 193, 2. 4. To suspect, to apprehend, Mâlat. 69, 19; Man. 7, 188. 5. To fear, Utt. Râmach. 62, 4.—With निस् *nis*, *niḥçaṅkita* (rather *çaṅkita* with *nis*), 1. Not hesitating, Pañch. 217, 12. 2. Careless, ib. 161, 16.—With परि *pari*, To suspect, MBh. 3, 10356; with *doshena*, of a crime or sin, Nal. 24, 26. *pariçaṅkita*, 1. Suspected, Chr. 54, 15. 2. Suspecting, Chr. 18, 36. 3. Fearful, Lass. 2. ed. 61, 32.—With वि *vi*, 1. To doubt, MBh. 1, 2966. 2. To suspect, Çâk. d. 114. 3. To fear, Mâlat. 70, 13; Pañch. ii. d. 178. *a-viçaṅkita*, adj. Fearless, Vikr. 81, 11.—With निर्वि *nis-vi*, *nirviçaṅkita* (rather *viçaṅkita* with *nis*), acc. °*tam*, adv. Without hesitation, Hariv. 7335.—With सम् *sam*, To suspect, MBh. 4, 568.—Cf. Lat. cunc + tari; A.S. hangian; Goth. and O.H.G. hugjan; Goth. hugs; A.S. hige, hyge, hogu, hygian, hyggan, hiegan, hogian; O.H.G. hugu.

शंकर *çaṁkara*, i. e. *çam-kṛi + a*, I. adj. 1. Causing happiness, Padmap. 2, 6. 2. Auspicious. II. m. 1. Çiva, Hariv. 15408; Vedântas. in Chr. 209, 20. 2. A proper name, Lass. 2. ed. 87, 16.

शङ्का *çaṅk + â*, f. 1. Doubt, uncertainty, Vedântas. in Chr. 217, 13 ; Kir. 5, 42 (at the end of a comp. adj., f. *kâ*) ; error, 5, 38. **2.** Presumption, Nal. 24, 3. **3.** Hope, Bhartṛ. 3, 5. **4.** Fear, Pañch. 238, 21 ; apprehension, Hit. i. d. 23, M.M.—**Comp.** *A-çaṅka*, adj. without fear, regard, Hit. i. d. 80, M.M. °*kam*, adv. courageously, Daçak. in Chr. 194, 11. *Nis-çaṅka*, adj. 1. without hesitation, Pañch. 24, 13 (regardless). 2. fearless, Pañch. 123, 25. °*kam-*, adv. without fear, Hit. ii. d. 163. *Vita-*, i.e. *vi-ita-*, adj. fearless. *Sa-*, adj. fearful, doubtful.

शङ्किन् *çaṅkin*, i. e. *çaṅk*, and *çaṅkâ*, + *in*, adj., f. *nî*, **1.** Fearful of, Râjat. 5, 144. **2.** Suspecting, Hit. iv. d. 101. **3.** Full of danger, Pañch. i. d. 216.

शङ्कु *çaṅk* + *u* (partly *çak* + *u*, cf. *çakti*), m. **1.** Fear. **2.** Çiva. **3.** Kâma. **4.** A demon. **5.** Poison. **6.** Sin. **7.** A pin, Hit. iv. d. 69 ; a pale, a style, Man. 8, 271 ; a stake. **8.** The trunk of a lopped tree. **9.** A dart, Utt. Râmach. 75, 12 ; a javelin, Pañch. 87, 12 (cf. Hiḍ. 2, 4) ; a weapon in general. **10.** A goose. **11.** An ant-hill. **12.** A skate. **13.** A number, ten billions. **14.** A tree, Shorea robusta.—**Comp.** *Tri-*, m. the name of a king, Hariv. 730. *Danta-*, n. an instrument for drawing out teeth, Suçr. 1, 26, 12. *Loha-*, m. 1. an iron pike. 2. a hell, Man. 4, 90.

शङ्कुर *çaṅk* + *ura*, adj. Formidable.

शङ्कुला *çaṅku* + *lâ*, f. A pair of scissors (cf. *danta-çaṅku*).

शङ्ख *çaṅkha*, I. m. and n. The conch-shell used as a vessel for offering libations, and for blowing as a horn, Pañch. 20, 8. **II.** m. **1.** A shell, Pañch. iv. d. 76 ; 158, 4. **2.** A military drum. **3.** The temple or temporal bone, Lass. 2. ed. 13, 13. **4.** An elephant's cheek. **5.** A large number, ten or a hundred billions. **6.** One of Kuvera's treasures, Pañch. ii. d. 12. **7.** A particular perfume.—**Comp.** *Mahâ-*, m. 1. the forehead. 2. a thousand millions. 3. one of Kuvera's treasures. *Sa-*, adj. with a conch-shell. *Saṁdhyâ-*, m. the conch proclaiming (by its sounding) the evening hour, Mâlat. 41, 16. *Sthûla-*, adj., f. *khâ*, having a large vulva, Lass. Pentap. 65, 16. *Hema-*, m. Vishṇu (cf. Pañch. 44, 15, sqq.).—Cf. κόγχη, κόλχος, κόχλος, κάλχη.

शङ्खक *çaṅkha* + *ka*, **I.** m. and n. **1.** The conch-shell. **2.** The temples, Yâjñ. 3, 93. **3.** Pain in the temples and forehead. **II.** n. A bracelet.

शङ्खध्म *çaṅkha-dhma* (vb. *dhmâ*), m. A shell-blower.

शङ्खिन् *çaṅkhin*, i. e. *çaṅkha* + *in*, **I.** adj. Having a shell or shells. **II.** m. **1.** The ocean. **2.** A shell-blower. **3.** A worker in shells. **4.** Vishṇu (cf. *hema-çaṅkha*). **III.** f. *inî*. **1.** One of the four classes into which females are divided. **2.** A female spirit.

† **शच्** *ÇACH*, i. 1, Âtm. To speak (cf. *çak*).

शचि and **शची** *çachî* (vb. *çak*, cf. *çakra*), f. **1.** The wife of Indra, Râm. 3, 54, 26 (*i*). **2.** *chi*, Strength, Chr. 296, 8 = Rigv. i. 112, 8.

शञ्च् *ÇAÑCH*, see *çvañch*.

† **शट्** *ÇAṬ*, i. 1, Par. **1.** To be diseased. **2.** To divide. **3.** To be dissolved. **4.** To be low-spirited. **5.** To go.—Cf. 2. *çaṭh*.

शटा *çaṭâ*, see *saṭâ*.

† 1. **शठ्** *ÇAṬH*, i. 1, Par. **1.** To deceive. **2.** To kill or hurt. **3.** To suffer pain. i. 10, Par. To be lazy.

† 2. **शठ्** *ÇAṬH*, **शट्** *ÇAṬ*, **शल्**

ÇAL, i. 10, Atm. To praise, to flatter.

† 3. शठ् *ÇAṬH*, श्वठ् *ÇVAṬH*, i. 10, *çaṭhaya*, *çvaṭhaya*, Par. **1.** To speak ill. **2.** To speak well. **3.** To be true.

† 4. शठ् *ÇAṬH*, श्वठ् *ÇVAṬH*, श्वण्ठ् *ÇVAṆṬH*, सठ् *SAṬH*, स्वठ् *SVAṬH*, i. 10, Par. **1.** To finish, to adorn. **2.** To leave unfinished or unadorned.

शठ *çaṭha*, probably akin to *çatru*, cf. *çatera*, perhaps a form of **çatra*, **I.** adj. Wicked, dishonest, perfidious, Lass. 31, 17; Hit. ii. d. 115. **II.** m. **1.** A rogue, a knave, Man. 7, 123. **2.** A false husband or lover, Lass. 45, 5; Çṛiṅgârat. 10; Mâlav. d. 55 (read *çaṭha*). **3.** An idler. **4.** A blockhead. **5.** A mediator.—**Comp.** *A-*, adj. honest, Man. 3, 246. *Danta-*, m. common lime, Ferronia elephantum Corr., and Averrhoa carambola Lin., Suçr. 1, 157, 5.

† शण् *ÇAṆ*, i. 1, Par. **1.** To give (cf. *çraṇ*). **2.** To move (?).

शण *çaṇa*, n. **1.** Hemp, MBh. 3, 16350. **2.** Bengal San, a plant from which a kind of hemp is prepared, Crotalaria juncea. **3.** (for **çarṇa*, i.e. *çri* + *na*), An arrow.—Cf. κάνναβις; O.H.G. hanaf; A.S. haenep (borrowed).

शणसूत्रमय *çaṇa-sûtra* + *maya*, adj., f. *yî*, Consisting of *çaṇa*-threads, Man. 2, 44.

शण्ठ *çaṇṭha*, m. An eunuch (cf. *çaṇḍa*).

† शण्ड् *ÇAṆḌ*, i. 1, Âtm. **1.** To disease. **2.** To collect.

शण्ड *çaṇḍa*, I. m. n. A collection of lotus flowers. **II.** m. **1.** An eunuch. **2.** An impotent man. **3.** A bull at liberty (cf. *çaṇṭha* and *çaṇḍha*).

शण्ढ *çaṇḍha*, m. **1.** An eunuch. **2.** An attendant on the women's apartments. **3.** A bull at liberty (cf. the last, *shaṇḍa*, and *shaṇḍha*).

शत *çata*, numeral, n. (also m., Nal. 15, 6, *çatâni çatâs*, ten thousand), A hundred, Chr. 28, 20 (pl.); nom. in the sense of an instr. (i.e. indecl.), Chr. 287, 7 = Rigv. i. 48, 7.—**Comp.** *Adhyardha-*, i.e. *adhi-ardha-*, I. n. a hundred and fifty. II. adj. consisting of a hundred and fifty, MBh. 1, 102. *Ardha-*, n. a hundred and fifty, Man. 8, 331. *Ashṭaçata*, i.e. *ashṭan-*, n. eight hundred, Yâjń. 1, 302. *Eka-*, n. a hundred and one; with *gavâm*, a hundred cows and one bull, Man. 11, 129 (cf. 127). *Tâvachchhata*, i.e. *tâvant-*, adj., f. *tî*, containing so many hundreds, Man. 1, 69. *Tri-*, I. n. three hundred, Râm. 1, 13, 31 Gorr. II. adj. three hundredth, MBh. 3, 12. *Daçaçata*, i.e. *daçan-*, n., and f. *tî*, a thousand, MBh. 3, 2658 (*ta*); Râjat. 5, 71 (*tî*). *Daçaraçmi-*, i.e. *daçan-*, adj. (having a thousand rays), epithet of the sun, Ragh. 8, 29. *Dvi-*, I. n. 1. two hundred. 2. hundred and two. II. adj. 1. amounting to two hundred, Man. 8, 257. 2. two hundredth, MBh. i. adhy. 200, sqq. *Pañchaçata*, i.e. *pañchan-*, I. n., and f. *tî*, five hundred, Man. 8, 384 (*ta*); Kathâs. 44, 77 (*tî*). II. adj. 1. five hundred, MBh. 3, 15723. 2. amounting to five hundred, Yâjń. 2, 301. 3. paying an amercement of five hundred, Man. 8, 376. *Paraḥçata*, i.e. *paras-*, adj., f. *tâ*, more than a hundred, MBh. 6, 4267.—Cf. Lat. centum; ἑ-κατόν (ἐν-κατόν); Goth. and A.S. hund.

शतक *çata* + *ka*, I. adj. Hundred. II. (m. ?), n. A century, a collection of a hundred stanzas, Bhartṛ. title.

शतखण्डमय *çata-khaṇḍa + maya*, adj. Consisting of a hundred pieces, Bhartṛ. 3, 16 (cf. *khaṇḍa*).

शतघ्नी *çataghnî*, i.e. *çata-han + î*, f. **1.** A kind of weapon, Arj. 6, 16. **2.** A female scorpion. **3.** A disease of the throat.

शततम *çata + tama*, ord. num., f. *mî*, Hundredth, Daçak. in Chr. 182, 15.—**Comp.** *Dvi-*, adj. two hundredth, Hariv. adhy. 200. *Tri-*, adj. 1. three hundredth, Hariv. adhy. 300. 2. hundred and third, Râm. ii. adhy. 103. *Chatuḥçatatama*, i.e. *chatur-*, adj. hundred and fourth, Râm. ii. adhy. 104. *Pañchaçatatama*, i.e. *pañchan-*, adj. hundred and fifth, Râm. ii. adhy. 105. *Navaçatatama*, i.e. *navan-*, adj. hundred and ninth, Râm. vi. adhy. 109. *Drâviṁçati-*. i.e. *dvi-viṁçati-*, adj. hundred and twenty-second, Râm. ii. adhy. 122 Gorr.

शतद्रु *çata-dru*, f. The name of a river, the Setlej, MBh. 1, 6753.

शतधा *çata + dhâ*, adv. **1.** In a hundred ways, hundred-fold, Man. 12, 115. **2.** In a hundred pieces, Pañch. 94, 16.

शतभिषज् *çata-bhishaj*, and **शतभिषा** *çatabhishâ* (a mutilation of *bhishaj*), f. A lunar mansion.

शतमान *çata-mâna*, m. and n. **1.** A *Pala* of silver, Man. 8, 137 (m.). **2.** A measure so termed.

शतयोजनवत् *çata-yojana + vat*, adv. As if a hundred *yojanas* large, Pañch. i. d. 447.

शतशस् *çata +ças*, adv. By hundreds, a hundred-fold, Chr. 30, 8; 36, 22.

शतशाखत्व *çata-çâkha + tva* (cf. *çâkhâ*), n. Condition of having many branches, of being much increased, Râjat. 5, 376.

शतसंघशस् *çata-saṁgha + ças*, adv. By hundreds, Arj. 10, 23.

शतिन् *çatin*, i.e. *çata + in*, **I.** adj. Consisting of hundreds, Chr. 291, 15 = Rigv. i. 64, 15. **II.** m. One who is possessed of a hundred, Pañch. v. d. 69.

शतेर *çatera* (cf. *çatru*), m. **1.** An enemy. **2.** Injury.

शत्त्रि *çattri*, m. An elephant.

शत्रु *çatru* (rather **शत्त्रु** *çattru*, i.e. probably *çad* or *çat*, for *çâtaya*, Caus. of *çad*, + *tru*, cf. Goth. hats; A.S. hate, héte; perhaps Lat. hod in odisse, hostis, and below), m. An enemy, a foe, Pañch. i. d. 131.—**Comp.** *Indra-*, m. Prahlâda, Ragh. 7, 32. *Krauñcha-*, m. the god of war, Mṛichchh. 173, 15. *Deva-*, m. 1. an Asura, MBh. 7, 6296. 2. a Râkshasa, Râm. 6, 36, 83. *Bahu-*, adj. having many enemies, Kathâs. 4, 106. *Vibudha-*, m. a demon, Vikr. d. 3. *Vṛitra-*, m. Indra.—Cf. ἔχθος, ἐχθρός, ὀχθέω.

शत्रुंसह *çatruṁsaha*, i.e. *çatru + m -sah + a*, adj. Bearing, or patient with an enemy.

शत्रुघ्न *çatru-ghna*, **I.** adj. Killing a foe. **II.** m. a proper name, Utt. Râmach. 31, 9.

शत्रुंजय *çatruṁjaya*, i.e. *çatru + m -ji + a*, **I.** adj. Subduing an enemy. **II.** m. **1.** A proper name, Draup. 2, 11. **2.** An elephant. **3.** The name of a mountain.

शत्रुतस् *çatru + tas*, adv. From any enemy, Nal. 14, 18.

शत्रुता *çatru + tâ*, f., and **शत्रुत्व**

çatru + *tva*, n. Enmity, hostility, Pañch. ii. d. 32; Châṇ. 19 in Berl. Monatsb. 1864, 408.

शत्वरी *çatvarî*, i.e. *çam* + *tvan* + *î* (cf. *çamanî*, s. v. *çamana*, *r* for *n*), f. The night.

शद् *ÇAD* substitutes in the pres., imperf., imperat., and potent. the pass. of *çî*, viz. *çîya*; in the remaining forms, Par. To fall, Bhaṭṭ. 17, 77 (*çîya*). Caus. I. *çâtaya* (probably a denomin., perhaps from an anomal. ptcple. of the pf. pass. *çâta* for *çatta*, cf. the substitution of a vowel long by nature for one long by position, and vice versâ in the Prâkṛ. languages), To fell, to throw down, Râm. 1, 66, 10. *çâtita*, Cut off, Râm. 1, 66, 12, Seramp. II. *çâdaya*, To drive, Pâṇ. vii. 3, 42.—With the prep. **प्र** *pra*, Caus. *çâtaya*, To break off, MBh. 1, 5561.—With **वि** *vi*, Caus. *çâtaya*, To break to pieces, MBh. 3, 11971. —With **सम्** *sam*, Caus. *çâtaya*, The same, MBh. 3, 865.—Cf. Lat. cadere.

शद *çad* + *a*, also (but wrongly)

सद *sada*, m. Any edible vegetable product, as fruits, Man. 8, 151; 241 (with *s*).

शद्रि *çad* + *ri*, I. m. **1.** A cloud. **2.** An elephant. **3.** Arjuna. **II.** f. Lightning.

शनकैस् *çanakais*, i. e. *çana* + *ka*, instr. pl. (cf. *çanais*), adv. **1.** By degrees, gradually, Man. 7, 172. **2.** In every case that arises, Man. 7, 116. **3.** Mildly, Çiç. 9, 26; Chr. 41, 5.

शनि *çani* (cf. *çanais*), and **शनैश्चर** *çanaiçchara*, i.e. *çanais-chara*, m. The planet Saturn, Pañch. 50, 19 (*çanaiçchara*); Râm. 2, 52, 15 (*çanaiçchara*).

शनैस् *çanais* (probably for *çamnais*, instr. pl. of an old ptcple. pf. pass. of *çam*), adv. (properly 'With intervals of quiet'). **1.** Hesitating, slowly, Vikr. 71, 18; stealthily, Vikr. d. 56. **2.** Mildly, Chr. 32, 27. **3.** Successively, by little and little, Râjat. 5, 470; at will, independently. **4.** Doubled, *çanaiḥ-çanais*, adv. By little and little, Man. 3, 233; successively, Pañch. 212, 1; step by step, 35, 8.

शंताति *çaṁtâti*, i.e. *çam* + *tâti*, f. Happiness, yielding bliss, Chr. 297, 20 = Rigv. i. 112, 20.

शप् *ÇAP*, i. 1 and 4, Par. Âtm. (the original signification was probably 'To cry aloud'), **1.** To execrate, to curse, Man. 3, 58. **2.** With the dat., To revile, Bhaṭṭ. 8, 33. **3.** To swear, Man. 8, 110. **4.** To assure by an oath, Râm. 2, 11, 8. Caus. **1.** To cause to swear, Man. 8, 113 (with the instr. of the object by which one is sworn). **2.** To conjure; *çapitâsi jîvitena*, You are conjured by the life of, Mâlat. 129, 10.—With the prep. **अभि** *abhi*, To execrate, Râm. 2, 41, 3.—With **परि** *pari*, The same, Bhaṭṭ. 4, 33.—Cf. probably κόμπος; cf. the frequent. *çaṁçap*.

शप *çap* + *a*, m. **1.** An imprecation. **2.** An oath.

शपथ *çap* + *atha*, m. **1.** An imprecation, curse, Pañch. 62, 2; cursing. **2.** An oath, asseveration by oath or ordeal, Man. 8, 109; 190; Pañch. i. d. 130. **3.** Conjuration, Daçak. in Chr. 194, 8.

शपन *çap* + *ana*, n. **1.** A curse. **2.** An oath.

शफ *çapha*, m. and n. **1.** A hoof in general, Man. 10, 89. **2.** A horse's hoof. **3.** The root of a tree.—**Comp.** *Eka-*, adj. and sbst. any animal whose hoof is not cloven, Man. 10, 89. *Dvi-*, adj. and sbst. any cloven-footed animal,

Man. 11, 168. *Mukha-*, adj. foul-mouthed, scurrilous. — Cf. O. H. G. huof; A.S. hóf, The hoof of a horse.

शफर *çapha+ra*, and सफर *saphara*, m., and f. *rî*, A small fish, Cyprinus Sophore, Pañch. ii. d. 87 (*ra*); Bhartṛ. 3, 94 (*rî*).

शबल *çabala=çavala*, q. cf.

शब्द् *ÇABD*, i. 10 (rather a denomin. derived from *çabda*), *çabdaya* and *çabdâpaya*, Par. **1.** To sound, Çiç. 11, 47; to bray, Pañch. 224, 9. **2.** To call, MBh. 3, 14400. **3.** To address, Râm. 2, 59, 7 (*çabdâpaya*). Ptcple. pf. pass. *çabdita*, n. Braying (of an ass), Pañch. 249, 6.—With the prep. अभि *abhi*, To declare, Man. 6, 82. —With सम् *sam*, To say, MBh. 1, 3215.

शब्द *çabda*, i.e. *çap-da* (vb. *dâ*), m. **1.** Sound, Pañch. 129, 15; noise, Pañch. 123, 24. **2.** A word, Vikr. d. 1. **3.** Grammar, Pañch. 4, 17; Daçak. in Chr. 180, 8.—**Comp.** *Jaya-*, m. 1. a shout of victory. 2. the exclamation *jaya*, victory, Vikr. d. 35. *Tâla-*, m. 1. noise produced by falling coco-nuts, Hariv. 3715. 2. noise produced by clapping the hands, applause, ib. 4111. *Niḥçabda*, i.e. *nis-*, adj. I. adj. soundless, noiseless, Megh. 112 (without speaking); Râm. 5, 3, 47. II. n. silence, Râm. 4, 59, 3. *Sa-çabda*, adj. proclaimed, Râjat. 5, 361. °*dam*, adv. with loud noise, Bhartṛ. 2, 86. *Sâdhu-*, m. a cry of ‘Good.’

शब्दज *çabda-ja*, adj. Produced by words, by verbal communication, Bhâshâp. 51.

शब्दन *çabd+ana*, I. adj. Sounding, sonorous. II. n. Uttering sounds.

शब्दाय *ÇABDÂYA*, a denomin. derived from *çabda* with *ya*, Âtm. To sound, to cry, Pañch. 254, 21; to bray, Pañch. 249, 5.

1. शम् *ÇAM*, i. 4, *çâmya*, Par. (the original signification is ‘To get tired’), **1.** To cease, Man, 2, 94. **2.** To grow calm, to be appeased, MBh. 2, 1936; to grow satisfied and pacified, Râjat. 5, 400. **3.** To be calm, undisturbed, MBh. 1, 6362. **4.** To sacrifice, Chr. 292, 12=Rigv. i. 85, 12; Chr. 292, 8=Rigv. i. 86, 8. Ptcple. of the pf. pass. *çânta*. **1.** Hushed, stilled (as wind). **2.** Ceased, Hit. 80, 21; extinguished, Kir. 17, 16. **3.** Allayed, alleviated. **4.** Calm, undisturbed, Utt. Râmach. 7, 7; tranquil, pacified, free from passions, Pañch. i. d. 181; content, Hit. i. d. 142, M.M. **5.** Meek, humble, Chr. 48, 10. **6.** Purified, cleansed. **7.** Repelled, MBh. 1, 212. **8.** °*tam*, adv. **a.** Enough, Utt. Râmach. 71, 2. **b.** A prohibitive word, implying negation, Utt. Râmach. 114, 1 (it must not befall), aversion, disgust, fie, for shame, heaven forbid, Çâk. 67, 13; Daçak. in Chr. 200, 13; hush, Utt. Râmach. 10, 1. **9.** Killed, MBh. 1, 7523. m. An ascetic. n. Appeasing, pacifying. f. *tâ*, A proper name, Utt. Râmach. 103, 3; 173, 9. Caus., and i. 10, I. *çamaya*. **1.** To cause to cease, to extinguish, Megh. 54; Hit. i. d. 87, M.M. **2.** To tame, Vikr. d. 156; to appease, Vedântas. in Chr. 218, 6. **3.** To remove. MBh. 5, 238; to avert, Çâk. 7, 16. **4.** To subdue, MBh. 3, 14620. **5.** To desist, Johns. Sel. 48, 84. **II.** *çâmaya*, Âtm. To look at or inspect.—With the prep. उप *upa*, **1.** To cease, MBh, 4, 1775. **2.** To grow quiet, MBh. 3, 1008. Caus. *çâmaya*, **1.** To allay, Daçak. in Chr. 184, 16; 17. **2.** To kill, MBh. 3, 8541.—With अभ्युप *abhi-upa*, *abhyupaçânta*, Appeased, Ṛit. 1, 1.—

With नि *ni*, **1.** To see, MBh. 2, 1740. **2.** To hear, Râm. 2, 44, 25. *niçânta*, Quiet, patient. n. A house, a dwelling, Ragh. 16, 40. Caus. *çâmaya*, **1.** To see, Râm. 1, 2, 6. **2.** To hear, 2, 57, 21.—With अभिनि *abhi-ni*, Caus. *çâmaya*, To perceive, Daçak. 201, 14. —With विनि *vi-ni*, To hear, MBh. 3, 1878.—With संनि *sam-ni*, To hear, MBh. 2, 1658. Caus. *çâmaya*, To summon, Chr. 52, 10.—With परि *pari*, Caus. *çamaya*, To allay, Gît. 7, 20.—With प्र *pra*, **1.** To cease, Râm. 2, 40, 33; to fade, Man. 4, 186. **2.** To be restrained, Pańch. i. d. 357; to become extinguished, Pańch. iii. d. 54. **3.** To be appeased, soothed, Chr. 22, 14; Pańch. i. d. 315. **4.** To grow calm, MBh. 2, 1941. **5.** To heal, Pańch. 253, 23. *praçânta*, **1.** Ceased, Utt. Râmach. 148, 16 (withdrawn). **2.** Dead, Râjat. 5, 21. **3.** Calmed, tranquillised, Nal. 26, 35; Vedântas. in Chr. 203, 21. **4.** Tamed, Lass. 53, 15. **5.** Relieved. Caus. I. *çamaya*. **1.** To allay, MBh. 2, 12978; to soothe, Man. 8, 391. **2.** To extinguish, MBh. 1, 8156. **3.** To kill, MBh. 2, 2031. II. *çâmaya*, To conquer, MBh. 3, 12196.—With सम् *sam*, *samçânta*, Extinguished, Râm. 2, 66, 1. Caus. *çamaya*, To allay, Râm. 2, 98, 1; to settle, Pańch. i. d. 421.—Cf. κάμνω (cf. ved. *çam*, ii. 9, *çamnâ*), σιδηρο-κμής, κημός (cf. *çamyâ*); O.H.G. chamo.

2. शम् *çam*, I. (sbst.), Work, Chr., 293, 5=Rigv. i. 87, 5. II. indecl. **1.** Happy, happily, auspiciously. **2.** Hail, happiness, Bhâg. P. 1, 17, 34; 8, 3, 23; Nalod. 3, 46.

शम *çam+a*, m. **1.** Rest, quiet, Çâk. d. 96; tranquillity. **2.** Disregarding the objects of sense, Vedântas. in Chr. 203, 19. **3.** Quiet of mind, the absence of passion, Pańch. i. d. 181. **4.** Final happiness. **5.** Cure, Utt. Râmach. 144, 13; convalescence. **6.** The hand. **7.** Abuse, imprecation.

शमक *çam+aka*, adj. sbst. Pacifying, a pacifier.

शमथ *çam+atha*, m. **1.** Quiet, tranquillity of mind, absence of passion. **2.** A counsellor.

शमन *çam+ana*, I. n. **1.** Calmness. **2.** End; with *yâ*, To be destroyed, Pańch. iii. 31, v.r. (cf. my translation and Böhtl. Ind. Spr. 1868). **3.** Immolation. **4.** Hurt, injury. **5.** Abuse, malediction. II. m. **1.** An antelope. **2.** Yama. III. f. *ni*, The night.

शमल *çamala*, n. Impurity, Bhâg. P. 2, 8, 5; calamity, 1, 13, 31.

शमि and मी *çamî*, f. I. A legume or pod. II. *mî*. **1.** A tree, Acacia Suma Roxb., Pańch. 94, 1; Ragh. 3, 9. **2.** A shrub, Serratula anthelmintica. III. A large stick, Man. 8, 237 (Sch.). —**Comp.** *Mahâ-çamî*, f. a large Acacia Suma, Pańch. 97, 15.

शमिन् *çamin*, i.e. *çama+in*, adj. Tranquil, tranquillised, Utt. Râmach. 16, 6.

शम्पा *çampâ*, f. Lightning.

शम्ब् *ÇAMB*, see *çarb* and *samb*.

शम्बर *çambara*, and सम्बर *sambara*, I. m. **1.** The name of a demon, Chr. 297, 14=Rigv. i. 112, 14. **2.** A mountain. **3.** A sort of deer. **4.** A fish. **5.** War. II. n. **1.** Water. **2.** A religious observance.

शम्बल *çambala*, I. (m. and) n. **1.**

Stock for travelling expenses. **2.** A bank, a shore. **3.** Envy. **II.** f. *lî*, A procuress (cf. *sambala*).

शम्बु *çambu* (cf. the next), m. A bivalve shell.

शम्बूक *çambûka* (borrowed from σαμβύκη), **I.** m. (and f. *kâ*), A bivalve shell. **II.** m. **1.** A conch-shell. **2.** A snail. **3.** The edge of the frontal protuberance of an elephant. **4.** The name of a Daitya. **5.** A proper name, Utt. Râmach. 42, 1.

शम्भु *çam-bhu* (vb. *bhû*), m. **1.** Çiva, Pańch. i. d. 175. **2.** Brahman. **3.** A sage man. **4.** A *Siddha*, a demi-divine being.

शम्या *çam+yâ*, f. **1.** The pin of a yoke, Kâtyâyana S. in Journ. of the German Oriental Society, ix. xxxvii. **2.** A sacrificial vessel, ib. **3.** A staff.

शम्व *çamva*, n. The iron end of a pestle.

शय *çaya*, i.e. *çî+a*, **I.** adj. Asleep, sleeping. **II.** m. **1.** Sleep. **2.** A couch. **3.** A snake, boa-constrictor. — **Comp.** *Guhâ-*, I. adj. 1. reposing in the heart, Bhâg. P. 3, 28, 19. 2. haunting caves, Suçr. 1, 200, 7. II. m. 1. a tiger. 2. Vishṇu. *Divâ-*, adj. sleeping by day, Ragh. 19, 34. *Nitya-*, adj. sleeping always, MBh. 3, 10415.—Cf. ὀρέσ-κοιος.

शयथ *çayatha*, i.e. *çî+atha*, **I.** adj. Sleepy. **II.** m. **1.** Death. **2.** A snake, boa-constrictor.

शयन *çayana*, i.e. *çî+ana*, n. **1.** Sleeping, reposing, Utt. Râmach. 28, 1; sleep, Hit. pr. d. 28, M.M. **2.** A bed, a couch, Vikr. d. 51 (*kusuma-*, of flowers).

शयानक *çayâna+ka* (vb. *çî*), m. The boa-constrictor.

शयालु *çayâlu*, *çaya+âlu*, **I.** adj. Sleepy. **II.** m. **1.** A snake, boa-constrictor. **2.** A dog.

ऽशयिन् *-çayin*, i.e. *çî+in*, adj. Reposing, Daçak. in Chr. 199, 7.

शयु *çayu*, i.e. *çî+u*, m. **1.** A snake, boa-constrictor. **2.** A proper name, Chr. 297, 16=Rigv. i. 112, 16.

शयुन *çayuna* (see the last), m. The boa-constrictor.

शय्या *çayyâ*, i.e. *çî+yâ*, f. A bed, a couch, Pańch. 138, 11.—**Comp.** *Adhaḥçayya*, i.e. *adhas-*, I. adj. sleeping on the ground, Râm. 5, 66, 13. II. f. *yâ*, sleeping on a low bed, Man. 2, 108. *Garbha-*, f. the womb, MBh. 12, 6758. *Pṛithak-*, f. sleeping apart, Hit. ii. d. 52. *Bhû-*, f. lying on the ground, Pańch. i. d. 301. *Mahâ-*, f. a throne. *Vîra-*, f. a certain posture, Lass. 2. ed. 70, 55.

शय्यापालत्व *çayyâ-pâla+tva*, n. The office of guarding the bed (of a king), Pańch. 63, 22.

शर *çara*, **I.** m. **1.** A sort of reed, Saccharum sara, Man. 8, 247; a reed, Pańch. 140, 25. **2.** An arrow (i.e. *çṛî+a*), Pańch. 224, 11. **3.** The cream of slightly curdled milk, Mâlav. d. 43 (cream, cf. *sara*). **II.** n. Water.—**Comp.** *A-yugma-* (having an odd number of arrows), m. Kâmadeva, Daçak. in Chr. 190, 22. *Kusuma-* (having flowers instead of arrows), m. epithet of Kâma, Kathâs. 26, 277. *Pańchaçara*, i.e. *pańchan-* (having five arrows), m. Kâma, Prab. 72, 11. *Pushpa-*, m. Kâma. *Sa-*, adj. furnished with arrows. *Hari-*, m. Çiva.

शरज *çara-ja*, n. Fresh butter.

शरट *çaraṭa*, see *saraṭa*.

शरण *çaraṇa*, n. I. (akin to *çṛî*), **1.**

A house, Pańch. i. d. 69; habitation, Lass. 2. ed. 67, 26. **2.** Refuge, Hit. i. d. 189, M.M.; protection, Pańch. 90, 5; 141, 11; 175, 12; help, Vikr. 19, 17; a protector. **II.** (vb. *çṛî + ana*), Killing.—**Comp.** *A-*, adj. without a refuge, helpless, Utt. Râmach. 74, 10; Hit. 90, 1, M.M. *Açaraṇî-kṛita*, made helpless, Pańch. i. d. 241. *Agni-*, n. the sanctuary where the sacred fire is kept, Vikr. 35, 2.

शरणि *çaraṇi* (akin to *çṛî*), f. **1.** A row, a line. **2.** A road, a path.

शरण्य *çaraṇya*, i.e. *çaraṇa + ya*, **I.** adj. **1.** Needing protection, Lass. 2. ed. 90, 50; helpless, poor, miserable. **2.** Yielding protection, helping, Utt. Râmach. 42, 3; Sâv. 1, 2; Chr. 17, 25. **II.** n. **1.** A house. **2.** Refuge, protection, a protector. **3.** (i.e. *çṛî + ana + ya*), Injury, hurt.

शरद् *çarad*, and **शरदा** *çaradâ* (probably from *çṛî*), f. **1.** The autumn, Pańch. v. d. 42 (*rad*). **2.** A year, Utt. Râmach. 11, 8 (*rad*).—**Comp.** *Pariṇata-çarad*, i.e. *pari-nata-* (vb. *nam*), f. the latter part of autumn, Megh. 109.

शरदिज *çarad + i-ja*, adj. Produced in autumn, Utt. Râmach. 53, 18.

शरद्वन्त् *çarad + vant*, m. A proper name, Johns. Sel. 59, 176.

शरधि *çaradhi*, i.e. *çara-dhâ* (cf. *nidhi*), m. A quiver, Vikr. d. 18.

शरन्मेघवत् *çaranmeghavat*, i.e. *çarad-megha + vat*, adv. Like clouds of autumn, Hit. d. 91.

शरभ *çarabha* (cf. *karabha*), m. **1.** A fabulous animal with eight legs, stronger than a lion, Megh. 55. **2.** A young elephant. **3.** A camel. **4.** A grasshopper (cf. *çalabha*). **5.** A locust, Ṛit. 1, 23.—Cf. perhaps κάραβος; A.S. crabba.

शरमय *çara + maya*, adj., f. *yî*, Made or consisting of *çara* grass.

शरयु and **यू** *çara + yû* (better *sarayû*, q. cf.), f. The name of a river.

शरल *çarala* (cf. *sarala*), **I.** adj. **1.** Upright, Pańch. iii. d. 69. **2.** Fraudulent (?). **II.** m. A sort of pine, Râm. 5, 17, 15.

शरवणोद्भव *çaravaṇodbhava*, and **शरवणभव** *çaravaṇabhava*, i.e. *çara-vana-ud-bhû + a*, or *-vana-bhava*, m. A name of the god of war, Megh. 46 (*°vaṇabh°*).

शरवाणि *çaravâṇi*, m. **1.** The head of an arrow. **2.** The maker of arrows. **3.** A foot-soldier (probably an anomal. derivation from *çara + van*).

शरव्य *çara + vya* (or *çaru + ya?*), n. A butt, a mark for arrows, Çâk. d. 156; aim, Ragh. 11, 27.

शराटि *çarâṭi*, **शराडि** *çarâḍi*, **शराति** *çarâti*, **शरारि** *çarâri*, and **शरालि** *çarâli*, f. A bird, Turdus ginginianus.

शराय *ÇARÂYA*, a denomin. derived from *çara* with *ya*, Âtm. To become an arrow, Çṛiṅgârat. 13.

शरारि *çarâri*, **शरालि** *çarâli*, see *çarâṭi*.

शरारु *çarâru* (vb. *çṛî*), adj. Hurtful, mischievous.

शराव *çarâva*, m. and n. (ÇKD.), **1.** A lid, a cover. **2.** A shallow cup or dish, Hit. 114, 22; Pańch. 174, 14; Man. 6, 56; a tray, Vikr. 45, 13; a vessel (figurat. *nishṭhivana-*, A spitting-box), Bhartṛ. 1, 91. **3.** A measure equal to two *Kuḍavas*.—**Comp.** *Çaktu-*, m. a pot full of flour of barley, Hit. 115, 2.

शरासन *çarâsana*, i.e. *çara-asana*, n. **1.** Shooting arrows. **2.** A bow, Vikr. d. 70.

शरि *çari*, i.e. *çṛî + i*, adj. Hurtful.

शरिमन् and **शरीमन्** *çarîman*, m. Bringing forth.

शरीर *çarîra* (vb. *çṛî*), n. **1.** The body, Pańch. iii. d. 96. **2.** Life, Hit. iii. d. 103.—**Comp.** *A-*, m. Kâma, Çiç. 9, 61. *Linga-*, n. the primary body, Vedântas. in Chr. 206, 21. *Çesha-*, n. the remaining body, i.e. all the other parts of the body, Pańch. 38, 8. *Sûkshma-*, n. atom-like body, a Vedântic term, Vedântas. in Chr. 208, 5.—Cf. perhaps A.S. hold, cadaver.

शरीरज *çarîra-ja*, I. adj. Produced by the body. II. m. **1.** A son. **2.** Disease. **3.** Kâma.

शरीरिन् *çarîrin*, i.e. *çarîra + in*, I. adj., f. *riṇî*. **1.** Embodied, Utt. Râmach. 53, 12. **2.** Living, Chr. 20, 20 (*nahi vâṇâ mayotsṛishṭâḥ sajjanti çarîriṇâm̃ kâyeshu*, For the arrows which I have shot do not stick in the bodies of living beings, i.e. all I hit with my arrows must die). **II.** m. **1.** A sentient being, Râjat. 5, 20; Pańch. iii. d. 90; a man, Pańch. ii. d. 107. **2.** An embodied spirit, Man. 1, 53; 6, 64. **3.** The soul, Bhag. 2, 18; Bhâshâp. 26.—**Comp.** *A-*, adj. incorporeal, Utt. Râmach. 39, 19.

शरु *çaru*, i.e. *çṛî + u* (or rather *çar + van*, cf. *κεραυν + ός*), m. **1.** An arrow. **2.** The thunderbolt of Indra. **3.** Any weapon. **4.** Passion, anger. —Cf. Goth. hairus.

शर्करा *çarkarâ* (probably from vb. *çṛî*, but cf. *karkara*), f. **1.** A potsherd. **2.** Gravel. **3.** Stone, Râjat. 5, 432. **4.** A part. **5.** A soil abounding in stony fragments. **6.** Clayed or candied sugar, Pańch. i. d. 423; 185, 21; Lass. 79, 16.—**Comp.** *Guḍa-*, f. sugar, Suçr. 2, 457, 5. *Niḥçarkara*, i.e. *nis-*, adj. free from stones, Râm. 1, 2, 6 Gorr. *Maṇi-çankha-çarkara*, adj. having shells and gravel consisting of jewels, Râm. 2, 63, 36, ed. Seramp. *Vṛihat-tuhinaçarkara*, i.e. *vṛihant-tuhina-*, adj. full of great pieces of ice, Râjat. 3, 362. —Cf. Lat. calculus, calx; *κρόκη*, *κροκάλη*, *κάχληξ*, etc.

शर्करावन्त् *çarkarâ + vant*, and **शर्करिल** *çarkarila*, i.e. *çarkarâ + ila*, adj., f. *vatî*, *lâ*, Full of stony particles.

शर्ध *çardha*, i.e. *çṛidh + a*, m. **1.** A fart. **2.** A troop, Chr. 290, 1 = Rigv. i. 64, 1.

शर्धंजह *çardham̃jaha*, i.e. *çardha + m-jaha* (the latter is a mutilation of *jahat*, the ptcple. pres. of *hâ*), m. Any leguminous pulse (causing flatulence), as beans.

† **शर्ब्** *ÇARB*, i. 1, Par. I. To kill. II. and **शम्ब्** *ÇAMB*, To go (cf. *çarv*).

शर्मन् *çarman* (vb. *çri*, cf. *caraṇa*), n. **1.** Blessing, Chr. 292, 12 = Rigv. i. 85, 12 (ved. *çarma* for *çarmâṇi*). **2.** Happiness, delight, Indr. 3, 9; Draup. 8, 23.—**Comp.** A. *Çarman* may be added at the end of all Brâhmaṇa names, as *Deva-*, *Vishṇu-*, m., MBh. 1, 2049; Hit. 11, 4, M.M. B. *A-*, n. misery, Kir. 12, 25.

शर्मवन्त् *çarmavant*, i.e. *çarman + vant*, adj., f. *vatî*, Happy, auspicious, Man. 2, 32.

शर्मिष्ठा *çarmishṭhâ*, i.e. superl. of the last, f. A proper name, the wife of Yayâti, Çâk. d. 82; Mâlav. 19, 11.

शर्या *çaryâ*, i.e. *çṛî + yâ*, f. Night.

शर्यात *çaryâta*, m. A proper name, Chr. 297, 17=Rigv. i. 112, 17.

† **शर्व्** *ÇARV*, **सर्व्** *SARV*, i. 1, Par. To kill (cf. *çṛî* and the next).

शर्व *çarva*, i.e. *çṛî + va* (cf. *çaru*), I. m. A name of Çiva, Pańch. ii. d. 169; Hariv. 15408. II. f. *çarvâṇî*, Çiva's wife.

शर्वट *çarvaṭa*, m. A proper name, Râjat. 5, 413.

शर्वरी *çarvarî*, i. e. *çṛî + van + î* (with *r* for *n*, cf. *çaru*), f. 1. Night, Man. 1, 66. 2. A woman. 3. Turmeric.—Cf. probably as akin, Κέρβερος.

शर्वरीक *çarvarî + ka*, adj. Hurtful, mischievous.

शल् *ÇAL*, i. 1, Âtm. 1. To shake, to tremble (cf. *chal*). 2. To cover. i. 1, Par. To go, to run. Cf. *çval* and *çaṭh*. — With the prep. **उद्** *ud*, i. 1, Par. To start up, Çiç. 3, 37. Ptcple. of the pf. pass. *uchchhalita*. 1. Starting up, bubbling up, Pańch. i. d. 148. 2. Uncovered, Vikr. 57, 19. — With **प्रोद्** *pra-ud*, To spirt out, Çiç. 2, 66.

शल *çala*, probably *çṛî + a* (with *l* for *r*), I. m. and n. The quill of a porcupine. II. m. 1. A dart. 2. A kind of field. 3. Brahman.

शलक *çalaka*, m. A spider; Pańch. iii. d. 179, read *çalâkâm̃*.

शलभ *çalabha* (cf. *çarabha*), m. 1. A grasshopper, Pańch. i. d. 369; iv. d. 58 (cf. *patańga*). 2. A locust, Arj. 7, 24; Chr. 34, 13.

शलल *çalala* (cf. *çala*), n., and f. *lî*, The quill of a porcupine, Pâraskara, Gṛ. S. ii. 1, in Journ. of the German Oriental Society, vii. 532 (*lî*).

शलाका *çalâkâ* (cf. *çala*), f. 1. A javelin. 2. An arrow. 3. A small stake, rod, the bar of a cage, Pańch. iii. d. 179; a rib of an umbrella, etc. 4. A fibrous stick used as a brush or pencil, Suçr. 1, 33, 18; a pencil, Ragh. 7, 8. 5. A porcupine. 6. A piece of ivory used in particular games, a domino, MBh. 5, 1225 (read °*kâ-dhûrtân*, Sharpers). 7. A bone. 8. A bird, Turdus gosalica.— **Comp.** *Ayas-kânta-*, f. a magnetised needle, Mâlat. 14, 15. *Niḥçalâka*, i. e. *nis-*, adj. (properly, free from the birds called Turdus gosalica), lonely, Man. 7, 147. *Vam̃ça-*, f. 1. the bambu pipe that forms the body of the lute. 2. any small bambu pin or stake, as the bar of a cage.

शलाटु *çalâṭu*, adj. Unripe.

शल्क *çalka*, probably *çṛî + ka* (with *l* for *r*), n. 1. A part. 2. The bark of a tree. 3. The scale of a fish.—**Comp.** *Mahâ-*, m. a prawn or shrimp, Man. 3, 272. *Sa-*, adj. scaly, Man. 5, 16.

† **शल्भ्** *ÇALBH*, i. 1, Âtm. To boast.

शल्य *çalya*, i.e. *çala + ya*, I. m. and n. 1. A dart, a javelin. 2. An arrow, Utt. Râmach. 46, 14; Chr. 30, 1 (m.). II. m. 1. A peg, a pin. 2. A porcupine. 3. A thorny shrub, Vangueria spinosa. 4. A boundary. 5. The name of a king, Johns. Sel. 50, 98. III. n. 1. Any stake or thorn, Bhartṛ. 2, 97. 2. An iron crow. 3. Any extraneous substance which has lodged in the body, as an arrow or thorn. 4

Difficulty. **5.** Poison. **6.** Sin. **7.** Abuse. —Comp. *Nis-*, adj. free from an arrow, MBh. 6, 3375. *°yam*, adv. free from pain or care, Daçak. in Chr. 194, 23. *Vi-*, adj. 1. free from thorns or spikes, Râm. 6, 71, 24. 2. free from pain or care. *Sa-*, adj. 1. pierced by a thorn or dart. 2. pierced, Vikr. d. 29. 3. troublesome, difficult.—Cf. *κῆλα*, pl.

शल्यक *çalya + ka*, m. **1.** A thorn, a stake. **2.** A dart, a pike. **3.** A hedgehog, Man. 12, 65. **4.** A porcupine, ib. 5, 18; Bhâg. P. 3, 10, 22.

शल्यवन्त् *çalya + vant*, adj. **1.** Shooting arrows, one who has shot an arrow, Man. 9, 44. **2.** Set with stakes. **3.** Harassed with difficulties.

शल्लक *çallaka* (cf. *çalka* and *çalya*), **I.** m. A plant, Bignonia indica. **II.** f. *kî*. **1.** A porcupine. **2.** The gum olibanum tree, Boswellia thurifera, Vikr. d. 107. **III.** n. Bark, rind.

शल्व *çalva*, m. The name of a country.

शव् *ÇAV*, i. 1, Par. **1.** To go. **2.** To alter, to change, to destroy.

शव *çava*, I. m. and n. A dead body, Man. 4, 108; Pańch. v. d. 24 (m.); Kathâs. 4, 107 (m.). II. n. Water.

शवर *çavara*, m. **1.** A barbarian tribe, a Çavara, Nalod. 3, 37. **2.** f. *rî*, A female of that tribe, Utt. Râmach. 19, 14. **3.** Çiva. **4.** Water. — Comp. *Smara-*, m. the *Çavara*-like (i.e. cruel) god of love, Bhartṛ. 1, 94.

शवल *çavala*, I. adj. **1.** Variegated, of a variegated colour, Mâlat. 145, 12; brown or yellow, Vikr. d. 109 (cf. Wilson, Spec. of the Theatre of the Hind. 2. ed. i. 250, n.). **2.** Imitative. **3.** Articulated, Râjat. 5, 68 (divided, viz. by rivers). II. f. *lî*. **1.** A brindled cow. **2.** The cow of plenty, Vaçishṭha's cow, Râm. 1, 52, 21. **III.** n. Water.

शवलत्व *çavala + tva*, n. Alternation, Mâlat. 161, 5.

शवस् *çavas*, i.e. *çu* (=*çvi*), + *as*, n. **1.** Power, strength, Chr. 290, 8 = Rigv. i. 64, 8. **2.** A corpse.—Comp. *Satya-*, adj. possessed of real strength, Chr. 292, 8 = Rigv. i. 86, 8.

† **शश्** *ÇAÇ* (originally *ças*, cf. *çaça* and N.G. hast, Eng. to hasten, *ç* for *s* by assimilation), i. 1, Par. To jump, to move by leaping. Pres. ptcple. *çaçant*, Kir. 15, 5.

शश *çaç + a* (originally *çasa*, cf. O.H.G. haso; A.S. hara), m. **1.** A hare, Pańch. ii. d. 79; or rabbit. **2.** The spots on the moon, supposed to resemble the figure of a hare (cf. *çaça-dhara*, sqq.). **3.** Gum myrrh. **4.** A tree, Symplocos racemosa.

शशक *çaça + ka*, m. A hare, Hit. ii. d. 116.

शशधर *çaça-dhara*, **शशभृत्** *çaça-bhṛi + t*, **शशाङ्क** *çaçâṅka*, i.e. *çaça-aṅka*, and **शशिन्** *çaçin*, i.e. *çaça + in*, m. The moon, Bhartṛ. 1, 40 (*dhara*); Pańch. i. d. 107 (*çaçâṅka*); Vikr. d. 8 (*çaçin*); 109 (*çaçin*); see *çaça*.

शश्वन्त् *çaçvant* (for original *sa-çvant*, vb. *çvi*; cf. *ἅπας* and *viçva*, *çâçvata*), acc. n. *vat*, adv. **1.** Perpetually, Megh. 56; Hit. i. d. 211, M.M. **2.** Again and again.—Cf. *πᾶς*, i.e. mutilated *ἅπας*.

† **शष्** *ÇASH*, i. 1, Par. To hurt.

शष्कुल *çashkula*, I. m. A plant, Galedupa arborea Roxb. II. f. *lî*. **1.** The outer ear, Yâjń. 3, 96. **2.** Rice or barley water. **3.** A sort of pie.

शष्प *çashpa*, and **शस्प** *çaspa*, Pańch. 9, 6 (probably from vb. *ças*; cf. *vi-ças* and *çastra*, properly, grass which may be cut), n. 1. Young grass, Ragh. 2, 26; Vikr. d. 120 (read *çashpa* instead of *çashya*, Boll., and *çasya*, Calc.). 2. Loss of intellect.—Cf. Lat. cespes, i.e. cespo + vit = *çaspa* + *vant*, Endowed with young grass.

शष्पभुज् *çashpa-bhuj*, adj. sbst. A beast feeding on grass, Pańch. 102, 4.

शस् *ÇAS* (akin to *çam*, cf. e.g. *yas* and *yam*), i. 1, Par. To hurt, to kill, MBh. 3, 1638; cf. *sas*.—With the prep. **अभि** *abhi*, To hurt, Râm. 2, 11, 16 (figurat. To overpower by deceit); *abhiçasta*, Hurt, Man. 11, 112.—With **प्र** *pra*, *praçasta*, Destroyed, removed, MBh. 12, 5067. — With **वि** *vi*, 1. To dissect, Râm. 1, 13, 35. 2. To sacrifice, MBh. 3, 10495. 3. To kill, Nal. 11, 28. *viçasita*, 1. Cut, dissected. 2. Hurt, killed.—Cf. Lat. hostia; Goth. hunsl; A.S. husel.

शसन *ças+ana*, n. Immolation.

शस्त्र *ças+tra*, I. n. A sword, a scimitar, Pańch. 34, 15; Chr. 18, 33; 2. II. f. *trî*, A knife, Bhartṛ. 1, 89. III. n. 1. A weapon in general, Vikr. 87, 2; Pańch. 263, 6; Nal. 11, 28 (an arrow). 2. Iron. 3. Steel. 4. A hymn.—**Comp.** *Ati-*, adj. surpassing weapons, Ragh. 12, 73. *Nis-*, adj. disarmed, unarmed, Râjat. 5, 406. *Nyasta-*, i.e. *ni-asta-*, adj. one who has laid down his weapons, epithet of the Manes, Man. 3, 192. *Mahâ-*, n. an excellent weapon, Chr. 25, 53. *Vi-*, adj. disarmed, unarmed.—Cf. Lat. castrare.

शस्त्रधर *çastra-dhara*, and **शस्त्रभृत्** *çastra-bhṛi+t*, m. A warrior, Chr. 13, 5 (*-bhṛit*).

शस्त्रास्त्रभृत्त्व *çastrâstrabhṛittva*, i.e. *çastra-astra-bhṛi+t+tva*, n. Bearing arms for striking and throwing, Man. 10, 79.

ऽशस्त्रिक *-çastrika*, substituted for *çastra*, as latter part of a comp. adj., Daçak. in Chr. 189, 6 in *kaṇṭha-nyasta-*, Having put a knife to (his) throat, and 201, 10, *a-lakshya-* (my) sword not being noticed (properly against grammar, which prescribes *çastraka* with *a*, but perhaps for *çastrin+ka*).

शस्त्रिन् *çastrin*, i.e. *çastra+in*, adj., f. *iṇî*, Armed, Râjat. 5, 58.

शस्प *çaspa*, see *çashpa*.

शस्य *çasya*, see *çaṁs*.

शाक *çâka*, partly *çak+a*, I. (m. and) n. A potherb, any vegetable, Man. 2, 246; Hit. i. d. 67, M.M. II. m. 1. Power. 2. One of the seven *Dvîpas*. 3. An era, especially that of Çâlivâhana, beginning seventy-six or seventy-eight years after the Christian.—**Comp.** *Utpala-*, m. the name of a plant, Râjat. 5, 49. *Kâla-*, n. Ocimum sanctum, Man. 3, 272. *Tikta-*, m. 1. a bitter vegetable, Râjat. 5, 49 (?). 2. the name of several plants. *Patra-*, m. a potherb, Man. 12, 65.

शाकट *çâkaṭa*, i.e. *çakaṭa+a*, I. adj. Relating to a cart. II. m. A draught ox.

शाकटीन *çâkaṭîna*, i.e. *çakaṭa+îna*, I. adj. Relating to a cart. II. m. A cart-load as a measure of weight or value.

शाकल *çâkala*, adj. Epithet of a kind of sacrifice, Man. 11, 200; cf. 256.

शाकलहोमीय *çâkalahomîya*, i.e. *çâkala-homa+îya*, adj. Belonging to the *Çâkalahoma*, Man. 11, 256 (cf. the last).

शाकशाकट *çâkaçâkaṭa,* and **शाकशाकिन** *çâkaçâkina* (cf. *çâka*), n. A field of vegetables, a kitchen garden.

शाकिनी *çâkinî,* i.e. *çâka+in+î,* f. A female divinity of an inferior class, Pańch. 241, 1.

शाकुन *çâkuna,* i.e. *çakuna+a,* adj. 1. Of or relating to birds, Man. 3, 268. 2. Portentous.

शाकुनिक *çâkunika,* i.e. *çakuna+ika,* I. adj. Of or relating to birds. II. m. A fowler, Man. 8, 260; Pańch. iii. d. 158.

शाक्त *çâkta,* and **शाक्त्य** *çâktya,* i.e. *çakti+a* or *ya,* m. A worshipper of the female principle, Lass. 2. ed. 87, 9.

शाक्तीक *çâktîka,* i.e. *çakti+îka,* m. A spearman.

शाक्त्य *çâktya,* see *çâkta.*

शाक्य *çâkya,* m. Buddha, the founder of the Bauddha faith, Daçak. in Chr. 191, 15.

† **शाख्** *ÇÂKH,* i. 1, Par. To pervade, to embrace.

शाखा *çâkhâ,* f. 1. The branch of a tree, Pańch. 148, 5. 2. An arm. 3. Any part of an animal devoid of sensibility, as a horn. 4. A division, a sect. 5. A subdivision of the Vedas, according to the different schools and redactions of the holy writings, Windischmann, Sankara, 112. 6. A part, Mâlav. d. 29.—Comp. *Tri-çâkha,* adj., f. *khî,* consisting of three wrinkles (viz. a frown), MBh. 8, 4336. *Skandha-,* f. the principal branch of a tree.

शाखाभृत् *çâkhâ-bhṛi+t,* m. A tree, Kir. 5, 37.

शाखिन् *çâkhin,* i.e. *çâkhâ+in,* I. adj., f. *nî,* Having branches, branched, literally and figuratively. II. m. 1. A tree, Böhtl. Ind. Spr. 187. 2. A Veda.

शाङ्खिक *çâṅkhika,* i.e. *çaṅkha+ika,* I. adj. Relating to a conch-shell. II. m. 1. A shell-cutter. 2. A shell-blower.

शाट *çâṭa,* m., and f. *ṭî,* and **शाटक** *çâṭaka,* m. and n. 1. A petticoat, Pańch. i. d. 160 (*ṭaka*); Râm. 2, 32, 21 (*ṭî*); a gown, Mṛichchh. 49, 11. 2. (*ṭî*), Cloth, Bhâg. P. 9, 9, 7. 3. (*ṭa*), A garment, Böhtl. Ind. Spr. 1210.—Comp. *Sthûla-çâṭî,* or *-çâṭaka,* m., and *ṭakâ, ṭikâ,* f. coarse cloth.

शाठ्य *çâṭhya,* i.e. *çaṭha+ya,* n. 1. Deceit, Hit. i. d. 99, M.M. 2. Wickedness. 3. Perfidy, hatred, Bhartṛ. 2, 19.

† **शाड्** *ÇÂḌ,* or **शाल्** *ÇÂL,* i. 1, Âtm. To praise.

शाण *çâṇa,* A. i.e. *çaṇa+a,* I. adj. Made of Bengal San, Man. 2, 41. II. f. *ṇî.* 1. Ragged garment. 2. A new unseamed and single breadth of cloth, given to the religious student at his investiture. III. n. Coarse cloth, canvass. B. (from vb. *ço,* cf. *çâna*), m., and f. *ṇî.* 1. A whet or grindstone, Bhartṛ. 2, 36 (read *çâṇo°*). 2. A touchstone.

शाण्डिल्य *çâṇḍilya,* i.e. *çaṇḍila,* a proper name, *+ya,* patronym., f. *lî* (Pańch. 122, 1), Descended from Çaṇḍila, Pańch. ii. d. 83. m. The name of a Muni, Vedântas. in Chr. 202, 18.

शातकुम्भ *çâtakumbha,* i. e. *çata-kumbha+a,* n. Gold, Çiç. 9, 9.

शातकुम्भमय *çâtakumbha+maya,* adj., f. *yî,* Golden, Arj. 9, 25.

शातन *çâtana,* I. n. Withering, becoming thin (cf. *çâta,* s.v. *ço*). II. i.e.

çâtaya, Caus. of *çad,* + *ana,* at the end of a comp. adj. Cutting off, Ragh. 3, 42 (v.r., cf. *çâtin*).

शातभिष *çâtabhisha,* or **शातभिषज** *çâtabhishaja,* i.e. *çatabhishâ,* or *çatabhishaj,* + *a,* m. One who is born during the lunar mansion called *Çatabhishâ* or *Çatabhishaj,* Vârt. 2, ad Pâṇ. iv. 2, 8; cf. iv. 3, 36.

शातमन्यव *çâtamanyava,* i.e. *çata-manyu,* a name of Indra, + *a,* adj. Belonging to Indra, Kir. 13, 38.

शातिन् *çâtin,* i.e. *çâtaya,* Caus. of *çad,* + *in,* adj. Cutting off, Ragh. 3, 42 (v.r., cf. *çâtana*).

शात्रव *çâtrava,* i.e. *çatru* + *a,* I. m. An enemy, MBh. 8, 1523. II. n. 1. Enmity. 2. A multitude of enemies.

शाद *çâda,* i.e. *çada* + *a,* m. 1. Young grass. 2. Mud.

शाद्वल *çâdvala,* i. e. *çâda* + *vala,* I. adj. 1. Covered with young grass, Vikr. 57, 18; Râm. 3, 50, 14. 2. Green, Kâçîkh. 32, 50, and Aufrecht, Ujjvalad. 255, n. II. sbst. (n.) A place covered with grass, Kir. 7, 26.

† **शान्** *ÇÂN* (properly a denomin. derived from *çâna*), used only in the anomal. desider. *çîçâṁsa,* Par. Âtm. To whet, to sharpen.

शान *çâna,* i. e. *ço* + *na,* m. 1. A grindstone. 2. A touchstone.—Cf. A.S. haenan, lapidare.

शानैश्चर *çânaiçchara,* i.e. *çanaiç-chara* + *a,* adj. Falling on a Saturday, Lass. 16, 16.

शान्तनव *çântanava,* i.e. *çântanu* + *a,* patronym., m. The son of Çântanu, i.e. Bhîshma, Chr. 4, 15.

शान्तनु *çântanu,* m. The name of a king, Chr. 3, 4.

शान्ति *çânti,* i. e. *çam* + *ti,* f. 1. Quiet, the absence of passion, and indifference to objects of pleasure or pain, Hit. 78, 8, M.M.; iii. d. 4. 2. Felicity, Lass. 96, 12. 3. Rest, repose, Mâlat. 87, 6. 4. Ceasing, Hit. iii. d. 88. 5. Causing to cease, Mâlat. 128, 8; remission, alleviation, soothing, Çṛiṅgârat. 14; Çâk. 81, 11; Vikr. d. 24. 6. Appeasing (the stomach), Bhartṛ. 2, 23. 7. Expiatory rites to avert evil, Râm. 1, 11, 14. 8. Preservation, Pañch. 89, 5; 90, 4.

शान्त्व् *ÇÂNTV,* and (worse, although very frequent), **सान्त्व्** *SÂNTV,* i. 10 (rather a denomin. derived from the next), Par. (in epic poetry also Âtm., MBh. 2, 2428), 1. To pacify, Man. 7, 172 (with *s*). 2. To comfort, to console, Mâlat. 146, 3 (with *s*); MBh. 4, 436 (with *s*). 3. To address mildly, Man. 8, 79 (with *s*); Chr. 38, 7 (with *ç*). 4. To conciliate, Râm. 1, 38, 5 (with *s*). —With the prep. **अभि** *abhi,* To comfort, Râm. 2, 32, 39 (with *ç*).—With **उप** *upa,* To comfort, MBh. 3, 14330 (with *s*).—With **परि** *pari,* To console, Râm. 2, 23, 42 (with *ç*).

शान्त्व *çântva,* and **सान्त्व** *sântva* (Man. 8, 391), i.e. *çam* + *tva,* n. 1. Conciliation. 2. Comforting, consoling. 3. Mildness, Man. 8, 391 (*s*); Chr. 42, 9 (*ç*). 4. Mild speech, Râm. 2, 35, 23; MBh. 5, 2650 (*sântva*). 5. Peaceable way, Pañch. iii. d. 26 (*sântva*); Lass. 45, 14 (*ç*).

शाप *çâpa,* i.e. *çap* + *a,* m. 1. Abuse. 2. Oath. 3. Curse, Pañch. 186, 14.

शाब्द *çâbda,* i.e. *çabda* + *a,* I. adj. 1. Sonorous, sounding. 2. Relating to or derived from words, Bhâshâp. 80. 3. Nominal. II. f. *dî,* Sarasvatî.

शाब्दिक *çâbdika*, i.e. *çabda* + *ika*, I. adj. Relating to sounds or words. II. m. A grammarian.

शामन् *çâman* (vb. *çam*, cf. *sâman*), n. Conciliation, appeasing.

शामन *çâmana*, i.e. *çam*, anomal. Caus., + *ana*, n. 1. Killing. 2. Tranquillity. 3. End; with *yâ*, To be destroyed, Pańch. iii. 81 (but cf. my transl.).

शामित्र *çâmitra*, *çam* + *tra* (see the last), n. 1. A deadly blow, Mṛichchh. 161, 11. 2. Sacrificing. 3. Ticing cattle. 4. A sacrificial vessel.

शाम्बूक *çâmbûka* = *çambûka*, q. cf.

शाम्भव *çâmbhava*, i.e. *çambhu* + *a*, I. adj. Belonging to Çiva, Pańch. i. d. 175. II. m. 1. Çiva. 2. A worshipper of Çiva. 3. A sort of poison. III. f. *vî*, Pârvatî.

शायक *çâyaka*, see *sâyaka*.

शायिन् *çâyin*, i.e. *çî* + *in*, adj., f. *nî*, Lying down, lying, Daçak. in Chr. 188, 15; living, Hit. i. d. 138, M.M.—Comp. *Ûrdhva-*, m. a name of Çiva, MBh. 13, 1160. *Eka-*, adj. resting ever on the same seat, Lass. 2. ed. 70, 53. *Prâsâda-*, adj., f. *nî*, one who had slept in a palace, Hiḍ. 1, 34. *Yoga-*, adj. absorbed in meditation, Râjat. 5, 100. *Sthaṇḍila-*, m. a devotee who sleeps on ground prepared for a sacrifice.

† शार् *ÇÂR*, सार् *SÂR*, i. 10, Par. To be weak (cf. *çṛî*).

शार *çâra*, I. adj. 1. Variegated (in colour), Daçak. in Chr. 180, 1 (of hair, mixed with grey and white). 2. Yellow. II. m. 1. Hurting (vb. *çṛî*). 2. A mixture of blue and yellow, a green. 3. Variegating. 4. Air, wind (cf. *sâra*). 5. A piece or man at chess, backgammon, Daçak. in Chr. 185, 24 (cf. *sâra*). III. f. *rî*. 1. An arrow (vb. *çṛî*, cf. *çara*), Chr. 297, 16=Rigv. i. 112, 16. 2. Kuça grass.—Comp. *Kṛishṇa-*, adj. blue-black, Megh. 48, read *-çâra* (Sch.).

शारङ्ग *çâraṅga* (cf. the last and *sâraṅga*), I. adj. Variegated, spotted. II. m. 1. A deer. 2. An elephant. 3. The *Châtaka*, Cuculus melanoleucus. 4. A peacock. 5. A large bee. III. f. *gî*. 1. A sort of fiddle. 2. The wife of Mandapâla, Man. 9, 23.

शारद *çârada*, i.e. *çarad* + *a*, I. adj., f. *dî*. 1. Autumnal, Nal. 13, 44; Lass. 91, 15. 2. Produced or growing in the autumn, Man. 6, 11. 3. New. II. m. 1. Grain or rice ripening in the autumn. 2. A sort of kidney bean. 3. Autumnal sickness. 4. Autumnal sunshine. 5. A year. III. f. *dâ*. 1. Sarasvatî, Lass. 38, 7. 2. A title of Durgâ. 3. A sort of guitar. IV. f. *dî*, The day of full moon in the month *Kârttika*.

शारद्वत *çâradvata*, i.e. *çaradvant* + *a*, I. adj. Descended from Çaradvant, Johns. Sel. 20, 94. II. m. A proper name, Çâk. 63, 2.

शारि *çâri* (cf. *çâra*), I. m. 1. A piece or man at chess, draughts, etc. 2. An elephant's housings. 3. Fraud. II. m., f. *ri* or *rî*, A bird, Gracula religiosa.

शारिका *çârikâ*, i.e. *çâri* + *ka*, f. 1. A bird, Gracula religiosa and Turdus salica, Lass. 20, 1 (cf. *sârikâ*). 2. A bow or stick for playing any stringed musical instrument.

शारीर *çârîra*, i.e. *çarîra* + *a*, I. adj. 1. Corporeal, Bhag. 17, 14; relating to animal bodies, Man. 5, 110. 2. Spiritual, incorporate. II. n. 1. Excrement, Man. 11, 202. 2. The soul whilst incorporate.

शारीरक *çârîra+ka*, and **शारीरिक** *çârîrika*, i.e. *çarîra+ika*, adj. **1.** Corporeal. **2.** Incorporate; cf. *çârîraka-sûtra*.

शार्कक *çârkaka* (cf. *çarkarâ*), m. **1.** Clayed or candied sugar. **2.** Cream, the froth of milk. **3.** A lump of meat.

शार्कर *çârkara*, i.e. *çarkarâ+a*, I. adj. **1.** Stony. **2.** Sugary. II. m. The froth of milk, cream.

शार्गाल *çârgâla*, i.e. *çṛigâla+a*, adj., f. *lî*, Belonging to a jackal, MBh. 13, 411.

शार्ङ्ग *çârṅga*, i.e. *çṛiṅga+a*, I. adj. Horny, made of horn, etc. II. m. (n.?), **1.** A bow, Çâk. 94, 2. **2.** The bow of Vishṇu. **3.** The name of a bird.

शार्ङ्गिन् *çârṅgin*, i.e. *çârṅga+in*, m. **1.** An archer. **2.** Vishṇu, Megh. 47.

शार्दूल *çârdûla*, m. **1.** A tiger, Nal. 12, 129. **2.** A Râkshasa. **3.** A sort of bird. **4.** (as latter part of comp. words), Best, pre-eminent; e.g. *muni-*, m. A pre-eminent sage, Lass. 49, 15; *râjaçârdûla*, i.e. *râjan-*, m. A pre-eminent king, Râm. 3, 49, 28.

शार्व *çârva+a*, i.e. *çarva+a*, adj. Belonging to Çiva, Bhartṛ. 2, 10.

शार्वर *çârvara*, i.e. *çarvarî+a*, I. adj. **1.** Nocturnal. **2.** Mischievous, pernicious. II. m. Darkness. III. f. *rî*, Night.

† **शाल्** *ÇÂL*, see *çâḍ*.

शाल *çâla* (cf. *sâla*), I. m. **1.** A tree, Shorea robusta (ÇKD.), MBh. 9, 3239; 14, 2521. **2.** A fish, Ophiocephalus wrahl Ham., Hiḍ. 2, 18. **3.** Çâlivâhana. II. f. *lâ*. **1.** A large branch of a tree. **2.** A hall. **3.** A stable, Hit. i. d. 135, M.M. **4.** A house.—Comp. *Apûpa-*, f. a bake-house, Man. 9, 264. *Açva-*, f. a stable, Nal. 19, 11. *Açva-chalana-*, f. a stable for riding horses, Pañch. 252, 21. *Gândharva-*, f. a music-room, Kathâs. 12, 31. *Chatuḥçâla*, i.e. *chatur-*, I. adj. possessing four halls, Pañch. 252, 17. II. n. a square formed by four houses, Râm. 3, 23, 10. *Chandra-*, f. an apartment on the house-top, Ragh. 13, 40. *Chitra-*, f. a hall adorned with pictures, a picture-gallery, Râm. 3, 61, 16. *Nartana-*, f. a dancing-room, MBh. 4, 696. *Patnî-*, f. a room erected near the place of a sacrifice for the women and sacrificial implements, MBh. 12, 3648. *Parṇa-*, f. 1. an arbour, Râm. 3, 6, 15. 2. the name of a district inhabited by anchorites, MBh. 13, 3398. *Pâka-*, f. the kitchen, Lass. 81, 5. *Raṅga-*, f. a hall for public exhibition. *Ratha-*, f. a coach-house, Nal. 21, 29. *Çilpa-*, n., and f. *lâ*, a workshop. *Sûda-*, f. a kitchen.—Cf. A.S. heal, A hall.

शालभञ्जी *çâlabhañjî*, and **शालभञ्जिका** *çâlabhañjikâ*, i.e. *çâla-bhañj +a+î*, and *+ka*, f. **1.** A doll. **2.** A kind of play in the east of India.

शालाजिर *çâlâjira*, m. and n. A hollow earthen cup.

शालार *çâlâra*, n. **1.** A ladder. **2.** The claw of an elephant. **3.** A bird-cage.

शालि *çâli*, m. **1.** Rice, Pañch. 163, 23. **2.** The civet or polecat.

शालिक *çâlika*, i.e. *çâlâ+ika*, I. adj. Relating or belonging to the Shorea robusta, a hall, etc. II. m. **1.** A weaver. **2.** A village of artificers. **3.** A tax.

शालिता *çâlitâ*, i.e. *çâlin+tâ*, f. 1. Possessing. 2. Confidence in.

शालिन् *çâlin*, i.e. *çâlâ+in*, I. adj., f. *nî*. 1. Belonging to a house, domestic. 2. Endowed with, Kathâs. 46, 107; Kir. 5, 32; possessed of, having, Pańch. v. d. 12. 3. Shining or resplendent with. II. f. *nî*, A proper name, Lass. 39, 8.—Comp. *Abhimâna-*, adj. proud. *Jala-ja-*, adj. full of fishes, MBh. 2, 1813. *Naya-*, adj. conversant with politics, Kir. 5, 24. *Bâhu-*, m. a proper name. *Vîrya-*, adj. strong, heroic.

शालिहोत्र *çâlihotra*, m. 1. The name of a writer on veterinary medicine, Nal. 19, 28; Pańch. 253, 22; 255, 4. 2. A horse.

शालिहोत्रज्ञ *çâlihotra-jńa*, adj. Knowing (the precepts of) Çâlihotra, Pańch. 255, 1.

शालीन *çâlîna*, i.e. *çâlâ+îna*, I. adj. 1. Ashamed, bashful, humble, Nalod. 2, 3; Ragh. 6, 81; Mâlav. 51, 7 (cf. *çâlînikaraṇa*, Humbling, Pâṇ. 1, 3, 70). 2. Like. II. m. An opulent householder.

शालु *çâlu*, I. m. 1. A frog. 2. An astringent substance. 3. A sort of perfume. II. n. The root of the water lily.

शालूक *çâlûka* (cf. the last), n. The root of the esculent water lily.—Comp. *Kaṇṭha-*, n. a swelling in the throat, Suçr. 1, 306, 14.

शालूर *çâlûra* (cf. *çâlu*), m. A frog.

शालेय *çâleya*, i.e. *çâli+eya*, adj. Fit for rice.

शाल्मलि and **ली** *çâlmalî*, f. 1. The silk cotton tree, Bombax heptaphyllum, Man. 8, 246. 2. One of the seven *Dvîpas*. 3. *lî*, A hell, Man. 4, 90.—Comp. *Kûṭa-*, f. a fabulous thorny rod of the cotton tree for torturing the wicked in hell, MBh. 18, 84.

शाल्व *çâlva*, i.e. *çalva+a*, m. 1. pl. The inhabitants of Çalva, Sâv. 2, 7; Chr. 5, 6; 18, 34; 35. 2. The king of the Çâlvas, ib. 14, 26.

शाल्वेय *çâlveya*, i.e. *çalva+eya*, m. pl. The inhabitants of Çalva, Draup. 1, 6.

शाव *çâva*, I. i.e. *çava+a*, adj. 1. Relating to, or produced by, a dead body, Man. 5, 59. 2. Dead, Sâv. 5, 61. II. (akin to *çvi*, cf. *çiçu*), m. The young of any animal, Utt. Râmach. 122, 12 (*siṁha-*, A lion's cub).

शावक *çâva+ka*, m. The young of any animal, Hit. 39, 4, M.M.

शावर *çâvara*, i.e. *çavara+a*, I. adj. Low, vile. II. m. 1. Fault. 2. Sin, wickedness.

शाश्वत *çâçvata*, i.e. *çaçvant+a*, I. adj., f. *tî*. 1. All, Utt. Râmach. 36, 7; MBh. 12, 9192. 2. Eternal, Hit. ii. d. 60; perpetual, Böhtl. Ind. Spr. 101 (with *na*, perishable); °*tam*, adv. Constantly, Mâlat. 3, 5. II. m. 1. A name of Vyâsa. 2. Çiva. 3. The sun. III. f. *tî*, The earth. IV. n. Heaven.—Comp. *A-*, adj. short, Pańch. 4, 16. *Pari-*, adj. eternal, MBh. 5, 4574.

शाष्कुल *çâshkula* (anomal. for *çaushkula*, q. cf.), adj. Eating flesh or fish.

शास् *ÇÂS* (for *çaças*, i.e. *çaṁs*, ii. 3); the base of many formations is *çish* for *çis* (or rather *çiças*, i.e. *çaṁs*, ii. 3, with *i* in the reduplication), ii. 2, Par. (in epic poetry also Âtm., MBh. 1, 4993), 1. To teach, Bhag. 2, 7; pass. *çishya*, To learn, Pańch. 4, 20;

94, 10. **2.** To report, to proclaim, Man. 11, 82. **3.** To command, Ragh. 15, 79 (Calc.). **4.** To govern, Man. 7, 18. **5.** To punish, Man. 4, 175 ; 8, 314. Ptcple. of the pf. pass. *çishṭa.* **1.** Disciplined. **2.** Docile. **3.** Good, MBh. 1, 6845. **4.** Learned, Man. 3, 39. **Comp.** *A-*, adj. wicked, MBh. 1, 6845. Ptcple. of the fut. pass. *çishya*, m. A pupil, Vikr. 35, 1. **Comp.** *A-*, adj. indocile, Pańch. i. d. 433. *Upa-*, m. a pupil of a pupil, Prab. 28, 3. Caus. To punish, Hit. 65, 18 (*çâsita*). *çâsita*, Governed. **Comp.** *Mâtṛi-*, m. a fool. *Su-*, adj. well-governed, Hit. i. d. 21, M.M.—With the prep. अनु *anu*, **1.** To teach, Râjat. 5, 400 ; to instruct, Çâk. 55, 18. **2.** To speak to, to address, MBh. 4, 98. **3.** To order, Man. 9, 233 ; Vikr. 70, 13 ; 86, 19 (acc. of the pers.). **4.** To govern, MBh. 1, 4124. **5.** To punish, Man. 11, 99.—With समनु *sam-anu*, To govern, Nal. 12, 49.—With आ *â*, I. Par. **1.** To report, Bhaṭṭ. 6, 27. **2.** To command, Bhaṭṭ. 6, 4. II. Âtm. (in epic poetry also Par., Arj. 5, 19). **1.** To pray for benefits to (dat.), Man. 3, 80. **2.** To pray, Bhaṭṭ. 5, 16. **3.** To wish, Utt. Râmach. 7, 15 ; MBh. 3, 12430. **4.** To hope, Çâk. 112, 3. Ptcple. of the fut. pass. *âçâsya*, Desirable. n. Wish, blessing, Ragh. 5, 34. **Comp.** *An-*, adj. not to be desired, Ragh. 4, 44.—With उप *upa*, see *çishya* above. —With प्र *pra*, **1.** To command, MBh. 2, 2433. **2.** To govern, Man. 9, 66. **3.** To punish, Chr. 16, 14.

शासन *çâs + ana*, n. **1.** Governing, chastisement, Böhtl. Ind. Spr. 873. **2.** An order, Râm. 3, 51, 8 ; Vikr. d. 155 ; precept, Nal. 26, 9 ; edict, Nal. 2, 10. **3.** A royal grant of land or privileges, Pańch. 4, 25. **4.** A deed, a written contract. **5.** A *çâstra* or scripture. **6.** The government of the passions. **7.** Instruction, Johns. Sel. 57, 165.—**Comp.** *Kûṭa-*, n. a forged royal edict, Man. 9, 232. *Tâmra-*, n. an edict engraved on a copper plate, Daçak. 20, 15. *Dus-*, m. a proper name, MBh. 1, 2447. *Dharma-*, n. a code of law, MBh. 1, 2950. *Para-*, n. the order of another, Pańch. i. d. 300 (cf. Böhtl. Ind. Spr. 3292). *Pura-*, m. (the chastiser of Pura), epithet of Çiva, Kumâras. 7, 30. *Bhîma-*, m. Yama. *Mahâ-*, a minister, Lass. 67, 10 (? cf. n.).

शासितृ *çâs + itṛi*, m., f. *trî*, and n. Who or what orders, commands ; a governor, a king, Çâk. d. 24.

शास्ति *çâs + ti*, f. Punishment inflicted by royal command.

शास्तृ *çâs + tṛi*, m., f. *trî*, and n. **1.** Who or what orders, a ruler. **2.** A teacher.

शास्त्र *çâs + tra*, n. **1.** An order. **2.** A precept, Pańch. 141, 13. **3.** Scripture, institutes of religion, law, science, learning in general, Hit. pr. d. 10, M.M. ; Bhartṛ. 2, 12 ; Chr. 5, 5. **4.** A work of religious or scientific character, Man. 1, 58 ; Hit. pr. d. 6, M.M. ; a collection, a treatise, a book, Pańch. pr. d. 3.—**Comp.** *Chalachchhâstra*, i.e. *chalant-* (vb. *chal*), adj. one whose governing is staggering, unsteady, Lass. 53, 11. *Jńâna-*, n. a work on soothsaying, Lass. 36, 14. *Tarka-*, n. logic, MBh. 12, 9678. *Dharma-*, n. 1. a book treating of duty, Hit. 19, 8, M.M. 2. the body of law, Man. title, 2, 10. *Naya-* and *Nîti-*, n. 1. the science of political conduct, Râm. 3, 56, 18 ; MBh. 1, 5567. 2. works on polity, Pańch. pr. d. 2. *Yathâ-çâstra + m*, adv. as the law ordains, Man. 2, 70. *Çabda-*, n. rules of grammar,

Pańch. 4, 17. *Haya-*, n. art of training or treating horses, Chr. 25, 53. *Hetu-*, n. a philosophical (=heretical) book, Man. 2, 11.

शास्त्रकृत् *çâstra+kṛi+t,* m. **1.** An author of a *çâstra,* Vedântas. in Chr. 215, 17. **2.** An author in general. **3.** A Ṛishi.

शास्त्रज्ञ *çâstra-jña,* adj. **1.** Knowing the institutes of religion, etc., Pańch. i. d. 385. **2.** Knowing by books, a theorist, Hit. iii. d. 54 (*karmasv adṛishṭakarmâ yaḥ çâstrajño pi sa muhyati,* He who has not tested his skill by works, although knowing it by books, makes mistakes).

शास्त्रतस् *çâstra+tas,* n. According to the sacred authorities.

शास्त्रवत् *çâstra+vat,* adv. Like the holy writings, Hit. iii. d. 68.

शास्त्रवन्त् *çâstra+vant,* adj. Skilled in the holy writings, Pańch. iii. d. 270.

शाहि *çâhi,* m. The name of a dynasty, Râjat. 5, 154.

शि *ÇI,* † ii. 5, Par. Âtm. To sharpen (cf. *ço*).

शिंशपा *çiṁçapâ,* (**शिंशिपा** *çiṁçipâ,* Lass. 4, 10; 14; 5, 6), f. Two trees, Dalbergia Siçu and the Açoka tree, Pańch. 249, 24.

शिक्य *çikya,* n., and f. *yâ,* **1.** The string suspended from either end of a pole to receive a burthen. **2.** The burthen so carried. **3.** The strings of a balance.

शिक्ष् *çiksh,* see *çak,* desider.

शिक्षा *çikshâ,* i.e. *çiksha,* desider. of *çak,+a,* f. **1.** Learning, Johns. Sel. 8, 3; Râjat. 5, 318; study. **2.** One of the six Vedâṅgas, treating of pronunciation, Madhusûdana in Weber, Ind. St. i. 16. **3.** Modesty.—Comp. *Upa-*, f. desire of learning, Mṛichchh. 17, 11. *Gaja-*, f. training of elephants, MBh. 1, 4355.

शिखण्ड *çikhaṇḍa* (cf. *çikhâ*), m. **1.** The tail of a peacock, Vikr. d. 81. **2.** Locks of hair left at the time of tonsure, hair, Daçak. in Chr. 179, 15; 180, 1.

शिखण्डक *çikhaṇḍa+ka,* m. **1.** The tail of a peacock. **2.** The lock of hair, or crest, left on the crown of the head, Utt. Râmach. 105, 5; Çâk. 59, 17 (Prâkṛ.).

शिखण्डिक *çikhaṇḍika,* **I.** i.e. *çikhaṇḍin+ka,* m. A cock. **II.** i.e. *çikhaṇḍa+ka,* f. *kâ,* A lock of hair on the crown of the head.

शिखण्डिन् *çikhaṇḍin,* i.e. *çikhaṇḍa+in,* **I.** m. **1.** A peacock, Utt. Râmach. 65, 9. **2.** A peacock's tail. **3.** A cock. **4.** An arrow. **5.** A Ṛishi. **6.** The son of Drupada, who had been before a girl, Chr. 3, 1. **II.** f. *ní,* The daughter of Drupada, who was metamorphosed into a man, Chr. 52, 13.—Comp. *Chitra-*, m. pl. the seven Ṛishis, MBh. 12, 12722. *Sa-*, adj. with Çikhaṇḍin, Chr. 54, 9.

शिखर *çikhara* (cf. *çikhâ*), m. and n. **1.** Summit, Pańch. 9, 7; end. **2.** The summit of a mountain, Bhartṛ. 2, 91; Vikr. 10, 6. **3.** The top of a tree. **4.** The edge or a point of a sword. **5.** Horripilation. **6.** The armpit. **7.** A gem of a bright red colour; the bud of the Arabian jasmine, Megh. 80 (Sch.).—Comp. *Tri-*, adj. having three summits, the name of a mountain, Râm. 4, 44, 50.

शिखरिन् *çikharin,* i.e. *çikhara+*

in, I. adj. **1.** Crested, peaked, pointed. **2.** Resembling the buds of the Arabian jasmine, Râm. 3, 52, 27. **II.** m. **1.** A mountain, Râm. 3, 55, 44. **2.** A tree. **3.** A stronghold. **4.** The lapwing. **II.** f. *iṇî*. **1.** A line of hair extending across the navel. **2.** An excellent woman. **3.** A dish of curds and sugar with spices, Vikr. 42, 7 (Prâkṛ.). **4.** Arabian jasmine.

शिखा *çikhâ*, f. **1.** Point, top, Râm. 3, 49, 34; end, Çâk. d. 14; Ragh. 16, 48 (at the end of a comp. adj.; Sch. filaments). **2.** A crest, Râm. 3, 53, 60. **3.** A peacock's crest. **4.** A lock of hair on the crown of the head, Vikr. d. 124 (head). **5.** Flame, Pańch. i. d. 319. **6.** A ray of light. **7.** Chief. **8.** A branch. —Comp. *Agni-çikha*, I. adj. as hot as fire, Râm. 6, 30, 27. II. f. *khâ*, flame. *Uchchhikha*, i.e. *ud-çikha*, adj. blazing upwards or brightly, Utt. Râmach. 65, 8. *Tri-çikha*, adj., f. *khâ*, having the shape of a trident, Pańch. 220, 1. *Dîpa-*, f. the flame of a lamp, Kathâs. 18, 77. *Dîpta-çikha*, adj. blazing, Râm. 3, 53, 60. *Stana-*, f. a nipple.

शिखावत् *çikhâ + vat*, adv. Like a crest, Pańch. 121, 3.

शिखावन्त् *çikhâ + vant*, adj., f. *vatî*, Crested.

शिखावल *çikhâ + vala*, I. adj., f. *lî*. **1.** Crested. **2.** Burnt, Cṛiṅgârat. 16. II. m. A peacock, Lass. 2. ed. 91, 51.

शिखिन् *çikhin*, i.e. *çikhâ + in*, I. adj. **1.** Crested, MBh. 6, 71. **2.** Having a lock of hair on the top of the head, Râm. 3, 52, 9. **II.** m. **1.** A cock. **2.** A peacock, Vikr. d. 41. **3.** A religious mendicant. **4.** A mountain. Râjat. 5, 15. **5.** An arrow. **6.** A bull. **7.** A horse. **8.** Fire, Râm. 3, 55, 11; Pańch. iv. d. 76 (but cf. also Böhtl. Ind. Spr. 125). **9.** A lamp. **10.** Ketu, the personified descending node, Pańch. i. d. 240 (see my transl.).—**Comp.** *Çastra-*, adj. proud of (the practice of) weapons, Utt. Râmach. 149, 14.

शिग्रु *çigru*, m. **1.** A tree, Morunga guilandina. **2.** A potherb.

शिग्रुक *çigru + ka*, m. A particular plant (cf. the last), Man 6, 14.

† **शिङ्ख्** *ÇIṄKH*, i. 1, Par. To go, to move.

शिङ्घ् *ÇIṄGH*, i. 1, Par. To smell. —With the prep. **उप** *upa*, To kiss, Bhaṭṭ. 17, 95.

शिङ्घाण *çiṅghâṇa*, I. m. Froth, foam. II. n. **1.** The mucus of the nose. **2.** Rust of iron. **3.** A glass vessel.

शिङ्घाणक *çiṅghâṇa + ka*, m. Phlegm.

शिञ्ज् *ÇIŃJ*, ii. 2, Âtm. To tinkle, Bhaṭṭ. 14, 4; Megh. 77 (Par.). Ptcple. of the pf. pass. *çiñjita*, Tinkling, Râm. 1, 9, 17. n. Tinkling, Ragh. 4, 56; of metallic ornaments worn as chains, rings, etc., Vikr. d. 93.

शिञ्ज *çiñj + a*, I. m. Tinkling. II. f. *jâ*, A bow-string.

शिञ्जिन् *çiñj + in*, I. adj. Tinkling. II. f. *nî*. **1.** A bow-string. **2.** Metallic rings worn round the toes.

† **शिट्** *ÇIṬ*, **सिट्** *SIṬ*, i. 1, Par. To disrespect.

शितता *çita + tâ* (see *ço*), f. Sharpness, Çiç. 9, 66.

शिताभ्र *çitâbhra*, see *sitâbhra*.

शिति *çiti*, I. adj. **1.** Black, dark blue, Vikr. d. 151; Bhâg. P. 4, 4, 18. **2.** White. II. m. The *bhûrja* or birch.

शिथिल *çithila* (cf. *çlath*), adj. **1.** Loose, Vikr. d. 115; Pańch. ii. d. 143;

loosened, Megh. 69. **2.** Flaccid, faded, Çâk. d. 41. **3.** Feeble, languid, Bhartṛ. 2, 22. **4.** Ineffective. **5.** Relaxed, dissolved, Daçak. in Chr. 199, 5. **6.** Not very careful, Pańch. ii. d. 82. **7.** Not rigidly observed. **8.** Loosely retained. **9.** Abandoned, Ragh. 2, 41 (*°li kṛi*, To abandon).—Comp. *A-*, adj. tight, close, Utt. Râmach. 15, 16.

शिथिलता *çithila + tâ*, f. **1.** Looseness, state of dissolution, Pańch. 30, 11. **2.** Relaxedness, relaxation. **3.** Want of energy, Pańch. iv. d. 7.

शिथिलय *ÇITHILAYA*, a denomin. derived from *çithila*, Par. To loosen, to make loose, Çâk. 9, 21. Ptcple. of the pf. pass. *çithilita* (or *çithila + ita*). **1.** Loosened, loosed, loose, Çâk. d. 57. **2.** Relaxed, dissolved, Daçak. in Chr. 184, 8.

शिनि *çini*, m. pl. The name of a class of Kshatriyas.

शिफा *çiphâ*, f. **1.** A fibrous root. **2.** A lash with a whip, Man. 8, 369; 9, 230. **3.** A river. **4.** A mother.

शिम्बि and **बी** *çimbî*, f. A legume, a pod, Mâlat. 145, 20.

शिर *çira*, **I.** i.e. curtailed *çiras*, n. **1.** The head. **2.** The root of the pepper plant. **II.** f. *râ* (cf. *sirâ*), Any vessel of the body, really, or supposed to be of a tubular form, as a nerve, Râm. 5, 32, 11; a vein.—**Comp.** *Tri-*, I. adj. having three points, MBh. 13, 7379. II. m. the name of a Râkshasa, Bhâg. P. 9, 10, 9.

शिरःस्थ *çiraḥstha*, i. e. *çiras-stha*, adj. Borne on the head, Pańch. v. d. 36.

शिरस् *çiras* (for original *çaras*, cf. Zend. *çara*, and *çîrsha*), n. (the base of some cases is optionally *çîrshan*, i.e. *çiras + an*), **1.** The head, Pańch. iii. d. 193; *çirasâ pra-ṇi-pat*, To reverence by inclining one's head, Vikr. 3, 12; *çirasâ kṛi*, To bear on one's head, Böhtl. Ind. Spr. 1847. **2.** The top of a mountain, Kir. 5, 17; of a tree. **3.** Chief, principal.—**Comp.** *A-*, adj. headless, Man. 9, 237. *Abhra-*, n. a head represented by the sky, Çiç. 9, 8. *Açva-*, I. n. the head of a horse, MBh. 3, 3083. II. adj. having the head of a horse, ib. 12, 13100. III. m. a proper name, ib. 1, 2531. *Uchchaiḥçiras*, i.e. *uchchais-*, adj. m. a man of high rank, Kumâras. 1, 12. *Kapâla-*, Râm. 2, 54, 30 (=2, 54, 32 Gorr., where *kalâpa-*) ? perhaps a name of Çiva. *Kûrcha-*, n. the upper part of the palm and ball of the foot, Suçr. 1, 345, 9. *Tri-*, I. adj. having three heads, MBh. 5, 229. II. m. the name of an Asura and a Râkshasa, ib. 9, 1755; Râm. 3, 29, 32. *Dvi-*, adj. having two heads, Pańch. 251, 24. *Bhuja-*, n. the shoulder. *Mṛiga-*, n. the fifth lunar mansion. *Çiçu-mâra-*, n. a part of the heaven studded with stars, the north-east point.—Cf. κάρα, κάρηνον, κρανίον; Lat. cere- in cerebrum, and cer- in cervix, (vix from vincire, cf. *çirodharâ*); A.S. haernes.

शिरसिज *çiras + i-ja*, and **शिरसिरुह्** *çiras + i-ruh*, m. The hair of the head, Kir. 10, 52 (*-ja*).

शिरस्क *çiras + ka*, **I.** n. **1.** A helmet. **2.** A turban, a cap. **II.** f. *kâ*, A palanquin.

शिरस्त्र *çiras-tra* (vb. *trâ*), and **शिरस्त्राण** *çiras-trâṇa*, n. **1.** A helmet, Râjat. 5, 342; Ragh. 4, 64. **2.** A turban, a cap.

शिराल *çirâ + la* (see *çira*), **I.** adj., f. *lâ*. **1.** Veiny, showing the veins, Kâçîkh. 37, 14; Bhaṭṭ. 2, 30. **2.** Showing the tendons. II. n. An acid fruit, Averrhoa carambola.

शिरि *çiri*, i.e. *çṛî + i*, m. 1. A sword. 2. An arrow. 3. A murderer. 4. A locust.

शिरीष *çirîsha* (akin to the last), I. m. A tree, Acacia sirisa, Bhartṛ. 2, 6. II. n. Its flower, Çâk. d. 145.

शिरोधरा *çirodharâ*, i.e. *çiras-dhṛi + a*, f. The neck, Daçak. in Chr. 198, 23 (read °*çirodharoddeça*°). — Comp. *Mahâ-kâya-çirodhara*, adj. having a great body and neck, Râm. 3, 55, 2.

शिरोधि *çirodhi*, i.e. *çiras-dhâ* (cf. *nidhi*), f. The neck.

शिरोरुह् *çiroruh*, i.e. *çiras-ruh*, and

शिरोरुह *çiroruha*, i.e. *çiras-ruh + a*, m. Hair, Pańch. iii. d. 193 (*ha*).

† शिल् *ÇIL*, सिल् *SIL*, i. 6, Par. To glean (cf. the next).

शिल *çila*, A. n. Gleaning ears of corn, Man. 3, 100; 10, 112. B. i.e. probably *ço + la*, I. f. *lâ*. 1. A stone, Pańch. 100, 18; a rock, Vikr. d. 49. 2. A flat stone on which condiments are ground. 3. Arsenic. II. f. *lâ* and *li*. 1. A stone or beam placed across a post or pillar. 2. The timber of a door frame. III. f. *li*. 1. A dart, an arrow, Ragh. 7, 62. 2. An earth-worm. — Comp. *Gaṇḍa-çilâ*, f. a large rock, Bhâg. P. 3, 13, 22. *Jâta-rûpa-çila*, m. the name of a (golden) mountain, Râm. 4, 14, 52. *Tîrtha-çilâ*, f. stone steps leading to a bathing-place, Çṛiṅgârat. 1 (read °*lam*, at the end of a comp. adj.). *Badhya-*, f. *lâ*, rock of execution, Pańch. 52, 2. *Manaḥçila*, i.e. *manas-*, m., and f. *lâ*, red arsenic. *Svalpa-çilâ*, i.e. *su-alpa-*, f. a very small stone.

शिलाटक *çilâṭaka*, m. 1. A room on the top of a house. 2. A hole.

शिलि and ली *çili* (cf. *çili*, under *çila*), f. The lower timber of a door.

शिलीन्ध्र *çilîndhra*, I. m. 1. A sort of tree. 2. A kind of fish. II. f. *rî*. 1. Clay, earth. 2. A small earthworm (cf. *çili*, under *çila*). 3. A sort of bird. III. n. 1. Hail (cf. *çilâ*). 2. A mushroom, Megh. 11. 3. The flower of the plantain tree.

शिलीपद *çilîpada* (a dialect. form of *çlîpada*, q. cf.), m. A morbid enlargement of the leg, Lass. 94, 10.

शिल्प *çilpa*, n. 1. Proficiency in any manual or mechanical art, or profession; art, Pańch. i. d. 4, 446; Bhâg. P. 3, 23, 17; Chr. 51, 1; Daçak. in Chr. 180, 12. 2. A sort of spoon used at sacrifices to throw the butter into the fire.—Comp. *Kṛita-*, adj. one who has attained a knowledge of his art, Yâjń. 2, 184.

शिल्पिक *çilpika*, i.e. *çilpa + ika*, I. adj. Manual, mechanic. II. n. 1. Handicraft. 2. (and शिल्पक *çilpa + ka*), A sort of drama.

शिल्पिन् *çilpin*, i.e. *çilpa + in*, I. adj. Belonging or relating to a mechanical profession or art. II. m., f. *nî*, and n. An artificer, a mechanic, Pańch. 10, 6; Johns. Sel. 9, 11.

शिव *çiva* (probably akin to *çavas*), I. adj. 1. Prosperous, Hit. 68, 17; auspicious, Mâlat. 6, 12; happy. 2. Right, Nal. 20, 17. 3. Comparat. *çivatara*, Very complacent, Utt. Râmach. 145, 2. II. m. 1. Çiva, a deity of the Hindu triad, Kir. 5, 21; dual, Çiva and his wife, ib. 5, 40. 2. The phallic emblem of Çiva. 3. An auspicious planetary conjunction. 4. The Vedas. 5. One of the astronomical periods termed *Yogas*. 6. A pillar to which cattle are tied. 7. A sort of perfume. III. f. *vâ.* **1.** Durgâ, the wife of Çiva. **2.** The female jackal, Sâv. 5, 75. **3.** The name of several plants. **IV.** n. **1.** Happiness, Arj. 5, 19; bliss, Mâlat. 160, 14. **2.** Wellbeing, Pańch. 16, 5. **3.** Final emancipation from separate existence. **4.** Water. **5.** Sea or fossile salt.—**Comp.** *A-*, I. adj. inauspicious, Râm. 3, 29, 11. II. n. ill-luck, ib. 3, 30, 3. *Sadâ-*, m. Çiva.

शिवंकर *çivam̃kara*, i.e. *çiva* + *m-kṛi* + *a*, adj. Auspicious, conferring happiness.

सिवताति *çiva* + *tâti*, f. Benevolence, Mâlat. 160, 4.

शिवि *çivi*, m. **1.** A beast of prey. **2.** The name of a king, Sâv. 2, 17; MBh. 13, 2046, sqq.; pl. his descendants, Draup. 8, 3.

शिविका *çivikâ*, f. **1.** A palanquin, a litter, Râm. 2, 60, 76, Seramp. **2.** A tent, Johns. Sel. 9, 12; a marquee. **3.** A proper name, MBh. 3, 13155.

शिविर *çivira*, I. m. The name of a tribe (?), Râjat. 5, 176. **II.** n. **1.** A camp. **2.** A royal camp or residence. **3.** A guard or defence for the soldiers. **4.** A sort of grain.

शिशिर *çiçira* (akin to *ço*, cf. the ved. inflection of this vb.), I. adj. Cold, cool, Vikr. d. 41; comparat. Very cool, refreshing, Pańch. 9, 4. **II.** (m. and) n. **1.** Cold, frost, Megh. 81. **2.** Coolness, Vikr. 19, 17 (of a wood). **3.** The cold season, Pańch. v. d. 4.

शिशु *çiçu*, i. e. reduplic. *çvi*, m. **1.** The young of man or any animal, Vikr. d. 121; Pańch. 160, 4; a child, Pańch. i. d. 241; a calf, Pańch. 182, 12; a pup, etc. **2.** A boy. **3.** A pupil.

शिशुक *çiçu* + *ka*, m. **1.** A child, Pańch. ii. d. 200. **2.** A porpoise.

शिशुता *çiçu* + *tâ*, f., **शिशुत्व** *çiçu* + *tva*, n. Childhood, Utt. Râmach. 107, 6; Pańch. 220, 10.

शिश्न *çiçna*, m. The penis.

† 1. **शिष्** *ÇISH*, i. 1, Par. To hurt, to kill.

2. **शिष्** *ÇISH*, ii. 7, *çinash*, *çim̃sh*, Par. To leave; pass. To be left, MBh. 2, 1964. Pteple. of the pf. pass. *çishṭa*. **1.** Left, remaining. **2.** Also sbst. Chief, Hit. 100, 15. **Comp.** *Vishama-*, adj. unfair (division). Caus. *çeshaya*, To leave, to spare, MBh. 3, 14760.—With the prep. **अव** *ava*, pass. To be left, MBh. 3, 2276. *avaçishṭa*, Remaining, Hit. 61, 4, M.M.; remainder, Man. 3, 116; Hit. 103, 14 (*avaçishṭa-bala*, adj. With the rest of [my] army). Caus. *avaçeshita* (perhaps *avaçesha* + *ita*), Left, spared, MBh. 1, 5129. — With **समव** *sam-ava*, Caus. pass. *samavaçeshita*, Left, spared, MBh. 1, 6337. — With **उद्** *ud*, *uchchhishṭa*, **1.** Left, remainder, Daçak. in Chr. 197, 8. **2.** Left behind, Râjat. 5, 11. **3.** One who has a remnant of food in his mouth, Man. 2, 56; 4, 75. n. Remains, remainder of food, Man. 5, 140.—With **निस्** *nis*, Caus. *niḥçeshita* (perhaps rather *niḥçesha*, i.e. *nis-çesha*, + *ita*), **1.** Used up entirely (without leaving any part), Râm. 1, 65, 6. **2.** Exterminated, Pańch. 201, 22 (cf. my translation, n. 1210).—With **परि** *pari*, Caus. To leave, Bhaṭṭ. 17, 93; with *na*, To destroy, Ragh. 12, 79.—With **वि** *vi*, To distinguish, to make distinguished, to augment, Mâlat. 71, 8. Pass. **1.** To be distinguished, Ragh. 17, 62. **2.** To prefer, with abl. and instr., MBh. 3,

14735. Pass. a. To be better than, Man. 2, 83; Böhtl. Ind. Spr. 1672 (*mûrkha-sahasreṇa prâjńa eka vi çishyate*, One wise man is better than a thousand fools); to be of more weight, Râm. 2, 35, 8. b. To be most preferable, best, Hit. iii. d. 50; to be pre-eminent, Man. 9, 297. *viçishṭa*, 1. Having distinctive and exclusive properties, Bhâshâp. 132. 2. Especial. 3. Endowed with, possessed of. 4. Distinguished, Hit. pr. 42, M.M.; superior, pre-eminent, Chr. 28, 15; best, Bhag. 1, 7. Ptcple. of the fut. pass. *viçeshya*. 1. What is determinable or to be distinguished, Bhâshâp. 131. 2. Principal, primary, chief. m. A substantive. n. The subject of a predicate. Caus. 1. To distinguish, MBh. 3, 16449. 2. To surpass, Chr. 44, 2. 3. To adorn, Mṛichchh. 59, 14. *viçeshita*, 1. Distinguished, separated. 2. Excellent.—With प्रवि *pra-vi*, To increase, Utt. Râmach. 102, 5.—With प्रतिवि *prati-vi*, *prativiçishṭa*, Better than (with abl.), MBh. 1, 4684.—Cf. Lat. quæso, quæro, quæstor, perhaps cura; Goth. qvisteins, qvistjan, fra-qvisteins, fra-qvistjan, fra-qvistnan, us-qvistjan, based on a noun qvist= * *çish* + *ti*, Leaving, abandoning; also us-haista, Poor.

शिष्टि *çishṭi*, i. e. *çâs* + *ti*, f. An order.

शिष्यता *çishya* + *tâ* (see *çâs*), f. The state of a pupil, Pańch. 34, 11.

शी *ÇÎ* (cf. *çad*), ii. 2, Âtm. (in epic poetry also Par., MBh. 5, 63), 1. To lie (as on the ground), Daçak. in Chr. 187, 11. 2. To lie down, 187, 6. 3. To repose, MBh. 1, 5033. 4. To sleep, Man. 2, 163. Ptcple. of the pf. pass. *çayita*, Lying, Çiç. 9, 39. Ptcple. of the fut. pass. *çayanîya*, Fit for sleeping, lying on, Utt. Râmach. 67, 3. n. A couch. Caus. *çâyaya*, 1. To cause to lie, to throw, Daçak. in Chr. 190, 22. 2. To put, Râm. 2, 66, 16.—With the prep. अति *ati*, 1. To surpass, Ragh. 5, 14 (Calc.). 2. To sleep longer than (acc.), MBh. 3, 14686. Comp. ptcple. of the fut. pass. *an-ati-çayanîya*, adj. Not to be surpassed, Kir. 5, 52.—With अधि *adhi*, 1. To lie down on (acc.), Râm. 2, 88, 12. 2. To sleep on, Ragh. 5, 28 (Calc.). 3. To sleep, Pańch. 26, 25. 4. To inhabit, Bhaṭṭ. 10, 35.—With अनु *anu*, To lie down, to sleep, near, Daçak. in Chr. 184, 4.—With आ *â*, To sleep on, Vikr. d. 41.—With उप *upa*, To lie near (with acc.), Lass. 2. ed. 70, 51.—With निस् *nis*, in *niḥçayâna* (rather *çayâna* with *nis*, adj.), Not sleeping, Bhâg. P. 3, 9, 10.—With प्रति *prati*, To sleep opposite to (acc.), MBh. 3, 16300.—With सम् *sam*, *saṁçayâna*, and *saṁçayita*, Dubious, Chr. 31, 32 (Hit. iv. d. 19, read *saṁçayitam*).—Cf. κεῖμαι, κεῖται (=*çete*), κοίτη, κοιμάω, κῶμα, κώμη; Lat. quies, quiesco, civis; O.H.G. hîwî, matrimonium; A.S. hiwa, familia; O.H.G. hîwo, m. hîwa, f. conjux; hîwjan, hîjan, nubere; Goth. hêthjô (=κοίτη), haithi, campus, haims; O.H.G. haim; A.S. ham, haeman (cf. κοιμάω).

1. शीक् *ÇÎK* or सीक् *SÎK* (probably better, cf. *sich*), i. 1, Âtm. To sprinkle, Bhaṭṭ. 14, 76.

† 2. शीक् *ÇÎK*, सीक् *SÎK*, i. 1, Âtm. To go, to move. i. 1, and 10, Par. 1. To be angry. 2. To endure patiently. 3. To touch.

† 3. शीक् *ÇÎK*, i. 10, Par. To speak, to shine.

शीकर *çikara* (cf. 1. *çik*), I. m. 1. A drop of water, Ragh. 16, 62; of rain, Çâk. d. 166. 2. Thin rain, Ṛit. 1, 15; Kir. 5, 15 (also *sîkara*, MBh. 14, 2201). 3. Spray, Mâlat. 147, 14. II. n. A sort of pine, or its resin.—Comp. *Kara-* and *karin-*, m. water expelled by an elephant's trunk, Kir. 16, 9.

शीकरिन् *çîkarin*, i.e. *çikara + in*, adj. Sprinkling, Utt. Râmach. 63, 5.

शीघ्र *çighra*, adj. 1. Quick, speedy, Vikr. d. 140 (*mandala-çighra-châra*, Turning round quickly). 2. Violent, Pańch. iii. d. 52. 3. °*ram*, adv. Swiftly, Pańch. 128, 4. Comparat. °*ratara + m*, adv. As quickly as possible, Pańch. 88, 6.—Cf. A.S. higian, To make haste; κιχάνω.

शीत् *çit*, An imitative sound expressing pleasure, Bhartṛ. 1, 49 (cf. *sît*), and trembling, Böhtl. Ind. Spr. 738.

शीत *çita* (probably an old ptcple. pf. pass. of *ço*), I. adj. 1. Cold, Hit. i. d. 79, M.M.; chilly. 2. Apathetic. 3. Idle. 4. Stupid. II. n. 1. Coldness, Pańch. 169, 14. 2. Water.—Comp. *A-*, adj. hot, Bhâshâp. 25.

शीतता *çita + tâ*, f. Coldness, Pańch. i. d. 287.

शीतल *çita + la*, I. adj. Cold, cool, Pańch. ii. d. 58; figurat., Vikr. d. 90. Comparat. °*latara*, Cooler, Çiç. 9, 4. II. m. 1. The moon. 2. A sort of camphor. III. m., f. *lâ*, and *li*, and n. The name of several plants. IV. n. 1. Coldness. 2. A pearl.—Comp. *A-*, adj. hot, Çiç. 9, 86. *Ati-*, adj. very cool, Hit. iii. d. 45. *Su-*, adj. very cool, Hit. i. d. 96, M.M. *Hima-*, adj. very cold.

शीत्कार *çit-kâra*, m. 1. Making the sound *çit*, sighing on account of pleasure. 2. A frown, Amar. 31 (Sch.).—Comp. *Sa-çithâra + m*, adv. with sighs, Vikr. d. 103.

शीधु *çidhu*, m. and n. Rum distilled from molasses, intoxicating spirits, Çiç. 9, 87; wine, Böhtl. Ind. Spr. 3322 (cf. *sîdhu*).

शीन *çina*, see *çyai*.

† **शीभ्** *ÇÎBH*, i. 1, Âtm. To boast.

शीर *çi + ra*, m. A snake, boa-constricter, Pańch. 203, 6.

शीर्णता *çirṇa + tâ*, f., and **शीर्णत्व** *çirṇa + tva*, n. (vb. *çṛî*), Emaciation, withering.

शीर्वि *çirvi*, i.e. *çṛî + vi*, adj. Hurtful, destructive.

शीर्ष *çirsha*, i.e. curtailed *çirshan* (cf. *çiras*), n. The head, Utt. Râmach. 40, 2 (*-chhedya*, adj. One who must be beheaded), Bhartṛ. 2, 27.—Comp. *Go-*, I. adj. shaped like a cow's head, MBh. 7, 8097. II. n. a kind of sandal, Râm. 4, 41, 59. *Tri-*, adj. having three heads, MBh. 1, 2162. *Daçaçirsha*, i.e. *daçan-*, m. 1. a name of Râvaṇa, Râm. 4, 10, 22. 2. a spell, ib. 1, 30, 5. *Pańcha-*, adj. having five heads, Bhâg. P. 4, 25, 21. *Pûrva-*, adj., f. *shâ*, with the head turned to the east, MBh. 13, 463. *Mṛiga-*, m. the fifth lunar mansion, Lass. 16, 18.—Cf. probably O.H.G. and A.S. hals; Lat. collum; see *çiras*.

शीर्षक *çirsha + ka*, I. m. Râhu. II. n. 1. The skull. 2. A helmet. 3. Judgment, sentence.—Comp. *Sthûla -çirshikâ*, f. a small ant with a large head.

शीर्षण्य *çirshaṇya*, i.e. *çirshan + ya*, I. m. Clean and unentangled hair. II. n. A helmet.

शीर्षन् *çirshan* (see *çiras*), A substitute for *çiras*, as latter part of some comp. words, and in some derivatives; e.g. *sahasra-*, adj. Thousand-headed, Johns. Sel. 91, 38.

शील् *ÇÎL* (probably a denomin. derived from the next), i. 1, Par. **1.** † To meditate. **2.** To adore, to worship. Caus., and i. 10, Par. **1.** To make, Gît. 9, 6. **2.** To practise, Mṛichchh. 34, 19. **3.** To visit, Gît. 7, 4. **4.** To worship, MBh. 1, 3207. **5.** To put on, to dress, Gît. 5, 11. **6.** † To repeat. **7.** † To surpass. Ptcple. of the pf. pass. *çîlita*, Skilled, conversant.

शील *çîla*, i.e. **A.** *çish + la* (m. and) n. **1.** Nature, quality, MBh. 1, 4054. **2.** Disposition, inclination, character, Pańch. i. d. 282; a good character, Pańch. v. d. 2. **3.** Moral practice, Man. 2, 6. **4.** Good conduct, Johns. Sel. 13, 45. **5.** Virtue, Bhartṛ. 2, 77. **6.** Beauty. **B.** *çî + la*, m. A large snake.—Comp. *A-*, adj. wicked, Kir. 11, 25. *Abhivâdana-*, adj. one who habitually salutes, Man. 2, 121. *Guṇa-*, adj. virtuous, Hit. i. d. 182. *Dâna-*, adj. liberal, Yâjń. 3, 48. *Dus-*, adj. wicked, Râm. 3, 2, 23. *Duḥkha-*, adj. austere, MBh. 4, 277. *Dharma-*, adj. just, virtuous, Indr. 1, 22. *Puṇya-*, adj. virtuous, MBh. 5, 6011. *Mâṁsa-*, adj. fleshy. *Mṛigayâ-*, adj. attached to hunting. *Yajńa-*, adj. sbst. a sacrificer, Man. 11, 20. *Vi-*, adj. not observing approved usages, Man. 5, 154. *Vishama-*, adj. uneven, difficult. *Çânti-*, m. a proper name, Lass. 2, 4. *Sâdhu-*, adj. virtuous. *Su-*, I. adj. 1. well disposed, of good disposition. 2. well made, Pańch. ii. d. 74. II. f. *lâ*, the wife of Yama. *Snâna-*, adj. bathing, observing ablutions, Hit. 18, 7, M.M.

शीलतस् *çîla + tas*, adv. **1.** By natural disposition, Pańch. i. d. 288. **2.** Concerning the character, Daçak. in Chr. 186, 8.

ऽशीलता *-çîla + tâ*, f. in *tyâga-*, Generosity, Hit. i. d. 104, M.M. *çâlina-*, f. Bashfulness, Utt. Râmach. 173, 4.

शीलवन्त् *çîla + vant*, adj., f. *vatî*, Of a good disposition, Ragh. 10, 71.—Comp. *Çruti-*, adj. one who is learned in the Vedas, Man. 3, 27.

शीवन् *çî + van*, **I.** m. The boa-constrictor. **II.** f. *varî*, An iguana.

शु *ÇU*, see *sru*.

† **शुक्** *ÇUK*, i. 1, Par. To go.

शुक *çuka*, **I.** m. **1.** A parrot, Vikr. d. 41. **2.** A proper name. **II.** m. and n. The name of several plants. **III.** n. **1.** A turban. **2.** The hem of a cloth. **3.** Cloth. **4.** A sort of perfume.—Comp. *Gṛiha-*, m. 1. a parrot kept in a house, Amar. 13. 2. a poet maintained by a prince, Râjat. 5, 31.

शुक्त *çukta*, **I.** adj. **1.** Sour, acid. **2.** Harsh. **3.** i.e. 2. *çuch + ta*, Clean, pure. **II.** n. **1.** A preparation which has become acid by undergoing fermentation, as vinegar, etc., Man. 2, 177; 4, 211; 11, 153. **2.** Sour gruel. **3.** Flesh.

शुक्तक *çukta + ka* (n.), Sour eructation, Man. 4, 121 (Lois.).

शुक्ति *çukti*, i.e. 2. *çuch + ti*, f. **1.** A pearl oyster, Pańch. i. d. 280. **2.** A conch. **3.** A small shell. **4.** A portion of the skull used as a cup. **5.** A curl or feather on a horse's neck or breast. **6.** A disease of the cornea. **7.** A sort of perfume. **8.** A weight of two *karshas*.—Comp. *Mahâ-*, f. the pearl oyster.

शुक्तिज *çukti-ja* (vb. *jan*), n. A pearl.

शुक्र *çukra*, i.e. 2. *çuch + ra*, **I.** adj. **1.** Resplendent, Chr. 288, 14 = Rigv. i. 48, 14. **2.** Pure, Windischmann, Sankara, 68. **II.** m. **1.** A name of Agni. **2.** The planet Venus, Pańch. pr. d. 3.

3. The month Jyeshṭha (May—June), Hiḍ. 1, 10. III. n. 1. Semen virile, Vedântas. in Chr. 207, 13; MBh. 1, 2434; male and female strength, Man. 3, 49. 2. A morbid affection of the iris.

शुक्रल *çukra + la*, adj. Spermatic, augmenting the seminal secretion.

शुक्ल *çukla*, i.e. 2.*çuch + la*, I. adj. White, Pańch. i. d. 39; bright, i. d. 104; Man. 1, 66 (with *paksha*, the fortnight of the month in which the moon increases). II. m. 1. White (the colour). 2. One of the astronomical *Yogas*. 3. The light half of the month from new to full moon, Bhag. 8, 24; Râjat. 5, 412. III. f. *lâ*, A name of Sarasvatî. IV. n. 1. Silver. 2. Fresh butter. 3. A disease of the cornea. —Comp. *Pańchaçukla*, i.e. *pańchan-*, m. a certain poisonous insect, Suçr. 2, 288, 7. *Mahâ-çuklâ*, f. Sarasvatî.

शुक्लाभिजातीय *çuklâbhijâtîya*, i.e. *çukla-abhi-jan + ti + îya*, adj. Of a pure race, Râm. 6, 10, 24.

शुक्षि *çukshi*, m. Wind.

शुङ्ग *çuṅga*, I. m. The Indian fig-tree, Windischmann, Sankara, 179. II. f. *gâ*, The sheath of a young bud (cf. Atharv.-Ved. viii. 7, 4, at the end of a comp. adj.).

1. शुच् *ÇUCH*, i. 1, Par. (in epic poetry also Âtm., MBh. 4, 488), 1. To be afflicted, to grieve, Man. 3, 57. 2. To grieve for, to bewail, Pańch. i. d. 379. 3. To regret, to repent, Pańch. 118, 6. 4. To be absorbed in deep meditation, Lass. 2. ed. 42, 11, cf. 9. Ptcple. of the pf. pass. *çuchita*, Sad, lamenting. Comp. ptcple. of the fut. pass. *a-çochya*, adj. Not to be grieved for, Pańch. i. d. 379; 475. Caus. 1. To afflict, MBh. 4, 581. 2. To bewail, MBh. 1, 5649.—With the prep. अनु *anu*, To bewail, Bhag. 2, 11; Pańch. i. d. 475. Caus. The same, MBh. 2, 2594.—With परि *pari*, 1. To be much afflicted, MBh. 1, 4025. 2. To bewail, MBh. 3, 13656.—With अनुप्र *anu-pra*, To bewail, MBh. 1, 3229.—Cf. Goth. hiufan, queri; A.S. heaf, heofian; O.H.G. huvo, ulula.

2. शुच् *ÇUCH*, i. 4, Par. Âtm. 1. To shine, to be pure (ved.). 2. † To be wet. 3. † To be fetid. Ptcple of the fut. pass. *çochya*. 1. To be purified. 2. Wicked, Bhâg. P. 1, 17, 6. Comp. *A-*, adj. innocent, ib. Caus. To make pure, Kathâs. 19, 84, *dûshitam̃ triṇa-toyâdi pratiyogair açochayat*, He made pure (i.e. he restored to their former state), by antidotes, food, water, etc., which were spoiled (i.e. poisoned).

3. शुच् 1.*çuch*, f. 1. Sorrow, Hit. i. d. 133, M.M.; grief, Daçak. in Chr. 187, 14. 2. Calamity.

शुचन्ति *çuchanti*, m. A proper name, Chr. 296, 7=Rigv. i. 112, 7.

शुचि 2.*çuch + i*, I. adj. 1. White, resplendent, Böhtl. Ind. Spr. 3322. 2. Clear (as a jewel), Utt. Râmach. 35, 18. 3. Gentle (cf. *çuchi-smita*, s.v. *smi*). 4. Clean, Bhartṛ. 2, 17; purified. 5. Pure, Man. 1, 76; pious. 6. Exempt from passion. 7. Honest, upright, Râm. 3, 53, 12; Pańch. 191, 13. 8. Free from fault, Pańch. i. d. 215. II. m. 1. White (the colour). 2. Purity, virtue, correctness. 3. Purification by ablution. 4. Judicial acquittal. 5. A faithful and tried minister. 6. The month Jyeshṭha (May—June), and Âshâḍha (June—July), i.e. the hot season, Ragh. 3, 3; Râjat. 5, 477; Hiḍ. 1, 10. 7. The sun. 8. The moon. 9. Fire. 10. The planet Venus. 11. Çiva. 12. A Brâhmaṇa. 13. Oblation to fire at the first feeding of an infant.—**Comp.** *A-*, adj. impure, Hit. ii. d. 24. *Upadhâ-*, adj. free from deceit, Hit. iii. d. 16.

शुचित्व *çuchi + tva*, n. Purity, Hit. i. d. 95, M.M.

† **शुच्य्** *ÇUCHY*, **चुच्य्** *CHUCHY*, i. 1, Par. To express or squeeze out. *çukta*, see s.v.

शुटीरता **çuṭîra + tâ*, and **शुटीर्य** *çuṭîrya*, i.e. **çuṭîra + ya*, n. Heroism, prowess.

† **शुठ्** *ÇUṬH*, i. 1, Par. **1.** To be lame. **2.** To prevent. i. 10, Par. To be lazy (cf. 1. *çaṭh*).

† **शुण्ठ्** *ÇUṆṬH*, i. 1, Par. To be lame. i. 1 and 10, Par. To be dried or desiccated.

शुण्ठि, ठी *çuṇṭhî*, f., and **शुण्ठ्य** *çuṇṭhya*, n. Dry ginger, Pañch. 262, 13 (*ya*).

† **शुण्ड्** *ÇUṆḌ*, i. 1, Par. **1.** To break. **2.** To vex, to torment.

शुण्ड *çuṇḍa*, I. m. The exudation from an elephant's temples. **II.** f. *ḍâ*. **1.** Spirituous liquor. **2.** A tavern. **3.** An elephant's trunk, Pañch. 165, 1. **4.** The stalk of the lotus. **5.** A whore.

शुण्डक *çuṇḍaka* (cf. the last), m. A distiller.

शुण्डार *çuṇḍâra* (cf. *çuṇḍa*), m. **1.** A distiller. **2.** An elephant's trunk, Mahâvîrach. 17, 7.

शुण्डिका *çuṇḍikâ*, f. The soft palate. —**Comp.** *Gala-*, f. 1. the uvula or the soft palate, Yâjñ. 3, 98. 2. swelling of the kernels of the throat, Suçr. 1, 90, 16.

शुण्डी *çuṇḍî* in *kaṇṭha-*, f. Swelling of the kernels of the throat, Suçr. 1, 306, 5 (cf. the last).

शुद्धता *çuddha + tâ* (vb. *çudh*), f. Purity, Pañch. iv. d. 76.

शुद्धान्त *çuddhânta*, i.e. *çuddha -anta*, m. **1.** The private or women's apartments, Vikr. d. 43; Utt. Râmach. 25, 4 (*-chârin*, m., add. s.v. *chârin*, A servant of the private apartments). **2.** The king's wife or concubine.

शुद्धि *çuddhi*, i.e. *çudh + ti*, f. **1.** Cleaning, cleansing. **2.** Purity, purification, Pañch. iii. d. 119. **3.** Correctness, truth, Mâlat. 50, 14; certainty, Lass. 22, 11. **4.** Acquittal. **5.** Covering (of expenses), Pañch. 251, 16.—**Comp.** *Agni-*, f. purification by fire, passing the fiery ordeal, Utt. Râmach. 5, 1. *Dravya-*, f. purification of inanimate things, Man. 5, 57. *Vaira-*, f. revenge.

शुध् *ÇUDH* (probably for original *çvadh*), i. 4, Par. **1.** To be purified, Man. 3, 132; Pañch. i. d. 307. **2.** To become pure, Man. 5, 63. Ptcple. of the pf. pass. *çuddha*. **1.** Pure, Hit. d. 78, M.M. **2.** White. **3.** Faultless, genuine, Mâlav. d. 30. **4.** Innocent. **5.** Acquitted. **6.** Authorised. **7.** Alone, Megh. 88; only, mere, simple. **8.** Whetted. n. **1.** Pure spirit. **2.** Rock-salt. **Comp.** *A-*, adj. impure, wicked, Pañch. i. d. 335. *Ati-*, very pure, Hit. i. d. 198, M.M. Ptcple. of the pf. act. *çuddhavant*, f. *vatî*; nom. pl. *vatjas*, Man. 11, 249, designates a holy text beginning *çuddhavatyas*. Caus. **1.** To purify, Man. 9, 282. **2.** To explain, Vedântas. in Chr. 215, 4. **3.** To examine, to investigate, Pañch. 142, 11. *çodhita*, Purified, excused, Man. 8, 202.—With the prep. **परि** *pari*, Caus. **1.** To clean, to secure, Râm. 2, 31, 25. **2.** To solve, to explain, Gît. 12, 28.—With **वि** *vi*, To be purified, Man. 5, 66. *viçuddha*, **1.** Pure, Pañch. pr. d. 9. **2.** Faultless, Mâlav. 21, 8; Hit. pr. d. 23, M.M. (*vaṁça-*, regarding the bambu, of which it is made, viz. a bow). **3.** White, Ṛit. 6, 34. **4.** Corrected. **5.** Pious, virtuous. **6.** Humble, modest. **7.** Settled, Man. 8, 201. **Comp.** *A-*, adj. wicked, Râjat. 5, 315. Caus. To purify, MBh. 3, 15979.—With सम् *sam*, *saṁçuddha*, **1.** Purified, expiated, Bhag. 6, 45. **2.** Clean. **3.** Refined. **4.** Acquitted (as a debt, or of a crime). Caus. **1.** To purify, Râjat. 5, 89. **2.** To secure, Man. 7, 185. **3.** To cover (as expenses), MBh. 2, 204. **4.** To examine, Man. 7, 219.—Cf. *çundh* ; καθαρός ; probably Lat. castus, O.H.G. haitar, serenus.

† शुन् *ÇUN*, i. 6, Par. To go.

शुन *çuna*, i.e. *çvan + a*, m. A dog. *çunî*, see s.v. *çvan*.

शुनक *çuna + ka*, m. A dog, a young dog, Râm. 1, 61, 17.

शुनःशेप *çunaḥçepa* (ved.), and **शुनःशेफ** *çunaḥçepha* (Râm. 1, 61, 19), i.e. *çvan + as-çepa*, or *-çepha*, m. A proper name.

शुनाशीर *çunâçîra*, and **शुनासीर** *çunâsîra* (so in the Vedas), m. Indra.

शुनि *çuni*, i.e. *çvan + i*, m. A dog.

शुन्ध् *ÇUNDH* (cf. *çudh*), i. 1, Par. To purify. Âtm. To be purified. Caus., or i. 10, To purify.

शुन्ध्यु *çundh + yu*, I. adj. Purifying, Chr. 289, 9 = Rigv. i. 50, 9. II. m. A name of Agni.

1. **शुभ्** *ÇUBH* (probably for original *çvabh*, cf. *çudh* ; see also *çumbh*, s.v. 2. *çubh*), i. 1, Âtm., i. 6, Par. **1.** To shine, Chr. 40, 9. **2.** To be splendid, Râm. 2, 47, 17. **3.** To be beautiful, MBh. 4, 49. **4.** To be gay or happy, Pańch. iii. d. 226. **5.** † To hurt, to kill. Ved. infin. *çubhe*, Chr. 290, 4 = Rigv. i. 64, 4. Caus. *çobhaya*, To cause to shine, to adorn, Râm. 2, 96, 31. Ved. Caus. *çubhaya*, Chr. 291, 3 = Rigv. i. 85, 3. *çobhita*, Trimmed, Hit. iii. d. 27. — With the prep. उप *upa*, To shine, Pańch. i. d. 85. Caus. To adorn, Râm. 1, 5, 16 ; Pańch. 159, 20.—With वि *vi*, To shine, Hit. ii. d. 71.—With सम् *sam*, Caus. To adorn, Ṛit. 6, 23.

†2. **शुभ्** *ÇUBH*, **शुम्भ्** *ÇUMBH*, **सुभ्** *SUBH*, **सुम्भ्** *SUMBH*, i. 1, Par. **1.** To speak, to shine. **2.** To kill, to hurt.

शुभ *çubh + a*, I. adj., f. *bhâ*. **1.** Splendid, Lass. 2. ed. 72, 5 ; beautiful, Pańch. iii. d. 185. Comparat. *çubhatara*, Very beautiful, Pańch. 226, 5. **2.** Distinguished, Lass. 2. ed. 59, 10. **3.** Learned. **4.** Happy, Hit. i. d. 5, M.M. ; good, Pańch. iii. d. 106 ; virtuous, i. d. 150. II. m. One of the astrological Yogas. III. f. *bhâ*. **1.** A female friend of the goddess Umâ, Râm. 3, 52, 26. **2.** Bambu manna. **3.** Bent grass. IV. n. Happiness, hail, Hit. 54, 17.—**Comp.** *A-*, adj. 1. wicked, Pańch. i. d. 403. 2. inauspicious, Lass. 16, 19. *Çubhâçubha*, i. e. *çubha-a-çubha*, adj. good or wicked, Pańch. ii. d. 18.

शुभंभावुक *çubhaṁbhâvuka*, i. e. *çubha + m-bhû + uka*, adj. Resplendent, Lass. 67, 7.

शुभंयु *çubhaṁyu*, i.e. *çubha + m + yu*, adj. Happy, prosperous, Ragh. 8, 6.

शुभ्र *çubh + ra*, I. adj. **1.** White, Megh. 53 ; Lass. 4, 17. **2.** Shining, bright, Chr. 291, 3 = Rigv. i. 85, 3 ; Pańch. i. d. 252. II. m. **1.** White (the colour). **2.** Sandal, Padmap. 3, 4. III. f. *râ*. **1.** The Ganges. **2.** Crystal.

3. Bambu manna. **IV.** n. 1. Silver. 2. Talc.—Comp. *Mahâ-*, n. silver.

शुभ्रत्व *çubhra + tva*, n. Whiteness, Böhtl. Ind. Spr. 1915.

शुभ्रि *çubh + ri*, m. Brahman.

शुम्भ् *ÇUMBH* (cf. 2. *çubh*), i. 6, Par. (ved. also Âtm.), To shine. —With the prep. अभि *abhi*, Âtm. To assume as ornament, to adorn one's self with (acc.), Chr. 295, 10 = Rigv. i. 92, 10. — With प्र *pra*, Âtm. To adorn one's self carefully, Chr. 291, 1 = Rigv. i. 85, 1.—Cf. probably, A.S. camb; O.H.G. kamp; κομψός.

† शुल्क् *ÇULK*, i. 10, Par. 1. To create. 2. To gain. 3. To abandon. 4. To speak (cf. *çvalk*).

शुल्क *çulka*, m. and n. 1. Toll, tax, duty, Man. 10, 120. 2. Money given at the purchase of anything, to ratify the bargain. 3. Money given to the parents of the bride, originally as purchase-price, cf. MBh. 13, 2422, sqq. and 4530; Man. 3, 51. 4. A nuptial present, Man. 9, 93. 5. The profits of household labour, care of milch cattle, etc., when considered as the legal property of the wife. 6. Price, Daçak. in Chr. 180, 15.—Comp. *Guṇa-*, *Dhana-*, *Vîrya-*, adj., f. *kâ*, having as its price, i.e. to be purchased by, good qualities, money, prowess, Daçak. in Chr. 190, 24; 191, 1, and Chr. 4, 14.

शुल्व *çulva*, n. 1. Copper. 2. A rope. 3. Institute, law. 4. A sacrificial observance. 5. A quantity of water.

शुल्वारि *çulvâri*, m. Sulphur.

शुश्रूषक *çuçrûshaka*, i.e. *çuçrûsha*, desider. of *çru*, + *aka*, **I.** adj. Obedient, Lass. 41, 14. **II.** m. A servant.

शुश्रूषण *çuçrûshaṇa*, i.e. *çuçrûsha*, see the last, + *ana*, n. Obedience, MBh. 1, 741.

शुश्रूषा *çuçrûshâ*, i.e. *çuçrûsha*, see the last, + *a*, f. 1. Wishing to hear. 2. Obedience, Lass. 41, 7. 3. Service, Man. 1, 91; 2, 112; Pańch. 214, 19; reverence, Man. 2, 229. 4. Speaking. — Comp. *Agni-*, f. attention to the sacred fires, Man. 2, 248. *Charaṇa-*, f. prostration, Râm. 3, 14, 8. *Pari-*, f. complete obedience, Lass. 41, 15. *Pâda-*, f. obedience, Hariv. 12585.

शुश्रूषु *çuçrûshu*, i.e. *çuçrûsha*, see the last, + *u*, adj. Obedient, attentive, Man. 2, 109; MBh. 1, 740.

शुष् *ÇUSH* (for *sush*, and that for original *sus*; *ç* for *s*, by the assimilating influence of *sh*), i. 4, Par. (in epic poetry also Âtm., Râm. 2, 96, 34), 1. To become dry, literally and figuratively, Râm. 2, 69, 19; MBh. 2, 1685; 3, 591. 2. To be withered, to be afflicted, Draup. 6, 11. Ptcple. of the pf. pass. *çushka*. 1. Dried up, Pańch. 51, 5; dry, Pańch. ii. d. 96. 2. Causeless, Pańch. 172, 1. 3. Unprofitable. 4. Offensive, Man. 11, 35. Caus. 1. To dry up, Pańch, i. d. 117; MBh. 3, 189. 2. To emaciate, Man. 6, 24. 3. To destroy, Gît. 12, 5.—With the prep. उद् *ud*, Caus. 1. To dry up, Râm. 2, 64, 65. 2. To emaciate, Chr. 57, 23.—With समुद् *sam-ud*, To become dried up, Bhaṭṭ. 16, 17.—With उप *upa*, Caus. 1. To dry up, MBh. 3, 12874. 2. To emaciate, MBh. 1, 4624.—With परि *pari*, 1. To become dried up and withered, Râm. 2, 30, 25. 2. To be afflicted, Chr. 12, 25. *pari-*

çushka, **1.** Completely dry, Râm. 2, 59, 9. **2.** Withered. **3.** Emaciated, Râm. 4, 16, 35. Caus. To emaciate, Pańch. 182, 11.—With वि *vi, viçushka,* **1.** Very dry, thirsty, Ṛit. 1, 15. **2.** Withered, Mâlat. 78, 4. Caus. To dry up, MBh. 3, 10767.—With सम् *sam,* To be dried up, MBh. 1, 8230. *sam̃-çushka,* Completely dry, Ṛit. 1, 22. Caus. To dry up, Ragh. 6, 36.—Cf. *σαυσαρός, σαυκός* (=*çushka* for *sus+ka*), *σαυχμός, αὐχμός, σαχνός, αὔω, αὖος, αὐστηρός*; Lat. siccus (=*çushka* for *sus+ka*); Goth. siuk; A.S. seoc, seac, sioc, sic; O.H.G. siuh, siuchî, siuhjan; Goth. sauht; A.S. and O.H.G. suht.

शुष *çush+a,* m., and **शुषि** or **षी** *çush+î,* **1.** Drying. **2.** A hole in the ground.

शुषिर *çush+ira,* I. adj. Perforated (cf. *çusha*). II. m. **1.** Fire. **2.** A rat. III. n. **1.** A hole. **2.** A wind instrument.

शुषिल *çush+ila,* m. Wind.

शुष्क *çushka,* see *çush.*

शुष्कल *çushka+la,* m., f. *lâ,* and *lî,* and n. Dry flesh.

शुष्ण *çushṇa,* i.e. *çush+na,* m. **1.** The sun. **2.** Fire.

शुष्म *çush+ma,* I. adj. Strong, Chr. 291, 14=Rigv. i. 64, 14. II. m. **1.** The sun. **2.** Fire. **3.** Wind. III. n. Light.—Comp. *An-anta-,* adj. always roaring, Chr. 290, 10=Rigv. i. 64, 10.

शुष्मन् *çush+man,* I. m. Fire. II. n. **1.** Light, lustre. **2.** Strength.

शुष्मिन् *çushmin,* i.e. *çushma+in,* adj. Strong, Hiḍ. 1, 13.

शूक *çûka,* m. and n. **1.** The awn of barley. **2.** A bristle, a spicula. **3.** Compassion.—Comp. *Çasya-,* n. the beard of corn. *Çita* (or *sita-*), m. 1. barley. 2. wheat.

शूकर *çûkara,* m. A hog, Hit. 57, 12, M.M. f. *rî,* A sow. Cf. *sûkara.*

शूद्र *çûdra,* I. m. A man of the fourth caste, Man. 1, 31; 116; Hit. iv. d. 21. II. f. *râ,* A woman of that caste. III. f. *rî,* or *râṇî,* The wife of a Çûdra.—Comp. *Mahâ-,* m. a cowherd. f. *rî,* a milk-woman.

शूद्रक *çûdra+ka,* m. A proper name, Lass. 28, 9.

शूद्रता *çûdra+tâ,* f., and **शूद्रत्व** *çûdra+tva,* n. The nature or condition of a Çûdra, Man. 2, 168 (*tva*).

शून *çûna,* I. see *çvi.* II. (cf. *sûna*), f. *nâ.* **1.** A slaughter-house, Man. 4, 85; Mâlav. 25, 2; cf. the next. **2.** The soft palate.

शूनाचक्रध्वजवन्त् *çûnâ-chakra-dhvaja+vant,* adj. One who has a slaughter-house, or an oil-press, or a vintner's flag, Man. 4, 84.

शूनास्थ *çûnâ-stha,* adj. Being in, brought from, a slaughter-house, Man. 11, 155.

शून्य *çûnya* (probably for original *çvanya,* vb. *çvi*), I. adj. **1.** Empty, void, Vikr. 66, 1; vacant, Mâlat. 11, 8; ruined, Râm. 2, 13, 16. **2.** Deprived of, with instr., Bhâshâp. 69 (read *çûnyâ siddhir*); Vikr. d. 130 (as former part of a comp. Without, Pańch. 208, 22; figurat., Böhtl. Ind. Spr. 249). **3.** Unsuspicious, Râm. 3, 50, 24. **4.** Unmeaning, indifferent, Pańch. 117, 14. **5.** Lonely, Pańch. 231, 18 (*çûnye,* secretly); desert, Râm. 3, 51, 17 (n. in the lonely place). II. f. *yâ,* A hollow reed. III. n. **1.** A vacuum. **2.** Heaven. **3.** A dot.

4. A cypher. **5.** Absolute vacuity or rather nonentity, a principle of the Bauddha metaphysics, Vedântas. in Chr. 211, 14.—**Comp.** *A-*, adj. full, performed, Çâk. 24, 16. *Anyathâ-siddhi-*, adj. free from superfluous determination (as a cause), Bhâshâp. 15. *Pari-*, adj. completely empty, or void of, Ragh. 8, 65; 19, 6. *Sarva-*, adj. completely empty, Hit. i. d. 125, M.M.—Cf. κενεός, κεννός, κενός.

शून्यता *çûnya + tâ*, f., and **शून्यत्व** *çûnya + tva*, n. **1.** Emptiness, Lass. 72, 10 (*tâ*). **2.** Unreality.—**Comp.** *Mâtṛi-*, f. condition of having no mother, Chân. 49 in Berl. Monatsb. 1864, 410.

शून्यवत् *çûnya + vat*, adv. Like a cypher, annihilated, Daçak. in. Chr. 183, 22.

† **शूर्** *ÇÛR*, **सूर्** *SÛR*, i. 4, Âtm. **1.** To hurt or kill. **2.** To be firm. i. 10 (rather a denomin. derived from the next), Âtm. **1.** To be valiant. **2.** To make great exertion. *visûrita*, see s.v.

शूर *çûra*, i.e. **çavan* (for *çavas*), + *a* (with *r* for *n*), m. **1.** A hero, Hit. i. d. 71, M.M. **2.** The sun. **3.** A lion. **4.** A boar. **5.** A proper name, Râjat. 5, 32; 46.—**Comp.** *Piṇḍi-* (see *piṇḍa*), m. a hero at dinner. *Sva-bhâva-*, adj. containing men who are naturally heroes, Hit. iii. d. 87.—Cf. κοῦρος, κόρος, probably κῦρος, κοίρανος.

शूरता *çûra + tâ*, f. Prowess, heroism, Hit. iii. d. 44.

शूरसेनक *çûrasena + ka* (see *senâ*), m. pl. A people and country about Mathurâ, Man. 2, 19.

शूरसेनज *çûrasena-ja* (see *senâ*), m. An inhabitant of Çûrasena, Man. 7, 194.

† **शूर्प्** *ÇÛRP*, i. 10 (rather a denomin. derived from the next), Par. To measure.

शूर्प *çûrpa* (and probably better **सूर्प** *sûrpa*, q. cf.), **I.** m. and n. A winnowing basket, Man. 5, 117. **II.** m. A measure of two *Droṇas*. **III.** f. *pî*. **1.** A small winnowing basket, a toy for children. **2.** A proper name.

शूर्पक *çûrpaka*, m. A demon, the enemy of Kâma.

† **शूल्** *ÇÛL*, i. 1 (rather a denomin. derived from the next), Par. **1.** To be sick. **2.** To make a loud noise. **3.** To impale.

शूल *çûla* (cf. *ço*), **I.** m. and n. **1.** A pike, a dart, a weapon, Sund. 1, 24; Râm. 5, 53, 53. **2.** An iron pin or spit. **3.** A banner. **4.** Sharp pain, Daçak. in Chr. 190, 19; Lass. 31, 18: especially in the belly, as colic, Râjat. 5, 53. **5.** Death. **II.** f. *lâ*. **1.** A stake for impaling criminals, Pañch. 238, 1. **2.** A whore.—**Comp.** *A-kâṇḍa-* (m. n.), sudden colic, Râjat. 5, 53. *Karṇa-*, m. and n. earache, Suçr. 1, 55, 4. *Kukshi-*, m. colic, ib. 1, 219, 11. *Tri-*, **I.** n. a trident, Râm. 5, 37, 38. **II.** m. Çiva. *Danta-* (m. and n.), toothache, MBh. 12, 11267.

शूलक *çûla + ka*, m. A restive horse.

शूलिक *çûlika*, i.e. *çûla + ika*, **I.** adj. Roasted on a spit (ÇKD.). **II.** m. A hare.

शूलिन् *çûlin*, i.e. *çûla + in*, **I.** adj. Suffering sharp pain. **II.** m. **1.** A spearman. **2.** A stake-bearer. **3.** Çiva, Bhartṛ. 2, 52.—**Comp.** *Tri-*, **I.** n. Çiva. **II.** f. *nî*, Durgâ, Hariv. 9428.

शूल्य *çûlya*, i.e. *çûlâ+ya*, I. adj. **1.** Roasted on a spit, Bhaṭṭ. 4, 9. **2.** Deserving impalement. II. n. Roasted meat.

शूष् *ÇÛSH*, see *sûsh*.

शृगाल *çṛigâla*, I. m. **1.** A jackal, Hit. 52, 4, M.M. **2.** A rogue. **3.** A coward. **4.** A demon. **5.** Krishṇa. II. f. *lî*. **1.** A she-jackal, Pańch. 220, 9. **2.** A fox.

शृगालिका *çṛigâlikâ*, i.e. *çṛigâlî+ka*, f. **1.** A female jackal, Pańch. 226, 20. **2.** A fox. **3.** A proper name, Daçak. in Chr. 194, 9.

शृङ्खल *çṛiṅkhala*, m., f. *lâ*, and n. **1.** A chain, Daçak. in Chr. 190, 12 (*lâ*). **2.** A belt worn round a man's body. —Comp. *Uchchṛiṅkhala*, i.e. *ud-*, adj. ungovernable, Hit. iii. d. 97. *Chhinna-*, adj. (vb. *chhid*), having broken (his) chain (viz. an elephant), Daçak. in Chr. 190, 9. *Vi-*, adj. unfettered, unrestrained, dissolute, Bhartṛ. 2, 49.

शृङ्ग *çṛiṅga*, probably *çara+m-ga* (cf. *çṛî*), I. n. **1.** A horn, Pańch. 9, 7; a horn-like vessel, Ragh. 16, 70. **2.** The top of a mountain, Bhartṛ. 2, 77; Daçak. in Chr. 188, 21 (*udaya-achala-indra-padmarâga-çṛiṅga-kalpa*, As if it [viz. the sun] was the ruby top of the mountain *Udaya*); summit of a building, Pańch. 10, 8. **3.** Height, dignity. **4.** Sovereignty. **5.** A mark. **6.** A lotus. **7.** An artificial fountain. II. f. *gî*. **1.** A fish, a sort of silurus. **2.** A sort of drug. **3.** A sort of gold used for making trinkets.—Comp. *A-*, adj. having no horns, Râjat. 5, 460. *Ṛiksâmaçṛiṅga*, i.e. *ṛich-sâman-*, m. a name of Vishṇu, Râm. 6, 102, 17. *Eka-*, I. m. 1. epithet of Vishṇu, Râm. 6, 102, 13. 2. pl. a class of Manes, MBh. 2, 463. II. f. *gâ*, a proper name, Hariv. 987. *Chatuḥçṛ°*, i.e. *chatur-*, m. the name of a mountain, Bhâg. P. 5, 20, 15. *Prabâla-maṇi-*, adj. having horns of coral and jewels, Râm. 3, 49, 21. *Sa-*, adj. possessed of a horn, Chr. 40, 9.—Cf. as akin, κέρας; Lat. cornu; Goth. haurn; A.S. horn.

शृङ्गवेर *çṛiṅgavera*, I. n. Ginger. II. Name of a town, Utt. Râmach. 14, 10.

शृङ्गाट *çṛiṅgâṭa*, and **शृङ्गाटक** *çṛiṅgâṭa+ka*, n. A place where four roads meet.

शृङ्गार *çṛiṅgâra* (from *çṛiṅga*, cf. the next), I. m. **1.** Copulation, coition, Pańch. i. d. 191. **2.** Love, Vikr. d. 9; as an object of poetical description. **3.** (m. or n. ?), Elegant dress (properly, a dress for amorous purposes), Pańch. 36, 18 (cf. my transl. n. 173). **4.** Marks made with red lead on an elephant's head and trunk. **5.** Mark in general, Lass. 69, 5 (at the end of a comp. adj.). II. n. **1.** Red lead. **2.** Cloves. **3.** Fragrant powder for the dress or person.

शृङ्गारक *çṛiṅgâra+ka*, adj. Horned.

शृङ्गिण *çṛiṅgiṇa*, i.e. *çṛiṅgin+a*, m. A ram.

शृङ्गिन् *çṛiṅgin*, i.e. *çṛiṅga+in*, I. adj., f. *iṇî*. **1.** Horned, Hit. i. d. 18, M.M. **2.** Crested, peaked. II. m. **1.** A mountain. **2.** A tree. **3.** An elephant. III. f. *iṇî*, A cow.—Comp. *Prabâla-maṇi-*, i.e. *prabâlamaṇiçṛiṅga+in*, adj. having horns of coral and jewels, Râm. 3, 49, 4.

शृणि *çṛiṇi* (vb. *çṛî*), f. The hook for goading an elephant, Hit. ii. d. 155.

शृध् *ÇṚIDH*, i. 1, Âtm., and in the aor., fut., and condit. also Par. To fart. i. 1, Par. Âtm. † To wet, to moisten. i. 10, To insult (by breaking wind against, or by defiling with excrements).—With the prep. **अव** *ava*, To break wind against somebody, Man. 8, 282.—Cf. *çakṛit*.

शृधू *çṛidh+û*, f. The anus.

शॄ *ÇṚÎ*, ii. 9, *çṛiṇâ*, *ṇî*, Par. **1.** To hurt, to wound, Kir. 14, 13. **2.** Pass. To be broken, to split in pieces, MBh. 3, 591 (with the termination of the Par.). Ptcple. of the pf. pass. *çîrṇa*. **1.** Broken, Pańch. i. d. 387; MBh. i. d. 267. **2.** Withered, Megh. 30. **3.** Wasted, decayed, Mâlat. 79, 18 (*antar-*, Mouldering in it, viz. its water). **4.** Slender, thin. —With the prep. अव *ava*, pass. To be dissolved, to spread, Râm. 1, 31, 44, Seramp. (Schlegel, 1, 38, 14, v.r.).—With परि *pari*, pass. To be broken, to split, MBh. 3, 11141.—With वि *vi*, pass. **1.** To be broken, Man. 8, 408. **2.** To be destroyed, MBh. 1, 3726. **3.** To go asunder, to slip away, Man. 2, 74. **4.** To fade away, Bhartṛ. 2, 25; Hit. iv. d. 42. *viçîrṇa*, **1.** Broken, Pańch. 80, 9. **2.** Divided, Megh. 19. **3.** Withered, decayed. **4.** Wasted, dispersed, Nal. 13, 17.—Cf. A.S. hyrt; κέρας; Lat. cornu; Goth. haurn; A.S. horn; κεραός; Lat. cervus; A.S. heorot, heort; κλάω, κλῆρος, κολοβός, probably κορύνη; Goth. hairus, A sword; perhaps O.H.G. bi-hal, bipennis; Lat. clava, quiris, probably in-columis; cf. *çaru*, *çṛiñga*.

शेखर *çekhara* (from *çikhara*, with aff. *a*, for regular *çaikhara*), m. **1.** A crest, a diadem, Mâlat. 145, 8; Lass. 13, 6 (at the end of a comp. adj.); chief, Chaurap. 45 (read *çekhara*). **2.** A garland of flowers worn on the crown of the head, Ṛit. 1, 6. **3.** A proper name, Lass. n. ad 67, 10.—**Comp.** *Indu-*, *Chandra-*, and *Çaçiçekhara*, i.e. *çaçin-*, m. Çiva (having the moon as crest, wearing the moon on his head), Kathâs. 4, 22 (*indu-*); Hit. 116, 6 (*chandra-*).

शेप *çepa*, शेफ *çepha*, and सेफ *sepha*, m. The penis.

शेपस् *çepas*, and शेफस् *çephas*, n. **1.** The penis. **2.** A testicle.

शेपाल *çepâla*=*çevâla*.

शेमुषी *çemushi* (properly fem. of the ptcple. of the red. pf. of *çam*) f. Understanding.

शेल् *ÇEL*, see *sel*.

शेलु *çelu*, m. **1.** A small tree, Cordia myxa. **2.** A kind of fruit, Man. 5, 6.

† शेव् *ÇEV*, i. 1, Âtm. To worship (cf. *sev*).

शेव *çeva*, **I.** m. **1.** A snake (vb. *çî*). **2.** Happiness. **II.** acc. *vam*, indecl. Hail, homage, an exclamation or salutation addressed to the deities. **III.** n., and f. *vâ*, The penis (cf. *çepa*).

शेवधि *çevadhi* i.e. *çeva-dhâ* (cf. *nidhi*), m. A treasure, Mâlat. 103, 10; also *sevadhi*, q. cf.

शेवाल *çevâla*, शैवल and शैवाल *çaivâla*, m. n. The green moss-like substance growing on the surface of water, duck-weed (Vallisneria? cf. *çepâla* and *çaiva*), Pańch. 188, 12 (*çaivala*); Çâk. d. 19 (*çaivala*); Râm. 2, 46, 32, Seramp. (*çaivâla*).

शेष *çesha*, i.e. *çish+a*, **I.** adj. Remaining, Man. 1, 102; 3, 47; Megh. 31; other, Pańch. 123, 13; all the other, Vikr. d. 52. **II.** m. and n. **1.** Remainder, residue, Pańch. iii. d. 256; 51, 11 (*vija-çesha-mâtra*, Even a residue of seed); Daçak. in Chr. 184, 24 (at the end of a comp. adj.). **2.** What is omitted, Man. 8, 320; 322 (*çeshe*, for less). **III.** m. **1.** Killing, destroying, finishing. **2.** End, Pańch. 55, 6. **3.** The king of the serpent race, at once the couch and canopy of Vishṇu, and the upholder of the world, Bhartṛ. 2, 28. **4.** A name of Baladeva. **IV.** f.

shâ, Flowers and other things that have been offered to an idol (and are then distributed amongst the worshippers), Sâv. 1, 27.—**Comp. A.** as former part of comp. words, often: remaining, cf. *çesha-çarîra, çesha-bhâga.* **B.** *A-*, adj., f. *shâ,* entire, all, every, Mâlat. 2, 3; Ragh. 3, 65; Pańch. 163, 7. acc. *sham,* instr. *shena,* and adv. *sha+tas,* entirely, Kumâras. 5, 82; Bhag. 10, 16; Man. 1, 59. *Âlekhya-*, adj. (of whom is left only a likeness), dead, Ragh. 14, 15. *Kârya-*, n. the completion of a business, or affair begun, Man. 3, 157. *Jiva-*, adj. having saved only the bare life, Pańch. 160, 2. *Deva-*, n. the remainder of an offering to a deity, MBh. 13, 2019. *Nâma-çesha,* i.e. *nâman-*, adj., f. *shâ,* 1. one of whom only the name is left, Utt. Râmach. 37, 18. 2. dead. *Nih-çesha,* i.e. *nis-*, adj., f. *shâ,* 1. without leaving a residue, without sparing anybody or anything, completely destroyed, Pańch. iii. d. 256; MBh. 2, 1531. 2. all, whole, Pańch. i. d. 21. °*sham, sha+tas,* adv. completely, Kathâs. 24, 83. *Malamallaka-*, adj. one to whom is left nothing but a small piece of cloth to cover his privities, Daçak. in Chr. 184, 24. *Vaças-*, adj. dead. *Vâkya-*, m. the remainder of one's speech, Vikr. 35, 8 (i.e. you will say). *Smriti-*, adj., f. *shâ,* that of which is left nothing but remembrance, Râjat. 5, 189. *Hata-*, adj. the remainder of the killed, i.e. those who had avoided being killed, Pańch. 122, 24.

शै *ÇAI,* see *çrâ.*

शैक्य *çaikya,* i.e. *çikya+a,* adj. Placed between the ropes of a porter's yoke.

शैच्य *çaikshya,* i.e. *çikshâ+ya,* n. Learning, skill, Johns. Sel. 48, 84.

शैख *çaikha,* m. The offspring of an outcaste Brâhmaṇa, Man. 10, 21.

शैखावत्य *çaikhâvatya,* m. A proper name, Chr. 9, 39.

शैत्य *çaitya,* i.e. *çita+ya,* n. Coldness, Pańch. ii. d. 160.

शैथिल्य *çaithilya,* i.e. *çithila+ya,* n. 1. Looseness, laxity, Bhâg. P. 5, 7, 11. 2. Flaccidity. 3. Weakness, Çâk. 110, 15; cowardice, Daçak. in Chr. 188, 11. 4. Smallness, Hit. 62, 22. 5. Relaxation of rule or connexion. 6. Inattention, Pańch. 118, 8.

शैनेय *çaineya,* probably *çini+eya,* m. Satyaki, the charioteer of Kṛishṇa, MBh. 7, 7242.

शैल *çaila,* i.e. *çilâ+a,* I. adj. 1. Stony, Arj. 8, 10; rocky. 2. Mountainous, mountaineer. **II.** m. 1. A mountain, Man. 1, 27; Vikr. 10, 6. 2. A dike, Pańch. i. d. 115. **III.** n. 1. Bitumen. 2. Storax.—**Comp.** *Krîḍâ-*, m. a pleasure mountain, Megh. 61. *Târkshya-*, n. a kind of collyrium, Suçr. 2, 66, 9. *Tuhina-*, m. the Himâlaya, Kathâs. 22, 255. *Pańchaçaila,* i.e. *pańçhan-*, m. the name of a mountain, Mârk. P. 55, 8. *Badarî-* (see *vadarî*), n. a part of the Himâlaya range. *Mantha-*, m. the mount Mandara. *Mahâ-*, m. a great mountain, Bhartṛ. 2, 56.

शैलज *çaila-ja,* adj. Produced in or on mountains.—**Comp.** *Hima-*, f. *jâ,* Pârvatî.

शैलमय *çaila+maya,* adj., f. *yî,* Rocky, consisting of stones, Râjat. 5, 103.

शैलाट *çailâṭa,* i.e. *çaila-aṭ+a,* m. 1. A mountaineer, a barbarian. 2. A lion. 3. Crystal. 4. An idol.

शैलालिन् *çailâlin,* i.e. **çailâla+*

in, from *çilâlin* (a proper name), m. (properly a follower of the art taught by Çilâlin), An actor, a mime.

शैलूष *çailûsha*, i.e. *çilûsha* (a proper name), + *a*, m. **1.** An actor, a public dancer, Man. 4, 214. **2.** The master of the band, or one who beats time. **3.** A rogue, a cheat. **4.** A tree, Aegle marmelos.

शैलेय *çaileya*, i. e. *çaila* + *eya*, I. adj. **1.** Produced in the mountains. **2.** Mountainous, mountaineer. II. m. A bee, Ṛit. 6, 25. III. f. *yî*, Pârvatî. IV. n. **1.** Rock-salt. **2.** Benzoin or storax. **3.** A kind of vegetable perfume.

शैल्य *çailya*, i.e. *çilâ* + *ya*, n. Stoniness, hardness.

शैव *çaiva*, i.e. *çiva* + *a*, I. adj. Relating, belonging, to Çiva, Râm. 1, 66, 19. II. m. A worshipper of Çiva. III. n. A plant, Vallisneria octandra.

शैवता *çaiva* + *tâ*, f. Worship of Çiva, Râjat. 5, 43.

शैवल and शैवाल *caivâla*, see *çevâla*.

शैवालक *çaivâla* + *ka*, A substitute for *çaivâla*, at the end of a Bhvr. comp., Çriṅgârat. 1.

शैव्य *çaivya*, I. i.e. *çiva* + *ya*, adj. Relating to Çiva. II. m. **1.** One of the horses of Kṛishṇa. **2.** i.e. *çivi* + *ya*, A tribe of the Çivis. **3.** A proper name. III. f. *yâ*, A proper name, Sâv. 6, 2.

शैशव *çaiçava*, i.e. *çiçu* + *a*, n. Childhood, Man. 8, 27.

शैशिर *çaiçira*, i.e. *çiçira* + *a*, I. adj. Belonging to the cold season, Böhtl. Ind. Spr. 738. II. m. The name of a mountain, Arj. 3, 10.

शो ÇO, † i. 4, *çya* (the original form was *aç* + *ya*; cf. Lat. acies, acus, acer, acidus; ἀκή, ἀκμή, ἄκρος, ἀκόνη, ἄκων; Goth. aqvizi; A.S. acas; Sskr. *açra*, *açri*, *açru*, *açman*, *açva*, *ashṭra*, etc.), Par.; ved. ii. 3, *çiçâ*, *çiçi*, Par. Âtm. To sharpen, Lass. 98, 15 = Rigv. v. 9, 5 (cf. *çi*). Ptcple. of the pf. pass. I. *çâta*. **1.** Sharpened, sharp, Râjat. 5, 407. **2.** Handsome. **3.** Happy. **4.** Thin, Ragh. 10, 70; feeble. n. Joy, happiness. II. *çita*. **1.** Sharpened, sharp, Chr. 29, 35. **2.** Thin, emaciated. **3.** Feeble. —With the prep. आ *â*, ii. 3, To incite, Lass. 101, 15 = Rigv. vii. 16, 6.—With नि *ni*, I. *niçâta*, Sharpened, sharp, Bhâg. P. 3, 19, 14; polished, burnished. II. *niçità*, Sharpened, sharp, Chr. 29, 27; figurat., Pańch. i. d. 201. n. Iron. Comp. *Su-niçita*, adj. very sharp, Chr. 29, 32.—With सम् *sam*, *saṁçita*, **1.** Certain, certified, established. **2.** Completed, finished, Chr. 9, 38; 45, 16 (cf. *saṁçita-vrata*). **3.** Completing, attentive in completing, Johns. Sel. 1, 1.—Cf. also (see above), ἀκωκή, ἀκρέμων, ἀκριβής, ὄκρις, ἄκανος, ἄκανθα, ἄκορνα, ὀξύς (i.e. ὀκ + τυ), ὄξος, ἄχωρ (i.e. ἀκ + Ϝαν), ἄχυρον, ἄχερδος, αἰχμή; Lat. aculeus, cătus (= *çâta*), tri-que + trus, cos, cautes, citus (= *çita*), probably ciere, cio, cieo (= *çyâmi*); Goth. ahana, probably O.H.G. hvezjan; A.S. hwettan (a denomin.); Goth. hvôtjan.

शोक *çoka*, i. e. 1. *çuch* + *a*, m. Sorrow, grief, Pańch. 103, 2.—Comp. *A-*, see s.v. *Tri-*, m. the name of a Ṛishi, Chr. 297, 13 = Rigv. i. 112, 13. *Niḥç°*, i.e. *nis-* and *Vi-*, adj. free from sorrow, Hariv. 14227 (*nis-*). *Vîta-*, i.e. *vi-ita-*, I. adj. free from sorrow. II. m. the Açoka tree. *Sa-*, adj. sorrowful, Hit. 77, 1; sad, Ṛit. 6, 16. *°kam*, adv.

sorrowfully, Vikr. 52, 18. *Hṛichchhoka*, i.e. *hṛid-*, and *Hṛidaya-*, m. heartache, a pang.

शोकवन्त् *çoka + vant*, adj., f. *vatí*, Sorrowful, Chr. 17, 25.

शोचन *çochana*, i.e. 1. *çuch + ana*, I. adj. Sorrowing. II. n. Sorrow, grief.

शोचिष्केश *çochishkeça*, i.e. *çochis -keça*, I. adj. Having (rays of) light as hair, epithet of the sun, Chr. 289, 8 = Rigv. i. 50, 8. II. m. Fire.

शोचिस् *çochis*, i.e. 2. *çuch + is*, n. Light, splendour, Chr. 288, 14 = Rigv. i. 88, 14; Kâvya Pr. 70, 13.—Comp. *Çukra-*, adj. possessed of a resplendent lustre, Lass. 102, 7 = Rigv. vii. 14, 1.

शोठ *çoṭha* (perhaps a form of a lost *çush + ta*), adj. (ÇKD.), sbst. **1.** Foolish, a blockhead. **2.** Idle, an idler. **3.** A rogue. **4.** A low man. **5.** A sinner, a criminal.

† **शोण्** *ÇOṆ*, i. 1, Par. **1.** To become red (rather a denomin. derived from the next). **2.** To go, to move. *çoṇita*, see s.v.

शोण *çoṇa*, i.e. probably (although already in the Vedas), *sa-varṇa*, I. adj. **1.** Crimson, of a crimson colour, of chesnut colour, Vedântas. in Chr. 214, 11. **2.** Red in the face, from passion, etc. II. m. **1.** Crimson, the colour of the red lotus. **2.** A horse of a reddish or bright chesnut colour, Vedântas. in Chr. 214, 10. **3.** Fire. **4.** A red sort of sugar-cane. **5.** The name of a river. **6.** A flower, Bignonia indica. III. n. **1.** Blood. **2.** Red lead

शोणित *çoṇita*, i.e. *coṇa + ita*, I. adj. Red, crimson, Ragh. 2, 39. II. n. **1.** Blood, Pańch. iii. d. 32. **2.** Saffron.—Comp. *Jîva-*, n. living, i.e. sound blood, Suçr. 2, 193, 9. *Pûya-*, n. purulent blood, Man. 3, 180.

शोणिमन् *çoṇiman*, i. e. *coṇa + iman*, m. Redness, Gît. 12, 13.

शोथ *çotha*, i.e. *çû* (for *çvi*), *+ tha*, m. Swelling from disease.

शोधन *çodhana*, i.e. *çudh + ana*, I. adj. Cleaning, purifying. II. m. The lime. III. f. *ní*, A broom. IV. n. **1.** Cleaning, removing what may be prejudicial, Hit. 97, 15; purifying. **2.** Expiation, Man. 11, 125. **3.** Punishment, Man. 1, 115. **4.** Correcting from faults. **5.** Rooting up, Man. 9, 253. **6.** Precise determination, Vedântas. in Chr. 212, 11. **7.** The refining of metals. **8.** Payment, acquittal. **9.** Fæces, ordure. **10.** Green vitriol.

ऽशोधिन् *-çodhin*, i. e. *çudh + in*, adj., f. *ní*, Requiting, Daçak. in Chr. 190, 14.

शोफ *çopha* (vb. *çvi*, cf. *çotha*), m. Intumescence. — Comp. *Danta-*, m. swelling of the gum, Suçr. 1, 116, 7.

शोभ *çobha*, i.e. *çubh + a*, I. adj. **1.** Bright. **2.** Handsome. II. f. *bhâ*. **1.** Splendour, Megh. 60; Daçak. in Chr. 183, 4 (at the end of a comp. adj., f. *bhâ*). **2.** Light. **3.** Beauty, Hit. ii. d. 148.

शोभन *çobhana*, i.e. *çubh + ana*, I. adj., f. *ná*. **1.** Splendid. **2.** Beautiful. Râm. 4, 44, 38; ironically, Pańch. 216, 8. **3.** Propitious, Pańch. 143, 23; 155, 21 (n. with *na*, Misfortune, Pańch. 175, 18). **4.** Virtuous. **5.** Good, Pańch. 126, 20. **6.** Richly dressed. II. m. **1.** A planet. **2.** Burnt offering for auspicious results. III. n. **1.** Shining, being splendid. **2.** A lotus.—Comp. *Vana-*, n. a lotus.

ऽशोभिन् *-çobhin*, i.e. *çubh* and *çobhá*,

+ *in*, adj., f. *nî*, **1.** Shining, Vikr. d. 137; Râjat. 5, 358; Megh. 58. **2.** Exceeding, Râjat. 5, 384.—**Comp.** *Smita-* (vb. *smi*), adj., f. *nî*, smiling beautifully, Lass. 2. ed. 55, 66.

शोष *çosha*, i. e. *çush* + *a*, m. **1.** Drying up, Pańch. 51, 5; 159, 15. **2.** Exsiccation, ib. 76, 11. **3.** Pulmonary consumption.—**Comp.** *Tâlu-*, m. morbid dryness of the palate, Suçr. 1, 306, 3. *Dus-*, adj. difficult to be dried up, MBh. 8, 656. *Pari-*, m. complete drying up or shrivelling, Râm. 4, 15, 34.

शोषण *çoshaṇa*, i.e. *çush* + *ana*, **I.** adj. Drying up, causing to fade, Çâk. d. 58. **II.** m. One of the arrows of Kâma, Lass. 7, 3. **III.** n. Drying up, Lass. 2. ed. 91, 61; Pańch. 27, 1 (*vṛithâ-çarîra-*, Useless mortifying one's self).

ऽशोषिन् *-çoshin*, i. e. *çush* + *in*, Drying up, in *hṛidaya-kusuma-*, adj. Causing (her) flower-like heart to fade, Utt. Râmach. 53, 16.

शौक *çauka*, i. e. *çuka* + *a*, n. A flock of parrots.

शौक्तेय *çaukteya*, i.e. *çukti* + *eya*, n. A pearl.

शौक्ल्य *çauklya*, i.e. *çukla* + *ya*, n. Whiteness.

शौङ्गेय *çauńgeya*, m. Garuḍa, Daçak. in Chr. 200, 12 (cf. Wilson, Daçak. p. 93, n. 2).

शौच *çaucha*, i.e. *çuchi* + *a*, n. **1.** Purity, Râjat. 5, 11; cleanness, Pańch. iii. d. 112. **2.** Honesty, Pańch. v. d. 2. **3.** Purification, Man. 2, 69; cleaning (of vessels), Pańch. ii. d. 109, cf. Böhtl. Ind. Spr. 3029.—**Comp.** *A-*, n. 1. impurity, Man. 11, 183. 2. perfidy, Lass. 21, 9. *Artha-*, n. purity in acquiring wealth, honesty, Man. 5, 106.

शौचत्व *çaucha* + *tva*, n., in *a-*, Impurity, Hit. i. d. 194, M.M.

शौचेय *çaucheya*, i.e. *çuchi* + *eya*, m. A washerman.

† **शौट्** *ÇAUṬ*, **शौड्** *ÇAUḌ*, i. 1, Par. To be proud.

शौटीर *çauṭîra* (i.e. **çuṭîra* + *a*, cf. *çuṭîratâ*), adj. Proud. m. **1.** A hero, Râm. 3, 48, 4. **2.** An ascetic who has given up worldly pursuits. **3.** An upstart.

शौटीर्य *çauṭîrya*, i.e. *çauṭîra* (or **çuṭîra*, see the last), + *ya*, n. **1.** Pride. **2.** Heroism.

शौड् *ÇAUḌ*, see *çauṭ*.

शौण्ड *çauṇḍa*, i.e. *çuṇḍa* + *a*, adj. **1.** Drunk, intoxicated. **2.** Addicted to liquor, Draup. 6, 5.—**Comp.** *Dâna-*, adj. exceedingly liberal, Râjat. 6, 87.

शौण्डिक *çauṇḍika*, i.e. *çuṇḍa* + *ika*, **I.** m. A distiller and vendor of spirituous liquors, Man. 4, 216. **II.** f. *kî*. A female keeper of a tavern, Böhtl. Ind. Spr. 3355.

शौण्डिकेय *çauṇḍikeya*, i. e. *çauṇḍika* + *eya*, m. A demon, Journ. of the German Oriental Society, vii. 531, 16.

शौन *çauna*, i.e. *çûnâ* + *a* (n.), Meat kept at a slaughter-house, Man. 5, 13.

शौनक *çaunaka*, m. A proper name, Man. 3, 16.

शौनिक *çaunika*, i.e. *çûnâ* + *ika*, m. **1.** A butcher, Man. 4, 86. **2.** A poulterer, a vendor of flesh of birds. **3.** Chase, hunting.

शौर्य *çaurya*, i.e. *çûra* + *ya*, n. Prowess, heroism, Pańch. iii. d. 53; 238, 22.

शौल्किक *çaulkika*, i.e. *çulka* + *ika*, m. Superintendent of tolls or customs.

शौल्विक *çaulvika*, i.e. *çulva* + *ika*, m. A coppersmith.

शौवस्तिक *çauvastika*, i.e. *çvastya* + *ika*, adj. Of, or belonging to, to-morrow.

शौष्कल *çaushkala*, i. e. *çushkala* + *a*, I. adj. Eating flesh. II. m. A vendor of flesh (ÇKD.).

श्चुत् *ÇCHUT*, and 1. **श्च्युत्** *ÇCHYUT* (derived from a noun based on *çchyu*, cf. *chyu*), i. 1, Par. To ooze, to drop, Kir. 5, 29 (*çchyut*); to distill, Mâlat. 81, 13 (*çchut*). Ptcple. of the pf. pass. *çchyutita*. **1.** Shed, sprinkled. **2.** Dropping, flowing.—With the prep. **उप** *upa*, To drop, Chr. 293, 2 = Rigv. i. 87, 2 (*çchut*).—With **नि** *ni*, *çchut*, To drop down, Mâlat. 128, 5.—With **प्र** *pra*, To distill, Mâlat. 24, 3; Bhaṭṭ. 14, 79 (*çchut*).—Cf. Goth. skevjan (= *çchu*); skura; A.S. scur.

2. **ऽश्च्युत्** *-çchyut*, latter part of comp. words, adj. Shedding, *jala-* (water), Kir. 5, 9.

श्नथ् *ÇNATH*, i. 1, Par. To hurt, to kill, to destroy.—Cf. Goth. snithan; A.S. snidhan.

श्मशान *çmaçâna*, i.e. probably *çman* (for *çam* + *an*, cf. κμης in σιδηρο-κμής), *-çayana*, n. A cemetery, Pańch. v. d. 6.—Comp. *Pâreçmaçânam*, i.e. *pâra* + *i-çmaçâna* + *m*, adv. beyond the cemetery, Mâlat. 79, 19.

श्मश्रु *çmaçru*, n. The beard, Pańch. 182, 10.—Comp. *Rakta-* (vb. *rańj*), adj. having a red beard, Hiḍ. 3, 27. *Sa-*, f. a woman with a beard. *Sita-*, adj. silvery-bearded.

श्मश्रुल *çmaçru* + *la*, adj. Having a beard, Ragh. 4, 63; one who lets grow his beard, Man. 11, 105.

† **श्मील्** *ÇMÎL*, **स्मील्** *SMÎL* (cf. *mîl*), i. 1, Par. To wink, to contract the eyelids.

श्यान *çyâna*, see *çyai*.

श्याम *çyâma* (probably from *çvi*, cf. *çyeta*), I. adj., f. *mâ*. **1.** Green. **2.** Dark-blue, Vikr. d. 26. **3.** Black, Bhartṛ. 2, 14; 36 (dry ?); shady, Utt. Râmach. 42, 8. **4.** Brown, Hiḍ. 2, 25; Nal. 12, 50; 18, 11. **II.** m. **1.** Green, black (the colour). **2.** A cloud. **3.** The *kokila* or Indian cuckoo. **4.** A sacred fig-tree at *Prayâga*, Utt. Râmach. 15, 11; cf. Wilson, Hind. Theat. 2. ed. i. 302, n. †. **5.** Thorn-apple. **III.** m., and f. *mâ*, A sort of grain, Panicum frumentaceum. **IV.** f. *mâ*. **1.** Night. **2.** Shade, shadow. **3.** The female of the Indian cuckoo, Pańch. 157, 4. **4.** A cow. **5.** Durgâ. **6.** A married woman before she has borne children. **7.** A plant, commonly Priyańgu, Megh. 102; and name of several others. **V.** n. **1.** Pepper. **2.** Sea salt.—Cf. κύανος.

श्यामल *çyâma* + *la*, I. adj., f. *lâ*, Of a dark-blue or black colour, Daçak. in Chr. 190, 13; blackish, Mâlat. 145, 10. **II.** m. **1.** Black (the colour). **2.** Pepper. **3.** The religious fig-tree. **4.** A large bee. **III.** f. *lâ*, Pârvatî.

श्यामाक *çyâmâka* (cf. *çyâma*), m. A sort of grain, Panicum frumentaceum, Çâk. d. 89.

श्यामाय *ÇYAMÂYA*, a denomin. derived from *çyâma* with *ya*, Âtm. To become black, to prove impure (as gold, cf. the next), Mâlav. d. 30.

श्यामिका *çyâmikâ*, i.e. *çyâma* + *ka*, f. Impurity (of gold), Ragh. 1, 10.

श्यामित *çyâmita*, i.e. *çyâma+ita*, adj. Blackened, discoloured, Kir. 16, 2.

श्याल *çyâla*, see *syâla*.

श्यालक *çyâla+ka*, m. A miserable brother-in-law, Chân. 80 in Berl. Monatsb. 1864, 412.

श्याव *çyâva* (akin to *çyâma*), adj. Of a brown colour, livid, Daçak. in Chr. 187, 13.

श्येत *çyeta* (probably from *çvi* in *çvit*, cf. *çveta* and Zend. *çpi* in *çpi+tama*, *çpi+ti*), I. adj., f. *tâ* and *çyenî*, White, Kir. 5, 31. II. m. White (the colour).

श्येन *çyena* (akin to the last), I. m. **1.** White (the colour). **2.** A hawk, Pańch. 188, 15. II. f. *nî*, A female hawk.

श्यै *ÇYAI*, i. 1, Âtm. † To go. Ptcple. of the pf. pass. I. *çyâna*, Thick, viscous, adhesive. II. *çîna*, Thick, congealed.—With the prep. **आ** *â*, To dry up, Ragh. 17, 37. *âçyâna*, **1.** Dry, Ragh. 4, 24. **2.** A little dry (i.e. *çyâna*, with *â*), Kumâras. 7, 9.—With **प्रति** *prati*, *pratiçîna*, Melted, fluid, oozing.

श्यैनंपाता *çyainampâtâ*, i.e. *çyena+m-pat+a+a*, f. Hawking, hunting.

† **श्रङ्क्** *ÇRAŃK*, **स्रङ्क्** *SRAŃK*, **श्लङ्क्** *ÇLAŃK*, i. 1, Âtm. To go.

† **श्रङ्ग्** *ÇRAŃG*, **श्लङ्ग्** *ÇLAŃG*, **श्वङ्ग्** *ÇVAŃG*, **स्वङ्ग्** *SVAŃG*, i. 1, Par. To go.

श्रण् *ÇRAṆ*, i. 1 and 10, Par. To give, to present.—With the prep. **वि** *vi*, i. 10, To distribute, to give, Ragh. 14, 15. *viçrâṇita*, Given away, Daçak. in Chr. 194, 2.

श्रत् *çrat*, perhaps properly *çrath*, a prefix combined and compounded with *dhâ*, and in the Vedas with *kri*, and their derivatives, and implying faith.—Cf. Lat. cred in credo, for cred-do; see *dhâ*, p. 437.

श्रथ् *ÇRATH*, i. 1 and 10, Par., and **श्रन्थ्** ii. 9, *çrathnâ*, *nî*, and i. 1 and 10, Par. **1.** To tie (ved. ii. 9). **2.** To untie, to loosen (ved. ii. 9). **3.** † To kill. *çranth*, i. 1, Âtm. To be loose. *çrath*, i. 10, Par. I. † *çrâthaya*, **1.** To apply diligently. **2.** To delight frequently. II. *çrathaya*, † To be loose.—Cf. κλώθω, κάλαθος; Lat. crates, rete, restis; Goth. af-hlathan; O.H.G. and A.S. hládan; O.H.G. hlast; A.S. hlaest.

श्रथन *çrath+ana*, n. **1.** Tieing. **2.** Untieing.

श्रद्दधानता *çraddadhâna + tâ* (ptcple. pres. of *çrat-dhâ*), f. Faith, Man. 7, 86.

श्रद्ध *çraddha*, i.e. *çrat-dhâ*, n., and f. *dhâ*. **1.** Faith, Man. 3, 202 (f.); Bhag. 6, 37 (f.). **2.** Trust, intimacy, Râjat. 5, 285. **3.** Respect, reverence, Pańch. 265, 15 (f.). **4.** Purity. **5.** Wish, hope, Bhartr̥. 1, 89.—**Comp.** *A-çraddhâ*, f. want of faith, Man. 4, 225. *Yathâ-çraddha+m*, adv. confidently, without reserve, Nal. 4, 1.

श्रद्धामय *çraddhâ+maya*, adj., f. *yî*, Full of faith, Bhag. 17, 3.

श्रद्धालु *çraddhâ + lu*, I. adj. **1.** Faithful. **2.** Wishing, desirous. II. f. A pregnant woman longing for anything.

श्रद्धावन्त् *çraddhâ+vant*, adj., f. *vatî*, Believing, having faith, Bhag. 3, 31.

श्रद्धेयत्व *çraddheya+tva* (ptcple. of the fut. pass. of *çrat-dhâ*), n. Trustworthiness, Pańch. 162, 2.

श्रन्थ् *çranth*, see *çrath*.

श्रन्थ *çranth+a*, m. **1.** Tieing. **2.** Untieing. **3.** Vishṇu.

श्रन्थन *çranth+ana*, n. **1.** Tieing. **2.** Stringing flowers. **3.** Loosening. **4.** Killing.

श्रम् *ÇRAM*, i. 4, *çrâmya*, Par. **1.** To exert one's self, Lass. 2. ed. 66, 18. **2.** To perform acts of religious austerity, to undergo mortification or penance. **3.** To be wearied, Megh. 97. **4.** † To be distressed. Ptcple. of the pf. pass. *çrânta*. **1.** Wearied, fatigued, tired, Vikr. 67, 2. **2.** Calmed. m. An ascetic. **Comp.** *A-çrânta+m*, adv. indefatigably, Utt. Râmach. 148, 7. *Ati-*, adj. very fatigued, Pańch. 52, 4.—With the prep. **परि** *pari*, *pariçrânta*, **1.** Having performed acts of religious austerity, MBh. 3, 10002. **2.** Fatigued, Man. 4, 99. **3.** Exhausted, MBh. 1, 7626. **4.** Overcome with distress, Mâlat. 154, 10.—With **वि** *vi*, **1.** To repose, Hit. iv. d. 67; Râm. 1, 62, 1. **2.** To go to rest, Vikr. 40, 2. **3.** To cease, Pańch. 220, 25 (with ptcple. in the signification of an infin.). *viçrânta*, **1.** Reposed, Hit. 77, 1; reposing, Pańch. 222, 1; having reposed, Hit. 99, 5. **2.** Ceased, Vikr. d. 130; desisting from. **3.** Calm, composed, Utt. Râmach. 3, 1. Caus. *çramaya* (and in epic poetry *çrâmaya*), To let repose, MBh. 3, 11004.—Cf. perhaps A.S. hearm, grief, and O.H.G. râmen, râmjan, intendere.

श्रम *çram + a*, m. **1.** Exertion, Pańch. 226, 25; labour, toil, Pańch. 134, 14; taking pains, Chr. 22, 20; with *kṛi*, To study, Man. 2, 168. **2.** Military exercise. **3.** Fatigue, weariness, Hid. 1, 19; Kir. 5, 28; Utt. Râmach. 158, 10 (*-ambu*, Perspiration).—**Comp.** *A-*, m. absence of weariness, Ragh. 2, 67. *Ati-*, m. great fatigue, Çâk. d. 103. *Kṛita-*, adj. tired, Hit. iii. d. 110. *Khyâta-vyâkaraṇa-*, m. renowned for his study of grammar, Râjat. 5, 29. *Jita-*, adj. not suffering from fatigue, Hit. iii. d. 87. *Matta-ibha-kumbha-vidalana-kṛita-*, adj. one who has ever endeavoured to tear to pieces the frontal globes of furious elephants, Pańch. i. d. 351. *Vṛithâ-*, m. vain exertion, Pańch. 116, 25. *Sa-*, adj. wearied, fatigued.

श्रमण *çramaṇa*, i.e. *çram+ana*, I. adj. **1.** Following a low business. **2.** Base. **II.** m. **1.** An ascetic, a Bauddha friar, Râjat. 5, 427. **2.** A religious mendicant, Râm. 1, 13, 13. **III.** f. *ṇâ*. **1.** A female mendicant; also *ṇî*, Râm. 2, 38, 5. **2.** A woman of low caste or business. **3.** A handsome woman.

श्रमणाय *ÇRAMAṆÂYA*, a denomin. derived from the last with *ya*, Âtm. To become a beggar, Böhtl. Ind. Spr. 787.

श्रमिन् *çram+in*, and *çrama+in*, adj. **1.** Laborious, diligent. **2.** Wearying.

श्रम्भ् *ÇRAMBH*, **स्रम्भ्** *SRAMBH*, i. 1, Âtm. † To be careless.—With the prep. **वि** *vi*, To entrust, to confide. Ptcple. of the pf. pass. *viçrabdha*. **1.** Confided, entrusted, MBh. 3, 2161. **2.** Confided in. **3.** Confident, fearless, Pańch. 75, 9. **4.** Firm, Chr. 32, 30. **5.** Tranquil, patient. **6.** Lowlyminded. Acc. °*dham*, adv. **1.** Without hesitation, Man. 8, 417. **2.** Without fear, Râm. 3, 49, 33. **3.** Quietly, Daçak. in Chr. 199, 6.

श्रयण *çrayaṇa,* i.e. *çri + ana,* n. Refuge, protection.

श्रव *çrava,* m., i.e. **1.** *çru + a,* The ear. **2.** (Wrongly for *srava*), Oozing, dripping.—**Comp.** *Karṇa-,* adj. perceivable by the ear, Man. 4, 102. *Su-dus-,* m. very ill fame, Utt. Râmach. 166, 2.

श्रवण *çravaṇa,* i.e. *çru + ana,* I. m. and n. The ear, Hit. i. d. 193, M.M. **II.** m., and f. *ṇâ,* The twenty-third lunar asterism. **III.** n. **1.** Hearing, Pañch. 188, 10. **2.** Study, Vedântas. in Chr. 216, 2; learning, Mâlat. 6, 5. —**Comp.** *Ugra-,* adj. dreadful to hear, Johns. Sel. 96, 79.

श्रवस् *çravas,* i.e. *çru + as,* n. **1.** The ear. **2.** Renown, wealth, Chr. 294, 8 = Rigv. i. 92, 8.—**Comp.** *Uch-chaiḥçravas,* i. e. *uchchais-,* m. a fabulous horse, MBh. 1, 366. *Cha-kshuḥçravas,* i. e. *chakshus-,* m. a snake, MBh. 12, 13803. *Dirgha-,* adj. widely renowned, Chr. 297, 11 = Rigv. i. 112, 11. *Deva-,* m. a proper name, Hariv. 1461 (Θεοκλῆς). *Pṛithu-,* I. adj. widely renowned, Bhâg. P. 4, 15, 4. II. a proper name. *Vishṭara-,* m. Vishṇu. *Vṛiddha-* (vb. *vṛidh*), m. Indra. *Su-,* adj. famous, Chr. 288, 2 = Rigv. i. 49, 2 (cf. εὐκλεής).—Cf. κλέος.

श्रवस्यु *çravas + yu,* adj. Desirous of renown or wealth, Chr. 292, 8 = Rigv. i. 85, 8.

श्रवाय्य *çravâyya,* m. An animal destined for sacrifice.

श्रविष्ठा *çravishṭhâ* (f. of a superl. based on *çravas,* in the signification 'wealth'), f. A lunar asterism (= *dha-nishṭhâ*).

श्रा *ÇRÂ,* † ii. 2, Par., **श्रै** *ÇRAI* († **स्रै** *SRAI,* † **शै** *ÇAI*), † i. 1, *çrâya,* Par. **1.** To boil, to cook, to mature, to ripen. **2.** † To sweat; cf. *çrî.* Ptcple. of the pf. pass. I. *çrâṇa.* **1.** Boiled, dressed. **2.** Moist, wet. f. *ṇâ,* Rice-grnel. **II.** *çrita,* Cooked, ved. and Râm. 2, 56, 24, Schlegel (but Gorr. 2, 56, 26, *çṛita*). **III.** *çṛita,* Boiled, Man. 11, 147. Caus. *çrapaya* and † *çrápaya.* To cook, MBh. 3, 5038.—Cf. κρίβανος, κρίβανον, κλίβανος, κρι-βάνη, κράμβος, καρπός, κάρφω, κάρδοπος, probably κραῦρος, perhaps κέραμος, κέρ-νον; Lat. cremare, carbo, probably calere, cinis; Goth. hauri, hlaibs; A.S. heordh, hláf, haerefaest, haerfest, Ripe.

श्राद्ध *çrâddha,* i. e. *çraddhâ + a,* I. adj. Faithful. **II.** n. **1.** A funeral ceremony and worship of the Manes, consisting of offerings to the gods and Manes, and gifts and food to the relations and assisting Brâhmaṇas, Man. 1, 112; 3, 81; 82; 204; Pañch. ii. d. 101. **2.** Gifts given at the *çrâddha,* Lass. 89, 1.—**Comp.** *Vṛiddhi-,* n. a sacrifice to progenitors on any prosperous occasion, as a birth of a son, etc.

श्राद्धिक *çrâddhika,* i. e. *çrâddha + ika,* I. adj. **1.** Relating to an obsequial offering. **2.** n. A present given at a *çrâddha,* Man. 4, 116. **II.** m., f. *kî,* n. The object, receiver, or enjoyer of an obsequial oblation.

श्रान्ति *çrânti,* i. e. *çram + ti,* f. Weariness.

श्राम् *ÇRÂM,* v.r. of *grâm.*

श्राम *çrâma,* i.e. *çram + a,* m. **1.** A temporary shed. **2.** Time. **3.** A month.

श्राय *çrâya,* I. *çri + a,* m. Refuge,

protection. II. *çrî+a*, adj. Sacred, or belonging, to the goddess *Çrî*.

श्रावक *çrâvaka*, i.e. *çru*, Caus., + *aka*, m. **1.** The name of a class of the Bauddha votaries; a lay votary of the Bauddha religion, Pańch. 236, 19. **2.** A pupil, Mâlat, 174, 4.

श्रावण *çrâvaṇa*, i.e. **A.** *çravaṇa+a*, I. adj. Born or produced under the asterism *Çravanâ*. **II.** m. The name of a month (July—August). **III.** f. *ṇî*. **1.** The day of full moon in the month Çrâvaṇa, Man. 4, 95. **2.** The name of one of the domestic sacrifices (*pâka-yajńa*), Journ. of the German Oriental Society, vii. 527. **B.** *çru*, Caus., +*ana*, n. Causing to hear.—**Comp.** *Satya-*, n. taking an oath, Pańch. 97, 17.

श्रावणिक *çrâvaṇika*, i.e. *çrâvaṇa+ika*, m. The month *Çrâvaṇa*.

श्रि *ÇRI*, i. 1, Par. Âtm. (the original signification is probably 'To cling to,' 'To lean'), **1.** To go to, Ragh. 3, 70 (Calc.); to come, Vikr. d. 112. **2.** To enter, MBh. 5, 1741. **3.** To obtain, Chr. 294, 2=Rigv. i. 92, 2. **4.** To undergo, Râjat. 5, 132 (with the abstract *ânukûlyam*, 'To become inclined,' read *açiçriyan*). **5.** To serve (ved.). Ptcple of the pf. pass. *çrita*. **1.** Cherished, protected, fled for refuge. **2.** Served, worshipped. **3.** Joined with, contiguous to. **4.** Sitting on, Lass. 2. ed. 89, 37. **5.** Covered. **6.** Having. —With the prep. **अधि** *adhi*, To ascend; with *çayanam*, To go to rest, Daçak. in Chr. 188, 20. *adhiçrita*, **1.** Trespassing, being out of, Pańch. 291, 11 (v.r.). **2.** Placed. **3.** Received. **4.** Included.—With **समधि** *sam-adhi*, To approach, Nal. 23, 12.—With **अभि** *abhi*, To have recourse to, MBh. 1, 8274.—With **आ** *â*, **1.** To go to, Pańch. 188, 18; Chr. 46, 19; to retire in (acc.), Vikr. d. 155. **2.** With a word implying, 'Ground, earth,' To fall to, Chr. 32, 25. **3.** To enter, Râm. 2, 67, 5; with *ratham*, To mount, MBh. 1, 8187. **4.** To undergo, Hit. 75, 17; Râjat. 5, 130; *mitrabhâram âçritya*, Having become friends, Pańch. 141, 19; to take, Utt. Râmach. 88, 2. **5.** To have recourse to, MBh. 3, 13069; absol. *âçritya*, By help, by means of, Çâk. 4, 12. **6.** To use, Lass. 85, 7. **7.** To seek, Hit. ii. d. 127. **8.** To choose, Hit. 75, 10. **9.** To obtain, Pańch. 94, 24. **10.** To follow, Bhartṛ. 2, 33. **11.** To inhabit, Man. 7, 72. **12.** To depend upon, Man. 1, 17. **13.** To assist, MBh. 1, 5916. *âçrita*, **1.** Having recourse to; with *ahaṁkâram*, Having grown presumptuous, Pańch. 76, 20; using, Johns. Sel. 38, 27. **2.** Having attained, Pańch. 76, 8. **3.** Having assumed, Johns. Sel. 94, 56. **4.** Following, Man. 5, 90; practising. **5.** Inhabiting. **6.** Being, Râm. 3, 49, 33. **7.** Receiving anything as an inherent or integral part. **8.** Inherent, Bhâshâp. 85. **9.** Taking one's station, Râjat. 5, 286. **10.** A dependent, Hit. 30, 10, M.M.; Kumâras. 3, 1. **Comp.** *An-eka-*, adj. inherent in many, Bhâshâp. 88. *Para-*, adj. dependent, Hit. ii. d. 20.—With **अन्वा** *anu-â*, To go to, Râm. 2, 84, 7.—With **अपा** *apa-â*, To resort to, to have recourse to, MBh. 1, 651 (*an-apâçritya*, without the help of).—With **व्यपा** *vi-apa-â*, To have recourse to, Bhag. 9, 32.—With **उपा** *upa-â*, **1.** To go to, MBh. 1, 5918. **2.** To have recourse to, Bhag. 4, 10. *upâçritya*, By aid, Man. 9, 316. Ptcple. of the pf. pass. *upâçrita*. **1.** Supporting. **2.** Relying upon. **Comp.** *An-*, adj. not relied upon, used as support, Utt. Râmach.

24, 7.—With समुपा *sam-upa-â*, To have recourse to, MBh. 2, 618. *samupâçrita*, Having resorted to, Râjat. 5, 141.—With समा *sam-â*, **1.** To go to, MBh. 1, 59, 27; to approach; with *âsanam*, to sit down, Pańch. i. d. 283. **2.** To enter, Man. 6, 2. **3.** To occupy, Pańch. 136, 8; to obtain, i. d. 417. **4.** To have recourse to, Pańch. 154, 15; *samâçritya*, by aid, Man. 3, 77. **5.** To confide in, Man. 7, 70. *samâçrita*, **1.** Fled for refuge, protected. **2.** Having assumed, Chr. 29, 25. **3.** Joined, Râjat. 5, 248. **4.** Depending on, Pańch. iii. d. 62.—With उद् *ud*, **1.** Âtm. To rise, MBh. 4, 1018. **2.** Par. To raise, Râm. 2, 66, 17. *uchchhrita*, **1.** Produced. **2.** Lifted up, Hit. ii. d. 154. **3.** High, Kir. 5, 1. **4.** Rising, MBh. 3, 2437. **5.** Increased in size or bulk. **6.** Prosperous. **7.** Left, abandoned. **8.** Deprived, Pańch. v. d. 11 (*phala-*, Will not be fulfilled). Comp. *Ati-*, excessively elevated, Hit. ii. d. 120.—With अभ्युद् *abhi-ud*, *abhyuchchhrita*, Raised, Draup. 8, 20.—With प्रोद् *pra-ud*, *prochchhrita*, High, Mṛichchh. 76, 21.—With समुद् *sam-ud*, *samuchchhrita*, **1.** Raised, MBh. 3, 8064. **2.** Lofty, Hit. ii. d. 84.—With उप *upa*, To come to, to hit, MBh. 3, 10456.—With विनिस् *vi-nis*, To come out, Sâv. 6, 14.—With प्र *pra*, *praçrita*, Modest, humble, well-behaved, Indr. 1, 10.—With संप्र *sam-pra*, *sampraçrita*, The same, Râm. 2, 70, 11.—With सम् *sam*, **1.** To unite, Mâlat. 15, 2 (Âtm.). **2.** To go to, MBh. 3, 13053. **3.** To attain, to get, Man. 10, 60. **4.** To have recourse to, MBh. 2, 128; Pańch. 155, 21; to flee to, Hit. iii. d. 147. **5.** To seek, Râm. 1, 1, 6. **6.** To depend upon, Râm. 2, 60, 20. **7.** To inhabit, Man. 2, 24. *samçrita*, **1.** Having gone for refuge to (acc.), Pańch. iii. d. 129. **2.** Come for refuge, Çâk. d. 104. **3.** Protected, supported. **4.** Joined, Râjat. 5, 335. m. An attendant, Man. 4, 179.—With अभिसम् *abhi-sam*, *abhisamçrita*, Having gone to, Lass. 2. ed. 76, 54 (went to).—Cf. *çaraṇa*, and Goth. hulth; A.S. hold; perhaps Goth. hail; A.S. hál; perhaps Lat. clemens; to the original signification seem to belong, κλίνω, κλισία, κλιτύς; Lat. in-clinare, clivus; Goth. hlains, hleithra, hlija; A.S. hlynian, hlidh.

ऽश्रित् *-çri+t*, latter part of comp. adj. Reaching, rising to; cf. *nabhaḥçrit.*

श्रियपुत्र *çriyaputra*, erroneously for *priyaputra*, m. A kind of bird, Lass. 52, 20, see 2. ed. p. 112.

श्रियस् *çriyas*, probably *çri+as* (cf. 2. *çrî* and ved. *bhiyas*, n.), Happiness, Chr. 293, 6=Rigv. i. 87, 6 (cf. 293, 3= Rigv. i. 88, 3).

† श्रिष् *ÇRISH*, श्लिष् *ÇLISH*, i. 1, Par. To burn (cf. *çrâ*).

1. श्री *ÇRÎ* (cf. *çrâ*), ii. 9, *çrîṇâ*, *ṇî*, Par. Âtm. **1.** To cook, to burn. **2.** To mix.—Cf. probably κίρνημι, κεράω, κεράννυμι, κικράω, etc.; Lat. pin-cerna.

2. श्री *çrî* (either from *çrâ*, To ripen, cf. Lat. Ceres, or from *çri*, To approach for protection), f. **1.** The deity of plenty and prosperity, the wife of Vishṇu, Râm. 3, 52, 22. **2.** Fortune, Vikr. d. 161; 162; success, happiness, prosperity, Chr. 291, 12=Rigv. i. 64, 12; highest dignity, Chr. 291, 2=Rigv. i. 85, 2 (pl.); royal bliss, power, Vikr. d. 76; Pańch. i. d. 271; well-being, Pańch. i. d. 292; favour, Chr. 294, 6=

Rigv. i. 92, 6. **3.** Wealth, property, Kir. 14, 13. **4.** Beauty, Vikr. d. 26. **5.** Light, splendour, Pańch. v. d. 4. **6.** Glory, Pańch. iii. d. 259. **7.** Intellect. **8.** Decoration. **9.** A name of Sarasvatî. **10.** A tree, Pinus longifolia. **11.** Cloves. **12.** A prefix to the names of deities, and revered persons, and books, implying, Holy, illustrious, famous; e.g. *Çrî-vishṇu,* The holy deity, Vishṇu; *Çrî-râma; Çrî-bhâgavata-purâṇa,* The holy Bhâgavata-Purâṇa, cf. Râjat. 5, 30; 426; Lass. 45, 12; 66, 16; 67, 4; Bhartṛ. p. 21, l. 1.—**Comp.** *Apa-,* adj. deprived of beauty, Çiç. 11, 64. *Jaya-,* f. the goddess of victory, Râjat. 2, 64. *Mahâ-,* f. epithet of Lakshmî.

ऽश्रीक -*çrî+ka,* a substitute for *çrî* at the end of comp. adj.; e.g. *niḥçrîka,* i.e. *nis-,* adj. **1.** Unfortunate, MBh. 5, 533. **2.** Deprived of beauty, light, ib. 14, 476. *puṇya-,* Endowed with a pure royal majesty, Utt. Râmach. 105, 5. *vi-gata-,* adj. Unfortunate.

श्रीमन्त् *çrî+mant,* I. adj., f. *matî.* **1.** Fortunate, Hit. 54, 20. **2.** Wealthy. **3.** Famous, Pańch. iii. d. 238. **4.** Beautiful, Mâlat. 148, 8; Chr. 27, 6. II. m. **1.** Vishṇu. **2.** Çiva. **3.** Kuvera.

श्रील *çrî+la,* adj. **1.** Fortunate. **2.** Wealthy.

श्रीवत्सकिन् *çrîvatsakin,* i. e. *çrî-vatsa+ka+in,* m. A horse having a curl of hair on his breast and face.

1. **श्रु** *ÇRU,* ii. 5, *çriṇu,* Par. (in epic poetry also Âtm., MBh. 1, 386), **1.** To hear, Man. 5, 75; Chr. 292, 2=Rigv. i. 86, 2 (ved. *çriṇutâ*); Chr. 288, 10=Rigv. i. 48, 10 (*çrudhi,* imperat. aor.). **2.** To be attentive, Man. 1, 4. **3.** To be obedient, Bhag. 18, 58. *çruta,* **1.** Understood. **2.** Called, Lass. 2. ed. 61, 28. n. **1.** The object of hearing, that which is heard. **2.** Sacred learning, Man. 2, 149; Bhartṛ. 2, 55. **Comp.** *Ku-* and *Dus-,* adj. imperfectly heard, Pańch. v. d. 1 (*ku-*); Râm. 3, 41, 10 (*dus-*). *Bahu-,* adj. having learned much, Hit. i. d. 25, M.M. Desider. *çuçrûsha,* Âtm. **1.** To wish to hear, MBh. 3, 13248; to wish to learn, Bhâg. P. 2, 9, 40. **2.** To obey, Indr. 5, 34. **3.** To attend dutifully, Man. 4, 244. **4.** To serve, Man. 10, 100. **5.** To worship, Râm. 1, 8, 10. Ptcple. of the pf. pass. *çuçrûshita,* Served, Pańch. 118, 24. Caus. *çrâvaya,* **1.** To cause to hear, i.e. to speak, to say, Râm. 2, 3, 31. **2.** To propound, Man. 1, 59. **3.** To inform, Râm. 1, 17, 18. **4.** To report, MBh. 1, 6518.—With the prep. **अनु** *anu,* To hear, Man. 9, 100; pass. To be told, Pańch. 3, 10. Desider. To obey, Râm. 2, 8, 18.—With **आ** *â,* To hear, Chr. 292, 5=Rigv. i. 86, 5 (*çroshantu,* imperat. of the aor.). Caus. To report, MBh. 3, 15260.—With **समा** *sam-â,* To promise, Râm. 2, 76, 3, Seramp.—With **उप** *upa,* **1.** To be attentive, Chr. 11, 18. **2.** To hear, Utt. Râmach. 40, 3; MBh. 2, 1244; with abl. To hear from, Vikr. 11, 15.—With **समुप** *sam-upa,* To hear, MBh. 1, 384.—With **परि** *pari,* To hear, MBh. 1, 3754.—With **प्रति** *prati,* To promise, Râm. 1, 16, 8.—With **संप्रति** *sam-prati,* Caus. To remind one of his promise, Râm. 2, 107, 5.—With **वि** *vi,* pass. **1.** To be heard round about, Râm. 1, 13, 13. **2.** To become famous, Hit. pr. d. 20, M.M. *viçruta,* **1.** Told round about, celebrated, Daçak. in Chr. 179, 12. **2.** Heard, attended to, Amar. 15. **3.** Known. **4.** Famous, Râm. 3, 53, 32. **5.** Pleased, happy. Caus. **1.** To cry aloud, MBh. 1, 6287. **2.** To fill with noise, to pervade, MBh.

3, 16556. **3.** To report, MBh. 3, 12266. —With अभिवि *abhi-vi, abhiviçruta,* Celebrated, MBh. 1, 2718.—With सम् *sam,* **1.** To hear, MBh. 1, 1627. **2.** Âtm. To promise, MBh. 3, 2143. Caus. **1.** To cause to be heard, to cry, Pańch. 172, 25. **2.** To report, MBh. 5, 560.—Cf. κλύω, κλυτός (=*çruta*), κλέος (=*çravas*), ἀ-κροάομαι; Lat. clutus, cliens, probably aus-cultare, laudo (for claus-do, cf. *çravas*); Goth. hrôtheigs, hliuma; A.S. hlúd, hlyd, hlowan (Causal), hlyn, hlyrian (?), hliosa, hlyst, hlystan; O.H.G. hliumunt (=ved. *çromanta*), hlôsên.

2. श्रु *ÇRU,* see *sru.*

श्रुतर्य *çrutarya,* m. A proper name, Chr. 296, 9=Rigv. i. 112, 9.

श्रुतवन्त् *çruta + vant,* adj., f. *vatî,* Instructed in sacred learning, Bhartṛ. 2, 33.

श्रुति *çru + ti,* f. **1.** Hearing, Indr. 2, 5. **2.** An ear, Vikr. d. 56. **3.** Report, Johns. Sel. 53, 127. **4.** The Vedas, the revealed law, Hit. i. d. 31, M.M.; Pańch. 167, 1. **5.** A holy text, Man. 2, 15; 11; 33; Vedântas. in Chr. 203, 5.—**Comp.** *A-,* f. 1. not hearing, Utt. Râmach. 69, 11. 2. oblivion. *Çhakshuḥçruti,* i.e. *chakshus-,* m. a snake, Râjat. 5, 1. *Pûrṇa-* (vb. *prî*), adj. having the ears filled. *Yathâ-,* adv. conformable to the precepts of the Vedas, Çâk. d. 152.

श्रुतिमन्त् *çruti + mant,* adj., f. *matî,* Hearing, Bhag. 13, 13.

श्रुती *çrutî,* Râm. 3, 55, 34, for *çruti,* on account of the metre.

श्रुव *çruva,* incorrectly for *sruva,* m. **1.** A sacrificial ladle to pour *ghṛita* on the fire of a sacrifice, Râm. 6, 96, 12. **2.** Sacrifice, Râm. 2, 62, 26.

श्रूयमाणत्व *çrûyamâṇa* (ptcple. pres. pass. of *çru*), + *tva,* n. Condition of being heard, Vedântas. in Chr. 214, 9.

श्रेक् *ÇREK,* see *srek.*

श्रेणि *çreṇi,* i.e. *çri + ni,* m., f., and *ṇî,* f. **1.** A line, a row, Lass. 67, 10; 69, 8. **2.** A troop, Utt. Râmach. 117, 6; Chr. 34, 13 (*ṇî*); Bhartṛ. 2, 28 (*ṇî*; *bhuvana-,* all the worlds); ib. 71 (*ṇî*; *upakâra-,* plenty of benefits); Râjat. 5, 331 (*çiras-çreṇi,* a great quantity of heads). **3.** A company of artisans following the same business, Bhâg. P. 9, 10, 38. **4.** A corporation, Man. 8, 41. **5.** A bucket, a baling vessel.—**Comp.** *Pada-,* f. footsteps, Kathâs. 33, 113.

श्रेयंस् *çreyaṁs,* akin to *çrî,* I. Comparat. of *praçasya* (see *çaṁs*). **1.** Better, Hit. iii. d. 3. **2.** Best, Pańch. iii. d. 55; excellent, most beloved, Hit. iii. d. 34. acc. n. *yas,* adv. Well, most excellent; with *na,* Rather—than, Râm. 3, 48, 16. II. f. *yasî,* The name of several plants. III. n. *yas.* **1.** Prosperity, Pańch. 182, 1; fortune, Vikr. 68, 7 (pl.); happiness, Pańch. i. d. 344; Kir. 5, 49 (pl.). **2.** Final happiness. **3.** Virtue. **4.** An act leading to the chief temporal good, Man. 3, 223, 224.—**Comp.** *A-,* n. evil, Chr. 23, 30.

ऽश्रेयस -*çreyas + a,* in *nis-,* n. Final beatitude, Man. 1, 117; 12, 83; 104. 2. *çras-,* I. adj. Happy. II. °*sam,* adv. Well. III. n. **1.** Happiness. **2.** Brahman.

श्रेयस्कर *çreyaskara,* i.e. *çreyaṁs -kṛi + a,* adj. **1.** Effecting happiness, Pańch. 73, 19. **2.** Ensuring felicity, Man. 7, 88. **3.** Making better. **4.** Propitious.

श्रेयस्त्व *çreyastva,* i.e. *çreyaṁs + tva,* n. **1.** Superiority, Man. 10, 66. **2.** Final beatitude.

श्रेष्ठ *çreshṭha,* I. Superl. of *çreyaṁs.*

1. Best, excellent, Lass. 40, 6; of a higher rank, Pańch. iii. d. 219. 2. Oldest, senior. 3. Superl. *çreshṭha*+*tama*, The very best, Hit. iii. d. 87. II. m. 1. A king. 2. A Brâhmaṇa. 3. Kuvera. III. n. Cow's milk.—Comp. *Kuru-*, *Bharata-*, *Bhṛigu-*, m. an excellent descendant of Kuru, Bharata, Bhṛigu, Chr. 17, 32; 41, 6; 26, 74. *Muni-*, m. an excellent sage, Lass. 48, 3. *Varṇa-*, adj. being of the best caste, Hit. iv. d. 21.

श्रेष्ठता *çreshṭha*+*tâ*, f. Superiority, eminence, Man. 4, 245.

श्रेष्ठिन् *çreshṭhin*, i.e. *çreshṭha*+*in*, I. adj. Best. II. m. 1. An artist eminent by birth. 2. The head of a body of persons following the same business, Pańch. 234, 6; i. d. 14, read °*thî*; Daçak. in Chr. 184, 12.

श्रै *ÇRAI*, see *çrâ*.

श्रैष्ठ्य *çraishṭhya*, i.e. *çreshṭha*+*ya*, n. Superiority, Man. 1, 100; 12, 38.

† श्रोण् *ÇROṆ*, श्लोण् *ÇLOṆ*, i. 1, Par. To accumulate.

श्रोण *çroṇa*, adj. Lame, Chr. 296, 8 = Rigv. i. 112, 8.

श्रोणि *çroṇi*, m., f., and *ṇî*, f. 1. The hips and loins, buttocks, Vikr. d. 100 (*ṇî*); Megh. 80 (*ṇî*). 2. A road, a way. — Comp. *Pṛithu-çroṇî*, adj., f. having large buttocks, Indr. 5, 5. *Mahâ-kaṭi-taṭa-çroṇî*, adj. having large hips and buttocks, Indr. 2, 32. *Su-çroṇî*, adj., f. καλλίπυγος, Lass. 52, 2. —Cf. Lat. clunis; κλόνις.

श्रोतस् *çrotas*, i.e. *çru*+*tas*, n. 1. The ear. 2. An organ of sense; the trunk of an elephant as his special organ, Megh. 43 (Sch.). 3. Erroneously for *srotas*. 4. *çrotam*, Padmap. 8, 11, must be changed to *çrautam*.

श्रोतृ *çrotṛi*, i.e. *çru*+*tṛi*, m., f. *trî*, and n. Hearing, a hearer, Hit. ii. d. 128.

श्रोत्र *çrotra*, i.e. *çru*+*tra*, n. The ear, Pańch. v. d. 15.—Cf. A.S. hleodhor.

श्रोत्रिय *çrotriya*, i.e. *çrotra*+*iya*, I. adj. Modest, well-behaved. II. m. 1. A Brâhmaṇa conversant with the Vedas, Man. 2, 134 (cf. Sch. ad Çâk. d. 128). 2. One who observes the religious precepts, Pańch. 110, 24.—Comp. *A-*, adj. without learned Brâhmaṇas, Pańch. ii. d. 101. *Mantriçrotriya*, i.e. *mantrin-*, m. a *çrotriya*-like minister, Pańch. 25, 13.

श्रौत *çrauta*, i.e. *çruta*+*a*, I. adj. 1. Relating to the ear, hearing. 2. Relating to sacred learning, or the Vedas, Padmap. 8, 11 (see *çrotas*). 3. Prescribed by the Vedas, Çâk. 61, 12. II. n. Any observance ordained by the Vedas.

श्रौषट् *çraushaṭ*, anomal. old conjunct. of the aor. of *çru* (cf. *vashaṭ*), indecl. An exclamation used in making an offering to the Manes or gods.

श्लक्ष्ण *çlakshṇa*, adj. 1. Small, slender, thin, Lass. 2. ed. 60, 19. 2. Smooth, even, soft, Nal. 5, 5; Man. 8, 396; polished, Râm. 1, 13, 32, Seramp. 3. Mild, amiable, Nal. 8, 12. 4. Honest.

श्लक्ष्णय *ÇLAKSHṆAYA*, a denomin. derived from *çlakshṇa*, Par. To make thin or small, Pâṇ. iii. 1, 21.

श्लङ्क् *ÇLAṄK*, see *çraṅk*.

श्लङ्ग् *ÇLAṄG*, see *çraṅg*.

श्लथ् *ÇLATH*, i. 1, and † 10, Par. 1. To be relaxed, to open, Bhâg. P. 8, 12, 21. 2. To be weak (cf. *çrath*).—

With the prep. वि *vi*, To be relaxed, Bhâg. P. 6, 1, 60.

श्लथ *çlath + a*, adj. **1.** Untied. **2.** Relaxed, Bhartṛ. 1, 25; loose, Vikr. d. 146; flaccid, Ṛit. 6, 8. **3.** Dishevelled (hair).—**Comp.** *A-pari-çlatha + m*, adv. very tightly, Utt. Râmach. 147, 8.

† **श्लाख्** *ÇLÂKH*, i. 1, Par. To pervade.

श्लाघ् *ÇLÂGH*, i. 1, Âtm. (in epic poetry also Par., MBh. 3, 13306), **1.** To flatter, Bhaṭṭ. 8, 72. **2.** To praise, MBh. I. 1.; *çlâghya*, Praiseworthy, Râm. 3, 55, 16. **3.** To boast, Daçak. in Chr. 183, 20. *çlâghya*, Honourable, ib. 186, 21. Caus. To approve, Hit. 61, 6.—Cf. κρήγυον, probably κόλαξ.

श्लाघा *çlâgh + â*, f. **1.** Flattery. **2.** Praise, Pańch. iii. d. 33; Böhtl. Ind. Spr. 1155. **3.** Boasting, Vikr. 56, 15. **4.** Service. **5.** Wish, desire.—**Comp.** *Sa-çlâgha + m*, adv. praising, Vikr. 52, 7.

ऽश्लाघिन् *-çlâgh + in*, adj., in *raṇa-*, Chr. 20, 19, Praising, desiring combat (cf. the last).

श्लिकु *çliku*, I. m. A servant. II. n. (?), Astronomy.

1. **श्लिष्** *ÇLISH*, i. 4, Par. (in epic poetry also Âtm., MBh. 1, 3040); the original signification seems to have been, To adhere (cf. *çri*). **1.** To embrace, Gît. 1, 44. **2.** To tie, Hit. i. d. 83. **3.** To join, Daçak. in Chr. 198, 19. *çlishṭa*, Touched by, clung or adhered to, leaning on, Râm. 2, 68, 22, Seramp. **Comp.** *Su-*, adj. 1. well fastened, Hit. i. d. 87, M.M. 2. well strung, Mâlat. 18, 4. † i. 10, Par. To unite.—With the prep. आ *â*, **1.** To embrace, Râm. 2, 96, 22. **2.** To approach, Arj. 6, 12. —With उपा *upa-â*, *upâçlishṭa*, Having embraced, Lass. 2. ed. 73, 23.—With समा *sam-â*, **1.** To embrace, MBh. 3, 10043. **2.** To bring near, Arj. 6, 8.— With स्वा *su-â*, To embrace tightly, Man. 11, 103.—With उप *upa*, **1.** To embrace, MBh. 4, 515. **2.** With *urasâ*, To press against one's breast, Daçak. in Chr. 188, 6. Caus. **1.** To hold near, Vikr. 78, 11. **2.** To stop, Vikr. 10, 16. —With वि *vi*, To burst, Bhaṭṭ. 14, 67. *viçlishṭa*, Separated, disunited. Caus. **1.** To separate, Megh. 7. **2.** To disunite, Pańch. 42, 7.—With सम् *sam*, with *urasâ*, To press against one's breast, Râm. 1, 10, 28. *saṁçlishṭa*, **1.** Close together, adjoining, touching. **2.** United, joined, Pańch. ii. d. 136. **3.** Endowed, Pańch. 143, 8. **4.** Embraced. Caus. To join, MBh. 2, 735.

2. **श्लिष्** *ÇLISH*, see *çrish*.

श्लीपद *çlîpada*, i. e. probably *çlish -pada*, n. Morbid enlargement of the legs (cf. *çilîpada* and the next).

श्लीपदिन् *çlîpadin*, i.e. *çlîpada + in*, adj. Club-footed, Man. 3, 165.

श्लील *çlîla*, i.e. *çri + la* (cf. *çrîla*), adj. Prosperous.—**Comp.** *A-*, adj. 1. coarse, vulgar. 2. abusive. n. 1. rustic language. 2. untruth. 3. low abuse, Daçak. in Chr. 185, 23.

श्लेष *çlesha*, i.e. *çlish + a*, m. **1.** Embracing, an embrace, Utt. Râmach. 153, 4. **2.** Union. **3.** Association. **4.** Paronomasia.

श्लेष्मक *çleshmaka*, i.e. *çleshman + ka*, m. Phlegm.

श्लेष्मण *çleshmaṇa*, i.e. *çleshman + a*, adj. Phlegmatic.

श्लेष्मन् *çleshman*, i.e. *çlish + man*, m.

The phlegmatic humour, mucus, Man. 4, 132; Pańch. iii. d. 60.

श्लेष्मल *çleshmala*, i.e. *çleshman* + *a* (with *l* for *n*), adj. Phlegmatic.

श्लेष्मात *çleshmâta* (akin to the last), m. A small tree, Cordia latifolia.

श्लेष्मातक *çleshmâta* + *ka* (m.), A tree, Cordia myxa, Man. 6, 14; cf. Râm. 1, 13, 28 (°**कमय** *ka* + *maya*, adj. Made of *çleshmâtaka*).

† **श्लोक्** *ÇLOK* (rather a denomin. derived from the next), i. 1, Âtm. **1.** To compose verses. **2.** To be composed. **3.** To acquire. **4.** To abandon.

श्लोक *çloka*, i.e. *çru* + *ka*, m. **1.** Fame. **2.** A verse, Pańch. 106, 8; a saying, Chr. 22, 24.—**Comp.** *Puṇya-*, I. adj. well-famed, Bhâg. P. 1, 12, 18. II. m. 1. a name of Nala, Nal. 7, 18. 2. epithet of Yudhishṭhira and Vishṇu. III. f. *kâ*, a name of Damayantî and Sîtâ.

श्लोण् *ÇLOṆ*, see *çroṇ*.

श्वक्रीडिन् *çvakriḍin*, i.e. *çvan-kriḍâ* + *in*, m. A breeder of sporting dogs, Man. 3, 164.

श्वघ्निन् *çvaghnin* (? nom. sing. *ghnî*), m. A gamester, Chr. 295, 10 = Rigv. i. 92, 10.

† **श्वङ्क्** *ÇVAŃK*, or **स्वङ्क्** *SVAŃK*, i. 1, Âtm. To go, to move.

श्वङ्ग् *ÇVAŃG*, see *çrańg*.

श्वच् *ÇVACH*, see *çvańch*.

श्वज् *ÇVAJ*, see the next.

श्वञ्च् *ÇVAŃCH* (ved.), † **श्वच्** *ÇVACH*, † **श्चञ्च्** *ÇAŃCH*, † **श्वज्** *ÇVAJ*, † **श्वञ्ज्** *ÇVAŃJ*, i. 1, Âtm. To go.

श्वञ्ज् *ÇVAŃJ*, see the last.

श्वठ् *ÇVAṬH*, and **श्वण्ठ्** *ÇVAṆṬH*, see 4. *çaṭh*.

श्वन् *çvan* (probably from *çri*), I. m. A dog, Hit. i. d. 112, M.M. II. f. *çunî*, A bitch.—**Comp.** *Deva-çunî*, f. the bitch of the gods, *Saramâ*, MBh. 1, 671. *Vana-çvan*, m. 1. a jackal. 2. a tiger. 3. a civet or polecat.—Cf. κύων, ἀλ-κυών; Lat. canis, catulus (based on *çvant*, the original form of *çvan*); Goth. hunds (based on *çvant*); A.S. hund.

श्वनर *çvanara*, i.e. *çvan-nara*, m. A base fellow.

श्वपच् *çvapach*, i.e. *çvan-pach*, m. and f. A dog-feeder, Man. 3, 92.

श्वपच *çvapacha*, i.e. *çvan-pach* + *a*, m., and f. *châ*, **1.** A dog-feeder. **2.** A man or woman of a low caste, Râjat. 5, 390; 404.

श्वपाक *çvapâka*, i.e. *çvan-pach* + *a*, I. m. **1.** A man of a low and outcaste tribe, Râjat. 5, 217; 382. **2.** The son of a *Kshattṛi* by an *Ugrâ* woman, Man. 10, 19. II. f. *kî*, A woman of a low or outcaste tribe, Râjat. 5, 390.

† **श्वभ्र्** *ÇVABHR*, i. 10, Par. **1.** To go. **2.** To live in distress. **3.** To make a hole, to pierce (cf. the next).

श्वभ्र *çvabhra*, n. A hole, Vikr. d. 18.

श्वयथु *çvayathu*, i.e. *çvi* + *athu*, m. Swelling, intumescence.

श्वयीची *çvayîchî*, i.e. probably *çvi* + *a-ańch*, f. (?), A disease (tumefaction).

† श्वर्त् *ÇVART*, or स्वर्त् *SVART*, i. 10, Par. **1.** To go. **2.** To live in distress.

† श्वल् *ÇVAL*, श्वल्ल् *ÇVALL*, i. 1, Par. To run.

† श्वल्क् *ÇVALK*, i. 10, Par. To speak; cf. *çulk*.

श्वल्ल् *ÇVALL*, see *çval*.

श्ववन्त् *çvavant*, i.e. *çvan + vant*, m. A dog-feeder, Man. 4, 216.

श्वशुर *çvaçura* (for original *svaçura*; *ç* for *s* by the assimilating influence of the following *ç*), I. m. **1.** A father-in-law, a wife's or husband's father, Râm. 3, 53, 5. **2.** du. A father and mother-in-law. II. f. *cvaçrû*, A mother-in-law, Sâv. 3, 20; Râjat. 5, 245.—Cf. Lat. socer, socrus; Goth. svaihra; A.S. sweger, sweor; ἑκυρός.

श्वशुरक *çvaçura + ka*, m. A father-in-law, Pańch. 130, 1.

श्वशुर्य *çvaçurya*, i.e. *çvaçura + ya*, m. A brother-in-law.

श्वश्रू *çvaçrû*, see *çvaçura*.

1. श्वस् *ÇVAS*, ii. 2 (but potent. very often, according to i. 1, *çvaset*), Par. (in epic poetry also Âtm., MBh. 3, 690); the original signification seems to have been 'To pant.' **1.** To breathe, Hit. i. d. 150. **2.** To sigh, Râm. 2, 22, 1. **3.** To hiss, MBh. 4, 2040. **4.** † To kill. Ptcple. pf. pass. *çvasita*. **1.** Breathing. **2.** Sighing. n. **1.** Breathing. **2.** Breath. **3.** Sighing, Çiç. 9, 65; sigh, Mâlat. 11, 9. Caus. To (cause to breathe easily, i.e. to) re-create, Râm. 2, 84, 18.—With the prep. आ *â*, **1.** To fetch breath, to revive, MBh. 2, 17. **2.** To recover, Mâlat. 64, 4. **3.** To take courage, MBh. 3, 690. **4.** To sigh, Bhaṭṭ. 9, 56. I. *âçvasita*, Encouraged, cheered, consoled. II. *âçvasta*, Re-created, MBh. 3, 13150. Caus. **1.** To cause to fetch breath, to cause to recover, MBh. 1, 5406; to refresh, Pańch. 104, 7. **2.** To inspire with courage, Bhag. 11, 30; with hope, Vikr. d. 50. **3.** To console, Râm. 2, 75, 39. **4.** To soothe, to reconcile, Hit. 57, 7. *âçvâsita*, Blessed, Vikr. d. 154.—With पर्या *pari-â*, Caus. To console, MBh. 3, 11006. —With प्रत्या *prati-â*, **1.** To respire, Râm. 2, 51, 2. **2.** To take courage again, Ragh. 7, 74. *pratyâçvasta*, Recollected, Râm. 1, 67, 20; re-created, Megh. 96.—With समा *sam-â*, **1.** To recover, Vikr. 7, 6. **2.** To calm one's self, Nal. 11, 73. **3.** To take courage, Hit. 103, 18. **4.** To take confidence, Mâlat. 20, 10; to confide in, MBh. 3, 16098. *samâçvasta*, Full of confidence, Man. 7, 59. Caus. **1.** To encourage, Râm. 1, 17, 29. **2.** To console, MBh. 3, 2679. **3.** To calm, Hit. 90, 21.—With उद् *ud*, **1.** To exhale, Mâlat, 12, 15. **2.** To breathe, Man. 3, 72. **3.** To pant, MBh. 3, 15690. **4.** To expand, to open (as a flower), Vikr. d. 57; Mâlav. d. 31. **5.** To sigh, Bhaṭṭ. 6, 120. **6.** To heave, to rise, Vikr. d. 6. *uchchhvasita*, **1.** Swollen (figurat.), Megh. 98. **2.** n. Loosening, Megh. 69. **3.** n. Breath, Çâk. 31, 10. Caus. To refresh, Ṛit. 6, 8, v.r. *uchchhvâsita*, **1.** Made loose, Megh. 59. **2.** Fatigued, ib. 71.—With नि *ni*, **1.** To sigh, MBh. 3, 2376. **2.** To hiss, Râm. 3, 53, 55.—With विनि *vi-ni*, To sigh heavily, Pańch. iv. d. 5.—With निस् *nis*, To sigh, Vikr. 21, 14; Râm. 2, 57, 11.—With विनिस् *vi-nis*, To sigh heavily, Râm. 2, 85, 19.—With वि *vi*, **1.** To

confide, Mṛichchh. 63, 24. **2.** To put one's trust in, with gen. and loc., Hit. i. d. 85. **3.** To be fearless, Bhaṭṭ. 2, 25. I. *viçvasita* and *viçvasta*, Trusted, confided in. II. *viçvasta*, **1.** Confided, deserving confidence, Hit. iii. d. 128. **2.** Faithful. **3.** Bold, Râjat. 5, 405. **4.** Full of confidence, fearless, Hiḍ. 2, 25; without any suspicion, Pańch. 33, 8. **Comp.** *Su-*, adj. 1. confidential. 2. without any suspicion, Pańch. 34, 25. Caus. To inspire with confidence, Pańch. 33, 7.—With अभिवि *abhi-vi*, Caus. To inspire with confidence, MBh. 3, 10021.—With परिवि *pari-vi*, To confide completely, to be fearless, MBh. 3, 11451. Caus. To console, Râm. 2, 30, 26.—Cf. Lat. queri, ques+tus; A.S. hweosan, difficulter respirare, and perhaps hysian, hyst, gist.

2. **श्वस्** *çvas*, probably from *çvi* in *çvit*, adv. **1.** To-morrow, Hit. iv. d. 126. **2.** Future, e.g. as former part in *çvas-çreyasa*, and *çvas+tana*, and cf. *çvovasîya*. — **Comp.** *Paraçvas*, incorrectly for *parahçvas*, i.e. *paras-*, adv. The day after to-morrow, Pańch. ed. orn. 41, 10.—Cf. Lat. cras.

श्वसन 1.*çvas+ana*, I. m. **1.** Air, wind, breath, Çiç. 9, 52; Kir. 10, 34. **2.** A plant, Vangueria spinosa. II. n. **1.** Breathing, MBh. 8, 4205. **2.** Sighing.

श्वस्तन 2.*çvas+tana*, adj., f. *nî*, **1.** What will be to-morrow. **2.** Future. —Cf. Lat. crastinus.

श्वस्त्य 2.*çvas+tya*, adj. What will be to-morrow.

श्वान *çvâna*, i.e. *çvan+a*, I. m. A dog, Pańch. iii. d. 118. II. f. *nî*, A bitch.

श्वापद *çvâpada*, i.e. *çvan-pada+a*, I. adj. Ferocious, relating to a beast of prey. II. m. A beast of prey, Pańch. ii. d. 124; Lass. 53, 15.

श्वाविध् *çvâvidh*, i. e. *çvan-vyadh*, m. A porcupine, Man. 5, 18; 12, 65.

श्वास *çvâsa*, i.e. 1.*çvas+a*, m. **1.** Breathing, Pańch. ii. d. 173. **2.** Breath, Râjat. 5, 183. **3.** Air, wind. **4.** Sighing.—**Comp.** *Chhinna-* (vb. *chhid*), I. adj. one who breathes at irregular intervals, Suçr. 1, 115, 17. II. m. a kind of asthma, ib. 2, 294, 7.

श्वि *ÇVI*, i. 1, Par. **1.** To swell, Bhaṭṭ. 6, 19. **2.** To increase; ved. *çûçuvaṁs*, anomal. ptcple. of the red. pf. Large, Chr. 291, 15=Rigv. i. 92, 15. **3.** † To go. Ptcple. of the pf. pass. *çûna*. **1.** Swelled, swollen, Suçr. 2, 134, 3. **2.** Increased. **3.** Morbidly swollen.—With the prep. उद् *ud*, *uchchhûna*, **1.** Swollen, Megh. 82; Râjat. 5, 271; turgid. **2.** Lofty, high. **3.** Fat, bulky.—With प्रोद् *pra-ud*, *prochchhûna*, Swelled, swollen.—Cf. κίων, κίω, κινέω; κύω, κῦμα, ἐγ-κισσάω, κίσσα, κύαμος, κοῖλος, κύλα, κύτος, κυτίς, κύαθος, κῶνος, κηκίς and κίκυς (based on the frequent.); Lat. cuneus, cumulus, super-cilia, crescere; Goth. us-hulon; A.S. hol; see *çûnya*.

श्वित् *ÇVIT* (an old denomin. based on a vb. *çvi*, cf. Zend. *çpi-tama*, etc.), i. 1, Âtm. (ved. also Par.), To be white. —With the prep. वि *vi*, To shine, Chr. 295, 12=Rigv. i. 92, 12 (*açvait*, ved. aor.).

श्वित्र *çvitra* (perhaps better *çvittra*, i.e. *çvit+tra*, or from the lost vb. *çvi* [cf. *çvit*], with *tra*, as *chi+tra* from *chi*), n. White leprosy (Atharva-V. iii. 27, 6).

श्वित्रिन् *çvitrin*, i.e. *çvitra* + *in*, adj., f. *inî*, Subject to leprosy, Man. 3, 7.

श्विन्द् *ÇVIND* (akin to *çvi* in *çvit*), † i. 1, Âtm. To be white. Ptcple. of the red. pf. *çiçvidâna*. **1.** Innocent. **2.** Guilty.—Cf. probably κνδνός, κνδρός, κῦδος; Goth. hveits; A.S. hvît; O.H.G. hwîz; Goth. hvaitei; A.S. hvaete; O.H.G. hwaizi, hiza, haiz; A.S. hat; (O.H.G. hei, perhaps from *çvi* without the final *nd*).

श्वेत *çveta* (i.e. *çvit* + *a*, or from *çvi* in *çvit*, *çvind*), I. adj., f. *tâ* and *nî*, White, Pańch. 60, 24; wearing a white dress, Pańch. iii. d. 73. II. m., and f. *tâ*, A small white shell used as a coin. III. m. **1.** White (the colour). **2.** A white cloud. **3.** The planet Venus. **4.** A fabulous range of mountains. **5.** One of the *Dvîpas*, or divisions of the world. **6.** A couch. **7.** Cumin seed. IV. f. *tâ*. **1.** Crystal. **2.** Candied sugar. **3.** The name of several plants. V. n. Silver. —Comp. *Mahâ-*, f. *tâ*, 1. Sarasvatî. 2. candied sugar. 3. the name of two plants.

श्वैत्र्य *çvaitrya*, i.e. *çvitra* + *ya*, n. Leprosy, Man. 11, 51.

श्वोवसीय *çvovasîya*, and **श्वोवसीयस** *çvovasîyasa*, i.e. curtailed from *çvas* *-vasîyas* (comparat. of *vasu*), or with aff. *a*, I. adj. Fortunate, auspicious. II. *-vasîya*, n. Happiness, Daçak. in Chr. 179, 19.

ष SH.

ऽष *-sha*, see *pańchasha*.

षट्क *shaṭka*, i.e. *shash* + *ka*, I. adj. Six, sixfold. II. n. An aggregate of six, Pańch, 5, 12; Bhâshâp. 31.—Comp. *Ûrmi-*, n. the six waves (human infirmities), which obstruct the course of quiet life, viz. grief, ignorance, old age, death, hunger, and thirst, Lass. 58, 9 (where thus to be corrected).

षट्चरण *shaṭcharaṇa*, i.e. *shash* *-charaṇa*, m. A bee, Çâk. d. 23.

षट्पद *shaṭpada*, i.e. *shash-pada*, m. A bee, Man. 7, 129; Vikr. d. 41.

षट्पदज्य *shaṭpada-jya* (see *jyâ*), adj. The string of which consists of bees, epithet of the bow of Kâma, Megh. 72.

षडङ्घ्रि *shaḍanghri*, i.e. *shash-anghri*, m. A bee, Bhartṛ. 1, 78.

षड्ज *shaḍja*, i.e. *shash-ja*, m. The fourth note of the Hindu gamut, Ragh. 1, 39.

षड्धा *shaḍdhâ* (?), i.e. *shash* + *dhâ*, adv. In six ways (see *shoḍhâ*).

षण्ड *shaṇḍa*, I. m. **1.** A bull at liberty. **2.** An eunuch. **3.** A wood, a thicket, Megh. 20. **4.** A multitude. II. m. and n. A quantity of lotuses.—Comp. *Kamala-*, n. a multitude of lotuses, Lass. 2. ed. 46, 27. *Taru-* and *Druma-*, n. a group of trees, Pańch. 10, 4; Râm. 4, 13, 13 (*taru-*); 4, 13, 12 (*druma-*). *Padma-*, n. a quantity of lotuses, ib. 3, 76, 15 (cf. *çaṇḍa*, *çaṇḍha*, *shaṇḍha*, and *khaṇḍa*).

षण्डक *shaṇḍa* + *ka*, m. An eunuch, MBh. 4, 52.

षण्ढ *shaṇḍha*, m. An eunuch, Man. 2, 158 (cf. the last).

षष् *shash*, for original *svaksh*, numeral adj. Six, Man. 1, 16; cf. *shash-bhâga*.—Comp. *Dvi-*, twelve, Bhâg. P. 4, 1, 7.—Cf. Lat. sex; ἕξ, Fέξ; Goth. saihs; A.S. seox, six, sex.

ऽषष्ट -*shashṭa*, i.e. *shashṭi*+*a*, ord. num. Sixtieth.—Comp. *Eka-*, sixty-first. *Ekona-*, i.e. *eka-ûna-*, fifty-ninth. *Dvâ-* and *Dvi-*, sixty-second. *Tri-*, sixty-third. *Chatuḥsh°* i. e. *chatur-*, sixty-fourth. *Pañchash°*, i.e. *pañchan-*, sixty-fifth, etc., MBh. xii. adhy. 61, sqq.

षष्टि *shashṭi*, i.e. *shash*+*ti*, numeral, f. Sixty, Chr. 28, 20.—Comp. *Eka-*, f. sixty-one, Bhâg. P. 6, 6, 29. *Dvâ-* and *Dvi-*, f. sixty-two, MBh. xii. 162; i. adhy. 162. *Chatuḥsh°*, i.e. *chatur-*, f. sixty-four, Man. 8, 338. *Pañchash°*, i.e. *pañchan-*, f. sixty-five, MBh. xii. adhy. 165.

षष्टिक *shashṭi*+*ka*, I. adj. Bought with sixty. II. m., and f. *kâ*, A kind of rice of quick growth.

षष्टिक्य *shashṭikya*, i.e. *shashṭika*+*ya*, adj. Fit for the rice called *shashṭika* (see the last).

षष्टितम *shashṭi*+*tama*, ord. num., f. *mî*, Sixtieth, Râm. v. sarg. 60.—Comp. *Eka-*, sixty-first, Râm. v. sarg. 61. *Dvâ-* and *Dvi-*, sixty-second, Râm. iv. sarg. 62; v. adhy. 62. *Tri-*, sixty-third, MBh. i. adhy. 63. *Chatuḥsh°*, i. e. *chatur-*, sixty-fourth, Râm. vi. sarg. 64. *Pañchash°*, i. e. *panchan-*, sixty-fifth, MBh. ii. adhy. 65. *Navash°*, i.e. *navan-*, sixty-ninth, Râm. vi. sarg. 69.

षष्टिधा *shashṭi*+*dhâ*, adv. In sixty ways.—Comp. *Tri-*, adv. in sixty-three parts, Suçr. 1, 153, 18.

षष्ठ *shashṭha*, i.e. *shash*+*tha*, I. ord. num., f. *ṭhî*, Sixth, Vikr. d. 20. II. f. *ṭhâ*. 1. Durgâ. 2. The sixth day of the lunar fortnight.—Comp. *Mâtṛi-*, adj. six, inclusively of the mother, Hiḍ. 1, 1.—Cf. Lat. sextus; Goth. saihsta; A.S. sixta; ἕκτος.

षष्ठक *shashṭha*+*ka*, adj. Sixth.

षष्ठान्नकालता *shashṭhânnakâlatâ*, i.e. *shashṭha-anna-kâla*+*tâ*, f. Eating only at the time of the sixth meal, i.e. on the evening of every third day, Man. 11, 200.

षाडव *shâḍava* (derived anomal. from the nom. of *shash*), m. 1. Sentiment. 2. Music.

षाड्गुण्य *shâḍguṇya*, i.e. *shash-guṇa*+*ya*, n. An aggregate of six, six articles, Man. 7, 58; six measures, 7, 167; six kinds of behaving against an enemy, Pañch. 154, 9.

षाण्मासिक *shâṇmâsika*, i.e. *shash-mâsa*+*ika*, adj. 1. Relating to six months, come to pass six months ago, Bṛihaspati ap. Cowell, Kusumâñjali transl. p. 65, n. †. 2. Half-yearly, Man. 7, 126.

षिड्ग *shiḍga*, m. An inconstant lover, a gallant.

षुक्क् *SHUKK*, see *shvask*.

षोडन्त् *shoḍant*, i.e. *shash-dant*, m. A young ox, or one with six teeth.

षोडश *shoḍaça*, i.e. *shoḍaçan*+*a*, or curtailed, ord. num., f. *çî*, Sixteenth, Pañch. ii. d. 58.—Comp. *Pari-*, full sixteen, Nal. 26, 2. *Vṛishabha-* (having a bull as sixteenth, i.e.) fifteen cows and a bull, Man. 9, 124, v.r. (cf. Lois.).

षोडशक *shoḍaçaka*, i.e. *shoḍaçan*+*ka*, adj. Consisting of sixteen, Hit. iv. d. 107.

षोडशन् *shoḍaçan*, i. e. *shash-daçan*, numeral adj. Sixteen, Daçak. in Chr. 186, 3; 182, 9.

षोढा *shoḍha*, i.e. *shash*+*dhâ*, adv. In six ways, sixfold, Yâjñ. 3, 84.

ष्टम्भ् *SHṬAMBH*, see *stambh*.

ष्ठ्यै *SHṬYAI*, see *styai.*

ष्ठिव् † *SHṬHIV*, i. 1, *shṭhîva*, and i. 4, *shṭhîvya*, and ष्ठीव् *SHṬHÎV*, i. 1, Par. To spit, Bhaṭṭ. 12, 18. Ptcple. of the pf. pass. *shṭhyûta*, Ejected, as saliva.—With the prep. नि *ni*, To spit, Man. 5, 145. *nishṭhyûta*, Spit out, Râjat. 5, 462 (*kûrcha-âbhâshaṇa-*, Spit out, i. e. uttered, with boasting words); ejected, ib. 96. n. Saliva, Man. 4, 132.—With अवनि *ava-ni*, To spit on, Man. 8, 282.—With निस् *nis*, To sketch, Daçak. in Chr. 199, 18. *niḥshṭhyûta*, Distilled, Çâk. d. 80.—Cf. probably σίαλον, σίαλος, στυγέω, στύξ, etc., σπῖλος, σπιλόω, ψύττω, πτύω, ἐπι-φθύζω; Lat. spuere; Goth. speivan; A.S. spiwan; O.H.G. spîchilla; cf. *kshiv.*

ष्ठीवन *shṭhîv + ana*, n. **1.** Spitting. **2.** Spittle, Man. 4, 156; 5, 123.—**Comp.** *Kûrcha-*, n. boasting speech, Râjat. 5, 462 (cf. the last).

† ष्वस्क् *SHVASK*, ष्वष्क् *SHVASHK*, ष्वक्क् *SHVAKK*, षुक्क् *SHUKK*, स्वस्क् *SVASK*, i. 1, Âtm. To go.

स *S.*

स *sa*, originally 'One.' I. See *tad*; in the Vedas appears also the loc. *sasmin.* II. As former part of comp. nouns. **1.** With; see *sa-kamala*, adj. With lotus flowers. **2.** The same, like, equal; see *sa-dharman*, adj. Of the same caste, etc.—Cf. σ in σήμερον, ὁ, ἡ, οἱ, αἱ, ἑ in ἕεις, εἷς (i.e. ἑ-Fενς), ἁ- (e.g. in ἁ-πλοῦς), ἀ- (e.g. in ἀδελφός), ὀ- (e.g. in ὄ-πατρος); Lat. sum=eum, sam=eam, -sum, sem- in semper, sim- in simplex; Goth. sa, so, A.S. se, seo.

संयत् *saṁyat*, i.e. *sam-yam + t*, m. and f. War, battle, Chr. 36, 17.

संयन्तृ *saṁyantṛi*, i. e. *sam-yam + tṛi*, m., f. *trî*, and n. Constraining, a constrainer.

संयम *saṁyama*, i.e. *sam-yam + a*, m. **1.** Restraining, Man. 2, 88. **2.** Restraint, forbearance. **3.** Abstaining, Bhartṛ. 2, 60. **4.** Avoiding the infliction of pain on others, compassionateness, Çâk. d. 177.—**Comp.** *Vâksaṁyama*, i.e. *vâch-*, m. modesty, Bhartṛ. 2, 80.

संयमन *saṁyamana*, i.e. *sam-yam + ana*, I. m. A ruler, Sâv. 5, 65. II. n. **1.** Restraining, Sâv. 3, 20. **2.** Self-denial or control, forbearance. **3.** A religious vow or obligation. **4.** Holding, detaining. **5.** Drawing in, Çâk. 5, 12. **6.** A cluster of four houses. III. f. *nî*, The capital of Yama.

संयमिन् *saṁyamin*, i.e. I. *sam-yam + in*, adj. Who or what restrains, subdues; abstaining, Bhag. 2, 69. II. *saṁyama + in*, m. One who subdues his passions, a sage.

संयात्रा *saṁyâtrâ*, i.e. *sam-yâ + tra*, f. Travelling into another island or continent, voyaging.

संयान *saṁyâna*, i.e. *sam-yâ + ana*, n. Going together.

संयाम *saṁyâma*, i.e. *sam-yam + a*, m. **1.** Restraint. **2.** Self-control, forbearance. **3.** Abstaining from giving pain to others.

संयाव *saṁyâva*, i.e. *sam-yu + a*, m. A thin cake of unleavened bread fried with melted butter, Man. 5, 7.

संयुग *saṁyuga*, i.e. *sam-yuj + a*, m. War, battle, Chr. 33, 4; Râjat. 5, 424.

संयुज् *saṁyuj*, i.e. *sam-yuj*, adj. **1.** Joined. **2.** Endowed with good qualities.

संयोग *saṁyoga*, i. e. *sam-yuj+a*, m. **1.** Connexion, Man. 3, 157; Râm. 3, 49, 20; Chr. 38, 15 (*saṁyogam enasâ na prâpsyase*, You will not incur guilt). **2.** Junction, Bhâshâp. 3; adherence, accession, Pañch. ii. d. 146. **3.** A kind of alliance where both parties unite only for one object, but attack with united power, Hit. iv. d. 115. **4.** Union, being, living, with, Megh. 85; 88.

संयोजन *saṁyojana*, i.e. *sam-yuj+ana*, n. **1.** Joining, uniting, Vedântas. in Chr. 208, 20; Daçak. in Chr. 281, 2. **2.** Copulation, coition.

संरक्षण *saṁrakshaṇa*, i.e. *sam-raksh+ana*, n. **1.** Protecting, guarding, Pañch. 129, 2; protection, Johns. Sel. 95, 71. **2.** Saving, Man. 6, 68.

संरम्भ *saṁrambha*, i.e. *sam-rabh+a*, m. **1.** Beginning, Vikr. d. 61. **2.** Wrath, Vikr. d. 115; rage, anger, Vikr. d. 39. **3.** Pride, arrogance. **4.** Agitation, Râjat. 5, 334.

संरम्भिन् *saṁrambhin*, i.e. *saṁrambha+in*, adj. **1.** Angry. **2.** Proud. **3.** Agitated.

संराधन *saṁrâdhana*, i.e. *sam-râdh+ana*, n. **1.** Propitiation. **2.** Perfect meditation, Windischmann, Sankara, 173.

संराव *saṁrâva*, i.e. *sam-ru+a*, m. Sound, noise.

संरोध *saṁrodha*, i.e. *sam-rudh+a*, m. **1.** Hindering, stopping, Pañch. 162, 11; Mâlat. 79, 18. **2.** Impediment. **3.** Check, curb. **4.** Fetter.—**Comp.** *Kâla-*, m. expiry of the time (for which something has been pledged), Man. 8, 143.

संलय *saṁlaya*, i. e. *sam-lî+a*, m. Sleep.

संलाप *saṁlâpa*, i.e. *sam-lap+a*, m. Conversation, Hit. i. d. 38, M.M.

संलोडन *saṁloḍana*, i. e. *sam-loḍ+ana*, n. Making mad, MBh. 1, 1397.

संवत् *saṁvat*, probably *sam-*vat* (cf. *parut*), indecl. **1.** A year. **2.** A year of *Vikramâditya's* era. — Cf. ἔτος, ἐνιαυτός.

संवत्सर *saṁvatsara*, i. e. *sam-vat-sara*, m. A year, Râm. 3, 55, 19; Pañch. 186, 20.—**Comp.** *Pari-*, m. a full year, Man. 3, 119.

संवदन *saṁvadana*, i.e. *sam-vad+ana*, I. n., and f. *nâ* (cf. the next). **1.** Subduing by charms or magical drugs. **2.** A charm. **II.** n. **1.** Communication of tidings. **2.** Sight, seeing.

संवनन *saṁvanana*, i.e. *sam-van+ana*, n. **1.** Subduing by charms or magical drugs; a means of securing, Ragh. 16, 74. **2.** Fascination, charming, Râjat. 5, 188.

संवरण *saṁvaraṇa*, i.e. *sam-vṛi+ana*, n. Concealing, Vikr. 79, 5; secret, Mâlat. 174, 7; pretext, Mâlat. 7, 1.

संवर्त *saṁvarta*, i.e. *sam-vṛit+a*, m. **1.** Destruction of the universe, Johns. Sel. 91, 35. **2.** A cloud. **3.** Multitude, Mâlat. 166, 12. **4.** Being. **5.** Beleric myrobalan. **6.** The name of a Muni.

संवर्तक *saṁvarta+ka*, m. **1.** Submarine fire, Bhartṛ. 2, 68. **2.** Baladeva. **3.** The plough of Baladeva.

संवर्ति *saṁvarti*, and **संवर्तिका** *saṁvartikâ* (vb. *vṛit*), f. The new leaf of a water lily.

संवर्धक *saṁvardhaka*, i.e *sam-vṛidh*

+*aka*, adj. Augmenting, augmentative.

संवर्धन *saṁvardhana*, i.e. *sam-vṛidh* +*ana*, n. **1.** Increasing, thriving, increase, Vikr. 49, 16; happiness, Vikr. 57, 2. **2.** Bearing up, nourishing and developing, Daçak. in Chr. 180, 4.

संवर्षण *saṁvarshaṇa*, i.e. *sam-vṛish* +*ana*, or rather *sam-varshana*, n. Abundance of rain, Lass. 27, 2.

संवलन *saṁvalana*, i.e. *sam-val*+ *ana*, n. Mixture, Mâlat. 167, 5.

संवसथ *saṁvasatha*, i.e. *sam-* 1.*vas* +*atha*, m. A village.

संवाद *saṁvâda*, i.e. *sam-vad*+*a*, m. **1.** Conversation, Pañch. 118, 25. **2.** Communication of intelligence, information, Mâlat. 80, 5. **3.** Assent, agreement, Mâlav. 72, 8. **4.** Conformity, correspondence, sameness.

संवादिन् *saṁvâdin*, i.e. *sam-vad*+ *in*, adj., *f. nî*, Corresponding, Utt. Râmach. 154, 10.

संवास *saṁvâsa*, i.e. *sam-* 1.*vas*+*a*, m. **1.** Dwelling together, Pañch. 196, 15. **2.** Society, union, Hit. iv. d. 65. **3.** A house. **4.** An open space within or without a town for the meeting of the townsmen.

संवाह *saṁvâha*, m., i.e. *sam-vâh*+*a*, **1.** Rubbing the body. **2.** An attendant employed to rub and knead the body. **3.** Extortion, Râjat. 5, 175.

संवाहक *saṁvâhaka*, i.e. *sam-vâh*+ *aka*, m. An attendant employed to rub and knead the body.

संवाहन *saṁvâhana*, i.e. *sam-vâh*+ *ana*, n. **1.** Bearing, carrying, Utt. Râmach. 15, 15. **2.** Rubbing and kneading the body, Megh. 94; stroking, touching, Mâlat. 150, 10. **3.** Extortion, Râjat. 5, 191.

संविज्ञान *saṁvijñâna*, i.e. *sam-vi* -*jñâ*+*ana*, n. Knowledge, Utt. Râmach. 35, 1.

संवित्ति *saṁvitti*, i.e. *sam-vid*+*ti*, f. **1.** Perception, knowledge, Kir. 11, 34; 16, 32. **2.** Recollection of a thing or person previously known. **3.** Reconciliation, accommodation.

संविद् *saṁvid*, i.e. *sam-vid*, f. **1.** Contract, agreement, Man. 8, 5; Pañch. ii. d. 60. **2.** Promise, MBh. 1, 1223. **3.** Intellect. **4.** Knowledge, Mâlat. 100, 10; Kir. 18, 42. **5.** Name, appellation. **6.** Sign, signal. **7.** A watch-word, a battle-cry. **8.** Battle. **9.** Institute. **10.** Pleasing. **11.** Hemp. —**Comp.** *Na-*, f. want of consciousness, Bhartṛ. 1, 27, v. r.

संविधा *saṁvidhâ*, i.e. *sam-vi-dhâ*, f. **1.** Arrangement, food, Ragh. 14, 17. **2.** Kind of living, Ragh. 1, 94.

संविधान *saṁvidhâna*, i.e. *sam-vi* -*dhâ*+*ana*, n. Mode, Mâlat. 34, 11; rite.

संविधानक *saṁvidhâna* + *ka*, n. Strange, surprising occurrence, Utt. Râmach. 87, 11.

संविभाग *saṁvibhâga*, i.e. *sam-vi* -*bhaj*+*a*, m. **1.** Distributing, Daçak. in Chr. 185, 22. **2.** Apportioning, giving a portion, Man. 4, 32; Pañch. ii. d. 25. **3.** Communication, Mâlat. 128, 12. **4.** Part, share.

संविभागिन् *saṁvibhâgin*, i.e. *saṁvibhâga* + *in*, adj. Partaking, Pañch. 243, 24.

संवीक्षण *saṁvîkshaṇa*, i.e. *sam-vi* -*îksh*+*ana*, n. Search, inquiry.

संवृति *saṁvṛiti*, i.e. *sam-vṛi*+*ti*, f. Concealment, Kir. 10, 44.

संवेग *saṁvega*, i.e. *sam-vij+a*, m. **1.** Haste proceeding from fear, Utt. Râmach. 51, 14. **2.** Speed, Utt. Râmach. 26, 12 (*tîvra-*, adj. Wounding quickly). **3.** Vehemence, Utt. Râmach. 95, 5.

संवेद *saṁveda*, i.e. *sam-vid+a*, m. Perception, consciousness.

संवेदन *saṁvedana*, i.e. *sam-vid+ana*, n. Perceiving, suffering, Utt. Râmach. 30, 1.

संवेश *saṁveça*, i.e. *sam-viç+a*, m. **1.** Copulation. **2.** A chair. **3.** Sleeping, sleep. **4.** Dreaming, a dream.

संवेशक *saṁveçaka*, see *grihasaṁv°*.

संव्यवहार *saṁvyavahâra*, i.e. *sam-vi-ava-hṛi+a*, m. **1.** Relation to each other, Pañch. i. d. 316. **2.** Business, Man. 8, 131.

संव्यान *saṁvyâna*, i.e. *sam-vye+ana*, n. **1.** Cloth, vesture. **2.** Covering. **3.** An upper garment, Kir. 4, 28.

संशप्तक *saṁçaptaka*, i.e. *sam-çapta+ka* (vb. *çap*), m. **1.** A soldier sworn never to recede, and stationed to prevent the flight of the rest. **2.** A brother in arms.

संशमन *saṁçamana*, i.e. *sam-çam+ana*, in *pâpa-*, adj. Removing sin, Râm. 2, 56, 28.

संशय *saṁçaya*, i.e. *sam-çî+a*, m. **1.** Doubt, Hit. pr. d. 10, M.M.; uncertainty; very often with *na*, to be sure, Pañch. i. d. 256. **2.** Possibility, Hit. ii. d. 160. **3.** Danger, Râm. 3, 51, 13.—Comp. *A-*, 1. m. absence of doubt, to be sure, Râm. 5, 23, 25. 2. *°yam*, adv. undoubtedly, Pañch. i. d. 406. *Artha-*, adj. one whose solvency is doubtful, Daçak. in Chr. 181, 2. *Nis-*, adj. 1. doubtless, Brâhmaṇav. 2, 30. 2. resolute, MBh. 5, 7080. 3. *°yam*, adv. undoubtedly, certainly, MBh. 3, 1243. *Prâṇa-*, m. danger of life, Pañch. 130, 5. *Vi-saṁçaya+m*, adv. undoubtedly, Pañch. ii. d. 119. *Sa-*, adj. doubtful.

संशयालु *saṁçayâlu*, i.e. *saṁçaya+âlu*, adj. Dubious.

संशयितृ *saṁçayitṛi*, i.e. *sam-çî+tṛi*, m., f. *trî*, and n. Dubious, sceptical, a sceptic.

संशुद्धि *saṁçuddhi*, i.e. *sam-çudh+ti*, f. **1.** Cleaning the body. **2.** Purification, Bhag. 16, 1. **3.** Correction. **4.** Acquittal of debt. **5.** Acquittance of charge or crime.

संशोधन *saṁçodhana*, i.e. *sam-çudh+ana*, n. **1.** Cleaning. **2.** Purifying. **3.** Correcting. **4.** Refining. **5.** Discharging, paying.

संश्छत् *saṁçchat*, i.e. *sam-chat*, m. A juggler, a conjuror.

संश्छाय *SAṀÇCHÂYA*, a denomin. derived from *saṁçchat*, Âtm. To conjure, to juggle.

संश्रय *saṁçraya*, i.e. *sam-çri+a*, m. **1.** Refuge, a dwelling-place, Pañch. 155, 23; having become the dwelling-place, being possessed by, Nal. 20, 41. **2.** Asylum. **3.** Protection, Çâk. d. 177. **4.** Seeking protection (Man. 7, 160), or the alliance of a powerful prince, Pañch. 154, 10. **5.** Alliance, Pañch. 154, 20.—Comp. *Anyonya-*, m. supporting each other, Böhtl. Ind. Spr. 2150. *Eka-*, m. I. union, Pañch. iii. d. 52. II. adj. united, Pañch. iii. d. 49. *Kashṭa-*, adj. accompanied by pains, Pañch. i. d. 179. *Bhuja-*, m. taking refuge to one's arms, help of arms, Lass. 2. ed. 68, 33.

संश्रव *saṁçrava*, i.e. *sam-çru+a*, m. **1.** Hearing, Mâlat. 48, 17. **2.** Agreement. **3.** Promise.—**Comp.** *A-*, m. the not being audible ; loc. *ve*, out of hearing, Man. 2, 203.

संश्रवण *saṁçravaṇa*, i.e. *sam-çru* + *ana*, n. The ear, Râm. 6, 23, 7.

संश्लेष *saṁçlesha*, i.e. *sam-çlish* + *a*, m. **1.** Embracing, embrace, Çâk. d. 124. **2.** Union, Windischmann, Sankara, 152 ; contact, association, Lass. 24, 7.—**Comp.** *A-ghaṭita-*, adj., f. *shâ*, impossible to be closely joined, Pañch. 203, 4.

संश्लेषण *saṁçleshaṇa*, i.e. *sam-çlish* + *ana*, n. Means of binding together, Utt. Râmach. 65, 2.

संसक्ति *saṁsakti*, i.e. *sam-sañj* + *ti*, f. **1.** Tieing, fastening. **2.** Union. **3.** Proximity. **4.** Intimacy, acquaintance. **5.** Addiction to, devotion.

संसद् *saṁsad*, i.e. *sam-sad*, f. **1.** An assembly, Pañch. 19, 14. **2.** Court of justice, Man. 8, 52.

संसरण *saṁsaraṇa*, i. e. *sam-sṛi* + *ana*, n. **1.** Going, proceeding. **2.** Going unobstructedly. **3.** The unresisted march of troops. **4.** The beginning of war or battle. **5.** A highway. **6.** A resting-place for passengers near the gates of a city. **7.** Birth, the production of living beings. **8.** The world.

संसर्ग *saṁsarga*, i.e. *sam-sṛij* + *a*, m. **1.** Mixture, Hit. i. d. 5, M.M. **2.** Touching, contact, Çâk. d. 3 ; Pañch. i. d. 280. **3.** Union, Hit. pr. d. 41, M.M. **4.** Acquaintance, familiarity, intercourse, Pañch. iii. d. 234 ; Daçak. in Chr. 196, 3. **5.** Sensual attachment, Man. 6, 72.

संसर्गतस् *saṁsarga* + *tas*, adv. By union and intercourse, Bhartṛ. 2, 57.

संसर्गिन् *saṁsargin*, i.e. *saṁsarga* + *in*, adj., f. *iṇî*, adj. **1.** In contact with, united, connected, Châṇ. 106 in Berl. Monatsb. 1864, 413. **2.** Familiar, acquainted.

संसर्जन *saṁsarjana*, i. e. *sam-sṛij* + *ana*, n. **1.** Abandoning, leaving. **2.** Voiding.

संसर्प *saṁsarpa*, i.e. *sam-sṛip* + *a*, m. **1.** Creeping. **2.** Gliding.

संसार *saṁsâra*, i.e. *sam-sṛi* + *a*, m. **1.** Transmigration, Man. 12, 40. **2.** Mundane existence, Pañch. 165, 17. **3.** The world, Hit. pr. d. 14, M.M.—**Comp.** *Â-*, adj. always changing, Kathâs. 5, 103. °*ram*, adv. till the end of the world, Râjat. 5, 119.

संसारिन् *saṁsârin*, i.e. *saṁsâra* + *in*, I. adj., f. *iṇî*, Mundane, worldly. II. m. An animal or sentient being, a man, Mâlat. 140, 9.

संसिद्धि *saṁsiddhi*, i.e. *sam-sidh* + *ti*, f. **1.** Perfection, Bhag. 3, 20 ; Pañch. 4, 21. **2.** Obtaining, Kathâs. 13, 166. **3.** Natural disposition, nature.

संसृति *saṁsṛiti*, i.e. *sam-sṛi* + *ti*, f. **1.** Current, stream. **2.** Course, Bhâg. P. 3, 9, 9. **3.** Transmigration, Bhâg. P. 5, 18, 14. **4.** The world.

संसृष्टत्व *saṁsṛishṭa* + *tva* (vb. *sṛij*), n. **1.** Union. **2.** (In law), The voluntary co-residence of father and son, or brothers, after partition of property.

संसृष्टि *saṁsṛishṭi*, i.e. *sam-sṛij* + *ti*, f. **1.** Uniting. **2.** Collecting. **3.** Living together in one family.

संसेक *saṁseka*, i.e. *sam-sich* + *a*, m. Moistening, Râjat. 5, 271.

संसेवन *saṁsevana*, i.e. *sam-sev* + *ana*, n. Waiting on, serving.

संसेवा *saṁsevâ*, i.e. *sam-sev+a*, f. Service, Râjat. 5, 15.

संस्कर्तृ *saṁskartṛi*, i.e. *sam-kṛi+tṛi*, m., f. *trî*, and n. Who or what completes, initiates, Utt. Râmach. 170, 8; dresses (as meat), Man. 5, 51.

संस्कार *saṁskâra*, i.e. *sam-kṛi+a*, m. **1.** Completing. **2.** Perfecting, perfection, Utt. Râmach. 135, 6. **3.** Embellishment, decoration, Daçak. in Chr. 181, 19; Pańch. 185, 25; ornament, Mâlat. 126, 9. **4.** Institution and education, Man. 1, 111. **5.** Purification. **6.** A purificatory rite, Man. 2, 26; 27; Vedântas. in Chr. 219, 13. **7.** Ceremony in general, Man. 3, 43. **8.** The investiture with the holy cord, Man. 11, 150. **9.** Consecration (of a king), Man. 7, 2. **10.** Obsequies, Lass. 17, 11. **11.** Purity. **12.** Preparing as an article of medicine or food. **13.** Impression, form, mould, Çâk. d. 133 (Sch. a polishing stone). **14.** The power of memory, Kathâs. 7, 19. **15.** Apprehension, conception, Râjat. 5, 228; resolution, Hit. 112, 5 (*vi-smṛita-pûrva-*, adj. Forgetting his former resolution). **16.** The self-reproductive quality (Ballantyne, i.e. vitality, elasticity, and mental impression), Bhâshâp. 29; 156.—**Comp.** *Agni-*, m. 1. consecration of fire. 2. burning of the dead body, Man. 5, 69. *Dus-*, m. bad inclination, Râjat. 5, 228. *Keça-*, m. dressing the hair, Megh. 33. *Pâtra-*, m. cleaning a vessel that has been used. *Punaḥsaṁskâra*, i.e. *punar-*, m. renewed investiture, Man. 11, 150. *Çarîra-*, m. 1. adorning the person. 2. purification of the body by various ceremonies, initiation, etc., Man. 2, 26.

संस्क्रिया *saṁskriyâ*, i.e. *sam-kṛi+yâ*, f. **1.** Any purificatory rite. **2.** Funeral ceremonies, as burning the dead body.

संस्त् *SAṀST*, see *sas*.

संस्तम्भ *saṁstambha*, i.e. *sam-stambh+a*, m. **1.** Fixing, making firm (as a post). **2.** Confirming. **3.** Stop. **4.** Paralysis.

संस्तर *saṁstara*, i.e. *sam-stṛi+a*, m. **1.** A couch, a bed, Pańch. 117, 12; a layer, MBh. 1, 4708. **2.** Sacrifice, Râm. 1, 13, 23.

संस्तरण *saṁstaraṇa*, i.e. *sam-stṛi+ana*, n. Strewing, Çâk. 31, 6.

संस्तव *saṁstava*, i.e. *sam-stu+a*, m. **1.** Praise, Pańch. iv. d. 60. **2.** Acquaintance, Kir. 4, 22, 25.

संस्ताव *saṁstâva*, i.e. *sam-stu+a*, m. **1.** Hymning in chorus, the repetition of the verses of the Veda by a number of Brâhmaṇas. **2.** The place occupied at a sacrifice by the singing Brâhmaṇas.

संस्तुति *saṁstuti*, i.e. *sam-stu+ti*, f. Praise.

संस्त्याय *saṁstyâya*, i.e. *sam-styai+a*, m. **1.** Assemblage, heap. **2.** Vicinity. **3.** Spreading, diffusion. **4.** A house, Mâlat. 23, 11.

संस्थ *saṁstha*, **A.** i.e. *sam-stha*, **I.** adj. **1.** Standing, being, Pańch. i. d. 231 (*maṇḍala-*, in the disc, viz. of the sun); ii. d. 157. **2.** Staying with, associated. **3.** Stationary, fixed. **4.** Living, Pańch. 94, 2; iii. d. 226. **5.** Lasting, Lass. 42, 15. **II.** m. **1.** An inhabitant. **2.** A countryman. **3.** A spy. **B.** i.e. *sam-sthâ*, f. **1.** An assembly. **2.** Condition of being, situation, Bhâg. P. 5, 20, 38. **3.** Appearance. **4.** Form. **5.** Occupation, Man. 1, 21. **6.** Continuance in the right way, correct conduct. **7.** A sort of sacrifice. **8.** Stay, stop. **9.** A royal ordinance. **10.** End. **11.** Death. **12.** Destruction.—**Comp.** *Dûra-*, adj. distant, Megh. 3. *Dhara-*, adj. having the form of a mountain, Kir. 15, 12. *Phala-*, adj. bearing fruit, Brâhmaṇav. 3, 13. *Brâhmaṇa-*, adj. belonging to Brâhmaṇas, Man. 8, 325. *Sva-*, f. absorption in one's own self, Bhâg. P. 6, 4, 26.

संस्थान *saṁsthâna*, i.e. *sam-sthâ + ana*, n. **1.** A heap, a quantity. **2.** The aggregation of the primitive atoms. **3.** Position, Vedântas. in Chr. 217, 17; form, figure, shape, Çâk. d. 126. **4.** Fabrication, construction. **5.** A vicinity. **6.** Standing, being, Hit. ii. d. 90 (but cf. Böhtl. Ind. Spr. 59). **7.** A common place of abode. **8.** A place where four roads meet, an open place (?), Râm. 2, 65, 32, Scramp. **9.** Any place, Man. 8, 371; a station, 9, 261. **10.** A mark, a spot, a sign. **11.** Death.

संस्थापन *saṁsthâpana*, i. e. *sam -sthâ*, Caus., *+ana*, n. **1.** Collecting. **2.** Placing. **3.** Establishing, Bhag. 4, 8; fixing, Lass. 2. ed. 87, 14. **4.** A regulation, Man. 8, 402.

संस्थास्नु *saṁsthâsnu*, i.e. *sam-sthâ + snu*, adj. Immovable, MBh. 7, 372.

संस्थिति *saṁsthiti*, i.e. *sam-sthâ + ti*, f. **1.** Staying together, Hit. i. d. 38, M.M. **2.** Accumulation, heap. **3.** Contiguity. **4.** Abiding, Hit. i. d. 104, M.M.; abode, Man. 6, 90. **5.** State of life. **6.** Duration, Hit. i. d. 42, M.M. **7.** Restraint, Man. 9, 14. **8.** Death.

संस्पर्श *saṁsparça*, i.e. *sam-spriç + a*, m. **1.** Touching, Râm. 3, 49, 44; contact, Pañch. 198, 13; mixture, 250, 4. **2.** Being touched, being affected, Pañch. 93, 1. **3.** Perception, sense.—**Comp.** *Duḥkha-*, adj. of whom or of which the touch causes pain, MBh. 5, 2046.

संस्पृश् *saṁspriç*, i.e. *sam-spriç*, adj. Touching, Amar. 23.

संस्फोट *saṁsphoṭa*, i.e. *sam-sphuṭ + a*, m. War, battle.

संस्मरण *saṁsmaraṇa*, i.e. *sam-smṛi + ana*, n. Remembering.

संस्मृति *saṁsmṛiti*, i.e. *sam-smṛi + ti*, f. Remembrance, Kir. 18, 27.

संस्राव *saṁsrâva*, i.e. *sam-sru + a*, m. Flowing.—**Comp.** *Karṇa-*, m. suppuration of the ear, Suçr. 2, 362, 4.

संहतजानुक *saṁhata-jânu + ka* (vb. *han*), adj. Knock-kneed.

संहतता *saṁhata + tâ*, f., and **संहतत्व** *saṁhata + tva*, n. (vb. *han*), **1.** Close approximation, contact, Çiç. 9. 44 (*tâ*, and agreement). **2.** Compactness. **3.** Combination. **4.** Union, Hit. iv. d. 26 (*tva*); agreement (see **1.**).

संहति *saṁhati*, i.e. *sam-han + ti*, f. **1.** Combination, Hit. i. d. 34, M.M.; union, agreement, Râjat. 5, 247 (at the end of a comp. adj.). **2.** Assemblage, heap, multitude, Kir. 5, 4; bulk, 12, 10. **3.** Compactness.—**Comp.** *Ari-*, f. multitude of enemies, Nalod. 4, 46. *Bhinna-* (vb. *bhid*), adj. disunited, Râjat. 5, 260. *Çastra-*, f. an arsenal. *Hima-*, f. ice and snow.

संहनन *saṁhanana*, i.e. *sam-han + ana*, I. m. A destroyer, a conqueror, MBh. 3, 13300. II. n. **1.** Rubbing the body. **2.** Compactness, inflexibility, MBh. 1, 7022. **3.** Strength. **4.** Body, Utt. Râmach. 152, 12. **5.** Agreement, MBh. 12, 2420.—**Comp.** *Siṁha-*, adj. 1. of lion strength. 2. handsome and well shaped.

संहरण *saṁharaṇa*, i.e. *sam-hṛi + ana*, n. **1.** Collecting. **2.** Restraining. **3.** Destroying, Utt. Râmach.

148, 17 (at the end of a comp. adj.). 4. Taking.

संहर्तृ *saṁhartṛi,* i.e. *sam-hṛi+tṛi,* m., f. *tri,* and n. A destroyer, Vikr. d. 145.

संहर्ष *saṁharsha,* m., i.e. I. *sam-hṛish +a.* 1. Pleasure, joy. 2. Erection of the hair of the body. II. for *saṁgharsha.* 1. Rubbing. 2. Envy. 3. Wind.

संहात *saṁhâta* (probably for *saṁghâta,* q. cf., which is also a v.r.), m. One of the hells, Man. 4, 8.

संहार *saṁhâra,* i.e. *sam-hṛi+a,* m. 1. Collection, comprehensive description, in *ṛitu-,* of the (six) seasons, title of a poem, Lass. 60, 1. 2. Abridgment. 3. Restraining. 4. Destruction (of the world), Man. 1, 80. 5. Practice, Râm. 1, 30, 2; skill.—Comp. *Sa-,* adj. with charms for restraining (magical weapons), Johns. Sel. 4, 22.

संहूति *saṁhûti,* i.e. *sam-hve+ti,* f. Clamour, tumultuous exclamation.

सकलवर्ण *sa-ka-la-varṇa,* adj. Endowed with the letters *ka* and *la* (viz. *kalaha*), i.e. Quarrelling, Nalod. 2, 14.

सकाकोल *sa-kâkola,* m. One of the hells, Man. 4, 89.

सकाश *sakâça,* probably *sa-*kâça* (vb. *kâç*), m. Vicinity, presence, Nal. 1, 21; Pañch. 66, 10; acc. and loc. To, Pañch. 23, 1; Chr. 6, 6; Pañch. 55, 19. Abl. From, Pañch. 220, 14.—Comp. *Yûtha-pati-sakâça + m,* acc. To the chief of the herd, Pañch. 160, 24.

सकृत् *sa-kṛi + t,* adv. 1. Once, Vikr. d. 10. 2. At once, Vedântas. in Chr. 217, 5. 3. With, together. Cf. *çakṛit.* — Comp. *A-,* adv. repeatedly, Pañch. iii. d. 116; Chr. 30, 37.

सक्ति *sakti,* i.e. *sañj+ti,* f. 1. Contact. 2. Junction, Kir. 5, 46. 3. Addiction to, attachment. — Comp. *Ati-,* f. closest union, Çiç. 9, 7.

सक्तिमन्त् *sakti+mant,* adj., f. *mati,* Attached.—Comp. *Ati-,* adj. too much attached, Hit. iv. d. 31.

सक्तु *saktu,* see *çaktu.*

सक्तुल *saktu+la,* adj. Containing flour.

सक्थन् *sakthan,* see the next.

सक्थि *sakthi,* probably *sañj+than,* n.; the base of some cases is *sakthan,* 1. The thigh. 2. A bone. 3. The frame of a cart.

ऽसख *-sakha,* a substitute for *sakhi* at the end of comp. words; e.g. *nara-,* m. Friend of Nârâyana, Vikr. d. 3. *priya-,* I. m. 1. A dear friend, Chr. 13, 12. 2. A tree, Mimosa catechu. II. f. *khî,* A female friend, Utt. Râmach. 61, 13. *balabhid-,* m. Friend of Indra, Çâk. 27, 23. *madirâ-,* m. The mango, Mangifera Indica. *madhu-,* m. Kâma. *marut-,* m. 1. Indra. 2. Fire, Ragh. 2, 10. *vasanta-,* m. 1. Friend of spring, Vikr. 31, 18. 2. Kâma. *vâyu-,* m. Fire. *smara-,* m. The moon.

सखि *sakhi,* i.e. probably *sa-* 1. *kshi,* I. m. 1. An associate, Pañch. iii. d. 56; a companion, 265, 3. 2. A friend, Vikr. 12, 1. II. f. *khî,* A female friend, Vikr. 8, 2; Pañch. 258, 9.—Cf. Lat. socius.

सखित्व *sakhi+tva,* n. Friendship, Pañch. 60, 4.

सख्य *sakhya,* i.e. *sakhi+ya,* n. 1. Friendship, Hit. 38, 4, M.M. 2. Equality, Man. 2, 134.

† **सग्** *SAG,* i. 1, Par. To cover.

सगर *sa-gara,* **1.** adj. Poisonous. **2.** The name of a king, whose great-grandson brought the Ganges from heaven to the earth, Pańch. iii. d. 269; Râm. 1, 40, sqq. Gorr.; Daçak. in Chr. 197, 21.

सगर्भ्य *sagarbhya,* i.e. *sa-garbha* + *ya,* m. A brother by the same father and mother; cf. *garbha.*

सगुडशृङ्गक *sa-guḍa-çṛiṅga* + *ka,* adj., f. *gikâ,* Endowed with cupolas, MBh. 3, 643.

सघ् *SAGH,* ii. 5, Par. **1.** † To hurt, to kill. **2.** To bear (cf. *sah*).

संकर *saṁkara,* i.e. *sam-kṛi* + *a,* m. **1.** Mixing, blending, Râjat. 5, 377. **2.** The union of a man with a woman of a higher caste, Man. 5, 89; culpable mixture, Râm. 1, 6, 17. **3.** A mixed or degraded caste. **4.** Dust, sweepings. **5.** The crackling of flame.

संकरिन् *saṁkarin,* i.e. *sam-kṛi* + *in,* adj. Produced by culpable mixture of castes, Lass. Pentap. 66, 36.

संकरीकरण *saṁkarîkaraṇa,* i. e. *saṁkara-kṛi* + *ana,* n. **1.** Mixing, blending. **2.** Causing loss of caste, Man. 11, 63. **3.** Confusion either in kind, number, or arrangement.

संकर्षण *saṁkarshaṇa,* i.e. *sam-kṛish* + *ana,* I. n. **1.** Attracting. **2.** Ploughing. **II.** m. **1.** Baladeva, brother of Krishṇa, Johns. Sel. 55, 140; Râjat. 5, 112. **2.** Name of another man, Lass. 2. ed. 88, 24.

संकलन *saṁkalana,* i.e. *sam-kal* + *ana,* I. n., and f. *nâ.* **1.** Heaping. **2.** Junction, collision, Kir. 18, 8. **3.** Blending, intermixture. **II.** n. Addition.

संकल्प *saṁkalpa,* i.e. *sam-klip* + *a,* m. **1.** Will, Vedântas. in Chr. 207, 1; Hit. 54, 8, M.M. **2.** Wish, Megh. 100; desire, Mâlat. 125, 4. **3.** Mind, Nal. 24, 50. **4.** A solemn vow, Chr. 48, 5. **5.** Expectation of advantage from a holy work, Man. 2, 3. — **Comp.** *Dhṛita-,* adj., f. *pâ,* resolved (to, with loc.), Chr. 45, 10. *Pâpa-,* adj. ill-intentioned, Râm. 2, 74, 28. *Çiva-* (m.), the name of a hymn, Man. 11, 250. *Siddha-,* adj. one who has obtained his wishes, Daçak. in Chr. 193, 23. *Hṛishṭa-,* adj. contented, glad, Nal. 24, 50.

संकल्पज *saṁkalpa-ja,* I. adj. Proceeding from hope of advantage. **II.** m. Kâma, Johns. Sel. 45, 68.

संकसुक *saṁkasuka,* i.e. *sam-kas* + *uka,* adj. **1.** Unsteady, fickle. **2.** Uncertain, doubtful. **3.** Feeble, weak. **4.** Wicked. — **Comp.** *A-,* adj. firm, steady (in mind), Man. 6, 43, v.r.

संकार *saṁkâra,* i.e. *sam-kṛi* + *a,* I. m. **1.** Dust, sweepings. **2.** The crackling of flame. **II.** f. *ri,* A girl recently deflowered.

ऽसंकाश *-saṁkâça,* i.e. *sam-kâç* + *a,* latter part of comp. adj. Like, similar; e.g. *gaja-,* adj. Resembling elephants, Chr. 4, 18. *mṛityu-,* adj. death-like, ib. 39, 8. *adbhuta-,* adj. well-nigh marvellous, Johns. Sel. 36, 6.

संकीर्तन *saṁkîrtana,* i.e. *sam-kṛit* + *ana,* n., and f. *nâ,* **1.** Praising. **2.** Glorification. **3.** Honour.

संकुल *saṁkula* (cf. *kula*), adj., f. *lâ,* **1.** Crowded, Pańch. 43, 4. **2.** Filled with, Bhâg. P. 4, 25, 14; full, 1, 9, 41. **3.** Mixed, Nal. 13, 13. **4.** Perplexed, Hit. iii. d. 107. **5.** n. Throng, Mâlat. 19, 5.

संकेत् *SAṀKET* (cf. *kit*), i. 10 (rather a denomin. derived from the next), Par. **1.** To invite. **2.** † To advise. **3.** To fix or appoint a time. Comp. ptcple. of the pf. pass. (or rather *saṁketa + ita*), *a-saṁketita*, adj. Without agreement, Daçak. in Chr. 199, 11.

संकेत *saṁketa*, i.e. *sam-kit + a*, m. **1.** Sign, Lass. 2. ed. 5, 20. **2.** Gesture, gesticulation. **3.** Appointment, agreement, convention, Daçak. in Chr. 186, 24; Pańch. 26, 3. **4.** Condition, the circumstances under which anything is effected.

संकेतक *saṁketa + ka*(m.), and **संकेतन** *saṁketana*, i.e. *sam-kit + ana*, n. Appointment, a rendezvous, Kathâs. 4, 37 (*ka*); Pańch. 129, 1 (*ka*); Lass. 2. ed. 20, 14 (*na*).

संकोच *saṁkocha*, i.e. *sam-kuch + a*, I. m. **1.** Contracting, contraction, Pańch. iii. d. 20 (*kaurmaṁ saṁkocham âsthâya*, Contracting himself like a tortoise). **2.** Diminution, Pańch. i. d. 105. **3.** Fear, Râjat. 5, 14. **4.** Shutting, closing (as a flower), Naish. 22, 43 (Sch.). **5.** Tieing, binding. **6.** A fish, Raia Sancara Ham. **II.** n. Saffron.

संक्रन्दन *saṁkrandana*, i. e. *sam-krand + ana*, m. Indra.

संक्रम and **संक्राम** *saṁkrăma*, i.e. *sam-kram + a*, I. m. and n. **1.** Difficult progress, making way through almost impervious passes. **2.** The means of effecting such a passage, a causeway, a bridge, Man. 9, 285 (*rǎ*). **3.** Means of attaining, Pańch. iv. d. 2 (*rǎ*). **II.** m. **1.** Concurrence. **2.** Going. **3.** Traversing.—**Comp.** *Sûrya-saṁkrama*, m. the passage of the sun from one sign to another.

संक्रमण *saṁkramaṇa*, i.e. *sam-kram + ana*, n. **1.** Concurrence. **2.** Passing from one point to another, transition from one body into another, Pańch. 48, 16; Lass. 26, 4. **3.** The day at which begins the sun's progress to the north of the equator, the summer solstice. —**Comp.** *Garbha-*, n. entering in a womb, MBh. 14, 472.

संक्रान्ति *saṁkrânti*, i.e. *sam-kram + ti*, f. **1.** Union, Mâlat. 153, 17; Utt. Râmach. 63, 4 (imbibing). **2.** Passage from one point to another. **3.** The passage of the sun or planetary bodies from one sign of the zodiac to another. **4.** Proceeding, Mâlav. d. 15; 18. **5.** Imitation. **6.** Reflection.—**Comp.** *Uttarâyaṇa-*, i.e. *uttara-ayana-*, f. the sun's entrance into its northern journey, Pańch. 119, 1. *Sûrya-*, f. the sun's entrance into a new sign.

संक्राम *saṁkrâma*, see *saṁkrama*.

संक्लेद *saṁkleda*, i.e. *sam-klid + a*, m. **1.** Moisture, wet, damp. **2.** The rudiment of the fœtus, its form in the first month after conception, Yâjń. 3, 75.

संक्षय *saṁkshaya*, i.e. *sam-kshi + a*, m. **1.** Complete consumption, Pańch. 47, 10. **2.** Loss, Râjat. 5, 385. **3.** Destroying, Pańch. i. d. 256; destruction, Pańch. 104, 18; iii. d. 13. **4.** The destruction of the world, Chr. 34, 8. **5.** End, Chr. 30, 38.

संक्षिप्ति *saṁkshipti*, i.e. *sam-kship + ti*, f. **1.** Abridgment. **2.** Throwing. **3.** Sending. **4.** Ambuscade.

संक्षेप *saṁkshepa*, i.e. *sam-kship + a*, m. **1.** Throwing together; instr. *eṇa*, In all, Man. 7, 157. **2.** Abridgment, MBh. 1, 102; Pańch. 4, 17; iii. d. 103 (*pât*, in a few words). **3.** Conciseness. **4.** Throwing. **5.** Sending. **6.** Taking away. **7.** Assisting in another's duty.

संक्षेपतस् *saṁkshepa + tas*, adv. Concisely, Arj. 1, 13; Sâv. 2, 20.

संक्षोभ *saṁkshobha*, i.e. *sam-kshubh*

+*a*, m. **1.** Shaking, Vikr. d. 12. **2.** Trembling, Indr. 5, 9. **3.** Agitation. **4.** Overturning. **5.** Pride.

संख्य *saṁkhya,* i.e. *sam-khyâ,* **I.** n. War, battle, Râm. 3, 54, 28. **II.** f. *yâ,* **1.** Number in general, Pańch. 156, 6; *saṁkhyayâ parivarjita,* Without number, innumerable, Pańch. ii. d. 62. **2.** A numeral. **3.** Reflection, deliberation. **4.** Intellect. **5.** Manner, Râjat. 5, 172. —**Comp.** *A-*, adj., f. *yâ,* innumerable, Pańch. 122, 7. *Kula-*, f. being numbered among, belonging to eminent families, Man. 3, 66. *Go-*, m. a cowherd, MBh. 4, 284. *Daçârdha-*, i.e. *daçan-ardha-*, adj. five, Johns. Sel. 52, 113. *Çata-saṁkhya,* adj. numbering a hundred, Böhtl. Ind. Spr. 911. *Sahasra-*, f. a thousand, Kir. 5, 34.

संख्यता *saṁkhya+tâ,* f. **1.** Number. **2.** Numeration, counting.

संख्यातस् *saṁkhyâ+tas,* adv. = abl. sing. of *saṁkhyâ,* Bhâshâp. 110.

संख्यान *saṁkhyâna,* i.e. *sam-khyâ+ana,* n. **1.** Numbering, enumeration, Man. 8, 400. **2.** Reckoning.

संख्यावन्त् *saṁkhyâ+vant,* **I.** adj., f. *vatî.* **1.** Having number, numbered. **2.** Intelligent. **II.** m. A learned Brâhmaṇa, a teacher.

सङ्ग *sańga,* i.e. *sam-ga* (vb. *gam*), and *sańj+a,* m. **1.** Joining, uniting, Pańch. 187, 6. **2.** Meeting, Utt. Râmach. 33, 6. **3.** Confluence of rivers. **4.** Touch, Mâlat. 170, 3. **5.** Association, Hit. i. d. 202, M.M.; Pańch. i. d. 224; keeping company, Bhartṛ. 2, 34; intercourse, friendship, love (*kântâ-*, of one's wife), Pańch. v. d. 83. **6.** Attaching, Ragh. 2, 42 (an arrow, i.e. throwing). **7.** Attachment, Böhtl. Ind. Spr. 600; Pańch. i. d. 194; worldly attachment, Bhag. 2, 48. **8.** Desire, cupidity, Indr. 4, 3; Daçak. in Chr. 181, 3.—**Comp.** *A-*, I. m. 1. non-attachment, not being attached to, Man. 6, 75. 2. a proper name, Hariv. 9207. II. adj. 1. unfastened, MBh. 2, 944. 2. unimpeded, Ragh. 3, 63 (Mallin., ed. Calc. v.r.). *Dus-*, m. bad inclination, Bhâg. P. 1, 10, 11. *Nis-*, I. adj. 1. unimpeded, MBh. 5, 2371. 2. disinterested, free from desire, self-interest, Hit. i. d. 187, M.M.; indifferent, Prab. 110, 16. II. °*gam,* adv. without hesitation, Râm. 2, 21, 12. *Mukta-* (vb. *much*), adj. disinterested. *Yathâ-sańga+m,* adv. so as to be adapted, Nal. 23, 9 (the door lifts itself as much as is necessary for his entering it without bowing). *Satsańga,* i.e. *sant-* (vb. 1. *as*), I. m. association with the good. II. adj. good, pious, Utt. Râmach. 41, 12.

संगति *saṁgati,* i.e. *sam-gam+ti,* f. **1.** Meeting, Pańch. iv. d. 20. **2.** Chance, Brâhmaṇav. 1, 2. **3.** Union, Johns. Sel. 37, 19; association, Pańch. iii. d. 55. **4.** Intercourse, Pańch. 60, 9; sexual intercourse, Daçak. in Chr. 182, 13. **5.** Frequenting. **6.** Questioning for further information.

संगम *saṁgama,* i.e. *sam-gam+a,* m. **1.** Meeting, Pańch. iii. d. 127; acquiring, Pańch. ii. d. 197. **2.** Confluence of rivers, Utt. Râmach. 49, 5. **3.** Association, attendance, Hit. i. d. 113, M.M.; union, Vikr. d. 33; Pańch. ii. d. 184; company, Böhtl. Ind. Spr. 1212. **4.** Touch, Hit. iii. d. 20; mixture.—**Comp.** *Tvad-*, m. union with thee, Vikr. d. 61.

संगमन *saṁgamana,* i.e. *sam-gam+ana,* n. Meeting, Utt. Râmach. 144, 6.

संगमनीय *saṁgamanîya,* i.e. *saṁgamana+îya,* adj. Causing reunion, Vikr. d. 128.

संगर *saṁgara,* i.e. *sam-gṛî+a,* **I.** m. **1.** Agreement. **2.** Promise, Indr.

4, 12. **3.** A transaction of sale. **4.** War, battle, Man. 4, 121 ; Bhartṛ. 2, 85. **5.** Misfortune. **6.** Poison (cf. *gara*). **II.** n. The fruit of the Çamî tree.—**Comp.** *Satya-* and *Sthira-*, adj. true, veracious, Indr. 4, 12 (*sthira*).

संगाद् *saṁgâda*, i.e. *sam-gad+a*, m. Conversation, Mârk. P. 35, 21.

सङ्गिन् *saṅgin*, i.e. *saṅga+in*, adj., f. *ni*, **1.** Uniting with. **2.** Attached, devoted to, Bhag. 3, 26. **3.** Lustful, libidinous.

संगीतक *saṁgîtaka*, i. e. *sam-gîta* (vb. *gai*), *+ka* (cf. *gîtaka*, n.), A public entertainment consisting of songs, dancing, and music, Daçak. in Chr. 190, 8 ; Lass. 68, 4 (a drama).

संगीति *saṁgîti*, i.e. *sam-gai+ti*, f. **1.** The science of music and dancing. **2.** Discourse.

संगोपन *saṁgopana*, i.e. *sam-gup+ana*, n. Hiding, concealment.

संग्रह *saṁgraha*, i.e. *sam-grah+a*, m. **1.** Collection, Pañch. ii. d. 176 ; conjunction, Bhâshâp. 133 ; totality, Bhag. 18, 18.. **2.** A place where anything is kept. **3.** Quantity. **4.** A compilation, an abridgment, Bhag. 8, 11. **5.** A catalogue. **6.** Clenching the fist, clenching, grasp, Hit. iv. d. 13. **7.** Effort. **8.** Restraining, Lass. 2, 1. **9.** Governing, Man. 7, 113. **10.** Protecting, protection, Man. 8, 311. **11.** Propitiating, attaching, Pañch. i. d. 330 (*kurvanti saṁgraham*, Attach to themselves) ; Râjat. 5, 295 ; encouraging, Man. 3, 138. **12.** Assent, promise. **13.** Taking, seizing, Râjat. 5, 274 ; mentioning, Hit. ii. d. 57. **14.** Elevation, loftiness.—**Comp.** *Dâra-*, m. marrying, Chr. 51, 8. *Dharma-*, m. a collection of merit, of good actions, Pañch. iii. d. 96 (*kartavyaḥ*, one must do many good actions) ; Chr. 28, 23. *Madhyama-*, m. intriguing with another man's wife. *Sâra-*, adj. containing the essence, Châṇ. 2 in Berl. Monatsb. 1864, p. 407.

संग्रहण *saṁgrahaṇa*, i.e. *sam-grah+aṇa*, **I.** n. **1.** Collecting, compiling. **2.** Enchasing, Hit. ii. d. 71. **3.** Sexual intercourse. **4.** Adultery, Man. 8, 72 ; cf. 6 ; 356, sqq. **5.** Taking. **6.** Accepting. **7.** Hope. **II.** f. *ṇî*, Dysentery.—**Comp.** *Pâṇi-*, n. shaking hands as a token of promise, Râm. 4, 34, 23. *Strî-*, n. adultery, Man. 8, 6.

† **संग्राम्** *SAṀGRÂM*, i. 10 (or rather a denomin. derived from the next), Âtm. (Par.), To fight, to make war.

संग्राम *saṁgrâma*, i.e. *sam-grah+ma*, m. **1.** War, battle, Hit. 75, 17 ; fighting, Pañch. 238, 22. **2.** A proper name, Râjat. 5, 305 ; 423.

संग्राह *saṁgrâha*, i.e. *sam-grah+a*, m. **1.** Clenching the fist. **2.** The fist. **3.** The gripe of a shield. **4.** Seizing forcibly.

संघ *saṁgha*, i.e. *sam-han*, m. **1.** Multitude, Indr. 1, 36. **2.** Flock, Hariv. 8788. **3.** Quantity. **4.** Inhabitants, Man. 8, 219.

संघट्ट *saṁghaṭṭa*, i.e. *sam-ghaṭṭ+a*, **I.** m. **1.** Friction, Megh. 54 ; rubbing. **2.** Embracing. **3.** Clashing together, Mâlat. 74, 13 ; collision, Pañch. 35, 5 ; shock, Mâlat. 144, 11. **4.** Meeting, encounter. **II.** f. *ṭâ*, A large creeper.—**Comp.** *A-*, m. having no rival, Ragh. 14, 86.

संघट्टन *saṁghaṭṭana*, i.e. *sam-ghaṭṭ+ana*, n. **1.** Rubbing together. **2.** Collision, Pañch. 165, 8. **3.** Close contact. **4.** The intertwining of wrestlers. **5.** Union, Lass. 24, 8 (erroneously, °*ghaḍḍana*); cohesion. **6.** Collecting, Râjat. 5, 340. **7.** Meeting.

संघड्डन *saṁghaḍḍana*, Lass. 24, 8, read *saṁghaṭṭana*.

संघर्ष *saṁgarsha*, i.e. *sam-ghṛish* + *a*, m. **1.** Trituration, rubbing, grinding, friction, MBh. 1, 1134; Râjat, 5, 477. **2.** Collision, Râm. 1, 26, 10. **3.** Emulation, Daçak. in Chr. 183, 19; envy. **4.** Going gently, gliding.—**Comp.** *Danta-*, m. gnashing the teeth, Mârk. P. 34, 72.

संघर्षिन् *saṁgharshin*, i. e. *sam -ghṛish* or *saṁgharsha*, + *in*, adj. Emulating, Mâlav. 13, 14.

संघशस् *saṁgha* + *ças*, adj. **1.** By troops. **2.** Collectively.—**Comp.** *Çata-*, adv. by troops of hundreds, Indr. 1, 36.

संघाटिका *saṁghâṭikâ*, i.e. *saṁghâṭî* + *ka*, f. **1.** A couple. **2.** A procuress. **3.** Smell. **4.** A plant, Trapa bispinosa.

संघाटी *saṁghâṭî* (*sam* and vb. *han*), f., in the comp. *bhikshu-*, f. The garb of a mendicant.

संघात *saṁghâta*, i. e. *sam-han*, Caus., + *a*, m. **1.** Association, connexion, Bhartṛ. 2, 56 (*çilâ-*, properly, of a stone, i.e. its strong structure, a hard stone). **2.** Assemblage, multitude, Pańch. 157, 24; Râjat. 5, 260; cluster, Mâlat. 153, 8. **3.** Killing, striking. **4.** A division of Tartarus. **5.** Phlegm.

संघातवन्त् *saṁghâta* + *vant*, adj. Having, or connected with, many, Pańch. iii. d. 57.—**Comp.** *Bhrâtṛi-*, i.e. *bhrâtṛisaṁghâta* + *vant*, m. having many brothers, Pańch. iii. d. 8.

सच् *SACH*, i. 1, Âtm., and Par. Âtm.; ved. ii. 3, ***sishach*** and *saçch* (i.e. *sasach*), **1.** To follow. **2.** To obey. **3.** To favour. **4.** To honour, Chr. 291, 12 = Rigv. i. 64, 12. **5.** To cause to flow, Chr. 296, 9 = Rigv. i. 112, 9. Comp. ptcple. of the pres. *a-saçchant* and *a-saçchat* (Not obeying, not ceding), not ceasing, inexhaustible, Chr. 296, 2 = Rigv. i. 112, 2.—Cf. Lat. sequi, secundus, secus, sequior, sacer; ἕπομαι, ἕσπετο (for σεσπ = ved. *saçch*), ὁπλότερος, ἑκάς.

सचि *sach* + *i*, m. Friendship.

सचिव *sachi* + *va*, m. **1.** A friend, a companion, Râjat. 5, 341. **2.** A minister, a counsellor, Râm. 3, 53, 4; Kâm. Nîtis. 4, 28, sqq.; Pańch. 155, 5. —**Comp.** See *Ku-*. *Dhî-*, m. a counsellor, Râjat. 2, 67. *Narmasachiva*, i.e. *narman-*, m. a prince's companion, whose business it is to amuse him by jokes, Kâm. Nîtis. 5, 20; a favourite, Mâlat. 37, 4.

सचिवता *sachiva* + *tâ*, f. The office of a minister, Râjat. 5, 389.

सच्चिदानन्द *sachchidânanda*, i. e. *sant* (vb. 1. *as*), *-chit-ânanda*, n. Brahman, or the Supreme Spirit, Vedântas. in Chr. 202, 3.

सजुस् *sajus*, i.e. *sa-jush*, I. adj. sbst. Associated, a companion. II. *sajûs*, adv. With, together with (with the instr.).

1. **सज्ज्** *SAJJ*, see *sańj*.

† 2. **सज्ज्** *SAJJ*, **सञ्च्** *SAŃCH* (**सञ्ज्** *SAŃJ*), i. 1, Par. To go, to move.

सज्ज 1. *sajj* + *a*, I. adj. **1.** Armed. **2.** Fortified. **3.** Got ready, Chr. 30, 3; 31, 18; prepared, Pańch. ii. d. 200 (cf. my transl.). **4.** Ornamented. **5.**

Dressed. II. f. *jâ*. **1.** Armour. **2.** Dress.

सज्जता *sajja* + *tâ*, f. Readiness, Daçak. in Chr. 181, 3.

सज्जन *sajjana*, i.e. **A.** *sant* (vb. 1. *as*), -*jana*, adj. **1.** Respectable. **2.** Good, virtuous, Bhartṛ. 2, 46; 50. **B.** 1. *sajj* + *ana*, I. (m., f. *nâ*), n. **1.** Fastening, Man. 2, 63. **2.** Arming. **3.** Dressing. **4.** Preparing. II. n. **1.** A guard. **2.** A ferry. III. f. *nâ*, Caparisoning an elephant, Govardh. Âryâ Sapt. 370, d.

सज्जित *sajjita*, i.e. *sajja* + *ita*, adj. **1.** Prepared, Pańch. i. d. 173; 197, 25. **2.** Armed. **3.** Dressed, ornamented.

सज्य *sa-jya* (see *jyâ*), adj. Strung (as a bow), Johns. Sel. 39, 31.

सञ्च् *SAŃCH*, see 2. *sajj*.

सञ्चक *sańchaka* (m.?), Stamp, and disc (of the moon), Naish. 22, 47; 48 (Sch. ad 47).

संचय *saṁchaya*, i.e. *sam-chi* + *a*, m. **1.** Collection, Man. 4, 3. **2.** Heaping up, accumulation, Pańch. ii. d. 158; Hit. i. d. 159, M.M. **3.** Being constructed, built, Pańch. 33, 6. **4.** Heap, Pańch. 175, 2 (*kâshṭha*-, pl. A funeral pile). **5.** Multitude, Mâlat. 14, 6; quantity, Pańch. ii. d. 142.—**Comp.** *Ati*-, m. excessive accumulation, Hit. i. d. 159, M.M.

संचयन *saṁchayana*, i.e. *sam-chi* + *ana*, n. **1.** Gathering up, Man. 5, 59; putting together, Pańch. 244, 2. **2.** Collecting the ashes and bones of a body which has been burned.

ऽसंचयिक -*saṁchayika* in *mâsa*-, i.e. *mâsa-saṁchayin* + *ka*, adj. One who gathers enough for a month, Man. 6, 18.

संचयिन् *saṁchayin*, i.e. *sam-chi* + *in*, adj., f. *nî*, Who or what collects.

संचर *saṁchara*, i.e. *sam-char* + *a*, m. **1.** A defile, any narrow or difficult pass, a road along the edge of a mountain, or a bridge, etc. **2.** Difficult passage. **3.** A road. **4.** The body. **5.** Killing.—**Comp.** *Mûrti*-, adj. embodied, Utt. Râmach. 145, 12.

संचरण *saṁcharaṇa*, i.e. *sam-char* + *ana*, n. **1.** Going, Mâlat. 15, 12. **2.** Setting in motion, use, Pańch. 44, 17 (perhaps it must be changed to *saṁchâraṇa*, q. cf.).

संचलन *saṁchalana*, i.e. *sam-chal* + *ana*, n., and f. *nâ*, Trembling, shaking, Mâlat. 147, 12; Kir. 18, 8.

संचलनाडि *saṁchalanâḍi*, i.e. *sam-chal* + *a-nâḍi*, f. Artery, pulse, Râm. 2, 50, 13, Seramp.

संचार *saṁchâra*, i.e. *sam-char* + *a*, m. **1.** Difficult progress. **2.** Difficulty, distress. **3.** Going, Râm. 3, 52, 34; motion, Bhartṛ. 1, 11. **4.** Course, Utt. Râmach. 42, 16 (of life). **5.** Contagion. **6.** Setting in motion, Bhâshâp. 151. **7.** Leading. **8.** Inciting. **9.** A gem supposed to be in the head of a serpent.—**Comp.** *Duḥkha*-, adj. passing in a disagreeable manner, Râm. 3, 22, 10. *Dus*-, adj., f. *râ*, difficult to be passed, Pańch. i. d. 189. *Nis*-, adj. 1. not walking, staying at home, Râjat. 6, 125. 2. motionless, quiet, Mâlat. 126, 6. *Pâtra*-, m. perhaps, arranging the vessels after dinner, MBh. 12, 9975 (perhaps to be corrected to *pâtrasaṁskâra*). *Bhûta*-, I. m. possession by evil spirits. II. f. *rî*, fire in a forest.

संचारक *saṁchâraka*, i.e. *sam-char*, Caus., + *aka*, I. m. A leader, Hit. ii. d. 123. II. f. *rikâ*. **1.** A female messenger, a bawd. **2.** A pair. **3.** Smell.

संचारण *saṁchâraṇa*, i.e. *sam-char*, Caus., + *ana*, n. **1.** Setting in motion (cf. *saṁcharaṇa*). **2.** Impelling. **3.** Leading.

संचारिन् *saṁchârin*, i.e. *sam-char*, and *saṁchâra*, + *in*, I. adj., f. *iṇî*. **1.** Moving, Kumâras. 3, 54. **2.** Fickle, unsteady, changeable. **3.** Difficult. **4.** Putting in motion. **5.** Contagious. **6.** Hereditary (as disease). II. m. Incense. —**Comp.** *Bhûta-saṁchâriṇî*, f. fire in a forest.

1. **सञ्ज्** *SAṄJ*, i. 1, *saja*, Par. The pass. *sajya* has become very often *sajja*, which in epic poetry appears with the terminations of the Par. (MBh. 1, 7694), whence *sajj* has begun to be considered as a radical vb., To adhere, Ragh. 4, 47; Chr. 20, 20; *nahi vâṇâ mayotsṛishṭâḥ sajjantîha çarîriṇâṁ kâyeshu*, literally, 'For the arrows cast by me do not stick to the bodies of living men,' i.e. 'all those who are hit by my arrows will die.' Pass. **1.** To be attached, MBh. 3, 63. **2.** To become attached, Man. 6, 55. Ptcple. of the pf. pass. *sakta*. **1.** Attached, Man. 7, 30. **2.** Devoted. **3.** Diligent, intent on. **4.** Impending, Pañch. 186, 24. **5.** Belonging, Pañch. 222, 13; related, 89, 18. **6.** Concerning, Pañch. 221, 14. **Comp.** *A*-, adj. not attached, Pañch. ii. d. 130. Caus. To pimp, Man. 8, 362 (*sajjaya*).—With the prep. **अति** *ati, shaṅj*; *ati-sakta* (i.e *sakta* with *ati*), Exceedingly attached, Daçak. in Chr. 181, 21.—With **व्यति** *vi-ati*, **1.** Par. To connect mutually, Utt. Râmach. 146, 8. **2.** Âtm. To change, Daçak. in Chr. 186, 3. *vyatishakta*, Intermarrying, Man. 10, 25.—With **अनु** *anu, shaṅj*, To cling, to cleave, Daçak. in Chr. 182, 15. Pass. To be attached to, Bhag. 6, 4.—With **अभि** *abhi, shaṅj*, To humiliate, MBh. 3, 1090.—With **अव** *ava*, To suspend, Râm. 3, 53, 52. *avasakta*, **1.** Hanging, MBh. 1, 1692. **2.** Taken hold of, and pervaded, Çiç. 9, 7.—With **आ** *â*, **1.** To fix, to put on, MBh. 3, 16125. **2.** To entrust, MBh. 1, 1955. Pass. To be attached or fettered, Çâk. d. 74. *âsakta*, **1.** Attached, Râm. 3, 50, 9. **2.** Intent on, occupied, Pañch. 27, 9; zealously following. **3.** Trusting to. **4.** Eternal. **5.** °*tam*, adv. Eternally. Caus. *saṅjaya*, To cause to be attached, Ragh. 6, 83.—With **व्या** *vi-â*, *vyâsakta*, Occupied, Vikr. 60, 6.—With **समा** *sam-â*, **1.** To attach, MBh. 1, 4418. **2.** To entrust, to resign to, Man. 4, 257. *samâsakta*, **1.** Attached, Râm. 2, 64, 9. **2.** Joined. **3.** Combined. **4.** Marked, affected by.—With **उद्** *ud*, To attach, Mâlat. 172, 13. *utsakta*, Attached, Râjat. 5, 127.—With **नि** *ni*, *nishakta*, Fixed, Daçak. in Chr. 199, 3. —With **प्र** *pra*, To attach one's self, Daçak. in Chr. 183, 3. Pass. **1.** To be strongly addicted, Man. 4, 16. **2.** To be relevant, to apply, Bhâshâp. 61. *prasakta*, **1.** Attached to, Pañch. ii. d. 3. **2.** Fettered, Pañch. i. d. 208. **3.** Engaged in, Pañch. 197, 25. **4.** Connected with. **5.** Obtained. **6.** Employed. **7.** Continual, Mâlat. 70, 19; eternal. **8.** Opened, expanded, Utt. Râmach. 118, 5. **9.** °*tam*, adv. Continually.—With **अतिप्र** *ati-pra* in *atiprasakta*, i. e. *prasakta* with *ati*, Too much attached, Pañch. i. d. 201.—With **अनुप्र** *anu-pra*, *anuprasakta*, Attached, Çiç. 9, 63.—With **वि** *vi*, *vishakta*, **1.** Hung up, Çâk. d. 31. **2.** Adhering closely, firmly rooted, Daçak. in Chr. 183, 23; Utt. Râmach. 94, 12. **3.** In contact with.—With

सञ्ज् *sam*, pass. **1.** To adhere, MBh. 3, 17228. **2.** To be entwined, MBh. 2, 917. **3.** To be connected, Râm. 2, 25, 37. *saṁsakta*, **1.** Attached to, Pañch. i. d. 192; attached, Mâlat. 145, 11. **2.** Tied, connected, Râjat. 5, 366. **3.** Restrained, Nal. 13, 21. **4.** Endowed with. **5.** Joined, linked together. **6.** Contiguous.—Cf. σάττω (for σαγγω), σαγή, σάγμα, σακτός, σάκτωρ, probably σάκκος, σάκτας.

2. **सञ्ज्** *SAÑJ*, see 2. *sajj.*

सञ्ज *sañja*, m. **1.** Brahman. **2.** Çiva.

सञ्जतर *sañjatara*, n. The name of a city, Pañch. 118, 22.

संजनन *saṁjanana*, i.e. *sam-jan + ana*, n. **1.** Begetting. **2.** Producing, Lass. 2. ed. 60, 20.

संजीव *saṁjîva*, i.e. *sam-jîv + a*, adj. Living, Râm. 6, 26, 5.

संजीवक *saṁjîvaka*, i. e. *sam-jîv + aka*, m. A proper name, Hit. 58, 15.

संजीवन *saṁjîvana*, i.e. *sam-jîv + ana*, I. n. **1.** Animating, bringing to life, Pañch. 244, 4; reanimating, Utt. Râmach. 51, 9; life-restoring, Mâlat. 167, 4. **2.** A hell, Man. 4, 89. **3.** A cluster of four houses. II. f. *nî*, A kind of elixir, Lass. 79, 15.

संजीविन् *saṁjîvin*, i. e. *sam-jîv + in*, f. *nî*, Reanimating, Lass. 18, 13 (perhaps to be changed into *saṁjîvanî*, cf. *jîvana* and the last).

संज्ञ *saṁjña*, i. e. *sam-jânu*, adj. Knock-kneed.

ऽसंज्ञक *-saṁjña + ka*, a substitute for *saṁjñâ*, at the end of comp. adj., or sbst. based on them; e.g. *âsana-*, adj. Called *âsana*, Pañch. 154, 8. *ravi-*, n. Copper.

संज्ञा *saṁjñâ*, i.e. *sam-jñâ*, f. **1.** Consciousness, Vikr. 71, 20; Chr. 31, 18. **2.** Intellect, mind, Daçak. in Chr. 197, 1. **3.** Thought. **4.** Knowledge, Bhag. 1, 7. **5.** Sign, Vikr. 47, 12; gesticulation. **6.** Name, appellation, Hit. iv. d. 88.—**Comp.** *Antaḥsaṁjña*, i.e. *antar-*, adj. possessed of internal consciousness, Man. 1, 49. *Kṛita-*, adj. 1. ready-minded. 2. distinguished by appropriate marks, Man. 7, 190. *A-kṛita-*, adj. irresolute, MBh. 14, 588. *Gata-*, adj. bereft of sense, Indr. 5, 21. *Jîva-*, adj. called life, Man. 12, 13. *Nis-*, adj. deprived of consciousness, Râm. 3, 62, 25. *Vi-*, adj. 1. lifeless, 2. bereft of sense. *Sûrya-saṁjña*, n. saffron. *Soma-*, n. camphor.

संज्ञावन्त् *saṁjñâ + vant*, adj. **1.** Recovered after insensibility. **2.** Having a name.

संज्ञित *saṁjñita*, i.e. *saṁjñâ + ita*, adj. Called, Râm. 1, 39, 4; Lass. 16, 16 (at the end of a comp.).—**Comp.** *Kara-*, adj. called tax, Man. 7, 137.

संज्ञु *saṁjñu*, i. e. *sam-jânu*, adj. Knock-kneed.

संज्वर *saṁjvara*, i.e. *sam-jvar + a*, m. **1.** Fever. **2.** Heat, burning, scorching, a burn.—**Comp.** *A-*, adj. without indignation, Man. 4, 185.

संज्वरवन्त् *saṁjvara + vant*, adj., f. *vatî*, Hot, Mâlat. 154, 16.

† **सट्** *SAṬ*, i. 1, Par. To be a part or portion.

सट *saṭa* (cf. *jaṭa*), m., f. *ṭâ* (also **शटा** *çaṭâ*, Padmap. 16, 97), and n. **1.** An ascetic's clotted hair, Bhâg. P. 7, 8, 32 (*ṭâ*). **2.** A braid of hair, Draup. 9, 9 (*ṭâ*); a mane, Çiç. 1, 47; bristles (of a boar), Ragh. 9, 60. **3.** A crest.

† सट्ट् *SAṬṬ*, i. 10, Par. **1.** To kill, to injure. **2.** To be strong. **3.** To give. **4.** To dwell.

सठ् *SAṬH*, see 4. *çaṭh*.

सतत *sa-tata* (vb. *tan*), I. adj. Continual, eternal. II. °*tam*, adv. Continually, eternally, always, Pañch. 182, 9; Hit. i. d. 41, M.M. When former part of a comp. the final *m* is dropped; e.g. *satata-yâyin*, Taking place continually, Man. 1, 50; Bhartṛ. 2, 46 (*satata-durgata*, i.e. *-dus-gata*, Ever poor.)

सततग *satata-ga*, m. Wind, Hiḍ. 1, 8.

सति *sati*, i.e. *san* + *ti*, f. **1.** Gift, giving. **2.** End, destruction.

सतीत्व *satîtva*, i.e. *sant* (ptcple. pres. of 1. *as*), + *î* + *tva*, n. Virtuousness or purity in a wife, chastity, Pañch. iii. d. 204.

सतीन *satîna*, and सतीनक *satîna* + *ka*, m. Peas, or a particular kind of pulse (cf. *satîla*).

सतीर्थ्य *satîrthya*, i.e. *sa-tîrtha* + *ya*, m. A fellow student.

सतील *satîla*, I. m. **1.** A bambu. **2.** Air, wind. II. m., and f. *lâ*, Peas, or a particular kind of pulse (cf. *satîna*).

सतीलक *satîla* + *ka*, m. Pulse in general, or of a particular kind.

सत्कर्मन् *satkarman*, i.e. *sant* (ptcple. pres. of 1. *as*), *-karman*, n. **1.** A good act. **2.** Virtue. **3.** Hospitality. **4.** Funeral obsequies. **5.** Expiation.

सत्कार *satkâra*, i.e. *sant* (see the last), *-kâra*, m. **1.** Reverence, Sâv. 3, 20, b.; attention, Pañch. i. d. 84. **2.** Hospitality, hospitable reception, Hit. 60, 1, M.M. **3.** A meal, a festival, Man. 3, 59. **4.** Care, Sâv. 3, 20, a.—**Comp.** *A-*, m. injury, MBh. 1, 6355. *Atithi-*, m. hospitable treatment, Çâk. 7, 15 (corr. °*hâ*°).

सत्क्रिया *satkriyâ*, i.e. *sant-kriyâ* (see *satkarman*), f. **1.** Good action, Bhartṛ. 2, 96. **2.** Doing good, charity, virtue, Çâk. d. 112. **3.** Worship. **4.** Respectful treatment, Kir. 1, 12. **5.** Hospitality, Man. 3, 126. **6.** Funeral or obsequial ceremonies. **7.** Any purificatory ceremony.—**Comp.** *Anta-*, f. funeral ceremonies, Râjat. 5, 224.

सत्ता *sattâ*, i.e. *sant* (ptcple pres. of 1. *as*), + *tâ*, f. **1.** Existence, being, reality, Bhâshâp. 7. **2.** Goodness, excellence.

सत्तावन्त् *sattâ* + *vant*, adj., f. *vatî*, Possessing reality, Bhâshâp. 13.

सत्त्र *sattra*, and सत्र *satra*, n., i.e. I. *sad* + *tra*. **1.** A sacrifice, Utt. Râmach. 4, 1. **2.** Liberality, munificence. II. perhaps *sa-trâ*. **1.** Covering, concealing, a hiding-place, Daçak. in Chr. 190, 10 (*tad-dṛishṭi-vibhrama-'utpala-vana-sattra-apâçraya*, adj. Concealed in the play of her looks, which seemed as it were the covert of a wood of lotuses). **2.** Fraud, cheating. **3.** A house. **4.** Wealth. **5.** A wood, a forest, Kir. 13, 9. **6.** A tank.—**Comp.** *Dîrgha-*, n. 1. a Soma sacrifice of long continuance, MBh. 3, 5051. 2. the name of a place of pilgrimage, ib. 5050. *Deva-*, n. a long-lasting sacrifice in honour of the gods, MBh. 3, 8188. *Pañchasattra*, i.e. *pañchan-*, n. the name of a locality, Râjat. 5, 155. *Brahmasattra*, i.e. *brahman-*, n. 1. what must be read constantly, Man. 2, 106. 2. teaching the Veda, Man. 4, 9.

सत्त्रिन् *sattrin*, i.e. *sattra* + *in*, m. **1.** One constantly performing sacrifice, occupied with a sacrifice, Man. 5, 93.

2. A priest superintending a sacrifice. **3.** A liberal housekeeper. **4.** An ambassador.—**Comp.** *Dîrgha-*, i.e. *dirghasattra + in*, adj. one who performs a long sacrifice, Bhâg. P. 1, 4, 1.

सत्त्व *sattva*, i.e. *sant* (ptcple. pres. of 1. *as*), + *tva*, **I.** m. and n. **1.** An animal, Pańch. 69, 5 (n.); Hit. 56, 20; Lass. 2. ed. 44, 8 (m.); a beast, Ragh. 15, 15; a monster, Râm. 1, 40, 20. **2.** A being, Pańch. 165, 9; Râm. 3, 55, 48 (n.). **II.** n. **1.** Being, existence. **2.** Life, Çâk. d. 42. **3.** Nature, natural property, Hit. ii. d. 39; character, 100, 6. **4.** Essence, true essence, Bhag. 2, 45; 10, 36. **5.** Certainty, Vedântas. in Chr. 204, 17. **6.** Breath. **7.** Mind, Draup. 7, 15. **8.** Strength, power, Hit. 67, 5, M.M.; courage, Hit. ii. d. 78. **9.** Self-possession, Arj. 6, 20. **10.** A demon, a goblin. **11.** The quality of goodness, Man. 8, 40; virtue, Lass. 2. ed. 44, 2.—**Comp.** *A-*, **I.** n. non-existence. **II.** adj. without energy, Râm. 6, 89, 2. *A-dîna-*, adj. happy, Draup. 2, 13. *Âpanna-* (vb. *pad*), adj., f. *vâ*, pregnant, Çâk. 65, 9. *Gata-* (vb. *gam*), adj. lifeless, Nal. 16, 30. *Deva-*, adj. having the nature of a deity, Râm. 2, 1, 29 Gorr. *Nis-*, adj. 1. deprived of living beings, Pańch. 55, 8. 2. deprived of strength, Hit. i. d. 133, M.M. (*niḥ-sattva + tâ*, f. misery, Mâlat. 79, 12). *Bodhi-*, m. a Bauddha saint. *Ati-bodhi-sattva*, adj. surpassing a Bodhisattva, Mâlat. 171, 9 (corr. *dhi*). *Mahâ-*, adj. good, virtuous, Hit. 100, 12. *Mûḍha-* (vb. *muh*), adj. insane, silly, Draup. 7, 15. *Sa-*, f. *vâ*, pregnant, a pregnant woman, Ragh. 3, 9.

सत्त्ववन्त् *sattva + vant*, adj., f. *vatî*, and sbst. **1.** Living, a living being, Râm. 1, 41, 8. **2.** Endowed with, possessed of, the true essence, Bhag. 10, 36. **3.** Endowed with strength, magnanimous, Bhartr̥. 2, 31. **4.** Natural.

सत्त्वस्थ *sattva-stha* (vb. *sthâ*), adj. **1.** Existing in the nature of things. **2.** Animate. **3.** Inherent in animals. **4.** Good, excellent. **5.** Performing well, Mâlav. 20, 9.

सत्त्वोत्साहवन्त् *sattvotsâhavant*, i.e. *sattva-utsâha + vant*, adj., f. *vatî*, Endowed with courage and energy, Pańch. iii. d. 238.

सत्प्रतिपक्षिता *satpratipakshitâ*, i.e. *sant-pratipaksha + in + tâ* (cf. *satpratipaksha*, under *pratipaksha*), f. Condition of containing two opposite sets of premises, Bhâshâp. 76.

सत्य *satya*, i.e. *sant* (ptcple. pres. of 1. *as*), + *ya*, **I.** adj. **1.** True, Kathâs. 4, 104; superl. *satyatama*, Quite true, Hit. 87, 7, M.M.; realised, Chr. 48, 11; *satyaṁ kr̥i*, To fulfil, Râm. 3, 53, 8. **2.** Sincere, Lass. 2. ed. 29, 19; honest. **II.** °*yam*, adv. **1.** Truly, Vikr. 71, 18; indeed, Râjat. 5, 86; yes, Man. 11, 196. **2.** A particle of interrogation. **III.** m. **1.** Râmachandra. **2.** The uppermost of the seven worlds, the abode of Brahman. **IV.** f. *yâ*. **1.** Veracity. **2.** Sîtâ. **V.** n. **1.** Truth, Râm. 3, 53, 20. **2.** An oath, Chr. 58, 3; Pańch. 97, 17. **3.** Demonstrated conclusion. **4.** The first Yuga, the golden age.—**Comp.** *A-*, **I.** adj. untrue, false, MBh. 3, 14133. **II.** n. untruth, Man. 11, 69.—Cf. ἐτεός; A.S. for-sodh, Forsooth.

सत्यक *satya + ka*, **I.** adj. True, veracious. **II.** n. Ratification of a bargain.

सत्यंकार *satyaṁkâra*, i.e. *satya + m -kr̥i + a*, m. Ratification of a bargain.

सत्यजित् *satya-ji + t*, m. A proper name, Johns. Sel. 29, 38.

सत्यता *satya + tâ*, f. **1.** Truth, trueness, Râjat. 5, 27 (they ascended living to the truly highest abode of Hara). **2.** Veracity, Hit. i. d. 95, M.M. – **Comp.**

Nis-, f. want of veracity, Hit. i. d. 97, M.M.

सत्यवन्त् *satya* + *vant*, I. adj., f. *vatî*, True, practising truth. II. m. A proper name. III. f. *vatî*, A proper name, Chr. 3, 6.

सत्यापन *satyâpana*, i.e. *satyâpaya* (a denomin. derived from *satya*), + *ana*, n., and f. *nâ*, Ratification of a bargain.

† **सत्र्** *SATR*, i. 10, Âtm. **1.** To accomplish, or to extend. **2.** To connect.

सत्र *satra*, see *sattra*.

सत्रा *sa* + *trâ*, prep. (with instr.), With, together with.

सत्रिन् *satrin*, **सत्व** *satva*, see *sattrin*, *sattva*.

सत्वन् *satvan*, m. A warrior, Chr. 290, 2 = Rigv. i. 64, 2.

सथूत्कार *sa-thût* (an imitative sound), *-kâra*, n. Sputtering in speech.

1. **सद्** *SAD*, i. 1 and 6, *sîda* (for *sisada*), Par. (in epic poetry also Atm., MBh. 1, 5184), **1.** To sink down, to lie, Râm. 3, 74, 31. **2.** To sit down (ved.). **3.** To become helpless, Man. 4, 191; to be in distress, Pańch. ii. d. 24. **4.** To be impeded, Man. 9, 94. **5.** To be low-spirited, dejected, MBh. 1, 2061; Hit. iii. d. 6. **6.** To decay, to perish, Man. 4, 34; Hit. ii. d. 75. Ptcple. of the pf. pass. *sanna*. **1.** Lying motionless, Man. 6, 56; still. **2.** Shrunk, diminished. **3.** Gone, lost, Kir. 3, 38. **4.** Dispirited. **5.** Oppressed, Kumâras. 7, 85. **6.** Spoiled, Ragh. 19, 19. Caus. *sâdaya*, **1.** To throw down, Draup. 8, 29. **2.** To afflict, MBh. 3, 50. **3.** To destroy, Vikr. d. 42. *sâdita*, **1.** Exterminated. **2.** Exhausted. **3.** Decayed. **4.** Broken. **5.** Distressed, Kir. 14, 57. **6.** Drawn. — With the prep. **अव** *ava*, **1.** To wither, to perish gradually, MBh. 3, 2674; to perish, Daçak. in Chr. 193, 10. **2.** To be exhausted, to pine, Man. 4, 187. **3.** To be afflicted, Sâv. 5, 47. *avasanna*, **1.** Ended, Hit. 14, 6, M.M. **2.** Languid, weak, Daçak. in Chr. 194, 12. **3.** Dispirited, unhappy, Chân. 65 in Berl. Monatsb. 1864, 411. **4.** Bent. **5.** Separated. **6.** Nonsuited. Caus. **1.** To destroy, Bhag. 6, 5. **2.** To mitigate, Çâk. d. 103. Comp. absol. *an-avasâdya*, Without desponding, Daçak. in Chr. 189, 9.—With **व्यव** *vi-ava*, **1.** To sink down, MBh. 3, 713. **2.** To perish, MBh. 3, 823.—With **समव** *sam-ava*, *samavasanna*, Sorrowful, MBh. 2, 956.—With **आ** *â*, To sit down, Chr. 291, 6 = Rigv. i. 85, 6. i. 1 and 10, *sâdaya*, **1.** To approach, Râm. 2, 56, 33; to come to, Pańch. 127, 17; 247, 8 (*râtrim âsâdya*, at night); to reach, Hit. pr. d. 47, M.M.; to overtake, Vikr. 6, 7. **2.** To attack, Râm. 1, 21, 12. **3.** To find, Man. 4, 227. **4.** To obtain, Vikr. 73, 4; MBh. 3, 10472; with *garvam*, To become proud, Pańch. 26, 3. *âsanna*, Near, Hit. 84, 7, M.M. **Comp.** *Mahâ-*, m. Kuvera. *âsâdita*, **1.** Gone to, reached. **2.** Obtained, Daçak. in Chr. 196, 5. **3.** Spread. **4.** Effected. **Comp.** *An-âsâdita*, adj. not tested, Hit. iii. d. 41 (but cf. Böhtl. Ind. Spr. 3202). Absol. *âsâdya*, **1.** Having found, Hit. iv. d. 60 (*kâryam*, a motive, i.e. if it is one's interest). **2.** Agreeably to, Man. 8, 324.—With **अभ्या** *abhi-â*, **1.** To step on, Kir. 5, 52. **2.** To obtain, MBh. 3, 17101.—With **प्रत्या** *prati-â*, To be near, Kir. 11, 36. *pratyâsanna*, Near, Pańch. 10, 9; imminent, Hit. 115, 15. —With **समा** *sam-â*, **1.** To approach,

Chr. 58, 10. **2.** To encounter, to meet with, Pańch. 120, 9; MBh. 2, 553. **3.** To attack, MBh. 1, 5453. **4.** To find, Pańch. 87, 7; MBh. 1, 2846. **5.** To obtain (*chetanâm*, To recover), Pańch. 58, 19. *samâsâdita*, **1.** Attained. **2.** Obtained, Pańch. 69, 16. **3.** Finished, performed.—With उद् *ud*, **1.** To perish, Bhag. 3, 24. **2.** † To ascend. Caus. **1.** To destroy, Râm. 5, 3, 21. **2.** To draw forth, Man. 9, 267.—With प्रोद् *pra-ud*, Caus. **1.** To destroy, to remove, MBh. 2, 235. **2.** To draw forth, Man. 9, 261.—With समुद् *sam-ud*, Caus. To destroy, MBh. 3, 8832.—With उप *upa*, **1.** To approach. **2.** To worship, Lass. 100, 1 = Rigv. vii. 15, 1.—With नि *ni*, **1.** To sit down, Râm. 1, 20, 14; Pańch. 8, 18 (to fall down); to plunge, Vikr. d. 41. **2.** To be afflicted, MBh. 3, 333. *Nishaṇṇa*, **1.** Sitting, Daçak. in Chr. 184, 7. **2.** Placed in. **3.** Reclined, supported, Vikr. 64, 12. **4.** Gone to. Caus. To cause to sit down, to kneel, Mâlat. 91, 9.—With संनि *sam-ni*, **1.** To sink down, Chr. 31, 15. **2.** To sit down, MBh. 1, 8077 (*saṁnishîdatuḥ*, corr. °*shedatuḥ*).—With प्र *pra*, **1.** To be propitious, gracious, Vikr. d. 39 (for the transition to this signification, cf. inclined, Lat. propensus, Germ. geneigt); to favour, MBh. 1, 1259. **2.** To be soothed, Vikr. 72, 5; Hit. ii. d. 150. **3.** To be calm, Man. 2, 54; to be glad, Mâlat. 46, 12. **4.** To become clear, Man. 6, 67. *prasanna*, **1.** Favourable, soothed, Pańch. 223, 9; kind, Vikr. d. 53; propitious, Chr. 39, 5. **2.** Quiet, Daçak. in Chr. 200, 6. **3.** Pleased. **4.** Clear, Nal. 12, 112. **5.** True, Mâlat. 20, 3. f. *nâ*, Spirituous liquor. Caus. **1.** To propitiate, Vikr. d. 54; Râm. 1, 66, 24. **2.** To soothe, Man. 11, 205. **3.** To solicit, to beg, Râm. 1, 45, 9 Gorr.; to beg pardon, Pańch. 223, 11. *prasâdita*, **1.** Worshipped. **2.** Reconciled, Chr. 42, 15. **3.** Cleansed, purified.—With अभिप्र *abhi-pra*, Caus. To soothe, MBh. 3, 14063.—With संप्र *sam-pra*, To be soothed, Râm. 2, 26, 34. Caus. To propitiate, MBh. 3, 14039.—With वि *vi*, **1.** To be exhausted, MBh. 3, 448. **2.** To be afflicted, Bhag. 1, 28. **3.** To be sorrowful, MBh. 3, 3075. **4.** To despair, Hit. 82, 18. *vishaṇṇa*, Dejected, Vikr. 43, 2; sad, Râm. 1, 40, 24; desponding, spiritless. **Comp.** *Su-*, adj. very sad, Râm. 3, 50, 28. Caus. To afflict, Râm. 2, 53, 31.—With सम् *sam*, To be in distress, Pańch. ii. d. 24; to pine, Man. 4. 33.—Cf. ὁδός, probably, Goth. sinths; A.S. in-sidhian, To enter (=*sâdaya*?); οὐδος, ἔδεθλον; Lat. solum; ἕδος, ἕζομαι; Lat. sedeo; Goth. sitan; A.S. on-settan, sittan; ἵζω (=*sid*+*yâmi*); Lat. sidere, probably de-sidero, sella (i.e. sed+la); Goth. sitls; O.H.G. sezal; A.S. sadl, sadel; O.H.G. satul; ἱδρύω.

2. ऽसद् *-sad*, latter part of comp. words, Sitting, dwelling; e.g. *aranya-*, adj. Living in forests, Utt. Râmach. 133, 6. *âçrama-*, m. An anchorite, Çâk. 28, 11. *gagaṇa-*, m. An inhabitant of the air, Çiç. 4, 53.

सद *sada*, see *çada*.

सदन *sad*+*ana*, n. **1.** A house, Pańch. ii. d. 64; a palace, Pańch. i. d. 352. **2.** Decaying, perishing. **3.** Exhaustion. **4.** Water.—**Comp.** *Râjasadana*, i.e. *râjan-*, m. a palace.

सदस् *sad*+*as*, n. **1.** Seat, abode, Chr. 291, 2 = Rigv. i. 85, 2. **2.** (and m.), Assembly, Hit. i. d. 32, M.M.—Cf. ἕδος.

सदसदात्मक *sadasadâtmaka*, i. e. *sant* (ptcple. pres. of 1. *as*), *-a-sant -âtman* + *ka*, adj. Being both existent and not existent, Man. 1, 11; 74.

सदस्य *sadas* + *ya*, m. **1.** An assistant at a sacrifice, Çâk. 32, 11. **2.** Any person present or belonging to an assembly, Râm. 1, 13, 23.

सदा *sa* + *dâ*, adv. Always, Pańch. i. d. 48.

सदातन *sadâ* + *tana*, **I.** adj. Eternal. **II.** m. Vishṇu.

सदानन्द *sadânanda*, i. e. *sadâ-ânanda*, **I.** adj. Always happy. **II.** m. A proper name, Vedântas. in Chr. 219, 16.

सदृक्ष *sadṛiksha*, i.e. *sa-dṛiç* + *sa*, and **सदृश्** *sa-dṛiç*, adj. Like, similar.

सदृश *sa-dṛiç* + *a*, adj., f. *çî*, **1.** Like, Vikr. 36, 10; similar, Pańch. 165, 18; of the same rank, Pańch. iii. d. 219. **2.** Conformable, Çâk. 7, 4; fit, Hit. ii. d. 47; proper, right, suitable, Utt. Râmach. 166, 6. **3.** Worthy, Utt. Râmach. 41, 6.—**Comp.** *A-*, adj. unbecoming, Râm. 3, 49, 10. *An-anya-*, adj. not having their like, surpassing all others, Pańch. 4, 24.

सद्मन् *sad* + *man*, n. **1.** A house, a dwelling, Kir. 5, 30. **2.** A temple, Râjat. 5, 158 (read *çûra-sadm°*). **3.** Water.—**Comp.** *Deva-*, n. the seat of the gods, MBh. 1, 3687. *Bhoga-*, n. the zenana. *Sura-*, n. heaven.

सद्यस् *sadyas*, i.e. *sa-div* + *as* (abl.-gen. of *div*), adv. **1.** To-day, Utt. Râmach. 90, 7. **2.** Instantly, Pańch. 175, 1; in an instant, on a sudden, Vikr. d. 154.

सद्यस्क *sadyas* + *ka*, adj. New, recent.

सद्रु *sad* + *ru*, adj. **1.** Resting, staying. **2.** Going.—Cf. probably ἱδρυ in ἱδρύνω.

सद्वंद्व *sa-dvańdva*, adj. Litigating, disunited, Hit. iii. d. 34.

सद्वसथ *sadvasatha*, i.e. *sant* (ptcple. pres. of 1. *as*), *-vas* + *atha*, m. A village.

सधिस् *sadhis*, m. An ox.

सध्र्यञ्च् *sadhryańch*, i.e. *sa* + *trâ -ańch* (*t* changed to *dh*, by the influence of *r*, and *â* to *i*, in analogy with the change of final *â* before *as*, *kṛi*, *bhû*), **I.** adj., f. *richî*, Accompanying, a companion. **II.** f. *richî*, A woman's female friend. **III.** *°yak*, adv. Together with, Bhâg. P. 2, 7, 48 (united with themselves).

सन् *SAN*, i. 1, Par., ii. 8, Par. Âtm. **1.** † To honour. **2.** To obtain. **3.** To give. Desider. *sishâsa*, To wish to obtain (aid), Chr. 296, 5. = Rigv. i. 112, 5.

सनत् *sanat*, see the next.

सनद् *sa* + *na* + *d* (properly acc. sing. n. of *sa* + *na*, adj. ved. Old, eternal (see *sanâtana*), adv. Always.—Cf. Goth. sins, ἕνη; Goth. sineigs; Lat. senex.

सना *sa* + *nâ* (properly an old instr. sing. of *sana*; cf. *sanad*), adv. Always, perpetually.—Cf. A.S. sin.

सनात् *sanât* (abl. sing. of *sana*, see the last), adv. Always, perpetually, Bhâg. P. 2, 7, 5.

सनातन *sanâ* + *tana*, **I.** adj., f. *nî*. **1.** Perpetual, eternal, Man. 1, 7; Pańch. ii. d. 112. **2.** Firm, permanent. **3.** Primeval, Man. 1, 22 (ordained from the beginning); 3, 284. **II.** m. Vishṇu, Bhaṭṭ. 1, 1; Çiva, Brahman. **III.** f. *nî*, Lakshmî, Durgâ, Sarasvatî.—Cf. Goth. sinteins, sinteino.

सनाथता *sa-nâtha+tâ*, f. State of having a protector, Pańch. iii. d. 221.

सनि *san + i*, I. m. **1.** Worship, service. **2.** Giving, donation. II. m., f., and *nî*, f. A respectful solicitation. III. f. *nî*, A quarter or point of the compass.

सनिष्ठेव *sanishṭheva*, i.e. *sa-ni-shṭhiv +a*, n. Speech uttered with saliva.

सनुतर् *sanutar*, probably *sânu+tar*, adv. In a concealing manner, Chr. 295, 11=Rigv. i. 92, 11.

सन्त् *sant*, see 1. *as*.

संतक्षण *saṁtakshaṇa*, i.e. *sam-taksh +ana*, n. Sarcastic language, scoff, Daçak. in Chr. 180, 24.

संतति *saṁtati*, i.e. *sam-tan+ti*, f. **1.** Continuity, Mâlat. 14, 16. **2.** Continuous line, line, Pańch. 182, 17. **3.** Extent, multitude, Kir. 5, 17. **4.** Race, lineage. **5.** Offspring, Utt. Râmach. 166, 8; Hit. 67, 9; a son, a daughter.—Comp. *Kula-*, f. propagation of family, Man. 5, 159.

संतर्पण *saṁtarpaṇa*, i.e. *sam-tṛip+ana*, n. **1.** Satiating. **2.** Satisfying. **3.** Gratifying, delighting, Utt. Râmach. 23, 13; Mâlat. 95, 7.

संतान *saṁtâna*, i.e. *sam-tan+a*, m. (n., Draup. 5, 88), **1.** Spreading, Utt. Râmach. 50, 10; Hit. i. d. 206, M.M. (extending their influence from one existence to another); extension, Çâk. d. 167. **2.** Being spread, having grown, Utt. Râmach. 97, 13 (*-vâhin*, old). **3.** Family, race, lineage, Draup. 5, 88. **4.** Progeny, Man. 3, 15. **5.** A son, a daughter, Hit. iv. d. 109. **6.** One of the trees of heaven.

संतानिका *saṁtânikâ*, i.e. *saṁtâna +ka*, f. **1.** Froth. **2.** Cream. **3.** A cobweb. **4.** The blade of a knife or sword.

संताप *saṁtâpa*, i.e. *sam-tap+a*, m. **1.** Heat, Mâlat. 17, 9 (figurat.); fire, Utt. Râmach. 141, 10; Pańch. i. d. 392. **2.** Affliction, Pańch. ii. d. 59. **3.** Pain, Vikr. 55, 20; distress. **4.** Passion. **5.** Repentance, Pańch. v. d. 16. **6.** Penance, Kir. 5, 50.

संतापन *saṁtâpana*, i. e. *sam-tap*, Caus., *+ana*, I. adj. Burning. II. m. One of the arrows of Kâmadeva. III. n. **1.** Burning. **2.** Paining, afflicting. **3.** Exciting passion.

सन्ति *san+ti*, f. **1.** End, destruction. **2.** Gift, giving.

संतोष *saṁtosha*, i. e. *sam-tush+a*, m. **1.** Contentedness, Pańch. ii. d. 163; satisfaction; with *kṛi*, To be satisfied, Pańch. 136, 12; to be content, Pańch. 139, 17. **2.** Joy. **3.** Thumb and fore-finger.—Comp. *A-*, m. pain, Mâlat. 94, 10.

संतोषण *saṁtoshaṇa*, i.e. *sam-tush +ana*, n. **1.** Pleasing. **2.** Comforting.

संतोषवन्त् *saṁtosha+vant*, adj., f. *vatî*, Content.—Comp. *A-*, adj. not content, Pańch. ii. d. 163.

संत्रास *saṁtrâsa*, i.e. *sam-tras+a*, m. Fear, Johns. Sel. 27, 16; Râjat. 5, 224.

संदंश *saṁdaṁça*, i.e. *sam-daṁç+a*, m. A pair of tongs, Pańch. 52, 8 (*sva-daçana-*, His claws which are like a pair of nippers).

संदंशक *saṁdaṁça+ka*, I. m. A pair of tongs, Daçak. in Chr. 186, 10. II. f. *çikâ*. **1.** A pair of nippers, or small shears or tongs. **2.** A vice.

संदर्भ *saṁdarbha*, i.e. *sam-dṛibh+*

a, m. **1.** Weaving garlands. **2.** Stringing, collecting. **3.** Uniting, mixture, Utt. Râmach. 170, 2. **4.** Work, Utt. Râmach. 111, 3.

संदर्शन *saṁdarçana*, i.e. *sam-dṛiç* + *ana*, n. **1.** Seeing each other, meeting, Pañch. 109, 22; 161, 14. **2.** Looking, sight, presence, Chr. 25, 60. **3.** Consideration, Hit. 129, 10. **4.** Appearance, Vikr. 78, 19; *saṁdarçanaṁ gam*, To appear, Pañch. 235, 10. **5.** Vision, Megh. 105. **6.** Showing.

संदान *saṁdâna*, i.e. I. *sam-* 3. *dâ* + *ana*, n. A rope, a cord (especially for tieing cattle). II. *sam-dâna*, m. The elephant's temples, or part whence the ichorous fluid issues.

संदानित *saṁdânita*, i.e. *saṁdâna* + *ita*, adj. Bound, Mâlav. 41, 13.

संदानिनी *saṁdâninî*, i.e. *saṁdâna* + *in* + *î*, f. A cow-house.

संदाव *saṁdâva* (cf. *dûta*, *dûra*; but probably it is rather a Prâkṛit form of *saṁdrâva*), m. Flight.

संदीपन *saṁdîpana*, i.e. *sam-dîp* + *ana*, I. n. Inflaming, Ṛit. 1, 12; inflammation (of wrath), Utt. Râmach. 116, 10. II. m. One of Kâmadeva's arrows, Lass. 7, 3.

संदूषण *saṁdûshaṇa*, i.e. *sam-dush*, Caus., + *ana*, n. A vice which causes infamy, Man. 9, 13.

संदेश *saṁdeça*, i.e. *sam-diç* + *a*, m. **1.** Information, news, tidings, Pañch. 162, 3; Kathâs. 17, 161. **2.** Commission, Megh. 97. **3.** Command, Vikr. 86, 17.

संदेशक *saṁdeça* + *ka* (m.), n. Information, Pañch. 51, 21.

संदेशहर *saṁdeçahara*, and **संदेशहारक** *saṁdeçahâraka*, i.e. *saṁdeça* -*hṛi* + *a*, and -*hṛi*, Caus., + *aka*, m. A messenger.

संदेह *saṁdeha*, i.e. *sam-dih* + *a*, m. **1.** Doubt, Pañch. iv. d. 25; uncertainty. **2.** Danger, Pañch. i. d. 192.—Comp. *Nis-*, I. adj. doubtless. II. °*ham*, adv. undoubtedly, Somad. Nal. 127.

संदेहदोलास्थ *saṁdeha-dolâ-stha*, adj. Moved by doubt, as by a swing, Hit. iv. d. 18.

संदोह *saṁdoha*, i.e. *sam-duh* + *a*, m. Assemblage, multitude.

संद्राव *saṁdrâva*, i.e. *sam-dru* + *a*, m. Flight.

संधा *saṁdhâ*, i.e. *sam-dhâ*, f. **1.** Agreement, promise, Daçak. in Chr. 195, 19. **2.** Intimate union. **3.** State, condition. **4.** Stipulation, Lass. 2. ed. 91, 54. **5.** Steadiness, fixedness. **6.** Twilight.—Comp. *Jala-saṁdha*, m. a proper name, Johns. Sel. 24, 6. *Jarâ-saṁdha*, m. a proper name, ib. 49, 91. *Satya-saṁdha*, I. adj. 1. veracious, adhering to truth, Chr. 12, 1. 2. faithful to his promise, Man. 7, 31. II. m. 1. Bharata. 2. Janamejaya. III. f. *dhâ*, Draupadî. *A-satya-saṁdha*, adj. treacherous, Hit. i. d. 78, M.M.

संधान *saṁdhâna*, i.e. *sam-dhâ* + *ana*, I. n. **1.** Uniting, Hit. iii. d. 119 (*bhinna-* [vb. *bhid*], Uniting what is disunited); joining. **2.** Fixing (the arrow to the bow), Çâk. d. 52. **3.** Tieing, binding. **4.** Peace, alliance. **5.** Association, union, Pañch. iii. d. 10; Çâk. d. 9. **6.** Company. **7.** Mixing. **8.** A relish, something eaten to excite thirst. **9.** Pickles. **10.** Sour rice-gruel. **11.** Spirituous liquor. **12.** Supporting. **13.** Receiving. **14.** Contracting the skin, etc., by astringent applications. **II.** n., and f. *nî*, Distillation. **III.** f. *ni*, A foundry.—**Comp.** *Ati-*, n. deceit (v.r. *abhi-*, better), Çâk. d. 121. *Abhi-*, n. 1. speech, Râm. 5, 51, 21. 2. deceit, Ragh. 17, 76. *Dus-*, adj. difficult to be united, Hit. i. d. 91, M.M.

संधानित *saṁdhanita*, i.e. *saṁdhâna + ita*, adj. **1.** Strung together. **2.** Bound, tied.

संधि *saṁdhi*, i.e. *sam-dhâ* (cf. *nidhi*), m. **1.** Union, junction, Pañch. 210, 13; Megh. 59 (joint, structure of a mountain). **2.** Alliance, Man. 7, 163. **3.** Peace, Man. 7, 56. **4.** Making peace, a treaty, Hit. i. d. 87, M.M. **5.** A joint, an articulation of the body, Ṛit. 1, 7; Hit. iv. d. 63 (but cf. Böhtl. Ind. Spr. 1842). **6.** A fold, Pañch. 62, 13. **7.** The euphonic union of the final and initial letters of words or parts of a comp. **8.** An interval, a pause or rest. **9.** A period at the expiration of each Yuga or age, MBh. 12, 12953. **10.** A hole, a chasm, especially in a wall, for felonious purposes, a breach, Man. 9, 276; Daçak. in Chr. 186, 12. **11.** Breaking, dividing, division, Lass. 87, 5. **12.** The vulva.—**Comp.** *Kapâla-*, m. a peace on equal terms, Hit. iv. d. 108. *Dhruva-*, m. a proper name, Râm. 1, 70, 26 Gorr. *Pada-*, m. =**7.** Râm. 1, 3, 60 Gorr. *Parvasaṁdhi*, i.e. *parvan-*, m. the time of the periodic change of the moon, MBh. 3, 11647. *Sam-gata-* (vb. *gam*), m. a peace concluded after having before made friendship, Hit. iv. d. 109. *Saṁtâna-*, m. a peace concluded after having given one's daughter (in marriage), Hit. iv. d. 109. *Sama-*, f. alliance or peace on equal terms. *Su-kara-*, adj. easy to be joined or united, Pañch. ii. d. 36.

संधित *saṁdhita*, i.e. *saṁdhâ* and *saṁdhi*, + *ita*, **I.** adj. **1.** Tied, bound, Man. 8, 342. **2.** United, Pañch. i. d. 130; reconciled. **3.** Pickled. **II.** n. Pickles. —**Comp.** *A-*, adj. unbound, Man. 8, 342. *Ati-*, see under *dhâ*. *Sama-*, adj. 1. allied on equal terms (cf. the last). 2. bound equally. *Su-*, adj. well reconciled, Pañch. iii. d. 24.

ऽसंधितस् *saṁdhi + tas*, in *sama-*, adv. From an alliance on equal terms, Hit. iv. d. 108.

संधिनी *saṁdhinî*, i.e. *saṁdha + in + î*, f. **1.** A cow with calf, or one which has taken a bull, Man. 5, 8. **2.** One who is milked unseasonably.

संधुक्षण *saṁdhukshaṇa*, i.e. *sam-dhuksh + ana*, n. Inflaming, Daçak. in Chr. 180, 23.

संध्या *saṁdhyâ*, f., i.e. **I.** *saṁdhi + ya*, **1.** Twilight, either morning or evening, Man. 2, 101; Râm. 3, 51, 5; Pañch. i. d. 198; evening, Mâlat. 41, 16. **2.** The period between the expiration of one Yuga, or age, and the commencement of another, Man. 1, 69. **3.** Holy rites of morning, noon, and evening, Man. 2, 69. **4.** Evening prayer, Vikr. 37, 9; MBh. 1, 1890. **5.** Promise, agreement. **6.** Joining, union. **7.** Boundary. **8.** A particular flower. **9.** The name of a river. **II.** *sam-dhyai*, Reflection.—**Comp.** *Agra-*, f. dawn, Çâk. d. 78 (v.r.). *Upa-saṁdhya + m*, adv. near twilight, Çiç. 9, 5. *Tri-saṁdhya*, n. morning, noon, and evening, MBh. 3, 4063. *Sa-saṁdhya*, adj. 1. vespertine. 2. with the period following the end of a Yuga (see **2.**), Man. 1, 70 (see the next).

संध्यांश *saṁdhyâṁça*, i.e. *saṁdhyâ-aṁça*, m. **1.** Twilight. **2.** The period at the end of each Yuga, Man. 1, 70 (*saṁdhyâṁça* is perhaps especially the twilight following the expiring Yuga, and *saṁdhyâ* that which precedes the commencing Yuga).

संध्यातृ *saṁdhyâtṛi*, Man. 8, 342, m. One who binds, v.r. *saṁdâtṛi*, better.

संध्यात्व *saṁdhyâ + tva*, n. The time of twilight and devotion, Daçak. in Chr. 184, 2.

संनति *saṁnati*, i.e. *sam-nam + ti*, f. **1.** Reverence, reverential salutation. **2.** Humility, Râm. 1, 46, 9. **3.** Sound.

संनय *saṁnaya*, i.e. *sam-nî + a*, m. **1.** Multitude, Johns. Sel. 53, 126; number, quantity. **2.** Rear, rear-guard.

संनहन *saṁnahana*, i.e. *sam-nah + ana*, n. Arming, preparing, making one's self ready, Râm. 4, 15, 20.—Comp. *Sarva-*, n. assembling a complete army.

संनाम *saṁnâma*, i.e. *sam-nam + a*, m. Worship, Nalod. 1, 3.

संनाह *saṁnâha*, i.e. *sam-nah + a*, m. Armour, mail, Johns. Sel. 26, 10.—Comp. *Vi-*, adj. without a coat of mail, Man. 7, 92. *Sarva-*, 1. arming or assembling a complete army. 2. the Universal Spirit.

संनाह्य *saṁnâhya*, i.e. *saṁnâha + ya*, m. A war elephant.

संनिकर्ष *saṁnikarsha*, i.e. *sam-ni -kṛish + a*, m. **1.** Connection, relation, Bhâshâp. 62, 131. **2.** Nearness, proximity, Utt. Râmach. 151, 11; Pańch. i. d. 157.

संनिकर्षण *saṁnikarshaṇa*, i.e. *sam--ni-kṛish + ana*, n. **1.** Approximation, approaching. **2.** Proximity.

संनिधातृ *saṁnidhâtṛi*, i.e. *sam-ni dhâ + tṛi*, m. **1.** A receiver of stolen goods, Man. 9, 278. **2.** One who places near, who introduces, the name of a court officer, Pańch. 156, 17.

संनिधान *saṁnidhâna*, i.e. *sam-ni -dhâ + ana*, n., and **संनिधि** *saṁnidhi*, i.e. *sam-nidhâ* (cf. *nidhi*), m. **1.** Proximity, Hit. pr. d. 41, M.M. (*dhâna*); Pańch. v. d. 42 (*dhi*). **2.** Perceptibility, appearance, presence, Vikr. 19, 1 (*dhâna*); Hit. i. d. 113, M.M. (*dhi*); Bhartṛ. 2, 99 (*saṁnidhi-ratna-pûrṇa*, Full of jewels in close neighbourhood, i.e. round about himself, easily to be caught). **3.** Placing, depositing, a receptacle, Pańch. i. d. 204 (*dhâna*). **4.** Receiving, taking charge of.—Comp. *Kula-saṁnidhi*, m. the presence of a company, Man. 8, 194.

संनिपात *saṁnipâta*, i.e. *sam-ni-pat + a*, m. **1.** Contact, collision, Bhâshâp. 116; Kir. 5, 36. **2.** Assemblage, multitude. **3.** Morbid state of the three humours, Pańch. i. d. 193. **4.** Alighting, descending. **5.** Arrival. **6.** Union, junction. **7.** Mixture, Megh. 5; miscellaneous collection.

संनिबन्धन *saṁnibandhana*, i.e. *sam -ni-bandh + ana*, n. Tieing fast.

संनिभ *saṁnibha*, i.e. *sam-ni-bhâ*, adj. Like, similar, Pańch. i. d. 374; iii. d. 140.

संनियन्तृ *saṁniyantṛi*, i.e. *sam-ni -yam + tṛi*, m., f. *trî*, and n. Who or what chastises, Man. 9, 320.

संनिवृत्ति *saṁnivṛitti*, i.e. *sam-ni -vṛit + ti*, f. **1.** Return, Çâk. d. 137. **2.** Restraint, forbearance.

संनिवेश *saṁniveça*, i.e. *sam-ni-viç + a*, m. **1.** An open place, either in a town or its vicinity, where the people take exercise; place, Ragh. 6, 19. **2.** Assemblage, multitude, Ragh. 16, 11 (? v.r.). **3.** Vicinity. **4.** Junction, union, Mâlat. 18, 5. **5.** Causing to enter, putting in. 6. Construction, Daçak. in Chr. 198, 13 (*kanyâ-pura-*, of the gynæceum); fabrication, Mâlat. 151, 21.—Comp. *Bhûmi-*, m. the shape, face of a region, Utt. Râmach. 47, 4. *Samâja-*, m. a building for an assembly, Utt. Râmach. 161, 9.

संन्यसन *saṁnyasana*, i. e. *sam-ni -2. as + ana*, n. 1. Abandonment of all worldly affections and possessions, Bhag. 3, 4. 2. Entrusting to.

संन्यास *saṁnyâsa*, i.e. *sam-ni-2. as + a*, m. 1. Abandonment. 2. Abandonment of all worldly affections and possessions, and fixing one's mind only on the Supreme Spirit, Man. 1, 114; 5, 108. 3. Deposit, trust. 4. Stake (in game), Nal. 26, 5. 5. Sudden death. 6. Indian spikenard.

ऽसंन्यासिक *-saṁnyâsika*, i.e. *saṁnyâsin + ka*, in *veda-*, m. An ascetic according to the Veda, Man. 6, 86.

संन्यासिन् *saṁnyâsin*, i.e. *saṁnyâsa + in*, m. 1. One who has abandoned all worldly affections, etc. (see *saṁnyâsa*), Bhag. 5, 3; Lass. 48, 15. 2. The Brâhmaṇa of the fourth order, the religious mendicant. 3. An ascetic.

सन्मातुर *sanmâtura*, i.e. *sant-mâtṛi + a*, m. The son of a virtuous mother.

सन्मान *sanmâna*, i.e. *sant-mâna*, m. Respect for the good.

सप् *SAP*, i. 1, Par. 1. To connect. 2. To worship. — Cf. σέβομαι, σέβας, σεμνός, perhaps ἅπτω (doubtful on account of ἑάφθη, ἄαπτος).

सपत्न *sapatna*, i.e. *sa-patnî + a*, I. adj., f. *nâ*, Hostile, Pañch. i. d. 318. II. m. A foe, Man. 4, 174; cf. *patnî*. —Comp. *A-*, and *nis-*, adj. 1. without a rival, Vikr. d. 85 (*nis-*). 2. uncontested, MBh. 3, 4093 (*a-*).

सपत्राकरण *sapatrâ-kṛi + ana*, n., and **सपत्राकृति** *sapatrâ-kṛi + ti*, f. (cf. *sapatrâ-kṛi*, p. 209), Affliction, excessive agony.

सपदि *sa-pad + i*, adv. 1. Instantly, Pañch. 198, 3. 2. Quickly.

सपर्य *SAPARYA*, a denomin. derived from a lost noun *sapas* = σέβας, in the form **sapan* (with *r* for *n*), with *ya*, Par. To worship (ved.).

सपर्या *saparyâ*, i.e. *saparya + a*, f. Worship, Utt. Râmach. 16, 13.

सपिण्डता *sa-piṇḍa + tâ*, f. The condition of being a *Sapiṇḍa*, Man. 5, 60 (see *sa-piṇḍa*).

सप्तक *saptaka*, i.e. *saptan + ka*, I. adj. 1. Containing seven, Man. 11, 52. 2. Seven. 3. Seventh. II. n. A collection of seven verses, Man. 11, 255. III. f. *ki*, A woman's girdle.—Comp. *Saptasaptaka*, i. e. *saptan-*, n. forty-nine (winds), Râm. 3, 53, 41.

ऽसप्तत *-saptata*, i.e. *saptati + a*, ord. num., f. *tî*, Seventieth; e. g. *eka-*, Seventy-first, MBh. xii. adhy. 71. *dvâ-* or *dvi-*, Seventy-second, MBh. xii. adhy. 72 (*dvâ*); i. adhy. 72 (*dvi*). *tri-*, Seventy-third, ib. xii. adhy. 73. *Chatuḥsaptata*, i. e. *chatur-*, Seventy-fourth, MBh. xii. adhy. 74. *Pañchasaptata*, i.e. *pañchan-*, Seventy-fifth, ib. i. adhy. 75.

सप्तति *saptati*, i.e. *saptan + ti*, numeral, f. Seventy, Man. 1, 79.—Comp. *Eka-*, f. seventy-one, Man. 1, 79. *Dvâ-* or *Dvi-*, f. seventy-two, MBh. xii. adhy. 172 (*dvâ*); Man. 7, 157 (*dvi*). *Pañchas°*, i.e. *pañchan-*, f. seventy-five, MBh. xii. adhy. 175. *Saptas°*, i. e. *saptan-*, f. seventy-seven, Râjat. 5, 221. *Çuka-*, f. seventy tales of a parrot, title of a work, Lass. 38, 6.

सप्ततितम *saptati + tama*, ord. num., f. *mî*, Seventieth, MBh. xii. adhy. 70. —**Comp.** *Dvi-*, seventy-second. *Tri-*, seventy-third, MBh. ii. adhy. 73. *Chatuḥs°*, i.e. *chatur-*, seventy-fourth, Râm. vi. sarga 74. *Navas°*, i.e. *navan-*, seventy-ninth, Râm. vi. sarga 79.

सप्तदश *saptadaça*, i. e. *saptadaçan + a*, or curtailed, ord. num., f. *çî*, Seventeenth, MBh. iv. adhy. 17.

सप्तदशन् *saptadaçan*, i.e. *saptan-daçan*, numeral adj. Seventeen, MBh. v. adhy. 117.

सप्तधा *saptadhâ*, i.e. *saptan + dhâ*, adv. In seven ways, sevenfold.—**Comp.** *Dvi-*, adv. in fourteen parts, Bhâg. P. 3, 10, 8.

सप्तन् *saptan*, numeral adj. Seven, Man. 1, 19.—**Comp.** *Tri-*, adj. twenty-one, MBh. 9, 664. *Pańchasaptan*, i.e. *pańchan-*, adj. thirty-five, Mârk. P. 76, 12. *Saptasaptan*, i.e. *saptan-*, adj. seven and seven (seven ancestors and seven descendants), Man. 1, 105.—Cf. ἑπτά; Lat. septem; Goth. sibun; A.S. seqfon.

सप्तम *saptama*, i.e. *saptan + ma*, **I.** ord. num., f. *mî*, Seventh, MBh. iv. adhy. 7; Lass. 2. ed. 13, 12 (the seventh lunar mansion). **II.** f. *mî*, The seventh day of the fortnight, Râjat. 5, 221.—Cf. Lat. septimus; ἕβδομος.

सप्तर्षि *saptarshi*, i.e. *saptan-ṛishi*, m. pl. **1.** The seven Ṛishis or great saints, *Marîchi*, *Atri*, etc. **2.** The constellation Ursa major.

सप्तला *saptalâ*, f. The name of several plants, e.g. the trumpet-flower, Bignonia suaveolens.

सप्ति *sap + ti*, m. **1.** A span (of horses), united like a span, Chr. 291, 1 = Rigv. i. 85, 1. **2.** A horse.—**Comp.** *Saptasapti*, i. e. *saptan-*, m. the sun (properly, drawn by seven horses), Kir. 5, 34. *Sita-*, m. Arjuna, Kir. 13, 19.

सफर *saphara*, see *çaphara*; **सफल** *saphala*, see *sa-phala*.

सबाध् *sa-bâdh*, adj. Striking with fear, Chr. 290, 8 = Rigv. i. 64, 8.

सभक्तिकम् *sa-bhakti + ka + m*, adv. Respectfully, Lass. 41, 9.

सभा *sabhâ*, f. **1.** An assembly, Man. 8, 11; council, Râm. 2, 63, 36, Seramp. **2.** A much frequented place, Man. 9, 264. **3.** A court of justice, Man. 8, 12; Pańch. iii. d. 109. **4.** A house. **5.** A palace, Johns. Sel. 94, 57; Râjat. 5, 391. —**Comp.** *Râjasabhâ*, i. e. *râjan-*, f. a royal assembly, a court, Lass. 2, 2. *Strî-sabha*, n. an assembly of females. *Hrasva-sabhâ*, f. a small hall; cf. *sabhya*.

सभाज् *SABHÂJ*, i. 10 (rather a denomin. derived from a noun, **sabhâj*, i. e. *sa-bhaj*), Par. **1.** To serve, to worship, Râm. 5, 8, 20. **2.** To honour, to beautify, Utt. Râmach. 105, 5. **3.** † To exhilarate. **4.** † To show.

सभाजन *sabhâj + ana*, n. **1.** Courtesy, politeness. **2.** Honour, Mâlav. 74, 10 (thanks).

सभासद् *sabhâ-sad*, and **सभासद** *sabhâ-sad + a*, m. **1.** An assistant at an assembly, Râm. 2, 5, 24 (*sad*); Pańch. i. d. 336 (*sada*). **2.** A judge, Man. 8, 12 (*sad*).

सभास्तार *sabhâstâra*, i. e. *sabhâ-â-stṛi + a*, m. An assistant at an assembly, MBh. 2, 1787.

सभिक *sabhika*, i.e. *sabhâ + ika*, m. The keeper of a gaming-house, Daçak. in Chr. 185, 20; Mṛichchh. 33, 24.

सभ्य *sabhya*, i.e. *sabhâ + ya*, **I.** adj.

1. Relating to an assembly, fit for it, Ragh. 1, 55; polite, Pańch. i. d. 294 (cf. Bhartṛ. 3, 57; *sabhya-itara*, vulgar). **2.** Trusted, faithful. **II.** m. **1.** An assistant at an assembly of scholars, Râjat. 5, 32; of courtiers, 86; of judges, Pańch. 40, 23. **2.** A person of honourable parentage, Bhaṭṭ. 1, 13. **3.** The keeper of a gaming-house. **4.** The servant of a keeper of a gaming-house (?), Daçak. in Chr. 186, 4.—Cf. O.H.G. sibba; A.S. sib, sibbe, ge-sib; Goth. trasti-sibja, adoptatio, ga-sibjôn, reconciliare, un-sibja, iniqua; O.H.G. sibbi, sibbo, ga-sibbo, ga-sibbôt.

सभ्यता *sabhya* + *tâ*, f. Politeness.

† 1. **सम्** *SAM*, **स्तम्** *STAM*, i. 1, Par. **1.** To be unconfused. **2.** To be confused. i. 10, *samaya*, *stamaya*, Par. To be confused.

2. **सम्** *sa* + *m* (acc. sing. n. of *sa*), **1.** prep. With, only in the Veda, Chr. 290, 8 = Rigv. i. 64, 8. **2.** Combined and compounded with verbs and their derivatives, and compounded with nouns, With, together, much, very, wholly, beautifully. When followed by a prefix, it is generally without a special signification; e.g. *sam-ud-kship*, Pańch. 43, 8.

सम *sa* + *ma*, **I.** adj. **1.** Even, plain, Çâk. 5, 14; Pańch. ii. d. 188. **2.** Same, Hit. 116, 18. **3.** Equal, MBh. 10, 622; *samaṅ kṛi*, To balance, to pay, Man. 8, 177. **4.** Convenient, Böhtl. Ind. Spr. 1880; Nalod. 4, 8 (voice, neither too low nor too loud). **5.** Straight, Çâk. d. 9. **6.** Looking on unmoved, (with gen. and loc.), MBh. 1, 1061; 1942. **7.** Impartial, indifferent, Lass. 6, 16. **8.** Mean, common, Man. 7, 85; Hit. pr. d. 42, M.M. (not pre-eminent). **9.** Like, similar, Chr. 8, 27 (*mayâ*, Like myself). **10.** Good, Chr. 12, 28; virtuous. **11.** A purchaser at a fair price, Man. 9, 287. **12.** Full, complete. **13.** All, whole, entire (follows the pronominal declension). **II.** °*mam*, **A.** adv. **1.** With (with instr.), Râjat. 5, 216; together, Çiç. 9, 24; Vikr. 88, 17. **2.** Equally, Hit. iii. d. 49; Vedântas. in Chr. 208, 18. **3.** Like, Johns. Sel. 15, 55 (with loc. ?). **4.** In the same way, Çiç. 9, 44. **5.** Conformable to, Pańch. 25, 14. **6.** Entirely, ib. 63, 1. **B.** prep. (with instr.), With, Hit. i. d. 79, M.M.; together with, Pańch. ii. d. 200. **III.** f. *mâ*, A year, Man. 4, 26. **IV.** n. Level plain, Man. 1, 24.—**Comp.** *A*-, 1. uneven, Kir. 5, 7. 2. unequal, Man. 10, 73. 3. incomparable, Kathâs. 23, 32. *Chatuḥsama*, i.e. *chatur*-, adj. having four even or smooth (members of the body), Râm. 5, 32, 13.—Cf. Goth. sama, and sama-, e.g. in sama-frathjis; A.S. same, sam-; Goth. samana; A.S. somne, samne; Goth. samath; A.S. sámod; Goth. sums, and A.S. sum, quidam; Lat. similis, simul, semel, sem-per, singuli; ὁμός, ὁμοῖος, ὅμοιος, ὁμαλός, ἁμᾶ, ἅμα, μία, μέν (cf. *sa*).

समक्षम् *sam-aksha* + *m*, adv. Eye to eye, in presence of, Çâk. 97, 10; Hit. 99, 10; Mâlat. 47, 3.

समग्र *sam-agra*, adj. **1.** Entire, complete, Megh. 57; full, Hiḍ. 3, 13. **2.** All, Râm. 3, 49, 37.—**Comp.** *A*-, adj. not full-grown, Vikr. d. 124.

समचित्तत्व *sama-chitta* + *tva*, n. **1.** Equanimity. **2.** Indifference.

समज *sam-aj* + *a*, **I.** m. **1.** A multitude of beasts. **2.** A number of blockheads. **II.** n. A forest.

समज्ञा *sama-jñâ*, f. Fame, reputation.

समज्या *sam-aj* + *yâ*, f. An assembly.

समञ्जस *samańjasa*, i.e. *sam-ańjas*

(cf. *añjasâ*), + *a*, I. adj. **1.** Proper, right, fit, Johns. Sel. 5, 28 (*na-ati-*, Not very proper, f. *sâ*; MBh. 1, 5832, f. *sî*). **2.** Correct, true. **3.** Virtuous, good, Kir. 14, 12. **4.** Experienced. II. n. **1.** Propriety. **2.** Correct evidence, Man. 8, 256.—**Comp.** *A-*, I. adj. unfit, unskilled, Utt. Râmach. 95, 12; incorrect, Mâlat. 162, 10. II. *sam*, adv. unbecomingly, MBh. 2, 2100. III. n. impropriety, an abominable act, Pañch. in Weber, Ind. St. iii. 371, 15.

समता *sama* + *tâ*, f. **1.** Sameness, similarity. **2.** Equality, Pañch. ii. d. 90 (*sva-jâti-samatâm gata*, Grown equal to his kind). **3.** State of a common (not pre-eminent) person, Hit. pr. d. 42, M.M. **4.** Equanimity, Man. 6, 44. **5.** Right decision, Man. 8, 178. **6.** Perfectness, Pañch. v. d. 83.

समतिक्रम *sam-ati-kram* + *a*, m. **1.** Transgressing. **2.** Omission, Man. 11, 203.

समत्व *sama* + *tva*, n. **1.** Equality, Bhag, 2, 48. **2.** Identity, Pañch. i. d. 468.

समधिक *sam-adhika*, adj. **1.** Exceeding, Megh. 100. **2.** Abundant, plentiful, Utt. Râmach. 90, 4.

समन *samana*, probably *sam-an* + *a*, m. **1.** Zeal. **2.** A diligent man, Chr. 287, 6=Rigv. i. 48, 6.

समनुज्ञान *samanujñâna*, i.e. *sam-anu-jñâ* + *ana*, n. **1.** Assent. **2.** Permission.

समनुव्रत *sam-anu-vrata*, adj. Entirely devoted to, Nal. 13, 55 (with acc.).

समन्त *sam-anta*, I. adj. **1.** From every part, Böhtl. Ind. Spr. 1446; entire. **2.** All. II. Abl. *tât*, adv. **1.** From every part, Pañch. 51, 18. **2.** All round, on every side, Mâlat. 158, 4; Pañch. 230, 16; Chr. 4, 20. **3.** Completely, Pañch. 148, 12. III. m. Limit, boundary.

समन्ततस् *samanta* + *tas*, adv. **1.** All round, on every side, Hit. ii. d. 158. **2.** Wholly, Man. 3, 58.

समन्वय *samanvaya*, i.e. *sam-anu-i* + *a*, m. **1.** Natural succession. **2.** Connected sequence, consequence, Lass. 2. ed. 46, 31. **3.** Conjunction with each other, Bhâg. P. 3, 26, 49.

समभिसरण *samabhisaraṇa*, i. e. *sam-abhi-sṛi* + *ana*, n. **1.** Approaching. **2.** Seeking. **3.** Endeavouring to gain.

समभिहार *samabhihâra*, i. e. *sam-abhi-hṛi* + *a*, m. **1.** Repetition. **2.** Excess, surplus.

सममय *sama* + *maya*, adj., f. *yî*, Proceeding from the same cause.

समय *samaya*, i.e. *sam-i* + *a*, m. **1.** Agreement, Pañch. 193, 13; treaty, Pañch. 24, 25; contract, bargain. **2.** Engagement, Chr. 58, 2; appointment. **3.** Religious obligation, Böhtl. Ind. Spr. 304. **4.** Established moral or ceremonial custom, Chr. 19, 4. **5.** Rule, Man. 9, 273; law, Hit. ii. d. 45, M.M. **6.** Condition, Nal. 13, 67. **7.** Order, instruction. **8.** Oath, Sâv. 4, 17. **9.** Sign, hint, indication. **10.** Proper time for anything, season, Kir. 2, 28. **11.** Opportunity, leisure. **12.** Time, Vikr. 56, 1; Pañch. 229, 10. **13.** Same time, Chr. 7, 15. **14.** Limit, boundary. **15.** Demonstrated conclusion, and conclusion in general, Daçak. in Chr. 180, 8.—**Comp.** *Ṛitu-*, m. season proper for conception, Pañch. 74, 18. *Yathâ-samaya* + *m*, adv. according to established custom, Johns. Sel. 10, 20. *Lagna-*, m. auspicious time, Pañch. 129, 16.

समया *samayâ*, adv. and prep. with

acc., I. (old instr. of *sama*). **1.** Within, midst. **2.** Near, Vârt. ad Pâṇ. ii. 3, 2; Nalod. 4, 8. **II.** (old instr. of *samaya*). **1.** At a fixed time. **2.** Seasonably, in due time.—Cf. ἁμᾷ, ἅμα.

समयाध्युषित *samayâdhyushita*, i.e. *samaya-adhyushita* (vb. 1. *vas*, with *adhi*), n. A time at which neither stars nor sun are visible, Man. 2, 15.

समर *samara*, i.e. *sam-ṛi+a*, **I.** m. and n. War, battle, Hit. 106, 10. **II.** m. A proper name, Râjat. 5, 25.

समर्थ *sam-artha*, **I.** adj., f. *thâ*. **1.** Proper, fit, Pañch. 169, 10. **2.** Allowed, Man. 4, 186. **3.** Made proper, prepared, Pañch. 121, 24. **4.** Able, Hit. 31, 3, M.M.; adequate to. **5.** Strong, powerful, Pañch. iii. d. 54. **6.** Connected in sense. **II.** m. The construction of words.—**Comp.** *A-*, adj. 1. not adequate, Vedântas. in Chr. 215, 11. 2. unable, Hit. 32, 4, M.M. *Ati-*, adj. very strong, Hit. 83, 13.

समर्थता *samartha+tâ*, f. **1.** Adequacy. **2.** Ability. **3.** Strength, power. **4.** Signification of terms.

समर्थन *sam-arth+ana*, m. **1.** Reconciling differences, allaying a dispute. **2.** Perseverance in an arduous undertaking. **3.** Deliberation, deciding on the propriety or impropriety of anything. **4.** Objecting, objection.

समर्धक *samardhaka*, i. e. *sam-ṛidh +aka*, adj. Granting a boon.

समर्पण *samarpaṇa*, i.e. *sam-ṛi*, Caus., *+ana*, n. Delivering, consigning, handing over, Kathâs. 4, 109; Râjat. 5, 299.

समवतार *samavatâra*, i.e. *sam-ava -tṛî+a*, m. A place of pilgrimage at a sacred stream, Kir. 5, 7.

समवस्था *sam-ava-sthâ*, f. State, Çâk. 39, 20.

समवाय *samavâya*, i.e. *sam-ava-i+a*, m. **1.** Multitude, Pañch. 130, 7; aggregate; meeting, Daçak. in Chr. 180, 14. **2.** Assembly, Man. 4, 108. **3.** Intimate and constant relation, Bhâshâp. 1, 58; as of yarn and the cloth made of it, the individual and its species, etc. **4.** Intimate union, Çâk. 108, 10; union, Pañch. i. d. 376.

समवायिन् *samavâyin*, i.e. *sama-vâya+in*, **I.** adj. **1.** Aggregated. **2.** Connected intimately, Bhâshâp. 16; 17. **II.** n. Intimate and inseparable cause, as thread of cloth.—**Comp.** *A-*, adj. the non-intimate cause, as the conjunction of two halves for a jar, Sch. ad Bhâshâp. 17.

समष्टि *samashṭi*, i.e. *sam-aksh+ti*, f. Totality, Vedântas. in Chr. 204, 13.

समसन *sam-as+ana*, n. **1.** Combination. **2.** Formation of compound terms. **3.** Contraction.

समस्थ *sama-stha*, adj. **1.** Even. **2.** Like, similar.

समस्या *sam- 2.as+yâ* (fem. of the ptcple. fut. pass. of *sam- 2.as*), f. **1.** The part of a stanza given to another person to complete it. **2.** The giving to another person part of a stanza, and requiring him to complete it.

समांश *samâṁça*, i.e. *sama-aṁça*, **I.** m. An equal part. **II.** adj. Entitled to an equal share.

समांशिन् *samâṁçin*, i.e. *samâṁça +in*, adj. sbst. A co-heir, entitled to an equal share.

समांसमीना *samâṁsamînâ*, i.e. *samâ+m-samâ+m+îna* (see *sama*), f. A cow bearing a calf every year.

समाकर्षिन् *samâkarshin*, i. e. *sam-â-krish* + *a* + *in*, I. adj. Possessing a diffusive fragrance. II. m., f. *ṇî*, n. A scent spreading afar, Amarakosha.

समाकार *samâkâra*, i.e. *sama-âkâra*, adj. Like in appearance, Pańch. i. d. 211.

समाकुलत्व *sam-âkula* + *tva*, n. Agitation, anxiety.

समाख्या *sam-â-khyâ*, f. **1.** Fame. **2.** Name.

समागति *samâgati*, i.e. *sam-â-gam* + *ti*, f. **1.** Arrival. **2.** Union. **3.** Meeting. **4.** (i.e. *sama-âgati*), Similar progress or condition.

समागम *sam-â-gam* + *a*, m. **1.** Arrival, Vikr. 10, 21 (return); approach. **2.** Union, Vikr. d. 29; junction, Pańch. 128, 3; assembly, Pańch. 196, 16. **3.** Association, intercourse, Hit. pr. d. 42, M.M. **4.** Encountering, meeting, Pańch. 161, 12.—**Comp.** *Dhûrta-*, m. the assemblage of rogues, title of a drama, Lass. 66, 1.

समाघात *samâghâta*, i. e. *sam-â-han*, Caus., + *a*, m. **1.** War, battle. **2.** Killing.

समाचार *samâchâra*, i.e. I. *sam-â-char* + *a*, m. **1.** Proper practice or conduct, MBh. 5, 2688; Pańch. 24, 10. **2.** Proceeding, conduct, Draup. 9, 17. **3.** Going, way, Pańch. 109, 11. **4.** Information, report. II. *sama-âchâra*, adj. Equal in virtuous conduct, Pańch. iii. d. 140.—**Comp.** *Moksha-kriyâ-*, adj. affording a way for liberating, Pańch. 109, 11. *Vṛithâ-kula-*, adj. descended from a low family and ill-behaved, Johns. Sel. 20, 97. *Sâdhu-*, adj. well-behaved, Pańch. 41, 17.

समाज *samâja*, i. e. *sam-aj* + *a*, m. **1.** A multitude, MBh. 1, 5698; a number. **2.** An assembly, Pańch. 158, 7. **3.** A convivial meeting. **4.** An elephant.—**Comp.** *Dyûta-*, m. an assembly of gamesters, Daçak. in Chr. 185, 16. *Prekshâ-*, m. the crowd at theatres, Man. 9, 84.

समाजिक *samâjika*, i. e. *samâja* + *ika*, m. A spectator, Mâlat. 4, 14.

समादान *samâdâna*, i.e. *sam-â-dâ* + *ana*, n. **1.** Receiving suitable donations. **2.** Taking. **3.** The daily observances of the *Jaina* sect.

समादेश *samâdeça*, i.e. *sam-â-diç* + *a*, m. Advice, Pańch. i. d. 261.

समाधान *samâdhâna*, i.e. *sam-â-dhâ* + *ana*, n. **1.** Restraining the senses and confining the mind to contemplation on the true nature of spirit, Vedântas. in Chr. 203, 13, cf. 18; contemplation, Daçak. in Chr. 182, 5. **2.** Promising, declaring.

समाधि *samâdhi*, i.e. *sam-â-dhâ* (cf. *nidhi*), m. **1.** Composing or reconciling differences. **2.** Storing corn. **3.** The joint of the neck, Kir. 16, 21. **4.** A tomb. **5.** Agreement, promise. **6.** Requital. **7.** Restraining the senses and confining the mind to contemplation on the true nature of spirit, Vedântas. in Chr. 203, 18; 216, 1, cf. 217, 21; contemplation, Bhâg. P. 5, 18, 1; devotion, Pańch. 162, 24. **8.** A religious vow or obligation, Kumâras. 3, 24. **9.** Silence. **10.** Demonstrated conclusion. **11.** Attempting impossibilities.

समाधिन् *samâdhin*, i.e. *samâdhi* + *in*, adj. Absorbed in contemplation, meditating, Bhag. 4, 24.

समाधिस्थ *samâdhi-stha*, adj. Devoted to meditation, Pańch. 162, 23.

समान A. i.e. *sa-mâna*, I. adj., f. *nâ* and *nî*. **1.** Like, similar, equal, Vikr. d. 110; Pańch. ii. d. 26. **2.** Same, Chr.

295, 10=Rigv. i. 92, 10; Man. 7, 163; Vedântas. in Chr. 208, 21; one, uniform. **3.** Good, virtuous. **4.** Honoured, Lass. 1, 12. **II.** *am*, adv. Equally (with instr.), Kir. 18, 4. **III.** m. A friend, Nalod. 2, 16. **B.** i.e. *sam-an+a*, m. One of the vital airs, that which is essential to digestion, Vedântas. in Chr. 207, 12.

समानता *samâna+tâ*, f. **1.** Sameness, equality. **2.** Community of kind or quality.

समानोदर्य *samânodarya*, i.e. *samâna-udara + ya*, m. A brother of whole blood.

समापक *sam-âp + aka*, adj. **1.** Finishing, completing. **2.** Killing.

समापन *sam-âp+ana*, n. **1.** Conclusion, completion, Man. 5, 88. **2.** A section, a chapter. **3.** Profound meditation. **4.** Acquisition. **5.** Killing.

समापिपयिषु *samâpipayishu*, i. e. *sam-âpipayisha* (desider. of the Caus. of *âp*), *+u*, adj. Wishing to complete, MBh. 1, 6872.

समाप्ति *sam-âp + ti*, f. **1.** End, Man. 2, 244. **2.** Perfection, accomplishment, Râm. 2, 43, 31; Bhartṛ. 3, 98. **3.** Reconciling differences, putting an end to disputes.

समाप्तिक *samâpti+ka*, **I.** adj. **1.** Completing, final. **2.** One who has finished the whole, Man. 3, 145. **II.** m. **1.** A finisher. **2.** One who has completed a whole course of holy study.

समाम्नाय *samâmnâya*, i.e. *sam-â-mnâ+a*, m. Enumeration, Prâtiç. ed. Regnier, Journ. As. 1856, p. 187.—Comp. *Paçu-*, m. works on animal sacrifices, Utt. Râmach. 114, 6.

समाय *samâya*, i.e. *sam-i + a*, m. **1.** A visit. **2.** Arrival, Mâlat. 170, 2.

समायोग *samâyoga*, i. e. *sam-â-yuj +a*, m. **1.** Union, Lass. 2. ed. 65, 6; junction, connection. **2.** Aiming with (a bow), Râm. 1, 67, 10. **3.** Heap, multitude. **4.** Cause, motive, object.

समारम्भ *samârambha*, i. e. *sam-â-rabh+a*, m. **1.** Commencement, beginning, Pańch. ii. d. 196. **2.** Undertaking, Chr. 7, 14; Pańch. 183, 2. **3.** Using, Pańch. ii. d. 146. **4.** An unguent, Sch. Çâk. ap. Böhtl. 211, ad 18.

समारम्भण *samârambhaṇa*, i. e. *sam-â-rabh+ana*, n. =*samâlambhana*, q. cf.

समाराधन *sam-â-râdh + ana*, n. Winning, gratifying, Ragh. 18, 10.

समारोपण *samâropaṇa*, i.e. *sam-â-ruh*, Caus., *+ana*, n. Placing or fixing in or on.

समारोह *samâroha*, i.e. *sam-â-ruh +a*, m. **1.** Ascending. **2.** Riding upon. **3.** Agreeing.

समालम्बन *sam-â-lamb + ana*, n. Resting upon, being supported by.

समालम्भ *samâlambha*, m., and

समालम्भन *samâlambhana*, n., i. e. *sam-â-labh+a*, or *ana*, **1.** Smearing the body with coloured perfumes, cf. Böhtl. ad Çâk. 48, 18. **2.** *samâlambha*, Seizing (for a sacrifice), MBh. 2, 864.

समावर्तन *samâvartana*, i.e. *sam-â-vṛit+ana*, n. A pupil's return home after having finished his religious studies, Man. 2, 108.

समावाय *samâvâya*, i.e. *sam-â-ava-i+a*, m. **1.** Integral aggregation, totality, Bhâg. P. 2, 8, 14. **2.** Association. **3.** A multitude.

समावास *samâvâsa*, i.e. *sam-â-1.vas*

+*a*, m. A dwelling-place, Pañch. 160, 3.

समावेश *samâveça*, i.e. *sam-â-viç* +*a*, m. **1.** Entrance. **2.** Possession by evil spirits. **3.** Affection, passion.

समाश्रय *samâçraya*, i.e. *sam-â-çri* +*a*, m. **1.** Refuge. **2.** Seeking protection. **3.** Protection. **4.** A dwelling-place, Pañch. 126, 2; iii. d. 94.

समाश्लेष *samâçlesha*, i.e. *sam-â-çlish* +*a*, m. Embrace, Mâlat. 158, 12.

समाश्वास *samâçvâsa*, i. e. *sam-â -çvas*+*a*, m. Trust, belief.

समाश्वासन *samâçvâsana*, i.e. *sam-â -çvas*, Caus., +*ana*, n. **1.** Recreating, recreation, Pañch. 162, 18. **2.** Consolation, Vikr. 26, 17.

समास *samâsa*, i.e. *sam-* **2.** *as*+*a*, m. **1.** Aggregation. **2.** Composition of words, Pâṇ. ii. 1, 3. **3.** Composition of differences. **4.** Contraction, conciseness; °*sena*, instr. Succinctly, Man. 2, 25; Lass. 2. ed. 49, 6.

समासक्ति *samâsakti*, i.e. *sam-â-sañj* +*ti*, f. **1.** Union. **2.** Comprehension. **3.** Affection, attachment.

समासज्जन *samâsajjana*, i.e. *sam -â-sañj* + *ana*, n. Joining, uniting, union, contact.

समासतस् *samâsa*+*tas*, adv. Succinctly, Man. 1, 68; Vikr. 19, 10.

समासवन्त् *samâsa*+*vant*, I. adj., f. *vatî*. **1.** Compounded. **2.** Abridged. II. m. A tree, Cedrela Tunna.

समास्थ *samâstha*, i.e. *sama-â-stha* (cf. *âsthâ*), adj. Being happy, Chr. 10, 8.

समाहरण *samâharaṇa*, i.e. *sam-â -hṛi*+*ana*, n. Uniting, collecting, composition.

समाहर्तृ *samâhartṛi*, i.e. *sam-â-hṛi* +*tṛi*, m., f. *trî*, and n. **1.** Habituated to acquire, Man. 7, 60. **2.** A collector (of taxes or duties ?), Pañch. 156, 17.

समाहार *samâhâra*, i.e. *sam-â-hṛi*+*a*, m. **1.** Collection, aggregation, Mâlat. 155, 8. **2.** Contraction, abridgment.

समाहृति *sam-â-hṛi*+*ti*, f. Abridgment, compilation.

समाह्वय *samâhvaya*, i.e. *sam-â-hve* + *a*, m. **1.** Calling out. **2.** War, battle. **3.** The conflict of animals or birds for sport, cockfighting, etc., Man. 9, 223; 221.

समाह्वान *samâhvâna*, i. e. *sam-â -hve*+*ana*, n. **1.** Calling, Pañch. 193, 17. **2.** Challenge, Nal. 7, 8.

समित् *sam-i* + *t*, f. War, battle, Kâvya Pr. p. 67, 2.

समिता *samitâ*, f. Wheat, flour.—Cf. *samîda* and σεμίδαλις; Lat. simila, similago; it appears also in the Coptic samit and Arab. samîd, and is probably borrowed from the Greek.

समिति i.e. I. *sam-i*+*ti*, f. **1.** Meeting, union. **2.** Assembly, Nal. 5, 7; company, **3.** Likeness, equality. **4.** War, battle. II. *sam-iti*, indecl. A holy verse beginning with *sam*, Man. 11, 119.

समितिंजय *samitiñjaya*, i.e. *samiti* +*m-ji*+*a*, adj. Conquering, i.e. eminent in, the assembly, Râm. 2, 71, 29, Seramp.

समिध् *samidh*, i. e. *sam-indh*, f. Fuel, wood, Çâk. 7, 9; grass, Vedântas. in Chr. 204, 6 (*Kuça*).

समिन्धन *sam-indh*+*ana*, n. Fuel, Bhaṭṭ. 2, 23.

समिर *samira*, see *samîra*.

समीक *samîka*, probably *samyañch* + *a*, n. War, battle.

समीकरण *samîkaraṇa*, i.e. *sama-kṛi* + *ana*, n. **1.** Equalising. **2.** Assimilation, digestion, Vedântas. in Chr. 207, 13.

समीक्ष *sam-îksh* + *a*, I. f. *kshâ*. **1.** Investigation, search. **2.** Looking, inspection, sight. **3.** Understanding, intellect. **4.** Nature, essential nature. II. n. The *Sâṅkhya* system of philosophy (cf. Çiç. 2, 59, where *samîkshya*).—Comp. *A-samîksha* + *m*, adv. inconsiderately, Hit. 43, 22 (former part of a compound, without the final *m*, but v.r. *a-samîkshya-kârin*, probably to be preferred, Acting without due deliberation).

समीच *samîcha*, i.e. *samyañch* + *a*, I. m. The ocean. II. f. *chî*, A doe.

समीचीन *samîchîna*, i.e. *samyañch* + *îna*, I. adj. **1.** Right, correct. **2.** True. **3.** Fit, proper, Pañch. 229, 1. II. n. Truth, Bhâg. P. 2, 4, 4.

समीद *samîda*, m. Fine wheat flour; cf. *samitâ*.

समीन *samîna*, i.e. *samâ* + *îna* (see *sama*), adj. **1.** Yearly, annual. **2.** Hired for a year. **3.** A year hence.

समीप *samîpa*, i. e. *sam-âp* + *a*, I. adj. Near, at hand. II. n. Proximity, vicinity, Pañch. 81, 17; 167, 7; loc. *pe*, To, Pañch. 83, 25.

समीपतस् *samîpa* + *tas*, adv. Before, near.—Comp. *Asmad-*, i. e. *asmatsamîpa* + *tas*, adv. in our presence, Nal. 6, 4. *Deva-râja-*, adv. in the presence of the king of the gods, Arj. 2, 9.

समीपस्थ *samîpa-stha*, adj. Placed, or situated, or living near, Lass. 2. ed. 44, 3.

समीर and **समिर** *samîra*, i.e. *sam* -*îr* + *a*, m. Air, wind, Bhâg. P. 8, 24, 36; Prab. 80, 3.

समीरण *samîraṇa*, i.e. *sam-îr* + *ana*, I. m. **1.** Air, Mâlat. 148, 20; wind, Arj. 4, 7. **2.** A traveller. **3.** A plant, commonly Maruvaka. II. n. Throwing.

समुक्षण *samukshaṇa*, i.e. *sam-uksh* + *ana*, n. Shedding, Mâlat. 48, 18.

समुच्चय *samuchchaya*, i. e. *sam-ud* -*chi* + *a*, m. **1.** Collection, Chân. 2 in Berl. Monatsb. 1864, 407. **2.** Conjunction of words or sentences.

समुच्छेद *samuchchheda*, i.e. *sam-ud* -*chhid* + *a*, m. Destroying, destruction, Kir. 11, 69.

समुच्छ्रय *samuchchhraya*, i.e. *sam* -*ud-çri* + *a*, m. **1.** Height, elevation. **2.** Opposition, enmity.

समुच्छ्राय *samuchchhrâya*, i.e. *sam* -*ud-çri* + *a*, m. Height, elevation.

समुत्कर्ष *samutkarsha*, i. e. *sam-ud* -*kṛish* + *a*, m. Boasting one's self as being of a high tribe, Man. 11, 55.

समुत्क्रम *samutkrama*, i.e. *sam-ud* -*kram* + *a*, m. Rise, assent.

समुत्क्रोश *samutkroça*, i. e. *sam-ud* -*kruç* + *a*, m. **1.** Crying aloud. **2.** An osprey.

समुत्थ *sâmuttha*, i.e. *sam-ud-stha*, adj. **1.** Rising, Chr. 33, 34; getting up. **2.** Born, produced, Man. 8, 353. **3.** Occasioned, occurring.

समुत्थान *samûtthâna*, i.e. *sam-ud* -*sthâ* + *ana*, n. **1.** Rising, getting up. **2.** Increase (as of size or wealth), Râm. 3, 49, 49. **3.** Healing a wound, perfect cure, Man. 8, 287. **4.** Symptom of disease. **5.** Performance of work, occupation. **6.** With *sambhûya*, Partnership, Man. 8, 4.

समुत्पत्ति *samutpatti,* i. e. *sam-ud -pad+ti,* f. **1.** Origin, Man. 1, 111; production, birth. **2.** Formation, Man. 5, 49. **3.** Occurrence, existence, Man. 6, 65.

समुत्पिञ्ज *samutpiñja,* i.e. *sam-ud -piñj+a,* and **समुत्पिञ्जल** *samutpiñja+la,* I. adj. Excessively confused. II. m. An army in great disorder.

समुत्पिञ्जलक *samutpiñjala+ka,* m. Excessive confusion, Johns. Sel. 13, 44.

समुत्पीडन *samutpîḍana,* i.e. *sam -ud-pîḍ+ana,* n. Pressing, Lass. 87, 16.

समुत्सर्ग *samutsarga,* i. e. *sam-ud -sṛij+a,* m. **1.** Abandoning. **2.** Giving. **3.** Voiding of excrements, Man. 4, 50.

समुत्सारण *samutsâraṇa,* i.e. *sam-ud -sṛi,* Caus., *+ana,* n. Pursuing, hunting, Çâk. 22, 1 (Prâkṛ.).

समुत्सुक *sam-utsuka,* adj. **1.** Regretting, sorrowful, longing, Vikr. d. 10; 13. **2.** Agitated, Lass. 2. ed. 62, 42.—Comp. *Pari-,* adj. very agitated, Râm. 2, 65, 11.

समुत्सुकत्व *samutsuka+tva,* n. Longing, desire, Ṛit. 6, 15.

समुत्सुकय *SAMUTSUKAYA,* denomin. of *sam-utsuka,* Par. To cause to long for, Kir. 11, 81.

समुत्सेध *samutsedha,* i. e. *sam-ud -sidh+a,* m. Height, elevation, Râm. 6, 2, 7.—Comp. *Haima-chitra-,* adj., f. *dhâ,* enchased with golden pictures, Draup. 8, 4.

समुदय and **समुदाय** *samudâya,* i.e. *sam-ud-i+a,* m. **1.** Rising (as of the sun), rise. **2.** A day. **3.** Effort. **4.** Revenue, Man. 7, 56 (*ă*). **5.** Multitude, Pańch. 82, 5 (*â*); number, heap, Utt. Râmach. 145, 8; Chr. 53, 5 (*samudayam balânâm kṛitvâ,* Having collected his armies). **6.** War, battle. **7.** The rear or reserve of an army.

समुदागम *sam-ud-â-gam+a,* m. Knowledge.

समुदाचार *samudâchâra,* i.e. *sam -ud-â-char+a,* m. **1.** Intention, purpose, design. **2.** Proper, or right usage (address), Çâk. 67, 9 (Prâkṛ.).

समुदाय *samudâya,* see *samudaya.*

समुदीरण *samudîraṇa,* i.e. *sam-ud -îr+ana,* n. **1.** Declaring, speaking, pronouncing, Dev. 4, 7. **2.** Repeating.

समुद्ग *samudga,* i.e. I. *sam-ud-ga,* adj. **1.** Who or what rises. **2.** Who or what pervades. II. *sa-mudga,* m. A covered box, a casket.

समुद्गक *samudga+ka,* m. A covered box, a casket, Daçak. in Chr. 196, 8.

समुद्देश *samuddeça,* i.e. *sam-ud-diç +a,* m. **1.** Pointing out. **2.** Describing. **3.** Particularising.

समुद्धरण *samuddharaṇa,* i.e. *sam -ud-hṛi+ana,* n. **1.** Taking out. **2.** Eradicating. **3.** Drawing up. **4.** Food vomited or thrown up. **5.** Extricating, lifting out.

समुद्धर्तृ *samuddhartṛi,* i.e. *sam-ud -hṛi+tṛi,* m., f. *trî,* and n. **1.** Who or what takes out, pulls out, etc. **2.** A deliverer, a redeemer.

समुद्भव *samudbhava,* i. e. *sam-ud -bhû+a,* m. Origin, Man. 6, 61.—Comp. *Kula-,* adj. descended from a high family, Hit. 7, 21 (v.r.). *Majja-samudbhava,* i.e. *majjan-,* n. semen genitale. *Mad-bandhana-,* adj. caused by (the binding of me, i.e.) my bondage, Pańch. iii. d. 162. *Vahni-dâha-,* adj., f. *vâ,* produced by burning, Pańch. v. d. 66. *Sârtha-bhraṁça-,* adj. beginning with the loss of the caravan, Pańch. 68, 21.

समुद्यम *sam-ud-yam + a*, m. **1.** Lifting up, Chr. 29,. 25. **2.** Effort, exertion, Bhag. 1, 22. **3.** Commencing, onset.

समुद्र *samudra*, i.e. **I.** *sam-und + ra*, m. A sea, the ocean, Pańch. 157, 25; Vikr. 68, 6. **II.** *sa-mudra* (cf. *mudrâ*), adj. Sealed, Man. 8, 188.—**Comp.** *Kshâra-*, m. the sea of salt, Bhâg. P. 5, 17, 6. *Kshîra-*, m. the sea of milk, Pańch. 44, 21. *Saṁsâra-*, m. the ocean-like world, ib. 33, 15.

समुद्रग *samudra-ga*, **I.** m. **1.** A trader by sea. **2.** A seaman. **II.** f. *gâ*, A river.

समुद्रज *samudra-ja*, adj. Born from the sea, Pańch. i. d. 88.

समुद्रारु *samudrâru* (from *samudra*), m. **1.** A shark. **2.** A large fabulous fish. **3.** Râma's bridge.

समुद्वाह *samudvâha*, i.e. *sam-ud-vah + a*, m. Nuptials, Sâv. 3, 15.

समुद्वेग *samudvega*, i.e. *sam-uḍ-vij + a*, m. Fear, Râm. 3, 55, 18.

समुन्दन *sam-und + ana*, n. Wetness.

समुन्नति *samunnati*, i.e. *sam-ud-nam + ti*, f. **1.** Height, elevation, Hit. pr. d. 14, M.M. **2.** Rank, dignity. **3.** Pride. **4.** Increase, prosperity, Kir. 2, 21. **5.** Lifting up.

समुन्मूलन *samunmûlana*, i.e. *sam-ud-mûl + ana*, n. Unrooting, destruction, Utt. Râmach. 31, 9.

समुपजोषम् *samupajosham*, i. e. *sam-upa-jush + a + m*, adv. Happily.

समुपवेशन *samupaveçana*, i.e. *sam-upa-viç + ana*, n. A building, Utt. Râmach. 161, 10.

समुपार्जन *samupârjana*, i.e. *sam-upa-arj + ana*, n. Reconciliation, Man. 7, 152.

समूर *samûra*, and **समूरु** *samûru*, m. A kind of deer.

समूह *samûha*, i.e. *sam-ûh*, or *vah*, *+ a*, m. Assemblage, multitude, Çâk. d. 31; Vedântas. in Chr. 204, 10.—**Comp.** *Dâyâda-*, m. all the kinsmen, Pańch. 222, 7. *Çastra-*, n. (?), an arsenal.

समूहन *samûhana*, i.e. *sam-ûh*, or *vah*, *+ ana*, **I.** n. Collection, plenty, Man. 4, 102. **II.** f. *nî*, A broom.

समृद्धि *samṛiddhi*, i.e. *sam-ṛidh + ti*, f. **1.** Thriving, increase, Ragh. 8, 13 (at the end of a comp. adj.); gain, Pańch. 134, 8. **2.** Prosperity, Hit. i. d. 209, M.M.; well-being, Bhartṛ. 2, 34. **3.** Supremacy, power. **4.** Wealth, Pańch. ii. d. 71.—**Comp.** *A-*, f. misfortune, Man. 4, 137.

ऽसमृद्धिन् *-samṛiddhin*, i.e. *sam-ṛiddha + in* (vb. *ṛidh*), adj., f. *nî*, Possessing plenty (of), Râm. 5, 53, 3.

समोकस् *sam-okas*, adj. Endowed, Chr. 290, 10 = Rigv. i. 64, 10.

समोदक *samodaka*, i.e. *sama-udaka*, n. A mixture of half butter-milk and half water.

संपत्ति *saṁpatti*, i.e. *sam-pad + ti*, f. Prosperity, Hit. i. d. 141, M.M.; success, Lass. 3, 20; power.—**Comp.** *A-*, f. non-succeeding, Man. 12, 36. *Dhana-*, f. wealth, Hit. pr. d. 11, M.M. *Rûpa-*, f. beauty.

संपद् *saṁpad*, i.e. *sam-pad*, f. **1.** Success, Hit. i. d. 183, M.M.; prosperity, Hit. i. d. 32, M.M. **2.** Blessing, Çâk. d. 189. **3.** Wealth, Çâk. 91, 13;

power, Megh. 54. 4. Accomplishment, Mâlat. 104, 17; perfection, excellence, Hit. iii. d. 53; Çiç. 9, 1 (*abhitâpa-*, Most violent heat, excess of heat). 5. Advancement in good qualities, Vedântas. in Chr. 203, 7. 6. Adornment, Bhâg. P. 4, 25, 18. 7. Fate, Bhag. 16, 3; 4. 8. A necklace of pearls. 9. A treasure, Man. 3, 255; Râjat. 5, 231.

संपराय *sam̃parâya*, i.e. *sam-parâ-i+a*, m. 1. War, battle, Daçak. in Chr. 201, 2. 2. Calamity. 3. Futurity. 4. A son.

संपरिशोषण *sam̃pariçoshaṇa*, i.e. *sam-pari-çush+ana*, n. Emaciation, Râm. 2, 10, 30.

संपर्क *sam̃parka*, i.e. *sam-pṛich+a*, m. 1. Mixture. 2. Copulation. 3. Union, Vikr. d. 13; Pańch. iii. d. 58. 4. Contact, Megh. 26.

संपर्किन् *sam̃parkin*, i.e. *sam̃parka+in*, adj., f. *iṇî*, 1. Blended, mixed. 2. United with. 3. In contact with.

संपर्कीय *sam̃parkîya*, i.e. *sam̃parka+îya*, adj. Liable to come in contact.

संपाक *sam̃pâka*, i.e. *sam-pach+a*, I. adj. 1. Reasoning, a reasoner. 2. Impudent. 3. Lecherous, libertine. 4. Small, little. II. m. A tree, Cassia fistula.

संपात *sam̃pâta*, i.e. *sam-pat+a*, m. 1. Concurrence, falling against each other, Johns. Sel. 58, 170; butting together, Pańch. 35, 7. 2. Meeting, Daçak. in Chr. 188, 15. 3. Descending, falling down, Bhartṛ. 2, 29; Vikr. 85, 20 (flashing); Daçak. in Chr. 186, 15 (flashing). 4. Alighting (as a bird), flying (of arrows), Bhag. 1, 20. 5. A special mode of flight (of birds), Pańch. ii. d. 57. 6. Going, moving, Utt. Râmach. 22, 8. 7. Being removed, Man. 6, 56. 8. The son of Garuda, a fabulous bird. —Comp. *Dhârâ-*, m. a shower of rain, Prab. 87, 9. *Nis-*, adj. impassable, Hariv. 4286. *Vṛishṭi-*, m. a shower of rain, Râjat. 5, 275.

संपाति *sam̃pâti*, i.e. *sam-pat+i*, m. A fabulous bird, Mahâvîrach. 74, 1.

संपातिन् *sam̃pâtin*, i.e. *sam-pat+in*, adj., f. *nî*, Falling together, Utt. Râmach. 40, 11.

संपादन *sam̃pâdana*, i.e. *sam-pad*, Caus. *+ana*, n. 1. Accomplishing, Vikr. 37, 7 (*vrata-*, The completion of a vow); effecting, making, Pańch. 133, 1. 2. Cleansing, Man. 3, 255. 3. Attaining. 4. Acquiring.

संपीड *sam̃piḍa*, i.e. *sam-pîḍ+a*, I. m. 1. Pain, torture. 2. Agitating, Kir. 7, 12. 3. Sending. II. f. *ḍâ*, Torment, Man. 12, 76.

संपीडन *sam̃piḍana*, i.e. *sam-pîḍ+ana*, n. 1. Pressing. 2. Castigation, punishment. 3. Sending.

संपीति *sam̃pîti*, i.e. *sam-pâ+ti*, f. Drinking in company.

संपुट *sam̃puṭa* (cf. *puṭa*), m. 1. Cavity, Bhâg. P. 1, 11, 2; Ṛit. 1, 21. 2. A covered box. 3. A flower, commonly Kuruvaka.

संपुटक *sam̃puṭa+ka*, I. m. A casket. II. f. *ṭikâ*, A box filled with ornaments, Pańch. ii. d. 177.

संपूजन *sam̃pûjana*, i.e. *sam-pûj+ana*, n. Treating with respect, reverence, Man. 3, 137.

संप्रक्षालन *sam̃prakshâlana*, i.e. *sam-pra-kshal*, Caus., *+ana*, n. Inundation, Matsyop. 28.

संप्रणेतृ *sam̃praṇetṛi*, i.e. *sam-pra-nî*

+*tṛi*, m. **1.** A judge, Man. 7, 26. **2.** A ruler.

संप्रतापन *sampratâpana*, i.e. *sam-pra-tap*, Caus., +*ana*, n. **1.** Heating, burning. **2.** Afflicting. **3.** One of the hells, Man. 4, 89.

संप्रति *samprati*, i.e. *sam-prati*, adv. Now, at this time, Pańch. 172, 9; Vikr. d. 15.

संप्रतिपत्ति *sampratipatti*, i.e. *sam-prati-pad*+*ti*, f. **1.** Agreement. **2.** Admission. **3.** Co-operation. **4.** Presence, company. **5.** Assault. **6.** Doing, performing.

संप्रतिरोधक *sampratirodhaka*, i.e. *sam-prati-rudh*+*aka*, n. Durance, actual confinement.

संप्रतीति *sampratîti*, i.e. *sam-prati-i*+*ti*, f. Fame, notoriety, Kir. 3, 43.

संप्रदातृ *sampradâtṛi*, i.e. *sam-pra-dâ*+*tṛi*, m. A giver, Man. 9, 186.

संप्रदान *sampradâna*, i.e. *sam-pra-dâ*+*ana*, n. **1.** Giving, gift, Hit. iv. d. 108. **2.** Bestowing in marriage, Man. 7, 152.

संप्रदाय *sampradâya*, i.e. *sam-pra-dâ*+*a*, m. **1.** Traditional doctrine, Utt. Râmach. 39, 12 (*datta-divya-astra-*, adj. Possessed of the traditional knowledge of the celestial arms); Râjat. 5, 139. **2.** A peculiar doctrine and exclusive worship of one divinity.

संप्रधारणा *sampradhâraṇâ*, i.e. *sam-pra-dhṛi*, Caus., +*ana*, f. Deliberation, determining the propriety or impropriety of anything.

संप्रमोष *sampramosha*, i.e. *sam-pra-mush*+*a*, m. Suppression, Bhâg. P. 6, 4, 26.

संप्रयोग *samprayoga*, i.e. *sam-pra-yuj*+*a*, m. **1.** Union, Mâlat. 36, 8; copulation, connexion. **2.** Mutual relation, proportion. **3.** Order, natural series. **4.** Magic.

संप्रयोगिन् *samprayogin*, i.e. *samprayoga*+*in*, m. **1.** A joiner. **2.** A libertine. **3.** A catamite. **4.** A conjuror.

संप्रवेश *sampraveça*, i.e. *sam-pra-viç*+*a*, m. Entrance, Râjat. 5, 235.

संप्रश्न *sampraçna*, i.e. *sam-prachh*+*na*, m. Asking, question, Hit. ii. d. 56.

संप्रसाद *samprasâda*, i.e. *sam-pra-sad*+*a*, m. **1.** Favour, grace, Utt. Râmach. 42, 5. **2.** Serenity, Windischmann, Sankara, 171.

संप्रहार *samprahâra*, i.e. *sam-pra-hṛi*+*a*, m. **1.** Striking, wounding. **2.** War, battle, Çâk. 98, 14. **3.** Going, motion.—Comp. *Dvandva-*, m. a single combat, Utt. Râmach. 121, 8.

संप्राप्ति *samprâpti*, i.e. *sam-pra-âp*+*ti*, f. **1.** Obtaining, Pańch. 5, 10; acquisition, ib. 104, 1. **2.** Gaining, Man. 7, 208.

संप्रीति *samprîti*, i.e. *sam-prî*+*ti*, **1.** Attachment, affection, Man. 3, 113. **2.** Friendly assent, 8, 146. **3.** Delight.

संप्रेषण *sampreshaṇa*, i.e. *sam-pra-1. ish*+*ana*, n. Sending, Man. 7, 153.

संप्लव *samplava*, i.e. *sam-plu*+*a*, m. **1.** Surge, Râm. 1, 32, 17. **2.** Submerging, submersion, Hariv. 12375; inundation. **3.** Falling on all sides, Man. 4, 103; ruin, Hit. i. d. 72, M.M. (but cf. Böhtl. Ind. Spr. 458).

संफाल *samphâla*, i.e. *sam-sphal*+*a*, m. A ram.

† **सम्ब्** *SAMB*, **शम्ब्** *ÇAMB*,

साम्ब् *SÂMB*, i. 10, Par. To connect. —Cf. *sarb.*

संबन्ध *sambandha*, i.e. *sam-bandh* + *a*, **1.** Connexion, union, Man. 3, 157; Utt. Râmach. 27, 15 (*mad-*, with me); Vedântas. in Chr. 202, 9 (of intimately united subjects, cf. 204, 1; 212, 19; 21). **2.** Relationship, Pańch. ii. d. 106; relation, Hit. i. d. 157, M.M. (*asyedam iti sambandho hânau duḥkhena gamyate*, The proprietary connection between them is ascertained only by his grief in losing it). **3.** Fitness, propriety. **4.** Success, prosperity.—**Comp.** *Saptati-*, m. a collection of seventy tales, Lass. 40, 12. *Su-*, adj. well joined, Pańch. ii. d. 136. *Strî-*, m. marriage.

संबन्धक *sambandha* + *ka*, I. adj. **1.** Relating, concerning. **2.** Fit, suitable, Chr. 55, 7. **3.** m. (viz. *saṁdhi*), Proceeding from relationship, name of a kind of alliance, Hit. iv. d. 123. II. m. A friend, Râm. 1, 12, 21.

संबन्धिन् *sambandhin*, i.e. *sambandha* + *in*, adj. and sbst., f. *nî*, **1.** Connected with, Pańch. iii. d. 141; inherent, Vedântas. in Chr. 214, 2; referring to, Daçak. in Chr. 181, 22. **2.** Related, Man. 2, 132; 4, 179; a relation by marriage, Utt. Râmach. 12, 4; 98, 3. **3.** Belonging to, Pańch. 121, 25. **4.** Possessing good qualities.

सम्बर *sambara*, see *çambara.*

सम्बल *sambala*, I. (m.), n. Stock for travelling expenses. II. n. Water (cf. *çambala*, *çambara*).

संबाध *sambâdha*, i.e. *sam-bâdh* + *a*, I. m. **1.** Being thronged, Hariv. 2677. **2.** Pressing on, pressure, Johns. Sel. 60, 185. **3.** Difficulty, Mârk. P. 21, 1. **4.** The road to Tartarus. **5.** The vulva. **6.** Fear. II. adj., f. *dhâ* (Râm. 1, 40, 22, Schlegel; 2, 65, 33, Seramp.; Çakuntalop. ap. Chezy, ii. 29). **1.** Narrow. **2.** Crowded, Ragh. 12, 67. **3.** Blocked up, Pańch. i. d. 427 (cf. Böhtl. Ind. Spr. 1446); impassable.—**Comp.** *A-*, adj. 1. large, MBh. 2, 345. 2. lonely, Kir. 3, 53. *Abhi-*, adj., f. *dhâ*, very narrow. *Â-*, adj. crowded, full of, Râm. 5, 23, 21. *Nis-*, adj. 1. large, Suçr. 1, 241, 7. 2. shortest (properly, without any obstruction), Daçak. in Chr. 186, 16. *Çara-*, adj., f. *dhâ*, covered with arrows, Utt. Râmach. 117, 2. *Hastyaçvaratha-*, i.e. *hastin-açva-ratha-*, adj., f. *dhâ*, crowded by elephants, horses, and carriages, Râm. 3, 54, 16.

संबाधन *sambâdhana*, i.e. *sam-bâdh* + *ana*, n. **1.** Obstructing, Pańch. i. d. 427 (but cf. Böhtl. Ind. Spr. 1446). **2.** A barrier, a gate. **3.** A door-keeper. **4.** The point of a stake or spit.

संबुद्धि *sambuddhi*, i.e. *sam-budh* + *ti*, f. **1.** Calling, or calling to. **2.** (In grammar), The vocative case, Pâṇ. 2, 3, 49.

संबोध *sambodha*, i.e. *sam-budh* + *a*, m. Instructing, informing.

संबोधन *sambodhana*, i.e. *sam-budh* + *ana*, **1.** Calling. **2.** Addressing, Chr. 38, 16. **3.** (In grammar), The vocative case (see *sambuddhi*).

संभव *sambhava*, i.e. *sam-bhû* + *a*, m. **1.** Mixing, union. **2.** Adaptation, appropriateness. **3.** Adequacy, ability. **4.** Possibility. **5.** Compatibility, consistency. **6.** Agreement. **7.** Acquaintance. **8.** Destruction, loss. **9.** Springing up, Hit. iv. d. 72; origin, Man. 1, 116; birth, Mâlat. 156, 6; Pańch. 263, 23; production, Hit. 16, 5, M.M. **10.** Producing and rearing, Man. 2, 227. **11.** Cause, motive, Pańch. i. d. 328 (*grahaṇa-*, of taking, viz. the life of a dependent).—**Comp.** *A-*, I. m. 1.

non-existence, Böhtl. Ind. Spr. 872; impossibility, Pañch. ii. d. 4. **2.** omission, Man. 11, 27. **II.** adj. impossible, Hit. i. d. 27, M.M. *Apunaḥsambhava*, i.e. *a-punar-*, adj., f. *vâ*, not rising again, Râjat. 1, 161. *Asthi-*, I. adj. produced by the bones, MBh. 1, 1514. II. m. the marrow. *Âtmasambhava-*, i.e. *âtman-*, I. m. a son, Râm. 5, 18, 27. II. f. *vâ*, a daughter, ib. 3, 20, 22. *Ûru-*, adj., f. *vâ*, produced from the thigh, Vikr. 8, 17. *Kumbha-*, adj., m. epithet of Agastya, Bhâg. P, 6, 3, 35. *Garbha-*, m. the production of an embryo, pregnancy, Yâjú. 1, 69. *Dadhi-*, adj. prepared of milk, Man. 5, 10. *Deva-yajana-*, adj., f. *vâ*, sprung up from a place prepared for a sacrifice, Utt. Râmach. 10, 4. *Padma-*, adj., m. epithet of Brahman, Hariv. 3233. *Paulomî-*, adj. born from Paulomî, Vikr. d. 152. *Mânusha-*, adj. coming from a man, Pañch. 141, 3. *Viçâla-kula-*, adj. sprung from an illustrious race, Hit. pr. d. 39, M.M. *Sura-ari-*, adj. caused by an enemy of the gods, Vikr. d. 5.

संभार *sambhâra*, i.e. *sam-bhṛi+a*, m. **1.** Maintaining, supporting. **2.** Apparatus, things required for any act or affair, Râm. 1, 11, 13; Pañch. 157, 22. **3.** Provision, getting everything ready. **4.** Completion, Mâlat. 171, 5. **5.** Fullness, wealth, Nal. 26, 24. **6.** Multitude, heap, quantity, Utt. Râmach. 141, 8; Pañch. i. d. 35; Râjat. 5, 273.

संभावन *sambhâvana*, i.e. *sam-bhû*, Caus., *+ana*, n., and f. *nâ*, **1.** Adequacy, ability. **2.** Fitness. **3.** Possibility. **4.** Doubt. **5.** Considering, Ragh. 5, 28 (f.); reflecting. **6.** Review, Pañch. 218, 6 (f.). **7.** Thought, Mâlav. 38, 15 (Prâkṛ.). **8.** Worship, Pañch. 264, 4; honour, Râjat. 5, 328. **9.** Love, Çâk. d. 163 (f.).—Comp. *Sarpatva-*, f. imagination of being a snake, mistaking for a snake, Vedântas. in Chr. 206, 7.

संभाष *sambhâsha*, i.e. *sam-bhâsh +a*, I. m. Conversation, Man. 2, 195; in *sneha-*, Kind conversation, Pañch. 51, 23. **II.** f. **1.** Greeting, Hit. i. d. 38, M.M. **2.** A criminal connexion, Man. 8, 363. **3.** Contract, agreement. **4.** War-cry, watch-word. — Comp. *Madhura-sambhâsha*, adj. discoursing agreeably, Chr. 53, 2.

संभाषण *sambhâshaṇa*, i. e. *sam-bhâsh + ana*, n. **1.** Conversation, Lass. 41, 17. **2.** Sexual intercourse, Lass. 10, 20. **3.** War-cry, watchword.

संभूति *sambhûti*, i.e. *sam-bhû+ti*, f. **1.** Combination. **2.** Birth, Man. 2, 147. **3.** Origin, Râjat. 5, 73; production. — Comp. *Garbha-*, f. pregnancy, Kathâs. 5, 61.

संभृति *sambhṛiti*, i.e. *sam-bhṛi+ti*, f. **1.** Support, nourishment. **2.** Preparation, provision. **3.** Plenitude, fullness.

संभेद *sambheda*, i.e. *sam-bhid+a*, m. **1.** Breaking, splitting. **2.** Union, mixture, Mâlat. 167, 4. **3.** The confluence of two rivers, Man. 8, 356, or the junction of a river with the sea.

संभोग *sambhoga*, i.e. *sam-bhuj+a*, m. **1.** Enjoyment, Pañch. ii. d. 67; sensual enjoyment, Râjat. 5, 230. **2.** Coition, Megh. 94; copulation. **3.** A catamite. **4.** Use, occupation, Man. 8, 200.—Comp. *A-*, m. non-enjoyment, Hit. i. d. 156, M.M.

संभोजन *sambhojana*, i.e. *sam-bhuj +ana*, I. adj., f. *nî*, Convivial, Man. 3, 141. **II.** n. A meal.

संभ्रम *sambhrama*, i.e. *sam-bhram +a*, m. **1.** Turning round, revolving. **2.** Haste, MBh. 1, 764. **3.** Confusion arising from fear, joy, haste, etc.; cheerful quickness, Bhartṛ. 2, 54; zeal, Râjat. 5, 306. **4.** Fear, alarm, Man. 4, 118; Pańch. 52, 16. **5.** Error, ignorance. **6.** Reverence, Hit. iv. d. 103 (but cf. Böhtl. Ind. Spr. 3337).—**Comp.** *A-* and *nis-*, adj. unembarrassed, Râjat. 5, 82; 4, 94. *Sa-sambhrama* +*m*, adv. 1. hastily, Çâk. 6, 15; Pańch. 198, 9. 2. in confusion, Çâk. 40, 18; perplexed, Pańch. 140, 24. 3. in fear, Vikr. 25, 20. *Su-*, m. great haste, Hit. pr. d. 15, M.M.

संभ्रमभृत् *saṁbhrama-bhṛi+t*, adj. Embarrassed, Çiç. 9, 71.

संमति *saṁmati*, i.e. *sam-man+ti*, f. **1.** Agreement. **2.** Approbation, Pańch. 229, 1. **3.** Regard, respect, Kir. 10, 36. **4.** Real knowledge. **5.** Wish, desire.

संमद *saṁmada*, i. e. *sam-mad+a*, m. Joy, Mâlat. 77, 11; happiness, Govardh. Âryâ Saptaçatî, 275, d.

संमर्द *saṁmarda*, i.e. *sam-mṛid+a*, m. **1.** Friction, rubbing. **2.** War, battle, Kathâs. 3, 66. **3.** Trampling on, treading on, Râjat. 5, 57.

संमाद *saṁmâda*, i.e. *sam-mad+a*, m. Intoxication, frenzy.

संमान *saṁmâna*, i.e. I. *sam-man* +*a*, n. (Wils. and thus Hit. ii. d. 132, but Böhtl. Ind. Spr. 2755 corrects °*naḥ*, m.; the n. is against the general rule), Respect, honour, Man. 2, 162. II. *sam-mâ+ana*, n. Measure. —**Comp.** *A-*, m. no honour, Böhtl. Ind. Spr. 164.

संमार्जक *saṁmârjaka*, i.e. *sam-mṛij* +*aka*, m. A sweeper.

संमार्जन *saṁmârjana*, i.e. *sam-mṛij* +*ana*, I. n. Cleaning, purifying, sweeping, Pańch. 27, 5; 26, 22. II. f. *nî*, A broom.

संमिश्र *saṁmiçra*, i.e. *sam-miçra*, adj. Mixed, blended, joined.

संमिश्ल *saṁmiçla* (=the last, with *l* for *r*), adj. Endowed, Chr. 290, 10= Rigv. i. 64, 10.

संमुखीन *saṁmukhîna*, i. e. *sam -mukha+îna*, adj. Before, in front of.

संमूर्छन *saṁmûrchhana*, i. e. *sam -murchh+ana*, n. **1.** Uniform, or universal expansion, or permeation. **2.** Increasing. **3.** Height. **4.** Fainting, insensibility.

संमेलन *saṁmelana*, i. e. *sam-mil+ ana*, n. Union, Utt. Râmach. 177, 9.

संमोद *saṁmoda*, i.e. *sam-mud+a*, m. Pleasure, delight.

संमोह *saṁmoha*, i.e. *sam-muh+a*, m. **1.** Beguilement, fascination. **2.** Stupefaction, Utt. Râmach. 107, 8. **3.** Folly. **4.** Illusion of mind, Man. 7, 12. **5.** Ignorance. **6.** Fainting.

सम्यञ्च् *saṁyańch*, i. e. *sama-ańch* (the final *a* of *sama* is changed to *i*, as before *as*, *kṛi*, *bhû*), I. adj., f. *michî*. **1.** Going with, accompanying. **2.** Same, common, uniform. **3.** Accurate, correct. **4.** Right, true. **5.** Pleasant, agreeable. II. acc. sing. n. *yak*, adv. **1.** Properly, fitly, rightly, Man. 2, 14; well, Pańch. 134, 7; Vikr. 39, 7. **2.** Duly, Man. 3, 76; Pańch. 128, 17. **3.** By honourable means, Man. 7, 60. **4.** Distinctly, Man. 2, 101; Pańch. 167, 6. **5.** Wholly, completely, Pańch. 72, 17. **6.** Comprehensively, Man. 2, 89. **7.** With, Nal. 9, 8. **8.** Together, Lass. 98, 14=Rigv. v. 9, 5.

सम्राज् *sam-râj*, m. A paramount sovereign, one who rules over other princes, and has performed the Râjasûya sacrifice; a sovereign, Râjat. 5, 135.

† सय् *SAY*, i. 1, Âtm. To go.

सर *sara*, i.e. *sṛi+a*, I. adj. Who or what goes. II. m. 1. Going. 2. An arrow (? see *çara*). 3. The coagulum of curds or milk. 4. Salt, saltness. III. m., and f. *râ* or *rî*, A waterfall. IV. n. 1. Water. 2. A pond, a lake, Pańch. 131, 15.—Comp. *Maṇi-*, m. a necklace, Utt. Râmach. 18, 6. *Mauktika-*, m. a string of pearls, Utt. Râmach. 24, 13.—Cf. Lat. serum; ὀῤῥός, ὀρός; Lat. sal; Goth. salt; A.S. sealt; ἅλς; Lat. salum, insula; ἔναλος; A.S. siringie.

सरक *saraka*, i.e. *sṛi+aka*, I. adj. Going, moving. II. m. and n. 1. A continuous line of road. 2. Spirituous liquor. 3. Drinking spirits. 4. A drinking vessel. 5. Distribution of spirits. III. n. 1. Going. 2. A lake. 3. Heaven.—Comp. *Tri-*, n. a mixture of three spirituous liquors, Çiç. 10, 12.

सरघा *saraghâ*, f. A bee, Ragh. 4, 63.

सरज *sara-ja*, n. Fresh butter.

सरट् *saraṭ*, m. 1. Air, wind. 2. A cloud. 3. A lizard. 4. (ved.), A bee, Chr. 297, 21=Rigv. i. 112, 21.

सरट *saraṭa*, and शरट *çaraṭa*, m. The gecko, Lacerta gecko, Man. 12, 57 (with *s*).

सरटि *saraṭi*, m. 1. Wind. 2. A cloud (cf. *saraṭ*).

सरण *saraṇa*, i.e. *sṛi+ana*, I. adj. Who or what goes. II. n. 1. Going. 2. Oxidised iron. III. f. *ṇâ* and *ṇi*, A plant, Pæderia fetida.

सरणि and णी *saraṇi*, i.e. *sṛi+ana +i*, f. 1. A path, a road. 2. A straight or continuous line. 3. A disease of the throat. Cf. the last.

सरण्ड *saraṇḍa*, m. 1. A bird. 2. A rogue. 3. A sort of ornament.

सरण्यु *saraṇyu* (vb. *sṛi+aṇa+ya+u*), m. 1. Air, wind. 2. Water. 3. A cloud.—Cf. Ἐριννύς.

सरमा *saramâ*, f. 1. The bitch of the gods, MBh. 1, 671. 2. The daughter of Daksha, Vishṇu P. 122, n. 19. 3. The wife of Râvaṇa's brother.

सरयु *sarayu* (vb. *sṛi*), I. m. Air, wind. II. f., also यू *yû*, The name of a river, Râm. 2, 49, 15 (*yû*).

सरल *sarala* (vb. *sṛi*), I. adj. 1. Straight, Pańch. ii. d. 189. 2. Upright, honest, Mâlat. 38, 1. II. m. A sort of pine, Pinus longifolia Roxb., Megh. 54.

सरस् *saras*, i.e. *sṛi+as* (cf. *sara*), I. n., and f. *sî*. 1. A large pond, Pańch. 159, 14 (*ras*); Kir. 12, 51 (*rasî*). 2. A piece of water in which the lotus grows. II. n. Water.—Comp. *Karpûra-*, *Tṛiṇa-vindu-*, n. names of lakes, Hit. 84, 13, M.M. (*karpûra-*); MBh. 3, 15365 (*tṛiṇavindu-*). *Nabhas-*, n. clouds, sky, Râm. 5, 55, 4. *Hima-*, n. cold water, Mâlat. 17, 9.—Cf. O.N. sir, saer, sior (sea); A.S. sirendac.

सरस *sarasa*, i.e. *saras+a*, and *sa-rasa*, I. n. 1. A pond. 2. (or m. ?), Alchemy, Râjat. 4, 247. 3. A substitute for *saras* at the end of some comp. words. II. adj. 1. Tasty, juicy, Megh. 14. 2. Beautiful, charming, Mâlat. 51, 5: Bhartṛ. 1, 6; agreeable, Ṛit. 1, 2. 3. New, Çiç. 9, 85. 4. Impassioned. 5. °*sam*, adv. Enraptured, Vikr. 57, 11.

सरसिज *saras+i-ja*, n. A lotus, Kir. 5, 39.

सरसीरुह *sarasi-ruh+a* (see *saras*), n. A lotus, Mâlat. 169, 9.

सरस्वन्त् *saras+vant*, I. adj. **1.** Juicy, sapid. **2.** Elegant. **3.** Sentimental. II. m. **1.** The ocean. **2.** A male river. **3.** A buffalo. III. f. *vatî*. **1.** The wife of Brahman, the goddess of speech and eloquence, Râjat. 5, 415; of wisdom, Vikr. d. 162. **2.** The wife of a Muni. **3.** An excellent woman. **4.** Speech, Hit. 116, 8; Ragh. 15, 46, ed. Calc.; Râm. 1, 2, 34 (? modulation); the faculty or its exercise. **5.** A river. **6.** The name of a river, Chr. 20, 24. **7.** A crow.

सरागता *sa-râga+tâ*, f. State of being coloured or red, Pańch. i. d. 194.

सरि *sari*, i.e. *sṛi+i*, f. A waterfall.

सरित् *sarit*, i.e. *sṛi+it* (for *sarant*, ptcple. pres.), f. **1.** A river, Man. 1, 24; Vikr. 68, 5 (*paramârtha-*, Indeed a river). **2.** Thread.—**Comp.** *Ku-*, f. a rivulet, Pańch. ii. d. 92. *Dyu-*, f. the celestial Gańgâ, Bhartṛ. 3, 85.

सरिमन् and **सरीमन्** *sarîman* (vb. *sṛi*), m. Wind.

सरीसृप *sarîsṛip* (frequent. of *sṛip*), +*a*, m. A snake.

सरोगिता *sarogitâ*, i.e. *sa-roga+in+tâ*, f. Sickliness, Hit. ii. d. 4.

सरोज *saroja*, i.e. *saras-ja*, n. A lotus, Çiç. 9, 30; 65.

सरोजिन् *sarojin*, i. e. *saroja+in*, I. m. Brahman. II. f. *nî*. **1.** A lotus, Bhartṛ. 1, 100. **2.** A multitude of lotuses. **3.** A pond abounding in lotuses.

सरोरुह् *saroruh*, and **सरोरुह** *saroruha*, n., and **-रुहिणी** *-ruhiṇî*, f., i.e. *saras-ruh*, and *-ruh+a*, and +*in* +*î*, A lotus, Lass. 73, 15 (*ha*); Utt. Râmach. 24, 1 (*ha*); Kir. 4, 34 (*hiṇî*).

सर्ग *sarga*, i. e. *sṛij + a*, m. **1.** Abandoning, letting go. **2.** Creation, Man. 1, 27. **3.** Natural property, nature, Bhag. 5, 19. **4.** Certainty. **5.** Tendency of a thing. **6.** Assent, agreement. **7.** Effort, will, Ragh. 3, 51. **8.** A chapter, Râm. i. sarga 1, sqq.; a book, Çiç. 1, sqq. **9.** Voiding, as of excrement.—**Comp.** *Âdi-*, m. first creation, MBh. 14, 1095. *Tri-*, m. the threefold production (of qualities), Bhâg. P. 1, 1, 1.

† **सर्ज्** *SARJ*, i. 1, Par. To gain (cf. *arj*).

सर्ज *sarja*, m. **1.** A tree, Shorea robusta, Mâlat. 148, 14. **2.** Another tree, Pentaptera arjuna. **3.** The resinous exudation of the Shorea robusta, MBh. 1, 5723.

सर्जन *sarjana*, i.e. *sṛij+ana*, n. **1.** Abandoning. **2.** Creating. **3.** Voiding. **4.** The rear or reserve of an army.

सर्जू *sarjû*, i. e. *sṛij+û*, I. m. A merchant. II. f. **1.** Lightning. **2.** A necklace. **3.** Going, following.

सर्प *sarpa*, i.e. *sṛip+a*, I. m. **1.** Sliding motion. **2.** A snake, Man. 1, 37; Pańch. iii. d. 46. II. f. *pî*, The female of the snake.—**Comp.** *Kâla-*, and *Kṛishṇa-*, m. a particular snake, Coluber Naga, Lass. 16, 11; Pańch. i. d. 233.—Cf. Lat. serpens, ἑρπετός.

सर्पण *sarpaṇa*, i.e. *sṛip+ana*, n. **1.** Gliding, going. **2.** The slow flight of an arrow nearly parallel to the ground.

सर्पभुज् *sarpa-bhuj*, m. **1.** A peacock. **2.** A crane. **3.** A large snake.

सर्पिन् *sarpin*, i.e. *sṛip + in*, I. adj., f.

iṇî. **1.** Gliding, creeping. **2.** Moving, Kir. 5, 35. II. f. *iṇî.* **1.** A female serpent, Pańch. 210, 12. **2.** A small medicinal shrub.—Comp. *Pîṭha-*, m. a cripple, Man. 8, 394.

सर्पिष्मन्त् *sarpishmant*, i.e. *sarpis + mant*, adj., f. *matî*, Seasoned with clarified butter, Utt. Râmach. 90, 9.

सर्पिस् *sarpis*, i.e. *sṛip + is*, n. Clarified butter, Pańch. iii. d. 27.

† **सर्ब्** *SARB*, **सम्ब्** *SAMB*, i. 1, Par. To go.

सर्म *sarma*, i.e. *sṛi + ma*, m. Going.

सर्व् *SARV*, see *çarv.*

सर्व *sarva*, probably *sa + tra + va*, I. adj., f. *vâ.* **1.** All, Nal. 17, 50. **2.** Every, Megh. 20; 91. **3.** Whole, entire, Pańch. 53, 24. II. m. Vishṇu, Çiva. —Cf. ὅλος; Lat. soll-ennis, soll-ers, salvus, salus (= ved. *sarva + tâti*, ὁλότης).

सर्वंसह *sarvaṁsaha*, i.e. *sarva + m -sah + a*, I. adj. **1.** All-sustaining. **2.** Patient, enduring. II. f. *hâ*, The earth, Govardh. Âryâ Saptaçatî, 163, d.

सर्वक *sarva + ka*, adj. All, every.

सर्वकर्मीण *sarvakarmîṇa*, i.e. *sarva -karman + îna*, adj. Performing, or conversant with, every business.

सर्वग *sarva-ga*, I. adj. All-pervading. II. m. **1.** Brahman. **2.** Çiva. **3.** Soul, spirit. III. n. Water.

सर्वगतत्व *sarva-gata + tva* (vb. *gam*), n. Omnipresence, Bhâshâp. 25.

सर्वगुह्यमय *sarva-guhya + maya* (vb. *guh*), adj. Made up of all mystery, Johns. Sel. 23, 117.

सर्वंकष *sarvaṁkasha*, i.e. *sarva + m -kash + a*, I. adj. All-pervading, all-subduing, Mâlat. 14, 19. II. m. A rogue.

सर्वजित् *sarva-ji + t*, adj. **1.** All-subduing, irresistible. **2.** All-surpassing.

सर्वज्ञ *sarva-jña*, I. adj. Omniscient, Hit. 129, 9; Bhartṛ. 2, 8. II. m. Çiva. — Comp. *A-*, adj. not omniscient, Râjat. 5, 317.

सर्वज्ञानमय *sarva-jñâna + maya*, adj., f. *yî*, Containing every knowledge, Man. 2, 7.

सर्वतस् *sarva + tas*, adv., and prep. with the acc., Siddh. K. 36, a. **1.** From every quarter, Man. 2, 240; from every part, Pańch. iii. d. 51; from everybody, i. d. 156 (cf. Böhtl. Ind. Spr. 1031). **2.** In every direction, Nal. 1, 25. **3.** Round about, Chr. 4, 19. **4.** Wholly, entirely.

सर्वतेजोमय *sarvatejomaya*, i.e. *sarva-tejas + maya*, adj., f. *yî*, Containing every splendour, Man. 7, 11.

सर्वतोदिक्क *sarvatodikka*, i.e. *sarvatas-diç + ka*, adj. Diffused over all quarters, Râjat. 5, 262.

सर्वतोदिशम् *sarvatodiçam*, i.e. *sarvatas-diç + a + m*, adv. To every quarter (of the world), Nal. 16, 5.

सर्वत्र *sarva + tra*, I. = loc. of *sarva*, Châṇ. 48 in Berl. Monatsb. 1864, 410. II. adv. **1.** In all places, everywhere, Pańch. ii. d. 125. **2.** At all times, always, Vikr. 30, 14; 39, 14.

सर्वथा *sarva + thâ*, adv. **1.** In all ways, by all means, Pańch. 161, 13; with *na*, Not at all, Mâlat. 154, 13. **2.** At every time, Man. 2, 15. **3.** Certainly, Vikr. 32, 8. **4.** Exceeding, mostly, completely, Hit. 81, 22.

सर्वदा *sarva + dâ*, adv. At all times,

always, Râm. 6, 10, 23; Pańch. ii. d. 25.

सर्वदेवमय *sarva-deva + maya*, adj., f. *yî*, Made of, or comprising all, the gods, Pańch. i. d. 136.

सर्वधुरावह *sarva-dhurâ-vah + a*, and **सर्वधुरीण** *sarva-dhurîṇa*, m. An ox fit for any carriage or draught.

सर्वंदम *sarvaṁdama*, i.e. *sarva + m -dam + a*, m. A name of Bharata.

सर्वभूतकृत् *sarva-bhûta-kṛi + t*, adj. Who or what causes all that exists, Man. 1, 18.

सर्वभूतमय *sarva-bhûta + maya*, adj. I. Comprising all beings, Man. 1, 7. II. m. The supreme Spirit.

सर्वभूतात्मन् *sarvabhûtâtman*, i.e. *sarva-bhûta-âtman*, m. The universal all-pervading Spirit, Man. 1, 54.

सर्वमय *sarva + maya*, adj., f. *yî*, General, universal, comprehensive.

सर्वमेध्यत्व *sarva-medhya + tva*, n. Perfect purity, Böhtl. Ind. Spr. 3296 = Pańch. iii. d. 212.

सर्वर्तुक *sarvartuka*, i.e. *sarva-ṛitu + ka*, adj. Fit for, or inhabitable in, every season, Man. 7, 76.

सर्वशस् *sarva + ças*, adv. **1.** Universally, everywhere, Johns. Sel. 29, 34. **2.** All together, Chr. 37, 1; Nal. 2, 22; 12, 85.

सर्वसिद्धार्थ *sarvasiddhârtha*, i. e. *sarva-siddha* (vb. *sidh*), *-artha*, adj. Having every wish attained, Man. 1, 83.

सर्वाङ्गीण *sarvâṅgîṇa*, i. e. *sarva -aṅga + îna*, adj. **1.** Spreading through the whole body, spread over all the limbs, Vikr. d. 51; thrilling through the whole body, d. 149. **2.** Relating to the Aṅgas or parts of science collectively.

सर्वान्नीन *sarvânnîna*, i. e. *sarva -anna + îna*, adj. Eating all sorts of food.

सर्षप *sarshapa*, I. m. **1.** A sort of mustard, Sinapis dichotoma, Windischmann, Sankara, 165. **2.** A small measure of weight, a mustard seed so considered. **3.** A sort of poison. **II.** f. *pî*, A small bird.—**Comp.** *Gaura-*, m. 1. white mustard, Sinapis glauca, Man. 5, 120; Suçr. 1, 16, 10. 2. a measure of weight, Man. 8, 133. *Râjasarshapa*, i.e. *râjan-*, m. 1. mustard. 2. a measure of weight, Man. 8, 133.

† **सल्** *SAL*, i. 1, Par. To go (cf. *sṛi*).

सलिल *salila* (vb. *sṛi*, cf. *sara*), n. Water, Pańch. 165, 7.—**Comp.** *Antaḥsalila*, i.e. *antar-*, adj., f. *lâ*, containing water, Ragh. 3, 9. *A-gâdha-*, adj. having bottomless water, Pańch. ii. d. 21. *Nayana-*, n. tears, Megh. 40; 88. *Niḥsalila*, i.e. *nis-*, adj. deprived of water, Râjat. 1, 33.

सलिलपूरवत् *salila-pûra + vat*, adv. Like a large quantity of water, Pańch. ii. d. 42.

सलिलस्थलचर *salila-sthala-chara*, adj. sbst. Living in water and on the land, Pańch. 131, 12.

सलिलेशय *salileçaya*, i.e. *salila + i + çî + a*, adj. Lying in water, Lass. 50, 7.

सलोकता *sa-loka + tâ*, f. Condition of dwelling in the same world as, Man. 11, 220.

सव *sava*, i.e. *su*, and *sû*, *+ a*, I. m. **1.** Sacrifice. **2.** Offspring. **3.** The sun. **4.** The moon. **II.** n. **1.** Sprinkling the Soma, or juice of the acid Asclepias. **2.** The juice of flowers. **3.** Water.—**Comp.** *Go-*, m. a kind of sacrifice, Man. 11, 74.

सवन *savana*, i.e. *su*, and *sû*, + *ana*, I. m. The moon. II. n. **1.** Extracting and drinking the Soma, or juice of the acid Asclepias. **2.** A sacrifice, Râm. 1, 13, 5. **3.** Bearing children, bringing forth young.

सवितृ *savitṛi*, i.e. *sû* + *tṛi*, I. m. The sun, Vikr. d. 20. II. f. *trî*, A mother. III. adj. Causing, Kir. 3, 5.

सवृद्धिक *sa-vṛiddhi* + *ka*, adj. Bearing interest.

सव्य *savya*, adj. **1.** Left, left hand, Pańch. i. d. 86. **2.** Southern, south. **3.** Backward, reverse, contrary. — **Comp.** *Apa-*, I. adj. right (not left), Man. 3, 214; *apasavyam̃ kṛi*, to keep the right side towards one, ib. II. *apasavyam*, adv. from the left to the right, Man. 3, 279.—Cf. σκαιός; Lat. scævus, probably also sinister.

सव्यतस् *savya* + *tas*, adv. On one's left hand, Chr. 34, 14.

सव्यसाचिन् *savyasâchin*, perhaps *savya-sa-ańch* + *in* (cf. *sâchi*), m. (Drawing the bow with his left hand), a name of Arjuna, Pańch. iii. d. 237.

सव्येष्टृ *savyeshṭhṛi*, i.e. *savya* + *i* *-sthâr* (*sthâr* for *sthân*, with *r* for *n*, and *sthân* for *sthânt*, old ptcple. pres. of *sthâ*), m. A charioteer.

सश्च् *SAÇCH*, see *sach*.

सस् *SAS*, † **शस्** *ÇAS*, † **संस्त्** *SAM̃ST*, † **शंस्त्** *ÇAM̃ST*, ii. 2, Par. To sleep.

सस्य *sasya*, n. **1.** Fruit, Nal. 24, 52 (at the end of a comp. adj., f. *yâ*). **2.** Corn, grain, Man. 4, 26 (cf. *çasya*, under *çam̃s*). **3.** A weapon (cf. *ças*). **4.** A quality, an excellence (cf. *çam̃s*). —Cf. perhaps εἶα, ἤϊον.

सस्यक *sasya* + *ka*, I. adj. Possessed of all good qualities. II. n. **1.** A sort of precious stone. **2.** A sword.

1. **सह्** *SAH* (probably a combination of two originally different verbs, viz. *sah*, 'to conquer,' cf. *sahas*, and *sa* *-vah*, 'to bear,' cf. infin. *soḍhum* = *sa-voḍhum*, ptcple. of the pf. pass. *soḍha* = *sa-ûḍha*), i. 1, Âtm. (also Par.), and † i. 10, Par. **1.** To bear, Vikr. d. 135; Böhtl. Ind. Spr. 997 (Par.); to undergo, Man. 2, 227. **2.** To endure, Bhartṛ. 2, 30. **3.** To allow, Pańch. 135, 7 (Par.). **4.** To forbear (with gen.), Bhag. 11, 44. **5.** To be patient, to wait, Ragh. 5, 25. **6.** To be able to resist, to oppose, to conquer, Râm. 1, 22, 21. **7.** To stop, Râm. 2, 24, 27. **8.** To be able (with infin.), Hit. ii. d. 139. Comp. ptcple. of the pres. *a-sahamâna*, adj. Not able to endure, Pańch. 221, 1. Ptcple. of the pf. pass. *soḍha*. **1.** Borne, endured. **2.** Patient, enduring. *sahita*, see s.v. Ptcple. of the fut. pass. *sahya*. **1.** Equal or adequate to, Pańch. ii. d. 200 (but cf. my transl. n. 907). **2.** Sweet, agreeable; see also s.v. **Comp.** *A-sahya*, adj. 1. insupportable, Ṛit. 1. 10. 2. unconquerable, Ragh. 18, 24.—With the prep. **अभि** *abhi*, absol. *abhishahya*, Forcibly, Man. 8, 367. — With **उद्** *ud*, **1.** To make an effort or exertion, Bhaṭṭ. 19, 16. **2.** To dare, Pańch. 22, 1; with acc., To dare to pursue, Nal. 4, 16. **3.** To be able (with infin. and dat. of an abstract noun), Râm. 3, 51, 17; MBh. 3, 16543 (*paribhogâya*, To enjoy). — With **अभ्युद्** *abhi-ud*, To be able, to wish, Ragh. 5, 22.—With **प्रोद्** *pra*

-ud, Caus. To incite, to instigate, Râm. 2, 9, 46.—With समुद् *sam-ud*, Caus. To incite, MBh. 2, 1412.—With प्र *pra*, **1.** To make an effort, Pañch. iii. d. 51. **2.** To endure, Utt. Râmach. 148, 5; absolut. *prasahya*, Violently, Man. 8, 235. **3.** To overpower, Râm. 2, 51, 7. **4.** To be able (with infin.), MBh. 1, 4842. — With अभिप्र *abhi-pra*, To be able, Kir. 12, 18.—With प्रति *prati*, To sustain, Râm. 1, 37, 8. —With वि *vi*, **1.** To sustain, Ragh. 4, 49. **2.** To suffer, Râm. 2, 61, 4. **3.** To endure, Râm. 2, 12, 106. **4.** To be able to resist, MBh. 5, 2021. **5.** To determine. Ptcple. of the fut. pass. *vishahya*, Possible, Arj. 5, 9. **Comp.** *A-*, adj. not being able to be determined or ascertained, Man. 8, 265. *Durvishahya*, i.e. *dus-*, adj., f. *yâ*, difficult to be sustained.—Cf. ἔχω, ἕξω, ἔσχον, ἐχυρός, σχέσις, ἰσχάνω, ὑπισχνέομαι, σχολή; see *sahas* and *sahya*.

† 2. सह् *SAH*, i. 4, Par. **1.** To bear. **2.** To satisfy. **3.** To delight.

1. सह *sah + a*, I. adj. **1.** Bearing, Bhartṛ. 2, 68. **2.** Suffering. **3.** Enduring, Pañch. iii. d. 178 (*çîta-vâta-âtapa-*, Enduring coldness, wind, and heat). **4.** Patient. **5.** Able, Vikr. 78, 10; Çiç. 9, 51. II. m. and n. Strength, power. III. m. The month Mârgaçîrsha (November—December). IV. f. *hâ*. **1.** The earth. **2.** The name of several plants.—**Comp.** *A-*, adj. 1. not able to support, Kathâs. 9, 37. 2. impatient, 6, 114. 3. unable, Hit. ii. d. 120 (*bharasya*, to bear). *A-kâla-*, adj. unable to be maintained a long time, Hit. iii. d. 135. *Niḥsaha*, i.e. *nis-*, adj. 1. unable to bear, Kathâs. 17, 9. 2. powerless, Gît. 2, 17. *Mahâ-*, I. adj. much-enduring. II. f. *hâ*, the name of several plants. *Çatru-*, adj. enduring an enemy. *Sarva-*, adj. enduring everything, very patient, Hit. i. d. 63, M.M. *Sva-kârya-*, adj. able to do one's duty, Vikr. d. 156.

2. सह *saha*, i.e. *sa + dhâ* (with *h* for *dh* as often, and the final shortened, cf. *tra* for *trâ*, *sadha*, ved.), **1.** adv. as former part of comp. words, With, united, common, like, complete (e.g. *sahakârin*). **2.** prep. With (with instr., Râm. 3, 55, 41; epic also with dat., Chr. 13, 15; with abl., Chân. 105 in Berl. Monatsb. 1864, 413).—Cf. probably Lat. sōdā + lis.

सहक *sah + aka*, adj. Enduring, Nalod. 2, 14.

सहकार i.e. I. *sa-ha-kâra*, adj. Endowed with the letter *ha*, i.e. the vocative particle, i.e. calling, Nalod. 2, 14. II. 2. *saha-kâra*, m. A fragrant sort of mango, Vikr. d. 25.

सहकारिता *sahakâritâ*, i.e. *sahakârin + tâ*, f. Co-operation, assistance.

सहकारिन् *saha-kârin*, adj., f. *iṇî*, Co-operating, assisting, Bhâshâp. 80.

सहकृत् *saha-kṛi + t*, and सहकृत्वन् *saha-kṛi + tvan*, adj. sbst. Assisting, an assister.

सहचर *saha-char + a*, I. m. A companion, Pañch. 243, 3; a friend, 43, 4. II. f. *rî*, A companion, a wife, Vikr. d. 102.

सहचार *sahachâra*, i.e. *saha-char + a*, m. The accompaniment of the middle term by the major, Bhâshâp. 136.

सहचारिन् *saha-chârin*, m. A companion, a friend, Pañch. 43, 1 (*paras-param ativa*, Very dear to each other).

सहज *saha-ja,* I. adj. **1.** Born or produced with, together, Johns. Sel. 16, 66. **2.** Innate, Indr. 4, 7. **3.** Natural, Hit. 87, 12; Pańch. 110, 15. II. m. **1.** A brother of whole blood. **2.** The natural state or disposition.

सहजन्या *saha-janyâ* (see *janya*), f. The name of an Apsaras, Vikr. 51, 4.

सहदेव *saha-deva,* I. m. The youngest of the five Pâṇḍava princes. II. f. *vâ* and *vî,* The name of several plants, Pańch. 157, 23 (*vî*).

सहधर्म *saha-dharma,* m. Community of duty.

सहधर्मचारिन् *sahadharma-chârin,* I. m. A husband, Çâk. 111, 12. II. f. *iṇî,* A legitimate wife, ib. 5; Utt. Râmach. 85, 12.

सहधर्मिन् *sahadharmin,* i.e. *saha-dharma + in,* I. adj., f. *iṇî.* **1.** Following the same law. **2.** Having same or like properties. II. f. *iṇî,* A woman married according to the ritual of the Vedas.

सहन *sah + ana,* I. adj. Enduring. II. n. Bearing, enduring.—Comp. *A-*, adj., f. *nâ,* 1. unable to bear or endure, Kathâs. 15, 87. 2. jealous, Vikr. d. 55.

सहपांसुकिल *saha-pâṁsu-kila* (*kila,* Play, Hemach.), and **सहपांसुक्रीडन** *saha-pâṁsu-krîḍana,* adj. sbst. m. (properly, One who has played with another in the sand, i.e. in his childhood), a friend from childhood, Mûlat. 151, 17 (*-krîḍana*).

सहस् *sah + as,* I. m. **1.** The month Mârgaçîrsha (Nov.—Dec.). **2.** The winter season. II. n. **1.** ved. Victory, strength, Lass. 101, 10=Rigv. vii. 16, 4; power. **2.** instr. *sâ,* adv. **a.** Without consideration, precipitately, Hit. iv. d. 97; quickly, Râm. 3, 54, 9. **b.** On a sudden, Pańch. 222, 23; Çâk. d. 9; at once, Pańch. 182, 14; with (?), Johns. Sel. 46, l. 1 (perhaps corr. *saha châps°*). **3.** Light.—Cf. Goth. sigis; A.S. sigor, sige.

सहस्य *sahas + ya,* m. The month Pausha (Dec.—Jan.), Pâṇ. iv. 4, 128.

सहस्र *sahasra,* numeral, n. A thousand, Pańch. 130, 16.—Comp. *Paraḥsahasra,* i.e. *paras-*, adj., f. *râ,* more than a thousand, Utt. Râmach. 11, 8.

सहस्रकृत्वस् *sahasra-kṛitvas,* adv. **1.** A thousand times, Man. 2, 79. **2.** Repeatedly.

सहस्रतय *sahasra + taya,* I. adj. Thousandfold. II. n. A thousand, Çiç. 9, 80.

सहस्रधा *sahasra + dhâ,* adv. In a thousand ways, thousandfold, Kir. 5, 17; in a thousand pieces, Pańch. 190, 10.

सहस्रमीळ्ह *sahasra-mîḷha* (ved. for *mîḍha,* vb. *mih*), adj. Yielding a thousand treasures, Chr. 296, 10= Rigv. i. 112, 10.

सहस्रशस् *sahasra + ças,* adv. By a thousand, or thousands, Pańch. i. d. 262; thousandfold.—Comp. *Çata-*, adv. by hundreds of thousands, by myriads, Johns. Sel. 11, 27.

सहस्रिन् *sahasrin,* i.e. *sahasra + in,* I. adj., f. *iṇî.* **1.** Having a thousand, Pańch. v. d. 69. **2.** Consisting of thousands, Chr. 291, 15=Rigv. i. 64, 15. **3.** (A fine) amounting to a thousand, Man. 8, 376. II. m. **1.** A body of a thousand men. **2.** Commander or prefect of a thousand.

सहस्वन्त् *sahas + vant,* adj., f. *vatî,*

Powerful, Lass. 99, 2=Rigv. v. 9, 7 (ved. voc. °*vas*).

सहाय *sahâya*, probably *saha-i+a*, m. **1.** A companion, Pańch. 221, 22. **2.** An adherent. **3.** A helper, Lass. 52, 1. **4.** An ally, Daçak. in Chr. 201, 1. **5.** The ruddy goose, Anas casarca. **6.** A sort of drug and perfume.—**Comp.** *A-*, adj. one who has no assistant, Man. 7, 30; no allies, Pańch. iii. d. 54. *Karinî-*, adj. with his female elephant, Vikr. 64, 2. *Dus-*, adj. abandoned, MBh. 5, 1861. *Dharma-*, m. a companion for fulfilling religious duties, Sâh. D. 37, 2. *Madhu-*, m. Kâmadeva, the god of love. *Vachana-*, m. a companion for conversation, Pańch. 221, 22.

ऽसहायक *-sahâya+ka*, instead of *sahâya*, at the end of a comp. adj., in *nârâyaṇa-*, Accompanied by Nârâyaṇa, Johns. Sel. 90, 29.

सहायता *sahâya+tâ*, f., and **सहायत्व** *sahâya+tva*, n. **1.** A multitude of companions. **2.** Companionship, union, Pańch. 59, 10 (*tva*). **3.** Help, Pańch. 154, 17 (*tva*).

सहायवन्त् *sahâya+vant*, adj., f. *vatî*, **1.** Having a companion, Pańch. i. d. 97; Hit. iv. d. 18 ('in the true sense of the word'). **2.** Assisted, befriended.—**Comp.** *A-*, adj. alone, Man. 6, 42.

सहित *sahita*, i.e. 2. *saha+ita*, adj. **1.** Accompanied by; at the end of comp. words, With, Hit. 61, 4. **2.** With (with instr.), Chr. 23, 32. **3.** Associated, Chr. 62, 52. pl. All, Lass. 2. ed. 61, 30. —**Comp.** *Karṇa-*, adj. with the ears, Pańch. 217, 5.

सहिष्णु *sah+ishṇu*, adj. **1.** Able to support, Çâk. d. 37. **2.** Patient, Kir. 2, 50; resigned.—**Comp.** *A-*, adj. **1.** unable to bear, Mâlat. 144, 4. **2.** unable, Hit. 126, 17. **3.** envious, Hit. 85, 8.

सहिष्णुता *sahishṇu+tâ*, f. **1.** Ability to support, Vedântas. in Chr. 203, 17. **2.** Patience, resignation.—**Comp.** *A-*, f. envy, Bhartṛ. 2, 42.

सहुरि *sah+uri*, I. m. The sun. II. f. The earth.

सहोढ *sahoḍha*, i.e. *saha-ûḍha* (vb. *vah*), m. **1.** The son of a pregnant bride, Man. 9, 160. **2.** A thief caught with stolen property upon him.

सहोर *sahora*, i.e. probably *saha+van+a*, with *r* for *n*, adj. Good, excellent.

सह्य *sahya*, **A.** See *sah*. **B.** i.e. *saha+ya*, I. adj. Powerful, strong. II. n. **1.** Health, convalescence. **2.** Assistance, Râm. 6, 3, 26. **C.** m. The name of a range of mountains, Kir. 18, 5.—Cf. perhaps σαυ and σω in σαώτερος, σῶος, σωτήρ, σώζω, σῶκος; Lat. sanus, but questionable on account of A.S. sund; O.H.G. ga-sunt (perhaps=*saha+vant*).

सांयात्रिक *sâm̃yâtrika*, i.e. *sam̃yâtrâ+ika*, m. A merchant who trades by sea, Pańch. i. d. 220.

सांयुगीन *sâm̃yugîna*, i.e. *sam̃yuga+îna*, I. adj. Skilled in war, Vikr. 87, 2; warlike, Ragh. 11, 30. II. m. **1.** A soldier skilled in war. **2.** An able leader.

सांराविण *sâm̃râviṇa*, i.e. *sam-ru+in+a*, n. Shout, Mâlat. 77, 12.

सांवत्सर *sâm̃vatsara*, i.e. *sam̃vatsara+a*, I. adj. Annual, perennial. II. m. An almanac-maker, an astrologer, Kâm. Nîtis. 4, 33; Pańch. iii. d. 67.—**Comp.** *Ati-*, adj., f. *rî*, going beyond a year, Man. 8, 153.

सांवत्सरिक *sâṁvatsarika*, i.e. *saṁvatsara+ika*, I. adj. Yearly, Man. 7, 80. II. m. An astrologer, Pańch, 156, 21.

सांवादिक *sâṁvâdika*, i.e. *saṁvâda+ika*, m. A logician.

सांवृत्तिक *sâṁvṛittika*, *saṁvṛitti+ika*, Phenomenal, illusory.

सांशयिक *sâṁçayika*, i.e. *saṁçaya+ika*, adj. 1. Dubious, Pańch. iii. d. 11. 2. Irresolute.

सांसारिक *sâṁsârika*, i.e. *saṁsâra+ika*, adj. Worldly, Utt. Râmach, 45, 12.

सांसिद्धिक *sâṁsiddhika*, i.e. *saṁsiddhi+ika*, adj. 1. Belonging to a thing's nature, innate, Bhâshâp. 38. 2. Effected naturally, spontaneous, Sânkhya Aph. iii. 20. 3. Effected by supernatural means, as spells, etc. ib. v. 111.

सांस्थानिक *sâṁsthânika*, i.e. *saṁsthâna+ika*, m. An inhabitant or native of the same place.

साकम् *sâkam*, i.e. *sa-ańch+a+m* (cf. *sâchi*), I. adv. At the same time, together, Chr. 290, 4=Rigv. i. 64, 4. II. prep. With (with instr.), Kâvya Prak. 103, 6.

साकल्य *sâkalya*, i. e. *sa-kala* (see *kalâ*), *+ya*, n. 1. Totality, Nalod. 3, 19 ; instr. *yena*, Completely, Man. 12, 25. 2. The whole, all.

साकेत *sâketa*, n. A name of Ayodhya, Ragh. 13, 79.

साकेतक *sâketa+ka*, m. An inhabitant of Sâketa, Çâk. 90, 23 (Prâkṛ.).

साक्तुक *sâktuka*, i.e. *saktu+ka*, I. m. Barley. II. n. A quantity of fried grain.

साक्षतम् *sâkshatam*, i.e. *sa-a-kshata* (vb. *kshaṇ*), *+m*, adv. Uninterruptedly, Lass. 66, 4.

साक्षात् *sâkshât*, abl. sing. of *sa-aksha*, adv. 1. In presence, Nal. 24, 13 (in their presence, being present); before, eye to eye, Indr. 2, 16. 2. From (cf. *sakâçât*, s.v. *sakâça*), Arj. 1, 12. 3. Manifestly, evidently, visibly, Man. 2, 237 ; Pańch. 46, 6 ; Nal. 1, 4 (*sakshâd -iva manuḥ*, like an embodied Manu); with one's own eyes, Pańch. 197, 12. 4. Openly, Mâlat. 6, 13. 5. As, like.

साक्षात्कार *sâkshât-kâra*, m. Perception, Vedântas. in Chr. 215, 24 ; Bhâshâp. 84.

ऽसाक्षिक *sâkshika*, i.e. *sâkshin+ka*, a substitute for *sâkshin*, when latter part of comp. adj. ; e.g. *a-*, adj. Where there was no witness, Man. 8, 109. *agni-*, adj. Having fire or Agni as witness, Râm. 4, 7, 4.

साक्षिता *sâkshitâ*, i.e. *sâkshin+tâ*, f. Testimony, evidence, Man. 8, 80.

साक्षिन् *sâkshin*, i.e. *sa-aksha+in*, I. adj., f. *iṇî*. 1. Witnessing, having witnessed, Hit. iv. d. 62. 2. Attesting. II. m. A witness, Pańch. iii. d. 93 ; with gen. and loc., Pâṇ. ii. 3, 39. —Comp. *Kûṭa-* and *Dus-*, m. a false witness, Yâjú. 2, 77 (*kûṭa-*); Râm. 3, 18, 34 (*dus-*).

साक्षिमन्त् *sâkshimant*, i.e. *sâkshin+mant*, adj., f. *matî*, Having or requiring witness.

साक्ष्य *sâkshya*, i.e. *sâkshin+ya*, n. 1. Evidence, Man. 8, 82. 2. Giving evidence, 8, 62 ; testimony, MBh. 5, 1225.

साखेय *sâkheya*, i.e. *sakhi + eya*, adj. Friendly.

सागर *sâgara* (cf. *sagara*), m. **1.** The ocean, Pańch. i. d. 240. **2.** A kind of deer.—**Comp.** *Kshira-*, m. the sea of milk, Bhâg. P. 8, 5, 11. *Pûrva-*, m. the eastern sea, Ragh. 4, 32. *Buddhi-*, m. a proper name, or rather, plenty of wisdom, or having plenty of wisdom, Lass. 6, 2.

सागरग *sâgara-ga* (vb. *gam*), f. The Gaṅgâ or Ganges, Chr. 47, 34.

साग्र *sâgra*, i.e. *sa-agra* (*agra*, adj. Excessive, Gramm.), adj. With a surplus, more than, Râm. 5, 7, 28 ; 4, 8, 47.

साङ्कर्य *sâṅkarya*, i.e. *saṁkara + ya*, n. **1.** Mixture. **2.** The concurrence of various properties in one subject.

साङ्काश्या *sâṅkâçyâ*, i.e. *saṁkâça + ya*, f. Name of a town, Râm. 1, 70, 3.

साङ्क्षेपिक *sâṅkshepika*, i.e. *saṁkshepa + ika*, adj. Short, summary.

साङ्ख्य *sâṅkhya*, i.e. *saṁkhya + a*, **I.** adj. **1.** Numeral, relating to number. **2.** Deliberating, reasoning, Bhag. 3, 3. **3.** Rational, discriminative. **II.** m. The Sâṅkhya system of philosophy, Bhâg. P. 5, 18, 33; Bhag. 2, 39.

साङ्ग *sâṅga*, i.e. *sa-aṅga*, adj. **1.** With the members, divisions. **2.** Complete, finished, Utt. Râmach. 166, 2.

साङ्गतिक *sâṅgatika*, i.e. *saṁgati + ika*, **I.** adj. Associating. **II.** m. **1.** A visitor. **2.** One who comes on business, Man. 3, 103.

साङ्ग्रामिक *sâṅgrâmika*, i.e. *saṁgrâma + ika*, adj., f. *kâ*, Relating to war, Utt. Râmach. 114, 6 ; Pańch. i. d. 103 ; warlike, martial.

साचि *sâchi*, i.e. loc. sing. of *sa-ańch*, adv. Crookedly, awry, Kir. 10, 57.

साचिव्य *sâchivya*, i.e. *sachiva + ya*, n. **1.** Friendship. **2.** Ministership, Pańch. 13, 4.

साजात्य *sâjâtya*, i.e. *sa-jâti + ya*, n. Community of genus, Bhâshâp. 166.

† **साट्** *SÂṬ*, i. 10, Par. To make manifest.

साति *sâti*, i.e. *san + ti* and *so + ti*, f. **1.** Gaining, acquisition, Chr. 297, 22=Rigv. i. 112, 15. **2.** Gift, giving. **3.** End, conclusion. **4.** Destruction. **5.** Sharp pain.—**Comp.** *Vâja-*, f. gain of food, Chr. 298, 24=Rigv. i. 112, 24.

सात्त्विक *sâttvika*, i.e. *sattva + ika*, **I.** adj. **1.** Endowed with the quality *sattva*, i.e. the best of qualities, Man. 3, 263. **2.** Endowed with goodness, Man. 12, 40. **3.** Relating, belonging to, or proceeding from, that quality, Bhag. 7, 12 ; Man. 12, 31. **4.** Good, honest, true, Hit. i. d. 15, M.M. ; sincere, Mâlat. 16, 3. **II.** m. Brahman.

सात्यकि *sâtyaki*, m. The charioteer of Kṛishṇa.

सात्यवत *sâtyavata*, i.e. *satyavatî* (see *satyavant*), + *a*, metronym., m. The son of Satyavatî, i.e. Vyâsa.

सात्वत *sâtvata*, i. e. probably *sâtvant + a*, **I.** m. **1.** Vishṇu. **2.** Baladeva. **3.** The son of an outcaste Vaiçya, Man. 10, 23. **4.** pl. The name of a people. **II.** f. *tî*, A proper name.

सात्वन्त् *sâtvant*, m. **1.** A follower, a worshipper. **2.** A man of the Yâdava tribe, Bhâg. P. 8, 5, 13.

साद *sâda*, m., i.e. **A.** *sad + a*, **1.** Perishing, decay, Nalod. 2, 26 ; 3, 24 ; Vikr. d. 44 (*a-paksha-*, Not being deprived of its wings). **2.** Weariness, exhaustion, Ragh. 8, 57 ; Çiç. 9, 77. **3.** Pain, Nalod. 2, 26. **B.** Purity, Padmap.

8, 20; cleanness.—**Comp.** *Kara-*, m. sinking down of one's arms, and setting or disappearing of the sun's rays, Pańch. i. d. 194.]

सादन *sâdana*, i. e. *sad*, Caus., +*ana*, n. **1.** Dispelling. **2.** Destroying. **3.** Wearying. **4.** Exhaustion. **5.** A house, a dwelling, Hiḍ. 4, 7.—**Comp.** *Yama-*, n. the palace of Yama i.e. Tartarus, Lass. 17, 3.

सादि *sâdi*, i.e. *sad*+*i*, m. A charioteer.

सादिन् *sâdin*, i.e. *sad-in*, I. adj. Destroying, Râm. 2, 34, 37. II. m. One who rides on a horse or elephant, or is mounted in a car, Johns. Sel. 26, 8; Râjat. 5, 451.—**Comp.** *Açva-*, m. a horseman, Ragh. 7, 44.

सादृश्य *sâdṛiçya*, i.e. *sadṛiça*+*ya*, n. **1.** Resemblance, similarity, Kir. 5, 26; Bhâshâp. 78. **2.** A likeness, Megh. 83.

साद्यस्क *sâdyaska*, i.e. *sadyas*+*ka*, adj. Quick, instantaneous.

साध् *SADH* (i.e. probably *so-dhâ*), ii. 5, Par. **1.** To finish, to accomplish. **2.** To conquer, Hit. iii. d. 40. † i. 4, Par. To be completed or accomplished (cf. *sidh*). Caus. (also of *sidh*, q. cf.), **1.** To bring to a conclusion, to accomplish, Daçak. in Chr. 197, 24; Hit. i. d. 1. **2.** To prepare for heaven, Man. 2, 248. **3.** To secure, Man. 7, 173. **4.** To effect, to perform, MBh. 5, 117. **5.** To overcome, Hit. 59, 21; to conquer, MBh. 1, 7435; to kill, Pańch. 211, 12. **6.** To obtain, Man. 6, 75. **7.** To recover a debt, Man. 8, 176. **8.** To learn, Ragh. 10, 29. **9.** To set out, to go away, Çâk. 7, 19; to fly, Mâlat. 126, 5; to proceed, Vikr. 60, 13. Ptcple. of the pf. pass. *sâdhita*. **1.** Accomplished, Daçak. in Chr. 197, 24. **2.** Mastered, Kathâs. 46, 118; obtained, Daçak. in Chr. 189, 11. **3.** Successful, Lass. 3, 16. **4.** Recovered (as a debt). **5.** Fulfilled, discharged. **6.** Punished, Pańch. 257, 4; punished by fine. **7.** Awarded (as the thing or fine). **8.** Awarded to or in favour of (as the person to whom the fine is to be paid). Ptcple. of the fut. pass. *sâdhya*. **1.** What must or will be accomplished, Hit. pr. d. 1. **2.** Practicable, Daçak. in Chr. 190, 23. **3.** Conquerable, Pańch. i. d. 244. **4.** To be mastered, Pańch. i. d. 73; Çiç. 5, 49. **5.** Able to be destroyed, Pańch. 194, 19. **6.** To be inferred or concluded, Bhâshâp. 137. **7.** To be cured, curable. m. A class of inferior deity, Man. 3, 195. n. **1.** Accomplishment, perfection. **2.** (In logic), The major term in a syllogism, Siddh. Mukt. 62, 3. **Comp.** *A-*, adj. 1. unattainable, Pańch. i. d. 223. 2. intractable, Hit. ii. d. 98. *Âyâsa-*, adj. scarcely to be settled, Pańch. i. d. 421. *Duḥsâdhya*, i.e. *dus-*, adj. 1. difficult to be accomplished, Pańch. ii. d. 26. 2. difficult to be conquered, Pańch. 56, 10. 3. difficult to be cured, Hariv. 16132.

—With the prep. **उप** *upa*, *upasâdhita*, Subdued, Pańch. iii. d. 249.—With **परि** *pari*, Caus. To settle, Man. 8, 187.—With **प्र** *pra*, Caus. **1.** To further, Pańch. i. d. 407. **2.** To accomplish, Pańch. i. d. 140. **3.** To dress, Çâk. 49, 21. **4.** To acquire, Pańch. i. d. 2. **5.** To subdue, Man. 7, 103. *prasâdhita*, **1.** Accomplished, done. **2.** Ornamented, decorated, Daçak. in Chr. 180, 10. *prasâdhya*, **1.** What may be done. **2.** To be destroyed, defeated. **Comp.** *Dushprasâdhya*, i.e. *dus-*, adj. difficult to be defeated, Kâm. Nîtis. 10, 38.—With **संप्र** *sam-pra*, Caus. To settle, Hit. iv.

d. 117.—With सम् *sam*, Caus. **1.** Âtm. To be successful, MBh. 3, 1478. **2.** To endow with, Râm. 2, 36, 9. **3.** To destroy, MBh. 3, 1683. **4.** To extinguish, MBh. 1, 2841. **5.** To obtain, Man. 2, 100. **6.** To cause to be paid, 8, 213. **7.** To regain, 8, 50. —Cf. probably Goth. sandjan ; A.S. sendan.

साधक *sâdh + aka*, **I.** adj., f. *dhikâ*, **1.** Accomplishing. **2.** Helping, Indr. 5, 56. **3.** Magical, Pañch. 241, 2 ; an adept, Mâlat. 74, 6 ; 9, 7 (Prâkṛ.). **II.** f. *ikâ*, Deep sleep (=*sushupti*, a vedantic term).—**Comp.** *Uttara-*, m. one who accomplishes what remains, an assistant, Lass. 3, 20. *Kârya-*, adj., f. *dhikâ*, accomplishing one's aim, Hit. i. d. 34, M.M.

साधन *sâdh + ana*, n. **1.** Accomplishing, Hit. iv. d. 98 (*sâdhya-*, What must be accomplished, i.e. one's aim). **2.** Advancement, Man. 4, 196. **3.** A means of accomplishing, Pañch. i. d. 8. **4.** Wealth. **5.** A part of an army, Utt. Râmach. 39, 12. **6.** Instrument. **7.** Cause, efficient cause, Man. 11, 237 ; source of prosperity, Man. 12, 100. **8.** Subduing by charms, Pañch. 241, 2. **9.** Killing, destroying, Kir. 14, 17. **10.** Obsequies. **11.** Authority. **12.** Proof, substantiation. **13.** The *hetu* or middle term in an inference. **14.** Enforcement of the delivery of anything, of payment, especially juridically, Daçak. in Chr. 180, 20 ; 185, 21. **15.** Medicament, drug. **16.** Matter, materials, that of which anything is composed. **17.** Substance, thing. **18.** The penis, Sâh. D. 212, 19. **19.** Going. **20.** Following, profit, Pañch. 86, 24. **21.** Good works, Windischmann, Sankara, 97. **22.** Friendship.—**Comp.** *A-*, adj. having no means, Hit. i. d. 1, M.M. *Tri-*, adj., f. *nâ*, having a threefold origin, Ragh. 3, 13 (viz. majesty, perseverance, and counsel). *Mantra-*, n. a magical performance, Lass. 3, 16 (*ghora-*, dele ऽ before *ghora*). *Lekhana-*, n. writing materials, Çâk. 37, 9 (Prâkṛ.). *Sâdhya-*, n. effecting what is to be done, Hit. iv. d. 98. *Siddha-*, I. m. white mustard. II. n. 1. the performance of magical rites. 2. the materials employed in magical or alchemical processes.

साधनता *sâdhana + tâ*, f., and **साधनत्व** *sâdhana + tva*, n. State or condition of being a means to a desired end, Bhâshâp. 146 (*tva*); 147 (*tâ*).—**Comp.** *Bahu-sâdhanatâ*, f. possessing many expedients, Çiç. 9, 6.

साधन्त *sâdhant + a* (vb. *sâdh*), m. A beggar.

साधर्म्य *sâdharmya*, i.e. *sa-dharma + ya*, **1.** Community, equality, of duty, Vikr. 65, 12. **2.** Community of properties, common character, Bhâshâp. 12, 28 ; likeness, Kusumâñj. 3, 9.

साधारण *sâdhâraṇa*, i.e. *sa-dhâraṇa + a*, adj. **1.** Belonging to many, common, Bhâshâp. 71 ; equal, Vikr. d. 34. **2.** Like, similar, Lass. 85, 10.—**Comp.** *A-*, adj. 1. not common, Bhâshâp. 72. 2. unparalleled, Hit. 32, 8, M.M. 3. excessive, Daçak. in Chr. 183, 17.

साधारणत्व *sâdhâraṇa + tva*, and **साधारण्य** *sâdhâraṇya*, i.e. *sâdhâraṇa + ya*, n. Community, universality, general law, Journ. of the German Oriental Society, ix. xxxix. 10.

साधिमन् *sâdhiman*, i.e. *sâdhu + iman*, m. Goodness, excellence.

साधिष्ठ *sâdhishṭha*, **साधीयंस्** *sâdhiyaṁs*, see *vâḍha* and the next.

साधु *sâdh+u*, I. adj., f. *dhu* and *dhvî*, comparat. *sâdhîyañs*, superl. *sâdhishṭha*, **1.** Perfect, Çâk. d. 2. **2.** Fit, proper, right. **3.** Good, Hit. i. d. 11, M.M.; kind, Pańch. iv. d. 72; virtuous, pure. **4.** Excellent. **5.** Beautiful, pleasing. **II.** acc. sing. *dhu*, adv. **1.** Well, Çâk. d. 11; Vikr. 6, 6. **2.** Indeed, Vikr. 20, 9. **3.** With instr., prohibiting, Enough, away with, Pańch. v. d. 40. **III.** m. **1.** A Muni or sage. **2.** An honest man, Pańch. 67, 6. **3.** A usurer, Hit. 111, 1; a merchant, Hit. 65, 9. **IV.** f. *dhu* and *dhvî*, A chaste, virtuous woman. — **Comp.** *A-*, adj. wicked, Kir. 14, 12; 21; unpleasant, Kir. 1, 4. *Sarva-*, adv. quite well, Hit. 127, 14.

साधुता *sâdhu+tâ*, f., and **साधुत्व** *sâdhu+tva*, n. **1.** Correctness, Utt. Râmach. 4, 10 (*tva*). **2.** Goodness, Pańch. i. d. 277 (*tva*); Daçak. in Chr. 187, 23 (*tâ*).—**Comp.** *A-sâdhutva*, n. wickedness, Hit. iii. d. 48.

साधुंमन्य *sâdhummanya*, i.e. *sâdhu+m-man+ya*, adj. Thinking one's self virtuous.

साधुशीलत्व *sâdhu-çîla+tva*, n. Virtuous disposition, Hit. i. d. 85, M.M.

साध्य *sâdhya*, **1.** See *sâdh*. **2.** i.e. *sâdhya+a*, adj. Belonging to the Sâdhyas, a class of inferior deity, Arj. 4, 30.

साध्यता *sâdhya+tâ*, f. in *a-*, State of not being able to be overcome, Pańch. i. d. 245.

साध्यवन्त् *sâdhya+vant* (vb. *sâdh*), I. adj., f. *vatî*, Comprehending that which is to be proved. II. m. (In law), The party on whom rests the onus probandi. **III.** n. That in which the *sâdhya* or major term resides (i.e. the *paksha* and its *sapaksha's*), Bhâshâp. 67; 73.

साध्वस *sâdhvasa*, probably *sa-dhvañs+a+a*, n. **1.** Fear, terror, Vikr. d. 56; Mâlav. 20, 9; 53, 21; Çâk. 12, 21. **2.** Perturbation, Bhâg. P. 1, 11, 19. **3.** Torpor, Utt. Râmach. 80, 10.—**Comp.** *Ati-*, m. too great fear, Hit. iii. d. 123. *Niḥsâdhvasa*, i.e. *nis-*, adj. 1. fearless, Hariv. 8709. 2. bold, Râm. 1, 64, 16 Gorr. *Sa-*, adj., f. *sâ*, alarmed, frightened, timid, Vikr. 28, 10. °*sam*, adv., 28, 14.

सानसि *sânasi*, m. (?), f. (?), Gold.

सानु *sânu*, probably *so+nu*, m. and n. **1.** End, point, the top of a mountain, Mâlat. 145, 10. **2.** Level ground on the top or edge of a mountain, table-land, Bhâg. P. 4, 25, 13. **3.** A forest. **4.** A shoot, a sprout. **5.** A road. **6.** A gale of wind. **7.** A learned man, a sage. **8.** The sun.—**Comp.** *Antaḥsânu*, i.e. *antar-*, adv. on a table-land, Kir. 5, 36.

सानुमन्त् *sânu+mant*, I. m. A mountain, Vikr. d. 76. **II.** f. *matî*, The name of an Apsaras, Çâk. 77, 1.

सान्तपन *sântapana*, i.e. *sam-tap+ana+a*, n. A sort of penance, Man. 11, 212; 5, 20; 11, 129.—**Comp.** *Mahâ-*, n. a severer sort of penance.

सान्तानिक *sântânika*, i.e. *samtâna+ika*, I. adj. **1.** Expansive. **2.** Relating to posterity. **3.** Belonging to the heavenly tree, *samtâna*, Kir. 18, 20. **II.** m. A Brâhmaṇa intending to marry for the sake of issue, Man. 11, 1.

सान्त्व् *SÂNTV*, and **सान्त्व** *sântva* see *çântv*, *çântva*.

सान्त्वन *sântv+ana*, I. n. **1.** Conciliation, reconcilement. **2.** Appeasing, Râjat. 5, 345 (at the end of a comp. adj.). **II.** n., and f. *nâ*. **1.** Speaking kindly and in a conciliatory manner. **2.** Mildness, Daçak. in Chr. 185, 21 (n.);

kind or deceiving words, Pañch. iv. d. 1 (n. pl.). **3.** Friendly salutation and enquiry.

सान्दृष्टिक *sândṛishṭika*, i. e. *sam-dṛiç+ti+ika*, m. Immediate consequence.

सान्द्र *sândra*, I. adj. **1.** Thick, coarse, gross, Chaurap. 12; Ṛit. 1, 20; intense, Çiç. 9, 15; 22. **2.** Stout, robust. **3.** Much, abundant, Mâlat. 60, 18. **4.** Vehement, Böhtl. Ind. Spr. 830; Daçak. in Chr. 190, 8; Ragh. 7, 11; *sândratara*, Increased, Çiç. 9, 37. **5.** Clustering, collected. **6.** Compact, but having interstices. **7.** Unctuous, oily, Kâvya Prak. 62, 11. **8.** Soft, bland. **9.** Pleasing, agreeable, Mâlat. 127, 12; Megh. 97 (v.r.). **II.** n. **1.** A thicket, a wood. **2.** A heap, a cluster.—Cf. probably *ἁδρός*.

सान्धिविग्रहिक *sândhivigrahika*, i.e. *saṁdhi-vigraha+ika*, m. Prime minister (who decides peace and war), Lass. 2. ed. 16, 9; Sâh. D. 7, 8.

सान्ध्य *sândhya*, i. e. *saṁdhyâ+a*, adj. Relating to twilight or the evening, Kir. 5, 8; Çiç. 9, 15.

सान्नहनिक *sânnahanika*, i.e. *saṁnahana+ika*, I. adj. **1.** Bearing or putting on armour. **2.** Calling to arms. **II.** m. An armour-bearer.

सान्नाय्य *sânnâyya*, i.e. probably *sam-nâyya* (ptcple. of the fut. pass. of the Caus. of *nî*), *+a*, n. The thing to be offered with fire, Pâṇ. iii. 1, 129.

सान्निध्य *sânnidhya*, i.e. *saṁnidhi+ya*, n. **1.** Vicinity, Pañch. 258, 7. **2.** Presence, Man. 8, 87; attendance, Hit. 53, 12. **3.** °*yam*, adv. Near, Indr. 5, 24. —Comp. *A-*, n. absence, Râm. 3, 55, 50.

सान्निध्यतस् *sânnidhya+tas*, adv. From the proximity, Mâlat. 48, 8.

सान्निपातिक *sânnipâtika*, i.e. *saṁnipâta+ika*, adj. **1.** Complicated (as disease), relating to the morbid state of the three humours collectively, Hit. iii. d. 119. **2.** Miscellaneous, promiscuous, collective.

सान्न्यासिक *sânnyâsika*, i.e. *saṁnyâsa+ika*, m. A beggar.

सापत्न *sâpatna*, i.e. *sa-patnî+a*, adj. Born from another wife, Râm. 3, 53, 30.

सापत्न्य *sâpatnya*, i.e. **A.** *sapatna+ya*, I. m. An enemy. **II.** n. Ambition, Râm. 1, 45, 16. **B.** *sa-patnî+ya*, n. Plurality of wives, or the condition of the wife of one who has other wives.

सापिण्ड्य *sâpiṇḍya*, i.e. *sa-piṇḍa+ya*, n. Kindred, connexion, by presenting offerings to the same Manes.

साप्तपद *sâptapada*, i.e. *saptan-pada+a*, adj. Produced by seven steps (walked together), Pañch. ii. d. 47; Sâv. 5, 22.

साप्तपदीन *sâptapadîna*, i.e. *sâptapada+îna*, n. Friendship, Kumâras. 5, 39.

साप्तपौरुष *sâptapaurusha*, i.e. *saptan-purusha+a*, adj., f. *shî*, Comprising seven generations, Man. 3, 146.

साफल्य *sâphalya*, i.e. *sa-phala+ya*, n. **1.** Productiveness, fruitfulness, Hit. ii. d. 21. **2.** Advantage, Man. 12, 93. **3.** State of earning the fruit, Mâlat. 72, 9 (at the end of a Bahuvr.).

† **साम्** *SÂM*, i. 10 (rather a denomin. derived from *sâman*), Par. To conciliate, to appease.

सामग्र्य *sâmagrya*, i.e. *samagra+ya*, n., and f. *grî*, **1.** Entireness, wholeness, the whole, Bhâshâp. 63 (*grî*); Râm. 2, 70, 45, Seramp. (read *prâ-*

ṇasâmagryam). **2.** Perfection, Pańch. 109, 10 (*grî*). **3.** Stock, Hit. 130, 1 (*grî*); effects. **4.** Implements, apparatus, Pańch. iii. d. 129 (*grî*); utensils, 250, 5 (*grî*). **5.** Train, retinue, Hit. 98, 11 (*grî*).

सामज *sâmaja*, I. i.e. *sâman* + *ja*, adj. Producing from or produced by the Sâma-Veda. II. m. An elephant.

सामञ्जस्य *sâmańjasya*, i.e. *samańjasa* + *ya*, n. Fitness.

सामन् *sâman*, probably for *çâman* (cf. *çântva*, *sântvana*), i.e. *çam* + *man*, n. **1.** Calming, Nalod. 1, 41. **2.** Conciliation. **3.** Speaking kindly, Böhtl. Ind. Spr. 1847. **4.** Mildness, Man. 8, 187; instr. *mnâ*, Willingly, voluntarily, Pańch. iv. d. 27. **5.** Negotiation, Man. 7, 107. **6.** Peaceable way, Pańch. i. d. 421; Chr. 20, 17. **7.** The name of the third Veda, the Sâma-Veda, Man. 1, 23. **8.** Song, Bhag. 10, 35; Indr. 2, 28.—**Comp.** *Jyeshṭha-*, I. n. the name of a particular song (of the Sâma-Veda), Man. 3, 185. II. m. one who sings this song, Yâjń. 1, 219. *Tri-*, adj. one who sings three verses (of the Sâma-Veda), or the song called *triḥsâman* (?), MBh. 12, 3638. *Su-*, n. good negotiation, Pańch. iii. 21.

सामन्त *sâmanta*, i.e. *samanta* + *a*, I. adj. **1.** Limitative. **2.** Bordering, neighbouring, Man. 8, 259. **3.** Universal, Ragh. 5, 28 (Sch.). II. m. **1.** A neighbour, Man. 7, 69; Pańch. iii. d. 91. **2.** The chief of a district, a (tributary) king, Mâlat. 102, 6; Râjat. 5, 223; Vikr. d. 60. **3.** A leader, a general, Râm. 1, 20, 12; a champion, Râjat. 5, 249. III. n. Neighbourhood.

सामयिक *sâmayika*, i.e. *samaya* + *ika*, adj. **1.** According to agreement, exact. **2.** Conventional, customary. **3.** Seasonable.—**Comp.** *A-*, unseasonable, Kir. 2, 40.

सामर्थ्य *sâmarthya*, i.e. *samartha* + *ya*, n. **1.** Fitness, Râjat. 5, 308. **2.** Adequacy, Pańch. i. d. 215 (that which is adequate, but cf. Böhtl. Ind. Spr. 1873, v.r.); being entitled, Böhtl. Ind. Spr. 3027. **3.** Profit, Râm. 2, 61, 44, Seramp. **4.** Ability, Pańch. 263, 7. **5.** Strength, Râjat. 5, 384; power, Hit. ii. d. 140; fortitude, Bhag. 2, 36. **6.** Mutual relation of words. **7.** Sense of words.—**Comp.** *A-*, n. weakness, Pańch. 69, 3. *Niḥsâmarthya*, i.e. *nis-*, adj. unfit, MBh. 5, 4587. *Hîna-darçanu-* (vb. *hâ*), adj. blind, Râjat. 5, 219.

सामर्षता *sâmarshatâ*, i.e. *sa-a-marsha* + *tâ*, f. Wrath, Ragh. 7, 41.

सामवायिक *sâmavâyika*, i.e. *samavâya* + *ika*, m. **1.** The chief of a company or corporation. **2.** A principal minister.

सामाजिक *sâmâjika*, i.e. *samâja* + *a*, m. An assistant or spectator at an assembly, Mâlav. 17, 23.

सामानाधिकरण्य *sâmânâdhikaraṇya*, i.e. *samâna-adhikaraṇa* + *ya*, n. **1.** Common office. **2.** The condition of relating to the same object, Vedântas. in Chr. 212, 21. **3.** The residing in the same substratum or subject, Kusumâńj. 14, 20.

सामान्य *sâmânya*, i.e. *samâna* + *ya*, I. adj. **1.** Common, Hit. i. d. 157, M.M.; Nal. 13, 17; in common, Pańch. 264, 2; base, Râjat. 5, 197; *sâmânyatara*, Very insignificant, not dexterous, Pańch. 133, 1. **2.** Equal, Çâk. d. 92. **3.** Generic. **4.** General, universal, whole. II. n. **1.** Totality. **2.** Public affairs, Man. 7, 56. **3.** Equanimity, Hit. i. d. 95, M.M. **4.** Common property, Hit. pr. d. 25, M.M. **5.** Kind, genus, or species, Bhâshâp. 1; 7; 63. **6.** Identity, Vedântas. in Chr. 210, 11. **III.** f. *yâ*, A whore.—**Comp.** *A-* and *nis-*, adj. uncommon, extraordinary, Pañch. 115, 7; Râjat. 4,371. *An-anya-nârî-*, adj. having no intercourse with other women, Vikr. d. 59. *A-loka-*, adj. uncommon, Mâlat. 6, 8. *Sarva-*, adj. common to all.

सामासिक *sâmâsika*, i.e. *samâsa* + *ika*, adj. **1.** Compounded, Bhag. 10, 33; composite. **2.** Comprehensive, comprising the whole, Man. 7, 180; 10, 63. **3.** Summary, brief.

सामि *sâmi*, i.e. a form of the old instr. **sâmyâ* of *sâmya* (cf. *âdi* for *âdya*), adv. **1.** Half. **2.** Blameably.—Cf. O.H.G. sâmi-, A.S. sâm-, e.g. in O.H.G. sâmi-quek, A.S. sâm-cucc; Lat. semi-, ἡμι, ἥμισυς.

सामिधेन्य *sâmidhenya*, i. e. *sam -idhenya* (an old ptcple. of the fut. pass. of *indh*), + *a*, **I.** m. A mantra or mystical prayer. **II.** f. *nî*. **1.** Fuel. **2.** A prayer used on adding fuel to the sacrificial fire.

सामीप्य *sâmîpya* i.e. *samîpa* + *ya*, **I.** m. A neighbour, Sâv. 2, 8. **II.** n. Proximity.

सामुद्र *sâmudra*, i.e. *samudra* + *a*, **I.** adj. Marine, sea-born. **II.** m. A mariner, a voyager. **III.** n. **1.** Sea-salt. **2.** Cuttle-fish bone. **3.** (i.e. *sa -mudra* + *a*, see *mudrâ*), A spot or mark on the body (cf. the next).

सामुद्रिक *sâmudrika*, i.e. *sa* + *mudra* (cf. *mudrâ*), + *ika*, **I.** adj. Relating to spots on the body, or the good or ill fortune supposed to be indicated by them. **II.** m. An interpreter of spots on the body.

साम्पराय *sâmparâya*, i.e *sam̃parâya* + *a* **I.** adj. Warlike (?), MBh. 1, 723. **II.** (n.), **1.** Future, MBh. 1, 1921. **2.** Future life, Bhâg. P. 8, 19, 2.

साम्परायिक *sâmparâyika*, i.e. *sam̃parâya* + *ika*, **I.** adj. **1.** Relating to war, military, Man. 7, 185; warlike, Ragh. 17, 62. **2.** Calamitous. **3.** Future, relating to a future state, Man. 11, 30. **II.** n. War, battle.

साम्प्रतम् *sâmpratam*, i.e. *sam̃prati* + *a* + *m*, adv. **1.** Now, at this time, Pañch. 161, 18. **2.** Seasonably, fitly, properly.—**Comp.** *A-sâmprata*, adj. unbecoming, Pañch. i. d. 275. °*tam*, adv. unbecomingly, Hit. iii. d. 111.

साम्प्रतिक *sâmpratika*, i.e. *samprati* + *ika*, adj. Suitable, Utt. Râmach. 73, 3.

साम्प्रदायिक *sâmpradâyika*, i. e. *sam̃pradâya* + *ika*, adj. Belonging to traditional doctrine, transferred by traditional doctrine, Utt. Râmach. 155, 8 (*a-*, with *nahi*, Their tradition will not die out, they are hereditary).

साम्ब् *SÂMB*, see *samb*.

साम्बवती *sâmbavatî*, A proper name, Râjat. 5, 295.

साम्य *sâmya*, i.e. *sama* + *ya*, n. **1.** Equality, Man. 11, 195. **2.** Equability, Bhag. 6, 33. **3.** Harmony, Daçak. in Chr. 180, 4. **4.** Likeness, similarity, Kir. 17, 51.—**Comp.** *Tri-*, n. equality of the three fundamental qualities, Bhâg. P. 2, 7, 40.

साम्राज्य *sâmrâjya*, i.e. *samrâj* + *ya*, n. Imperial rule, Man. 8, 387; sovereignty, Pañch. 42, 14; Râjat. 5, 49; 151.

साम्राज्यकृत् *sâmrâjya-kṛi* + *t*, adj. One who gains imperial rule, Man. 8, 387.

साय *sâya*, **A.** i.e. *so+a*, **I.** m. **1.** End. **2.** Evening, Vikr. 77, 12. **B.** m. An arrow. **II.** acc. *yam*, adv. Evening, in the evening, Pańch. iii. d. 159. **III.** loc. *ye*, adv. In the evening.—**Comp.** *Ati-sâyam*, adv. too late, Man. 4, 62.—Cf. Lat. sērus, sērum.

सायक *sâya+ka* (and **शायक** *çâyaka*), m. **1.** An arrow, Pańch. 120, 10. **2.** A sword.—**Comp.** *A-sama-* and *Pushpa-*, m. Kâma, the god of love, Kathâs. 15, 2; Lass. 66, 11.

सायकमय *sâyaka + maya*, adj. Consisting in arrows, MBh. 4, 1853.

सायन्तन *sâyantana*, i.e. *sâya+m+tana*, adj., f. *nî*, Belonging to the evening, vespertine, Pańch. 229, 10; Bhâg. P. 3, 20, 37.

सायुज्य *sâyujya*, i.e. *sa-yuj+ya*, n. **1.** Intimate union, identification. **2.** Similarity, likeness.—**Comp.** *Râja-sâyujya*, i.e. *râjan-*, n. royalty.

सार् *SÂR*, see *çâr*.

सार *sâra*, perhaps *sṛi+a*, with 'cream,' II. **9.** as first signification, I. adj. **1.** Essential, Hit. iv. d. 71. **2.** Excellent, best, Daçak. in Chr. 194, 22; Pańch. i. d. 284; Hit. iii. d. 89. **3.** Hard, Çâk. d. 10. **4.** Irrefragable (as an argument), proved, Man. 9, 262. **II.** m. (and n.). **1.** The pith or sap of trees. **2.** The essence of anything, the essential or vital part of it, Hit. ii. d. 126; Pańch. 49, 4. **3.** Nectar, Bhâg. P. 7, 6, 25. **4.** The substance or material part (of a book, speech, etc.), Pańch. pr. d. 3; 10 (n.). **5.** Marrow, Ragh. 10, 10. **6.** Strength, vigour, Hit. 104, 7; affluence, Hit. i. d. 90, M.M. (*artha-*, of wealth, cf. **IV. 2.**). **7.** Prowess, heroism. **8.** Firmness, hardness. **9.** The coagulum of curds, cream. **10.** Fresh butter. **11.** Air, wind (cf. *çâra*). **12.** Disease, pus, Hit. ii. d. 101 (and wealth). **III.** m., and f. *rî*, A man at chess, backgammon (cf. *çâra*). **IV.** n. **1.** Water. **2.** Wealth, Man. 8, 126; Daçak. in Chr. 189, 3 (at the end of a comp. adj.). **3.** Fitness. **4.** Steel. **5.** (In rhetoric), Climax. **V.** f. *râ*, Kuça grass. **VI.** f. *rî*, Turdus Salica Buch. —**Comp.** *A-*, adj. 1. sapless, Hit. iv. d. 87. 2. insipid, Daçak. in Chr. 188, 2; vain, Pańch. 165, 17. 3. weak, Pańch. i. d. 376. 4. bad, Man. 8, 202. 5. poor, Daçak. in Chr. 180, 23. *Sâra-a-*, m. 1. strength and weakness, Hit. 104, 7. 2. excellence or defect, Man. 9, 331. 3. substance and emptiness. *Agra-*, f. *râ*, a method of numbering, by which one may sum up the sand of a hundred Koṭis of Gańgâ rivers, Lalit. 141 (cf. Archimedes' method). *Adri-*, m. iron. *Antaḥsâra*, i.e. *antar-*, I. m. and n. 1. the inward pus and wealth, Hit. ii. d. 101. 2. own worth, Châṇ. 69 in Berl. Monatsb. 1864, 411. II. adj. 1. having inward essence, full of strength, Pańch. i. d. 142. 2. heavy, ponderous. *Artha-*, m. important motive, Pańch. ii. d. 46. *Açmasâra*, i.e. *açman-*, m. iron, Suçr. 2, 531, 4. *Eka-*, m. only essence, Bhartṛ. 2, 1. *Kṛishṇa-* (cf. *çâra*), I. adj. of a blue-black colour, Râm. 5, 32, 47. II. m. 1. the black-pied antelope, Man. 2, 23; Vikr. d. 120. 2. the name of several plants. *Giri-*, m. 1. iron. 2. tin. *Ghana-*, m. camphor, Lass. 92, 8. *Chandana-*, m. the best sandal, Râm. 2, 20, 43 Gorr. *Tvaksâra*, i.e. *tvach-*, m. reed, Man. 10, 37. *Dṛishṭa-*, adj. one of whom the strength is tested, Kâm. Nîtis. 8, 67. *Nis-abhibhava-*, adj. having the highest excellence, i.e. than which there is nothing better, Bhartṛ. 2, 54 (but cf. also Böhtl. Ind. Spr. 1859). *Niḥsâra*, i.e. *nis-*, adj., f. *râ*, 1. sapless, Suçr. 1, 20, 16; Châṇ. 66 in Berl. Monatsb. 1864, 411. 2. powerless, insignificant, Pańch. i. d. 421. 3. insipid. 4. vain, perishable, Hit. iv. d. 71. *Prâṇa-*, adj. having the marrow of life, Çâk. d. 37. *Vajra-*, I. adj. having the vigour of a thunderbolt, Pańch. 58, 10. II. m. a proper name, Râjat. 5, 226. *Vedânta-*, m. the essence of the Vedânta philosophy, Vedântas. title, in Chr. 202, 1. *Çilâ-*, m. iron. *Çaila-*, adj. firm as a rock, Kir. 10, 14. *Sa-kala-artha-çâstra-*, adj. containing the essence of precepts about all things, Pańch. pr. d. 3. *Sattva-*, m. excellence of strength, i.e. the most powerful, Utt. Râmach. 151, 1. *Su-*, m. 1. a kind of jewel or crystal (?), MBh. 7, 672. 2. Mimosa catechu. *Sva-anubhûti-eka-sâra-*, adj. whose only essence consists in enjoying himself, Bhartṛ. 2, 1.—Cf. *sara*; Goth. sêls; A.S. sel, sael.

सारङ्ग *sâraṅga* (cf. *çâraṅga*), I. adj. Variegated, spotted. II. m. **1.** Variegated colour. **2.** A lion. **3.** An elephant. **4.** A deer, Vikr. 68, 9; Çâk. 5, 5. **5.** The Châtaka, Cuculus melanoleucus, Megh. 21. **6.** The Indian cuckoo. **7.** A kind of crane. **8.** A peacock. **9.** A large bee, Nalod. 1, 44. **10.** A cloud. **11.** A tree. **12.** A parasol. **13.** A garment. **14.** Hair. **15.** A lotus. **16.** A flower. **17.** A conch-shell. **18.** A jewel. **19.** Gold. **20.** A bow. **21.** Kâmadeva, the god of love. **22.** Sandal. **23.** Camphor. III. f. *gî*, A sort of fiddle.—**Comp.** *Krishṇa-*, I. adj. black-pied. II. m. the black-pied antelope, Çâk. 61, 14 (v. r.).

सारण *sâraṇa*, i.e. *sṛi*, Caus., + *ana*, m. Dysentery.

सारणि and **णी** *sâraṇî* i.e. *sṛi* + *ana* + *i*, f. A canal, a water-conduit.

सारतस् *sâra* + *tas*, adv. **1.** Essentially. **2.** Vigorously. **3.** Concerning (their) wealth, fortune, Daçak. in Chr. 186, 8; in proportion to the value, Man. 8, 405.

सारता *sâra* + *tâ*, f. **1.** Essence, Pańch. ii. d. 84. **2.** Substance. **3.** Strength. **4.** Highest degree, Râjat. 5, 400.—**Comp.** *A-*, f. fragility, Ragh. 8, 50. *Sâra-a-*, f. strong and weak points, Pańch. 58, 9.

सारथि *sârathi*, i.e. *sa-ratha* + *i*, m. A charioteer, Bhâshâp. 49.—**Comp.** *Ku-*, m. a bad charioteer, Lass. 53, 11. *Dharma-*, a proper name, Bhâg. P. 9, 17, 11. *Pârshṇi-*, m. du. the two charioteers who govern the outer horses attached to the extremities of the axle-tree, MBh. 1, 5490. *Madhu-*, m. Kâmadeva, the god of love.

सारथ्य *sârathya*, i.e. *sârathi* + *ya*, n. Charioteership, charioteering, Chr. 27, 9.—**Comp.** *Açva-*, n. management of horses and cars, Man. 10, 47.

सारफल्गुत्व *sâra-phalgu* + *tva*, n. Importance and non-importance, the proportional importance, Man. 9, 56.

सारमेय *sârameya*, i.e. *saramâ* + *eya*, I. m. A dog, Pańch. 110, 23. II. f. *yî*, A bitch.—Cf. probably Ἑρμείας.

सारवत्ता *sâravattâ*, i.e. *sâravant* + *tâ*, f. Hardness, Ragh. 3, 63.

सारवन्त् *sâra* + *vant*, adj., f. *vatî*, **1.** Substantial, having pith, substance. **2.** Fertile, Hit. iv. d. 121.

सारस *sârasa*, i.e. *saras* + *a*, I. adj. Relating or belonging to a lake, Nalod. 2, 40. II. m., and f. *sî*, The Indian crane, male and female, Ardea sibirica, Râm. 3, 53, 58; Pańch. 82, 6; ii. d. 102 (cf. my transl.); a bird in general, Nalod. 2, 10. III. m. The moon. IV. n. A lotus, Chaurap. 44.—**Comp.** *Râja-sârasa*, i.e. *râjan-*, m. a peacock.

सारसन *sârasana*, i.e. *sa-rasana + a*, n. A girdle, Kir. 18, 32.

सारस्वत *sârasvata*, i.e. *sarasvant + î + a*, I. adj., f. *tî*. **1.** Relating to the goddess Sarasvatî. **2.** Relating or belonging to the river Sarasvatî, Megh. 50. **3.** Eloquent. II. m. **1.** A staff of the Vilva tree. **2.** The name of a country; pl. its people.

सारापराधतस् *sârâparâdhatas*, i.e. *sâra-aparâdha + tas*, adv. Conformably to the proved crimes, Man. 9, 262.

सारिका *sârikâ*, f. A bird, Turdus Salica and Gracula religiosa (cf. *çârikâ*), Pańch. iv. d. 51; Megh. 83.

ऽसारिन् *-sârin*, i.e. I. *sṛi + in*, adj. Going; *pûrva-*, Going in front, being the first, MBh. 5, 142. II. *sâra + in*, adj. Having the essence or substance of, Nal. 12, 59.

सारूप्य *sârûpya*, i.e. *sa-rûpa + ya*, n. **1.** Identity of form. **2.** Conformity, Man. 4, 18. **3.** Close resemblance.

सारूप्यतस् *sârûpya + tas*, adv. In consequence of the identity, Mâlat. 76, 20.

सार्थ *sârtha*, i.e. *sa-artha*, I. adj. **1.** Opulent. **2.** Of like meaning. **3.** Significant. II. m. **1.** A caravan, Pańch. 8, 21. **2.** A troop, Râjat. 5, 374. **3.** A multitude in general, Lass. 66, 17; Çák. 32, 6.—**Comp.** *Eka-sârtha + m*, together, Johns. Sel. 36, 6. *Bhańga-*, adj. fraudulent.

सार्थिक *sârthika*, i.e. *sârtha + ika*, m. A merchant, Pańch. 8, 20.

सार्धम् *sârdham*, i.e. *sa-ardha + m*, prep. (with instr.), With, Man. 1, 27; Pańch. i. d. 61; iii. d. 74.

सार्पिष *sârpisha*, and **सार्पिष्क** *sârpishka*, i. e. *sarpis + a*, or *ka*, adj. Dressed with clarified butter.

सार्पी *sârpî*, see the next.

सार्प्य *sârpya*, i.e. *sarpa + ya*, I. adj. Relating to a snake. II. f. *pî*, The ninth lunar mansion.

सार्वकामिक *sârvakâmika*, i.e. *sarva-kâma + ika*, adj. Satisfying every wish, Kir. 18, 25.

सार्वकालिक *sârvakâlika*, i.e. *sarva-kâla + ika*, adj., f. *kî*, Of all times or seasons, everlasting, MBh. 1, 7648.

सार्वजनिक *sârvajanika*, and **सार्वजनीन** *sârvajanîna*, i.e. *sarva-jana + ika*, or *îna*, adj. Relating, or belonging, or suited, to all men.

सार्वदैवत्य *sârvadaivatya*, i.e. *sarva-devata + ya*, adj. Presided over by, or sacred to, all the gods.

सार्वभौतिक *sârvabhautika*, i.e. *sarva-bhûta + ika*, adj. **1.** Belonging or relating to all elements, beings. **2.** Comprising all animated beings, Man. 12, 51.

सार्वभौम *sârvabhauma*, i.e. *sarva-bhûmi + a*, I. adj. Relating to, or consisting of, the whole earth. II. m. **1.** An universal monarch. **2.** The elephant of the northern quarter. **3.** A proper name, Bhâg. P. 9, 22, 10.

सार्वलौकिक *sârvalaukika*, i.e. *sarva-loka + ika*, adj. Prevailing through the universe, Mâlat. 7, 5.

सार्ववर्णिक *sârvavarṇika*, i.e. *sarva-varṇa + ika*, adj. **1.** Of every kind, Man. 2, 244. **2.** Belonging to every tribe.

सार्ववेदस *sârvavedasa*, i.e. *sarva-vedas + a*, m. One who gives away all his wealth at a sacred rite, Man. 11, 1.

सार्ववेद्य *sârvavedya*, i.e. *sarva-veda*

+*ya*, m. A Brâhmaṇa conversant with all the Vedas.

सार्षप *sârshapa*, i.e. *sarshapa* + *a*, I. adj. Made of or from mustard. II. n. Mustard oil.

सार्ष्टिता *sârshṭitâ*, perhaps *sa-ṛish* + *ti* + *tâ*, f. Equality, Man. 4, 232.

साल *sâla* (cf. *çâla*), I. m. 1. A wall surrounding a building, a wall in general, Daçak. in Chr. 201, 1. 2. A tree, Shorea robusta, Man. 8, 246. 3. A tree in general. 4. A fish, Ophiocephalus Wrahl. II. f. *lâ*, A house.

सालभञ्जिका *sâla-bhañj* + *ikâ*, f. A doll, a puppet.

सालोक्य *sâlokya*, i.e. *sa-loka* + *ya*, n. Habitation with, Man. 4, 231; MBh. 3, 11184.

साल्व *sâlva*, m. 1. = *çâlva*. 2. The name of a demon.

साल्वहन् *sâlva-han*, m. Vishṇu (the slayer of Sâlva).

सावधानता *sâvadhânatâ*, i. e. *sa-avadhâna* + *tâ*, f. Carefulness, Pañch. 34, 23.

सावन *sâvana*, i.e. *su*, Caus., + *ana*, m. 1. An employer of priests for a sacrifice. 2. The ceremonies by which a sacrifice is terminated. 3. Varuṇa. 4. A month of thirty solar days.

सावर्णि *sâvarṇi*, i.e. *sa-varṇa* + *i*, m. The eighth Manu, Bhâg. P. 8, 13, 11. — Comp. *Indra-*, the fourteenth Manu, ib. 34. *Daksha-*, m. the ninth Manu, ib. 18. *Deva-*, m. the thirteenth Manu, ib. 31. *Dharma-*, m. the eleventh Manu, ib. 25. *Brahman-*, m. the tenth Manu, ib. 21. *Rudra-*, m. the twelfth Manu, ib. 28.

सावर्ण्य *sâvarṇya*, i.e. *sa-varṇa* + *ya*, n. Identity of caste.

सावित्र *sâvitra*, i.e. *savitṛi* + *a*, I. adj. 1. Descended from the sun, Utt. Râmach. 132, 3. 2. Belonging to the dynasty descended from the sun, ib. 27, 13. II. m. 1. The sun. 2. Çiva. 3. A Vasu or demigod so called. 4. Karṇa, child of the sun. 5. One of the Nakshatras, or lunar asterisms, Johns. Sel. 15, 62. III. f. *trî*. 1. A beam of light, a cluster of solar rays. 2. Umâ, the wife of Çiva, Sâv. 1, 7. 3. A proper name, Sâv. 1, 21. 4. The name of the most holy verse of the Rigv. (iii. 62, 11), Man. 2, 77; 11, 191. 5. The ceremony of investiture with the sacrificial string, Man. 2, 38. IV. n. The sacrificial string.

साष्टाङ्गम् *sâshṭâṅgam*, i.e. *sa-ashṭan-aṅga* + *m*, adv. With a humble prostration (touching the earth with eight parts of the body, viz. the forehead, breast, both shoulders, hands, and feet), Pañch. 33, 12.

सास्ना *sâsnâ*, f. The dewlap of an ox, Sâh. D. 10, 3.

साहचर्य *sâhacharya*, i.e. *saha-chara* + *ya*, n. Company, association, congregation, Mâlat. 6, 2.

साहस *sâhasa*, i. e. *sahas* + *a*, n. (and m., Man. 8, 138), 1. Violence, Man. 8, 345. 2. Oppression, cruelty, Çiç. 9, 59. 3. Punishment, Man. 8, 120. 4. Rape, ravishment. 5. Hatred. 6. Boldness, daring, Hit. ii. d. 3; Pañch. 135, 8; courage, Mâlat. 75, 12. 7. Rashness, Hit. iii. d. 115; Hit. 100, 3. 8. Suicide, Pañch. 135, 6; Daçak. in Chr. 189, 7.—Comp. *Vishama-*, n. temerity.

साहसिक *sâhasika*, adj., i.e. *sâhasa* + *ika*, I. adj., f. *kî*. 1. Using force or violence, Man. 8, 344. 2. Rapacious. 3. Cruel, Mâlat. 9, 5. 4. Inflicted as punishment. 5. Perpetrated by violence. 6. Bold, daring. 7. Rash, Mâlat.

64, 4; impetuous. **II.** m. A robber, Pańch. i. d. 390.—**Comp.** *A-*, adj., f. *kî*, being of a mild disposition, Çiç. 9, 59. *Ati-*, adj. very bold, daring, Pańch. 241, 3. *A-sama-*, adj. who has not his match in boldness, Lass. 4, 17. *Mahâ-*, m. 1. an assaulter. 2. a robber.

साहसिकता *sâhasika + tâ*, f. in *mahâ-*, Great boldness, Pańch. 129, 22.

साहस्र *sâhasra*, i.e. *sahasra + a*, **I.** adj. **1.** Relating or belonging to a thousand. **2.** Bought with a thousand. **3.** Paid per thousand, as interest, duty. **4.** A thousandfold, a thousand times better, Man. 2, 85. **II.** m. An army or detachment, a thousand strong. **III.** n. An aggregate of many thousands.—**Comp.** *Daçasâhasra*, i.e. *daçan-*, I. adj. consisting of ten thousand, MBh. 4, 289. II. n. ten thousand, Hariv. 13900. *Dvâdaçasâhasra*, i.e. *dvâdaçan-*, adj. consisting of twelve thousand, Man. 1, 71. *Çata-*, adj. consisting of a hundred thousand, a hundred thousandfold, Man. 7, 85.

साहायक *sâhâyaka*, i.e. *sahâya + ka* (? perhaps it is to be read *sâhâyyaka*), n. Assistance, Râjat. 5, 307.

साहाय्य *sâhâyya*, i.e. *sahâya + ya*, n. **1.** Friendship. **2.** Alliance. **3.** Help, Pańch. ii. d. 13.

साहित्य *sâhitya*, i.e. *sahita + ya*, **I.** n., and f. *hitî*, Society, connexion, combination. **II.** n. Poetry, Böhtl. Ind. Spr. 3250.

साह्वय *sâhvaya*, i.e. *sa-âhvaya*, m. Fighting animals for sport or money. —Cf. *âhvaya*.

सि *SI*, ii. 5 and 9, Par. Âtm. To bind. Ptcple. of the pf. pass. *sita*, Bound, surrounded, Chr. 296, 5 = Rigv. i. 112, 5; cf. s.v. *sita*.—With the prep. **प्र** *pra*, *prasita*, **1.** Bound. **2.** Attached to. **3.** Diligent, attentive.—Cf. *siman*; σειρά; O.H.G. sail; A.S. sal, laqueus, sael, saelan, sicran, syrwan; Goth. in-sailjan, illaqueare; O.H.G. saito; A.S. sad, laqueus.

सिंह *simha*, **I.** m. **1.** A lion, Pańch. 218, 22. **2.** The sign Leo. **3.** As latter part of comp. words, Preeminent; e.g. *purusha-*, m. (properly, a lion-like man), A hero, Hit. pr. d. 31, M.M. *râjasimha*, i.e. *râjan-*, m. A great king, Hit. iii. d. 121. **II.** f. *hî*, A lioness, Râm. 3, 53, 46; Pańch. 218, 22.

सिंहल *simha + la*, **I.** n. **1.** Tin. **2.** Brass. **3.** Cassia bark. **II.** n., and f. *lâ*, Ceylon, Hit. 63, 10 (*la*).

सिंहान *simhâna*, n. **1.** Rust of iron. **2.** The mucus of the nose.

सिंहाय *SIMHÂYA*, a denomin. derived from *simha* with *ya*, Âtm. To behave like a lion, Hit. iii. 134.

सिंहासनस्थ *simhâsanastha*, i. e. *simha-âsana-stha*, adj. Sitting on the throne, Pańch. 195, 11.

सिंहिका *simhikâ*, i.e. *simhî + ka*, f. The mother of Râhu.

सिकत *sikata*, **I.** m. pl. Sand. **II.** f. *tâ*. **1.** Sandy soil. **2.** Sand, Vikr. d. 79 (pl.); Pańch. ii. d. 62. **3.** Gravel or stone (the disease).

सिकतामय *sikatâ + maya*, adj., f. *yî*, **सिकतावन्त्** *sikatâ + vant*, adj., f. *vatî*, and **सिकतिल** *sikatila*, i.e. *sikatâ + ila*, adj. Sandy, Bhartṛ. 3, 49 (*tila*, see Böhtl. Ind. Spr. 2721).

सिक्थ *siktha*, i. e. *sich + tha*. **I.** m. **1.** Boiled rice. **2.** A lump or ball of boiled rice, Skanda P., Kâçîkh. 81, 38. II. n. **1.** Beeswax. **2.** Indigo.

सिक्थक *siktha + ka*, n. Beeswax.—Comp. *Madhu-*, n. a sort of poison.

सिच् *SICH*, i. 6, *siñcha*, Par. Âtm. **1.** To sprinkle, MBh. 1, 8153. **2.** To discharge, Man. 11, 170; with *çukram*, To lose semen, 2, 181. **3.** To pour in, Bhartṛ. 2, 20.—With the prep. **अभि** *abhi, shich*, **1.** To besprinkle, Râm. 1, 38, 14; to wet, Pañch. 50, 9. **2.** To pour upon, Megh. 49. **3.** To inaugurate by sprinkling with sacred water, to initiate, Râm. 1, 1, 79; Vikr. d. 161. Âtm. To be inaugurated, MBh. 3, 14423. Caus. To cause to be inaugurated, MBh. 1, 3117.—With **अव** *ava, avasikta*, Sprinkled, MBh. 1, 7730.—With **आ** *â*, Caus. To order to be dropped in, Man. 8, 272.—With **उद्** *ud*, To make haughty, Ragh. 17, 43. *utsikta*, **1.** Sprinkled. **2.** Overflowing, abounding, Râm. 1, 21, 13. **3.** Haughty, Kathâs. 18, 86. **4.** Mad, Man. 8, 71.—With **नि** *ni, shich*, To sprinkle, Vikr. d. 23; Ragh. 3, 26. Caus. To cause to be sprinkled, Râm. 2, 63, 9.—With **परि** *pari, shich*, **1.** To sprinkle round about, Pañch. iii. d. 26. **2.** To sprinkle, MBh. 1, 4500.—With **प्र** *pra*, i. 4, To flow away, MBh. 3, 14767. *prasikta*, Sprinkled, Utt. Râmach. 58, 4.—With **सम्** *sam, saṁsikta*, **1.** Sprinkled, Râm. 1, 5, 8. **2.** Moistened, Pañch. iii. d. 33.—Cf. O.H.G. sîhan, colare, seihjan, mingere, probably Goth. saivs; O.H.G. seo, gi-sich; Lat. stilla (for stic-la; cf. strau in O.H.G. straum = Sskr. *sro*, vb. *sru*); *στίλη*, probably *ἰκμάς*, *σίκυς*.

सिचय *sichaya*, m. Cloth, Vikr. d. 7.

सिट् *SIṬ*, see *çiṭ*.

सित *sita*, I. (cf. *si* and *so*), adj. White, Vikr. d. 53; Pañch. 158, 3. II. m. **1.** White (the colour). **2.** The light half of the month from new to full moon, Râjat. 5, 327. **3.** The planet Venus. **4.** An arrow. III. f. *tâ*. **1.** Candied sugar. **2.** Moonlight. **3.** A handsome woman. **4.** Spirituous liquor. **5.** The name of several plants. IV. n. **1.** Silver. **2.** Sandal.—Comp. *A-*, adj., f. *tâ* and *asiknî*, I. adj. 1. black, Râm. 2, 96, 19. 2. the black half of the month from full to new moon, Pañch. ed. orn. i. d. 139. II. m. 1. black (the colour). 2. a proper name, MBh. 1, 106. III. f. *tâ*, a proper name, Hariv. 120. *Sita-a-*, I. adj. white and black. II. m. a name of Baladeva.

सिताभ्र *sitâbhra*, i.e. *sita-abhra*, m. and n. (also **सिताभ** *sitâbha*, a dialect. form, m., and **सिताभ्रक** *sitâbhra* + *ka*, n.), Camphor (Indr. 1, 6, *sitâbhra*, White clouds; MBh. 13, 836, *çitâbhra*, White-clouded).

सितिमन् *sitiman*, i.e. *sita* + *iman*, m. Whiteness, Çiç. 1, 25.

सिद्धान्त *siddhânta*, i.e. *siddha-anta*, m. Demonstrated conclusion, established truth, reliable doctrine; doctrine, Lass. 2. ed. 90, 40.

सिद्धार्थ *siddhârtha*, i. e. *siddha -artha*, I. adj. One who has obtained his aim, Chr. 62, 60; successful. II. m. White mustard, Pañch. 158, 3.—Comp. *A-*, adj. unfortunate, Râm. 3, 55, 20.

सिद्धि *siddhi*, i. e. *sidh* + *ti*, f. **1.** Accomplishment, Vedântas. in Chr. 202, 4; Hit. ii. d. 13; fulfilment, Vikr. d. 28 (read *abhimukhîshviva*, in the ed.

of Bollens). **2.** Success, Böhtl. Ind. Spr. 3255; prosperity, well-being, Pańch. i. d. 432. **3.** Use, Pańch. ii. d. 93 (*na siddhyai*, useless). **4.** Final emancipation, supreme felicity, Man. 2, 93. **5.** The fruit of the adoration of the gods or of ascetic austerities. **6.** The acquisition of supernatural powers by magical means, magical power, Pańch. 241, 3. **7.** A magical shoe, which is supposed to convey the bearer wherever he likes. **8.** A medicinal root. **9.** Indisputable conclusion, decision, Pańch. iii. d. 91. **10.** Validity. **11.** Knowledge, Vedântas. in Chr. 202, 8; understanding, intellect, Râm. 5, 18, 13. **12.** Acquittance, discharge (of debt). **13.** Concealment.—**Comp.** *A-*, f. 1. imperfect accomplishment, failure, Böhtl. Ind. Spr. 3255. 2. want of proof, conclusion not warranted by the premises, Bhâshâp. 74. *Âçraya-a-*, *Svarûpa-a-*, *Vyâpyatva-a-*, f. forms of *asiddhi*, or fallacious inference, Bhâshâp. 74–76. *Ati-*, f. excessive accomplishment, Râm. 4, 57, 10. *Anyathâ-*, f. establishing wrongly, especially assigning superfluous causes, Bhâshâp. 15. *Mahâ-*, f. magical power, Lass. 3, 17. *Yajńa-*, f. due performance of sacrifice, Man. 1, 23. *Rasa-*, f. knowledge of alchemy. *Vighâta-*, and *Vighna-*, f. removing obstacles. *Sâdhya-*, f. 1. completion. 2. establishing what is to be proved. *Sâmasiddhi*, i.e. *sâman-*, f. the art of accomplishing something in a peaceable way, Pańch. 91, 17.

1. सिध् *SIDH* (i.e. probably *so -dhâ*, cf. *sâdh*), i. 4, Par. (in epic poetry also Âtm., MBh. 3, 12025), **1.** To be accomplished, Pańch. i. d. 2. **2.** To reach, Çâk. d. 38 (with loc.). **3.** To attain one's aim, Pańch. i. d. 131. **4.** To succeed, Daçak. in Chr. 198, 3. **5.** To be established, Hit. 84, 17; to be valid, Man. 8, 74; 163. **6.** Pass. To be concluded, Bhâshâp. 77. Ptcple. of the pf. pass. *siddha*. **1.** Accomplished, Hit. i. d. 31, M.M. (*prakṛiti-*, by nature, i.e. natural; n. true nature, Bhartṛ. 2, 42); effected, settled, Pańch. i. d. 424. **2.** Succeeded, Pańch. 44, 10; successful, Pańch. v. d. 77. **3.** Liberated, emancipated. **4.** Endowed with supernatural powers. **5.** Prepared, compounded (in medicine). **6.** Ready (as money), Hit. ii. d. 92. **7.** Cooked, dressed, Man. 3, 84; Pańch. 116, 22. **8.** Subdued, acquired, by magical power, Lass. 2. ed. 3, 3; Kathâs. 18, 177; gained, Pańch. 250, 12. **9.** Demonstrated, proved. **10.** Judged, decided, Utt. Râmach. 10, 8. **11.** Valid, deemed right, Mâlat. 160, 5. **12.** Celebrated, famous. **13.** Shining, splendid. **14.** Eternal. **15.** Initiated in alchemy or magic, magical, Pańch. 241, 6. **16.** Discharged, settled (as a debt). m. **1.** A sort of demigod, Pańch. 242, 5. **2.** A wise man, Hit. ii. d. 98. **3.** An ascetic who has attained one or all of his purposes. **4.** A magician, Pańch. 242, 21. n. Sea salt. **Comp.** *A-*, adj. 1. unaccomplished. 2. imperfect. 3. unproven. 4. unripe. *Anyathâ-*, adj. wrongly established, especially used of superfluous causes, Bhâshâp. 20. *Rasa-*, I. adj. accomplished in poetry, Bhartṛ. 2, 21. II. m. an alchemist. *A-vi-hita-* (vb. *dhâ*), adj. not artificial, innate, Utt. Râmach. 154, 3. *Saṁkalpa-*, adj. endowed with supernatural powers by energy, Chr. 58, 4. *Suvarṇa-*, m. an adept who has acquired gold (by magical means), Pańch. 243, 1, sqq. Caus. *sedhaya* and *sâdhaya*, see *sâdh*. —With the prep. प्र *pra*, **1.** To be acquired, Man. 11, 237. **2.** To succeed, Bhag. 3, 8. **3.** To be known, Man. 12, 97. *prasiddha*, **1.** Celebrated, famous, Pańch. 127, 20; Lass. 49, 17. **2.** Known, Daçak. in Chr. 193, 11. **3.**

Adorned.—With सम् *sam,* To attain beatitude, Man. 2, 87. *saṁsiddha,* One who has attained beatitude, Lass. 49, 9.

2. सिध् *SIDH,* i. 1, Par. (in epic poetry also Âtm., MBh. 3, 15643), **1.** To command. **2.** To restrain, Lass. 101, 1 = Rigv. vii. 15, 10. **3.** To ordain. **4.** † To do an auspicious act. **5.** † To go. *siddha,* see s.v. 1. *sidh.*—With the prep. अप *apa,* To remove, Man. 11, 198.—With नि *ni, shidh,* **1.** To remove, Râjat. 5, 56. **2.** To prohibit, MBh. 1, 279. **3.** To forbid, Man. 8, 361; Pañch. 160, 25. Caus. To prohibit, Pañch. 160, 25.—With प्रति *prati, shidh,* **1.** To prevent, Pañch. 171, 25. **2.** To restrain, Man. 2, 206. **3.** To forbid, Man. 8, 361. Caus. **1.** To restrain, MBh. 1, 1594. **2.** To keep off, Chr. 31, 9.—With विप्रति *vi-prati, vipratishiddha,* Contradicted, containing contradiction, Utt. Râmach. 146, 7.

सिध्म *sidhma,* and सिध्मन् *sidhman,* n. Leprosy.

सिध्मल *sidhma + la,* and सिध्मवन्त् *sidhma + vant,* adj. Affected with leprosy.

सिध्य *sidhya,* m. The asterism Pushya.

सिध्र *sidh + ra,* adj. Perfect, good.

सिध्रकावण *sidhrakâvaṇa,* i.e. *sidhra + ka-vana,* n. One of the celestial gardens.

सिनीवाली *sinîvâlî,* f. A name of the day of new moon, Journ. of the German Oriental Society, ix. lviii. 68.

सिन्दुक *sinduka* (probably vb. *syand*), m. A small tree, Vitex negundo.

सिन्दुवार *sinduvâra* (cf. *sinduka*), m. A small tree, Vitex negundo, Pañch. 105, 3.

सिन्दूर *sindûra* (vb. *syand* ?), I. m. A sort of tree. II. f. *rî.* **1.** Red clothes. **2.** The name of two plants. III. n. Red lead, minium, Ṛit. 1, 24; Kathâs. 23, 78 (red colour).

सिन्धु *sindhu* (probably from vb. *syand*), I. m. **1.** The Indus, Râjat. 5, 215. **2.** The ocean, Pañch. i. d. 117. **3.** The country along the Indus; m. pl. Its inhabitants, Draup. 1, 6. **4.** The juice that exudes from an elephant's temples. **5.** An elephant. II. f. A river in general, Çâk. d. 117; Râjat. 5, 112.—Comp. *Dyu-,* f. the Gaṅgâ, Kathâs. 4, 137. *Soma-,* m. Vishṇu.

सिन्धुज *sindhu-ja,* I. adj. **1.** River or sea-born. **2.** Born in Sindhu. II. n. Rock-salt.

सिन्धुर *sindhu + ra,* m. An elephant.

सिन्व् *SINV,* see *ninv.*

सिप्र *sipra,* I. m. **1.** Perspiration, sweat. **2.** The moon. II. f. *râ.* **1.** A woman's zone. **2.** A female buffalo. **3.** A river near Oujein, Pañch. 240, 11; Megh. 32.

सिभ् *SIBH,* see *sṛibh.*

सिम *sima* (akin to *sama*), adj. Every, all, entire.

सिम्भ् *SIMBH,* see *sṛimbh.*

सिर *sira* (vb. *si* ?), I. m. The root of long pepper. II. f. *râ.* **1.** Any tubular vessel of the body, as a vein, a nerve, Suçr. 1, 267, 13. **2.** A bucket, a baling vessel.

सिल् *SIL,* see *çil.*

सिव् *SIV*, i. 4, *sivya*, Par. **1.** To sew. **2.** To unite, Utt. Râmach. 128, 5. Ptcple. of the pf. pass. *syûta.* **1.** Sewn, Mâlat. 77, 4; stitched, joined, made, Prab. 116, 8. **2.** Pierced by a fishing-hook. —With the prep. अनु *anu*, *anusyûta*, **1.** Sewn on (cf. *anusyûtatva*). **2.** Closely attached to. **3.** Uninterrupted.—Cf. *si*; Goth. siujan; A.S. siwian; O.H.G. siut, suila, saum; A.S. seam, limbus; O.N. saumr, sutura; Lat. suere, Con-sus, Con-sualia; κασ-σύω, probably ὑμήν and Ὑμήν (cf. *sivanî*, s.v. *sivana*).

सिषाधयिषा *sishâdhayishâ*, i. e. *sishâdhayisha*, desider. of the causal of *sâdh* and *sidh*, +*a*, f. Wish or purpose to effect, to prove, Bhâshâp. 69.

सिसृक्षा *sisṛikshâ*, i. e. *sisṛiksha*, desider. of *sṛij*, +*a*, f. Wish or purpose to create, Man. 1, 75.

सिसृक्षु *sisṛikshu*, i. e. *sisṛiksha*, desider. of *sṛij*, +*u*, adj. Wishing or purposing to create, Man. 1, 8.

सीक् *SÎK*, see 1. 2. *çîk*.

सीकर *sîkara*, see *çîkara*.

सीता *sîtâ* (vb. *si*), f. **1.** A furrow, the track of the ploughshare. **2.** Husbandry, Man. 9, 293. **3.** Name of a goddess, wife of Indra, presiding over fruits, etc., Pâraskara Gṛ. S. in Journ. of the German Oriental Society, vii. 538, 17. **4.** The wife of Râma, Râm. 5, 48, 19. **5.** Lakshmî. **6.** Umâ. **7.** One of the fabulous branches of the Gangâ. **8.** Spirituous liquor.—Cf. *sîtya*.

सीत् *sît* (cf. *çît*), an imitative sound, expressing sighing, shivering with cold, murmuring, Râjat. 1, 213; cf. Nalod. 2, 62, Sch.

सीत्य *sîtya*, i.e. *sîta*+*ya*, **I.** adj. Tilled, ploughed. **II.** n. Corn, grain. —Cf. probably σῖτος.

सीद *sîda*, see 1. *sad*.

सीधु *sîdhu*, m. Spirit distilled from molasses, Ṛit. 6, 33; Indr. 5, 13.

सीमन् *sîman*, i.e. *si* or *siv*+*man*, and सीमा *sîmâ*, f. **1.** A boundary, Böhtl. Ind. Spr. 461; a limit, a landmark, Man. 8, 149; 255; Pañch. i. d. 104 (*man* and *mâ*); skirt, Utt. Râmach. 43, 6 (*man*). **2.** Observance of due bounds in morals, Bhaṭṭ. 1, 6; Nalod. 3, 28. **3.** A field. **4.** The nape of the neck. **5.** The scrotum.—Comp. *Niḥsîman*, i.e. *nis-*, adj. boundless, Bhartṛ. 2, 28.—Cf. ἵμας; O.S. sîmo, laqueus.

सीमन्त *sîmanta*, i.e. **sîmant*, the original form of *sîman*, +*a*, **I.** m. A separation of the hair on each side, so as to leave a distinct line on the top of the head, Megh. 66. **II.** m. and n. The head. **III.** m. or n. A landmark (?), Lass. 41, 7.

सीमन्तित *sîmantita*, i.e. ptcple. pf. pass. of a denomin. *SÎMANTAYA*, derived from *sîmanta*, Marked by a line, Kir. 4, 18.

सीमन्तिनी *sîmantinî*, i.e. *sîmanta* +*in*+*î*, f. A woman, Hit. ii. d. 6.

सीमा *sîmâ*, see *sîman*.

सीर *sîra* (vb. *si*, cf. *sîtâ*), m. **1.** A plough, Megh. 16. **2.** The sun.

सीरिन् *sîrin*, i.e. *sîra* + *in*, m. Baladeva, Çiç. 2, 2.—Comp. *Ardha-*, i.e. *ardhasîra*+*in*, m. A cultivator who takes half the crop for his labour, Yâjñ. 1, 166.

सीवन *sîvana*, i.e. *siv*+*ana*, **I.** n. Sewing, stitching. **II.** f. *nî*, The frenum of the prepuce.

सीस *sîsa*, **सीसक** *sîsa+ka*, and **सीसपत्रक** *sîsa-patra+ka*, n. Lead, Man. 5, 114 (*saka*).

1. **सु** *SU*, i. 1, and ii. 2, Par., and **सू** *SÛ*, i. 4, *sûya* (properly pass. refl. of *su*), and ii. 2, Âtm. **1.** To beget, Man. 10, 32. **2.** To bear, to bring forth, Man. 10, 39; Pańch. pr. d. 5. ii. 5, *sunu*, Par. Âtm. (the act of expressing the Soma juice being compared to the act of generating, cf. Rigv. i. 28), To express the Soma juice, Chr. 294, 3=Rigv. i, 92, 3. Ptcple. of the pf. pass. **I.** *suta*, **1.** m. A son, Pańch. i. d. 185. **2.** f. *tâ*, A daughter, Chr. 3, 9. **3.** m. pl. Children, Man. 2, 28. **Comp.** *Giri-*, f. *tâ*, Pârvatî, Pańch. i. d. 175. *Jahnu-*, f. *tâ*, the Gangâ, MBh. 1, 3913. *Jîva-*, adj. one who has living children, Bhâg. P. 6, 19, 25. *Dâra-*, m. wife and son, Yâjń. 2, 175. *Dâsî-*, m. a base man, Râjat. 5, 179. *Dharma-*, m. (the son of the god Dharma), epithet of Yudhishṭhira, Bhâg. P. 1, 7, 49. *Bhû-* and *Mahî-*, m. the planet Mars. *Bhṛigu-*, m. 1. Çukra or Venus. 2. Paraçurâma. *Râdhâ-*, m. Karṇa. *Çaila-*, f. *tâ*, Pârvatî, Vikr. d. 128. **II.** *sûta*, **1.** Engendered. **2.** Born. f. *tâ*, **1.** A daughter, Pańch. 181, 5. **2.** A woman lying in; see s.v. **Comp.** *Sûra-*, m. Aruṇa, the dawn. **III.** *sûna*, **1.** Born, produced. **2.** Blown, budded (as a flower). m. A son, Pańch. 198, 2. f. *nâ*, A daughter. n. **1.** Bringing forth, parturition. **2.** A flower.—With the prep. **अभि** *abhi*, *shu*, **1.** To express the Soma juice, Râm. 1, 13, 5 (cf. Schlegel's translation). **2.** To extract juice, Man. 5, 10. **3.** To sprinkle, Bhaṭṭ. 9, 90.—With **उद्** *ud*, ii. 5, To agitate, Bhâg. P. 3, 20, 35 (cf. 2. *sû*).—With **प्र** *pra*, **1.** To beget, Man. 10, 30. **2.** To bring forth, Man. 4, 44. **3.** Pass. To be brought forth, Man. 10, 36; with the termination of the Par. (i. 4, Par.), MBh. 12, 5687. *prasûta*, **1.** Engendered, Hit. pr. d. 23, M.M. **2.** Born, Pańch. 45, 2. **3.** Produced, Chr. 294, 8=Rigv. i. 92, 8. **4.** Engendering, Man. 3, 19. **5.** Having brought forth, delivered, Hit. 72, 14; Utt. Râmach. 52, 1 (she has brought forth). **Comp.** *A-*, adj. one who has not brought forth, Böhtl. Ind. Spr. 809. *Kula-*, adj. descended from a respectable family, Pańch. pr. d. 6. *prasûna*, Born, produced. n. **1.** A bud, a blossom, Utt. Râmach. 129, 12; flower, Mâlat. 57, 13. **2.** Fruit. **Comp.** *Visa-*, n. a lotus.—With **संप्र** *sam-pra*, **1.** To beget, Man. 10, 33. **2.** Pass. To be brought forth, MBh. 3, 12978 (with the termination of the Par.).—Cf. *ὕω*, *υἱός*, *ὑστέρα*; Goth. sunus; A.S. sunu (cf. *sûnu*).

2. **सु** *SU*, i. 1, and ii. 2, Par. † To possess power or supremacy (cf. the last).

3. **सु** *SU*, i. 1, Par. Âtm. † To go.

4. **सु** *su* (for original *vasu*, cf. *εὖ*; *ἐΰς*; *ἑάων* = Zend. *vańhvãm* = Sskr. **vasvâm*), **I.** adv. ved. Beautifully, Chr. 296, 1=Rigv. i. 112, 1. **II.** Very seldom combined and compounded with a verbum finitum; e.g. Pańch. i. d. 205, but cf. Böhtl. Ind. Spr. 647; but very often with nouns, **1.** Good, well, Râm. 3, 53, 6; Ṛit. 6, 2; Lass. 15, 5. **2.** Beautiful, beautifully, Râm. 3, 52, 35. **3.** Much, very, Chr. 4, 12. **4.** Easily, Daçak. in Chr. 185, 2. Comparat. *sutarâm*, **1.** Better. **2.** With *na*, Very badly, Pańch. 199, 24; with *mâ*, In no way, Megh. 108. **3.** More, Çiç. 9, 67; Pańch. 163, 3. **4.** Exceedingly, Çiç. 9, 55. **5.** Consequently, of course.—Cf. *εὖ*.

सुकालिन् *sukâlin*, probably *su* -2. *kâla* + *in*, m. pl. The Manes of the Çûdras, Man. 3, 197.

सुकृत् *su-kṛi* + *t*, adj. **1.** Virtuous, pious, Chr. 294, 3=Rigv. i. 92, 3; Pańch. ii. d. 170. **2.** Fortunate.

सुख् *SUKH*, i. 10, *sukhaya* (rather a denomin. derived from the next), Par. To make happy, to comfort, Megh. 86; to delight, Vikr. d. 61; MBh. 3, 181; Hit. i. d. 96, M.M. *sukhita* (ptcple. pf. pass., or *sukha* + *ita*), Pleased, Vikr. 59, 1; happy, Çâk. d. 99. n. Happiness, Mâlav. 33, 3.

सुख *su-kha*, **I.** adj. **1.** Happy. **2.** Joyful, Ṛit. 6, 2. **3.** Agreeable, sweet, Chr. 16, 15; Râm. 3, 55, 45. **4.** Virtuous, pious. **5.** Easy, Pańch. 211, 10. **II.** *kham*, adv. **1.** And *sukhena*, Joyfully, Nal. 17, 18; Pańch. 53, 7; iii. d. 79; well, Pańch. iii. d. 164; Vikr. 65, 17 (*sukham âstâm̃ bhavân*, Farewell). **2.** Placidly, Man. 1, 54. **3.** Willingly, Bhartṛ. 2, 49; Indr. 4, 18; with following *na punar*, Rather . . . than, Bhartṛ. 2, 100 (*tejasvinaḥ sukham asûn api sam̃ tyajanti . . . na punaḥ pratijńâm*, The virtuous renounce even life rather than break a promise). **4.** And *sukhena*, Easily, Bhartṛ. 2, 3; Pańch. 52, 20; 48, 2. **III.** n. **1.** Happiness, Pańch. 184, 2. **2.** Joy, MBh. 12, 12427. **3.** Pleasure, Vikr. d. 49; Pańch. 216, 10; alleviation, Pańch. iv. d. 19. **4.** Easiness, see **II. 4. 5.** Paradise. **6.** Water. —**Comp.** *A*-, I. adj. 1. unhappy, MBh. 1, 3984. 2. difficult, Kir. 5, 49. II. n. distress, Pańch. ii. d. 191. *A-nirde-çya*- (vb. *diç*), adj. having inexpressible pleasure, Vikr. d. 59. *Antaḥsukha*, i.e. *antar*-, adj. one who derives his happiness from his soul, Bhag. 5, 24. *Grâma*- and *Grâmya*-, n. pleasure of common people, sexual intercourse, MBh. 5, 3225; 3226. *Nis*-, adj. sad, MBh. 5, 2379. *Yathâ-sukha* + *m*, adv. 1. happily, Hit. 95, 1, M.M. 2. willingly, Nal. 23, 9.

सुखद *sukha-da*, **I.** adj. Affording pleasure, Pańch. ii. d. 2. **II.** f. *dâ*, A courtesan of Indra's heaven. **III.** n. The seat of Vishṇu.

सुखमय *sukha* + *maya*, adj., f. *yî*, Full, or consisting of happiness.

सुखस्थ *sukha-stha* (vb. *sthâ*), adj. Happy, Pańch. i. d. 406.

सुखिन् *sukhin*, i.e. *sukha* + *in*, **I.** adj., f. *nî*. **1.** Happy, Pańch. 262, 10. **2.** Glad, Hit. 78, 3. **3.** Pleasant. **4.** Comfortable (corpulent), Hit. 106, 16. **II.** m. A religious ascetic.

सुखोद्य *sukhodya*, i. e. *sukha-udya* (ptcple. of the fut. pass. of *vad*), adj. To be uttered agreeably, Man. 2, 33.

सुग *su-ga*, **I.** adj. **1.** Going well. **2.** Graceful. **3.** Well rid of. **4.** Plain, intelligible. **5.** Easy of access, Pańch. ii. d. 151. **II.** n. Fæces, ordure.

सुगोपा *su-gopâ* (*gopâ*, ved.=*gopa*), adj. Having a good protector, Chr. 292, 1=Rigv. i. 86, 1.

सुग्म्य *sugmya*, i.e. *su-gam* + *a* + *ya*, adj. Yielding happiness, Chr. 288, 13=Rigv. i. 48, 13.

सुचेलक *su-chela* + *ka*, m. Cloth or fine cloth.

सुजनता *su-jana* + *tâ*, f., सुजनत्व *su-jana* + *tva*, n. **1.** Goodness, Bhartṛ. 2, 99 (*upa yâti sujanatâm*, becomes a good person, a friend). **2.** Benevolence, Bhartṛ. 2, 80 (*tâ*).

† सुट्ट् *SUṬṬ*, i. 10, Par. **1.** To disregard. **2.** To be small.

सुतवन्त् *suta* + *vant* (vb. 1. *su*), **I.**

adj. Having children. II. m. **1.** The father of a son. **2.** A drinker of the Soma juice.

सुतिन् *sutin*, i.e. *suta + in* (vb. 1. *su*), I. adj., f. *nî*, Having a child or children, Pańch. pr. d. 7. II. m. A father. III. f. *nî*, A mother.

सुत्वन् *su + tvan*, m. **1.** An offerer or drinker of the Soma juice, Bhaṭṭ. 4, 12, Sch. **2.** A student who has performed his ablutions subsequent or preparatory to a sacrifice.

सुदानु *su-dâ + nu*, adj. Munificent, Chr. 290, 6 = Rigv. i. 64, 6.

सुदामन् *su-dâ + man*, m. **1.** A cloud. **2.** A mountain. **3.** The sea.

सुदास् *sudâs*, and (but wrongly) **सुदास** *sudâsa*, m. The name of a king, Chr. 297, 19 = Rigv. i. 112, 19; Man. 7, 41 (cf. Lois.).

सुदुस्तर *sudustara*, i.e. *su-dus-tṛî + a*, adj. Very difficult to be crossed, Hit. i. d. 4, M.M.

सुधा *su-dhâ*, and *-dhe + a*, f. **1.** Plaster, mortar, Râm. 2, 80, 13; Daçak. in Chr. 199, 18. **2.** A brick, Chr. 57, 22. **3.** The beverage of the gods, nectar, Pańch. v. d. 42. **4.** The nectar of flowers. **5.** Juice. **6.** Water. **7.** Lightning. **8.** The name of several plants.

सुधाद्रव *SUDHÂDRAVA*, a denomin. derived from *sudhâ-drava*, Par. To flow like nectar, Lass. 67, 15.

सुधामय *sudhâ + maya*, I. adj., f. *yî*, **1.** Made of plaster. **2.** Consisting of nectar. II. m. A palace, a mansion, a brick or stone building.

सुधाहर *sudhâ-hara*, and **सुधाहृत्** *sudhâ-hṛi + t*, m. Garuḍa, a fabulous bird.

सुनाशीर *sunâçîra*, and **सुनासीर** *sunâsîra*, m. Indra.

सुन्द *sunda*, m. A proper name, Râm. 3, 48, 19.

सुन्दर *sundara*, I. adj., f. *rî*, Handsome, Pańch. 184, 14; Draup. 1, 15; charming, Kathâs. 22, 103; right, Pańch. 130, 4; 164, 11. Comparat. °*ratara + m*, adv. Very well, Pańch. 88, 15. II. m. Kâma, the god of love. III. f. *rî*. **1.** A handsome woman, Râm. 3, 52, 29. **2.** Turmeric. **3.** A small timber tree, Heritiera minor.—**Comp.** *A-*, adj. disagreeable, Hit. ii. d. 49. *Ati-*, adj., f. *rî*, very beautiful, Draup. 1, 13. *Sura-*, f. *rî*, an Apsaras or courtesan of heaven, Kir. 5, 28. *Sura-loka-*, f. *rî*, 1. a celestial woman, Vikr. d. 21. 2. a name of Durgâ, Râjat. 5, 100.

सुन्दरक *sundara + ka*, m. A proper name, Daçak. in Chr. 184, 13.

सुन्दरंमन्य *sundaraṁmanya*, i. e. *sundara + m-man + ya*, adj. Thinking himself handsome, Daçak. in Chr. 195, 12.

सुपिश् *su-piç*, adj. Graceful, Chr. 290, 8 = Rigv. i. 64, 8.

सुप्ति *supti*, i.e. *svap + ti*, f. **1.** Sleeping, sleep. **2.** Drowsiness. **3.** Numbness, insensibility. **4.** Confidence, trust. — **Comp.** *Sama-*, f. universal sleep, the end of a Kalpa, and destruction of the world.

सुभ् *SUBH*, see 2. *çubh*.

सुभाषितमय *su-bhâshita* (vb. *bhâsh*), + *maya*, adj. Consisting in fine speeches, Pańch. ii. d. 176.

सुभ्रु *subhru*, see *bhrû*.

सुम *suma*, probably 1. *su + ma* (cf.

sûna, prasûna, s.v. 1.*su*), n. A flower, Châṇ. 24 in Berl. Monatsb. 1864, 408.

सुमर *sumara*, i.e. *su-mṛi+a*, adj. Easy to die, Râm. 2, 57, 20 Gorr.

सुम्न 4.*su+mna*, n. A hymn.—Cf. ὕμνος.

सुम्नयु *sumnayu*, i.e. *sumna+yu*, a ved. denomin., +*u*, m. A chanter of hymns.

सुम्भ् *SUMBH*, see 2.*çubh*.

सुयन्त्रितत्व *su-yantrita+tva* (vb. *yantr*), n. State of being well bound, Pańch. 146, 25 (cf. my transl.).

सुयोधन *suyodhana*, i.e. *su-yudh+ana*, m. A name of Duryodhana (easy to be fought), Hiḍ. 4, 58.

सुय्य *suyya*, I. m. A proper name, Râjat. 5, 72. II. f. *yâ*, A proper name, ib. 74.

† **सुर्** *SUR*, i. 6, Par. **1.** To possess superhuman power. **2.** To shine.

सुर *sura*, i.e. 2.*svar+a*, I. m. **1.** The sun, Pańch. iii. d. 69. **2.** A god, Pańch. iii. d. 211; Vikr. d. 48. **3.** A sage. II. f. *râ* and *rî*. **1.** Spirituous liquor, Pańch. i. d. 338 (*râ*). **2.** A drinking vessel. **3.** A snake.

सुरद्विष् *sura-dvish*, m. An Asura or demon.

सुरभि *su-rabh+i*, I. adj. **1.** Fragrant, Vikr. d. 105; sweet-smelling. **2.** Pleasing. **3.** Handsome. **4.** Friendly. **5.** Good. **6.** Wise. **7.** Celebrated. II. m. **1.** A fragrance, a perfume. **2.** Spring, Kir. 10, 30. **3.** The month Chaitra (March—April). **4.** Resin. **5.** The Michelia Champaca. **6.** Nutmeg. III. f. *bhî*. **1.** The earth. **2.** The cow of plenty, Lass. 2. ed. 89, 36 (ई); Megh. 46. **3.** A cow. **4.** Spirituous liquor. **5.** The name of several plants. **IV.** n. **1.** Gold. **2.** Sulphur.

सुरभिकन्दर *surabhi-kandara*, m. Name of a mountain, Vikr. 65, 18.

सुरभित *surabhita*, i. e. *surabhi+ita*, adj. Perfumed, Megh. 53.

सुराप *surâ-pa* (vb. 1.*pâ*), adj., f. *pî*, Drinking spirits, one who habitually drinks spirits, Man. 5, 90; Pańch. iv. d. 11.

सुरासव *surâsava*, i.e. *surâ-âsava*, n. Spirituous liquor, MBh. 13, 4737.

सुरुङ्गा *suruṅgâ* (borrowed from σύριγξ), f. A hole made underground, or through the walls of a building, a mine, Daçak. in Chr. 197, 18.

सुरुच् *su-ruch*, adj. Very shining, Chr. 296, 1=Rigv. i. 112, 1.

सुरेन्द्रवती *surendravatî*, i.e. *sura-indra+vant+î*, f. A proper name, Râjat. 5, 225.

सुलभ *su-labh+a*, adj. **1.** Of easy acquisition, easy to be found, Pańch. ii. d. 171; easy to be got, Pańch. iii. d. 262; easy to be perceived, Vikr. d. 26. **2.** Easy to be effected. **3.** Easy. —Comp. *A-*, adj. not easy to be obtained, Vikr. 19, 2; Hit. i. d. 184, M.M.

सुवर्चल *su-varch+ala*, I. m. A country so named. II. f. *lâ*. **1.** The wife of the sun. **2.** Linseed.—Comp. *Brahmasuvarchalâ*, i.e. *brahman-*, f. a plant, an infusion of which is used as an expiatory means, Man. 11, 150.

सुवर्चस *su-varchas+a*, adj. Shining brightly, Sâv. 5, 38.

सुवर्णमय *su-varṇa+maya*, adj., f. *yî*, Golden, Pańch. 192, 16.

सुविद *su-vid+a*, m. A guard or attendant on the womens' apartment.

सुविदत्र *su-vid+atra*, n. A household.

सुविदल्ल *suvidalla*, I. n. A haram. II. f. *lâ*, A woman.

सुवृक्ति *suvṛikti*, i.e. *su-vṛij+ti*, f. A hymn, Chr. 290, 1=Rigv. i. 64, 1.

सुशंस *su-çaṁs+a*, adj. Well-praising, a good praiser, Lass. 101, 15=Rigv. vii. 16, 6.

सुशमी *su-çam+î* (?), m. A good acquirer (?), Lass. 101, 6 (so to be read instead of *suçarmâ*)=Rigv. vii. 16, 2.

सुशीम *suçîma*, see *sushîma*.

सुषंसद् *sushaṁsad*, i.e. *su-saṁsad*, adj. Endowed with a comfortable house, Chr. 296, 7=Rigv. i. 112, 7.

सुषम *sushama*, i.e. *su-sama*, I. adj. **1.** Same, even. **2.** Beautiful. **3.** All. II. f. *mâ*, Exquisite beauty.

सुषि *sushi*, **सुषिर** *sushira*=*çushi*, *çushira*.

सुषीम *sushîma*, also (better, cf. *çîta*),

सुशीम *suçîma*, I. adj. **1.** Cold. **2.** Pleasant. **3.** Intense, Daçak. 106, 6, cf. Wils., n. II. m. **1.** Cold. **2.** The moon gem. **3.** A sort of snake.

सुषुप्त *sushupta*, i.e. *su-supta* (vb. *svap*), adj. Fast asleep.

सुषुप्ति *sushupti*, i.e. *su-supti*, f. Deep sleep, insensibility, Vedântas. in Chr. 204, 22.

सुषुम्णा *sushumṇâ*, f. An artery, Bhâg. P. 2, 2, 24 (Sch).

सुष्टुति *sushṭuti*, i.e. *su-stuti*, f. A beautiful hymn, Lass. 99, 5=Rigv. iii. 62, 7.

सुष्ठु *sushṭhu*, i.e. *su-sthâ+u*, adv. **1.** Well, Hit. 73, 21; Vikr. 60, 6; excellently. **2.** Much, very much.

सुस्थ *su-stha* (vb. *sthâ*), adj. **1.** Being well, healthy, Hit. iii. d. 119; Man. 4, 142. **2.** Happy, Utt. Râmach. 16, 13.

† **सुह्** *SUH*, (in signification 1, 2, for *sukh*, q. cf.), i. 4, Par. **1.** To satisfy, to delight. **2.** To be pleased. **3.** To bear, to endure (cf. *sah*).

सुहृत्ता *suhṛittâ*, i.e. *su-hṛid+tâ*, f. Friendship.

सुह्म *suhma*, m. pl. Name of a people, Ragh. 4, 35.

1. **सू** *SÛ*, see 1. *su*.

2. **सू** *SÛ*, i. 6, Par. **1.** To cast, to send. **2.** To incite, to impel. Ptcple. of the pf. pass. *sûta*. **1.** Sent, dispatched. **2.** Gone, departed, Pañch. 176, 4; see s.v.; see 1. *su* with *ud*.—Cf. perhaps *σεύω*, *σοῦμαι*; Lat. sævus.

3. **सू** *sû*, A. (1. *sû*), I. f. Birth. II. As latter part of comp. words, **1.** Bringing forth, yielding; e.g. *kâma-*, adj. Yielding wishes, Ragh. 5, 33. **2.** A father. *kumâra-*, m. A name of Agni, father of Kumâra, the god of war, MBh. 2, 1148. **3.** One who has brought forth. *jîva-*, adj. f. One who has borne a living child, MBh. 1, 7353. f. A mother. *vichitravîrya-*, f. The mother of Vichitravîrya. B. (2. *sû*), in *sa-asu-*, adj. Having arrows, Kir. 15, 5.

सूक 2. *sû+ka*, m. **1.** An arrow. **2.** Air, wind.

सूकर *sû-kara*, I. m. **1.** A hog (see *çûkara*). **2.** The hog-deer. **3.** A potter. II. f. *rî*, A sort of moss,

Lycopodium imbricatum.—With the first part cf. Lat. sus; σῦς, ὗς, σύαινα; O.H.G. sû; A.S; sugu; Goth. svein; A.S. swin.

सूक्त *sûkta*, i.e. *su-ukta* (vb. *vach*), I. adj. Well or properly said. II. n. 1. A hymn. 2. A sentence, Pańch. 266, 5. 3. pl. Seducing words, MBh. 8, 2037.

सूक्ति *sûkti*, i.e. *su-ukti*, f. Kind speech, Râjat. 5, 188.

सूक्ष्म *sûkshma*, i. e. perhaps *su-kshâma* (but cf. also *sûch*), I. adj. 1. Little, small, Pańch. i. d. 254; Bhartṛ. 2, 90. 2. Atomic, atom-like, Man. 1, 7; 22. 3. Fine, delicate, tender, Râm. 3, 49, 8; 52, 9; Pańch. i. d. 395. 4. Subtle, exact, Pańch. 62, 12. °*mam*, adv. Attentively, Utt. Râmach. 154, 10. II. m. 1. An atom. 2. Clearing-nut plant, Strychnos potatorum. III. f. *mâ*. 1. A kind of jasmine. 2. Small cardamoms. 3. A sort of perfume. IV. n. 1. Fine thread. 2. The supreme soul. 3. Subtlety, craft. 4. Fraud.—Comp. *Su-*, adj. very small, Pańch. ii. d. 42.

सूक्ष्मता *sûkshma* + *tâ*, f. Subtlety, the subtle essence, Man. 6, 65.

सूक्ष्मत्व *sûkshma* + *tva*, n. Fineness, subtilty, Bhag. 13, 15.

सूक्ष्मदर्शिता *sûkshmadarçitâ*, i.e. *sûkshma-darçin* + *tâ*, f. Acuteness, wisdom, Mâlav. 21, 17.

सूच् *SÛCH*, i. 10 (properly a denomin. derived from *sûchi*, and signifying originally 'To point out'), Par. 1. To indicate, to show (by a gesture), Çâk. 8, 17; Vikr. 7, 4. 2. To prove, MBh. 8, 2706. 3. To betray, Ragh. 17, 50. 4. To espy, to see, Çâk. d. 14; to trace out, Vikr. 57, 5. 5. To hear, Çâk. 52, 11.—With the prep. अभि *abhi*, To indicate, Nal. 23, 18.—With सम् *sam*, 1. To indicate, Pańch. 158, 7. 2. To prove, Hit. iv. d. 72.

सूच *sûcha* (akin to *sûchi*), I. m. The shoot of Kuça grass. II. f. *châ*. 1. Piercing. 2. (cf. *sûch*), Gesticulation. 3. Light.

सूचक *sûch* + *aka*, I. adj. Indicative, Johns. Sel. 15, 59. II. m. 1. A spy, an informer. 2. A teacher. 3. A dog. 4. A crow. 5. A cat. 6. A detractor, Man. 4, 71; 11, 50. 7. A scoundrel. 8. An imp. 9. The manager or chief actor of a company.—Comp. *Visha-*, m. the Greek partridge, Perdix rufa.

सूचन *sûch* + *ana*, I. m. 1. Informing, information. 2. Teaching, describing. II. f. *nâ*. 1. Piercing (cf. *sûchi*). 2. Conveying any intimation by signs, gesticulation. 3. Wickedness.

सूचि and **सूची** *sûchi*, *î* (probably akin to *siv*, cf. *sûtra*), f. 1. Piercing. 2. A needle, Râm. 3, 53, 50; Megh. 24 (*chi*); Hit. 98, 22 (*chi*). 3. (cf. *sûch*), Indication of a feeling by signs. 4. A mode of dancing, MBh. 7, 3383 (?). 5. A mode of array, a sharp file or column. 6. A cone.

सूचिक *sûchi* + *ka*, I. m. A tailor. II. f. *kâ*. 1. A needle. 2. An elephant's trunk.

सूचिता *sûchi* + *tâ*, f. Needle-work.

सूत *sûta*, I. cf. 1. *su* and 2. *sû*. II. m. A. i.e. probably 2. *sû* + *tṛi* (cf. *nâpita*). 1. A charioteer, Vikr. 5, 4. 2. The son of a Kshattriya by a Brâhmaṇî wife, Man. 10, 10. 3. A bard, Johns. Sel. 37, 16. B. 1. A carpenter. 2. The sun. III. m. and n. Quicksilver.—

Comp. *Sa-*, adj. with the charioteer, Chr. 34, 11.

सूतक *sûta+ka* (see vb. 1. *su*), I. n. **1.** Birth, Man. 4, 112; 5, 58; cf. 4, 110 (birth of Râhu=causing an eclipse). **2.** Impurity from child-birth, Lass. 76, 7. II. m. and n. Quicksilver. III. f. *kâ* and *tikâ*, A woman recently delivered, Man. 4, 212.

सूतत्व *sûta+tva*, n. The art of a charioteer, Nal. 22, 12.

सूति A. *sû+ti*, (see vb. 1. *su*), f. **1.** Birth, production. **2.** Offspring. **3.** Source, Kir. 2, 56. B. i.e. *siv+ti*, f. Sewing.—Comp. *Mṛityu-*, f. a crab.

सूत्या 1. *sû+tyâ*, f. **1.** Drinking the Soma juice. **2.** Religious ablution.

सूत्र् *SÛTR*, i. 10 (rather a denomin. derived from the next), Par. **1.** To bind, to string. **2.** † To unbind, to loosen. Ptcple. of the pf. pass. *sûtrita*. **1.** Strung. **2.** Arranged in the form of *sûtras*, Lass. 2. ed. 89, 34. **3.** Arranged. **4.** Ruled, prescribed (in the Sûtras), Râjat. 5, 477.—With the prep. आ *â*, *âsûtrita*, Attached, Râjat. 5, 482.

सूत्र *sûtra*, i.e. *siv + tra*, n. **1.** A thread, Hit. 65, 13. **2.** Fibre, Vikr. d. 19. **3.** A string, Vikr. d. 140; the holy string, d. 157. **4.** A rule in morals or science, a short aphorism, e.g. the rules of Pâṇini. **5.** An opinion or decree in law. — Comp. *Kaṭi-*, n. a zone, Bhâg. P. 5, 3, 4. *Kaṇṭha-*, n. a kind of embracing, Ragh. 19, 32. *Kalpa-*, n. a *sûtra* or rule concerning ritual. *Kâla-*, n. the name of a hell, Man. 3, 249. *Dîrgha-*, adj. irresolute, Pańch. 245, 23 (*dîrgha-sûtra+tâ*, f. procrastination, Râm. 2, 72, 96, Seramp). *A-dîrgha-*, adj. resolute. *Dharma-*, I. n. a work on law, Utt. Râmach. 71, 12. II. m. a proper name, Bhâg. P. 9, 22, 16. *Brahmasûtra*, i.e. *brahman-*, n. title of a vedantic work, Lass. 2. ed. 87, 14 (see *çârîraka-*). *Mâna-*, n. 1. a chain of gold or silver worn round the loins. 2. a thread for measuring, Daçak. in Chr. 186, 11. *Mûla-*, n. a principal precept, Châṇ. 3 in Berl. Monatsb. 1864, p. 407. *Yajńa-*, n. the sacrificial cord. *Çârîraka-*, n. statement concerning the embodied spirit, i.e. the *Brahmasûtras* of Bâdarâyaṇa, Vedântas. in Chr. 202, 7. *Sâvitrî-*, n. the sacrificial cord. *Hasta-*, n. a bracelet.

सूत्रकार *sûtra-kâra*, m. An author of a work containing rules, precepts, Utt. Râmach. 92, 6.—Comp. *Taurya-trika-*, m. author of the rules concerning vocal and instrumental music and dancing, ib. 111, 4.

सूत्रण *sûtraṇa*, i.e. *sûtr+ana*, n. **1.** Stringing. **2.** Arranging.

सूत्रधार *sûtra-dhâra*, m. **1.** A carpenter, Hit. 49, 12. **2.** The manager or principal actor of a company, Vikr. 3, 12. **3.** The author of a set of rules. **4.** Indra.

सूत्रभिद् *sûtra-bhid*, m. A tailor.

सूत्रमध्यभू *sûtra-madhya-bhû*, m. Incense.

सूत्रला *sûtra+lâ*, f. A spindle or distaff.

सूत्रामन् *sûtrâman*, i.e. *su-trâman*, m. Indra (cf. *trâman*).

सूत्रिका *sûtrikâ*, i.e. *sûtra+ka*, f. A kind of dish (or cake), Pańch. 245, 22.

सूत्रिन् *sûtrin*, i.e. *sûtra+in*, I. adj.,

f. *iṇî*, Having threads, rules. **II.** m. A crow.

सूद् *SÛD*, † i. 1, Âtm. **1.** To kill, to hurt. **2.** To distill. **3.** To eject. Caus., or i. 10, Par. **1.** To incite (ved.). **2.** To kill, MBh. 1, 2833; Pańch. 48, 3; ii. d. 39. **3.** † To distill. **4.** † To eject. **5.** † To promise.—With the prep. अभि *abhi*, Caus. To kill, Râm. 1, 27, 19.—With नि *ni*, Caus. To kill, MBh. 1, 1339.—With विनि *vi-ni*, To kill, MBh. 3, 8814.—With संनि *sam-ni*, To kill, MBh. 3, 8742.—Cf. *συδ* in *παν-συδίῃ πασ-συδί* (see 2. *sû*).

सूद *sûd+a*, m. **1.** A cook, Râm. 3, 28, 27. **2.** Seasoning. **3.** Anything seasoned. **4.** Split peas. **5.** Mud.

सूदन *sûd+ana*, I. adj. Destructive, a destroyer, Johns. Sel. 16, 67; 22, 116. II. n. Destroying, Nal. 12, 126.—Comp. *Krauńcha-*, m. a name of the god of war, Suçr. 2, 386, 10. *Bala-*, m. a name of Indra, Lass. 50, 17. *Madhu-*, m. Vishṇu.

सून *sûna*, I. See 1. *su*. **II.** adj. Empty (wrongly for *çûna*, see *çvi*). **III.** f. *nâ* (cf. *çûna*). **1.** A shambles or slaughter-house, a place or utensil of slaughter, Man. 3, 68. **2.** Hurting, killing, Bhâg. P. 1, 17, 38. **3.** The uvula. **4.** A zone. **5.** A river. **6.** The mumps. **7.** A ray.

सूनरी *sûnarî*, i.e. *su-nara+î*, adj. f. A respectable woman, Chr. 287, 5= Rigv. i. 48, 5.

सूनिन् *sûnin*, i.e. *sûnâ+in*, m. **1.** A butcher. **2.** A hunter.

सूनु *sû+nu* (see vb. 1. *su*), **I.** m. **1.** A son, Vikr. d. 145. **2.** A younger brother. **3.** The sun. **II.** f. *nû*, A daughter.—Cf. Goth sunus; A.S. sunu.

सूनृत *sûnṛita*, probably based on *su-nṛi+tâ*, **I.** f. *tâ*, Excellent song, Chr. 287, 2=Rigv. i. 48, 2; Chr. 294, 7 =Rigv. i. 92, 7. **II.** adj. *ta*, f. *tâ*. **1.** True and agreeable, Utt. Râmach. 135, 4. **2.** Auspicious. **3.** Gentle, Hit. i. d. 59, M.M.; kind, Çâk. 13, 1. **4.** Dear to. **III.** n. Agreeable and true discourse or speech.

सूनृतावन्त् *sûnṛitâvant*, i.e. *sûnṛita +vant*, adj., f. *vatî*, Abounding in excellent songs, Chr. 295, 14=Rigv. i. 92, 14.

सून्मद and **सून्माद** i.e. *su-unmâda*, adj. Mad, crazy.

सूप *sûpa*, m. **1.** Broth, Man. 3, 226; soup. **2.** Sauce. **3.** A cook. **4.** A vessel. **5.** An arrow.—Cf. O.H.G. suf; O.N. sup; A.S. supan; O.H.G. sûfan, saufjan.

सूपकार *sûpa-kâra*, m. A cook, Pańch. 253, 15.

सूम *sû+ma* (see vb. 1. *su*), m. **1.** Milk. **2.** Water. **3.** Sky.

सूर् *SÛR*, see *çûr*.

सूर *sûra*, i.e. 2. *svar+a*, m. **1.** The sun, Chr. 289, 2; 9=Rigv. i. 50, 2; 9. **2.** A wise man, Chr. 292, 5=Rigv. i. 86, 5. **3.** A teacher.

सूरण *sûraṇa*, m. An esculent root.

सूरत *sûrata*, i.e. *su-rata* (see *ram*), adj. **1.** Compassionate, tender. **2.** Calm, tranquil.

सूरि *sûri*, i.e. 2. *svar+i* (or rather curtailed *sûrin*), m. **1.** The sun. **2.** A wise man, Chr. 287, 4=Rigv. i. 48, 4; Pańch. i. d. 71. **3.** A teacher.

सूरिन् *sûrin*, i.e. *sûra+in*, **I.** adj. Wise. **II.** m. A learned man, a teacher.

† **सूर्क्ष्** *SÛRKSH*, i. 1, Par. **1.** To respect. **2.** To disregard.

सूर्क्षण *sûrkshaṇa*, i.e. *sûrksh + ana*, n. Disrespect.

† **सूर्क्ष्य्** *SÛRKSHY*, i. 1, Par. **1.** To envy. **2.** To disregard.

सूर्क्ष्य *sûrkshya*, m. A kind of bean.

सूर्प *sûrpa* (cf. *çûrpa*), m. A winnowing basket, Yâjñ. 1, 285; Pańch. 121, 19.—Cf. probably O.H.G. swarb, gurges; N.N.L. zwerven, vagari; Goth. svairban; O.H.G. swerban (To dry something, originally, by swinging it in the open air).

सूर्मि and **सूर्मी** *sûrmî*, f. **1.** An iron image (of a woman), Man. 11, 103. **2.** The pillar of a house.—**Comp.** *Tapta-sûrmi*, f. the name of a hell, Bhâg. P. 5, 26, 7.

सूर्य *sûrya*, i.e. 2. *svar*, or rather **savar* (for original **savan*), +*ya*, **I.** m. **1.** The sun, Pańch. 37, 20. **2.** Gigantic swallow-wort. **3.** The son of Bali. **II.** f. *yâ*. **1.** The wife of the sun. **2.** A new bride. **3.** A bitter gourd. —**Comp.** *Prati-sûrya+m*, adv. opposite to the sun; *pratisûrya*, see s.v.—Cf. ἀβέλιος (for ἀϝέλιος = **savar+ya*), ἠέλιος, ἥλιος; Goth. sauil; Lat. sol; Goth. sunna (=**savan+ya*), sunno; A.S. sunna, sunne, sun.

सूर्यज *sûrya-ja*, **I.** m. **1.** Karṇa. **2.** Sugrîva. **II.** f. *jâ*, The Yamunâ river.

सूर्यभक्तक *sûrya-bhakta + ka* (see *bhaj*), m. **1.** A worshipper of the sun. **2.** A flower, Pentapetes phœnicea.

सूर्योढ *sûryoḍha*, i.e. *sûrya-ûḍha* (vb. *vah*), **I.** adj. One who comes after sunset, Pańch. 35, 16; i. d. 186. **II.** m. An evening guest.

† **सूष्** *SÛSH* (cf. 1. *su*), **शूष्** *ÇÛSH*, i. 1, Par. To bring forth, to bear.

सृ *SṚI*, i. 1, and ii. 3, *sisṛi*, Par. **1.** To flow, to flow to, Chr. 292, 5 = Rigv. i. 86, 5 (*sasrushîs*, ved. for *sasrushyas*). **2.** To blow, Megh. 54. **3.** To go, MBh. 1, 169, 6; to go to, 3, 2728. Caus., or i. 10, Par. **1.** To extend. **2.** To move, to touch, Megh. 84. **3.** To remove, Megh. 89.—With the prep. **अति** *ati*, Caus. To extend, MBh. 3, 665. — With **अनु** *anu*, **1.** To follow, Man. 11, 77; to pursue, Pańch. 227, 23. **2.** To go to, Megh. 31. **3.** To return to, Pańch. 137, 12. *anusṛita*, Accompanied, Utt. Râmach. 90, 9. Caus. To pursue, MBh. 1, 4309.—With **अप** *apa*, To retire, Pańch. iii. d. 40; 220, 13; to withdraw, Hit. 18, 18. Caus. To order to withdraw, Man. 7, 149; to remove, Pańch. 15, 25.—With **अभि** *abhi*, **1.** To go to, Daçak. in Chr. 187, 1; to approach, MBh. 1, 3002. **2.** To attack, MBh. 1, 1175. Caus. To meet, Mṛichchh. 121, 14.—With **अत्यभि** *ati-abhi*, To pass, MBh. 1, 3854.—With **उद्** *ud*, Caus. **1.** To cause to go out, to call out, Chr. 53, 22. **2.** To expel, MBh. 3, 14872; to drive away, Bhartṛ. 1, 18.—With **प्रोद्** *pra-ud*, Caus. **1.** To offer, Hit. ii. d. 154. **2.** To urge on, to incite, MBh. 3, 10620.—With **समुद्** *sam-ud*, Caus. To give, Prab. 116, 7.—With **उप** *upa*, **1.** To approach, Çâk. 12, 14; Vikr. 11, 11; with *âsanam*, To sit down, Vikr. 46, 20. **2.** To visit,

Vikr. d. 3; Daçak. in Chr. 192, 16.—With नि ni, nisṛita, 1. (= niḥsṛita), Gone forth, disappeared, Râjat. 4, 566. 2. f. tâ, A plant, Ipomœa Turpethum.—With निस् nis, 1. To slip or to go forth or out, Hit. 29, 5, M.M.; 44, 7, M.M. 2. To depart, Man. 6, 4. a-niḥsarant, adj. Not being able to withdraw, Pańch. 195, 8. niḥsṛita, 1. Gone out, having left (abl.), Hit. iii. d. 133. 2. Broken forth, Çiç. 9, 25. Caus. 1. To cause to go out, MBh. 3, 12995. 2. To drive away, to expel, Pańch. 227, 9.—With विनिस् vi-nis, viniḥsṛita, Gone forth or out, issued forth, Man. 4, 165; Vikr. d. 43.—With परि pari, To flow round, MBh. 3, 10983.—With प्र pra, 1. To proceed, Râm. 2, 59, 10; to pass, Vikr. d. 63. 2. To spring up, Pańch. iii. d. 258. 3. To break forth, Mâlat. 24, 17. 4. To increase, Pańch. iii. d. 2. 5. To extend, Ṛit. 1, 25. prasṛita, 1. Gone. 2. Spread. 3. Stretched. 4. Long. 5. Swift. 6. Modest, Râm. 3, 52, 21. 7. Attached to, occupied. 8. Appointed. m. The palm of the hand. f. tâ, The leg. n. A measure of two *Palas*. Comparat. prasṛitatara, Excessive, Daçak. in Chr. 194, 16. Comp. *Panchavinduprasṛita*, i.e. panchan-vindu-, n. a kind of dancing motion, Daçak. 145, 13. Caus. 1. To stretch forward or out, MBh. 3, 845; Pańch. 53, 6. 2. To spread, Pańch. 105, 1; 157, 25; 174, 11. 3. To open wide, Mṛichchh. 35, 17. 4. To expose for sale, Man. 5, 129.—With विप्र vi-pra, To spread, Ragh. 16, 3.—With प्रति prati, Caus. 1. To replace, Çâk. d. 61. 2. To remove, Vikr. d. 47. pratisârita, 1. Repelled. 2. Dressed (as a wound).—With वि vi, 1. To spread, Çiç. 9, 19. 2. To return, Çiç. 9, 37. visṛita, 1. Spread. 2. Drawn (as a bowstring), Kir. 10, 53. 3. Uttered, Daçak. in Chr. 200, 22. Caus. To extend, Râm. 1, 42, 6. visârita, 1. Set on foot. 2. Effected.—With सम् sam, To obtain, Man. 12, 70. Caus. To cause to revolve, Man. 12, 124.—With अनुसम् anu-sam, Caus. To dismiss, MBh. 3, 11552.—Cf. ὁρμή, ὁρμάω, etc., σάλος, σάλα, σαλεύω; Lat. salio, saltare (A.S. saltian, borrowed); ἅλλομαι, also ἰάλλω (rather than to ṛi, p. 136), probably also Lat. serere; ἁρμός, ὅρμος, ἕρμα; A.S. serian, to set in order (Caus., cf. also Lat. serere).

सृक sṛi + ka, m. 1. A lotus. 2. Air, wind. 3. An arrow (cf. sṛiga).

सृक्कन् sṛikkan, सृक्क sṛikka, सृक्वन् sṛikvan, सृक्व sṛikva, i.e. sṛij + van (anomal.), n. The corner of the mouth, Pańch. 55, 7 (*kkan*); 262, 20 (cf. my transl.).—Comp. *Visha-*, m. a wasp.

सृग sṛiga, i.e. probably sṛij + a, m. A short arrow.

सृज् SṚIJ (akin to sṛi), i. 6, Par. (in epic poetry also Âtm., Ram. 1, 16, 6), and † i. 4, Âtm. 1. To let flow, to let loose, Râm. 1, 44, 38. 2. To effuse, to shed (ved.). 3. To create, Man. 1, 25; 41; with gen. in the sense of the dat., Hit. pr. d. 27, M.M. (to destinate). 4. To beget, Râm. 1, 16, 9. 5. To cast, Chr. 32, 23. 6. To put on, to place, Nal. 5, 28. Ptcple. of the pf. pass. sṛishṭa. 1. Abandoned. 2. Connected. 3. Adorned. 4. Much, many. Comp. *A-*, adj. uninterrupted, Daçak. in Chr. 184, 7.—With the prep. अति ati, 1. To leave, MBh. 3, 431. 2. To give (with gen.), Râm. 2, 18, 23; Vikr.

d. 15. **3.** To remit.—With व्यप *vi-apa*, To abandon, MBh. 3, 16104.—With अभि *abhi*, To give, Râm. 1, 9, 63.—With अव *ava*, **1.** To let loose, Man. 1, 8; Matsyop. 23. **2.** To cast, MBh. 1, 1973. **3.** To give (one his life), Nal. 26, 23.—With व्यव *vi-ava*, **1.** To throw, MBh. 3, 14253. **2.** To put down, MBh. 3, 10438.—With समव *sam-ava*, **1.** To abandon, MBh. 1, 6749. **2.** To throw, MBh. 3, 1586.—With समा *sam-â*, **1.** To place on, MBh. 1, 1703. **2.** To commit, Man. 9, 323.—With उद् *ud*, **1.** To shed, Chr. 12, 28. **2.** To let loose, Chr. 36, 21; Pańch. 224, 4. **3.** To abandon, Man. 6, 16; Vikr. 37, 8; Daçak. in Chr. 194, 23. **4.** To shoot, figurat., Pańch. i. d. 219 (cf. my transl.); to cast, Chr. 20, 20. **5.** To throw away, Vikr. d. 94; 70, 8. **6.** To dismiss, MBh. 3, 2093. **7.** To give up, Man. 8, 144. **8.** To decline, Man. 8, 170. **9.** To repudiate, Pańch. iii. d. 210; 170, 25.—With समुद् *sam-ud*, **1.** To shed, Râm. 2, 44, 21. **2.** To let loose, to leave, Pańch. 226, 23. **3.** To cast, Man. 4, 56. **4.** To put off, Chr. 30, 4. **5.** To place, Man. 3, 244. **6.** To dismiss (without punishment), Man. 8, 347. **7.** To lose, MBh. 3, 8750.—With उप *upa*, *upasṛishṭa*, **1.** Connected to. **2.** Swarming, Man. 4, 61. **3.** Seized by, possessed by (evil demons), Râm. 2, 47, 1, Seramp. **4.** Assailed, Bhâg. P. 4, 12, 16. **5.** Eclipsed, Man. 4, 37. n. Coition.—With नि *ni*, *nisṛishṭa*, **1.** Delivered. **2.** Emancipated, Man. 8, 419. **3.** Centrical. **Comp.** *A*-, adj. not allowed, Man. 2, 205.—With संनि *sam-ni*, *saṁnisṛishṭa*, Committed, MBh. 1, 7134.—With प्र *pra*, **1.** To abandon, MBh. 3, 1080. **2.** To injure, MBh. 2, 856.—With प्रति *prati*, *pratisṛishṭa*, **1.** Sent. **2.** Given. **3.** Celebrated.—With वि *vi*, **1.** To shed, Daçak. in Chr. 193, 7. **2.** To let loose, Râm. 1, 44, 13; to abandon, Bhâg. P. 6, 9, 38. **3.** To create, to produce, Man. 1, 11. **4.** To drop, Man. 9, 282. **5.** To send, Chr. 54, 12. **6.** To let fall, Utt. Râmach. 41, 3; to cast, MBh. 4, 1856; to throw away, Böhtl. Ind. Spr. 2876. **7.** To repudiate, Pańch. 200, 4. **8.** To utter, to sound, Râm. 3, 51, 20. **9.** To give, Râm. 2, 36, 8 (with gen. instead of dat.); Utt. Râmach. 111, 5. *visṛishṭa*, **1.** Abandoned, Daçak. in Chr. 183, 14. **2.** Given away. **3.** Dismissed. **4.** Expelled. Caus. **1.** To shed, Ṛit. 6, 12, v.r. **2.** To dismiss, Pańch. 214, 3; Chr. 14, 25. **3.** To spare, MBh. 1, 8362. **4.** To repudiate, MBh. 3, 1860. **5.** To put off, Chr. 42, 14. *visarjita*, **1.** Abandoned, Hit. ii. d. 17. **2.** Given away.—With सम् *sam*, pass. **1.** To mix, Ragh. 5, 69. **2.** To meet with (instr.), Ragh. 13, 73. **3.** To converse with one, Daçak. in Chr. 196, 6. *saṁsṛishṭa*, **1.** United, composed, Man. 1, 56. **2.** Reunited, Man. 9, 212. **3.** Connected as partners. **4.** Dressed in clean clothes. **5.** Involved in.

सृञ्जय *sṛińjaya*, m. **1.** A people, Johns. Sel. 29, 34. **2.** A proper name, Chr. 13, 7; 15, 28.

सृणि *sṛiṇi*, I. m. **1.** An enemy. **2.** The moon. II. m., f., and *ṇî*, f. A hook to drive an elephant.

सृणीका *sṛiṇikâ*, f. Saliva.

सृति *sṛi+ti*, f. **1.** Gliding, Man. 6, 63. **2.** Going, proceeding. **3.** A road, Bhag. 8, 27. **4.** Hurting. See *ku*-. —Cf. Lat. sors.

सृत्वन् *sṛitvan*, m. The creator.

सृदाकु *sṛidâku*, I. m. **1.** Fire. **2.** Wind. **3.** Indra's thunderbolt. **4.** The disc of the sun. II. f. A river.

सृप् *SṚIP* (akin to *sṛi*), i. 1, Par. (in epic poetry also Âtm., Râm. 2, 96, 9), **1.** To creep, Râm. 2, 59, 10. **2.** To go, to move, Hit. 30, 3.—With the prep. व्यति *vi-ati*, To move to and fro, MBh. 4, 1042.—With अनु *anu*, To approach, MBh. 1, 6201.—With अप *apa*, **1.** To go away, MBh. 3, 14112. **2.** To run away, Râm. 2, 29, 4. **3.** To deviate from, Pańch. iii. d. 241 (*apasarpya*, anomal., or erroneously for *apasṛipya*). **4.** To espy, Utt. Râmach. 25, 5 (*paura-jânapadân*, the inhabitants of the town and district).—With व्यप *vi-apa*, To run away, MBh. 4, 1899.—With उद् *ud*, To rise, Nal. 23, 9 (cf. *yathâsaṃgam*, under *sanga*).—With समुद् *sam-ud*, To rise, Ragh. 6, 8.—With उप *upa*, **1.** To go near, to approach, Chr. 61, 40. **2.** To undergo, Hit. ii. d. 175. **3.** To go forth, Pańch. 159, 23; Man. 9, 269. **4.** To move, Hit. iv. d. 27.—With समुप *sam-upa*, To approach, MBh. 1, 6450.—With परि *pari*, To go to and fro, Râm. 3, 52, 48.—With प्र *pra*, To proceed, Pańch. 120, 9. *prasṛipta*, Come forth, Utt. Râmach. 27, 6.—With वि *vi*, **1.** To sneak about, Pańch. ii. d. 48; to fly about, Hit. 16, 3, M.M. **2.** To spread, Mâlat. 32, 4. **3.** To disperse, Nal. 1, 25. **4.** To flow to and fro on (acc.), Utt. Râmach. 18, 7. **5.** To wind, to meander, Râm. 1, 44, 17. **6.** To run away, MBh. 1, 8286.—With सम् *sam*, **1.** To flow, Megh. 29. **2.** To glide, to move, Megh. 52.—Cf. Lat. serpere; ἕρπω; A.S. slipan.

सृपाट *sṛipâṭa*, m., and f. *ṭi*, A measure.

सृपाटिका *sṛipâṭikâ*, f. The beak of a bird.

सृप्र *sṛip+ra*, m. The moon.

† सृभ् *SṚIBH*, सृम्भ् *SṚIMBH*, सिभ् *SIBH*, सिम्भ् *SIMBH*, स्रिभ् *SRIBH*, स्रिम्भ् *SRIMBH*, i. 1, Par. To kill, to hurt.

सृमर *sṛi+mara*, I. adj. Going. II. m. A young deer, Râm. 3, 49, 24.

सृम्भ् *SṚIMBH*, see *sṛibh*.

सृष्टि *sṛishṭi*, i. e. *sṛij + ti*, f. **1.** Creation, Vikr. 8, 18; Man. 1, 25; with *âdyâ*, Çâk. d. 1, The first creation, i.e. water. **2.** Nature. **3.** A liberal gift, Man. 3, 255.

सॄ *SṜÎ*, see *svṛi*.

सेक् *SEK*, see *srek*.

सेक *seka*, i.e. *sich + a*, m. **1.** Sprinkling, Hit. ii. d. 132; Kir. 5, 26; a drop (? of fire), Pańch. i. d. 416. **2.** Seminal fluid.—**Comp.** *Amṛita-*, m. sprinkling with the beverage of the gods, Hit. ii. d. 132 (*phalanty amṛitaseke 'pi na pathyâni vishadrumâḥ*, 'Poisonous trees, although sprinkled with nectar, do not bear healthy fruits').

सेकिम *sekima* (vb. *sich*), n. A radish.

सेक्तृ *sektṛi*, i.e. *sich + tṛi*, I. m., f. *trî*, and n. Who or what sprinkles. II. m. A husband.

सेत्र *sehtra*, i.e. *sich* + *tra*, n. A bucket.

सेचक *sechaka*, i.e. *sich*+*aka*, I. adj. Sprinkling. II. m. A cloud.

सेचन *sechana*, i.e. *sich*+*ana*, I. n. **1.** Sprinkling, watering, Çâk. 8, 23. **2.** Dripping. II. n., and f. *ní*, A bucket.—**Comp.** *Agni-*, n. spirituous liquor (?), Pańch. ii. d. 165 (Böhtl. Ind. Spr. 2772 reads *sevanaiḥ*).

सेटु *seṭu*, m. **1.** The water melon. **2.** A kind of cucumber.

सेतु *setu*, i. e. *si*+*tu*, m. **1.** A mound, a bank, a dike, Râjat. 5, 91; figurat. Means of protecting (the law and institutes), Bhâg. P. 3, 1, 36; 3, 21, 54. **2.** A high causeway in fields. **3.** A landmark, Man. 8, 245. **4.** A pass, a defile. **5.** Figurat. Law, Bhâg. P. 3, 9, 19. **6.** A bridge, Pańch. i. d. 115 (cf. my transl.). **7.** The islands between India and Ceylon (cf. *Nala-setu*), Lass. 2. ed. 92, 66. **8.** A tree, Tapia cratæva.—**Comp.** *Dharma-*, m. a dike for the protection of right, Hariv. 11315. *A-pâshaṇḍa-dharma-setu*, m. a dike for the protection of right free from heresy, Bhâg. P. 5, 26, 22. *Nala-*, m. the bridge constructed by the monkey Nala, name of the islands between India and Ceylon, Râm. 6, 108, 16.

सेत्र *setra*, i.e. *si*+*tra*, n. A ligament or fetter.

सेना *senâ*, i. e. *si*+*na*, f. **1.** An army, Vikr. 11, 16. **2.** The wife of Kârttikeya, the god of war.—**Comp.** I. At the end of Tatpurusha comp. it may become n.; e.g. *brâhmaṇa-senâ*, f., or *-sena*, n., Pâṇ. ii. 4, 25. II. *Indra-* and *Chitra-sena*, m. proper names, Draup. 8, 15; Indr. 3, 8. *Chitra-senâ*, f. a proper name, Indr. 2, 30. *Deva-*, I. f. an army of celestials, MBh. 3, 14245. II. m. *Deva-sena*, a proper name, Kathâs. 15, 63. III. f. *nâ*, a proper name, MBh. 3, 14257. *Mahâ-*, I. adj. having a great army, Chr. 52, 12. II. m. 1. a general. 2. Kârttikeya, the god of war, Vikr. d. 161. *Yajña-*, m. a proper name, Johns. Sel. 26, 11. *Rûpa-sena*, m. a proper name, Lass. 19, 12. *Vira-sena*, m. the father of Nala, Nal. 1, 1. *Çûra-sena*, m. 1. a country about Mathura, Man. 7, 193. 2. a proper name. 3. pl. m., and also **॰नकाः** *°nakâḥ*, the inhabitants, Man. 2, 19.

सेनानी *senâ-ní*, m. **1.** A general, Hit. iii. d. 69. **2.** Kârttikeya, the god of war, Kir. 15, 7.

सेफ *sepha*, see *çepa*.

सेराह *serâha*, m. A horse of a milk-white colour.

सेल् *SEL*, † **शेल्** *ÇEL*, i. 1, Par. To go or move.—With the prep. **अति** *ati*, Caus. To oblige to make excessive marches, Hit. iii. d. 91.

सेव् *SEV* (akin to *sap*), i. 1, Par. Atm. **1.** To follow, to apply one's self to, Man. 6, 35. **2.** To study, MBh. 3, 27. **3.** To practise, Man. 6, 29; to do, Ragh. 17, 49. **4.** To enjoy, Hit. i. d. 172, M.M. (cherish); Pańch. v. d. 24; carnally, Man. 8, 365; to love, Hit. 87, 1. **5.** To inhabit, MBh. 3, 2402. **6.** To tarry somewhere (with acc.), Man. 4, 131. **7.** To frequent, Pańch. i. d. 9; Lass. 39, 7; to search, Vikr. d. 41. **8.** To stand at, to guard, Hit. 98, 18. **9.** To serve, to gratify, Ragh. 11, 11. **10.** To honour, Man. 7, 38; to worship, Hit. ii. d. 27. *sevita*, **1.** Pursued, used. **2.** Protected. **3.** Frequented, Hit. i. d. 150, M.M. Comp.

A-, adj. not frequented, Hit. i. d. 144, M.M. *Su-*, adj. well served, Hit. i. d. 21, M.M. *sevya*, **1.** To be taken care of. **2.** Venerable; with *jana*, Master, Vikr. d. 39. m., f. *yâ*, and n. Names of plants. **Comp.** *A-*, adj. 1. not deserving to be served, Pańch. i. d. 286. 2. not deserving to be visited, Pańch. 31, 1. *Dus-*, adj. difficult to be treated, MBh. 13, 2225. Caus. To worship, Hit. ii. d. 33.—With the prep. **आ** *â*, **1.** To practise, Mṛichchh. 35, 6. **2.** To employ for smearing with, Ṛit. 6, 12 (v.r.). **3.** To enjoy, Vikr. 67, 3; MBh. 3, 16564.—With **समा** *sam-â*, To practise, Man. 11, 174. *samâsevita*, Served.—With **उप** *upa*, **1.** To apply one's self to, to practise, MBh. 2, 159. **2.** To perform, MBh. 13, 7567. **3.** To enjoy, MBh. 3, 15382. **4.** To serve, to honour, Man. 4, 133. **5.** To haunt, Pańch. i. d. 279. *upasevita*, Smeared, Râm. 2, 100, 33.—With **अभ्युप** *abhi-upa*, To observe, MBh. 3, 13432.—With **समुप** *sam-upa*, To enjoy, Râm. 1, 35, 23.—With **नि** *ni*, *shev*, **1.** To pursue, to attach one's self to, Hit. i. d. 209, M.M. **2.** To practise, Man. 4, 155. **3.** To employ, Çiç. 9, 68. **4.** To enjoy, MBh. 3, 11877. **5.** To inhabit, Pańch. 31, 1; Râm. 1, 31, 21. **6.** To observe, Çâk. d. 26. **7.** To attend, Man. 9, 300.—With **सम्** *sam*, To worship, Kir. 18, 24.

सेवक **A.** *sev + aka*, **I.** adj. Servile, dependent. **II.** m. A servant, Pańch. 217, 25; Râjat. 5, 51 (read *deva sevakaḥ*, 'O king, a servant of the minister Çûra, hold by him like a son . . .'). **B.** i.e. *siv + aka*, A sack.—**Comp.** *Kula-*, m. an excellent servant, Pańch. i. d. 399.

सेवधि *sevadhi*, also *çevadhi*, q. cf., m. **1.** A divine treasure owned by Kuvera, the god of wealth. **2.** A treasure, Man. 2, 114.

सेवन *sevana*, i.e. *siv* and *sev + ana*, **I.** n. **1.** Sewing, stitching. **2.** A sack. **3.** Following, being addicted to, haunting, Pańch. 241, 1; practising, Hit. ii. d. 32; using, 217, 23. **4.** Enjoying, dallying with, Man. 11, 178. **5.** Service, Râjat. 5, 368. **II.** f. *nî*, A needle.—**Comp.** *Kâma-*, n. wantonness, Lass. 40, 12. *Kṛishi-*, n. husbandry, Bhartṛ. 2, 91. *Tunna-* (vb. *tud*), f. *nî*, the suture of a wound, Suçr. 1, 93, 18.

सेवा *sev + â*, f. **1.** Service, Man. 4, 5; Vikr. d. 42. **2.** Servitude, Hit. i. d. 136, M.M. **3.** Practice, Râjat. 5, 280. **4.** Worship, Bhag. 4, 34. **5.** Homage, Râjat. 5, 154.—**Comp.** *A-*, f. avoiding to serve, Man. 2, 96. *Vâra-*, f. 1. harlotry. 2. a set of courtesans. *Strî-*, f. libertinism. *Hîna-* (vb. *hâ*), f. serving a low person, Böhtl. Ind. Spr. 3355.

सेवित्व *sevitva*, i.e. *sevin + tva*, n. **1.** Staying, inhabiting, Bhag. 13, 10. **2.** Serving, devotion.

सेविन् *sev + in*, adj. **1.** Pursuing, practising. **2.** Serving. **3.** Honouring, Man. 7, 38. **4.** Dwelling, Vikr. 64, 1.—**Comp.** *Dviṭsevin*, i.e. *dvish-*, m. a traitor, Man. 9, 232.

सेव्यता *sevya + tâ* (vb. *sev*), f. **1.** State of being honoured, Ṛit. 1, 2; Hit. ii. d. 89 (cf. Böhtl. Ind. Spr. 1304). **2.** Rank, eminence, worth, Mâlat. 46, 10.

† **सै** *SAI*, i. 1, Par. To waste or decline.

सैंह *saiṁha*, i.e. *siṁha + a*, adj., f. *hî*, **1.** Inherent in a lion, Hit. i. d. 174, M.M. **2.** Lion-like.

सैंहिक *saiṁhika*, **I.** i.e. *siṁha + ika*,

adj. Lion-like. II. i.e. *siṁhikâ + a*, metronym., m. Râhu.

सैंह्किकेय *saiṁhikeya*, i.e. *siṁhikâ + eya*, metronym., m. Râhu.

सैकत *saikata*, i.e. *sikatâ + a*, I. adj. Sandy. II. n. 1. A sand-bank, Çâk. d. 144. 2. A bank, a shore, Ragh. 5, 8.

सैकतिक *saikatika*, i.e. *sikatâ + ika*, I. adj. Living in doubt and error. II. m. A religious mendicant. III. n. A thread worn to secure good fortune.

सैद्धान्तिक *saiddhântika*, i. e. *siddhânta + ika*, adj. Relating to a demonstrated truth, knowing the truth.

सैनापत्य *sainâpatya*, i.e. *senâ-pati + ya*, n. The command of an army, Man. 12, 100; generalship, Vikr. d. 161.

सैनिक *sainika*, i. e. *senâ + ika*, I. adj. Belonging or relating to an army. II. m. 1. A soldier, Hit. ii. d. 82; Râjat. 5, 430. 2. A guard, a picket. 3. A body of forces in array.

सैन्धव *saindhava*, i. e. *sindhu + a*, I. adj. 1. Marine. 2. Produced or born in Sindh, Johns. Sel. 96, 73. II. m. and n. Rock-salt. III. m. 1. A horse. 2. pl. The people of the country along the Indus, Draup. 6, 6.

सैन्धवक *saindhava + ka*, adj. Relating to the Saindhavas (see the last); with *nṛipa*, their king, Draup. 8, 42.

सैन्य *sainya*, i.e. *senâ + ya*, I. m. 1. A soldier, Râjat. 5, 216. 2. A guard. II. n. An army, Hit. iii. d. 79.—Comp. *Sa-*, adj. with the army, Râjat. 5, 323.

सैरन्ध्री *sairandhrî*, i.e. *sîra + m -dhṛi + a + a*, f. 1. A female artist, a female servant, Nal. 13, 55; Pañch. iii. d. 240. 2. Epithet and name of Draupadî.

सैरिक *sairika*, i.e. *sîra + ika*, I. adj. 1. Relating to a plough. 2. Having furrows. II. m. 1. A ploughman. 2. A plough-ox.

सैरिन्ध्र *sairindhra*, for *sairandhra*, see *sairandhrî* and cf. *saudâminî*, I. m. 1. A menial servant. 2. The son of a Dasyu by an Ayogava female, Man. 10, 32. II. f. *dhrî* (cf. *sairandhrî*), 1. A female servant. 2. Draupadî.

सैरिभ *sairibha* (akin to *sîra*, cf. *sairika*), m. 1. A buffalo. 2. Indra's heaven.

सैसक *saisaka*, i.e. *sîsaka + a*, adj. Leaden, Man. 11, 133.

सो *SO*, i. 4, *sya* (probably akin to 2. *as*, of which the base of the present is *asya*), Par. To destroy. Ptcple. of the pf. pass. *sita*, Finished, completed, destroyed; see s. v.—With the prep. अव *ava*, 1. To let fly, Rigv. i. 104, 1. 2. To fail, Kir. 16, 17. *avasita*, Completed, Çâk. 3, 6; finished, Vikr. 37, 9. Comp. *Dus-*, adj. difficult to be comprehended, Bhâg. P. 6, 16, 47. Caus. *sâyaya*, To cause to be completed, Ragh. 5, 76.—With अध्यव *adhi-ava*, 1. To practise, Hit. 42, 10, M.M. 2. To be able, Çiç. 9, 76. 3. To determine, MBh. 3, 16254. 4. To reflect, Çâk. d. 115, v.r.—With पर्यव *pari-ava*, To endeavour, Naish. 6, 23. *paryavasita*, 1. Finished, Utt. Râmach. 29, 10. 2. Resolved, Mâlat. 75, 3. 3. Perished, lost, Mâlat. 149, 6. 4. With *lokântaram*, Gone in another world, Utt. Râmach. 172, 4.—With प्रत्यव *prati-ava*, *pratya-*

vasita, Eaten.—With व्यव *vi-ava,* **1.** To effectuate, to be able, Megh. 29. **2.** To establish, Man. 12, 113. **3.** To determine, Megh. 112. **4.** To reflect, Çâk. d. 115. **5.** To believe, Râm. 2, 12, 71. **6.** To wish, Çâk. d. 17. Anomal. pres. *sâmi,* MBh. 3, 16808; potent. *seyam,* 1, 4163; fut. *sishyâmi,* 1, 6118; absol. *vyavasya,* 1, 5926. *vyavasita,* **1.** Resolved, Mâlat. 21, 10. **2.** Energetic, persevering, Vikr. 57, 2; endeavouring, Vikr. d. 125. **3.** Tricked, cheated. n. Certainty. Caus. *sâyaya,* To embolden, Kir. 1, 28.—With संव्यव *sam-vi-ava,* To decree, Man. 7, 13.—With वि *vi,* To distill, Chr. 291, 5=Rigv. i. 85, 5.

सोढृ *sodhṛi,* i.e. *sah + tṛi,* m., f. *ḍhrî,* and n. **1.** Enduring, patient. **2.** Powerful, able.

सोत्साहता *sotsâhatâ,* i.e. *sa-utsâha + tâ,* f. Energy, Kathâs. 25, 296 (read *sot°*).

सोदर्य *sodarya,* i.e. *sa-udara + ya,* m. A brother of whole blood, Man. 9, 212; Pañch. iv. d. 6 (cf. Böhtl. Ind. Spr. 542).

सोनह *sonaha,* m. Garlic.

सोपाक *sopâka,* perhaps an anomal. form of *çvapâka,* m. The son of a Chaṇḍâla by a Pukkasî female, Man. 10, 38.—Comp. *Pâṇḍu-,* m. the son of a Chaṇḍâla by a Vaidehî female, Man. 10, 37.

सोपाधिक *sopâdhika,* i.e. *sa-upâdhi + ka,* adj. Special, limited by a condition.

सोपान *sopâna,* n. Stairs, steps, Kathâs. 26, 283; a ladder, Vikr. 39, 4; MBh. 5, 1017.—Comp. *Sukhârohaṇa-,* i.e. *sukha-ârohaṇa-,* adj. having stairs ea sy as ce nt, MBh. 2,1281.

सोपानत्क *sopânatka,* i.e. *sa-upânah + ka,* adj. With sandals, Man. 3, 238.

सोम *soma,* i.e. 1. *su + ma,* **I.** m. **1.** The acid juice of the Sarcostema viminalis, Chr. 292, 10=Rigv. i. 85, 10; Bhag. 9, 20. **2.** Sarcostema viminalis, MBh. 14, 274; Pañch. i. d. 346; personified, Pañch. iii. d. 111; 112. **3.** Nectar, the beverage of the immortals. **4.** Water. **5.** The moon, Chr. 27, 8. **6.** Kuvera, the god of wealth; Yama, the god of death; Çiva. **7.** Air, wind, **8.** Camphor. **9.** A mountainous range. **II.** n. **1.** Rice-gruel. **2.** Sky.—Comp. *Nṛi-,* m. a distinguished man (properly, a moon-like man), Ragh. 5, 59.

सोमक *soma + ka,* m. **1.** Grandfather of Drupada. **2.** pl. Name of the whole family, Johns. Sel. 42, 51; Chr. 3, 2.

सोमज *soma-ja,* n. Milk.

सोमन् *soman* (cf. *soma*), m. The moon.

सोमप and **सोमपा** *soma-pâ,* m. **1.** One that drinks the juice of the moon-plant; the performer of a sacrifice. **2.** The Manes of the Brâhmaṇas, Man. 3, 197.

सोमपीतिन् *somapîtin,* i.e. *soma -pîti + in,* m. A drinker of the Soma juice.

सोमभू *soma-bhû,* m. The son of Soma, Budha, the regent of Mercury.

सोमवन्त् *soma + vant,* adj., f. *vatî,* Possessing Soma (with *diç,* the region of the Himâlaya, cf. Sch. ad Kumâras. 1, 17), Râm. 1, 41, 21.

सोमसद् *soma-sad,* m. The name of the Manes of the Sâdhyas, Man. 3, 195.

सोमाल *somâla,* properly a Prâkṛ. word for Sskr. *sukumâra,* Vararuchi, ii. 30, ed. Cowell, adj. Soft.

सोमिन् *somin*, i.e. *soma* + *in*, m. A performer of a Soma sacrifice, Chr. 288, 1 = Rigv. i. 49, 1.

सोल्लुण्ठ *sollunṭha*, m., and **सोल्लुण्ठन** *sollunṭhana*, n., i.e. *sa-ud-lunṭh* + *a*, or *ana*, Irony.

सौकर *saukara*, i.e. *sûkara* + *a*, adj. **1.** Relating to a hog, Kir. 12, 53. **2.** Hoggish, swinish.

सौकर्य *saukarya*, i.e. *su-kara* and *sûkara* + *ya*, n. **1.** Ease of effecting anything. **2.** Easy and extempore preparation of food or medicine. **3.** Hoggishness.

सौकुमार्य *saukumârya*, i.e. *su-kumâra* + *ya*, n. **1.** Youthfulness, Râm. 3, 52, 36. **2.** Tenderness, Mâlat. 57, 11. **3.** Delicacy, Daçak. in Chr. 188, 10.

सौक्ष्म्य *saukshmya*, i.e. *sûkshma* + *ya*, n. **1.** Minuteness. **2.** Subtilty, Bhag. 13, 32.

सौखशायिक *saukhaçâyika*, i.e. *sukha-çâyin* + *ika*, and **सौखशायनिक** *saukhaçâyanika*, i.e. *sukha-çayana* + *ika*, adj. Asking if one has slept well, Râm. 2, 12, 36 Gorr.; Ragh. 10, 14 (cf. Siddh. K. 83, b. 1).

सौखसुप्तिक *saukhasuptika*, i.e. *sukha-supti* + *ika*, m. A bard who wakes a prince in the morning with music and song.

सौख्य *saukhya*, i.e. *sukha* + *ya*, n. Pleasure, Pañch. 3, 15; happiness, Pañch. ii. d. 17.

सौगत *saugata*, i.e. *su-gata* + *a* (vb. *gam*), m. **1.** A follower of the Bauddha faith, Lass. 2. ed. 88, 28; Çiç. 2, 28. **2.** A heretic.

सौगन्ध *saugandha*, i.e. *su-gandha* + *a*, n. **1.** A fragrant grass. **2.** Fragrance.

सौगन्धिक *saugandhika*, i.e. *saugandha* + *ika*, I. adj. Fragrant, Nal. 13. 2. II. m. **1.** A dealer in perfumes. **2.** Sulphur. III. n. **1.** The white water lily, Indr. 2, 2. **2.** A fragrant grass. **3.** A ruby.

सौगन्ध्य *saugandhya*, i.e. *su-gandha* + *ya*, n. Fragrance.—Comp. *Tri-*, n. three spices, Suçr. 1, 162, 12.

सौचि *sauchi*, and **सौचिक** *sauchika*, i.e. *sûchi* + *i* (?), or *ika*, m. A tailor.

सौजन्य *saujanya*, i.e. *su-jana* + *ya*, n. **1.** Goodness, Utt. Râmach. 60, 4; magnanimousness, Râjat. 5, 192; generosity, Mâlat. 66, 2. **2.** Kindness, compassion, benevolence, Bhartṛ. 2, 45; clemency, Mâlat. 140, 10. **3.** Friendship.

सौति *sauti*, i.e. *sûta* + *i*, m. A proper name, Lass. 2. ed. 71, l. 3, bel.

सौत्य *sautya*, i.e. *sûta* + *ya*, n. Charioteership, Nalod. 4, 9.

सौत्र *sautra*, i.e. *sûtra* + *a*, I. adj. According to rule or precept. II. m. **1.** A Brâhmaṇa. **2.** A radical which is no verbal root.

सौत्रामणी *sautrâmaṇî*, i.e. *sû-trâman* + *a*, f. A kind of sacrifice, Journ. of the German Oriental Society, vii. 527.

सौदर्य *saudarya*, i.e. *sa* + *udara* + *ya*, adj. Entered into fraternity with, Daçak. in Chr. 189, 8.

सौदामनी *saudâmanî*, and **सौदामिनी** *saudâminî*, i.e. *sudâman* + *a* (in *saudâminî*, *a* is irregularly changed to *i*, as in *sairindhra*), f. **1.** Lightning, Daçak. in Chr. 199, 8 (*mini*). **2.** One of the Apsaras. **3.** A proper name, Mâlat. 144, 1 (*minî*).

सौदाम्नी *saudâmni*, i.e. *sudâman* + *a*, f. Lightning (cf. the last).

सौदायिक *saudâyika*, i.e. *su-dâya* +*ika*, adj. Received by a woman as a nuptial gift.

सौदास *saudâsa*, i.e. *sudâs*+*a*, patronym., m. The son of Sudâs, Lass. 2. ed. 67, 28.

सौध *saudha*, i.e. *sudhâ*+*a*, n. **1.** A mansion, a palace, Pañch. 128, 8. **2.** Silver. **3.** Opal.

सौधातकि *saudhâtaki*, i.e. *su-dhâtṛi* +*aka*+*i* (cf. Pâṇ. iv. 1, 97), m. A proper name, Utt. Râmach. 90, 3.

सौन *sauna*, i.e. *sûnâ*+*a*, I. Relating to a slaughter-house. II. n. Butchers' meat.

सौनधर्म्य *saunadharmya*, i.e. *sauna -dharma*+*ya*, n. Bloody hatred, MBh. 5, 715.

सौनन्द *saunanda*, i.e. *su-nanda*+*a*, n. The club of Baladeva.

सौनिक *saunika*, i.e. *sûnâ*+*ika*, m. **1.** A butcher, Bhâg. P. 5, 26, 31. **2.** A vendor of the flesh of beasts or birds, Utt. Râmach. 29, 4.

सौन्दर्य *saundarya*, i. e. *sundara*+ *ya*, n. Beauty, loveliness, Mâlat. 155, 17; Hit. ii. d. 148; Râjat. 5, 148; 381.

सौपर्ण *sauparṇa*, i.e. *su-parṇa*+*a*, I. adj. Belonging or relating to Garuḍa, Utt. Râmach. 132, 9. **II.** n. **1.** The emerald. **2.** Dry ginger.—**Comp.** *Ati-*, adj. surpassing that (viz. the power) of Garuḍa, Râm. 4, 58, 33.

सौपर्णेय *sauparṇeya*, i.e. *suparṇâ* (see *parṇa*), + *eya*, m. Garuḍa, a fabulous bird.

सौप्तिक *sauptika*, i.e. *supti*+*ika*, I. adj. Somnolent, somniferous. **II.** n. Nocturnal combat, MBh. 10, title.

सौबल *saubala*, i. e. *su-bala* + *a* (patronym., MBh. 1, 5655), m. A proper name, Indr. 3, 9.

सौभ *saubha*, I. m. The name of a people, Chr. 14, 24; 18, 35. **II.** n. The city of Hariçchandra, suspended in mid-air.

सौभग *saubhaga*, i.e. *su-bhaga*+*a*, n. **1.** A gift of fortune, riches, Chr. 288, 9; 295, 15=Rigv. i. 48, 9; 92, 15. **2.** Welfare, MBh. 1, 724.

सौभद्र *saubhadra*, i.e. *su-bhadrâ* (a proper name, f.), +*a*, metronym., m. The son of Subhadrâ, MBh. 1, 1947; cf. Wils. Vishṇu P. 460.

सौभागिनेय *saubhâgineya*, from *subhagâ*+*in*+*î*+*eya* (see *bhaga*), m. The son of an auspicious mother.

सौभाग्य *saubhâgya*, i.e. *su-bhaga*+ *ya*, n. **1.** Good fortune, auspiciousness, Megh. 30; Nal. 1, 10; Râjat. 5, 230; 282. **2.** Beauty, charm, Ṛit. 6, 3; Utt. Râmach. 155, 4. **3.** Red lead.

सौभ्रात्र *saubhrâtra*, i.e. *su-bhrâtṛi* +*a*, n. Brotherly affection, fraternity, MBh. 3, 355.

सौमनस *saumanasa*, i.e. *su-manas* +*a*, I. adj. **1.** Pleasing. **2.** Flowery. II. n. Pleasure, satisfaction, Chr. 294, 6=Rigv. i. 92, 6.

सौमनस्य *saumanasya*, i.e. *su-manas* +*ya*, n. Enjoyment, satisfaction.

सौमिक *saumika*, i. e. *soma* + *iha*, I. adj. **1.** Performed with the Soma juice, Man. 4, 26; relating to it. **2.** Lunar. II. f. *kî*, A sacrifice performed on the day of full moon.

सौमित्र and **सौमित्रि** *saumitra*,

and *tri*, i.e. *sumitrâ* (see *mitra*), + *a*, or *i*, metronym., m. Lakshmaṇa, Râm. 3, 49, 11 (*tri*).

सौमेधिक *saumedhika*, i.e. *su-medhâ* + *ika*, m. A sage, a seer.

सौमेरुक *saumeruka*, i.e. *su-meru* + *ka*, n. Gold.

सौम्य *saumya*, i.e. *soma* + *ya*, I. adj., f. *mî*. **1.** Handsome, Sâv. 1, 14; pleasing, excellent, Man. 2, 125; used in addressing, Dear, Daçak. in Chr. 184, 11; Draup. 1, 14; Megh. 50; 84. **2.** Strong, Pañch. 169, 6. **3.** Placid, mild, Râm. 3, 52, 51; 55, 3. **4.** Sacred to the moon. II. m. **1.** Budha, regent of Mercury. **2.** One of the Khaṇḍas, or divisions of the continent. **3.** A class of Pitṛis or Manes, Man. 3, 199. **4.** pl. Five stars in Orion's head. III. f. *yâ*, The Soma plant, Sarcostema viminalis, and several others.

सौम्यता *saumya* + *tâ*, f., and **सौम्यत्व** *saumya* + *tva*, n. **1.** Beauty. **2.** Gentleness, Indr. 5, 7 (*tâ*). **3.** Benevolence, Bhag. 17, 16 (*tva*).

सौर *saura*, i. e. *sûrya*, and *surâ*, + *a*, I. adj., f. *rî*. **1.** Solar, Pañch. iii. d. 187. **2.** Sacred to Sûrya, i. e. the sun, Man. 5, 86. **3.** Celestial. **4.** Spirituous. II. m. **1.** A solar month. **2.** A solar day. **3.** The planet Saturn. III. f. *rî*, The wife of the sun.

सौरथ *sauratha*, i. e. *su-ratha* + *a*, m. A hero, MBh. 3, 13300.

सौरभ *saurabha*, i. e. *su-rabhî* + *a*, I. adj. Fragrant. II. f. *bhî*, A cow, Brâhmaṇav. 1, 12. III. n. Fragrance.

सौरभेय *saurabheya*, i.e. *surabhî* + *eya*, I. m. An ox. II. f. *yî*, A cow.

सौरभ्य *saurabhya*, i.e. *surabhi* + *ya*, I. m. Kuvera, the god of wealth. II. n. **1.** Fragrance, Lass. 92, 8. **2.** Pleasingness, beauty. **3.** Fame.

सौरसैन्धव *saurasaindhava*, i.e. *sura-sindhu* + *a*, adj. Relating to the Gaṅgâ.

सौराष्ट्रक *saurâshṭraka*, i.e. *surâshṭra* + *ka* (see *râshṭra*), n. A sort of white or bell-metal.

सौरि *sauri*, i.e. *sûrya* + *i*, m. Saturn.

सौरिक *saurika*, i.e. *surâ* + *ika*, I. adj. **1.** Celestial. **2.** Spirituous. **3.** Due for liquors, Man. 8, 159. II. m. **1.** Heaven. **2.** A vendor of spirituous liquors.

सौवर्चल *sauvarchala*, i. e. *suvarchala* + *a*, n. **1.** *Sochal* salt. **2.** Natron, alkali.

सौवर्ण *sauvarṇa*, i.e. *su-varṇa* + *a*, adj. **1.** Golden, Pañch. 174, 22. **2.** Weighing a *suvarṇa* (see *suvarṇa* under *varṇa*).

ऽसौवर्णिक *-sauvarṇika*, i.e. *su-varṇa* (see *varṇa*), + *ika*, in *chatuḥsauvarṇika*, i.e. *chatur-*, adj. Weighing four *suvarṇas* (see the last), Man. 8, 137.

सौवस्तिक *sauvastika*, i.e. *svasti* + *ika*, I. adj. Benedictory. II. m. A family priest.

सौविद *sauvida*, i.e. *suvida* + *a*, and **सौविदल्ल** *sauvidalla*, i.e. *suvidalla* + *a*, m. A guard or attendant on the womens' apartment, Sâh. D. 281, 1 (*-dalla*).

सौवीर *sauvîra*, i.e. *su-vîra* + *a*, I. m. **1.** The name of a country. **2.** pl. Its inhabitants, Draup. 4, 12; 8, 27. **3.** The king of the Sauvîras, ib. 4, 7. II. n. **1.** The fruit of the jujube. **2.** Antimony. **3.** Sour gruel.—Comp. *Sindhu-*, m. pl. name of a people, Râm. 1, 12, 25.

सौवीरक *sauvîra* + *ka*, m. An inhabitant of Sauvîra, Râm. 3, 53, 56.

सौष्ठव *saushṭhava*, i.e. *sushṭhu + a*, n. **1.** Excellence, beauty, Mâlav. 20, 3. **2.** Excess. **3.** Fleetness, MBh. 1, 5368 (read *saushṭhavena*); lightness, suppleness, Mâlav. 14, 9. **4.** A part of a drama.—Comp. *A-*, adj. disarrayed, Mâlat. 11, 8. *Sa-*, adj. 1. excellent. 2. quick.

सौहार्द *sauhârda*, and सौहार्द्य *sauhârdya*, i.e. *su-hṛid + a* or *ya*, n. **1.** Affection, Mâlat. 2, 18 (*da*). **2.** Friendship, Hit. i. d. 99, M.M. (*da*).

सौहित्य *sauhitya*, i.e. *su-hita + ya* (vb. *dhâ*), n. **1.** Satiety, satisfaction. **2.** Fullness.—Comp. *Ati-*, n. excessive satiety, Man. 4, 62.

सौहृद *sauhṛida*, and सौहृद्य *sauhṛidya*, i.e. *su-hṛid + a* or *ya*, n. Friendship, Vikr. d. 10 (*da*); Pańch. ii. d. 130 (*da*). (Pańch. v. d. 19, *sauhṛida*, A friend,—perhaps a misreading.)—Comp. *Dṛiḍha-sauhṛida*, adj. having true friendship, Pańch. 239, 13. *Vigata-sneha-sauhṛida* (vb. *gam*), adj. abandoning love and friendship, Sund. 4, 17.

1. स्कन्द् *SKAND*, i. 1, Par. **1.** To jump. **2.** To jump upwards, to ascend. **3.** To burst out, MBh. 1, 5105. **4.** To jump downward, to drop, to fall, Bhaṭṭ. 22, 11. **5.** To perish, Man. 7, 84. Ptcple. of the pf. pass. *skanna*. **1.** Trickled down, Râm. 1, 38, 27. **2.** Sprinkled, MBh. 1, 2434. **3.** Fallen. Caus. **1.** To emit (the seminal fluid), Man. 2, 180; 9, 150. **2.** To neglect. Man. 6, 9.—With the prep. अव *ava*, To assail, to besiege, Çiç. 1, 51.—With अभ्यव *abhi-ava*, To jump out, MBh. 4, 810.—With समव *sam-ava*, Caus. To assail, Man. 7, 196.—With आ *â*, To assail, Mâlat. 151, 9; Bhaṭṭ. 17, 11.—With समा *sam-â*, To assail, Bhaṭṭ. 16, 10.—With परि *pari*, *shand* and *shkand*, To spring about, Bhaṭṭ. 9, 75.—With प्र *pra*, **1.** To spring forward, MBh. 1, 134; to spring down, 3, 15587. **2.** To burst forth, MBh. 1, 2380. *praskanna*, Fallen. m. A sinner, one who has violated the usages of his caste. Caus. To cross (a river), MBh. 4, 1971.—Cf. Lat. scandere; σκάνδαλον, σχαστήρ (χ for κ by the influence of σ), probably σκάζω.

† 2. स्कन्द् *SKAND*, स्कन्ध् *SKANDH*, i. 10, Par. To collect.

3. स्कन्द् *SKAND*, see *skund*.

स्कन्द 1. *skand + a*, m. **1.** Skanda or Kârttikeya, the god of war, Megh. 44. **2.** A king. **3.** The body. **4.** The bank of a river. **5.** A clever man (cf. *skandha*). **6.** A proper name, Râjat. 5, 417 (or *Ghrâṇaskanda*).

स्कन्दक *skanda + ka*, m. A soldier, Râjat. 5, 174.

स्कन्दन *skand + ana*, n. **1.** Effusion. **2.** Purging. **3.** Going.

स्कन्ध् *SKANDH*, see 2. *skand*.

स्कन्ध *skhandha*, I. m. **1.** The shoulder, Pańch. 144, 23. **2.** The body, Mâlat. 84, 17. **3.** The trunk of a tree, Pańch. iii. d. 149. **4.** A branch, Pańch. 134, 5. **5.** A branch of human knowledge. **6.** A book, Bhâg. P. i. ii., etc. **7.** The five objects of sense. **8.** The five forms of mundane consciousness, in the Bauddha philosophy, Çiç. 2, 26; cf. Burnouf, Introd. à l'Hist. du Buddh. 475. **9.** A road. **10.** Part of an army. **11.** War. **12.** A multitude. **13.** An agreement. **14.** A king. **15.** A wise or learned man. **16.** A heron. II. f. *dhâ*. **1.** A branch. **2.** A creeper.—Comp. *Kâla-*, m. the name of several plants, e.g. Diospyros embryopteris

Pers., Suçr. 1, 138, 3. *Mahâ-pṛishṭha-gala-*, adj. having a large back, neck, and shoulders, Hiḍ. 2, 4. *Râjaskandha*, i.e. *râjan-*, m. a horse. *Vishâṇa-ud-nâmita-* (vb. *nam*), adj. whose shoulders reach to his horns, Hit. iii. d. 144 (but cf. Böhtl. Ind. Spr. 932). *Vishâṇa-ud-likhita-*, adj. whose shoulders are slit up by horns, i.e. brave, Böhtl. Ind. Spr. 932. *Vṛisha-*, adj. having the shoulders of a bull, Râm. 3, 55, 4. *Skandha-* (repeated), m. every shoulder, Kâm. Nîtis. 9, 19 (where the visarga must be erased), Hit. iv. d. 122, v.r.—Cf. A.S. sculdor, sculder; O.H.G. scultarra; probably σπάθη; Lat. scapula (for old scaphula, cf. rufus, s.v. *rudhira*, and rutilus, ib. for old ruthilus).

स्कन्धस् *skandhas*, n. **1.** The shoulder. **2.** The trunk of a tree (cf. the last).

स्कन्धावार *skandhâvâra*, i.e. *skandha-â-vṛi+a*, m. **1.** An army, or division of it attached to the king. **2.** A royal residence. **3.** A camp, Hit. 107, 21; MBh. 1, 6950.

स्कन्धिक *skandhika*, i.e. *skandha+ika*, m. An ox of burthen.

स्कन्धिन् *skandhin*, i.e. *skandha+in*, m. A tree.

स्कन्धोपनेय *skandhopaneya*, i.e. *skandha-upa-neya* (vb. *nî*), adj. m. (viz. *saṁdhi*), A form of peace-offering in which fruit or grain is presented as token of submission, Hit. iv. d. 122.

स्कम्भ् *SKAMBH*, i. 1, Âtm., ii. 5, *skabhnu* and 9, *skabhnâ, nî*, Par. **1.** To make firm (to create), Bhâg. P. 2, 7, 40. **2.** To support (ved.). **3.** To stop, to obstruct, to impede.—With the prep. **वि** *vi*, Caus. *vishkambhita*, **1.** Impeded, shown away, Pańch. 29, 6. **2.** Obstructed, precluded, Pańch. 56, 10.—Cf. *stambh* and *stamba*; Lat. scabellum, scamnum; Goth. ga-skapjan, ga-skafts; A.S. scapen, sceápan, sceaft; O.H.G. scafan, scafôn, scoppôn, to stop; probably σκῆπτρον, σκήπτω, σκίμπτω.

स्कु *SKU*, ii. 5, *skunu*, and 9, *skunâ, nî*, Par. Âtm. **1.** † To go by leaps. **2.** To cover, Bhaṭṭ. 17, 82. **3.** † To lift. **4.** † To approach.—With **प्रति** *prati*, To cover in one's turn, Bhaṭṭ. 17, 82.—Cf. Lat. ob-scurus, scutum, corium, cavere, cautus, causa; probably A.S. scuva, umbra; Goth. skôh; A.S. scoh, sceo; O.H.G. scur, tugurium; A.S. scúnian; O.H.G. skiuhan; also A.S. scawian, sceawian, to see (concerning the signification, cf. *vṛi*, ὁράω); ἐπι-σκύνιον, σκῦτος.

† **स्कुन्द्** *SKUND*, **स्कन्द्** *SKAND*, i. 1, Âtm. **1.** To jump or go by leaps. **2.** To raise (cf. 1. *skand*).

† **स्कुम्भ्** *SKUMBH*, ii. 5, *skubhnu*, and 9, *skubhnâ, nî*, Par. **1.** To stop or hinder. **2.** To hold; cf. *skambh*.

स्खद् *SKHAD*, i. 1, Âtm. **1.** To cut. **2.** To hurt or kill. **3.** To discomfit, to defeat. **4.** To fatigue, to exhaust. **5.** To destroy. **6.** To make firm.—Cf. *kshad*.

स्खल् *SKHAL*, i. 1, Par. **1.** To stumble, to tumble, Hit. iii. d. 132. **2.** To fall, Mâlat. 73, 2. **3.** To stutter, Mâlat. 162, 10; to hesitate, Hit. ii. d. 63. **4.** To err, to fail, Râm. 1, 13, 10. **5.** To disappear, Çriṅgârat. 7. *skhalita*, **1.** Shaken, Mâlat. 148, 15. **2.** Shaking, wavering. **3.** Staggering, Çiç. 9, 78; interrupted, faltering, Utt. Râmach. 70, 6; stammering, ib. 95, 12. **4.** Fluctuating, Pańch. 188, 10. **5.** Drunk. **6.** Hesitating. **7.** Slipped, fallen. **8.** Stopped, Çâk. d. 131; obstructed, Vikr.

d. 49. **9.** Confounded, Çâk. d. 132; Çiç. 9, 83. n. **1.** Tumbling, Pańch. i. d. 316; ii. d. 188; falling. **2.** Deviating from virtue, fault, Vikr. d. 89; sin, d. 115. **3.** Stratagem. **Comp.** *A-*, adj. not stumbled, Pańch. ii. d. 188.—With the prep. प्र *pra*, **1.** To stagger, Arj. 8, 14. **2.** To tumble, Pańch. 36, 16.—Cf. *chhala*; Lat. scelus, culpa; Goth. skula, skulan; A.S. sceal, sculan, scyld; cf. also *sphar*, *sphur*, *sphal*, *sphul*, which may be originally identical.

स्खलन *skhal + ana*, n. **1.** Stumbling. **2.** Falling, Chaurap. 13; Utt. Râmach. 44, 13 (flowing through). **3.** Falling from virtue. **4.** Tripping in speech. **5.** Falling together. **6.** Rubbing, Çiç. 9, 52.

† **स्खुड्** *SKHUḌ*, i. 6, Par. To cover (v.r.).

| **स्तक्** *STAK*, i. 1, Par. To resist.

स्तन् *STAN*, i. 1, Par. To sound, to sigh. i. 10, To thunder, Chr. 290, 6=Rigv. i. 64, 6. *stanita*, n. **1.** Thunder, Man. 4, 103. **2.** The noise of clapping the hands. **Comp.** *Sa-vidyut-*, adj. with lightning and thunder.—With the prep. नि *ni*, *shṭan*, **1.** To sigh, MBh. 3, 14060. **2.** To bewail, Râm. 2, 77, 8.—Cf στένω; Icel. stynja; N.H.G. stöhnen; Lat. tonare (cf. ved. *tan + yatu = stanayitnu*, thunder), tonitru; A.S. thunor.

स्तन *stana*, m. The nipple, the female breast, Vikr. d. 7; Pańch. ii. d. 98.—**Comp.** *Gala-*, I. m. a small fleshy process resembling nipples, hanging from the throat of some species of the Bengal goat, Pańch. iii. d. 265. II. f. *nî*, a she-goat. *Tri-*, adj., f. *nî*, having three breasts, Pańch. v. d. 77. *Prasnuta-*, adj., f. *nî*, from whose breast drops milk, Râjat. 5, 76; Utt. Râmach. 64, 10 (a token of maternal love, cf. Arji Bordschi, in the German Journal, Ausland, 1858, p. 823; Stan. Julien, Mém. sur les Contrées Occident., par Hiouen Thsang. ii. 152). *Saṁhata-* (vb. *han*), adj., f. *nî*, whose breasts are very contiguous to each other, Râm. 3, 52, 35.

स्तनन *stan + ana*, n. **1.** Sound. **2.** Groaning. **3.** The grumbling of clouds.

स्तनंधय *stanaṁdhaya*, i.e. *stana + m-dhe + a*, I. adj. Suckling, Mâlat. 164, 11 (read *dṛishṭas tanayaḥ st°*). II. m., and f. *yâ* and *yî*, An infant, Ragh. 14, 78.

स्तनयित्नु *stanayitnu*, i.e. *stan*, i. 10, + *itnu*, m. **1.** Thunder, Utt. Râmach. 122, 12. **2.** Lightning, Utt. Râmach. 55, 8. **3.** A cloud. **4.** Sickness. **5.** Death.

स्तन्य *stanya*, i.e. *stana + ya*, n. Milk, Pańch. 238, 7.

स्तब्धता *stabdha + tâ* (vb. *stambh*), f. Stubbornness, MBh. 5, 1536.

स्तब्धत्व *stabdha + tva*, n. in *a-*, Unsteadiness, Hit. i. d. 98, M.M.

स्तब्धीकरण *stabdhîkaraṇa*, i.e. *stabdha-kṛi + ana*, n. Making rigid, paralysing.

स्तब्धीभाव *stabdhîbhâva*, i.e. *stabdha-bhû + a*, m. Growing stiff, torpidity, Vedântas. in Chr. 218, 1.

स्तम् *STAM*, see *sam*.

स्तम्ब *stamba* (cf. *stambh*), I. m. **1.** A post to which an elephant is tied. **2.** A mountain. **3.** A shrub. **4.** A clump of grass, a cluster, Pańch. 140, 25. II. n. **1.** A post. **2.** Stupidity insensibility.—Comp. *Kuça-*, m. 1. a cluster of Kuça grass, Bhâg. P. 5, 20, 13. 2. the name of a place of pilgrimage, MBh. 13, 1714. *Brahmastamba*, i.e. *brahman-*, m. the world, Mahâvîrach. 51, 4; 86, 21. *Çara-*, m. a clump of reeds, Pañch. 140, 25.—Cf. A.S. stapel, a prop.

स्तम्बकरि *stambakari*, m. Corn or rice.

स्तम्बघ्न *stambaghna*, i.e. *stamba-han* + *a*, I. adj. Turf-destroying. II. m. 1. A hoe. 2. A sickle.

स्तम्बेरम *stamberama*, i.e. *stamba* + *i-ram* + *a*, m. An elephant, Ragh. 5, 72.

स्तम्भ् *STAMBH*, ii. 5, *stabhnu*, and 9, *stabhnâ, ni*, Par. 1. To make firm (to create), ved. 2. To stop, to make immovable, Bhaṭṭ. 17, 45. 3. To oppose, to hurtle, Arj. 6, 13. i. 1, Âtm. To become immovable, Bhaṭṭ. 14, 55. Ptcple. of the pf. pass. *stabdha*, 1. Stopped, blocked up. 2. Immovable, MBh. 3, 2214. 3. Firm, Utt. Râmach. 76, 1; hard, Pañch. 190, 17; rigid, Daçak. in Chr. 187, 13; stiff, Hit. 51, 8, M.M. 4. Hard-hearted, Hit. iv. d. 102. 5. Stubborn, Bhag. 18, 28. 6. Coarse, Bhâg. P. 4, 2, 8. 7. Stupid, Çriṅgârat. 21. 8. Insensible. 9. Indifferent, Hit. ii. d. 104. 10. Paralysed. Caus. 1. To support, MBh. 3, 827. 2. To make immovable, Utt. Râmach. 148, 10; to stop, MBh. 3, 10378. *stambhita*, 1. Stopped, contained, Megh. 61; constrained, Mâlat. 140, 4. 2. Stupified, paralysed, Râm. 1, 75, 17; insensible, Utt. Râmach. 159, 3.—With the prep. **अव** *ava*, after which the initial *st* becomes *shṭ*, 1. To bind, Böhtl. Chr. 229, verse 178. 2. To rest on, Mahâvîrach. 74, 5. 3. To rely on, Bhag. 9, 8. *avashṭabdha*, 1. Supported. 2. Stopped. 3. Paralysed. 4. Opposed. 5. Near, Bhaṭṭ. 9, 72. 6. Hanging from. 7. Surpassed, overcome. 8. Bound. 9. Wrapped up.—With **पर्यव** *pari-ava*, 1. To surround, Mâlat. 86, 4; 8. 2. To surround and oppose, Utt. Râmach. 122, 18.—With **समव** *sam-ava*, To encourage, Chr. 29, 34.—With **उद्** *ud*, Caus. *uttambhaya*, To cherish, support, Kir. 2, 48. *uttambhita*, 1. Supported, upheld. 2. Erect, Utt. Râmach. 60, 3. 3. Stopped.—With **नि** *ni*, *nistabdha*, Stopped. Comp. *A-*, adj. unconquered, Bhaṭṭ. 9, 89.—With **प्रति** *prati*, I. *pratistabdha*, Stopped. Comp. *A-*, adj. unconquered, Bhaṭṭ. 9, 82. II. *pratishṭabdha*, Stopped, obstructed.—With **वि** *vi*, *shṭambh*, 1. To fix (to create), MBh. 1, 6694; with *pâdau*, to stand immovable, Hit. ii. d. 120. 2. To stop, MBh. 3, 2123; to restrain, Chr. 29, 36. *vishṭabdha*, 1. Fixed, well supported, Man. 9, 296. 2. Placed in or upon. 3. Hindered. 4. Made motionless. Caus. To stop, to restrain, MBh. 3, 10314. *vishṭambhita*, Stopped, Çâk. d. 106.—With **सम्** *sam*, 1. To support, Bhag. 3, 43. 2. To corroborate, Râm. 2, 14, 13. 3. To stop, Râm. 2, 63, 47. 4. To hurtle, Pañch. 190, 15. *saṁstabdha*, 1. Made firm. 2. Corroborated. 3. Stopped. Caus. 1. To corroborate, Râm. 2, 34, 53. 2. To make immovable, MBh. 1, 7291.—With **अभिसम्** *abhi-sam*, To corroborate, Râm. 2, 64, 11.—Cf. στέμφυλον, στέμβω (cf. *stamba*); O.H.G. stamphôn; O.N. stôfn; O.H.G. stam; A.S. stemn (based on *stambh* + *na*).

स्तम्भ *stambh* + *a*, m. 1. A post, a pillar, Hit. 49, 11; Pañch. i. d. 142. 2. A stem, Hit. iv. d. 71 (*kadali-*, adj. Having the stem of a *kadali*, i.e. faintly supported). 3. Obstruction.

4. Stupefaction, Kir. 12, 28. **5.** Stupidity. **6.** Insensibility, Bhartṛ. 3, 6. **7.** Coldness, Mâlat. 80, 7. **8.** Paralysis, Mâlat. 21, 7.—**Comp.** *Niḥstambha*, i.e. *nis-*, adj. without pillars, Kâm. Nîtis. 11, 66. *Netra-*, m. rigidity of the eyes, Suçr. 2, 232, 4. *Sa-vâshpa-stambha + m*, adv. suppressing tears, Utt. Râmach. 45, 5. *Smara-*, m. the penis. —Cf. A.S. steb, a trunk (of a tree).

स्तम्भक *stambh + aka*, adj. Restraining, Râm. 1, 30, 9.

स्तम्भकर *stambha-kara*, m. A fence.

स्तम्भन *stambh + ana*, I. m. One of Kâma's arrows. II. n. **1.** Supporting, holding upright, Pańch. i. d. 405. **2.** Stopping. **3.** Suppressing the use of the faculties by magic.

ऽस्तम्भिन् *-stambh + in*, adj. Restraining, Nalod. 1, 53.

स्तर *stara*, i.e. *stṛî + a*, I. m. **1.** A layer. **2.** A bed. II. f. *rî*, Smoke. —**Comp.** *Sa-*, m. a bed of leaves.

स्तरिमन् and **स्तरीमन्** *starîman*, i.e. *stṛî + îman*, m. A bed.

स्तव *stava*, i.e. *stu + a*, m. **1.** Praising, MBh. 13, 7662. **2.** Praise.

स्तवक *stavaka* i.e. *stu + aka*, m. **1.** Praise. **2.** A panegyrist. **3.** A cluster of blossoms, Pańch. iii. d. 155 ; Vikr. d. 125 ; a designation of chapters in the Kusumâńjali. **4.** A multitude.—**Comp.** *Kusuma-*, m. a nosegay, Bhartṛ. 2, 25.

स्तवकित *stavakita*, i.e. *stavaka + ita*, adj. Full of blossoms. —**Comp.** *Abhinava-kusuma-stavaka + ita*, adj. having clusters of fresh blossoms, Vikr. d. 119. *Nârî-dṛiç-niraja-*, adj. having as (i.e. instead of) clusters of blossoms the lotus-like eyes of the women, Râjat. 5, 480.

स्तवन *stavana*, i.e. *stu + ana*, n. Praising, a hymn, Brahmav. 2, 83.

† **स्तिघ्** *STIGH*, ii. 5, Âtm. **1.** To ascend. **2.** To assail.—Cf. Goth. steigan ; A.S. stígan, staeger, a stair ; O.H.G. steigal ; A.S. sticol ; *στείχω, στίχη, στοῖχος*.

† **स्तिप्** *STIP*, **स्तेप्** *STEP*, i. 1, Âtm. To ooze, to drop.

स्तिभि *stibhi*, m. The ocean.

स्तिम् *STIM*, † **स्तीम्** *STÎM*, i. 4, Par. To be wet. *stimita*, **1.** Wet, Mâlat. 16, 5 ; Râjat. 5, 481. **2.** Immovable, Ragh. 1, 73 ; Râm. 3, 52, 12 (adv.) ; steady, fixed (of the eye), Megh. 37 (Sch.) ; benumbed, Mâlat. 12, 2. **3.** Soft, Çâk. d. 192. **4.** Unsteady, tossing, Mâlat. 50, 13 ; trembling, Mâlav. d. 27 (? rather, immovable *vâmaṁ saṁdhi-stimita-valayam*, The left hand, of which the bracelet is immovable, on account of the contact or support (of the hip). n. Moisture, Pańch. i. d. 35.

स्तिमितत्व *stimita + tva* (see the last), n. Absence of motion, absorption, Mâlat. 47, 2.

स्तीर्वि *stirvi*, i.e. *stṛî + vi*, m. An officiating priest at a sacrifice.

स्तु *STU*, ii. 2, Par. Âtm. **1.** To praise, Râm. 2, 65, 53 ; ved. Âtm. To be praised, Chr. 294, 7 = Rigv. i. 92, 7 (*stave* instead of *stavate*, i. 1). **2.** To worship by hymns, MBh. 1, 721.—With the prep. **अभि** *abhi*, *shṭu*, To praise, Pańch. 172, 14.—With **समभि** *sam-abhi*, To praise, Râm. 1, 14, 26.—With **प्र** *pra*, **1.** To praise, Mâlat. 76, 13. **2.** To begin, Utt. Râmach. 162, 10 ;

Mâlav. 13, 21. **3.** To say, to report, Hit. 100, 16. *prastuta*, **1.** Praised. **2.** Declared, Mâlat. 16, 15; vowed, Hit. 120, 21. **3.** Approached. **4.** Desired, expected. **5.** Prepared, ready, being at hand, Hit, 87, 21. **6.** Done. **7.** Made of. **Comp.** *A-*, adj. 1. extraneous. 2. unsuitable, Pañch. 36, 23; cf. i. d. 193. *Yathâ-prastuta + m*, adv. conformably to the circumstances, Mâlat. 146, 3. Caus. To cause to begin, MBh. 1, 6. *prastâvita*, Caused to be told, Mâlat. 47, 1.—With वि *vi, shṭu*, To praise, MBh. 1, 7056.—With सम् *sam*, To praise, Indr. 2, 9. *saṁstavâna*, Eloquent. *saṁstuta*, **1.** Praised, Râjat. 5, 9. **2.** Known, Utt. Râmach, 76, 2. Comp. *A-*, 1. disagreeing, Çâk. d. 33. 2. unfit, Pañch. i. d. 41 (but cf. v.r., Böhtl. Ind. Spr. 404).—With अभिसम् *abhi-sam*, To praise, MBh. 3, 12709.—With परिसम् *pari-sam*, To praise, MBh. 1, 2122.—Cf. perhaps Æol. στύμα, στόμα (questionable, on account of Zend. *çtaman*, the muzzle).

† स्तुच् *STUCH*, i. 1, Âtm. To be clear, to be propitious.

ऽस्तुत् *-stu + t*, latter part of comp. words, Praising; e.g. *chhandas-*, adj. Praising by hymns, Bhâg. P. 5, 20, 8.

स्तुति *stu + ti*, f. Praise, Sund. 2, 4; Utt. Râmach. 136, 6.—**Comp.** *Nis-*, adj. without praising (anything,) MBh. 12, 8832.

स्तुनक *stunaka*, m. A goat.

स्तुभ् *STUBH*, **1.** (i.e. *stu-bhâ*), i. 1, Par. To praise. **2.** † i. 1, Âtm. To stupify, to be stupified; cf. *stumbh*. Caus. ved. To praise, Chr. 294, 6 = Rigv. i. 88, 6.—With प्रति *prati, shṭubh*, ved. To praise, ib.

स्तुभ *stubha*, m. A he-goat.

† स्तुम्भ् *STUMBH*, ii. 5, *stubhnu*, and 9, *stubhnâ, ni* (cf. *stambh*), Par. **1.** To stop (cf. Rigv. v. 54, 1). **2.** To stupify. **3.** To expel.—Cf. στύφω, στυφελός, στυμνός, στυφεδανός, and τυφεδανός; probably τυφλός, τυφώδης; perhaps O.H.G. stumph, stumbal; A.S. stypel; Goth. and A.S. dumb.

† स्तूप् *STÛP*, i. 4 and 10, Par. To heap, to pile.

स्तूप *stûpa*, m. **1.** A heap, a pile, a Bauddha construction for keeping holy relics. **2.** A funeral pile.

1. स्तृ *STṚI*, ii. 5, *stṛiṇu*, and स्तॄ *STṜÎ*, ii. 9, *stṛiṇâ, ṇi*, Par. Âtm. **1.** To spread, to expand. **2.** To cover, Ragh. 7, 55. Caus. To cover, Bhaṭṭ. 15, 48.—With the prep. अव *ava*, To cover, to fill, Kir. 14, 29.—With आ *â*, **1.** To spread, MBh. 3, 15142. **2.** To cover, Daçak. in Chr. 179, 15. *âstaraṇîya*, n. A cover, a carpet, Râm. 5, 11, 19.—With समा *sam-â*, To cover (fire with water, i.e. to extinguish), MBh. 1, 1495.—With उप *upa*, ptcple. pf. pass. *upastîrṇa*, Arranged, MBh. 2, 2033.—With परि *pari*, **1.** To spread, Râm. 3, 49, 9. **2.** To arrange, MBh. 1, 69, 75. **3.** To cover, Çiç. 9, 18.—With प्र *pra, prastṛita*, Disappeared.—With वि *vi*, To spread, Man. 1, 51; 7, 33. *vistṛita*, **1.** Diffused. **2.** Diffuse. **3.** Wide opened, MBh. 3, 12905. **4.** Broad, Matsyop. 13; ample, Nalod. 3, 14. *vistîrṇa*, Large, great, Pañch. 51, 20; iii. d. 264. **Comp.** *Su-vistîrṇa*, adj. very large, Hit. 79, 13. Caus. **1.** To cause to spread, Pañch. 171, 3. **2.** To extend, Man. 7, 188.—

With सम् *sam*, **1.** To spread, MBh. 1, 7163. **2.** To cover, MBh. 2, 1774.—Cf. *στόρνυμι, στορεύς, στρώννυμι, στλεγγίς*; Lat. sternere, strages, struere, stringo; O.H.G. sturm; A.S. stearm, storm; strene, lectus; Goth. straujan; A.S. streowian, sternere; A.S. strion, thesaurus, strionan; O.H.G. sterbjan (old Caus.), interficere, sterban; A.S. steorfian, steorfan, mori; strec; O.H.G. strac; A.S. streccan, a-stregdan, a-strican, probably stregan, stredan; ge-strangian, To strengthen, etc.

2. स्तृ *STṚI*, see *spṛi*.

3. स्तृ *stṛi*, probably 2. *as* + *tṛi*, A star, Chr. 293, 1 = Rigv. i. 87, 1.—Cf. *ἀστήρ, τεῖρος*, Æol. *τέῤῥος*; Goth. stairno; A.S. steorra; Lat. stella (see *târa*).

† स्तृक्ष् *STṚIKSH*, i. 1. Par. To go.

† स्तृह् *STṚIH*, स्तृंह् *STṚÎH*, i. 6, Par. To hurt, to kill.

स्तॄ *STṚÎ*, see *stṛi*; स्तृंह् *STṚÎH*, see *stṛih*.

स्तेन् *STEN*, i. 10 (rather a denomin. derived from the next), Par. To steal, Man. 4, 256; 8, 333.

स्तेन *stena*, m. A thief, Man. 8, 197.—Cf. probably *στερέω*; Goth. stilan; A.S. stelan, stal, stalian, stalu.

† स्तेप् *STEP*, i. 10, Par. To throw; see *stip*.

स्तेम *stema*, i.e. *stim* + *a*, m. Wetness.

स्तेय *steya*, perhaps anomal. *stena* + *ya*, n. Theft, robbery, Man. 2, 116; Vikr. d. 139.—Comp. *A*-, n. not stealing, Vedântas. in Chr. 217, 15.

स्तेयिन् *steyin*, i.e. *steya* + *in*, m. A thief, Man. 9, 235.

स्तै *STAI*, see *snai*.

स्तैन *staina*, and स्तैन्य *stainya*, i.e. *stena* + *a*, or *ya*, n. Theft, robbery.

स्तोक *stoka*, **I.** adj. **1.** Little, Pańch. 263, 25; short, Pańch. 245, 13; small, few, Pańch. 31, 5. **2.** Low, Bhartṛ. 2, 10. **II.** °*kam*, adv. **1.** A little, Pańch. 170, 6. **2.** Cf. *bahutaram*, see *bahu*. **III.** m. **1.** The Châtaka, Cuculus melanoleucus. **2.** A drop of water.—Comp. *A*-, adj. much, Mâlat. 161, 2.

स्तोकक *stoka* + *ka*, m. The Châtaka, Cuculus melanoleucus, Man. 12, 67.

स्तोतृ *stotṛi*, i.e. *stu* + *tṛi*, m., f. *trî*, n. Praising, a praiser, Chr. 297, 11 = Rigv. i. 112, 11.

स्तोत्र *stotra*, i.e. *stu* + *tra*, n. Praise, Lass. 53, 17; Râjat. 5, 351.—Comp. *Anyathâ*-, n. ironical praise, Yâjń. 2, 204.

स्तोभ *stobha*, i.e. *stumbh*, and *stubh* + *a*, m. **1.** Stopping. **2.** Contumely. **3.** Latter part of the name of some verses of the Sâmaveda.

† स्तोम् *STOM*, i. 10 (a denomin. derived from the next), Par. To praise.

स्तोम *stoma*, i.e. partly *stu* + *ma*, **I.** m. **1.** Praise, Chr. 288, 14 = Rigv. i. 48, 14. **2.** Sacrifice. **3.** A heap, a quantity, multitude, Utt. Râmach. 31, 7. **II.** n. **1.** The head. **2.** Wealth. **3.** Grain. **4.** A stick bound with iron. **III.** adj. Crooked.—Comp. *Vrâtya*-, m. a sacrifice to recover the rights forfeited by an improper delay of the investiture.

स्त्येन *styena* (cf. *stena*), m. **1.** A thief. **2.** Nectar.

स्त्यै *STYAI*, ष्ट्यै *SHṬYAI*, i. 1, Par.

1. To be collected or joined. 2. Pass. To increase, Utt. Râmach. 45, 3 (to spread round about). 3. To sound. Ptcple. of the pf. pass. *styâna*, 1. Thick, gross, bulky. 2. Soft, bland. n. 1. Thickness. 2. Idleness. 3. Echo, Utt. Râmach. 45, 2.—With प्र *pra*, ptcple. of the pf. pass. *prastita* and *prastîma*. 1. Crowded, clustering. 2. Sounded.—Cf. probably στειός; Lat. stipare (Caus.).

स्त्री *strî*, probably 1. *sû*+*tṛi*+*î*, f. 1. A woman, Pańch. iii. d. 61. 2. A female in general, Draup. 4, 4.—Comp. *Amara-*, f. an Apsaras, Kir. 10, 15. *Kula-*, f. a respectable or chaste woman, Böhtl. Ind. Spr. 277; Daçak. in Chr. 191, 6. *Su-kula-*, f. a respectable woman, Châṇ. 36 in Berl. Monatsb. 1864, 409. *Paṇa-* and *Paṇya-*, f. a courtesan, Mṛichchh. 127, 20; Pańch. iii. d. 61. *Su-*, f. a brave wife, Böhtl. Ind. Spr. 1155. *Sura-*, f. an Apsaras, a nymph, Vikr. d. 3.

ऽस्त्रीक *-strî*+*ka*, a substitute for *strî*, at the end of a comp. adj.; e.g. *sa-*, adj. With women, Çâk. 61, 7.

स्त्रीता *strî*+*tâ*, f., and **स्त्रीत्व** *strî*+*tva*, n. Womanhood, Chr. 52, 19 (*tva*).

स्त्रीपुंस *strî-pums*+*a*, m. Wife and husband, Man. 1, 115.

स्त्रीपूर्विन् *strîpûrvin*, i.e. *strî-pûrva* +*in*, adj. One who has been at first a female, Chr. 63, 61.

स्त्रीमन्त् *strî*+*mant*, m. A husband.

स्त्रैण *straiṇa*, i.e. *strî*+*na*, I. adj. Female, feminine. II. n. 1. Womanhood, Utt. Râmach. 100, 8. 2. The female sex, Bhartṛ. suppl. 24 (Sch., children). — Comp. *Bhûyishṭha-dvija-bâla-vṛiddha-vikala-straiṇa*, adj. consisting for the greatest part of Brâhmaṇas, children, old and sick persons, and women, Utt. Râmach. 114, 2.

स्थ *stha* (vb. *sthâ*), adj. Staying, abiding; e.g. *garbha-*, Being in the womb, Hit. pr. d. 27, M.M. *jana-*, adj. Living amongst men, Bhâg. P. 7, 15, 56. *jala-*, adj. Existing in water, Râm. 4, 13, 10. *taṭa-*, adj. 1. Standing on the shore. 2. Indifferent, Utt. Râmach. 60, 2. *dûra-*, adj. Standing aloof, Man. 2, 202. *bhû-tala-*, adj. Standing, being on the surface of the earth, Pańch. 106, 6. *yauvana-*, adj., f. *thâ*, Marriageable, Sâv. 1, 22.

स्थग् *STHAG*, i. 1, Par. To cover, Çiç. 9, 21. *sthagita*, Hidden, covered, Kir. 14, 31; Râjat. 5, 415 (*Sarasvatî sthagitâ*, 'Sarasvatî has hidden herself,' i.e. I can scarcely find words). Caus. 1. To cover, Mâlat. 7, 8; to veil, Mâlat. 149, 15. 2. To cause inability of perceiving anything, Utt. Râmach. 78, 2. —Cf. στέγω, στέγη, τέγη; Lat. tegere; O.H.G. dakjan; A.S. theccan, thaca.

स्थग *sthag*+*a*, I. adj. 1. Cheating, a rogue. 2. Shameless. II. f. *gî*, A betel box.

स्थगन *sthag*+*ana*, n. Covering.

स्थगिका *sthagikâ*, i.e. *sthaga*+*kâ*, f. 1. A courtesan, Çukas. Narr. 7, MS. 2. The office of the betel-bearer, Pańch. v.r. of the MSS. H., I., and K., ad Kos. 63, 23.

स्थगु *sthagu*, m. A hump on the back.

स्थण्डिल *sthaṇḍila*, n. 1. A square place prepared for a sacrifice, MBh. 13, 6550; Râjat. 6, 87. 2. A barren field. 3. A heap of clods, Man. 10, 71. 4. A boundary, a landmark, Bhaṭṭ. 3, 41.

स्थण्डिलसितक *sthaṇḍilasitaka* (cf. *sthaṇḍila*), n. An altar.

स्थण्डिलेशय *sthaṇḍileçaya*, i.e. *sthaṇḍila* + *i-çaya*, m. A devotee sleeping on a place prepared for a sacrifice, Lass. 2. ed. 49, 11.

स्थपति *sthapati*, i.e. *sthâ*, Caus., + *ati*, and perhaps *stha-pati*, I. m. **1.** An architect, Pańch. 10, 4. **2.** A carpenter, a wheelwright, Râm. 2, 63, 2, Seramp. **3.** The performer of the Vṛihaspati sacrifice, MBh. 1, 2029. **4.** A charioteer. **5.** A king or chief. **6.** A guard or attendant of the womens' apartment. II. adj. Chief, best.—**Comp.** *Pushkara-*, m. a name of Çiva, MBh. 13, 1207 (erroneously written *puskara-*).

स्थपुट *sthapuṭa*, adj. **1.** Distressed. **2.** Bent with pain, Mâlat. 78, 17.

† **स्थल्** *STHAL* (akin to *sthâ*, cf. the next), i. 1, Par. To stand or be firm.—Cf. O.H.G. stallan, stellan.

स्थल *sthal* + *a*, or rather *sthâ* + *la*, I. n., and f. *lî*. **1.** Firm or dry ground, Hit. i. d. 89, M.M. (*la*). **2.** Place, Vikr. d. 79 (*lî*); Pańch. 161, 15 (*la*). **II.** n., and f. *lâ*, A spot drained and raised. **III.** n. **1.** A mound, a terrace, Megh. 67. **2.** A tent. **3.** Point, topic.—**Comp.** *Adri-kṛita-*, f. *lî*, an Apsaras. *Kuça-*, n., and f. *lî*, names of towns, MBh. 2, 614 (*lî*). *Kḷipta-harmya-sthala*, adj., f. *lî*, of which the ground of the palaces was made, Bhâg. P. 4, 25, 15. *Gaṇḍa-*, n., and f. *lî*, 1. the cheek, Çṛingârat. 7 (*la*); Daçak. in Chr. 199, 2 (*lî*). 2. an elephant's temple, Pańch. i. d. 139. *Jaghana-sthalî*, f. the buttocks, Çiç. 9, 45. *Prasava-*, f. *lî*, a mother. *Maru-*, n. a desert, Hit. i. d. 10, M.M.; 80, 7. *Mahâ-*, f. *lî*, the earth. *Vakshas-*, n. breast, Hit. iv. d. 130.—Cf. O.H.G. stal, stall; A.S. stal, stael; O.H.G. stullan; Goth. ga-stalds; O.H.G. stelza, stolz; also A.S. stillan, stille.

स्थलकमल *sthala-kamala*, n., and *-kamalinî*, f. A shrub, Hibiscus mutabilis, Megh. 90.

स्थलज *sthala-ja*, adj. **1.** Growing on earth, Man. 6, 13. **2.** Terrestrial.

स्थलता *sthala* + *tâ*, in *çushka-sthala* + *tâ*, f. Dryness, Pańch. 84, 19; 79, 13.

स्थलेशय *sthaleçaya*, i.e. *sthala* + *i-çaya*, m. An amphibious animal.

स्थवि *sthavi*, probably vb. *sthâ* (see the next), m. A weaver.

स्थविर *sthavira*, probably for *sthâvara*, cf. *sthâvira*, I. adj., f. *râ*. **1.** Fixed, firm. **2.** Old, Daçak. in Chr. 200, 12. **II.** m. **1.** An old man. **2.** A beggar. **3.** Brahman.

स्थविष्ठ *sthavishṭha*, **स्थवीयंस्** *sthavîyaṁs*, see *sthûla*.

स्था *STHÂ*, i. 1, *tishṭha*, Par., and in some significations only Âtm., but in epic poetry Âtm. as well as Par., against the rules of the Gramm. **1.** To stand, Hit. i. d. 97; with *jânubhyâm*, To kneel, Vikr. 63, 6; with *çâsane*, To obey, Vikr. d. 155. **2.** To cease to move, to stand still, to stop, Vikr. d. 20; Râm. 1, 60, 19; to wait, Vikr. 88, 17; to be restrained, Man. 7, 108. **3.** To stay, MBh. 2, 732; to abide, Man. 7, 37 (*çâsane*, He may abide by their decision). Impers. pass., Hit. 46, 2, MM.; Lass. 56, 2, *sthîyatâm*, It may be abided, viz. by you, i.e. you may abide. **4.** With instr. To practise, to use what the instrumental expresses, Pańch. 31, 18 (*sâmâdibhis*, To use conciliatory speech, etc.); 76, 20 (*maunavratena*, To be silent). **5.** To be, Man. 8, 158; to exist, Man. 7, 8. **6.** To remain, Lass.

51, 25; Man. 4, 111; to stand at one's side, Hit. i. d. 72, M.M. **7.** With an absol. it implies duration of the action expressed by the absol.; e.g. *yâ sthitâ vyâpya,* Which ever fills, Çâk. d. 1; Vikr. 14, 5 (*parikramyopariçya sthita,* After having walked up and down, he sits down and remains sitting). **8.** To be at hand, Man. 5, 104; Hit. 50, 21. **9.** Âtm. To stand firm, MBh. 1, 5558. Ptcple. of the pf. pass. *sthita.* **1.** Got up, risen. **2.** Standing, Chr. 17, 24. **3.** Steady, firm, immovable. **4.** Upright, virtuous. **5.** Stayed, stopped. **6.** Desisted, Pañch. v. d. 40 (from singing). **7.** Having lived (*sukhe,* happily), Pañch. ii. d. 95; *katham̃ sthitâsi,* How did you do? Vikr. 72, 6; living, Râm. 3, 53, 59. **8.** Being, Daçak. in Chr. 191, 11; Pañch. 149, 13 (*evam̃ sthite,* The matter being thus); Pañch. 136, 3 (*lambamânau yathâ sthitau,* How they hang down). **9.** Established, determined, Chr. 28, 17. **10.** Agreed, promised. **Comp.** *Evam-,* adj. so conditioned, Pañch. 87, 19. *Taṭa-,* adj. indifferent, Utt. Râmach. 156, 8. *Dus-,* adj. unsteady, Bhâg. P. 1, 5, 14. n. indecent kind of standing, MBh. 12, 3084. *Su-,* adj. 1. living well. 2. being well. 3. safe, Mâlat. 86, 12. *A-su-,* adj. not being well, dejected, Hit. iii. d. 108. Ptcple. fut. pass. *stheya,* **1.** To be fixed or determined. **2.** To be placed. m. **1.** A judge, an arbitrator, Hit. iv. d. 1. **2.** A domestic priest. **Comp.** *Uchchaiḥstheya,* i. e. *uchchais-,* n. standing upright, Bhartṛ. 2, 61. *Dus-,* n. difficult standing, MBh. 12, 11090. Caus. *sthâpaya,* **1.** To place, Vikr. 78, 7; Hit. i. d. 112. **2.** To establish, Râm. 3, 54, 19. **3.** To restrain, to stop, Çâk. 6, 16; Vikr. 10, 19. **4.** To keep, Man. 7, 44. **5.** To cause to exist, to found, Man. 1, 62. **6.** To cause to be durable, Lass. 2. ed. 67, 21. **7.** To let live, Hit. 121, 14. **8.** To give in marriage, MBh. 1, 2576.—With the prep. अधि *adhi,* Par. (in epic poetry also Âtm.), **1.** To stand on, Man. 4, 78; MBh. 2, 2541, *çiraḥ pâdenâdhi sthâsyâmi,* I shall put my foot on his head. **2.** To be supported, to rest on, Râm. 1, 34, 34. **3.** To stay, MBh. 1, 3572. **4.** To remain, Chr. 32, 31, *çarâ antarâdhishṭhitâḥ,* The arrows remained in the sky. **5.** To inhabit, MBh. 3, 12198. **6.** To stand, MBh. 1, 8325. **7.** To be, MBh. 1, 2867. **8.** To command, Man. 7, 114; to govern, Râm. 2, 1, 25; to lead, Utt. Râmach. 91, 8. **9.** To pass over, Râm. 1, 31, 19. **10.** To surpass, MBh. 3, 14652; to overcome, Bhaṭṭ. 9, 72. **11.** To ascend to, Chr. 288, 2 = Rigv. i. 49, 2. **12.** To do; with *prasâdam,* To show favour, Mâlat. 140, 11. *adhishṭhita* (and *dhishṭhita*), **1.** Guided, Utt. Râmach. 3, 7. **2.** Fixed, established, Pañch. 29, 7. **3.** Occupied, Hit. 56, 20. **4.** Overpowered, Pañch. 30, 5. **5.** Guarded, Utt. Râmach. 38, 13. **6.** Presiding, Pañch. 97, 1. **7.** Standing, MBh. 13, 235. **Comp.** *Dus-,* adj. wrongly performed, MBh. 7, 3314. n. remaining unbecomingly in some place, MBh. 12, 3084.—With समधि *sam-adhi,* To administer, MBh. 2, 199.—With अनु *anu,* **1.** To stand near, Man. 11, 111. **2.** To follow, to obey, Man. 2, 9. **3.** To remain, Lass. 56, 10. **4.** To execute, to perform, Râm. 1, 12, 3; to do, Pañch. 192, 10; to act, Vikr. 24, 7; to practise, Daçak. in Chr. 182, 6. **5.** To govern, Draup. 4, 12. *anushṭhita,* **1.** Agreed to, done accordingly. **2.** Done, Râm. 1, 51, 6; *tathâ-anushṭhite,* Afterwards, thereupon, Pañch. 43, 14; 42, 2; 37, 22. n. Action, Pañch. 43, 15. Desider. *tishṭhâsa,* To wish to imitate, Daçak. in Chr. 191, 6.—With अव *ava,* Âtm. **1.** To withdraw, Hit. 47, 22. **2.** To stand firm, Vedântas. in Chr. 218, 5; to keep ground, Böhtl. Ind. Spr. 70 (= Hit. ii. d. 120, v.r.); to stand ready, Pańch. 91, 6 (with dat., for). **3.** To be decided, Çâk. 23, 11. **4.** To remain, Man. 8, 145; Pańch. 127, 17. **5.** To be present, MBh. 1, 4826. **6.** To stay; *kim atrâvasthâya mayâ kartavyam*, What shall I do here? Hit. 59, 1, M.M.; with instr. To practise, Pańch. 50, 13 (cf. the simple vb). *avasthita*, **1.** Standing, Vikr. d. 160; Râjat. 5, 49. **2.** Abiding, remaining firm, Râm. 3, 50, 15. **3.** Steady, Man. 7, 60. **4.** Being, Pańch. 180, 20 (*evam avasthite*, Matters being in this state). *yathâvasthita*, As it was, Pańch. 196, 18. °*tam*, adv. Truly (as it happened), Pańch. 237, 19. **5.** Engaged in, prosecuting. **Comp.** *An-*, adj. 1. unsteady, changed, Utt. Râmach. 47, 4. 2. fickle, unchaste, Râm. 5, 51, 10; Man. 11, 138. Caus. **1.** To cause to stand, to place, Hit. 61, 4, M.M. **2.** To cause to stay, to leave, Vikr. 35, 3.—With **पर्यव** *pari-ava*, Âtm. **1.** To rely on, MBh. 1, 4029. **2.** To exist everywhere, Bhag. 2, 65.—With **प्रत्यव** *prati-ava*, To stand opposite, Sund. 3, 24. Caus. To collect; with *âtmânam*, To recover, Vikr. 8, 1.—With **व्यव** *vi-ava*, *vyavasthita*, **1.** Separated, going away, Pańch. 57, 9, *agre*, He took the head. **2.** Extracted. **3.** Constant, Lass. 2. ed. 39, 10. **4.** Declared. **5.** Appointed. **6.** Fixed, Man. 10, 68; based, Mâlat. 70, 7. **7.** Depending on, Hit. iv. d. 98. **8.** Staying, having rested at the same place, Chr. 20, 1. **9.** Restrained, Utt. Râmach. 135, 8 (*-vishaya*, Of which the sphere is restrained to one alone). **10.** Standing, Chr. 27, 1; Pańch. 229, 21 (*agre*, Was standing in front of him). **11.** With *vâkye*, Obeying, Râm. 3, 51, 35. **12.** Existing, Pańch. 76, 23. **13.** One who has agreed, Man. 8, 156. Caus. **1.** To establish, Daçak. in Chr. 184, 19. **2.** To perform, Ragh. 14, 53.—With **समव** *sam-ava*, *samavasthita*, **1.** Ready, MBh. 3, 633. **2.** Standing immovable, Vikr. d. 4. Caus. **1.** To stop (a chariot), MBh. 3, 887. **2.** To found (a tribe), MBh. 1, 4365.—With **आ** *â*, **1.** To be near at hand, Man. 9, 87. **2.** To stand on, Chr. 290, 9 = Rigv. i. 64, 9; to sit on, MBh. 3, 11776. **3.** To stay, to remain, Hit. 95, 1, M.M. **4.** To walk toward, Man. 11, 104. **5.** To turn to; *apayânam âsthita*, Turning to withdraw, i.e. being about to withdraw, Çiç. 9, 84; *kâm̃ buddhim âsthâya*, What did you think (when . . .)? Chr. 21, 5. **6.** To ascend, MBh. 1, 3677 (a chariot). **7.** To assume, Pańch. iii. d. 20; Râm. 3, 50, 26 (a shape). **8.** To apply, MBh. 3, 11964 (a weapon); Man. 2, 88 (care). **9.** To observe, Man. 7, 226; with *vrittim*, To behave, Man. 2, 133. **10.** To perform, Man. 2, 103; MBh. 3, 8514 (religious austerities). **11.** To act, to behave, Nal. 9, 8. *âsthita*, **1.** Standing on (with acc.), Chr. 36, 16. **2.** Stayed. **3.** Occupied. **4.** Applied to, having recourse to, having assumed, Râm. 3, 50, 26. **5.** Undergone, Lass. 2. ed. 90, 49. **6.** Spread. **7.** Observing, following, Man. 5, 36. **8.** Practising, exhibiting, Lass. 53, 17; with acc., Vikr. d. 130 (absorbed in).—With **उपा** *upa-â*, Âtm. To approach carnally, MBh. 3, 10754.—With **समुपा** *sam-upa-â*, To observe (a law), MBh. 1, 7452.—With **समा** *sam-â*, **1.** To undergo, Chr. 49, 4 (*samâsthitas tapo ghoram*, He performed great austerities). **2.** To apply, MBh. 3, 11967; with *vrittim*, To act, Man. 4, 2; with *yogam*, To exert one's self, Man. 7, 44. **3.** To perform, Râm. 1, 56, 24. *samâsthita*, Seated.—With **उद्** *ud*, **1.** To get up, to rise, Râm. 2, 72, 24; Vikr. 31, 18; *uttishṭhamâna*, Being about to rise, Pańch. i. d. 408. *utthâya-utthâya*,

Whenever one rises, Hit. i. d. 3, M.M. **2.** To rouse one's self, Bhag. 2, 3. Ptcple. pf. pass. *utthita.* **1.** Rising, Lass. 2. ed. 46, 23. **2.** Arising (as revenue), Hit. iv. d. 121. Caus. **1.** To lead away (one's wife from her father's house), Lass. 22, 1 (cf. 24, 9). **2.** To lift; Hit. 91, 13, M.M.; to raise, Râm. 2, 72, 23 (a fallen person); to lift out, Hit. 21, 7, M.M. **3.** To arouse, MBh. 1, 1887. **4.** To reanimate, MBh. 1, 3297. —With अनूद् *anu-ud,* To rise after one, Ragh. 2, 24.—With अभ्युद् *abhi-ud,* **1.** To rise, Daçak. in Chr. 185, 14. **2.** To rise to (with acc.), Utt. Râmach. 83, 5.—With प्रत्युद् *prati-ud,* To rise to salute, Man. 2, 119.—With व्युद् *vi-ud,* To incite, MBh. 1, 7404.—With समुद् *sam-ud,* **1.** To rise together, Chr. 13, 7. **2.** To rise, Sâv. 1, 8. **3.** To return to life, MBh. 3, 16574. *samutthita,* **1.** Swollen up, Râm. 3, 49, 51. **2.** Arisen, produced, Pańch. 57, 15. Caus. **1.** To raise, MBh. 1, 6588. **2.** To reanimate, Râm. 1, 1, 85.—With उप *upa,* **1.** To stand near, Râm. 1, 13, 38; to be imminent, Pańch. 86, 25. **2.** To stand opposite, Man. 2, 48. **3.** To be at hand, MBh. 3, 11671. **4.** To serve, Râm. 1, 16, 28; to wait on, Çâk. 3, 12; Vikr. 3, 8 (Âtm.); to salute, Mâlat. 2, 3 (Âtm.). **5.** To oblige (by presents), Ragh. 18, 21. **6.** To adore, MBh. 1, 4405. **7.** To embrace, MBh. 3, 10754. **8.** To approach, Râm. 1, 25, 4; to arrive at, Man. 3, 76. **9.** To fall to one's share, Pańch. 194, 5; MBh. 3, 3043. *upasthita,* **1.** Arrived, come, Man. 3, 103. **2.** Staying, standing by or near, Hit. 47, 2, M.M. **3.** Near, Râm. 2, 51, 18; impending, Hit. i. d. 3, M.M. **4.** Caused. **5.** Got. **6.** Felt. **7.** Cleansed. **8.** Done. **9.** Known. Caus. **1.** To bring near, Çâk. 28, 9; to order to be brought, Utt. Râmach. 22, 8. **2.** To supply, Râm. 1, 26, 2 (a ship). **3.** To place, Râm. 2, 3, 18.—With अभ्युप *abhi-upa,* To adore, Bhâg. P. 5, 7, 12. *abhyupasthita,* Accompanied, MBh. 3, 16132.—With पर्युप *pari-upa,* **1.** To surround, Râm. 2, 64, 1. **2.** To wait on, Râm. 2, 32, 15. *paryupasthita,* Imminent, MBh. 3, 13027.—With प्रत्युप *prati-upa, pratyupasthita,* **1.** Imminent, MBh. 3, 1920. **2.** Present, Utt. Râmach. 156, 14.—With समुप *sam-upa,* **1.** To approach, Chr. 7, 17; Pańch. ii. d. 13. **2.** To fall in the way, Hit. 76, 8, M.M. **3.** To send, Çâk, d. 43. *samupasthita,* Imminent, Chr. 5, 4.—With नि *ni, nishṭhita,* **1.** Firm, fixed. **2.** Certain. **3.** Staying in, Bhag. 13, 17. **4.** Versed in, Râm. 1, 12, 20. **5.** Engaged in.—With परिनि *pari-ni, parinishṭhita,* Very skilled in, Râm. 1, 9, 8. Caus. *parinishṭhâpita,* Taught, Utt. Râmach. 35, 10.—With परि *pari,* To stand round about, to surround, Pańch. 51, 19. *parishṭhita,* Standing, Lass. 23, 6.—With प्र *pra,* Âtm. (in epic poetry also Par.), **1.** To set out, Vikr. 12, 10; to depart (with the acc., to), MBh. 3, 2401. **2.** To come, Vikr. 37, 17. *prasthita,* Set out, Çâk. 7, 9. **Comp.** *Pûrva-,* adj. set out before, Vikr. 6, 6. Caus. **1.** To push on, Râjat. 5, 415. **2.** To induce to retire, Hit. 130, 10. **3.** To send away, Râm. 2, 9, 2; to despatch, Hit. 88, 8, M.M.; to dismiss, MBh. 3, 2716.—With प्रत्यभिप्र *prati-abhi-pra,* Âtm. To depart, MBh. 1, 683.—With विप्र *vi-pra,* Âtm. **1.** To depart, MBh. 1, 8140. **2.** To spread, MBh. 1, 3709. —With संप्र *sam-pra,* Âtm. To depart,

MBh. 2, 1198. *samprasthita*, **1.** Departed, MBh. 3, 8540. **2.** Being about to set off, Râm. 2, 38, 13.—With प्रति *prati*, **1.** To stand firm, to be supported, Pańch. i. d. 93. **2.** To depend upon, MBh. 1, 6190. **3.** To stay, MBh. 3, 11855. *pratishṭhita*, **1.** Fixed, Pańch. i. d. 93; staying, Pańch. iii. d. 214. **2.** Secured, acquired. **3.** Supported, Man. 8, 163. **4.** Placed. **5.** Married. **6.** Comprised. **7.** Infixed, present, Bhag. 3, 15. **8.** Applied, Man. 8, 226. **9.** Applicable. **10.** Completed, done, Pańch. 86, 20. **11.** Consecrated. **12.** Famous (rather *pratishṭhâ+ita*), Nal. 22, 12. **13.** Valued. **Comp.** *Su-*, 1. well rooted, Pańch. iii. d. 51. 2. well set up, well consecrated, Hit. pr. d. 45, M.M. 3. celebrated. Caus. **1.** To set up, to erect, Râjat. 5, 38. **2.** To place, Chr. 12, 28. **3.** To offer, Man. 3, 135. *pratishṭhâpita*, Appointed, Daçak. in Chr. 200, 20.—With संप्रति *sam-prati*, To rest on, MBh. 1, 8359.—With वि *vi*, Âtm. (in epic poetry also Par.), **1.** To spread, Chr. 294, 5=Rigv. i. 92, 5. **2.** To stand apart, to stand, MBh. 1, 6559. *vishṭhita*, Stopping, Râm. 3, 52, 11.—With सम् *sam*, Âtm. (in epic poetry also Par.), **1.** To stand close together, MBh. 3, 15716. **2.** To stand on, to be on, Bhartṛ. 2. 57. **3.** To agree, to conform to, Mṛichchh. 15, 12. **4.** To be completed, Man. 5, 98. **5.** To exist, to live, Pańch. 96, 13. **6.** To perish, Daçak. in Chr. 181, 9. *saṁsthita*, **1.** Heaped, covered (painted ?), Râm. 5, 10, 4. **2.** Frequented, Man. 8, 371. **3.** Contiguous. **4.** Like. **5.** Placed in or on, Pańch. i. d. 105 (*niyoga-*, Being in office). **6.** Residing, Pańch. 60, 24. **7.** Lying, Hit. iv. d. 130. **8.** Abiding, Lass. 53, 9. **9.** Fixed. **10.** Stopped, MBh. 3, 1763. **11.** Concluded. **12.** Dead, Man. 3, 247. **Comp.** *Su-*, I. very contiguous (to each other), Râm. 3, 52, 28. 2. well situated. 3. being well. 4. well defined, circumscribed. Caus. **1.** To collect, to compose, Vikr. 29, 15 (one's self.) **2.** To place, Pańch. 174, 21. **3.** To subject, Man. 9, 2. **4.** To restrain, to stop. **5.** To kill, MBh. 1, 4610. *saṁsthâpita*, **1.** Accumulated. **2.** Restrained. **3.** Fixed, established. —With परिसम् *pari-sam*, *parisaṁsthita*, Standing together round about, MBh. 1, 4827.—Cf. *ἵστημι, ἔστην, σταμίν, στῆμα, στήμων, στάμνος, ἱστός, ἐπίσταμαι, στήλη, σταθερός, σταθμός, στῆθος, σθένος, τόπος* (from the Caus.); Lat. stare, sistere, stamen, stupere (Caus.), stupidus; cf. *sthûla*; O.H.G. stân, stên; Goth. and A.S. standan (frequent.); O.H.G. standa; A.S. stidh, stand, cupellus; stadhelian; O.H.G. stat, locus; stat, stad, ripa; tur-studil; A.S. studu, postis; O.H.G. stunt; A.S. stund; A.S. staef (based on the Caus.), stif, stifian (or to *styai* ?). On nouns like *sthavi*, etc., are based *σταυρός, στύω, στῦλος, στόα*; Goth. staujan, stôjan; O.H.G. stauuan; cf. also A.S. stow, etc.

स्थाणु *sthâṇu* (vb. *sthâ*), I. adj. Firm, steady, fixed, immovable, Chr. 46, 20; MBh. 1, 7291. II. m. and n. The trunk of a tree, Man. 9, 44; Bhâshâp. 128. III. m. **1.** A stake, a post, Pańch. i. d. 55. **2.** A spear. **3.** A nest of white ants. **4.** Çiva, Vikr. d. 1; Râm. 3, 53, 60.

स्थाणुवत् *sthâṇu+vat*, adv. Like a post, Pańch. i. d. 55.

स्थाण्डिल *sthâṇḍila*, i.e. *sthaṇḍila+a*, m. **1.** An ascetic who sleeps on the place prepared for a sacrifice. **2.** A religious mendicant.

स्थातृ *sthâ+tṛi*, m., f. *tri*, and n. Who or what stands.—Cf. Lat. stator.

स्थान *sthâna*, i.e. *sthâ + ana*, **I.** n. **1.** Staying, Lass. 28, 10; stay, state, Utt. Râmach. 51, 5; Man. 7, 56 (forces); position, Hit. i. d. 51, M.M. **2.** Middle state, as neither loss nor gain (equality), calmness, Râm. 3, 52, 2 (corr. *nahi me jîvitam̃ sthâne*, My life, i.e. my whole being, is disquieted). **3.** Firmness of troops. **4.** Keeping in array. **5.** Halt. **6.** Place, Pańch. 133, 5; 37, 8; a holy place, Chr. 46, 26; the right place, Hit. ii. d. 70. **7.** Country, Hit. i. d. 169, M.M. **8.** An altar, Vikr. d. 43. **9.** An open place in a town. **10.** A dwelling-place, Hit. iii. d. 5; house, Chr. 60, 37; Cṛiṅgârat. 11. **11.** A town. **12.** Office, Râjat. 5, 297. **13.** The part of an actor, Vikr. 3, 9. **14.** Degree, rank, Hit. i. d. 168, M.M. **15.** Object, Man. 2, 136; Pańch. 82, 12. **16.** Likeness. **17.** Intimation (cf. *sthânaka*), Lass. 7, 5. **18.** Interval. **II.** loc. *ne*, adv. **1.** Fitly, properly, justly, Vikr. 8, 16; in the right moment, Çâk. 37, 34. **2.** Sometimes, MBh. 1, 6845. **3.** Because. **4.** Instead, Pańch. 37, 21. **5.** Like, as, Pańch. 52, 1; 55, 22.—**Comp.** *A-sthâna*, n. unsuitable, wrong place, Pańch. 10, 10. *An-uchita-*, n. the same, Pańch. 64, 8. *Asmad-*, n. our place; loc. *ne*, instead of us (me), Pańch. 83, 19. *Uchchais-*, n. elevation in rank, Man. 7, 121. *Eka-*, n. same place; loc. *ne*, together, Pańch. 85, 22. *Karmasthâna*, i.e. *karman-*, n. a government building, Râjat. 5, 166. *Kopa-*, n. an object of wrath, i.e. easy to be injured, Lass. 41, 4. *Jana-*, n. the name of a wood, Utt. Râmach. 17, 12. *Janmasthâna*, i.e. *janman-*, n. birthplace, home, Pańch. 247, 4. *Tadîya-*, n. its place, Vikr. 71, 11. *Dhana-*, n. treasury, Râjat. 4, 621. *Dharma-adhikaraṇa-*, n. court of justice, Pańch. 40, 22. *Prasava-*, n. a nest, Pańch. 74, 25. *Badhya-*, or *vadhya-* (vb. *vadh*), n. place of execution, Pańch. 41, 15. *Bandhana-*, n. a stable, Pańch. 224, 8. *Bhaksha-*, n. state of being (one's) food, Pańch. 131, 2 (*bhakshasthâne sthitam api*, although you are destined to be his food). *Yathâ-sthâna + m*, adv. instantly, Pańch. in Weber, Ind. St. iii. 373, 4. *Vibhishikâ-*, n. object, or means, of frightening, Pańch. 160, 21. *Viçvâsa-*, **I.** n. an object or person of trust. **II.** *viçvâsasthâne*, adv. as hostage, Pańch. 55, 22. *Vîra-*, n. a certain posture, Lass. 2. ed. 70, 55. *Vyańjana-sthâne*, loc. as condiment (*karomi*, I shall use), Pańch. 52, 1. *Çulka-*, n. any object of toll or duty, Man. 8, 398. *Sam̃keta-*, n. 1. place of assignation. 2. a sign, an intimation, Lass. 7, 5. *Sura-*, n. a temple, Hit. iii. d. 36. *Siddhi-*, n. name of a country, Lass. 40, 19. *Hṛidaya-*, n. the breast.—Cf. *δύστηνος* (i.e. *δυσ-στηνος*), *ἄ-στηνος*, *ἀ-στήν*, *ἀσταίνω*, *δυσταίνω*.

स्थानक *sthâna + ka*, n. **1.** A town. **2.** A basin of water at the root of a tree, **3.** A bubble on spirits or wine. **4.** A kind of speaking (addressing ?), Vikr. 64, 21.—**Comp.** *Patâkâ-*, n. intimation of an episode in a drama, Daçar. 1, 14.

स्थानासनविहारवन्त् *sthânâsana-vihâravant*, adj. *sthâna-âsana-vihâra + vant*, adj, Occupying the station, seat, and place of religious exercises (of his preceptor), Man. 2, 248.

स्थानिक *sthânika*, i.e. *sthâna + ika*, **I.** adj. Local. **II.** m. The governor of a place.

स्थानिन् *sthânin*, i.e. *sthâna + in*, adj. Having a place or situation, permanent.

स्थानीय *sthânîya*, i.e. *sthâna + îya*, **I.** adj. Relating or suitable to any place. **II.** n. A city.—**Comp.** *Avatam̃sa-*, adj., f. *yâ*, taking the place of a crest, i.e. being, as it were, the ornament, Daçak. in Chr. 179, 14. *Kaṇṭha-*, adj. having its place in the throat, Vedântas. in Chr. 207, 11.

स्थापक *sthâpaka,* i.e. *sthâ,* Caus., + *aka,* I. adj. Causing to stand, placing, fixing, ordering. II. m. 1. A stage manager. 2. The founder of a temple. —Comp. *Sthiti-,* I. adj. who or what fixes (cf. *sthiti*). II. m. (n., Wils.), elasticity, Bhâshâp. 95; 156 (cf. *sthiti*).

स्थापत्य *sthâpatya,* i.e. *sthapati* + *ya,* I. m. A guard of the womens' apartments. II. n. Architecture, building, erecting, Râm. 1, 12, 6.

स्थापन *sthâpana,* i.e. *sthâ,* Caus., + *ana,* I. n. 1. Placing, Naish. 22, 45, Sch.; fixing, erecting, founding. 2. Concentrating one's thoughts upon the object of meditation. 3. Ordering. 4. A habitation. 5. A ceremony performed when the mother perceives the first signs of living conception. II. f. *nâ,* Stage management. III. f. *nî,* A plant, Cissampelos hexandra.

स्थामन् *sthâ* + *man,* n. Strength, power.

स्थायिन् *sthâyin,* i.e. *sthâ* + *in,* adj., f. *nî,* 1. Staying, lasting, Hit. i. d. 48, M.M. 2. Firm, steady, unchangeable, Pańch. i. d. 39.—Comp. *A-,* adj. not permanent, Bhartṛ. 2, 83. *Puras-,* adj. standing before one's eyes, Böhtl. Ind. Spr. 1212. *Vana-,* I. adj. abiding in a wood. II. m. a hermit.

स्थायुक *sthâyuka,* i.e. *sthâ* + *uka,* I. adj. Steady, stationary. II. m. The overseer of a village.

स्थाल *sthâ* + *la,* I. n. A plate, a dish, Râjat. 5, 46. II. f. *lî,* A pot, Pańch. 262, 16.

स्थावर *sthâ* + *vara* (i. e. *van* + *a,* with *r* for *n*), I. adj. 1. Fixed, stable, immovable, Man. 1, 40; 41; 5, 28. 2. Stationary (guards), Man. 9, 266. 3. Established, regular. II. m. A mountain, Bhag. 10, 25. III. n. 1. A bowstring. 2. Real estate. 3. A heirloom.

स्थावरता *sthâvara* + *tâ,* f. Immobility, Man. 12, 9 (a vegetable or mineral form).

स्थाविर *sthâvira,* i.e. *sthâ* + *van* + *a,* with *i* for *a,* and *r* for *n,* n. Old age, Man. 9, 3 (adj. Old, Hit. i. d. 119, M.M.; but cf. Böhtl. Ind. Spr. 1774).

स्थासक *sthâsaka* (vb. *sthâ*), m. 1. A bubble of any fluid (cf. *sthânaka*). 2. Smearing the body with fragrant unguents.

स्थासु *sthâsu,* vb. *sthâ,* n. Bodily strength or capability.

स्थास्नु *sthâ* + *snu,* adj. 1. Firm, immovable, Man. 1, 56. 2. Durable, eternal, Kir. 2, 19.

स्थिक *sthika,* i.e. *sthâ* + *ka,* m. A buttock.

स्थिति *sthiti,* i. e. *sthâ* + *ti,* f. 1. Standing, Mâlat. 160, 6; staying, stay, Man. 11, 237. 2. Living, doing well, Böhtl. Ind. Spr. 1125. 3. Residence, Utt. Râmach. 5, 1. 4. Remaining, Pańch. pr. d. 8 (*garbhe,* in the womb, i. e. not being brought forth). 5. Keeping, i. d. 159 (but cf. v.r. Böhtl. Ind. Spr. 1561). 6. Being fixed, duration, Vikr. d. 153; a firm position, Pańch. i. d. 220. 7. State, Chân. 90 in Berl. Monatsb. 1864, 412; condition, Pańch. 124, 4; natural state (cf. *-sthâpaka,* Bhâshâp. 95, properly 'restoring the natural state'). 8. Correctness of conduct, Kir. 11, 54. 9. Honour, Mâlat. 152, 20; dignity, Nal. 12, 10. 10. Stop, cessation. 11. Limit, boundary. 12. A sure decision, Man. 2, 225; a settled rule, 3, 120; a maxim, Hit. 50, 9, M.M. 13. Order, decree.—

Comp. *A-bhinna-* (vb. *bhid*), adj. not swerving from the right path, Çâk. d. 107. *Prithak-*, f. separation, Vikr. d. 102. *Maṭha-*, f. staying in a college of priests, Pańch. ii. d. 66 (read *maṭhasthityâ*). *Râjya-*, f. staying in government, being a king, Pańch. 251, 9. *Su-*, f. 1. welfare. 2. health.

स्थितिमन्त् *sthiti + mant*, adj., f. *matî*, **1.** Firm, stable, Vikr. d. 160. **2.** Virtuous, Man. 9, 74.

स्थिर *sthira*, i.e. *sthâ + ra*, **I.** adj., comparat. *stheyaṁs*, superl. *stheshṭha*. **1.** Firm, Vikr. d. 1; fixed, immovable, Bhag. 6, 33 (*sthirî kṛi*, To stop, Pańch. 258, 20). **2.** Permanent, Vikr. d. 109; Chr. 291, 15 = Rigv. i. 64, 15; eternal, Megh. 56. **3.** Hard, Utt. Râmach. 30, 2; solid, strong, Indr. 1, 18. **4.** Steady, Mâlat. 175, 6; free from passion, Bhartṛ. 2, 44. **5.** Cool, collected, Lass. 43, 17. **6.** Convinced, sure, Chr. 53, 25. **7.** Constant, determined, Chr. 43, 28. **8.** Faithful, Pańch. 107, 11. **II.** m. **1.** A deity. **2.** Final emancipation. **3.** A mountain. **4.** A tree. **5.** A bull. **6.** Kârttikeya, the god of war. **7.** Saturn. **III.** f. *râ*. **1.** The earth. **2.** Silk-cotton tree, and two other plants. — **Comp.** *A-sthira*, adj. 1. inconstant, Hit. iii. d. 106. 2. weak, Man. 8, 77. — Cf. *στηρίζω*, *στερεός*, *στεῤῥός*, *στελεόν*; Lat. stolidus, stultus; O.H.G. starên; A.S. starian; O.H.G. storrên, stornên, starh; A.S. stare; O.H.G. ga-starkên, starhjan, etc.

स्थिरता *sthira + tâ*, f. **1.** Firmness, Çâk. d. 90; stability; *sthiratâṁ nî*, To secure, Pańch. 97, 14. **2.** Moral firmness. **3.** Fortitude.

स्थिरत्व *sthira + tva*, n. Firmness, steadiness, Johns. Sel. 12, 30. — **Comp.** *A-*, n. inconstancy, Man. 8, 77.

† **स्थुड्** *STHUḌ*, i. 6, To cover.

स्थूणा *sthûṇâ* (vb. *sthâ*, based on *sthâ + va°*, cf. the next), f. **1.** A pillar, a post, Pańch. 37, 6. **2.** An iron image. **3.** An anvil. **4.** A disease. — **Comp.** *Veçmasthûṇâ*, i.e. *veçman-*, f. the main post of a house.

स्थूर *sthûra*, i.e. *sthâ + vara* (cf. the next), m. A man.

स्थूरिन् *sthûrin*, i.e. *sthûra* (in the signification of **sthava* in *sthavîyaṁs*, cf. *sthûla* and *sthûlin*), + *in*, m. A pack-horse. — Cf. Zend. *çtaora* (= *sthûra*, or rather *sthaura*, cf. *sthaurin*), A beast of burden; Goth. stiurs; A.S. steor; *ταῦρος*; cf. also *sthûla*, and O.H.G. stiuri, fortis; A.S. stor; O.H.G. stur, magnus.

† **स्थूल्** *STHÛL*, i. 10 (a denomin. derived from the next), Par. To become big or bulky.

स्थूल *sthûla* = *sthûra* (with *l* for *r*), but in the original signification of its base, *sthâ + vara*, **I.** adj., comparat. *sthûlatara* and *sthavîyaṁs*, superl. *sthûlatama* and *sthavishṭha*. **1.** Great, large, Râjat. 5, 12; Megh. 47; Pańch. i. d. 373; *sthûlatara*, Very large, Pańch. 134, 5. **2.** Bulky, Vedântas. in Chr. 204, 22; fat. **3.** Powerful, Pańch. 168, 25. **4.** Clumsy. **5.** Coarse, Pańch. 133, 1. **6.** Stupid. **II.** m. The jack tree. **III.** f. *lâ*. **1.** A sort of pepper. **2.** A pumpkin gourd. **IV.** n. **1.** A heap. **2.** A tent. — **Comp.** *Ati-*, adj. 1. very big, Râm. 5, 10, 17. 2. too clumsy, Suçr. 1, 25, 21. *Muktâ-*, adj. as large as pearls, Megh. 105.

स्थूलता *sthûla + tâ*, f. **1.** Coarseness, bulkiness, Pańch. i. d. 205. **2.** Stupidity.

स्थूलिन् *sthûlin* (cf. *sthûrin*), m. A camel.

स्थेयंस् *stheyaṁs*, **स्थेष्ठ** *stheshṭha*, see *sthira*.

स्थैर्य *sthairya*, i.e. *sthira + ya*, n. **1.** Firmness, stability, staying continually, Pańch. 225, 22. **2.** Constancy, Pańch. iii. d. 102. **3.** Patience, Pańch. iii. d. 238. — Comp. *A-*, n. perishableness, Râjat. 5, 381.

स्थौर *sthaura*, i. e. *sthûra* (but in the signification of *sthûla* and *sthûrin*, q. cf.), *+a*, n. **1.** Strength, power. **2.** A load for a horse or ass.

स्थौरिन् *sthaurin*, i.e. *sthaura + in* (cf. *sthûrin*), m. **1.** A pack-horse. **2.** A strong horse.

स्थौललक्ष्य *sthaulalakshya*, i. e. *sthûla-laksha + ya*, n. Incessant liberality, Man. 7, 211.

स्थौलशीर्ष *sthaulaçîrsha*, i. e. *sthûla-çîrsha + a*, adj. Large-headed.

स्थौल्य *sthaulya*, i.e. *sthûla + ya*, n. Largeness, bulk.

स्नपन *snapana*, i. e. *snâ*, Caus., *+ana*, n. **1.** Washing. **2.** Bathing, ablution, Çiç. 8, 70.

स्नव *snava*, i.e. *snu + a*, m. Oozing, dripping.

† **स्नस्** *SNAS*, i. 1 and 4, Par. **1.** To eject. **2.** To eat (?).

स्नसा *snasâ*, f. A tendon, a muscle. — Cf. perhaps O.H.G. snôr, snuor, see *snâva*.

स्ना *SNÂ*, ii. 2, Par. (in epic poetry also Âtm., MBh. 3, 7072), **1.** To bathe, Man. 4, 82; anomal. potent. *snâyîta*, MBh. 3, 7072. **2.** To perform the ceremony of bathing when leaving the house of one's spiritual preceptor, Man. 2, 245. *snâta*, **1.** Bathed, having bathed, Râjat. 5, 391; Daçak. in Chr. 188, 20. **2.** Purified, Mahâv. 77, 2; pure. m. (One whose spiritual instruction is finished, see **2.**), an initiated householder. Comp. *Mṛita-*, adj. 1. bathed after mourning. 2. dying immediately after ablution. *Su-*, I. adj. very clean, Lass. 24, 4. II. m. a student who has performed his ablutions preparatory or subsequent to a sacrifice. Caus. *snăpaya*, **1.** To wash, to cleanse, Daçak. in Chr. 200, 7 (*â*); Megh. 44 (*ă*). **2.** To weep for (?), Utt. Râmach. 69, 1 (*ă*). *snapita*, **1.** Bathed, Mâlat. 60, 10. **2.** Moistened, Kir. 5, 44; 47. — With **अप** *apa*, *apasnâta*, Bathed after mourning, Râm. 2, 42, 22. — With **नि** *ni*, *nishṇâta*, **1.** Perfect, superior. **2.** Learned, MBh. 1, 3988; skilful, conversant, Çâk. 65, 18. **3.** Given to, Mâlat. 37, 3. **4.** (In law), Agreed upon, Mâlat. 174, 13. *ati-nishṇâta*, Very conversant, Daçak. in Chr. 190, 19. — With **प्रति** *prati*, **1.** *pratisnâta*, Bathed. **2.** *pratishṇâta*, Pure. Comp. *Su-pratishṇâta*, adj. certain. — Cf. ναρός, νᾶμα, νοτίς, νῆσος, νίπτω; Lat. nare; Goth. nadr; A.S. naeddre, nedre; O.H.G. nacho; see *nau*.

स्नातक *snâta + ka* (vb. *snâ*), m. A Brâhmaṇa just returned from the mansion of his preceptor, Man. 2, 138 (cf. *snâ*); an initiated householder, Lass. 71, 1; a Brâhmaṇa in his second *âçrama* (order of life), Man. 1, 113; Hit. 123, 19. — Comp. *Vidyâ-*, *Vidyâ-vrata-*, and *Vrata-*, m. a Brâhmaṇa who has completed his studentship.

स्नान *snâna*, i.e. *snâ + ana*, n. **1.** Bathing, Pańch. 100, 8. **2.** Purification by bathing, Man. 1, 111; Pańch. iii. d. 120. **3.** Anything used in it, as water, perfumed powder, etc., Ṛit. 1, 4; Megh. 34, Sch. — Comp. *Tris-*, n. bathing three times a day, Kâm. Nîtis. 2, 28. *Dus-*, n. inauspicious bathing, Hariv. 3413. *Mṛita-*, n. funeral ablution.

स्नानीय *snânîya*, adj. Ablutionary, fit for bathing in, or to be used in bathing, Mâlav. d. 87; Ragh. 16, 21.

स्नापक *snâpaka*, i. e. *snâ*, Caus., + *aka*, m. A servant who supplies or applies bathing water, Râm. 2, 64, 12, Seramp.

स्नापन *snâpana*, i. e. *snâ*, Caus., + *ana*, Bathing, Man. 2, 209.

स्नायिन् *snâyin*, i.e. *snâ* + *in*, adj., f. *nî*, Bathing, Man. 11, 214.—**Comp.** *Nitya-*, adj. constantly bathing, Hit. 40, 10, M.M.

स्नायु *snâyu* (probably a form of *snâva*, for *snâu*), f. **1.** A tendon, Man. 8, 234; Pańch. 182, 17; a muscle, Bhartṛ. 2, 23. **2.** The string of a bow, Pańch. 121, 1.

स्नायुमय *snâyu* + *maya*, adj., f. *yî*, Made of tendons, Pańch. 144, 14.

स्नाव *snâva*, m. A tendon, a muscle. —Cf. probably O.H.G. senwa; A.S. sinu, sinw, senw.

स्निग्धता *snigdha* + *tâ* (vb. *snih*), f. **1.** Affection. **2.** Unctuousness.

† स्निट् *SNIṬ*, i. 10, Par. **1.** To go. **2.** To love (cf. *snih*).

स्निह् *SNIH*, i. 4, Par. (properly, To be viscous, easy to be attached to), To bear affection to, Çâk. 102, 6 (to this boy). Ptcple. of the pf. pass. *snigdha*. **1.** Oily, unctuous, smooth, Râjat. 5, 319. **2.** Wet, Megh. 16 (Sch.). **3.** Resplendent, Vikr. d. 70 (*kanaka -nikasha-*, like a streak of pure gold). **4.** Agreeable, Megh. 65. **5.** Coarse. **6.** Thick, dense, Megh. 1. **7.** Cooling, emollient. **8.** Attached, Hit. ii. d. 151; kind, well affected, Man. 7, 32; 120; loving, Pańch. i. d. 317. m. **1.** A friend, Pańch. ii. d. 178. **2.** Two kinds of pine. f. *dhâ*, Marrow. n. **1.** Oil, Megh. 60. **2.** Beeswax. **3.** Light. **4.** Thickness. † i. 10, Par. To be unctuous.—With अति *ati*, *atisnigdha*, Very smooth, Râm. 3, 49, 36.—With उप *upa*, Caus. To cause to love, to fascinate, Utt. Râmach. 34, 18.—With प्र *pra*, *prasnigdha*, Very oily, Çâk. d. 14.

1. स्नु *SNU*, ii. 2, Par. To distill, to flow.—With प्र *pra*, To pour forth, Râm. 2, 64, 55, Seramp. *prasnuta*, Dropping, Râjat. 5, 76 (cf. s.v. *stana*). —Cf. Æol. ναύω, νάω; Goth. snivan; A.S. sniwan; O.H.G. sniutan; A.S. snytan; probably also Goth. sniumjan, sniumundo; O. H. G. sniumi; A.S. sneome.

2. स्नु *snu*, probably *so* + *nu* (cf. *sânu*), m. and n. Table-land.

स्नुतस् *snutas* (for *snâyu* + *tas*), adv. From the muscles, Bhâg. P. 3, 12, 45.

स्नुषा *snushâ*, f. **1.** A daughter-in-law, Utt. Râmach. 15, 8. **2.** The milk-hedge plant.—Cf. O.H.G. snur; A.S. snóru; Lat. nurus; νυός.

† स्नुस् *SNUS*, i. 4, Par. To eat, or to be invisible, or to take (?).

† स्नुह् *SNUH*, i. 4, Par. To vomit.

स्नेह *sneha*, i.e. *snih* + *a*, m. **1.** Oil, Ragh. 4, 75; unguent, grease, Megh. 93; Râm. 2, 64, 68. **2.** Moisture, the corporeal fluids, Man. 12, 120. **3.** Oiliness, viscidity, Bhâshâp. 4; 86. **4.** Affection, love, Pańch. ii. d. 178; Megh. 111 (plur., read *snehân âhuḥ*).—**Comp.** *Nis-*, adj., f. *hâ*, 1. not oily, Man. 5, 87. 2. void of affection, Pańch. iv. d. 47. 3. free from desire, MBh. 13, 1658. 4. not treated affectionately, Pańch. i. d. 94. 5. abhorred, Somad. Nal. 71. *Mastaka-*, m. the brain. *Vi-gata-* (vb. *gam*), adj. void of affection, Sund. 4, 17. *Sa-sneha*, adj. affectionate, Hit. iv. d. 74. °*ham*, adv. affectionately, Pańch. 187, 8.

स्नेहन् *snehan* (vb. *snih*), m. A sort of disease.

स्नेहन *snehana*, i.e. *snih+ana*, n. 1. Anointing. 2. Unctuousness. 3. An unguent, an emollient.

स्नेहभू *sneha-bhû*, m. The phlegmatic humour.

स्नेहवन्त् *sneha+vant*, adj., f. *vatî*, Possessed of affection.—Comp. *A-*, deprived of affection, Pańch. i. d. 310.

स्नेहित *snehita*, i. e. *sneha+ita*, I. adj. 1. Kind, affectionate. 2. Beloved. II. m. A friend.

स्नेहिन् *snehin*, i. e. *sneha+in*, I. adj. 1. Affectionate. 2. Oily. II. m. 1. A friend. 2. A painter.

स्नै *SNAI*, † स्तै *STAI*, i. 1, Par. To dress, to adorn.

स्नैग्ध्य *snaigdhya*, i. e. *snigdha+ya* (vb. *snih*), n. 1. Affectionateness. 2. Oiliness.

स्पन्द् *SPAND*, i. 1, Âtm. To tremble, Mṛichchh. 105, 12. *spandita*, 1. Throbbing, Vikr. d. 50; beating. 2. Gone. n. Pulsation.—With the prep. परि *pari*, To tremble, Râm. 2, 14, 12.—With वि *vi*, To struggle, MBh. 3, 445.—Cf. σφενδόνη, σφεδανός, σφοδρός, σφόδρα (φ by the influence of σ); Lat. funda.

स्पन्द *spand + a*, m. Trembling, motion, Bhâshâp. 158.—Comp. *A-*, adj. immovable, Utt. Râmach. 125, 13; Râjat. 5, 364. *Sparça-*, m. a frog.

स्पन्दन *spand+ana*, n. 1. Quivering, trembling (Bhâshâp. 6, read *spandano*°). 2. Throbbing, Mâlat. 5, 3. 3. Quickening of the child in the womb. 4. Going.—Comp. *Garbha-a-*, n. immobility of the child in the womb, Suçr. 1, 49, 15.

स्पन्दिन् *spand+in*, adj. 1. Quivering, Râjat. 5, 1. 2. Palpitating (as an eye), Megh. 93 (with *upari-*, above).

स्परितृ *sparitṛi*, i.e. *spṛi+tṛi*, m., f. *trî*, and n. The active cause of pain, an enemy, a disease.

स्पर्ध् *SPARDH* (i. e. *spṛi-dhâ*), i. 1, Âtm. (in epic poetry also Par., MBh. 5, 170), 1. To contend with, to contest, MBh. 1, 205. 2. To emulate, to vie, Pańch. v. d. 50; to envy, Râm. 2, 60, 65, Seramp. 3. To be equal, MBh. 1, 4991. *spardhita*, Contended with, envied, defied.—With वि *vi*, To vie, MBh. 1, 1088.—Cf. Goth. spaurds; A.S. spyrd; O.H.G. spurt, stadium (originally certamen); probably also A.S. flit, ge-flit, strife; see *spṛih*.

स्पर्ध *spardh+a*, I. adj. Emulous, envious. II. f. *dhâ*. 1. Emulation, envy, jealousy, Johns. Sel. 45, 68; Râjat. 5, 285. 2. Successive elevation. 3. Sameness.—Comp. *Vi-spardhâ*, f. absence of envy, MBh. 5, 1602.

स्पर्धिन् *spardhin*, i. e. *spardhâ + in*, adj, 1. Rivalling, Pańch. ed. orn. 3, 5. 2. Emulating, Ragh. 13, 13. 3. Envious. 4. Proud.

† स्पर्श् *SPARÇ*, स्पश् *SPAÇ*, i. 10, Par. 1. To take. 2. To embrace (cf. *spṛiç*).

स्पर्श *sparça*, i.e. *spṛiç+a*, I. m. 1. Touch, Vikr. 47, 12; feeling, Man.

1, 76; Vedântas. in Chr. 208, 23; Bhâshâp. 3; touching, Çâk. d. 27; Mâlav. 29, 13; contact, Bhag. 2, 14. **2.** Sexual intercourse, Râjat. 5, 401. **3.** Gift, donation. **4.** The thing touching. **5.** Air, wind, Arj. 5, 14. **6.** The agent of pain, as sickness (Daçak. in Chr. 190, 19, *çiras-çûla-*, headache, or literally, 'the perceiving as of a sharp spear in my head'). **7.** Morbid heat. **II.** f. *çâ*, A wanton woman.—**Comp.** *Dus-*, adj. 1. of difficult or disagreeable touch, MBh. 13, 2109. 2. affecting disagreeably, Bhâg. P. 3, 17, 5 (of wind). *Sama-*, adj. literally, having the same contact, i.e. 1. wounding like, Chr. 39, 5. 2. the touching of which has the same effect, viz. to defile, Pańch. iii. d. 118.

स्पर्शक *sparçaka*, i.e. *spṛiç + aka*, adj. Touching, a toucher.

स्पर्शता *sparça + tâ*, f. Touching, Çâk. d. 169.

स्पर्शन *sparçana*, i. e. *spṛiç + ana*, **I.** m. Wind. **II.** n. **1.** Touching, Pańch. 163, 5. **2.** Sensation, Man. 12, 120. **3.** Gift, donation.—**Comp.** *A-*, n. not touching, Pańch. ii. d. 167.

स्पर्शवन्त् *sparça + vant*, adj., f. *vatí*, **1.** Palpable, Bhâshâp. 25. **2.** Smooth, soft, Kumâras. 1, 56.

स्पर्ष् *SPARSH*, see *parsh*.

स्पर्ष्टृ *sparshṭṛi*, i.e. *spṛiç + tṛi*, m. **1.** The agent of pain. **2.** Morbid heat.

1. **स्पश्** *SPAÇ*, † **पश्** *PAÇ*, † **पष्** *PASH*, † **पस्** *PAS*, i. 1, Par. Âtm. **1.** † To obstruct. **2.** To string together. **3.** To begin.

2. **स्पश्** *SPAÇ*, see *sparç*.

स्पश *spaç + a* (see *dṛiç*), m. **1.** A spy, Man. 8, 116 (v.r. see Lois.; read in Kull. commentary *chârabhûta*, and cf. the vedic designation of Agni as *dûta*, messenger); Pańch. 156, 21. **2.** A secret agent. **3.** War. **4.** Fighting with a dangerous animal.

स्पष्ट *spashṭa*, i.e. the ptcple. pf. pass. of *spaç* (see *dṛiç*), **1.** Evident, Vedântas. in Chr. 211, 18. **2.** Clear, able to see (not blind), Pańch. 262, 24. **3.** Intelligible. **4.** *ṭam*, adv. a. Distinctly, Lass. 2. ed. 34, 20. b. Looking in the face, Böhtl. Ind. Spr. 396.—**Comp.** *A-*, adj. indistinct, Vedântas. in Chr. 205, 5. *Vi-*, see s.v.—Cf. Lat. con-spectus.

स्पार्ह *spârha*, i. e. *spṛihâ + a*, adj. Desirable, Lass. 100, 9=Rigv. vii. 15, 5.

स्पृ *SPṚI*, † **स्तृ** *STṚI*, † **स्मृ** *SMṚI*, ii. 5, Par. **1.** † To gratify. **2.** To protect. **3.** † To live.

1. **स्पृश्** *SPṚIÇ*, i. 6, Par. (in epic poetry also Âtm.), **1.** To touch, Râm. 2, 42, 6; 3, 53, 47; with *adbhis*, To sprinkle with water, Man. 2, 60; with *hastam anyonyam*, To shake hands with each other, Vikr. 11, 14. **2.** To reach, to attain, Lass. 2. ed. 78, 72. **3.** Pass. To be seized, Daçak. in Chr. 194, 5 (by inebriation or frenzy). **4.** To obtain, to undergo, MBh. 3, 318. *spṛishṭa*, **1.** Touched, Bhartṛ. 2, 36. **2.** Felt. **3.** Defiled, Lass. 2. ed. 67, 31. **Comp.** *Çvaspṛishṭa*, i. e. *çvan-*, adj. touched by a dog, defiled. Comp. ptcple. of the fut pass. *a-spṛiçya*, not to be touched, Râjat. 5, 401. Caus. **1.** To order to touch, Man. 8, 114. **2.** To give, Man. 11, 135.—With **अप** *apa*, in *apo paspṛiçya*, MBh. 1, 764, To touch water for ablution, i.e. to rinse one's mouth, is probably preserved as an archaism for *apa upaspṛiçya*, see *upa-spṛiç*.—With **उप** *upa*, **1.** To

touch, Chr. 36, 14; *dantais dantân*, To gnash the teeth, Nal. 7, 3; with and without *adbhis*, To sprinkle with water, Man. 4, 143; 5, 138. **2.** To rinse one's mouth (as ablution), Man. 2, 53. **3.** To bathe, Man. 5, 62.—With पर्युप *pari-upa*, To touch or to use for ablution, MBh. 3, 165.—With समुप *sam-upa*, **1.** The same, MBh. 3, 8022. **2.** To bathe, MBh. 3, 10530.—With परि *pari*, To touch, Râm. 1, 9, 38.—With सम् *sam*, **1.** To touch, Man. 3, 178; with *adbhis*, To sprinkle with water, Man. 2, 53. **2.** To perceive, Râjat. 5, 375. *saṁsprishṭa*, Touched, Hit. ii. d. 16.—With अभिसम् *abhi-sam*, To bathe, MBh. 3, 8080.—With परिसम् *pari-sam*, To touch, to stroke, MBh. 3, 1457.

2. स्पृश् *spṛiç*, adj. Who or what touches, touching, Râjat. 5, 343; 475 (having).—**Comp.** *Diva-*, and *Nabhas-*, adj. touching or reaching to the heavens, MBh. 1, 2854; 11, 133. *Praṇaya-*, adj. affectionate, Mâlat. 76, 4.

स्पृश *spriç + a*, erroneous reading, Man. 8, 116 (see *spaça*).—**Comp.** *Dus-*, adj. of disagreeable touch, Hariv. 3654. *Nabhas-*, adj. touching the heavens, Bhag. 11, 24 (may belong also to *nabhaḥ-spṛiç*).

स्पृष्टि *spṛishṭi*, i.e. *spṛiç + ti*, f. Touch, feeling.

स्पृष्टिन् *spṛishṭin*, i.e. *spṛishṭa* (vb. *spṛiç*), *+ in*, adj. One who has touched, Man. 5, 85.

स्पृह् *SPṚIH*, i. 10, *spṛihaya* (old Caus. of *spardh*, with *h* for *dh*, and *ṛi* for *ar*), Par., with dat. and gen. **1.** To envy, Pañch. 137, 16. **2.** To desire, to long for, Râm. 3, 53, 39; Çâk. 103, 4.—Cf. probably σπέρχομαι; Lat. spero, spes; O.H.G. spulgen.

स्पृहणीयता *spṛihaṇîya + tâ* (vb. *spṛih*), f. Condition of being worthy to be desired, Utt. Râmach. 160, 3.

स्पृहणीयत्व *spṛihaṇîya + tva* (vb. *spṛih*), n. Enviableness, Râjat. 5, 336.

स्पृहयाय्य *spṛihayâyya* (vb. *spṛih*), adj. Desiring.

स्पृहा *spṛih + â*, f. Wish, desire, Hit. ii. d. 121; Pañch. 131, 19 (read *spṛihâṁ*).—**Comp.** *A-gata-*, adj., f. *hâ*, not having attained one's desire, Böhtl. Ind. Spr. 1156. *Nis-*, *Vi-gata-* (vb. *gam*), and *Vita-*, i.e. *vi-ita-*, adj., f. *hâ*, free from wish or desire, Pañch. iii. d. 84 (*nis-*); Kir. 3, 12 (*vîta-*). *Sa-*, adj., f. *hâ*, desirous, Kir. 14, 36. °*ham*, adv. passionately longing, Çâk. 11, 19; Vikr. 13, 18.

† स्पॄ *SPṚÎ*, ii. 9, *spṛiṇâ*, *ṇî*, Par. To hurt, to kill.

स्प्रष्टृ *sprashṭṛi*, i.e. *spṛiç + tṛi*, **I.** m., f. *ṭrî*, n. Who or what touches. **II.** m. **1.** The agent of pain, as a disease. **2.** Morbid heat.

स्फट् *SPHAṬ*, see *sphuṭ*, *sphiṭṭ*, *sphuḍ*.

स्फट *sphaṭa* (cf. *sphuṭ*), **I.** m., and f. *ṭâ*, A snake's expanded hood. **II.** f. *ṭî*, Alum.

स्फटिक *sphaṭika*, probably for *spashṭika*, i.e. *spashṭa + ika*, (properly, transparent), m. Crystal, Hit. ii. d. 157; Kir. 5, 31.

स्फटिकमय *sphaṭika + maya*, adj., f. *yî*, Made of crystal.

स्फण्ट् *SPHAṆṬ*, see *sphaṇḍ*, *sphuṭ*, *sphiṭṭ*, *sphuḍ*.

† स्फण्ड् *SPHAṆḌ*, स्फुण्ड् *SPHUṆḌ*, स्फण्ट् *SPHAṆṬ*, स्फुण्ट् *SPHUṆṬ*, i. 10, Par. To jest or joke with.

स्फर् *SPHAR*, see *sphur*.

स्फरण *spharaṇa*, i.e. *sphar* + *ana*, n. Trembling, throbbing.

स्फल् *SPHAL*, see *sphul*.

स्फाटिक *sphâṭika*, i.e *sphaṭika* + *a*, adj. Crystalline, Râm. 5, 9, 17.

स्फाति *sphâti*, i.e. *sphây* + *ti*, f. **1.** Swelling, intumescence. **2.** Increase.

स्फाय् *SPHÂY*, i. 1, Âtm. (properly pass. of a lost vb. *span*, *ph* for *p*, by the influence of *s*), To swell, to become bulky, to increase, Bhaṭṭ. 14, 109. Ptcple. of the pf. pass. **I.** *sphâta*, Swollen, enlarged. **II.** *sphîta*, **1.** Swollen, enlarged, large, Nal. 24, 37; Daçak. in Chr. 180, 11; thick, Mâlat. 75, 21. **2.** Abounding, Lass. 1, 8 (abounding in taste, i. e. elegant); much, many. **3.** Successful, risen in rank. **4.** Affected by hereditary disease. Caus. *sphâvaya* (for original *sphâpaya*), To augment, Bhaṭṭ. 12, 76. —Cf. O.H.G. spannan (originally, To draw); O.H.G. and A.S. spanan; Goth. and A.S. spinnan; σπάω, ἀ-σπάζομαι, ἀγαπάω (i.e. ἀγαν-σπαω); Lat. spatium, patere (a denomin. derived from *pă-to, old ptcple. pf. pass.); probably also A.S. spówan (cf. Caus.); spédan; Goth. spêd.

स्फार *sphâra*, i.e. *sphây* + *ra* and *sphar* + *a*, **I.** adj. **1.** Large, Mâlat. 81, 14; great, Kathâs. 7, 19; Pañch. v. d. 22; spreading, Bhartṛ. 3, 85 (cf. *sphârî-bhû*). **2.** Loud. **II.** m. **1.** Quivering, throbbing. **2.** Twanging, as of a bowstring. **3.** A bubble or flaw in gold.—Cf. σφαῖρα (i.e. σφαρια).

स्फारण *sphâraṇa*, i.e. *sphur*, Caus., + *ana*, n., and स्फाल *sphâla*, i.e. *sphul* + *a*, m. Trembling, throbbing.

स्फालन *sphâlana*, i.e. *sphul*, Caus., + *ana*, n. **1.** Quivering, shaking. **2.** Rubbing, friction.

स्फिच् *sphich*, f. A buttock, Man. 8, 281.—Comp. *Bṛihatsphich*, i.e. *bṛihant-*, m. a proper name, Pañch. 117, 13. *Lamba-*, adj. having large buttocks, Hiḍ. 2, 3.—Cf. O.H.G. spech; A.S. spic (the buttocks being the fattest parts of the body).

† स्फिट् *SPHIṬ*, i. 10, Par. **1.** To despise. **2.** To love. **3.** See the next.

† स्फिट्ट् *SPHIṬṬ*, स्फिट् *SPHIṬ*, स्फट् *SPHAṬ*, i. 10, Par. To kill.

स्फिर *sphira*, i.e. *sphây* + *ra* (cf. *sphâra*), adj., comparat. *spheyaṁs*, superl. *sphesh̤ṭha*, **1.** Large. **2.** Much, many.

स्फीति *sphîti*, i.e. *sphây* + *ti*, Increase, prosperity.

स्फुट् *SPHUṬ* (akin to *sphur*, *sphul*; probably for original **spart*; O.H.G. spaltan; Engl. split), i. 6, Par., and † i. 1, Âtm. **1.** (also † i. 1, Par., and † स्फुण्ट् *SPHUṆṬ*, स्फट् *SPHAṬ*, † स्फण्ट् *SPHAṆṬ*, i. 1, Par.), To burst, Utt. Râmach. 77, 15; MBh. 1, 3023. **2.** To open, to expand (as a flower), Pañch. i. d. 152. **3.** To disperse, to run away, Bhaṭṭ. 10, 8. *sphuṭita*, **1.** Burst, broken, destroyed, Pañch. 98, 1; 254, 23 (cf. 42, 10). **2.** Splay (as feet), Pañch. 104, 15. Caus., or i. 10, **1.** *sphoṭaya*, To break, to divide, to tear open, Pañch. 87, 7; to destroy, Pañch. 42, 10. **2.** † *sphuṭaya*,

To burst, to appear. **3.** *sphâṭaya*, *sphâṭita*, Cleft, Hit. 49, 11. — With आ *â*, Caus., or i. 10, *sphoṭaya*, **1.** To cause to sound, MBh. 3, 11139. **2.** To strike, Lass. 30, 18; especially one's own arm with the hand (perhaps rather, to snap the fingers, cf. *sphoṭana*), Man. 4, 64. **3.** To pat, MBh. 3, 1780.—With प्र *pra*, Caus., or i. 10, To pierce, MBh. 4, 2100.

स्फुट *sphuṭ+a*, and perhaps at the same time a form of *spashṭa*, with *u*, by the influence of the labial, *ph* by that of *s*, cf. *sphaṭika*, I. adj. **1.** Broken, rent. **2.** Opened, expanded (as a flower), Utt. Râmach. 81, 5. **3.** Spread. **4.** Loud, Râm. 6, 8, 45. **5.** Manifest, evident, Kir. 11, 44. **6.** Plain, distinct, Pańch. iii. d. 109, i. d. 180 (without duplicity). **7.** White, bright, Bhartṛ. 3, 23. **8.** Known. II. *ṭam*, adv. Distinctly, Pańch. 167, 15; evidently, Hit. iii. d. 89; certainly, Nalod. 2, 41. III. f. *ṭâ*, A snake's expanded hood, Pańch. iii. 135.—Comp. *Ati-pari-*, adj. very distinct; with *na*, half concealed, Çâk. d. 110.

स्फुटता *sphuṭa+tâ*, f. Perspicuity, Kir. 2, 27.

स्फुटन *sphuṭ+ana*, n. **1.** Tearing, rending. **2.** Opening, expanding.

स्फुटार्थ *sphuṭârtha*, i. e. *sphuṭa-artha*, adj. Intelligible, obvious.

स्फुटि and **स्फुटी** *sphuṭ + î*, f. **1.** Kibe, swelling of the feet. **2.** A sort of melon.

स्फुटिका *sphuṭikâ*, i.e. *sphuṭ+aka*, f. A small piece (?), Daçak. in Chr. 199, 17.

† **स्फुट्ट्** *SPHUṬṬ*, i. 10, Par. To slight, to despise.

† **स्फुड्** *SPHUḌ*, i. 6, Par. To cover.

स्फुण्ट् *SPHUṆṬ*, see *sphaṇḍ*, *sphuṭ*.

† **स्फुण्ड्** *SPHUṆḌ*, i. 1, Âtm. To open, to expand (cf. *sphuṭ*); see *sphaṇḍ*.

स्फुत्कार *sphut-kâra* (*sphut*, an imitative sound), m. Crackling, burning.

स्फुर् *SPHUR*, also **स्फर्** *SPHAR*, (which appears only in the Caus. and derivative nouns; nevertheless, it is the original form, its *a* being changed to *u* by the combined influence of the preceding labial and the accent of the sixth conj. cl.), i. 6, Par. **1.** To tremble, MBh. 3, 1867; to palpitate, Mṛichchh. 143, 14; to throb, Mâlat. 5, 5. **2.** To struggle, Pańch. iii. d. 123; to rebound, Johns. Sel. 48, 83. **3.** To break forth, Gît. 11, 1; Hit. ii. d. 59 (*puraḥ sphurant*, Springing up before one's eyes). **4.** To flash, to shine, to sparkle, Gît. 10, 6; Hit. ii. d. 52; Pańch. i. d. 33; Vikr. d. 136. **5.** To destroy (ved.). *sphurita*, **1.** Shaken. **2.** Trembling, Pańch. 64, 15; throbbing. **3.** Glittering, Megh. 15; shining, Mâlat. 40, 10. **4.** Swollen. n. **1.** Trembling, motion, MBh. 1, 1258. **2.** Throbbing of the eyelids, the quivering of the lip, Kumâras. 7, 18. Caus. *sphâraya*, and † *sphoraya*, To cast, Lass. 66, 8. *sphârita*, **1.** Throbbing, Mâlat. 60, 12. **2.** Spread, large, Böhtl. Ind. Spr. 552.—With अभि *abhi*, *abhisphurita*, **1.** Expanded, in full bloom. **2.** Known.—With परि *pari*, *parisphurita*, **1.** Glanced. **2.** Glancing. **3.** Expanded, Utt. Râmach. 72, 10.—With प्र *pra*, To tremble, MBh. 3, 11498. *prasphurita*, **1.** Trembling, Johns. Sel. 22, 112. **2.** Swollen, Pańch. 220, 1. **3.**

Budded.—With वि *vi*, **1.** To tremble, MBh. 3, 15639. **2.** To struggle, MBh. 1, 6001. **3.** To glitter, Kathâs. 26, 283. *visphurita*, **1.** Tremulous, shaken, Utt. Râmach. 117, 10. **2.** Swollen, enlarged. Caus. *sphâraya*, **1.** To draw (a bow), Râm. 3, 30, 28; Kir. 17, 24. **2.** To cause to flash, MBh. 3, 404. *visphârita*, **1.** Trembling. **2.** Flashing, Râm. 1, 54, 19. **3.** Twanged or drawn, as a bowstring, Kir. 14, 31. **4.** Evident.—Cf. σπαίρω (i.e. σπαρ + jω; the Sskr. *ph* is produced by the influence of *s*), ἀσπαίρω, probably σπείρω, σπέρμα, σποράς; the ved. use shows that hither belong also A.S. spurnan; σφυρόν; A.S. spura; probably Lat. sperno. Cf. *skhal*.

स्फुर *sphur + a*, m. **1.** Trembling, Pañch. iii. d. 237; throbbing. **2.** Swelling. **3.** A shield.

स्फुरण *sphuraṇa*, i.e. *sphur + ana*, n. **1.** Trembling, Bhâg. P. 3, 26, 29 (trembling appearance). **2.** Quivering of the lips, throbbing of the eyes. **3.** Expansion of the mind, Pañch. 42, 6. **4.** Breaking forth, flashing, Megh. 28; glittering, Mâlat. 143, 5.

† स्फुर्छ् *SPHURCHH* (i.e. *sphur + chh*), स्वुर्छ् *SVURCHH*, i. 1, *sphûrchchha*, *svûrchchha*, Par. **1.** To expand. **2.** To forget.

स्फुर्ज् *SPHURJ* (i.e. *sphur + j*), i. 1, *sphûrja*, Par. To thunder, Bhaṭṭ. 15, 41.—With वि *vi*, *visphûrjita*, Resounding (as arrows), Bhâg. P. 2, 7, 25. n. **1.** Roar (of the wind), Arj. 8, 6 (read *sphûrj*°). **2.** Increase, Ragh. 13, 12, Calc. Sch.—Cf. Lat. spargo; A.S. sprecan; spraecan, sprengan, sprincan, springan.

स्फुल् *SPHUL* (originally = *sphur*), also स्फल् *SPHAL*, which, like *sphar*, appears only in the Caus. and derivative nouns, i. 6, Par. **1.** † To tremble, to throb. **2.** † To appear. **3.** † To collect.—With आ *â*, Caus. *sphâlaya*, **1.** To strike, Utt. Râmach. 123, 4; Ragh. 16, 13; to touch, Utt. Râmach. 150, 8 (?). **2.** To crush, Pañch. 93, 17.—With वि *vi*, To move cheerfully, Bhaṭṭ. 9, 76.—Cf. σφάλλω (Caus.); O.H.G. fallan; A.S. feallan; Lat. fallere. Cf. *skhal*.

स्फुल *sphul + a*, n. A tent.

स्फुलन *sphul + ana*, n. Trembling, throbbing.

स्फुलिङ्ग *sphuliṅga*, probably *sphul + a + m-ga*, m., f. *gâ*, n. A spark of fire, Vikr. d. 125.—**Comp.** *Vi-*, m. 1. the same. 2. a sort of poison.

स्फुलिङ्गिन् *sphuliṅgin*, adj., f. *nî*, Having sparks of fire, Mârk. P. 99, 57.

स्फूर्ज *sphûrja*, i.e. *sphurj + a*, m. **1.** The sound of thunder. **2.** Indra's thunderbolt.

स्फूर्जथु *sphûrjathu*, i.e. *sphurj + athu*, m. A thunderclap, Mahâvîrach. 124, 1.

स्फूर्ति *sphûrti*, i. e. *sphur + ti*, f. Shaking, Bhartṛ. 3, 34; throbbing, Windischmann, Sankara, 12.

स्फूर्तिमन्त् *sphûrti + mant*, adj., f. *matî*, **1.** Tremulous. **2.** Kind-hearted.

स्फेयंस् *spheyaṁs*, स्फेष्ठ *spheshṭha*, see *sphira*.

स्फोट *sphoṭa*, i.e. *sphuṭ + a*, **I.** m. **1.** Bursting, breaking. **2.** A tumour, a boil, Suçr. 2, 383, 10. **3.** The eternal sound, in the Pûrva Mîmâṁsâ. **II.** f. *ṭâ*, The hood of the snake.—**Comp.** *Muktâ-*, m. a pearl-oyster.

स्फोटन *sphoṭana*, i.e. *sphuṭ + ana*, **I.** n. **1.** Breaking, Pañch. 81, 8;

tearing. **2.** Fidgeting with the hand, snapping the fingers. **II.** f. *ni*, A gimblet, an auger.

स्फ्य *sphya*, n. An implement used in sacrifices, shaped like a spit, Man. 5, 117; cf. Journ. of the German Oriental Society, ix. xxxvi.

स्वृ *SBṚÎ*, see *svṛi*.

स्म *sma*, an old case (probably the instr. sing. n.) of *sama*; a particle. **1.** A present and ptcple. of the pres. followed by it have generally a past sense; e. g. *prati vasataḥ sma*, They dwelt, Pańch. 43, 1; *kathayantau sma . . . âsâtâm*, Chr. 16, 20, They were sitting and told. **2.** Preceded by *mâ*, sometimes after a present, and in the Ved., after particles, it has no distinct signification; *mâ sma kârshis*, Do not, Chr. 41, 4; *charanti sma*, They go, Indr. 1, 23; *adha sma*, Lass. 98, 14= Rigv. v. 9, 5.

स्मय *smaya*, i.e. *smi*+*a*, m. **1.** Surprise, astonishment. **2.** Arrogance, pride, Bhartṛ. 3, 2; Râjat. 5, 4.

स्मर *smara*, i.e. *smṛi*+*a*, m. **1.** Recollection. **2.** Love, Hit. 86, 4, M.M. **3.** Kâma, the god of love, Pańch. 226, 1; Çâk. d. 119 (and at the same time, perhaps, Remembrance).—**Comp.** *Jâti-*, adj., f. *râ*, one who remembers or knows his former existences, MBh. 3, 8180. *Dus-*, adj. disagreeable to be remembered, Utt. Râmach. 157, 14.

स्मरण *smaraṇa*, i.e. *smṛi*+*ana*, n. **1.** Remembering, Hit. ii. d. 56; remembrance, Pańch. 208, 14. **2.** Memory, **3.** Regretting.—**Comp.** *Jâti-*, n. Remembering one's former existences, MBh. 12, 6256.

स्मरवीथिका *smara-vîthi*+*kâ*, f. A harlot.

स्मर्तृ *smartṛi*, i.e. *smṛi*+*tṛi*, m., f. *trî*, n. Who or what remembers, Bhâg. P. 1, 15, 18.

स्मारण *smâraṇa*, i.e. *smṛi*, Caus., +*ana*, n. Calling to mind, causing to remember.

स्मार्त *smârta*, i.e. *smṛiti*+*a*, **I.** adj. **1.** Memorial, relating to memory. **2.** Within memory. **3.** Recorded in the *Smṛitis*, or codes of law, Man. 1, 108. **4.** Following or professing the law books. **II.** m. A Brâhmaṇa following the revealed law; one who knows the traditional law, Pańch. i. d. 283.

स्मि *SMI*, i. 1, Âtm. (in epic poetry also Par., Chr. 27, 1), To smile, Chr. 27, 3. *smita*, **1.** Smiling, Pańch. i. d. 152. **2.** Blown (as a flower), Pańch. i. d. 152. n. A smile, Vikr. 13, 4. **Comp.** *Çuchi-*, adj. smiled, smiling sweetly, Râm. 3, 49, 22. *Sa-*, adj. smiling; °*tam*, adv., Vikr. 28, 12; Râm. 3, 49, 51. *Su-*, adj. smiling. f. *tâ*, a woman with a smiling countenance. † i. 10, Âtm. To despise. **Frequent.** *seshmîya*, To suffer from convulsions, to tremble, Mâlav. 47, 5.—With **अभि** *abhi*, To smile, MBh. 3, 8237.—With **उद्** *ud*, To smile, MBh. 1, 7059. *utsmâyitvâ* (Râm. 1, 1, 63), is an anomalous form either for *utsmâyayitvâ*, Caus. 'To make a mock of, to insult,' or for *utsmitvâ*, and then to be changed to *utsmayitvâ*, 'To burst into laughter.' —With **अभ्युद्** *abhi-ud*, To smile, Chr. 44, 35.—With **वि** *vi*, **1.** To be surprised, Râm. 3, 49, 3. **2.** To admire. **3.** To be proud, Man. 4, 236. *vismita*, Astonished, perplexed, Hit. 56, 18. **Comp.** *Su-*, adj. much surprised, Pańch. 41, 21. **Caus.** *smâpaya*, To cause to be surprised, Ragh. 2, 33.—Cf. *smera* and O.H.G. smielan; A.S. smaere, smirk;

Lat. mirari; probably *σμοιός, μέμφομαι* (Caus.), *μῶμος*.

† **स्मिट्** *SMIṬ* (akin to *smi*), i. 10, Par. **1.** To despise. **2.** To love. **3.** To go.

स्मील् *SMÎL*, see *çmîl.*

1. **स्मृ** *SMṚI*, i. 1, Par. (in epic poetry also Âtm., MBh. 1, 3005), **1.** To remember (with acc. and gen.), Vikr. 29, 16; Chr. 20, 17; with the second fut. in the sense of past time, Çiç. 1, 68, *smarati—hanishyati*, You remember having killed. **2.** To desire, to long for (with gen.), MBh. 3, 12281. **3.** To record, to declare, Pañch. i. d. 36. *smṛita*, **1.** Recollected. **2.** Recorded, Chr. 52, 11. **3.** Said (according to traditional doctrine), Man. 1, 20. **4.** Allowed (according to tradition), Man. 3, 13. **5.** Called, Man. 1, 10. Comp. ptcple. of the fut. pass. *smara-smarya*, m. An ass. Caus. I. *smâraya*, **1.** To cause to remember, MBh. 2, 2484; with gen., Kir. 6, 13 (*smăraya*). **2.** To give information, Mâlat. 8, 9. **II.** *smăraya*, To cause to remember with grief, Vikr. d. 78.—With **अनु** *anu*, **1.** To call to mind, Man. 2, 217; to remember, Bhâg. P. 4, 30, 28 (pass.) **2.** To invoke, Pañch. 258, 25. Caus. *smăraya*, To cause to remember with sorrow, Kir. 5, 14.—With **अप** *apa*, To forget, Mâlat. 161, 2.—With **वि** *vi*, To forget, MBh. 3, 15705; Çâk. 37, 4. Caus. *smâraya*, To cause to forget, Vikr. d. 59.—With **सम्** *sam*, To remember, Man. 4, 149. Caus. *smâraya*, To cause to remember, MBh. 2, 2537.—With **अनुसम्** *anu-sam*, **1.** To remember, MBh. 1, 6911. **2.** To long for, MBh. 4, 149.—With **अभिसम्** *abhi-sam*, To remember, MBh. 3, 15758.—Cf. *μάρτυρ, μέριμνα, μέρμερος*; Lat. memor; O.H.G. mâri; Goth. mêrjan, meritha; A.S. maelan, mal, ge-maered, maerdh, a -maerian, maersian, meldian; Goth. maurnan; A.S. murnan.

2. **स्मृ** *SMṚI*, see *spṛi.*

स्मृति *smṛi* + *ti*, f. **1.** Recollection, remembrance, memory, Hit. iv. d. 96; Bhag. 2, 63; Bhâshâp. 47; Râjat. 5, 5; Utt. Râmach. 100, 14. **2.** The body of law, as delivered originally by tradition; tradition, Man. 2, 6; Pañch. 164, 20. **3.** A law book. **4.** A passage concerning law, Vedântas. in Chr. 203, 2. **5.** Understanding. **6.** Desire, wish.

स्मृतिमन्त् *smṛiti* + *mant*, adj., f. *matî*, **1.** Remembering, having recovered one's recollection, Çâk. 112, 16. **2.** Having a good memory, Man. 7, 64.

स्मेर *smera*, i.e. *smi* + *ra*, I. adj. **1.** Smiling, Kâvya Prak. 121, 5; Ratnâv. p. 35, 10 (2. ed.). **2.** Blown (as a flower), blooming, Bhartṛ. 1, 35; opened, Mâlat. 16, 10. **3.** Evident. **II.** m. Evidence, appearance.

स्यद *syada*, i.e. *syand* + *a*, m. Speed, Nalod. 4, 6.

स्यन्द् *SYAND*, i. 1, Âtm., and in the aor., fut., and condit., Par. **1.** To drop, to distill, Lass. 59, 5. **2.** To flow, MBh. 1, 3990. **3.** To run, Nal. 13, 10. —With the prep. **अभि** *abhi* (*shyand* and *syand*), To rain on, Utt. Râmach. 16, 10; 133, 9 (*hṛidayam̃ snehena*, To flow, to melt with love).—With **नि** *ni* (*shyand* and *syand*), To flow, Bhâg. P. 6, 9, 38.

स्यन्दन *syand* + *ana*, I. adj. Quick, Kir. 15, 16. **II.** m. **1.** A war chariot, Hit. iii. d. 81. **2.** Air. **3.** A tree,

Dalbergia ougeinensis, Nal. 12, 3. **III.** f. *ni,* Saliva. **IV.** n. **1.** Oozing, Bhâshâp. 6; 155. **2.** Water. **3.** Going swiftly.

स्यन्दनिका *syandanikâ,* i.e. *syandanî + ka,* f. A drop of saliva, Râm. 3, 53, 56.

स्यन्दिन् *syand + in,* **I.** adj., f. *nî.* **1.** Oozing, trickling, Utt. Râmach. 23, 3. **2.** Going. **II.** f. *nî.* **1.** Saliva. **2.** A cow bearing twins.—**Comp.** *Sudhâ-,* adj. flowing with nectar, Bhartṛ. 2, 6.

† **स्यम्** *SYAM,* i. 1, Par. **1.** To sound. **2.** To go. i. 10, Âtm. To consider, to think.

स्यमन्तक *syamantaka,* m. The gem worn by Kṛishṇa.

स्यमीक *syamîka,* **I.** m. **1.** An ant-hill. **2.** A particular tree. **3.** Time. **4.** Cloud. **II.** f. *kâ,* Indigo.

स्याल *syâla,* and **श्याल** *çyâla,* **I.** m. **1.** A wife's brother, Bhag. 1, 34 (*ç*). **2.** The favourite of a king, Râjat. 5, 451 (? *ç*). **II.** f. *lî,* A wife's sister.—Cf. ἀέλιοι.

स्यूति *syûti,* i.e. *siv + ti,* f. **1.** Sewing, needle-work. **2.** A sack. **3.** Offspring.

स्यून *syûna,* i.e. *siv + na,* m. **1.** A ray of light. **2.** The sun. **3.** A sack.

स्यूम *syûma,* i.e. *siv + ma,* m. A ray of light; cf. *syûma-raçmi.*

स्योत *syota,* vb. *siv,* m. A sack.

स्योन *syona,* **A.** adj. Handsome, pleasing. **B.** (vb. *siv*), **I.** m. **1.** A ray of light. **2.** The sun. **3.** A sack. **II.** n. Happiness.

स्रंश् *SRAṀÇ,* v.r. of the next.

1. **स्रंस्** *SRAṀS,* i. 1, Âtm. To fall down, Bhag. 1, 30; to fall asunder, Utt. Râmach. 77, 15. Ptcple. of the pf. pass. *srasta.* **1.** Fallen, Daçak. in Chr. 196, 20. **2.** Hanging down, Çâk. d. 29. **3.** Loosened. **4.** Separated. Caus. **1.** To cause to fall from, Bhartṛ. 1, 49. **2.** To move, Ragh. 6, 75. Ptcple. pf. pass. *sraṁsita,* Caused to be loosened, Utt. Râmach. 40, 12.—With the prep. **आ** *â, âsrasta,* Fallen off, MBh. 4, 777.—With **वि** *vi, visrasta,* The same, Arj. 10, 64. Caus. To cause to drop, Mahâvîrach. 73, 17.

2. **स्रंस्** *SRAṀS,* v.r. of *çrambh.*

स्रंसिन् *sraṁs + in,* **I.** adj., f. *nî.* **1.** Falling, Mâlat. 79, 3; being loosened, Çâk. d. 29. **2.** Hanging down, pendulous. **II.** m. A tree, commonly *Pilu.*

† **स्रंह्** *SRAṀH,* i. 1, Âtm. To confide (cf. *çrambh*).

स्रग्विन् *sragvin,* i.e. *sraj + vin,* adj., f. *nî,* Bearing a chaplet, Man. 2, 167.

स्रङ्क् *SRAṄK,* see *çraṅk.*

स्रज् *sraj,* vb. *sṛij,* f. A chaplet, a wreath of flowers, a garland, Böhtl. Ind. Spr. 3322; Vedântas. in Chr. 203, 10.

स्रम्भ् *SRAMBH,* see *çrambh.*

स्रव *srava,* i.e. *sru + a,* **I.** m. **1.** Oozing, trickling, flowing, Lass. 2. ed. 59, 5. **2.** A drop, Hiḍ. 2, 9. **3.** A fountain. **II.** f. *vâ,* A plant, Sanseviera zeylanica.—**Comp.** *Giri-,* f. *vâ,* a mountain stream, MBh. 13, 6362.—Cf. ῥόος.

स्रवण *sravaṇa,* i.e. *sru + ana,* n. **1.** Oozing, flowing. **2.** Sweat. **3.** Urine.

स्रवन्त *sravanta,* i.e. *sravant,* ptcple. pres. of *sru,* + *a,* adj. Dropping, Pañch. i. d. 346.

स्रष्टृ *srashṭṛi,* i.e. *sṛij + tṛi,* m. **1.** A creator, Man. 1, 33; MBh. 7, 2864; Vikr. d. 159. **2.** A maker, author, Râjat. 4, 655. **3.** Brahman. **4.** Çiva.

स्रस्तर *srastara,* i.e. probably *sraṁs + tṛi + a,* or *+ tra,* n. A bed, Kâvya Pr. 68, 4 (Prâkṛ.).

स्राक् *srâk,* vb. *sṛi,* probably *sara -añch,* cf. *drâk,* acc. sing. n., adv. Quickly.

स्राव *srâva,* i.e. *sru + a,* m. Oozing, flowing.—**Comp.** *Garbha-,* m. miscarriage, abortment, Pañch. pr. d. 8. *Nâsâ-,* m. catarrh, Suçr. 2, 371, 14. *Lâlâ-,* m. a spider.

स्रिध् *SRIDH,* i. 1, Par. **1.** To injure, to assail (ved.). **2.** To be injured (ved.).—Cf. O.H.G. stritan, strit; A.S. stridh; Lat. stlis, lis.

स्रिध् *sridh,* An enemy, Chr. 87, 8 =Rigv. i. 48, 8.

स्रिभ् *SRIBH,* **स्रिम्भ्** *SRIMBH,* see *sṛibh.*

† **स्रिव्** *SRIV,* i. 4, *srîvya,* Par. **1.** To go. **2.** To dry.

स्रु *SRU* (cf. *sṛi*), **श्रु** *ÇRU* (bad), † **श्रु** *ÇU,* i. 1, Par. **1.** To flow, Râm. 2, 63, 18; Man. 4, 122. **2.** To slip away, Man. 4, 74; to perish, MBh. 2, 932. **3.** To be divulged, to transpire, Daçak. in Chr. 198, 3. **4.** To let flow, Râm. 2, 91, 15; to shed, MBh. 1, 1485. *sruta,* Flowing, dropping, Çiç. 9, 15. Caus. *srâvaya,* To cause to flow, Man. 4, 169.—With **निस्** *nis,* Caus. To cause to flow off, to empty, MBh. 3, 13164.—With **परि** *pari,* **1.** To flow round about, Mâlat. 169, 3. **2.** To flow, MBh. 3, 2966. *parisruta,* Oozed, trickled. f. *tâ,* Vinous or distilled liquor.—With **प्र** *pra,* **1.** To flow forth, MBh. 3, 8127. **2.** To let flow, Râm. 2, 48, 13; Hit. i. d. 177, M.M. (to yield, viz. milk). *prasruta,* **1.** Oozed, dropped. **2.** Dropping, Kir. 4, 10. **Comp.** *Tri-,* m. (an elephant in rut), of whom the juice breaks forth at three places of his forehead, Râm. 2, 26, 18 Gorr.—With **वि** *vi,* To shed, MBh. 3, 825. *visruta,* **1.** Flowing, Râm. 1, 34, 9. **2.** Dropped. **3.** Spread. Caus. *visrâvita,* **1.** Caused to flow. **2.** Bled. — Cf. O. H. G. straum; A.S. streám; O.H.G. sliumo, slunic, slunigên; ῥέω, ῥυθμός, Στρύμων.

स्रुघ्नी *srughni,* probably *sruch-han + a,* f. Natron, alkali.

स्रुच् *sruch,* i.e. *sru-añch,* f. A sort of ladle to pour clarified butter on a sacrificial fire, Draup. 6, 20; Journ. of the German Oriental Society, ix. xli. 4; 20.

ऽस्रुत् *-sru + t,* adj. Flowing, distilling; e.g. *amṛita-,* adj. Distilling nectar, Çiç. 9, 68.

स्रुति *sru + ti,* f. **1.** Oozing, distilling; Kir. 5, 44. **2.** Exudation, resin, Megh. 106. **3.** Stream, Râjat. 5, 111.

स्रुव *sruva,* i.e. *sru + a* (cf. *çruva*), **I.** m., and f. *vâ,* A sacrificial ladle to pour *ghṛita* on a sacrificial fire, Journ. of the German Oriental Society, ix. viii. **II.** f. *vâ,* The name of two plants.

स्रू *srû* (vb. *sru*), f. **1.** A sacrificial ladle, Râm. 1, 60, 12. **2.** A cascade.

† **स्रेक्** *SREK,* **सेक्** *SEK,* **श्रेक्** *ÇREK,* **स्वेक्** *SVEK,* i. 1, Âtm. To go.

स्रै *SRAI,* see *çrâ.*

स्रोत *srota,* i.e. curtailed *srotas,* n. A rapid stream.—Comp. *Çushka-,* adj.,

f. *tâ*, of whom the water is dried up, Nal. 16, 14.

स्रोतस् *srotas*, i.e. *sru* + *tas*, n. 1. A current, stream, Vikr. d. 24. 2. The course of water, Mâlat. 79, 18. 3. A torrent, Mâlat. 60, 11; a river. 4. A wave, Çâk. d. 50. 5. A spring. 6. Water. 7. An organ of sense (? cf. *çrotas* and Mallinâtha ad Megh. 43), MBh. 1, 814.—Comp. *Ud-*, and *Ûrdhva-*, adj. the course (of life) of which is going upwards, Bhâg. P. 3, 10, 18; MBh. 14, 1054. *Garga-*, n. the name of a place of pilgrimage, MBh. 9, 2132. *Tiryaksrotas*, i.e. *tiryañch-*, m. the course (of life) of which is going athwart, the animals, Mârk. P. 47, 18. *Tri-*, adj. having three courses, epithet of the Gangâ, Çâk. d. 165. *Mûla-*, n. principal current, Râjat. 5, 96.

स्रोतस्य *srotas* + *ya*, m. 1. Çiva. 2. A thief.

स्रोतस्वती *srotasvati*, and **स्रोतस्विनी** *srotasvinî*, i.e. *srotas* + *vant*, or *vin*, + *î*, f. A river.

स्रोतोवह् *srotovah*, and **स्रोतोवहा** *srotovahâ*, i.e. *srotas-vah*, or *vah*, + *a*, f. A river, Çâk. d. 50 (*vah*); 143 (*vahâ*); Vikr. 67, 4 (*vahâ*).

स्व *sva*, I. pron. refl. One's own self, Vedântas. in Chr. 210, 13; Man. 8, 85; especially as former part of comp. words, e.g. *sva-gata*, adj. Kept to one's self, apart; adv. *svagatam*, 1. Speaking to himself, Pañch. 27, 11. 2. Aside (in theatrical language), Vikr. 30, 8. II. adj., f. *svâ*. 1. Own, Pañch. i. d. 369; 226, 14 (my); Vikr. 27, 3 (thy); Hit. i. d. 16, M.M. (his). 2. Of one's own tribe, Man. 3, 13. III. m. 1. Soul, Nalod. 3, 30. 2. A kinsman, Man. 2, 109. IV. n. Property, wealth, Daçak. in Chr. 196, 13; Hit. 65, 17 (*hrita-sarva-*, adj. Robbed of all his property).—Comp. *Deva-*, n. property of the gods, Man. 11, 20. *Nis-*, adj. 1. deprived of property, Man. 9, 231. 2. poor, Pañch. ii. d. 97. *Para-*, n. another person's property, Man. 7, 123. *Yathâ-sva* + *m*, adv. 1. properly. 2. individually, Kir. 14, 43. *Sarva-*, n. 1. the whole property, Pañch. iii. d. 132. 2. the whole essence of anything, Pañch. 111, 6; iii. d. 104.—Cf. Lat. se, suus; Goth. sve, sik, seina; A.S. sín; σφί, ἕ, εἷο, ἑός; A.S. swa.

स्वक *sva* + *ka*, adj., f. *kâ*, Own, Pañch. iii. d. 203.

स्वकीय *svakîya*, i.e. *svaka* + *îya*, adj. 1. Own, Pañch. 187, 12; his, ib. 42, 2. 2. Of one's own family.

स्वङ्ग् *SVAṄG*, see *çrang*.

स्वच्छक *svachchhaka*, i.e. *su-achchha* + *ka*, adj. White, beautiful, Pañch. i. d. 225 (pure = harmless ?).

स्वज *sva-ja*, I. adj. Self-born or produced. II. m. 1. A son. 2. Perspiration. III. f. *jâ*, A daughter. IV. n. Blood.

स्वजनाय *SVAJANÂYA*, a denomin. derived from *sva-jana* with *ya*, Âtm. To become a relation, Pañch. i. d. 5.

स्वञ्ज् *SVAÑJ*, (probably from *sva*), i. 1, *svaja*, Âtm. (also Par., MBh. 4, 513), To embrace, MBh. 3, 2999.—With **परि** *pari*, *shvañj*, To embrace, Vikr. 11, 3.—With **अभिपरि** *abhi-pari*, To embrace, Râm. 2, 44, 10.—With **संपरि** *sam-pari*, To embrace, MBh. 1, 3307. —With **सम्** *sam*, To embrace, Chr. 32, 27.

स्वठ् *SVAṬH*, see 3. 4. *çaṭh*.

स्वतन्त्र *sva-tantra*, see *tantra*.

स्वतन्त्रता *sva-tantra* + *tâ*, f. 1. Independence, Man. 5, 148. **2.** Wilfulness.

स्वतस् *sva + tas*, adv. **1.** By one's own self, MBh. 3, 10051; Daçak. in Chr. 180, 15. **2.** Of itself, Bhâshâp. 135. **3.** Out of one's own property, Man. 8, 166; 408.

स्वता *sva + tâ*, f. Relation to one's own self, Çâk. d. 35.

स्वत्र *sva-tra* (vb. *trâ*), I. adj. Self-preserving. II. m. A blind man.

स्वत्व *sva + tva*, n. **1.** Self-existence. **2.** Independence. **3.** Ownership, proprietary right.

स्वद् *SVAD*, i.e. probably *su-ad*,

स्वाद् *SVÂD*, i. 1, Âtm. **1.** To taste, to eat, MBh. 1, 3362. **2.** To please, to be liked, Çiç. 10, 23. *svâdanîya*, Savoury, Indr. 1, 26. i. 10, Par. **1.** To taste, Bhaṭṭ. 7, 40. **2.** † To cut.—With **आ** *â*, To taste, to eat, Râm. 1, 9, 36. Comp. ptcple. pf. pass., *an-âsvâdita*, adj. Not tasted, not touched, Çâk. d. 43. *âsvâdya*, Savoury, Hit. pr. d. 47, M.M. n. Cookery, Daçak. in Chr. 180, 7 (?). Comp. *Nis-*, adj. yielding no enjoyment, Râm. 2, 36, 12. *âsvâdanîya*. Comp. *Amṛita-*, adj. as pleasant to the taste as nectar, MBh. 3, 1740. i. 10, **1.** To taste, Pañch. 35, 3. **2.** To eat, Pañch. 214, 22. —Cf. A.S. swaesend, Food; ἀνδάνω, εὔαδε, ἕαδα, ἑδανός, and ἡδονή (and see *svâdu*).

स्वदन *svad + ana*, n. Eating.

स्वधा *sva-dhâ*, I. f. **1.** Spontaneity, Chr. 290, 4=Rigv. i. 64, 4 (they are produced without an external cause). **2.** Self-will, strength, Chr. 294, 6= Rigv. i. 88, 6. **3.** A personification of Mâya, or worldly illusion. **4.** The food offered to deceased ancestors, Man. 9, 127. **5.** A nymph, the food of the Manes personified. II. indecl. An exclamation or blessing used on presenting an oblation to the Manes, Man. 3, 252.—Cf. Lat. suetus; Goth. sidus; A.S. sidu, siodo; ἔθος, ἦθος.

स्वधाभुज् *svadhâ-bhuj*, m. **1.** A deified ancestor. **2.** A deity.

स्वधिति *svadhiti*, m. and f., also **ती** *tî*, An axe.

स्वधितीवन्त् *svadhitî + vant*, adj. Armed with an axe, Chr. 293, 2=Rigv. i. 88, 2.

स्वन् *SVAN*, i. 1, Par. To sound, e.g. to sing, Râm. 2, 65, 5. Ptcple. of the pf. pass. I. *svanita*, Sounding. n. The noise of thunder. II. *svânta*, Sounded. Caus. *svănaya*, † **1.** To cause to sound. **2.** † To sound. **3.** and *svânaya*, † To adorn.—With the prep. **अव** *ava*, or **वि** *vi*, To make a noise when eating; in this signification the vb. is changed to *shvaṇ*.—With **नि** *ni*, *nisvanita*, n. Noise, MBh. 7, 324. —Cf. Lat. sonare.

स्वन *svan + a*, m. Sound, Nal. 25, 5. —Comp. *Kara-*, m. the sound produced by clapping the hands, Râm. 5, 83, 5. *Dus-*, adj. sounding disagreeably, MBh. 5, 7241. *Mañju-*, adj., f. *nâ*, sweet-sounding, Vikr. 60, 12. *Mahâ-*, I. adj. loud-sounding, Nal. 21, 5. II. m. 1. a loud sound. 2. a kind of drum. *Mahâ-megha-*, adj. having the sound of a large cloud, Indr. 1, 5.—Cf. Lat. sonus.

स्वनि *svan + i*, m. Sound, Mahâv. 132, 19.

ऽस्वनिक *-svanika* in *pâṇi-*, i.e. *pâṇi -svana + ika*, m. One who claps the hands, MBh. 12, 1899.

स्वप् *SVAP*, ii. 2 (i. 1, Man. 4, 99), Par. (in epic poetry also Âtm., MBh. 3, 15993), **1.** To sleep, Man. 1, 25. **2.** To fall asleep, MBh. 2, 2027. **3.** To lie down to sleep, to go to bed, Man. 4, 99. **4.** To lie down, to extend one's self, Man. 11, 103. **5.** To lie, MBh. 4, 1674. **6.** To be dead, Bhaṭṭ. 18, 11. Ptcple. of the pf. pass. *supta*. **1.** Having slept, Sâv. 5, 64. **2.** Sleeping, Vikr. d. 135. **3.** Senseless. n. Sleep. Comp. *Divâ-*, adj. sleeping at day, Hit. iii. d. 110.—With the prep. **अव** *ava*, To sleep, Râm. 2, 56, 1.—With **प्र** *pra*, To fall asleep, Hit. 50, 2. *prasupta*, **1.** Beginning to sleep, Pańch. 134, 6; gone to bed, Pańch. 117, 12. **2.** Fallen asleep, Chr. 38, 6. **3.** Slept, Sâv. 5, 65. **4.** Sleeping, Daçak. in Chr. 199, 6.—With **संप्र** *sam-pra*, To sleep, MBh. 1, 955.—With **सम्** *sam*, To sleep, MBh. 1, 5967.—Cf. Lat. sopire (Caus.); A.S. swefian; O.H.G. suabjan, suebjan; ὕπαρ; see *svapna*, also with *l* for *v* (cf. *çvas*); Goth. slêpan; A.S. slápan.

स्वपन *svap + ana*, n. **1.** Sleeping, Hit. iii. d. 75. **2.** Sleep.—Comp. *Divâ-*, n. sleeping by day, Suçr. 1, 330, 8.

स्वप्तुकाम *svaptukâma*, i.e. *svaptum -kâma* (vb. *svap*), adj. Wishing to sleep, Johns. Sel. 91, 38.

स्वप्न *svap + na*, m. **1.** Sleep, Vedântas. in Chr. 208, 6. **2.** Indolence, Man. 12, 33. **3.** Dreaming. **4.** A dream, Vikr. d. 29; Pańch. 134, 6.—Comp. *Jâgratsvapna*, i.e. *jâgrant-*, m. waking and sleeping, Man. 1, 57. *Divâ-*, m. sleeping by day, Man. 7, 47. *Dus-*, m. an inauspicious dream, Râm. 2, 71, 23 Gorr. *Su-*, m. a lucky dream.—Cf. A.S. swefn; Lat. somnus; ὕπνος.

स्वप्नज् *svapna-j* (*j*, from vb. *jan*), adj. Sleeping, asleep, MBh. 3, 10648.

स्वप्नज *svapna-ja*, adj. Produced by a dream, Megh. 88.

स्वभावज *sva-bhâva-ja*, adj. **1.** Become by one's own nature, Hit. i. d. 205, M.M. **2.** Innate, Hit. i. d. 194, M.M.

स्वभावतस् *sva-bhâva + tas*, adv. By one's own nature, Pańch. 166, 15.

स्वभू *sva-bhû*, m. **1.** Vishṇu. **2.** Brahman.

स्वयंवर *svayaṁvara*, i.e. *svayam -vara*, I. m. The public choice of a husband by a princess, Nal. 2, 8. II. f. *râ*, A girl choosing her husband, Man. 9, 92.

स्वयम् *svayam* (from *sva*), indecl. **1.** Reflective pronoun of the three persons: Self, myself, Pańch. 163, 19; himself, Pańch. iii. d. 114; one's self, Hit. ii. d. 23; by himself, Mâlat. 70, 5. **2.** Spontaneously, Bhartṛ. 2, 82; Pańch. 230, 15. **3.** Of one's own accord, Pańch. v. d. 49.

स्वयंभू *svayaṁbhû*, i.e. *svayam-bhû* (existing by himself, not created), m. **1.** Brahman, Man. 1, 3; 94; Vishṇu, Çiva, Pańch. i. d. 422 (?). **2.** Time. **3.** Love.

† 1. **स्वर्** *SVAR* (**सुर्** *SUR*), i. 10, *svaraya* (*suraya*), To blame.

2. **स्वर्** *svar*, i.e. *sû + an* (with *r* for *n*), I. n. (Rigv. i. 105, 3), The sun, Chr. 289, 5 = Rigv. i. 50, 5. II. indecl. **1.** Splendour. **2.** Heaven, Bhag. 9, 20; Râjat. 5, 8. **3.** Paradise. **4.** A mystical word, signifying the space between the sun and polar star, Man. 2, 76; Vedântas. in Chr. 209, 1.

स्वर *svara*, i.e. *svṛi + a*, m. **1.** Sound, Pańch. 82, 17; voice, Pańch.

v. d. 83. **2.** Snoring. **3.** A note in music, Pańch. v. d. 43. **4.** A vowel. **5.** Accent, Sâv. 5, 25.—**Comp.** *A-*, adj. low, indistinct, Râm. 2, 42, 26. *Târa-*, m. loud sound or voice, Pańch. 97, 19; 107, 5. *Bhinna-* (vb. *bhid*), adj. 1. faltering in speech. 2. hoarse. *Mahâ-*, adj. crying aloud, Râm. 3, 55, 32. *Vi-*, adj. discordant, inharmonious. *Su-*, adj. loud, Chr. 12, 28.

स्वरित *svarita*, i.e. *svara + ita*, **I.** adj. **1.** Articulated. **2.** Sounded as a note. **3.** Accented. **II.** m. The circumflex accent.

स्वरु *svaru*, m., i.e. **I.** *svṛi + u*, **1.** Indra's thunderbolt. **2.** An arrow. **II. 1.** Sunshine. **2.** A sacrifice. **3.** A kind of scorpion. **4.** Shavings of the sacrificial post. **5.** The sacrificial post, Chr. 294, 5 = Rigv. i. 92, 5.

स्वरूपता *sva-rûpa + tâ*, f. **1.** Natural state. **2.** Handsomeness.

स्वर्ग *svar-ga*, m. Heaven, Indra's paradise, Bhartṛ. 2, 85; Vikr. d. 59; Pańch. i. d. 248.—**Comp.** *Bhû-*, m. the mountain Sumeru.

स्वर्गजित् *svarga-ji + t*, adj. Obtaining or ensuring paradise.

स्वर्गद *svarga-da* (vb. *dâ*), adj. Procuring paradise, Pańch. i. d. 283.

स्वर्गिन् *svarga + in*, m. **1.** A deity, Çâk. d. 193; Megh. 31. **2.** (In law), Dead.

स्वर्गीय *svargîya*, i.e. *svarga + îya*, adj. Heavenly, divine.

स्वर्ग्य *svargya*, i.e. *svarga + ya*, adj. **1.** Heavenly. **2.** Procuring a place in heaven, Man. 3, 106.—**Comp.** *A-*, adj. prejudicial to heavenly beatitude, Man. 2, 57.

स्वर्जित् *svar-ji + t* (m.), A peculiar sacrifice, Man. 11, 74 (cf. *svargajit*).

स्वर्ण *svarṇa*, i.e. *su-varṇa*, n. Gold, Bhâg. P. 4, 25, 14; a gold coin, Kathâs. 22, 97.—**Comp.** *Kûṭa-*, n. counterfeit gold, Yâjń. 2, 297.

स्वर्णक *svarṇa + ka*, adj. Golden.

स्वर्णकृत् *svarṇa-kṛi + t*, m. A goldsmith.

स्वर्णज *svarṇa-ja*, n. Tin.

स्वर्णदी *svarṇadî*, i.e. *svar-nadî*, f. The Gańgâ.

स्वर्त् *SVART*, see *çvart*.

† **स्वर्द्** *SVARD*, i. 1, Âtm. To taste.

† **स्वल्** *SVAL*, i. 1, Par. To go.

स्वल्पक *svalpaka*, i.e. *su-alpa + ka*, adj. **1.** Little. **2.** Few.

स्वल्पशिलाय *SVALPAÇILÂYA*, a denomin. derived from *su-alpa-çilâ*, with *ya*, Âtm. To become a little stone, Bhartṛ. 2, 78.

स्ववीर्यतस् *sva-vîrya + tas*, adv. Conformably to one's power, Pańch. i. d. 460.

स्वसृ *svasṛi*, i.e. probably *sva-strî*, f. A sister, Hiḍ. 1, 31; Chr. 295, 11 = Rigv. i. 92, 11 (the night).—**Comp.** *Yama-*, f. the Yamunâ river.—Cf. Goth. svistar; A.S. sweoster, swuster, syster; Lat. soror, con-sobrinus.

स्वसृत् *sva-sṛi + t*, adj. Going or moving at one's own will, Chr. 294, 11 = Rigv. i. 64, 11.

स्वस्क् *SVASK*, see *shvash*.

स्वस्ति *svasti*, i.e. *su-1. as + ti*, **I.** f. Welfare, blessing, Lass. 102, 12 = Rigv.

vii. 14, 3. **II.** indecl. **1.** A particle of benediction, bliss, hail! happiness, in the sense of a nomin., Chr. 36, 16; Vikr. 87, 19; Râm. 3, 51, 37; or acc., Nal. 12, 120. **2.** A term of sanction or approbation, so be it!

स्वस्तिक *svasti + ka*, **I.** m. and n. A temple of a particular form, with a portico in front. **II.** m. **1.** Any auspicious object. **2.** The meeting of four roads. **3.** A palace having a portico on three sides. **4.** A mystical mark, Mâlat. 73, 15 (at the end of a Bahuvr. comp. f. *kâ*); a cross. **5.** The crossing of the arms. **6.** A particular kind of posture, Vedântas. in Chr. 217, 17. **7.** A kind of cake. **8.** A libertine. **9.** Garlic.—**Comp.** *Padma-*, m. or n. a mystical mark consisting of lotus flowers, Râm. 5, 10, 4 (Sch. a four-cornered sort of painting).

स्वस्तिमन्त् *svasti + mant*, adj., f. *mati*, Happy.

स्वस्त्ययन *svastyayana*, i.e. *svasti -ayana*, **I.** adj. Auspicious, producing happiness, Man. 1, 106. **II.** n. The recitation of holy texts for the averting of evil, Man. 5, 152; benediction, Chr. 25, 51 (*kṛita-svastyayana*, adj. After having received benedictions).

स्वस्थ *sva-stha*, adj., f. *thâ*, **1.** Relying upon one's self, resolute, Pańch. 106, 22; firm, Pańch. ii. d. 88. **2.** Content, Pańch. 56, 2. **3.** Well, safe, Mâlat. 63, 12; healthy, Man. 7, 226. **4.** Self-sufficient, independent, Nal. 2, 1 (*Damayantî na svasthâ babhûva Nalam prati*, Damayantî was dependent with regard to Nala, i.e. she was in love with Nala).—**Comp.** *A-*, adj., f. *thâ*, 1. not firm, Böhtl. Ind. Spr. 936. 2. ill, suffering, Çâk. 31, 9. 3. dependent, enamoured, Nal. 2, 5.

स्वस्थता *svastha + tâ*, f. Well-being, health, Pańch. 159, 17.

स्वस्रीय *svasrîya*, i.e. *svasṛi + îya*, **I.** m. A sister's son, Man. 3, 148. **II.** f. *yâ*, A sister's daughter, Man. 11, 171.

स्वहस्तिका *svahastikâ* (v.r. *suh°*), i.e. *sva-* (or *su*), *-hasta + ka*, f. An axe (?), Pańch. 122, 10; 123, 15.

स्वाच्छन्द्य *svâchchhandya*, i.e. *sva -chhanda + ya*, n. Independence, wilfulness; abl. Voluntarily, Man. 3, 31.

स्वातन्त्र्य *svâtantrya*, i.e. *sva-tantra + ya*, n. **1.** Independence, Man. 9, 3; Bhartṛ. 3, 92. **2.** Wilfulness, Man. 5, 147 (mere pleasure, Jones).

स्वाति or **स्वाती** *svâti*, f. **1.** One of the wives of the sun. **2.** The star Arcturus, or fifteenth lunar asterism. **3.** An auspicious constellation, Bhartṛ. 2, 57. **4.** A sword.

स्वाद् *SVÂD*, see *svad*.

स्वाद *svâd + a*, m. **1.** Tasting, eating, Pańch. 253, 18; drinking. **2.** Taste.—**Comp.** *Vi-*, adj. insipid.

स्वादिन् *svâd + in*, adj. Tasting, drinking, Nalod. 3, 4.

स्वादिमन् *svâdiman*, i.e. *svâdu + iman*, m. Sweetness.

स्वादु *svâd + u*, **I.** adj., comparat. *svâdîyaṁs*, superl. *svâdishṭha*, **1.** Grateful to the palate. **2.** Sweet, Pańch. v. d. 88; *svâdishṭha*, with abl. Sweeter, Bhartṛ. 3, 97. **3.** Agreeable. **4.** Handsome. **II.** *du*, adv. Sweetly. **III.** m. **1.** Sweetness, Megh. 25 (? n.). **2.** Molasses. **3.** A medicinal root. **IV.** f. *du*, or *dvî*, A grape.—**Comp.** *Nis-*, adj. unsweet, Hit. 77, 1, M.M.—Cf. A.S. swét, swaes; Goth. suts; O.H.G. suozi; Lat. suavis (i.e. svâdu + i), suadere; ἡδύς.

स्वाधीनता *svâdhînatâ*, i. e. *sva-adhîna + tâ*, f. Independence.

स्वाध्यायवन्त् *svâdhyâyavant*, i.e. *sva-adhyâya + vant*, m. A student of the Vedas, Johns. Sel. 36, 12.

स्वाध्यायिन् *svâdhyâyin*, i.e. *sva-adhyâya + in*, **1.** A student of the Vedas. **2.** A tradesman.

स्वान *svâna*, i.e. *svan + a*, m. Sound.

स्वान्त *svânta*, **I.** See *svan*. **II.** i.e. *sva-anta*, n. **1.** The mind, Vedântas. in Chr. 202, 12; Bhartṛ. 3, 92. **2.** A cavern.

स्वाप *svâpa*, i.e. *svap + a*, m. **1.** Sleeping, Utt. Râmach. 24, 7; sleep. **2.** Sleepiness. **3.** Loss of sensation. **4.** The sleep of a limb. **5.** Ignorance. **6.** Dream.—**Comp.** *Divâ-*, m. sleeping by day, Suçr. 1, 330, 5.

स्वापतेय *svâpateya*, i.e. *sva-pati + eya*, n. Wealth, MBh. 1, 1781; Pańch. ii. d. 166.

स्वाभाविक *svâbhâvika*, i.e. *sva-bhâva + ika*, adj. Being by one's own nature, inherent, natural, Man. 3, 46; Pańch. 66, 10; 110, 21.

ऽस्वामिक *-svâmika*, i.e. *svâmin + ka*, a substitute for *svâmin*, when latter part of a comp. adj.; e.g. *pranashta-* (so to be read instead of *praṇashṭa*, Man. 8, 30), adj. That of which it is not known whether its owner is alive or dead.

स्वामित्व *svâmitva*, i.e. *svâmin + tva*, n. **1.** Ownership. **2.** Sovereignty, Pańch. 163, 14.

स्वामिन् *svâmin*, i.e. *sva + min*, m. **1.** A proprietor. **2.** A master, Pańch. i. d. 328. **3.** A sovereign, Hit. 3, 4, M.M. **4.** A husband, Hit. 87, 9, M.M.; a lover. **5.** A spiritual preceptor. **6.** A learned Brâhmaṇa. **7.** Vishṇu, Çiva, Kârttikeya, the god of war, Garuḍa, a fabulous bird. **8.** In comp. it signifies often a sanctuary built by, or in honour of, those who are denoted in the former part of the comp.; e.g. *avanti-*, m. a sanctuary built by Avantivarman, Râjat. 5, 45. *abhimanyu-*, m. A sanctuary built in commemoration of Abhimanyu, Râjat. 6, 299. *dharma-*, m. A sanctuary built by Dharma, Râjat. 4, 696. *vishṇu-*, A sanctuary built in honour of Vishṇu, Râjat. 5, 99.—**Comp.** *A-*, m. one who is not owner, Man. 8, 4. *Ku-*, m. a wicked master, Pańch. 73, 11. *Go-*, m. 1. the owner of cattle, Man. 8, 231. 2. a holy man, used after proper names, as a honorary title. *Jagat-*, m. the lord of the universe, Prab. 99, 8. *Jaya-*, m. the lord of victory, epithet of Çiva, Râjat. 5, 448. *Raṇa-*, m. the lord of battles, epithet of Çiva, Râjat. 5, 394. *Çiva-*, m. a proper name, Râjat. 5, 34.

स्वाम्य *svâmya*, i.e. *svâmin + ya*, n. **1.** Ownership. **2.** Mastership. **3.** Supremacy, Hit. 84, 7; dominion, Dev. 1, 8. **4.** Marital dominion, Man. 5, 152.

स्वायम्भुव *svâyambhuva*, i.e. *svayam̃-bhû + a*, **I.** adj. **1.** Relating to Brahman. **2.** Descended from Brahman. **II.** m. The son of Brahman, Çâk. d. 168; epithet of the first Manu, Man. 1, 61; 63.

स्वायुज् *svâyuj*, i.e. *su*, or *sva*, *-â-yuj*, adj. Easily yoked, or putting themselves spontaneously to the chariot, Chr. 294, 2 = Rigv. i. 92, 2.

स्वाराज् *svârâj*, i. e. *svar-râj*, m. Indra.

स्वाराज्य *svârâjya*, n., i.e. **I.** *sva-râj + ya*, The state of Brahman, union with Brahman, final felicity, Man. 12, 91. II. *svârâj+ya*, Indra's heaven.

स्वारोचिष *svârochisha*, i. e. *sva-rochis+a*, m. The second Manu, Man. 1, 62.

स्वार्थिक *svârthika*, i.e. *sva-artha+ika*, adj. 1. Done with one's own property. 2. Having one's own object. 3. Having its literal meaning.

स्वास्थ्य *svâsthya*, i. e. *svastha+ya*, n. 1. Health, Pańch. 183, 22. 2. Content. 3. Happiness, Pańch. ii. d. 165. 4. Self-reliance, firmness, Pańch. ii. d. 170 (with *vraj*, To recover).

स्वाहा *svâhâ*, I. indecl. An exclamation on offering to the gods. II. f. A personification of the preceding as the wife of fire, Ragh. 1, 56.

1. स्विद् *SVID*, i. 4, Par. To perspire, to sweat, Gît. 10, 16. i. 1, Âtm. 1. † To be greasy or unctuous. 2. † To be disturbed. 3. † To shed. Ptcple. of the pf. pass. I. *svidita*, 1. Sweated, melted. 2. Perspiring. II. *svinna*, Sweating, Lass. 59, 6. Caus. 1. To cause to perspire; *svedya*, What must be treated by sudorific means, Böhtl. Ind. Spr. 890. 2. To warm, Hit. ii. d. 131. *svedita*, Sweated, heated.—With प्र *pra*, *prasvinna*, and *prasvedita*, 1. Perspiring, covered with perspiration, Râm. 2, 100, 35 (*svinna*). 2. Heated; *prasvedita* (also 3.), Hot, causing perspiration.—Cf. Goth. sveitan; A.S. swaetan; O.H.G. svizzan, sueizjan (Caus.); ἱδρώς, σίδηρος; Lat. sudor, sudare.

2. स्विद् *svid*, i.e. *su-id*, 1. A particle used in an interrogation, Perhaps, Kir. 12, 15; 14, 60; after *kim*, MBh. 3, 10648; after *uta* and *utâho* (see *uta*), Or, Pańch. 41, 1; 142, 5. 2. An exclamation of doubt or surprise.

स्विष्टकृत् *svishṭakrit*, i. e. *su-ishṭa* (vb. *yaj*), *-kṛi+t*, The name of a divinity, the fire of the good sacrifice, Man. 3, 86.

स्वीकरण *svîkaraṇa*, i. e. *sva-kṛi+ana*, n. 1. Assenting. 2. Promising. 3. Marriage, Çâk. 66, 17.

स्वीकार *svîkâra*, i.e. *sva-kṛi+a*, m. 1. Assent. 2. Promise.

स्वीय *svîya*, i.e. *sva+îya*, I. adj. Own, Pańch. ii. d. 80. II. f. *yâ*, A faithful wife.—Cf. ἑός, σφέος, σφός.

स्वुर्छ् *SVURCHH*, see *sphurchh*.

स्वृ *SVṚI*, i. 1, Par. 1. To sound. 2. To praise (ved.). 3. To be pained. 4. † To go. Caus. To sing, Chr. 294, 5 = Rigv. i. 88, 5 (*sasvar*, ved. aor.).—With सम् *sam*, Âtm. To pain, Bhaṭṭ. 9, 28.—Cf. Lat. susurro, absurdus, surdus (properly, Suffering from humming in the ears), sorex; σύριγξ, ὕραξ, ὕρον; probably Goth. svaran; A.S. swaran, swerian, and-swar, answer; probably Lat. sorbere; ῥοφέω (from the sound of drinking; cf. Zend. *qar* = Sskr. *svar*, properly, To smack; cf. *ava* and *vi*, with *svan*, also *vishvaṇana*, *vishvâṇa*).

† स्वॄ *SVṜÎ*, स्बॄ *SBṜÎ*, सॄ *SṜÎ*, ii. 9, *svṛiṇâ*, *sbṛiṇâ*, *sṛiṇâ*, *ṇi*, Par. To hurt, to kill.

स्वेक् *SVEK*, see *srek*.

स्वेच्छातस् *svechchhâtas*, i. e. *sva-ichchhâ+tas*, adv. Conformably to one's wish, Hit. 69, 19.

स्वेद *sveda*, i.e. *svid+a*, m. 1. Perspiration, sweat, Vikr. 27, 2. 2. Hot moisture, Vedântas. in Chr. 209, 5. 3. Warmth. 4. Hot work, labour, Chr. 292, 8 = Rigv. i. 86, 8. 5. Vapour.—Comp. *Sa-*, I. adj. perspiring, exuding,

Râjat. 5, 343. II. f. *dâ*, a virgin deflowered. — Cf. O.H.G. sueiz; A.S. swát.

स्वेदन *svedana*, i.e. *svid + ana*, I. n. **1.** Perspiration. **2.** Causing to perspire, warming, Hit. ii. d. 130. **3.** A sudorific. II. f. *-nî*, An iron plate used for cooking and frying.

स्वेदनिक *svedanika*, i.e. *svedanî + ka*, f. An iron plate for cooking and frying.

स्वैर *svaira* (from *sva* and *ir*), I. adj. **1.** Self-willed, Pańch. 31, 3; of one's own accord, Râm. 3, 52, 27 (without the permission of her husband); unrestrained. **2.** Slow, or refractory, Nal. 21, 13; Sâv. 5, 98. **3.** Dependent on one's will, unimportant, MBh. 1, 1726; 1921; 3, 15573. II. *ram*, adv. **1.** With one's own will, assent, Râm. 3, 52, 27; Utt. Râmach. 29, 6; Kathâs. 22, 99. **2.** Of one's own accord, Râjat. 5, 411. III. n. Wilfulness.

स्वैरता *svaira + tâ*, and **स्वैरिता** *svairitâ*, i.e. *svairin + tâ*, f. Wilfulness, Lass. 2. ed. 19, 18 (*ra*).

स्वैरिन् *svairin*, i.e. *svaira + in*, I. adj., f. *iṇî*, Self-willed, wanton, Lass. 42, 13. II. f. *iṇî*, An unchaste woman, Pańch. 129, 1; Râjat. 5, 316.

ह *H.*

1. **ह** *ha*, **1.** = ved. *gha*, Lass. 98, 2 = Rigv. vi. 64, 5. **2.** A particle laying a stress on the preceding word (as γέ), or without a distinct signification, Man. 9, 28; Chr. 12, 2; 25, 62; *na ha*, Not indeed, Man. 9, 270; used very often after the red. pf. (Râm. 3, 52, 53), and imperf., Pâṇ. iii. 2, 116. **3.** A vocative particle, Ho! holloa! **4.** A particle of reproach. — Cf. Lat. ha, ho, hi, in hic, hæc, hoc; Goth. prefix, ga-; A.S. ge-; see *gha*.

2. **ऽह** *-ha* (vb. *han*), at the end of comp. adj. Killing, Pâṇ. iii. 2, 49.

हंस् *HAṀS*, a denomin. derived from the next, Par. To behave like a swan, Lass. 67, 15.

हंस *haṁsa*, I. m. **1.** A goose, a gander, a swan, a phœnicopteros, Vikr. d. 95; Man. 3, 10; it is the vehicle of Brahman. **2.** A sort of horse. **3.** The sun. **4.** A devotee. **5.** A liberal prince. **6.** One of the vital breaths. **7.** Brahman, Vishṇu, Çiva, Kâma, the god of love. **8.** (In composition), Best, excellent. II. f. *sî*. **1.** A goose. **2.** A proper name, Râjat. 5, 359.—**Comp.** *Para-*, and *Parama-*, m. an ascetic who has subdued all his senses, MBh. 13, 6478 (*parama*). *Râjahaṁsa*, i.e. *râjan-*, m. 1. an excellent king. 2. m., f. *sî*, a white goose with red legs and bill, Vikr. d. 19; a flamingo, Hit. 79, 7. 3. a drake.—Cf. O.H.G. gans; A.S. gós, gandra; Lat. anser; χήν.

हंसक *haṁsa + ka*, m. **1.** The flamingo. **2.** An ornament for the feet.

हंसकाकीय *hâṁsakâkîya*, i.e. *haṁsa-kâka + îya*, adj. Relating to the goose and the crow (a fable), MBh. 1, 543.

हंसपदिका *haṁsapadikâ*, i.e. *haṁsa-pada + î + ka*, f. A proper name, Çâk. 59, 15.

हंसिका *haṁsikâ*, i.e. *haṁsî + ka*, f. A goose, Nalod. 2, 40.

हंहो *haṁho*, **1.** An interjection of calling, Chaurap. 22; Ho! holloa! Pańch. 192, 12; Vikr. 61, 12. **2.** A particle of contempt.

हञ्जा *hañjâ*, and **हञ्जे** *hañje*, A vocative particle used in addressing a female attendant (in theatrical language), Sâh. D. 172, 13.

† हट् *HAṬ*, i. 1, Par. To shine.

हट्ट *haṭṭa*, I. m. A market, a fair, Pańch. 262, 15. II. f. *ṭi*, A petty market.

† हठ् *HAṬH*, i. 1, Par. **1.** To jump. **2.** To treat with violence. **3.** To bind to a post.

हठ *haṭha*, perhaps a dialect. form of *hasta*, I. m. **1.** Violence, Râm. 5, 85, 11; abl. *ṭhât*, By force, Pańch. 138, 1. **2.** Rapine. II. m., f. *ṭhî*, A plant, Pistia stratiotes.

हडिक *haḍika*, and हड्डक *haḍḍaka*, m. A sweeper, a servant of the lowest caste.

हड्ड *haḍḍa*, n. A bone.

हड्डक *haḍḍaka*, see *haḍika*.

हड्डज *haḍḍa-ja*, n. Marrow.

हण्डे *haṇḍe*, used like *hańjâ*, q. cf.

हतक *hata+ka* (vb. *han*), I. adj. Miserable (?), Mâlat. 87, 3. II. m. A coward, Utt. Râmach. 30, 7.

हताश *hatâça*, i.e. *hata-âça*, (see *han* and *âçâ*), m. **1.** Hopeless, desponding. **2.** Weak. **3.** Barren. **4.** Cruel, merciless. **5.** Vile, wicked, Vikr. 8, 9 (Prâkṛ.).

हति *hati*, i.e. *han+ti*, f. **1.** Striking; in *hala-*, f. Ploughing. **2.** Destroying, removing, Bhartṛ. 3, 100. — Cf. A.S. dynt; see *han*.

हत्नु *hatnu*, i.e. *han+tnu*, m. **1.** A weapon. **2.** Sickness.

हत्य *hatya*, i.e. *han+tya*, n., and f. *yâ*, Killing, Chr. 297, 14 = Rigv. i. 112, 14 (n.); Pańch. i. d. 306 (I read *tasya hatyâ tadutthânâ*, The murder of that man has its origin in this person, i.e. his death is caused by that person, by trusting to whom he has found it; but cf. also Böhtl. Ind. Spr. 2850); 221, 14 (f.).—Comp. *Go-*, f. killing a cow, Man. 11, 115. *Brahmahatyâ*, i.e. *brahman-*, f. killing a Brâhmaṇa, Hit. i. d. 184. *Bhrûṇa-*, f. murder of an unborn child, Râm. 2, 47, 41, Seramp. *Vîra-*, f. the slaughter of a man (Jones, 'a son'), Man. 11, 41. *Strî-*, f. the crime of having killed a woman, Pańch. 216, 17.

हथ *hatha*, i.e. *han+tha*, m. A man in despondency.

हद् *HAD*, i. 1, Âtm. To evacuate, as fæces. Ptcplc. pf. pass. *hanna*, Passed, as ordure. — Cf. χέζω, χόδος; probably O.H.G scizan; A.S. scitan.

हन् *HAN*, probably for original *dhan*, ii. 2, Par. (in epic poetry also Âtm., Râm. 1, 45, 49), ved., i. 1, *jighna*; some verbal forms are derived also, or only, from बध् *BADH*, or वध् *VADH*, **1.** To strike, MBh. 1, 6706; to peck, Hit. 81, 21. **2.** To wound, to hurt, Man. 10, 84; to injure, Pańch. iii. d. 50 (*badhyante*, pass.), to overturn (right), Man. 8, 15. **3.** To kill, Râm. 2, 78, 22; pass. *badh*, with the termination of the Par., MBh. 2, 8765. **4.** To destroy, Man. 8, 14; *mâ hato 'badhît*, 8, 15 (blot out the '). **5.** To remove (darkness), Hit. pr. d. 17, M.M.; (impurity), Man. 2, 102. **6.** To impede, Râjat. 5, 253. **7.** † To go. Ptcple. of the pf. pass. *hata*. **1.** Killed, Chr. 62, 51. **2.** Utterly ruined, Çâk. d. 22. **3.** Ended. **4.** Lost, Chr. 32, 28. **5.** Deprived of, without, especially when former part of comp. adj.; e.g. *hata-sâdhvasa*, adj. Fearless, cf. also Kir.

5, 49; Sâv. 5, 17. **6.** Disappointed. **7.** Worthless, Böhtl. Ind. Spr. 809. **8.** (In arithmetic), Multiplied. n. **1.** Hurting, killing. **2.** Multiplication. **Comp.** *A-*, adj. 1. not beaten (as a drum). 2. unwashed, MBh. 2, 99. 3. new, Râm. 2, 3, 10. n. new cloth (properly, 'not yet washed'). *Manohata*, i. e. *manas-*, adj. disappointed. Ptcple. of the fut. pass. *badhya*. **1.** Deserving death, Vikr. d. 144. **2.** Condemned to death. **Comp.** *Âtmavadhyâ*, i. e. *âtman-*, f. suicide, MBh. 1, 6227. Frequent. *jaṁghan*, To strike repeatedly, Chr. 293, 2=Rigv. i. 88, 2. Desider. *jighâṁsa*, To wish or to be inclined to kill, Man. 5, 3; Johns. Sel. 54, 135 (Âtm.). Caus. *ghâtaya*, properly a denomin. derived from *ghâta*, To cause to be killed, Bhag. 2, 21 (*kaṁ ghâtayati hanti kam*, Whom will he kill by means of others or by his own hand?). *ghâtavya* (anomal. for *ghâtayitavya*, or *hantavya*?), Deserving death, Mâlav. 9, 9. *ghâtya*, To be killed, Pańch. 194, 6 (*sukha-*, Easy to be killed).—With अप *apa*, **1.** To remove (sin), Man. 6, 96. **2.** To take away, Bhartṛ. 2, 15 (probably is to be read *apahartum*).—With अभि *abhi*, **1.** To assail, Daçak. in Chr. 194, 11. **2.** To strike, Man. 11, 206; anomal. *abhy aghnam*, Arj. 7, 6. **3.** To cast on, Utt. Râmach. 117, 3. **4.** To kill, MBh. 3, 12108. *abhihata*, **1.** Struck, Chr. 40, 9. **2.** Subdued. **3.** (In medicine), Obstructed. **4.** (In arithmetic), Multiplied.—With अव *ava*, To kick (*anyonyaṁ jânubhis*, each other with the knees, in wrestling), MBh. 2, 915.—With आ *â*, Âtm., when without object, or the object being a member, **1.** To strike, Dev. 9, 27; Râm. 3, 50, 20. **2.** To beat (a kettle-drum), Megh. 67. **3.** Âtm. To kill one's self, Daçak. in Chr. 190, 12. *âhata*, **1.** Struck, Pańch. v. d. 4; injured, killed. **2.** Understood, known. **3.** Uttered falsely. **4.** Multiplied. m. A drum. n. **1.** Old cloth. **2.** Assertion of an impossibility. **Comp.** *An-*, adj. without being beaten (as drums), Chr. 37, 25.—With अभ्या *abhi-â*, **1.** To strike, MBh. 1, 8223. **2.** To wound, Chr. 43, 25. *abhyâhata*, **1.** Killed. **2.** Obstructed, impeded.—With प्रत्या *prati-â*, To drive back, Chr. 31, 11 (Âtm.).—With व्या *vi-â*, **1.** To obstruct, to impede, Râm. 2, 10, 32. **2.** To delay, Ragh. 9, 54. *a-vyâhata*, Unimpeded, Pańch. 16, 1. Caus. To obstruct, MBh. 1, 8109.—With समा *sam-â*, **1.** To join, Arj. 3, 40. **2.** To strike, Pańch. i. d. 339; MBh. 1, 6291. **3.** To beat (a kettle-drum), MBh. 1, 7941. **4.** To kill, Râm. 1, 32, 17. *samâhata*, **1.** Struck, Hit. iii. d. 147 (*nîti-mantra-pavanaiḥ*, Struck by the counsels of good policy as by storms). **2.** Wounded.—With उद् *ud*, ved. *jighna*, To throw up, Chr. 290, 11=Rigv. i. 64, 11. *uddhata*, **1.** Thrown up (as dust), Çâk. d. 8; (as the sea), Johns. Sel. 28, 27. **2.** Raised, Ṛit. 1, 10; moved, Pańch. 21, 2. **3.** Intense, Pańch. 93, 2. **4.** Puffed up, haughty, Utt. Râmach. 151, 2; Böhtl. Ind. Spr. 2375. **5.** Ill-behaved, rude. **6.** Râm. 2, 53, 32, read *uddhṛitau*, with Gorr. 39. **Comp.** *An-*, adj. not proud, Râm. 2, 6, 22. *Madu-*, adj. drunk, mad, Pańch. 254, 8.—With समुद् *sam-ud*, *samuddhata*, **1.** Risen, Utt. Râmach. 124, 10. **2.** Proud, Çiç. 2, 117; Kir. 5, 15.—With उप *upa*, **1.** To scratch, MBh. 2, 2123 (you scratch as a cat its nourisher). **2.** To touch, Man. 9, 208. **3.** To strike, Mâlat. 160, 18. **4.** To kill, Kathâs. 26, 140;

Utt. Râmach. 176, 8. *upahata*, **1.** Injured, spoiled, Vikr. d. 127. **2.** Assailed, Çṛiṅgârat. 12. **3.** Pained, afflicted, Ṛit. 1, 15; *dâridra-*, adj. Afflicted by poverty, Pańch. 119, 5; *apâya-upahata-antar-âtman*, adj. One whose heart is discouraged by misfortune, Hit. iii. d. 115. **4.** Struck by lightning, etc., by the rays of the sun, Kir. 5, 48. **5.** Destroyed. **6.** Infected, polluted, tarnished, Çâk. d. 191. **7.** Impure. **Comp.** *An-*, adj. approved, Bhartṛ. 2, 60.—With नि *ni*, **1.** To strike, MBh. 3, 11953. **2.** To kill, Hit. iii. d. 116. **3.** To destroy, Hit. i. d. 42, M.M. **4.** To disregard, Hit. pr. d. 31, M.M. *nihata*, **1.** Struck down, Lass. 2. ed. 78, 70. **2.** Killed, Kir. 14, 14. **3.** Infixed, attached, Râm. 2, 82, 16.—With परिणि *pari-ni*, To strike, MBh. 3, 12261 (has *ni*).—With विनि *vi-ni*, **1.** To pat, Râm. 1, 9, 16. **2.** To kill, Pańch. i. d. 347. **3.** To destroy, Hit. iv. d. 37; to remove (darkness), MBh. 1, 85.—With निस् *nis*, **1.** To drag out (of one's house), Râjat. 5, 432. **2.** To remove, Suçr. 1, 100, 16.—With परा *parâ*, To push on, MBh. 3, 1288 (the clouds were pushed on by the violence of the wind). *parâhata*, **1.** Struck. **2.** Assailed. n. Strike, Mâlat. 140, 15.—With परि *pari*, *parihata*, Lost, Gît. 5, 13. **Comp.** *A-*, adj. not avoided, Çâk. 69, 2 (v.r. probably is to be read *aparihṛita*).—With प्र *pra*, *prahata*, **1.** Struck, wounded. **2.** Beaten (as a drum), Megh. 65. **3.** Killed. **4.** Repelled. **5.** Overcome. **6.** Spread, expanded. **7.** Contiguous. **8.** Learned, accomplished. Absol. *prabadhya*, Being killed, Pańch. iii. d. 269.—With विप्र *vi-pra*, *a-viprahata*, adj. Not distant, Râm. 1, 26, 12.—With प्रति *prati*, **1.** To return a blow, MBh. 3, 1091. **2.** To drive back, Çâk. d. 50; to remove, Vikr. d. 20. **3.** To disown, Çâk. d. 191. **4.** To keep off, Çâk. d. 13; to prevent, Mâlat. 174, 6. **5.** To oppose, to resist, Arj. 10, 20. *pratihata*, **1.** Obstructed, Mâlat. 156, 9. **2.** Repulsed, Arj. 8, 11; averted, Çâk. 91, 15. **3.** Hated. **4.** Struck. **5.** Disappointed. **6.** Sent, dispatched. **7.** Overthrown, fallen. **8.** Tied, bound. **Comp.** *A-*, adj. 1. uninjured, Hit. i. d. 126, M.M. 2. unfailing, Mâlat. 86, 3.—With वि *vi*, **1.** To strike, Arj. 10, 23. **2.** To afflict, MBh. 2, 151; Râm. 3, 79, 28. **3.** To kill, Pańch. 86, 23; MBh. 3, 11117. **4.** To destroy, Man. 7, 27. **5.** To interrupt, Mâlav. d. 33. **6.** To separate, Mâlat. 163, 3. **7.** To obstruct, to impede, Pańch. iii. d. 232; Bhartṛ. 2, 73. **8.** To deny, to refuse, Ragh. 11, 2. *vihata*, Opposed, resisted. **Comp.** *A-*, adj. irresistible, Megh. 10. Caus. To cause to be destroyed, Hit. iii. d. 109.—With सम् *sam*, To put together, to close (one's hands), Man. 2, 71. *saṁhata*, **1.** Joined, combined, Hit. i. d. 36, M.M. **2.** Collected, Indr. 1, 6; keeping together, Hit. iii. d. 125. **3.** Closely allied, Man. 7, 66. **4.** Closed, shut. **5.** Compact, Râm. 3, 52, 25. **6.** Strong-knit, Draup. 7, 9 (the forehead by frowning); well-limbed. **7.** Combining, acting together. **8.** Struck, wounded, killed. **Comp.** *A-*, adj. disagreeing, Pańch. v. d. 86. *Su-*, adj. well-compacted, well-knit.—With अभिसम् *abhi-sam*, To unite, MBh. 2, 800.—Cf. θάνατος, θείνω, θνήσκω; Goth. dauths, dauthus; A.S. deád, deadh; dydan, to kill; Lat. fen-d in offendere, infestus, probably fessus, fatigare (cf. rutilus, s.v. *rudhira*, latere, s.v. *rah*, etc.); with *badh*, cf. πάθος, πάσχω;

Lat. patior; perhaps A. S. beado, battle; bytl, a hammer; also Goth. du-ginnan; A.S. a-ginnan.

ऽहन् *-han*, latter part of comp. words, f. *ghnî*, Killing, having killed, etc.; e.g. *chakshurhan*, i.e. *chakshus-*, adj. Killing by a glance of his eye, MBh. 13, 2156. *pitṛi-*, m. A parricide, Râjat. 5, 447. *brahmahan*, i.e. *brahman-*, m. The slayer of a Brâhmaṇa, Man. 11, 101; 128 (anomal. gen. *-haṇas* instead of *ghnas*). *yajña-*, adj. Sacrifice-destroying, a name of Çiva, Johns. Sel. 96, 78. *vîrahan* and *vṛitrahan*, see s.vv. *haya-grîva-* (see *grîvâ*), m. Vishṇu.

हन *han+a*, I. m. A killer. II. Latter part of comp. words, Killing; e.g. *kshatriya-haṇa*, m. A destroyer of the Kshatriyas, MBh. 5, 7116. *vîra-haṇa*, adj., f. *ṇî*, Hero-killing, MBh. 9, 3238.

हनन *han + ana*, n. 1. Striking, Mâlat. 85, 7. 2. Injuring. 3. Killing. 4. Multiplication.

हनु I. *hanu* (vb. 1. *hâ*? cf. A.S. gôma, the jaws), m., f. also **नू** *nû* (and n.), The jaw. II. *han+u*, f. 1. A weapon. 2. Sickness. 3. Death. 4. A sort of vegetable perfume.—Cf. γένυς; Lat. gena; Goth. kinnus; A.S. cinn, cyn.

हनुमन्त् and **हनूमन्त्** *hanû+mant*, I. adj. Having large jaws. II. m. The monkey chief, Hanumant, Utt. Râmach. 20, 8 (*û*); Mahâv. 114, 17 (*ŭ*).

हनूष *hanûsha* (derived from *hanu*), m. A Râkshasa or demon.

हन्त *hanta*, I. An inceptive particle, Lass. 2. ed. 69, 44. II. An interjection. 1. Of grief, pity, Alas! Mâlat. 24, 6; Utt. Râmach. 13, 17. 2. Of pleasure, Vikr. 10, 9; Utt. Râmach. 37, 5; joy, ib. 39, 15. 3. Of hurry, Çṛiṅgârat. 14. 4. Of surprise, Utt. Râmach. 142, 10.

हन्तकार *hanta-kâra*, m. Rice to be given to a guest.

हन्तु *han+tu*, m. 1. Death. 2. A bull.

हन्तृ *han+tṛi*, m. 1. A murderer, Man. 5, 34. 2. A thief, a robber. 3. One who injures, Hit. i. d. 76, M.M. (*kârya-*, another's interest).—Comp. *Dharma-*, f. *trî*, one who overturns the law, MBh. 1, 2440. *Vighna-*, m. a destroyer of obstacles, Châṇ. 97 in Berl. Monatsb. 1864, 413.

हम् *ham*, An interjection of wrath.

हम्भा *hambhâ* (an imitative sound), f. The lowing of kine, Râm. 1, 54, 18; 55, 2.

† **हम्म्** *HAMM*, i. 1, Par. To go.

† **हय्** *HAY*, i. 1, Par. 1. To go. 2. To worship. 3. To sound. 4. To be weary.

हय *haya*, i.e. *hi+a*, I. m. 1. A horse, Vikr. d. 4. 2. A man of a particular class. 3. Indra. II. f. *yî*, A mare.—Comp. *Hari-*, m. 1. Indra, Johns. Sel. 19, 88. 2. the sun. 3. Skanda, the god of war. 4. Gaṇeça.

हयंकष *hayaṁkasha*, i.e. *haya+m-kash + a*, m. 1. A charioteer. 2. Indra's charioteer.

हयन *hayana*, i.e. *hi+ana*, I. m. A year. II. n. A covered carriage.

हर *hara*, i.e. *hṛi+a*, I. adj. Taking, Pañch. i. d. 278; seizing, carrying, Kir. 5, 50; depriving of (*vibhrama-*, surpassing the beauty), Bhartṛ. 1, 5. **II.** m. **1.** Çiva, Vikr. d. 48. **2.** Agni. **3.** An ass (cf. *khara*).—Comp. *Aṁça-*, m. a co-heir, Yâjń. 2, 132; 133. *Mûla-*, adj. uprooting (viz. happiness), Man. 8, 353. *Riktha-*, m. an heir, ib. 9, 185. *Sarva-pâpa-*, adj. removing, or the remover of, all sin. *Smara-*, m. Çiva, Kâvya. Prak. 103, 14.

हरक *haraka*, i.e. *hṛi* + *aka*, m. **1.** A taker. **2.** A rogue. **3.** A person of reflection. **4.** Çiva.

हरण *haraṇa*, i.e. *hṛi* + *ana*, **I.** m. The hand. **II.** n. **1.** Taking, seizing, Pańch. iv. d. 28; carrying away, Pańch. ii. d. 111; 112; removing, Hit. ii. d. 155; stealing, Man. 8, 323. **2.** Withholding, Hit. iii. d. 90. **3.** Annulling, disregarding, Râjat. 5, 180. **4.** The arm. **5.** Accepting. **6.** A special gift, as a nuptial present. **7.** Semen virile. **8.** Gold. **9.** Boiling water.—Comp. *Kâla-*, n. delaying, Utt. Râmach. 125, 4. *Go-*, n. stealing cattle, Pańch. i. d. 281. *Strî-*, n. carrying off a woman, ravishment.

हरि *hari* (curtailed *harit*), **I.** adj. **1.** Green. **2.** Tawny. **3.** Yellow, Indr. 1, 7; Arj. 4, 12. **II.** m. **1.** Green, tawny, yellow, the colour. **2.** Vishṇu or Kṛishṇa, Hit. pr. d. 28, M.M.; Pańch. pr. d. 1. **3.** Indra, Çâk. d. 156. **4.** Çiva. **5.** Yama. **6.** The sun, Mâlat. 149, 1. **7.** The moon. **8.** A ray of light. **9.** Fire. **10.** Wind. **11.** A horse (of Indra; cf. the ved. use of *harit*, and Çâk. 6, 5); Arj. 4, 32. **12.** A lion, Vikr. d. 16. **13.** A parrot. **14.** The Indian cuckoo. **15.** A peacock. **16.** A goose. **17.** An ape, Utt. Râmach. 84, 9. **18.** A frog. **19.** A snake. **20.** One of the *varshas*, or divisions, into which the continent is divided.—Comp. *Nara-*, and *Nṛi-*, m. Vishṇu, in his fourth avatâra, as a lion-headed man, Bhâg. P. 5, 18, 7; 7, 8, 27. —Cf. A.S. growan; O.H.G. grôen, grôni; A.S. groen, grene; also geal, gealla; Lat. gilvus; χολή, and probably χλόα; cf. *harit*.

हरिक *hari* + *ka*, m. A horse of a yellowish-blue tint.

हरिण (akin to *harit*, cf. *hari*), **I.** adj., f. *ṇî*, Yellowish-white, MBh. 13, 5893; Râjat. 5, 482. **II.** m. **1.** Yellowish-white (the colour). **2.** White. **3.** A deer, an antelope, Pańch. 140, 23. **4.** A goose. **5.** Vishṇu, Çiva. **6.** A minor division of the world. **III.** f. *ṇî*. **1.** A doe, Megh. 80; 102. **2.** Yellow jasmine. **3.** A beautiful woman. **4.** A golden image, Râjat. 5, 15.

हरिणक *hariṇa* + *ka*, m. A deer, Çâk. d. 10; Utt. Râmach. 67, 5.

हरिणाय *HARIṆÂYA*, a denomin. derived from *hariṇa*, with *ya*, Âtm. To become a deer, Çṛiṅgârat. 13.

हरित् *harit* (for original *harant*, cf. *hiraṇa*), **I.** adj. Green. **II.** m. **1.** Green, the colour. **2.** A horse of the sun (properly, his rays), Chr. 287, 8 = Rigv. i. 50, 8. **3.** A lion. **4.** The sun, Çâk. 6, 5. **5.** Vishṇu. **6.** Kidney bean. **III.** m. and n. Grass. **IV.** f. **1.** A quarter, or point of the compass, Çiç, 9, 28. **2.** Turmeric. — Cf. χάριτες; Goth. gulth; A.S. gold (see *hari*, Yellow, and *hiraṇa*); akin is also Goth. glitmunjan, To shine; cf. also χόρτος, Goth. gras; A.S. graes.

हरित *harita*, **I.** adj., f. *tâ*, or *iṇî* (cf. *hariṇa*), **1.** Green, Megh. 21; Hit. i. d. 178, M.M. (in *haritî-kṛita*, adj. Made green). **2.** Dark blue, Kir. 5, 38. **3.** Grassy. **II.** m. **1.** Green, the colour. **2.** A lion. **III.** f. *tâ*. **1.** Bent grass. **2.** Turmeric. **3.** A brown grape.

हरिताल *haritâla*, i.e. *harita* + *âla*, **I.** n. Yellow orpiment. **II.** f. *lî*. **1.**

Bent grass. 2. A line in the sky. 3. A sort of creeper.

हरितालक *haritâla+ka*, I. m. The green pigeon. II. f. *likâ*. 1. A sort of grass. 2. The fourth lunar day of the month Bhadra. III. n. Theatrical decoration of the person.

हरिदश्व *haridaçva*, i.e. *harit-açva*, m. The sun, Kir. 2, 46.

हरिद्रा *haridrâ*, f. Turmeric, Sch. ad Vikr. d. 53; MBh. 3, 12880; Râjat. 5, 381.

हरिन्मणि *harinmaṇi*, i.e. *harit-maṇi*, m. An emerald, Kir. 6, 23; 14, 41.

हरिभुज् *hari-bhuj*, m. A snake (properly, eating frogs).

हरिमन् *hariman*, m. I. i.e. *hari+iman*, Paleness, Chr. 289, 11=Rigv. i. 50, 11. II. i.e. *hṛi+iman*, Time.

हरिय *hariya* (derived from *hari*), m. A horse of yellow colour.

हरिले *harile*, A term of calling a female slave (in theatrical language).

हरिवन्त् *hari+vant*, m. Indra.

हरिश्चन्द्र *hari-çchand + ra* (see *chand*), m. The name of a king.

हरिहेतिहूति *hari-heti-hûti* (*hari-heti*, The weapon of Vishṇu, i. e. *chakra*, the discus, and *hûti=vâha*), m.=*chakra-vâka*, A kind of duck, Çiç. 9, 15.

हरीतक *harîtaka* (derived from *harit*), m., f. *kî*, Yellow or chebulic myrobalan, Terminalia Chebula, Lass. 2. ed. 51, 33 (*ka*).

हरेणु *hareṇu*, I. m. Peas, pulse. II. f. 1. A sort of drug and perfume. 2. A reputable woman.

हर्तृ *hartṛi*, i. e. *hṛi+tṛi*, m., f. *trî*, and n. 1. One who takes, seizes, a robber, Man. 8, 342. 2. One who brings, Mâlat. 150, 10.—Comp. *Bhaya-*, m. a remover of fear. *Çalya-*, m. a weeder, Râm. 5, 28, 6.

हर्मन् *harman*, n. Yawning.

हर्मित *harmita*, adj. 1. Thrown. 2. Burned (cf. *gharma*). 3. Yawned (cf. the last).

हर्म्य *harmya*, n. A palace, Vikr. d. 56; a mansion, a house, Pańch. ii. d. 63.—Comp. *Maṇi-*, n. a pavilion of gems, Vikr. 38, 11.

हर्य् *HARY*, i. 1, Par. 1. To take, ved., cf. *hṛi*. 2. † To go. 3. † To desire. 4. † To be weary.—Cf. χαίρω, γέλως, γελάω; Goth. gailjan, gôljan; A.S. gal, gagol; see *hṛi*, and cf. *hṛish*.

हर्यत *haryata*, m. A horse.

हर्यश्व *haryaçva*, i.e. *hari-açva*, m. Indra.

हर्ष *harsha*, i.e. *hṛish+a*, I. adj., f. *shâ*, Delighted, happy, Mâlav. 60, 5. II. m. Joy, Daçak. in Chr. 183, 12; exultation, Hit. i. d. 32, M.M.; happiness, Pańch. iii. d. 188.—Comp. *Upâtta-*, i.e. *upa-â-datta-* (vb. *dâ*), adj. joyful, Ṛit. 6, 21. *Danta-*, m. 1. a morbid affection of the teeth, Suçr. 1, 305, 3. 2. chattering of the teeth. *Romaharsha*, i.e. *roman-*, m. horripilation. *Sa-harsha+m*, adv. cheerfully, Vikr. 6, 1. *Sanna-* (vb. *sad*), adj. destitute of joy.

हर्षक *harshaka*, i.e. *hṛish+aka*, I. adj. Delighting. II. m. The name of a mountain.

हर्षण *harshaṇa*, i.e. *hṛish+ana*, I. adj. Delighting. II. m. 1. A cause of pleasure. 2. A morbid affection of the eyes. III. n. Rejoicing.—Comp.

Romaharshaṇa, i. e. *roman-,* I. adj. causing the hair to stand erect, terrible, Râm. 1, 30, 17. II. n. horripilation, caused by pleasure. *Lomaharshaṇa,* i.e. *loman-,* I. adj. causing horripilation or delight, Chr. 39, 2; Utt. Râmach. 42, 18. II. n. horripilation. *A-loman-,* adj. causing displeasure, Râm. 3, 51, 31.

हर्षयित्नु *harshayitnu,* i. e. *hṛish,* Caus., *+tnu,* I. adj. Delighting. II. m. A child. III. (m. ?), Gold.

हर्षुल *harshula,* i. e. *hṛish+ula,* I. adj. Delighted, Râjat. 5, 473. II. m. **1.** A lover. **2.** A deer.

† **हल्** *HAL,* i. 1, Par. To plough.

हल *hala,* I. m. A plough, Gît. 1, 12. II. f. *lâ.* **1.** The earth. **2.** Vinous liquor. **3.** Water. See *halâ,* s.v.

हलभृत् *hala-bhṛi+t,* I. adj. Having a plough. II. m. Balarâma, Megh. 60.

हलहलाशब्द *halahalâ-çabda* (*halahalâ,* imitative sound), m. **1.** Shout, Râm. 2, 60, 68, Seramp; 2, 13, 29 Gorr. **2.** Tumult, noise, Chr. 41, 1.

हला *halâ,* a vocative particle, addressed to a female friend (in theatrical language), Çâk. 9, 7 (Prâkṛ.); cf. *hala.*

हलाह *halâha,* m. A horse of mixed colour.

हलाहल *halâhala,* m. and n. A sort of poison, Pañch. 105, 6. Cf. *hâlahala.*

हलि *hali,* m. (?), **1.** A furrow. **2.** Agriculture.

हलिन् *halin,* i.e. *hala+in,* m. **1.** A ploughman. **2.** Balarâma.

हलीमक *halîmaka,* i. e. *harîman+ka,* with *l* for *r,* and *i* lengthened, n. A sort of jaundice.

हल्य *halya,* i. e. *hala+ya,* I. adj. Ploughed. II. f. *yâ,* A multitude of ploughs.

हल्लीष *hallîsha,* and **हल्लीस** *hallîsa,* n. **1.** A dance performed by women in a circle. **2.** A minor dramatic entertainment.

हव *hava,* m., I. *hu+a,* m. Sacrifice, oblation. II. *hve* (q. cf.), *+a,* **1.** Calling, Chr. 288, 10=Rigv. i. 48, 10; 292, 2=Rigv. i. 86, 2. **2.** Challenging. **3.** Order.

हवन *havana,* i. e. *hu+ana,* I. n. Sacrifice. II. f. *nî,* A hole in the ground for receiving the sacrificial fire.

हवस् *havas,* i.e. *hve+as,* n. Praise, Chr. 291, 12=Rigv. i. 64, 12.

हवित्री *havitrî,* i.e. *hu+tra,* f. A hole in the ground for keeping the sacrificial fire.

हविर्भुज् *havirbhuj,* i.e. *havis-bhuj,* m. **1.** Fire, Çiç. 1, 2. **2.** The name of the Manes of the Kshatriyas, Man. 3, 197.

हविष्मन्त् *havishmant,* i.e. *havis+mant,* adj. With oblations, Lass. 98, 6 =Rigv. v. 9, 1.

हविष्य *havishya,* i.e. *havis+ya,* n. **1.** Clarified butter. **2.** The same with rice. **3.** An oblation, Man. 3, 256. **4.** Wild grains, Man. 11, 77; 106.

हविष्यन्तीय *havishyantîya,* The name of a holy text, Man. 11, 250.

हविष्यभुज् *havishya-bhuj,* m. Fire.

हविस् *havis,* i. e. *hu+is,* n. **1.** Clarified butter, Bhag. 4, 24. **2.** An oblation, sacrifice, Lass. 100, 1=Rigv. vii. 15, 1; Çâk. d. 1.

हव्यवाह *havya-vâha*, **हव्यवाहन** *havya-vâhana*, **हव्याश** *havyâça*, i. e. *havya-aç+a*, and **हव्याशन** *havyâça-na*, i.e. *havya-açana*, m. Fire, Draup. 2, 10 (*vâha*); Râm. 3, 51, 29 (*vâhana*); Râjat. 5, 416 (*âça*).

हस् *HAS*, i. 1, Par. **1.** To laugh, Daçak. in Chr. 185, 24; to smile, Lass. 2. ed. 53, 48. **2.** To laugh at (with acc.), Çiç. 1, 71. *hasita*, **1.** Smiling. **2.** Blown (as a flower). n. **1.** Laughter, jesting, Kir. 13, 47. **2.** Smiling, Böhtl. Ind. Spr. 396. **3.** The bow of Kâma, the god of love. *hâsya*, Laughable, ridiculous, Pańch. i. d. 356. n. **1.** Laughter, mirth. **2.** Amusement, Man. 9, 227. **3.** Jest, Pańch. 209, 16; Râm. 2, 69, 5. **4.** Ridicule, Hit. pr. d. 7, M.M. Frequent. *jâhas*, *jâhasya*, To smile very much, MBh. 3, 14650. Caus. *hâsaya*, To cause to laugh, Kumâras. 7, 95.—With **व्यति** *vi-ati*, Par. To laugh at each other.—With **अप** *apa*, To laugh at, Râm. 2, 35, 21. Caus. To ridicule, 1, 34, 17.—With **अव** *ava*, **1.** To laugh, Pańch. 191, 3; to smile, Lass. 2. ed. 55, 74. **2.** To laugh at, ridicule, MBh. 3, 11181. *avahâsya*, Ridiculous, Râm. 4, 14, 31.—With **उप** *upa*, To mock, Mṛichchh. 49, 10.—With **प्र** *pra*, **1.** To laugh, Pańch. 216, 10; Râm. 1, 2, 23. **2.** To mock, Nal. 12, 117. *prahasita*, Laughing, cheerful, Pańch. 36, 2. n. Laughter, mirth. Caus. *prahâsita*, Caused to laugh, Daçak. in Chr. 196, 24.—With **संप्र** *sam-pra*, To laugh, MBh. 1, 3431.—With **वि** *vi*, **1.** To laugh, Vikr. 12, 20; Lass. 73, 9; Pańch. 74, 15 (*vihasyamâna*, perhaps corr. °*hasamâna*, but also irreg.). **2.** To smile, Çâk. 17, 8. **3.** To laugh at, MBh. 1, 4762. *vihasita*, n. A gentle laugh.—With **संवि** *sam-vi*, To laugh, Mṛichchh. 85, 14.—Cf. probably Lat. histrio; perhaps τωθεία, τωθάζω, frequentative.

हस *has+a*, m. **1.** Laughter. **2.** Derision, Padmap. 16, 82.

हसन *has+ana*, I. n. Laughter. II. f. *nî*, A fire-pan.

हसन्तिका *hasantikâ*, i.e. *hasanti+ka*, f. A fire-pan.

हसन्ती *hasanti* (ptcple. pres. f. of *has*), f. A fire-pan.

हस्त *hasta*, I. m. **1.** The hand, Vikr. 27, 3. **2.** An elephant's trunk, Megh. 14; Hiḍ. 3, 9. **3.** A multitude, after words signifying 'hair.' **4.** A cubit, or measure extending from the elbow to the little finger, Böhtl. Ind. Spr. 3348. II. m., f. *tâ*, The thirteenth lunar asterism. III. n. A bellows.—**Comp.** *A-*, adj. without hands, Man. 5, 29. *Agra-*, m. 1. the tip of the extended hand, Râm. 2, 23, 4. 2. the tip of an elephant's trunk, Vikr. d. 107. *Apa-*, n. 1. taking away. 2. stealing. *Kapota-*, m. a mode of joining the hands, as token of reverence, Çâk. 78, 9. *Kṛita-*, adj. 1. skilled in archery, MBh. 4, 1843. 2. dexterous, clever. *Keça-*, m. a tuft of hair, MBh. 3, 1822. *Khaḍga-*, adj. bearing a sword, Lass. 26, 17. *Gala-*, m. throttling, Kathâs. 4, 68. *Jâla-*, adj. with a net or nets in (his or their) hands, Pańch. 104, 14; 246, 14. *Daṇḍa-*, I. adj. bearing a staff, MBh. 6, 4959. II. m. 1. a staff-bearer. 2. a door-keeper. *Dhanus-vyagra-*, adj., f. *tâ*, holding a bow in one's hand, Vikr. 77, 4. *Pâça-*, adj. bearing a noose in his hand, Râm. 3, 54, 9. *Mukta-* (vb. *much*), adj. liberal,

Hit. iii. d. 121. *A-mukta-*, adj., f. *tâ*, economical, Man. 5, 150. *Laghu-*, I. adj. ready, or light-handed. II. m. a good archer. *Vi-*, adj. confounded, bewildered, Ragh. 5, 49. *Çûla-*, adj. armed with a lance, Sund. 1, 14. *Çûla-mudgara-*, adj. armed with clubs and lances, Sund. 2, 3. *Sthûla-*, m. the fore part of an elephant's trunk, Megh. 14. *Srasta-* (vb. *sraṁs*), adj. relaxing one's hold. *Sva-*, m. own hand, handwriting, letter, Vikr. d. 38 (*dayitâ-sneha-*, a love-letter of one's mistress).—Cf. Goth. handu; A.S. hand; Lat. pre-hendere; χανδάνω.

हस्तवन्त् *hasta+vant*, adj. **1.** Endowed with hands, Böhtl. Ind. Spr. 1106. **2.** Dexterous, Daçak. in Chr. 197, 18.

हस्तस्थ *hasta-stha*, adj. Being in one's hand, Hit. ii. d. 170.

हस्तिन् *hasta+in*, I. m. An elephant, Hit. i. d. 17, M.M. II. f. *nî*. **1.** A female elephant. **2.** A class of women. **3.** A drug and perfume.—**Comp.** *Gandha-*, m. a kind of elephant (in rut?), Râm. 5, 73, 26. *Jala-*, m. a large aquatic animal (the crocodile?), Pańch. 51, 9.

हस्तिनापुर *hastinâpura*, **हस्तिनीपुर** *hastinipura* (from *hastin*, with *pura*), n. Ancient Delhi, Hit. 81, 11 (*nâ*).

हस्तिप *hastipa*, and **हस्तिपक** *hastipaka*, i.e. *hastin-pa*, and *-pa+ka*, m. **1.** An elephant-driver, Hit. ii. d. 83 (*paka*). **2.** An elephant-keeper.

हस्त्य *hastya*, i.e. *hasta+ya*, adj. **1.** Given with the hand. **2.** Done with the hand.—**Comp.** *Su-*, adj. clever, skilful, Chr. 290, 1=Rigv. i. 64, 1.

हस्र *has+ra*, m. A fool.

हहा *hahâ*, m. A Gandharva, MBh. 13, 7639.

1. **हा** *HÂ*, ii. 3, *jihâ*, Âtm. **1.** To give way (ved.). **2.** To go, Kir. 13, 23.—With **उद्** *ud*, **1.** To rise, Daçak. in Chr. 183, 13 (Râm. 2, 71, 12, Schl. read *urjihân°*, with Gorr. 2, 73, 10). **2.** To raise, Bhaṭṭ. 3, 47. **3.** To leave, Mâlat. 163, 11.—With **उप** *upa*, To descend, Çiç. 1, 37.—With **सम्** *sam*, To obtain, Nalod. 1, 54.—Cf. χήμη, χάσις, χαίνω, χαλάω; Lat. in-hiare, hiscere; O.H.G. gîên, ginên, geinôn; A.S. ginan, cinan, geonan, gynian, ganian.

2. **हा** *HÂ* (akin to the last), ii. 3, *jahâ*, Par. **1.** To abandon, to leave, MBh. 3, 12339; to forsake, Man. 6, 42. **2.** To avoid, Pańch. iii. d. 71. **3.** To remove, MBh. 1, 2301. **4.** To resign, Bhag. 2, 50. **5.** To let fall, Hit. ii. d. 120. **6.** To lose, Râm. 2, 63, 50. Pass. *hîya*, **1.** To be forsaken, Man. 6, 42. **2.** To be lost, Pańch. ii. d. 6. **3.** To be deprived, Man. 3, 17; 5, 161. **4.** To be omitted, MBh. 1, 6424. **5.** To become weary or weak, MBh. 1, 6291. **6.** To be lowered, Hit. pr. 42. **7.** To fail (in a lawsuit), Man. 8, 56; cf. Pańch. 166, 18. Ptcple. of the pf. pass. *hîna*. **1.** Deprived, Man. 8, 232; Râm. 3, 51, 40. **2.** Free from. **3.** Wasted, decayed, feeble, Pańch. iii. d. 133. **4.** Deficient, defective. **5.** Lower, less, Man. 2, 194. **6.** Blameable, vile, bad, low, Man. 3, 107. m. An objectionable witness. **Comp.** *Pâda-hînât*, abl., adv. on a sudden, Suçr. 2, 145, 12. *Phala-*, adj. yielding no profit, Pańch. i. d. 168. Absol. *hitvâ*, Neglecting, without regarding, Hit. iv. d. 17. Desider. *jihâsa*, To wish to leave, Daçak. in Chr. 188, 8. Caus. *hâpaya*, **1.** To cause to want, to refuse, MBh. 3, 1463. **2.** To omit, Man. 3, 71.—With **अप** *apa*, To leave, Vikr. 33, 13; Nal. 24, 11. Absol. *apahâya*, Besides,

Ragh. 6, 19 (whom did Lakshmî worship besides him?).—With अव *ava*, pass. To be left, MBh. 3, 11558.—With व्यव *vi-ava*, To abandon, MBh. 3, 13661.—With अपा *apa-â*, **1.** To leave, MBh. 1, 4946. **2.** To pass by, MBh. 3, 2963 (=Nal. 24, 13, Bopp., *apahâya*, against the metre). Absol. *apâhâya*, Except (except immortality, speak what you wish for), MBh. 3, 11982 (=Arj. 3, 47, Bopp., *apahâya*, against the metre). —With नि *ni*, *nihina*, Low, vile.—With परि *pari*, pass. **1.** To decrease, MBh. 3, 12858; with *aṅgais*, Çâk. 34, 12 (Prâkṛ. Thy limbs become thinner). **2.** To be wanting, Râm. 1, 2, 16 (act so that nothing may be wanting); to be unacquainted with, Mâlat. 69, 18. **3.** To be deprived, Man. 9, 254. **4.** To be lost, Hit. ii. d. 68. **5.** To be avoided, Hit. ii. d. 54. **6.** To be omitted, to be sinned, MBh. 2, 2460 (with the termination of the Par.). *parihîṇa*, **1.** Deprived, Bhâshâp. 14. **2.** Waned, decayed. Caus. To abandon, Man. 8, 206.—With प्र *pra*, **1.** To leave, MBh. 1, 4620. **2.** Pass. To be lost, to perish, Man. 4, 41; to be relinquished, Kir. 14, 13.—With विप्र *vi-pra*, *viprahîṇa*, **1.** Abandoned, Chr. 8, 27 (read *ṇâ*). **2.** Deprived, MBh. 1, 8142.—With वि *vi*, To abandon, Lass. 2. ed. 77, 65; to leave, Çâk. d. 67; Vikr. d. 41. *vihîna*, **1.** Deprived, void of, without, Bhartṛ. 2, 17; Râm. 2, 52, 37; Pańch. iii. d. 24. **2.** Free from, Ragh. 18, 13. **Comp.** *Pṛichchhâ-*, adj. one who has not asked, Pańch. i. d. 438. Caus. *vihâpita*, **1.** Given. **2.** Extorted. n. Gift.—With प्रवि *pra-vi*, To neglect, to disdain, Pańch. iv. d. 36.—Cf. χῆρος, χωρίς, χῆτος, χατέω; Goth. gaidv, giban; A.S. gifan (=*hâpaya*, cf. *vihâpita*), gafol, gaefel, gif; Engl. if; Lat. habere.

3. हा *hâ*, an interj. **1.** Of pain, weariness, grief, Ah! Mâlat. 153, 21; Râm. 3, 50, 22; 55, 35; sorrow, Woe! Vikr. 61, 7. **2.** Of joy. **3.** Of reproach, Râm. 3, 51, 25. **4.** Of wrath, Mâlat. 82, 5. Repeated, हाहा *hâ-hâ*, interjection of, **1.** Surprise. **2.** Grief, Pańch. 35, 10.

हाटक *hâṭaka*, I. adj. Golden, Râm. 3, 49, 8. II. n. Gold, Pańch. 184, 16.

हाटकमय *hâṭaka+maya*, adj., f. *yî*, Made of gold.

हात्र *hâ+tra* (vb. ?), n. Wages.

हान *hâna*, i.e. 2. *hâ+ana*, n. **1.** Relinquishing. **2.** Prowess.

हानि 2. *hâ+ni*, f. **1.** Abandonment, Bhag. 2, 65. **2.** Privation, absence, Pańch. v. d. 83. **3.** Diminution, neglecting, Utt. Râmach. 86, 10. **4.** Loss, Hit. i. d. 157, M.M. **5.** Want, Râjat. 5, 179.—Comp. *Tejas-*, f. loss of splendour and of power, Pańch. i. d. 194. *Vîrya-*, f. 1. loss of vigour or courage. 2. impotence. *Svatva-*, f. forfeiture of proprietary right.

हानिकर *hânikara*, i.e. *hâni-kṛi+a*, adj. Prejudicial, Pańch. i. d. 99.

हान्त्र *hântra* (हान्द्र *hândra*), i.e. probably *han+tra*, n. Dying, death.

हायन *hâyana*, i.e. *hayana+a*, I. m. and n. A year, Man. 2, 154. II. m. **1.** A flame. **2.** A sort of rice.—Comp. *Eka-*, adj. one year old, Man. 11, 136. *Tri-hâyaṇa*, adj., f. *ṇî*, three years old, MBh. 3, 14854. *Shashṭi-*, I. adj. sixty years old, Hiḍ. 4, 23. II. m. an elephant.

हार् *HÂR*, a denomin. derived from the next, Par. To behave or be like a string of pearls, Lass. 67, 16.

हार *hâra*, i.e. partly *hṛi+a*, I. adj. Who or what takes. II. m. 1. Taking. 2. A porter. 3. A string of pearls, Pańch. 52, 22; 53, 1. 4. War, battle. —Comp. *Jala-*, m., f. *rî*, one who carries water, Hariv. 3400. *Preta-*, i.e. *pra -ita-*, m. one who carries a corpse, a near kinsman, Man. 5, 65. *Sarva-sva-*, m. seizure or confiscation of all one's property, Man. 9, 242; 8, 399.

हारक *hâraka*, i.e. *hṛi+aka*, I. adj. Taking, drawing upon one's self, Man. 8, 308. II. m. 1. A thief, a plunderer, Râjat. 5, 451. 2. A rogue. 3. i.e. *hâra+ka*, A string of pearls, Pańch. 176, 3.—Comp. *Maṇḍa-*, m. a distiller.

हारहूर *hârahûra*, I. m. Vinous liquor. II. f. *râ*, A grape.

हारि *hâri*, I. i.e. *hṛi+i*, adj. Handsome. II. f. 1. A caravan. 2. Defeat in war or gambling. III. f. *rî*, A pearl.

हारिकण्ठ *hârikaṇṭha*, cf. *hârî*, s.v. *hâri*, and *kaṇṭha*, I. adj. Wearing a necklace. II. m. The Indian cuckoo.

हारिण *hâriṇa*, i.e. *hariṇa+a*, adj. Relating to deer, Man. 3, 268 (venison).

हारिणिक *hâriṇika*, i.e. *hariṇa+ika*, m. A hunter.

हारित *hârita*, i.e. *harit+a*, m. 1. Green, the colour. 2. The green pigeon, Lass. 2. ed. 52, 34.

हारिद्र *hâridra*, i.e. *haridrâ + a*, I. adj. 1. Stained with turmeric. 2. Yellow. II. m. 1. Yellow, the colour. 2. The Kadamba tree.

हारिद्रव *hâridrava*, m. A tree, Curcuma zanthorizon, Chr. 289, 12= Rigv. i. 50, 12.

हारिन् *hârin*, i.e. *hṛi+in*, adj., f. *iṇî*, 1. Taking, Man. 8, 308. 2. Robbing, Pańch. i. d. 31. 3. Agitating (with gen.), Man. 12, 28. 4. Captivating, Çâk. d. 5; charming, Pańch. i. d. 303; Daçak. in Chr. 196, 19; delighting, Böhtl. Ind. Spr. 3288. 5. Pleasant, Kathâs. 22, 103. 6. Bringing, Çâk. 61, 9.—Comp. *Riktha-*, I. adj. taking or inheriting property. II. m. 1. an heir. 2. a maternal uncle. *Roga-*, m. a physician. *Strî-*, m. one who carries off a woman.

हारीत *hârîta* (cf. *hârita*), m. 1. The green pigeon, Ragh. 4, 46. 2. A Muni, author of a law book. 3. A rogue.

हारीतक *hârîta+ka*, m. The green pigeon (ÇKD.), Pańch. 158, 21.

हार्द *hârda*, i.e. *hṛid + a*, n. 1. Affection, love, Vikr. d. 148; kindness. 2. Will, Bhâg. P. 1, 7, 55.—Comp. *Sa-*, adj. affectionate, tender, Çiç. 9, 69.

हाल *hâla*, I. i.e. *hala+a*, m. 1. A plough. 2. Balarâma, Çâlivâhana. II. f. *lâ*, Spirituous liquor, Pańch. i. d. 62. III. f. *lî*, A wife's younger sister.

हालहल, हालहाल, हालाहल, *hâlâhâla*, n. A sort of poison, Pańch. i. d. 62 (*hâlâhala*, cf. Böhtl. Ind. Spr. 1261). Cf. *halâhala*.

हालिक *hâlika*, i.e. *hala+ika*, adj. Belonging or relating to a plough, as a cultivator, a peasant, Pańch. 225, 22; cattle.

हालिनी *hâlinî*, f. A sort of lizard.

हालु *hâlu*, m. A tooth.

हाव *hâva*, i.e. *hve+a*, m. 1. Calling.

2. Coquetry, dalliance, Indr. 2, 32; cf. Bharata, ap. Sch. ad Nalod. 2, 55.

हास *hâsa*, i.e. *has + a*, m. **1.** Laughing, Hit. ii. d. 56. **2.** Joy, Nalod. 1, 31. **3.** Derision, Râm. 1, 3, 19. — **Comp.** *Antar-*, m. an inward or suppressed laugh, Pańch. 187, 1. *Mahâ-*, m. a horse-laugh. *Pushpa-*, m. 1. a flower-garden (?), Hariv. 12395. 2. a name of Vishṇu. 3. a proper name. *Mam̃sa-*, f. *sâ*, skin. *Sa-*, adj. smiling, Lass. 66, 5; °*sam*, adv. scornfully, Utt. Râmach. 136, 1.

हासक *hâsaka*, i. e. *has*, Caus., + *aka*, **I.** m. A buffoon. **II.** f. *sikâ*, Laughter.

हासिन् *hâsin*, i. e. *has + in*, and *hâsa + in*, adj., f. *nî*, Laughing, smiling, Râjat. 5, 449; Râm. 3, 52, 31 (*châru-*, sweetly).

हास्त *hâsta*, i. e. *hasta + a*, adj. Formed by the hands (with *mukula = ańjali*, humble salutation), Nalod. 1, 38.

हास्तिक *hâstika*, i.e. *hastin + ka*, **I.** m. A rider on an elephant. **II.** n. A herd of elephants.

हास्तिन *hâstina*, i. e. *hastin + a*, **I.** adj. As big as an elephant. **II.** n. Hastinâpura.

हास्तिनपुर *hâstina-pura*, n. Ancient Delhi, Chr. 5, 23. Cf. *hastinâpura*.

हास्यता *hâsya + tâ* (vb. *has*), f. Condition of being ridiculous, Pańch. ii. d. 29; Râjat. 5, 144; Pańch. v. d. 33 (°*tâm̃ yâ*, To grow ridiculous).

हाहस् *hâhas*, and **हाहा** *hâhâ*, m. A Gandharva (cf. *hahâ*).

हाहाकार *hâ-hâ-kâra*, m. **1.** Lamentation. **2.** The uproar of battle, Lass. 2. ed. 78, 71.

1. **हि** *HI*, ii. 5, *hinu*, Par. **1.** To go. **2.** To send. **3.** To discharge, as an arrow from a bow, to throw, Bhaṭṭ. 14, 36. — With **प्र** *pra*, *hiṇu*, **1.** To send, Pańch. 161, 19; Daçak. in Chr. 184, 19. **2.** To discharge, to throw, Chr. 40, 12 (anomal. °*hiṇvam*). *prahita*, **1.** Dispatched, Hit. 92, 20. **2.** Stretched out, extended. — With **अनुप्र** *anu-pra*, *anuprahita*, Dispatched after (something), Utt. Râmach. 39, 13.

2. **हि** *hi*, **I.** A particle, **1.** Because, Utt. Râmach. 167, 8; for, Chr. 4, 16; on account of; with preceding *tathâ*, Namely, to wit, Çâk. d. 31; Pańch. 221, 6. **2.** Assuredly (assertion), Matsyop. 22; Chr. 288, 11 = Rigv. i. 48, 11. **3.** Indeed (interrogation), Hiḍ. 3, 17. **4.** But, Chr. 10, 2; Daçak. in Chr. 180, 20. **II.** An interjection, **1.** Of grief, Ah! alas! **2.** Of envy and hurry.

हिंस् *HIM̃S* (an anomal. desider. of *han*), i. 1, and ii. 7, *hinas*, *him̃s*, Par. **1.** To strike, Bhaṭṭ. 17, 13. **2.** To hurt, Man. 7, 73. **3.** To kill, Man. 5, 42. **4.** To destroy, Vikr. d. 16; Pańch. i. d. 342. Ptcple. of the pf. pass. *him̃sita*, n. Injury, Pańch. v. d. 70. Caus., or i. 10, Par. To kill, MBh. 3, 13030. — With **आ** *â*, To kill, Man. 7, 20, v.r. — With **उप** *upa*, **1.** To hurt, Man. 7, 73. **2.** To injure, Man. 11, 26. — With **प्रति** *prati*, *pratihim̃sita*, n. Requital of an injury, Pańch. v. d. 70. — With **वि** *vi*, **1.** To injure, Râm. 2, 56, 39, Scramp. **2.** To damage (grain), Man. 8, 238.

हिंसक *him̃s + aka*, **I.** adj. **1.** Mischievous, injurious, noxious, Pańch. iii. d. 106. **2.** One who has injured, Pańch. i. d. 342. **II.** m. **1.** A beast of prey. **2.** An enemy. **3.** A Brâhmaṇa skilled in the Atharva-Veda (cf. *hiṁsâ*).—**Comp.** *A-*, adj. innoxious, harmless, Man. 5, 45.

हिंसन *hiṁs + ana*, n. **1.** Slaying, Man. 10, 78. **2.** Injury, ib. 2, 177.

हिंसा *hiṁs + â*, f. **1.** Injuring, Man. 8, 255; injury, mischief, Râm. 3, 51, 20. **2.** Spoiling, Man. 11, 63. **3.** Incantation; in *hiṁsâ-karman*, Employment of mystical texts for malevolent purposes. **4.** Killing, murder, Bhâg. P. 2, 6, 8; Pañch. 60, 6.—**Comp.** *A-*, f. 1. not hurt, Man. 5, 44. 2. not injuring, 6, 75. 3. not giving pain, Man. 2, 159. 4. benevolence, Hit. 43, 1, M.M.

हिंसारु *hiṁsâ + ru*, m. A tiger.

हिंसालु *hiṁsâ + lu*, adj. Mischievous.

हिंसालुक *hiṁsâlu + ka*, I. adj. Mischievous. II. m. A mischievous dog.

हिंसीर *hiṁsîra* (vb. *hiṁs*), m. **1.** A tiger. **2.** A villain.

हिंस्र *hiṁs + ra*, I. adj. **1.** One who delights in mischief, Man. 3, 164; mischievous, destroying, Man. 9, 310. **2.** Terrible. **3.** Cruel, Hit. ii. d. 174. II. m. **1.** A beast of prey, Ragh. 2, 62. **2.** Çiva. III. f. *râ*. **1.** A vein. **2.** The name of three plants.—**Comp.** *A-*, adj. not injuring (any living being), Man. 4, 246. *Hiṁsra-a-*, n. noxious and innocent, Man. 1, 29.

† **हिक्** *HIKK*, i. 1, Par. To hiccough. i. 10, Âtm., v.r. of *kishk*.

हिक्का *hikkâ*, f. Hiccough, Lass. 17, 4; Râm. 6, 28, 26.

हिङ्गु *hiṅgu*, m. Assafœtida.

हिञ्जीर *hiñjîra*, m. A rope for an elephant's feet.

हिट् *HIṬ*, see *biṭ*.

हिडिम्ब *hiḍimba*, I. m. The name of a Râkshasa, Hiḍ. 2, 1 (read *hiḍ°*). II. f. *bâ*, His sister, ib. 15 (read *hiḍ°*).

हिण्ड् *HIṆḌ*, i. 1, Âtm. **1.** To go. **2.** To disregard.—With **आ** *â*, To ramble, Çâk. 20, 5 (Prâkṛ.).—With **परि** *pari*, Daçak. 151, 6 (anomal. *pary ahiṇḍata*, which Wilson translates, 'They were deserted').

हिण्डक *hiṇḍ + aka*, see *râtrihiṇḍaka*.

हिण्डन *hiṇḍ + ana*, n. **1.** Wandering. **2.** Copulation. **3.** Writing.

हिण्डिक *hiṇḍika*, m. An astrologer.

हिण्डी *hiṇḍî*, f. Durgâ.

हिण्डीर *hiṇḍîra*, I. m. Cuttle-fish bone, Sâh. D. 287, 16. II. n. A pomegranate.

हित *hita*, I. Ptcple. pf. pass. of *dhâ* and *hi* (q. cf.). II. f. *tâ*, A causeway, a dike, Man. 9, 274.

हितकर *hita-kara*, I. adj. Kind, favourable. II. m. A benefactor.

हितकृत् *hita-kṛi + t*, adj. Useful, Pañch. i. d. 109.

हितप्रणी *hitapraṇi*, i.e. *hita-pra-ṇi*, m. A spy.

हितवन्त् *hita + vant*, adj., f. *vatî*, **1.** Friendly. **2.** Useful, Hit. iii. d. 98.

हिन्दोल *hindola*, and **हिन्दोलक** *hindola + ka*, m. A swing (cf. *dul*, *andolaya*), Çṛiṅgârat. 9.

† **हिन्दोलय** *HINDOLAYA* (a denomin. derived from *hindola*), Par. To swing.

† **हिन्व्** *HINV*, i. 1, Par. To satisfy or please (cf. *dhinv*).

हिम *hima* (i.e. lost *hyam + a*), I. adj.

Cold, Bhâg. P. 4, 25, 18. II. n. 1. Frost, snow, Pańch. 169, 14. 2. Cold, Pańch. iii. d. 165; coolness, Mâlat. 100, 4. 3. Fresh butter. 4. Tin. 5. A pearl. 6. A lotus. 7. Sandal-wood. III. m. 1. The moon. 2. The Himâlaya mountain. 3. Sandal. 4. Camphor. IV. f. *mâ*. 1. Winter (a year), Chr. 291, 14=Rigv. i. 64, 14. 2. Small cardamoms. 3. A fragrant grass, Cyperus. 4. A perfume.—Cf. Lat. hiems, hibernus (for himernus); χιών.

हिमकर *hima-kara*, I. adj. Frigorific, cold. II. m. 1. The moon, Lass. 92, 7. 2. Camphor.

हिमज *hima-ja*, I. adj. 1. Produced by cold. 2. Produced in the Himâlaya. II. f. *jâ*, Pârvatî.

हिमवन्त् *hima+vant*, I. adj., f. *vatî*, Cold. II. m. Himâlaya, Vikr. d. 160; Râjat. 5, 152.

हिमानी *himânî*, i. e. *hima+î*, f. Great frost, a mass of snow, Nalod. 2, 5; Kir. 4, 12.

हिमालय *himâlaya*, i.e. *hima-âlaya*, m. The Himâlaya range of mountains, Kumâras. 1, 1.

हिमिका *himikâ*, i.e. *hima+ka*, f. Hoar-frost.

हिम्य *himya*, i.e. *hima+ya*, adj. Frozen, snowy, cold.

हिरण *hiraṇa* (i.e. **haran+a*, cf. *harit*), n. 1. Gold. 2. A cowry (a small coin). 3. Semen virile.

हिरण्मय *hiraṇmaya*, probably *hiraṇa+maya*, I. adj., f. *yî*, Golden, MBh. 7, 2266; Utt. Râmach. 39, 6. II. m. Brahman. III. n. One of the divisions of the continent.

हिरण्य *hiraṇya*, probably *hiraṇa+ya*, n. 1. Gold, Pańch. iii. d. 15; Man. 2, 29 (a golden spoon). 2. Silver. 3. Wealth. 4. A cowry (a small coin). 5. Substance. 6. Imperishable matter. 7. Semen virile.—Comp. *Go-*, n. kine and gold, MBh. 2, 1833.

हिरण्यक *hiraṇya+ka*, m. A proper name, Hit. 28, 8, M.M.

हिरण्यकशिपुहन् *hiraṇya-kaçipu-han*, m. Vishṇu.

हिरण्यबाहु *hiraṇya-bâhu*, and

हिरण्यवाह *hiraṇya-vâha*, m. 1. The river Sone. 2. Çiva.

हिरण्यवन्त् *hiraṇya+vant*, adj., f. *vatî*, Abounding in gold, Chr. 295, 16=Rigv. i. 92, 16.

हिरुक् *hiruk*, indecl. 1. Without, except. 2. Amongst. 3. Near.

† **हिल्** *HIL*, i. 6, Par. To express (amorous) inclination, to dally.

हिल्लोलय *HILLOLAYA* (v.r. of *hindolaya*).

हिष्क् *HISHK*, v.r. of *kishk*.

हिहि *hihi*, an interj. of surprise.

ऽहीनक *-hîna+ka* (vb. 2. *hâ*), in *karapâdaika-*, i.e. *kara-pâda-eka-*, adj. Losing a hand and a foot, Yâjń. 2, 274.

ऽहीनत्व *-hîna+tva* (vb. 2. *hâ*), in *utsâha-çakti-*, n. Want of the power of exertion, Hit. iv. d. 36. *putra-*, n. Condition of having no son, Chân. 49 in Berl. Monatsb. 1864, 410. *buddhi-*, n. Want of understanding, Hit. ii. d. 99.

हीर *hîra* (partly for *hâra*, q. cf.), I. m. 1. Indra's thunderbolt. 2. A necklace. 3. A lion. 4. A snake. 5. Çiva. II. f. *râ*. 1. Lakshmî. 2.

An ant. **3.** A cockroach. **III.** n. A diamond.

हीलुक *hîluka*, n. Rum.

हीही *hîhî*, indecl. **1.** An interjection of laughter, Hee! hee! **2.** Of surprise, Ah!

ऌ *HU*, ii. 3, *juhu*, Par. **1.** To sacrifice, Man. 4, 206. **2.** To worship by oblations, Man. 2, 186. *huta*, **1.** Sacrificed, Bhartṛ. 2, 67. **2.** One to whom is sacrificed, Sâv. 1, 21. n. Oblation. **Comp.** *A-huta*, adj. not sacrificed (=*japa*), divine study, Man. 3, 74. Ptcple. of the fut. pass. *havya*, Fit to be offered. n. **1.** An offering to the gods, Man. 1, 94; 95. **2.** Clarified butter, Kir. 1, 22. Caus. To cause to worship, Râm. 2, 25, 25.—With **आ** *â*, *âhuta*, Worshipped by sacrifices, Lass. 100, 14 = Rigv. vii. 15, 7. *âhavanîya*, m. (viz. *agni*), The sacrificial fire, Man. 2, 231.—With **अभ्युद्** *abhi-ud*, To worship by sacrifices, Ragh. 1, 53.—With **प्र** *pra*, *prahuta*, m. (viz. *yajña*), Sacrificial food offered to spirits, Man. 3, 73. n. Offering to spirits. **Comp.** *A-prahuta*, adj. not sacrificed before, Bhâg. P. 5, 26, 18.—Cf. χέω; Goth. giutan; A.S. geotan; Lat. fundere.

ऌंकार *huṁkâra*, i.e. *hum* (an imitative sound), *-kâra*, m. **1.** Uttering a menacing sound, Râjat. 5, 345. **2.** Roaring, bellowing, Pañch. 162, 25 (of an elephant). **3.** Twang (of a bow), Çâk. d. 52.

ऌंकृत *huṁkṛita*, i. e. *hum-kṛita* (vb. *kṛi*), **I.** adj. Uttered as an incantation. **II.** n. **1.** Incantation. **2.** Roar (of the thunder), Mâlat. 151, 2.

† **ऌड्** *HUḌ*, i. 6, Par. **1.** To collect, **2.** To dive. **3.** See *hûḍ*.

ऌड *huḍa*, and **ऌडु** *huḍu*, m. A ram, MBh. 3, 640 (*ḍa* ?); Pañch. i. d. 216 (*ḍu*).—**Comp.** *Sa-huḍa*, adj., f. *ḍâ*, MBh. 3, 640, with rams (for fighting ?).

ऌडुक्क *huḍukka*, m. **1.** A gallinule. **2.** A drunken man. **3.** A kind of drum. **4.** A stick bound with iron. **5.** The bar of a door.

† **ऌण्ड्** *HUṆḌ*, i. 1, Par. **1.** To collect. **2.** To select. **3.** See *bhuṇḍ*.

ऌण्ड *huṇḍa*, m. **1.** A tiger. **2.** A ram. **3.** A village hog. **4.** An imp. **5.** A blockhead.

ऌण्डिका *huṇḍikâ*, f. Assignment, order (given for the maintenance of soldiers), Râjat. 5, 265 (cf. Troyer and *huṇḍ*).

ऌतभुज् *huta-bhuj* (vb. *hu*), m. Agni, or fire, Vikr. d. 8; Utt. Râmach. 123, 1.

ऌतवह *huta-vah* + *a* (vb. *hu*), m. Fire, Pañch. 182, 17.

ऌताश *hutâça*, i.e. *huta*-2. *aç* + *a*, m. Fire, Johns. Sel. 22, 111.

ऌताशनवन्त् *hutâçanavant*, i.e. *huta-açana* + *vant*, adj., f. *vatî*, Endowed with the sacred fire, Çâk. d. 75.

ऌम् *hum*, an interj. **1.** Of remembering, Ah! Utt. Râmach. 136, 14. **2.** Of repulse, Away! **3.** Of interrogation, Hey? **4.** Of assent, Yes. **5.** Of doubt. **6.** A mystical syllable used in incantations (cf. *huṁkâra*, *huṁkṛita*).

† **ऌर्च्** *HURCHH* (properly, *hvṛi* + *chh*; cf. *ṛi* + *chh*, s.v. *ṛi*, *gachh*, s.v. *gam*, etc.), i. 1, Par. To be crooked, to go crookedly.—Cf. Goth. vraiqs; probably Lat. quercus, ob-liquus; λοξός (old ptcple. pf. pass.).

† हुल् *HUL*, i. 1, Par. 1. To go. 2. To cover. 3. To kill.

हुलहुली *hulahulî*, f. Inarticulate sounds of pleasure made by women.

हुष्कपुर *hushka* (probably the name of a Scythian tribe), *-pura*, n., Râjat. 5, 258.

हुहु and हुहू *huhû* (probably from an anomal. frequent. of *hve*), m. A Gandharva, Indr. 2, 14 (*hu*); MBh. 13, 7639 (*hû*).

हू *hû*, an interjection of calling, of contempt, of pride, and of weeping.

हूंकार *hûm̐kâra*, i.e. *hûm-kâra*, 1. Uttering the sound *hûm*, Dev. 6, 9; as injury, Man. 11, 204. 2. Roaring, Kathâs. 4, 24.

हूंकृति *hûm̐kṛiti*, i.e. *hûm-kṛiti* (cf. the last), f. 1. Making *hûm*, sound of a sleeping person, Kathâs. 3, 64, at the end of a comp. adj. 2. Injury, Nalod. 2, 5.

† हूड् *HÛḌ*, होड् *HOḌ*, हुड् *HUḌ*, हौड् *HAUḌ*, हूड् *HRÛḌ*, हुड् *HRUḌ*, ह्रौड् *HRAUḌ*, i. 1, Par. To go.

हूति *hûti*, i.e. *hve + ti*, f. 1. Calling. 2. Challenging.—Comp. *Deva-*, f. 1. invocation of the gods, Lass. 102, 7 = Rigv. vii. 14, 1. 2. *Deva-hûti*, the name of a spell, Bhâg. P. 9, 24, 31. 3. a proper name. *Su-puru-*, adj. very much invoked, Bhâg. P. 6, 9, 30. *Pûrva-*, f. former invocation, Lass. 98, 2 = Rigv. vi. 64, 5.

हूम् *hûm*, an interj. (cf. *hum*), 1. Of doubt, Humph! ha! 2. Of interrogation, Hey? 3. Of assent, Yes. 4. Of anger, fear. 5. Of laughing, Lass. 80, 1 (Prâkṛ.). 6. Of reproach, contempt, Lass. 2. ed. 48, 47; equivalent to 'Be silent,' Tush! 7. Of aversion. 8. A mystical syllable. Cf. *hûm̐kâra*, *hûm̐kṛiti*.

हूरव *hû+rava* (*hû*, an imitative sound), m. A jackal.

हृ *HṚI* (for original *bhṛi*, which still appears in the signification of *hṛi* in the Vedas; cf. *bhṛi*. The original signification, 'to bring,' becomes, on the one side, 'to carry to,' on the other, 'to carry away'). i. 1, Par. Âtm. † ii. 3, *jihṛi*, Par. 1. To convey, Megh. 7. 2. To offer, Man. 3, 121. 3. To direct or discharge (an arrow), Chr. 37, 29. 4. To take, to fetch, Sâv. 5, 103. 5. To retain, Hit. 90, 9. 6. To seize, to carry away, Vikr. d. 38; Bhag. 2, 67 (his understanding is carried away, as a ship by the wind). 7. To cut off (the head), MBh. 3, 10184. 8. To steal, to rob, Râm. 1, 1, 51; to charm, Vikr. d. 85. 9. To acquire, Bhartṛ. 3, 97; to gain, Hit. iv. d. 103. 10. To put off, Man. 4, 74. 11. To accept, to inherit, Man. 9, 131. Ptcple. of the pf. pass. *hṛita*, Captivated, Çâk. d. 5. Ptcple. of the fut. pass. *hârya* (Lass. 98, 12, read *hvârya*). Comp. *A-hârya*, 1. not to be seized or confiscated, Man. 9, 189. 2. not to be brought back, Daçak. in Chr. 181, 8 (*sâ ched ahâryaniçchayâ*, 'if she cannot be induced to change her mind'). 3. not to be gained (by bribes), incapable of perfidy, Man. 7, 217. Desider. *jihîrsha*, To wish to rob, MBh. 1, 7480. Caus. *hâraya*, 1. To cause to take, i.e. to give, Pañch. iv. d. 47; to give away, i. d. 296; to cause to drink, Râjat. 5, 368. 2. To send, Megh. 4. *hârita*, 1. Lost, Lass. 21, 19. 2. Fascinated, Râjat. 5, 367.—With अनु *anu*, To imitate, Gît. 8, 4.—With अप *apa*, 1. To take away, Pañch. i. d. 352; to rob, Ragh. 9, 7; Vikr. 11, 5. **2.** To captivate, Lass. 69, 10. **3.** To take off, Man. 4, 55. **4.** To remove, MBh. 3, 719. *apahṛita*, Seized (by sleep), Nal. 10, 7. Caus. *apahârita*, Caused or ordered to be robbed, Râm. 1, 42, 2.—With व्यप *vi-apa*, **1.** To remove, MBh. 3, 870. **2.** To cut off, MBh. 2, 1584.—With अभि *abhi*, To remove, to cut off, MBh. 3, 14610. Caus. To attack, Draup. 8, 5.—With अव *ava*, To put off, MBh. 4, 1304. *avahṛita*, **1.** Taken off, back, or away, seized, stolen. **2.** Fined. *avahârya*, **1.** Recoverable, to be restored, Man. 8, 145. **2.** To be fined, Man. 8, 198.—With अभ्यव *abhi-ava*, To eat, Bhâg. P. 5, 9, 12. *abhyavahârya*, see s.v. Caus. **1.** To cause to eat, Daçak. in Chr. 200, 8. **2.** To cause to resist, MBh. 3, 16369.—With प्रत्यव *prati-ava*, Caus. To suspend or to interrupt again, Chr. 37, 30.—With व्यव *vi-ava*, **1.** To waste away, Mâlat. 153, 21. **2.** To distinguish, to name, Vedântas. in Chr. 204, 13. **3.** To act, Hit. 62, 9; MBh. 3, 12861; to behave, Mâlat. 7, 7. **4.** To litigate, Daçak. in Chr. 190, 2. **5.** To fight, MBh. 4, 1870. **6.** To obtain, MBh. 3, 1462 (satisfaction). *vyavahârya*, **1.** To be observed as a duty. **2.** Subject to legal process.—With आ *â*, **1.** To carry, Man. 2, 182. **2.** To offer (a sacrifice), Râm. 6, 113, 10; Man. 6, 10. **3.** To give, Man. 2, 245. **4.** To fetch, Nal. 20, 5. **5.** To rob, Nal. 26, 7. **6.** To get, Man. 9, 190 (to bring forth a son). **7.** To enjoy, Lass. 70, 14. **8.** To eat, MBh. 3, 54; 57. **9.** To destroy, Mâlat. 153, 12. *âhṛita*, **1.** Brought, Hit. iii. d. 6. **2.** Collected, Pañch. 263, 22. **3.** Made captive, Man. 8, 415 (*dhvaja-*, under a standard, or in battle, a kind of slave). *âhârya*, **1.** Producible (*an-*, Not producible, Man. 8, 202). **2.** Removable. Desider. To wish to recover, MBh. 1, 6247. Caus. **1.** To cause to hold, Man. 8, 114. **2.** To cause to be paid, MBh. 2, 987; to collect (duties), Man. 7, 80. **3.** To apply, Hiḍ. 4, 48. **4.** To show (as anger), Râm. 1, 60, 19; (joy), Chr. 58, 11. **5.** To eat, Lass. 29, 14.—With अन्वा *anu-â*, *anvâhârya*, see s.v.—With अभ्या *abhi-â*, To offer, MBh. 1, 3733.—With उदा *ud-â*, **1.** To utter, Man. 11, 96; to pronounce, 2, 199; to call, Vikr. d. 88. **2.** To tell, MBh. 3, 2190. **3.** To require, Mâlat. 2, 15. *udâhṛita*, **1.** Called, named, Kir. 11, 72. **2.** Said, Chr. 42, 12. **3.** Illustrated. **4.** Predicated, Bhâshâp. 14.—With प्रत्युदा *prati-ud-â*, To answer, Râm. 1, 52, 10.—With समुदा *sam-ud-â*, *samudâhṛita*, **1.** Uttered, Râm. 1, 14, 23. **2.** Declared. **3.** Illustrated, recorded, Man. 1, 50.—With उपा *upa-â*, **1.** To offer, MBh. 1, 758 (cf. Man. 2, 245). **2.** To employ, MBh. 3, 1353. *upâhṛita*, **1.** Taken, got, Râjat. 5, 444. **2.** Prepared, cultivated (?), Râm. 5, 110.—With प्रत्या *prati-â*, **1.** To recover, MBh. 3, 8655. **2.** To utter, MBh. 3, 2177 (a speech). **3.** To cry, Draup. 6, 7. **4.** To report, Chr. 45, 14. *pratyâhṛita*, **1.** Resumed. **2.** Restrained. **3.** Withheld.—With व्या *vi-â*, **1.** To explain, declare, MBh. 3, 12466; Vikr. 55, 21. **2.** To report, Pañch. 30, 8. **3.** To tell, Râm. 2, 53, 5. **4.** To speak, Râm. 1, 48, 1; to address (acc.), Pañch. 109, 18. **5.** To utter, to pronounce, Bhag. 8, 13. **6.** To answer, Râm. 2, 93, 8.—With अभिव्या *abhi-vi-â*, Caus. To pronounce, Man. 2, 172.—With प्रव्या

pra-vi-â, **1.** To foretell, MBh. 1, 7240. **2.** To roar, MBh. 3, 15673.—With समा *sam-â*, **1.** To restore (to its former condition), Man. 8, 319. **2.** To collect, to assemble, MBh. 1, 6951. **3.** To offer, Râm. 1, 58, 4. **4.** To destroy, Bhag. 11, 32. *samâhṛita*, **1.** Accepted. **2.** Compiled. **3.** Much, Pańch. 171, 11. —With उद् *ud*, **1.** To take out, Ragh. 2, 30 (an arrow out of the quiver); to draw out of (abl.), Hit. iii. d. 30; from, Hit. 39, 2, M.M. **2.** To lift up, MBh. 1, 3299. **3.** To pluck up, Man. 7, 110. **4.** To pull out, MBh. 3, 11186; to exterminate, Böhtl. Ind. Spr. 483; to destroy, MBh. 3, 221. **5.** To hold out, to extend, Man. 4, 58. **6.** To raise, to extol, MBh. 1, 4923. **7.** To corroborate, Bhag. 6, 5 (cf. Daçak. in Chr. 189, 9). **8.** To deliver from (abl.), Vikr. d. 94; to save, MBh. 2, 2293; Pańch. i. d. 403. *uddhṛita*, **1.** Thrown up. **2.** Vomited. **3.** Separated. **4.** Divided. **5.** Recovered. **6.** Uncovered. **7.** Dispersed. **8.** Extracted, Man. 4, 62. In the Pańchatantra occurs *uddharita* instead of *uddhṛita*, Saved, Pańch. 114, 7; 141, 10; cf. my translation, n. 753. Desider. To wish to relieve, Man. 4, 251. Caus. **1.** To order to pull out, Ragh. 9, 78. **2.** To lift up, MBh. 3, 10946.—With अभ्युद् *abhi-ud*, To further, Pańch. iii. d. 246. *abhyuddhṛita*, **1.** Taken out. **2.** Destined, Mṛichchh. 61, 3. Caus. To snatch away, MBh. 3, 13326.—With प्रोद् *pra-ud*, **1.** To lift up, Râm. 2, 110, 4. **2.** To fetch (water), Ṛit. 1, 23. **3.** To save, Lass. 2. ed. 88, 21.—With समुद् *sam-ud*, **1.** To take out, Sâv. 5, 17. **2.** To pick up, Böhtl. Ind. Spr. 2262. **3.** To lift up, MBh. 3, 10946. **4.** To extol, MBh. 1, 4271. **5.** To favour, Pańch. 188, 1. **6.** To destroy, Ṛit. 1, 20; MBh. 1, 3821. *samuddhṛita*, **1.** Thrown up (as food). **2.** Extricated, lifted out. **3.** Divided, set apart, deducted, Man. 9, 116. **4.** Seized.—With उप *upa*, **1.** To bring, Daçak. in Chr. 196, 18. **2.** To offer, Çâk. 118, 4; with *pûjâm*, To honour, Râm. 1, 51, 5. **3.** To sacrifice, Mâlat. 75, 6. **4.** To destroy, MBh. 2, 861. Desider. To wish to offer, MBh. 2, 862. Caus. To cause to be offered, Râm. 1, 20, 9.—With समुप *sam-upa*, To offer, to perform (a sacrifice), Râm. 1, 40, 2.—With निस् *nis*, **1.** To draw from, Man. 7, 4. **2.** To export (wares), Man. 8, 399. **3.** To carry out (a corpse), Man. 5, 91; 10, 55. **4.** To pull out, MBh. 3, 6033. **5.** To mix (the clothes of one person with those of another), Man. 8, 396. *nirhṛita*, Extracted.—With परि *pari*, **1.** To pass by (a place for paying custom), Man. 8, 400. **2.** To shun, Hit. i. d. 75. **3.** To avoid, Pańch. 261, 5; Megh. 14. **4.** To conceal, Mṛichchh. 14, 3. **5.** To leave, to spare, Râm. 2, 48, 10 (Gorr. v.r. 2, 45, 26). *parihṛita*, Quitted, Râjat. 5, 190. *parihârya*, To be separated, Kathâs. 39, 32. **Comp.** *A*-, adj. unavoidable, Bhag. 2, 27.—With प्र *pra*, **1.** To direct, Çâk. d. 11. **2.** To strike, Man. 8, 300. **3.** To assail (with dat.), Chr. 28, 24; (with gen.), 25 (read *pra hare*); to attack, Pańch. 149, 1. Ptcple. of the pres. *praharant*, m. A warrior, Chr. 35, 2. *prahṛita*, Seized. n. Striking, killing.—With संप्र *sam-pra*, To fight, MBh. 3, 15167.—With वि *vi*, **1.** To remove, to wipe off (a tear), Çâk. 49, 19. **2.** To change, Johns. Sel. 5, 31. **3.** To alternate (between standing and sitting), Man. 6, 22. **4.** To ramble for pleasure, Megh. 61; to ramble, Pańch. 197, 22. **5.** To divert one's self, Man.

7, 221. **6.** To pass (as time), Man. 6, 33. **7.** To live, MBh. 4, 27. *vihṛita*, **1.** Expanded. **2.** Sported. n. Reluctance (in a female) to avow her feelings to her lover.—With **सम्** *sam*, **1.** To contract, Bhag. 2, 58 (as the tortoise contracts its limbs). **2.** To clench (the fist), MBh. 3, 11517. **3.** To abridge, Ragh. 10, 33. **4.** To seize, MBh. 3, 18. **5.** To draw away (the curtain of a theatre), Mâlav. d. 22. **6.** To take back, Çâk. d. 131; to put aside, Utt. Râmach. 148, 12. **7.** To withhold, Hit. i. d. 60, M.M. **8.** To destroy, MBh. 1, 241. **9.** To restrain (as wrath), Nal. 6, 14; (fear), Mâlat. 125, 1. **10.** To take, Man. 9, 113; 8, 188; 189. **11.** To conciliate, MBh. 1, 5996. *saṁhṛita*, Scattered. **Comp.** *A-*, adj. unrestrained, perpetual, Utt. Râmach. 2, 9.—With **उपसम्** *upa-sam*, **1.** To take back, Çâk. 94, 20. **2.** To withhold, Hit. i. d. 58, M.M. **3.** To collect, MBh. 1, 7206.—With **समुपसम्** *sam-upa-sam*, To stop, Utt. Râmach. 144, 4.—With **प्रतिसम्** *prati-sam*, **1.** To take back, Ragh. 9, 57; to draw back, Çâk. d. 11. **2.** To retract, Râm. 2, 22, 10. *prati-saṁhṛita*, **1.** Compressed. **2.** Checked, Çiç. 2, 15. **3.** Comprehended, included. Caus. To retract, Râm. 2, 22, 26.—Cf. probably Lat. co-hors; heres; χείρ, χράομαι, κίχρημι (cf. *jiharmi*); Goth. geiro, gairôn, gairnjan; A.S. georn, avidus, geornian, to yearn; Engl. yare; cf. *hary*.

हृच्छय *hṛichchhaya*, i.e. *hṛid-çî + a*, m. Kâma, the god of love, and love, Indr. 5, 44; Nal. 1, 17; Bhâg. P. 3, 14, 7.

हृणीय *HṚIṆÎYA*, (properly a denomin. derived from a lost noun, **hṛiṇa*, akin to *harit*, *hiraṇa*, with *ya*), Âtm. **1.** To be angry. **2.** To be ashamed. — Cf. O.H.G. galla; A.S. gealla; χολή; Lat. fel, bilis.

हृणीया *hṛiṇîyâ*, i.e *hṛiṇîya + a*, f. **1.** Censure, reproach. **2.** Bashfulness.

हृति *hṛi + ti*, f. Robbing, Râjat. 5, 190.

हृद् *hṛid*, n. **1.** The heart, Hit. 77, 3, M.M.; Pañch. i. d. 151 (former part of a comp.). **2.** The mind.—**Comp.** *Dus-*, I. adj. wicked, MBh. 3, 17300. II. m. an enemy, MBh. 4, 82. *Su-*, I. adj. loving, Pañch. i. d. 294; superl. *suhṛittama*, very fond (of each other), Hit. i. d. 1, M.M. II. m. 1. a friend, Vikr. 11, 13. 2. an ally. *A-su-*, adj. hostile, Râjat. 5, 191. *Kim-su-*, m. a bad friend, Hit. ii. d. 31 (read *kiṁ-suhṛid*); cf. Kir. 1, 5. *Makhâsu-*, i.e. *makha-a-su-*, m. Çiva. *Madhu-su-*, m. Kâmadeva.—Cf. Goth. hairto; A.S. heorte; Lat. cor, cordis; κέαρ, κῆρ.

हृदय *hṛidaya*, n. (cf. the last), **1.** The heart, Vikr. d. 7. **2.** The mind, Pañch. i. d. 198. **3.** Knowledge, Nal. 14, 21.—**Comp.** *A-karṇa-*, adj. deprived of ears and heart, Pañch. iv. d. 33. *Ayas-*, adj. iron-hearted, Ragh. 9, 9. *Bhîru-*, m. a deer. *Rikti-kṛita-* (vb. *rich*), adj. deprived of (its) heart, Pañch. 89, 2. *Çûnya-*, adj. unsuspecting, unsuspicious, Pañch. 208, 22. *Sa-*, I. adj. 1. along with the heart, Vikr. 71, 13. 2. compassionate, Râm. 2, 13, 16. II. m. a wise man, Böhtl. Ind. Spr. 1265. *Su-*, adj. good-hearted. *Hariṇa-*, adj. fearful.—Cf. καρδία.

हृदयंगम *hṛidayaṁgama*, i.e. *hṛidaya + m-gam + a*, adj. **1.** Affecting. **2.** Touching the heart, sweet, Ragh. 19, 13. **3.** Dear, Utt. Râmach. 103, 5; Râjat. 5, 79.

हृदयच्छिद् *hṛidayachchhid*, i. e. *hṛidaya-chhid*, adj. Heart-piercing, Chr. 36, 20.

हृदयवन्त् *hṛidaya + vant*, adj., f. *vatî*, and हृदयालु *hṛidayâlu*, i.e. *hṛidaya + âlu*, adj. Good-hearted, kind.

हृदयविध् *hṛidayavidh*, i. e. *hṛidaya-vyadh*, adj. Heart-piercing.

हृदयस्थ *hṛidaya-stha*, adj. Cherished in the heart, Pańch. 46, 19.

हृदयिक *hṛidayika*, i.e. *hṛidayin + ka*, adj., and हृदयिन् *hṛidayin*, i. e. *hṛidaya + in*, adj., f. *nî*, Good-hearted.

हृदिस्पृश् *hṛid + i-spṛiç*, adj. Beloved.

हृद्य *hṛid + ya*, I. adj. 1. Produced in or from the heart. 2. Dear, Bhag. 17, 8. 3. Affectionate. 4. Pleasant, Râm. 3, 52, 25; Kathâs. 26, 283. 5. Savoury, Man. 3, 227. II. m. A Mantra or verse for effecting fascination. III. f. *yâ*, A medicinal root. IV. n. Cassia bark.

हृल्लास *hṛillâsa*, i.e. *hṛid-las + a*, m. 1. Hiccough. 2. Heart-ache, Mâlat. 57, 9 (Sch. = *hṛidaya-çochaka* and *hṛidaya-avasâda*).

हृष् *HṚISH* (originally *bhṛish*), i. 4, Par. (in epic poetry also Âtm., MBh. 2, 1219), 1. To bristle, to be erect (as hair, especially of the body, a token of fear, or, more commonly, of pleasure), MBh. 2, 1757; Râm. 3, 50, 27. 2. To be glad, Daçak. in Chr. 197, 6. † i. 1, Par. To lie, to affirm falsely. Ptcple. of the pf. pass. I. *hṛishita* and *hṛishṭa*. 1. Having the hair of the body erect with pleasure, Râm. 3, 50, 27 (*hṛishṭa*); MBh. 4, 1245 (*hṛishita*); with fear, Râm. 2, 9, 34 Gorr. 2. Standing erect (of flowers), Nal. 23, 17 (*hṛishita*). 3. Pleased, Vikr. 75, 1 (*hṛishṭa*). 4. Astonished 5. Disappointed, deceived. II. *hṛishṭa*, Smiling. Caus. 1. To delight, Chr. 27, 10. 2. To be glad, Man. 6, 57. *harshita*, Delighted, Pańch. 146, 22.—With नि *ni*, *nihṛishṭa*, Pleased, Daçak. in Chr. 198, 4.—With परि *pari*, Caus. To delight much, MBh. 3, 887.—With संपरि *sam-pari*, Caus. To delight completely, or much, MBh. 3, 17470.—With प्र *pra*, To be very glad, Bhag. 5, 20; *prahṛishṭa*, Very glad, Pańch. 241, 23. Caus. To delight, Hit. iv. d. 9; *praharshita*, Very delighted, Pańch. 241, 16.—With संप्र *sam-pra*, *saṁprahṛishṭa*, 1. Erect (viz. the hair of the body), MBh. 3, 3061. 2. Pleased, MBh. 1, 3107. Caus. *saṁ-praharshita*, Much delighted, MBh. 3, 11829.—With सम् *sam*, To be glad, MBh. 2, 941. *saṁhṛishṭa-româṅga*, i.e. *-roman-aṅga*, adj. literally, 'Having a body, the hair of which stood erect,' Râm. 3, 55, 5.—With अतिसम् *ati-sam*, *atisaṁhṛishṭa*, Very glad, Lass. 2. ed. 47, 40.—With परिसम् *pari-sam*, *parisaṁhṛishṭa*, Very pleased, Râm. 3, 49, 11.—With प्रतिसम् *prati-sam*, To be glad, Râm. 3, 49, 11.—Cf. φρίσσω, φρίξ; O.H.G. burst; A.S. byrst, bristl, forst, frost, gelu; frysan; a-grísan, gerst, gryre; Lat. horrere, Hersilia; probably χέρσος, χήρ.

हृषीक *hṛish + îka*, n. Any organ of sense.—Comp. *Dus-*, adj. having defective organs of sense, MBh. 3, 13951.

हृषीकेश *hṛishîkeça*, i. e. *hṛishîka-îça*, m. Kṛishṇa or Vishṇu, Râm. 1, 45, 30; Râjat. 5, 100.

हृष्टवत् *hṛishṭavat*, i. e. *hṛishṭa +*

vant, acc. sing. n., adv. Cheerfully, Johns. Sel. 59, 179.

हृष्टि *hṛishṭi,* i.e. *hṛish + ti,* f. Joy, Mâlat. 82, 4; delight, pleasure.

हे *he,* 1. A vocative particle, Lass. 8, 18. 2. An interjection expressing envy or malice, He! Pańch. 37, 23; disapprobation, Bhartṛ. 2, 96.

हेक्का *hekkâ,* f. Hiccough (cf. *hikkâ*).

† हेट् *HEṬ* (?), हेठ् *HEṬH,* i. 1, Âtm. and Par. 1. To be wicked. 2. To vex or harass, to hurt; see *heḍh.*

हेठ *heṭha,* m. 1. Hindering, obstructing. 2. Hurting, injury.

हेड् *HEḌ* (हेल् *HEL*), i. 1, Âtm. To disregard; *a-heḍamâna,* adj. Careful, Râm. 2, 68, 22. † i. 1, Par. To surround, to attire.

हेडज *heḍ+a-ja,* m. Anger.

† हेढ् *HEḌH,* हेठ् *HEṬH,* ii. 9, *heḍhṇâ, heṭhṇâ, ṇî,* Par. 1. To be born again. 2. To produce happiness or purity.

हेति *heti,* i.e. *hi+ti,* f. 1. A weapon, Pańch. i. d. 236. 2. A ray of the sun. 3. Flame.—Comp. *Çvâsa-,* f. sleep.

ऽहेतिक *-heti+ka,* a substitute for *heti,* when latter part of comp. words; e.g. *çakti-,* m. A spearman.

हेतिमन्त् *heti+mant,* adj., f. *matî,* in *hari-,* Illuminated by the sun, Mâlat. 149, 1.

हेतु *hetu,* perhaps *hi+tu* (properly, Impulse, Chr. 18, 2), 1. Motive; abl., on account of, Râm. 3, 49, 39; in order to, Hit. i. d. 173, M.M.; dat. *mṛityu -hetave,* In order to kill, Bhâg. P. 7, 1, 41. 2. Origin. 3. Cause, Hit. i. d. 42, M.M.; reason, Pańch. i. d. 417; proof, Lass. 2. ed. 65, 2. 4. Means, Hit. 114, 7; Râjat. 5, 310; prize, 5, 71. 5. Condition, Draup. 9, 10; law, Hit. ii. d. 10. 6. The reason or middle term in an inference, Bhâshâp. 68. 7. *hetau,* loc. By reason of. 8. Logic, Daçak. in Chr. 180, 8.—Comp. *Nis-,* adj. having no cause, MBh. 12, 3277.

हेतुक *hetu+ka,* I. adj. 1. Relating to the cause. 2. Causal, instrumental. II. m. 1. An active cause, an instrument, Hit. 55, 5. 2. A logician, Man. 12, 111.—Comp. *Bhaya-,* adj. dangerous, Hit. 85, 1, M.M. *Sa-,* adj. 1. produced by a cause, Bhâshâp. 100. 2. with the motive, Râjat. 5, 54 (Çûra knowing that he had retired, and also his motive for it).

हेतुता *hetu+tâ,* f., and हेतुत्व *hetu +tva,* n. Causation, the state of being a cause, Hit. i. d. 29, M.M. (*tâ*); Râjat. 5, 292; 388 (*tâ*); Bhâshâp. 146, 147 (*tva*). — Comp. *Nimitta-hetu+tva,* n. the being an instrumental cause, Bhâshâp. 16.

हेतुमन्त् *hetu+mant,* adj. 1. Having a cause; that in which the reason or middle term resides (i.e. the *paksha*), Bhâshâp. 68. 2. Accompanied by arguments, Râm. 3, 53, 20. 3. Attacked by arguments, MBh. 12, 597 (perhaps it is to be read *hi* instead of *'pi,* then it would be, Skilled in logic).

हेम *hema,* I. m. A horse of dark colour. II. n. Gold (cf. *heman*).

हेमक *hema+ka* (n.), Gold, Râm. 3, 49, 20.

हेमकार *hema-kâra,* m. A goldsmith, Man. 9, 292.

हेमन् *heman,* I. m. Winter (ÇKD.). II. n. Gold, Ragh. 1, 10, Naish. 52; Vikr. d. 140 (or *hema*).—Cf. χειμών; with ρ for ν, χειμέρ + ιος.

हेमन्त *hemanta* (i.e. **hemant,* original form of ***heman***, + *a*), m. (and n.), The cold season, winter, about November—December, Pańch. 94, 2.—Cf. *χεῖμα*.

हेममय *hema* + *maya*, adj., f. *yî*, Golden, Râm. 3, 49, 6.

हेमल *hema* + *la*, m. **1.** A goldsmith. **2.** A touchstone. **3.** A lizard.

हेमवन्त् *hema* + *vant*, adj., f. *vatî*, Golden, Râm. 3, 50, 2.

हेमवल *hemavala* (probably from *hema*), n. A pearl.

हेरम्ब *heramba*, m. **1.** Gaṇeça, Mâlat. 144, 21. **2.** A buffalo. **3.** A proud hero.

हेरिक *herika*, m. A spy.

हेरुक *heruka*, m. An attendant on Çiva.

हेल् *HEL*, see *heḍ*.

हेलन *hel* + *ana*, n. **1.** Disregard, Bhâg. P. 1, 19, 2. **2.** Dalliance.

हेला *hel* + *â*, f. **1.** Sport, Ratnâv. 2. ed. 17, 11. **2.** Contempt, Çiç. 2, 48. **3.** Dallying, lascivious endearment, delight, Mâlat. 157, 19. **4.** Manner, Neriosengh, see Gött. Gel. Anz. 1861, p. 1837. **5.** instr. *layâ* (properly, Sportively, easily; cf. *lîlâ*), At once, Pańch. ii. d. 80; 106, 1; 134, 13; 168, 6; Râjat. 5, 84.—Comp. *Eka-*, f. instr. at once, Pańch. 256, 24. *Sa-*, adj. sportive.

हेलि *hel* + *i*, m. **1.** The sun (borrowed from ἥλιος), Bhavishyap., see Aufrecht, Ujjvalad. 267, n. **2.** Embracing.

हेलुदिन्न *helu-diṇṇa* (*helu*, The name of a village, and *diṇṇa*, the Prâkṛit. form for *datta*), adj. Presented with the village *Helu*, Râjat. 5, 397.

हेष् *HESH*, i. 1, Âtm. To neigh as a horse, Pańch. iv. d. 49. *heshita*, n. Neighing, Episod. MBh. de Çakuntala, ed. Chezy, 1, 16.—Cf. probably Lat. hinnire, hinnulus; γίννος; but cf. also *hresh*.

हेषा *hesh* + *â*, f. Neighing (as a horse, or braying, as an ass), Kir. 16, 8.

हेषाय *HESHÂYA*, a denomin. derived from *heshâ* with *ya*, Âtm. To neigh, Pańch. 254, 25.

हेषिन् *hesh* + *in*, m. A horse.

है *hai*, A vocative particle.

हैतुक *haituka*, i.e. *hetuka* + *a*, I. adj. Causal, causative. **II.** m. **1.** A follower of the Mîmâṁsâ doctrines. **2.** A sceptic, a sophist, Man. 4, 30.—Comp. *Kâma-*, adj. caused by arbitrariness, i.e. by accident, Bhag. 16, 8.

हैतुक्य *haitukya*, i. e. *haituka* + *ya*, in the comp. *a-*, n. Want of selfish motives, Bhâg. P. 3, 29, 12.

हैम *haima*, i.e. *heman* + *a*, I. adj. **1.** Cold. **2.** Golden, Vikr. d. 157. **II.** n. Hoar-frost. **III.** f. *mî*, Yellow jasmine.

हैमन *haimana*, i.e. *heman* + *a*, I. adj., f. *nî*, Winterly, MBh. 2, 2669; Kir. 17, 12. **II.** m. The month Mârgaçîrsha. **III.** n. Winter.

हैमन्त *haimanta*, and **हैमन्तिक** *haimantika*, i.e. *hemanta* + *a*, or *ika*, I. adj. Wintry. **II.** n. Winter.

हैमल *haima* + *la*, n. Winter.

हैमवत *haimavata*, i.e. *himavant* + *a*, I. adj., f. *tî*, Belonging to the Himâlaya mountain, Draup. 5, 5. **II.** m.

A sort of poison. III. f. *ti.* 1. Pârvatî. 2. Several plants. IV. n. India.

हैयंगवीन *haiyam̃gavîna,* i.e. *hyas + a + m-go + îna,* n. Fresh butter (prepared a day before it is used), Ragh. 1, 45.

हैरण्यगर्भ *hairaṇyagarbha,* i. e. *hiraṇya-garbha + a,* patronym., m. A son of Brahman, Man. 3, 194.

हैरण्यवासस् *hairaṇyavâsas,* i. e. *hiraṇya + a-vâsas,* m. An arrow, MBh. 4, 2071.

हैरिक *hairika,* m. A thief.

हैहय *haihaya,* m. 1. The name of a people, Chr. 34, 12. 2. A prince.

हो *ho,* A vocative particle, Kir. 15, 20.

† होड् *HOḌ,* i. 1, Âtm. To disregard; see *hûd.*

होड *hoḍa,* m. A raft.

होडृ *hoḍṛi,* m. A robber.

होढ *hoḍha,* I. adj. Stolen. II. n. Stolen goods, Man. 9, 270.

होतृ *hotṛi,* i.e. I. *hu + tṛi,* m., f. *trî,* and n. Sacrificing, a sacrificer, Çâk. d. 1; Bhartṛ. 2, 47. II. *hu,* or *hve + tṛi* (cf. *hve*), m. A priest who, at sacrifice, recites the hymns of the Rigveda.

होत्र *hotra,* i.e. *hu + tra,* n. 1. A burnt-offering. 2. An oblation of clarified butter.—Comp. *Agni-,* n. 1. a ceremony consisting in oblations to consecrated fire, Man. 4, 25. 2. the consecrated fire, Man. 5, 167. *Vîti-,* m. 1. Agni. 2. the sun. *Çâli-,* see s.v.

होत्रीय *hotrîya,* i. e. *hotra + îya,* I. m. A priest offering an oblation. II. n. A place where oblations are offered.

होम *homa,* i.e. *hu + ma,* m. An oblation of clarified butter, a sacrifice, Chr. 60, 36 (corr. *datta-*); Pañch. i. d. 347.—Comp. *Japa-,* m. the oblation consisting in prayers, Man. 10, 111. *Darvî-,* m. oblation with a spoon, MBh. 2, 537 (*vî*). *Huta-* (vb. *hu*), m. a Brâhmaṇa who has offered an oblation. (n.), an oblation.

होमन् *homan,* i. e. *hu + man,* n. An oblation of clarified butter.

होमवन्त् *homa + vant,* adj., f. *vatî,* Having performed sacrifice.

होमि *homi,* i.e. *hu + mi,* m. 1. Fire. 2. Clarified butter. 3. Water.

होमिन् *homin,* i.e. *homa + in,* m. A priest who makes an oblation of clarified butter.

होरा *horâ* (borrowed from ὥρα), f. 1. The rising of a sign of the zodiac. 2. An hour. 3. A line. 4. A work on astrology.

होहौ *hohau,* and हौ *hau,* interj. of calling.

हौड् *HAUḌ,* see *hûd.*

हौतृक *hautṛika,* i.e. *hotṛi + ka,* adj. Relating to the priest called *hotṛi.*

हौम्य *haumya,* i.e. *homa + ya,* n. Clarified butter.

ह्नु *HNU,* ii. 2, Âtm. 1. To take away, Bhaṭṭ. 15, 88. 2. To conceal one's self, Pâṇ. i. 4, 34.—With अप *apa,* 1. To conceal, Naish. 1, 49. 2. To deny, to disclaim, Man. 8, 53.—

With नि *ni*, To deny, Man. 8, 59. — With अतिनि *ati-ni*, To deny strongly, Daçak. in Chr. 193, 9.—With अपनि *apa-ni*, To conceal, Mâlat. 16, 14.—Cf. Lat. ab-nuere, nutare, gnavus, navare, i-gnavus, se-gnis, niti, nictare, con-nivere; Goth. hneivan, hnaivs; A.S. hnigan; ἀνα-νεύω, νεύω, νυστάζω, νυθός, etc.

† ह्मल् *HMAL*, i. 1, Par. To shake.

ह्यस् *hyas*, i.e. perhaps *ha-dyas* (cf. *sadyas*), adv. Yesterday.—Cf. Lat. hes+ternus, heri; Goth. gis+tra; A.S. gyrstan; χθές.

ह्यस्तन *hyas+tana*, adj., f. *nî*, and

ह्यस्त्य *hyas+tya*, adj. Of yesterday, Chr. 39, 4 (*tana*).

† ह्रग् *HRAG*, ह्लग् *HLAG*, i. 1, Par. To cover.

ह्रद *hrada*, probably *hrâd+a*, m. 1. A large piece of water, Utt. Râmach. 53, 9; a deep lake, Pańch. 159, 14. 2. A ray of light.—Comp. *Gańgâ-*, *Tîrtha-mahâ-*, *Râma-*, m. names of holy ponds, MBh. 3, 7047 (*gańgâ-*); 13, 7645 (*tîrthamahâ-*); Chr. 46, 28 (*râma-*). *Çata-*, f. *dâ*, 1. lightning, Vikr. 66, 1. 2. the thunderbolt.

ह्रदिनी *hradinî*, i.e. *hrada+in+î*, f. 1. A river, Bhâg. P. 6, 4, 41. 2. Lightning.

ह्रप् *HRAP*, see *hlap*.

ह्रस् *HRAS*, i. 1, Par. 1. † To sound (cf. *ras*). 2. To become small, to be lessened, Man. 1, 83. Caus. *hrâsaya*, To diminish, Man. 11, 216.

ह्रसिमन् *hrasiman*, i.e. *hrasva+iman*, m. Shortness.

ह्रस्व *hras+va*, I. adj., comparat. *hrasîyaṁs*, superl. *hrasishṭha*, 1. Short, Johns. Sel. 15, 53; Bhâshâp. 109. 2. Small, Johns. Sel. 51, 107. 3. Low, Nal. 23, 9. II. m. A dwarf.—Cf. χέρηϊ, χερείων, χείρων, χείριστος; perhaps Lat. brevis.

ह्रस्वक *hrasva+ka*, adj. Small, Râm. 2, 117, 13 Gorr.

ह्राद् *HRAD*, i. 1, Âtm. To sound inarticulately (as a drum), Bhaṭṭ. 14, 4; to roar (as thunder), Kâçinâtha apud Wilkins.—Cf. χλάζω, κέχλαδα (see *hlâd*), probably χάλαζα; Lat. grando; perhaps χέραδος, etc.; Goth. grêtan; A.S. graetan.

ह्राद *hrâd+a*, m. Noise, Kir. 16, 8.

ह्रादिन् *hrâd+in*, I. adj., f. *nî*, Sounding. II. f. *nî*. 1. Lightning. 2. Indra's thunderbolt. 3. A river. 4. The olibanum tree.

ह्रास *hrâsa*, i.e. *hras+a*, m. Sound. 2. Decrease, Man. 1, 85.

ह्री *HRÎ* (cf. *hriṇîya*), ii. 3, *jihrî*, Par. To be ashamed, Ragh. 15, 44. Ptcple. of the pf. pass. *hrîṇa*, and *hrîta*, Ashamed, bashful, modest, Nal. 13, 30 (*hrîta*). Caus. *hrepaya*, To put to blush, to confound, Kir. 11, 64.—With सम् *sam*, *saṁhrîṇa*, Ashamed.—Cf. probably O.H.G. hriuwan; A.S. hreówan.

ह्री *hrî*, f. Shame, Hit. i. d. 133, M.M.; bashfulness, Pańch. i. d. 185; personified, Râm. 3, 52, 26.

ह्रीका *hrî+kâ*, f. 1. Bashfulness, modesty. 2. Fear.—Comp. *Nis-*, adj. bold, MBh. 7, 4806.

ह्रीकु *hrî+ku*, adj. Bashful, modest.

† ह्रीछ् *HRÎCHH* (i.e. *hrî + chh*;

cf. *hurchh*), i. 1, Par. To be ashamed or modest.

ह्रीमन्त् *hrî + mant*, adj., f. *matî*, Bashful, modest, Bhartṛ. 2, 44.

हुड्, ह्रूड् *HRŪD*, see *hûḍ*.

† ह्रेप् *HREP*, i. 1, Âtm. To go.

ह्रेपण *hrepaṇa*, i.e. *hrî*, Caus., + *ana*, n. Putting to shame.

ह्रेष् *HRESH*, i. 1, Âtm. 1. To neigh as a horse, MBh. 2. † To go. *hreshita*, n. Neighing, MBh. 3, 11764. Caus. To neigh, MBh. 3, 11764.—Cf. *ras*; O.H.G. hros; A.S. hors; χρόμη, χρεμίζω.

ह्रेषा *hresh + â*, f. Neighing as a horse.

ह्रेषुक *hreshuka*, MBh. 3, 8871, An instrument for digging with (?).

ह्रौड् *HRAUḌ*, see *hûḍ*.

ह्लग् *HLAG*, see *hrag*.

† ह्लप् *HLAP*, ह्रप् *HRAP*, i. 10, Par. To speak (cf. *klap* and *lap*).

† ह्लस् *HLAS*, i. 1, Par. To sound (cf. *hras*).

ह्लाद् *HLÂD*, i. 1, Âtm. To be glad or delighted, MBh. 1, 3036. Caus. To delight, Râm. 2, 44, 10.—With आ *â*, Caus. To delight, Nal. 21, 8.—With प्र *pra*, To be delighted, Kir. 11, 8. Ptcple. of the pf. pass. *prahlanna*, Pleased, glad. Caus. To delight, Râm. 1, 9, 56; Pañch. ii. d. 63; Vikr. d. 149 (Âtm.). *prahlâdita*, Rejoiced.—Cf. κέχλαδα, καχλάζω; A.S. glaed, glad, gladian; O.H.G. glat, splendens (cf. *hrâdini*, *hlâdinî*).

ह्लाद *hlâd + a*, m. Pleasure, joy.

ह्लादिन् *hlâdin*, i.e. *hlâd + in*, and *hlâda + in*, I. adj., f. *nî*. 1. Delighting, Ṛit. 6, 29. 2. Happy, glad. II. f. *nî*. 1. Lightning. 2. Indra's thunderbolt.

ह्लीका *hlîkâ = hrîkâ*.

ह्लीकु *hlîku*, I. (= *hrîku*), adj. Bashful, modest. II. m. 1. Tin. 2. Lac.

ह्वल् *HVAL* (cf. *hvṛi*), i. 1, Par. To move, to shake, to tremble, Bhaṭṭ. 9, 8. Caus. To cause to tremble, Bhaṭṭ. 6, 45.—With वि *vi*, To stagger, to be agitated, Râm. 2, 13, 4. *vihvalita*, Staggering, Râm. 1, 9, 15.

ह्वान *hvâna*, i.e. *hve + ana*, n. Cry. —Comp. *Ku-*, n. disagreeable cry, Bhâg. P. 1, 14, 14.

ह्वृ *HVṚI* (originally *dhvṛi*, q. cf.),

ह्वॄ *HVṚÎ*, i. 1, and ii. 9, *hvṛiṇâ*, *ṇî*, Par. To be crooked.—Cf. Lat. curvus, varus; κυρτός, κύρβεις; Goth. hvairban; A.S. hwearfian (Caus.), hwerfa, hweorfan; hwealf, hwealfa; ἐρέφω.

ह्वे *HVE*, i. 1, Par. Âtm. (in the Vedas also हू *HÛ*), 1. To call, Râm. 2, 34, 11; Chr. 289, 4 = Rigv. i. 49, 4 (*ahûshata*, ved. aor.); Chr. 288, 14 = Rigv. i. 48, 14 (*juhûre*, ved. red. pf.). 2. To name, Kumâras. 1, 26. 3. To invoke, MBh. 1, 4944. 4. To challenge, to vie with (with acc.), MBh. 3, 1823 (*çaçinaṁ hvayantî*, Vying with the moon). Ptcple. of the pf. pass. *hûta*, Summoned, invited. Comp. *Puru-*, adj. invoked by many, or much invoked.—With आ *â*, I. Par. (in epic poetry also Âtm., Râm. 2, 91, 12). 1. To call, Râm. 2, 58, 1. 2. To invoke, Râm. 2, 91, 12; Lass. 101, 3 = Rigv. vii. 16, 1 (*â huve*, ved. pres.); Lass. 101, 7 = Rigv. vii. 16, 3 (*â juhvâna*, ptcple. pf. pass.). 3. To invite, Man. 3, 27.

4. To convoke, Hit. 82, 16. **II.** Âtm. **1.** To challenge, MBh. 2, 879; Chr. 26, 74 (*âhvayâm âsa*, anomal. pf.), 37, 10 (*âhvayâna*, anomal. ptcple. pres.). **2.** To emulate. Caus. *hvâyaya*, To order to call, Râm. 2, 89, 3.—With उपा *upa-â*, Âtm. To challenge, MBh. 2, 1785.—With समा *sam-â*, **1.** To convoke, Pańch. 82, 6; Râm. 1, 8, 18. **2.** To call, Pańch. 210, 10; MBh. 3, 8549. **3.** To challenge, MBh. 2, 1518. *samâhûta*, Convoked, Daçak. in Chr. 191, 19. —With नि *ni*, To call down (from heaven), Chr. 298, 24 = Rigv. i. 112, 24. —With प्र *pra*, To call, Utt. Râmach. 146, 2.—Cf. O.H.G. hweion; Goth. vôpjan (probably the regular Caus.); A.S. hweóp (cry, called out), and wepan; probably also cygan (3. conj., cl. *juhû*); βοή, βοάω, probably ἀΰω and ἰωή; Lat. re-boare, and perhaps vovere, vōtum.

ADDENDA AND CORRIGENDA.

PAGE

1, A, 2 below, add. *A-hima-aṁçu*, m. the sun, Kir. 12, 15.

1, B, 3 bel., add. as akin, A.S. ange, enge.

2, B, 21, add. *Mallika-aksha*, m. = *mallika* and *mallikâkhya*, q. cf.

2, B, 23, add. after Indra, Vikr. d. 35.

5, A, 9 (*agresara*), add. Preceding, Mâlat. 155, 3.

5, A, 19 (*agh*), add. Cf. *aṁh*, *agha*, and Goth. us-aglian, probably ogan; A.S. oga, oht, ege, eige, egesa.

5, A, 3 bel., add. *Vṛisha-aṅka*, m. Çiva, Ragh. 3, 23.

5, B, 15, add. अङ्कुराय *AṄKURÂ-YA*, a denomin. derived from *aṅkura*, with *ya*, Âtm. To shoot up, to thrive, Böhtl. Ind. Spr. 3095.

5, B, 15 (*aṅkuça*), add. as akin, A.S. angel.

6, A, 15, add. after devotees, Mâlat. 74, 18.

6, A, 29, add. after casarca, Vikr. d. 100.

13, A, 7 bel. (*ad*), add. A.S. aet, aes; O.H.G. az; A.S. fretan, of-aet; O.H.G. ob-az.

14, A, 24 (*adha*), add. Cf. ἔνθα (see *adhara* and *adhas*); Lat. indu; A.S. and.

14, B, 25 (*adhas*), add. Lat. inde.

14, B, 3, bel., dele 'Cf. Lat. ad' (Cf. add. ad p. 100, *idam*); add. Cf. A.S. ed-, e.g. in ed-niwan.

PAGE

16, B, 19, add. *Kṛita-adhivâsa*, adj. perfumed, Ṛit. 6, 32.

17, A, 5, corr. 1 (for I.).

18, B, 3 (*an-*), add. A.S. an-, e.g. in an-aedhelan; in-, e.g. in in·cudh; and on-, e.g. in on-rihtwis.

22, B, 27, add. अनुप्लव *anuplava*, i. e. *anu-plu* + *a*, m. A follower.—Comp. *Sa-*, adj. with his retinue, Ragh. 13, 75.

25, A, 1, bel., add. अनुष्टुभ् *anushṭubh*, i. e. *anu-stubh*, f. Name of a metre.

26, B, 7 (*anokaha*), add. after tree, Mâlat. 145, 12; Utt. Râmach. 16, 8.

27, A, 2 (*anta*), add. *Niçâ-anta*, m. the end of the night, dawn, Man. 4, 99.

27, A, 14 (*antaḥpura*), add. 4. Wives in general, Daçak. in Chr. 182, 9.

27, A, 25, add. *Madana-antaka*, n. the destroyer of the god of love (i.e. Çiva), Bhartṛ. 3, 83.

27, B, 9 bel., corr. odher.

29, B, 11 bel., add. A.S. ael- in ael-theodige; elles.

31, A, 19, add. अन्वीक्षा *anvîkshâ*, i.e. *anu-îksh* + *a*, f. Reflection.

31, A, 3 bel., dele aqua, and Goth. ahva, A.S. ewe.

31, B, 8, add. A.S. aeftar, aeftan, aeft, aefen, aefer, eft.

PAGE

31, B, 25 (*apakâra*), add. (after Injury), evil, misfortune, Mâlat. 88, 2.

33, A, 1 bel., add. अपरतस् *apara+tas*, adv. Another time, Utt. Râmach. 42, 7.

34, A, 5, add. अपरोक्षय *APAROKSHAYA*, To make visible, see p. 530, *paroksha*.

34, B, 3, add. after individual, Mâlat. 83, 2.

35, A, 3, add. अपहस्तित *apahastita*, ptcple. pf. pass. of a denomin. *APAHASTAYA*, derived from *apa-hasta*, Lost, scorned (?), Mâlat. 149, 9.

37, A, 13 (*abhi*), add. A.S. bi, be.

37, B, 33 (*abhijńa*), add. II. f. *ńâ*, A divine faculty attributed to Buddha; and l. 34, add. *Shash-*, adj. one who attributes six divine faculties (to Buddha), Lass. 2. ed. 90, 39.

40, B, 26, add. अभिलास *abhilâsa*, अभिलासिन् *abhilâsin* = *abhilâsha*, °*shin*, Megh. 109; 76.

43, A, 4, add. (after Near), till, Mâlat. 78, 1.

44, B, 19, add. **1.** before Unable, and **2.** One who does not submit, Pańch. i. d. 370. **3.** Angry, MBh. 1, 1736; 2007.

45, B, 12, add. अम्बरचर *ambara-chara*, m. A bird, Pańch. i. d. 350.

46, A, 15, corr. Matsyop.

46, A, 24, add. A.S. ysen, aeren.

47, B, 11, add. Comp. *An-arâla*, adj. straight, Utt. Râmach, 63, 6; Mâlat. 153, 19.

48, B, 15, add. Cf. probably as akin, A.S. lúcan, To lock.

49, B, 3 bel., corr. Ind.

50, A, 2 bel., add. *Anubaddha* (vb. *bandh*), *-artha*, m. wealthy, Daçak. in Chr. 181, 1.

52, A, 14, corr. *ardhabhâskara*, instead of *ardha-bhâskara*.

PAGE

53, A, 3, add. Cf. probably as akin, ὄρρος; A.S. aers, ears.

54, A, 22 (*alarka*), add. (after **2.**), A mad dog. **3.**

55, A, 30 (*ava*), add. αὖταρ; A.S. awdher, audhar, adhar (= comparat. of *ava*); Lat. auster (cf. ved. *avas* and *avâchî*, f. of *avâńch*, The south).

56, B, 4 bel. add. (after **2.**), Watching, Böhtl. Ind. Spr. 1610.

58, B, 25, add. (after **2.**), Staying, Hit. ii. p. 93, 7, M.M. **3.**

60, A, 19, add. *Etad-avastha*, adj. such a, Vikr. d. 135. l. 20, add. *Bâla-avastha*, adj. young, Vikr. d. 156.

60, B, 14, corr. A.S. eaw, and add. eowed.

60, B, 14, add. अविपर्यय *AVIPARYAYA*, a denomin. derived from *a-viparyaya*, Par. Not to fail, not to be disappointed, Mâlat. 107, 4.

62, A, 6 (*açmantaka*), add. I. m. A plant, hog-plum, Mâlat. 145, 20; cf. Wils. Th. of the Hind. 2. ed. ii. 98, n. II. n.

62, B, 16, Cf. Böhtl. Ind. Spr. 1095, n., who maintains the signification 'female mule' also in this case.

63, A, 21, corr. A.S. achta.

64, A, 10, add. A.S. scó.

64, B, 17, add. (after 24, 45), with *gaṇanayâ*, To reckon up one by one, Megh. 85.

65, A, 20, add. see *vâṇâsana*.

66, B, 27, add. Goth. af-aikan.

67, B, 11, add. ἔγχελυς; Lat. anguilla; A.S. ael.

68, A, 32, add. cf. *pushpâkara*.

69, A, 4 bel., add. (after 141), intentively, Mâlat. 80, 3; significantly, ib. 62, 4.

70, A, 9, corr. Kumâras.

70, A, 13, add. आक्षेपण *âkshepaṇa*, i.e. *â-kship+ana*, I. adj. Destroying, Mâlat. 160, 13. II. n. Pushing, Suçr. 1, 300, 5; 9.

70, A, 34, add. आख्यातुकाम *âkhyâ*

PAGE

tukâma, i.e. *â-khyâtum-kâma* (vb. *khyâ*), adj., f. *mâ*, Wishing to tell, Mâlat. 49, 14.

77, B, 28 (*âdhâra*), add. (after **2.**), A receptacle, Suçr. 1, 78, 18. **3.** and corr. the following num. Cf. *vidyâdhâra*.

79, A, 5, add. **आनुयात्रिक** *ânuyâtrika*, i.e. *anu-yâtrâ+ika*, m. A companion, Utt. Râmach. 111, 12.

79, A, 16, add. **आनुष्टुभ** *ânushṭubha*, i. e. *anushṭubh* (see Add. ad p. 25), *+a*, adj. Composed in the metre Anushṭubh, Utt. Râmach. 36, 6.

79, A, 27 (*ântara*), add. **I.** adj. Inward, Utt. Râmach. 34, 18. **II.** m.

79, A, 2 bel., add. **आन्वीक्षिकी** *ânvîkshikî*, i.e. *anvîkshâ* (see Add. ad p. 31), *+ika*, f. Logic, Mâlat. 41, 6.

79, B, 21, add. (before 136), 5.

80, B, 20 (*âp*), add. A.S. efnan (cf. ved. *apnas*); perhaps A.S. efst (cf. the ved. desider. *aps*).

81, B, 16, add. **आवुत्त** *âbutta*, m. A sister's husband (in theatrical language), Utt. Râmach. 7, 6.

84, B, 17, add. A.S. aa, ae, á.

85, A, 20, add. *Nihita-ârambha* (vb. *dhâ*), adj. formed, Megh. 85 (*hṛidi*, imagined).

85, A, 31, 32, dele O.H.G. âla, etc. (on account of A.S. awul).

87, B, 22, add. **आलर्क** *âlarka*, i. e. *alarka* (see Add. ad p. 54), *+a*, adj. Coming from a mad dog (as poison), Utt. Râmach. 27, 6.

88, B, 16, add. *Sa-âvaraṇa*, adj. clandestine, Ragh. 19, 16.

90, B, 3, add. *Bhikshâ-âçitva*, n. eating alms, Hit. i. d. 134, M.M.

91, A, 22 (*âçraya*), add. (after 95, 14), a means, Bhartṛ. 2, 34 (*pravâsâçrayât*, by going abroad).

92, A, 3, corr. *âstâm̃*.

PAGE

92, A, 1 bel., corr. MBh.

93, A, 1, corr. 3. a kind of posture (cf. Sch. ad Ragh. 13, 52; Stenzler, ad Kumâras. 3, 45); Man. . . .

93, A, 5, add. **आसन्नतरता** *â-sanna+tara+tâ* (vb. *sad*), f. Greater proximity, Hit. iv. d. 64.

95, A, 33, add. **आह्वायक** *âhvâyaka*, i.e. *â-hve+aka*, adj. One who calls, Utt. Râmach. 122, 6.

96, A, 26, add. (after *antarita*, **1.**), Entered, Hit. iii. d. 60 (*chara-*, Being inwardly, i. e. really, a spy, not an ambassador). **2.** Plunged. . . .

97, B, 2, bel. add. (after *vi-pari*), To fail, Mâlat. 88, 12; 13.

98, A, 14, add. (after 16), n. Opinion, Daçak. in Chr. 182, 2.

98, A, 1 bel., corr. MBh.

98, B, 2, add. A.S. iedon.

100, A, 19, add. (after 16), Concerning the difference of *idam* and *tad*, cf. Vedântas. in Chr. 213, 2.

100, A, 25, add. Lat. ita; the old accus. n. of the pronom. base *a* appears in Zend. *aṭ*; Lat. ad; Goth. at; A.S. aet; Engl. at.

101, A, 8 bel., corr. *îvant*.

102, A, 2 bel., add. (after *ishṭakâ*), i.e. *ishṭa* (vb. *yaj*, cf. Weber, in Journ. of the German Oriental Society, xviii. 264), *+ka*.

102, B, 25, add. (after **1.**), *=asmin*, Utt. Râmach. 116, 1. **2.** . . .

104, B, 18, add. Comp. absolutive, *a-samîkshya*, Without having perceived, Böhtl. Ind. Spr. 905.

105, B, 33, add. (after *îrshy*), Jealousy.

106, A, 12, add. Goth. aihts; A.S. aeht, Property.

108, A, 10, add. Cf. O.H.G. waskan; A.S. wacsan, waescan (*uksh* for original *vaksh* or *vask*).

108, B, 11 (*samuchita*), add. **2.** Proper, suitable, Megh. 113.

PAGE

108, B, 22, add. Cf. probably Goth. auhuma, auhumists.

108, B, 5 bel., add. (after **2.**), m.

111, A, 2, add. With प्रति *prati*, *pratyuthaṇṭhita*, Expecting with desire, Pañch. 209, 18.

114, A, 11, add. *Pûra-utpîḍa*, m. excessive plenty of water, Utt. Râmach. 73, 5.

115, B, 2, add. A.S. ytan, yte, b-utan, a-b-útan.

116, A, 12, add. A.S. waetan, waet, waeta, waeter.

116, A, 12 bel., corr. *Karuṇâ-*.

116, A, 6 bel., add. (after lord), Ragh. 8, 16.

118, A, 4, add. उद्दीपक *ud-dîp + aka*, adj. Illuminating, Chân. 25 in Berl. Monatsb. 1864, 408.

118, B, 21, add. उद्ध्य *uddhya*, i.e. probably *ud* (for *uda*), *-dhi* (from *dhâ*), *+ya*, m. A river, Ragh. 11, 8.

119, B, 10, add. उद्र *udra*, i.e. *und +ra*, m. An aquatic animal, an udder.—Cf. ὕδρος, ὕδρα; A.S. oter.

120, B, 28, add. see *manas*, p. 683, B, 6 bel.

121, A, 24, corr. (after **2.**), Twinkling, Megh. 79 (*vidyudunmeshadṛishṭi*, a lightning-flash glance, i.e. a lightning instead of a twinkling look).

121, B, 4, add. A.S. ufan, b-ufan, and up, upp.

122, A, 2 bel., add. उपगान *upagâna*, i.e. *upa-gai + ana*, n. Song, Mâlav. 20, 15.

122, A, 12, corr. MBh. (for Râm.).

124, A, 28, add. (after 165), **2.** Support; and l. 30, *Sva-upadhi* (m.?), a fixed star, Padmap. 16, 101.

126, B, 5, dele ved.

128, B, 19, add. **Comp.** *Mantra-*, m. encouragement by counsel, Hit. ii. p. 102, 4, M.M.

129, A, 7, add. (after **1.**), An offering, MBh. 14, 1913.

129, B, 8, add. **4.** Surname, Utt. Râmach. 2, 4.

130, B, 3 bel., add. A.S. bá.

131, A, 30, corr. *-uras + ka*.

131, B, 17, add. उलप *ulapa*, m. (n.), **1.** A creeper, Mâlat. 144, 14. **2.** A reed, Saccharum cylindricum.

132, B, 29, add. as akin, A.S. east, eastan, easter.

133, B, 25, add. A.S. wana, wanian, wenian.

134, A, 29, corr. Skandap.

134, B, 16, corr. wull (for vull).

135, A, 21, add. **Comp.** *Schaḍûshaṇa*, i.e. *shash-*, n. six spices.

135, B, 29, add. (after **2.**), Left, Mâlat. 146, 19. **3.**

136, B, 1, dele ἰάλλω.

136, B, 4, add. probably Lat. arma; A.S. earm, brachium; earnian, aernian (=ἄρνυμαι).

137, A, 20, add. Goth. rahtôn; A.S. un-ge-reclice.

138, B, 4, add. (after please), **4.** To worship, Mâlat. 84, 16.

139, B, 23, add. probably A.S. aeg, aegdher (=*ekatara*), egdher.

142, A, 23, corr. Brâhmaṇav.

142, A, 30, add. (after *ṛidh*), cf. *medinî*, *vetana*.

142, B, 16, corr. an (for ân), and add. A.S. ain, aen.

144, A, 7, add. ऐदम्पर्य *aidamparya*, i.e. *idam-para + ya*, n. Main point, Mâlat. 37, 4.

145, B, 7, add. Cf. Goth. vegs; A.S. waegh.

145, B, 29, add. ओजाय *OJÂYA*, a denomin. derived from *ojas* with *ya*, Âtm. To exert one's self, Bhaṭṭ. 5, 76. Ptcple. pf. pass. *ojâyita*, Proved strong, Utt. Râmach. 135, 13.

ADDENDA AND CORRIGENDA.

PAGE

146, B, 2 bel., add. see *bimboshṭha*, p. 633.

151, A, 21, add. see *Vikaṭa*, p. 844.

151, A, 25, add. (after narrow), Mâlat. 77, 20.

151, A, 27, add. (after name), *Ati-sam-kaṭa*, adj. very dangerous, Mâlat. 103, 19.

151, A, 2 bel., add. (after m.), and f. *nâ*, Mâlat. 77, 12.

152, A, 7, add. कठोरय *KAṬHORAYA*, a denomin. derived from *kaṭhora*, Par. To strengthen, Mâlat. 157, 6.

153, A, 1, add. *Kimnara-kanṭha*, adj., f. *ṭhî*, having the voice of a Kimnara, Mâlat. 128, 17.

153, A, 11, add. (after Çiva), Râm. 1, 75, 14.

153, B, 9, add. कण्डूल *kaṇḍû+la*, adj. Itchy, itching, Utt. Râmach. 40, 11.

155, A, 19, add. (after anthers), cf. Wils. Th. of the Hind. 2. ed. ii. 80, n.

156, A, 12, add. Comp. *Surabhi-kandara*, m. name of a mountain, Vikr. 65, 18.

158, B, 21 and 28, see *Sthalakamala* and *-kamalinî*, p. 1074.

159, B, 14, add. कम्र *kam+ra*, adj. Charming, beautiful, Mâlat. 152, 14.

160, B, 7 bel., add. Mâlat. 159, 9 (*v*).

163, B, 34, add. कर्त *karta*, i.e. 1. *kṛit+a*, m. Separation; in *a-*, m. Non-separation, Bhâg. P. 2, 7, 48.

164, A, 1 bel., add. कर्दमित *kardamita*, i.e. *kardama+ita*, adj. Soiled, Mâlat. 153, 10.

164, B, 1 bel., add. 2. A blacksmith, Hit. ii. d. 11, M.M.

165, B, 33, add. *Sûtra-karman*, n. carpentry, Râm. 2, 63, 1, Seramp.

172, B, 3, add. 2. Happened by chance (?), Mâlat. 84, 7.

PAGE

177, A, 32, add. काम्पिल्ल *kâmpilla*, m. Name of a plant, Mâlat. 152, 14.

185, A, 23, add. कास्मरी *kâsmarî* = *kâçmarî*, Mâlat. 145, 19.

185, A, 30, add. Goth. skeinan; A.S. scinan (cf. *chi* in *chitra*, for original **skitra*, and *kit*, *ketu*).

187, A, 34, corr. hwa, and add. hwaet (=ved. *kad*).

189, A, 18 (*kîlita*), add. 2. Pinned, Mâlat. 77, 3.

190, A, 7 bel., add. (after *kuch+a*), and कुचक *kucha+ka*, Daçak. in Chr. 198, 23.

192, A, 7, add. कुट्टाक *kuṭṭâka* (cf. *kuṭṭ*), adj., f. *kî*, Pounding, grinding, Mâlat. 85, 18.

192, A, 17, add. कुड्मलित *kuṭmalita*, i.e. *kuṭmala+ita*, adj. Opened, Mâlat. 152, 18.

193, B, 14, add. कुतस्त्य *kutas + tya*, adj. Whence coming, undecided whence, Utt. Râmach. 55, 7; 106, 3.

193, B, 4 bel., add. A.S. hwaeder, hwaer, hwar, and probably cor in ael-cor, elsewhere.

194, B, 1, corr. कुन्ति.

195, A, 7, add. Lat. caupo (Goth. kaupôn; A.S. be-cypdh, ceapian, borrowed); κάπηλος.

197, A, 16, add. कुर्पास *kurpâsa*, and कुर्प°.

200, A, 9, dele 'probably *ku-smi+a*.'

200, A, 7 bel. With *kuh*=κεύθω cf. A.S. hydan, hyde; Lat. custos, cutis (?); Goth. huzd.

200, B, 4, add. (after 2.), An interval, Nalod. 3, 32. 3.

201, B, 14, add. (after mountains), Vikr. d. 11.

202, A, 11 (*kûrcha*), add. 3. Boasting, Râjat. 5, 462.

PAGE

204, A, 31, add. With *ambu*, becoming अम्बू *ambû*, *ambûkṛita*, **1.** Accompanied by spitting, Utt. Râmach. 45, 2. **2.** Spit on, Mâlat. 145, 15.

208, A, 11, add. (after *praguṇî*), **1.** To make straight, to cause to grow. Mâlat. 164, 2. **2.**

208, A, 1 bel., add. With फेत् *phet*, in *phetkṛita*, n. Howling, Çatr. 14, 29.

208, B, 2, add. With *bhasman-râçi*, becoming भस्मराशी *bhasmarâçî*, To reduce to a heap of ashes, Râm. 1, 41, 30,

208, B, 6, add. With *mukula*, becoming मुकुली *mukulî*, *mukulîkṛita*, Put together (viz. the hands, in token of reverence), Lass. 2. ed. 86, 2.

208, B, 4 bel., add. With *vidheya* (vb. *dhâ*), becoming विधेयी *vidheyî*, To make compliant, to conquer, Mâlat. 16, 14.

209, A, 14, add. **2.** To abandon, Ragh. 2, 41; cf. *çithila*, p. 948.

213, A, 12, add. A.S. wyrm.

215, B, 3 bel., corr. Contracted (for stretched out).

217, B, 10, add. (after corpus), A.S. hrif.

218, A, 14, add. (after love), Vikr. d. 21.

221, B, 2, add. (after bird), the lapwing, and Mâlat. 145, 19; cf. Wilson. Th. of the Hind. 2. ed. ii. 97, n.

227, B, 8, add. *saṁkrânta*, Concurring (well-supporting an intrigue), Mâlat. 107, 3.

229, B, 26, add. (after hillock), or wall, Megh. 2.

233, B, 15, add. A.S. scedhan.

237, A, 10, add. A.S. scaenan. With the Caus. cf. Lat. scabo; A.S. scafan, scaefere, probably as akin, A.S. sceáp; σκάπτω.

238, B, 24, add. क्षिप्रकारिता *kshiprakâritâ*, i.e. *kshipra-kârin* + *tâ*, f. Rashness, Utt. Râmach. 113, 5.

240, A, 25, add. Goth. af-sciuban, of which the labial is regular.

249, A, 9, add. (before 219), Pañch.

250, A, 6 bel., add. (after *gaṇḍa*), a form of *grantha*; cf. *gaṇḍa-bhedaka*, p. 667.

251, A, 32, add. A.S. cwaedhan.

251, A, 43, add. Cf. probably A.S. codhe, Disease.

252, B, 19, add. Cf. with *gambhîra*, as akin, A.S. comb, vallis.

253, A, 24, add. (after 3014), **2.** m. Buddha.

253, A, 44, add. (after Buddha), **2.** A follower of the Bauddha religion, Lass. 2. ed. 86, 3.

256, A, 30, add. A.S. gán.

257, B, 11, corr. *garda-bha* (vb. *bhá*; with *garda* cf. A.S. colt).

259, A, 18, dele etc., and add. A.S. ciolaen, ciolon.

264, A, 27, add. βόμβος.

265, B, 24, add. गुणगुणाय *GUṆA-GUṆÂYA*, a denomin. derived from *guṇa-guṇa* with *ya*, Âtm. To be multiplied, Utt. Râmach. 143, 1.

266, B, 9, add. (after 76), *gupta* may be added after all Vaiçya names, Colebr. Ess. i. 278.

268, B, 4 bel., add. Cf. γάργαρον.

269, A, 13, add. A.S. graedig.

269, A, 33, add. **2.** A proper name, Utt. Râmach. 96, 7; 99, 5.

270, B, 26, add. A.S. gelan, perhaps be-galian, gyllan.

277, B, 2 bel., add. A.S. grapian.

278, A, 16, 17, corr. Çrut.

278, A, 2 bel., add. *Dhûma-graha*, m. Rahu, Mâlat. 38, 10.

281, B, 2, add. (after *ghaṭṭ*), or rather a form of *grath*.

281, B, 32, add. *vighaṭita*, Separated, Mâlat. 19, 5 (disappeared).

ADDENDA AND CORRIGENDA.

PAGE

282, B, 4 bel., add. **2.** Dense, Mâlat. 155, 12.

283, A, 11, add. Goth. varmjan; perhaps A.S. waelm, welm, wylm (or rather to *jval*?).

286, B, 1 bel., add. probably A.S. hrenian, To scent.

287, B, 22, add. (after *chakra*), probably from *kram*, reduplicated.

288, A, 6, add. *Shaḍadhikadaçanâḍî-chakra*, i.e. *shash-adhika-daçan-nâḍî-*, the disc of the sixteen tubular vessels, Mâlat. 74, 2 (the heart).

290, A, 4, add. (after **2.**), To overflow, Pańch. 74, 22 (cf. my translation, n. 350). **3.** and change the following numerals.

294, B, 10 bel., corr. Çâk.

296, B, 3, add. πέλομαι and cf. *parichara*, p. 520.

297, A, 5, add. *A-charama*, adj. new, young, Utt. Râmach. 125, 1.

299, A, 3, add. (after immovable), Vikr. d. 5.

301, A, 17, add. (after *châmuṇḍa*), i.e. *chaṇḍa-muṇḍa*, cf. Wilson, Th. of the Hind. 2. ed. ii. 57, n.

301, A. 26, add. (after foot), 2. a foot soldier, Utt. Râmach. 130, 5; and corr. 3. a walk, Megh. 61.

301, B, 1 bel., corr. *Brahmachârin.*

302, A, 2, add. *Çuddhânta-chârin*, s.v. *çuddhânta*, p. 955.

302, A, 25, add. II. f. *châlanî*, A sieve. —Cf. τηλία; Lat. colum.

302, A, 27, add. Cf. probably κίσσα.

303, A, 2, add. A. S. a-hafen, haeftan.

309, A, 18, add. A.S. scyndan; Icel. skunda (*chud* for original *skud*).

311, B, 16, add. (after **1.**), Motion, Lass. 2. ed. 62, 48. **2.**

311, B, 17, corr. **3.** and add. Behaviour, Lass. 2. ed. 49, 6. **4.**

313, A, 2, add. (after **3.**), Defraudation, Pańch. 222, 3. **4.**

313, B, 22, add. (after drop), Utt. Râmach. 75, 9.

314, B, 20, add. A.S. scad, scadu, sceád.

318, A, 3 bel., add. **2.** To besmear, Mâlat. 152, 10 (corr. *kapolam*).

320, B, 27, add. A.S. cwidh.

320, B, 31, add. A.S. caelan, celan, calian.

322, B, 8, add. γόνος, γουνός.

322, B, 12, add. A.S. cnosl.

324, A, 13, add. (after existence), Châṇ. 15 in Berl. Monatsb. 1864, 408.

324, A, 20, add. (after war), Ragh. 3, 23.

325, A, 8, add. *Râjajambû*, i.e. *râjan-*, f. name of a tree, Vikr. d. 90.

325, A, 20, add. see Add. ad p. 957, A, 13, 14.

330, B, 29, corr. जाम्बु°.

331, B, 28, add. ऽजाह *-jâha* (probably from the frequent. of *hâ*), n. Root; e. g. *karṇa-*, n. The root of the ear, Mâlat. 76, 10.

333, B, 6 bel., add. (after crooked), Kir. 6, 2.

335, A, 21, add. *Bandhu-jiva*, m. A flower, Pentapteris phœnicea, Ragh. 11, 25.

336, B, 3, add. A.S. cis, cist, costian, cyst.

337, A, 26, add. (after Expanded), Mâlat. 171, 12.

337, A, 27, add. (after wantoned), **3.** Proceeded (from), Mâlat. 170, 13; ib. (after Wish), Mâlat. 87, 4; Häberl. Anth. 238, 2.

338, B, 33, add. A.S. corn; perhaps grindan, greot, grut, gryt.

340, A, 30, add. A.S. cunnan, conne, cudh (=*jńâta*), cydhan.

341, A, 15, add. γω in γωρυτός, and ज्यानि *jyâ+ni*, f. Loss, Mâlat. 153, 4.

343, A, 26, add. N.H.G. Qualm, qualmen.

343, B, 23, add. झणझणाय *JHAṆAJHAṆÂYA*, a denomin.

PAGE

derived from *jhanajhana* with *ya*, Âtm. To tinkle, Mâlat. 15, 12. Ptcple. pf. pass. *jhanajhaṇâyita*, n. Tinkling, Utt. Râmach. 120, 13.

344, B, 23, add. (after m.), 1. The sound *ṭam*, produced by speed, Utt. Râmach. 119, 13. 2.

345, A, 6, add. (after go), Mâlat. 145, 19.

345, A, 4 bel., add. (after 21), 5. To afflict, Mâlat. 48, 17.

345, B, 6, add. 3. Excellence, Utt. Râmach. 150, 2.

345, B, 18, add. डामरत्व *ḍâmara*+*tva*, n. Honour, Mâlat. 74, 14.

345, B, 33, add. 2. A fool, Mâlat. 84, 13.

348, B, 28, add. Goth. thar; A. S. thaeder, thider, thar, thaer.

349, A, 22, add. see Add. ad p. 100, A, 19.

349, B, 4, add. तदानींतन *tadânîṁtana*, i.e. *tadânim*+*tana*, adj. Coeval, Utt. Râmach. 2, 7.

351, B, 33, add. n. Independence, Hit. ii. d. 121.

356, A, 17, add. 3. Tossed, Mâlat. 147, 2.

357, A, 5, add. तरुणय *TARUṆA-YA*, a denomin. derived from *taruṇa*, Par. To bring forth, Mâlat. 75, 22.

357, B, 7, add. Goth. threihan; A.S. thringan.

358, A, 3, add. perhaps A.S. thracian, thraec.

358, A, 6 bel., add. (after Then), Mâlat. 69, 18.

360, B, 9, add. Mâlat. 75, 19.

364, A, 10, add. to overpower, Mâlat. 152, 8 (corr. *vachanaṁ*).

365, B, 15, add. 2. Poison, Hit. iii. d. 60.

367, B, 17, add. Cf. Goth. thiubs; A.S. theof.

368, B, 7, add. (after 10588), to drive to and fro, as in a scale while weighing, i.e. to drive astray from the way, Megh. 20.

369, B, 4, add. (after adj.), 1. not satisfied, Hit. i. d. 24, M.M. 2. . . .; change 'ib.' to 'Böhtl. Ind. Spr. 277.'

369, B, 16, add. A.S. thystre, thystrian, theostre, theosterlic.

371, B, 6 bel., add. Cf. perhaps, Goth. thraskan; A.S. therscan (old desider.).

373, A, 9, add. A.S. thearl, thearm, thirel, thirlian, thole, tholian, thaelian, for-thyldian.

376, B, 2, add. Cf. perhaps τρέχω; Goth. thragjan; A.S. thrag.

376, B, 17, corr. drifan, and add. A.S. drefan.

378, A, 31, add. Cf. τρεῖς; Lat. tres; Goth. threis; A.S. threo, thry, thri.

382, B, 28, add. A.S. tux, tusk.

382, B, 2 bel., add. *Vṛisha-daṁçaka*, m. a cat.

383, B, 5, add. A.S. teso.

384, A, 13, add. A.S. taengan, To hasten.

389, B, 17, add. (after 9), 2. To divide, Mâlat. 127, 9.

393, B, 33, add. A.S. tidhe, tidhian.

394, A, 5, add. A.S. tian, To tie.

395, B, 4, add. *Vidyut-dâman*, n. a garland, a mass, of lightnings, Megh. 28.

396, A, 33, add. II. f. *dârikâ*, A daughter, Hit. iv. d. 109.

402, A, 16, add. A.S. tier (for tiher).

402, B, 24, add. A.S. teging.

405, A, 2, add. A.S. tynan.

405, B, 30, add. दुन्दुमा *dundumâ*, f. Sound, Sch. ad Utt. Râmach. 140, 2.

दुन्दुमाय *DUNDUMÂYA*, a denomin. derived from the last with *yâ*. Ptcple. pf. pass. *dundumâyita*, n. Sound, Utt. Râmach. 140, 2.

407, A, 30, add. दुर्मनाय *DURMA-*

PAGE

NÂYA, a denomin. derived from *dus-manas* with *yâ*, Âtm. To be sad.—With अति *ati*, To grieve excessively, Mâlat. 69, 13.—With परि *pari*, ptcple. pf. pass. *paridurmanâyita*, Very sad, Utt. Râmach. 77, 10.

407, A, 35, add. दुर्मर्यादता *durmaryâdatâ*, i. e. *dus-maryâda* (see *maryâdâ*), + *tâ*, f. Wickedness, Utt. Râmach. 113, 4.

408, B, 8, add. **2.** Embarrassed, Hit. ii. d. 64.

410, A, 10, add. A.S. tucian; τεύχω.

412, A, 27, add. Cf. perhaps A.S. tearflian.

414, B, 19, add. A.S. telga, telgon.

415, A, 26, add. A.S. tirian, tilian, To till; perhaps daru, daere, dael, daradh.

421, B, 2 bel., add. द्रढय *DRAḌHAYA*, a denomin. derived from *dṛiḍha* (see *dṛiṁh*), Par. To confirm, Utt. Râmach. 47, 8; 100, 7.

424, B, 3 bel., add. A.S. trucian.

429, B, 2, add. धक् *dhak* (vb. *dah*), indecl. An exclamation of wrath, Utt. Râmach. 113, 7.

437, A, 18, add. Comp. ptcple. fut. pass. *a-çraddheya*, adj. Incredible, Pańch. 79, 16.

441, B, 31, add. (after *dhik*), probably from *dah*, cf. *dhak*.

442, B, 1, add. (after man), Pańch. i. d. 314.

443, A, 8, add. *Mantridhura*, i.e. *mantrin-*, adj. able to hold the office of a counsellor, Râm. 2, 72, 50, Seramp.

445, A, 12, add. धूम्या *dhûmyâ*, i.e. *dhûma* + *ya*, f. Thick smoke, Mâlat. 75, 21.

448, A, 20, add. A.S. thriste; cf. Swed. dristig, Icel. dreiss.

450, B, 25, add. A.S. truwa.

PAGE

451, B, 9 bel., add. Cf. perhaps A.S. weoce.

452, B, 12, add. (after **2.**), Gives the opposite signification; e.g. *na pushyati*, Diminishes, Çâk. d. 18; *na na pushyati*, Increases, ib. 10, 6. **3.** and change the following num.

457, B, 8 bel., add. *unnâmita*, Heightened, reaching to, Hit. iii. d. 144 (M.M. iii. d. 146, v.r.).

458, A, 12, add. **5.** Following, Vikr. d. 62. **6.** Having befallen, ib. d. 73.

463, B, 9, add. A.S. nestan.

463, B, 8 bel., dele 'i.e. *naga* + *a*' and write 'probably for original *snâga*=A.S. snaca; cf. A.S. snican, akin to *snâ*.'

464, A, 12, add. Cf. A.S. snaegel.

465, A, 16, add. *Çakti-nâtha*, m. Çiva, Mâlat. 74, 5.

468, B, 17, corr. A.S. naese, and add. naesse.

470, A, 12, add. **2.** An arbour, Mâlat. 41, 15.

470, A, 19, add. (before निकुरुम्ब) 'निकुरम्ब *nikuramba* (Mâlat. 157, 11), and.'

475, B, 11, add. **2.** A fish, Vârt. 4, ad Pâṇ. i. 1, 68.

483, A, 30, add. निविडय *NIVIḌAYA*, a denomin. derived from *niviḍa* (Par.), To make tight, Mâlat. 73, 12.

484, A, 17, add. निशुम्भ *ni-çumbh* + *a*, m. **1.** Killing, Mâlat. 81, 8. **2.** The name of a Dânava.

489, A, 32, add. *pariṇîta*, n. Marriage, Utt. Râmach. 39, 3 (For shame! also remarried!).

492, A, 8, add. **4.** To pass away, to forget, Mâlat. 157, 7.

493, B, 27, add. (after *nepathya*), probably for *narpathya* (cf. *vetana*), i.e. *nṛi-pathya*.

493, A, 31, add. **4.** Dress, Mâlat. 103, 15.

495, A, 2, add. Utt. Râmach. 60, 2.

PAGE

495, B, 27, add. natural, Mâlat. 160, 5.

501, B, 8 bel., add. (after 15), a dark veil, Hit. ii. p. 62, 9, M.M.

501, B, 2 bel., add. *Jala-paṭala*, n. a cloud, Hit. 80, 15.

502, A, 4 bel., add. (after tiara), Mâlat. 150, 7; cf. Wilson, Th. of the Hind. 2. ed. ii. 102, n.

502, B, 3, add. (after condiments), Ragh. 18, 16.

502, B, 22, add. (after *spashṭa*), cf. *vispashṭa*.

503, B, 2, add. पणयितृ *paṇayitṛi*, i.e. *paṇ*, Caus., + *tṛi*, m. A seller, Mâlat. 75, 15.

508, A, 2 bel., add. *Lekha-patra*, n. a letter, Mâlat. 172, 7.

508, B, 1, add. (after parrot), Lass. 2. ed. 51, 34.

508, B, 5, add. *Sahasra-patra*, n. a lotus, Ragh. 7, 11.

512, B, 16, add. *Mekhalâ-pada*, n. the hip and loins. *Mekhalâ-guṇa-*, n. the same, Ragh. 9, 26.

524, B, 22, corr. *pari-barha* (for *pari-barh + a*), Surrounding like a peacock's tail.

526, A, 11, add. परिमाथिन् *pari-mâthin*, i.e. *pari-math + in*, adj. Torturing, Mâlat. 24, 7.

527, B, 8, add. 2. i.e. *pari-vâs + a*, m. Perfume, Mâlat. 157, 12.

529, A, 1 bel., add. (after 68), read *parisaraiç*, and cf. Schütz' translation; *parisara* being retained, the signification is 'circumference.'

533, A, 25, add. *Çarad-parvan*, n. the new moon of the first autumnal month, Lass. 2. ed. 88, 26.

537, B, 7, add. पाकल *pâka + la*, m. Fever of elephants. — **Comp.** *Kûṭa-*, m. bilious fever, Mâlat. 24, 9 (Böhtlingk and Roth have *kûṭapâlaka*).

538, A, 32, add. II. f. *pâñchâlikâ*, A doll, Mâlat. 164, 3 (*danta-*, of ivory).

538, B, 15, add. पाटलवती *pâṭala-vatî*, i.e. *pâṭala + vant + î*, f. Name of a river, Mâlat. 155, 2.

545, A, 21, add. पारित *pârita*, i.e. *pâra + ita* (?), adj. Inverted, Mâlat. 144, 11.

549, B, 17, add. Cf. Lat. pix; πίσσα; and probably Lat. piscis; Goth. fisks; AS. fisc. For the signification cf. *pichchhila*.

554, A, 7, add. (after *pîṭha*), i.e. probably *api-stha*.

554, A, 27 dele (after impudent), Daçak. in Chr. 180, 13, and put it l. 29, after courtesans.

558, A, 17, add. *Ku-putra*, m. a wicked son, Böhtl. Ind. Spr. 547.

558, A, 4 bel., add. *Su-putra-*, m. a good son, Böhtl. Ind. Spr. 551.

561, A, 6, add. (after First), Bhartṛ. 2, 67; and (after Soon), Megh. 83.

566, A, 19, add. *Dṛishṭi-pûta*, adj. ascertained as pure by one's own eye, Böhtl. Ind. Spr. 1232. *Vastra-*, adj. purified by a cloth, ib.

567, A, 24, corr. पूतन *pûtana*, I. m. A kind of demon, Mâlat. 78, 6. II. f. *nâ*. 1. Yellow . . .

567, A, 32, add. *Ugra-pûti*, adj. stinking horribly, Mâlat. 78, 16.

568, A, 6 bel., add. (after bird), Pelecanus fusicollis, Mâlat. 145, 20; cf. Wilson, Th. of the Hind. 2. ed. ii. 98, n.

570, A, 12, add. *pârita*, see s.v. Add. ad p. 545.

576, B, 7, add. (after *puṇḍarîka + a*), I. adj. Consisting of lotus flowers, Mâlat. 60, 10. II. m. . .

583, A, 4, add. प्रगुणन *praguṇana*, i.e. *praguṇaya* (see Add. ad A, 5), + *ana*, n. Putting right, Mâlat. 158, 13.

583, A, 5, corr. प्रगुणय *PRAGU-*

PAGE

NAYA, a denomin. derived from *praguṇa*, To make straight. Ptcple. pf. pass. *praguṇita*, Made . . .

593, A, 2 bel., add. प्रतिमल्ल *prati-malla*, m. A rival, Mâlat. 81, 10.

598, B, 7, add. प्रत्याशत्व *pratyâça-tva*, i.e. *prati-âça* + *tva* (see *âçâ*), n. Hope, Mâlat. 146, 20.

598, B, 9, add. (after Hope), Mâlat. 149, 6.

599, A, 16, add. *Nishpratyûha*, i.e. *nis-*, adj. irremediable, Mâlat. 158, 10.

599, A, 6 bel., add. A.S. a-bredian.

599, A, 2 bel., add. (after 132), gives to the present the signification of a preterite: *samarthaye yat prathamam*, What I judged first.

601, B, 19, dele 'or,' and add. (after action), Mâlat. 88, 11.

605, A, 29, add. प्ररोचन *prarocha-na*, i.e. *pra-ruch*, Caus., + *ana*, I. adj., f. *nî*, Stimulating, seducing, Kathâs. 17, 124. II. n. 1. Stimulating, Mâlat. 6, 8. 2. Seducing, Prab. 100, 19. III. n., and f. *nâ*, Praising, Sâh. D. 388.

609, B, 24, add. प्रसादिन् *prasâdin*, i.e. *prasâda* + *in*, adj. Serene, Mâlat. 169, 8.

610, B, 8, add. प्रस्ताविक *prastâvi-ka*, i.e. *prastâva* + *ika*, in *A-*, adj., f. *kî*, Inopportune, Mâlat. 39, 7 (perhaps corr. *aprâst°*).

611, B, 11, add. प्रहासिन् *prahâsin*, i.e. *pra-has* + *in*, adj. Smiling, Mâlat. 148, 6.

612, B, 2, add. प्राचण्ड्य *prâchaṇḍya*, i.e. *prachaṇḍa* + *ya*, n. Violence, Mâlat. 61, 9.

614, A, 11, add. प्रादोषिक *prâdo-shika*, i.e. *pradosha* + *ika*, adj. Vespertine, Mâlat. 79, 5.

PAGE

616, A, 8, add. 2. Dew, Megh. 40 (*prâleya-açra*, Tear-like dew, i.e. dew instead of tears).

616, B, 25, add. प्राशस्त्य *prâçastya*, i.e. *pra-çasta* (vb. *çaṁs*), + *ya*, n. Excellence, value, Mâlat. 93, 8.

621, B, 3 bel., add. (after 8), cf. Wilson, Th. of the Hind. 2. ed. ii. 53.

623, A, 11, add. (after 1395), II. m. An eunuch, Râm. 1, 48, 27.

623, B, 10, add. (after Priyaṅgu), Ragh. 8, 60.

623, B, 12, add. फलेग्रहि *phalegra-hi*, i.e. *phala* + *i-grah* + *i*, adj. Fruitful, Mâlat. 155, 13.

624, A, 1 bel., add. फेत् *phet*, A sound imitative of howling; in *phet-kâra*, m. Roaring, Bhâg. P. 3, 17, 5; *phetkârin*, i.e. *phet-kṛi* + *in*, adj. Howling, Prab. 85, 13.

624, B, 12, add. फेनिका *phenikâ*, i.e. *phena* + *ka*, f. Froth rising from treacle, Skandap. Kâçîkh. 4, 95.

626, B, 20, add. (after body), Lass. 2. ed. 39, 16.

627, B, 6 bel., add. (after ichneumon), Lass. 2. ed. 41, 3.

628, A, 19, add. (after leaf), Ragh. 6, 17.

629, A, 11, add. (after *valâka*), and बलाकिन् *balâkin*, see s. v. *valâkin*.

629, B, 14, add. (after *balibha*), Bhaṭṭ. 4, 16.

629, B, 16, add. बलीमन्त् *balî* + *mant*, adj., f. *matî*, Curled, Ragh. 8, 52.

630, B, 12, add. (after month), MBh. 1, 1292.

633, A, 8 bel., add. (after Disgust), Mâlat. 78, 14.

PAGE

633, A, 2, add. *Sa-bîbhatsa + m*, adv. with abhorrence, Mâlat. 61, 7.

636, B, 5 bel., add. (after God), Lass. 2. ed. 57, 84.

636, B, 16, add. *Sa-brahmaṇya*, m. Kârttikeya (guardian of the Brâhmaṇas), Lass. 2. ed. 88, 27.

637, A, 8 bel., add. ब्रह्मिष्ठ *brahmishṭha*, i.e. I. Superlative of *brahman + vant*, One who knows very well the Supreme Spirit, Ragh. 18, 27. II. m. A proper name, ib.

640, A, 2, add. (after wave), Ragh. 16, 63, Calc.

640, A, 35, corr. 63 (for 36), and add. Stenzler.

641, A, 5 bel., add. (after soldier), Râm. 1, 54, 3; Padmap. 16, 56.

643, B, 23, add. (after mime), Mâlat. 2, 12.

645, A, 13, add. (after 10), existence, incarnation, Padmap. 16, 148.

645, B, 30, add. (after become), Megh. 60.

645, B, 33, add. भविष्णु *bhavishṇu*, i.e. *bhû + ishṇu*, adj. **1.** Actually being, Bhaṭṭ. 3, 1. **2.** Being well.

646, B, 28, add. (after Daybreak), Ragh. 5, 69.

646, B, 6, bel., add. (after Splendour), Nalod. 1, 17.

646, B, 6 bel., add. भाक्त *bhâkta*, i.e. *bhakti + a*, m. A follower, Ragh. 11, 2, Stenzler (Calc. v.r.).

649, A, 8, add. (after *mânini*), proud, Brahmav. P. 2, 85.

649, A, 20, add. *Prâgbhâra*,' i. e. *prâñch-bhâra*, m. 1. bending, inclination. 2. a multitude, Prab. 5, 8. 3. top, Mâlat. 148, 7.

650, B, 10 bel., add. (after be), MBh. 1, 928.

651, A, 33, add. (after 239), Ptcple. fut. pass. *bhâshya*, n. A commentary, Lass. 2. ed. 87, 14.

653, A, 13, add. (after 104), II. f. *bhikshuṇi*, A Bauddha nun, Burnouf, Introd. à l'Hist. du Buddh. 278.

653, B, 31, add. (after river), Ragh. 11, 8.

654, A, 20, add. (after severed), **3.** Broken up (in the temples of an elephant in rut), Lass. 2. ed. 46, 24.

654, B, 12, add. (after Brittle), Mâlat. 69, 4.

655, A, 1 bel., add. भीमन्त् 2. *bhi + mant*, adj., f. *mati*, Fearful, Nalod. 1, 16.

656, A, 6 bel., corr. (after *Ku-*, n.) a general term for the lowest sorts of grain unfit for offering, Lass. 2. ed. p. viii.

659, A, 9, dele † (before To purify), and add. (after it), Bhâg. P. 3, 14, 45.

659, A, 30, add. i. 10, *anu-bhâvaya*, To purify, Bhâg. P. 3, 14, 47.

661, B, 8, add. With *valaya*, becoming वलयी *valayî*, *valayî-bhûta*, Serving as a bracelet, surrounding, Kir. 13, 30.

663, B, 30, add. *Aksha-bhûmi*, f. a board on which dice are cast, Daçak. in Chr. 185, 18.

664, A, 13, add. (after stage), theatrical dress, Mâlat. 4, 6.

666, A, 33, add. (after Hire), **2.** Treating (viz. medical), Ragh. 3, 12.

666, B, 8 bel., add.—Comp. *A-bhettṛi*, m. One who trespasses not, who observes, Ragh. 3, 27.

669, A, 20, add. (after Mars), **2.** Falling on Tuesday, Lass. 16, 16.

669, B, 27, add. (after Fallen), Lass. 2. ed. 61, 27.

670, A, 9 bel., add. (after 20), Mâlat. 17, 10.

671, A, 2, add. (after 6), MBh. 1, 1122.

671, A, 4 bel., add. (after Splendid), Ragh. 16, 69.

672, B, 10, add (after priest), cf. Râm. 2, 65, 39, Seramp.

675, B, 11, add. (after feel), Mâlat. 15, 10; Brahmav. P. 2, 13.

PAGE

676, A, 7, add. (after **3.**), An amulet, Lass. 2. ed. 91, 53. **4.** and corr. the following num.

676, A, 35, add. (after jeweller), Râm. 2, 64, 12, Seramp.

678, A, 7 bel., add. (after passion), Ragh. 3, 60.

678, B, 10 bel., add. (after 7669), n. Buttermilk, Lass. Pentap. 65, 19.

679, A, 4, add. **4.** Killed, Mâlat. 62, 2.

679, A, 14, add. (after 28), **2.** Name of a weapon, Râm. 1, 29, 11.

680, A, 1, add. (after liquor), Lass. 2. ed. 87, 9.

680, A, 31, add. (after Beeswax), **6.** (n. ?), Name of a weapon, Râm. 1, 29, 16.

680, A, 15, add. (after bard), **2.** A tree, Bassia latifolia, Râm. 2, 69, 8, Seramp.

681, A, 35, add. II. f. *tî*, Name of a river, Mâlat. 145, 5.

681, B, 8 bel., add. (after 129), **3.** instr. *madhyena*, Through, with acc., Râm. 2, 68, 12; 13.

685, A, 36, add. **मनोहरतरत्व** *mano-hara+tara+tva*, n. Greater beauty, Mâlat. 35, 2.

687, A, 5, add. (after **2.**), Hesitating, Mâlat. 130, 1. **3.** and corr. the following num.

687, B, 4, add. **3.** *mandara+m*, adv. Sluggishly, Lass. 2. ed. 54, 62.

687, B, 31, add. **मन्दारिता** *mandâ-ritâ*, f., i.e. I. *manda-ari+tâ*, Having foolish enemies, Nalod. 2, 22. II. *mandâra+in+tâ*, Plenty of Mandâra trees, ib.

688, A, 34, add. *Çata-manyu*, m. Indra, Bhaṭṭ. 1, 5.

688, B, 14, add. **3.** A demon, carpenter of the Daityas, Nalod. 2, 24.

689, A, 12, add. (after Pepper), Ragh. 4, 46 (the tree, *î*, Calc. v.r.).

690, A, 7, add. **मर्मत्र** *marmatra*, i.e. *marman-trâ*, n. A coat of mail (?), Râm. 2, 67, 61, Seramp.

PAGE

690, B, 2, add. (after rectitude), Lass. 2. ed. 87, 10. **4.** Rule of life, ib. 88, 28.

690, B, 24, add. **मर्शन** *marçana*, i.e. *mriç + ana*, n. Explication, Bhâg. P. 3, 32, 34.

691, A, 1, add. (after Dirty), Lass. 2. ed. 32, 12.

691, A, 34, dele Lass. 38, 17.

691, B, 1 bel., add. (after *mallikâ-khya*), Mâlat. 147, 18; (*mallikâ-khya* is probably a phonetical change of *mallikâksha*).

692, A, 22, add. *mashi* or *mashî*, Kathâs. 8, 3.

692, B, 3 bel., add. (after 24), *mahita*, Honoured, Ragh. 5, 25.

693, A, 14, add. (after festival), Nalod. 2, 9.

693, B, 6, add. **महात्म्य** *mahâtmya*, i.e. *mahâ-âtman + ya*, adj. Magnanimous, Padmap. 2, 14.

694, A, 10, add. **महिता** *mahitâ*, i.e. *mahin + tâ*, f. Festivity, Nalod. 4, 28.

694, A, 12, add. **महिन्** *mahin*, i.e. *maha + in*, adj. Festive, Nalod. 2, 5; 64.

694, B, 20, add. (after woman), Nalod. 2, 59.

694, B, 21, add. **महोक्षता** *mahoksha-tâ*, i.e. *mahâ-ukshan + tâ*, f. Age of a bull, Ragh. 3, 32.

695, B, 14, add. 4. **मा** *mâ*, f. A name of Lakshmî, Nalod. 4, 8. — **Comp.** *Sa-ma*, adj., f. *mâ*, happy, ib. 2, 23.

696, A, 3, corr. **माकन्द** *mâkanda*, I. m. The mango tree, Böhtl. Ind. Spr. 1769. II. f. *dî*. **1.** Emblic myrobalan. **2.** Yellow sanders. **3.** The name . . . .

696, A, 4, add. **माकर** *mâkara*, i.e. *makara + a*, adj. Full of Makaras, Nalod. 3, 45.

PAGE

697, B, 24, add. I. *mâtrishvaseya*, adj. Brought forth by mothers who are sisters, Râm. 1, 45, 16.

699, A, 30, add. माधवीय *mâdhavîya*, i.e. *mâdhava* (a proper name), +*îya*, adj. 1. Relating to Mâdhava, Mâlat. 151, 5. 2. Composed by Mâdhava, Lass. 2. ed. 93, 1.

700, A, 17, add. मानना *mân+anâ*, f. Worship, Nalod. 2, 23.

701, A, 27, add. (after adj.), 1. Relating to love, Mâlat. 35, 5. 2.

701, A, 31, add. II. f. *mâpanâ*, Measuring, marking a place for a sacrifice, MBh. 1, 2030.

701, A, 1 bel., add. (after Mine), Mâlat. 49, 19.

701, B, 4, add. (after cheat), Padmap. 16, 29.

701, B, 10 bel., add. (after juggler), Râgh. 10, 46 (*v*).

702, A, 10, add. मायूरिक *mâyûrika*, i.e. *mayûra+ika*, m. A hunter or killer of peacocks; Râm. 2, 64, 12, Seramp. has, probably erroneously, *mâyuraka*, One who catches and tames peacocks.

702, A, 14, add. (after love), Nalod. 1, 17.

702, A, 7 bel., add. मारव *mârava*, i.e. *maru+a*, adj. Sterile, Nalod. 1, 41; 3, 35.

मारवन्त् *mâra+vant*, adj. Full of love, Nalod. 1, 41.

704, A, 1 bel., add. मालय *mâlaya*, i.e. *malaya + a*, adj. Coming from the Malaya mountains, Nalod. 2, 56.

706, B, 10, corr. मित्र *mitra*, i.e. probably *smi+tra*.

706, B, 24, corr. मित्रता *mitra+tâ*, and मित्रत्व *mitra+tva*.

PAGE

706, B, 27, corr. मित्रयु *mitra+yu*.

706, B, 31, corr. मित्रवन्त् *mitra + vant*.

707, A, 5 bel., add. (after 11), Caus. *melaya*, To congregate, Lass. 2. ed. 89, 32.

707, B, 30, add. (after Sweetmeat), Lass. 2. ed. 59, 6.

709, B, 18 (*mukula*), Cf. *hâsta*, p. 1113.

709, B, 20, corr. मुकुलय *MUKULAYA*, a denomin. derived from *mukula*, Par. To cause to shut, Bhartr̥. 1, 54. Ptcple. pf. pass. *mukulita*, 1. Half . . .

709, B, 22, add. 3. Shut, Böhtl. Ind. Spr. 461.

709, B, 22, add. मुकुलिन् *mukulin*, i.e. *mukula+in*, adj. Budded, Mâlat. 51, 4.

711, A, 9, add. (after fire), MBh. 1, 1220.

711, B, 28, corr. मुखरय *MUKHARAYA*, a denomin. derived from *mukhara*, Par. To make noisy. Ptcple. pf. pass. *mukharita*, 1. Made resounding, Mâlat. 1, 7. 2. Sounding . . .

711, B, 1 bel., add. (after 14), 2. A dancing girl, Bhâg. P. 1, 11, 20.

717, A, 9 bel., add. (after 17), 2. Insensible, Mâlat. 149, 7.

717, A, 5 bel., add. (after *vi*), Pass. To be disturbed, Lass. 2. ed. 62, 40.

719, B, 7 bel., add. (after mus), mustela.

721, B, 1 bel., add. मृतपा *mr̥ita-pâ* (vb. *mr̥i*), m. A man of the lowest caste who, for a subsistence, collects dead men's clothes, conveys dead bodies to be burnt, executes criminals, etc., Râm. 1, 46, 19, Seramp.

724, A, 2, add. (after 5), To repent (?).

724, B, 14, add. (after tail), Mâlat. 90, 6.

PAGE

725, A, 8, add. (after Unctuous), Mâlat. 77, 9; and (after Smooth), Gît. 1, 1.

727, B, 10, add. मोट्टायित *moṭṭâyita*, n. One of the states of love: Languishing with remembrance of the lover, Bharata, 7 in Sch. ad Nalod. 2, 55.

727, B, 19, add. III. f. *modakî*, Name of a weapon, Râm. 1, 29, 8.

730, B, 1, add. (after consumption), Ragh. 19, 50 (*man*).

734, B, 7, add. (after Restraining), 6. Instr. *treṇa*, Violently, Lass. 2. ed. 73, 21.

734, B, 32, add. (before An artisan), Acquainted with machinery, Râm. 2, 63, 1, Seramp.

735, A, 2, add. यन्त्रिन् *yantr + in*, adj. Tormenting, Râm. 1, 1, 74.

735, A, 6 bel., add. (after Long), tall, Râm. 1, 67, 4.

737, A, 24, add. 2. A veil, Bhâg. P. 1, 8, 19.

738, A, 12 bel., add. Caus. *pra-yâsita*, n. Fatigue, Mâlat. 153, 6.

741, A, 10, add. (after 2.), A road, Râm. 3, 65, 55, Seramp.

741, B, 3, add. (after Kṛishṇa), Nalod. 1, 1.

741, B, 10, add. f. *çî*.

742, A, 5, add. (after time), Nalod. 2, 18 (*nâ*).

742, B, 18, add. (after sacrifices), Bhaṭṭ. 2, 20; devout, Râm. 2, 56, 13, Seramp.

यायावर *yâyâ* (frequent. of *yâ*), + *vara*, m. 1. A horse fit for the Açvamedha sacrifice, Pâṇ. iii. 2, 176; cf. Bhaṭṭ. 2, 20. 2. A Brâhmaṇa who has preserved his household fire. 3. A vagrant mendicant, a saint, MBh. 1, 1030.

742, B, 24, add. (after 3.), Going to. *manas-*, adj. Touching the heart, Brahmav. P. 1, 40.

743, B, 14, add. (after Mixed), Lass. 2. ed. 65, 9.

PAGE

743, B, 30, add. (after 2.), Adaptedness, Mâlat. 3, 11. 3. and corr. the following num.

745, B, 21, add. (after 2.), Intent on, Lass. 2. ed. 68, 36.

748, B, 3 bel., add. (after trophy), Ragh. 8, 36.

753, B, 26, add. (after 284), Miserable, Mâlat. 78, 17.

754, B, 21, add. *Vi-raja*, adj. free from dust, MBh. 1, 722.

754, B, 4 bel., add. (after Turmeric), Naish. 22, 49 (and, Night).

756, B, 10, add. (after 109), to jingle, Mâlat. 74, 18.

756, B, 29, add. रणत्कार *raṇat-kâra* (vb. *raṇ*), m. Sound, Mâlat. 15, 14; 74, 14; 86, 16.

756, B, 32, add. (after Desire), Mâlat. 24, 19.

758, A, 3 bel., add. (after Tooth), Nalod. 2, 8.

758, B, 15, add. (after Vishṇu), MBh. 1, 2099.

759, B, 4, corr. *Sa-rabhasa*, 1. adj. passionate, Bhartṛ. 1, 47. 2. °*ram*, adv. . . .

760, B, 14, add. (after 1.), Joy, Padmap. 16, 144. 2. and change the following num.

760, B, 27, add. (after Wife), Nalod. 2, 14.

761, A, 22, add. रराटी *rarâṭî* (cf. *lalâṭa*), f. The forehead, Bhâg. P. 2, 1, 28.

761, B, 7 bel., add. *anu-rasita*, n. Cry, Mâlat. 145, 15.

762, A, 31, add. (after earth), Nalod. 2, 10.

762, B, 17, add. (after adj.), 1. solid, Bhaṭṭ. 2, 32. 2. insipid, Bhartṛ. 1, 51. 3 . . .

763, A, 19, add. रसाल *rasâla*, i.e. *rasa* + *âla*, I. m. 1. The sugar cane. 2. The mango tree. 3. The jack tree. 4. The olibanum tree. 5. Wheat. II. f. *lâ*. 1. The tongue. 2. Bent

PAGE

grass. **3.** A flower, Hedysarum gangeticum. **4.** A grape. **5.** Curds mixed up with sugar and spices (also n. ? cf. Râm. 2, 67, 58, Seramp.). III. n. **1.** Frankincense. **2.** Gum myrrh.

763, A, 22, add. (after **3.**), Delighted, Mâlat. 102, 8. **4.**

763, A, 32, add. **रसिन्** *rasin*, i.e. *rasa* + *in*, adj. Impassioned, Nalod. 2, 39.

763, B, 14, put the article **रहस्** after **रहःस्थ**, and between them **रहण** *rahaṇa*, i.e. *rah* + *ana*, n. Separation, Nalod. 2, 14.

764, B, 29, add. *Chakshûrâgin*, i.e. *chakshus-*, adj., f. *iṇi*, enjoying one's eyes, Mâlat. 19, 11.

766, B, 6 bel., add. **राजिल** *râjila*, m. A sort of snake, Ragh. 11, 27.

768, A, 2 bel., add. **राधावन्त्** *râdhâvant*, i.e. *râdh* + *a* (f.), + *vant*, adj. Full of wealth, Nalod. 3, 50.

768, B, 7, add. (after Beautiful), Padmap. 16, 10.

768, B, 16, add. **रामणीयक** *râmaṇîyaka*, i.e. *ramaṇîya* (vb. *ram*), + *ka*, adj. Beautiful, Mâlat. 14, 1.

770, A, 7, dele 'Mixed,' and 'I propose —Made;' and add. i.e. *rechita*, with *â*, adj. A little crooked; cf. also Mâlat. 68, 9.

770, A, 1 bel., corr. Nalod. (for Nal.).

771, A, 25, add. (after 33), **2.** Consolation, Nalod. 3, 45.

771, B, 3, add. (after ed.), ii.

772, B, 12, add. *Hiṁsâ-ruchi*, adj. one who likes bloody work, Mâlat. 84, 14.

780, A, 24, add. (after Plantain), **5.** A worker in glass, Râm. 2, 64, 12, Seramp.

781, B, 20, add. (after tree), Mâlat. 78, 13; 152, 16.

PAGE

782, B, 17, add. (after dye), **3.** A spot of lac, Kathâs. 3, 71.

783, A, 13, add. (after *âlakshya*), n. A meteor, Mâlat. 78, 4; Çâk. d. 176; it is . . .

784, A, 31, add. **लक्ष्मि** *lakshmi*, for *lakshmî*, on account of the metre, Râm. 1, 19, 20; 21.

791, A, 2 bel., add. (after river), Mâlat. 144, 12.

792, A, 12, add. (after 137), **3.** A brilliant action, Mâlat. 171, 9.

792, B, 29, add.—Comp. *Go-lâṅgula*, m. a kind of ape, Mâlat. 152, 10.

800, A, 1 bel., corr. 7 (for 17).

802, A, 10, add. (after 111), *Stabdha-lochana* (vb. *stambh*), adj. having unwinking eyes, as a god, Wilson, Th. of the Hind. 2. ed. i. 23, n.

806, B, 7, add. *a-vâchya*, n. Blameable discourse.

807, B, 12, add. Goth. aukan, vôkrs.

809, A, 6, add. **3.** (*bhî*), A tent, MBh. 1, 796.

809, B, 10, add. (after **2.**), Horror, Mâlat. 61, 12. **3.** and corr. the following num.

809, B, 32, add. (after steer), a calf, Ragh. 3, 32.

811, B, 20, add. (after 1, a), **3.** A young wife in general, Mahâv. 76, 21.

819, A, 7 bel., add. *Nideça-vartin*, adj. obedient to the command, Mâlat. 87, 14.

821, B, 3 bel., add. (after **2.**), Zone, sign of a woman being no widow, Bhaṭṭ. 3, 22, Sch. **3.**

822, A, 22, add. **वलाकिन्** *valâkin*, i.e. *valâka* + *in*, also *bal°*, adj., f. *nî*, Full of cranes, Ragh. 11, 15 (Stenzler, *b*).

823, A, 10, add. (after herdsman), Râm. 2, 75, 61, Seramp.

823, A, 4 bel., add. *Bhujaṅga-valli*, f. serpents instead of creepers, Mâlat. 1, 13.

PAGE

824, A, 32, add. **वशंवद** *vaça+m-vad+a*, adj. Compliant, subjected, Mâlat. 165, 12 (Prâkṛ.).

824, A, 33, corr. *vaçaṁvada+tva*.

831, A, 19, add. **10.** After an interrogative pronoun, and followed by *na*, Every, all, Bhartṛ. 2, 24 (*mṛitaḥ ko vâ na jâyate*, Every dead person is born again); Megh. 8, 5 (*ke vâ na syuḥ paribhavapadaṁ nishphalârambhayatnâḥ*, All those who exert themselves in vain undertakings are objects of contempt).

840, A, 19, add. (after 551), n. Perfume, Mâlat. 148, 14.

846, B, 9, add. *Mahâ-mâṁsa-vikraya*, m. selling man's flesh, Mâlat. 72, 10 (i.e. performing horrid mysteries).

847, B, 16, add. *Saṁdhi-vigraha*, m. peace, war (i.e. a public office; cf. *sândhivigrahika*), Daçak. in Chr. 182, 20.

864, B, 12, add. (after 23), 2. staggering, Ṛit. 6, 11.

PAGE

898, B, 5 bel., add. as akin, A.S. windan; Lat. vitta; A.S. waetl.

911, A, 10, add. (after 12), clearness, Mâlat. 17, 7.

922, B, 31, add. (after bee), Bhâg. P. 3, 8, 31.

926, B, 19, add. (after **3.**), Royal power, Ragh. 3, 13. **4.** and corr. the following num.

946, B, 5 bel., add. **8.** (or f. *râ* ?), Name of a weapon, Râm. 1, 29, 8.

949, A, 4 bel., add. (after arsenic), Ragh. 12, 80 (m.).

957, A, 13, 14, dele A.S. camb, and O.H.G. kamp. They belong rather to *jambha*, the comb being formed like a row of teeth.

963, B, 12 bel., add. A.S. aechir, ear.

988, A, 24, add. **संह्रादिन्** *saṁhrâdin*, i. e. *sam-hrâd+in*, adj, f. *nî*, Noisy, Kir. 18, 19.